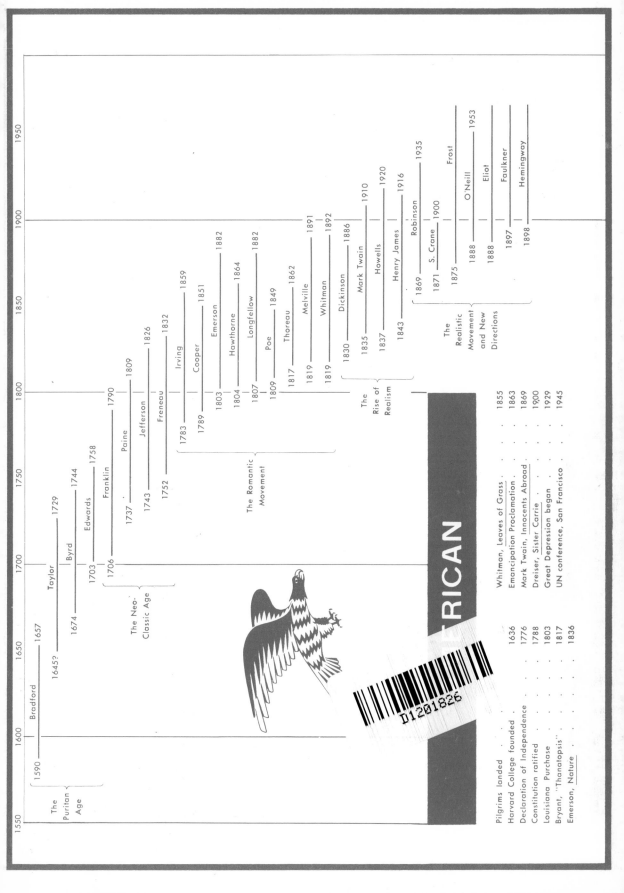

AMERICAN

■ ■

POETRY AND PROSE

New Shorter Edition

Edited by NORMAN FOERSTER

and ROBERT FALK

of the University of California, Los Angeles

HOUGHTON MIFFLIN COMPANY BOSTON The Riverside Press Cambridge

Acknowledgment is made for permission to reprint the following materials, alphabetically listed by authors:

HENRY ADAMS   From *The Education of Henry Adams,* by Henry Adams. Copyright 1918 by The Massachusetts Historical Society. Copyright 1946 by Charles Francis Adams. Reprinted by permission of Houghton Mifflin Company.

SHERWOOD ANDERSON   "Queer," from *Winesburg, Ohio* by Sherwood Anderson. Copyright 1919 by B. W. Huebsch, 1947 by Eleanor Copenhaver Anderson. Reprinted by permission of The Viking Press, Inc.

IRVING BABBITT   "The Critic and American Life," from *On Being Creative and Other Essays* by Irving Babbitt. Copyright 1932 by Irving Babbitt. Reprinted by permission of Houghton Mifflin Company.

WILLIAM BRADFORD   Selections reprinted from *Of Plymouth Plantation* by William Bradford, edited by Samuel Eliot Morison, by permission of Alfred A. Knopf, Inc. Copyright 1952 by Samuel Eliot Morison.

CLEANTH BROOKS   "The Waste Land: An Analysis," from *Modern Poetry and the Tradition* by Cleanth Brooks; reprinted by permission of The University of North Carolina Press.

WILLIAM BYRD   From the *Secret Diary of William Byrd of Westover, 1709–1712,* edited by Louis B. Wright and Marion Tinling. Copyright 1941 by Louis B. Wright and Marion Tinling.

WILLA CATHER   "Neighbor Rosicky," reprinted from *Obscure Destinies* by Willa Cather, by permission of Alfred A. Knopf, Inc. Copyright 1930, 1932 by Willa Cather.

MALCOLM COWLEY   "William Faulkner's Legend of the South," copyright 1945 by Malcolm Cowley; reprinted by permission of the author.

HART CRANE   From *The Collected Poems of Hart Crane.* By permission of Liveright Publishers, New York. Copyright 1933 by Liveright, Inc.

E. E. CUMMINGS   #20 (a wind has blown), #30 (in Just-spring), #31 (Buffalo Bill's defunct), copyright, 1923, 1950, by E. E. Cummings; #225 (somewhere i have never travelled), copyright, 1931, 1958, by E. E. Cummings; #312 (may my heart always), copyright, 1938, by E. E. Cummings; XXXIX (all ignorance), copyright, 1944, by E. E. Cummings; all reprinted from *Poems 1923-1954* by E. E. Cummings by permission of Harcourt, Brace and Company, Inc.

EMILY DICKINSON   Poems reprinted by permission of the publishers from *The Poems of Emily Dickinson*, edited by Thomas H. Johnson. Cambridge, Mass.: The Belknap Press of Harvard University Press, Copyright, 1955, by The President and Fellows of Harvard College.

"The First Day's Night," from *Unpublished Poems of Emily Dickinson*, edited by Martha Dickinson Bianchi and Alfred Leete Hampson, by permission of Little, Brown & Co.; copyright 1935 by Martha Dickinson Bianchi.

Four letters reprinted by permission of the publishers from *The Letters of Emily Dickinson*, edited by Thomas H. Johnson and Theodora V. W. Ward. Cambridge, Mass.: The Belknap Press of Harvard University Press, Copyright, 1958, by The President and Fellows of Harvard College.

THEODORE DREISER   "The Lost Phoebe," from *Free and Other Stories* by Theodore Dreiser. Copyright 1918 by Liveright, Inc.

T. S. ELIOT   Selections from *Collected Poems 1909-1935* by T. S. Eliot, copyright, 1936, by Harcourt, Brace and Company, Inc. Reprinted by permission also of Faber and Faber Ltd.

From "The Dry Salvages" in *Four Quartets*, copyright, 1943, by T. S. Eliot. Reprinted by permission of Harcourt, Brace and Company, Inc. and of Faber and Faber Ltd.

"The Metaphysical Poets," from *Selected Essays 1917-1932* by T. S. Eliot, copyright, 1932, by Harcourt, Brace and Company, Inc. Reprinted by permission also of Faber and Faber Ltd.

"Literature and the Modern World," by T. S. Eliot, from *American Prefaces*, November, 1935. Copyright 1935 by the State University of Iowa.

WILLIAM FAULKNER   "Dry September," William Faulkner. Copyright 1930 and renewed 1958 by William Faulkner. Reprinted from *Collected Stories of William Faulkner* by permission of Random House, Inc.

"The Bear," from *Go Down, Moses*. Copyright 1942 by William Faulkner. Reprinted by permission of Random House, Inc.

F. SCOTT FITZGERALD   "May Day," by F. Scott Fitzgerald. Copyright 1920 Smart Set, Inc.; renewal copyright 1948 Frances Scott Fitzgerald Lanahan. Reprinted from *Tales of the Jazz Age* by F. Scott Fitzgerald by permission of Charles Scribner's Sons.

ROBERT FROST   From *Complete Poems of Robert Frost*. Copyright, 1930, 1939, 1943, 1947, 1949, by Henry Holt and Company, Inc. Copyright, 1936, 1942, 1945, 1948, by Robert Frost. By permission of the publishers.

ERNEST HEMINGWAY   "A Clean, Well-Lighted Place," by Ernest Hemingway. Copyright 1933 Charles Scribner's Sons. Reprinted from *Winner Take Nothing* by Ernest Hemingway by permission of Charles Scribner's Sons.

HENRY JAMES   "The Death of the Lion," from *Terminations* by Henry James. Copyright 1895 by Harper & Brothers. Copyright 1922 by Henry James. Reprinted by permission of Harper & Brothers.

"The Real Thing," from *The Real Thing and Other Stories* by Henry James. Copyright 1907 by The Macmillan Company, and reprinted with their permission.

"Maud-Evelyn," from *The Soft Side* by Henry James. Copyright 1922 by The Macmillan Company, and reprinted with their permission.

"The Art of Fiction," by Henry James, reprinted with the permission of The Macmillan Company.

Selection from *Hawthorne* by Henry James, reprinted with the permission of Macmillan & Company Ltd.

ROBINSON JEFFERS   "Roan Stallion," Robinson Jeffers. Copyright 1925 and renewed 1953 by Robinson Jeffers. Reprinted from *Selected Poetry of Robinson Jeffers* by permission of Random House, Inc.

"Gale in April" and "To the Stone-Cutters," Robinson Jeffers. Copyright 1924 and renewed 1951 by Robinson Jeffers. Reprinted from *Roan Stallion, Tamar and Other Poems* by Robinson Jeffers, with permission of Random House, Inc.

SINCLAIR LEWIS   From *The Man Who Knew Coolidge* by Sinclair Lewis, copyright, 1928, by Harcourt, Brace and Company, Inc.; renewed, 1955, by Michael Lewis. Reprinted by permission of the publishers.

JOHN A. AND ALAN LOMAX   "Sweet Betsy from Pike," "Swing Low, Sweet Chariot" and "Casey Jones," collected, adapted & arranged by John A. & Alan Lomax; copyright 1934 by John A. & Alan Lomax in the book *American Ballads and Folk Songs;* copyright assigned 1958 to Ludlow Music, Inc., New York; used by permission. "Whoopee Ti Yi Yo, Git Along, Little Dogies," collected, adapted & arranged by John A. & Alan Lomax; copyright 1938 by John A. & Alan Lomax in the book *Cowboy Songs & Other Frontier Ballads;* copyright assigned 1958 to Ludlow Music, Inc., New York; used by permission. "Go Down Moses" and "Bury Me Not on the Lone Prairie," collected, adapted & arranged by John A. & Alan Lomax; copyright 1947 by John A. & Alan Lomax in the book *Folk Song: USA;* copyright assigned 1958 to Ludlow Music, Inc., New York; used by permission.

ARCHIBALD MACLEISH   "Ars Poetica," "You, Andrew Marvell," "American Letter," and selections from "Frescoes for Mr. Rockefeller's City," from *Poems 1924-1933*, by Archibald MacLeish. Copyright 1933 by Houghton Mifflin Company.

"Speech to Those Who Say Comrade" and "Pole Star," from *Public Speech* by Archibald MacLeish. Copyright, 1936, by Archibald MacLeish. Reprinted by permission of Rinehart & Company, Inc., New York, Publishers.

HERMAN MELVILLE "Billy Budd," reprinted by permission of the publishers from *Melville's Billy Budd,* edited by Frederic Barron Freeman. Cambridge, Mass.: Harvard University Press, Copyright, 1948, 1956, by The President and Fellows of Harvard College.

H. L. MENCKEN "Footnote on Criticism," reprinted from *A Mencken Chrestomathy* by H. L. Mencken, by permission of Alfred A. Knopf, Inc. Copyright 1922, 1949 by Alfred A. Knopf, Inc.

MARIANNE MOORE "The Steeple-Jack," from Marianne Moore, *Selected Poems.* Copyright 1935 by The Macmillan Company and used with their permission.

"In Distrust of Merits," from Marianne Moore, *Nevertheless.* Copyright 1944 by The Macmillan Company and used with their permission.

EUGENE O'NEILL "The Emperor Jones," Eugene O'Neill. Copyright 1921 and renewed 1948 by Eugene O'Neill. Reprinted from *Nine Plays by Eugene O'Neill* by permission of Random House, Inc.

KATHERINE ANNE PORTER "María Concepción," from *Flowering Judas and Other Stories,* copyright, 1930, 1935, 1958, by Katherine Anne Porter. Reprinted by permission of Harcourt, Brace and Company, Inc.

EZRA POUND From *Personae, The Collected Poems of Ezra Pound.* Copyright 1926 by Ezra Pound. Reprinted by permission of New Directions.

From *The Cantos of Ezra Pound.* Copyright 1934, 1937, 1940, 1948 by Ezra Pound. Reprinted by permission of New Directions.

EDWIN ARLINGTON ROBINSON "Isaac and Archibald," "Ben Jonson Entertains a Man from Stratford," "The Man Against the Sky," "Flammonde," "Cassandra," "Mr. Flood's Party," "Karma," from *Collected Poems of Edwin Arlington Robinson,* copyright 1935, 1937 by The Macmillan Company and used with their permission.

"Miniver Cheevy," copyright 1907 Charles Scribner's Sons; renewal copyright 1935. Reprinted from *The Town Down the River* by Edwin Arlington Robinson by permission of Charles Scribner's Sons.

"For a Dead Lady," from *The Town Down the River* by Edwin Arlington Robinson; copyright 1910 by Charles Scribner's Sons, 1938 by Ruth Nivison. Reprinted with the permission of Charles Scribner's Sons.

"The Children of the Night," "George Crabbe," "John Evereldown," "Cliff Klingenhagen," "Richard Cory," "Luke Havergal," and "Credo," from *The Children of the Night* by Edwin Arlington Robinson, published by Charles Scribner's Sons.

CARL SANDBURG "Nocturne in a Deserted Brickyard," "Fog," "Chicago," and "I Am the People, the Mob," from *Chicago Poems* by Carl Sandburg. Copyright, 1916, by Henry Holt and Company, Inc. Copyright, 1944, by Carl Sandburg. By permission of the publishers.

"Cool Tombs" and "Grass," from *Cornhuskers* by Carl Sandburg. Copyright, 1918, by Henry Holt and Company, Inc. Copyright, 1946, by Carl Sandburg. By permission of the publishers.

Selections from *The People, Yes* by Carl Sandburg, copyright, 1936, by Harcourt, Brace and Company, Inc.

WALLACE STEVENS Poems reprinted from *The Collected Poems of Wallace Stevens,* by permission of Alfred A. Knopf, Inc. Copyright 1923, 1931, 1935, 1936, 1937, 1942, 1954 by Wallace Stevens.

EDWARD TAYLOR Selections from *The Poetical Works of Edward Taylor,* edited by Thomas H. Johnson. Copyright Rockland Editions. Copyright 1943, Princeton University Press edition.

"Upon a Wasp Chilled with Cold," from an article by Thomas H. Johnson, copyright 1943 by the *New England Quarterly.*

LIONEL TRILLING "Freud and Literature," from *The Liberal Imagination* by Lionel Trilling. Copyright 1940, 1947 by Lionel Trilling. Reprinted by permission of The Viking Press, Inc.

EDITH WHARTON "The Choice," reprinted from *Xingu* by Edith Wharton: copyright 1916 Charles Scribner's Sons; renewal copyright 1944 Elisina Tyler. Used by permission of Charles Scribner's Sons.

WILLIAM CARLOS WILLIAMS From *Al Que Quiere.* Copyright 1909, 1934 by W. C. Williams.

EDMUND WILSON "Symbolism," reprinted from *Axel's Castle* by Edmund Wilson: copyright 1931 Charles Scribner's Sons; renewal copyright © 1959 Edmund Wilson. Used by permission of Charles Scribner's Sons.

THOMAS WOLFE Selections from *You Can't Go Home Again* by Thomas Wolfe. Copyright 1934, 1937, 1938, 1939, 1940 by Maxwell Perkins as Executor. Reprinted by permission of the publisher, Harper & Brothers.

PREFACE

American literature deserves to be studied as the finest expression of an idealized national myth or tradition which is as difficult to define as it is valuable to possess. Without such a tradition a people might rapidly become absorbed in the mass pressure for lesser and easier goals. We have endeavored to place the best literature of this tradition in its proper cultural and historical background, including the important influences of European thought and the American scene. We have tried to present it in such a way that the student will find his own emotional and intellectual discovery of it encouraged and stimulated. It has been a fundamental aim to avoid usurping the prerogative of teacher and student to interpret and evaluate the literature for themselves.

Three years ago, when the more detailed and inclusive Fourth Edition was published, the editor's preface stated that the book was "designed to serve both the historical and the critical approaches to our literature." The present New Shorter Edition has carried on this purpose, combining the methods of historical scholarship with the more recent aesthetic and analytical criticism. We have sought to provide a significant historical framework *and* useful critical commentary without allowing either to dominate and leaving room for the instructor to place the emphasis where he prefers.

The Text. Designed for a general, introductory course in American literature, as well as for the increasing number of single-semester or quarter offerings in various limited aspects, the present edition contains in one volume a generous representation of the masters while still retaining the broad outline and development of our literature from its beginnings. One of our organizing principles has been to preserve the best of the major authors together with adequate selections from lesser writers in whose work the student may see certain trends of thought and expression not always apparent from a reading of masterpieces alone.

The eight leading writers of the nineteenth century have come through almost unscathed from the larger edition, with few omissions, and only minor cuts in such longer works as "Nature," "Song of Myself," and "Old Times on the Mississippi." In the twentieth century, where omissions and inclusions are the most problematical, we have been careful to guide our own judgments by the best recent critical taste and opinion. Within the restrictions of copyright availability, we have tried to represent by at least one or two characteristic pieces the work of the writers of fiction who seem most likely to endure. In verse, it was possible to include full selections from widely recognized figures like Frost and Eliot and still add several poems of Pound and extend "Hugh Selwyn Mauberley" to the length of the entire Part I. Otherwise, aside from necessary reductions of space, the recent poetry section remains substantially the same as in the Complete Edition.

The principal change from the 1957 edition is in the section on modern criticism. Malcolm Cowley, Lionel Trilling, and Cleanth Brooks have been included to broaden the representation of recent critical approaches. While exemplifying the points of view of these newer critics, we have chosen essays that serve to illuminate such complex contemporaries as Eliot and Faulkner and such controversial topics as the influence of Freud and of symbolism upon literature. In the work of Faulkner, we have had to omit the long fourth section of "The Bear." His "Dry September" is, however, a new addition.

✤ *Periods and Movements.* The division into basic intellectual and historical periods — Puritanism, Neo-Classicism, Romanticism, and Realism — has remained as the shaping principle of the book, and the introductions elucidating these periods and movements have been changed only by reducing portions of their illustrative detail. Social and political backgrounds have been abridged in favor of the discussions of literary methods, types, and individual authors. The prevailing "literary tone" of the Fourth Edition has thus been further accentuated.

✤ *Notes and Bibliographies.* As in the Fourth Edition the notes immediately precede the text. However, in two instances, Eliot and Pound, it has seemed desirable to have footnotes explaining the allusions to remote literary names and places and the many literary echoes in such poems as "The Waste Land," "Ash Wednesday," "Hugh Selwyn Mauberley," and "The Cantos." The biographical sketches have been brought up to date. Some have been slightly expanded. All names, dates of composition, references, and other historical data have been checked. The suggestions for "further reading" have been scanned for their most recent relevance, and a completely revised "Guide to Scholarship," based on the 1957 version prepared by Roger B. Stein, has been appended.

✤ *Acknowledgments.* The editors are grateful once again to all those friends and colleagues, scattered throughout the nation, whose assistance, invaluable in the larger work, is of course reflected in the New Shorter Edition. The editors wish also to acknowledge the careful reading and correction of the notes to Pound and Eliot by Professor John Espey of the University of California, Los Angeles.

NORMAN FOERSTER
ROBERT FALK

CONTENTS

THE PURITAN AGE

THE NEO-CLASSIC AGE

THE ROMANTIC MOVEMENT

THE RISE OF REALISM

THE REALISTIC MOVEMENT AND
NEW DIRECTIONS

AMERICAN POETRY AND PROSE

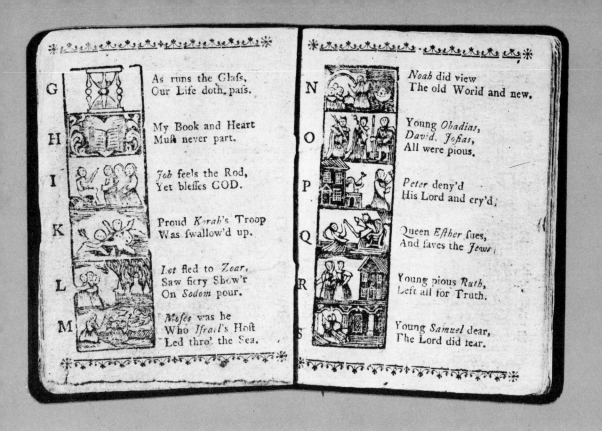

G	As runs the Glaſs, Our Life doth paſs.	N	Noah did view The old World and new.
H	My Book and Heart Muſt never part.	O	Young Obadias, David, Joſias, All were pious.
I	Job feels the Rod, Yet bleſſes GOD.	P	Peter deny'd His Lord and cry'd.
K	Proud Korah's Troop Was ſwallow'd up.	Q	Queen Eſther ſues, And ſaves the Jews.
L	Lot fled to Zoar, Saw fiery Show'r On Sodom pour.	R	Young pious Ruth, Left all for Truth.
M	Moſes was he Who Iſrael's Hoſt Led thro' the Sea.	S	Young Samuel dear, The Lord did fear.

Pages from "The New England Primer," a schoolbook popular in all the colonies

THE PURITAN AGE

The Word of God as the Law of Man

"Man should not glory in himself, but alone in God" — EDWARDS

It was the Puritans of the seventeenth century who, more than any other early colonists, affected deeply the national character in later times. And it was they who wrote most of the literature of the first colonial century. These are reasons enough to speak of this century and part of the next as a "Puritan Age."

Why did so many Puritans leave their homes in "the best island in the universe" (the phrase is Cotton Mather's) and begin life over again in a dark primeval forest, establishing the fron-

tier of Europe 3,000 miles across the turbulent Atlantic? Whatever motive we may choose to emphasize, most of them thought of themselves as refugees from tyranny and persecution.

A radical group came first, the small band of Pilgrims who founded Plymouth in 1620. They were poor and humble and devout — "cobblers, tailors, feltmakers, and such-like trash," the bishop of London chose to characterize them. Ten years later came the founders of the Massachusetts Bay Colony, a large band of conserva-

3

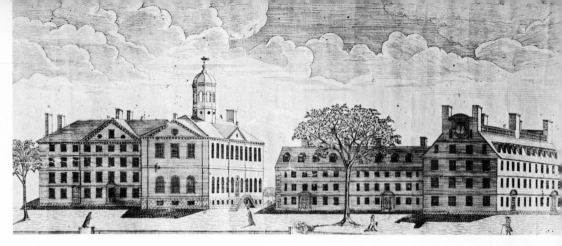

tive Puritans, led by landed gentry, wealthy merchants, university graduates. Their fleet of eleven ships carried livestock, tools, and a full assortment of supplies. With them began a great migration that lasted throughout two decades of turmoil in the mother country. During these years (1620–1640) the Puritans spread along the coast from Maine almost to what is now surburban New York. By 1640, when Virginia had 8,000 white people, New England had 14,000, chiefly in Massachusetts. Then the influx of new settlers almost ceased. For the next half century the hardy and prolific Puritans were free to develop their own government, economy, and way of life virtually undisturbed by the authorities in England. After the arrival of a Governor-General in 1686 it began to be clear that the independence they had enjoyed in isolation would have to yield, if gradually, to royal insistence on imperial control. But by this time they had given to New England a special character which in some aspects is evident to the present day.

🎔 *A Holy Commonwealth.* The kind of government that the seventeenth-century Puritans wanted, as their aims grew clear, was a theocracy: a Holy Commonwealth governed by God or God's representatives. The clergy were the representatives. They were men of vigorous intellect, deeply learned in theology, Hebrew and Greek. Church and state being closely united, the clergy guided the magistrates. Together they were determined to see to it that the welfare of their Christian society was not to be subverted. They had given up much to come to America and they proposed to have and keep the sort of colony they wanted. Nonconformists in England, in Massachusetts they bristled at any suggestion of nonconformity to their rigid and angular conceptions. Quakers, for example, were banished and, if they returned, executed.

Harvard, like many early American colleges, was founded for the training of ministers. Michael Wigglesworth, Edward Taylor, Cotton Mather, and Samuel Sewall were among her seventeenth-century graduates.

Cotton Mather

Samuel Sewall

Puritan Child, 1670

This charming portrait by an unknown painter — the subject is one Margaret Gibbs — suggests the religious and moral sternness of certain levels of colonial society, and the child's elaborate costume attests to the Puritan love of finery.

Along with intolerance, however, the administration possessed qualities we can readily admire, such as willingness to accept an undesired office, a strong sense of justice and order, a remarkable probity of conduct. "I have found no record," says the historian Morison, "of malfeasance in public life in any New England colony or state, before the nineteenth century — there have been plenty since the religious sanction evaporated."

The Puritans came from the middle and lower classes. In the absence of an aristocracy such as England had, they accorded primacy to the wealthier and more cultivated merchants and landowners. Below them came the smaller merchants, storekeepers, farmers, artisans, mechanics, fishermen, free day laborers, and indentured servants and slaves (Indian slaves, a few Negroes). A fussy concern for social distinctions is well illustrated by the seating arrangements in church, which were based upon the class, age, and special qualifications of each person and upon the relative prestige of the seats themselves ("the fore seat in the front gallery shall be equal in dignity with the second seat in the body"). There was of course no leisure class; work, diligence, and thrift were regarded as godly virtues, as by middle-class Englishmen generally. They gave redoubled emphasis, in their frontier situation, to the view expressed, for example, by Richard Baxter in England: "If God show you a way in which you may lawfully get more than in another way (without wrong to your soul or to any other), if you refuse this, and choose the less gainful way, you cross one of the ends of your calling, and you refuse to be God's steward." With the help of oxen and wooden plows they wrested wheat and Indian corn from the poor soil, but the economy depended increasingly upon lumbering, shipbuilding, fishing, and commerce. Particu-

(*continued on page 7*)

Jonathan Edwards

In a time of growing worldliness, Edwards, philosopher, theologian, and preacher, made the last and greatest statement of New England Calvinism. Along with a powerful intellect, he possessed a mystical love of God and a poetic feeling for nature.

"Wilhelmina Byrd,"
by Charles Bridges

Daughter of the accomplished and
fashionable William Byrd of Westover, Wilhelmina enjoyed the fruits
of her father's vast land holdings and
his extensive trade in tobacco, slaves,
and rum. Customs in Virginia differed widely from those in the northern
colonies.

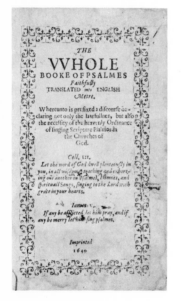

Title Page, "Bay Psalm Book," 1640

The first book printed in America was done by Stephen Day on the
premises of Harvard College. Psalm-singing was the only church music
considered by the Puritans to have scriptural authority, but their first
metrical version of the psalms, while accurate and singable, was so awkward that it reflected little of the poetic beauty of the originals.

"Quaker Meeting," from an
Early Book Illustration

The Society of Friends, living in spiritual
love and quietness, followed a religion simple and personal, alien to the ceremonious
and priestly. Persecuted for their nonconformity, they established their own colony
in Pennsylvania, which was to become the
cultural center of early America.

larly lucrative was the trade in rum and in slaves (Negroes were carried from Africa to the West Indies, later to the Southern plantations).

GOD AS THE MEASURE

The early New Englanders did not use themselves as a measure of essential reality: they used God. Man they looked upon as not self-sufficient but wholly dependent. They were not rationalists, because they found human reason, unaided, an inadequate guide. They were not romanticists, because they deeply distrusted emotional desire and private intuition. They were not what *we* call realists, because they held ordinary, or matter-of-fact, or scientific reality to be something on the surface of life, not at its heart. Their psychology is a very old one, quite unlike the Freudian, behavioristic, and other interpretations typical of our time. The salient fact about human nature they held to be the soul, the image of God, individually created by God, infused into the body. In the great chain of being, man alone has the "rational soul," which contains the capacities of the lower forms of life, such as the senses and appetites, and adds to them the special human faculties, reason which guides and will which chooses.

In the Fall, man became entirely incapable of virtue save through the operation of divine grace. Owing to the corruption of his reason, of his will, of all his faculties, notably imagination and the affections, man lay open to the perversions of sin. He could be restored to health only by the ministration of grace — "holy sparks of Heavenly fire" which might kindle him at any moment, inflame his higher nature, renew head and heart simultaneously. The sparks might come in various ways: an experience of bereavement, any affliction, any providential deliverance, but most commonly through the enkindling words of a minister of the Gospel. One can see how this might happen if the preacher were like John Cotton, a "living, breathing Bible" as he was described by the first graduate of Harvard. But so vital a presence was not necessary. "Whatsoever any faithful minister shall speak out of the Word," said Hooker, "that is also the voice of Christ."

The "Word" out of which the minister speaks is the Word of God, revealed in the Bible. In the Bible, God told man not all, but all that is needful for man to know. Beyond his declared will God has his secret will, not to be fathomed by his creatures; but his declared will, showing us our duties, is enough. We are to conceive of the Bible as a rule by which to measure ourselves and our essential knowledge and proper action, a rule superior to any that human experience might devise. "Crook not God's rules to the experience of men (which is fallible, and many times corrupt), but bring men unto the rule."

Open any of the typical books of the Puritans and you will come upon passages affirming that God or Providence, not erring man, is the final measure. Thus Urian Oakes, onetime president of Harvard: "The successes and events of undertakings and affairs are not determined infallibly by the greatest sufficiency of men, or second causes, but by the counsel and Providence of God ordering and governing time and chance according to his own good pleasure." Or: "See what a poor, dependent nothing-creature proud man is. . . . Man saith, he will do this and that: but he must ask God leave first. He saith, Today or tomorrow I will go to such a place, and buy and sell, and get gain; whereas he knows not what shall be." A merchant, soldier, scholar, or minister, however rationally he may strive, cannot prosper "unless God give him success." A good statesman aims at justice, but it must be the justice of one who fears God, "owns his commission to be from Him," "is a student in the law of God, and meditates in it day and night."

To the Puritans the Bible was a complete body of laws, bringing the spiritual life into relation not only with theology and ethics but all knowledge and all conduct. Anglicans and Puritans agreed in holding that scripture should be harmonious with human reason. To make this possible the Anglicans sought to reduce the doctrines required by scripture to a bare minimum, while the Puritans, extending scripture to cover the whole of life, undertook to show that the entire Bible, from beginning to end, is reasonable. In consequence of this literal and legalistic interpretation, scriptural chapter-and-verse buttressed every proposition in books of theology, science, politics, morals, even had a place in poetry and love letters.

Calvinism. The Puritans claimed the right of the individual to read and interpret the Bible for himself. Yet in the fundamentals of their faith they usually found themselves in large agreement with the teachings of John Calvin, the French Protestant reformer of Geneva. The five points of Calvinism may be stated as follows: First, God elects individuals to be saved. Second, He designs complete redemption only for those elect. Third, fallen man is himself incapable of true faith and repentance. Fourth, God's grace is sufficient for the salvation of the elect. Fifth, a soul once regenerated is never ultimately lost. When the Puritans of New England agreed with Calvin, they did so not because Calvin was authoritative for them but because his teachings seemed confirmed by the Bible and experience.

The Puritan faith made life anything but dull. It produced a high excitement. The world was the setting for a great drama, the drama of man in relation to God and Satan, to Heaven and Hell. It was the drama of the individual human soul, facing unspeakable bliss or unspeakable torment. It was also the drama of the Christian society. Having come to America as to a promised land, the Puritans thought of themselves as a chosen people. In the Holy Commonwealth, the Bible was the constitution, only church members were citizens, and God's ministers guided the state. The more this corporate blessedness was subverted by Satan — acting through the Indians, the witches, and the internal conflicts of the churches — the more passionately was it believed in and propagated. But not even such strenuous leaders as Increase and Cotton Mather could halt the forces of disintegration, and in the failure of Jonathan Edwards and the Great Awakening the whole Calvinistic structure was finally doomed. It was not disproved; it was merely abandoned.

All along, Calvinism had met with opposition of various sorts. In the early years it was shaken by antinomianism, till Anne Hutchinson was banished for sundry heresies, among them the doctrine that God reveals himself directly to individual persons, which ran counter to the Calvinist teaching that God's final revelation was the Bible. Another heresy was the doctrine of Arminianism that salvation could depend on "good works," that is, moral living, which was rejected by the orthodox on the ground that it diminished God's sovereignty — made man a bit uppish In these and other dissenting opinions we can now see that the age was moving, however gradually, away from the concept of a strictly God-centered world toward the man-centered world of the eighteenth century. It was moving from dependence of man on God to dependence of man on himself, from humility toward Providence to pride in human powers. For a new age was coming on, with new beliefs and interests, almost the opposite of Puritan orthodoxy. A rising secular spirit was assuming

or proclaiming that the proper study of mankind is man, that man is not inherently evil but naturally good, and that he is not an exile awaiting the time of felicity (or damnation) but a reasonable creature engaged in the pursuit of happiness in this pleasant world.

Today, we feel less comfortable in the Puritan age than in the age of reason that followed, less at home with Winthrop and Cotton Mather than with Franklin and Jefferson. And yet — the scholarly editors of *The Puritans* conclude — "we are terribly aware once more, thanks to the revelation of psychologists and the events of recent political history, that men are not perfect or essentially good. The Puritan description of them, we have been reluctantly compelled to admit, is closer to what we have witnessed than the description given in Jeffersonian democracy or in transcendentalism."

PURITAN LITERATURE

Settlers of the Atlantic frontier, builders of commonwealths, men of morals and religion, the Puritans were otherwise absorbed than in the production of *belles-lettres*. Yet they did write a considerable amount of prose, much more than the colonists to the south, and more verse than one would expect. We shall have an opportunity to follow the course of their writings chronologically, from Bradford's journal on the Pilgrim settlement to Jonathan Edwards' defence of Calvinism in the increasingly alien eighteenth century — he died in the year when Franklin published "The Way to Wealth." But here, instead of proceeding in the order of time, let us glance at the literature with reference to the types or forms commonly used. They were: historical writings, sermons, and poetry.

❧❧ *Historical Writings.* Historical writings were motivated by a desire to record what had happened or was happening in a very "New" England. Often they consisted of little more than chronicles or annals, setting down contemporary events as Bradford did for the Plymouth plantation and Winthrop for Massachusetts Bay. The scope of other historical works may be suggested by a few titles: Nathaniel Morton's *New England's Memorial*, William Wood's *New England's Prospect* (its natural features), Edward Johnson's *History of New England* (covering 1628–1652), William Hubbard's *Narrative of the Troubles with the Indians*, and the most famous historical work of the period, Cotton Mather's *Magnalia Christi*

Americana, or The Ecclesiastical History of New England (covering 1620–1698).

It goes without saying that such books do not illustrate our modern attempt to write objective or scientific history. The New Englanders generally wrote what may be called providential history. That is, they interpreted their matter in the light of the theory that the key to history is Providence, the direct divine guidance of the world. Following a tradition that goes back to St. Augustine and classical antiquity, they believed that the great, commanding reality in life is the operation of God's will, in general and in detail. The art of history, consequently, must show this through things that have happened, must bring out the high meaning of particular events and the general sequence of events.

Along with history there were other forms of narrative record. Thus, within the loose structure of his ecclesiastical history of New England, Cotton Mather included a large number of biographies. The Puritans also wrote autobiographies, such as the "Personal Narrative" of Jonathan Edwards, and no end of diaries. Practically all Puritans who could write kept a diary, as a record of constant self-examination. The center of concern was the course not of the outer life, but of the inner. Every fluctuation of inner condition, every temptation, doubt, bewilderment, struggle, every moment of insight or ecstasy, of deep humility or resurgence of pride (if only pride in being humble) was of absorbing interest to men and women uncertain whether their hearts had indeed been visited by grace, whether they were truly progressing in their pilgrimage toward the Celestial City.

Diarists had little or nothing to say of their mundane affairs, their vocations, their practical decisions, how people dealt with each other, behaved, dressed, etc. To this there is one notable exception, a late Puritan, Samuel Sewall. His life span carried him from the middle of the seventeenth century through the first third of the eighteenth, and his diary reflects the spirit of the changing times. The earlier entries record the usual self-examination, but as time went on this Yankee judge found it worth while to set down more and more details of a worldly sort, with a sense of the picturesque and a personal flavor that give his pages "human interest."

Sermons. Most of the published prose of the Puritan age consisted of sermons and controversial writings. These were central in the intellectual life which the clergy controlled. In our own time the map of life is drawn for us by scientists, journalists, novelists, by the producers of motion pictures and television, but in Puritan New England it was virtually the clergy alone who performed this function. In addition to providing leadership in church and state, they were the writing class. Various aspects of church and state, of theology and church government, of moral and practical needs in a Christian society were subjects of many treatises and tracts. They were written by such men as Roger Williams, Nathaniel Ward, John Cotton, Thomas Hooker, Increase Mather, Cotton Mather, and later, at their best, by Jonathan Edwards. These ministers and scores of others also published numerous sermons.

Sermons, in fact, may be taken as the typical form of Puritan literature. To most people today, seventeenth-century sermons might seem alien and unmeaning, but to the congregations who heard or read them they were often absorbingly important, given close attention, discussed, reconsidered. They provided spiritual enlightenment by means of intellectual stimulation. A sermon was an argument built like a lawyer's brief, with major divisions, headings, and subheadings. After the elucidation of the text came a direct, dry statement of the "Doctrine." Then came the demonstration or proof, in which the reasons and often the sub-reasons were numbered 1, 2, 3, etc. The points were given a logical order, but without transition between them. Doctrine was followed by "Use" or application, again in 1, 2, 3 fashion. There was no peroration or climactic oratory; the sermon simply ended when the argument was complete.

Thus the Puritan sermon was addressed primarily to the logical faculty. It was intended to convince the reason, not excite the imagination; to instruct the mind, not stir the passions. It was quite different from the rich, harmonious oratory of Anglican pulpits in the mother country. The general effect aimed at was called "plainness." Thomas Hooker, perhaps the greatest of New England preachers, said, "I have accounted it the chiefest part of judicious learning to make a hard point easy and familiar in explication." The language was to be fit, not fancy, for "fitness of words," as another writer conceived, "puts wheels to the chariots to carry them to the mind." If (as here) a metaphor or simile was used, it was not to adorn the homespun of the discourse or to divert or dazzle the listener, but simply to make the teaching clear or vital. Often we find abstractions made concrete by means of homely images drawn from farming, fishing, village life, and other familiar concerns. Only rarely do we come upon a passage where language and rhythm are finely molded by poetic feeling. Such a passage occurs in an election day sermon by William Hubbard in 1676. The divine principle of Order he finds in the goodly fabric of our world, and in the invisible heavens where the Almighty has reared his mansion place, and, between the two, in the skies within our ken:

> . . . the firmament, the pavement of that glorious mansion place, although it be the roof of this lower world, may we not there see one star differing from another in glory? There is placed the Sun, the lord and ruler of the day, as well as the Moon, that rules the night, together with the stars, as the common-people of that upper region, who yet do immediately veil their glory, and withdraw their light, when their bridegroom cometh forth of his chamber.

The poet Coleridge would have enjoyed this, if we may judge from his own famous sentence about the moon and the stars in the prose gloss to "The Ancient Mariner."

🕮 *Poetry.* The Puritans published little poetry: a very few books of verse, the rest dispersed in almanacs, biographies, funeral sermons, etc. This was not because they wrote little, for they wrote much; but most of what they wrote was circulated in manuscript or simply preserved in private or not even preserved. What does this mean?

It cannot be that they who wrote so much were hostile to poetry. Heirs of the Renaissance, the Puritans valued the ancient classics, esteemed such moderns as Spenser, Sidney, and (later) Milton, and of course were in sympathy with the Renaissance belief in the ethical foundation of poetry. With such a tradition behind them, and living intensely in the present, they had, it would seem, a situation favorable to a high order of religious poetry. For their failure to publish a body of epic and lyric poetry we must look for reasons other than hostility. One has already been suggested: they were too absorbed in the practical demands of settlement. At the same time they were too absorbed in an austere religion, which made them fearful of the dangers latent in the senses and passions that poetry cultivates; also, in their zeal for solid substance of thought, they undervalued aesthetic expression. Again, they had no public familiar with literary art to address themselves to, and, as likely as not, they simply had a deficiency of talent.

Certainly they made an ominous beginning! In the *Bay Psalm Book* three ministers joined in a literal translation of the Psalms, not even intended to be "poetry" but rather material to be adjusted to the tunes sung in the churches. Two lines will suffice to show the dreadful result:

> The Lord to me a shepherd is,
> want therefore shall not I.

The subordination of aesthetic quality to sound doctrine is strikingly shown by the "best-seller" of Puritan verse, Wigglesworth's *Day of Doom.* It is not devoid of poetic power, but on the whole is little more than versified Calvinism which the pious could readily learn by heart. Within a hundred years it went through ten editions. There is vastly more merit in the work of Anne Bradstreet. Though she was given to imitating an unfortunate model, she had an effectively simple way of her own. We can see that she was capable of a free genuine expression, though she refrained from going beyond the limits set by decorum.

But the one poet who plainly emerges above the rest of the Puritans is Edward Taylor, who published only a little but left in manuscript a large collection of verse virtually unknown till the twentieth century. He is our seventeenth-century "Metaphysical," reminiscent of Donne, Crashaw, and other English poets of the time. T. S. Eliot has defined "metaphysical" poetry in terms of sudden juxtapositions of thought, "conceits," and "the elaboration of a figure of speech to the farthest stage to which ingenuity can carry it." In imagery ranging from common experience (spinning cloth, kneading bread) to more abstract symbols such as the "rose" in "The Reflection," Taylor's best verse illustrates that quality of intellectuality and of unity fusing together heterogeneous material which Eliot finds typical of the seventeenth-century English metaphysical school. Most surprising are passages where the imagery attains a frank, sensuous warmth which, as Kenneth Murdock suggests, might well have seemed to many Puritans dangerous, a warmth more to be expected in an Anglican than in a Puritan poet. In this respect, and in his many allusions to censers, altars, jewelry, incense, and music, Taylor is by no means the orthodox Puritan. His poetry has faults of syntax, metrical crudity, and occasional incoherence, but in its complexity of thought, paradox, and indirection, we recognize qualities frequently associated with modern verse.

PURITANS

William Bradford [1590–1657]

William Bradford was the son of a farmer and a shopkeeper's daughter in Yorkshire, England. As a boy of twelve he became a devoted student of the Bible. He joined a Puritan group that met at the house of William Brewster, and stayed with it, despite family opposition, when it formed a Separatist congregation, i.e. one that withdrew wholly from the Established Church of England. He was among the Separatists who migrated to Holland, where he became a weaver, learned Dutch and some Latin and Hebrew, and built up a library which he took to America.

When the 180-ton *Mayflower* sailed, Bradford was one of about a hundred Separatists and non-Separatist workers (whom he calls "strangers") who made the venture. With him went his first wife Dorothy, who, while he was absent exploring Cape Cod, fell overboard and was drowned — or, as a modern historian puts it, perhaps "took her own life, after gazing for six weeks at the barren sand dunes of Cape Cod." Death was to be a familiar visitor at the Plymouth plantation: by summer half of the colonists were gone.

When John Carver died in the first spring, Bradford, then only thirty-one, was chosen to succeed him as governor of Plymouth. He was re-elected to this position thirty times, serving without salary the first eighteen years. By the end of the first decade, through the arrival of other ships the community numbered about three hundred. By the time Bradford stopped writing his annals in 1650 its population was still under a thousand. In 1691 Plymouth Plantation was merged with the Massachusetts Bay Colony.

In his declining years Bradford tried to read the Old Testament in Hebrew, that he might see "the ancient oracles of God in their native beauty." At his death his possessions included a red waistcoat, a violet cloak, and a large silver beer bowl.

Two hundred years after his death the long-lost manuscript of his journal turned up and was first published. Many historians and literary scholars, in England and America, have agreed in prizing *Of Plymouth Plantation* as one of the great prose works of the seventeenth century. It deals with small-scale but momentous events, giving us an inside view of the life and the fortunes of the little colony. To our troubled generation, as S. E. Morison has summed it up, it is "a story of a simple people inspired by an ardent faith to a dauntless courage in danger, a resourcefulness in dealing with new problems, an impregnable fortitude in adversity, that exalts and heartens one in an age of uncertainty, when courage falters and faith grows dim."

The book is written in a "plain style" as honest and modest as the author himself. Often clumsy and pedestrian, it occasionally breaks through to disciplined ease, or memorable vividness, or quiet elevation. In diction, idiom, and rhythm it belongs to its period, the period of the men who made the King James translation of the Bible.

Further reading: *Of Plymouth Plantation*, ed. S. E. Morison, 1952. Bradford Smith, *Bradford of Plymouth*, 1951. E. F. Bradford, "Conscious Art in Bradford's *History of Plymouth Plantation*," *New England Quarterly*, April 1928.

From *Of Plymouth Plantation*

(w.[1] 1630–50)

A long introduction concerns the departure of the Separatists from England, their life for more than a decade in Holland, the decision to remove to America, the voyage in the *Mayflower*, and the landing. The main body of the work is in the form of annals recording the history of the colony from the settlement in 1620 through the year 1646.

The economic "communism" of the colony, an expedient demanded by the investing capitalists in England for a term of seven years, was reluctantly accepted by the Pilgrims and was abandoned in the third year.

[Arrival at Cape Cod]

After long beating at sea they fell with that land which is called Cape Cod; the which being made and certainly known to be it, they were not a little joyful. After some deliberation had amongst themselves and with the master of the ship, they tacked about and resolved to stand for the southward (the wind and weather being fair) to find some place about Hudson's River for their habitation. But after they had sailed that course about half the day, they fell amongst dangerous shoals and roaring breakers, and they were so far entangled therewith as they conceived themselves in great danger; and the wind shrinking upon them withal, they resolved to bear up again for the Cape and thought themselves happy to get out of those dangers before night overtook them, as by God's good providence they did. And the next day they got into the Cape Harbor where they rid in safety.

A word or two by the way of this cape. It was thus first named by Captain Gosnold and his company, Anno 1602, and after by Captain Smith was called Cape James; but it retains the former name amongst seamen. Also, that point which first showed those dangerous shoals unto

---

[1] A "w" before the date of a selection indicates that the year is that in which the piece was written. Otherwise the years are those of publication.

---

them they called Point Care, and Tucker's Terrour; but the French and Dutch to this day call it Malabar by reason of those perilous shoals and the losses they have suffered there.

Being thus arrived in a good harbor, and brought safe to land, they fell upon their knees and blessed the God of Heaven who had brought them over the vast and furious ocean, and delivered them from all the perils and miseries thereof, again to set their feet on the firm and stable earth, their proper element. And no marvel if they were thus joyful, seeing wise Seneca was so affected with sailing a few miles on the coast of his own Italy, as he affirmed, that he had rather remain twenty years on his way by land than pass by sea to any place in a short time, so tedious and dreadful was the same unto him.

But here I cannot but stay and make a pause, and stand half amazed at this poor people's present condition; and so I think will the reader, too, when he well considers the same. Being thus passed the vast ocean, and a sea of troubles before in their preparation (as may be remembered by that which went before), they had now no friends to welcome them nor inns to entertain or refresh their weatherbeaten bodies; no houses or much less towns to repair to, to seek for succour. It is recorded in Scripture as a mercy to the Apostle and his shipwrecked company, that the barbarians showed them no small kindness in refreshing them, but these savage barbarians, when they met with them (as after will appear) were readier to fill their sides full of arrows than otherwise. And for the season it was winter, and they that know the winters of that country know them to be sharp and violent, and subject to cruel and fierce storms, dangerous to travel to known places, much more to search an unknown coast. Besides, what could they see but a hideous and desolate wilderness, full of wild beasts and wild men — and what multitudes there might be of them they knew not. Neither could they, as it were, go up to the top of Pisgah to view from this wilderness a more goodly country to feed their hopes; for which way soever they turned their eyes (save upward to the heavens) they could have little solace or content in respect of any outward objects. For summer being done, all things stand upon them with a weatherbeaten face, and the whole country, full of woods and thickets, represented a wild and savage hue. If they looked behind them, there was the mighty ocean which they had passed and was now as a main bar and gulf to separate them from all the civil parts of the world. If it be said they had a ship to succour them, it is true; but what heard they daily from the master and company? But that with speed they should look out a place (with their shallop) where they would be, at some near distance; for the season was such as he would not stir from thence till a safe harbor was discovered by them, where they would be, and he might go without danger; and that victuals consumed apace but he must and would keep sufficient for themselves and their return. Yea, it was muttered by some that if they got not a place in time, they would turn them and their goods ashore and leave them. Let it also be considered what weak hopes of supply and succour they left behind them, that might bear up their minds in this sad condition and trials they were under; and they could not but be very small. It is true, indeed, the affections and love of their brethren at Leyden was cordial and entire towards them, but they had little power to help them or themselves; and how the case stood between them and the merchants at their coming away hath already been declared.

What could now sustain them but the Spirit of God and His grace? May not and ought not the children of these fathers rightly say: "Our fathers were Englishmen which came over this great ocean, and were ready to perish in this wilderness; but they cried unto the Lord, and He heard their voice and looked on their adversity," etc. "Let them therefore praise the Lord, because He is good: and His mercies endure forever." "Yea, let them which have been redeemed of the Lord, shew how He hath delivered them from the hand of the oppressor. When they wandered in the desert wilderness out of the way, and found no city to dwell in, both hungry and thirsty, their soul was overwhelmed in them. Let them confess before the Lord His lovingkindness and His wonderful works before the sons of men."***

I shall a little return back, and begin with a combination made by them before they came ashore; being the first foundation of their government in this place. Occasioned partly by the discontented and mutinous speeches that some of the strangers amongst them had let fall from them in the ship: That when they came ashore they would use their own liberty, for none had power to command them, the patent they had being for Virginia and not for New England, which belonged to another government, with which the Virginia Company had nothing to do. And partly that such an act by them done, this their condition considered, might be as firm as any patent, and in some respects more sure.

The form was as followeth:

IN THE NAME OF GOD, AMEN.

We whose names are underwritten, the loyal subjects of our dread Sovereign Lord King James, by the Grace of God of Great Britain, France, and Ireland King, Defender of the Faith, etc.

Having undertaken, for the Glory of God and advancement of the Christian Faith and Honour of our King and Country, a Voyage to plant the First Colony in the Northern Parts of Virginia, do by these presents solemnly and mutually in the presence of God and one of another, Covenant and Combine ourselves together into a Civil Body Politic, for our better ordering and preservation and furtherance of the ends aforesaid; and by virtue hereof to enact, constitute and frame such just and equal Laws, Ordinances, Acts, Constitutions and Offices, from time to time, as shall be thought most meet and convenient for the general good of the Colony, unto which we promise all due submission and obedience. In witness whereof we have hereunder subscribed our names at Cape Cod, the 11th of November, in the year of the reign of our Sovereign Lord King James, of England, France and Ireland the eighteenth, and of Scotland the fifty-fourth. Anno Domini 1620.

After this they chose, or rather confirmed, Mr. John Carver (a man godly and well approved amongst them) their Governor for that year.***

[First Spring, First Thanksgiving]

They now began to dispatch the ship away which brought them over, which lay till about this time, or the beginning of April. The reason on their part why she stayed so long, was the necessity and danger that lay upon them; for it was well towards the end of December before she could land anything here, or they able to receive anything ashore. Afterwards, the 14th of January, the house which they had made for a general rendezvous by casualty fell afire, and some were fain to retire aboard for shelter; then the sickness began to fall sore amongst them, and the weather so bad as they could not make much sooner any dispatch. Again, the Governor and chief of them, seeing so many die and fall down sick daily, thought it no wisdom to send away the ship, their condition considered and the danger they stood in from the Indians, till they could procure some shelter; and therefore thought it better to draw some more charge upon themselves and friends than hazard all. The master and seamen likewise, though before they hasted the passengers ashore to be gone, now many of their men being dead, and of the ablest of them (as is before noted), and of the rest many lay sick and weak; the master durst not put to sea till he saw his men begin to recover, and the heart of winter over.

Afterwards they (as many as were able) began to plant their corn, in which service Squanto stood them in great stead, showing them both the manner how to set it, and after how to dress and tend it. Also he told them, except they got fish and set with it in these old grounds it would come to nothing. And he showed them that in the middle of April they should have store enough come up the brook by which they began to build, and taught them how to take it, and where to get other provisions necessary for them. All which they found true by trial and experience. Some English seed they sowed, as wheat and pease, but it came not to good, either by the badness of the seed or lateness of the season or both, or some other defect.

In this month of April, whilst they were busy about their seed, their Governor (Mr. John Carver) came out of the field very sick, it being a hot day. He complained greatly of his head and lay down, and within a few hours his senses failed, so as he never spake more till he died, which was within a few days after. Whose death was much lamented and caused great heaviness amongst them, as there was cause. He was buried in the best manner they could, with some volleys of shot by all that bore arms. And his wife, being a weak woman, died within five or six weeks after him.

Shortly after, William Bradford was chosen Governor in his stead, and being not recovered of his illness, in which he had been near the point of death, Isaac Allerton was chosen to be an assistant unto him who, by renewed election every year, continued sundry years together. Which I here note once for all.

May 12 was the first marriage in this place which, according to the laudable custom of the Low Countries, in which they had lived, was thought most requisite to be performed by the magistrate, as being a civil thing, upon which many questions about inheritances do depend, with other things most proper to their cognizance and most consonant to the Scriptures (Ruth iv) and nowhere found in the Gospel to be laid on the ministers as a part of their office.***

They began now to gather in the small harvest they had, and to fit up their houses and dwellings against winter, being all well recovered in health and strength and had all things in good plenty. For as some were thus employed in affairs abroad, others were exercised in fishing, about cod and bass and other fish, of which they took good store, of which every family had their portion. All the summer there was no want; and now began to come in store of fowl, as winter approached, of which this place did abound when they came first (but afterward decreased by degrees). And besides waterfowl there was great store of wild turkeys, of which they took many, besides venison, etc. Besides they had about a peck a meal a week to a person, or now since harvest, Indian corn to that proportion. Which made many afterwards write so largely of their plenty here to their friends in England, which were not feigned but true reports.

[Communal Farming Fails]

All this while no supply was heard of, neither knew they when they might expect any. So they began to think how they might raise as much corn as they could, and obtain a better crop than they had done, that they might not still thus languish in misery. At length, after much debate of things, the Governor (with the advice of the chiefest amongst them) gave way that they should set corn every man for his own particular, and in that regard trust to themselves; in all other things to go on in the general way as before. And so assigned to every family a parcel of land, according to the proportion of their number, for that end, only for present use (but made no division for inheritance) and ranged all boys and youth under some family. This had very good success, for it made all hands very industrious, so as much more corn was planted than otherwise would have been by any means the Governor or any other could use, and saved him a great deal of trouble, and gave far better content. The women now went willingly into the field, and took their little ones with them to set corn; which before would allege weakness and inability; whom to have compelled would have been thought great tyranny and oppression.

The experience that was had in this common course and condition, tried sundry years and that amongst godly and sober men, may well evince the vanity of that conceit of Plato's and other ancients applauded by some of later times; that the taking away of property and bringing in community into a commonwealth would make them happy and flourishing; as if they were wiser than God. For this community (so far as it was) was found to breed much confusion and discontent and retard much employment that would have been to their benefit and comfort. For the young men, that were most able and fit for labour and service, did repine that they should spend their time and strength to work for other men's wives and children without any recompense. The strong, or man of parts, had no more in division of victuals and clothes than he that was weak and not able to do a quarter the other could; this was thought injustice. The aged and graver men to be ranked and equalized in labours and victuals, clothes, etc., with the meaner and younger sort, thought it some indignity and disrespect unto them. And for men's wives to be commanded to do service for other men, as dressing their meat, washing their clothes, etc., they deemed it a kind of slavery, neither could many husbands well brook it. Upon the point all being to have alike, and all to do alike, they thought themselves in the like condition, and one as good as another; and so, if it did not cut off those relations that God hath set amongst men, yet it did at least much diminish and take off the mutual respects that should be preserved amongst them. And would have been worse if they had been men of another condition. Let none object this is men's corruption, and nothing to the course itself. I answer, seeing all men have this corruption in them, God in His wisdom saw another course fitter for them.***

[Dancing and Frisking and Worse]

There came over one Captain Wollaston (a man of pretty parts) and with him three or four more of some eminency, who brought with them a great many servants, with provisions and other implements for to begin a plantation. And pitched themselves in a place within the Massachusetts which they called after their Captain's name, Mount Wollaston. Amongst whom was one Mr. Morton, who it should seem had some small adventure of his own or other men's amongst them, but had little respect amongst them, and was slighted by the meanest servants. Having continued there some time, and not finding things to answer their expectations nor profit to arise as they looked for, Captain Wollaston takes a great part of the servants and transports them to Virginia, where he puts them off at good rates, selling their time to other men; and writes back to one Mr. Rasdall (one of his chief partners and accounted their merchant) to bring another part of them to Virginia likewise, intending to put them off there as he had done the rest. And he, with the consent of the said Rasdall, appointed one Fitcher to be his Lieutenant and govern the remains of the Plantation till he or Rasdall returned to take further order thereabout. But this Morton abovesaid, having more craft than honesty (who had been a kind of pettifogger of Furnival's Inn) in the others' absence watches an opportunity (commons being but hard amongst them) and got some strong drink and other junkets and made them a feast; and after they were merry, he began to tell them he would give them good counsel. "You see," saith he, "that many of your fellows are carried to Virginia, and if you stay till this Rasdall return, you will also be carried away and sold for slaves with the rest. Therefore I would advise you to thrust out this Lieutenant Fitcher, and I, having a part in the Plantation, will receive you as my partners and consociates; so may you be free from service, and we will converse, plant, trade, and live together as equals and support and protect one another," or to like effect. This counsel was easily received, so they took opportunity and thrust Lieutenant Fitcher out o' doors, and would suffer him to come no more amongst them, but forced him to seek bread to eat and other relief from his neighbours till he could get passage for England.

After this they fell to great licentiousness and led a dissolute life, pouring out themselves into all profaneness. And Morton became Lord of Misrule, and maintained (as it were) a School of Atheism. And after they had got some goods into their hands, and got much by trading with the Indians, they spent it as vainly in quaffing and drinking, both wine and strong waters in great excess (and, as some reported) £10 worth in a morning. They also set up a maypole, drinking and dancing about it many days together, inviting the Indian women for their consorts, dancing and frisking together like so many fairies, or furies, rather; and worse practices. As if they had anew revived and celebrated the feasts of the Roman goddess Flora, or the beastly practices of the mad Bacchanalians. Morton likewise, to show his poetry composed sundry rhymes and verses, some tending to lasciviousness, and others to the detraction and scandal of some persons, which he affixed to this idle or idol maypole. They changed also the name of their place, and instead of calling it Mount Wollaston they call it Merry-mount, as if this jollity would have lasted ever. But this continued not long, for after Morton was sent for England (as follows to be declared) shortly after came over that worthy gentleman Mr. John Endecott, who brought over a patent under the broad seal for the government of the Massachusetts. Who, visiting those parts, caused that maypole to be cut down and rebuked them for their profaneness and admonished them to look there should be better walking. So they or others now changed the name of their place again and called it Mount Dagon.

Now to maintain this riotous prodigality and profuse excess, Morton, thinking himself lawless, and hearing what gain the French and fishermen made by trading of pieces, powder and shot to the Indians, he as the head of this consortship began the practice of the same in these parts. And first he taught them how to use them, to charge and discharge, and what proportion of powder to give the piece, according to the size or bigness of the same; and what shot to use for fowl and what for deer. And having thus instructed them, he employed some of them to hunt and fowl for him, so as they became far more active in that employment than any of the English, by reason of their swiftness of foot and nimbleness of body, being also quick-sighted and by continual exercise well knowing the haunts of all sorts of game. So as when they saw the execution that a piece would do, and the benefit that might come by the same, they became mad (as it were) after them and would not stick to give any price they could attain to for them; accounting their bows and arrows but baubles in comparison of them.

And here I may take occasion to bewail the mischief that this wicked man began in these parts, and which since, base covetousness prevailing in men that should know better, has now at length got the upper hand and made this thing common, notwithstanding any laws to the contrary. So as the Indians are full of pieces all over, both fowling pieces, muskets, pistols, etc. They have also their moulds to make shot of all sorts, as musket bullets, pistol bullets, swan and goose shot, and of smaller sorts. Yea some have seen them have their screw-plates to make screw-pins themselves when they want them, with sundry other implements, wherewith they are ordinarily better fitted and furnished than the English themselves. Yea, it is well known that they will have powder and shot when the English want it nor cannot get it; and that in a time of war or danger, as experience hath manifested, that when lead hath been scarce and men for their own defense would gladly have given a groat a pound, which is dear enough, yet hath it been bought up and sent to other places and sold to such as trade it with the Indians at 12d the pound. And it is like they give 3s or 4s the pound, for they will have it at any rate. And these things have been done in the same times when some of their neighbours and friends are daily killed by the Indians, or are in danger thereof and live but at the Indians' mercy. Yea some, as they have acquainted them with all other things, have told them how gunpowder is made, and all the materials in it, and that they are to be had in their own land; and I am confident, could they attain to make saltpeter, they would teach them to make powder.

O, the horribleness of this villainy! How many both Dutch and English have been lately slain by those Indians thus furnished, and no remedy provided; nay, the evil more increased, and the blood of their brethren sold for gain (as is to be feared) and in what danger all these colonies are in is too well known. O that princes and parliaments would take some timely order to prevent this mischief and at length to suppress it by some exemplary punishment upon some of these gain-thirsty murderers, for they deserve no better title, before their colonies in these parts be overthrown by these barbarous savages thus armed with their own weapons, by these evil instruments and traitors to their neighbours and country! But I have forgot myself and have been too long in this digression; but now to return.

This Morton having thus taught them the use of pieces, he sold them all he could spare, and he and his consorts determined to send for many out of England and had by some of the ships sent for above a score. The which being known, and his neighbours meeting the Indians in the woods armed with guns in this sort, it was a terror unto them who lived stragglingly and were of no strength in any place. And other places (though more remote) saw this mischief would quickly spread over all, if not prevented. Besides, they saw they should keep no servants, for Morton would entertain any, how vile soever, and all the scum of the country or any discontents would flock to him from all places, if this nest was not broken. And they should stand in more fear of their lives and goods in short time from this wicked and debased crew than from the savages themselves.

So sundry of the chief of the straggling plantations, meeting together, agreed by mutual consent to solicit those of Plymouth (who were then of more strength than them all) to join with them to prevent the further growth of this mischief, and suppress Morton and his consorts before they grew to further head and strength. Those that joined in this action, and after contributed to the charge of sending him for England, were from Piscataqua, Naumkeag, Winnisimmet, Wessagusset, Nantasket and other places where any English were seated. Those of Plymouth being thus sought to by their messengers and letters, and weighing both their reasons and the common danger, were willing to afford them their help though themselves had least cause of fear or hurt. So, to be short, they first resolved jointly to write to him, and in a friendly and neighbourly way to admonish him to forbear those courses, and sent a messenger with their letters to bring his answer.

But he was so high as he scorned all advice, and asked who had to do with him, he had and would trade pieces with the Indians, in despite of all, with many other scurrilous terms full of disdain. They sent to him a second time and bade him be better advised and more temperate in his terms, for the country could not bear the injury he did. It was against their common safety and against the King's proclamation. He answered in high terms as before; and that the King's proclamation was no law, demanding what penalty was upon it. It was answered, more than he could bear — His Majesty's displeasure. But insolently he persisted and said the King was dead and his displeasure with him, and many the like things. And threatened withal that if any came to molest him, let them look to themselves for he would prepare for them.

Upon which they saw there was no way but to take him by force; and having so far proceeded, now to give over would make him far more haughty and insolent. So they mutually resolved to proceed, and obtained of the Governor of Plymouth to send Captain Standish and some other aid with him, to take Morton by force. The which accordingly was done. But they found him to stand stiffly in his defense, having made fast his doors, armed his consorts, set divers dishes of powder and bullets ready on the table; and if they had not been overarmed with drink, more hurt might have been done. They summoned him to yield, but he kept his house and they could get nothing but scoffs and scorns from him. But at length, fearing they would do some violence to the house, he and some of his crew came out, but not to yield but to shoot; but they were so steeled with drink as their pieces were too heavy for them. Himself with a carbine, overcharged and almost half filled with powder and shot, as was after found, had thought to have shot Captain Standish; but he stepped to him and put by his piece and took him. Neither was there any hurt done to any of either side, save that one was so drunk that he ran his own nose upon the point of a sword that one held before him, as he entered the house; but he lost but a little of his hot blood.

Morton they brought away to Plymouth, where he was kept till a ship went from the Isle of Shoals for England, with which he was sent to the Council of New England, and letters written to give them information of his course and carriage. And also one was sent at their common charge to inform their Honours more particularly and to prosecute against him. But he fooled of the messenger, after he was gone from hence, and though he went for England yet nothing was done to him, not so much as rebuked, for aught was heard, but returned the next year. Some of the worst of the company were dispersed and some of the more modest kept the house till he should be heard from. But I have been too long about so unworthy a person, and bad a cause.***

[Pequot War, and a Murder]

In the fore part of this year [1637], the Pequots fell openly upon the English at Connecticut, in the lower parts of the river, and slew sundry of them as they were at work in the fields, both men and women, to the great terrour of the rest, and went away in great pride and triumph, with many high threats. They also assaulted a fort at the river's mouth, though strong and well defended; and though they did not there prevail, yet it struck them with much fear and astonishment to see their bold attempts in the face of danger. Which made them in all places to stand upon their guard and to prepare for resistance, and earnestly to solicit their friends and confederates in the Bay of Massachusetts to send them speedy aid, for they looked for more forcible assaults. Mr. Vane, being then Governor, writ from their General Court to them here to join with them in this war. To which they were cordially willing, but took opportunity to write to them about some former things, as well as present, considerable hereabout. The which will best appear in the Governor's answer, which he returned to the same, which I shall here insert.

In the meantime, the Pequots, especially in the winter before, sought to make peace with the Narragansetts, and used very pernicious arguments to move them thereunto: as that the English were strangers and began to overspread their country, and would deprive them thereof in time, if they were suffered to grow and increase. And if the Narragansetts did assist the English to subdue them, they did but make way for their own overthrow, for if they were rooted out, the English would soon take occasion to subjugate them. And if they would hearken to them they should not need to fear the strength of the English, for they would not come to open battle with them but fire their houses, kill their cattle, and lie in ambush for them as they went abroad upon their occasions; and all this they might easily do without any or little danger to themselves. The which course being held, they well saw the English could not long subsist but they would either be starved with hunger or be forced to forsake the country. With many the like things; insomuch that the Narragansetts were once wavering and were half minded to have made peace with them, and joined against the English. But again, when they considered how much wrong they had received from the Pequots, and what an opportunity they now had by the help of the English to right themselves; revenge was so sweet unto them as it prevailed above all the rest, so as they resolved to join with the English against them, and did.

The Court here agreed forthwith to send fifty men at their own charge; and with as much speed as possibly they could, got them armed and had made them ready under sufficient leaders, and provided a bark to carry them provisions and tend upon them for all occasions. But when they were ready to march, with a supply from the Bay, they had word to stay; for the enemy was as good as vanquished and there would be no need.

I shall not take upon me exactly to describe their proceedings in these things, because I expect it will be fully done by themselves who best know the carriage and circumstances of things. I shall therefore but touch them in general. From Connecticut, who were most sensible of the hurt sustained and the present danger, they set out a party of men, and another party met them from the Bay, at Narragansetts', who were to join with them. The Narragansetts were earnest to be gone before the English were well rested and refreshed, especially some of them which came last. It should seem their desire was to come upon the enemy suddenly and undiscovered. There was a bark of this place, newly put in there, which was come from Connecticut, who did encourage them to lay hold of the Indians' forwardness, and to show as great forwardness as they, for it would encourage them, and expedition might prove to their great advantage. So they went on, and so ordered their march as the Indians brought them to a fort of the enemy's (in which most of their chief men were) before day. They approached the same with great silence and surrounded it both with English and Indians, that they might not break out; and so assaulted them with great courage, shooting amongst them, and entered the fort with all speed. And those that first entered found sharp resistance from the enemy who both shot at and grappled with them; others ran into their houses and brought out fire and set them on fire, which soon took in their mat; and standing close together, with the wind all was quickly on a flame, and thereby more were burnt to death than was otherwise slain. It burnt their bowstrings and made them unserviceable; those that scaped the fire were slain with the sword, some hewed to pieces, others run through with their rapiers, so as they were quickly dispatched and very few escaped. It was conceived they thus destroyed about 400 at this time. It was a fearful sight to see them thus frying in the fire and the streams of blood quenching the same, and horrible was the stink and scent thereof; but the victory seemed a sweet sacrifice, and they gave the praise thereof to God, who had wrought so wonderfully for them, thus to enclose their enemies in their hands and give them so speedy a victory over so proud and insulting an enemy.***

This year [1638], Mr. Thomas Prence was chosen Governor.

Amongst other enormities that fell out amongst them; this year three men were after due trial executed for robbery and murder which they had committed. Their names were these: Arthur Peach, Thomas Jackson and Richard Stinnings. There was a fourth, Daniel Cross, who was also guilty, but he escaped away and could not be found.

This Arthur Peach was the chief of them, and the ringleader of all the rest. He was a lusty and a desperate young man, and had been one of the soldiers in the Pequot War and had done as good service as the most there, and one of the forwardest in any attempt. And being now out of means and loath to work, and falling to idle courses and company, he intended to go to the Dutch plantation; and had allured these three, being other men's servants and apprentices, to go with him. But another cause there was also of his secret going away in this manner. He was not only run into debt, but he had got a maid with child (which was not known till after his death), a man's servant in the town, and fear of punishment made him get away. The other three complotting with him ran away from their masters in the night, and could not be heard of; for they went not the ordinary way, but shaped such a course as they thought to avoid the pursuit of any. But falling into the way that lieth between the Bay of Massachusetts and the Narragansetts, and being disposed to rest themselves, struck fire and took tobacco, a little out of the way by the wayside.

At length there came a Narragansett Indian by, who had been in the Bay a-trading, and had both cloth and beads about him — they had met him the day before, and he was now returning. Peach called him to drink tobacco with them, and he came and sat down with them. Peach told the other he would kill him and take what he had from him, but they were something afraid. But he said, "Hang him, rogue, he had killed many of them." So they let him alone to do as he would. And when he saw his time, he took a rapier and ran him through the body once or twice and took from him five fathom of wampum and three coats of cloth and went their way, leaving him for dead. But he scrambled away when they were gone, and made shift to get home, but died within a few days after. By which means they were discovered. And by subtlety the Indians took them; for they, desiring a canoe to set them over a water, not thinking their fact had been known, by the sachem's command they were carried to Aquidneck Island and there accused of the murder, and were examined and committed upon it by the English there.

The Indians sent for Mr. Williams and made a grievous complaint; his friends and kindred were ready to rise in arms and provoke the rest thereunto, some conceiving they should now find the Pequots' words true, that the English would fall upon them. But Mr. Williams pacified them and told them they should see justice done upon the offenders, and went to the man and took Mr. James, a physician, with him. The man told him who did it, and in what manner it was done; but the physician found his wounds mortal and that he could not live, as he after testified upon oath before the jury in open court. And so he died shortly after, as both Mr. Williams, Mr. James and some Indians testified in court.

The Government in the Bay were acquainted with it but referred it hither because it was done in this jurisdiction; but pressed by all means that justice might be done in it, or else the country must rise and see justice done; otherwise it would raise a war. Yet some of the rude and ignorant sort murmured that any English should be put to death for the Indians. So at last they of the Island [Rhode Island] brought them hither, and being often examined and the evidence produced, they all in the end freely confessed in effect all that the Indian accused them of, and that they had done it in the manner aforesaid. And so, upon the forementioned evidence, were cast by the jury and condemned, and executed for the same, September 4. And some of the Narragansett Indians and of the party's friends were present when it was done, which gave them and all the country good satisfaction. But it was a matter of much sadness to them here, and was the second execution which they had since they came; being both for wilful murder, as hath been before related. Thus much of this matter.

John Winthrop [1588-1649]

What Bradford was to Plymouth, Winthrop was to Massachusetts Bay.

After a brief course at Trinity College, Cambridge, Winthrop became a prominent lawyer. He was lord of the manor of Groton, but spent much time in London. He went through the spiritual experience associated with Puritanism, and came to be widely acquainted with leaders of the Puritan party. He took an active part in the formation of the Massachusetts Bay Company, was appointed governor, and in 1630 sailed with a fleet of small vessels for the New World. This was a large migration: there were about seven hundred Puritan gentlemen, yeomen, and indentured servants, contrasting in "quality" as well as numbers with the little band of humble farmers and artisans who had settled at Plymouth a decade earlier. The expedition was well planned, well equipped, well led. In the words of the historians Beard: "Rich in this world's goods, rich in the religious learning of the schools, imbued with a firm belief in the proper subordination of the lower ranks, and endowed with a charter of self-government, the directors of the Massachusetts Company embarked on their great experiment."

By autumn, Winthrop with many of his closer associates settled in Boston, where he built a great house and lived till his death. He was governor or deputy governor for nineteen years, spending much of his private fortune in public service.

Further reading: *Journal*, ed. J. K. Hosmer, 1908. A chapter in S. E. Morison, *Builders of the Bay Colony*, 1930. S. Gray, "The Political Thought of John Winthrop," *New England Quarterly*, 1930.

From Christian Experience

✄ Fundamentally a practical man with a marked talent for leadership, Winthrop was also deeply religious. On his forty-ninth birthday he wrote this account of his spiritual experience following his first marriage at "about 18" (actually, seventeen). It well illustrates the Puritan agonized conscience.

[A Happiness Better than All the World]

About 18 years of age (being a man in stature, and understanding as my parents conceived me) I married into a family under Mr. Culverwell his ministry in Essex; and living there sometimes I first found the ministry of the Word to come home to my heart with power (for in all before I found only light), and after that I found the like in the ministry of many others. So as there began to be some change which I perceived in myself, and others took notice of. Now I began to come under strong exercises of conscience (yet by fits only). I could no longer dally with religion. God put my soul to sad tasks sometimes, which yet the flesh would shake off, and outwear still. I had withal many sweet invitations, which I would willingly have entertained, but the flesh would not give up her interest. The merciful Lord would not thus be answered, but notwithstanding all my stubbornness and unkind rejections of mercy, he left me not till he had overcome my heart to give up itself to him, and to bid farewell to all the world, and until my heart could answer, "Lord! what wilt thou have me do?"

Now came I to some peace and comfort in God and in his ways, my chief delight was therein. I loved a Christian and the very ground he went upon. I honored a faithful minister in my heart and could have kissed his feet: Now

I grew full of zeal (which outran my knowledge and carried me sometimes beyond my calling), and very liberal to any good work. I had an unsatiable thirst after the word of God and could not miss a good sermon, though many miles off, especially of such as did search deep into the conscience. I had also a great striving in my heart to draw others to God. It pitied my heart to see men so little to regard their souls, and to despise that happiness which I knew to be better than all the world besides, which stirred me up to take any opportunity to draw men to God, and by success in my endeavors I took much encouragement hereunto. But these affections were not constant, but very unsettled. By these occasions I grew to be of some note for religion (which did not a little puff me up) and divers would come to me for advice in cases of conscience; — and if I heard of any that were in trouble of mind I usually went to comfort them; so that upon the bent of my spirit this way and the success I found of my endeavors, I gave up myself to the study of Divinity, and intended to enter into the ministry, if my friends had not diverted me.

But as I grew into employment and credit thereby, so I grew also in pride of my gifts, and under temptations which set me on work to look to my evidence more narrowly than I had done before (for the great change which God had wrought in me, and the general approbation of good ministers and other Christians, kept me from making any great question of my good estate), though my secret corruptions, and some tremblings of heart (which was greatest when I was among the most godly persons) put me to some plunges; but especially when I perceived a great decay in my zeal and love, etc. And hearing sometimes of better assurance by the seal of the Spirit, which I also knew by the word of God, but could not, nor durst say that ever I had it; and finding by reading of Mr. Perkin's and other books, that a reprobate might (in appearance) attain to as much as I had done; finding withal much hollowness and vain glory in my heart, I began to grow very sad, and knew not what to do: I was ashamed to open my case to any minister that knew me; I feared it would shame myself and religion also, that such an eminent professor as I was accounted, should discover such corruptions as I found in myself; and had in all this time attained no better evidence of salvation; and [if] I should prove a hypocrite, it was too late to begin anew: I should never repent in truth; having repented so oft as I had done. It was like Hell to me to think of that in Hebr. 6. Yet I should sometimes propound questions afar off to such of the most godly ministers as I met, which gave me ease for the present, but my heart could not find where to rest; but I grew very sad and melancholy; and now to hear others applaud me, was a dart through my liver; for still I feared I was not sound at the root, and sometimes I had thoughts of breaking from my profession, and proclaim myself an hypocrite. But these troubles came not all at once but by fits, for sometimes I should find refreshing in prayer, and sometimes in the love that I had had to the Saints.

Letters to (and from) His Wife

After burying two wives, Winthrop was married in 1618 to Margaret, daughter of Sir John Tyndall, of Great Maplestead, Essex. She bore him eight children (in all he had fifteen). A year after Winthrop sailed she followed him to America.

Some Old Puritan Love Letters: John and Margaret Winthrop afford intimate glimpses of the Puritan heart and faith. The letters given below were written when the Winthrops had been married a decade.

MY MOST SWEET HUSBAND,

How dearly welcome thy kind letter was to me, I am not able to express. The sweetness of it did much refresh me. What can be more pleasing to a wife, than to hear of the welfare of her best beloved, and how he is pleased with her poor endeavors! I blush to hear myself commended, knowing my own wants. But it is your love that conceives the best, and makes all things seem better than they are. I wish that I may be always pleasing to thee, and that those comforts we have in each other may be daily increased, as far as they be pleasing to God. I will use that speech to thee, that Abigail did to David, I will be a servant to wash the feet of my lord. I will do any service wherein I may please my good husband. I confess I cannot do enough for thee; but thou art pleased to accept the will for the deed, and rest contented.

I have many reasons to make me love thee, whereof I will name two: First, because thou lovest God; and, secondly, because that thou lovest me. If these two were wanting, all the rest would be eclipsed. But I must leave this discourse, and go about my household affairs. I am a bad housewife to be so long from them;

but I must needs borrow a little time to talk with thee, my sweet heart. The term is more than half done. I hope thy business draws to an end. It will be but two or three weeks before I see thee, though they be long ones. God will bring us together in his good time; for which time I shall pray. I thank the Lord, we are all in health. We are very glad to hear so good news of our son Henry. The Lord make us thankful for all his mercies to us and ours. And thus, with my mother's and my own best love to yourself and all the rest, I shall leave scribbling. The weather being cold, makes me make haste. Farewell, my good husband; the Lord keep thee.

Your obedient wife,

MARGARET WINTHROP.

GROTON [ENGLAND]. *November 22* [1628].

[P.S.] I have not yet received the box; but I will send for it. I send up a turkey and some cheese. I pray send my son Forth such a knife as mine is. Mrs. Hugen would pray you to buy a cake for the boys.

I did dine at Groton Hall yesterday; they are in health, and remember their love. We did wish you there, but that would not bring you, and I could not be merry without thee. Mr. Lee and his wife were there; they remember their love. Our neighbor Cole and goodman Newton have been sick, but somewhat amended again. I fear thy cheese will not prove so good as thou didst expect. I have sent it all, for we could not cut it.

MY FAITHFUL AND DEAR WIFE,

It pleaseth God, that thou shouldst once again hear from me before our departure, and I hope this shall come safe to thy hands. I know it will be a great refreshing to thee. And blessed be his mercy, that I can write thee so good news, that we are all in very good health, and, having tried our ship's entertainment now more than a week, we find it agree very well with us. Our boys are well and cheerful, and have no mind of home. They lie both with me, and sleep as soundly in a rug (for we use no sheets here) as ever they did at Groton; and so I do myself, (I praise God). The wind hath been against us this week and more; but this day it has come fair to the north, so as we are preparing (by God's assistance) to set sail in the morning. We have only four ships ready, and some two or three Hollanders go along with us. The rest of our fleet (being seven ships) will not be ready this sennight. We have spent now two Sabbaths on shipboard very comfortably, (God be praised), and are daily more and more encouraged to look for the Lord's presence to go along with us. Henry Kingsbury hath a child or two in the Talbot sick of the measles, but like to do well. One of my men had them at Hampton, but he was soon well again. We are, in all our eleven ships, about seven hundred persons, passengers, and two hundred and forty cows, and about sixty horses. The ship, which went from Plimouth, carried about one hundred and forty persons, and the ship, which goes from Bristowe, carrieth about eighty persons. And now (my sweet soul) I must once again take my last farewell of thee in Old England. It goeth very near to my heart to leave thee; but I know to whom I have committed thee, even to him who loves thee much better than any husband can, who hath taken account of the hairs of thy head, and puts all thy tears in his bottle, who can, and (if it be for his glory) will bring us together again with peace and comfort. Oh, how it refresheth my heart, to think, that I shall yet again see thy sweet face in the land of the living! — that lovely countenance, that I have so much delighted in, and beheld with so great content! I have hitherto been so taken up with business, as I could seldom look back to my former happiness; but now, when I shall be at some leisure, I shall not avoid the remembrance of thee, nor the grief for thy absence. Thou hast thy share with me, but I hope the course we have agreed upon will be some ease to us both. Mondays and Fridays, at five of the clock at night, we shall meet in spirit till we meet in person. Yet, if all these hopes should fail, blessed be our God, that we are assured we shall meet one day, if not as husband and wife, yet in a better condition. Let that stay and comfort thy heart. Neither can the sea drown thy husband, nor enemies destroy, nor any adversary deprive thee of thy husband or children. Therefore I will only take thee now and my sweet children in mine arms, and kiss and embrace you all, and so leave you with my God. Farewell, farewell. I bless you all in the name of the Lord Jesus. I salute my daughter Winth. Matt. Nan. and the rest, and all my good neighbors and friends. Pray all for us. Farewell. Commend my blessing to my son John. I cannot now write to him; but tell him I have committed thee and thine to him. Labor to draw him yet nearer to God, and he will be

the surer staff of comfort to thee. I cannot
name the rest of my good friends, but thou
canst supply it. I wrote, a week since, to thee
and Mr. Leigh, and divers others.

                    Thine wheresoever,
                                JO. WINTHROP.
    From aboard the *Arbella,* riding at the
COWES, *March 28, 1630.*

Journal

Winthrop began his journal at Southampton,
when the ship *Arbella* was preparing to embark, and
continued till shortly before his death. Although he
was less gifted than Bradford as a writer, his journal
is a valuable record.

[Control of Wages and Prices]

[1633] The scarcity of workmen had caused
them to raise their wages to an excessive rate,
so as a carpenter would have three shillings the
day, a labourer two shillings and sixpence, etc.;
and accordingly those who had commodities to
sell advanced their prices sometimes double to
that they cost in England, so as it grew to a
general complaint, which the court, taking
knowledge of, as also of some further evils,
which were springing out of the excessive rates
of wages, they made an order, that carpenters,
masons, etc. should take but two shillings the
day, and labourers but eighteen pence, and that
no commodity should be sold at above four
pence in the shilling more than it cost for ready
money in England; oil, wine etc. cheese, in
regard of the hazard of bringing, etc. [excepted].
The evils which were springing etc. were, 1.
Many spent much time idly, etc. because they
could get as much in four days as would keep
them a week. 2. They spent much in tobacco
and strong waters, etc. which was a great waste
to the commonwealth, which, by reason of so
many foreign commodities expended, could not
have subsisted to this time, but that it was
supplied by the cattle and corn, which were sold
to new comers at very dear rates, viz. corn at six
shillings the bushel, a cow at £20, — yea, some
at £24, some £26, — a mare at £35, an ewe goat
at 3 or 4 £; and yet many cattle were every year
brought out of England, and some from Virginia. Soon after order was taken for prices of
commodities, viz. not to exceed the rate of four
pence in the shilling above the price in England,
except cheese and liquors, etc.

[Harvard Commencement]

[1642] Nine bachelors commenced at Cambridge; they were young men of good hope, and
performed their acts, so as gave good proof of
their proficiency in the tongues and arts. The
general court had settled a government or super-
intendency over the college, viz., all the magistrates and elders over the six nearest churches
and the president, or the greatest part of these.
Most of them were now present at this first
commencement, and dined at the college with
the scholars' ordinary commons, which was done
of purpose for the students' encouragement, etc.,
and it gave good content to all.

    At this commencement, complaint was made
to the governors of two young men, of good
quality, lately come out of England, for foul
misbehavior, in swearing and ribaldry speeches,
etc., for which, though they were adulti, they
were corrected in the college, and sequestered,
etc., for a time.

[Trial for Adultery]

[1644] At this court of assistants, one James
Britton, a man ill affected both to our church
discipline and civil government, and one Mary
Latham, a proper young woman about 18 years
of age, whose father was a godly man and had
brought her up well, was condemned to die for
adultery, upon a law formerly made and published in print. It was thus occasioned and
discovered. This woman, being rejected by a
young man whom she had an affection unto,
vowed she would marry the next that came to
her, and accordingly, against her friends' minds,
she matched with an ancient man who had
neither honesty nor ability, and one whom she
had no affection unto. Whereupon, soon after
she was married, divers young men solicited her
chastity, and drawing her into bad company,
and giving her wine and other gifts, easily prevailed with her, and among others this Britton.
But God smiting him with a deadly palsy and
fearful horror of conscience withal, he could not
keep secret, but discovered this, and other the
like with other women, and was forced to
acknowledge the justice of God in that having
often called others fools, etc., for confessing
against themselves, he was now forced to do the
like. The woman dwelt now in Plymouth patent,
and one of the magistrates there, hearing she
was detected, etc., sent her to us. Upon her

examination, she confessed he did attempt the fact, but did not commit it, and witness was produced that testified (which they both confessed) that in the evening of a day of humiliation through the country for England, etc., a company met at Britton's and there continued drinking sack, etc., till late in the night, and then Britton and the woman were seen upon the ground together, a little from the house. It was reported also that she did frequently abuse her husband, setting a knife to his breast and threatening to kill him, calling him old rogue and cuckold, and said she would make him wear horns as big as a bull. And yet some of the magistrates thought the evidence not sufficient against her, because there were not two direct witnesses; but the jury cast her, and then she confessed the fact, and accused twelve others, whereof two were married men. Five of these were apprehended and committed (the rest were gone), but denying it, and there being no other witness against them than the testimony of a condemned person, there could be no proceeding against them. The woman proved very penitent, and had deep apprehension of the foulness of her sin, and at length attained to hope of pardon by the blood of Christ, and was willing to die in satisfaction to justice. The man also was very much cast down for his sins, but was loth to die, and petitioned the general court for his life, but they would not grant it, though some of the magistrates spake much for it, and questioned the letter, whether adultery was death by God's law now. This Britton had been a professor in England, but coming hither he opposed our church government, etc., and grew dissolute, losing both power and profession of godliness.

They were both executed, they both died very penitently, especially the woman, who had some comfortable hope of pardon of her sin, and gave good exhortation to all young maids to be obedient to their parents, and to take heed of evil company, etc.

[A Little Speech on Liberty]

꿋꿋 The charter of the colony left undefined the powers of the magistrates and of the freemen. In the view of a rising democratic element in the commonwealth, Governor Winthrop often seemed arbitrary. Winthrop himself took it for granted that the true ruler is God, that the supreme law or constitution is God's absolute will as expressed in the Bible, and that

it was the responsibility of the magistrates to fulfill the absolute will of God.

"From this conception of the absolute nature of law," as Parrington says, "came the famous discussion of liberty and authority, known as the 'little speech,' which is the most highly praised of Winthrop's utterances. In a certain police-court matter that had loosed the class prejudices of all parties, he had held against the popular feeling, and was impeached before the general court. Upon his acquittal he rose and addressed the court in words which he afterwards set down in his journal. No other episode in his varied career reveals so well the admirable poise of the man — the dignity, the self-control, the fair-mindedness, despite an attack that hurt him to the quick."

[1645] Then was the deputy governor [Winthrop] desired by the court to go up and take his place again upon the bench, which he did accordingly, and the court being about to arise, he desired leave for a little speech, which was to this effect.

I suppose something may be expected from me, upon this charge that has befallen me, which moves me to speak now to you; yet I intend not to intermeddle in the proceedings of the court, or with any of the persons concerned therein. Only I bless God, that I see an issue of this troublesome business. I also acknowledge the justice of the court, and, for mine own part, I am well satisfied, I was publicly charged, and I am publicly and legally acquitted, which is all I did expect or desire. And though this be sufficient for my justification before men, yet not so before the God, who hath seen so much amiss in my dispensations (and even in this affair) as calls me to be humble. For to be publicly and criminally charged in this court, is matter of humiliation (and I desire to make a right use of it), notwithstanding I be thus acquitted. If her father had spit in her face (saith the Lord concerning Miriam), should she not have been ashamed seven days? Shame had lien upon her, whatever the occasion had been. I am unwilling to stay you from your urgent affairs, yet give me leave (upon this special occasion) to speak a little more to this assembly. It may be of some good use, to inform and rectify the judgments of some of the people, and may prevent such distempers as have arisen amongst us.

The great questions that have troubled the country, are about the authority of the magistrates and the liberty of the people. It is yourselves who have called us to this office, and being called by you, we have our authority from God, in way of an ordinance, such as hath the image of God eminently stamped upon it, the contempt and violation whereof hath been vindicated with examples of divine vengeance. I entreat you to consider, that when you choose magistrates, you take them from among yourselves, men subject to like passions as you are. Therefore when you see infirmities in us, you should reflect upon your own, and that would make you bear the more with us, and not be severe censurers of the failings of your magistrates, when you have continual experience of the like infirmities in yourselves and others. We account him a good servant, who breaks not his covenant. The covenant between you and us is the oath you have taken of us, which is to this purpose, that we shall govern you and judge your causes by the rules of God's laws and our own, according to our best skill. When you agree with a workman to build you a ship or house, etc., he undertakes as well for his skill as for his faithfulness, for it is his profession, and you pay him for both. But when you call one to be a magistrate, he doth not profess nor undertake to have sufficient skill for that office, nor can you furnish him with gifts, etc. therefore you must run the hazard of his skill and ability. But if he fail in faithfulness, which by his oath he is bound unto, that he must answer for. If it fall out that the case be clear to common apprehension, and the rule clear, also, if he transgress here, the error is not in the skill, but in the evil of the will: it must be required of him. But if the case be doubtful, or the rule doubtful, to men of such understanding and parts as your magistrates are, if your magistrates should err here, yourselves must bear it.

For the other point concerning liberty, I observe a great mistake in the country about that. There is a twofold liberty, natural (I mean as our nature is now corrupt) and civil or federal. The first is common to man with beasts and other creatures. By this, man, as he stands in relation to man simply, hath liberty to do what he lists; it is a liberty to evil as well as to good. This liberty is incompatible and inconsistent with authority, and cannot endure the least restraint of the most just authority. The exercise and maintaining of this liberty makes men grow more evil, and in time to be worse than brute beasts: *omnes sumus licentia deteriores* [we are all weakened by liberty]. This is that great enemy of truth and peace, that wild beast, which all the ordinances of God are bent against, to restrain and subdue it. The other kind of liberty I call civil or federal, it may also be termed moral, in reference to the covenant between God and man, in the moral law, and the politic covenants and constitutions, amongst men themselves. This liberty is the proper end and object of authority, and cannot subsist without it; and it is a liberty to that only which is good, just, and honest. This liberty you are to stand for, with the hazard, not only of your goods, but of your lives, if need be. Whatsoever crosseth this, is not authority, but a distemper thereof. This liberty is maintained and exercised in a way of subjection to authority; it is of the same kind of liberty wherewith Christ hath made us free. The woman's own choice makes such a man her husband; yet being so chosen, he is her lord, and she is to be subject to him, yet in a way of liberty, not of bondage; and a true wife accounts her subjection her honor and freedom, and would not think her condition safe and free, but in her subjection to her husband's authority. Such is the liberty of the church under the authority of Christ, her king and husband; his yoke is so easy and sweet to her as a bride's ornaments; and if through frowardness or wantonness, etc. she shake it off, at any time, she is at no rest in her spirit, until she take it up again; and whether her lord smiles upon her, and embraceth her in his arms, or whether he frowns, or rebukes, or smites her, she apprehends the sweetness of his love in all, and is refreshed, supported and instructed by every such dispensation of his authority over her. On the other side, ye know who they are that complain of this yoke and say, let us break their bands, etc. we will not have this man to rule over us. Even so, brethren, it will be between you and your magistrates. If you stand for your natural corrupt liberties, and will do what is good in your own eyes, you will not endure the least weight of authority, but will murmur, and oppose, and be always striving to shake off that yoke; but if you will be satisfied to enjoy such civil and lawful liberties, such as Christ allows you, then will you quietly and cheerfully submit unto that authority which is set over you, in all the administrations of it, for your good. Wherein, if we fail at any time, we hope we shall be willing (by God's assistance) to hearken to good advice from any of you, or in any other way of God; so shall your liberties be preserved, in upholding the honor and power of authority amongst you.

Anne Bradstreet [1612–1672]

Born in England, the writer of the first considerable verse in America was the daughter of Thomas Dudley, steward to the Earl of Lincoln. She was educated amid surroundings of wealth; at one time she had eight tutors, and a large library was always at her disposal. At the age of sixteen she married Simon Bradstreet, a Cambridge graduate, and a year later they sailed with John Winthrop for Massachusetts. Her father and her husband both became governors of the colony.

Mrs. Bradstreet was the mother of eight children. She was a loving wife and a busy hostess, but in spite of her large family, illness, and untold duties she managed to write verse enough to fill a volume of 400 pages. This book, published anonymously in London in 1650, bore the title: *THE TENTH MUSE Lately sprung up in America. Severall Poems, compiled with great variety of Wit and Learning, full of delight. Wherein especially is contained a compleat discourse and description of the Four Elements, Constitutions, Ages of Man, Seasons of the Year. Together with an exact epitome of the Four Monarchies, viz. The Assyrian, Persian, Grecian, Roman. Also a Dialogue between Old England and New, concerning the late troubles. With divers other pleasant and serious Poems. By a Gentlewoman in those parts.*

In her later work, which did not appear till the second edition of her poems in 1678, she is less dominated by literary masters — such as Du Bartas, Sidney, and Spenser — and is more truly herself, a real person, an admirable Puritan woman who has found a voice and, in ample modesty, has dared to use it. Our selections are from this later and better work.

Further reading: *Works*, ed. J. H. Ellis, 1867, 1932. S. E. Morison, *Builders of the Bay Colony*, 1930.

The Author to Her Book

(1678)

Anne Bradstreet wrote poems for her own satisfaction. But without her knowledge, a brother-in-law, "less wise than true," took them to a London publisher and had them "expos'd to public view" in cold type. Her book was labeled with a foolish title. Readers of that day if not of ours were well aware that in Greek mythology there were nine muses or goddesses of poetry, song, etc. The hapless Mrs. Bradstreet was thus *The Tenth Muse Lately Sprung up in America!*

She planned a revised edition "in better dress," which was finally published in Boston eight years after her death. It included new poems, among them "The Author to Her Book" and nearly all the others given below.

Thou ill-form'd offspring of my feeble brain,
Who after birth did'st by my side remain,
Till snatcht from thence by friends, less wise
    than true
Who thee abroad expos'd to public view,   4
Made thee in rags, halting to th' press to trudge,
Where errors were not lessened (all may judge).
At thy return my blushing was not small,
My rambling brat (in print) should mother call.
I cast thee by as one unfit for light,
Thy visage was so irksome in my sight;   10
Yet being mine own, at length affection would
Thy blemishes amend, if so I could:
I wash'd thy face, but more defects I saw,
And rubbing off a spot, still made a flaw.
I stretcht thy joints to make thee even feet,   15
Yet still thou run'st more hobbling than is meet;

In better dress to trim thee was my mind,
But nought save home-spun cloth, i' th' house
    I find.
In this array, 'mongst vulgars mayst thou roam,
In critics' hands beware thou dost not come; 20
And take thy way where yet thou art not known,
If for thy father asked, say, thou hadst none:
And for thy mother, she alas is poor,
Which caus'd her thus to send thee out of door.

The Flesh and the Spirit

(1678)

"Many times," Mrs. Bradstreet confessed, "hath
Satan troubled me concerning the verity of the
scriptures, many times by atheism how I could know
whether there was a God." Like other people she
had her doubts, and felt herself drawn in opposite
directions by the claims of two sides of human nature. For her conception of this conflict she was
presumably indebted to the eighth chapter of St.
Paul's Epistle to the Romans, and for the form, to
the convention of the debate, a popular literary type
in the Middle Ages (*The Owl and the Nightingale*,
The Debate of the Body and the Soul, etc.).

Today (as for nearly two centuries past) the usual
dualism is that of the individual and society. For the
Puritans (as for St. Paul and Christianity generally)
it was an internal struggle between two aspects of
the self. In the poem, these aspects are the flesh —
the natural self begotten by Adam — and the spirit
— the self that comes "from above." They are in
"deadly feud." Each sister states what she objects
to in the other's values, and what values she herself
believes in. As might be expected, Spirit gets the
last word, and she rises to a climax in rapt, symbolical language suggested by Revelation 21:2, "the holy
city, new Jerusalem, coming down from God out of
heaven, prepared as a bride adorned by her husband."
Line 2, "lacrym flood": a stream of tears.

In secret place where once I stood,
Close by the banks of lacrym flood,
I heard two sisters reason on
Things that are past and things to come.
One Flesh was called, who had her eye 5
On worldly wealth and vanity;
The other Spirit, who did rear
Her thoughts unto a higher sphere.
"Sister," quoth *Flesh*, "what livest thou on —
Nothing but meditation? 10
Doth contemplation feed thee, so
Regardlessly to let earth go?
Can speculation satisfy

Notion without reality?
Dost dream of things beyond the moon, 15
And dost thou hope to dwell there soon?
Hast treasures there laid up in store
That all in the world thou countest poor?
Art fancy sick, or turned a sot,
To catch at shadows which are not? 20
Come, come, I'll show unto thy sense
Industry hath its recompense.
What canst desire but thou mayst see
True substance in variety?
Dost honor like? Acquire the same, 25
As some to their immortal fame,
And trophies to thy name erect
Which wearing time shall ne'er deject.
For riches dost thou long full sore?
Behold enough of precious store; 30
Earth hath more silver, pearls, and gold
Than eyes can see or hands can hold.
Affectest thou pleasure? Take thy fill;
Earth hath enough of what you will.
Then let not go what thou mayst find 35
For things unknown, only in mind."

Spirit: "Be still, thou unregenerate part;
Disturb no more my settled heart,
For I have vowed, and so will do,
Thee as a foe still to pursue, 40
And combat with thee will and must
Until I see thee laid in the dust.
Sisters we are, yea, twins we be,
Yet deadly feud 'twixt thee and me;
For from one father are we not. 45
Thou by old Adam was begot,
But my arise is from above,
Whence my dear Father I do love.
Thou speakest me fair, but hatest me sore;
Thy flattering shows I'll trust no more. 50
How oft thy slave hast thou me made
When I believed what thou hast said,
And never had more cause of woe
Than when I did what thou bad'st do.
I'll stop mine ears at these thy charms, 55
And count them for my deadly harms.
Thy sinful pleasures I do hate,
Thy riches are to me no bait,
Thine honors do nor will I love,
For my ambition lies above. 60
My greatest honor it shall be
When I am victor over thee,
And triumph shall, with laurel head,
When thou my captive shalt be led.
How I do live thou needst not scoff, 65
For I have meat thou knowst not of:

The hidden manna I do eat,
The word of life it is my meat.
My thoughts do yield me more content
Than can thy hours in pleasure spent.   70
Nor are they shadows which I catch,
Nor fancies vain at which I snatch,
But reach at things that are so high,
Beyond thy dull capacity.
Eternal substance I do see,   75
With which enrichéd I would be;
Mine eye doth pierce the heavens, and see
What is invisible to thee.
My garments are not silk or gold,
Nor such like trash which earth doth hold,   80
But royal robes I shall have on,
More glorious than the glistering sun.
My crown not diamonds, pearls, and gold,
But such as angels' heads enfold.
The city where I hope to dwell   85
There's none on earth can parallel:
The stately walls, both high and strong,
Are made of precious jasper stone;
The gates of pearl both rich and clear,
And angels are for porters there;   90
The streets thereof transparent gold,
Such as no eye did e'er behold;
A crystal river there doth run,
Which doth proceed from the Lamb's throne;
Of life there are the waters sure,   95
Which shall remain for ever pure;
Of sun or moon they have no need,
For glory doth from God proceed —
No candle there, nor yet torch-light,
For there shall be no darksome night.   100
From sickness and infirmity
For evermore they shall be free,
Nor withering age shall e'er come there,
But beauty shall be bright and clear.
This city pure is not for thee,   105
For things unclean there shall not be.
If I of Heaven may have my fill,
Take thou the world, and all that will.''

Contemplations
(1678)

Mrs. Bradstreet's most famous but not best
poem is a descriptive-didactic production of 33 stanzas, of which a selection may suffice for the modern
reader. Is it fair to say that her pictures of nature
are appreciative but unmagical, her moralizings earnest
but commonplace? Are there signs of her more
simple, natural style?

1

Some time now past in the autumnal tide,
When Phoebus wanted but one hour to bed,
The trees all richly clad, yet void of pride,
Were gilded o'er by his rich golden head;
Their leaves and fruits seemed painted, but was
     true,   5
Of green, of red, of yellow, mixèd hue;
Rapt were my senses at this delectable view.

2

I wist not what to wish. "Yet sure,"
     thought I,
"If so much excellence abide below,
How excellent is He that dwells on high?   10
Whose power and beauty by His works we know!
Sure He is goodness, wisdom, glory, light,
That hath this underworld so richly dight.''
More heaven than earth was here, no winter and
     no night.

3

Then on a stately oak I cast mine eye,   15
Whose ruffling top the clouds seemed to aspire;
"How long since thou wast in thine infancy?
Thy strength and stature, more thy years admire.
Hath hundred winters passed since thou wast
     born,   19
Or thousand since thou brak'st thy shell of horn?
If so, all these as nought eternity doth scorn.''

4

Then higher on the glistering sun I gazed,
Whose beams was shaded by the leafy tree;
The more I looked the more I grew amazed,
And softly said, "What glory's like to thee?   25
Soul of this world, this universe's eye,
No wonder some made thee a deity;
Had I not better known, alas, the same had I.

5

"Thou as a bridegroom from thy chamber
     rushes
And, as a strong man, joys to run a race.   30
The morn doth usher thee with smiles and
     blushes,
The earth reflects her glances in thy face.
Birds, insects, animals, with vegetive,
Thy heart from death and dullness doth revive,
And in the darksome womb of fruitful nature
     dive.   35

6

"Thy swift annual and diurnal course,

Thy daily straight and yearly oblique path,
Thy pleasing fervor and thy scorching force,
All mortals here the feeling knowledge hath.
Thy presence makes it day, thy absence
night,   40
Quaternal seasons causèd by thy might.
Hail, creature, full of sweetness, beauty, and
delight!

7

"Art thou so full of glory that no eye
Hath strength thy shining rays once to hold?
And is thy splendid throne erect so high   45
As to approach it can no earthly mould?
How full of glory then must thy Creator be,
Who gave this bright light luster unto thee!
Admired, adored forever be that majesty!"

8

Silent, alone, where none or saw or heard,   50
In pathless paths I led my wand'ring feet;
My humble eyes to lofty skies I reared;
To sing some song my mazèd Muse thought
meet;
My great Creator I would magnify,
That nature had thus deckèd liberally.   55
But ah, and ah, again, my imbecility!

9

I heard the merry grasshopper then sing,
The black-clad cricket bear a second part;
They kept one tune and played on the same
string,
Seeming to glory in their little art.   60
Shall creatures abject thus their voices raise,
And in their kind resound their Maker's praise,
Whilst I, as mute, can warble forth no higher
lays?***

31

The mariner that on smooth waves doth glide
Sings merrily and steers his bark with ease,   65
As if he had command of wind and tide,
And now become great master of the seas;
But suddenly a storm spoils all the sport
And makes him long for a more quiet port
Which 'gainst all adverse winds may serve for
fort.   70

32

So he that faileth in this world of pleasure,
Feeding on sweets, that never bit of th' sour,

That's full of friends, of honor, and of
treasure,
Fond fool, he takes this earth ev'n for heaven's
bower.
But sad affliction comes and makes him see   75
Here's neither honor, wealth, nor safety;
Only above is found all with security.

33

O time, the fatal wrack of mortal things,
That draws oblivion's curtains over kings;
Their sumptuous monuments, men know them
not;   80
Their names without a record are forgot;
Their parts, their ports, their pomp's all laid in
th' dust;
Nor wit nor gold nor buildings 'scape time's
rust.
But he whose name is graved in the white stone
Shall last and shine when all of these are
gone.   85

To My Dear and Loving Husband

(1678)

strong humanity of P.

Mrs. Bradstreet's best poems, to our modern taste, are the short domestic pieces, those concerning her mother, her husband, her children, her house. In these, whether she writes directly or figuratively, her thought and feeling strike us as genuine and unforced.

They are mostly written with disciplined order. In "To My Dear and Loving Husband," for instance, the first two couplets give a direct statement on the human level, the next two employ figures (gold mines, riches of the Orient, rivers), the last two give a direct statement culminating on the level of the eternal. Meaning is communicated through the simplest words, generally monosyllabic.

If ever two were one, then surely we.
If ever man were lov'd by wife, then thee;
If ever wife was happy in a man,
Compare with me ye women if you can.
I prize thy love more than whole mines of
gold,   5
Or all the riches that the East doth hold.
My love is such that rivers cannot quench,
Nor aught but love from thee give recompence.
Thy love is such I can no way repay,
The heavens reward thee manifold I pray.   10
Then while we live, in love let's so persever,
That when we live no more, we may live ever.

Edward Taylor [1645?–1729]

personal expression of emotions

The most richly endowed of the colonial poets, Edward Taylor wrote his verse, apparently, as a personal expression of emotions which the restraints of Puritan life and custom denied to him. Only his friends read it, and it was not discovered until the present century when a modern scholar published an edition in 1939. The small but impressively "modern" body of his work is now thought to be the most distinguished poetry written in America during the age of the Puritans in the seventeenth century.

Taylor was born near Coventry, England, and emigrated to Boston in 1668, probably as a result of the religious persecutions in 1662 which forced conformity upon dissenters, of whom he was one. A young and eager scholar, he entered Harvard through the influence of Increase Mather, the prominent clergyman, and others to whom he had brought letters of introduction. Trained for the ministry, he accepted a call to the village of Westfield on the Massachusetts frontier. Here, for the remaining fifty-eight years of his life, he served his pastorate and community in a career of usefulness and sermonizing. The accounts of his life show that he was a man of affection and sympathetic emotions toward his fellows, well liked by his friends, "of small stature, but firm; of quick passions, yet serious and grave," as he is described by a grandson, President Stiles of Yale. He was twice married and the father of thirteen children. In 1720 Harvard honored him with a degree of Master of Arts. He died in 1729.

The poetry of Taylor, when finally printed, gave America a "metaphysical" poet at the very time when the work of Eliot and Pound was bringing about a revival of interest in Donne, Vaughan, Crashaw, and others of the English metaphysical school. Taylor's work, though seldom achieving the subtlety and complexity of the best of Donne, nevertheless belongs clearly to that tradition and indicates his own familiarity with the methods and poems of his English contemporaries. Like them he liked to yoke together violent opposites, form verse "conceits," and indulge playfully his delight in everyday life and his intense spiritual yearning for union with God. Even the severe doctrines of the New England Calvinists were softened in his striking analogies of Grace, Sin, Election, and Regeneration with commonplace activities of life such as kneading bread, weaving cloth, or drinking beer. It has been said that his reason for withholding the poems from publication during his lifetime lay in their joyousness and sensuous pleasure which ran counter to characteristic colonial New England attitudes. The two extremes of his poetic language are its realism and its religious mysticism. How successfully he was able to combine them may well be a measure of his individual poems and his work as a whole.

Further reading: *Poetical Works*, ed. T. H. Johnson. T. H. Johnson, life in *Dictionary of American Biography*, Supplement I, page 681. W. C. Brown, "Edward Taylor: an American 'Metaphysical,'" *American Literature*, November, 1944. R. H. Pearce, "Edward Taylor: The Poet as Puritan," *New England Quarterly*, March, 1950.

The Preface

(w. 1682?)

This is a fresh, poetic vision of the world created and formed in grandeur and beauty by Almighty God. The poem may be compared with the account of creation at the beginning of the Bible. Taylor's various allusions to human arts and crafts (lathe, bellows, furnace, mould, etc.) serve to contrast the small creative powers of man with the boundless Might that made all things from a void — "spake all things from nothing." The contrast is deepened at the end by the reference to the fall of man ("sin").

Line 4, "riggaled," grooved; 10, "smaragdine," emerald; 30, "squitchen," may mean switch; 35, "fet," an old form of fetched.

Infinity, when all things it beheld,
In nothing, and of nothing all did build,
Upon what base was fixed the lathe wherein
He turned this globe and riggaled it so trim?
Who blew the bellows of His furnace vast?   5
Or held the mould wherein the world was cast?
Who laid its corner-stone? Or whose command?
Where stand the pillars upon which it stands?
Who laced and filleted the earth so fine
With rivers like green ribbons smaragdine?   10
Who made the seas its selvedge, and it locks
Like a quilt ball within a silver box?
Who spread its canopy? Or curtains spun?
Who in this bowling alley bowled the sun?
Who made it always when it rises, set: 15
To go at once both down and up to get?
Who the curtain rods made for this tapestry?
Who hung the twinkling lanthorns in the sky?
Who? who did this? or who is he? Why, know
It's only Might Almighty this did do.   20
His hand hath made this noble work which
      stands
His glorious handiwork not made by hands.
Who spake all things from nothing; and with
      ease
Can speak all things to nothing, if He please.
Whose little finger at His pleasure can   25
Out mete ten thousand worlds with half a span.
Whose might almighty can by half a look
Root up the rocks and rock the hills by th' roots.
Can take this mighty world up in His hand
And shake it like a squitchen or a wand.   30
Whose single frown will make the heavens shake
Like as an aspen leaf the wind makes quake.
Oh! what a might is this! Whose single frown
Doth shake the world as it would shake it down?
Which all from nothing fet, from nothing
      all;   35

Hath all on nothing set, lets nothing fall.
Gave all to nothing man indeed, whereby
Through nothing man all might Him glorify.
In nothing is embossed the brightest gem
More precious than all preciousness in them.   40
But nothing man did throw down all by sin,
And darkened that lightsome gem in him,
      That now His brightest diamond is grown
      Darker by far than any coal-pit stone.

The Soul's Admiration

If man is all unworthiness, if he is unfit to sing God's praise in this world, how can he hope to sing it in heaven? "Sing" leads the poet to develop his whole theme musically (with string and wind instruments as well as voice).

Line 15, consents: harmony; 18, quavers: eighth notes; 19, kit: miniature violin; 33, heft: raise; 34, stob: stop.

What, I such praises sing! How can it be?
      Shall I in heaven sing?
What, I, that scarce durst hope to see,
      Lord, such a thing?
      Though nothing is too hard for Thee,   5
      One hope hereof seems hard to me.

What, can I ever tune those melodies,
      Who have no tune at all,
Not knowing where to stop nor rise,
      Nor when to fall?   10
      To sing Thy praise I am unfit;
      I have not learned my gamut yet.

But should these praises on stringed instruments
      Be sweetly tuned? I find
I nonplussed am, for no consents   15
      I ever mind.
      My tongue is neither quill nor bow,
      Nor can my fingers quavers show.

But was it otherwise, I have no kit;
      Which though I had, I could   20
Not tune the strings, which soon would slip
      Though others should.
      But should they not, I cannot play,
      But for an F should strike an A.

And should Thy praise upon wind instruments
      Sound all o'er heaven shrill?   26
My breath will hardly through such vents
      A whistle fill.

Which though it should, it's past my spell
   By stops and falls to sound it well.   30

How should I then join in such exercise?
   One sight of Thee'll entice
Mine eyes to heft, whose ecstasies
   Will stob my voice.
Hereby mine eyes will bind my tongue   35
   Unless Thou, Lord, do cut the thong.

What use of useless me then there, poor snake?
   There saints and angels sing
Thy praise in full career, which make
   The heavens to ring.   40
Yet if Thou wilt, Thou canst me raise
   With angels bright to sing Thy praise.

The Joy of Church Fellowship

In contrast with the poet's sense of human inadequacy (the preceding poem), we have here a
picture of the joy of the elect on earth, the saints
"encoached for heaven," singing as they ride to
glory. Even the saints are not quite perfect: they get
out of harmony (line 13) and some walk (line 27)
instead of riding. But the joy and the glory, insisted
upon by the refrain closing each stanza, dominate.

In heaven soaring up I dropt an ear
   On earth, and, oh! sweet melody!
And listening found it was the saints who were
   Encoached for heaven that sang for joy.
   For in Christ's coach they sweetly sing   5
   As they to glory ride therein.

Oh, joyous hearts! Enfired with holy flame!
   Is speech thus tasselèd with praise?
Will not your inward fire of joy contain,
   That it in open flames doth blaze?   10
   For in Christ's coach saints sweetly sing
   As they to glory ride therein.

And if a string do slip by chance, they soon
   Do screw it up again, whereby
They set it in a more melodious tune   15
   And a diviner harmony.
   For in Christ's coach they sweetly sing
   As they to glory ride therein.

In all their acts public and private, nay
   And secret too, they praise impart;   20
But in their acts divine and worship, they
   With hymns do offer up their heart.
   Thus in Christ's coach they sweetly sing
   As they to glory ride therein.

Some few not in; and some, whose time and
   place   25
   Block up this coach's way, do go
As travellers afoot, and so do trace
   The road that gives them right thereto.
   While in this coach these sweetly sing
   As they to glory ride therein.   30

Upon a Wasp Chilled with Cold

To the wasp renewing itself in the warmth of
the sun-god, the poet gives more lines than to himself. "Her" (not "its") movements are detailed with
an acute and sympathetic observation, a warmly sensuous imagination, that may remind the modern reader
of Keats. But Taylor is intent, as usual, upon spiritual
analogies. For example, the humming wasp offers
thanks, the poet would pipe God's praise; the wasp
sails home to her nest, the poet would climb into
Heaven.

"Torpedo," in line 2, is the electric ray or numb-
fish. Near the end, "fustian" is a kind of cloth.
"Furr'd," in the last line, may mean "coated" or
"filled," according to T. H. Johnson.

The Bear that breathes the Northern blast
Did numb, torpedo-like, a wasp
Whose stiffened limbs encramped, lay bathing
In Sol's warm breath and shine as saving,
Which with her hands she chafes and slams   5
Rubbing her legs, shanks, thighs, and hands.
Her pretty toes and fingers' ends
Nipped with this breath, she out extends
Unto the sun, in great desire
To warm her digits at that fire: 10
Doth hold her temples in this state
Where pulse doth beat, and head doth ache:
Doth turn, and stretch her body small,
Doth comb her velvet capital
As if her little brain-pan were   15
A volume of choice precepts clear:
As if her satin jacket hot
Contained apothecary's shop
Of Nature's receipts, that prevails
To remedy all her sad ails,   20
As if her velvet helmet high
Did turret rationality.
She fans her wing up to the wind
As if her petticoat were lined
With reason's fleece, and hoises sail   25
And humming flies in thankful gale
Unto her dun curled palace hall,
Her warm thanks offering for all.

Lord, clear my misted sight that I
May hence view thy Divinity, 30
Some sparks whereof thou up dost hasp
Within this little downy wasp,
In whose small corporation we
A school and a schoolmaster see:
Where we may learn, and easily find 35
A nimble spirit, bravely mind
Her work in ev'ry limb: and lace
It up neat with a vital grace,
Acting each part though ne'er so small,
Here of this fustian animal, 40
Till I enravished climb into
The Godhead on this ladder do:
Where all my pipes inspired upraise
An Heavenly music, furr'd with praise.

Upon a Spider Catching a Fly

Taylor gives his parable a setting, appropriately, in the world of predatory animals: the spider, wasp, and fly. A spider spares a wasp, an "aspish" creature, because the wasp by nature is capable of matching the spider's stratagems. The fly is less lucky. Animals that are not endowed by Mother Nature with protective equipment should avoid the spider's web, for they will surely be destroyed.

In like manner Hell's Spider spins his web to tangle the race of Adam, who by nature are venomous creatures also, but with this difference. In the animal world are some creatures whose protection has been built in, as it were, by Nature. The arrangement is useful, for they can expect no other salvation. Such is not so in the world of man. Though no man has power to win his own salvation, yet all are free to seek the grace of God which, when communicated, will break the spider's web and afford eternal salvation. Thus Taylor, in darting, nervous rhythms and with sharp detail poses the issue of man's struggle, and envisions the manner by which salvation may be won. (Note prepared by Thomas H. Johnson.)

Line 8, "whorl pins": the flywheel of a spindle is suggested by the whirling motion of the spider's legs. "Hasp": fasten the thread.

Thou sorrow, venom elf:
  Is this thy play,
To spin a web out of thyself
  To catch a fly?
    For why? 5

I saw a pettish wasp
  Fall foul therein:
Whom yet thy whorl pins did not hasp
  Lest he should fling
    His sting. 10

But as afraid, remote
  Didst stand hereat,
And with thy little fingers stroke
  And gently tap
    His back. 15

Thus gently him didst treat
  Lest he should pet,
And in a froppish, aspish heat
  Should greatly fret
    Thy net. 20

Whereas the silly fly,
  Caught by its leg,
Thou by the throat took'st hastily,
  And 'hind the head
    Bite dead. 25

This goes to pot, that not
  Nature doth call.
Strive not above what strength hath got,
  Lest in the brawl
    Thou fall. 30

This fray seems thus to us:
  Hell's Spider gets
His intrails spun to whip cords thus,
  And wove to nets,
    And sets. 35

To tangle Adam's race
  In's stratagems
To their destructions, spoil'd, made base
  By venom things,
    Damn'd Sins. 40

But mighty, Gracious Lord,
  Communicate
Thy Grace to break the cord; afford
  Us Glory's gate
    And state. 45

We'll nightingale sing like,
  When percht on high
In Glory's cage, thy glory, bright:
  Yea, thankfully,
    For joy. 50

Housewifery

(1685?)

This poem, and the one that follows it, illustrate Taylor's capacity to develop a "conceit," or extended metaphor, with ingenious precision. Here, as Austin Warren says, he "tidily analogizes the Christian life to all the instruments and processes of clothmaking, — the spinning-wheel, the distaff, the reel, the loom, the web, the fulling mills, till the robes of salvation are ready for the pious wearing." To a poet born in a weaving district in England, this analogy came naturally, as did the various technical terms, those named above and also "flyers" (revolving arms in a spinning-wheel), "quills" (spindles), "fulling mills" (where cloth was processed) and "pinked" (perforated with ornamental patterns).

Thus the Christian life is conceived as an art, a making. The making of a Christian prospers with the operations of grace. Essentially the poem is a prayer ("Make me, O Lord . . ."), ending with a vision of fulfillment in "glory."

Make me, O Lord, Thy spinning-wheel complete.
   Thy holy Word my distaff make for me;
Make mine affections Thy swift flyers neat;
   And make my soul Thy holy spool to be;
     My conversation make to be Thy reel,   5
And reel the yarn thereon spun of Thy wheel.

Make me Thy loom then; knit therein this
     twine;
   And make Thy Holy Spirit, Lord, wind quills;
Then weave the web Thyself. The yarn is fine.
   Thine ordinances make my fulling mills.   10
   Then dye the same in heavenly colors choice,
   All pinked with varnished flowers of paradise.

Then clothe therewith mine understanding, will,
   Affections, judgment, conscience, memory,
My words and actions, that their shine may fill
   My ways with glory and Thee glorify.   16
   Then mine apparel shall display before Ye
That I am clothed in holy robes for glory.

The Ebb and Flow

When first Thou on me, Lord, wroughtest
     Thy sweet print,
   My heart was made Thy tinder box.
My 'ffections were Thy tinder in't,
   Where fell Thy sparks by drops.
These holy sparks of heavenly fire that came   5
Did ever catch and often out would flame.

But now my heart is made Thy censer trim,
   Full of Thy golden altar's fire,
   To offer up sweet incense in
     Unto Thyself entire: 10

I find my tinder scarce Thy sparks can feel
That drop out from Thy holy flint and steel.

Hence doubts out-bud for fear Thy fire in me
   Is a mocking ignis fatuus;
     Or lest Thine altar's fire out be   15
     It's hid in ashes thus.
Yet when the bellows of Thy spirit blow
Away mine ashes, then Thy fire doth glow.

The Reflection

(w. 1688)

The textual image is from the Song of Solomon, 2:1: "I am the rose of Sharon." The poem is "a brilliant piece in which, after Taylor's frequent fashion, each stanza is allotted its own conceit, while the textual image, the rose, appears and reappears. . . . Christ, as the Rose, offers his sacramental presence: he *sits rose at table-head*, and carves a morsel of what is at once meat, bread, flower, and supreme value." (Austin Warren.)
In line 35, "sprindge" means spread out.

Lord, art Thou at the table-head above
   Meat, medicine, sweetness, sparkling
     beauties, to
Enamour souls with flaming flakes of love,
   And not my trencher nor my cup o'er-
     flow?
Ben't I a bidden guest? Oh! sweat, mine
     eye,   5
O'erflow with tears. Oh! draw thy foun-
     tains dry.

Shall I not smell Thy sweet, oh! Sharon's rose?
   Shall not mine eye salute Thy beauty?
     Why?
Shall Thy sweet leaves their beauteous sweets
     upclose?
   As half-ashamed my sight should on them
     lie?   10
   Woe's me! For this my sighs shall be in
     grain,
   Offered on sorrow's altar for the same.

Had not my soul's (Thy conduit) pipes stopped
     been
   With mud, what ravishment would'st
     Thou convey?
Let grace's golden spade dig till the spring   15
   Of tears arise, and clear this filth away.
   Lord, let Thy spirit raise my sighings till

These pipes my soul do with Thy sweetness
fill.

Earth once was paradise of heaven below,
   Till ink-faced sin had it with poison
    stocked,   20
And chased this paradise away into
   Heaven's upmost loft and it in glory
    locked.
   But Thou, sweet Lord, hast with Thy
    golden key
   Unlocked the door and made a golden day.

Once at Thy feast I saw Thee pearl-like
   stand   25
   'Tween heaven and earth, where heaven's
    bright glory all
In streams fell on Thee as a floodgate, and
   Like sun beams through Thee on the world
    to fall.
   Oh! sugar-sweet then! My dear sweet Lord,
    I see
   Saints' heaven-lost happiness restored by
    Thee.   30

Shall heaven and earth's bright glory all up-lie
   Like sun beams bundled in the sun in
    Thee?
Dost Thou sit rose at table-head, where I
   Do sit, and carv'st no morsel sweet for
    me?
   So much before, so little now! Springdge,
    Lord,   35
   Thy rosy leaves, and me their glee afford.

Shall not Thy rose my garden fresh perfume?
Shall not Thy beauty my dull heart assail?
Shall not Thy golden gleams run through this
   gloom?
   Shall my black velvet mask Thy fair face
    veil?   40
   Pass o'er my faults. Shine forth, bright sun:
    arise!
   Enthrone Thy rosy-self within mine eyes.

The Experience

(w. 1687)

Taylor's experience is "sweet though short." In holy communion he has come nearer God than he ever thought to be. It was as if a divine flame had inflamed him, and he saw his nature one with that of God and the Christ.

Oh! that I always breath'd in such an air,
   As I sucked in, feeding on sweet content!
Disht up unto my soul ev'n in that pray'r
   Poured out to God over last Sacrament.
What beam of light wrapt up my sight to find
Me nearer God than ere came in my mind? 6

Most strange it was! But yet more strange that
   shine
   Which fill'd my soul then to the brim to spy
My nature with thy nature all Divine   9
   Together joined in Him that's Thou, and I.
Flesh of my flesh, bone of my bone: there's run
   Thy Godhead, and my manhood in thy Son.

Oh! that that flame which thou didst on me cast
   Might me enflame, and lighten ev'rywhere.
Then heaven to me would be less at last   15
   So much of heaven I should have while here.
   Oh! Sweet though short! I'll not forget the
    same.
   My nearness, Lord, to thee did me enflame.

I'll claim my right: Give place, ye Angels bright.
   Ye further from the Godhead stand than I. 20
My nature is your Lord; and doth unite
   Better than yours unto the Deity.
   God's throne is first and mine is next; to you
   Only the place of waiting-men is due.

Oh! that my heart thy golden harp might be 25
   Well tun'd by glorious Grace, that ev'ry string
Screw'd to the highest pitch, might unto thee
   All praises wrapt in sweetest music bring.
   I praise thee, Lord, and better praise thee
    would
   If what I had, my heart might ever hold. 30

Samuel Sewall [1652–1730]

Born in England, brought to America when nine years old, graduated from Harvard ten years later, Samuel Sewall prepared for the ministry but entered public life. From 1692 to 1728 he served as judge of the supreme court of the colony, and during the last ten years of the term as chief justice. In 1693, while judge of the probate court, he was appointed to the court which tried the witchcraft cases, and concurred in sentencing nineteen to be hanged. Although he acted in all sincerity at the time, his conscience smote him later, and in January, 1697, he stood with bowed head before the congregation of the Old South Church during the reading of a prepared confession of guilt. He died in 1730, respected and loved.

On December 3, 1673, he began to keep a diary and wrote in it faithfully until October 13, 1729. He had no thought of publication — indeed, the diary was not published until a hundred and fifty years later — and the book gives us a valuable picture of colonial life as well as an interesting revelation of the author. "Samuel Sewall, Yankee," Parrington calls him, and explains: "not American as yet like Franklin, and no longer wholly English like Winthrop, far from democratic and yet no tory, he was the progenitor of a practical race that was to spread the gospel of economic individualism across the continent."

Further reading: *Samuel Sewall's Diary*, abridged, ed. Mark Van Doren, 1927.

From his *Diary*

[Courtship of Madam Winthrop]

May 26. [1720] About midnight my dear wife expired to our great astonishment, especially 5 mine. May the Sovereign Lord pardon my sin, and sanctify to me this very extraordinary, awful dispensation.

May 29. God having in his holy Sovereignty put my wife out of the fore-seat, I apprehended 10 I had cause to be ashamed of my sin, and to loath myself for it; and retired into my Pew.*** I put up a Note to this purpose: Samuel Sewall, deprived of his wife by a very sudden and awful stroke, desires prayers that God would sanctify 15 the same to himself, and children, and family. Writ and sent three; to the South, Old, and Mr. Colman's church.

Sept. 5. Going to son Sewall's I there meet with Madam Winthrop, told her I was glad 20 to meet her there, had not seen her a great while; gave her Mr. Home's Sermon.

Sept. 30. Daughter Sewall acquaints Madam Winthrop that if she pleased to be within at 3 P.M., I would wait on her. She answered she would be at home.

Oct. 1. Saturday. I dine at Mr. Stoddard's; from thence I went to Madam Winthrop's just at 3. Spake to her, saying my loving wife died so soon and suddenly, 'twas hardly convenient for me to think of marrying again; however, I came to this resolution, that I would not make my court to any person without first consulting with her. Had a pleasant discourse about 7 (seven) single persons sitting in the fore-seat September 29th, viz., Madam Rebecca Dudley, Katherine Winthrop, Bridget Usher, Deliverance Legg, Rebecca Lloyd, Lydia Colman, Elizabeth Bellingham. She propounded one and another for me; but none would do; said Mrs. Lloyd was about her age.

Oct. 3. Waited on Madam Winthrop again; 'twas a little while before she came in. Her daughter Noyes being there alone with me, I said I hoped my waiting on her mother would not be disagreeable to her. She answered she should not be against that that might be for her comfort. I saluted her, and told her I perceived I must shortly wish her a good time (her mother had told me she was with child and within a month or two of her time). By and by in came Mr. Airs, chaplain of the Castle, and hanged up his hat, which I was a little startled at, it seeming as if he was to lodge there. At last Madam Winthrop came too. After a considerable time I went up to her and said if it might not be inconvenient, I desired to speak with her. She assented, and spake of going into another room; but Mr. Airs and Mrs. Noyes presently rose up and went out, leaving us there alone. Then I ushered in discourse from the names in the fore-seat; at last I prayed that Katherine [Mrs. Winthrop] might be the person assigned for me. She instantly took it up in the way of denial, as if she had catched at an opportunity to do it, saying she could not do it before she was asked. Said that was her mind unless she should change it, which she believed she should not; could not leave her children. I expressed my sorrow that she should do it so speedily, prayed her consideration, and asked her when I should wait on her again. She setting no time, I mentioned that day sennight. Gave her Mr. Willard's *Fountain*, opened with the little print and verses, saying I hoped if we did well read that book, we should meet together hereafter, if we did not now. She took the book and put it in her pocket. Took leave.

Oct. 5. Midweek. I dined with the court; from thence went and visited Cousin Jonathan's wife, lying in with her little Betty. Gave the nurse 2ˢ. Although I had appointed to wait upon her, Madam Winthrop, next Monday, yet I went from my cousin Sewall's thither about 3 P.M. The nurse told me Madam dined abroad at her daughter Noyes's, they were to go out together. I asked for the maid, who was not within. Gave Katee a penny and a kiss, and came away. Accompanied my son and daughter Cooper in their remove to their new house. Went to tell Joseph, and Mr. Belcher saw me by the South Meetinghouse though 'twas duskish, and said I had been at house-warming (he had been at our house). Invited me to drink a glass of wine at his house at 7, and eat part of the pasty provided for the commissioners' voyage to Casco Bay. His Excellency, Madam Belcher, S.S., Col. Fitch, Mr. D. Oliver, Mr. Anthony Stoddard, Mr. Welsteed, Mr. White, Mr. Belcher sat down. At coming home gave us of the cake and gingerbread to carry away. 'Twas about ten before we got home; Mr. Oliver and I waited on the Governor to his gate; and then Mr. Oliver would wait on me home.

Oct. 6. Lecture day. Mr. Cutler, president of the Connecticut college, preached in Dr. C. Mather's turn. He made an excellent discourse from Heb. 11:14: "For they that say such things, declare plainly that they seek a country." Brother Odlin, Son Sewall of Brookline, and Mary Hirst dine with me. I asked Mary of Madam Lord, Mr. Oliver and wife, and bid her present my service to them. October 6th. A little after 6 P.M. I went to Madam Winthrop's. She was not within. I gave Sarah Chickering the maid 2ˢ, Juno, who brought in wood, 1ˢ. Afterward the nurse came in; I gave her 18ᵈ, having no other small bill. After a while Dr. Noyes came in with his mother, and quickly after his wife came in; they sat talking, I think, till eight o'clock. I said I feared I might be some interruption to their business; Dr. Noyes replied pleasantly he feared they might be an interruption to me, and went away. Madam seemed to harp upon the same string. Must take care of her children; could not leave that house and neighborhood where she had dwelt so long. I told her she might do her children as much or more good by bestowing what she laid out in housekeeping, upon them. Said her son would be of age the 7th of August. I said it might be inconvenient for her to dwell with her daughter-in-law, who must be mistress of the house. I gave her a piece of Mr. Belcher's cake and gingerbread wrapped up in a clean sheet of paper; told her of her father's kindness to me when treasurer, and I constable. My daughter Judith was gone from me and I was more lonesome — might help to forward one another in our journey to Canaan. Mr. Eyre came within the door; I saluted him, asked how Mr. Clark did, and he went away. I took leave about 9 o'clock. I told [her] I came now to refresh her memory as to Monday night; said she had not forgot it. In discourse with her, I asked leave to speak with her sister; I meant to gain Madam Mico's favor to persuade her sister. She seemed surprised and displeased, and said she was in the same condition.

Oct. 7. Friday. I gather the quinces. Gave Mr. Jonathan Simson and Mrs. Fifield, each of them, a funeral sermon.

Cousin Abiel Hobart comes to us. Mr. Short, having received his £40, returns home.

Mr. Cooper visits me, thanks me for my cheese.

Oct. 8. Mr. Short returns not till this day.

Oct. 9. Mr. Sewall preaches very well from Acts 2:24 of the resurrection of Christ. One woman taken into church; one child baptized.

Oct. 10. Examine Mr. Briggs his account; said they could not find Mr. Whittemore. Mr. Willard offered to answer for him. But I showed the necessity of his being here; and appointed Wednesday, 10 o'clock; and ordered notice to be given to the auditors, to pray their assistance.

In the evening I visited Madam Winthrop, who treated me with a great deal of courtesy; wine, marmalade. I gave her a *News-Letter* about the Thanksgiving; proposals, for sake of the verses for David Jeffries. She tells me Dr. Increase Mather visited her this day, in Mr. Hutchinson's coach.

It seems Dr. Cotton Mather's chimney fell afire yesterday, so as to interrupt the Assembly A.M. Mr. Cutler ceased preaching ¼ of an hour.

Oct. 11. I writ a few lines to Madam Winthrop to this purpose: "Madam, These wait on you with Mr. Mayhew's sermon, and account of the state of the Indians on Martha's Vineyard. I thank you for your unmerited favors of yesterday; and hope to have the happiness of waiting on you tomorrow before eight o'clock after noon. I pray God to keep you, and give you a joyful entrance upon the two hundred and twenty-ninth year of Christopher Columbus his discovery; and take leave, who am, Madam, your humble servant.   S.S."

Sent this by Deacon Green, who delivered it to Sarah Chickering, her mistress not being at home.

Oct. 12. Give Mr. Whittemore and Willard their oath to Dr. Mather's inventory. Visit Mr. Cooper. Go to the meeting at the Widow Emon's; Mr. Manly prayed, I read half Mr. Henry's 12th chapter of *The Lord's Supper.* Sung 1, 2, 3, 4, 5, 10, and 12th verses of the 30th Psalm. Brother Franklin concluded with prayer. At Madam Winthrop's steps I took leave of Capt. Hill, etc.

Mrs. Anne Cotton came to door ('twas before 8), said Madam Winthrop was within, directed me into the little room, where she was full of work behind a stand; Mrs. Cotton came in and stood. Madam Winthrop pointed to her to set me a chair. Madam Winthrop's countenance

was much changed from what 'twas on Monday, looked dark and lowering. At last the work (black stuff or silk) was taken away; I got my chair in place, had some converse, but very cold and indifferent to what 'twas before. Asked her to acquit me of rudeness if I drew off her glove. Inquiring the reason, I told her 'twas great odds between handling a dead goat and a living lady. Got it off. I told her I had one petition to ask of her — that was that she would take off the negative she laid on me the third of October; she readily answered she could not, and enlarged upon it; she told me of it so soon as she could; could not leave her house, children, neighbors, business. I told her she might do some good to help and support me. Mentioning Mrs. Gookin (Nath.), the Widow Weld was spoken of; said I had visited Mrs. Denison. I told her, "Yes!" Afterward I said if after a first and second vagary she would accept of me returning, her victorious kindness and good will would be very obliging. She thanked me for my book (Mr. Mayhew's sermon), but said not a word of the letter. When she insisted on the negative, I prayed there might be no more thunder and lightning, I should not sleep all night. I gave her Dr. Preston, *The Church's Marriage and the Church's Carriage*, which cost me 6s at the sale. The door standing open, Mr. Airs came in, hung up his hat, and sat down. After a while, Madam Winthrop moving, he went out. John Eyre looked in; I said, "How do ye?" or, "Your servant, Mr. Eyre," but heard no word from him. Sarah filled a glass of wine; she drank to me, I to her; she sent Juno home with me with a good lantern; I gave her 6d and bid her thank her mistress. In some of our discourse, I told her I had rather go to the stone house adjoining to her than to come to her against her mind. Told her the reason why I came every other night was lest I should drink too deep draughts of pleasure. She had talked of canary; her kisses were to me better than the best canary. Explained the expression concerning Columbus.

Oct. 13. I tell my son and daughter Sewall that the weather was not so fair as I apprehended. Mr. Sewall preached very well in Mr. Wadsworth's turn. Mr. Williams of Weston and Mr. Odlin dine with us. Text was the excellency of the knowledge of Christ.

Friday, October 14. Made a dinner for my son and daughter Cooper. At table in the best room were Sister Stoddard, Sister Cooper, His Excellency, Mrs. Hannah Cooper, Brother Stoddard,

S.S., Mr. Joseph Sewall, Mr. Cooper, Mr. Sewall of Brookline, Mrs. Rand, Mrs. Gerrish, daughter of Brookline. Mr. Gerrish, Clark, and Rand sat at a side table.

Oct. 15. I dine on fish and oil at Mr. Stoddard's. Capt. Hill wished me joy of my proceedings, i.e., with M —. Winthrop; Sister Cooper applauded it, spake of visiting her; I said her complaisance of her visit would be obliging to me.

Oct. 16. Lord's Day. I upbraided myself that could be so solicitous about earthly things, and so cold and indifferent as to the love of Christ, who is altogether lovely. Mr. Prince administered. Dined at my son's with Mr. Cutler and Mr. Shurtleff. Mr. Cutler preaches in the afternoon from Ezek. 16:30: "How weak is thy heart." Son reads the order for the Thanksgiving.

Oct. 17. Monday. Give Mr. Daniel Willard and Mr. Pelatiah Whittemore their oaths to their accounts, and Mr. John Briggs to his, as they are attorneys to Dr. Cotton Mather, administrator to the estate of Nathan Howell, deceased. In the evening I visited Madam Winthrop, who treated me courteously, but not in clean linen as sometimes. She said she did not know whether I would come again or no. I asked her how she could so impute inconstancy to me. (I had not visited her since Wednesday night, being unable to get over the indisposition received by the treatment received that night, and I *must* in it seemed to sound like a made piece of formality.) Gave her this day's *Gazette*. Heard David Jeffries say the Lord's Prayer, and some other portions of the Scriptures. He came to the door and asked me to go into chamber where his grandmother was tending little Katee, to whom she had given physic; but I chose to sit below. Dr. Noyes and his wife came in and sat a considerable time; had been visiting Son and Daughter Cooper. Juno came home with me.

Oct. 18. Visited Madam Mico, who came to me in a splendid dress. I said, "It may be you have heard of my visiting Madam Winthrop," her sister. She answered, her sister had told her of it. I asked her good will in the affair. She answered, if her sister were for it, she should not hinder it. I gave her Mr. Homes's sermon. She gave me a glass of canary, entertained me with good discourse and a respectful remembrance of my first wife. I took leave.

Oct. 19. Midweek. Visited Madam Winthrop; Sarah told me she was at Mr. Walley's, would not come home till late. I gave her Hannah 3 oranges with her duty, not knowing whether I should find her or no. Was ready to go home; but said if I knew she was there, I would go thither. Sarah seemed to speak with pretty good courage she would be there. I went and found her there, with Mr. Walley and his wife in the little room below. At 7 o'clock I mentioned going home; at 8 I put on my coat and quickly waited on her home. She found occasion to speak loud to the servant, as if she had a mind to be known. Was courteous to me, but took occasion to speak pretty earnestly about my keeping a coach. I said 'twould cost £100 per annum; she said 'twould cost but £40. Spake much against John Winthrop, his false-heartedness. Mr. Eyre came in and sat a while; I offered him Dr. Incr. Mather's *Sermons*, whereof Mr. Appleton's ordination sermon was one; said he had them already. I said I would give him another. Exit. Came away somewhat late.

Oct. 20. Mr. Colman preaches from Luke 15:10: "Joy among the angels"; made an excellent discourse.

At council, Col. Townsend spake to me of my hood: should get a wig. I said 'twas my chief ornament; I wore it for sake of the day. Brother Odlin, and Sam, Mary, and Jane Hirst dine with us. Promised to wait on the Governor about 7. Madam Winthrop not being at lecture, I went thither first; found her very serene with her daughter Noyes, Mrs. Dering, and the Widow Shipreeve, sitting at a little table, she in her armed chair. She drank to me, and I to Mrs. Noyes. After a while prayed the favor to speak with her. She took one of the candles and went into the best room, closed the shutters, sat down upon the couch. She told me Madam Usher had been there, and said the coach must be set on wheels, and not by rusting. She spake something of my needing a wig. Asked me what her sister said to me. I told her she said if her sister were for it, she would not hinder it. But I told her she did not say she would be glad to have me for her brother. Said, "I shall keep you in the cold"; and asked her if she would be within tomorrow night, for we had had but a running feat. She said she could not tell whether she should or no. I took leave. As were drinking at the Governor's, he said in England the ladies minded little more than that they might have money, and coaches to ride in. I said, "And New England brooks its name."

At which Mr. Dudley smiled. Governor said they were not quite so bad here.

Oct. 21. Friday. My son the minister came to me P.M. by appointment and we pray one for another in the old chamber, more especially respecting my courtship. About 6 o'clock I go to Madam Winthrop's; Sarah told me her mistress was gone out, but did not tell me whither she went. She presently ordered me a fire; so I went in, having Dr. Sibb's *Bowels* with me to read. I read the two first sermons; still nobody came in. At last about 9 o'clock Mr. John Eyre came in; I took the opportunity to say to him as I had done to Mrs. Noyes before, that I hoped my visiting his mother would not be disagreeable to him; he answered me with much respect. When 'twas after 9 o'clock he of himself said he would go and call her, she was but at one of his brothers'; a while after I heard Madam Winthrop's voice, inquiring something about John. After a good while and clapping the garden door twice or thrice, she came in. I mentioned something of the lateness; she bantered me, and said I was later. She received me courteously. I asked when our proceedings should be made public; she said they were like to be no more public than they were already. Offered me no wine that I remember. I rose up at 11 o'clock to come away, saying I would put on my coat; she offered not to help me. I prayed her that Juno might light me home; she opened the shutter and said 'twas pretty light abroad, Juno was weary and gone to bed. So I came home by star light as well as I could. At my first coming in, I gave Sarah five shillings. I writ Mr. Eyre his name in his book with the date October 21, 1720. It cost me 8ˢ. *Jehovah jireh!* [God will provide.] Madam told me she had visited M. Mico, Wendell, and William Clark of the South [Church].

Oct. 22. Daughter Cooper visited me before my going out of town, stayed till about sunset. I brought her, going near as far as the Orange-tree. Coming back, near Leg's Corner, little David Jeffries saw me, and looking upon me very lovingly, asked me if I was going to see his grandmother. I said, "Not to-night." Gave him a penny and bid him present my service to his grandmother.

Oct. 24. I went in the hackney coach through the Common, stopped at Madam Winthrop's (had told her I would take my departure from thence). Sarah came to the door with Katee in her arms; but I did not think to take notice of the child. Called her mistress. I told her, being encouraged by David Jeffries' loving eyes and sweet words, I was come to inquire whether she could find in her heart to leave that house and neighborhood, and go and dwell with me at the South End; I think she said softly, "Not yet." I told her it did not lie in my lands to keep a coach. If I should, I should be in danger to be brought to keep company with her neighbor Brooker (he was a little before sent to prison for debt). Told her I had an antipathy against those who would pretend to give themselves, but nothing of their estate. I would a proportion of my estate with myself. And I supposed she would do so. As to a periwig, my best and greatest Friend, I could not possibly have a greater, began to find me with hair before I was born, and had continued to do so ever since; and I could not find in my heart to go to another. She commended the book I gave her, Dr. Preston, *The Church Marriage;* quoted him saying 'twas inconvenient keeping out of a fashion commonly used. I said the time and tide did circumscribe my visit. She gave me a dram of black-cherry brandy, and gave me a lump of the sugar that was in it. She wished me a good journey. I prayed God to keep her, and came away. Had a very pleasant journey to Salem.

Oct. 25. Sent a letter of it to my son by Wakefield, who delivered it not till Wednesday; so he visited her not till Friday P.M. and then presented my service to her.

Oct. 27. Kept the Thanksgiving at Salem. Mr. Fisk preached very well from Ephes. 5:20: "Giving thanks always." Dine at Col. Brown's.

Oct. 29. Hold court in the morn. Had a pleasant journey home a little before sunset.

Oct. 30. Mrs. Phillips and her son sit in their pew.

Oct. 31. She proves her husband's will. At night I visited Madam Winthrop about 6 P.M. They told me she was gone to Madam Mico's. I went thither and found she was gone; so returned to her house, read the epistles to the Galatians, Ephesians in Mr. Eyre's Latin Bible. After the clock struck 8, I began to read the 103 Psalm. Mr. Wendell came in from his warehouse. Asked me if I were alone. Spake very kindly to me, offered me to call Madam Winthrop. I told him she would be angry, had been at Mrs. Mico's; he helped me on with my coat, and I came home; left the *Gazette* in the Bible, which told Sarah of, bid her present my service to Mrs. Winthrop, and tell her I had been to wait on her if she had been at home.

Nov. 1. I was so taken up that I could not go if I would.

Nov. 2. Midweek. Went again, and found Mrs. Alden there, who quickly went out. Gave her about ½ pound of sugar almonds, cost 3ˢ per £. Carried them on Monday. She seemed pleased with them, asked what they cost. Spake of giving her a hundred pounds per annum if I died before her. Asked her what sum she would give me, if she should die first. Said I would give her time to consider of it. She said she heard as if I had given all to my children by deeds of gift. I told her 'twas a mistake, Point Judith was mine, etc. That in England, I owned, my father's desire was that it should go to my eldest son; 'twas £20 per annum; she thought 'twas forty. I think when I seemed to excuse pressing this, she seemed to think 'twas best to speak of it; a long winter was coming on. Gave me a glass or two of canary.

Nov. 4. Friday. Went again about 7 o'clock; found there Mr. John Walley and his wife; sat discoursing pleasantly. Madam W. served comfits to us. After a while a table was spread, and supper was set. I urged Mr. Walley to crave a blessing; but he put it upon me. About 9 they went away. I asked Madam what fashioned necklace I should present her with; she said, "None at all." I asked her whereabout we left off last time, mentioned what I had offered to give her, asked her what she would give me; she said she could not change her condition, she had said so from the beginning, could not be so far from her children, the lecture. Quoted the Apostle Paul affirming that a single life was better than a married. I answered that was for the present distress. Said she had not pleasure in things of that nature as formerly. I said, "You are the fitter to make me a wife." If she held in that mind, I must go home and bewail my rashness in making more haste than good speed. However, considering the supper, I desired her to be within next Monday night, if we lived so long. Assented. She charged me with saying that she must put away Juno if she came to me; I utterly

denied it, it never came in my heart; yet she insisted upon it, saying it came in upon discourse about the Indian woman that obtained her freedom this court. About 10 I said I would not disturb the good orders of her house, and came away. She not seeming pleased with my coming away. Spake to her about David Jeffries; had not seen him.

Monday, Nov. 7. My son prayed in the old chamber. Our time had been taken up by Son and Daughter Cooper's visit, so that I only read the 130th and 143rd Psalm. 'Twas on the account of my courtship. I went to Mad. Winthrop; found her rocking her little Katee in the cradle. I excused my coming so late (near eight). She set me an armed chair and cushion; and so the cradle was between her armed chair and mine. Gave her the remnant of my almonds; she did not eat of them as before, but laid them away; I said I came to enquire whether she had altered her mind since Friday, or remained of the same mind still. She said, "Thereabouts." I told her I loved her, and was so fond as to think that she loved me. She said [she] had a great respect for me. I told her I had made her an offer without asking any advice; she had so many to advise with that 'twas a hindrance. The fire was come to one short brand besides the block, which brand was set up in end; at last it fell to pieces, and no recruit was made. She gave me a glass of wine. I think I repeated again that I would go home and bewail my rashness in making more haste than good speed. I would endeavor to contain myself, and not go on to solicit her to do that which she could not consent to. Took leave of her. As came down the steps she bid me have a care. Treated me courteously. Told her she had entered the 4th year of her widowhood. I had given her the *News-Letter* before. I did not bid her draw off her glove as sometime I had done. Her dress was not so clean as sometime it had been. *Jehovah jireh!*

Midweek, Nov. 9. Dine at Brother Stoddard's; were so kind as to inquire of me if they should invite Madam Winthrop; I answered "No."

Jonathan Edwards [1703–1758]

Born at East Windsor, Connecticut, Edwards was the only son of a minister who had ten daughters. In the meadow behind the parsonage young Jonathan built the booth where he and his boy companions meditated and prayed. Prepared at home by his father, he entered Yale, graduated before he was seventeen, and then spent two years in the study of theology. After eight months of preaching in a Presbyterian church in New York, he was back in New Haven as a tutor in Yale. Three years later, in 1727, he became colleague pastor in the church of his grandfather, Solomon Stoddard, at Northampton, Massachusetts, and thither he brought his bride, Sarah Pierrepont, whom he had known in New Haven and of whom he had written a charming description when she was thirteen (see below).

Upon the death of his grandfather, Edwards was left in sole charge of the Northampton church, said to be the largest and wealthiest in the colony outside Boston. As preacher he attained a great reputation. A restrained intensity made his delivery highly effective. He preached many kinds of sermons in addition to the kind for which he is, unfortunately, best remembered — the revivalist discourses such as his terrible *Sinners in the Hands of an Angry God*. This was one of the high spots in the Great Awakening, which began in Northampton in 1734, lasted for fifteen years, spread till it covered the colonies from Maine to Georgia. In time Edwards's parishioners began to rebel openly against the rigor of his doctrines, and in 1750 he was finally dismissed by his church. "I am now thrown upon the wide ocean of the world," he wrote, "and know not what will become of me, and my numerous and chargeable family." (He had twelve children.)

The next year Edwards became pastor at Stockbridge, on the Massachusetts frontier, a settlement composed largely of Indians. His years as missionary gave him leisure enough to pursue his metaphysical speculations and to engage in controversial writing. The fruits of his labor were four impressive treatises, first his most famous book, on Freedom of Will, then others on Original Sin, on the Nature of True Virtue, on the End for which God Created the World. His half dozen years at Stockbridge ended in 1757, when he reluctantly gave up his studies to become president of the College of New Jersey, now Princeton. Inaugurated in January, he died in March of smallpox, a disease frequent in the colonies. As he lay dying he sent the following message to his wife: "Tell her," he said, "that the uncommon union which has so long subsisted between us has been of such a nature as I trust is spiritual, and therefore will continue forever." Poet and mystic, he was still a cautious logician to the end.

Further reading: *Jonathan Edwards: Representative Selections*, ed. C. H. Faust and T. H. Johnson, 1935. Perry Miller, *Jonathan Edwards*, 1949. E. H. Cady, "The Artistry of Jonathan Edwards," *New England Quarterly*, March 1949.

Sarah Pierrepont

(w. 1723)

She was thirteen when Edwards wrote this; he was twenty. They were married four years later. According to a minister not without wit, Mrs. Edwards was said to have learned a shorter way to heaven than her husband.

They say there is a young lady in [New Haven] who is beloved of that Great Being, who made and rules the world, and that there are certain seasons in which this Great Being, in some way or other invisible, comes to her and fills her mind with exceeding sweet delight, and that she hardly cares for anything, except to meditate on him — that she expects after a while to be received up where he is, to be raised up out of the world and caught up into heaven; being assured that he loves her too well to let her remain at a distance from him always. There she is to dwell with him, and to be ravished with his love and delight forever. Therefore, if you present all the world before her, with the richest of its treasures, she disregards it and cares not for it, and is unmindful of any pain or affliction. She has a strange sweetness in her mind, and singular purity in her affections; is most just and conscientious in all her conduct; and you could not persuade her to do any thing wrong or sinful, if you would give her all the world, lest she should offend this Great Being. She is of a wonderful sweetness, calmness and universal benevolence of mind; especially after this Great God has manifested himself to her mind. She will sometimes go about from place to place, singing sweetly; and seems to be always full of joy and pleasure; and no one knows for what. She loves to be alone, walking in the fields and groves, and seems to have some one invisible always conversing with her.

Personal Narrative

(w. 1743)

I had a variety of concerns and exercises about my soul from my childhood; but had two more remarkable seasons of awakening, before I met with that change by which I was brought to those new dispositions, and that new sense of things, that I have since had. The first time was when I was a boy, some years before I went to college, at a time of remarkable awakening in my father's congregation. I was then very much affected for many months, and concerned about the things of religion, and my soul's salvation; and was abundant in duties. I used to pray five times a day in secret, and to spend much time in religious talk with other boys, and used to meet with them to pray together. I experienced I know not what kind of delight in religion. My mind was much engaged in it, and had much self-righteous pleasure; and it was my delight to abound in religious duties. I with some of my schoolmates joined together, and built a booth in a swamp, in a very retired spot, for a place of prayer. And besides, I had particular secret places of my own in the woods, where I used to retire by myself; and was from time to time much affected. My affections seemed to be lively and easily moved, and I seemed to be in my element when engaged in religious duties. And I am ready to think, many are deceived with such affections, and such a kind of delight as I then had in religion, and mistake it for grace.

But in process of time, my convictions and affections wore off; and I entirely lost all those affections and delights and left off secret prayer, at least to any constant performance of it; and returned like a dog to his vomit, and went on in the ways of sin. Indeed I was at times very uneasy, especially towards the latter part of my time at college; when it pleased God, to seize me with the pleurisy; in which he brought me nigh to the grave, and shook me over the pit of hell. And yet, it was not long after my recovery, before I fell again into my old ways of sin. But God would not suffer me to go on with my quietness; I had great and violent inward struggles, till, after many conflicts, with wicked inclinations, repeated resolutions, and bonds that I laid myself under by a kind of vows to God, I was brought wholly to break off all former wicked ways, and all ways of known outward sin; and to apply myself to seek salvation, and practice many religious duties; but without that kind of affection and delight which I had formerly experienced. My concern now wrought more by inward struggles and conflicts, and self-reflections. I made seeking my salvation the main business of my life. But yet, it seems to me, I sought after a miserable manner; which has made me sometimes since to question, whether ever it issued in that which was saving; being ready to doubt, whether such miserable seeking ever succeeded. I was indeed brought to seek salvation in a manner that I never was before; I felt a spirit to part with all things in the world, for an interest in Christ. — My concern continued and prevailed, with many exercising thoughts and inward struggles; but yet it never seemed to be proper to express that concern by the name of terror.

From my childhood up, my mind had been full of objections against the doctrine of God's sovereignty, in choosing whom he would to eternal life, and rejecting whom he pleased; leaving them eternally to perish, and be everlastingly tormented in hell. It used to appear like a horrible doctrine to me. But I remember the time very well, when I seemed to be convinced, and fully satisfied, as to this sovereignty of God, and his justice in thus eternally disposing of men, according to his sovereign pleasure. But never could give an account, how, or by what means, I was thus convinced, not in the least imagining at the time, nor a long time after, that there was any extraordinary influence of God's Spirit in it; but only that now I saw further, and my reason apprehended the justice and reasonableness of it. However, my mind rested in it; and it put an end to all those cavils and objections. And there has been a wonderful alteration in my mind, with respect to the doctrine of God's sovereignty, from that day to this; so that I scarce ever have found so much as the rising of an objection against it, in the most absolute sense, in God's shewing mercy to whom he will shew mercy, and hardening whom he will. God's absolute sovereignty and justice, with respect to salvation and damnation, is what my mind seems to rest assured of, as much as of any thing that I see with my eyes; at least it is so at times. But I have often, since that first conviction, had quite another kind of sense of God's sovereignty than I had then. I have often since had not only a conviction, but a delightful conviction. The doctrine has very often appeared exceeding pleasant, bright, and sweet.

Absolute sovereignty is what I love to ascribe to God. But my first conviction was not so.

The first instance that I remember of that sort of inward, sweet delight in God and divine things that I have lived much in since, was on reading those words, 1 Tim. i: 17. *Now unto the King eternal, immortal, invisible, the only wise God, be honor and glory forever and ever, Amen.* As I read the words, there came into my soul, and was as it were diffused through it, a sense of the glory of the Divine Being; a new sense, quite different from any thing I ever experienced before. Never any words of scripture seemed to me as these words did. I thought within myself, how excellent a being that was, and how happy I should be, if I might enjoy that God, and be wrapt up in heaven, and be as it were swallowed up in him forever! I kept saying, and as it were singing over these words of scripture to myself; and went to pray

to God that I might enjoy him, and prayed in a manner quite different from what I used to do; with a new sort of affection. But it never came into my thought, that there was any thing spiritual, or of a saving nature in this.

From about that time, I began to have a new kind of apprehensions and ideas of Christ, and the work of redemption, and the glorious way of salvation by him. An inward, sweet sense of these things, at times, came into my heart; and my soul was led away in pleasant views and contemplations of them. And my mind was greatly engaged to spend my time in reading and meditating on Christ, on the beauty and excellency of his person, and the lovely way of salvation by free grace in him. I found no books so delightful to me, as those that treated of these subjects. Those words, Cant. ii: 1, used to be abundantly with me, *I am the Rose of Sharon, and the Lily of the valleys.* The words seemed to me, sweetly to represent the loveliness and beauty of Jesus Christ. The whole book of Canticles used to be pleasant to me, and I used to be much in reading it, about that time; and found, from time to time, an inward sweetness, that would carry me away, in my contemplations. This I know not how to express otherwise, than by a calm, sweet abstraction of soul from all the concerns of this world; and sometimes a kind of vision, or fixed ideas and imaginations, of being alone in the mountains, or some solitary wilderness, far from all mankind, sweetly conversing with Christ, and wrapt and swallowed up in God. The sense I had of divine things, would often of a sudden kindle up, as it were, a sweet burning in my heart; an ardor of soul, that I know not how to express.

Not long after I began to experience these things, I gave an account to my father of some things that had passed in my mind. I was pretty much affected by the discourse we had together; and when the discourse was ended, I walked abroad alone, in a solitary place in my father's pasture for contemplation. And as I was walking there and looking up on the sky and clouds, there came into my mind so sweet a sense of the glorious *majesty* and *grace* of God, that I know not how to express. I seemed to see them both in a sweet conjunction; majesty and meekness joined together; it was a gentle, and holy majesty; and also a majestic meekness; a high, great, and holy gentleness.

After this my sense of divine things gradually increased, and became more and more lively, and had more of that inward sweetness. The appearance of every thing was altered; there seemed to be, as it were, a calm, sweet cast, or appearance of divine glory, in almost every thing. God's excellence, his wisdom, his purity and love, seemed to appear in every thing; in the sun, moon, and stars; in the clouds, and blue sky; in the grass, flowers, trees; in the water, and all nature; which used greatly to fix my mind. I often used to sit and view the moon for continuance; and in the day, spent much time in viewing the clouds and sky, to behold the sweet glory of God in these things; in the mean time, singing forth, with a low voice; my contemplations of the Creator and Redeemer. And scarce any thing, among all the works of nature, was so delightful to me as thunder and lightning; formerly, nothing had been so terrible to me. Before, I used to be uncommonly terrified with thunder, and to be struck with terror when I saw a thunder storm rising; but now, on the contrary, it rejoiced me. I felt God, so to speak, at the first appearance of a thunder storm; and used to take the opportunity, at such times, to fix myself in order to view the clouds, and see the lightnings play, and hear the majestic and awful voice of God's thunder, which oftentimes was exceedingly entertaining, leading me to sweet contemplations of my great and glorious God. While thus engaged, it always seemed natural to me to sing, or chant for my meditations; or, to speak my thoughts in soliloquies with a singing voice.

I felt then great satisfaction, as to my good state; but that did not content me. I had vehement longings of soul after God and Christ, and after more holiness, wherewith my heart seemed to be full, and ready to break; which often brought to my mind the words of the Psalmist, Psal. cxix:28: *My soul breaketh for the longing it hath.* I often felt a mourning and lamenting in my heart, that I had not turned to God sooner, that I might have had more time to grow in grace. My mind was greatly fixed on divine things; almost perpetually in the contemplation of them. I spent most of my time in thinking of divine things, year after year; often walking alone in the woods, and solitary places, for meditation, soliloquy, and prayer, and converse with God; and it was always my manner, at such times, to sing forth my contemplations. I was almost constantly in ejaculatory prayer, wherever I was. Prayer seemed to be natural to me, as the breath by which the inward burnings of my heart had vent. The delights which I now felt in the things of religion, were of an exceedingly different kind from those before mentioned, that I had when a boy; and what I then had no more notion of, than one born blind has of pleasant and beautiful colors. They were of a more inward, pure, soul-animating and refreshing nature. Those former delights never reached the heart; and did not arise from any sight of the divine excellency of the things of God; or any taste of the soul-satisfying and life-giving good there is in them.

My sense of divine things seemed gradually to increase, until I went to preach at New York, which was about a year and a half after they began; and while I was there, I felt them, very sensibly, in a higher degree than I had done before. My longings after God and holiness, were much increased. Pure and humble, holy and heavenly Christianity, appeared exceedingly amiable to me. I felt a burning desire to be in every thing a complete Christian; and conform to the blessed image of Christ; and that I might live, in all things, according to the pure and blessed rules of the gospel. I had an eager thirsting after progress in these things; which put me upon pursuing and pressing after them. It was my continual strife day and night, and constant inquiry, how I should *be* more holy, and *live* more holily, and more becoming a child of God, and a disciple of Christ. I now sought an increase of grace and holiness, and a holy life, with much more earnestness, than ever I sought grace before I had it. I used to be continually examining myself, and studying and contriving for likely ways and means, how I should live holily, with far greater diligence and earnestness, than ever I pursued any thing in my life; but yet with too great a dependence on my own strength; which afterwards proved a great damage to me. My experience had not then taught me, as it has done since, my extreme feebleness and impotence, every manner of way; and the bottomless depths of secret corruption and deceit there was in my heart. However, I went on with my eager pursuit after more holiness, and conformity to Christ.

The heaven I desired was a heaven of holiness; to be with God, and to spend my eternity in divine love, and holy communion with Christ. My mind was very much taken up with contemplations on heaven, and the enjoyments there, and living there in perfect holiness, humility and love. And it used at that time to appear a great part of the happiness of heaven, that there the saints could express their love to Christ. It appeared to me a great clog and burden, that what I felt within, I could not express as I desired. The inward ardor of my soul, seemed to be hindered and pent up, and could not freely flame out as it would. I used often to think, how in heaven this principle should freely and fully vent and express itself. Heaven appeared exceedingly delightful, as a world of love; and that all happiness consisted in living in pure, humble, heavenly, divine love.

I remember the thoughts I used then to have of holiness; and said sometimes to myself, "I do certainly know that I love holiness, such as the gospel prescribes." It appeared to me, that there was nothing in it but what was ravishingly lovely; the highest beauty and amiableness — a *divine* beauty; far purer than any thing here upon earth; and that every thing else was like mire and defilement, in comparison of it.

Holiness, as I then wrote down some of my contemplations on it, appeared to me to be of a sweet, pleasant, charming, serene, calm nature; which brought an inexpressible purity, brightness, peacefulness and ravishment to the soul. In other words, that it made the soul like a field or garden of God, with all manner of pleasant flowers; all pleasant, delightful, and undisturbed; enjoying a sweet calm, and the gently vivifying beams of the sun. The soul of a true Christian, as I then wrote my meditations, appeared like such a little white flower as we see in the spring of the year; low and humble on the ground, opening its bosom to receive the pleasant beams of the sun's glory; rejoicing as it were in a calm rapture; diffusing around a sweet fragrancy; standing peacefully and lovingly, in the midst of other flowers round about; all in like manner opening their bosoms, to drink in the light of the sun. There was no part of creature holiness, that I had so great a sense of its loveliness, as humility, brokenness of heart and poverty of spirit; and there was nothing that I so earnestly longed for. My heart panted after this, to lie low before God, as in the dust; that I might be nothing, and that God might be ALL, that I might become as a little child.

While at New York, I was sometimes much affected with reflections on my past life, considering how late it was before I began to be truly religious; and how wickedly I had lived till then; and once so as to weep abundantly, and for a considerable time together.

On January 12, 1723, I made a solemn dedication of myself to God, and wrote it down; giving up myself, and all that I had to God; to be for the future in no respect my own; to act as one that had no right to himself, in any respect. And solemnly vowed to take God for my whole portion and felicity; looking on nothing else as any part of my happiness, nor acting as if it were; and his law for the constant rule of my obedience; engaging to fight with all my might, against the world, the flesh and the devil, to the end of my life. But I have reason to be infinitely humbled, when I consider how much I have failed of answering my obligation.

I had then abundance of sweet religious conversation in the family where I lived, with Mr. John Smith and his pious mother. My heart was knit in affection to those in whom were appearances of true piety; and I could bear the thoughts of no other companions, but such as were holy, and the disciples of the blessed Jesus. I had great longings for the advancement of Christ's kingdom in the world; and my secret prayer used to be, in great part, taken up in praying for it. If I heard the least hint of any thing that happened, in any part of the world, that appeared, in some respect or other, to have a favorable aspect on the interest of Christ's kingdom, my soul eagerly catched at it; and it would much animate and refresh me. I used to be eager to read public news letters, mainly for that end; to see if I could not find some news favorable to the interest of religion in the world.

I very frequently used to retire into a solitary place, on the banks of Hudson's river, at some distance from the city, for contemplation on divine things, and secret converse with God; and had many sweet hours there. Sometimes Mr. Smith and I walked there together, to converse on the things of God; and our conversation used to turn much on the advancement of Christ's kingdom in the world, and the glorious things that God would accomplish for his church in the latter days. I had then, and at other times, the greatest delight in the holy scriptures, of any book whatsoever. Oftentimes in reading it, every word seemed to touch my heart. I felt a harmony between something in my heart, and those sweet and powerful words. I seemed often to see so much light exhibited by every sentence, and such a refreshing food communicated, that I could not get along in reading; often dwelling long on one sentence, to see the wonders contained in it; and yet almost every sentence seemed to be full of wonders.

I came away from New York in the month of April, 1723, and had a most bitter parting with Madam Smith and her son. My heart seemed to sink within me at leaving the family and city, where I had enjoyed so many sweet and pleasant days. I went from New York to Weathersfield, by water, and as I sailed away, I kept sight of the city as long as I could. However, that night, after this sorrowful parting, I was greatly comforted in God at Westchester, where we went ashore to lodge; and had a pleasant time of it all the voyage to Saybrook. It was sweet to me to think of meeting dear Christians in heaven, where we should never part more. At Saybrook we went ashore to lodge, on Saturday, and there kept the Sabbath; where I had a sweet and refreshing season, walking alone in the fields.

After I came home to Windsor, I remained much in a like frame of mind, as when at New York; only sometimes I felt my heart ready to sink with the thoughts of my friends at New York. My support was in contemplations on the heavenly state; as I find in my Diary of May 1, 1723. It was a comfort to think of that state, where there is fulness of joy; where reigns heavenly, calm, and delightful love, without alloy; where there are continually the dearest expressions of this love; where is the enjoyment of the persons loved, without ever parting; where those persons who appear so lovely in this world, will really be inexpressibly more lovely and full of love to us. And how sweetly will the mutual lovers join together to sing the praises of God and the Lamb! How will it fill us with joy to think, that this enjoyment, these sweet exercises will never cease, but will last to all eternity! I continued much in the same frame, in the general, as when at New York, till I went to New Haven as tutor to the college; particularly once at Bolton, on a journey from Boston, while walking out alone in the fields. After I went to New Haven I sunk in religion; my mind being diverted from my eager pursuits after holiness, by some affairs that greatly perplexed and distracted my thoughts.

In September, 1725, I was taken ill at New Haven, and while endeavoring to go home to Windsor, was so ill at the North Village, that I could go no further; where I lay sick for about a quarter of a year. In this sickness God was pleased to visit me again with the sweet influences of his Spirit. My mind was greatly engaged there in divine, pleasant contemplations, and longings of soul. I observed that those who watched with me, would often be looking out wishfully for the morning; which brought to my mind those words of the Psalmist, and which my soul with delight made its own language, *My soul waiteth for the Lord, more than they that watch for the morning, I say, more than they that watch for the morning;* and when the light of day came in at the windows, it refreshed my soul from one morning to another. It seemed to be some image of the light of God's glory.

I remember, about that time, I used greatly to long for the conversion of some that I was concerned with; I could gladly honor them, and with delight be a servant to them, and lie at their feet, if they were but truly holy. But, some time after this, I was again greatly diverted in my mind with some temporal concerns that exceedingly took up my thoughts, greatly to the wounding of my soul; and went on through various exercises, that it would be tedious to relate, which gave me much more experience of my own heart, than ever I had before.

Since I came to this town, I have often had sweet complacency in God, in views of his glorious perfections and the excellency of Jesus Christ. God has appeared to me a glorious and lovely being, chiefly on the account of his holiness. The holiness of God has always appeared to me the most lovely of all his attributes. The doctrines of God's absolute sovereignty, and free grace, in shewing mercy to whom he would shew mercy; and man's absolute dependence on the operations of God's Holy Spirit, have very often appeared to me as sweet and glorious doctrines. These doctrines have been much my delight. God's sovereignty has ever appeared to me, great part of his glory. It has often been my delight to approach God, and adore him as a sovereign God, and ask sovereign mercy of him.

I have loved the doctrines of the gospel; they have been to my soul like green pastures. The gospel has seemed to me the richest treasure; the treasure that I have most desired, and longed that it might dwell richly in me. The way of salvation by Christ has appeared, in a general way, glorious and excellent, most pleasant and most beautiful. It has often seemed to me, that it would in a great measure spoil heaven, to receive it in any other way. That text has often been affecting and delightful to me. Isa. xxxii:

2. *A man shall be an hiding place from the wind, and a covert from the tempest, etc.*

It has often appeared to me delightful, to be united to Christ; to have him for my head, and to be a member of his body; also to have Christ for my teacher and prophet. I very often think with sweetness, and longings, and pantings of soul, of being a little child, taking hold of Christ, to be led by him through the wilderness of this world. That text, Matth. xviii: 3, has often been sweet to me, *except ye be converted and become as little children, etc.* I love to think of coming to Christ, to receive salvation of him, poor in spirit, and quite empty of self, humbly exalting him alone; cut off entirely from my own root, in order to grow into, and out of Christ; to have God in Christ to be all in all; and to live by faith on the Son of God, a life of humble unfeigned confidence in him. That scripture has often been sweet to me, Psal. cxv: 1. *Not unto us, O Lord, not unto us, but to thy name give glory, for thy mercy and for thy truth's sake.* And those words of Christ, Luke x: 21. *In that hour Jesus rejoiced in spirit, and said, I thank thee, O Father, Lord of heaven and earth, that thou hast hid these things from the wise and prudent, and hast revealed them unto babes; even so, Father, for so it seemed good in thy sight.* That sovereignty of God which Christ rejoiced in, seemed to me worthy of such joy; and that rejoicing seemed to show the excellency of Christ, and of what spirit he was.

Sometimes, only mentioning a single word caused my heart to burn within me; or only seeing the name of Christ, or the name of some attribute of God. And God has appeared glorious to me, on account of the Trinity. It has made me have exalting thoughts of God, that he subsists in three persons; Father, Son and Holy Ghost. The sweetest joys and delights I have experienced, have not been those that have arisen from a hope of my own good state; but in a direct view of the glorious things of the gospel. When I enjoy this sweetness, it seems to carry me above the thoughts of my own estate; it seems at such times a loss that I cannot bear, to take off my eye from the glorious pleasant object I behold without me, to turn my eye in upon myself, and my own good estate.

My heart has been much on the advancement of Christ's kingdom in the world. The histories of the past advancement of Christ's kingdom have been sweet to me. When I have read histories of past ages, the pleasantest thing in all my reading has been, to read of the kingdom of Christ being promoted. And when I have expected, in my reading, to come to any such thing, I have rejoiced in the prospect, all the way as I read. And my mind has been much entertained and delighted with the scripture promises and prophecies, which relate to the future glorious advancement of Christ's kingdom upon earth.

I have sometimes had a sense of the excellent fulness of Christ, and his meetness and suitableness as a Saviour; whereby he has appeared to me, far above all, the chief of ten thousands. His blood and atonement have appeared sweet, and his righteousness sweet; which was always accompanied with ardency of spirit; and inward strugglings and breathings, and groanings that cannot be uttered, to be emptied of myself, and swallowed up in Christ.

Once as I rode out into the woods for my health, in 1737, having alighted from my horse in a retired place, as my manner commonly has been, to walk for divine contemplation and prayer, I had a view that for me was extraordinary, of the glory of the Son of God, as Mediator between God and man, and his wonderful, great, full, pure and sweet grace and love, and meek and gentle condescension. This grace that appeared so calm and sweet, appeared also great above the heavens. The person of Christ appeared ineffably excellent with an excellency great enough to swallow up all thought and conception — which continued, as near as I can judge, about an hour; which kept me the greater part of the time in a flood of tears, and weeping aloud. I felt an ardency of soul to be, what I know not otherwise how to express, emptied and annihilated; to lie in the dust, and to be full of Christ alone; to love him with a holy and pure love; to trust in him; to live upon him; to serve and follow him; and to be perfectly sanctified and made pure, with a divine and heavenly purity. I have, several other times, had views very much of the same nature, and which have had the same effects.

I have many times had a sense of the glory of the third person in the Trinity, in his office of Sanctifier; in his holy operations, communicating divine light and life to the soul. God, in the communications of his Holy Spirit, has appeared as an infinite fountain of divine glory and sweetness; being full, and sufficient to fill and satisfy the soul; pouring forth itself in sweet communications; like the sun in its glory, sweetly and pleasantly diffusing light and life. And I have sometimes had an affecting sense of the excellency of the word of God, as a word of life; as the light of life; a sweet, excellent, life-giving word; accompanied with a thirsting after that word; that it might dwell richly in my heart.

Often, since I lived in this town, I have had very affecting views of my own sinfulness and vileness; very frequently to such a degree as to hold me in a kind of loud weeping, sometimes for a considerable time together; so that I have often been forced to shut myself up. I have had a vastly greater sense of my own wickedness, and the badness of my own heart, than ever I had before my conversion. It has often appeared to me, that if God should mark iniquity against me, I should appear the very worst of all mankind; of all that have been, since the beginning of the world to this time; and that I should have by far the lowest place in hell. When others, that have come to talk with me about their soul concerns, have expressed the sense they have had of their own wickedness, by saying that it seemed to them, that they were as bad as the devil himself; I thought their expression seemed exceedingly faint and feeble, to represent my wickedness.

My wickedness, as I am in myself, has long appeared to me perfectly ineffable, and swallowing up all thought and imagination; like an infinite deluge, or mountains over my head. I know not how to express better what my sins appear to me to be, than by heaping infinite upon infinite, and multiplying infinite by infinite. Very often, for these many years, these expressions are in my mind, and in my mouth, "Infinite upon infinite — Infinite upon infinite!" When I look into my heart, and take a view of my wickedness, it looks like an abyss infinitely deeper than hell. And it appears to me, that were it not for free grace, exalted and raised up to the infinite height of all the fulness and glory of the great Jehovah, and the arm of his power and grace stretched forth in all the majesty of his power, and in all the glory of his sovereignty, I should appear sunk down in my sins below hell itself; far beyond the sight of every thing, but the eye of sovereign grace, that can pierce even down to such a depth. And yet, it seems to me, that my conviction of sin is exceedingly small, and faint; it is enough to amaze me, that I have no more sense of my sin. I know certainly, that I have very little sense of my sinfulness. When I have had turns of weeping and crying for my

sins, I thought I knew at the time, that my repentance was nothing to my sin.

I have greatly longed of late, for a broken heart, and to lie low before God; and, when I ask for humility, I cannot bear the thoughts of being no more humble than other Christians. It seems to me, that though their degrees of humility may be suitable for them, yet it would be a vile self-exaltation to me, not to be the lowest in humility of all mankind. Others speak of their longing to be "humbled to the dust"; that may be a proper expression for them, but I always think of myself, that I ought, and it is an expression that has long been natural for me to use in prayer, "to lie infinitely low before God." And it is affecting to think, how ignorant I was, when a young Christian, of the bottomless, infinite depths of wickedness, pride, hypocrisy and deceit, left in my heart.

I have a much greater sense of my universal, exceeding dependence on God's grace and strength, and mere good pleasure, of late, than I used formerly to have; and have experienced more of an abhorrence of my own righteousness. The very thought of any joy arising in me, on any consideration of my own amiableness, performances, or experiences or any goodness of heart or life, is nauseous and detestable to me. And yet I am greatly afflicted with a proud and self-righteous spirit, much more sensibly than I used to be formerly. I see that serpent rising and putting forth its head continually, every where, all around me.

Though it seems to me, that, in some respects, I was a far better Christian, for two or three years after my first conversion, than I am now; and lived in a more constant delight and pleasure; yet, of late years, I have had a more full and constant sense of the absolute sovereignty of God, and a delight in that sovereignty; and have had more of a sense of the glory of Christ, as a Mediator revealed in the gospel. On one Saturday night, in particular, I had such a discovery of the excellency of the gospel above all other doctrines, that I could not but say to myself, "This is my chosen light, my chosen doctrine;" and of Christ, "This is my chosen Prophet." It appeared sweet, beyond all expression, to follow Christ, and to be taught, and enlightened, and instructed by him; to learn of him, and live to him. Another Saturday night, (January, 1739) I had such a sense, how sweet and blessed a thing it was to walk in the way of duty; to do that which was right and meet to be done, and

agreeable to the holy mind of God; and it caused
me to break forth into a kind of loud weeping,
which held me some time, so that I was forced
to shut myself up, and fasten the doors. I could
not but, as it were, cry out, "How happy are 5
they which do that which is right in the sight
of God! They are blessed indeed, they are the
happy ones!" I had, at the same time, a very
affecting sense, how meet and suitable it was
that God should govern the world, and order 10
all things according to his own pleasure; and I
rejoiced in it, that God reigned, and that his
will was done.

Passages from Sermons

❧ The Rev. Mr. Edwards — a tall, spare man with
a large forehead, clear piercing eyes, and thin, set
lips — read his sermons with the assurance of the 20
dedicated, and needed no pulpit arts. In literary style
his sermons are plain, precise, compact, fresh and
vigorous, devoid of rhetorical decoration, pedantry,
or any other affectation. While shorter, they differ
little in structure from earlier New England sermons.
Edwards begins with the Exposition of the text, pro- 25
ceeds to the Doctrine, which he develops under logical
divisions, and concludes with the Application (also
called Use or Improvement), which he develops
similarly.

The selections given here represent, respectively, 30
Edwards's basic doctrine of divine sovereignty, his
poetic intuition of a divine light that adds sweetness
and beauty to holiness, and his vision of divine wrath
and the unspeakable misery awaiting the unregenerate.

God Glorified in Man's Dependence

(1731)

❧ When only twenty-seven, Edwards was invited
to preach in Boston in the "Public Lecture." With 40
this sermon, his first published work, began his reputation as a theologian.

"Edwards does not seek to show that an instinct
of dependence is rooted in the soul, forming an essential element in the human consciousness, or that its 45
development is important to a complete human culture. He looks at his subject from the divine point
of view, not from the human. Human dependence is
both true and desirable, because it tends to humiliate
man and to promote the glory of God. But none the 50
less was Edwards's sermon an epochal one. Those
who listened to it must have felt that a great champion had appeared to defend the old discredited
theology. . . . It was the preacher's challenge to the
age — to the fashionable Arminianism which was

denying or ignoring the divine sovereignty, which was
magnifying man at the expense of God, which was
cheapening the gift of divine grace by extending it
to all, instead of the few whom God had chosen"
(A. V. G. Allen).

The selection is less than the first half of the
sermon.

There is an absolute and universal dependence of the redeemed on God. The nature and
contrivance of our redemption is such, that the
redeemed are in every thing directly, immediately, and entirely dependent on God: They are
dependent on him for all, and are dependent on
him every way.

The several ways wherein the dependence of 15
one being may be upon another for its good, and
wherein the redeemed of Jesus Christ depend on
God for all their good, are these, *viz.* That they
have all their good of him, and that they have
all through him, and that they have all in him:
That he is the *cause* and original whence all
their good comes, therein it is *of* him; and that
he is the *medium* by which it is obtained and
conveyed, therein they have it *through* him; and
that he is the *good itself* given and conveyed, 25
therein it is *in* him. Now those that are redeemed by Jesus Christ do, in all these respects,
very directly and entirely depend on God for
their all.

First, The redeemed have all their good *of* 30
God. God is the great *author* of it. He is the
first cause of it; and not only so, but he is the
only proper cause. It is of God that we have
our Redeemer. It is God that has provided a
Savior for us. Jesus Christ is not only of God 35
in his person, as he is the only begotten Son of
God, but he is from God, as we are concerned
in him, and in his office of Mediator. He is the
gift of God to us: God chose and anointed him,
appointed him his work, and sent him into the 40
world. And as it is God that *gives,* so it is God
that *accepts* the Savior. He gives the purchaser,
and he affords the thing purchased.

It is of God that Christ becomes ours, that
we are brought to him and are united to him. It 45
is of God that we receive faith to close with him,
that we may have an interest in him. Eph. ii: 8.
"For by grace ye are saved, through faith; and
that not of yourselves, it is the gift of God."
It is of God that we actually receive all the 50
benefits that Christ has purchased. It is God
that pardons and justifies, and delivers from
going down to hell; and into his favor the redeemed are received, when they are justified.

So it is God that delivers from the dominion of sin, cleanses us from our filthiness, and changes us from our deformity. It is of God that the redeemed receive all their true excellency, wisdom, and holiness: and that two ways, viz. as the Holy Ghost by whom these things are immediately wrought is from God, proceeds from him, and is sent by him; and also as the Holy Ghost himself is God, by whose operation and indwelling the knowledge of God and divine things, a holy disposition and all grace, are conferred and upheld. And though means are made use of in conferring grace on men's souls, yet it is of God that we have these means of grace, and it is he that makes them effectual. It is of God that we have the holy scriptures: they are his word. It is of God that we have ordinances, and their efficacy depends on the immediate influence of his Spirit. The ministers of the gospel are sent of God, and all their sufficiency is of him. — 2 Cor. iv: 7. "We have this treasure in earthen vessels, that the excellency of the power may be of God, and not of us." Their success depends entirely and absolutely on the immediate blessing and influence of God.

1. The redeemed have all from the *grace* of God. It was of mere grace that God gave us his only begotten Son. The grace is great in proportion to the excellency of what is given. The gift was infinitely precious, because it was of a person infinitely worthy, a person of infinite glory; and also because it was of a person infinitely near and dear to God. The grace is great in proportion to the benefit we have given us in him. The benefit is doubly infinite, in that in him we have deliverance from an infinite, because an eternal misery, and do also receive eternal joy and glory. The grace in bestowing this gift is great in proportion to our unworthiness to whom it is given; instead of deserving such a gift, we merited infinitely ill of God's hands. The grace is great according to the manner of giving, or in proportion to the humiliation and expense of the method and means by which a way is made for our having the gift. He gave him to dwell amongst us; he gave him to us incarnate, or in our nature; and in the like though sinless infirmities. He gave him to us in a low and afflicted state; and not only so, but as slain, that he might be a feast for our souls.

The grace of God in bestowing this gift is most free. It was what God was under no obligation to bestow. He might have rejected fallen man, as he did the fallen angels. It was what we never did any thing to merit; it was given while we were yet enemies, and before we had so much as repented. It was from the love of God who saw no excellency in us to attract it; and it was without expectation of ever being requited for it. — And it is from mere grace that the benefits of Christ are applied to such and such particular persons. Those that are called and sanctified are to attribute it alone to the good pleasure of God's goodness by which they are distinguished. He is sovereign, and hath mercy on whom he will have mercy.

Man hath now a greater dependence on the grace of God than he had before the fall. He depends on free goodness of God for much more than he did then. Then he depended on God's goodness for conferring the reward of perfect obedience; for God was not obliged to promise and bestow that reward. But now we are dependent on the grace of God for much more; we stand in need of grace, not only to bestow glory upon us, but to deliver us from hell and eternal wrath. Under the first covenant we depended on God's goodness to give us the reward of righteousness; and so we do now: But we stand in need of God's free and sovereign grace to give us that righteousness; to pardon our sin, and release us from the guilt and infinite demerit of it.

And as we are dependent on the goodness of God for more now than under the first covenant, so we are dependent on a much greater, more free and wonderful goodness. We are now more dependent on God's arbitrary and sovereign good pleasure. We were in our first estate dependent on God for holiness. We had our original righteousness from him; but then holiness was not bestowed in such a way of sovereign good pleasure as it is now. Man was created holy, for it became God to create holy all his reasonable creatures. It would have been a disparagement to the holiness of God's nature, if he had made an intelligent creature unholy. But now when fallen man is made holy, it is from mere and arbitrary grace: God may for ever deny holiness to the fallen creature if he pleases, without any disparagement to any of his perfections.

And we are not only indeed more dependent on the grace of God, but our dependence is much more conspicuous, because our own insufficiency and helplessness in ourselves is much more apparent in our fallen and undone state, than it was before we were either sinful or miserable. We are more apparently dependent on God for holiness, because we are first sinful, and utterly polluted, and afterward holy. So the production of the effect is sensible, and its derivation from God more obvious. If man was ever holy and always was so, it would not be so apparent, that he had not holiness necessarily, as an inseparable qualification of human nature. So we are more apparently dependent on free grace for the favor of God, for we are first justly the objects of his displeasure, and afterward are received into favor. We are more apparently dependent on God for happiness, being first miserable, and afterward happy. It is more apparently free and without merit in us, because we are actually without any kind of excellency to merit, if there could be any such thing as merit in creature-excellency. And we are not only without any true excellency, but are full of, and wholly defiled with, that which is infinitely odious. All our good is more apparently from God, because we are first naked and wholly without any good, and afterward enriched with all good.

2. We receive all from the *power* of God. Man's redemption is often spoken of as a work of wonderful power as well as grace. The great power of God appears in bringing a sinner from his low state from the depth of sin and misery, to such an exalted state of holiness and happiness. Eph. i: 19. "And what is the exceeding greatness of his power to us-ward who believe, according to the working of his mighty power."

We are dependent on God's power through every step of our redemption. We are dependent on the power of God to convert us, and give faith in Jesus Christ, and the new nature. It is a work of creation: "If any man be in Christ, he is a new creature," 2 Cor. v: 17. "We are created in Christ Jesus," Eph. ii: 10. The fallen creature cannot attain to true holiness, but by being created again, Eph. iv: 24. "And that ye put on the new man, which after God is created in righteousness and true holiness." It is a raising from the dead, Colos. ii: 12, 13. "Wherein also ye are risen with him through the faith of the operation of God, who hath raised him from the dead." Yea, it is a more glorious work of power than mere creation, or raising a dead body to life, in that the effect attained is greater and more excellent. That holy and happy being, and spiritual life which is produced in the work of conversion, is a far

greater and more glorious effect, than mere being and life. And the state from whence the change is made — a death in sin, a total corruption of nature, and depth of misery — is far more remote from the state attained, than mere death or non-entity.

It is by God's power also that we are preserved in a state of grace. 1 Pet. i: 5. "Who are kept by the power of God through faith unto salvation." As grace is at first from God, so it is continually from him, and is maintained by him, as much as light in the atmosphere is all day long from the sun, as well as at first dawning, or at sun-rising. — Men are dependent on the power of God for every exercise of grace, and for carrying on that work in the heart, for subduing sin and corruption, increasing holy principles, and enabling to bring forth fruit in good works. Man is dependent on divine power in bringing grace to its perfection, in making the soul completely amiable in Christ's glorious likeness, and filling of it with a satisfying joy and blessedness; and for the raising of the body to life, and to such a perfect state, that it shall be suitable for a habitation and organ for a soul so perfected and blessed. These are the most glorious effects of the power of God, that are seen in the series of God's acts with respect to the creatures.

Man was dependent on the power of God in his first estate, but he is more dependent on his power now; he needs God's power to do more things for him, and depends on a more wonderful exercise of his power. It was an effect of the power of God to make man holy at the first; but more remarkably so now, because there is a great deal of opposition and difficulty in the way. It is a more glorious effect of power to make that holy that was so depraved, and under the dominion of sin, than to confer holiness on that which before had nothing of the contrary. It is a more glorious work of power to rescue a soul out of the hands of the devil, and from the powers of darkness, and to bring it into a state of salvation, than to confer holiness where there was no prepossession or opposition. Luke xi: 21, 22. "When a strong man armed keepeth his palace, his goods are in peace; but when a stronger than he shall come upon him, and overcome him, he taketh from him all his armor wherein he trusted, and divideth his spoils." So it is a more glorious work of power to uphold a soul in a state of grace and holiness, and to carry it on till it is brought to glory, when there is so much sin remaining in the heart resisting, and

Satan with all his might opposing, than it would have been to have kept man from falling at first, when Satan had nothing in man. — Thus we have shown how the redeemed are dependent on God for all their good, as they have all of him.

Secondly, They are also dependent on God for all, as they have all *through* him. God is the medium of it, as well as the author and fountain of it. All we have, wisdom, the pardon of sin, deliverance from hell, acceptance into God's favor, grace and holiness, true comfort and happiness, eternal life and glory, is from God by a Mediator; and this Mediator is God; which Mediator we have an absolute dependence upon, as he through whom we receive all. So that here is another way wherein we have our dependence on God for all good. God not only gives us the Mediator, and accepts his mediation, and of his power and grace bestows the things purchased by the Mediator; but he the Mediator is God.

Our blessings are what we have by purchase; and the purchase is made of God, the blessings are purchased of him, and God gives the purchaser; and not only so, but God is the purchaser. Yea, God is both the purchaser and the price; for Christ who is God, purchased these blessings for us, by offering up himself as the price of our salvation. He purchased eternal life by the sacrifice of himself. Heb. vii: 27. "He offered up himself." And chap. ix: 26. "He hath appeared to take away sin by the sacrifice of himself." Indeed it was the human nature that was offered; but it was the same person with the divine, and therefore was an infinite price.

As we thus have our good through God, we have a dependence on him in a respect that man in his first estate had not. Man was to have eternal life then through his own righteousness; so that he had partly a dependence upon what was in himself; for we have a dependence upon that through which we have our good, as well as that from which we have it: and though man's righteousness that he then depended on was indeed from God, yet it was his own, it was inherent in himself; so that his dependence was not so *immediately* on God. But now the righteousness that we are dependent on is not in ourselves, but in God. We are saved through the righteousness of Christ: he *is made unto us righteousness*; and therefore is prophesied of, Jer. xxiii: 6, under that name, "the Lord our righteousness." In that the righteousness we are justified by is the righteousness of Christ, it is the righteousness of God. 2 Cor. v: 21. "That

we might be made the righteousness of God in him." — Thus in redemption we have not only all things of God, but by and through him, 1 Cor. viii: 6. "But to us there is but one God, the Father, of whom are all things, and we in him; and one Lord Jesus Christ, by whom are all things, and we by him."

A Divine and Supernatural Light
(1734)

The extended title is *A Divine and Supernatural Light Immediately Imparted to the Soul by the Spirit of God.* The conception brings to mind the "Inner Light" of Edwards's Quaker contemporaries (such as Woolman, page 61). It also prefigures the intuition of Emerson and other Transcendentalists in the next century that "a light shines through us," even though Emerson's thought is vastly different from that of Edwards.

In the following passage Edwards tries to show what spiritual light is, and how it is given by God. Though the light comes directly from God, the Bible, as the revealed Word of God, is still indispensable, for "a person cannot have spiritual light without the Word."

2. This spiritual and divine light does not consist in any impression made upon the imagination. It is no impression upon the mind, as though one saw any thing with the bodily eyes: it is no imagination or idea of an outward light or glory, or any beauty of form or countenance, or a visible lustre or brightness of any object. The imagination may be strongly impressed with such things; but this is not spiritual light. Indeed when the mind has a lively discovery of spiritual things, and is greatly affected by the power of divine light, it may, and probably very commonly doth, much affect the imagination; so that impressions of an outward beauty or brightness may accompany those spiritual discoveries. But spiritual light is not that impression upon the imagination, but an exceeding different thing from it. Natural men may have lively impressions on their imaginations; and we cannot determine but the devil, who transforms himself into an angel of light, may cause imaginations of an outward beauty, or visible glory, and of sounds and speeches, and other such things; but these are things of a vastly inferior nature to spiritual light.

3. This spiritual light is not the suggesting of any new truths or propositions not contained in

the word of God. This suggesting of new truths or doctrines to the mind, independent of any antecedent revelation of those propositions, either in word or writing, is inspiration; such as the prophets and apostles had, and such as some enthusiasts pretend to. But this spiritual light that I am speaking of, is quite a different thing from inspiration: it reveals no new doctrine, it suggests no new proposition to the mind, it teaches no new thing of God, or Christ, or another world, not taught in the Bible, but only gives a due apprehension of those things that are taught in the word of God.

4. It is not every affecting view that men have of the things of religion that is this spiritual and divine light. Men by mere principles of nature are capable of being affected with things that have a special relation to religion as well as other things. A person by mere nature, for instance, may be liable to be affected with the story of Jesus Christ, and the sufferings he underwent, as well as by any other tragical story: he may be the more affected with it from the interest he conceives mankind to have in it: yea, he may be affected with it without believing it; as well as a man may be affected with what he reads in a romance, or sees acted in a stage play. He may be affected with a lively and eloquent description of many pleasant things that attend the state of the blessed in heaven, as well as his imagination be entertained by a romantic description of the pleasantness of fairy land, or the like. And that common belief of the truth of the things of religion, that persons may have from education or otherwise, may help forward their affection. We read in Scripture of many that were greatly affected with things of a religious nature, who yet are there represented as wholly graceless, and many of them very ill men. A person therefore may have affecting views of the things of religion, and yet be very destitute of spiritual light. Flesh and blood may be the author of this: one man may give another an affecting view of divine things with but common assistance: but God alone can give a spiritual discovery of them.

But I proceed to show,

SECONDLY, Positively what this spiritual and divine light is.

And it may be thus described: a true sense of the divine excellency of the things revealed in the word of God, and a conviction of the truth and reality of them thence arising.

This spiritual light primarily consists in the former of these, viz., a real sense and apprehension of the divine excellency of things revealed in the word of God. A spiritual and saving conviction of the truth and reality of these things, arises from such a sight of their divine excellency and glory; so that this conviction of their truth is an effect and natural consequence of this sight of their divine glory. There is therefore in this spiritual light,

1. A true sense of the divine and superlative excellency of the things of religion; a real sense of the excellency of God and Jesus Christ, and of the work of redemption, and the ways and works of God revealed in the gospel. There is a divine and superlative glory in these things; an excellency that is of a vastly higher kind, and more sublime nature than in other things; a glory greatly distinguishing them from all that is earthly and temporal. He that is spiritually enlightened truly apprehends and sees it, or has a sense of it. He does not merely rationally believe that God is glorious, but he has a sense of the gloriousness of God in his heart. There is not only a rational belief that God is holy, and that holiness is a good thing, but there is a sense of the loveliness of God's holiness. There is not only a speculatively judging that God is gracious, but a sense how amiable God is upon that account, or a sense of the beauty of this divine attribute.

There is a twofold understanding or knowledge of good that God has made the mind of man capable of. The first, that which is merely speculative and notional; as when a person only speculatively judges that any thing is, which, by the agreement of mankind, is called good or excellent, viz., that which is most to general advantage, and between which and a reward there is a suitableness, and the like. And the other is, that which consists in the sense of the heart: as when there is a sense of the beauty, amiableness, or sweetness of a thing; so that the heart is sensible of pleasure and delight in the presence of the idea of it. In the former is exercised merely the speculative faculty, or the understanding, strictly so called, or as spoken of in distinction from the will or disposition of the soul. In the latter, the will, or inclination, or heart, is mainly concerned.

Thus there is a difference between having an opinion, that God is holy and gracious, and having a sense of the loveliness and beauty of that holiness and grace. There is a difference between having a rational judgment that honey is sweet, and having a sense of its sweetness. A man may have the former, that knows not how honey tastes; but a man cannot have the latter unless he has an idea of the taste of honey in his mind. So there is a difference between believing that a person is beautiful, and having a sense of his beauty. The former may be obtained by hearsay, but the latter only by seeing the countenance. There is a wide difference between mere speculative rational judging any thing to be excellent, and having a sense of its sweetness and beauty. The former rests only in the head, speculation only is concerned in it; but the heart is concerned in the latter. When the heart is sensible of the beauty and amiableness of a thing, it necessarily feels pleasure in the apprehension. It is implied in a person's being heartily sensible of the loveliness of a thing, that the idea of it is sweet and pleasant to his soul; which is a far different thing from having a rational opinion that it is excellent.

2. There arises from this sense of divine excellency of things contained in the word of God, a conviction of the truth and reality of them; and that either directly or indirectly.

First, Indirectly, and that two ways.

1. As the prejudices that are in the heart, against the truth of divine things, are hereby removed; so that the mind becomes susceptive of the due force of rational arguments for their truth. The mind of man is naturally full of prejudices against the truth of divine things: it is full of enmity against the doctrines of the gospel; which is a disadvantage to those arguments that prove their truth, and causes them to lose their force upon the mind. But when a person has discovered to him the divine excellency of Christian doctrines, this destroys the enmity, removes those prejudices, and sanctifies the reason, and causes it to lie open to the force of arguments for their truth.

Hence was the different effect that Christ's miracles had to convince the disciples from what they had to convince the Scribes and Pharisees. Not that they had a stronger reason, or had their reason more improved; but their reason was sanctified, and those blinding prejudices, that the Scribes and Pharisees were under, were removed by the sense they had of the excellency of Christ and his doctrine.

2. It not only removes the hindrances of reason, but positively helps reason. It makes even the speculative notions the more lively. It engages the attention of the mind, with the more

fixedness and intenseness to that kind of objects; which causes it to have a clearer view of them, and enables it more clearly to see their mutual relations, and occasions it to take more notice of them. The ideas themselves that otherwise are dim and obscure, are by this means impressed with the greater strength, and have a light cast upon them; so that the mind can better judge of them. As he that beholds the objects on the face of the earth, when the light of the sun is cast upon them, is under greater advantage to discern them in their true forms and mutual relations, than he that sees them in a dim starlight or twilight.

The mind having a sensibleness of the excellency of divine objects, dwells upon them with delight; and the powers of the soul are more awakened and enlivened to employ themselves in the contemplation of them, and exert themselves more fully and much more to the purpose. The beauty and sweetness of the objects draws on the faculties, and draws forth their exercises: so that reason itself is under far greater advantages for its proper and free exercises, and to attain its proper end, free of darkness and delusion. But,

SECONDLY. A true sense of the divine excellency of the things of God's word doth more directly and immediately convince of the truth of them; and that because the excellency of these things is so superlative. There is a beauty in them that is so divine and godlike, that is greatly and evidently distinguishing of them from things merely human, or that men are the inventors and authors of; a glory that is so high and great, that when clearly seen, commands assent to their divinity and reality. When there is an actual and lively discovery of this beauty and excellency, it will not allow of any such thought as that it is a human work, or the fruit of men's invention. This evidence that they that are spiritually enlightened have of the truth of the things of religion, is a kind of intuitive and immediate evidence. They believe the doctrines of God's word to be divine, because they see divinity in them; i.e., they see a divine, and transcendent, and most evidently distinguishing glory in them; such a glory as, if clearly seen, does not leave room to doubt of their being of God, and not of men.

Such a conviction of the truth of religion as this, arising, these ways, from a sense of the divine excellency of them, is that true spiritual conviction that there is in saving faith. And this original of it, is that by which it is most essentially distinguished from that common assent, which unregenerate men are capable of.

II. I proceed now to the second thing proposed, viz., to show how this light is immediately given by God, and not obtained by natural means. And here,

1. It is not intended that the natural faculties are not made use of in it. The natural faculties are the subject of this light: and they are the subject in such a manner, that they are not merely passive, but active in it; the acts and exercises of man's understanding are concerned and made use of in it. God, in letting in this light into the soul, deals with man according to his nature, or as a rational creature; and makes use of his human faculties. But yet this light is not the less immediately from God for that; though the faculties are made use of, it is as the subject and not as the cause; and that acting of the faculties in it, is not the cause, but is either implied in the thing itself (in the light that is imparted) or is the consequence of it. As the use that we make of our eyes in beholding various objects, when the sun arises, is not the cause of the light that discovers those objects to us.

2. It is not intended that outward means have no concern in this affair. As I have observed already, it is not in this affair, as it is in inspiration, where new truths are suggested: for here is by this light only given a due apprehension of the same truths that are revealed in the word of God; and therefore it is not given without the word. The gospel is made use of in this affair: this light is the light of the glorious gospel of Christ, 2 Cor. iv: 4. The gospel is as a glass, by which this light conveyed to us, 1 Cor. xiii: 12. Now we see through a glass. — But,

3. When it is said that this light is given immediately by God, and not obtained by natural means, hereby is intended, that it is given by God without making use of any means that operate by their own power, or a natural force. God makes use of means; but it is not as mediate causes to produce this effect. They are not truly any second causes of it; but it is produced by God immediately. The word of God is no proper cause of this effect: it does not operate by any natural force in it. The word of God is only made use of to convey to the mind the subject matter of this saving instruction: and this indeed it doth convey to us by natural force or influence. It conveys to our minds these and those doctrines; it is the cause of the notion of

them in our heads, but not of the sense of the divine excellency of them in our hearts. Indeed a person cannot have spiritual light without the word. But that does not argue, that the word properly causes that light. The mind cannot see the excellency of any doctrine, unless that doctrine be first in the mind; but the seeing of the excellency of the doctrine may be immediately from the Spirit of God; though the conveying of the doctrine or proposition itself may be by the word. So that the notions that are the subject matter of this light, are conveyed to the mind by the word of God; but that due sense of the heart, wherein this light formally consists, is immediately by the Spirit of God. As for instance, that notion that there is a Christ, and that Christ is holy and gracious, is conveyed to the mind by the word of God: but the sense of the excellency of Christ by reason of that holiness and grace, is nevertheless immediately the work of the Holy Spirit.

Sinners in the Hands of an Angry God
(1741)

🪶 A short passage from the famous sermon that Edwards delivered at Enfield, Connecticut, will serve to illustrate the revivalist type of sermon associated with the Great Awakening. Intent, as he said, upon "awakening unconverted persons in this congregation," he chose as his grim text Deut. 32, 35: "Their foot shall slide in due time."

Edwards developed his "awful subject" with dramatic art as well as his usual logical force. He spoke (or rather read) with undemonstrative dignity, yet with such effect that, according to a minister who was present, "There was such a breathing of distress, and weeping, that the preacher was obliged to speak to the people and desire silence, that he might be heard."

Your wickedness makes you as it were heavy as lead, and to tend downwards with great weight and pressure towards hell; and if God should let you go, you would immediately sink and swiftly descend and plunge into the bottomless gulf, and your healthy constitution, and your own care and prudence, and best contrivance, and all your righteousness, would have no more influence to uphold you and keep you out of hell than a spider's web would have to stop a falling rock. Were it not that so is the sovereign pleasure of God, the earth would not bear you one moment; for you are a burden to it; the creation groans with you; the creature is made subject to the bondage of your corruption, not willingly; the sun don't willingly shine upon you to give you light to serve sin and Satan; the earth don't willingly yield her increase to satisfy your lusts; nor is it willingly a stage for your wickedness to be acted upon; the air don't willingly serve you for breath to maintain the flame of life in your vitals, while you spend your life in the service of God's enemies. God's creatures are good, and were made for men to serve God with, and don't willingly subserve to any other purpose, and groan when they are abused to purposes so directly contrary to their nature and end. And the world would spew you out, were it not for the sovereign hand of him who hath subjected it in hope. There are the black clouds of God's wrath now hanging directly over your heads, full of the dreadful storm, and big with thunder; and were it not for the restraining hand of God, it would immediately burst forth upon you. The sovereign pleasure of God, for the present, stays his rough wind; otherwise it would come with fury, and your destruction would come like a whirlwind, and you would be like the chaff of the summer threshing floor.

The wrath of God is like great waters that are dammed for the present; they increase more and more, and rise higher and higher, till an outlet is given; and the longer the stream is stopped, the more rapid and mighty is its course, when once it is let loose. 'Tis true, that judgment against your evil work has not been executed hitherto; the floods of God's vengeance have been withheld; but your guilt in the mean time is constantly increasing, and you are every day treasuring up more wrath; the waters are continually rising, and waxing more and more mighty; and there is nothing but the mere pleasure of God that holds the waters back, that are unwilling to be stopped, and press hard to go forward. If God should only withdraw his hand from the floodgate, it would immediately fly open, and the fiery floods of the fierceness and wrath of God would rush forth with inconceivable fury, and would come upon you with omnipotent power; and if your strength were ten thousand times greater than it is, yea, ten thousand times greater than the strength of the stoutest, sturdiest devil in hell, it would be nothing to withstand or endure it.

The bow of God's wrath is bent, and the arrow made ready on the string, and justice bends the arrow at your heart, and strains the bow, and it is nothing but the mere pleasure of God, and that of an angry God, without any promise or obligation at all, that keeps the arrow one moment from being made drunk with your blood.

Thus are all you that never passed under a great change of heart by the mighty power of the Spirit of God upon your souls; all that were never born again, and made new creatures, and raised from being dead in sin to a state of new and before altogether unexperienced light and life, (however you may have reformed your life in many things, and may have had religious affections, and may keep up a form of religion in your families and closets, and in the house of God, and may be strict in it), you are thus in the hands of an angry God; 'tis nothing but his mere pleasure that keeps you from being this moment swallowed up in everlasting destruction.

However unconvinced you may now be of the truth of what you hear, by and by you will be fully convinced of it. Those that are gone from being in the like circumstances with you see that it was so with them; for destruction came suddenly upon most of them; when they expected nothing of it, and while they were saying, Peace and safety: now they see, that those things that they depended on for peace and safety were nothing but thin air and empty shadows.

The God that holds you over the pit of hell, much as one holds a spider or some loathsome insect over the fire, abhors you, and is dreadfully provoked; his wrath towards you burns like fire; he looks upon you as worthy of nothing else, but to be cast into the fire; he is of purer eyes than to bear to have you in his sight; you are ten thousand times so abominable in his eyes, as the most hateful and venomous serpent is in ours. You have offended him infinitely more than ever a stubborn rebel did his prince: and yet it is nothing but his hand that holds you from falling into the fire every moment. 'Tis ascribed to nothing else, that you did not go to hell the last night; that you was suffered to awake again in this world after you closed your eyes to sleep; and there is no other reason to be given why you have not dropped into hell since you arose in the morning, but that God's hand has held you up. There is no other reason to be given why you han't gone to hell since you have sat here in the house of God, provoking his pure eyes by your sinful wicked manner of attending his solemn worship. Yea, there is nothing else that is to be given as a reason why you don't this very moment drop down into hell.

O sinner! consider the fearful danger you are in. 'Tis a great furnace of wrath, a wide and bottomless pit, full of the fire of wrath, that you are held over in the hand of that God whose wrath is provoked and incensed as much against you as against many of the damned in hell. You hang by a slender thread, with the flames of divine wrath flashing about it, and ready every moment to singe it and burn it asunder; and you have no interest in any Mediator, and nothing to lay hold of to save yourself, nothing to keep off the flames of wrath, nothing of your own, nothing that you ever have done, nothing that you can do, to induce God to spare you one moment.

From *Religious Affections*

(1746)

🞛 This treatise corrects misapprehensions that may arise from the sermon "Sinners in the Hands of an Angry God." Edwards was as ready as anyone else to deplore much of the religious enthusiasm of the Great Awakening, and would certainly have condemned many of the revivalists from his day down to ours. At the same time, "to despise and cry down all religious affections" was, he held, a fundamental blunder.

Exactly wherein he believed the blunder to lie is made clear enough in the following passages, in which this man of intellect set forth the claims of the heart. "Light without heat," he declares, would reduce religion to "a mere lifeless formality" — which it was rapidly becoming in the Age of Reason in which he lived.

2. The Author of the human nature has not only given affections to men, but has made them very much the spring of men's actions. As the affections do not only necessarily belong to the human nature, but are a very great part of it; so (inasmuch as by regeneration persons are renewed in the whole man, and sanctified throughout) holy affections do not only necessarily belong to true religion, but are a very great part of it. And as true religion is of a practical nature, and God hath so constituted the human nature, that the affections are very much the spring of men's actions, this also shows, that true religion must consist very much in the affections.

Such is man's nature, that he is very inactive, any otherwise than he is influenced by some affection, either love or hatred, desire, hope, fear, or some other. These affections we see to be the springs that set men agoing, in all the affairs of life, and engage them in all their pursuits: these are the things that put men forward in all their worldly business; and especially are men excited and animated by these, in all affairs wherein they are earnestly engaged, and which they pursue with vigor. We see the world of mankind to be exceeding busy and active; and the affections of men are the springs of the motion: take away all love and hatred, all hope and fear, all anger, zeal, and affectionate desire, and the world would be in a great measure motionless and dead; there would be no such thing as activity amongst mankind, or any earnest pursuit whatsoever. It is affection that engages the covetous man, and him that is greedy of worldly profits, in his pursuits; and it is by the affections that the ambitious man is put forward in his pursuit of worldly glory; and it is the affections also that actuate the voluptuous man, in his pursuit of pleasure and sensual delights: the world continues, from age to age, in a continual commotion and agitation, in a pursuit of these things; but take away all affection, and the spring of all this motion would be gone, and the motion itself would cease. And as in worldly things, worldly affections are very much the spring of men's motion and action; so in religious matters, the spring of their actions is very much religious affection: he that has doctrinal knowledge and speculation only, without affection, never is engaged in the business of religion.

3. Nothing is more manifest in fact, than that the things of religion take hold of men's souls, no further than they affect them. There are multitudes that often hear the word of God, and therein hear of those things that are infinitely great and important, and that most nearly concern them, and all that is heard seems to be wholly ineffectual upon them, and to make no alteration in their disposition or behavior; and the reason is, they are not affected with what they hear. There are many that often hear of the glorious perfections of God, his almighty power and boundless wisdom, his infinite majesty, and that holiness of God, by which he is of purer eyes than to behold evil, and cannot look on iniquity, and the heavens are not pure in his sight, and of God's infinite goodness and

mercy, and hear of the great works of God's wisdom, power and goodness, wherein there appear the admirable manifestations of these perfections; they hear particularly of the unspeakable love of God and Christ, and of the great things that Christ has done and suffered, and of the great things of another world, of eternal misery in bearing the fierceness and wrath of Almighty God, and of endless blessedness and glory in the presence of God, and the enjoyment of his dear love; they also hear the peremptory commands of God, and his gracious counsels and warnings, and the sweet invitations of the gospel; I say, they often hear these things and yet remain as they were before, with no sensible alteration in them, either in heart or practice, because they are not affected with what they hear; and ever will be so till they are affected. — I am bold to assert, that there never was any considerable change wrought in the mind or conversation of any person, by any thing of a religious nature, that ever he read, heard or saw, that had not his affections moved. Never was a natural man engaged earnestly to seek his salvation; never were any such brought to cry after wisdom, and lift up their voice for understanding, and to wrestle with God in prayer for mercy; and never was one humbled, and brought to the foot of God, from any thing that ever he heard or imagined of his own unworthiness and deserving of God's displeasure; nor was ever one induced to fly for refuge unto Christ, while his heart remained unaffected. Nor was there ever a saint awakened out of a cold, lifeless frame, or recovered from a declining state in religion, and brought back from a lamentable departure from God, without having his heart affected. And in a word, there never was any thing considerable brought to pass in the heart or life of any man living, by the things of religion, that had not his heart deeply affected by those things.***

Of late, instead of esteeming and admiring all religious affections without distinction, it is a thing much more prevalent, to reject and discard all without distinction. Herein appears the subtilty of Satan. While he saw that affections were much in vogue, knowing the greater part of the land were not versed in such things, and had not had much experience of great religious affections to enable them to judge well of them, and distinguish between true and false; then he knew he could best play his game, by sowing tares amongst the wheat, and mingling false affections with the works of God's Spirit: he knew this to be a likely way to delude and eternally ruin many souls, and greatly to wound religion in the saints, and entangle them in a dreadful wilderness, and by and by, to bring all religion into disrepute.

But now, when the ill consequences of these false affections appear, and it is become very apparent, that some of those emotions which made a glaring show, and were by many greatly admired, were in reality nothing; the devil sees it to be for his interest to go another way to work, and to endeavor to his utmost to propagate and establish a persuasion, that all affections and sensible emotions of the mind, in things of religion, are nothing at all to be regarded, but are rather to be avoided, and carefully guarded against, as things of a pernicious tendency. This he knows is the way to bring all religion to a mere lifeless formality, and effectually shut out the power of godliness, and every thing which is spiritual, and to have all true Christianity turned out of doors. For although to true religion there must indeed be something else besides affection; yet true religion consists so much in the affections, that there can be no true religion without them. He who has no religious affection, is in a state of spiritual death, and is wholly destitute of the powerful, quickening, saving influences of the Spirit of God upon his heart. As there is no true religion where there is nothing else but affection, so there is no true religion where there is no religious affection. As on the one hand, there must be light in the understanding, as well as an affected fervent heart; where there is heat without light, there can be nothing divine or heavenly in that heart; so on the other hand, where there is a kind of light without heat, a head stored with notions and speculations, with a cold and unaffected heart, there can be nothing divine in that light, that knowledge is no true spiritual knowledge of divine things. If the great things of religion are rightly understood, they will affect the heart. The reason why men are not affected by such infinitely great, important, glorious, and wonderful things, as they often hear and read of, in the word of God, is undoubtedly because they are blind; if they were not so, it would be impossible, and utterly inconsistent with human nature, that their hearts should be otherwise than strongly impressed, and greatly moved by such things.

This manner of slighting all religious affections, is the way exceedingly to harden the hearts of men, and to encourage them in their stupidity and senselessness, and to keep them in a state of spiritual death as long as they live, and bring them at last to death eternal. The prevailing prejudice against religious affections at this day, in the land, is apparently of awful effect to harden the hearts of sinners, and damp the graces of many of the saints, and stun the life and power of religion, and preclude the effect of ordinances, and hold us down in a state of dulness and apathy, and undoubtedly causes many persons greatly to offend God, in entertaining mean and low thoughts of the extraordinary work he has lately wrought in this land.

And for persons to despise and cry down all religious affections, is the way to shut all religion out of their own hearts, and to make thorough work in ruining their souls.

They who condemn high affections in others, are certainly not likely to have high affections themselves. And let it be considered, that they who have but little religious affection, have certainly but little religion. And they who condemn others for their religious affections, and have none themselves, have no religion.

There are false affections, and there are true. A man's having much affection, does not prove that he has any true religion: but if he has no affection, it proves that he has no true religion. The right way, is not to reject all affections, nor to approve all; but to distinguish between affections, approving some, and rejecting others; separating between the wheat and the chaff, the gold and the dross, the precious and the vile.

2. If it be so, that true religion lies much in the affections, hence we may infer, that such means are to be desired, as have much of a tendency to move the affections. Such books, and such a way of preaching the word, and administration of ordinances, and such a way of worshipping God in prayer, and singing praises, is much to be desired, as has a tendency deeply to affect the hearts of those who attend these means.

Such a kind of means would formerly have been highly approved of, and applauded by the generality of the people of the land, as the most excellent and profitable, and having the greatest tendency to promote the ends of the means of grace. But the prevailing taste seems of late strangely to be altered: that pathetical manner of praying and preaching, which would formerly have been admired and extolled, and that for this reason, because it had such a tendency to move the affections, now, in great multitudes, immediately excites disgust, and moves no other affections than those of displeasure and contempt.

Perhaps, formerly the generality (at least of the common people) were in the extreme, of looking too much to an affectionate address, in public performances: but now, a very great part of the people seem to have gone far into a contrary extreme. Indeed there may be such means, as may have a great tendency to stir up the passions of weak and ignorant persons, and yet have no great tendency to benefit their souls: for though they may have a tendency to excite affections, they may have little or none to excite gracious affections, or any affections tending to grace. But undoubtedly, if the things of religion, in the means used, are treated according to their nature, and exhibited truly, so as tends to convey just apprehensions, and a right judgment of them; the more they have a tendency to move the affections the better.

QUAKER

John Woolman [1720–1772]

Persecuted in seventeenth-century Massachusetts, the Friends throve in New Jersey and especially in the colony of William Penn. In contrast with the Puritans (who did not like people that contrasted with them), the Friends avoided a rigid creed, formal worship, and the leadership of trained ministers. While accepting the Bible as the revealed Word of God, they held each individual competent to understand the teachings of Christ and to lead a Christian life by virtue of direct access to the Holy Spirit. They sought to follow simply, humbly, utterly, the guidance of the Inner Light, which led them toward plain living, peace of mind, and love of all men.

For an insight into the heart of the Friends, we have the journal of a wandering preacher of the eighteenth century. Born in New Jersey, John Woolman received an elementary school education, read much in his father's library, worked as a shopkeeper's apprentice, and became a tailor and merchant. He began preaching at twenty-one and in an itinerant way continued through the rest of his life. In 1772 he went as delegate from the Pennsylvania Friends to those in the north of England, but died of smallpox in York.

His journal has been beloved by many. Whittier called it "a classic of the inner life." Channing said it was "beyond comparison the sweetest and purest autobiography in the language." In England, Charles Lamb advised his readers to get the writings of Woolman "by heart," and Crabb Robinson said: "His is a schöne Seele, a beautiful soul. An illiterate tailor, he writes in a style of the most exquisite purity and grace. His moral qualities are transferred to his writings."

Further reading: *The Journals and Essays of John Woolman*, ed., with a biographical introduction, by A. M. Gummere, 1922. Janet Whitney, *John Woolman, American Quaker*, 1942.

From his *Journal*

(w. 1756–72)

[A Young Quaker's Inward Life]

I have often felt a motion of love to leave some hints of my experience of the goodness of God; and pursuant thereto, in the thirty-sixth year of my age, I begin this work.

I was born in Northampton, in Burlington county, in West Jersey, in the year of our Lord 1720; and before I was seven years old I began to be acquainted with the operations of Divine love. Through the care of my parents, I was taught to read near as soon as I was capable of it; and as I went from school one seventh-day, I remember, while my companions went to play by the way, I went forward out of sight, and sitting down, I read the twenty-second chapter of the Revelation: "He showed me a pure river of water of life, clear as crystal, proceeding out of the throne of God and of the lamb," etc.; and in the reading of it, my mind was drawn to seek after that pure habitation, which, I then believed, God had prepared for his servants. The place where I sat, and the sweetness that attended my mind, remain fresh in my memory.

This, and the like gracious visitations, had that effect upon me, that when boys used ill language, it troubled me, and through the continued mercies of God, I was preserved from it. The pious instructions of my parents were often fresh in my mind when I happened to be among wicked children, and were of use to me.

My parents having a large family of children, used frequently, on first days after meeting, to put us to read in the Holy Scriptures, or some religious books, one after another, the rest sitting by without much conversation; which I have since often thought was a good practice. From what I had read and heard, I believed there had been, in past ages, people who walked in uprightness before God, in a degree exceeding any that I knew or heard of, now living; and the apprehension of there being less steadiness and firmness amongst people in this age than in past ages, often troubled me while I was still young.

I had a dream about the ninth year of my age as follows. I saw the moon rise near the west, and run a regular course eastward, so swift that in about a quarter of an hour she reached our meridian; when there descended from her a small cloud on a direct line to the earth, which lighted on a pleasant green about twenty yards from the door of my father's house (in which I thought I stood) and was immediately turned into a beautiful green tree. The moon appeared to run on with equal swiftness, and soon set in the east, at which time the sun arose at the place where it commonly doth in the summer, and shining with full radiance in a serene air, it appeared as pleasant a morning as ever I saw.

All this time I stood still in the door, in an awful frame of mind, and observed that as heat increased by the rising sun, it wrought so powerfully on the little green tree, that the leaves gradually withered, and before noon it appeared dry and dead. There then appeared a being, small of size, moving swift from the north southward, called a "*Sun Worm*."

Though I was a child, this dream was instructive to me.

Another thing remarkable in my childhood was, that once, as I went to a neighbor's house, I saw, on the way, a robin sitting on her nest; and as I came near she went off, but having young ones, flew about, and with many cries expressed her concern for them. I stood and threw stones at her, till one striking her, she fell down dead. At first I was pleased with the exploit; but after a few minutes was seized with horror, as having, in a sportive way, killed an innocent creature while she was careful for her young. I beheld her lying dead, and thought those young ones, for which she was so careful, must now perish for want of their dam to nourish them; and after some painful considerations on the subject, I climbed up the tree, took all the young birds, and killed them — supposing that better than to leave them to pine away and die miserably; and believed, in this case, that Scripture proverb was fulfilled, "The tender mercies of the wicked are cruel." I then went on my errand, but, for some hours, could think of little else but the cruelties I had committed, and was much troubled. Thus He, whose tender mercies are over all his works, hath placed that in the human mind, which incites to exercise goodness towards every living creature, and this being singly attended to, people become tender-hearted and sympathizing; but being frequently and totally rejected, the mind shuts itself up in a contrary disposition.

About the twelfth year of my age, my father being abroad, my mother reproved me for some misconduct, to which I made an undutiful reply; and the next first-day, as I was with my father returning from meeting, he told me he understood I had behaved amiss to my mother, and advised me to be more careful in future. I knew myself blamable, and in shame and confusion remained silent. Being thus awakened to a sense of my wickedness, I felt remorse in my mind, and getting home, I retired and prayed to the Lord to forgive me; and do not remember that I ever, after that, spoke unhandsomely to either of my parents, however foolish in some other things.

Having attained the age of sixteen, I began to love wanton company; and though I was preserved from profane language or scandalous conduct, still I perceived a plant in me which produced much wild grapes. Yet my merciful Father forsook me not utterly, but at times, through his grace, I was brought seriously to consider my ways; and the sight of my backsliding affected me with sorrow; but for want of rightly attending to the reproofs of instruction, vanity was added to vanity, and repentance. Upon the whole, my mind was more and more alienated from the Truth, and I hastened towards destruction. While I meditate on the gulf towards which I travelled, and reflect on my youthful disobedience, my heart is affected with sorrow.

Advancing in age, the number of my acquaintance increased, and thereby my way grew more difficult. Though I had heretofore found comfort in reading the Holy Scriptures, and thinking on heavenly things, I was now estranged therefrom. I knew I was going from the flock of Christ, and had no resolution to return; hence serious reflections were uneasy to me, and youthful vanities and diversions my greatest pleasure. Running in this road I found many like myself; and we associated in that which is reverse to true friendship. But in this swift race it pleased God to visit me with sickness, so that I doubted of recovering; and then did darkness, horror, and amazement, with full force seize me, even when my pain and distress of body was very great. I thought it would have been better for me never to have had a being, than to see the day which I now saw. I was filled with confusion; and in great affliction, both of mind and body, I lay and bewailed myself. I had not confidence to lift up my cries to God, whom I had thus offended; but in a deep sense of my great folly, I was humbled before him: and at length, that Word which is as a fire and a hammer, broke and dissolved my rebellious heart, and then my cries were put up in contrition; and in the multitude of his mercies I found inward relief, and felt a close engagement, that if he was pleased to restore my health, I might walk humbly before him.

After my recovery, this exercise remained with me a considerable time; but by degrees, giving way to youthful vanities, they gained strength, and getting with wanton young people I lost ground. The Lord had been very gracious, and spoke peace to me in the time of my distress; and I now most ungratefully turned again to folly; on which account, at times, I felt sharp reproof, but did not get low enough to cry for help. I was not so hardy as to commit things scandalous; but to exceed in vanity and promote mirth, was my chief study. Still I retained a love and esteem for pious people; and their company brought an awe upon me. My dear parents several times admonished me in the fear of the Lord, and their admonition entered into my heart, and had a good effect for a season; but not getting deep enough to pray rightly, the tempter, when he came, found entrance. I remember once, having spent a part of a day in wantonness, as I went to bed at night, there lay in a window near my bed a Bible, which I opened, and first cast my eye on the text, "we lie down in our shame, and our confusion covers us"; this I knew to be my case; and meeting with so unexpected a reproof, I was somewhat affected with it, and went to bed under remorse of conscience; which I soon cast off again.

Thus time passed on: my heart was replenished with mirth and wantonness, while pleasing scenes of vanity were presented to my imagination, till I attained the age of eighteen years, near which time I felt the judgments of God in my soul like a consuming fire, and looking over my past life, the prospect was moving. I was often sad, and longed to be delivered from those vanities; then, again, my heart was strongly inclined to them, and there was in me a sore conflict. At times I turned to folly; and then again, sorrow and confusion took hold of me. In a while, I resolved totally to leave off some of my vanities; but there was a secret reserve in my heart, of the more refined part of them, and I was not low enough to find true peace. Thus for some months, I had great troubles and disquiet, there remaining in me an unsubjected will, which rendered my labors fruitless, till at length, through the merciful continuance of heavenly visitations, I was made to bow down in spirit before the Lord. I remember one evening I had spent some time in reading a pious author; and walking out alone, I humbly prayed to the Lord for his help, that I might be delivered from those vanities which so ensnared me. Thus, being brought low, he helped me, and as I learned to bear the Cross, I felt refreshment to come from his presence, but not keeping in that strength which gave victory, I lost ground again, the sense of which greatly afflicted me; and I sought deserts and lonely places, and there with tears did confess my sins to God, and humbly craved help of him. And I may say with reverence, he was near to me in my troubles, and in those times of humiliation opened my ear to discipline. I was now led to look seriously at the means by which I was drawn from the pure truth, and learned this, that if I would live in the life which the faithful servants of God lived in, I must not go into company as heretofore, in my own will; but all the cravings of sense must be governed by a Divine principle. In times of sorrow and abasement, these instructions were sealed up me, and I felt the power of Christ prevail over all selfish desires, so that I was preserved in a good degree of steadiness; and being young, and believing, at that time, that a single life was best for me, I was strengthened to keep from such company as had often been a snare to me.

I kept steady to meetings; spent first-days in the afternoon chiefly in reading the Scriptures, and other good books; and was early convinced in my mind that true religion consisted in an inward life, wherein the heart doth love and reverence God the Creator, and learn to exercise true justice and goodness, not only toward all men, but also toward the brute creatures. That as the mind was moved by an inward principle to love God as an invisible, incomprehensible Being, by the same principle it was moved to love him in all his manifestations in the visible world. That, as by his breath the flame of life was kindled in all animal and sensible creatures, to say we love God as unseen, and, at the same time, exercise cruelty toward the least creature moving by his life, or by life derived from him, was a contradiction in itself.

I found no narrowness respecting sects and opinions; but believed that sincere, upright-hearted people, in every society, who truly love God, were accepted of him.

As I lived under the Cross, and simply followed the openings of Truth, my mind, from day to day, was more enlightened; my former acquaintance were left to judge of me as they would, for I found it safest for me to live in private, and to keep these things sealed up in my own breast. While I silently ponder on that change which was wrought in me, I find no language equal to it, nor any means to convey to another a clear idea of it. I looked upon the works of God in this visible creation, and an awfulness covered me; my heart was tender, and often contrite, and a universal love to my fellow-creatures increased in me. This will be understood by such who have trodden in the same path.

[Uneasiness as to Slavery]

✣ In 1746 Woolman and a friend made a journey to Virginia and North Carolina, traveling about 1500 miles. His comment on slavery, printed below, foreshadows his *Essay on Some Considerations on the Keeping of Negroes*, 1754, 1762, a significant document in the early phase of anti-slavery agitation.

Two things were remarkable to me in this journey. First, in regard to my entertainment: when I eat, drank, and lodged free-cost, with people who lived in ease on the hard toil of their slaves, I felt uneasy; and as my mind was inward to the Lord, I found, from place to place, this uneasiness return upon me, at times, through the whole visit. Where the masters bore a good share of the burthen, and lived frugally, so that their servants were well provided for, and their labor moderate, I felt more easy; but where they lived in a costly way, and laid heavy burthens on their slaves, my exercise was often great, and I frequently had conversation with them, in private, concerning it. Secondly, this trade of importing slaves from their native country being much encouraged amongst them, and the white people and their children so generally living without much labor, was frequently the subject of my serious thought; and I saw in these Southern provinces so many vices and corruptions, increased by this trade and this way of life, that it appeared to me as a dark gloominess hanging over the land; and though now many willingly run into it, yet in future the consequences will be grievous to posterity. I express it as it hath appeared to me, not at once, or twice, but as a matter fixed on my mind.

[A Plain Way of Living]

Until the year 1756, I continued to retail goods, besides following my trade as a tailor; about which time I grew uneasy on account of my business growing too cumbersome. I began with selling trimmings for garments, and from thence proceeded to sell cloths and linens; and at length, having got a considerable shop of goods, my trade increased every year, and the road to large business appeared open: but I felt a stop in my mind.

Through the mercies of the Almighty, I had, in a good degree, learned to be content with a plain way of living. I had but a small family; and on serious reflection, I believed Truth did not require me to engage in many cumbering affairs. It had generally been my practice to buy and sell things really useful. Things that served chiefly to please the vain mind in people, I was not easy to trade in; seldom did it, and whenever I did, I found it to weaken me as a Christian.

The increase of business became my burthen; for though my natural inclination was toward merchandise, yet I believed Truth required me to live more free from outward cumbers. There was now a strife in my mind betwixt the two, and in this exercise my prayers were put up to the Lord, who graciously heard me, and gave me a heart resigned to his holy will; I then lessened my outward business; and as I had opportunity, told my customers of my intention, that they might consider what shop to turn to; and so in a while, wholly laid down merchandise, following my trade as a tailor, myself only, having no prentice. I also had a nursery of apple trees, in which I spent a good deal of time hoeing, grafting, trimming, and inoculating.

In merchandise it is the custom, where I lived, to sell chiefly on credit, and poor people often get in debt; and when payment is expected, having not wherewith to pay, and so their creditors often sue for it at law. Having often observed occurrences of this kind, I found it good for me to advise poor people to take such goods as were most useful and not costly.

In the time of trading, I had an opportunity of seeing that a too liberal use of spirituous liquors, and the custom of wearing too costly apparel, led some people into great inconveniences; and these two things appear to be often connected one with the other; for by not attending to that use of things which is consistent with universal righteousness, there is an increase of labor which extends beyond what our heavenly Father intends for us; and by great labor, and often by much sweating in the heat, there is, even among such who are not drunkards, a craving of some liquor to revive the spirits; that, partly by the luxurious drinking of some, and partly by the drinking of others, led to it through immoderate labor, very great quantities of rum are annually expended in our colonies; of which we should have no need, did we steadily attend to pure wisdom.

Where men take pleasure in feeling their minds elevated with strong drink, and so indulge this appetite as to disorder their understanding, neglect their duty as members in a family or civil society, and cast off all pretence to religion, their case is much to be pitied; and

where such whose lives are for the most part regular, and whose examples have a strong influence on the minds of others, adhere to some customs which powerfully draw toward the use of more strong liquor than pure wisdom directeth the use of; this also, as it hinders the spreading of the spirit of meekness, and strengthens the hands of the more excessive drinkers, is a case to be lamented.

As the least degree of luxury hath some connection with evil, for those who profess to be disciples of Christ, and are looked upon as leaders of the people, to have that mind in them which was also in Him, and so stand separate from every wrong way, is a means of help to the weaker. As I have sometimes been much spent in the heat, and taken spirits to revive me, I have found by experience that the mind is not so calm in such circumstances, nor so fitly disposed for Divine meditation, as when all such extremes are avoided; and I have felt an increasing care to attend to that Holy Spirit which sets right bounds to our desires, and leads those who faithfully follow it to apply all the gifts of Divine Providence to the purposes for which they were intended. Did such who have the care of great estates, attend with singleness of heart to this heavenly Instructor, which so opens and enlarges the mind that men love their neighbors as themselves, they would have wisdom given them to manage, without ever finding occasion to employ some people in the luxuries of life, or to make it necessary for others to labor too hard; but for want of regarding steadily this principle of Divine love, a selfish spirit takes place in the minds of people, which is attended with darkness and manifold confusions in the world.

In the course of my trading, being somewhat affected at the various law suits about collecting money which I saw going forward, on applying to a constable he gave me a list of his proceedings for one year, as follows: to wit, served 267 warrants, 193 summonses, and 17 executions!

Though trading in things useful is an honest employ, yet, through the great number of superfluities which are commonly bought and sold, and through the corruptions of the times, they who apply to merchandize for a living have great need to be well experienced in that precept which the prophet Jeremiah laid down for Baruc, his scribe: "Seekest thou great things for thyself? seek them not."

ANGLICAN GENTLEMAN

William **B**yrd [1674–1744]

Gentleman planter from Virginia, slaveholder and landowner, wealthy tobacco grower, William Byrd represents a way of colonial life in America greatly different from the stern moral code of New England. In his secret diary, Byrd reveals the daily round of his activities on the plantation at Westover on the James River — visiting, dancing, drinking, controlling the servants, reading Greek and Hebrew, quarreling with his wife. An element of worldliness characterizes the planting aristocracy of Virginia, a love of amusement, luxury, fine houses, fashionable furniture, books, ornaments, and clothes in the mode. Yet along with the hunting, fishing, card-playing, and horse-racing, the claims of religion were always in the background. The plantation owner like Byrd was bred to a sense of duty and leadership toward his household, acting as the spiritual as well as the secular head of his small community. The Anglican Church inspired in him a sense of decorum and a reverence for religion unlike that of Massachusetts in its greater sense of tradition, ceremony, and ease of conscience.

Byrd was the author of *A Progress to the Mines*, *A Journey to the Land of Eden*, and *The History of the Dividing Line*, books written in the form of notes or diaries of trips he made to survey lands he owned or establish boundary lines. His writing is straightforward, earthy, and shrewd in observation of people and places. He describes the sluggard life of North Carolina planters with evident distaste, or the love habits of Indian women with curiosity and relish. But writing was only one of many interests of this dilettante scholar and traveler. He moved freely in London society. Devoted to the theater, he knew the Restoration dramatists Congreve, Rowe, and Wycherley. An eager collector of books, Byrd built up a library of over 3,600 titles, the largest in Virginia. It included history, biography, and travels (more than 250 works); books of law, medicine, and divinity (about 150 each); books of science, mathematics, architecture, painting, philosophy, agriculture, distillery, and cooking; Greek and Latin authors in the original (nearly 300); and English literature, especially the Elizabethan and Restoration dramatists.

A blend of worldliness, cultural interests, gentility, and class responsibility, Byrd's life reveals much of the way sophisticated Anglican culture was transferred to the colonial frontier. As a statesman he was an early example of the later gentlemen of Virginia who were leaders of the American Revolution and spokesmen of the Age of Reason. He represented Virginia three times at the court of England, took part in the colony's long dispute with Governor Spotswood, and founded Richmond and Petersburg. In 1709 Byrd became a member of the Council of State, the aristocratic group that virtually governed Virginia. In 1728 he served as one of the commissioners to settle the boundary dispute between Virginia and North Carolina. At his death he was president of the Council of State.

Further reading: *The Writings of William Byrd*, ed. J. S. Bassett, 1901. L. B. Wright, *The First Gentlemen of Virginia*, 1940. R. C. Beatty, *William Byrd of Westover*, 1932.

From *Secret Diary*

For his own eyes only, Byrd kept a shorthand diary somewhat resembling that of Pepys in England. Undiscovered till our own times, a diary for 1709– 1712 was published in 1941, one for 1739–1741 in 1942. Our selections are from the former. They provide interesting glimpses of Byrd's life at Westover.

[Life of a Virginia Gentleman]

Dec. 25, 1709. I rose at 7 o'clock and ate milk for breakfast. I neglected to say my prayers because of my company. I ate milk for breakfast. About 11 o'clock the rest of the company ate some broiled turkey for their breakfast. Then we went to church, notwithstanding it rained a little, where Mr. Anderson preached a good sermon for the occasion. I received the sacrament with great devoutness. After church the same company went to dine with me and I ate roast beef for dinner. In the afternoon Dick Randolph and Mr. Jackson went away and Mr. Jackson rode sidelong like a woman. Then we took a walk about the plantation, but a great fog soon drove us into the house again. In the evening we were merry with nonsense and so were my servants. I said my prayers shortly and had good health, good thoughts, and good humor, thanks be to God Almighty.

Dec. 29. I rose at 5 o'clock and read two chapters in Hebrew and some Greek in Cassius. I said my prayers and ate milk for breakfast. I danced my dance. About 9 o'clock I ate again some chocolate with the company. Then we took a walk and I slid on skates, notwithstanding there was a thaw. Then we returned and played at billiards till dinner. I ate boiled beef for dinner. In the afternoon we played at billiards again and in the evening took another walk and gave Mr. Isham Randolph two bits to venture on the ice. He ventured and the ice broke with him and took him up to the mid-leg. Then we came home and played a little at whisk, but I was so sleepy we soon left off.

March 31, 1710. I rose at 7 o'clock and read some Greek in bed. I said my prayers and ate milk for breakfast. Then about 8 o'clock we got a-horseback and rode to Mr. Harrison's and found him very ill but sensible. Here I met Mr. Bland who brought me several letters from England and among the rest 2 from Colonel Blakiston who had endeavored to procure the Government of Virginia for me at the price of 1000 pounds of my Lady Orkney and that my Lord [agreed], but the Duke of Marlborough declared that no one but soldiers should have the government of a plantation so I was disappointed. God's will be done. From hence I came home where I found all well, thank God. I ate fish for dinner. In the afternoon I went again with my wife to Mr. Harrison's who continued very bad so that I resolved to stay with him all night, which I did with Mr. Anderson and Nat Burwell. He was in the same bad condition till he vomited and then he was more easy. In the morning early I returned home and went to bed. It is remarkable that Mrs. Burwell dreamed this night that she saw a person that with money scales weighed time and declared that there was no more than 18 pennies worth of time to come, which seems to be a dream with some significance either concerning the world or a sick person. In my letters from England I learned that the Bishop of Worcester was of opinion that in the year 1715 the city of Rome would be burnt to the ground, that before the year 1745 the popish religion would be rooted out of the world, that before the year 1790 the Jews and Gentiles would be converted to the Christianity and then would begin the millennium.

April 10. I rose at 6 o'clock and wrote several letters to my overseers. I sent early to inquire after Mr. Harrison and received word that he died about 4 o'clock this morning, which completed the 18th day of his sickness, according to Mrs. Burwell's dream exactly. Just before his death he was sensible and desired Mrs. Lee with importunity to open the door because he wanted to go out and could not go till the door was open and as soon as the door was opened he died. The country has lost a very useful man and who was both an advantage and an ornament to it, and I have lost a good neighbor, but God's will be done. I said my prayers and ate caudle for breakfast. I danced my dance. My wife rode to Mrs. Harrison's to comfort her and to assure her that I should be always ready to do her all manner of service. My wife returned before dinner. I ate tripe for dinner. In the afternoon we played at piquet. Then I prepared my matters for the General Court. It rained, with the wind at northeast, and it was very cold, and in the night it snowed.

May 23. I rose at 5 o'clock and read 2 chapters in Hebrew and some Greek in Anacreon. The children were a little better, thank God. I said my prayers and ate milk and strawberries for breakfast. I danced my dance. My daughter was very ill, but the boy had lost his fever, thank God. I settled some accounts and wrote some commonplace. I ate hashed shoat for dinner. In the afternoon Evie had a sweat that worked pretty well, but not long enough, for which I was out of humor with my wife. I read some Italian and some news and then took a walk about the plantation. When I returned I had a great quarrel with my wife, in which she was to blame altogether; however, I made the first step to the reconciliation, to [which] she with difficulty consented.

June 15. I rose at 5 o'clock and read a chapter in Hebrew and some Greek in Thucydides. I said my prayers and ate milk for breakfast. The weather was very hot. I wrote a letter to England. I ate some broiled pork for dinner. In the afternoon my gripes returned on me and continued till the evening with some violence. Hot things did it no good but in the evening I drank some warm milk from the cow which eased me immediately. It rained this afternoon very hard with a little wind and thunder. This hindered my walking anywhere but in the garden. I foretold by my cellar stinking that it would rain. I impute my gripes to cherry wine, or else pulling my coat off about noon. I said my prayers and had good thoughts, good humor, but indifferent good health, thank God Almighty.

June 16. I rose at 5 o'clock and drank some milk warm from the cow. I read a chapter in Hebrew and some Greek in Thucydides. I said my prayers and danced my dance. About 10 o'clock Captain Drury Stith and his wife came

to make us a visit, notwithstanding it was very hot. I was glad to see them because I think them excellent people. We played at billiards till dinner. I ate boiled pork. In the afternoon we passed away the time pleasantly till about 6 o'clock and then they went home. In the evening I took a walk with my wife. We made a little cider of the G-n-t-n apples, which yielded but little juice. I was better of my gripes, thank God. I neglected to say my prayers but had good health, good thoughts, and good humor, thank God Almighty.

June 17. I rose at 5 o'clock and drank some milk hot from the cow. I read a chapter in Hebrew and some Greek in Thucydides. I said my prayers and danced my dance. About 8 o'clock Mr. Anderson came on his way over the river. He told me the quarrel was made up between Parson Slater and his vestry without coming to trial. He stayed about half an hour. Colonel Hill sent his man with a basket of apricots, of which my wife ate twelve immediately and I ate eight which however did not make my gripes return. I set my closet right. I ate tongue and chicken for dinner. In the afternoon I caused L-s-n to be whipped for beating his wife and Jenny was whipped for being his whore. In the evening the sloop came from Appomatox with tobacco. I took a walk about the plantation. I said my prayers and drank some new milk from the cow. I had good health, good thoughts, and good humor, thanks be to God Almighty.

June 18. I rose at 5 o'clock and drank some new milk from the cow. I read a chapter in Hebrew and some Greek in Thucydides. I said my prayers. It was extremely hot. I read a sermon in Dr. Tillotson about angels. I wrote a letter to Williamsburg to send by my sloop which I sent for rum, wine, and sugar from thence and that this might come safely I resolved to send Bannister with the sloop. I ate chicken for dinner but very little because I had no appetite. In the afternoon my wife told me a dream she had two nights. She thought she saw a scroll in the sky in form of a light cloud with writing on it. It ran extremely fast from west to east with great swiftness. The writing she could not read but there was a woman before her that told her there would be a great dearth because of want of rain and after that a pestilence for that the seasons were changed and time inverted. Mr. James Burwell and Charles Doyley came and in the evening I took a walk with them. Our nurse went away in the sloop. I said my prayers and had good health, good thoughts, and good humor, thanks be to God Almighty.

June 19. I rose at 5 o'clock and read a chapter in Hebrew and some Greek in Thucydides. I drank some warm milk from the cow. I said my prayers and danced my dance. About 10 o'clock came Isham Randolph and Mr. Finney to see us. They told me Colonel Randolph was very ill and very melancholy. We played at billiards till dinner. I ate fish for dinner. In the afternoon Mr. Stith came over with my cousin Berkeley, who all stayed here till the evening and then they all went away but Mr. Finney. In the evening we took a walk. Mr. Finney is a sensible man and good natured. He told me that Major Allen died on Thursday last. In our walk we met Mr. C—s who came home with us. I neglected to say my prayers but had good health, good thoughts, and good humor, thank God Almighty.

June 20. I rose at 5 o'clock and drank milk from the cow. I read a chapter in Hebrew and some Greek in Thucydides. I said my prayers and danced my dance. Mr. Finney returned home without any breakfast but I gave him some strong water. Colonel Hill sent us another present of apricots. I wrote a letter to England. I ate five apricots which put my belly out of order. I ate roast mutton for dinner. In the afternoon my belly was griped. I played with my wife at piquet and then I ordered the boat to carry us to my cousin Harrison's where we found my cousin Berkeley and Jimmy Burwell. I was out of order in my belly. About 8 o'clock we returned home where we found all well, thank God. I said my prayers and had good health, good thoughts, and good humor, thanks be to God Almighty.

June 21. I rose at 5 o'clock and drank milk from the cow. I read a chapter in Hebrew and some Greek in Thucydides. I said my prayers and danced my dance. My wife was indisposed. I sent Tom to Appomattox to desire Mr. Mumford to go to the outcry of my uncle's estate. About five nights since I dreamed I saw a flaming star in the air at which I was much frightened and called some others to see it but when they came it disappeared. I fear this portends some judgment to this country or at least to myself. I ate roast mutton for dinner. In the afternoon I settled the closet. About 5 o'clock I received an express from Mr. Clayton that the Governor, Colonel Spotswood, with two men-of-war arrived last night at Kiquotan with several other ships.

I sent word of this to Mrs. Harrison and then prepared to go to Williamsburg tomorrow. In the evening I took a walk about the plantation. I said my prayers and had good thoughts, good humor, and good health, thank God Almighty.

July 9. About 11 o'clock we went to church and had a good sermon. After church I invited nobody home because I design to break that custom, that my people may go to church. I ate boiled pork for dinner. In the afternoon my wife and I had a terrible quarrel about the things she had come in [i.e. her goods from England], but at length she submitted because she was in the wrong. For my part I kept my temper very well.

July 15. About 7 o'clock the Negro Betty that ran away was brought home. My wife against my will caused little Jenny to be burned with a hot iron, for which I quarreled with her. It was so hot today that I did not intend to go to the launching of Colonel Hill's ship, but about 9 o'clock the Colonel was so kind as to come and call us. My wife would not go at first but with much entreaty she at last consented. About 12 o'clock we went and found abundance of company at the ship, and about one she was launched and went off very well, notwithstanding several had believed the contrary.

Sept. 20. I rose at 6 o'clock but read nothing because I prepared for the Governor's coming in the evening. I neglected to say my prayers but ate milk for breakfast. I settled several things in my library. All the wood was removed from the place where it used to lay to a better place. I sent John to kill some blue wing and he had good luck. I ate some boiled beef for dinner. In the afternoon all things were put into the best order because Captain Burbydge sent word that the Governor would be here at 4 o'clock but he did not come till 5. Captain Burbydge sent his boat for him and fired as he came up the river. I received at the landing with Mr. C—s and gave him 3 guns. Mr. Clayton and Mr. Robinson came with him. After he had drunk some wine he walked in the garden and in the library till it was dark. Then he went to supper and ate some blue wing. After supper we sat and talked till 9 o'clock.

Sept. 21. I rose at 6 o'clock and read nothing but got ready to receive the company. About 8 o'clock the Governor came down. I offered him some of my fine water [?]. Then we had milk tea and bread and butter for breakfast. The Governor was pleased with everything and very complaisant. About 10 o'clock Captain Stith came and soon after him Colonel Hill, Mr. Anderson and several others of the militia officers. The Governor was extremely courteous to them. About 12 o'clock Mr. Clayton went to Mrs. Harrison's and then orders were given to bring all the men into the pasture to muster. Just as we got on our horses it began to rain hard; however this did not discourage the Governor but away we rode to the men. It rained half an hour and the Governor mustered them all the while and he presented me to the people to be their Colonel and commander-in-chief. About 3 o'clock we returned to the house and as many of the officers as could sit at the table stayed to dine with the Governor, and the rest went to take part of the hogshead [of punch] in the churchyard. We had a good dinner, well served, with which the Governor seemed to be well pleased. I ate venison for dinner. In the evening all the company went away and we took a walk and found a comic freak of a man that was drunk that hung on the pales. Then we went home and played at piquet and I won the pool. About 9 the Governor went to bed.

Feb. 5, 1711. I rose about eight o'clock and found my cold still worse. I said my prayers and ate milk and potatoes for breakfast. My wife and I quarreled about her pulling her brows. She threatened she would not go to Williamsburg if she might not pull them; I refused, however, and got the better of her and maintained my authority.

Nov. 23. It was very cold this morning. About 11 o'clock I went to the coffeehouse where the Governor also came and from thence we went to the capitol and read the bill concerning ports the first time. We stayed till 3 o'clock and then went to dinner to Marot's but could get none there and therefore Colonel Lewis and I dined with Colonel Duke and I ate broiled chicken for dinner. After dinner we went to Colonel Carter's room where we had a bowl of punch of French brandy and oranges. We talked very lewdly and were almost drunk and in that condition we went to the coffeehouse and played at dice and I lost £12. We stayed at the coffeehouse till almost 4 o'clock in the morning talking with Major Harrison.

Dec. 29. I rose about 7 o'clock and read two chapters in Hebrew and some Greek in Lucian. I said my prayers and ate boiled milk for breakfast. I had abundance of talk with Mr. G-r-l about the affairs of Falling Creek and he told me some of his wants and so did George Smith,

which I endeavored to supply as well as I could. I gave John G-r-l leave to go visit his mother. Poor old Jane died this morning about 9 o'clock and I caused her to be buried as soon as possible because she stank very much. It was not very cold today. I danced my dance. Mr. G-r-l and George Smith went away about 12 o'clock. I ate some broiled goose for dinner. In the afternoon I set my razor, and then went out to shoot with bow and arrow till the evening and then I ran to breathe myself and looked over everything. At night I read some Latin in Terence till about 10 o'clock. I said my prayers and had good health, good thoughts, and good humor, thank God Almighty.

Dec. 30. I rose about 7 o'clock and read a chapter in Hebrew and three chapters in the Greek Testament. I said my prayers very devoutly and ate boiled milk for breakfast. The weather was very clear and warm so that my wife walked out with Mrs. Dunn and forgot dinner, for which I had a little quarrel with her and another afterwards because I was not willing to let her have a book out of the library. About 12 o'clock came Mr. Bland from Williamsburg but brought no news. He stayed to dinner and I ate some roast beef. In the afternoon we sat and talked till about 4 o'clock and then I caused my people to set him over the river and then I walked with the women about the plantation till they were very weary. At night we ate some eggs and drank some Virginia beer and talked very gravely without reading anything. However I said my prayers and spoke with all my people. I had good health, good thoughts, and good humor, thank God Almighty. I danced my dance in the morning.

Dec. 31. I rose about 7 o'clock and read a chapter in Hebrew and six leaves in Lucian. I said my prayers and ate boiled milk for breakfast. The weather continued warm and clear. I settled my accounts and wrote several things till dinner. I danced my dance. I ate some turkey and chine for dinner. In the afternoon I weighed some money and then read some Latin in Terence and then Mr. Mumford came and told me my man Tony had been very sick but he was recovered again, thank God. He told me Robin Bolling had been like to die and that he denied that he was the first to mention the imposition on skins which he certainly did. Then he and I took a walk about the plantation. When I returned I was out of humor to find the Negroes all at work in our chambers. At night I ate some broiled turkey with Mr. Mumford and we talked and were merry all the evening. I said my prayers and had good health, good thoughts, and good humor, thank God Almighty. My wife and I had a terrible quarrel about whipping Eugene while Mr. Mumford was there but she had a mind to show her authority before company but I would not suffer it, which she took very ill; however for peace sake I made the first advance towards a reconciliation which I obtained with some difficulty and after abundance of crying. However it spoiled the mirth of the evening, but I was not conscious that I was to blame in that quarrel.

Jan. 1, 1712. I lay abed till 9 o'clock this morning to bring my wife into temper again and rogered her by way of reconciliation. I read nothing because Mr. Mumford was here, nor did I say my prayers, for the same reason. However I ate boiled milk for breakfast, and after my wife tempted me to eat some pancakes with her. Mr. Mumford and I went to shoot with our bows and arrows but shot nothing, and afterwards we played at billiards till dinner, and when we came we found Ben Harrison there, who dined with us. I ate some partridge for dinner. In the afternoon we played at billiards again and I won two bits. I had a letter from Colonel Duke by H-e the bricklayer who came to offer his services to work for me. Mr. Mumford went away in the evening and John Bannister with him to see his mother. I took a walk about the plantation and at night we drank some mead of my wife's making which was very good. I gave the people some cider and a dram to the Negroes. I read some Latin in Terence and had good health, good thoughts, and good humor, thank God Almighty. I said my prayers.

History of the Dividing Line

𝕏 Surveying the disputed boundary line between Virginia and North Carolina was an arduous undertaking. Byrd's narrative, presumably intended for publication, remained in manuscript form till 1841, nearly a century after his death. In 1929 a rougher version, *A Secret History of the Line*, appeared. The selections below are from the more finished version. Byrd's fresh, lively style, with its flashes of wit, causes us to regard lightly his exaggerations and prejudices.

[The Dismal Swamp]

March 12, 1728. Our landlord had a tolerable good house and clean furniture, and yet we could not be tempted to lodge in it. We chose rather to lie in the open field, for fear of growing too tender. A clear sky, spangled with stars, was our canopy which, being the last thing we saw before we fell asleep, gave us magnificent dreams. The truth of it is, we took so much pleasure in that natural kind of lodging that I think at the foot of the account mankind are great losers by the luxury of feather beds and warm apartments.

The curiosity of beholding so new and withal so sweet a method of encamping, brought one of the senators of North Carolina to make us a midnight visit. But he was so very clamorous in his commendations of it that the sentinel, not seeing his quality, either through his habit or behavior, had like to have treated him roughly. After excusing the unseasonableness of his visit, and letting us know he was a Parliament man, he swore he was so taken with our lodging that he would set fire to his house as soon as he got home, and teach his wife and children to lie, like us, in the open field.

March 14. Before nine of the clock this morning, the provisions, bedding, and other necessaries, were made up into packs for the men to carry on their shoulders into the Dismal. They were victualed for eight days at full allowance, nobody doubting but that would be abundantly sufficient to carry them through that inhospitable place; nor indeed was it possible for the poor fellows to stagger under more. As it was, their loads weighed from 60 to 70 pounds, in just proportion to the strength of those who were to bear them.

'Twould have been unconscionable to have saddled them with burthens heavier than that, when they were to lug them through a filthy bog which was hardly practicable with no burthen at all. Besides this luggage at their backs, they were obliged to measure the distance, mark the trees, and clear the way for the surveyors every step they went. It was really a pleasure to see with how much cheerfulness they undertook, and with how much spirit they went through all this drudgery. For their greater safety, the commissioners took care to furnish them with Peruvian bark, rhubarb, and hipocoacanah, in case they might happen, in that wet journey, to be taken with fevers or fluxes.

Although there was no need of example to inflame persons already so cheerful, yet, to enter the people with better grace, the author and two more of the commissioners accompanied them half a mile into the Dismal. The skirts of it were thinly planted with dwarf reeds and gall bushes but, when we got into the Dismal itself, we found the reeds grew there much taller and closer and, to mend the matter, was so interlaced with bamboo briars that there was no scuffling through them without the help of pioneers. At the same time, we found the ground moist and trembling under our feet like a quagmire, insomuch that it was an easy matter to run a ten-foot pole up to the head in it, without exerting any uncommon strength to do it.

Two of the men, whose burthens were the least cumbersome, had orders to march before with their tomahawks and clear the way, in order to make an opening for the surveyors. By their assistance we made a shift to push the line half a mile in three hours, and then reached a small piece of firm land about 100 yards wide standing up above the rest like an island. Here the people were glad to lay down their loads and take a little refreshment, while the happy man whose lot it was to carry the jug of rum began already, like Aesop's breadcarriers, to find it grow a good deal lighter.

After reposing about an hour, the commissioners recommended vigor and constancy to their fellow travelers, by whom they were answered with three cheerful huzzas in token of obedience. This ceremony was no sooner over but they took up their burthens and attended the motion of the surveyors who, though they worked with all their might, could reach but one mile farther, the same obstacles still attending them which they had met with in the morning.

However small this distance may seem to such as are used to travel at their ease, yet our poor men, who were obliged to work with an unwieldy load at their backs, had reason to think it a long way; especially in a bog where they had no firm footing, but every step made a deep impression, which was instantly filled with water. At the same time they were laboring with their hands to cut down the reeds, which were ten feet high, their legs were hampered with the briars. Besides, the weather happened to be very warm, and the tallness of the reeds kept off every friendly breeze from coming to refresh them. And, indeed, it was a little provoking to hear the wind whistling among the branches of the white cedars, which grew here and there amongst the reeds, and at the same time not have the comfort to feel the least breath of it.

In the meantime the three commissioners returned out of the Dismal the same way they went in and, having joined their brethren, proceeded that night as far as Mr. Wilson's.

This worthy person lives within sight of the Dismal, in the skirts whereof his stocks range and maintain themselves all the winter, and yet he knew as little of it as he did of *Terra Australis Incognita* [Unknown Southern Land]. He told us a Canterbury tale of a North Briton whose curiosity spurred him a long way into this great desert, as he called it, near 20 years ago, but he having no compass, nor seeing the sun for several days together, wandered about till he was almost famished; but at last he bethought himself of a secret his countrymen make use of to pilot themselves in a dark day.

He took a fat louse out of his collar and exposed it to the open day on a piece of white paper which he brought along with him for his journal. The poor insect, having no eyelids, turned himself about till he found the darkest part of the heavens, and so made the best of his way towards the north. By this direction he steered himself safe out, and gave such a frightful account of the monsters he saw and the distresses he underwent, that no mortal since has been hardy enough to go upon the like dangerous discovery.

[The Alligator]

In Santee river, as in several others of Carolina, a small kind of alligator is frequently seen, which perfumes the water with a musky smell. They seldom exceed eight feet in length in these parts, whereas, near the Equinoctial, they come up to twelve or fourteen. And the heat of the climate don't only make them bigger, but more fierce and voracious. They watch the cattle there when they come to drink and cool themselves in the river; and because they are not able to drag them into the deep water, they make up by stratagem what they want in force. They swallow great stones, the weight of which being added to their strength, enables them to tug a moderate cow under water, and as soon as they have drowned her, they discharge the stones out of their maw and then feast upon the carcass. However, as fierce and strong as these monsters are, the Indians will surprise them napping as they float upon the surface, get astride upon their necks, then whip a short piece of wood like a truncheon into their jaws, and holding the ends with their two hands, hinder them from diving by keeping their mouths open, and when they are almost spent, they will make to the shore, where their riders knock them on the head and eat them. This amphibious animal is a smaller kind of crocodile, having the same shape exactly, only the crocodile of the Nile is twice as long, being when full grown from 20 to 30 feet. This enormous length is the more to be wondered at, because the crocodile is hatched from an egg very little larger than that of a goose. It has a long head, which it can open very wide, with very sharp and strong teeth. Their eyes are small, their legs short, with claws upon their feet. Their tail makes half the length of their body, and the whole is guarded with hard impenetrable scales, except the belly, which is much softer and smoother. They keep much upon the land in the day time, but towards the evening retire into the water to avoid the cold dews of the night. They run pretty fast right forward, but are very awkward and slow in turning, by reason of their unwieldy length. It is an error that they have no tongue, without which they could hardly swallow their food; but in eating they move the upper jaw only, contrary to all other animals. The way of catching them in Egypt is, with a strong hook fixt to the end of a chain, and baited with a joint of pork, which they are very fond of. But a live hog is generally tied near, the cry of which allures them to the hook. This account of the crocodile will agree in most particulars with the alligator, only the bigness of the last cannot entitle it to the name of "Leviathan," which Job gave formerly to the crocodile, and not to the whale, as some interpreters would make us believe.

[Plantation Life in North Carolina]

March 25. The air was chilled this morning with a smart north-west wind, which favored the Dismalites in their dirty march. They returned by the path they had made in coming out, and with great industry arrived in the evening at the spot where the Line had been discontinued.

After so long and laborious a journey, they were glad to repose themselves on their couches of cypress-bark, where their sleep was as sweet as it would have been on a bed of Finland down.

In the mean time, we who stayed behind had nothing to do, but to make the best observations we could upon that part of the country. The soil of our landlord's plantation, though none of the best, seemed more fertile than any thereabouts, where the ground is near as sandy as the deserts of Africa, and consequently barren. The road leading from thence to Edenton, being in distance about 27 miles, lies upon a ridge called Sandy Ridge, which is so wretchedly poor that it will not bring potatoes.

The pines in this part of the country are of a different species from those that grow in Virginia: their bearded leaves are much longer and their cones much larger. Each cell contains a seed of the size and figure of a black-eyed pea, which, shedding in November, is very good mast for hogs, and fattens them in a short time.

The smallest of these pines are full of cones, which are eight or nine inches long, and each affords commonly 60 or 70 seeds. This kind of mast has the advantage of all other by being more constant, and less liable to be nipped by the frost or eaten by the caterpillars. The trees also abound more with turpentine, and consequently yield more tar than either the yellow or the white pine; and for the same reason make more durable timber for building. The inhabitants hereabouts pick up knots of lightwood in abundance, which they burn into tar, and then carry it to Norfolk or Nansimond for a market. The tar made in this method is the less valuable because it is said to burn the cordage, though it is full as good for all other uses as that made in Sweden and Muscovy.

Surely there is no place in the world where the inhabitants live with less labor than in North Carolina. It approaches nearer to the description of Lubberland than any other, by the great felicity of the climate, the easiness of raising provisions, and the slothfulness of the people.

Indian corn is of so great increase that a little pains will subsist a very large family with bread, and then they may have meat without any pains at all, by the help of low grounds, and the great variety of mast that grows on the high land. The men for their parts, just like the Indians, impose all the work upon the poor women. They make their wives rise out of their beds early in the morning, at the same time that they lie and snore till the sun has run one-third of his course and dispersed all the unwholesome damps. Then, after stretching and yawning for half an hour, they light their pipes, and, under the protection of a cloud of smoke, venture out into the open air; though, if it happens to be never so little cold, they quickly return shivering into the chimney corner. When the weather is mild, they stand leaning with both their arms upon the cornfield fence, and gravely consider whether they had best go and take a small heat at the hoe: but generally find reasons to put it off till another time.

Thus they loiter away their lives, like Solomon's sluggard, with their arms across, and at the winding up of the year scarcely have bread to eat.

To speak the truth, 'tis a thorough aversion to labor that makes people file off to North Carolina, where plenty and a warm sun confirm them in their disposition to laziness for their whole lives.

[A Visit to the Indians]

April 7.*** In the morning we dispatched a runner to the Nottoway Town, to let the Indians know we intended them a visit that evening, and our honest landlord was so kind as to be our pilot thither, being about 4 miles from his house.

Accordingly in the afternoon we marched in good order to the town, where the female scouts, stationed on an eminence for that purpose, had no sooner spied us, but they gave notice of our approach to their fellow-citizens by continual whoops and cries, which could not possibly have been more dismal at the sight of their most implacable enemies.

This signal assembled all their great men, who received us in a body, and conducted us into the fort. This fort was a square piece of ground, inclosed with substantial puncheons, or strong palisades, about ten feet high, and leaning a little outwards, to make a scalade more difficult.***

The young men had painted themselves in a hideous manner, not so much for ornament as terror. In that frightful equipage they entertained us with sundry war-dances, wherein they endeavored to look as formidable as possible. The instrument they danced to was an Indian-drum, that is, a large gourd with a skin braced tort over the mouth of it. The dancers all sang to this music, keeping exact time with their feet, while their heads and arms were screwed into a thousand menacing postures.

Upon this occasion the ladies had arrayed themselves in all their finery. They were wrapt in their red and blue match-coats, thrown so negligently about them that their mahogany skins appeared in several parts, like the Lacedaemonian damsels of old. Their hair was braided with white and blue peak, and hung gracefully in a large roll upon their shoulders.

This peak consists of small cylinders cut out of a conque-shell, drilled through and strung like beads. It serves them both for money and jewels, the blue being of much greater value than the white, for the same reason that Ethiopian mistresses in France are dearer than French, because they are more scarce. The women wear necklaces and bracelets of these precious materials, when they have a mind to appear lovely. Though their complexions be a little sad-colored, yet their shapes are very straight and well proportioned. Their faces are seldom handsome, yet they have an air of innocence and bashfulness, that with a little less dirt would not fail to make them desirable. Such charms might have had their full effect upon men who had been so long deprived of female conversation, but that the whole winter's soil was so crusted on the skins of those dark angels, that it required a very strong appetite to approach them. The bear's oil, with which they anoint their persons all over, makes their skins soft, and at the same time protects them from every species of vermin that use to be troublesome to other uncleanly people.

We were unluckily so many that they could not well make us the complement of bed-fellows, according to the Indian rules of hospitality, though a grave matron whispered one of the Commissioners very civilly in the ear, that if her daughter had been but one year older, she should have been at his devotion.

It is by no means a loss of reputation among the Indians, for damsels that are single to have intrigues with the men; on the contrary, they count it an argument of superior merit to be liked by a great number of gallants. However, like the ladies that game they are a little mercenary in their amours, and seldom bestow their favors out of stark love and kindness. But after these women have once appropriated their charms by marriage, they are from thenceforth faithful to their vows, and will hardly ever be tempted by an agreeable gallant, or be provoked by a brutal or even by a fumbling husband to go astray.

Group of buildings in the classical manner: Girard Institute, Philadelphia

THE NEO–CLASSIC AGE

Human Reason and Natural Order

❦

"All, nature made, in reason's sight
Is order all and all is right."
— FRENEAU

In the eighteenth century the faith of the Puritans subsided. Jonathan Edwards, it is true, carried it far into the century — made a last great stand in defence of a lost cause. But the world in which he lived had already turned to new interests, adopted a new outlook on life. Broadly speaking the eighteenth century was dedicated not to religion but to science and politics. Its leaders were no longer Christian ministers like Mather and Edwards but natural philosophers like Franklin and Jefferson. The change was profound; in many respects the old and the new were opposite.

Otherworldliness gave way to worldliness. A divine, a God-centered world became a human, a man-centered world. Life guided by the Holy Bible became life guided by human reason. No longer was the world a place where Providence, ever present and ever active, controlled everything that happened, even trivial events. To the eye of reason the world was now part of a machine universe which, once set in motion, had run of its own accord ever since. God himself, no longer a person, a father to be loved and feared, became a remote and impersonal intelligence, a "First Cause" that started the machine and left it to operate in perfect order according to mathematical and physical laws. And Jesus, Son of God, became Jesus, son of man.

The proper study of mankind was no longer God but man. Man had been a spiritual being in a fleshly form, but now, according to a new psychology, he must be thought of as coming into the world devoid of ideas and moral principles, as if he were a blank piece of paper to be written on by sense experience. In place of the old view that just a few souls are "elect," chosen for salvation in eternity, came the view that all men are entitled to share in the "pursuit of happiness" in their own time. Government by an aristocracy of birth and wealth was beginning to be altered by emphasis on leadership by those naturally best, regardless of class — a leadership subject to the consent of the governed. The evils of civilization were now explained, not by the old doctrine of original sin (Adam's fall) but by the effect of an unsound social environment. The relief of man's estate might be expected to come not so much from religion as from science, education, and politics, by which the environment could be improved.

It goes without saying that these contrasts have been rather too sharply drawn. The difference between two ages is always complex. We know how highly the Puritans esteemed human reason, and science as well. And we must bear in mind that, while the new outlook was common in the intellectual class that set the tone for the new age, the great majority of the population was ready to accept only certain features of the new order. A large number of people, in fact, clung to old beliefs and values with hardly any change.

So long as we remember that all periods are complex, particularly to those living in them,

(continued on page 79)

Classic Interior

The stately Greek style of many American interiors reflected the spirit of the Age of Reason.

Tavern Sign, 1773

Sign probably from the Yellow House, Rocky Hill, Connecticut, a wayside tavern popular in the early days of stagecoach travel.

"Charles Calvert and Colored Slave"

Charles was a direct descendant of Maryland's founder. Painting is by John Hesselius (1728–1778), for many years the leading artist of Maryland.

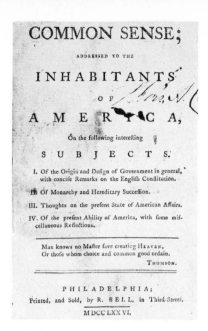

Title Page, Common Sense, 1776

Thomas Paine's *Common Sense* stated simply and effectively the American case for independence. The pamphlet sold over 100,000 copies within three months of its publication and had much to do with the eventual break with England.

Benjamin Franklin

Franklin, epitome of the Age of Reason, had this profile drawn for the frontispiece of his *Political, Miscellaneous, and Philosophical Pieces*, published when he was seventy-three.

"Congress Voting Independence," by Robert Edge Pine, completed by Edward Savage, 1788

Congress appointed a committee consisting of John Adams, Benjamin Franklin, Thomas Jefferson, Robert R. Livingston, and Roger Sherman to draft a declaration of independence. The committee presented its resolution to the delegates assembled in Philadelphia on July 2, 1776, and two days later Congress formally adopted the document.

"Paul Revere," by John Singleton Copley

Distinguished Boston patriot, engraver, and silversmith, Revere is largely remembered through Longfellow's poem for his famous ride from Charlestown to Lexington to announce the approach of British troops. Revere designed the first issue of Continental money and the first official seal for the federated colonies.

First American Playbill

The production *Venice Preserv'd*, written by the English dramatist Otway, was staged at the Nassau Street Theatre, New York, in 1752. The first American play, Thomas Godfrey's *The Prince of Parthia*, was not produced until 1767.

Philadelphia Salon

The art of conversation was important in the cultural life of early Philadelphia. In this sketch by Benjamin West, Francis Hopkinson — lawyer, author, musician, and designer of the American flag — is conversing with a lady, possibly Elizabeth Graeme, a leading hostess of the day.

we may sensibly choose a unifying name to apply to the period we are now concerned with. In point of time it was, roughly, the *Eighteenth Century*. In politics, it was the *Revolutionary Period*. In terms of ideas, attitudes, values, it was the *Age of Reason*. In relation to literary art, the subject of our study, it was the *Neo-Classic Age*. This age, in turning away from the Puritan view of life, gave primary allegiance to that Classical culture which for the Puritans had been secondary. For much that it valued most, it found its best examples in the humanistic world of the Greeks, man-centered and rational, and in the civilization of the Romans, with their sense of law, order, and dignity.

REASON AS THE MEASURE

How did it come about that faith in human reason gradually suppressed the beliefs and exaltations of the Puritan Age? Why did men give up their hard-won sureness and security? Why were the men and women of the new age so different from John and Margaret Winthrop ("Our God . . . will be our God to the end, to carry us along through this course of our pilgrimage") or from Jonathan and Sarah Edwards ("sweetly conversing with Christ, and wrapt and swallowed up in God")? What did mere reason — cold reason that chills the heart — have to offer that was so attractive?

Rationalism, developing in Europe, looked not to the Bible but to the realm of nature. Nature, said Galileo (1564–1642), can be known only by one who understands her language — the language of mathematics. A little later Descartes, French founder of modern philosophy, affirmed that mathematical knowledge might become the source of all other knowledge, and conceived that the entire world of matter, including animal life (and even man, except for his power of reason) is determined by the laws of physics. The universe as a whole is simply a stupendous machine. Then Descartes' sketch of a machine universe was filled out scientifically by Isaac Newton in one of the most influential books of the world, the *Principia Mathematica* (1687). He proved to a fascinated generation that the falling apple and the stars in their courses obey the same laws of gravitation and motion. The order of nature is apparently a mathematical harmony, its laws uniform, fixed, undeviating. The universe is a perpetual motion machine, self-regulating, operating in time and space.

To us in the twentieth century, dominated by concepts of evolutionary change and relativity, this mathematical vision of a fixed mechanical order of things has lost its power of enchantment. But to the educated public of the Age of Reason the work of Newton became a new Bible. Its dazzling reception is suggested by the lines of Alexander Pope:

Nature and Nature's laws lay hid in night:
God said, *Let Newton be!* and all was light.

To explain such a response we must look into the inferences that thinking men drew. A generation weary of religious conflict and political disorder, they needed blueprints for a sane and solid reconstruction, such as Newton seemed to offer. Gladly they embraced a new faith. They believed that the clear light of truth was no longer to be blurred by the chaotic, the abnormal, the irrational. Nature itself is rational and orderly throughout. Perfection comes from perfection: the exquisite order of the universe must be the masterpiece of God, the supreme artist. Natural law is held to be the authoritative word of God. Nature — Reason — Science: these were now almost interchangeable with each other and with God. Surely for man, as a part of the "stupendous whole," here was an idea worthy of trust. We need only seek, it seems, in all fields of thought and life, that which is *natural*, that which is *reasonable*, that which is in harmony with *science* (clear and distinct demonstration) and with *God* (the First Cause of all subsequent causes and effects).

To do this we must cast aside all traditions that are blind, irrational, superstitious, fanatical. We are not to be sparing in our criticism of the traditions of Christianity, or of absolute monarchy, or whatever else has been handed down to us. For such criticism we have some helpful standards. Since the laws of science are uniform, we are to look for the *universal*, i.e. ideals and customs always and everywhere the same, despite superficial variety. For example, we should consider the Orient as well as our Western world, to determine what they have in common. What is national may be mere prejudice; our view should be cosmopolitan. We are also to look to the *primitive*, not as an "escape" to indulge our emotions, but as that stage of society, whether actual or theoretical, in which things were still rational, not yet twisted out of shape by human error or refined almost past recognition. The clear simplicities of that early time have a validity self-evident to our minds. By faithful reasoning from axiomatic truths we can assure an enlightenment and happiness that man has never known. Let us drop the partial and see the whole; let us abandon the artificial and return to the natural and rational; let us penetrate to the very nature of things! As Tom Paine made bold to declare, the Creation itself is "the Word of God," and science is the medium by which "man can see God, as it were, face to face."

This is a religious affirmation. It goes far beyond the starting point, the mathematics and physics of Newton, and well beyond a mere trust in reason. Many of the intellectuals most remote from orthodox Christianity were religious, in an eighteenth century way, believing in what was called natural religion or deism.

🙖 *Deism.* Natural religion, as opposed to revealed religion, denied the authority of any religious beliefs not held everywhere, in all times, by all men. Thus, it could not admit the divinity of Christ or the doctrine of the Trinity. When all such doctrines had been rejected, what remained? What doctrines could unaided human reason establish as universally valid? What beliefs are agreeable to nature and science? They might be stated as follows: First, there is an all-powerful God. Second, man is required to live virtuously. Third, in a future life the virtuous will be rewarded, the wicked punished. This simple creed was acceptable to deists and orthodox Christians alike. The orthodox could subscribe to natural religion while claiming that revealed religion was necessary to complete it; deists could subscribe to it as sufficient by itself. Both in England and America deism appealed strongly to the more intellectual classes. In America it represented in varying degrees the view of men like Franklin, Washington, Jefferson, Ethan Allen, Paine, Freneau. Radical deists like Paine harshly attacked the most cherished beliefs of the orthodox; the orthodox sometimes countered by condemning deism as outright atheism.

It was not atheism, because it provided for a God — of a sort. God was to be put in his place — outside the range of human experience, outside our world; absent from, not present within us and the world. God was the creative mind that designed the universe and set the machine going with a stock of laws assuring order, but thereafter not meddling in the world's affairs, nor concerning himself more for man than for his other creations. This First Cause of all things is discoverable, by human reason, through the rational processes of nature. In

ruling God out of the world, thoroughgoing deists of course threw out all divine interference through the miraculous and the providential, but others sometimes used the idea of Providence at least conventionally. And there were even those, like Shaftesbury and Pope, who, despite their deistic views, inconsistently brought God back into the world, as in Pope's familiar lines:

> All are but parts of one stupendous whole,
> Whose body Nature is, and God the soul.

A concept like this helped to prepare the way for romanticism, for the "Presences of Nature" worshipped by Wordsworth and by Emerson and Thoreau after him. But the concept is clearly contrary to the mechanical interpretation of the universe that is a usual mark of deism. As for man, deism employed the view of human nature worked out by the philosophical school of John Locke.

It was the sober theory of Locke that man's experience through the five senses is basic, that his response to sensory stimuli causes him to form simple ideas, these in turn building up in his mind into more and more complex ideas, so that all that we know really goes back to the senses. Evidently men do not come into the world predestined by a class-conscious God who provides one way for the elect and another way for the masses. Nor is it the nature of man to come into the world with a mind already stocked with ideas, latent ideas that become plain with experience. To use Locke's term, there are no "innate ideas." The mind at birth is simply a blank. Everything written on it comes later. And the writing is done by environment, by the institutions and customs of the state, the church, the school, the economic system, etc. If these were sound and rational, the results would be good.

Increasingly associated with the religion of reason was a belief in progress (not to be confused with our idea of organic evolution). Belief in progress had grown out of the new science, of which Bacon was the prophet and Newton the Messiah. With justified pride, many men came to feel that there would be endless progress in scientific knowledge and material conveniences. From this they passed on to a more questionable belief in social progress. Could not a new social science improve the environment by changing the institutions, above all education, and soon bring on a society enlightened, wise, and prosperous? In this way was not man perfectible? We should not look backward but forward. The Golden Age lies not in the ancient past but in the future. There can be, there will be, a Heaven on earth! Such was the faith of many intellectuals in England, and in America as well. Typically, an American named Chipman affirmed that man is nothing less than "a being capable of improvement, in a progression of which he knows not the limits." Faith in progress blended easily with the optimism of a frontier land of opportunity, and in the nineteenth century was to receive fresh impetus through the idea of evolution.

The religion of reason was strongly opposed. While it was spreading, from the second decade to the end of the eighteenth century, the two leading orthodox churches — the Congregational (Calvinist) and the Anglican — were well entrenched, though weakening by deist infiltration and attrition. A more formidable opponent was the counter-offensive of the Revivalist movement. Religious feeling revolted against worldliness and skepticism. In contrast to the serene common sense of Franklin and the acid rationalism of Paine, we must place the emotional explosions of revivals, with their visions and trances, their weeping and swooning. They occurred from Massachusetts to Georgia, and by 1800 crossed the mountains into Kentucky and Tennessee. They throve especially among the lower classes and at the frontier. In the early nineteenth century, Methodists, Baptists, Presbyterians, and others had assured the establishment of Protestant evangelism as the dominant religion of America. Even the colleges changed, almost suddenly. According to Lyman Beecher, who entered Yale in 1793, "The college was in a most ungodly state. The college church was almost extinct. Most of the students were skeptical, and rowdies were plenty. Wine and liquors were kept in many rooms; intemperance, profanity, gambling, and licentiousness were common. I hardly know how I escaped. . . . That was the day of the infidelity of the Tom Paine school." But in 1802, Benjamin Silliman, then a Yale tutor, converted in the great revival of that year, was able to write to his mother: "It would delight your heart, my dear mother, to see how the trophies of the Cross are multiplied in this institution. Yale College is a little temple: prayer and praise seem to be the delight of the greater part of the students, while those who are still unfeeling are awed into respectful silence."

While the religion of reason was still thriving, it was strongest in the cities — especially Philadelphia, where colonial culture attained its fullest expression.

Science. Philadelphia was also the scientific center of the colonies. Among its prominent men were David Rittenhouse, a farm boy who became an astronomer, John Bartram the botanist, and Morgan, Rush, Shippen and other leaders in medicine. How broadly based and democratic the scientific life was is suggested by the Junto, a discussion group led by Franklin. In the group were young men like Godfrey the glazier, Scull the surveyor, Parsons the shoemaker, Maugridge the joiner, men who could apply their skills to making instruments essential to science; also Breintnall, the Quaker merchant, who could establish relations with scientists abroad. Ready to help the group was the aristocrat James Logan, who loved the ancient classics but also collected in his mansion a superb scientific library.

The most famous "natural philosopher" of the city was of course the ingenious Dr. Franklin himself. Today most people picture Franklin the scientist as a bespectacled colonial flying a kite during a thunderstorm. While the identity of lightning and electricity was his most celebrated discovery, he was in fact fruitful in more than a dozen fields of research. Again and again he regretted that circumstances kept pushing him into political life and away from the investigation of nature. Truly did Tom Paine say of him: "His mind was ever young; his temper ever serene; science, that never grows gray, was always his mistress." Wedded to public service, he yet served his scientific mistress so well that his contemporaries were inclined to hail him as a second Newton. Along with his quiet passion for study, Franklin entertained a deistic outlook on life, but was too moderate and prudent to display it militantly like Paine. Instead, he went to church. In his heart he agreed with his scientific associate Bartram that "It is through the telescope I see God in his glory."

MAKING THIRTEEN CLOCKS STRIKE TOGETHER

The golden age of colonial culture, flowering in the creative brilliance of Philadelphia, in the charming, studied elegance of the Virginia capital at Williamsburg, and in other centers on the coast from Boston to Charleston, was succeeded by a period of political ferment that culminated in revolution and a new nation.

From the political confusion of the period two men emerge who seem about as indispensable as Washington himself — the radical Jefferson and the conservative Hamilton.

Jefferson. Thomas Jefferson has remained a symbol of the democratic faith to this day, in foreign countries as well as America. The son of a middle-class father and aristocratic mother, himself aristocratic in temper and tastes, he was persistently and increasingly democratic in his political thought. His cultural attainments were early recognized. Said John Adams: "Mr. Jefferson came into Congress in June, 1775, and brought with him a reputation for literature, science, and a happy talent of composition." A year later, when only thirty-three, he was chosen to head the committee that drafted the Declaration of Independence.

To the ringing generalities of the Declaration, Jefferson tried to give concrete meaning and effect by sponsoring measures toward a free, individualistic society in his own state. One was a reform of the laws of inheritance, to distribute land more widely and abolish the aristocracy of birth and wealth. Another disestablished the church in Virginia — "Almighty God has created the mind free" and how can man be truly free unless he has liberty of spirit? Another urged a universal system of education, since Jefferson held that republican government cannot be maintained unless the people's minds are improved. He early advocated the emancipation of Negro slaves, and worked for it till his death. He held freedom of speech and of the press to be indispensable for popular government. State rights he favored not for the sake of the states, but for the sake of individuals, on the ground that the state, as a smaller unit than the nation, is better qualified to assure the liberty of individuals.

This does not exhaust the list of reforms and devices that Jefferson supported in the interest of "a government truly republican." Characteristically, he deplored the "witch-hunt" (the term is his) for radicals and liberals during the Adams administration. And characteristically, at the time of the adoption of the Constitution, he was reconciled only when it was clear that a Bill of Rights would be immediately attached. Typical, too, was his assertion of a right of protest by violence: "a little rebellion, now and then, is a good thing, and as necessary in the political world as storms in the physical."

Plainly, Jefferson's democracy was focused upon the individual. Living in a farming state and a farmer himself, he was strongly drawn by the agrarian philosophy current in his time: the vision of an agricultural society of individuals, virtuous, free, and proud. In a way common among farmers, he distrusted government, especially government from a national center — "Were we directed from Washington when to sow, and when to reap, we should soon want bread." His resentment at government was the greater when it came from the imperial authority in London. He had a nature peculiarly suited to his momentous task in the Declaration of Independence, and to his role as a perennial foe of tyranny. Yet his reliance upon the free individual involved the risk of having no government at all but only anarchy, so that a modern historical scholar was constrained to say that "Had we attempted to follow Jefferson completely, the nation might not only not have continued but not have survived its first decade."

Hamilton. Had we, on the other hand, attempted to follow Hamilton completely, the nation might have had a government like that of eighteenth-century England, monarchical and aristocratic, or like the "Leviathan" state of Hobbes, highly centralized and authoritative, which in our time we call the totalitarian state. Yet this must not blind us to his immense contribution. Hamilton had much to do with the fact that there was a nation at all, and that it did survive. During the war, the government of the sovereign colonies through their Congress was so feeble that in 1780 Hamilton could say of the army: "It is now a mob rather than an army; without clothing, without provision, without morals, without discipline." In the same year, even before the weak Articles of Confederation had been adopted, he proposed the Constitutional Convention which eventually met half a dozen years later. Hamilton was quite right in observing to Washington that "The centrifugal is much stronger than the centripetal force in these States; the seeds of disunion much more numerous than those of union." In the happy phrase of John Adams, the problem was to make thirteen clocks strike together. This was also the view of Franklin, who had warned long before that if the colonies did not hang together they would hang separately.

While we can easily see now, as Hamilton did then, the need of a strong central government to assure union and stability in peace and war, we are not likely to share Hamilton's in-

tense fear of democracy. Yet he was only saying what nearly all eighteenth-century gentlemen
were thinking when he argued before the convention:

> All communities divide themselves into the
> few and the many. The first are the rich and
> well born, the other the mass of the people. The
> voice of the people has been said to be the voice
> of God; and, however generally this maxim has
> been quoted and believed, it is not true to fact.
> The people are turbulent and changing; they
> seldom judge or determine right.

As a realist (cynic?) answering the idealist
(dreamer?) Hamilton went so far, on another
occasion, as to exclaim, "The people! — the
people is a great beast!"

The Constitution did not give Hamilton what
he had proposed: a president and senate chosen
for life, together with state governors appointed
by the president for life. But he supported it
as an acceptable compromise. At least "the
imprudence of democracy" was to be curbed in
some measure by a system of checks and balances. According to Woodrow Wilson, among
others, this elaborate arrangement of political
forces opposed to each other but producing an
equilibrium while they kept moving is to be
accounted for ultimately by the Newtonian
physics. The physical universe being an intricate mechanism like a watch, it seemed possible for human reason to devise a carefully
balanced political watch. The instrument did
provide a way to balk a hasty and impulsive
popular will, and reconciled state and nation
by means of federation. In 1760 an English
traveler had opined that "fire and water are
not more heterogeneous than the different
colonies." Yet before the 1800's federation
was a durable fact, and by the middle 1900's
success in the New World seriously suggested
federal union in the Old — a United States of
Europe.

Was Hamilton actually so zealous for union
and stability or was he primarily intent upon
government in the interest of the capitalist
class? The question is still debated by historians. At least we may say with assurance that,
as Jefferson had seen that an agricultural society
would make for free individuals, Hamilton saw
that an industrial society would make for firm
government. He thus helped form the middle-
class capitalist state that we know. America
was to be less and less a nation of Jefferson's
small farmers, more and more a nation of "Big
Business" developed by industrialists and financiers.

A CULTURAL ANCHOR: THE CLASSICAL TRADITION

People who divorce themselves from one tradition have usually become attached to another.
The aristocratic and the educated classes of the
eighteenth century, gradually alienated from the
tradition of Christian devotion, found more and
more satisfaction in the more worldly tradition
of Classical humanism. The Puritan Age had
prized but subordinated the classics; the Neo-
Classic Age found in them the main cultural
anchor of its rationalism, its unbounded belief
that human reason is competent to deal with
the world and life. Had not the Greeks and
the Romans lived a life so rational, so clear-
eyed, so moderate and sane, that they set a
standard for all time? Even if pure reason was
the ultimate authority, were not reason and the
ancients essentially the same? Pure reason had
triumphed in Newton, scientist of the physical
universe, and in Locke, scientist of man, but
far behind these modern thinkers lay a whole
world of wisdom and beauty, a constant source
of guidance and delight. The history, philosophy, and literature of the ancients did not seem
remote or antiquated, but intimately present
because permanently enlightening.

Before entering college at the age of fourteen
or fifteen, American students in this period were
expected to be able to speak in Latin, and in
college they were fined for not speaking in
Latin, except during recreation. Latin was the
language of most of their textbooks and lectures. The New Testament in Greek was required for admission, and in Greek they also
studied Homer and Longinus. In Latin the
chief authors were Cicero, Vergil, and Horace.
A continued interest in the classics after college was usual. "Every accomplished gentleman," says Wertenbaker, "was supposed to
know his Homer and his Ovid, and in conversation was put to shame if he failed to recognize
a quotation from either." Self-made men like
Franklin, without benefit of college, derived
more from the ancient world than one would
expect, but the more typical Founding Fathers
meditated long and deeply on the ancient
patterns of democracy and republics, and
Jefferson was only expressing a frequent view of
his time when he said of ancient literature:
"The Greeks and Romans have left us the
present models which exist of fine composition,
whether we examine them as works of reason,
or style, or fancy. . . . To read the Latin and
Greek authors in their original is a sublime
luxury." In their literary taste the men of the

Age of Reason felt themselves to be descendants not of Chaucer, Spenser, and Shakespeare, but of Homer, Sophocles, Vergil, and Horace.

To pass from ancient to contemporary literature did not then mean, as it would today, a vast cultural leap, for contemporary writers purported, in the main, to imitate the ancients. The tradition coming down from the Greeks and Romans had been rationalized and formalized into a new classicism, first in seventeenth-century France, then in eighteenth-century England. Because the culture of America was English, American readers relied heavily upon such masters of the Neo-Classic Age as Addison, Steele, Pope, Swift and Dr. Johnson. The authoritarian confidence of neo-classicism, lingering among Federalists into the nineteenth century, was well expressed by a literary minister of Boston, Theodore Dehon, who said: "It is with literature as with government. Neither is a subject of perpetual experiment. The principles of both are fixed."

🌿 *Poetry*. Modern poetry, to Americans of the period, meant chiefly the sort of verse written in England by Alexander Pope and his followers. Pope reigned supreme on our side of the Atlantic through the eighteenth century and beyond. Early in the century Mather Byles compared him to Homer. Even James Russell Lowell, who was born in 1819 and belongs in the next period, could say, "I was brought up in the old superstition that he was the greatest poet that ever lived." Critics extolled Pope for his ethical sentiments, his keen satire, and the "musick" of his verse. William Bentley, in Salem, inserted in his commonplace book these lines describing the work of the master:

> Though gay as mirth, as curious thought sedate,
> As elegance polite, as power elate;
> Profound as reason, and as justice clear;
> Soft as compassion, yet as truth severe;
> As bounty copious, as persuasion sweet,
> Like nature various, and like art complete.

To eighteenth-century Americans it seemed that Pope's poetry harmonized with life as they were trying to live it: a poetry of rationality, clarity, moderation, elegance, decorum. It was, in truth, a poetry well suited to the age of the minuet, of salons, of formal gardens, of Georgian and Classical architecture. The fashionable verse form was the heroic couplet as perfected by Pope, regular, brilliant, neatly phrased, faultlessly groomed — should not poetic truth, like

ladies and gentlemen, be dressed to advantage? The substance beneath should be unchanging Nature — that is, human nature as it always is. The art of poetry, like the art of politics, should express universal, self-evident truths:

> . . . Nature to advantage drest,
> What oft was thought, but ne'er so well exprest,
> Something whose truth convinc'd at sight we find.

When they themselves composed verse, Americans followed, awkwardly, the English style of the day. New England's poets in the 1730's, says H. B. Parkes, "described Harvard commencements in the style of 'The Rape of the Lock,' or else they sang of the charms of Woman and the delights of Marriage in the borrowed strains of Matthew Prior. John Adams [the Rev. John Adams] gave Pope a Puritan coloring, putting psalms into heroic couplets and describing Cotton Mather's entry into heaven, surrounded by attendant angels, chubby and florid as on a Versailles ceiling." Some better things in the neo-classic vein were achieved late in the period by the Connecticut Wits (discussed at page 163), but most of their work was superficially patriotic, ineptly ambitious, and dull. On the whole, American neo-classic verse showed so little original power that there is hardly occasion to attempt here an account of its development, though we shall have something to say presently of Freneau as a transitional figure between neo-classicism and romanticism.

🌿 *Prose*. The prose was excellent. In that "age of prose and reason" (as Matthew Arnold called the eighteenth century) Americans learned to write an admirable prose of reason — a prose of statement and argument, not of description and narration — a prose serving practical rather than aesthetic ends. It reflected the discipline of twenty years of discussion before the Revolution, when the streets, taverns, and homes of America were filled with talk of politics, local and imperial. By 1775 it was possible for the elder William Pitt, speaking in the House of Lords, to say of the political papers coming from America: "For solidity of reasoning, force of sagacity, and wisdom of conclusion, no nation or body of men can stand in preference to the General Congress in Philadelphia." During the Revolutionary period alone, political pamphlets came pouring from the presses till they reached an estimated 2,000. Sometimes these little books had public readings, in a militia camp or at meetings of the Sons of Liberty; sometimes they had public burnings, if written by loyalists. A good example of the radical pamphlets is Paine's *Common Sense,* which argued that the colonists, having gone so far, must embrace freedom. This brilliantly conceived piece of propaganda was greeted with enthusiasm by leaders and public alike, sold over 100,000 copies within three months, and had much to do with the eventual break with England. But the masterpiece of all this political writing was Jefferson's Declaration of Independence. The colonies had a writer equal to the greatest occasion of the century. After independence had been achieved and the dark critical years had offered the challenge met by the Constitution, came another distinguished work of civic literature: *The Federalist,* written in support of the Constitution by Hamilton with the aid of Madison and Jay.

The leading prose writer of the period, however, was Benjamin Franklin. An able political writer, he often showed a waggish or satirical turn of mind. Like his political, his non-political writings were intended in one way or another to serve a useful purpose. They included his Almanac, his scientific works, and the earliest masterpiece of American literature — his *Autobiography.* This guarded yet intimate revelation of a personality comes to us refreshingly from a period when attention was fixed on ideas and principles and on men in general rather than on the individual and his experiences. Franklin also wrote periodical essays, with a didactic purpose, in the manner of the English *Spectator,* and tried his hand at "bagatelles," informal essays with a French wit and urbanity. And he was America's best letter-writer (with Jefferson next after him) in a century that excelled in the letter as a supplement to the art of conversation.

Writers in America as in England were now employing a new prose style. In England style had been reshaped, for an age of science and politics, in the interest of greater clarity and simplicity. Earlier English prose had abounded in involved sentence structure, complicated parentheses, Latinized diction, fantastic phrasing, pedantry, luxuriance — at its worst "a glaring chaos and wild heap." A new pattern was forming when in 1667, as Thomas Sprat tells us, the Royal Society expected its members to use "a close, naked, natural way of speaking; positive expressions, clear senses, a native easiness, bringing all things as near the mathematical plainness as they can." The new prose was perfected by Dryden, with a fine balance of ease and energy, and later polished by Addison. America imported not only the ideas of the eighteenth century but the neo-classic style of Addison, Swift, Goldsmith, and the rest. One can readily see the movement toward order, lucidity, precision, ease, and simplicity by contrasting the writings of Cotton Mather and Franklin.

Freneau. Sentimentalism, a literary mood composed of feeling and "fancy," began to develop in the midst of the Age of Reason. Evident in the "Gothic" novels of Charles Brockden Brown and the melodramatic play, the new attitude indicated a transition toward romanticism as illustrated in the leading poet of the period, Philip Freneau, poised, so to speak, between two centuries. As a deist he subscribed, like Tom Paine, to the religion of reason. As a democrat he was, again like Paine, an ardent radical. Feeling called upon to make poetry as well as prose serve politics, he devoted a large proportion of his verse to the cause of, first, American independence, next the French Revolution, and then the party of Jefferson, commonly using the method of satire. But his real interest and talent lay elsewhere. He preferred to write poetry rather than versified propaganda, and managed to write enough of it to show what he could do. While retaining much that was typical of the neo-classic regime, such as direct moralizing, conventional diction ("vernal showers"), and facile personification ("Liberty, Celestial Maid"), he could also write simply and naturally, sometimes with delicate precision. In his lyrical poems he is akin to such English "pre-romantics" as Gray, Collins, and Cowper. As they pointed toward Wordsworth and Coleridge, so he toward Bryant and Poe. Thus, in "The Wild Honeysuckle" there is a sensitive response to nature, in "The Beauties of Vera Cruz" freshness of sensuous appeal and the charm of the strange and remote, in "The House of Night" the ability to invest the horrible and the supernatural with imaginative energy. By writing of this sort Freneau takes us to the threshold of a new literary age, an age of romanticism.

THE AGE OF REASON INCARNATE

Benjamin Franklin [1706–1790]

Franklin represented more fully than any other one man the worldly temper of the eighteenth century: its common sense and rationalism, its science and deism, its political concerns and humanitarian activities, its clear and simple neo-classical prose style. His fame during his latter years was universal. An enemy of kings and friend of democracy, "he snatched lightning from the sky and the sceptre from tyrants." For Europeans, especially the French, he was a world citizen, "the first American." In his own country he has been mythologized as the earliest case of "rags-to-riches" success, and his shrewd Poor Richard maxims on how to get ahead have become part of the native folklore.

A reputation as great as Franklin's has not been without its detractors, however. His versatility and accomplishments are admittedly great, but his prudential wisdom and calculated self-aggrandizement, his utilitarianism and opportunism have been unfavorably contrasted to the sincerity, idealism, and religious devotion of an Edwards or a John Woolman. D. H. Lawrence did not like him or his moralism; Mark Twain burlesqued his maxims; he has been called the first Babbitt and a precursor of Puritan-capitalism.

Son of a tallow chandler and soap boiler, Ben was early apprenticed in his brother's printing shop, but at the age of seventeen he left his home in Boston for New York and Philadelphia because, as he said, he was "pointed out with horror by good people as an infidel or atheist." Freedom of religion and freedom of the press seemed more easily attained in the city of the Quakers. There he rapidly became a civic leader, sponsoring and organizing the Junto, a philosophical discussion group, and many cultural as well as practical projects. The most famous "natural philosopher" of this scientific center, he was most celebrated for his discovery of the identity of lightning and electricity, but he was likewise interested in medicine, astronomy, physics, oceanography, and meteorology. Everything roused his curiosity and study, if only the most comfortable way to lie in bed. A scholar and a seeker after knowledge, he was also eager to see science applied to the service of mankind: the long list of his own inventions ranges from the "Franklin stove" and the lightning rod to an improved type of paving block.

In his autobiography Franklin has given us an interesting and revealing account of his earlier years. The unfinished narrative ends abruptly, however, with his arrival in London, in 1757, as agent for the colony of Pennsylvania. Thirty-three years of his long life remained, and he was active to the end. From 1757 to 1775 he was the principal representative of the American point of view in England, reluctantly coming to believe that the colonies were being forced into rebellion. Returning home to serve in the Continental Congress, he was on the committee that drafted the Declaration of Independence. Next he was sent to France, where he succeeded in securing the alliance that was to assure American victory in the war. When victory came, he took part in negotiating the Treaty of Paris. Back in America again, he served as president of the Executive Council of Pennsylvania, and became a member of the Constitutional Convention. It is evident that in the long and stormy transition from colonies to nation Franklin's services were constantly in request. His devotion, energy, astuteness, and solidity made him one of the foremost Founding Fathers.

Self-educated and self-made, Franklin became remarkably versatile. We can think of him as a writer and publisher, a scientist and inventor, a philosopher, soldier, civic leader, postmaster, statesman and diplomat. He was equally remarkable, despite his provincial origin, for his cosmopolitanism. He moved with ease in the currents of life in eighteenth-century England, and was even tempted to stay and make it his home. In France his admiring friends included men like Lafayette, Mirabeau, Buffon, Robespierre, Voltaire. At a public session of the Academy of Sciences, Franklin sat on the platform with Voltaire, the illustrious leader of the Age of Reason, and those present were not satisfied till the two famous old men had embraced and kissed *á la Française*. Yet he remained a good Yankee, in plain Quaker garb and great fur cap, with a walking-stick in place of a sword. As Preserved Smith has said, "In the formative period of modern democracy, he was the typical democrat. In the adolescence of America, he was the representative American."

Further reading: *Benjamin Franklin: Representative Selections*, ed. F. L. Mott and C. E. Jorgenson, 1936. Carl Van Doren, *Benjamin Franklin*, 1938.

From his *Autobiography*

(w. 1771–1789)

🖝 "Prose writing," said Franklin, "was a principal means of my advancement." He wrote enough, in fact, to make up ten volumes in modern editions. Virtually all of it was intended to be useful in one way or another. Even his *Autobiography* was begun, at least, with a practical purpose: addressing it to his son William, governor of New Jersey, the elderly Franklin sought to inform him and later members of the family of the facts about his life, in the hope that they might find worthy of imitation some of the means he used toward affluence, reputation, and happiness.

The autobiography introduces us at once to the charm and vigor of Franklin's writings. In the neo-classical way, he learned to write by imitation of models — primarily, he tells us, the *Spectator* papers of Addison. But he must have found congenial the whole development of English prose following the Royal Society's call for "a close, naked, natural way of speaking," especially the prose of Defoe and Swift. He himself said: "The words used should be the most expressive that the language affords, provided

that they are the most generally understood. Nothing should be expressed in two words that can be as well expressed in one; that is, no synonyms should be used, or very rarely, but the whole should be as short as possible, consistent with clearness; the words should be so placed as to be agreeable to the ear in reading; summarily it should be smooth, clear, and short, for the contrary qualities are displeasing."

[Family]

This obscure family of ours was early in the Reformation, and continued Protestants through the reign of Queen Mary, when they were sometimes in danger of trouble on account of their zeal against popery. They had got an English Bible, and to conceal and secure it, it was fastened open with tapes under and within the frame of a joint-stool. When my great-great-grandfather read it to his family, he turned up the joint-stool upon his knees, turning over the leaves then under the tapes. One of the children stood at the door to give notice if he saw the apparitor coming, who was an officer of the spiritual court. In that case the stool was turned down again upon its feet, when the Bible remained concealed under it as before. This anecdote I had from my uncle Benjamin. The family continued all of the Church of England till about the end of Charles the Second's reign, when some of the ministers that had been outed for non-conformity holding conventicles in Northamptonshire, Benjamin and Josiah adhered to them, and so continued all their lives: the rest of the family remained with the Episcopal Church.

Josiah, my father, married young, and carried his wife and three children into New England, about 1682. The conventicles having been forbidden by law, and frequently disturbed, induced some considerable men of his acquaintance to remove to that country, and he was prevailed with to accompany them thither, where they expected to enjoy their mode of religion with freedom. By the same wife he had four children more born there, and by a second wife ten more, in all seventeen; of which I remember thirteen sitting at one time at his table, who all grew up to be men and women, and married; I was the youngest son, and the youngest child but two, and was born in Boston, New England. My mother, the second wife, was Abiah Folger, daughter of Peter Folger, one of the first settlers of New England, of whom honorable mention is made by Cotton Mather, in his church history of that country, entitled Magnalia Christi Americana, as *"a godly, learned Englishman,"* if I remember the words rightly. I have heard that he wrote sundry small occasional pieces, but only one of them was printed, which I saw now many years since. It was written in 1675, in the homespun verse of that time and people, and addressed to those then concerned in the government there. It was in favor of liberty of conscience, and in behalf of the Baptists, Quakers, and other sectaries that had been under persecution, ascribing the Indian wars, and other distresses that had befallen the country, to that persecution, as so many judgments of God to punish so heinous an offense, and exhorting a repeal of those uncharitable laws.

[A Bookish Inclination]

My elder brothers were all put apprentices to different trades. I was put to the grammar-school at eight years of age, my father intending to devote me, as the tithe of his sons, to the service of the Church. My early readiness in learning to read (which must have been very early, as I do not remember when I could not read), and the opinion of all his friends, that I should certainly make a good scholar, encouraged him in this purpose of his. My uncle Benjamin, too, approved of it, and proposed to give me all his short-hand volumes of sermons, I suppose as a stock to set up with, if I would learn his character. I continued, however, at the grammar-school not quite one year, though in that time I had risen gradually from the middle of the class of that year to be the head of it, and farther was removed into the next class above it, in order to go with that into the third at the end of the year. But my father, in the meantime, from a view of the expense of a college education, which having so large a family he could not well afford, and the mean living many so educated were afterwards able to obtain — reasons that he gave to his friends in my hearing — altered his first intention, took me from the grammar-school, and sent me to a school for writing and arithmetic, kept by a then famous man, Mr. George Brownell, very successful in his profession generally, and that by mild, encouraging methods. Under him I acquired fair writing pretty soon, but I failed in the arithmetic, and made no progress in it. At ten years old I was taken home to assist my father in his business, which was that of a tallow-chandler and soap-boiler; a business he was not bred to, but had assumed on his arrival in New England, and on finding his dying trade would not maintain his family, being in little request. Accordingly, I was employed in cutting wick for the candles, filling the dipping mold and the molds for cast candles, attending the shop, going of errands, etc.***

From a child I was fond of reading, and all the little money that came into my hands was ever laid out in books. Pleased with the *Pilgrim's Progress,* my first collection was of John Bunyan's works in separate little volumes. I afterward sold them to enable me to buy R. Burton's *Historical Collections;* they were small chapmen's books, and cheap, 40 or 50 in all. My father's little library consisted chiefly of books in polemic divinity, most of which I read, and have since often regretted that, at a time when I had such a thirst for knowledge, more proper books had not fallen in my way, since it was now resolved I should not be a clergyman. Plutarch's *Lives* there was, in which I read abundantly, and I still think that time spent to great advantage. There was also a book of Defoe's, called an *Essay on Projects,* and another of Dr. Mather's, called *Essays to do Good,* which perhaps gave me a turn of thinking that had an influence on some of the principal future events of my life.

This bookish inclination at length determined my father to make me a printer, though he had already one son (James) of that profession. In 1717 my brother James returned from England with a press and letters to set up his business in Boston. I liked it much better than that of my father, but still had a hankering for the sea. To prevent the apprehended effect of such an inclination, my father was impatient to have me bound to my brother. I stood out some time, but at last was persuaded, and signed the indentures when I was yet but twelve years old. I was to serve as an apprentice till I was twenty-one years of age, only I was to be allowed journeyman's wages during the last year. In a little time I made great proficiency in the business, and became a useful hand to my brother. I now had access to better books. An acquaintance with the apprentices of booksellers enabled me sometimes to borrow a small one, which I was careful to return soon and clean. Often I sat up in my room reading the greatest part of the night, when the book was borrowed in the evening and to be returned early in the morning, lest it should be missed or wanted.

And after some time an ingenious tradesman, Mr. Matthew Adams, who had a pretty collection of books, and who frequented our printing-house, took notice of me, invited me to his library, and very kindly lent me such books as I chose to read. I now took a fancy to poetry, and made some little pieces; my brother, thinking it might turn to account, encouraged me, and put me on composing occasional ballads. One was called *The Lighthouse Tragedy,* and contained an account of the drowning of Captain Worthilake, with his two daughters: the other was a sailor's song, on the taking of *Teach* (or blackbeard) the pirate. They were wretched stuff, in the Grub-street-ballad style; and when they were printed he sent me about the town to sell them. The first sold wonderfully; the event being recent, having made a great noise. This flattered my vanity; but my father discouraged me by ridiculing my performances, and telling me verse-makers were generally beggars. So I escaped being a poet, most probably a very bad one; but as prose writing has been of great use to me in the course of my life, and was a principal means of my advancement, I shall tell you how, in such a situation, I acquired what little ability I have in that way.

There was another bookish lad in the town, John Collins by name, with whom I was intimately acquainted. We sometimes disputed, and very fond we were of argument, and very desirous of confuting one another, which disputatious turn, by the way, is apt to become a very bad habit, making people often extremely disagreeable in company by the contradiction that is necessary to bring it into practice; and thence, besides souring and spoiling the conversation, is productive of disgusts and, perhaps, enmities where you may have occasion for friendship. I had caught it by reading my father's books of dispute about religion. Persons of good sense, I have since observed, seldom fall into it, except lawyers, university men, and men of all sorts that have been bred at Edinburgh.

A question was once, somehow or other, started between Collins and me, of the propriety of educating the female sex in learning, and their abilities for study. He was of opinion that it was improper, and that they were naturally unequal to it. I took the contrary side, perhaps a little for dispute's sake. He was naturally more eloquent, had a ready plenty of words; and sometimes, as I thought, bore me down more by his fluency than by the strength of his reasons. As we parted without settling the point, and were not to see one another again for some time, I sat down to put my arguments in writing, which I copied fair and sent to him. He answered, and I replied. Three or four letters of a side had passed, when my father happened to find my papers and read them. Without entering into the discussion, he took occasion to talk to me about the manner of my writing; observed that, though I had the advantage of my antagonist in correct spelling and pointing (which I owed to the printing-house), I fell far short in elegance of expression, in method and in perspicuity, of which he convinced me by several instances. I saw the justice of his remarks, and thence grew more attentive to the manner in writing, and determined to endeavor at improvement.

About this time I met with an odd volume of the *Spectator.* It was the third. I had never before seen any of them. I bought it, read it over and over, and was much delighted with it. I thought the writing excellent, and wished, if possible, to imitate it. With this view I took some of the papers, and, making short hints of the sentiment in each sentence, laid them by a few days, and then, without looking at the book, tried to complete the papers again, by expressing each hinted sentiment at length, and as fully as it had been expressed before, in any suitable words that should come to hand. Then I compared my *Spectator* with the original, discovered some of my faults, and corrected them. But I found I wanted a stock of words, or a readiness in recollecting and using them, which I thought I should have acquired before that time if I had gone on making verses; since the continual occasion for words of the same import, but of different length, to suit the measure, or of different sound for the rhyme, would have laid me under a constant necessity of searching for variety, and also have tended to fix that variety in my mind, and make me master of it. Therefore I took some of the tales and turned them into verse; and, after a time, when I had pretty well forgotten the prose, turned them back again. I also sometimes jumbled my collections of hints into confusion, and after some weeks endeavored to reduce them into the best order, before I began to form the full sentences and complete the paper. This was to teach me method in the arrangement of thoughts. By comparing my work afterwards with the original, I discovered my faults and amended them; but I sometimes had the pleasure of fancying that, in certain particulars of small import, I had been lucky enough to improve the method or the language, and this encouraged me to think I might possibly in time come to be a tolerable English writer, of which I was extremely ambitious. My time for these exercises and for reading was at night, after work or before it began in the morning, or on Sundays, when I contrived to be in the printing-house alone, evading as much as I could the common attendance on public worship which my father used to exact on me when I was under his care, and which indeed I still thought a duty, though I could not, as it seemed to me, afford time to practise it.

When about 16 years of age I happened to meet with a book, written by one Tryon, recommending a vegetable diet. I determined to go into it. My brother, being yet unmarried, did not keep house, but boarded himself and his apprentices in another family. My refusing to eat flesh occasioned an inconveniency, and I was frequently chid for my singularity. I made myself acquainted with Tryon's manner of preparing some of his dishes, such as boiling potatoes or rice, making hasty pudding, and a few others, and then proposed to my brother, that if he would give me, weekly, half the money he paid for my board, I would board myself. He instantly agreed to it, and I presently found that I could save half what he paid me. This was an additional fund for buying books. But I had another advantage in it. My brother and the rest going from the printing-house to their meals, I remained there alone, and, despatching presently my light repast, which often was no more than a bisquit or a slice of bread, a handful of raisins or a tart from the pastry-cook's, and a glass of water, had the rest of the time till their return for study, in which I made the greater progress, from that greater clearness of head and quicker apprehension which usually attend temperance in eating and drinking.

And now it was that, being on some occasion made ashamed of my ignorance in figures, which I had twice failed in learning when at school, I took Cocker's book of Arithmetic, and went through the whole by myself with great ease. I also read Seller's and Shermy's books of Navigation, and became acquainted with the little geometry they contain; but never proceeded far in that science. And I read about this time Locke *On Human Understanding*, and the *Art of Thinking*, by Messrs. du Port Royal.

While I was intent on improving my language, I met with an English grammar (I think it was Greenwood's), at the end of which there were two little sketches of the arts of rhetoric and logic, the latter finishing with a specimen of a dispute in the Socratic method; and soon after I procured Xenophon's *Memorable Things of Socrates*, wherein there are many instances of the same method. I was charmed with it, adopted it, dropt my abrupt contradiction and positive argumentation, and put on the humble inquirer and doubter. And being then, from reading Shaftesbury and Collins, become a real doubter in many points of our religious doctrine, I found this method safest for myself and very embarrassing to those against whom I used it; therefore I took a delight in it, practised it continually, and grew very artful and expert in drawing people, even of superior knowledge, into concessions, the consequences of which they did not foresee, entangling them in difficulties out of which they could not extricate themselves, and so obtaining victories that neither myself nor my cause always deserved. I continued this method some few years, but gradually left it, retaining only the habit of expressing myself in terms of modest diffidence; never using, when I advanced anything that may possibly be disputed, the words *certainly, undoubtedly,* or any others that give the air of positiveness to an opinion, but rather say, I conceive or apprehend a thing to be so and so; it appears to me, or *I should think it so or so,* for such and such reasons; or *I imagine it to be so;* or *it is so, if I am not mistaken.* This habit, I believe, has been of great advantage to me when I have had occasion to inculcate my opinions, and persuade men into measures that I have been from time to time engaged in promoting; and, as the chief ends of conversation are to *inform* or to be *informed,* to *please* or to *persuade,* I wish well-meaning, sensible men would not lessen their power of doing good by a positive, assuming manner, that seldom fails to disgust, tends to create opposition, and to defeat everyone of those purposes for which speech was given to us, to wit, giving or receiving information or pleasure. For, if you would inform, a positive and dogmatical manner in advancing your sentiments may provoke contradiction and prevent a candid attention. If you wish information and improvement from the knowledge of others, and yet at the same time express yourself as firmly fixed in your present opinions, modest, sensible men, who do not love disputation, will probably leave you undisturbed in the possession of your error. And by such a manner, you can seldom hope to recommend yourself in *pleasing* your hearers, or to persuade those whose concurrence you desire. Pope says, judiciously:

Men should be taught as if you taught them not,
And things unknown propos'd as things forgot;

farther recommending to us

To speak, tho' sure, with seeming diffidence.

[I Became a Deist]

Before I enter upon my public appearance in business, it may be well to let you know the then state of my mind with regard to my principles and morals, that you may see how far those influenced the future events of my life. My parents had early given me religious impressions, and brought me through my childhood piously in the Dissenting way. But I was scarce fifteen, when, after doubting by turns of several points, as I found them disputed in the different books I read, I began to doubt of Revelation itself. Some books against Deism fell into my hands; they were said to be the substance of sermons preached at Boyle's Lectures. It happened that they wrought an effect on me quite contrary to what was intended by them; for the arguments of the Deists, which were quoted to be refuted, appeared to me much stronger than the refutations; in short, I soon became a thorough Deist. My arguments perverted some others, particularly Collins and Ralph; but, each of them having afterwards wronged me greatly without the least compunction, and recollecting Keith's conduct towards me (who was another freethinker), and my own towards Vernon and Miss Read, which at times gave me great trouble, I began to suspect that this doctrine, though it might be true, was not very useful. My London pamphlet, which had for its motto these lines of Dryden:

Whatever is, is right. Though purblind man
Sees but a part o' the chain, the nearest link:
His eyes not carrying to the equal beam,
That poises all above;

and from the attributes of God, his infinite wisdom, goodness and power, concluded that nothing could possibly be wrong in the world, and that vice and virtue were empty distinctions, no such things existing, appeared now not so clever a performance as I once thought it; and I doubted whether some error had not insinuated itself unperceived into my argument, so as to infect all that followed, as is common in metaphysical reasonings.

I grew convinced that *truth, sincerity* and *integrity* in dealings between man and man were of the utmost importance to the felicity of life; and I formed written resolutions, which still remain in my journal book, to practice them ever while I lived. Revelation had indeed no weight with me, as such; but I entertained an opinion that, though certain actions might not be bad *because* they were forbidden by it, or good *because* it commanded them, yet probably these actions might be forbidden *because* they were bad for us, or commanded *because* they were beneficial to us, in their own natures, all the circumstances of things considered. And this persuasion, with the kind hand of Providence, or some guardian angel, or accidental favorable circumstances and situations, or all together, preserved me, through this dangerous time of youth, and the hazardous situations I was sometimes in among strangers, remote from the eye and advice of my father, without any willful gross immorality or injustice, that might have been expected from my want of religion. I say willful, because the instances I have mentioned had something of *necessity* in them, from my youth, inexperience, and the knavery of others. I had therefore a tolerable character to begin with; I valued it properly, and determined to preserve it.***

I had been religiously educated as a Presbyterian; and though some of the dogmas of that persuasion, such as *the eternal decrees of God*, *election*, *reprobation*, etc., appeared to me unintelligible, others doubtful, and I early absented myself from the public assemblies of the sect, Sunday being my studying day, I never was without some religious principles. I never doubted, for instance, the existence of the Deity; that He made the world, and governed it by his Providence; that the most acceptable service of God was the doing good to man; that our souls are immortal; and that all crime will be punished, and virtue rewarded, either here or hereafter. These I esteemed the essentials of every religion; and being to be found in all the religions we had in our country, I respected them all, though with different degrees of respect, as I found them more or less mixed with other articles, which, without any tendency to inspire, promote, or confirm morality, served principally to divide us, and make us unfriendly to one another. This respect to all, with an opinion that the worst had some good effects, induced me to avoid all discourse that might tend to lessen the good opinion another might have of his own religion; and as our province increased in people, and new places of worship were continually wanted, and generally erected by voluntary contribution, my mite for such purpose, whatever might be the sect, was never refused.

Though I seldom attended any public worship, I had still an opinion of its propriety, and of its utility when rightly conducted, and I regularly paid my annual subscription for the support of the only Presbyterian minister or meeting we had in Philadelphia. He used to visit me sometimes as a friend, and admonish me to attend his administrations, and I was now and then prevailed on to do so, once for five Sundays successively. Had he been in my opinion a good preacher, perhaps I might have continued, notwithstanding the occasion I had for the Sunday's leisure in my course of study; but his discourses were chiefly either polemic arguments, or explications of the peculiar doctrines of our sect, and were all to me very dry, uninteresting, and unedifying, since not a single moral principle was inculcated or enforced, their aim seeming to be rather to make us Presbyterians than good citizens.

At length he took for his text that verse of the fourth chapter of Philippians, *"Finally, brethren, whatsoever things are true, honest, just, pure, lovely, or of good report, if there be any virtue, or any praise, think on these things."* And I imagined, in a sermon on such a text, we could not miss of having some morality. But he confined himself to five points only, as meant by the apostle, viz.: 1. Keeping holy the Sabbath day. 2. Being diligent in reading the holy Scriptures. 3. Attending duly the public worship. 4. Partaking of the Sacrament. 5. Paying a due respect to God's ministers. These might be all good things; but as they were not the kind of good things that I expected from that text, I despaired of ever meeting with them from any other, was disgusted, and attended his preaching no more. I had some years before composed a little Liturgy, or form of prayer, for my own private use (viz., in 1728), entitled, *Articles of Belief and Acts of Religion*. I returned to the use of this, and went no more to the public assemblies. My conduct might be blameable, but I leave it, without attempting further to excuse it; my present purpose being to relate facts, and not to make apologies for them.

It was about this time [between 1731 and 1733] I conceived the bold and arduous project of arriving at moral perfection. I wished to live without committing any fault at any time; I would conquer all that either natural inclination, custom, or company might lead me into. As I knew, or thought I knew, what was right and wrong, I did not see why I might not always do the one and avoid the other. But I soon found I had undertaken a task of more difficulty than I had imagined. While my care was employed in guarding against one fault, I was often surprised by another; habit took the advantage of inattention; inclination was sometimes too strong for reason. I concluded, at length, that the mere speculative conviction that it was our interest to be completely virtuous, was not sufficient to prevent our slipping; and that the contrary habits must be broken, and good ones acquired and established, before we can have any dependence on a steady, uniform rectitude of conduct. For this purpose I therefore contrived the following method.

In the various enumerations of the moral virtues I had met with in my reading, I found the catalogue more or less numerous, as different writers included more or fewer ideas under the same name. Temperance, for example, was by some confined to eating and drinking, while by others it was extended to mean the moderating every other pleasure, appetite, inclination, or passion, bodily or mental, even to our avarice and ambition. I proposed to myself, for the sake of clearness, to use rather more names, with fewer ideas annexed to each, than a few names with more ideas; and I included under thirteen names of virtues all that at that time occurred to me as necessary or desirable, and annexed to each a short precept, which fully expressed the extent I gave to its meaning.

These names of virtues, with their precepts, were:

1. TEMPERANCE.
Eat not to dullness; drink not to elevation.

2. SILENCE.
Speak not but what may benefit others or yourself; avoid trifling conversation.

3. ORDER.
Let all your things have their places; let each part of your business have its time.

4. RESOLUTION.
Resolve to perform what you ought; perform without fail what you resolve.

5. FRUGALITY.
Make no expense but to do good to others or yourself; *i.e.*, waste nothing.

6. INDUSTRY.
Lose no time; be always employed in something useful; cut off all unnecessary actions.

7. SINCERITY.
Use no hurtful deceit; think innocently and justly, and, if you speak, speak accordingly.

8. JUSTICE.
Wrong none by doing injuries, or omitting the benefits that are your duty.

9. MODERATION.
Avoid extremes; forbear resenting injuries so much as you think they deserve.

10. CLEANLINESS.
Tolerate no uncleanliness in body, clothes, or habitation.

11. TRANQUILLITY.
Be not disturbed at trifles, or at accidents common or unavoidable.

12. CHASTITY.
Rarely use venery but for health or offspring, never to dullness, weakness, or the injury of your own or another's peace or reputation.

13. HUMILITY.
Imitate Jesus and Socrates.

My intention being to acquire the *habitude* of all these virtues, I judged it would be well not to distract my attention by attempting the whole at once, but to fix it on one of them at a time; and, when I should be master of that, then to proceed to another, and so on, till I should have gone through the thirteen; and, as the previous acquisition of some might facilitate the acquisition of certain others, I arranged them with that view, as they stand above. Temperance first, as it tends to procure that coolness and clearness of head, which is so necessary where constant vigilance was to be kept up, and guard maintained against the unremitting attraction of ancient habits, and the force of perpetual temptations. This being acquired and established, Silence would be more easy; and my desire being to gain knowledge at the same time that I improved in virtue, and considering that in conversation it was obtained rather by the use of the ears than of the tongue, and therefore wishing to break a habit I was getting into of prattling, punning, and joking, which only made me acceptable to trifling company, I gave *Silence* the second place. This and the next, *Order*, I expected would allow me more time for attending to my project and my studies. *Resolution*, once become habitual, would keep me firm in my endeavors to obtain all the subsequent virtues; *Frugality* and *Industry* freeing me from my remaining debt, and producing affluence and independence, would make more easy the practice of *Sincerity* and *Justice*, etc., etc. Conceiving then, that, agreeably to the advice of Pythagoras in his Golden Verses, daily examination would be necessary, I contrived the following method for conducting that examination.

I made a little book, in which I allotted a page for each of the virtues. I ruled each page with red ink, so as to have seven columns, one for each day of the week, marking each column with a letter for the day. I crossed these columns with thirteen red lines, marking the beginning of each line with the first letter of one of the virtues, on which line, and in its proper column, I might mark, by a little black spot, every fault I found upon examination to have been committed respecting that virtue upon that day.

Form of the pages.

TEMPERANCE.						
EAT NOT TO DULLNESS; DRINK NOT TO ELEVATION.						
	S.	M.	T.	W.	T.	F.	S.
T.							
S.	*	*		*		*	
O.	* *	*	*	*		*	*	*
R.				*		*	
F.		*			*		
I.			*				
S.							
J.							
M.							
C.							
T.							
C.							
H.							

I determined to give a week's strict attention to each of the virtues successively. Thus, in the first week, my great guard was to avoid every the least offence against *Temperance*, leaving the other virtues to their ordinary chance, only marking every evening the faults of the day. Thus, if in the first week I could keep my first line, marked T, clear of spots, I supposed the habit of that virtue so much strengthened, and its opposite weakened, that I might venture extending my attention to include the next, and for the following week keep both lines clear of spots. Proceeding thus to the last, I could go through a course complete in thirteen weeks, and four courses in a year. And like him who, having a garden to weed, does not attempt to eradicate all the bad herbs at once, which would exceed his reach and his strength, but works on one of the beds at a time, and, having accomplished the first, proceeds to a second, so I should have, I hoped, the encouraging pleasure of seeing on my pages the progress I made in virtue, by clearing successively my lines of their spots, till in the end, by a number of courses, I should be happy in viewing a clean book, after a thirteen weeks' daily examination.

This my little book had for its motto these lines from Addison's *Cato:*

Here will I hold. If there's a power above us
(And that there is, all nature cries aloud
Thro' all her works), He must delight in virtue;
And that which He delights in must be happy.

Another from Cicero,

O vitæ Philosophia dux! O virtutum indagatrix expultrixque vitiorum! Unus dies, bene et ex præceptis tuis actus, peccanti immortalitati est anteponendus.
[O Philosophy, leader of life! O inducer of virtues and expeller of vices. One day well spent on account of your precepts ought to be preferred to a sinful immortality.]

Another from the Proverbs of Solomon, speaking of wisdom or virtue:

Length of days is in her right hand, and in her left hand riches and honor. Her ways are ways of pleasantness, and all her paths are peace. iii. 16, 17.

And conceiving God to be the fountain of wisdom, I thought it right and necessary to solicit his assistance for obtaining it; to this end I formed the following little prayer, which was prefixed to my tables of examination, for daily use:

> O powerful Goodness! bountiful Father! merciful Guide! Increase in me that wisdom which discovers my truest interest. Strengthen my resolutions to perform what that wisdom dictates. Accept my kind offices to thy other children as the only return in my power for thy continual favours to me.

I used also sometimes a little prayer which I took from Thomson's Poems, viz.:

> Father of light and life, thou Good Supreme!
> O teach me what is good; teach me Thyself!
> Save me from folly, vanity, and vice,
> From every low pursuit; and fill my soul
> With knowledge, conscious peace, and virtue pure;
> Sacred, substantial, never-fading bliss!

The precept of *Order* requiring that *every part of my business should have its allotted time*, one page in my little book contained the following scheme of employment for the twenty-four hours of a natural day.

THE MORNING. *Question.* What good shall I do this day?	5 6 7	Rise, wash, and address *Powerful Goodness!* Contrive day's business, and take the resolution of the day; prosecute the present study, and breakfast.
	8 9 10 11	Work.
NOON.	12 1	Read, or overlook my accounts, and dine.
	2 3 4 5	Work.
EVENING. *Question.* What good have I done to-day?	6 7 8 9 10 11 12	Put things in their places. Supper. Music or diversion, or conversation. Examination of the day.
NIGHT.	1 2 3 4	Sleep.

I entered upon the execution of this plan for self-examination, and continued it with occasional intermissions for some time. I was surprised to find myself so much fuller of faults than I had imagined; but I had the satisfaction of seeing them diminish. To avoid the trouble of renewing now and then my little book, which, by scraping out the marks on the paper of old faults to make room for new ones in a new course, became full of holes, I transferred my tables and precepts to the ivory leaves of a memorandum book, on which the lines were drawn with red ink, that made a durable stain, and on those lines I marked my faults with a black-lead pencil, which marks I could easily wipe out with a wet sponge. After a while I went through one course only in a year, and afterward only one in several years, till at length I omitted them entirely, being employed in voyages and business abroad, with a multiplicity of affairs that interfered; but I always carried my little book with me.

My scheme of ORDER gave me the most trouble; and I found that, though it might be practicable where a man's business was such as to leave him the disposition of his time, that of a journeyman printer, for instance, it was not possible to be exactly observed by a master, who must mix with the world, and often receive people of business at their own hours. *Order*, too, with regard to places for things, papers, etc., I found extremely difficult to acquire. I had not been early accustomed to it, and, having an exceeding good memory, I was not so sensible of the inconvenience attending want of method. This article, therefore, cost me so much painful attention, and my faults in it vexed me so much, and I made so little progress in amendment, and had such frequent relapses, that I was almost ready to give up the attempt, and content myself with a faulty character in that respect, like the man who, in buying an ax of a smith, my neighbor, desired to have the whole of its surface as bright as the edge. The smith consented to grind it bright for him if he would turn the wheel; he turned, while the smith pressed the broad face of the ax hard and heavily on the stone, which made the turning of it very fatiguing. The man came every now and then from the wheel to see how the work went on, and at length would take his ax as it was, without farther grinding. "No," said the smith, "turn on, turn on; we shall have it bright by-and-by; as yet, it is only speckled." "Yes," says the man, *"but I like a speckled ax best."* And I believe this may have been the case with many, who, having, for want of some such means as I employed, found the difficulty of obtaining good and breaking bad habits in other points of vice and virtue, have given up the struggle, and concluded that *"a speckled ax was best"*; for something, that pretended to be reason, was every now and then suggesting to me that such extreme nicety as I exacted of myself might be a kind of foppery in morals, which, if it were known, would make me ridiculous; that a perfect character might be attended with the inconvenience of being envied and hated; and that a benevolent man should allow a few faults in himself, to keep his friends in countenance.

In truth, I found myself incorrigible with respect to Order; and now I am grown old, and my memory bad, I feel very sensibly the want of it. But, on the whole, though I never arrived at the perfection I had been so ambitious of obtaining, but fell far short of it, yet I was, by the endeavor, a better and a happier man than I otherwise should have been if I had not attempted it; as those who aim at perfect writing by imitating the engraved copies, though they never reach the wished-for excellence of those copies, their hand is mended by the endeavor, and is tolerable while it continues fair and legible.

It may be well my posterity should be informed that to this little artifice, with the blessing of God, their ancestor owed the constant felicity of his life, down to his 79th year, in which this is written. What reverses may attend the remainder is in the hand of Providence; but, if they arrive, the reflection on past happiness enjoyed ought to help his bearing them with more resignation. To Temperance he ascribes his long-continued health, and what is still left to him of a good constitution; to Industry and Frugality, the early easiness of his circumstances and acquisition of his fortune, with all that knowledge that enabled him to be a useful citizen, and obtained for him some degree of reputation among the learned; to Sincerity and Justice, the confidence of his country, and the honorable employs it conferred upon him; and to the joint influence of the whole mass of the virtues, even in the imperfect state he was able to acquire them, all that evenness of temper, and that cheerfulness in conversation, which makes his company still sought for, and agreeable even to his younger acquaintance. I hope, therefore, that some of my descendants may follow the example and reap the benefit.

It will be remarked that, though my scheme was not wholly without religion, there was in it no mark of any of the distinguishing tenets of any particular sect. I had purposely avoided them; for, being fully persuaded of the utility and excellency of my method, and that it might be serviceable to people in all religions, and intending some time or other to publish it, I would not have anything in it that should prejudice any one, of any sect, against it. I purposed writing a little comment on each virtue, in which I would have shown the advantages of possessing it, and the mischiefs attending its opposite vice; and I should have called my book THE ART OF VIRTUE, because it would have shown the means and manner of obtaining virtue, which would have distinguished it from the mere exhortation to be good, that does not instruct and indicate the means, but is like the apostle's man of verbal charity, who only without showing to the naked and hungry how or where they might get clothes or victuals exhorted them to be fed and clothed. — James ii. 15, 16.

But it so happened that my intention of writing and publishing this comment was never fulfilled. I did, indeed, from time to time, put down short hints of the sentiments, reasonings, etc., to be made use of in it, some of which I have still by me; but the necessary close attention to private business in the earlier part of my life, and public business since, have occasioned my postponing it; for, it being connected in my mind with *a great and extensive project*, that required the whole man to execute, and which an unforeseen succession of employs prevented my attending to, it has hitherto remained unfinished.

In this piece it was my design to explain and enforce this doctrine, that vicious actions are not hurtful because they are forbidden, but forbidden because they are hurtful, the nature of man alone considered; that it was, therefore, every one's interest to be virtuous who wished to be happy even in this world; and I should, from this circumstance (there being always in the world a number of rich merchants, nobility, states, and princes, who have need of honest instruments for the management of their affairs, and such being so rare), have endeavored to convince young persons that no qualities were so likely to make a poor man's fortune as those of probity and integrity.

My list of virtues contained at first but twelve; but a Quaker friend having kindly informed me that I was generally thought proud; that my pride showed itself frequently in conversation; that I was not content with being in the right when discussing any point, but was overbearing, and rather insolent, of which he convinced me by mentioning several instances; I determined endeavoring to cure myself, if I could, of this vice or folly among the rest, and I added *Humility* to my list, giving an extensive meaning to the word.

I cannot boast of much success in acquiring the *reality* of this virtue, but I had a good deal with regard to the *appearance* of it. I made it a rule to forbear all direct contradiction to the sentiments of others, and all positive assertion of my own. I even forbid myself, agreeably to the old laws of our Junto, the use of every word or expression in the language that imported a fixed opinion, such as *certainly, undoubtedly,* etc., and I adopted, instead of them, *I conceive, I apprehend,* or *I imagine* a thing to be so or so; or it *so appears to me at present.* When another asserted something that I thought an error, I denied myself the pleasure of contradicting him abruptly, and of showing immediately some absurdity in his proposition; and in answering I began by observing that in certain cases or circumstances his opinion would be right, but in the present case there *appeared* or *seemed* to me some difference, etc. I soon found the advantage of this change in my manner; the conversations I engaged in went on more pleasantly. The modest way in which I proposed my opinions procured them a readier reception and less contradiction; I had less mortification when I was found to be in the wrong, and I more easily prevailed with others to give up their mistakes and join with me when I happened to be in the right.

And this mode, which I at first put on with some violence to natural inclination, became at length so easy, and so habitual to me, that perhaps for these fifty years past no one has ever heard a dogmatical expression escape me. And to this habit (after my character of integrity) I think it principally owing that I had early so much weight with my fellow-citizens when I proposed new institutions, or alterations in the old, and so much influence in public councils when I became a member; for I was but a bad speaker, never eloquent, subject to much hesitation in my choice of words, hardly correct in language, and yet I generally carried my points.

In reality, there is, perhaps, no one of our natural passions so hard to subdue as *pride.* Disguise it, struggle with it, beat it down, stifle it, mortify it as much as one pleases, it is still alive, and will every now and then peep out and show itself; you will see it, perhaps, often in this history; for, even if I could conceive that I had completely overcome it, I should probably be proud of my humility.

Having mentioned a *great and extensive project* which I had conceived, it seems proper that some account should be here given of that project and its object. Its first rise in my mind appears in the following little paper, accidentally preserved, viz.:

Observations on my reading history, in Library, May 19th, 1731.

That the great affairs of the world, the wars, revolutions, etc., are carried on and affected by parties.

That the view of these parties is their present general interest, or what they take to be such.

That the different views of these different parties occasion all confusion.

That while a party is carrying on a general design, each man has his particular private interest in view.

That as soon as a party has gained its general point, each member becomes intent upon his particular interest; which, thwarting others, breaks that party into divisions, and occasions more confusion.

That few in public affairs act from a mere view of the good of their country, whatever they may pretend; and, though their actings bring real good to their country, yet men primarily considered that their own and their country's interest was united, and did not act from a principle of benevolence.

That fewer still, in public affairs, act with a view to the good of mankind.

There seems to me at present to be great occasion for raising a United Party for Virtue, by forming the virtuous and good men of all nations into a regular body, to be governed by suitable, good, and wise rules, which good and wise men may probably be more unanimous in their obedience to, than common people are to common laws.

I at present think that whoever attempts this aright, and is well qualified, cannot fail of pleasing God, and of meeting with success.   B. F.

Revolving this project in my mind, as to be undertaken hereafter, when my circumstances should afford me the necessary leisure, I put down from time to time, on pieces of paper, such thoughts as occurred to me respecting it. Most of these are lost; but I find one purporting to be the substance of an intended creed, containing, as I thought, the essentials of every known religion, and being free of everything that might shock the professors of any religion. It is expressed in these words, viz.:

That there is one God, who made all things. 5

That He governs the world by his providence.

That He ought to be worshipped by adoration, prayer, and thanksgiving.

But that the most acceptable service of God is do- 10 ing good to man.

That the soul is immortal.

And that God will certainly reward virtue and punish vice, either here or hereafter.

My ideas at that time were that the sect 15 should be begun and spread at first among young and single men only; that each person to be initiated should not only declare his assent to such creed, but should have exercised himself with the thirteen weeks' examination and prac- 20 tice of the virtues, as in the before-mentioned model; that the existence of such a society should be kept a secret, till it was become considerable, to prevent solicitations for the admission of improper persons, but that the mem- 25 bers should each of them search among his acquaintance for ingenuous, well-disposed youths, to whom, with prudent caution, the scheme should be gradually communicated; that the members should engage to afford their advice, 30 assistance, and support to each other in promoting one another's interests, business, and advancement in life; that, for distinction, we should be called *The Society of the Free and Easy*: free, as being, by the general practice and 35 habit of the virtues, free from the dominion of vice; and particularly by the practice of industry and frugality, free from debt, which exposes a man to confinement, and a species of slavery to his creditors. 40

This is as much as I can now recollect of the project, except that I communicated it in part to two young men, who adopted it with some enthusiasm; but my then narrow circumstances, and the necessity I was under of sticking close to 45 my business, occasioned my postponing the further prosecution of it at that time; and my multifarious occupations, public and private, induced me to continue postponing, so that it has been omitted till I have no longer strength 50 or activity left sufficient for such an enterprise; though I am still of opinion that it was a practicable scheme, and might have been very useful, by forming a great number of good

citizens; and I was not discouraged by the seeming magnitude of the undertaking, as I have always thought that one man of tolerable abilities may work great changes, and accomplish great affairs among mankind, if he first forms a 5 good plan, and, cutting off all amusements or other employments that would divert his attention, makes the execution of that same plan his sole study and business.

[The Reverend Mr. Whitefield]

In 1739 arrived among us from Ireland the Reverend Mr. Whitefield, who had made himself remarkable there as an itinerant preacher. He was at first permitted to preach in some of our churches; but the clergy, taking a dislike to him, soon refused him their pulpits, and he was obliged to preach in the fields. The multitudes of all sects and denominations that attended his sermons were enormous, and it was matter of speculation to me, who was one of the number, to observe the extraordinary influence of his oratory on his hearers, and how much they admired and respected him, notwithstanding his common abuse of them, by assuring them they were naturally *half beasts and half devils*. It was wonderful to see the change soon made in the manners of our inhabitants. From being thoughtless or indifferent about religion, it seemed as if all the world were growing religious, so that one could not walk through the town in an evening without hearing psalms sung in different families of every street.

And it being found inconvenient to assemble in the open air, subject to its inclemencies, the building of a house to meet in was no sooner proposed, and persons appointed to receive contributions, but sufficient sums were soon received to procure the ground and erect the building, which was one hundred feet long and seventy broad, about the size of Westminster Hall; and the work was carried on with such spirit as to be finished in a much shorter time than could have been expected. Both house and ground were vested in trustees, expressly for the use of any preacher of any religious persuasion who might desire to say something to the people at Philadelphia; the design in building not being to accommodate any particular sect, but the inhabitants in general; so that even if the Mufti of Constantinople were to send a missionary to preach Mohammedanism to us, he would find a pulpit at his service.

Mr. Whitefield, in leaving us, went preaching all the way through the colonies to Georgia. The settlement of that province had lately been begun, but, instead of being made with hardy, industrious husbandmen accustomed to labor, the only people fit for such an enterprise, it was with families of broken shop-keepers and other insolvent debtors, many of indolent and idle habits, taken out of the jails, who, being set down in the woods, unqualified for clearing land, and unable to endure the hardships of a new settlement, perished in numbers, leaving many helpless children unprovided for. The sight of their miserable situation inspired the benevolent heart of Mr. Whitefield with the idea of building an Orphan House there, in which they might be supported and educated. Returning northward, he preached up this charity, and made large collections, for his eloquence had a wonderful power over the hearts and purses of his hearers, of which I myself was an instance.

I did not disapprove of the design, but, as Georgia was then destitute of materials and workmen, and it was proposed to send them from Philadelphia at a great expense, I thought it would have been better to have built the house here, and brought the children to it. This I advised; but he was resolute in his first project, rejected my counsel, and I therefore refused to contribute. I happened soon after to attend one of his sermons, in the course of which I perceived he intended to finish with a collection, and I silently resolved he should get nothing from me. I had in my pocket a handful of copper money, three or four silver dollars, and five pistoles in gold. As he proceeded I began to soften, and concluded to give the coppers. Another stroke of his oratory made me ashamed of that, and determined me to give the silver; and he finished so admirably, that I emptied my pocket wholly into the collector's dish, gold and all. At this sermon there was also one of our club, who, being of my sentiments respecting the building in Georgia, and suspecting a collection might be intended, had, by precaution, emptied his pockets before he came from home. Towards the conclusion of the discourse, however, he felt a strong desire to give, and applied to a neighbor, who stood near him, to borrow some money for the purpose. The application was unfortunately [made] to perhaps the only man in the company who had the firmness not to be affected by the preacher. His answer was, "At any other time, Friend Hopkinson, I would lend to thee freely; but not now, for thee seems to be out of thy right senses."

Some of Mr. Whitefield's enemies affected to suppose that he would apply these collections to his own private emolument; but I, who was intimately acquainted with him (being employed in printing his Sermons and Journals, etc.), never had the least suspicion of his integrity, but am to this day decidedly of opinion that he was in all his conduct a perfectly *honest man*; and methinks my testimony in his favor ought to have the more weight, as we had no religious connection. He used, indeed, sometimes to pray for my conversion, but never had the satisfaction of believing that his prayers were heard. Ours was a mere civil friendship, sincere on both sides, and lasted to his death.

The following instance will show something of the terms on which we stood. Upon one of his arrivals from England at Boston he wrote to me that he should come soon to Philadelphia, but knew not where he could lodge when there, as he understood his old friend and host, Mr. Benezet, was removed to Germantown. My answer was, "You know my house; if you can make shift with its scanty accommodations, you will be most heartily welcome." He replied, that if I made that kind offer for Christ's sake, I should not miss of a reward. And I returned, "Don't let me be mistaken; it was not for Christ's sake, but for your sake." One of our common acquaintance jocosely remarked, that, knowing it to be the custom of the saints, when they received any favor, to shift the burden of the obligation from off their own shoulders, and place it in heaven, I had contrived to fix it on earth.

The last time I saw Mr. Whitefield was in London, when he consulted me about his Orphan House concern, and his purpose of appropriating it to the establishment of a college.

He had a loud and clear voice, and articulated his words and sentences so perfectly, that he might be heard and understood at a great distance, especially as his auditories, however numerous, observed the most exact silence. He preached one evening from the top of the Court-house steps, which are in the middle of Market-street, and on the west side of Second-street, which crosses it at right angles. Both streets were filled with his hearers to a considerable distance. Being among the hindmost in Market-street, I had the curiosity to learn how far he could be heard, by retiring backwards

down the street towards the river; and I found
his voice distinct till I came near Front-street,
when some noise in that street obscured it.
Imagining then a semicircle, of which my distance should be the radius, and that it were
filled with auditors, to each of whom I allowed
two square feet, I computed that he might well
be heard by more than thirty thousand. This
reconciled me to the newspaper accounts of his
having preached to twenty-five thousand people
in the fields, and to the ancient histories of
generals haranguing whole armies, of which I
had sometimes doubted.

By hearing him often, I came to distinguish
easily between sermons newly composed, and
those which he had often preached in the course
of his travels. His delivery of the latter was so
improved by frequent repetitions that every
accent, every emphasis, every modulation of
voice was so perfectly well turned and well
placed that, without being interested in the
subject, one could not help being pleased with
the discourse, a pleasure of much the same kind
with that received from an excellent piece of
music. This is an advantage itinerant preachers
have over those who are stationary, as the latter
cannot well improve their delivery of a sermon
by so many rehearsals.

The Way to Wealth

(1758)

"In 1732 I first published my Almanac, under
the name of *Richard Saunders*; it was continued by
me about twenty-five years, commonly called *Poor
Richard's Almanac*. I endeavored to make it both
entertaining and useful, and it accordingly came to
be in such demand that I reaped considerable profit
from it, vending annually near ten thousand. And
observing that it was generally read, scarce any
neighborhood in the province being without it, I
considered it as a proper vehicle for conveying instruction among the common people, who bought
scarcely any other books; I therefore filled all the
little spaces that occurred between the remarkable
days in the calendar with proverbial sentences, chiefly
such as inculcated industry and frugality, as the
means of procuring wealth, and thereby securing
virtue; it being more difficult for a man in want, to
act always honestly, as, to use here one of those
proverbs, *it is hard for an empty sack to stand upright*.

"These proverbs, which contained the wisdom of
many ages and nations, I assembled and formed into
a connected discourse prefixed to the Almanac of

175[8], as the harangue of a wise old man to the
people attending an auction. The bringing all these
scattered counsels thus into a focus enabled them to
make greater impression. The piece, being universally
approved, was copied in all the newspapers of the
[American] Continent; reprinted in Britain on a broad
side, to be stuck up in houses; two translations were
made of it in French; and great numbers bought by
the clergy and gentry, to distribute gratis among their
poor parishioners and tenants. In Pennsylvania, . . .
some thought it had its share of influence in producing that growing plenty of money which was
observable for several years after its publication."
(Franklin, *Autobiography*.)

COURTEOUS READER,

I have heard that nothing gives an author so
great pleasure as to find his works respectfully
quoted by other learned authors. This pleasure
I have seldom enjoyed; for though I have been,
if I may say it without vanity, an eminent author of almanacs annually now a full quarter
of a century, my brother authors in the same
way, for what reason I know not, have ever been
very sparing in their applauses; and no other author has taken the least notice of me; so that,
did not my writings produce me some *solid pudding*, the great deficiency of praise would have
quite discouraged me.

I concluded at length that the people were
the best judges of my merit, for they buy my
works; and besides, in my rambles where I am
not personally known, I have frequently heard
one or other of my adages repeated, with "as
Poor Richard says" at the end on't. This gave
me some satisfaction, as it showed not only that
my instructions were regarded, but discovered
likewise some respect for my authority; and I
own that, to encourage the practice of remembering and repeating those wise sentences, I have
sometimes *quoted myself* with great gravity.

Judge, then, how much I must have been
gratified by an incident I am going to relate to
you. I stopped my horse lately where a great
number of people were collected at a vendue of
merchant goods. The hour of sale not being
come, they were conversing on the badness of
the times, and one of the company called to a
plain, clean old man with white locks: "Pray,
Father Abraham, what think you of the times?
Won't these heavy taxes quite ruin the country?
How shall we be ever able to pay them? What
would you advise us to?" Father Abraham stood
up and replied, "If you'd have my advice, I'll
give it you in short, for 'A word to the wise is

enough,' and 'Many words won't fill a bushel,' as Poor Richard says." They joined in desiring him to speak his mind, and gathering round him, he proceeded as follows:

"Friends," says he, "and neighbors, the taxes are indeed very heavy, and if those laid on by the government were the only ones we had to pay, we might more easily discharge them; but we have many others, and much more grievous to some of us. We are taxed twice as much by our idleness, three times as much by our pride, and four times as much by our folly; and from these taxes the commissioners cannot ease or deliver us by allowing an abatement. However, let us hearken to good advice, and something may be done for us; 'God helps them that help themselves,' as Poor Richard says in his almanac of 1733.

"It would be thought a hard government that should tax its people one-tenth part of their time, to be employed in its service. But idleness taxes many of us much more, if we reckon all that is spent in absolute sloth, or doing of nothing, with that which is spent in idle employments or amusements that amount to nothing. Sloth, by bringing on diseases, absolutely shortens life. 'Sloth, like rust, consumes faster than labor wears; while the used key is always bright,' as Poor Richard says. 'But dost thou love life? Then do not squander time; for that's the stuff life is made of,' as Poor Richard says. How much more than is necessary do we spend in sleep, forgetting that 'The sleeping fox catches no poultry,' and that 'There will be sleeping enough in the grave,' as Poor Richard says.

" 'If time be of all things the most precious, wasting time must be,' as Poor Richard says, 'the greatest prodigality'; since, as he elsewhere tells us, 'Lost time is never found again'; and 'What we call time enough always proves little enough." Let us then up and be doing, and doing to the purpose; so by diligence shall we do more with less perplexity. 'Sloth makes all things difficult, but industry all easy,' as Poor Richard says; and 'He that riseth late must trot all day, and shall scarce overtake his business at night'; while 'Laziness travels so slowly that poverty soon overtakes him,' as we read in Poor Richard, who adds, 'Drive thy business, let not that drive thee'; and 'Early to bed, and early to rise, makes a man healthy, wealthy, and wise.'

"So what signifies wishing and hoping for better times? We may make these times better if we bestir ourselves. 'Industry need not wish,'

as Poor Richard says, and 'He that lives upon hope will die fasting.' 'There are no gains without pains'; 'Then help, hands, for I have no lands,' or if I have, they are smartly taxed. And, as Poor Richard likewise observes, 'He that hath a trade hath an estate; and he that hath a calling, hath an office of profit and honor'; but then the trade must be worked at, and the calling well followed, or neither the estate nor the office will enable us to pay our taxes. If we are industrious, we shall never starve; for, as Poor Richard says, 'At the working man's house hunger looks in but dares not enter.' Nor will the bailiff or the constable enter, for 'Industry pays debts, while despair increaseth them,' says Poor Richard. What though you have found no treasure, nor has any rich relation left you a legacy, 'Diligence is the mother of good luck,' as Poor Richard says, and 'God gives all things to industry.' 'Then plough deep while sluggards sleep, and you shall have corn to sell and to keep,' says Poor Dick. Work while it is called today, for you know not how much you may be hindered tomorrow, which makes Poor Richard say, 'One today is worth two tomorrows,' and farther, 'Have you somewhat to do tomorrow, do it today.' If you were a servant, would you not be ashamed that a good master should catch you idle? Are you then your own master, 'Be ashamed to catch yourself idle,' as Poor Dick says. When there is so much to be done for yourself, your family, your country, and your gracious King, be up by peep of day; 'Let not the sun look down and say, "Inglorious here he lies." ' Handle your tools without mittens; remember that 'The cat in gloves catches no mice,' as Poor Richard says. 'Tis true there is much to be done, and perhaps you are weakhanded; but stick to it steadily, and you will see great effects, for 'Constant dropping wears away stones,' and 'By diligence and patience the mouse ate in two the cable'; and 'Little strokes fell great oaks,' as Poor Richard says in his almanac — the year I cannot just now remember.

"Methinks I hear some of you say, 'Must a man afford himself no leisure?' I will tell thee, my friend, what Poor Richard says: 'Employ thy time well, if thou meanest to gain leisure'; and, 'Since thou art not sure of a minute, throw not away an hour.' Leisure is time for doing something useful; this leisure the diligent man will obtain, but the lazy man never; so that, as Poor Richard says, 'A life of leisure and a life of laziness are two things.' Do you imagine that sloth will afford you more comfort than labor? No, for as Poor Richard says, 'Trouble springs from idleness, and grievous toil from needless ease.' 'Many, without labor, would live by their wits only, but they break for want of stock.' Whereas industry gives comfort, and plenty, and respect: 'Fly pleasures, and they'll follow you.' 'The diligent spinner has a large shift'; and, 'Now I have a sheep and a cow, everybody bids me good morrow'; all which is well said by Poor Richard.

"But with our industry we must likewise be steady, settled, and careful, and oversee our own affairs with our own eyes, and not trust too much to others; for, as Poor Richard says,

'I never saw an oft-removèd tree,
Nor yet an oft-removèd family,
That throve so well as those that settled be.'

And again, 'Three removes is as bad as a fire'; and again, 'Keep thy shop, and thy shop will keep thee'; and again, 'If you would have your business done, go; if not, send.' And again,

'He that by the plough would thrive
Himself must either hold or drive.'

And again, 'The eye of a master will do more work than his hands'; and again, 'Want of care does us more damage than want of knowledge'; and again, 'Not to oversee workmen is to leave them your purse open.' Trusting too much to others' care is the ruin of many; for, as the almanac says, 'In the affairs of this world men are saved not by faith but by the want of it'; but a man's own care is profitable; for, saith Poor Dick, 'Learning is to the studious, and riches to the careful, as well as power to the bold, and heaven to the virtuous'; and farther, 'If you would have a faithful servant and one that you like, serve yourself.' And again, he adviseth to circumspection and care, even in the smallest matters, because sometimes 'A little neglect may breed great mischief'; adding: 'For want of a nail the shoe was lost; for want of a shoe the horse was lost; and for want of a horse the rider was lost, being overtaken and slain by the enemy; all for want of care about a horseshoe nail.'

"So much for industry, my friends, and attention to one's own business; but to these we must add frugality if we would make our industry more certainly successful. A man may, if he knows not how to save as he gets, keep his nose all his life to the grindstone, and die not worth a groat at last. 'A fat kitchen makes a lean will,' as Poor Richard says; and

'Many estates are spent in the getting,
Since women for tea forsook spinning and knit-
    ting,
And men for punch forsook hewing and split-
    ting.'

'If you would be wealthy,' says he in another almanac, 'think of saving as well as of getting: the Indies have not made Spain rich, because her outgoes are greater than her incomes.'

"Away then with your expensive follies, and you will not then have so much cause to complain of hard times, heavy taxes, and chargeable families; for, as Poor Dick says,

'Women and wine, game and deceit
Make the wealth small and the wants great.'

And farther, 'What maintains one vice would bring up two children.' You may think, perhaps, that a little tea, or a little punch now and then, diet a little more costly, clothes a little finer, and a little entertainment now and then can be no great matter; but remember what Poor Richard says, 'Many a little makes a mickle'; and farther, 'Beware of little expenses; a small leak will sink a great ship'; and again, 'Who dainties love, shall beggars prove'; and moreover, 'Fools make feasts, and wise men eat them.'

"Here you are all got together at this vendue of fineries and knickknacks. You call them goods; but if you do not take care, they will prove evils to some of you. You expect they will be sold cheap, and perhaps they may for less than they cost; but if you have no occasion for them, they must be dear to you. Remember what Poor Richard says, 'Buy what thou hast no need of, and ere long thou shalt sell thy necessaries.' And again, 'At a great pennyworth pause a while.' He means that perhaps the cheapness is apparent only, and not real; or the bargain, by straitening thee in thy business, may do thee more harm than good. For in another place he says, 'Many have been ruined by buying good pennyworths.' Again, Poor Richard says, ' 'Tis foolish to lay out money in a purchase of repentance'; and yet this folly is practiced every day at vendues for want of minding the almanac. 'Wise men,' as Poor Dick says, 'learn by others' harms, fools scarcely by their own'; but *felix quem faciunt aliena pericula cautum.* ["Fortunate he whom another's dangers render cautious."] Many a one, for the sake of finery on the back, have gone with a hungry belly and half starved their families. 'Silks and satins, scarlet and velvets,' as Poor Richard says, 'put out the kitchen fire.'

"These are not the necessaries of life; they can scarcely be called the conveniences; and yet, only because they look pretty, how many want to have them! The artificial wants of mankind thus become more numerous than the natural; and, as Poor Dick says, 'For one poor person, there are an hundred indigent.' By these and other extravagancies the genteel are reduced to poverty and forced to borrow of those whom they formerly despised, but who through industry and frugality have maintained their standing; in which case it appears plainly that 'A ploughman on his legs is higher than a gentleman on his knees,' as Poor Richard says. Perhaps they have had a small estate left them, which they knew not the getting of; they think 'tis day and will never be night, that a little to be spent out of so much is not worth minding. 'A child and a fool,' as Poor Richard says, 'imagine twenty shillings and twenty years can never be spent'; but 'Always taking out of the meal-tub, and never putting in, soon comes to the bottom'; then as Poor Dick says, 'When the well's dry, they know the worth of water.' But this they might have known before if they had taken his advice. 'If you would know the value of money, go and try to borrow some'; or 'He that goes a-borrowing goes a-sorrowing'; and indeed so does he that lends to such people, when he goes to get it again. Poor Dick farther advises, and says,

'Fond pride of dress is sure a very curse;
E'er fancy you consult, consult your purse.'

And again, 'Pride is as loud a beggar as want, and a great deal more saucy.' When you have bought one fine thing, you must buy ten more, that your appearance may be all of a piece; but Poor Dick says, ' 'Tis easier to suppress the first desire than to satisfy all that follow it.' And 'tis as truly folly for the poor to ape the rich as for the frog to swell in order to equal the ox.

'Great estates may venture more,
But little boats should keep near shore.'

'Tis, however, a folly soon punished; for 'Pride that dines on vanity sups on contempt,' as Poor Richard says. And in another place, 'Pride breakfasted with plenty, dined with poverty, and supped with infamy.' And after all, of what use is this pride of appearance, for which so much is suffered? It cannot promote health, or ease pain; it makes no increase of merit in the person; it creates envy, it hastens misfortune.

'What is a butterfly? At best
He's but a caterpillar drest.
The gaudy fop's his picture just,'

as Poor Richard says.

"But what madness must it be to run in debt for these superfluities! We are offered by the terms of this vendue six months' credit; and that perhaps has induced some of us to attend it, because we cannot spare the ready money and hope now to be fine without it. But, ah, think what you do when you run in debt; you give to another power over your liberty! If you cannot pay at the time, you will be ashamed to see your creditor; you will be in fear when you speak to him; you will make poor pitiful sneaking excuses, and by degrees come to lose your veracity, and sink into base downright lying; for, as Poor Richard says, 'The second vice is lying, the first is running in debt.' And again, to the same purpose, 'Lying rides upon debt's back.' Whereas a free-born Englishman ought not to be ashamed or afraid to see or speak to any man living. But poverty often deprives a man of all spirit and virtue: ' 'Tis hard for an empty bag to stand upright,' as Poor Richard truly says.

"What would you think of that prince or that government who should issue an edict forbidding you to dress like a gentleman or a gentlewoman on pain of imprisonment or servitude? Would you not say that you were free, have a right to dress as you please, and that such an edict would be a breach of your privileges, and such a government tyrannical? And yet you are about to put yourself under that tyranny, when you run in debt for such dress! Your creditor has authority at his pleasure to deprive you of your liberty by confining you in gaol for life, or to sell you as a servant, if you should not be able to pay him! When you have got your bargain, you may perhaps think little of payment; but 'Creditors,' Poor Richard tells us, 'have better memories than debtors'; and in another place says, 'Creditors are a superstitious sect, great observers of set days and times.' The day comes round before you are aware, and the demand is made before you are prepared to satisfy it; or, if you bear your debt in mind, the term which at first seemed so long will, as it lessens, appear extremely short. Time will seem to have added wings to his heels as well as shoulders. 'Those have a short Lent,' saith Poor Richard, 'who owe money to be paid at Easter.' Then since, as he says, 'The borrower is a slave to the lender, and the debtor to the creditor,' disdain the chain, preserve your freedom; and maintain your independency. Be industrious and free; be frugal and free. At present, perhaps, you may think yourself in thriving circumstances, and that you can bear a little extravagance without injury; but,

'For age and want, save while you may;
No morning sun lasts a whole day,'

as Poor Richard says. Gain may be temporary and uncertain, but ever while you live expense is constant and certain; and ' 'Tis easier to build two chimneys than to keep one in fuel,' as Poor Richard says. So, 'Rather go to bed supperless than rise in debt.'

'Get what you can, and what you get hold;
'Tis the stone that will turn all your lead into
    gold,'

as poor Richard says. And when you have got the philosopher's stone, sure you will no longer complain of bad times or the difficulty of paying taxes.

"This doctrine, my friends, is reason and wisdom; but after all, do not depend too much upon your own industry, and frugality, and prudence, though excellent things, for they may all be blasted without the blessing of Heaven; and therefore ask that blessing humbly, and be not uncharitable to those that at present seem to want it, but comfort and help them. Remember, Job suffered, and was afterwards prosperous.

"And now to conclude, 'Experience keeps a dear school, but fools will learn in no other, and scarce in that'; for it is true, 'We may give advice, but we cannot give conduct,' as Poor Richard says. However, remember this: 'They that won't be counselled can't be helped,' as Poor Richard says; and farther, that 'If you will not hear reason, she'll surely rap your knuckles.' "

Thus the old gentleman ended his harangue.

The people heard it and approved the doctrine, and immediately practiced the contrary, just as if it had been a common sermon; for the vendue opened, and they began to buy extravagantly, notwithstanding all his cautions and their own fear of taxes. I found the good man had thoroughly studied my almanacs and digested all I had dropped on these topics during the course of five and twenty years. The frequent mention he made of me must have tired anyone else, but my vanity was wonderfully delighted with it, though I was conscious that not a tenth part of the wisdom was my own which he ascribed to me, but rather the gleanings I had made of the sense of all ages and nations. However, I resolved to be the better for the echo of it; and though I had at first determined to buy stuff for a new coat, I went away resolved to wear my old one a little longer. Reader, if thou wilt do the same, thy profit will be as great as mine. I am, as ever, thine to serve thee,

RICHARD SAUNDERS.

Rules by Which a Great Empire May Be Reduced to a Small One

(1773)

Like the Declaration of Independence three years later, this paper and the *Edict by the King of Prussia* present the case of the colonies against Great Britain.

Franklin excelled in irony, from the playful to the bitter. Here it is bitter. Tongue in cheek, he writes with grim humor.

An ancient sage boasted, that, though he could not fiddle, he knew how to make a *great city* of a *little one*. The science that I, a modern simpleton, am about to communicate, is the very reverse.

I address myself to all ministers who have the management of extensive dominions, which from their very greatness are become troublesome to govern, because the multiplicity of their affairs leaves no time for *fiddling*.

I. In the first place, gentlemen, you are to consider, that a great empire, like a great cake, is most easily diminished at the edges. Turn your attention, therefore, first to your *remotest* provinces; that, as you get rid of them, the next may follow in order.

II. That the possibility of this separation may always exist, take special care the provinces are never incorporated with the mother country; that they do not enjoy the same common rights, the same privileges in commerce; and that they are governed by *severer* laws, all of *your enacting*, without allowing them any share in the choice of the legislators. By carefully making and preserving such distinctions, you will (to keep to my simile of the cake) act like a wise gingerbread-baker, who, to facilitate a division, cuts his dough half through in those places where, when baked, he would have it *broken to pieces*.

III. Those remote provinces have perhaps been acquired, purchased, or conquered, at the *sole expense* of the settlers, or their ancestors, without the aid of the mother country. If this should happen to increase her *strength*, by their growing numbers, ready to join in her wars, her *commerce*, by their growing demand for her manufactures; or her *naval power*, by greater employment for her ships and seamen, they may probably suppose some merit in this, and that it entitles them to some favor; you are therefore to *forget it all, or resent it*, as if they had done you injury. If they happen to be zealous whigs, friends of liberty, nurtured in revolution principles, *remember all that* to their prejudice, and resolve to punish it; for such principles, after a revolution is thoroughly established, are of *no more use*; they are even *odious* and *abominable*.

IV. However peaceably your colonies have submitted to your government, shown their affection to your interests, and patiently borne their grievances, you are to *suppose* them always inclined to revolt, and treat them accordingly. Quarter troops among them, who by their insolence may *provoke* the rising of mobs, and by their bullets and bayonets *suppress* them. By this means, like the husband who uses his wife ill *from suspicion*, you may in time convert your *suspicions* into *realities*.

V. Remote provinces must have *governors* and *judges*, to represent the Royal Person, and execute everywhere the delegated parts of his office and authority. You ministers know, that much of the strength of government depends on the *opinion* of the people, and much of that opinion on the *choice of rulers* placed immediately over them. If you send them wise and good men for governors, who study the interest of the colonists, and advance their prosperity, they will think their King wise and good, and that he wishes the welfare of his subjects. If

you send them learned and upright men for judges, they will think him a lover of justice. This may attach your provinces more to his government. You are therefore to be careful whom you recommend for those offices. If you can find prodigals, who have ruined their fortunes, broken gamesters or stock-jobbers, these may do well as *governors*; for they will probably be rapacious, and provoke the people by their extortions. Wrangling proctors and pettifogging lawyers, too, are not amiss, for they will be for ever disputing and quarrelling with their little parliaments. If withal they should be ignorant, wrong-headed, and insolent, so much the better. Attornies' clerks and Newgate solicitors will do for *Chief Justices*, especially if they hold their places *during your pleasure*; and all will contribute to impress those ideas of your government, that are proper for a people *you would wish to renounce it*.

VI. To confirm these impressions, and strike them deeper, whenever the injured come to the capital with complaints of maladministration, oppression, or injustice, punish such suitors with long delay, enormous expense, and a final judgment in favor of the oppressor. This will have an admirable effect every way. The trouble of future complaints will be prevented, and governors and judges will be encouraged to farther acts of oppression and injustice; and thence the people may become more disaffected, and at length desperate.

VII. When such governors have crammed their coffers, and made themselves so odious to the people that they can no longer remain among them, with safety to their persons, *recall and reward* them with pensions. You may make them *baronets* too, if that respectable order should not think fit to resent it. All will contribute to encourage new governors in the same practice, and make the supreme government *detestable*.

VIII. If, when you are engaged in war, your colonies should vie in liberal aids of men and money against the common enemy, upon your simple requisition, and give far beyond their abilities, reflect that a penny taken from them by your power is more honorable to you, than a pound presented by their benevolence; despise therefore their voluntary grants, and resolve to harass them with novel taxes. They will probably complain to your Parliaments that they are taxed by a body in which they have no representative, and that this is contrary to common right. They will petition for redress. Let the Parliaments flout their claims, reject their petitions, refuse even to suffer the reading of them, and treat the petitioners with the utmost contempt. Nothing can have a better effect in producing the alienation proposed; for though many can forgive injuries, *none ever forgave contempt*.

IX. In laying these taxes, never regard the heavy burthens those remote people already undergo, in defending their own frontiers, supporting their own provincial governments, making new roads, building bridges, churches, and other public edifices, which in old countries have been done to your hands by your ancestors, but which occasion constant calls and demands on the purses of a new people. Forget the *restraints* you lay on their trade for *your own* benefit, and the advantage a *monopoly* of this trade gives your exacting merchants. Think nothing of the wealth those merchants and your manufacturers acquire by the colony commerce; their increased ability thereby to pay taxes at home; their accumulating, in the price of their commodities, most of those taxes, and so levying them from their consuming customers; all this, and the employment and support of thousands of your poor by the colonists, you are *entirely to forget*. But remember to make your arbitrary tax more grievous to your provinces, by public declarations importing that your power of taxing them has *no limits*; so that when you take from them without their consent one shilling in the pound, you have a clear right to the other nineteen. This will probably weaken every idea of *security in their property*, and convince them, that under such a government they *have nothing they can call their own*; which can scarce fail of producing the *happiest consequences!*

X. Possibly, indeed, some of them might still comfort themselves, and say, "Though we have no property, we have yet *something* left that is valuable; we have constitutional *liberty*, both of person and of conscience. This King, these Lords, and these Commons, who it seems are too remote from us to know us, and feel for us, cannot take from us our *Habeas Corpus* right, or our right of trial *by a jury of our neighbors*; they cannot deprive us of the exercise of our religion, alter our ecclesiastical constitution, and compel us to be Papists, if they please, or Mahometans." To annihilate this comfort, begin by laws to perplex their commerce with infinite regulations, impossible to be remembered and observed; ordain seizures of their property for every failure; take away the trial of such property by jury, and give it to arbitrary judges of your own appointing, and of the lowest characters in the country, whose salaries and emoluments are to arise out of the duties or condemnations, and whose appointments are *during pleasure*. Then let there be a formal declaration of both Houses, that opposition to your edicts is *treason*, and that any person suspected of treason in the provinces may, according to some obsolete law, be seized and sent to the metropolis of the empire for trial; and pass an act, that those there charged with certain other offences shall be sent away in chains from their friends and country to be tried in the same manner for felony. Then erect a new Court of Inquisition among them, accompanied by an armed force, with instructions to transport all such suspected persons; to be ruined by the expense, if they bring over evidences to prove their innocence, or be found guilty and hanged, if they cannot afford it. And, lest the people should think you cannot possibly go any farther, pass another solemn declaratory act, "that King, Lords, Commons had, hath, and of right ought to have, full power and authority to make statutes of sufficient force and validity to bind the unrepresented provinces IN ALL CASES WHATSOEVER." This will include *spiritual* with temporal, and, taken together, must operate wonderfully to your purpose: by convincing them, that they are at present under a power something like that spoken of in the scriptures, which can not only *kill their bodies*, but *damn their souls* to all eternity, by compelling them, if it pleases, *to worship the Devil*.

XI. To make your taxes more odious, and more likely to procure resistance, send from the capital a board of officers to superintend the collection, composed of the most *indiscreet, ill-bred*, and *insolent* you can find. Let these have large salaries out of the extorted revenue, and live in open, grating luxury upon the sweat and blood of the industrious; whom they are to worry continually with groundless and expensive prosecutions before the above-mentioned arbitrary revenue judges; *all at the cost of the party prosecuted*, though acquitted, because *the King is to pay no costs*. Let these men, *by your order*, be exempted from all the common taxes and burthens of the province, though they and their property are protected by its laws. If any revenue officers are *suspected* of the least tenderness for the people, discard them. If others are justly complained of, protect and reward them. If any of the under officers behave so as to provoke the people to drub them, promote those to better offices: this will encourage others to procure for themselves such profitable drubbings, by multiplying and enlarging such provocations, and *all will work towards the end you aim at*.

XII. Another way to make your tax odious, is to misapply the produce of it. If it was originally appropriated for the *defence* of the provinces, the better support of government, and the administration of justice, where it may be *necessary*, then apply none of it to that *defence*, but bestow it where it is *not necessary*, in augmented salaries or pensions to every governor, who has distinguished himself by his enmity to the people, and by calumniating them to their sovereign. This will make them pay it more unwillingly, and be more apt to quarrel with those that collect it and those that imposed it, who will quarrel again with them, and all shall contribute to your *main purpose*, of making them *weary of your government*.

XIII. If the people of any province have been accustomed to support their own governors and judges to satisfaction, you are to apprehend that such governors and judges may be thereby influenced to treat the people kindly, and to do them justice. This is another reason for applying part of that revenue in larger shares to such governors and judges, given, as their commissions are, *during your pleasure* only; forbidding them to take any salaries from their provinces; that thus the people may no longer hope any kindness from their governors, or (in Crown cases) any justice from their judges. And, as the money thus misapplied in one province is extorted from all, probably *all will resent the misapplication*.

XIV. If the parliaments of your provinces should dare to claim rights, or complain of your administration, order them to be harassed with *repeated dissolutions*. If the same men are continually returned by new elections, adjourn their meetings to some country village, where they cannot be accommodated, and there keep them *during pleasure*; for this, you know, is your PREROGATIVE; and an excellent one it is, as you may manage it to promote discontents among the people, diminish their respect, and *increase their disaffection*.

XV. Convert the brave, honest officers of your *navy* into pimping tide-waiters and colony officers of the *customs*. Let those who in time of war fought gallantly in defence of the commerce of their countrymen, in peace be taught to prey upon it. Let them learn to be corrupted by great and real smugglers; but (to show their diligence) scour with armed boats every bay, harbor, river, creek, cove, or nook throughout the coast of your colonies; stop and detain every coaster, every wood-boat, every fisherman, tumble their cargoes and even their ballast inside out and upside down; and, if a penn'orth of pins is found un-entered, let the whole be seized and confiscated. Thus shall the trade of your colonists suffer more from their friends in time of peace, than it did from their enemies in war. Then let these boats' crews land upon every farm in their way, rob the orchards, steal the pigs and the poultry, and insult the inhabitants. If the injured and exasperated farmers, unable to procure other justice, should attack the aggressors, drub them, and burn their boats; you are to call this *high treason and rebellion*, order fleets and armies into their country, and threaten to carry all the offenders three thousand miles to be hanged, drawn, and quartered. *O! this will work admirably!*

XVI. If you are told of discontents in your colonies, never believe that they are general, or that you have given occasion for them; therefore do not think of applying any remedy, or of changing any offensive measure. Redress no grievance, lest they should be encouraged to demand the redress of some other grievance. Grant no request that is just and reasonable, lest they should make another that is unreasonable. Take all your informations of the state of the colonies from your governors and officers in enmity with them. Encourage and reward these *leasing-makers*; secrete their lying accusations, lest they should be confuted; but act upon them as the clearest evidence; and believe nothing you hear from the friends of the people; suppose all *their* complaints to be invented and promoted by a few factious demagogues, whom if you could catch and hang, all would be quiet. Catch and hang a few of them accordingly; and the *blood of the martyrs* shall *work miracles* in favor of your purpose.

XVII. If you see *rival nations* rejoicing at the prospect of your disunion with your provinces, and endeavoring to promote it; if they translate, publish, and applaud all the complaints of your discontented colonists, at the same time privately stimulating you to severer measures, let not that *alarm* or offend you. Why should it, since you all mean *the same thing?*

XVIII. If any colony should at their own charge erect a fortress to secure their port against the fleets of a foreign enemy, get your governor to betray that fortress into your hands. Never think of paying what it cost the country, for that would look, at least, like some regard for justice; but turn it into a citadel to awe the inhabitants and curb their commerce. If they should have lodged in such fortress the very arms they bought and used to aid you in your conquests, seize them all; it will provoke like *ingratitude* added to *robbery*. One admirable effect of these operations will be, to discourage every other colony from erecting such defences, and so your enemies may more easily invade them; to the great disgrace of your government, and of course *the furtherance of your project.*

XIX. Send armies into their country under pretence of protecting the inhabitants; but, instead of garrisoning the forts on their frontiers with those troops, to prevent incursions, demolish those forts, and order the troops into the heart of the country, that the savages may be encouraged to attack the frontiers, and that the troops may be protected by the inhabitants. This will seem to proceed from your ill will or your ignorance, and contribute farther to produce and strengthen an opinion among them, *that you are no longer fit to govern them.*

XX. Lastly, invest the general of your army in the provinces, with great and unconstitutional powers, and free him from the control of even your own civil governors. Let him have troops enow under his command, with all the fortresses in his possession; and who knows but (like some provincial generals in the Roman empire, and encouraged by the universal discontent you have produced) he may take it into his head to set up for himself? If he should, and you have carefully practised these few *excellent rules* of mine, take my word for it, all the provinces will immediately join him; and you will that day (if you have not done it sooner) get rid of the trouble of governing them, and all the *plagues* attending their *commerce* and connection from henceforth and for ever.

Q. E. D.

An Edict by the King of Prussia

(1773)

The ancient German settlements in Britain, compared with the English settlements in America, suggested to Franklin one of his clever hoaxes. In a letter to his son he reports: "What made it the more noticed here was, that people in reading it were, as the phrase is, taken in, till they had got half through it, and imagined it a real edict, to which mistake I suppose the King of Prussia's *character* must have contributed."

We have long wondered here at the supineness of the English nation, under the Prussian impositions upon its trade entering our port. We did not, till lately, know the claims, ancient and modern, that hang over that nation, and therefore could not suspect that it might submit to those impositions from a sense of duty, or from principles of equity. The following Edict, just made public, may, if serious, throw some light upon this matter:

"FREDERICK, by the grace of God, King of Prussia, etc. etc. etc. to all present and to come, Health. The peace now enjoyed throughout our dominions, having afforded us leisure to apply ourselves to the regulation of commerce, the improvement of our finances, and at the same time the easing our domestic subjects in their taxes: For these causes and other good considerations us thereunto moving, we hereby make known, that, after having deliberated these affairs in our council, present our dear brothers, and other great officers of the state, members of the same, we, of our certain knowledge, full power, and authority royal, have made and issued this present Edict, viz.

"Whereas it is well known to all the world, that the first German settlements made in the island of Britain were by colonies of people, subjects to our renowned ducal ancestors, and drawn from their dominions, under the conduct of Hengist, Horsa, Hella, Uffa, Cerdicus, Ida, and others; and that the said colonies have flourished under the protection of our august house, for ages past; have never been emancipated therefrom; and yet have hitherto yielded little profit to the same: And whereas we ourself have in the last war fought for and defended the said colonies, against the power of France, and thereby enabled them to make conquests from the said power in America; for which we have not yet received adequate compensation: And whereas it is just and expedient that a revenue should be raised from the said colonies in Britain, towards our indemnification; and that those who are descendants of our ancient subjects, and thence still owe us due obedience, should contribute to the replenishing of our royal coffers, as they must have done, had their ancestors remained in the territories now to us appertaining: We do therefore hereby ordain and command, that, from and after the date of these presents, there shall be levied, and paid to our officers of the customs, on all goods, wares, and merchandizes, and on all grain and other produce of the earth, exported from the said island of Britain, and on all goods of whatever kind imported into the same, a duty of four and a half per cent. ad valorem, for the use of us and our successors. And that the said duty may more effectually be collected, we do hereby ordain, that all ships or vessels bound from Great-Britain to any other part of the world, or from any other part of the world to Great-Britain, shall in their respective voyages touch at our port of Koningsberg, there to be unladen, searched, and charged with the said duties.

"And whereas there hath been from time to time discovered in the said island of Great-Britain, by our colonists there, many mines or beds of iron stone; and sundry subjects of our ancient dominion, skilful in converting the said stone into metal, have in times past transported themselves thither, carrying with them and communicating that art; and the inhabitants of the said island, presuming that they had a natural right to make the best use they could of the natural productions of their country, for their own benefit, have not only built furnaces for smelting the said stone into iron, but have erected plating forges, slitting mills, and steel furnaces, for the more convenient manufacturing of the same, thereby endangering a diminution of the said manufacture in our ancient dominion; we do therefore hereby farther ordain, that, from and after the date hereof, no mill or other engine for slitting or rolling of iron, or any plating forge to work with a tilt-hammer, or any furnace for making steel, shall be erected or continued in the said island of Great-Britain: And the Lord-Lieutenant of every country in the said island is hereby commanded, on information of any such erection within his county, to order and by force to cause the same to be abated and destroyed, as he shall answer the neglect thereof to us at his peril. But we are

nevertheless graciously pleased to permit the inhabitants of the said island to transport their iron into Prussia, there to be manufactured, and to them returned, they paying our Prussian subjects for the workmanship, with all the costs of commission, freight, and risk, coming and returning, any thing herein contained to the contrary notwithstanding.

"We do not, however, think fit to extend this our indulgence to the article of wool; but meaning to encourage not only the manufacturing of woolen cloth, but also the raising of wool, in our ancient dominions; and to prevent both, as much as may be, in our said island, we do hereby absolutely forbid the transportation of wool from thence even to the mother-country, Prussia; And that those islanders may be farther and more effectually restrained in making any advantage of their own wool, in the way of manufacture, we command that none shall be carried out of one country into another, nor shall any worsted, bay, or woollen-yarn, cloth, says, bays, kerseys, serges, frizes, druggets, cloth-serges, shalloons, or any other drapery stuffs, or woollen manufactures whatsoever, made up or mixed with wool in any of the said counties, be carried into any other county, or be water-borne even across the smallest river or creek, on penalty of forfeiture of the same, together with the boats, carriages, horses, etc. that shall be employed in removing them. Nevertheless, our loving subjects there are hereby permitted (if they think proper) to use all their wool as manure, for the improvement of their lands.

"And whereas the art and mystery of making hats hath arrived at great perfection in Prussia; and the making of hats by our remoter subjects ought to be as much as possible restrained: And forasmuch as the islanders before mentioned, being in possession of wool, beaver and other furs, have presumptuously conceived they had a right to make some advantage thereof, by manufacturing the same into hats, to the prejudice of our domestic manufacture: We do therefore hereby strictly command and ordain, that no hats or felts whatsoever, dyed or undyed, finished or unfinished, shall be loaden or put into or upon any vessel, cart, carriage, or horse, to be transported or conveyed out of one county in the said island into another county, or to any other place whatsoever, by any person or persons whatsoever, on pain of forfeiting the same, with a penalty of five hundred pounds sterling for every offence.

Nor shall any hat-maker, in any of the said counties, employ more than two apprentices, on penalty of five pounds sterling per month: we intending hereby that such hatmakers, being so restrained, both in the production and sale of their commodity, may find no advantage in continuing their business. But, lest the said islanders should suffer inconveniency by the want of hats, we are farther graciously pleased to permit them to send their beaver furs to Prussia; and we also permit hats made thereof to be exported from Prussia to Britain; the people thus favored to pay all costs and charges of manufacturing, interest, commission to our merchants, insurance and freight going and returning, as in the case of iron.

"And lastly, being willing farther to favor our said colonies in Britain, we do hereby also ordain and command, that all the thieves, highway and street robbers, house-breakers, forgerers, murderers, s—d—tes, and villains of every denomination, who have forfeited their lives to the law in Prussia, but whom we, in our great clemency, do not think fit here to hang, shall be emptied out of our goals into the said island of Great-Britain, for the better peopling of that country.

"We flatter ourselves, that these our royal regulations and commands will be thought just and reasonable by our much favored colonists in England; the said regulations being copied from their own statutes, of 10 and 11 Will. III. c. 10. — 5 Geo. II. c. 22 — 23 Geo. II c. 29 — 4 Geo. I. c. 11. and from other equitable laws made by their parliaments, or from instructions given by their Princes, or from resolutions of both Houses, entered into for the good government of their own colonies in Ireland and America.

"And all persons in the said island are hereby cautioned not to oppose in any wise the execution of this our Edict, or any part thereof, such opposition being high-treason; of which all who are suspected shall be transported in fetters from Britain to Prussia, there to be tried and executed according to the Prussian law.

"Such is our pleasure.

"Given at Potsdam, this twenty-fifth day of the month of August, One thousand seven hundred and seventy-three, and in the thirty-third year of our reign.

"By the King, in his Council.

"Rechtmaessig, Sec."

Some take this Edict to be merely one of the King's *jeux d'esprit:* others suppose it serious, and that he means a quarrel with England; but all here think the assertion it concludes with, "that these regulations are copied from acts of the English parliament respecting their colonies," a very injurious one; it being impossible to believe, that a people distinguished for their love of liberty, a nation so wise, so liberal in its sentiments, so just and equitable towards its neighbors, should, from mean and injudicious views of petty immediate profit, treat its own children in a manner so arbitrary and tyrannical!

The Ephemera

An Emblem of Human Life

(w. 1778)

This little fable and also the *Dialogue between Franklin and the Gout* are examples of the *bagatelles* (from the Italian *bagata*, a trifle) which *le grand Franklin* threw off while in Paris.

The Ephemera, said S. P. Sherman, "proves that this great eighteenth-century rationalist had a fancy" — "the classic Muse of eighteenth-century art which summons the rosy Loves and Desires to sport among the courtiers and philosophers and the wasp-waisted ladies." In such a mood of light elegance the one-time chandler's son wrote this mellow essay-letter, originally in French, for his "dear friend" Madame Brillon. The Moulin Joly of the opening sentence, he explained elsewhere, was a little island in the Seine where he could spend a summer day "in the pleasing society of the ingenious, learned, and very polite persons who inhabit it. At the time when the letter was written, all conversations at Paris were filled with disputes about the music of Gluck and Piccini, a German and Italian musician, who divided the town into violent parties."

You may remember, my dear friend, that when we lately spent that happy day in the delightful garden and sweet society of the Moulin Joly, I stopt a little in one of our walks, and staid some time behind the company. We had been shown numberless skeletons of a kind of little fly, called an ephemera, whose successive generations, we were told, were bred and expired within the day. I happened to see a living company of them on a leaf, who appeared to be engaged in conversation. You know I understand all the inferior animal tongues; my too great application of the study of them is the best excuse I can give for the little progress I have made in your charming language. I listened through curiosity to the discourse of these little creatures; but as they, in their national vivacity, spoke three or four together, I could make but little of their conversation. I found, however, by some broken expressions that I heard now and then, they were disputing warmly on the merits of two foreign musicians, one a *cousin* [gnat], the other a *moscheto* [mosquito]; in which dispute they spent their time, seemingly as regardless of the shortness of life as if they had been sure of living a month. Happy people! thought I, you live certainly under a wise, just, and mild government, since you have no public grievances to complain of, nor any subject of contention but the perfections and imperfections of foreign music. I turned my head from them to an old grey-headed one, who was single on another leaf, and talking to himself. Being amused with his soliloquy, I put it down in writing, in hopes it will likewise amuse her to whom I am so much indebted for the most pleasing of all amusements, her delicious company and heavenly harmony.

"It was," said he, "the opinion of learned philosophers of our race, who lived and flourished long before my time, that this vast world, the Moulin Joly, could not itself subsist more than eighteen hours; and I think there was some foundation for that opinion, since, by the apparent motion of the great luminary that gives life to all nature, and which in my time has evidently declined considerably towards the ocean at the end of our earth, it must then finish its course, be extinguished in the waters that surround us, and leave the world in cold and darkness, necessarily producing universal death and destruction. I have lived seven of those hours, a great age, being no less than four hundred and twenty minutes of time. How very few of us continue so long! I have seen generations born, flourish, and expire. My present friends are the children and grandchildren of the friends of my youth, who are now, alas, no more! And I must soon follow them; for, by the course of nature, though still in health, I cannot expect to live above seven or eight minutes longer. What now avails all my toil and labor, in amassing honey-dew on this leaf, which I cannot live to enjoy! What the political struggles I have been engaged in, for the good of my compatriot inhabitants of this bush, or my philosophical studies for the benefit of our race in general! for, in politics, what can laws do without morals? Our present race of ephemeræ

will in a course of minutes become corrupt, like those of other and older bushes, and consequently as wretched. And in philosophy how small our progress! Alas! art is long, and life is short! My friends would comfort me with the idea of a name, they say, I shall leave behind me, and they tell me I have lived long enough to nature and to glory. But what will fame be to an ephemera who no longer exists? And what will become of all history in the eighteenth hour, when the world itself, even the whole Moulin Joly, shall come to its end, and be buried in universal ruin?"

To me, after all my eager pursuits, no solid pleasures now remain, but the reflection of a long life spent in meaning well, the sensible conversation of a few good lady ephemeræ, and now and then a kind smile and a tune from the ever amiable *Brillante*.

B. FRANKLIN.

Dialogue Between Franklin and the Gout

Midnight, October 22, 1780.

FRANKLIN. Eh! Oh! Eh! What have I done to merit these cruel sufferings?

GOUT. Many things; you have ate and drank too freely, and too much indulged those legs of yours in their indolence.

FRANKLIN. Who is that accuses me?

GOUT. It is I, even I, the Gout.

FRANKLIN. What! my enemy in person?

GOUT. No, not your enemy.

FRANKLIN. I repeat it; my enemy; for you would not only torment my body to death, but ruin my good name; you reproach me as a glutton and a tippler; now all the world, that knows me, will allow that I am neither the one nor the other.

GOUT. The world may think as it pleases; it is always very complaisant to itself, and sometimes to its friends; but I very well know that the quantity of meat and drink proper for a man, who takes a reasonable degree of exercise, would be too much for another, who never takes any.

FRANKLIN. I take — Eh! Oh! — as much exercise — Eh! — as I can, Madam Gout. You know my sedentary state, and on that account, it would seem, Madam Gout, as if you might spare me a little, seeing it is not altogether my own fault.

GOUT. Not a jot; your rhetoric and your politeness are thrown away; your apology avails nothing. If your situation in life is a sedentary one, your amusements, your recreations, at least, should be active. You ought to walk or ride; or, if the weather prevents that, play at billiards. But let us examine your course of life. While the mornings are long, and you have leisure to go abroad, what do you do? Why, instead of gaining an appetite for breakfast, by salutary exercise, you amuse yourself, with books, pamphlets, or newspapers, which commonly are not worth the reading. Yet you eat an inordinate breakfast, four dishes of tea, with cream, and one or two buttered toasts, with slices of hung beef, which I fancy are not things the most easily digested. Immediately afterward you sit down to write at your desk, or converse with persons who apply to you on business. Thus the time passes till one, without any kind of bodily exercise. But all this I could pardon, in regard, as you say, to your sedentary condition. But what is your practice after dinner? Walking in the beautiful gardens of those friends, with whom you have dined, would be the choice of men of sense; yours is to be fixed down to chess, where you are found engaged for two or three hours! This is your perpetual recreation, which is the least eligible of any for a sedentary man, because, instead of accelerating the motion of the fluids, the rigid attention it requires helps to retard the circulation and obstruct internal secretions. Wrapt in the speculations of this wretched game, you destroy your constitution. What can be expected from such a course of living, but a body replete with stagnant humors, ready to fall a prey to all kinds of dangerous maladies, if I, the Gout, did not occasionally bring you relief by agitating those humors, and so purifying or dissipating them? If it was in some nook or alley in Paris, deprived of walks, that you played awhile at chess after dinner, this might be excusable; but the same taste prevails with you in Passy, Auteuil, Montmartre, or Sanoy, places where there are the finest gardens and walks, a pure air, beautiful women, and most agreeable and instructive conversation; all which you might enjoy by frequenting the walks. But these are rejected for this abominable game of chess. Fie, then, Mr. Franklin! But amidst my instructions, I had almost forgot to administer my wholesome corrections; so take that twinge, — and that.

FRANKLIN. Oh! Eh! Oh! Ohhh! As much instruction as you please, Madam Gout, and as many reproaches; but pray, Madam, a truce with your corrections!

GOUT. No, Sir, no, — I will not abate a particle of what is so much for your good, — therefore —

FRANKLIN. Oh! Ehhh! — It is not fair to say I take no exercise, when I do very often, going out to dine and returning in my carriage.

GOUT. That, of all imaginable exercises, is the most slight and insignificant, if you allude to the motion of a carriage suspended on springs. By observing the degree of heat obtained by different kinds of motion, we may form an estimate of the quantity of exercise given by each. Thus, for example, if you turn out to walk in winter with cold feet, in an hour's time you will be in a glow all over; ride on horseback, the same effect will scarcely be perceived by four hours' round trotting; but if you loll in a carriage, such as you have mentioned, you may travel all day, and gladly enter the last inn to warm your feet by a fire. Flatter yourself then no longer, that half an hour's airing in your carriage deserves the name of exercise. Providence has appointed few to roll in carriages, while he has given to all a pair of legs, which are machines infinitely more commodious and serviceable. Be grateful, then, and make a proper use of yours. Would you know how they forward the circulation of your fluids, in the very action of transporting you from place to place; observe when you walk, that all your weight is alternately thrown from one leg to the other; this occasions a great pressure on the vessels of the foot, and repels their contents; when relieved, by the weight being thrown on the other foot, the vessels of the first are allowed to replenish, and, by a return of this weight, this repulsion again succeeds; thus accelerating the circulation of the blood. The heat produced in any given time, depends on the degree of this acceleration; the fluids are shaken, the humors attenuated, the secretions facilitated, and all goes well; the cheeks are ruddy, and health is established. Behold your fair friend at Auteuil, a lady who received from bounteous nature more really useful science, than half a dozen such pretenders to philosophy as you have been able to extract from all your books. When she honors you with a visit, it is on foot. She walks all hours of the day, and leaves indolence, and its concomitant maladies, to be endured by her horses. In this see at once the preservative of her health and personal charms. But when you go to Auteuil, you must have your charge, though it is no further from Passy to Auteuil than from Auteuil to Passy.

FRANKLIN. Your reasonings grow very tiresome.

GOUT. I stand corrected. I will be silent and continue my office; take that, and that.

FRANKLIN. Oh! Ohh! Talk on, I pray you!

GOUT. No, no; I have a good number of twinges for you tonight, and you may be sure of some more tomorrow.

FRANKLIN. What, with such a fever! I shall go distracted. Oh! Eh! Can no one bear it for me?

GOUT. Ask that of your horses; they have served you faithfully.

FRANKLIN. How can you so cruelly sport with my torments?

GOUT. Sport! I am very serious. I have here a list of offences against your own health distinctly written, and can justify every stroke inflicted on you.

FRANKLIN. Read it then.

GOUT. It is too long a detail; but I will briefly mention some particulars.

FRANKLIN. Proceed. I am all attention.

GOUT. Do you remember how often you have promised yourself, the following morning, a walk in the grove of Boulogne, in the garden de la Muette, or in your own garden, and have violated your promise, alleging, at one time, it was too cold, at another too warm, too windy, too moist, or what else you pleased; when in truth it was too nothing, but your insuperable love of ease?

FRANKLIN. That I confess may have happened occasionally, probably ten times in a year.

GOUT. Your confession is very far short of the truth; the gross amount is one hundred and ninety-nine times.

FRANKLIN. Is it possible?

GOUT. So possible, that it is fact; you may rely on the accuracy of my statement. You know M. Brillon's gardens, and what fine walks they contain; you know the handsome flight of an hundred steps, which lead from the terrace above to the lawn below. You have been in the practice of visiting this amiable family twice a week, after dinner, and it is a maxim of your own, that "a man may take as much exercise in walking a mile, up and down stairs, as in ten on level ground." What an

opportunity was here for you to have had exercise in both these ways! Did you embrace it, and how often?

FRANKLIN. I cannot immediately answer that question.

GOUT. I will do it for you; not once.

FRANKLIN. Not once?

GOUT. Even so. During the summer you went there at six o'clock. You found the charming lady, with her lovely children and friends, eager to walk with you, and entertain you with their agreeable conversation; and what has been your choice? Why to sit on the terrace, satisfying yourself with the fine prospect, and passing your eye over the beauties of the garden below, without taking one step to descend and walk about in them. On the contrary, you call for tea and the chess-board; and lo! you are occupied in your seat till nine o'clock, and that besides two hours' play after dinner; and then, instead of walking home, which would have bestirred you a little, you step into your carriage. How absurd to suppose that all this carelessness can be reconcilable with health, without my interposition!

FRANKLIN. I am convinced now of the justness of Poor Richard's remark, that "Our debts and our sins are always greater than we think for."

GOUT. So it is. You philosophers are sages in your maxims, and fools in your conduct.

FRANKLIN. But do you charge among my crimes, that I return in a carriage from Mr. Brillon's?

GOUT. Certainly; for, having been seated all the while, you cannot object the fatigue of the day, and cannot want therefore the relief of a carriage.

FRANKLIN. What then would you have me do with my carriage?

GOUT. Burn it if you choose; you would at least get heat out of it once in this way; or, if you dislike that proposal, here's another for you; observe the poor peasants, who work in the vineyards and grounds about the villages of Passy, Auteuil, Chaillot, etc.; you may find every day, among these deserving creatures, four or five old men and women, bent and perhaps crippled by weight of years, and too long and too great labor. After a most fatiguing day, these people have to trudge a mile or two to their smoky huts. Order your coachman to set them down. This is an act that will be good for your soul; and, at the same time, after your visit to the Brillons, if you return on foot, that will be good for your body.

FRANKLIN. Ah! how tiresome you are!

GOUT. Well, then, to my office; it should not be forgotten that I am your physician. There.

FRANKLIN. Ohhh! what a devil of a physician!

GOUT. How ungrateful you are to say so! Is it not I who, in the character of your physician, have saved you from the palsy, dropsy, and apoplexy? one or other of which would have done for you long ago, but for me.

FRANKLIN. I submit, and thank you for the past, but entreat the discontinuance of your visits for the future; for, in my mind, one had better die than be cured so dolefully. Permit me just to hint, that I have also not been unfriendly to *you*. I never feed physician or quack of any kind, to enter the list against you; if then you do not leave me to my repose, it may be said you are ungrateful too.

GOUT. I can scarcely acknowledge that as any objection. As to quacks, I despise them; they may kill you indeed, but cannot injure me. And, as to regular physicians, they are at last convinced that the gout, in such a subject as you are, is no disease, but a remedy; and wherefore cure a remedy? — but to our business, — there.

FRANKLIN. Oh, oh! — for Heaven's sake leave me! and I promise faithfully never more to play at chess, but to take exercise daily, and live temperately.

GOUT. I know you too well. You promise fair; but, after a few months of good health, you will return to your old habits; your fine promises will be forgotten like the forms of last year's clouds. Let us then finish the account, and I will go. But I leave you with an assurance of visiting you again at a proper time and place; for my object is your good, and you are sensible now that I am your *real friend*.

Letters

[Faith, Hope, and Charity Upside Down]

London, September 16, 1758.

DEAR SISTER,

I received your favor of June 17. I wonder you have had no letter from me since my being in England. I have wrote you at least two, and I think a third before this, and what was next to waiting on you in person, sent you my picture. In June last I sent Benny a trunk of books, and wrote to him; I hope they are come to hand, and that he meets with encouragement in his business. I congratulate you on the conquest of Cape Breton, and hope as your people took it by praying, the first time, you will now pray that it may never be given up again, which you then forgot. Billy is well, but in the country. I left him at Tunbridge Wells, where we spent a fortnight, and he is now gone with some company to see Portsmouth. We have been together over a great part of England this summer, and among other places, visited the town our father was born in, and found some relations in that part of the country still living.

Our cousin Jane Franklin, daughter of our uncle John, died about a year ago. We saw her husband, Robert Page, who gave us some old letters to his wife, from uncle Benjamin. In one of them, dated Boston, July 4, 1732, he writes that your uncle Josiah has a daughter Jane, about twelve years old, a good-humoured child. So keep up to your character, and don't be angry when you have no letters. In a little book he sent her, called "None but Christ," he wrote an acrostick on her name, which for namesake's sake, as well as the good advice it contains, I transcribe and send you, viz.

"Illuminated from on high,
And shining brightly in your sphere,
Ne'er faint, but keep a steady eye,
Expecting endless pleasures there.

"Flee vice as you'd a serpent flee;
Raise *faith* and *hope* three stories higher,
And let Christ's endless love to thee
Ne'er cease to make thy love aspire.
Kindness of heart by words express,
Let your obedience be sincere,
In prayer and praise your God address,
Nor cease, till he can cease to hear."

After professing truly that I had a great esteem and veneration for the pious author, permit me a little to play the commentator and critic on these lines. The meaning of *three stories higher* seems somewhat obscure. You are to understand, then, that *faith*, *hope*, and *charity* have been called the three steps of Jacob's ladder, reaching from earth to heaven; our author calls them *stories*, likening religion to a building, and these are the three stories of the Christian edifice. Thus improvement in religion is called *building up* and *edification*. *Faith* is then the ground floor, *hope* is up one pair of stairs. My dear beloved Jenny, don't delight so much to dwell in those lower rooms, but get as fast as you can into the garret, for in truth the best room in the house is *charity*. For my part, I wish the house was turned upside down; 'tis so difficult (when one is fat) to go up stairs; and not only so, but I imagine *hope* and *faith* may be more firmly built upon *charity*, than *charity* upon *faith* and *hope*. However that may be, I think it the better reading to say —

"Raise faith and hope one story higher."

Correct it boldly, and I'll support the alteration; for, when you are up two stories already, if you raise your building three stories higher you will make five in all, which is two more than there should be, you expose your upper rooms more to the winds and storms; and, besides, I am afraid the foundation will hardly bear them, unless indeed you build with such light stuff as straw and stubble, and that, you know, won't stand fire. Again, where the author says,

"Kindness of heart by words express,"

strike out *words*, and put in *deeds*. The world is too full of compliments already. They are the rank growth of every soil, and choke the good plants of benevolence, and beneficence; nor do I pretend to be the first in this comparison of words and actions to plants; you may remember an ancient poet, whose works we have all studied and copied at school long ago.

"A man of words and not of deeds
Is like a garden full of weeds."

'Tis a pity that good works, among some sorts of people, are so little valued, and good words admired in their stead: I mean seemingly pious discourses, instead of humane benevolent actions. Those they almost put out of countenance, by calling morality *rotten morality*, righteousness *ragged righteousness*, and even filthy rags — and when you mention virtue, pucker up their noses as if they smelt a stink; at the same time that they eagerly snuff up an empty canting harangue, as if it was a posey of the choicest flowers: So they have inverted the good old verse, and say now

"A man of deeds and not of words
Is like a garden full of ——"

I have forgot the rhyme, but remember 'tis something the very reverse of perfume. So much by way of commentary.

My wife will let you see my letter, containing an account of our travels, which I would have you read to sister Dowse, and give my love to her. I have no thoughts of returning till next year, and then may possibly have the pleasure of seeing you and yours; taking Boston in my way home. My love to brother and all your children, concludes at this time from, dear Jenny, your affectionate brother,

B. FRANKLIN.

[To Mrs. Jane Mecom]

[A Deistic Creed]

Franklin died on 17 April 1790, little more than a month after writing this letter to Rev. Ezra Stiles, President of Yale, known both as theologian and as Newtonian scientist. Franklin's final statement of his religion is a mild and tolerant deism expressed in his best urbane and witty style. It follows closely the beliefs of Lord Herbert of Cherbury, the English philosopher who approached religion from a purely rational viewpoint. Franklin's creed should be compared with the more extreme form of deism of Paine's *Age of Reason*.

Philadelphia, March 9, 1790.
REVEREND AND DEAR SIR,

I received your kind letter of January 28, and am glad you have at length received the portrait of Governor Yale from his family, and deposited it in the College Library. He was a great and good man, and had the merit of doing infinite service to your country by his munificence to that institution. The Honor you propose doing me by placing mine in the same room with his, is much too great for my deserts; but you always had a partiality for me, and to that it must be ascribed. I am however too much obliged to Yale College, the first learned society that took notice of me and adorned me with its honors, to refuse a request that comes from it through so esteemed a friend. But I do not think any one of the portraits you mention, as in my possession, worthy of the place and company you propose to place it in. You have an excellent artist lately arrived. If he will undertake to make one for you, I shall cheerfully pay the expense; but he must not delay setting about it, or I may slip through his fingers, for I am now in my eighty-fifth year, and very infirm.

I send with this a very learned work, as it seems to me, on the ancient Samaritan coins, lately printed in Spain, and at least curious for the beauty of the impression. Please to accept it for your College Library. I have subscribed for the Encyclopædia now printing here, with the intention of presenting it to the College. I shall probably depart before the work is finished, but shall leave directions for its continuance to the end. With this you will receive some of the first numbers.

You desire to know something of my religion. It is the first time I have been questioned upon it. But I cannot take your curiosity amiss, and shall endeavor in a few words to gratify it. Here is my creed. I believe in one God, Creator of the Universe. That he governs it by his Providence. That he ought to be worshipped. That the most acceptable service we render to him is doing good to his other children. That the soul of man is immortal, and will be treated with justice in another life respecting its conduct in this. These I take to be the fundamental principles of all sound religion, and I regard them as you do in whatever sect I meet with them.

As to Jesus of Nazareth, my opinion of whom you particularly desire, I think the system of morals and his religion, as he left them to us, the best the world ever saw or is likely to see; but I apprehend it has received various corrupting changes, and I have, with most of the present dissenters in England, some doubts as to his divinity; though it is a question I do not dogmatize upon, having never studied it, and think it needless to busy myself with it now, when I expect soon an opportunity of knowing the truth with less trouble. I see no harm, however, in its being believed, if that belief has the good consequence, as probably it has, of making his doctrine more respected and better observed; especially as I do not perceive, that the Supreme takes it amiss, by distinguishing the unbelievers in his government of the world with any peculiar marks of his displeasure.

I shall only add, respecting myself, that, having experienced the goodness of that Being in conducting me prosperously through a long life, I have no doubt of its continuance in the next, though without the smallest conceit of meriting such goodness. My sentiments on this head you will see in the copy of an old letter enclosed, which I wrote in answer to one from a zealous religionist, whom I had relieved in a paralytic case by electricity, and who, being afraid I should grow proud upon it, sent me his serious though rather impertinent caution. I send you also the copy of another letter, which will show something of my disposition relating to religion. With great and sincere esteem and affection, I am, Your obliged old friend and most obedient humble servant

B. FRANKLIN

P.S. Had not your College some present of books from the King of France? Please to let me know, if you had an expectation given you of more, and the nature of that expectation? I have a reason for the enquiry.

I confide, that you will not expose me to criticism and censure by publishing any part of this communication to you. I have ever let others enjoy their religious sentiments, without reflecting on them for those that appeared to me unsupportable and even absurd. All sects here, and we have a great variety, have experienced my good will in assisting them with subscriptions for building their new places of worship; and, as I have never opposed any of their doctrines, I hope to go out of the world in peace with them all.

AGRARIAN SENTIMENTALIST

St. Jean de Crèvecoeur [1735–1813]

Born in France, near Caen in Normandy, Crèvecoeur went to England when he was nineteen, then on to the New World. In Canada he served in the army under Montcalm till he was wounded when the British took Quebec. In 1765 he became a naturalized citizen of New York, taking the name of John Hector St. John. Surveyor and trader, he traveled widely in the colonies and explored the region between the Great Lakes and the Ohio. Taking an American wife he settled on a farm in Orange County, New York, and there spent idyllic years till the Revolution brought civil war.

Unwilling to join either party in the Revolution, he was suspected by both, and in 1780 sailed for England, where he sold his *Letters from an American Farmer* to a publisher, and the next year was in France. He became the protégé of the Countess d'Houdetot, Rousseau's former mistress, enjoyed the life of the Paris salons, translated his *Letters* into French, was elected a member of the Académie des Sciences. Thanks to his friends and Franklin, he was appointed French consul to New York, but upon his return to America found that the Indians had burned his house and killed his wife; two missing children turned up the next year in Boston. The last twenty-three years of his life he spent in Europe. Crèvecoeur's fame rests on *Letters from an American Farmer*. Some further letters, suggesting Tory sympathies, appeared only in 1925, with the title *Sketches of Eighteenth Century America*.

Further reading: *Letters from an American Farmer*, ed. W. P. Trent and L. Lewisohn, 1904. *Sketches of Eighteenth Century America*. ed. H. L. Bourdin, R. H. Gabriel, S. T. Williams, 1925. J. P. Mitchell, *St. Jean de Crèvecoeur*, 1916. G. Chinard, "The American Dream," a contribution to *Literary History of the United States*, I, 1948.

From *Letters from an American Farmer*

(1782)

These letters — really essays — were written in America "for the information of a friend in England," chiefly before the Revolution, and were published as the work of "J. Hector St. John, a Farmer in Pennsylvania." Having an agrarian outlook akin to that of Franklin and Jefferson, he extolled the virtues of simple living in a natural environment. Whether depressed or joyous, this "farmer of feelings" was given to dropping into sentimentalism, indulging in copious but shallow emotionality, making no secret of the fact that things readily "dilate his heart" or cause "involuntary tears." The first three essays give a broad and enthusiastic characterization of American rural life. The next six focus on Nantucket, Martha's Vineyard, and Charleston. Then come a nature essay, an account of a visit, and a concluding essay on "Distresses of a Frontier Man" — distresses incident to the growing Revolution.

The essay below, printed in excerpt, makes clear an attitude of high importance throughout American history and literature. Commonly spoken of as the *American Dream*, it is the aspiration to a land in which every man might find life full of opportunity for self-development, unhampered by the restrictions of the Old World. As K. B. Murdock has said: "Crèvecoeur not only wrote the first full-length definition of 'an American' in our literature, but expressed better than anyone had done before the fact and the dream which inspired many of the founders of a new nation, many of the pioneers who opened a new continent, and many of the leaders who eventually made the United States a world power."

What is an American?

I wish I could be acquainted with the feelings and thoughts which must agitate the heart and present themselves to the mind of an enlightened Englishman, when he first lands on this continent. He must greatly rejoice that he lived at a time to see this fair country discovered and settled; he must necessarily feel a share of national pride, when he views the chain of settlement which embellishes these extended shores. When he says to himself, this is the work of my countrymen, who, when convulsed by factions, afflicted by a variety of miseries and wants, restless and impatient, took refuge here. They brought along with them their national genius, to which they principally owe what liberty they enjoy, and what substance they possess. Here he sees the industry of his native country displayed in a new manner, and traces in their works the embryos of all the arts, sciences, and ingenuity which flourish in Europe. Here he beholds fair cities, substantial villages, extensive fields, an immense country filled with decent houses, good roads, orchards, meadows, and bridges, where an hundred years ago all was wild, woody, and uncultivated! What a train of pleasing ideas this fair spectacle must suggest; it is a prospect which must inspire a good citizen with the most heartfelt pleasure. The difficulty consists in the manner of viewing so extensive a scene. He is arrived on a new continent; a modern society offers itself to his contemplation, different from what he had hitherto seen. It is not composed, as in Europe, of great lords who possess everything, and of a herd of people who have nothing. Here are no aristocratical families, no courts, no kings, no bishops, no ecclesiastical dominion, no invisible power giving to a few a very visible one; no great manufac-

turers employing thousands, no great refinements of luxury. The rich and the poor are not so far removed from each other as they are in Europe. Some few towns excepted, we are all tillers of the earth, from Nova Scotia to West Florida. We are a people of cultivators, scattered over an immense territory, communicating with each other by means of good roads and navigable rivers, united by the silken bands of mild government, all respecting the laws, without dreading their power, because they are equitable. We are all animated with the spirit of an industry which is unfettered and unrestrained, because each person works for himself. If he travels through our rural districts he views not the hostile castle, and the haughty mansion, contrasted with the clay-built hut and miserable cabin, where cattle and men help to keep each other warm, and dwell in meanness, smoke, and indigence. A pleasing uniformity of decent competence appears throughout our habitations. The meanest of our log-houses is a dry and comfortable habitation. Lawyer or merchant are the fairest titles our towns afford; that of a farmer is the only appellation of the rural inhabitants of our country. It must take some time ere he can reconcile himself to our dictionary, which is but short in words of dignity, and names of honor. There, on a Sunday, he sees a congregation of respectable farmers and their wives, all clad in neat homespun, well mounted, or riding in their own humble wagons. There is not among them an esquire, saving the unlettered magistrate. There he sees a parson as simple as his flock, a farmer who does not riot on the labor of others. We have no princes, for whom we toil, starve, and bleed: we are the most perfect society now existing in the world. Here man is free as he ought to be; nor is this pleasing equality so transitory as many others are. Many ages will not see the shores of our great lakes replenished with inland nations, nor the unknown bounds of North America entirely peopled. Who can tell how far it extends? Who can tell the millions of men whom it will feed and contain? for no European foot has as yet travelled half the extent of this mighty continent!

The next wish of this traveller will be to know whence came all these people? They are a mixture of English, Scotch, Irish, French, Dutch, Germans, and Swedes. From this promiscuous breed, that race now called Americans have arisen. The eastern provinces must indeed be excepted, as being the unmixed descendants of Englishmen. I have heard many wish that they had been more intermixed also: for my part, I am no wisher, and think it much better as it has happened. They exhibit a most conspicuous figure in this great and variegated picture; they too enter for a great share in the pleasing perspective displayed in these thirteen provinces. I know it is fashionable to reflect on them, but I respect them for what they have done; for the accuracy and wisdom with which they have settled their territory; for the decency of their manners; for their early love of letters; their ancient college, the first in this hemisphere; for their industry; which to me who am but a farmer, is the criterion of everything. There never was a people, situated as they are, who with so ungrateful a soil have done more in so short a time. Do you think that the monarchial ingredients which are more prevalent in other governments, have purged them from all foul stains? Their histories assert the contrary.

In this great American asylum, the poor of Europe have by some means met together, and in consequence of various causes, to what purpose should they ask one another what countrymen they are? Alas, two thirds of them had no country. Can a wretch who wanders about, who works and starves, whose life is a continual scene of sore affliction or pinching penury; can that man call England or any other kingdom his country? A country that had no bread for him, whose fields procured him no harvest, who met with nothing but the frowns of the rich, the severity of the laws, with jails and punishments; who owned not a single foot of the extensive surface of this planet? No! urged by a variety of motives, here they came. Everything has tended to regenerate them; new laws, a new mode of living, a new social system; here they are become men: in Europe they were as so many useless plants, wanting vegetative mould, and refreshing showers; they withered, and were mowed down by want, hunger, and war; but now by the power of transportation, like all other plants they have taken root and flourished! Formerly they were not numbered in any civil lists of their country, except in those of the poor; here they rank as citizens. By what invisible power has this surprising metamorphosis been performed? By that of the laws and that of their industry. The laws, the indulgent laws, protect them as they arrive, stamping on them the symbol of adoption; they receive ample rewards for their labors; these accumulated rewards procure them lands; those lands confer on them the title of free-men, and to that title every benefit is affixed which men can possibly require. This is the great operation daily performed by our laws. From whence proceed these laws? From our government. Whence the government? It is derived from the original genius and strong desire of the people ratified and confirmed by the crown. This is the great chain which links us all, this is the picture which every province exhibits, Nova Scotia excepted. There the crown has done all; either there were no people who had genius, or it was not much attended to: the consequence is that the province is very thinly inhabited indeed; the power of the crown in conjunction with the musketos has prevented men from settling there. Yet some parts of it flourished once, and it contained a mild harmless set of people. But for the fault of a few leaders, the whole were banished. The greatest political error the crown ever committed in America, was to cut off men from a country which wanted nothing but men!

What attachment can a poor European emigrant have for a country where he had nothing? The knowledge of the language, the love of a few kindred as poor as himself, were the only cords that tied him: his country is now that which gives him land, bread, protection, and consequence. *Ubi panis ibi patria* [Where bread is, there is a fatherland] is the motto of all emigrants. What then is the American, this new man? He is either an European, or the descendant of an European, hence that strange mixture of blood, which you will find in no other country. I could point out to you a family whose grandfather was an Englishman, whose wife was Dutch, whose son married a French woman, and whose present four sons have now four wives of different nations. *He* is an American, who, leaving behind him all his ancient prejudices and manners, receives new ones from the new mode of life he has embraced, the new government he obeys, and the new rank he holds. He becomes an American by being received in the broad lap of our great *Alma Mater*. Here individuals of all nations are melted into a new race of men, whose labors and posterity will one day cause great changes in the world. Americans are the western pilgrims, who are carrying along with them that great mass of arts, sciences, vigor, and industry which began long since in the east; they will finish the great circle. The

Americans were once scattered all over Europe; here they are incorporated into one of the finest systems of population which has ever appeared, and which will hereafter become distinct by the power of the different climates they inhabit. The American ought therefore to love this country much better than that wherein either he or his forefathers were born. Here the rewards of his industry follow with equal steps the progress of his labor; his labor is founded on the basis of nature, *self-interest*; can it want a stronger allurement? Wives and children, who before in vain demanded of him a morsel of bread, now, fat and frolicsome, gladly help their father to clear those fields whence exuberant crops are to arise to feed and to clothe them all; without any part being claimed, either by a despotic prince, a rich abbot, or a mighty lord. Here religion demands but little of him; a small voluntary salary to the minister, and gratitude to God; can he refuse these? The American is a new man, who acts upon new principles; he must therefore entertain new ideas, and form new opinions. From involuntary idleness, servile dependence, penury, and useless labor, he has passed to toils of a very different nature, rewarded by ample subsistence. — This is an American.***

Men are like plants; the goodness and flavor of the fruit proceeds from the peculiar soil and exposition in which they grow. We are nothing but what we derive from the air we breathe, the climate we inhabit, the government we obey, the system of religion we profess, and the nature of our employment. Here you will find but few crimes; these have acquired as yet no root among us.***

Those who live near the sea, feed more on fish than on flesh, and often encounter that boisterous element. This renders them more bold and enterprising; this leads them to neglect the confined occupations of the land. They see and converse with a variety of people; their intercourse with mankind becomes extensive. The sea inspires them with a love of traffic, a desire of transporting produce from one place to another; and leads them to a variety of resources which supply the place of labor. Those who inhabit the middle settlements, by far the most numerous, must be very different; the simple cultivation of the earth purifies them, but the indulgences of the government, the soft remonstrances of religion, the rank of independent freeholders, must necessarily inspire them with

sentiments very little known in Europe among people of the same class. What do I say? Europe has no such class of men; the early knowledge they acquire, the early bargains they make, give them a great degree of sagacity. As freemen they will be litigious; pride and obstinacy are often the cause of law suits; the nature of our laws and governments may be another. As citizens it is easy to imagine that they will carefully read the newspapers, enter into every political disquisition, freely blame or censure governors and others. As farmers they will be careful and anxious to get as much as they can, because what they get is their own. As northern men they will love the cheerful cup. As Christians, religion curbs them not in their opinions; the general indulgence leaves every one to think for themselves in spiritual matters; the laws inspect our actions, our thoughts are left to God. Industry, good living, selfishness, litigiousness, country politics, the pride of freemen, religious indifference, are their characteristics. If you recede still farther from the sea, you will come into more modern settlements; they exhibit the same strong lineaments, in a ruder appearance. Religion seems to have still less influence, and their manners are less improved.

Now we arrive near the great woods, near the last inhabited districts; there men seem to be placed still farther beyond the reach of government, which in some measure leaves them to themselves. How can it pervade every corner; as they were driven there by misfortunes, necessity of beginnings, desire of acquiring large tracts of land, idleness, frequent want of economy, ancient debts; the re-union of such people does not afford a very pleasing spectacle. When discord, want of unity and friendship; when either drunkenness or idleness prevail in such remote districts; contention, inactivity, and wretchedness must ensue. There are not the same remedies to these evils as in a long established community. The few magistrates they have, are in general little better than the rest; they are often in a perfect state of war; that of man against man, sometimes decided by blows, sometimes by means of the law; that of man against every wild inhabitant of these venerable woods, of which they are come to dispossess them. There men appear to be no better than carnivorous animals of a superior rank, living on the flesh of wild animals when they can catch them, and when they are not able, they subsist on grain. He who would wish to see America in its proper light, and have a true idea of its feeble beginnings and barbarous rudiments, must visit our extended line of frontiers where the last settlers dwell, and where he may see the first labors of settlement, the mode of clearing the earth, in all their different appearances; where men are wholly left dependent on their native tempers, and on the spur of uncertain industry, which often fails when not sanctified by the efficacy of a few moral rules. There, remote from the power of example and check of shame, many families exhibit the most hideous parts of our society. They are a kind of forlorn hope, preceding by ten or twelve years the most respectable army of veterans which come after them. In that space, prosperity will polish some, vice and the law will drive off the rest, who uniting again with others like themselves will recede still farther; making room for more industrious people, who will finish their improvements, convert the loghouse into a convenient habitation, and rejoicing that the first heavy labors are finished, will change in a few years that hitherto barbarous country into a fine fertile, well regulated district. Such is our progress, such is the march of the Europeans toward the interior parts of this continent. In all societies there are off-casts; this impure part serves as our precursors or pioneers; my father himself was one of that class, but he came upon honest principles, and was therefore one of the few who held fast; by good conduct and temperance, he transmitted to me his fair inheritance, when not above one in fourteen of his contemporaries had the same good fortune.

Forty years ago this smiling country was thus inhabited; it is now purged, a general decency of manners prevails throughout, and such has been the fate of our best countries.***

As I have endeavored to show you how Europeans become Americans; it may not be disagreeable to show you likewise how the various Christian sects introduced, wear out, and how religious indifference becomes prevalent.***

Let us suppose you and I to be travelling; we observe that in this house, to the right, lives a Catholic, who prays to God as he has been taught, and believes in transubstantiation; he works and raises wheat, he has a large family of children, all hale and robust; his belief, his prayers offend nobody. About one mile farther on the same road, his next neighbor may be a good honest plodding German Lutheran, who addresses himself to the same God, the God of all, agreeably to the modes he has been educated in, and believes in consubstantiation; by so doing he scandalizes nobody; he also works in his fields, embellishes the earth, clears swamps, etc. What has the world to do with his Lutheran principles? He persecutes nobody, and nobody persecutes him, he visits his neighbors, and his neighbors visit him. Next to him lives a seceder, the most enthusiastic of all sectaries; his zeal is hot and fiery, but separated as he is from others of the same complexion, he has no congregation of his own to resort to, where he might cabal and mingle religious pride with worldly obstinacy. He likewise raises good crops, his house is handsomely painted, his orchard is one of the fairest in the neighborhood. How does it concern the welfare of the country, or of the province at large, what this man's religious sentiments are, or really whether he has any at all? He is a good farmer, he is a sober, peaceable, good citizen: William Penn himself would not wish for more. This is the visible character, the invisible one is only guessed at, and is nobody's business. Next again lives a Low Dutchman, who implicitly believes the rules laid down by the synod of Dort. He conceives no other idea of a clergyman than that of an hired man; if he does his work well he will pay him the stipulated sum; if not he will dismiss him, and do without his sermons, and let his church be shut up for years. But notwithstanding this coarse idea, you will find his house and farm to be the neatest in all the country; and you will judge by his wagon and fat horses, that he thinks more of the affairs of this world than of those of the next. He is sober and laborious, therefore he is all he ought to be as to the affairs of this life; as for those of the next, he must trust to the great Creator. Each of these people instruct their children as well as they can, but these instructions are feeble compared to those which are given to the youth of the poorest class in Europe. Their children will therefore grow up less zealous and more indifferent in matters of religion than their parents. The foolish vanity, or rather the fury of making proselytes, is unknown here; they have no time, the seasons call for all their attention, and thus in a few years, this mixed neighborhood will exhibit a strange religious medley, that will be neither pure Catholicism nor pure Calvinism. A very perceptible indifference even in the first generation, will become apparent; and it may happen that the daughter of the Catholic will marry the son of the seceder, and settle by themselves at a distance from their parents. What religious education will they give their children? A very imperfect one. If there happens to be in the neighborhood any place of worship, we will suppose a Quaker's meeting; rather than not show their fine clothes, they will go to it, and some of them may perhaps attach themselves to that society. Others will remain in a perfect state of indifference; the children of these zealous parents will not be able to tell what their religious principles are, and their grandchildren still less. The neighborhood of a place of worship generally leads them to it, and the action of going thither is the strongest evidence they can give of their attachment to any sect. The Quakers are the only people who retain a fondness for their own mode of worship; for be they ever so far separated from each other, they hold a sort of communion with the society, and seldom depart from its rules, at least in this country. Thus all sects are mixed as well as all nations; thus religious indifference is imperceptibly disseminated from one end of the continent to the other; which is at present one of the strongest characteristics of the Americans. Where this will reach no one can tell, perhaps it may leave a vacuum fit to receive other systems. Persecution, religious pride, the love of contradiction, are the food of what the world commonly calls religion. These motives have ceased here; zeal in Europe is confined; here it evaporates in the great distance it has to travel; there it is a grain of powder inclosed, here it burns away in the open air, and consumes without effect.***

There is no wonder that this country has so many charms, and presents to Europeans so many temptations to remain in it. A traveller in Europe becomes a stranger as soon as he quits his own kingdom; but it is otherwise here. We know, properly speaking, no strangers; this is every person's country; the variety of our soils, situations, climates, governments, and produce, hath something which must please everybody. No sooner does an European arrive, no matter of what condition, than his eyes are opened upon the fair prospect; he hears his language spoke, he retraces many of his own country manners, he perpetually hears the names of families and towns with which he is acquainted; he sees happiness and prosperity in all places disseminated; he meets with hospitality, kindness, and plenty everywhere; he beholds hardly any poor, he seldom hears of punishments and executions; and he wonders at the elegance of our towns, those miracles of industry and freedom. He cannot admire enough our rural districts, our convenient roads, good taverns, and our many accommodations; he involuntarily loves a country where everything is so lovely. When in England, he was a mere Englishman; here he stands on a larger portion of the globe, not less than its fourth part, and may see the productions of the north, in iron and naval stores; the provisions of Ireland, the grain of Egypt, the indigo, the rice of China. He does not find, as in Europe, a crowded society, where every place is over-stocked; he does not feel that perpetual collision of parties, that difficulty of beginning, that contention which oversets so many. There is room for everybody in America; has he any particular talent, or industry? he exerts it in order to procure a livelihood, and it succeeds. Is he a merchant? the avenues of trade are infinite; is he eminent in any respect? he will be employed and respected. Does he love a country life? pleasant farms present themselves; he may purchase what he wants, and thereby become an American farmer. Is he a laborer, sober and industrious? he need not go many miles, nor receive many informations before he will be hired, well fed at the table of his employer, and paid four or five times more than he can get in Europe. Does he want uncultivated lands? thousands of acres present themselves, which he may purchase cheap. Whatever be his talents or inclinations, if they are moderate, he may satisfy them. I do not mean that every one who comes will grow rich in a little time; no, but he may procure an easy, decent maintenance, by his industry. Instead of starving he will be fed, instead of being idle he will have employment; and these are riches enough for such men as come over here. The rich stay in Europe, it is only the middling and the poor that emigrate. Would you wish to travel in independent idleness, from north to south, you will find easy access, and the most cheerful reception at every house; society without ostentation, good cheer without pride, and every decent diversion which the country affords, with little expense. It is no wonder that the European who has lived here a few years, is desirous to remain; Europe with all its pomp, is not to be compared to this continent, for men of middle stations, or laborers.

An European, when he first arrives, seems limited in his intentions, as well as in his views; but he very suddenly alters his scale; two hundred miles formerly appeared a very great distance, it is now but a trifle; he no sooner breathes our air than he forms schemes, and embarks in designs he never would have thought of in his own country. There the plentitude of society confines many useful ideas, and often extinguishes the most laudable schemes which here ripen into maturity. Thus Europeans become Americans.

But how is this accomplished in that crowd of low, indigent people, who flock here every year from all parts of Europe? I will tell you; they no sooner arrive than they immediately feel the good effects of that plenty of provisions we possess: they fare on our best food, and they are kindly entertained: their talents, character, and peculiar industry are immediately inquired into; they find countrymen everywhere disseminated, let them come from whatever part of Europe. Let me select one as an epitome of the rest; he is hired, he goes to work, and works moderately; instead of being employed by a haughty person, he finds himself with his equal, placed at the substantial table of the farmer, or else at an inferior one as good; his wages are high, his bed is not like that bed of sorrow on which he used to lie: if he behaves with propriety, and is faithful, he is caressed, and becomes as it were a member of the family. He begins to feel the effects of a sort of resurrection; hitherto he had not lived, but simply vegetated; he now feels himself a man, because he is treated as such; the laws of his own country had overlooked him in his insignificancy; the laws of this cover him with their mantle. Judge what an alteration there must arise in the mind and thoughts of this man; he begins to forget his former servitude and dependence, his heart involuntarily swells and glows; this first swell inspires him with those new thoughts which constitute an American. What love can he entertain for a country where his existence was a burthen to him; if he is a generous good man, the love of this new adoptive parent will sink deep into his heart. He looks around, and sees many a prosperous person, who but a few years before was as poor as himself. This encourages him much, he begins to form some little scheme, the first, alas, he ever formed in his life. If he is wise he thus spends two or three years, in which time he acquires knowledge, the use of tools, the modes of working the lands, felling trees, etc. This prepares the foundation of a good name, the most useful acquisition he can make. He is encouraged, he has gained friends; he is advised and directed, he feels bold, he purchases some land; he gives all the money he has brought over, as well as what he has earned, and trusts to the God of harvests for the discharge of the rest. His good name procures him credit. He is now possessed of the deed, conveying to him and his posterity the fee simple and absolute property of two hundred acres of land, situated on such a river. What an epoch in this man's life! He is become a freeholder, from perhaps a German boor — he is now an American, a Pennsylvanian, an English subject. He is naturalized, his name is enrolled with those of the other citizens of the province. Instead of being a vagrant, he has a place of residence; he is called the inhabitant of such a county, or of such a district, and for the first time in his life counts for something; for hitherto he has been a cypher. I only repeat what I have heard many say, and no wonder their hearts should glow, and be agitated with a multitude of feelings, not easy to describe. From nothing to start into being; from a servant to the rank of a master; from being the slave of some despotic prince, to become a free man, invested with lands, to which every municipal blessing is annexed! What a change indeed! It is in consequence of that change that he becomes an American. This great metamorphosis has a double effect, it extinguishes all his European prejudices, he forgets that mechanism of subordination, that servility of disposition which poverty had taught him; and sometimes he is apt to forget too much, often passing from one extreme to the other. If he is a good man, he forms schemes of future prosperity, he proposes to educate his children better than he has been educated himself; he thinks of future modes of conduct, feels an ardor to labor he never felt before. Pride steps in and leads him to everything that the laws do not forbid: he respects them; with a heartfelt gratitude he looks toward the east, toward that insular government from whose wisdom all his new felicity is derived, and under whose wings and protection he now lives.***

*** It is of very little importance how, and in what manner an indigent man arrives; for if he is but sober, honest, and industrious, he has nothing more to ask of heaven. Let him go to work, he will have opportunities enough to earn a comfortable support, and even the means of procuring some land; which ought to be the utmost wish of every person who has health and hands to work. I knew a man who came to this country, in the literal sense of the expression, stark naked; I think he was a Frenchman, and a sailor on board an English man-of-war. Being discontented, he had stripped himself and swam ashore; where, finding clothes and friends, he settled afterwards at Maraneck, in the county of Chester in the province of New York: he married and left a good farm to each of his sons. I knew another person who was but twelve years old when he was taken on the frontiers of Canada, by the Indians; at his arrival at Albany he was purchased by a gentleman, who generously bound him apprentice to a tailor. He lived to the age of ninety, and left behind him a fine estate and a numerous family, all well settled; many of them I am acquainted with. — Where is then the industrious European who ought to despair?

After a foreigner from any part of Europe is arrived, and become a citizen; let him devoutly listen to the voice of our great parent, which says to him, "Welcome to my shores, distressed 5 European; bless the hour in which thou didst see my verdant fields, my fair navigable rivers, and my green mountains! — If thou wilt work, I have bread for thee; if thou wilt be honest, sober, and industrious, I have greater rewards to 10 confer on thee — ease and independence. I will give thee fields to feed and clothe thee; a comfortable fireside to sit by, and tell thy children by what means thou hast prospered; and a decent bed to repose on. I shall endow thee 15 beside with the immunities of a freeman. If thou wilt carefully educate thy children, teach them gratitude to God, and reverence to that government, that philanthropic government, which has collected here so many men and made 20 them happy.***

DEISM AND REVOLUTION

Thomas Paine [1737-1809]

Franklin once said, "Where liberty is, there is my country." Paine's response was typical: "Where liberty is not, there is mine."

When Tom Paine, an Englishman, came to America in the momentous year 1774, he was already thirty-seven years old. Up to this time he had floundered about — been corset-maker, grocer, exciseman, schoolteacher, tobacconist. The net result: bankruptcy, plus a broken marriage. Meeting Franklin, who thought well of his mental capacity, he got a letter of introduction and sailed for America.

In Philadelphia he found himself. He began by writing for the *Pennsylvania Magazine* on such eighteenth-century themes as women's rights, the evils of slavery, kindness to animals. After little more than a year he suddenly showed himself a propagandist of genius, an important force in American history, through two electrifying pamphlets. The first was *Common Sense*, issued in January 1776, a bold and ringing call for complete independence from England. After independence was declared in July, Paine served in the Continental Army. Presently the American forces were retreating across New Jersey, and Philadelphia was in panic. At this juncture Paine wrote the first of *The Crisis* pamphlets, read to the troops before the victory at Trenton. It did much to preserve army morale through the dismal winter of 1776–77. That Paine's services to the Revolution were beyond calculation is indicated well enough by the testimony of both Washington and Jefferson.

When independence was achieved and the American Republic established, the French Revolution gave this militant radical another opportunity. Paine witnessed the early events of the French Revolution, and associated himself with radicals in both France and England. Charged with treason in England, he escaped across the Channel, held office in the revolutionary party, had the courage to oppose the execution of the King, spent ten months in prison before the American ambassador, James Monroe, secured his release. Meanwhile Burke in England, in 1790, had published his *Reflections on the Revolution in France*, a masterly statement of conservatism, and Paine in the next two years had published his answer, *The Rights of Man*, a masterly statement of radicalism. This was followed by *The Age of Reason* (Part I, 1794; Part II, 1796), a coarse and slashing attack on traditional Christianity and an affirmation of his own deistical beliefs. It did much to make him unpopular in America, where he lived from 1802 till his death.

Further reading: *Thomas Paine: Representative Selections*, ed. H. H. Clark 1944. M. D. Conway, *The Life of Thomas Paine*, 2 vols., 1892.

From Common Sense

(January 10, 1776)

☙ There had been fighting at Lexington, Bunker Hill, Quebec. England had proclaimed a state of rebellion. With perfect timing and shrewd appeals to various groups, Paine now called upon the country to recognize that independence was both necessary and desirable.

The pamphlet contained seventy-nine pages. The third chapter is given here, without abridgement.

Thoughts on the Present State of American Affairs

In the following pages I offer nothing more than simple facts, plain arguments, and common sense; and have no other preliminaries to settle with the reader, than that he will divest himself of prejudice and prepossession, and suffer his reason and his feeling to determine for themselves; that he will put on, or rather that he will not put off, the true character of a man, and generously enlarge his views beyond the present day.

Volumes have been written on the subject of the struggle between England and America. Men of all ranks have embarked in the controversy, from different motives, and with various designs; but all have been ineffectual, and the period of debate is closed. Arms, as the last resource, must decide the contest; the appeal was the choice of the King, and the continent hath accepted the challenge.

It has been reported of the late Mr. Pelham (who, though an able minister was not without his faults) that on his being attacked in the House of Commons, on the score that his measures were only of a temporary kind, replied, "they will last my time." Should a thought so fatal and unmanly possess the colonies in the present contest, the name of ancestors will be remembered by future generations with detestation.

The sun never shone on a cause of greater worth. 'Tis not the affair of a city, a county, a province, or a kingdom, but of a continent — of at least one eighth part of the habitable globe. 'Tis not the concern of a day, a year, or an age; posterity are virtually involved in the contest, and will be more or less affected even to the end of time, by the proceedings now. Now is the seedtime of continental union, faith, and honor. The least fracture now will be like a name engraved with the point of a pin on the tender rind of a young oak; the wound will enlarge with the tree, and posterity read it in full grown characters.

By referring the matter from argument to arms, a new area for politics is struck; a new method of thinking hath arisen. All plans, proposals, etc., prior to the nineteenth of April, i.e., to the commencement of hostilities, are like the almanacs of last year; which, though proper then, are superseded and useless now. Whatever was advanced by the advocates on either side of the question then, terminated in one and the same point, viz., a union with Great Britain; the only difference between the parties was the method of effecting it; the one proposing force, the other friendship; but it hath so far happened that the first has failed, and the second has withdrawn her influence.

As much hath been said of the advantages of reconciliation, which, like an agreeable dream, hath passed away and left us as we were, it is but right that we should examine the contrary side of the argument, and inquire into some of the many material injuries which these colonies sustain, and always will sustain, by being connected with and dependent on Great Britain. To examine that connection and dependence, on the principles of nature and common sense, to see what we have to trust to, if separated, and what we are to expect, if dependent.

I have heard it asserted by some, that as America has flourished under her former connection with Great Britain, the same connection is necessary towards her future happiness, and will always have the same effect. Nothing can be more fallacious than this kind of argument. We may as well assert that because a child has thrived upon milk, that it is never to have meat, or that the first twenty years of our lives is to become a precedent for the next twenty. But even this is admitting more than is true, for I answer roundly that America would have flourished as much, and probably much more, had no European power taken any notice of her. The articles of commerce by which she has enriched herself, are the necessaries of life, and will always have a market while eating is the custom of Europe.

But she has protected us, say some. That she hath engrossed us is true, and defended the continent at our expense as well as her own, is admitted; and she would have defended Turkey from the same motives, viz., for the sake of trade and dominion.

Alas! we have been long led away by ancient prejudices, and made large sacrifices to superstition. We have boasted the protection of Great Britain, without considering that her motive was interest not attachment; and that she did not protect us from our enemies on our account, but from her enemies on her own account, from those who had no quarrel with us on any other account, and who will always be our enemies on the same account. Let Britain waive her pretensions to the continent, or the continent throw off the dependence, and we should be at peace with France and Spain, were they at war with Britain. The miseries of Hanover's last war ought to warn us against connections.

It hath lately been asserted in Parliament, that the colonies have no relation to each other but through the parent country, i.e., that Pennsylvania and the Jerseys, and so on for the rest, are sister colonies by the way of England; this is certainly a very roundabout way of proving relationship, but it is the nearest and only true way of proving enemyship, if I may so call it. France and Spain never were, nor perhaps ever will be, our enemies as Americans, but as our being the subjects of Great Britain.

But Britain is the parent country, say some. Then the more shame upon her conduct. Even brutes do not devour their young, nor savages make war upon their families; wherefore, the assertion, if true, turns to her reproach; but it happens not to be true, or only partly so, and the phrase, *parent* or *mother* country, hath been jesuitically adopted by the King and his parasites, with a low papistical design of gaining an unfair bias on the credulous weakness of our minds. Europe and not England is the parent country of America. This new World hath been the asylum for the persecuted lovers of civil and religious liberty from *every part* of Europe. Hither have they fled, not from the tender embraces of the mother, but from the cruelty of the monster; and it is so far true of England, that the same tyranny which drove the first emigrants from home, pursues their descendants still.

In this extensive quarter of the Globe, we forget the narrow limits of three hundred and sixty miles (the extent of England) and carry our friendship on a larger scale; we claim brotherhood with every European Christian, and triumph in the generosity of the sentiment.

It is pleasant to observe by what regular gradations we surmount local prejudices, as we enlarge our acquaintance with the world. A man born in any town in England divided into parishes, will naturally associate most with his fellow parishioners (because their interests in many cases will be common) and distinguish him by the name of neighbor; if he meet him but a few miles from home, he drops the narrow idea of a street, and salutes him by the name of townsman; if he travel out of the county, and meets him in any other, he forgets the minor divisions of street and town, and calls him countryman, i.e., county-man; but if in their foreign excursions they should associate in France or any other part of Europe, their local remembrance would be enlarged into that of Englishmen. And by a just parity of reasoning, all Europeans meeting in America, or any other quarter of the globe, are countrymen; for England, Holland, Germany, or Sweden, when compared with the whole, stand in the same places on the larger scale which the divisions of street, town, and county do on the smaller one; distinctions too limited, for continental minds. Not one third of the inhabitants, even of this province [Pennsylvania], are of English descent. Wherefore, I reprobate the phrase of parent or mother country applied to England only, as being false, selfish, narrow, and ungenerous.

But, admittting that we were all of English descent, what does it amount to? Nothing. Britain, being now an open enemy, extinguishes every other name and title, and to say that reconciliation is our duty, is truly farcical. The first king of England, of the present line (William the Conqueror) was a Frenchman, and half the peers of England are descendants from the same country; wherefore, by the same method of reasoning, England ought to be governed by France.

Much hath been said of the united strength of Britain and the colonies, that in conjunction they might bid defiance to the world. But this is mere presumption; the fate of war is uncertain, neither do the expressions mean anything; for this continent would never suffer itself to be drained of inhabitants to support the British arms in either Asia, Africa, or Europe.

Besides, what have we to do with setting the world at defiance? Our plan is commerce, and that, well attended to, will secure us the peace and friendship of all Europe; because it is the interest of all Europe to have America a free port. Her trade will always be a protection, and her barrenness of gold and silver secure her from invaders.

I challenge the warmest advocate for reconciliation to show a single advantage that this continent can reap by being connected with Great Britain. I repeat the challenge; not a single advantage is derived. Our corn will fetch its price in any market in Europe, and our imported goods must be paid for, buy them where we will.

But the injuries and disadvantages which we

sustain by that connection, are without number; and our duty to mankind at large, as well as to ourselves, instructs us to renounce the alliance; because any submission to or dependence on Great Britain tends directly to involve this continent in European war and quarrels; and sets us at variance with nations who would otherwise seek our friendship, and against whom we have neither anger nor complaint. As Europe is our market for trade, we ought to form no partial connection with any part of it. It is the true interest of America to steer clear of European contentions, which she never can do, while, by her dependence on Britain, she is made the make-weight in the scale of British politics.

Europe is too thickly planted with kingdoms to be long at peace, and whenever a war breaks out between England and any foreign power, the trade of America goes to ruin, because of her connection with Britain. The next war may not turn out like the last, and should it not, the advocates for reconciliation now will be wishing for separation then, because neutrality, in that case, would be a safer convoy than a man-of-war. Everything that is right or natural pleads for separation. The blood of the slain, the weeping voice of nature cries, "'Tis time to part." Even the distance at which the Almighty hath placed England and America is a strong and natural proof that the authority of the one over the other was never the design of Heaven. The time likewise at which the continent was discovered, adds weight to the argument, and the manner in which it was peopled increases the force of it. The Reformation was preceded by the discovery of America, as if the Almighty graciously meant to open a sanctuary to the persecuted in future years, when home should afford neither friendship nor safety.

The authority of Great Britain over this Continent is a form of government which sooner or later must have an end. And a serious mind can draw no true pleasure by looking forward, under the painful and positive conviction that what he calls "the present constitution" is merely temporary. As parents, we can have no joy, knowing that *this government* is not sufficiently lasting to insure anything which we may bequeath to posterity. And by a plain method of argument, as we are running the next generation into debt, we ought to do the work of it, otherwise we use them meanly and pitifully. In order to discover the line of our duty rightly, we should take our children in our hand, and fix our station a few years farther into life; that eminence will present a prospect which a few present fears and prejudices conceal from our sight.

Though I would carefully avoid giving unnecessary offence, yet I am inclined to believe, that all those who espouse the doctrine of reconciliation may be included within the following descriptions.

Interested men, who are not to be trusted, weak men who *cannot* see, prejudiced men who *will not* see, and a certain set of moderate men who think better of the European world than it deserves; and this last class, by an ill-judged deliberation, will be the cause of more calamities to this continent than all the other three.

It is the good fortune of many to live distant from the scene of present sorrow; the evil is not sufficiently brought to *their* doors to make *them* feel the precariousness with which all American property is possessed. But let our imaginations transport us a few moments to Boston; that seat of wretchedness will teach us wisdom, and instruct us for ever to renounce a power in whom we can have no trust. The inhabitants of that unfortunate city who but a few months ago were in ease and affluence, have now no other alternative than to stay and starve, or turn out to beg. Endangered by the fire of their friends if they continue within the city, and plundered by the soldiery if they leave it, in their present situation they are prisoners without the hope of redemption, and in a general attack for their relief they would be exposed to the fury of both armies.

Men of passive tempers look somewhat lightly over the offences of Great Britain, and, still hoping for the best, are apt to call out, *come, come, we shall be friends again for all this*. But examine the passions and feelings of mankind: bring the doctrine of reconciliation to the touchstone of nature, and then tell me whether you can hereafter love, honor, and faithfully serve the power that hath carried fire and sword into your land? If you cannot do all these, then are you only deceiving yourselves, and by your delay bringing ruin upon posterity. Your future connection with Britain, whom you can neither love nor honor, will be forced and unnatural, and being formed only on the plan of present convenience, will in a little time fall into a relapse more wretched than the first. But if you say, you can still pass the violations over, then I ask, Hath your house been burnt? Hath your property been destroyed before your face? Are

your wife and children destitute of a bed to lie on, or bread to live on? Have you lost a parent or child by their hands, and yourself the ruined and wretched survivor? If you have not, then are you not a judge of those who have. But if you have, and can still shake hands with the murderers, then are you unworthy the name of husband, father, friend, or lover, and whatever may be your rank or title in life, you have the heart of a coward, and the spirit of a sycophant.

This is not inflaming or exaggerating matters, but trying them by those feelings and affections which nature justifies, and without which we should be incapable of discharging the social duties of life, or enjoying the felicities of it. I mean not to exhibit horror for the purpose of provoking revenge, but to awaken us from fatal and unmanly slumbers, that we may pursue determinately some fixed object. 'Tis not in the power of Britain or of Europe to conquer America, if she doth not conquer herself by *delay* and *timidity*. The present winter is worth an age if rightly employed, but if lost or neglected the whole continent will partake of the misfortune; and there is no punishment which that man doth not deserve, be he who, or what, or where he will, that may be the means of sacrificing a season so precious and useful.

'Tis repugnant to reason, to the universal order of things; to all examples from former ages, to suppose that this continent can long remain subject to any external power. The most sanguine in Britain doth not think so. The utmost stretch of human wisdom cannot, at this time, compass a plan, short of separation, which can promise the continent even a year's security. Reconciliation is *now* a fallacious dream. Nature has deserted the connection, and art cannot supply her place. For, as Milton wisely expresses, "never can true reconcilement grow where wounds of deadly hate have pierced so deep."

Every quiet method for peace hath been ineffectual. Our prayers have been rejected with disdain; and have tended to convince us that nothing flatters vanity or confirms obstinacy in Kings more than repeated petitioning — and nothing hath contributed more than that very measure to make the Kings of Europe absolute. Witness Denmark and Sweden. Wherefore, since nothing but blows will do, for God's sake let us come to a final separation, and not leave the next generation to be cutting throats under the violated unmeaning names of parent and child.

To say they will never attempt it again is idle and visionary; we thought so at the repeal of the stamp act, yet a year or two undeceived us; as well may we suppose that nations which have been once defeated will never renew the quarrel.

As to government matters, 'tis not in the power of Britain to do this Continent justice: the business of it will soon be too weighty and intricate to be managed with any tolerable degree of convenience, by a power so distant from us, and so very ignorant of us; for if they cannot conquer us they cannot govern us. To be always running three or four thousand miles with a tale or a petition, waiting four or five months for an answer, which, when obtained, requires five or six more to explain it in, will in a few years be looked upon as folly and childishness. — There was a time when it was proper, and there is a proper time for it to cease.

Small islands not capable of protecting themselves, are the proper objects for government to take under their care; but there is something absurd in supposing a Continent to be perpetually governed by an island. In no instance hath nature made the satellite larger than its primary planet; and as England and America, with respect to each other, reverse the common order of nature, it is evident that they belong to different systems. England to Europe: America to itself.

I am not induced by motives of pride, party or resentment to espouse the doctrine of separation and independence; I am clearly, positively, and conscientiously persuaded that 'tis the true interest of this continent to be so; that everything short of *that* is mere patchwork, that it can afford no lasting felicity — that it is leaving the sword to our children, and shrinking back at a time when a little more, a little further, would have rendered this continent the glory of the earth.

As Britain hath not manifested the least inclination towards a compromise, we may be assured that no terms can be obtained worthy the acceptance of the continent, or any ways equal to the expense of blood and treasure we have been already put to.

The object contended for ought always to bear some just proportion to the expense. The removal of North, or the whole detestable junto, is a matter unworthy the millions we have expended. A temporary stoppage of trade was an inconvenience, which would have sufficiently balanced the repeal of all the acts complained of, had such repeals been obtained; but if the whole continent must take up arms, if every man must be a soldier, 'tis scarcely worth our while to fight against a contemptible ministry only. Dearly, dearly do we pay for the repeal of the acts, if that is all we fight for; for, in a just estimation 'tis as great a folly to pay a bunker-hill price for law as for land. As I have always considered the independency of this continent, as an event which sooner or later must arrive, so from the late rapid progress of the Continent to maturity, the event cannot be far off. Wherefore, on the breaking out of hostilities, it was not worth the while to have disputed a matter which time would have finally redressed, unless we meant to be in earnest: otherwise it is like wasting an estate on a suit at law, to regulate the trespasses of a tenant whose lease is just expiring. No man was a warmer wisher for a reconciliation than myself, before the fatal nineteenth of April, 1775, but the moment the event of that day was made known, I rejected the hardened, sullen-tempered Pharaoh of England for ever; and disdain the wretch, that with the pretended title of FATHER OF HIS PEOPLE can unfeelingly hear of their slaughter, and composedly sleep with their blood upon his soul.

But admitting that matters were now made up, what would be the event? I answer, the ruin of the continent. And that for several reasons.

First. The powers of governing still remaining in the hands of the king, he will have a negative over the whole legislation of this continent. And as he hath shown himself such an inveterate enemy to liberty, and discovered such a thirst for arbitrary power, is he, or is he not, a proper person to say to these Colonies, *You shall make no laws but what I please?* And is there any inhabitant of America so ignorant as not to know, that according to what is called the *present Constitution*, this continent can make no laws but what the king gives leave to; and is there any man so unwise as not to see, that (considering what has happened) he will suffer no law to be made here but such as suits his purpose? We may be as effectually enslaved by the want of laws in America, as by submitting to laws made for us in England. After matters are made up (as it is called) can there be any doubt, but the whole power of the crown will be exerted to keep this continent as low and humble as possible? Instead of going forward we shall go backward, or be perpetually quarrelling, or ridiculously petitioning. — We are already greater than the King wishes us to be, and will he not hereafter endeavor to make us less? To bring the matter to one point, Is the power who is jealous of our prosperity, a proper power to govern us? Whoever says No, to this question, is an Independent, for independency means no more than this, whether we shall make our own laws, or, whether the King, the greatest enemy this continent hath, or can have, shall tell us *"there shall be no laws but such as I like."*

But the King, you'll say, has a negative in England; the people there can make no laws without his consent. In point of right and good order, it is something very ridiculous that a youth of twenty-one (which hath often happened) shall say to several millions of people older and wiser than himself, "I forbid this or that act of yours to be law." But in this place I decline this sort of reply, though I will never cease to expose the absurdity of it, and only answer that England being the King's residence, and America not so, makes quite another case. The King's negative here is ten times more dangerous and fatal than it can be in England; for *there* he will scarcely refuse his consent to a bill for putting England into as strong a state of defence as possible, and in America he would never suffer such a bill to be passed.

America is only a secondary object in the system of British politics, England consults the good of *this* country no further than it answers her *own* purpose. Wherefore, her own interest leads her to suppress the growth of *ours*, in every case which doth not promote *her* advantage, or in the least interfere with it. A pretty state we should soon be in under such a second-hand government, considering what has happened! Men do not change from enemies to friends by the alteration of a name: And in order to show that reconciliation *now* is a dangerous doctrine, I affirm, *that it would be policy in the king at this time to repeal the acts, for the sake of reinstating himself in the government of the provinces*; in order that HE MAY ACCOMPLISH BY CRAFT AND SUBTLETY, IN THE LONG RUN, WHAT HE CANNOT DO BY FORCE AND VIOLENCE IN THE SHORT ONE. Reconciliation and ruin are nearly related.

Secondly. — That as even the best terms which we can expect to obtain can amount to no more than a temporary expedient, or a kind of government by guardianship, which can last no longer than till the Colonies come of age, so the general face and state of things in the interim will be unsettled and unpromising. Emigrants of property will not choose to come to a country whose form of government hangs but by a thread, and who is every day tottering on the brink of commotion and disturbance. And numbers of the present inhabitants would lay hold of the interval to dispose of their effects, and quit the continent.

But the most powerful of all arguments is, that nothing but independence, i.e. a continental form of government, can keep the peace of the continent and preserve it inviolate from civil wars. I dread the event of a reconciliation with Britain *now*, as it is more than probable that it will be followed by a revolt somewhere or other, the consequences of which may be far more fatal than all malice of Britain.

Thousands are already ruined by British barbarity (thousands more will probably suffer the same fate). Those men have other feelings than us who have nothing suffered. All they *now* possess is liberty; what they have before enjoyed is sacrificed to its service, and having nothing more to lose they disdain submission. Besides, the general temper of the colonies towards a British government will be like that of a youth who is nearly out of his time; they will care very little about her. And a government which cannot preserve the peace is no government at all, and in that case we pay our money for nothing; and pray what is it that Britain can do, whose power will be wholly on paper, should a civil tumult break out the very day after reconciliation? I have heard some men say, many of whom I believe spoke without thinking, that they dreaded an independence, fearing that it would produce civil wars. It is but seldom that our first thoughts are truly correct, and that is the case here; for there is ten times more to dread from a patched up connection than from independence. I make the sufferer's case my own, and I protest, that were I driven from house and home, my property destroyed, and my circumstances ruined, that as a man, sensible of injuries, I could never relish the doctrine of reconciliation, or consider myself bound thereby.

The colonies have manifested such a spirit of good order and obedience to continental government, as is sufficient to make every reasonable person easy and happy on that head. No man can assign the least pretence for his fears, on any other grounds, than such as are truly childish and ridiculous, viz., that one colony will be striving for superiority over another.

Where there are no distinctions there can be no superiority; perfect equality affords no temptation. The Republics of Europe are all (and we may say always) in peace. Holland and Switzerland are without wars, foreign or domestic. Monarchical governments, it is true, are never long at rest: the crown itself is a temptation to enterprising ruffians at *home*; and that degree of pride and insolence ever attendant on regal authority, swells into a rupture with foreign powers in instances where a republican government, by being formed on more natural principles, would negotiate the mistake.

If there is any true cause of fear regarding independence, it is because no plan is yet laid down. Men do not see their way out. — Wherefore, as an opening into that business I offer the following hints; at the same time modestly affirming, that I have no other opinion of them myself, than that they may be the means of giving rise to something better. Could the straggling thoughts of individuals be collected, they would frequently form materials for wise and able men to improve into useful matter.

Let the assemblies be annual, with a president only. The representation more equal, their business wholly domestic, and subject to the authority of a Continental Congress.

Let each Colony be divided into six, eight, or ten, convenient districts, each district to send a proper number of Delegates to Congress, so that each Colony send at least thirty. The whole number in Congress will be at least 390. Each Congress to sit and to choose a President by the following method. When the Delegates are met, let a colony be taken from the whole thirteen Colonies by lot, after which let the Congress choose (by ballot) a president from out of the Delegates of that province. In the next Congress, let a Colony be taken by lot from twelve only, omitting that Colony from which the president was taken in the former Congress, and so proceeding on till the whole thirteen shall have had their proper rotation. And in order that nothing may pass into a law but what is satisfactorily just, not less than three fifths of the Congress to be called a majority. He that will promote discord, under a government so equally formed as this, would have joined Lucifer in his revolt.

But as there is a peculiar delicacy from whom, or in what manner, this business must first arise, and as it seems more agreeable and consistent that it should come from some intermediate body between the governed and the governors, that is, between the Congress and the People, Let a CONTINENTAL CONFERENCE be held in the following manner, and for the following purpose.

A Committee of twenty-six members of Congress, *viz.* Two for each colony. Two members from each house or Assembly, or Provincial convention; and five Representatives of the people at large, to be chosen in the capital city or town of each Province, for, and in behalf of the whole Province, by as many qualified voters as shall think proper to attend from all parts of the Province for that purpose; or, if more convenient, the Representatives may be chosen in two or three of the most populous parts thereof. In this CONFERENCE, thus assembled, will be united the two grand principles of business, *knowledge* and *power*. The members of Congress, Assemblies, or Conventions, by having had experience in national concerns, will be able and useful counsellors, and the whole, being impowered by the people, will have a truly legal authority.

The conferring members being met, let their business be to frame a CONTINENTAL CHARTER, or Charter of the United Colonies (answering to what is called the Magna Charta of England), fixing the number and manner of choosing members of Congress, Members of Assembly, with their date of sitting; and drawing the line of business and jurisdiction between them. Always remembering, that our strength is continental, not provincial. Securing freedom and property to all men, and above all things, the free exercise of religion, according to the dictates of conscience; with such other matter as it is necessary for a charter to contain. Immediately after which, the said conference to dissolve, and the bodies which shall be chosen comfortable to the said charter, to be the legislators and governors of this continent for the time being. Whose peace and happiness, may God preserve. AMEN.

Should any body of men be hereafter delegated for this or some similar purpose, I offer them the following extracts from that wise observer on governments, Dragonetti. "The science," says he, "of the politician consists in fixing the true point of happiness and freedom. Those men would deserve the gratitude of ages, who should discover a mode of government that contained the greatest sum of individual happiness, with the least national expense."

But where, say some, is the king of America? I'll tell you, friend, he reigns above, and doth not make havoc of mankind like the Royal Brute of Great Britain. Yet that we may not appear to be defective even in earthly honors, let a day be solemnly set apart for proclaiming the Charter; let it be brought forth placed on the divine law, the Word of God; let a Crown be placed thereon, by which the world may know, that so far as we approve of monarchy, that in America THE LAW IS KING. For as in absolute governments the king is law, so in free countries the law *ought* to BE king, and there ought to be no other. But lest any ill use should afterwards arise, let the Crown at the conclusion of the ceremony be demolished, and scattered among the People whose right it is.

A government of our own is our natural right: and when a man seriously reflects on the precariousness of human affairs, he will become convinced, that it is infinitely wiser and faster, to form a Constitution of our own in a cool deliberate manner, while we have it in our power, than to trust such an interesting event to time and chance. If we omit it now, some Massanello may hereafter arise, who, laying hold of popular disquietudes, may collect together the desperate and the discontented, and by assuming to themselves the powers of government, finally sweep away the liberties of the continent like a deluge. Should the government of America return again into the hands of Britain, the tottering situation of things will be a temptation for some desperate adventurer to try his fortune; and in such a case, what relief can Britain give? Ere she could hear the news, the fatal business might be done; and ourselves suffering like the wretched Britons under the oppression of the conqueror. Ye that oppose independence now, ye know not what ye do; ye are opening a door to eternal tyranny, by keeping vacant the seat of government. There are thousands and tens of thousands, who would think it glorious to expel from the continent that barbarous and hellish power, which hath stirred up the Indians and the Negroes to destroy us; the cruelty hath a double guilt, it is dealing brutally by us, and treacherously by them.

To talk of friendship with those in whom our reason forbids us to have faith, and our affections wounded through a thousand pores instruct us to detest, is madness and folly. Every day wears out the little remains of kindred between us and them; and can there be any reason to hope, that as the relationship expires, the affection will increase, or that we shall agree better when we have ten times more and greater concerns to quarrel over than ever?

Ye that tell us of harmony and reconciliation, can ye restore to us the time that is past? Can ye give to prostitution its former innocence? neither can ye reconcile Britain and America. The last cord now is broken, the people of England are presenting addresses against us. There are injuries which nature cannot forgive; she would cease to be nature if she did. As well can the lover forgive the ravisher of his mistress, as the continent forgive the murders of Britain. The Almighty hath implanted in us these inextinguishable feelings for good and wise purposes. They are the guardians of his image in our hearts. They distinguish us from the herd of common animals. The social compact would dissolve, and justice be extirpated from the earth, or have only a casual existence, were we callous to the touches of affection. The robber and the murderer would often escape unpunished, did not the injuries which our tempers sustain provoke us into justice.

O ye that love mankind! Ye that dare oppose not only the tyranny but the tyrant, stand forth! Every spot of the old world is over-run with oppression. Freedom hath been hunted round the globe. Asia and Africa have long expelled her. — Europe regards her like a stranger, and England hath given her warning to depart. O receive the fugitive, and prepare in time an asylum for mankind.

From *The Crisis*

(*December 19, 1776*)

[*The Times That Try Men's Souls*]

These are the times that try men's souls. The summer soldier and the sunshine patriot will, in this crisis, shrink from the service of their country; but he that stands it *now*, deserves the love and thanks of man and woman. Tyranny, like hell, is not easily conquered; yet we have this consolation with us, that the harder the conflict, the more glorious the triumph. What we obtain too cheap, we esteem too lightly: it is dearness only that gives every thing its value. Heaven knows how to put a proper price upon its goods; and it would be strange indeed if so celestial an article as FREEDOM should not be highly rated. Britain, with an army to enforce her tyranny, has declared that she has a right (*not only to* TAX) but "to BIND *us in* CASES WHATSOEVER," and if being *bound in that manner* is not slavery, then there is not such a thing as slavery upon earth. Even the expression is impious; for so unlimited a power can belong only to God.

Whether the independence of the continent was declared too soon, or delayed too long, I will not now enter into as an argument; my own simple opinion is, that had it been eight months earlier, it would have been much better. We did not make a proper use of last winter, neither could we, while we were in a dependent state. However, the fault, if it were one, was all our own; we have none to blame but ourselves. But no great deal is lost yet. All that Howe has been doing for this month past, is rather a ravage than a conquest, which the spirit of the Jerseys, a year ago, would have quickly repulsed, and which time and a little resolution will soon recover.

I have as little superstition in me as any man living, but my secret opinion has ever been, and still is, that God Almighty will not give up a people to military destruction, or leave them unsupportedly to perish, who have so earnestly and so repeatedly sought to avoid the calamities of war, by every decent method which wisdom could invent. Neither have I so much of the infidel in me, as to suppose that He has relinquished the government of the world, and given us up to the care of devils; and as I do not, I cannot see on what grounds the king of Britain can look up to heaven for help against us: a common murderer, a highwayman, or a housebreaker, has as good a pretence as he.

'Tis surprising to see how rapidly a panic will sometimes run through a country. All nations and ages have been subject to them: Britain has trembled like an ague at the report of a French fleet of flat bottomed boats; and in the fourteenth century the whole English army, after ravaging the kingdom of France, was driven back like men petrified with fear; and this brave exploit was performed by a few broken forces collected and headed by a woman, Joan of Arc. Would that heaven might inspire some Jersey maid to spirit up her countrymen, and save her fair fellow sufferers from ravage and ravishment! Yet panics, in some cases, have their uses; they produce as much good as hurt. Their duration is always short; the mind soon grows through them, and acquires a firmer habit than before. But their peculiar advantage is, that they are

the touchstones of sincerity and hypocrisy, and bring things and men to light, which might otherwise have lain forever undiscovered. In fact, they have the same effect on secret traitors, which an imaginary apparition would have upon a private murderer. They sift out the hidden thoughts of man, and hold them up in public to the world. Many a disguised tory has lately shown his head, that shall penitentially solemnize with curses the day on which Howe arrived upon the Delaware.

As I was with the troops at Fort Lee, and marched with them to the edge of Pennsylvania, I am well acquainted with many circumstances which those who live at a distance know but little or nothing of. Our situation there was exceedingly cramped, the place being a narrow neck of land between the North River and the Hackensack. Our force was inconsiderable, being not one fourth so great as Howe could bring against us. We had no army at hand to have relieved the garrison, had we shut ourselves up and stood on our defence. Our ammunition, light artillery, and the best part of our stores, had been removed, on the apprehension that Howe would endeavor to penetrate the Jerseys, in which case Fort Lee could be of no use to us; for it must occur to every thinking man, whether in the army or not, that these kind of field forts are only for temporary purposes, and last in use no longer than the enemy directs his force against the particular object, which such forts are raised to defend. Such was our situation and condition at Fort Lee on the morning of the 20th of November, when an officer arrived with information that the enemy with 200 boats had landed about seven miles above: Major General Green, who commanded the garrison, immediately ordered them under arms, and sent express to General Washington at the town of Hackensack, distant by the way of the ferry = six miles. Our first object was to secure the bridge over the Hackensack, which laid up the river between the enemy and us, about six miles from us, and three from them. General Washington arrived in about three quarters of an hour, and marched at the head of the troops towards the bridge, which place I expected we should have a brush for; however, they did not choose to dispute it with us, and the greatest part of our troops went over the bridge, the rest over the ferry except some which passed at a mill on a small creek, between the bridge and the ferry, and made their way through some marshy grounds up to the town of Hackensack, and there passed the river. We brought off as much baggage as the wagons could contain, the rest was lost. The simple object was to bring off the garrison, and march them on till they could be strengthened by the Jersey or Pennsylvania militia, so as to be enabled to make a stand. We staid four days at Newark, collected our outposts with some of the Jersey militia, and marched out twice to meet the enemy, on being informed that they were advancing, though our numbers were greatly inferior to theirs. Howe, in my little opinion, committed a great error in generalship in not throwing a body of forces off from Staten Island through Amboy, by which means he might have seized all our stores at Brunswick, and intercepted our march into Pennsylvania; but if we believe the power of hell to be limited, we must likewise believe that their agents are under some providential control.

I shall not now attempt to give all the particulars of our retreat to the Delaware; suffice it for the present to say, that both officers and men, though greatly harassed and fatigued, frequently without rest, covering, or provision, the inevitable consequences of a long retreat, bore it with a manly and martial spirit. All their wishes centered in one, which was, that the country would turn out and help them to drive the enemy back. Voltaire has remarked that King William never appeared to full advantage but in difficulties and in action; the same remark may be made on General Washington, for the character fits him. There is a natural firmness in some minds which cannot be unlocked by trifles, but which, when unlocked, discovers a cabinet of fortitude; and I reckon it among those kind of public blessings, which we do not immediately see, that God hath blessed him with uninterrupted health, and given him a mind that can even flourish upon care.

I shall conclude this paper with some miscellaneous remarks on the state of our affairs; and shall begin with asking the following question, Why is it that the enemy have left the New-England provinces, and made these middle ones the seat of war? The answer is easy: New-England is not infested with tories, and we are. I have been tender in raising the cry against these men, and used numberless arguments to show them their danger, but it will not do to sacrifice a world either to their folly or their baseness. The period is now arrived, in which either they or we must change our sentiments, or one or

both must fall. And what is a tory? Good God! what is he? I should not be afraid to go with a hundred whigs against a thousand tories, were they to attempt to get into arms. Every tory is a coward; for servile, slavish, self-interested fear is the foundation of toryism; and a man under such influence, though he may be cruel, never can be brave.

But, before the line of irrecoverable separation be drawn between us, let us reason the matter together: Your conduct is an invitation to the enemy, yet not one in a thousand of you has heart enough to join him. Howe is as much deceived by you as the American cause is injured by you. He expects you will all take up arms, and flock to his standard, with muskets on your shoulders. Your opinions are of no use to him, unless you support him personally, for 'tis soldiers, and not tories, that he wants.

I once felt all that kind of anger, which a man ought to feel, against the mean principles that are held by the tories: a noted one who kept a tavern at Amboy, was standing at his door, with as pretty a child in his hand, about eight or nine years old, as ever I saw, and after speaking his mind as freely as he thought was prudent, finished with this unfatherly expression, "*Well! give me peace in my day.*" Not a man lives on the continent but fully believes that a separation must some time or other finally take place, and a generous parent should have said, "*If there must be trouble, let it be in my day, that my child may have peace;*" and this single reflection, well applied, is sufficient to awaken every man to duty. Not a place upon earth might be so happy as America. Her situation is remote from all the wrangling world, and she has nothing to do but to trade with them. A man can distinguish himself between temper and principle, and I am as confident, as I am that God governs the world, that America will never be happy till she gets clear of foreign dominion. Wars, without ceasing, will break out till that period arrives, and the continent must in the end be conqueror; for though the flame of liberty may sometimes cease to shine, the coal can never expire.

America did not, nor does not want force; but she wanted a proper application of that force. Wisdom is not the purchase of a day, and it is no wonder that we should err at the first setting off. From an excess of tenderness, we were unwilling to raise an army, and trusted our cause to the temporary defence of a well-meaning militia. A summer's experience has now taught us better; yet with those troops, while they were collected, we were able to set bounds to the progress of the enemy, and, thank God! they are again assembling. I always considered militia as the best troops in the world for a sudden exertion, but they will not do for a long campaign. Howe, it is probable, will make an attempt on this city [Philadelphia]; should he fail on this side the Delaware, he is ruined. If he succeeds, our cause is not ruined. He stakes all on his side against a part on ours; admitting he succeeds, the consequences will be that armies from both ends of the continent will march to assist their suffering friends in the middle states; for he cannot go everywhere, it is impossible. I consider Howe as the greatest enemy the tories have; he is bringing war into their country, which, had it not been for him and partly for themselves, they had been clear of. Should he now be expelled, I wish with all the devotion of a Christian, that the names of whig and tory may never more be mentioned; but should the tories give him encouragement to come, or assistance if he come, I as sincerely wish that our next year's arms may expel them from the continent, and the Congress appropriate their possessions to the relief of those who have suffered in well-doing. A single successful battle next year will settle the whole. America could carry on a two years' war by the confiscation of the property of disaffected persons, and be made happy by their expulsion. Say not that this is revenge, call it rather the soft resentment of a suffering people, who, having no object in view but the GOOD of ALL, have staked their OWN ALL upon a seemingly doubtful event. Yet it is folly to argue against determined hardness; eloquence may strike the ear, and the language of sorrow draw forth the tear of compassion, but nothing can reach the heart that is steeled with prejudice.

Quitting this class of men, I turn with the warm ardor of a friend to those who have nobly stood, and are yet determined to stand the matter out. I call not upon a few, but upon all: not in THIS state or THAT state, but on EVERY state: up and help us; lay your shoulders to the wheel; better have too much force than too little, when so great an object is at stake. Let it be told to the future world that in the depth of winter, when nothing but hope and virtue could survive, that the city and country, alarmed at one common danger, came forth to meet and to repulse it. Say not that thousands are gone, turn out your tens of thousands; throw not the burden of the day upon Providence, but *"show your faith by your works,"* that God may bless you. It matters not where you live, or what rank of life you hold, the evil or the blessing will reach you all. The far and the near, the home counties and the back, the rich and the poor, will suffer or rejoice alike. The heart that feels not now is dead; the blood of his children will curse his cowardice, who shrinks back at a time when a little might have saved the whole, and made *them* happy. I love the man that can smile in trouble, that can gather strength from distress, and grow brave by reflection. 'Tis the business of little minds to shrink; but he whose heart is firm, and whose conscience approves his conduct, will pursue his principles unto death. My own line of reasoning is to myself as straight and clear as a ray of light. Not all the treasures of the world, so far as I believe, could have induced me to support an offensive war, for I think it murder; but if a thief breaks into my house, burns and destroys my property, and kills or threatens to kill me, or those that are in it, and to *"bind me in all cases whatsoever"* to his absolute will, am I to suffer it? What signifies it to me, whether he who does it is a king or a common man; my countryman or not my countryman; whether it be done by an individual villain, or an army of them? If we reason to the root of things we shall find no difference; neither can any just cause be assigned why we should punish in the one case and pardon in the other. Let them call me rebel and welcome, I feel no concern from it; but I should suffer the misery of devils, were I to make a whore of my soul by swearing allegiance to one whose character is that of a sottish, stupid, stubborn, worthless, brutish man. I conceive likewise a horrid idea in receiving mercy from a being, who at the last day shall be shrieking to the rocks and mountains to cover him, and fleeing with terror from the orphan, the widow, and the slain of America.

There are cases which cannot be overdone by language, and this is one. There are persons, too, who see not the full extent of the evil which threatens them; they solace themselves with hopes that the enemy, if he succeed, will be merciful. It is the madness of folly, to expect mercy from those who have refused to do justice; and even mercy, where conquest is the object, is only a trick of war. The cunning of the fox is as murderous as the violence of the wolf, and we ought to guard equally against both. Howe's first object is, partly by threats and partly by promises, to terrify or seduce the people to deliver up their arms and receive mercy. The ministry recommended the same plan to Gage, and this is what the tories call making their peace, *"a peace which passeth all understanding,"* indeed! A peace which would be the immediate forerunner of a worse ruin than any we have yet thought of. Ye men of Pennsylvania, do reason upon these things! Were the back counties to give up their arms, they would fall an easy prey to the Indians, who are all armed: this perhaps is what some tories would not be sorry for. Were the home counties to deliver up their arms, they would be exposed to the resentment of the back counties, who would then have it in their power to chastise their defection at pleasure. And were any one state to give up its arms, THAT state must be garrisoned by all Howe's army of Britons and Hessians to preserve it from the anger of the rest. Mutual fear is the principal link in the chain of mutual love, and woe be to that state that breaks the compact. Howe is mercifully inviting you to barbarous destruction, and men must be either rogues or fools that will not see it. I dwell not upon the vapors of imagination; I bring reason to your ears, and, in language as plain as A, B, C, hold up truth to your eyes.

I thank *God* that I fear not. I see no real cause for fear. I know our situation well, and can see the way out of it. While our army was collected, Howe dared not risk a battle; and it is no credit to him that he decamped from the White Plains, and waited a mean opportunity to ravage the defenceless Jerseys; but it is great credit to us that, with a handful of men, we sustained an orderly retreat for near an hundred miles, brought off our ammunition, all our field-pieces, the greatest part of our stores, and had four rivers to pass. None can say that our retreat was precipitate, for we were near three weeks in performing it, that the country might have time to come in. Twice we marched back to meet the enemy, and remained out till dark. The sign of fear was not seen in our camp, and had not some of the cowardly and disaffected inhabitants spread false alarms through the country, the Jerseys had never been ravaged. Once more we are again collected and collecting, our new army at both ends of the continent is recruiting fast, and we shall be able to open the next campaign with sixty thousand men, well armed and clothed. This is our situation, and who will may know it. By perseverance and fortitude we have the prospect of a glorious issue; by cowardice and submission, the sad choice of a variety of evils — a ravaged country — a depopulated city — habitations without safety, and slavery, without hope — our homes turned into barracks and bawdy-houses for Hessians, and a future race to provide for, whose fathers we shall doubt of. Look on this picture and weep over it! and if there yet remains one thoughtless wretch who believes it not, let him suffer it unlamented.

COMMON SENSE

From *The Age of Reason*

Being an Investigation of True and of Fabulous Theology

(1794–96)

✤ *The Age of Reason* is the most famous, or notorious, statement of radical deism. It "was scattered the length and breadth of the land. . . . The democratic clubs and the deistical societies used it as a textbook. College students swallowed it whole, to the great alarm of their preceptors; and humble men in villages from New Hampshire to Georgia and beyond the Alleghenies discussed it by tavern candlelight. The storm of criticism which the book brought forth for the time only seemed to feed the fire, nor did the epithets cast on Paine slow down the conflagration. He was abused as a filthy atheist, a dissolute drunkard, a malignant blasphemer, a superficial reasoner" (Curti, *The Growth of American Thought*).

However one may today deplore the obvious defects of Paine's attack on Christianity, *The Age of Reason* is historically an important work, essential to an understanding of the time in which it was written.

TO MY FELLOW-CITIZENS OF THE
UNITED STATES OF AMERICA

I put the following work under your protection. It contains my opinion upon religion. You will do me the justice to remember that I have always strenuously supported the right of every man to his own opinion, however different that opinion might be to mine. He who denies to another this right makes a slave of himself to his present opinion, because he precludes himself the right of changing it.

The most formidable weapon against errors of every kind is reason. I have never used any other, and I trust I never shall.

Your affectionate friend and fellow citizen,

THOMAS PAINE

[A Deist's Belief]

It has been my intention, for several years past, to publish my thoughts upon religion; I am well aware of the difficulties that attend the subject, and from that consideration, had reserved it to a more advanced period of life. I intended it to be the last offering I should make to my fellow-citizens of all nations, and that at a time when the purity of the motive that induced me to it, could not admit of a question, even by those who might disapprove the work.

The circumstance that has now taken place in France of the total abolition of the whole national order of priesthood and of everything appertaining to compulsive systems of religion, and compulsive articles of faith, has not only precipitated my intention, but rendered a work of this kind exceedingly necessary, lest, in the general wreck of superstition, of false systems of government, and false theology, we lose sight of morality, of humanity, and of the theology that is true.

As several of my colleagues, and others of my fellow-citizens of France, have given me the example of making their voluntary and individual profession of faith, I also will make mine; and I do this with all that sincerity and frankness with which the mind of man communicates with itself.

I believe in one God, and no more; and I hope for happiness beyond this life.

I believe in the equality of man; and I believe that religious duties consist in doing justice, loving mercy, and endeavoring to make our fellow creatures happy.

But, lest it should be supposed that I believe many other things in addition to these, I shall, in the progress of this work, declare the things I do not believe, and my reasons for not believing them.

I do not believe in the creed professed by the Jewish church, by the Roman church, by the Greek church, by the Turkish church, by the Protestant church, nor by any church that I know of. My own mind is my own church.

All national institutions of churches, whether Jewish, Christian, or Turkish, appear to me no other than human inventions, set up to terrify and enslave mankind, and monopolize power and profit.***

Soon after I published the pamphlet, COM-MON SENSE, in America I saw the exceeding probability that a revolution in the system of govern-ment would be followed by a revolution in the system of religion. The adulterous connection of church and state, wherever it had taken place, whether Jewish, Christian, or Turkish, had so effectually prohibited, by pains and penalties, every discussion upon established creeds and upon first principles of religion, that until the system of government should be changed those subjects could not be brought fairly and openly before the world; but that whenever this should be done, a revolution in the system of religion would follow. Human inventions and priest-craft would be detected, and man would return to the pure, unmixed, and unadulterated belief of one God, and no more.

[Revelation]

Every national church or religion has established itself by pretending some special mission from God communicated to certain individuals. The Jews have their Moses; the Christians their Jesus Christ, their apostles and saints; and the Turks their Mahomet, as if the way to God was not open to every man alike.

Each of those churches show certain books, which they call *revelation*, or the word of God. The Jews say, that their word of God was given by God to Moses, face to face; the Christians say, their word of God came by divine inspiration; and the Turks say, that their word of God (the Koran) was brought by an angel from Heaven. Each of those churches accuse the other of unbelief; and, for my own part, I disbelieve them all.

As it is necessary to affix right ideas to words, I will, before I proceed further into the subject, offer some other observations on the word *revelation*. Revelation when applied to religion, means something communicated *immediately* from God to man.

No one will deny or dispute the power of the Almighty to make such a communication, if he pleases. But admitting, for the sake of a case, that something has been revealed to a certain person, and not revealed to any other person, it is revelation to that person only. When he tells it to a second person, a second to a third, a third to a fourth, and so on, it ceases to be a revelation to all those persons. It is revelation to the first person only, and *hearsay* to every other, and, consequently, they are not obliged to believe it.

It is a contradiction in terms and ideas to call anything a revelation that comes to us at second-hand, either verbally or in writing. Revelation is necessarily limited to the first communication. — After this, it is only an account of something which that person says was a revelation made to him; and though he may find himself obliged to believe it, it cannot be incumbent on me to believe it in the same manner, for it was not a revelation made to *me*, and I have only his word for it that it was made to *him*.

When Moses told the children of Israel that he received the two tables of the commandments from the hands of God, they were not obliged to believe him, because they had no other authority for it than his telling them so; and I have no other authority for it than some historian telling me so. The commandments carry no internal evidence of divinity with them; they contain some good moral precepts such as any man qualified to be a lawgiver, or a legislator, could produce himself, without having recourse to supernatural intervention.

When I am told that the Koran was written in Heaven, and brought to Mahomet by an angel, the account comes too near the same kind of hearsay evidence and second-hand authority as the former. I did not see the angel myself, and, therefore, I have a right not to believe it.

When also I am told that a woman called the Virgin Mary, said, or gave out, that she was with child without any cohabitation with a man, and that her betrothed husband, Joseph, said that an angel told him so, I have a right to believe them or not; such a circumstance required a much stronger evidence than their bare word for it; but we have not even this — for neither Joseph nor Mary wrote any such matter themselves; it is only reported by others that *they said so* — it is hearsay upon hearsay, and I do not choose to rest my belief upon such evidence.

It is, however, not difficult to account for the credit that was given to the story of Jesus Christ being the son of God. He was born when the heathen mythology had still some fashion and repute in the world, and that mythology had prepared the people for the belief of such a story. Almost all the extraordinary men that lived under the heathen mythology were reputed to be the sons of some of their gods. It was not a new thing, at that time, to believe a man to have been celestially begotten; the intercourse of gods with women was then a matter of familiar opinion. Their Jupiter, according to their accounts, had cohabited with hundreds; the story therefore had nothing in it either new, wonderful or obscene; it was conformable to the opinions that then prevailed among the people called Gentiles, or Mythologists, and it was those people only that believed it. The Jews, who had kept strictly to the belief of one God, and no more, and who had always rejected the heathen mythology, never credited the story.

It is curious to observe how the theory of what is called the Christian Church sprung out of the tail of heathen mythology. A direct incorporation took place in the first instance, by making the reputed founder to be celestially begotten. The trinity of gods that then followed was no other than a reduction of the former plurality, which was about twenty or thirty thousand; the statue of Mary succeeded the statue of Diana of Ephesus; the deification of heroes changed into the canonization of saints; the mythologists had gods for everything; the Christian Mythologists had saints for everything; the church became as crowded with the one, as the pantheon had been with the other; and Rome was the place of both. The Christian theory is little else than the idolatry of the ancient Mythologists, accommodated to the purposes of power and revenue; and it yet remains to reason and philosophy to abolish the amphibious fraud.

[The Order of Nature]

But some perhaps will say — Are we to have no word of God — no revelation? I answer, Yes: there is a word of God; there is a revelation.

THE WORD OF GOD IS THE CREATION WE BEHOLD: And it is in *this word,* which no human invention can counterfeit or alter, that God speaketh universally to man.

Human language is local and changeable, and is therefore incapable of being used as the means of unchangeable and universal information. The idea that God sent Jesus Christ to publish, as they say, the glad tidings to all nations, from one end of the earth to the other, is consistent only with the ignorance of those who knew nothing of the extent of the world, and who believed, as those world-saviours believed, and continued to believe, for several centuries (and that in contradiction to the discoveries of philosophers and the experience of navigators), that the earth was flat like a trencher; and that a man might walk to the end of it.

But how was Jesus Christ to make anything known to all nations? He could speak but one language, which was Hebrew; and there are in the world several hundred languages. Scarcely any two nations speak the same language, or understand each other; and as to translations, every man who knows anything of languages, knows that it was impossible to translate from one language to another, not only without losing a great part of the original, but frequently of mistaking the sense; and besides all this, the art of printing was wholly unknown at the time Christ lived.

It is always necessary that the means that are to accomplish any end, be equal to the accomplishment of that end, or the end cannot be accomplished. It is in this, that the difference between finite and infinite power and wisdom discovers itself. Man frequently fails in accomplishing his ends, from a natural inability of the power to the purpose; and frequently from the want of wisdom to apply power properly. But it is impossible for infinite power and wisdom to fail as man faileth. The means it useth are always equal to the end; but human language, more especially as there is not an universal language, is incapable of being used as an universal means of unchangeable and uniform information, and therefore it is not the means that God useth in manifesting himself universally to man.

It is only in the CREATION that all our ideas and conceptions of a *word of God* can unite. The Creation speaketh an universal language, independently of human speech or human language, multiplied and various as they be. It is an ever-existing original, which every man can read. It cannot be forged; it cannot be counterfeited; it cannot be lost; it cannot be altered; it cannot be suppressed. It does not depend upon the will of man whether it shall be published or not; it publishes itself from one end of the earth to the other. It preaches to all nations and to all worlds; and this *word of God* reveals to man all that is necessary for man to know of God.

Do we want to contemplate his power? We see it in the unchangeable order by which the incomprehensible whole is governed. Do we want to contemplate his munificence? We see it in the abundance with which he fills the earth. Do we want to contemplate his mercy? We see it in his not withholding that abundance even from the unthankful. In fine, do we want to know what God is? Search not the book called the Scripture, which any human hand might make, but the scripture called the Creation.

[God and Human Reason]

The only idea man can affix to the name of God, is that of a *first cause*, the cause of all things. And, incomprehensible and difficult as it is for a man to conceive what a first cause is, he arrives at the belief of it, from the tenfold greater difficulty of disbelieving it. It is difficult beyond description to conceive that space can have no end; but it is more difficult to conceive an end. It is difficult beyond the power of man to conceive an eternal duration of what we call time; but it is more impossible to conceive a time when there shall be no time.

In like manner of reasoning, everything we behold carries in itself the internal evidence that it did not make itself. Every man is an evidence to himself that he did not make himself; neither could his father make himself, nor his grandfather, nor any of his race; neither could any tree, plant, or animal make itself; and it is the conviction arising from this evidence, that carries us on, as it were, by necessity, to the belief of a first cause eternally existing, of a nature totally different to any material existence we know of, and by the power of which all things exist; and this first cause, man calls God.

It is only by the exercise of reason that man can discover God. Take away that reason, and he would be incapable of understanding any thing; and, in this case it would be just as consistent to read even the book called the Bible to a horse as to a man. How then is it that those people pretend to reject reason?

Almost the only parts in the book called the Bible, that convey to us any idea of God, are some chapters in Job, and the 19th Psalm; I recollect no other. Those parts are true *deistical* compositions; for they treat of the *Deity* through his works. They take the book of Creation as the word of God, they refer to no other book, and all the inferences they make are drawn from that volume.

I insert in this place the 19th Psalm, as paraphrased into English verse by Addison. I recollect not the prose, and where I write this I have not the opportunity of seeing it.

The spacious firmament on high,
With all the blue etherial sky,
And spangled heavens, a shining frame,
Their great original proclaim.
The unwearied sun, from day to day,   5
Does his Creator's power display,
And publishes to every land,
The work of an Almighty hand.
Soon as the evening shades prevail,
The moon takes up the wondrous tale,
And nightly to the list'ning earth,   10
Repeats the story of her birth;
Whilst all the stars that round her burn,
And all the planets, in their turn,
Confirm the tidings as they roll,
And spread the truth from pole to pole.   15
What though in solemn silence all
Move round this dark terrestrial ball;
What though no real voice, nor sound,
Amidst their radiant orbs be found,
In reason's ear they all rejoice,   20
And utter forth a glorious voice,
Forever singing as they shine,
THE HAND THAT MADE US IS DIVINE.

What more does man want to know, than
that the hand or power that made these things   25
is Divine, is Omnipotent? Let him believe this
with the force it is impossible to repel, if he
permits his reason to act, and his rule of moral
life will follow of course.

The allusions in Job have, all of them, the   30
same tendency with this Psalm; that of deducing
or proving a truth that would be otherwise
unknown, from truths already known.

I recollect not enough of the passages in Job
to insert them correctly: but there is one occurs   35
to me that is applicable to the subject I am
speaking upon. "Canst thou by searching find
out God? Canst thou find out the Almighty
to perfection?"

I know not how the printers have pointed   40
this passage, for I keep no Bible; but it contains two distinct questions that admit of distinct
answers.

First — Canst thou by searching find out
God? Yes; because, in the first place, I know   45
I did not make myself, and yet I have existence;
and by *searching* into the nature of other things,
I find that no other thing could make itself;
and yet millions of other things exist; therefore
it is that I know, by positive conclusion result-   50
ing from this search, that there is a power
superior to all those things, and that power is
God.

Secondly — Canst thou find out the Almighty to *perfection?* No; not only because the
power and wisdom He has manifested in the
structure of the Creation that I behold is to me
incomprehensible, but because even this manifestation, great as it is, is probably but a small
display of that immensity of power and wisdom,
by which millions of other worlds to me invisible
by their distance, were created and continue to
exist.

It is evident that both of these questions are
put to the reason of the person to whom they
are supposed to have been addressed; and it is
only by admitting the first question to be answered affirmatively, that the second could follow. It would have been unnecessary, and even
absurd, to have put a second question, more
difficult than the first, if the first question had
been answered negatively. The two questions
have different objects; the first refers to the
existence of God, the second to his attributes;
reason can discover the one, but it falls infinitely
short in discovering the whole of the other.

I recollect not a single passage in all the
writings ascribed to the men called apostles,
that convey any idea of what God is. Those
writings are chiefly controversial; and the subject
they dwell upon, that of a man dying in agony
on a cross, is better suited to the gloomy genius
of a monk in a cell, by whom it is not impossible
they were written, than to any man breathing
the open air of the Creation. The only passage
that occurs to me, that has any reference to the
works of God, by which only his power and
wisdom can be known, is related to have been
spoken by Jesus Christ, as a remedy against
distrustful care. "Behold the lilies of the field,
they toil not, neither do they spin." This, however, is far inferior to the allusions in Job and
in the 19th Psalm; but it is similar in idea, and
the modesty of the imagery is correspondent to
the modesty of the man.

[The World-Machine]

We can know God only through his works.
We cannot have a conception of any one attribute but by following some principle that leads
to it. We have only a confused idea of his
powers if we have not the means of comprehending something of its immensity. We can have
no idea of his wisdom but by knowing the order
and manner in which it acts. The principles of
science lead to this knowledge; for the Creator

of man is the Creator of science; and it is through that medium that man can see God, as it were, face to face.

Could a man be placed in a situation and endowed with the power of vision to behold at one view, and to contemplate deliberately, the structure of the universe; to mark the movements of the several planets, the cause of their varying appearances, the unerring order in which they revolve, even to the remotest comet; their connection and dependence on each other; and to know the system of laws established by the Creator that governs and regulates the whole; he would then conceive, far beyond what any church theology can teach him, the power, the wisdom, the vastness, the munificence of the Creator. He would then see that all the knowledge man has of science, and that all the mechanical arts by which he renders his situation comfortable here, are derived from that source; his mind, exalted by the scene and convinced by the fact, would increase in gratitude as it increased in knowledge; his religion or his worship would become united with his improvement as a man; any employment he followed that had connection with the principles of the creation, as everything of agriculture, of science, and of the mechanical arts has, would teach him more of God and of the gratitude he owes to him than any theological Christian sermon he now hears. Great objects inspire great thoughts; great munificence excites great gratitude; but the groveling tales and doctrines of the Bible and the Testament are fit only to excite contempt.

Though man cannot arrive, at least in this life, at the actual scene I have described, he can demonstrate it because he has a knowledge of the principles upon which the creation is constructed. We know that the greatest works can be represented in model, and that the universe can be represented by the same means. The same principles by which we measure an inch or an acre of ground will measure to millions in extent. A circle of an inch diameter has the same geometrical properties as a circle that would circumscribe the universe. The same properties of a triangle that will demonstrate upon paper the course of a ship will do it on the ocean, and when applied to what are called the heavenly bodies, will ascertain to a minute the time of an eclipse, though those bodies are millions of miles distant from us. This knowledge is of divine origin, and it is from the Bible of the creation that man has learned it, and not from the stupid Bible of the church that teacheth man nothing.

All the knowledge man has of science and of machinery, by the aid of which his existence is rendered comfortable upon earth, and without which he would be scarcely distinguishable in appearance and condition from a common animal, comes from the great machine and structure of the universe. The constant and unwearied observations of our ancestors upon the movements and revolutions of the heavenly bodies, in what are supposed to have been the early ages of the world, have brought this knowledge upon earth. It is not Moses and the prophets, nor Jesus Christ, nor his apostles, that have done it. The Almighty is the great mechanic of the creation; the first philosopher and original teacher of all science. Let us then learn to reverence our master, and not forget the labor of our ancestors.

Had we at this day no knowledge of machinery, and were it possible that man could have a view, as I have before described, of the structure and machinery of the universe, he would soon conceive the idea of constructing some at least of the mechanical works we now have; and the idea so conceived would progressively advance in practice. Or could a model of the universe, such as is called an orrery, be presented before him and put in motion, his mind would arrive at the same idea. Such an object and such a subject would, while it improved him in knowledge useful to himself as a man and a member of society, as well as entertaining, afford far better matter for impressing him with a knowledge of and a belief in the Creator, and of the reverence and gratitude that a man owes to him, than the stupid texts of the Bible and the Testament, from which, be the talents of the preacher what they may, only stupid sermons can be preached. If man must preach, let him preach something that is edifying, and from the texts that are known to be true.

The Bible of the Creation is inexhaustible in texts. Every part of the science, whether connected with the geometry of the universe, with the systems of animal and vegetable life, or with the properties of inanimate matter, is a text as well for devotion as for philosophy — for gratitude as for human improvement. It will perhaps be said that if such a revolution in the system of religion takes place, every preacher ought to be a philosopher. *Most certainly*; and every house of devotion a school of science.

It has been by wandering from the immutable laws of science and the light of reason, and setting up an invented thing called revealed religion, that so many wild and blasphemous conceits have been formed of the Almighty. The Jews have made him the assassin of the human species, to make room for the religion of the Jews. The Christians have made him the murderer of himself, and the founder of a new religion to supersede and expel the Jewish religion. And to find pretense and admission for these things, they must have supposed his power or his wisdom imperfect, or his will changeable; and the changeableness of the will is the imperfection of the judgment. The philosopher knows that the laws of the Creator have never changed with respect either to the principles of science or the properties of matter. Why, then, is it to be supposed they have changed with respect to man?

I here close the subject. I have shown in all the foregoing parts of this work that the Bible and Testament are impositions and forgeries; and I leave the evidence I have produced in proof of it to be refuted, if anyone can do it; and I leave the ideas that are suggested in the conclusion of the work to rest on the mind of the reader; certain, as I am, that when opinions are free either in matters of government or religion, truth will finally and powerfully prevail.

BUILDING A NEW NATION

Thomas Jefferson [1743–1826]

Three freedoms — political, religious, and intellectual — were, according to Jefferson, his dearest aims. At least they were the aims of the three achievements which he selected for the epitaph he wrote: HERE WAS BURIED THOMAS JEFFERSON, AUTHOR OF THE DECLARATION OF INDEPENDENCE, THE STATUTE OF VIRGINIA FOR RELIGIOUS FREEDOM, AND FATHER OF THE UNIVERSITY OF VIRGINIA.

The events of his life, already touched upon in the introduction (page 82), are in any case too familiar for extended outline here. Educated at the College of William and Mary, law student and practising lawyer for a time, he was almost constantly in the political service of his state and nation from 1769, when he entered the Virginia House of Burgesses, until 1809, when he retired from the Presidency after declining a third term. He served with distinction as a member of the Continental Congress, as a governor of Virginia (1779–81), as minister to France (1784–89), Secretary of State under Washington (1789–94), Vice-President (1797–1801), and President (1801–1809). In his later years he retired to his beautiful home, Monticello, and through a telescope watched the building of the University of Virginia. He died on July 4, 1826, the fiftieth anniversary of the adoption of his Declaration.

Further reading: *The Life and Selected Writings of Thomas Jefferson*, ed. A. Koch and W. Peden, Modern Library, 1944. G. Chinard, *Thomas Jefferson, the Apostle of Americanism*, 1929. D. Malone, *Jefferson, the Virginian*, 1948, *Jefferson and the Rights of Man*, 1951. H. M. Jones, *The Pursuit of Happiness*, 1953.

Declaration of Independence

(1776)

This brief document is perhaps the supreme ex- 5
ample of "useful" prose in American literature, comparable only with the Gettysburg Address. Each
served, at the time, a great purpose. Together, they
serve, today, a great purpose: they are the spiritual
constitution of the United States.

The situation out of which the Declaration arose 10
is too well known to need elaboration here. As head
of the drafting committee, Jefferson was aware that
he was not to present any original arguments or
principles. He followed, as Carl Becker puts it, "the
accepted premises, the preconceptions, of most 15
eighteenth century thinking, not only in America,
but also in England and France." In ideas and even
in phrasing, the famous preamble of the Declaration
is filled with echoes of the works of Locke and other
writers, as well as current documents passed from
hand to hand. An example of the latter is the 20
Virginia Bill of Rights, by George Mason, adopted
while Jefferson was at work on his own document.

To see what Jefferson accomplished we need only
contrast the exalted tension of his phrasing with the
relaxed prosiness of Mason. For instance, Mason 25
wrote: "All men are by nature equally free and independent, and have certain inherent rights, . . .
namely, the enjoyment of life and liberty, with the
means of acquiring and possessing property, and
pursuing and obtaining happiness and safety."
The Story of the Declaration of Independence has 30
been told by Dumas Malone, 1954.

When in the course of human events it becomes necessary for one people to dissolve the
political bands which have connected them with 35
another, and to assume among the powers of the
earth, the separate and equal station to which
the laws of Nature and of Nature's God entitle
them, a decent respect to the opinions of mankind requires that they should declare the causes 40
which impel them to the separation. — We hold
these truths to be self-evident, that all men are
created equal, that they are endowed by their
creator with certain unalienable rights, that
among these are life, liberty, and the pursuit of 45
happiness. — That to secure these rights, governments are instituted among men, deriving
their just powers from the consent of the governed, — That whenever any form of government becomes destructive of these ends, it is the
right of the people to alter or to abolish it, and
to institute new government, laying its foundation on such principles and organizing its powers
in such form, as to them shall seem most likely
to effect their safety and happiness. Prudence,
indeed, will dictate that governments long established should not be changed for light and transient causes; and accordingly all experience hath
shown that mankind are more disposed to suffer,
while evils are sufferable, than to right themselves by abolishing the forms to which they are
accustomed. But when a long train of abuses
and usurpations, pursuing invariably the same
object evinces a design to reduce them under
absolute despotism, it is their right, it is their
duty, to throw off such government, and to provide new guards for their future security. —
Such has been the patient sufferance of these
colonies; and such is now the necessity which
constrains them to alter their former systems of
government. The history of the present King of
Great Britain is a history of repeated injuries and
usurpations, all having in direct object the
establishment of an absolute tyranny over these
states. To prove this, let facts be submitted to a
candid world. — He has refused his assent to
laws, the most wholesome and necessary for the
public good. — He has forbidden his governors
to pass laws of immediate and pressing importance, unless suspended in their operation till his
assent should be obtained; and when so suspended, he has utterly neglected to attend to
them. — He has refused to pass other laws for
the accommodation of large districts of people,
unless those people would relinquish the right of
representation in the legislature, a right inestimable to them and formidable to tyrants only.
— He has called together legislative bodies at
places unusual, uncomfortable, and distant from
the depository of their public records, for the
sole purpose of fatiguing them into compliance
with his measures. — He has dissolved representative houses repeatedly, for opposing with
manly firmness his invasions on the rights of the

people. — He has refused for a long time, after such dissolutions, to cause others to be elected; whereby the legislative powers, incapable of annihilation, have returned to the people at large for their exercise; the state remaining in the meantime exposed to all the dangers of invasion from without, and convulsions within. — He has endeavored to prevent the population of these states; for that purpose obstructing the laws for naturalization of foreigners; refusing to pass others to encourage their migrations hither, and raising the conditions of new appropriations of lands. — He has obstructed the administration of justice, by refusing his assent to laws for establishing judiciary powers. — He has made judges dependent on his will alone, for the tenure of their offices, and the amount and payment of their salaries. — He has erected a multitude of new offices, and sent hither swarms of officers to harass our people, and eat out their substance. — He has kept among us, in times of peace, standing armies without the consent of our legislatures. — He has affected to render the military independent of and superior to the civil power. — He has combined with others to subject us to a jurisdiction foreign to our constitution, and unacknowledged by our laws; giving his assent to their acts of pretended legislation: — For quartering large bodies of armed troops among us: — For protecting them, by a mock trial, from punishment for any murders which they should commit on the inhabitants of these states: — For cutting off our trade with all parts of the world: — For imposing taxes on us without our consent: — For depriving us in many cases of the benefits of trial by jury: — For transporting us beyond seas to be tried for pretended offences: — For abolishing the free system of English laws in a neighboring province, establishing therein an arbitrary government, and enlarging its boundaries so as to render it at once an example and fit instrument for introducing the same absolute rule into these colonies: — For taking away our charters, abolishing our most valuable laws, and altering fundamentally the forms of our governments: — For suspending our own legislatures, and declaring themselves invested with power to legislate for us in all cases whatsoever. — He has abdicated government here, by declaring us out of his protection and waging war against us: — He has plundered our seas, ravaged our coasts, burnt our towns, and destroyed the lives of our people. — He is at this time transporting large armies of foreign mercenaries to complete the works of death, desolation and tyranny, already begun with circumstances of cruelty and perfidy scarcely paralleled in the most barbarous ages, and totally unworthy the head of a civilized nation. — He has constrained our fellow citizens taken captive on the high seas to bear arms against their country, to become the executioners of their friends and brethren, or to fall themselves by their hands. — He has excited domestic insurrections amongst us, and has endeavored to bring on the inhabitants of our frontiers, the merciless Indian savages, whose known rule of warfare, is an undistinguished destruction of all ages, sexes and conditions. In every stage of these oppressions we have petitioned for redress in the most humble terms: Our repeated petitions have been answered only by repeated injury. A prince whose character is thus marked by every act which may define a tyrant, is unfit to be the ruler of a free people. Nor have we been wanting in attentions to our British brethren. We have warned them from time to time of attempts by their legislature to extend an unwarrantable jurisdiction over us. We have reminded them of the circumstances of our emigration and settlement here. We have appealed to their native justice and magnanimity, and we have conjured them by the ties of our common kindred to disavow these usurpations, which would inevitably interrupt our connections and correspondence. They too have been deaf to the voice of justice and of consanguinity. We must, therefore, acquiesce in the necessity, which denounces our separation, and hold them, as we hold the rest of mankind, enemies in war, in peace friends. —

We, THEREFORE, the representatives of the United States of America, in General Congress assembled, appealing to the Supreme Judge of the world for the rectitude of our intentions, do, in the name and by authority of the good people of these colonies, solemnly publish and declare, That these United Colonies are, and of right ought to be FREE AND INDEPENDENT STATES; that they are absolved from all allegiance to the British crown, and that all political connection between them and the State of Great Britain, is and ought to be totally dissolved; and that as free and independent states, they have full power to levy war, conclude peace, contract alliances, establish commerce, and to do all other acts and things which independent states may of right do. — And for the support of this declaration, with a firm reliance on the

protection of divine providence, we mutually
pledge to each other our lives, our fortunes and
our sacred honor.

From *Notes on Virginia*

(1784)

According to G. B. Goode, Jefferson's *Notes on
Virginia* was "the most important scientific work yet
published in America," "the first comprehensive treatise upon the topography, natural history, and natural resources of one of the states." The student of
American literature will however be more concerned
with passages, like those below, on social and political
matters.

[No Dictators]

In December 1776, our circumstances being
much distressed, it was proposed in the house
of delegates to create a *dictator,* invested with
every power legislative, executive, and judiciary,
civil and military, of life and of death, over our
persons and over our properties; and in June
1781, again under calamity, the same proposition
was repeated, and wanted a few votes only of
being passed. One who entered into this contest from a pure love of liberty, and a sense of
injured rights, who determined to make every
sacrifice, and to meet every danger, for the re-
establishment of those rights on a firm basis,
who did not mean to expend his blood and substance for the wretched purpose of changing this
matter for that, but to place the powers of governing him in a plurality of hands of his own
choice, so that the corrupt will of no one man
might in future oppress him, must stand confounded and dismayed when he is told, that a
considerable portion of that plurality had meditated the surrender of them into a single hand,
and, in lieu of a limited monarch, to deliver him
over to a despotic one! How must he find his
efforts and sacrifices abused and baffled, if he
may still, by a single vote, be laid prostrate at the
feet of one man!

In God's name, from whence have they derived this power? Is it from our ancient laws?
None such can be produced. Is it from any
principle in our new Constitution expressed or
implied? Every lineament of that expressed or
implied is in full opposition to it. Its fundamental principle is, that the State shall be governed as a commonwealth. It provides a republican organization, proscribes under the name of
prerogative the exercise of all powers undefined
by the laws; places on this basis the whole system
of our laws; and by consolidating them together,
chooses that they shall be left to stand or fall
together, never providing for any circumstances,
nor admitting that such could arise, wherein
either should be suspended; no, not for a moment. Our ancient laws expressly declare, that
those who are but delegates themselves shall not
delegate to others powers which require judgment and integrity in their exercise. Or was this
proposition moved on a supposed right in the
movers, of abandoning their posts in a moment
of distress? The same laws forbid the abandonment of that post, even on ordinary occasions;
and much more a transfer of their powers into
other hands and other forms, without consulting
the people. They never admit the idea that
these, like sheep or cattle, may be given from
hand to hand without an appeal to their own
will. Was it from the necessity of the case?
Necessities which dissolve a government do not
convey its authority to an oligarchy or a monarchy. They throw back, into the hands of the
people, the powers they had delegated, and
leave them as individuals to shift for themselves.
A leader may offer, but not impose himself, nor
be imposed on them. Much less can their necks
be submitted to his sword, their breath be held
at his will or caprice. The necessity which
should operate these tremendous effects should
at least be palpable and irresistible. Yet in both
instances, where it was feared, or pretended with
us, it was belied by the event. It was belied,
too, by the preceding experience of our sister
States, several of whom had grappled through
greater difficulties without abandoning their
forms of government. When the proposition
was first made, Massachusetts had found even
the government of committees sufficient to carry
them through an invasion. But we at the time
of that proposition were under no invasion.
When the second was made, there had been
added to this example those of Rhode Island,
New York, New Jersey, and Pennsylvania, in all
of which the republican form had been found
equal to the task of carrying them through the
severest trials. In this State alone did there exist so little virtue, that fear was to be fixed in
the hearts of the people, and to become the
motive of their exertions, and the principle of
their government? The very thought alone was
treason against the people; was treason against

mankind in general; as riveting forever the chains which bow down their necks, by giving to their oppressors a proof, which they would have trumpeted through the universe of the imbecility of republican government, in times of pressing danger, to shield them from harm. Those who assume the right of giving away the reins of government in any case, must be sure that the herd, whom they hand on to the rods and hatchet of the dictator, will lay their necks on the block when he shall nod to them. But if our assemblies supposed such a resignation in the people, I hope they mistook their character. I am of opinion, that the government, instead of being braced and invigorated for greater exertions under the difficulties, would have been thrown back upon the bungling machinery of county committees for administration, till a convention could have been called, and its wheels again set into regular motion. What a cruel moment was this for creating such an embarrassment, for putting to the proof the attachment of our countrymen to republican government!

[Religious Freedom]

By our own act of assembly of 1705, c. 30, if a person brought up in the Christian religion denies the being of a God, or the Trinity, or asserts there are more gods than one, or denies the Christian religion to be true, or the scriptures to be of divine authority, he is punishable on the first offence by incapacity to hold any office or employment ecclesiastical, civil, or military; on the second by disability to sue, to take any gift or legacy, to be guardian, executor, or administrator, and by three years' imprisonment without bail. A father's right to the custody of his own children being founded in law on his right of guardianship, this being taken away, they may of course be severed from him, and put by the authority of a court into more orthodox hands. This is a summary view of that religious slavery under which a people have been willing to remain, who have lavished their lives and fortunes for the establishment of their civil freedom. The error seems not sufficiently eradicated, that the operations of the mind, as well as the acts of the body, are subject to the coercion of the laws. But our rulers can have authority over such natural rights, only as we have submitted to them. The rights of conscience we never submitted, we could not submit. We are answerable for them to our God. The legitimate powers of government extend to such acts only as are injurious to others. But it does me no injury for my neighbor to say there are twenty gods, or no god. It neither picks my pocket nor breaks my leg. If it be said, his testimony in a court of justice cannot be relied on, reject it then, and be the stigma on him. Constraint may make him worse by making him a hypocrite, but it will never make him a truer man. It may fix him obstinately in his errors, but will not cure them. Reason and free inquiry are the only effectual agents against error. Give a loose to them, they will support the true religion by bringing every false one to their tribunal, to the test of their investigation. They are the natural enemies of error, and of error only. Had not the Roman government permitted free inquiry, Christianity could never have been introduced. Had not free inquiry been indulged, at the era of the Reformation, the corruptions of Christianity could not have been purged away. If it be restrained now, the present corruptions will be protected, and new ones encouraged. Was the government to prescribe to us our medicine and diet, our bodies would be in such keeping as our souls are now. Thus in France the emetic was once forbidden as a medicine, and the potato as an article of food. Government is just as infallible, too, when it fixes systems in physics. Galileo was sent to the Inquisition for affirming that the earth was a sphere; the government had declared it to be as flat as a trencher, and Galileo was obliged to adjure his error. This error, however, at length prevailed, the earth became a globe, and Descartes declared it was whirled round its axis by a vortex. The government in which he lived was wise enough to see that this was no question of civil jurisdiction, or we should all have been involved by authority in vortices. In fact, the vortices have been exploded, and the Newtonian principle of gravitation is now more firmly established, on the basis of reason, than it would be were the government to step in, and to make it an article of necessary faith. Reason and experiment have been indulged, and error has fled before them.

It is error alone which needs the support of government. Truth can stand by itself. Subject opinion to coercion: whom will you make your inquisitors? Fallible men; men governed by bad passions, by private as well as public reasons. And why subject it to coercion? To produce uniformity. But is uniformity of opinion desirable? No more than of face and stature. Introduce the bed of Procrustes then, and as there is danger that the large men may beat the small, make us all of a size, by lopping the former and stretching the latter. Difference of opinion is advantageous in religion. The several sects perform the office of a *censor morum* over each other. Is uniformity attainable? Millions of innocent men, women, and children, since the introduction of Christianity, have been burnt, tortured, fined, imprisoned; yet we have not advanced one inch towards uniformity. What has been the effect of coercion? To make one-half the world fools, and the other half hypocrites. To support roguery and error all over the earth. Let us reflect that it is inhabited by a thousand millions of people. That these profess probably a thousand different systems of religion. That ours is but one of that thousand. That if there be but one right, and ours that one, we should wish to see the nine hundred and ninety-nine wandering sects gathered into the fold of truth. But against such a majority we cannot effect this by force. Reason and persuasion are the only practicable instruments. To make way for these, free inquiry must be indulged; and how can we wish others to indulge it while we refuse it ourselves?

But every state, says an inquisitor, has established some religion. No two, say I, have established the same. Is this a proof of the infallibility of establishments? Our sister States of Pennsylvania and New York, however, have long subsisted without any establishment at all. The experiment was new and doubtful when they made it. It has answered beyond conception. They flourish infinitely. Religion is well supported; of various kinds, indeed, but all good enough; all sufficient to preserve peace and order; or if a sect arises whose tenets would subvert morals, good sense has fair play, and reasons and laughs it out of doors, without suffering the State to be troubled with it. They do not hang more malefactors than we do. They are not more disturbed with religious dissensions. On the contrary, their harmony is unparalleled, and can be ascribed to nothing but their unbounded tolerance, because there is no other circumstance in which they differ from every nation on earth. They have made the happy discovery, that the way to silence religious disputes, is to take no notice of them. Let us too give this experiment fair play, and get rid, while we may, of those tyrannical laws.

[Negro Slavery]

There must doubtless be an unhappy influence on the manners of our people produced by the existence of slavery among us. The whole commerce between master and slave is a perpetual exercise of the most boisterous passions, the most unremitting despotism on the one part, and degrading submissions on the other. Our children see this, and learn to imitate it; for man is an imitative animal. This quality is the germ of all education in him. From his cradle to his grave he is learning to do what he sees others do. If a parent could find no motive either in his philanthropy or his self-love, for restraining the intemperance of passion towards his slave, it should always be a sufficient one that his child is present. But generally it is not sufficient. The parent storms, the child looks on, catches the lineaments of wrath, puts on the same airs in the circle of smaller slaves, gives a loose to the worst of passions, and thus nursed, educated, and daily exercised in tyranny, cannot but be stamped by it with odious peculiarities. The man must be a prodigy who can retain his manners and morals undepraved by such circumstances. And with what execration should the statesman be loaded, who, permitting one-half the citizens thus to trample on the rights of the other, transforms those into despots, and these into enemies, destroys the morals of the one part, and the *amor patriæ* of the other. For if a slave can have a country in this world, it must be any other in preference to that in which he is born to live and labor for another; in which he must lock up the faculties of his nature, contribute as far as depends on his individual endeavors to the evanishment of the human race, or entails his own miserable condition on the endless generations proceeding from him. With the morals of the people, their industry also is destroyed. For in a warm climate, no man will labor for himself who can make another labor for him. This is so true, that of the proprietors of slaves a very small proportion indeed are ever seen to labor. And can the liberties of a nation be thought secure when we have removed their only firm basis, a conviction in the minds of the people that these liberties are of the gift of God? That they are not to be violated but with His wrath? Indeed I tremble for my country when I reflect that God is just; that his justice cannot sleep forever; that considering numbers, nature and natural means only, a revolution of the wheel of fortune, an exchange of situation is among possible events; that it may become probable by supernatural interference! The Almighty has no attribute which can take side with us in such a contest. But it is impossible to be temperate and to pursue this subject through the various considerations of policy, of morals, of history natural and civil. We must be contented to hope they will force their way into every one's mind. I think a change already perceptible, since the origin of the present revolution. The spirit of the master is abating, that of the slave rising from the dust, his condition mollifying, the way I hope preparing, under the auspices of heaven, for a total emancipation, and that this is disposed, in the order of events, to be with the consent of the masters, rather than by their extirpation.

First Inaugural Address

(1801)

Friends and Fellow-Citizens:

Called upon to undertake the duties of the first executive office of our country, I avail myself of the presence of that portion of my fellow-citizens which is here assembled, to express my grateful thanks for the favor with which they have been pleased to look towards me, to declare a sincere consciousness that the task is above my talents, and that I approach it with those anxious and awful presentiments which the greatness of the charge and the weakness of my powers so justly inspire. A rising nation spread over a wide and fruitful land, traversing all the seas with the rich productions of their industry, engaged in commerce with nations who feel power and forget right, advancing rapidly to destinies beyond the reach of mortal eye; when I contemplate these transcendent objects, and see the honor, the happiness, and the hopes of this beloved country committed to the issue and the auspices of this day, I shrink from the contemplation, and humble myself before the magnitude of the undertaking.

Utterly, indeed, should I despair, did not the presence of many whom I here see remind me that in the other high authorities provided by our constitution I shall find resources of wisdom, of virtue, and of zeal on which to rely under all difficulties. To you then, gentlemen, who are charged with the sovereign functions of legislation, and to those associated with you, I look with encouragement for that guidance and support which may enable us to steer with safety the vessel in which we are all embarked, amidst the conflicting elements of a troubled sea.

During the contest of opinion through which we have passed, the animation of discussions and of exertions has sometimes worn an aspect which might impose on strangers unused to think freely and to speak and to write what they think. But this being now decided by the voice of the nation, announced according to the rules of the Constitution, all will, of course, arrange themselves under the will of the law, and unite in common efforts for the common good. All too will bear in mind this sacred principle, that though the will of the majority is in all cases to prevail, that will, to be rightful, must be reasonable; that the minority possess their equal rights, which equal laws must protect, and to violate would be oppression. Let us then, fellow-citizens, unite with one heart and one mind; let us restore to social intercourse that harmony and affection without which liberty, and even life itself, are but dreary things. And let us reflect that having banished from our land that religious intolerance under which mankind so long bled and suffered, we have yet gained little if we countenance a political intolerance as despotic, as wicked, and capable of as bitter and bloody persecutions. During the throes and convulsions of the ancient world, during the agonizing spasms of infuriated man, seeking through blood and slaughter this long-lost liberty, it was not wonderful that the agitation of the billows should reach even this distant and peaceful shore; that this should be more felt and feared by some and less by others; and should divide opinions as to measures of safety. But every difference of opinion is not a difference of principle. We have called by different names brethren of the same principle. We are all Republicans; we are all Federalists. If there be any among us who would wish to dissolve this Union, or to change its republican form, let them stand undisturbed as monuments of the safety with which error of opinion may be tolerated, where reason is left free to combat it. I know, indeed, that some honest men have feared that a republican government cannot be strong; that this Government is not strong enough. But would the honest patriot, in the full tide of successful experiment, abandon a government which has so far kept us free and firm, on the theoretic and visonary fear that this Government, the world's best hope, may by possibility want energy to preserve itself? I trust not. I believe this, on the contrary, the strongest government on earth. I believe it the only one where every man at the call of the law would fly to the standard of the law; would meet invasions of the public order as his own personal concern. Sometimes it is said that man cannot be trusted with the government of himself. Can he then, be trusted with the government of others? Or have we found angels in the form of kings to govern him? Let history answer this question.

Let us then, pursue with courage and confidence our own federal and republican principles, our attachment to union and representative government. Kindly separated by nature and a wide ocean from the exterminating havoc of one quarter of the globe; too high-minded to endure the degradations of the others; possessing a chosen country, with room for our descendants to the hundredth and thousandth generation; entertaining a due sense of our equal right to the use of our own faculties, to the acquisitions of our own industry, to honor and confidence from our fellow-citizens, resulting not from birth, but from our actions and their sense of them; enlightened by a benign religion, professed indeed and practiced in various forms yet all of them inculcating honesty, truth, temperance, gratitude, and the love of man, acknowledging and adoring an overruling Providence, which by all its dispensations proves that it delights in the happiness of man here and his greater happiness hereafter: with all these blessings, what more is necessary to make us a happy and a prosperous people? Still one thing more, fellow-citizens — a wise and frugal government, which shall restrain men from injuring one another, shall leave them otherwise free to regulate their own pursuits of industry and improvement, and shall not take from the mouth of labor the bread it has earned. This is the sum of good government; and this is necessary to close the circle of our felicities.

About to enter, fellow-citizens, on the exercise of duties which comprehend everything dear and valuable to you, it is proper you should understand what I deem the essential principle of this government, and consequently those which ought to shape its administration. I will compress them in the narrowest compass they will bear, stating the general principle but not all its limitations. Equal and exact justice to all men of whatever state or persuasion, religious or political; peace, commerce and honest friendship with all nations, entangling alliances with none; the support of the state governments in all their rights, as the most competent administrations for our domestic concerns, and the surest bulwarks against anti-republican tendencies; the preservation of the general government in its whole constitutional vigor, as the sheet-anchor of our peace at home and safety abroad; a jealous care of the right of election by the people; a mild and safe corrective of abuses which are lopped by the sword of revolution, where peaceable remedies are unprovided; absolute acquiescence in the decisions of the majority, the vital principle of republics, from which is no appeal but to force, the vital principle and immediate parent of despotism; a well-disciplined militia, our best reliance in peace and for the first moments of war, till regulars may relieve them; the supremacy of the civil over the military authority — economy in the public expense, that labor might be lightly burdened; the honest payment of our debts, and sacred preservation of the public faith; encouragement of agriculture, and of commerce as its handmaid; the diffusion of information and arraignment of all abuses at the bar of the public reason; freedom of religion, freedom of the press, and freedom of person, under the protection of the habeas corpus; and trial by juries impartially selected. These principles form the bright constellation which has gone before us, and guided our steps through an age of revolution and reformation. The wisdom of our sages and blood of our heroes have been devoted to their attainment; they should be the creed of our political faith; the text of civic instruction; the touchstone by which to try the services of those we trust; and should we wander from them in moments of error or alarm, let us hasten to retrace our steps and to regain the road which alone leads to peace, liberty, and safety.

I repair then, fellow-citizens, to the post which you have assigned me. With experience enough in subordinate stations to know the difficulties of this, the greatest of all, I have learned to expect that it will rarely fall to the lot of imperfect man to retire from this station with the reputation and the favor which bring him into it. Without pretentions to that high confidence you reposed in our first and greatest revolutionary character, whose preëminent services had entitled him to the first place in his country's love, and had destined for him the fairest page in the volume of faithful history, I ask so much confidence only as may give firmness and effect to the legal administration of your affairs. I shall often go wrong through defect of judgment. When right, I shall often be thought wrong by those whose positions will not command a view of the whole ground. I ask your indulgence for my own errors, which will never be intentional; and your support against the errors of others who may condemn what they would not, if seen in all its parts. The approbation implied by your suffrage is a great consolation to me for the past; and my future solicitude will be to retain the good opinion of those who have bestowed it in advance, to conciliate that of others by doing them all the good in my power, and to be instrumental to the happiness and freedom of all.

Relying then on the patronage of your good-will, I advance with obedience to the work, ready to retire from it whenever you become sensible how much better choice it is in your power to make. And may that Infinite Power which rules the destinies of the universe lead our councils to what is best, and give them a favorable issue for your peace and prosperity.

Letters

[Advice to a Young Daughter]

Written to Martha when she was eleven years old.

ANNAPOLIS, November 28, 1783.

DEAR PATSY:

After four days' journey, I arrived here without any accident, and in as good health as when I left Philadelphia. The conviction that you would be more improved in the situation I have placed you than if still with me, has solaced me on my parting with you, which my love for you has rendered a difficult thing. The acquirements which I hope you will make under the tutors I have provided for you will render you more worthy of my love; and if they cannot increase it, they will prevent its diminution. Consider the good lady who has taken you under her roof, who has undertaken to see that you perform all your exercises, and to admonish

you in all those wanderings from what is right or what is clever, to which your inexperience would expose you: consider her, I say, as your mother, as the only person to whom, since the loss with which Heaven has pleased to afflict you, you can now look up; and that her displeasure or disapprobation, on any occasion, will be an immense misfortune, which should you be so unhappy as to incur by any unguarded act, think no concession too much to regain her good-will. With respect to the distribution of your time, the following is what I should approve:

From 8 to 10, practice music.

From 10 to 1, dance one day and draw another.

From 1 to 2, draw on the day you dance, and write a letter next day.

From 3 to 4, read French.

From 4 to 5, exercise yourself in music.

From 5 till bed-time, read English, write, etc.

Communicate this plan to Mrs. Hopkinson, and if she approves of it, pursue it. As long as Mrs. Trist remains in Philadelphia, cultivate her affection. She has been a valuable friend to you, and her good sense and good heart make her valued by all who know her, and by nobody on earth more than me. I expect you will write me every post. Inform me what books you read, what tunes you learn, and enclose me your best copy of every lesson in drawing. Write also one letter a week either to your Aunt Eppes, your Aunt Skipwith, your Aunt Carr, or the little lady from whom I now enclose a letter, and always put the letter you so write under cover to me. Take care that you never spell a word wrong. Always before you write a word, consider how it is spelt, and if you do not remember it, turn to a dictionary. It produces great praise to a lady to spell well. I have placed my happiness on seeing you good and accomplished; and no distress this world can now bring on me equal that of your disappointing my hopes. If you love me, then strive to be good under every situation and to all living creatures, and to acquire those accomplishments which I have put in your power, and which will go far towards ensuring you the warmest love of your affectionate father.

ANNAPOLIS, Dec. 22, 1783.

***I omitted to advise you on the subject of dress, which I know you are a little apt to neglect. I do not wish you to be gaily clothed at this time of life, but what you wear should be fine of its kind. But above all things and at all times let your clothes be clean, whole, and properly put on. Do not fancy you must wear them till the dirt is visible to the eye. You will be the last who is sensible of this. Some ladies think they may, under the privileges of the *dishabillé*, be loose and negligent of their dress in the morning. But be you, from the moment you rise till you go to bed, as cleanly and properly dressed as at the hours of dinner or tea. A lady who has been seen as a sloven or a slut in the morning, will never efface the impression she has made, with all the dress and pageantry she can afterwards involve herself in. Nothing is so disgusting to our sex as a want of cleanliness and delicacy in yours. I hope, therefore, the moment you rise from bed, your first work will be to dress yourself in such style, as that you may be seen by any gentleman without his being able to discover a pin amiss, or any other circumstance of neatness wanting.

[Reason is the Only Oracle]

Written to a favorite nephew, Peter Carr, age seventeen, an undergraduate at the College of William and Mary, about a quarter of a century after Jefferson's own student days there. With a plan of study Jefferson wrote a long letter, including the following advice concerning religion.

Religion. Your reason is now mature enough to examine this object. In the first place, divest yourself of all bias in favor of novelty and singularity of opinion. Indulge them in any other subject, rather than that of religion. It is too important, and the consequences of error may be too serious. On the other hand, shake off all the fears and servile prejudices, under which weak minds are servilely crouched. Fix reason firmly in her seat, and call to her tribunal every fact, every opinion. Question with boldness even the existence of a God; because, if there be one, he must more approve of the homage of reason, than that of blindfolded fear. You will naturally examine first, the religion of your own country. Read the Bible, then, as you would read Livy or Tacitus. The facts which are within the ordinary course of nature, you will believe on the authority of the writer, as you do those of the same kind in Livy and Tacitus. The testimony of the writer weighs in their favor, in one scale, and their not being

against the laws of nature, does not weigh against them. But those facts in the Bible which contradict the laws of nature must be examined with more care, and under a variety of faces. Here you must recur to the pretensions of the writer to inspiration from God. Examine upon what evidence his pretensions are founded, and whether that evidence is so strong, as that its falsehood would be more improbable than a change in the laws of nature, in the case he relates. For example, in the book of Joshua, we are told, the sun stood still several hours. Were we to read that fact in Livy or Tacitus, we should class it with their showers of blood, speaking of statues, beasts, etc. But it is said, that the writer of that book was inspired. Examine, therefore, candidly, what evidence there is of his having been inspired. The pretension is entitled to your inquiry, because millions believe it. On the other hand, you are astronomer enough to know how contrary it is to the law of nature that a body revolving on its axis, as the earth does, should have stopped, should not, by that sudden stoppage, have prostrated animals, trees, buildings, and should after a certain time have resumed its revolution, and that without a second general prostration. Is this arrest of the earth's motion, or the evidence which affirms it, most within the law of probabilities?

You will next read the New Testament. It is the history of a personage called Jesus. Keep in your eye the opposite pretensions: 1, of those who say he was begotten by God, born of a virgin, suspended and reversed the laws of nature at will, and ascended bodily into heaven; and 2, of those who say he was a man of illegitimate birth, of a benevolent heart, enthusiastic mind, who set out without pretensions to divinity, ended in believing them, and was punished capitally for sedition, by being gibbeted, according to the Roman law, which punished the first commission of that offence by whipping, and the second by exile; or death *in furca* [i.e. by crucifixion]. See this Law in the Digest, Lib. 48, tit. 19.28.3 and Lipsius Lib. 2. de cruce, cap. 2. These questions are examined in the books I have mentioned, under the head of Religion, and several others. They will assist you in your inquiries; but keep your reason firmly on the watch in reading them all. Do not be frightened from this inquiry by any fear of its consequences. If it ends in a belief that there is no God, you will find incitements to virtue in the comfort and pleasantness you feel in its exercise, and the love of others which it will procure you. If you find reason to believe there is a God, a consciousness that you are acting under his eye, and that he approves you, will be a vast additional incitement; if that there be a future state, the hope of a happy existence in that increases the appetite to deserve it; if that Jesus was also a God, you will be comforted by a belief of his aid in love. In fine, I repeat, you must lay aside all prejudice on both sides, and neither believe nor reject anything, because any other persons, or description of persons, have rejected or believed it. Your own reason is the only oracle given you by heaven, and you are answerable, not for the rightness, but uprightness of the decision. I forgot to observe, when speaking of the New Testament, that you should read all the histories of Christ, as well of those whom a council of ecclesiastics have decided for us, to be Pseudo-evangelists, as those they named Evangelists. Because these Pseudo-evangelists pretended to inspiration, as much as the others, and you are to judge their pretensions by your own reason, and not by the reason of those ecclesiastics. Most of these are lost. There are some, however, still extant, collected by Fabricius, which I will endeavor to get and send you.

[Thrown on a Wide World]

Jefferson, now sixty-five, wrote a long letter to his grandson Thomas Jefferson Randolph (in Philadelphia for his education), blending advice and reminiscence.

The three men of high standing mentioned by Jefferson are worthy of notice. Professor Small was elsewhere described by Jefferson as "Dr. Wm. Small of Scotland, . . . a man profound in most of the useful branches of science" and of "correct and gentlemanly manners." Wythe was the best Classical scholar in the colony, later the leading member of the Virginia bar. "No man," said Jefferson, "ever left behind him a character more venerated." Peyton Randolph, a kinsman to Jefferson, was one of the most popular of Virginians, later the first president of the Continental Congress. Young Jefferson's acceptability as a companion of men like these was a major factor in his development.

WASHINGTON, November 24, 1808.
MY DEAR JEFFERSON, —
Your situation, thrown at such a distance from us, and alone, cannot but give us all great anxieties for you. As much has been secured for you, by your particular position and the acquaintance to which you have been recommended, as could be done towards shielding you from the dangers which surround you. But thrown on a wide world, among entire strangers, without a friend or guardian to advise, so young too, and with so little experience of mankind, your dangers are great, and still your safety must rest on yourself. A determination never to do what is wrong, prudence and good humor, will go far towards securing to you the estimation of the world. When I recollect that at fourteen years of age, the whole care and direction of myself was thrown on myself entirely, without a relation or friend qualified to advise or guide me, and recollect the various sorts of bad company with which I associated from time to time, I am astonished I did not turn off with some of them, and become as worthless to society as they were. I had the good fortune to become acquainted very early with some characters of very high standing, and to feel the incessant wish that I could ever become what they were. Under temptations and difficulties, I would ask myself, what would Dr. Small, Mr. Wythe, Peyton Randolph do in this situation? What course in it will insure me their approbation? I am certain that this mode of deciding on my conduct tended more to its correctness than any reasoning powers I possessed. Knowing the even and dignified line they pursued, I could never doubt for a moment which of two courses would be in character for them. Whereas, seeking the same object through a process of moral reasoning, and with the jaundiced eye of youth, I should often have erred. From the circumstances of my position, I was often thrown into the society of horse-racers, card-players, fox-hunters, scientific and professional men, and of dignified men; and many a time have I asked myself, in the enthusiastic moment of the death of a fox, the victory of a favorite horse, the issue of a question eloquently argued at the bar, or in the great council of the nation, — well, which of these kinds of reputation should I prefer? That of a horse-jockey? a fox-hunter? an orator? or the honest advocate of my country's rights? Be assured, my dear Jefferson, that these little returns into ourselves, this self-catechising habit, is not trifling nor useless, but leads to the prudent selection and steady pursuit of what is right.

[Aristocracy, Natural versus Artificial]

Written to John Adams. Adams, the Massachu etts Federalist, and Jefferson, the Virginia Republican, long estranged, were drawn into friendly correspondence again in 1812. It is a mellow and thoughtful correspondence between two old men disciplined by intense experience in the great period when modern democracy arose.

MONTICELLO, October 28, 1813.

***I agree with you that there is a natural aristocracy among men. The grounds of this are virtue and talents. Formerly, bodily powers gave place among the aristoi. But since the invention of gunpowder has armed the weak as well as the strong with missile death, bodily strength, like beauty, good humor, politeness and other accomplishments, has become but an auxiliary ground for distinction. There is also an artificial aristocracy, founded on wealth and birth, without either virtue or talents; for with these it would belong to the first class. The natural aristocracy I consider as the most precious gift of nature, for the instruction, the trusts, and government of society. And indeed, it would have been inconsistent in creation to have formed man for the social state, and not to have provided virtue and wisdom enough to manage the concerns of the society. May we not even say, that that form of government is the best, which provides the most effectually for a pure selection of these natural aristoi into the offices of government? The artificial aristocracy is a mischievous ingredient in government, and provision should be made to prevent its ascendency. On the question, what is the best provision, you and I differ; but we differ as rational friends, using the free exercise of our own reason, and mutually indulging its errors. You think it best to put the pseudo-aristoi into a separate chamber of legislation, where they may be hindered from doing mischief by their co-ordinate branches, and where, also, they may be a protection to wealth against the agrarian and plundering enterprises of the majority of the people. I think that to give them power in order to prevent them from doing mischief, is arming them for it, and increasing instead of remedying the evil. For if the co-ordinate branches can arrest their action, so may they that of the co-ordinates. Mischief may be done negatively as well as positively. Of this, a cabal in the Senate of the United States has furnished many proofs. Nor do I believe them necessary

to protect the wealthy; because enough of these will find their way into every branch of the legislation, to protect themselves. From fifteen to twenty legislatures of our own, in action for thirty years past, have proved that no fears of an equalization of property are to be apprehended from them. I think the best remedy is exactly that provided by all our constitutions, to leave to the citizens the free election and separation of the aristoi from the pseudo-aristoi, of the wheat from the chaff. In general they will elect the really good and wise. In some instances, wealth may corrupt, and birth blind them; but not in sufficient degree to endanger the society.

It is probable that our difference of opinion may, in some measure, be produced by a difference of character in those among whom we live. From what I have seen of Massachusetts and Connecticut myself, and still more from what I have heard, and the character given of the former by yourself, who know them so much better, there seems to be in those two States a traditionary reverence for certain families, which has rendered the offices of the government nearly hereditary in those families. I presume that from an early period of your history, members of those families happening to possess virtue and talents, have honestly exercised them for the good of the people, and by their services have endeared their names to them. In coupling Connecticut with you, I mean it politically only, not morally. For having made the Bible the common law of their land, they seemed to have modeled their morality on the story of Jacob and Laban. But although this hereditary succession to office with you, may, in some degree, be founded in real family merit, yet in a much higher degree, it has proceeded from your strict alliance of Church and State. These families are canonized in the eyes of the people on common principles, "you tickle me, and I will tickle you." In Virginia we have nothing of this. Our clergy, before the revolution, having been secured against rivalship by fixed salaries, did not give themselves the trouble of acquiring influence over the people. Of wealth, there were great accumulations in particular families, handed down from generation to generation, under the English law of entails. But the only object of ambition for the wealthy was a seat in the King's Council. All their court then was paid to the crown and its creatures; and they Philipized in all collisions between the King and the people. Hence they were unpopular; and that unpopularity continues attached to their names. A Randolph, a Carter, or a Burwell must have great personal superiority over a common competitor to be elected by the people even at this day. At the first session of our legislature after the Declaration of Independence, we passed a law abolishing entails. And this was followed by one abolishing the privilege of primogeniture, and dividing the lands of intestates equally among all their children, or other representatives. These laws, drawn by myself, laid the ax to the foot of pseudo-aristocracy. And had another which I prepared been adopted by the legislature, our work would have been complete. It was a bill for the more general diffusion of learning. This proposed to divide every county into wards of five or six miles square, like your townships; to establish in each ward a free school for reading, writing and common arithmetic; to provide for the annual selection of the best subjects from these schools, who might receive, at the public expense, a higher degree of education at a district school; and from these district schools to select a certain number of the most promising subjects, to be completed at an University, where all the useful sciences should be taught. Worth and genius would thus have been sought out from every condition of life, and completely prepared by education for defeating the competition of wealth and birth for public trusts. My proposition had, for a further object, to impart to these wards those portions of self-government for which they are best qualified, by confiding to them the care of their poor, their roads, police, elections, the nomination of jurors, administration of justice in small cases, elementary exercises of militia; in short, to have made them little republics, with a warden at the head of each, for all those concerns which, being under their eye, they would better manage than the larger republics of the county or State. A general call of ward meetings by their wardens on the same day through the State, would at any time produce the genuine sense of the people on any required point, and would enable the State to act in mass, as your people have so often done, and with so much effect by their town meetings. The law for religious freedom, which made a part of this system, having put down the aristocracy of the clergy, and restored to the citizen the freedom of the mind, and those of entails and descents nurturing an

equality of condition among them, this on education would have raised the mass of the people to the high ground of moral respectability necessary to their own safety, and to orderly government; and would have completed the great object of qualifying them to select the veritable aristoi, for the trusts of government, to the exclusion of the pseudalists; and the same Theognis who has furnished the epigraphs of your two letters, assures us that "Ουδεμιαν πω, Κυρν', αγαθοι πολιν ωλεσαν ανδρες." [Not any state, Curnus, have good men yet destroyed.]

Although this law has not yet been acted on but in a small and inefficient degree, it is still considered as before the legislature, with other bills of the revised code, not yet taken up, and I have great hope that some patriotic spirit will, at a favorable moment, call it up, and make it the key-stone of the arch of our government.

With respect to aristocracy, we should further consider, that before the establishment of the American States, nothing was known to history but the man of the old world, crowded within limits either small or overcharged, and steeped in the vices which that situation generates. A government adapted to such men would be one thing; but a very different one, that for the man of these States. Here every one may have land to labor for himself, if he chooses; or, preferring the exercise of any other industry, may exact for it such compensation as not only to afford a comfortable subsistence, but wherewith to provide a cessation from labor in old age. Every one, by his property, or by his satisfactory situation, is interested in the support of law and order. And such men may safely and advantageously reserve to themselves a wholesome control over their public affairs, and a degree of freedom, which, in the hands of the *canaille* of the cities of Europe, would be instantly perverted to the demolition and destruction of everything public and private. The history of the last twenty-five years of France, and of the last forty years in America, nay of its last two hundred years, proves the truth of both parts of this observation.

But even in Europe a change has sensibly taken place in the mind of man. Science had liberated the ideas of those who read and reflect, and the American example had kindled feelings of right in the people. An insurrection has consequently begun, of science, talents, and courage, against rank and birth, which have fallen into contempt. It has failed in its first effort, because the mobs of the cities, the instrument used for its accomplishment, debased by ignorance, poverty and vice, could not be restrained to rational action. But the world will recover from the panic of this first catastrophe. Science is progressive and talents and enterprise on the alert. Resort may be had to the people of the country, a more governable power from their principles and subordination; and rank and birth and tinsel-aristocracy will finally shrink into insignificance even there. This, however, we have no right to meddle with. It suffices for us, if the moral and physical condition of our own citizens qualifies them to select the able and good for the direction of their government, with a recurrence of elections at such short periods as will enable them to displace an unfaithful servant, before the mischief he meditates may be irremediable.

I have thus stated my opinion on a point on which we differ, not with a view to controversy, for we are both too old to change opinions which are the result of a long life of inquiry and reflection; but on the suggestions of a former letter of yours, that we ought not to die before we have explained ourselves to each other. We acted in perfect harmony, through a long and perilous contest for our liberty and independence. A constitution has been acquired, which, though neither of us thinks perfect, yet both consider as competent to render our fellow citizens the happiest and the securest on whom the sun has ever shone. If we do not think exactly alike as to its imperfections, it matters little to our country, which, after devoting to it long lives of disinterested labor, we have delivered over to our successors in life, who will be able to take care of it and of themselves.

[An Aristocrat]

MONTICELLO, JANUARY 2, 1814.

***I think I knew General Washington intimately and thoroughly; and were I called on to delineate his character, it should be in terms like these.

His mind was great and powerful, without being of the very first order; his penetration strong, though not so acute as that of a Newton, Bacon, or Locke; and as far as he saw, no judgment was ever sounder. It was slow in operation, being little aided by invention or imagination, but sure in conclusion. Hence the common remark of his officers, of the advantage he derived from councils of war, where hearing all suggestions, he selected whatever was best; and certainly no general ever planned his battles more judiciously. But if deranged during the course of the action, if any member of his plan was dislocated by sudden circumstances, he was slow in re-adjustment. The consequence was, that he often failed in the field, and rarely against an enemy in station, as at Boston and York. He was incapable of fear, meeting personal dangers with the calmest unconcern. Perhaps the strongest feature in his character was prudence, never acting until every circumstance, every consideration, was maturely weighed; refraining if he saw a doubt, but, when once decided, going through with his purpose, whatever obstacles opposed. His integrity was most pure, his justice the most inflexible I have ever known, no motives of interest or consanguinity, of friendship or hatred, being able to bias his decision. He was, indeed, in every sense of the words, a wise, a good, and a great man. His temper was naturally high toned; but reflection and resolution had obtained a firm and habitual ascendency over it. If ever, however, it broke its bonds, he was most tremendous in his wrath. In his expenses he was honorable, but exact; liberal in contributions to whatever promised utility; but frowning and unyielding on all visionary projects and all unworthy projects and all unworthy calls on his charity. His heart was not warm in its affections; but he exactly calculated every man's value, and gave him a solid esteem proportioned to it. His person, you know, was fine, his stature exactly what one would wish, his deportment easy, erect and noble; the best horseman of his age, and the most graceful figure that could be seen on horseback. Although in the circle of his friends, where he might be unreserved with safety, he took a free share in conversation, his colloquial talents were not above mediocrity, possessing neither copiousness of ideas, nor fluency of words. In public, when called on for a sudden opinion, he was unready, short and embarrassed. Yet he wrote readily, rather diffusely, in an easy and correct style. This he had acquired by conversation with the world, for his education was merely reading, writing, and common arithmetic, to which he added surveying at a later day. His time was employed in action chiefly, reading little, and that only in agriculture and English history. His correspondence became necessarily extensive, and, with journalizing his agricultural proceedings, occupied most of his leisure hours within doors. On the whole, his character was, in its mass, perfect, in nothing bad, in few points indifferent; and it may truly be said, that never did nature and fortune combine more perfectly to make a man great, and to place him in the same constellation with whatever worthies have merited from man an everlasting remembrance. For his was the singular destiny and merit of leading the armies of his country successfully through an arduous war, for the establishment of its independence; of conducting its councils through the birth of a government, new in its forms and principles, until it had settled down into a quiet and orderly train; and of scrupulously obeying the laws through the whole of his career, civil and military, of which the history of the world furnishes no other example.***

[To Dr. Walter Jones]

Alexander Hamilton [1757–1804] and
James Madison [1751–1836]

Hamilton's political point of view has been indicated in the general introduction, page 82. Son of a Scottish merchant, Hamilton was born in the West Indies and in 1772 sent to New Jersey and New York to complete his education. As a student of seventeen in King's College (now Columbia) he entered the political controversy by writing pamphlets answering the brilliant Tory cleric, Samuel Seabury. In the Revolution he served on the staff of General Washington. A member of the Constitutional Convention, he endorsed its work by writing more than half of *The Federalist* papers. As first Secretary of the Treasury, supported by President Washington and by Congress, he virtually directed the new administration in its task of making the Constitution work. He declined the office of Chief Justice of the Supreme Court in favor of a distinguished law practice. He died early in consequence of a duel with Aaron Burr.

Further reading: *Alexander Hamilton and Thomas Jefferson: Representative Selections*, ed. F. C. Prescott, 1934. N. Schachner, *Alexander Hamilton*, 1946.

James Madison, fourth President of the United States, was brought up on a plantation in Virginia and educated at the College of New Jersey (now Princeton), where his classmates included the poet Freneau. With the coming of the Revolution he held political office in Virginia and in the Continental Congress. In the Constitutional Convention, 1787, he used his subtle, penetrating mind and deep knowledge of history and politics to such advantage that he earned the name of "father of the Constitution." When the new government was set up, he was in the House of Representatives, taking a leading part in the framing of the Bill of Rights then added to the Constitution. After 1800 he served under Jefferson as Secretary of State, and became Jefferson's successor to the Presidency, serving for two terms. From the point of view of the Federalists, the luckless War of 1812 was "Mr. Madison's War."

Further reading: I. Brant, *James Madison, Father of the Constitution*, 1950.

From *The Federalist*

(1787–1788)

Jefferson had been only thirty-three when he drafted the Declaration of Independence. Now, more than a decade later, he was in Paris as minister to France when other brilliant young men were active in the Philadelphia convention that drafted the Constitution. Among them were Madison, thirty-six years old, and Hamilton, only thirty.

The task of the Constitutional Convention was to reform a government that could not govern, the flimsy central government set up under the Articles of Confederation. When the "wise and good men" who labored throughout a hot summer in Philadelphia had finished their work, Jefferson rejoiced that the American States had "set the world a beautiful example of a government reformed by reason alone, without bloodshed."

Since ratification was uncertain, especially in New York, Madison and Hamilton decided to engage in propaganda. The result was *The Federalist* papers which they wrote together (a few were by John Jay), signing themselves "Publius." These eighty-five papers appeared as letters in New York newspapers, and promptly afterward as a book in two volumes. Whatever their original value in their particular time and place, Jefferson, viewing the work in a large perspective, declared that *The Federalist* was "the best commentary on the principles of government which ever was written." The superlative is debatable, but the world has agreed that Hamilton and Madison achieved a perennially suggestive classic of political literature.

Their manner of writing was well described by Hamilton when he said: "Our communications should be calm, reasoning, and serious, showing steady resolution more than feeling, having force in the idea rather than in the expression." Yet this force could not have existed without expression, in language clear, orderly, temperate, impersonal, dignified, appealing to quiet reason and abounding, like the Constitution itself, in checks and balances. Perhaps Number 10, as A. H. Quinn suggests, best "illustrates the right of *The Federalist* to be called literature."

The papers that follow are Number 23 and 10.

[A Strong Central Government. Hamilton]

The necessity of a Constitution, at least equally energetic with the one proposed, to the preservation of the Union, is the point at the examination of which we are now arrived.

This inquiry will naturally divide itself into three branches — the objects to be provided for by the federal government, the quantity of power necessary to the accomplishment of those objects, the persons upon whom that power ought to operate. Its distribution and organization will properly claim our attention under the succeeding head.

The principal purposes to be answered by union are these — the common defence of the members; the preservation of the public peace, as well against internal convulsions as external attacks; the regulation of commerce with other nations and between the States; the superintendence of our intercourse, political and commercial, with foreign countries.

The authorities essential to the common defence are these: to raise armies; to build and equip fleets; to prescribe rules for the government of both; to direct their operations; to provide for their support. These powers ought to exist without limitation, *because it is impossible to forsee or define the extent and variety of national exigencies, or the correspondent extent and variety of the means which may be necessary to satisfy them.* The circumstances that endanger the safety of nations are infinite, and for this reason no constitutional shackles can wisely be imposed on the power to which the care of it is committed. This power ought to be co-extensive with all the possible combinations of such circumstances; and ought to be under the direction of the same councils which are appointed to preside over the common defence.

This is one of those truths which, to a correct and unprejudiced mind, carries its own evidence along with it; and may be obscured, but cannot be made plainer by argument or reasoning. It rests upon axioms as simple as they are universal; the *means* ought to be proportioned to the *end*; the persons, from whose agency the attainment of any *end* is expected, ought to possess the *means* by which it is to be attained.

Whether there ought to be a federal government entrusted with the care of the common defence, is a question in the first instance open for discussion; but the moment it is decided in the affirmative, it will follow, that that government ought to be clothed with all the powers requisite to complete execution of its trust. And unless it can be shown that the circumstances which may affect the public safety are reducible within certain determinate limits; unless the contrary of this position can be fairly and rationally disputed, it must be admitted, as a necessary consequence, that there can be no limitation of that authority which is to provide for the defence and protection of the community, in any matter essential to its efficacy — that is, in any matter essential to the *formation, direction,* or *support* of the NATIONAL FORCES.

Defective as the present Confederation has been proved to be, this principle appears to have been fully recognized by the framers of it; though they have not made proper or adequate provision for its exercise. Congress have an unlimited discretion to make requisitions of men and money; to govern the army and navy; to direct their operations. As their requisitions are made constitutionally binding upon the States, who are in fact under the most solemn obligation to furnish the supplies required of them, the intention evidently was, that the United States should command whatever resources were by them judged requisite to the "common defence and general welfare." It was presumed that a sense of their true interests, and a regard to the dictates of good faith, would be found sufficient pledges for the punctual performance of the duty of the members to the federal head.

The experiment has, however, demonstrated that this expectation was ill-founded and illusory; and the observations, made under the last head, will, I imagine, have sufficed to convince the impartial and discerning, that there is an absolute necessity for an entire change in the first principles of the system; that if we are in earnest about giving the Union energy and duration, we must abandon the vain project of legislating upon the States in their collective capacities; we must extend the laws of the federal government to the individual citizens of America; we must discard the fallacious scheme of quotas and requisitions, as equally impracticable and unjust. The result from all this is that the Union ought to be invested with full power to levy troops; to build and equip fleets; and to raise the revenues which will be required for the formation and support of an army and navy, in the customary and ordinary modes practised in other governments.

If the circumstances of our country are such as to demand a compound instead of a simple, a confederate instead of a sole, government, the essential point which will remain to be adjusted will be to discriminate the OBJECTS, as far as it can be done, which shall appertain to the different provinces or departments of power; allowing to each the most ample authority for

fulfilling the objects committed to its charge. Shall the Union be constituted the guardian of the common safety? Are fleets and armies and revenues necessary to this purpose? The government of the Union must be empowered to pass all laws, and to make all regulations which have relation to them. The same must be the case in respect to commerce, and to every other matter to which its jurisdiction is permitted to extend. Is the administration of justice between the citizens of the same State the proper department of the local governments? These must possess all the authorities which are connected with this object, and with every other that may be allotted to their particular cognizance and direction. Not to confer in each case a degree of power commensurate to the end, would be to violate the most obvious rules of prudence and propriety, and improvidently to trust the great interests of the nation to hands which are disabled from managing them with vigor and success.

Who so likely to make suitable provisions for the public defence as that body to which the guardianship of the public safety is confided; which, as the center of information, will best understand the extent and urgency of the dangers that threaten; as the representative of the WHOLE, will feel itself most deeply interested in the preservation of every part; which, from the responsibility implied in the duty assigned to it, will be most sensibly impressed with the necessity of proper exertions; and which, by the extension of its authority throughout the States, can alone establish uniformity and concert in the plans and measures by which the common safety is to be secured? Is there not a manifest inconsistency in devolving upon the federal government the care of the general defence, and leaving in the State governments the *effective* powers by which it is to be provided for? Is not a want of co-operation the infallible consequence of such a system? And will not weakness, disorder, an undue distribution of the burdens and calamities of war, an unnecessary and intolerable increase of expense, be its natural and inevitable concomitants? Have we not had unequivocal experience of its effects in the course of the revolution which we have just accomplished?

Every view we may take of the subject, as candid inquirers after truth, will serve to convince us, that it is both unwise and dangerous to deny the federal government an unconfined authority, as to all those objects which are intrusted to its management. It will indeed deserve the most vigilant and careful attention of the people, to see that it be modelled in such a manner as to admit of its being safely vested with the requisite powers. If any plan which has been, or may be, offered to our consideration, should not, upon a dispassionate inspection, be found to answer this description, it ought to be rejected. A government, the constitution of which renders it unfit to be trusted with all the powers which a free people *ought to delegate to any government*, would be an unsafe and improper depositary of the NATIONAL INTERESTS. Wherever THESE can with propriety be confided, the coincident powers may safely accompany them. This is the true result of all just reasoning upon the subject. And the adversaries of the plan promulgated by the convention ought to have confined themselves to showing that the internal structure of the proposed government was such as to render it unworthy of the confidence of the people. They ought not to have wandered into inflammatory declamations and unmeaning cavils about the extent of the powers. The POWERS are not too extensive for the OBJECTS of federal administration, or, in other words, for the management of our NATIONAL INTERESTS; nor can any satisfactory argument be framed to show that they are chargeable with such an excess. If it be true, as has been insinuated by some of the writers on the other side, that the difficulty arises from the nature of the thing, and that the extent of the country will not permit us to form a government in which such ample powers can safely be reposed, it would prove that we ought to contract our views, and resort to the expedient of separate confederacies, which will move within more practicable spheres. For the absurdity must continually stare us in the face of confiding to a government the direction of the most essential national interests, without daring to trust it to the authorities which are indispensable to their proper and efficient management. Let us not attempt to reconcile contradictions, but firmly embrace a rational alternative.

I trust, however, that the impracticability of one general system cannot be shown. I am greatly mistaken, if anything of weight has yet been advanced of this tendency; and I flatter myself that the observations which have been made in the course of these papers have served to place the reverse of that position in as clear a light as any matter still in the womb of time and experience can be susceptible of. This, at all events, must be evident, that the very difficulty itself, drawn from the extent of the country, is the strongest argument in favor of an energetic government; for any other can certainly never preserve the Union of so large an empire. If we embrace the tenets of those who oppose the adoption of the proposed Constitution, as the standard of our political creed, we cannot fail to verify the gloomy doctrines which predict the impracticability of a national system pervading entire limits of the present Confederacy.

[Interests and Passions of Majorities and Minorities. Madison]

Among the numerous advantages promised by a well-constructed union, none deserves to be more accurately developed than its tendency to break and control the violence of faction. The friend of popular governments never finds himself so much alarmed for their character and fate as when he contemplates their propensity to this dangerous vice. He will not fail, therefore, to set a due value on any plan which, without violating the principles to which he is attached, provides a proper cure for it. The instability, injustice, and confusion introduced into the public councils have, in truth, been the mortal diseases under which popular governments have everywhere perished; as they continue to be the favorite and fruitful topics from which the adversaries to liberty derive their most specious declamations. The valuable improvements made by the American constitutions on the popular models, both ancient and modern, cannot certainly be too much admired; but it would be an unwarrantable partiality, to contend that they have as effectually obviated the danger on this side as was wished and expected. Complaints are everywhere heard from our most considerate and virtuous citizens, equally the friends of public and private faith and of public and personal liberty, that our governments are too unstable; that the public good is disregarded in the conflicts of rival parties; and that measures are too often decided, not according to the rules of justice, and the rights of the minor party, but by the superior force of an interested and overbearing majority. However anxiously we may wish that these complaints had no foundation, the evidence of known facts will not permit us to deny that they are in some degree true. It will be found, indeed, on a candid review of our situation, that some of the distresses under which we labor have been erroneously charged on the operation of our governments; but it will be found, at the same time, that other causes will not alone account for many of our heaviest misfortunes; and, particularly, for that prevailing and increasing distrust of public engagements, and alarm for private rights, which are echoed from one end of the continent to the other. These must be chiefly, if not wholly, effects of the unsteadiness and injustice with which a factious spirit has tainted our public administrations.

By a faction, I understand a number of citizens, whether amounting to a majority or minority of the whole, who are united and actuated by some common impulse of passion, or of interest, adverse to the rights of other citizens or to the permanent and aggregate interests of the community.

There are two methods of curing the mischiefs of faction: the one, by removing its causes; the other, by controlling its effects.

There are again two methods of removing the causes of faction: the one, by destroying the liberty which is essential to its existence; the other, by giving to every citizen the same opinions, the same passions, and the same interests.

It could never be more truly said of the first remedy, that it was worse than the disease. Liberty is to faction what air is to fire, an aliment without which it instantly expires. But it could not be less folly to abolish liberty, which is essential to political life, because it nourishes faction, than it would be to wish the annihilation of air, which is essential to animal life, because it imparts to fire its destructive agency.

The second expedient is as impracticable as the first would be unwise. As long as the reason of man continues fallible, and he is at liberty to exercise it, different opinions will be formed. As long as the connection subsists between his reason and his self-love, his opinions and his passions will have a reciprocal influence on each other; and the former will be objects to which the latter will attach themselves. The diversity in the faculties of men, from which the rights of property originate, is not less an insuperable obstacle to a uniformity of interests. The protection of these faculties is the first object of government. From the protection of different and unequal faculties of acquiring property, the possession of different degrees and kinds of property immediately results; and from the influence of these on the sentiments and views of the respective proprietors ensues a division of the society into different interests and parties.

The latent causes of faction are thus sown in the nature of man; and we see them everywhere brought into different degrees of activity, according to the different circumstances of civil society. A zeal for different opinions concerning religion, concerning government and many other points, as well of speculation as of practice; an attachment to different leaders ambitiously contending for pre-eminence and power, or to persons of other descriptions whose fortunes have been interesting to the human passions, have, in turn, divided mankind into parties, inflamed them with mutual animosity, and rendered them much more disposed to vex and oppress each other, than to co-operate for their common good. So strong is this propensity of mankind to fall into mutual animosities, that where no substantial occasion presents itself, the most frivolous and fanciful distinctions have been sufficient to kindle their unfriendly passions and excite their most violent conflicts. But the most common and durable source of factions has been the various and unequal distribution of property. Those who hold and those who are without property have ever formed distinct interests in society. Those who are creditors and those who are debtors fall under a like discrimination. A landed interest, a manufacturing interest, a mercantile interest, a moneyed interest, with many lesser interests, grow up of necessity in civilized nations, and divide them into different classes, actuated by different sentiments and views. The regulation of these various and interfering interests forms the principal task of modern legislation, and involves the spirit of party and faction in the necessary and ordinary operations of the government.

No man is allowed to be a judge in his own cause; because his interest would certainly bias his judgment and, not improbably, corrupt his integrity. With equal, nay, with greater reason, a body of men are unfit to be both judges and parties at the same time; yet what are many of the most important acts of legislation, but so many judicial determinations, not indeed concerning the rights of single persons, but concerning the rights of large bodies of citizens? and what are the different classes of legislators, but advocates and parties to the causes which they determine? Is a law proposed concerning private debts? — it is a question to which the creditors are parties on one side, and the debtors on the other. Justice ought to hold the balance between them. Yet the parties are, and must be, themselves the judges; and the most numerous party, or, in other words, the most powerful faction, must be expected to prevail. Shall domestic manufactures be encouraged, and in what degree by restrictions on foreign manufactures? are questions which would be differently decided by the landed and the manufacturing classes, and probably by neither with a sole regard to justice and the public good. The apportionment of taxes on the various descriptions of property is an act which seems to require the most exact impartiality; yet there is, perhaps, no legislative act in which greater opportunity and temptation are given to a predominant party, to trample on the rules of justice. Every shilling with which they overburden the inferior number is a shilling saved to their own pockets.

It is in vain to say that enlightened statesmen will be able to adjust these clashing interests and render them all subservient to the public good. Enlightened statesmen will not always be at the helm; nor, in many cases, can such an adjustment be made at all, without taking into view indirect and remote considerations, which will rarely prevail over the immediate interest which one party may find in disregarding the rights of another or the good of the whole.

The inference to which we are brought is that the causes of faction cannot be removed, and that relief is only to be sought in the means of controlling its effects.

If a faction consists of less than a majority, relief is supplied by the republican principle, which enables the majority to defeat its sinister views by regular vote. It may clog the administration, it may convulse the society; but it will be unable to execute and mask its violence under the forms of the Constitution. When a majority is included in a faction, the form of popular government, on the other hand, enables it to sacrifice to its ruling passion or interest both the public good and the rights of other citizens. To secure the public good, and private rights, against the danger of such a faction, and at the same time to preserve the spirit and the form of popular government, is then the great object to which our inquiries are directed. Let me add that it is the great *desideratum*, by which alone this form of government can be rescued from the opprobrium under which it has so long labored, and be recommended to the esteem and adoption of mankind.

By what means is this object attainable? Evidently by one of two only. Either the existence of the same passion or interest in a majority, at the same time, must be prevented; or the majority, having such coexistent passion or interest, must be rendered, by their number and local situation, unable to concert and carry into effect schemes of oppression. If the impulse and the opportunity be suffered to coincide, we well know that neither moral nor religious motives can be relied on as an adequate control. They are not found to be such on the injustice and violence of individuals, and lose their efficacy in proportion to the number combined together; that is, in proportion as their efficacy becomes needful.

From this view of the subject it may be concluded that a pure democracy, by which I mean a society consisting of a small number of citizens, who assemble and administer the government in person, can admit of no cure for the mischiefs of faction. A common passion or interest will, in almost every case, be felt by a majority of the whole; a communication and concert results from the form of government itself; and there is nothing to check the inducements to sacrifice the weaker party or an obnoxious individual. Hence it is that such democracies have ever been spectacles of turbulence and contention; have ever been found incompatible with personal security, or the rights of property, and have in general been as short in their lives as they have been violent in their deaths. Theoretic politicians, who have patronized this species of government, have erroneously supposed that by reducing mankind to a perfect equality in their political rights, they would at the same time be perfectly equalized and assimilated in their possessions, their opinions, and their passions.

A republic, by which I mean a government in which the scheme of representation takes place, opens a different prospect, and promises the cure for which we are seeking. Let us examine the points in which it varies from pure democracy, and we shall comprehend both the nature of the cure and the efficacy which it must derive from the union.

The two great points of difference between a democracy and a republic are: First, the delegation of the government, in the latter, to a small number of citizens elected by the rest; secondly, the greater number of citizens, and greater sphere of country, over which the latter may be extended.

The effect of the first difference is, on the one hand, to refine and enlarge the public views, by passing them through the medium of a chosen body of citizens, whose wisdom may best discern the true interest of their country, and whose patriotism and love of justice will be least likely to sacrifice it to temporary or partial considerations. Under such a regulation, it may well happen that the public voice, pronounced by the representatives of the people, will be more consonant to the public good than if pronounced by the people themselves, convened for the purpose. On the other hand, the effect may be inverted. Men of factious tempers, of local prejudices, or of sinister designs, may by intrigue, by corruption, or by other means, first obtain the suffrages, and then betray the interests of the people. The question resulting is, whether small or extensive republics are most favorable to the election of proper guardians of the public weal; and it is clearly decided in favor of the latter by two obvious considerations.

In the first place, it is to be remarked that, however small the republic may be, the representatives must be raised to a certain number, in order to guard against the cabals of a few; and that, however large it may be, they must be limited to a certain number, in order to guard against the confusion of a multitude. Hence, the number of representatives in the two cases not being in proportion to that of the constituents, and being proportionally greatest in the small republic, it follows that if the proportion of fit characters be not less in the large than in the small republic, the former will present a greater option, and consequently a greater probability of a fit choice.

In the next place, as each representative will be chosen by a greater number of citizens in the large than in the small republic, it will be more difficult for unworthy candidates to practise with success the vicious arts by which elections are too often carried; and the suffrages of the people, being more free, will be more likely to center in men who possess the most attractive merit and the most diffusive and established characters.

It must be confessed that in this as in most other cases, there is a mean, on both sides of which inconveniences will be found to lie. By enlarging too much the number of electors, you render the representative too little acquainted with all their local circumstances and lesser interests; as by reducing it too much, you render him unduly attached to these, and too little fit to comprehend and pursue great and national objects. The federal Constitution forms a happy combination in this respect; the great and aggregate interests being referred to the national, the local and particular to the state legislatures.

The other point of difference is, the greater number of citizens and extent of territory which may be brought within the compass of republican than of democratic government; and it is this circumstance principally which renders factious combination less to be dreaded in the former than in the latter. The smaller the society, the fewer probably will be the distinct parties and interests composing it; the fewer the distinct parties and interests, the more frequently will a majority be found of the same party; and the smaller the number of individuals composing a majority, and the smaller the compass within which they are placed, the more easily will they concert and execute their plans of oppression. Extend the sphere, and you take in a greater variety of parties and interests; you make it less probable that a majority of the whole will have a common motive to invade the rights of other citizens; or if such a common motive exists, it will be more difficult for all who feel it to discover their own strength, and to act in unison with each other. Besides other impediments, it may be remarked that where there is a consciousness of unjust or dishonorable purposes, communication is always checked by distrust, in proportion to the number whose concurrence is necessary.

Hence it clearly appears that the same advantage which a republic has over a democracy, in controlling the effects of faction, is enjoyed by a large over a small republic — is enjoyed by the Union over the States composing it. Does the advantage consist in the substitution of representatives, whose enlightened views and virtuous sentiments render them superior to local prejudices, and to schemes of injustice? It will not be denied that the representation of the Union will be most likely to possess these requisite endowments. Does it consist in the greater security afforded by a greater variety of parties, against the event of any one party being able to outnumber and oppress the rest? In an equal degree does the increased variety of parties, comprised within the Union, increase this security. Does it, in fine, consist in the greater obstacles opposed to the concert and accomplishment of the secret wishes of an unjust and interested majority? Here, again, the extent of the Union gives it the most palpable advantage.

The influence of factious leaders may kindle a flame within their particular States, but will be unable to spread a general conflagration through the other States. A religious sect may degenerate into a political faction in a part of the confederacy; but the variety of sects dispersed over the entire face of it must secure the national councils against any danger from that source. A rage for paper money, for an abolition of debts, for an equal division of property, or for any other improper and wicked project will be less apt to pervade the whole body of the Union than a particular member of it; in the same proportion as such a malady is more likely to taint a particular county or district than an entire State.

In the extent and proper structure of the Union, therefore, we behold a republican remedy for the diseases most incident to republican government. And according to the degree of pleasure and pride we feel in being republicans, ought to be our zeal in cherishing the spirit and supporting the character of federalists.

THE CONNECTICUT WITS

Looking backward from the year 1818, William Cullen Bryant wrote a critical sketch of early American literature. Before the Revolution, he pointed out, colonial Americans were naturally content to participate in the literary fame of the nation of which they were a part: the literature of England was a literature for Americans too. With the coming of political independence, however, as Bryant goes on to say, "the general ambition to distinguish ourselves as a nation was not without an effect on our literature. It seems to us that it is from this time only that we can be said to have poets of our own." The best example of "a pervading spirit of *nationality*" he finds in a group of Connecticut poets, whose work he proceeds to view at some length, taking just the right attitude — sympathy with what they were trying to do, firm recognition of their limited success.

The Connecticut poets named by Bryant were Trumbull, Dwight, Barlow, Humphreys, and Hopkins, though he could have included a number of others. They were sometimes called Yale Poets; all five just mentioned were Yale undergraduates in the 1760's and 1770's. More often they were called Hartford Wits, because in the 1780's they came to be associated with that Connecticut town. A more or less coherent school of writers, they collaborated in various combinations in such undertakings as *The Anarchiad*, *The Echo*, and other poems, in addition to what they published individually. Though they had begun as clever young men interested in literature and the arts, they found themselves drawn into the absorbing currents of political affairs, and eventually the three leading members became a judge, a college president, a diplomat. Nearly all were conservatives — Federalists in politics, Calvinists in religion.

Devoted to the literature of their day, the Connecticut Wits reflected the neo-classical taste of the period (see the introduction, page 84). With the usual time lag between English and American cultural movements, they imitated especially the poets of the earlier eighteenth century. Though they used American subject matter, they used it in the English fashion, wishing to "shine with Pope" and his school. Characteristically, their verse form was the Popean five-foot rhyming couplet, though some of their best work was in the crisper four-foot line. They liked their poems long, even attempting the epic, a form suited to their nationalistic aim, and adopting Miltonic conventions of method and style. Unconcerned with self-revelation, they wanted to be objective, descriptive, narrative, didactic, satirical. Satire appealed to them as a form inviting sharp perception and bright expression, though their comic spirit rarely reached the level needed for intellectual laughter. But they were even less successful in serious poetry, generally succumbing to diffuseness, sheer rhetoric, and artificial sublimity. Courageous and enthusiastic, they were weak in self-criticism, nor were they helped by the uncritical reputation for genius which they enjoyed in their own time. Yet their frequent use of American materials in English forms shows a strong urge, and a genuine step, toward establishing a native elegant tradition.

John Trumbull [1750–1831]

Trumbull came of a distinguished Connecticut family — among his relatives were Governor Jonathan Trumbull and the painter John Trumbull. His father was a minister and trustee of Yale College. When only seven years old, we are told, the boy passed the Yale entrance examinations. Entering six years later, he proceeded to the A.B. and A.M. degrees, gave a valedictory oration called *An Essay on the Use and Advantages of the Fine Arts*, served Yale as a tutor, helped to modernize the curriculum by introducing English literature. He was admitted to the Connecticut bar in 1773, worked for a time in the law office of John Adams in Boston, then practiced the law in New Haven and later in Hartford.

Meanwhile he was interested all along in writing, his taste formed by such authors as Addison, Samuel Butler, Pope, Swift, Charles Churchill. In verse his favorite form was the eight-syllable couplet, managed with a good deal of ingenuity in *The Progress of Dullness*, which grew out of his long years at Yale, and in his immensely popular satire *M'Fingal*, inspired by the Revolution. After his removal to Hartford in 1781, he was a member of the coterie of Wits and took part in writing *The Anarchiad*. But more and more his limited energies were consumed by his legal career. He finally became judge of the Supreme Court of Connecticut.

Further reading: *The Connecticut Wits*, ed. V. L. Parrington, 1926. Alexander Cowie, *John Trumbull, Connecticut Wit*, 1936, and "John Trumbull as a Critic of Poetry," *New England Quarterly*, 1938.

From *The Progress of Dullness*

(1772–1773)

👥 This satire on the academic life struck home in its day and can still be read with interest. It suggests that dullness is by no means a necessary bar to success in college — or in the ministry. In the main, the point is made fictionally. A slender story, in three Parts, is built around three characters, whose names sufficiently indicate their human shortcomings: Tom Brainless, Dick Hairbrain (not included in our selections; all he learned in college was unbelief), and Harriet Simper. After Harriet has been dropped by Hairbrain, the Rev. Mr. Brainless presents himself to her, providentially.

In the second verse-paragraph below, *non paravi* is Latin for "unprepared"; *tardes* and *egresses* are terms for coming late and leaving early. Tully, a few lines farther, is Cicero.

[Tom Brainless as Student and Preacher]

Two years thus spent in gathering knowledge,
The lad sets forth t'unlade at college,
While down his sire and priest attend him,
To introduce and recommend him;
Or if detain'd, a letter's sent   5
Of much apocryphal content,
To set him forth, how dull soever,
As very learn'd and very clever;
A genius of the first emission,
With burning love for erudition;   10
So studious he'll outwatch the moon
And think the planets set too soon.
He had but little time to fit in;
Examination too must frighten.
Depend upon't he must do well,   15
He knows much more than he can tell;
Admit him, and in little space
He'll beat his rivals in the race;
His father's incomes are but small,
He comes now, if he come at all.   20
So said, so done, at college now
He enters well, no matter how;
New scenes awhile his fancy please,
But all must yield to love of ease.
In the same round condemn'd each day,   25
To study, read, recite and pray;
To make his hours of business double —
He can't endure th' increasing trouble;
And finds at length, as times grow pressing,
All plagues are easier than his lesson.   30
With sleepy eyes and count'nance heavy,
With much excuse of *non paravi*,
Much absence, *tardes* and *egresses*,
The college-evil on him seizes.
Then ev'ry book, which ought to please,   35
Stirs up the seeds of dire disease;
Greek spoils his eyes, the print's so fine,
Grown dim with study, or with wine;
Of Tully's Latin much afraid,
Each page, he calls the doctor's aid;   40
While geometry, with lines so crooked,
Sprains all his wits to overlook it.
His sickness puts on every name

Its cause and uses still the same;
'Tis tooth-ache, cholic, gout or stone,   45
With phases various as the moon;
But though through all the body spread,
Still makes its cap'tal seat, the head.
In all diseases, 'tis expected,
The weakest parts be most infected.   50

* * *

Now in the desk, with solemn air,
Our hero makes his audience stare;
Asserts with all dogmatic boldness,
Where impudence is yoked to dullness;
Reads o'er his notes with halting pace,   55
Mask'd in the stiffness of his face;
With gestures such as might become
Those statues once that spoke at Rome,
Or Livy's ox, that to the state
Declared the oracles of fate,   60
In awkward tones, not said, nor sung,
Slow rumbling o'er the falt'ring tongue,
Two hours his drawling speech holds on,
And names it preaching, when he's done.
With roving tired, he fixes down   65
For life, in some unsettled town.
People and priest full well agree,
For why — they know no more than he.
Vast tracts of unknown land he gains,
Better than those the moon contains;   70
There deals in preaching and in prayer,
And starves on sixty pounds a year,
And culls his texts, and tills his farms,
Does little good, and little harm;
On Sunday, in his best array,   75
Deals forth the dullness of the day,
And while above he spends his breath,
The yawning audience nod beneath.
Thus glib-tongued Merc'ry in his hand
Stretch'd forth the sleep-compelling wand,   80
Each eye in endless doze to keep —
The God of speaking, and of sleep.

[Harriet Simper Has Her Day]

A judge of modes in silks and satins,
From tassels down to clogs and pattens;
A genius, that can calculate   85
When modes of dress are out of date,
Cast the nativity with ease
Of gowns, and sacks and negligees,
And tell, exact to half a minute,
What's out of fashion and what's in it;   90
And scanning all with curious eye,
Minutest faults in dresses spy;

(So in nice points of sight, a flea
Sees atoms better far than we;)
A patriot too, she greatly labours,   95
To spread her arts among her neighbours,
Holds correspondences to learn
What facts the female world concern,
To gain authentic state-reports
Of varied modes in distant courts,   100
The present state and swift decays
Of tuckers, handkerchiefs, and stays,
The colour'd silk that beauty wraps,
And all the rise and fall of caps.
Then shines, a pattern to the fair,   105
Of mien, address and modish air,
Of every new, affected grace,
That plays the eye, or decks the face,
The artful smile, that beauty warms,
And all the hypocrisy of charms.   110
    On Sunday, see the haughty maid
In all the glare of dress array'd,
Deck'd in her most fantastic gown,
Because a stranger's come to town.
Heedless at church she spends the day,   115
For homelier folks may serve to pray,
And for devotion those may go,
Who can have nothing else to do.
Beauties at church must spend their care in
Far other work, than pious hearing;   120
They've beaux to conquer, belles to rival;
To make them serious were uncivil.
For, like the preacher, they each Sunday
Must do their whole week's work in one day.
    As though they meant to take by blows   125
Th' opposing galleries of beaux,
To church the female squadron move,
All arm'd with weapons used in love.
Like coloured ensigns gay and fair,
High caps rise floating in the air;   130
Bright silk its varied radiance flings,
And streamers wave in kissing-strings;
Each bears th' artill'ry of her charms,
Like training bands at viewing arms.
    So once, in fear of Indian beating,   135
Our grandsires bore their guns to meeting,
Each man equipp'd on Sunday morn,
With psalm-book, shot and powder-horn;
And look'd in form, as all must grant,
Like th' ancient, true church militant;   140
Or fierce, like modern deep divines,
Who fight with quills, like porcupines.
    Or let us turn the style and see
Our belles assembled o'er their tea;
Where folly sweetens ev'ry theme,   145
And scandal serves for sugar'd cream.

"And did you hear the news? (they cry)
The court wear caps full three feet high,
Built gay with wire, and at the end on't,
Red tassels streaming like a pendant.   150
Well sure, it must be vastly pretty;
'Tis all the fashion in the city.
And were you at the ball last night?
Well, Chloe look'd like any fright;
Her day is over for a toast;   155
She'd now do best to act a ghost.
You saw our Fanny; envy must own
She figures, since she came from Boston.
Good company improves one's air —
I think the troops were station'd there.   160
Poor Cœlia ventured to the place;
The small-pox quite has spoil'd her face,
A sad affair, we all confest:
But providence knows what is best.
Poor Dolly, too, that writ the letter   165
Of love to Dick; but Dick knew better;
A secret that; you'll not disclose it;
There's not a person living knows it.
Sylvia shone out, no peacock finer;
I wonder what the fops see in her.   170
Perhaps 'tis true what Harry maintains,
She mends on intimate acquaintance."
    Yet that we fairly may proceed,
We own that ladies sometimes read,
And grieve, that reading is confin'd   175
To books that poison all the mind;
Novels and plays (where shines display'd
A world that nature never made),
Which swell their hopes with airy fancies,
And amorous follies of romances;   180
Inspire with dreams the witless maiden
On flowery vales and fields Arcadian,
And constant hearts no chance can sever,
And mortal loves, that last for ever.
    For while she reads romance, the fair one   185
Fails not to think herself the heroine;
For every glance, or smile, or grace,
She finds resemblance in her face,
Expects the world to fall before her,
And every fop she meets adore her.   190
Thus HARRIET reads, and reading really
Believes herself a young Pamela,
The high-wrought whim, the tender strain
Elate her mind and turn her brain:
Before her glass, with smiling grace,   195
She views the wonders of her face;
There stands in admiration moveless,
And hopes a Grandison, or Lovelace.
    Then shines she forth, and round her hovers,
The powder'd swarm of bowing lovers;   200

By flames of love attracted thither,
Fops, scholars, dunces, cits, together.
No lamp exposed in nightly skies,
E'er gather'd such a swarm of flies;
Or flame in tube electric draws   205
Such thronging multitudes of straws.
(For I shall still take similes
From fire electric when I please.)
    With vast confusion swells the sound,
When all the coxcombs flutter round.   210
What undulation wide of bows!
What gentle oaths and am'rous vows!
What double entendres all so smart!
What sighs hot-piping from the heart!
What jealous leers! what angry brawls   215
To gain the lady's hand at balls!
What billet-doux, brimful of flame!
Acrostics lined with HARRIET's name!
What compliments, o'er-strained with telling
Sad lies of Venus and of Helen!   220
What wits half-crack'd with commonplaces
On angels, goddesses and graces!
On fires of love what witty puns!
What similes of stars and suns!
What cringing, dancing, ogling, sighing,   225
What languishing for love, and dying!
                *   *   *
    Poor Harriet now hath had her day;
No more the beaux confess her sway;
New beauties push her from the stage;
She trembles at th' approach of age,   230
And starts to view the alter'd face,
That wrinkles at her in her glass:
So Satan, in the monk's tradition,
Fear'd, when he met his apparition.
    At length her name each coxcomb cancels   235
From standing lists of toasts and angels;
And slighted where she shone before,
A grace and goddess now no more,
Despised by all, and doom'd to meet
Her lovers at her rival's feet,   240
She flies assemblies, shuns the ball,
And cries out, vanity, on all;
Affects to scorn the tinsel-shows
Of glittering belles and gaudy beaux;
Nor longer hopes to hide by dress   245
The tracks of age upon her face.
Now careless grown of airs polite,
Her noonday nightcap meets the sight;
Her hair uncomb'd collects together,
With ornaments of many a feather;   250
Her stays for easiness thrown by,
Her rumpled handkerchief awry,
A careless figure half undress'd,

(The reader's wits may guess the rest;)
All points of dress and neatness carried,   255
As though she'd been a twelvemonth married;
She spends her breath, as years prevail,
At this sad wicked world to rail,
To slander all her sex *impromptu*,
And wonder what the times will come to.   260

[An Amorous Temper]

    Tom Brainless, at the close of last year,
Had been six years a rev'rend Pastor,
And now resolved, to smooth his life,
To seek the blessing of a wife.
His brethren saw his amorous temper,   265
And recommended fair Miss Simper,
Who fond, they heard, of sacred truth,
Had left her levities of youth,
Grown fit for ministerial union,
And grave, as Christian's wife in Bunyan.   270
    On this he rigg'd him in his best,
And got his old grey wig new dress'd,
Fix'd on his suit of sable stuffs,
And brush'd the powder from his cuffs,
With black silk stockings, yet in being,   275
The same he took his first degree in;
Procured a horse of breed from Europe,
And learn'd to mount him by the stirrup,
And set forth fierce to court the maid;
His white-hair'd Deacon went for aid;   280
And on the right, in solemn mode,
The Reverend Mr. Brainless rode.
Thus grave, the courtly pair advance,
Like knight and squire in famed romance.
The priest then bow'd in sober gesture,   285
And all in scripture terms address'd her;
He'd found, for reasons amply known,
It was not good to be alone,
And thought his duty led to trying
The great command of multiplying;   290
So with submission, by her leave,
He'd come to look him out an Eve,
And hoped, in pilgrimage of life,
To find an helpmate in a wife,
A wife discreet and fair withal,   295
To make amends for Adam's fall.
    In short, the bargain finish'd soon
A reverend Doctor made them one.
    And now the joyful people rouse all
To celebrate their priest's espousal;   300
And first, by kind agreement set,
In case their priest a wife could get,
The parish vote him five pounds clear,

T' increase his salary every year.
Then swift the tag-rag gentry come   305
To welcome Madam Brainless home;
Wish their good Parson joy; with pride
In order round salute the bride;

At home, at visits and at meetings,
To Madam all allow precedence;   310
Greet her at church with rev'rence due,
And next the pulpit fix her pew.

Timothy Dwight [1752–1817]

opposed deism + demo
conservative

One of Yale's greatest presidents, Dwight was a grandson of Jonathan Edwards, and
was born in Northampton, Massachusetts, the scene of Edwards's revivals. He took
his degree at Yale in 1769 and, with Trumbull, became a tutor there. Within the
next few years he wrote *The Conquest of Canaan*, an allegorical epic which is unread-
able today, using the heroic couplet of Pope's Homer and filling the poem, as Leon
Howard observes, with "eighteenth century Americans with Hebrew names who talked
like Milton's angels and fought like prehistoric Greeks."

In 1777–78 Dwight was a chaplain in the army. In 1783 he became pastor of the
church at Greenfield, where he was agreeably associated with the other Hartford Wits.
In later years his publications included *The Triumph of Infidelity*, in which, as Calvinist and Federalist, he opposed deism and democracy, and *Greenfield Hill*, a long
descriptive and didactic poem in the eighteenth-century manner.

Further reading: *The Connecticut Wits*, ed. V. L. Parrington, 1926. C. E. Cuning-
ham, *Timothy Dwight*, 1942.

From *Greenfield Hill*

(1794)

🦋 An attractive exercise rather than a piece of
creative art, *Greenfield Hill* was originally intended
"to imitate, in the several parts, the manner of as
many British poets." Though Dwight gave up this
preposterous plan, he did plainly imitate a variety of
poets of neo-classical England: Denham (*Cooper's
Hill*), Pope, Thomson, Beattie, Dyer, Gray, Goldsmith, etc. As Lewis Leary remarks dryly, "The scene
is perhaps less familiar to one who knows New England than to one with some acquaintance among the
poets of England."

Dwight did manage to convey, however, his love
of the Connecticut landscape and of the life about
him as he saw it with the eyes of an agrarian Federalist. He made this clear in Part II, "The Flourishing Village," frankly adapted from Goldsmith's *Deserted Village*. Here he designed, as he said, "to illustrate the effects of a state of property which is the

counterpart to that so beautifully exhibited by Dr.
Goldsmith in *The Deserted Village*. That excellent
writer, in the most interesting manner, displays the
wretched condition of the many, where enormous
wealth, splendor, and luxury constitute the state of
the few. In this imperfect attempt, the writer wished
to exhibit the blessings which flow from an equal
division of property and a general competence."

Goldsmith's poem had begun:
"Sweet Auburn! loveliest village of the plain".

[Sweet Simplicity]

Fair Verna! loveliest village of the west;
Of every joy, and every charm, possess'd;
How pleas'd amid thy varied walks I rove,
Sweet, cheerful walks of innocence, and love,
And o'er thy smiling prospects cast my eyes,   5
And see the seats of peace, and pleasure, rise,
And hear the voice of Industry resound,

And mark the smile of Competence, around!
Hail, happy village! O'er thy cheerful lawns,
With earliest beauty, spring delighted dawns;   10
The northward sun begins his vernal smile;
The spring-bird carols o'er the cressy rill:
The shower, that patters in the ruffled stream,
The ploughboy's voice, that chides the lingering
 team,
The bee, industrious, with his busy song,   15
The woodman's axe, the distant groves among,
The waggon, rattling down the rugged steep,
The light wind, lulling every care to sleep,
All these, with mingled music, from below,
Deceive intruding sorrow, as I go.   20
 How pleas'd, fond Recollection, with a smile,
Surveys the varied round of wintery toil!
How pleas'd, amid the flowers, that scent the
 plain,
Recalls the vanish'd frost, and sleeted rain;   24
The chilling damp, the ice-endangering street,
And treacherous earth that slump'd beneath the
 feet.

Yet even stern winter's glooms could joy in-
 spire:
Then social circles grac'd the nutwood fire;
The axe resounded, at the sunny door;
The swain, industrious, trimm'd his flaxen
 store,   30
Or thresh'd, with vigorous flail, the bounding
 wheat,
His poultry round him pilfering for their
 meat;
Or slid his firewood on the creaking snow;
Or bore his produce to the main below;
Or o'er his rich returns exulting laugh'd;   35
Or pledg'd the healthful orchard's sparkling
 draught:
While, on his board, for friends and neighbours
 spread,
The turkey smok'd, his busy housewife fed;
And Hospitality look'd smiling round,
And leisure told his tale, with gleeful sound.   40

Then too, the rough road hid beneath the
 sleigh,
The distant friend despis'd a length of way,
And join'd the warm embrace, and mingling
 smile,
And told of all his bliss, and all his toil;
And, many a month elaps'd, was pleas'd to
 view   45
How well the household far'd, the children
 grew;

While tales of sympathy deceiv'd the hour,
And sleep, amus'd, resign'd his wonted power.

 Yes! let the proud despise, the rich deride,
These humble joys, to Competence allied: 50
To me, they bloom, all fragrant to my heart,
Nor ask the pomp of wealth, nor gloss of
 art.
As a bird, in prison long confin'd,
Springs from his open'd cage, and mounts the
 wind,
Thro' fields of flowers, and fragrance, gaily
 flies,   55
Or re-assumes his birth-right, in the skies:
Unprison'd thus from artificial joys,
Where pomp fatigues, and fussful fashion cloys,
The soul, reviving, loves to wander free
Thro' native scenes of sweet simplicity;   60
Thro' Peace' low vale, where Pleasure lingers
 long,
And every songster tunes his sweetest song,
And Zephyr hastes, to breathe his first perfume,
And Autumn stays, to drop his latest bloom:
'Till grown mature, and gathering strength to
 roam,   65
She lifts her lengthen'd wings, and seeks her
 home.

 But now the wintery glooms are vanish'd all;
The lingering drift behind the shady wall;
The dark-brown spots, that patch'd the snowy
 field;
The surly frost, that every bud conceal'd;   70
The russet veil, the way with slime o'er-spread,
And all the saddening scenes of March are fled.
 Sweet-smiling village! loveliest of the hills!
How green thy groves! How pure thy glassy
 rills!   74
With what new joy, I walk thy verdant streets!
How often pause, to breathe thy gale of sweets;
To mark thy well-built walls! thy budding fields!
And every charm, that rural nature yields;
And every joy, to Competence allied,
And every good, that Virtue gains from
 Pride!   80
 No griping landlord here alarms the door,
To halve, for rent, the poor man's little store.
No haughty owner drives the humble swain
To some far refuge from his dread domain;
Nor wastes, upon his robe of useless pride,   85
The wealth, which shivering thousands want
 beside;
Nor in one palace sings a hundred cots;
Nor in one manor drowns a thousand lots;

Nor, on one table, spread for death and pain,
Devours what would a village well sustain.   90

O Competence, thou bless'd by Heaven's
  decree,
How well exchang'd is empty pride for thee!
Oft to thy cot my feet delighted turn,
To meet thy cheerful smile, at peep of morn;
To join thy toils, that bid the earth look gay;   95
To mark thy sports, that hail the eve of May;
To see thy ruddy children, at thy board,
And share thy temperate meal, and frugal hoard;
And every joy, by winning prattlers giv'n,
And every earnest of a future Heaven.   100

[Two Ways of Visiting]

Ye Muses! dames of dignified renown,
Rever'd alike in country, and in town,
Your bard the mysteries of a visit show;
For sure your Ladyships those mysteries know:
What is it then, obliging Sisters! say,   5
The debt of social visiting to pay?

'Tis not to toil before the idol pier;
To shine the first in fashion's lunar sphere;
By sad engagements forc'd, abroad to roam,   9
And dread to find the expecting fair, at home!
To stop at thirty doors, in half a day,
Drop the gilt card, and proudly roll away;
To alight, and yield the hand, with nice parade;
Up stairs to rustle in the stiff brocade;   14
Swim thro' the drawing room, with studied air;
Catch the pink'd beau, and shade the rival fair;
To sit, to curb, to toss, with bridled mien,
Mince the scant speech, and lose a glance be-
  tween;
Unfurl the fan, display the snowy arm,
And ope, with each new motion, some new
  charm: 20
Or sit, in silent solitude, to spy
Each little failing, with malignant eye;
Or chatter, with incessancy of tongue,
Careless, if kind, or cruel, right, or wrong;
To trill of us, and ours, of mine, and me,   25
Our house, our coach, our friends, our family,
While all th' excluded circle sit in pain,
And glance their cool contempt, or keen disdain:
T' inhale, from proud Nanking, a sip of tea,
And wave a curtsey trim, and flirt away;   30

Or waste, at cards, peace, temper, health and life,
Begin with sullenness, and end in strife,
Lose the rich feast, by friendly converse given,
And backward turn from happiness, and heaven.

It is, in decent habit, plain and neat,   35
To spend a few choice hours, in converse sweet;
Careless of forms, to act th' unstudied part,
To mix in friendship, and to blend the heart;
To choose those happy themes, which all must
  feel,
The moral duties, and the household weal,   40
The tale of sympathy, the kind design,
Where rich affections soften, and refine;
T' amuse, to be amus'd, to bless, be bless'd,
And tune to harmony the common breast;   44
To cheer, with mild good-humor's sprightly ray,
And smooth life's passage, o'er its thorny way;
To circle round the hospitable board,
And taste each good, our generous climes afford;
To court a quick return, with accents kind,
And leave, at parting, some regret behind.   50

Such, here, the social intercourse is found;
So slides the year, in smooth enjoyment, round.

Thrice bless'd the life, in this glad region
  spent,
In peace, in competence, and still content;
Where bright, and brighter, all things daily
  smile,   55
And rare and scanty, flow the streams of ill;
Where undecaying youth sits blooming round,
And Spring looks lovely on the happy ground;
Improvement glows, along life's cheerful way,
And with soft lustre makes the passage gay.   60
Thus oft, on yonder Sound, when evening gales
Breath'd o'er th' expanse, and gently fill'd the
  sails,
The world was still, the heavens were dress'd
  in smiles,
And the clear moon-beam tipp'd the distant
  isles,
On the blue plain a lucid image gave,   65
And capp'd, with silver light, each little wave;
The silent splendour, floating at our side,
Mov'd as we mov'd, and wanton'd on the tide;
While shadowy points, and havens, meet the
  eye,
And the faint-glimmering landmark told us
  home was nigh.   70

FROM CLASSIC TO ROMANTIC

Philip Freneau [1752–1832]

[handwritten margin notes: imaginatory romantic nature power of fancy short lyric satire]

Sea-captain, farmer, editor, as well as author, Freneau was born of French Huguenot and Scottish stock in New York. When he was ten the family moved to a large New Jersey estate, Mount Pleasant, within sight of the ocean. At Princeton he was associated with Madison, the future statesman and president, and Brackenridge, later the author of the novel *Modern Chivalry*. His own interests were already vital in both political (Whig) and literary concerns, and the two interests fused in the commencement poem which he and Brackenridge wrote on *The Rising Glory of America* (1772):

> This is the land of every joyous sound,
> Of liberty and life, sweet liberty!
> Without whose aid the noblest genius fails,
> And Science irretrievably must die.

After college Freneau's activities and movements were too varied to be stated specifically in a brief account. He did some school-teaching, he visited and dreamed in the West Indies, he returned and enlisted in the Revolutionary forces, he nearly died in a British prison ship; he served as captain of various freight ships, he was appointed by Jefferson as clerk of foreign languages, he edited the *Freeman's Journal* and other newspapers, conducted a farm, and lost his life at eighty in a blizzard.

Though he wrote verse persistently, circumstances were on the whole against him. Much of his verse was propaganda in the service of the Revolutionary cause and later the cause of Jeffersonian democracy, not the kind of poetry he was naturally drawn to, and he often wrote it while anger still clouded his vision. A large part of his energy, besides, was consumed in newspaper work. He managed to antagonize Washington, who called him "that rascal Freneau," and even disturbed Jefferson, though Jefferson thought so well of his partisan paper, the *National Gazette*, as to affirm that it had "saved our constitution which was galloping fast into monarchy." He spent much time writing essays, some six hundred in all. Freneau's poetry also suffered from the want of an audience that could respond to his best work and draw him out. The public preferred him when he wrote on the level of newspaper verse.

That Freneau's poetry marks the transition from the eighteenth century to the nineteenth century has already been indicated (page 85). His more significant work falls into two broad divisions. He was neo-classic in his satires, following as his masters Dryden, Churchill, and Peter Pindar, and ranging from burlesque to bitter invective. As a satirist he might seem to belong with the Connecticut Wits, but he dismissed them as aristocrats no better than the "old, defunct Tories of 1775."

The other division of his poetry, comprising nearly all of his best work, may be called pre-romantic. Some of it is descriptive, like the exotic "Beauties of Santa Cruz," or descriptive and narrative, like the Gothic "House of Night." It attained its highest level, however, in the short lyric, simple and telling in the manner of Collins and Gray, foreshadowing the poets of the romantic revival, while the themes handled were American. His hatred of England was less productive than his love of his own land.

Further reading: *Poems of Freneau*, ed. H. H. Clark, 1929. Prose writings, ed. Philip Marsh, 1955. Lewis Leary, *That Rascal Freneau: A Study in Literary Failure*, 1941.

To the Memory of the Brave Americans

Under General Greene, in South Carolina
Who Fell in the Action of September 8, 1781.

(w. 1781)

At Eutaw Springs the valiant died;
   Their limbs with dust are covered o'er —
Weep on, ye springs, your tearful tide;
   How many heroes are no more!

If in this wreck of ruin, they   5
   Can yet be thought to claim a tear,
O smite your gentle breast, and say
   The friends of freedom slumber here!

Thou, who shalt trace this bloody plain,
   If goodness rules thy generous breast,   10
Sigh for the wasted rural reign;
   Sigh for the shepherds, sunk to rest!

Stranger, their humble graves adorn;
   You too may fall, and ask a tear;
'Tis not the beauty of the morn   15
   That proves the evening shall be clear. —

They saw their injured country's woe;
   The flaming town, the wasted field;
Then rushed to meet the insulting foe;
   They took the spear — but left the shield. 20

Led by the conquering genius, Greene,
   The Britons they compelled to fly;
None distant viewed the fatal plain,
   None grieved, in such a cause to die —

But, like the Parthian, famed of old,   25
   Who, flying, still their arrows threw,
These routed Britons, full as bold,
   Retreated, and retreating slew.

Now rest in peace, our patriot band;
   Though far from nature's limits thrown, 30
We trust they find a happier land,
   A brighter sunshine of their own.

The Hurricane

The following poem was inspired by an actual experience at sea. It was published with a note: "In that violent hurricane at Jamaica, on the night of the 30th of July, 1784, in which no more than eight out of 150 sail of vessels, in the ports of Kingston and Port-Royal, were saved, Captain Freneau was at sea, and arrived at Kingston next morning a mere wreck. On that occasion, the following beautiful lines were penned."

In this poem Freneau relies upon the neo-classic "grandeur of generality" more than upon the concrete particularity of his romantic vein.

Happy the man who, safe on shore,
   Now trims, at home, his evening fire;
Unmoved, he hears the tempests roar,
   That on the tufted groves expire:
Alas! on us they doubly fall,   5
Our feeble bark must bear them all.

Now to their haunts the birds retreat,
   The squirrel seeks his hollow tree,
Wolves in their shaded caverns meet,
   All, all are blest but wretched we —   10
Foredoomed a stranger to repose,
No rest the unsettled ocean knows.

While o'er the dark abyss we roam,
   Perhaps, with last departing gleam,
We saw the sun descend in gloom,   15
   No more to see his morning beam;
But buried low, by far too deep,
On coral beds, unpitied, sleep!

But what a strange, uncoasted strand
   Is that, where fate permits no day —   20
No charts have we to mark that land,
   No compass to direct that way —
What Pilot shall explore that realm,
What new Columbus take the helm!

While death and darkness both surround,   25
   And tempests rage with lawless power,
Of friendship's voice I hear no sound,

No comfort in this dreadful hour —
What friendship can in tempests be,
What comfort on this raging sea?   30

The bark, accustomed to obey,
No more the trembling pilots guide:
Alone she gropes her trackless way,
While mountains burst on either side —
Thus, skill and science both must fall;   35
And ruin is the lot of all.

The Wild Honeysuckle

(w. 1786)

In a secluded spot at Charleston, South Carolina, Freneau came upon a flowering shrub, probably
the white swamp honeysuckle, and perhaps recalled
the flower of Gray's famous elegy,

> ". . . born to blush unseen,
> And waste its sweetness. . . ."

He proceeded to write in his own way, not in a
derivative neo-classical way, the best American poem
of nature before Bryant. Neglected in its time, it
is generally admired today more than any other of
Freneau's poems.

The theme is the evanescence of beauty. With
muted wonder the poet comes upon a fair and fragrant flower hidden in a shady retreat, and contemplates the simple terms of its existence, the "mere
idea" of a flower, as he wrote at first, or, as he happily revised, the "frail duration." No reader is likely
to miss the relevance to the lot of human kind,
though Freneau leaves it wholly unexpressed. It will
be noted, also, that he speaks to the flower in the
second person (you, thee, thy) as if it were indeed a
person, with a tender intimacy (too tender?), unro-
mantically subordinating himself ("I" occurs but
once). In the first two stanzas he speaks of its setting, where it flourishes under the fostering care of
nature; in the last two, of the unpitying Autumn in
which it must fade and disappear. Flaws in the poem
are forgotten when we reach the firm and tense concluding line.

Fair flower, that dost so comely grow,
Hid in this silent, dull retreat,
Untouched thy honied blossoms blow,
Unseen thy little branches greet;
No roving foot shall crush thee here,   5
No busy hand provoke a tear.

By Nature's self in white arrayed,
She bade thee shun the vulgar eye,
And planted here the guardian shade,

And sent soft waters murmuring by;   10
Thus quietly thy summer goes,
Thy days declining to repose.

Smit with those charms, that must decay,
I grieve to see your future doom;
They died — nor were those flowers more gay,
The flowers that did in Eden bloom: 16
Unpitying frosts, and Autumn's power
Shall leave no vestige of this flower.

From morning suns and evening dews
At first thy little being came: 20
If nothing once, you nothing lose,
For when you die you are the same;
The space between, is but an hour,
The frail duration of a flower.

The Indian Student

or, Force of Nature

(w. 1778)

Was the American Indian a mere savage, utterly barbaric? Or was he the "noble savage," simpler
and happier than civilized man, as pictured in the
primitivistic theory widely current in eighteenth-century Europe?

As R. H. Pearce made clear in The Savages of
America (1953), Freneau could not reconcile his
faith in civilization with his faith in the noble savage. But plainly he liked to think of the Indian as
free, honest, natural. As he asserted roundly in a
late poem, "The child of Nature is the better man."

From Susquehanna's farthest springs
Where savage tribes pursue their game,
(His blanket tied with yellow strings,)
A shepherd of the forest came.

Not long before, a wandering priest   5
Expressed his wish, with visage sad —
"Ah, why (he cried) in Satan's waste,
Ah, why detain so fine a lad?

"In white-man's land there stands a town
Where learning may be purchased low —   10
Exchange his blanket for a gown,
And let the lad to college go." —

From long debate the council rose,
And viewing Shalum's tricks with joy
To Cambridge Hall, o'er wastes of snows,   15
They sent the copper-colored boy.

One generous chief a bow supplied,
This gave a shaft, and that a skin;
The feathers, in vermillion dyed,
Himself did from a turkey win: 20

Thus dressed so gay, he took his way
O'er barren hills, alone, alone!
His guide a star, he wandered far,
His pillow every night a stone.

At last he came, with foot so lame,   25
Where learned men talk heathen Greek,
And Hebrew lore is gabbled o'er,
To please the Muses, — twice a week.

Awhile he writ, awhile he read,
Awhile he conned their grammar rules —   30
(An Indian savage so well bred
Great credit promised to the schools.)

Some thought he would in *law* excel,
Some said in *physic* he would shine;
And one that knew him, passing well,   35
Beheld, in him, a sound Divine.

But those of more discerning eye
Even then could other prospects show,
And saw him lay his *Virgil* by
To wander with his *dearer* bow.   40

The tedious hours of study spent,
The heavy-moulded lecture done,
He to the woods a hunting went,
Through lonely wastes he walked, he run.

No mystic wonders fired his mind;   45
He sought to gain no learned degree,
But only sense enough to find
The squirrel in the hollow tree.

The shady bank, the purling stream,
The woody wild his heart possessed,   50
The dewy lawn, his morning dream
In fancy's gayest colours dressed.

"And why (he cried) did I forsake
My native wood for gloomy walls;
The silver stream, the limpid lake   55
For musty books and college halls.

"A little could my wants supply —
Can wealth and honor give me more;
Or, will the sylvan god deny
The humble treat he gave before?   60

"Let seraphs gain the bright abode,
And heaven's sublimest mansions see —
I only bow to NATURE'S GOD —
The land of shades will do for me.

"These dreadful secrets of the sky   65
Alarm my soul with chilling fear —
Do planets in their orbits fly?
And is the earth, indeed, a sphere?

"Let planets still their course pursue,
And comets to the CENTRE run —   70
In HIM my faithful friend I view,
The image of my God — the SUN.

"Where Nature's ancient forests grow,
And mingled laurel never fades,
My heart is fixed; — and I must go   75
To die among my native shades."

He spoke and to the western springs
(His gown discharged, his money spent,
His blanket tied with yellow strings)
The shepherd of the forest went.   80

The Indian Burying Ground

(w. 1788)

Freneau provided a note for this poem: "The North American Indians bury their dead in a sitting posture; decorating the corpse with wampum, the images of birds, quadrupeds, etc., and (if that of a warrior) with bows, arrows, tomahawks, and other military weapons." An analysis of the poem by George Arms is in *The Explicator*, May 1944.

In spite of all the learned have said,
  I still my old opinion keep;
The posture, that we give the dead,
  Points out the soul's eternal sleep.

Not so the ancients of these lands —   5
  The Indian, when from life released,
Again is seated with his friends,
  And shares again the joyous feast.

His imaged birds, and painted bowl,
  And venison, for a journey dressed,   10
Bespeak the nature of the soul,
  Activity, that knows no rest.

His bow, for action ready bent,
  And arrows, with a head of stone,

Can only mean that life is spent,   15
  And not the old ideas gone.

Thou, stranger, that shalt come this way,
  No fraud upon the dead commit —
Observe the swelling turf, and say
  They do not lie, but here they sit.   20

Here still a lofty rock remains,
  On which the curious eye may trace
(Now wasted, half, by wearing rains)
  The fancies of a ruder race.

Here still an aged elm aspires,   25
  Beneath whose far-projecting shade
(And which the shepherd still admires)
  The children of the forest played!

There oft a restless Indian queen
  (Pale Shebah, with her braided hair)   30
And many a barbarous form is seen
  To chide the man that lingers there.

By midnight moons, o'er moistening dews;
  In habit for the chase arrayed,
The hunter still the deer pursues,   35
  The hunter and the deer, a shade!

And long shall timorous fancy see
  The painted chief, and pointed spear,
And Reason's self shall bow the knee
  To shadows and delusions here.   40

To an Author

(1788)

✖️ Freneau was only too well aware of the handi-
caps confronting the American poet in the eighteenth
century: "this fantastic century," in which "rigid
Reason reigns alone" and "lovely Fancy has no play,"
this time of disorder and armed conflict ("An age
employed in edging steel"), a time with no room for
solitude, or leisure, or love, or "poetic raptures." A
poet could hardly find other poets to emulate, or
even win the attention of hostile critics! The only
acceptable kind of verse seemed to be satire, which
Freneau pictured as one of the nine Muses, the "least
engaging" one. Yet even in stating his complaints
he contrived to write in a poetic style fresh, vigorous,
and disciplined.

Your leaves bound up compact and fair,
In neat array at length prepare
To pass their hour on learning's stage,

To meet the surly critic's rage;   4
The statesman's slight, the smatterer's sneer —
Were these, indeed, your only fear,
You might be tranquil and resigned:
What most should touch your fluttering mind
Is that few critics will be found
To sift your works, and deal the wound.   10

Thus, when one fleeting year is past
On some bye-shelf your book is cast —
Another comes, with something new,
And drives you fairly out of view:
With some to praise, but more to blame,   15
The mind returns to — whence it came;
And some alive, who scarce could read
Will publish satires on the dead.

Thrice happy Dryden, who could meet
Some rival bard in every street!   20
When all were bent on writing well
It was some credit to excel: —

Thrice happy Dryden, who could find
A Milbourne for his sport designed —
And Pope, who saw the harmless rage   25
Of Dennis bursting o'er his page
Might justly spurn the critic's aim,
Who only helped to swell his fame.

On these bleak climes by Fortune thrown,
Where rigid Reason reigns alone,   30
Where lovely Fancy has no sway,
Nor magic forms about us play —
Nor nature takes her summer hue
Tell me, what has the muse to do? —

An age employed in edging steel   35
Can no poetic raptures feel;
No solitude's attracting power,
No leisure of the noon day hour,
No shaded stream, no quiet grove
Can this fantastic century move;   40

The muse of love in no request —
Go — try your fortune with the rest,
One of the nine you should engage,
To meet the follies of the age: —

On one, we fear, your choice must fall —   45
The least engaging of them all —
Her visage stern — an angry style —
A clouded brow — malicious smile —
A mind on murdered victims placed —
She, only she, can please the taste!   50

On a Honey Bee

Drinking from a Glass of Wine and Drowned Therein

(1809)

Thou, born to sip the lake or spring,
Or quaff the waters of the stream,
Why hither come on vagrant wing? —
Does Bacchus tempting seem —
Did he, for you, this glass prepare? —   5
Will I admit you to a share?

Did storms harass or foes perplex,
Did wasps or king-birds bring dismay —
Did wars distress, or labours vex,
Or did you miss your way? —   10
A better seat you could not take
Than on the margin of this lake.

Welcome! — I hail you to my glass:
All welcome, here, you find;
Here let the cloud of trouble pass,   15
Here, be all care resigned. —
This fluid never fails to please,
And drown the griefs of men or bees.

What forced you here, we cannot know;
And you will scarcely tell —   20
But cheery we would have you go
And bid a glad farewell:
On lighter wings we bid you fly,
Your dart will now all foes defy.

Yet take not, oh! too deep a drink,   25
And in this ocean die;
Here bigger bees than you might sink,
Even bees full six feet high.
Like Pharaoh, then, you would be said
To perish in a sea of red.   30

Do as you please, your will is mine;
Enjoy it without fear —
And your grave will be this glass of wine,
Your epitaph — a tear —
Go, take your seat in Charon's boat,   35
We'll tell the hive, you died afloat.

To a Caty-Did

(1815)

In a branch of willow hid
Sings the evening Caty-did:

From the lofty locust bough
Feeding on a drop of dew,
In her suit of green arrayed   5
Hear her singing in the shade
    Caty-did, Caty-did, Caty-did!

While upon a leaf you tread,
Or repose your little head,
On your sheet of shadows laid,   10
All the day you nothing said:
Half the night your cheery tongue
Reveled out its little song,
    Nothing else but Caty-did.

From your lodgings on the leaf   15
Did you utter joy or grief? —
Did you only mean to say,
I have had my summer's day,
And am passing, soon, away
To the grave of Caty-did: —   20
    Poor, unhappy Caty-did!

But you would have uttered more
Had you known of nature's power —
From the world when you retreat,
And a leaf's your winding sheet,   25
Long before your spirit fled,
Who can tell but nature said,
Live again, my Caty-did!
    Live and chatter, Caty-did.

Tell me, what did Caty do?   30
Did she mean to trouble you? —
Why was Caty not forbid
To trouble little Caty-did? —
Wrong indeed at you to fling,
Hurting no one while you sing   35
    Caty-did! Caty-did! Caty-did!

Why continue to complain?
Caty tells me, she again
Will not give you plague or pain: —
Caty says you may be hid   40
Caty will not go to bed
While you sing us Caty-did.
    Caty-did! Caty-did! Caty-did!

But while singing, you forgot
To tell us what did Caty not: 45
Caty did not think of cold,
Flocks retiring to the fold,
Winter, with his wrinkles old,
Winter, that yourself foretold
When you gave us Caty-did.   50

Stay securely in your nest;
Caty now will do her best,
All she can to make you blest;
But, you want no human aid —
Nature, when she formed you, said,   55
"Independent you are made,
My dear little Caty-did:
Soon yourself must disappear
With the verdure of the year, —"
And to go, we know not where,   60
    With your song of Caty-did.

On the Uniformity and Perfection of Nature

(1815)

This poem and the one that follows are direct statements of Freneau's deism, published after the movement had declined. With a compactness and enthusiasm suited to a verse statement, Freneau presents a familiar set of concepts and attitudes: the First Cause, reason, nature, the Newtonian world machine, law and order, optimism ("all is right," "heaven below"), a religion of truth and goodness and tolerance.

On one fix'd point all nature moves,
Nor deviates from the track she loves;
Her system, drawn from reason's source,
She scorns to change her wonted course.

Could she descend from that great plan   5
To work unusual things for man,
To suit the insect of an hour —
This would betray a want of power,

Unsettled in its first design
And erring, when it did combine   10
The parts that form the vast machine,
The figures sketch'd on nature's scene.

Perfections of the great first cause
Submit to no contracted laws,
But all-sufficient, all-supreme,   15
Include no trivial views in them.

Who looks through nature with an eye
That would the scheme of heaven descry,
Observes her constant, still the same,
In all her laws, through all her frame.   20

No imperfection can be found
In all that is, above, around, —
All, nature made, in reason's sight
Is order all and all is right.

On the Religion of Nature

(1815)

The power that gives with liberal hand
  The blessings man enjoys, while here,
And scatters through a smiling land
  The abundant products of the year;
    That power of nature, ever bless'd,   5
    Bestow'd religion with the rest.

Born with ourselves, her early sway
  Inclines the tender mind to take
The path of right, fair virtue's way
  Its own felicity to make.   10
    This universally extends
    And leads to no mysterious ends.

Religion, such as nature taught,
  With all divine perfection suits;
Had all mankind this system sought   15
  Sophists would cease their vain disputes,
    And from this source would nations know
    All that can make their heaven below.

This deals not curses on mankind,
  Or dooms them to perpetual grief,   20
If from its aid no joys they find,
  It damns them not for unbelief;
    Upon a more exalted plan
    Creatress nature dealt with man —

Joy to the day, when all agree   25
  On such grand systems to proceed,
From fraud, design, and error free,
  And which to truth and goodness lead:
    Then persecution will retreat
    And man's religion be complete.   30

Durand's "Kindred Spirits" portrays Bryant and Cole and their romantic kinship with nature.

THE ROMANTIC MOVEMENT

Individualism in Feeling and Imagination

"The world exists for you. . . . Build therefore your own world" — EMERSON

The broad facts of American romanticism may be outlined briefly. Its revolt: against the rationalism that dominated the eighteenth century and lingered among the Unitarians. Its affirmation: the supremacy of the heart, the inner life of the self. Its environment: expansive, optimistic young America from about 1820 to the Civil War. Its development in literary centers: Transcendental Concord and elsewhere in the East and South, with a few of its chief writers, Poe, Melville, and Whitman, more or less apart from any group. If we do not attempt to present a set definition of romanticism, this is because its complexities have eluded all scholarly efforts to enclose it in an acceptable formula. But we cannot ignore the complexities. The significance of the literature of the period will be clearer if we make some attempt to ex-

179

plore and describe the romantic quest, without constantly stopping to qualify our statements. It will be clearer, too, if we frequently turn, as our writers did, to European examples.

THE ROMANTIC QUEST

Romantic Individualism. "Individualism in feeling and imagination" will perhaps serve as a label for the confusing elements entering into romantic literature, but only an analysis will make such a label really useful. The individualism demanded by the romantics was something other than the rational individualism of the age of Franklin and Jefferson. Jefferson had said: "Fix reason firmly in her seat, and call to her tribunal every fact, every opinion. . . . Neither believe nor reject anything because other persons . . . have rejected or believed it. Your own reason is the only oracle given you by heaven." The romantics shared this hostility to authority, but not the deference to reason. They boldly unfixed reason from her seat, and declared that the true oracle is intuition — something they knew without reasoning, something that satisfied the instincts of the heart. The individualism they proclaimed was that of the whole self, in which the affirmation of the feelings and imagination seemed to be central.

"Trust thyself: every heart vibrates to that iron string," said Emerson. He said: "If the single man plant himself indomitably on his instincts, and there abide, the huge world will come round to him." He said: "Whoso would be a man, must be a non-conformist." He said: "The root and seed of democracy is the doctrine, Judge for yourself. Reverence thyself."

Now, self-reliance has been justified in two opposite ways — because all men are different from each other, and because they are all alike. The view that they are different has been associated with romanticism ever since Rousseau began his *Confessions* by declaring that he was made unlike anybody he had ever seen; different, if not better. All men, it seems, are born free and different, and each should be himself and pursue happiness in his own way. "Is it not

the chief disgrace in the world," asked Emerson, "not to yield that peculiar fruit which each man was created to bear?" The dignity of man requires that a man insist on himself and never imitate other men. In the same vein Walt Whitman speaks of the thought that comes to us, a thought calm "like the stars, shining eternal. This is the thought of identity — yours for you, as mine for me." A man, says Whitman, has his "own central idea and purpose," grows from it and to it. While he may gather and absorb influences from outside, he must never imperil "the precious idiocrasy and special nativity and intention that he is, the man's self." This idea of the uniqueness of every man runs, as an assumption if not an assertion, all through the Romantic Movement, anticipating our modern scientific study of "individual differences."

In direct contrast is the idea of the Neo-Classic Age that all men are basically the same: not the uniqueness of men but the unity of man, not the particular man but the universal man. The two views do not, of course, exclude each other, but simply emphasize two aspects of humanity. Both views are common in this period, both the romantic sense of difference or novelty and the old classical sense — going back to Socrates and Plato — of sameness or universality. We have quoted Emerson's doctrine of uniqueness, but actually his prevailing emphasis was on unity, though in the end he gave unity itself, as we shall see, a romantic twist. In a *Dial* paper he directly contrasted the two views, and left no doubt as to his choice of emphasis. There is, he said, a healthy subjectivism and an unhealthy subjectivism. The dan-

Lyceum Lecture: Clinton Hall, New York

Local lyceums numbered about 3,000 in 1834, attesting to the universality of the cultural movement. Ralph Waldo Emerson was a popular speaker at such lectures.

ger of subjectivism is shown when it is indulged by the narrow-minded and the selfish, in whom it is a form of personal vanity, or escape from inner sickness. This is the "abominable self." On the other hand, there is an impersonal subjectivism. "A man may say I, and never refer to himself as an individual. . . . The great man, even whilst he relates a private fact personal to him, is really leading us away from him to an universal experience." The reason is, "that there is One Mind, and that all the powers and privileges which lie in any, lie in all." This last quotation, it will be observed, sums up the central drift of essay after essay in Emerson's best-known writings. Thus, in *Essays, First Series*, Emerson prefixed a motto in which he says (as he wants us to say):

> I am owner of the sphere,
> Of the seven stars and the solar year,
> Of Caesar's hand, and Plato's brain,
> Of Lord Christ's heart, and Shakespeare's strain.

Whitman later said much the same thing, beginning his "Song of Myself" with a line that looks purely personal till the second line makes it universal:

> I celebrate myself, and sing myself,
> And what I assume you shall assume.

Harmonious though this kind of thought is with the classical tradition, it takes on, we feel, a romantic cast. Perhaps it is the focus on the ego — the inflated ego — the very notion of a "Song of Myself" in place of say Pope's "Essay on Man." Or we may say it is the bold pride of the romantic instead of the ethical modera-

(*continued on page 183*)

Nathaniel Hawthorne

Ever aloof from Emersonian optimism, Hawthorne brooded on the enigma of evil.

Thoreau's Walden Pond Hut

Drawn by Henry Thoreau's sister Sophia, this sketch appeared on the title page of the first edition of *Walden*.

Southern Cotton Plantation, from a Currier and Ives Print

Agriculture and politics occupied the mind of the South during the era of the Cotton Kingdom, yet a small coterie of writers flourished in Charleston in the decade before the war; among them were Simms, Timrod, Hayne, and J. M. Legaré.

Walt Whitman

Whitman's free-and-easy and unadorned poetry was illustrated, in the first edition of *Leaves of Grass*, with this portrait of the nonchalant and self-sufficient Walt in workingman's clothes.

"Sperm Whaling: The Capture," by Benjamin Russell

Melville brought to his novels a wide knowledge and experience in whaling, and an imagination which worked wonders on the facts of his own voyages. He was always obsessed with the problem of evil in the universe, and his narratives often created a mood of grim realism and disaster.

tion inculcated by a classical author like Homer or Sophocles. Or we may say, rather, that a romantic optimism, a too ready slipping into illusion, causes a certain blindness to the facts of life. In sober truth, few individuals who plant themselves indomitably on their instincts will find the huge world coming round to them. Emerson, as usual, suggests his own corrective, remarking upon the "yawning difference" "between men as they ought to be and as they are." His doubts that men have it in their power to bring into being all that is latent but buried in them, begin early in his writings and multiply and deepen as he moves on to scan the meaning of Experience, of Illusions, of Fate. He had called genius "a larger imbibing of the common heart," or "a large infusion of Deity," but his efforts to encourage and confidently call forth in every man the vast riches of humanity — to democratize genius, so to speak — were typical only of transcendentalism in its flushed heyday.

Before doubt grew upon him, Emerson accepted the view of modern philosophy, as he understood it, that "The individual is the world. . . . Every man for himself." He believed that the individual, by employing his inner powers, can create a spiritual world for himself. In the highly transcendental flights of the early book on *Nature*, he often reminds us of the German romantic outlook. Novalis, the mystic of the German school, asserted that life is not something given us but something made by us; it is not imposed on us from without, we shape it from within. The self, as Spirit, creates its own world. This is also Emerson's assertion in the rapturous last paragraph of *Nature*. Here the individual self is conceived as having divine powers of creation. In his journal Emerson says that "God is in every man" and speaks of "the omnipotence that animates my clay." This is strong language. The God within is omnipotent, not a mere spark or breath as in the Christian tradition. Within us — "*there* is the celestial host," he says in an early sermon. He writes an essay on the Over-Soul, toward which we owe "perfect humility," but its "beatitude is all accessible to us," and "the simplest person who in his integrity worships God, becomes God." It is not surprising that such opinions gave offense to many of Emerson's Christian contemporaries. The unity of man had become the unity or identity of man and God. Each self, fully self-reliant, was divine. Not a transcendent God, or human reason, but the spiritual individual now seemed to be the measure.

It was the *feeling* individual, rather, with most romantics. Not developing their outlook, like Emerson, ministerially, they placed at the center of the self feeling and imagination. They sought every kind of experience and responded with sensuous warmth, trusting the heart wherever it led.

❦ *Feeling.* Feeling — love — the heart: these were bepraised in the romantic period as reason had been in the neo-classic. For a hundred years sentimentalism, reacting against the rule of reason, had proclaimed the goodness of human nature, the virtue of the man of feeling. In the romantic triumph this sentimentalism was changed into something rich and strange. Feeling became far more genuine, complicated, and interesting. It was still at war with the eighteenth-century kind of reason: "that false secondary power," Wordsworth called it, "by which we multiply distinctions," an analytic power by which we divide and divide vital reality till we "break down all grandeur." Feeling, a synthetic power, preserves vital reality, the meaning of things in their wholeness.

Romanticism restored to literature the emotional vitality of the Renaissance, interrupted by the long reign of neo- and pseudo-classicism. But now, in literature as in life, feeling was far more introverted and personal. It was individual joy, rapture, love, longing, regret, fear, hope, faith, enthusiasm, despair, an auto-registration of moods. These feelings were experienced with the keen sensibility and tumult of a youthful spirit — most romantics died early or became less romantic. The feeling perhaps most typical, internationally, was that of longing (in German, *Sehnsucht*), a vague longing for love, beauty, the infinite. The poetry of ancient classicism was the poetry of enjoyment, said A. W. Schlegel, and that of romanticism is the poetry of desire, a desire that can never be satisfied, an indefinite desire that must end in melancholy.

The romantic absorption in feeling is easily illustrated. There was Byron, for instance, who bore through Europe the pageant of his bleeding heart. There was Keats, haunted by shapes of beauty in myth and nature, who said in a famous letter: "I am certain of nothing but of the holiness of the heart's affections, and the truth of the imagination. . . . O for a life of sensations rather than thoughts!" There was Shelley, who aspired to an ideal Platonic realm of "love, and beauty, and delight," sometimes envisaged as a

world far from ours,
Where music and moonlight and feeling
Are one.

There was Poe, with "a thirst unquenchable," "no mere appreciation of the Beauty before us — but a wild effort to reach the Beauty above." This was in his verse; in his prose, on the other hand, he explored "terror, or passion, or horror, or a multitude of such other points." There was Longfellow, who called himself "a dreamer of dreams," who had drunk deeply of European romanticism, and spoke the language of the heart gently and happily, though not without an undertone of melancholy. And to name one more, a very different voice, there was Whitman, caresser of all life, even of death. "I am he that aches with love." "I know of nothing else but miracles." In his glowing acceptance of the universe Whitman reconciled all opposites. Body and soul, good and evil, man and nature, man and God — he blended them all in an emotional synthesis.

Is the romantic, then, like the sentimentalist, a man of feeling instead of a man of reason or of action? Basically, perhaps; and yet we must at once recognize a great difference. The feeling of the sentimentalist is weak and shallow; that of the romantic, stronger and deeper. The sentimentalist luxuriates in feeling for its own sake; the romantic, while he may often do this, is engaged in a quest of high truth through imagination. He believes in feeling as a value; he believes also that its value depends on an exertion of imagination. This is one of his key words, an old word which he used in a new way that has been common ever since. Before the romantic period, imagination had been synonymous with memory, a calling up of things past, or, by extension, a creation of something new by a recombination of things remembered. But now it transcended these old uses, came to be thought of as an instrument of insight into a truth above the field of the senses. Truth, it was held, lies in feeling, but it is the imagination that finds it. The really vital meanings of human life cannot be approached by the systematic and external operations of science, but only by an immediate emotional perception, warm flashes of intuition or imagination, a knowledge from within the human spirit.

Imagination. The concept of imagination is so important that it will be worth while to review a famous statement of it. In his preface to *Lyrical Ballads* Wordsworth announced that the object of this new departure in poetry was to take situations from common life — in which "the essential passions of the heart" are clearest — and "to throw over them a certain coloring of imagination, whereby ordinary things should be presented to the mind in an unusual aspect." That is, the poetic mind does not see nature and life prosaically, as literal fact, but throws over them (as Coleridge put it in one of his poems),

A light, a glory, a fair luminous cloud
Enveloping the earth.

How does this happen? First, something that the poet sees or experiences stirs an emotion in him. Secondly, this emotion is recollected in the tranquillity of meditation, till the actual emotion has become a poetic emotion. Thirdly, this poetic emotion, now grown powerful, spontaneously overflows in expression. So far the poet. Other persons, reading the poem, have their feelings strengthened and purified. Most readers, belonging to "the poor loveless ever-anxious crowd," as Coleridge calls them, need to be awakened from "the lethargy of custom" and to see life freshly with eyes of wonder. As moonlight gives an ordinary and familiar scene or experience a new and richer meaning, so the romantic imagination, shedding the light of the human spirit, adds, says Wordsworth,

the gleam,
The light that never was, on sea or land,
The consecration and the poet's dream.

The views of the two poets are so close that we may speak of the Wordsworth-Coleridge concept of imagination. Again and again, from Bryant to Whitman, we are reminded of it in American criticism. Poe, for example, maintains that it is not the business of the poet to express passion — what we have called the "actual emotion" — but to "elevate the soul" by an image of Supernal Beauty. In an imaginative poem, he says, at every stroke of the lyre we hear a ghostly echo; in every glimpse of beauty "we catch, through long and wild vistas, dim bewildering visions of a far more ethereal beauty *beyond*." Poetry should have "the *vagueness* of exaltation," "a certain wild license and *indefiniteness*": "the atmosphere of the mystic," a "breath of faëry." Poe was obviously following, in his own way, the theory as well as the practice of Coleridge and Shelley.

The romantic imagination was not equally

satisfactory to all the leaders of the American movement. Lowell, especially, became highly suspicious of "cloud-castles," and called for wisdom, judgment, reason to steady and guide the poet, as in the ethical imagination of the Greeks and Shakespeare and the spiritual imagination of his beloved Dante. While he complained that Wordsworth could not see "beyond the limits of his own consciousness and experience," he held that Dante, though himself the protagonist of the *Divine Comedy*, had for his theme not a man but man, whose highest end was to "climb through every phase of human experience to that transcendental and supersensual region where the true, the good, and the beautiful blend in the white light of God." Deploring the irresponsibility to which the romantic imagination was inclined, Lowell also condemned its frequent morbidity or "liver-complaint." So did Walt Whitman, and more significantly, because the ground of his criticism was an optimism just as characteristically romantic as the pessimism he brushed aside. Of the modern tendency "to turn everything to pathos, ennui, morbidity, dissatisfaction, death," Whitman remarked abruptly: "I call this thing in our modern literature delirium tremens." Its presence in the wholesome air of the New World he attributed to the influence of the decadent Old World. "Europe, with all its glories," is "a vast abnormal ward or hysterical sick-chamber."

The German romantic critic Schlegel attributed melancholy to the Christian religion: it had made man an exile longing for his distant home. We have noted what deism, that acid solvent, did to the Christian religion. But the melancholy survived. As faith subsided and man was thrown back upon himself, the feeling of longing was left without any tangible object. As Coleridge said, "The moderns revere the infinite and affect the indefinite as the vehicle of the infinite." Certainly the indefinite occupies a large place in romanticism, both in the values of living and in the means of artistic expression. Whereas mathematics had seemed the appropriate guide for the clarity demanded by rationalism, so now music — music as feeling rather than form — seemed the natural language for the vague exaltation of romanticism. To the German poet Novalis, for example, music is "an impression of immediate assurance, an intuition, a vision of truest and most intimate life." In the same vein Poe suggested that "It is in Music, perhaps, that the soul most clearly attains the great end for which, when inspired by the Po-

etic Sentiment, it struggles — the creation of supernal Beauty." Verse, to Poe, was "an inferior and less capable Music." Yet it must be added that Poe, like the Concord writers who eulogized music, and Whitman as well, had only the scantiest understanding of the art. Only in Lanier do we come upon a romantic who knew the discipline of music, while holding, like Poe, that

> Man's love ascends
> To finer and diviner ends
> Than man's mere thought e'er comprehends.
>
> . . . .
>
> Music is love in search of a word.

Like the indefinite, the remote and strange attracted the romantic imagination. " 'Tis distance lends enchantment to the view." Perhaps no one has put so neatly the contrast between things near when seen with merely realistic eyes and things remote when seen by the idealizing imagination, as Emerson contrived to do in a single sentence: "Every ship is romantic, save that we are sailing in." But it was Poe who most deliberately cultivated the addition of strangeness to beauty, in prose as well as verse. Attracted, as Hawthorne was also, by the horrors and mysteries that the "Gothic" writers of the sentimental movement had exploited so crudely, he made them shapes of beauty, as in "The Fall of the House of Usher." To the humdrum actual world he opposed visions of Dream-Land, the Valley of Many-Colored Grass, or "ultimate dim Thule."

In the German school the divorce from the actual world was carried so far that the fairy tale (*Märchen*) was esteemed by the group as a whole and written by Tieck and Novalis. Its dream-world seemed to offer a deeper reality — as many students of the Freudian psychology might agree. More representative of German romanticism, however, was its preference of past to present — a remote native past: "Blessed be thy golden age, Nüremberg!" Following the same impulse, Longfellow was to find inspiration in the Middle Ages, and in the German romantic writers as well. Irving's imagination was similarly captured by early Spain: "It is a romantic country," he said, its romance "chiefly derived from the brilliant regions of the East, and from the high-minded school of Saracenic chivalry."

To some of the Transcendentalists, Asia counted far more than did the European Middle Ages. Emerson found Asia rich in suggestions of a spiritual view of life, which he looked for, one is tempted to add, everywhere save in the Christian tradition. Once he came to know the sages and poets of the Orient, they were never long absent from his writings. Thoreau's interest was more studious. He immersed himself, as in bracing waters, in the Bhagavad-Gita, the Vedas, the Vishnu Purana, the Institute of Menu. He liked to speak of the "Scriptures of the Nations," by which he meant "the collected Scriptures or Sacred Writings of the several nations, the Chinese, the Hindoos, the Persians, the Hebrews, and others," which, printed together, would make the true Bible. With delight he received from an English friend the "royal gift" of twenty-four volumes "almost exclusively relating to ancient Hindoo literature, and scarcely one to be bought in America." The next year, on meeting Walt Whitman, who struck him as "wonderfully like the Orientals," he asked whether he had read them. "No," replied Whitman, "tell me about them." And for Whitman too the "mystic Orient" became important.

✦ The American Past. Whatever inspiration our writers found in foreign lands, they derived most of their subject-matter from America — an America more or less remote. Like the Germans they went back to the native past. A nationalistic, self-reliant America must use what past it had. It must grow from roots in its own soil, even though that soil was poor when compared (as by Irving) with Europe's "storied and poetical associations." To Emerson at sea, homeward bound from the Old World, "America, my country" was a

> Land without history, . . .
> No castles, no cathedrals, and no kings;
> Land of the forest. . . .

Yet the mother land of our writers was not to be disowned, but prized for herself and for whatever she could offer her children. From Irving to Whitman, American writers explored their domestic heritage.

Columbus was the subject of a biography by Irving, and the Dutch of New Amsterdam were pictured in his rollicking Knickerbocker's History and the best of his short tales. The Puritan background became foreground in the fine art of Hawthorne's Scarlet Letter and of short pieces like "The Maypole of Merry Mount" and "Young Goodman Brown." In the period of the Revolution we have, among other things,

the life of Washington by Irving and The Spy by Cooper. The Indians appear in Cooper and in Simms, in Longfellow's Hiawatha, in the historical writing of Parkman. Whitman gives numerous glimpses of the American past. These are only examples. Through the writers named, and others, one could reconstruct, however inadequately, the first two centuries of American experience.

While our writers in the romantic period chose to recreate much of the older America, they correspondingly slighted contemporary themes, though there were important exceptions such as Lowell's Biglow Papers and Melville's Moby Dick. They were even more aloof from the present when dealing with the European scene, making it remote in time as well as place. Thus, Irving romantically closed his eyes to the England of the Industrial Revolution, with its factories, mines, and social problems, preferring Westminster Abbey, Stratford-on-Avon, and picturesque byways. Even Emerson, shifting his focus from America and the present, wrote a book on English Traits and found all of his Representative Men in Europe.

Meanwhile, it should be added, romantic Europe reciprocally found inspiration in America, which had for it the charms of the exotic, the primitive, and the democratic. This influence in reverse has been summed up by Merle Curti. Into the catchall of European romanticism, he says,

> had gone enthusiasm for the noble savage, the mysteries of the American wilderness, the primitive in general. The cult of simplicity and the state of equality which the Americans, particularly frontiersmen and Quakers, presumably exemplified were other quarries from which the imagination and sentiment could secure foundation stones for the Romantic structure. Thus, the picturesque, strange, and fantastic phenomena of the terrestrial paradise beyond the Atlantic gave to Romanticists the very stuff of dreams. Herder, Goethe, Chateaubriand, Byron, Wordsworth, Blake, and Coleridge, among many others, were deeply in debt to America.

✦ Nature. To the Americans the terrestrial paradise was home. "Never need an American," said Irving, "look beyond his own country for the sublime and beautiful of natural scenery." To Irving nature was just scenery, but to our more typical romantics it was a spiritual resource valid when religion had faded, a living being (not Newton's machine) speaking to the soul in a language that feeling and imagination could understand. Nature, the near thing, was indubitably American, but the new attitude toward it came with the romantic impulse from abroad. Among the early European enthusiasts for wild nature had been Rousseau. To him nature was both a standard of simplicity and virtue and a refuge from harsh actuality. The introspective, complicated Germans went further, and fell into an ambiguity from which romanticism never quite extricated itself. On the one hand, it seemed to them, nature is a personality, a friend, let us say a divine friend, that sympathizes with man's sorrow, works upon his feelings, speaks to him of beauty, freedom, peace, happiness, touches him with intimations of high truth. On the other hand, when nature comes alive in this manner, it is really man — the poetically endowed man — who gives the life he seems to receive. Does man perhaps, as Wordsworth suggests, half create and half perceive?

However this mystery may be resolved, the essential fact, for romanticism, remains the kinship of man and nature. We strike it at once, in the opening lines of the first great poem in the American movement, Bryant's "Thanatopsis":

To him who in the love of Nature holds
Communion with her visible forms, she speaks
A various language.

It was Emerson who formulated most carefully, in his book on *Nature*, the relation of the inner and outer worlds. "The lover of nature," he says, "is he whose inward and outward senses are still truly adjusted to each other." In the fields and woods he finds himself, with delight, "not alone and unacknowledged. They nod to me, and I to them." "It is certain that the power to produce this delight does not reside in nature, but in man, or in a harmony of both," though actually, as Emerson goes on, the human soul seems to be swallowing up nature, assimilating the Not Me to the Me. The harmony of the two, in his theory, depends on the relation of correspondence. "Every appearance in nature corresponds to some state of the mind." He gives familiar examples: an enraged man is a lion, a firm one is a rock, light and darkness are knowledge and ignorance. But "Every natural fact is a symbol of some spiritual fact." In *Nature* Emerson thought of all these symbols as fixed and permanent; later, as changing and transitory — so many brief illuminations. But the important thing is that corre-

spondence meant for him what Providence had meant to his Puritan ancestors; that nature, to the sensitive human spirit, was a revelation taking the place of the Bible. Emerson might have made much of the one Puritan, Jonathan Edwards, who had glimpsed this possibility. Had he had access to *Images or Shadows of Divine Things* he would have read with wide open eyes:

Why is it not rational to suppose that the corporeal and visible world should be designedly made and constituted in analogy to the more spiritual, noble, and real world? It is certainly agreeable to what is apparently the method of God's working.

To feel kinship with nature in her gentler aspects was not difficult. One could be at home where nature invited the domesticities of hedgerow, orchard, pasture, woodlot — a more or less humanized nature. But what of wild nature? This was America's original distinction. Stretching westward from the ocean, even beyond the Father of Waters, was this "land of the forest." It powerfully affected the imagination of many of our romantic writers. Even Irving, with his face toward the Old World, remembers America's "trackless forests, where vegetation puts forth all its magnificence." "The mighty forest" dominates Bryant's "Thanatopsis," "A Forest Hymn," and other poems. Cooper gave a full picture of it: the ancient woods with soaring trees, the black mystery at night, the lakes and mountains, here and there human figures swallowed up in the landscape. Hawthorne restored the old Puritan forest, as in a famous scene of *The Scarlet Letter*, or in the sinister adventures of Young Goodman Brown "in the heart of the dark wilderness." Emerson thought of calling his first collected essays *Forest Essays*, and worshipped the pine gods in "Wood Notes."

But it was Thoreau who best communicated the tonic freedom of the forest, its wildness and beauty in large and small. In *The Maine Woods* he described a nature "savage and awful, though beautiful." *Walden* bore as a sub-title *Life in the Woods*; the life was that of wild creatures and plants as well as his own among them. To get to the heart of reality, it seemed to Thoreau, he must enter deeply into the wild. True, the inner spiritual reality was for him as for Emerson final. Yet, by the doctrine of correspondence, the inner was closely bound up with the outer reality. When the mood of wildness was on, he could "eat the brown earth," or desire to seize and devour a woodchuck raw. He loved rainstorms, and enjoyed wading in cold, bracing swamps — "a sort of baptism." As he might have put it, the Wild made him wild. But such adventures in feeling were matched by an intellectual conviction: that all civilization refers back to primitive nature and from time to time must return to its source of vitality, or decay and die. This was symbolized for him in the old fable of Romulus and Remus. The children of the Roman Empire, not being suckled by wolves, had to yield place to the northern barbarians who were. The continent of America, he goes on to say, is the she-wolf of our time. Here the moribund civilization of Europe can be reinvigorated and found a new Rome. We need not be surprised that Thoreau rejoiced when he read Whitman's "very brave and American" *Leaves of Grass:* "Though rude, and sometimes ineffectual, it is a great primitive poem, — an alarum or trumpet-note ringing through the American camp."

The Common Man. With Whitman we come to one more object of romantic enthusiasm: the common man. He is the natural, earthy man. Everything, says Whitman, "comes out of the dirt — everything: everything comes out of the people, the everyday people, the people as you find them and leave them: not university people, not F.F.V. people." The People, yes the People — this has been the cry of the modern world ever since the eighteenth century. Then, as Emerson noted, such poets as Goldsmith (*The Deserted Village*), Burns ("The Cotter's Saturday Night"), and Cowper (*The Task*) had begun to celebrate plain folk and wholesome rustic living. But it was Wordsworth who most memorably celebrated not only the natural world but the common man who lived in it, beginning with the "underprivileged" people of the *Lyrical Ballads* and rising to a climax in the shepherd poem "Michael."

In America, where the equalitarian spirit of the frontier was added to the democratic ideology inherited from the eighteenth century, writers like Bryant, Cooper, and Hawthorne were sympathetic toward the Jacksonian revolution, and Emerson (as Whitman recognized) formed a view of life basically democratic despite his patrician origin and training. No one placed a higher valuation than Emerson on the latent powers of every man: "Each man shall feel the world is his, and man shall treat with man as a sovereign state with a sovereign state." In the

main he presented his thought abstractly, as the titles of his essays indicate, leaving to others a more concrete, flesh-and-blood representation. Thus, it was Whittier who gave the dignity of verse to farmers, lumbermen, and shoemakers, and who in *Snow-Bound* dwelt with loving memory upon what Emerson had called "the meaning of household life." It was Whittier also who most passionately espoused the cause of the common man made slave, though Emerson, Thoreau, Longfellow, and Lowell also took part, each in his own way.

But the cause of the common man belonged especially to Whitman. In him the currents of romantic individualism and humanitarian altruism ran strong and ran together, blending self-pride and universal sympathy. Son of a carpenter, brought up in the country and in the "village" of Brooklyn, Whitman lived his life outside the circles of gentility and learning. Common people were, for him, the "divine average," the promise of a future America leading the modern world. United in a "universal democratic comradeship," in "adhesiveness or love, that fuses, ties and aggregates, making the races comrades, and fraternizing all," they must equally possess self-pride, "a rich, luxuriant, varied personalism," "the pride and centripetal isolation of a human being in himself." With Emerson, he conceived that greatness was for each individual, waiting only to be claimed. How far he was inclined to carry romantic egoism is indicated by a notebook entry: "If I walk with Jah in Heaven and he assume to be intrinsically greater than I it offends me, and I shall certainly withdraw from Heaven."

Here was a poet of the people, by the people, and for the people. Ironically, the people themselves preferred a poet like Longfellow.

LITERARY ART

"Trust your genius." The romantics trusted it in art, as in life. For them the essence of literary art, like the essence of living, was self-expression.

Self-Expression. This meant a pivotal change in the concept of literature. The new concept can be made clearer by glancing back at the old. Through the ages, from Plato and Aristotle down to Dr. Johnson, the classical mind had viewed literature as an imitation of life, a representation of the actions of men. The object was to picture men not as they are "actually" but as they are "ideally." That is, a character in an epic or drama should seem more than an actual man, for too much of such a man is personal, local, and transient. In addition to being "himself," a character should represent his type (the general nature of a warrior, a poet, a man of ambition, loyalty, deceit, etc.) and, above the type, should suggest the universal man, the ideal which human nature is striving to attain but never actually does attain. Examples are Hector and Odysseus, Oedipus and Antigone, Hamlet and Cordelia. In these extensions above the actual, the poet's imagination is guided by reason and moral insight toward a reality higher than the mere facts of life. It never occurs to the poet to exploit his personal and subjective experience.

The romantics rejected this literary theory. The theory, and still more the practice, had been distorted and diminished during the long reign of neo- and pseudo-classicism by the development of conventions and rules. The time seemed ripe for a fresh start. For the old concept of literature as an *imitation* the romantics substituted the concept of literature as an *expression*. It might be the expression of a state of society, or of a national spirit, but characteristically it was assumed to be an expression of self, of the writer's own personality and experience in the world as he knew it or chose to make it. Literature became largely confessional — personal, autobiographic, lyrical. The epic, in any proper sense of the word, disappeared. The drama was transformed, but could not thrive in so subjective an era. Often the novel, as in Goethe's *Wilhelm Meister*, presented characters straining toward self-culture and fulfillment. The familiar essay became far more personal, as in Lamb. For the first time in the history of literature, the lyric became the typical kind of poetry. The romantic revival was indeed a period of great lyrical poetry, expressing keen and subtle sense impressions and an immense range of emotions — every variety of joy, of ecstasy, of love, of yearning, of regret — with a spontaneity and intensity reminiscent of the Renaissance. Small wonder that Emerson, while aware of the Puritan in himself, exclaimed approvingly, "This writing is blood-warm." The same emphasis on self, on its adventures in the realm of the senses and feelings, appeared in the typical art of the period — music. P. H. Lang has said of Chopin, for example, that he "spoke of himself and to himself: he composed confessions."

Life and art tended, in romanticism, to be identical. Should not the poet's life be poetic, and his poetry be a living thing — himself in words? What life might be is shown not by the practical and prudential crowd, whose existence is almost a death-in-life, but by the poet, who lives creatively and freely, building his inner world of beauty and high meaning. His very life — his inner life — is a poem. And his poetry is the verbal externalization of his inner life, in a word himself. Thus, the poetry of Byron is Byron, and Goethe valued it with enthusiasm as the expression of a great personality. Even Wordsworth, though far more objective, established his name by the autobiographical *Prelude* and by innumerable short pieces that recorded his personal responses to the outer world, his own perceptions, intimations, visions, moods.

This closeness to personal experience is characteristic of the poetry of Bryant, Poe, Emerson, Longfellow, and many other American writers. Our best example is Walt Whitman. Glancing backward from old age, he himself described *Leaves of Grass* as "an attempt, from first to last, to put a *Person*, a human being (myself, in the latter half of the Nineteenth Century, in America), freely, fully and truly on record." The book was a memorable contribution to that art of the self which is typical of the Romantic Movement. Wherein it is so different from the great books of the ages will be clear if we ask: How much of Homer is there in Homer's poetry — how much of Shakespeare in his — how much, even, of Milton in his? But Goethe was vastly more personal than these, and the German romantics were personal on principle. It was Novalis who declared, "The novel is a life in the form of a book." And Whitman went one step further:

> Camerado, this is no book,
> Who touches this touches a man.

Organic Form. The idea that a work of literary art grows out of experience and expresses a life lived brings us to the doctrine of organic form. This favorite romantic doctrine was not new but renovated. In Greek thought we find it as early as Plato, who said that a work of art should be like a living creature. After the middle of the eighteenth century it was affirmed by Edward Young, in whose view a work of original genius "may be said to be of a vegetable nature; it grows, it is not made." Here was an idea highly appropriate to romanticism. As the universe is not a machine but a living entity, so a work of art is not a mechanical construction but an organic structure. Like A. W. Schlegel in Germany, Coleridge wrote: "The organic form is innate; it shapes, as it develops itself from within, and its fullness of development is one and the same with the perfection of its outward form. Such as the life is, such is the form." Mechanical form, on the other hand, is consciously imposed from the outside: "The form is mechanic when on any given material we impress a predetermined form, . . . as when to a mass of wet clay we give whatever shape we wish it to retain when hardened."

Pursuing this biological analogy, romanticism conceives of any excellent work of art as a structure growing in an environment, developing from a living germ. Each part has its proper function, and all the parts work together as a unit. Among the parts that may enter into the complex unity and harmony of a particular work of art are diction, rhythm, image, symbol, ideas, attitude, tone, setting, character, incident, etc. Thus a successful poem, says Coleridge, offers "such delight from the *whole*, as is compatible with a distinct gratification from each component part." The parts "mutually support and explain each other." Successful poetry, in his view, cannot be written by deliberate effort; the organic principle applies to the poet as well as the poem — he is born and not made, though he can cultivate his gift.

Among American writers Emerson made the fullest use of the organic view of art. The difference between mechanical construction and organic form, he writes in his journal,

is the difference between the carpenter who makes a box, and the mother who bears a child. The box was all in the carpenter; but the child was not all in the parents. They knew no more of the child's formation than they did of their own. They were merely channels through which the child's nature flowed from quite another and eternal power, and the child is as much a wonder to them as to any.

Using the Platonic idea of inspiration, Emerson conceives that the eternal power expresses itself in the poet's intuition, and the poet's intuition expresses itself in the words and music of the poem. Spirit gives the divine hint to the poet, and the poet passes it on to all men, in a form that is excellent in proportion as it is determined by the hint itself, not arbitrarily devised by the poet. "For it is not meters, but a meter-making argument that makes a poem — a thought so passionate and alive that like the spirit of a plant or an animal it has an architec-

ture of its own, and adorns nature with a new thing." Like all beauty, it has "fitness," a perfect adaptation of means to end. Form is not "outside embellishment" as the eighteenth century seemed to think, but already dictated by content. "A verse is not a vehicle to carry a sentence as a jewel is carried in a case: the verse must be alive, and inseparable from its contents, as the soul of man inspires and directs the body." The superior poem cannot be analyzed; you cannot separate word and thought. But in the inferior poem they fall apart, and you can distinguish between the vague thought and the awkward or conventional expression. Strictly, in the ideal poem, "There is always a right word, and every other than that is wrong." To Shakespeare writing his plays, his thought must have come with the authority of familiar truth, "as if it were already a proverb and not hereafter to become one."

Evidently the organic principle could be used to explain any aspect of creation: the man of genius, the intuition that flashed upon his inward eye, the shaping spirit of his imagination, the expression of his vision in an aesthetic order governing even the word. Not only order but disorder, according to A. W. Schlegel. Classical art, he said, reflects "a world submitted to a beautiful order," but romantic art responds to "the secret attraction to a chaos which lies concealed in the very bosom of the ordered universe and is perpetually striving after new and marvellous births." A paradox of romanticism was its revolt against order — though all art has form, and form is order. Yet the wish to escape restraints may explain the presence in romantic art of so much that is experimental, uneven, disproportionate, pretentious, inconsistent, fragmentary, or simply careless. We might attribute romantic disorder to the stress placed upon the values of living rather than the values of art, which made the search for beauty a quest of the poetic life rather than the patient and loving production of works of art. When they did concentrate upon an artifact, the romantics were inclined to value content more than form, despite the theory that the two are inseparable. The wonder is that they nevertheless produced so many shapes of beauty that are contemplated with pleasure today, notably, in our own literature, *Moby Dick,* which confronts the chaos of life with a powerful aesthetic control, and *The Scarlet Letter,* in which the problem of evil is treated with the tight economy and perfect harmony of mature art.

Tight economy and perfect harmony were

deliberately chosen as aesthetic goals in the conscious art of Poe. In this he was closer to the classicists than the romantics. Here was one theorist who, in contrast to Emerson and Whitman, had scant use for the organic view of art, that form grows naturally out of idea, and at times embraced a view almost mechanical. In theory and practice alike, he believed that art should be rational. Yet he was not wholly a classicist. He himself reported, in romantic terms, "My life has been *whim* — impulse — passion — a longing for solitude — a scorn of all things present in an earnest desire for the future." If that was his life, his life and his art were anything but identical. To him the natural man was the rational man: "Man's chief idiosyncracy being reason, it follows that his savage condition — his condition of action *without* reason — is his *un*natural state." Writing a poem or story is a kind of action, requiring in high degree the powers of causality, i.e., a perception of the causes needed to produce a desired effect. Imagination is "never otherwise than analytic." Originality is not "a mere matter of impulse or inspiration" but rather a matter of purposeful construction: "To originate is carefully, patiently, and understandingly to combine." In his view art is almost a mathematical logic. In many of his tales he used mathematics or discussed its nature, and he was absorbed in problems and puzzles of all sorts, from cryptography to plagiarism, some of which he presented in a new art form, the detective story.

The end of art, Poe holds, is pleasure. In order that pleasure may be intense, a work of art must have unity. As in the classical theory, he calls for unity of action or plot. Plot is like a building "so dependently constructed that to change the position of a single brick is to overthrow the entire fabric." Too often story writers seem to begin their stories without knowing how they are to end; they should begin at the end. When a work is complete, with a well defined beginning, middle, and end, it produces, for a few readers, the pleasure of "totality of beauty," though most readers will respond only to the intensity of the predetermined end. When plot is not the main interest, Poe invokes the romantic unity of tone, or atmosphere, as in "The Masque of the Red Death," — "*tone*, by means of which alone, an old subject, even when developed through hackneyed incidents, or thoughts, may be made to produce a fully original effect." As a strict unity of some sort is essential for intensity of pleasure, so, argues

Poe, is a due brevity. A particular emotional or "psychal" excitement is to be created. But all excitement is transient. In fiction it cannot be sustained for more than an hour; in poetry not even that is possible.

Beauty, for Poe, is the special province of poetry. Poetry is not a mere transcript of the concrete beauties we perceive through the senses — the waving grain, the sighing nightwind, the scent of the violet — or even such interior beauties as noble thoughts or unworldly motives. It is nothing less than an aspiration in which earthly passions are transformed, an aspiration for supernal Beauty. It is not an excitement of feeling, but an "elevating excitement of the Soul," which makes all the feelings of ordinary life seem insignificant. At every stroke of the lyre, "we catch, through long and wild vistas, dim bewildering visions of a far more ethereal beauty *beyond*."

Symbolism.

Though Poe was exceptional in displaying his thought concerning external form, we may infer that most romantic writers reflected upon technical problems far more than their published works show. For example, even if some of them had little to say about symbolism, they were generally agreed that it is an invaluable artistic method for expressing a complex and difficult kind of meaning.

Through the symbol, as they conceived, the indefinite could be suggested through a concrete representation, and the abstract thus made tangible. Instead of using familiar symbols such as the crown of monarchy and the cross of Christianity, a writer could devise fresh ones of his own choosing. Some might be made obvious to any reader; others might be left vague, stimulating the imagination to find the most fitting abstract equivalent. Symbolism is not the same as allegory. In an allegory there is a fixed and coherent system of signs, whereas a symbol can stand alone, serve a temporary purpose — a flash of illumination. It may appear once or repeatedly, and the same image may at various times represent quite different things. A good example of a symbol is the ethereal dreammaiden, in Rousseau, Novalis, Shelley, Poe, Melville.

A symbol dominates the masterpiece of Hawthorne, from title — *The Scarlet Letter* — to the very end. And as he showed in one short tale after another, his mind characteristically brooded upon or played with symbols, often with a tantalizing ambiguity. Reality, he felt, was something far too complex and uncertain to be set down in terms of reason and denotative statement. This is why Melville declared that in reading Hawthorne, "It is not the brain that can test such a man; it is only the heart."

Melville himself well exemplified his own belief that "You must have plenty of sea-room to tell the Truth in." There is plenty of sea-room in *Moby Dick*, a work that owed something to Hawthorne's deep probings, Carlyle's flashes of insight, Shakespeare's grappling with the essence of things, but mainly grew out of his own experience and speculation. Symbols irradiate the whole fable, help to bind it together. Some are used only to enlighten details of the action. The same image may symbolize quite different things in different contexts. The sea can suggest mystery, the source of life, its end, an alien element, or a friendly one. And readers interpreting with both brain and heart are by no means always agreed as to what is symbolized. Like Hawthorne, unlike most romantics, Melville was obsessed with the problem of evil in the universe. To the ship's captain with the Old Testament name of Ahab, the monstrous White Whale symbolizes "that intangible malignity which has been from the beginning; to whose dominion even the modern Christians ascribe one-half of the worlds . . . all the subtle demonisms of life and thought; all evil. . . ." Hating the inscrutable, — "be the white whale agent, or be the white whale principal," — Ahab defies the universe. "I'd strike the sun if it insulted me. . . . Who's over me?"

Poetic Style. Turning now to the question of style, in poetry and prose, we shall find relatively little on the subject in the writings of the two great innovators: Wordsworth in England and Whitman in America. Like romantic writers in general, they were more absorbed in "life values" than in "art values."

In the well-known preface to *Lyrical Ballads* the question of poetic style is mainly a matter of language and diction. As the term ballad implies, Wordsworth did not propose to abandon the long established conventions of meter and rhyme. But he attacked with vigor the neo-classic convention of a "poetic diction" apart from the diction of prose and of actual speech. He pointed out that in early times, writers, feeling powerfully, used a daring and figurative language, but that in later times (apparently the eighteenth century) they maintained this language without feeling powerfully. They used it mechanically, unconcerned about the contrast between the heightened language and their low-keyed feelings. Wordsworth gives an example from Gray:

> In vain to me the smiling mornings shine,
> And reddening Phoebus lifts his golden fire;
> The birds in vain their amorous descant join
> Or cheerful fields resume their green attire.

Such language he finds artificial and gaudy, without the urgency of genuine feeling. To restore vitality, to bring expression close to real life once more, Wordsworth proposes the experiment of employing "a selection of the real language of men in a state of vivid sensation." It is not to be the language of gentlemen or of the craft of poets, but a "plainer and more emphatic language" suited to "humble and rustic life." Incidentally, he will have scant use for the personifications (Hope, Peace, and the like, with capital letters) by means of which poets had sought an easy elevation. What he wishes to do, in short, is to write like "a man speaking to men."

By the time of Emerson and Longfellow this "blood-warm" manner of writing was common. Poetry was much closer to the currents of real life, its language more concrete, its verse freed from the stylized heroic couplet and diversified to serve many ends. Yet romanticism itself tended to form a poetic diction and style of its own, a vague and too readily flowing eloquence. We can see this style beginning in Wordsworth and Coleridge, established as a pattern by Byron and Shelley, followed in varying degrees by Bryant, Poe, Whittier, Longfellow, and Lowell. Its weaknesses are nowhere more evident than in the noble "Commemoration Ode" of Lowell in 1865. To the bold, independent mind of Walt Whitman, however, romantic verse seemed anything but an inevitable expression of modern democratic America. Rhyme for example, — "venerable and heavenly forms of chiming versification" — he regarded as fitting for the feudal order, not for the democratic.

We have already observed how Whitman felt that the genius of the United States lay "most in the common people," as he declared in his 1855 preface. The true meaning of simplicity, the "art of art," was perhaps suggested to him by the natural man, the "indescribable freshness and unconsciousness about an illiterate person." But simplicity was suggested even more, in his preface (as in the title *Leaves of Grass*), by lower orders of life: "To speak in literature with the perfect rectitude and insouciance of the movements of animals and the unimpeachableness of the sentiment of trees in the woods and grass by the roadside is the flawless triumph of art." For such simple communication he will need "new free forms" of expression: "The cleanest expression is that which finds no sphere worthy of itself and makes one." In his own poems Whitman proceeded (with hints from various sources including Biblical verse) to create a new form, which came to be called free verse, avowedly if not always actually dispensing with poetic diction, personification, rhyme, stanza, and meter. He retained only the verse line, which, on the organic principle, should tally the substance expressed. The result might be called a free-and-easy, unadorned poetry, fitly illustrated by the daguerreotype used in the first edition — Walt in workingman's clothes, nonchalant and self-sufficient, "me imperturbe." Here was a poetry intended, more truly than in Wordsworth's theory, to be the natural speech of a man speaking to men, an exalted conversational medium. Similar experiments were later to be made by Robert Frost, Carl Sandburg, T. S. Eliot.

Prose Style. The new view of life also brought a new way of writing prose. The prose desired by the Neo-classic Age had had the formal clarity and order of a Greek temple. Proper words were in proper places, and unity, proportion, and balance produced a design that appealed to the mind. In the Romantic Movement, on the other hand, prose had a more flowing contour, like that of romantic music, appealing to the senses and emotions. There is another significant contrast. Neo-classic prose was thought of as a *human* medium, essentially the same for all who wrote. (In practice, this implied writing with the easy dignity of eighteenth-century gentlemen.) But when emphasis was shifted from the samenesses of men to their differences, it was also shifted from social communication to self-expression. Style became, consciously or unconsciously, a more *personal* medium: the mirror of a man's peculiar individuality, the echo of his uniqueness, the flavor of his special sensibility.

A good American example of what style meant under romantic auspices is offered by Thoreau. Like Poe and Hawthorne, he wrote a prose blending the old virtues of rational design and the new virtues of emotional imagery and color expressed in terms of a distinct personality. Few writers give us so strong a sense of their own essence. Prominent in the author of *Walden* are his disciplined integrity, his play of mind,

his love of beauty, features of his writing that also enter into his conscious reflections on style.

Often he speaks of style in organic terms, as when he says, "It is not in man to determine what his style shall be." But this means no resting on his oars. Only by sustained effort can a man learn to write well, for "Every sentence is the result of a long probation." Mind, body, and senses, he says, must work together: "Expression is the act of a whole man." A writer needs intercourse with men and things, and especially labor with his hands, which is "the best method of removing palaver and sentimentality out of one's style." Calluses on the hands will have much to do with the writing of "tougher truth" and the firmness of his sentences. As Thoreau says finely, "A sentence should read as if its author, had he held a plow instead of a pen, could have drawn a furrow deep and straight to the end." He liked to speak with the homely reality of the farmer, being suspicious of genteel literary men and college professors, so often "weak and flimsy." With Puritan integrity and Yankee common sense he proclaims that "the one great rule of composition — and if I were a professor of rhetoric I should insist on this — is to *speak the truth.*"

Nothing is harder than perfect truth, honesty, candor, but if a writer can achieve it, "the rest will follow." Of the rest he says little, but for him, judging from his writing, it included color and warmth, surprise of the mind, a loving precision in shaping the thought, and a "concentrated and nutty" quality — his own was somewhat acrid, like an acorn. Surprise came from the use of paradox, conceits, puns, sundry kinds of wit and humor. Color and warmth came from keen senses and health, faithful observation, sensitive imagery, sympathetic response to the theme. With his reserved temperament, Thoreau generally avoided speaking directly of beauty, but it is prominent in one illuminating passage, which sums up his own notion of prose style:

In writing, conversation should be folded many times thick. It is the height of art that, on the first persual, plain common sense should appear; on the second, severe truth; and on a third, beauty; and, having these warrants for its depth and reality, we may then enjoy the beauty for evermore.

Both in life and in art, the extremes of romanticism were avoided in England and the

United States. In these countries there was little of the extravagance, the chaos, the license of German romanticism. Though the English had largely started the movement, they were restrained, as in other periods, by their common-sense aversion to extremes and their respect for tradition. In America the strongest restraint came from the old Puritan culture, its discipline still effective even when the sanctioning beliefs had evaporated, as one can readily see in men like Emerson and Hawthorne. At the same time common sense, Anglo-Saxon and Yankee, had a sobering effect on men like Emerson, Thoreau, and Lowell. Furthermore, the romantic revolt was moderate because American rationalism and neo-classicism had been moderate, and because the way to a romantic outlook had been gradually prepared by the fluid frontier of a land of opportunity, and by the democratic revolution that preceded the French Revolution by about 20 years. The heady ideas of European romanticism came to a nation of free men accustomed to belief in human dignity and habituated to self-control no less than to self-assertion.

EARLIER ROMANTICS

Washington Irving [1783–1859]

"America was ready for a man of letters," says Stanley Williams: "the lights were on; the audience assembled." The applause that Irving received was enthusiastic, both in America and in England. He was one of the most successful authors of his time in either country, delighting a large general public and at the same time winning the admiration of fellow writers like Sir Walter Scott in Britain and Poe and Hawthorne in the United States. The respect in which he was held was partly owing to the man himself, with his warm friendliness of nature, his good sense, his urbanity, his gay spirits, his integrity as an artist, his love of both the Old World and the New. Thackeray described him as "a gentleman who, though himself born in no very high sphere, was most finished, polished, easy, witty, quiet; and, socially, the equal of the most refined Europeans." England gave him an honorary degree from Oxford and the medal of the Royal Society of Literature. America made him ambassador to Spain.

Of middle class parentage, son of a Scotch father and English mother, Washington Irving was born in New York. As the story goes, his Scotch nurse presented him to General Washington (who had just driven the British from the city), saying, "Please your honor, here's a bairn was named after you." A gifted child, but delicate, he had little schooling. Later he studied in law offices, but without zeal, and he never practiced much. He was immune to his Presbyterian and commercial home environment, preferring social gatherings and the theater. At age twenty-one, threatened with tuberculosis, he traveled in England, France, and Italy. After two years abroad he resumed his pleasant way of life in New York, and presently wrote, with others, a series of *Salmagundi* papers on the social life of the city, in the manner of the English *Spectator* and from a conservative point of view that he never abandoned. In 1809 he suffered a tragic experience in the death of his fiancée. (He remained unmarried all his life.) But he pressed on, in the same year, to the publication of his highly successful *Knickerbocker's History of New York,* a burlesque narrative that gave the city — barring a few old Dutch families — a good laugh.

In 1815, in the prime of life, he went to England on business, quite unaware that he was to remain abroad for seventeen years and return in middle age. Within three years his brothers' hardware firm, of which he had become a member, fell into bankruptcy, and Irving was spurred into adopting literature as a profession, in his case a lucrative one. *The Sketch Book,* which contains some of his finest work, first appeared in installments in the United States, and was republished in England in book form. It was soon followed by *Bracebridge Hall* and *Tales of a Traveller.* After visiting Spain, he wrote *The Alhambra,* which came out in 1832, the year of his return to America after his long immersion in the Old World. He had now given his country what it dearly wanted, a writer highly respected in Europe.

He returned to America at the top of his powers, yet apparently written out. The first major American writer was also the first of many who, for one reason or another, ended their significant contributions early. There is little vitality in Irving's writings of his last quarter century — they reflect a shift to history and biography, which had social prestige — such as his several frontier narratives or his biographies of Oliver Goldsmith and George Washington, the latter in five volumes. In this final period he went abroad once more, as Minister to Spain. After holding the post for three years he settled down for the remainder of his life at Sunnyside, his country estate near Tarrytown on the Hudson.

Further reading: *The Sketch Book; The Alhambra. Washington Irving* (American Writers Series), ed. H. A. Pochmann, 1934. Stanley Williams, *The Life of Washington Irving,* 2 vols., 1935.

From *Knickerbocker's History of New York*

(1809)

Diedrich Knickerbocker was Irving's pen name for his comic history. Many years later he summarized his purpose: "The main object of my work . . . was to embody the traditions of the city in an amusing form; to illustrate its local humors, customs, and peculiarities; to clothe home scenes and places and familiar names with those imaginative and whimsical associations so seldom met with in our new country, but which live like charms and spells about the cities of the old world, binding the heart of the native inhabitant to his home. . . ."

In this work Irving is not without kinship with the romantic writers of Europe. Like them, he loves to travel in the obscure past, especially the local past, with its "peculiar and racy customs." In this respect he may be compared, for example, with his friend Sir Walter Scott. At the same time he is plainly related with the English humorists of the eighteenth century

— as Scott, among others, recognized, when he said he had "never read anything so closely resembling the style of Dean Swift. . . . I think, too, there are passages which indicate that the author possesses powers of a different kind, and has some touches which remind me of Sterne." He combines the eighteenth-century tenderness of sympathy with the eighteenth-century bent for satire.

Irving's satire is directed against pedantic historians, the heroic poem, and persons and events during the Dutch period and in his own time as well. William the Testy is a caricature of Jefferson (especially his foreign policy) from a Federalist point of view. To readers familiar with great authors, the method of parody offers amusing reminders of Homer, Malory, Cervantes, Fielding, Swift, and various others.

A youthful masterpiece — Irving was only twenty-six when it was published — the book is remarkable for its spontaneous high spirits, good-natured irreverence, and vitality of imagination. Its perennial appeal, says W. F. Taylor, "lies in something more than a clever intermingling of burlesque, mock-heroics, caricature, and satire. Primarily it can be traced to the imagination of the master artist, which creates, out of the meager outlines of early colonial history, a romantic world of legend, grotesquely humorous, it is true, but full of warm, breathing life. In his attempts to embody the traditions of his city in an amusing form, Irving met with a success which must have astonished even himself. Within forty years after the *History* was published, Knickerbocker insurance companies, Knickerbocker steamboats, omnibuses, bakeries, ice factories, and magazines were all profiting by the fame of an old Dutch historian who had never lived at all, except in the imagination of Washington Irving. The Knickerbocker legend had become part of the national heritage."

The Golden Reign of Wouter Van Twiller

CHAPTER I

Of the Renowned Wouter Van Twiller, His Unparalleled Virtues — as Likewise His Unutterable Wisdom in the Law-Case of Wandle Schoonhoven and Barent Bleecker — and the Great Admiration of the Public Thereat

Grievous and very much to be commiserated is the task of the feeling historian, who writes the history of his native land. If it fall to his lot to be the recorder of calamity or crime, the mournful page is watered with his tears; nor can he recall the most prosperous and blissful era, without a melancholy sigh at the reflection that it has passed away forever! I know not whether it be owing to an immoderate love for the simplicity of former times, or to that certain tenderness of heart incident to all sentimental historians; but I candidly confess that I cannot look back on the happier days of our city, which I now describe, without great dejection of spirit. With faltering hand do I withdraw the curtain of oblivion, that veils the modest merit of our venerable ancestors, and as their figures rise to my mental vision, humble myself before their mighty shades.

Such are my feelings when I revisit the family mansion of the Knickerbockers, and spend a lonely hour in the chamber where hang the portraits of my forefathers, shrouded in dust, like the forms they represent. With pious reverence do I gaze on the countenances of those renowned burghers, who have preceded me in the steady march of existence, — whose sober and temperate blood now meanders through my veins, flowing slower and slower in

its feeble conduits, until its current shall soon be stopped forever!

These, I say to myself, are but frail memorials of the mighty men who flourished in the days of the patriarchs; but who, alas, have long since mouldered in that tomb towards which my steps are insensibly and irresistibly hastening! As I pace the darkened chamber and lose myself in melancholy musings, the shadowy images around me almost seem to steal once more into existence, — their countenances to assume the animation of life, — their eyes to pursue me in every movement! Carried away by the delusions of fancy, I almost imagine myself surrounded by the shades of the departed, and holding sweet converse with the worthies of antiquity! Ah, hapless Diedrich! born in a degenerate age, abandoned to the buffetings of fortune, — a stranger and a weary pilgrim in thy native land, — blest with no weeping wife, nor family of helpless children, but doomed to wander neglected through those crowded streets, and elbowed by foreign upstarts from those fair abodes where once thine ancestors held sovereign empire!

Let me not, however, lose the historian in the man, nor suffer the doting recollections of age to overcome me, while dwelling with fond garrulity on the virtuous days of the patriarchs, — on those sweet days of simplicity and ease, which never more will dawn on the lovely island of Manna-hata.

These melancholy reflections have been forced from me by the growing wealth and importance of New Amsterdam, which, I plainly perceive, are to involve it in all kinds of perils and disasters. Already, as I observed at the close of my last book, they had awakened the attentions of the mother-country. The usual mark of protection shown by mother-countries to wealthy colonies was forthwith manifested; a governor being sent out to rule over the province, and squeeze out of it as much revenue as possible. The arrival of a governor of course put an end to the protectorate of Oloffe the Dreamer. He appears, however, to have dreamt to some purpose during his sway, as we find him afterwards living as a patroon on a great landed estate on the banks of the Hudson; having virtually forfeited all right to his ancient appellation of Kortlandt or Lackland.

It was in the year of our Lord 1629 that Mynheer Wouter Van Twiller was appointed governor of the province of Nieuw Nederlandts, under the commission and control of their High Mightinesses the Lords States General of the United Netherlands, and the privileged West India Company.

This renowned old gentleman arrived at New Amsterdam in the merry month of June, the sweetest month in all the year; when dan Apollo seems to dance up the transparent firmament, — when the robin, the thrush, and a thousand other wanton songsters, make the woods to resound with amorous ditties, and the luxurious little boblincon revels among the clover-blossoms of the meadows, — all which happy coincidence persuaded the old dames of New Amsterdam who were skilled in the art of foretelling events, that this was to be a happy and prosperous administration.

The renowned Wouter (or Walter) Van Twiller was descended from a long line of Dutch burgomasters, who had successively dozed away their lives, and grown fat upon the bench of magistracy in Rotterdam; and who had comported themselves with such singular wisdom and proprietry, that they were never either heard or talked of — which, next to being universally applauded, should be the object of ambition of all magistrates and rulers. There are two opposite ways by which some men make a figure in the world: one, by talking faster than they think, and the other, by holding their tongues and not thinking at all. By the first, many a smatterer acquires the reputation of a man of quick parts; by the other, many a dunderpate, like the owl, the stupidest of birds, comes to be considered the very type of wisdom. This, by the way, is a casual remark, which I would not, for the universe, have it thought I apply to Governor Van Twiller. It is true he was a man shut up within himself, like an oyster, and rarely spoke except in monosyllables; but then it was allowed he seldom said a foolish thing. So invincible was his gravity that he was never known to laugh or even to smile through the whole course of a long and prosperous life. Nay, if a joke were uttered in his presence, that set light-minded hearers in a roar, it was observed to throw him into a state of perplexity. Sometimes he would deign to inquire into the matter, and when, after much explanation, the joke was made as plain as a pike-staff, he would continue to smoke his pipe in silence, and at length, knocking out the ashes, would exclaim, "Well! I see nothing in all that to laugh about."

With all his reflective habits, he never made up his mind on a subject. His adherents accounted for this by the astonishing magnitude of his ideas. He conceived every subject on so grand a scale that he had not room in his head to turn it over and examine both sides of it. Certain it is, that, if any matter were propounded to him on which ordinary mortals would rashly determine at first glance, he would put on a vague, mysterious look, shake his capacious head, smoke some time in profound silence, and at length observe, that "he had his doubts about the matter"; which gained him the reputation of a man slow of belief and not easily imposed upon. What is more, it gained him a lasting name; for to this habit of the mind has been attributed his surname of Twiller; which is said to be a corruption of the original Twijfler, or, in plain English, *Doubter*.

The person of this illustrious old gentleman was formed and proportioned, as though it had been moulded by the hands of some cunning Dutch statuary, as a model of majesty and lordly grandeur. He was exactly five feet six inches in height, and six feet five inches in circumference. His head was a perfect sphere, and of such stupendous dimensions, that dame Nature, with all her sex's ingenuity, would have been puzzled to construct a neck capable of supporting it; wherefore she wisely declined the attempt, and settled it firmly on the top of his backbone, just between the shoulders. His body was oblong and particularly capacious at bottom; which was wisely ordered by Providence, seeing that he was a man of sedentary habits, and very averse to the idle labor of walking. His legs were short, but sturdy in proportion to the weight they had to sustain; so that when erect he had not a little the appearance of a beer-barrel on skids. His face, that infallible index of the mind, presented a vast expanse, unfurrowed by any of those lines and angles which disfigure the human countenance with what is termed expression. Two small gray eyes twinkled feebly in the midst, like two stars of lesser magnitude in a hazy firmament, and his full-fed cheeks, which seemed to have taken toll of everything that went into his mouth, were curiously mottled and streaked with dusky red, like a spitzenberg apple.

His habits were as regular as his person. He daily took his four stated meals, appropriating exactly an hour to each; he smoked and doubted eight hours, and he slept the remaining twelve of the four-and-twenty. Such was the renowned Wouter Van Twiller, — a true philosopher, for his mind was either elevated above, or tranquilly settled below, the cares and perplexities of this world. He had lived in it for years, without feeling the least curiosity to know whether the sun revolved round it, or it round the sun; and he had watched, for at least half a century, the smoke curling from his pipe to the ceiling, without once troubling his head with any of those numerous theories by which a philosopher would have perplexed his brain, in accounting for its rising above the surrounding atmosphere.

In his council he presided with great state and solemnity. He sat in a huge chair of solid oak, hewn in the celebrated forest of the Hague, fabricated by an experienced timmerman of Amsterdam, and curiously carved about the arms and feet, into exact imitations of gigantic eagle's claws. Instead of a sceptre, he swayed a long Turkish pipe, wrought with jasmin and amber, which had been presented to a stadt-holder of Holland at the conclusion of a treaty with one of the petty Barbary powers. In this stately chair would he sit, and this magnificent pipe would he smoke, shaking his right knee with a constant motion, and fixing his eye for hours together upon a little print of Amster-dam, which hung in a black frame against the opposite wall of the council-chamber. Nay, it has even been said, that when any deliberation of extraordinary length and intricacy was on the carpet, the renowned Wouter would shut his eyes for full two hours at a time, that he might not be disturbed by external objects; and at such times the internal commotion of his mind was evinced by certain regular guttural sounds, which his admirers declared were merely the noise of conflict, made by his contending doubts and opinions.

It is with infinite difficulty I have been en-abled to collect these biographical anecdotes of the great man under consideration. The facts respecting him were so scattered and vague, and divers of them so questionable in point of authenticity, that I have had to give up the search after many, and decline the admission of still more, which would have tended to heighten the coloring of his portrait.

I have been the more anxious to delineate fully the person and habits of Wouter Van Twiller, from the consideration that he was not only the first, but also the best governor that ever presided over this ancient and respectable province, and so tranquil and benevolent was his reign, that I do not find throughout the whole of it a single instance of any offender being brought to punishment, — a most induti-able sign of a merciful governor, and a case unparalleled, excepting in the reign of the illus-trious King Log, from whom, it is hinted, the renowned Van Twiller was a lineal descendant.

The very outset of the career of this excellent magistrate was distinguished by an example of legal acumen, that gave flattering presage of a wise and equitable administration. The morn-ing after he had been installed in office, and at the moment that he was making his breakfast from a prodigious earthen dish, filled with milk and Indian pudding, he was interrupted by the appearance of Wandle Schoonhoven, a very important old burgher of New Amsterdam, who complained bitterly of one Barent Bleecker, inasmuch as he refused to come to a settlement of accounts, seeing that there was a heavy balance in favor of the said Wandle. Governor Van Twiller, as I have already observed, was a man of few words; he was likewise a mortal enemy to multiplying writings — or being dis-turbed at his breakfast. Having listened atten-tively to the statement of Wandle Schoonhoven, giving an occasional grunt, as he shovelled a spoonful of Indian pudding into his mouth, — either as a sign that he relished the dish, or comprehended the story, — he called unto him his constable, and pulling out of his breeches-pocket a huge jack-knife, dispatched it after the defendant as a summons, accompanied by his tobacco-box as a warrant.

This summary process was as effectual in those simple days as was the seal-ring of the great Haroun Alraschild among the true be-lievers. The two parties being confronted before him, each produced a book of accounts, written in a language and character that would have puzzled any but a High-Dutch commentator, or a learned decipherer of Egyptian obelisks. The sage Wouter took them one after the other, and having poised them in his hands, and attentively counted over the number of leaves, fell straightway into a very great doubt, and smoked for half an hour without saying a word; at length, laying his finger beside his nose, and shutting his eyes for a moment, with the air of a man who has just caught a subtle idea by the tail, he slowly took his pipe from his mouth, puffed forth a column of tobacco-smoke, and with marvellous gravity and solemnity pronounced, that, having carefully counted over the leaves and weighed the books, it was found, that one was just as thick and as heavy as the other: therefore, it was the final opinion of the court, that the accounts were equally balanced: therefore, Wandle should give Barent a receipt, and Barent should give Wandle a receipt, and the constable should pay the costs.

This decision, being straightway made known, diffused general joy throughout New Amsterdam, for the people immediately perceived that they had a very wise and equitable magistrate to rule over them. But its happiest effect was, that not another lawsuit took place throughout the whole of his administration; and the office of constable fell into such decay, that there was not one of those losel scouts known in the province for many years. I am the more particular in dwelling on this transaction, not only because I deem it one of the most sage and righteous judgments on record, and well worthy the attention of modern magistrates, but because it was a miraculous event in the history of the renowned Wouter — being the only time he was ever known to come to a decision in the whole course of his life.

CHAPTER II

Containing Some Account of the Grand Council of New Amsterdam, as also Divers Especial Good Philosophical Reasons Why an Alderman Should Be Fat — with Other Particulars Touching the State of the Province

In treating of the early governors of the province, I must caution my readers against confounding them, in point of dignity and power, with those worthy gentlemen who are whimsically denominated governors in this enlightened republic, — a set of unhappy victims of popularity, who are, in fact, the most dependent, hen-pecked beings in the community; doomed to bear the secret goadings and corrections of their own party, and the sneers and revilings of the whole world beside; set up, like geese at Christmas holidays, to be pelted and shot at by every whipster and vagabond in the land. On the contrary, the Dutch governors enjoyed that uncontrolled authority vested in all commanders of distant colonies or territories. They were, in a manner, absolute despots in their little domains, lording it, if so disposed, over both law and gospel, and accountable to

none but the mother-country; which it is well known is astonishingly deaf to all complaints against its governors, provided they discharge the main duty of their station — squeezing out a good revenue. This hint will be of importance, to prevent my readers from being seized with doubt and incredulity, whenever, in the course of this authentic history, they encounter the uncommon circumstance of a governor acting with independence, and in opposition to the opinions of the multitude.

To assist the doubtful Wouter in the arduous business of legislation, a board of magistrates was appointed, which presided immediately over the police. This potent body consisted of a schout or bailiff, with powers between those of the present mayor and sheriff; five burgermeesters, who were equivalent to aldermen; and five schepens, who officiated as scrubs, subdevils, or bottleholders to the burgermeesters, in the same manner as do assistant aldermen to their principals at the present day, — it being their duty to fill the pipes of the lordly burgermeesters, hunt the markets for delicacies for corporation dinners, and to discharge such other little offices of kindness as were occasionally required. It was, moreover, tacitly understood, though not specifically enjoined, that they should consider themselves as butts for the blunt wits of the burgermeesters, and should laugh most heartily at all their jokes; but this last was a duty as rarely called in action in those days as it is at present, and was shortly remitted, in consequence of the tragical death of a fat little schepen, who actually died of suffocation in an unsuccessful effort to force a laugh at one of burgermeester Van Zandt's best jokes.

In return for these humble services, they were permitted to say *yes* and *no* at the councilboard, and to have that enviable privilege, the run of the public kitchen, — being graciously permitted to eat, and drink, and smoke, at all those snug junketings and public gormandizings for which the ancient magistrates were equally famous with their modern successors. The post of schepen, therefore, like that of assistant alderman, was eagerly coveted by all your burghers of a certain description, who have a huge relish for good feeling, and an humble ambition to be great men in a small way, — who thirst after a little brief authority, that shall render them the terror of the alms-house and the bridewell, — that shall enable them to lord it over obsequious poverty, vagrant vice, outcast prostitution, and hunger-driven dishonesty, — that shall give to their beck a houndlike pack of catchpolls and bumbailiffs — tenfold greater rogues than the culprits they hunt down! My readers will excuse this sudden warmth, which I confess is unbecoming of a grave historian, — but I have a mortal antipathy to catchpolls, bumbailiffs, and little-great men.

The ancient magistrates of this city correspond with those of the present time no less in form, magnitude, and intellect, than in prerogative and privilege. The burgomasters, like our aldermen, were generally chosen by weight, — and not only the weight of the body, but likewise the weight of the head. It is a maxim practically observed in all honest, plain-thinking, regular cities, that an alderman should be fat, — and the wisdom of this can be proved to a certainty. That the body is in some measure an image of the mind, or rather that the mind is moulded to the body, like melted lead to the clay in which it is cast, has been insisted on by many philosophers, who have made human nature their peculiar study; for, as a learned gentleman of our own city observes, "there is a constant relation between the moral character of all intelligent creatures and their physical constitution, between their habits and the structure of their bodies." Thus we see that a lean, spare, diminutive body is generally accompanied by a petulant, restless, meddling mind: either the mind wears down the body, by its continual motion, or else the body, not affording the mind sufficient house-room, keeps it continually in a state of fretfulness, tossing and worrying about from the uneasiness of its situation. Whereas your round, sleek, fat, unwieldy periphery is ever attended by a mind like itself, tranquil, torpid, and at ease; and we may always observe, that your well-fed, robustious burghers are in general very tenacious of their ease and comfort, being great enemies to noise, discord, and disturbance, — and surely none are more likely to study the public tranquillity than those who are so careful of their own. Who ever hears of fat men heading a riot, or herding together in turbulent mobs? — no — no. It is your lean, hungry men who are continually worrying society, and setting the whole community by the ears.

The divine Plato, whose doctrines are not sufficiently attended to by philosophers of the present age, allows to every man three souls: one, immortal and rational, seated in the brain, that it may overlook and regulate the body; a second,

consisting of the surly and irascible passions, which, like belligerent powers, lie encamped around the heart; a third, mortal and sensual, destitute of reason, gross and brutal in its propensities, and enchained in the belly, that it may not disturb the divine soul by its ravenous howlings. Now, according to this excellent theory, what can be more clear than that your fat alderman is most likely to have the most regular and well-conditioned mind. His head is like a huge spherical chamber, containing a prodigious mass of soft brains, whereon the rational soul lies softly and snugly couched, as on a feather-bed; and the eyes, which are the windows of the bed-chamber, are usually half closed, that its slumberings may not be disturbed by external objects. A mind thus comfortably lodged, and protected from disturbance, is manifestly most likely to perform its functions with regularity and ease. By dint of good feeding, moreover, the mortal and malignant soul, which is confined in the belly, and which, by its raging and roaring, puts the irritable soul in the neighborhood of the heart in an intolerable passion and thus renders men crusty and quarrelsome when hungry, is completely pacified, silenced, and put to rest, — whereupon a host of honest, good-fellow qualities and kind-hearted affections, which had lain perdue, slyly peeping out of the loop-holes of the heart, finding this Cerberus asleep, do pluck up their spirits, turn out one and all in their holiday suits, and gambol up and down the diaphragm, — disposing their possessor to laughter, good-humor, and a thousand friendly offices towards his fellow-mortals.

As a board of magistrates, formed on this principle, think but very little, they are the less likely to differ and wrangle about favorite opinions; and as they generally transact business upon a hearty dinner, they are naturally disposed to be lenient and indulgent in the administration of their duties. Charlemagne was conscious of this, and therefore ordered in his cartularies, that no judge should hold a court of justice, except in the morning, on an empty stomach. — A pitiful rule, which I can never forgive, and which I warrant bore hard upon all the poor culprits in the kingdom. The more enlightened and humane generation of the present day have taken an opposite course, and have so managed that the aldermen are the best-fed men in the community; feasting lustily on the fat things of the land, and gorging so heartily on oysters and turtles, that in process of time they acquire the activity of the one, and the form, the waddle, and the green fat of the other. The consequence is, as I have just said, these luxurious feastings do produce such a dulcet equanimity and repose of the soul, rational and irrational, that their transactions are proverbial for unvarying monotony; and the profound laws which they enact in their dozing moments, amid the labors of digestion, are quietly suffered to remain as dead letters, and never enforced, when awake. In a word, your fair, round-bellied burgomaster, like a full-fed mastiff, dozes quietly at the house-door, always at home, and always at hand to watch over its safety; but as to electing a lean, meddling candidate to the office, as has now and then been done, I would as lief put a greyhound to watch the house, or a race-horse to draw an ox-wagon.

The burgomasters, then, as I have already mentioned, were wisely chosen by weight, and the schepens, or assistant aldermen, were appointed to attend upon them and help them eat; but the latter, in the course of time, when they had been fed and fattened into sufficient bulk of body and drowsiness of brain, became very eligible candidates for the burgomasters' chairs, having fairly eaten themselves into office, as a mouse eats his way into a comfortable lodgment in a goodly, blue-nosed, skimmed-milk, New-England cheese.

Nothing could equal the profound deliberations that took place between the renowned Wouter and these his worthy compeers, unless it be the sage divans of some of our modern corporations. They would sit for hours, smoking and dozing over public affairs, without speaking a word to interrupt that perfect stillness so necessary to deep reflection. Under the sober sway of Wouter Van Twiller and these his worthy coadjutors, the infant settlement waxed vigorous apace, gradually emerging from the swamps and forests, and exhibiting that mingled appearance of town and country, customary in new cities, and which at this day may be witnessed in the city of Washington, — that immense metropolis, which makes so glorious an appearance on paper.

It was a pleasing sight, in those times, to behold the honest burgher, like a patriarch of yore, seated on the bench at the door of his white-washed house, under the shade of some gigantic sycamore or overhanging willow. Here would he smoke his pipe of a sultry afternoon, enjoying the soft southern breeze, and listening with silent gratulation to the clucking of his hens, the cackling of his geese, and the sonorous grunting of his swine, — that combination of farm-yard melody which may truly be said to have a silver sound, inasmuch as it conveys a certain assurance of profitable marketing.

The modern spectator, who wanders through the streets of this populous city, can scarcely form an idea of the different appearance they presented in the primitive days of the Doubter. The busy hum of multitudes, the shouts of revelry, the rumbling equipages of fashion, the rattling of accursed carts, and all the spirit-grieving sounds of brawling commerce, were unknown in the settlement of New Amsterdam. The grass grew quietly in the highways; the bleating sheep and frolicsome calves sported about the verdant ridge, where now the Broadway loungers take their morning stroll; the cunning fox or ravenous wolf skulked in the woods, where now are to be seen the dens of Gomez and his righteous fraternity of money-brokers; and flocks of vociferous geese cackled about the fields where now the great Tammany wigwam and the patriotic tavern of Martling echo with the wranglings of the mob.

In these good times did a true and enviable equality of rank and property prevail, equally removed from the arrogance of wealth, and the servility and heart-burnings of repining poverty; and, what in my mind is still more conducive to tranquillity and harmony among friends, a happy equality of intellect was likewise to be seen. The minds of the good burghers of New Amsterdam seemed all to have been cast in one mould, and to be those honest, blunt minds, which, like certain manufacturers, are made by the gross, and considered as exceedingly good for common use.

Thus it happens that your true dull minds are generally preferred for public employ, and especially promoted to city honors; your keen intellects, like razors, being considered too sharp for common service. I know that it is common to rail at the unequal distribution of riches, as the great source of jealousies, broils, and heart-breakings; whereas, for my part, I verily believe it is the sad inequality of intellect that prevails, that embroils communities more than anything else; and I have remarked that your knowing people, who are so much wiser than anybody else, are eternally keeping society in a ferment. Happily for New Amsterdam, nothing of the kind was known within its walls; the very words of learning, education, taste, and talents were unheard of; a bright genius was an animal unknown, and a blue-stocking lady would have been regarded with as much wonder as a horned frog or a fiery dragon. No man, in fact, seemed to know more than his neighbor, nor any man to know more than an honest man ought to know, who has nobody's business to mind but his own; the parson and the council clerk were the only men that could read in the community, and the sage Van Twiller always signed his name with a cross.

Thrice happy and ever to be envied little Burgh! existing in all the security of harmless insignificance, — unnoticed and unenvied by the world, without ambition, without vain-glory, without riches, without learning, and all their train of carking cares; — and as of yore, in the better days of man, the deities were wont to visit him on earth and bless his rural habitations, so, we are told, in the sylvan days of New Amsterdam, the good St. Nicholas would often make his appearance in his beloved city, of a holiday afternoon, riding jollily among the tree-tops, or over the roofs of the houses, now and then drawing forth magnificent presents from his breeches-pockets, and dropping them down the chimneys of his favorites. Whereas, in these degenerate days of iron and brass, he never shows us the light of his countenance, nor ever visits us, save one night in the year, when he rattles down the chimneys of the descendants of patriarchs, confining his presents merely to the children, in token of the degeneracy of the parents.

Such are the comfortable and thriving effects of a fat government. The province of the New Netherlands, destitute of wealth, possessed a sweet tranquillity that wealth could never purchase. There were neither public commotions, nor private quarrels; neither parties, nor sects, nor schisms; neither persecutions, nor trials, nor punishments; nor were there counsellors, attorneys, catchpolls, or hangmen. Every man attended to what little business he was lucky enough to have, or neglected it if he pleased, without asking the opinion of his neighbor. In those days nobody meddled with concerns above his comprehension; nor thrust his nose into other people's affairs; nor neglected to correct his own conduct, and reform his own character, in his zeal to pull to pieces the characters of others; — but, in a word, every respectable citizen ate when he was not hungry, drank when he was not thirsty, and went regularly to bed when the sun set and the fowls went to roost, whether he was sleepy or not; all which tended so remarkably to the population of the settlement, that I am told every dutiful wife throughout New Amsterdam made a point of enriching her husband with at least one child a year, and very often a brace, — this superabundance of good things clearly constituting the true luxury of life, according to the favorite Dutch maxim, that "more than enough constitutes a feast." Everything, therefore, went on exactly as it should do, and in the usual words employed by historians to express the welfare of a country, "the profoundest *tranquillity* and *repose* reigned throughout the province."

Chapter III

How the Town of New Amsterdam Arose out of Mud, and Came to Be Marvellously Polished and Polite — Together with a Picture of the Manners of Our Great-Great-Grandfathers

Manifold are the tastes and dispositions of the enlightened *literati*, who turn over the pages of history. Some there be whose hearts are brimful of the yeast of courage, and whose bosoms do work, and swell, and foam, with untried valor, like a barrel of new cider, or a train-band captain, fresh from under the hands of his tailor. This doughty class of readers can be satisfied with nothing but bloody battles, and horrible encounters; they must be continually storming forts, sacking cities, springing mines, marching up to the muzzles of cannon, charging bayonet through every page, and revelling in gun-powder and carnage. Others, who are of a less martial, but equally ardent imagination, and who, withal, are a little given to the marvellous, will dwell with wondrous satisfaction on descriptions of prodigies, unheard-of events, hair-breadth escapes, hardy adventures, and all those astonishing narrations which just amble along the boundary-line of possibility. A third class, who, not to speak slightly of them, are of a lighter turn, and skim over the records of past times, as they do over the edifying pages of a novel, merely for relaxation and innocent amusement, do singularly delight in treasons, executions, Sabine rapes, Tarquin outrages, conflagrations, murders, and all the other catalogue of hideous crimes, which, like cayenne in cookery, do give a pungency and flavor to the dull detail of history. While a fourth class, of more philosophic habits, do diligently pore over the musty chronicles of time, to investigate the operations of the human kind, and watch the gradual changes in men and manners, effected by the progress of knowledge, the vicissitudes of events, or the influence of situation.

If the three first classes find but little wherewithal to solace themselves in the tranquil reign of Wouter Van Twiller, I entreat them to exert their patience for a while, and bear with the tedious picture of happiness, prosperity, and peace, which my duty as a faithful historian obliges me to draw; and I promise them, that, as soon as I can possibly alight on anything horrible, uncommon, or impossible, it shall go hard, but I will make it afford them entertainment. This being premised, I turn with great complacency to the fourth class of my readers, who are men, or, if possible, women after my own heart; grave, philosophical, and investigating; fond of analyzing characters, of taking a start from first causes, and so hunting a nation down, through all the mazes of innovation and improvement. Such will naturally be anxious to witness the first development of the newly-hatched colony, and the primitive manners and customs prevalent among its inhabitants, during the halcyon reign of Van Twiller, or the Doubter.

I will not grieve their patience, however, by describing minutely the increase and improvement of New Amsterdam. Their own imaginations will doubtless present to them the good burghers, like so many painstaking and persevering beavers, slowly and surely pursuing their labors: they will behold the prosperous transformation from the rude log hut to the stately Dutch mansion, with brick front, glazed windows, and tiled roof; from the tangled thicket to the luxuriant cabbage-garden; and from the skulking Indian to the ponderous burgomaster. In a word, they will picture to themselves the steady, silent and undeviating march of prosperity incident to a city destitute of pride or ambition, cherished by a fat government, and whose citizens do nothing in a hurry.

The sage council, as has been mentioned in a preceding chapter, not being able to determine upon any plan for the building of their city, — the cows, in a laudable fit of patriotism, took it under their peculiar charge, and, as they went to and from pasture, established paths through the bushes, on each side of which the good folks built their houses, — which is one cause of the rambling and picturesque turns and labyrinths which distinguish certain streets of New York at this very day.

The houses of the higher class were generally constructed of wood, excepting the gable end which was of small, black and yellow Dutch bricks, and always faced on the street, as our ancestors, like their descendants, were very much given to outward show, and were noted for putting the best leg foremost. The house was always furnished with abundance of large doors and small windows on every floor, the date of its erection was curiously designated by iron figures on the front, and on the top of the roof was perched a fierce little weathercock, to let the family into the important secret which way the wind blew.

These, like the weathercocks on the tops of our steeples, pointed so many different ways, that every man could have a wind to his mind; — the most stanch and loyal citizens, however, always went according to the weathercock on the top of the governor's house, which was certainly the most correct, as he had a trusty servant employed every morning to climb up and set it to the right quarter.

In those good days of simplicity and sunshine, a passion for cleanliness was the leading principle in domestic economy, and the universal test of an able housewife, — a character which formed the utmost ambition of our unenlightened grandmothers. The front-door was never opened, except on marriages, funerals, New-Year's days, the festival of St. Nicholas, or some such great occasion. It was ornamented with a gorgeous brass knocker, curiously wrought, sometimes in the device of a dog, and sometimes of a lion's head, and was daily burnished with such religious zeal, that it was ofttimes worn out by the very precautions taken for its preservation. The whole house was constantly in a state of inundation, under the discipline of mops and brooms and scrubbing-brushes; and the good housewives of those days were a kind of amphibious animal, delighting exceedingly to be dabbling in water, — insomuch that an historian of the day gravely tells us, that many of his townswomen grew to have webbed fingers like unto a duck; and some of them, he had little doubt, could the matter be examined into, would be found to have the tails of mermaids, — but this I look upon to be a mere sport of fancy, or, what is worse, a wilful misrepresentation.

The grand parlor was the sanctum sanctorum, where the passion for cleaning was indulged without control. In this sacred apartment no one was permitted to enter, excepting the mistress and her confidential maid, who visited it once a week, for the purpose of giving it a thorough cleaning, and putting things to rights, — always taking the precaution of leaving their shoes at the door, and entering devoutly on their stocking-feet. After scrubbing the floor, sprinkling it with fine white sand, which was curiously stroked into angles and curves and rhomboids with a broom, — after washing the windows, rubbing and polishing the furniture, and putting a new bunch of evergreens in the fireplace, — the window-shutters were again closed to keep out the flies, and the room carefully locked up until the revolution of time brought round the weekly cleaning-day.

As to the family, they always entered in at the gate, and most generally lived in the kitchen. To have seen a numerous household assembled round the fire, one would have imagined that he was transported back to those happy days of primeval simplicity, which float before our imaginations like golden visions. The fireplaces were of a truly patriarchal magnitude, where the whole family, old and young, master and servant, black and white, nay, even the very cat and dog, enjoyed a community of privilege, and had each a right to a corner. Here the old burgher would sit in perfect silence, puffing his pipe, looking in the fire with half-shut eyes, and thinking of nothing for hours together; the goede vrouw, on the opposite side, would employ herself diligently in spinning yarn, or knitting stockings. The young folks would crowd around the hearth, listening with breathless attention to some old crone of a negro, who was the oracle of the family, and who, perched like a raven in a corner of the chimney, would croak forth for a long winter afternoon a string of incredible stories about New-England witches, — grisly ghosts, horses without heads, — and hairbreadth escapes, and bloody encounters among the Indians.

In those happy days a well-regulated family always rose with the dawn, dined at eleven, and went to bed at sunset. Dinner was invariably a private meal, and the fat old burghers showed incontestable signs of disapprobation and uneasiness at being surprised by a visit from a neighbor on such occasions. But though our worthy ancestors were thus singularly averse to giving dinners, yet they kept up the social bands of intimacy by occasional banquetings, called tea-parties.

These fashionable parties were generally confined to the higher classes, or noblesse, that is to say, such as kept their own cows, and drove their own wagons. The company commonly assembled at three o'clock, and went away about six, unless it was in winter-time, when the fashionable hours were a little earlier, that the ladies might get home before dark. The tea-table was crowned with a huge earthen dish, well stored with slices of fat pork, fried brown, cut up into morsels, and swimming in gravy. The company being seated round the genial board, and each furnished with a fork, evinced their dexterity in launching at the fattest pieces in this mighty dish, — in much the same manner as sailors harpoon porpoises at sea, or our Indians spear salmon in the lakes. Sometimes the table was graced with immense apple-pies, or saucers full of preserved peaches and pears; but it was always sure to boast an enormous dish of balls of sweetened dough, fried in hog's fat, and called doughnuts, or olykoeks, — a delicious kind of cake, at present scarce known in this city, except in genuine Dutch families.

The tea was served out of a majestic Delft tea-pot, ornamented with paintings of fat little Dutch shepherds and shepherdesses tending pigs with boats sailing in the air, and houses built in the clouds, and sundry other ingenious Dutch fantasies. The beaux distinguished themselves by their adroitness in replenishing this pot from a huge copper tea-kettle, which would have made the pigmy macaronies of these degenerate days sweat merely to look at it. To sweeten the beverage, a lump of sugar was laid beside each cup, and the company alternately nibbled and sipped with great decorum, until an improvement was introduced by a shrewd and economic old lady, which was to suspend a large lump directly over the tea-table, by a string from the ceiling, so that it could be swung from mouth to mouth, — an ingenious expedient, which is still kept up by some families in Albany, but which prevails without exception in Communipaw, Bergen, Flatbush, and all our uncontaminated Dutch villages.

At these primitive tea-parties the utmost propriety and dignity of deportment prevailed. No flirting nor coquetting, — no gambling of old ladies, nor hoyden chattering and romping of young ones, — no self-satisfied struttings of wealthy gentlemen, with their brains in their pockets, nor amusing conceits and monkey divertisements of smart young gentlemen, with no brains at all. On the contrary, the young ladies seated themselves demurely in their rush-bottomed chairs, and knit their own woollen stockings; nor ever opened their lips excepting to say *yah, Mynheer,* or, *yah, yah, Vrouw,* to any question that was asked them; behaving in all things like decent, well-educated damsels. As to the gentlemen, each of them tranquilly smoked his pipe, and seemed lost in contemplation of the blue and white tiles with which the fireplaces were decorated; wherein sundry passages of Scripture were piously portrayed: Tobit and his dog figured to great advantage; Haman swung conspicuously on his gibbet; and Jonah appeared most manfully bouncing out of the whale, like Harlequin through a barrel of fire.

The parties broke up without noise and without confusion. They were carried home by their own carriages, that is to say, by the vehicles nature had provided them, excepting such of the wealthy as could afford to keep a wagon. The gentlemen gallantly attended their fair ones to their respective abodes, and took leave of them with a hearty smack at the door: which, as it was an established piece of etiquette, done in perfect simplicity and honesty of heart, occasioned no scandal at that time, nor should it at the present; — if our great-grandfathers approved of the custom, it would argue a great want of deference in their descendants to say a word against it.

Chapter IV

Containing Further Particulars of the Golden Age, and What Constituted a Fine Lady and Gentleman in the Days of Walter the Doubter

In this dulcet period of my history, when the beauteous island of Manna-hata presented a scene, the very counterpart of those glowing pictures drawn of the golden reign of Saturn, there was, as I have before observed, a happy ignorance, a honest simplicity prevalent among its inhabitants, which, were I even able to depict, would be but little understood by the degenerate age for which I am doomed to write. Even the female sex, those arch innovators upon the tranquillity, the honesty, and gray-beard customs of society, seemed for a while to conduct themselves with incredible sobriety and comeliness.

Their hair, untortured by the abominations of art, was scrupulously pomatumed back from their foreheads with a candle, and covered with a little cap of quilted calico, which fitted exactly to their heads. Their petticoats of linsey-woolsey were striped with a variety of gorgeous dyes, — though I must confess these gallant garments were rather short, scarce reaching below the knee; but then they made up in the number, which generally equalled that of the gentleman's small-clothes; and what is still more praiseworthy, they were all of their own manufacture, — of which circumstance, as may well be supposed, they were not a little vain.

These were the honest days in which every woman staid at home, read the Bible, and wore pockets, — ay, and that too of a goodly size, fashioned with patchwork into many curious devices, and ostentatiously worn on the outside. These, in fact, were convenient receptacles, where all good housewives carefully stored away such things as they wished to have at hand; by which means they often came to be incredibly crammed; and I remember there was a story current, when I was a boy, that the lady of Wouter Van Twiller once had occasion to empty her right pocket in search of a wooden ladle, when the contents filled a couple of corn-baskets, and the utensil was discovered lying among some rubbish in one corner; — but we must not give too much faith to all these stories, the anecdotes of those remote periods being very subject to exaggeration.

Besides these notable pockets, they likewise wore scissors and pin-cushions suspended from their girdles by red ribands, or, among the more opulent and showy classes, by brass, and even silver chains, — indubitable tokens of thrifty housewives, and industrious spinsters. I cannot say much in vindication of the shortness of the petticoats; it doubtless was introduced for the purpose of giving the stockings a chance to be seen, which were generally of blue worsted, with magnificent red clocks, — or, perhaps, to display a well-turned ankle, and a neat, though serviceable foot, set off by a high-heeled leathern shoe, with a large and splendid silver buckle. Thus we find that the gentle sex in all ages have shown the same disposition to infringe a little upon the laws of decorum, in order to betray a lurking beauty, or gratify an innocent love of finery.

From the sketch here given, it will be seen that our good grandmothers differed considerably in their ideas of a fine figure from their scantily dressed descendants of the present day. A fine lady, in those times, waddled under more clothes, even on a fair summer's day, than would have clad the whole bevy of a modern ball-room. Nor were they the less admired by the gentlemen in consequence thereof. On the contrary, the greatness of a lover's passion seemed to increase in proportion to the magnitude of its object, — and a voluminous damsel, arrayed in a dozen of petticoats, was declared by a Low-Dutch sonneteer of the province to be radiant as a sunflower, and luxuriant as a full-blown cabbage. Certain it is, that in those days the heart of a lover could not contain more than one lady at a time; whereas the heart of a modern gallant has often room enough to accommodate half a dozen. The reason of which I conclude to be, that either the hearts of the gentlemen have grown larger, or the persons of the ladies smaller: this, however, is a question for physiologists to determine.

But there was a secret charm in these petticoats, which, no doubt, entered into the consideration of the prudent gallants. The wardrobe of a lady was in those days her only fortune; and she who had a good stock of petticoats and stockings was as absolutely an heiress as is a Kamtchatka damsel with a store of bear-skins, or a Lapland belle with a plenty of reindeer. The ladies, therefore, were very anxious to display these powerful attractions to the greatest advantage; and the best rooms in the house, instead of being adorned with caricatures of dame Nature, in water-colors and needle-work, were always hung round with abundance of homespun garments, the manufacture and the property of the females, — a piece of laudable ostentation that still prevails among the heiresses of our Dutch villages.

The gentleman, in fact, who figured in the circles of the gay world in these ancient times, corresponded, in most particulars, with the beauteous damsels whose smiles they were ambitious to deserve. True it is, in their merits would make but a very inconsiderable impression upon the heart of a modern fair: they neither drove their curricles, nor sported their tandems, for as yet those gaudy vehicles were not even dreamt of; neither did they distinguish themselves by their brilliancy at the table, and their consequent rencontres with watchmen, for our forefathers were of too pacific a disposition to need those guardians of the night, every soul throughout the town being sound asleep before nine o'clock. Neither did they establish their claims to gentility at the expense of their tailors, for as yet those offenders against the pockets of society, and the tranquillity of all aspiring young gentlemen, were unknown in New Amsterdam; every good housewife made the clothes of her husband and family, and even the goede vrouw of Van Twiller himself thought it no disparagement to cut out her husband's linsey-woolsey galligaskins.

Not but what there were some two or three youngsters who manifested the first dawning of what is called fire and spirit; who held all labor in contempt; skulked about docks and market-places; loitered in the sunshine; squandered what little money they could procure at hustle-cap and chuck-farthing; swore, boxed, fought cocks, and raced their neighbors' horses; in short, who promised to be the wonder, the talk, and abomination of the town, had not their stylish career been unfortunately cut short by an affair of honor with a whipping-post.

Far other, however, was the truly fashionable gentleman of those days: his dress, which served for both morning and evening, street and drawing-room, was a linsey-woolsey coat, made, perhaps, by the fair hands of the mistress of his affections, and gallantly bedecked with abundance of large brass buttons; half a score of breeches heightened the proportions of his figure; his shoes were decorated by enormous copper buckles: a low-crowned broad-rimmed hat overshadowed his burly visage; and his hair dangled down his back in a prodigious queue of eel-skin.

Thus equipped, he would manfully sally forth, with pipe in mouth, to besiege some fair damsel's obdurate heart, — not such a pipe, good reader, as that which Acis did sweetly tune in praise of his Galatea, but one of true Delft manufacture, and furnished with a charge of fragrant tobacco. With this would he resolutely set himself down before the fortress, and rarely failed, in the process of time, to smoke the fair enemy into a surrender, upon honorable terms.

Such was the happy reign of Wouter Van Twiller, celebrated in many a long-forgotten song as the real golden age, the rest being nothing but counterfeit copper-washed coin. In that delightful period, a sweet and holy calm reigned over the whole province. The burgomaster smoked his pipe in peace; the substantial solace of his domestic cares, after her daily toils were done, sat soberly at the door, with her arms crossed over her apron of snowy white, without being insulted with ribald street-walkers or vagabond boys, — those unlucky urchins who do so infest our streets, displaying, under the roses of youth, the thorns and briers of iniquity. Then it was that the lover with ten breeches, and the damsel with petticoats of half a score, indulged in all the innocent endearments of virtuous love, without fear and without reproach; for what had that virtue to fear, which was defended by a shield of good linsey-woolseys, equal at least to the seven bull-hides of the invincible Ajax?

Ah, blissful and never to be forgotten age! when everything was better than it has ever been since, or ever will be again, — when Buttermilk Channel was quite dry at low water, — when the shad in the Hudson were all salmon, — and when the moon shone with a pure and resplendent whiteness, instead of that melancholy yellow light which is the consequence of her sickening at the abominations she every night witnesses in this degenerate city!

Happy would it have been for New Amsterdam could it always have existed in this state of blissful ignorance and lowly simplicity; but, alas! the days of childhood are too sweet to last! Cities, like men, grow out of them in time, and are doomed alike to grow into the bustle, the cares, and miseries of the world. Let no man congratulate himself, when he beholds the child of his bosom or the city of his birth increasing in magnitude and importance, — let the history of his own life teach him the dangers of the one, and this excellent little history of Mann-hata convince him of the calamities of the other.

Chronicles of the Reign of William the Testy

CHAPTER I

Showing the Nature of History in General; Containing Farthermore the Universal Acquirements of William the Testy, and How a Man May Learn so Much as to Render Himself Good for Nothing

When the lofty Thucydides is about to enter upon his description of the plague that desolated Athens, one of his modern commentators assures the reader that the history is now going to be exceeding solemn, serious, and pathetic; and hints, with that air of chuckling gratulation with which a good dame draws forth a choice morsel from a cupboard to regale a favorite, that this plague will give his history a most agreeable variety.

In like manner did my heart leap within me, when I came to the dolorous dilemma of Fort Goed Hoop, which I at once perceived to be the forerunner of a series of great events and entertaining disasters. Such are the true subjects for the historic pen. For what is history, in fact, but a kind of Newgate calendar, a register of the crimes and miseries that man has inflicted on his fellow-man? It is a huge libel on human nature, to which we industriously add page after page, volume after volume, as if we were building up a monument to the honor, rather than the infamy of our species. If we turn over the pages of these chronicles that man has written of himself, what are the characters dignified by the appellation of great, and held up to the admiration of posterity? Tyrants, robbers, conquerors, renowned only for the magnitude of their misdeeds, and the stupendous wrongs and miseries they have inflicted on mankind — warriors, who have hired themselves to the trade of blood, not from motives of virtuous patriotism, or to protect the injured and defenceless, but merely to gain the vaunted glory of being adroit and successful in massacring their fellow-beings! What are the great events that constitute a glorious era? — The fall of empires — the desolation of happy countries — splendid cities smoking in their ruins — the proudest works of art tumbled in the dust — the shrieks and groans of whole nations ascending unto heaven!

It is thus the historian may be said to thrive on the miseries of mankind, like birds of prey which hover over the field of battle, to fatten on the mighty dead. It was observed by a great projector of inland lock navigation, that rivers, lakes, and oceans were only formed to feed canals. — In like manner I am tempted to believe that plots, conspiracies, wars, victories, and massacres, are ordained by Providence only as food for the historian.

It is a source of great delight to the philosopher, in studying the wonderful economy of nature, to trace the mutual dependencies of things, how they are created reciprocally for each other, and how the most noxious and apparently unnecessary animal has its uses. Thus those swarms of flies, which are so often execrated as useless vermin, are created for the sustenance of spiders — and spiders, on the other hand, are evidently made to devour flies. So those heroes who have been such scourges to the world, were bounteously provided as themes for the poet and historian, while the poet and the historian were destined to record the achievements of heroes!

These, and many similar reflections, naturally arose in my mind, as I took up my pen to commence the reign of William Kieft: for now the stream of our history, which hitherto has rolled in a tranquil current, is about to depart forever from its peaceful haunts, and brawl through many a turbulent and rugged scene.

As some sleek ox, sunk in the rich repose of a clover-field, dozing and chewing the cud, will bear repeated blows before it raises itself; so the province of Nieuw Nederlandts, having waxed fat under the drowsy reign of the Doubter, needed cuffs and kicks to rouse it into action. The reader will now witness the manner in which a peaceful community advances towards a state of war; which is apt to be like the approach of a horse to a drum, with much prancing and little progress, and too often with the wrong end foremost.

Wilhelmus Kieft, who, in 1634, ascended the gubernatorial chair (to borrow a favorite though clumsy appellation of modern phraseologists), was of a lofty descent, his father being inspector of wind-mills in the ancient town of Saardam; and our hero, we are told, when a boy, made very curious investigations into the nature and operation of these machines, which was one reason why he afterwards came to be so ingenious a governor. His name, according to the most authentic etymologists, was a corruption of Kyver; that is to say, a *wrangler* or *scolder*; and expressed the characteristic of his family, which, for nearly two centuries, had kept the windy town of Saardam in hot water, and produced more tartars and brimstones than any ten families in the place; and so truly did he inherit this family peculiarity, that he had not been a year in the government of the province, before he was universally denominated William the Testy. His appearance answered to his name. He was a brisk, wiry, waspish little old gentleman; such a one as may now and then be seen stumping about our city in a broad-skirted coat with huge buttons, a cocked hat stuck on the back of his head, and a cane as high as his chin. His face was broad, but his features were sharp; his cheeks were scorched into a dusky red, by two fiery little gray eyes; his nose turned up, and the corners of his mouth turned down, pretty much like the muzzle of an irritable pug-dog.

I have heard it observed by a profound adept in human physiology, that if a woman waxes fat with the progress of years, her tenure of life is somewhat precarious, but if haply she withers as she grows old, she lives forever. Such promised to be the case with William the Testy, who grew tough in proportion as he dried. He had withered, in fact, not through the process of years, but through the tropical fervor of his soul, which burnt like a vehement rush-light in his bosom; inciting him to incessant broils and bickerings. Ancient traditions speak much of his learning, and of the gallant inroads he had made into the dead languages, in which he had made captive a host of Greek nouns and Latin verbs; and brought off rich booty in ancient saws and apothegms; which he was wont to parade in his public harangues, as a triumphant general of yore, his *spolia opima*. Of metaphysics he knew enough to confound all hearers and himself into the bargain. In logic, he knew the whole family of syllogisms and dilemmas, and was so proud of his skill that he never suffered even a self-evident fact to pass unargued. It was observed, however, that he seldom got into an argument without getting into a perplexity, and then into a passion with his adversary for not being convinced gratis.

He had, moreover, skirmished smartly on the frontiers of several of the sciences, was fond of experimental philosophy, and prided himself upon inventions of all kinds. His abode, which he had fixed at a Bowerie or country-seat at a short distance from the city, just at what is now called Dutch-street, soon abounded with proofs of his ingenuity: patent smokejacks that required a horse to work them; Dutch ovens that roasted meat without fire; carts that went before the horses; weathercocks that turned against the wind; and other wrong-headed contrivances that astonished and confounded all beholders. The house, too, was beset with paralytic cats and dogs, the subjects of his experimental philosophy; and the yelling and yelping of the latter unhappy victims of science, while aiding in the pursuit of knowledge, soon gained for the place the name of "Dog's Misery," by which it continues to be known even at the present day.

It is in knowledge as in swimming; he who flounders and splashes on the surface, makes more noise, and attracts more attention, than the pearl-diver who quietly dives in quest of treasures to the bottom. The vast acquirements of the new governor were the theme of marvel among the simple burghers of New Amsterdam; he figured about the place as learned a man as a Bonze at Pekin, who has mastered one half of the Chinese alphabet: and was unanimously pronounced a "universal genius!"

I have known in my time many a genius of this stamp; but, to speak my mind freely, I never knew one who, for the ordinary purposes of life, was worth his weight in straw. In this respect, a little sound judgment and plain common sense is worth all the sparkling genius that ever wrote poetry or invented theories. Let us see how the universal acquirements of William the Testy aided him in the affairs of government.

CHAPTER II

How William the Testy Undertook to Conquer by Proclamation — How He Was a Great Man Abroad, but a Little Man in His Own House

No sooner had this bustling little potentate been blown by a whiff of fortune into the seat of government than he called his council together to make them a speech on the state of affairs.

Caius Gracchus, it is said, when he harangued the Roman populace, modulated his tone by an oratorical flute or pitchpipe; Wilhelmus Kieft, not having such an instrument at hand, availed himself of that musical organ or trump which nature has implanted in the midst of a man's face; in other words, he preluded his address by a sonorous blast of the nose; a preliminary flourish much in vogue among public orators.

He then commenced by expressing his humble sense of his utter unworthiness of the high post to which he had been appointed; which made some of the simple burghers wonder why he undertook it, not knowing that it is a point of etiquette with a public orator never to enter upon office without declaring himself unworthy to cross the threshold. He then proceeded in a manner highly classic and erudite to speak of government generally, and of the governments of ancient Greece in particular; together with the wars of Rome and Carthage; and the rise and fall of sundry outlandish empires which the worthy burghers had never read nor heard of. Having thus, after the manner of your learned orator, treated of things in general, he came by a natural, roundabout transition, to the matter in hand, namely, the daring aggressions of the Yankees.

As my readers are well aware of the advantage a potentate has of handling his enemies as he pleases in his speeches and bulletins, where he has the talk all on his own side, they may rest assured that William the Testy did not let such an opportunity escape of giving the Yankees what is called "a taste of his quality." In speaking of their inroads into the territories of their High Mightinesses, he compared them to the Gauls who desolated Rome; the Goths and Vandals who overran the fairest plains of Europe; but when he came to speak of the unparalleled audacity with which they of Weathersfield had advanced their patches up to the very walls of Fort Goed Hoop, and threatened to smother the garrison in onions, tears of rage started into his eyes, as though he nosed the very offence in question.

Having thus wrought up his tale to a climax, he assumed a most belligerent look, and assured the council that he had devised an instrument, potent in its effects, and which he trusted would soon drive the Yankees from the land. So saying, he thrust his hand into one of the deep pockets of his broadskirted coat and drew forth, not an infernal machine, but an instrument in writing, which he laid with great emphasis upon the table.

The burghers gazed at it for a time in silent awe, as a wary housewife does at a gun, fearful it may go off half-cocked. The document in question had a sinister look, it is true; it was crabbed in text, and from a broad red ribbon dangled the great seal of the province, about the size of a buckwheat pancake. Still, after all, it was but an instrument in writing. Herein, however, existed the wonder of the invention. The document in question was a PROCLAMATION, ordering the Yankees to depart instantly from the territories of their High Mightinesses under pain of suffering all the forfeitures and punishments in such case made and provided. It was on the moral effect of this formidable instrument that Wilhelmus Kieft calculated;

pledging his valor as a governor that, once fulminated against the Yankees, it would, in less than two months, drive every mother's son of them across the borders.

The council broke up in perfect wonder, and nothing was talked of for some time among the old men and women of New Amsterdam but the vast genius of the governor, and his new and cheap mode of fighting by proclamation.

As to Wilhelmus Kieft, having dispatched his proclamation to the frontiers, he put on his cocked hat and corduroy small-clothes, and mounting a tall raw-boned charger, trotted out to his rural retreat of Dog's Misery. Here, like the good Numa, he reposed from the toils of state, taking lessons in government, not from the nymph Egeria, but from the honored wife of his bosom; who was one of that class of females sent upon the earth a little after the flood, as a punishment for the sins of mankind, and commonly known by the appellation of *knowing women*. In fact, my duty as an historian obliges me to make known a circumstance which was a great secret at the time, and consequently was not a subject of scandal at more than half the tea-tables in New Amsterdam, but which like many other great secrets, has leaked out in the lapse of years — and this was, that Wilhelmus the Testy, though one of the most potent little men that ever breathed, yet submitted at home to a species of government, neither laid down in Aristotle nor Plato; in short, it partook of the nature of a pure, unmixed tyranny, and is familiarly denominated *petticoat government*. — An absolute sway, which, although exceedingly common in these modern days, was very rare among the ancients, if we may judge from the rout made about the domestic economy of honest Socrates; which is the only ancient case on record.

The great Kieft, however, warded off all the sneers and sarcasms of his particular friends, who are ever ready to joke with a man on sore points of the kind, by alleging that it was a government of his own election, to which he submitted through choice; adding at the same time a profound maxim which he had found in an ancient author, that "he who would aspire to *govern*, should first learn to *obey*."

CHAPTER III

In Which Are Recorded the Sage Projects of a Ruler of Universal Genius — The Art of

Fighting by Proclamation — And How that the Valiant Jacobus Van Curlet Came to Be Foully Dishonored at Fort Goed Hoop

Never was a more comprehensive, a more expeditious, or, what is still better, a more economical measure devised, than this of defeating the Yankees by proclamation — an expedient, likewise, so gentle and humane, there were ten chances to one in favor of its succeeding, — but then there was one chance to ten that it would not succeed — as the ill-natured fates would have it, that single chance carried the day! The proclamation was perfect in all its parts, well constructed, well written, well sealed, and well published — all that was wanting to insure its effect was, that the Yankees should stand in awe of it; but, provoking to relate, they treated it with the most absolute contempt, applied it to an unseemly purpose, and thus did the first warlike proclamation come to a shameful end — a fate which I am credibly informed has befallen but too many of its successors.

So far from abandoning the country, those varlets continued their encroachments, squatting along the green banks of the Varsche river, and founding Hartford, Stamford, New Haven, and other border towns. I have already shown how the onion patches of Pyquag were an eyesore to Jacobus Van Curlet and his garrison; but now these moss-troopers increased in their atrocities, kidnapping hogs, impounding horses, and sometimes grievously rib-roasting their owners. Our worthy forefathers could scarcely stir abroad without danger of being outjockeyed in horseflesh, or taken in in bargaining; while, in their absence, some daring Yankee peddler would penetrate to their household, and nearly ruin the good housewives with tin-ware and wooden bowls.

I am well aware of the perils which environ me in this part of my history. While raking, with curious hand but pious heart, among the mouldering remains of former days, anxious to draw therefrom the honey of wisdom, I may fare somewhat like that valiant worthy, Samson, who, in meddling with the carcass of a dead lion, drew a swarm of bees about his ears. Thus, while narrating the many misdeeds of the Yanokie or Yankee race, it is ten chances to one but I offend the morbid sensibilities of certain of their unreasonable descendants, who may fly out and raise such a buzzing about this unlucky head of mine, that I shall need the tough hide of an Achilles or an Orlando Furioso, to protect me from their stings.

Should such be the case, I should deeply and sincerely lament — not my misfortune in giv- 5 ing offence — but the wrong-headed perverseness of an ill-natured generation, in taking offence at any thing I say. That their ancestors did use my ancestors ill is true, and I am very sorry for it. I would, with all my heart, the fact 10 were otherwise; but as I am recording the sacred events of history, I'd not bate one nail's breadth of the honest truth, though I were sure the whole edition of my work would be bought up and burnt by the common hangman of 15 Connecticut. And in sooth, now that these testy gentlemen have drawn me out, I will make bold to go farther, and observe that this is one of the grand purposes for which we impartial historians are sent into the world — to redress 20 wrongs and render justice on the heads of the guilty. So that, though a powerful nation may wrong its neighbors with temporary impunity, yet sooner or later an historian springs up, who wreaks ample chastisement on it in return. 25

Thus these moss-troopers of the east little thought, I'll warrant it, while they were harassing the inoffensive province of Nieuw Nederlands, and driving its unhappy governor to his wit's end, that an historian would ever arise, 30 and give them their own, with interest. Since, then, I am but performing my bounden duty as an historian, in avenging the wrongs of our revered ancestors, I shall make no further apology, and, indeed, when it is considered that I 35 have all these ancient borderers of the east in my power, and at the mercy of my pen, I trust that it will be admitted I conduct myself with great humanity and moderation.

It was long before William the Testy could 40 be persuaded that his much vaunted war measure was ineffectual; on the contrary, he flew in a passion whenever it was doubted, swearing that though slow in operating, yet when it once began to work, it would soon purge the land of 45 these invaders. When convinced, at length, of the truth, like a shrewd physician, he attributed the failure to the quantity, not the quality of the medicine, and resolved to double the dose. He fulminated, therefore, a second proclamation 50 more vehement than the first, forbidding all intercourse with these Yankee intruders; ordering the Dutch burghers on the frontiers to buy none of their pacing horses, measly pork, apple sweetmeats, Weathersfield onions, or wooden 55

bowls, and to furnish them with no supplies of gin, gingerbread, or sourkrout.

Another interval elapsed, during which the last proclamation was as little regarded as the first, and the non-intercourse was especially set at naught by the young folks of both sexes, if we may judge by the active bundling which took place along the borders.

At length one day the inhabitants of New Amsterdam were aroused by a furious barking of dogs, great and small, and beheld, to their surprise, the whole garrison of Fort Goed Hoop straggling into town all tattered and wayworn, with Jacobus Van Curlet at their head, bringing the melancholy intelligence of the capture of Fort Goed Hoop by the Yankees.

The fate of this important fortress is an impressive warning to all military commanders. It was neither carried by storm nor famine; nor was it undermined; nor bombarded; nor set on fire by red-hot shot; but was taken by a stratagem no less singular than effectual, and which can never fail of success, whenever an opportunity occurs of putting it in practice.

It seems that the Yankees had received intelligence that the garrison of Jacobus Van Curlet had been reduced nearly one eighth by the death of two of his most corpulent soldiers, who had overeaten themselves on fat salmon caught in the Varsche river. A secret expedition was immediately set on foot to surprise the fortress. The crafty enemy knowing the habits of the garrison to sleep soundly after they had eaten their dinners and smoked their pipes, stole upon them at the noontide of a sultry summer's day, and surprised them in the midst of their slumbers.

In an instant the flag of their High Mightinesses was lowered, and the Yankee standard elevated in its stead, being a dried codfish, by way of a spread eagle. A strong garrison was appointed, of long-sided, hard-fisted Yankees, with Weathersfield onions for cockades and feathers. As to Jacobus Van Curlet and his men, they were seized by the nape of the neck, conducted to the gate, and one by one dismissed with a kick in the crupper, as Charles XII dismissed the heavy-bottomed Russians at the battle of Narva; Jacobus Van Curlet receiving two kicks in consideration of his official dignity.

Chapter IV

Containing the Fearful Wrath of William the Testy, and the Alarm of New Amsterdam —

How the Governor Did Strongly Fortify the City — of the Rise of Antony the Trumpeter, and the Windy Addition to the Armorial Bearings of New Amsterdam

Language cannot express the awful ire of William the Testy on hearing of the catastrophe at Fort Goed Hoop. For three good hours his rage was too great for words, or rather the words were too great for him, (being a very small man), and he was nearly choked by the misshapen, nine-cornered Dutch oaths and epithets which crowded at once into his gullet. At length his words found vent, and for three days he kept up a constant discharge, anathematizing the Yankees, man, woman, and child, for a set of dieven, schobbejacken, deugenieten, twistzoekeren, blaes-kaken, loosen-schalken, kakkenbedden, and a thousand other names, of which, unfortunately for posterity, history does not make mention. Finally, he swore that he would have nothing more to do with such a squatting, bundling, guessing, questioning, swapping, pumpkin-eating, molasses-daubing, shingle-splitting, cider-watering, horse-jockeying, notion-peddling crew — that they might stay at Fort Goed Hoop and rot, before he would dirty his hands by attempting to drive them away; in proof of which he ordered the new-raised troops to be marched forthwith into winter quarters, although it was not as yet quite midsummer. Great despondency now fell upon the city of New Amsterdam. It was feared that the conquerors of Fort Goed Hoop, flushed with victory and applebrandy, might march on to the capital, take it by storm, and annex the whole province to Connecticut. The name of Yankee became as terrible among the Nieuw Nederlanders as was that of Gaul among the ancient Romans; insomuch that the good wives of the Manhattoes used it as a bugbear wherewith to frighten their unruly children.

Everybody clamored around the governor, imploring him to put the city in a complete posture of defence, and he listened to their clamors. Nobody could accuse William the Testy of being idle in time of danger, or at any other time. He was never idle, but then he was often busy to very little purpose. When a youngling he had been impressed with the words of Solomon, "Go to the ant, thou sluggard, observe her ways and be wise," in conformity to which he had ever been of a restless, ant-like turn; hurrying hither and thither, nobody knew why or wherefore, busying himself about small matters with an air of great importance and anxiety, and toiling at a grain of mustard-seed in the full conviction that he was moving a mountain. In the present instance, he called in all his inventive powers to his aid, and was continually pondering over plans, making diagrams, and worrying about with a troop of workmen and projectors at his heels. At length, after a world of consultation and contrivance, his plans of defence ended in rearing a great flag-staff in the center of the fort, and perching a wind-mill on each bastion.

These warlike preparations in some measure allayed the public alarm, especially after an additional means of securing the safety of the city had been suggested by the governor's lady. It has already been hinted in this most authentic history, that in the domestic establishment of William the Testy "the gray mare was the better horse"; in other words, that his wife "ruled the roast," and, in governing the governor, governed the province, which might thus be said to be under petticoat government.

Now it came to pass, that about this time there lived in the Manhattoes a jolly, robustious trumpeter, named Antony Van Corlear, famous for his long wind; and who, as the story goes, could twang so potently upon his instrument, that the effect upon all within hearing was like that ascribed to the Scotch bagpipe when it sings right lustily i' the nose.

This sounder of brass was moreover a lusty bachelor, with a pleasant, burly visage, a long nose, and huge whiskers. He had his little *bowerie,* or retreat in the country, where he led a roystering life, giving dances to the wives and daughters of the burghers of the Manhattoes, insomuch that he became a prodigious favorite with all the women, young and old. He is said to have been the first to collect that famous toll levied on the fair sex at Kissing Bridge, on the highway to Hellgate.

To this sturdy bachelor the eyes of all the women were turned in this time of darkness and peril, as the very man to second and carry out the plans of defence of the governor. A kind of petticoat council was forthwith held at the government house, at which the governor's lady presided; and this lady, as has been hinted, being all potent with the governor, the result of these councils was the elevation of Antony the Trumpeter to the post of commandant of wind-mills and champion of New Amsterdam.

The city being thus fortified and garrisoned, it would have done one's heart good to see the governor snapping his fingers and fidgeting with delight, as the trumpeter strutted up and down the ramparts twanging defiance to the whole Yankee race, as does a modern editor to all the principalities and powers on the other side 5 of the Atlantic. In the hands of Antony Van Corlear this windy instrument appeared to him as potent as the horn of the paladin Astolpho, or even the more classic horn of Alecto; nay, he had almost the temerity to compare it with 10 the rams' horns celebrated in holy writ, at the very sound of which the walls of Jericho fell down.

Be all this as it may, the apprehension of hostilities from the east gradually died away. 15 The Yankees made no further invasion; nay, they declared they had only taken possession of Fort Goed Hoop as being erected within their territories. So far from manifesting hostility, they continued to throng to New Amsterdam 20 with the most innocent countenances imaginable, filling the market with their notions, being as ready to trade with the Nederlanders as ever — and not a whit more prone to get to the windward of them in a bargain. 25

The old wives of the Manhattoes who took tea with the governor's lady attributed all this affected moderation to the awe inspired by the military preparations of the governor, and the windy prowess of Antony the Trumpeter. 30

There were not wanting illiberal minds, however, who sneered at the governor for thinking to defend his city as he governed it, by mere wind; but William Kieft was not to be jeered out of his wind-mills — he had seen them 35 perched upon the ramparts of his native city of Saardam, and was persuaded they were connected with the great science of defence; nay, so much piqued was he by having them made a matter of ridicule, that he introduced them into 40 the arms of the city, where they remain to this day, quartered with the ancient beaver of the Manhattoes, an emblem and momento of his policy.

I must not omit to mention that certain wise 45 old burghers of the Manhattoes, skilful in expounding signs and mysteries, after events have come to pass, consider this early intrusion of the wind-mill into the escutcheon of our city, which before had been wholly occupied by the 50 beaver, as portentous of its after fortune, when the quiet Dutchman would be elbowed aside by the enterprising Yankee, and patient industry overtopped by windy speculation.

From *The Sketch Book*
(1819–1920)

The Sketch Book marks the maturity of Irving as an artist. His literary orientation came largely from such English writers of the eighteenth century as Fielding, Sterne, Goldsmith, and such romantics, in Britain and Germany, as Scott, Tieck, and Hoffman. He commanded an admirable prose style, long considered a model for youth in the schools. It is easy, natural, neatly turned in the neo-classic manner, not without romantic richness. Through it he conveyed an attitude toward life which is genial — warmly good-natured with a twinkle in the eye — and sometimes sentimental. He had none of the mental commotion of men like Coleridge, Carlyle, and Emerson. He was a man of quiet reverie (as he came to realize), not a man of ideas. Typical of him is a pleasantly melancholy sense of mutability, evanescence — the certainty of change, the brevity of life. Like Shakespeare's Hotspur, he felt that to spend that brevity basely would make it too long. For he had the humanistic attitude of the gentleman, compounded of solidity of character, honor, courtesy, kindliness, a high-minded disdain of the vulgar. In writing, he conceived it his business to please as an artist rather than instruct as a moralist.

The Sketch Book is composed of familiar essays with a few short stories. Chiefly it is an English sketch book, containing such observations as an American, bred in the English tradition, might make upon visiting the motherland, observations on the good old customs ("Rural Life in England," "The Christmas Dinner") and the famous old scenes and monuments ("Stratford-on-Avon," "Westminster Abbey"). But there are also half a dozen chapters on American themes, including the short tales "Rip Van Winkle" and "The Legend of Sleepy Hollow," the best things in a very uneven collection.

The Author's Account of Himself

After telling of his "roving passion" for the new and strange, Irving, in the last paragraph, warns us not to expect of him a philosophic interpretation but only a humble love of the picturesque. He presents himself as a tourist traveling pencil in hand (before the day of the camera) and sketching what interests him. Actually he was rather more the artist than this would imply. Since Washington Allston, the painter, had urged him to take up painting seriously, he must have shown some talent. He preferred to use literature as his medium, but largely for its pictorial capacities. His collection of essays and tales became, for him, an artist's portfolio or sketch book, and a pen name for the author was suggested by the artist's crayon — "Geoffrey Crayon, Gent."

I was always fond of visiting new scenes, and observing strange characters and manners. Even when a mere child I began my travels, and made many tours of discovery into foreign parts and unknown regions of my native city, to the frequent alarm of my parents, and the emolument of the town-crier. As I grew into boyhood, I extended the range of my observations. My holiday afternoons were spent in rambles about the surrounding country. I made myself familiar with all its places famous in history or fable. I knew every spot where a murder or robbery had been committed, or a ghost seen. I visited the neighboring villages, and added greatly to my stock of knowledge, by noting their habits and customs, and conversing with their sages and great men. I even journeyed one long summer's day to the summit of the most distant hill, whence I stretched my eye over many a mile of terra incognita, and was astonished to find how vast a globe I inhabited.

This rambling propensity strengthened with my years. Books of voyages and travels became my passion, and in devouring their contents, I neglected the regular exercises of the school. How wistfully would I wander about the pier-heads in fine weather, and watch the parting ships, bound to distant climes — with what longing eyes would I gaze after their lessening sails, and waft myself in imagination to the ends of the earth!

Further reading and thinking, though they brought this vague inclination into more reasonable bounds, only served to make it more decided. I visited various parts of my own country; and had I been merely a lover of fine scenery, I should have felt little desire to seek elsewhere its gratification; for on no country have the charms of nature been more prodigally lavished. Her mighty lakes, like oceans of liquid silver; her mountains, with their bright aerial tints; her valleys, teeming with wild fertility; her tremendous cataracts, thundering in their solitudes; her boundless plains, waving with spontaneous verdure; her broad deep rivers, rolling in solemn silence to the ocean; her trackless forests, where vegetation puts forth all its magnificence; her skies, kindling with the magic of summer clouds and glorious sunshine; —no, never need an American look beyond his own country for the sublime and beautiful of natural scenery.

But Europe held forth the charms of storied and poetical association. There were to be seen the masterpieces of art, the refinements of highly-cultivated society, the quaint peculiarities of ancient and local custom. My native country was full of youthful promise: Europe was rich in the accumulated treasures of age. Her very ruins told the history of times gone by, and every mouldering stone was a chronicle. I longed to wander over the scenes of renowned achievement — to tread, as it were, in the footsteps of antiquity — to loiter about the ruined castle — to meditate on the falling tower — to escape, in short, from the commonplace realities of the present, and lose myself among the shadowy grandeurs of the past.

I had, beside all this, an earnest desire to see the great men of the earth. We have, it is true, our great men in America: not a city but has an ample share of them. I have mingled among them in my time, and been almost withered by the shade into which they cast me; for there is nothing so baleful to a small man as the shade of a great one, particularly the great man of a city. But I was anxious to see the great men of Europe; for I had read in the works of the various philosophers, that all animals degenerated in America, and man among the number. A great man of Europe, thought I, must therefore be as superior to a great man of America, as a peak of the Alps to a highland of the Hudson; and in this idea I was confirmed, by observing the comparative importance and swelling magnitude of many English travellers among us, who, I was assured, were very little people in their own country. I will visit this land of wonders, thought I, and see the gigantic race from which I am degenerated.

It has been either my good or evil lot to have my roving passion gratified. I have wandered through different countries, and witnessed many of the shifting scenes of life. I cannot say that I have studied them with the eye of a philosopher; but rather with the sauntering gaze with which humble lovers of the picturesque stroll from the window of one print-shop to another; caught sometimes by the delineations of beauty, sometimes by the distortions of caricature, and sometimes by the loveliness of landscape. As it is the fashion for modern tourists to travel pencil in hand, and bring home their port-folios filled with sketches, I am disposed to get up a few for the entertainment of my friends. When, however, I look over the hints and memorandums I have taken down for the purpose, my heart almost fails me at finding how my idle humor has led me aside from the great objects studied by every regular traveller who would make a book. I fear I shall give equal disappointment with an unlucky landscape painter, who had travelled on the continent, but, following the bent of his vagrant inclination, had sketched in nooks, and corners and by-places. His sketch-book was accordingly crowded with cottages, and landscapes, and obscure ruins; but he had neglected to paint St. Peter's, or the Coliseum; the cascade of Terni, or the bay of Naples; and had not a single glacier or volcano in his whole collection.

Rip Van Winkle

Irving's conception of the short story as a literary form was expressed in a letter written a few years after *The Sketch Book:* "For my part I consider a story merely as a frame on which to stretch my materials. It is the play of thought, and sentiment and language; the weaving in of characters, lightly yet expressively delineated; the familiar and faithful exhibition of scenes in common life; and the half concealed vein of humor that is often playing through the whole — these are among what I aim at. . . . There is a constant activity of thought and a nicety of execution required in writings of the kind, more than the world appears to imagine."

This may seem a rather easygoing, rambling technique to readers habituated to the short story as Poe and Maupassant later wrote it, but that it can be used in great fiction was shown long ago by Chaucer in his *Canterbury Tales.* Both in this story and in "The Legend of Sleepy Hollow" Irving begins in the essay manner and on this leisurely foundation builds a series of incidents focusing upon a particular character. His plots were of the kind cultivated by the "Gothic" tale, the tale of terror. As he handled it, it became, in the phrase of O. S. Coad, "sportive Gothic." With much skill he transplanted to an American scene old folk legends which he had come upon in his reading of the German romantics, telling them with tongue in cheek.

The scenery of the opening passage of "Rip Van Winkle" is the Catskill country, soon to inspire America's first landscape painting, the Hudson River School of Cole, Durant, and others. In a disarmingly leisurely fashion Irving begins with the mountains, passes to the village, to its houses, to Rip and his family and dog, and then, setting and character attended to, unfolds the incidents of the action. "Moral" the story has none, yet Irving seems to suggest his characteristic fondness for an old, rural, stable society. After sleeping through the period of the Revolution, Rip awakes in a "busy, bustling, disputatious" young America in which tranquillity and idle-

ness no longer appear to be values. His bewilderment has been easily understood by many who have since lived through the breathless changes of an industrial civilization.

By Woden, God of Saxons,
From whenne comes Wensday, that is Wodens-
  day.
Truth is a thing that ever I will keep
Unto thylke day in which I creep into
My sepulchre.
                                    CARTWRIGHT.

Whoever has made a voyage up the Hudson must remember the Kaatskill Mountains. They are a dismembered branch of the great Appalachian family, and are seen away to the west of the river, swelling up to a noble height, and lording it over the surrounding country. Every change of season, every change of weather, indeed every hour of the day, produces some change in the magical hues and shapes of these mountains, and they are regarded by all the good wives, far and near, as perfect barometers. When the weather is fair and settled, they are clothed in blue and purple, and print their bold outlines on the clear evening sky; but sometimes when the rest of the landscape is cloudless they will gather a hood of gray vapors about their summits, which, in the last rays of the setting sun, will glow and light up like a crown of glory.

At the foot of these fairy mountains, the voyager may have descried the light smoke curling up from a village, whose shingle-roofs gleam among the trees, just where the blue tints of the upland melt away into the fresh green of the nearer landscape. It is a little village of great antiquity, having been founded by some of the Dutch colonists in the early times of the province, just about the beginning of the government of the good Peter Stuyvesant, (may he rest in peace!) and there were some of the houses of the original settlers standing within a few years, built of small yellow bricks brought from Holland, having latticed windows and gable fronts, surmounted with weathercocks.

In the same village, and in one of these very houses (which, to tell the precise truth, was sadly time-worn and weather-beaten), there lived many years since, while the country was yet a province of Great Britain, a simple, good-natured fellow, of the name of Rip Van Winkle. He was a descendant of the Van Winkles who figured so gallantly in the chivalrous days of

Peter Stuyvesant, and accompanied him to the siege of Fort Christina. He inherited, however, but little of the martial character of his ancestors. I have observed that he was a simple, good-natured man; he was, moreover, a kind neighbor, and an obedient henpecked husband. Indeed, to the latter circumstance might be owing that meekness of spirit which gained him such universal popularity; for those men are most apt to be obsequious and conciliating abroad, who are under the discipline of shrews at home. Their tempers, doubtless, are rendered pliant and malleable in the fiery furnace of domestic tribulation; and a curtain lecture is worth all the sermons in the world for teaching the virtues of patience and long-suffering. A termagant wife may, therefore, in some respects be considered a tolerable blessing, and if so, Rip Van Winkle was thrice blessed.

Certain it is, that he was a great favorite among all the good wives of the village, who, as usual with the amiable sex, took his part in all family squabbles; and never failed, whenever they talked those matters over in their evening gossipings, to lay all the blame on Dame Van Winkle. The children of the village, too, would shout with joy whenever he approached. He assisted at their sports, made their playthings, taught them to fly kites and shoot marbles, and told them long stories of ghosts, witches, and Indians. Whenever he went dodging about the village, he was surrounded by a troop of them, hanging on his skirts, clambering on his back, and playing a thousand tricks on him with impunity; and not a dog would bark at him throughout the neighborhood.

The great error in Rip's composition was an insuperable aversion to all kinds of profitable labor. It could not be from the want of assiduity or perseverance; for he would sit on a wet rock, with a rod as long and heavy as a Tartar's lance, and fish all day without a murmur, even though he should not be encouraged by a single nibble. He would carry a fowling-piece on his shoulder for hours together, trudging through woods and swamps, and up hill and down dale, to shoot a few squirrels or wild pigeons. He would never refuse to assist a neighbor, even in the roughest toil, and was a foremost man at all country frolics for husking Indian corn, or building stone-fences; the women of the village, too, used to employ him to run their errands, and to do such little odd jobs as their less obliging husbands would not do for them. In a word, Rip was ready to attend to anybody's business but his own; but as to doing family duty, and keeping his farm in order, he found it impossible.

In fact, he declared it was of no use to work on his farm; it was the most pestilent little piece of ground in the whole country; everything about it went wrong, and would go wrong, in spite of him. His fences were continually falling to pieces; his cow would either go astray or get among the cabbages; weeds were sure to grow quicker in his fields than anywhere else; the rain always made a point of setting in just as he had some outdoor work to do; so that though his patrimonial estate had dwindled away under his management, acre by acre, until there was little more left than a mere patch of Indian corn and potatoes, yet it was the worst-conditioned farm in the neighborhood.

His children, too, were as ragged and wild as if they belonged to nobody. His son Rip, an urchin begotten in his own likeness, promised to inherit the habits, with the old clothes of his father. He was generally seen trooping like a colt at his mother's heels, equipped in a pair of his father's cast-off galli-gaskins, which he had much ado to hold up with one hand, as a fine lady does her train in bad weather.

Rip Van Winkle, however, was one of those happy mortals, of foolish, well-oiled dispositions, who take the world easy, eat white bread or brown, whichever can be got with least thought or trouble, and would rather starve on a penny than work for a pound. If left to himself, he would have whistled life away in perfect contentment; but his wife kept continually dinning in his ears about his idleness, his carelessness, and the ruin he was bringing on his family. Morning, noon, and night her tongue was incessantly going, and everything he said or did was sure to produce a torrent of household eloquence. Rip had but one way of replying to all lectures of the kind, and that, by frequent use, had grown into a habit. He shrugged his shoulders, shook his head, cast up his eyes, but said nothing. This, however, always provoked a fresh volley from his wife; so that he was fain to draw off his forces, and take to the outside of the house — the only side which, in truth, belongs to a henpecked husband.

Rip's sole domestic adherent was his dog Wolf, who was as much henpecked as his master; for Dame Van Winkle regarded them as companions in idleness, and even looked upon Wolf with an evil eye, as the cause of his master's going so often astray. True it is, in all points of spirit befitting an honorable dog, he was as courageous an animal as ever scoured the woods — but what courage can withstand the ever-during and all-besetting terrors of a woman's tongue? The moment Wolf entered the house his crest fell, his tail drooped to the ground, or curled between his legs, he sneaked about with a gallows air, casting many a sidelong glance at Dame Van Winkle, and at the least flourish of a broomstick or ladle he would fly to the door with yelping precipitation.

Times grew worse and worse with Rip Van Winkle as years of matrimony rolled on; a tart temper never mellows with age, and a sharp tongue is the only edged tool that grows keener with constant use. For a long while he used to console himself, when driven from home, by frequenting a kind of perpetual club of the sages, philosophers, and other idle personages of the village; which held its sessions on a bench before a small inn, designated by a rubicund portrait of His Majesty George the Third. Here they used to sit in the shade through a long lazy summer's day, talking listlessly over village gossip, or telling endless sleepy stories about nothing. But it would have been worth any statesman's money to have heard the profound discussions that sometimes took place, when by chance an old newspaper fell into their hands, from some passing traveller. How solemnly they would listen to the contents, as drawled out by Derrick Van Bummel, the school-master, a dapper learned little man, who was not to be daunted by the most gigantic word in the dictionary; and how sagely they would deliberate upon public events some months after they had taken place.

The opinions of this junto were completely controlled by Nicholas Vedder, a patriarch of the village, and landlord of the inn, at the door of which he took his seat from morning till night, just moving sufficiently to avoid the sun and keep in the shade of a large tree; so that the neighbors could tell the hour by his movements as accurately as by a sundial. It is true he was rarely heard to speak, but smoked his pipe incessantly. His adherents, however (for every great man has his adherents), perfectly understood him, and knew how to gather his opinions. When anything that was read or related displeased him, he was observed to smoke his pipe vehemently, and to send forth short, frequent and angry puffs; but when pleased, he would inhale the smoke slowly and tranquilly, and emit it in light and placid clouds; and sometimes, taking the pipe from his mouth, and letting the fragrant vapor curl about his nose, would gravely nod his head in token of perfect approbation.

From even this stronghold the unlucky Rip was at length routed by his termagant wife, who would suddenly break in upon the tranquillity of the assemblage and call the members all to naught; nor was that august personage, Nicholas Vedder himself, sacred from the daring tongue of this terrible virago, who charged him outright with encouraging her husband in habits of idleness.

Poor Rip was at last reduced almost to despair; and his only alternative, to escape from the labor of the farm and clamor of his wife, was to take gun in hand and stroll away into the woods. Here he would sometimes seat himself at the foot of a tree, and share the contents of his wallet with Wolf, with whom he sympathized as a fellow-sufferer in persecution. "Poor Wolf," he would say, "thy mistress leads thee a dog's life of it; but never mind, my lad, whilst I live thou shalt never want a friend to stand by thee!" Wolf would wag his tail, look wistfully in his master's face, and if dogs can feel pity I verily believe he reciprocated the sentiment with all his heart.

In a long ramble of the kind on a fine autumnal day, Rip had unconsciously scrambled to one of the highest parts of the Kaatskill Mountains. He was after his favorite sport of squirrel shooting, and the still solitudes had echoed and reëchoed with the reports of his gun. Panting and fatigued, he threw himself, late in the afternoon, on a green knoll, covered with mountain herbage, that crowned the brow of a precipice. From an opening between the trees he could overlook all the lower country for many a mile of rich woodland. He saw at a distance the lordly Hudson, far, far below him, moving on its silent but majestic course, with the reflection of a purple cloud, or the sail of a lagging bark, here and there sleeping on its glassy bosom, and at last losing itself in the blue highlands.

On the other side he looked down into a deep mountain glen, wild, lonely, and shagged, the bottom filled with fragments from the impending cliffs, and scarcely lighted by the reflected rays of the setting sun. For some time Rip lay musing on this scene; evening was gradually advancing; the mountains began to throw their long blue shadows over the valleys; he saw that it would be dark long before he could reach the village, and he heaved a heavy sigh when he thought of encountering the terrors of Dame Van Winkle.

As he was about to descend, he heard a voice from a distance, hallooing, "Rip Van Winkle! Rip Van Winkle!" He looked round, but could see nothing but a crow winging its solitary flight across the mountain. He thought his fancy must have deceived him, and turned again to descend, when he heard the same cry ring through the still evening air: "Rip Van Winkle! Rip Van Winkle!" — at the same time Wolf bristled up his back, and giving a low growl, skulked to his master's side, looking fearfully down into the glen. Rip now felt a vague apprehension stealing over him; he looked anxiously in the same direction, and perceived a strange figure slowly toiling up the rocks, and bending under the weight of something he carried on his back. He was surprised to see any human being in this lonely and unfrequented place; but supposing it to be some one of the neighborhood in need of his assistance, he hastened down to yield it.

On nearer approach he was still more surprised at the singularity of the stranger's appearance. He was a short, square-built old fellow, with thick bushy hair, and a grizzled beard. His dress was of the antique Dutch fashion: a cloth jerkin strapped round the waist, several pair of breeches, the outer one of ample volume, decorated with rows of buttons down the sides, and bunches at the knees. He bore on his shoulder a stout keg, that seemed full of liquor, and made signs for Rip to approach and assist him with the load. Though rather shy and distrustful of this new acquaintance, Rip complied with his usual alacrity; and mutually relieving one another, they clambered up a narrow gully, apparently the dry bed of a mountain torrent. As they ascended, Rip every now and then heard long rolling peals like distant thunder, that seemed to issue out of a deep ravine, or rather cleft, between lofty rocks, toward which their rugged path conducted. He paused for a moment, but supposing it to be the muttering of one of those transient thundershowers which often take place in mountain heights, he proceeded. Passing through the ravine, they came to a hollow, like a small amphitheatre, surrounded by perpendicular precipices, over the brinks of which impending trees shot their branches, so that you only caught glimpses of the azure sky and the bright evening cloud. During the whole time Rip and his companion had labored on in silence; for though the former marvelled greatly what could be the object of carrying a keg of liquor up this wild mountain, yet there was something strange and incomprehensible about the unknown, that inspired awe and checked familiarity.

On entering the amphitheatre, new objects of wonder presented themselves. On a level spot in the center was a company of odd-looking personages playing at ninepins. They were dressed in a quaint outlandish fashion; some wore short doublets, others jerkins, with long knives in their belts, and most of them had enormous breeches of similar style with that of the guide's. Their visages, too, were peculiar; one had a large beard, broad face, and small piggish eyes, the face of another seemed to consist entirely of nose, and was surmounted by a white sugarloaf hat, set off with a little red cock's tail. They all had beards, of various shapes and colors. There was one who seemed to be the commander. He was a stout old gentleman, with a weather-beaten countenance; he wore a laced doublet, broad belt and hanger, highcrowned hat and feather, red stockings, and high-heeled shoes, with roses in them. The whole group reminded Rip of the figures in an old Flemish painting in the parlor of Dominie Van Shaick, the village parson, which had been brought over from Holland at the time of the settlement.

What seemed particularly odd to Rip was, that though these folks were evidently amusing themselves, yet they maintained the gravest faces, the most mysterious silence, and were, withal, the most melancholy party of pleasure he had ever witnessed. Nothing interrupted the stillness of the scene but the noise of the balls, which, whenever they were rolled, echoed along the mountains like rumbling peals of thunder.

As Rip and his companion approached them, they suddenly desisted from their play, and stared at him with such fixed, statue-like gaze, and such strange, uncouth, lack-lustre countenances, that his heart turned within him, and his knees smote together. His companion now emptied the contents of the keg into large flagons, and made signs to him to wait upon the company. He obeyed with fear and trembling; they quaffed the liquor in profound silence, and then returned to their game.

By degrees Rip's awe and apprehension subsided. He even ventured, when no eye was fixed upon him, to taste the beverage, which he found had much of the flavor of excellent Hollands. He was naturally a thirsty soul, and was soon tempted to repeat the draught. One taste provoked another; and he reiterated his visits to the flagon so often that at length his senses were overpowered, his eyes swam in his head, his head gradually declined, and he fell into a deep sleep.

On waking, he found himself on the green knoll whence he had first seen the old man of the glen. He rubbed his eyes — it was a bright, sunny morning. The birds were hopping and twittering among the bushes, and the eagle was wheeling aloft, and breasting the pure mountain breeze. "Surely," thought Rip, "I have not slept here all night." He recalled the occurrences before he fell asleep. The strange man with a keg of liquor — the mountain ravine — the wild retreat among the rocks — the woe-begone party at nine-pins — the flagon — "Oh! that flagon! that wicked flagon!" thought Rip — "what excuse shall I make to Dame Van Winkle?"

He looked round for his gun, but in place of the clean, well-oiled fowling-piece, he found an old firelock lying by him, the barrel incrusted with rust, the lock falling off, and the stock worm-eaten. He now suspected that the grave roisters of the mountain had put a trick upon him, and, having dosed him with liquor, had robbed him of his gun. Wolf, too, had disappeared, but he might have strayed away after a squirrel or partridge. He whistled after him, and shouted his name, but all in vain; the echoes repeated his whistle and shout, but no dog was to be seen.

He determined to revisit the scene of the last evening's gambol, and if he met with any of the party, to demand his dog and gun. As he rose to walk, he found himself stiff in the joints, and wanting in his usual activity. "These mountain beds do not agree with me," thought Rip, "and if this frolic should lay me up with a fit of the rheumatism, I shall have a blessed time with Dame Van Winkle." With some difficulty he got down into the glen: he found the gully up which he and his companion had ascended the preceding evening; but to his astonishment a mountain stream was now foaming down it, leaping from rock to rock, and filling the glen with babbling murmurs. He, however, made shift to scramble up its sides, working his toilsome way through thickets of birch, sassafras, and witch-hazel, and sometimes tripped up or entangled by the wild grapevines that twisted their coils or tendrils from tree to tree, and spread a kind of network in his path.

At length he reached to where the ravine had opened through the cliffs to the amphitheatre; but no traces of such opening remained. The rocks presented a high, impenetrable wall, over which the torrent came tumbling in a sheet of feathery foam, and fell into a broad, deep basin, black from the shadows of the surrounding forest. Here, then, poor Rip was brought to a stand. He again called and whistled after his dog; he was only answered by the cawing of a flock of idle crows, sporting high in air about a dry tree that overhung a sunny precipice; and who, secure in their elevation, seemed to look down and scoff at the poor man's perplexities. What was to be done? the morning was passing away, and Rip felt famished for want of his breakfast. He grieved to give up his dog and gun; he dreaded to meet his wife; but it would not do to starve among the mountains. He shook his head, shouldered the rusty firelock, and, with a heart full of trouble and anxiety, turned his steps homeward.

As he approached the village he met a number of people, but none whom he knew, which somewhat surprised him, for he had thought himself acquainted with every one in the country round. Their dress, too, was of a different fashion from that to which he was accustomed. They all stared at him with equal marks of surprise, and whenever they cast their eyes upon him, invariably stroked their chins. The constant recurrence of this gesture induced Rip, involuntarily, to do the same, when, to his astonishment, he found his beard had grown a foot long!

He had now entered the skirts of the village. A troop of strange children ran at his heels, hooting after him, and pointing at his gray beard. The dogs, too, not one of which he recognized for an old acquaintance, barked at him as he passed. The very village was altered; it was larger and more populous. There were rows of houses which he had never seen before, and those which had been his familiar haunts had disappeared. Strange names were over the doors — strange faces at the windows, — everything was strange. His mind now misgave him; he began to doubt whether both he and the world around him were not bewitched. Surely this was his native village, which he had left but the day before. There stood the Kaatskill Mountains — there ran the silver Hudson at a distance — there was every hill and dale precisely as it had always been — Rip was sorely perplexed — "That flagon last night," thought he, "has addled my poor head sadly!"

It was with some difficulty that he found the way to his own house, which he approached with silent awe, expecting every moment to hear the shrill voice of Dame Van Winkle. He found the house gone to decay — the roof fallen in, the windows shattered, and the doors off the hinges. A half-starved dog that looked like Wolf was skulking about it. Rip called him by name, but the cur snarled, showed his teeth, and passed on. This was an unkind cut indeed — "My very dog," sighed poor Rip, "has forgotten me!"

He entered the house, which, to tell the truth, Dame Van Winkle had always kept in neat order. It was empty, forlorn, and apparently abandoned. This desolateness overcame all his connubial fears — he called loudly for his wife and children — the lonely chambers rang for a moment with his voice, and then again all was silence.

He now hurried forth, and hastened to his old resort, the village inn — but it, too, was gone. A large, rickety wooden building stood in its place, with great gaping windows, some of them broken and mended with old hats and petticoats, and over the door was painted, "The Union Hotel, by Jonathan Doolittle." Instead of the great tree that used to shelter the quiet little Dutch inn of yore, there now was reared a tall naked pole, with something on the top that looked like a red night-cap, and from it was fluttering a flag, on which was a singular assemblage of stars and stripes — all this was strange and incomprehensible. He recognized on the sign, however, the ruby face of King George, under which he had smoked so many a peaceful pipe; but even this was singularly metamorphosed. The red coat was changed for one of blue and buff, a sword was held in the hand instead of a sceptre, the head was decorated with a cocked hat, and underneath was painted in large characters, GENERAL WASHINGTON.

There was, as usual, a crowd of folk about the door, but none that Rip recollected. The very character of the people seemed changed. There was a busy, bustling, disputatious tone about it, instead of the accustomed phlegm and drowsy tranquillity. He looked in vain for the sage Nicholas Vedder, with his broad face, double chin, and fair long pipe, uttering clouds of tobacco-smoke instead of idle speeches; or Van Bummel, the schoolmaster, doling forth the contents of an ancient newspaper. In place of these, a lean, bilious-looking fellow, with his pockets full of handbills, was haranguing vehemently about rights of citizens — elections — members of congress — liberty — Bunker's Hill — heroes of seventy-six — and other words, which were a perfect Babylonish jargon to the bewildered Van Winkle.

The appearance of Rip, with his long grizzled beard, his rusty fowling-piece, his uncouth dress, and an army of women and children at his heels, soon attracted the attention of the tavern-politicians. They crowded round him, eyeing him from head to foot with great curiosity. The orator bustled up to him, and, drawing him partly aside, inquired "on which side he voted?" Rip stared in vacant stupidity. Another short but busy little fellow pulled him by the arm, and, rising on tiptoe, inquired in his ear, "Whether he was Federal or Democrat?" Rip was equally at a loss to comprehend the question; when a knowing, self-important old gentleman, in a sharp cocked hat, made his way through the crowd, putting them to the right and left with his elbows as he passed, and planting himself before Van Winkle, with one arm akimbo, the other resting on his cane, his keen eyes and sharp hat penetrating, as it were, into his very soul, demanded in an austere tone, "what brought him to the election with a gun on his shoulder, and a mob at his heels, and whether he meant to breed a riot in the village?" — "Alas! gentlemen," cried Rip, somewhat dismayed, "I am a poor quiet man, a native of the place, and a loyal subject of the king, God bless him!"

Here a general shout burst from the bystanders — "A tory! a tory! a spy! a refugee! hustle him! away with him!" It was with great difficulty that the self-important man in the cocked hat restored order; and, having assumed a tenfold austerity of brow, demanded again of the unknown culprit what he came there for, and whom he was seeking? The poor man humbly assured him that he meant no harm, but merely came there in search of some of his neighbors, who used to keep about the tavern.

"Well — who are they? — name them."

Rip bethought himself a moment, and inquired, "Where's Nicholas Vedder?"

There was a silence for a little while, when an old man replied, in a thin, piping voice: "Nicholas Vedder! why, he is dead and gone 5 these eighteen years! There was a wooden tombstone in the churchyard that used to tell all about him, but that is rotten and gone too."

"Where's Brom Dutcher?"

"Oh, he went off to the army in the begin- 10 ning of the war; some say he was killed at the storming of Stony Point — others say he was drowned in a squall at the foot of Antony's Nose. I don't know — he never came back again." 15

"Where's Van Bummel, the schoolmaster?"

"He went off to the wars too, was a great militia general, and is now in Congress."

Rip's heart died away at hearing of these sad changes in his home and friends, and 20 finding himself thus alone in the world. Every answer puzzled him too, by treating of such enormous lapses of time, and of matters which he could not understand: war — Congress — Stony Point; he had no courage to ask after any 25 more friends, but cried out in despair, "Does nobody here know Rip Van Winkle?"

"Oh, Rip Van Winkle!" exclaimed two or three, "Oh, to be sure! that's Rip Van Winkle yonder, leaning against the tree." 30

Rip looked, and beheld a precise counterpart of himself, as he went up the mountain: apparently as lazy, and certainly as ragged. The poor fellow was now completely confounded. He doubted his own identity, and whether he 35 was himself or another man. In the midst of his bewilderment, the man in the cocked hat demanded who he was, and what was his name?

"God knows," exclaimed he, at his wit's end; "I'm not myself — I'm somebody else — 40 that's me yonder — no — that's somebody else got into my shoes — I was myself, last night, but I fell asleep on the mountain and they've changed my gun, and everything's changed, and I'm changed, and I can't tell what's my name, 45 or who I am!"

The bystanders began now to look at each other, nod, wink significantly, and tap their fingers against their foreheads. There was a whisper, also, about securing the gun, and keep- 50 ing the old fellow from doing mischief, at the very suggestion of which the self-important man in the cocked hat retired with some precipitation. At this critical moment a fresh, comely

woman pressed through the throng to get a peep at the gray-bearded man. She had a chubby child in her arms, which, frightened at his looks, began to cry. "Hush, Rip," cried she, "hush, you little fool; the old man won't hurt you." The name of the child, the air of the mother, the tone of her voice, all awakened a train of recollections in his mind. "What is your name, my good woman?" asked he.

"Judith Gardenier."

"And your father's name?"

"Ah, poor man, Rip Van Winkle was his name, but it's twenty years since he went away from home with his gun, and never has been heard of since, — his dog came home without him, but whether he shot himself, or was carried away by the Indians, nobody can tell. I was then but a little girl."

Rip had but one question more to ask; and he put it with a faltering voice:

"Where's your mother?"

"Oh, she too died but a short time since; she broke a blood-vessel in a fit of passion at a New England peddler."

There was a drop of comfort, at least, in this intelligence. The honest man could contain himself no longer. He caught his daughter and her child in his arms. "I am your father!" cried he — "Young Rip Van Winkle once — old Rip Van Winkle now! Does nobody know poor Rip Van Winkle?"

All stood amazed, until an old woman, tottering out from among the crowd, put her hand to her brow, and peering under it in his face for a moment, exclaimed, "Sure enough it is Rip Van Winkle — it is himself! Welcome home again, old neighbor — Why, where have you been these twenty long years?"

Rip's story was soon told, for the whole twenty years had been to him but as one night. The neighbors stared when they heard it; some were seen to wink at each other, and put their tongues in their cheeks; and the self-important man in the cocked hat, who, when the alarm was over, had returned to the field, screwed down the corners of his mouth, and shook his head — upon which there was a general shaking of the head throughout the assemblage.

It was determined, however, to take the opinion of old Peter Vanderdonk, who was seen slowly advancing up the road. He was a descendant of the historian of that name, who wrote one of the earliest accounts of the province. Peter was the most ancient inhabitant of the village, and well versed in all the wonderful events and traditions of the neighborhood. He recollected Rip at once and corroborated his story in the most satisfactory manner. He assured the company that it was a fact, handed down from his ancestor the historian, that the Kaatskill Mountains had always been haunted by strange beings. That it was affirmed that the great Hendrick Hudson, the first discoverer of the river and country, kept a kind of vigil there every twenty years, with his crew of the Half-moon; being permitted in this way to revisit the scenes of his enterprise, and keep a guardian eye upon the river and the great city called by his name. That his father had once seen them in their old Dutch dresses playing at ninepins in a hollow of the mountain; and that he himself had heard, one summer afternoon, the sound of their balls like distant peals of thunder.

To make a long story short, the company broke up, and returned to the more important concerns of the election. Rip's daughter took him home to live with her; she had a snug well-furnished house, and a stout cheery farmer for a husband, whom Rip recollected for one of the urchins that used to climb upon his back. As to Rip's son and heir, who was the ditto of himself, seen leaning against the tree, he was employed to work on the farm, but evinced an hereditary disposition to attend to anything else but his business.

Rip now resumed his old walks and habits; he soon found many of his former cronies, though all rather the worse for the wear and tear of time, and preferred making friends among the rising generation, with whom he soon grew into great favor.

Having nothing to do at home, and being arrived at that happy age when a man can be idle with impunity, he took his place once more on the bench at the inn door, and was reverenced as one of the patriarchs of the village, and a chronicle of the old times "before the war." It was some time before he could get into the regular track of gossip, or could be made to comprehend the strange events that had taken place during his torpor. How that there had been a revolutionary war — that the country had thrown off the yoke of old England — and that, instead of being a subject of his Majesty George the Third, he was now a free citizen of the United States. Rip, in fact, was no politician; the changes of states and empires made but little impression on him; but there was one species of despotism under which he had long groaned, and that was — petticoat government. Happily that was at an end; he had got his neck out of the yoke of matrimony, and could go in and out whenever he pleased, without dreading the tyranny of Dame Van Winkle. Whenever her name was mentioned, however, he shook his head, shrugged his shoulders, and cast up his eyes, which might pass either for an expression of resignation to his fate, or joy at his deliverance.

He used to tell his story to every stranger that arrived at Mr. Doolittle's hotel. He was observed, at first, to vary on some points every time he told it, which was, doubtless, owing to his having so recently awaked. It at last settled down precisely to the tale I have related, and not a man, woman, or child in the neighborhood but knew it by heart. Some always pretended to doubt the reality of it, and insisted that Rip had been out of his head, and that this was one point on which he always remained flighty. The old Dutch inhabitants, however, almost universally gave it full credit. Even to this day they never hear a thunder-storm of a summer afternoon about the Kaatskill, but they say Hendrick Hudson and his crew are at their game of ninepins; and it is a common wish of all henpecked husbands in the neighborhood, when life hangs heavy on their hands, that they might have a quieting draught out of Rip Van Winkle's flagon.

James Fenimore Cooper [1789-1851]

Cooper belonged to New York — city and upstate. Though born in Burlington, New Jersey, he was little over a year old when taken to a frontier settlement at Cooperstown, New York, about one hundred fifty miles from Manhattan. At Cooperstown his Federalist father, Judge Cooper, owned thousands of acres, built a dwelling, and later a mansion called Otsego Hall. The boy was sent to Albany to be tutored by an English gentleman. At Yale, in his junior year, he was dismissed from college because of a prank. For some years he served as foremast hand on a merchant ship and as midshipman in the navy. Then he married and resigned from the navy. His wife was Susan DeLancey, daughter of a wealthy Tory family. He now assumed his inherited role as country gentleman, living in Westchester County, New York (later, in the city).

He drifted into authorship. To prove to his wife that he could write a better book than the English society novel he had been reading aloud to her, he produced a novel, of the same type, published as *Precaution*. Though conventionally sentimental, it served to set him upon his distinguished career in literature. It was followed by a romance of the American Revolution, *The Spy* (1821), the best novel yet written in America, highly popular at home and abroad.

From this success Cooper proceeded to a romanticized exploitation of the frontier life he had known as a boy: his famous series of novels known as the Leather-Stocking Tales. They are *The Pioneers* (1823), *The Last of the Mohicans* (1826), *The Prairie* (1827), *The Pathfinder* (1840), and *The Deerslayer* (1841). As the great character of *The Spy* had been a patriotic peddler, unhandsome in appearance but heroic of soul, so the central character of the Leather-Stocking Tales was one Natty Bumppo, a noble scout (there were noble savages too), who "stands as a protest, on behalf of simplicity and perfect freedom, against encroaching law and order." As civilization advances, Natty carries his virtues into the deeper forest, but at last is sought down and compelled to yield the battle. Though these books do not enthrall today as they did in the nineteenth century, they represent, like Scott's Waverley Novels, no mean achievement. What Cooper contributed to American literature can be understood only by reading at least one of them.

His life in New York furnished him with two great characters, Birch (*The Spy*) and Leather-Stocking. His experiences before the mast furnished him with another, Long Tom Coffin, in *The Pilot* (1824).

Between 1826 and 1833 Cooper lived in Europe, becoming absorbed in social and political philosophy, largely under the influence of Lafayette. A democrat by warm conviction, Cooper was an aristocrat by birth and training, and wished to preserve the aristocratic principle as a safeguard against the tyranny of pure democracy. His outlook was akin to that of Jefferson in an earlier America. But the Jacksonian revolution, occurring while he was abroad, reflected a national temper resentful of his stand. As R. E. Spiller has said, "He was firmly convinced that his countrymen had slipped from their first fine vision of the good life, that American facts were not keeping pace with American opinions nor opinions with facts, that Europeans understood neither American facts nor American opinions, and that he had been specially appointed to set everyone straight about everything." Much of his time and energy went into libel suits — generally successful — against persons who had defamed his character.

This interest led Cooper to write a number of novels of social criticism, such as *Satanstoe* (1945), *The Chainbearer* (1846), and *The Redskins* (1846). It also caused him to write such non-fictional works as *Notions of the Americans* (1828), *A Letter to His Countrymen* (1834), *Gleanings in Europe* (1837, 1838), and *The American Democrat* (1838), which represent a side of Cooper not revealed in the Leather-Stocking Tales.

Further reading: One of the Leather-Stocking Tales. *James Fenimore Cooper* (American Writers Series), 1936, ed. R. E. Spiller. T. R. Lounsbury, *James Fenimore Cooper* (life), 1882. R. E. Spiller, *Fenimore Cooper, Critic of His Times*, 1931.

From *Notions of the Americans*

(1828)

[American Literature]

In the verbal conflict between England and the new republic, Cooper took an active part, beginning with *Notions of the Americans*. Replying anonymously to unfavorable criticism, he here used a semi-fictional device: presented his views in the form of letters from an intelligent English gentleman traveling in the United States. As an essay toward better international understanding, the work had little success.

The passage given here was, for its time, an acute account of the literary situation in the United States. The absence of an international copyright to which Cooper refers — "the fact that an American publisher can get an English work without money" — favored the publication of English rather than American books. This conditioning factor in American literature was not remedied till the last decade of the century.

Compared to the books that are printed and read, those of native origin are few indeed. The principal reason of this poverty of original writers, is owing to the circumstance that men are not yet driven to their wits for bread. The United States are the first nation that possessed institutions, and, of course, distinctive opinions of its own, that was ever dependent on a foreign people for its literature. Speaking the same language as the English, and long in the habit of importing their books from the mother country, the revolution effected no immediate change in the nature of their studies, or mental amusements. The works were reprinted, it is true, for the purposes of economy, but they still continued English. Had the latter nation used this powerful engine with tolerable address, I think

they would have secured such an ally in this country as would have rendered their own decline not only more secure, but as illustrious as had been their rise. There are many theories entertained as to the effect produced in this country by the falsehoods and jealous calumnies which have been undeniably uttered in the mother country, by means of the press, concerning her republican descendant. It is my own opinion that, like all other ridiculous absurdities, they have defeated themselves, and that they are now more laughed at and derided, even here, than resented. By all that I can learn, twenty years ago, the Americans were, perhaps, far too much disposed to receive the opinions and to adopt the prejudices of their relatives; whereas, I think it is very apparent that they are now beginning to receive them with singular distrust. It is not worth our while to enter further into this subject, except as it has had, or is likely to have, an influence on the national literature.

It is quite obvious, that, so far as taste and forms alone are concerned, the literature of England and that of America must be fashioned after the same models. The authors, previously to the revolution, are common property, and it is quite idle to say that the American has not just as good a right to claim Milton, and Shakespeare, and all the old masters of the language, for his countrymen, as an Englishman. The Americans having continued to cultivate, and to cultivate extensively, an acquaintance with the writers of the mother country, since the separation, it is evident they must have kept pace with the trifling changes of the day. The only peculiarity that can, or ought to be expected in their literature, is that which is connected with the promulgation of their distinctive political opinions. They have not been remiss in this duty, as any one may see, who chooses to examine their books.***

The literature of the United States has, indeed, two powerful obstacles to conquer before (to use a mercantile expression) it can ever enter the markets of its own country on terms of perfect equality with that of England. Solitary and individual works of genius may, indeed, be occasionally brought to light, under the impulses of the high feeling which has conceived them; but, I fear, a good, wholesome, profitable and continued pecuniary support, is the applause that talent most craves. The fact, that an American publisher can get an English work without money, must for a few years longer, (unless legislative protection shall be extended to their own authors), have a tendency to repress a national literature. No man will pay a writer for an epic, a tragedy, a sonnet, a history, or a romance, when he can get a work of equal merit for nothing. I have conversed with those who are conversant on the subject, and, I confess, I have been astonished at the information they imparted.

A capital American publisher has assured me that there are not a dozen writers in this country whose works he should feel confidence in publishing at all, while he reprints hundreds of English books without the least hesitation. This preference is by no means so much owing to any difference in merit, as to the fact that, when the price of the original author is to be added to the uniform hazard which accompanies all literary speculations, the risk becomes too great. The general taste of the reading world in this country is better than that of England. The fact is both proved and explained by the circumstances that thousands of works that are printed and read in the mother country, are not printed and read here. The publisher on this side of the Atlantic has the advantage of seeing the reviews of every book he wishes to reprint, and, what is of far more importance, he knows, with the exception of books that he is sure of selling, by means of a name, the decision of the English critics before he makes his choice. Nine times in ten, popularity, which is all he looks for, is a sufficient test of general merit. Thus, while you find every English work of character, or notoriety, on the shelves of an American book-store, you may ask in vain for most of the trash that is so greedily devoured in the circulating libraries of the mother country, and which would be just as eagerly devoured here, had not a better taste been treated by a compelled abstinence. That taste must now be overcome before such works could be sold at all.

When I say that books are not rejected here, from any want of talent in the writers, perhaps I ought to explain. I wish to express something a little different. Talent is sure of too many avenues to wealth and honors, in America, to seek, unnecessarily, an unknown and hazardous path. It is better paid in the ordinary pursuits of life, than it would be likely to be paid by an adventure in which an extraordinary and skilful, because practised, foreign competition is certain. Perhaps high talent does not often make the trial with the American bookseller; but it is precisely for the reason I have named.

The second obstacle against which American literature has to contend, is in the poverty of materials. There is scarcely an ore which contributes to the wealth of the author, that is found, here, in veins as rich as in Europe. There are no annals for the historian; no follies (beyond the most vulgar and commonplace) for the satirist; no manners for the dramatist; no obscure fictions for the writer of romance; no gross and hardy offences against decorum for the moralist; nor any of the rich artificial auxiliaries of poetry. The weakest hand can extract a spark from the flint, but it would baffle the strength of a giant to attempt kindling a flame with a pudding-stone. I very well know there are theorists who assume that the society and institutions of this country are, or ought to be, particularly favorable to novelties and variety. But the experience of one month, in these States, is sufficient to show any observant man the falsity of their position. The effect of a promiscuous assemblage anywhere, is to create a standard of deportment; and great liberty permits every one to aim at its attainment. I have never seen a nation so much alike in my life, as the people of the United States, and what is more, they are not only like each other, but they are remarkably like that which common sense tells them they ought to resemble. No doubt, traits of character that are a little peculiar, without, however, being either very poetical, or very rich, are to be found in remote districts; but they are rare, and not always happy exceptions. In short, it is not possible to conceive a state of society in which more of the attributes of plain good sense, or fewer of the artificial absurdities of life, are to be found, than here. There is no costume for the peasant (there is scarcely a peasant at all), no wig for the judge, no baton for the general, no diadem for the chief magistrate. The darkest ages of their history are illuminated by the light of truth; the utmost efforts of their chivalry are limited by 5 the laws of God; and even the deeds of their sages and heroes are to be sung in a language that would differ but little from a version of the ten commandments. However useful and respectable all this may be in actual life, it indi- 10 cates but one direction to the man of genius.

Preface to the Leather-Stocking Tales

(1850)

❧ Nearly a decade after the last of the Leather-Stocking Tales, Cooper brought out a revised edition of the series of five novels. For it he wrote this preface, with breadth and judgment if not finesse. He places the novels both in the order written and the order of time of action. He states his intention in delineating his central character, Leather-Stocking. And he defends his favorable pictures of Indian character.

In his discussion of his Indians it will be noted that Cooper rejects the kinds of treatment now known as realistic and naturalistic. Instead he invokes the privilege of the romancer to elevate or idealize his characters. At the end, in leaning upon the example of Homer, he leaves unexamined the question whether idealism meant the same thing in classicism and romanticism.

This series of Stories, which has obtained the name of The Leather-Stocking Tales, has been 35 written in a very desultory and inartificial manner. The order in which the several books appeared was essentially different from that in which they would have been presented to the world, had the regular course of their incidents 40 been consulted. In The Pioneers, the first of the series written, the Leather-Stocking is represented as already old, and driven from his early haunts in the forest, by the sound of the axe, and the smoke of the settler. The Last of the 45 Mohicans, the next book in the order of publication, carried the readers back to a much earlier period in the history of our hero, representing him as middle-aged, and in the fullest vigor of manhood. In The Prairie, his career terminates, 50 and he is laid in his grave. There, it was originally the intention to leave him, in the expectation that, as in the case of the human mass, he would soon be forgotten. But a latent regard for

this character induced the author to resuscitate him in The Pathfinder, a book that was not long after succeeded by The Deerslayer, thus completing the series as it now exists.

While the five books that have been written were originally published in the order just mentioned, that of the incidents, insomuch as they are connected with the career of their principal character, is, as has been stated, very different. 10 Taking the life of the Leather-Stocking as a guide, The Deerslayer should have been the opening book, for in that work he is seen just emerging into manhood; to be succeeded by The Last of the Mohicans, The Pathfinder, The 15 Pioneers, and The Prairie. This arrangement embraces the order of events, though far from being that in which the books at first appeared. The Pioneers was published in 1822; The Deerslayer in 1841; making the interval between 20 them nineteen years. Whether these progressive years have had a tendency to lessen the value of the last-named book by lessening the native fire of its author, or of adding somewhat in the way of improved taste and a more matured judgment, 25 is for others to decide.

If anything from the pen of the writer of these romances is at all to outlive himself, it is, unquestionably, the series of The Leather-Stocking Tales. To say this, is not to predict a very 30 lasting reputation for the series itself, but simply to express the belief it will outlast any, or all, of the works from the same hand.

It is undeniable that the desultory manner in which The Leather-Stocking Tales were written, has, in a measure, impaired their harmony, and otherwise lessened their interest. This is proved by the fate of the two books last published, though probably the two most worthy an enlightened and cultivated reader's notice. If 40 the facts could be ascertained, it is probable the result would show that of all those (in America, in particular) who have read the three first books of the series, not one in ten has a knowledge of the existence even of the two last. Several 45 causes have tended to produce this result. The long interval of time between the appearance of The Prairie and that of The Pathfinder, was itself a reason why the later books of the series should be overlooked. There was no longer novelty to attract attention, and the interest was materially impaired by the manner in which events were necessarily anticipated, in laying the last of the series first before the world. With the generation that is now coming on the stage this fault will be partially removed by the edition contained in the present work, in which the several tales will be arranged solely in reference to their connection with each other.

The author has often been asked if he had any original in his mind, for the character of Leather-Stocking. In a physical sense, different individuals known to the writer in early life, certainly presented themselves as models, through his recollections; but in a moral sense this man of the forest is purely a creation. The idea of delineating a character that possessed little of civilization but its highest principles as they are exhibited in the uneducated, and all of savage life that is not incompatible with these great rules of conduct, is perhaps natural to the situation in which Natty was placed. He is too proud of his origin to sink into the condition of the wild Indian, and too much a man of the woods not to imbibe as much as was at all desirable, from his friends and companions. In a moral point of view it was the intention to illustrate the effect of seed scattered by the way side. To use his own language, his "gifts" were "white gifts," and he was not disposed to bring on them discredit. On the other hand, removed from nearly all the temptations of civilized life, placed in the best associations of that which is deemed savage, and favorably disposed by nature to improve such advantages, it appeared to the writer that his hero was a fit subject to represent the better qualities of both conditions, without pushing either to extremes.

There was no violent stretch of the imagination, perhaps, in supposing one of civilized associations in childhood, retaining many of his earliest lessons amid the scenes of the forest. Had these early impressions, however, not been sustained by continued, though casual connection with men of his own color, if not of his own caste, all our information goes to show he would soon have lost every trace of his origin. It is believed that sufficient attention was paid to the particular circumstances in which this individual was placed to justify the picture of his qualities that has been drawn. The Delawares early attracted the attention of missionaries, and were a tribe unusually influenced by their precepts and example. In many instances they became Christians, and cases occurred in which their subsequent lives gave proof of the efficacy of the great moral changes that had taken place within them.

A leading character in a work of fiction has a fair right to the aid which can be obtained from a poetical view of the subject. It is in this view, rather than in one more strictly circumstantial, that Leather-Stocking has been drawn. The imagination has no great task in portraying to itself a being removed from the every-day inducements to err, which abound in civilized life, while he retains the best and simplest of his early impressions; who sees God in the forest; hears him in the winds; bows to him in the firmament that o'ercanopies all; submits to his sway in a humble belief of his justice and mercy; in a word, a being who finds the impress of the Deity in all the works of nature, without any of the blots produced by the expedients, and passion, and mistakes of man. This is the most that has been attempted in the character of Leather-Stocking. Had this been done without any of the drawbacks of humanity, the picture would have been, in all probability, more pleasing than just. In order to preserve the *vraisemblable* [probable], therefore, traits derived from the prejudices, tastes, and even the weaknesses of his youth, have been mixed up with these higher qualities and longings, in a way, it is hoped, to represent a reasonable picture of human nature, without offering to the spectator a "monster of goodness."

It has been objected to these books that they give a more favorable picture of the red man than he deserves. The writer apprehends that much of this objection arises from the habits of those who have made it. One of his critics, on the appearance of the first work in which Indian character was portrayed, objected that its "characters were Indians of the school of Heckewelder, rather than of the school of nature." These words quite probably contain the substance of the true answer to the objection. Heckewelder was an ardent, benevolent missionary, bent on the good of the red man, and seeing in him one who had the soul, reason, and characteristics of a fellow-being. The critic is understood to have been a very distinguished agent of the government, one very familiar with Indians, as they are seen at the councils to treat for the sale of their lands, where little or none of their domestic qualities come in play, and where, indeed, their evil passions are known to have the fullest scope. As just would it be to draw conclusions of the general state of American society from the scenes of the capital, as to suppose that the negotiating of one of these treaties is a fair picture of Indian life.

It is the privilege of all writers of fiction, more particularly when their works aspire to the elevation of romances, to present the *beau-idéal* [model of excellence] of their characters to the reader. This it is which constitutes poetry, and to suppose that the red man is to be repre- sented only in the squalid misery or in the de- graded moral state that certainly more or less belongs to his condition, is, we apprehend, tak- ing a very narrow view of an author's privileges. Such criticism would have deprived the world of even Homer.

William Cullen Bryant [1794–1878]

In an autobiographical account of his early years Bryant tells of his birth at Cum- mington, in the Berkshire Hills of Massachusetts, on November 3, 1794; of his father, a poetry-loving physician, his mother, descended from John and Priscilla Alden, and his maternal grandfather, a devout Calvinist in whose home he spent much of his child- hood; of his experience in country activities — fishing, cornhusking, making maple syrup and cider; of his enthusiasm over Pope's translation of the *Iliad*, of his own first writing of verse, and his Popean political satire "The Embargo," attacking Jefferson, published in 1808; of his one year at Williams College, his law studies, and his admission to the bar; and of his reading just prior to the composition of "Thanatopsis."

The reception accorded "Thanatopsis," and the success of other early writings, lost Massachusetts a lawyer and gave America a man of letters. "Ah, Phillips, you have been imposed upon," said R. H. Dana to one of the editors of the *North American Review* who showed him the newly-submitted manuscript of "Thanatopsis." "No one on this side of the Atlantic is capable of writing such verses." In 1821 Bryant read the Phi Beta Kappa poem at Harvard and published his first important volume of verse. In 1825 he abandoned the practice of law and removed to New York to edit the *New York Review*. The following year he became assistant editor of the *New York Evening Post*, and three years later, in 1829, he began fifty years as editor in chief and part owner.

Bryant's long life in New York was primarily that of one of the great editors of Ameri- can journalism in a period when taste, highmindedness, and dignity were valued. A liberal, he supported such causes as free speech, free trade, collective bargaining, and the abolition of slavery. Investing his *Post* profits, he acquired a fortune. He made six voyages to Europe, delivered many addresses on public affairs and on the arts, trans- lated the *Iliad* and *Odyssey* into English blank verse, published several more volumes of his own verse.

Bryant's literary reputation continues to rest on a few poems, minor classics of American verse, whose intrinsic qualities have outlasted their historical importance as early expressions of romanticism. Lowell's rather damaging couplet in "A Fable for Critics" dismissing him as "cool and dignified" as an "iceberg" should be read along- side the concluding judgment that Bryant was the only poet of his day who knew "How much grace, strength, and dignity lie in Repose." "To a Waterfowl," for many readers, still merits the opinion of Matthew Arnold as the finest poem of its length in the English language. Bryant's poetry counted most in the earlier years, from 1821 to 1832, years when it was natural for a poet to face two ways, toward the eighteenth-century taste which was declining and the romantic which was advancing. One can see in him, as his art developed, a conflict between, on the one hand, the examples of Thomson,

Cowper, and the graveyard poets, and on the other, the examples of Byron and Words-worth. Had he merely imitated, he would not have merited our attention; he assimilated, rather, what he could use, while achieving his own poetic vision and technique.

Further reading: *Poetical Works. William Cullen Bryant* (American Writers Series), ed. by Tremaine McDowell, 1935. Biographies by John Bigelow, 1890, and W. A. Bradley, 1905.

Thanatopsis
(w. *1811–21*)

✦ Not since the time of Edward Taylor had New England shown an imaginative vitality comparable with that of the young Bryant in this poem. Between the two, Calvinistic orthodoxy had declined, despite the Great Awakening, and the intellectual climate had been changed by deism and Unitarianism. Notwithstanding Bryant's Calvinistic boyhood, his poem on death is not recognizably Christian in any sense.

He probably started writing this famous poem when he was a youth of sixteen. Originally it began "Yet a few days" and ended "make their bed with thee" (lines 18–66 of the poem as we now have it). In this form it was sent by his father to the *North American Review*, along with another poem on death the boy had written. The editors, assuming that the two poems were one, so published them in September, 1817, under the Greek title "Thanatopsis" ("View of Death"). In 1821 Bryant substituted lines 1–17 (present version) for the poem that had been mistakenly included, and at the end added lines 66–81 (present version).

In the ten years between the original beginning and the final completion, the young poet had naturally changed. He had begun in a manner reminiscent of modern deism and ancient stoicism, and in the poetic tradition of the English pre-romantics of the graveyard school such as Henry Kirke White and Robert Blair. Then he prefixed an introduction, possibly suggested by the poet Akenside's phrase "Then Nature speaks her genuine language" as well as by Wordsworth's celebration of nature. Because of this introduction, the voice that speaks in the long middle section of the poem is no longer the poet's "better genius," as it had been in the original poem, but the voice of Nature. At the same time, in the added conclusion, he gave to the whole poem a moralizing turn.

As might be expected, adjustment of such different parts to each other was far from perfect. Nature is glad, beautiful, sympathetic (introduction), yet she tells her lover that he will soon lie in the cold ground, since the whole earth is "the great tomb of man" (middle part). Meanwhile he should so live that he will be prepared to meet death serenely, "sustained and soothed By an unfaltering trust" —

in what? If this confusion troubles few readers, it is mainly because Bryant has such a compelling vision of the universality of death in time and the world. He invests it with a certain grandeur, which comes from the conception itself and also from his elevated stoical attitude, the breadth of his imagery, the solemn strength of his blank verse, and the sureness of his feeling for language.

To him who in the love of Nature holds
Communion with her visible forms, she speaks
A various language: for his gayer hours
She has a voice of gladness, and a smile
And eloquence of beauty, and she glides   5
Into his darker musings, with a mild
And healing sympathy that steals away
Their sharpness ere he is aware. When thoughts
Of the last bitter hour come like a blight
Over thy spirit, and sad images   10
Of the stern agony, and shroud, and pall,
And breathless darkness, and the narrow house,
Make thee to shudder and grow sick at heart, —
Go forth under the open sky and list   14
To Nature's teachings, while from all around —
Earth and her waters and the depths of air —
Comes a still voice:
                    Yet a few days, and thee
The all-beholding sun shall see no more
In all his course; nor yet in the cold ground,
Where thy pale form was laid with many tears,
Nor in the embrace of ocean, shall exist   21
Thy image. Earth, that nourished thee, shall claim
Thy growth, to be resolved to earth again,
And, lost each human trace, surrendering up
Thine individual being, shalt thou go   25
To mix for ever with the elements,
To be a brother to the insensible rock
And to the sluggish clod, which the rude swain
Turns with his share and treads upon; the oak
Shall send his roots abroad and pierce thy mould.   30

Yet not to thine eternal resting-place
Shalt thou retire alone, nor couldst thou wish

Couch more magnificent. Thou shalt lie down
With patriarchs of the infant world, with kings,
The powerful of the earth, the wise, the good,
Fair forms, and hoary seers of ages past,   36
All in one mighty sepulchre. The hills
Rock-ribbed and ancient as the sun; the vales
Stretching in pensive quietness between;
The venerable woods, rivers that move   40
In majesty, and the complaining brooks
That make the meadows green; and, poured
        round all,
Old Ocean's gray and melancholy waste, —
Are but the solemn decorations all
Of the great tomb of man. The golden sun,   45
The planets, all the infinite host of heaven,
Are shining on the sad abodes of death,
Through the still lapse of ages. All that tread
The globe are but a handful to the tribes
That slumber in its bosom. Take the wings   50
Of morning, pierce the Barcan wilderness,
Or lose thyself in the continuous woods
Where rolls the Oregon, and hears no sound
Save his own dashings; yet the dead are there,
And millions in those solitudes, since first   55
The flight of years began, have laid them down
In their last sleep: the dead reign there alone.
So shalt thou rest; and what if thou withdraw
In silence from the living, and no friend
Take note of thy departure? All that breathe   60
Will share thy destiny. The gay will laugh
When thou art gone, the solemn brood of
        care
Plod on, and each one as before will chase
His favorite phantom; yet all these shall leave
Their mirth and their employments, and shall
        come   65
And make their bed with thee. As the long train
Of ages glide away, the sons of men —
The youth in life's green spring, and he who
        goes
In the full strength of years, matron and maid,
The speechless babe, and the gray-headed
        man —   70
Shall one by one be gathered to thy side
By those who in their turn shall follow them.

    So live, that when thy summons comes to
        join
The innumerable caravan which moves
To that mysterious realm where each shall take
His chamber in the silent halls of death,   76
Thou go not, like the quarry-slave at night,
Scourged to his dungeon, but, sustained and
        soothed

By an unfaltering trust, approach thy grave
Like one who wraps the drapery of his couch   80
About him and lies down to pleasant dreams.

The Yellow Violet

(w. 1814)

While a law student Bryant came upon the poems of Wordsworth in *Lyrical Ballads*. According to R. H. Dana, "He said that, upon opening the book, a thousand springs seemed to gush up at once in his heart, and the face of Nature, of a sudden, to change into a strange freshness and life." The effect upon his own poetry we have already noted in the opening passage of "Thanatopsis." It appears again in his poem on the yellow violet, which may be compared with Wordsworth's "To the Daisy" ("In youth from rock to rock"). Preceding Wordsworth's poem was Burns's "To a Mountain Daisy." In America, Freneau had written "The Wild Honeysuckle" (see page 173).

In Bryant's poem one can see the conflict between the roundabout phrases of neo-classic verse (as in line 30) and the direct language commonly sought in romantic verse. It is worthwhile also to consider the structure of the poem (is it appropriate to the theme? is it compact or discursive?), the question of sentimentalism (is it avoided?), the justification, if any, of the "moral."

When beechen buds begin to swell,
    And woods the bluebird's warble know,
The yellow violet's modest bell
    Peeps from the last year's leaves below.

Ere russet fields their green resume,   5
    Sweet flower, I love, in forest bare,
To meet thee, when thy faint perfume
    Alone is in the virgin air.

Of all her train, the hands of Spring
    First plant thee in the watery mould,   10
And I have seen thee blossoming
    Beside the snow-bank's edges cold.

Thy parent sun, who bade thee view
    Pale skies, and chilling moisture sip,
Has bathed thee in his own bright hue,   15
    And streaked with jet thy glowing lip.

Yet slight thy form, and low thy seat,
    And earthward bent thy gentle eye,
Unapt the passing view to meet,
    When loftier flowers are flaunting nigh.   20

Oft, in the sunless April day,
 Thy early smile has stayed my walk;
But midst the gorgeous blooms of May,
 I passed thee on thy humble stalk.

So they, who climb to wealth, forget   25
 The friends in darker fortunes tried.
I copied them — but I regret
 That I should ape the ways of pride.

And when again the genial hour
 Awakes the painted tribes of light, 30
I'll not o'erlook the modest flower
 That made the woods of April bright.

Inscription for the Entrance to a Wood

(w. 1815)

First published along with "Thanatopsis" in the same issue of the *North American Review*, this poem carries further the conception of nature in "Thanatopsis" as full of pleasure and as communicating to man a healing sympathy. In this respect Bryant is at one with Wordsworth. But he does not share Wordsworth's pantheistic feeling of a divine presence in nature, or call himself a "worshipper of Nature." The word *God* does not appear in Wordsworth's "Tintern Abbey," or in Bryant's "Thanatopsis" but it does appear in this "Inscription" — and with a specific Christian reference. The "primal curse" (line 11) that fell upon sinning man in Paradise fell also upon the unsinning earth: "And unto Adam he said, Because thou hast hearkened unto the voice of thy wife, and hast eaten of the tree, . . . cursed is the ground for thy sake" (Genesis 3:17).

Stranger, if thou hast learned a truth which needs
No school of long experience, that the world
Is full of guilt and misery, and hast seen
Enough of all its sorrows, crimes, and cares
To tire thee of it, enter this wild wood 5
And view the haunts of Nature. The calm shade
Shall bring a kindred calm; and the sweet breeze,
That makes the green leaves dance, shall waft a balm
To thy sick heart. Thou wilt find nothing here
Of all that pained thee in the haunts of men 10
And made thee loathe thy life. The primal curse
Fell, it is true, upon the unsinning earth,
But not in vengeance. God hath yoked to guilt
Her pale tormentor, misery. Hence these shades

Are still the abodes of gladness: the thick roof 15
Of green and stirring branches is alive
And musical with birds, that sing and sport
In wantonness of spirit; while, below,
The squirrel, with raised paws and form erect,
Chirps merrily. Throngs of insects in the shade 20
Try their thin wings and dance in the warm beam
That waked them into life. Even the green trees
Partake the deep contentment; as they bend
To the soft winds, the sun from the blue sky
Looks in and sheds a blessing on the scene. 25
Scarce less the cleft-born wild-flower seems to enjoy
Existence than the wingèd plunderer
That sucks its sweets. The mossy rocks themselves,
And the old and ponderous trunks of prostrate trees
That lead from knoll to knoll a causey rude 30
Or bridge the sunken brook, and their dark roots,
With all their earth upon them, twisting high,
Breathe fixed tranquillity. The rivulet
Sends forth glad sounds, and, tripping o'er its bed
Of pebbly sands or leaping down the rocks, 35
Seems with continuous laughter to rejoice
In its own being. Softly tread the marge,
Lest from her midway perch thou scare the wren
That dips her bill in water. The cool wind,
That stirs the stream in play, shall come to thee, 40
Like one that loves thee nor will let thee pass
Ungreeted, and shall give its light embrace.

To a Waterfowl

(w. 1815)

Bryant was only twenty-one when he wrote this lyric. Though he lived to an eighty-fourth year, he never wrote so well again. It came out of a specific situation. One day in December, Bryant walked to Plainfield, Mass., to inquire into opportunities there for beginning the practice of law. He "says in a letter that he felt, as he walked up the hills, very forlorn and desolate indeed, not knowing what was to become of him in the big world. . . . The sun had already set, leaving behind it one of those brilliant seas of chrysolite and opal which often flood the New England skies; and while he was looking upon the rosy splendor with rapt admiration, a solitary bird made wing along the illuminated horizon. He watched the lone wanderer until it was lost in the distance, asking himself whither it had come and to what far home it was flying. When he went to the house where he was to stop for the night, his mind was still full of what he had seen and felt, and he wrote those lines. . . ." (P. Godwin).

From the point of view of poetic taste in our time, the conclusion poses a question. Is the "lesson" merely appended, extraneous, so that it damages the poem's unity, or does it grow out of the rest of the poem naturally, completing a true whole? If the last stanza were omitted (and the preceding stanza altered to avoid the idea of a lesson), what would the poem gain or lose?

Whither, midst falling dew,
While glow the heavens with the last steps of day,
Far through their rosy depths dost thou pursue
Thy solitary way?

Vainly the fowler's eye   5
Might mark thy distant flight to do thee wrong,
As, darkly seen against the crimson sky,
Thy figure floats along.

Seek'st thou the plashy brink
Of weedy lake or marge of river wide,   10
Or where the rocking billows rise and sink
On the chafed ocean-side?

There is a Power whose care
Teaches thy way along that pathless coast —
The desert and illimitable air, —   15
Lone wandering, but not lost.

All day thy wings have fanned,
At that far height, the cold thin atmosphere,
Yet stoop not, weary, to the welcome land,
Though the dark night is near.   20

And soon that toil shall end:
Soon shalt thou find a summer home, and rest,
And scream among thy fellows; reeds shall bend,
Soon, o'er thy sheltered nest.

Thou'rt gone, the abyss of heaven   25
Hath swallowed up thy form; yet, on my heart
Deeply has sunk the lesson thou hast given,
And shall not soon depart.

He who, from zone to zone,
Guides through the boundless sky thy certain flight,   30
In the long way that I must tread alone
Will lead my steps aright.

Green River

(w. 1818)

At Great Barrington, Mass., Bryant often sought relief from his legal preoccupation in the beauty and peace of the country along the river. Apparently the lively rhythm was intended to suit the gayety of his mood.

When breezes are soft and skies are fair,
I steal an hour from study and care,
And hie me away to the woodland scene,
Where wanders the stream with waters of green;
As if the bright fringe of herbs on its brink,   5
Had given their stain to the wave they drink;
And they, whose meadows it murmurs through,
Have named the stream from its own fair hue.

Yet pure its waters — its shallows are bright
With colored pebbles and sparkles of light.   10
And clear the depths where its eddies play,
And dimples deepen and whirl away,
And the plane-tree's speckled arms o'ershoot
The swifter current that mines its root,
Through whose shifting leaves, as you walk the hill,   15
The quivering glimmer of sun and rill,
With a sudden flash on the eye is thrown,
Like the ray that streams from the diamond-stone.
Oh, loveliest there the spring days come,
With blossoms, and birds, and wild-bees' hum;
The flowers of summer are fairest there,   21
And freshest the breath of the summer air;
And sweetest the golden autumn day
In silence and sunshine glides away.

Yet fair as thou art, thou shun'st to glide,
Beautiful stream! by the village side;   26
But windest away from haunts of men,
To quiet valley and shaded glen;
And forest, and meadow, and slope of hill,
Around thee, are lonely, lovely, and still.   30
Lonely — save when, by thy rippling tides,
From thicket to thicket the angler glides;
Or the simpler comes with basket and book,
For herbs of power on thy banks to look;
Or haply, some idle dreamer, like me,   35
To wander, and muse, and gaze on thee.
Still — save the chirp of birds that feed

On the river cherry and seedy reed,
And thy own mild music gushing out
With mellow murmur and fairy shout,   40
From dawn, to the blush of another day,
Like traveller singing along his way.

    That fairy music I never hear,
Nor gaze on those waters so green and clear,
And mark them winding away from sight,   45
Darkened with shade or flashing with light,
While o'er them the vine to its thicket clings,
And the zephyr stoops to freshen his wings,
But I wish that fate had left me free
To wander these quiet haunts with thee,   50
Till the eating cares of earth should depart,
And the peace of the scene pass into my heart;
And I envy the stream, as it glides along,
Through its beautiful banks in a trance of song.

    Though forced to drudge for the dregs of
      men,   55
And scrawl strange words with the barbarous
      pen,
And mingle among the jostling crowd,
Where the sons of strife are subtle and loud —
I often come to this quiet place,
To breathe the airs that ruffle thy face,   60
And gaze upon thee in silent dream,
For in thy lonely and lovely stream,
An image of that calm life appears,
That won my heart in my greener years.

A Winter Piece

(w. 1820)

Also written at Great Barrington. However indebted to Wordsworth, Bryant himself was in various ways similar to the English poet and his poetry arose from genuine experience.

    The time has been that these wild solitudes,
Yet beautiful as wild, were trod by me
Oftener than now; and when the ills of life
Had chafed my spirit — when the unsteady
    pulse
Beat with strange flutterings — I would wander
    forth   5
And seek the woods. The sunshine on my path
Was to me as a friend. The swelling hills,
The quiet dells retiring far between,
With gentle invitation to explore
Their windings, were a calm society   10

That talked with me and soothed me. Then the
    chant
Of birds, and chime of brooks, and soft caress
Of the fresh sylvan air, made me forget
The thoughts that broke my peace, and I began
To gather simples by the fountain's brink,   15
And lose myself in day-dreams. While I stood
In nature's loneliness, I was with one
With whom I early grew familiar, one
Who never had a frown for me, whose voice
Never rebuked me for the hours I stole   20
From cares I loved not, but of which the world
Deems highest, to converse with her. When
    shrieked
The bleak November winds, and smote the
    woods,
And the brown fields were herbless, and the
    shades,
That met above the merry rivulet,   25
Were spoiled, I sought, I loved them still, —
    they seemed
Like old companions in adversity.
Still there was beauty in my walks; the brook,
Bordered with sparkling frost-work, was as gay
As with its fringe of summer flowers. Afar,   30
The village with its spires, the path of streams,
And dim receding valleys, hid before
By interposing trees, lay visible
Through the bare grove, and my familiar haunts
Seemed new to me. Nor was I slow to come   35
Among them, when the clouds, from their still
    skirts,
Had shaken down on earth the feathery snow,
And all was white. The pure keen air abroad,
Albeit it breathed no scent of herb, nor heard
Love-call of bird nor merry hum of bee,   40
Was not the air of death. Bright mosses crept
Over the spotted trunks, and the close buds,
That lay along the boughs, instinct with life,
Patient, and waiting the soft breath of Spring,
Feared not the piercing spirit of the North.   45
The snow-bird twittered on the beechen bough,
And 'neath the hemlock, whose thick branches
    bent
Beneath its bright cold burden, and kept dry
A circle, on the earth, of withered leaves,
The partridge found a shelter. Through the snow
The rabbit sprang away. The lighter track   51
Of fox, and the raccoon's broad path were there,
Crossing each other. From his hollow tree,
The squirrel was abroad, gathering the nuts
Just fallen, that asked the winter cold and
    sway   55
Of winter blast, to shake them from their hold.

But winter has yet brighter scenes, — he
  boasts
Splendors beyond what gorgeous summer knows;
Or autumn, with his many fruits, and woods
All flushed with many hues. Come, when the
  rains   60
Have glazed the snow, and clothed the trees with
  ice;
While the slant sun of February pours
Into the bowers a flood of light. Approach!
The encrusted surface shall upbear thy steps,
And the broad arching portals of the grove   65
Welcome thy entering. Look! the massy trunks
Are cased in pure crystal, each light spray,
Nodding and tinkling in the breath of heaven,
Is studded with its trembling water-drops,   69
That stream with rainbow radiance as they move.
But round the parent stem the long low boughs
Bend, in a glittering ring, and arbors hide
The grassy floor. Oh! you might deem the spot
The spacious cavern of the virgin mine,
Deep in the womb of earth — where the gems
  grow,   75
And diamonds put forth radiant rods and bud
With amethyst and topaz — and the place
Lit up, most royally, with the pure beam
That dwells in them. Or haply the vast hall
Of fairy palace, that outlasts the night,   80
And fades not in the glory of the sun; —
Where crystal columns send forth slender shafts
And crossing arches; and fantastic aisles
Wind from the sight in brightness, and are lost
Among the crowded pillars. Raise thine eye, —
Thou seest no cavern roof, no palace vault;   86
There the blue sky and the white drifting cloud
Look in. Again the wildered fancy dreams
Of spouting fountains, frozen as they rose,
And fixed, with all their branching jets, in air,
And all their sluices sealed. All, all is light; 91
Light without shade. But all shall pass away
With the next sun. From numberless vast
  trunks,
Loosened, the crashing ice shall make a sound
Like the far roar of rivers, and the eve   95
Shall close o'er the brown woods as it was wont.

   And it is pleasant, when the noisy streams
Are just set free, and milder suns melt off
The plashy snow, save only the firm drift   99
In the deep glen or the close shade of pines, —
'Tis pleasant to behold the wreaths of smoke
Roll up among the maples of the hill,
Where the shrill sound of youthful voices wakes
The shriller echo, as the clear pure lymph,   104

That from the wounded trees, in twinkling
  drops,
Falls, 'mid the golden brightness of the morn,
Is gathered in with brimming pails, and oft,
Wielded by sturdy hands, the stroke of axe
Makes the woods ring. Along the quiet air
Come and float calmly off the soft light clouds,
Such as you see in summer, and the winds   111
Scarce stir the branches. Lodged in sunny cleft,
Where the cold breezes come not, bloom alone
The little wind-flower, whose just opened eye
Is blue as the spring heaven it gazes at —   115
Startling the loiterer in the naked groves
With unexpected beauty, for the time
Of blossoms and green leaves is yet afar.
And ere it comes, the encountering winds shall
  oft
Muster their wrath again, and rapid clouds   120
Shade heaven, and bounding on the frozen earth
Shall fall their volleyed stores, rounded like hail,
And white like snow, and the loud North again
Shall buffet the vexed forests in his rage.

O Fairest of the Rural Maids
(w. 1820)

🎏 This poem Bryant addressed to Frances Fair-
child a year before their marriage. It may be compared with Wordsworth's "Three Years She Grew
in Sun and Shower."

O fairest of the rural maids!
Thy birth was in the forest shades;
Green boughs, and glimpses of the sky,
Were all that met thine infant eye.

Thy sports, thy wanderings, when a child, 5
Were ever in the sylvan wild;
And all the beauty of the place
Is in thy heart and on thy face.

The twilight of the trees and rocks
Is in the light shade of thy locks;   10
Thy step is as the wind, that weaves
Its playful way among the leaves.

Thine eyes are springs, in whose serene
And silent waters heaven is seen;
Their lashes are the herbs that look   15
On their young figures in the brook.

The forest depths, by foot unpressed,
Are not more sinless than thy breast;

The holy peace, that fills the air
Of those calm solitudes, is there.   20

A Forest Hymn

(w. 1825)

The last poem written by Bryant in Great Barrington before removing to New York. In "this great
city" he was to lose his intimate contact with nature.
In fact nearly twenty years passed before he regained
it by living several days a week at an old country
mansion on Long Island.

As if he foresaw the alienation to come, he wrote
a poem which, more fully than any other, expresses
what nature meant to him. He called it a hymn; it
is, rather, a reflective blank-verse poem in which he
self-consciously analyzes his ideas and feelings. It is
composed of an introduction and three paragraphs
concerning different aspects of his relation to nature
as the work of God.

Much of the poem reminds us of Wordsworth.
Especially (as Tremaine McDowell has pointed out)
do lines 38–47 seem very close to "Tintern Abbey,"
lines 95–102. Here Bryant even shares Wordsworth's
feeling of a divine *presence* in nature. But he does
not repeat the emotional abandon of Wordsworth's
famous poem. Bryant's deity, even if present, im-
manent, in nature, is still the transcendent "Father"
and "Maker" of the old Puritans, and still, as in
deism, the Creator who revealed himself in the order
of nature (note "witness" in line 53, together with
the last two lines of the poem). There is also a
passage in which Bryant repeats his old conception
of nature as the great tomb of man. A prevailing
emphasis on the "tranquillity" of nature (in Wordsworth, "quietness" and "tranquil restoration") is
offset by recognition of "the mad unchained elements" that "scare the world."

The result is hardly a unified attitude. In sum we
may say that the poem has some features that conform to Christianity, and more that are deistic and
romantic. Thus Bryant's romanticism is cautious and
restrained.

The groves were God's first temples. Ere man
        learned
To hew the shaft, and lay the architrave,
And spread the roof above them — ere he
        framed
The lofty vault, to gather and roll back
The sound of anthems; in the darkling wood,
Amid the cool and silence, he knelt down,   6
And offered to the Mightiest solemn thanks
And supplication. For his simple heart
Might not resist the sacred influence
Which, from the stilly twilight of the place,   10

And from the gray old trunks that high in
        heaven
Mingled their mossy boughs, and from the
        sound
Of the invisible breath that swayed at once
All their green tops, stole over him, and bowed
His spirit with the thought of boundless power
And inaccessible majesty. Ah, why   16
Should we, in the world's riper years, neglect
God's ancient sanctuaries, and adore
Only among the crowd, and under roofs
That our frail hands have raised? Let me, at
        least,   20
Here, in the shadow of this aged wood,
Offer one hymn — thrice happy, if it find
Acceptance in His ear.

                    Father, thy hand
Hath reared these venerable columns, thou
Didst weave this verdant roof. Thou didst look
        down   25
Upon the naked earth, and, forthwith, rose
All these fair ranks of trees. They, in thy sun,
Budded, and shook their green leaves in thy
        breeze,
And shot toward heaven. The century-living
        crow
Whose birth was in their tops, grew old and
        died   30
Among their branches, till at last they stood,
As now they stand, massy and tall and dark,
Fit shrine for humble worshipper to hold
Communion with his Maker. These dim vaults,
These winding isles, of human pomp or pride
Report not; no fantastic carvings show   36
The boast of our vain race to change the form
Of thy fair works. But thou art here — thou
        fill'st
The solitude. Thou art in the soft winds,
That run along the summit of these trees   40
In music; thou art in the cooler breath,
That from the inmost darkness of the place,
Comes, scarcely felt; the barky trunks, the
        ground,
The fresh moist ground, are all instinct with
        thee.
Here is continual worship: Nature, here,   45
In the tranquillity that thou dost love,
Enjoys thy presence. Noiselessly around,
From perch to perch, the solitary bird
Passes; and yon clear spring, that midst its herbs
Wells softly forth and, wandering, steeps the
        roots   50
Of half the mighty forest, tells no tale

Of all the good it does. Thou hast not left
Thyself without a witness, in the shades,
Of thy perfections. Grandeur, strength, and
    grace
Are here to speak of thee. This mighty oak, 55
By whose immovable stem I stand and seem
Almost annihilated — not a prince,
In all that proud old world beyond the deep,
E'er wore his crown as loftily as he 59
Wears the green coronal of leaves with which
Thy hand has graced him. Nestled at his root
Is beauty such as blooms not in the glare
Of the broad sun: that delicate forest flower,
With scented breath and look so like a smile,
Seems, as it issues from the shapeless mould,
An emanation of the indwelling Life, 66
A visible token of the upholding Love,
That are the soul of this great universe.

My heart is awed within me when I think
Of the great miracle that still goes on, 70
In silence, round me — the perpetual work
Of thy creation, finished, yet renewed
Forever. Written on thy works I read
The lesson of thy own eternity:
Lo, all grow old and die; but see, again, 75
How on the faltering footsteps of decay
Youth presses, ever gay and beautiful youth
In all its beautiful forms. These lofty trees
Wave not less proudly that their ancestors
Moulder beneath them. Oh, there is not lost 80
One of earth's charms: upon her bosom yet,
After the flight of untold centuries,
The freshness of her far beginning lies
And yet shall lie. Life mocks the idle hate
Of his arch-enemy, Death; yea, seats himself 85
Upon the tyrant's throne, the sepulchre,
And of the triumphs of his ghastly foe
Makes his own nourishment; for he came forth
From thine own bosom, and shall have no end.

There have been holy men who hid them-
    selves 90
Deep in the woody wilderness, and gave
Their lives to thought and prayer, till they out-
    lived
The generation born with them, nor seemed
Less aged than the hoary trees and rocks
Around them; and there have been holy men 95
Who deemed it were not well to pass life thus.
But let me often to these solitudes
Retire, and in thy presence reassure
My feeble virtue. Here its enemies,
The passions, at thy plainer footsteps shrink 100

And tremble and are still. O God! when thou
Dost scare the world with tempests, set on fire
The heavens with falling thunderbolts, or fill
With all the waters of the firmament
The swift dark whirlwind that uproots the
    woods 105
And drowns the villages; when, at thy call,
Uprises the great deep and throws himself
Upon the continent and overwhelms
Its cities; who forgets not, at the sight
Of these tremendous tokens of thy power, 110
His pride, and lays his strifes and follies by?
Oh, from these sterner aspects of thy face
Spare me and mine, nor let us need the wrath
Of the mad unchained elements to teach
Who rules them. Be it ours to meditate 115
In these calm shades thy milder majesty,
And to the beautiful order of thy works
Learn to conform the order of our lives.

To Cole, the Painter, Departing
for Europe

(w. 1829)

🙐 With the romantic spirit came the first group
of landscape painters, the Hudson River School led
by the English-born Thomas Cole, a close friend of
Bryant's. Together poet and painter made walking
tours in the Catskill mountains, as in the painting by
Durand (see page 179).

Thine eyes shall see the light of distant skies;
    Yet, COLE! thy heart shall bear to Europe's
        strand
    A living image of our own bright land,
Such as upon thy glorious canvas lies; 4
Lone lakes — savannas where the bison roves —
    Rocks rich with summer garlands — solemn
        streams —
    Skies, where the desert eagle wheels and
        screams —
Spring bloom and autumn blaze of boundless
    groves.
Fair scenes shall greet thee where thou goest —
    fair, 9
    But different — everywhere the trace of men,
Paths, homes, graves, ruins, from the lowest glen
To where life shrinks from the fierce Alpine
    air —
    Gaze on them, till the tears shall dim thy
        sight,
    But keep that earlier, wilder image bright.

ROMANTIC ARTIST

Edgar Allan Poe [1809-1849]

[handwritten annotation: end of art is pleasure — work needs unity of action or tone — beauty — meaning not imp.]

"The saddest and the strangest figure in American literary history," Killis Campbell called Poe. "Few writers have lived a life so full of struggle and disappointment, and none have lived and died more completely out of sympathy with their times." His macabre poetry and prose was equaled in strangeness by the circumstances of his life and the mystery of his death. He has become one of the most controversial figures of American literature; and he has had enemies and defenders of equal virulence ever since Griswold published the notorious memoir of his death in the *New York Tribune* of October 9, 1849, inspired, no doubt, by envy.

> Edgar Allan Poe is dead. He died in Baltimore the day before yesterday. This announcement will startle many, but few will be grieved by it. The poet was known personally or by reputation, in all this country; he has readers in England, and in several of the states of continental Europe; but he had few or no friends; and the regrets for his death will be suggested principally by the consideration that in him literary art has lost one of its most brilliant, but erratic stars.

Edgar Poe was the child of itinerant actors. Within less than three years after his birth in Boston, his father, David Poe, Jr., had deserted his family, and his mother, Elizabeth Arnold Poe, had died in poverty at Richmond, Virginia. It may well be that the sight of his mother dying of tuberculosis made an impression that eventually transmuted itself into fictional forms (Berenice, Morella, Eleanora, Ligeia). The child Edgar was taken into the home of a Richmond merchant, Allan, whose name Poe later added to his own. He was never formally adopted, and his relations with his foster parents were never happy. From 1815 to 1820 he studied at schools in England, and during the next five years in Richmond. In February 1826 he entered the University of Virginia, where he soon acquired heavy gambling debts and a reputation as a hard drinker, so that he was taken out of the University by Allan in December of the same year. Over the settlement of the debts they had the last and bitterest of many quarrels, and in 1827 Poe ran away and enlisted, in Boston, as a private in the U. S. Army under the name of Edgar A. Perry. In Boston, too, he brought out his first book, a thin little volume called *Tamerlane and Other Poems.*

Within two years the young soldier had found time to produce another book of poems, *Al Aaraaf, Tamerlane, and Minor Poems,* and had risen to the rank of sergeant-major. With Allan's help, he secured appointment to West Point, where he entered in July 1830. Less than eight months later he deliberately got himself dismissed for neglect of duty. From this time on Poe was dependent on his pen for a livelihood.

A volume of poems issued in 1831 showed a new sureness: here were "Israfel," "To Helen," "The City in the Sea." The next four years he spent mostly in Baltimore, writing poems and stories. In 1833 the *Baltimore Saturday Visitor* awarded him a prize of $100 for the best short story submitted in its contest. It was one of his few financial successes. He was never to rise above poverty and want. In 1835 he removed to Richmond and became editor of the *Southern Literary Messenger*, an able and successful editor noted for his caustic book reviews in a day when criticism was indulgent. With an assured salary, he proceeded to marry his cousin, Virginia Clemm, a girl of thirteen. The next year he quit the *Messenger*, partly because he felt his salary was less than he deserved.

He spent a year in New York, then settled in Philadelphia, and became editor of *Graham's Magazine*. His *Tales of the Grotesque and Arabesque* were published in 1840, and in 1843 "The Gold Bug" won him another $100 prize. His wife was ill, he dreaded her death, he drank, he could not make a decent living. In 1844 he returned to New York to seek new opportunities.

The next year "The Raven" brought him fame and ten dollars. He was editor of the *Broadway Journal* for two years, till it failed. In 1847 he was working on *Eureka: an Essay on the Material and Spiritual Universe*, and his wife was dying. The rest of his story is one of poverty, intoxication, frequent illness, mistaken love affairs, and fine poems. In 1848 he attempted suicide with laudanum. In 1849 he visited Richmond for the last time, and became engaged to a sweetheart of his youth, now a wealthy widow. The remaining events are obscure. In Baltimore he was found unconscious at a ward polling place, and died four days later at age 40.

Such are the chief external facts of his life. It is still difficult to say just what sort of person the man himself was. Poe made a bad mistake when he chose as his literary executor Reverend Rufus W. Griswold, an editor and compiler. Griswold wrote a memoir in which, by a combination of truth, half-truth, and lies he made Poe look something like a devil. Before long Poe's defenders pictured him as virtually a saint. The sordid story and the romantic legend were equally unsatisfactory. Partisanship has often dogged even the efforts of careful scholars to give us a convincing portrait.

At the same time critical opinion of Poe's writings has tended toward the extremes of enthusiasm and distaste. The Irish poet Yeats judged Poe to be "always and for all lands a great lyric poet," and many French authors, such as Maupassant, Baudelaire, and Valéry, have extolled him as an original artist of high distinction. In France, indeed, Poe has generally been hailed as the founder of modern poetry, especially Symbolist poetry. In the United States, on the other hand, he has been disparaged or dismissed by writers in many camps. Emerson once summed him up as "the jingle man." Henry James pronounced an enthusiasm for Poe's work as "the mark of a decidedly primitive stage of reflection." Latterly even our poets and critics in the Symbolist tradition have been inclined to disown him as vague, disorderly, and monotonous. In this situation, the student of Poe is challenged to form his opinion carefully.

Some account of Poe's view of literary art is given in the period introduction, page 191. His writings fall into three main types, poetry, the short story, and literary criticism, which are illustrated in the selections that follow.

Further reading: *The Poems of Edgar Allan Poe*, ed. Killis Campbell, 1917. *Poe's Short Stories*, ed. Killis Campbell, 1927. *Selections from the Critical Writings of Edgar Allan Poe*, ed. F. C. Prescott, 1909. *Edgar Allan Poe* (American Writers Series), ed. M. Alterton and H. Craig, 1935. A. H. Quinn, *Edgar Allan Poe: A Critical Biography*, 1941. Allen Tate, "The Angelic Imagination," *Kenyon Review*, Summer 1952.

Romance

(1829)

Poe chose this poem as the preface to a group of his poems published in 1829, and as the introduction to the entire volume of 1831.

Romance, who loves to nod and sing,
With drowsy head and folded wing,
Among the green leaves as they shake
Far down within some shadowy lake,
To me a painted paroquet   5
Hath been — a most familiar bird —
Taught me my alphabet to say —
To lisp my very earliest words
While in the wild wood I did lie,
A child — with a most knowing eye.   10

Of late, eternal Condor years
So shake the very Heaven on high
With tumult as they thunder by,
I have no time for idle cares
Through gazing on the unquiet sky.   15
And when an hour with calmer wings
Its down upon my spirit flings —
That little time with lyre and rhyme
To while away — forbidden things!
My heart would feel to be a crime   20
Unless it trembled with the strings.

To Science

(1829)

Here Poe enlarges upon his complaint, in "Al Aaraaf," that

> "the breath
> Of science dims the mirror of our joy."

His subject is not natural science but rather metaphysics, or philosophy in general. He deplores the invasion of the province of poetry by philosophy, having in mind Keats's protest, in *Lamia*, against "cold philosophy," which empties the haunted air and unweaves the rainbow. Poe defends the poetic, myth-making imagination (Diana, Hamadryad) which had enthralled Keats.

Science! true daughter of Old Time thou art!
Who alterest all things with thy peering eyes.
Why preyest thou thus upon the poet's heart.
Vulture, whose wings are dull realities?
How should he love thee? or how deem thee
          wise,   5
Who wouldst not leave him in his wandering
To seek for treasure in the jewelled skies,
Albeit he soared with an undaunted wing?

Hast thou not dragged Diana from her car?
And driven the Hamadryad from the wood   10
To seek a shelter in some happier star?
Hast thou not torn the Naiad from her flood,
The Elfin from the green grass, and from me
The summer dream beneath the tamarind tree?

A Dream Within a Dream

(1827, 1829, 1849)

Take this kiss upon the brow!
And, in parting from you now,
Thus much let me avow —
You are not wrong, who deem
That my days have been a dream;   5
Yet if hope has flown away
In a night, or in a day,
In a vision, or in none,
Is it therefore the less *gone*?
All that we see or seem   10
Is but a dream within a dream.

I stand amid the roar
Of a surf-tormented shore,
And I hold within my hand
Grains of the golden sand —   15
How few! yet how they creep
Through my fingers to the deep,
While I weep — while I weep!
O God! can I not grasp
Them with a tighter clasp?   20
O God! can I not save
One from the pitiless wave?
Is *all* that we see or seem
But a dream within a dream?

To Helen

(1831, 1845)

Poe said that this poem was inspired by Mrs. Jane Stanard, of Richmond, mother of a school friend. She died in 1824, when he was fifteen. In letters, Poe later spoke of her as "the first purely ideal love of my soul," and as "an angel to my forlorn and darkened nature." From his early wanderings on the sea of life she brought him to his home port — to an exalted sense of security.

Yet the Helen of the poem is not a flesh-and-blood but a romantically idealized image, a symbol of beauty in a land of heart's desire. Like Keats and Shelley, Poe expresses a yearning, a nostalgia, for a realm of serene beauty in life, in myth, in art, first and best given expression by the ancient Greeks.

Thus while the feeling in this famous poem is romantic, the pictures and allusions are classical: the name Helen, her "classic face," "hyacinth hair" (as in Homer; Poe describes it in "Ligeia," see page 261), "Naiad airs," "statue-like," "agate lamp," "psyche" ("Soul," the Greek princess loved by Cupid). Greece and Rome are summed up in lines 9 and 10. Compare an earlier version:

> "To the beauty of fair Greece
> And the grandeur of old Rome."

"Nicéan" in line 2, as Douglas Bush says, is "a romantically vague allusion which has exercised scholars"; it has various possible classical associations but may remain, as Poe perhaps intended, remote and strange.

Helen, thy beauty is to me
  Like those Nicéan barks of yore,
That gently, o'er a perfumed sea,
  The weary, way-worn wanderer bore
  To his own native shore.   5

On desperate seas long wont to roam,
  Thy hyacinth hair, thy classic face,
Thy Naiad airs have brought me home
  To the glory that was Greece
  And the grandeur that was Rome.   10

Lo! in yon brilliant window-niche
  How statue-like I see thee stand,
The agate lamp within thy hand!
  Ah, Psyche, from the regions which
  Are Holy Land!   15

Israfel

(1831)

☙ Poe's note: "And the angel Israfel, whose heart-strings are a lute, and who has the sweetest voice of all God's creatures. — KORAN." Apparently Poe quoted not the Koran itself but Sale's Discourse on the Koran, inserting from Béranger the phrase about the heart-strings.

In this poem beauty is allied not to serenity as in "To Helen" but to "ecstasies," "burning measures," and the imagery is suggested not by the ancient classical world but by the Mohammedan religion. The angel Israfel illustrates in heavenly perfection that "union of Poetry with Music" which Poe extolled in an essay on poetry. Even the lightning ("leyin") pauses to listen.

No such ecstasy of song is possible for the poet in our "world of sweets and sours" — we know how pronounced the sours were in Poe's experience. He can but aspire, earthly poetry being only, as Poe says in the essay, "a wild effort to reach the Beauty above." He himself affords no better example than the present poem. Here, as his biographer Woodberry says, "rings out the lyric burst, the first pure song of the poet, the notes most clear and liquid and soaring of all he ever sang." It may be compared with Shelley's "To a Skylark."

In Heaven a spirit doth dwell
  "Whose heart-strings are a lute;"
None sing so wildly well
As the angel Israfel,
And the giddy stars (so legends tell)   5
Ceasing their hymns, attend the spell
  Of his voice, all mute.

Tottering above
  In her highest noon,
  The enamoured moon   10
Blushes with love,
  While, to listen, the red levin
  (With the rapid Pleiads, even,
  Which were seven,)
  Pauses in Heaven.   15

And they say (the starry choir
  And the other listening things)
That Israfeli's fire
Is owing to that lyre
By which he sits and sings —   20
The trembling living wire
Of those unusual strings.

But the skies that angel trod,
  Where deep thoughts are a duty —
Where Love's a grown-up God —   25
  Where the Houri glances are
Imbued with all the beauty
  Which we worship in a star.

Therefore, thou art not wrong,
  Israfeli, who despisest   30
An unimpassioned song;
To thee the laurels belong,
  Best bard, because the wisest!
Merrily live, and long!

The ecstasies above   35
  With thy burning measures suit —
Thy grief, thy joy, thy hate, thy love,
  With the fervour of thy lute —
  Well may the stars be mute!

Yes, Heaven is thine; but this   40
  Is a world of sweets and sours;
  Our flowers are merely — flowers,

And the shadow of thy perfect bliss
  Is the sunshine of ours.

If I could dwell   45
Where Israfel
  Hath dwelt, and he where I,
He might not sing so wildly well
  A mortal melody,
While a bolder note than this might swell   50
  From my lyre within the sky.

The City in the Sea

(1831, 1845)

The earlier titles Poe used for this poem indicate aspects of its meaning: "The Doomed City," "The City of Sin," "The City in the Sea: a Prophecy."

Death and horror had been the theme of Freneau's "House of Night" many years earlier. Poe now carried the "Gothic" poem to perfection through his selective, constructive imagination and his verse technique. He was concerned with a purely aesthetic effect uncomplicated by any moral or religious aims.

The literary and traditional materials that Poe worked with have been well absorbed into the structure. They include poems by Coleridge, Byron, and Shelley, sundry passages in the Bible, and legends and records of sunken cities. (Details on these may be found in Killis Campbell's *Poems of Edgar Allan Poe* and in an article by Louise Pound in *American Literature*, March, 1934.)

Lo! Death has reared himself a throne
In a strange city lying alone
Far down within the dim West,
Where the good and the bad and the worst and
      the best
Have gone to their eternal rest.   5
There shrines and palaces and towers
(Time-eaten towers that tremble not!)
Resemble nothing that is ours.
Around, by lifting winds forgot,
Resignedly beneath the sky   10
The melancholy waters lie.

No rays from the holy heaven come down
On the long night-time of that town;
But light from out the lurid sea
Streams up the turrets silently —   15
Gleams up the pinnacles far and free —
Up domes — up spires — up kingly halls —
Up fanes — up Babylon-like walls —
Up shadowy long-forgotten bowers
Of sculptured ivy and stone flowers —   20

Up many and many a marvelous shrine
Whose wreathéd friezes intertwine
The viol, the violet, and the vine.

Resignedly beneath the sky
The melancholy waters lie.   25
So blend the turrets and shadows there
That all seem pendulous in air,
While from a proud tower in the town
Death looks gigantically down.

There open fanes and gaping graves   30
Yawn level with the luminous waves;
But not the riches there that lie
In each idol's diamond eye —
Not the gayly-jewelled dead
Tempt the waters from their bed;   35
For no ripples curl, alas!
Along that wilderness of glass —
No swellings tell that winds may be
Upon some far-off happier sea —
No heavings hint that winds have been   40
On seas less hideously serene.

But lo, a stir is in the air!
The wave — there is a movement there!
As if the towers had thrust aside,
In slightly sinking, the dull tide —   45
As if their tops had feebly given
A void within the filmy Heaven.
The waves have now a redder glow —
The hours are breathing faint and low —
And when, amid no earthly moans,   50
Down, down that town shall settle hence,
Hell, rising from a thousand thrones,
Shall do it reverence.

Lenore

(1831, 1843, 1845)

The name Lenore may have come from Bürger's famous romantic ballad "Lenore," which Scott and others had translated from the German.

The poem is a good example of Poe's view that the death of a young and beautiful woman is a peculiarly poetic theme. Elegies, he once said, should express "not so much the tone of passion, as of a gentle but melancholy regret, interwoven with a pleasant sense of the natural loveliness surrounding the lost in the tomb, and a memory of her human beauty when alive. . . . or, better still, utter the notes of triumph. I have endeavored to carry out this latter idea in some verses which I have called 'Lenore.' "

The first and third stanzas are spoken by the false

friends of the dead Lenore, the second and fourth (with quotation marks) by her lover, Guy De Vere.

Line 1, "golden bowl": see Ecclesiastes xii:6. Line 13: the Latin is a confessional word — "We have sinned."

Ah, broken is the golden bowl! the spirit flown
    forever!
Let the bell toll! — a saintly soul floats on the
    Stygian river;
And, Guy De Vere, hast *thou* no tear? — weep
    now or never more!
See! on yon drear and rigid bier low lies thy
    love, Lenore!
Come! let the burial rite be read — the fu-
    neral song be sung! —   5
An anthem for the queenliest dead that ever
    died so young —
A dirge for her the doubly dead in that she died
    so young.

"Wretches! ye loved her for her wealth and
    ye hated her for her pride,
"And when she fell in feeble health, ye blessed
    her — that she died!
"How *shall* the ritual, then, be read? — the re-
    quiem how be sung   10
"By you — by yours, the evil eye, — by yours,
    the slanderous tongue
"That did to death the innocence that died,
    and died so young?"

Peccavimus; but rave not thus! and let a Sab-
    bath song
Go up to God so solemnly the dead may feel
    no wrong!
The sweet Lenore hath "gone before," with
    Hope, that flew beside,   15
Leaving thee wild for the dear child that should
    have been thy bride —
For her, the fair and *debonair*, that now so
    lowly lies,
The life upon her yellow hair but not within
    her eyes —
The life still there, upon her hair — the death
    upon her eyes.

"Avaunt! to-night my heart is light. No dirge
    will I upraise.   20
"But waft the angel on her flight with a pæan
    of old days!
"'Let *no* bell toll! — lest her sweet soul, amid
    its hallowed mirth,
"Should catch the note, as it doth float up from
    the damnèd Earth.

"To friends above, from fiends below, the in-
    dignant ghost is riven —
"From Hell unto a high estate far up within the
    heaven —   25
"From grief and groan, to a golden throne, be-
    side the King of Heaven."

The Valley of Unrest

(1831, 1845)

🕮 The situation of the *Once* passage at the beginning may remind one of the empty town in the
fourth stanza of Keats's "Ode on a Grecian Urn."
Now, perhaps the valley is, as Campbell says, "the
temporary abiding-place of the wicked after death,
though the poet is careful not to make this explicit."
The signs of unrest — e.g., trees stirred without wind
— are given an eerie, supernatural quality.

Once it smiled a silent dell
Where the people did not dwell;
They had gone unto the wars,
Trusting to the mild-eyed stars,
Nightly, from their azure towers,   5
To keep watch above the flowers,
In the midst of which all day
The red sun-light lazily lay.
Now each visitor shall confess
The sad valley's restlessness.   10
Nothing there is motionless —
Nothing save the airs that brood
Over the magic solitude.
Ah, by no wind are stirred those trees
That palpitate like the chill seas   15
Around the misty Hebrides!
Ah, by no wind those clouds are driven
That rustle through the unquiet Heaven
Uneasily, from morn till even,
Over the violets there that lie   20
In myriad types of the human eye —
Over the lilies there that wave
And weep above a nameless grave!
They wave: — from out their fragrant tops
Eternal dews come down in drops.   25
They weep: — from off their delicate stems
Perennial tears descend in gems.

The Sleeper

(1831, 1845)

🕮 "The Sleeper" belongs to the group of seven
poems concerning the world of spirits, further represented in this book by "The City in the Sea," "The
Valley of Unrest," and "Dream-Land."

The poem also belongs, like "Lenore" (above), to the group touching upon the death of a beautiful woman. Later poems in this group are "To One in Paradise," "The Raven," "Ulalume," and "Annabel Lee," all of which are printed below.

In the present poem the scene seems to be the death-chamber, from which the body will soon be taken to a chamber "more holy," the family tomb.

At midnight, in the month of June,
I stand beneath the mystic moon.
An opiate vapor, dewy, dim,
Exhales from out her golden rim,
And, softly dripping, drop by drop,   5
Upon the quiet mountain top,
Steals drowsily and musically
Into the universal valley.
The rosemary nods upon the grave;
The lily lolls upon the wave;   10
Wrapping the fog about its breast,
The ruin moulders into rest;
Looking like Lethe, see! the lake
A conscious slumber seems to take,
And would not, for the world, awake.   15
All Beauty sleeps! — and lo! where lies
Irene, with her Destinies!

Oh, lady bright! can it be right —
This window open to the night?
The wanton airs, from the tree-top,   20
Laughingly through the lattice drop —
The bodiless airs, a wizard rout,
Flit through thy chamber in and out,
And wave the curtain canopy
So fitfully — so fearfully —   25
Above the closed and fringèd lid
'Neath which thy slumb'ring soul lies hid,
That, o'er the floor and down the wall,
Like ghosts the shadows rise and fall!
Oh, lady dear, hast thou no fear?   30
Why and what art thou dreaming here?
Sure thou art come o'er far-off seas,
A wonder to these garden trees!
Strange is thy pallor! strange thy dress!
Strange, above all, thy length of tress,   35
And this all solemn silentness!

The lady sleeps! Oh, may her sleep,
Which is enduring, so be deep!
Heaven have her in its sacred keep!
This chamber changed for one more holy,   40
This bed for one more melancholy,
I pray to God that she may lie
Forever with unopened eye,

While the pale sheeted ghosts go by!

My love, she sleeps! Oh, may her sleep,   45
As it is lasting, so be deep!
Soft may the worms about her creep!
Far in the forest, dim and old,
For her may some tall vault unfold —
Some vault that oft hath flung its black   50
And wingèd panels fluttering back,
Triumphant, o'er the crested palls,
Of her grand family funerals —

Some sepulchre, remote, alone,
Against whose portal she hath thrown,   55
In childhood, many an idle stone —
Some tomb from out whose sounding door
She ne'er shall force an echo more,
Thrilling to think, poor child of sin!
It was the dead who groaned within.   60

To One in Paradise

(1834, 1845)

Thou wast that all to me, love,
    For which my soul did pine —
A green isle in the sea, love,
    A fountain and a shrine,
All wreathed with fairy fruits and flowers,   5
    And all the flowers were mine.

Ah, dream too bright to last!
    Ah, starry Hope! that didst arise
But to be overcast!
    A voice from out the Future cries,   10
"On! on!" — but o'er the Past
    (Dim gulf!) my spirit hovering lies
Mute, motionless, aghast!

For, alas! alas! with me
    The light of Life is o'er!   15
No more — no more — no more —
    (Such language holds the solemn sea
To the sands upon the shore)
    Shall bloom the thunder-blasted tree,
Or the stricken eagle soar!   20

And all my days are trances,
    And all my nightly dreams
Are where thy grey eye glances,
    And where thy footstep gleams —
In what ethereal dances,   25
    By what eternal streams.

Dream-Land

(1844)

🐝 Here the rhythmic pattern and the use of repetition artfully modified prepare us for the Poe of "The Raven" and "Ulalume."

On the attraction of romantic writers to the strange and remote, see the introduction, page 185. "Ultimate" is used in the sense of farthest, as in the Latin *ultima Thule*. Thule was the Greek and Latin name for the northernmost land, but came to be used for any very distant region — even, as here by Poe, a region outside space and time.

By a route obscure and lonely,
Haunted by ill angels only,
Where an Eidolon, named NIGHT,
On a black throne reigns upright,
I have reached these lands but newly   5
From an ultimate dim Thule —
From a wild weird clime that lieth, sublime,
    Out of SPACE — out of TIME.

Bottomless vales and boundless floods,
And chasms, and caves, and Titan woods, 10
With forms that no man can discover
For the tears that drip all over;
Mountains toppling evermore
Into seas without a shore;
Seas that restlessly aspire,   15
Surging, unto skies of fire;
Lakes that endlessly outspread
Their lone waters — lone and dead, —
Their still waters — still and chilly
With the snows of the lolling lily.   20

By the lakes that thus outspread
Their lone waters, lone and dead, —
Their sad waters, sad and chilly
With the snows of the lolling lily, —

By the mountains — near the river   25
Murmuring lowly, murmuring ever, —
By the grey woods, — by the swamp
Where the toad and the newt encamp, —
By the dismal tarns and pools
    Where dwell the Ghouls, —   30
By each spot the most unholy —
In each nook most melancholy, —
There the traveller meets, aghast,
Sheeted Memories of the Past —
Shrouded forms that start and sigh   35
As they pass the wanderer by —
White-robed forms of friends long given,
In agony, to the Earth — and Heaven.

For the heart whose woes are legion
'Tis a peaceful, soothing region —   40
For the spirit that walks in shadow
'Tis — oh 'tis an Eldorado!
But the traveller, travelling through it,
May not — dare not openly view it;
Never its mysteries are exposed   45
To the weak human eye unclosed;
So wills its King, who hath forbid
The uplifting of the fringéd lid;
And thus the sad Soul that here passes
Beholds it but through darkened glasses. 50

By a route obscure and lonely,
Haunted by ill angels only,
Where an Eidolon, named NIGHT,
On a black throne reigns upright,
I have wandered home but newly   55
From this ultimate dim Thule.

The Raven

(1845)

🐝 There is a pet raven named Grip in Dickens's *Barnaby Rudge*. In reviewing the novel, Poe felt that Dickens might have made more of the bird: "Its croakings might have been *prophetically* heard in the course of the drama. Its character might have performed, in regard to that of the idiot, much the same part as, in music, the accompaniment in respect to the air." Here perhaps was the germ of the poem. In his metrical form, Poe may have been influenced by the verse of Thomas Holley Chivers (a matter that has been much debated), and was almost certainly indebted to *Lady Geraldine's Courtship* by Elizabeth Barrett Browning, to whom he dedicated *The Raven and Other Poems*. For example, Poe's line 13 is close to Mrs. Browning's

"With a murmurous stir uncertain, in the air the
    purple curtain. . . ."

The question of Poe's originality in the poem and the truth of his account of how it was written are discussed in the note to "The Philosophy of Composition" (page 250). The poem and that essay should be read together.

"The Raven" was first published in the New York *Evening Mirror*, January 29, 1845.

In Line 41, "Pallas" is Pallas Athene, goddess of wisdom. Line 89, "balm in Gilead": see Jeremiah viii:22. Line 93, "Aidenn" is the Mohammedan paradise.

Once upon a midnight dreary, while I pondered, weak and weary,

Over many a quaint and curious volume of forgotten lore —
While I nodded, nearly napping, suddenly
there came a tapping,
As of some one gently rapping, rapping at my
chamber door.
" 'Tis some visitor," I muttered, "tapping at my
chamber door —   5
Only this and nothing more."

Ah, distinctly I remember it was in the bleak
December;
And each separate dying ember wrought its
ghost upon the floor.
Eagerly I wished the morrow; — vainly I had
sought to borrow
From my books surcease of sorrow — sorrow
for the lost Lenore —   10
For the rare and radiant maiden whom the
angels name Lenore —
Nameless *here* for evermore.

And the silken, sad, uncertain rustling of each
purple curtain
Thrilled me — filled me with fantastic terrors
never felt before;
So that now, to still the beating of my heart,
I stood repeating   15
" 'Tis some visitor entreating entrance at my
chamber door —
Some late visitor entreating entrance at my
chamber door; —
This it is and nothing more."

Presently my soul grew stronger; hesitating then
no longer,
"Sir," said I, "or Madam, truly your forgiveness
I implore;   20
But the fact is I was napping, and so gently
you came rapping,
And so faintly you came tapping, tapping at my
chamber door,
That I scarce was sure I heard you" — here I
opened wide the door; —
Darkness there and nothing more.

Deep into that darkness peering, long I stood
there wondering, fearing,   25
Doubting, dreaming dreams no mortal ever
dared to dream before;
But the silence was unbroken, and the stillness gave no token,
And the only word there spoken was the whispered word, "Lenore!"

This I whispered, and an echo murmured back
the word "Lenore!"
Merely this and nothing more.   30

Back into the chamber turning, all my soul
within me burning,
Soon again I heard a tapping somewhat louder
than before.
"Surely," said I, "surely that is something at
my window lattice;
Let me see, then, what thereat is, and this
mystery explore —
Let my heart be still a moment and this mystery
explore; —   35
'Tis the wind and nothing more!"

Open here I flung the shutter, when, with many
a flirt and flutter
In there stepped a stately Raven of the saintly
days of yore.
Not the least obeisance made he; not a minute
stopped or stayed he;
But, with mien of lord or lady, perched above
my chamber door —
Perched upon a bust of Pallas just above my
chamber door —   40
Perched, and sat, and nothing more.

Then this ebony bird beguiling my sad fancy
into smiling,
By the grave and stern decorum of the counte-
nance it wore,
"Though thy crest be shorn and shaven, thou,"
I said, "art sure no craven,   45
Ghastly grim and ancient Raven wandering
from the Nightly shore —
Tell me what thy lordly name is on the Night's
Plutonian shore!"
Quoth the Raven, "Nevermore."

Much I marvelled this ungainly fowl to hear
discourse so plainly,
Though its answer little meaning — little relevancy bore;   50
For we cannot help agreeing that no living
human being
Ever yet was blessed with seeing bird above his
chamber door —
Bird or beast upon the sculptured bust above
his chamber door,
With such name as "Nevermore."

But the Raven, sitting lonely on the placid bust,
spoke only   55

That one word, as if his soul in that one word
    he did outpour.
Nothing farther then he uttered — not a feather
    then he fluttered —
Till I scarcely more than muttered "Other
    friends have flown before —
On the morrow *he* will leave me, as my hopes
    have flown before."
    Then the bird said "Nevermore."   60

Startled at the stillness broken by reply so aptly
    spoken,
"Doubtless," said I, "what it utters is its only
    stock and store
Caught from some unhappy master whom un-
    merciful Disaster
Followed fast and followed faster till his songs
    one burden bore —
Till the dirges of his Hope that melancholy
    burden bore   65
    Of 'Never — nevermore.' "

But the Raven still beguiling all my fancy into
    smiling,
Straight I wheeled a cushioned seat in front
    of bird, and bust and door;
Then, upon the velvet sinking, I betook myself
    to linking
Fancy unto fancy, thinking what this ominous
    bird of yore —   70
What this grim, ungainly, ghastly, gaunt, and
    ominous bird of yore
    Meant in croaking "Nevermore."

This I sat engaged in guessing, but no syllable
    expressing
To the fowl whose fiery eyes now burned into
    my bosom's core;
This and more I sat divining, with my head at
    ease reclining   75
On the cushion's velvet lining that the lamplight
    gloated o'er,
But whose velvet violet lining with the lamp-
    light gloating o'er,
    She shall press, ah, nevermore!

Then, methought, the air grew denser, per-
    fumed from an unseen censer
Swung by Seraphim whose foot-falls tinkled on
    the tufted floor.   80
"Wretch," I cried, "thy God hath lent thee
    — by these angels he hath sent thee
Respite — respite and nepenthe from thy mem-
    ories of Lenore;

Quaff, oh quaff this kind nepenthe and forget
    this lost Lenore!"
    Quoth the Raven "Nevermore."

"Prophet!" said I, "thing of evil! prophet still,
    if bird or devil! —   85
Whether Tempter sent, or whether tempest
    tossed thee here ashore,
Desolate yet all undaunted, on this desert land
    enchanted —
On this home by Horror haunted — tell me
    truly, I implore —
Is there — *is* there balm in Gilead? — tell me
    — tell me, I implore!"
    Quoth the Raven "Nevermore."   90

"Prophet!" said I, "thing of evil! — prophet
    still, if bird or devil!
By that Heaven that bends above us — by that
    God we both adore —
Tell this soul with sorrow laden if, within the
    distant Aidenn,
It shall clasp a sainted maiden whom the angels
    name Lenore —
Clasp a rare and radiant maiden whom the
    angels name Lenore."   95
    Quoth the Raven "Nevermore."

"Be that word our sign of parting, bird or fiend!"
    I shrieked, upstarting —
"Get thee back into the tempest and the Night's
    Plutonian shore!
Leave no black plume as a token of that lie
    thy soul hath spoken!
Leave my loneliness unbroken! — quit the bust
    above my door!   100
Take thy beak from out my heart, and take thy
    form from off my door!"
    Quoth the Raven "Nevermore."

And the Raven, never flitting, still is sitting,
    still is sitting
On the pallid bust of Pallas just above my
    chamber door;
And his eyes have all the seeming of a demon's
    that is dreaming,   105
And the lamp-light o'er him streaming
    throws his shadow on the floor;
And my soul from out that shadow that lies
    floating on the floor
    Shall be lifted — nevermore!

Ulalume

(1847)

Many readers enjoy this poem, as Poe perhaps enjoyed writing it, primarily for its mood and tone as conveyed by sound and image. The romantic landscape, the direct appeal of word associations, the insistent, hypnotic repetitions in changing contexts as in the art of music, the bold expression of emotions restrained by reticence (e.g., the word *death* appears nowhere), — such aesthetic elements are interwoven with fine art, or artifice. A close reading reveals many interesting features. What is the effect, for instance, of so many *l* sounds, from title to end, coming as they do in all the lines closing stanzas and sometimes in clusters (lines 49 and 50, 80 and 81)? Again, what is the effect of so many Latinized adjectives of three to five syllables (immemorial, sulphurous, senescent, liquescent, nebulous, miraculous, duplicate, bediamonded)?

As a dramatic vehicle, Poe adopted the "debate," an old device noted in connection with Mrs. Bradstreet's "The Flesh and the Spirit" (page 27). In "Ulalume" the opposition is essentially the same: flesh and spirit, the sensuous and emotional self versus a deeper, truer self. Poe's conception is less Christian, however, than romantic, allied with the notion of a "double," a *Doppelgänger*, familiar in the Romantic Movement. Contributing to the romantic atmosphere are the place names, Auber, Wier, Yaanek, invented by Poe, and absorbed harmoniously into this atmosphere are symbols from Classical myth, Psyche, Diana, Lethe, Sibyl. The chaste moon-goddess Diana of Roman mythology is contrasted with the warmer Phoenician Astarte, goddess of the moon and earthly love.

The poet's emotional self — "my heart was volcanic" — desires relief in "Hope and in Beauty," offered to him by an earthly love. Psyche, mistrustful, warns him, urges flight, but cannot overcome his enthusiasm. Then they suddenly confront the tomb of his lost love, and the poet is shocked by memory of the "dread burden" he had brought there exactly one year before. In the full renewal of his grief and devotion, the allurement of Astarte is gone. Body and soul, now speaking in unison, realize that the bediamonded crescent was a false promise of happiness.

The skies they were ashen and sober;
   The leaves they were crispèd and sere —
   The leaves they were withering and sere;
It was night in the lonesome October
   Of my most immemorial year;   5
It was hard by the dim lake of Auber,
   In the misty mid region of Weir —
It was down by the dank tarn of Auber,
   In the ghoul-haunted woodland of Weir.

Here once, through an alley Titanic,   10
   Of cypress, I roamed with my Soul —
   Of cypress, with Psyche, my Soul.
These were days when my heart was volcanic
   As the scoriac rivers that roll —
   As the lavas that restlessly roll   15
Their sulphurous currents down Yaanek
   In the ultimate climes of the pole —
That groan as they roll down Mount Yaanek
   In the realms of the boreal pole.

Our talk had been serious and sober,   20
   But our thoughts they were palsied and sere —
   Our memories were treacherous and sere —
For we knew not the month was October,
   And we marked not the night of the year —
   (Ah, night of all nights in the year!)   25
We noted not the dim lake of Auber —
   (Though once we have journeyed down here) —
Remembered not the dank tarn of Auber,
   Nor the ghoul-haunted woodland of Weir.

And now, as the night was senescent   30
   And star-dials pointed to morn —
   As the star-dials hinted of morn —
At the end of our path a liquescent
   And nebulous lustre was born,
Out of which a miraculous crescent   35
   Arose with a duplicate horn —
Astarte's bediamonded crescent
   Distinct with its duplicate horn.

And I said — "She is warmer than Dian:
   She rolls through an ether of sighs —   40
   She revels in a region of sighs:
She has seen that the tears are not dry on
   These cheeks, where the worm never dies,
And has come past the stars of the Lion
   To point us the path to the skies —   45
   To the Lethean peace of the skies —
Come up, in despite of the Lion,
   To shine on us with her bright eyes —
Come up through the lair of the Lion,
   With love in her luminous eyes."   50

But Psyche, uplifting her finger,
   Said — "Sadly this star I mistrust —
   Her pallor I strangely mistrust: —
Oh, hasten! — oh, let us not linger!
   Oh, fly! — let us fly! — for we must."   55
In terror she spoke, letting sink her
   Wings until they trailed in the dust —

In agony sobbed, letting sink her
   Plumes till they trailed in the dust —
   Till they sorrowfully trailed in the dust.   60

I replied — "This is nothing but dreaming:
   Let us on by this tremulous light!
   Let us bathe in this crystalline light!
Its Sibyllic splendor is beaming
   With Hope and in Beauty to-night: —   65
See! — it flickers up the sky through the night!
Ah, we safely may trust to its gleaming,
   And be sure it will lead us aright —
We safely may trust to a gleaming
   That cannot but guide us aright,   70
   Since it flickers up to Heaven through the
      night."

Thus I pacified Psyche and kissed her,
   And tempted her out of her gloom —
   And conquered her scruples and gloom;
And we passed to the end of the vista,   75
   But were stopped by the door of a tomb —
   By the door of a legended tomb;
And I said — "What is written, sweet sister,
   On the door of this legended tomb?"
   She replied — "Ulalume — Ulalume —   80
   'Tis the vault of thy lost Ulalume!"

Then my heart it grew ashen and sober
   As the leaves that were crispèd and sere —
   As the leaves that were withering and sere,
And I cried — "It was surely October   85
   On *this* very night of last year
   That I journeyed — I journeyed down
      here —
   That I brought a dread burden down here —
   On this night of all nights in the year,
Ah, what demon has tempted me here?   90
Well I know, now, this dim lake of Auber —
   This misty mid region of Weir —
Well I know, now, this dank tarn of Auber,
   This ghoul-haunted woodland of Weir."

Said we, then — the two, then: "Ah, can it   95
   Have been that the woodlandish ghouls —
   The pitiful, the merciful ghouls —
To bar up our way and to ban it
   From the secret that lies in these wolds —
   From the thing that lies hidden in these
      wolds —   100
Have drawn up the spectre of a planet
   From the limbo of lunary souls —
This sinfully scintillant planet
   From the Hell of the planetary souls?"

For Annie

(w. 1849)

For Mrs. Annie Richmond, of Lowell, Massachusetts, a friend of Poe's.

Thank Heaven! the crisis —
   The danger is past,
And the lingering illness
   Is over at last —
And the fever called "Living"   5
   Is conquered at last.

Sadly, I know
   I am shorn of my strength,
And no muscle I move
   As I lie at full length —   10
But no matter! — I feel
   I am better at length.

And I rest so composedly
   Now, in my bed,
That any beholder   15
   Might fancy me dead —
Might start at beholding me,
   Thinking me dead.

The moaning and groaning,
   The sighing and sobbing,   20
Are quieted now,
   With that horrible throbbing
At heart: — ah that horrible,
   Horrible throbbing!

The sickness — the nausea —   25
   The pitiless pain —
Have ceased with the fever
   That maddened my brain —
With the fever called "Living"
   That burned in my brain.   30

And oh! of all tortures
   That torture the worst
Has abated — the terrible
   Torture of thirst
For the napthaline river   35
   Of Passion accurst: —
I have drank of a water
   That quenches all thirst: —

Of a water that flows,
   With a lullaby sound,   40
From a spring but a very few
   Feet under ground —

From a cavern not very far
  Down under ground.

And ah! let it never   45
  Be foolishly said
That my room it is gloomy
  And narrow my bed;
For a man never slept
  In a different bed —   50
And, to sleep, you must slumber
  In just such a bed.

My tantalized spirit
  Here blandly reposes,
Forgetting, or never   55
  Regretting, its roses —
Its old agitations
  Of myrtles and roses:

For now, while so quietly
  Lying, it fancies   60
A holier odor
  About it, of pansies —
A rosemary odor,
  Commingled with pansies —
With rue and the beautiful   65
  Puritan pansies.

And so it lies happily,
  Bathing in many
A dream of the truth
  And the beauty of Annie —   70
Drowned in a bath
  Of the tresses of Annie.

She tenderly kissed me,
  She fondly caressed,
And then I fell gently   75
  To sleep on her breast —
Deeply to sleep
  From the heaven of her breast.

When the light was extinguished,
  She covered me warm,   80
And she prayed to the angels
  To keep me from harm —
To the queen of the angels
  To shield me from harm.

And I lie so composedly,   85
  Now, in my bed,
(Knowing her love)
  That you fancy me dead —
And I rest so contentedly,

Now, in my bed,   90
  (With her love at my breast)
That you fancy me dead —
  That you shudder to look at me.
Thinking me dead: —

But my heart it is brighter   95
  Than all of the many
Stars of the sky,
  For it sparkles with Annie —
It glows with the light
  Of the love of my Annie —   100
With the thought of the light
  Of the eyes of my Annie.

Annabel Lee

(1849)

Commonly held to have been written in memory of Virginia Clemm, Poe's "child-wife."

It was many and many a year ago,
  In a kingdom by the sea,
That a maiden there lived whom you may know
  By the name of ANNABEL LEE;
And this maiden she lived with no other thought
  Than to love and be loved by me.   6

I was a child and she was a child,
  In this kingdom by the sea,
But we loved with a love that was more than
    love —
  I and my ANNABEL LEE —   10
With a love that the wingèd seraphs of heaven
  Coveted her and me.

And this was the reason that, long ago,
  In this kingdom by the sea,
A wind blew out of a cloud, chilling   15
  My beautiful ANNABEL LEE;
So that her high-born kinsmen came
  And bore her away from me,
To shut her up in a sepulchre
  In this kingdom by the sea.   20

The angels, not half so happy in heaven,
  Went envying her and me —
Yes! — that was the reason (as all men know,
  In this kingdom by the sea)
That the wind came out of the cloud by night, 25
  Chilling and killing my ANNABEL LEE.

But our love it was stronger by far than the
    love
Of those who were older than we —
Of many far wiser than we —
And neither the angels in heaven above,   30
  Nor the demons down under the sea,
Can ever dissever my soul from the soul
  Of the beautiful ANNABEL LEE:

For the moon never beams, without bringing
    me dreams
Of the beautiful ANNABEL LEE;   35
And the stars never rise, but I feel the bright
    eyes
Of the beautiful ANNABEL LEE:
And so, all the night-tide, I lie down by the
    side
Of my darling — my darling — my life and my
    bride,
  In the sepulchre there by the sea —   40
  In her tomb by the sounding sea.

Eldorado

(w. 1849)

After the discovery of gold in 1848, California was often spoken of as Eldorado (Spanish, "the gilded"). Poe uses the word here very broadly, to represent a quest of the ideal — finally attainable, if at all, only beyond death.

Gaily bedight
A gallant knight,
In sunshine and in shadow,
Had journeyed long,
Singing a song,   5
In search of Eldorado.

But he grew old —
This knight so bold —
And o'er his heart a shadow
Fell as he found   10
No spot of ground
That looked like Eldorado.

And, as his strength
Failed him at length,
He met a pilgrim shadow —   15
  "Shadow," said he,
  "Where can it be —
This land of Eldorado?"

"Over the Mountains
Of the Moon,   20
Down the Valley of the Shadow.
Ride, boldly ride,"
The shade replied, —
"If you seek for Eldorado."

The Philosophy of Composition

(1846)

Students of Poe have questioned the literal accuracy of this account of how he wrote "The Raven," giving these reasons for skepticism:

1. Poe's love of a hoax or *tour de force*,
2. his omission of debt to Dickens' *Barnaby Rudge* for the idea of a raven as an unreasoning creature to utter the refrain,
3. a raven of ill-omen appeared in a poem in *Fraser's* magazine in 1839, just at the time Poe began ruminating his poem,
4. Poe himself had used "nevermore" and "no more" in earlier poems,
5. Poe revised his poem in as many as sixteen manuscript forms, and it was printed in four different states.

T. H. Chivers, who accused Poe of borrowing "The Raven" from his "To Allegra Florence in Heaven," had written in 1841 (four years before "The Raven" was published) a poem with these lines:

While the world lay round me sleeping
  I alone for Isadore
Patient Vigils lonely keeping,
Someone said to me while weeping:
  "Why this grief forever more?"

Poe had reviewed the poems of W. W. Lord in which the poet wrote:

And the aged beldames napping
Dreamed of gently rapping, rapping,
With a hammer gently tapping . . .

But whatever light the famous Chivers controversy may throw on Poe's assertion that he wrote "The Raven" with "the precision and rigid consequence of a mathematical problem," the essay does interestingly reveal Poe's rejection of the romantic view that literary works, especially poems, are written unconsciously in a state of inspiration. The ratiocinative side of Poe's mind, the quality shown in his love of detective tales, codes, anagrams, and cryptograms, is instanced in this essay which he called his best "specimen of analysis." Likewise, it is the clearest example of Poe's theories as to the proper length, theme, tone, and dramatic structure of a lyric poem.

Charles Dickens, in a note now lying before me, alluding to an examination I once made of the mechanism of *Barnaby Rudge*, says — "By the way, are you aware that Godwin wrote his *Caleb Williams* backwards? He first involved his hero in a web of difficulties, forming the second volume, and then, for the first, cast about him for some mode of accounting for what had been done."

I cannot think this the *precise* mode of procedure on the part of Godwin — and indeed what he himself acknowledges, is not altogether in accordance with Mr. Dickens' idea — but the author of *Caleb Williams* was too good an artist not to perceive the advantage derivable from at least a somewhat similar process. Nothing is more clear than that every plot, worth the name, must be elaborated to its *dénouement* before anything be attempted with the pen. It is only with the *dénouement* constantly in view that we can give a plot its indispensable air of consequence, or causation, by making the incidents, and especially the tone at all points, tend to the development of the intention.

There is a radical error, I think, in the usual mode of constructing a story. Either history affords a thesis — or one is suggested by an incident of the day — or, at best, the author sets himself to work in the combination of striking events to form merely the basis of his narrative — designing, generally, to fill in with description, dialogue, or autorial comment, whatever crevices of fact, or action, may, from page to page, render themselves apparent.

I prefer commencing with the consideration of an *effect*. Keeping originality *always* in view — for he is false to himself who ventures to dispense with so obvious and so easily attainable a source of interest — I say to myself, in the first place, "Of the innumerable effects, or impressions, of which the heart, the intellect, or (more generally) the soul is susceptible, what one shall I, on the present occasion, select?" Having chosen a novel, first, and secondly, a vivid effect, I consider whether it can be best wrought by incident or tone — whether by ordinary incidents and peculiar tone, or the converse, or by peculiarity both of incident and tone — afterward looking about me (or rather within) for such combinations of event, or tone, as shall best aid me in the construction of the effect.

I have often thought how interesting a magazine paper might be written by any author who would — that is to say who could — detail, step by step, the processes by which any one of his compositions attained its ultimate point of completion. Why such a paper has never been given to the world, I am much at a loss to say — but, perhaps, the autorial vanity has had more to do with the omission than any one other cause. Most writers — poets in especial — prefer having it understood that they compose by a species of fine frenzy — an ecstatic intuition — and would positively shudder at letting the public take a peep behind the scenes, at the elaborate and vacillating crudities of thought — at the true purposes seized only at the last moment — at the innumerable glimpses of idea that arrived not at the maturity of full view — at the fully matured fancies discarded in despair as unmanageable — at the cautious selections and rejections — at the painful erasures and interpolations — in a word, at the wheels and pinions — the tackle for scene-shifting — the step-ladders and demon-traps — the cock's feathers, the red paint and the black patches, which, in ninety-nine cases out of the hundred, constitute the properties of the literary *histrio*.

I am aware, on the other hand, that the case is by no means common, in which an author is at all in condition to retrace the steps by which his conclusions have been attained. In general, suggestions, having arisen pell-mell, are pursued and forgotten in a similar manner.

For my own part, I have neither sympathy with the repugnance alluded to, nor, at any time the least difficulty in recalling to mind the progressive steps of any of my compositions; and, since the interest of an analysis, or reconstruction, such as I have considered a *desideratum*, is quite independent of any real or fancied interest in the thing analyzed, it will not be regarded as a breach of decorum on my part to show the *modus operandi* by which some one of my own works was put together. I select "The Raven," as most generally known. It is my design to render it manifest that no one point in its composition is referable either to accident or intuition — that the work proceeded, step by step, to its completion with the precision and rigid consequence of a mathematical problem.

Let us dismiss, as irrelevant to the poem, *per se*, the circumstance — or say the necessity — which, in the first place, gave rise to the intention of composing *a* poem that should suit at once the popular and the critical taste.

We commence, then, with this intention.

The initial consideration was that of extent. If any literary work is too long to be read at one sitting, we must be content to dispense with the immensely important effect derivable from unity of impression — for, if two sittings be required, the affairs of the world interfere, and everything like totality is at once destroyed. But since, *ceteris paribus*, no poet can afford to dispense with *anything* that may advance his design, it but remains to be seen whether there is, in extent, any advantage to counterbalance the loss of unity which attends it. Here I say no, at once. What we term a long poem is, in fact, merely a succession of brief ones — that is to say, of brief poetical effects. It is needless to demonstrate that a poem is such, only inasmuch as it intensely excites, by elevating, the soul; and all intense excitements are, through a psychal necessity, brief. For this reason, at least one half of the *Paradise Lost* is essentially prose — a succession of poetical excitements interspersed, *inevitably*, with corresponding depressions — the whole being deprived, through the extremeness of its length, of the vastly important artistic element, totality, or unity, of effect.

It appears evident, then, that there is a distinct limit, as regards length, to all works of literary art — the limit of a single sitting — and that, although in certain classes of prose composition, such as *Robinson Crusoe* (demanding no unity), this limit may be advantageously overpassed, it can never properly be overpassed in a poem. Within this limit, the extent of a poem may be made to bear mathematical relation to its merit — in other words, to the excitement or elevation — again in other words, to the degree of the true poetical effect which it is capable of inducing; for it is clear that the brevity must be in direct ratio of the intensity of the intended effect: — this, with one proviso — that a certain degree of duration is absolutely requisite for the production of any effect at all.

Holding in view these considerations, as well as that degree of excitement which I deemed not above the popular, while not below the critical, taste, I reached at once what I conceived the proper *length* for my intended poem — a length of about one hundred lines. It is, in fact, a hundred and eight.

My next thought concerned the choice of an impression, or effect, to be conveyed: and here I may as well observe that, throughout the construction, I kept steadily in view the design of rendering the work *universally* appreciable. I should be carried too far out of my immediate topic were I to demonstrate a point upon which I have repeatedly insisted, and which, with the poetical, stands not in the slightest need of demonstration — the point, I mean, that Beauty is the sole legitimate province of the poem. A few words, however, in elucidation of my real meaning, which some of my friends have evinced a disposition to misrepresent. That pleasure which is at once the most intense, the most elevating, and the most pure, is I believe, found in the contemplation of the beautiful. When, indeed, men speak of Beauty, they mean, precisely, not a quality, as is supposed, but an effect — they refer, in short, just to that intense and pure elevation of *soul* — *not* of intellect, or of heart — upon which I have commented, and which is experienced in consequence of contemplating "the beautiful." Now I designate Beauty as the province of the poem, merely because it is an obvious rule of Art that effects should be made to spring from direct causes — that objects should be attained through means best adapted for their attainment — no one as yet having been weak enough to deny that the peculiar elevation alluded to is *most readily* attained in the poem. Now the object Truth, or the satisfaction of the intellect, and the object Passion, or the excitement of the heart, are, although attainable, to a certain extent, in poetry, far more readily attainable in prose. Truth, in fact, demands a precision, and Passion a *homeliness* (the truly passionate will comprehend me) which are absolutely antagonistic to that Beauty which, I maintain, is the excitement, or pleasurable elevation, of the soul. It by no means follows from any thing here said, that passion, or even truth, may not be introduced, and even profitably introduced, into a poem — for they may serve in elucidation, or aid the general effect, as do discords in music, by contrast — but the true artist will always contrive, first, to tone them into proper subservience to the predominant aim, and, secondly, to enveil them, as far as possible, in that Beauty which is the atmosphere and the essence of the poem.

Regarding, then, Beauty as my province, my next question referred to the *tone* of its highest manifestation — and all experience has shown that this tone is one of *sadness*. Beauty of whatever kind, in its supreme development, invariably excites the sensitive soul to tears. Melancholy is thus the most legitimate of all the poetical tones.

The length, the province, and the tone, being thus determined, I betook myself to ordinary induction, with the view of obtaining some artistic piquancy which might serve me as a key-note in the construction of the poem — some pivot upon which the whole structure might turn. In carefully thinking over all the usual artistic effects — or more properly *points*, in the theatrical sense — I did not fail to perceive immediately that no one had been so universally employed as that of the *refrain*. The universality of its employment sufficed to assure me of its intrinsic value, and spared me the necessity of submitting it to analysis. I considered it, however, with regard to its susceptibility of improvement, and soon saw it to be in a primitive condition. As commonly used, the *refrain*, or burden, not only is limited to lyric verse, but depends for its impression upon the force of monotone — both in sound and thought. The pleasure is deduced solely from the sense of identity — of repetition. I resolved to diversify, and so heighten, the effect, by adhering, in general, to the monotone of sound, while I continually varied that of thought: that is to say, I determined to produce continuously novel effects, by the variation *of the application* of the *refrain* — the *refrain* itself remaining, for the most part, unvaried.

These points being settled, I next bethought me of the *nature* of my *refrain*. Since its application was to be repeatedly varied, it was clear that the *refrain* itself must be brief, for there would have been an insurmountable difficulty in frequent variations of application in any sentence of length. In proportion to the brevity of the sentence, would, of course, be the facility of the variation. This led me at once to a single word as the best *refrain*.

The question now arose as to the *character* of the word. Having made up my mind to a *refrain*, the division of the poem into stanzas was, of course, a corollary: the *refrain* forming the close of each stanza. That such a close, to have force, must be sonorous and susceptible of protracted emphasis, admitted no doubt: and these considerations inevitably led me to the long *o* as the most sonorous vowel, in connection with *r* as the most producible consonant.

The sound of the *refrain* being thus determined, it became necessary to select a word embodying this sound, and at the same time in the fullest possible keeping with that melancholy which I had predetermined as the tone of the poem. In such a search it would have been absolutely impossible to overlook the word "Nevermore." In fact, it was the very first which presented itself.

The next *desideratum* was a pretext for the continuous use of the one word "nevermore." In observing the difficulty which I at once found in inventing a sufficiently plausible reason for its continuous repetition, I did not fail to perceive that this difficulty arose solely from the pre-assumption that the word was to be so continuously or monotonously spoken by a *human* being — I did not fail to perceive, in short, that the difficulty lay in the reconciliation of this monotony with the exercise of reason on the part of the creature repeating the word. Here, then, immediately arose the idea of a *non-*reasoning creature capable of speech; and, very naturally, a parrot, in the first instance, suggested itself, but was superseded forthwith by a Raven, as equally capable of speech, and infinitely more in keeping with the intended *tone*.

I had now gone so far as the conception of a Raven — the bird of ill omen — monotonously repeating the one word, "Nevermore," at the conclusion of each stanza, in a poem of melancholy tone, and in length about one hundred lines. Now, never losing sight of the object *supremeness*, or perfection, at all points, I asked myself — "Of all melancholy topics, what, according to the *universal* understanding of mankind, is the *most* melancholy?" Death — was the obvious reply. "And when," I said, "is this most melancholy of topics most poetical?" From what I have already explained at some length, the answer, here also, is obvious — "When it most closely allies itself to *Beauty*: the death, then, of a beautiful woman is, unquestionably, the most poetical topic in the world — and equally is it beyond doubt that the lips best suited for such topic are those of a bereaved lover."

I had now to combine the two ideas, of a lover lamenting his deceased mistress and a Raven continuously repeating the word "Nevermore." — I had to combine these, bearing in mind my design of varying, at every turn, the *application* of the word repeated; but the only intelligible mode of such combination is that of imagining the Raven employing the word in answer to the queries of the lover. And here it was that I saw at once the opportunity afforded for the effect on which I had been depending — that is to say, the effect of the *variation of application*. I saw that I could make the first query propounded by the lover — the first query to which the Raven should reply "Nevermore" — that I could make this first query a commonplace one — the second less so — the third still less, and so on — until at length the lover, startled from his original *nonchalance* by the melancholy character of the word itself — by its frequent repetition — and by a consideration of the ominous reputation of the fowl that uttered it — is at length excited to superstition, and wildly propounds queries of a far different character — queries whose solution he has passionately at heart — propounds them half in superstition and half in that species of despair which delights in self-torture — propounds them not altogether because he believes in the prophetic or demoniac character of the bird (which, reason assures him, is merely repeating a lesson learned by rote) but because he experiences a frenzied pleasure in so modeling his questions as to receive from the *expected* "Nevermore" the most delicious because the most intolerable of sorrow. Perceiving the opportunity thus afforded me — or, more strictly, thus forced upon me in the progress of the construction — I first established in mind the climax, or concluding query — that query to which "Nevermore" should be in the last place an answer — that in reply to which this word "Nevermore" should involve the utmost conceivable amount of sorrow and despair.

Here then the poem may be said to have its beginning — at the end, where all works of art should begin — for it was here, at this point of my preconsiderations, that I first put pen to paper in the composition of the stanza:

"Prophet," said I, "thing of evil! prophet still if bird
    or devil!
By that heaven that bends above us — by what God
    we both adore,
Tell this soul with sorrow laden, if within the distant
    Aidenn,
It shall clasp a sainted maiden whom the angels
    name Lenore —
Clasp a rare and radiant maiden whom the angels
    name Lenore."
    Quoth the raven "Nevermore."

I composed this stanza, at this point, first that, by establishing the climax, I might the better vary and graduate, as regards seriousness and importance, the preceding queries of the lover — and, secondly, that I might definitely settle the rhythm, the metre, and the length and general arrangement of the stanza — as well as graduate the stanzas which were to precede, so that none of them might surpass this in rhythmical effect. Had I been able, in the subsequent composition, to construct more vigorous stanzas, I should, without scruple, have purposely enfeebled them, so as not to interfere with the climacteric effect.

And here I may as well say a few words of the versification. My first object (as usual) was originality. The extent to which this has been neglected, in versification, is one of the most unaccountable things in the world. Admitting that there is little possibility of variety in mere *rhythm*, it is still clear that the possible varieties of metre and stanza are absolutely infinite — and yet, *for centuries, no man, in verse, has ever done, or ever seemed to think of doing, an original thing*. The fact is, that originality (unless in minds of very unusual force) is by no means a matter, as some suppose, of impulse or intuition. In general, to be found, it must be elaborately sought, and although a positive merit of the highest class, demands in its attainment less of invention than negation.

Of course, I pretend to no originality in either the rhythm or metre of the "Raven." The former is trochaic — the latter is octameter acatalectic, alternating with heptameter catalectic repeated in the *refrain* of the fifth verse, and terminating with tetrameter catalectic. Less pedantically — the feet employed throughout (trochees) consist of a long syllable followed by a short: the first line of the stanza consists of eight of these feet — the second of seven and a half (in effect two-thirds) — the third of eight — the fourth of seven and a half — the fifth the same — the sixth three and a half. Now, each of these lines, taken individually, has been employed before, and what originality the "Raven" has, is in their *combination into stanza*; nothing even remotely approaching this combination has ever been attempted. The effect of this originality of combination is aided by other unusual, and some altogether novel effects, arising from an extension of the application of the principles of rhyme and alliteration.

The next point to be considered was the mode of bringing together the lover and the Raven — and the first branch of this consideration was the *locale*. For this the most natural suggestion might seem to be a forest, or the fields — but it has always appeared to me that a close *circumscription of space* is absolutely necessary to the effect of insulated incident: — it has the force of a frame to a picture. It has an indisputable moral power in keeping concentrated the attention, and, of course, must not be confounded with mere unity of place.

I determined, then, to place the lover in his chamber — in a chamber rendered sacred to him by memories of her who had frequented it. The room is represented as richly furnished — this in mere pursuance of the ideas I have already explained on the subject of Beauty, as the sole true poetical thesis.

The *locale* being thus determined, I had now to introduce the bird — and the thought of introducing him through the window, was inevitable. The idea of making the lover suppose, in the first instance, that the flapping of the wings of the bird against the shutter, is a "tapping" at the door, originated in a wish to increase, by prolonging, the reader's curiosity, and in a desire to admit the incidental effect arising from the lover's throwing open the door, finding all dark, and thence adopting the half-fancy that it was the spirit of his mistress that knocked.

I made the night tempestuous, first, to account for the Raven's seeking admission, and secondly, for the effect of contrast with the (physical) serenity within the chamber.

I made the bird alight on the bust of Pallas, also for the effect of contrast between the marble and the plumage — it being understood that the bust was absolutely *suggested* by the bird — the bust of *Pallas* being chosen, first, as most in keeping with the scholarship of the lover, and, secondly, for the sonorousness of the word, Pallas, itself.

About the middle of the poem, also, I have availed myself of the force of contrast, with a view of deepening the ultimate impression. For example, an air of the fantastic — approaching as nearly to the ludicrous as was admissible — is given to the Raven's entrance. He comes in "with many a flirt and flutter."

Not the *least obeisance made he* — not a moment
   stopped or stayed he,
But with mien of lord or lady, perched above my
   chamber door.

In the two stanzas which follow, the design is more obviously carried out: —

Then this ebony bird beguiling my sad fancy into
   smiling
By the *grave and stern decorum of the countenance
   it wore*,
"Though thy *crest be shorn and shaven* thou," I said,
   "art sure no craven,
Ghastly grim and ancient Raven wandering from
   the nightly shore —
Tell me what thy lordly name is on the Night's
   Plutonian shore?"
   Quoth the Raven "Nevermore."

Much I marvelled *this ungainly fowl* to hear discourse so plainly
Though its answer little meaning — little relevancy
   bore;
For we cannot help agreeing that no living human
   being
*Ever yet was blessed with seeing bird above his cham-
   ber door* —
*Bird or beast upon the sculptured bust above his
   chamber door,*
   With such name as "Nevermore."

The effect of the *dénouement* being thus provided for, I immediately drop the fantastic for a tone of the most profound seriousness: — this tone commencing in the stanza directly following the one last quoted, with the line,

But the Raven, sitting lonely on that placid bust,
   spoke only, etc.

From this epoch the lover no longer jests — no longer sees anything even of the fantastic in the Raven's demeanor. He speaks of him as a "grim, ungainly, ghastly, gaunt, and ominous bird of yore," and feels the "fiery eyes" burning into his "bosom's core." This revolution of thought, or fancy, on the lover's part, is intended to induce a similar one on the part of the reader — to bring the mind into a proper frame for the *dénouement* — which is now brought about as rapidly and as *directly* as possible.

With the *dénouement* proper — with the Raven's reply, "Nevermore," to the lover's final demand if he shall meet his mistress in another world — the poem, in its obvious phase, that of a simple narrative, may be said to have its completion. So far, everything is within the limits of the accountable — of the real. A raven, having learned by rote the single word "Nevermore," and having escaped from the custody of its owner, is driven at midnight, through the violence of a storm, to seek admission at a window from which a light still gleams — the chamber-window of a student, occupied half in poring over a volume, half in dreaming of a beloved mistress deceased. The casement being thrown open at the fluttering of the bird's wings, the bird itself perches on the most convenient seat out of the immediate reach of the student, who, amused by the incident and the oddity of the visitor's demeanor, demands of it, in jest and without looking for a reply, its name. The raven addressed, answers with its customary word, "Nevermore" — a word which finds immediate echo in the melancholy heart of the student, who, giving utterance aloud to certain thoughts suggested by the occasion, is again startled by the fowl's repetition of "Nevermore." The student now guesses the state of the case, but is impelled, as I have before explained, by the human thirst for self-torture, and in part by superstition, to propound such queries to the bird as will bring him, the lover, the most of the luxury of sorrow, through the anticipated answer "Nevermore." With the indulgence, to the extreme, of this self-torture, the narration, in what I have termed its first or obvious phase, has a natural termination, and so far there has been no overstepping of the limits of the real.

But in subjects so handled, however skilfully, or with however vivid an array of incident, there is always a certain hardness or nakedness, which repels the artistical eye. Two things are invariably required — first, some amount of complexity, or more properly, adaptation; and, secondly, some amount of suggestiveness — some undercurrent, however indefinite, of meaning. It is this latter, in especial, which imparts to a work of art so much of that *richness* (to borrow from colloquy a forcible term) which we are too fond of confounding with *the ideal*. It is the *excess* of the suggested meaning — it is the rendering this the upper instead of the undercurrent of the theme — which turns into prose (and that of the very flattest kind) the so called poetry of the so called transcendentalists.

Holding these opinions, I added the two concluding stanzas of the poem — their suggestiveness being thus made to pervade all the narrative which has preceded them. The undercurrent of meaning is rendered first apparent in the lines —

"Take thy beak from out *my heart*, and take thy
    form from off my door!"
Quoth the Raven "Nevermore!"

It will be observed the words, "from out my heart," involve the first metaphorical expression in the poem. They, with the answer, "Nevermore," dispose the mind to seek a moral in all that has been previously narrated. The reader begins now to regard the Raven as emblematical — but it is not until the very last line of the very last stanza, that the intention of making him emblematical of *Mournful and Never-ending Remembrance* is permitted distinctly to be seen:

And the Raven, never flitting, still is sitting, still is
    sitting,
On the pallid bust of Pallas, just above my chamber
    door;
And his eyes have all the seeming of a demon's that
    is dreaming,
And the lamplight o'er him streaming throws his
    shadow on the floor;
And my soul *from out that shadow* that lies floating
    on the floor
    Shall be lifted — nevermore.

Hawthorne's Twice-Told Tales
(1842)

🖅 In the preceding essay Poe was engaged in theoretical criticism, discussing various aspects of his theory of literature. But he also wrote a great bulk of practical criticism, discussing particular authors and books, with a high degree of independence, honesty, and insight. The two kinds often overlap, as in his essay on Hawthorne, where he is reviewing the second edition of *Twice-Told Tales* and at the same time setting forth his theory of the short story.

The essay may be most profitably read at this point for the light which it sheds upon his own fiction, examples of which are printed directly after this selection. Some of his essential ideas on literary art have already been touched upon in the period introduction.

We said a few hurried words about Mr. Hawthorne in our last number, with the design of speaking more fully in the present. We are still, however, pressed for room, and must necessarily discuss his volumes more briefly and more at random than their high merits deserve.

The book professes to be a collection of *tales*, yet is, in two respects, misnamed. These pieces are now in their third republication, and, of course, are thrice-told. Moreover, they are by no means *all* tales, either in the ordinary or in the legitimate understanding of the term. Many of them are pure essays; for example, "Sights from a Steeple," "Sunday at Home," "Little Annie's Ramble," "A Rill from the Town Pump," "The Toll-Gatherer's Day," "The Haunted Mind," "The Sister Years," "Snow-Flakes," "Night Sketches," and "Foot-Prints on the Sea-Shore." We mention these matters chiefly on account of their discrepancy with that marked precision and finish by which the body of the work is distinguished.

Of the essays just named, we must be content to speak in brief. They are each and all beautiful, without being characterized by the polish and adaptation so visible in the tales proper. A painter would at once note their leading or predominant feature, and style it *repose*. There is no attempt at effect. All is quiet, thoughtful, subdued. Yet this repose may exist simultaneously with high originality of thought; and Mr. Hawthorne has demonstrated the fact. At every turn we meet with novel combinations; yet these combinations never surpass the limits of the quiet. We are soothed as we read; and withal is a calm astonishment that ideas so apparently obvious have never occurred or been presented to us before. Herein our author differs materially from Lamb or Hunt or Hazlitt — who, with vivid originality of manner and expression, have less of the true novelty of thought than is generally supposed, and whose originality, at best, has an uneasy and meretricious quaintness, replete with startling effects unfounded in nature, and inducing trains of reflection which lead to no satisfactory result. The Essays of Hawthorne have much of the character of Irving, with more of originality, and less of finish; while, compared with the Spectator, they have a vast superiority at all points. The Spectator, Mr. Irving, and Mr. Hawthorne have in common that tranquil and subdued manner which we have chosen to denominate *repose*; but, in the case of the two former, this repose is attained rather by the absence of novel combination, or of originality, than otherwise, and consists chiefly in the calm, quiet, unostentatious expression of commonplace thoughts, in an unambitious, unadulterated Saxon. In them, by strong effort, we are made to conceive the absence of all. In the essays before us the absence of effort is too obvious to be mistaken, and a strong undercurrent of *suggestion* runs continuously beneath the upper stream of the tranquil thesis. In short, these effusions of Mr. Hawthorne are the product of a truly imagina-tive intellect, restrained, and in some measure repressed, by fastidiousness of taste, by constitutional melancholy, and by indolence.

But it is of his tales that we desire principally to speak. The tale proper, in our opinion, affords unquestionably the fairest field for the exercise of the loftiest talent, which can be afforded by the wide domains of mere prose. Were we bidden to say how the highest genius could be most advantageously employed for the best display of its own powers, we should answer, without hesitation — in the composition of a rhymed poem, not to exceed in length what might be perused in an hour. Within this limit alone can the highest order of true poetry exist. We need only here say, upon this topic, that, in almost all classes of composition, the unity of effect or impression is a point of the greatest importance. It is clear, moreover, that this unity cannot be thoroughly preserved in productions whose perusal cannot be completed at one sitting. We may continue the reading of a prose composition, from the very nature of prose itself, much longer than we can persevere, to any good purpose, in the perusal of a poem. This latter, if truly fulfilling the demands of the poetic sentiment, induces an exaltation of the soul which cannot be long sustained. All high excitements are necessarily transient. Thus a long poem is a paradox. And, without unity of impression, the deepest effects cannot be brought about. Epics were the offspring of an imperfect sense of Art, and their reign is no more. A poem *too* brief may produce a vivid, but never an intense or enduring impression. Without a certain continuity of effort — without a certain duration or repetition of purpose — the soul is never deeply moved. There must be the dropping of the water upon the rock. De Béranger has wrought brilliant things — pungent and spirit-stirring — but, like all immassive bodies, they lack *momentum*, and thus fail to satisfy the Poetic Sentiment. They sparkle and excite, but, from want of continuity, fail deeply to impress. Extreme brevity will degenerate into epigrammatism; but the sin of extreme length is even more unpardonable. *In medio tutissimus ibis.* [You travel most safely the middle road.]

Were we called upon, however, to designate that class of composition which, next to such a poem as we have suggested, should best fulfill the demands of high genius — should offer it the most advantageous field of exertion — we should unhesitatingly speak of the prose tale, as Mr. Hawthorne has here exemplified it. We allude to the short prose narrative, requiring from a half-hour to one or two hours in its perusal. The ordinary novel is objectionable, from its length, for reasons already stated in substance. As it cannot be read at one sitting, it deprives itself, of course, of the immense force derivable from *totality*. Worldly interests intervening during the pauses of perusal, modify, annul, or counteract, in a greater or less degree, the impressions of the book. But simple cessation in reading would, of itself, be sufficient to destroy the true unity. In the brief tale, however, the author is enabled to carry out the fulness of his intention, be it what it may. During the hour of perusal the soul of the reader is at the writer's control. There are no external or extrinsic influences — resulting from weariness or interruption.

A skillful literary artist has constructed a tale. If wise, he has not fashioned his thoughts to accommodate his incidents; but having conceived, with deliberate care, a certain unique or single *effect* to be wrought out, he then invents such incidents — he then combines such events as may best aid him in establishing this preconceived effect. If his very initial sentence tend not to the outbringing of this effect, then he has failed in his first step. In the whole composition there should be no word written, of which the tendency, direct or indirect, is not to the one pre-established design. And by such means, with such care and skill, a picture is at length painted which leaves in the mind of him who contemplates it with a kindred art, a sense of the fullest satisfaction. The idea of the tale has been presented unblemished, because undisturbed; and this is an end unattainable by the novel. Undue brevity is just as exceptionable here as in the poem; but undue length is yet more to be avoided.

We have said that the tale has a point of superiority even over the poem. In fact, while the *rhythm* of this latter is an essential aid in the development of the poem's highest idea — the idea of the Beautiful — the artificialities of this rhythm are an inseparable bar to the development of all points of thought or expression which have their basis in *Truth*. But Truth is often, and in very great degree, the aim of the tale. Some of the finest tales are tales of ratiocination. Thus the field of this species of composition, if not in so elevated a region on the

mountain of Mind, is a table-land of far vaster extent than the domain of the mere poem. Its products are never so rich, but infinitely more numerous, and more appreciable by the mass of mankind. The writer of the prose tale, in short, may bring to his theme a vast variety of modes or inflections of thought and expression — (the ratiocinative, for example, the sarcastic, or the humorous) which are not only antagonistical to the nature of the poem, but absolutely forbidden by one of its most peculiar and indispensable adjuncts; we allude, of course, to rhythm. It may be added here, *par parenthèse*, that the author who aims at the purely beautiful in a prose tale is laboring at a great disadvantage. For Beauty can be better treated in the poem. Not so with terror, or passion, or horror, or a multitude of such other points. And here it will be seen how full of prejudice are the usual animadversions against those *tales of effect*, many fine examples of which were found in the earlier numbers of *Blackwood*. The impressions produced were wrought in a legitimate sphere of action, and constituted a legitimate although sometimes an exaggerated interest. They were relished by every man of genius: although there were found many men of genius who condemned them without just ground. The true critic will but demand that the design intended be accomplished, to the fullest extent, by the means most advantageously applicable.

We have very few American tales of real merit — we may say, indeed, none, with the exception of *The Tales of a Traveller* of Washington Irving, and these *Twice-Told Tales* of Mr. Hawthorne. Some of the pieces of Mr. John Neal abound in vigor and originality; but, in general, his compositions of this class are excessively diffuse, extravagant, and indicative of an imperfect sentiment of Art. Articles at random are, now and then, met with in our periodicals which might be advantageously compared with the best effusions of the British Magazines; but, upon the whole, we are far behind our progenitors in this department of literature.

Of Mr. Hawthorne's tales we should say, emphatically, that they belong to the highest region of Art — an Art subservient to genius of a very lofty order. We had supposed, with good reason for so supposing, that he had been thrust into his present position by one of the impudent *cliques* which beset our literature, and whose pretensions it is our full purpose to expose at the earliest opportunity; but we have been most agreeably mistaken. We know of few compositions which the critic can more honestly commend than these *Twice-Told Tales*. As Americans, we feel proud of the book.

Mr. Hawthorne's distinctive trait is invention, creation, imagination, originality — a trait which, in the literature of fiction, is positively worth all the rest. But the nature of the originality, so far as regards its manifestation in letters, is but imperfectly understood. The inventive or original mind as frequently displays itself in novelty of *tone* as in novelty of matter. Mr. Hawthorne is original at *all* points.

It would be a matter of some difficulty to designate the best of these tales; we repeat that, without exception, they are beautiful. "Wakefield" is remarkable for the skill with which an old idea — a well-known incident — is worked up or discussed. A man of whims conceives the purpose of quitting his wife and residing *incognito*, for twenty years, in her immediate neighborhood. Something of this kind actually happened in London. The force of Mr. Hawthorne's tale lies in the analysis of the motives which must or might have impelled the husband to such folly, in the first instance, with the possible causes of his perseverance. Upon this thesis a sketch of singular power has been constructed.

"The Wedding Knell" is full of the boldest imagination — an imagination fully controlled by taste. The most captious critic could find no flaw in this production.

"The Minister's Black Veil" is a masterly composition, of which the sole defect is that to the rabble its exquisite skill will be *caviare*. The *obvious* meaning of this article will be found to smother its insinuated one. The *moral* put into the mouth of the dying minister will be supposed to convey the *true* import of the narrative; and that a crime of dark dye (having reference to the "young lady") has been committed, is a point which only minds congenial with that of the author will perceive.

"Mr. Higginbotham's Catastrophe" is vividly original, and managed most dexterously.

"Dr. Heidegger's Experiment" is exceedingly well imagined, and executed with surpassing ability. The artist breathes in every line of it.

"The White Old Maid" is objectionable even more than the "Minister's Black Veil," on the score of its mysticism. Even with the thoughtful and analytic, there will be much trouble in penetrating its entire import.

"The Hollow of the Three Hills" we would quote in full had we space; — not as evincing higher talent than any of the other pieces, but as affording an excellent example of the author's peculiar ability. The subject is commonplace. A witch subjects the Distant and the Past to the view of a mourner. It has been the fashion to describe, in such cases, a mirror in which the images of the absent appear; or a cloud of smoke is made to arise, and thence the figures are gradually unfolded. Mr. Hawthorne has wonderfully heightened his effect by making the ear, in place of the eye, the medium by which the fantasy is conveyed. The head of the mourner is enveloped in the cloak of the witch, and within its magic folds there arise sounds which have an all-sufficient intelligence. Throughout this article also, the artist is conspicuous — not more in positive than in negative merits. Not only is all done that should be done, but (what perhaps is an end with more difficulty attained) there is nothing done which should not be. Every word *tells*, and there is not a word which does *not* tell.

In "Howe's Masquerade" we observe something which resembles plagiarism — but which *may be* a very flattering coincidence of thought. We quote the passage in question.

[Quotation.] [1]

The idea here is, that the figure in the cloak is the phantom or reduplication of Sir William Howe; but in an article called "William Wilson," one of the *Tales of the Grotesque and Arabesque*, we have not only the same idea, but the same idea similarly presented in several respects. We quote two paragraphs, which our readers may compare with what has been already given. We have italicized, above, the immediate particulars of resemblance.

[Quotation.] [1]

Here it will be observed that, not only are the two general conceptions identical, but there are various *points* of similarity. In each case the figure seen is the wraith or duplication of the beholder. In each case the scene is a masquerade. In each case the figure is cloaked. In each, there is a quarrel — that is to say, angry words pass between the parties. In each the beholder is enraged. In each the cloak and sword fall upon the floor. The "villain, unmuffle your-

[1] Omitted here, as in the text of the Virginia edition.

self," of Mr. H. is precisely paralleled by a passage at page 56 of "William Wilson."

In the way of objection we have scarcely a word to say of these tales. There is, perhaps, a somewhat too general or prevalent *tone* — a tone of melancholy and mysticism. The subjects are insufficiently varied. There is not so much of *versatility* evinced as we might well be warranted in expecting from the high powers of Mr. Hawthorne. But beyond these trivial exceptions we have really none to make. The style is purity itself. Force abounds. High imagination gleams from every page. Mr. Hawthorne is a man of the truest genius. We only regret that the limits of our Magazine will not permit us to pay him that full tribute of commendation, which, under other circumstances, we should be so eager to pay.

Ligeia

(1838)

❧ From Shelley and Keats to Baudelaire, romantics associated beauty and death. As Victor Hugo linked them in a sonnet, they were "two sisters" with the "same enigma." For Poe the connection was more mysterious and more complex, and the death of a beloved woman is a recurring theme — see "The Fall of the House of Usher" as well as this story. The significance of these deaths for Poe has been variously interpreted. G. E. Woodberry, in his biography, took the simple view that the Lady Ligeia was to Poe an "airwoven divinity," and that her return to life in the dead body of her successor showed "the awful might of the soul in the victory of its will over death and the eternity of its love." A different interpretation was advanced by Mario Praz in *The Romantic Agony*, a study of erotic sensibility. Many of Poe's tales, he says, represent symbolically the "thirst for unrealizable love," and "the desire for that complete fusion with the beloved being which ends in vampirism." D. H. Lawrence, English novelist and often astute critic, felt that this desire for total possession in the hero is a thing of evil and that Ligeia felt a "horror at his probing, horror at being vamped by his consciousness," though she wanted to be "vamped." Finally, the American poet Allen Tate has agreed with Lawrence that Poe's heroes never desire possession in a physical or even a normal way, but he goes further and argues that "the destruction works both ways"; that the vampire-wish to possess reflects a lack of vitality — even a death-wish — in the hero (and the writer); and that the dehumanized and possessed lady acts in turn to possess her destroyer.

The story contains a number of allusions which Poe hardly expected the reader to recognize. Many of them are little more than decorative and do not clarify or enrich the meaning. It may be worth noting, however, that in the paragraph beginning "For eyes we have no models" (page 261) is a reference to a proverb that came from the Greek philosopher Democritus: "Truth lies at the bottom of a well."

And the will therein lieth, which dieth not. Who knoweth the mysteries of the will, with its vigor? For God is but a great will pervading all things by nature of its intentness. Man doth not yield himself to the angels, nor unto death utterly, save only through the weakness of his feeble will.

JOSEPH GLANVILL

I cannot, for my soul, remember how, when, or even precisely where, I first became acquainted with the lady Ligeia. Long years have since elapsed, and my memory is feeble through much suffering. Or, perhaps, I cannot *now* bring these points to mind, because, in truth, the character of my beloved, her rare learning, her singular yet placid cast of beauty, and the thrilling and enthralling eloquence of her low musical language, made their way into my heart by paces so steadily and stealthily progressive that they have been unnoticed and unknown. Yet I believe that I met her first and most frequently in some large, old, decaying city near the Rhine. Of her family — I have surely heard her speak. That it is of a remotely ancient date cannot be doubted. Ligeia! Ligeia! Buried in studies of a nature more than all else adapted to deaden impressions of the outward world, it is by that sweet word alone — by Ligeia — that I bring before mine eyes in fancy the image of her who is no more. And now, while I write, a recollection flashes upon me that I have *never known* the paternal name of her who was my friend and my betrothed, and who became the partner of my studies, and finally the wife of my bosom. Was it a playful charge on the part of my Ligeia? or was it a test of my strength of affection, that I should institute no inquiries upon this point? or was it rather a caprice of my own — a wildly romantic offering on the shrine of the most passionate devotion? I but indistinctly recall the fact itself — what wonder that I have utterly forgotten the circumstances which originated or attended it? And, indeed, if ever that spirit which is entitled *Romance* — if ever she, the wan and the misty-winged Ashtophet of idolatrous Egypt, presided, as they tell, over marriages ill-omened, then most surely she presided over mine.

There is one dear topic, however, on which my memory fails me not. It is the *person* of Ligeia. In stature she was tall, somewhat slender, and, in her latter days, even emaciated. I would in vain attempt to portray the majesty, the quiet case, of her demeanor, or the incomprehensible lightness and elasticity of her footfall. She came and departed as a shadow. I was never made aware of her entrance into my closed study, save by the dear music of her low sweet voice, as she placed her marble hand upon my shoulder. In beauty of face no maiden ever equalled her. It was the radiance of an opium-dream — an airy and spirit-lifting vision more wildly divine than the fantasies which hovered about the slumbering souls of the daughters of Delos. Yet her features were not of that regular mold which we have been falsely taught to worship in the classical labors of the heathen. "There is no exquisite beauty," says Bacon, Lord Verulam, speaking truly of all the forms and genera of beauty, "without some *strangeness* in the proportion." Yet, although I saw that the features of Ligeia were not of a classic regularity — although I perceived that her loveliness was indeed "exquisite," and felt that there was much of "strangeness" pervading it, yet I have tried in vain to detect the irregularity and to trace home my own perception of "the strange." I examined the contour of the lofty and pale forehead: it was faultless — how cold indeed that word when applied to a majesty so divine! — the skin rivalling the purest ivory, the commanding extent and repose, the gentle prominence of the regions above the temples; and then the raven-black, the glossy, the luxuriant, and naturally-curling tresses, setting forth the full force of the Homeric epithet, "hyacinthine"! I looked at the delicate outlines of the nose — and nowhere but in the graceful medallions of the Hebrews had I beheld a similar perfection. There were the same luxurious smoothness of surface, the same scarcely perceptible tendency to the aquiline, the same harmoniously curved nostrils speaking the free spirit. I regarded the sweet mouth. Here was indeed the triumph of all things heavenly — the magnificent turn of the short upper lip — the soft, voluptuous slumber of the under — the dimples which sported, and the color which spoke — the teeth glancing back, with a brilliance almost startling, every ray of the holy light which fell upon them in her serene and placid, yet most exultingly radiant of all smiles. I scrutinized the formation of the chin: and here, too, I found the gentleness of breadth, the softness and the majesty, the fulness and the spirituality, of the Greek — the contour which the god Apollo revealed but in a dream to Cleomenes, the son of the Athenian. And then I peered into the large eyes of Ligeia.

For eyes we have no models in the remotely antique. It might have been, too, that in these eyes of my beloved lay the secret to which Lord Verulam alludes. They were, I must believe, far larger than the ordinary eyes of our own race. They were even fuller than the fullest of the gazelle eyes of the tribe of the valley of Nourjahad. Yet it was only at intervals — in moments of intense excitement — that this peculiarity became more than slightly noticeable in Ligeia. And at such moments was her beauty — in my heated fancy thus it appeared perhaps — the beauty of beings either above or apart from the earth, the beauty of the fabulous Houri of the Turk. The hue of the orbs was the most brilliant of black, and, far over them, hung jetty lashes of great length. The brows, slightly irregular in outline, had the same tint. The "strangeness," however, which I found in the eyes, was of a nature distinct from the formation, or the color, or the brilliancy of the features, and must, after all, be referred to the *expression*. Ah, word of no meaning! behind whose vast latitude of mere sound we intrench our ignorance of so much of the spiritual. The expression of the eyes of Ligeia! How for long hours have I pondered upon it! How have I, through the whole of a midsummer night, struggled to fathom it! What was it — that something more profound than the well of Democritus — which lay far within the pupils of my beloved? What *was* it? I was possessed with a passion to discover. Those eyes! those large, those shining, those divine orbs! they became to me twin stars of Leda, and I to them devoutest of astrologers.

There is no point, among the many incomprehensible anomalies of the science of mind, more thrillingly exciting than the fact — never, I believe, noticed in the schools — that in our endeavors to recall to memory something long forgotten, we often find ourselves *upon the very verge* of remembrance, without being able, in the end, to remember. And thus how frequently, in my intense scrutiny of Ligeia's eyes, have I felt approaching the full knowledge of their expression — felt it approaching, yet not quite be mine, and so at length entirely depart! And (strange, oh strangest mystery of all!) I found, in the commonest objects of the universe, a circle of analogies to that expression. I mean to say that, subsequently to the period when Ligeia's beauty passed into my spirit, there dwelling as in a shrine, I derived, from many existences in the material world, a sentiment such as I felt always aroused within me by her large and luminous orbs. Yet not the more could I define that sentiment, or analyze, or even steadily view it. I recognized it, let me repeat, sometimes in the survey of a rapidly growing vine — in the contemplation of a moth, a butterfly, a chrysalis, a stream of running water. I have felt it in the ocean; in the falling of a meteor. I have felt it in the glances of unusually aged people. And there are one or two stars in heaven (one especially, a star of the sixth magnitude, double and changeable, to be found near the large star in Lyra), in a telescopic scrutiny of which I have been made aware of the feeling. I have been filled with it by certain sounds from stringed instruments, and not unfrequently by passages from books. Among innumerable other instances, I well remember something in a volume of Joseph Glanvill, which (perhaps merely from its quaintness — who shall say?) never failed to inspire me with the sentiment: "And the will therein lieth, which dieth not. Who knoweth the mysteries of the will, with its vigor? For God is but a great will pervading all things by nature of its intentness. Man doth not yield him to the angels, nor unto death utterly, save only through the weakness of his feeble will."

Length of years and subsequent reflection have enabled me to trace, indeed, some remote connection between this passage in the English moralist and a portion of the character of Ligeia. An *intensity* in thought, action, or speech, was possibly, in her, a result, or at least an index, of that gigantic volition which, during our long intercourse, failed to give other and more immediate evidence of its existence. Of all the women whom I have ever known, she, the outwardly calm, the ever-placid Ligeia, was the most violently a prey to the tumultuous vultures of stern passion. And of such passion I could form no estimate, save by the miraculous expansion of those eyes which at once so delighted and appalled me — by the almost magical melody, modulation, distinctness, and placidity of her very low voice — and by the fierce energy (rendered doubly effective by contrast with her manner of utterance) of the wild words which she habitually uttered.

I have spoken of the learning of Ligeia: it was immense — such as I have never known in woman. In the classical tongues was she deeply proficient, and as far as my own acquaintance extended in regard to the modern dialects of Europe, I have never known her at fault. Indeed upon any theme of the most admired, because simply the most abstruse of the boasted erudition of the academy, have I *ever* found Ligeia at fault? How singularly, how thrillingly, this one point in the nature of my wife has forced itself, at this late period only, upon my attention! I said her knowledge was such as I have never known in woman — but where breathes the man who has traversed, and successfully, *all* the wide areas of moral, physical, and mathematical science? I saw not then what I now clearly perceive, that the acquisitions of Ligeia were gigantic, were astounding; yet I was sufficiently aware of her infinite supremacy to resign myself, with a child-like confidence, to her guidance through the chaotic world of metaphysical investigation at which I was most busily occupied during the earlier years of our marriage. With how vast a triumph, with how vivid a delight, with how much of all that is ethereal in hope, did I *feel*, as she bent over me in studies but little sought — but less known — that delicious vista by slow degrees expanding before me, down whose long, gorgeous, and all untrodden path, I might at length pass onward to the goal of a wisdom too divinely precious not to be forbidden!

How poignant, then, must have been the grief with which, after some years, I beheld my well-grounded expectations take wings to themselves and fly away! Without Ligeia I was but as a child groping benighted. Her presence, her readings alone, rendered vividly luminous the many mysteries of the transcendentalism in which we were immersed. Wanting the radiant lustre of her eyes, letters, lambent and golden, grew duller than Saturnian lead. And now those eyes shone less and less frequently upon the pages over which I pored. Ligeia grew ill. The wild eyes blazed with a too-too glorious effulgence; the pale fingers became of the transparent waxen hue of the grave; and the blue veins upon the lofty forehead swelled and sank impetuously with the tides of the most gentle emotion. I

saw that she must die — and I struggled desperately in spirit with the grim Azrael. And the
struggles of the passionate wife were, to my astonishment, even more energetic than my own.
There had been much in her stern nature to 5
impress me with the belief that, to her, death
would have come without its terrors; but not
so. Words are impotent to convey any just idea
of the fierceness of resistance with which she
wrestled with the Shadow. I groaned in anguish 10
at the pitiable spectacle. I would have soothed
— I would have reasoned; but, in the intensity
of her wild desire for life — for life — *but* for
life — solace and reason were alike the uttermost of folly. Yet not until the last instance, 15
amid the most convulsive writhings of her fierce
spirit, was shaken the external placidity of her
demeanor. Her voice grew more gentle — grew
more low — yet I would not wish to dwell upon
the wild meaning of the quietly uttered words. 20
My brain reeled as I hearkened, entranced, to a
melody more than mortal — to assumptions and
aspirations which mortality had never before
known.

That she loved me I should not have doubted; 25
and I might have been easily aware that, in a
bosom such as hers, love would have reigned no
ordinary passion. But in death only was I fully
impressed with the strength of her affection. For
long hours, detaining my hand, would she pour 30
out before me the overflowing of a heart whose
more than passionate devotion amounted to
idolatry. How had I deserved to be so blessed
by such confessions? How had I deserved to be
so cursed with the removal of my beloved in the 35
hour of her making them? But upon this subject
I cannot bear to dilate. Let me say only, that
in Ligeia's more than womanly abandonment
to a love, alas! all unmerited, all unworthily bestowed, I at length recognized the principle of 40
her longing, with so wildly earnest a desire, for
the life which was now fleeing so rapidly away.
It is this wild longing, it is this eager vehemence
of desire for life — *but* for life, that I have no
power to portray, no utterance capable of ex- 45
pressing.

At high noon of the night in which she departed, beckoning me peremptorily to her side,
she bade me repeat certain verses composed by
herself not many days before. I obeyed her. 50
They were these:

Lo! 'tis a gala night
Within the lonesome latter years!

An angel throng, bewinged, bedight
In veils, and drowned in tears,
Sit in a theatre, to see
A play of hopes and fears,
While the orchestra breathes fitfully
The music of the spheres.

Mimes, in the form of God on high,
Mutter and mumble low,
And hither and thither fly —
Mere puppets they, who come and go
At bidding of vast formless things
That shift the scenery to and fro,
Flapping from out their condor wings
Invisible Woe!

That motley drama — oh, be sure
It shall not be forgot!
With its Phantom chased for evermore,
By a crowd that seize it not,
Through a circle that ever returneth in
To the self-same spot,
And much of Madness, and more of Sin,
And Horror the soul of the plot.

But see, amid the mimic rout
A crawling shape intrude!
A blood-red thing that writhes from out
The scenic solitude!
It writhes — it writhes! with mortal pangs
The mimes become its food,
And seraphs sob at vermin fangs
In human gore imbued.

Out — out are the lights — out all!
And over each quivering form
The curtain, a funeral pall,
Comes down with the rush of a storm,
While the angels, all pallid and wan,
Uprising, unveiling, affirm
That the play is the tragedy, "Man,"
And its hero, the Conqueror Worm.

"O God!" half shrieked Ligeia, leaping to her
feet and extending her arms aloft with a spasmodic movement, as I made an end of these
lines — "O God! O Divine Father! shall these
things be undeviatingly so? shall this Conqueror
be not once conquered? Are we not part and
parcel in Thee? Who — who knoweth the mysteries of the will with its vigor? 'Man doth not
yield him to the angels, *nor unto death utterly*
save only through the weakness of his feeble
will.' "

And now, as if exhausted with emotion, she
suffered her white arms to fall, and returned
solemnly to her bed of death. And as she
breathed her last sighs, there came mingled

with them a low murmur from her lips. I bent to them my ear, and distinguished, again, the concluding words of the passage in Glanvill: "*Man doth not yield him to the angels, nor unto death utterly, save only through the weakness of his feeble will.*"

She died: and I, crushed into the very dust with sorrow, could no longer endure the lonely desolation of my dwelling in the dim and decaying city by the Rhine. I had no lack of what the world calls wealth. Ligeia had brought me far more, very far more, than ordinarily falls to the lot of mortals. After a few months, therefore, of weary and aimless wandering, I purchased, and put in some repair, an abbey, which I shall not name, in one of the wildest and least frequented portions of fair England. The gloomy and dreary grandeur of the building, the almost savage aspect of the domain, the many melancholy and time-honored memories connected with both, had much in unison with the feelings of utter abandonment which had driven me into that remote and unsocial region of the country. Yet although the external abbey, with its verdant decay hanging about it, suffered but little alteration, I gave way with a child-like perversity, and perchance with a faint hope of alleviating my sorrows, to a display of more than regal magnificence within. For such follies, even in childhood, I had imbibed a taste, and now they came back to me as if in the dotage of grief. Alas, I feel how much even of incipient madness might have been discovered in the gorgeous and fantastic draperies, in the solemn carvings of Egypt, in the wild cornices and furniture, in the Bedlam patterns of the carpets of tufted gold! I had become a bounden slave in the trammels of opium, and my labors and my orders had taken a coloring from my dreams. But these absurdities I must not pause to detail. Let me speak only of that one chamber, ever accursed, whither, in a moment of mental alienation, I led from the altar as my bride — as the successor of the unforgotten Ligeia — the fair-haired and blue-eyed Lady Rowena Trevanion, of Tremaine.

There is no individual portion of the architecture and decoration of that bridal chamber which is not now visibly before me. Where were the souls of the haughty family of the bride, when, through thirst of gold, they permitted to pass the threshold of an apartment *so* bedecked, a maiden and a daughter so beloved? I have said that I minutely remember the details of the chamber — yet I am sadly forgetful on topics of deep moment; and here there was no system, no keeping, in the fantastic display, to take hold upon the memory. The room lay in a high turret of the castellated abbey, was pentagonal in shape, and of capacious size. Occupying the whole southern face of the pentagon was the sole window — an immense sheet of unbroken glass from Venice — a single pane, and tinted of a leaden hue, so that the rays of either the sun or moon, passing through it, fell with a ghastly lustre on the objects within. Over the upper portion of this huge window extended the trellis-work of an aged vine, which clambered up the massy walls of the turret. The ceiling, of gloomy-looking oak, was excessively lofty, vaulted, and elaborately fretted with the wildest and most grotesque specimens of a semi-Gothic, semi-Druidical device. From out the most central recess of this melancholy vaulting depended, by a single chain of gold with long links, a huge censer of the same metal, Saracenic in pattern, and with many perforations so contrived that there writhed in and out of them, as if endued with a serpent vitality, a continual succession of parti-colored fires.

Some few ottomans and golden candelabra, of Eastern figure, were in various stations about; and there was the couch, too — the bridal couch — of an Indian model, and low, and sculptured of solid ebony, with a pall-like canopy above. In each of the angles of the chamber stood on end a gigantic sarcophagus of black granite, from the tombs of the kings over against Luxor, with their aged lids full of immemorial sculpture. But in the draping of the apartment lay, alas! the chief fantasy of all. The lofty walls, gigantic in height, even unproportionably so, were hung from summit to foot, in vast folds, with a heavy and massive-looking tapestry — tapestry of a material which was found alike as a carpet on the floor, as a covering for the ottomans and the ebony bed, as a canopy for the bed, and as the gorgeous volutes of the curtains which partially shaded the window. The material was the richest cloth of gold. It was spotted all over, at irregular intervals, with arabesque figures, about a foot in diameter, and wrought upon the cloth in patterns of the most jetty black. But these figures partook of the true character of the arabesque only when regarded from a single point of view. By a contrivance now common, and indeed traceable to a very remote period of antiquity, they were made changeable in aspect. To one entering the room, they bore the appearance of simple monstrosities; but upon a farther advance, this appearance gradually departed; and, step by step, as the visitor moved his station in the chamber, he saw himself surrounded by an endless succession of the ghastly forms which belong to the superstition of the Norman, or arise in the guilty slumbers of the monk. The phantasmagoric effect was vastly heightened by the artificial introduction of a strong continual current of wind behind the draperies, giving a hideous and uneasy animation to the whole.

In halls such as these, in a bridal chamber such as this, I passed, with the Lady of Tremaine, the unhallowed hours of the first month of our marriage — passed them with but little disquietude. That my wife dreaded the fierce moodiness of my temper — that she shunned me, and loved me but little — I could not help perceiving; but it gave me rather pleasure than otherwise. I loathed her with a hatred belonging more to demon than to man. My memory flew back (oh, with what intensity of regret!) to Ligeia, the beloved, the august, the beautiful, the entombed. I revelled in recollections of her purity, of her wisdom, of her lofty, her ethereal nature, of her passionate, her idolatrous love. Now, then, did my spirit fully and freely burn with more than all the fires of her own. In the excitement of my opium dreams (for I was habitually fettered in the shackles of the drug), I would call aloud upon her name, during the silence of the night, or among the sheltered recesses of the glens by day, as if, through the wild eagerness, the solemn passion, the consuming ardor of my longing for the departed, I could restore her to the pathway she had abandoned — ah, *could* it be forever? — upon the earth.

About the commencement of the second month of the marriage, the Lady Rowena was attacked with sudden illness, from which her recovery was slow. The fever which consumed her, rendered her nights uneasy; and in her perturbed state of half-slumber, she spoke of sounds, and of motions, in and about the chamber of the turret, which I concluded had no origin save in the distemper of her fancy, or perhaps in the phantasmagoric influences of the chamber itself. She became at length convalescent — finally, well. Yet but a brief period elapsed, ere a second more violent disorder again threw her upon a bed of suffering; and from this attack her frame, at all times feeble, never altogether recovered. Her illnesses were, after this epoch,

of alarming character, and of more alarming recurrence, defying alike the knowledge and the great exertions of her physicians. With the increase of the chronic disease, which had thus apparently taken too sure hold upon her constitution to be eradicated by human means, I could not fail to observe a similar increase in the nervous irritation of her temperament, and in her excitability by trivial causes of fear. She spoke again, and now more frequently and pertinaciously, of the sounds — of the slight sounds — and of the unusual motions among the tapestries, to which she had formerly alluded.

One night, near the closing in of September, she pressed this distressing subject with more than usual emphasis upon my attention. She had just awakened from an unquiet slumber, and I had been watching, with feelings half of anxiety, half of vague terror, the workings of her emaciated countenance. I sat by the side of her ebony bed, upon one of the ottomans of India. She partly arose, and spoke, in an earnest low whisper, of sounds which she *then* heard, but which I could not hear — of motions which she *then* saw, but which I could not perceive. The wind was rushing hurriedly behind the tapestries, and I wished to show her (what, let me confess it, I could not *all* believe) that those almost inarticulate breathings, and those very gentle variations of the figures upon the wall, were but the natural effects of that customary rushing of the wind. But a deadly pallor, overspreading her face, had proved to me that my exertions to reassure her would be fruitless. She appeared to be fainting, and no attendants were within call. I remembered where was deposited a decanter of light wine which had been ordered by her physicians, and hastened across the chamber to procure it. But, as I stepped beneath the light of the censer, two circumstances of a startling nature attracted my attention. I had felt that some palpable although invisible object had passed lightly by my person; and I saw that there lay upon the golden carpet, in the very middle of the rich lustre thrown from the censer, a shadow — a faint, indefinite shadow of angelic aspect — such as might be fancied for the shadow of a shade. But I was wild with the excitement of an immoderate dose of opium, and heeded these things but little, nor spoke of them to Rowena. Having found the wine, I recrossed the chamber, and poured out a gobletful, which I held to the lips of the fainting lady. She had now partially recovered, however, and took the vessel herself, while I sank upon an ottoman near me, with my eyes fastened upon her person. It was then that I became distinctly aware of a gentle footfall upon the carpet, and near the couch; and in a second thereafter, as Rowena was in the act of raising the wine to her lips, I saw, or may have dreamed that I saw, fall within the goblet, as if from some invisible spring in the atmosphere of the room, three or four large drops of a brilliant and ruby-colored fluid. If this I saw — not so Rowena. She swallowed the wine unhesitatingly, and I forbore to speak to her of a circumstance which must after all, I considered, have been but the suggestion of a vivid imagination, rendered morbidly active by the terror of the lady, by the opium, and by the hour.

Yet I cannot conceal it from my own perception that, immediately subsequent to the fall of the ruby-drops, a rapid change for the worse took place in the disorder of my wife; so that, on the third subsequent night, the hands of her menials prepared her for the tomb, and on the fourth, I sat alone, with her shrouded body, in that fantastic chamber which had received her as my bride. Wild visions, opium-engendered, flitted shadow-like before me. I gazed with unquiet eye upon the sarcophagi in the angles of the room, upon the varying figures of the drapery, and upon the writhing of the particolored fires in the censer overhead. My eyes then fell, as I called to mind the circumstances of a former night, to the spot beneath the glare of the censer where I had seen the faint traces of the shadow. It was there, however, no longer; and breathing with greater freedom, I turned my glances to the pallid and rigid figure upon the bed. Then rushed upon me a thousand memories of Ligeia — and then came back upon my heart, with the turbulent violence of a flood, the whole of that unutterable woe with which I had regarded *her* thus enshrouded. The night waned; and still, with a bosom full of bitter thoughts of the one only and supremely beloved, I remained gazing upon the body of Rowena.

It might have been midnight, or perhaps earlier, or later, for I had taken no note of time, when a sob, low, gentle, but very distinct, startled me from my revery. I *felt* that it came from the bed of ebony — the bed of death. I listened in an agony of superstitious terror — but there was no repetition of the sound. I strained my vision to detect any motion in the corpse — but there was not the slightest perceptible. Yet I could not have been deceived. I *had* heard the noise, however faint, and my soul was awakened within me. I resolutely and perseveringly kept my attention riveted upon the body. Many minutes elapsed before any circumstance occurred tending to throw light upon the mystery. At length it became evident that a slight, a very feeble, and barely noticeable tinge of color had flushed up within the cheeks, and along the sunken small veins of the eyelids. Through a species of unutterable horror and awe, for which the language of mortality has no sufficiently energetic expression, I felt my heart cease to beat, my limbs grow rigid where I sat. Yet a sense of duty finally operated to restore my self-possession. I could no longer doubt that we had been precipitate in our preparations — that Rowena still lived. It was necessary that some immediate exertion be made; yet the turret was altogether apart from the portion of the abbey tenanted by the servants — there were none within call — I had no means of summoning them to my aid without leaving the room for many minutes — and this I could not venture to do. I therefore struggled alone in my endeavors to call back the spirit still hovering. In a short period it was certain, however, that a relapse had taken place; the color disappeared from both eyelid and cheek, leaving a wanness even more than that of marble; the lips became doubly shrivelled and pinched up in the ghastly expression of death; a repulsive clamminess and coldness overspread rapidly the surface of the body; and all the usual rigorous stiffness immediately supervened. I fell back with a shudder upon the couch from which I had been so startlingly aroused, and again gave myself up to passionate waking visions of Ligeia.

An hour thus elapsed, when (could it be possible?) I was a second time aware of some vague sound issuing from the region of the bed. I listened — in extremity of horror. The sound came again — it was a sigh. Rushing to the corpse, I saw — distinctly saw — a tremor upon the lips. In a minute afterwards they relaxed, disclosing a bright line of the pearly teeth. Amazement now struggled in my bosom with the profound awe which had hitherto reigned there alone. I felt that my vision grew dim, that my reason wandered; and it was only by a violent effort that I at length succeeded in nerving myself to the task which duty thus once more had pointed out. There was now a partial glow upon the forehead and upon the cheek and throat; a perceptible warmth pervaded the whole frame; there was even a slight pulsation at the heart. The lady *lived*; and with redoubled ardor I betook myself to the task of restoration. I chafed and bathed the temples and the hands, and used every exertion which experience, and no little medical reading, could suggest. But in vain. Suddenly, the color fled, the pulsation ceased, the lips resumed the expression of the dead, and, in an instant afterward, the whole body took upon itself the icy chilliness, the livid hue, the intense rigidity, the sunken outline, and all the loathsome peculiarities of that which has been, for many days, a tenant of the tomb.

And again I sunk into visions of Ligeia — and again (what marvel that I shudder while I write?) *again* there reached my ears a low sob from the region of the ebony bed. But why shall I minutely detail the unspeakable horrors of that night? Why shall I pause to relate how, time after time, until near the period of the gray dawn, this hideous drama of revivification was repeated; how each terrific relapse was only into a sterner and apparently more irredeemable death; how each agony wore the aspect of a struggle with some invisible foe; and how each struggle was succeeded by I know not what of wild change in the personal appearance of the corpse? Let me hurry to a conclusion.

The greater part of the fearful night had worn away, and she who had been dead, once again stirred — and now more vigorously than hitherto, although arousing from a dissolution more appalling in its utter helplessness than any. I had long ceased to struggle or to move, and remained sitting rigidly upon the ottoman, a helpless prey to a whirl of violent emotions, of which extreme awe was perhaps the least terrible, the least consuming. The corpse, I repeat, stirred, and now more vigorously than before. The hues of life flushed up with unwonted energy into the countenance — the limbs relaxed — and, save that the eyelids were yet pressed heavily together, and that the bandages and draperies of the grave still imparted their charnel character to the figure, I might have dreamed that Rowena had indeed shaken off, utterly, the fetters of Death. But if this idea was not, even then, altogether adopted, I could at least doubt no longer, when, arising from the bed, tottering, with feeble steps, with closed eyes, and with the manner of one bewildered in a dream, the thing that was enshrouded advanced bodily and palpably into the middle of the apartment.

I trembled not — I stirred not — for a crowd of unutterable fancies connected with the air, the stature, the demeanor of the figure, rushing hurriedly through my brain, had paralyzed — had chilled me into stone. I stirred not — but gazed upon the apparition. There was a mad disorder in my thoughts — a tumult unappeasable. Could it, indeed, be the *living* Rowena who confronted me? Could it indeed be Rowena *at all* — the fair-haired, the blue-eyed Lady Rowena Trevanion of Tremaine? Why, *why* should I doubt it? The bandage lay heavily about the mouth — but then might it not be the mouth of the breathing Lady of Tremaine? And the cheeks — there were the roses as in her noon of life — yes, these might indeed be the fair cheeks of the living Lady of Tremaine. And the chin, with its dimples, as in health, might it not be hers? but *had she then grown taller since her malady?* What inexpressible madness seized me with that thought? One bound, and I had reached her feet! Shrinking from my touch, she let fall from her head the ghastly cerements which had confined it, and there streamed forth, into the rushing atmosphere of the chamber, huge masses of long and dishevelled hair; *it was blacker than the raven wings of the midnight!* And now slowly opened *the eyes* of the figure which stood before me. "Here then, at least," I shrieked aloud, "can I never — can I never be mistaken — these are the full, and the black, and the wild eyes — of my lost love — of the lady — of the Lady Ligeia."

The Fall of the House of Usher

(1839)

"The tempestuous loveliness of terror" — the phrase is the poet Shelley's — is well exemplified by "The Fall of the House of Usher."

English eighteenth-century Gothic romances, such as Walpole's *Castle of Otranto* and Mrs. Radcliffe's *Mysteries of Udolpho*, had been crudely melodramatic. By 1796, Coleridge had complained that he was "wearied with fiends, incomprehensible characters, with shrieks, murders, and subterranean dungeons," though he was himself about to use such material — and refine it magically — in the poem "Christabel." In America, the Gothic novels of

Charles Brockden Brown, who died in 1810, had been followed by the playful terrors of Irving's tales, and were now transcended, in a serious use of the tradition, by the concentrated tales of Poe and Hawthorne.

"The grim phantasm, FEAR" (which all human beings face) dominates this story, from the foreboding opening paragraph to the terrible conclusion. By stages it grows upon the narrator, with whom we tend to identify ourselves. His inner disturbance is contrasted with the habitual rationality suggested by the measured pace of the style. He makes credible the central fear of the story, that of the romantic Roderick, "the hopeless and the frail," "a bounden slave" to fear. His is "a mind haunted by phantasms — a disordered brain." While he is drawn, impotent toward death, his sister Madeline has a superhuman will to live, shown in an improbable action of which we read with a willing suspension of disbelief.

The story has the unity of a closed circle. Inside, everything contributes to the effect of terror. The oppressive autumn day at the beginning, the ancient mansion and family both on the verge of collapse, the friend who is gradually unnerved, the passion of the elements of nature — all these, and all details, are drawn together as by a centripetal force. The very scene is isolated, has "no affinity with the air of heaven." To unity of design is added unity of atmosphere. Within this tight, rounded story we experience the pleasure of form, even though it is a form of gloom, degeneration, desolation, ruin — of the grim phantasm, fear.

Heading the story is a motto: "His heart is a lute held up; as soon as it is touched it resounds." This we may remember when we come to the characterization of Usher, with his "morbid acuteness of the senses" and "excessive nervous agitation." Cf. "Israfel," line 2 and note.

> Son cœur est un luth suspendu;
> Sitôt qu'on le touche il résonne.
>
> BÉRANGER

During the whole of a dull, dark, and soundless day in the autumn of the year, when the clouds hung oppressively low in the heavens, I had been passing alone, on horseback, through a singularly dreary tract of country; and at length found myself, as the shades of the evening drew on, within view of the melancholy House of Usher. I know not how it was — but, with the first glimpse of the building, a sense of insufferable gloom pervaded my spirit. I say insufferable; for the feeling was unrelieved by any of that half-pleasurable, because poetic, sentiment with which the mind usually receives even the sternest natural images of the desolate or terrible. I looked upon the scene before me — upon the mere house, and the simple landscape features of the domain, upon the bleak walls, upon the vacant eye-like windows, upon a few rank sedges, and upon a few white trunks of decayed trees — with an utter depression of soul which I can compare to no earthly sensation more properly than to the after-dream of the reveller upon opium; the bitter lapse into everyday life, the hideous dropping off of the veil. There was an iciness, a sinking, a sickening of the heart, an unredeemed dreariness of thought which no goading of the imagination could torture into aught of the sublime. What was it — I paused to think — what was it that so unnerved me in the contemplation of the House of Usher? It was a mystery all insoluble; nor could I grapple with the shadowy fancies that crowded upon me as I pondered. I was forced to fall back upon the unsatisfactory conclusion, that while, beyond doubt, there *are* combinations of very simple natural objects which have the power of thus affecting us, still the analysis of this power lies among considerations beyond our depth. It was possible, I reflected, that a mere different arrangement of the particulars of the scene, of the details of the picture, would be sufficient to modify, or perhaps to annihilate, its capacity for sorrowful impression; and acting upon this idea, I reined my horse to the precipitous brink of a black and lurid tarn that lay in unruffled lustre by the dwelling, and gazed down — but with a shudder even more thrilling than before — upon the remodelled and inverted images of the gray sedge, and the ghastly tree-stems, and the vacant and eye-like windows.

Nevertheless, in this mansion of gloom I now proposed to myself a sojourn of some weeks. Its proprietor, Roderick Usher, had been one of my boon companions in boyhood; but many years had elapsed since our last meeting. A letter, however, had lately reached me in a distant part of the country — a letter from him — which in its wildly importunate nature had admitted of no other than a personal reply. The MS. gave evidence of nervous agitation. The writer spoke of acute bodily illness, of a mental disorder which oppressed him, and of an earnest desire to see me, as his best and indeed his only personal friend, with a view of attempting, by the cheerfulness of my society, some alleviation of his malady. It was the manner in which all this, and much more, was said — it was the apparent *heart* that went with his request —

which allowed me no room for hesitation; and I accordingly obeyed forthwith what I still considered a very singular summons.

Although as boys we had been even intimate associates, yet I really knew little of my friend. His reserve had been always excessive and habitual. I was aware, however, that his very ancient family had been noted, time out of mind, for a peculiar sensibility of temperament, displaying itself, through long ages, in many works of exalted art, and manifested of late in repeated deeds of munificent yet unobtrusive charity, as well as in a passionate devotion to the intricacies, perhaps even more than to the orthodox and easily recognizable beauties, of musical science. I had learned, too, the very remarkable fact that the stem of the Usher race, all time-honored as it was, had put forth at no period any enduring branch; in other words, that the entire family lay in the direct line of descent, and had always, with very trifling and very temporary variation, so lain. It was this deficiency, I considered, while running over in thought the perfect keeping of the character of the premises with the accredited character of the people, and while speculating upon the possible influence which the one, in the long lapse of centuries, might have exercised upon the other — it was this deficiency, perhaps of collateral issue, and the consequent undeviating transmission from sire to son of the patrimony with the name, which had, at length, so identified the two as to merge the original title of the estate in the quaint and equivocal appellation of the "House of Usher" — an appellation which seemed to include, in the minds of the peasantry who used it, both the family and the family mansion.

I have said that the sole effect of my somewhat childish experiment, that of looking down within the tarn, had been to deepen the first singular impression. There can be no doubt that the consciousness of the rapid increase of my superstition — for why should I not so term it? — served mainly to accelerate the increase itself. Such, I have long known, is the paradoxical law of all sentiments having terror as a basis. And it might have been for this reason only, that, when I again uplifted my eyes to the house itself, from its image in the pool, there grew in my mind a strange fancy — a fancy so ridiculous, indeed, that I but mention it to show the vivid force of the sensations which oppressed me. I had so worked upon my imagination as really

to believe that about the whole mansion and domain there hung an atmosphere peculiar to themselves and their immediate vicinity: an atmosphere which had no affinity with the air of heaven, but which had reeked up from the decayed trees, and the gray wall, and the silent tarn: a pestilent and mystic vapor, dull, sluggish, faintly discernible, and leaden-hued.

Shaking off from my spirit what *must* have been a dream, I scanned more narrowly the real aspect of the building. Its principal feature seemed to be that of an excessive antiquity. The discoloration of ages had been great. Minute fungi overspread the whole exterior, hanging in a fine tangled webwork from the eaves. Yet all this was apart from any extraordinary dilapidation. No portion of the masonry had fallen; and there appeared to be a wild inconsistency between its still perfect adaptation of parts and the crumbling condition of the individual stones. In this there was much that reminded me of the specious totality of old wood-work which has rotted for long years in some neglected vault, with no disturbance from the breath of the external air. Beyond this indication of extensive decay, however, the fabric gave little token of instability. Perhaps the eye of a scrutinizing observer might have discovered a barely perceptible fissure, which, extending from the roof of the building in front, made its way down the wall in a zigzag direction, until it became lost in the sullen waters of the tarn.

Noticing these things, I rode over a short causeway to the house. A servant in waiting took my horse, and I entered the Gothic archway of the hall. A valet, of stealthy step, thence conducted me, in silence, through many dark and intricate passages in my progress to the studio of his master. Much that I encountered on the way contributed, I know not how, to heighten the vague sentiments of which I have already spoken. While the objects around me — while the carvings of the ceilings, the sombre tapestries of the walls, the ebon blackness of the floors, and the phantasmagoric armorial trophies which rattled as I strode, were but matters to which, or to such as which, I had been accustomed from my infancy — while I hesitated not to acknowledge how familiar was all this — I still wondered to find how unfamiliar were the fancies which ordinary images were stirring up. On one of the staircases, I met the physician of the family. His countenance, I thought, wore a mingled expression of low cunning and perplexity. He accosted me with trepidation and passed on. The valet now threw open a door and ushered me into the presence of his master.

The room in which I found myself was very large and lofty. The windows were long, narrow, and pointed, and at so vast a distance from the black oaken floor as to be altogether inaccessible from within. Feeble gleams of encrimsoned light made their way through the trellised panes, and served to render sufficiently distinct the more prominent objects around; the eye, however, struggled in vain to reach the remoter angles of the chamber, or the recesses of the vaulted and fretted ceiling. Dark draperies hung upon the walls. The general furniture was profuse, comfortless, antique, and tattered. Many books and musical instruments lay scattered about, but failed to give any vitality to the scene. I felt that I breathed an atmosphere of sorrow. An air of stern, deep, and irredeemable gloom hung over and pervaded all.

Upon my entrance, Usher arose from a sofa on which he had been lying at full length, and greeted me with a vivacious warmth which had much in it, I at first thought, of an overdone cordiality — of the constrained effort of the *ennuyé* man of the world. A glance, however, at his countenance convinced me of his perfect sincerity. We sat down; and for some moments, while he spoke not, I gazed upon him with a feeling half of pity, half of awe. Surely man had never before so terribly altered, in so brief a period, as had Roderick Usher! It was with difficulty that I could bring myself to admit the identity of the wan being before me with the companion of my early boyhood. Yet the character of his face had been at all times remarkable. A cadaverousness of complexion; an eye large, liquid, and luminous beyond comparison; lips somewhat thin and very pallid, but of a surpassingly beautiful curve; a nose of a delicate Hebrew model, but with a breadth of nostril unusual in similar formations; a finely moulded chin, speaking, in its want of prominence, of a want of moral energy; hair of a more than web-like softness and tenuity; these features, with an inordinate expansion above the regions of the temple, made up altogether a countenance not easily to be forgotten. And now in the mere exaggeration of the prevailing character of these features, and of the expression they were wont to convey, lay so much of change that I doubted to whom I spoke. The now

ghastly pallor of the skin, and the now miraculous lustre of the eye, above all things startled and even awed me. The silken hair, too, had been suffered to grow all unheeded, and as, in its wild gossamer texture, it floated rather than fell about the face, I could not, even with effort, connect its arabesque expression with any idea of simple humanity.

In the manner of my friend I was at once struck with an incoherence, an inconsistency; and I soon found this to arise from a series of feeble and futile struggles to overcome an habitual trepidancy, an excessive nervous agitation. For something of this nature I had indeed been prepared, no less by his letter than by reminiscences of certain boyish traits, and by conclusions deduced from his peculiar physical conformation and temperament. His action was alternately vivacious and sullen. His voice varied rapidly from a tremendous indecision (when the animal spirits seemed utterly in abeyance) to that species of energetic concision — that abrupt, weighty, unhurried, and hollow-sounding enunciation — that leaden, self-balanced and perfectly modulated guttural utterance — which may be observed in the lost drunkard, or the irreclaimable eater of opium, during the periods of his most intense excitement.

It was thus that he spoke of the object of my visit, of his earnest desire to see me, and of the solace he expected me to afford him. He entered, at some length, into what he conceived to be the nature of his malady. It was, he said, a constitutional and a family evil, and one for which he despaired to find a remedy — a mere nervous affection, he immediately added, which would undoubtedly soon pass off. It displayed itself in a host of unnatural sensations. Some of these, as he detailed them, interested and bewildered me; although, perhaps, the terms and the general manner of the narration had their weight. He suffered much from a morbid acuteness of the senses; the most insipid food was alone endurable; he could wear only garments of certain texture; the odors of all flowers were oppressive; his eyes were tortured by even a faint light; and there were but peculiar sounds, and these from stringed instruments, which did not inspire him with horror.

To an anomalous species of terror I found him a bounden slave. "I shall perish," said he, "I *must* perish in this deplorable folly. Thus, thus, and not otherwise, shall I be lost. I dread the events of the future, not in themselves, but in their results. I shudder at the thought of any, even the most trivial, incident, which may operate upon this intolerable agitation of soul. I have, indeed, no abhorrence of danger, except in its absolute effect — in terror. In this unnerved — in this pitiable condition, I feel that the period will sooner or later arrive when I must abandon life and reason together, in some struggle with the grim phantasm, FEAR."

I learned moreover at intervals, and through broken and equivocal hints, another singular feature of his mental condition. He was enchained by certain superstitious impressions in regard to the dwelling which he tenanted, and whence, for many years, he had never ventured forth — in regard to an influence whose suppositious force was conveyed in terms too shadowy here to be restated — an influence which some peculiarities in the mere form and substance of his family mansion, had, by dint of long sufferance, he said, obtained over his spirit — an effect which the physique of the gray walls and turrets, and of the dim tarn into which they all looked down, had, at length, brought about upon the morale of his existence.

He admitted, however, although with hesitation, that much of the peculiar gloom which thus afflicted him could be traced to a more natural and far more palpable origin — to the severe and long-continued illness, indeed to the evidently approaching dissolution, of a tenderly beloved sister — his sole companion for long years, his last and only relative on earth. "Her decease," he said, with a bitterness which I can never forget, "would leave him (him the hopeless and the frail) the last of the ancient race of the Ushers." While he spoke the lady Madeline (for so was she called) passed slowly through a remote portion of the apartment, and, without having noticed my presence, disappeared. I regarded her with an utter astonishment not unmingled with dread, and yet I found it impossible to account for such feelings. A sensation of stupor oppressed me, as my eyes followed her retreating steps. When a door, at length, closed upon her, my glance sought instinctively and eagerly the countenance of the brother; but he had buried his face in his hands, and I could only perceive that a far more than ordinary wanness had overspread the emaciated fingers through which trickled many passionate tears.

The disease of the lady Madeline had long baffled the skill of her physicians. A settled apathy, a gradual wasting away of the person, and frequent although transient affections of a partially cataleptical character, were the unusual diagnosis. Hitherto she had steadily borne up against the pressure of her malady, and had not betaken herself finally to bed; but, on the closing in of the evening of my arrival at the house, she succumbed (as her brother told me at night with inexpressible agitation) to the prostrating power of the destroyer; and I learned that the glimpse I had obtained of her person would thus probably be the last I should obtain — that the lady, at least while living, would be seen by me no more.

For several days ensuing, her name was unmentioned by either Usher or myself; and during this period I was busied in earnest endeavors to alleviate the melancholy of my friend. We painted and read together; or I listened, as if in a dream, to the wild improvisations of his speaking guitar. And thus, as a closer and still closer intimacy admitted me more unreservedly into the recesses of his spirit, the more bitterly did I perceive the futility of all attempt at cheering a mind from which darkness, as if an inherent positive quality, poured forth upon all objects of the moral and physical universe, in one unceasing radiation of gloom.

I shall ever bear about me a memory of the many solemn hours I thus spent alone with the master of the House of Usher. Yet I should fail in any attempt to convey an idea of the exact character of the studies, or of the occupations, in which he involved me, or led me the way. An excited and highly distempered ideality threw a sulphureous lustre over all. His long improvised dirges will ring forever in my ears. Among other things, I hold painfully in mind a certain singular perversion and amplification of the wild air of the last waltz of Von Weber. From the paintings over which his elaborate fancy brooded, and which grew, touch by touch, into vaguenesses at which I shuddered the more thrillingly because I shuddered knowing not why; — from these paintings (vivid as their images now are before me) I would in vain endeavor to educe more than a small portion which should lie within the compass of merely written words. By the utter simplicity, by the nakedness of his designs, he arrested and overawed attention. If ever mortal painted an idea, that mortal was Roderick Usher. For me at least, in the circumstances then surrounding me, there arose, out of the pure abstractions which the hypochondriac contrived to throw upon his canvas, an intensity of intolerable awe, no shadow of which felt I ever yet in the contemplation of the certainly glowing yet too concrete reveries of Fuseli.

One of the phantasmagoric conceptions of my friend, partaking not so rigidly of the spirit of abstraction, may be shadowed forth, although feebly, in words. A small picture presented the interior of an immensely long and rectangular vault or tunnel, with low walls, smooth, white, and without interruption or device. Certain accessory points of the design served well to convey the idea that this excavation lay at an exceeding depth below the surface of the earth. No outlet was observed in any portion of its vast extent, and no torch or other artificial source of light was discernible; yet a flood of intense rays rolled throughout, and bathed the whole in a ghastly and inappropriate splendor.

I have just spoken of that morbid condition of the auditory nerve which rendered all music intolerable to the sufferer, with the exception of certain effects of stringed instruments. It was, perhaps, the narrow limits to which he thus confined himself upon the guitar, which gave birth, in great measure, to the fantastic character of his performances. But the fervid *facility* of his impromptus could not be so accounted for. They must have been, and were, in the notes, as well as in the words of his wild fantasias (for he not unfrequently accompanied himself with rhymed verbal improvisations), the result of that intense mental collectedness and concentration to which I have previously alluded as observable only in particular moments of the highest artificial excitement. The words of one of these rhapsodies I have easily remembered. I was, perhaps, the more forcibly impressed with it, as he gave it, because, in the under or mystic current of its meaning, I fancied that I perceived, and for the first time, a full consciousness, on the part of Usher, of the tottering of his lofty reason upon her throne. The verses, which were entitled "The Haunted Palace," ran very nearly, if not accurately, thus:

I

In the greenest of our valleys
    By good angels tenanted,
Once a fair and stately palace —
    Radiant palace — reared its head.
In the monarch Thought's dominion,
    It stood there!

Never seraph spread a pinion
    Over fabric half so fair!

II

Banners yellow, glorious, golden,
    On its roof did float and flow,
(This — all this — was in the olden
    Time long ago)
And every gentle air that dallied,
    In that sweet day,
Along the ramparts plumed and pallid,
    A wingèd odor went away.

III

Wanderers in that happy valley,
    Through two luminous windows, saw
Spirits moving musically
    To a lute's well-tunèd law,
Round about a throne where, sitting,
    Porphyrogene!
In state his glory well befitting,
    The ruler of the realm was seen.

IV

And all with pearl and ruby glowing
    Was the fair palace door,
Through which came flowing, flowing, flowing
    And sparkling evermore,
A troop of Echoes, whose sweet duty
    Was but to sing,
In voices of surpassing beauty,
    The wit and wisdom of their king.

V

But evil things, in robes of sorrow,
    Assailed the monarch's high estate.
(Ah, let us mourn! — for never morrow
    Shall dawn upon him, desolate!)
And round about his home the glory
    That blushed and bloomed
Is but a dim-remembered story
    Of the old time entombed.

VI

And travellers, now, within that valley,
    Through the red-litten windows see
Vast forms that move fantastically
    To a discordant melody;
While, like a ghastly rapid river,
    Through the pale door
A hideous throng rush out forever,
    And laugh — but smile no more.

I well remember that suggestions arising from this ballad led us into a train of thought, wherein there became manifest an opinion of Usher's which I mention not so much on account of its novelty, (for other men [1] have thought thus), as on account of the pertinacity with which he maintained it. This opinion, in its general form, was that of the sentience of all vegetable things. But in his disordered fancy the idea had assumed a more daring character, and trespassed, under certain conditions, upon the kingdom of inorganization. I lack words to express the full extent, or the earnest *abandon* of his persuasion. The belief, however, was connected (as I have previously hinted) with the gray stones of the home of his forefathers. The conditions of the sentience had been here, he imagined, fulfilled in the method of collocation of these stones — in the order of their arrangement, as well as in that of the many fungi which overspread them, and of the decayed trees which stood around — above all, in the long undisturbed endurance of this arrangement, and in its reduplication in the still waters of the tarn. Its evidence — the evidence of the sentience — was to be seen, he said (and I here started as he spoke), in the gradual yet certain condensation of an atmosphere of their own about the waters and the walls. The result was discoverable, he added, in that silent, yet importunate and terrible influence which for centuries had moulded the destinies of his family, and which made *him* what I now saw him — what he was. Such opinions need no comment, and I will make none.

Our books — the books which, for years, had formed no small portion of the mental existence of the invalid — were, as might be supposed, in strict keeping with this character of phantasm. We pored together over such works as the *Ververt* and *Chartreuse* of Gresset; the *Belphegor* of Machiavelli; the *Heaven and Hell* of Swedenborg; the *Subterranean Voyage of Nicholas Klimm* by Holberg; the *Chiromancy* of Robert Flud, of Jean D'Indaginé, and of De la Chambre; the *Journey into the Blue Distance* of Tieck; and the *City of the Sun* of Campanella. One favorite volume was a small octavo edition of the *Directorium Inquisitorum* by the Dominican Eymeric de Gironne; and there were passages in Pomponius Mela, about the old African Satyrs and Ægipans, over which Usher would sit dreaming for hours. His chief delight, however, was found in the perusal of an exceedingly rare and curious book in quarto Gothic —

[1] Watson, Dr. Percival, Spallanzani, and especially the Bishop of Llandaff. — See *Chemical Essays*, vol. v. [Poe's note.]

the manual of a forgotten church — the *Vigilæ Mortuorum Secundum Chorum Ecclesiæ Maguntinæ.*[2]

I could not help thinking of the wild ritual of this work, and of its probable influence upon the hypochondriac, when one evening, having informed me abruptly that the lady Madeline was no more, he stated his intention of preserving her corpse for a fortnight (previously to its final interment), in one of the numerous vaults within the main walls of the building. The worldly reason, however, assigned for this singular proceeding, was one which I did not feel at liberty to dispute. The brother had been led to his resolution (so he told me) by consideration of the unusual character of the malady of the deceased, of certain obtrusive and eager inquiries on the part of her medical men, and of the remote and exposed situation of the burial-ground of the family. I will not deny that when I called to mind the sinister countenance of the person whom I met upon the staircase, on the day of my arrival at the house, I had no desire to oppose what I regarded as at best but a harmless, and by no means an unnatural precaution.

At the request of Usher, I personally aided him in the arrangements for the temporary entombment. The body having been encoffined, we two alone bore it to its rest. The vault in which we placed it (and which had been so long unopened that our torches, half smothered in its oppressive atmosphere, gave us little opportunity for investigation) was small, damp, and entirely without means of admission for light; lying, at great depth, immediately beneath that portion of the building in which was my own sleeping apartment. It had been used, apparently, in remote feudal times, for the worst purposes of a donjon-keep, and in later days as a place of deposit for powder, or some other highly combustible substance, as a portion of its floor, and the whole interior of a long archway through which we reached it, were carefully sheathed with copper. The door, of massive iron, had been, also, similarly protected. Its immense weight caused an unusually sharp grating sound, as it moved upon its hinges.

Having deposited our mournful burden upon tressels within this region of horror, we partially turned aside the yet unscrewed lid of the coffin, and looked upon the face of the tenant. A

[2] Vigils for the Dead according to the Choir of the Church of Mayence.

striking similitude between the brother and sister now first arrested my attention; and Usher, divining, perhaps, my thoughts, murmured out some few words from which I learned that the deceased and himself had been twins, and that sympathies of a scarcely intelligible nature had always existed between them. Our glances, however, rested not long upon the dead — for we could not regard her unawed. The disease which had thus entombed the lady in the maturity of youth, had left, as usual in all maladies of a strictly cataleptical character, the mockery of a faint blush upon the bosom and the face, and that suspiciously lingering smile upon the lip which is so terrible in death. We replaced and screwed down the lid, and, having secured the door of iron, made our way, with toil, into the scarcely less gloomy apartments of the upper portion of the house.

And now, some days of bitter grief having elapsed, an observable change came over the features of the mental disorder of my friend. His ordinary manner had vanished. His ordinary occupations were neglected or forgotten. He roamed from chamber to chamber with hurried, unequal, and objectless step. The pallor of his countenance had assumed, if possible, a more ghastly hue — but the luminousness of his eye had utterly gone out. The once occasional huskiness of his tone was heard no more; and a tremulous quaver, as if of extreme terror, habitually characterized his utterance. There were times, indeed, when I thought his unceasingly agitated mind was laboring with some oppressive secret, to divulge which he struggled for the necessary courage. At times, again, I was obliged to resolve all into the mere inexplicable vagaries of madness, for I beheld him gazing upon vacancy for long hours, in an attitude of the profoundest attention, as if listening to some imaginary sound. It was no wonder that his condition terrified — that it infected me. I felt creeping upon me, by slow yet certain degrees, the wild influences of his own fantastic yet impressive superstitions.

It was, especially, upon retiring to bed late in the night of the seventh or eighth day after the placing of the lady Madeline within the donjon, that I experienced the full power of such feelings. Sleep came not near my couch, while the hours waned and waned away. I struggled to reason off the nervousness which had dominion over me. I endeavored to believe that much, if not all, of what I felt was due to the bewilder-

ing influence of the gloomy furniture of the room — of the dark and tattered draperies which, tortured into motion by the breath of a rising tempest, swayed fitfully to and fro upon the walls, and rustled uneasily about the decorations of the bed. But my efforts were fruitless. An irrepressible tremor gradually pervaded my frame; and at length there sat upon my very heart an incubus of utterly causeless alarm. Shaking this off with a gasp and a struggle, I uplifted myself upon the pillows, and, peering earnestly within the intense darkness of the chamber, hearkened — I know not why, except that an instinctive spirit prompted me — to certain low and indefinite sounds which came, through the pauses of the storm, at long intervals, I knew not whence. Overpowered by an intense sentiment of horror, unaccountable yet endurable, I threw on my clothes with haste (for I felt that I should sleep no more during the night), and endeavored to arouse myself from the pitiable condition into which I had fallen, by pacing rapidly to and fro through the apartment.

I had taken but few turns in this manner, when a light step on an adjoining staircase arrested my attention. I presently recognized it as that of Usher. In an instant afterward he rapped with a gentle touch at my door, and entered, bearing a lamp. His countenance was, as usual, cadaverously wan — but, moreover, there was a species of mad hilarity in his eyes — an evidently restrained hysteria in his whole demeanor. His air appalled me — but anything was preferable to the solitude which I had so long endured, and I even welcomed his presence as a relief.

"And you have not seen it?" he said abruptly, after having stared about him for some moments in silence — "you have not then seen it? — but, stay! you shall." Thus speaking, and having carefully shaded his lamp, he hurried to one of the casements, and threw it freely open to the storm.

The impetuous fury of the entering gust nearly lifted us from our feet. It was, indeed, a tempestuous yet sternly beautiful night, and one wildly singular in its terror and its beauty. A whirlwind had apparently collected its force in our vicinity; for there were frequent and violent alterations in the direction of the wind; and the exceeding density of the clouds (which hung so low as to press upon the turrets of the house) did not prevent our perceiving the lifelike velocity with which they flew careering from all points against each other, without passing away into the distance. I say that even their exceeding density did not prevent our perceiving this; yet we had no glimpse of the moon or stars, nor was there any flashing forth of the lightning. But the under surfaces of the huge masses of agitated vapor, as well as all terrestrial objects immediately around us, were glowing in the unnatural light of a faintly luminous and distinctly visible gaseous exhalation which hung about and enshrouded the mansion.

"You must not — you shall not behold this!" said I, shudderingly, to Usher, as I led him with a gentle violence from the window to a seat. "These appearances, which bewilder you, are merely electrical phenomena not uncommon — or it may be that they have their ghastly origin in the rank miasma of the tarn. Let us close this casement; the air is chilling and dangerous to your frame. Here is one of your favorite romances. I will read, and you shall listen; — and so we will pass away this terrible night together."

The antique volume which I had taken up was the *Mad Trist* of Sir Launcelot Canning; but I had called it a favorite of Usher's more in sad jest than in earnest; for, in truth, there is little in its uncouth and unimaginative prolixity which could have had interest for the lofty and spiritual ideality of my friend. It was, however, the only book immediately at hand; and I indulged a vague hope that the excitement which now agitated the hypochondriac might find relief (for the history of mental disorder is full of similar anomalies) even in the extremeness of the folly which I should read. Could I have judged, indeed, by the wild overstrained air of vivacity with which he hearkened, or apparently hearkened, to the words of the tale, I might well have congratulated myself upon the success of my design.

I had arrived at that well-known portion of the story where Ethelred, the hero of the *Trist*, having sought in vain for peaceable admission into the dwelling of the hermit, proceeds to make good an entrance by force. Here, it will be remembered, the words of the narrative run thus:

And Ethelred, who was by nature of a doughty heart, and who was now mighty withal, on account of the powerfulness of the wine which he had drunken, waited no longer to hold parley with the hermit, who, in sooth, was of an obstinate and mal-iceful turn, but, feeling the rain upon his shoulders, and fearing the rising of the tempest, uplifted his mace outright, and with blows made quickly room in the plankings of the door for his gauntleted hand; and now pulling therewith sturdily, he so cracked, and ripped, and tore all asunder, that the noise of the dry and hollow-sounding wood alarmed and reverberated throughout the forest.

At the termination of this sentence I started, and for a moment paused; for it appeared to me (although I at once concluded that my excited fancy had deceived me) — it appeared to me that from some very remote portion of the mansion there came, indistinctly, to my ears, what might have been, in its exact similarity of character, the echo (but a stifled and dull one certainly) of the very cracking and ripping sound which Sir Launcelot had so particularly described. It was, beyond doubt, the coincidence alone which had arrested my attention; for, amid the rattling of the sashes of the casements, and the ordinary commingled noises of the still increasing storm, the sound, in itself, had nothing, surely, which should have interested or disturbed me. I continued the story:

But the good champion Ethelred, now entering within the door, was sore enraged and amazed to perceive no signal of the maliceful hermit; but, in the stead thereof, a dragon of a scaly and prodigious demeanor, and of a fiery tongue, which sate in guard before a palace of gold, with a floor of silver; and upon the wall there hung a shield of shining brass with this legend enwritten —

Who entereth herein, a conqueror hath bin;
Who slayeth the dragon, the shield he shall win.

And Ethelred uplifted his mace, and struck upon the head of the dragon, which fell before him, and gave up his pesty breath, with a shriek so horrid and harsh, and withal so piercing, that Ethelred had fain to close his ears with his hands against the dreadful noise of it, the like whereof was never before heard.

Here again I paused abruptly, and now with a feeling of wild amazement; for there could be no doubt whatever that, in this instance, I did actually hear (although from what direction it proceeded I found it impossible to say) a low and apparently distant, but harsh, protracted, and most unusual screaming or grating sound — the exact counterpart of what my fancy had already conjured up for the dragon's unnatural shriek as described by the romancer.

Oppressed, as I certainly was, upon the occurrence of this second and most extraordinary coincidence, by a thousand conflicting sensations, in which wonder and extreme terror were predominant, I still retained sufficient presence of mind to avoid exciting, by any observation, the sensitive nervousness of my companion. I was by no means certain that he had noticed the sounds in question; although, assuredly, a strange alteration had during the last few minutes taken place in his demeanor. From a position fronting my own, he had gradually brought round his chair, so as to sit with his face to the door of the chamber; and thus I could but partially perceive his features, although I saw that his lips trembled as if he were murmuring inaudibly. His head had dropped upon his breast — yet I knew that he was not asleep, from the wide and rigid opening of the eye as I caught a glance of it in profile. The motion of his body, too, was at variance with this idea — for he rocked from side to side with a gentle yet constant and uniform sway. Having rapidly taken notice of all this, I resumed the narrative of Sir Launcelot, which thus proceeded:

And now, the champion, having escaped from the terrible fury of the dragon, bethinking himself of the brazen shield, and of the breaking up of the enchantment which was upon it, removed the carcass from out of the way before him, and approached valorously over the silver pavement of the castle to where the shield was upon the wall; which in sooth tarried not for his full coming; but fell down at his feet upon the silver floor, with a mighty great and terrible ringing sound.

No sooner had these syllables passed my lips, than — as if a shield of brass had indeed, at the moment, fallen heavily upon a floor of silver — I became aware of a distinct, hollow, metallic and clangorous yet apparently muffled reverberation. Completely unnerved, I leaped to my feet; but the measured rocking movement of Usher was undisturbed. I rushed to the chair in which he sat. His eyes were bent fixedly before him, and throughout his whole countenance there reigned a stony rigidity. But as I placed my hand upon his shoulder, there came a strong shudder over his whole person; a sickly smile quivered about his lips; and I saw that he spoke in a low, hurried, and gibbering murmur, as if unconscious of my presence. Bending closely over him, I at length drank in the hideous import of his words.

"Not hear it? — yes, I hear it, and *have* heard it. Long — long — long — many minutes, many hours, many days, have I heard it — yet I dared not — oh, pity me, miserable wretch that I am! — I dared not — I *dared* not speak! *We have put her living in the tomb!* Said I not that my senses were acute? I *now* tell you that I heard her first feeble movements in the hollow coffin. I heard them — many, many days ago — yet I dared not — *I dared not speak!* And now — to-night — Ethelred — ha! ha! — the breaking of the hermit's door, and the death-cry of the dragon, and the clangor of the shield! — say, rather, the rending of her coffin, and the grating of the iron hinges of her prison, and her struggles within the coppered archway of the vault! Oh, whither shall I fly? Will she not be here anon? Is she not hurrying to upbraid me for my haste? Have I not heard her footstep on the stair? Do I not distinguish that heavy and horrible beating of her heart? Madman!" — here he sprang furiously to his feet, and shrieked out his syllables, as if in the effort he were giving up his soul — "*Madman! I tell you that she now stands without the door!*"

As if in the superhuman energy of his utterance there had been found the potency of a spell, the huge antique panels to which the speaker pointed threw slowly back, upon the instant, their ponderous and ebony jaws. It was the work of the rushing gust — but then without those doors there *did* stand the lofty and enshrouded figure of the lady Madeline of Usher. There was blood upon her white robes, and the evidence of some bitter struggle upon every portion of her emaciated frame. For a moment she remained trembling and reeling to and fro upon the threshold — then, with a low moaning cry, fell heavily inward upon the person of her brother, and, in her violent and now final death agonies, bore him to the floor a corpse, and a victim to the terrors he had anticipated.

From that chamber, and from that mansion, I fled aghast. The storm was still abroad in all its wrath as I found myself crossing the old causeway. Suddenly there shot along the path a wild light, and I turned to see whence a gleam so unusual could have issued; for the vast house and its shadows were alone behind me. The radiance was that of the full, setting, and blood-red moon, which now shone vividly through that once barely discernible fissure, of which I have before spoken as extending from the roof of the building, in a zigzag direction, to the base. While I gazed, this fissure rapidly widened — there came a fierce breath of the whirlwind — the entire orb of the satellite burst at once upon my sight — my brain reeled as I saw the mighty walls rushing asunder — there was a long tumultuous shouting sound like the voice of a thousand waters — and the deep and dank tarn at my feet closed sullenly and silently over the fragments of the "*House of Usher.*"

The Purloined Letter
(1845)

✣ Very different from the tales of tone or atmosphere are the "tales of ratiocination," or detective stories. "The Purloined Letter" is one of a series concerning M. Dupin, the prototype of Conan Doyle's Sherlock Holmes.

The quotation at the end may be translated: "So deadly a scheme, if it is not worthy of Atreus, is at least worthy of Thyestes." In Greek legend, Thyestes seduced the wife of his brother Atreus; and Atreus, in revenge, killed Thyestes' sons and served them to their father at a banquet.

Nil sapientiae odiosius acumine nimio.[1]
SENECA.

At Paris, just after dark one gusty evening in the autumn of 18—, I was enjoying the twofold luxury of meditation and a meerschaum, in company with my friend C. Auguste Dupin, in his little back library, or book-closet, *au troisième, No. 33, Rue Dunôt, Faubourg St. Germain.* For one hour at least we had maintained a profound silence; while each, to any casual observer, might have seemed intently and exclusively occupied with the curling eddies of smoke that oppressed the atmosphere of the chamber. For myself, however, I was mentally discussing certain topics which had formed matter for conversation between us at an earlier period of the evening; I mean the affair of the Rue Morgue, and the mystery attending the murder of Marie Rogêt. I looked upon it, therefore, as something of a coincidence, when the door of our apartment was thrown open and admitted our old acquaintance, Monsieur G—, the Prefect of the Parisian police.

We gave him a hearty welcome; for there was nearly half as much of the entertaining as of the

[1] "No part of wisdom is more odious than too great acumen."

contemptible about the man, and we had not seen him for several years. We had been sitting in the dark, and Dupin now arose for the purpose of lighting a lamp, but sat down again, without doing so, upon G—'s saying that he had called to consult us, or rather to ask the opinion of my friend, about some official business which had occasioned a great deal of trouble.

"If it is any point requiring reflection," observed Dupin, as he forebore to enkindle the wick, "we shall examine it to better purpose in the dark."

"That is another of your odd notions," said the Prefect, who had a fashion of calling every thing "odd" that was beyond his comprehension, and thus lived amid an absolute legion of "oddities."

"Very true," said Dupin, as he supplied his visitor with a pipe, and rolled towards him a comfortable chair.

"And what is the difficulty now?" I asked. "Nothing more in the assassination way, I hope?"

"Oh no; nothing of that nature. The fact is, the business is *very* simple indeed, and I make no doubt that we can manage it sufficiently well ourselves; but then I thought Dupin would like to hear the details of it, because it is so excessively *odd.*"

"Simple and odd," said Dupin.

"Why, yes; and not exactly that, either. The fact is, we have all been a good deal puzzled because the affair *is* so simple, and yet baffles us altogether."

"Perhaps it is the very simplicity of the thing which puts you at fault," said my friend.

"What nonsense you *do* talk!" replied the Prefect, laughing heartily.

"Perhaps the mystery is a little *too* plain," said Dupin.

"Oh, good heavens! who ever heard of such an idea?"

"A little *too* self-evident."

"Ha! ha! ha! — ha! ha! ha! — ho! ho! ho!" — roared our visitor, profoundly amused, "oh, Dupin, you will be the death of me yet!"

"And what, after all, *is* the matter on hand?" I asked.

"Why, I will tell you," replied the Prefect, as he gave a long, steady, and contemplative puff, and settled himself in his chair. "I will tell you in a few words; but, before I begin, let me caution you that this is an affair demanding the greatest secrecy, and that I should most probably lose the position I now hold, were it known that I confided it to any one."

"Proceed," said I.

"Or not," said Dupin.

"Well, then; I have received personal infor- 5 mation, from a very high quarter, that a certain document of the last importance has been purloined from the royal apartments. The individual who purloined it is known; this beyond a doubt; he was seen to take it. It is known, 10 also, that it still remains in his possession."

"How is this known?" asked Dupin.

"It is clearly inferred," replied the Prefect, "from the nature of the document, and from the non-appearance of certain results which 15 would at once arise from its passing *out* of the robber's possession; — that is to say, from his employing it as he must design in the end to employ it."

"Be a little more explicit," I said. 20

"Well, I may venture so far as to say that the paper gives its holder a certain power in a certain quarter where such power is immensely valuable." The Prefect was fond of the cant of diplomacy. 25

"Still I do not quite understand," said Dupin.

"No? Well; the disclosure of the document to a third person who shall be nameless would bring in question the honor of a personage of most exalted station; and this fact gives the 30 holder of the document an ascendancy over the illustrious personage whose honor and peace are so jeopardized."

"But this ascendancy," I interposed, "would depend upon the robber's knowledge of the 35 loser's knowledge of the robber. Who would dare — "

"The thief," said G—, "is the Minister D—, who dares all things, those unbecoming as well as those becoming a man. The method 40 of the theft was not less ingenious than bold. The document in question — a letter, to be frank — had been received by the personage robbed while alone in the royal *boudoir*. During its perusal she was suddenly interrupted by the 45 entrance of the other exalted personage from whom especially it was her wish to conceal it. After a hurried and vain endeavor to thrust it in a drawer, she was forced to place it, open as it was, upon a table. The address, however, 50 was uppermost, and, the contents thus unexposed, the letter escaped notice. At this juncture enters the Minister D—. His lynx eye immediately perceives the paper, recognizes the handwriting of the address, observes the confusion of the personage addressed, and fathoms her secret. After some business transactions, hurried through in his ordinary manner, he produces a letter somewhat similar to the one in question, opens it, pretends to read it, and then places it in close juxtaposition to the other. Again he converses, for some fifteen minutes, upon the public affairs. At length, in taking leave, he takes also from the table the letter to which he had no claim. Its rightful owner saw, but, of course, dared not call attention to the act, in the presence of the third personage who stood at her elbow. The Minister decamped; leaving his own letter — one of no importance — upon the table."

"Here, then," said Dupin to me, "you have precisely what you demand to make the ascendancy complete — the robber's knowledge of the loser's knowledge of the robber."

"Yes," replied the Prefect; "and the power thus attained has, for some months past, been wielded, for political purposes, to a very dangerous extent. The personage robbed is more thoroughly convinced, every day, of the necessity of reclaiming her letter. But this, of course, cannot be done openly. In fine, driven to despair, she has committed the matter to me."

"Than whom," said Dupin, amid a perfect whirlwind of smoke, "no more sagacious agent could, I suppose, be desired, or even imagined."

"You flatter me," replied the Prefect; "but it is possible that some such opinion may have been entertained."

"It is clear," said I, "as you observe, that the letter is still in possession of the Minister; since it is this possession, and not any employment of the letter, which bestows the power. With the employment the power departs."

"True," said G—; "and upon this conviction I proceeded. My first care was to make thorough search of the Minister's hotel; and here my chief embarrassment lay in the necessity of searching without his knowledge. Beyond all things, I have been warned of the danger which would result from giving him reason to suspect our design."

"But," said I, "you are quite *au fait* in these investigations. The Parisian police have done this thing often before."

"Oh yes; and for this reason I did not despair. The habits of the Minister gave me, too, a great advantage. He is frequently absent from home all night. His servants are by no means numerous. They sleep at a distance from their master's apartment, and, being chiefly Neapolitans, are readily made drunk. I have keys, as you know, with which I can open any chamber or cabinet in Paris. For three months a night has not passed, during the greater part of which I have not been engaged, personally, in ransacking the D— Hôtel. My honor is interested, and, to mention a great secret, the reward is enormous. So I did not abandon the search until I had become fully satisfied that the thief is a more astute man than myself. I fancy that I have investigated every nook and corner of the premises in which it is possible that the paper can be concealed."

"But is it not possible," I suggested, "that although the letter may be in the possession of the Minister, as it unquestionably is, he may have concealed it elsewhere than upon his own premises?"

"This is barely possible," said Dupin. "The present peculiar condition of affairs at court, and especially of those intrigues in which D— is known to be involved, would render the instant availability of the document — its susceptibility of being produced at a moment's notice — a point of nearly equal importance with its possession."

"Its susceptibility of being produced?" said I.

"That is to say, of being *destroyed*," said Dupin.

"True," I observed; "the paper is clearly then upon the premises. As for its being upon the person of the Minister, we may consider that as out of the question."

"Entirely," said the Prefect. "He has been twice waylaid, as if by footpads, and his person rigorously searched under my own inspection."

"You might have spared yourself this trouble," said Dupin. "D—, I presume, is not altogether a fool, and, if not, must have anticipated these waylayings, as a matter of course."

"Not *altogether* a fool," said G—, "but then he's a poet, which I take to be only one remove from a fool."

"True," said Dupin, after a long and thoughtful whiff from his meerschaum, "although I have been guilty of certain doggerel myself."

"Suppose you detail," said I, "the particulars of your search."

"Why the fact is, we took our time, and we searched *every where*. I have had long experience in these affairs. I took the entire building, room by room; devoting the nights of a whole week to each. We examined, first, the furniture of each apartment. We opened every possible drawer; and I presume you know that, to a properly trained police agent, such a thing as a *secret* drawer is impossible. Any man is a dolt who permits a 'secret' drawer to escape him in a search of this kind. The thing is *so* plain. There is a certain amount of bulk — a space — to be accounted for in every cabinet. Then we have accurate rules. The fiftieth part of a line could not escape us. After the cabinets we took the chairs. The cushions we probed with the fine long needles you have seen me employ. From the tables we removed the tops."

"Why so?"

"Sometimes the top of a table, or other similarly arranged piece of furniture, is removed by the person wishing to conceal an article; then the leg is excavated, the article deposited within the cavity, and the top replaced. The bottoms and tops of bed-posts are employed in the same way."

"But could not the cavity be detected by sounding?" I asked.

"By no means, if, when the article is deposited, a sufficient wadding of cotton be placed around it. Besides, in our case, we were obliged to proceed without noise."

"But you could not have removed — you could not have taken to pieces *all* articles of furniture in which it would have been possible to make a deposit in the manner you mention. A letter may be compressed into a thin spiral roll, not differing much in shape or bulk from a large knitting-needle, and in this form it might be inserted into the rung of a chair, for example. You did not take to pieces all the chairs?"

"Certainly not; but we did better — we examined the rungs of every chair in the hotel, and, indeed, the jointings of every description of furniture, by the aid of a most powerful microscope. Had there been any traces of recent disturbance we should not have failed to detect it instantly. A single grain of gimlet-dust, for example, would have been as obvious as an apple. Any disorder in the glueing — any unusual gaping in the joints — would have sufficed to insure detection."

"I presume you looked to the mirrors, between the boards and the plates, and you probed the beds and the bed-clothes, as well as the curtains and carpets."

"That of course; and when we had absolutely completed every particle of the furniture in this way, then we examined the house itself. We divided its entire surface into compartments, which we numbered, so that none might be missed; then we scrutinized each individual square inch throughout the premises, including the two houses immediately adjoining, with the microscope, as before."

"The two houses adjoining!" I exclaimed; "you must have had a great deal of trouble."

"We had; but the reward offered is prodigious."

"You include the *grounds* about the houses?"

"All the grounds are paved with brick. They gave us comparatively little trouble. We examined the moss between the bricks, and found it undisturbed."

"You looked among D—'s papers, of course, and into the books of the library?"

"Certainly; we opened every package and parcel; we not only opened every book, but we turned over every leaf in each volume, not contenting ourselves with a mere shake, according to the fashion of some of our police officers. We also measured the thickness of every book-*cover*, with the most accurate admeasurement, and applied to each the most jealous scrutiny of the microscope. Had any of the bindings been recently meddled with, it would have been utterly impossible that the fact should have escaped observation. Some five or six volumes, just from the hands of the binder, we carefully probed, longitudinally, with the needles."

"You explored the floors beneath the carpets?"

"Beyond doubt. We removed every carpet, and examined the boards with the microscope."

"And the paper on the walls?"

"Yes."

"You looked into the cellars?"

"We did."

"Then," I said, "you have been making a miscalculation, and the letter is *not* upon the premises, as you suppose."

"I fear you are right there," said the Prefect. "And now, Dupin, what would you advise me to do?"

"To make a thorough re-search of the premises."

"That is absolutely needless," replied G—. "I am not more sure that I breathe than I am that the letter is not at the Hôtel."

"I have no better advice to give you," said Dupin. "You have, of course, an accurate description of the letter?"

"Oh yes!" — And here the Prefect, produc-

ing a memorandum-book, proceeded to read aloud a minute account of the internal, and especially of the external appearance of the missing document. Soon after finishing the perusal of this description, he took his departure, more entirely depressed in spirits than I had ever known the good gentleman before.

In about a month afterwards he paid us another visit, and found us occupied very nearly as before. He took a pipe and a chair and entered into some ordinary conversation. At length I said, —

"Well, but G—, what of the purloined letter? I presume you have at last made up your mind that there is no such thing as overreaching the Minister?"

"Confound him, say I — yes; I made the reexamination, however, as Dupin suggested — but it was all labor lost, as I knew it would be."

"How much was the reward offered, did you say?" asked Dupin.

"Why, a very great deal — a *very* liberal reward — I don't like to say how much, precisely; but one thing I *will* say, that I wouldn't mind giving my individual cheque for fifty thousand francs to any one who could obtain me that letter. The fact is, it is becoming of more and more importance every day; and the reward has been lately doubled. If it were trebled, however, I could do no more than I have done."

"Why, yes," said Dupin, drawlingly, between the whiffs of his meerschaum, "I really — think, G—, you have not exerted yourself — to the utmost in this matter. You might — do a little more, I think, eh?"

"How? — in what way?"

"Why — puff, puff — you might — puff, puff — employ counsel in the matter, eh? — puff, puff, puff. Do you remember the story they tell of Abernethy?"

"No; hang Abernethy!"

"To be sure! hang him and welcome. But, once upon a time, a certain rich miser conceived the design of sponging upon this Abernethy for a medical opinion. Getting up, for this purpose, an ordinary conversation in a private company, he insinuated his case to his physician, as that of an imaginary individual.

"'We will suppose,' said the miser, 'that his symptoms are such and such; now, doctor, what would *you* have directed him to take?'"

"'Take!' said Abernethy, 'why, take *advice*, to be sure.'"

"But," said the Prefect, a little discomposed,

"I am *perfectly* willing to take advice, and to pay for it. I would *really* give fifty thousand francs to any one who would aid me in the matter."

"In that case," replied Dupin, opening a drawer, and producing a cheque-book, "you may as well fill me up a cheque for the amount mentioned. When you have signed it, I will hand you the letter."

I was astounded. The Prefect appeared absolutely thunder-stricken. For some minutes he remained speechless and motionless, looking incredulously at my friend with open mouth, and eyes that seemed starting from their sockets; then, apparently recovering himself in some measure, he seized a pen, and after several pauses and vacant stares, finally filled up and signed a cheque for fifty thousand francs, and handed it across the table to Dupin. The latter examined it carefully and deposited it in his pocket-book; then, unlocking an *escritoire*, took thence a letter and gave it to the Prefect. This functionary grasped it in a perfect agony of joy, opened it with a trembling hand, cast a rapid glance at its contents, and then, scrambling and struggling to the door, rushed at length unceremoniously from the room and from the house, without having uttered a syllable since Dupin had requested him to fill up the cheque.

When he had gone, my friend entered into some explanations.

"The Parisian police," he said, "are exceedingly able in their way. They are persevering, ingenious, cunning, and thoroughly versed in the knowledge which their duties seem chiefly to demand. Thus, when G— detailed to us his mode of searching the premises at the Hôtel D—, I felt entire confidence in his having made a satisfactory investigation — so far as his labors extended."

"So far as his labors extended?" said I.

"Yes," said Dupin. "The measures adopted were not only the best of their kind, but carried out to absolute perfection. Had the letter been deposited within the range of their search, these fellows would, beyond a question, have found it."

I merely laughed — but he seemed quite serious in all that he said.

"The measures, then," he continued, "were good in their kind, and well executed; their defect lay in their being inapplicable to the case, and to the man. A certain set of highly ingenious resources are, with the Prefect, a sort of Procrustean bed, to which he forcibly adapts his designs. But he perpetually errs by being too deep or too shallow, for the matter in hand; and many a schoolboy is a better reasoner than he. I knew one about eight years of age, whose success at guessing in the game of 'even and odd' attracted universal admiration. This game is simple, and is played with marbles. One player holds in his hand a number of these toys, and demands of another whether that number is even or odd. If the guess is right, the guesser wins one; if wrong, he loses one. The boy to whom I allude won all the marbles of the school. Of course he had some principle of guessing; and this lay in mere observation and admeasurement of the astuteness of his opponents. For example, an arrant simpleton is his opponent, and, holding up his closed hand, asks, 'are they even or odd?' Our schoolboy replies, 'odd,' and loses; but upon the second trial he wins, for he then says to himself, 'the simpleton had them even upon the first trial, and his amount of cunning is just sufficient to make him have them odd upon the second; I will therefore guess odd'; — he guesses odd, and wins. Now, with a simpleton a degree above the first, he would have reasoned thus: 'This fellow finds that in the first instance I guessed odd, and, in the second, he will propose to himself upon the first impulse, a simple variation from even to odd, as did the first simpleton; but then a second thought will suggest that this is too simple a variation, and finally he will decide upon putting it even as before. I will therefore guess even'; — he guesses even, and wins. Now this mode of reasoning in the schoolboy, whom his fellows termed 'lucky,' — what, in its last analysis, is it?"

"It is merely," I said, "an identification of the reasoner's intellect with that of his opponent."

"It is," said Dupin; "and, upon inquiring of the boy by what means he effected the *thorough* identification in which his success consisted, I received answer as follows: 'When I wish to find out how wise, or how stupid, or how good, or how wicked is any one, or what are his thoughts at the moment, I fashion the expression of my face, as accurately as possible, in accordance with the expression of his, and then wait to see what thoughts or sentiments arise in my mind or heart, as if to match or correspond with the expression.' This response of the schoolboy lies at the bottom of all the spurious profundity which has been attributed to Rochefoucauld, to La Bougive, to Machiavelli, and to Campanella."

"And the identification," I said, "of the reasoner's intellect with that of his opponent, depends, if I understand you aright, upon the accuracy with which the opponent's intellect is admeasured."

"For its practical value it depends upon this," replied Dupin; "and the Prefect and his cohort fail so frequently, first, by default of this identification, and, secondly, by ill-admeasurement, or rather through non-admeasurement of the intellect with which they are engaged. They consider only their *own* ideas of ingenuity; and, in searching for anything hidden, advert only to the modes in which *they* would have hidden it. They are right in this much — that their own ingenuity is a faithful representative of that of *the mass*; but when the cunning of the individual felon is diverse in character from their own, the felon foils them, of course. This always happens when it is above their own, and very usually when it is below. They have no variation of principle in their investigations; at best, when urged by some unusual emergency — by some extraordinary reward — they extend or exaggerate their old modes of *practice*, without touching their principles. What, for example, in this case of D—, has been done to vary the principle of action? What is all this boring, and probing, and sounding, and scrutinizing with the microscope, and dividing the surface of the building into registered square inches — what is it all but an exaggeration *of the application* of the one principle or set of principles of search, which are based upon the one set of notions regarding human ingenuity, to which the Prefect, in the long routine of his duty, has been accustomed? Do you not see he has taken it for granted that *all* men proceed to conceal a letter — not exactly in a gimlet-hole bored in a chairleg — but, at least, in *some* out-of-the-way hole or corner suggested by the same tenor of thought which would urge a man to secrete a letter in a gimlet-hole bored in a chair-leg? And do you not see also, that such *recherchés* nooks for concealment are adapted only for ordinary occasions, and would be adopted only by ordinary intellects; for, in all cases of concealment, a disposal of the article concealed — a disposal of it in this *recherché* manner — is, in the very first instance, presumable and presumed; and thus its discovery depends, not at all upon the acumen, but altogether upon the mere care, patience, and determination of the seekers; and where the case is of importance — or, what amounts to the same thing in the policial eyes, when the reward is of magnitude, — the qualities in question have *never* been known to fail? You will now understand what I meant in suggesting that, had the purloined letter been hidden any where within the limits of the Prefect's examination — in other words, had the principle of its concealment been comprehended within the principles of the Prefect — its discovery would have been a matter altogether beyond question. This functionary, however, has been thoroughly mystified; and the remote source of his defeat lies in the supposition that the Minister is a fool, because he has acquired renown as a poet. All fools are poets; this the Prefect *feels*; and he is merely guilty of a *non distributio medii*[1] in thence inferring that all poets are fools."

"But is this really the poet?" I asked. "There are two brothers, I know; and both have attained reputation in letters. The Minister I believe has written learnedly on the Differential Calculus. He is a mathematician, and no poet."

"You are mistaken; I know him well; he is both. As poet *and* mathematician, he would reason well; as mere mathematician, he could not have reasoned at all, and thus would have been at the mercy of the Prefect."

"You surprise me," I said, "by these opinions, which have been contradicted by the voice of the world. You do not mean to set at naught the well-digested idea of centuries. The mathematical reason has long been regarded as *the* reason *par excellence*."

" '*Il y a à parier*,' " replied Dupin, quoting from Chamfort, " '*que toute idée publique, toute convention reçue, est une sottise, car elle a convenu au plus grand nombre.*'[2] The mathematicians, I grant you, have done their best to promulgate the popular error to which you allude, and which is none the less an error for its promulgation as truth. With an art worthy a better cause, for example, they have insinuated the term 'analysis' into application to algebra. The French are the originators of this particular deception; but if a term is of any importance — if words derive any value from applicability — then 'analysis' conveys 'algebra' about as much as, in Latin, '*ambitus*' implies 'ambition,' '*religio*' 'religion,' or '*homines honesti*' a set of honorable men."

[1] Undistributed middle.

[2] "I'll wager, that every idea which is generally held, every set convention, is a stupidity; for it has suited the majority."

"You have a quarrel on hand, I see," said I, "with some of the algebraists of Paris; but proceed."

"I dispute the availability, and thus the value, of that reason which is cultivated in any especial form other than the abstractly logical. I dispute, in particular, the reason educed by mathematical study. The mathematics are the science of form and quantity; mathematical reasoning is merely logic applied to observation upon form and quantity. The great error lies in supposing that even the truths of what is called *pure* algebra, are abstract or general truths. And this error is so egregious that I am confounded at the universality with which it has been received. Mathematical axioms are *not* axioms of general truth. What is true of *relation* — of form and quantity — is often grossly false in regard to morals, for example. In this latter science it is very usually *un*true that the aggregated parts are equal to the whole. In chemistry also the axiom fails. In the consideration of motive it fails; for two motives, each of a given value, have not, necessarily, a value when united, equal to the sum of their values apart. There are numerous other mathematical truths which are only truths within the limits of *relation*. But the mathematician argues, from his *finite truths*, through habit, as if they were of an absolutely general applicability — as the world indeed imagines them to be. Bryant, in his very learned 'Mythology,' mentions an analogous source of error, when he says that 'although the Pagan fables are not believed, yet we forget ourselves continually, and make inferences from them as existing realities.' With the algebraists, however, who are Pagans themselves, the 'Pagan fables' *are* believed, and the inferences are made, not so much through lapse of memory, as through an unaccountable addling of the brains. In short, I never yet encountered the mere mathematician who could be trusted out of equal roots, or one who did not clandestinely hold it as a point of his faith that $x^2 + px$ was absolutely and unconditionally equal to q. Say to one of these gentlemen, by way of experiment, if you please, that you believe occasions may occur where $x^2 + px$ is *not* altogether equal to q, and, having made him understand what you mean, get out of his reach as speedily as convenient, for, beyond doubt, he will endeavor to knock you down.

"I mean to say," continued Dupin, while I merely laughed at his last observations, "that

if the Minister had been no more than a mathematician, the Prefect would have been under no necessity of giving me this check. I knew him, however, as both mathematician and poet, and my measures were adapted to his capacity, with reference to the circumstances by which he was surrounded. I knew him as a courtier, too, and as a bold *intriguant*. Such a man, I considered, could not fail to be aware of the ordinary policial modes of action. He could not have failed to anticipate — and events have proved that he did not fail to anticipate — the waylayings to which he was subjected. He must have foreseen, I reflected, the secret investigations of his premises. His frequent absences from home at night, which were hailed by the Prefect as certain aids to his success, I regarded only as *ruses*, to afford opportunity for thorough search to the police, and thus the sooner to impress them with the conviction to which G—, in fact, did finally arrive — the conviction that the letter was not upon the premises. I felt, also, that the whole train of thought, which I was at some pains in detailing to you just now, concerning the invariable principal of policial action in searches for articles concealed — I felt that this whole train of thought would necessarily pass through the mind of the Minister. It would imperatively lead him to despise all the ordinary *nooks* of concealment. *He* could not, I reflected, be so weak as not to see that the most intricate and remote recess of his hotel would be as open as his commonest closets to the eyes, to the probes, to the gimlets, and to the microscopes of the Prefect. I saw, in fine, that he would be driven, as a matter of course, to *simplicity*, if not deliberately induced to it as a matter of choice. You will remember, perhaps, how desperately the Prefect laughed when I suggested, upon our first interview, that it was just possible this mystery troubled him so much on account of its being so *very* self-evident."

"Yes," said I, "I remember his merriment well. I really thought he would have fallen into convulsions."

"The material world," continued Dupin, "abounds with the very strict analogies to the immaterial; and thus some color of truth has been given to the rhetorical dogma, that metaphor, or simile, may be made to strengthen an argument, as well as to embellish a description. The principle of the *vis inertiæ*,[1] for example, seems to be identical in physics and metaphysics.

[1] Force of inertia.

It is not more true in the former, that a large body is with more difficulty set in motion than a smaller one, and that its subsequent *momentum* is commensurate with this difficulty, than it is, in the latter, that intellects of the vaster capacity, while more forcible, more constant, and more eventful in their movements than those of inferior grade, are yet the less readily moved, and more embarrassed and full of hesitation in the first few steps of their progress. Again: have you ever noticed which of the street signs, over the shop doors, are the most attractive of attention?"

"I have never given the matter a thought," I said.

"There is a game of puzzles," he resumed, "which is played upon a map. One party playing requires another to find a given word — the name of town, river, state or empire — any word, in short, upon the motley and perplexed surface of the chart. A novice in the game generally seeks to embarrass his opponents by giving them the most minutely lettered names; but the adept selects such words as stretch, in large characters, from one end of the chart to the other. These, like the over-largely lettered signs and placards of the street, escape observation by dint of being excessively obvious; and here the physical oversight is precisely analogous with the moral inapprehension by which the intellect suffers to pass unnoticed those considerations which are too obtrusively and too palpably self-evident. But this is a point, it appears, somewhat above or beneath the understanding of the Prefect. He never once thought it probable, or possible, that the Minister had deposited the letter immediately beneath the nose of the whole world, by way of best preventing any portion of that world from perceiving it.

"But the more I reflected upon the daring, dashing, and discriminating ingenuity of D—; upon the fact that the document must always have been *at hand*, if he intended to use it to good purpose; and upon the decisive evidence, obtained by the Prefect, that it was not hidden within the limits of that dignitary's ordinary search — the more satisfied I became that, to conceal this letter, the Minister had resorted to the comprehensive and sagacious expedient of not attempting to conceal it at all.

"Full of these ideas, I prepared myself with a pair of green spectacles, and called one fine morning, quite by accident, at the Ministerial hotel. I found G— at home, yawning, lounging, and dawdling, as usual, and pretending to

be in the last extremity of *ennui*. He is, perhaps, the most really energetic human being now alive — but that is only when nobody sees him.

"To be even with him, I complained of my weak eyes, and lamented the necessity of the spectacles, under cover of which I cautiously and thoroughly surveyed the apartment, while seemingly intent only upon the conversation of my host.

"I paid especial attention to a large writing-table near which he sat, and upon which lay confusedly some miscellaneous letters and other papers, with one or two musical instruments and a few books. Here, however, after a long and very deliberate scrutiny, I saw nothing to excite particular suspicion.

"At length my eyes, in going the circuit of the room, fell upon a trumpery filigree card-rack of pasteboard, that hung dangling by a dirty blue ribbon, from a little brass knob just beneath the middle of the mantel-piece. In this rack, which had three or four compartments, were five or six visiting cards and a solitary letter. This last was much soiled and crumpled. It was torn nearly in two, across the middle — as if a design, in the first instance, to tear it entirely up as worthless, had been altered, or stayed, in the second. It had a large black seal, bearing the D— cipher *very* conspicuously, and was addressed, in a diminutive female hand, to D—, the Minister, himself. It was thrust carelessly, and even, as it seemed, contemptuously, into one of the upper divisions of the rack.

"No sooner had I glanced at this letter, than I concluded it to be that of which I was in search. To be sure, it was, to all appearance, radically different from the one of which the Prefect had read us so minute a description. Here the seal was large and black, with the D— cipher; there it was small and red, with the ducal arms of the S— family. Here, the address, to the Minister, was diminutive and feminine; there the superscription, to a certain royal personage, was markedly bold and decided; the size alone formed a point of correspondence. But, then, the *radicalness* of these differences, which was excessive; the dirt; the soiled and torn condition of the paper, so inconsistent with the *true* methodical habits of D—, and so suggestive of a design to delude the beholder into an idea of the worthlessness of the document; — these things, together with the hyperobtrusive situation of this document, full in the view of every visitor, and thus exactly in accordance with the conclusions to which I had previously arrived;

these things, I say, were strongly corroborative of suspicion, in one who came with the intention to suspect.

"I protracted my visit as long as possible, and, while I maintained a most animated discussion with the Minister, on a topic which I knew well had never failed to interest and excite him, I kept my attention really riveted upon the letter. In this examination, I committed to memory its external appearance and arrangement in the rack; and also fell, at length, upon a discovery which set at rest whatever trivial doubt I might have entertained. In scrutinizing the edges of the paper, I observed them to be more *chafed* than seemed necessary. They presented the *broken* appearance which is manifested when a stiff paper, having been once folded and pressed with a folder, is refolded in a reversed direction, in the same creases or edges which had formed the original fold. This discovery was sufficient. It was clear to me that the letter had been turned, as a glove, inside out, re-directed, and resealed. I bade the Minister good morning, and took my departure at once, leaving a gold snuff-box upon the table.

"The next morning I called for the snuff-box, when we resumed, quite eagerly, the conversation of the preceding day. While thus engaged, however, a loud report, as if of a pistol, was heard immediately beneath the windows of the hotel, and was succeeded by a series of fearful screams, and the shoutings of a mob. D— rushed to a casement, threw it open, and looked out. In the meantime, I stepped to the card-rack, took the letter, and put it in my pocket, and replaced it by a *fac-simile* (so far as regards externals), which I had carefully prepared at my lodgings; imitating the D— cipher, very readily, by means of a seal formed of bread.

"The disturbance in the street had been occasioned by the frantic behavior of a man with a musket. He had fired it among a crowd of women and children. It proved, however, to have been without ball, and the fellow was suffered to go his way as a lunatic or a drunkard. When he had gone, D— came from the window, whither I had followed him immediately upon securing the object in view. Soon afterwards I bade him farewell. The pretended lunatic was a man in my own pay."

"But what purpose had you," I asked, "in replacing the letter by a *fac-simile*? Would it not have been better, at the first visit, to have seized it openly, and departed?"

"D—," replied Dupin, "is a desperate man, and a man of nerve. His hotel, too, is not without attendants devoted to his interests. Had I made the wild attempt you suggest, I might never have left the Ministerial presence alive. The good people of Paris might have heard of me no more. But I had an object apart from these considerations. You know my political prepossessions. In this matter, I act as a partisan of the lady concerned. For eighteen months the Minister has had her in his power. She has now him in hers — since, being unaware that the letter is not in his possession, he will proceed with his exactions as if it was. Thus will he inevitably commit himself, at once, to his political destruction. His downfall, too, will not be more precipitate than awkward. It is all very well to talk about the *facilis descensus Averni*;[1] but in all kinds of climbing, as Catalani said of singing, it is far more easy to get up than to come down. In the present instance I have no sympathy — at least no pity — for him who descends. He is that *monstrum horrendum*,[2] an unprincipled man of genius. I confess, however, that I should like very well to know the precise character of his thoughts, when, being defied by her whom the Prefect terms 'a certain personage,' he is reduced to opening the letter which I left for him in the card-rack."

"How? did you put any thing particular in it?"

"Why — it did not seem altogether right to leave the interior blank — that would have been insulting. D—, at Vienna once, did me an evil turn, which I told him, quite good-humoredly, that I should remember. So, as I knew he would feel some curiosity in regard to the identity of the person who had outwitted him, I thought it a pity not to give him a clue. He is well acquainted with my MS., and I just copied into the middle of the blank sheet the words —

"— *Un dessein si funeste,
S'il n'est digne d'Atrée, est digne de Thyeste.*

They are to be found in Crébillon's 'Atrée.'"

The Cask of Amontillado
(1846)

This story of revenge illustrates admirably Poe's doctrines of unity and economy. The theme is announced in the first sentence and sustained undeviatingly to the last ("May he rest in peace."). While

1 "Easy descent to Hades."
2 "Horrible monster."

the plot is very simple, some intellectual complexity
is attained through irony: the meaning of an act or
speech is often contrary to that seemingly indicated.

The thousand injuries of Fortunato I had
borne as I best could, but when he ventured
upon insult I vowed revenge. You, who so well
know the nature of my soul, will not suppose,
however, that I gave utterance to a threat.
At length I would be avenged; this was a point
definitely settled — but the very definitiveness
with which it was resolved precluded the idea
of risk. I must not only punish but punish
with impunity. A wrong is unredressed when
retribution overtakes its redresser. It is equally
unredressed when the avenger fails to make
himself felt as such to him who has done the
wrong.

It must be understood that neither by word
nor deed had I given Fortunato cause to doubt
my good will. I continued, as was my wont,
to smile in his face, and he did not perceive
that my smile *now* was at the thought of his
immolation.

He had a weak point — this Fortunato —
although in other regards he was a man to be
respected and even feared. He prided himself
on his connoisseurship in wine. Few Italians
have the true virtuoso spirit. For the most part
their enthusiasm is adopted to suit the time
and opportunity, to practise imposture upon
the British and Austrian *millionaires*. In painting and gemmary, Fortunato, like his countrymen, was a quack, but in the matter of old wines
he was sincere. In this respect I did not differ
from him materially; — I was skilful in the
Italian vintages myself, and bought largely
whenever I could.

It was about dusk, one evening during the
supreme madness of the carnival season, that I
encountered my friend. He accosted me with
excessive warmth, for he had been drinking
much. The man wore motley. He had on a
tight-fitting parti-striped dress, and his head was
surmounted by the conical cap and bells. I
was so pleased to see him that I thought I
should never have done wringing his hand.

I said to him — "My dear Fortunato, you are
luckily met. How remarkably well you are looking today. But I have received a pipe of what
passes for Amontillado, and I have my doubts."

"How?" said he. "Amontillado? A pipe?
Impossible! And in the middle of the carnival!"

"I have my doubts," I replied; "and I was

silly enough to pay the full Amontillado price
without consulting you in the matter. You
were not to be found, and I was fearful of losing
a bargain."

"Amontillado!"

"I have my doubts."

"Amontillado!"

"And I must satisfy them."

"Amontillado!"

"As you are engaged, I am on my way to
Luchresi. If any one has a critical turn it is he.
He will tell me —"

"Luchresi cannot tell Amontillado from
Sherry."

"And yet some fools will have it that his taste
is a match for your own."

"Come, let us go."

"Whither?"

"To your vaults."

"My friend, no; I will not impose upon your
good nature. I perceive you have an engagement. Luchresi —"

"I have no engagement; — come."

"My friend, no. It is not the engagement,
but the severe cold with which I perceive you
are afflicted. The vaults are insufferably damp.
They are encrusted with nitre."

"Let us go, nevertheless. The cold is merely
nothing. Amontillado! You have been imposed
upon. And as for Luchresi, he cannot distinguish Sherry from Amontillado."

Thus speaking, Fortunato possessed himself
of my arm; and putting on a mask of black silk
and drawing a *roquelaire* closely about my person, I suffered him to hurry me to my palazzo.

There were no attendants at home; they had
absconded to make merry in honor of the time.
I had told them that I should not return until
the morning, and had given them explicit orders not to stir from the house. These orders
were sufficient, I well knew, to insure their immediate disappearance, one and all, as soon as
my back was turned.

I took from their sconces two flambeaux, and
giving one to Fortunato, bowed him through
several suites of rooms to the archway that led
into the vaults. I passed down a long and
winding staircase, requesting him to be cautious
as he followed. We came at length to the foot
of the descent, and stood together upon the
damp ground of the catacombs of the Montresors.

The gait of my friend was unsteady, and the
bells upon his cap jingled as he strode.

"The pipe," he said.

"It is farther on," I said; "but observe the white web-work which gleams from these cavern walls."

He turned towards me, and looked into my eyes with two filmy orbs that distilled the rheum of intoxication.

"Nitre?" he asked, at length.

"Nitre," I replied. "How long have you had that cough?"

"Ugh! ugh! ugh! — ugh! ugh! ugh! — ugh! ugh! ugh! — ugh! ugh! ugh! — ugh! ugh! ugh!"

My poor friend found it impossible to reply for many minutes.

"It is nothing," he said, at last.

"Come," I said, with decision, "we will go back; your health is precious. You are rich, respected, admired, beloved; you are happy, as once I was. You are a man to be missed. For me it is no matter. We will go back; you will be ill, and I cannot be responsible. Besides, there is Luchresi —"

"Enough," he said; "the cough is a mere nothing; it will not kill me. I shall not die of a cough."

"True — true," I replied; "and, indeed, I had no intention of alarming you unnecessarily — but you should use all proper caution. A draught of this Medoc will defend us from the damps."

Here I knocked off the neck of a bottle which I drew from a long row of its fellows that lay upon the mould.

"Drink," I said, presenting him the wine.

He raised it to his lips with a leer. He paused and nodded to me familiarly, while his bells jingled.

"I drink," he said "to the buried that repose around us."

"And I to your long life."

He again took my arm, and we proceeded.

"These vaults," he said, "are extensive."

"The Montresors," I replied, "were a great and numerous family."

"I forget your arms."

"A huge human foot d'or, in a field azure; the foot crushes a serpent rampant whose fangs are imbedded in the heel."

"And the motto?"

"*Nemo me impune lacessit.*" [1]

"Good!" he said.

The wine sparkled in his eyes and the bells jingled. My own fancy grew warm with the Medoc. We had passed through long walls of

[1] "No one can harm me with impunity."

piled skeletons, with casks and puncheons intermingling, into the inmost recesses of the catacombs. I paused again, and this time I made bold to seize Fortunato by an arm above the elbow.

"The nitre!" I said: "see, it increases. It hangs like moss upon the vaults. We are below the river's bed. The drops of moisture trickle among the bones. Come, we will go back ere it is too late. Your cough —"

"It is nothing," he said; "let us go on. But first, another draught of the Medoc."

I broke and reached him a flagon of De Grâve. He emptied it at a breath. His eyes flashed with a fierce light. He laughed and threw the bottle upwards with a gesticulation I did not understand.

I looked at him in surprise. He repeated the movement — a grotesque one.

"You do not comprehend?" he said.

"Not I," I replied.

"Then you are not of the brotherhood."

"How?"

"You are not of the masons."

"Yes, yes," I said; "yes, yes."

"You? Impossible! A mason?"

"A mason," I replied.

"A sign," he said, "a sign."

"It is this," I answered, producing from beneath the folds of my *roquelaire* a trowel.

"You jest," he exclaimed, recoiling a few paces. "But let us proceed to the Amontillado."

"Be it so," I said, replacing the tool beneath the cloak and again offering him my arm. He leaned upon it heavily. We continued our route in search of the Amontillado. We passed through a range of low arches, descended, passed on, and descending again, arrived at a deep crypt, in which the foulness of the air caused our flambeaux rather to glow than flame.

At the most remote end of the crypt there appeared another less spacious. Its walls had been lined with human remains, piled to the vault overhead, in the fashion of the great catacombs of Paris. Three sides of this interior crypt were still ornamented in this manner. From the fourth side the bones had been thrown down, and lay promiscuously upon the earth, forming at one point a mound of some size. Within the wall thus exposed by the displacing of the bones, we perceived a still interior crypt or recess, in depth about four feet, in width three, in height six or seven. It seemed to have been constructed for no especial use within itself, but formed merely the interval between two of the colossal supports of the roof of the catacombs, and was backed by one of their circumscribing walls of solid granite.

It was in vain that Fortunato, uplifting his dull torch, endeavored to pry into the depth of the recess. Its termination the feeble light did not enable us to see.

"Proceed," I said; "herein is the Amontillado. As for Luchresi — "

"He is an ignoramus," interrupted my friend, as he stepped unsteadily forward, while I followed immediately at his heels. In an instant he had reached the extremity of the niche, and finding his progress arrested by the rock, stood stupidly bewildered. A moment more and I had fettered him to the granite. In its surface were two iron staples, distant from each other about two feet, horizontally. From one of these depended a short chain, from the other a padlock. Throwing the links about his waist, it was but the work of a few seconds to secure it. He was too much astounded to resist. Withdrawing the key I stepped back from the recess.

"Pass your hand," I said, "over the wall; you cannot help feeling the nitre. Indeed, it is *very* damp. Once more let me *implore* you to return. No? Then I must positively leave you. But I must first render you all the little attentions in my power."

"The Amontillado!" ejaculated my friend, not yet recovered from his astonishment.

"True," I replied; "the Amontillado."

As I said these words I busied myself among the pile of bones of which I have before spoken. Throwing them aside, I soon uncovered a quantity of building stone and mortar. With these materials and with the aid of my trowel, I began vigorously to wall up the entrance of the niche.

I had scarcely laid the first tier of the masonry when I discovered that the intoxication of Fortunato had in a great measure worn off. The earliest indication I had of this was a low moaning cry from the depth of the recess. It was *not* the cry of a drunken man. There was then a long and obstinate silence. I laid the second tier, and the third, and the fourth; and then I heard the furious vibrations of the chain. The noise lasted for several minutes, during which, that I might hearken to it with the more satisfaction, I ceased my labors and sat down upon the bones. When at last the clanking subsided, I resumed the trowel, and finished without interruption the fifth, the sixth, and the seventh

tier. The wall was now nearly upon a level with my breast. I again paused, and holding the flambeaux over the mason-work, threw a few feeble rays upon the figure within.

A succession of loud and shrill screams, bursting suddenly from the throat of the chained form, seemed to thrust me violently back. For a brief moment I hesitated, I trembled. Unsheathing my rapier, I began to grope with it about the recess; but the thought of an instant reassured me. I placed my hand upon the solid fabric of the catacombs, and felt satisfied. I reapproached the wall; I replied to the yells of him who clamored. I re-echoed, I aided, I surpassed them in volume and in strength. I did this, and the clamorer grew still.

It was now midnight, and my task was drawing to a close. I had completed the eighth, the ninth and the tenth tier. I had finished a portion of the last and the eleventh; there remained but a single stone to be fitted and plastered in. I struggled with its weight; I placed it partially in its destined position. But now there came from out the niche a low laugh that erected the hairs upon my head. It was succeeded by a sad voice, which I had difficulty in recognizing as that of the noble Fortunato. The voice said —

"Ha! ha! ha! — he! he! he! — a very good joke, indeed — an excellent jest. We will have many a rich laugh about it at the palazzo — he he! he! — over our wine — he! he! he!"

"The Amontillado!" I said.

"He! he! he! — he! he! he! — yes, the Amontillado. But is it not getting late? Will not they be awaiting us at the palazzo, the Lady Fortunato and the rest? Let us be gone."

"Yes," I said, "let us be gone."

"*For the love of God, Montresor!*"

"Yes," I said, "for the love of God!"

But to these words I hearkened in vain for a reply. I grew impatient. I called aloud —

"Fortunato!"

No answer. I called again —

"Fortunato!"

No answer still. I thrust a torch through the remaining aperture and let it fall within. There came forth in return only a jingling of the bells. My heart grew sick; it was the dampness of the catacombs that made it so. I hastened to make an end of my labor. I forced the last stone into its position; I plastered it up. Against the new masonry I re-erected the old rampart of bones. For the half of a century no mortal has disturbed them. *In pace requiescat!*

ROMANTICISM ON PURITAN SOIL

Ralph Waldo Emerson [1803–1882]

[handwritten margin note: art for moral's sake / says a poem shows the / poet's argument / meaning imp.]

Like Poe, Emerson was born in Boston. "His soul received its bent," said Charles Eliot Norton, "from the innocent America of before 1830," an America that had a "confident, sweet, morning spirit." (In the opinion of Norton, who was professor of the history of fine art at Harvard in Emerson's later years, the mood of young America limited his mind, encouraged him in an optimism that became a bigotry.)

Along with the buoyant optimism of the new nation, Emerson had the moral enthusiasm of his Puritan heritage. While Poe was the son of wandering actors, grew up in Virginia, and became an advocate of art for art's sake, Emerson was the son of a Unitarian minister, was shaped by his Massachusetts ancestry and environment, and believed in art for life's sake — or morals' sake. Behind him stretched impressively a long line of ministers of the Gospel. His own father, William Emerson, was minister of the First Church, Unitarian, in Boston. He died when the boy was not quite eight years old. Thereafter the widow (Ruth Haskins Emerson) and her four boys attended the church of William Ellery Channing. Mrs. Emerson was a highly competent mother. His Aunt Mary Moody Emerson was a pious and stimulating woman who held before him, as he put it later, an "immeasurably high standard." He was brought up in poverty; at times he and a brother had to share the use of a winter overcoat. Yet all four managed to go through Harvard. Emerson was messenger for the president, and waited on table; he graduated at the middle of his class. To help his brother William, he spent the next three years in teaching, shyly, in a school for young ladies.

He entered the Harvard divinity school in 1825, his studies handicapped by physical ailments, the care of a brother temporarily insane, and the need of more school teaching. His license to preach, given late in 1826, implied not so much a proof of capacity as a vote of confidence. At this juncture a new ailment, in the lungs, sent him to South Carolina and Florida for a long winter. In 1829 he became pastor of the Second Church, the church of the Mathers, now Unitarian, and in the same year married Ellen Tucker — "17 years old," he reported, "and very beautiful, by universal consent," but of delicate health. Within less than a year and a half her life was taken by tuberculosis. The white plague was almost a family institution: it brought death also to Emerson's two younger brothers, and dogged his own career for about six years, years in what he called the house of Pain.

He was also struggling in the house of doubt. First — as early as 1824 — he had questioned whether the ministry, after all, was his true vocation. His love of eloquence boded well for his preaching, but was he not lacking in self-confidence among men, in warmth of heart, in moral worth? As time went on he questioned not so much his own fitness as the Christian ministry itself. Did not even the Unitarian church involve restraints upon the free spiritual life? And was it not a worship of dead forms rather than a vital faith? "The profession," he said, in his journal "is antiquated." In December 1832 he resigned his charge. Disagreement with his congregation over celebration of the Lord's Supper was only the immediate occasion. Bereaved, ill, and adrift in the world, he sailed for Europe on Christmas Day.

When he returned in the following September, he had regained his health and won a new assurance. In the course of his travels, from Italy to Scotland, he had seen his contemporary heroes — Landor, Coleridge, Carlyle, Wordsworth — and found them "all deficient, all these four . . . in insight into religious truth. They have no idea of that species of moral truth which I call the first philosophy." He must have meant that he had a better idea of it himself. In November he began giving lectures. In the next year he settled in Concord, thenceforth his home. In 1835 he married Lydia Jackson. In 1836 his son Waldo was born, and his book *Nature* was published.

With this book he launched what turned out to be a series of three great Transcendental challenges. In them we can see the interplay of many forces: the old Puritan spirit, the deistic tendency of Unitarianism, an optimistic nationalism, the doctrines of the Platonic tradition, the impulse of the Romantic Movement. In *Nature* the challenge lay mainly in the field of philosophy. In the address on the American Scholar it was mainly in literature — the fit education of the writer. In his Divinity School address it was in religion. Emerson's years of frustration and groping were at an end. In place of the "antiquated" faith of his fathers, he had achieved a new faith of his own, vital if unorthodox.

He had also achieved a new vocation — that of the lecturer. Two of the three challenges were lectures. His love of eloquence, frustrated when he resigned his pulpit, found expression on the public lecture platform. Why he became one of the most popular lecturers in America is suggested by Lowell's essay "Emerson the Lecturer" (printed in this volume). In this way he nearly doubled the income he received from the estate of his first wife. He gave hundreds upon hundreds of lectures, ranging repeatedly as far as the West, even beyond the Mississippi. Cheerfully he bore the hardships of travel in those days, and temperatures of 20 below zero. "This climate and people are a new test for the wares of a man of letters."

As a man of letters, he mostly arrived at his published results indirectly, writing in his private journal, writing lectures based largely on his journal, finally writing essays based on both journal and lectures and publishing them as books. His most famous books were the *Essays* of 1841 and a second series in 1844. Most of the essays dealt with abstractions, such as Self-Reliance, Compensation, Love, The Over-Soul, The Poet, Manners, Politics, and were suggestive and inspirational rather than closely reasoned. These two volumes came with the flood-tide of Transcendentalism, far more memorably registered in them than in the four years' run of *The Dial*, the periodical organ of the movement edited by Margaret Fuller and Emerson.

In many of the essays his faith in the religion of the self was at its height, but in a few, such as that on Experience, we begin to see the later Emerson, forced by growing experience to recognize that man is not always a god but a creature limited by heredity, temperament, circumstance, suffering. The later Emerson appears in some of the poems, in *Representative Men* (1850), in *English Traits* (1856), most notably in the essays of *The Conduct of Life* (1860). His old optimism still shone, but the bright light of his faith did not blind him to the dark realities of the human lot.

In his own day and long after, Emerson was regarded as a Yankee Plato, or, in the phrase of Oliver Wendell Holmes, as "a winged Franklin" — "a soaring nature, ballasted with sense." In the cynical period between two world wars, his wings were often clipped by those critics who complained, not without justification, of his bland optimism, or his insistent preaching, or his rhetorical eloquence, or his intangible pantheism and mysticism, or his indifference to reason. In the years that have followed, he has impressed scholars with his important place in the development of American civilization, and interested critics in his qualities of mind and personality, especially in his "psychological ambivalence," i.e. his effort to perceive sharply, and keep himself poised between, the conflicting elements of life, such as free will and fate.

Further reading: *Essays, First Series, Second Series; Representative Men; The Conduct of Life.* R. L. Rusk, *The Life of Ralph Waldo Emerson*, 1949. S. E. Whicher, *Freedom and Fate: an Inner Life of Ralph Waldo Emerson*, 1953. V. C. Hopkins, *Spires of Form: a Study of Emerson's Aesthetic Theory*, 1951.

From his *Journals*

We have noted that the journals were Emerson's "savings bank," material for his addresses and essays. They were also a typical expression of the man. It has even been suggested, by Austin Warren, that his writings as a whole were a sort of journal. "After the fashion of his Puritan ancestors in England and New England, he is a self-analyst, a diarist . . . not primarily a 'maker,' either of poetry or philosophy, but a self-explorer."

He began his journals in 1820, when he was a junior in college, and continued for fifty-five years. When they were published, they made a set of ten substantial volumes, from which, in 1926, Bliss Perry extracted *The Heart of Emerson's Journals*. In its first sixteen months, this book of selections had a sale of over 43,000 copies. To the skeptical 1920's Emerson the believer was interesting because of his keen and independent mind, his effort to explore his experience honestly, without any meekness toward conventional opinions. As he said in an entry written when he was twenty years old, "I see no reason why I should bow my head to man, or cringe in my demeanor." In this respect he was close to the spirit of John Adams and Thomas Jefferson, whose funeral solemnities he attended in Faneuil Hall three years later. He did not propose to be a slave even to his own pedigree.

(age 21)

It is my own humor to despise pedigree. I was educated to prize it. The kind Aunt whose cares instructed my youth (and whom may God reward), told me oft the virtues of her and mine ancestors. They have been clergymen for many generations, and the piety of all and the eloquence of many is yet praised in the Churches. But the dead sleep in their moonless night; my business is with the living.

(age 28)

A sect or party is an elegant incognito devised to save a man from the vexation of thinking.

(age 29)

The hour of decision. It seems not worth while for them who charge others with exalting forms above the moon to fear forms themselves with extravagant dislike.*** I know very well that it is a bad sign in a man to be too conscientious, and stick at gnats. The most desperate scoundrels have been the over-refiners. Without accommodation society is impracticable. But this ordinance [the Lord's Supper] is esteemed the most sacred of religious institutions, and I cannot go habitually to an institution which they esteem holiest with indifference and dislike. [*White Mountains, July 15, 1832*]

Sailed from Boston for Malta, December 25, 1832, in Brig Jasper, Captain Ellis, 235 tons, laden with logwood, mahogany, tobacco, sugar, coffee, beeswax, cheese, etc.

The good Captain rejoices much in my ignorance. He confounded me the other day about the book in the Bible where God was not mentioned, and last night upon St. Paul's shipwreck. Yet I comforted myself at midnight with *Lycidas*. What marble beauty in that classic pastoral.

Perhaps it is a pernicious mistake, yet, rightly seen, I believe it is sound philosophy, that wherever we go, whatever we do, self is the sole subject we study and learn. Montaigne said, himself was all he knew. Myself is much more than

I know, and yet I know nothing else. The chemist experiments upon his new salt by trying its affinity to all the various substances he can command, arbitrarily selected, and thereby discloses the most wonderful properties in his subject. And I bring myself to sea, to Malta, to Italy, to find new affinities between me and my fellow men, to observe narrowly the affections, weaknesses, surprises, hopes, doubts, which new sides of the panorama shall call forth in me. Mean, sneakingly mean, would be this philosophy, a reptile unworthy of the name, if *self* be used in the low sense, but as self means Devil, so it means God.

I have been to the Opera, and thought three *taris*, the price of a ticket, rather too much for the whistle. It is doubtless a vice to turn one's eyes inward too much, but I am my own comedy and tragedy. [*Sicily*]

Tonight I heard the *Miserere* sung in St. Peter's and with less effect than yesterday. But what a temple! When night was settling down upon it and a long religious procession moved through a part of the church, I got an idea of its immensity such as I had not before. You walk about on its ample, marble pavement as you would on a common, so free are you of your neighbors; and throngs of people are lost upon it. And what beautiful lights and shades on its mighty gilded arches and vaults and far windows and brave columns, and its rich-clad priests that look as if they were the pictures come down from the walls and walking. [*Rome*]

I ought not to forget the ballet between the acts. Goethe laughs at those who force every work of art into the narrow circle of their own prejudices and cannot admire a picture as a picture, and a tune as a tune. So I was willing to look at this as a ballet, and to see that it was admirable, but I could not help feeling the while that it were better for mankind if there were no such dancers. I have since learned God's decision on the same, in the fact that all the *ballerine* are nearly idiotic.

(age 30)

I collect nothing that can be touched or tasted or smelled, neither cameo, painting, nor medallion; nothing in my trunk but old clothes; but I value much the growing picture which the ages have painted and which I reverently survey.

Pray what brought you here, grave sir? the moving Boulevard seems to say. [*Paris*]

I went this evening into Frascati's, long the most noted of the gambling houses or hells of Paris.

Went into St. Paul's, where service was saying. Poor church. [*London*]

I thank the Great God who has led me through this European scene, this last schoolroom in which he has pleased to instruct me, from Malta's isle, through Sicily, through Italy, through Switzerland, through France, through England, through Scotland, in safety and pleasure, and has now brought me to the shore and the ship that steers westward. He has shown me the men I wished to see, — Landor, Coleridge, Carlyle, Wordsworth; he has thereby comforted and confirmed me in my convictions. Many things I owe to the sight of these men. I shall judge more justly, less timidly, of wise men forevermore. [*Liverpool*]

The men of Europe will say, Expound; let us hear what it is that is to convince the faithful and at the same time the philosopher? Let us hear this new thing. It is very old. It is the old revelation, that perfect beauty is perfect goodness, it is the development of the wonderful congruities of the moral law of human nature. Let me enumerate a few of the remarkable properties of that nature. A man contains all that is needful to his government within himself. He is made a law unto himself. All real good or evil that can befall him must be from himself. He only can do himself any good or any harm. Nothing can be given to him or taken from him but always there is a compensation. There is a correspondence between the human soul and everything that exists in the world; more properly, everything that is known to man. Instead of studying things without the principles of them, all may be penetrated unto within him. Every act puts the agent in a new condition. The purpose of life seems to be to acquaint a man with himself. He is not to live to the future as described to him, but to live to the real future by living to the real present. The highest revelation is that God is in every man.

(age 31)

Hail to the quiet fields of my fathers! Not

wholly unattended by supernatural friendship and favor, let me come hither. Bless my purposes as they are simple and virtuous. Coleridge's fine letter (in London *Literary Gazette*, September 13, 1834) comes in aid of the very thoughts I was revolving. And be it so. Henceforth I design not to utter any speech, poem, or book that is not entirely and peculiarly my work. I will say at public lectures, and the like, those things which I have meditated for their own sake, and not for the first time with a view to that occasion. (*Concord, November 15, 1834.*)

(age 32)

You affirm that the moral development contains all the intellectual, and that Jesus was the perfect man. I bow in reverence unfeigned before that benign man. I know more, hope more, am more, because he has lived. But, if you tell me that in your opinion he has fulfilled all the conditions of man's existence, carried out to the utmost, at least by implication, all man's powers, I suspend my assent. I do not see in him cheerfulness: I do not see in him the love of natural science: I see in him no kindness for art; I see in him nothing of Socrates, of Laplace, of Shakespeare. The perfect man should remind us of all great men. Do you ask me if I would rather resemble Jesus than any other man? If I should say Yes, I should suspect myself of superstition.

I bought my house and two acres six rods of land of John T. Coolidge for 3,500 dollars.

I was married to Lydia Jackson.

(age 33)

Transcendentalism means, says our accomplished Mrs. B., with a wave of her hand, *a little beyond.*

The grey present, the white future.

Pleasant walk yesterday, the most pleasant of days. At Walden Pond I found a new musical instrument which I call the ice-harp. A thin coat of ice covered a part of the pond, but melted around the edge of the shore. I threw a stone upon the ice which rebounded with a shrill sound, and falling again and again, repeated the note with pleasing modulation. I thought at first it was the "peep, peep" of a bird I had scared. I was so taken with the music that I threw down my stick and spent twenty minutes in throwing stones single or in handfuls on this crystal drum.

Margaret Fuller left us yesterday morning. Among other things that make her visit valuable and memorable, this is not the least, that she gave me five or six lessons in German pronunciation, never by my offer and rather against my will each time, so that now, spite of myself, I shall always have to thank her for a great convenience — which she foresaw.

(age 35)

The unbelief of the age is attested by the loud condemnation of trifles. Look at the silly religious papers. Let a minister wear a cane, or a white hat, go to a theatre, or avoid a Sunday School, let a school-book with a Calvinistic sentence or a Sunday School book without one be heard of, and instantly all the old grannies squeak and gibber and do what they call "sounding an alarm," from Bangor to Mobile. Alike nice and squeamish is its ear. You must on no account say "stink" or "Damn."

"Seek ye first the kingdom of God, and all these things shall be added unto you." What! Art! Hamlets? Ballads?

A College. — My College should have Allston, Greenough, Bryant, Irving, Webster, Alcott, summoned for its domestic professors. And if I must send abroad (and, if we send for dancers and singers and actors, why not at the same prices for scholars?), Carlyle, Hallam, Campbell, should come and read lectures on History, Poetry, Letters. I would bid my men come for the love of God and man, promising them an open field and a boundless opportunity, and they should make their own terms. Then I would open my lecture rooms to the wide nation; and they should pay, each man, a fee that should give my professor a remuneration fit and noble. Then I should see the lecture-room, the college, filled with life and hope. Students would come from afar; for who would not ride a hundred miles to hear some one of these men giving his selectest thoughts to those who received them with joy? I should see living learning; the Muse once more in the eye and cheek of the youth.

(age 36)

Nature will not have us fret or fume. When

we come out of the Caucus or the Abolition Convention or the Temperance Meeting, she says to us, "So hot, my little Sir!" I fear the criticism of the sun and moon.

I know no means of calming the fret and perturbation into which too much sitting, too much talking, brings me, so perfect as labor. I have no animal spirits; therefore, when surprised by company and kept in a chair for many hours, my heart sinks, my brow is clouded and I think I will run for Acton woods, and live with the squirrels henceforward. But my garden is nearer, and my good hoe, as it bites the ground, revenges my wrongs, and I have less lust to bite my enemies. I confess I work at first with a little venom, lay to a little unnecessary strength. But by smoothing the rough hillocks, I smooth my temper; by extracting the long roots of the piper-grass, I draw out my own splinters; and in a short time I can hear the bobolink's song and see the blessed deluge of light and color that rolls around me.

What Possibilities! — In the country church, I see the cousins of Napoleon, of Wellington, of Wilberforce, of Bentham, of Humboldt. A little air and sunshine, an hour of need, a provoking society, would call out the right fire from these slumbering peasants.

On Sunday we heard sulphurous Calvinism. The preacher railed at Lord Byron. I thought Lord Byron's vice better than Rev. Mr. M.'s virtue.

When I was thirteen years old, my Uncle Samuel Ripley one day asked me, "How is it, Ralph, that all the boys dislike you and quarrel with you, whilst the grown people are fond of you?" Now am I thirty-six and the fact is reversed, — the old people suspect and dislike me, and the young love me.

(age 37)

Yesterday George and Sophia Ripley, Margaret Fuller and Alcott discussed here the Social Plans [Brook Farm]. I wished to be convinced, to be thawed, to be made nobly mad by the kindlings before my eye of a new dawn of human piety. But this scheme was arithmetic and comfort: this was a hint borrowed from the Tremont House and United States Hotel; a rage in our poverty and politics to live rich and

gentlemanlike, an anchor to leeward against a change of weather; a prudent forecast on the probable issue of the great questions of Pauperism and Poverty. And not once could I be inflamed, but sat aloof and thoughtless; my voice faltered and fell. It was not the cave of persecution which is the palace of spiritual power, but only a room in the Astor House hired for the Transcendentalists. I do not wish to remove from my present prison to a prison a little larger. I wish to break all prisons. I have not yet conquered my own house. It irks and repents me. Shall I raise the siege of this hencoop, and march baffled away to a pretended siege of Babylon? It seems to me that so to do were to dodge the problem I am set to solve, and to hide my impotency in the thick of a crowd. I can see too, afar, — that I should not find myself more than now, — no, not so much, in that select, but not by me selected, fraternity. Moreover, to join this body would be to traverse all my long trumpeted theory, and the instinct which spoke from it, that one man is a counterpoise to a city, — that a man is stronger than a city, that his solitude is more prevalent and beneficent than the concert of crowds.

(age 38)

I remember, when a child, in the pew on Sundays amusing myself with saying over common words as "black," "white," "board," etc., twenty or thirty times, until the word lost all meaning and fixedness, and I began to doubt which was the right name for the thing, when I saw that neither had any natural relation, but all were arbitrary. It was a child's first lesson in Idealism.

At Cambridge, the last Wednesday, I met twenty members of my college class and spent the day with them. Governor Kent of Maine presided, Upham, Quincy, Lowell, Gardner, Loring, Gorham, Motte, Wood, Blood, Cheney, Withington, Bulfinch, Reed, Burton, Stetson, Lane, Angier, Hilliard, Farnsworth, Dexter, Emerson. It was strange how fast the company returned to their old relation, and the whole mass of college nonsense came back in a flood. They all associated perfectly, were a unit for the day — men who now never meet. Each resumed his old place. The change in them was really very little in twenty years, although every man present was married, and all but one fathers. I too resumed my old place and found myself as of old a spectator rather than a fellow. I drank a great deal of wine (for me) with the wish to raise my spirits to the pitch of good fellowship, but wine produced on me its old effect, and I grew graver with every glass. Indignation and eloquence will excite me, but wine does not.

I saw in Boston Fanny Elssler in the ballet of *Nathalie*.*** The chief beauty is in the extreme grace of her movement, the variety and nature of her attitude, the winning fun and spirit of all her little coquetries, the beautiful erectness of her body, and the freedom and determination which she can so easily assume, and, what struck me much, the air of perfect sympathy with the house.***

I should not think of danger to young women stepping with their father or brother out of happy and guarded parlors into this theatre to return in a few hours to the same; but I can easily suppose that it is not the safest resort for college boys who have left metaphysics, conic sections, or Tacitus to see these tripping satin slippers, and they may not forget this graceful, silvery swimmer when they have retreated again to their baccalaureate cells.

It is a great satisfaction to see the best in each kind, and as a good student of the world, I desire to let pass nothing that is excellent in its own kind unseen, unheard.

The *Dial* is to be sustained or ended, and I must settle the question, it seems, of its life or death. I wish it to live, but do not wish to be its life. Neither do I like to put it in the hands of the Humanity and Reform Men, because they trample on letters and poetry; nor in the hands of the Scholars, for they are dead and dry.

Alcott sees the law of man truer and farther than any one ever did. Unhappily, his conversation never loses sight of his own personality. He never quotes; he never refers; his only illustration is his own biography. His topic yesterday is Alcott on the 17th October; today, Alcott on the 18th October; tomorrow, on the 19th. So will it be always. The poet, rapt into future times or into deeps of nature admired for themselves, lost in their law, cheers us with a lively charm; but this noble genius discredits genius to me. I do not want any more such persons to exist.

If I go into the churches in these days, I usually find the preacher in proportion to his intelligence to be cunning, so that the whole institution sounds hollow. X, the ablest of all the Unitarian clergy, spread popular traps all over the lecture which I heard in the Odeon. But in the days of the Pilgrims and the Puritans, the preachers were the victims of the same faith with which they whipped and persecuted other men, and their sermons are strong, imaginative, fervid, and every word a cube of stone.

(age 39)

I hear with pleasure that a young girl in the midst of rich, decorous Unitarian friends in Boston is well-nigh persuaded to join the Roman Catholic Church. Her friends, who are also my friends, lamented to me the growth of this inclination. But I told them that I think she is to be greatly congratulated on the event. She has lived in great poverty of events. In form and years a woman, she is still a child, having had no experiences, and although of a fine, liberal, susceptible, expanding nature, has never yet found any worthy object of attention; has not been in love, not been called out by any taste, except lately by music, and sadly wants adequate objects. In this church, perhaps, she shall find what she needs, in a power to call out the slumbering religious sentiment. It is unfortunate that the guide who has led her into this path is a young girl of a lively, forcible, but quite external character, who teaches her the historical argument for the Catholic faith. I told A. that I hoped she would not be misled by attaching any importance to that. If the offices of the church attracted her, if its beautiful forms and humane spirit draw her, if St. Augustine and St. Bernard, Jesus and Madonna, cathedral music and masses, then go, for thy dear heart's sake, but do not go out of this icehouse of Unitarianism, all external, into an icehouse again of external. At all events, I charged her to pay no regard to dissenters, but to suck that orange thoroughly.

It is greatest to believe and to hope well of the world, because he who does so quits the world of experience, and makes the world he lives in.

(age 41)

Be an opener of doors for such as come after thee, and do not try to make the universe a blind alley.

There is not the slightest probability that the college will foster an eminent talent in any youth. If he refuses prayers and recitations, they will torment and traduce and expel him, though he were Newton or Dante.

Even for those whom I really love I have not animal spirits.

I like man, but not men.

(age 43)

Eager, solicitous, hungry, rabid, busy-bodied America attempting many things, vain, ambitious to feel thy own existence, and convince others of thy talent, by attempting and hastily accomplishing much; yes, catch thy breath and correct thyself, and failing here, prosper out there; speed and fever are never greatness; but reliance and serenity and waiting.

The Superstitions of our Age:
The fear of Catholicism;
The fear of pauperism;
The fear of immigration;
The fear of manufacturing interests;
The fear of radicalism or democracy;
And faith in the steam engine.

(age 46)

Love is temporary and ends with marriage. Marriage is the perfection which love aimed at, ignorant of what it sought. Marriage is a good known only to the parties, — a relation of perfect understanding, aid, contentment, possession of themselves and of the world, — which dwarfs love to green fruit.

(age 48)

This filthy enactment (The Fugitive Slave Law) was made in the nineteenth century, by people who could read and write. I will not obey it, by God.

(age 52)

A *practical man* is the hobby of the age. Well, when I read German philosophy, or wrote verses, I was willing to concede there might be too much of these, and that the Western pioneer with axe on his shoulder, and still moving West as the settlements approached him, had his merits.

Whipple said of the author of "Leaves of Grass" that he had every leaf but the fig leaf.

(age 59)

Why has never the poorest country college offered me a professorship of rhetoric? I think I could have taught an orator, though I am none.

I like people who can do things. When Edward and I struggled in vain to drag our big calf into the barn, the Irish girl put her finger into the calf's mouth, and led her in directly.

(age 60)

I went to Dartmouth College, and found the same old Granny system which I met there twenty-five years ago. The President has an aversion to emulation, as injurious to the character of the pupils. He therefore forbids the election of members into the two literary societies by merit, but arranges that the first scholar alphabetically on the list shall be assigned to the Adelphi, and the second to the Mathesians, and the third to the Adelphi, and the fourth to the Mathesians; and so on. Every student belonging to the one or the other. "Well, but there is a first scholar in the class, is there not, and he has the first oration at Commencement?" "Oh, no, the parts are assigned by lot." The amiable student who explained it added that it tended to remove disagreeable excitement from the societies. I answered, "Certainly, and it would remove more if there were no college at all." I recommended morphine in liberal doses at the College Commons.

(age 65)

A man never gets acquainted with himself, but is always a surprise. We get daily news of the world within, as well as of the world outside, and not less of the central than of the surface facts. A new thought is awaiting him every morning.

(age 66)

Dr. Hedge tells us that the Indian asked John Eliot, "Why God did not kill the Devil?" One would like to know what was Eliot's answer.

(age 67)

In Yosemite, grandeur of these mountains perhaps unmatched in the globe; for here they strip themselves like athletes for exhibition, and stand perpendicular granite walls, showing their entire height, and wearing a liberty cap of snow on their head.

At the request of Galen Clark, our host at Mariposa, and who is, by State appointment, the protector of the trees, and who went with us to the Mammoth Groves, I selected a Sequoia Gigantea, near Galen's Hospice, in the presence of our party, and named it *Samoset*, in memory of the first Indian ally of the Plymouth Colony, and I gave Mr. Clark directions to procure a tin plate, and have the inscription painted thereon in the usual form of the named trees: and paid him its cost.

(age 59–69)

A man's style is his mind's voice. Wooden minds, wooden voices.

Fate.*** Even the chickens running up and down, and pecking at each spot and at each other as ridden by chicken nature, seem ever and anon to have a pause of consideration, then hurry on again to be chickens. Men have more pause.

(age 70)

Egypt. Mrs. Helen Bell, it seems, was asked, "What do you think the Sphinx said to Mr. Emerson?" "Why," replied Mrs. Bell, "the Sphinx probably said to him, 'You're another.'"

America, My Country
(w. 1833)

If it is true, as John Jay Chapman said, that "Emerson has America in his mind's eye all the time," we may appropriately begin the reading of his poetry with these unfinished lines. He wrote them in a note-book but never published them. They now appear in the *Journals.*

About to sail from Liverpool at the end of his first visit abroad, Emerson remarked in his diary that it is England's "best merit to my eye that it is the most resembling country to America which the world contains." In the same entry he says: "I am thankful that I am an American as I am thankful that I am a man." In mid-Atlantic, he expressed, in homespun verse, affection for his plain Yankee-land. In his desire to see truly the contrast between Old World and New, he emphasizes America's lacks (by negatives, from "unpeopled" in line 3 to "no kings" at the end) and, after the "my" of the first line, never refers to himself. What is perhaps dearest to him is stated in lines 35 and 36.

America, my country, can the mind
Embrace in its affections realms so vast
(Unpeopled, yet the land of men to be)
As the great oceans that wash thee enclose?
'Tis an ambitious charity that makes   5
Its arms meet round —
And yet, the sages say, the preference
Of our own cabin to a stranger's wealth,
The insidious love and hate that curls the lip
Of the frank Yankee in the tenements   10
Of ducal and of royal rank abroad,
His supercilious ignorance
Of heraldry and ceremony,
And his tenacious recollection
Amid the colored treasuries of art   15
That circle the Louvre or the Pitti house, —
Tuscany's unrivalled boast, —
Of the brave steamboats of New York,
The Boston Common, and the Hadley farms
Washed by Connecticut;   20
Yea, if the ruddy Englishman speak true,
Of the vast Roman church, and underneath
The frescoed sky of its majestic dome,
The American will count the cost
And build the shrine with dollars in his head; 25
And all he asks, arrived in Italy,
Has the star-bearing squadron left Leghorn?
Land without history, land lying all
In the plain daylight of the temperate zone,
          Thy plain acts   30
Without exaggeration done in day;
Thy interests contested by their manifold
          good sense,
In their own clothes without the ornament
Of bannered army harnessed in uniform.
Land where — and 'tis in Europe counted a
          reproach —   35
Where man asks questions for which man was
          made.
A land without nobility, or wigs, or debt,
No castles, no cathedrals, and no kings;
Land of the forest.

The Rhodora:
On Being Asked, Whence is the Flower?
(w. 1834)

Emerson chooses to write about a flower of the American forest (as Freneau and Bryant had done before him) rather than the rose or violet of English poetry. His "redbird" of the forest was presumably the scarlet tanager.

Beauty, says Emerson, needs no "excuse." Later he formulated this idea in philosophical terms (see *Nature*, page 316, beginning "This element I call an ultimate end"). When, as in the experience of this poem, he is in the presence of beauty, it seems supreme. But generally he speaks of other ultimate ends; it is equally true for him that goodness needs no excuse, that truth needs no excuse. Unlike Poe, he associates "an interchangeable Truth, Beauty, and Goodness, each wholly interfused in the other," "the eternal trinity of Truth, Goodness, and Beauty, each in its perfection including the three."

In May, when sea-winds pierced our solitudes,
I found the fresh Rhodora in the woods,
Spreading its leafless blooms in a damp nook,
To please the desert and the sluggish brook.
The purple petals, fallen in the pool,   5
Made the black water with their beauty gay;
Here might the redbird come his plumes to
      cool,
And court the flower that cheapens his array.
Rhodora! if the sages ask thee why
This charm is wasted on the earth and sky,   10
Tell them, dear, that if eyes were made for see-
      ing,
Then Beauty is its own excuse for being:
Why thou wert there, O rival of the rose!
I never thought to ask, I never knew:
But, in my simple ignorance, suppose   15
The self-same Power that brought me there
      brought you.

Each and All
(w. 1834?)

The topic is nothing less than the universe, the "perfect whole." The universe (Latin, "turned into one"), like unity in art, is a whole made up of related parts. This fundamental concept appeared in early Greek philosophy; Emerson wrote, in 1834, a poem on Xenophanes to which he originally gave the Greek title *En kai pan* (The One and the All). He probably knew Goethe's poem "Eins und Alles" (One and All), and he certainly read in Coleridge of the "universal law," of "the relation of each to the other, of each to all, and of all to each."

As in "The Rhodora," Emerson here chooses to view the universe in its aspect of Beauty. He wishes to convey to the reader an awareness that each particular beauty (of person or thing, of sight or sound, etc.) is part of the total Beauty, and derives its charm from its organic relationship with the whole. The germ of the poem was probably an 1834 journal entry where he had stated this abstraction in

connection with a parable. "I remember when I was a boy going upon the beach and being charmed with the colors and forms of the shells. I picked up many and put them in my pocket. When I got home I could find nothing that I gathered — nothing but some dry, ugly mussel and snail shells. Thence I learned that Composition was more important than the beauty of individual forms to Effect. On the shore they lay wet and social, by the sea and under the sky."

Another journal passage, perhaps a memory of his European trip, gave him the beginning of his poem: "The shepherd or the beggar [the "clown," i.e. rustic, of the poem] in his red cloak little knows what a charm he gives to the wide landscape that charms you on the mountain-top and whereof he makes the most agreeable feature, and I [know] no more the part my individuality plays in the All."

The poem opens with this and three other separate situations, the meaning of which is crystallized in the statement of lines 11 and 12. Then come three experiences of enchantment and disillusion — the sparrow, the shells, the maiden. Beauty seems a cheat of the immature; is not truth more to be desired? (Lines 37–39.) The answer, romantically conceived, is given in the rest of the poem. With Emerson, however, the answer represents a poetic mood rather than his prevailing outlook. Oddly enough, the setting of the poem — the place where the poet has these thoughts — is withheld till we come to this concluding passage, line 40.

There are various awkwardnesses in images, movement of thought and feeling, pattern of meter and rhyme. Yet the lack of conventional design and finish is offset by an intriguing unexpectedness, growing out of free perception. Emerson's "rough" technique will prepare us for Whitman, Emily Dickinson, and many poets of the twentieth century.

Little thinks, in the field, yon red-cloaked clown
Of thee from the hill-top looking down;
The heifer that lows in the upland farm,
Far-heard, lows not thine ear to charm;
The sexton, tolling his bell at noon,   5
Deems not that great Napoleon
Stops his horse, and lists with delight,
Whilst his files sweep round yon Alpine height;
Nor knowest thou what argument
Thy life to thy neighbor's creed has lent.   10
All are needed by each one;
Nothing is fair or good alone.
I thought the sparrow's note from heaven,
Singing at dawn on the alder bough;
I brought him home, in his nest, at even;   15
He sings the song, but it cheers not now,
For I did not bring home the river and sky; —
He sang to my ear, — they sang to my eye.

The delicate shells lay on the shore;
The bubbles of the latest wave   20
Fresh pearls to their enamel gave,
And the bellowing of the savage sea
Greeted their safe escape to me.
I wiped away the weeds and foam,
I fetched my sea-born treasures home;   25
But the poor, unsightly, noisome things
Had left their beauty on the shore
With the sun and the sand and the wild uproar.
The lover watched his graceful maid,
As 'mid the virgin train she strayed,   30
Nor knew her beauty's best attire
Was woven still by the snow-white choir.
At last she came to his hermitage,
Like the bird from the woodlands to the cage; —
The gay enchantment was undone,   35
A gentle wife, but fairy none.
Then I said, "I covet truth;
Beauty is unripe childhood's cheat;
I leave it behind with the games of youth:" —
As I spoke, beneath my feet   40
The ground-pine curled its pretty wreath,
Running over the club-moss burrs;
I inhaled the violet's breath;
Around me stood the oaks and firs;
Pine-cones and acorns lay on the ground;   45
Over me soared the eternal sky,
Full of light and of deity;
Again I saw, again I heard,
The rolling river, the morning bird; —
Beauty through my senses stole;   50
I yielded myself to the perfect whole.

Concord Hymn

Sung at the Completion of the Battle Monument, July 4, 1837

This poem, in which Emerson wrote a line heard round the world, is so familiar that it is difficult to read freshly, difficult to do justice to its stately design, its quiet compactness, its genuine feeling beneath simple words. These decorous sentences seem representative rather than personal, American rather than Emersonian. This is why the poem is not far — despite the distance in time — from Freneau's "To the Memory of the Brave Americans" (page 172). It was written, not to be spoken by the poet, but to be sung by the people assembled at the monument, to the tune of "Old Hundred."

Why Emerson was capable of so sure an utterance will be clearer if we recall his lines "America, My Country" (page 297), and note that, two years before the hymn, he had delivered a "Historical

Discourse at Concord," for the two hundredth anniversary of his ancestral town, a discourse lasting an hour and three quarters! For this he had prepared himself by interviewing survivors of the fight at Concord and by reading (his table groaning with books) with something like a scholar's zeal. The poem was no casual performance.

By the rude bridge that arched the flood,
  Their flag to April's breeze unfurled,
Here once the embattled farmers stood
  And fired the shot heard round the world.

The foe long since in silence slept;   5
  Alike the conqueror silent sleeps;
And Time the ruined bridge has swept
  Down the dark stream which seaward creeps.

On this green bank, by this soft stream,
  We set to-day a votive stone;   10
That memory may their deed redeem,
  When, like our sires, our sons are gone.

Spirit, that made those heroes dare
  To die, and leave their children free,
Bid Time and Nature gently spare   15
  The shaft we raise to them and thee.

The Humble-Bee

(w. 1837?)

Burly, dozing humble-bee,
Where thou art is clime for me.
Let them sail for Porto Rique,
Far-off hearts through seas to seek;
I will follow thee alone,   5
Thou animated torrid zone!
Zigzag steerer, desert cheerer,
Let me chase thy waving lines;
Keep me nearer, me thy hearer,
Singing over shrubs and vines.   10

Insect lover of the sun,
Joy of thy dominion!
Sailor of the atmosphere;
Swimmer through the waves of air;
Voyager of light and noon;   15
Epicurean of June;
Wait, I prithee, till I come
Within earshot of thy hum, —
All without is martyrdom.

When the south wind, in May days,   20
With a net of shining haze

Silvers the horizon wall,
And with softness touching all,
Tints the human countenance
With a color of romance,   25
And infusing subtle heats,
Turns the sod to violets,
Thou, in sunny solitudes,
Rover of the underwoods,
The green silence dost displace   30
With thy mellow, breezy bass.

Hot midsummer's petted crone,
Sweet to me thy drowsy tone
Tells of countless sunny hours,
Long days, and solid banks of flowers;   35
Of gulfs of sweetness without bound
In Indian wildernesses found;
Of Syrian peace, immortal leisure,
Firmest cheer, and bird-like pleasure.

Aught unsavory or unclean   40
Hath my insect never seen;
But violets and bilberry bells,
Maple-sap and daffodels,
Grass with green flag half-mast high,
Succory to match the sky,   45
Columbine with horn of honey,
Scented fern, and agrimony,
Clover, catchfly, adder's-tongue
And brier-roses, dwelt among;
All beside was unknown waste,   50
All was picture as he passed.

Wiser far than human seer,
Yellow-breeched philosopher!
Seeing only what is fair,
Sipping only what is sweet,   55
Thou dost mock at fate and care,
Leave the chaff, and take the wheat.
When the fierce northwestern blast
Cools sea and land so far and fast,
Thou already slumberest deep;   60
Woe and want thou canst outsleep;
Want and woe, which torture us,
Thy sleep makes ridiculous.

The Problem

(w. 1839)

✣ Seven years before, Emerson had made his
decision to abandon the minister's vocation. But the
problem he had faced continued to haunt him. It is
stated clearly in the journal:

"I dislike to be a clergyman and refuse to be one. Yet
how rich a music would be to me a holy clergyman
in my town. It seems to me he cannot be a man,
quite and whole; yet how plain is the need of one,
and how high, yes, highest is the function. Here is
division of labor that I like not: a man must sacrifice
his manhood for the social good. Something is
wrong; I see not what."

In the poem, the problem is almost lost to view,
because the argument is so one-sided. The case
against the ministry remains to the end unstated.
The case *for* it is this argument:

What could be higher than the office of a minister,
who speaks for and from God? From a divine source
— "the vast soul," "the heart of nature" — come all
religious expressions, whether oracles, litanies, Bible,
statues (the Jove of Phidias), churches and temples,
monuments (Pyramids), the Church Fathers, or
eloquent divines. In all there is an organic necessity,
like that in nature — the woodbird's nest, the sea-
shell, the pine's needles, the growing grass.

I like a church; I like a cowl;
I love a prophet of the soul;
And on my heart monastic aisles
Fall like sweet strains, or pensive smiles;
Yet not for all his faith can see   5
Would I that cowlèd churchman be.

Why should the vest on him allure,
Which I could not on me endure?

Not from a vain or shallow thought
His awful Jove young Phidias brought;   10
Never from lips of cunning fell
The thrilling Delphic oracle;
Out from the heart of nature rolled
The burdens of the Bible old;
The litanies of nations came,   15
Like the volcano's tongue of flame,
Up from the burning core below, —
The canticles of love and woe:
The hand that rounded Peter's dome
And groined the aisles of Christian Rome   20
Wrought in a sad sincerity:
Himself from God he could not free;
He builded better than he knew; —
The conscious stone to beauty grew.

Know'st thou what wove yon woodbird's nest   25
Of leaves, and feathers from her breast?
Or how the fish outbuilt her shell,
Painting with morn her annual cell?
Or how the sacred pine-tree adds
To her old leaves new myriads?   30
Such and so grew these holy piles,

Whilst love and terror laid the tiles.
Earth proudly wears the Parthenon,
As the best gem upon her zone,
And Morning opes with haste her lids   35
To gaze upon the Pyramids;
O'er England's abbeys bends the sky,
As on its friends, with kindred eye;
For out of Thought's interior sphere
These wonders rose to upper air;   40
And Nature gladly gave them place,
Adopted them into her race,
And granted them an equal date
With Andes and with Ararat.

These temples grew as grows the grass;   45
Art might obey, but not surpass.
The passive Master lent his hand
To the vast soul that o'er him planned;
And the same power that reared the shrine
Bestrode the tribes that knelt within.   50
Ever the fiery Pentecost
Girds with one flame the countless host,
Trances the heart through chanting choirs,
And through the priest the mind inspires.
The word unto the prophet spoken   55
Was writ on tables yet unbroken;
The word by seers or sibyls told,
In groves of oak, or fanes of gold,
Still floats upon the morning wind,
Still whispers to the willing mind.   60
One accent of the Holy Ghost
The heedless world hath never lost.
I know what say the fathers wise, —
The Book itself before me lies,
Old *Chrysostom*, best Augustine,   65
And he who blent both in his line,
The younger *Golden Lips* or mines,
Taylor, the Shakespeare of divines.
His words are music in my ear,
I see this cowlèd portrait dear;   70
And yet, for all his faith could see,
I would not the good bishop be.

Woodnotes, I

(1840)

Wordsworth, one of Emerson's masters, characteristically conferred upon nature his own solemnity, and made her seem old. Emerson, tempering his seriousness with a sprightly mood and rhythm, made her seem young. In his journal of the time of this poem is a recurrent romantic irresponsibility. "My life is a May game, I will live as I like. I defy your strait-laced, weary, social ways and modes.

Blue is the sky, green the fields and groves, fresh the springs, glad the rivers. . . ." "I wish to write such rhymes as shall not suggest a restraint, but contrariwise the wildest freedom."

In regard to nature lore, Emerson always deferred to his young friend Thoreau, who had reached manhood only a year or two before this poem was written. Thoreau is almost certainly the "forest seer" of the passage beginning at line 30.

1

When the pine tosses its cones
To the song of its waterfall tones,
Who speeds to the woodland walks?
To birds and trees who talks?
Cæsar of his leafy Rome,   5
There the poet is at home.
He goes to the river-side, —
Not hook nor line hath he;
He stands in the meadows wide, —
Nor gun nor scythe to see.   10
Sure some god his eye enchants:
What he knows nobody wants.
In the wood he travels glad,
Without better fortune had,
Melancholy without bad.   15
Knowledge this man prizes best
Seems fantastic to the rest:
Pondering shadows, colors, clouds,
Grass-buds and caterpillar-shrouds,
Boughs on which the wild bees settle,   20
Tints that spot the violet's petal,
Why Nature loves the number five,
And why the star-form she repeats:
Lover of all things alive,
Wonderer at all he meets,   25
Wonderer chiefly at himself,
Who can tell him what he is?
Or how meet in human elf
Coming and past eternities?

2

And such I knew, a forest seer,   30
A minstrel of the natural year,
Foreteller of the vernal ides,
Wise harbinger of spheres and tides,
A lover true, who knew by heart
Each joy the mountain dales impart;   35
It seemed that Nature could not raise
A plant in any secret place,
In quaking bog, on snowy hill,
Beneath the grass that shades the rill,
Under the snow, between the rocks,   40
In damp fields known to bird and fox,
But he would come in the very hour

It opened in its virgin bower,
As if a sunbeam showed the place,
And tell its long-descended race. 45
It seemed as if the breezes brought him,
It seemed as if the sparrows taught him;
As if by secret sight he knew
Where, in far fields, the orchis grew.
Many haps fall in the field 50
Seldom seen by wishful eyes,
But all her shows did Nature yield,
To please and win this pilgrim wise.
He saw the partridge drum in the woods;
He heard the woodcock's evening hymn; 55
He found the tawny thrushes' broods;
And the shy hawk did wait for him;
What others did at distance hear,
And guessed within the thicket's gloom,
Was shown to this philosopher, 60
And at his bidding seemed to come.

3

In unploughed Maine he sought the lumberers'
gang 62
Where from a hundred lakes young rivers sprang;
He trode the unplanted forest floor, whereon
The all-seeing sun for ages hath not shone; 65
Where feeds the moose, and walks the surly bear,
And up the tall mast runs the woodpecker.
He saw beneath dim aisles, in odorous beds,
The slight Linnæa hang its twin-born heads,
And blessed the monument of the man of
flowers, 70
Which breathes his sweet fame through the
northern bowers.
He heard, when in the grove, at intervals,
With sudden roar the aged pine-tree falls, —
One crash, the death-hymn of the perfect tree,
Declares the close of its green century. 75
Low lies the plant to whose creation went
Sweet influence from every element;
Whose living towers the years conspired to build,
Whose giddy top the morning loved to gild.
Through these green tents, by eldest Nature
dressed, 80
He roamed, content alike with man and beast.
Where darkness found him he lay glad at night;
There the red morning touched him with its
light.
Three moons his great heart him a hermit made,
So long he roved at will the boundless shade. 85
The timid it concerns to ask their way,
And fear what foe in caves and swamps can stray,
To make no step until the event is known,
And ills to come as evils past bemoan.

Not so the wise; no coward watch he keeps 90
To spy what danger on his pathway creeps;
Go where he will, the wise man is at home,
His hearth the earth, — his hall the azure dome;
Where his clear spirit leads him, there's his road
By God's own light illumined and foreshowed.

4

'Twas one of the charmèd days 96
When the genius of God doth flow;
The wind may alter twenty ways,
A tempest cannot blow;
It may blow north, it still is warm; 100
Or south, it still is clear;
Or east, it smells like a clover-farm;
Or west, no thunder fear.
The musing peasant, lowly great,
Beside the forest water sate; 105
The rope-like pine-roots crosswise grown
Composed the network of his throne;
The wide lake, edged with sand and grass,
Was burnished to a floor of glass,
Painted with shadows green and proud 110
Of the tree and of the cloud.
He was the heart of all the scene;
On him the sun looked more serene;
To hill and cloud his face was known, —
It seemed the likeness of their own; 115
They knew by secret sympathy
The public child of earth and sky.
"You ask," he said, "what guide
Me through trackless thickets led,
Through thick-stemmed woodlands rough and
wide, 120
I found the water's bed.
The watercourses were my guide;
I travelled grateful by their side,
Or through their channel dry;
They led me through the thicket damp, 125
Through brake and fern, the beavers' camp,
Through beds of granite cut my road,
And their resistless friendship showed.
The falling waters led me,
The foodful waters fed me, 130
And brought me to the lowest land,
Unerring to the ocean sand.
The moss upon the forest bark
Was pole-star when the night was dark;
The purple berries in the wood 135
Supplied me necessary food;
For Nature ever faithful is
To such as trust her faithfulness.
When the forest shall mislead me,
When the night and morning lie, 140

When sea and land refuse to feed me,
'Twill be time enough to die;
Then will yet my mother yield
A pillow in her greenest field,
Nor the June flowers scorn to cover   145
The clay of their departed lover."

The Snow-Storm

(1841)

Announced by all the trumpets of the sky,
Arrives the snow, and, driving o'er the fields,
Seems nowhere to alight: the whited air
Hides hills and woods, the river, and the
     heaven,
And veils the farm-house at the garden's end. 5
The sled and traveller stopped, the courier's feet
Delayed, all friends shut out, the housemates sit
Around the radiant fireplace, enclosed
In a tumultuous privacy of storm.

Come see the north wind's masonry.   10
Out of an unseen quarry evermore
Furnished with tile, the fierce artificer
Curves his white bastions with projected roof
Round every windward stake, or tree, or door.
Speeding the myriad-handed, his wild work 15
So fanciful, so savage, nought cares he
For number or proportion. Mockingly,
On coop or kennel he hangs Parian wreaths;
A swan-like form invests the hidden thorn;
Fills up the farmer's lane from wall to wall, 20
Maugre the farmer's sighs; and at the gate
A tapering turret overtops the work.
And when his hours are numbered, and the
     world
Is all his own, retiring, as he were not,
Leaves, when the sun appears, astonished Art 25
To mimic in slow structures, stone by stone,
Built in an age, the mad wind's night-work,
The frolic architecture of the snow.

Grace

(1842)

Gayly romantic in "Woodnotes," Emerson
could be soberly Christian, even Puritan, as in
"Grace." In this poem, which he wrote in his copy
of Milton's Prose Works, life is not a May game,
nor are social ways and modes strait-laced and
wearisome. Instead of wild freedom, divine grace.
Man is weak, needs defences against himself, such
as those in line 3, provided by God. In two lines

later omitted, lines in harmony with traditional
Christianity, Emerson found these defences

". . . props to my tottering conscience,
     Hedges to my soul from Satan's creeping feet."

In his journal he had much earlier (March 1833)
confessed the same sense of man's dependence, giving
a different set of aids to virtue: "I think now that we
need all the advantages we can get, that our virtue
wants all the crutches; that we must avail ourselves
of our strength, and weakness, and want of appetite,
and press of affairs, and of calculation, and of fear,
as well as of the just and sublime considerations of
the love of God and of self-respect."

How much, preventing God! how much I owe
To the defences thou hast round me set:
Example, custom, fear, occasion slow, —
These scornèd bondmen were my parapet.
I dare not peep over this parapet   5
To gauge with glance the roaring gulf below,
The depths of sin to which I had descended,
Had not these me against myself defended.

Ode

Inscribed to W. H. Channing

(1846)

Which is the better way to improve society —
the reform of its institutions or the renovation of its
members? To Emerson the answer seemed clear:
"The criticism and attack on institutions, which we
have witnessed, has made one thing plain, that society
gains nothing whilst a man, not himself renovated,
attempts to renovate things around him." As he said
in compact verse:

"He who feeds men serveth few;
     He serves all who dares be true."

William Henry Channing, nephew of the great
Unitarian leader, was a minister and humanitarian
who espoused such causes as Fourierism and aboli-
tionism. To this good friend Emerson addressed his
ode in reply to those who deplored his own aloofness
from humanitarian movements, especially the anti-
slavery movement. Actually, as a citizen, Emerson
spoke out against the institution of Negro slavery.
But as a "scholar" (writer, man of letters) he held
to his conviction that American society was a slave
to materialism, that it could not be improved by
external measures, that the remedy lay in an inner
change, an awakening of the individual to truth, and
love, and discipline.

Emerson's reply to the reformers is developed in

four stages. *Lines 1–11:* He, like any individual, has his chosen work to do; for him it centers in his study. *Lines 12–43:* The method of politics fails. Note his bitter comment on the Mexican war; on the Fugitive Slave Law that subverted even the freedom-loving mountaineer (Contoocook is a New Hampshire river, Agiochook is an Indian name for the White Mountains); on the willingness to destroy the Union (secession of the North to dissociate itself from slavery). *Lines 44–70:* Let man serve law for man, not law for thing. Concentration on things betrays the dignity of man, unkings him; let him concentrate instead on friendship, love, truth, harmony. *Lines 71–97:* The over-god, joining right and might in his good time, is sure to bring good out of evil.

What is the effect of the staccato rhythm — the short, abrupt lines, the packed phrases? What advantages has the poem over a prose discourse following the same plan of development?

Though loath to grieve
The evil time's sole patriot,
I cannot leave
My honeyed thought
For the priest's cant,   5
Or the statesman's rant.

If I refuse
My study for their politique,
Which at the best is trick,
The angry Muse   10
Puts confusion in my brain.

But who is he that prates
Of the culture of mankind,
Of better arts and life?
Go, blindworm, go,   15
Behold the famous States
Harrying Mexico
With rifle and with knife!

Or who, with accent bolder,
Dare praise the freedom-loving mountaineer?   20
I found by thee, O rushing Contoocook!
And in thy valleys, Agiochook!
The jackals of the negro-holder.

The God who made New Hampshire
Taunted the lofty land   25
With little men: —
Small bat and wren
House in the oak: —

If earth-fire cleave
The upheaved land, and bury the folk,   30
The southern crocodile would grieve.

Virtue palters; Right is hence;
Freedom praised, but hid;
Funeral eloquence
Rattles the coffin-lid.   35

What boots thy zeal,
O glowing friend,
That would indignant rend
The northland from the south?
Wherefore? to what good end?   40
Boston Bay and Bunker Hill
Would serve things still; —
Things are of the snake.

The horseman serves the horse,
The neatherd serves the neat,   45
The merchant serves the purse,
The eater serves his meat;
'Tis the day of the chattel,
Web to weave, and corn to grind;
Things are in the saddle,   50
And ride mankind.

There are two laws discrete,
Not reconciled, —
Law for man, and law for thing;
The last builds town and fleet,   55
But it runs wild,
And doth the man unking.

'Tis fit the forest fall,
The steep be graded,
The mountain tunnelled,   60
The sand shaded,
The orchard planted,
The glebe tilled,
The prairie granted,
The steamer built.   65

Let man serve law for man;
Live for friendship, live for love,
For truth's and harmony's behoof;
The state may follow how it can,
As Olympus follows Jove.   70

Yet do not I implore
The wrinkled shopman to my sounding woods,
Nor bid the unwilling senator
Ask votes of thrushes in the solitudes.
Every one to his chosen work; —   75
Foolish hands may mix and mar;
Wise and sure the issues are.
Round they roll till dark is light,
Sex to sex, and even to odd; —

The over-god   80
Who marries Right to Might,
Who peoples, unpeoples, —
He who exterminates
Races by stronger races,
Black by white faces, —   85
Knows to bring honey
Out of the lion;
Grafts gentlest scion
On pirate and Turk.
The Cossack eats Poland,   90
Like stolen fruit;
Her last noble is ruined,
Her last poet mute:
Straight, into double band
The victors divide;   95
Half for freedom strike and stand; —
The astonished Muse finds thousands at her
    side.

Merlin

(w. 1846)

❧ In medieval romance Merlin was bard, prophet,
magician, counselor of King Arthur. Emerson used
the name, with some of its romantic connotations, to
represent himself, as poet, ideally.

1

Thy trivial harp will never please
Or fill my craving ear;
Its chords should ring as blows the breeze,
Free, peremptory, clear.
No jingling serenader's art,   5
Nor tinkle of piano strings,
Can make the wild blood start
In its mystic springs.
The kingly bard
Must smite the chords rudely and hard,   10
As with hammer or with mace;
That they may render back
Artful thunder, which conveys
Secrets of the solar track,
Sparks of the supersolar blaze.   15
Merlin's blows are strokes of fate,
Chiming with the forest tone,
When boughs buffet boughs in the wood;
Chiming with the gasp and moan
Of the ice-imprisoned flood;   20
With the pulse of manly hearts;
With the voice of orators;
With the din of city arts;
With the cannonades of wars;

With the marches of the brave;   25
And prayers of might from martyrs' cave.

Great is the art,
Great be the manners, of the bard.
He shall not his brain encumber
With the coil of rhythm and number;   30
But, leaving the rule and pale forethought,
He shall aye climb
For his rhyme.
"Pass in, pass in," the angels say,
"In to the upper doors,   35
Nor count compartments of the floors,
But mount to paradise
By the stairway of surprise."

Blameless master of the games,
King of sport that never shames,   40
He shall daily joy dispense
Hid in song's sweet influence.
Forms more cheerly live and go,
What time the subtle mind
Sings aloud the tune whereto   45
Their pulses beat,
And march their feet,
And their members are combined.

By Sybarites beguiled,
He shall no task decline;   50
Merlin's mighty line
Extremes of nature reconciled, —
Bereaved a tyrant of his will,
And made the lion mild.
Songs can the tempest still,   55
Scattered on the stormy air,
Mould the year to fair increase,
And bring in poetic peace.

He shall not seek to weave,
In weak, unhappy times,   60
Efficacious rhymes;
Wait his returning strength,
Bird that from the nadir's floor
To the zenith's top can soar, —
The soaring orbit of the muse exceeds that jour-
    ney's length.   65
Nor profane affect to hit
Or compass that, by meddling wit,
Which only the propitious mind
Publishes when 'tis inclined.
There are open hours   70
When the God's will sallies free,
And the dull idiot might see
The flowing fortunes of a thousand years; —

Sudden, at unawares,
Self-moved, fly-to the doors,   75
Nor sword of angels could reveal
What they conceal.

2

The rhyme of the poet
Modulates the king's affairs;
Balance-loving Nature   80
Made all things in pairs.
To every foot its antipode;
Each color with its counter glowed;
To every tone beat answering tones,
Higher or graver;   85
Flavor gladly blends with flavor;
Leaf answers leaf upon the bough;
And match the paired cotyledons.
Hands to hands, and feet to feet,
In one body grooms and brides;   90
Eldest rite, two married sides
In every mortal meet.
Light's far furnace shines,
Smelting balls and bars,
Forging double stars,   95
Glittering twins and trines.
The animals are sick with love,
Lovesick with rhyme;
Each with all propitious Time
Into chorus wove.   100
Like the dancers' ordered band,
Thoughts come also hand in hand;
In equal couples mated,
Or else alternated;
Adding by their mutual gage,   105
One to other, health and age.
Solitary fancies go
Short-lived wandering to and fro,
Most like to bachelors,
Or an ungiven maid,   110
Not ancestors,
With no posterity to make the lie afraid,
Or keep truth undecayed.
Perfect-paired as eagle's wings,
Justice is the rhyme of things;   115
Trade and counting use
The self-same tuneful muse;
And Nemesis,
Who with even matches odd.
Who athwart space redresses   120
The partial wrong,
Fills the just period,
And finishes the song.

Subtle rhymes, with ruin rife,

Murmur in the house of life,   125
Sung by the Sisters as they spin;
In perfect time and measure they
Build and unbuild our echoing clay.
As the two twilights of the day
Fold us music-drunken in.   130

Bacchus
(w. 1846)

🦋 Romantic poetry often feeds upon itself —
poetry is written about poetry, since the best life is
held to be poetic. For example, Keats, in his ode to
a nightingale, calls for a "draught" from the spring
of the Muses, so that, intoxicated with Poesy, he may
escape from life's fever. He craves not the wine of
"Bacchus" but the "true" wine, typified in the deathless "music" of the bird. Though Emerson's poem
is very different, he too calls for a "draught," not
of the wine of "Bacchus" but the "true" wine, which
is poetry — "music." Inspired by this joy-giving,
form-making power, he would enter into the meaning
of life and nature, experience reality in its pristine,
dazzling freshness.

Through the ages, the concept of poetic inspiration
has been associated with Plato — as it was by Emerson when, in a copy of his own *Poems*, he wrote as
a motto for "Bacchus" a sentence from the *Phaedrus:*
"The man who is his own master knocks in vain at
the door of poetry." Emerson wishes to be "assimilated" by a draught of the wine of inspiration. Notice
that it is "the remembering wine" of the grape, not
the forgetting juice of the lote (lotus). Like Wordsworth in his great ode on immortality, he turns to
Plato's doctrine of recollection. Most of life is a
forgetting of the high truth we inwardly know, the
truth we have brought, as it were, from a previous
state of existence. What Emerson calls "use" (habit,
custom) erects "walls" between the poet and this
truth. The promise of his days brings only disappointment, "despair." He desires the compensation that
poetic inspiration might bring, the wine of the vine
growing in a timeless region, "in the silver hills of
heaven." It might renew his memories, restore him to
the level of true being, enable him to write as one
present on "the first day" when all was new.
(Cf. Goethe's *Faust:* "herrlich wie am ersten Tag,"
"bright as on the first day," i.e. at Creation.)

Bring me wine, but wine which never grew
In the belly of the grape,
Or grew on vine whose tap-roots, reaching
          through
Under the Andes to the Cape,
Suffered no savor of the earth to scape.   5

Let its grapes the morn salute
From a nocturnal root,
Which feels the acrid juice
Of Styx and Erebus;
And turns the woe of Night,   10
By its own craft, to a more rich delight.

We buy ashes for bread;
We buy diluted wine;
Give me of the true, —
Whose ample leaves and tendrils curled   15
Among the silver hills of heaven,
Draw everlasting dew;
Wine of wine,
Blood of the world,
Form of forms, and mould of statures,   20
That I intoxicated,
And by the draught assimilated,
May float at pleasure through all natures;
The bird-language rightly spell,
And that which roses say so well.   25
Wine that is shed
Like the torrents of the sun
Up the horizon walls,
Or like the Atlantic streams, which run
When the South Sea calls.   30

Water and bread,
Food which needs no transmuting,
Rainbow-flowering, wisdom-fruiting
Wine which is already man,
Food which teach and reason can.   35

Wine which Music is, —
Music and wine are one, —
That I, drinking this,
Shall hear far Chaos talk with me;
Kings unborn shall walk with me;   40
And the poor grass shall plot and plan
What it will do when it is man.
Quickened so, will I unlock
Every crypt of every rock.

I thank the joyful juice   45
For all I know; —
Winds of remembering
Of the ancient being blow,
And seeming-solid walls of use
Open and flow.   50

Pour, Bacchus! the remembering wine;
Retrieve the loss of me and mine!
Vine for vine be antidote,
And the grape requite the lote!

Haste to cure the old despair, —   55
Reason in Nature's lotus drenched,
The memory of ages quenched;
Give them again to shine;
Let wine repair what this undid;

And where the infection slid,   60
A dazzling memory revive;
Refresh the faded tints,
Recut the aged prints,
And write my old adventures with the pen
Which on the first day drew,   65
Upon the tablets blue,
The dancing Pleiads and eternal men.

Give All to Love

(1847)

Emerson wrote several poems about love, rather than love poems. In "Give All to Love" there is, in three stanzas, an abandon such as might be expected of the author of "Bacchus." As R. L. Rusk has summed up the poem: "It opened with one of Emerson's most uninhibited recommendations of love but ended with the cool advice that stoical self-reliance be kept alive underneath the passion, ready to play its part in case of need, and with the equally assured declaration of faith in compensation should the beloved be lost." What might be the "gods" of the last line?

Give all to love;
Obey thy heart;
Friends, kindred, days,
Estate, good-fame,
Plans, credit and the Muse, —   5
Nothing refuse.
'Tis a brave master;
Let it have scope:
Follow it utterly,
Hope beyond hope: 10
High and more high
It dives into noon,
With wing unspent,
Untold intent;
But it is a god,   15
Knows its own path
And the outlets of the sky.

It was never for the mean;
It requireth courage stout,
Souls above doubt,   20
Valor unbending,
It will reward, —

They shall return
More than they were,
And ever ascending.   25

Leave all for love;
Yet, hear me, yet,
One word more thy heart behoved,
One pulse more of firm endeavor, —
Keep thee to-day,   30
To-morrow, forever,
Free as an Arab
Of thy beloved.

Cling with life to the maid;
But when the surprise,   35
First vague shadow of surmise
Flits across her bosom young,
Of a joy apart from thee,
Free be she, fancy-free;
Nor thou detain her vesture's hem,   40
Nor the palest rose she flung
From her summer diadem.

Though thou loved her as thyself,
As a self of purer clay,
Though her parting dims the days,   45
Stealing grace from all alive;
Heartily know,
When half-gods go,
The gods arrive.

Hamatreya

(1847)

Emerson here adapted to his own poetical use a passage from the Hindu *Vishnu Parana* which he had copied into his journal: "These, and other kings who with perishable frames have possessed this ever-enduring world, and who, blinded with deceptive notions of individual occupation, have indulged the feeling that suggests 'This earth is mine, — it is my son's, — it belongs to my dynasty,' — have all passed away. So, many who reigned before them, many who succeeded them, and many who are yet to come, have ceased or will cease to be. Earth laughs, as if smiling with autumnal flowers to behold her kings unable to effect the subjugation of themselves. I will repeat to you, Maitreya, [Emerson's Hamatreya] the stanzas that were chanted by Earth."

The names in the first line of the poem are those of the first settlers of Concord.

Bulkeley, Hunt, Willard, Hosmer, Meriam, Flint

Possessed the land which rendered to their toil
Hay, corn, roots, hemp, flax, apples, wool and
    wood.
Each of these landlords walked amidst his farm,
Saying, "'Tis mine, my children's and my
    name's.   5
How sweet the west wind sounds in my own
    trees!
How graceful climb those shadows on my hill!
I fancy these pure waters and the flags
Know me, as does my dog: we sympathize;
And, I affirm, my actions smack of the soil." 10

Where are these men? Asleep beneath their
    grounds:
And strangers, fond as they, their furrows
    plough.
Earth laughs in flowers, to see her boastful boys
Earth-proud, proud of the earth which is not
    theirs;
Who steer the plough, but cannot steer their
    feet   15
Clear of the grave.
They added ridge to valley, brook to pond,
And sighed for all that bounded their domain;
"This suits me for a pasture; that's my park;
We must have clay, lime, gravel, granite-ledge,
And misty lowland, where to go for peat.   21
The land is well, — lies fairly to the south.
'Tis good, when you have crossed the sea and
    back,
To find the sitfast acres where you left them."
Ah! the hot owner sees not Death, who adds   25
Him to his land, a lump of mould the more.
Hear what the Earth says:

EARTH-SONG

"Mine and yours;
Mine, not yours.
Earth endures;   30
Stars abide —
Shine down in the old sea;
Old are the shores;
But where are old men?
I who have seen much,   35
Such have I never seen.

"The lawyer's deed
Ran sure,
In tail,
To them, and to their heirs   40
Who shall succeed,
Without fail,
Forevermore.

"Here is the land,
Shaggy with wood,   45
With its old valley,
Mound and flood.
But the heritors? —
Fled like the flood's foam.
The lawyer, and the laws,   50
And the kingdom,
Clean swept herefrom.

"They called me theirs,
Who so controlled me;
Yet every one   55
Wished to stay, and is gone,
How am I theirs,
If they cannot hold me,
But I hold them?"

When I heard the Earth-song   60
I was no longer brave;
My avarice cooled
Like lust in the chill of the grave.

Days

(w. 1851)

Eleven years earlier, he had written to Margaret Fuller: "Heaven walks among us ordinarily muffled in such triple or tenfold disguises that the wisest are deceived and no one suspects the days to be gods." In 1847, on the eve of his birthday, he wrote in his journal: "The days come and go like muffled and veiled figures sent from a distant friendly party, but they say nothing, and if we do not use the gifts they bring, they carry them as silently away."

When, after several more years, he finally wrote and revised the poem, it had an absolute rightness. It translated into the medium of high poetry the old Puritan dread of the waste of God's gift of time, that earnestness which Longfellow had expressed on a low plane in "A Psalm of Life," with all its singsong banalities ("Time is fleeting," "Let us, then, be up and doing," etc.).

In Emerson's poem time is not a vague abstraction. Silent and muffled like Mohammedan friars, the daughters of Time deceive us by disguising their divinity. As they march past, they offer to each of us gifts, from diadems (another Oriental touch) to bundles of sticks, from bread to the sky. We have free will to choose. In the second half of the poem Emerson becomes still more concrete, instances himself and a single Day. In his garden, under interwoven branches, he watched the pomp (solemn procession) and took from the Day only a few trifles. As the Day departed he saw, too late, under her hair band, her scorn at his choice.

The poem has the impact of a rich brevity. There are only eleven lines, four sentences, but into them Emerson has packed, with a sure ease, a fascinating picture, a dramatic moment, a striking parable, an implied judgment, a solemn tone and adagio movement. Agreeing in advance with many of his most discriminating readers, Emerson regarded this as perhaps his best poem.

Daughters of Time, the hypocritic Days,
Muffled and dumb like barefoot dervishes,
And marching single in an endless file,
Bring diadems and fagots in their hands.
To each they offer gifts after his will,   5
Bread, kingdoms, stars, and sky that holds them
        all.
I, in my pleachèd garden, watched the pomp,
Forgot my morning wishes, hastily
Took a few herbs and apples, and the Day
Turned and departed silent. I, too late,   10
Under her solemn fillet saw the scorn.

Two Rivers

(w. 1856)

By the doctrine of correspondence, the river flowing through the meadows is a symbol of the unbounded Spirit that flows through all things: through the river itself, all of nature, and man, and time.

Thy summer voice, Musketaquit,
Repeats the music of the rain;
But sweeter rivers pulsing flit
Through thee, as thou through Concord Plain.

Thou in thy narrow banks are pent: 5
The stream I love unbounded goes
Through flood and sea and firmament;
Through light, through life, it forward flows.

I see the inundation sweet,
I hear the spending of the stream   10
Through years, through men, through Nature
        fleet,
Through love and thought, through power and
        dream.

Musketaquit, a goblin strong,
Of shard and flint makes jewels gay;
They lose their grief who hear his song,   15
And where he winds is the day of day.

So forth and brighter fares my stream, —
Who drink it shall not thirst again;
No darkness stains its equal gleam
And ages drop in it like rain.   20

Brahma

(w. 1856)

🙦 Why Emerson was attracted to Oriental
thought, as well as to Plato and Neo-Platonism, may
be seen in his essay on Plato. "In all nations there
are minds which incline to dwell in the conception
of the fundamental Unity. . . . This tendency finds
its highest expression in the religious writings of the
East, and chiefly in the Indian Scriptures."

In its day "Brahma" was ridiculed as incomprehensible. But its difficulties would have vanished, as
Emerson remarked, if readers had mentally altered
Brahma to Jehovah. Its ideas may be stated readily
enough in an outline:

Stanza 1: The soul of a man cannot be slain; it is
transformed. *Stanzas 2 and 3:* There is an identity
of being. All things — sunlight and shadow, past
and present, good and evil, the skeptic's doubt and
the Brahmin's hymn — share the deepest reality, are
manifestations of the Universal Soul. *Stanza 4:*
Limited gods desire in vain the abidingness which
belongs only to the Universal Soul, the Absolute.

Emerson conveys the sense not by the theological
abstractions one would expect in prose, but by a
poetical blending of ideas and images, as in the
parables and verbal paradoxes (e.g. he who loses his
life shall find it) of the New Testament. This is
made especially natural by the device of imputing the
words to the god Brahma.

If the red slayer think he slays,
  Or if the slain think he is slain,
They know not well the subtle ways
  I keep, and pass, and turn again.

Far or forgot to me is near;   5
  Shadow and sunlight are the same;
The vanished gods to me appear;
  And one to me are shame and fame.

They reckon ill who leave me out;
  When me they fly, I am the wings;   10
I am the doubter and the doubt,
  And I the hymn the Brahmin sings.

The strong gods pine for my abode,
  And pine in vain the sacred Seven;
But thou, meek lover of the good!   15
  Find me, and turn thy back on heaven.

Seashore

(w. 1857)

I heard or seemed to hear the chiding Sea
Say, Pilgrim, why so late and slow to come?
Am I not always here, thy summer home?
Is not my voice thy music, morn and eve?
My breath thy healthful climate in the heats,   5
My touch thy antidote, my bay thy bath?
Was ever building like my terraces?
Was ever couch magnificent as mine?
Lie on the warm rock-ledges, and there learn
A little hut suffices like a town.   10
I make your sculptured architecture vain,
Vain beside mine. I drive my wedges home,
And carve the coastwise mountain into caves.
Lo! here is Rome and Nineveh and Thebes,
Karnak and Pyramid and Giant's Stairs   15
Half piled or prostrate; and my newest slab
Older than all thy race.

                              Behold the Sea,
The opaline, the plentiful and strong,
Yet beautiful as is the rose in June,
Fresh as the trickling rainbow of July;   20
Sea full of food, the nourisher of kinds,
Purger of earth, and medicine of men;
Creating a sweet climate by my breath,
Washing out harms and griefs from memory,
And, in my mathematic ebb and flow,   25
Giving a hint of that which changes not.
Rich are the sea-gods: — who gives gifts but
            they?
They grope the sea for pearls, but more than
            pearls:
They pluck Force thence, and give it to the wise.
For every wave is wealth to Dædalus,   30
Wealth to the cunning artist who can work
This matchless strength. Where shall he find,
            O waves!
A load your Atlas shoulders cannot lift?

  I with my hammer pounding evermore
The rocky coast, smite Andes into dust,   35
Strewing my bed, and, in another age,
Rebuild a continent of better men.
Then I unbar the doors: my paths lead out
The exodus of nations: I disperse   39
Men to all shores that front the hoary main.

  I too have arts and sorceries;
Illusion dwells forever with the wave.
I know what spells are laid. Leave me to deal
With credulous and imaginative man;

For, though he scoop my water in his palm,   45
A few rods off he deems it gems and clouds.
Planting strange fruits and sunshine on the
    shore,
I make some coast alluring, some lone isle,
To distant men, who must go there, or die.

Terminus

(w. 1860)

It is time to be old
To take in sail:
The god of bounds,
Came to me in his fatal rounds
And said: "No more!   5
No farther spread
Thy broad ambitious branches and thy root.
Fancy departs: no more invent;
Contract thy firmament
To compass of a tent.   10
There's not enough for this and that,
Make thy option which of two;
Economize the failing river,
Not the less revere the Giver;
Leave the many and hold the few.   15
Timely wise, accept the terms,
Soften the fall with wary foot;
Still plan and smile,
And, fault of novel germs,
Mature the unfallen fruit.   20
Curse, if thou wilt, thy sires,
Bad husbands of their fires,
Who, when they gave thee breath,
Failed to bequeath
The needful sinew stark as once,   25
The Baresark marrow to thy bones,
But left a legacy of ebbing veins,
Inconstant heat and nerveless reins;
Amid the Muses left thee deaf and dumb,
Amid the gladiators halt and numb."   30

As the bird trims her to the gale,
I trim myself to the storm of time;
I man the rudder, reef the sail,
Obey the voice at eve obeyed at prime: 5
"Lowly faithful, banish fear,   35
Right onward drive unharmed;
The port, well worth the cruise, is near,
And every wave is charmed."
    10

Nature

(1836)

⚑ Blue, like the sky, a little book of 92 pages
appeared quietly, anonymously, in an edition of
only five hundred copies, in Boston, September
1836, less than two weeks before the first meeting
of the Transcendentalist Club. It was in effect
the manifesto of the Transcendental movement. It
was also the summation of Emerson's previous
thinking, and a ground-plan for his future work.
It stated the case for a philosophy of idealism
suggested to Emerson by the romantic Coleridge
and, behind him, by the new German philosophers,
and eighteenth-century Berkeley, and the seventeenth-century Cambridge Platonists, and the remoter tradition leading back to Plotinus and
finally Plato.

The book is not easy reading. Despite a show of
method, it is the work of a mind impatient of close
logical thinking. Emerson does not attempt, in the
manner of philosophers, carefully to build a demonstration. He throws out affirmations supported by
images rather than arguments, and appeals for an
instinctive response rather than rational assent. As
Oliver Wendell Holmes said, "Nature is a reflective
prose poem. It is divided into eight chapters, which
might almost as well have been called cantos. Beginning simply enough, it took more and more the
character of a rhapsody."

Introduction

⚑ In the spirit of the romantic revolt, Emerson dis-
parages the past and its traditions, champions the
present and originality. Instead of groping "among
the dry bones of the past," let us remember that
"There are new lands, new men, new thoughts."
Instead of a poetry and philosophy of "tradition,"
let us have "an original relation to the universe."

We shall inquire into the purposes and values of
nature, the entire Not Me (external nature, human
bodies, one's own body — everything but the Soul).

Our age is retrospective. It builds the sepul-
chres of the fathers. It writes biographies, histories, and criticism. The foregoing generations
beheld God and nature face to face; we, through
their eyes. Why should not we also enjoy an
original relation to the universe? Why should
not we have a poetry and philosophy of insight
and not of tradition, and a religion by revelation
to us, and not the history of theirs? Embosomed
for a season in nature, whose floods of life stream
around and through us, and invite us, by the
powers they supply, to action proportioned to
nature, why should we grope among the dry

bones of the past, or put the living generation into masquerade out of its faded wardrobe? The sun shines to-day also. There is more wool and flax in the fields. There are new lands, new men, new thoughts. Let us demand our own works and laws and worship.

Undoubtedly we have no questions to ask which are unanswerable. We must trust the perfection of the creation so far as to believe that whatever curiosity the order of things has awakened in our minds, the order of things can satisfy. Every man's condition is a solution in hieroglyphic to those inquiries he would put. He acts it as life, before he apprehends it as truth. In like manner, nature is already, in its forms and tendencies, describing its own design. Let us interrogate the great apparition that shines so peacefully around us. Let us inquire, to what end is nature?

All science has one aim, namely, to find a theory of nature. We have theories of races and of functions, but scarcely yet a remote approach to an idea of creation. We are now so far from the road to truth, that religious teachers dispute and hate each other, and speculative men are esteemed unsound and frivolous. But to a sound judgment, the most abstract truth is the most practical. Whenever a true theory appears, it will be its own evidence. Its test is, that it will explain all phenomena. Now many are thought not only unexplained but inexplicable; as language, sleep, madness, dreams, beasts, sex.

Philosophically considered, the universe is composed of Nature and the Soul. Strictly speaking, therefore, all that is separate from us, all which Philosophy distinguishes as the NOT ME, that is, both nature and art, all other men and my own body, must be ranked under this name, NATURE. In enumerating the values of nature and casting up their sum, I shall use the word in both senses; — in its common and in its philosophical import. In inquiries so general as our present one, the inaccuracy is not material; no confusion of thought will occur. Nature, in the common sense, refers to essences unchanged by man; space, the air, the river, the leaf. Art is applied to the mixture of his will with the same things, as in a house, a canal, a statue, a picture. But his operations taken together are so insignificant, a little chipping, baking, patching, and washing, that in an impression so grand as that of the world on the human mind, they do not vary the result.

I. Nature

❧ If we have not lost the responsiveness of the child, we feel in the presence of nature a strong delight. This delight comes not from nature but from spirit, or the harmony of nature and spirit.

In this chapter Emerson touches upon the dominant idea of his book: that nature is a symbol of the inner life of man and a symbol of the divine Being.

To go into solitude, a man needs to retire as much from his chamber as from society. I am not solitary whilst I read and write, though nobody is with me. But if a man would be alone, let him look at the stars. The rays that come from those heavenly worlds will separate between him and what he touches. One might think the atmosphere was made transparent with this design, to give man, in the heavenly bodies, the perpetual presence of the sublime. Seen in the streets of cities, how great they are! If the stars should appear one night in a thousand years, how would men believe and adore; and preserve for many generations the remembrance of the city of God which had been shown! But every night come out these envoys of beauty, and light the universe with their admonishing smile.

The stars awaken a certain reverence, because though always present, they are inaccessible; but all natural objects make a kindred impression, when the mind is open to their influence. Nature never wears a mean appearance. Neither does the wisest man extort her secret, and lose his curiosity by finding out all her perfection. Nature never became a toy to a wise spirit. The flowers, the animals, the mountains, reflected the wisdom of his best hour, as much as they had delighted the simplicity of his childhood.

When we speak of nature in this manner, we have a distinct but most poetical sense in the mind. We mean the integrity of impression made by manifold natural objects. It is this which distinguishes the stick of timber of the wood-cutter, from the tree of the poet. The charming landscape which I saw this morning is indubitably made up of some twenty or thirty farms. Miller owns this field, Locke that, and Manning the woodland beyond. But none of them owns the landscape. There is a property in the horizon which no man has but he whose eye can integrate all the parts, that is, the poet. This is the best part of these men's farms, yet to this their warranty-deeds give no title.

To speak truly, few adult persons can see nature. Most persons do not see the sun. At least they have a very superficial seeing. The sun illuminates only the eye of the man, but shines into the eye and the heart of the child. The lover of nature is he whose inward and outward senses are still truly adjusted to each other; who has retained the spirit of infancy even into the era of manhood. His intercourse with heaven and earth becomes part of his daily food. In the presence of nature a wild delight runs through the man, in spite of real sorrows. Nature says, — he is my creature, and maugre all his impertinent griefs, he shall be glad with me. Not the sun or the summer alone, but every hour and season yields its tribute of delight; for every hour and change corresponds to and authorizes a different state of the mind, from breathless noon to grimmest midnight. Nature is a setting that fits equally well a comic or a mourning piece. In good health, the air is a cordial of incredible virtue. Crossing a bare common, in snow puddles, at twilight, under a clouded sky, without having in my thoughts any occurrence of special good fortune, I have enjoyed a perfect exhilaration. I am glad to the brink of fear. In the woods, too, a man casts off his years, as the snake his slough, and at what period soever of life, is always a child. In the woods is perpetual youth. Within these plantations of God, a decorum and sanctity reign, a perennial festival is dressed, and the guest sees not how he should tire of them in a thousand years. In the woods, we return to reason and faith. There I feel that nothing can befall me in life, — no disgrace, no calamity (leaving me my eyes), which nature cannot repair. Standing on the bare ground, — my head bathed by the blithe air, and uplifted into infinite space, — all mean egotism vanishes. I become a transparent eye-ball; I am nothing; I see all; the currents of the Universal Being circulate through me. I am part or parcel of God. The name of the nearest friend sounds then foreign and accidental: to be brothers, to be acquaintances, master or servant, is then a trifle and a disturbance. I am the lover of uncontained and immortal beauty. In the wilderness, I find something more dear and connate than in streets or villages. In the tranquil landscape, and especially in the distant line of the horizon, man beholds somewhat as beautiful as his own nature.

The greatest delight which the fields and woods minister is the suggestion of an occult relation between man and the vegetable. I am not alone and unacknowledged. They nod to me, and I to them. The waving of the boughs in the storm is new to me and old. It takes me by surprise, and yet is not unknown. Its effect is like that of a higher thought or a better emotion coming over me, when I deemed I was thinking justly or doing right.

Yet it is certain that the power to produce this delight does not reside in nature, but in man, or in a harmony of both. It is necessary to use these pleasures with great temperance. For nature is not always tricked in holiday attire, but the same scene which yesterday breathed perfume and glittered as for the frolic of the nymphs, is overspread with melancholy to-day. Nature always wears the colors of the spirit. To a man laboring under calamity, the heat of his own fire hath sadness in it. Then there is a kind of contempt of the landscape felt by him who has just lost by death a dear friend. The sky is less grand as it shuts down over less worth in the population.

II. Commodity

Among the uses and values of nature the most obvious is commodity, the practical advantages that impress all men: nature's wind, rain, etc., and man's ships, canals, etc. In his useful arts man employs nature as material.

Whoever considers the final cause of the world will discern a multitude of uses that enter as parts into that result. They all admit of being thrown into one of the following classes: Commodity; Beauty; Language; and Discipline.

Under the general name of commodity, I rank all those advantages which our senses owe to nature. This, of course, is a benefit which is temporary and mediate, not ultimate, like its service to the soul. Yet although low, it is perfect in its kind, and is the only use of nature which all men apprehend. The misery of man appears like childish petulance, when we explore the steady and prodigal provision that has been made for his support and delight on this green ball which floats him through the heavens. What angels invented these splendid ornaments, these rich conveniences, this ocean of air above, this ocean of water beneath, this firmament of earth between? this zodiac of lights, this tent of dropping clouds, this striped coat of climates, this fourfold year? Beasts, fire, water, stones, and corn serve him. The field is at once his floor, his workyard, his play-ground, his garden.

> More servants wait on man
> Than he'll take notice of.

Nature, in its ministry to man, is not only the material, but is also the process and the result. All the parts incessantly work into each other's hands for the profit of man. The wind sows the seed; the sun evaporates the sea; the wind blows the vapor to the field; the ice, on the other side of the planet, condenses rain on this; the rain feeds the plant; the plant feeds the animal; and thus the endless circulations of the divine charity nourish man.

The useful arts are reproductions or new combinations by the wit of man, of the same natural benefactors. He no longer waits for favoring gales, but by means of steam, he realizes the fable of Æolus's bag, and carries the two and thirty winds in the boiler of his boat. To diminish friction, he paves the road with iron bars, and, mounting a coach with a ship-load of men, animals, and merchandise behind him, he darts through the country, from town to town, like an eagle or a swallow through the air. By the aggregate of these aids, how is the face of the world changed, from the era of Noah to that of Napoleon! The private poor man hath cities, ships, canals, bridges, built for him. He goes to the post-office, and the human race run on his errands; to the book-shop, and the human race read and write of all that happens, for him; to the court-house, and nations repair his wrongs. He sets his house upon the road, and the human race go forth every morning, and shovel out the snow, and cut a path for him.

But there is no need of specifying particulars in this class of uses. The catalogue is endless, and the examples so obvious, that I shall leave them to the reader's reflection, with the general remark, that this mercenary benefit is one which has respect to a farther good. A man is fed, not that he may be fed, but that he may work.

III. Beauty

First among the nobler uses of nature, serving our non-physical being, is beauty. (1) We delight in the aesthetic perception of nature's forms — sunset, moonrise, the morning wind, all the changes of the seasons. (2) We perceive a higher beauty, relating nature to the human will, to virtue, to great action. (3) We perceive, also, a beauty sought by the intellect. The mind, desiring new forms of beauty, creates them. Poet, painter, etc. take the works of nature and from them distill works of fine art.

A nobler want of man is served by nature, namely, the love of Beauty.

The ancient Greeks called the world κόσμος, beauty. Such is the constitution of all things, or such the plastic power of the human eye, that the primary forms, as the sky, the mountain, the tree, the animal, give us a delight in and for themselves; a pleasure arising from outline, color, motion, and grouping. This seems partly owing to the eye itself. The eye is the best of artists. By the mutual action of its structure and of the laws of light, perspective is produced, which integrates every mass of objects, of what character soever, into a well colored and shaded globe, so that where the particular objects are mean and unaffecting, the landscape which they compose is round and symmetrical. And as the eye is the best composer, so light is the first of painters. There is no object so foul that intense light will not make beautiful. And the stimulus it affords to the sense, and a sort of infinitude which it hath, like space and time, make all matter gay. Even the corpse has its own beauty. But besides this general grace diffused over nature, almost all the individual forms are agreeable to the eye, as is proved by our endless imitations of some of them, as the acorn, the grape, the pine-cone, the wheat-ear, the egg, the wings and forms of most birds, the lion's claw, the serpent, the butterfly, seashells, flames, clouds, buds, leaves, and the forms of many trees, as the palm.

For better consideration, we may distribute the aspects of Beauty in a threefold manner.

1. First, the simple perception of natural forms is a delight. The influence of the forms and actions in nature is so needful to man, that, in its lowest functions, it seems to lie on the confines of commodity and beauty. To the body and mind which have been cramped by noxious work or company, nature is medicinal and restores their tone. The tradesman, the attorney comes out of the din and craft of the street and sees the sky and the woods, and is a man again. In their eternal calm, he finds himself. The health of the eye seems to demand a horizon. We are never tired, so long as we can see far enough.

But in other hours, Nature satisfies by its loveliness, and without any mixture of corporeal benefit. I see the spectacle of morning from the hill-top over against my house, from day-break to sun-rise, with emotions which an angel might share. The long slender bars of cloud float like fishes in the sea of crimson light. From the earth, as a shore, I look out into that silent sea. I seem to partake its rapid transformations; the active enchantment reaches my dust, and I dilate and conspire with the morning wind. How does Nature deify us with a few and cheap elements! Give me health and a day, and I will make the pomp of emperors ridiculous. The dawn is my Assyria; the sunset and moon-rise my Paphos, and unimaginable realms of faerie; broad noon shall be my England of the senses and the understanding; the night shall be my Germany of mystic philosophy and dreams.

Not less excellent, except for our less susceptibility in the afternoon, was the charm, last evening, of a January sunset. The western clouds divided and subdivided themselves into pink flakes modulated with tints of unspeakable softness, and the air had so much life and sweetness that it was a pain to come within doors. What was it that nature would say? Was there no meaning in the live repose of the valley behind the mill, and which Homer or Shakespeare could not reform for me in words? The leafless trees become spires of flame in the sunset, with the blue east for their background, and the stars of the dead calices of flowers, and every withered stem and stubble rimed with frost, contribute something to the mute music.

The inhabitants of cities suppose that the country landscape is pleasant only half the year. I please myself with the graces of the winter scenery, and believe that we are as much touched by it as by the genial influences of summer. To the attentive eye, each moment of the year has its own beauty, and in the same field, it beholds, every hour, a picture which was never seen before, and which shall never be seen again. The heavens change every moment, and reflect their glory or gloom on the plains beneath. The state of the crop in the surrounding farms alters the expression of the earth from week to week. The succession of native plants in the pastures and roadsides, which makes the silent clock by which time tells the summer hours, will make even the divisions of the day sensible to a keen observer. The tribes of birds and insects, like the plants punctual to their time, follow each other, and the year has room for all. By watercourses, the variety is greater. In July, the blue pontederia or pickerel-weed blooms in large beds in the shallow parts of our pleasant river, and swarms with yellow butterflies in continual motion. Art cannot rival this pomp of purple and gold. Indeed the river is a perpetual gala, and boasts each month a new ornament.

But this beauty of Nature which is seen and felt as beauty, is the least part. The shows of day, the dewy morning, the rainbow, mountains, orchards in blossom, stars, moonlight, shadows in still water, and the like, if too eagerly hunted, become shows merely, and mock us with their unreality. Go out of the house to see the moon, and 'tis mere tinsel; it will not please as when its light shines upon your necessary journey. The beauty that shimmers in the yellow afternoons of October, who ever could clutch it? Go forth to find it, and it is gone; 'tis only a mirage as you look from the windows of diligence.

2. The presence of a higher, namely, of the spiritual element is essential to its perfection. The high and divine beauty which can be loved without effeminacy, is that which is found in combination with the human will. Beauty is the mark God sets upon virtue. Every natural action is graceful. Every heroic act is also decent, and causes the place and the bystanders to shine. We are taught by great actions that the universe is the property of every individual in it. Every rational creature has all nature for his dowry and estate. It is his, if he will. He may divest himself of it; he may creep into a corner, and abdicate his kingdom, as most men do, but he is entitled to the world by his constitution. In proportion to the energy of his thought and will, he takes up the world into himself. "All those things for which men plough, build, or sail, obey virtue," said Sallust. "The winds and waves," said Gibbon, "are always on the side of the ablest navigators." So are the sun and moon and all the stars of heaven. When a noble act is done, — perchance in a scene of great natural beauty; when Leonidas and his three hundred martyrs consume one day in dying, and the sun and moon come each and look at them once in the steep defile of Thermopylæ; when Arnold Winkelried, in the high Alps, under the shadow of the avalanche, gathers in his side a sheaf of Austrian spears to break the line for his comrades; are not these heroes entitled to add the beauty of the scene to the beauty of the deed? When the bark of Columbus nears the shore of America; — before it, the

beach lined with savages, fleeing out of all their huts of cane; the sea behind; and the purple mountains of the Indian Archipelago around, can we separate the man from the living picture? Does not the New World clothe his form with her palm-groves and savannahs as fit drapery? Ever does natural beauty steal in like air, and envelope great actions. When Sir Harry Vane was dragged up the Tower-hill, sitting on a sled, to suffer death as the champion of the English laws, one of the multitude cried out to him, "You never sate on so glorious a seat!" Charles II, to intimidate the citizens of London, caused the patriot Lord Russell to be drawn in an open coach through the principal streets of the city on his way to the scaffold. "But," his biographer says, "the multitude imagined they saw liberty and virtue sitting by his side." In private places, among sordid objects, an act of truth or heroism seems at once to draw to itself the sky as its temple, the sun as its candle. Nature stretches out her arms to embrace man, only let his thoughts be of equal greatness. Willingly does she follow his steps with the rose and the violet, and bend her lines of grandeur and grace to the decoration of her darling child. Only let his thoughts be of equal scope, and the frame will suit the picture. A virtuous man is in unison with her works, and makes the central figure of the visible sphere. Homer, Pindar, Socrates, Phocion, associate themselves fitly in our memory with the geography and climate of Greece. The visible heavens and earth sympathize with Jesus. And in common life whosoever has seen a person of powerful character and happy genius, will have remarked how easily he took all things along with him, — the persons, the opinions, and the day, and nature became ancillary to a man.

3. There is still another aspect under which the beauty of the world may be viewed, namely, as it becomes an object of the intellect. Beside the relation of things to virtue, they have a relation to thought. The intellect searches out the absolute order of things as they stand in the mind of God, and without the colors of affection. The intellectual and the active powers seem to succeed each other, and the exclusive activity of the one generates the exclusive activity of the other. There is something unfriendly in each to the other, but they are like the alternate periods of feeding and working in animals; each prepares and will be followed by the other. Therefore does beauty, which, in relation to actions, as we have seen, comes unsought, and comes because it is unsought, remain for the apprehension and pursuit of the intellect; and then again, in its turn, of the active power. Nothing divine dies. All good is eternally reproductive. The beauty of nature reforms itself in the mind, and not for barren contemplation, but for new creation.

All men are in some degree impressed by the face of the world; some men even to delight. This love of beauty is Taste. Others have the same love in such excess, that, not content with admiring, they seek to embody it in new forms. The creation of beauty is Art.

The production of a work of art throws a light upon the mystery of humanity. A work of art is an abstract or epitome of the world. It is the result or expression of nature, in miniature. For although the works of nature are innumerable and all different, the result or the expression of them all is similar and single. Nature is a sea of forms radically alike and even unique. A leaf, a sunbeam, a landscape, the ocean, make an analogous impression on the mind. What is common to them all, — that perfectness and harmony, is beauty. The standard of beauty is the entire circuit of natural forms, — the totality of nature; which the Italians expressed by defining beauty "il più nell' uno [many in one]." Nothing is quite beautiful alone; nothing but is beautiful in the whole. A single object is only so far beautiful as it suggests this universal grace. The poet, the painter, the sculptor, the musician, the architect, seek each to concentrate this radiance of the world on one point, and each in his several work to satisfy the love of beauty which stimulates him to produce. Thus is Art a nature passed through the alembic of man. Thus in art does Nature work through the will of a man filled with the beauty of her first works.

The world thus exists to the soul to satisfy the desire of beauty. This element I call an ultimate end. No reason can be asked or given why the soul seeks beauty. Beauty, in its largest and profoundest sense, is one expression for the universe. God is the all-fair. Truth, and goodness, and beauty, are but different faces of the same All. But beauty in nature is not ultimate. It is the herald of inward and eternal beauty, and is not alone a solid and satisfactory good. It must stand as a part, and not as yet the last or highest expression of the final cause of Nature.

IV. Language

Nature is the medium of thought. (1) All our words for moral and intellectual facts, if traced to their roots, are found based on some material appearance. (2) and (3) There is a correspondence between natural facts and spiritual facts. Natural facts are symbols of spiritual facts. The chapter should be read with care.

Language is a third use which Nature subserves to man. Nature is the vehicle of thought, and in a simple, double, and threefold degree.

1. Words are signs of natural facts.
2. Particular natural facts are symbols of particular spiritual facts.
3. Nature is the symbol of spirit.

1. Words are signs of natural facts. The use of natural history is to give us aid in supernatural history; the use of the outer creation, to give us language for the beings and changes of the inward creation. Every word which is used to express a moral or intellectual fact, if traced to its root, is found to be borrowed from some material appearance. *Right* means *straight*; *wrong* means *twisted*. *Spirit* primarily means *wind*; *transgression*, the crossing of a *line*; *supercilious*, the *raising of the eyebrow*. We say the *heart* to express emotion, the *head* to denote thought; and *thought* and *emotion* are words borrowed from sensible things, and now appropriated to spiritual nature. Most of the process by which this transformation is made, is hidden from us in the remote time when language was framed; but the same tendency may be daily observed in children. Children and savages use only nouns or names of things, which they convert into verbs, and apply to analogous mental acts.

2. But this origin of all words that convey a spiritual import, — so conspicuous a fact in this history of language, — is our least debt to nature. It is not words only that are emblematic; it is things which are emblematic. Every natural fact is a symbol of some spiritual fact. Every appearance in nature corresponds to some state of the mind, and that state of the mind can only be described by presenting that natural appearance as its picture. An enraged man is a lion, a cunning man is a fox, a firm man is a rock, a learned man is a torch. A lamb is innocence; a snake is subtle spite; flowers express to us the delicate affections. Light and darkness are our familiar expression for knowledge and ignorance; and heat for love. Visible distance behind and before us, is respectively our image of memory and hope. Who looks upon a river in a meditative hour and is not reminded of the flux of all things? Throw a stone into the stream, and the circles that propagate themselves are the beautiful type of all influence. Man is conscious of a universal soul within or behind his individual life, wherein, as in a firmament, the natures of Justice, Truth, Love, Freedom, arise and shine. The universal soul he calls Reason: it is not mine, or thine, or his, but we are its; we are its property and men. And the blue sky in which the private earth is buried, the sky with its eternal calm, and full of everlasting orbs, is the type of Reason. That which intellectually considered we call Reason, considered in relation to nature, we call Spirit. Spirit is the Creator. Spirit hath life in itself. And man in all ages and countries embodies it in his language as the FATHER.

It is easily seen that there is nothing lucky or capricious in these analogies, but that they are constant, and pervade nature. These are not the dreams of a few poets, here and there, but man is an analogist, and studies relations in all objects. He is placed in the center of beings, and a ray of relation passes from every other being to him. And neither can man be understood without these objects, nor these objects without man. All the facts in natural history taken by themselves, have no value, but are barren, like a single sex. But marry it to human history, and it is full of life. Whole floras, all Linnæus' and Buffon's volumes, are dry catalogues of facts; but the most trivial of these facts, the habit of a plant, the organs, or work, or noise of an insect, applied to the illustration of a fact in intellectual philosophy, or in any way associated to human nature, affects us in the most lively and agreeable manner. The seed of a plant, — to what affecting analogies in the nature of man is that little fruit made use of, in all discourse, up to the voice of Paul, who calls the human corpse a seed, — "It is sown a natural body; it is raised a spiritual body." The motion of the earth round its axis and round the sun, makes the day and the year. These are certain amounts of brute light and heat. But is there no intent of an analogy between man's life and the seasons? And do the seasons gain no grandeur or pathos from that analogy? The instincts of the ant are very unimportant considered as the ant's; but the moment a ray of relation is seen to extend from it to man, and the little drudge is seen to be a monitor, a little body with a mighty heart, then all its habits, even that said to be recently observed, that it never sleeps, become sublime.

Because of this radical correspondence between visible things and human thoughts, savages, who have only what is necessary, converse in figures. As we go back in history, language becomes more picturesque, until its infancy, when it is all poetry; or all spiritual facts are represented by natural symbols. The same symbols are found to make the original elements of all languages. It has moreover been observed, that the idioms of all languages approach each other in passages of the greatest eloquence and power. And as this is the first language, so is it the last. This immediate dependence of language upon nature, this conversion of an outward phenomenon into a type of somewhat in human life, never loses its power to affect us. It is this which gives that piquancy to the conversation of a strong-natured farmer or backwoodsman, which all men relish.

A man's power to connect his thought with its proper symbol, and so to utter it, depends on the simplicity of his character, that is, upon his love of truth and his desire to communicate it without loss. The corruption of man is followed by the corruption of language. When simplicity of character and the sovereignty of ideas is broken up by the prevalence of secondary desires, — the desire of riches, of pleasure, of power, and of praise, — and duplicity and falsehood take place of simplicity and truth, the power over nature as an interpreter of the will is in a degree lost; new imagery ceases to be created, and old words are perverted to stand for things which are not; a paper currency is employed, when there is no bullion in the vaults. In due time the fraud is manifest, and words lose all power to stimulate the understanding or the affections. Hundreds of writers may be found in every long-civilized nation who for a short time believe and make others believe that they see and utter truths, who do not of themselves clothe one thought in its natural garment, but who feed unconsciously on the language created by the primary writers of the country, those, namely, who hold primarily on nature.

But wise men pierce this rotten diction and fasten words again to visible things; so that picturesque language is at once a commanding certificate that he who employs it is a man in alliance with truth and God. The moment our discourse rises above the ground line of familiar facts and is inflamed with passion or exalted by thought, it clothes itself in images. A man conversing in earnest, if he watch his intellectual processes, will find that a material image more or less luminous arises in his mind, contemporaneous with every thought, which furnishes the vestment of the thought. Hence, good writing and brilliant discourse are perpetual allegories. This imagery is spontaneous. It is the blending of experience with the present action of the mind. It is proper creation. It is the working of the Original Cause through the instruments he has already made.

These facts may suggest the advantage which the country-life possesses, for a powerful mind, over the artificial and curtailed life of cities. We know more from nature than we can at will communicate. Its light flows into the mind evermore, and we forget its presence. The poet, the orator, bred in the woods, whose senses have been nourished by their fair and appeasing changes, year after year, without design and without heed, — shall not lose their lesson altogether, in the roar of cities or the broil of politics. Long hereafter, amidst agitation and terror in national council, — in the hour of revolution, — these solemn images shall reappear in their morning lustre, as fit symbols and words of the thoughts which the passing events shall awaken. At the call of a noble sentiment, again the woods wave, the pines murmur, the river rolls and shines, and the cattle low upon the mountains, as he saw and heard them in his infancy. And with these forms, the spells of persuasion, the keys of power are put into his hands.

3. We are thus assisted by natural objects in the expression of particular meanings. But how great a language to convey such pepper-corn informations! Did it need such noble races of creatures, this profusion of forms, this host of orbs in heaven, to furnish man with the dictionary and grammar of his municipal speech? Whilst we use this grand cipher to expedite the affairs of our pot and kettle, we feel that we have not yet put it to its use, neither are able. We are like travellers using the cinders of a volcano to roast their eggs. Whilst we see that it always stands ready to clothe what we would say, we cannot avoid the question whether the characters are not significant of themselves.

Have mountains, and waves, and skies, no significance but what we consciously give them when we employ them as emblems of our thoughts? The world is emblematic. Parts of speech are metaphors, because the whole of nature is a metaphor of the human mind. The laws of moral nature answer to those of matter as face to face in a glass. "The visible world and the relation of its parts, is the dial plate of the invisible." The axioms of physics translate the laws of ethics. Thus, "the whole is greater than its part"; "reaction is equal to action"; "the smallest weight may be made to lift the greatest, the difference of weight being compensated by time"; and many the like propositions, which have an ethical as well as physical sense. These propositions have a much more extensive and universal sense when applied to human life, than when confined to technical use.

In like manner, the memorable words of history and the proverbs of nations consist usually of a natural fact, selected as a picture or parable of a moral truth. Thus: A rolling stone gathers no moss; A bird in the hand is worth two in the bush; A cripple in the right way will beat a racer in the wrong; Make hay while the sun shines: 'Tis hard to carry a full cup even; Vinegar is the son of wine; The last ounce broke the camel's back; Long-lived trees make roots first; — and the like. In their primary sense these are trivial facts, but we repeat them for the value of their analogical import. What is true of proverbs, is true of all fables, parables, and allegories.

This relation between the mind and matter is not fancied by some poet, but stands in the will of God, and so is free to be known by all men. It appears to men, or it does not appear. When in fortunate hours we ponder this miracle, the wise man doubts if at all other times he is not blind and deaf;

> Can these things be,
> And overcome us like a summer's cloud,
> Without our special wonder?

for the universe becomes transparent, and the light of higher laws than its own shines through it. It is the standing problem which has exercised the wonder and the study of every fine genius since the world began; from the era of the Egyptians and the Brahmins to that of Pythagoras, of Plato, of Bacon, of Leibnitz, of Swedenborg. There sits the Sphinx at the roadside, and from age to age, as each prophet comes by, he tries his fortune at reading her riddle. There seems to be a necessity in spirit to manifest itself in material forms; and day and night, river and storm, beast and bird, acid and alkali, pre-exist in necessary Ideas in the mind of God, and are what they are by virtue of preceding affections in the world of spirit. A fact is the end or last issue of spirit. The visible creation is the terminus or the circumference of the invisible world. "Material objects," said a French philosopher, "are necessarily kinds of *scoriæ* of the substantial thoughts of the Creator, which must always preserve an exact relation to their first origin; in other words, visible nature must have a spiritual and moral side."

This doctrine is abstruse, and though the images of "garment," "scoriæ," "mirror," etc., may stimulate the fancy, we must summon the aid of subtler and more vital expositors to make it plain. "Every scripture is to be interpreted by the same spirit which gave it forth," — is the fundamental law of criticism. A life in harmony with Nature, the love of truth and of virtue, will purge the eyes to understand her text. By degrees we may come to know the primitive sense of the permanent objects of nature, so that the world shall be to us an open book, and every form significant of its hidden life and final cause.

A new interest surprises us, whilst, under the view now suggested, we contemplate the fearful extent and multitude of objects; since "every object rightly seen, unlocks a new faculty of the soul." That which was unconscious truth, becomes, when interpreted and defined in an object, a part of the domain of knowledge, — a new weapon in the magazine of power.

* * * * *

[The remaining four sections of Nature may be summarized briefly. They do not add to the essential theme, the ideal theory of nature, but Emerson continues to state, more strongly than before, that the mind of man—a reflection of the mind of God—contains within itself the essential reality and that the seeming permanence of external nature is an illusion.

Section V, "Discipline," combines the Kantian distinction between the Understanding and the Reason with the Platonic concept of the central Unity (Emerson called it Oversoul or Moral Law) of the universe which underlies the variety

of nature. The Understanding (rational perception, derived from the senses) is a secondary
power by which man adds, measures, divides,
etc., while Reason is a superior power by which
man possesses the vision to grasp the moral law
and to see the unity beneath the variety of things.

Section VI, "Idealism," proposes the idea,
hinted at throughout the earlier parts of Nature,
that nature does not outwardly exist, but is instead phenomenon, not substance. Its only excuse for existence is as "discipline" to man to
apprise him of the fact that his own mind is
stable, while outward things are fluid and changing. The poet, being a superior man, most easily
conforms things to his thought and makes all
objects serve his mood and his passion. Poetry,
philosophy, religion, ethics—even science—all
conspire to cast doubt upon the existence of
matter.

Section VII, "Spirit," is a brief chapter emphasizing again that spirit, or God, is present
behind nature and that man, "the creator in the
finite," has access to the entire mind of God.
Emerson believes that through "purification" of
the soul man can better understand the divine
mind (he does not attempt to define the process
of purification) and that "as we degenerate" we
become strangers in nature and aliens from God.

Section VIII, "Prospects," is interesting as a
manifestation of Emerson's poetic side. Here he
abandons the attempt to "demonstrate" his
theory of nature and breaks into a kind of poetic-
prose which, as he says, "a certain poet sang to
me." This Orphic poet, perhaps a friend and
idealist like Bronson Alcott, or merely a disguise
for himself, speaks in prophetic strain and mystic
accent of man's descent from his former godlike
estate. "A man is a god in ruins." The essay
concludes on this note, that man is, for the most
part, blind to his own divine potential and only
here and there—as in the history of Jesus Christ
or the abolition of slavery or in religious miracles
or in the wisdom of children—does Reason throw
its gleams of light into the common darkness. In
conclusion Emerson once again calls upon his
Orphic poet who speaks to man: "Nature is not
fixed but fluid. Spirit alters, moulds, makes it.
. . . Know then that the world exists for you.
. . . Build therefore your own world. As fast as
you conform your life to the pure idea in your
mind, that will unfold its great proportions."

The student will do well to compare this
theme with that of "Self-Reliance" and other of
Emerson's essays in which, in the last analysis, he
teaches over and over the same doctrine, namely,
that "the highest revelation is that God is in
every man."]

The American Scholar
(Phi Beta Kappa Address at Harvard, 1837)

Scarcely a year after Nature came another
challenge, this time concerning "the study of letters." By "the studious classes," or "scholars," Emerson meant poets, orators, writers of biography and
history, philosophers, actors, clergy — he mentions
them all in this address. Thus he could think of
himself, in his study, as an American scholar, a free
man thinking and writing. And he could think of
himself as a scholar when on the lecture platform,
engaged in "public labor," a scholar in action.

Holding this conception of the scholar "in the
right state," Emerson attacked the wrong type, in
theory and practice. In theory the conventional
scholar was a specialist, a "thinker," not "Man Thinking." In practice he was "decent, indolent, complaisant," not "free and brave." This was an awkward criticism to present on so decorous an occasion.
But Emerson spoke out, as his audience knew he
would. "What crowded and breathless aisles," exclaimed Lowell long afterward, "what windows clustering with eager heads, what enthusiasm of approval,
what grim silence of foregone dissent!" A typical
elderly conservative found the address "misty,
dreamy, unintelligible." But Emerson spoke to the
hearts of the young, reaching depths they had not
been aware of. "The young men went out from it,"
said Oliver Wendell Holmes, "as if a prophet had
been proclaiming to them 'Thus saith the Lord.'"
In time if not at once, Holmes realized (as did
Lowell) that "This grand oration was our intellectual
Declaration of Independence."

Earlier announcements of our cultural self-reliance
had been premature or superficial; Emerson's was
timely and profound. It was profound because the
independent mind, as he conceived, rested upon
principles not simply national but universal, valid
for all men. And it was timely because the hope
which romanticism had encouraged in the few could
be offered to the educated public at a moment when
its wise and courageous leadership was badly needed.
"The present generation," Emerson had written in his
journal, "is bankrupt of principles and hope, as of
property." It was the time of the panic of 1837, the
most severe business panic the country had yet known.
It was a time of economic fear that accented the
timidity and conformity in all realms of thought,
political, moral, religious, educational. Tocqueville,

the French author of a remarkable study of *Democracy in America*, reported that "Freedom of opinion does not exist in America," and an English observer, Harriet Martineau, concluded that "subservience to opinion at that time seemed a sort of mania." Far from leading the way with courage and wisdom, the scholar class, as Emerson described it, had itself succumbed to timidity and conformity. He felt obliged to state the case for self-reliance strongly, even exaggeratedly, in order to awaken a response.

As in *Nature*, Emerson built his composition formally; one can see this clearly by outlining it. At the same time, as R. L. Rusk has said, "His sentences were quick, powerful thrusts, and almost every stroke opened the way for another." This is true of the many passages in which the style was heightened by strong feeling. Yet the speech — an hour and a quarter long — was effective largely because of the contrast between the intensity of these passages and the quiet mood and slower movement of others. The contrast is evident even within the first paragraph.

I greet you on the recommencement of our literary year. Our anniversary is one of hope, and, perhaps, not enough of labor. We do not meet for games of strength or skill, for the recitation of histories, tragedies, and odes, like the ancient Greeks; for parliaments of love and poesy, like the Troubadours; nor for the advancement of science, like our contemporaries in the British and European capitals. Thus far, our holiday has been simply a friendly sign of the survival of the love of letters amongst a people too busy to give to letters any more. As such it is precious as the sign of an indestructible instinct. Perhaps the time is already come when it ought to be, and will be, something else; when the sluggard intellect of this continent will look from under its iron lids and fill the postponed expectation of the world with something better than the exertions of mechanical skill. Our day of dependence, our long apprenticeship to the learning of other lands, draws to a close. The millions that around us are rushing into life, cannot always be fed on the sere remains of foreign harvests. Events, actions arise, that must be sung, that will sing themselves. Who can doubt that poetry will revive and lead in a new age, as the star in the constellation Harp, which now flames in our zenith, astronomers announce, shall one day be the pole-star for a thousand years?

In this hope I accept the topic which not only usage but the nature of our association seem to prescribe to this day, — the AMERICAN SCHOLAR. Year by year we come up hither to read one more chapter of his biography. Let us inquire what light new days and events have thrown on his character and his hopes.

It is one of those fables which out of an unknown antiquity convey an unlooked-for wisdom, that the gods, in the beginning, divided Man into men, that he might be more helpful to himself; just as the hand was divided into fingers, the better to answer its end.

The old fable covers a doctrine ever new and sublime; that there is One Man, — present to all particular men only partially, or through one faculty; and that you must take the whole society to find the whole man. Man is not a farmer, or a professor, or an engineer, but he is all. Man is priest, and scholar, and statesman, and producer, and soldier. In the *divided* or social state these functions are parcelled out to individuals, each of whom aims to do his stint of the joint work, whilst each other performs his. The fable implies that the individual, to possess himself, must sometimes return from his own labor to embrace all the other laborers. But, unfortunately, this original unit, this fountain of power, has been so distributed to multitudes, has been so minutely subdivided and peddled out, that it is spilled into drops, and cannot be gathered. The state of society is one in which the members have suffered amputation from the trunk, and strut about so many walking monsters, — a good finger, a neck, a stomach, an elbow, but never a man.

Man is thus metamorphosed into a thing, into many things. The planter, who is Man sent out into the field to gather food, is seldom cheered by an idea of the true dignity of his ministry. He sees his bushel and his cart, and nothing beyond, and sinks into the farmer, instead of Man on the farm. The tradesman scarcely ever gives an ideal worth to his work, but is ridden by the routine of his craft, and the soul is subject to dollars. The priest becomes a form; the attorney a statute-book; the mechanic a machine; the sailor a rope of the ship.

In this distribution of functions the scholar is the delegated intellect. In the right state he is *Man Thinking*. In the degenerate state, when the victim of society, he tends to become a mere thinker, or still worse, the parrot of other men's thinking.

In this view of him, as Man Thinking, the theory of his office is contained. Him Nature solicits with all her placid, all her monitory pictures; him the past instructs; him the future invites. Is not indeed every man a student, and do not all things exist for the student's behoof? And, finally is not the true scholar the only true master? But the old oracle said, "All things have two handles: beware of the wrong one." In life, too often, the scholar errs with mankind and forfeits his privilege. Let us see him in his school, and consider him in reference to the main influences he receives.

I. The first in time and the first in importance of the influences upon the mind is that of nature. Every day, the sun; and, after the sunset, night and her stars. Ever the winds blow; ever the grass grows. Every day, men and women, conversing, beholding and beholden. The scholar is he of all men whom this spectacle most engages. He must settle its value in his mind. What is nature to him? There is never a beginning, there is never an end, to the inexplicable continuity of this web of God, but always circular power returning into itself. Therein it resembles his own spirit, whose beginning, whose ending, he never can find, — so entire, so boundless. Far too as her splendors shine, system on system shooting like rays, upward, downward, without center, without circumference, — in the mass and in the particle. Nature hastens to render account of herself to the mind. Classification begins. To the young mind every thing is individual, stands by itself. By and by, it finds how to join two things and see in them one nature; then three, then three thousand; and so, tyrannized over by its own unifying instinct, it goes on tying things together, diminishing anomalies, discovering roots running under ground whereby contrary and remote things cohere and flower out from one stem. It presently learns that since the dawn of history there has been a constant accumulation and classifying of facts. But what is classification but the perceiving that these objects are not chaotic, and are not foreign, but have a law which is also a law of the human mind? The astronomer discovers that geometry, a pure abstraction of the human mind, is the measure of planetary motion. The chemist finds proportions and intelligible method throughout matter; and science is nothing but the finding of analogy, identity, in the most remote parts. The ambitious soul sits down before each refractory fact; one after another reduces all strange constitutions, all new powers, to their class and their law, and

goes on forever to animate the last fibre of organization, the outskirts of nature, by insight.

Thus to him, to this school-boy under the bending dome of day, is suggested that he and it proceed from one root; one is leaf and one is flower; relation, sympathy, stirring in every vein. And what is that root? Is not that the soul of his soul? A thought too bold; a dream too wild. Yet when this spiritual light shall have revealed the law of more earthly natures, — when he has learned to worship the soul, and to see that the natural philosophy that now is, is only the first gropings of its gigantic hand, he shall look forward to an ever expanding knowledge as to a becoming creator. He shall see that nature is the opposite of the soul, answering to it part for part. One is seal and one is print. Its beauty is the beauty of his own mind. Its laws are the laws of his own mind. Nature then becomes to him the measure of his attainments. So much of nature as he is ignorant of, so much of his own mind does he not yet possess. And, in fine, the ancient precept, "Know thyself," and the modern precept, "Study nature," become at last one maxim.

II. The next great influence into the spirit of the scholar is the mind of the Past, — in whatever form, whether of literature, of art, of institutions, that mind is inscribed. Books are the best type of the influence of the past, and perhaps we shall get at the truth, — learn the amount of this influence more conveniently, — by considering their value alone.

The theory of books is noble. The scholar of the first age received into him the world around; brooded thereon; gave it the new arrangement of his own mind, and uttered it again. It came into him life; it went out from him truth. It came to him short-lived actions; it went out from him immortal thoughts. It came to him business; it went from him poetry. It was a dead fact; now, it is quick thought. It can stand, and it can go. It now endures, it now flies, it now inspires. Precisely in proportion to the depth of mind from which it issued, so high does it soar, so long does it sing.

Or, I might say, it depends on how far the process had gone, of transmuting life into truth. In proportion to the completeness of the distillation, so will the purity and imperishableness of the product be. But none is quite perfect. As no air-pump can by any means make a perfect vacuum, so neither can any artist entirely exclude the conventional, the local, the perishable from his book, or write a book of pure thought, that shall be as efficient, in all respects, to a remote posterity, as to contemporaries, or rather to the second age. Each age, it is found, must write its own books; or rather, each generation for the next succeeding. The books of an older period will not fit this.

Yet hence arises a grave mischief. The sacredness which attaches to the act of creation, the act of thought, is transferred to the record. The poet chanting was felt to be a divine man: henceforth the chant is divine also. The writer was a just and wise spirit: henceforward it is settled the book is perfect; as love of the hero corrupts into worship of his statue. Instantly the book becomes noxious: the guide is a tyrant. The sluggish and perverted mind of the multitude, slow to open to the incursions of Reason, having once so opened, having once received this book, stands upon it, and makes an outcry if it is disparaged. Colleges are built on it. Books are written on it by thinkers, not by Man Thinking; by men of talent, that is, who start wrong, who set out from accepted dogmas, not from their own sight of principles. Meek young men grow up in libraries, believing it their duty to accept the views which Cicero, which Locke, which Bacon, have given; forgetful that Cicero, Locke, and Bacon were only young men in libraries when they wrote these books.

Hence, instead of Man Thinking, we have the bookworm. Hence the book-learned class, who value books, as such; not as related to nature and the human constitution, but as making a sort of Third Estate with the world and the soul. Hence the restorers of readings, the emendators, the bibliomaniacs of all degrees.

Books are the best of things, well used; abused, among the worst. What is the right use? What is the one end which all means go to effect? They are for nothing but to inspire. I had better never see a book than to be warped by its attraction clean out of my own orbit, and made a satellite instead of a system. The one thing in the world, of value, is the active soul. This every man is entitled to; this every man contains within him, although in almost all men obstructed, and as yet unborn. The soul active sees absolute truth and utters truth, or creates. In this action it is genius; not the privilege of here and there a favorite, but the sound estate of every man. In its essence, it is progressive. The book, the college, the school of art, the institu-

tion of any kind, stop with some past utterance of genius. This is good, say they, — let us hold by this. They pin me down. They look backward and not forward. But genius looks forward: the eyes of man are set in his forehead, not in his hindhead: man hopes: genius creates. Whatever talents may be, if the man create not, the pure efflux of the Deity is not his; — cinders and smoke there may be, but not yet flame. There are creative manners, there are creative actions, and creative words; manners, actions, words, that is, indicative of no custom or authority, but springing spontaneous from the mind's own sense of good and fair.

On the other part, instead of being its own seer, let it receive from another mind its truth, though it were in torrents of light, without periods of solitude, inquest, and self-recovery, and a fatal disservice is done. Genius is always sufficiently the enemy of genius by over-influence. The literature of every nation bears me witness. The English dramatic poets have Shakespearized now for two hundred years.

Undoubtedly there is a right way of reading, so it be sternly subordinated. Man Thinking must not be subdued by his instruments. Books are for the scholar's idle times. When he can read God directly, the hour is too precious to be wasted in other men's transcripts of their readings. But when the intervals of darkness come, as come they must, — when the sun is hid and the stars withdraw their shining, — we repair to the lamps which were kindled by their ray, to guide our steps to the East again, where the dawn is. We hear, that we may speak. The Arabian proverb says, "A fig tree, looking on a fig tree, becometh fruitful."

It is remarkable, the character of the pleasure we derive from the best books. They impress us with the conviction that one nature wrote and the same reads. We read the verses of one of the great English poets, of Chaucer, of Marvell, of Dryden, with the most modern joy, — with a pleasure, I mean, which is in great part caused by the abstraction of all *time* from their verses. There is some awe mixed with the joy of our surprise, when this poet, who lived in some past world, two or three hundred years ago, says that which lies close to my own soul, that which I also had well-nigh thought and said. But for the evidence thence afforded to the philosophical doctrine of the identity of all minds, we should suppose some preëstablished harmony, some foresight of souls that were to be, and some preparation of stores for their future wants, like the fact observed in insects, who lay up food before death for the young grub they shall never see.

I would not be hurried by any love of system, by any exaggeration of instincts, to underrate the Book. We all know, that as the human body can be nourished on any food, though it were boiled grass and the broth of shoes, so the human mind can be fed by any knowledge. And great and heroic men have existed who had almost no other information than by the printed page. I only would say that it needs a strong head to bear that diet. One must be an inventor to read well. As the proverb says, "He that would bring home the wealth of the Indies, must carry out the wealth of the Indies." There is then creative reading as well as creative writing. When the mind is braced by labor and invention, the page of whatever book we read becomes luminous with manifold allusion. Every sentence is doubly significant, and the sense of our author is as broad as the world. We then see, what is always true, that as the seer's hour of vision is short and rare among heavy days and months, so is its record, perchance the least part of his volume. The discerning will read, in his Plato or Shakespeare, only that least part, — only the authentic utterances of the oracle; — all the rest he rejects, were it never so many times Plato's and Shakespeare's.

Of course there is a portion of reading quite indispensable to a wise man. History and exact science he must learn by laborious reading. Colleges, in like manner, have their indispensable office, — to teach elements. But they can only highly serve us when they aim not to drill, but to create; when they gather from far every ray of various genius to their hospitable halls, and by the concentrated fires, set the hearts of their youth on flame. Thought and knowledge are natures in which apparatus and pretension avail nothing. Gowns and pecuniary foundations, though of towns of gold, can never countervail the least sentence or syllable of wit. Forget this, and our American colleges will recede in their public importance, whilst they grow richer every year.

III. There goes in the world a notion that the scholar should be a recluse, a valetudinarian, — as unfit for any handiwork or public labor as a pen-knife for an axe. The so-called "practical men" sneer at speculative men, as if, because

they speculate or *see*, they could do nothing. I have heard it said that the clergy, — who are always, more universally than any other class, the scholars of their day, — are addressed as women; that the rough, spontaneous conversation of men they do not hear, but only a mincing and diluted speech. They are often virtually disfranchised; and indeed there are advocates for their celibacy. As far as this is true of the studious classes, it is not just and wise. Action is with the scholar subordinate, but it is essential. Without it he is not yet man. Without it thought can never ripen into truth. Whilst the world hangs before the eye as a cloud of beauty, we cannot even see its beauty. Inaction is cowardice, but there can be no scholar without the heroic mind. The preamble of thought, the transition through which it passes from the unconscious to the conscious, is action. Only so much do I know, as I have lived. Instantly we know whose words are loaded with life, and whose not.

The world, — this shadow of the soul, or *other me*, — lies wide around. Its attractions are the keys which unlock my thoughts and make me acquainted with myself. I run eagerly into this resounding tumult. I grasp the hands of those next me, and take my place in the ring to suffer and to work, taught by an instinct that so shall the dumb abyss be vocal with speech. I pierce its order; I dissipate its fear; I dispose of it within the circuit of my expanding life. So much only of life as I know by experience, so much of the wilderness have I vanquished and planted, or so far have I extended my being, my dominion. I do not see how any man can afford, for the sake of his nerves and his nap, to spare any action in which he can partake. It is pearls and rubies to his discourse. Drudgery, calamity, exasperation, want, are instructors in eloquence and wisdom. The true scholar grudges every opportunity of action past by, as a loss of power. It is the raw material out of which the intellect moulds her splendid products. A strange process too, this by which experience is converted into thought, as a mulberry leaf is converted into satin. The manufacture goes forward at all hours.

The actions and events of our childhood and youth are now matters of calmest observation. They lie like fair pictures in the air. Not so with our recent actions, — with the business which we now have in hand. On this we are quite unable to speculate. Our affections as yet circulate through it. We no more feel or know it than we feel the feet, or the hand, or the brain of our body. The new deed is yet a part of life, — remains for a time immersed in our unconscious life. In some contemplative hour it detaches itself from the life like a ripe fruit, to become a thought of the mind. Instantly it is raised, transfigured; the corruptible has put on incorruption. Henceforth it is an object of beauty, however base its origin and neighborhood. Observe too the impossibility of antedating this act. In its grub state, it cannot fly, it cannot shine, it is a dull grub. But suddenly, without observation, the selfsame thing unfurls beautiful wings, and is an angel of wisdom. So is there no fact, no event, in our private history, which shall not, sooner or later, lose its adhesive, inert form, and astonish us by soaring from our body into the empyrean. Cradle and infancy, school and playground, the fear of boys, and dogs, and ferules, the love of little maids and berries, and many another fact that once filled the whole sky, are gone already; friend and relative, profession and party, town and country, nation and world, must also soar and sing.

Of course, he who has put forth his total strength in fit actions has the richest return of wisdom. I will not shut myself out of this globe of action, and transplant an oak into a flowerpot, there to hunger and pine; nor trust the revenue of some single faculty, and exhaust one vein of thought, much like those Savoyards, who, getting their livelihood by carving shepherds, shepherdesses, and smoking Dutchmen, for all Europe, went out one day to the mountain to find stock, and discovered that they had whittled up the last of their pine-trees. Authors we have, in numbers, who have written out their vein, and who, moved by a commendable prudence, sail for Greece or Palestine, follow the trapper into the prairie, or ramble round Algiers, to replenish their merchantable stock.

If it were only for a vocabulary, the scholar would be covetous of action. Life is our dictionary. Years are well spent in country labors; in town; in the insight into trades and manufactures; in frank intercourse with many men and women; in science; in art; to the one end of mastering in all their facts a language by which to illustrate and embody our perceptions. I learn immediately from any speaker how much he has already lived, through the poverty or the splendor of his speech. Life lies behind us as the quarry from whence we get tiles and copestones

for the masonry of to-day. This is the way to learn grammar. Colleges and books only copy the language which the field and the work-yard made.

But the final value of action, like that of books, and better than books, is that it is a resource. That great principle of Undulation in nature, that shows itself in the inspiring and expiring of the breath; in desire and satiety; in the ebb and flow of the sea; in day and night; in heat and cold; and, as yet more deeply ingrained in every atom and every fluid, is known to us under the name of Polarity, — these "fits of easy transmission and reflection," as Newton called them, are the law of nature because they are the law of spirit.

The mind now thinks, now acts, and each fit reproduces the other. When the artist has exhausted his materials, when the fancy no longer paints, when thoughts are no longer apprehended and books are a weariness, — he has always the resource *to live.* Character is higher than intellect. Thinking is the function. Living is the functionary. The stream retreats to its source. A great soul will be strong to live, as well as strong to think. Does he lack organ or medium to impart his truth? He can still fall back on this elemental force of living them. This is a total act. Thinking is a partial act. Let the grandeur of justice shine in his affairs. Let the beauty of affection cheer his lowly roof. Those "far from fame," who dwell and act with him, will feel the force of his constitution in the doings and passages of the day better than it can be measured by any public and designed display. Time shall teach him that the scholar loses no hour which the man lives. Herein he unfolds the sacred germ of his instinct, screened from influence. What is lost in seemliness is gained in strength. Not out of those on whom systems of education have exhausted their culture, comes the helpful giant to destroy the old or to build the new, but out of unhandselled savage nature; out of terrible Druids and Berserkers come at last Alfred and Shakespeare.

I hear therefore with joy whatever is beginning to be said of the dignity and necessity of labor to every citizen. There is virtue yet in the hoe and the spade, for learned as well as for unlearned hands. And labor is everywhere welcome; always we are invited to work; only be this limitation observed, that a man shall not for the sake of wider activity sacrifice any opinion to the popular judgments and modes of action.

I have now spoken of the education of the scholar by nature, by books, and by action. It remains to say somewhat of his duties.

They are such as become Man Thinking. They may all be comprised in self-trust. The office of the scholar is to cheer, to raise, and to guide men by showing them facts amidst appearances. He plies the slow, unhonored, and unpaid task of observation. Flamsteed and Herschel, in their glazed observatories, may catalogue the stars with the praise of all men, and the results being splendid and useful, honor is sure. But he, in his private observatory, cataloguing obscure and nebulous stars of the human mind, which as yet no man has thought of as such, — watching days and months sometimes for a few facts; correcting still his old records; — must relinquish display and immediate fame. In the long period of his preparation he must betray often an ignorance and shiftlessness in popular arts, incurring the disdain of the able who shoulder him aside. Long he must stammer in his speech; often forego the living for the dead. Worse yet, he must accept — how often! — poverty and solitude. For the ease and pleasure of treading the old road, accepting the fashions, the education, the religion of society, he takes the cross of making his own, and, of course, the self-accusation, the faint heart, the frequent uncertainty and loss of time, which are the nettles and tangling vines in the way of the self-relying and self-directed; and the state of virtual hostility in which he seems to stand to society, and especially to educated society. For all this loss and scorn, what offset? He is to find consolation in exercising the highest functions of human nature. He is one who raises himself from private considerations and breathes and lives on public and illustrious thoughts. He is the world's eye. He is the world's heart. He is to resist the vulgar prosperity that retrogrades ever to barbarism, by preserving and communicating heroic sentiments, noble biographies, melodious verse, and the conclusions of history. Whatsoever oracles the human heart, in all emergencies, in all solemn hours, has uttered as its commentary on the world of actions, — these he shall receive and impart. And whatsoever new verdict Reason from her inviolable seat pronounces on the passing men and events of today, — this he shall hear and promulgate.

These being his functions, it becomes him to feel all confidence in himself, and to defer never to the popular cry. He and he only knows the world. The world of any moment is the merest appearance. Some great decorum, some fetish of a government, some ephemeral trade, or war, or man, is cried up by half mankind and cried down by the other half, as if all depended on this particular up or down. The odds are that the whole question is not worth the poorest thought which the scholar has lost in listening to the controversy. Let him not quit his belief that a popgun is a popgun, though the ancient and honorable of the earth affirm it to be the crack of doom. In silence, in steadiness, in severe abstraction, let him hold by himself; add observation to observation, patient of neglect, patient of reproach, and bide his own time, — happy enough if he can satisfy himself alone that this day he has seen something truly. Success treads on every right step. For the instinct is sure, that prompts him to tell his brother what he thinks. He then learns that in going down into the secrets of his own mind he has descended into the secrets of all minds. He learns that he who has mastered any law in his private thoughts, is master to that extent of all men whose language he speaks, and of all into whose language his own can be translated. The poet, in utter solitude remembering his spontaneous thoughts and recording them, is found to have recorded that which men in crowded cities find true for them also. The orator distrusts at first the fitness of his frank confessions, his want of knowledge of the persons he addresses, until he finds that he is the complement of his hearers; — that they drink his words because he fulfils for them their own nature; the deeper he dives into his privatest, secretest presentiment, to his wonder he finds this is the most acceptable, most public, and universally true. The people delight in it; the better part of every man feels, This is my music; this myself.

In self-trust all the virtues are comprehended. Free should the scholar be, — free and brave. Free even to the definition of freedom, "without any hindrance that does not arise out of his own constitution." Brave; for fear is a thing which a scholar by his very function puts behind him. Fear always springs from ignorance. It is a shame to him if his tranquility, amid dangerous times, arise from the presumption that like children and women his is a protected class; or if he seek a temporary peace by the diversion of his thoughts from politics or vexed questions, hiding his head like an ostrich in the flowering bushes, peeping into microscopes, and turning rhymes, as a boy whistles to keep his courage up. So is the danger a danger still; so is the fear worse. Manlike let him turn and face it. Let him look into its eye and search its nature, inspect its origin, — see the whelping of this lion, — which lies no great way back; he will then find in himself a perfect comprehension of its nature and extent; he will have made his hands meet on the other side, and can henceforth defy it and pass on superior. The world is his who can see through its pretension. What deafness, what stone-blind custom, what overgrown error you behold is there only by sufferance, — by your sufferance. See it to be a lie, and you have already dealt it its mortal blow.

Yes, we are the cowed, — we the trustless. It is a mischievous notion that we are come late into nature; that the world was finished a long time ago. As the world was plastic and fluid in the hands of God, so it is ever to so much of his attributes as we bring to it. To ignorance and sin, it is flint. They adapt themselves to it as they may; but in proportion as a man has any thing in him divine, the firmament flows before him and takes his signet and form. Not he is great who can alter matter, but he who can alter my state of mind. They are the kings of the world who give the color of their present thought to all nature and all art, and persuade men by the cheerful serenity of their carrying the matter, that this thing which they do is the apple which the ages have desired to pluck, now at last ripe, and inviting nations to the harvest. The great man makes the great thing. Wherever Macdonald sits, there is the head of the table. Linnæus makes botany the most alluring of studies, and wins it from the farmer and the herb-woman; Davy, chemistry; and Cuvier, fossils. The day is always his who works in it with serenity and great aims. The unstable estimates of men crowd to him whose mind is filled with a truth, as the heaped waves of the Atlantic follow the moon.

For this self-trust, the reason is deeper than can be fathomed, — darker than can be enlightened. I might not carry with me the feeling of my audience in stating my own belief. But I have already shown the ground of my hope, in adverting to the doctrine that man is one. I believe man has been wronged; he has wronged himself. He has almost lost the light that can lead him back to his prerogatives. Men are become of no account. Men in history, men in the world of to-day, are bugs, are spawn, and are called "the mass" and "the herd." In a century, in a millennium, one or two men; that is to say, one or two approximations to the right state of every man. All the rest behold in the hero or the poet their own green and crude being, — ripened; yes, and are content to be less, so *that* may attain to its full stature. What a testimony, full of grandeur, full of pity, is borne to the demands of his own nature, by the poor clansman, the poor partisan, who rejoices in the glory of his chief. The poor and the low find some amends to their immense moral capacity, for their acquiescence in a political and social inferiority. They are content to be brushed like flies from the path of a great person, so that justice shall be done by him to that common nature which it is the dearest desire of all to see enlarged and glorified. They sun themselves in the great man's light, and feel it to be their own element. They cast the dignity of man from their downtrod selves upon the shoulders of a hero, and will perish to add one drop of blood to make that great heart beat, those giant sinews combat and conquer. He lives for us, and we live in him.

Men such as they are, very naturally seek money or power; and power because it is as good as money, — the "spoils," so called, "of office." And why not? for they aspire to the highest, and this, in their sleep-walking, they dream is highest. Wake them and they shall quit the false good and leap to the true, and leave governments to clerks and desks. This revolution is to be wrought by the gradual domestication of the idea of Culture. The main enterprise of the world for splendor, for extent, is the upbuilding of a man. Here are the materials strewn along the ground. The private life of one man shall be a more illustrious monarchy, more formidable to its enemy, more sweet and serene in its influence to its friend, than any kingdom in history. For a man, rightly viewed, comprehendeth the particular natures of all men. Each philosopher, each bard, each actor has only done for me, as by a delegate, what one day I can do for myself. The books which once we valued more than the apple of the eye, we have quite exhausted. What is that but saying that we have come up with the point of view which the universal mind took through the eyes of one scribe; we have been that man, and have passed on. First, one, then another, we drain all cisterns, and waxing greater by all these supplies, we crave a better and more abundant food.

The man has never lived that can feed us ever. The human mind cannot be enshrined in a person who shall set a barrier on any one side to this unbounded, unboundable empire. It is one central fire, which, flaming now out of the lips of Etna, lightens the capes of Sicily, and now out of the throat of Vesuvius, illuminates the towers and vineyards of Naples. It is one light which beams out of a thousand stars. It is one soul which animates all men.

But I have dwelt perhaps tediously upon this abstraction of the Scholar. I ought not to delay longer to add what I have to say of nearer reference to the time and to this country.

Historically, there is thought to be a difference in the ideas which predominate over successive epochs, and there are data for marking the genius of the Classic, of the Romantic, and now of the Reflective or Philosophical age. With the views I have intimated of the oneness or the identity of the mind through all individuals, I do not much dwell on these differences. In fact, I believe each individual passes through all three. The boy is a Greek; the youth, romantic; the adult, reflective. I deny not, however, that a revolution in the leading idea may be distinctly enough traced.

Our age is bewailed as the age of Introversion. Must that needs be evil? We, it seems, are critical; we are embarrassed with second thoughts; we cannot enjoy any thing for hankering to know whereof the pleasure consists; we are lined with eyes; we see with our feet; the time is infected with Hamlet's unhappiness,

Sicklied o'er with the pale cast of thought.

It is so bad then? Sight is the last thing to be pitied. Would we be blind? Do we fear lest we should outsee nature and God, and drink truth dry? I look upon the discontent of the literary class as a mere announcement of the fact that they find themselves not in the state of mind of their fathers, and regret the coming state as untried; as a boy dreads the water before he has learned that he can swim. If there is any period one would desire to be born in, is it not the age of Revolution; when the old and the new stand side by side and admit of being compared; when the energies of all men are searched by fear and by hope; when the historic glories of the old can be compensated by the rich possibilities of the new era? This time, like all times, is a very good one, if we but know what to do with it.

I read with some joy of the auspicious signs of the coming days, as they glimmer already through poetry and art, through philosophy and science, through church and state.

One of these signs is the fact that the same movement which effected the elevation of what was called the lowest class in the state, assumed in literature a very marked and as benign an aspect. Instead of the sublime and beautiful, the near, the low, the common, was explored and poetized. That which had been negligently trodden under foot by those who were harnessing and provisioning themselves for long journeys into far countries, is suddenly found to be richer than all foreign parts. The literature of the poor, the feelings of the child, the philosophy of the street, the meaning of household life, are the topics of the time. It is a great stride. It is a sign — is it not? — of new vigor when the extremities are made active, when currents of warm life run into the hands and the feet. I ask not for the great, the remote, the romantic; what is doing in Italy or Arabia; what is Greek art, or Provençal minstrelsy; I embrace the common, I explore and sit at the feet of the familiar, the low. Give me insight into to-day, and you may have the antique and future worlds. What would we really know the meaning of? The meal in the firkin; the milk in the pan; the ballad in the street; the news of the boat; the glance of the eye; the form and the gait of the body; — show me the ultimate reason of these matters; show me the sublime presence of the highest spiritual cause lurking, as always it does lurk, in these suburbs and extremities of nature; let me see every trifle bristling with the polarity that ranges it instantly on an eternal law; and the shop, the plough, and the ledger referred to the like cause by which light undulates and poets sing; — and the world lies no longer a dull miscellany and lumber-room, but has form and order; there is no trifle, there is no puzzle, but one design unites and animates the farthest pinnacle and the lowest trench.

This idea has inspired the genius of Goldsmith, Burns, Cowper, and, in a newer time, of Goethe, Wordsworth, and Carlyle. This idea they have differently followed and with various success. In contrast with their writing, the style of Pope, of Johnson, of Gibbon, looks cold and pedantic. This writing is blood-warm. Man is surprised to find that things near are not less beautiful and wondrous than things remote. The near explains the far. The drop is a small ocean. A man is related to all nature. This perception of the worth of the vulgar is fruitful in discoveries. Goethe, in this very thing the most modern of the moderns, has shown us as none ever did, the genius of the ancients.

There is one man of genius who has done much for this philosophy of life, whose literary value has never yet been rightly estimated; — I mean Emanuel Swedenborg. The most imaginative of men, yet writing with the precision of a mathematician, he endeavored to engraft a purely philosophical Ethics on the popular Christianity of his time. Such an attempt of course must have difficulty which no genius could surmount. But he saw and showed the connection between nature and the affections of the soul. He pierced the emblematic or spiritual character of the visible, audible, tangible world. Especially did his shade-loving muse hover over and interpret the lower parts of nature; he showed the mysterious bond that allies moral evil to the foul material forms, and has given in epical parables a theory of insanity, of beasts, of unclean and fearful things.

Another sign of our times, also marked by an analogous political movement, is the new importance given to the single person. Every thing that tends to insulate the individual, — to surround him with barriers of natural respect, so that each man shall feel the world is his, and man shall treat with man as a sovereign state with a sovereign state, — tends to true union as well as greatness. "I learned," said the melancholy Pestalozzi, "that no man in God's wide earth is either willing or able to help any other man." Help must come from the bosom alone. The scholar is that man who must take up into himself all the ability of the time, all the contributions of the past, all the hopes of the future. He must be an university of knowledges. If there be one lesson more than another which should pierce his ear, it is, The world is nothing, the man is all; in yourself is the law of all nature, and you know not yet how a globule of sap ascends; in yourself slumbers the whole of Reason; it is for you to know all; it is for you to dare all. Mr. President and Gentlemen, this confidence in the unsearched might of man belongs, by all motives, by all prophecy, by all preparation, to the American Scholar. We have listened too long to the courtly muses of Europe. The spirit of the American freeman is

already suspected to be timid, imitative, tame. Public and private avarice make the air we breathe thick and fat. The scholar is decent, indolent, complaisant. See already the tragic consequence. The mind of this country, taught to aim at low objects, eats upon itself. There is no work for any but the decorous and the complaisant. Young men of the fairest promise, who begin life upon our shores, inflated by the mountain winds, shined upon by all the stars of God, find the earth below not in unison with these, but are hindered from action by the disgust which the principles on which business is managed inspire, and turn drudges, or die of disgust, some of them suicides. What is the remedy? They did not yet see, and thousands of young men as hopeful now crowding to the barriers for the career do not yet see, that if the single man plant himself indomitably on his instincts, and there abide, the huge world will come round to him. Patience, — patience; with the shades of all the good and great for company; and for solace the perspective of your own infinite life; and for work the study and the communication of principles, the making those instincts prevalent, the conversion of the world. Is it not the chief disgrace in the world, not to be an unit; — not to be reckoned one character; — not to yield that peculiar fruit which each man was created to bear, but to be reckoned in the gross, in the hundred, or the thousand, of the party, the section, to which we belong; and our opinion predicted geographically, as the north, or the south? Not so, brothers and friends, — please God, ours shall not be so. We will walk on our own feet; we will work with our own hands; we will speak our own minds. The study of letters shall be no longer a name for pity, for doubt, and for sensual indulgence. The dread of man and the love of man shall be a wall of defence and a wreath of joy around all. A nation of men will for the first time exist, because each believes himself inspired by the Divine Soul which also inspires all men.

Self-Reliance

(1841)

Among all the essays of Emerson, the favorite is still that on self-reliance, even in the century of "the Masses" and "the Welfare State." In this essay, a good society is a society of good individuals, and the only fundamental reform is the reform of one's self. The aims and effects of those known as reformers and humanitarians are superficial, and social progress is an illusion. Conformity, the virtue most widely valued, is the means by which free men are intimidated into slavery to society.

In affirming self-reliance vs. conformity, independence vs. subjection, the individual vs. society, Emerson had behind him an immense amount of American experience, including the settlement of New England by non-conformists, the stand of Roger Williams in favor of the individual conscience, the Inner Light of the Quakers, the passion of Jefferson for all freedoms, the Jacksonian assertion of the common man. Emerson's was a democratic individualism, not aristocratic in the manner of Goethe and Carlyle, who espoused self-culture for the few, obedience or hero-worship for the many. At the same time it was a spiritual individualism deeply related to European traditions reaching far back to early Christianity and the philosophy of Plato.

Although his thought was sustained by these backgrounds, Emerson chose to emphasize, in various passages, the spirit of romanticism current in his own time. This would seem to explain why, when asking "Who is the Trustee?" implied by self-trust, he gave such ambiguous answers as Self, Intuition, Spontaneity, Instinct, holding off God till the next paragraph. It may also explain why he failed to provide, in the essay, the safeguards of humility upon which, in another mood, he reflected in "Grace" (see the poem and the note, page 303). As if bent on avoiding a too ministerial approach that might defeat his purpose, he availed himself of the rebellious spirit, the attitude of self-absorption, and the unguarded language of romanticism. In this provocative way he might shock the convention-ridden reader into a realization of his loss of manhood.

In the preceding selection, Emerson's art was that of the orator adapting his speech to a dignified occasion. Now he is an informal essayist, using the old techniques of Montaigne (personal) and Bacon (aphoristic), two of his favorite writers. Instead of the charming chattiness of a romantic like Charles Lamb, he has an electric and tonic quality that is his own — "Emersonian." He is still, in a sense, addressing an audience ("you"), and he is still in a sense ministerial, seeking to stir unused depths in the listener's experience. Full of his subject and purpose, he sustains them through a lengthy discourse, repeating his main point — "trust thyself" — in many statements and over-statements, testing it by many applications to situations in life, alerting the reader by changes in tone and attitude. The essay is studded with pithy, quotable epigrams and with telling metaphors. And the diction, as Lowell said, is at once rich and homely, "like home-spun cloth-of-gold."

I read the other day some verses written by an eminent painter which were original and not conventional. The soul always hears an admonition in such lines, let the subject be what it may. The sentiment they instil is of more value than any thought they may contain. To believe your own thought, to believe that what is true for you in your private heart is true for all men, — that is genius. Speak your latent conviction, and it shall be the universal sense; for the inmost in due time becomes the outmost, and our first thought is rendered back to us by the trumpets of the Last Judgment. Familiar as the voice of the mind is to each, the highest merit we ascribe to Moses, Plato, and Milton is that they set at naught books and traditions, and spoke not what men, but what *they* thought. A man should learn to detect and watch that gleam of light which flashes across his mind from within, more than the lustre of the firmament of bards and sages. Yet he dismisses without notice his thought, because it is his. In every work of genius we recognize our own rejected thoughts; they come back to us with a certain alienated majesty. Great works of art have no more affecting lesson for us than this. They teach us to abide by our spontaneous impression with good-humored inflexibility then most when the whole cry of voices is on the other side. Else to-morrow a stranger will say with masterly good sense precisely what we have thought and felt all the time, and we shall be forced to take with shame our own opinion from another.

There is a time in every man's education when he arrives at the conviction that envy is ignorance; that imitation is suicide; that he must take himself for better for worse as his portion; that though the wide universe is full of good, no kernel of nourishing corn can come to him but through his toil bestowed on that plot of ground which is given to him to till. The power which resides in him is new in nature, and none but he knows what that is which he can do, nor does he know until he has tried. Not for nothing one face, one character, one fact, makes much impression on him and another none. This sculpture in the memory is not without preëstablished harmony. The eye was placed where one ray should fall, that it might testify of that particular ray. We but half express ourselves, and are ashamed of that divine idea which each of us represents. It may be safely trusted as proportionate and of good issues, so it be faithfully imparted, but God will not have his work made manifest by cowards. A man is relieved and gay when he has put his heart into his work and done his best; but what he has said or done otherwise shall give him no peace. It is a deliverance which does not deliver. In the attempt his genius deserts him; no muse befriends; no invention, no hope.

Trust thyself: every heart vibrates to that iron string. Accept the place the divine providence has found for you, the society of your contemporaries, the connection of events. Great men have always done so, and confided themselves childlike to the genius of their age, betraying their perception that the absolutely trustworthy was seated at their heart, working through their hands, predominating in all their being. And we are now men, and must accept in the highest mind the same transcendent destiny; and not minors and invalids in a protected corner, not cowards fleeing before a revolution, but guides, redeemers, and benefactors, obeying the Almighty effort and advancing on Chaos and the Dark.

What pretty oracles nature yields us on this text in the face and behavior of children, babes, and even brutes! That divided and rebel mind, that distrust of a sentiment because our arithmetic has computed the strength and means opposed to our purpose, these have not. Their mind being whole, their eye is as yet unconquered, and when we look in their faces we are disconcerted. Infancy conforms to nobody; all conform to it; so that one babe commonly makes four or five out of the adults who prattle and play to it. So God has armed youth and puberty and manhood no less with its own piquancy and charm, and made it enviable and gracious and its claims not to be put by, if it will stand by itself. Do not think the youth has no force, because he cannot speak to you and me. Hark! in the next room his voice is sufficiently clear and emphatic. It seems he knows how to speak to his contemporaries. Bashful or bold then, he will know how to make us seniors very unnecessary.

The nonchalance of boys who are sure of a dinner, and would disdain as much as a lord to do or say aught to conciliate one, is the healthy attitude of human nature. A boy is in the parlor what the pit is in the playhouse; independent, irresponsible, looking out from his corner on such people and facts as pass by, he tries and sentences them on their merits, in the swift, summary ways of boys, as good, bad, interesting, silly, eloquent, troublesome. He cumbers himself never about consequences, about interests; he gives an independent, genuine verdict. You must court him; he does not court you. But the man is as it were clapped into jail by his consciousness. As soon as he has once acted or spoken with *éclat* he is a committed person, watched by the sympathy or the hatred of hundreds whose affections must now enter into his account. There is no Lethe for this. Ah, that he could pass again into his neutrality! Who can thus avoid all pledges and, having observed, observe again from the same unaffected, unbiased, unbribable, unaffrighted innocence, — must always be formidable. He would utter opinions on all passing affairs, which being seen to be not private but necessary, would sink like darts into the ear of men and put them in fear.

These are the voices which we hear in solitude, but they grow faint and inaudible as we enter into the world. Society everywhere is in conspiracy against the manhood of every one of its members. Society is a joint-stock company, in which the members agree, for the better securing of his bread to each shareholder, to surrender the liberty and culture of the eater. The virtue in most request is conformity. Self-reliance is its aversion. It loves not realities and creators, but names and customs.

Whoso would be a man, must be a nonconformist. He who would gather immortal palms must not be hindered by the name of goodness, but must explore if it be goodness. Nothing is at last sacred but the integrity of your own mind. Absolve you to yourself, and you shall have the suffrage of the world. I remember an answer which when quite young I was prompted to make to a valued adviser who was wont to importune me with the dear old doctrines of the church. On my saying, "What have I to do with the sacredness of traditions, if I live wholly from within?" my friend suggested, — "But these impulses may be from below, not from above." I replied, "They do not seem to me to be such; but if I am the Devil's child, I will live then from the Devil." No law can be sacred to me but that of my nature. Good and bad are but names very readily transferable to that or this; the only right is what is after my constitution; the only wrong what is against it. A man is to carry himself in the presence of all opposition as if everything were titular and ephemeral but he. I am ashamed to think how easily we capitulate to badges and names, to large societies and dead institutions. Every decent and well-spoken individual affects and sways me more than is right. I ought to go upright and vital, and speak the rude truth in all ways. If malice and vanity wear the coat of philanthropy, shall that pass? If an angry bigot assumes this bountiful cause of Abolition, and comes to me with his last news from Barbadoes, why should I not say to him, "Go love thy infant; love thy woodchopper; be good-natured and modest; have that grace; and never varnish your hard, uncharitable ambition with this incredible tenderness for black folk a thousand miles off. Thy love afar is spite at home." Rough and graceless would be such greeting, but truth is handsomer than the affectation of love. Your goodness must have some edge to it, — else it is none. The doctrine of hatred must be preached, as the counteraction of the doctrine of love, when that pules and whines. I shun father and mother and wife and brother when my genius calls me. I would write on the lintels of the doorpost, Whim. I hope it is somewhat better than whim at last, but we cannot spend the day in explanation. Expect me not to show cause why I seek or why I exclude company. Then again, do not tell me, as a good man did to-day, of my obligation to put all poor men in good situations. Are they my poor? I tell thee, thou foolish philanthropist, that I grudge the dollar, the dime, the cent I give to such men as do not belong to me and to whom I do not belong. There is a class of persons to whom by all spiritual affinity I am bought and sold; for them I will go to prison if need be; but your miscellaneous popular charities; the education at college of fools; the building of meeting-houses to the vain end to which many now stand; alms to sots, and the thousand-fold Relief Societies; — though I confess with shame I sometimes succumb and give the dollar, it is a wicked dollar, which by and by I shall have the manhood to withhold.

Virtues are, in the popular estimate, rather the exception than the rule. There is the man and his virtues. Men do what is called a good action, as some piece of courage or charity, much as they would pay a fine in expiation of daily non-appearance on parade. Their works are done as an apology or extenuation of their living in the world, — as invalids and the insane pay a high board. Their virtues are penances. I do not wish to expiate, but to live. My life is for itself and not for a spectacle. I much prefer that it should be of a lower strain, so it be genuine and equal, than that it should be glittering and unsteady. I wish it to be sound and sweet, and not to need diet and bleeding. I ask primary evidence that you are a man and refuse this appeal from the man to his actions. I know that for myself it makes no difference whether I do or forbear those actions which are reckoned excellent. I cannot consent to pay for a privilege where I have intrinsic right. Few and mean as my gifts may be, I actually am, and do not need for my own assurance or the assurance of my fellows any secondary testimony.

What I must do is all that concerns me, not what the people think. This rule, equally arduous in actual and in intellectual life, may serve for the whole distinction between greatness and meanness. It is the harder because you will always find those who think they know what is your duty better than you know it. It is easy in the world to live after the world's opinion; it is easy in solitude to live after our own; but the great man is he who in the midst of the crowd keeps with perfect sweetness the independence of solitude.

The objection to conforming to usages that have become dead to you is that it scatters your force. It loses your time and blurs the impression of your character. If you maintain a dead church, contribute to a dead Bible-society, vote with a great party either for the government or against it, spread your table like base housekeepers, — under all these screens I have difficulty to detect the precise man you are: and of course so much force is withdrawn from all your proper life. But do your work, and I shall know you. Do your work, and you shall reinforce yourself. A man must consider what a blindman's-buff is this game of conformity. If I know your sect I anticipate your argument. I hear a preacher announce for his text and topic the expediency of one of the institutions of his church. Do I not know beforehand that not possibly can he say a new and spontaneous word? Do I not know that with all this ostentation of grounds of the institution he will do no such thing? Do I not know that he is pledged to himself not to look but at one side, the permitted side, not as a man, but as a parish minister? He is a retained attorney, and these airs of the bench are the emptiest affectation. Well, most men have bound their eyes with one or another handkerchief, and attached themselves to some one of these communities of opinion. This conformity makes them not false in a few particulars, authors of a few lies, but false in all particulars. Their every truth is not quite true. Their two is not the real two, their four not the real four; so that every word they say chagrins us and we know not where to begin to set them right. Meantime nature is not slow to equip us in the prison-uniform of the party to which we adhere. We come to wear one cut of face and figure, and acquire by degrees the gentlest asinine expression. There is a mortifying experience in particular, which does not fail to wreak itself also in the general history; I mean the "foolish face of praise," the forced smile which we put on in company where we do not feel at ease, in answer to conversation which does not interest us. The muscles, not spontaneously moved but moved by a low usurping wilfulness, grow tight about the outline of the face, with the most disagreeable sensation.

For nonconformity the world whips you with its displeasure. And therefore a man must know how to estimate a sour face. The by-standers look askance on him in the public street or in the friend's parlor. If this aversion had its origin in contempt and resistance like his own he might well go home with a sad countenance; but the sour faces of the multitude, like their sweet faces, have no deep cause, but are put on and off as the wind blows and a newspaper directs. Yet is the discontent of the multitude more formidable than that of the senate and the college. It is easy enough for a firm man who knows the world to brook the rage of the cultivated classes. Their rage is decorous and prudent for they are timid, as being very vulnerable themselves. But when to their feminine rage the indignation of the people is added, when the ignorant and the poor are aroused, when the unintelligent brute force that lies at the bottom of society is made to growl and mow, it needs the habit of magnanimity and religion to treat it godlike as a trifle of no concernment.

The other terror that scares us from self-trust is our consistency; a reverence for our past act or word because the eyes of others have no other data for computing our orbit than our past acts, and we are loth to disappoint them.

But why should you keep your head over your shoulder? Why drag about this corpse of your memory, lest you contradict somewhat you have stated in this or that public place? Suppose you should contradict yourself; what then? It seems to be a rule of wisdom never to rely on your memory alone, scarcely even in acts of pure memory, but to bring the past for judgment into the thousand-eyed present, and live ever in a new day. In your metaphysics you have denied personality to the Deity, yet when the devout motions of the soul come, yield to them heart and life, though they should clothe God with shape and color. Leave your theory, as Joseph his coat in the hand of the harlot, and flee.

A foolish consistency is the hobgoblin of little minds, adored by little statesmen and philosophers and divines. With consistency a great soul has simply nothing to do. He may as well concern himself with his shadow on the wall. Speak what you think now in hard words and to-morrow speak what to-morrow thinks in hard words again, though it contradict everything you said to-day. — "Ah, so you shall be sure to be misunderstood." — Is it so bad then to be misunderstood? Pythagoras was misunderstood, and Socrates, and Jesus, and Luther, and Copernicus, and Galileo, and Newton, and every pure and wise spirit that ever took flesh. To be great is to be misunderstood.

I suppose no man can violate his nature. All the sallies of his will are rounded in by the law of his being, as the inequalities of Andes and Himmaleh are insignificant in the curve of the sphere. Nor does it matter how you gauge and try him. A character is like an acrostic or Alexandrian stanza; — read it forward, backward, or across, it still spells the same thing. In this pleasing contrite woodlife which God allows me, let me record day by day my honest thought without prospect or retrospect, and I cannot doubt, it will be found symmetrical, though I mean it not and see it not. My book should smell of pines and resound with the hum of insects. The swallow over my window should interweave that thread or straw he carries in his bill into my web also. We pass for what we are. Character teaches above our wills. Men imagine that they communicate their virtue or vice only by overt actions, and do not see that virtue or vice emit a breath every moment.

There will be an agreement in whatever variety of actions, so they be each honest and natural in their hour. For of one will, the actions will be harmonious, however unlike they seem. These varieties are lost sight of at a little distance, at a little height of thought. One tendency unites them all. The voyage of the best ship is a zigzag line of a hundred tacks. See the line from a sufficient distance, and it straightens itself to the average tendency. Your genuine action will explain itself and will explain your other genuine actions. Your conformity explains nothing. Act singly, and what you have already done singly will justify you now. Greatness appeals to the future. If I can be firm enough to-day to do right and scorn eyes, I must have done so much right before as to defend me now. Be it how it will, do right now. Always scorn appearances and you always may. The force of character is cumulative. All the foregone days of virtue work their health into this. What makes the majesty of the heroes of the senate and the field, which so fills the imagination? The consciousness of a train of great days and victories behind. They shed a united light on the advancing actor. He is attended as by a visible escort of angels. That is it which throws thunder into Chatham's voice, and dignity into Washington's port, and America into Adams's eye. Honor is venerable to us because it is no ephemera. It is always ancient virtue. We worship it to-day because it is not of to-day. We love it and pay it homage because it is not a trap for our love and homage, but is self-dependent, self-derived, and therefore of an old immaculate pedigree, even if shown in a young person.

I hope in these days we have heard the last of conformity and consistency. Let the words be gazetted and ridiculous henceforward. Instead of the gong for dinner, let us hear a whistle from the Spartan fife. Let us never bow and apologize more. A great man is coming to eat at my house. I do not wish to please him; I wish that he should wish to please me. I will stand here for humanity, and though I would make it kind, I would make it true. Let us affront and reprimand the smooth mediocrity and squalid contentment of the times, and hurl in the face of custom and trade and office, the fact which is the upshot of all history, that there is a great responsible Thinker and Actor working wherever a man works; that a true man belongs to no other time or place, but is the center of things. Where he is there is nature. He measures you and all men and all events. Ordinarily, everybody in society reminds us of somewhat else, or of some other person. Character, reality, reminds you of nothing else; it takes place of the whole creation. The man must be so much that he must make all circumstances indifferent. Every true man is a cause,

a country, and an age; requires infinite spaces and numbers and time fully to accomplish his design; — and posterity seem to follow his steps as a train of clients. A man Cæsar is born, and for ages after we have a Roman Empire. Christ is born, and millions of minds so grow and cleave to his genius that he is confounded with virtue and the possible of man. An institution is the lengthened shadow of one man; as, Monachism, of the Hermit Antony; the Reformation, of Luther; Quakerism, of Fox; Methodism, of Wesley; Abolition, of Clarkson. Scipio, Milton called "the height of Rome"; and all history resolves itself very easily into the biography of a few stout and earnest persons.

Let a man then know his worth, and keep things under his feet. Let him not peep or steal, or skulk up and down with the air of a charity-boy, a bastard, or an interloper in the world which exists for him. But the man in the street, finding no worth in himself which corresponds to the force which built a tower or sculptured a marble god, feels poor when he looks on these. To him a palace, a statue, or a costly book have an alien and forbidding air, much like a gay equipage, and seem to say like that, "Who are you, Sir?" Yet they are all his, suitors for his notice, petitioners to his faculties that they will come out and take possession. The picture waits for my verdict; it is not to command me, but I am to settle its claims to praise. That popular fable of the sot who was picked up dead-drunk in the street, carried to the duke's house, washed and dressed and laid in the duke's bed, and, on his waking, treated with all obsequious ceremony like the duke, and assured that he had been insane, owes its popularity to the fact that it symbolizes so well the state of man, who is in the world a sort of sot, but now and then wakes up, exercises his reason and finds himself a true prince.

Our reading is mendicant and sycophantic. In history our imagination plays us false. Kingdom and lordship, power and estate, are a gaudier vocabulary than private John and Edward in a small house and common day's work; but the things of life are the same to both; the sum total of both is the same. Why all this deference to Alfred and Scanderbeg and Gustavus? Suppose they were virtuous; did they wear out virtue? As great a stake depends on your private act to-day as followed their public and renowned steps. When private men shall act with original views, the lustre will be transferred from the actions of kings to those of gentlemen.

The world has been instructed by its kings, who have so magnetized the eyes of nations. It has been taught by this colossal symbol the mutual reverence that is due from man to man. The joyful loyalty with which men have everywhere suffered the king, the noble, or the great proprietor to walk among them by a law of his own, make his own scale of men and things and reverse theirs, pay for benefits not with money but with honor, and represent the law in his person, was the hieroglyphic by which they obscurely signified their consciousness of their own right and comeliness, the right of every man.

The magnetism which all original action exerts is explained when we inquire the reason of self-trust. Who is the Trustee? What is the aboriginal Self, on which a universal reliance may be grounded? What is the nature and power of that science-baffling star, without parallax, without calculable elements, which shoots a ray of beauty even into trivial and impure actions, if the least mark of independence appear? The inquiry leads us to that source, at once the essence of genius, of virtue, and of life, which we call Spontaneity or Instinct. We denote this primary wisdom as Intuition, whilst all later teachings are tuitions. In that deep force, the last fact behind which analysis cannot go, all things find their common origin. For the sense of being which in calm hours rises, we know not how, in the soul, is not diverse from things, from space, from light, from time, from man, but one with them and proceeds obviously from the same source whence their life and being also proceed. We first share the life by which things exist and afterwards see them as appearances in nature and forget that we have shared their cause. Here is the fountain of action and of thought. Here are the lungs of that inspiration which giveth man wisdom and which cannot be denied without impiety and atheism. We lie in the lap of immense intelligence, which makes us receivers of its truth and organs of its activity. When we discern justice, when we discern truth, we do nothing of ourselves, but allow a passage to its beams. If we ask whence this comes, if we seek to pry into the soul that causes, all philosophy is at fault. Its presence or its absence is all we can affirm. Every man discriminates between the voluntary acts of his mind and his involuntary perceptions, and knows that to his involuntary perceptions a perfect

faith is due. He may err in the expression of them, but he knows that these things are so, like day and night, not to be disputed. My wilful actions and acquisitions are but roving; — the idlest reverie, the faintest native emotion, command my curiosity and respect. Thoughtless people contradict as readily the statement of perceptions as of opinions, or rather much more readily; for they do not distinguish between perception and notion. They fancy that I choose to see this or that thing. But perception is not whimsical, but fatal. If I see a trait, my children will see it after me, and in course of time all mankind, — although it may chance that no one has seen it before me. For my perception of it is as much a fact as the sun.

The relations of the soul to the divine spirit are so pure that it is profane to seek to interpose helps. It must be that when God speaketh he should communicate, not one thing, but all things; should fill the world with his voice; should scatter forth light, nature, time, souls, from the center of the present thought; and new date and new create the whole. Whenever a mind is simple and receives a divine wisdom, old things pass away, — means, teachers, texts, temples fall; it lives now, and absorbs past and future into the present hour. All things are made sacred by relation to it, — one as much as another. All things are dissolved to their center by their cause, and in the universal miracle petty and particular miracles disappear. If therefore a man claims to know and speak of God and carries you backward to the phraseology of some old mouldered nation in another country, in another world, believe him not. Is the acorn better than the oak which is its fulness and completion? Is the parent better than the child into whom he has cast his ripened being? Whence then this worship of the past? The centuries are conspirators against the sanity and authority of the soul. Time and space are but physiological colors which the eye makes, but the soul is light: where it is, is day; where it was, is night; and history is an impertinence and an injury if it be anything more than a cheerful apologue or parable of my being and becoming.

Man is timid and apologetic; he is no longer upright; he dares not say "I think," "I am," but quotes some saint or sage. He is ashamed before the blade of grass or the blowing rose. These roses under my window make no reference to former roses or to better ones; they are for what they are; they exist with God to-day. There is no time for them. There is simply the rose; it is perfect in every moment of its existence. Before a leaf-bud has burst, its whole life acts; in the full-blown flower there is no more; in the leafless root there is no less. Its nature is satisfied and it satisfies nature in all moments alike. But man postpones or remembers; he does not live in the present, but with reverted eye laments the past, or, heedless of the riches that surround him, stands on tiptoe to foresee the future. He cannot be happy and strong until he too lives with nature in the present, above time.

This should be plain enough. Yet see what strong intellects dare not yet hear God himself unless he speaks the phraseology of I know not what David, or Jeremiah, or Paul. We shall not always set so great a price on a few texts, on a few lives. We are like children who repeat by rote the sentences of grandames and tutors, and, as they grow older, of the men of talents and character they chance to see, — painfully recollecting the exact words they spoke; afterwards, when they come into the point of view which those had who uttered these sayings, they understand them and are willing to let the words go; for at any time they can use words as good when occasion comes. If we live truly, we shall see truly. It is as easy for the strong man to be strong, as it is for the weak to be weak. When we have new perception, we shall gladly disburden the memory of its hoarded treasures as old rubbish. When a man lives with God, his voice shall be as sweet as the murmur of the brook and the rustle of the corn.

And now at last the highest truth on this subject remains unsaid; probably cannot be said: for all that we say is the far-off remembering of the intuition. That thought by what I can now nearest approach to say it, is this. When good is near you, when you have life in yourself, it is not by any known or accustomed way; you shall not discern the footprints of any other; you shall not see face of man; you shall not hear any name; — the way, the thought, the good, shall be wholly strange and new. It shall exclude example and experience. You take the way from man, not to man. All persons that ever existed are its forgotten ministers. Fear and hope are alike beneath it. There is somewhat low even in hope. In the hour of vision there is nothing that can be called gratitude, nor properly joy. The soul raised over passion be-

holds identity and eternal causation, perceives the self-existence of Truth and Right, and calms itself with knowing that all things go well. Vast spaces of nature, the Atlantic Ocean, the South Sea; long intervals of time, years, centuries, are of no account. This which I think and feel underlay every former state of life and circumstances, as it does underlie my present, and what is called life and what is called death.

Life only avails, not the having lived. Power ceases in the instant of repose; it resides in the moment of transition from a past to a new state, in the shooting of the gulf, in the darting to an aim. This one fact the world hates; that the soul *becomes*; for that forever degrades the past, turns all riches to poverty, all reputation to a shame, confounds the saint with the rogue, shoves Jesus and Judas equally aside. Why then do we prate of self-reliance? Inasmuch as the soul is present there will be power not confident but agent. To talk of reliance is a poor external way of speaking. Speak rather of that which relies because it works and is. Who has more obedience than I masters me, though he should not raise his finger. Round him I must revolve by the gravitation of spirits. We fancy it rhetoric when we speak of eminent virtue. We do not yet see that virtue is Height, and that a man or a company of men, plastic and permeable to principles, by the law of nature must overpower and ride all cities, nations, kings, rich men, poets, who are not.

This is the ultimate fact which we so quickly reach on this, as on every topic, the resolution of all into the ever-blessed ONE. Self-existence is the attribute of the Supreme Cause, and it constitutes the measure of good by the degree in which it enters into all lower forms. All things real are so by so much virtue as they contain. Commerce, husbandry, hunting, whaling, war, eloquence, personal weight, are somewhat, and engage my respect as examples of its presence and impure action. I see the same law working in nature for conservation and growth. Power is, in nature, the essential measure of right. Nature suffers nothing to remain in her kingdoms which cannot help itself. The genesis and maturation of a planet, its poise and orbit, the bended tree recovering itself from the strong wind, the vital resources of every animal and vegetable, are demonstrations of the self-sufficing and therefore self-relying soul.

Thus all concentrates: let us not rove; let us sit at home with the cause. Let us stun and astonish the intruding rabble of men and books and institutions by a simple declaration of the divine fact. Bid the invaders take the shoes from off their feet, for God is here within. Let our simplicity judge them, and our docility to our own law demonstrate the poverty of nature and fortune beside our native riches.

But now we are a mob. Man does not stand in awe of man, nor is his genius admonished to stay at home, to put itself in communication with the internal ocean, but it goes abroad to beg a cup of water of the urns of other men. We must go alone. I like the silent church before the service begins, better than any preaching. How far off, how cool, how chaste the persons look, begirt each one with a precinct or sanctuary! So let us always sit. Why should we assume the faults of our friend, or wife, or father, or child, because they sit around our hearth, or are said to have the same blood? All men have my blood and I all men's. Not for that will I adopt their petulance or folly, even to the extent of being ashamed of it. But your isolation must not be mechanical, but spiritual, that is, must be elevation. At times the whole world seems to be in conspiracy to importune you with emphatic trifles. Friend, climate, child, sickness, fear, want, charity, all knock at once at thy closet door and say, — "Come out unto us." But keep thy state; come not into their confusion. The power men possess to annoy me I give them by a weak curiosity. No man can come near me but through my act. "What we love that we have, but by desire we bereave ourselves of the love."

If we cannot at once rise to the sanctities of obedience and faith, let us at least resist our temptations; let us enter into the state of war and wake Thor and Woden, courage and constancy, in our Saxon breasts. This is to be done in our smooth times by speaking the truth. Check this lying hospitality and lying affection. Live no longer to the expectation of these deceived and deceiving people with whom we converse. Say to them, "Oh father, O mother, O wife, O brother, O friend, I have lived with you after appearances hitherto. Henceforward I am the truth's. Be it known unto you that henceforward I obey no law less than the eternal law. I will have no covenants but proximities. I shall endeavor to nourish my parents, to support my family, to be the chaste husband of one wife, — but these relations I must fill after a new and unprecedented way. I appeal from your customs. I must be myself. I cannot break myself any longer for you, or you. If you can love me for what I am, we shall be the happier. If you cannot, I will still seek to deserve that you should. I will not hide my tastes or aversions. I will so trust that what is deep is holy, that I will do strongly before the sun and moon whatever inly rejoices me and the heart appoints. If you are noble, I will love you; if you are not, I will not hurt you and myself by hypocritical attentions. If you are true, but not in the same truth with me, cleave to your companions; I will seek my own. I do this not selfishly but humbly and truly. It is alike your interest, and mine, and all men's, however long we have dwelt in lies, to live in truth. Does this sound harsh to-day? You will soon love what is dictated by your nature as well as mine, and if we follow the truth it will bring us out safe at last." — But so may you give these friends pain. Yes, but I cannot sell my liberty and my power, to save their sensibility. Besides, all persons have their moments of reason, when they look out into the region of absolute truth; then will they justify me and do the same thing.

The populace think that your rejection of popular standards is a rejection of all standard, and mere antinomianism; and the bold sensualist will use the name of philosophy to gild his crimes. But the law of consciousness abides. There are two confessionals, in one or the other of which we must be shriven. You may fulfil your round of duties by clearing yourself in the *direct*, or in the *reflex* way. Consider whether you have satisfied your relations to father, mother, cousin, neighbor, town, cat and dog — whether any of these can upbraid you. But I may also neglect this reflex standard and absolve me to myself. I have my own stern claims and perfect circle. It denies the name of duty to many offices that are called duties. But if I can discharge its debts it enables me to dispense with the popular code. If any one imagines that this law is lax, let him keep its commandment one day.

And truly it demands something godlike in him who has cast off the common motives of humanity and has ventured to trust himself for a taskmaster. High be his heart, faithful his will, clear his sight, that he may in good earnest be doctrine, society, law, to himself, that a simple purpose may be to him as strong as iron necessity is to others!

If any man consider the present aspects of

what is called by distinction *society*, he will
see the need of these ethics. The sinew and
heart of man seem to be drawn out, and we are
become timorous, desponding whimperers. We
are afraid of truth, afraid of fortune, afraid of 5
death, and afraid of each other. Our age yields
no great and perfect persons. We want men
and women who shall renovate life and our
social state, but we see that most natures are
insolvent, cannot satisfy their own wants, have 10
an ambition out of all proportion to their practical force and do lean and beg day and night
continually. Our housekeeping is mendicant,
our arts, our occupations, our marriages, our
religion we have not chosen, but society has 15
chosen for us. We are parlor soldiers. We shun
the rugged battle of fate, where strength is born.

If our young men miscarry in their first enterprises they lose all heart. If the young merchant
fails, men say he is *ruined*. If the finest genius 20
studies at one of our colleges and is not installed
in an office within one year afterwards in the
cities or suburbs of Boston or New York, it seems
to his friends and to himself that he is right in
being disheartened and in complaining the rest 25
of his life. A sturdy lad from New Hampshire
or Vermont, who in turn tries all the professions,
who *teams it, farms it, peddles*, keeps a school,
preaches, edits a newspaper, goes to Congress,
buys a township, and so forth, in successive 30
years, and always like a cat falls on his feet, is
worth a hundred of these city dolls. He walks
abreast with his days and feels no shame in not
"studying a profession," for he does not postpone
his life, but lives already. He has not one chance, 35
but a hundred chances. Let a Stoic open the
resources of man and tell men they are not leaning willows, but can and must detach themselves;
that with the exercise of self-trust, new powers
shall appear; that a man is the word made flesh, 40
born to shed healing to the nations; that he
should be ashamed of our compassion, and that
the moment he acts from himself, tossing the
laws, the books, idolatries and customs out of
the window, we pity him no more but thank and 45
revere him; — and that teacher shall restore the
life of man to splendor and make his name dear
to all history.

It is easy to see that a greater self-reliance
must work a revolution in all the offices and 50
relations of men; in their religion; in their education; in their pursuits; in their modes of living;
in their association; in their property; in their speculative views.

1. In what prayers do men allow themselves!
That which they call a holy office is not so much
as brave and manly. Prayer looks abroad and
asks for some foreign addition to come through
some foreign virtue, and loses itself in endless
mazes of natural and supernatural, and medi-
atorial and miraculous. Prayer that craves a
particular commodity, anything less than all
good, is vicious. Prayer is the contemplation of
the facts of life from the highest point of view.
It is the soliloquy of a beholding and jubilant
soul. It is the spirit of God pronouncing his
works good. But prayer as a means to effect a
private end is meanness and theft. It supposes
dualism and not unity in nature and consciousness. As soon as the man is at one with God,
he will not beg. He will then see prayer in all
action. The prayer of the farmer kneeling in
his field to weed it, the prayer of the rower kneeling with the stroke of his oar, are true prayers
heard throughout nature, though for cheap ends.
Caratach, in Fletcher's *Bonduca*, when admonished to inquire the mind of the god Audate,
replies, —

His hidden meaning lies in our endeavors;
Our valors are our best gods.

Another sort of false prayers are our regrets.
Discontent is the want of self-reliance: it is
infirmity of will. Regret calamities if you can
thereby help the sufferer; if not attend your own
work and already the evil begins to be repaired.
Our sympathy is just as base. We come to them
who weep foolishly and sit down and cry for
company, instead of imparting to them truth
and health in rough electric shocks, putting
them once more in communication with their
own reason. The secret of fortune is joy in our
hands. Welcome evermore to gods and men is
the self-helping man. For him all doors are
flung wide; him all tongues greet, all honors
crown, all eyes follow with desire. Our love goes
out to him and embraces him because he did not
need it. We solicitously and apologetically
caress and celebrate him because he held on his
way and scorned our disapprobation. The gods
love him because men hated him. "To the
persevering mortal," said Zoroaster, "the blessed
Immortals are swift."

As men's prayers are a disease of the will, so
are their creeds a disease of the intellect. They
say with those foolish Israelites, "Let not God
speak to us, lest we die. Speak thou, speak any

man with us, and we will obey." Everywhere I am hindered of meeting God in my brother, because he has shut his own temple doors and recites fables merely of his brother's, or his brother's brother's God. Every new mind is a new classification. If it prove a mind of uncommon activity and power, a Locke, a Lavoisier, a Hutton, a Bentham, a Fourier, it imposes its classification on other men, and lo! a new system. In proportion to the depth of the thought, and so to the number of the objects it touches and brings within reach of the pupil, is his complacency. But chiefly is this apparent in creeds and churches, which are also classifications of some powerful mind acting on the elemental thought of duty and man's relation to the Highest. Such is Calvinism, Quakerism, Swedenborgism. The pupil takes the same delight in subordinating everything to the new terminology as a girl who has just learned botany in seeing a new earth and new seasons thereby. It will happen for a time that the pupil will find his intellectual power has grown by the study of his master's mind. But in all unbalanced minds the classification is idolized, passes for the end and not for a speedily exhaustible means, so that the walls of the system blend to their eye in the remote horizon with the walls of the universe; the luminaries of heaven seem to them hung on the arch their master built. They cannot imagine how you aliens have any right to see, — how you can see; "It must be somehow that you stole the light from us." They do not yet perceive that light, unsystematic, indomitable, will break into any cabin, even into theirs. Let them chirp awhile and call it their own. If they are honest and do well, presently their neat new pinfold will be too strait and low, will crack, will lean, will rot and vanish, and the immortal light, all young, and joyful, million-orbed, million-colored, will beam over the universe as on the first morning.

2. It is for want of self-culture that the superstition of Travelling, whose idols are Italy, England, Egypt, retains its fascination for all educated Americans. They who made England, Italy, or Greece venerable in the imagination, did so by sticking fast where they were, like an axis of the earth. In manly hours we feel that duty is our place. The soul is no traveller; the wise man stays at home, and when his necessities, his duties, on any occasion call him from his house, or into foreign lands, he is at home still and shall make men sensible by the expression of his countenance that he goes, the missionary of wisdom and virtue, and visits cities and men like a sovereign and not like an interloper or a valet.

I have no churlish objection to the circumnavigation of the globe for the purposes of art, of study, and benevolence, so that the man is first domesticated, or does not go abroad with the hope of finding somewhat greater than he knows. He who travels to be amused, or to get somewhat which he does not carry, travels away from himself, and grows old even in youth among old things. In Thebes, in Palmyra, his will and mind have become old and dilapidated as they. He carries ruins to ruins.

Travelling is a fool's paradise. Our first journeys discover to us the indifference of places. At home I dream that at Naples, at Rome, I can be intoxicated with beauty and lose my sadness. I pack my trunk, embrace my friends, embark on the sea and at last wake up in Naples, and there beside me is the stern fact, the sad self, unrelenting, identical, that I fled from. I seek the Vatican and the palaces. I affect to be intoxicated with sights and suggestions, but I am not intoxicated. My giant goes with me wherever I go.

3. But the rage of travelling is a symptom of a deeper unsoundness affecting the whole intellectual action. The intellect is vagabond, and our system of education fosters restlessness. Our minds travel when our bodies are forced to stay at home. We imitate; and what is imitation but the travelling of the mind? Our houses are built with foreign taste; our shelves are garnished with foreign ornaments; our opinions, our tastes, our faculties lean, and follow the Past and the Distant. The soul created the arts wherever they have flourished. It was in his own mind that the artist sought his model. It was an application of his own thought to the thing to be done and the conditions to be observed. And why need we copy the Doric or the Gothic model? Beauty, convenience, grandeur of thought and quaint expression are as near to us as to any, and if the American artist will study with hope and love the precise thing to be done by him, considering the climate, the soil, the length of the day, the wants of the people, the habit and form of the government, he will create a house in which all these will find themselves fitted, and taste and sentiment will be satisfied also.

Insist on yourself; never imitate. Your own gift you can present every moment with the cumulative force of a whole life's cultivation; but of the adopted talent of another you have only an extemporaneous half possession. That which each can do best, none but his Maker can teach him. No man yet knows what it is, nor can, till that person has exhibited it. Where is the master who could have taught Shakspeare? Where is the master who could have instructed Franklin, or Washington, or Bacon, or Newton? Every great man is a unique. The Scipionism of Scipio is precisely that part he could not borrow. Shakspeare will never be made by the study of Shakspeare. Do that which is assigned you, and you cannot hope too much or dare too much. There is at this moment for you an utterance brave and grand as that of the colossal chisel of Phidias, or trowel of the Egyptians, or the pen of Moses or Dante, but different from all these. Not possibly will the soul, all rich, all eloquent, with thousand-cloven tongue, deign to repeat itself; but if you can hear what these patriarchs say, surely you can reply to them in the same pitch of voice; for the ear and the tongue are two organs of one nature. Abide in the simple and noble regions of thy life, obey thy heart, and thou shall reproduce the Foreworld again.

4. As our Religion, our Education, our Art look abroad, so does our spirit of society. All men plume themselves on the improvement of society, and no man improves.

Society never advances. It recedes as fast on one side as it gains on the other. It undergoes continual changes; it is barbarous, it is civilized, it is christianized, it is rich, it is scientific; but this change is not amelioration. For everything that is given something is taken. Society acquires new arts and loses old instincts. What a contrast between the well-clad, reading, writing, thinking American, with a watch, a pencil, and a bill of exchange in his pocket, and the naked New Zealander, whose property is a club, a spear, a mat, and an undivided twentieth of a shed to sleep under! But compare the health of the two men and you shall see that the white man has lost his aboriginal strength. If the traveller tell us truly, strike the savage with a broad-axe and in a day or two the flesh shall unite and heal as if you struck the blow into soft pitch, and the same blow shall send the white to his grave.

The civilized man has built a coach, but has lost the use of his feet. He is supported on crutches, but lacks so much support of muscle. He has a fine Geneva watch, but he fails of the skill to tell the hour by the sun. A Greenwich nautical almanac he has, and so being sure of the information when he wants it, the man in the street does not know a star in the sky. The solstice he does not observe; the equinox he knows as little; and the whole bright calendar of the year is without a dial in his mind. His note-books impair his memory; his libraries overload his wit; the insurance-office increases the number of accidents; and it may be a question whether machinery does not encumber; whether we have not lost by refinement some energy, by a Christianity, entrenched in establishments and forms, some vigor of wild virtue. For every Stoic was a Stoic; but in Christendom where is the Christian?

There is no more deviation in the moral standard than in the standard of height or bulk. No greater men are now than ever were. A singular equality may be observed between the great men of the first and of the last ages; nor can all the science, art, religion, and philosophy of the nineteenth century avail to educate greater men than Plutarch's heroes, three or four and twenty centuries ago. Not in time is the race progressive. Phocion, Socrates, Anaxagoras, Diogenes, are great men, but they leave no class. He who is really of their class will not be called by their name, but will be his own man, and in his turn the founder of a sect. The arts and inventions of each period are only its costume and do not invigorate men. The harm of the improved machinery may compensate its good. Hudson and Behring accomplished so much in their fishing-boats as to astonish Parry and Franklin, whose equipment exhausted the resources of science and art. Galileo, with an opera-glass, discovered a more splendid series of celestial phenomena than any one since. Columbus found the New World in an undecked boat. It is curious to see the periodical disuse and perishing of means and machinery which were introduced with loud laudation a few years or centuries before. The great genius returns to essential man. We reckoned the improvements of the art of war among the triumphs of science, and yet Napoleon conquered Europe by the bivouac, which consisted of falling back on naked valor and disencumbering it of all aids. The Emperor held it impossible to make a perfect army, says Las Cases, "without abolishing our arms, magazines, commissaries, and carriages, until, in imitation of the Roman custom, the soldier should receive his supply of corn, grind it in his handmill and bake his bread himself."

Society is a wave. The wave moves onward, but the water of which it is composed does not. The same particle does not rise from the valley to the ridge. Its unity is only phenomenal. The persons who make up a nation to-day, next year die, and their experience dies with them.

And so the reliance on Property, including the reliance on governments which protect it, is the want of self-reliance. Men have looked away from themselves and at things so long that they have come to esteem the religious, learned, and civil institutions as guards of property, and they deprecate assaults on these, because they feel them to be assaults on property. They measure their esteem of each other by what each has, and not by what each is. But a cultivated man becomes ashamed of his property, out of new respect for his nature. Especially he hates what he has if he see that it is accidental, — came to him by inheritance, or gift, or crime; then he feels that it is not having; it does not belong to him, has no root in him and merely lies there because no revolution or no robber takes it away. But that which a man is, does always by necessity acquire; and what the man acquires, is living property, which does not wait the beck of rulers, or mobs, or revolutions, or fire, or storm, or bankruptcies, but perpetually renews itself wherever the man breathes. "Thy lot or portion of life," said the Caliph Ali, "is seeking after thee; therefore be at rest from seeking after it." Our dependence on these foreign goods leads us to our slavish respect for numbers. The political parties meet in numerous conventions; the greater the concourse and with each new uproar of announcement, The delega-

tion from Essex! The Democrats from New Hampshire! The Whigs of Maine! the young patriot feels himself stronger than before by a new thousand of eyes and arms. In like manner the reformers summon conventions and vote and resolve in multitude. Not so, O friends! will the God deign to enter and inhabit you, but by a method precisely the reverse. It is only as a man puts off all foreign support and stands alone that I see him to be strong and to prevail. He is weaker by every recruit to his banner. Is not a man better than a town? Ask nothing of men, and, in the endless mutation, thou only firm column must presently appear the upholder of all that surrounds thee. He who knows that power is inborn, that he is weak because he has looked for good out of him and elsewhere, and, so perceiving, throws himself unhesitatingly on his thought, instantly rights himself, stands in the erect position, commands his limbs, works miracles; just as a man who stands on his feet is stronger than a man who stands on his head.

So use all that is called Fortune. Most men gamble with her, and gain all, and lose all, as her wheel rolls. But do thou leave as unlawful these winnings, and deal with Cause and Effect, the chancellors of God. In the Will work and acquire, and thou hast chained the wheel of Chance, and shall sit hereafter out of fear from her rotations. A political victory, a rise of rents, the recovery of your sick or the return of your absent friend, or some other favorable event raises your spirits, and you think good days are preparing for you. Do not believe it. Nothing can bring you peace but yourself. Nothing can bring you peace but the triumph of principles.

Thoreau

(1862)

❦ "It was a pleasure and a privilege to walk with him," said Emerson of his Concord friend, fourteen years his junior. The rest of the Emerson family enjoyed him when, at times, he lived in the household, and he enjoyed them (see the letters, page 351). As we have noted, Thoreau was almost certainly the "forest seer" of the poem "Woodnotes." Soon after his death, he was the subject of this engaging prose portrait, one of the best essays ever written on Thoreau.

Henry David Thoreau was the last male descendant of a French ancestor who came to this country from the Isle of Guernsey. His character exhibited occasional traits drawn from this blood, in singular combination with a very strong Saxon genius.

He was born in Concord, Massachusetts, on the 12th of July, 1817. He was graduated at Harvard College in 1837, but without any literary distinction. An iconoclast in literature, he seldom thanked colleges for their service to him, holding them in small esteem, whilst yet his debt to them was important. After leaving the University, he joined his brother in teaching a private school, which he soon renounced. His father was a manufacturer of lead-pencils, and Henry applied himself for a time to this craft, believing he could make a better pencil than was then in use. After completing his experiments, he exhibited his work to chemists and artists in Boston, and having obtained their certificates to its excellence and to its equality with the best London manufacture, he returned home contented. His friends congratulated him that he had now opened his way to fortune. But he replied that he should never make another pencil. "Why should I? I would not do again what I have done once." He resumed his endless walks and miscellaneous studies, making every day some new acquaintance with Nature, though as yet never speaking of zoölogy or botany, since, though very studious of natural facts, he was incurious of technical and textual science.

At this time, a strong, healthy youth, fresh from college, whilst all his companions were choosing their profession, or eager to begin some lucrative employment, it was inevitable that his thoughts should be exercised on the same question, and it required rare decision to refuse all the accustomed paths and keep his solitary freedom at the cost of disappointing the natural expectations of his family and friends: all the more difficult that he had a perfect probity, was exact in securing his own independence, and in holding every man to the like duty. But Thoreau never faltered. He was a born protestant. He declined to give up his large ambition of knowledge and action for any narrow craft or profession, aiming at a much more comprehensive calling, the art of living well. If he slighted and defied the opinions of others, it was only that he was more intent to reconcile his practice with his own belief. Never idle or self-indulgent, he preferred, when he wanted money, earning it by some piece of manual labor agreeable to him, as building a boat or a fence, planting, grafting, surveying, or other short work, to any long engagements. With his hardy habits and few wants, his skill in woodcraft, and his powerful arithmetic, he was very competent to live in any part of the world. It would cost him less time to supply his wants than another. He was therefore secure of his leisure.

A natural skill for mensuration, growing out of his mathematical knowledge and his habit of ascertaining the measures and distances of objects which interested him, the size of trees, the depth and extent of ponds and rivers, the height of mountains, and the air-line distance of his favorite summits, — this, and his intimate knowledge of the territory about Concord, made him drift into the profession of land-surveyor. It had the advantage for him that it led him continually into new and secluded grounds, and helped his studies of Nature. His accuracy and skill in this work were readily appreciated, and he found all the employment he wanted.

He could easily solve the problems of the surveyor, but he was daily beset with graver questions, which he manfully confronted. He interrogated every custom, and wished to settle all his practice on an ideal foundation. He was a protestant à outrance, and few lives contain so many renunciations. He was bred to no profession; he never married; he lived alone; he never went to church; he never voted; he refused to pay a tax to the State; he ate no flesh, he drank no wine, he never knew the use of tobacco; and, though a naturalist, he used neither trap nor gun. He chose, wisely no doubt for himself, to be the bachelor of thought and Nature. He had no talent for wealth, and knew how to be poor without the least hint of squalor or inelegance. Perhaps he fell into his way of living without forecasting it much, but approved it with later wisdom. "I am often reminded," he wrote in his journal, "that if I had bestowed on me the wealth of Croesus, my aims must be still the same, and my means essentially the same." He had no temptations to fight against, — no appetites, no passions, no taste for elegant trifles. A fine house, dress, the manners and talk of highly cultivated people, were all thrown away on him. He much preferred a good Indian, and considered these refinements as impediments to conversation, wishing to meet his companion on the simplest terms. He declined invitations to dinner-parties, because there each was in every one's way, and he could not meet the individuals to any purpose. "They make their pride," he said, "in making their dinner cost much; I make my pride in making my dinner cost little." When asked at table what dish he preferred, he answered, "The nearest." He did not like the taste of wine, and never had a vice in his life. He said, "I have a faint recollection of pleasure derived from smoking dried lily-stems, before I was a man. I had commonly a supply of these. I have never smoked anything more noxious."

He chose to be rich by making his wants few, and supplying them himself. In his travels, he used the railroad only to get over so much country as was unimportant to the present purpose, walking hundreds of miles, avoiding taverns, buying a lodging in farmers' and fishermen's houses, as cheaper, and more agreeable to him, and because there he could better find the men and the information he wanted.

There was somewhat military in his nature, not to be subdued, always manly and able, but rarely tender, as if he did not feel himself except in opposition. He wanted a fallacy to oppose, a blunder to pillory, I may say required a little sense of victory, a roll of the drum, to call his powers into full exercise. It cost him nothing to say No; indeed he found it much easier than to say Yes. It seemed as if his first instinct on hearing a proposition was to controvert it, so impatient was he of the limitations of our daily thought. This habit, of course, is a little chilling to the social affections; and though the companion would in the end acquit him of any malice or untruth, yet it mars conversation. Hence, no equal companion stood in affectionate relations with one so pure and guileless.

"I love Henry," said one of his friends, "but I cannot like him; and as for taking his arm, I should as soon think of taking the arm of an elm-tree."

Yet, hermit and stoic as he was, he was really fond of sympathy, and threw himself heartily and childlike into the company of young people whom he loved, and whom he delighted to entertain, as he only could, with the varied and endless anecdotes of his experiences by field and river; and he was always ready to lead a huckleberry-party or a search for chestnuts or grapes. Talking, one day, of a public discourse, Henry remarked that whatever succeeded with the audience was bad. I said, "Who would not like to write something which all can read, like *Robinson Crusoe?* and who does not see with regret that his page is not solid with a right materialistic treatment, which delights everybody?" Henry objected, of course, and vaunted the better lectures which reached only a few persons. But, at supper, a young girl, understanding that he was to lecture at the Lyceum, sharply asked him "whether his lecture would be a nice, interesting story, such as she wished to hear, or whether it was one of those old philosophical things that she did not care about." Henry turned to her, and bethought himself, and, I saw, was trying to believe that he had matter that might fit her and her brother, who were to sit up and go to the lecture, if it was a good one for them.

He was a speaker and actor of the truth, born such, and was ever running into dramatic situations from this cause. In any circumstance it interested all bystanders to know what part Henry would take, and what he would say; and he did not disappoint expectation, but used an original judgment on each emergency. In 1845 he built himself a small framed house on the shores of Walden Pond, and lived there two years alone, a life of labor and study. This action was quite native and fit for him. No one who knew him would tax him with affectation. He was more unlike his neighbors in his thought than in his action. As soon as he had exhausted the advantages of that solitude, he abandoned it. In 1847, not approving some uses to which the public expenditure was applied, he refused to pay his town tax, and was put in jail. A friend paid the tax for him, and he was released. The like annoyance was threatened the next year. But as his friends paid the tax, notwithstanding his protest, I believe he ceased to resist. No opposition or ridicule had any weight with him. He coldly and fully stated his opinion without affecting to believe that it was the opinion of the company. It was of no consequence if every one present held the opposite opinion. On one occasion he went to the University Library to procure some books. The librarian refused to lend them. Mr. Thoreau repaired to the President, who stated to him the rules and usages, which permitted the loan of books to resident graduates, to clergymen who were alumni, and to some others resident within a circle of ten miles' radius from the College. Mr. Thoreau explained to the President that the railroad had destroyed the old scale of distances, — that the library was useless, yes, and President and College useless, on the terms of his rules, — that the one benefit he owed to the College was its library, — that, at this moment, not only his want of books was imperative but he wanted a large number of books, and assured him that he, Thoreau, and not the librarian, was the proper custodian of these. In short, the President found the petitioner so formidable, and the rules getting to look so ridiculous, that he ended by giving him a privilege which in his hands proved unlimited thereafter.

No truer American existed than Thoreau. His preference of his country and condition was genuine, and his aversation from English and European manners and tastes almost reached contempt. He listened impatiently to news or *bon-mots* gleaned from London circles; and though he tried to be civil, these anecdotes fatigued him. The men were all imitating each other, and on a small mould. Why can they not live as far apart as possible, and each be a man by himself? What he sought was the most energetic nature; and he wished to go to Oregon, not to London. "In every part of Great Britain," he wrote in his diary, "are discovered traces of the Romans, their funereal urns, their camps, their dwellings. But New England, at least, is not based on any Roman ruins. We have not to lay the foundations of our houses on the ashes of a former civilization."

But idealist as he was, standing for abolition of slavery, abolition of tariffs, almost for abolition of government, it is needless to say he found himself not only unrepresented in actual politics, but almost equally opposed to every class of reformers. Yet he paid the tribute of his uniform respect to the Anti-slavery party. One man, whose personal acquaintance he had formed, he honored with exceptional regard. Before the first friendly word had been spoken for Captain John Brown, he sent notices to most houses in Concord that he would speak in a public hall on the condition and character of John Brown, on Sunday evening, and invited all people to come. The Republican Committee, the Abolitionist Committee, sent him word that it was premature and not advisable. He replied, — "I did not send to you for advice, but to announce that I am to speak." The hall was filled at an early hour by people of all parties, and his earnest eulogy of the hero was heard by all respectfully, by many with a sympathy that surprised themselves.

It was said of Plotinus that he was ashamed of his body, and 'tis very likely he had good reason for it, — that his body was a bad servant, and he had not skill in dealing with the material world, as happens often to men of abstract intellect. But Mr. Thoreau was equipped with a most adapted and serviceable body. He was of short stature, firmly built, of light complexion, with strong, serious blue eyes, and a grave aspect, — his face covered in the late years with a becoming beard. His senses were acute, his frame well-knit and hardy, his hands strong and skillful in the use of tools. And there was a wonderful fitness of body and mind. He could pace sixteen rods more accurately than another man could measure them with rod and chain. He could find his path in the woods at night, he said, better by his feet than his eyes. He could estimate the measure of a tree very well by his eye; he could estimate the weight of a calf or a pig, like a dealer. From a box containing a bushel or more of loose pencils, he could take up with his hands fast enough just a dozen pencils at every grasp. He was a good swimmer, runner, skater, boatman, and would probably outwalk most countrymen in a day's journey. And the relation of body to mind was still finer than we have indicated. He said he wanted every stride his legs made. The length of his walk uniformly made the length of his writing. If shut up in the house he did not write at all.

He had a strong common sense, like that which Rose Flammock, the weaver's daughter in Scott's romance, commends in her father, as resembling a yardstick, which, whilst it measures dowlas and diaper, can equally well measure tapestry and cloth of gold. He had always a new resource. When I was planting forest trees, and had procured half a peck of acorns, he said that only a small portion of them would be sound, and proceeded to examine them and select the sound ones. But finding this took time, he said, "I think if you put them all into water the good ones will sink"; which experiment we tried with success. He could plan a garden or a house or a barn; would have been competent to lead a "Pacific Exploring Expedition"; could give judicious counsel in the gravest private or public affairs.

He lived for the day, not cumbered and mortified by his memory. If he brought you yesterday a new proposition, he would bring you today another not less revolutionary. A very industrious man, and setting, like all highly organized men, a high value on his time, he seemed the only man of leisure in town, always ready for any excursion that promised well, or for conversation prolonged into late hours. His trenchant sense was never stopped by his rules of daily prudence, but was always up to the new occasion. He liked and used the simplest food, yet, when some one urged a vegetable diet, Thoreau thought all diets a very small matter, saying that "the man who shoots the buffalo lives better than the man who boards at the Graham House." He said, "You can sleep near the railroad, and never be disturbed: Nature knows very well what sounds are worth attending to, and has made up her mind not to hear the railroad-whistle. But things respect the devout mind, and a mental ecstasy was never interrupted." He noted what repeatedly befell him, that, after receiving from a distance a rare plant, he would presently find the same in his own haunts. And those pieces of luck which happen only to good players happened to him. One day, walking with a stranger, who inquired where Indian arrow-heads could be found, he replied, "Everywhere," and, stooping forward, picked one on the instant from the ground. At Mount Washington, in Tuckerman's Ravine, Thoreau had a bad fall, and sprained his foot. As he was in the act of getting up from his fall, he saw for the first time the leaves of the *Arnica mollis*.

His robust common sense, armed with stout hands, keen perceptions, and strong will, cannot yet account for the superiority which shone in his simple and hidden life. I must add the cardinal fact, that there was excellent wisdom in him, proper to a rare class of men, which showed him the material world as a means and symbol. This discovery, which sometimes yields to poets a certain casual and interrupted light, serving for the ornament of their writing, was in him an unsleeping insight; and whatever faults or obstructions of temperament might cloud it, he was not disobedient to the heavenly vision. In his youth he said, one day, "The other world is all my art; my pencils will draw no other; my jackknife will cut nothing else; I do not use it as a means." This was the muse and genius that ruled his opinions, conversation, studies, work, and course of life. This made him a searching judge of men. At first glance he measured his companion, and, though insensible to some fine traits of culture, could very well report his weight and caliber. And this made the impression of genius which his conversation sometimes gave.

He understood the matter in hand at a glance, and saw the limitations and poverty of those he talked with, so that nothing seemed concealed from such terrible eyes. I have repeatedly known young men of sensibility converted in a moment to the belief that this was the man they were in search of, the man of men, who could tell them all they should do. His own dealing with them was never affectionate, but superior, didactic, scorning their petty ways, — very slowly conceding, or not conceding at all, the promise of his society at their houses, or even at his own. "Would he not walk with them?" "He did not know. There was nothing so important to him as his walk; he had no walks to throw away on company." Visits were offered him from respectful parties, but he declined them. Admiring friends offered to carry him at their own cost to the Yellowstone River, — to the West Indies, — to South America. But though nothing could be more grave or considerate than his refusals, they remind one, in quite new relations, of that fop Brummell's reply to the gentleman who offered him his carriage in a shower, "But where will *you* ride, then?" — and what accusing silences, and what searching and irresistible speeches, battering down all defenses, his companions can remember!

Mr. Thoreau dedicated his genius with such entire love to the fields, hills, and waters of his native town that he made them known and interesting to all reading Americans, and to people over the sea. The river on whose banks he was born and died he knew from its springs to its confluence with the Merrimack. He had made summer and winter observations on it for many years, and at every hour of the day and night. The result of the recent survey of the Water Commissioners appointed by the State of Massachusetts he had reached by his private experiments, several years earlier. Every fact which occurs in the bed, on the banks, or in the air over it; the fishes, and their spawning and nests, their manners, their food; the shad-flies which fill the air on a certain evening once a year, and which are snapped at by the fishes so ravenously that many of these die of reple-tion; the conical heaps of small stones on the river-shallows, the huge nests of small fishes, one of which will sometimes overfill a cart; the birds which frequent the stream, heron, duck, sheldrake, loon, osprey; the snake, muskrat, otter, woodchuck, and fox, on the banks; the turtle, frog, hyla, and cricket, which made the banks vocal, — were all known to him, and, as it were, townsmen and fellow-creatures; so that he felt an absurdity or violence in any narrative of one of these by itself apart, and still more of its dimensions on an inch-rule, or in the exhibition of its skeleton, or the specimen of a squirrel or a bird in brandy. He liked to speak of the manners of the river, as itself a lawful creature, yet with exactness, and always to an observed fact. As he knew the river, so the ponds in this region.

One of the weapons he used, more impor-tant to him than microscope or alcohol-receiver to other investigators, was a whim which grew on him by indulgence, yet appeared in gravest statement, namely, of extolling his own town and neighborhood as the most favored center for natural observation. He remarked that the flora of Massachusetts embraced almost all the important plants of America, — most of the oaks, most of the willows, the best pines, the ash, the maple, the beech, the nuts. He returned Kane's "Arctic Voyage" to a friend of whom he had borrowed it, with the remark, that "most of the phenomena noted might be observed in Concord." He seemed a little envious of the Pole, for the coincident sunrise and sunset, or five minutes' day after six months: a splendid fact, which Annursnuc had never afforded him. He found red snow in one of his walks, and told me that he expected to find yet the *Victoria regia* in Concord. He was the attorney of the indigenous plants, and owned to a preference of the weeds to the imported plants, as of the Indian to the civilized man, and noticed, with pleasure, that the willow bean-poles of his neigh-bor had grown more than his beans. "See these weeds," he said, "which have been hoed at by a million farmers all spring and summer, and yet have prevailed, and just now come out tri-umphant over all lanes, pastures, fields, and gardens, such is their vigor. We have insulted them with low names, too, — as Pigweed, Wormwood, Chickweed, Shad-blossom." He says, "They have brave names, too, — Ambrosia, Stellaria, Amelanchier, Amaranth, etc."

I think his fancy for referring everything to the meridian of Concord did not grow out of any ignorance or depreciation of other longitudes or latitudes, but was rather a playful expression of his conviction of the indifferency of all places, and that the best place for each is where he stands. He expressed it once in this wise: "I think nothing is to be hoped from you, if this bit of mould under your feet is not sweeter to you to eat than any other in this world, or in any world."

The other weapon with which he conquered all obstacles in science was patience. He knew how to sit immovable, a part of the rock he rested on, until the bird, the reptile, the fish, which had retired from him, should come back and resume its habits, nay, moved by curiosity, should come to him and watch him.

It was a pleasure and a privilege to walk with him. He knew the country like a fox or a bird, and passed through it as freely by paths of his own. He knew every track in the snow or on the ground, and what creature had taken this path before him. One must submit abjectly to such a guide, and the reward was great. Under his arm he carried an old music-book to press plants; in his pocket, his diary and pencil, a spy-glass for birds, microscope, jack-knife, and twine. He wore a straw hat, stout shoes, strong gray trou-sers, to brave scrub-oaks and smilax, and to climb a tree for a hawk's or a squirrel's nest. He waded into the pool for the water-plants, and his strong legs were no insignificant part of his armor. On the day I speak of he looked for the Meny-anthes, detected it across the wide pool, and, on examination of the florets, decided that it had been in flower five days. He drew out of his breast-pocket his diary, and read the names of all the plants that should bloom on this day, whereof he kept account as a banker when his notes fall due. The Cypripedium not due till tomorrow. He thought that, if waked up from a trance, in this swamp, he could tell by the plants what time of the year it was within two days. The redstart was flying about, and presently the fine grosbeaks, whose brilliant scarlet "makes the rash gazer wipe his eye," and whose fine clear note Thoreau compared to that of a tanager which has got rid of its hoarseness. Presently he heard a note which he called that of the night-warbler, a bird he had never identified, had been in search of twelve years, which always, when he saw it, was in the act of diving down into a tree or bush, and which it was in vain to seek; the only bird which sings indifferently by night and by day. I told him he must beware of finding and booking it, lest life should have nothing more to show him. He said, "What you seek in vain for, half your life, one day you come full upon, all the family at dinner. You seek it like a dream, and as soon as you find it you become its prey."

His interest in the flower or the bird lay very deep in his mind, was connected with Nature,—and the meaning of Nature was never attempted to be defined by him. He would not offer a memoir of his observations to the Natural History Society. "Why should I? To detach the description from its connections in my mind would make it no longer true or valuable to me: and they do not wish what belongs to it." His power of observation seemed to indicate additional senses. He saw as with microscope, heard as with ear-trumpet, and his memory was a photographic register of all he saw and heard. And yet none knew better than he that it is not the fact that imports, but the impression or effect of the fact on your mind. Every fact lay in glory in his mind, a type of the order and beauty of the whole.

His determination on Natural History was organic. He confessed that he sometimes felt like a hound or a panther, and, if born among Indians, would have been a fell hunter. But, restrained by his Massachusetts culture, he played out the game in this mild form of botany and ichthyology. His intimacy with animals suggested what Thomas Fuller records of Butler the apiologist, that "either he had told the bees things or the bees had told him." Snakes coiled round his legs; the fishes swam into his hand, and he took them out of the water; he pulled the woodchuck out of its hole by the tail, and took the foxes under his protection from the hunters. Our naturalist had perfect magnanimity; he had no secrets: he would carry you to the heron's haunt, or even to his most prized botanical swamp,—possibly knowing that you could never find it again, yet willing to take his risks.

No college ever offered him a diploma, or a professor's chair; no academy made him its corresponding secretary, its discoverer or even its member. Perhaps these learned bodies feared the satire of his presence. Yet so much knowledge of Nature's secret and genius few others possessed; none in a more large and religious synthesis. For not a particle of respect had he to the opinions of any man or body of men, but homage solely to the truth itself; and as he discovered everywhere among doctors some leaning of courtesy, it discredited them. He grew to be revered and admired by his townsmen, who had at first known him only as an oddity. The farmers who employed him as a surveyor soon discovered his rare accuracy and skill, his knowledge of their lands, of trees, of birds, of Indian remains and the like, which enabled him to tell every farmer more than he knew before of his own farm; so that he began to feel a little as if Mr. Thoreau had better rights in his land than he. They felt, too, the superiority of character which addressed all men with a native authority.

Indian relics abound in Concord — arrowheads, stone chisels, pestles and fragments of pottery; and on the riverbank, large heaps of clam-shells and ashes mark spots which the savages frequented. These, and every circumstance touching the Indian, were important in his eyes. His visits to Maine were chiefly for love of the Indian. He had the satisfaction of seeing the manufacture of the bark canoe, as well as of trying his hand in its management on the rapids. He was inquisitive about the making of the stone arrowhead, and in his last days charged a youth setting out for the Rocky Mountains to find an Indian who could tell him that: "It was well worth a visit to California to learn it." Occasionally, a small party of Penobscot Indians would visit Concord, and pitch their tents for a few weeks in summer on the river-bank. He failed not to make acquaintance with the best of them; though he well knew that asking questions of Indians is like catechizing beavers and rabbits. In his last visit to Maine he had great satisfaction from Joseph Polis, an intelligent Indian of Oldtown, who was his guide for some weeks.

He was equally interested in every natural fact. The depth of his perception found likeness of law throughout Nature, and I know not any genius who so swiftly inferred universal law from the single fact. He was no pedant of a department. His eye was open to beauty, and his ear to music. He found these, not in rare conditions, but wheresoever he went. He thought the best of music was in single strains; and he found poetic suggestion in the humming of the telegraph-wire.

His poetry might be bad or good; he no doubt wanted a lyric facility and technical skill, but he had the source of poetry in his spiritual perception. He was a good reader and critic, and his judgment on poetry was to the ground of it. He could not be deceived as to the presence or absence of the poetic element in any composition, and his thirst for this made him negligent and perhaps scornful of superficial graces. He would pass by many delicate rhythms, but he would have detected every live stanza or line in a volume and knew very well where to find an equal poetic charm in prose. He was so enamoured of the spiritual beauty that he held all actual written poems in very light esteem in the comparison. He admired Æschylus and Pindar; but when some one was commending them, he said that Æschylus and the Greeks, in describing Apollo and Orpheus, had given no song, or no good one. "They ought not to have moved trees, but to have chanted to the gods such a hymn as would have sung all their old ideas out of their heads, and new ones in." His own verses are often rude and defective. The gold does not yet run pure, is drossy and crude. The thyme and marjoram are not yet honey. But if he want lyric fineness and technical merits, if he have not the poetic temperament, he never lacks the causal thought, showing that his genius was better than his talent. He knew the worth of the Imagination for the uplifting and consolation of human life, and liked to throw every thought into a symbol. The fact you tell is of no value, but only the impression. For this reason his presence was poetic, always piqued the curiosity to know more deeply the secrets of his mind. He had many reserves, an unwillingness to exhibit to profane eyes what was still sacred in his own, and knew well how to throw a poetic veil over his experience. All readers of Walden will remember his mythical record of his disappointments:

"I long ago lost a hound, a bay horse and a turtle-dove, and am still on their trail. Many are the travellers I have spoken concerning them, describing their tracks, and what calls they answered to. I have met one or two who have heard the hound, and the tramp of the horse, and even seen the dove disappear behind a cloud; and they seemed as anxious to recover them as if they had lost them themselves."

His riddles were worth the reading, and I confide that if at any time I do not understand the expression, it is yet just. Such was the wealth of his truth that it was not worth his while to use words in vain. His poem entitled "Sympathy" reveals the tenderness under that triple steel of stoicism, and the intellectual subtilty it could animate. His classic poem on "Smoke" suggests Simonides, but is better than any poem of Simonides. His biography is in his verses. His habitual thought makes all his poetry a hymn to the Cause of causes, the Spirit which vivifies and controls his own:

I hearing get, who had but ears,
And sight, who had but eyes before;
I moments live, who lived but years,
And truth discern, who knew but learning's lore.

And still more in these religious lines:

Now chiefly is my natal hour,
And only now my prime of life;
I will not doubt the love untold,
Which not my worth nor want have bought,
Which wooed me young, and wooes me old,
And to this evening hath me brought.

Whilst he used in his writings a certain petulance of remark in reference to churches or churchmen, he was a person of a rare, tender and absolute religion, a person incapable of any profanation, by act or by thought. Of course, the same isolation which belonged to his original thinking and living detached him from the social religious forms. This is neither to be censured nor regretted. Aristotle long ago explained it, when he said, "One who surpasses his fellow citizens in virtue is no longer a part of the city. Their law is not for him, since he is a law to himself."

Thoreau was sincerity itself, and might fortify the convictions of prophets in the ethical laws by his holy living. It was an affirmative experience which refused to be set aside. A truth-speaker he, capable of the most deep and strict conversation; a physician to the wounds of any soul; a friend, knowing not only the secret of friendship, but almost worshipped by those few persons who resorted to him as their confessor and prophet, and knew the deep value of his mind and great heart. He thought that without religion or devotion of some kind nothing great was ever accomplished: and he thought that the bigoted sectarian had better bear this in mind.

His virtues, of course, sometimes ran into extremes. It was easy to trace to the inexorable demand on all for exact truth that austerity which made this willing hermit more solitary even than he wished. Himself of a perfect probity, he required not less of others. He had a disgust at crime, and no worldly success would cover it. He detected paltering as readily in dignified and prosperous persons as in beggars, and with equal scorn. Such dangerous frankness was in his dealing that his admirers called him "that terrible Thoreau," as if he spoke when silent, and was still present when he had departed. I think the severity of his ideal interfered to deprive him of a healthy sufficiency of human society.

The habit of a realist to find things the reverse of their appearance inclined him to put every statement in a paradox. A certain habit of antagonism defaced his earlier writings, — a trick of rhetoric not quite outgrown in his later, of substituting for the obvious word and thought its diametrical opposite. He praised wild mountains and winter forests for their domestic air, in snow and ice he would find sultriness, and commended the wilderness for resembling Rome and Paris. "It was so dry, that you might call it wet."

The tendency to magnify the moment, to read all the laws of Nature in the one object or one combination under your eye, is of course comic to those who do not share the philosopher's perception of identity. To him there was no such thing as size. The pond was a small ocean; the Atlantic, a large Walden Pond. He referred every minute fact to cosmical laws. Though he meant to be just, he seemed haunted by a certain chronic assumption that the science of the day pretended completeness, and he had just found out that the *savans* had neglected to discriminate a particular botanical variety, had failed to describe the seeds or count the sepals. "That is to say," we replied, "the blockheads were not born in Concord; but who said they were? It was their unspeakable misfortune to be born in London, or Paris, or Rome; but poor fellows, they did what they could, considering that they never saw Bateman's Pond, or Nine-Acre Corner, or Becky Stow's Swamp; be-

sides, what were you sent into the world for, but to add this observation?"

Had his genius been only contemplative, he had been fitted to his life, but with his energy and practical ability he seemed born for great enterprise and for command; and I so much regret the loss of his rare powers of action, that I cannot help counting it a fault in him that he had no ambition. Wanting this, instead of engineering for all America, he was the captain of a huckleberry-party. Pounding beans is good to the end of pounding empires one of these days; but if, at the end of years, it is still only beans!

But these foibles, real or apparent, were fast vanishing in the incessant growth of a spirit so robust and wise, and which effaced its defeats with new triumphs. His study of Nature was a perpetual ornament to him, and inspired his friends with curiosity to see the world through his eyes, and to hear his adventures. They possessed every kind of interest.

He had many elegancies of his own, whilst he scoffed at conventional elegance. Thus, he could not bear to hear the sound of his own steps, the grit of gravel; and therefore never willingly walked in the road, but in the grass, on mountains and in woods. His senses were acute, and he remarked that by night every dwelling-house gives out bad air, like a slaughterhouse. He liked the pure fragrance of melilot. He honored certain plants with special regard, and, over all, the pond-lily, — then, the gentian, and the *Mikania scandens*, and "life-everlasting," and a bass-tree which he visited every year when it bloomed, in the middle of July. He thought the scent a more oracular inquisition than the sight, — more oracular and trustworthy. The scent, of course, reveals what is concealed from the other senses. By it he detected earthliness. He delighted in echoes, and said they were almost the only kind of kindred voices that he heard. He loved Nature so well, was so happy in her solitude, that he became very jealous of cities and the sad work which their refinements and artifices made with man and his dwelling. The axe was always destroying his forest. "Thank God," he said, "they cannot cut down the clouds!" "All kinds of figures are drawn on the blue ground with this fibrous white paint."

I subjoin a few sentences taken from his unpublished manuscripts, not only as records of his thought and feeling, but for their power of description and literary excellence:

"Some circumstantial evidence is very strong, as when you find a trout in the milk."

"The chub is a soft fish, and tastes like boiled brown paper salted."

"The youth gets together his materials to build a bridge to the moon, or, perchance, a palace or temple on the earth, and, at length the middle-aged man concludes to build a wood-shed with them."

"The locust z-ing."

"Devil's-needles zigzagging along the Nut-Meadow brook."

"Sugar is not so sweet to the palate as sound to the healthy ear."

"I put on some hemlock-boughs, and the rich salt crackling of their leaves was like mustard to the ear, the crackling of uncountable regiments. Dead trees love the fire."

"The bluebird carries the sky on his back."

"The tanager flies through the green foliage as if it would ignite the leaves."

"If I wish for a horse-hair for my compass-sight I must go to the stable; but the hair-bird, with her sharp eyes, goes to the road."

"Immortal water, alive even to the superficies."

"Fire is the most tolerable third party."

"Nature made ferns for pure leaves, to show what she could do in that line."

"No tree has so fair a bole and so handsome an instep as the beech."

"How did these beautiful rainbow-tints get into the shell of the fresh-water clam, buried in the mud at the bottom of our dark river?"

"Hard are the times when the infant's shoes are second-foot."

"We are strictly confined to our men to whom we give liberty."

"Nothing is so much to be feared as fear. Atheism may comparatively be popular with God himself."

"Of what significance the things you can forget? A little thought is sexton to all the world."

"How can we expect a harvest of thought who have not had a seed-time of character?"

"Only he can be trusted with gifts who can present a face of bronze to expectations."

"I ask to be melted. You can only ask of the metals that they be tender to the fire that melts them. To nought else can they be tender."

There is a flower known to botanists, one of the same genus with our summer plant called "Life-Everlasting," a *Gnaphalium* like that, which grows on the most inaccessible cliffs of the Tyrolese mountains, where the chamois dare hardly venture, and which the hunter, tempted by its beauty, and by his love (for it is immensely valued by the Swiss maidens), climbs the cliffs to gather, and is sometimes found dead at the foot, with the flower in his hand. It is called by botanists the *Gnaphalium leontopodium*, but by the Swiss *Edelweisse*, which signifies *Noble Purity*. Thoreau seemed to me living in the hope to gather this plant, which belonged to him of right. The scale on which his studies proceeded was so large as to require longevity, and we were the less prepared for his sudden disappearance. The country knows not yet, or in the least part, how great a son it has lost. It seems an injury that he should leave in the midst his broken task which none else can finish, a kind of indignity to so noble a soul that he should depart out of Nature before yet he has been really shown to his peers for what he is. But he, at least, is content. His soul was made for the noblest society; he had in a short life exhausted the capabilities of this world; wherever there is knowledge, wherever there is virtue, wherever there is beauty, he will find a home.

Henry David Thoreau [1817–1862]

To Emerson's biographical sketch of Thoreau it may be worth while to add an account in the manner of *Who's Who*.

Born in Concord, Massachusetts, son of John Thoreau, pencil maker, and Cynthia Dunbar; attended the village academy; at Harvard, mastered Greek and read widely on his own account in English literature; graduated in 1837, the year of "The American

Scholar," and thereafter was associated with Emerson; did some teaching, and began giving lectures; contributed to *The Dial*, both verse and prose; tutored William Emerson's children on Staten Island; lived for a time at Walden Pond; published in 1849 the first of his two books, *A Week on the Concord and Merrimac Rivers*; five years later published *Walden*; published essays gathered into books after his death (*The Maine Woods, A Yankee in Canada*, and *Cape Cod*); journeyed to Minnesota in search of health; died of tuberculosis in Concord the next year, age forty-four; between his return from college and his death had been away from Concord less than a year in all.

Some general comments on Thoreau's writings are given in the period introduction, page 193.

Further reading: *Walden; A Week on the Concord and Merrimac Rivers*. H. S. Canby, *Thoreau* (biography), 1939. B. V. Crawford (ed.), *Henry David Thoreau* (American Writers Series), 1934; Walter Harding (ed.), *Thoreau, A Century of Criticism*, 1954.

Letters to Emerson

When Emerson made his second trip to Europe, he left in his household Henry Thoreau, as man of all work and guardian for Lidian and the children. Thoreau's reports, below, reveal a genial human quality that alleviates the austere tendency of his published writings.

CONCORD, *November 14, 1847*

DEAR FRIEND, — I am but a poor neighbor to you here, — a very poor companion am I. I understand that very well, but that need not prevent my *writing* to you now. I have almost never written letters in my life, yet I think I can write as good ones as I frequently see, so I shall not hesitate to write this, such as it may be, knowing that you will welcome anything that reminds you of Concord.

I have banked up the young trees against the winter and the mice, and I will look out, in my careless way, to see when a pale is loose or a nail drops out of its place. The broad gaps, at least, I will occupy. I heartily wish I could be of good service to this household. But I, who have only used these ten digits so long to solve the problem of a living, how can I? The world is a cow that is hard to milk, — life does not come so easy, — and oh, how thinly it is watered ere we get it! But the young bunting calf, he will get at it. There is no way so direct. This is to earn one's living by the sweat of his brow. It is a little like joining a community, this life, to such a hermit as I am; and as I don't keep the accounts, I don't know whether the experiment will succeed or fail finally. At any rate, it is good for society, so I do not regret my transient nor my permanent share in it.

Lidian [Mrs. Emerson] and I make very good housekeepers. She is a very dear sister to me. Ellen and Edith and Eddy and Aunty Brown keep up the tragedy and comedy and tragic-comedy of life as usual. The two former have not forgotten their old acquaintance; even Edith carries a young memory in her head, I find. Eddy can teach us all how to pronounce. If you should discover any rare hoard of wooden or pewter horses, I have no doubt he will know how to appreciate it. He occasionally surveys mankind from my shoulders as wisely as ever Johnson did. I respect him not a little, though it is I that lift him up so unceremoniously. And sometimes I have to set him down again in a hurry, according to his "mere will and good pleasure." He very seriously asked me, the other day, "Mr. Thoreau, will you be my father?" I am occasionally Mr. Rough-and-tumble with him that I may not miss *him*, and lest he should miss *you* too much. So you must come back soon, or you will be superseded.

Alcott has heard that I laughed, and so set the people laughing, at his arbor, though I never laughed louder than when I was on the ridge-pole. But now I have not laughed for a long time, it is so serious. He is very grave to look at. But, not knowing all this, I strove innocently enough, the other day, to engage his attention to my mathematics. "Did you ever study geometry, the relation of straight lines to curves, the transition from the finite to the infinite? Fine things about it in Newton and Leibnitz." But he would hear none of it, — men of taste preferred the natural curve. Ah, he is a crooked stick himself. He is getting on now so many *knots* an hour. There is one knot at present occupying the point of highest elevation, — the present highest point; and as many knots as are not handsome, I presume, are thrown down and cast into the pines. Pray show him this if you meet him anywhere in London, for I cannot make him hear much plainer words here. He forgets that I am neither old nor young, nor anything in particular, and behaves as if I had still some of the animal heat in me. As for the building, I feel a little oppressed when I come near it. It has no great disposition to be beautiful; it is certainly a wonderful structure, on the whole, and the fame of the architect will endure as long as it shall stand. I should not show you this side alone, if I did not suspect that Lidian had done complete justice to the other.

Mr. [Edmund] Hosmer has been working at a tannery in Stow for a fortnight, though he has just now come home sick. It seems that he was a tanner in his youth, and so he has made up his mind a little at last. This comes of reading the New Testament. Wasn't one of the Apostles a tanner? Mrs. Hosmer remains here, and John looks stout enough to fill his own shoes and his father's too.

Mr. Blood and his company have at length seen the stars through the great telescope, and he told me that he thought it was worth the while. Mr. Peirce made him wait till the crowd had dispersed (it was a Saturday evening), and then was quite polite, — conversed with him, and showed him the micrometer, etc.; and he said Mr. Blood's glass was large enough for all ordinary astronomical work. [Rev.] Mr. Frost and Dr. [Josiah] Bartlett seemed disappointed that there was no greater difference between the Cambridge glass and the Concord one. They used only a power of 400. Mr. Blood tells me that he is too old to study the calculus or higher mathematics. At Cambridge they think that they have discovered traces of another satellite to Neptune. They have been obliged to exclude the public altogether, at last. The very dust which they raised, "which is filled with minute crystals," etc., as professors declare, having to be wiped off the glasses, would ere long wear them away. It is true enough, Cambridge college [Harvard] is really beginning to wake up and redeem its character and overtake the age.

I see by the catalogue that they are about establishing a scientific school in connection with the university, at which any one above eighteen, on paying one hundred dollars annually (Mr. Lawrence's fifty thousand dollars will probably diminish this sum), may be instructed in the highest branches of science, — in astronomy, "theoretical and practical, with the use of the instruments" (so the great Yankee astronomer may be born without delay), in mechanics and engineering to the last degree. Agassiz will ere long commence his lectures in the zoölogical department. A chemistry class has already been formed under the direction of Professor Horsford. A new and adequate building for the purpose is already being erected. They have been foolish enough to put at the end of all this earnest the old joke of a diploma. Let every sheep keep but his own skin, I say.

I have had a tragic correspondence, for the most part all on one side, with Miss ——. She did really wish to — I hesitate to write — marry me. That is the way they spell it. Of course I did not write a deliberate answer. How could I deliberate upon it? I sent back as distinct a *no* as I have learned to pronounce after considerable practice, and I trust that this *no* has succeeded. Indeed, I wished that it might burst, like hollow shot, after it had struck and buried itself and made itself felt there. *There was no other way.* I really had anticipated no such foe as this in my career.

I suppose you will like to hear of my book, though I have nothing worth writing about it. Indeed, for the last month or two I have forgotten it, but shall certainly remember it again. Wiley & Putnam, Munroe, the Harpers, and Crosby & Nichols have all declined printing it with the least risk to themselves; but Wiley & Putnam will print it in their series, and any of them anywhere, at *my* risk. If I liked the book well enough, I should not delay; but for the present I am indifferent. I believe this is, after all, the course you advised, — to let it lie.

I do not know what to say of myself. I sit before my green desk, in the chamber at the head of the stairs, and attend to my thinking, sometimes more, sometimes less distinctly. I am not unwilling to think great thoughts if there are any in the wind, but what they are I am not sure. They suffice to keep me awake while the day lasts, at any rate. Perhaps they will redeem some portion of the night ere long.

I can imagine you astonishing, bewildering,

confounding, and sometimes delighting John Bull with your Yankee notions, and that he begins to take a pride in the relationship at last; introduced to all the stars of England in succession, after the lecture, until you pine to thrust your head once more into a genuine and unquestionable nebula, if there be any left. I trust a common man will be the most uncommon to you before you return to these parts. I have thought there was some advantage even in death, by which we "mingle with the herd of common men."

Hugh [the gardener] still has his eye on the Walden *agellum*, and orchards are waving there in the windy future for him. That's the where-I'll-go-next, thinks he; but no important steps are yet taken. He reminds me occasionally of this open secret of his, with which the very season seems to labor, and affirms seriously that as to his wants — wood, stone, or timber — I know better than he. That is a clincher which I shall have to avoid to some extent; but I fear that it is a wrought nail and will not break. Unfortunately, the day after cattle-show — the day after small beer — he was among the missing, but not long this time. The Ethiopian cannot change his skin nor the leopard his spots, nor indeed Hugh — his Hugh.

As I walked over Conantum, the other afternoon, I saw a fair column of smoke rising from the woods directly over my house that was (as I judged), and already began to conjecture if my deed of sale would not be made invalid by this. But it turned out to be John Richardson's young wood, on the southeast of your field. It was burnt nearly all over, and up to the rails and the road. It was set on fire, no doubt, by the same Lucifer that lighted Brook's lot before. So you see that your small lot is comparatively safe for this season, the back fire having been already set for you.

They have been choosing between John Keys and Sam Staples, if the world wants to know it, as representative of this town, and Staples is chosen. The candidates for governor — think of my writing this to you! — were Governor Briggs and General Cushing, and Briggs is elected, though the Democrats have gained. Ain't I a brave boy to know so much of politics for the nonce? But I shouldn't have known it if Coombs hadn't told me. They have had a peace meeting here, — I shouldn't think of telling you if I didn't know anything would do for the English market, — and some men, Deacon Brown at the head, have signed a long pledge, swearing that they will "treat all mankind as brothers henceforth." I think I shall wait and see how they treat me first. I think that Nature meant kindly when she made our brothers few. However, my voice is still for peace. So good-by, and a truce to all joking, my dear friend, from

H. D. T.

Concord, *February 23, 1848*

Dear Waldo, — For I think I have heard that that is your name, — my letter which was put last into the leathern bag arrived first. Whatever I may *call* you, I know you better than I know your name, and what becomes of the fittest name if in any sense you are here with him who *calls*, and not there simply to be called?

I believe I never thanked you for your lectures, one and all, which I heard formerly read here in Concord. I *know* I never have. There was some excellent reason each time why I did not; but it will never be too late. I have that advantage, at least, over you in my education.

Lidian is too unwell to write to you; so I must tell you what I can about the children and herself. I am afraid she has not told you how unwell she is, — or to-day perhaps we may say has been. She has been confined to her chamber four or five weeks, and three or four weeks, at least, to her bed, with the jaundice. The doctor, who comes once a day, does not let her read (nor can she now) nor *hear* much reading. She has written her letters to you, till recently, sitting up in bed, but he said he would not come again if she did so. She has Abby and Almira to take care of her, and Mrs. Brown to read to her; and I also, occasionally, have something to read or to say. The doctor says she must not expect to "take any comfort of her life" for a week or two yet. She wishes me to say that she has written two long and full letters to you about the household economies, etc., which she hopes have not been delayed. The children are quite well and full of spirits, and are going through a regular course of picture-seeing, with commentary by me, every evening, for Eddy's behoof. All the Annuals and "Diadems" are in requisition, and Eddy is forward to exclaim, when the hour arrives, "Now for the demdems!" I overheard this dialogue when Frank [Brown] came down to breakfast the other morning.

Eddy. "Why, Frank, I am astonished that

you should leave your boots in the dining-room."

Frank. "I guess you mean *surprised,* don't you?"

Eddy. "No, boots!"

"If Waldo were here," said he, the other night, at bedtime, "we'd be four going upstairs." Would he like to tell papa anything? No, not anything; but finally, yes, he would, — that one of the white horses in his new barouche is broken! Ellen and Edith will perhaps speak for themselves, as I hear something about letters to be written by them.

Mr. Alcott seems to be reading well this winter: Plato, Montaigne, Ben Jonson, Beaumont and Fletcher, Sir Thomas Browne, etc., etc., "I believe I have read them all now, or nearly all," — those English authors. He is rallying for another foray with his pen, in his latter years, not discouraged by the past, into that crowd of unexpressed ideas of his, that undisciplined Parthian army, which, as soon as a Roman soldier would face, retreats on all hands, occasionally firing backwards; easily routed, not easily subdued, hovering on the skirts of society. Another summer shall not be devoted to the raising of vegetables (Arbors?) which rot in the cellar for want of consumers; but perchance to the arrangement of the material, the brain-crop which the winter has furnished. I have good talks with him. His respect for Carlyle has been steadily increasing for some time. He has read him with new sympathy and appreciation.

I see Channing often. He also goes often to Alcott's, and confesses that he has made a discovery in him, and gives vent to his admiration or his confusion in characteristic exaggeration; but between this extreme and that you may get a fair report, and draw an inference if you can. Sometimes he will ride a broomstick still, though there is nothing to keep him, or it, up but a certain centrifugal force of whim, which is soon spent, and there lies your stick, not worth picking up to sweep an oven with now. His accustomed path is strewn with them. But then again, and perhaps for the most part, he sits on the Cliffs amid the lichens, or flits past on noiseless pinion, like the barred owl in the daytime, as wise and unobserved. He brought me a poem the other day, for me, on Walden Hermitage: not remarkable.

Lectures begin to multiply on my desk. I have one on Friendship which is new, and the materials of some others. I read one last week

to the Lyceum, on The Rights and Duties of the Individual in Relation to Government, — much to Mr. Alcott's satisfaction.

Joel Britton has failed and gone into chancery, but the woods continue to fall before the axes of other men. Neighbor Coombs was lately found dead in the woods near Goose Pond, with his half-empty jug, after he had been rioting a week. Hugh, by the last accounts, was still in Worcester County. Mr. Hosmer, who is himself again, and living in Concord, has just hauled the rest of your wood, amounting to about ten and a half cords.

The newspapers say that they have printed a pirated edition of your Essays in England. Is it as bad as they say, and undisguised and unmitigated piracy? I thought that the printed scrap would entertain Carlyle, notwithstanding its history. If this generation will see out of its hind-head, why then you may turn your back on its forehead. Will you forward it to him for me?

This stands written in your day-book: "September 3d. Received of Boston Savings Bank, on account of Charles Lane, his deposit with interest, $131.33. 16th. Received of Joseph Palmer, on account of Charles Lane, three hundred twenty-three $^{23}/_{100}$ dollars, being the balance of a note on demand for four hundred dollars, with interest, $323.36."

If you have any directions to give about the trees, you must not forget that spring will soon be upon us.

Farewell. From your friend,

HENRY THOREAU

From his *Journals*

🐝 As published in 1906, Thoreau's journal occupies fourteen volumes. A large proportion is little more than a record of observations of nature, of interest to him but of scant scientific or literary interest to the reader. One example: (August 1, 1854, the year of *Walden*) "Meadow-haying begun for a week. Erechthites, begun for four or five days in Moore's Swamp. Two turtle doves in the stubble beyond. *Hieracium Canadense,* apparently a day or two. Do not see stamens or thyme-leaved pinweed, but *perhaps* petals. Ground-nut well out."

On the other hand, the journal also contains much that could be used, and often was used, as material for lectures and books. Entries of this eminently readable sort follow.

(1841, 1850)

I seem to see somewhat more of my own kith and kin in the lichens on the rocks than in any books. It does seem as if mine were a peculiarly wild nature, which so yearns toward all wildness.***

In literature it is only the wild that attracts us. Dullness is only another name for tameness. It is the untamed, uncivilized, free, and wild thinking in Hamlet, in the Iliad, and in all the scriptures and mythologies that delights us, — not learned in the schools, not refined and polished by art. A truly good book is something as wildly natural and primitive, mysterious and marvellous, ambrosial and fertile, as a fungus or a lichen. Suppose the muskrat or beaver were to turn his views to literature, what fresh views of nature would he present! The fault of our books and other deeds is that they are too humane. I want something speaking in some measure to the condition of muskrats and skunk-cabbage as well as of men, — not merely to a pining and complaining coterie of philanthropists.

(1851)

It is the fault of some excellent writers — De Quincey's first impressions on seeing London suggest it to me — that they express themselves with too great fullness and detail. They give the most faithful, natural, and lifelike account of their sensations, mental and physical, but they lack moderation and sententiousness. They do not affect us by an ineffectual earnestness and a reserve of meaning, like a stutterer; they say all they mean. Their sentences are not concentrated and nutty. Sentences which suggest far more than they say, which have an atmosphere about them, which do not merely report an old, but make a new, impression; sentences which suggest as many things and are as durable as a Roman aqueduct; to frame these, that is the *art* of writing. Sentences which are expensive, towards which so many volumes, so much life, went; which lie like boulders on the page, up and down or across; which contain the seed of other sentences, not mere repetition, but creation; which a man might sell his grounds and castles to build. If De Quincey had suggested each of his pages in a sentence and passed on, it would have been far more excellent writing.

His style is nowhere kinked and knotted up into something hard and significant, which you could swallow like a diamond, without digesting.

The glorious sandy banks far and near, caving and sliding, — far sandy slopes, the forts of the land, — where you see the naked flesh of New England, her garment being blown aside like that of the priests (of the Levites?) when they ascend to the altar. Seen through this November sky, these sands are dear to me, worth all the gold of California, suggesting Pactolus, while the Saxonville factory-bell sounds o'er the woods. That sound perchance it is that whets my vision. The shore suggests the seashore, and two objects at a distance near the shore look like seals on a sand-bar. Dear to me to lie in, this sand; fit to preserve the bones of a race for thousands of years to come. And this is my home, my native soil; and I am a New-Englander. Of thee, O earth, are my bone and sinew made; to thee, O sun, am I brother. It must be the largest lake in Middlesex. To this dust my body will gladly return as to its origin. Here have I my habitat. I am of thee.

(1852)

As I turned round the corner of Hubbard's Grove, saw a woodchuck, the first of the season, in the middle of the field, six or seven rods from the fence which bounds the wood, and twenty rods distant. I ran along the fence and cut him off, or rather overtook him, though he started at the same time. When I was only a rod and a half off, he stopped, and I did the same; then he ran again, and I ran up within three feet of him, when he stopped again, the fence being between us. I squatted down and surveyed him at my leisure. His eyes were dull black and rather inobvious, with a faint chestnut (?) iris, with but little expression and that more of resignation than of anger. The general aspect was a coarse grayish brown, a sort of grisel(?). A lighter brown next the skin, then black or very dark brown and tipped with whitish rather loosely. The head between a squirrel and a bear, flat on the top and dark brown, and darker still or black on the tip of the nose. The whiskers black, two inches long. The ears very small and roundish, set far back and nearly buried in the fur. Black feet, with long and slender claws for digging. It appeared to tremble, or perchance shivered with cold. When I moved, it gritted its teeth quite loud, sometimes striking the under jaw against the other chatteringly, sometimes grinding one jaw on the other, yet as if more from instinct than anger. Whichever way I turned, that way it headed. I took a twig a foot long and touched its snout, at which it started forward and bit the stick, lessening the distance between us to two feet, and still it held all the ground it gained. I played with it tenderly a while with the stick, trying to open its gritting jaws. Ever its long incisors, two above and two below, were presented. But I thought it would go to sleep if I stayed long enough. It did not sit upright as sometimes, but *standing* on its fore feet with its head down, *i.e.* half sitting, half standing. We sat looking at one another about half an hour, till we began to feel mesmeric influences.

When I was tired, I moved away, wishing to see him run, but I could not start him. He would not stir as long as I was looking at him or could see him. I walked round him; he turned as fast and fronted me still. I sat down by his side within a foot. I talked to him *quasi* forest lingo, baby-talk, at any rate in a conciliatory tone, and thought that I had some influence on him. He gritted his teeth less. I chewed checkerberry leaves and presented them to his nose at last without a grit; though I saw that by so much gritting of the teeth he had worn them rapidly and they were covered with a fine white powder, which, if you measured it thus, would have made his anger terrible. He did not mind any noise I might make. With a little stick I lifted one of his paws to examine it, and held it up at pleasure. I turned him over to see what color he was beneath (darker or more purely brown), though he turned himself back again sooner than I could have wished. His tail was also all brown, though not very dark, rat-tail like, with loose hairs standing out on all sides like a caterpillar brush. He had a rather mild look. I spoke kindly to him. I reached checkerberry leaves to his mouth. I stretched my hands over him, though he turned up his head and still gritted a little. I laid my hand on him, but immediately took it off again, instinct not being wholly overcome. If I had had a few fresh bean leaves, thus in advance of the season, I am sure I should have tamed him completely. It was a frizzly tail. His is a humble, terrestrial color like the partridge's, well concealed where dead wiry grass rises above darker brown or chestnut dead leaves, — a modest color. If I had had some food, I should have ended with stroking him at my leisure.

Could easily have wrapped him in my handkerchief. He was not fat nor particularly lean. I finally had to leave him without seeing him move from the place. A large, clumsy, burrowing squirrel. *Arctomys,* bearmouse. I respect him as one of the natives. He lives there, by his color and habits so naturalized amid the dry leaves, the withered grass, and the bushes. A sound nap, too, he has enjoyed in his native fields, the past winter. I think I might learn some wisdom of him. His ancestors have lived here longer than mine. He is more thoroughly acclimated and naturalized than I. Bean leaves the red man raised for him, but he can do without them.

(1854)

There is no such thing as pure *objective* observation. Your observation, to be interesting, *i.e.* to be significant, must be *subjective.* The sum of what the writer of whatever class has to report is simply some human experience, whether he be poet or philosopher or man of science. The man of most science is the man most alive, whose life is the greatest event. Senses that take cognizance of outward things merely are of no avail. It matters not where or how far you travel, — the farther commonly the worse, — but how much alive you are. If it is possible to conceive of an event outside to humanity, it is not of the slightest significance, though it were the explosion of a planet. Every important worker will report what life there is in him. It makes no odds into what seeming deserts the poet is born. Though all his neighbors pronounce it a Sahara, it will be a paradise to him; for the desert which we see is the result of the barrenness of our experience. No mere willful activity whatever, whether in writing verses or collecting statistics, will produce true poetry or science. If you are really a sick man, it is indeed to be regretted, for you cannot accomplish so much as if you were well. All that a man has to say or do that can possibly concern mankind, is in some shape or other to tell the story of his love, — to sing, and, if he is fortunate and keeps alive, he will be forever in love. This alone is to be alive to the extremities. It is a pity that this divine creature should ever suffer from cold feet; a still greater pity that the coldness so often reaches to his heart. I look over the report of the doings of a scientific association and am surprised that there is so little life to be reported; I am put off with a parcel of dry technical terms. Anything living is easily and naturally expressed in popular language. I cannot help suspecting that the life of these learned professors has been almost as inhuman and wooden as a rain-gauge or self-registering magnetic machine. They communicate no fact which rises to the temperature of blood-heat. It doesn't all amount to one rhyme.

This earth which is spread out like a map around me is but the lining of my inmost soul exposed.

I have brought home a half-bushel of grapes to scent my chamber with. It is impossible to get them home in a basket with all their rich bloom on them, which, no less than the form of the clusters, makes their beauty. As I paddled home with my basket of grapes in the bow, every now and then their perfume was wafted to me in the stern, and I thought that I was passing a richly laden vine on shore. Some goldfinches twitter over, while I am pulling down the vines from the birch-tops. The ripest rattle off and strew the ground before I reach the clusters, or, while I am standing on tiptoe and endeavoring gently to break the rough peduncle, the petiole of a leaf gets entangled in the bunch and I am compelled to strip them all off loosely.

(1855)

What a strong and hearty but reckless, hit-or-miss style had some of the early writers of New England, like Josselyn and William Wood and others elsewhere in those days; as if they spoke with a relish, smacking their lips like a coach-whip, caring more to speak heartily than scientifically true. They are not to be caught napping by the wonders of Nature in a new country, and perhaps are often more ready to appreciate them than she is to exhibit them. They give you one piece of nature, at any rate, and that is themselves. (Cotton Mather, too, has a rich phrase.) They use a strong, coarse, homely speech which cannot always be found in the dictionary, nor sometimes be heard in polite society, but which brings you very near to the thing itself described. The strong new soil speaks through them. I have just been reading some in Wood's "New England's Prospect." He speaks a good word for New England, indeed will come very near lying for her, and when he doubts the justness of his praise, he brings it out not the less

roundly; as who cares if it is not so? we love her not the less for all that. Certainly that generation stood nearer to nature, nearer to the facts, than this, and hence their books have more life in them.

(1856)

When it was proposed to me to go abroad, rub off some rust, and *better my condition* in a worldly sense, I fear lest my life will lose some of its homeliness. If these fields and streams and woods, the phenomena of nature here, and the simple occupations of the inhabitants should cease to interest and inspire me, no culture or wealth would atone for the loss. I fear the dissipation that travelling, going into society, even the best, the enjoyment of intellectual luxuries, imply. If Paris is much in your mind, if it is more and more to you, Concord is less and less, and yet it would be a wretched bargain to accept the proudest Paris in exchange for my native village. At best, Paris could only be a school in which to learn to live here, a stepping-stone to Concord, a school in which to fit for this university. I wish so to live ever as to derive my satisfactions and inspirations from the commonest events, every-day phenomena, so that what my senses hourly perceive, my daily walk, the conversation of my neighbors, may inspire me, and I may dream of no heaven but that which lies about me. A man may acquire a taste for wine or brandy, and so lose his love for water, but should we not pity him?

I see the old pale-faced farmer out again on his sled now for the five-thousandth time, — Cyrus Hubbard, a man of a certain New England probity and worth, immortal and natural, like a natural product, like the sweetness of a nut, like the toughness of hickory. He, too, is a redeemer for me. How superior actually to the faith he professes! He is not an office-seeker. What an institution, what a revelation is a man! We are wont foolishly to think that the creed which a man professes is more significant than the fact he is. It matters not how hard the conditions seemed, how mean the world, for a man is a prevalent force and a new law himself. He is a system whose law is to be observed. The old farmer condescends to countenance still this nature and order of things. It is a great encouragement that an honest man makes this world his abode.

(1857)

These regular phenomena of the seasons get at last to be — they were *at first*, of course — simply and plainly phenomena or phases of my life. The seasons and all their changes are in me. I see not a dead eel or floating snake, or a gull, but it rounds my life and is like a line or accent in its poem. Almost I believe the Concord would not rise and overflow its banks again, were I not here. After a while I learn what my moods and seasons are. I would have nothing subtracted. I can imagine nothing added. My moods are thus periodical, not two days in my year alike. The perfect correspondence of Nature to man, so that he is at home in her!

(1859)

Time will soon destroy the works of famous painters and sculptors, but the Indian arrowhead will balk his efforts and Eternity will have to come to his aid. They are not fossil bones, but, as it were, fossil thoughts, forever reminding me of the mind that shaped them. I would fain know that I am treading in the tracks of human game, — that I am on the trail of mind, — and these little reminders never fail to set me right. When I see these signs I know that the subtle spirits that made them are not far off, into whatever form transmuted. What if you do plow and hoe amid them, and swear that not one stone shall be left upon another? They are only the less like to break in that case. When you turn up one layer you bury another so much the more securely. They are at peace with rust. This arrow-headed character promises to outlast all others. The larger pestles and axes may, perchance, grow scarce and be broken, but the arrowhead shall, perhaps, never cease to wing its way through the ages to eternity. It was originally winged for but a short flight, but it still, to my mind's eye, wings it way through the ages, bearing a message from the hand that shot it. Myriads of arrowpoints lie sleeping in the skin of the revolving earth, while meteors revolve in space. The footprint, the mind-print of the oldest men. When some Vandal chieftain has razed to the earth the British Museum, and, perchance, the winged bulls from Ninevah shall have lost most if not all of their features, the arrowheads which the museum contains will, perhaps, find themselves at home again in familiar dust, and resume their shining in new springs upon the bared surface of the earth then,

to be picked up for the thousandth time by the shepherd or savage that may be wandering there, and once more suggest their story to him.

There was a remarkable sunset, I think the 25th of October. The sunset sky reached quite from west to east, and it was the most varied in its forms and colors of any that I remember to have seen. At one time the clouds were most softly and delicately rippled, like the ripple-marks on sand. But it was hard for me to see its beauty then, when my mind was filled with Captain Brown. So great a wrong as his fate implied overshadowed all beauty in the world.

Civil Disobedience
(w. 1847)

As is suggested by the last selection from the *Journals*, above, Thoreau, individualist and lover of beauty, could not ignore the great public problem of slavery. His house in Concord was a station on the underground railroad. He knew and admired Captain John Brown, and spoke for him even though public opinion was virtually solid against Brown. This was in 1859.

More than a decade earlier, during the Mexican war, he had written "Resistance to Civil Government," later entitled "Civil Disobedience." It was a protest against slavery: "I cannot for an instant recognize that political organization as *my* government which is the *slave's* government also." At the same time it was a general protest against any form of political injustice and an affirmation of the obligation of passive resistance. Thoreau's brave statement, published in *Aesthetic Papers*, a collection of essays edited by Elizabeth Peabody, "attracted no attention at the time, but has since gone round the world. It was Gandhi's source-book in his Indian campaign for Civil Resistance, and has been read and pondered by thousands who hope to find some way to resist seemingly irresistible force." (H. S. Canby).

I heartily accept the motto, — "That government is best which governs least"; and I should like to see it acted up to more rapidly and systematically. Carried out, it finally amounts to this, which also I believe, — "That government is best which governs not at all"; and when men are prepared for it, that will be the kind of government which they will have. Government is at best but an expedient; but most governments are usually, and all governments are sometimes, inexpedient. The objections which have been brought against a standing army, and they are many and weighty, and deserve to prevail, may also at last be brought against a standing government. The standing army is only an arm of the standing government. The government itself, which is only the mode which the people have chosen to execute their will, is equally liable to be abused and perverted before the people can act through it. Witness the present Mexican war, the work of comparatively a few individuals using the standing government as their tool; for, in the outset, the people would not have consented to this measure.

This American government, — what is it but a tradition, though a recent one, endeavoring to transmit itself unimpaired to posterity, but each instant losing some of its integrity? It has not the vitality and force of a single living man; for a single man can bend it to his will. It is a sort of wooden gun to the people themselves. But it is not the less necessary for this; for the people must have some complicated machinery or other, and hear its din, to satisfy that idea of government which they have. Governments show thus how successfully men can be imposed on, even impose on themselves, for their own advantage. It is excellent, we must all allow. Yet this government never of itself furthered any enterprise, but by the alacrity with which it got out of its way. *It* does not keep the country free. *It* does not settle the West. *It* does not educate. The character inherent in the American people has done all that has been accomplished; and it would have done somewhat more, if the government had not sometimes got in its way. For government is an expedient by which men would fain succeed in letting one another alone; and, as has been said, when it is most expedient, the governed are most let alone by it. Trade and commerce, if they were not made of India-rubber, would never manage to bounce over the obstacles which legislators are continually putting in their way; and, if one were to judge these men wholly by the effects of their actions and not partly by their intentions, they would deserve to be classed and punished with those mischievous persons who put obstructions on the railroads.

But, to speak practically and as a citizen, unlike those who call themselves no-government men, I ask for, not at once no government, but *at once* a better government. Let every man make known what kind of government would command his respect, and that will be one step toward obtaining it.

After all, the practical reason why, when the power is once in the hands of the people, a majority are permitted, and for a long period continue, to rule is not because they are most likely to be in the right, nor because this seems fairest to the minority, but because they are physically the strongest. But a government in which the majority rule in all cases cannot be based on justice, even as far as men understand it. Can there not be a government in which majorities do not virtually decide right and wrong, but conscience? — in which majorities decide only those questions to which the rule of expediency is applicable? Must the citizen ever for a moment, or in the least degree, resign his conscience to the legislator? Why has every man a conscience, then? I think that we should be men first, and subjects afterward. It is not desirable to cultivate a respect for the law, so much as for the right. The only obligation which I have a right to assume is to do at any time what I think right. It is truly enough said that a corporation has no conscience; but a corporation of conscientious men is a corporation *with* a conscience. Law never made men a whit more just; and, by means of their respect for it, even the well-disposed are daily made the agents of injustice. A common and natural result of an undue respect for law is, that you may see a file of soldiers, colonel, captain, corporal, privates, powder-monkeys, and all, marching in admirable order over hill and dale to the wars, against their wills, ay, against their common sense and consciences, which makes it very steep marching indeed, and produces a palpitation of the heart. They have no doubt that it is a damnable business in which they are concerned; they are all peaceably inclined. Now, what are they? Men at all? or small movable forts and magazines, at the service of some unscrupulous man in power? Visit the Navy-Yard, and behold a marine, such a man as an American government can make, or such as it can make a man with its black arts, — a mere shadow and reminiscence of humanity, a man laid out alive and standing, and already, as one may say, buried under arms with funeral accompaniments, though it may be

Not a drum was heard, not a funeral note,
    As his corse to the rampart we hurried;
Not a soldier discharged his farewell shot
    O'er the grave where our hero we buried.

The mass of men serve the state thus, not as men mainly, but as machines, with their bodies. They are the standing army, and the militia, jailers, constables, posse comitatus, etc. In most cases there is no free exercise whatever of the judgment or of the moral sense; but they put themselves on a level with wood and earth and stones; and wooden men can perhaps be manufactured that will serve the purpose as well. Such command no more respect than men of straw or a lump of dirt. They have the same sort of worth only as horses and dogs. Yet such as these even are commonly esteemed good citizens. Others — as most legislators, politicians, lawyers, ministers, and office-holders — serve the state chiefly with their heads; and, as they rarely make any moral distinctions, they are as likely to serve the Devil, without *intending* it, as God. A very few, as heroes, patriots, martyrs, reformers in the great sense, and *men*, serve the state with their consciences also, and so necessarily resist it for the most part; and they are commonly treated as enemies by it. A wise man will only be useful as a man, and will not submit to be "clay," and "stop a hole to keep the wind away," but leave that office to his dust at least:

I am too high-born to be propertied,
To be a secondary at control,
Or useful serving-man and instrument
To any sovereign state throughout the world.

He who gives himself entirely to his fellow-men appears to them useless and selfish; but he who gives himself partially to them is pronounced a benefactor and philanthropist.

How does it become a man to behave toward this American government today? I answer, that he cannot without disgrace be associated with it. I cannot for an instant recognize that political organization as *my* government which is the *slave's* government also.

All men recognize the right of revolution; that is, the right to refuse allegiance to, and to resist, the government, when its tyranny or its inefficiency are great and unendurable. But almost all say that such is not the case now. But such was the case, they think, in the Revolution of '75. If one were to tell me that this was a bad government because it taxed certain foreign commodities brought to its ports, it is most probable that I should not make an ado about it, for I can do without them. All machines have their friction; and possibly this does enough good to counterbalance the evil. At any rate, it is a great evil to make a stir about it. But when the friction comes to have its machine, and oppression and robbery are organized, I say, let us not have such a machine any longer. In other words, when a sixth of the population of a nation which has undertaken to be the refuge of liberty are slaves, and a whole country is unjustly overrun and conquered by a foreign army, and subjected to military law, I think that it is not too soon for honest men to rebel and revolutionize. What makes this duty the more urgent is the fact that the country so overrun is not our own, but ours is the invading army.

Paley, a common authority with many on moral questions, in his chapter on the "Duty of Submission to Civil Government," resolves all civil obligation into expediency; and he proceeds to say, "that so long as the interest of the whole society requires it, that is, so long as the established government cannot be resisted or changed without public inconveniency, it is the will of God that the established government be obeyed, and no longer. . . . This principle being admitted, the justice of every particular case of resistance is reduced to a computation of the quantity of the danger and grievance on the one side, and of the probability and expense of redressing it on the other." Of this, he says, every man shall judge for himself. But Paley appears never to have contemplated those cases to which the rule of expediency does not apply, in which a people, as well as an individual, must do justice, cost what it may. If I have unjustly wrested a plank from a drowning man, I must restore it to him though I drown myself. This, according to Paley, would be inconvenient. But he that would save his life, in such a case, shall lose it. This people must cease to hold slaves, and to make war on Mexico, though it cost them their existence as a people.

In their practice, nations agree with Paley; but does any one think that Massachusetts does exactly what is right at the present crisis?

A drab of state, a cloth-o'-silver slut,
To have her train borne up, and her soul trail in the dirt.

Practically speaking, the opponents to a reform in Massachusetts are not a hundred thousand politicians at the South, but a hundred thousand merchants and farmers here, who are more interested in commerce and agriculture than they are in humanity, and are not prepared to do justice to the slave and to Mexico, *cost what it may.* I quarrel not with far-off foes, but with those who, near at home, co-operate with, and do the bidding of, those far away, and without whom the latter would be harmless. We are accustomed to say, that the mass of men are unprepared; but improvement is slow, because the few are not materially wiser or better than the many. It is not so important that many should be as good as you, as that there be some absolute goodness somewhere; for that will leaven the whole lump. There are thousands who are *in opinion* opposed to slavery and to the war, who yet in effect do nothing to put an end to them; who, esteeming themselves children of Washington and Franklin, sit down with their hands in their pockets, and say that they know not what to do, and do nothing; who even postpone the question of freedom to the question of free-trade, and quietly read the prices-current along with the latest advices from Mexico, after dinner, and, it may be, fall asleep over them both. What is the price-current of an honest man and patriot to-day? They hesitate, and they regret, and sometimes they petition; but they do nothing in earnest and with effect. They will wait, well disposed, for others to remedy the evil, that they may no longer have it to regret. At most, they give only a cheap vote, and a feeble countenance and God-speed, to the right, as it goes by them. There are nine hundred and ninety-nine patrons of virtue to one virtuous man. But it is easier to deal with the real possessor of a thing than with the temporary guardian of it.

All voting is a sort of gaming, like checkers or backgammon, with a slight moral tinge to it, a playing with right and wrong, with moral questions; and betting naturally accompanies it. The character of the voters is not staked. I cast my vote, perchance, as I think right; but I am not vitally concerned that that right should prevail. I am willing to leave it to the majority. Its obligation, therefore, never exceeds that of expediency. Even voting *for the right* is *doing* nothing for it. It is only expressing to men feebly your desire that it should prevail. A wise man will not leave the right to the mercy of chance nor wish it to prevail through the power of the majority. There is but little virtue in the action of masses of men. When the majority shall at length vote for the abolition of slavery, it will be because they are indifferent to slavery, or because there is but little slavery left to be abolished by their vote. *They* will then be the

only slaves. Only *his* vote can hasten the abolition of slavery who asserts his own freedom by his vote.

I hear of a convention to be held at Baltimore, or elsewhere, for the selection of a candidate for the Presidency, made up chiefly of editors, and men who are politicians by profession; but I think, what is it to any independent, intelligent, and respectable man what decision they may come to? Shall we not have the advantage of his wisdom and honesty, nevertheless? Can we not count upon some independent votes? Are there not many individuals in the country who do not attend conventions? But no: I find that the respectable man, so called, has immediately drifted from his position, and despairs of his country, when his country has more reason to despair of him. He forthwith adopts one of the candidates thus selected as the only *available* one, thus proving that he is himself *available* for any purposes of the demagogue. His vote is of no more worth than that of any unprincipled foreigner or hireling native, who may have been bought. O for a man who is a *man,* and, as my neighbor says, has a bone in his back which you cannot pass your hand through! Our statistics are at fault: the population has been returned too large. How many *men* are there to a square thousand miles in this country? Hardly one. Does not America offer any inducement for men to settle here? The American has dwindled into an Odd Fellow, — one who may be known by the development of his organ of gregariousness, and a manifest lack of intellect and cheerful self-reliance; whose first and chief concern, on coming into the world, is to see that the Almshouses are in good repair; and, before yet he has lawfully donned the virile garb, to collect a fund for the support of the widows and orphans that may be; who, in short, ventures to live only by the aid of the Mutual Insurance company, which has promised to bury him decently.

It is not a man's duty, as a matter of course, to devote himself to the eradication of any, even the most enormous wrong; he may still properly have other concerns to engage him; but it is his duty, at least, to wash his hands of it, and, if he gives it no thought longer, not to give it practically his support. If I devote myself to other pursuits and contemplations, I must first see, at least, that I do not pursue them sitting upon another man's shoulders. I must get off him first, that he may pursue his contemplations too. See what gross inconsistency is tolerated. I have heard some of my townsmen say, "I should like to have them order me out to help put down an insurrection of the slaves, or to march to Mexico; — see if I would go"; and yet 5 these very men have each, directly by their allegiance, and so indirectly, at least, by their money, furnished a substitute. The soldier is applauded who refuses to serve in an unjust war by those who do not refuse to sustain the unjust govern- 10 ment which makes the war; is applauded by those whose own act and authority he disregards and sets at naught; as if the state were penitent to that degree that it hired one to scourge it while it sinned, but not to that degree that it 15 left off sinning for a moment. Thus, under the name of Order and Civil Government, we are all made at last to pay homage to and support our own meanness. After the first blush of sin comes its indifference; and from immoral it becomes, 20 as it were, unmoral, and not quite unnecessary to that life which we have made.

The broadest and most prevalent error requires the most disinterested virtue to sustain it. The slight reproach to which the virtue of pa- 25 triotism is commonly liable, the noble are most likely to incur. Those who, while they disapprove of the character and measures of a government, yield to it their allegiance and support are undoubtedly its most conscientious sup- 30 porters, and so frequently the most serious obstacles to reform. Some are petitioning the state to dissolve the Union, to disregard the requisitions of the President. Why do they not dissolve it themselves, — the union between them- 35 selves and the state, — and refuse to pay their quota into its treasury? Do not they stand in the same relation to the state that the state does to the Union? And have not the same reasons prevented the state from resisting the Union 40 which have prevented them from resisting the state?

How can a man be satisfied to entertain an opinion merely, and enjoy it? Is there any enjoyment in it, if his opinion is that he is ag- 45 grieved? If you are cheated out of a single dollar by your neighbor, you do not rest satisfied with knowing that you are cheated, or with saying that you are cheated, or even with petitioning him to pay you your due; but you 50 take effectual steps at once to obtain the full amount, and see that you are never cheated again. Action from principle, the perception and the performance of right, changes things

and relations; it is essentially revolutionary, and does not consist wholly with anything which was. It not only divides states and churches, it divides families; ay, it divides the individual, separating the diabolical in him from the divine. 5

Unjust laws exist: shall we be content to obey them, or shall we endeavor to amend them, and obey them until we have succeeded, or shall we transgress them at once? Men generally, under such a government as this, think that they ought 10 to wait until they have persuaded the majority to alter them. They think that, if they should resist, the remedy would be worse than the evil. But it is the fault of the government itself that the remedy is worse than the evil. It makes it 15 worse. Why is it not more apt to anticipate and provide for reform? Why does it not cherish its wise minority? Why does it cry and resist before it is hurt? Why does it not encourage its citizens to be on the alert to point out its faults, 20 and do better than it would have them? Why does it always crucify Christ, and excommunicate Copernicus and Luther, and pronounce Washington and Franklin rebels?

One would think that a deliberate and prac- 25 tical denial of its authority was the only offense never contemplated by government; else, why has it not assigned its definite, its suitable and proportionate penalty? If a man who has no property refuses but once to earn nine shillings 30 for the state, he is put in prison for a period unlimited by any law that I know, and determined only by the discretion of those who placed him there; but if he should steal ninety times nine shillings from the state, he is soon permitted 35 to go at large again.

If the injustice is part of the necessary friction of the machine of government, let it go, let it go: perchance it will wear smooth, — certainly the machine will wear out. If the injustice 40 has a spring, or a pulley, or a rope, or a crank, exclusively for itself, then perhaps you may consider whether the remedy will not be worse than the evil; but if it is of such a nature that it requires you to be the agent of injustice to an- 45 other, then, I say, break the law. Let your life be a counter friction to stop the machine. What I have to do is to see, at any rate, that I do not lend myself to the wrong which I condemn.

As for adopting the ways which the state has 50 provided for remedying the evil, I know not of such ways. They take too much time, and a man's life will be gone. I have other affairs to attend to. I came into this world, not chiefly to make this a good place to live in, but to live in it, be it good or bad. A man has not everything to do, but something; and because he cannot do *everything*, it is not necessary that he should do *something* wrong. It is not my business to be petitioning the Governor or the Legislature any more than it is theirs to petition me; and if they should not hear my petition, what should I do then? But in this case the state has provided no way: its very Constitution is the evil. This may seem to be harsh and stubborn and unconciliatory; but it is to treat with the utmost kindness and consideration the only spirit that can appreciate or deserves it. So is all change for the better, like birth and death, which convulse the body.

I do not hesitate to say, that those who call themselves Abolitionists should at once effectually withdraw their support, both in person and property, from the government of Massachusetts, and not wait till they constitute a majority of one, before they suffer the right to prevail through them. I think that it is enough if they have God on their side, without waiting for that other one. Moreover, any man more right than his neighbors constitutes a majority of one already.

I meet this American government, or its representative, the state government, directly, and face to face, once a year — no more — in the person of its tax-gatherer; this is the only mode in which a man situated as I am necessarily meets it; and it then says distinctly, Recognize me; and the simplest, the most effectual, and, in the present posture of affairs, the indispensablest mode of treating with it on this head, of expressing your little satisfaction with and love for it is to deny it then. My civil neighbor, the tax-gatherer, is the very man I have to deal with, — for it is, after all, with men and not with parchment that I quarrel, — and he has voluntarily chosen to be an agent of the government. How shall he ever know well what he is and does as an officer of the government, or as a man, until he is obliged to consider whether he shall treat me, his neighbor, for whom he has respect, as a neighbor and well-disposed man, or as a maniac and disturber of the peace, and see if he can get over this obstruction to his neighborliness without a ruder and more impetuous thought or speech corresponding with his action. I know this well, that if one thousand, if one hundred, if ten men whom I could name, — if ten *honest* men only, — ay, if *one* HONEST

man, in this State of Massachusetts, *ceasing to hold slaves*, were actually to withdraw from this copartnership, and be locked up in the county jail therefor, it would be the abolition of slavery in America. For it matters not how small the beginning may seem to be: what is once well done is done forever. But we love better to talk about it: that we say is our mission. Reform keeps many scores of newspapers in its service, but not one man. If my esteemed neighbor, the State's ambassador, who will devote his days to the settlement of the question of human rights in the Council Chamber, instead of being threatened with the prisons of Carolina, were to sit down the prisoner of Massachusetts, that State which is so anxious to foist the sin of slavery upon her sister, — though at present she can discover only an act of inhospitality to be the ground of a quarrel with her, — the Legislature would not wholly waive the subject the following winter.

Under a government which imprisons any unjustly, the true place for a just man is also a prison. The proper place today, the only place which Massachusetts has provided for her freer and less desponding spirits, is in her prisons, to be put out and locked out of the State by her own act, as they have already put themselves out by their principles. It is there that the fugitive slave, and the Mexican prisoner on parole, and the Indian come to plead the wrongs of his race should find them; on that separate, but more free and honorable ground, where the State places those who are not *with* her, but *against* her, — the only house in a slave State in which a free man can abide with honor. If any think that their influence would be lost there, and their voices no longer afflict the ear of the State, that they would not be as an enemy within its walls, they do not know by how much truth is stronger than error, nor how much more eloquently and effectively he can combat injustice who has experienced a little in his own person. Cast your whole vote, not a strip of paper merely, but your whole influence. A minority is powerless while it conforms to the majority; it is not even a minority then; but it is irresistible when it clogs by its whole weight. If the alternative is to keep all just men in prison, or give up war and slavery, the State will not hesitate which to choose. If a thousand men were not to pay their tax-bills this year, that would not be a violent and bloody measure, as it would be to pay them, and enable the State to commit violence and shed innocent blood. This is, in fact, the definition of a peaceable revolution, if any such is possible. If the tax-gatherer, or any other public officer, asks me, as one has done, "But what shall I do?" my answer is, "If you really wish to do anything, resign your office." When the subject has refused allegiance, and the officer has resigned his office, then the revolution is accomplished. But even suppose blood should flow. Is there not a sort of blood shed when the conscience is wounded? Through this wound a man's real manhood and immortality flow out, and he bleeds to an everlasting death. I see this blood flowing now.

I have contemplated the imprisonment of the offender, rather than the seizure of his goods, — though both will serve the same purpose, — because they who assert the purest right, and consequently are most dangerous to a corrupt State, commonly have not spent much time in accumulating property. To such the State renders comparatively small service, and a slight tax is wont to appear exorbitant, particularly if they are obliged to earn it by special labor with their hands. If there were one who lived wholly without the use of money, the State itself would hesitate to demand it of him. But the rich man — not to make any invidious comparison — is always sold to the institution which makes him rich. Absolutely speaking, the more money, the less virtue; for money comes between a man and his objects, and obtains them for him; and it was certainly no great virtue to obtain it. It puts to rest many questions which he would otherwise be taxed to answer; while the only new question which it puts is the hard but superfluous one, how to spend it. Thus his moral ground is taken from under his feet. The opportunities of living are diminished in proportion as what are called the "means" are increased. The best thing a man can do for his culture when he is rich is to endeavor to carry out those schemes which he entertained when he was poor. Christ answered the Herodians according to their condition. "Show me the tribute-money," said he; — and one took a penny out of his pocket; — if you use money which has the image of Cæsar on it, and which he has made current and valuable, that is, *if you are men of the State,* and gladly enjoy the advantages of Cæsar's government, then pay him back some of his own when he demands it. "Render therefore to Cæsar that which is Cæsar's, and to God those things which are God's," — leaving them no wiser than before as to which was which; for they did not wish to know.

When I converse with the freest of my neighbors, I perceive that, whatever they may say about the magnitude and seriousness of the question, and their regard for the public tranquillity, the long and the short of the matter is, that they cannot spare the protection of the existing government, and they dread the consequences to their property and families of disobedience to it. For my own part, I should not like to think that I rely on the protection of the State. But, if I deny the authority of the State when it presents its tax-bill, it will soon take and waste all my property, and so harass me and my children without end. This is hard. This makes it impossible for a man to live honestly, and at the same time comfortably, in outward respects. It will not be worth the while to accumulate property; that would be sure to go again. You must hire or squat somewhere, and raise but a small crop, and eat that soon. You must live within yourself, and depend upon yourself always tucked up and ready for a start, and not have many affairs. A man may grow rich in Turkey even, if he will be in all respects a good subject of the Turkish government. Confucius said: "If a state is governed by the principles of reason, poverty and misery are subjects of shame; if a state is not governed by the principles of reason, riches and honors are the subjects of shame." No: until I want the protection of Massachusetts to be extended to me in some distant Southern port, where my liberty is endangered, or until I am bent solely on building up an estate at home by peaceful enterprise, I can afford to refuse allegiance to Massachusetts, and her right to my property and life. It costs me less in every sense to incur the penalty of disobedience to the State than it would to obey. I should feel as if I were worth less in that case.

Some years ago, the State met me in behalf of the Church, and commanded me to pay a certain sum toward the support of a clergyman whose preaching my father attended, but never I myself. "Pay," it said, "or be locked up in the jail." I declined to pay. But, unfortunately, another man saw fit to pay it. I did not see why the schoolmaster should be taxed to support the priest, and not the priest the schoolmaster; for I was not the State's schoolmaster, but I supported myself by voluntary subscription. I did not see why the lyceum should not present its tax-bill, and have the State to back its demand, as well as the Church. However, at the request of the selectmen, I condescended to make some such statement as this in writing: — "Know all men by these presents, that I, Henry Thoreau, do not wish to be regarded as a member of any incorporated society which I have not joined." This I gave to the town clerk; and he has it. The State, having thus learned that I did not wish to be regarded as a member of that church, has never made a like demand on me since; though it said that it must adhere to its original presumption that time. If I had known how to name them, I should then have signed off in detail from all the societies which I never signed on to; but I did not know where to find a complete list.

I have paid no poll-tax for six years. I was put into a jail once on this account, for one night; and, as I stood considering the walls of solid stone, two or three feet thick, the door of wood and iron, a foot thick, and the iron grating which strained the light, I could not help being struck with the foolishness of that institution which treated me as if I were mere flesh and blood and bones, to be locked up. I wondered that it should have concluded at length that this was the best use it could put me to, and had never thought to avail itself of my services in some way. I saw that, if there was a wall of stone between me and my townsmen, there was a still more difficult one to climb or break through before they could get to be as free as I was. I did not for a moment feel confined, and the walls seemed a great waste of stone and mortar. I felt as if I alone of all my townsmen had paid my tax. They plainly did not know how to treat me, but behaved like persons who are underbred. In every threat and in every compliment there was a blunder; for they thought that my chief desire was to stand the other side of that stone wall. I could not but smile to see how industriously they locked the door on my meditations, which followed them out again without let or hindrance, and *they* were really all that was dangerous. As they could not reach me, they had resolved to punish my body; just as boys, if they cannot come at some person against whom they have a spite, will abuse his dog. I saw that the State was half-witted, that it was timid as a lone woman with her silver spoons, and that it did not know its friends from its foes, and I lost all my remaining respect for it, and pitied it.

Thus the State never intentionally confronts a man's sense, intellectual or moral, but only his body, his senses. It is not armed with superior wit or honesty, but with superior physical strength. I was not born to be forced. I will breathe after my own fashion. Let us see who is the strongest. What force has a multitude? They only can force me who obey a higher law than I. They force me to become like themselves. I do not hear of *men* being *forced* to live this way or that by masses of men. What sort of life were that to live? When I meet a government which says to me, "Your money or your life," why should I be in haste to give it my money? It may be in a great strait, and not know what to do: I cannot help that. It must help itself; do as I do. It is not worth the while to snivel about it. I am not responsible for the successful working of the machinery of society. I am not the son of the engineer. I perceive that, when an acorn and a chestnut fall side by side, the one does not remain inert to make way for the other, but both obey their own laws, and spring and grow and flourish as best they can, till one, perchance, overshadows and destroys the other. If a plant cannot live according to its nature, it dies; and so a man.

The night in prison was novel and interesting enough. The prisoners in their shirtsleeves were enjoying a chat and the evening air in the doorway, when I entered. But the jailer said, "Come, boys, it is time to lock up"; and so they dispersed, and I heard the sound of their steps returning into the hollow apartments. My room-mate was introduced to me by the jailer as "a first-rate fellow and a clever man." When the door was locked, he showed me where to hang my hat, and how he managed matters there. The rooms were whitewashed once a month; and this one, at least, was the whitest, most simply furnished, and probably the neatest apartment in the town. He naturally wanted to know where I came from, and what brought me there; and, when I had told him, I asked him in my turn how he came there, presuming him to be an honest man, of course; and, as the world goes, I believe he was. "Why," said he, "they accuse me of burning a barn; but I never did it." As near as I could discover, he had probably gone to bed in a barn when drunk, and smoked his pipe there; and so a barn was burnt. He had the reputation of being a clever man, had been there some three months waiting for his trial to come on, and would have to wait as much longer; but he was quite domesticated and contented, since he got his board for nothing, and thought that he was well treated.

He occupied one window, and I the other; and I saw that if one stayed there long, his principal business would be to look out the window. I had soon read all the tracts that were left there, and examined where former prisoners had broken out, and where a grate had been sawed off, and heard the history of the various occupants of that room; for I found that even here there was a history and a gossip which never circulated beyond the walls of the jail. Probably this is the only house in the town where verses are composed, which are afterward printed in a circular form, but not published. I was shown quite a long list of verses which were composed by some young men who had been detected in an attempt to escape, who avenged themselves by singing them.

I pumped my fellow-prisoner as dry as I could, for fear I should never see him again; but at length he showed me which was my bed, and left me to blow out the lamp.

It was like traveling into a far country, such as I had never expected to behold, to lie there for one night. It seemed to me that I never had heard the town-clock strike before, nor the evening sounds of the village; for we slept with the windows open, which were inside the grating. It was to see my native village in the light of the Middle Ages, and our Concord was turned into a Rhine stream, and visions of knights and castles passed before me. They were the voices of old burghers that I heard in the streets. I was an involuntary spectator and auditor of whatever was done and said in the kitchen of the adjacent village-inn, — a wholly new and rare experience to me. It was a closer view of my native town. I was fairly inside of it. I never had seen its institutions before. This is one of its peculiar institutions; for it is a shire town. I began to comprehend what its inhabitants were about.

In the morning, our breakfasts were put through the hole in the door, in small oblong-square tin pans, made to fit, and holding a pint of chocolate, with brown bread, and an iron spoon. When they called for the vessels again, I was green enough to return what bread I had left; but my comrade seized it, and said that I should lay that up for lunch or dinner. Soon after he was let out to work at haying in a neigh-

boring field, whither he went every day, and would not be back till noon; so he bade me good-day, saying that he doubted if he should see me again.

When I came out of prison, — for some one interfered, and paid that tax, — I did not perceive that great changes had taken place on the common, such as he observed who went in a youth and emerged a tottering and gray-headed man; and yet a change had to my eyes come over the scene, — the town, and State, and country, — greater than any that mere time could effect. I saw yet more distinctly the State in which I lived. I saw to what extent the people among whom I lived could be trusted as good neighbors and friends; that their friendship was for summer weather only; that they did not greatly propose to do right; that they were a distinct race from me by their prejudices and superstitions, as the Chinamen and Malays are; that in their sacrifices to humanity they ran no risks, not even to their property; that after all they were not so noble but they treated the thief as he had treated them, and hoped, by a certain outward observance and a few prayers, and by walking in a particular straight though useless path from time to time, to save their souls. This may be to judge my neighbors harshly; for I believe that many of them are not aware that they have such an institution as the jail in their village.

It was formerly the custom in our village, when a poor debtor came out of jail, for his acquaintances to salute him, looking through their fingers, which were crossed to represent the grating of a jail window, "How do ye do?" My neighbors did not thus salute me, but first looked at me, and then at one another, as if I had returned from a long journey. I was put into jail as I was going to the shoemaker's to get a shoe which was mended. When I was let out the next morning, I proceeded to finish my errand, and, having put on my mended shoe, joined a huckleberry party, who were impatient to put themselves under my conduct; and in half an hour, — for the horse was soon tackled, — was in the midst of a huckleberry field, on one of our highest hills, two miles off, and then the State was nowhere to be seen.

This is the whole history of "My prisons."

I have never declined paying the highway tax, because I am as desirous of being a good neighbor as I am of being a bad subject; and as for supporting schools, I am doing my part to educate my fellow-countrymen now. It is for no particular item in the tax-bill that I refuse to pay it. I simply wish to refuse allegiance to the State, to withdraw and stand aloof from it effectually. I do not care to trace the course of my dollar, if I could, till it buys a man or a musket to shoot one with, — the dollar is innocent, — but I am concerned to trace the effects of my allegiance. In fact, I quietly declare war with the State, after my fashion, though I will still make what use and get what advantage of her I can, as is usual in such cases.

If others pay the tax which is demanded of me, from a sympathy with the State, they do but what they have already done in their own case, or rather they abet injustice to a greater extent than the State requires. If they pay the tax from a mistaken interest in the individual taxed, to save his property, or prevent his going to jail, it is because they have not considered wisely how far they let their private feelings interfere with the public good.

This, then, is my position at present. But one cannot be too much on his guard in such a case, lest his action be biased by obstinacy or an undue regard for the opinions of men. Let him see that he does only what belongs to himself and to the hour.

I think sometimes, Why, this people mean well, they are only ignorant; they would do better if they knew how: why give your neighbors this pain to treat you as they are not inclined to? But I think again, This is no reason why I should do as they do, or permit others to suffer much greater pain of a different kind. Again, I sometimes say to myself, When many millions of men, without heat, without ill will, without personal feeling of any kind, demand of you a few shillings only, without the possibility, such is their constitution, of retracing or altering their present demand, and without the possibility, on your side, of appeal to any other millions, why expose yourself to this overwhelming brute force? You do not resist cold and hunger, the winds and the waves, thus obstinately; you quietly submit to a thousand similar necessities. You do not put your head into the fire. But just in proportion as I regard this as not wholly a brute force, but partly a human force, and consider that I have relations to those millions as to so many millions of men, and not of mere brute or inanimate things, I see that appeal is possible, first and instantaneously, from

them to the Maker of them, and, secondly, from them to themselves. But if I put my head deliberately into the fire, there is no appeal to fire or to the Maker of fire, and I have only myself to blame. If I could convince myself that I have any right to be satisfied with men as they are, and to treat them accordingly, and not according, in some respects, to my requisitions and expectations of what they and I ought to be, then, like a good Mussulman and fatalist, I should endeavor to be satisfied with things as they are, and say it is the will of God. And, above all, there is this difference between resisting this and a purely brute or natural force, that I can resist this with some effect; but I cannot expect, like Orpheus, to change the nature of the rocks and trees and beasts.

I do not wish to quarrel with any man or nation. I do not wish to split hairs, to make fine distinctions, or set myself up as better than my neighbors. I seek rather, I may say, even an excuse for conforming to the laws of the land. I am but too ready to conform to them. Indeed, I have reason to suspect myself on this head; and each year, as the tax-gatherer comes round, I find myself disposed to review the acts and position of the general and State governments, and the spirit of the people, to discover a pretext for conformity.

> We must affect our country as our parents,
> And if at any time we alienate
> Our love or industry from doing it honor,
> We must respect effects and teach the soul
> Matter of conscience and religion
> And not desire of rule or benefit.

I believe that the State will soon be able to take all my work of this sort out of my hands, and then I shall be no better a patriot than my fellow-countrymen. Seen from a lower point of view, the Constitution, with all its faults, is very good; the law and the courts are very respectable; even this State and this American government are, in many respects, very admirable, and rare things, to be thankful for, such as a great many have described them; but seen from a point of view a little higher, they are what I have described them; seen from a higher still, and the highest, who shall say what they are, or that they are worth looking at or thinking of at all?

However, the government does not concern me much, and I shall bestow the fewest possible thoughts on it. It is not many moments that I live under a government, even in this world. If a man is thought-free, fancy-free, imagination-free, that which *is not* never for a long time appearing *to be* to him, unwise rulers or reformers cannot fatally interrupt him.

I know that most men think differently from myself; but those whose lives are by profession devoted to the study of these or kindred subjects content me as little as any. Statesmen and legislators, standing so completely within the institution, never distinctly and nakedly behold it. They speak of moving society, but have no resting-place without it. They may be men of a certain experience and discrimination, and have no doubt invented ingenious and even useful systems, for which we sincerely thank them; but all their wit and usefulness lie within certain not very wide limits. They are wont to forget that the world is not governed by policy and expediency. Webster never goes behind government, and so cannot speak with authority about it. His words are wisdom to those legislators who contemplate no essential reform in the existing government; but for thinkers, and those who legislate for all time, he never once glances at the subject. I know of those whose serene and wise speculations on this theme would soon reveal the limits of his mind's range and hospitality. Yet, compared with the cheap professions of most reformers, and the still cheaper wisdom and eloquence of politicians in general, his are almost the only sensible and valuable words, and we thank Heaven for him. Comparatively, he is always strong, original, and, above all, practical. Still, his quality is not wisdom, but prudence. The lawyer's truth is not Truth, but consistency or a consistent expediency. Truth is always in harmony with herself, and is not concerned chiefly to reveal the justice that may consist with wrong-doing. He well deserves to be called, as he has been called, the Defender of the Constitution. There are really no blows to be given by him but defensive ones. He is not a leader, but a follower. His leaders are the men of '87. "I have never made an effort," he says, "and never propose to make an effort; I have never countenanced an effort, and never mean to countenance an effort, to disturb the arrangement as originally made, by which the various States came into the Union." Still thinking of the sanction which the Constitution gives to slavery, he says, "Because it was a part of the original compact, — let it stand." Notwithstanding his special acuteness and ability,

he is unable to take a fact out of its merely political relations, and behold it as it lies absolutely to be disposed of by the intellect, — what, for instance, it behooves a man to do here in America to-day with regard to slavery, — but ventures, or is driven, to make some such desperate answer as the following, while professing to speak absolutely, and as a private man, — from which what new and singular code of social duties might be inferred? "The manner," says he, "in which the governments of those States where slavery exists are to regulate it is for their own consideration, under their responsibility to their constituents, to the general laws of propriety, humanity, and justice, and to God. Associations formed elsewhere, springing from a feeling of humanity, or any other cause, have nothing whatever to do with it. They have never received any encouragement from me, and they never will."

They who know of no purer sources of truth, who have traced up its stream no higher, stand, and wisely stand, by the Bible and the Constitution, and drink at it there with reverence and humility; but they who behold where it comes trickling into this lake or that pool, gird up their loins once more, and continue their pilgrimage toward its fountain-head.

No man with a genius for legislation has appeared in America. They are rare in the history of the world. There are orators, politicians, and eloquent men, by the thousand; but the speaker has not yet opened his mouth to speak who is capable of settling the much-vexed questions of the day. We love eloquence for its own sake, and not for any truth which it may utter, or any heroism it may inspire. Our legislators have not yet learned the comparative value of free-trade and of freedom, of union, and of rectitude, to a nation. They have no genius or talent for comparatively humble questions of taxation and finance, commerce and manufactures and agriculture. If we were left solely to the wordy wit of legislators in Congress for our guidance, uncorrected by the seasonable experience and the effectual complaints of the people, America would not long retain her rank among the nations. For eighteen hundred years, though perchance I have no right to say it, the New Testament has been written; yet where is the legislator who has wisdom and practical talent enough to avail himself of the light which it sheds on the science of legislation?

The authority of government, even such as

I am willing to submit to, — for I will cheerfully obey those who know and can do better than I, and in many things even those who neither know nor can do so well, — is still an impure one: to be strictly just, it must have the sanction and consent of the governed. It can have no pure right over my person and property but what I conceded to it. The progress from an absolute to a limited monarchy, from a limited monarchy to a democracy, is a progress toward a true respect for the individual. Even the Chinese philosopher was wise enough to regard the individual as the basis of the empire. Is a democracy, such as we know it, the last improvement possible in government? Is it not possible to take a step further towards recognizing and organizing the rights of man? There will never be a really free and enlightened State until the State comes to recognize the individual as a higher and independent power, from which all its own power and authority are derived, and treats him accordingly. I please myself with imagining a State at last which can afford to be just to all men, and to treat the individual with respect as a neighbor; which even would not think it inconsistent with its own repose if a few were to live aloof from it, not meddling with it, nor embraced by it, who fulfilled all the duties of neighbors and fellow-men. A State which bore this kind of fruit, and suffered it to drop off as fast as it ripened, would prepare the way for a still more perfect and glorious State, which also I have imagined, but not yet anywhere seen.

From *Walden*
(1854)

The reputation of Thoreau's masterpiece has grown apace in the twentieth century. The first edition, 2000 copies, probably more than sufficed till the death of Thoreau eight years later. Misrepresentation of his motives and actions by James Russell Lowell and Robert Louis Stevenson hindered the growth of his fame for decades. But during the literary revival that set in about 1912, especially after the centenary of Thoreau in 1917, he became a major American author. *Walden* was reprinted in the Modern Library, the Penguin Library, and similar series. Reasons for this popular success have been plausibly suggested by Randall Stewart, namely, "that the modern emphasis upon efficient writing has resulted in a new appreciation of his 'vigorous and pithy' prose; that the compensatory need of nature in a nation of city dwellers has led to the

discovery of his matchless colloquies with nature; that many readers, pinched by economic depression, have found wholesome lessons in his philosophy of economy; and that those who oppose the authoritarian state have been fortified by his insistence upon the rights and responsibilities of the individual citizen."

Walden has four main aspects, is almost four simultaneous books. First, it is an account of actual experience by a remarkable personality. A young man, not yet twenty-eight, undertakes in March 1845 an experiment in living, with a view to discovering what is really important to him and what is not. This aspect is indicated by the sub-title, *Life in the Woods*. Thoreau writes of his building and furnishing of the hut, his simple housekeeping, his "seven miles" of beans, his observation of what is around him, his visits and visitors, his reading, reflection, and revery.

The book is also a study of nature: of the lake known as Walden Pond, in summer and in winter, of such animals as the fox and muskrat, birds such as the loon and thrasher, of frogs and turtles, ants and wasps, pickerel and perch, the ground-nut and the pine tree, of rain storms and snow storms and the whole moving picture of the seasons. Close observation in the spirit of science is united with a living literary language.

The book is a social study, a view of modern society as seen by a critical and radical individualist. Men are no longer free and creative. They have been enslaved by labor and the division of labor. The Industrial Revolution has tended to produce a mechanized, standardized, and conformist society destructive of simplicity, naturalness, integrity, depth, and contentment. (A fascinating contrast is offered by the individualism of *Walden* and the socialism of Bellamy's *Looking Backward*, a novel published in 1888.) One should note that Thoreau does not claim universal validity for his way of life, but earnestly urges the reader to "find and pursue *his own way*," not some way derived from ancestors or contemporaries.

Finally, the book is a work of art, a group of substantially unified essays in which the personal experience, the study of nature, and the study of society are closely interrelated. We may even say that there is a rough equivalent of the dramatic elements of character (Thoreau and the villagers), plot (the unfolding of the experiment), and setting (nature and modern society). As for time, the actual time was two years, two months, and two days, but, the two years being "similar," they are represented in the book with the unity of a single year, from spring to spring. Yet "Time is but the stream I go a-fishing in. . . . Its thin current slides away, but eternity remains." The tone of the book is set by the sense of eternity, that which does not slide away but remains, that which is timeless, universal, absolute.

Of the eighteen essays, four are given below, all save the first one complete.

Economy

When I wrote the following pages, or rather the bulk of them, I lived alone, in the woods, a mile from any neighbor, in a house which I had built myself, on the shore of Walden Pond, in Concord, Massachusetts, and earned my living by the labor of my hands only. I lived there two years and two months. At present I am a sojourner in civilized life again.

I should not obtrude my affairs so much on the notice of my readers if very particular inquiries had not been made by my townsmen concerning my mode of life, which some would call impertinent, though they do not appear to me at all impertinent, but, considering the circumstances, very natural and pertinent. Some have asked what I got to eat; if I did not feel lonesome; if I was not afraid; and the like. Others have been curious to learn what portion of my income I devoted to charitable purposes; and some, who have large families, how many poor children I maintained. I will therefore ask those of my readers who feel no particular interest in me to pardon me if I undertake to answer some of these questions in this book. In most books, the *I*, or first person, is omitted; in this it will be retained; that, in respect to egotism, is the main difference. We commonly do not remember that it is, after all, always the first person that is speaking. I should not talk so much about myself if there were anybody else whom I knew as well. Unfortunately, I am confined to this theme by the narrowness of my experience. Moreover, I, on my side, require of every writer, first or last, a simple and sincere account of his own life, and not merely what he has heard of other men's lives; some such accounts as he would send to his kindred from a distant land; for if he has lived sincerely, it must have been in a distant land to me. Perhaps these pages are more particularly addressed to poor students. As for the rest of my readers, they will accept such portions as apply to them. I trust that none will stretch the seams in putting on the coat, for it may do good service to him whom it fits.

I would fain say something, not so much concerning the Chinese and Sandwich Islanders, as you who read these pages, who are said to live in New England; something about your condition, especially your outward condition or circumstances in this world, in this town, what it is, whether it is necessary that it be as bad as it is, whether it cannot be improved as well as not. I have traveled a good deal in Concord; and everywhere, in shops, and offices, and fields, the inhabitants have appeared to me to be doing penance in a thousand remarkable ways. What I have heard of Brahmins sitting exposed to four fires and looking in the face of the sun; or hanging suspended, with their heads downward, over flames; or looking at the heavens over their shoulders "until it becomes impossible for them to resume their natural position, while from the twist of the neck nothing but liquids can pass into the stomach"; or dwelling, chained for life, at the foot of a tree; or measuring with their bodies, like caterpillars, the breadth of vast empires; or standing on one leg on the tops of pillars, — even these forms of conscious penance are hardly more incredible and astonishing than the scenes which I daily witness. The twelve labors of Hercules were trifling in comparison with those which my neighbors have undertaken; for they were only twelve, and had an end; but I could never see that these men slew or captured any monster or finished any labor. They have no friend Iolas to burn with a hot iron the root of the hydra's head, but as soon as one head is crushed, two spring up.

I see young men, my townsmen, whose misfortune it is to have inherited farms, houses, barns, cattle, and farming tools; for these are more easily acquired than got rid of. Better if they had been born in the open pasture and suckled by a wolf, that they might have seen with clearer eyes what field they were called to labor in. Who made them serfs of the soil? Why should they eat their sixty acres, when man is condemned to eat only his peck of dirt? Why should they begin digging their graves as soon as they are born? They have got to live a man's life, pushing all these things before them, and get on as well as they can. How many a poor immortal soul have I met well nigh crushed and smothered under its load, creeping down the road of life, pushing before it a barn seventy-five feet by forty, its Augean stables never cleansed, and one hundred acres of land tillage, mowing, pasture, and woodlot! The portionless, who struggle with no such unnecessary inherited encumbrances, find it labor enough to subdue and cultivate a few cubic feet of flesh.***

Near the end of March, 1845, I borrowed an axe and went down to the woods by Walden Pond, nearest to where I intended to build my house, and began to cut down some tall arrowy white pines, still in their youth, for timber. It is difficult to begin without borrowing, but perhaps it is the most generous course thus to permit your fellow-men to have an interest in your enterprise. The owner of the axe, as he released his hold on it, said that it was the apple of his eye; but I returned it sharper than I received it. It was a pleasant hillside where I worked, covered with pine woods, through which I looked out on the pond, and a small open field in the woods where pines and hickories were springing up. The ice in the pond was not yet dissolved, though there were some open spaces, and it was all dark colored and saturated with water. There were some slight flurries of snow during the days that I worked there; but for the most part when I came out on to the railroad, on my way home, its yellow sand heap stretched away gleaming in the hazy atmosphere, and the rails shone in the spring sun, and I heard the lark and pewee and other birds already come to commence another year with us. They were pleasant spring days, in which the winter of man's discontent was thawing as well as the earth, and the life that had lain torpid began to stretch itself. One day, when my axe had come off and I had cut a green hickory for a wedge, driving it with a stone, and had placed the whole to soak in a pond hole in order to swell the wood, I saw a striped snake run into the water, and he lay on the bottom, apparently without inconvenience, as long as I stayed there, or more than a quarter of an hour; perhaps because he had not yet fairly come out of the torpid state. It appeared to me that for a like reason men remain in their present low and primitive condition; but if they should feel the influence of the spring of springs arousing them, they would of necessity rise to a higher and more ethereal life. I had previously seen the snakes in frosty mornings in my path with portions of their bodies still numb and inflexible, waiting for the sun to thaw them. On the 1st of April it rained and melted the ice, and in the early part of the day, which was very foggy, I heard a stray goose groping about over the pond and cackling as if lost, or like the spirit of the fog.

So I went on for some days cutting and hewing timber, and also studs and rafters, all with my narrow axe, not having many communicable or scholar-like thoughts singing to myself, —

Men say they know many things;
But lo! they have taken wings, —
The arts and sciences,
And a thousand appliances;
The wind that blows
Is all that anybody knows.

I hewed the main timbers six inches square, most of the studs on two sides only, and the rafters and floor timbers on one side, leaving the rest of the bark on, so that they were just as straight and much stronger than sawed ones. Each stick was carefully mortised or tenoned by its stump, for I had borrowed other tools by this time. My days in the woods were not very long ones; yet I usually carried my dinner of bread and butter, and read the newspaper in which it was wrapped, at noon, sitting amid the green pine boughs which I had cut off, and to my bread was imparted some of their fragrance, for my hands were covered with a thick coat of pitch. Before I had done I was more the friend than the foe of the pine tree, though I had cut down some of them, having become better acquainted with it. Sometimes a rambler in the wood was attracted by the sound of my axe, and we chatted pleasantly over the chips which I had made.

By the middle of April, for I made no haste in my work, but rather made the most of it, my house was framed and ready for the raising. I had already bought the shanty of James Collins, an Irishman who worked on the Fitchburg Railroad, for boards. James Collins' shanty was considered an uncommonly fine one. When I called to see it he was not at home. I walked about the outside, at first unobserved from within, the window was so deep and high. It was of small dimensions, with a peaked cottage roof, and not much else to be seen, the dirt being raised five feet all around as if it were a compost heap. The roof was the soundest part, though a good deal warped and made brittle by the sun. Doorsill there was none, but a perennial passage for the hens under the door board. Mrs. C. came to the door and asked me to view it from the inside. The hens were driven in by my approach. It was dark, and had a dirt floor for the most part, dank, clammy, and aguish, only here a board and there a board which would not bear removal. She lighted a lamp to show me the inside of the roof and the walls, and also that the board floor extended under the bed, warning me not to step into the cellar, a sort of dust hole two feet deep. In her own words, they were "good boards over- head, good boards all around, and a good win- dow," — of two whole squares originally, only the cat had passed out that way lately. There was a stove, a bed, and a place to sit, an infant in the house where it was born, a silk parasol, gilt-framed looking-glass, and a patent new coffeemill nailed to an oak sapling, all told. The bargain was soon concluded, for James had in the meanwhile returned. I to pay four dollars and twenty-five cents tonight, he to vacate at five tomorrow morning, selling to nobody else meanwhile: I to take possession at six. It were well, he said, to be there early, and anticipate certain indistinct but wholly unjust claims on the score of ground rent and fuel. This he as- sured me was the only encumbrance. At six I passed him and his family on the road. One large bundle held their all, — bed, coffeemill, looking-glass, hens, — all but the cat; she took to the woods and became a wild cat, and, as I learned afterward, trod in a trap set for wood- chucks, and so became a dead cat at last.

I took down this dwelling the same morning, drawing the nails, and removed it to the pond side by small cartloads, spreading the boards on the grass there to bleach and warp back again in the sun. One early thrush gave me a note or two as I drove along the woodland path. I was informed treacherously by a young Pat- rick that neighbor Seeley, an Irishman, in the intervals of the carting, transferred the still tolerable straight, and drivable nails, staples, and spikes to his pocket, and then stood when I came back to pass the time of day, and look freshly up, unconcerned, with spring thoughts, at the devastation; there being a dearth of work, as he said. He was there to represent spectator- dom, and help make this seemingly insignificant event one with the removal of the gods of Troy.

I dug my cellar in the side of a hill sloping to the south, where a woodchuck had formerly dug his burrow, down through sumach and blackberry roots, and the lowest stain of vege- tation, six feet square by seven deep, to a fine sand where potatoes would not freeze in any winter. The sides were left shelving, and not stoned; but the sun having never shone on them, the sand still keeps its place. It was but two hours' work. I took particular pleasure

in this breaking of ground, for in almost all latitudes men dig into the earth for an equable temperature. Under the most splendid house in the city is still to be found the cellar where they store their roots as of old, and long after the superstructure has disappeared posterity remark its dent in the earth. The house is still but a sort of porch at the entrance of a burrow.

At length, in the beginning of May, with the help of some of my acquaintances, rather to im- prove so good an occasion for neighborliness than from any necessity, I set up the frame of my house. No man was ever more honored in the character of his raisers than I. They are destined, I trust, to assist at the raising of loftier structures one day. I began to occupy my house on the 4th of July, as soon as it was boarded and roofed, for the boards were carefully feather- edged and lapped, so that it was perfectly im- pervious to rain; but before boarding I laid the foundation of a chimney at one end, bring- ing two cartloads of stones up the hill from the pond in my rams. I built the chimney after my hoeing in the fall, before a fire became necessary for warmth, doing my cooking in the meanwhile out of doors on the ground, early in the morning: which mode I still think is in some respects more convenient and agreeable than the usual one. When it stormed before my bread was baked, I fixed a few boards over the fire, and sat under them to watch my loaf, and passed some pleasant hours in that way. In those days, when my hands were much em- ployed, I read but little, but the least scraps of paper which lay on the ground, my holder, or tablecloth, afforded me as much entertainment, in fact answered the same purpose as the Il- iad.***

Before winter I built a chimney, and shingled the sides of my house, which were already im- pervious to rain, with imperfect and sappy shingles made of the first slice of the log, whose edges I was obliged to straighten with a plane.

I have thus a tight shingled and plastered house, ten feet wide by fifteen long, and eight- feet posts, with a garret and a closet, a large window on each side, two trap doors, one door at the end, and a brick fireplace opposite. The exact cost of my house, paying the usual price for such materials as I used, but not counting the work, all of which was done by myself, was as follows; and I give the details because very few are able to tell exactly what their houses cost, and fewer still, if any, the separate cost of the various materials which compose them: —

Boards	$8.03½, mostly shanty boards.	
Refuse shingles for roof and sides....	4.00	
Laths	1.25	
Two secondhand windows with glass	2.43	
One thousand old brick	4.00	
Two casks of lime..	2.40	That was high.
Hair	.31	More than I needed.
Mantle-tree iron	.15	
Nails	3.90	
Hinges and screws...	.14	
Latch	.10	
Chalk	.01	
Transportation	1.40	I carried a good part on my back.
In all	$28.12½	

These are all the materials excepting the timber, stones, and sand, which I claimed by squatter's right. I have also a small wood-shed adjoining, made chiefly of the stuff which was left after building the house.

I intend to build me a house which will surpass any on the main street in Concord in grandeur and luxury, as soon as it pleases me as much and will cost me no more than my present one.

I thus found that the student who wishes for a shelter can obtain one for a lifetime at an expense not greater than the rent which he now pays annually. If I seem to boast more than is becoming, my excuse is that I brag for humanity rather than for myself; and my shortcomings and inconsistencies do not affect the truth of my statement. Notwithstanding much cant and hypocrisy, — chaff which I find it difficult to separate from my wheat, but for which I am as sorry as any man, — I will breathe freely and stretch myself in this respect, it is such a relief to both the moral and physical system; and I am resolved that I will not through humility become the devil's attorney. I will endeavor to speak a good word for the truth. At Cambridge College the mere rent of a student's room, which is only a little larger than my own, is thirty dollars each year, though the corporation had the advantage of building thirty-two side by side and under one roof, and the occupant suffers the inconvenience of many

and noisy neighbors, and perhaps a residence in the fourth story. I cannot but think that if we had more true wisdom in these respects, not only less education would be needed, because, forsooth, more would already have been acquired, but the pecuniary expense of getting an education would in a great measure vanish. Those conveniences which the student requires at Cambridge or elsewhere cost him or somebody else ten times as great a sacrifice of life as they would with proper management on both sides. Those things for which the most money is demanded are never the things which the student most wants. Tuition, for instance, is an important item in the term bill, while for the far more valuable education which he gets by associating with the most cultivated of his contemporaries no charge is made. The mode of founding a college is, commonly, to get up a subscription of dollars and cents, and then following blindly the principles of a division of labor to its extreme, a principle which should never be followed but with circumspection, — to call in a contractor who makes this a subject of speculation, and he employs Irishmen or other operatives actually to lay the foundations, while the students that are to be are said to be fitting themselves for it; and for these oversights successive generations have to pay. I think that it would be *better than this*, for the students, or those who desire to be benefited by it, even to lay the foundation themselves. The student who secures his coveted leisure and retirement by systematically shirking any labor necessary to man obtains but an ignoble and unprofitable leisure, defrauding himself of the experience which alone can make leisure fruitful. "But," says one, "you do not mean that the students should go to work with their hands instead of their heads?" I do not mean that exactly, but I mean something which he might think a good deal like that; I mean that they should not *play life*, or *study* it merely, *while* the community supports them at this expensive game, but earnestly *live* it from beginning to end. How could youths better learn to live than by at once trying the experiment of living? Methinks this would exercise their minds as much as mathematics. If I wished a boy to know something about the arts and sciences, for instance, I would not pursue the common course, which is merely to send him into the neighborhood of some professor, where anything is professed and practiced but the art of life: — to survey the world through a telescope or a microscope, and never with his natural eye; to study chemistry, and not learn how his bread is made, or mechanics, and not learn how it is earned; to discover new satellites to Neptune, and not detect the motes in his eyes, or to what vagabond he is a satellite himself; or to be devoured by the monsters that swarm all around him, while contemplating the monsters in a drop of vinegar. Which would have advanced the most at the end of a month, — the boy who had made his own jackknife from the ore which he had dug and smelted, reading as much as would be necessary for this, — or the boy who had attended the lectures on metallurgy at the Institute in the meanwhile, and had received a Rogers' penknife from his father? Which would be most likely to cut his fingers? . . . To my astonishment I was informed on leaving college that I had studied navigation! — why, if I had taken one turn down the harbor I should have known more about it. Even the *poor* student studies and is taught only *political* economy, while that economy of living which is synonymous with philosophy is not even sincerely professed in our colleges. The consequence is that while he is reading Adam Smith, Ricardo, and Say, he runs his father in debt irretrievably.***

Before I finished my house, wishing to earn ten or twelve dollars by some honest and agreeable method, in order to meet my unusual expenses, I planted about two acres and a half of light and sandy soil near it chiefly with beans, but also a small part with potatoes, corn, peas, and turnips. The whole lot contains eleven acres, mostly growing up to pines and hickories, and was sold the preceding season for eight dollars and eight cents an acre. One farmer said that it was "good for nothing but to raise cheeping squirrels on." I put no manure whatever on this land, not being the owner, but merely a squatter, and not expecting to cultivate so much again, and I did not quite hoe it all once. I got out several cords of stumps in plowing, which supplied me with fuel for a long time, and left small circles of virgin mold, easily distinguishable through the summer by the greater luxuriance of the beans there. The dead and for the most part unmerchantable wood behind my house, and the driftwood from the pond, have supplied the remainder of my fuel. I was obliged to hire a team and a man for the plowing, though I held the plow myself. My farm outgoes for the first season were, for implements, seed, work, etc., $14.72½. The seed corn was given me. This never costs anything to speak of, unless you plant more than enough. I got twelve bushels of beans, and eighteen bushels of potatoes, beside some peas and sweet corn. The yellow corn and turnips were too late to come to anything. My whole income from the farm was

	$23.44
Deducting the outgoes	14.72½
There are left......................	$ 8.71½

besides produce consumed and on hand at the time this estimate was made of the value of $4.50, — the amount on hand much more than balancing a little grass which I did not raise. All things considered, that is, considering the importance of a man's soul and of today, notwithstanding the short time occupied by my experiment, nay, partly even because of its transient character, I believe that that was doing better than any farmer in Concord did that year.

The next year I did better still, for I spaded up all the land which I required, about a third of an acre, and I learned from the experience of both years, not being in the least awed by many celebrated works on husbandry, Arthur Young among the rest, that if one would live simply and eat only the crop which he raised, and raise no more than he ate, and not exchange it for an insufficient quantity of more luxurious and expensive things, he would need to cultivate only a few rods of ground, and that it would be cheaper to spade up that than to use oxen to plow it, and to select a fresh spot from time to time than to manure the old, and he could do all his necessary farm work as it were with his left hand at odd hours in the summer; and thus he would not be tied to an ox, or horse, or cow, or pig, as at present. I desire to speak impartially on this point, and as one not interested in the success or failure of the present economical and social arrangements, I was more independent than any farmer in Concord, for I was not anchored to a house or farm, but could follow the bent of my genius, which is a very crooked one, every moment. Besides being better off than they already, if my house had been burned or my crops had failed, I should have been nearly as well off as before.***

By surveying, carpentry, and day-labor of various other kinds in the village in the meanwhile, for I have as many trades as fingers, I had earned $13.34. The expense of food for eight months, namely, from July 4th to March 1st, the time when these estimates were made, though I lived there more than two years, — not counting potatoes, a little green corn, and some peas, which I had raised, nor considering the value of what was on hand at the last date, was

Rice	$1.73½	
Molasses	1.73	Cheapest form of the saccharine.
Rye Meal	1.04¾	
Indian meal	.99¾	Cheaper than rye.
Pork	.22	
Flour	.88	Costs more than Indian meal, both money and trouble.
Sugar	.80	
Lard	.65	
Apples	.25	
Dried apples	.22	
Sweet potatoes	.10	
One pumpkin	.06	
One watermelon	.02	
Salt	.03	

All experiments which failed

Yes, I did eat $8.74, all told; but I should not thus unblushingly publish my guilt, if I did not know that most of my readers were equally guilty with myself, and that their deeds would look no better in print. The next year I sometimes caught a mess of fish for my dinner, and once I went so far as to slaughter a woodchuck which ravaged my beanfield, — effect his transmigration, as a Tartar would say, — and devour him, partly for experiment's sake; but though it afforded me a momentary enjoyment, notwithstanding a musky flavor, I saw that the longest use would not make that a good practice, however it might seem to have your woodchucks ready dressed by the village butcher.

Clothing and some incidental expenses within the same dates, though little can be inferred from this item, amounted to $8.40¾
Oil and some household utensils 2.00

So that all the pecuniary outgoes, excepting for washing and mending, which for the most part were done out of the house, and their bills have not yet been received, — and these are all and more than all the ways by which money necessarily goes out in this part of the world, — were

House	$28.12½
Farm, one year	14.72½
Food eight months	8.74
Clothing, etc., eight months	8.40¾
Oil, etc., eight months	2.00
In all	$61.99¾

I address myself now to those of my readers who have a living to get. And to meet this I have for farm produce sold

	$23.44
Earned by day-labor	13.34
In all	$36.78

which substracted from the sum of the outgoes leaves a balance of $25.21¾ on the one side, — this being very nearly the means with which I started, and the measure of expenses to be incurred, — and on the other, besides the leisure and independence and health thus secured, a comfortable house for me as long as I choose to occupy it.

These statistics, however accidental and therefore uninstructive they may appear, as they have a certain completeness, have a certain value also. Nothing was given me of which I have not rendered some account. It appears from the above estimate, that my food alone cost me in money about twenty-seven cents a week. It was for nearly two years after this, rye and Indian meal without yeast, potatoes, rice, a very little salt pork, molasses, and salt, and my drink, water. It was fit that I should live on rice, mainly, who loved so well the philosophy of India. To meet the objections of some inveterate cavilers, I may as well state that if I dined out occasionally, as I always had done, and I trust shall have opportunities to do again, it was frequently to the detriment of my domestic arrangements. But the dining out, being, as I have stated, a constant element, does not in the least affect a comparative statement like this.

I learned from my two years' experience that it would cost incredibly little trouble to obtain one's necessary food, even in this latitude; that a man may use as simple a diet as the animals, and yet retain health and strength. I have made a satisfactory dinner, satisfactory on several accounts, simply off a dish of purslane (*Portulaca oleracea*) which I gathered in my cornfield, boiled and salted. I give the Latin on account of the savoriness of the trivial name. And pray what more can a reasonable man desire, in peaceful times, in ordinary noons, than a sufficient number of ears of green sweet-corn boiled, with the addition of salt? Even the little variety that I used was a yielding to the demands of appetite, and not of health. Yet men have come to such a pass that they frequently starve, not for want of necessaries, but for want of luxuries; and I know a good woman who thinks that her son lost his life because he took to drinking water only.***

One young man of my acquaintance, who has inherited some acres, told me that he thought he should live as I did, *if he had the means*. I would not have any one adopt *my* mode of living on any account; for, besides that before he has fairly learned it I may have found out another for myself, I desire that there may be as many different persons in the world as possible; but I would have each one be very careful to find out and pursue *his own* way, and not his father's or his mother's or his neighbor's instead. The youth may build or plant or sail, only let him not be hindered from doing that which he tells me he would like to do. It is by a mathematical point only that we are wise, as the sailor or the fugitive slave keeps the polestar in his eye; but that is sufficient guidance for all our life. We may not arrive at our port within a calculable period, but we would preserve the true course.

Undoubtedly, in this case, what is true for one is truer still for a thousand, as a large house is not proportionally more expensive than a small one, since one roof may cover, one cellar underlie, and one wall separate several apartments. But for my part, I preferred the solitary dwelling. Moreover, it will commonly be cheaper to build the whole yourself than to convince another of the advantage of the common wall; and when you have done this, the common partition, to be much cheaper, must be a thin one, and that other may prove a bad neighbor, and also not keep his side in repair. The only coöperation which is commonly possible is exceedingly partial and superficial; and what little true coöperation there is, is as if it were not, being a harmony inaudible to men. If a man has faith he will coöperate with equal faith everywhere; if he has not faith, he will continue to live like the rest of the world, whatever company he is joined to. To coöperate, in the highest as well as the lowest sense, means *to get our living together*. I heard it proposed lately that two young men should travel together over the world, the one without money, earning his means as he went, before the mast and behind the plough, the other carrying a bill of exchange in his pocket. It was easy to see that they could not long be companions or coöperate, since one would not *operate* at all. They would part at the first interesting crisis in their adventures. Above all, as I have implied, the man who goes alone can start to-day; but he who travels with another must wait till that other is ready, and it may be a long time before they get off.

But all this is very selfish, I have heard some of my townsmen say. I confess that I have hitherto indulged very little in philanthropic enterprises. I have made some sacrifices to a sense of duty, and among others have sacrificed this pleasure also. There are those who have used all their arts to persuade me to undertake the support of some poor family in the town; and if I had nothing to do, — for the devil finds employment for the idle, — I might try my hand at some such pastime as that. However, when I have thought to indulge myself in this respect, and lay their Heaven under an obligation by maintaining certain poor persons in all respects as comfortably as I maintain myself, and have even ventured so far as to make them the offer, they have one and all unhesitatingly preferred to remain poor. While my townsmen and women are devoted in so many ways to the good of their fellows, I trust that one at least may be spared to other and less humane pursuits. You must have a genius for charity as well as for anything else. As for Doing-good, that is one of the professions which are full. Moreover, I have tried it fairly, and, strange as it may seem, am satisfied that it does not agree with my constitution. Probably I should not consciously and deliberately forsake my particular calling to do the good which society demands of me, to save the universe from annihilation; and I believe that a like but infinitely greater steadfastness elsewhere is all that now preserves it. But I would not stand between any man and his genius; and to him who does this work, which I decline, with his whole heart and soul and life, I would say, Persevere, even if the world call it doing evil, as it is most likely they will.

I am far from supposing that my case is a peculiar one; no doubt many of my readers would make a similar defence. At doing something, — I will not engage that my neighbors shall pronounce it good, — I do not hesitate to say that I should be a capital fellow to hire; but what that is, it is for my employer to find out. What *good* I do, in the common sense of that word, must be aside from my main path, and for the most part wholly unintended. Men say, practically, Begin where you are and such as you are, without aiming mainly to become of more worth, and with kindness aforethought go about doing good. If I were to preach at all in this strain, I should say rather, Set about being good. As if the sun should stop when he has kindled his fires up to the splendor of a moon or a star of the sixth magnitude, and go about like a Robin Goodfellow, peeping in at every cottage window, inspiring lunatics, and tainting meats, and making darkness visible, instead of steadily increasing his genial heat and beneficence till he is of such brightness that no mortal can look him in the face, and then, and in the meanwhile too, going about the world in his own orbit, doing it good, or rather, as a truer philosophy has discovered, the world going about him getting good. When Phaëton, wishing to prove his heavenly birth by his beneficence, had the sun's chariot but one day, and drove out of the beaten track, he burned several blocks of houses in the lower streets of heaven, and scorched the surface of the earth, and dried up every spring, and made the great desert of Sahara, till at length Jupiter hurled him headlong to the earth with a thunderbolt, and the sun, through grief at his death, did not shine for a year.

There is no odor so bad as that which arises from goodness tainted. It is human, it is divine, carrion. If I knew for a certainty that a man was coming to my house with the conscious design of doing me good, I should run for my life, as from that dry and parching wind of the African deserts called the simoom, which fills the mouth and nose and ears and eyes with dust till you are suffocated, for fear that I should get some of his good done to me, — some of its virus mingled with my blood. No, — in this case I would rather suffer evil the natural way. A man is not a good *man* to me because he will feed me if I should be starving, or warm me if I should be freezing, or pull me out of a ditch if I should ever fall into one. I can find you a Newfoundland dog that will do as much. Philanthropy is not love for one's fellow-man in the broadest sense. Howard was no doubt an exceedingly kind and worthy man in his way, and has his reward; but, comparatively speaking, what are a hundred Howards to *us*, if their philanthropy do not help *us* in our best estate, when we are most worthy to be helped? I never heard of a philanthropic meeting in which it was sincerely proposed to do any good to me, or the like of me.

The Jesuits were quite balked by those Indians who, being burned at the stake, suggested new modes of torture to their tormentors. Being superior to physical suffering, it sometimes chanced that they were superior to any consolation which the missionaries could offer; and the law to do as you would be done by fell with less persuasiveness on the ears of those who, for their part, did not care how they were done by, who loved their enemies after a new fashion, and came very near freely forgiving them all they did.

Be sure that you give the poor the aid they most need, though it be your example which leaves them far behind. If you give money, spend yourself with it, and do not merely abandon it to them. We make curious mistakes sometimes. Often the poor man is not so cold and hungry as he is dirty and ragged and gross. It is partly his taste, and not merely his misfortune. If you give him money, he will perhaps buy more rags with it. I was wont to pity the clumsy Irish laborers who cut ice on the pond, in such mean and ragged clothes, while I shivered in my more tidy and somewhat more fashionable garments, till, one bitter cold day, one who had slipped into the water came to my house to warm him, and I saw him strip off three pairs of pants and two pairs of stockings ere he got down to the skin, though they were dirty and ragged enough, it is true, and that he could afford to refuse the *extra* garments which I offered him, he had so many *intra* ones. This ducking was the very thing he needed. Then I began to pity myself, and I saw that it would be a greater charity to bestow on me a flannel shirt than a whole slop-shop on him. There are a thousand hacking at the branches of evil to one who is striking at the root, and it may be that he who bestows the largest amount of time and money on the needy is doing the most by his mode of life to produce that misery which he strives in vain to relieve. It is the pious slave-breeder devoting the proceeds of every tenth slave to buy a Sunday's liberty for the rest. Some show their kindness to the poor by employing them in their kitchens. Would they not be kinder if they employed themselves there? You boast of spending a tenth part of your income in charity; maybe you should spend the nine tenths so, and done with it. Society recovers only a tenth part of the property then. Is this owing to the generosity of him in whose possession it is found, or to the remissness of the officers of justice?

Philanthropy is almost the only virtue which is sufficiently appreciated by mankind. Nay, it is greatly overrated; and it is our selfishness which overrates it. A robust poor man, one sunny day here in Concord, praised a fellow-townsman to me, because, as he said, he was kind to the poor; meaning himself. The kind uncles and aunts of the race are more esteemed than its true spiritual fathers and mothers. I once heard a reverend lecturer on England, a man of learning and intelligence, after enumerating her scientific, literary, and political worthies, Shakspeare, Bacon, Cromwell, Milton, Newton, and others, speak next of her Christian heroes, whom, as if his profession required it of him, he elevated to a place far above all the rest, as the greatest of the great. They were Penn, Howard, and Mrs. Fry. Every one must feel the falsehood and cant of this. The last were not England's best men and women; only, perhaps, her best philanthropists.

I would not subtract anything from the praise that is due to philanthropy, but merely demand justice for all who by their lives and works are a blessing to mankind. I do not value chiefly a man's uprightness and benevolence, which are, as it were, his stem and leaves. Those plants of whose greenness withered we make herb tea for the sick, serve but a humble use, and are most employed by quacks. I want the flower and fruit of a man; that some fragrance be wafted over from him to me, and some ripeness flavor our intercourse. His goodness must not be a partial and transitory act, but a constant superfluity, which costs him nothing and of which he is unconscious. This is a charity which hides a multitude of sins. The philanthropist too often surrounds mankind with the remembrance of his own cast-off griefs as an atmosphere, and calls it sympathy. We should impart our courage, and not our despair, our health and ease, and not our disease, and take care that this does not spread by contagion. From what southern plains comes up the voice of wailing? Under what latitudes reside the heathen to whom we send light? Who is that intemperate and brutal man whom we would redeem? If anything ail a man, so that he does not perform his functions, if he have a pain in his bowels even, — for that is the seat of sympathy, — he forthwith sets about reforming — the world. Being a microcosm himself, he discovers, and it is a true discovery, and he is the man to make it, — that the world has been eating green apples; to his eyes, in fact, the globe itself is a great green apple, which there is danger awful to think of that the children of men will nibble before it is ripe; and straightway his drastic philanthropy seeks out the Esquimau and the Patagonian, and embraces the populous Indian and Chinese villages; and thus, by a few years of philanthropic activity, the powers in the meanwhile using him for their own ends, no doubt, he cures himself of his dyspepsia, the globe acquires a faint blush on one or both of its cheeks, as if it were beginning to be ripe, and life loses its crudity and is once more sweet and wholesome to live. I never dreamed of any enormity greater than I have committed. I never knew, and never shall know, a worse man than myself.

I believe that what so saddens the reformer is not his sympathy with his fellows in distress, but, though he be the holiest son of God, is his private ail. Let this be righted, let the spring come to him, the morning rise over his couch, and he will forsake his generous companions without apology. My excuse for not lecturing against the use of tobacco is that I never chewed it; that is a penalty which reformed tobacco-chewers have to pay; though there are things enough I have chewed, which I could lecture against. If you should ever be betrayed into any of these philanthropies, do not let your left hand know what your right hand does, for it is not worth knowing. Rescue the drowning and tie your shoe-strings. Take your time, and set about some free labor.

Our manners have been corrupted by communication with the saints. Our hymnbooks resound with a melodious cursing of God and enduring him forever. One would say that even the prophets and redeemers had rather consoled the fears than confirmed the hopes of man. There is nowhere recorded a simple and irrepressible satisfaction with the gift of life, any

memorable praise of God. All health and success does me good, however far off and withdrawn it may appear; all disease and failure
helps to make me sad and does me evil, however
much sympathy it may have with me or I with
it. If, then, we would indeed restore mankind
by truly Indian, botanic, magnetic, or natural
means, let us first be as simple and well as
Nature ourselves, dispel the clouds which hang
over our own brows, and take up a little life
into our pores. Do not stay to be an overseer of
the poor, but endeavor to become one of the
worthies of the world.

I read in the Gulistan, or Flower Garden,
of Sheik Sadi of Shiraz, that "They asked a
wise man, saying: Of the many celebrated trees
which the Most High God has created lofty and
umbrageous, they call none azad, or free, excepting the cypress, which bears no fruit; what
mystery is there in this? He replied: Each has
its appropriate produce, and appointed season,
during the continuance of which it is fresh and
blooming, and during their absence dry and
withered; to neither of which states is the cypress exposed, being always flourishing; and of
this nature are the azads, or religious inde-
pendents. — Fix not thy heart on that which is
transitory; for the Dijlah, or Tigris, will continue
to flow through Bagdad after the race of caliphs
is extinct: if thy hand has plenty, be liberal as
the date tree; but if it affords nothing to give
away, be an azad, or free man, like the cypress."

Where I Lived, and What I Lived For

At a certain season of our life we are accustomed to consider every spot as the possible
site of a house. I have thus surveyed the country
on every side within a dozen miles of where I
live. In imagination I have bought all the farms
in succession, for all were to be bought, and I
knew their price. I walked over each farmer's
premises, tasted his wild apples, discoursed on
husbandry with him, took his farm at his price,
at any price, mortgaging it to him in my mind;
even put a higher price on it, — took everything
but a deed of it, — took his word for his deed,
for I dearly love to talk, — cultivated it, and
him too to some extent, I trust, and withdrew
when I had enjoyed it long enough, leaving him
to carry it on. This experience entitled me to be
regarded as a sort of real-estate broker by my
friends. Wherever I sat, there I might live, and
the landscape radiated from me accordingly.

What is a house but a *sedes*, a seat? — better
if a country seat. I discovered many a site for
a house not likely to be soon improved, which
some might have thought too far from the village, but to my eyes the village was too far from
it. Well, there I might live, I said; and there I
did live, for an hour, a summer and a winter
life; saw how I could let the years run off, buffet
the winter through, and see the spring come in.
The future inhabitants of this region, wherever
they may place their houses, may be sure that
they have been anticipated. An afternoon
sufficed to lay out the land into orchard, woodlot, and pasture, and to decide what fine oaks or
pines should be left to stand before the door,
and whence each blasted tree could be seen to
the best advantage; and then I let it lie, fallow
perchance, for a man is rich in proportion to the
number of things which he can afford to let
alone.

My imagination carried me so far that I even
had the refusal of several farms, — the refusal
was all I wanted, — but I never got my fingers
burned by actual possession. The nearest that
I came to actual possession was when I bought
the Hollowell place, and had begun to sort my
seeds, and collected materials with which to
make a wheelbarrow to carry it on or off with;
but before the owner gave me a deed of it, his
wife — every man has such a wife — changed
her mind and wished to keep it, and he offered
me ten dollars to release him. Now, to speak
the truth, I had but ten cents in the world, and
it surpassed my arithmetic to tell, if I was that
man who had ten cents, or who had a farm,
or ten dollars, or all together. However, I let
him keep the ten dollars and the farm too, for
I had carried it far enough; or rather, to be
generous, I sold him the farm for just what I
gave for it, and, as he was not a rich man, made
him a present of ten dollars, and still had my
ten cents, and seeds, and materials for a wheelbarrow left. I found thus that I had been a rich
man without any damage to my poverty. But
I retained the landscape, and I have since
annually carried off what it yielded without a
wheelbarrow. With respect to landscapes, —

I am monarch of all I *survey*,
    My right there is none to dispute.

I have frequently seen a poet withdraw,
having enjoyed the most valuable part of a
farm, while the crusty farmer supposed that he

had got a few wild apples only. Why, the owner does not know it for many years when a poet has put his farm in rhyme, the most admirable kind of invisible fence, has fairly impounded it, milked it, skimmed it, and got all the cream, and left the farmer only the skimmed milk.

The real attractions of the Hollowell farm, to me, were: its complete retirement, being about two miles from the village, half a mile from the nearest neighbor, and separated from the highway by a broad field; its bounding on the river, which the owner said protected it by its fogs from frosts in the spring, though that was nothing to me; the gray color and ruinous state of the house and barn, and the dilapidated fences, which put such an interval between me and the last occupant; the hollow and lichen-covered apple trees, gnawed by rabbits, showing what kind of neighbors I should have; but above all the recollection I had of it from my earliest voyages up the river, when the house was concealed behind a dense grove of red maples, through which I heard the house-dog bark. I was in haste to buy it, before the proprietor finished getting out some rocks, cutting down the hollow apple trees, and grubbing up some young birches which had sprung up in the pasture, or, in short, had made any more of his improvements. To enjoy these advantages I was ready to carry it on; like Atlas, to take the world on my shoulders, — I never heard what compensation he received for that, — and do all those things which had no other motive or excuse but that I might pay for it and be un-molested in my possession of it; for I knew all the while that it would yield the most abundant crop of the kind I wanted, if I could only afford to let it alone. But it turned out as I have said.

All that I could say, then, with respect to farming on a large scale — I have always cultivated a garden — was, that I had had my seeds ready. Many think that seeds improve with age. I have no doubt that time discriminates between the good and the bad; and when at last I shall plant, I shall be less likely to be disappointed. But I would say to my fellows, once for all, As long as possible live free and uncommitted. It makes but little difference whether you are committed to a farm or the county jail.

Old Cato, whose *De Re Rustica* is my *Cultivator*, says, — and the only translation I have seen makes sheer nonsense of the passage, — "When you think of getting a farm turn it thus in your mind, not to buy greedily; nor spare your pains to look at it, and do not think it enough to go round it once. The oftener you go there the more it will please you, if it is good." I think I shall not buy greedily, but go round and round it as long as I live, and be buried in it first, that it may please me the more at last.

The present was my next experiment of this kind, which I purpose to describe more at length, for convenience putting the experience of two years into one. As I have said, I do not propose to write an ode to dejection, but to brag as lustily as chanticleer in the morning, standing on his roost, if only to wake my neighbors up.

When first I took up my abode in the woods, that is, began to spend my nights as well as days there, which, by accident, was on Independence Day, or the Fourth of July, 1845, my house was not finished for winter, but was merely a defence against the rain, without plastering or chimney, the wall being of rough, weather-stained boards, with wide chinks, which made it cool at night. The upright white hewn studs and freshly planed door and window casings gave it a clean and airy look, especially in the morning, when its timbers were saturated with dew, so that I fancied that by noon some sweet gum would exude from them. To my imagination it retained throughout the day more or less of this auroral character, reminding me of a certain house on a mountain which I had visited a year before. This was an airy and unplastered cabin, fit to entertain a travelling god, and where a goddess might trail her garments. The winds which passed over my dwelling were such as sweep over the ridges of mountains, bearing the broken strains, or celestial parts only, of terrestrial music. The morning wind forever blows, the poem of creation is uninterrupted: but few are the ears that hear it. Olympus is but the outside of the earth everywhere.

The only house I had been the owner of before, if I except a boat, was a tent, which I used occasionally when making excursions in the summer, and this is still rolled up in my garret; but the boat, after passing from hand to hand, has gone down the stream of time. With this more substantial shelter about me, I had made some progress toward settling in the world. This frame, so slightly clad, was a sort of crystallization around me, and reacted on the builder. It was suggestive somewhat as a picture in outlines. I did not need to go outdoors to take the air, for the atmosphere within had lost none of its freshness. It was not so much within-doors as behind a door where I sat, even in the rainiest weather. The Harivansa says, "An abode without birds is like a meat without seasoning." Such was not my abode, for I found myself suddenly neighbor to the birds; not by having imprisoned one, but having caged myself near them. I was not only nearer to some of those which commonly frequent the garden and the orchard, but to those wilder and more thrilling songsters of the forest which never, or rarely, serenade a villager, — the wood thrush, the veery, the scarlet tanager, the field sparrow, the whip-poor-will, and many others.

I was seated by the shore of a small pond, about a mile and a half south of the village of Concord and somewhat higher than it, in the midst of an extensive wood between that town and Lincoln, and about two miles south of that our only field known to fame, Concord Battle Ground; but I was so low in the woods that the opposite shore, half a mile off, like the rest covered with wood, was my most distant horizon. For the first week, whenever I looked out on the pond it impressed me like a tarn high up on the side of a mountain, its bottom far above the surface of other lakes, and, as the sun arose, I saw it throwing off its nightly clothing of mist, and here and there, by degrees, its soft ripples or its smooth reflecting surface was revealed, while the mists, like ghosts, were stealthily withdrawing in every direction into the woods, as at the breaking up of some nocturnal conventicle. The very dew seemed to hang upon the trees later into the day than usual, as on the sides of mountains.

This small lake was of most value as a neighbor in the intervals of a gentle rainstorm in August, when, both air and water being perfectly still, but the sky overcast, mid-afternoon had all the serenity of evening, and the wood thrush sang around, and was heard from shore to shore. A lake like this is never smoother than at such a time; and the clear portion of the air above it being shallow and darkened by clouds, the water, full of light and reflections, becomes a lower heaven itself so much the more important. From a hill-top near by, where the wood had been recently cut off, there was a pleasing vista southward across the pond, through a wide indentation in the hills which form the shore

there, where their opposite sides sloping toward each other suggested a stream flowing out in that direction through a wooded valley, but stream there was none. That way I looked between and over the near green hills to some distant and higher ones in the horizon, tinged with blue. Indeed, by standing on tiptoe I could catch a glimpse of some of the peaks of the still bluer and more distant mountain ranges in the northwest, those true-blue coins from heaven's own mint, and also of some portion of the village. But in other directions, even from this point, I could not see over or beyond the woods which surrounded me. It is well to have some water in your neighborhood, to give buoyancy to and float the earth. One value even of the smallest well is, that when you look into it you see that earth is not continent but insular. This is as important as that it keeps butter cool. When I looked across the pond from this peak toward the Sudbury meadows, which in time of flood I distinguished elevated perhaps by a mirage in their seething valley, like a coin in a basin, all the earth beyond the pond appeared like a thin crust insulated and floated even by this small sheet of intervening water, and I was reminded that this on which I dwelt was but *dry land*.

Though the view from my door was still more contracted, I did not feel crowded or confined in the least. There was pasture enough for my imagination. The low shrub oak plateau to which the opposite shore arose stretched away toward the prairies of the West and the steppes of Tartary, affording ample room for all the roving families of men. "There are none happy in the world but beings who enjoy freely a vast horizon," — said Damodara, when his herds required new and larger pastures.

Both place and time were changed, and I dwelt nearer to those parts of the universe and to those eras in history which had most attracted me. Where I lived was as far off as many a region viewed nightly by astronomers. We are wont to imagine rare and delectable places in some remote and more celestial corner of the system, behind the constellation of Cassiopeia's Chair, far from noise and disturbance. I discovered that my house actually had its site in such a withdrawn, but forever new and unprofaned, part of the universe. If it were worth the while to settle in those parts near to the Pleiades or the Hyades, to Aldebaran or Altair, then I was really there, or at an equal remoteness from the life which I had left behind, dwindled and twinkling with as fine a ray to my nearest neighbor, and to be seen only in moonless nights by him. Such was that part of creation where I had squatted; —

> There was a shepherd that did live,
>   And held his thoughts as high
> As where the mounts whereon his flocks
>   Did hourly feed him by.

What should we think of the shepherd's life if his flocks always wandered to higher pastures than his thoughts?

Every morning was a cheerful invitation to make my life of equal simplicity, and I may say innocence, with Nature herself. I have been as sincere a worshipper of Aurora as the Greeks. I got up early and bathed in the pond; that was a religious exercise, and one of the best things which I did. They say that characters were engraven on the bathing tub of King Tching-thang to this effect: "Renew thyself completely each day; do it again and again, and forever again." I can understand that. Morning brings back the heroic ages. I was as much affected by the faint hum of a mosquito making its invisible and unimaginable tour through my apartment at earliest dawn, when I was sitting with door and windows open, as I could be by any trumpet that ever sang of fame. It was Homer's requiem; itself an Iliad and Odyssey in the air, singing its own wrath and wanderings. There was something cosmical about it; a standing advertisement, till forbidden, of the everlasting vigor and fertility of the world. The morning, which is the most memorable season of the day, is the awakening hour. Then there is least somnolence in us; and for an hour, at least, some part of us awakes which slumbers all the rest of the day and night. Little is to be expected of that day, if it can be called a day, to which we are not awakened by our Genius, but by the mechanical nudgings of some servitor, are not awakened by our own newly acquired force and aspirations from within, accompanied by the undulations of celestial music, instead of factory bells, and a fragrance filling the air — to a higher life than we fell asleep from; and thus the darkness bear its fruit, and prove itself to be good, no less than the light. That man who does not believe that each day contains an earlier, more sacred, and auroral hour than he has yet profaned, has despaired of life, and is pursuing a descending and darkening way. After a partial cessation of his sensuous life, the soul of man, or its organs rather, are reinvigorated each day, and his Genius tries again what noble life it can make. All memorable events, I should say, transpire in morning time and in a morning atmosphere. The Vedas say, "All intelligences awake with the morning." Poetry and art, and the fairest and most memorable of the actions of men, date from such an hour. All poets and heroes, like Memnon, are the children of Aurora, and emit their music at sunrise. To him whose elastic and vigorous thought keeps pace with the sun, the day is a perpetual morning. It matters not what the clocks say or the attitudes and labors of men. Morning is when I am awake and there is a dawn in me. Moral reform is the effort to throw off sleep. Why is it that men give so poor an account of their day if they have not been slumbering? They are not such poor calculators. If they had not been overcome with drowsiness, they would have performed something. The millions are awake enough for physical labor; but only one in a million is awake enough for effective intellectual exertion, only one in a hundred millions to a poetic or divine life. To be awake is to be alive. I have never yet met a man who was quite awake. How could I have looked him in the face?

We must learn to reawaken and keep ourselves awake, not by mechanical aids, but by an infinite expectation of the dawn, which does not forsake us in our soundest sleep. I know of no more encouraging fact than the unquestionable ability of man to elevate his life by a conscious endeavor. It is something to be able to paint a particular picture, or to carve a statue, and so to make a few objects beautiful; but it is far more glorious to carve and paint the very atmosphere and medium through which we look, which morally we can do. To affect the quality of the day, that is the highest of arts. Every man is tasked to make his life, even in its details, worthy of the contemplation of his most elevated and critical hour. If we refused, or rather used up, such paltry information as we get, the oracles would distinctly inform us how this might be done.

I went to the woods because I wished to live deliberately, to front only the essential facts of life, and see if I could not learn what it had to teach, and not, when I came to die, discover that I had not lived. I did not wish to live what was not life, living is so dear; nor did I wish to practice resignation, unless it was quite necessary. I wanted to live deep and suck out all the marrow of life, to live so sturdily and Spartan-like as to put to rout all that was not life, to cut a broad swath and shave close, to drive life into a corner, and reduce it to its lowest terms, and, if it proved to be mean, why then to get the whole and genuine meanness of it, and publish its meanness to the world; or if it were sublime, to know it by experience, and be able to give a true account of it in my next excursion. For most men, it appears to me, are in a strange uncertainty about it, whether it is of the devil or of God, and have *somewhat hastily* concluded that it is the chief end of man here to "glorify God and enjoy him forever."

Still we live meanly, like ants; though the fable tells us that we were long ago changed into men; like pygmies we fight with cranes; it is error upon error, and clout upon clout, and our best virtue has for its occasion a superfluous and evitable wretchedness. Our life is frittered away by detail. An honest man has hardly need to count more than his ten fingers, or in extreme cases he may add his ten toes, and lump the rest. Simplicity, simplicity, simplicity! I say, let your affairs be as two or three, and not a hundred or a thousand; instead of a million count half a dozen, and keep your accounts on your thumbnail. In the midst of this chopping sea of civilized life, such are the clouds and storms and quicksands and thousand-and-one items to be allowed for, that a man has to live, if he would not founder and go to the bottom and not make his port at all, by dead reckoning, and he must be a great calculator indeed who succeeds. Simplify, simplify. Instead of three meals a day, if it be necessary eat but one; instead of a hundred dishes, five; and reduce other things in proportion. Our life is like a German Confederacy, made up of petty states, with its boundary forever fluctuating, so that even a German cannot tell you how it is bounded at any moment. The nation itself, with all its so-called internal improvements, which, by the way are all external and superficial, is just such an unwieldy and overgrown establishment, cluttered with furniture and tripped up by its own traps, ruined by luxury and heedless expense, by want of calculation and a worthy aim, as the million households in the land; and the only cure for it, as for them, is in a rigid economy, a stern and more than Spartan simplicity of life and elevation of purpose. It lives too fast. Men think

that it is essential that the *Nation* have commerce, and export ice, and talk through a telegraph, and ride thirty miles an hour, without a doubt, whether *they* do or not; but whether we should live like baboons or like men, is a little uncertain. If we do not get out sleepers, and forge rails, and devote days and nights to the work, but go to tinkering upon our *lives* to improve *them*, who will build railroads? And if railroads are not built, how shall we get to heaven in season? But if we stay at home and mind our business, who will want railroads? We do not ride on the railroad; it rides upon us. Did you ever think what those sleepers are that underlie the railroad? Each one is a man, an Irishman, or a Yankee man. The rails are laid on them, and they are covered with sand, and the cars run smoothly over them. They are sound sleepers, I assure you. And every few years a new lot is laid down and run over; so that, if some have the pleasure of riding on a rail, others have the misfortune to be ridden upon. And when they run over a man that is walking in his sleep, a super-numerary sleeper in the wrong position, and wake him up, they suddenly stop the cars, and make a hue and cry about it, as if this were an exception. I am glad to know that it takes a gang of men for every five miles to keep the sleepers down and level in their beds as it is, for this is a sign that they may sometime get up again.

Why should we live with such hurry and waste of life? We are determined to be starved before we are hungry. Men say that a stitch in time saves nine, and so they take a thousand stitches to-day to save nine tomorrow. As for *work*, we haven't any of any consequence. We have the Saint Vitus's dance, and cannot possibly keep our heads still. If I should only give a few pulls at the parish bell-rope, as for a fire, that is, without setting the bell, there is hardly a man on his farm in the outskirts of Concord, notwithstanding that press of engagements which was his excuse so many times this morning, nor a boy, nor a woman, I might almost say, but would forsake all and follow that sound, not mainly to save property from the flames, but, if we will confess the truth, much more to see it burn, since burn it must, and we, be it known, did not set it on fire, — or to see it put out, and have a hand in it, if that is done as handsomely; yes, even if it were the parish church itself. Hardly a man takes a half-hour's nap after dinner, but when he wakes he holds up his head and asks, "What's the news?" as if the rest of mankind had stood his sentinels. Some give directions to be waked every half-hour, doubtless for no other purpose; and then, to pay for it, they tell what they have dreamed. After a night's sleep the news is as indispensable as the breakfast. "Pray tell me anything new that has happened to a man anywhere on this globe," — and he reads it over his coffee and rolls, that a man has had his eyes gouged out this morning on the Wachito River; never dreaming the while that he lives in the dark unfathomed mammoth cave of this world, and has but the rudiment of an eye himself.

For my part, I could easily do without the post-office. I think that there are very few important communications made through it. To speak critically, I never received more than one or two letters in my life — I wrote this some years ago — that were worth the postage. The penny-post is, commonly, an institution through which you seriously offer a man that penny for his thoughts which is so often safely offered in jest. And I am sure that I never read any memorable news in a newspaper. If we read of one man robbed, or murdered, or killed by accident, or one house burned, or one vessel wrecked, or one steamboat blown up, or one cow run over on the Western Railroad, or one mad dog killed; or one lot of grasshoppers in the winter, — we never need read of another. One is enough. If you are acquainted with the principle, what do you care for a myriad instances and applications? To a philosopher all *news*, as it is called, is gossip, and they who edit and read it are old women over their tea. Yet not a few are greedy after this gossip. There was such a rush, as I hear, the other day at one of the offices to learn the foreign news by the last arrival, that several large squares of plate glass belonging to the establishment were broken by the pressure, — news which I seriously think a ready wit might write a twelvemonth, or twelve years, beforehand with sufficient accuracy. As for Spain, for instance, if you know how to throw in Don Carlos and the Infanta, and Don Pedro and Seville and Granada, from time to time in the right proportions, — they may have changed the names a little since I saw the papers, — and serve up a bullfight when other entertainments fail, it will be true to the letter, and give us as good an idea of the exact state or ruin of things in Spain as the most succinct and lucid reports under this

head in the newspapers: and as for England, almost the last significant scrap of news from that quarter was the revolution of 1649; and if you have learned the history of her crops for an average year, you never need attend to that thing again, unless your speculations are of a merely pecuniary character. If one may judge who rarely looks into the newspapers, nothing new does ever happen in foreign parts, a French revolution not excepted.

What news! how much more important to know what that is which was never old! "Kieou-he-yu (great dignitary of the state of Wei) sent a man to Khoung-tseu to know his news. Khoung-tseu caused the messenger to be seated near him, and questioned him in these terms: What is your master doing? The messenger answered with respect: My master desires to diminish the number of his faults, but he cannot come to the end of them. The messenger being gone, the philosopher remarked: What a worthy messenger! What a worthy messenger!" The preacher, instead of vexing the ears of drowsy farmers on their day of rest at the end of the week, — for Sunday is the fit conclusion of an ill-spent week, and not the fresh and brave beginning of a new one, — with this one other draggle-tail of a sermon, should shout with thundering voice, "Pause! Avast! Why so seeming fast, but deadly slow?"

Shams and delusions are esteemed for soundest truths, while reality is fabulous. If men would steadily observe realities only, and not allow themselves to be deluded, life, to compare it with such things as we know, would be like a fairy tale and the Arabian Nights' Entertainments. If we respected only what is inevitable and has a right to be, music and poetry would resound along the streets. When we are unhurried and wise, we perceive that only great and worthy things have any permanent and absolute existence, that petty fears and petty pleasures are but the shadow of the reality. This is always exhilarating and sublime. By closing the eyes and slumbering, and consenting to be deceived by shows, men establish and confirm their daily life of routine and habit everywhere, which still is built on purely illusory foundations. Children, who play life, discern its true law and relations more clearly than men, who fail to live it worthily, but who think that they are wiser by experience, that is, by failure. I have read in a Hindoo book, that "there was a king's son, who, being expelled in infancy from his native city, was brought up by a forester, and, growing up to maturity in that state, imagined himself to belong to the barbarous race with which he lived. One of his father's ministers having discovered him, revealed to him what he was, and the misconception of his character was removed, and he knew himself to be a prince. So soul," continues the Hindoo philosopher, "from the circumstances in which it is placed, mistakes its own character, until the truth is revealed to it by some holy teacher, and then it knows itself to be *Brahme*." I perceive that we inhabitants of New England live this mean life that we do because our vision does not penetrate the surface of things. We think that that *is* which *appears* to be. If a man should walk through this town and see only the reality, where, think you, would the "Milldam" go to? If he should give us an account of the realities he beheld there, we should not recognize the place in his description. Look at a meeting-house, or a courthouse, or a jail, or a shop, or a dwelling-house, and say what that thing really is before a true gaze, and they would all go to pieces in your account of them. Men esteem truth remote, in the outskirts of the system, behind the farthest star, before Adam and after the last man. In eternity there is indeed something true and sublime. But all these times and places and occasions are now and here. God himself culminates in the present moment, and will never be more divine in the lapse of all the ages. And we are enabled to apprehend at all what is sublime and noble only by the perpetual instilling and drenching of the reality that surrounds us. The universe constantly and obediently answers to our conceptions; whether we travel fast or slow, the track is laid for us. Let us spend our lives in conceiving then. The poet or the artist never yet had so fair and noble a design but some of his posterity at least could accomplish it.

Let us spend one day as deliberately as Nature, and not be thrown off the track by every nutshell and mosquito's wing that falls on the rails. Let us rise early and fast, or break fast, gently and without perturbation; let company come and let company go, let the bells ring and the children cry, — determined to make a day of it. Why should we knock under and go with the stream? Let us not be upset and overwhelmed in that terrible rapid and whirlpool called a dinner, situated in the meridian shallows. Weather this danger and you are safe, for the rest of the way is down hill. With unrelaxed nerves, with morning vigor, sail by it, looking another way, tied to the mast like Ulysses. If the engine whistles, let it whistle till it is hoarse for its pains. If the bell rings, why should we run? We will consider what kind of music they are like. Let us settle ourselves, and work and wedge our feet downward through the mud and slush of opinion, and prejudice, and tradition, and delusion, and appearance, that alluvion which covers the globe, through Paris and London, through New York and Boston and Concord, through Church and State, through poetry and philosophy and religion, till we come to a hard bottom and rocks in place, which we can call *reality*, and say, This is, and no mistake; and then begin, having a *point d'appui*, below freshet and frost and fire, a place where you might found a wall or a state, or set a lamp-post safely, or perhaps a gauge, not a Nilometer, but a Realometer, that future ages might know how deep a freshet of shams and appearances had gathered from time to time. If you stand right fronting and face to face to a fact, you will see the sun glimmer on both its surfaces, as if it were a cimeter, and feel its sweet edge dividing you through the heart and marrow, and so you will happily conclude your mortal career. Be it life or death, we crave only reality. If we are really dying, let us hear the rattle in our throats and feel cold in the extremities; if we are alive, let us go about our business.

Time is but the stream I go a-fishing in. I drink at it; but while I drink I see the sandy bottom and detect how shallow it is. Its thin current slides away, but eternity remains. I would drink deeper; fish in the sky, whose bottom is pebbly with stars. I cannot count one. I know not the first letter of the alphabet. I have always been regretting that I was not as wise as the day I was born. The intellect is a cleaver; it discerns and rifts its way into the secret of things. I do not wish to be any more busy with my hands than is necessary. My head is hands and feet. I feel all my best faculties concentrated in it. My instinct tells me that my head is an organ for burrowing, as some creatures use their snout and fore paws, and with it I would mine and burrow my way through these hills. I think that the richest vein is somewhere hereabouts; so by the divining-rod and thin rising vapors I judge; and here I will begin to mine.

Sounds

But while we are confined to books, though the most select and classic, and read only particular written languages, which are themselves but dialects and provincial, we are in danger of forgetting the language which all things and events speak without metaphor, which alone is copious and standard. Much is published, but little printed. The rays which stream through the shutter will be no longer remembered when the shutter is wholly removed. No method nor discipline can supersede the necessity of being forever on the alert. What is a course of history, or philosophy, or poetry, no matter how well selected, or the best society, or the most admirable routine of life, compared with the discipline of looking always at what is to be seen? Will you be a reader, a student merely, or a seer? Read your fate, see what is before you, and walk on into futurity.

I did not read books the first summer; I hoed beans. Nay, I often did better than this. There were times when I could not afford to sacrifice the bloom of the present moment to any work, whether of the head or hands. I love a broad margin to my life. Sometimes, in a summer morning, having taken my accustomed bath, I sat in my sunny doorway from sunrise till noon, rapt in a revery, amidst the pines and hickories and sumachs, in undisturbed solitude and stillness, while the birds sang around or flitted noiseless through the house, until by the sun falling in at my west window, or the noise of some traveller's wagon on the distant highway, I was reminded of the lapse of time. I grew in those seasons like corn in the night, and they were far better than any work of the hands would have been. They were not time subtracted from my life, but so much over and above my usual allowance. I realized what the Orientals mean by contemplation and the forsaking of works. For the most part, I minded not how the hours went. The day advanced as if to light some work of mine; it was morning, and lo, now it is evening, and nothing memorable is accomplished. Instead of singing like the birds, I silently smiled at my incessant good fortune. As the sparrow had its trill, sitting on the hickory before my door, so had I my chuckle or suppressed warble which he might hear out of my nest. My days were not days of the week, bearing the stamp of any heathen deity, nor were they minced into hours and fretted by the ticking of a clock; for I lived like the Puri Indians, of whom it is said that "for yesterday, to-day, and to-morrow they have only one word, and they express the variety of meaning by pointing backward for yesterday, forward for to-morrow, and overhead for the passing day." This was sheer idleness to my fellow-townsmen, no doubt; but if the birds and flowers had tried me by their standard, I should not have been found wanting. A man must find his occasions in himself, it is true. The natural day is very calm, and will hardly reprove his indolence.

I had this advantage, at least, in my mode of life, over those who were obliged to look abroad for amusement, to society and the theatre, that my life itself was become my amusement and never ceased to be novel. It was a drama of many scenes and without an end. If we were always indeed getting our living, and regulating our lives according to the last and best mode we had learned, we should never be troubled with ennui. Follow your genius closely and it will not fail to show you a fresh prospect every hour. Housework was a pleasant pastime. When my floor was dirty, I rose early, and, setting all my furniture out of doors on the grass, bed and bedstead making but one budget, dashed water on the floor, and sprinkled white sand from the pond on it, and then with a broom scrubbed it clean and white; and by the time the villagers had broken their fast the morning sun had dried my house sufficiently to allow me to move in again, and my meditations were almost uninterrupted. It was pleasant to see my whole household effects out on the grass, making a little pile like a gypsy's pack, and my three-legged table, from which I did not remove the books and pen and ink, standing amid the pines and hickories. They seemed glad to get out themselves, and as if unwilling to be brought in. I was sometimes tempted to stretch an awning over them and take my seat there. It was worth the while to see the sun shine on these things, and hear the free wind blow on them; so much more interesting most familiar objects look out doors than in the house. A bird sits on the next bough, life-everlasting grows under the table, and blackberry vines run round its legs; pine cones, chestnut burs, and strawberry leaves are strewn about. It looked as if this was the way these forms came to be transferred to our furniture, to tables, chairs and bedstead, —because they once stood in their midst.

My house was on the side of a hill, immediately on the edge of the larger wood, in the midst of a young forest of pitch pines and hickories, and half a dozen rods from the pond, to which a narrow footpath led down the hill. In my front yard grew the strawberry, blackberry, and life-everlasting, johnswort and goldenrod, shrub-oaks and sand-cherry, blueberry and ground-nut. Near the end of May, the sand-cherry (*cerasus pumila*) adorned the sides of the path with its delicate flowers arranged in umbels cylindrically about its short stems, which last, in the fall, weighed down with good-sized and handsome cherries, fell over in wreaths like rays on every side. I tasted them out of compliment to Nature, though they were scarcely palatable. The sumach (*rhus glabra*) grew luxuriantly about the house, pushing up through the embankment which I had made, and growing five or six feet the first season. Its broad pinnate tropical leaf was pleasant though strange to look on. The large buds, suddenly pushing out late in the spring from dry sticks which had seemed to be dead, developed themselves as by magic into graceful green and tender boughs, an inch in diameter; and sometimes, as I sat at my window, so heedlessly did they grow and tax their weak joints, I heard a fresh and tender bough suddenly fall like a fan to the ground, when there was not a breath of air stirring, broken off by its own weight. In August, the large masses of berries, which, when in flower, had attracted many wild bees, gradually assumed their bright velvety crimson hue, and by their weight again bent down and broke the tender limbs.

As I sit at my window this summer afternoon, hawks are circling about my clearing; the tantivy of wild pigeons, flying by twos and threes athwart my view, or perching restless on the white-pine boughs behind my house, gives a voice to the air; a fishhawk dimples the glassy surface of the pond and brings up a fish; a mink steals out of the marsh before my door and seizes a frog by the shore; the sedge is bending under the weight of the reed-birds flitting hither and thither; and for the last half hour I have heard the rattle of railroad cars, now dying away and then reviving like the beat of a partridge, conveying travellers from Boston to the country. For I did not live so out of the world as that boy who, as I hear, was put out to a farmer in the east part of the town, but erelong ran away and came home again, quite down at the heel

and homesick. He had never seen such a dull and out-of-the-way place; the folks were all gone off; why, you couldn't even hear the whistle! I doubt if there is such a place in Massachusetts now: —

In truth, our village has become a butt
For one of those fleet railroad shafts, and o'er
Our peaceful plain its soothing sound is — Concord.

The Fitchburg Railroad touches the pond about a hundred rods south of where I dwell. I usually go to the village along its causeway, and am, as it were, related to society by this link. The men on the freight trains, who go over the whole length of the road, bow to me as to an old acquaintance, they pass me so often, and apparently they take me for an employee; and so I am. I too would fain be a track-repairer somewhere in the orbit of the earth.

The whistle of the locomotive penetrates my woods summer and winter, sounding like the scream of a hawk sailing over some farmer's yard, informing me that many restless city merchants are arriving within the circle of the town, or adventurous country traders from the other side. As they come under one horizon, they shout their warning to get off the track to the other, heard sometimes through the circles of two towns. Here come your groceries, country; your rations, countrymen! Nor is there any man so independent on his farm that he can say them nay. And here's your pay for them! screams the countryman's whistle; timber like long battering rams going twenty miles an hour against the city's walls, and chairs enough to seat all the weary and heavy laden that dwell within them. With such huge and lumbering civility the country hands a chair to the city. All the Indian huckleberry hills are stripped, all the cranberry meadows are raked into the city. Up comes the cotton, down goes the woven cloth; up comes the silk, down goes the woolen; up come the books, but down goes the wit that writes them.

When I meet the engine with its train of cars moving off with planetary motion, — or, rather, like a comet, for the beholder knows not if with that velocity and with that direction it will ever revisit this system, since its orbit does not look like a returning curve, — with its steam cloud like a banner streaming behind in golden and silver wreaths, like many a downy cloud which I have seen, high in the heavens, unfolding its masses to the light, — as if this travelling demigod, this cloud-compeller, would erelong take the sunset sky for the livery of his train; when I hear the iron horse make the hills echo with his snort like thunder, shaking the earth with his feet, and breathing fire and smoke from his nostrils (what kind of winged horse or fiery dragon they will put into the new Mythology I don't know), it seems as if the earth had got a race now worthy to inhabit it. If all were as it seems, and men made the elements their servants for noble ends! If the cloud that hangs over the engine were the perspiration of heroic deeds, or as beneficent as that which floats over the farmer's fields, then the elements and Nature herself would cheerfully accompany men on their errands and be their escort.

I watch the passage of the morning cars with the same feeling that I do the rising of the sun, which is hardly more regular. Their train of clouds stretching far behind and rising higher and higher, going to heaven while the cars are going to Boston, conceals the sun for a minute and casts my distant field into the shade, a celestial train beside which the petty train of cars which hugs the earth is but the barb of the spear. The stabler of the iron horse was up early this winter morning by the light of the stars amid the mountains, to fodder and harness his steed. Fire, too, was awakened thus early to put the vital heat in him and get him off. If the enterprise were as innocent as it is early! If the snow lies deep, they strap on his snow-shoes, and with the giant plough plough a furrow from the mountains to the seaboard, in which the cars, like a following drill-barrow, sprinkle all the restless men and floating merchandise in the country for seed. All day the fire-steed flies over the country, stopping only that his master may rest, and I am awakened by his tramp and defiant snort at midnight, when in some remote glen in the woods he fronts the elements incased in ice and snow; and he will reach his stall only with the morning star, to start once more on his travels without rest or slumber. Or perchance, at evening, I hear him in his stable blowing off the superfluous energy of the day, that he may calm his nerves and cool his liver and brain for a few hours of iron slumber. If the enterprise were as heroic and commanding as it is protracted and unwearied!

Far through unfrequented woods on the confines of towns, where once only the hunter penetrated by day, in the darkest night dart

these bright saloons without the knowledge of their inhabitants; this moment stopping at some brilliant station-house in town or city, where a social crowd is gathered, the next in the Dismal Swamp, scaring the owl and fox. The startings and arrivals of the cars are now the epochs in the village day. They go and come with such regularity and precision, and their whistle can be heard so far, that the farmers set their clocks by them, and thus one well-conducted institution regulates a whole country. Have not men improved somewhat in punctuality since the railroad was invented? Do they not talk and think faster in the depot than they did in the stage-office? There is something electrifying in the atmosphere of the former place. I have been astonished at the miracles it has wrought; that some of my neighbors, who, I should have prophesied, once for all, would never get to Boston by so prompt a conveyance, are on hand when the bell rings. To do things "railroad fashion" is now the by-word; and it is worth the while to be warned so often and so sincerely by any power to get off its track. There is no stopping to read the riot act, no firing over the heads of the mob, in this case. We have constructed a fate, an *Atropos*, that never turns aside. (Let that be the name of your engine.) Men are advertised that at a certain hour and minute these bolts will be shot toward particular points of the compass; yet it interferes with no man's business, and the children go to school on the other track. We live the steadier for it. We are all educated thus to be sons of Tell. The air is full of invisible bolts. Every path but your own is the path of fate. Keep on your own track, then.

What recommends commerce to me is its enterprise and bravery. It does not clasp its hands and pray to Jupiter. I see these men every day go about their business with more or less courage and content, doing more even than they suspect, and perchance better employed than they could have consciously devised. I am less affected by their heroism who stood up for half an hour in the front line at Buena Vista, than by the steady and cheerful valor of the men who inhabit the snow-plough for their winter quarters; who have not merely the three o'clock in the morning courage, which Bonaparte thought was the rarest, but whose courage does not go to rest so early, who go to sleep only when the storm sleeps or the sinews of their iron steed are frozen. On this morning of the

Great Snow, perchance, which is still raging and chilling men's blood, I hear the muffled tone of their engine bell from out the fog bank of their chilled breath, which announces that the cars *are coming*, without long delay, notwith- standing the veto of a New England northeast snow-storm, and I behold the ploughmen cov- ered with snow and rime, their heads peering above the mould-board which is turning down other than daisies and the nests of field mice, like boulders of the Sierra Nevada, that occupy an outside place in the universe.

Commerce is unexpectedly confident and serene, alert, adventurous, and unwearied. It is very natural in its methods withal, far more so than many fantastic enterprises and sentimental experiments, and hence its singular success. I am refreshed and expanded when the freight train rattles past me, and I smell the stores which go dispensing their odors all the way from Long Wharf to Lake Champlain, remind- ing me of foreign parts, of coral reefs, and In- dian oceans, and tropical climes, and the extent of the globe. I feel more like a citizen of the world at the sight of the palm-leaf which will cover so many flaxen New England heads the next summer, the Manilla hemp and cocoa-nut husks, the old junk, gunny bags, scrap iron, and rusty nails. This carload of torn sails is more legible and interesting now than if they should be wrought into paper and printed books. Who can write so graphically the history of the storms they have weathered as these rents have done? They are proof-sheets which need no correction. Here goes lumber from the Maine woods, which did not go out to sea in the last freshet, risen four dollars on the thousand because of what did go out or was split up: pine, spruce, cedar, — first, second, third, and fourth qualities, so lately all of one quality, to wave over the bear, and moose, and caribou. Next rolls Thomaston lime, a prime lot, which will get far among the hills before it gets slacked. These rags in bales, of all hues and qualities, the lowest condition to which cotton and linen descend, the final result of dress, — of patterns which are now no longer cried up, unless it be in Milwaukee, as those splendid articles, English, French, or American prints, ginghams, muslins, etc., gath- ered from all quarters both of fashion and pov- erty, going to become paper of one color or a few shades only, on which forsooth will be writ- ten tales of real life, high and low, and founded on fact! This closed car smells of salt fish, the strong New England and commercial scent, re- minding me of the Grand Banks and the fish- eries. Who has not seen a salt fish, thoroughly cured for this world, so that nothing can spoil it, and putting the perseverance of the saints to the blush? with which you may sweep or pave the streets, and split your kindlings, and the teamster shelter himself and his lading against sun, wind, and rain behind it, — and the trader, as a Concord trader once did, hang it up by his door for a sign when he commences business, until at last his oldest customer cannot tell surely whether it be animal, vegetable, or min- eral, and yet it shall be as pure as a snowflake, and if it be put into a pot and boiled, will come out an excellent dun fish for a Saturday's din- ner. Next Spanish hides, with the tails still preserving their twist and the angle of elevation they had when the oxen that wore them were careering over the pampas of the Spanish main, — a type of all obstinacy, and evincing how al- most hopeless and incurable are all constitutional vices. I confess that, practically speaking, when I have learned a man's real disposition, I have no hopes of changing it for the better or worse in this state of existence. As the Orientals say, "A cur's tail may be warmed, and pressed, and bound round with ligatures, and after a twelve years' labor bestowed upon it, still it will retain its natural form." The only effectual cure for such inveteracies as these tails exhibit is to make glue of them, which I believe is what is usually done with them, and then they will stay put and stick. Here is a hogshead of molasses or of brandy directed to John Smith, Cuttingsville, Vermont, some trader among the Green Moun- tains, who imports for the farmers near his clearing, and now perchance stands over his bulk-head and thinks of the last arrivals on the coast, how they may affect the price for him, telling his customers this moment, as he has told them twenty times before this morning, that he expects some by the next train of prime quality. It is advertised in the Cuttingsville Times.

While these things go up other things come down. Warned by the whizzing sound, I look up from my book and see some tall pine, hewn on far northern hills, which has winged its way over the Green Mountains and the Connecticut, shot like an arrow through the township within ten minutes, and scarce another eye beholds it; going

to be the mast
Of some great ammiral.

And hark! here comes the cattle-train bearing the cattle of a thousand hills, sheepcots, stables, and cow-yards in the air, drovers with their sticks, and shepherd boys in the midst of their flocks, all but the mountain pastures, whirled along like leaves blown from the mountains by the September gales. The air is filled with the bleating of calves and sheep, and the hustling of oxen, as if a pastoral valley were going by. When the old bell-wether at the head rattles his bell, the mountains do indeed skip like rams and the little hills like lambs. A car-load of drovers, too, in the midst, on a level with their droves now, their vocation gone, but still clinging to their useless sticks as their badge of office. But their dogs, where are they? It is a stampede to them; they are quite thrown out; they have lost the scent. Methinks I hear them barking behind the Peterboro' Hills, or panting up the western slope of the Green Mountains. They will not be in at the death. Their vocation, too, is gone. Their fidelity and sagacity are below par now. They will slink back to their kennels in disgrace, or perchance run wild and strike a league with the wolf and the fox. So is your pastoral life whirled past and away. But the bell rings, and I must get off the track and let the cars go by:

What's the railroad to me?
I never go to see
Where it ends.
It fills a few hollows,
And makes banks for the swallows,
It sets the sand a-blowing,
And the blackberries a-growing,

but I cross it like a cart-path in the woods. I will not have my eyes put out and my ears spoiled by its smoke and steam and hissing.

Now that the cars are gone by and all the restless world with them, and the fishes in the pond no longer feel their rumbling, I am more alone than ever. For the rest of the long afternoon, perhaps, my meditations are interrupted only by the faint rattle of a carriage or team along the distant highway.

Sometimes, on Sundays, I heard the bells, the Lincoln, Acton, Bedford, or Concord bell, when the wind was favorable, a faint, sweet, and, as it were, natural melody, worth importing into the wilderness. At a sufficient distance over the woods this sound acquires a certain vibratory hum, as if the pine needles in the horizon were the strings of a harp which it swept. All sound heard at the greatest possible distance produces one and the same effect, a vibration of the universal lyre, just as the intervening atmosphere makes a distant ridge of earth interesting to our eyes by the azure tint it imparts to it. There came to me in this case a melody which the air had strained, and which had conversed with every leaf and needle of the wood, that portion of the sound which the elements had taken up and modulated and echoed from vale to vale. The echo is, to some extent, an original sound, and therein is the magic and charm of it. It is not merely a repetition of what was worth repeating in the bell, but partly the voice of the wood; the same trivial words and notes sung by a wood-nymph.

At evening, the distant lowing of some cow in the horizon beyond the woods sounded sweet and melodious, and at first I would mistake it for the voices of certain minstrels by whom I was sometimes serenaded, who might be straying over hill and dale; but soon I was not unpleasantly disappointed when it was prolonged into the cheap and natural music of the cow. I do not mean to be satirical, but to express my appreciation of those youths' singing, when I state that I perceived clearly that it was akin to the music of the cow, and they were at length one articulation of Nature.

Regularly at half-past seven, in one part of the summer, after the evening train had gone by, the whippoorwills chanted their vespers for half an hour, sitting on a stump by my door, or upon the ridge pole of the house. They would begin to sing almost with as much precision as a clock, within five minutes of a particular time, referred to the setting of the sun, every evening. I had a rare opportunity to become acquainted with their habits. Sometimes I heard four or five at once in different parts of the wood, by accident one a bar behind another, and so near me that I distinguished not only the cluck after each note, but often that singular buzzing sound like a fly in a spider's web, only proportionally louder. Sometimes one would circle round and round me in the woods a few feet distant as if tethered by a string, when probably I was near its eggs. They sang at intervals throughout the night, and were again as musical as ever just before and about dawn.

When other birds are still the screech owls

take up the strain, like mourning women their ancient u-lu-lu. Their dismal scream is truly Ben Jonsonian. Wise midnight hags! It is no honest and blunt tu-whit tu-who of the poets, but, without jesting, a most solemn grave-yard ditty, the mutual consolations of suicide lovers remembering the pangs and delights of supernal love in the infernal groves. Yet I love to hear their wailing, their doleful responses, trilled along the woodside; reminding me sometimes of music and singing birds; as if it were the dark and tearful side of music, the regrets and sighs that would fain be sung. They are the spirits, the low spirits and melancholy forebodings, of fallen souls that once in human shape night-walked the earth and did the deeds of darkness, now expiating their sins with their wailing hymns or threnodies in the scenery of their transgressions. They give me a new sense of the variety and capacity of that nature which is our common dwelling. *Oh-o-o-o-o that I never had been bor-r-r-rn!* sighs one on this side of the pond, and circles with the restlessness of despair to some new perch on the gray oaks. Then — *that I never had been bor-r-r-n!* echoes another on the farther side with tremulous sincerity, and — *bor-r-r-n!* come faintly from far in the Lincoln woods.

I was also serenaded by a hooting owl. Near at hand you could fancy it the most melancholy sound in Nature, as if she meant by this to stereotype and make permanent in her choir the dying moans of a human being, — some poor weak relic of mortality who has left hope behind, and howls like an animal, yet with human sobs, on entering the dark valley, made more awful by a certain gurgling melodiousness, — I find myself beginning with the letters *gl* when I try to imitate it, — expressive of a mind which has reached the gelatinous mildewy stage in the mortification of all healthy and courageous thought. It reminded me of ghouls and idiots and insane howlings. But now one answers from far woods in a strain made really melodious by distance, — *Hoo hoo hoo hoorer hoo;* and indeed for the most part it suggested only pleasing associations, whether heard by day or night, summer or winter.

I rejoice that there are owls. Let them do the idiotic and maniacal hooting for men. It is a sound admirably suited to swamps and twilight woods which no day illustrates, suggesting a vast and undeveloped nature which men have not recognized. They represent the stark twilight and unsatisfied thoughts which all have. All day the sun has shone on the surface of some savage swamp, where the single spruce stands hung with usnea lichens, and small hawks circulate above, and the chickadee lisps amid the evergreens, and the partridge and rabbit skulk beneath; but now a more dismal and fitting day dawns, and a different race of creatures awakes to express the meaning of Nature there.

Late in the evening I heard the distant rumbling of wagons over bridges, — a sound heard farther than almost any other at night, — the baying of dogs, and sometimes again the lowing of some disconsolate cow in a distant barn-yard. In the meanwhile all the shore rang with the trump of bullfrogs, the sturdy spirits of ancient wine-bibbers and wassailers, still unrepentant, trying to sing a catch in their Stygian lake, — if the Walden nymphs will pardon the comparison, for though there are almost no weeds, there are frogs there, — who would fain keep up the hilarious rules of their old festal tables, though their voices have waxed hoarse and solemnly grave, mocking at mirth, and the wine has lost its flavor, and become only liquor to distend their paunches, and sweet intoxication never comes to drown the memory of the past, but mere saturation and waterloggedness and distention. The most aldermanic, with his chin upon a heart-leaf, which serves for a napkin to his drooling chaps, under this northern shore quaffs a deep draught of the once scorned water, and passes round the cup with the ejaculation *tr-r-r-oonk, tr-r-r-onk, tr-r-roonk!* and straightway comes over the water from some distant cove the same password repeated, where the next in seniority and girth has gulped down to his mark; and when this observance has made the circuit of the shores, then ejaculates the master of ceremonies, with satisfaction, *tr-r-r-oonk!* and each in his turn repeats the same down to the least distended, leakiest, and flabbiest-paunched, that there be no mistake; and then the bowl goes round again and again, until the sun disperses the morning mist, and only the patriarch is not under the pond, but vainly bellowing *troonk* from time to time, and pausing for a reply.

I am not sure that I ever heard the sound of cock-crowing from my clearing, and I thought that it might be worth the while to keep a cockerel for his music merely, as a singing bird. The note of this once wild Indian pheasant is certainly the most remarkable of any bird's, and

if they could be naturalized without being domesticated, it would soon become the most
famous sound in our woods, surpassing the
clangor of the goose and the hooting of the owl;
and then imagine the cackling of the hens to 5
fill the pauses when their lords' clarions rested!
No wonder that man added this bird to his
tame stock, — to say nothing of the eggs and
drumsticks. To walk in a winter morning in a
wood where these birds abounded, their native 10
woods, and hear the wild cockerels crow on the
trees, clear and shrill for miles over the resounding earth, drowning the feebler notes of other
birds, — think of it! It would put nations on
the alert. Who would not be early to rise, and 15
rise earlier and earlier every successive day of
his life, till he became unspeakably healthy,
wealthy, and wise? This foreign bird's note is
celebrated by the poets of all countries along
with the notes of their native songsters. All 20
climates agree with brave Chanticleer. He is
more indigenous even than the natives. His
health is ever good, his lungs are sound, his
spirits never flag. Even the sailor on the Atlantic
and Pacific is awakened by his voice; but its 25
shrill sound never roused me from my slumbers.
I kept neither dog, cat, cow, pig, nor hens, so
that you would have said there was a deficiency
of domestic sound; neither the churn, nor the
spinning-wheel, nor even the singing of the 30
kettle, nor the hissing of the urn, nor children
crying, to comfort one. An old-fashioned man
would have lost his senses or died of ennui
before this. Not even rats in the wall, for they
were starved out, or rather were never baited 35
in, — only squirrels on the roof and under the
floor, a whippoorwill on the ridge pole, a blue-
jay screaming beneath the window, a hare or
woodchuck under the house, a screech-owl or
a cat-owl behind it, a flock of wild geese or a 40
laughing loon on the pond, and a fox to bark
in the night. Not even a lark or an oriole, those
mild plantation birds, ever visited my clearing.
No cockerels to crow nor hens to cackle in the
yard. No yard! but unfenced Nature reaching 45
up to your very sills. A young forest growing
up under your windows, and wild sumachs and
blackberry vines breaking through into your
cellar; sturdy pitch-pines rubbing and creaking
against the shingles for want of room, their 50
roots reaching quite under the house. Instead
of a scuttle or a blind blown off in the gale, —
a pine tree snapped off or torn up by the roots
behind your house for fuel. Instead of no path

to the front-yard gate in the Great Snow, —
no gate — no frontyard, — and no path to the
civilized world!

Conclusion

To the sick the doctors wisely recommend a
change of air and scenery. Thank Heaven, here
is not all the world. The buckeye does not grow
in New England, and the mockingbird is rarely
heard here. The wild goose is more of a cos-
mopolite than we; he breaks his fast in Canada,
takes a luncheon in the Ohio, and plumes himself for the night in a southern bayou. Even the
bison to some extent keeps pace with the seasons, cropping the pastures of the Colorado
only till a greener and sweeter grass awaits him
by the Yellowstone. Yet we think that if rail-
fences are pulled down, and stone-walls piled
up on our farms, bounds are henceforth set to
our lives and our fates decided. If you are chosen
town clerk, forsooth, you cannot go to Terra del
Fuego this summer; but you may go to the land
of infernal fire nevertheless. The universe is
wider than our views of it.

Yet we should oftener look over the tafferel
of our craft, like curious passengers, and not
make the voyage like stupid sailors picking
oakum. The other side of the globe is but the
home of our correspondent. Our voyage is only
great-circle sailing, and the doctors prescribe
for diseases of the skin merely. One hastens to
Southern Africa to chase the giraffe; but surely
that is not the game he would be after. How
long, pray, would a man hunt giraffes if he
could? Snipes and woodcocks also may afford
rare sport; but I trust it would be nobler game
to shoot one's self. —

> Direct your eye right inward, and you'll find
> A thousand regions in your mind
> Yet undiscovered. Travel them, and be
> Expert in home-cosmography.

What does Africa, — what does the West
stand for? Is not our own interior white on the
chart? black though it may prove, like the coast,
when discovered. Is it the source of the Nile,
or the Niger, or the Mississippi, or a Northwest
Passage around this continent, that we would
find? Are these the problems which most concern mankind? Is Franklin the only man who is
lost, that his wife should be so earnest to find
him? Does Mr. Grinnell know where he himself is? Be rather the Mungo Park, the Lewis

and Clarke and Frobisher, of your own streams and oceans; explore your own higher latitudes, — with shiploads of preserved meats to support you, if they be necessary; and pile the empty cans sky-high for a sign. Were preserved meats invented to preserve meat merely? Nay, be a Columbus to whole new continents and worlds within you, opening new channels, not of trade, but of thought. Every man is the lord of a realm beside which the earthly empire of the Czar is but a petty state, a hummock left by the ice. Yet some can be patriotic who have no *self*-respect, and sacrifice the greater to the less. They love the soil which makes their graves, but have no sympathy with the spirit which may still animate their clay. Patriotism is a maggot in their heads. What was the meaning of that South-Sea Exploring Expedition, with all its parade and expense, but an indirect recognition of the fact that there are continents and seas in the moral world, to which every man is an isthmus or an inlet, yet unexplored by him, but that it is easier to sail many thousand miles through cold and storm and cannibals, in a government ship, with five hundred men and boys to assist one, than it is to explore the private sea, the Atlantic and Pacific Ocean of one's being alone, —

> "Erret, et extremos alter scrutetur Iberos.
> Plus habet hic vitæ, plus habet ille viæ."

Let them wander and scrutinize the outlandish Australians.
I have more of God, they more of the road.

It is not worth the while to go round the world to count the cats in Zanzibar. Yet do this even till you can do better, and you may perhaps find some "Symmes' Hole" by which to get at the inside at last. England and France, Spain and Portugal, Gold Coast and Slave Coast, all front on this private sea; but no bark from them has ventured out sight of land, though it is without doubt the direct way to India. If you would learn to speak all tongues and conform to the customs of all nations, if you would travel farther than all travellers, be naturalized in all climes, and cause the Sphinx to dash her head against a stone, even obey the precept of the old philosopher, and Explore thyself. Herein are demanded the eye and the nerve. Only the defeated and deserters go to the wars, cowards that run away and enlist. Start now on that farthest western way, which does not pause at the Mississippi or the Pacific, nor conduct to-ward a wornout China or Japan, but leads on direct, a tangent to this sphere, summer and winter, day and night, sun down, moon down, and at last earth down too.

It is said that Mirabeau took to highway robbery "to ascertain what degree of resolution was necessary in order to place one's self in formal opposition to the most sacred laws of society." He declared that "a soldier who fights in the ranks does not require half so much courage as a foot-pad," — "that honor and religion have never stood in the way of a well-considered and a firm resolve." This was manly, as the world goes; and yet it was idle, if not desperate. A saner man would have found himself often enough "in formal opposition" to what are deemed "the most sacred laws of society," through obedience to yet more sacred laws, and so have tested his resolution without going out of his way. It is not for a man to put himself in such an attitude to society, but to maintain himself in whatever attitude he find himself through obedience to the laws of his being, which will never be one of opposition to a just government, if he should chance to meet with such.

I left the woods for as good a reason as I went there. Perhaps it seemed to me that I had several more lives to live, and could not spare any more time for that one. It is remarkable how easily and insensibly we fall into a particular route, and make a beaten track for ourselves. I had not lived there a week before my feet wore a path from my door to the pond-side; and though it is five or six years since I trod it, it is still quite distinct. It is true, I fear that others may have fallen into it, and so helped to keep it open. The surface of the earth is soft and impressible by the feet of men; and so with the paths which the mind travels. How worn and dusty, then, must be the highways of the world, how deep the ruts of tradition and conformity! I did not wish to take a cabin passage, but rather to go before the mast and on the deck of the world, for there I could best see the moonlight amid the mountains. I do not wish to go below now.

I learned this, at least, by my experiment: that if one advances confidently in the direction of his dreams, and endeavors to live the life which he has imagined, he will meet with a success unexpected in common hours. He will put some things behind, will pass an invisible boundary; new, universal, and more liberal laws will begin to establish themselves around and within him; or the old laws be expanded, and interpreted in his favor in a more liberal sense, and he will live with the license of a higher order of beings. In proportion as he simplifies his life, the laws of the universe will appear less complex, and solitude will not be solitude, nor poverty poverty, nor weakness weakness. If you have built castles in the air, your work need not be lost; that is where they should be. Now put the foundations under them.

It is a ridiculous demand which England and America make, that you shall speak so that they can understand you. Neither men nor toadstools grow so. As if that were important, and there were not enough to understand you without them. As if Nature could support but one order of understandings, could not sustain birds as well as quadrupeds, flying as well as creeping things, and *hish* and *whoa*, which Bright can understand, were the best English. As if there were safety in stupidity alone. I fear chiefly lest my expression may not be *extra-vagant* enough, may not wander far enough beyond the narrow limits of my daily experience, so as to be adequate to the truth of which I have been convinced. *Extravagance!* it depends on how you are yarded. The migrating buffalo which seeks new pastures in another latitude, is not extravagant like the cow which kicks over the pail, leaps the cowyard fence, and runs after her calf, in milking-time. I desire to speak somewhere *without* bounds; like a man in a waking moment, to men in their waking moments; for I am convinced that I cannot exaggerate enough even to lay the foundation of a true expression. Who that has heard a strain of music feared then lest he should speak extravagantly any more forever? In view of the future or possible, we should live quite laxly and undefined in front, our outlines dim and misty on that side; as our shadows reveal an insensible perspiration toward the sun. The volatile truth of our words should continually betray the inadequacy of the residual statement. Their truth is instantly *translated*; its literal monument alone remains. The words which express our faith and piety are not definite; yet they are significant and fragrant like frankincense to superior natures.

Why level downward to our dullest perception always, and praise that as common sense? The commonest sense is the sense of men asleep, which they express by snoring. Sometimes we are inclined to class those who are once-and-a-half-witted with the half-witted, be-cause we appreciate only a third part of their wit. Some would find fault with the morning-red, if they ever got up early enough. "They pretend," as I hear, "that the verses of Kabir have four different senses: illusion, spirit, intellect, and the exoteric doctrine of the Vedas"; but in this part of the world it is considered a ground for complaint if a man's writings admit of more than one interpretation. While England endeavors to cure the potato-rot, will not any endeavor to cure the brain-rot, which prevails so much more widely and fatally?

I do not suppose that I have attained to obscurity, but I should be proud if no more fatal fault were found with my pages on this score than was found with the Walden ice. Southern customers objected to its blue color, which is the evidence of its purity, as if it were muddy, and preferred the Cambridge ice, which is white, but tastes of weeds. The purity men love is like the mists which envelop the earth, and not like the azure ether beyond.

Some are dinning in our ears that we Americans, and moderns generally, are intellectual dwarfs compared with the ancients, or even the Elizabethan men. But what is that to the purpose? A living dog is better than a dead lion. Shall a man go and hang himself because he belongs to the race of pygmies, and not be the biggest pygmy that he can? Let every one mind his own business, and endeavor to be what he was made.

Why should we be in such desperate haste to succeed, and in such desperate enterprises? If a man does not keep pace with his companions, perhaps it is because he hears a different drummer. Let him step to the music which he hears, however measured or far away. It is not important that he should mature as soon as an apple tree or an oak. Shall he turn his spring into summer? If the condition of things which we were made for is not yet, what were any reality which we can substitute? We will not be shipwrecked on a vain reality. Shall we with pains erect a heaven of blue glass over ourselves, though when it is done we shall be sure to gaze still at the true ethereal heaven far above, as if the former were not?

There was an artist in the city of Kouroo who was disposed to strive after perfection. One day it came into his mind to make a staff. Having considered that in an imperfect work time is an ingredient, but into a perfect work time does not enter, he said to himself, It shall

be perfect in all respects, though I should do
nothing else in my life. He proceeded instantly
to the forest for wood, being resolved that it
should not be made of unsuitable material; and
as he searched for and rejected stick after stick, 5
his friends gradually deserted him, for they grew
old in their works and died, but he grew not
older by a moment. His singleness of purpose
and resolution, and his elevated piety, endowed
him, without his knowledge, with perennial 10
youth. As he made no compromise with Time,
Time kept out of his way, and only sighed at a
distance because he could not overcome him.
Before he had found a stock in all respects
suitable the city of Kouroo was a hoary ruin, 15
and he sat on one of its mounds to peel the
stick. Before he had given it the proper shape
the dynasty of the Candahars was at an end, and
with the point of the stick he wrote the name
of the last of that race in the sand, and then 20
resumed his work. By the time he had smoothed
and polished the staff Kalpa was no longer the
pole-star; and ere he had put on the ferule and
the head adorned with precious stones, Brahma
had awoke and slumbered many times. But 25
why do I stay to mention these things? When
the finishing stroke was put to his work, it
suddenly expanded before the eyes of the
astonished artist into the fairest of all the creations of Brahma. He had made a new system 30
in making a staff, a world with full and fair
proportions; in which, though the old cities and
dynasties had passed away, fairer and more
glorious ones had taken their places. And now
he saw by the heap of shavings still fresh at his 35
feet, that, for him and his work, the former
lapse of time had been an illusion, and that no
more time had elapsed than is required for a
single scintillation from the brain of Brahma to
fall on and inflame the tinder of a mortal brain. 40
The material was pure, and his art was pure;
how could the result be other than wonderful?

No face which we can give to a matter will
stead us so well at last as the truth. This alone
wears well. For the most part, we are not where 45
we are, but in a false position. Through an
infirmity of our natures, we suppose a case, and
put ourselves into it, and hence are in two cases
at the same time, and it is doubly difficult to
get out. In sane moments we regard only the 50
facts, the case that is. Say what you have to say,
not what you ought. Any truth is better than
make-believe. Tom Hyde, the tinker, standing
on the gallows, was asked if he had anything to
say. "Tell the tailors," said he, "to remember
to make a knot in their thread before they take
the first stitch." His companion's prayer is
forgotten.

However mean your life is, meet it and live it: 5
do not shun it and call it hard names. It is
not so bad as you are. It looks poorest when you
are richest. The fault-finder will find faults even
in paradise. Love your life, poor as it is. You
may perhaps have some pleasant, thrilling, 10
glorious hours, even in a poorhouse. The setting
sun is reflected from the windows of the alms-
house as brightly as from the rich man's abode;
the snow melts before its door as early in the
spring. I do not see but a quiet mind may live 15
as contentedly there, and have as cheering
thoughts, as in a palace. The town's poor seem
to me often to live the most independent lives
of any. Maybe they are simply great enough to
receive without misgiving. Most think that they 20
are above being supported by the town; but it
oftener happens that they are not above supporting themselves by dishonest means, which
should be disreputable. Cultivate poverty like
a garden herb, like sage. Do not trouble your- 25
self much to get new things, whether clothes or
friends. Turn the old; return to them. Things
do not change; we change. Sell your clothes
and keep your thoughts. God will see that you
do not want society. If I were confined to a 30
corner of a garret all my days, like a spider, the
world would be just as large to me while I had
my thoughts about me. The philosopher said:
"From an army of three divisions one can take
away its general, and put it in disorder; from 35
the man the most abject and vulgar one cannot
take away his thought." Do not seek so anxiously
to be developed, to subject yourself to many
influences to be played on; it is all dissipation.
Humility like darkness reveals the heavenly 40
lights. The shadows of poverty and meanness
gather around us, "and lo! creation widens to
our view." We are often reminded that if there
were bestowed on us the wealth of Crœsus, our
aims must still be the same, and our means 45
essentially the same. Moreover, if you are restricted in your range by poverty, if you cannot
buy books and newspapers, for instance, you are
but confined to the most significant and vital
experiences; you are compelled to deal with the 50
material which yields the most sugar and the
most starch. It is life near the bone where it is
sweetest. You are defended from being a trifler.
No man loses ever on a lower level by magna-

nimity on a higher. Superfluous wealth can buy superfluities only. Money is not required to buy one necessary of the soul.

I live in the angle of a leaden wall, into whose composition was poured a little alloy of bell metal. Often, in the repose of my midday, there reaches my ears a confused *tintinnabulum* from without. It is the noise of my contemporaries. My neighbors tell me of their adventures with famous gentlemen and ladies, what notabilities they met at the dinner-table; but I am no more interested in such things than in the contents of the *Daily Times*. The interest and the conversation are about costume and manners chiefly; but a goose is a goose still, dress it as you will. They tell me of California and Texas, of England and the Indies, of the Hon. Mr. — of Georgia or of Massachusetts, all transient and fleeting phenomena, till I am ready to leap from their court-yard like the Mameluke bey. I delight to come to my bearings, — not walk in procession with pomp and parade, in a conspicuous place, but to walk even with the Builder of the universe, if I may, — not to live in this restless, nervous, bustling, trivial Nineteenth Century, but stand or sit thoughtfully while it goes by. What are men celebrating? They are all on a committee of arrangements, and hourly expect speech from somebody. God is only the president of the day, and Webster is His orator. I love to weigh, to settle, to gravitate toward that which most strongly and rightfully attracts me; — not hang by the beam of the scale and try to weigh less, — not suppose a case, but take the case that is; to travel the only path I can, and that on which no power can resist me. It affords me no satisfaction to commence to spring an arch before I have got a solid foundation. Let us not play at kittly-benders. There is a solid bottom everywhere. We read that the traveller asked the boy if the swamp before him had a hard bottom. The boy replied that it had. But presently the traveller's horse sank in up to the girths, and he observed to the boy, "I thought you said this bog had a hard bottom." "So it has," answered the latter, "but you have not got half way to it yet." So it is with the bogs and quicksands of society; but he is an old boy that knows it. Only what is thought, said, or done at a certain rare coincidence is good. I would not be one of those who will foolishly drive a nail into mere lath and plastering; such a deed would keep me awake nights. Give me a hammer, and let me feel for the furring. Do not depend on the putty. Drive a nail home and clinch it so faithfully that you can wake up in the night and think of your work with satisfaction, — a work at which you would not be ashamed to invoke the Muse. So will help you God, and so only. Every nail driven should be as another rivet in the machine of the universe, you carrying on the work.

Rather than love, than money, than fame, give me truth. I sat at a table where were rich food and wine in abundance, and obsequious attendance, but sincerity and truth were not; and I went away hungry from the inhospitable board. The hospitality was as cold as the ices. I thought that there was no need of ice to freeze them. They talked to me of the age of the wine and the fame of the vintage; but I thought of an older, a newer, and purer wine, of a more glorious vintage, which they had not got, and could not buy. The style, the house and grounds and "entertainment," pass for nothing with me. I called on the king, but he made me wait in his hall, and conducted like a man incapacitated for hospitality. There was a man in my neighborhood who lived in a hollow tree. His manners were truly regal. I should have done better had I called on him.

How long shall we sit in our porticos practising idle and musty virtues, which any work would make impertinent? As if one were to begin the day with long-suffering, and hire a man to hoe his potatoes; and in the afternoon go forth to practise Christian meekness and charity with goodness aforethought! Consider the China pride and stagnant self-complacency of mankind. This generation inclines a little to congratulate itself on being the last of an illustrious line; and in Boston and London and Paris and Rome, thinking of its long descent, it speaks of its progress in art and science and literature with satisfaction. There are the Records of the Philosophical Societies, and the public Eulogies of *Great Men!* It is the good Adam contemplating his own virtue. "Yes, we have done great deeds, and sung divine songs, which shall never die," — that is, as long as *we* can remember them. The learned societies and great men of Assyria, — where are they? What youthful philosophers and experimentalists we are! There is not one of my readers who has yet lived a whole human life. These may be but the spring months in the life of the race. If we have had the seven-years' itch, we have not seen the seventeen-year locust yet in Concord. We are acquainted with a mere pellicle of the globe on which we live. Most have not delved six feet beneath the surface, nor leaped as many above it. We know not where we are. Besides, we are sound asleep nearly half our time. Yet we esteem ourselves wise, and have an established order on the surface. Truly, we are deep thinkers, we are ambitious spirits! As I stand over the insect crawling amid the pine needles on the forest floor, and endeavoring to conceal itself from my sight, and ask myself why it will cherish those humble thoughts and hide its head from me who might, perhaps, be its benefactor and impart to its race some cheering information, I am reminded of the greater Benefactor and Intelligence that stands over me, the human insect.

There is an incessant influx of novelty into the world, and yet we tolerate incredible dulness. I need only suggest what kind of sermons are still listened to in the most enlightened countries. There are such words as joy and sorrow, but they are only the burden of a psalm, sung with a nasal twang, while we believe in the ordinary and mean. We think that we can change our clothes only. It is said that the British Empire is very large and respectable, and that the United States are a first-rate power. We do not believe that a tide rises and falls behind every man which can float the British Empire like a chip, if he should ever harbor it in his mind. Who knows what sort of seventeen-year locust will next come out of the ground? The government of the world I live in was not framed, like that of Britain, in after-dinner conversations over the wine.

The life in us is like the water in the river. It may rise this year higher than man has ever known it, and flood the parched uplands; even this may be the eventful year, which will drown out all our muskrats. It was not always dry land where we dwell. I see far inland the banks which the stream anciently washed, before science began to record its freshets. Every one has heard the story which has gone the rounds of New England, of a strong and beautiful bug which came out of the dry leaf of an old table of apple-tree wood, which had stood in a farmer's kitchen for sixty years, first in Connecticut, and afterward in Massachusetts, — from an egg deposited in the living tree many years earlier still, as appeared by counting the annual layers beyond it; which was heard gnawing out for several weeks, hatched perchance by the heat of an urn. Who does not feel his faith

in a resurrection and immortality strengthened by hearing of this? Who knows what beautiful and winged life, whose egg has been buried for ages under many concentric layers of woodenness in the dead dry life of society, deposited at the first in the alburnum of the green and living tree, which has been gradually converted into the semblance of its well-seasoned tomb, — heard perchance gnawing out now for years by the astonished family of man, as they sat round the festive board, — may unexpectedly come forth from amidst society's most trivial and handselled furniture, to enjoy its perfect summer life at last!

I do not say that John or Jonathan will realize all this; but such is the character of that morrow which mere lapse of time can never make to dawn. The light which puts out our eyes is darkness to us. Only that day dawns to which we are awake. There is more day to dawn. The sun is but a morning star.

Sic Vita

(1841)

In "Sic Vita" ("Such is Life"), as often in Thoreau's verse, there are signs of stylistic absorption from English poets of the seventeenth century. At the same time Thoreau "anticipates the bold symbolism, airy impressionism, stringent realism, and restless inconsistencies of twentieth-century poetry" (H. W. Wells).

I am a parcel of vain strivings tied
   By a chance bond together,
Dangling this way and that, their links
   Were made so loose and wide,
      Methinks,
    For milder weather.

A bunch of violets without their roots,
   And sorrel intermixed,
Encircled by a wisp of straw
   Once coiled about their shoots,
      The law
    By which I'm fixed.

A nosegay which Time clutched from out
   Those fair Elysian fields,
With weeds and broken stems, in haste,
   Doth make the rabble rout
      That waste
    The day he yields.

And here I bloom for a short hour unseen,
   Drinking my juices up,   20
With no root in the land
   To keep my branches green,
      But stand
       In a bare cup.

Some tender buds were left upon my stem 25
   In mimicry of life,
But ah! the children will not know,
   Till time has withered them,
      The woe
   With which they're rife.   30

But now I see I was not plucked for naught,
   And after in life's vase
Of glass set while I might survive,
   But by a kind hand brought
      Alive   35
   To a strange place.

That stock thus thinned will soon redeem its
      hours,
And by another year,

Such as God knows, with freer air,
   More fruits and fairer flowers   40
      Will bear,
   While I droop here.

Smoke

Published in the *Dial*, April, 1843, and republished in *Walden*, in which it is introduced as follows: "When the villagers were lighting their fires beyond the horizon, I too gave notice to the various wild inhabitants of Walden vale, by a smoky streamer from my chimney, that I was awake."

Light-winged smoke, Icarian bird,
Melting thy pinions in thy upward flight,
Lark without song, and messenger of dawn,
Circling above the hamlets as thy nest;
Or else, departing dream, and shadowy form 5
Of midnight vision, gathering up thy skirts;
By night star-veiling, and by day
Darkening the light and blotting out the sun;
Go thou my incense upward from this hearth,
And ask the Gods to pardon this clear flame. 10

Nathaniel Hawthorne [1804–1864]

Of his Puritan ancestors Hawthorne said, "Strong traits of their nature have intertwined themselves with mine." In the beginning the Hathornes (as they spelled the name) were a prominent family of the seaport town of Salem. The first settler, William Hathorne — "grave, bearded, sable-cloaked and steeple-crowned," as Hawthorne pictured him — was a magistrate who took part in the persecution of the Quakers. His son John was a judge conspicuous in the Salem witch trials. In the eighteenth century the Hathornes were sea-captains — including Nathaniel's father, who died in Dutch Guiana when the boy was four years old.

The widow, at age twenty-eight, shut herself into her own room in a solitude that lasted most of the rest of her life, and the boy, like his two sisters, also fell into solitary ways. When the family went to live for some years at Lake Sebago in Maine, they took their old habits from the city to the wilderness. Nathaniel was normal enough, to be sure, while a student at Bowdoin College, Brunswick, Maine, where he established life-long friendships with Longfellow, Horatio Bridge, and Franklin Pierce, the future President of the United States. But, returned from college, he drifted into a seclusion that lasted twelve years. Near the end of this period he wrote to Longfellow: "I have secluded myself from society; and yet I never meant any such thing, nor dreamed what sort of life I was going to lead. I have made a captive of myself and put me into a dungeon; and now I cannot find the key to let myself out — and if the door were open, I should be almost afraid to come out." Actually, he did come out, in a raiding sort of fashion: by means of free passes on his uncle's stagecoach line he made a number of summer trips in New England, experiencing, he said, "as much of life as other people do in the whole year's round." But the bulk of his time he spent in dreaming and reflecting, in reading and writing. Under various assumed names, he published an undistinguished novel (*Fanshawe*) and sketches and stories partially collected, in 1837, in the first group of *Twice-Told Tales*. They did not describe what a later American writer called "the rich thicket of reality." As he said to Longfellow, with some over-statement, "I have seen so little of the world that I have nothing but thin air to concoct my stories of." But that little he commanded with an imaginative insight denied to most writers who have thrown themselves into the tumult of life.

Hawthorne's return to the "living world" (as he had called it in *Fanshawe*) came after he had met and fallen in love with Sophia Peabody. In 1838 he became engaged to her. In 1839–40 he served as weigher and gauger in the Boston Custom House, a position secured for him by his Democratic friends and lost through a change of political parties. Then, oddly enough, he became a member of the Brook Farm community. In 1842 he married and went to Concord, where, in the Old Manse, he spent four happy years. This was the period of the second collection of *Twice-Told Tales* and of *Mosses from an Old Manse*. Again he held a custom house position, this time in Salem, and again lost it through a change in administration. By this time he had the experience of fatherhood — a daughter Una, a son Julian. The family left Salem for good, removed to Lenox, to West Newton, to Concord.

Up to this time he had been a writer of sketches and short tales; now he took up the novel, or "romance": *The Scarlet Letter*, 1850; *The House of the Seven Gables*, 1851; *The Blithedale Romance*, 1853. At this juncture, too late for a full effect, he spent seven years in Europe. His friend Pierce, becoming President, nominated him consul at Liverpool. Resigning after three years, he toured the Continent, wrote *The Marble Faun* while living in Italy and in England, and returned to settle in The Wayside in Concord. Four years later, on a tour with Pierce, he died in New Hampshire.

Hawthorne felt strongly the impulse of the Romantic Movement: he shared its feeling for the strange and mysterious, its symbolical imagination and sportive fancy, and he turned to a regional past for much of his material. Yet he could not accept Transcendental optimism, nor did he celebrate nature, or the natural man, or the supremacy of beauty. Far deeper than his interest in the romanticism of his age was his feeling for the Christianity of New England in an earlier age. While he was skeptical of the Puritan theology and found the old intolerance repugnant, he agreed with his ancestors in focusing attention upon the problem of evil, the nature of sin, the contrast of pride and humility. Perversion, mystery, horror, and the like are never with him, as they were with Poe, merely materials for aesthetic use. On the other hand, he is not the moralist intent upon edification. Rather, he is a psychological type of literary artist, analyzing the inner life, the workings of the human heart and will, in a day when this could still be done as by Dante and Shakespeare (or Spenser and Bunyan, two of his favorites), without the help or the hindrance of the psychological science of the age of Freud. The best example is his own great book, his tragedy in the form of a novel, *The Scarlet Letter*.

Hawthorne's art is above all an art of symbols. Whether his story be a novel or a short tale, he works outward from some inner fact, some truth of the mind or soul, toward the concrete world, using a symbol, oftener a cluster of symbols, to link inner and outer and give body to his spiritual meaning. It may even seem, as W. C. Brownell said, that "everything means something else," or might mean various things. Are we to agree with Brownell and other able critics that this ambiguity is a defect in Hawthorne's art, a sign of weakness and confusion, or with R. H. Fogle and other recent able critics, that it is a source of strength, an enrichment of meaning and effect?

Further reading: *The Scarlet Letter, The House of the Seven Gables.* Henry James, Jr., *Hawthorne* (biography), 1879. Randall Stewart, *Nathaniel Hawthorne* (biography), 1948. Austin Warren (ed.), *Nathaniel Hawthorne* (American Writers Series), 1934. R. H. Fogle, *Hawthorne's Fiction*, 1952. H. H. Waggoner, *Hawthorne: A Critical Study*, 1955.

From his *Note-Books*

[Brook Farm]

The experimental community, Brook Farm, nine miles from Boston, lasted from 1841 to 1847. George Ripley was its leading spirit. Emerson — who never joined — described its ideal, "to combine cultivation of mind and heart with a reasonable amount of daily labor," but was inclined to sum up the reality as "a perpetual picnic." Hawthorne gave a fictional account of Brook Farm in *The Blithedale Romance*, as well as a notebook record of his actual experience there.

Brook Farm, Oak Hill, April 13th, 1841. — . . . Here I am in a polar Paradise! I know not how to interpret this aspect of nature, — whether it be of good or evil omen to our enterprise. But I reflect that the Plymouth pilgrims arrived in the midst of storm, and stepped ashore upon mountain snow-drifts; and, nevertheless, they prospered, and became a great people, — and doubtless it will be the same with us.

I have not yet taken my first lesson in agriculture, except that I went to see our cows foddered, yesterday afternoon. We have eight of our own; and the number is now increased by a transcendental heifer belonging to Miss Margaret Fuller. She is very fractious, I believe, and apt to kick over the milk-pail. . . . I intend to convert myself into a milkmaid this evening, but I pray Heaven that Mr. Ripley may be moved to assign me the kindliest cow in the herd, otherwise I shall perform my duty with fear and trembling.

I like my brethren in affliction very well; and, could you see us sitting round our table at meal-times, before the great kitchen fire, you would call it a cheerful sight. Mrs. B—— is a most comfortable woman to behold. She looks as if her ample person were stuffed full of tenderness, — indeed, as if she were all one great, kind heart. . . .

April 14th, 10 a. m. — . . . I did not milk the cows last night, because Mr. Ripley was afraid to trust them to my hands, or me to their horns, I know not which. But this morning I have done wonders. Before breakfast, I went out to the barn and began to chop hay for the cattle, and with such "righteous vehemence," as Mr. Ripley says, did I labor, that in the space of ten minutes I broke the machine. Then I brought wood and replenished the fires; and finally went down to breakfast, and ate up a huge mound of buckwheat cakes. After breakfast, Mr. Ripley put a four-pronged instrument into my hands, which he gave me to understand was called a pitchfork; and he and Mr. Farley being armed with similar weapons, we all three commenced a gallant attack upon a heap of manure. This office being concluded, and I having purified myself, I sit down to finish this letter. . . .

Miss Fuller's cow hooks the other cows, and has made herself ruler of the herd, and behaves in a very tyrannical manner. . . . I shall make an excellent husbandman, — I feel the original Adam reviving within me.

August 12th. — . . . I am very well, and not at all weary, for yesterday's rain gave us a holiday; and, moreover, the labors of the farm are not so pressing as they have been. And, joyful thought! in a little more than a fortnight I shall be free from my bondage, — . . . free to enjoy Nature, — free to think and feel! . . . Even my Custom House experience was not such a thraldom and weariness; my mind and heart were free. Oh, labor is the curse of the world, and nobody can meddle with it without becoming proportionally brutified! Is it a praiseworthy matter that I have spent five golden months in providing food for cows and horses? It is not so.

[Concord Friends]

After leaving the book at Mr. Emerson's I returned through the woods, and, entering Sleepy Hollow, I perceived a lady reclining near the path which bends along its verge. It was Margaret herself. She had been there the whole afternoon, meditating or reading; for she had a book in her hand, with some strange title, which I did not understand, and have forgotten. She said that nobody had broken her solitude, and was just giving utterance to a theory that no inhabitant of Concord ever visited Sleepy Hollow, when we saw a group of people entering the sacred precincts. Most of them followed a path which led them away from us; but an old man passed near us, and smiled to see Margaret reclining on the ground, and me sitting by her side. He made some remark about the beauty of the afternoon, and withdrew himself into the shadow of the wood. Then we talked about autumn, and about the pleasures of being lost in the woods, and about the crows, whose voices Margaret had heard, and about the experiences of early childhood, whose influence remains upon the character after the recollection of them has passed away; and about the sight of mountains from a distance, and the view from their summits; and about other matters of high and low philosophy. In the midst of our talk, we heard footsteps above us, on the high bank; and while the person was still hidden among the trees, he called to Margaret, of whom he had gotten a glimpse. Then he emerged from the green shade, and, behold! it was Mr. Emerson. He appeared to have had a pleasant time; for he said that there were Muses in the woods to-day, and whispers to be heard in the breezes. It being now nearly six o'clock, we separated, — Margaret and Mr. Emerson towards his home, and I towards mine. . . .

Last evening there was the most beautiful moonlight that ever hallowed this earthly world; and when I went to bathe in the river, which was as calm as death, it seemed like plunging down into the sky. But I had rather be on earth than even in the seventh heaven, just now.

Thursday, September 1st. — Mr. Thoreau dined with us yesterday. . . .

After dinner (at which we cut the first watermelon and muskmelon that our garden has grown), Mr. Thoreau and I walked up the bank of the river, and at a certain point he shouted for his boat. Forthwith a young man paddled it across, and Mr. Thoreau and I voyaged farther up the stream, which soon became more beautiful than any picture, with its dark and quiet sheet of water, half shaded, half sunny, between high and wooded banks. The late rains have swollen the stream so much that many trees are standing up to their knees, as it were, in the water, and boughs, which lately swung high in air, now dip and drink deep of the passing wave. As to the poor cardinals which glowed upon the bank a few days since, I could see only a few of their scarlet hats, peeping above the tide. Mr. Thoreau managed the boat so perfectly, either with two paddles or with one, that it seemed instinct with his own will, and to require no physical effort to guide it. He said that, when some Indians visited Concord a few years ago, he found that he had acquired, without a teacher, their precise method of propelling and steering a canoe. Nevertheless he was desirous of selling the boat of which he was so fit a pilot, and which was built by his own hands; so I agreed to take it, and accordingly became possessor of the Musketaquid. I wish I could acquire the aquatic skill of the original owner.

Saturday, April 8th. — After journalizing yesterday afternoon, I went out and sawed and split wood till tea-time, then studied German (translating "Lenore"), with an occasional glance at a beautiful sunset, which I could not enjoy sufficiently by myself to induce me to lay aside the book. After lamplight, finished "Lenore," and drowsed over Voltaire's "Candide," occasionally refreshing myself with a tune from Mr. Thoreau's musical-box, which he had left in my keeping.

[Hints for Stories]

A change from a gay young girl to an old woman; the melancholy events, the effects of which have clustered around her character, and gradually imbued it with their influence, till she becomes a lover of sick-chambers, taking pleasure in receiving dying breaths and in laying out the dead; also having her mind full of funeral reminiscences, and possessing more acquaintances beneath the burial turf than above it.

The scene of a story or sketch to be laid within the light of a street-lantern; the time, when the lamp is near going out; and the catastrophe to be simultaneous with the last flickering gleam.

In an old house, a mysterious knocking might be heard on the wall, where had formerly been a doorway, now bricked up.

A snake, taken into a man's stomach and nourished there from fifteen years to thirty-five, tormenting him most horribly. A type of envy or some other evil passion.

A Fancy Ball, in which the prominent American writers should appear, dressed in character.

An idle man's pleasures and occupations and thoughts during a day spent by the sea-shore; among them, that of sitting on the top of a cliff, and throwing stones at his own shadow, far below.

Meditations about the main gaspipe of a great city — if the supply were to be stopped, what would happen? How many different scenes it sheds light on? It might be made emblematical of something.

To poison a person or a party of persons with the sacramental wine.

The semblance of a human face to be formed on the side of a mountain, or in the fracture of a small stone, by a *lusus naturæ*. The face is an object of curiosity for years or centuries, and by and by a boy is born, whose features gradually assume the aspect of that portrait. At some critical juncture, the resemblance is found to be perfect. A prophecy may be connected.

My Kinsman, Major Molineux

(1832)

🎏 The introductory paragraph, in a sober historical style, should be read attentively for the light it eventually throws on the meaning of the story. What is the effect on the country boy of his search for his kinsman in a time of "high political excitement"?

After the kings of Great Britain had assumed the right of appointing the colonial governors, the measures of the latter seldom met with the ready and generous approbation which had been paid to those of their predecessors, under the original charters. The people looked with most jealous scrutiny to the exercise of power which did not emanate from themselves, and they usually rewarded their leaders with slender gratitude for the compliances by which, in softening their instructions from beyond the sea, they had incurred the reprehension of those who gave them. The annals of Massachusetts Bay will inform us, that of six governors in the space of about forty years from the surrender of the old charter, under James II, two were imprisoned by a popular insurrection; a third, as Hutchinson inclines to believe, was driven from the province by the whizzing of a musket-ball; a

fourth, in the opinion of the same historian, was hastened to his grave by continual bickerings with the House of Representatives, and the remaining two, as well as their successors, till the Revolution, were favored with few and brief intervals of peaceful sway. The inferior members of the court party, in times of high political excitement, led scarcely a more desirable life. These remarks may serve as a preface to the following adventures, which chanced upon a summer night, not far from a hundred years ago. The reader, in order to avoid a long and dry detail of colonial affairs, is requested to dispense with an account of the train of circumstances that had caused much temporary inflammation of the popular mind.

It was near nine o'clock of a moonlight evening, when a boat crossed the ferry with a single passenger, who had obtained his conveyance at that unusual hour by the promise of an extra fare. While he stood on the landing-place, searching in either pocket for the means of fulfilling his agreement, the ferryman lifted a lantern, by the aid of which, and the newly risen moon, he took a very accurate survey of the stranger's figure. He was a youth of barely eighteen years, evidently country-bred, and now, as it should seem, upon his first visit to town. He was clad in a coarse gray coat, well worn, but in excellent repair; his under garments were durably constructed of leather, and fitted tight to a pair of serviceable and well-shaped limbs; his stockings of blue yarn were the incontrovertible work of a mother or a sister; and on his head was a three-cornered hat, which in its better days had perhaps sheltered the graver brow of the lad's father. Under his left arm was a heavy cudgel formed of an oak sapling, and retaining a part of the hardened root; and his equipment was completed by a wallet, not so abundantly stocked as to incommode the vigorous shoulders on which it hung. Brown, curly hair, well-shaped features, and bright, cheerful eyes were nature's gifts, and worth all that art could have done for his adornment.

The youth, one of whose names was Robin, finally drew from his pocket the half of a little province bill of five shillings, which, in the depreciation in that sort of currency, did but satisfy the ferryman's demand, with the surplus of a sexangular piece of parchment, valued at three pence. He then walked forward into the town, with as light a step as if his day's journey had not already exceeded thirty miles, and with as eager an eye as if he were entering London city, instead of the little metropolis of a New England colony. Before Robin had proceeded far, however, it occurred to him that he knew not whither to direct his steps; so he paused, and looked up and down the narrow street, scrutinizing the small and mean wooden buildings that were scattered on either side.

"This low hovel cannot be my kinsman's dwelling," thought he, "nor yonder old house, where the moonlight enters at the broken casement; and truly I see none hereabouts that might be worthy of him. It would have been wise to inquire my way of the ferryman, and doubtless he would have gone with me, and earned a shilling from the Major for his pains. But the next man I meet will do as well."

He resumed his walk, and was glad to perceive that the street now became wider, and the houses more respectable in their appearance. He soon discerned a figure moving on moderately in advance, and hastened his steps to overtake it. As Robin drew nigh, he saw that the passenger was a man in years, with a full periwig of gray hair, a wide-skirted coat of dark cloth, and silk stockings rolled above his knees. He carried a long and polished cane, which he struck down perpendicularly before him at every step; and at regular intervals he uttered two successive hems, of a peculiarly solemn and sepulchral intonation. Having made these observations, Robin laid hold of the skirt of the old man's coat, just when the light from the open door and windows of a barber's shop fell upon both their figures.

"Good evening to you, honored sir," said he, making a low bow, and still retaining his hold of the skirt. "I pray you tell me whereabouts is the dwelling of my kinsman, Major Molineux."

The youth's question was uttered very loudly; and one of the barbers, whose razor was descending on a well-soaped chin, and another who was dressing a Ramillies wig, left their occupations, and came to the door. The citizen, in the mean time, turned a long-favored countenance upon Robin, and answered him in a tone of excessive anger and annoyance. His two sepulchral hems, however, broke into the very center of his rebuke, with most singular effect, like a thought of the cold grave obtruding among wrathful passions.

"Let go my garment, fellow! I tell you, I know not the man you speak of. What! I have authority, I have — hem, hem — authority; and if this be the respect you show for your betters, your feet shall be brought acquainted with the stocks by daylight, tomorrow morning!"

Robin released the old man's skirt, and hastened away, pursued by an ill-mannered roar of laughter from the barber's shop. He was at first considerably surprised by the result of his question, but, being a shrewd youth, soon thought himself able to account for the mystery.

"This is some country representative," was his conclusion, "who has never seen the inside of my kinsman's door, and lacks the breeding to answer a stranger civilly. The man is old, or verily — I might be tempted to turn back and smite him on the nose. Ah, Robin, Robin! even the barber's boys laugh at you for choosing such a guide! You will be wiser in time, friend Robin."

He now became entangled in a succession of crooked and narrow streets, which crossed each other, and meandered at no great distance from the water-side. The smell of tar was obvious to his nostrils, the masts of vessels pierced the moonlight above the tops of the buildings, and the numerous signs, which Robin paused to read, informed him that he was near the center of business. But the streets were empty, the shops were closed, and lights were visible only in the second stories of a few dwelling-houses. At length, on the corner of a narrow lane, through which he was passing, he beheld the broad countenance of a British hero swinging before the door of an inn, whence proceeded the voices of many guests. The casement of one of the lower windows was thrown back, and a very thin curtain permitted Robin to distinguish a party at supper, round a well-furnished table. The fragrance of the good cheer steamed forth into the outer air, and the youth could not fail to recollect that the last remnant of his travelling stock of provision had yielded to his morning appetite, and that noon had found and left him dinnerless.

"Oh, that a parchment three-penny might give me a right to sit down at yonder table!" said Robin, with a sigh. "But the Major will make me welcome to the best of his victuals; so I will even step boldly in, and inquire my way to his dwelling."

He entered the tavern, and was guided by the murmur of voices and the fumes of tobacco to the public-room. It was a long and low apartment, with oaken walls, grown dark in the continual smoke, and a floor which was thickly sanded, but of no immaculate purity. A number of persons — the larger part of whom appeared to be mariners, or in some way connected with the sea — occupied the wooden benches, or 5 leather-bottomed chairs, conversing on various matters, and occasionally lending their attention to some topic of general interest. Three or four little groups were draining as many bowls of punch, which the West India trade had long 10 since made a familiar drink in the colony. Others, who had the appearance of men who lived by regular and laborious handicraft, preferred the insulated bliss of an unshared potation, and became more taciturn under its 15 influence. Nearly all, in short, evinced a predilection for the Good Creature in some of its various shapes, for this is a vice to which, as Fast Day sermons of a hundred years ago will testify, we have a long hereditary claim. The 20 only guests to whom Robin's sympathies inclined him were two or three sheepish countrymen, who were using the inn somewhat after the fashion of a Turkish caravansary; they had gotten themselves into the darkest corner of the 25 room, and heedless of the Nicotian atmosphere, were supping on the bread of their own ovens, and the bacon cured in their own chimney-smoke. But though Robin felt a sort of brotherhood with these strangers, his eyes were attracted 30 from them to a person who stood near the door, holding whispered conversation with a group of ill-dressed associates. His features were separately striking almost to grotesqueness, and the whole face left a deep impression on the mem- 35 ory. The forehead bulged out into a double prominence, with a vale between; the nose came boldly forth in an irregular curve, and its bridge was of more than a finger's breadth; the eyebrows were deep and shaggy, and the eyes 40 glowed beneath them like fire in a cave.

While Robin deliberated of whom to inquire respecting his kinsman's dwelling, he was accosted by the innkeeper, a little man in a stained white apron, who had come to pay his pro- 45 fessional welcome to the stranger. Being in the second generation from a French Protestant, he seemed to have inherited the courtesy of his parent nation; but no variety of circumstances was ever known to change his voice from the 50 one shrill note in which he now addressed Robin.

"From the country, I presume, sir?" said he, with a profound bow. "Beg leave to congratu-

late you on your arrival, and trust you intend a long stay with us. Fine town here, sir, beautiful buildings, and much that may interest a stranger. May I hope for the honor of your commands in respect to supper?"

"The man sees a family likeness! the rogue has guessed that I am related to the Major!" thought Robin, who had hitherto experienced little superfluous civility.

All eyes were now turned on the country lad, standing at the door, in his worn three-cornered hat, gray coat, leather breeches, and blue yarn stockings, leaning on an oaken cudgel, and bearing a wallet on his back.

Robin replied to the courteous innkeeper, with such an assumption of confidence as befitted the Major's relative. "My honest friend," he said, "I shall make it a point to patronize your house on some occasion, when" — here he could not help lowering his voice — "when I may have more than a parchment three-pence in my pocket. My present business," continued he, speaking with lofty confidence, "is merely to inquire my way to the dwelling of my kinsman, Major Molineux."

There was a sudden and general movement in the room, which Robin interpreted as expressing the eagerness of each individual to become his guide. But the innkeeper turned his eyes to a written paper on the wall, which he read, or seemed to read, with occasional recurrences to the young man's figure.

"What have we here?" said he, breaking his speech into little dry fragments. "Left the house of the subscriber, bounden servant, Hezekiah Mudge, — had on, when he went away, gray coat, leather breeches, master's third-best hat. One pound currency reward to whosoever shall lodge him in any jail of the providence.' Better trudge, boy; better trudge!"

Robin had begun to draw his hand towards the lighter end of the oak cudgel, but a strange hostility in every countenance induced him to relinquish his purpose of breaking the courteous innkeeper's head. As he turned to leave the room, he encountered a sneering glance from the bold-featured personage whom he had before noticed; and no sooner was he beyond the door, than he heard a general laugh, in which the innkeeper's voice might be distinguished, like the dropping of small stones into a kettle.

"Now, is it not strange," thought Robin, with his usual shrewdness, — "is it not strange that the confession of an empty pocket should outweigh the name of my kinsman, Major Molineux? Oh, if I had one of those grinning rascals in the woods, where I and my oak sapling grew up together, I would teach him that my arm is heavy though my purse be light!"

On turning the corner of the narrow lane, Robin found himself in a spacious street, with an unbroken line of lofty houses on each side, and a steepled building at the upper end, whence the ringing of a bell announced the hour of nine. The light of the moon, and the lamps from the numerous shop-windows, discovered people promenading on the pavement, and amongst them Robin had hoped to recognize his hitherto inscrutable relative. The result of his former inquiries made him unwilling to hazard another, in a scene of such publicity, and he determined to walk slowly and silently up the street, thrusting his face close to that of every elderly gentleman, in search of the Major's lineaments. In his progress, Robin encountered many gay and gallant figures. Embroidered garments of showy colors, enormous periwigs, gold-laced hats, and silver-hilted swords glided past him and dazzled his optics. Travelled youths, imitators of the European fine gentlemen of the period, trod jauntily along, half dancing to the fashionable tunes which they hummed, and making poor Robin ashamed of his quiet and natural gait. At length, after many pauses to examine the gorgeous display of goods in the shop-windows, and after suffering some rebukes for the impertinence of his scrutiny into people's faces, the Major's kinsman found himself near the steepled building, still unsuccessful in his search. As yet, however, he had seen only one side of the thronged street; so Robin crossed, and continued the same sort of inquisition down the opposite pavement, with stronger hopes than the philosopher seeking an honest man, but with no better fortune. He had arrived about midway towards the lower end, from which his course began, when he overheard the approach of some one who struck down a cane on the flag-stones at every step, uttering at regular intervals, two sepulchral hems.

"Mercy on us!" quoth Robin, recognizing the sound.

Turning a corner, which chanced to be close at his right hand, he hastened to pursue his researches in some other part of the town. His patience now was wearing low, and he seemed to feel more fatigue from his rambles since he crossed the ferry, than from his journey of several days on the other side. Hunger also pleaded loudly within him, and Robin began to balance the propriety of demanding, violently, and with lifted cudgel, the necessary guidance from the first solitary passenger whom he should meet. While a resolution to this effect was gaining strength, he entered a street of mean appearance, on either side of which a row of ill-built houses was straggling towards the harbor. The moonlight fell upon no passenger along the whole extent, but in the third domicile which Robin passed there was a half-open door, and his keen glance detected a woman's garment within.

"My luck may be better here," said he to himself.

Accordingly, he approached the door, and beheld it shut closer as he did so; yet an open space remained, sufficing for the fair occupant to observe the stranger, without a corresponding display on her part. All that Robin could discern was a strip of scarlet petticoat, and the occasional sparkle of an eye, as if the moonbeams were trembling on some bright thing.

"Pretty mistress," for I may call her so with a good conscience, thought the shrewd youth, since I know nothing to the contrary, — "my sweet pretty mistress, will you be kind enough to tell me whereabouts I must seek the dwelling of my kinsman, Major Molineux?"

Robin's voice was plaintive and winning, and the female, seeing nothing to be shunned in the handsome country youth, thrust open the door, and came forth into the moonlight. She was a dainty little figure, with a white neck, round arms, and a slender waist, at the extremity of which her scarlet petticoat jutted out over a hoop, as if she were standing in a balloon. Moreover, her face was oval and pretty, her hair dark beneath the little cap, and her bright eyes possessed a sly freedom, which triumphed over those of Robin.

"Major Molineux dwells here," said this fair woman.

Now, her voice was the sweetest Robin had heard that night, yet he could not help doubting whether that sweet voice spoke Gospel truth. He looked up and down the mean street, and then surveyed the house before which they stood. It was a small, dark edifice of two stories, the second of which projected over the lower floor, and the front apartment had the aspect of a shop for petty commodities.

"Now, truly, I am in luck," replied Robin,

cunningly, "and so indeed is my kinsman, the Major, in having so pretty a housekeeper. But I prithee trouble him to step to the door; I will deliver him a message from his friends in the country, and then go back to my lodgings at the inn."

"Nay, the Major has been abed this hour or more," said the lady of the scarlet petticoat; "and it would be to little purpose to disturb him to-night, seeing his evening draught was of the strongest. But he is a kind-hearted man, and it would be as much as my life's worth to let a kinsman of his turn away from the door. You are the good old gentleman's very picture, and I could swear that was his rainy-weather hat. Also he has garments very much resembling those leather small-clothes. But come in, I pray, for I bid you hearty welcome in his name."

So saying, the fair and hospitable dame took our hero by the hand; and the touch was light, and the force was gentleness, and though Robin read in her eyes what he did not hear in her words, yet the slender-waisted woman in the scarlet petticoat proved stronger than the athletic country youth. She had drawn his half-willing footsteps nearly to the threshold, when the opening of a door in the neighborhood startled the Major's housekeeper, and, leaving the Major's kinsman, she vanished speedily into her own domicile. A heavy yawn preceded the appearance of a man, who, like the Moonshine of Pyramus and Thisbe, carried a lantern, needlessly aiding his sister luminary in the heavens. As he walked sleepily up the street, he turned his broad, dull face on Robin, and displayed a long staff, spiked at the end.

"Home, vagabond, home!" said the watchman, in accents that seemed to fall asleep as soon as they were uttered. "Home, or we'll set you in the stocks by peep of day!"

"This is the second hint of the kind," thought Robin. "I wish they would end my difficulties, by setting me there to-night."

Nevertheless, the youth felt an instinctive antipathy towards the guardian of midnight order, which at first prevented him from asking his usual question. But just when the man was about to vanish behind the corner, Robin resolved not to lose the opportunity, and shouted lustily after him, —

"I say, friend! will you guide me to the house of my kinsman, Major Molineux?"

The watchman made no reply, but turned the corner and was gone; yet Robin seemed to hear the sound of drowsy laughter stealing along the solitary street. At that moment, also, a pleasant titter saluted him from the open window above his head; he looked up, and caught the sparkle of a saucy eye; a round arm beckoned to him, and next he heard light footsteps descending the staircase within. But Robin, being of the household of a New England clergyman, was a good youth, as well as a shrewd one; so he resisted temptation, and fled away.

He now roamed desperately, and at random, through the town, almost ready to believe that a spell was on him, like that by which a wizard of his country had once kept three pursuers wandering, a whole winter night, within twenty paces of the cottage which they sought. The streets lay before him, strange and desolate, and the lights were extinguished in almost every house. Twice, however, little parties of men, among whom Robin distinguished individuals in outlandish attire, came hurrying along; but, though on both occasions, they paused to address him, such intercourse did not at all enlighten his perplexity. They did but utter a few words in some language of which Robin knew nothing, and perceiving his inability to answer, bestowed a curse upon him in plain English and hastened away. Finally, the lad determined to knock at the door of every mansion that might appear worthy to be occupied by his kinsman, trusting that perseverance would overcome the fatality that had hitherto thwarted him. Firm in this resolve, he was passing beneath the walls of a church, which formed the corner of two streets, when, as he turned into the shade of its steeple, he encountered a bulky stranger, muffled in a cloak. The man was proceeding with the speed of earnest business, but Robin planted himself full before him, holding the oak cudgel with both hands across his body as a bar to further passage.

"Halt, honest man, and answer me a question," said he, very resolutely. "Tell me, this instant, whereabouts is the dwelling of my kinsman, Major Molineux!"

"Keep your tongue between your teeth, fool, and let me pass!" said a deep, gruff voice, which Robin partly remembered. "Let me pass, or I'll strike you to the earth!"

"No, no, neighbor!" cried Robin, flourishing his cudgel, and then thrusting its larger end close to the man's muffled face. "No, no, I'm not the fool you take me for, nor do you pass till I have an answer to my question. Whereabouts is the dwelling of my kinsman, Major Molineux?"

The stranger, instead of attempting to force his passage, stepped back into the moonlight, unmuffled his face, and stared full into that of Robin.

"Watch here an hour, and Major Molineux will pass by," said he.

Robin gazed with dismay and astonishment on the unprecedented physiognomy of the speaker. The forehead with its double promi- nence, the broad hooked nose, the shaggy eye- brows, and fiery eyes were those which he had noticed at the inn, but the man's complexion had undergone a singular, or, more properly, a twofold change. One side of the face blazed an intense red, while the other was black as mid- night, the division line being in the broad bridge of the nose; and a mouth which seemed to extend from ear to ear was black or red, in con- trast to the color of the cheek. The effect was as if two individual devils, a fiend of fire and a fiend of darkness, had united themselves to form this infernal visage. The stranger grinned in Robin's face, muffled his party-colored features, and was out of sight in a moment.

"Strange things we travellers see!" ejaculated Robin.

He seated himself, however, upon the steps of the church-door, resolving to wait the ap- pointed time for his kinsman. A few moments were consumed in philosophical speculations upon the species of man who had just left him; but having settled this point shrewdly, rationally, and satisfactorily, he was compelled to look else- where for his amusement. And first he threw his eyes along the street. It was of more respectable appearance than most of those into which he had wandered; and the moon, creating, like the imaginative power, a beautiful strangeness in familiar objects, gave something of romance to a scene that might not have possessed it in the light of day. The irregular and often quaint architecture of the houses, some of whose roofs were broken into numerous little peaks, while others ascended, steep and narrow, into a single point, and others again were square; the pure snow-white of some of their complexions, the aged darkness of others, and the thousand spark- lings, reflected from bright substances in the walls of many; these matters engaged Robin's attention for a while, and then began to grow wearisome. Next he endeavored to define the forms of distant objects, starting away, with almost ghostly indistinctness, just as his eye

appeared to grasp them; and finally he took a minute survey of an edifice which stood on the opposite side of the street, directly in front of the church-door, where he was stationed. It was a large, square mansion, distinguished from its neighbors by a balcony, which rested on tall pillars, and by an elaborate Gothic window, communicating therewith.

"Perhaps this is the very house I have been seeking," thought Robin.

Then he strove to speed away the time, by listening to a murmur which swept continually along the street, yet was scarcely audible, except to an unaccustomed ear like his; it was a low, dull, dreamy sound, compounded of many noises, each of which was at too great a distance to be separately heard. Robin marvelled at this snore of a sleeping town, and marvelled more whenever its continuity was broken by now and then a distant shout, apparently loud where it originated. But altogether it was a sleep-inspir- ing sound, and, to shake off its drowsy influence, Robin arose, and climbed a window-frame, that he might view the interior of the church. There the moonbeams came trembling in, and fell down upon the deserted pews, and extended along the quiet aisles. A fainter yet more awful radiance was hovering around the pulpit, and one solitary ray had dared to rest upon the open page of the great Bible. Had nature, in that deep hour, become a worshipper in the house which man had builded? Or was that heavenly light the visible sanctity of the place, — visible because no earthly and impure feet were within the walls? The scene made Robin's heart shiver with a sensation of loneliness stronger than he had ever felt in the remotest depths of his native woods; so he turned away and sat down again before the door. There were graves around the church, and now an uneasy thought obtruded into Robin's breast. What if the object of his search, which had been so often and so strangely thwarted, were all the time mouldering in his shroud? What if his kinsman should glide through yonder gate, and nod and smile to him in dimly passing by?

"Oh, that any breathing thing were here with me!" said Robin.

Recalling his thoughts from this uncomfort- able track, he sent them over forest, hill, and stream, and attempted to imagine how that eve- ning of ambiguity and weariness had been spent by his father's household. He pictured them assembled at the door, beneath the tree, the great old tree, which had been spared for its huge twisted trunk and venerable shade, when a thousand leafy brethren fell. There, at the going down of the summer sun, it was his father's custom to perform domestic worship, that the neighbors might come and join with him like brothers of the family, and that the wayfaring man might pause to drink at that fountain, and keep his heart pure by freshening the memory of home. Robin distinguished the seat of every individual of the little audience; he saw the good man in the midst, holding the Scriptures in the golden light that fell from the western clouds; he beheld him close the book and all rise up to pray. He heard the old thanksgivings for daily mercies, the old supplications for their continuance, to which he had so often listened in weariness, but which were now among his dear remembrances. He perceived the slight inequality of his father's voice when he came to speak of the absent one; he noted how his mother turned her face to the broad and knotted trunk; how his elder brother scorned, because the beard was rough upon his upper lip, to permit his features to be moved; how the younger sister drew down a low hanging branch before her eyes; and how the little one of all, whose sports had hitherto broken the decorum of the scene, understood the prayer for her playmate, and burst into clamorous grief. Then he saw them go in at the door; and when Robin would have entered also, the latch tinkled into its place, and he was excluded from his home.

"Am I here, or there?" cried Robin, starting; for all at once, when his thoughts had become visible and audible in a dream, the long, wide, solitary street shone out before him.

He aroused himself, and endeavored to fix his attention steadily upon the large edifice which he had surveyed before. But still his mind kept vibrating between fancy and reality; by turns, the pillars of the balcony lengthened into the tall, bare stems of pines, dwindled down to human figures, settled again into their true shape and size, and then commenced a new succession of changes. For a single moment, when he deemed himself awake, he could have sworn that a visage — one which he seemed to remember, yet could not absolutely name as his kinsman's — was looking towards him from the Gothic window. A deeper sleep wrestled with and nearly overcame him, but fled at the sound of footsteps along the opposite pavement. Robin rubbed his eyes, discerned a man passing at the foot of the balcony, and addressed him in a loud, peevish, and lamentable cry.

"Hallo, friend! must I wait here all night for my kinsman, Major Molineux?"

The sleeping echoes awoke, and answered the voice; and the passenger, barely able to discern a figure sitting in the oblique shade of the steeple, traversed the street to obtain a nearer view. He was himself a gentleman in his prime, of open, intelligent, cheerful, and altogether prepossessing countenance. Perceiving a country youth, apparently homeless and without friends, he accosted him in a tone of real kindness, which had become strange to Robin's ears.

"Well, my good lad, why are you sitting here?" inquired he. "Can I be of service to you in any way?"

"I am afraid not, sir," replied Robin, despondingly; "yet I shall take it kindly, if you'll answer me a single question. I've been searching, half the night, for one Major Molineux; now, sir, is there really such a person in these parts, or am I dreaming?"

"Major Molineux! The name is not altogether strange to me," said the gentleman, smiling. "Have you any objection to telling me the nature of your business with him?"

Then Robin briefly related that his father was a clergyman, settled on a small salary, at a long distance back in the country, and that he and Major Molineux were brothers' children. The Major, having inherited riches, and acquired civil and military rank, had visited his cousin, in great pomp, a year or two before; had manifested much interest in Robin and an elder brother, and, being childless himself, had thrown out hints respecting the future establishment of one of them in life. The elder brother was destined to succeed to the farm which his father cultivated in the interval of sacred duties; it was therefore determined that Robin should profit by his kinsman's generous intentions, especially as he seemed to be rather the favorite, and was thought to possess other necessary endowments.

"For I have the name of being a shrewd youth," observed Robin, in this part of his story.

"I doubt not you deserve it," replied his new friend, good-naturedly; "but pray proceed."

"Well, sir, being nearly eighteen years old, and well grown, as you see," continued Robin, drawing himself up to his full height, "I thought it high time to begin in the world. So my mother and sister put me in handsome trim, and my father gave me half the remnant of his last year's salary, and five days ago I started for this place, to pay the Major a visit. But, would you believe it, sir! I crossed the ferry a little after dark, and have yet found nobody that would show me the way to his dwelling; only, an hour or two since, I was told to wait here, and Major Molineux would pass by."

"Can you describe the man who told you this?" inquired the gentleman.

"Oh, he was a very ill-favored fellow, sir," replied Robin, "with two great bumps on his forehead, a hook nose, fiery eyes; and, what struck me as the strangest, his face was of two different colors. Do you happen to know such a man, sir?"

"Not intimately," answered the stranger, "but I chanced to meet him a little time previous to your stopping me. I believe you may trust his word, and that the Major will very shortly pass through this street. In the mean time, as I have a singular curiosity to witness your meeting, I will sit down here upon the steps and bear you company."

He seated himself accordingly, and soon engaged his companion in animated discourse. It was but of brief continuance, however, for a noise of shouting, which had long been remotely audible, drew so much nearer that Robin inquired its cause.

"What may be the meaning of this uproar?" asked he. "Truly, if your town be always as noisy, I shall find little sleep while I am an inhabitant."

"Why, indeed, friend Robin, there do appear to be three or four riotous fellows abroad to-night," replied the gentleman. "You must not expect all the stillness of your native woods here in our streets. But the watch will shortly be at the heels of these lads and" —

"Ay, and set them in the stocks by peep of day," interrupted Robin, recollecting his own encounter with the drowsy lantern-bearer. "But, dear sir, if I may trust my ears, an army of watchmen would never make head against such a multitude of rioters. There were at least a thousand voices went up to make that one shout."

"May not a man have several voices, Robin, as well as two complexions?" said his friend.

"Perhaps a man may; but Heaven forbid that a woman should!" responded the shrewd youth, thinking of the seductive tones of the Major's housekeeper.

The sounds of a trumpet in some neighboring street now became so evident and continual, that Robin's curiosity was strongly excited. In addition to the shouts, he heard frequent bursts from many instruments of discord, and a wild and confused laughter filled up the intervals. Robin rose from the steps, and looked wistfully towards a point whither people seemed to be hastening.

"Surely some prodigious merry-making is going on," exclaimed he. "I have laughed very little since I left home, sir, and should be sorry to lose an opportunity. Shall we step round the corner by that darkish house, and take our share of the fun?"

"Sit down again, sit down, good Robin," replied the gentleman, laying his hand on the skirt of the gray coat. "You forget that we must wait here for your kinsman; and there is reason to believe that he will pass by, in the course of a very few moments."

The near approach of the uproar had now disturbed the neighborhood; windows flew open on all sides; and many heads, in the attire of the pillow, and confused by sleep suddenly broken, were protruded to the gaze of whoever had leisure to observe them. Eager voices hailed each other from house to house, all demanding the explanation, which not a soul could give. Half-dressed men hurried towards the unknown commotion, stumbling as they went over the stone steps that thrust themselves into the narrow footwalk. The shouts, the laughter, and the tuneless bray, the antipodes of music, came onwards with increasing din, till scattered individuals, and then denser bodies, began to appear round a corner at the distance of a hundred yards.

"Will you recognize your kinsman, if he passes in this crowd?" inquired the gentleman.

"Indeed, I can't warrant it, sir; but I'll take my stand here, and keep a bright lookout," answered Robin, descending to the outer edge of the pavement.

A mighty stream of people now emptied into the street, and came rolling slowly towards the church. A single horseman wheeled the corner in the midst of them, and close behind him came a band of fearful wind-instruments, sending forth a fresher discord now that no intervening buildings kept it from the ear. Then a redder light disturbed the moonbeams, and a dense multitude of torches shone along the street, concealing, by their glare, whatever object they illuminated. The single horseman, clad in a military dress, and bearing a drawn sword, rode onward as the leader, and, by his fierce and variegated countenance, appeared like war personified; the red of one cheek was an emblem of fire and sword; the blackness of the other betokened the mourning that attends them. In his train were wild figures in the Indian dress, and many fantastic shapes without a model, giving the whole march a visionary air, as if a dream had broken forth from some feverish brain, and were sweeping visibly through the midnight streets. A mass of people, inactive, except as applauding spectators, hemmed the procession in; and several women ran along the sidewalk, piercing the confusion of heavier sounds with their shrill voices of mirth or terror.

"The double-faced fellow has his eye upon me," muttered Robin, with an indefinite but an uncomfortable idea that he was himself to bear a part in the pageantry.

The leader turned himself in the saddle, and fixed his glance full upon the country youth, as the steed went slowly by. When Robin had freed his eyes from those fiery ones, the musicians were passing before him, and the torches were close at hand; but the unsteady brightness of the latter formed a veil which he could not penetrate. The rattling of wheels over the stones sometimes found its way to his ear, and confused traces of a human form appeared at intervals, and then melted into the vivid light. A moment more, and the leader thundered a command to halt: the trumpets vomited a horrid breath, and then held their peace; the shouts and laughter of the people died away, and there remained only a universal hum, allied to silence. Right before Robin's eyes was an uncovered cart. There the torches blazed the brightest, there the moon shone out like day, and there, in tar-and-feathery dignity, sat his kinsman, Major Molineux!

He was an elderly man, of large and majestic person, and strong, square features, betokening a steady soul; but steady as it was, his enemies had found means to shake it. His face was pale as death, and far more ghastly; the broad forehead was contracted in his agony, so that his eyebrows formed one grizzled line; his eyes were red and wild, and the foam hung white upon his quivering lip. His whole frame was agitated by a quick and continual tremor, which his pride strove to quell, even in those circumstances of overwhelming humiliation. But perhaps the bitterest pang of all was when his eyes

met those of Robin; for he evidently knew him on the instant, as the youth stood witnessing the foul disgrace of a head grown gray in honor. They stared at each other in silence, and Robin's knees shook, and his hair bristled, with a mixture of pity and terror. Soon, however, a bewildering excitement began to seize upon his mind; the preceding adventures of the night, the unexpected appearance of the crowd, the torches, the confused din and the hush that followed, the spectre of his kinsman reviled by that great multitude, — all this, and, more than all, a perception of tremendous ridicule in the whole scene, affected him with a sort of mental inebriety. At that moment a voice of sluggish merriment saluted Robin's ears; he turned instinctively, and just behind the corner of the church stood the lantern-bearer, rubbing his eyes, and drowsily enjoying the lad's amazement. Then he heard a peal of laughter like the ringing of silvery bells; a woman twitched his arm, a saucy eye met his, and he saw the lady of the scarlet petticoat. A sharp, dry cachinnation appealed to his memory, and standing on tiptoe in the crowd, with his white apron over his head, he beheld the courteous little innkeeper. And lastly, there sailed over the heads of the multitude a great, broad laugh, broken in the midst by two sepulchral hems; thus, "Haw, haw, haw, — hem, hem, — haw, haw, haw, haw!"

The sound proceeded from the balcony of the opposite edifice, and thither Robin turned his eyes. In front of the Gothic window stood the old citizen, wrapped in a wide gown, his gray periwig exchanged for a nightcap, which was thrust back from his forehead, and his silk stockings hanging about his legs. He supported himself on his polished cane in a fit of convulsive merriment, which manifested itself on his solemn old features like a funny inscription on a tombstone. Then Robin seemed to hear the voices of the barbers, of the guests of the inn, and of all who had made sport of him that night. The contagion was spreading among the multitude, when all at once, it seized upon Robin, and he sent forth a shout of laughter that echoed through the street — every man shook his sides, every man emptied his lungs, but Robin's shout was the loudest there. The cloud-spirits peeped from their silvery islands, as the congregated mirth went roaring up the sky! The Man in the Moon heard the far bellow. "Oho," quoth he, "the old earth is frolicsome tonight!"

When there was a momentary calm in that

tempestuous sea of sound, the leader gave the sign, the procession resumed its march. On they went, like fiends that throng in mockery around some dead potentate, mighty no more, but majestic still in his agony. On they went, in counterfeited pomp, in senseless uproar, in frenzied merriment, trampling all on an old man's heart. On swept the tumult, and left a silent street behind.

"Well, Robin, are you dreaming?" inquired the gentleman, laying his hand on the youth's shoulder.

Robin started, and withdrew his arm from the stone post to which he had instinctively clung, as the living stream rolled by him. His cheek was somewhat pale, and his eye not quite as lively as in the earlier part of the evening.

"Will you be kind enough to show me the way to the ferry?" said he, after a moment's pause.

"You have, then, adopted a new subject of inquiry?" observed his companion, with a smile.

"Why, yes, sir," replied Robin, rather dryly. "Thanks to you, and to my other friends, I have at last met my kinsman, and he will scarce desire to see my face again. I begin to grow weary of a town life, sir. Will you show me the way to the ferry?"

"No, my good friend Robin,—not tonight, at least," said the gentleman. "Some few days hence, if you wish it, I will speed you on your journey. Or, if you prefer to remain with us, perhaps, as you are a shrewd youth, you may rise in the world without the help of your kinsman, Major Molineux."

Roger Malvin's Burial
(1832)

A favorite with college students, this story has often been undervalued by critics. Henry James, however, in his life of Hawthorne, named it among three "little masterpieces" — the other two being "Young Goodman Brown" and "Rappaccini's Daughter."

In reading Hawthorne's stories, we are not to expect them to be like those typical of our own time. As Walter Havighurst has said: "The modern story deals with mind and feelings, but not with a soul. It is a rare thing to find the personal conscience at work in our short fiction. We have people working out their compulsions, but seldom are we made conscious of the hard choice between good and evil. Hawthorne was a moral writer, always pondering, always making distinctions. He had a moral humility and a moral

anxiousness that led him to explore, again and again, the dark fact of human guilt and the isolation that it imposes."

In "Roger Malvin's Burial" a historical incident involves problems invested with a universal human interest. How does evil come about? Why does not Reuben Bourne send help? Why does he conceal what has happened? What is the effect of concealment on him? Is it chance that he eventually returns to the very spot where he left Roger Malvin? Is his shooting of his own boy purely an accident? Was his abandonment of Malvin an act calling for expiation, or was it morally justified? Finally, why does not Hawthorne give the reader clear answers to such questions?

One of the few incidents of Indian warfare naturally susceptible of the moonlight of romance was that expedition undertaken for the defence of the frontiers in the year 1725, which resulted in the well-remembered "Lovell's Fight." Imagination, by casting certain circumstances judicially into the shade, may see much to admire in the heroism of a little band who gave battle to twice their number in the heart of the enemy's country. The open bravery displayed by both parties was in accordance with civilized ideas of valor; and chivalry itself might not blush to record the deeds of one or two individuals. The battle, though so fatal to those who fought, was not unfortunate in its consequences to the country; for it broke the strength of a tribe and conduced to the peace which subsisted during several ensuing years. History and tradition are unusually minute in their memorials of this affair; and the captain of a scouting party of frontier men has acquired as actual a military renown as many a victorious leader of thousands. Some of the incidents contained in the following pages will be recognized, nothwithstanding the substitution of fictitious names, but such as have heard, from old men's lips, the fate of the few combatants who were in a condition to retreat after "Lovell's Fight."

The early sunbeams hovered cheerfully upon the tree-tops, beneath which two weary and wounded men had stretched their limbs the night before. Their bed of withered oak leaves was strewn upon the small level space, at the foot of a rock, situated near the summit of one of the gentle swells by which the face of the country is there diversified. The mass of granite, rearing its smooth, flat surface fifteen or twenty feet above their heads, was not unlike a gigantic gravestone, upon which the veins seemed to form an inscription in forgotten characters. On a tract of several acres around this rock, oaks and other hardwood trees had supplied the place of the pines, which were the usual growth of the land; and a young and vigorous sapling stood close beside the travellers.

The severe wound of the elder man had probably deprived him of sleep; for, so soon as the first ray of sunshine rested on the top of the highest tree, he reared himself painfully from his recumbent posture and sat erect. The deep lines of his countenance and the scattered gray of his hair marked him as past the middle age; but his muscular frame would, but for the effects of his wound, have been as capable of sustaining fatigue as in the early vigor of life. Languor and exhaustion now sat upon his haggard features; and the despairing glance which he sent forward through the depths of the forest proved his own conviction that his pilgrimage was at an end. He next turned his eyes to the companion who reclined by his side. The youth — for he had scarcely attained the years of manhood — lay, with his head upon his arm, in the embrace of an unquiet sleep, which a thrill of pain from his wounds seemed each moment on the point of breaking. His right hand grasped a musket; and, to judge from the violent action of his features, his slumbers were bringing back a vision of the conflict of which he was one of the few survivors. A shout — deep and loud in his dreaming fancy — found its way in an imperfect murmur to his lips; and, starting even at the slight sound of his own voice, he suddenly awoke. The first act of reviving recollection was to make anxious inquiries respecting the condition of his wounded fellow-traveller. The latter shook his head.

"Reuben, my boy," said he, "this rock beneath which we sit will serve for an old hunter's gravestone. There is many and many a long mile of howling wilderness before us yet; nor would it avail me anything if the smoke of my own chimney were but on the other side of that swell of land. The Indian bullet was deadlier than I thought."

"You are weary with our three days' travel," replied the youth, "and a little longer rest will recruit you. Sit you here while I search the woods for the herbs and roots that must be our sustenance; and having eaten, you shall lean on me, and we will turn our faces homeward. I doubt not that, with my help, you can attain to some one of the frontier garrisons."

"There is not two days' life in me, Reuben," said the other, calmly, "and I will no longer burden you with my useless body, when you can scarcely support your own. Your wounds are deep and your strength is failing fast; yet, if you hasten onward alone, you may be preserved. For me there is no hope, and I will await death here."

"If it must be so, I will remain and watch by you," said Reuben, resolutely.

"No, my son, no," rejoined his companion. "Let the wish of a dying man have weight with you; give me one grasp of your hand, and get you hence. Think you that my last moments will be eased by the thought that I leave you to die a more lingering death? I have loved you like a father, Reuben; and at a time like this I should have something of a father's authority. I charge you to be gone that I may die in peace."

"And because you have been a father to me, should I therefore leave you to perish and to lie unburied in the wilderness?" exclaimed the youth. "No; if your end be in truth approaching, I will watch by you and receive your parting words. I will dig a grave here by the rock, in which, if my weakness overcome me, we will rest together; or, if Heaven gives me strength, I will seek my way home."

"In the cities and wherever men dwell," replied the other, "they bury their dead in the earth; they hide them from the sight of the living; but here, where no step may pass perhaps for a hundred years, wherefore should I not rest beneath the open sky, covered only by the oak leaves when the autumn winds shall strew them? And for a monument, here is this gray rock, on which my dying hand shall carve the name of Roger Malvin; and the traveller in days to come will know that here sleeps a hunter and a warrior. Tarry not, then, for a folly like this, but hasten away, if not for your own sake, for hers who will else be desolate."

Malvin spoke the last few words in faltering voice, and their effect upon his companion was strongly visible. They reminded him that there were other and less questionable duties than that of sharing the fate of a man whom his death could not benefit. Nor can it be affirmed that no selfish feeling strove to enter Reuben's heart, though the consciousness made him more earnestly resist his companion's entreaties.

"How terrible to wait the slow approach of death in this solitude!" exclaimed he. "A brave man does not shrink in the battle; and, when friends stand round the bed, even women may die composedly; but here"—

"I shall not shrink even here, Reuben Bourne," interrupted Malvin. "I am a man of no weak heart, and if I were, there is a surer support than that of earthly friends. You are young, and life is dear to you. Your last moments will need comfort far more than mine; and when you have laid me in the earth, and are alone, and night is settling on the forest, you will feel all the bitterness of the death that may now be escaped. But I will urge no selfish motive to your generous nature. Leave me for my sake, that, having said a prayer for your safety, I may have space to settle my account undisturbed by worldly sorrows."

"And your daughter,—how shall I dare to meet her eye?" exclaimed Reuben. "She will ask the fate of her father, whose life I vowed to defend with my own. Must I tell her that he travelled three days' march with me from the field of battle and that then I left him to perish in the wilderness? Were it not better to lie down and die by your side than to return safe and say this to Dorcas?"

"Tell my daughter," said Roger Malvin, "that, though yourself sore wounded, and weak, and weary, you led my tottering footsteps many a mile, and left me only at my earnest entreaty, because I would not have your blood upon my soul. Tell her that through pain and danger you were faithful, and that, if your lifeblood could have saved me, it would have flowed to its last drop; and tell her that you will be something dearer than a father, and that my blessing is with you both, and that my dying eyes can see a long and pleasant path in which you will journey together."

As Malvin spoke he almost raised himself from the ground, and the energy of his concluding words seemed to fill the wild and lonely forest with a vision of happiness; but, when he sank exhausted upon his bed of oak leaves, the light which had kindled in Reuben's eye was quenched. He felt as if it were both sin and folly to think of happiness at such a moment. His companion watched his changing countenance, and sought with generous art to wile him to his own good.

"Perhaps I deceive myself in regard to the time I have to live," he resumed. "It may be that, with speedy assistance, I might recover of my wound. The foremost fugitives must, ere this, have carried tidings of our fatal battle to the frontiers, and parties will be out to succor those in like condition with ourselves. Should you meet one of these and guide them hither, who can tell but that I may sit by my own fireside again?"

A mournful smile strayed across the features of the dying man as he insinuated that unfounded hope,—which, however, was not without its effect on Reuben. No merely selfish motive, nor even the desolate condition of Dorcas, could have induced him to desert his companion at such a moment—but his wishes seized on the thought that Malvin's life might be preserved, and his sanguine nature heightened almost to certainty the remote possibility of procuring human aid.

"Surely there is reason, weighty reason, to hope that friends are not far distant," he said, half aloud. "There fled one coward, unwounded, in the beginning of the fight, and most probably he made good speed. Every true man on the frontier would shoulder his musket at the news; and, though no party may range so far into the woods as this, I shall perhaps encounter them in one day's march. Counsel me faithfully," he added, turning to Malvin, in distrust of his own motives. "Were your situation mine, would you desert me while life remained?"

"It is now twenty years," replied Roger Malvin,—sighing, however, as he secretly acknowledged the wide dissimilarity between the two cases,—"it is now twenty years since I escaped with one dear friend from Indian captivity near Montreal. We journeyed many days through the woods, till at length overcome with hunger and weariness, my friend lay down and besought me to leave him; for he knew that, if I remained, we both must perish; and, with but little hope of obtaining succor, I heaped a pillow of dry leaves beneath his head and hastened on."

"And did you return in time to save him?" asked Reuben hanging on Malvin's words as if they were to be prophetic of his own success.

"I did," answered the other. "I came upon the camp of a hunting party before sunset of the same day. I guided them to the spot where my comrade was expecting death; and he is now a hale and hearty man upon his own farm, far within the frontiers, while I lie wounded here in the depths of the wilderness."

This example, powerful in affecting Reuben's decision, was aided, unconsciously to himself, by the hidden strength of many another motive.

Roger Malvin perceived that the victory was nearly won.

"Now, go, my son, and Heaven prosper you!" he said. "Turn not back with your friends when you meet them, lest your wounds and weariness overcome you; but send hitherward two or three, that may be spared, to search for me; and believe me, Reuben, my heart will be lighter with every step you take towards home." Yet there was, perhaps, a change both in his countenance and voice as he spoke thus; for, after all, it was a ghastly fate to be left expiring in the wilderness.

Reuben Bourne, but half convinced that he was acting rightly, at length raised himself from the ground and prepared himself for his departure. And first, though contrary to Malvin's wishes, he collected a stock of roots and herbs, which had been their only food during the last two days. This useless supply he placed within reach of the dying man, for whom, also, he swept together a bed of dry oak leaves. Then climbing to the summit of the rock, which on one side was rough and broken, he bent the oak sapling downward, and bound his handkerchief to the topmost branch. This precaution was not unnecessary to direct any who might come in search of Malvin; for every part of the rock, except its broad, smooth front, was concealed at a little distance by the dense undergrowth of the forest. The handkerchief had been the bandage of a wound upon Reuben's arm; and, as he bound it to the tree, he vowed by the blood that stained it that he would return, either to save his companion's life or to lay his body in the grave. He then descended, and stood, with downcast eyes, to receive Roger Malvin's parting words.

The experience of the latter suggested much and minute advice respecting the youth's journey through the trackless forest. Upon this subject he spoke with calm earnestness, as if he were sending Reuben to the battle or the chase while he himself remained secure at home, and not as if the human countenance that was about to leave him were the last he would ever behold. But his firmness was shaken before he concluded.

"Carry my blessing to Dorcas, and say that my last prayer shall be for her and you. Bid her to have no hard thoughts because you left me here," — Reuben's heart smote him, — "for that your life would not have weighed with you if its sacrifice could have done me good. She will marry you after she has mourned a little

while for her father; and Heaven grant you long and happy days, and may your children's children stand round your death bed! And, Reuben," he added, as the weakness of mortality made its way at last, "return, when your wounds are healed and your weariness refreshed, — return to this wild rock, and lay my bones in the grave, and say a prayer over them."

An almost superstititous regard, arising perhaps from the customs of the Indians, whose war was with the dead as well as the living, was paid by the frontier inhabitants to the rites of the sepulture; and there are many instances of the sacrifice of life in the attempt to bury those who had fallen by the "sword of the wilderness." Reuben, therefore, left the full importance of the promise which he most solemnly made to return and perform Roger Malvin's obsequies. It was remarkable that the latter, speaking his whole heart in his parting words, no longer endeavored to persuade the youth that even the speediest succor might avail to the preservation of his life. Reuben was internally convinced that he should see Malvin's living face no more. His generous nature would fain have delayed him, at whatever risk, till the dying scene were past; but the desire of existence and the hope of happiness had strengthened in his heart, and he was unable to resist them.

"It is enough," said Roger Malvin, having listened to Reuben's promise. "Go, and God speed you!"

The youth pressed his hand in silence, turned, and was departing. His slow and faltering steps, however, had borne him but a little way before Malvin's voice recalled him.

"Reuben, Reuben," said he, faintly; and Reuben returned and knelt down by the dying man.

"Raise me, and let me lean against the rock," was his last request. "My face will be turned towards home, and I shall see you a moment longer as you pass among the trees."

Reuben, having made the desired alteration in his companion's posture, again began his solitary pilgrimage. He walked more hastily at first than was consistent with his strength; for a sort of guilty feeling, which sometimes torments men in their most justifiable acts, caused him to seek concealment from Malvin's eyes; but after he had trodden far upon the rustling leaves he crept back, impelled by a wild and painful curiosity, and, sheltered by the earthly roots of an uptorn tree, gazed earnestly at the desolate man. The morning sun was unclouded, and the trees and shrubs imbibed the sweet air of the month of May; yet there seemed a gloom on Nature's face, as if she sympathized with mortal pain and sorrow. Roger Malvin's hands were uplifted in a fervent prayer, some of the words of which stole through the stillness of the woods and entered Reuben's heart, torturing it with an unutterable pang. They were the broken accents of a petition for his own happiness and that of Dorcas; and, as the youth listened, conscience, or something in its similitude, pleaded strongly with him to return and lie down again by the rock. He felt how hard was the doom of the kind and generous being whom he had deserted in his extremity. Death would come like the slow approach of a corpse, stealing gradually towards him through the forest, and showing its ghastly and motionless features from behind a nearer and yet a nearer tree. But such must have been Reuben's own fate had he tarried another sunset; and who shall impute blame to him if he shrink from so useless a sacrifice? As he gave a parting look, a breeze waved the little banner upon the sapling oak and reminded Reuben of his vow.

Many circumstances combined to retard the wounded traveller in his way to the frontiers. On the second day the clouds, gathering densely over the sky, precluded the possibility of regulating his course by the position of the sun; and he knew not but that every effort of his almost exhausted strength was removing him farther from the home he sought. His scanty sustenance was supplied by the berries and other spontaneous products of the forest. Herds of deer, it is true, sometimes bounded past him, and partridges frequently whirred up before his footsteps; but his ammunition had been expended in the fight, and he had no means of slaying them. His wounds, irritated by the constant exertion in which lay the only hope of life, wore away his strength and at intervals confused his reason. But, even in the wanderings of intellect, Reuben's young heart clung strongly to existence; and it was only through absolute incapacity of motion that he at last sank down beneath a tree, compelled there to await death.

In this situation he was discovered by a party who, upon the first intelligence of the fight, had been despatched to the relief of the survivors. They conveyed him to the nearest settlement, which chanced to be that of his own residence.

Dorcas, in the simplicity of the olden time, watched by the bedside of her wounded lover, and administered all those comforts that are in the sole gift of woman's heart and hand. During several days Reuben's recollection strayed drowsily among the perils and hardships through which he had passed, and he was incapable of returning definite answers to the inquiries with which many were eager to harass him. No authentic particulars of the battle had yet been circulated; nor could mothers, wives, and children tell whether their loved ones were detained by captivity or by the stronger chain of death. Dorcas nourished her apprehensions in silence till one afternoon when Reuben awoke from an unquiet sleep, and seemed to recognize her more perfectly than at any previous time. She saw that his intellect had become composed, and she could no longer restrain her filial anxiety.

"My father, Reuben?" she began; but the change in her lover's countenance made her pause.

The youth shrank as if with a bitter pain, and the blood gushed vividly into his wan and hollow cheeks. His first impulse was to cover his face; but, apparently with a desperate effort, he half raised himself and spoke vehemently, defending himself against an imaginary accusation.

"Your father was sore wounded in the battle, Dorcas; and he bade me not burden myself with him, but only to lead him to the lakeside, that he might quench his thirst and die. But I would not desert the old man in his extremity, and, though bleeding myself, I supported him; I gave him half my strength, and led him away with me. For three days we journeyed on together, and your father was sustained beyond my hopes, but, awaking at sunrise on the fourth day, I found him faint and exhausted; he was unable to proceed; his life had ebbed away fast; and —"

"He died!" exclaimed Dorcas, faintly.

Reuben felt it impossible to acknowledge that his selfish love of life had hurried him away before her father's fate was decided. He spoke not; he only bowed his head; and, between shame and exhaustion, sank back and hid his face in the pillow. Dorcas wept when her fears were thus confirmed; but the shock, as it had been long anticipated, was on that account the less violent.

"You dug a grave for my poor father in the

wilderness, Reuben?" was the question by which her filial piety manifested itself.

"My hands were weak; but I did what I could," replied the youth in a smothered tone. "There stands a noble tombstone above his head; and I would to Heaven I slept as soundly as he!"

Dorcas, perceiving the wildness of his latter words, inquired no further at the time; but her heart found ease in the thought that Roger Malvin had not lacked such funeral rites as it was possible to bestow. The tale of Reuben's courage and fidelity lost nothing when she communicated it to her friends; and the poor youth, tottering from his sick chamber to breathe the sunny air, experienced from every tongue the miserable and humiliating torture of unmerited praise. All acknowledged that he might worthily demand the hand of the fair maiden to whose father he had been "faithful unto death"; and, as my tale is not of love, it shall suffice to say that in the space of a few months Reuben became the husband of Dorcas Malvin. During the marriage ceremony the bride was covered with blushes, but the bridegroom's face was pale.

There was now in the breast of Reuben Bourne an incommunicable thought — something which he was to conceal most heedfully from her whom he most loved and trusted. He regretted, deeply and bitterly, the moral cowardice that had restrained his words when he was about to disclose the truth to Dorcas; but pride, the fear of losing her affection, the dread of universal scorn, forbade him to rectify this falsehood. He felt that for leaving Roger Malvin he deserved no censure. His presence, the gratuitous sacrifice of his own life, would have added only another and a needless agony to the last moments of the dying man; but concealment had imparted to a justifiable act much of the secret effect of guilt; and Reuben, while reason told him that he had done right, experienced in no small degree the mental horrors which punish the perpetrator of undiscovered crime. By a certain association of ideas, he at times almost imagined himself a murderer. For years, also, a thought would occasionally recur, which, though he perceived all its folly and extravagance, he had not power to banish from his mind. It was a haunting and torturing fancy that his father-in-law was yet sitting at the foot of the rock, on the withered forest leaves, alive, and awaiting his pledged assistance. These mental deceptions, however, came and went, nor did he ever mistake them for realities; but in the calmest and clearest moods of his mind he was conscious that he had a deep vow unredeemed, and that an unburied corpse was calling to him out of the wilderness. Yet such was the consequence of his prevarication that he could not obey the call. It was now too late to require the assistance of Roger Malvin's friends in performing his long-deferred sepulture; and superstitious fears, of which none were more susceptible than the people of the outward settlements, forbade Reuben to go alone. Neither did he know where in the pathless and illimitable forest to seek that smooth and lettered rock at the base of which the body lay: his remembrance of every portion of his travel thence was indistinct, and the latter part had left no impression upon his mind. There was, however, a continual impulse, a voice audible only to himself, commanding him to go forth and redeem his vow; and he had a strange impression that, were he to make the trial, he would be led straight to Malvin's bones. But year after year that summons, unheard but felt, was disobeyed. His one secret thought became like a chain binding down his spirit and like a serpent gnawing into his heart; and he was transformed into a sad and downcast yet irritable man.

In the course of a few years after their marriage changes began to be visible in the external prosperity of Reuben and Dorcas. The only riches of the former had been his stout heart and strong arm; but the latter, her father's sole heiress, had made her husband master of a farm, under older cultivation, larger, and better stocked than most of the frontier establishments. Reuben Bourne, however, was a neglectful husbandman; and, while the lands of the other settlers became annually more fruitful, his deteriorated in the same proportion. The discouragements to agriculture were greatly lessened by the cessation of Indian war, during which men held the plough in one hand and the musket in the other, and were fortunate if the products of their dangerous labor were not destroyed, either in the field or in the barn, by the savage enemy. But Reuben did not profit by the altered condition of the country; nor can it be denied that his intervals of industrious attention to his affairs were but scantily rewarded with success. The irritability by which he had recently become distinguished was another cause of his declining prosperity, as it occasioned frequent quarrels in his unavoidable intercourse with the neighboring settlers. The results of these were innumerable lawsuits; for the people of New England, in the earliest stages and wildest circumstances of the country, adopted, whenever attainable, the legal mode of deciding their differences. To be brief, the world did not go well with Reuben Bourne; and, though not till many years after his marriage, he was finally a ruined man, with but one remaining expedient against the evil fate that had pursued him. He was to throw sunlight into some deep recess of the forest, and seek subsistence from the virgin bosom of the wilderness.

The only child of Reuben and Dorcas was a son, now arrived at the age of fifteen years, beautiful in youth, and giving promise of a glorious manhood. He was peculiarly qualified for, and already began to excel in, the wild accomplishments of frontier life. His foot was fleet, his aim true, his apprehension quick, his heart glad and high; and all who anticipated the return of Indian war spoke of Cyrus Bourne as a future leader in the land. The boy was loved by his father with a deep and silent strength, as if whatever was good and happy in his own nature had been transferred to his child, carrying his affections with it. Even Dorcas, though loving and beloved, was far less dear to him; for Reuben's secret thoughts and insulated emotions had gradually made him a selfish man, and he could no longer love deeply except where he saw or imagined some reflection or likeness of his own mind. In Cyrus, he recognized what he had himself been in other days; and at intervals he seemed to partake of the boy's spirit, and to be revived with a fresh and happy life. Reuben was accompanied by his son in the expedition, for the purpose of selecting a tract of land and felling and burning the timber, which necessarily preceded the removal of the household gods. Two months of autumn were thus occupied after which Reuben Bourne and his young hunter returned to spend their last winter in the settlements.

It was early in the month of May that the little family snapped asunder whatever tendrils of affections had clung to inanimate objects, and bade farewell to the few who, in the blight of fortune, called themselves their friends. The sadness of the parting moment had, to each of the pilgrims, its peculiar alleviations. Reuben,

a moody man, and misanthropic because unhappy, strode onward with his usual stern brow and downcast eye, feeling few regrets and disdaining to acknowledge any. Dorcas, while she wept abundantly over the broken ties by which her simple and affectionate nature had bound itself to everything, felt that the inhabitants of her innermost heart moved on with her, and that all else would be supplied wherever she might go. And the boy dashed one tear-drop from his eye, and thought of the adventurous pleasures of the untrodden forest.

Oh, who, in the enthusiasm of a daydream, has not wished that he were a wanderer in a world of summer wilderness, with one fair and gentle being hanging lightly on his arms? In youth his free and exulting step would know no barrier but the rolling ocean or the snow-topped mountains; a calmer manhood would choose a home where Nature had strewn a double wealth in the vale of some transparent stream; and when hoary age, after long, long years of that pure life, stole on and found him there, it would find him the father of a race, the patriarch of a people, the founder of a mighty nation yet to be. When death, like the sweet sleep which we welcome after a day of happiness, came over him, his far descendants would mourn over the venerated dust. Enveloped by tradition in mysterious attributes, the men of future generations would call him godlike; and remote posterity would see him standing, dimly glorious, far up the valley of a hundred centuries.

The tangled and gloomy forest through which the personages of my tale were wandering differed widely from the dreamer's land of fantasy; yet there was something in their way of life that Nature asserted as her own, and the gnawing cares which went with them from the world were all that now obstructed their happiness. One stout and shaggy steed, the bearer of all their wealth, did not shrink from the added weight of Dorcas; although her hardy breeding sustained her, during the latter part of each day's journey, by her husband's side. Reuben and his son, their muskets on their shoulders and their axes slung behind them, kept an unwearied pace, each watching with a hunter's eye for the game that supplied their food. When hunger bade, they halted and prepared their meal on the bank of some unpolluted forest brook, which, as they knelt down with thirsty lips to drink, murmured a sweet unwillingness, like a maiden at love's first kiss. They slept beneath a hut of branches, and awoke at peep of light refreshed for the toils of another day. Dorcas and the boy went on joyously, and even Reuben's spirit shone at intervals with an outward gladness; but inwardly there was a cold, cold sorrow, which he compared to the snowdrifts lying deep in the glens and hollows of the rivulets while the leaves were brightly green above.

Cyrus Bourne was sufficiently skilled in the travel of the woods to observe that his father did not adhere to the course they had pursued in their expedition of the preceding autumn. They were now keeping farther to the north, striking out more directly from the settlements, and into a region of which savage beasts and savage men were as yet the sole possessors. The boy sometimes hinted his opinions upon the subject, and Reuben listened attentively, and once or twice altered the direction of their march in accordance with his son's counsel; but, having so done, he seemed ill at ease. His quick and wandering glances were sent forward, apparently in search of enemies lurking behind the tree trunks; and, seeing nothing there, he would cast his eyes backwards as if in fear of some pursuer. Cyrus, perceiving that his father gradually resumed the old direction, forbore to interfere; nor, though something began to weigh upon his heart, did his adventurous nature permit him to regret the increased length and the mystery of their way.

On the afternoon of the fifth day they halted, and made their simple encampment nearly an hour before sunset. The face of the country, for the last few miles, had been diversified by swells of land resembling huge waves of a petrified sea; and in one of the corresponding hollows, a wild and romantic spot, had the family reared their hut and kindled their fire. There is something chilling, and yet heart-warming, in the thought of these three, united by strong bands of love and insulated from all that breathe beside. The dark and gloomy pines looked down upon them, and, as the wind swept through their tops, a pitying sound was heard in the forest; or did those old trees groan in fear that men were come to lay the axe to their roots at last? Reuben and his son, while Dorcas made ready their meal, proposed to wander out in search of game, of which that day's march had afforded no supply. The boy, promising not to quit the vicinity of the encampment,

bounded off with a step as light and elastic as that of the deer he hoped to slay; while his father, feeling a transient happiness as he gazed after him, was about to pursue an opposite direction. Dorcas, in the meanwhile, had seated herself near their fire of fallen branches, upon the mossgrown and mouldering trunk of a tree uprooted years before. Her employment, diversified by an occasional glance at the pot, now beginning to simmer over the blaze, was the perusal of the current year's Massachusetts Almanac, which, with the exception of an old black-letter Bible, comprised all the literary wealth of the family. None pay a greater regard to arbitrary divisions of time than those who are excluded from society; and Dorcas mentioned, as if the information were of importance, that it was now the twelfth of May. Her husband started.

"The twelfth of May! I should remember it well," muttered he, while many thoughts occasioned a momentary confusion in his mind. "Where am I? Whither am I wandering? Where did I leave him?"

Dorcas, too well accustomed to her husband's wayward moods to note any peculiarity of demeanor, now laid aside the almanac and addressed him in that mournful tone which the tender hearted appropriate to griefs long cold and dead.

"It was near this time of the month, eighteen years ago, that my poor father left this world for a better. He had a kind arm to hold his head and a kind voice to cheer him, Reuben, in his last moments; and the thought of the faithful care you took of him has comforted me many a time since. Oh, death would have been awful to a solitary man in a wild place like this!"

"Pray Heaven, Dorcas," said Reuben, in a broken voice, — "pray Heaven that neither of us three dies solitary and lies unburied in this howling wilderness!" And he hastened away, leaving her to watch the fire beneath the gloomy pines.

Reuben Bourne's rapid pace gradually slackened as the pang, unintentionally inflicted by the words of Dorcas, became less acute. Many strange reflections, however, thronged upon him; and, straying onward rather like a sleep walker than a hunter, it was attributable to no care of his own that his devious course kept him in the vicinity of the encampment. His steps were imperceptibly led almost in a circle; nor did he observe that he was on the verge of a tract of land heavily timbered, but not with pine-trees. The place of the latter was here supplied by oaks and other of the harder woods; and around their roots clustered a dense and bushy undergrowth, leaving, however, barren spaces between the trees, thick strewn with withered leaves. Whenever the rustling of the branches or the creaking of the trunks made a sound, as if the forest were waking from slumber, Reuben instinctively raised the musket that rested on his arm, and cast a quick, sharp glance on every side; but, convinced by a partial observation that no animal was near, he would again give himself up to his thoughts. He was musing on the strange influence that had led him away from his premeditated course, and so far into the depths of the wilderness. Unable to penetrate to the secret place of his soul where his motives lay hidden, he believed that a supernatural voice had called him onward, and that a supernatural power had obstructed his retreat. He trusted that it was Heaven's intent to afford him an opportunity of expiating his sin; he hoped that he might find the bones so long unburied; and that, having laid the earth over them, peace would throw its sunlight into the sepulchre of his heart. From these thoughts he was aroused by a rustling in the forest at some distance from the spot to which he had wandered. Perceiving the motion of some object behind a thick veil of undergrowth, he fired, with the instinct of a hunter and the aim of a practiced marksman. A low moan, which told his success, and by which even animals can express their dying agony, was unheeded by Reuben Bourne. What were the recollections now breaking upon him?

The thicket into which Reuben had fired was near the summit of a swell of land, and was clustered around the base of a rock, which, in the shape and smoothness of one of its surfaces, was not unlike a gigantic gravestone. As if reflected in a mirror, its likeness was in Reuben's memory. He even recognized the veins which seemed to form an inscription in forgotten characters: everything remained the same, except that a thick covert of bushes shrouded the lower part of the rock, and would have hidden Roger Malvin had he still been sitting there. Yet in the next moment Reuben's eye was caught by another change that time had effected since he last stood where he was now standing again behind the earthy roots of the uptorn tree. The sapling to which he had bound the blood-stained symbol of his vow had increased and strengthened into an oak, far indeed from its maturity, but with no mean spread of shadowy branches. There was one singularity observable in this tree which made Reuben tremble. The middle and lower branches were in luxuriant life, and an excess of vegetation had fringed the trunk almost to the ground; but a blight had apparently stricken the upper part of the oak, and the very topmost bough was withered, sapless, and utterly dead. Reuben remembered how the little banner had fluttered on that topmost bough, when it was green and lovely, eighteen years before. Whose guilt had blasted it?

Dorcas, after the departure of the two hunters, continued her preparations for their evening repast. Her sylvan table was the moss-covered trunk of a large fallen tree, on the broadest part of which she had spread a snow-white cloth and arranged what were left of the bright pewter vessels that had been her pride in the settlements. It had a strange aspect, that one little spot of homely comfort in the desolate heart of Nature. The sunshine yet lingered upon the higher branches of the trees that grew on rising ground; but the shadows of evening had deepened into the hollow where the encampment was made, and the firelight began to redden as it gleamed up the tall trunks of the pines or hovered on the dense and obscure mass of foliage that circled round the spot. The heart of Dorcas was not sad; for she felt that it was better to journey in the wilderness with two whom she loved than to be a lonely woman in a crowd that cared not for her. As she busied herself in arranging seats of mouldering wood, covered with leaves, for Reuben and her son, her voice danced through the gloomy forest in the measure of a song that she had learned in youth. The rude melody, the production of a bard who won no name, was descriptive of a winter evening in a frontier cottage, when, secured from savage inroad by the high-piled snow-drifts, the family rejoiced by their own fireside. The whole song possessed the nameless charm peculiar to unborrowed thought, but four continually-recurring lines shone out from the rest like the blaze of the hearth whose joys they celebrated. Into them, working magic with a few simple words, the poet had instilled the very essence of domestic love and household happiness, and they were poetry and picture joined in one. As Dorcas sang, the walls of her forsaken home seemed to encircle her; she no longer saw the gloomy pines, nor heard the wind which still, as she began each verse, sent a heavy breath through the branches, and died away in a hollow moan from the burden of the song. She was aroused by the report of a gun in the vicinity of the encampment; and either the sudden sound, or her loneliness by the glowing fire, caused her to tremble violently. The next moment she laughed in the pride of a mother's heart.

"My beautiful young hunter! My boy has slain a deer!" she exclaimed, recollecting that in the direction whence the shot proceeded Cyrus had gone to the chase.

She waited a reasonable time to hear her son's light step bounding over the rustling leaves to tell of his success. But he did not immediately appear; and she sent her cheerful voice among the trees in search of him.

"Cyrus! Cyrus!"

His coming was still delayed; and she determined, as the report had apparently been very near, to seek for him in person. Her assistance, also, might be necessary in bringing home the venison which she flattered herself he had obtained. She therefore set forward, directing her steps by the long-past sound, and singing as she went, in order that the boy might be aware of her approach and run to meet her. From behind the trunk of every tree, and from every hiding-place in the thick foliage of the undergrowth, she hoped to discover the countenance of her son, laughing with the sportive mischief that is born of affection. The sun was now beneath the horizon, and the light that came down among the leaves was sufficiently dim to create many illusions in her expecting fancy. Several times she seemed indistinctly to see his face gazing out from among the leaves; and once she imagined that he stood beckoning to her at the base of a craggy rock. Keeping her eyes on this object, however, it proved to be no more than the trunk of an oak fringed to the very ground with little branches, one of which, thrust out farther than the rest, was shaken by the breeze. Making her way round the foot of the rock, she suddenly found herself close to her husband, who had approached in another direction. Leaning upon the butt of his gun, the muzzle of which rested upon the withered leaves, he was apparently absorbed in the contemplation of some object at his feet.

"How is this, Reuben? Have you slain the deer and fallen asleep over him?" exclaimed Dorcas, laughing cheerfully, on her first slight observation of his posture and appearance.

He stirred not, neither did he turn his eyes towards her; and a cold, shuddering fear, indefinite in its source and object, began to creep into her blood. She now perceived that her husband's face was ghastly pale, and his features were rigid, as if incapable of assuming any other expression than the strong despair which had hardened upon them. He gave not the slightest evidence that he was aware of her approach.

"For the love of Heaven, Reuben, speak to me!" cried Dorcas; and the strange sound of her own voice affrighted her even more than the dead silence.

Her husband started, stared into her face, drew her to the front of the rock, and pointed with his finger.

Oh, there lay the boy, asleep, but dreamless, upon the fallen forest leaves! His cheek rested upon his arm — his curled locks were thrown back from his brow — his limbs were slightly relaxed. Had a sudden weariness overcome the youthful hunter? Would his mother's voice arouse him? She knew that it was death.

"This broad rock is the gravestone of your near kindred, Dorcas," said her husband. "Your tears will fall at once over your father and your son."

She heard him not. With one wild shriek, that seemed to force its way from the sufferer's inmost soul, she sank insensible by the side of her dead boy. At that moment the withered topmost bough of the oak loosened itself in the stilly air, and fell in soft, light fragments upon the leaves, upon Reuben, upon his wife and child, and upon Roger Malvin's bones. Then Reuben's heart was stricken, and the tears gushed out like water from a rock. The vow that the wounded youth had made the blighted man had come to redeem. His sin was expiated, — the curse was gone from him; and in the hour when he had shed blood dearer to him than his own, a prayer, the first for years, went up to Heaven from the lips of Reuben Bourne.

The Maypole of Merry Mount

(1835)

🙢 "Hawthorne felt the continuity of the present with the past, the sense that his own life and attitudes were inexplicable without a knowledge of the ancestral mind" (Austin Warren). This knowledge he gained by wide reading in the Puritan Age, including even the local histories of various Massachusetts towns and volumes from the *Collections* of the Massachusetts Historical Society.

In what he called "the grave pages of our New England annalists" he found Bradford's account of the doings at Merry Mount, which should be compared (see page 15) with Hawthorne's. In the simple story that he has made of the incident Hawthorne indicates, not obtrusively, his own attitude toward Cavalier jollity and Puritan gloom.

Bright were the days at Merry Mount, when the Maypole was the banner staff of that gay colony! They who reared it, should their banner be triumphant, were to pour sunshine over New England's rugged hills, and scatter flower seeds throughout the soil. Jollity and gloom were contending for an empire. Midsummer eve had come, bringing deep verdure to the forest, and roses in her lap, of a more vivid hue than the tender buds of Spring. But May, or her mirthful spirit, dwelt all the year round at Merry Mount, sporting with the Summer months, and revelling with Autumn, and basking in the glow of Winter's fireside. Through a world of toil and care she flitted with a dreamlike smile, and came hither to find a home among the lightsome hearts of Merry Mount.

Never had the Maypole been so gayly decked as at sunset on midsummer eve. This venerated emblem was a pine-tree, which had preserved the slender grace of youth, while it equalled the loftiest height of the old wood monarchs. From its top streamed a silken banner, colored like the rainbow. Down nearly to the ground the pole was dressed with birchen boughs, and others of the liveliest green, and some with silvery leaves, fastened by ribbons that fluttered in fantastic knots of twenty different colors, but no sad ones. Garden flowers, and blossoms of the wilderness, laughed gladly forth amid the verdure, so fresh and dewy that they must have grown by magic on that happy pinetree. Where this green and flowery splendor terminated, the shaft of the Maypole was stained with the seven brilliant hues of the banner at its top. On the lowest green bough hung an abundant wreath of roses, some that had been gathered in the sunniest spots of the forest, and others, of still richer blush, which the colonists had reared from English seed. O, people of the Golden Age, the chief of your husbandry was to raise flowers!

But what was the wild throng that stood hand in hand about the Maypole? It could not be that the fauns and nymphs, when driven from their classic groves and homes of ancient fable, had sought refuge, as all the persecuted did, in the fresh woods of the West. These were Gothic monsters, though perhaps of Grecian ancestry. On the shoulders of a comely youth uprose the head and branching antlers of a stag; a second, human in all other points, had the grim visage of a wolf; a third, still with the trunk and limbs of a mortal man, showed the beard and horns of a venerable he-goat. There was the likeness of a bear erect, brute in all but his hind legs, which were adorned with pink silk stockings. And here again almost as wondrous, stood a real bear of the dark forest, lending each of his fore paws to the grasp of a human hand, and as ready for the dance as any in that circle. His inferior nature rose half way, to meet his companions as they stooped. Other faces wore the similitude of man or woman, but distorted or extravagant, with red noses pendulous before their mouths, which seemed of awful depth, and stretched from ear to ear in an eternal fit of laughter. Here might be seen the Salvage Man, well known in heraldry, hairy as a baboon, and girdled with green leaves. By his side, a noble figure, but still a counterfeit, appeared an Indian hunter, with feathery crest and wampum belt. Many of this strange company wore foolscaps, and had little bells appended to their garments, tinkling with a silvery sound, responsive to the inaudible music of their gleesome spirits. Some youths and maidens were of soberer garb, yet well maintained their places in the irregular throng by the expression of wild revelry upon their features. Such were the colonists of Merry Mount, as they stood in the broad smile of sunset round their venerated Maypole.

Had a wanderer, bewildered in the melancholy forest, heard their mirth, and stolen a half-affrighted glance, he might have fancied them the crew of Comus, some already transformed to brutes, some midway between man and beast, and the others rioting in the flow of tipsy jollity that foreran the change. But a band of Puritans, who watched the scene, invisible themselves, compared the masques to those devils and ruined souls with whom their superstition peopled the black wilderness.

Within the ring of monsters appeared the two airiest forms that had ever trodden on any more solid footing than a purple and golden cloud. One was a youth in glistening apparel, with a scarf of the rainbow pattern crosswise on his breast. His right hand held a gilded staff, the ensign of high dignity among the revellers, and his left grasped the slender fingers of a fair maiden, not less gayly decorated than himself. Bright roses glowed in contrast with the dark and glossy curls of each, and were scattered round their feet, or had sprung up spontaneously there. Behind this lightsome couple, so close to the Maypole that its boughs shaded his jovial face, stood the figure of an English priest, canonically dressed, yet decked with flowers, in heathen fashion, and wearing a chaplet of the native vine leaves. By the riot of his rolling eye, and the pagan decorations of his holy garb, he seemed the wildest monster there, and the very Comus of the crew.

"Votaries of the Maypole," cried the flower-decked priest, "merrily, all day long, have the woods echoed to your mirth. But be this your merriest hour, my hearts! Lo, here stand the Lord and Lady of the May, whom I, a clerk of Oxford, and high priest of Merry Mount, am presently to join in holy matrimony. Up with your nimble spirits, ye morris-dancers, green men, and glee maidens, bears and wolves, and horned gentlemen! Come; a chorus now, rich with the old mirth of Merry England, and the wilder glee of this fresh forest; and then a dance, to show the youthful pair what life is made of, and how airily they should go through it! All ye that love the Maypole, lend your voices to the nuptial song of the Lord and Lady of the May!"

This wedlock was more serious than most affairs of Merry Mount, whence jest and delusion, trick and fantasy, kept up a continual carnival. The Lord and Lady of the May, though their titles must be laid down at sunset, were really and truly to be partners for the dance of life, beginning the measure that same bright eve. The wreath of roses, that hung from the lowest green bough of the Maypole, had been twined for them, and would be thrown over both their heads, in symbol of their flowery union. When the priest had spoken, therefore, a riotous uproar burst from the rout of monstrous figures.

"Begin you the stave, reverend Sir," cried they all; "and never did the woods ring to such a merry peal as we of the Maypole shall send up!"

Immediately a prelude of pipe, cithern, and viol, touched with practised minstrelsy, began to play from a neighboring thicket, in such a mirthful cadence that the boughs of the Maypole quivered to the sound. But the May Lord, he of the gilded staff, chancing to look into his Lady's eyes, was wonder struck at the almost pensive glance that met his own.

"Edith, sweet Lady of the May," whispered he reproachfully, "is yon wreath of roses a garland to hang above our graves, that you look so sad? O, Edith, this is our golden time! Tarnish it not by any pensive shadow of the mind; for it may be that nothing of futurity will be brighter than the mere remembrance of what is now passing."

"That was the very thought that saddened me! How came it in your mind too?" said Edith, in a still lower tone than he, for it was high treason to be sad at Merry Mount. "Therefore do I sigh amid this festive music. And besides, dear Edgar, I struggle as with a dream, and fancy that these shapes of our jovial friends are visionary, and their mirth unreal, and that we are no true Lord and Lady of the May. What is the mystery in my heart?"

Just then, as if a spell had loosened them down came a little shower of withering rose leaves from the Maypole. Alas, for the young lovers! No sooner had their hearts glowed with real passion than they were sensible of something vague and unsubstantial in their former pleasures, and felt a dreary presentiment of inevitable change. From the moment that they truly loved, they had subjected themselves to earth's doom of care and sorrow, and troubled joy, and had no more a home at Merry Mount. That was Edith's mystery. Now leave we the priest to marry them, and the masquers to sport round the Maypole, till the last sunbeam be withdrawn from its summit, and the shadows of the forest mingle gloomily in the dance. Meanwhile, we may discover who these gay people were.

Two hundred years ago, and more, the old world and its inhabitants became mutually weary of each other. Men voyaged by thousands to the West: some to barter glass beads, and such like jewels, for the furs of the Indian hunter; some to conquer virgin empires; and one stern band to pray. But none of these motives had much weight with the colonists of Merry Mount. Their leaders were men who had sported so long with life, that when Thought and Wisdom came, even these unwelcome guests were led astray by the crowd of vanities which they should have put to flight. Erring Thought and perverted Wisdom were made to put on masques, and play the fool. The men of whom we speak, after losing the heart's fresh gayety, imagined a wild philosophy of pleasure, and came hither to act out their latest daydream. They gathered followers from all that giddy tribe whose whole life is like the festal days of soberer men. In their train were minstrels, not unknown in London streets: wandering players, whose theatres had been the halls of noblemen; mummers, rope-dancers, and mountebanks, who would long be missed at wakes, church ales, and fairs; in a word, mirth makers of every sort, such as abounded in that age, but now began to be discountenanced by the rapid growth of Puritanism. Light had their footsteps been on land, and as lightly they came across the sea. Many had been maddened by their previous troubles into a gay despair; others were as madly gay in the flush of youth, like the May Lord and his Lady; but whatever might be the quality of their mirth, old and young were gay at Merry Mount. The young deemed themselves happy. The elder spirits, if they knew that mirth was but the counterfeit of happiness, yet followed the false shadow wilfully, because at least her garments glittered brightest. Sworn triflers of a lifetime, they would not venture among the sober truths of life not even to be truly blest.

All the hereditary pastimes of Old England were transplanted hither. The King of Christmas was duly crowned, and the Lord of Misrule bore potent sway. On the Eve of St. John, they felled whole acres of the forest to make bonfires, and danced by the blaze all night, crowned with garlands, and throwing flowers into the flame. At harvest time, though their crop was of the smallest, they made an image with the sheaves of Indian corn, and wreathed it with autumnal garlands, and bore it home triumphantly. But what chiefly characterized the colonists of Merry Mount was their veneration for the Maypole. It has made their true history a poet's tale. Spring decked the hallowed emblem with young blossoms and fresh green boughs; Summer brought roses of the deepest blush, and the perfected foliage of the forest; Autumn enriched it with that red and yellow gorgeousness which converts each wildwood leaf into a painted flower; and Winter silvered it with sleet, and hung it round with icicles, till it flashed in the cold sunshine, itself a frozen sunbeam. Thus each alternate season did homage to the Maypole, and paid it a tribute of its own richest splendor. Its votaries danced round it, once, at least, in every month; sometimes they called it their religion, or their altar; but always, it was the banner staff of Merry Mount.

Unfortunately, there were men in the new world of a sterner faith than these Maypole worshippers. Not far from Merry Mount was a settlement of Puritans, most dismal wretches, who said their prayers before daylight, and then wrought in the forest or the cornfield till evening made it prayer time again. Their weapons were always at hand to shoot down the straggling savage. When they met in conclave, it was never to keep up the old English mirth, but to hear sermons three hours long, or to proclaim bounties on the heads of wolves and the scalps of Indians. Their festivals were fast days, and their chief pastime the singing of psalms. Woe to the youth or maiden who did but dream of a dance! The selectman nodded to the constable; and there sat the light-heeled reprobate in the stocks; or if he danced, it was round the whipping-post, which might be termed the Puritan Maypole.

A party of these grim Puritans, toiling through the difficult woods, each with a horseload of iron armor to burden his footsteps, would sometimes draw near the sunny precincts of Merry Mount. There were the silken colonists, sporting round their Maypole: perhaps teaching a bear to dance, or striving to communicate their mirth to the grave Indian; or masquerading in the skins of deer and wolves, which they had hunted for that especial purpose. Often, the whole colony were playing at blindman's buff, magistrates and all, with their eyes bandaged, except a single scapegoat, whom the blinded sinners pursued by the tinkling of the bells at his garments. Once, it is said, they were seen following a flower-decked corpse, with merriment and festive music, to his grave. But did the dead man laugh? In their quietest times, they sang ballads and told tales, for the edification of their pious visitors; or perplexed them with juggling tricks; or grinned at them through horse collars; and when sport itself grew wearisome, they made game of their own stupidity, and began a yawning match. At the very least of these enormities, the men of iron shook their heads and frowned so darkly that the revellers looked up, imagining that a momentary cloud had overcast the sunshine, which was to be perpetual there. On the other hand, the Puritans affirmed that, when a psalm was pealing from their place of worship, the echo which the forest sent them back seemed often like the chorus of a jolly catch, closing with a roar of laughter. Who but the fiend, and his bond slaves, the crew of Merry Mount, had thus disturbed them? In due time, a feud arose, stern and bitter on one side, and as serious on the other as anything could be among such light spirits as had sworn allegiance to the Maypole. The future complexion of New England was involved in this important quarrel. Should the grizzly saints establish their jurisdiction over the gay sinners, then would their spirits darken all the clime and make it a land of clouded visages, of hard toil, of sermon and psalm forever. But should the banner staff of Merry Mount be fortunate, sunshine would break upon the hills, and flowers would beautify the forest, and late posterity do homage to the Maypole.

After these authentic passages from history, we return to the nuptials of the Lord and Lady of the May. Alas! we have delayed too long, and must darken our tale too suddenly. As we glance again at the Maypole, a solitary sunbeam is fading from the summit, and leaves only a faint, golden tinge blended with the hues of the rainbow banner. Even that dim light is now withdrawn, relinquishing the whole domain of Merry Mount to the evening gloom, which has rushed so instantaneously from the black surrounding woods. But some of these black shadows have rushed forth in human shape.

Yes, with the setting sun, the last day of mirth had passed from Merry Mount. The ring of gay masquers was disordered and broken; the stag lowered his antlers in dismay; the wolf grew weaker than a lamb; the bells of the morris-dancers tinkled with tremulous affright. The Puritans had played a characteristic part in the Maypole mummeries. Their darksome figures were intermixed with the wild shapes of their foes, and made the scene a picture of the moment, when waking thoughts start up amid the scattered fantasies of a dream. The leader of the hostile party stood in the center of the circle, while the route of monsters cowered around him, like evil spirits in the presence of a dread magician. No fantastic foolery could look him in the face. So stern was the energy of his aspect, that the whole man, visage, frame and soul, seemed wrought of iron, gifted with

life and thought, yet all of one substance with his headpiece and breastplace. It was the Puritan of Puritans; it was Endicott himself!

"Stand off, priest of Baal!" said he, with a grim frown, and laying no reverent hand upon the surplice. "I know thee, Blackstone! [1] Thou art the man who couldst not abide the rule even of thine own corrupted church, and hast come hither to preach iniquity, and to give example of it in thy life. But now shall it be seen that the Lord hath sanctified this wilderness for his peculiar people. Woe unto them that would defile it! And first, for this flower-decked abomination, the altar of thy worship!"

And with his keen sword Endicott assaulted the hallowed Maypole. Nor long did it resist his arm. It groaned with a dismal sound; it showered leaves and rosebuds upon the remorseless enthusiast; and finally, with all its green boughs and ribbons and flowers, symbolic of departed pleasures, down fell the banner staff of Merry Mount. As it sank, tradition says, the evening sky grew darker, and the woods threw forth a more sombre shadow.

"There," cried Endicott, looking triumphantly on his work, "there lies the only Maypole in New England! The thought is strong within me that, by its fall, is shadowed forth the fate of light and idle mirth makers, amongst us and our posterity. Amen, saith John Endicott."

"Amen!" echoed his followers.

But the votaries of the Maypole gave one groan for their idol. At the sound, the Puritan leader glanced at the crew of Comus, each a figure of broad mirth, yet, at this moment, strangely expressive of sorrow and dismay.

"Valiant captain," quoth Peter Palfrey, the Ancient of the band, "what order shall be taken with the prisoners?"

"I thought not to repent me of cutting down a Maypole," replied Endicott, "yet now I could find in my heart to plant it again, and give each of these bestial pagans one other dance round their idol. It would have served rarely for a whipping-post!"

"But there are pine-trees enow," suggested the lieutenant.

"True, good Ancient," said the leader. "Wherefore, bind the heathen crew, and bestow

[1] Did Governor Endicott speak less positively, we should suspect a mistake here. The Rev. Mr. Blackstone, though an eccentric, is not known to have been an immoral man. We rather doubt his identity with the priest of Merry Mount. [*Author's note.*]

on them a small matter of stripes apiece, as earnest of our future justice. Set some of the rogues in the stocks to rest themselves, so soon as Providence shall bring us to one of our own well-ordered settlements, where such accommo- dations may be found. Further penalties, such as branding and cropping of ears, shall be thought of hereafter."

"How many stripes for the priest?" inquired Ancient Palfrey.

"None as yet," answered Endicott, bending his iron frown upon the culprit. "It must be for the Great and General Court to determine, whether stripes and long imprisonment, and other grievous penalty, may atone for his trans- gressions. Let him look to himself! For such as violate our civil order, it may be permitted us to show mercy. But woe to the wretch that troubleth our religion!"

"And this dancing bear," resumed the officer. "Must he share the stripes of his fellows?"

"Shoot him through the head!" said the energetic Puritan. "I suspect witchcraft in the beast."

"Here be a couple of shining ones," continued Peter Palfrey, pointing his weapon at the Lord and Lady of the May. "They seem to be of high station among these misdoers. Methinks their dignity will not be fitted with less than a double share of stripes."

Endicott rested on his sword, and closely surveyed the dress and aspect of the hapless pair. There they stood, pale, downcast, and apprehensive. Yet there was an air of mutual support, and of pure affection, seeking aid and giving it, that showed them to be man and wife, with the sanction of a priest upon their love. The youth, in the peril of the moment, had dropped his gilded staff, and thrown his arm about the Lady of the May, who leaned against his breast, too lightly to burden him, but with weight enough to express that their destinies were linked together, for good or evil. They looked first at each other, and then into the grim captain's face. There they stood, in the first hour of wedlock, while the idle pleasures, of which their companions were the emblems, had given place to the sternest cares of life, personified by the dark Puritans. But never had their youthful beauty seemed so pure and high as when its glow was chastened by adversity.

"Youth," said Endicott, "ye stand in an evil case, thou and thy maiden wife. Make ready presently, for I am minded that ye shall both have a token to remember your wedding day!"

"Stern man," cried the May Lord, "how can I move thee? Were the means at hand, I would resist to the death. Being powerless, I entreat! Do with me as thou wilt, but let Edith go untouched!"

"Not so," replied the immitigable zealot. "We are not wont to show an idle courtesy to that sex, which requireth the stricter discipline. What sayest thou, maid? Shall thy silken bridegroom suffer thy share of the penalty, besides his own?"

"Be it death," said Edith, "and lay it all on me!"

Truly, as Endicott had said, the poor lovers stood in woful case. Their foes were triumphant, their friends captive and abased, their home desolate, the benighted wilderness around them, and a rigorous destiny, in the shape of the Puri- tan leader, their only guide. Yet the deepening twilight could not altogether conceal that the iron man was softened; he smiled at the fair spectacle of early love; he almost sighed for the inevitable blight of early hopes.

"The troubles of life have come hastily on this young couple," observed Endicott, "We will see how they comport themselves under their present trials ere we burden them with greater. If, among the spoil, there be any gar- ments of a more decent fashion, let them be put upon this May Lord and his Lady, instead of their glistening vanities. Look to it, some of you."

"And shall not the youth's hair be cut?" asked Peter Palfrey, looking with abhorrence at the lovelock and long glossy curls of the young man.

"Crop it forthwith, and that in the true pumpkinshell fashion," answered the captain. "Then bring them along with us, but more gently than their fellows. There be qualities in the youth, which may make him valiant to fight, and sober to toil, and pious to pray; and in the maiden, that may fit her to become a mother in our Israel, bringing up babes in better nurture than her own hath been. Nor think ye, young ones, that they are the happiest, even in our lifetime of a moment, who misspend it in dancing round a Maypole!"

And Endicott, the severest Puritan of all who laid the rock foundation of New England, lifted the wreath of roses from the ruin of the May- pole, and threw it, with his own gauntleted hand, over the heads of the Lord and Lady of the May. It was a deed of prophecy. As the moral gloom of the world overpowers all systematic gayety, even so was their home of wild mirth made desolate amid the sad forest. They returned to it no more. But as their flowery garland was wreathed of the brightest roses that had grown there, so, in the tie that united them, were intertwined all the purest and best of their early joys. They went heavenward, supporting each other along the difficult path which it was their lot to tread, and never wasted one regretful thought on the vanities of Merry Mount.

Young Goodman Brown

(1835)

✷ Among the persons sentenced to death by Judge Hathorne in the Salem witch trials of 1692 were Goody Cloyse and Goody Cory, who figure in this story. To many contemporaries of Hawthorne's ancestor, witchcraft was a terrible menace. To Hawthorne himself, it was local history and a theme for the art of fiction — an opportunity to image forth the fraternity of Evil. His material he found largely in a work published in the year after the trials, Cotton Mather's *Wonders of the Invisible World: Being an Account of the Trials of Several Witches, Lately Executed in New-England*. And his technique for this and other stories Hawthorne found in the conventions of Gothic romance or tale of terror, which he refined and psychologized, focusing upon interior experience.

This vigorous and closely worked story moves within bounds fixed by one night (sunset to "early sunshine"), by a journey from Salem village into the forest and back again, and by the desolating workings of moral doubt. Did Young Goodman Brown dream the events, or are they to be taken as actual? Hawthorne will not say. This calculated ambiguity of the whole encloses many ambiguities in the conduct of the story. Again and again the reader is offered double meanings, invited to make his choice or suspend his judgment. Is this an aesthetic virtue, a suggestion of the final elusiveness of all human experience, or is it a defect, a destruction of the illusion of reality at which art aims?

In either view, one must recognize Hawthorne's firm command of his artistic intention, shown "in the lucid simplicity of the basic action; in the skilful foreshadowing by which the plot is bound together; in balance of episode and scene; in the continuous use of contrast; in the firmness and selectivity of Hawthorne's pictorial composition; in the carefully arranged climactic order of incident and tone; in the detachment and irony of Hawthorne's attitude; and finally in the purity, the grave formality, and the rhetorical balance of the style" (R. H. Fogle).

Young Goodman Brown came forth at sunset into the street at Salem village; but put his head back, after crossing the threshold, to exchange a parting kiss with his young wife. And Faith, as the wife was aptly named, thrust her own pretty head into the street, letting the wind play with the pink ribbons of her cap while she called to Goodman Brown.

"Dearest heart," whispered she, softly and rather sadly, when her lips were close to his ear, "prithee put off your journey until sunrise and sleep in your own bed to-night. A lone woman is troubled with such dreams and such thoughts that she's afeard of herself sometimes. Pray tarry with me this night, dear husband, of all nights in the year."

"My love and my Faith," replied young Goodman Brown, "of all nights in the year, this one night must I tarry away from thee. My journey, as thou callest it, forth and back again, must needs be done 'twixt now and sunrise. What, my sweet wife, dost thou doubt me already, and we but three months married?"

"Then God bless you!" said Faith, with the pink ribbons; "and may you find all well when you come back."

"Amen!" cried Goodman Brown. "Say thy prayers, dear Faith, and go to bed at dusk, and no harm will come to thee."

So they parted; and the young man pursued his way until, being about to turn the corner by the meeting-house, he looked back and saw the head of Faith still peeping after him with a melancholy air, in spite of her pink ribbons.

"Poor little Faith!" thought he, for his heart smote him, "What a wretch am I to leave her on such an errand! She talks of dreams, too. Methought as she spoke there was trouble in her face, as if a dream had warned her what work is to be done to-night. But no, no; 'twould kill her to think it. Well, she's a blessed angel on earth; and after this one night I'll cling to her skirts and follow her to heaven."

With this excellent resolve for the future, Goodman Brown felt himself justified in making more haste on his present evil purpose. He had taken a dreary road, darkened by all the gloomiest trees of the forest, which barely stood aside to let the narrow path creep through, and closed immediately behind. It was all as lonely as could be; and there is this peculiarity in such a solitude, that the traveller knows not who may be concealed by the innumerable trunks and the thick boughs overhead; so that with lonely footsteps he may yet be passing through an unseen multitude.

"There may be a devilish Indian behind every tree," said Goodman Brown to himself; and he glanced fearfully behind him as he added, "What if the devil himself should be at my very elbow!"

His head being turned back, he passed a crook of the road, and, looking forward again, beheld the figure of a man, in grave and decent attire, seated at the foot of an old tree. He arose at Goodman Brown's approach and walked onward side by side with him.

"You are late, Goodman Brown," said he. "The clock of the Old South was striking as I came through Boston, and that is full fifteen minutes agone."

"Faith kept me back a while," replied the young man, with a tremor in his voice, caused by the sudden appearance of his companion, though not wholly unexpected.

It was now deep dusk in the forest, and deepest in that part of it where these two were journeying. As nearly as could be discerned, the second traveller was about fifty years old, apparently in the same rank of life as Goodman Brown, and bearing a considerable resemblance to him, though perhaps more in expression than features. Still they might have been taken for father and son. And yet, though the elder person was as simply clad as the younger, and as simple in manner too, he had an indescribable air of one who knew the world, and who would not have felt abashed at the governor's dinner table or in King William's court, were it possible that his affairs should call him thither. But the only thing about him that could be fixed upon as remarkable was his staff, which bore the likeness of a great black snake, so curiously wrought that it might almost be seen to twist and wriggle itself like a living serpent. This, of course, must have been an ocular deception, assisted by the uncertain light.

"Come, Goodman Brown," cried his fellow-traveller, "this is a dull pace for the beginning of a journey. Take my staff, if you are so soon weary."

"Friend," said the other, exchanging his slow pace for a full stop, "having kept covenant by meeting thee here, it is my purpose now to return whence I came. I have scruples touching the matter thou wot'st of."

"Sayest thou so?" replied he of the serpent, smiling apart. "Let us walk on, nevertheless, reasoning as we go; and if I convince thee not thou shalt turn back. We are but a little way in the forest yet."

"Too far! too far!" exclaimed the goodman, unconsciously resuming his walk. "My father never went into the woods on such an errand, nor his father before him. We have been a race of honest men and good Christians since the days of the martyrs; and shall I be the first of the name of Brown that ever took his path and kept" —

"Such company, thou wouldst say," observed the elder person, interpreting his pause. "Well said, Goodman Brown! I have been as well acquainted with your family as with ever a one among the Puritans; and that's no trifle to say. I helped your grandfather, the constable, when he lashed the Quaker woman so smartly through the streets of Salem; and it was I that brought your father a pitch-pine knot, kindled at my own hearth, to set fire to an Indian village, in King Philip's war. They were my good friends, both; and many a pleasant walk have we had along this path, and returned merrily after midnight. I would fain be friends with you for their sake."

"If it be as thou sayest," replied Goodman Brown, "I marvel they never spoke of these matters; or, verily, I marvel not, seeing that the least rumor of the sort would have driven them from New England. We are a people of prayer, and good works to boot, and abide no such wickedness."

"Wickedness or not," said the traveller with the twisted staff, "I have a very general acquaintance here in New England. The deacons of many a church have drunk the communion wine with me; the selectmen of divers towns make me their chairman; and a majority of the Great and General Court are firm supporters of my interest. The governor and I, too — But these are state secrets."

"Can this be so?" cried Goodman Brown, with a stare of amazement at his undisturbed companion. "Howbeit, I have nothing to do with the governor and council; they have their own ways, and are no rule for a simple husbandman like me. But, were I to go on with thee, how should I meet the eye of that good old man, our minister, at Salem village? Oh, his voice would make me tremble both Sabbath day and lecture day."

Thus far the elder traveller had listened with due gravity; but now burst into a fit of irrepressible mirth, shaking himself so violently that his snake-like staff actually seemed to wriggle in sympathy.

"Ha! ha! ha!" shouted he again and again; then composing himself, "Well, go on, Goodman Brown, go on; but, prithee, don't kill me with laughing."

"Well, then, to end the matter at once," said Goodman Brown, considerably nettled, "there is my wife, Faith. It would break her dear little heart; and I'd rather break my own."

"Nay, if that be the case," answered the other, "e'en go thy ways, Goodman Brown. I would not for twenty old women like the one hobbling before us that Faith should come to any harm."

As he spoke he pointed his staff at a female figure on the path, in whom Goodman Brown recognized a very pious and exemplary dame, who had taught him his catechism in youth, and was still his moral and spiritual adviser, jointly with the minister and Deacon Gookin.

"A marvel, truly, that Goody Cloyse should be so far in the wilderness at nightfall," said he. "But with your leave, friend, I shall take a cut through the woods until we have left this Christian woman behind. Being a stranger to you, she might ask whom I was consorting with and whither I was going."

"Be it so," said his fellow-traveller. "Betake you to the woods, and let me keep the path."

Accordingly the young man turned aside, but took care to watch his companion, who advanced softly along the road until he had come within a staff's length of the old dame. She, meanwhile, was making the best of her way, with singular speed for so aged a woman, and mumbling some indistinct words — a prayer, doubtless — as she went. The traveller put forth his staff and touched her withered neck with what seemed the serpent's tail.

"The devil!" screamed the pious old lady.

"Then Goody Cloyse knows her old friend?" observed the traveller, confronting her and leaning on his writhing stick.

"Ah, forsooth, and is it your worship indeed?" cried the good dame. "Yea, truly is it, and in the very image of my old gossip, Goodman Brown, the grandfather of the silly fellow that now is. But — would your worship believe it? — my broomstick hath strangely disappeared, stolen, as I suspect, by that unhanged witch, Goody Cory, and that, too, when I was all anointed with the juice of smallage, and cinquefoil, and wolf's bane —"

"Mingled with fine wheat and the fat of a new-born babe," said the shape of old Goodman Brown.

"Ah, your worship knows the recipe," cried the old lady, cackling aloud. "So, as I was saying, being all ready for the meeting, and no horse to ride on, I made up my mind to foot it; for they tell me there is a nice young man to be taken into communion to-night. But now your good worship will lend me your arm, and we shall be there in a twinkling."

"That can hardly be," answered her friend. "I may not spare you my arm, Goody Cloyse; but here is my staff, if you will."

So saying, he threw it down at her feet, where, perhaps, it assumed life, being one of the rods which its owner had formerly lent to the Egyptian magi. Of this fact, however, Goodman Brown could not take cognizance. He had cast up his eyes in astonishment, and, looking down again, beheld neither Goody Cloyse nor the serpentine staff, but his fellow-traveller alone, who waited for him as calmly as if nothing had happened.

"That old woman taught me my catechism," said the young man; and there was a world of meaning in this simple comment.

They continued to walk onward, while the elder traveller exhorted his companion to make good speed and persevere in the path, discoursing so aptly that his arguments seemed rather to spring up in the bosom of his auditor than to be suggested by himself. As they went, he plucked a branch of maple to serve for a walking stick, and began to strip it of the twigs and little boughs, which were wet with evening dew. The moment his fingers touched them they became strangely withered and dried up as with a week's sunshine. Thus the pair proceeded, at a good free pace, until suddenly, in a gloomy hollow of the road, Goodman Brown sat himself down on the stump of a tree and refused to go any farther.

"Friend," said he, stubbornly, "my mind is made up. Not another step will I budge on this errand. What if a wretched old woman do choose to go to the devil when I thought she was going to heaven: is that any reason why I should quit my dear Faith and go after her?"

"You will think better of this by and by," said his acquaintance, composedly. "Sit here and rest yourself a while; and when you feel like moving again, there is my staff to help you along."

Without more words, he threw his companion the maple stick, and was as speedily out of sight as if he had vanished into the gloom. The young man sat a few moments by the roadside, applauding himself greatly, and thinking with how clear a conscience he should meet the minister in his morning walk, nor shrink from the eye of good old Deacon Gookin. And what calm sleep would be his that very night, which was to have been spent so wickedly, but so purely and sweetly now, in the arms of Faith! Amidst these pleasant and praiseworthy meditations, Goodman Brown heard the tramp of horses along the road, and deemed it advisable to conceal himself within the verge of the forest, conscious of the guilty purpose that had brought him thither, though now so happily turned from it.

On came the hoof tramps and the voices of the riders, two grave old voices, conversing soberly as they drew near. These mingled sounds appeared to pass along the road, within a few yards of the young man's hiding-place; but, owing doubtless to the depth of the gloom at that particular spot, neither the travellers nor their steeds were visible. Though their figures brushed the small boughs by the wayside, it could not be seen that they intercepted, even for a moment, the faint gleam from the strip of bright sky athwart which they must have passed. Goodman Brown alternately crouched and stood on tiptoe, pulling aside the branches and thrusting forth his head as far as he durst without discerning so much as a shadow. It vexed him the more, because he could have sworn, were such a thing possible, that he recognized the voices of the minister and Deacon Gookin, jogging along quietly, as they were wont to do, when bound to some ordination or ecclesiastical council. While yet within hearing, one of the riders stopped to pluck a switch.

"Of the two, reverend sir," said the voice like the deacon's, "I had rather miss an ordination dinner than to-night's meeting. They tell me that some of our community are to be here from Falmouth and beyond, and others from Connecticut and Rhode Island, besides several of the Indian powwows, who, after their fashion know almost as much deviltry as the best of us. Moreover, there is a goodly young woman to be taken into communion."

"Mighty well, Deacon Gookin!" replied the solemn old tones of the minister. "Spur up, or we shall be late. Nothing can be done, you know, until I get on the ground."

The hoofs clattered again; and the voices, talking so strangely in the empty air, passed on through the forest, where no church had ever been gathered or solitary Christian prayed. Whither, then, could these holy men be journeying so deep into the heathen wilderness? Young Goodman Brown caught hold of a tree for support, being ready to sink down on the ground, faint and overburdened with the heavy sickness of his heart. He looked up to the sky, doubting whether there really was a heaven above him. Yet there was the blue arch, and the stars brightening in it.

"With heaven above and Faith below, I will yet stand firm against the devil!" cried Goodman Brown.

While he still gazed upward into the deep arch of the firmament and had lifted his hands to pray, a cloud, though no wind was stirring, hurried across the zenith and hid the brightening stars. The blue sky was still visible, except directly overhead, where this black mass of cloud was sweeping swiftly northward. Aloft in the air, as if from the depths of the cloud, came a confused and doubtful sound of voices. Once the listener fancied that he could distinguish the accents of townspeople of his own, men and women, both pious and ungodly, many of whom he had met at the communion table, and had seen others rioting at the tavern. The next moment, so indistinct were the sounds, he doubted whether he had heard aught but the murmur of the old forest, whispering without a wind. Then came a stronger swell of those familiar tones, heard daily in the sunshine at Salem village, but never until now from a cloud of night. There was one voice, of a young woman, uttering lamentations, yet with an uncertain sorrow, and entreating for some favor, which, perhaps, it would grieve her to obtain; and all the unseen multitude, both saints and sinners, seemed to encourage her onward.

"Faith!" shouted Goodman Brown, in a voice of agony and desperation; and the echoes of the forest mocked him, crying, "Faith! Faith!" as if bewildered wretches were seeking her all through the wilderness.

The cry of grief, rage, and terror was yet piercing the night, when the unhappy husband held his breath for a response. There was a scream, drowned immediately in a louder murmur of voices, fading into far-off laughter, as the dark cloud swept away, leaving the clear and silent sky above Goodman Brown. But something fluttered lightly down through the air and caught on the branch of a tree. The young man seized it, and beheld a pink ribbon.

"My Faith is gone!" cried he, after one stupefied moment. "There is no good on earth; and sin is but a name. Come, devil; for to thee is this world given."

And, maddened with despair, so that he laughed loud and long, did Goodman Brown grasp his staff and set forth again, at such a rate that he seemed to fly along the forest path rather than to walk or run. The road grew wilder and drearier and more faintly traced, and vanished at length, leaving him in the heart of the dark wilderness, still rushing onward with the instinct that guides mortal man to evil. The whole forest was peopled with frightful sounds — the creaking of the trees, the howling of wild beasts, and the yell of Indians; while sometimes the wind tolled like a distant church bell, and sometimes gave a broad roar around the traveller, as if all Nature were laughing him to scorn. But he was himself the chief horror of the scene, and shrank not from its other horrors.

"Ha! ha! ha!" roared Goodman Brown when the wind laughed at him. "Let us hear which will laugh loudest. Think not to frighten me with your deviltry. Come witch, come wizard, come Indian powwow, come devil himself, and here comes Goodman Brown. You may as well fear him as he fear you."

In truth, all through the haunted forest there could be nothing more frightful than the figure of Goodman Brown. On he flew among the black pines, brandishing his staff with frenzied gestures, now giving vent to an inspiration of horrid blasphemy, and now shouting forth such laughter as set all the echoes of the forest laughing like demons around him. The fiend in his own shape is less hideous than when he rages in the breast of man. Thus sped the demoniac on his course, until, quivering among the trees, he saw a red light before him, as when the felled trunks and branches of a clearing have been set on fire, and throw up their lurid blaze against the sky, at the hour of midnight. He paused, in a lull of the tempest that had driven him onward, and heard the swell of what seemed a hymn, rolling solemnly from a distance with the weight of many voices. He knew the tune; it was a familiar one in the choir of the village meeting-house. The verse died heavily away, and was lengthened by a chorus, not of human voices, but of all the sounds of the benighted

wilderness pealing in awful harmony together. Goodman Brown cried out, and his cry was lost to his own ear by its unison with the cry of the desert.

In the interval of silence he stole forward until the light glared full upon his eyes. At one extremity of an open space, hemmed in by the dark wall of the forest, arose a rock, bearing some rude, natural resemblance either to an altar or a pulpit, and surrounded by four blazing pines, their tops aflame, their stems untouched, like candles at an evening meeting. The mass of foliage that had over-grown the summit of the rock was all on fire, blazing high into the night and fitfully illuminating the whole field. Each pendent twig and leafy festoon was in a blaze. As the red light arose and fell, a numerous congregation alternately shone forth, then disappeared in shadow, and again grew, as it were, out of the darkness, peopling the heart of the solitary woods at once.

"A grave and dark-clad company," quoth Goodman Brown.

In truth they were such. Among them, quivering to and fro between gloom and splendor, appeared faces that would be seen next day at the council board of the province, and others which, Sabbath after Sabbath, looked devoutly heavenward, and benignantly over the crowded pews, from the holiest pulpits in the land. Some affirm that the lady of the governor was there. At least there were high dames well known to her, and wives of honored husbands, and widows, a great multitude, and ancient maidens, all of excellent repute, and fair young girls, who trembled lest their mothers should espy them. Either the sudden gleams of light flashing over the obscure field bedazzled Goodman Brown, or he recognized a score of the church members of Salem village famous for their especial sanctity. Good old Deacon Gookin had arrived, and waited at the skirts of that venerable saint, his revered pastor. But, irreverently consorting with these grave, reputable, and pious people, these elders of the church, these chaste dames and dewy virgins, there were men of dissolute lives and women of spotted fame, wretches given over to all mean and filthy vice, and suspected even of horrid crimes. It was strange to see that the good shrank not from the wicked, nor were the sinners abashed by the saints. Scattered also among their palefaced enemies were the Indian priests, or powwows, who had often scared their native forest with more hideous incantations than any known to English witchcraft.

"But where is Faith?" thought Goodman Brown; and, as hope came into his heart, he trembled.

Another verse of the hymn arose, a slow and mournful strain, such as the pious love, but joined to words which expressed all that our nature can conceive of sin, and darkly hinted at far more. Unfathomable to mere mortals is the lore of fiends. Verse after verse was sung; and still the chorus of the desert swelled between like the deepest tone of a mighty organ; and with the final peal of that dreadful anthem there came a sound, as if the roaring wind, the rushing streams, the howling beasts, and every other voice of the unconcerted wilderness were mingling and according with the voice of guilty man in homage to the prince of all. The four blazing pines threw up a loftier flame, and obscurely discovered shapes and visages of horror on the smoke wreaths above the impious assembly. At the same moment the fire on the rock shot redly forth and formed a glowing arch above its base, where now appeared a figure. With reverence be it spoken, the figure bore no slight similitude, both in garb and manner, to some grave divine of the New England churches.

"Bring forth the converts!" cried a voice that echoed through the field and rolled into the forest.

At the word, Goodman Brown stepped forth from the shadow of the trees and approached the congregation, with whom he felt a loathful brotherhood by the sympathy of all that was wicked in his heart. He could have well-nigh sworn that the shape of his own dead father beckoned him to advance, looking downward from a smoke wreath, while a woman, with dim features of despair, threw out her hand to warn him back. Was it his mother? But he had no power to retreat one step, nor to resist, even in thought, when the minister and good old Deacon Gookin seized his arms and led him to the blazing rock. Thither came also the slender form of a veiled female, led between Goody Cloyse, that pious teacher of the catechism, and Martha Carrier, who had received the devil's promise to be queen of hell. A rampant hag was she. And there stood the proselytes beneath the canopy of fire.

"Welcome, my children," said the dark figure, "to the communion of your race. Ye have found thus young your nature and your destiny. My children, look behind you!"

They turned; and flashing forth, as it were, in a sheet of flame, the fiend worshippers were seen; the smile of welcome gleamed darkly on every visage.

"There," resumed the sable form, "are all whom ye have reverenced from youth. Ye deemed them holier than yourselves, and shrank from your own sin, contrasting it with their lives of righteousness and prayerful aspirations heavenward. Yet here are they all in my worshipping assembly. This night it shall be granted you to know their secret deeds: how hoary-bearded elders of the church have whispered wanton words to the young maids of their households; how many a woman, eager for widow's weeds, has given her husband a drink at bedtime and let him sleep his last sleep in her bosom; how beardless youths have made haste to inherit their fathers' wealth; and how fair damsels — blush not, sweet ones — have dug little graves in the garden, and bidden me, the sole guest, to an infant's funeral. By the sympathy of your human hearts for sin ye shall scent out all the places — whether in church, bed-chamber, street, field, or forest — where crime has been committed, and shall exult to behold the whole earth one stain of guilt, one mighty bloody spot. Far more than this. It shall be yours to penetrate, in every bosom, the deep mystery of sin, the fountain of all wicked arts, and which inexhaustibly supplies more evil impulses than human power — than my power at its utmost — can make manifest in deeds. And now, my children, look upon each other."

They did so; and, by the blaze of the hell-kindled torches, the wretched man beheld his Faith, and the wife her husband, trembling before that unhallowed altar.

"Lo, there ye stand, my children," said the figure, in a deep and solemn tone, almost sad with its despairing awfulness, as if his once angelic nature could yet mourn for our miserable race. "Depending upon one another's hearts, ye had still hoped that virtue were not all a dream. Now are ye undeceived. Evil is the nature of mankind. Evil must be your only happiness. Welcome again, my children to the communion of your race."

"Welcome," repeated the fiend worshippers, in one cry of despair and triumph.

And there they stood, the only pair, as it seemed, who were yet hesitating on the verge of wickedness in this dark world. A basin was hollowed, naturally, in the rock. Did it contain water, reddened by the lurid light? or was it blood? or, perchance, a liquid flame? Herein did the shape of evil dip his hand and prepare to lay the mark of baptism upon their foreheads, that they might be partakers of the mystery of sin, more conscious of the secret guilt of others, both in deed and thought, than they could now be of their own. The husband cast one look at his pale wife, and Faith at him. What polluted wretches would the next glance show them to each other, shuddering alike at what they disclosed and what they saw!

"Faith! Faith!" cried the husband, "look up to heaven, and resist the wicked one."

Whether Faith obeyed he knew not. Hardly had he spoken when he found himself amid calm night and solitude, listening to a roar of the wind which died heavily away through the forest. He staggered against the rock, and felt it chill and damp; while a hanging twig, that had been all on fire, besprinkled his cheek with the coldest dew.

The next morning young Goodman Brown came slowly into the street of Salem village, staring around him like a bewildered man. The good old minister was taking a walk along the graveyard to get an appetite for breakfast and meditate his sermon, and bestowed a blessing, as he passed, on Goodman Brown. He shrank from the venerable saint as if to avoid an anathema. Old Deacon Gookin was at domestic worship, and the holy words of his prayer were heard through the open window. "What God doth the wizard pray to?" quoth Goodman Brown. Goody Cloyse, that excellent old Christian, stood in the early sunshine at her own lattice, catechizing a little girl who had brought her a pint of morning's milk. Goodman Brown snatched away the child as from the grasp of the fiend himself. Turning the corner by the meeting-house, he spied the head of Faith, with the pink ribbons, gazing anxiously forth, and bursting into such joy at sight of him that she skipped along the street and almost kissed her husband before the whole village. But Goodman Brown looked sternly and sadly into her face, and passed on without a greeting.

Had Goodman Brown fallen asleep in the forest and only dreamed a wild dream of a witch-meeting?

Be it so if you will; but, alas! it was a dream of evil omen for young Goodman Brown. A stern, a sad, a darkly meditative, a distrustful, if not a desperate man did he become from the

night of that fearful dream. On the Sabbath day, when the congregation were singing a holy psalm, he could not listen because an anthem of sin rushed loudly upon his ear and drowned all the blessed strain. When the minister spoke from the pulpit with power and fervid eloquence, and, with his hand on the open Bible, of the sacred truths of our religion, and of saint-like lives and triumphant deaths, and of future bliss or misery unutterable, then did Goodman Brown turn pale, dreading lest the roof should thunder down upon the gray blasphemer and his hearers. Often, waking suddenly at midnight, he shrank from the bosom of Faith; and at morning or eventide, when the family knelt down at prayer, he scowled and muttered to himself, and gazed sternly at his wife, and turned away. And when he had lived long, and was borne to his grave a hoary corpse, followed by Faith, an aged woman, and children and grandchildren, a goodly procession, besides neighbors not a few, they carved no hopeful verse upon his tombstone, for his dying hour was gloom.

The Artist of the Beautiful

(1844)

🦋 In this story Hawthorne dealt with the common romantic theme of the sensitive, idealistic artist in a practical and materialistic society. Note how Hawthorne works out the contrast through characters that embody it and through incidents that give it dramatic poignancy.

In European life and literature many romantic poets and artists, feeling misunderstood and isolated like Hawthorne's hero, contemplated or committed self-destruction. But Owen Warland, possessing "force of character" along with "delicacy," learns to recognize that "the reward of all high performance must be sought within itself." Self-reliant, "he must stand up against mankind and be his own sole disciple, both as respects his genius and the objects to which it is directed." What is truly valuable to an artist is not a material symbol but his inner vision of beauty.

An elderly man, with his pretty daughter on his arm, was passing along the street, and emerged from the gloom of the cloudy evening into the light that fell across the pavement from the window of a small shop. It was a projecting window; and on the inside were suspended a variety of watches, pinchbeck, silver, and one or two of gold, all with their faces turned from the streets, as if churlishly disinclined to inform the wayfarers what o'clock it was. Seated within the shop, sidelong to the window, with his pale face bent earnestly over some delicate piece of mechanism on which was thrown the concentrated lustre of a shade lamp, appeared a young man.

"What can Owen Warland be about?" muttered old Peter Hovenden, himself a retired watchmaker, and the former master of this same young man whose occupation he was now wondering at. "What can the fellow be about? These six months past I have never come by his shop without seeing him just as steadily at work as now. It would be a flight beyond his usual foolery to seek for the perpetual motion; and yet I know enough of my old business to be certain that what he is now so busy with is no part of the machinery of a watch."

"Perhaps, father," said Annie, without showing much interest in the question, "Owen is inventing a new kind of timekeeper. I am sure he has ingenuity enough."

"Poh, child! He has not the sort of ingenuity to invent anything better than a Dutch toy," answered her father, who had formerly been put to much vexation by Owen Warland's irregular genius. "A plague on such ingenuity! All the effect that ever I knew of it was to spoil the accuracy of some of the best watches in my shop. He would turn the sun out of its orbit and derange the whole course of time, if, as I said before, his ingenuity could grasp anything bigger than a child's toy!"

"Hush, father! He hears you!" whispered Annie, pressing the old man's arm. "His ears are as delicate as his feelings; and you know how easily disturbed they are. Do let us move on."

So Peter Hovenden and his daughter Annie plodded on without further conversation, until in a by-street of the town they found themselves passing the open door of a blacksmith's shop. Within was seen the forge, now blazing up and illuminating the high and dusky roof, and now confining its lustre to a narrow precinct of the coal-strewn floor, according as the breath of the bellows was puffed forth or again inhaled into its vast leathern lungs. In the intervals of brightness it was easy to distinguish objects in remote corners of the shop and the horseshoe that hung upon the wall; in the momentary gloom the fire seemed to be glimmering amidst the vagueness of uninclosed space. Moving about in this red glare and alternate dusk was the figure of the blacksmith, well worthy to be viewed in so picturesque an aspect of light and shade, where

the bright blaze struggled with the black night, as if each would have snatched his comely strength from the other. Anon he drew a white hot bar of iron from the coals, laid it on the anvil, uplifted his arm of might, and was soon enveloped in the myriads of sparks which the strokes of his hammer scattered into the surrounding gloom.

"Now, that is a pleasant sight," said the old watch-maker. "I know what it is to work in gold; but give me the worker in iron after all is said and done. He spends his labor upon a reality. What say you, daughter Annie?"

"Pray don't speak so loud, father," whispered Annie, "Robert Danforth will hear you."

"And what if he should hear me?" said Peter Hovenden. "I say again, it is a good and a wholesome thing to depend upon main strength and reality, and to earn one's bread with the bare and brawny arm of a blacksmith. A watchmaker gets his brain puzzled by his wheels within a wheel, or loses his health or the nicety of his eyesight, as was my case, and finds himself at middle age, or a little after, past labor at his own trade and fit for nothing else, yet too poor to live at his ease. So I say once again, give me main strength for my money. And then, how it takes the nonsense out of a man! Did you ever hear of a blacksmith being such a fool as Owen Warland yonder?"

"Well said, uncle Hovenden!" shouted Robert Danforth from the forge, in a full, deep, merry voice, that made the roof re-echo. "And what says Miss Annie to that doctrine? She, I suppose, will think it a genteeler business to tinker up a lady's watch than to forge a horseshoe or make a gridiron."

Annie drew her father onward without giving him time for reply.

But we must return to Owen Warland's shop, and spend more meditation upon his history and character than either Peter Hovenden, or probably his daughter Annie, or Owen's old schoolfellow, Robert Danforth, would have thought due to so slight a subject. From the time that his little fingers could grasp a penknife, Owen had been remarkable for a delicate ingenuity, which sometimes produced pretty shapes in wood, principally figures of flowers and birds, and sometimes seemed to aim at the hidden mysteries of mechanism. But it was always for purposes of grace, and never with any mockery of the useful. He did not, like the crowd of school-boy artisans, construct little windmills on the angle of a barn or watermills across the neighboring brook. Those who discovered such peculiarity in the boy as to think it worth their while to observe him closely, sometimes saw reason to suppose that he was attempting to imitate the beautiful movements of Nature as exemplified in the flight of birds or the activity of little animals. It seemed, in fact, a new development of the love of the beautiful, such as might have made him a poet, a painter, or a sculptor, and which was as completely refined from all utilitarian coarseness as it could have been in either of the fine arts. He looked with singular distaste at the stiff and regular processes of ordinary machinery. Being once carried to see a steam-engine, in the expectation that his intuitive comprehension of mechanical principles would be gratified, he turned pale and grew sick, as if something monstrous and unnatural had been presented to him. This horror was partly owing to the size and terrible energy of the iron laborer; for the character of Owen's mind was microscopic, and tended naturally to the minute, in accordance with his diminutive frame and the marvellous smallness and delicate power of his fingers. Not that his sense of beauty was thereby diminished into a sense of prettiness. The beautiful idea has no relation to size, and may be as perfectly developed in a space too minute for any but microscopic investigation as within the ample verge that is measured by the arc of the rainbow. But, at all events, this characteristic minuteness in his objects and accomplishments made the world even more incapable than it might otherwise have been of appreciating Owen Warland's genius. The boy's relatives saw nothing better to be done — as perhaps there was not — than to bind him apprentice to a watchmaker, hoping that his strange ingenuity might thus be regulated and put to utilitarian purposes.

Peter Hovenden's opinion of his apprentice has already been expressed. He could make nothing of the lad. Owen's apprehension of the professional mysteries, it is true, were inconceivably quick; but he altogether forgot or despised the grand object of a watchmaker's business, and cared no more for the measurement of time than if it had been merged into eternity. So long, however, as he remained under his old master's care, Owen's lack of sturdiness made it possible, by strict injunctions and sharp oversight, to restrain his creative eccentricity within bounds; but when his apprenticeship was served out, and he had taken the little shop which Peter Hovenden's failing eyesight compelled him to relinquish, then did people recognize how unfit a person was Owen Warland to lead old blind Father Time along his daily course. One of his most rational projects was to connect a musical operation with the machinery of his watches, so that all the harsh dissonances of life might be rendered tuneful, and each flitting moment fall into the abyss of the past in golden drops of harmony. If a family clock was intrusted to him for repair, — one of those tall, ancient clocks that have grown nearly allied to human nature by measuring out the lifetime of many generations, — he would take upon himself to arrange a dance or funeral procession of figures across its venerable face, representing twelve mirthful or melancholy hours. Several freaks of this kind quite destroyed the young watchmaker's credit with that steady and matter-of-fact class of people who hold the opinion that time is not to be trifled with, whether considered as the medium of advancement and prosperity in this world or preparation for the next. His custom rapidly diminished — a misfortune, however, that was probably reckoned among his better accidents by Owen Warland, who was becoming more and more absorbed in a secret occupation which drew all his science and manual dexterity into himself, and likewise gave full employment to the characteristic tendencies of his genius. This pursuit had already consumed many months.

After the old watchmaker and his pretty daughter had gazed at him out of the obscurity of the street, Owen Warland was seized with a fluttering of the nerves, which made his hand tremble too violently to proceed with such delicate labor as he was now engaged upon.

"It was Annie herself!" murmured he. "I should have known it, by this throbbing of my heart, before I heard her father's voice. Ah, how it throbs! I shall scarcely be able to work again on this exquisite mechanism to-night. Annie! dearest Annie! thou shouldst give firmness to my heart and hand, and not shake them thus; for if I strive to put the very spirit of beauty into form and give it motion, it is for thy sake alone. O throbbing heart, be quiet! If my labor be thus thwarted, there will come vague and unsatisfied dreams which will leave me spiritless to-morrow."

As he was endeavoring to settle himself again to his task, the shop door opened and gave admittance to no other than the stalwart figure which Peter Hovenden had paused to admire, as seen amid the light and shadow of the blacksmith's shop. Robert Danforth had brought a little anvil of his own manufacture, and peculiarly constructed, which the young artist had recently bespoken. Owen examined the article and pronounced it fashioned according to his wish.

"Why, yes," said Robert Danforth, his strong voice filling the shop as with the sound of a bass viol, "I consider myself equal to anything in the way of my own trade; though I should have made but a poor figure at yours with such a fist as this," added he, laughing, as he laid his vast hand beside the delicate one of Owen. "But what then? I put more main strength into one blow of my sledge hammer than all that you have expended since you were a 'prentice. Is not that the truth?"

"Very probably," answered the low and slender voice of Owen. "Strength is an earthly monster. I make no pretensions to it. My force, whatever there may be of it, is altogether spiritual."

"Well, but, Owen, what are you about?" asked his old school-fellow, still in such a hearty volume of tone that it made the artist shrink, especially as the question related to a subject so sacred as the absorbing dream of his imagination. "Folks do say that you are trying to discover the perpetual motion."

"The perpetual motion? Nonsense!" replied Owen Warland, with a movement of disgust; for he was full of little petulances. "It can never be discovered. It is a dream that may delude men whose brains are mystified with matter, but not me. Besides, if such a discovery were possible, it would not be worth my while to make it only to have the secret turned to such purposes as are now effected by steam and water power. I am not ambitious to be honored with the paternity of a new kind of cotton machine."

"That would be droll enough!" cried the blacksmith, breaking out into such an uproar of laughter that Owen himself and the bell glasses on his work-board quivered in unison. "No, no, Owen! No child of yours will have iron joints and sinews. Well, I won't hinder you any more. Good night, Owen, and success, and if you need any assistance, so far as a downright blow of hammer upon anvil will answer the purpose, I'm your man."

And with another laugh the man of main strength left the shop.

"How strange it is," whispered Owen Warland to himself, leaning his head upon his hand, "that all my musings, my purposes, my passion for the beautiful, my consciousness of power to create it, — a finer, more ethereal power, of which this earthly giant can have no conception, — all, all, look so vain and idle whenever my path is crossed by Robert Danforth! He would drive me mad were I to meet him often. His hard, brute force darkens and confuses the spiritual element within me; but I, too, will be strong in my own way. I will not yield to him."

He took from beneath a glass a piece of minute machinery, which he set in the condensed light of his lamp, and, looking intently at it through a magnifying glass, proceeded to operate with a delicate instrument of steel. In an instant, however, he fell back in his chair and clasped his hands, with a look of horror on his face that made its small features as impressive as those of a giant would have been.

"Heaven! What have I done?" exclaimed he. "The vapor, the influence of that brute force, — it has bewildered me and obscured my perception. I have made the very stroke — the fatal stroke — that I have dreaded from the first. It is all over — the toil of months, the object of my life. I am ruined!"

And there he sat, in strange despair, until his lamp flickered in the socket and left the Artist of the Beautiful in darkness.

Thus it is that ideas, which grow up within the imagination and appear so lovely to it and of a value beyond whatever men call valuable, are exposed to be shattered and annihilated by contact with the practical. It is requisite for the ideal artist to possess a force of character that seems hardly compatible with its delicacy; he must keep his faith in himself while the incredulous world assails him with its utter disbelief; he must stand up against mankind and be his own sole disciple, both as respects his genius and the objects to which it is directed.

For a time Owen Warland succumbed to this severe but inevitable test. He spent a few sluggish weeks with his head so continually resting in his hands that the towns-people had scarcely an opportunity to see his countenance. When at last it was again uplifted to the light of day, a cold, dull, nameless change was perceptible upon it. In the opinion of Peter Hovenden, however, and that order of sagacious understandings who think that life should be regulated, like clockwork, with leaden weights, the alteration was entirely for the better. Owen now, indeed, applied himself to business with dogged industry. It was marvellous to witness the obtuse gravity with which he would inspect the wheels of a great old silver watch; thereby delighting the owner, in whose fob it had been worn till he deemed it a portion of his own life, and was accordingly jealous of its treatment. In consequence of the good report thus acquired, Owen Warland was invited by the proper authorities to regulate the clock in the church steeple. He succeeded so admirably in this matter of public interest that the merchants gruffly acknowledged his merits on 'Change; the nurse whispered his praises as she gave the potion in the sick-chamber; the lover blessed him at the hour of appointed interview; and the town in general thanked Owen for the punctuality of dinner time. In a word, the heavy weight upon his spirits kept everything in order, not merely within his own system, but wheresoever the iron accents of the church clock were audible. It was a circumstance, though minute, yet characteristic of his present state, that, when employed to engrave names or initials on silver spoons, he now wrote the requisite letters in the plainest possible style, omitting a variety of fanciful flourishes that had heretofore distinguished his work in this kind.

One day, during the era of this happy transformation, old Peter Hovenden came to visit his former apprentice.

"Well, Owen," said he, "I am glad to hear such good accounts of you from all quarters, and especially from the town clock yonder, which speaks in your commendation every hour of the twenty-four. Only get rid altogether of your nonsensical trash about the beautiful, which I nor nobody else, nor yourself to boot, could ever understand, — only free yourself of that, and your success in life is as sure as daylight. Why, if you go on in this way, I should even venture to let you doctor this precious old watch of mine, though, except my daughter Annie, I have nothing else so valuable in the world."

"I should hardly dare touch it, sir," replied Owen, in a depressed tone; for he was weighed down by his old master's presence.

"In time," said the latter, — "in time, you will be capable of it."

The old watchmaker, with the freedom naturally consequent on his former authority, went on inspecting the work which Owen had in hand at the moment, together with other matters that were in progress. The artist, meanwhile, could scarcely lift his head. There was nothing so antipodal to his nature as this man's cold, unimaginative sagacity, by contact with which everything was converted into a dream except the densest matter of the physical world. Owen groaned in spirit and prayed fervently to be delivered from him.

"But what is this?" cried Peter Hovenden abruptly, taking up a dusty bell glass, beneath which appeared a mechanical something, as delicate and minute as the system of a butterfly's anatomy. "What have we here? Owen! Owen! there is witchcraft in these little chains, and wheels, and paddles. See! with one pinch of my finger and thumb I am going to deliver you from all future peril."

"For Heaven's sake," screamed Owen Warland, springing up with wonderful energy, "as you would not drive me mad, do not touch it! The slightest pressure of your finger would ruin me forever."

"Aha, young man! And is it so?" said the old watchmaker, looking at him with just enough of penetration to torture Owen's soul with the bitterness of worldly criticism. "Well, take your own course, but I warn you again that in this small piece of mechanism lives your evil spirit. Shall I exorcise him?"

"You are my evil spirit," answered Owen, much excited, — "you and the hard, coarse world! The leaden thoughts and the despondency that you fling upon me are my clogs, else I should long ago have achieved the task that I was created for."

Peter Hovenden shook his head, with the mixture of contempt and indignation which mankind, of whom he was partly a representative, deem themselves entitled to feel towards all simpletons who seek other prizes than the dusty one along the highway. He then took his leave, with an uplifted finger and a sneer upon his face that haunted the artist's dreams for many a night afterwards. At the time of his old master's visit, Owen was probably on the point of taking up the relinquished task; but, by this sinister event, he was thrown back into the state whence he had been slowly emerging.

But the innate tendency of his soul had only been accumulating fresh vigor during its apparent sluggishness. As the summer advanced he almost totally relinquished his business, and permitted Father Time, so far as the old gentleman was represented by the clocks and watches under his control, to stray at random through human life, making infinite confusion among the train of bewildered hours. He wasted the sunshine, as people said, in wandering through the woods and fields and along the banks of streams. There, like a child, he found amusement in chasing butterflies or watching the motions of water insects. There was something truly mysterious in the intentness with which he contemplated these living playthings as they sported on the breeze or examined the structure of an imperial insect whom he had imprisoned. The chase of butterflies was an apt emblem of the ideal pursuit in which he had spent so many golden hours; but would the beautiful idea ever be yielded to his hand like the butterfly that symbolized it? Sweet, doubtless, were these days, and congenial to the artist's soul. They were full of bright conceptions, which gleamed through his intellectual world as the butterflies gleamed through the outward atmosphere, and were real to him, for the instant, without the toil, and perplexity, and many disappointments of attempting to make them visible to the sensual eye. Alas that the artist, whether in poetry, or whatever other material, may not content himself with the inward enjoyment of the beautiful, but must chase the flitting mystery beyond the verge of his ethereal domain, and crush its frail being in seizing it with material grasp. Owen Warland felt the impulse to give external reality to his ideas as irresistibly as any of the poets or painters who have arrayed the world in a dimmer and fainter beauty, imperfectly copied from the richness of their visions.

The night was now his time for the slow progress of re-creating the one idea to which all his intellectual activity referred itself. Always at the approach of dusk he stole into the town, locked himself within his shop, and wrought with patient delicacy of touch for many hours. Sometimes he was startled by the rap of the watchman, who, when all the world should be asleep, had caught the gleam of lamplight through the crevices of Owen Warland's shutters. Daylight, to the morbid sensibility of his mind, seemed to have an intrusiveness that interfered with his pursuits. On cloudy and inclement days, therefore, he sat with his head upon his hands, muffling, as it were, his sensitive brain in a mist of indefinite musings; for it was a relief to escape from the sharp distinctness with which he was compelled to shape out his thoughts during his nightly toil.

From one of these fits of torpor he was aroused by the entrance of Annie Hovenden, who came into the shop with the freedom of a customer, and also with something of the familiarity of a childish friend. She had worn a hole through her silver thimble, and wanted Owen to repair it.

"But I don't know whether you will condescend to such a task," said she, laughing, "now that you are so taken up with the notion of putting spirit into machinery."

"Where did you get that idea, Annie?" said Owen, starting in surprise.

"Oh, out of my own head," answered she, "and from something that I heard you say, long ago, when you were but a boy and I a little child. But come; will you mend this poor thimble of mine?"

"Anything for your sake, Annie," said Owen Warland, — "anything, even were it to work at Robert Danforth's forge."

"And that would be a pretty sight!" retorted Annie, glancing with imperceptible slightness at the artist's small and slender frame. "Well, here is the thimble."

"But that is a strange idea of yours," said Owen, "about the spiritualization of matter."

And then the thought stole into his mind that this young girl possessed the gift to comprehend him better than all the world besides. And what a help and strength would it be to him in his lonely toil if he could gain the sympathy of the only being whom he loved! To persons whose pursuits are insulated from the common business of life — who are either in advance of mankind or apart from it — there often comes a sensation of moral cold that makes the spirit shiver as if it had reached the frozen solitudes around the pole. What the prophet, the poet, the reformer, the criminal, or any other man with human yearnings, but separated from the multitude by a peculiar lot, might feel, poor Owen felt.

"Annie," cried he, growing pale as death at the thought, "how gladly would I tell you the secret of my pursuit! You, methinks, would estimate it rightly. You, I know, would hear it with a reverence that I must not expect from the harsh material world."

"Would I not? to be sure I would!" replied Annie Hovenden, lightly laughing. "Come; explain to me quickly what is the meaning of this little whirligig, so delicately wrought that it might be a plaything for Queen Mab. See! I will put it in motion."

"Hold!" exclaimed Owen, "hold!"

Annie had but given the slightest possible touch, with the point of a needle, to the same minute portion of complicated machinery which has been more than once mentioned, when the artist seized her by the wrist with a force that made her scream aloud. She was affrighted at the convulsion of intense rage and anguish that writhed across his features. The next instant he let his head sink upon his hands.

"Go, Annie," murmured he; "I have deceived myself, and must suffer for it. I yearned for sympathy and thought, and fancied, and dreamed that you might give it me; but you lack the talisman, Annie, that should admit you into my secrets. That touch has undone the toils of months and the thought of a lifetime! It was not your fault, Annie; but you have ruined me!"

Poor Owen Warland! He had indeed erred, yet pardonably; for if any human spirit could have sufficiently reverenced the process so sacred in his eyes, it must have been a woman's. Even Annie Hovenden, possibly, might not have disappointed him had she been enlightened by the deep intelligence of love.

The artist spent the ensuing winter in a way that satisfied any persons who had hitherto retained a hopeful opinion of him that he was, in truth, irrevocably doomed to inutility as regarded the world, and to an evil destiny on his own part. The decease of a relative had put him in possession of a small inheritance. Thus freed from the necessity of toil, and having lost the steadfast influence of a great purpose, — great, at least, to him, — he abandoned himself to habits from which it might have been supposed the mere delicacy of his organization would have availed to secure him. But when the ethereal portion of a man of genius is obscured, the earthly part assumes an influence the more uncontrollable, because the character is now thrown off the balance to which Providence had so nicely adjusted it, and which, in coarser natures, is adjusted by some other method. Owen Warland made proof of whatever show of bliss may be found in riot. He looked at the world through the golden medium of wine, and contemplated the visions that bubble up so gaily around the brim of the glass,

and that people the air with shapes of pleasant madness, which so soon grow ghostly and forlorn. Even when this dismal and inevitable change had taken place, the young man might still have continued to quaff the cup of enchantments, though its vapor did but shroud life in gloom and fill the gloom with spectres that mocked at him. There was a certain irksomeness of spirit, which, being real, and the deepest sensation of which the artist was now conscious, was more intolerable than any fantastic miseries and horrors that the abuse of wine could summon up. In the latter case he could remember, even out of the midst of his trouble, that all was but a delusion; in the former, the heavy anguish was his actual life.

From this perilous state he was redeemed by an incident which more than one person witnessed, but of which the shrewdest could not explain or conjecture the operation on Owen Warland's mind. It was very simple. On a warm afternoon of spring, as the artist sat among his riotous companions with a glass of wine before him, a splendid butterfly flew in at the open window and fluttered about his head.

"Ah," exclaimed Owen, who had drank freely, "are you alive again, child of the sun and playmate of the summer breeze, after your dismal winter's nap? Then it is time for me to be at work!"

And, leaving his unempted glass upon the table, he departed and was never known to sip another drop of wine.

And now, again, he resumed his wanderings in the woods and fields. It might be fancied that the bright butterfly, which had come so spirit-like into the window as Owen sat with the rude revellers, was indeed a spirit commissioned to recall him to the pure, ideal life that had so etherealized him among men. It might be fancied that he went forth to seek this spirit in its sunny haunts; for still, as in the summer time gone by, he was seen to steal gently up wherever a butterfly had alighted, and lose himself in contemplation of it. When it took flight his eyes followed the winged vision, as if its airy track would show the path to heaven. But what could be the purpose of the unseasonable toil, which was again resumed, as the watchman knew by the lines of lamplight through the crevices of Owen Warland's shutters? The towns-people had one comprehensive explanation of all these singularities. Owen Warland had gone mad! How universally efficacious — how satisfactory, too, and soothing to the injured sensibility of narrowness and dulness — is this easy method of accounting for whatever lies beyond the world's most ordinary scope! From St. Paul's days down to our poor little Artist of the Beautiful, the same talisman had been applied to the elucidation of all mysteries in the words or deeds of men who spoke or acted too wisely or too well. In Owen Warland's case the judgment of his towns-people may have been correct. Perhaps he was mad. The lack of sympathy — that contrast between himself and his neighbors which took away the restraint of example — was enough to make him so. Or possibly he had caught just so much of the ethereal radiance as served to bewilder him, in an earthly sense, by its inter-mixture with the common daylight.

One evening, when the artist had returned from a customary ramble and had just thrown the lustre of his lamp on the delicate piece of work so often interrupted, but still taken up again, as if his fate were embodied in its mechanism, he was surprised by the entrance of old Peter Hovenden. Owen never met this man without a shrinking of the heart. Of all the world he was most terrible, by reason of a keen understanding which saw so distinctly what it did see, and disbelieved so uncompromisingly in what it could not see. On this occasion the old watchmaker had merely a gracious word or two to say.

"Owen, my lad," said he, "we must see you at my house to-morrow night."

The artist began to mutter some excuse.

"Oh, but it must be so," quoth Peter Hovenden, "for the sake of the days when you were one of the household. What, my boy! don't you know that my daughter Annie is engaged to Robert Danforth? We are making an entertainment, in our humble way, to celebrate the event."

"Ah!" said Owen.

That little monosyllable was all he uttered; its tone seemed cold and unconcerned to an ear like Peter Hovenden's; and yet there was in it the stifled outcry of the poor artist's heart, which he compressed within him like a man holding down an evil spirit. One slight outbreak, however, imperceptible to the old watchmaker, he allowed himself. Raising the instrument with which he was about to begin his work, he let it fall upon the little system of machinery that

had, anew, cost him months of thought and toil. It was shattered by the stroke!

Owen Warland's story would have been no tolerable representation of the troubled life of those who strive to create the beautiful, if, amid all other thwarting influences, love had not interposed to steal the cunning from his hand. Outwardly he had been no ardent or enterprising lover; the career of his passion had confined its tumults and vicissitudes so entirely within the artist's imagination that Annie herself had scarcely more than a woman's intuitive perception of it; but, in Owen's view, it covered the whole field of his life. Forgetful of the time when she had shown herself incapable of any deep response, he had persisted in connecting all his dreams of artistical success with Annie's image; she was the visible shape in which the spiritual power that he worshipped, and on whose altar he hoped to lay a not unworthy offering, was made manifest to him. Of course he had deceived himself; there were no such attributes in Annie Hovenden as his imagination had endowed her with. She, in the aspect which she wore to his inward vision, was as much a creature of his own as the mysterious piece of mechanism would be were it ever realized. Had he become convinced of his mistake through the medium of successful love, — had he won Annie to his bosom, and there beheld her fade from angel into ordinary woman, — the disappointment might have driven him back, with concentrated energy, upon his sole remaining object. On the other hand, had he found Annie what he fancied, his lot would have been so rich in beauty that out of its mere redundancy he might have wrought the beautiful into many a worthier type than he had toiled for; but the guise in which his sorrow came to him, the sense that the angel of his life had been snatched away and given to a rude man of earth and iron, who could neither need nor appreciate her ministrations, — this was the very perversity of fate that makes human existence appear too absurd and contradictory to be the scene of one other hope or one other fear. There was nothing left for Owen Warland but to sit down like a man that had been stunned.

He went through a fit of illness. After his recovery his small slender frame assumed an obtuser garniture of flesh than it had ever before worn. His thin cheeks became round; his delicate little hand, so spiritually fashioned to achieve fairy task-work, grew plumper than the hand of a thriving infant. His aspect had a childishness, such as might have induced a stranger to pat him on the head — pausing, however, in the act, to wonder what manner of child was here. It was as if the spirit had gone out of him, leaving the body to flourish in a sort of vegetable existence. Not that Owen Warland was idiotic. He could talk, and not irrationally. Somewhat of a babbler, indeed, did people begin to think him; for he was apt to discourse at wearisome length of marvels of mechanism that he had read about in books, but which he had learned to consider as absolutely fabulous. Among them he enumerated the Man of Brass, constructed by Albertus Magnus, and the Brazen Head of Friar Bacon; and, coming down to later times, the automata of a little coach and horses, which it was pretended had been manufactured for the Dauphin of France; together with an insect that buzzed about the ear like a living fly, and yet was but a contrivance of minute steel springs. There was a story, too, of a duck that waddled, and quacked, and ate; though, had any honest citizen purchased it for dinner, he would have found himself cheated with the mere mechanical apparition of a duck.

"But all these accounts," said Owen Warland, "I am now satisfied are mere impositions."

Then, in a mysterious way, he would confess that he once thought differently. In his idle and dreamy days he had considered it possible, in a certain sense, to spiritualize machinery, and to combine with the new species of life and motion thus produced a beauty that should attain to the ideal which Nature has proposed to herself in all her creatures, but has never taken pains to realize. He seemed, however, to retain no very distinct perception either of the process of achieving this object or of the design itself.

"I have thrown it all aside now," he would say. "It was a dream such as young men are always mystifying themselves with. Now that I have acquired a little common sense, it makes me laugh to think of it."

Poor, poor and fallen Owen Warland! These were the symptoms that he had ceased to be an inhabitant of the better sphere that lies unseen around us. He had lost his faith in the invisible, and now prided himself, as such unfortunates invariably do, in the wisdom which rejected much that even his eye could see, and trusted confidently in nothing but what his hand could touch. This is the calamity of men whose spiritual part dies out of them and leaves the grosser understanding to assimilate them more and more to the things of which alone it can take cognizance; but in Owen Warland the spirit was not dead nor passed away; it only slept.

How it awoke again is not recorded. Perhaps the torpid slumber was broken by a convulsive pain. Perhaps, as in a former instance, the butterfly came and hovered about his head and reinspired him, — as indeed this creature of the sunshine had always a mysterious mission for the artist, — reinspired him with the former purpose of his life. Whether it were pain or happiness that thrilled through his veins, his first impulse was to thank Heaven for rendering him again the being of thought, imagination, and keenest sensibility that he had long ceased to be.

"Now for my task," said he. "Never did I feel such strength for it as now."

Yet, strong as he felt himself, he was incited to toil the more diligently by an anxiety lest death should surprise him in the midst of his labors. This anxiety, perhaps, is common to all men who set their hearts upon anything so high, in their own view of it, that life becomes of importance only as conditional to its accomplishment. So long as we love life for itself, we seldom dread the losing it. When we desire life for the attainment of an object, we recognize the frailty of its texture. But, side by side with this sense of insecurity, there is a vital faith in our invulnerability to the shaft of death while engaged in any task that seems assigned by Providence as our proper thing to do, and which the world would have cause to mourn for should we leave it unaccomplished. Can the philosopher, big with the inspiration of an idea that is to reform mankind, believe that he is to be beckoned from this sensible existence at the very instant when he is mustering his breath to speak the word of light? Should he perish so, the weary ages may pass away — the world's, whose life sand may fall, drop by drop — before another intellect is prepared to develop the truth that might have been uttered then. But history affords many an example where the most precious spirit, at any particular epoch manifested in human shape, has gone hence untimely, without space allowed him, so far as mortal judgment could discern, to perform his mission on the earth. The prophet dies, and the man of torpid heart and sluggish brain lives on. The poet leaves his song half sung, or finishes it, beyond the scope of mortal ears, in a celestial choir. The painter — as Allston did — leaves half his conception on the canvas to sadden us with its imperfect beauty, and goes to picture forth the whole, if it be no irreverence to say so, in the hues of heaven. But rather such incomplete designs of this life will be perfected nowhere. This so frequent abortion of man's dearest projects must be taken as a proof that the deeds of earth, however etherealized by piety or genius, are without value, except as exercises and manifestations of the spirit. In heaven, all ordinary thought is higher and more melodious than Milton's song. Then, would he add another verse to any strain that he had left unfinished here?

But to return to Owen Warland. It was his fortune, good or ill, to achieve the purpose of his life. Pass we over a long space of intense thought, yearning effort, minute toil, and wasting anxiety, succeeded by an instant of solitary triumph: let all this be imagined; and then behold the artist, on a winter evening, seeking admittance to Robert Danforth's fireside circle. There he found the man of iron, with his massive substance thoroughly warmed and attempered by domestic influences. And there was Annie, too, now transformed into a matron, with much of her husband's plain and sturdy nature, but imbued, as Owen Warland still believed, with a finer grace, that might enable her to be the interpreter between strength and beauty. It happened, likewise, that old Peter Hovenden was a guest this evening at his daughter's fireside, and it was his well-remembered expression of keen, cold criticism that first encountered the artist's glance.

"My old friend Owen!" cried Robert Danforth, starting up, and compressing the artist's delicate fingers within a hand that was accustomed to gripe bars of iron. "This is kind and neighborly to come to us at last. I was afraid your perpetual motion had bewitched you out of the remembrance of old times."

"We are glad to see you," said Annie, while a blush reddened her matronly cheek. "It was not like a friend to stay from us so long."

"Well, Owen," inquired the old watchmaker, as his first greeting, "how comes on the beautiful? Have you created it at last?"

The artist did not immediately reply, being startled by the apparition of a young child of strength that was tumbling about on the carpet, — a little personage who had come mysteriously out of the infinite, but with something so sturdy and real in his composition that he seemed moulded out of the densest substance which earth could supply. This hopeful infant crawled towards the new-comer, and setting himself on end, as Robert Danforth expressed the posture, stared at Owen with a look of such sagacious observation that the mother could not help exchanging a proud glance with her husband. But the artist was disturbed by the child's look, as imagining a resemblance between it and Peter Hovenden's habitual expression. He could have fancied that the old watchmaker was compressed into this baby shape, and looking out of those baby eyes, and repeating, as he now did, the malicious question: —

"The beautiful, Owen! How comes on the beautiful? Have you succeeded in creating the beautiful?"

"I have succeeded," replied the artist, with a momentary light of triumph in his eyes and a smile of sunshine, yet steeped in such depth of thought that it was almost sadness. "Yes, my friends, it is the truth. I have succeeded."

"Indeed!" cried Annie, a look of maiden mirthfulness peeping out of her face again. "And is it lawful now, to inquire what the secret is?"

"Surely; it is to disclose it that I have come," answered Owen Warland. "You shall know, and see, and touch, and possess the secret! For, Annie, — if by that name I may still address the friend of my boyish years, — Annie, it is for your bridal gift that I have wrought this spiritualized mechanism, this harmony of motion, this mystery of beauty. It comes late, indeed; but it is as we go onward in life, when objects begin to lose their freshness of hue and our souls their delicacy of perception, that the spirit of beauty is most needed. If, — forgive me, Annie, — if you know how to value this gift, it can never come too late."

He produced, as he spoke, what seemed a jewel box. It was carved richly out of ebony by his own hand, and inlaid with a fanciful tracery of pearl, representing a boy in pursuit of a butterfly, which, elsewhere, had become a winged spirit, and was flying heavenward; while the boy, or youth, had found such efficacy in his strong desire that he ascended from earth to cloud, and from cloud to celestial atmosphere, to win the beautiful. This case of ebony the artist opened, and bade Annie place her finger on its edge. She did so, but almost screamed as a butterfly fluttered forth, and, alighting on her finger's tip, sat waving the ample magnificence of its purple and gold-speckled wings, as if in prelude to a flight. It is impossible to express by words the glory, the splendor, the delicate gorgeousness which were softened into the beauty of this object. Nature's ideal butterfly was here realized in all its perfection; not in the pattern of such faded insects as flit among earthly flowers, but of those which hover across the meads of paradise for child-angels and the spirits of departed infants to disport themselves with. The rich down was visible upon its wings; the lustre of its eyes seemed instinct with spirit. The firelight glimmered around this wonder — the candles gleamed upon it; but it glistened apparently by its own radiance, and illuminated the finger and outstretched hand on which it rested with a white gleam like that of precious stones. In its perfect beauty, the consideration of size was entirely lost. Had its wings overreached the firmament, the mind could not have been more filled or satisfied.

"Beautiful! beautiful!" exclaimed Annie. "Is it alive? Is it alive?"

"Alive? To be sure it is," answered her husband. "Do you suppose any mortal has skill enough to make a butterfly, or would put himself to the trouble of making one, when any child may catch a score of them in a summer's afternoon? Alive? Certainly! But this pretty box is undoubtedly of our friend Owen's manufacture; and really it does him credit."

At this moment the butterfly waved its wings anew, with a motion so absolutely lifelike that Annie was startled, and even awestricken; for, in spite of her husband's opinion, she could not satisfy herself whether it was indeed a living creature or a piece of wondrous mechanism.

"Is it alive?" she repeated, more earnestly than before.

"Judge for yourself," said Owen Warland, who stood gazing in her face with fixed attention.

The butterfly now flung itself upon the air, fluttered round Annie's head, and soared into a distant region of the parlor, still making itself perceptible to sight by the starry gleam in which the motion of its wings enveloped it. The infant on the floor followed its course with his sagacious little eyes. After flying about the room, it returned in a spiral curve and settled again on Annie's finger.

"But is it alive?" exclaimed she again; and the finger on which the gorgeous mystery had alighted was so tremulous that the butterfly was forced to balance himself with his wings. "Tell me if it be alive, or whether you created it."

"Wherefore ask who created it, so it be beautiful?" replied Owen Warland. "Alive? Yes, Annie; it may well be said to possess life, for it has absorbed my own being into itself; and in the secret of that butterfly, and in its beauty, — which is not merely outward, but deep as its whole system, — is represented the intellect, the imagination, the sensibility, the soul of an Artist of the Beautiful! Yes; I created it. But" — and here his countenance somewhat changed — "this butterfly is not now to me what it was when I beheld it afar off in the day-dreams of my youth."

"Be it what it may, it is a pretty plaything," said the blacksmith, grinning with childlike delight. "I wonder whether it would condescend to alight on such a great clumsy finger as mine? Hold it hither, Annie."

By the artist's direction, Annie touched her finger's tip to that of her husband; and, after a momentary delay, the butterfly fluttered from one to the other. It preluded a second flight by a similar, yet not precisely the same, waving of wings as in the first experiment; then, ascending from the blacksmith's stalwart finger, it rose in a gradually enlarging curve to the ceiling, made one wide sweep around the room, and returned with an undulating movement to the point whence it had started.

"Well, that does beat all nature!" cried Robert Danforth, bestowing the heartiest praise that he could find expression for; and, indeed, had he paused there, a man of finer words and nicer perception could not easily have said more. "That goes beyond me, I confess. But what then? There is more real use in one downright blow of my sledge hammer than in the whole five years' labor that our friend Owen has wasted on this butterfly."

Here the child clapped his hands and made a great babble of indistinct utterance, apparently demanding that the butterfly should be given him for a plaything.

Owen Warland, meanwhile, glanced sidelong at Annie, to discover whether she sympathized in her husband's estimate of the comparative value of the beautiful and the practical. There was, amid all her kindness towards himself, amid all the wonder and admiration with which she contemplated the marvelous work of his hands and incarnation of his idea, a secret scorn — too secret, perhaps, for her own consciousness, and perceptible only to such intuitive discernment as that of the artist. But Owen, in the latter stages of his pursuit, had risen out of the region in which such a discovery might have been torture. He knew that the world, and Annie as the representative of the world, whatever praise might be bestowed, could never say the fitting word nor feel the fitting sentiment which should be the perfect recompense of an artist who, symbolizing a lofty moral by a material trifle, — converting what was earthly to spiritual gold, — had won the beautiful into his handiwork. Not at this latest moment was he to learn that the reward of all high performance must be sought within itself, or sought in vain. There was, however, a view of the matter which Annie and her husband, and even Peter Hovenden, might fully have understood, and which would have satisfied them that the toil of years had here been worthily bestowed. Owen Warland might have told them that this butterfly, this plaything, this bridal gift of a poor watchmaker to a blacksmith's wife, was, in truth, a gem of art that a monarch would have purchased with honors and abundant wealth, and have treasured it among the jewels of his kingdom as the most unique and wondrous of them all. But the artist smiled and kept the secret to himself.

"Father," said Annie, thinking that a word of praise from the old watchmaker might gratify his former apprentice, "do come and admire this pretty butterfly."

"Let us see," said Peter Hovenden, rising from his chair, with a sneer upon his face that always made people doubt, as he himself did, in everything but a material existence. "Here is my finger for it to alight upon. I shall understand it better when once I have touched it."

But, to the increased astonishment of Annie, when the tip of her father's finger was pressed against that of her husband, on which the butterfly still rested, the insect drooped its wings and seemed on the point of falling to the floor. Even the bright spots of gold upon its wings and body, unless her eyes deceived her, grew dim, and the glowing purple took a dusky hue, and the starry lustre that gleamed around the blacksmith's hand became faint and vanished.

"It is dying! it is dying!" cried Annie, in alarm.

"It has been delicately wrought," said the artist, calmly. "As I told you, it has imbibed a spiritual essence—call it magnetism, or what you will. In an atmosphere of doubt and mockery its exquisite susceptibility suffers torture, as does the soul of him who instilled his own life into it. It has already lost its beauty; in a few moments more its mechanism would be irreparably injured."

"Take away your hand, father!" entreated Annie, turning pale. "Here is my child; let it rest on his innocent hand. There, perhaps, its life will revive and its colors grow brighter than ever."

Her father, with an acrid smile, withdrew his finger. The butterfly then appeared to recover the power of voluntary motion, while its hues assumed much of their original lustre, and the gleam of starlight, which was its most ethereal attribute, again formed a halo round about it. At first, when transferred from Robert Danforth's hand to the small finger of the child, this radiance grew so powerful that it positively threw the little fellow's shadow back against the wall. He, meanwhile, extended his plump hand as he had seen his father and mother do, and watched the waving of the insect's wings with infantine delight. Nevertheless, there was a certain odd expression of sagacity that made Owen Warland feel as if here were old Peter Hovenden, partially, and but partially, redeemed from his hard scepticism into childish faith.

"How wise the little monkey looks!" whispered Robert Danforth to his wife.

"I never saw such a look on a child's face," answered Annie, admiring her own infant, and with good reason, far more than the artistic butterfly. "The darling knows more of the mystery than we do."

As if the butterfly, like the artist, were conscious of something not entirely congenial in the child's nature, it alternately sparkled and grew dim. At length it arose from the small hand of the infant with an airy motion that seemed to bear it upward without an effort, as if the ethereal instincts with which its master's spirit had endowed it impelled this fair vision involuntarily to a higher sphere. Had there been no obstruction, it might have soared into the sky and grown immortal. But its lustre gleamed upon the ceiling; the exquisite texture of its wings brushed

against that earthly medium; and a sparkle or
two, as of stardust, floated downward and lay
glimmering on the carpet. Then the butterfly
came fluttering down, and, instead of returning
to the infant, was apparently attracted towards   5
the artist's hand.

"Not so! not so!" murmured Owen Warland,
as if his handiwork could have understood him.
"Thou hast gone forth out of thy master's heart.
There is no return for thee."   10

With a wavering movement, and emitting a
tremulous radiance, the butterfly struggled, as
it were, towards the infant, and was about to
alight upon his finger; but while it still hovered
in the air, the little child of strength, with his   15
grandsire's sharp and shrewd expression in his
face, made a snatch at the marvellous insect
and compressed it in his hand. Annie screamed.
Old Peter Hovenden burst into a cold and scornful laugh. The blacksmith, by main force, un-   20
closed the infant's hand, and found within the
palm a small heap of glittering fragments,
whence the mystery of beauty had fled forever.
And as for Owen Warland, he looked placidly
at what seemed the ruin of his life's labor, and   25
which was yet no ruin. He had caught a far
other butterfly than this. When the artist rose
high enough to achieve the beautiful, the symbol by which he made it perceptible to mortal
senses became of little value in his eyes while   30
his spirit possessed itself in the enjoyment of
the reality.

Rappaccini's Daughter

(1844)

🦋 Theme, setting, symbols, and style conspire to   35
make this story one of Hawthorne's warmest and
most appealing. It is, as F. O. Matthiessen remarked,
"a more incisively drawn companion piece to 'The
Birthmark'" (the story of a scientist who in his   40
passion for overcoming imperfection sacrificed human
life). It is also closely related, in general conception,
to "Ethan Brand" (the next selection, page 458).

As his notebooks show, Hawthorne had been read-   45
ing in Sir Thomas Browne: "A story there passeth of
an Indian King that sent unto Alexander a fair
woman fed with aconites and other poisons, with his
intent, either by converse or copulation complexion-
ally to destroy him." This notion of the communica-   50
tion of poison by a person inoculated with it provided
Hawthorne with part of his material for a story of an
Italian scientist and the love affair between the man's
daughter and a young student.

On the level of simplest meaning, the story is

rewarding enough. But much lies beneath the surface. As Hawthorne's narrative proceeds, it provokes
such challenging questions as these:

Is the testimony of Baglione, a rival of Rappaccini's, to be trusted? Did the young student see, or   5
merely imagine, the baleful effects of the poison on
the lizard — on the butterfly — on himself? Is Beatrice's avowal of innocence to be accepted? What
possibilities of interpretation are opened up by Hawthorne's question, "Was this garden, then, the Eden   10
of the present world?" Just what is the evil in the
garden, instilled in Giovanni by Beatrice? Is Beatrice
both good and evil? What boundless passion consumes Rappaccini? If head and heart are separated
and the scientific intellect functions alone, what price   15
must the scientist pay? Are we to understand that
evil is inevitable in any dedicated work for the advancement of knowledge, admirable though the aim
is? In what sense is the poisonous shrub Beatrice's
"sister"? What is the antidote of the poison, seem-   20
ingly the only possible escape from evil?

A young man, named Giovanni Guasconti,
came, very long ago, from the more southern
region of Italy, to pursue his studies at the
University of Padua. Giovanni, who had but   25
a scanty supply of gold ducats in his pocket, took
lodgings in a high and gloomy chamber of an
old edifice which looked not unworthy to have
been the palace of a Paduan noble, and which,
in fact, exhibited over its entrance the armorial   30
bearings of a family long since extinct. The
young stranger, who was not unstudied in the
great poem of his country, recollected that one
of the ancestors of this family, and perhaps an
occupant of this very mansion, had been pic-   35
tured by Dante as a partaker of the immortal
agonies of his Inferno. Their reminiscences and
associations, together with the tendency to
heartbreak natural to a young man for the first
time out of his native sphere, caused Giovanni   40
to sigh heavily as he looked around the desolate
and ill-furnished apartment.

"Holy Virgin, signor!" cried old Dame Lisabetta, who, won by the youth's remarkable
beauty of person, was kindly endeavoring to   45
give the chamber a habitable air, "what a sigh
was that to come out of a young man's heart!
Do you find this old mansion gloomy? For the
love of Heaven, then, put your head out of the
window, and you will see as bright sunshine as   50
you have left in Naples."

Guasconti mechanically did as the old woman
advised, but could not quite agree with her that
the Paduan sunshine was as cheerful as that
of southern Italy. Such as it was, however, it

fell upon a garden beneath the window, and expended its fostering influences on a variety of plants, which seemed to have been cultivated with exceeding care.

"Does this garden belong to the house?" asked Giovanni.

"Heaven forbid, signor, unless it were fruitful of better pot herbs than any that grow there now," answered old Lisabetta. "No; that garden is cultivated by the own hands of Signor Giacomo Rappaccini, the famous doctor, who, I warrant him, has been heard of as far as Naples. It is said that he distils these plants into medicines that are as potent as a charm. Oftentimes you may see the signor doctor at work, and perchance the signora, his daughter, too, gathering the strange flowers that grow in the garden."

The old woman had now done what she could for the aspect of the chamber; and, commending the young man to the protection of the saints, took her departure.

Giovanni still found no better occupation than to look down into the garden beneath his window. From its appearance, he judged it to be one of those botanic gardens which were of earlier date in Padua than elsewhere in Italy or in the world. Or, not improbably, it might once have been the pleasure-place of an opulent family; for there was the ruin of a marble fountain in the center sculptured with rare art, but so wofully shattered that it was impossible to trace the original design from the chaos of remaining fragments. The water, however, continued to gush and sparkle into the sunbeams as cheerfully as ever. A little gurgling sound ascended to the young man's window, and made him feel as if the fountain were an immortal spirit that sung its song unceasingly and without heeding the vicissitudes around it, while one century embodied it in marble and another scattered the perishable garniture on the soil. All about the pool into which the water subsided grew various plants, that seemed to require a plentiful supply of moisture for the nourishment of gigantic leaves, and, in some instances, flowers gorgeously magnificent. There was one shrub in particular, set in a marble vase in the midst of the pool, that bore a profusion of purple blossoms, each of which had the lustre and richness of a gem; and the whole together made a show so resplendent that it seemed enough to illuminate the garden, even had there been no sunshine. Every portion of the soil was peopled with plants and herbs, which, if less beautiful, still bore tokens of assiduous care, as if all had their individual virtues, known to the scientific mind that fostered them. Some were placed in urns, rich with old carving, and others in common garden pots; some crept serpent-like along the ground or climbed on high, using whatever means of ascent was offered them. One plant had wreathed itself round a statue of Vertumnus, which was thus quite veiled and shrouded in a drapery of hanging foliage, so happily arranged that it might have served a sculptor for a study.

While Giovanni stood at the window he heard a rustling behind a screen of leaves, and became aware that a person was at work in the garden. His figure soon emerged into view, and showed itself to be that of no common laborer, but a tall, emaciated, sallow, and sickly-looking man, dressed in a scholar's garb of black. He was beyond the middle term of life, with gray hair, a thin, gray beard, and a face singularly marked with intellect and cultivation, but which could never, even in his more youthful days, have expressed much warmth of heart.

Nothing could exceed the intentness with which this scientific gardener examined every shrub which grew in his path: it seemed as if he was looking into their inmost nature, making observations in regard to their creative essence, and discovering why one leaf grew in this shape and another in that, and wherefore such and such flowers differed among themselves in hue and perfume. Nevertheless, in spite of this deep intelligence on his part, there was no approach to intimacy between himself and these vegetable existences. On the contrary, he avoided their actual touch or the direct inhaling of their odors with a caution that impressed Giovanni most disagreeably; for the man's demeanor was that of one walking among malignant influences, such as savage beasts, or deadly snakes, or evil spirits, which, should he allow them one moment of license, would wreak upon him some terrible fatality. It was strangely frightful to the young man's imagination to see this air of insecurity in a person cultivating a garden, that most simple and innocent of human toils, and which had been alike the joy and labor of the unfallen parents of the race. Was this garden, then, the Eden of the present world? And this man, with such perception of harm in what his own hands caused to grow, — was he the Adam?

The distrustful gardener, while plucking away the dead leaves or pruning the too luxuriant growth of the shrubs, defended his hands with a pair of thick gloves. Nor were these his only armor. When, in his walk through the garden, he came to the magnificent plant that hung its purple gems beside the marble foun-tain, he placed a kind of mask over his mouth and nostrils, as if all this beauty did but conceal a deadlier malice; but, finding his task still too dangerous, he drew back, removed the mask, and called loudly, but in the infirm voice of a person affected with inward disease.

"Beatrice! Beatrice!"

"Here am I, my father. What would you?" cried a rich and youthful voice from the window of the opposite house — a voice as rich as a tropical sunset, and which made Giovanni, though he knew not why, think of deep hues of purple or crimson and of perfumes heavily delectable. "Are you in the garden?"

"Yes, Beatrice," answered the gardener, "and I need your help."

Soon there emerged from under a sculptured portal the figure of a young girl, arrayed with as much richness of taste as the most splendid of the flowers, beautiful as the day, and with a bloom so deep and vivid that one shade more would have been too much. She looked redun-dant with life, health, and energy; all of which attributes were bound down and compressed, as it were, and girdled tensely, in their luxuriance, by her virgin zone. Yet Giovanni's fancy must have grown morbid while he looked down into the garden; for the impression which the fair stranger made upon him was as if here were another flower, the human sister of those vege-table ones, as beautiful as they, more beautiful than the richest of them, but still to be touched only with a glove, nor to be approached without a mask. As Beatrice came down the garden path, it was observable that she handled and inhaled the odor of several of the plants which her father had most sedulously avoided.

"Here, Beatrice," said the latter, "see how many needful offices require to be done to our chief treasure. Yet, shattered as I am, my life might pay the penalty of approaching it so closely as circumstances demand. Henceforth, I fear, this plant must be consigned to your sole charge."

"And gladly will I undertake it," cried again the rich tones of the young lady, as she bent towards the magnificent plant and opened her arms as if to embrace it. "Yes, my sister, my splendor, it shall be Beatrice's task to nurse and serve thee; and thou shalt reward her with thy kisses and perfumed breath, which to her is as the breath of life."

Then, with all the tenderness in her manner that was so strikingly expressed in her words, she busied herself with such attentions as the plant seemed to require; and Giovanni, at his lofty window, rubbed his eyes and almost doubted whether it were a girl tending her favorite flower, or one sister performing the duties of affection to another. The scene soon terminated. Whether Dr. Rappaccini had finished his labors in the garden, or that his watchful eye had caught the stranger's face, he now took his daughter's arm and retired. Night was already closing in; oppressive exhalations seemed to proceed from the plants and steal upward past the open window; and Giovanni, closing the lattice, went to his couch and dreamed of a rich flower and beautiful girl. Flower and maiden were different, and yet the same, and fraught with some strange peril in either shape.

But there is an influence in the light of morning that tends to rectify whatever errors of fancy, or even of judgment, we may have incurred during the sun's decline, or among the shadows of the night, or in the less whole-some glow of moonshine. Giovanni's first move-ment, on starting from sleep, was to throw open the window and gaze down into the garden which his dreams had made so fertile of myster-ies. He was surprised and a little ashamed to find how real and matter-of-fact an affair it proved to be, in the first rays of the sun which gilded the dew-drops that hung upon leaf and blossom, and, while giving a brighter beauty to each rare flower, brought everything within the limits of ordinary experience. The young man rejoiced that, in the heart of the barren city, he had the privilege of overlooking this spot of lovely and luxuriant vegetation. It would serve, he said to himself, as a symbolic language to keep him in communion with Nature. Neither the sickly and thoughtworn Dr. Giacomo Rap-paccini, it is true, nor his brilliant daughter, were now visible; so that Giovanni could not determine how much of the singularity which he attributed to both was due to their own qualities and how much to his wonder-working fancy; but he was inclined to take a most rational view of the whole matter.

In the course of the day he paid his respects to Signor Pietro Baglioni, professor of medicine in the university, a physician of eminent repute, to whom Giovanni had brought a letter of introduction. The professor was an elderly personage, apparently of genial nature, and habits that might almost be called jovial. He kept the young man to dinner, and made himself very agreeable by the freedom and liveliness of his conversation, especially when warmed by a flask or two of Tuscan wine. Giovanni, conceiving that men of science, inhabitants of the same city, must needs be on familiar terms with one another, took an opportunity to mention the name of Dr. Rappaccini. But the professor did not respond with so much cordiality as he had anticipated.

"Ill would it become a teacher of the divine art of medicine," said Professor Pietro Baglioni, in answer to a question of Giovanni, "to withhold due and well-considered praise of a physician so eminently skilled as Rappaccini; but, on the other hand, I should answer it but scantily to my conscience were I to permit a worthy youth like yourself, Signor Giovanni, the son of an ancient friend, to imbibe erroneous ideas respecting a man who might hereafter chance to hold your life and death in his hands. The truth is, our worshipful Dr. Rappaccini has as much science as any member of the faculty — with perhaps one single exception — in Padua, or all Italy; but there are certain grave objections to his professional character."

"And what are they?" asked the young man.

"Has my friend Giovanni any disease of body or heart, that he is so inquisitive about physicians?" said the professor, with a smile. "But as for Rappaccini, it is said of him — and I, who know the man well, can answer for its truth — that he cares infinitely more for science than for mankind. His patients are interesting to him only as subjects for some new experiment. He would sacrifice human life, his own among the rest, or whatever else was dearest to him, for the sake of adding so much as a grain of mustard seed to the great heap of his accumulated knowledge."

"Methinks he is an awful man indeed," remarked Guasconti, mentally recalling the cold and purely intellectual aspect of Rappaccini. "And yet, worshipful professor, is it not a noble spirit? Are there many men capable of so spiritual a love of science?"

"God forbid," answered the professor, somewhat testily; "at least, unless they take sounder views of the healing art than those adopted by Rappaccini. It is his theory that all medicinal virtues are comprised within those substances which we term vegetable poisons. These he cultivates with his own hands, and is said even to have produced new varieties of poison, more horribly deleterious than Nature, without the assistance of this learned person, would ever have plagued the world withal. That the signor doctor does less mischief than might be expected with such dangerous substances is undeniable. Now and then, it must be owned, he has effected, or seemed to effect, a marvellous cure; but, to tell you my private mind, Signor Giovanni, he should receive little credit for such instances of success, — they being probably the work of chance, — but should be held strictly accountable for his failures, which may justly be considered his own work."

The youth might have taken Baglioni's opinions with many grains of allowance had he known that there was a professional warfare of long continuance between him and Dr. Rappaccini, in which the latter was generally thought to have gained the advantage. If the reader be inclined to judge for himself, we refer him to certain black-letter tracts on both sides, preserved in the medical department of the University of Padua.

"I know not, most learned professor," returned Giovanni, after musing on what had been said of Rappaccini's exclusive zeal for science, — "I know not how dearly this physician may love his art; but surely there is one object more dear to him. He has a daughter."

"Aha!" cried the professor, with a laugh. "So now our friend Giovanni's secret is out. You have heard of this daughter, whom all the young men in Padua are wild about, though not half a dozen have ever had the good hap to see her face. I know little of the Signora Beatrice save that Rappaccini is said to have instructed her deeply in his science, and that, young and beautiful as fame reports her, she is already qualified to fill a professor's chair. Perchance her father destines her for mine! Other absurd rumors there be, not worth talking about or listening to. So now, Signor Giovanni, drink off your glass of lachryma."

Guasconti returned to his lodgings somewhat heated with the wine he had quaffed, and which caused his brain to swim with strange fantasies in reference to Dr. Rappaccini and the beautiful Beatrice. On his way, happening to pass by a florist's he bought a fresh bouquet of flowers.

Ascending to his chamber, he seated himself near the window, but within the shadow thrown by the depth of the wall, so that he could look down into the garden with little risk of being discovered. All beneath his eye was a solitude. The strange plants were basking in the sunshine, and now and then nodding gently to one another, as if in acknowledgment of sympathy and kindred. In the midst, by the shattered fountain, grew the magnificent shrub, with its purple gems clustering all over it; they glowed in the air, and gleamed back again out of the depths of the pool, which thus seemed to overflow with colored radiance from the rich reflection that was steeped in it. At first, as we have said, the garden was a solitude. Soon, however, — as Giovanni had half hoped, half feared, would be the case, — a figure appeared beneath the antique sculptured portal, and came down between the rows of plants, inhaling their various perfumes as if she were one of those beings of old classic fable that lived upon sweet odors. On again beholding Beatrice, the young man was even startled to perceive how much her beauty exceeded his recollection of it; so brilliant, so vivid, was its character, that she glowed amid the sunlight, and, as Giovanni whispered to himself, positively illuminated the more shadowy intervals of the garden path. Her face being now more revealed than on the former occasion, he was struck by its expression of simplicity and sweetness, — qualities that had not entered into his idea of her character, and which made him ask anew what manner of mortal she might be. Nor did he fail again to observe, or imagine, an analogy between the beautiful girl and the gorgeous shrub that hung its gemlike flowers over the fountain, — a resemblance which Beatrice seemed to have indulged a fantastic humor in heightening, both by the arrangement of her dress and the selection of its hues.

Approaching the shrub, she threw open her arms, as with a passionate ardor, and drew its branches into an intimate embrace — so intimate that her features were hidden in its leafy bosom and her glistening ringlets all intermingled with the flowers.

"Give me thy breath, my sister," exclaimed Beatrice; "for I am faint with common air. And give me this flower of thine, which I separate with gentlest fingers from the stem and place it close beside my heart."

With these words the beautiful daughter of Rappaccini plucked one of the richest blossoms of the shrub, and was about to fasten it in her bosom. But now, unless Giovanni's draughts of wine had bewildered his senses, a singular incident occurred. A small orange-colored reptile, of the lizard or chameleon species, chanced to be creeping along the path, just at the feet of Beatrice. It appeared to Giovanni, — but, at the distance from which he gazed, he could scarcely have seen anything so minute, — it appeared to him, however, that a drop or two of moisture from the broken stem of the flower descended upon the lizard's head. For an instant the reptile contorted itself violently, and then lay motionless in the sunshine. Beatrice observed this remarkable phenomenon, and crossed herself, sadly, but without surprise; nor did she therefore hesitate to arrange the fatal flower in her bosom. There it blushed, and almost glimmered with the dazzling effect of a precious stone, adding to her dress and aspect the one appropriate charm which nothing else in the world could have supplied. But Giovanni, out of the shadow of his window, bent forward and shrank back, and murmured and trembled.

"Am I awake? Have I my senses?" said he to himself. "What is this being? Beautiful shall I call her, or inexpressibly terrible?"

Beatrice now strayed carelessly through the garden, approaching closer beneath Giovanni's window, so that he was compelled to thrust his head quite out of its concealment in order to gratify the intense and painful curiosity which she excited. At this moment there came a beautiful insect over the garden wall; it had, perhaps, wandered through the city, and found no flowers or verdure among those antique haunts of men until the heavy perfumes of Dr. Rappaccini's shrubs had lured it from afar. Without alighting on the flowers, this winged brightness seemed to be attracted by Beatrice, and lingered in the air and fluttered about her head. Now, here it could not be but that Giovanni Guasconti's eyes deceived him. Be that as it might, he fancied that, while Beatrice was gazing at the insect with childish delight, it grew faint and fell at her feet; its bright wings shivered; it was dead — from no cause that he could discern, unless it were the atmosphere of her breath. Again Beatrice crossed herself and sighed heavily as she bent over the dead insect.

An impulsive movement of Giovanni drew her eyes to the window. There she beheld the beautiful head of the young man — rather a Grecian than an Italian head, with fair, regular features, and a glistening of gold among his ringlets — gazing down upon her like a being that hovered in mid air. Scarcely knowing what he did, Giovanni threw down the bouquet which he had hitherto held in his hand.

"Signora," said he, "there are pure and healthful flowers. Wear them for the sake of Giovanni Guasconti."

"Thanks, signor," replied Beatrice, with her rich voice, that came forth as it were like a gush of music, and with a mirthful expression half childish and half woman-like. "I accept your gift, and would fain recompense it with this precious purple flower; but if I toss it into the air it will not reach you. So Signor Guasconti must even content himself with my thanks."

She lifted the bouquet from the ground, and then, as if inwardly ashamed at having stepped aside from her maidenly reserve to respond to a stranger's greeting, passed swiftly homeward through the garden. But few as the moments were, it seemed to Giovanni, when she was on the point of vanishing beneath the sculptured portal, that his beautiful bouquet was already beginning to wither in her grasp. It was an idle thought; there could be no possibility of distinguishing a faded flower from a fresh one at so great a distance.

For many days after this incident the young man avoided the window that looked into Dr. Rappaccini's garden, as if something ugly and monstrous would have blasted his eyesight had he been betrayed into a glance. He felt conscious of having put himself, to a certain extent, within the influence of an unintelligible power by the communication which he had opened with Beatrice. The wisest course would have been, if his heart were in any real danger, to quit his lodgings and Padua itself at once; the next wiser, to have accustomed himself, as far as possible, to the familiar and daylight view of Beatrice — thus bringing her rigidly and systematically within the limits of ordinary experience. Least of all, while avoiding her sight, ought Giovanni to have remained so near this extraordinary being that the proximity and possibility even of intercourse should give a kind of substance and reality to the wild vagaries which his imagination ran riot continually in producing. Guasconti had not a deep heart — or, at all events, its depths were not sounded now; but he had a quick fancy, and an ardent

southern temperament, which rose every instant to a higher fever pitch. Whether or no Beatrice possessed those terrible attributes, that fatal breath, the affinity with those so beautiful and deadly flowers which were indicated by what Giovanni had witnessed, she had at least instilled a fierce and subtle poison into his system. It was not love, although her rich beauty was a madness to him; nor horror, even while he fancied her spirit to be imbued with the same baneful essence that seemed to pervade her physical frame; but a wild offspring of both love and horror that had each parent in it, and burned like one and shivered like the other. Giovanni knew not what to dread; still less did he know what to hope; yet hope and dread kept a continual warfare in his breast, alternately vanquishing one another and starting up afresh to renew the contest. Blessed are all simple emotions, be they dark or bright! It is the lurid intermixture of the two that produces the illuminating blaze of the infernal regions.

Sometimes he endeavored to assuage the fever of his spirit by a rapid walk through the streets of Padua or beyond its gates: his footsteps kept time with the throbbings of his brain, so that the walk was apt to accelerate itself to a race. One day he found himself arrested; his arm was seized by a portly personage, who had turned back on recognizing the young man and expended much breath in overtaking him.

"Signor Giovanni! Stay, my young friend!" cried he. "Have you forgotten me? That might well be the case if I were as much altered as yourself."

It was Baglioni, whom Giovanni had avoided ever since their first meeting, from a doubt that the professor's sagacity would look too deeply into his secrets. Endeavoring to recover himself, he stared forth wildly from his inner world into the outer one and spoke like a man in a dream.

"Yes; I am Giovanni Guasconti. You are Professor Pietro Baglioni. Now let me pass!"

"Not yet, not yet, Signor Giovanni Guasconti," said the professor, smiling, but at the same time scrutinizing the youth with an earnest glance. "What! did I grow up side by side with your father? and shall his son pass me like a stranger in these old streets of Padua? Stand still, Signor Giovanni; for we must have a word or two before we part."

"Speedily, then, most worshipful professor, speedily," said Giovanni, with feverish impatience. "Does not your worship see that I am in haste?"

Now, while he was speaking there came a man in black along the street, stooping and moving feebly like a person in inferior health. His face was all overspread with a most sickly and sallow hue, but yet so pervaded with an expression of piercing and active intellect that an observer might easily have overlooked the merely physical attributes and have seen only this wonderful energy. As he passed, this person exchanged a cold and distant salutation with Baglioni, but fixed his eyes upon Giovanni with an intentness that seemed to bring out whatever was within him worthy of notice. Nevertheless, there was a peculiar quietness in the look, as if taking merely a speculative, not a human, interest in the young man.

"It is Dr. Rappaccini!" whispered the professor when the stranger had passed. "Has he ever seen your face before?"

"Not that I know," answered Giovanni, starting at the name.

"He *has* seen you! he must have seen you!" said Baglioni hastily. "For some purpose or other, this man of science is making a study of you. I know that look of his! It is the same that coldly illuminates his face as he bends over a bird, a mouse, or a butterfly, which, in pursuance of some experiment, he has killed by the perfume of a flower; a look as deep as Nature itself, but without Nature's warmth of love. Signor Giovanni, I will stake my life upon it, you are the subject of one of Rappaccini's experiments!"

"Will you make a fool of me?" cried Giovanni passionately. "*That*, signor professor, were an untoward experiment."

"Patience! patience!" replied the imperturbable professor. "I tell thee, my poor Giovanni, that Rappaccini has a scientific interest in thee. Thou hast fallen into fearful hands! And the Signora Beatrice, — what part does she act in this mystery?"

But Guasconti, finding Baglioni's pertinacity intolerable, here broke away, and was gone before the professor could again seize his arm. He looked after the young man intently and shook his head.

"This must not be," said Baglioni to himself. "The youth is the son of my old friend, and shall not come to any harm from which the arcana of medical science can preserve him. Besides, it is too insufferable an impertinence

in Rappaccini, thus to snatch the lad out of my own hands, as I may say, and make use of him for his infernal experiments. This daughter of his! It shall be looked to. Perchance, most learned Rappaccini, I may foil you where you little dream of it!"

Meanwhile Giovanni had pursued a circuitous route, and at length found himself at the door of his lodgings. As he crossed the threshold he was met by old Lisabetta, who smirked and smiled, and was evidently desirous to attract his attention; vainly, however, as the ebullition of his feelings had momentarily subsided into a cold and dull vacuity. He turned his eyes full upon the withered face that was puckering itself into a smile, but seemed to behold it not. The old dame, therefore, laid her grasp upon his cloak.

"Signor! signor!" whispered she, still with a smile over the whole breadth of her visage, so that it looked not unlike a grotesque carving in wood, darkened by centuries. "Listen, signor! There is a private entrance into the garden!"

"What do you say?" exclaimed Giovanni, turning quickly about, as if an inanimate thing should start into feverish life. "A private entrance into Dr. Rappaccini's garden?"

"Hush! hush! not so loud!" whispered Lisabetta, putting her hand over his mouth. "Yes; into the worshipful doctor's garden, where you may see all his fine shrubbery. Many a young man in Padua would give gold to be admitted among those flowers."

Giovanni put a piece of gold into her hand.

"Show me the way," said he.

A surmise, probably excited by his conversation with Baglioni, crossed his mind, that this interposition of old Lisabetta might perchance be connected with the intrigue, whatever were its nature, in which the professor seemed to suppose that Dr. Rappaccini was involving him. But such a suspicion, though it disturbed Giovanni, was inadequate to restrain him. The instant that he was aware of the possibility of approaching Beatrice, it seemed an absolute necessity of his existence to do so. It mattered not whether she were angel or demon; he was irrevocably within her sphere, and must obey the law that whirled him onward, in ever-lessening circles, towards a result which he did not attempt to foreshadow; and yet, strange to say, there came across him a sudden doubt whether this intense interest on his part were not delusory; whether it were really of so deep and positive a nature as to justify him in now thrusting himself into an incalculable position; whether it were not merely the fantasy of a young man's brain, only slightly or not at all connected with his heart.

He paused, hesitated, turned half about, but again went on. His withered guide led him along several obscure passages, and finally undid a door, through which, as it was opened, there came the sight and sound of rustling leaves, with the broken sunshine glimmering among them. Giovanni stepped forth, and forcing himself through the entanglement of a shrub that wreathed its tendrils over the hidden entrance, stood beneath his own window in the open area of Dr. Rappaccini's garden.

How often is it the case that, when impossibilities have come to pass and dreams have condensed their misty substance into tangible realities, we find ourselves calm, and even coldly self-possessed, amid circumstances which it would have been a delirium of joy or agony to anticipate! Fate delights to thwart us thus. Passion will choose his own time to rush upon the scene, and lingers sluggishly behind when an appropriate adjustment of events would seem to summon his appearance. So was it now with Giovanni. Day after day his pulses had throbbed with feverish blood at the improbable idea of an interview with Beatrice, and of standing with her, face to face, in this very garden, basking in the Oriental sunshine of her beauty, and snatching from her full gaze the mystery which he deemed the riddle of his own existence. But now there was a singular and untimely equanimity within his breast. He threw a glance around the garden to discover if Beatrice or her father were present, and, perceiving that he was alone, began a critical observation of the plants.

The aspect of one and all of them dissatisfied him; their gorgeousness seemed fierce, passionate, and even unnatural. There was hardly an individual shrub which a wanderer, straying by himself through a forest, would not have been startled to find growing wild, as if an unearthly face had glared at him out of the thicket. Several also would have shocked a delicate instinct by an appearance of artificialness indicating that there had been such commixture, and, as it were, adultery, of various vegetable species, that the production was no longer of God's making, but the monstrous offspring of man's depraved fancy, glowing with only an evil mockery of beauty. They were probably the result of experiment, which in one or two cases had succeeded in mingling plants individually lovely into a compound possessing the questionable and ominous character that distinguished the whole growth of the garden. In fine, Giovanni recognized but two or three plants in the collection, and those of a kind that he well knew to be poisonous. While busy with these contemplations he heard the rustling of a silken garment, and, turning, beheld Beatrice emerging from beneath the sculptured portal.

Giovanni had not considered with himself what should be his deportment; whether he should apologize for his intrusion into the garden, or assume that he was there with the privity at least, if not by the desire, of Dr. Rappaccini or his daughter; but Beatrice's manner placed him at his ease, although leaving him still in doubt by what agency he had gained admittance. She came lightly along the path and met him near the broken fountain. There was surprise in her face, but brightened by a simple and kind expression of pleasure.

"You are a connoisseur in flowers, signor," said Beatrice, with a smile, alluding to the bouquet which he had flung her from the window. "It is no marvel, therefore, if the sight of my father's rare collection has tempted you to take a nearer view. If he were here, he could tell you many strange and interesting facts as to the nature and habits of these shrubs; for he has spent a lifetime in such studies, and this garden is his world."

"And yourself, lady," observed Giovanni, "if fame says true, — you likewise are deeply skilled in the virtues indicated by these rich blossoms and these spicy perfumes. Would you deign to be my instructress, I should prove an apter scholar than if taught by Signor Rappaccini himself."

"Are there such idle rumors?" asked Beatrice, with the music of a pleasant laugh. "Do people say that I am skilled in my father's science of plants? What a jest is there! No; though I have grown up among these flowers, I know no more of them than their hues and perfume; and sometimes methinks I would fain rid myself of even that small knowledge. There are many flowers here, and those not the least brilliant, that shock and offend me when they meet my eye. But pray, signor, do not believe these stories about my science. Believe nothing of me save what you see with your own eyes."

"And must I believe all that I have seen with

my own eyes?" asked Giovanni, pointedly, while the recollection of former scenes made him shrink. "No, signora; you demand too little of me. Bid me believe nothing save what comes from your own lips."

It would appear that Beatrice understood him. There came a deep flush to her cheek; but she looked full into Giovanni's eyes, and responded to his gaze of uneasy suspicion with a queenlike haughtiness.

"I do so bid you, signor," she replied. "Forget whatever you may have fancied in regard to me. If true to the outward senses, still it may be false in its essence; but the words of Beatrice Rappaccini's lips are true from the depths of the heart outward. Those you may believe."

A fervor glowed in her whole aspect and beamed upon Giovanni's consciousness like the light of truth itself; but while she spoke there was a fragrance in the atmosphere around her, rich and delightful, though evanescent, yet which the young man, from an indefinable reluctance, scarcely dared to draw into his lungs. It might be the odor of the flowers. Could it be Beatrice's breath which thus embalmed her words with a strange richness, as if by steeping them in her heart? A faintness passed like a shadow over Giovanni and flitted away; he seemed to gaze through the beautiful girl's eyes into her transparent soul, and felt no more doubt or fear.

The tinge of passion that had colored Beatrice's manner vanished; she became gay, and appeared to derive a pure delight from her communion with the youth not unlike what the maiden of a lonely island might have felt conversing with a voyager from the civilized world. Evidently her experience of life had been confined within the limits of that garden. She talked now about matters as simple as the daylight or summer clouds, and now asked questions in reference to the city, or Giovanni's distant home, his friends, his mother, and his sisters — questions indicating such seclusion, and such lack of familiarity with modes and forms, that Giovanni responded as if to an infant. Her spirit gushed out before him like a fresh rill that was just catching its first glimpse of the sunlight and wondering at the reflections of earth and sky which were flung into its bosom. There came thoughts, too, from a deep source, and fantasies of a gemlike brilliancy, as if diamonds and rubies sparkled upward among the bubbles of the fountain. Ever and anon

there gleamed across the young man's mind a sense of wonder that he should be walking side by side with the being who had so wrought upon his imagination, whom he had idealized in such hues of terror, in whom he had positively witnessed such manifestations of dreadful attributes, — that he should be conversing with Beatrice like a brother, and should find her so human and so maidenlike. But such reflections were only momentary; the effect of her character was too real not to make itself familiar at once.

In this free intercourse they had strayed through the garden, and now, after many turns among its avenues, were come to the shattered fountain, beside which grew the magnificent shrub, with its treasury of glowing blossoms. A fragrance was diffused from it which Giovanni recognized as identical with that which he had attributed to Beatrice's breath, but incomparably more powerful. As her eyes fell upon it, Giovanni beheld her press her hand to her bosom as if her heart were throbbing suddenly and painfully.

"For the first time in my life," murmured she, addressing the shrub, "I had forgotten thee."

"I remember, signora," said Giovanni, "that you once promised to reward me with one of these living gems for the bouquet which I had the happy boldness to fling to your feet. Permit me now to pluck it as a memorial of this interview."

He made a step towards the shrub with extended hand; but Beatrice darted forward, uttering a shriek that went through his heart like a dagger. She caught his hand and drew it back with the whole force of her slender figure. Giovanni felt her touch thrilling through his fibres.

"Touch it not!" exclaimed she, in a voice of agony. "Not for thy life! It is fatal!"

Then, hiding her face, she fled from him and vanished beneath the sculptured portal. As Giovanni followed her with his eyes, he beheld the emaciated figure and pale intelligence of Dr. Rappaccini, who had been watching the scene, he knew not how long, within the shadow of the entrance.

No sooner was Guasconti alone in his chamber than the image of Beatrice came back to his passionate musings, invested with all the witchery that had been gathering around it ever since his first glimpse of her, and now likewise imbued with a tender warmth of girlish womanhood. She was human; her nature was endowed with all gentle and feminine qualities; she was worthiest to be worshipped; she was capable, surely, on her part, of the height and heroism of love. Those tokens which he had hitherto considered as proofs of a frightful peculiarity in her physical and moral system were now either forgotten, or, by the subtle sophistry of passion transmitted into a golden crown of enchantment, rendering Beatrice the more admirable by so much as she was the more unique. Whatever had looked ugly was now beautiful; or, if incapable of such a change, it stole away and hid itself among those shapeless half ideas which throng the dim region beyond the daylight of our perfect consciousness. Thus did he spend the night, nor fell asleep until the dawn had begun to awake the slumbering flowers in Dr. Rappaccini's garden, whither Giovanni's dreams doubtless led him. Up rose the sun in his due season, and, flinging his beams upon the young man's eyelids, awoke him to a sense of pain. When thoroughly aroused, he became sensible of a burning and tingling agony in his hand — in his right hand — the very hand which Beatrice had grasped in her own when he was on the point of plucking one of the gemlike flowers. On the back of that hand there was now a purple print like that of four small fingers, and the likeness of a slender thumb upon his wrist.

Oh, how stubbornly does love, — or even that cunning semblance of love which flourishes in the imagination, but strikes no depth of root into the heart, — how stubbornly does it hold its faith until the moment comes when it is doomed to vanish into thin mist! Giovanni wrapped a handkerchief about his hand and wondered what evil thing had stung him, and soon forgot his pain in a reverie of Beatrice.

After the first interview, a second was in the inevitable course of what we call fate. A third; a fourth; and a meeting with Beatrice in the garden was no longer an incident in Giovanni's daily life, but the whole space in which he might be said to live; for the anticipation and memory of that ecstatic hour made up the remainder. Nor was it otherwise with the daughter of Rappaccini. She watched for the youth's appearance, and flew to his side with confidence as unreserved as if they had been playmates from early infancy — as if they were such playmates still. If, by any unwonted chance, he failed to come at the appointed moment, she stood beneath the window and sent up the rich sweetness of her tones to float around him in his chamber and echo and reverberate throughout his heart: "Giovanni! Giovanni! Why tarriest thou? Come down!" And down he hastened into that Eden of poisonous flowers.

But, with all this intimate familiarity, there was still a reserve in Beatrice's demeanor, so rigidly and invariably sustained that the idea of infringing it scarcely occurred to his imagination. By all appreciable signs, they loved; they had looked love with eyes that conveyed the holy secret from the depths of one soul into the depths of the other, as if it were too sacred to be whispered by the way; they had even spoken love in those gushes of passion when their spirits darted forth in articulated breath like tongues of long-hidden flame; and yet there had been no seal of lips, no clasp of hands, nor any slightest caress such as love claims and hallows. He had never touched one of the gleaming ringlets of her hair; her garment — so marked was the physical barrier between them — had never been waved against him by a breeze. On the few occasions when Giovanni had seemed tempted to overstep the limit, Beatrice grew so sad, so stern, and withal wore such a look of desolate separation, shuddering at itself, that not a spoken word was requisite to repel him. At such times he was startled at the horrible suspicions that rose, monster-like, out of the caverns of his heart and stared him in the face; his love grew thin and faint as the morning mist; his doubts alone had substance. But, when Beatrice's face brightened again after the momentary shadow, she was transformed at once from the mysterious, questionable being whom he had watched with so much awe and horror; she was now the beautiful and unsophisticated girl whom he felt that his spirit knew with a certainty beyond all other knowledge.

A considerable time had now passed since Giovanni's last meeting with Baglioni. One morning, however, he was disagreeably surprised by a visit from the professor, whom he had scarcely thought of for whole weeks, and would willingly have forgotten still longer. Given up as he had long been to a pervading excitement, he could tolerate no companions except upon condition of their perfect sympathy with his present state of feeling. Such sympathy was not to be expected from Professor Baglioni.

The visitor chatted carelessly for a few moments about the gossip of the city and the university, and then took up another topic.

"I have been reading an old classic author lately," said he, "and met with a story that strangely interested me. Possibly you may remember it. It is of an Indian prince, who sent a beautiful woman as a present to Alexander the Great. She was as lovely as the dawn and gorgeous as the sunset; but what especially distinguished her was a certain rich perfume in her breath — richer than a garden of Persian roses. Alexander, as was natural to a youthful conqueror, fell in love at first sight with this magnificent stranger; but a certain sage physician, happening to be present, discovered a terrible secret in regard to her."

"And what was that?" asked Giovanni, turning his eyes downward to avoid those of the professor.

"That this lovely woman," continued Baglioni, with emphasis, "had been nourished with poisons from her birth upward, until her whole nature was so imbued with them that she herself had become the deadliest poison in existence. Poison was her element of life. With that rich perfume of her breath she blasted the very air. Her love would have been poison — her embrace death. Is not this a marvellous tale?"

"A childish fable," answered Giovanni, nervously, starting from his chair. "I marvel how your worship finds time to read such nonsense among your graver studies."

"By the by," said the professor, looking uneasily about him, "what singular fragrance is this in your apartment? Is it the perfume of your gloves? It is faint, but delicious; and yet, after all, by no means agreeable. Were I to breathe it long, methinks it would make me ill. It is like the breath of a flower; but I see no flowers in the chamber."

"Nor are there any," replied Giovanni, who had turned pale as the professor spoke; "nor, I think, is there any fragrance except in your worship's imagination. Odors, being a sort of element combined of the sensual and the spiritual, are apt to deceive us in this manner. The recollection of a perfume, the bare idea of it, may easily be mistaken for a present reality."

"Ay; but my sober imagination does not often play such tricks," said Baglioni; "and, were I to fancy any kind of odor, it would be that of some vile apothecary drug, wherewith my fingers are likely enough to be imbued. Our worshipful friend Rappaccini, as I have heard, tinctures his medicaments with odors richer than those of Araby. Doubtless, likewise, the fair and learned Signora Beatrice would minister to her patients with draughts as sweet as a maiden's breath; but woe to him that sips them!"

Giovanni's face evinced many contending emotions. The tone in which the professor alluded to the pure and lovely daughter of Rappaccini was a torture to his soul; and yet the intimation of a view of her character, opposite to his own, gave instantaneous distinctness to a thousand dim suspicions, which now grinned at him like so many demons. But he strove hard to quell them and to respond to Baglioni with a true lover's perfect faith.

"Signor professor," said he, "you were my father's friend; perchance, too, it is your purpose to act a friendly part towards his son. I would fain feel nothing towards you save respect and deference; but I pray you to observe, signor, that there is one subject on which we must not speak. You know not the Signora Beatrice. You cannot, therefore, estimate the wrong — the blasphemy, I may even say — that is offered to her character by a light or injurious word."

"Giovanni! my poor Giovanni!" answered the professor, with a calm expression of pity, "I know this wretched girl far better than yourself. You shall hear the truth in respect to the poisoner Rappaccini and his poisonous daughter; yes, poisonous as she is beautiful. Listen; for, even should you do violence to my gray hairs, it shall not silence me. That old fable of the Indian woman has become a truth by the deep and deadly science of Rappaccini and in the person of the lovely Beatrice."

Giovanni groaned and hid his face.

"Her father," continued Baglioni, "was not restrained by natural affection from offering up his child in this horrible manner as the victim of his insane zeal for science; for, let us do him justice, he is as true a man of science as ever distilled his own heart in an alembic. What, then, will be your fate? Beyond a doubt you are selected as the material of some new experiment. Perhaps the result is to be death; perhaps a fate more awful still. Rappaccini, with what he calls the interest of science before his eyes, will hesitate at nothing."

"It is a dream," muttered Giovanni to himself; "surely it is a dream."

"But," resumed the professor, "be of good

cheer, son of my friend. It is not yet too late for the rescue. Possibly we may even succeed in bringing back this miserable child within the limits of ordinary nature, from which her father's madness has estranged her. Behold this little silver vase! It was wrought by the hands of the renowned Benvenuto Cellini, and is well worthy to be a love gift to the fairest dame in Italy. But its contents are invaluable. One little sip of this antidote would have rendered the most virulent poisons of the Borgias innocuous. Doubt not that it will be as efficacious against those of Rappaccini. Bestow the vase, and the precious liquid within it, on your Beatrice, and hopefully await the result."

Baglioni laid a small, exquisitely wrought silver vial on the table and withdrew, leaving what he had said to produce its effects upon the young man's mind.

"We will thwart Rappaccini yet," thought he, chuckling to himself, as he descended the stairs; "but, let us confess the truth of him, he is a wonderful man — a wonderful man indeed; a vile empiric, however, in his practice, and therefore not to be tolerated by those who respect the good old rules of the medical profession."

Throughout Giovanni's whole acquaintance with Beatrice, he had occasionally, as we have said, been haunted by dark surmises as to her character; yet so thoroughly had she made herself felt by him as a simple, natural, most affectionate, and guileless creature, that the image now held up by Professor Baglioni looked as strange and incredible as if it were not in accordance with his own original conception. True, there were ugly recollections connected with his first glimpses of the beautiful girl; he could not quite forget the bouquet that withered in her grasp, and the insect that perished amid the sunny air, by no ostensible agency save the fragrance of her breath. These incidents, however, dissolving in the pure light of her character, had no longer the efficacy of facts, but were acknowledged as mistaken fantasies, by whatever testimony of the senses they might appear to be substantiated. There is something truer and more real than what we can see with the eyes and touch with the finger. On such better evidence had Giovanni founded his confidence in Beatrice, though rather by the necessary force of her high attributes than by any deep and generous faith on his part. But now his spirit was incapable of sustaining itself at the height to which the early enthusiasm of passion had exalted it; he fell down, grovelling among earthly doubts, and defiled therewith the pure whiteness of Beatrice's image. Not that he gave her up; he did but distrust. He resolved to institute some decisive test that should satisfy him, once for all, whether there were those dreadful peculiarities in her physical nature which could not be supposed to exist without some corresponding monstrosity of soul. His eyes, gazing down afar, might have deceived him as to the lizard, the insect, and the flowers; but if he could witness, at the distance of a few paces, the sudden blight of one fresh and healthful flower in Beatrice's hand, there would be room for no further question. With this idea he hastened to the florist's and purchased a bouquet that was still gemmed with the morning dew-drops.

It was now the customary hour of his daily interview with Beatrice. Before descending into the garden, Giovanni failed not to look at his figure in the mirror, — a vanity to be expected in a beautiful young man, yet, as displaying itself at that troubled and feverish moment, the token of a certain shallowness of feeling and insincerity of character. He did gaze, however, and said to himself that his features had never before possessed so rich a grace, nor his eyes such vivacity, nor his cheeks so warm a hue of superabundant life.

"At least," thought he, "her poison has not yet insinuated itself into my system. I am no flower to perish in her grasp."

With that thought he turned his eyes on the bouquet, which he had never once laid aside from his hand. A thrill of indefinable horror shot through his frame on perceiving that those dewy flowers were already beginning to droop; they wore the aspect of things that had been fresh and lovely yesterday. Giovanni grew white as marble, and stood motionless before the mirror, staring at his own reflection there as at the likeness of something frightful. He remembered Baglioni's remark about the fragrance that seemed to pervade the chamber. It must have been the poison in his breath! Then he shuddered — shuddered at himself. Recovering from his stupor, he began to watch with curious eye a spider that was busily at work hanging its web from the antique cornice of the apartment, crossing and recrossing the artful system of interwoven lines — as vigorous and active a spider as ever dangled from an old ceiling. Giovanni bent towards the insect, and emitted a deep, long breath. The spider suddenly ceased its toil; the web vibrated with a tremor originating in the body of the small artisan. Again Giovanni sent forth a breath, deeper, longer, and imbued with a venomous feeling out of his heart: he knew not whether he were wicked, or only desperate. The spider made a convulsive gripe with his limbs and hung dead across the window.

"Accursed! accursed!" muttered Giovanni, addressing himself. "Hast thou grown so poisonous that this deadly insect perishes by thy breath?"

At that moment a rich, sweet voice came floating up from the garden.

"Giovanni! Giovanni! It is past the hour! Why tarriest thou? Come down!"

"Yes," muttered Giovanni again. "She is the only being whom my breath may not slay! Would that it might!"

He rushed down, and in an instant was standing before the bright and loving eyes of Beatrice. A moment ago his wrath and despair had been so fierce that he could have desired nothing so much as to wither her by a glance; but with her actual presence there came influences which had too real an existence to be at once shaken off: recollections of the delicate and benign power of her feminine nature, which had so often enveloped him in a religious calm; recollections of many a holy and passionate outgush of her heart, when the pure fountain had been unsealed from its depths and made visible in its transparency to his mental eye; recollections which, had Giovanni known how to estimate them, would have assured him that all this ugly mystery was but an earthly illusion, and that, whatever mist of evil might seem to have gathered over her, the real Beatrice was a heavenly angel. Incapable as he was of such high faith, still her presence had not utterly lost its magic. Giovanni's rage was quelled into an aspect of sullen insensibility. Beatrice, with a quick spiritual sense, immediately felt that there was a gulf of blackness between them which neither he nor she could pass. They walked on together, sad and silent, and came thus to the marble fountain and to its pool of water on the ground, in the midst of which grew the shrub that bore gemlike blossoms. Giovanni was affrighted at the eager enjoyment — the appetite, as it were — with which he found himself inhaling the fragrance of the flowers.

"Beatrice," asked he, abruptly, "whence came this shrub?"

"My father created it," answered she, with simplicity.

"Created it! created it!" repeated Giovanni. "What mean you, Beatrice?"

"He is a man fearfully acquainted with the secrets of Nature," replied Beatrice; "and at the hour when I first drew breath, this plant sprang from the soil, the offspring of his science, of his intellect, while I was but his earthly child. Approach it not!" continued she, observing with terror that Giovanni was drawing nearer to the shrub. "It has qualities that you little dream of. But I, dearest Giovanni, — I grew up and blossomed with the plant and was nourished with its breath. It was my sister, and I loved it with a human affection; for, alas! — hast thou not suspected it? — there was an awful doom."

Here Giovanni frowned so darkly upon her that Beatrice paused and trembled. But her faith in his tenderness reassured her, and made her blush that she had doubted for an instant.

"There was an awful doom," she continued, "the effect of my father's fatal love of science, which estranged me from all society of my kind. Until Heaven sent thee, dearest Giovanni, oh, how lonely was thy poor Beatrice!"

"Was it a hard doom?" asked Giovanni fixing his eyes upon her.

"Only of late have I known how hard it was," answered she, tenderly. "Oh, yes; but my heart was torpid, and therefore quiet."

Giovanni's rage broke forth from his sullen gloom like a lightning flash out of a dark cloud.

"Accursed one!" cried he, with venomous scorn and anger. "And, finding thy solitude wearisome, thou has severed me likewise from all the warmth of life and enticed me into thy region of unspeakable horror!"

"Giovanni!" exclaimed Beatrice, turning her large bright eyes upon his face. The force of his words had not found its way into her mind; she was merely thunderstruck.

"Yes, poisonous thing!" repeated Giovanni, beside himself with passion. "Thou hast done it! Thou hast blasted me! Thou hast filled my veins with poison! Thou hast made me as hateful, as ugly, as loathsome and deadly a creature as thyself — a world's wonder of hideous monstrosity! Now, if our breath be happily as fatal to ourselves as to all others, let us join our lips in one kiss of unutterable hatred, and so die!"

"What has befallen me?" murmured Beatrice,

with a low moan out of her heart. "Holy Virgin, pity me, a poor heartbroken child!"

"Thou, — dost thou pray?" cried Giovanni, still with the same fiendish scorn. "Thy very prayers, as they come from thy lips, taint the atmosphere with death. Yes, yes; let us pray! Let us to church and dip our fingers in the holy water at the portal! They that come after us will perish as by a pestilence! Let us sign crosses in the air! It will be scattering curses abroad in the likeness of holy symbols!"

"Giovanni," said Beatrice, calmly, for her grief was beyond passion, "why dost thou join thyself with me thus in those terrible words? I, it is true, am the horrible thing thou namest me. But thou,— what hast thou to do, save with one other shudder at my hideous misery to go forth out of the garden and mingle with thy race, and forget that there ever crawled on earth such a monster as poor Beatrice?"

"Dost thou pretend ignorance?" asked Giovanni, scowling upon her. "Behold! this power have I gained from the pure daughter of Rappaccini."

There was a swarm of summer insects flitting through the air in search of the food promised by the flower odors of the fatal garden. They circled round Giovanni's head, and were evidently attracted towards him by the same influence which had drawn them for an instant within the sphere of several of the shrubs. He sent forth a breath among them, and smiled bitterly at Beatrice as at least a score of the insects fell dead upon the ground.

"I see it! I see it!" shrieked Beatrice. "It is my father's fatal science! No, no, Giovanni; it was not I! Never! never! I dreamed only to love thee and be with thee a little time, and so to let thee pass away, leaving but thine image in mine heart; for, Giovanni, believe it, though my body be nourished with poison, my spirit is God's creature, and craves love as its daily food. But my father, — he has united us in this fearful sympathy. Yes; spurn me, tread upon me, kill me! Oh, what is death after such words as thine? But it was not I. Not for a world of bliss would I have done it."

Giovanni's passion had exhausted itself in its outburst from his lips. There now came across him a sense, mournful, and not without tenderness, of the intimate and peculiar relationship between Beatrice and himself. They stood, as it were, in an utter solitude, which would be made none the less solitary by the densest throng of human life. Ought not, then, the desert of humanity around them to press this insulated pair closer together? If they should be cruel to one another, who was there to be kind to them? Besides, thought Giovanni, might there not still be a hope of his returning within the limits of ordinary nature, and leading Beatrice, the redeemed Beatrice, by the hand? O, weak, and selfish, and unworthy spirit, that could dream of an earthly union and earthly happiness as possible, after such deep love had been so bitterly wronged as was Beatrice's love by Giovanni's blighting words! No, no; there could be no such hope. She must pass heavily, with that broken heart, across the borders of Time — she must bathe her hurts in some fount of paradise, and forget her grief in the light of immortality, and *there* be well.

But Giovanni did not know it.

"Dear Beatrice," said he approaching her, while she shrank as always at his approach, but now with a different impulse, "dearest Beatrice, our fate is not yet so desperate. Behold! there is a medicine, potent as a wise physician has assured me, and almost divine in its efficacy. It is composed of ingredients the most opposite to those by which thy awful father has brought this calamity upon thee and me. It is distilled of blessed herbs. Shall we not quaff it together, and thus be purified from evil?"

"Give it me!" said Beatrice, extending her hand to receive the little silver vial which Giovanni took from his bosom. She added, with a peculiar emphasis, "I will drink; but do thou await the result."

She put Baglioni's antidote to her lips; and, at the same moment, the figure of Rappaccini emerged from the portal and came slowly towards the marble fountain. As he drew near, the pale man of science seemed to gaze with a triumphant expression at the beautiful youth and maiden, as might an artist who should spend his life in achieving a picture or a group of statuary and finally be satisfied with his success. He paused; his bent form grew erect with conscious power; he spread out his hands over them in the attitude of a father imploring a blessing upon his children; but those were the same hands that had thrown poison into the stream of their lives. Giovanni trembled. Beatrice shuddered nervously, and pressed her hand upon her heart.

"My daughter," said Rappaccini, "thou art no longer lonely in the world. Pluck one of those precious gems from thy sister shrub and bid thy bridegroom wear it in his bosom. It will not harm him now. My science and the sympathy between thee and him have so wrought within his system that he now stands apart from common men, as thou dost, daughter of my pride and triumph, from ordinary women. Pass on, then, through the world, most dear to one another and dreadful to all besides!"

"My father," said Beatrice, feebly, — and still as she spoke she kept her hand upon her heart, — "wherefore didst thou inflict this miserable doom upon thy child?"

"Miserable!" exclaimed Rappaccini. "What mean you, foolish girl? Dost thou deem it misery to be endowed with marvelous gifts against which no power nor strength could avail an enemy — misery, to be able to quell the mightiest with a breath — misery, to be as terrible as thou art beautiful? Wouldst thou, then, have preferred the condition of a weak woman, exposed to all evil and capable of none?"

"I would fain have been loved, not feared," murmured Beatrice, sinking down upon the ground. "But now it matters not. I am going, father, where the evil which thou hast striven to mingle with my being will pass away like a dream — like the fragrance of these poisonous flowers, which will no longer taint my breath among the flowers of Eden. Farewell, Giovanni! Thy words of hatred are like lead within my heart; but they, too, will fall away as I ascend. Oh, was there not, from the first, more poison in thy nature than in mine?"

To Beatrice, — so radically had her earthly part been wrought upon by Rappaccini's skill, — as poison had been life, so the powerful antidote was death; and thus the poor victim of man's ingenuity and of thwarted nature, and of the fatality that attends all such efforts of perverted wisdom, perished there, at the feet of her father and Giovanni. Just at that moment Professor Pietro Baglioni looked forth from the window, and called loudly, in a tone of triumph mixed with horror, to the thunderstricken man of science.

"Rappaccini! Rappaccini! and is *this* the upshot of your experiment!"

Ethan Brand
(1850)

🕊 The idea of an Unpardonable Sin, the theme of this story, goes back to the New Testament: "He that

shall blaspheme against the Holy Ghost hath never forgiveness, but is in danger of eternal damnation." (Mark 3: 28–29.)

The immediate germ of Hawthorne's story may be found in his notebooks, 1844: "The Unpardonable Sin might consist in a want of love and reverence for the Human Soul; in consequence of which the investigator pried into its dark depths, not with a hope or purpose of making it better, but from a cold philosophical curiosity — content that it should be wicked in whatever kind or degree, and only desiring to study it out. Would not this, in other words, be a separation of the intellect from the heart?" Another notebook entry reads: "The search of an investigator for the Unpardonable Sin — he at last finds it in his own heart and practice."

As Hawthorne conceives of human nature, a man should, ideally, maintain a balance between intellect and feeling. Ethan Brand (like Dr. Rappaccini) has long since lost this balance. His mind has been developed to the highest point; his heart has contracted, hardened, turned to stone. Intellectual pride and loss of human feeling have brought him to a bleak and terrible solitude, to alienation alike from his fellow human beings, Mother Earth, and God — a solitude signed and sealed in his final dramatic act.

The setting and some of the characters were suggested to Hawthorne by a summer holiday visit to North Adams, Massachusetts, as we learn from unrelated observations recorded in his notebook on Mt. Greylock, the lime-kiln, the lime-burner, Lawyer Haynes (Giles in the story), the showman with the diorama, the soap-boiler, little Joe and the dog. Such observations were brought together and melted into an aesthetic form dominated by the concept of a sin beyond mercy.

Readers in Hawthorne's time readily recognized his allusion, early in the story, to the Delectable Mountains of Bunyan's *Pilgrim's Progress*.

Bartram the lime-burner, a rough, heavy-looking man, begrimed with charcoal, sat watching his kiln, at nightfall, while his little son played at building houses with the scattered fragments of marble, when, on the hillside below them, they heard a roar of laughter, not mirthful, but slow, and even solemn, like a wind shaking the boughs of the forest.

"Father, what is that?" asked the little boy, leaving his play, and pressing betwixt his father's knees.

"Oh, some drunken man, I suppose," answered the lime-burner; "some merry fellow from the bar-room in the village, who dared not laugh loud enough within doors lest he should blow the roof of the house off. So here he is, shaking his jolly sides at the foot of Graylock."

"But, father," said the child, more sensitive than the obtuse, middle-aged clown, "he does not laugh like a man that is glad. So the noise frightens me!"

"Don't be a fool, child!" cried his father, gruffly. "You will never make a man, I do believe; there is too much of your mother in you. I have known the rustling of a leaf startle you. Hark! Here comes the merry fellow now. You shall see that there is no harm in him."

Bartram and his little son, while they were talking thus, sat watching the same lime-kiln that had been the scene of Ethan Brand's solitary and meditative life, before he began his search for the Unpardonable Sin. Many years, as we have seen, had now elapsed, since the portentous night when the IDEA was first developed. The kiln, however, on the mountain-side, stood unimpaired, and was in nothing changed since he had thrown his dark thoughts into the intense glow of its furnace, and melted them, as it were, into the one thought that took possession of his life. It was a rude, round, tower-like structure about twenty feet high, heavily built of rough stones, and with a hillock of earth heaped about the larger part of its circumference; so that the blocks and fragments of marble might be drawn by cart-loads, and thrown in at the top. There was an opening at the bottom of the tower, like an oven-mouth, but large enough to admit a man in a stooping posture, and provided with a massive iron door. With the smoke and jets of flame issuing from the chinks and crevices of this door, which seemed to give admittance into the hillside, it resembled nothing so much as the private entrance to the infernal regions, which the shepherds of the Delectable Mountains were accustomed to show to pilgrims.

There are many such lime-kilns in that tract of country, for the purpose of burning the white marble which composes a large part of the substance of the hills. Some of them, built years ago, and long deserted, with weeds growing in the vacant round of the interior, which is open to the sky, and grass and wild-flowers rooting themselves in the chinks of the stones, look already like relics of antiquity, and may yet be overspread with the lichens of centuries to come. Others, where the lime-burner still feeds his daily and night-long fire, afford points of interest to the wanderer among the hills, who seats himself on a log of wood or a fragment of marble, to hold a chat with the solitary man.

It is a lonesome, and, when the character is inclined to thought, may be an intensely thoughtful occupation; as it proved in the case of Ethan Brand, who had mused to such strange purpose, in days gone by, while the fire in this very kiln was burning.

The man who now watched the fire was of a different order, and troubled himself with no thoughts save the very few that were requisite to his business. At frequent intervals, he flung back the clashing weight of the iron door, and, turning his face from the insufferable glare, thrust in huge logs of oak, or stirred the immense brands with a long pole. Within the furnace were seen the curling and riotous flames, and the burning marble, almost molten with the intensity of heat; while without, the reflection of the fire quivered on the dark intricacy of the surrounding forest, and showed in the foreground a bright and ruddy little picture of the hut, the spring beside its door, the athletic and coal-begrimed figure of the lime-burner, and the half-frightened child, shrinking into the protection of his father's shadow. And when again the iron door was closed, then reappeared the tender light of the half-full moon, which vainly strove to trace out the indistinct shapes of the neighboring mountains; and, in the upper sky, there was a flitting congregation of clouds, still faintly tinged with the rosy sunset, though thus far down into the valley the sunshine had vanished long and long ago.

The little boy now crept still closer to his father, as footsteps were heard ascending the hillside, and a human form thrust aside the bushes that clustered beneath the trees.

"Halloo! who is it?" cried the lime-burner, vexed at his son's timidity, yet half infected by it. "Come forward, and show yourself, like a man, or I'll fling this chunk of marble at your head!"

"You offer me a rough welcome," said a gloomy voice, as the unknown man drew nigh. "Yet I neither claim nor desire a kinder one, even at my own fireside."

To obtain a distincter view, Bartram threw open the iron door of the kiln, whence immediately issued a gush of fierce light, that smote full upon the stranger's face and figure. To a careless eye there appeared nothing very remarkable in his aspect, which was that of a man in a coarse, brown, country-made suit of clothes, tall and thin, with the staff and heavy shoes of a wayfarer. As he advanced, he fixed his eyes — which were very bright — intently upon the brightness of the furnace, as if he beheld, or expected to behold, some object worthy of note within it.

"Good evening, stranger," said the lime-burner; "whence come you, so late in the day?"

"I come from my search," answered the wayfarer; "for, at last, it is finished."

"Drunk! — or crazy!" muttered Bartram to himself. "I shall have trouble with the fellow. The sooner I drive him away, the better."

The little boy, all in a tremble, whispered to his father, and begged him to shut the door of the kiln, so that there might not be so much light; for that there was something in the man's face which he was afraid to look at, yet could not look away from. And, indeed, even the lime-burner's dull and torpid sense began to be impressed by an indescribable something in that thin, rugged, thoughtful visage, with the grizzled hair hanging wildly about it, and those deeply sunken eyes, which gleamed like fires within the entrance of a mysterious cavern. But, as he closed the door, the stranger turned towards him, and spoke in a quiet, familiar way, that made Bartram feel as if he were a sane and sensible man, after all.

"Your task draws to an end, I see," said he. "This marble has already been burning three days. A few hours more will convert the stone to lime."

"Why, who are you?" exclaimed the lime-burner. "You seem as well acquainted with my business as I am myself."

"And well I may be," said the stranger; "for I followed the same craft many a long year, and here, too, on this very spot. But you are a new-comer in these parts. Did you never hear of Ethan Brand?"

"The man that went in search of the Unpardonable Sin?" asked Bartram, with a laugh.

"The same," answered the stranger. "He has found what he sought, and therefore he comes back again."

"What! then you are Ethan Brand himself?" cried the lime-burner, in amazement. "I am a new-comer here, as you say, and they call it eighteen years since you left the foot of Graylock. But, I can tell you, the good folks still talk about Ethan Brand, in the village yonder, and what a strange errand took him away from his lime-kiln. Well, and so you have found the Unpardonable Sin?"

"Even so!" said the stranger, calmly.

"If the question is a fair one," proceeded Bartram, "where might it be?"

Ethan Brand laid his finger on his own heart. "Here!" replied he.

And then, without mirth in his countenance, but as if moved by an involuntary recognition of the infinite absurdity of seeking throughout the world for what was the closest of all things to himself, and looking into every heart, save his own, for what was hidden in no other breast, he broke into a laugh of scorn. It was the same slow, heavy laugh, that had almost appalled the lime-burner when it heralded the wayfarer's approach.

The solitary mountain-side was made dismal by it. Laughter, when out of place, mistimed, or bursting forth from a disordered state of feeling, may be the most terrible modulation of the human voice. The laughter of one asleep, even if it be a little child, — the madman's laugh, — the wild, screaming laugh of a born idiot, — are sounds that we sometimes tremble to hear, and would always willingly forget. Poets have imagined no utterance of fiends or hobgoblins so fearfully appropriate as a laugh. And even the obtuse lime-burner felt his nerves shaken, as this strange man looked inward at his own heart, and burst into laughter that rolled away into the night, and was indistinctly reverberated among the hills.

"Joe," said he to his little son, "scamper down to the tavern in the village, and tell the jolly fellows that Ethan Brand has come back, and that he has found the Unpardonable Sin!"

The boy darted away on his errand, to which Ethan Brand made no objection, nor seemed hardly to notice it. He sat on a log of wood, looking steadfastly at the iron door of the kiln. When the child was out of sight, and his swift and light footsteps ceased to be heard treading first on the fallen leaves and then on the rocky mountain-path, the lime-burner began to regret his departure. He felt that the little fellow's presence had been a barrier between his guest and himself, and that he must now deal, heart to heart, with a man who, on his own confession, had committed the one only crime for which Heaven could afford no mercy. That crime, in its indistinct blackness, seemed to overshadow him. The lime-burner's own sins rose up within him, and made his memory riotous with a throng of evil shapes that asserted their kindred with the Master Sin, whatever it might be, which it was within the scope of man's corrupted nature to conceive and cherish. They were all of one family; they went to and fro between his breast and Ethan Brand's, and carried dark greetings from one to the other.

Then Bartram remembered the stories which had grown traditionary in reference to this strange man, who had come upon him like a shadow of the night, and was making himself at home in his old place, after so long absence that the dead people, dead and buried for years, would have had more right to be at home, in any familiar spot, than he. Ethan Brand, it was said, had conversed with Satan himself in the lurid blaze of this very kiln. The legend had been matter of mirth heretofore, but looked grisly now. According to this tale, before Ethan Brand departed on his search, he had been accustomed to evoke a fiend from the hot furnace of the lime-kiln, night after night, in order to confer with him about the Unpardonable Sin; the man and the fiend each laboring to frame the image of some mode of guilt which could neither be atoned for nor forgiven. And, with the first gleam of light upon the mountaintop, the fiend crept in at the iron door, there to abide the intensest element of fire, until again summoned forth to share in the dreadful task of extending man's possible guilt beyond the scope of Heaven's else infinite mercy.

While the lime-burner was struggling with the horror of these thoughts, Ethan Brand rose from the log, and flung open the door of the kiln. The action was in such accordance with the idea in Bartram's mind, that he almost expected to see the Evil One issue forth, red-hot, from the raging furnace.

"Hold! hold!" cried he, with a tremulous attempt to laugh; for he was ashamed of his fears, although they overmastered him. "Don't, for mercy's sake, bring out your Devil now!"

"Man!" sternly replied Ethan Brand, "what need have I of the Devil? I have left him behind me, on my track. It is with such half-way sinners as you that he busies himself. Fear not, because I open the door. I do but act by old custom, and am going to trim your fire, like a lime-burner, as I was once."

He stirred the vast coals, thrust in more wood, and bent forward to gaze into the hollow prison-house of the fire, regardless of the fierce glow that reddened upon his face. The lime-burner sat watching him, and half suspected this strange guest of a purpose, if not to evoke a fiend, at least to plunge bodily into the flames, and thus vanish from the sight of man. Ethan Brand, however, drew quietly back, and closed the door of the kiln.

"I have looked," said he, "into many a human heart that was seven times hotter with sinful passions than yonder furnace is with fire. But I found not there what I sought. No, not the Unpardonable Sin!"

"What is the Unpardonable Sin?" asked the lime-burner; and then he shrank farther from his companion, trembling lest his question should be answered.

"It is a sin that grew within my own breast," replied Ethan Brand, standing erect, with a pride that distinguishes all enthusiasts of his stamp. "A sin that grew nowhere else! The sin of an intellect that triumphed over the sense of brotherhood with man and reverence for God, and sacrificed everything to its own mighty claims! The only sin that deserves a recompense of immortal agony! Freely, were it to do again, would I incur the guilt. Unshrinkingly I accept the retribution!"

"The man's head is turned," muttered the lime-burner to himself. "He may be a sinner like the rest of us, — nothing more likely, — but, I'll be sworn, he is a madman too."

Nevertheless, he felt uncomfortable at his situation, alone with Ethan Brand on the wild mountain-side, and was right glad to hear the rough murmur of the tongues, and the footsteps of what seemed a pretty numerous party, stumbling over the stones and rustling through the underbrush. Soon appeared the whole lazy regiment that was wont to infest the village tavern, comprehending three or four individuals who had drunk flip beside the bar-room fire through all the winters, and smoked their pipes beneath the stoop through all the summers, since Ethan Brand's departure. Laughing boisterously, and mingling all their voices together in unceremonious talk, they now burst into the moonshine and narrow streaks of firelight that illuminated the open space before the lime-kiln. Bartram set the door ajar again, flooding the spot with light, that the whole company might get a fair view of Ethan Brand, and he of them.

There, among other old acquaintances, was a once ubiquitous man, now almost extinct, but whom we were formerly sure to encounter at the hotel of every thriving village throughout the country. It was the stage-agent. The present specimen of the genus was a wilted and smoke-dried man, wrinkled and red-nosed, in a smartly cut, brown, bobtailed coat, with brass buttons, who, for a length of time unknown, had kept his desk and corner in the bar-room, and was still puffing what seemed to be the same cigar that he had lighted twenty years before. He had great fame as a dry joker, though, perhaps, less on account of any intrinsic humor than from a certain flavor of brandy-toddy and tobacco-smoke, which impregnated all his ideas and expressions, as well as his person. Another well-remembered though strangely altered face was that of Lawyer Giles, as people still called him in courtesy; an elderly ragamuffin, in his soiled shirt-sleeves and tow-cloth trousers. This poor fellow had been an attorney, in what he called his better days, a sharp practitioner, and in great vogue among the village litigants; but flip, and sling, and toddy, and cocktails, imbibed at all hours, morning, noon, and night, had caused him to slide from intellectual to various kinds and degrees of bodily labor, till at last, to adopt his own phrase, he slid into a soap-vat. In other words, Giles was now a soap-boiler, in a small way. He had come to be but the fragment of a human being, a part of one foot having been chopped off by an axe, and an entire hand torn away by the devilish grip of a steam-engine. Yet, though the corporeal hand was gone, a spiritual member remained; for, stretching forth the stump, Giles steadfastly averred that he felt an invisible thumb and fingers with as vivid a sensation as before the real ones were amputated. A maimed and miserable wretch he was; but one, nevertheless, whom the world could not trample on, and had no right to scorn, either in this or any previous stage of his misfortunes, since he had still kept up the courage and spirit of a man, asked nothing in charity, and with his one hand — and that the left one — fought a stern battle against want and hostile circumstances.

Among the throng, too, came another personage, who, with certain points of similarity to Lawyer Giles, had many more of difference. It was the village doctor; a man of some fifty years, whom, at an earlier period of his life, we introduced as paying a professional visit to Ethan Brand during the latter's supposed insanity. He was now a purple-visaged, rude, and brutal, yet half-gentlemanly figure, with something wild, ruined, and desperate in his talk, and in all the details of his gesture and manners. Brandy possessed this man like an evil spirit, and made him as surly and savage as a wild beast, and as miserable as a lost soul; but there was supposed to be in him such wonderful skill, such native gifts of healing, beyond any which medical science could impart, that society caught hold of him, and would not let him sink out of its reach. So, swaying to and fro upon his horse, and grumbling thick accents at the bedside, he visited all the sick-chambers for miles about among the mountain towns, and sometimes raised a dying man, as it were, by miracle, or quite as often, no doubt, sent his patient to a grave that was dug many a year too soon. The doctor had an everlasting pipe in his mouth, and, as somebody said, in allusion to his habit of swearing, it was always alight with hell-fire.

These three worthies pressed forward, and greeted Ethan Brand each after his own fashion, earnestly inviting him to partake of the contents of a certain black bottle, in which, as they averred, he would find something far better worth seeking for than the Unpardonable Sin. No mind, which has wrought itself by intense and solitary meditation into a high state of enthusiasm, can endure the kind of contact with low and vulgar modes of thought and feeling to which Ethan Brand was now subjected. It made him doubt — and, strange to say, it was a painful doubt — whether he had indeed found the Unpardonable Sin, and found it within himself. The whole question on which he had exhausted life, and more than life, looked like a delusion.

"Leave me," he said bitterly, "ye brute beasts, that have made yourselves so, shrivelling up your souls with fiery liquors! I have done with you. Years and years ago, I groped into your hearts, and found nothing there for my purpose. Get ye gone!"

"Why, you uncivil scoundrel," cried the fierce doctor, "is that the way you respond to the kindness of your best friends? Then let me tell you the truth. You have no more found the Unpardonable Sin than yonder boy Joe has. You are but a crazy fellow, — I told you so twenty years ago, — neither better nor worse than a crazy fellow, and the fit companion of old Humphrey, here!"

He pointed to an old man, shabbily dressed, with long white hair, thin visage, and unsteady eyes. For some years past this aged person had been wandering about among the hills, inquiring of all travelers whom he met for his daughter. The girl, it seemed, had gone off with a company of circus-performers; and occasionally tidings of her came to the village, and fine stories were told of her glittering appearance as she rode on horseback in the ring, or performed marvelous feats on the tight-rope.

The white-haired father now approached Ethan Brand, and gazed unsteadily into his face.

"They tell me you have been all over the earth," said he, wringing his hands with earnestness. "You must have seen my daughter, for she makes a grand figure in the world, and everybody goes to see her. Did she send any word to her old father, or say when she was coming back?"

Ethan Brand's eye quailed beneath the old man's. That daughter, from whom he so earnestly desired a word of greeting, was the Esther of our tale, the very girl whom, with such cold and remorseless purpose, Ethan Brand had made the subject of a psychological experiment, and wasted, absorbed, and perhaps annihilated her soul in the process.

"Yes," murmured he, turning away from the hoary wanderer; "it is no delusion. There is an Unpardonable Sin!"

While these things were passing, a merry scene was going forward in the area of cheerful light, beside the spring and before the door of the hut. A number of the youth of the village, young men and girls, had hurried up the hillside, impelled by curiosity to see Ethan Brand, the hero of so many a legend familiar to their childhood. Finding nothing, however, very remarkable in his aspect, — nothing but a sunburnt wayfarer, in plain garb and dusty shoes, who sat looking into the fire as if he fancied pictures among the coals, — these young people speedily grew tired of observing him. As it happened, there was other amusement at hand. An old German Jew, traveling with a diorama on his back, was passing down the mountain-road towards the village just as the party turned aside from it, and, in hopes of eking out the profits of the day, the showman had kept them company to the lime-kiln.

"Come, old Dutchman," cried one of the young men, "let us see your pictures, if you can swear they are worth looking at!"

"Oh, yes, Captain," answered the Jew, — whether as a matter of courtesy or craft, he styled everybody Captain, — "I shall show you, indeed, some very superb pictures!"

So, placing his box in a proper position, he invited the young men and girls to look through the glass orifices of the machine, and proceeded to exhibit a series of the most outrageous scratchings and daubings, as specimens of the fine arts, that ever an itinerant showman had the face to impose upon his circle of spectators. The pictures were worn out, moreover, tattered, full of cracks and wrinkles, dingy with tobacco-smoke, and otherwise in a most pitiable condition. Some purported to be cities, public edifices, and ruined castles in Europe; others represented Napoleon's battles and Nelson's sea-fights; and in the midst of these would be seen a gigantic, brown, hairy hand, — which might have been mistaken for the Hand of Destiny, though, in truth, it was only the showman's, — pointing its forefinger to various scenes of the conflict, while its owner gave historical illustrations. When, with much merriment at its abominable deficiency of merit, the exhibition was concluded, the German bade little Joe put his head into the box. Viewed through the magnifying-glasses, the boy's round, rosy visage assumed the strangest imaginable aspect of an immense Titanic child, the mouth grinning broadly, and the eyes and every other feature overflowing with fun at the joke. Suddenly, however, that merry face turned pale, and its expression changed to horror, for this easily impressed and excitable child had become sensible that the eye of Ethan Brand was fixed upon him through the glass.

"You make the little man to be afraid, Captain," said the German Jew, turning up the dark and strong outline of his visage, from his stooping posture. "But look again, and, by chance, I shall cause you to see somewhat that is very fine, upon my word!"

Ethan Brand gazed into the box for an instant, and then starting back, looked fixedly at the German. What had he seen? Nothing, apparently; for a curious youth, who had peeped in almost at the same moment, beheld only a vacant space of canvas.

"I remember you now," muttered Ethan Brand to the showman.

"Ah, Captain," whispered the Jew of Nuremberg, with a dark smile, "I find it to be a heavy matter in my show-box, — this Unpardonable Sin! By my faith, Captain, it has wearied my shoulders, this long day, to carry it over the mountain."

"Peace," answered Ethan Brand, sternly, "or get thee into the furnace yonder!"

The Jew's exhibition had scarcely concluded,

when a great, elderly dog — who seemed to be his own master, as no person in the company laid claim to him — saw fit to render himself the object of public notice. Hitherto, he had shown himself a very quiet, well-disposed old dog, going round from one to another, and, by way of being sociable, offering his rough head to be patted by any kindly hand that would take so much trouble. But now, all of a sudden, this grave and venerable quadruped, of his own mere motion, and without the slightest suggestion from anybody else, began to run round after his tail, which, to heighten the absurdity of the proceeding, was a great deal shorter than it should have been. Never was seen such head-long eagerness in pursuit of an object that could not possibly be attained; never was heard such a tremendous outbreak of growling, snarling, barking, and snapping, — as if one end of the ridiculous brute's body were at deadly and most unforgivable enmity with the other. Faster and faster, round about went the cur; and faster and still faster fled the unapproachable brevity of his tail; and louder and fiercer grew his yells of rage and animosity; until, utterly exhausted, and as far from the goal as ever, the foolish old dog ceased his performance as suddenly as he had begun it. The next moment he was as mild, quiet, sensible, and respectable in his deportment, as when he first scraped acquaintance with the company.

As may be supposed, the exhibition was greeted with universal laughter, clapping of hands, and shouts of encore, to which the canine performer responded by wagging all that there was to wag of his tail, but appeared totally unable to repeat his very successful effort to amuse the spectators.

Meanwhile, Ethan Brand had resumed his seat upon the log, and moved, it might be, by a perception of some remote analogy between his own case and that of this self-pursuing cur, he broke into the awful laugh, which, more than any other token, expressed the condition of his inward being. From that moment, the merriment of the party was at an end; they stood aghast, dreading lest the inauspicious sound should be reverberated around the horizon, and that mountain would thunder it to mountain, and so the horror be prolonged upon their ears. Then, whispering one to another that it was late, — that the moon was almost down, — that the August night was growing chill, — they hurried homewards, leaving the lime-burner and little Joe to deal as they might with their unwelcome guest. Save for these three human beings, the open space on the hillside was a solitude, set in a vast gloom of forest. Beyond that darksome verge, the firelight glimmered on the stately trunks and almost black foliage of pines, intermixed with the lighter verdure of sapling oaks, maples, and poplars, while here and there lay the gigantic corpses of dead trees, decaying on the leaf-strewn soil. And it seemed to little Joe — a timorous and imaginative child — that the silent forest was holding its breath until some fearful thing should happen.

Ethan Brand thrust more wood into the fire, and closed the door of the kiln; then looking over his shoulder at the lime-burner and his son, he bade, rather than advised, them to retire to rest.

"For myself, I cannot sleep," said he. "I have matters that it concerns me to meditate upon. I will watch the fire, as I used to do in the old time."

"And call the Devil out of the furnace to keep you company, I suppose," muttered Bartram, who had been making intimate acquaintance with the black bottle above mentioned. "But watch, if you like, and call as many devils as you like! For my part, I shall be all the better for a snooze. Come, Joe!"

As the boy followed his father into the hut, he looked back at the wayfarer, and the tears came into his eyes, for his tender spirit had an intuition of the bleak and terrible loneliness in which this man had enveloped himself.

When they had gone, Ethan Brand sat listening to the crackling of the kindled wood, and looking at the little spirts of fire that issued through the chinks of the door. These trifles, however, once so familiar, had but the slightest hold of his attention, while deep within his mind he was reviewing the gradual but marvelous change that had been wrought upon him by the search to which he had devoted himself. He remembered how the night dew had fallen upon him, — how the dark forest had whispered to him, — how the stars had gleamed upon him, — a simple and loving man, watching his fire in the years gone by, and ever musing as it burned. He remembered with what tenderness, with what love and sympathy for mankind, and what pity for human guilt and woe, he had first begun to contemplate those ideas which afterwards became the inspiration of his life;

with what reverence he had then looked into the heart of man, viewing it as a temple originally divine, and, however desecrated, still to be held sacred by a brother; with what awful fear he had deprecated the success of his pursuit, and prayed that the Unpardonable Sin might never be revealed to him. Then ensued that vast intellectual development, which, in its progress, disturbed the counterpoise between his mind and heart. The Idea that possessed his life had operated as a means of education; it had gone on cultivating his powers to the highest point of which they were susceptible; it had raised him from the level of an unlettered laborer to stand on a star-lit eminence, whither the philosophers of the earth, laden with the lore of universities, might vainly strive to clamber after him. So much for the intellect! But where was the heart? That, indeed, had withered, — had contracted, — had hardened, — had perished! It had ceased to partake of the universal throb. He had lost his hold of the magnetic chain of humanity. He was no longer a brother-man, opening the chambers or the dungeons of our common nature by the key of holy sympathy, which gave him a right to share in all its secrets; he was now a cold observer, looking on mankind as the subject of his experiment, and, at length, converting man and woman to be his puppets, and pulling the wires that moved them to such degrees of crime as were demanded for his study.

Thus Ethan Brand became a fiend. He began to be so from the moment that his moral nature had ceased to keep the pace of improvement with his intellect. And now, as his highest effort and inevitable development, — as the bright and gorgeous flower, and rich, delicious fruit of his life's labor, — he had produced the Unpardonable Sin!

"What more have I to seek? what more to achieve?" said Ethan Brand to himself. "My task is done, and well done!"

Starting from the log with a certain alacrity in his gait and ascending the hillock of earth that was raised against the stone circumference of the lime-kiln, he thus reached the top of the structure. It was a space of perhaps ten feet across, from edge to edge, presenting a view of the upper surface of the immense mass of broken marble with which the kiln was heaped. All these innumerable blocks and fragments of marble were red-hot and vividly on fire, sending up great spouts of blue flame, which quivered aloft and danced madly, as within a magic circle, and sank and rose again, with continual and multitudinous activity. As the lonely man bent forward over this terrible body of fire, the blasting heat smote up against his person with a breath that, it might be supposed, would have scorched and shrivelled him up in a moment.

Ethan Brand stood erect, and raised his arms on high. The blue flames played upon his face, and imparted the wild and ghastly light which alone could have suited its expression; it was that of a fiend on the verge of plunging into his gulf of intensest torment.

"O Mother Earth," cried he, "who art no more my Mother, and into whose bosom this frame shall never be resolved! O mankind, whose brotherhood I have cast off, and trampled thy great heart beneath my feet! O stars of heaven, that shone on me of old, as if to light me onward and upward! — farewell all, and forever. Come, deadly element of Fire, — henceforth my familiar frame! Embrace me, as I do thee!"

That night the sound of a fearful peal of laughter rolled heavily through the sleep of the lime-burner and his little son; dim shapes of horror and anguish haunted their dreams, and seemed still present in the rude hovel, when they opened their eyes to the daylight.

"Up, boy, up!" cried the lime-burner, staring about him. "Thank Heaven, the night is gone, at last; and rather than pass such another, I would watch my lime-kiln, wide awake, for a twelvemonth. This Ethan Brand, with his humbug of an Unpardonable Sin, has done me no such mighty favor, in taking my place!"

He issued from the hut, followed by little Joe, who kept fast hold of his father's hand. The early sunshine was already pouring its gold upon the mountain-tops, and though the valleys were still in shadow, they smiled cheerfully in the promise of the bright day that was hastening onward. The village, completely shut in by hills, which swelled away gently about it, looked as if it had rested peacefully in the hollow of the great hand of Providence. Every dwelling was distinctly visible; the little spires of the two churches pointed upwards, and caught a foreglimmering of brightness from the sungilt skies upon their gilded weathercocks. The tavern was astir, and the figure of the old, smoke-dried stage-agent, cigar in mouth, was seen beneath the stoop. Old Graylock was glorified with a golden cloud upon his head. Scattered likewise over the breasts of the surrounding mountains, there were heaps of hoary mist, in fantastic shapes, some of them far down into the valley, others high up towards the summits, and still others, of the same family of mist or cloud, hovering in the gold radiance of the upper atmosphere. Stepping from one to another of the clouds that rested on the hills, and thence to the loftier brotherhood that sailed in air, it seemed almost as if a mortal man might thus ascend into the heavenly regions. Earth was so mingled with sky that it was a daydream to look at it.

To supply that charm of the familiar and homely, which Nature so readily adopts into a scene like this, the stage coach was rattling down the mountain-road, and the driver sounded his horn, while Echo caught up the notes, and intertwined them into a rich and varied and elaborate harmony, of which the original performer could lay claim to little share. The great hills played a concert among themselves, each contributing a strain of airy sweetness.

Little Joe's face brightened at once.

"Dear father," cried he, skipping cheerily to and fro, "that strange man is gone, and the sky and the mountains all seem glad of it!"

"Yes," growled the lime-burner, with an oath, "but he has let the fire go down, and no thanks to him if five hundred bushels of lime are not spoiled. If I catch the fellow hereabouts again, I shall feel like tossing him into the furnace!"

With his long pole in his hand, he ascended to the top of the kiln. After a moment's pause, he called to his son.

"Come up here, Joe!" said he.

So little Joe ran up the hillock, and stood by his father's side. The marble was all burnt into perfect, snow-white lime. But on its surface, in the midst of the circle, — snow-white too, and thoroughly converted into lime — lay a human skeleton, in the attitude of a person who, after long toil, lies down to long repose. Within the ribs — strange to say — was the shape of a human heart.

"Was the fellow's heart made of marble?" cried Bartram, in some perplexity at this phenomenon. "At any rate, it is burnt into what looks like special good lime; and, taking all the bones together, my kiln is half a bushel the richer for him."

So saying, the rude lime-burner lifted his pole, and, letting it fall upon the skeleton, the relics of Ethan Brand were crumbled into fragments.

Herman Melville [1819–1891]

Hawthorne had shown that great fiction could come out of long seclusion; Melville showed that it could come out of intense adventurous experience.

When Melville was born, his father, Allan Melville, of distinguished New England Scottish ancestry, was a cultivated gentleman-merchant in New York, dealing in French fabrics, hose, perfumes, and the like. During a business depression he became bankrupt, and in 1830 tried to rehabilitate himself in Albany. There, two· years later, he died, leaving Herman (a boy of thirteen) and seven other children. The widow, who had been Maria Gansevoort, of a notable New Netherland family, managed the domestic economy with skill. From parents in the Dutch Reformed Church she had acquired a piety that she sought to pass on to her children. In later years Melville retained a close knowledge of the Bible and a speculative awareness of the essential problems of religion. His formal schooling ended when he was only fifteen — after that he was educated by varied experience and wide reading.

He worked in a bank, he worked in a store, he worked on a farm, he did some teaching. Then, at age twenty, he had his first taste of sea life, shipping as a cabin-boy on a freighter, and, though he did not know it, beginning to gather the primary subject-matter of his fiction. On this voyage he sampled the hard life of the seaman, and saw, not the famed charms of the Old World, but the waterfront slums of vice-ridden Liverpool. After his return he taught school off and on, then submitted again to what he later called "the everlasting itch for things remote."

After a trip to Illinois in 1840, he shipped, early the next year, on the whaler *Acushnet* ("my Yale College and Harvard") bound for the South Seas, and, as it turned out, was away nearly four years. After eighteen months on the ship, he deserted, and with a companion lived in the society of cannibals, the Typees of the Marquesas Islands. Escaping on an Australian whaler to Tahiti, he shipped on another whaler that sailed in Japanese waters and eventually brought him to Honolulu. He joined the American navy, at length returned home on the frigate *United States*, and was discharged in Boston.

Graduated from the school of the sea, Melville entered the vocation of writing. He turned his wanderings into fiction, drawing into the net what he could find in books (such as Stewart's *A Visit to the South Seas* and Ames's *A Mariner's Sketches*). The result was a series of romances, varying in autobiographic content, all published within five years: *Typee* (1846), his life among the cannibals; *Omoo*, adventures in the South Seas; *Redburn*, the voyage to Liverpool; *Mardi*, the South Seas again, in an allegorical and satirical mode; *White-Jacket*, service in the navy; and *Moby Dick* (1851), life on a whaling ship.

In 1847, the year of the second of these books, he married Elizabeth Shaw, daughter of the chief justice of Massachusetts. For nearly three years he lived and wrote in New York (visiting London and Paris in winter 1849–50). Then he settled with his wife and first child — he was soon to be father to two sons and two daughters — at Pittsfield, Massachusetts. While Hawthorne, a few miles away at Lenox, was writing *The House of the Seven Gables*, Melville was deep in *Moby Dick, or The Whale*, a book "broiled," he told Hawthorne, "in hell-fire." In this book Melville did for the South Seas and the whalers what Cooper had done for the frontier and Mark Twain was to do for the great age of the Mississippi steamboats. More important, he created a fine story, an unforgettable character, an impressive wrestling with the problem of evil, and a rich, symphonic style. (On his use of symbols, see the period introduction, page 192.)

Melville had poured his best into *Moby Dick*, and felt that he had written himself out, though forty years of his life were still before him. For reasons not very clear, his art fell into a long decline. In 1852 he published *Pierre, or The Ambiguities*, a darkly symbolical study of good and evil, and then his last novels, *Israel Potter* and *The Confidence Man*. He tried shorter fiction in *The Piazza Tales*. He tried poetry: *Battle-Pieces and Aspects of the War* and *Clarel*. Then, surprisingly enough, late in life he achieved one more triumph — *Billy Budd*, a short novel left among his manuscripts and unpublished till 1924. Unlike Ahab and Pierre, his earlier heroes, Billy Budd, in tragic defeat, accepts the inscrutable law of life. In this attitude the young sailor perhaps represents the old author.

Once his writing career had turned awry, Melville could not expect to support his sizeable family by his pen. He received help from relatives, he tried lecturing, and in 1866 was appointed inspector of customs in New York, a post which he held for nearly twenty years. He died obscure.

The story of Melville's reputation is not without significance. Both in England and the United States he had once been popular as a writer of adventurous narratives of the South Seas. Then his new vein of symbolism and satire alienated his many readers. His masterpiece, *Moby Dick*, was dismissed in one journal as "so much trash," and when it was followed by *Pierre* another journal feared that he had gone "clean daft." In 1900 Barrett Wendell, in an extensive *Literary History of America*, gave Melville only one sentence, saying that he "began a career of literary promise, which never came to fruition"! As late as 1921, Carl Van Doren, in *The American Novel*, allotted Melville only a few pages, linking him with a group of minor novelists. Yet by this time Melville was at last receiving recognition as one of the greatest American writers. In a revised edition of *The American Novel* Van Doren found it natural to make Melville the subject of a separate, full-length, and enthusiastic chapter. How are we to account for so remarkable a revival? Evidently the disillusioned and rebellious 1920's, in both England and America, found a kindred spirit in the author of *Moby Dick*. The next decades responded both to his probing of the problem of evil in the world, and to his literary art, an art like that cultivated by many moderns, symbolical, ambiguous, at once deeply imaginative and witty.

Further reading: *Moby Dick*. Willard Thorp, *Herman Melville* (American Writers Series), 1938. Leon Howard, *Herman Melville: A Biography*, 1951. Richard Chase, *Herman Melville, A Critical Study*, 1949. C. R. Anderson, *Melville in the South Seas*, 1939. F. O. Matthiessen, *American Renaissance*, 1941 (Book 3).

The Great Art of Telling the Truth

🐦 In July 1850 Melville came upon Hawthorne's *Mosses from an Old Manse*. In excited admiration he wrote a review article, concealed his authorship by signing it as "By a Virginian," and had it printed in the *Literary World* after the middle of August. Between the two dates — on August 5 — Melville met Hawthorne for the first time and they soon became friends.

The following paragraphs from the article are interesting not only for what they say about Hawthorne, but also for what they reveal about Melville himself, especially his passionate desire to probe to "the very axis of reality." It happens that at this time he was writing his own great novel, *Moby Dick*, himself wrestling with "black" Truth. In his enthusiasm over the example of Hawthorne, he declares: "Hawthorne has dropped germinous seeds into my soul. He expands and deepens down, the more I contemplate him; and further and further shoots his strong New England roots in the hot soil of my Southern soul." When *Moby Dick* was published, it was dedicated to Nathaniel Hawthorne.

It is the least part of genius that attracts admiration. Where Hawthorne is known, he seems to be deemed a pleasant writer, with a pleasant style, — a sequestered, harmless man from whom any deep and weighty thing would hardly be anticipated — a man who means no meanings. But there is no man, in whom humor and love, like mountain peaks, soar to such a

rapt height as to receive the irradiations of the upper skies; — there is no man in whom humor and love are developed in that high form called genius; no such man can exist without also 5 possessing, as the indispensable complement of these, a great, deep intellect, which drops down into the universe like a plummet. Or, love and humor are only the eyes through which such an intellect views this world. The great beauty in 10 such a mind is but the product of its strength.***

Spite of all the Indian-summer sunlight on the hither side of Hawthorne's soul, the other side — like the dark half of the physical sphere 15 — is shrouded in a blackness, ten times black. But this darkness but gives more effect to the ever-moving dawn, that for ever advances through it, and circumnavigates his world. Whether Hawthorne has simply availed himself 20 of this mystical blackness as a means to the wondrous effects he makes it to produce in his lights and shades; or whether there really lurks in him, perhaps unknown to himself, a touch of Puritanic gloom, — this, I cannot altogether 25 tell. Certain it is, however, that this great power of blackness in him derives its force from its appeals to the Calvinistic sense of Innate Depravity and Original Sin, from whose visitations, in some shape or other, no deeply think-30 ing mind is always and wholly free. For, in certain moods, no man can weigh this world without throwing in something, somehow like Original Sin, to strike the uneven balance. At all events, perhaps no writer has ever wielded this terrific thought with greater terror than this same harmless Hawthorne. Still more: this black conceit pervades him through and through. You may be witched by his sunlight, — transported by the bright gildings in the skies he builds over you; but there is the blackness of darkness beyond; and even his bright gildings but fringe and play upon the edges of thunderclouds. In one word, the world is mistaken in this Nathaniel Hawthorne. He himself must often have smiled at its absurd misconception of him. He is immeasurably deeper than the plummet of the mere critic. For it is not the brain that can test such a man; it is only the heart. You cannot come to know greatness by inspecting it; there is no glimpse to be caught of it, except by intuition; you need not ring it, you but touch it, and you find it is gold.

Now, it is that blackness in Hawthorne, of which I have spoken, that so fixes and fascinates me. It may be, nevertheless, that it is too largely developed in him. Perhaps he does not give us a ray of his light for every shade of his dark. But however this may be, this blackness it is that furnishes the infinite obscure of his background, — that back-ground, against which Shakspeare plays his grandest conceits, the things that have made for Shakspeare his loftiest but most circumscribed renown, as the profoundest of thinkers. For by philosophers Shakspeare is not adored as the great man of tragedy and comedy. — "Off with his head; so much for Buckingham!" This sort of rant, interlined by another hand, brings down the house, — those mistaken souls, who dream of Shakspeare as a mere man of Richard-the-Third humps and Macbeth daggers. But it is those deep far-away things in him; those occasional flashings-forth of the intuitive Truth in him; those short, quick probings at the very axis of reality; — these are the things that make Shakspeare, Shakspeare. Through the mouths of the dark characters of Hamlet, Timon, Lear, and Iago, he craftily says, or sometimes insinuates the things which we feel to be so terrifically true, that it were all but madness for any good man, in his own proper character, to utter, or even hint of them. Tormented into desperation, Lear, the frantic king, tears off the mask, and speaks the same madness of vital truth. But, as I before said, it is the least part of genius that attracts admiration. And so, much of the blind, unbridled admiration that has been heaped upon Shakspeare, has been lavished upon the least part of him. And few of his endless commentators and critics seem to have remembered, or even perceived, that the immediate products of a great mind are not so great as that undeveloped and sometimes undevelopable yet dimly-discernible greatness, to which those immediate products are but the infallible indices. In Shakspeare's tomb lies infinitely more than Shakspeare ever wrote. And if I magnify Shakspeare, it is not so much for what he did do as for what he did not do, or refrained from doing. For in this world of lies, Truth is forced to fly like a scared white doe in the woodlands; and only by cunning glimpses will she reveal herself, as in Shakspeare and other masters of the great Art of Telling the Truth, — even though it be covertly and by snatches.

But if this view of the all-popular Shakspeare be seldom taken by his readers, and if very few who extol him have ever read him deeply, or perhaps, only have seen him on the tricky stage (which alone made, and is still making him his mere mob renown) — if few men have time, or patience, or palate, for the spiritual truth as it is in that great genius; — it is then no matter of surprise, that in a contemporaneous age, Nathaniel Hawthorne is a man as yet almost utterly mistaken among men. Here and there, in some quiet arm-chair in the noisy town, or some deep nook among the noiseless mountains, he may be appreciated for something of what he is. But unlike Shakspeare, who was forced to the contrary course by circumstances, Hawthorne (either from simple disinclination, or else from inaptitude) refrains from all the popularizing noise and show of broad farce and blood-besmeared tragedy; content with the still, rich utterance of a great intellect in repose, and which sends few thoughts into circulation, except they be arterialized at his large warm lungs, and expanded in his honest heart.

Bartleby the Scrivener

A Story of Wall Street

🦅 First published in *Putnam's Monthly* (1853), this story was one of the *Piazza Tales* written for the magazines at a period when Melville was discouraged at the neglect of his masterpiece, *Moby Dick*, and *Pierre*. Its Wall Street setting and Dickensian echoes show Melville in a more realistic vein than usual, and it is possible he is commenting in part on the indifference of the world of business toward a maladjusted individual. Bartleby is an enigmatic combination of exasperating stubbornness and pathetic passivity, unable to respond to the sympathy even of his well-disposed employer. It has been suggested that Melville was referring in the scrivener, a former "Dead Letter" clerk, to his own literary frustrations, but the reader should ascertain for himself whether the author identifies himself more with the lawyer than with Bartleby and to what extent this is a psychological study of negation.

I am a rather elderly man. The nature of my avocations, for the last thirty years, has brought me into more than ordinary contact with what would seem an interesting and somewhat singular set of men, of whom, as yet, nothing, that I know of, has ever been written — I mean, the law-copyists, or scriveners. I have known very many of them, professionally and privately, and, if I pleased, could relate divers histories, at which good-natured gentlemen might smile, and sentimental souls might weep. But I waive the biographies of all other scriveners, for a few passages in the life of Bartleby, who was a scrivener, the strangest I ever saw, or heard of. While, of other law-copyists, I might write the complete life, of Bartleby nothing of that sort can be done. I believe that no materials exist, for a full and satisfactory biography of this man. It is an irreparable loss to literature. Bartleby was one of those beings of whom nothing is ascertainable, except from the original sources, and, in his case, those are very small. What my own astonished eyes saw of Bartleby, *that* is all I know of him, except, indeed, one vague report, which will appear in the sequel.

Ere introducing the scrivener, as he first appeared to me, it is fit I make some mention of myself, my *employés*, my business, my chambers, and general surroundings; because some such description is indispensable to an adequate understanding of the chief character about to be presented. Imprimis: I am a man who, from his youth upwards, has been filled with a profound conviction that the easiest way of life is the best. Hence, though I belong to a profession proverbially energetic and nervous, even to turbulence, at times, yet nothing of that sort have I ever suffered to invade my peace. I am one of those unambitious lawyers who never address a jury, or in any way draw down public applause; but, in the cool tranquillity of a snug retreat, do a snug business among rich men's bonds, and mortgages, and title-deeds. All who know me, consider me an eminently *safe* man. The late John Jacob Astor, a personage little given to poetic enthusiasm, had no hesitation in pronouncing my first grand point to be prudence; my next, method. I do not speak it in vanity, but simply record the fact, that I was not unemployed in my profession by the late John Jacob Astor; a name which, I admit, I love to repeat; for it hath a rounded and orbicular sound to it, and rings like unto bullion. I will freely add, that I was not insensible to the late John Jacob Astor's good opinion.

Some time prior to the period at which this little history begins, my avocations had been largely increased. The good old office, now extinct in the State of New York, of a Master in Chancery, had been conferred upon me. It was not a very arduous office, but very pleasantly remunerative. I seldom lose my temper; much more seldom indulge in dangerous indignation at wrongs and outrages; but I must be permitted to be rash here and declare, that I consider the sudden and violent abrogation of the office of Master in Chancery, by the new Constitution, as a —— premature act; inasmuch as I had counted upon a life-lease of the profits, whereas I only received those of a few short years. But this is by the way.

My chambers were up stairs, at No. — Wall Street. At one end, they looked upon the white wall of the interior of a spacious skylight shaft, penetrating the building from top to bottom.

This view might have been considered rather tame than otherwise, deficient in what landscape painters call "life." But, if so, the view from the other end of my chambers offered, at least, a contrast, if nothing more. In that direction, my windows commanded an unobstructed view of a lofty brick wall, black by age and everlasting shade; which wall required no spy-glass to bring out its lurking beauties, but, for the benefit of all near-sighted spectators, was pushed up to within ten feet of my window-panes. Owing to the great height of the surrounding buildings, and my chambers being on the second floor, the interval between this wall and mine not a little resembled a huge square cistern.

At the period just preceding the advent of Bartleby, I had two persons as copyists in my employment, and a promising lad as an office-boy. First, Turkey; second, Nippers; third, Ginger Nut. These may seem names, the like of which are not usually found in the Directory. In truth, they were nicknames, mutually conferred upon each other by my three clerks, and were deemed expressive of their respective persons or characters. Turkey was a short, pursy Englishman, of about my own age — that is, somewhere not far from sixty. In the morning, one might say, his face was of a fine florid hue, but after twelve o'clock, meridian — his dinner hour — it blazed like a grate full of Christmas coals; and continued blazing — but, as it were, with a gradual wane — till six o'clock, P.M., or thereabouts; after which, I saw no more of the proprietor of the face, which, gaining its meridian with the sun, seemed to set with it, to rise, culminate, and decline the following day, with the like regularity and undiminished glory. There are many singular coincidences I have known in the course of my life, not the least among which was the fact, that, exactly when Turkey displayed his fullest beams from his red and radiant countenance, just then, too, at that critical moment, began the daily period when I considered his business capacities as seriously disturbed for the remainder of the twenty-four hours. Not that he was absolutely idle, or averse to business then; far from it. The difficulty was, he was apt to be altogether too energetic. There was a strange, inflamed, flurried, flighty recklessness of activity about him. He would be incautious in dipping his pen into his inkstand. All his blots upon my documents were dropped there after twelve o'clock, meridian. Indeed, not only would he be reckless, and sadly given to making blots in the afternoon, but, some days, he went further, and was rather noisy. At such times, too, his face flamed with augmented blazonry, as if cannel coal had been heaped on anthracite. He made an unpleasant racket with his chair; spilled his sand-box; in mending his pens, impatiently split them all to pieces, and threw them on the floor in a sudden passion; stood up, and leaned over his table, boxing his papers about in a most indecorous manner, very sad to behold in an elderly man like him. Nevertheless, as he was in many ways a most valuable person to me, and all the time before twelve o'clock, meridian, was

the quickest, steadiest creature, too, accomplishing a great deal of work in a style not easily to be matched — for these reasons, I was willing to overlook his eccentricities, though indeed, occasionally, I remonstrated with him. I did this very gently, however, because, though the civilest, nay, the blandest and most reverential of men in the morning, yet, in the afternoon, he was disposed, upon provocation, to be slightly rash with his tongue — in fact, insolent. Now, valuing his morning services as I did, and resolved not to lose them — yet, at the same time, made uncomfortable by his inflamed ways after twelve o'clock — and being a man of peace, unwilling by my admonitions to call forth unseemly retorts from him, I took upon me, one Saturday noon (he was always worse on Saturdays) to hint to him, very kindly, that, perhaps, now that he was growing old, it might be well to abridge his labors; in short, he need not come to my chambers after twelve o'clock, but, dinner over, had best go home to his lodgings, and rest himself till tea-time. But no; he insisted upon his afternoon devotions. His countenance became intolerably fervid, as he oratorically assured me — gesticulating with a long ruler at the other end of the room — that if his services in the morning were useful, how indispensable, then, in the afternoon?

"With submission, sir," said Turkey, on this occasion, "I consider myself your right-hand man. In the morning I but marshal and deploy my columns; but in the afternoon I put myself at their head, and gallantly charge the foe, thus" — and he made a violent thrust with the ruler.

"But the blots, Turkey," intimated I.

"True; but, with submission, sir, behold these hairs! I am getting old. Surely, sir, a blot or two of a warm afternoon is not to be severely urged against gray hairs. Old age — even if it blot the page — is honorable. With submission, sir, we *both* are getting old."

This appeal to my fellow-feeling was hardly to be resisted. At all events, I saw that go he would not. So, I made up my mind to let him stay, resolving, nevertheless, to see to it that, during the afternoon, he had to do with my less important papers.

Nippers, the second on my list, was a whiskered, sallow, and, upon the whole, rather piratical-looking young man, of about five-and-twenty. I always deemed him the victim of two evil powers — ambition and indigestion. The ambition was evinced by a certain impatience of the duties of a mere copyist, an unwarrantable usurpation of strictly professional affairs, such as the original drawing up of legal documents. The indigestion seemed betokened in an occasional nervous testiness and grinning irritability, causing the teeth to audibly grind together over mistakes committed in copying; unnecessary maledictions, hissed, rather than spoken, in the heat of business; and especially by a continual discontent with the height of the table where he worked. Though of a very ingenious mechanical turn, Nippers could never get this table to suit him. He put chips under it, blocks of various sorts, bits of pasteboard, and at last went so far as to attempt an exquisite adjustment, by final pieces of folded blotting-paper. But no invention would answer. If, for the sake of easing his back, he brought the table-lid at a sharp angle well up towards his chin, and wrote there like a man using the steep roof of a Dutch house for his desk, then he declared that it stopped the circulation in his arms. If now he lowered the table to his waistbands, and stooped over it in writing, then there was a sore aching in his back. In short, the truth of the matter was, Nippers knew not what he wanted. Or, if he wanted anything, it was to be rid of a scrivener's table altogether. Among the manifestations of his diseased ambition was a fondness he had for receiving visits from certain ambiguous-looking fellows in seedy coats, whom he called his clients. Indeed, I was aware that not only was he, at times, considerable of a ward-politician, but he occasionally did a little business at the Justices' courts, and was not unknown on the steps of the Tombs. I have good reason to believe, however, that one individual who called upon him at my chambers, and who, with a grand air, he insisted was his client, was no other than a dun, and the alleged title-deed, a bill. But, with all his failings, and the annoyances he caused me, Nippers, like his compatriot Turkey, was a very useful man to me; wrote a neat, swift hand; and when he chose, was not deficient in a gentlemanly sort of deportment. Added to this, he always dressed in a gentlemanly sort of way; and so, incidentally, reflected credit upon my chambers. Whereas, with respect to Turkey, I had much ado to keep him from being a reproach to me. His clothes were apt to look oily, and smell of eating-houses. He wore his pantaloons very loose and baggy in summer. His coats were execrable; his hat not to be handled. But while the hat was a thing of indifference to me, inasmuch

as his natural civility and deference, as a dependent Englishman, always led him to doff it the moment he entered the room, yet his coat was another matter. Concerning his coats, I reasoned with him; but with no effect. The truth was, I suppose, that a man with so small an income could not afford to sport such a lustrous face and a lustrous coat at one and the same time. As Nippers once observed, Turkey's money went chiefly for red ink. One winter day, I presented Turkey with a highly respectable-looking coat of my own — a padded gray coat, of a most comfortable warmth, and which buttoned straight up from the knee to the neck. I thought Turkey would appreciate the favor, and abate his rashness and obstreperousness of afternoons. But no; I verily believe that buttoning himself up in so downy and blanket-like a coat had a pernicious effect upon him — upon the same principle that too much oats are bad for horses. In fact, precisely as a rash, restive horse is said to feel his oats, so Turkey felt his coat. It made him insolent. He was a man whom prosperity harmed.

Though, concerning the self-indulgent habits of Turkey, I had my own private surmises, yet, touching Nippers, I was well persuaded that, whatever might be his faults in other respects, he was, at least, a temperate young man. But, indeed, nature herself seemed to have been his vintner, and, at his birth, charged him so thoroughly with an irritable, brandy-like disposition, that all subsequent potations were needless. When I consider how, amid the stillness of my chambers, Nippers would sometimes impatiently rise from his seat, and stooping over his table, spread his arms wide apart, seize the whole desk, and move it, and jerk it, with a grim, grinding motion on the floor, as if the table were a perverse volutary agent, intent on thwarting and vexing him, I plainly perceive that, for Nippers, brandy-and-water were altogether superfluous.

It was fortunate for me that, owing to its peculiar cause — indigestion — the irritability and consequent nervousness of Nippers were mainly observable in the morning, while in the afternoon he was comparatively mild. So that, Turkey's paroxysms only coming on about twelve o'clock, I never had to do with their eccentricities at one time. Their fits relieved each other, like guards. When Nippers's was on, Turkey's was off; and *vice versa*. This was a good natural arrangement, under the circumstances.

Ginger Nut, the third on my list, was a lad, some twelve years old. His father was a carman, ambitious of seeing his son on the bench instead of a cart, before he died. So he sent him to my office, as student at law, errand-boy, cleaner and sweeper, at the rate of one dollar a week. He had a little desk to himself, but he did not use it much. Upon inspection, the drawer exhibited a great array of the shells of various sorts of nuts. Indeed, to this quick-witted youth, the whole noble science of the law was contained in a nut-shell. Not the least among the employments of Ginger Nut, as well as one which he discharged with the most alacrity, was his duty as cake and apple purveyor for Turkey and Nippers. Copy-ing law-papers being proverbially a dry, husky sort of business, my two scriveners were fain to moisten their mouths very often with Spitzen-bergs, to be had at the numerous stalls nigh the Custom House and Post Office. Also, they sent Ginger Nut very frequently for that peculiar cake — small, flat, round, and very spicy — after which he had been named by them. Of a cold morning, when business was but dull, Turkey would gobble up scores of these cakes, as if they were mere wafers — indeed, they sell them at the rate of six or eight for a penny — the scrape of his pen blending with the crunching of the crisp particles in his mouth. Of all the fiery afternoon blunders and flurried rashnesses of Turkey, was his once moistening a ginger-cake between his lips, and clapping it on to a mort-gage, for a seal. I came within an ace of dismiss-ing him then. But he mollified me by making an oriental bow, and saying —

"With submission, sir, it was generous of me to find you in stationery on my own account."

Now my original business — that of a con-veyancer and title hunter, and drawer-up of recondite documents of all sorts — was consid-erably increased by receiving the Master's office. There was now great work for scriveners. Not only must I push the clerks already with me, but I must have additional help.

In answer to my advertisement, a motionless young man one morning stood upon my office threshold, the door being open, for it was sum-mer. I can see that figure now — pallidly neat, pitiably respectable, incurably forlorn! It was Bartleby.

After a few words touching his qualifications, I engaged him, glad to have among my corps of copyists a man of so singularly sedate an aspect, which I thought might operate beneficially upon the flighty temper of Turkey, and the fiery one of Nippers.

I should have stated before that ground-glass folding-doors divided my premises into two parts, one of which was occupied by my scriveners, the other by myself. Accordingly to my humor, I threw open these doors, or closed them. I re-solved to assign Bartleby a corner by the folding-doors, but on my side of them, so as to have this quiet man within easy call, in case any trifling thing was to be done. I placed his desk close up to a small side-window in that part of the room, a window which originally had afforded a lateral view of certain grimy backyards and bricks, but which, owing to subsequent erections, com-manded at present no view at all, though it gave some light. Within three feet of the panes was a wall, and the light came down from far above, between two lofty buildings, as from a very small opening in a dome. Still further to a satisfac-tory arrangement, I procured a high green fold-ing screen, which might entirely isolate Bartleby from my sight, though not remove him from my voice. And thus, in a manner, privacy and so-ciety were conjoined.

At first, Bartleby did an extraordinary quantity of writing. As if long famishing for something to copy, he seemed to gorge himself on my docu-ments. There was no pause for digestion. He ran a day and night line, copying by sunlight and by candle-light. I should have been quite delighted with his application, had he been cheerfully industrious. But he wrote on silently, palely, mechanically.

It is, of course, an indispensable part of a scrivener's business to verify the accuracy of his copy, word by word. Where there are two or more scriveners in an office, they assist each other in this examination, one reading from the copy, the other holding the original. It is a very dull, wearisome, and lethargic affair. I can readily imagine that, to some sanguine temperaments, it would be altogether intolerable. For example, I cannot credit that the mettlesome poet, Byron, would have contentedly sat down with Bartleby to examine a law document of, say five hundred pages, closely written in a crimpy hand.

Now and then, in the haste of business, it had been my habit to assist in comparing some brief document myself, calling Turkey or Nippers for this purpose. One object I had, in placing Bar-tleby so handy to me behind the screen, was, to avail myself of his services on such trivial occa-sions. It was on the third day, I think, of his being with me, and before any necessity had arisen for having his own writing examined, that, being much hurried to complete a small affair I had in hand, I abruptly called to Bartleby. In my haste and natural expectancy of instant compliance, I sat with my head bent over the original on my desk, and my right hand sideways, and somewhat nervously extended with the copy, so that, immediately upon emerging from his retreat, Bartleby might snatch it and proceed to business without the least delay.

In this very attitude did I sit when I called to him, rapidly stating what it was I wanted him to do — namely, to examine a small paper with me. Imagine my surprise, nay, my consternation, when, without moving from his privacy, Bartleby, in a singularly mild, firm voice, replied, "I would prefer not to."

I sat awhile in perfect silence, rallying my stunned faculties. Immediately it occurred to me that my ears had deceived me, or Bartleby had entirely misunderstood my meaning. I repeated my request in the clearest tone I could assume; but in quite as clear a one came the previous reply, "I would prefer not to."

"Prefer not to," echoed I, rising in high excitement, and crossing the room with a stride. "What do you mean? Are you moon-struck? I want you to help me compare this sheet here — take it," and I thrust it towards him.

"I would prefer not to," said he.

I looked at him steadfastly. His face was leanly composed; his gray eye dimly calm. Not a wrinkle of agitation rippled him. Had there been the least uneasiness, anger, impatience or impertinence in his manner; in other words, had there been anything ordinarily human about him, doubtless I should have violently dismissed him from the premises. But as it was, I should have as soon thought of turning my pale plaster-of-paris bust of Cicero out of doors. I stood gazing at him awhile, as he went on with his own writing, and then reseated myself at my desk. This is very strange, thought I. What had one best do? But my business hurried me. I concluded to forget the matter for the present, reserving it for my future leisure. So, calling Nippers from the other room, the paper was speedily examined.

A few days after this, Bartleby concluded four lengthy documents, being quadruplicates of a week's testimony taken before me in my High Court of Chancery. It became necessary to examine them. It was an important suit, and great accuracy was imperative. Having all things arranged, I called Turkey, Nippers and Ginger Nut, from the next room, meaning to place the four copies in the hands of my four clerks, while I should read from the original. Accordingly, Turkey, Nippers, and Ginger Nut had taken their seats in a row, each with his document in his hand, when I called to Bartleby to join this interesting group.

"Bartleby! quick, I am waiting."

I heard a slow scrape of his chair legs on the uncarpeted floor, and soon he appeared standing at the entrance of his hermitage.

"What is wanted?" said he, mildly.

"The copies, the copies," said I, hurriedly. "We are going to examine them. There" — and I held towards him the fourth quadruplicate.

"I would prefer not to," he said, and gently disappeared behind the screen.

For a few moments I was turned into a pillar of salt, standing at the head of my seated column of clerks. Recovering myself, I advanced towards the screen, and demanded the reason for such extraordinary conduct.

"Why do you refuse?"

"I would prefer not to."

With any other man I should have flown outright into a dreadful passion, scorned all further words, and thrust him ignominiously from my presence. But there was something about Bartleby that not only strangely disarmed me, but, in a wonderful manner, touched and disconcerted me. I began to reason with him.

"These are your own copies we are about to examine. It is labor saving to you, because one examination will answer for your four papers. It is common usage. Every copyist is bound to help examine his copy. Is it not so? Will you not speak? Answer!"

"I prefer not to," he replied in a flute-like tone. It seemed to me that, while I had been addressing him, he carefully revolved every statement that I made; fully comprehended the meaning; could not gainsay the irresistible conclusion; but, at the same time, some paramount consideration prevailed with him to reply as he did.

"You are decided, then, not to comply with my request — a request made according to common usage and common sense?"

He briefly gave me to understand, that on that point my judgment was sound. Yes: his decision was irreversible.

It is not seldom the case that, when a man is browbeaten in some unprecedented and violently unreasonable way, he begins to stagger in his own plainest faith. He begins, as it were, vaguely to surmise that, wonderful as it may be, all the justice and all the reason is on the other side. Accordingly, if any disinterested persons are present, he turns to them for some reinforcement for his own faltering mind.

"Turkey," I said, "what do you think of this? Am I not right?"

"With submission, sir," said Turkey, in his blandest tone, "I think that you are."

"Nippers," said I, "what do *you* think of it?"

"I think I should kick him out of the office."

(The reader of nice perceptions will here perceive that, it being morning, Turkey's answer is couched in polite and tranquil terms, but Nippers replies in ill-tempered ones. Or, to a repeat a previous sentence, Nippers's ugly mood was on duty, and Turkey's off.)

"Ginger Nut," said I, willing to enlist the smallest suffrage in my behalf, "what do *you* think of it?"

"I think, sir, he's a little *luny*," replied Ginger Nut, with a grin.

"You hear what they say," said I, turning towards the screen, "come forth and do your duty."

But he vouchsafed no reply. I pondered a moment in sore perplexity. But once more business hurried me. I determined again to postpone the consideration of this dilemma to my future leisure. With a little trouble we made out to examine the papers without Bartleby, though at every page or two Turkey deferentially dropped his opinion, that this proceeding was quite out of the common; while Nippers, twitching in his chair with a dyspeptic nervousness, ground out, between his set teeth, occasional hissing maledictions against the stubborn oaf behind the screen. And for his (Nippers's) part, this was the first and the last time he would do another man's business without pay.

Meanwhile Bartleby sat in his hermitage, oblivious to everything but his own peculiar business there.

Some days passed, the scrivener being employed upon another lengthy work. His late remarkable conduct led me to regard his ways narrowly. I observed that he never went to dinner; indeed, that he never went anywhere. As yet I had never, of my personal knowledge, known him to be outside of my office. He was a perpetual sentry in the corner. At about eleven o'clock though, in the morning, I noticed that Ginger Nut would advance toward the opening in Bartleby's screen, as if silently beckoned thither by a gesture invisible to me where I sat. The boy would then leave the office, jingling a few pence, and reappear with a handful of ginger-nuts, which he delivered in the hermitage, receiving two of the cakes for his trouble.

He lives, then, on ginger-nuts, thought I; never eats a dinner, properly speaking; he must be a vegetarian, then; but no; he never eats even vegetables, he eats nothing but ginger-nuts. My mind then ran on in reveries concerning the probable effects upon the human constitution of living entirely on ginger-nuts. Ginger-nuts are so called, because they contain ginger as one of their peculiar constituents, and the final flavoring one. Now, what was ginger? A hot, spicy thing. Was Bartleby hot and spicy? Not at all. Ginger, then, had no effect upon Bartleby. Probably he preferred it should have none.

Nothing so aggravates an earnest person as a passive resistance. If the individual so resisted be of a not inhumane temper, and the resisting one perfectly harmless in his passivity, then, in the better moods of the former, he will endeavor charitably to construe to his imagination what proves impossible to be solved by his judgment. Even so, for the most part, I regarded Bartleby and his ways. Poor fellow! thought I, he means no mischief; it is plain he intends no insolence; his aspect sufficiently evinces that his eccentricities are involuntary. He is useful to me. I can get along with him. If I turn him away, the chances are he will fall in with some less indulgent employer, and then he will be rudely treated, and perhaps driven forth miserably to starve. Yes. Here I can cheaply purchase a delicious self-approval. To befriend Bartleby; to humor him in his strange wilfulness, will cost me little or nothing, while I lay up in my soul what will eventually prove a sweet morsel for my conscience. But this mood was not invariable with me. The passiveness of Bartleby sometimes irritated me. I felt strangely goaded on to encounter him in new opposition — to elicit some angry spark from him answerable to my own. But, indeed, I might as well have essayed to strike fire with my knuckles against a bit of Windsor soap. But one afternoon the evil impulse in me mastered me, and the following little scene ensued:

"Bartleby," said I, "when those papers are all copied, I will compare them with you."

"I would prefer not to."

"How? Surely you do not mean to persist in that mulish vagary?"

No answer.

I threw open the folding-doors near by, and, turning upon Turkey and Nippers, exclaimed:

"Bartleby a second time says, he won't examine his papers. What do you think of it, Turkey?"

It was afternoon, be it remembered. Turkey sat glowing like a brass boiler; his bald head steaming; his hands reeling among his blotted papers.

"Think of it?" roared Turkey. "I think I'll just step behind his screen, and black his eyes for him!"

So saying, Turkey rose to his feet and threw his arms into a pugilistic position. He was hurrying away to make good his promise, when I detained him, alarmed at the effect of incautiously rousing Turkey's combativeness after dinner.

"Sit down, Turkey," said I, "and hear what Nippers has to say. What do you think of it, Nippers? Would I not be justified in immediately dismissing Bartleby?"

"Excuse me, that is for you to decide, sir. I think his conduct quite unusual, and, indeed, unjust, as regards Turkey and myself. But it may only be a passing whim."

"Ah," exclaimed I, "you have strangely changed your mind, then — you speak very gently of him now."

"All beer," cried Turkey; "gentleness is effects of beer — Nippers and I dined together to-day. You see how gentle *I* am, sir. Shall I go and black his eyes?"

"You refer to Bartleby, I suppose. No, not to-day, Turkey," I replied; "pray, put up your fists."

I closed the doors, and again advanced towards Bartleby. I felt additional incentives tempting me to my fate. I burned to be rebelled against again. I remembered that Bartleby never left the office.

"Bartleby," said I, "Ginger Nut is away; just step around to the Post Office, won't you?" (it was but a three minutes' walk) "and see if there is anything for me."

"I would prefer not to."

"You *will* not?"

"I *prefer* not."

I staggered to my desk, and sat there in a deep study. My blind inveteracy returned. Was there any other thing in which I could procure myself to be ignominiously repulsed by this lean, penniless wight? — my hired clerk? What added thing is there, perfectly reasonable, that he will be sure to refuse to do?

"Bartleby!"

No answer.

"Bartleby," in a louder tone.

No answer.

"Bartleby," I roared.

Like a very ghost, agreeably to the laws of magical invocation, at the third summons, he appeared at the entrance of his hermitage.

"Go to the next room, and tell Nippers to come to me."

"I prefer not to," he respectfully and slowly said, and mildly disappeared.

"Very good, Bartleby," said I, in a quiet sort of serenely-severe self-possessed tone, intimating the unalterable purpose of some terrible retribution very close at hand. At the moment I half intended something of the kind. But upon the whole, as it was drawing towards my dinner-hour, I thought it best to put on my hat and walk home for the day, suffering much from perplexity and distress of mind.

Shall I acknowledge it? The conclusion of this whole business was, that it soon became a fixed fact of my chambers, that a pale young scrivener, by the name of Bartleby, had a desk there; that he copied for me at the usual rate of four cents a folio (one hundred words); but he was permanently exempt from examining the work done by him, that duty being transferred to Turkey and Nippers, out of compliment, doubtless, to their superior acuteness; moreover, said Bartleby was never, on any account, to be dispatched on the most trivial errand of any sort; and that even if entreated to take upon him such a matter, it was generally understood that he would "prefer not to" — in other words, that he would refuse point-blank.

As days passed on, I became considerably reconciled to Bartleby. His steadiness, his freedom from all dissipation, his incessant industry (except when he chose to throw himself into a standing revery behind his screen), his great stillness, his unalterableness of demeanor under all circumstances, made him a valuable acquisition. One prime thing was this — *he was always there* — first in the morning, continually through the day, and the last at night. I had a singular confidence in his honesty. I felt my most precious papers perfectly safe in his hands. Sometimes, to be sure, I could not, for the very soul of me, avoid falling into sudden spasmodic passions with him. For it was exceeding difficult to bear in mind all the time those strange peculiarities, privileges, and unheard-of exemptions, forming the tacit stipulations on Bartleby's part under which he remained in my office. Now and then, in the eagerness of dispatching pressing business, I would inadvertently summon Bartleby, in a short, rapid tone, to put his finger, say, on the incipient tie of a bit of red tape with which I was about compressing some papers. Of course, from behind the screen the usual answer, "I prefer not to," was sure to come; and then, how could a human creature, with the common infirmities of our nature, refrain from bitterly exclaiming upon such perverseness — such unreasonableness? However, every added repulse of this sort which I received only tended to lessen the probability of my repeating the inadvertence.

Here it must be said, that, according to the custom of most legal gentlemen occupying chambers in densely-populated law buildings, there were several keys to my door. One was kept by a woman residing in the attic, which person weekly scrubbed and daily swept and dusted my apartments. Another was kept by Turkey for convenience sake. The third I sometimes carried in my own pocket. The fourth I knew not who had.

Now, one Sunday morning I happened to go to Trinity Church, to hear a celebrated preacher, and finding myself rather early on the ground I thought I would walk round to my chambers for a while. Luckily I had my key with me; but upon applying it to the lock, I found it resisted by something inserted from the inside. Quite surprised, I called out; when to my consternation a key was turned from within; and thrusting his lean visage at me, and holding the door ajar, the apparition of Bartleby appeared, in his shirt-sleeves, and otherwise in a strangely tattered deshabille, saying quietly that he was sorry, but he was deeply engaged just then, and — preferred not admitting me at present. In a brief word or two, he moreover added, that perhaps I had better walk round the block two or three times, and by that time he would probably have concluded his affairs.

Now, the utterly unsurmised appearance of Bartleby, tenanting my law-chambers of a Sunday morning, with his cadaverously gentlemanly *nonchalance*, yet withal firm and self-possessed, had such a strange effect upon me, that incontinently I slunk away from my own door, and did as desired. But not without sundry twinges of impotent rebellion against the mild effrontery of this unaccountable scrivener. Indeed, it was his wonderful mildness chiefly, which not only disarmed me, but unmanned me, as it were. For I consider that one, for the time, is a sort of unmanned when he tranquilly permits his hired clerk to dictate to him, and order him away from his own premises. Furthermore, I was full of uneasiness as to what Bartleby could possibly be doing in my office in his shirt-sleeves, and in an otherwise dismantled condition of a Sunday morning. Was anything amiss going on? Nay, that was out of the question. It was not to be thought of for a moment that Bartleby was an immoral person. But what could he be doing there? — copying? Nay again, whatever might be his eccentricities, Bartleby was an eminently decorous person. He would be the last man to sit down to his desk in any state approaching nudity. Besides, it was Sunday; and there was something about Bartleby that forbade the supposition that he would by any secular occupation violate the proprieties of the day.

Nevertheless, my mind was not pacified; and full of a restless curiosity, at last I returned to the door. Without hindrance I inserted my key, opened it, and entered. Bartleby was not to be seen. I looked round anxiously, peeped behind his screen; but it was very plain that he was gone. Upon more closely examining the place, I surmised that for an indefinite period Bartleby must have ate, dressed, and slept in my office, and that too without plate, mirror, or bed. The cushioned seat of a rickety old sofa in one corner bore the faint impress of a lean, reclining form. Rolled away under his desk, I found a blanket; under the empty grate, a blacking box and brush; on a chair, a tin basin, with soap and a ragged towel; in a newspaper a few crumbs of ginger-nuts and a morsel of cheese. Yes, thought I, it is evident enough that Bartleby has been making his home here, keeping bachelor's hall all by himself. Immediately then the thought came sweeping across me, what miserable friendlessness and loneliness are here revealed! His poverty is great; but his solitude, how horrible! Think of it. Of a Sunday, Wall Street is deserted as Petra; and every night of every day it is an emptiness. This building, too, which of week-days hums with industry and life, at nightfall echoes with sheer vacancy, and all through Sunday is forlorn. And here Bartleby makes his home; sole spectator of a solitude which he has seen all populous — a sort of innocent and transformed Marius brooding among the ruins of Carthage!

For the first time in my life a feeling of over-powering stinging melancholy seized me. Before, I had never experienced aught but a not un-pleasing sadness. The bond of a common humanity now drew me irresistibly to gloom. A fraternal melancholy! For both I and Bartleby were sons of Adam. I remembered the bright silks and sparkling faces I had seen that day, in gala trim, swan-like sailing down the Mississippi of Broadway; and I contrasted them with the pallid copyist, and thought to myself, Ah, happiness courts the light, so we deem the world is gay; but misery hides aloof, so we deem that misery there is none. These sad fancyings — chimeras, doubtless, of a sick and silly brain — led on to other and more special thoughts, concerning the eccentricities of Bartleby. Presentiments of strange discoveries hovered round me. The scrivener's pale form appeared to me laid out, among uncaring strangers, in its shivering winding-sheet.

Suddenly I was attracted by Bartleby's closed desk, the key in open sight left in the lock.

I mean no mischief, seek the gratification of no heartless curiosity, thought I; besides, the desk is mine, and its contents, too, so I will make bold to look within. Everything was methodically arranged, the papers smoothly placed. The pigeon-holes were deep, and removing the files of documents, I groped into their recesses. Presently I felt something there, and dragged it out. It was an old bandanna handkerchief, heavy and knotted. I opened it, and saw it was a saving's bank.

I now recalled all the quiet mysteries which I had noted in the man. I remembered that he never spoke but to answer; that, though at intervals he had considerable time to himself, yet I had never seen him reading — no, not even a newspaper; that for long periods he would stand looking out, at his pale window behind the screen, upon the dead brick wall; I was quite sure he never visited any refectory or eating-house; while his pale face clearly indicated that he never drank beer like Turkey, or tea and coffee even, like other men; that he never went anywhere in particular that I could learn; never went out for a walk, unless, indeed, that was the case at present; that he had declined telling who he was, or whence he came, or whether he had any relatives in the world; that though so thin and pale, he never complained of ill-health. And more than all, I remembered a certain unconscious air of pallid — how shall I call it? — of

pallid haughtiness, say, or rather an austere reserve about him, which had positively awed me into my tame compliance with his eccentricities, when I had feared to ask him to do the slightest incidental thing for me, even though I might know, from his long-continued motionlessness, that behind his screen he must be standing in one of those dead-wall reveries of his.

Revolving all these things, and coupling them with the recently discovered fact, that he made my office his constant abiding place and home, and not forgetful of his morbid moodiness; revolving all these things, a prudential feeling began to steal over me. My first emotions had been those of pure melancholy and sincerest pity; but just in proportion as the forlornness of Bartleby grew and grew to my imagination, did that same melancholy merge into fear, that pity into repulsion. So true it is, and so terrible, too, that up to a certain point the thought or sight of misery enlists our best affections; but, in certain special cases, beyond that point it does not. They err who would assert that invariably this is owing to the inherent selfishness of the human heart. It rather proceeds from a certain hopelessness of remedying excessive and organic ill. To a sensitive being, pity is not seldom pain. And when at last it is perceived that such pity cannot lead to effectual succor, common sense bids the soul be rid of it. What I saw that morning persuaded me that the scrivener was the victim of innate and incurable disorder. I might give alms to his body; but his body did not pain him; it was his soul that suffered, and his soul I could not reach.

I did not accomplish the purpose of going to Trinity Church that morning. Somehow, the things I had seen disqualified me for the time from church-going. I walked homeward, thinking what I would do with Bartleby. Finally, I resolved upon this — I would put certain calm questions to him the next morning, touching his history, etc., and if he declined to answer them openly and unreservedly (and I supposed he would prefer not), then to give him a twenty dollar bill over and above whatever I might owe him, and tell him his services were no longer required; but that if in any other way I could assist him, I would be happy to do so, especially if he desired to return to his native place, wherever that might me, I would willingly help to defray the expenses. Moreover, if, reaching home, he found himself at any time in want of aid, a letter from him would be sure of a reply.

The next morning came.

"Bartleby," said I, gently calling to him behind his screen.

No reply.

"Bartleby," said I, in a still gentler tone, "come here; I am not going to ask you to do anything you would prefer not to do — I simply wish to speak to you."

Upon this he noiselessly slid into view.

"Will you tell me, Bartleby, where you were born?"

"I would prefer not to."

"Will you tell me *anything* about yourself?"

"I would prefer not to."

"But what reasonable objection can you have to speak to me? I feel friendly towards you."

He did not look at me while I spoke, but kept his glance fixed upon my bust of Cicero, which, as I then sat, was directly behind me, some six inches above my head.

"What is your answer, Bartleby?" said I, after waiting a considerable time for a reply, during which his countenance remained immovable, only there was the faintest conceivable tremor of the white attenuated mouth.

"At present I prefer to give no answer," he said, and retired into his hermitage.

It was rather weak in me I confess, but his manner, on this occasion, nettled me. Not only did there seem to lurk in it a certain calm disdain, but his perverseness seemed ungrateful, considering the undeniable good usage and indulgence he had received from me.

Again I sat ruminating what I should do. Mortified as I was at his behavior, and resolved as I had been to dismiss him when I entered my office, nevertheless I strangely felt something superstitious knocking at my heart, and forbidding me to carry out my purpose, and denouncing me for a villain if I dared to breathe one bitter word against this forlornest of mankind. At last, familiarly drawing my chair behind his screen, I sat down and said: "Bartleby, never mind, then, about revealing your history; but let me entreat you, as a friend, to comply as far as may be with the usages of this office. Say now, you will help to examine papers to-morrow or next day: in short, say now, that in a day or two you will begin to be a little reasonable: — say so, Bartleby."

"At present I would prefer not to be a little reasonable," was his mildly cadaverous reply.

Just then the folding-doors opened, and Nippers approached. He seemed suffering from an unusually bad night's rest, induced by severer indigestion than common. He overheard those final words of Bartleby.

"*Prefer not,* eh?" gritted Nippers — "I'd *prefer* him, if I were you, sir," addressing me — "I'd *prefer* him; I'd give him preferences, the stubborn mule! What is it, sir, pray, that he *prefers* not to do now?"

Bartleby moved not a limb.

"Mr. Nippers," said I, "I'd prefer that you would withdraw for the present."

Somehow, of late, I had got into the way of involuntarily using this word "prefer" upon all sorts of not exactly suitable occasions. And I trembled to think that my contact with the scrivener had already and seriously affected me in a mental way. And what further and deeper aberration might it not yet produce? This apprehension had not been without efficacy in determining me to summary measures.

As Nippers, looking very sour and sulky, was departing, Turkey blandly and deferentially approached.

"With submission, sir," said he, "yesterday I was thinking about Bartleby here, and I think that if he would but prefer to take a quart of good ale every day, it would do much towards mending him, and enabling him to assist in examining his papers."

"So you have got the word, too," said I, slightly excited.

"With submission, what word, sir?" asked Turkey, respectfully crowding himself into the contracted space behind the screen, and by so doing, making me jostle the scrivener. "What word, sir?"

"I would prefer to be left alone here," said Bartleby, as if offended at being mobbed in his privacy.

"*That's* the word, Turkey," said I — "*that's* it."

"Oh, *prefer?* oh yes — queer word. I never use it myself. But, sir, as I was saying, if he would but prefer — "

"Turkey," interrupted I, "you will please withdraw."

"Oh certainly, sir, if you prefer that I should."

As he opened the folding-door to retire, Nippers at his desk caught a glimpse of me, and asked whether I would prefer to have a certain paper copied on blue paper or white. He did not in the least roguishly accent the word "prefer." It was plain that it involuntarily rolled from his tongue. I thought to myself, surely

I must get rid of a demented man, who already has in some degree turned the tongues, if not the heads of myself and clerks. But I thought it prudent not to break the dismission at once.

The next day I noticed that Bartleby did nothing but stand at his window in his dead-wall revery. Upon asking him why he did not write, he said that he had decided upon doing no more writing.

"Why, how now? what next?" exclaimed I, "do no more writing?"

"No more."

"And what is the reason?"

"Do you not see the reason for yourself?" he indifferently replied.

I looked steadfastly at him, and perceived that his eyes looked dull and glazed. Instantly it occurred to me, that his unexampled diligence in copying by his dim window for the first few weeks of his stay with me might have temporarily impaired his vision.

I was touched. I said something in condolence with him. I hinted that of course he did wisely in abstaining from writing for a while; and urged him to embrace that opportunity of taking wholesome exercise in the open air. This, however, he did not do. A few days after this, my other clerks being absent, and being in a great hurry to dispatch certain letters by the mail, I thought that, having nothing else earthly to do, Bartleby would surely be less inflexible than usual, and carry these letters to the post-office. But he blankly declined. So, much to my inconvenience, I went myself.

Still added days went by. Whether Bartleby's eyes improved or not, I could not say. To all appearance, I thought they did. But when I asked him if they did, he vouchsafed no answer. At all events, he would do no copying. At last, in reply to my urgings, he informed me that he had permanently given up copying.

"What!" exclaimed I; "suppose your eyes should get entirely well — better than ever before — would you not copy then?"

"I have given up copying," he answered, and slid aside.

He remained as ever, a fixture in my chamber. Nay — if that were possible — he became still more of a fixture than before. What was to be done? He would do nothing in the office; why should he stay there? In plain fact, he had now become a millstone to me, not only useless as a necklace, but afflictive to bear. Yet I was sorry for him. I speak less than truth when I say

that, on his own account, he occasioned me uneasiness. If he would but have named a single relative or friend, I would instantly have written, and urged their taking the poor fellow away to some convenient retreat. But he seemed alone, absolutely alone in the universe. A bit of wreck in the mid-Atlantic. At length, necessities connected with my business tyrannized over all other considerations. Decently as I could, I told Bartleby that in six days' time he must unconditionally leave the office. I warned him to take measures, in the interval, for procuring some other abode. I offered to assist him in this endeavor, if he himself would but take the first step towards a removal. "And when you finally quit me, Bartleby," added I, "I shall see that you go not away entirely unprovided. Six days from this hour, remember."

At the expiration of that period, I peeped behind the screen, and lo! Bartleby was there.

I buttoned up my coat, balanced myself; advanced slowly towards him, touched his shoulder, and said, "The time has come; you must quit this place; I am sorry for you; here is money; but you must go."

"I would prefer not," he replied, with his back still towards me.

"You *must*."

He remained silent.

Now I had an unbounded confidence in this man's common honesty. He had frequently restored to me sixpences and shillings carelessly dropped upon the floor, for I am apt to be very reckless in such shirt-button affairs. The proceeding, then, which followed will not be deemed extraordinary.

"Bartleby," said I, "I owe you twelve dollars on account; here are thirty-two; the odd twenty are yours — Will you take it?" and I handed the bills towards him.

But he made no motion.

"I will leave them here, then," putting them under a weight on the table. Then taking my hat and cane and going to the door, I tranquilly turned and added — "After you have removed your things from these offices, Bartleby, you will of course lock the door — since every one is now gone for the day but you — and if you please, slip your key underneath the mat, so that I may have it in the morning. I shall not see you again; so good-bye to you. If, hereafter, in your new place of abode, I can be of any service to you, do not fail to advise me by letter. Good-bye, Bartleby, and fare you well."

But he answered not a word; like the last column of some ruined temple, he remained standing mute and solitary in the middle of the otherwise deserted room.

As I walked home in a pensive mood, my vanity got the better of my pity. I could not but highly plume myself on my masterly management in getting rid of Bartleby. Masterly I call it, and such it must appear to any dispassionate thinker. The beauty of my procedure seemed to consist in its perfect quietness. There was no vulgar bullying, no bravado of any sort, no choleric hectoring, and striding to and fro across the apartment, jerking out vehement commands for Bartleby to bundle himself off with his beggarly traps. Nothing of the kind. Without loudly bidding Bartleby depart — as an inferior genius might have done — I *assumed* the ground that depart he must; and upon that assumption built all I had to say. The more I thought over my procedure, the more I was charmed with it. Nevertheless, next morning, upon awakening, I had my doubts — I had somehow slept off the fumes of vanity. One of the coolest and wisest hours a man has, is just after he awakes in the morning. My procedure seemed as sagacious as ever — but only in theory. How it would prove in practice — there was the rub. It was truly a beautiful thought to have assumed Bartleby's departure; but, after all, that assumption was simply my own, and none of Bartleby's. The great point was, not whether I had assumed that he would quit me, but whether he would prefer so to do. He was more a man of preferences than assumptions.

After breakfast, I walked down town, arguing the probabilities *pro* and *con*. One moment I thought it would prove a miserable failure, and Bartleby would be found all alive at my office as usual; the next moment it seemed certain that I should find his chair empty. And so I kept veering about. At the corner of Broadway and Canal Street, I saw quite an excited group of people standing in earnest conversation.

"I'll take odds he doesn't," said a voice as I passed.

"Doesn't go? — done!" said I, "put up your money."

I was instinctively putting my hand in my pocket to produce my own, when I remembered that this was an election day. The words I had overheard bore no reference to Bartleby, but to the success or non-success of some candidate for the mayoralty. In my intent frame of mind, I had, as it were, imagined that all Broadway shared in my excitement, and were debating the same question with me. I passed on, very thankful that the uproar of the street screened my momentary absent-mindedness.

As I had intended, I was earlier than usual at my office door. I stood listening for a moment. All was still. He must be gone. I tried the knob. The door was locked. Yes, my procedure had worked to a charm; he indeed must be vanished. Yet a certain melancholy mixed with this: I was almost sorry for my brilliant success. I was fumbling under the door mat for the key, which Bartleby was to have left there for me, when accidentally my knee knocked against a panel, producing a summoning sound, and in response a voice came to me from within — "Not yet; I am occupied."

It was Bartleby.

I was thunderstruck. For an instant I stood like the man who, pipe in mouth, was killed one cloudless afternoon long ago in Virginia, by summer lightning; at his own warm open window he was killed, and remained leaning out there upon the dreamy afternoon, till some one touched him, when he fell.

"Not gone!" I murmured at last. But again obeying that wondrous ascendancy which the inscrutable scrivener had over me, and from which ascendancy, for all my chafing, I could not completely escape, I slowly went down stairs and out into the street, and while walking round the block, considered what I should next do in this unheard-of perplexity. Turn the man out by an actual thrusting I could not; to drive him away by calling him hard names would not do; calling in the police was an unpleasant idea; and yet, permit him to enjoy his cadaverous triumph over me — this, too, I could not think of. What was to be done? or, if nothing could be done, was there anything further that I could *assume* in the matter? Yes, as before I had prospectively assumed that Bartleby would depart, so now I might retrospectively assume that departed he was. In the legitimate carrying out of this assumption, I might enter my office in a great hurry, and pretending not to see Bartleby at all, walk straight against him as if he were air. Such a proceeding would in a singular degree have the appearance of a home-thrust. It was hardly possible that Bartleby could withstand such an application of the doctrine of assumptions. But upon second thoughts the success of the plan seemed rather dubious. I re-

men, proceeded to my chambers, and, having but little furniture, everything was removed in a few hours. Throughout, the scrivener remained standing behind the screen, which I directed to be removed the last thing. It was withdrawn; and, being folded up like a huge folio, left him the motionless occupant of a naked room. I stood in the entry watching him a moment, while something from within me upbraided me.

I re-entered, with my hand in my pocket — and — and my heart in my mouth.

"Good-bye, Bartleby; I am going — good-bye, and God some way bless you; and take that," slipping something in his hand. But it dropped upon the floor, and then — strange to say — I tore myself from him whom I had so longed to be rid of.

Established in my new quarters, for a day or two I kept the door locked, and started at every footfall in the passages. When I returned to my rooms, after any little absence, I would pause at the threshold for an instant, and attentively listen, ere applying my key. But these fears were needless. Bartleby never came nigh me.

I thought all was going well, when a perturbed-looking stranger visited me, inquiring whether I was the person who had recently occupied room at No. — Wall Street.

Full of forebodings, I replied that I was.

"Then, sir," said the stranger, who proved a lawyer, "you are responsible for the man you left there. He refuses to do any copying; he refuses to do anything; he says he prefers not to; and he refuses to quit the premises."

"I am very sorry, sir," said I, with assumed tranquillity, but an inward tremor, "but, really, the man you allude to is nothing to me — he is no relation or apprentice of mine, that you should hold me responsible for him."

"In mercy's name, who is he?"

"I certainly cannot inform you. I know nothing about him. Formerly I employed him as a copyist; but he has done nothing for me now for some time past."

"I shall settle him, then — good morning, sir."

Several days passed, and I heard nothing more; and, though I often felt a charitable prompting to call at the place and see poor Bartleby, yet a certain squeamishness, of I know not what, withheld me.

All is over with him, by this time, thought I, at last, when, through another week, no further intelligence reached me. But, coming to my room the day after, I found several persons waiting at my door in a high state of nervous excitement.

"That's the man — here he comes," cried the foremost one, whom I recognized as the lawyer who had previously called upon me alone.

"You must take him away, sir, at once," cried a portly person among them, advancing upon me, and whom I knew to be the landlord of No. — Wall Street. "These gentlemen, my tenants, cannot stand it any longer; Mr. B——," pointing to the lawyer, "has turned him out of his room, and he now persists in haunting the building generally, sitting upon the banisters of the stairs by day, and sleeping in the entry by night. Everybody is concerned; clients are leaving the offices; some fears are entertained of a mob; something you must do, and that without delay."

Aghast at this torrent, I fell back before it, and would fain have locked myself in my new quarters. In vain I persisted that Bartleby was nothing to me — no more than to any one else. In vain — I was the last person known to have anything to do with him, and they held me to the terrible account. Fearful, then, of being exposed in the papers (as one person present obscurely threatened), I considered the matter, and, at length, said, that if the lawyer would give me a confidential interview with the scrivener, in his (the lawyer's) own room, I would, that afternoon, strive my best to rid them of the nuisance they complained of.

Going up stairs to my old haunt, there was Bartleby silently sitting upon the banister at the landing.

"What are you doing here, Bartleby?" said I.

"Sitting upon the banister," he mildly replied.

I motioned him into the lawyer's room, who then left us.

"Bartleby," said I, "are you aware that you are the cause of great tribulation to me, by persisting in occupying the entry after being dismissed from the office?"

No answer.

"Now one of two things must take place. Either you must do something, or something must be done to you. Now what sort of business would you like to engage in? Would you like to re-engage in copying for some one?"

"No; I would prefer not to make any change."

"Would you like a clerkship in a dry-goods store?"

"There is too much confinement about that. No, I would not like a clerkship; but I am not particular."

"Too much confinement," I cried, "why, you keep yourself confined all the time!"

"I would prefer not to take a clerkship," he rejoined, as if to settle that little item at once.

"How would a bar-tender's business suit you? There is no trying of the eye-sight in that."

"I would not like it all; though, as I said before, I am not particular."

His unwonted wordiness inspirited me. I returned to the charge.

"Well, then, would you like to travel through the country collecting bills for the merchants? That would improve your health."

"No, I would prefer to be doing something else."

"How, then, would going as a companion to Europe, to entertain some young gentleman with your conversation — how would that suit you?"

"Not at all. It does not strike me that there is anything definite about that. I like to be stationary. But I am not particular."

"Stationary you shall be, then," I cried, now losing all patience, and, for the first time in all my exasperating connection with him, fairly flying into a passion. "If you do not go away from these premises before night, I shall feel bound — indeed, I *am* bound — to — to — to quit the premises myself!" I rather absurdly concluded, knowing not with what possible threat to try to frighten his immobility into compliance. Despairing of all further efforts, I was precipitately leaving him, when a final thought occurred to me — one which had not been wholly unindulged before.

"Bartleby," said I, in the kindest tone I could assume under such exciting circumstances, "will you go home with me now — not to my office, but my dwelling — and remain there till we can conclude upon some convenient arrangement for you at our leisure? Come, let us start now, right away."

"No: at present I would prefer not to make any change at all."

I answered nothing; but, effectually dodging every one by the suddenness and rapidity of my flight, rushed from the building, ran up Wall Street towards Broadway, and, jumping into the first omnibus, was soon removed from pursuit. As soon as tranquillity returned, I distinctly perceived that I had now done all that I possibly could, both in respect to the demands of the landlord and his tenants, and with regard to my own desire and sense of duty, to benefit Bartleby, and shield him from rude persecution. I now strove to be entirely care-free and quiescent; and my conscience justified me in the attempt; though, indeed, it was not so successful as I could have wished. So fearful was I of being again hunted out by the incensed landlord and his exasperated tenants, that, surrendering my business to Nippers, for a few days, I drove about the upper part of the town and through the suburbs, in my rockaway; crossed over to Jersey City and Hoboken, and paid fugitive visits to Manhattanville and Astoria. In fact, I almost lived in my rockaway for the time.

When again I entered my office, lo, a note from the landlord lay upon the desk. I opened it with trembling hands. It informed me that the writer had sent to the police, and had Bartleby removed to the Tombs as a vagrant. Moreover, since I knew more about him than any one else, he wished me to appear at that place, and make a suitable statement of the facts. These tidings had a conflicting effect upon me. At first I was indignant; but, at last, almost approved. The landlord's energetic, summary disposition, had led him to adopt a procedure which I do not think I would have decided upon myself; and yet, as a last resort, under such peculiar circumstances, it seemed the only plan.

As I afterwards learned, the poor scrivener, when told that he must be conducted to the Tombs, offered not the slightest obstacle, but, in his pale, unmoving way, silently acquiesced.

Some of the compassionate and curious bystanders joined the party; and headed by one of the constables arm-in-arm with Bartleby, the silent procession filed its way through all the noise, and heat, and joy of the roaring thoroughfares at noon.

The same day I received the note, I went to the Tombs, or, to speak more properly, the Halls of Justice. Seeking the right officer, I stated the purpose of my call, and was informed that the individual I described was, indeed, within. I then assured the functionary that Bartleby was a perfectly honest man, and greatly to be compassionated, however unaccountably eccentric. I narrated all I knew, and closed by suggesting the idea of letting him remain in as indulgent confinement as possible, till something less harsh might be done —

though, indeed, I hardly knew what. At all events, if nothing else could be decided upon, the alms-house must receive him. I then begged to have an interview.

Being under no disgraceful charge, and quite serene and harmless in all his ways, they had permitted him freely to wander about the prison, and, especially, in the inclosed grass-platted yards thereof. And so I found him there, standing all alone in the quietest of the yards, his face towards a high wall, while all around, from the narrow slits of the jail windows, I thought I saw peering out upon him the eyes of murderers and thieves.

"Bartleby!"

"I know you," he said, without looking around — "and I want nothing to say to you."

"It was not I that brought you here, Bartleby," said I, keenly pained at his implied suspicion. "And to you, this should not be so vile a place. Nothing reproachful attaches to you by being here. And see, it is not so sad a place as one might think. Look, there is the sky, and here is the grass."

"I know where I am," he replied, but would say nothing more, and so I left him.

As I entered the corridor again, a broad meat-like man, in an apron, accosted me, and jerking his thumb over his shoulder, said — "Is that your friend?"

"Yes."

"Does he want to starve? If he does, let him live on the prison fare, that's all."

"Who are you?" asked I, not knowing what to make of such an unofficially speaking person in such a place.

"I am the grub-man. Such gentlemen as have friends here, hire me to provide them with something good to eat."

"Is this so?" said I, turning to the turnkey.

He said it was.

"Well, then," said I, slipping some silver into the grub-man's hands (for so they called him), "I want you to give particular attention to my friend there; let him have the best dinner you can get. And you must be as polite to him as possible."

"Introduce me, will you?" said the grub-man, looking at me with an expression which seemed to say he was all impatience for an opportunity to give a specimen of his breeding.

Thinking it would prove of benefit to the scrivener, I acquiesced; and, asking the grub-man his name, went up with him to Bartleby.

"Bartleby, this is a friend; you will find him very useful to you."

"Your sarvant, sir, your sarvant," said the grub-man, making a low salutation behind his apron. "Hope you find it pleasant here, sir; nice grounds — cool apartments — hope you'll stay with us some time — try to make it agreeable. What will you have for dinner to-day?"

"I prefer not to dine to-day," said Bartleby, turning away. "It would disagree with me; I am unused to dinners." So saying, he slowly moved to the other side of the inclosure, and took up a position fronting the dead-wall.

"How's this?" said the grub-man, addressing me with a stare of astonishment. "He's odd, ain't he?"

"I think he is a little deranged," said I, sadly.

"Deranged? deranged is it? Well, now, upon my word, I thought that friend of yourn was a gentleman forger; they are always pale and genteel-like, them forgers. I can't help pity 'em — can't help it, sir. Did you know Monroe Edwards?" he added, touchingly, and paused. Then, laying his hand piteously on my shoulder, sighed, "He died of consumption at Sing-Sing. So you weren't acquainted with Monroe?"

"No, I was never socially acquainted with any forgers. But I cannot stop longer. Look to my friend yonder. You will not lose by it. I will see you again."

Some few days after this, I again obtained admission to the Tombs, and went through the corridors in quest of Bartleby; but without finding him.

"I saw him coming from his cell not long ago," said a turnkey, "may be he's gone to loiter in the yards."

So I went in that direction.

"Are you looking for the silent man?" said another turnkey, passing me. "Yonder he lies — sleeping in the yard there. 'Tis not twenty minutes since I saw him lie down."

The yard was entirely quiet. It was not accessible to the common prisoners. The surrounding walls, of amazing thickness, kept off all sounds behind them. The Egyptian character of the masonry weighted upon me with its gloom. But a soft imprisoned turf grew under foot. The heart of the eternal pyramids, it seemed, wherein, by some strange magic, through the clefts, grass-seed, dropped by birds, had sprung.

Strangely huddled at the base of the wall, his knees drawn up, and lying on his side, his head touching the cold stones, I saw the wasted Bartleby. But nothing stirred. I paused; then went close up to him, stopped over, and saw that his dim eyes were open; otherwise he seemed profoundly sleeping. Something prompted me 5 to touch him. I felt his hand, when a tingling shiver ran up my arm and down my spine to my feet.

The round face of the grub-man peered upon me now. "His dinner is ready. Won't he dine 10 to-day, either? Or does he live without dining?"

"Lives without dining," said I, and closed the eyes.

"Eh! — He's asleep, ain't he?"

"With kings and counselors," murmured I. 15

There would seem little need for proceeding further in this history. Imagination will readily supply the meagre recital of poor Bartleby's interment. But, ere parting with the reader, let me say, that if this little narrative has sufficiently 20 interested him, to awaken curiosity as to who Bartleby was, and what manner of life he led prior to the present narrator's making his acquaintance, I can only reply, that in such curiosity I fully share, but am wholly unable to 25 gratify it. Yet here I hardly know whether I should divulge one little item of rumor, which came to my ear a few months after the scrivener's decease. Upon what basis it rested, I could never ascertain; and hence, how true it is 30 I cannot now tell. But, inasmuch as this vague report has not been without a certain suggestive interest to me, however sad, it may prove the same with others; and so I will briefly mention it. The report was this: that Bartleby had been 35 a subordinate clerk in the Dead Letter Office at Washington, from which he had been suddenly removed by a change in the administration. When I think over this rumor, hardly can I express the emotions which seize me. Dead 40 letters! does it not sound like dead men? Conceive a man by nature and misfortune prone to a pallid hopelessness, can any business seem more fitted to heighten it than that of continually handling these dead letters, and assort- 45 ing them for the flames? For by the cart-load they are annually burned. Sometimes from out the folded paper the pale clerk takes a ring — the finger it was meant for, perhaps, moulders in the grave; a banknote sent in swiftest charity 50 — he whom it would relieve, nor eats nor hungers any more; pardon for those who died despairing; hope for those who died unhoping; good tidings for those who died stifled by un-

relieved calamities. On errands of life, these letters speed to death.

Ah, Bartleby! Ah, humanity!

The Portent

(w. 1859)

Though the poetry of Melville has an ungainly tread and often slips or falls, it has interested some good readers in our time because of its "energy of mind."

Hanging from the beam,
  Slowly swaying (such the law),
Gaunt the shadow on your green,
  Shenandoah!
The cut is on the crown   **5**
(Lo, John Brown),
And the stabs shall heal no more.

Hidden in the cap
  Is the anguish none can draw;
So your future veils its face,   **10**
  Shenandoah!
But with streaming beard is shown
(Weird John Brown),
The meteor of the war.

Malvern Hill

(w. 1862)

Ye elms that wave on Malvern Hill
  In prime of morn and May,
Recall ye how McClellan's men
  Here stood at bay?
While deep within yon forest dim   **5**
  Our rigid comrades lay —
Some with the cartridge in their mouth,
Others with fixed arms lifted South —
  Invoking so
The cypress glades? Ah wilds of woe!   **10**

The spires of Richmond, late beheld
  Through rifts in musket-haze,
Were closed from view in clouds of dust
  On leaf-walled ways,
Where streamed our wagons in caravan;   **15**
  And the Seven Nights and Days
Of march and fast, retreat and fight,
Pinched our grimed faces to ghastly plight —
  Does the elm wood
Recall the haggard beards of blood?   **20**

The battle-smoked flag, with stars eclipsed,
  We followed (it never fell!) —
In silence husbanded our strength —
  Received their yell;
Till on this slope we patient turned   25
  With cannon ordered well;
Reverse we proved was not defeat;
  But ah, the sod what thousands meet! —
    Does Malvern Wood
Bethink itself, and muse and brood?   30

    We elms of Malvern Hill
    Remember everything;
    But sap the twig will fill:
    Wag the world how it will,
      Leaves must be green in Spring.   35

On the Grave of a
Young Cavalry Officer

Killed in the Valley of Virginia

Beauty and youth, with manners sweet, and
  friends —
  Gold, yet a mind not unenriched had he
Whom here low violets veil from eyes.
  But all these gifts transcended be:
His happier fortune in this mound you see.   5

Far Off-Shore

Look, the raft, a signal flying,
  Thin — a shred;
None upon the lashed spars lying,
  Quick or dead.

Cries the sea-fowl, hovering over,   5
  "Crew, the crew?"
And the billow, reckless, rover,
  Sweeps anew!

The Maldive Shark

About the Shark, phlegmatical one,
  Pale sot of the Maldive sea,
The sleek little pilot-fish, azure and slim,
  How alert in attendance be.
From his saw-pit of mouth, from his charnel of
  maw   5
They have nothing of harm to dread,
But liquidly glide on his ghastly flank

Or before his Gorgonian head;
Or lurk in the port of serrated teeth
In white triple tiers of glittering gates,   10
And there find a haven when peril's abroad,
An asylum in jaws of the Fates!
They are friends; and friendly they guide him
  to prey,
Yet never partake of the treat —
Eyes and brains to the dotard lethargic and
  dull,   15
Pale ravener of horrible meat.

Art

In placid hours well pleased we dream
Of many a brave unbodied scheme.
But form to lend, pulsed life create,
What unlike things must meet and mate:
A flame to melt — a wind to freeze;   5
Sad patience — joyous energies;
Humility — yet pride and scorn;
Instinct and study; love and hate;
Audacity — reverence. These must mate,
And fuse with Jacob's mystic heart,   10
To wrestle with the angel — Art.

Billy Budd
(w. 1888–1891)

Found among the author's papers after his
death, *Billy Budd* was first published in 1924, adding
to the new enthusiasm over Melville.

  Whatever the book may have owed to Melville's
memories of his early naval experience, and to reading done in 1888, it seems clear, as C. R. Anderson
has concluded, that "imaginative invention counts
for almost everything that makes it, as one critic
declares, a masterpiece in miniature."

  Unlike *Moby Dick*, this short novel has the serenity
associated with tragedy. All the principal characters
are largely conceived. Billy Budd, the handsome
young sailor, was more or less patterned upon a close
friend of Melville's seafaring days, Jack Chase, "that
great heart" to whom he dedicated the book. Billy
is as innocent as Adam in Paradise. One tragic flaw
he has, inability to speak when the occasion demands, which causes him to commit an unintended
crime. His enemy, as naturally depraved as Billy is
naturally good, is an officer who hates the pure-
hearted young man with a Satanic malignity. Captain Vere, while devoted to Billy as to a son, has the
hard role of a disinterested judge applying human law
in a martial court, even though divine law may

acquit "at the Last Assizes." Such are the commander's magnanimity, integrity, and love that Billy cries "God bless Captain Vere!" Is he, then, the hero? No, even though the crew echoes the cry, for, Melville assures us, "Billy alone must have been in their hearts, even as he was in their eyes."

The text given below is that edited by F. B. Freeman, revised by Miss Elizabeth Treeman from the original manuscript at Harvard. Some obvious slips in punctuation in Melville's manuscript have been corrected by the present editor.

Preface

The year 1797, the year of this narrative, belongs to a period which, as every thinker now feels, involved a crisis for Christendom not exceeded in its undetermined momentousness at the time by any other era whereof there is record. The opening proposition made by the Spirit of that Age involved rectification of the Old World's hereditary wrongs. In France, to some extent, this was bloodily effected. But what then? Straightway the Revolution itself became a wrong-doer, one more oppressive than the kings. Under Napoleon it enthroned upstart kings, and initiated that prolonged agony of continual war whose final throe was Waterloo. During those years not the wisest could have foreseen that the outcome of all would be what to some thinkers apparently it has since turned out to be — a political advance along nearly the whole line for Europeans.

Now, as elsewhere hinted, it was something caught from the Revolutionary Spirit that at Spithead emboldened the man-of-war's men to rise against real abuses, long-standing ones, and afterwards at the Nore to make inordinate and aggressive demands — successful resistance to which was confirmed only when the ringleaders were hung for an admonitory spectacle to the anchored fleet. Yet in a way analogous to the operation of the Revolution at large — the Great Mutiny, though by Englishmen naturally deemed monstrous at the time, doubtless gave the first latent prompting to most important reforms in the British navy.

1

In the time before steamships, or then more frequently than now, a stroller along the docks of any considerable sea-port would occasionally have his attention arrested by a group of bronzed mariners, man-of-war's men or merchant-sailors in holiday attire ashore on liberty. In certain instances they would flank, or, like a body-guard quite surround some superior figure of their own class, moving along with them like Aldebaran among the lesser lights of his constellation. That signal object was the "Handsome Sailor" of the less prosaic time alike of the military and merchant navies. With no perceptible trace of the vainglorious about him, rather with the off-hand unaffectedness of natural regality, he seemed to accept the spontaneous homage of his shipmates. A somewhat remarkable instance recurs to me. In Liverpool, now half a century ago I saw under the shadow of the great dingy street-wall of Prince's Dock (an obstruction long since removed) a common sailor, so intensely black that he must needs have been a native African of the unadulterate blood of Ham. A symmetric figure much above the average height. The two ends of a gay silk handkerchief thrown loose about the neck danced upon the displayed ebony of his chest; in his ears were big hoops of gold, and a Scotch Highland bonnet with a tartan band set off his shapely head.

It was a hot noon in July; and his face, lustrous with perspiration, beamed with barbaric good humor. In jovial sallies right and left, his white teeth flashing into view, he rollicked along, the center of a company of his shipmates. These were made up of such an assortment of tribes and complexions as would have well fitted them to be marched up by Anacharsis Cloots before the bar of the first French Assembly as Representatives of the Human Race. At each spontaneous tribute rendered by the wayfarers to this black pagod of a fellow — the tribute of a pause and stare, and less frequent an exclamation, — the motley retinue showed that they took that sort of pride in the evoker of it which the Assyrian priests doubtless showed for their grand sculptured Bull when the faithful prostrated themselves.

To return.

If in some cases a bit of a nautical Murat in setting forth his person ashore, the handsome sailor of the period in question evinced nothing of the dandified Billy-be-Damn, an amusing character all but extinct now, but occasionally to be encountered, and in a form yet more amusing than the original, at the tiller of the boats on the tempestuous Erie Canal or, more likely, vaporing in the groggeries along the tow-path. Invariably a proficient in his perilous calling, he was also more or less of a mighty boxer or wrestler. It was strength and beauty. Tales of his prowess were recited. Ashore he was the champion; afloat the spokesman; on every suitable occasion always foremost. Close-reefing topsails in a gale, there he was, astride the weather yard-arm-end, foot in the Flemish horse as "stirrup," both hands tugging at the "earring" as at a bridle, in very much the attitude of young Alexander curbing the fiery Bucephalus. A superb figure, tossed up as by the horns of Taurus against the thunderous sky, cheerily hallooing to the strenuous file along the spar.

The moral nature was seldom out of keeping with the physical make. Indeed, except as toned by the former, the comeliness and power, always attractive in masculine conjunction, hardly could have drawn the sort of honest homage the Handsome Sailor in some examples received from his less gifted associates.

Such a cynosure, at least in aspect, and something such too in nature, though with important variations made apparent as the story proceeds, was welkin-eyed Billy Budd, or Baby Budd as more familiarly under circumstances hereafter to be given he at last came to be called, aged twenty-one, a foretopman of the British fleet toward the close of the last decade of the eighteenth century. It was not very long prior to the time of the narration that follows that he had entered the King's Service, having been impressed on the Narrow Seas from a homeward-bound English merchantman into a seventy-four outward-bound, H.M.S. *Indomitable*; which ship, as was not unusual in those hurried days, having been obliged to put to sea short of her proper complement of men. Plump upon Billy at first sight in the gangway the boarding officer Lieutenant Ratcliffe pounced, even before the merchantman's crew was formally mustered on the quarter-deck for his deliberate inspection. And him only he elected. For whether it was because the other men when ranged before him showed to ill advantage after Billy, or whether he had some scruples in view of the merchantman being rather short-handed, however it might be, the officer contented himself with his first spontaneous choice. To the surprise of the ship's company, though much to the Lieutenant's satisfaction Billy made no demur. But, indeed, any demur would have been as idle as the protest of a goldfinch popped into a cage.

Noting this uncomplaining acquiescence, all but cheerful one might say, the shipmates turned a surprised glance of silent reproach at the sailor. The shipmaster was one of those worthy mortals found in every vocation even the humbler ones — the sort of person whom everybody agrees in calling "a respectable man." And — nor so strange to report as it may appear to be — though a ploughman of the troubled waters, life-long contending with the intractable elements, there was nothing this honest soul at heart loved better than simple peace and quiet. For the rest, he was fifty or thereabouts, a little inclined to corpulence, a prepossessing face, unwhiskered, and of an agreeable color — a rather full face, humanely intelligent in expression. On a fair day with a fair wind and all going well, a certain musical chime in his voice seemed to be the veritable unobstructed outcome of the innermost man. He had much prudence, much conscientiousness, and there were occasions when these virtues were the cause of overmuch disquietude in him. On a passage, so long as his craft was in any proximity to land, no sleep for Captain Graveling. He took to heart those serious responsibilities not so heavily borne by some shipmasters.

Now while Billy Budd was down in the forecastle getting his kit together, the *Indomitable's* lieutenant, burly and bluff, nowise disconcerted by Captain Graveling's omitting to proffer the customary hospitalities on an occasion so unwelcome to him, an omission simply caused by preoccupation of thought, unceremoniously invited himself into the cabin, and also to a flask from the spirit-locker, a receptacle which his experienced eye instantly discovered. In fact he was one of those sea-dogs in whom all the hardship and peril of naval life in the great prolonged wars of his time never impaired the natural instinct for sensuous enjoyment. His duty he always faithfully did; but duty is sometimes a dry obligation, and he was for irrigating its aridity, whensoever possible, with a fertilizing decoction of strong waters. For the cabin's proprietor there was nothing left but to play the part of the enforced host with whatever grace and alacrity were practicable. As necessary adjuncts to the flask, he silently placed tumbler and water-jug before the irrepressible guest. But excusing himself from partaking just then, he dismally watched the unembarrassed officer deliberately diluting his grog a little, then tossing it off in three swallows, pushing the empty tumbler away, yet not so far as to be beyond easy reach, at the same time settling himself in his seat and smacking his lips with high satisfaction, looking straight at the host.

These proceedings over, the Master broke the silence; and there lurked a rueful reproach in the tone of his voice; "Lieutenant, you are going to take my best man from me, the jewel of 'em."

"Yes, I know" rejoined the other, immediately drawing back the tumbler preliminary to a replenishing; "Yes, I know. Sorry."

"Beg pardon, but you don't understand, Lieutenant. See here now. Before I shipped that young fellow, my forecastle was a rat-pit of quarrels. It was black times, I tell you, aboard the 'Rights' here. I was worried to that degree my pipe had no comfort for me. But Billy came; and it was like a Catholic priest striking peace in an Irish shindy. Not that he preached to them or said or did anything in particular; but a virtue went out of him, sugaring the sour ones. They took to him like hornets to treacle; all but the buffer of the gang, the big shaggy chap with the fire-red whiskers. He indeed out of envy, perhaps, of the newcomer, and thinking such a 'sweet and pleasant fellow,' as he mockingly designated him to the others, could hardly have the spirit of a game-cock, must needs bestir himself in trying to get up an ugly row with him. Billy forebore with him and reasoned with him in a pleasant way — he is something like myself, lieutenant, to whom aught like a quarrel is hateful — but nothing served. So, in the second dog-watch one day the Red Whiskers in presence of the others, under pretence of showing Billy just whence a sirloin steak was cut — for the fellow had once been a butcher — insultingly gave him a dig under the ribs. Quick as lightning Billy let fly his arm. I dare say he never meant to do quite as much as he did, but anyhow he gave the burly fool a terrible drubbing. It took about half a minute, I should think. And, lord bless you, the lubber was astonished at the celerity. And will you believe, Lieutenant, the Red Whiskers now really loves Billy — loves him, or is the biggest hypocrite that I ever heard of. But they all love him. Some of 'em do his washing, darn his old trousers for him; the carpenter is at odd times making a pretty little chest of drawers for him. Anybody will do anything for Billy Budd; and it's the happy family here. But now, Lieutenant, if that young fellow goes — I know how it will be aboard the 'Rights.' Not again very soon shall I, coming up from dinner, lean over the capstan smoking a quiet pipe — no, not very soon again, I think. Ay, Lieutenant, you are going to take away the jewel of 'em; you are going to take away my peacemaker!" And with that the good soul had really some ado in checking a rising sob.

"Well," said the officer, who had listened with amused interest to all this, and now waxing merry with his tipple; "Well, blessed are the peacemakers, especially the fighting peacemakers! And such are the seventy-four beauties some of which you see poking their noses out of the port-holes of yonder war-ship lying-to for me" pointing thro' the cabin window at the Indomitable. "But courage! don't look so downhearted, man. Why, I pledge you in advance the royal approbation. Rest assured that His Majesty will be delighted to know that in a time when his hard tack is not sought for by sailors with such avidity as should be; a time also when some shipmasters privily resent the borrowing from them a tar or two for the service; His Majesty, I say, will be delighted to learn that one shipmaster at least cheerfully surrenders to the King, the flower of his flock, a sailor who with equal loyalty makes no dissent. — But where's my beauty? Ah," looking through the cabin's open door. "Here he comes; and, by Jove — lugging along his chest — Apollo with his portmanteau! — My man," stepping out to him, "you can't take that big box aboard a warship. The boxes there are mostly shot-boxes. Put your duds in a bag, lad. Boot and saddle for the cavalryman, bag and hammock for the man-of-war's man."

The transfer from chest to bag was made. And, after seeing his man into the cutter and then following him down, the lieutenant pushed off from the Rights-of-Man. That was the merchant-ship's name; tho' by her master and crew abbreviated in sailor fashion into The Rights. The hard-headed Dundee owner was a staunch admirer of Thomas Paine whose book in rejoinder to Burke's arraignment of the French Revolution had then been published for some time and had gone everywhere. In christening his vessel after the title of Paine's volume the man of Dundee was something like his contemporary shipowner, Stephen Girard of Philadelphia, whose sympathies, alike with his native land and its liberal philosophers, he evinced by naming his ships after Voltaire, Diderot, and so forth.

But now, when the boat swept under the

merchant-man's stern, and officer and oarsmen were noting — some bitterly and others with a grin, — the name emblazoned there; just then it was that the new recruit jumped up from the bow where the coxswain had directed him to sit, and waving his hat to his silent shipmates sorrowfully looking over at him from the taffrail, bade the lads a genial good-bye. Then, making a salutation as to the ship herself, "And, good-bye to you too, old *Rights of Man*."

"Down, Sir!" roared the lieutenant, instantly assuming all the rigor of his rank, though with difficulty repressing a smile.

To be sure, Billy's action was a terrible breach of naval decorum. But in that decorum he had never been instructed; in consideration of which the lieutenant would hardly have been so energetic in reproof but for the concluding farewell to the ship. This he rather took as meant to convey a covert sally on the new recruit's part, a sly slur at impressment in general, and that of himself in especial. And yet, more likely, if satire it was in effect, it was hardly so by intention, for Billy tho' happily endowed with a gayety of high health, youth, and a free heart, was yet by no means of a satirical turn. The will to it and the sinister dexterity were alike wanting. To deal in double meanings and insinuations of any sort was quite foreign to his nature.

As to his enforced enlistment, that he seemed to take pretty much as he was wont to take any vicissitude of weather. Like the animals, though no philosopher, he was, without knowing it, practically a fatalist. And it may be, that he rather liked this adventurous turn in his affairs, which promised an opening into novel scenes and martial excitements.

Aboard the *Indomitable* our merchant-sailor was forthwith rated as an able-seaman and assigned to the starboard watch of the fore-top. He was soon at home in the service, not at all disliked for his unpretentious good looks and a sort of genial happy-go-lucky air. No merrier man in his mess: in marked contrast to certain other individuals included like himself among the impressed portion of the ship's company; for these when not actively employed were sometimes, and more particularly in the last dog-watch when the drawing near of twilight induced revery, apt to fall into a saddish mood which in some partook of sullenness. But they were not so young as our foretopman, and no few of them must have known a hearth of some sort, others may have had wives and children left, too probably, in uncertain circumstances, and hardly any but must have had acknowledged kith and kin, while for Billy, as will shortly be seen, his entire family was practically invested in himself.

2

Though our new-made foretopman was well received in the top and on the gun-decks, hardly here was he that cynosure he had previously been among those minor ship's companies of the merchant marine, with which companies only had he hitherto consorted.

He was young; and despite his all but fully developed frame in aspect looked even younger than he really was, owing to a lingering adolescent expression in the as yet smooth face all but feminine in purity of natural complexion but where, thanks to his seagoing, the lily was quite suppressed and the rose had some ado visibly to flush through the tan.

To one essentially such a novice in the complexities of factitious life, the abrupt transition from his former and simpler sphere to the ampler and more knowing world of a great warship; this might well have abashed him had there been any conceit or vanity in his composition. Among her miscellaneous multitude, the *Indomitable* mustered several individuals who however inferior in grade were of no common natural stamp, sailors more signally susceptive of that air which continuous martial discipline and repeated presence in battle can in some degree impart even to the average man. As the *handsome sailor* Billy Budd's position aboard the seventy-four was something analogous to that of a rustic beauty transplanted from the provinces and brought into competition with the highborn dames of the court. But this change of circumstances he scarce noted. As little did he observe that something about him provoked an ambiguous smile in one or two harder faces among the blue-jackets. Nor less unaware was he of the peculiar favorable effect his person and demeanor had upon the more intelligent gentlemen of the quarter-deck. Nor could this well have been otherwise. Cast in a mould peculiar to the finest physical examples of those Englishmen in whom the Saxon strain would seem not at all to partake of any Norman or other admixture, he showed in face that humane look of reposeful good nature which the Greek sculptor in some instances gave to his heroic strong man, Hercules. But this again was subtly modified by another and pervasive quality. The ear, small and shapely, the arch of the foot, the curve in mouth and nostril, even the indurated hand dyed to the orange-tawny of the toucan's bill, a hand telling alike of the halyards and tar-bucket; but, above all, something in the mobile expression, and every chance attitude and movement, something suggestive of a mother eminently favored by Love and the Graces; all this strangely indicated a lineage in direct contradiction to his lot. The mysteriousness here, became less mysterious through a matter-of-fact elicited when Billy at the capstan was being formally mustered into the service. Asked by the officer, a small brisk little gentleman, as it chanced among other questions, his place of birth, he replied, "Please, Sir, I don't know."

"Don't know where you were born? — Who was your father?"

"God knows, Sir."

Struck by the straightforward simplicity of these replies, the officer next asked, "Do you know anything about your beginning?"

"No, Sir. But I have heard that I was found in a pretty silk-lined basket hanging one morning from the knocker of a good man's door in Bristol."

"*Found* say you? Well," throwing back his head and looking up and down the new recruit; "Well, it turns out to have been a pretty good find. Hope they'll find some more like you, my man; the fleet sadly needs them."

Yes, Billy Budd was a foundling, a presumable bye-blow, and, evidently, no ignoble one. Noble descent was as evident in him as in a blood horse.

For the rest, with little or no sharpness of faculty or any trace of the wisdom of the serpent, nor yet quite a dove, he possessed that kind and degree of intelligence going along with the unconventional rectitude of a sound human creature, one to whom not yet has been proffered the questionable apple of knowledge. He was illiterate; he could not read, but he could sing, and like the illiterate nightingale was sometimes the composer of his own song.

Of self-consciousness he seemed to have little or none, or about as much as we may reasonably impute to a dog of Saint Bernard's breed.

Habitually living with the elements and knowing little more of the land than as a beach, or, rather, that portion of the terraqueous globe providentially set apart for dance-houses doxies and tapsters, in short what sailors call a "fiddlers' green," his simple nature remained unsophisticated by those moral obliquities which are not in every case incompatible with that manufacturable thing known as respectability. But are sailors, frequenters of "fiddlers'-greens," without vices? No; but less often than with landsmen do their vices, so called, partake of crookedness of heart, seeming less to proceed from viciousness than exuberance of vitality after long constraint; frank manifestations in accordance with natural law. By his original constitution aided by the cooperating influences of his lot, Billy in many respects was little more than a sort of upright barbarian, much such perhaps as Adam presumably might have been ere the urbane Serpent wriggled himself into his company.

And here be it submitted that apparently going to corroborate the doctrine of man's fall, a doctrine now popularly ignored, it is observable that where certain virtues pristine and unadulterate peculiarly characterize anybody in the external uniform of civilization, they will upon scrutiny seem not to be derived from custom or convention, but rather to be out of keeping with these, as if indeed exceptionally transmitted from a period prior to Cain's city and citified man. The character marked by such qualities has to an unvitiated taste an untampered-with flavor like that of berries, while the man thoroughly civilized even in a fair specimen of the breed has to the same moral palate a questionable smack as of a compounded wine. To any stray inheritor of these primitive qualities found, like Caspar Hauser, wandering dazed in any Christian capital of our time the good-natured poet's famous invocation, near two thousand years ago, of the good rustic out of his latitude in the Rome of the Caesars, still appropriately holds: —

Honest and poor, faithful in word and thought
What has thee, Fabian, to the city brought.

Though our Handsome Sailor had as much of masculine beauty as one can expect anywhere to see; nevertheless, like the beautiful woman in one of Hawthorne's minor tales, there was just one thing amiss in him. No visible blemish indeed, as with the lady; no, but an occasional liability to a vocal defect. Though in the hour of elemental uproar or peril, he was everything that a sailor should be, yet under sudden provocation of strong heart-feeling his voice otherwise singularly musical, as if expressive of the harmony within, was apt to develop an organic hesitancy, in fact more or less of a stutter or even worse. In this particular Billy was a striking instance that the arch interferer, the envious marplot of Eden still has more or less to do with every human consignment to this planet of earth. In every case, one way or another he is sure to slip in his little card, as much as to remind us — I too have a hand here.

The avowal of such an imperfection in the Handsome Sailor should be evidence not alone that he is not presented as a conventional hero, but also that the story in which he is the main figure is no romance.

3

At the time of Billy Budd's arbitrary enlistment into the *Indomitable* that ship was on her way to join the Mediterranean fleet. No long time elapsed before the junction was effected. As one of that fleet the seventy-four participated in its movements, tho' at times on account of her superior sailing qualities, in the absence of frigates, despatched on separate duty as a scout and at times on less temporary service. But with all this the story has little concernment, restricted as it is to the inner life of one particular ship and the career of an individual sailor.

It was the summer of 1797. In the April of that year had occurred the commotion at Spithead followed in May by a second and yet more serious outbreak in the fleet at the Nore. The latter is known, and without exaggeration in the epithet, as the Great Mutiny. It was indeed a demonstration more menacing to England than the contemporary manifestoes and conquering and proselyting armies of the French Directory.

To the British Empire the Nore Mutiny was what a strike in the fire-brigade would be to London threatened by general arson. In a crisis when the kingdom might well have anticipated the famous signal that some years later published along the naval line of battle what it was that upon occasion England expected of Englishmen; *that* was the time when at the mastheads of the three-deckers and seventy-fours

moored in her own roadstead — a fleet, the right arm of a Power then all but the sole free conservative one of the Old World, the bluejackets, to be numbered by thousands, ran up with huzzas the British colors with the union and cross wiped out; by that cancellation transmuting the flag of founded law and freedom defined, into the enemy's red meteor of unbridled and unbounded revolt. Reasonable discontent growing out of practical grievances in the fleet had been ignited into irrational combustion as by live cinders blown across the Channel from France in flames.

The event converted into irony for a time those spirited strains of Dibdin — as a songwriter no mean auxiliary to the English Government at the European conjuncture — strains celebrating, among other things, the patriotic devotion of the British tar:

And as for my life, 'tis the King's!

Such an episode in the Island's grand naval story her naval historians naturally abridge; one of them (G. P. R. James) candidly acknowledging that fain would be pass it over did not "impartiality forbid fastidiousness." And yet his mention is less a narration than a reference, having to do hardly at all with details. Nor are these readily to be found in the libraries. Like some other events in every age befalling states everywhere including America, the Great Mutiny was of such character that national pride along with views of policy would fain shade it off into the historical background. Such events can not be ignored, but there is a considerate way of historically treating them. If a well-constituted individual refrains from blazoning aught amiss or calamitous in his family; a nation in the like circumstance may without reproach be equally discreet.

Though after parleyings between Government and the ring-leaders, and concessions by the former as to some glaring abuses, the first uprising — that at Spithead — with difficulty was put down, or matters for the time pacified; yet at the Nore the unforeseen renewal of insurrection on a yet larger scale, and emphasized in the conferences that ensued by demands deemed by the authorities not only inadmissible but aggressively insolent, indicated — if the Red Flag did not sufficiently do so — what was the spirit animating the men. Final suppression, however, there was; but only made possible perhaps by the unswerving loyalty of the marine corps and voluntary resumption of loyalty among influential sections of the crews.

To some extent the Nore Mutiny may be regarded as analogous to the distempering irruption of contagious fever in a frame constitutionally sound, and which anon throws it off.

At all events, of these thousands of mutineers were some of the tars who not so very long afterwards — whether wholly prompted thereto by patriotism, or pugnacious instinct, or by both, — helped to win a coronet for Nelson at the Nile, and the naval crown of crowns for him at Trafalgar. To the mutineers those battles and especially Trafalgar were a plenary absolution and a grand one: For all that goes to make up scenic naval display, heroic magnificence in arms, those battles especially Trafalgar stand unmatched in human annals.

4

Concerning "The greatest sailor since the world began." — Tennyson?

In this matter of writing, resolve as one may to keep to the main road, some by-paths have an enticement not readily to be withstood. I am going to err into such a by-path. If the reader will keep me company I shall be glad. At the least we can promise ourselves that pleasure which is wickedly said to be in sinning, for a literary sin the divergence will be.

Very likely it is no new remark that the inventions of our times have at last brought about a change in sea-warfare in degree corresponding to the revolution in all warfare effected by the original introduction from China into Europe of gunpowder. The first European fire-arm, a clumsy contrivance, was, as is well known, scouted by no few of the knights as a base implement, good enough peradventure for weavers too craven to stand up crossing steel with steel in frank fight. But as ashore knightly valor tho' shorn of its blazonry did not cease with the knights, neither on the seas though nowadays in encounters there a certain kind of displayed gallantry be fallen out of date as hardly applicable under changed circumstances, did the nobler qualities of such naval magnates as Don John of Austria, Doria, Van Tromp, Jean Bart, the long line of British Admirals and the American Decaturs of 1812 become obsolete with their wooden walls.

Nevertheless, to anybody who can hold the Present at its worth without being inappreciative of the Past, it may be forgiven, if to such an one the solitary old hulk at Portsmouth, Nelson's *Victory*, seems to float there, not alone as the decaying monument of a fame incorruptible, but also as a poetic reproach, softened by its picturesqueness, to the *Monitors* and yet mightier hulls of the European iron-clads. And this not altogether because such craft are unsightly, unavoidably lacking the symmetry and grand lines of the old battle-ships, but equally for other reasons.

There are some, perhaps, who while not altogether inaccessible to that poetic reproach just alluded to, may yet on behalf of the new order, be disposed to parry it; and this to the extent of iconoclasm, if need be. For example, prompted by the sight of the star inserted in the *Victory's* quarter-deck designating the spot where the Great Sailor fell, these martial utilitarians may suggest considerations implying that Nelson's ornate publication of his person in battle was not only unnecessary, but not military, nay, savored of foolhardiness and vanity. They may add, too, that at Trafalgar it was in effect nothing less than a challenge to death; and death came; and that but for his bravado the victorious Admiral might possibly have survived the battle, and so, instead of having his sagacious dying injunctions overruled by his immediate successor in command, he himself when the contest was decided might have brought his shattered fleet to anchor, a proceeding which might have averted the deplorable loss of life by shipwreck in the elemental tempest that followed the martial one.

Well, should we set aside the more disputable point whether for various reasons it was possible to anchor the fleet, then plausibly enough the Benthamites of war may urge the above.

But the *might-have-been* is but boggy ground to build on. And, certainly, in foresight as to the larger issue of an encounter, and anxious preparations for it — buoying the deadly way and mapping it out, as at Copenhagen — few commanders have been so painstakingly circumspect as this same reckless declarer of his person in fight.

Personal prudence even when dictated by quite other than selfish considerations surely is no special virtue in a military man; while an excessive love of glory, impassioning a less burning impulse, the honest sense of duty, is the first. If the name *Wellington* is not so much of a trumpet to the blood as the simpler name *Nelson*, the reason for this may perhaps be inferred from the above. Alfred in his funeral ode on the victor of Waterloo ventures not to call him the greatest soldier of all time, tho' in the same ode he invokes Nelson as "the greatest sailor since the world began."

At Trafalgar Nelson on the brink of opening the fight sat down and wrote his last brief will and testament. If under the presentiment of the most magnificent of all victories to be crowned by his own glorious death, a sort of priestly motive led him to dress his person in the jewelled vouchers of his own shining deeds; if thus to have adorned himself for the altar and the sacrifice were indeed vainglory, then affectation and fustian is each more heroic line in the great epics and dramas, since in such lines the poet but embodies in verse those exaltations of sentiment that a nature like Nelson, the opportunity being given, vitalizes into acts.

5

Yes, the outbreak at the Nore was put down. But not every grievance was redressed. If the contractors, for example, were no longer permitted to ply some practices peculiar to their tribe everywhere, such as providing shoddy cloth, rations not sound, or false in the measure, not the less impressment, for one thing, went on. By custom sanctioned for centuries, and judicially maintained by a Lord Chancellor as late as Mansfield, that mode of manning the fleet, a mode now fallen into a sort of abeyance but never formally renounced, it was not practicable to give up in those years. Its abrogation would have crippled the indispensable fleet, one wholly under canvas, no steam-power, its innumerable sails and thousands of cannon, everything in short, worked by muscle alone; a fleet the more insatiate in demand for men, because then multiplying its ships of all grades against contingencies present and to come of the convulsed Continent.

Discontent foreran the Two Mutinies, and more or less it lurkingly survived them. Hence it was not unreasonable to apprehend some return of trouble sporadic or general. One instance of such apprehensions: In the same year with this story, Nelson, then Vice Admiral Sir Horatio, being with the fleet off the Spanish coast, was directed by the Admiral in command to shift his pennant from the *Captain* to the *Theseus*; and for this reason: that the latter ship having newly arrived on the station from home where it had taken part in the Great Mutiny, danger was apprehended from the temper of the men; and it was thought that an officer like Nelson was the one, not indeed to terrorize the crew into base subjection, but to win them, by force of his mere presence back to an allegiance if not as enthusiastic as his own, yet as true. So it was that for a time on more than one quarter-deck anxiety did exist. At sea precautionary vigilance was strained against relapse. At short notice an engagement might come on. When it did, the lieutenants assigned to batteries felt it incumbent on them, in some instances, to stand with drawn swords behind the men working the guns.

6

But on board the seventy-four in which Billy now swung his hammock, very little in the manner of the men and nothing obvious in the demeanor of the officers would have suggested to an ordinary observer that the Great Mutiny was a recent event. In their general bearing and conduct the commissioned officers of a warship naturally take their tone from the commander, that is if he have that ascendancy of character that ought to be his.

Captain the Honorable Edward Fairfax Vere, to give his full title, was a bachelor of forty or thereabouts, a sailor of distinction even in a time prolific of renowned seamen. Though allied to the higher nobility his advancement had not been altogether owing to influences connected with that circumstance. He had seen much service, been in various engagements, always acquitting himself as an officer mindful of the welfare of his men, but never tolerating an infraction of discipline; thoroughly versed in the science of his profession, and intrepid to the verge of temerity, though never injudiciously so. For his gallantry in the West Indian waters as flag-lieutenant under Rodney in that Admiral's crowning victory over De Grasse, he was made a post-captain.

Ashore in the garb of a civilian scarce anyone would have taken him for a sailor, more especially that he never garnished unprofessional talk with nautical terms, and, grave in his bearing, evinced little appreciation of mere humor. It was not out of keeping with these traits that on a passage when nothing demanded his paramount action, he was the most undemonstrative of men. Any landsman observing this gentleman not conspicuous by his stature and wearing no pronounced insignia, emerging from his cabin to the open deck, and noting the silent deference of the officers retiring to leeward, might have taken him for the King's guest, a civilian aboard the King's-ship, some highly honorable discreet envoy on his way to an important post. But in fact this unobtrusiveness of demeanor may have proceeded from a certain unaffected modesty of manhood sometimes accompanying a resolute nature, a modesty evinced at all times not calling for pronounced action, and which shown in any rank of life suggests a virtue aristocratic in kind.

As with some others engaged in various departments of the world's more heroic activities, Captain Vere though practical enough upon occasion would at times betray a certain dreaminess of mood. Standing alone on the weatherside of the quarter deck, one hand holding by the rigging, he would absently gaze off at the blank sea. At the presentation to him then of some minor matter interrupting the current of his thoughts he would show more or less irascibility; but instantly he would control it.

In the navy he was popularly known by the appellation — Starry Vere. How such a designation happened to fall upon one who whatever his sturdy qualities was without any brilliant ones was in this wise: A favorite kinsman, Lord Denton, a free-hearted fellow, had been the first to meet and congratulate him upon his return to England from his West Indian cruise; and but the day previous turning over a copy of Andrew Marvell's poems, had lighted, not for the first time however, upon the lines entitled *Appleton House*, the name of one of the seats of their common ancestor, a hero in the German wars of the seventeenth century, in which poem occur the lines,

This 'tis to have been from the first
In a domestic heaven nursed,
Under the discipline severe
Of Fairfax and the starry Vere.

And so, upon embracing his cousin fresh from Rodney's great victory wherein he had played so gallant a part, brimming over with just family pride in the sailor of the house, he exuberantly exclaimed, "Give ye joy, Ed; give ye joy, my starry Vere!" This got currency, and the novel prefix serving in familiar parlance readily to distinguish the *Indomitable's* Captain from another Vere his senior, a distant relative, an officer of like rank in the navy, it remained permanently attached to the surname.

7

In view of the part the commander of the *Indomitable* plays in scenes shortly to follow, it may be well to fill out that sketch of him outlined in the previous chapter.

Aside from his qualities as a sea-officer Captain Vere was an exceptional character. Unlike no few of England's renowned sailors, long and arduous service with signal devotion to it, had not resulted in absorbing and *salting* the entire man. He had a marked leaning toward everything intellectual. He loved books, never going to sea without a newly replenished library, compact but of the best. The isolated leisure, in some cases so wearisome, falling at intervals to commanders even during a war-cruise, never was tedious to Captain Vere. With nothing of that literary taste which less heeds the thing conveyed than the vehicle, his bias was towards those books to which every serious mind of superior order occupying any active post of authority in the world, naturally inclines: books treating of actual men and events no matter of what era — history, biography and unconventional writers, who, free from cant and convention, like Montaigne, honestly and in the spirit of common sense philosophize upon realities.

In this line of reading he found confirmation of his own more reasoned thoughts — confirmation which he had vainly sought in social converse, so that as touching most fundamental topics, there had got to be established in him some positive convictions, which he forefelt would abide in him essentially unmodified so long as his intelligent part remained unimpaired. In view of the troubled period in which his lot was cast this was well for him. His settled convictions were as a dyke against those invading waters of novel opinion social political and otherwise, which carried away as in a torrent no few minds in those days, minds by nature not inferior to his own. While other members of that aristocracy to which by birth he belonged were incensed at the innovators mainly because their theories were inimical to the privileged classes, not alone Captain Vere disinterestedly opposed them because they seemed to him incapable of embodiment in lasting institutions, but at war with the peace of the world and the true welfare of mankind.

With minds less stored than his and less earnest, some officers of his rank, with whom at times he would necessarily consort, found him lacking in the companionable quality, a dry and bookish gentleman as they deemed. Upon any chance withdrawal from their company one would be apt to say to another, something like this: "Vere is a noble fellow, Starry Vere. Spite the gazettes, Sir Horatio" meaning him with the Lord title "is at bottom scarce a better seaman or fighter. But between you and me now don't you think there is a queer streak of the pedantic running thro' him? Yes, like the King's yarn in a coil of navy-rope?"

Some apparent ground there was for this sort of confidential criticism; since not only did the Captain's discourse never fall into the jocosely familiar, but in illustrating of any point touching the stirring personages and events of the time he would be as apt to cite some historic character or incident of antiquity as that he would cite from the moderns. He seemed unmindful of the circumstance that to his bluff company such remote allusions however pertinent they might really be were altogether alien to men whose reading was mainly confined to the journals. But considerateness in such matters is not easy to natures constituted like Captain Vere's. Their honesty prescribes to them directness, sometimes far-reaching like that of a migratory fowl that in its flight never heeds when it crosses a frontier.

8

The lieutenant and other commissioned gentlemen forming Captain Vere's staff it is not necessary here to particularize, nor needs it to make any mention of any of the warrant-officers. But among the petty-officers was one who having much to do with the story, may as well be forthwith introduced. His portrait I essay, but shall never hit it. This was John Claggart, the Master-at-arms. But that sea-title may to landsmen seem somewhat equivocal. Originally doubtless that petty-officer's function was the instruction of the men in the use of arms, sword or cutlas. But very long ago, owing to the advance in gunnery making hand-to-hand encounters less frequent and giving to nitre and sulphur the preeminence over steel, that function ceased; the master-at-arms of a great warship becoming a sort of Chief of Police charged among other matters with the duty of preserving order of the populous lower gun-decks.

Claggart was a man about five and thirty, somewhat spare and tall, yet of no ill figure upon the whole. His hand was too small and shapely to have been accustomed to hard toil. The face was a notable one; the features all except the chin cleanly cut as those on a Greek medallion; yet the chin, beardless as Tecumseh's, had something of strange protuberant heaviness in its make that recalled the prints of the Rev. Dr. Titus Oates, the historic deponent with the clerical drawl in the time of Charles II and the fraud of the alleged Popish Plot. It served Claggart in his office that his eye could cast a tutoring glance. His brow was of the sort phrenologically associated with more than average intellect; silken jet curls partly clustering over it, making a foil to the pallor below, a pallor tinged with a faint shade of amber akin to the hue of time-tinted marbles of old. This complexion, singularly contrasting with the red or deeply bronzed visages of the sailors, and in part the result of his official seclusion from the sunlight, tho' it was not exactly displeasing, nevertheless seemed to hint of something defective or abnormal in the constitution and blood. But his general aspect and manner were so suggestive of an education and career incongruous with his naval function that when not actively engaged in it he looked like a man of high quality, social and moral, who for reasons of his own was keeping incog. Nothing was known of his former life. It might be that he was an Englishman; and yet there lurked a bit of accent in his speech suggesting that possibly he was not such by birth, but through naturalization in early childhood. Among certain grizzled sea-gossips of the gun-decks and forecastle went a rumor perdue that the master-at-arms was a *chevalier* who had volunteered into the King's navy by way of compounding for some mysterious swindle whereof he had been arraigned at the King's Bench. The fact that nobody could substantiate this report was, of course, nothing against its secret currency. Such a rumor once started on the gun-decks in reference to almost anyone below the rank of a commissioned officer would, during the period assigned to this narrative, have seemed not altogether wanting in credibility to the tarry old wiseacres of a man-of-war crew. And indeed a man of Claggart's accomplishments, without prior nautical experience entering the navy at mature life, as he did, and necessarily allotted at the start to the lowest grade in it; a man too who never made allusion to his previous life ashore; these were circumstances which in the dearth of exact knowledge as to his true antecedents opened to the invidious a vague field for unfavorable surmise.

But the sailors' dog-watch gossip concerning him derived a vague plausibility from the fact that now for some period the British Navy could so little afford to be squeamish in the matter of keeping up the muster-rolls, that not only were press-gangs notoriously abroad both afloat and ashore, but there was little or no secret about another matter, namely that the London police were at liberty to capture any able-bodied suspect, any questionable fellow at large and summarily ship him to the dockyard or fleet. Furthermore, even among voluntary enlistments there were instances where the motive thereto partook neither of patriotic impulse nor yet of a random desire to experience a bit of sea-life and martial adventure. Insolvent debtors of minor grade, together with the promiscuous lame ducks of morality, found in the Navy a convenient and secure refuge. Secure, because once enlisted aboard a King's-Ship, they were as much in sanctuary, as the transgressor of the Middle Ages harboring himself under the shadow of the altar. Such sanctioned irregularities, which for obvious reasons the Government would hardly think to parade at the time and which consequently, and as affecting the least influential class of mankind, have all but dropped into oblivion, lend color to something for the truth whereof I do not vouch, and hence have some scruple in stating; something I remember having seen in print though the book I can not recall; but the same thing was personally communicated to me now more than forty years ago by an old pensioner in a cocked hat with whom I had a most interesting talk on the terrace at Greenwich, a Baltimore Negro, a Trafalgar man. It was to this effect: In the case of a warship short of hands whose speedy sailing was imperative, the deficient quota in lack of any other way of making it good, would be eked out by draughts culled direct from the jails. For reasons previously suggested it would not perhaps be easy at the present day directly to prove or disprove the allegation. But allowed as a verity,

how significant would it be of England's straits at the time confronted by those wars which like a flight of harpies rose shrieking from the din and dust of the fallen Bastille. That era appears measurably clear to us who look back at it, and but read of it. But to the grandfathers of us graybeards, the more thoughtful of them, the genius of it presented an aspect like that of Camoen's Spirit of the Cape, an eclipsing menace mysterious and prodigious. Nor was America exempt from apprehension. At the height of Napoleon's unexampled conquests, there were Americans who had fought at Bunker Hill who looked forward to the possibility that the Atlantic might prove no barrier against the ultimate schemes of this French upstart from the revolutionary chaos who seemed in act of fulfilling judgment prefigured in the Apocalypse.

But the less credence was to be given to the gun-deck talk touching Claggart, seeing that no man holding his office in a man-of-war can ever hope to be popular with the crew. Besides, in derogatory comments upon anyone against whom they have a grudge, or for any reason or no reason mislike, sailors are much like landsmen, they are apt to exaggerate or romance it.

About as much was really known to the *Indomitable's* tars of the master-at-arms' career before entering the service as an astronomer knows about a comet's travels prior to its first observable appearance in the sky. The verdict of the sea quidnuncs has been cited only by way of showing what sort of moral impression the man made upon rude uncultivated natures whose conceptions of human wickedness were necessarily of the narrowest, limited to ideas of vulgar rascality, — a thief among the swinging hammocks during a night-watch, or the man-brokers and land-sharks of the sea-ports.

It was no gossip, however, but fact, that though, as before hinted, Claggart upon his entrance into the navy was, as a novice, assigned to the least honorable section of a man-of-war's crew, embracing the drudgery, he did not long remain there.

The superior capacity he immediately evinced, his constitutional sobriety, ingratiating deference to superiors, together with a peculiar ferreting genius manifested on a singular occasion, all this capped by a certain austere patriotism abruptly advanced him to the position of master-at-arms.

Of this maritime Chief of Police the ship's-

corporals, so called, were the immediate subordinates, and compliant ones; and this, as is
to be noted in some business departments
ashore, almost to a degree inconsistent with
entire moral volition. His place put various 5
converging wires of underground influence
under the Chief's control, capable when
astutely worked thro' his understrappers of operating to the mysterious discomfort, if nothing
worse, of any of the sea-commonalty.   10

9

Life in the fore-top well agreed with Billy
Budd. There, when not actually engaged on 15
the yards yet higher aloft, the topmen, who as
such had been picked out for youth and activity, constituted an aerial club lounging at
ease against the smaller stun'sails rolled up into
cushions, spinning yarns like the lazy gods, and 20
frequently amused with what was going on in
the busy world of the decks below. No wonder
then that a young fellow of Billy's disposition
was well content in such society. Giving no
cause of offence to anybody, he was always 25
alert at a call. So in the merchant service it
had been with him. But now such a punctil-
iousness in duty was shown that his topmates
would sometimes good-naturedly laugh at him
for it. This heightened alacrity had its cause, 30
namely, the impression made upon him by the
first formal gangway-punishment he had ever
witnessed, which befell the day following his
impressment. It had been incurred by a little
fellow, young, a novice, an after-guardsman 35
absent from his assigned post when the ship was
being put about; a dereliction resulting in a
rather serious hitch to that manœuvre, one demanding instantaneous promptitude in letting
go and making fast. When Billy saw the cul- 40
prit's naked back under the scourge gridironed
with red welts, and worse; when he marked the
dire expression on the liberated man's face as
with his woolen shirt flung over him by the
executioner he rushed forward from the spot to 45
bury himself in the crowd, Billy was horrified.
He resolved that never through remissness
would he make himself liable to such a visita-
tion or do or omit aught that might merit even
verbal reproof. What then was his surprise and 50
concern when ultimately he found himself getting into petty trouble occasionally about such
matters as the stowage of his bag or something
amiss in his hammock, matters under the police

oversight of the ship's-corporals of the lower
decks, and which brought down on him a vague
threat from one of them.

So heedful in all things as he was, how
could this be? He could not understand it, and
it more than vexed him. When he spoke to his
young topmates about it they were either
lightly incredulous or found something comical
in his unconcealed anxiety. "Is it your bag,
Billy?" said one; "well, sew yourself up in it,
bully boy, and then you'll be sure to know if
anybody meddles with it."

Now there was a veteran aboard who because
his years began to disqualify him for more active
work had been recently assigned duty as main-
mast-man in his watch, looking to the gear be-
layed at the rail roundabout that great spar
near the deck. At off-times the foretopman had
picked up some acquaintance with him, and
now in his trouble it occurred to him that he
might be the sort of person to go to for wise
counsel. He was an old Dansker long angli-
cized in the service, of few words, many
wrinkles and some honorable scars. His wizened face, time-tinted and weather-stained to
the complexion of an antique parchment, was
here and there peppered blue by the chance
explosion of a gun-cartridge in action. He was
an *Agamemnon*-man; some two years prior to
the time of this story having served under
Nelson when but Sir Horatio in that ship immortal in naval memory, and which, dismantled and in part broken up to her bare ribs, is
seen a grand skeleton in Haydon's etching. As
one of a boarding-party from the *Agamemnon*
he had received a cut slantwise along one temple and cheek leaving a long pale scar like a
streak of dawn's light falling athwart the dark
visage. It was on account of that scar and the
affair in which it was known that he had received it, as well as from his blue-peppered
complexion that the Dansker went among the
Indomitable's crew by the name of "Board-her-
in-the-smoke."

Now the first time that his small weazel-eyes
happened to light on Billy Budd, a certain grim
internal merriment set all his ancient wrinkles
into antic play. Was it that his eccentric un-
sentimental old sapience primitive in its kind
saw or thought it saw something which in contrast with the war-ship's environment looked
oddly incongruous in the handsome sailor?
But after slyly studying him at intervals, the
old Merlin's equivocal merriment was modi-

fied; for now when the twain would meet, it would start in his face a quizzing sort of look, but it would be but momentary and sometimes replaced by an expression of speculative query as to what might eventually befall a nature like that, dropped into a world not without some mantraps and against whose subtleties simple courage lacking experience and address and without any touch of defensive ugliness, is of little avail; and where such innocence as man is capable of does yet in a moral emergency not always sharpen the faculties or enlighten the will.

However it was the Dansker in his ascetic way rather took to Billy. Nor was this only because of a certain philosophic interest in such a character. There was another cause. While the old man's eccentricities, sometimes bordering on the ursine, repelled the juniors, Billy, undeterred thereby, revering him as a salt hero would make advances, never passing the old *Agamemnon*-man without a salutation marked by that respect which is seldom lost on the aged however crabbed at times or whatever their station in life.

There was a vein of dry humor, or what not, in the mast-man; and, whether in freak of patriarchal irony touching Billy's youth and athletic frame, or for some other and more recondite reason, from the first in addressing him he always substituted Baby for Billy. The Dansker in fact being the originator of the name by which the foretopman eventually became known aboard ship.

Well then, in his mysterious little difficulty going in quest of the wrinkled one, Billy found him off duty in a dog-watch ruminating by himself seated on a shot-box of the upper gun-deck, now and then surveying with a somewhat cynical regard certain of the more swaggering promenaders there. Billy recounted his trouble, again wondering how it all happened. The salt seer attentively listened, accompanying the foretopman's recital with queer twitchings of his wrinkles and problematical little sparkles of his small ferret eyes. Making an end of his story, the foretopman asked, "And now, Dansker, do tell me what you think of it."

The old man, shoving up the front of his tarpaulin and deliberately rubbing the long slant scar at the point where it entered the thin hair, laconically said, "Baby Budd, *Jemmy Legs*" (meaning the master-at-arms) "is down on you."

"*Jemmy Legs!*" ejaculated Billy his welkin eyes expanding; "what for? Why he calls me *the sweet and pleasant young fellow,* they tell me."

"Does he so?" grinned the grizzled one; then said "Ay, Baby Lad, a sweet voice has *Jemmy Legs.*"

"No, not always. But to me he has. I seldom pass him but there comes a pleasant word."

"And that's because he's down upon you, Baby Budd."

Such reiteration along with the manner of it, incomprehensible to a novice, disturbed Billy almost as much as the mystery for which he had sought explanation. Something less unpleasingly oracular he tried to extract; but the old sea-Chiron thinking perhaps that for the nonce he had sufficiently instructed his young Achilles, pursed his lips, gathered all his wrinkles together and would commit himself to nothing further.

Years, and those experiences which befall certain shrewder men subordinated life-long to the will of superiors, all this had developed in the Dansker the pithy guarded cynicism that was his leading characteristic.

10

The next day an incident served to confirm Billy Budd in his incredulity as to the Dansker's strange summing up of the case submitted. The ship at noon going large before the wind was rolling on her course, and he below at dinner and engaged in some sportful talk with the members of his mess, chanced in a sudden lurch to spill the entire contents of his soup-pan upon the new scrubbed deck. Claggart, the Master-at-arms, official rattan in hand, happened to be passing along the battery in a bay of which the mess was lodged, and the greasy liquid streamed just across his path. Stepping over it, he was proceeding on his way without comment, since the matter was nothing to take notice of under the circumstances, when he happened to observe who it was that had done the spilling. His countenance changed. Pausing, he was about to ejaculate something hasty at the sailor, but checked himself, and pointing down to the streaming soup, playfully tapped him from behind with his rattan, saying in a low musical voice peculiar to him at times "Handsomely done, my lad! And handsome is as handsome did it too!" And with that passed on. Not noted by Billy as not coming within his view was the involuntary smile, or rather grimace, that accompanied Claggart's equivocal words. Aridly it drew down the thin corners of his shapely mouth. But everybody taking his remark as meant for humorous, and at which therefore as coming from a superior they were bound to laugh, "with counterfeited glee" acted accordingly; and Billy tickled, it may be, by the allusion to his being the handsome sailor, merrily joined in; then addressing his messmates exclaimed "There now, who says that Jemmy Legs is down on me!" "And who said he was, Beauty?" demanded one Donald with some surprise. Whereat the foretopman looked a little foolish recalling that it was only one person, Board-her-in-the-smoke, who had suggested what to him was the smoky idea that this master-at-arms was in any peculiar way hostile to him. Meantime that functionary resuming his path must have momentarily worn some expression less guarded than that of the bitter smile, and usurping the face from the heart, some distorting expression perhaps, for a drummer-boy heedlessly frolicking along from the opposite direction and chancing to come into light collision with his person was strangely disconcerted by his aspect. Nor was the impression lessened when the official impulsively giving him a sharp cut with the rattan, vehemently exclaimed "Look where you go!"

11

What was the matter with the master-at-arms? And, be the matter what it might, how could it have direct relation to Billy Budd with whom prior to the affair of the spilled soup he had never come into any special contact official or otherwise? What indeed could the trouble have to do with one so little inclined to give offence as the merchant-ship's *peacemaker*, even him who in Claggart's own phrase was "the sweet and pleasant young fellow"? Yes, why should *Jemmy Legs*, to borrow the Dansker's expression, be *down* on the Handsome Sailor? But, at heart and not for nothing, as the late chance encounter may indicate to the discerning, down on him, secretly down on him, he assuredly was.

Now to invent something touching the more private career of Claggart, something involving Billy Budd, of which something the latter should be wholly ignorant, some romantic incident implying that Claggart's knowledge of the young blue-jacket began at some period anterior to catching sight of him on board the seventy-four — all this, not so difficult to do, might avail in a way more or less interesting to account for whatever of enigma may appear to lurk in the case. But in fact there was nothing of the sort. And yet the cause, necessarily to be assumed as the sole one assignable, is in its very realism as much charged with that prime element of Radcliffian romance, *the mysterious,* as any that the ingenuity of the author of the *Mysteries of Udolpho* could devise. For what can more partake of the mysterious than an antipathy spontaneous and profound such as is evoked in certain exceptional mortals by the mere aspect of some other mortal, however harmless he may be? if not called forth by this very harmlessness itself.

Now there can exist no irritating juxtaposition of dissimilar personalities comparable to that which is possible aboard a great war-ship fully manned and at sea. There, every day among all ranks almost every man comes into more or less of contact with almost every other man. Wholly there to avoid even the sight of an aggravating object one must needs give it Jonah's toss or jump overboard himself. Imagine how all this might eventually operate on some peculiar human creature the direct reverse of a saint?

But for the adequate comprehending of Claggart by a normal nature these hints are insufficient. To pass from a normal nature to him one must cross "the deadly space between." And this is best done by indirection.

Long ago an honest scholar my senior, said to me in reference to one who like himself is now no more, a man so unimpeachably respectable that against him nothing was ever openly said tho' among the few something was whispered, "Yes, X—— is a nut not to be cracked by the tap of a lady's fan. You are aware that I am the adherent of no organized religion much less of any philosophy built into a system. Well, for all that, I think that to try and get into X——, enter his labyrinth and get out again, without a clue derived from some source other than what is known as *knowledge of the world* — that were hardly possible, at least for me."

"Why" said I, "X—— however singular a

study to some, is yet human, and knowledge of the world assuredly implies the knowledge of human nature, and in most of its varieties."

"Yes, but a superficial knowledge of it, serving ordinary purposes. But for anything deeper, I am not certain whether to know the world and to know human nature be not two distinct branches of knowledge, which while they may coexist in the same heart, yet either may exist with little or nothing of the other. Nay, in an average man of the world, his constant rubbing with it blunts that fine spiritual insight indispensable to the understanding of the essential in certain exceptional characters, whether evil ones or good. In a matter of some importance I have seen a girl wind an old lawyer about her little finger. Nor was it the dotage of senile love. Nothing of the sort. But he knew law better than he knew the girl's heart. Coke and Blackstone hardly shed so much light into obscure places as the Hebrew prophets. And who were they? Mostly recluses."

At the time my inexperience was such that I did not quite see the drift of all this. It may be that I see it now. And, indeed, if that lexicon which is based on Holy Writ were any longer popular, one might with less difficulty define and denominate certain phenomenal men. As it is, one must turn to some authority not liable to the charge of being tinctured with the Biblical element.

In a list of definitions included in the authentic translation of Plato, a list attributed to him, occurs this: "Natural Depravity: a depravity according to nature." A definition which tho' savoring of Calvinism, by no means involves Calvin's dogmas as to total mankind. Evidently its intent makes it applicable but to individuals. Not many are the examples of this depravity which the gallows and jail supply. At any rate for notable instances, since these have no vulgar alloy of the brute in them, but invariably are dominated by intellectuality, one must go elsewhere. Civilization, especially if of the austerer sort, is auspicious to it. It folds itself in the mantle of respectability. It has its certain negative virtues serving as silent auxiliaries. It never allows wine to get within its guard. It is not going too far to say that it is without vices or small sins. There is a phenomenal pride in it that excludes them from anything mercenary or avaricious. In short the depravity here meant partakes nothing of the sordid or sensual. It is serious, but free from

acerbity. Though no flatterer of mankind it never speaks ill of it.

But the thing which in eminent instances signalizes so exceptional a nature is this: though the man's even temper and discreet bearing would seem to intimate a mind peculiarly subject to the law of reason, not the less in his heart he would seem to riot in complete exemption from that law, having apparently little to do with reason further than to employ it as an ambidexter implement for effecting the irrational. That is to say: Toward the accomplishment of an aim which in wantonness of malignity would seem to partake of the insane, he will direct a cool judgement sagacious and sound.

These men are true madmen, and of the most dangerous sort, for their lunacy is not continuous but occasional, evoked by some special object; it is probably secretive, which is as much to say it is self-contained, so that when moreover, most active, it is to the average mind not distinguishable from sanity, and for the reason above suggested that whatever its aims may be, and the aim is never declared — the method and the outward proceeding are always perfectly rational.

Now something such an one was Claggart, in whom was the mania of an evil nature, not engendered by vicious training or corrupting books or licentious living, but born with him and innate, in short "a depravity according to nature."

12

Lawyers, Experts, Clergy
An Episode

By the way, can it be the phenomenon, disowned or at least concealed, that in some criminal cases puzzles the courts? For this cause have our juries at times not only to endure the prolonged contentions of lawyers with their fees, but also the yet more perplexing strife of the medical experts with theirs? — But why leave it to them? why not subpoena as well the clerical proficients? Their vocation bringing them into peculiar contact with so many human beings, and sometimes in their least guarded hour, in interviews very much more confidential than those of physician and patient; this would seem to qualify them to know something about those intricacies involved in the question of moral responsibility; whether in a given case, say, the crime proceeded from mania in the brain or rabies of the heart. As to any differences among themselves these clerical proficients might develop on the stand, these could hardly be greater than the direct contradictions exchanged between the remunerated medical experts.

Dark sayings are these, some will say. But why? Is it because they somewhat savor of Holy Writ in its phrase "mysteries of iniquity"? If they do, such savor was far from being intended, for little will it commend these pages to many a reader of to-day.

The point of the present story turning on the hidden nature of the master-at-arms has necessitated this chapter. With an added hint or two in connection with the incident at the mess, the resumed narrative must be left to vindicate, as it may, its own credibility.

13

Pale ire, envy and despair

That Claggart's figure was not amiss, and his face, save the chin, well moulded, has already been said. Of these favorable points he seemed not insensible, for he was not only neat but careful in his dress. But the form of Billy Budd was heroic; and if his face was without the intellectual look of the pallid Claggart's, not the less was it lit, like his, from within, though from a different source. The bonfire in his heart made luminous the rose-tan in his cheek.

In view of the marked contrast between the persons of the twain, it is more than probable that when the master-at-arms in the scene last given applied to the sailor the proverb *Handsome is as handsome does*; he there let escape an ironic inkling, not caught by the young sailors who heard it, as to what it was that had first moved him against Billy, namely, his significant personal beauty.

Now envy and antipathy, passions irreconcilable in reason, nevertheless in fact may spring conjoined like Chang and Eng in one birth. Is Envy then such a monster? Well, though many an arraigned mortal has in hopes of mitigated penalty pleaded guilty to horrible actions, did ever anybody seriously confess to envy? Something there is in it universally felt to be more shameful than even felonious crime. And

not only does everybody disown it but the better sort are inclined to incredulity when it is in earnest imputed to an intelligent man. But since its lodgement is in the heart not the brain, no degree of intellect supplies a guarantee against it. But Claggart's was no vulgar form of the passion. Nor, as directed toward Billy Budd did it partake of that streak of apprehensive jealousy that marred Saul's visage perturbedly brooding on the comely young David. Claggart's envy struck deeper. If askance he eyed the good looks, cheery health and frank enjoyment of young life in Billy Budd, it was because these went along with a nature that as Claggart magnetically felt, had in its simplicity never willed malice or experienced the reactionary bite of that serpent. To him, the spirit lodged within Billy, and looking out from his welkin eyes as from windows, that ineffability it was which made the dimple in his dyed cheek, suppled his joints, and dancing in his yellow curls made him preeminently the Handsome Sailor. One person excepted the master-at-arms was perhaps the only man in the ship intellectually capable of adequately appreciating the moral phenomenon presented in Billy Budd. And the insight but intensified his passion, which assuming various secret forms within him, at times assumed that of cynic disdain of innocence — To be nothing more than innocent! Yet in an æsthetic way he saw the charm of it, the courageous free-and-easy temper of it, and fain would have shared it, but he despaired of it.

With no power to annul the elemental evil in him, tho' readily enough he could hide it; apprehending the good, but powerless to be it; a nature like Claggart's surcharged with energy as such natures almost invariable are, what recourse is left to it but to recoil upon itself and like the scorpion for which the Creator alone is responsible, act out to the end the part allotted it.

14

Passion, and passion in its profoundest, is not a thing demanding a palatial stage whereon to play its part. Down among the groundlings, among the beggars and rakers of the garbage, profound passion is enacted. And the circumstances that provoke it, however trivial or mean, are no measure of its power. In the present instance the stage is a scrubbed gun-deck, and

which in some cases instinctively conveys to ignorant innocence an admonition of the proximity of the malign. He thought the Master-at-arms acted in a manner rather queer at times. That was all. But the occasional frank air and pleasant word went for what they purported to be, the young sailor never having heard as yet of the "too fair-spoken man."

Had the foretopman been conscious of having done or said anything to provoke the ill will of the official, it would have been different with him, and his sight might have been purged if not sharpened. As it was, innocence was his blinder.

So was it with him in yet another matter. Two minor officers — the Armorer and Captain of the Hold, with whom he had never exchanged a word, his position in the ship not bringing him into contact with them; these men now for the first began to cast upon Billy, when they chanced to encounter him, that peculiar glance which evidences that the man from whom it comes has been some way tampered with and to the prejudice of him upon whom the glance lights. Never did it occur to Billy as a thing to be noted or a thing suspicious, tho' he well knew the fact, that the Armorer and Captain of the Hold, with the ship's-yeoman, apothecary, and others of that grade, were by naval usage mess-mates of the master-at-arms, men with ears convenient to his confidential tongue.

But the general popularity that our *Handsome Sailor's* manly forwardness upon occasion, and irresistible good nature, indicating no mental superiority tending to excite an invidious feeling; this good will on the part of most of his shipmates made him the less to concern himself about such mute aspects toward him as those whereto allusion has just been made.

As to the afterguardsman, tho' Billy for reasons already given necessarily saw little of him, yet when the two did happen to meet, invariably came the fellow's off-hand cheerful recognition, sometimes accompanied by a passing pleasant word or two. Whatever that equivocal young person's original design may really have been, or the design of which he might have been the deputy, certain it was from his manner upon these occasions, that he had wholly dropped it.

It was as if his precocity of crookedness (and every vulgar villain is precocious) had for once deceived him, and the man he had sought to entrap as a simpleton had, through his very simplicity, ignorantly baffled him.

But shrewd ones may opine that it was hardly possible for Billy to refrain from going up to the afterguardsman and bluntly demanding to know his purpose in the initial interview, so abruptly closed in the fore-chains. Shrewd ones may also think it but natural in Billy to set about sounding some of the other impressed men of the ship in order to discover what basis, if any, there was for the emissary's obscure suggestions as to plotting disaffection aboard. Yes, shrewd may so think. But something more, or rather, something else than mere shrewdness is perhaps needful for the due understanding of such a character as Billy Budd's.

As to Claggart, the monomania in the man — if that indeed it were — as involuntarily disclosed by starts in the manifestations detailed, yet in general covered over by his self-contained and rational demeanor; this, like a subterranean fire was eating its way deeper and deeper in him. Something decisive must come of it.

19

After the mysterious interview in the fore-chains, the one so abruptly ended there by Billy, nothing especially german to the story occurred until the events now about to be narrated.

Elsewhere it has been said that in the lack of frigates (of course better sailers than line-of-battle ships) in the English squadron up the Straits at that period, the *Indomitable* was occasionally employed not only as an available substitute for a scout, but at times on detached service of more important kind. This was not alone because of her sailing qualities, not common in a ship of her rate, but quite as much, probably, that the character of her commander, it was thought, specially adapted him for any duty where under unforeseen difficulties a prompt initiative might have to be taken in some matter demanding knowledge and ability in addition to those qualities implied in good seamanship. It was on an expedition of the latter sort, a somewhat distant one, and when the *Indomitable* was almost at her furthest remove from the fleet that in the latter part of an afternoon-watch she unexpectedly came in sight of a ship of the enemy. It proved to be a frigate. The latter perceiving thro' the glass that the weight of men and metal would be heavily against her, invoking her light heels crowded sail to get away. After a chase urged almost against hope and lasting until about the middle of the first dog-watch, she signally succeeded in affecting her escape.

Not long after the pursuit had been given up, and ere the excitement incident thereto had altogether waned away, the Master-at-Arms ascending from his cavernous sphere made his appearance cap in hand by the mainmast respectfully waiting the notice of Captain Vere then solitary walking the weather-side of the quarter-deck, doubtless somewhat chafed at the failure of the pursuit. The spot where Claggart stood was the place allotted to men of lesser grades seeking some more particular interview with the officer-of-the-deck or the Captain himself. But from the latter it was not often that a sailor or petty-officer of those days would seek a hearing; only some exceptional cause, would, according to established custom have warranted that.

Presently, just as the Commander absorbed in his reflections was on the point of turning aft in his promenade, he became sensible of Claggart's presence, and saw the doffed cap held in deferential expectancy. Here be it said that Captain Vere's personal knowledge of this petty-officer had only begun at the time of the ship's last sailing from home, Claggart then for the first time, in transfer from a ship detained for repairs, supplying on board the *Indomitable* the place of a previous master-at-arms disabled and ashore.

No sooner did the Commander observe who it was that now deferentially stood awaiting his notice, than a peculiar expression came over him. It was not unlike that which uncontrollably will flit across the countenance of one at unawares encountering a person who though known to him indeed has hardly been long enough known for thorough knowledge, but something in whose aspect nevertheless now for the first provokes a vaguely repellent distaste. But coming to a stand, and resuming much of his wonted official manner, save that a sort of impatience lurked in the intonation of the opening word, he said "Well? what is it, Master-at-Arms?"

With the air of a subordinate grieved at the necessity of being a messenger of ill tidings, and while conscientiously determined to be frank, yet equally resolved upon shunning overstatement, Claggart at this invitation or rather summons to disburthen, spoke up. What he said, conveyed in the language of no uneducated man, was to the effect following if not altogether in these words, namely, that during the chase and preparations for the possible encounter he had seen enough to convince him that at least one sailor aboard was a dangerous character in a ship mustering some who not only had taken a guilty part in the late serious troubles, but others also who, like the man in question, had entered His Majesty's service under another form than enlistment.

At this point Captain Vere with some impatience, interrupted him: "Be direct, man; say impressed men."

Claggart made a gesture of subservience, and proceeded.

Quite lately he (Claggart) had begun to suspect that on the gun-decks some sort of movement prompted by the sailor in question was covertly going on, but he had not thought himself warranted in reporting the suspicion so long as it remained indistinct. But from what he had that afternoon observed in the man referred to the suspicion of something clandestine going on had advanced to a point less removed from certainty. He deeply felt, he added, the serious responsibility assumed in making a report involving such possible consequences to the individual mainly concerned, besides tending to augment those natural anxieties which every naval commander must feel in view of extraordinary outbreaks so recent as those which, he sorrowfully said it, it needed not to name.

Now at the first broaching of the matter Captain Vere taken by surprise could not wholly dissemble his disquietude. But as Claggart went on, the former's aspect changed into restiveness under something in the witness' manner in giving his testimony. However, he refrained from interrupting him. And Claggart, continuing, concluded with this:

"God forbid, your honor, that the *Indomitable's* should be the experience of the — "

"Never mind that!" here peremptorily broke in the superior, his face altering with anger, instinctively divining the ship that the other was about to name, one in which the Nore Mutiny had assumed a singularly tragical character that for a time jeopardized the life of its commander. Under the circumstances he was indignant at the purposed allusion. When the commissioned officers themselves were on all occasions very heedful how they referred to the recent events, for a petty-officer unnecessarily to allude to them in the presence of his Captain, this struck him as a most immodest presumption. Besides, to his quick sense of self-respect, it even looked under the circumstances something like an attempt to alarm him. Nor at first was he without some surprise that one who so far as he had hitherto come under his notice had shown considerable tact in his function should in this particular evince such lack of it.

But these thoughts and kindred dubious ones flitting across his mind were suddenly replaced by an intuitional surmise which though as yet obscure in form served practically to affect his reception of the ill tidings. Certain it is, that long versed in everything pertaining to the complicated gun-deck life, which like every other form of life, has its secret mines and dubious side, the side popularly disclaimed, Captain Vere did not permit himself to be unduly disturbed by the general tenor of his subordinate's report. Furthermore, if in view of recent events prompt action should be taken at the first palpable sign of recurring insubordination, for all that, not judicious would it be, he thought, to keep the idea of lingering disaffection alive by undue forwardness in crediting an informer even if his own subordinate and charged among other things with police surveillance of the crew. This feeling would not perhaps have so prevailed with him were it not that upon a prior occasion the patriotic zeal officially evinced by Claggart had somewhat irritated him as appearing rather supersensible and strained. Furthermore, something even in the official's self-possessed and somewhat ostentatious manner in making his specifications strangely reminded him of a bandsman, a perjurous witness in a capital case before a court-martial ashore of which when a lieutenant he Captain Vere had been a member.

Now the peremptory check given to Claggart in the matter of the arrested allusion was quickly followed up by this: "You say that there is at least one dangerous man aboard. Name him."

"William Budd. A foretopman, your honor—"

"William Budd" repeated Captain with unfeigned astonishment; "and mean you the man that Lieutenant Ratcliffe took from the merchantman not very long ago—the young fellow who seems to be so popular with the men—Billy, the Handsome Sailor, as they call him?"

"The same, your honor; but for all his youth and good looks, a deep one. Not for nothing does he insinuate himself into the good will of his shipmates, since at the least all hands will at a pinch say a good word for him at all hazards. Did Lieutenant Ratcliffe happen to tell your honor of that adroit fling of Budd's, jumping up in the cutter's bow under the merchantman's stern when he was being taken off? It is even masqued by that sort of good humored air that at heart he resents his impressment. You have but noted his fair cheek. A man-trap may be under his ruddy-tipped daisies."

Now the *Handsome Sailor* as a signal figure among the crew had naturally enough attracted the Captain's attention from the first. Tho' in general not very demonstrative to his officers, he had congratulated Lieutenant Ratcliffe upon his good fortune in lighting on such a fine specimen of the genus homo, who in the nude might have posed for a statue of young Adam before the Fall.

As to Billy's adieu to the ship *Rights-of-Man*, which the boarding lieutenant had indeed reported to him but in a deferential way more as a good story than aught else, Captain Vere, tho' mistakenly understanding it as a satiric sally, had but thought so much the better of the impressed man for it; as a military sailor, admiring the spirit that could take an arbitrary enlistment so merrily and sensibly. The foretopman's conduct, too, so far as it had fallen under the Captain's notice had confirmed the first happy augury, while the new recruit's qualities as a *sailor-man* seemed to be such that he had thought of recommending him to the executive officer for promotion to a place that would more frequently bring him under his own observation, namely, the captaincy of the mizzen-top, replacing there in the starboard watch a man not so young whom partly for that reason he deemed less fitted for the post. Be it parenthesized here that since the mizzen-top-men having not to handle such breadths of heavy canvas as the lower sails on the mainmast and fore-mast, a young man if of the right stuff not only seems best adapted to duty there, but in fact is generally selected for the captaincy of that top, and the company under him are light hands and often but striplings. In sum, Captain Vere had from the beginning deemed Billy Budd to be what in the naval parlance of the time was called a *"King's bargain,"* that is to say, for His Britannic Majesty's navy a capital investment at small outlay or none at all.

After a brief pause during which the reminiscences above mentioned passed vividly through his mind and he weighed the import of Claggart's last suggestion conveyed in the phrase "pitfall under the clover," and the more he weighed it the less reliance he felt in the informer's good faith. Suddenly he turned upon him and in a low voice: "Do you come to me, master-at-arms, with so foggy a tale? As to Budd, cite me an act or spoken word of his confirmatory of what you in general charge against him. Stay," drawing nearer to him "heed what you speak. Just now, and in a case like this, there is a yard-arm-end for the false-witness."

"Ah, your honor!" sighed Claggart mildly shaking his shapely head as in sad deprecation of such unmerited severity of tone. Then, bridling — erecting himself as in virtuous self-assertion, he circumstantially alleged certain words and acts, which collectively, if credited, led to presumptions mortally inculpating Budd. And for some of these averments, he added, substantiating proof was not far.

With gray eyes impatient and distrustful essaying to fathom to the bottom Claggart's calm violet ones, Captain Vere again heard him out; then for the moment stood ruminating. The mood he evinced, Claggart — himself for the time liberated from the other's scrutiny — steadily regarded with a look difficult to render, — a look curious of the operation of his tactics, a look such as might have been that of the spokesman of the envious children of Jacob deceptively imposing upon the troubled patriarch the blood-dyed coat of young Joseph.

Though something exceptional in the moral quality of Captain Vere made him, in earnest encounter with a fellow-man, a veritable touchstone of that man's essential nature, yet now as to Claggart and what was really going on in him his feeling partook less of intuitional conviction than of strong suspicion clogged by strange dubieties. The perplexity he evinced proceeded less from aught touching the man informed against — as Claggart doubtless opined — than from considerations how best to act in regard to the informer. At first indeed he was naturally for summoning that substantiation of his allegations which Claggart said was at hand. But such a proceeding would result in the matter at once getting abroad, which in the present stage of it, he thought, might undesirably affect the ship's company. If Claggart was a false witness, — that closed the affair. And therefore before trying the accusation, he would first practically test the accuser; and thought this could be done in a quiet undemonstrative way.

The measure he determined upon involved a shifting of the scene, a transfer to a place less exposed to observation than the broad quarter-deck. For although the few gun-room officers there at the time had, in due observance of naval etiquette, withdrawn to leeward the moment Captain Vere had begun his promenade on the deck's weather-side; and tho' during the colloquy with Claggart they of course ventured not to diminish the distance; and though throughout the interview Captain Vere's voice was far from high, and Claggart's silvery and low; and the wind in the cordage and the wash of the sea helped the more to put them beyond ear-shot; nevertheless, the interview's continuance already attracted observation from some topmen aloft and other sailors in the waist or further forward.

Having determined upon his measures, Captain Vere forthwith took action. Abruptly turning to Claggart he asked "Master-at-arms, is it now Budd's watch aloft?"

"No, your honor." Whereupon, "Mr. Wilkes!" summoning the nearest midshipman, "tell Albert to come to me." Albert was the Captain's hammock-boy, a sort of sea-valet in whose discretion and fidelity his master had much confidence. The lad appeared. "You know Budd the foretopman?"

"I do, Sir."

"Go find him. It is his watch off. Manage to tell him out of earshot that he is wanted aft. Contrive it that he speaks to nobody. Keep him in talk yourself. And not till you get well aft here, not till then let him know that the place where he is wanted is my cabin. You understand. Go. — Master-at-Arms, show yourself on the decks below, and when you think it time for Albert to be coming with his man, stand by quietly to follow the sailor in."

20

Now when the foretopman found himself closeted there, as it were, in the cabin with the Captain and Claggart, he was surprised enough. But it was a surprise unaccompanied by apprehension or distrust. To an immature nature essentially honest and humane, forewarning intimations of subtler danger from one's kind come tardily if at all. The only thing that took shape in the young sailor's mind was this: Yes, the Captain, I have always thought, looks kindly upon me. Wonder if he's going to make me coxswain. I should like that. And maybe now he is going to ask the master-at-arms about me.

"Shut the door there, sentry," said the commander; "stand without, and let nobody come in. — Now, master-at-arms, tell this man to his face what you told of him to me"; and stood prepared to scrutinize the mutually confronting visages.

With the measured step and calm collected air of an asylum-physician approaching in the public hall some patient beginning to show indications of a coming paroxysm, Claggart deliberately advanced within short range of Billy, and mesmerically looking him in the eye, briefly recapitulated the accusation.

Not at first did Billy take it in. When he did, the rose-tan of his cheek looked struck as by white leprosy. He stood like one impaled and gagged. Meanwhile the accuser's eyes removing not as yet from the blue dilated ones, underwent a phenomenal change, their wonted rich violet color blurring into a muddy purple. Those lights of human intelligence losing human expression, gelidly protruding like the alien eyes of certain uncatalogued creatures of the deep. The first mesmeric glance was one of serpent fascination; the last was as the hungry lurch of the torpedo-fish.

"Speak, man!" said Captain Vere to the transfixed one struck by his aspect even more than by Claggart's, "Speak! defend yourself." Which appeal caused but a strange dumb gesturing and gurgling in Billy; amazement at such an accusation so suddenly sprung on inexperienced nonage; this, and, it may be horror of the accuser, serving to bring out his lurking defect and in this instance for the time intensifying it into a convulsed tongue-tie; while the intent head and entire form straining forward in an agony of ineffectual eagerness to obey the injunction to speak and defend himself, gave an expression to the face like that of a condemned Vestal priestess in the moment of being buried alive, and in the first struggle against suffocation.

Though at the time Captain Vere was quite ignorant of Billy's liability to vocal impediment, he now immediately divined it, since vividly Billy's aspect recalled to him that of a bright young schoolmate of his whom he had once seen struck by much the same startling impotence in the act of eagerly rising in the class to be foremost in response to a testing question put to it by the master. Going close up to the young sailor, and laying a soothing hand on his shoulder, he said, "There is no hurry, my boy. Take your time, take your time." Contrary to the effect intended, these words so fatherly in tone, doubtless touching Billy's heart to the quick, prompted yet more violent efforts at utterance — efforts soon ending for the time in confirming the paralysis, and bringing to his face an expression which was as a crucifixion to behold. The next instant, quick as the flame from a discharged cannon at night, his right arm shot out, and Claggart dropped to the deck. Whether intentionally or but owing to the young athlete's superior height, the blow had taken effect full upon the forehead, so shapely and intellectual-looking a feature in the master-at-arms; so that the body fell over lengthwise, like a heavy plank tilted from erectness. A gasp or two, and he lay motionless.

"Fated boy," breathed Captain Vere in tone so low as to be almost a whisper, "what have you done! But here, help me."

The twain raised the felled one from the loins up into a sitting position. The spare form flexibly acquiesced, but inertly. It was like handling a dead snake. They lowered it back. Regaining erectness Captain Vere with one hand covering his face stood to all appearances as impassive as the object at his feet. Was he absorbed in taking in all the bearings of the event and what was best not only now at once to be done, but also in the sequel? Slowly he uncovered his face; and the effect was as if the moon emerging from eclipse should reappear with quite another aspect than that which had gone into hiding. The father in him, manifested towards Billy thus far in the scene, was replaced by the military disciplinarian. In his official tone he bade the foretopman retire to a state-room aft, (pointing it out) and there remain till thence summoned. This order Billy in silence mechanically obeyed. Then going to the cabin-door where it opened on the quarter-deck, Captain Vere said to the sentry without, "Tell somebody to send Albert here." When the lad appeared his master so contrived it that he should not catch sight of the prone one. "Albert," he said to him, "tell the Surgeon I wish to see him. You need not come back till called." When the Surgeon entered — a self-poised character of that grave sense and experience that hardly anything could take him aback, — Captain Vere advanced to meet him, thus unconsciously intercepting his view of Claggart and interrupting the other's wonted ceremonious salutation, said, "Nay, tell me how it is with yonder man," directing his attention to the prostrate one.

The Surgeon looked, and for all his self-command, somewhat startled at the abrupt revelation. On Claggart's always pallid complexion, thick black blood was now oozing from nostril and ear. To the gazer's professional eye it was unmistakably no living man that he saw.

"Is it so then?" said Captain Vere intently watching him. "I thought it. But verify it." Whereupon the customary tests confirmed the Surgeon's first glance, who now looking up in unfeigned concern, cast a look of intense inquisitiveness upon his superior. But Captain Vere, with one hand to his brow, was standing motionless. Suddenly, catching the Surgeon's arm convulsively, he exclaimed, pointing down to the body — "It is the divine judgment on Ananias! Look!"

Disturbed by the excited manner he had never before observed in the *Indomitable's* Captain, and as yet wholly ignorant of the affair, the prudent Surgeon nevertheless held his peace, only again looking an earnest interrogation as to what it was that had resulted in such a tragedy.

But Captain Vere was now again motionless standing absorbed in thought. But again starting, he vehemently exclaimed — "Struck dead by an angel of God! Yet the angel must hang!"

At these passionate interjections, mere incoherences to the listener as yet unapprised of the antecedents, the Surgeon was profoundly discomposed. But now as recollecting himself, Captain Vere in less harsh tone briefly related the circumstances leading up to the event.

"But come; we must despatch" he added.

"Help me to remove him (meaning the body) to yonder compartment," designating one opposite that where the foretopman remained immured. Anew disturbed by a request that as implying a desire for secrecy, seemed unaccountably strange to him, there was nothing for the subordinate to do but comply.

"Go now" said Captain Vere with something of his wonted manner — "Go now. I shall presently call a drum-head court. Tell the lieutenants what has happened, and tell Mr. Mordant," meaning the captain of marines, "and charge them to keep the matter to themselves."

21

Full of disquietude and misgiving the Surgeon left the cabin. Was Captain Vere suddenly affected in his mind, or was it but a transient excitement, brought about by so strange and extraordinary a happening? As to the drum-head court, it struck the Surgeon as impolitic, if nothing more. The thing to do, he thought, was to place Billy Budd in confinement and in a way dictated by usage, and postpone further action in so extraordinary a case, to such time as they should rejoin the squadron, and then refer it to the Admiral. He recalled the unwonted agitation of Captain Vere and his excited exclamations so at variance with his normal manner. Was he unhinged? But assuming that he is, it is not so susceptible of proof. What then can he do? No more trying situation is conceivable than that of an officer subordinate under a Captain whom he suspects to be, not mad indeed, but yet not quite unaffected in his intellect. To argue his order to him would be insolence. To resist him would be mutiny.

In obedience to Captain Vere he communicated what had happened to the lieutenants and captain of marines; saying nothing as to the Captain's state. They fully shared his own surprise and concern. Like him too they seemed to think that such a matter should be referred to the Admiral.

22

Who in the rainbow can draw the line where the violet tint ends and the orange tint begins? Distinctly we see the difference of the colors, but where exactly does the one first blendingly enter into the other? So with sanity and insanity. In pronounced cases there is no question about them. But in some supposed cases, in various degrees supposedly less pronounced, to draw the exact line of demarkation few will undertake tho' for a fee some professional experts will. There is nothing namable but that some men will undertake to do it for pay.

Whether Captain Vere, as the Surgeon professionally and privately surmised, was really the sudden victim of any degree of aberration, one must determine for himself by such light as this narrative may afford.

That the unhappy event which has been narrated could not have happened at a worse juncture was but too true. For it was close on the heel of the suppressed insurrections, an aftertime very critical to naval authority, demanding from every English sea-commander two qualities not readily interfusable — prudence and rigor. Moreover there was something crucial in the case.

In the jugglery of circumstances preceding and attending the event on board the *Indomitable* and in the light of that martial code whereby it was formally to be judged, innocence and guilt personified in Claggart and Budd in effect changed places. In a legal view the apparent victim of the tragedy was he who had sought to victimize a man blameless; and the indisputable deed of the latter, navally regarded, constituted the most heinous of military crimes. Yet more. The essential right and wrong involved in the matter, the clearer that might be, so much the worse for the responsibility of a loyal sea-commander inasmuch as he was not authorized to determine the matter on that primitive basis.

Small wonder then that the *Indomitable's* Captain though in general a man of rapid decision, felt that circumspectness not less than promptitude was necessary. Until he could decide upon his course, and in each detail; and not only so, but until the concluding measure was upon the point of being enacted, he deemed it advisable, in view of all the circumstances to guard as much as possible against publicity. Here he may or may not have erred. Certain it is however that subsequently in the confidential talk of more than one or two gunrooms and cabins he was not a little criticized by some officers, a fact imputed by his friends and vehemently by his cousin Jack Denton to professional jealousy of *Starry Vere*. Some imaginative ground for invidious comment

there was. The maintenance of secrecy in the matter, the confining all knowledge of it for a time to the place where the homicide occurred, the quarter-deck cabin; in these particulars lurked some resemblance to the policy adopted in those tragedies of the place which have occurred more than once in the capital founded by Peter the Barbarian.

The case indeed was such that fain would the *Indomitable's* captain have deferred taking any action whatever respecting it further than to keep the foretopman a close prisoner till the ship rejoined the squadron and then submitting the matter to the judgment of his Admiral.

But a true military officer is in one particular like a true monk. Not with more of self-abnegation will the latter keep his vows of monastic obedience than the former his vows of allegiance to martial duty.

Feeling that unless quick action was taken on it, the deed of the foretopman, so soon as it should be known on the gun-decks would tend to awaken any slumbering embers of the Nore among the crew, a sense of the urgency of the case overruled in Captain Vere every other consideration. But tho' a conscientious disciplinarian he was no lover of authority for mere authority's sake. Very far was he from embracing opportunities for monopolizing to himself the perils of moral responsibility, none at least that could properly be referred to an official superior or shared with him by his official equals or even subordinates. So thinking, he was glad it would not be at variance with usage to turn the matter over to a summary court of his own officers, reserving to himself as the one on whom the ultimate accountability would rest, the right of maintaining a supervision of it, or formally or informally interposing at need. Accordingly a drum-head court was summarily convened, he electing the individuals composing it, the First Lieutenant, the Captain of marines, and the Sailing Master.

In associating an officer of marines with the sea-lieutenants in a case having to do with a sailor the Commander perhaps deviated from general custom. He was prompted thereto by the circumstance that he took that soldier to be a judicious person, thoughtful, and not altogether incapable of grappling with a difficult case unprecedented in his prior experience. Yet even as to him he was not without some latent misgiving, for withal he was an extremely good-natured man, an enjoyer of his dinner, a sound sleeper, and inclined to obesity. A man who tho' he would always maintain his manhood in battle might not prove altogether reliable in a moral dilemma involving aught of the tragic. As to the First Lieutenant and the Sailing Master Captain Vere could not but be aware that though honest natures, of approved gallantry upon occasion, their intelligence was mostly confined to the matter of active seamanship and the fighting demands of their profession. The court was held in the same cabin where the unfortunate affair had taken place. The cabin, the Commander's, embraced the entire area under the poop-deck. Aft, and on either side was a small state-room; the one room temporarily a jail and the other a dead-house, and a yet smaller compartment leaving a space between, expanding forward into a goodly oblong of length coinciding with the ship's beam. A skylight of moderate dimension was overhead and at each end of the oblong space were two sashed port-hole windows easily convertible back into embrasures for short carronades.

All being quickly in readiness, Billy Budd was arraigned, Captain Vere necessarily appearing as the sole witness in the case, and as such temporarily sinking his rank, though singularly maintaining it in a matter apparently trivial, namely, that he testified from the ship's weather-side, with that object having caused the court to sit on the lee-side. Concisely he narrated all that had led up to the catastrophe, omitting nothing in Claggart's accusation and deposing as to the manner in which the prisoner had received it. At this testimony the three officers glanced with no little surprise at Billy Budd, the last man they would have suspected either of the mutinous design alleged by Claggart or the undeniable deed he himself had done.

The First Lieutenant, taking judicial primacy and turning toward the prisoner, said, "Captain Vere has spoken. Is it or is it not as Captain Vere says?" In response came syllables not so much impeded in the utterance as might have been anticipated. They were these: "Captain Vere tells the truth. It is just as Captain Vere says, but it not as the Master-at-Arms said. I have eaten the King's bread and I am true to the King."

"I believe you, my man" said the witness,

his voice indicating a suppressed emotion not otherwise betrayed.

"God will bless you for that, Your Honor!" not without stammering said Billy, and all but broke down. But immediately was recalled to self-control by another question, to which with the same emotional difficulty of utterance he said "No, there was no malice between us. I never bore malice against the Master-at-arms. I am sorry that he is dead. I did not mean to kill him. Could I have used my tongue I would not have struck him. But he foully lied to my face and in presence of my Captain, and I had to say something, and I could only say it with a blow, God help me!"

In the impulsive above-board manner of the frank one the court saw confirmed all that was implied in words that just previously had perplexed them, coming as they did from the testifier to the tragedy and promptly following Billy's impassioned disclaimer of mutinous intent — Captain Vere's words, "I believe you, my man."

Next it was asked of him whether he knew of or suspected aught savoring of incipient trouble (meaning mutiny, tho' the explicit term was avoided) going on in any section of the ship's company.

The reply lingered. This was naturally imputed by the court to the same vocal embarrassment which had retarded or obstructed previous answers. But in main it was otherwise here; the question immediately recalling to Billy's mind the interview with the after-guardsman in the fore-chains. But an innate repugnance to playing a part at all approaching that of an informer against one's own shipmates — the same erring sense of uninstructed honor which had stood in the way of his reporting the matter at the time though as a loyal man-of-war-man it was incumbent on him, and failure so to do if charged against him and proven, would have subjected him to the heaviest of penalties; this, with the blind feeling now his, that nothing really was being hatched, prevailed with him. When the answer came it was a negative.

"One question more," said the officer of marines now first speaking and with a troubled earnestness, "You tell us that what the Master-at-arms said against you was a lie. Now why should he have so lied, so maliciously lied, since you declare there was no malice between you?"

At that question unintentionally touching on

a spiritual sphere wholly obscure to Billy's thoughts, he was nonplussed, evincing a confusion indeed that some observers, such as can readily be imagined, would have construed into involuntary evidence of hidden guilt. Nevertheless he strove some way to answer, but all at once relinquished the vain endeavor, at the same time turning an appealing glance towards Captain Vere as deeming him his best helper and friend. Captain Vere who had been seated for a time rose to his feet, addressing the interrogator. "The question you put to him comes naturally enough. But how can he rightly answer it? or anybody else? unless indeed it be he who lies within there" designating the compartment where lay the corpse. "But the prone one there will not rise to our summons. In effect, tho', as it seems to me, the point you make is hardly material. Quite aside from any conceivable motive actuating the Master-at-arms, and irrespective of the provocation to the blow, a martial court must needs in the present case confine its attention to the blow's consequence, which consequence justly is to be deemed not otherwise than as the striker's deed."

This utterance the full significance of which it was not at all likely that Billy took in, nevertheless caused him to turn a wistful interrogative look toward the speaker, a look in its dumb expressiveness not unlike that which a dog of generous breed might turn upon his master seeking in his face some elucidation of a previous gesture ambiguous to the canine intelligence. Nor was the same utterance without marked effect upon the three officers, more especially the soldier. Couched in it seemed to them a meaning unanticipated, involving a prejudgement on the speaker's part. It served to augment a mental disturbance previously evident enough.

The soldier once more spoke; in a tone of suggestive dubiety addressing at once his associates and Captain Vere: "Nobody is present — none of the ship's company, I mean, who might shed lateral light, if any is to be had, upon what remains mysterious in this matter."

"That is thoughtfully put" said Captain Vere; "I see your drift. Ay, there is a mystery; but, to use a Scriptural phrase, it is 'a mystery of iniquity,' a matter for psychologic theologians to discuss. But what has a military court to do with it? Not to add that for us any possible investigation of it is cut off by the lasting tongue-tie of — him — in yonder," again designating the mortuary state-room "The prisoner's deed, — with that alone we have to do."

To this, and particularly the closing reiteration, the marine soldier knowing not how aptly to reply, sadly abstained from saying aught. The First Lieutenant who at the outset had not unnaturally assumed primacy in the court, now overrulingly instructed by a glance from Captain Vere, a glance more effective than words, resumed that primacy. Turning to the prisoner, "Budd," he said, and scarce in equable tones, "Budd, if you have aught further to say for yourself, say it now."

Upon this the young sailor turned another quick glance toward Captain Vere; then, as taking a hint from that aspect, a hint confirming his own instinct that silence was now best, replied to the Lieutenant "I have said all, Sir."

The marine — the same who had been the sentinel without the cabin-door at the time that the foretopman followed by the master-at-arms, entered it — he, standing by the sailor throughout these judicial proceedings, was now directed to take him back to the after compartment originally assigned to the prisoner and his custodian. As the twain disappeared from view, the three officers as partially liberated from some inward constraint associated with Billy's mere presence, simultaneously stirred in their seats. They exchanged looks of troubled indecision, yet feeling that decide they must and without long delay. As for Captain Vere, he for the time stood unconsciously with his back toward them, apparently in one of his absent fits, gazing out from a sashed port-hole to windward upon the monotonous blank of the twilight sea. But the court's silence continuing, broken only at moments by brief consultations in low earnest tones, this seemed to arm him and energize him. Turning, he to-and-fro paced the cabin athwart; in the returning ascent to windward, climbing the slant deck in the ship's lee roll; without knowing it symbolizing thus in his action a mind resolute to surmount difficulties even if against primitive instincts strong as the wind and the sea. Presently he came to a stand before the three. After scanning their faces he stood less as mustering his thoughts for expression, than as one inly deliberating how best to put them to well-meaning men not intellectually mature, men with whom it was necessary to demonstrate certain principles that were axioms to himself. Similar impatience as to talking is perhaps one reason that deters some minds from addressing any popular assemblies.

When speak he did, something both in the substance of what he said and his manner of saying it, showed the influence of unshared studies modifying and tempering the practical training of an active career. This, along with his phraseology now and then was suggestive of the grounds whereon rested that imputation of a certain pedantry socially alleged against him by certain naval men of wholly practical cast, captains who nevertheless would frankly concede that His Majesty's navy mustered no more efficient officer of their grade than *Starry Vere*.

What he said was to this effect: "Hitherto I have been but the witness, little more; and I should hardly think now to take another tone, that of your coadjutor, for the time, I did not perceive in you, — at the crisis too — a troubled hesitancy, proceeding, I doubt not from the clash of military duty with moral scruple — scruple vitalized by compassion. For the compassion how can I otherwise than share it. But, mindful of paramount obligations I strive against scruples that may tend to enervate decision. Not, gentlemen, that I hide from myself that the case is an exceptional one. Speculatively regarded, it well might be referred to a jury of casuists. But for us here acting not as casuists or moralists, it is a case practical, and under martial law practically to be dealt with.

"But your scruples: do they move as in a dusk? Challenge them. Make them advance and declare themselves. Come now: do they import something like this: If, mindless of palliating circumstances, we are bound to regard the death of the Master-at-Arms as the prisoner's deed, then does that deed constitute a capital crime whereof the penalty is a mortal one. But in natural justice is nothing but the prisoner's overt act to be considered? How can we adjudge to summary and shameful death a, fellow-creature innocent before God, and whom we feel to be so? — Does that state it aright? You sign sad assent. Well, I too feel that, the full force of that. It is Nature. But do these buttons that we wear attest that our allegiance is to Nature? No, to the King. Though the ocean, which is inviolate Nature primeval, tho' this be the element where we move and have our being as sailors, yet as the King's officers lies our duty in a sphere correspondingly natural? So little is that true, that in receiving our commissions we in the most important regards

ceased to be natural free-agents. When war is declared are we the commissioned fighters previously consulted? We fight at command. If our judgements approve the war, that is but coincidence. So in other particulars. So now. For suppose condemnation to follow these present proceedings. Would it be so much we ourselves that would condemn as it would be martial law operating through us? For that law and the rigor of it, we are not responsible. Our vowed responsibility is in this: That however pitilessly that law may operate, we nevertheless adhere to it and administer it.

"But the exceptional in the matter moves the hearts within you. Even so too is mine moved. But let not warm hearts betray heads that should be cool. Ashore in a criminal case will an upright judge allow himself off the bench to be waylaid by some tender kinswoman of the accused seeking to touch him with her tearful plea? Well the heart here denotes the feminine in man is as that piteous woman, and hard tho' it be she must here be ruled out."

He paused, earnestly studying them for a moment; then resumed.

"But something in your aspect seems to urge that it is not solely the heart that moves in you, but also the conscience, the private conscience. But tell me whether or not, occupying the position we do, private conscience should not yield to that imperial one formulated in the code under which alone we officially proceed?"

Here the three men moved in their seats, less convinced than agitated by the course of an argument troubling but the more the spontaneous conflict within.

Perceiving which, the speaker paused for a moment; then abruptly changing his tone, went on.

"To steady us a bit, let us recur to the facts. — In war-time at sea a man-of-war's-man strikes his superior in grade, and the blow kills. Apart from its effect the blow itself is, according to the Articles of War, a capital crime. Furthermore —"

"Ay, Sir!" emotionally broke in the officer of marines, "in one sense it was. But surely Budd purposed neither mutiny nor homicide."

"Surely not, my good man. And before a court less arbitrary and more merciful than a martial one, that plea would largely extenuate. At the Last Assizes it shall acquit. But how here? We proceed under the law of the Mutiny Act. In feature no child can resemble his father more than that Act resembles in spirit the thing from which it derives — War. In His Majesty's service — in this ship indeed — there are Englishmen forced to fight for the King against their will. Against their conscience, for aught we know. Tho' as their fellow-creatures some of us may appreciate their position, yet as navy officers, what reck we of it? Still less recks the enemy. Our impressed men he would fain cut down in the same swath with our volunteers. As regards the enemy's naval conscripts, some of whom may even share our own abhorrence of the regicidal French Directory, it is the same on our side. War looks but to the frontage, the appearance. And the Mutiny Act, War's child, takes after the father. Budd's intent or non-intent is nothing to the purpose.

"But while, put to it by those anxieties in you which I can not but respect, I only repeat myself — while thus strangely we prolong proceedings that should be summary — the enemy may be sighted and an engagement result. We must do; and one of two things must we do — condemn or let go."

"Can we convict and yet mitigate the penalty?" asked the junior lieutenant here speaking, and falteringly, for the first.

"Lieutenant, were that clearly lawful for us under the circumstances consider the consequences of such clemency. The people" (meaning the ship's company) "have native-sense; most of them are familiar with our naval usage and tradition; and how would they take it? Even could you explain to them — which our official position forbids — they, long moulded by arbitrary discipline have not that kind of intelligent responsiveness that might qualify them to comprehend and discriminate. No, to the people the foretopman's deed however it be worded in the announcement will be plain homicide committed in a flagrant act of mutiny. What penalty for that should follow, they know. But it does not follow. Why? they will ruminate. You know what sailors are. Will they not revert to the recent outbreak at the Nore? Ay. They know the well-founded alarm — the panic it struck throughout England. Your clement sentence they would account pusillanimous. They would think that we flinch, that we are afraid of them — afraid of practising a lawful rigor singularly demanded at this juncture lest it should provoke new troubles. What shame to us such a conjecture on their part, and how deadly to discipline.

You see then, whither prompted by duty and the law I steadfastly drive. But I beseech you, my friends, do not take me amiss. I feel as you do for this unfortunate boy. But did he know our hearts, I take him to be of that generous nature that he would feel even for us on whom in this military necessity so heavy a compulsion is laid."

With that, crossing the deck he resumed his place by the sashed port-hole, tacitly leaving the three to come to a decision. On the cabin's opposite side the troubled court sat silent. Loyal lieges, plain and practical, though at bottom they dissented from some points Captain Vere had put to them, they were without the faculty, hardly had the inclination to gainsay one whom they felt to be an earnest man, one too not less their superior in mind than in naval rank. But it is not improbable that even such of his words as were not without influence over them, less came home to them than his closing appeal to their instinct as sea-officers in the forethought he threw out as to the practical consequences to discipline, considering the unconfirmed tone of the fleet at the time, should a man-of-war's-man's violent killing at sea of a superior in grade be allowed to pass for aught else than a capital crime demanding prompt infliction of the penalty.

Not unlikely they were brought to something more or less akin to that harassed frame of mind which in the year 1842 actuated the commander of the U.S. brig-of-war *Somers* to resolve, under the so-called Articles of War, Articles modelled upon the English Mutiny Act, to resolve upon the execution at sea of a midshipman and two petty-officers as mutineers designing the seizure of the brig. Which resolution was carried out though in a time of peace and within not many days sail of home. An act vindicated by a naval court of inquiry subsequently convened ashore. History, and here cited without comment. True, the circumstances on board the *Somers* were different from those on board the *Indomitable*. But the urgency felt, well-warranted or otherwise, was much the same.

Says a writer whom few know, "Forty years after a battle it is easy for a non-combatant to reason about how it ought to have been fought. It is another thing personally and under fire to direct the fighting while involved in the obscuring smoke of it. Much so with respect to other emergencies involving considerations both practical and moral, and when it is imperative promptly to act. The greater the fog the more it imperils the steamer, and speed is put on tho' at the hazard of running somebody down. Little ween the snug card-players in the cabin of the responsibilities of the sleepless man on the bridge."

In brief, Billy Budd was formally convicted and sentenced to be hung at the yard-arm in the early morning-watch, it being now night. Otherwise, as is customary in such cases, the sentence would forthwith have been carried out. In war-time on the field or in the fleet, a mortal punishment decreed by a drum-head court — on the field sometimes decreed by but a nod from the General — follows without delay on the heel of conviction without appeal.

23

It was Captain Vere himself who of his own motion communicated the finding of the court to the prisoner; for that purpose going to the compartment where he was in custody and bidding the marine there to withdraw for the time.

Beyond the communication of the sentence what took place at this interview was never known. But in view of the character of the twain briefly closeted in that state-room, each radically sharing in the rarer qualities of our nature — so rare indeed as to be all but incredible to average minds however much cultivated — some conjectures may be ventured.

It would have been in consonance with the spirit of Captain Vere should he on this occasion have concealed nothing from the condemned one — should he indeed have frankly disclosed to him the part he himself had played in bringing about the decision, at the same time revealing his actuating motives. On Billy's side it is not improbable that such a confession would have been received in much the same spirit that prompted it. Not without a sort of joy indeed he might have appreciated the brave opinion of him implied in his Captain making such a confidant of him. Nor, as to the sentence itself could he have been insensible that it was imparted to him as to one not afraid to die. Even more may have been. Captain Vere in the end may have developed the passion sometimes latent under an exterior stoical or indifferent. He was old enough to have been Billy's father. The austere devotee of military duty letting himself melt back into

what remains primeval in our formalized humanity may in the end have caught Billy to his heart even as Abraham may have caught young Isaac on the brink of resolutely offering him up in obedience to the exacting behest. But there is no telling the sacrament, seldom if in any case revealed to the gadding world wherever under circumstances at all akin to those here attempted to be set forth two of great Nature's nobler order embrace. There is privacy at the time, inviolable to the survivor, and holy oblivion the sequel to each diviner magnanimity, providentially covers all at last.

The first to encounter Captain Vere in act of leaving the compartment was the senior Lieutenant. The face he beheld, for the moment one expressive of the agony of the strong, was to that officer, tho' a man of fifty, a startling revelation. That the condemned one suffered less than he who mainly had effected the condemnation was apparently indicated by the former's exclamation in the scene soon perforce to be touched upon.

24

Of a series of incidents within a brief term rapidly following each other, the adequate narration may take up a term less brief, especially if explanation or comment here and there seem requisite to the better understanding of such incidents. Between the entrance into the cabin of him who never left it alive, and him who when he did leave it left it as one condemned to die; between this and the closeted interview just given less than an hour and a half had elapsed. It was an interval long enough however to awaken speculations among no few of the ship's company as to what it was that could be detaining in the cabin the master-at-arms and the sailor; for a rumor that both of them had been seen to enter it and neither of them had been seen to emerge, this rumor had got abroad upon the gun-decks and in the tops; the people of a great warship being in one respect like villagers taking microscopic note of every outward movement or non-movement going on. When therefore in weather not at all tempestuous all hands were called in the second dog-watch, a summons under such circumstances not usual in those hours, the crew were not wholly unprepared for some announcement extraordinary, one having connection too with the continued absence of the two men from their wonted haunts.

There was a moderate sea at the time; and the moon, newly risen and near to being at its full, silvered the white spar-deck wherever not blotted by the clear-cut shadows horizontally thrown of fixtures and moving men. On either side the quarter-deck the marine guard under arms was drawn up; and Captain Vere standing in his place surrounded by all the wardroom officers, addressed his men. In so doing his manner showed neither more nor less than that properly pertaining to his supreme position aboard his own ship. In clear terms and concise he told them what had taken place in the cabin; that the master-at-arms was dead; that he who killed him had been already tried by a summary court and condemned to death; and that the execution would take place in the early morning watch. The word *mutiny* was not named in what he said. He refrained too from making the occasion an opportunity for any preachment as to the maintenance of discipline, thinking perhaps that under existing circumstances in the navy the consequence of violating discipline should be made to speak for itself.

Their captain's announcement was listened to by the throng of standing sailors in a dumbness like that of a seated congregation of believers in hell listening to the clergyman's announcement of his Calvinistic text.

At the close, however, a confused murmur went up. It began to wax. All but instantly, then, at a sign, it was pierced and suppressed by shrill whistles of the Boatswain and his Mates piping down one watch.

To be prepared for burial Claggart's body was delivered to certain petty-officers of his mess. And here, not to clog the sequel with lateral matters, it may be added that at a suitable hour, the Master-at-arms was committed to the sea with every funeral honor properly belonging to his naval grade.

In this proceeding as in every public one growing out of the tragedy strict adherence to usage was observed. Nor in any point could it have been at all deviated from, either with respect to Claggart or Billy Budd, without begetting undesirable speculations in the ship's company, sailors, and more particularly men-of-war's men, being of all men the greatest sticklers for usage.

For similar cause, all communication between Captain Vere and the condemned one ended with the closeted interview already given, the latter being now surrendered to the ordinary routine preliminary to the end. This transfer under guard from the Captain's quarters was effected without unusual precautions — at least no visible ones.

If possible not to let the men so much as surmise that their officers anticipate aught amiss from them is the tacit rule in a military ship. And the more that some sort of trouble should really be apprehended the more do the officers keep that apprehension to themselves; tho' not the less unostentatious vigilance may be augmented.

In the present instance the sentry placed over the prisoner had strict orders to let no one have communication with him but the Chaplain. And certain unobtrusive measures were taken absolutely to insure this point.

25

In a seventy-four of the old order the deck known as the upper gun-deck was the one covered by the spar-deck which last though not without its armament was for the most part exposed to the weather. In general it was at all hours free from hammocks; those of the crew swinging on the lower gun-deck, and berth-deck, the latter being not only a dormitory but also the place for the stowing of the sailors' bags, and on both sides lined with the large chests or movable pantries of the many messes of the men.

On the starboard side of the *Indomitable's* upper gun-deck, behold Billy Budd under sentry lying prone in irons in one of the bays formed by the regular spacing of the guns comprising the batteries on either side. All these pieces were of the heavier calibre of that period. Mounted on lumbering wooden carriages they were hampered with cumbersome harness of breeching and strong side-tackles for running them out. Guns and carriages, together with the long rammers and shorter lintstocks lodged in loops overhead — all these, as customary, were painted black; and the heavy hempen breechings tarred to the same tint, wore the like livery of the undertakers. In contrast with the funereal hue of these surroundings the prone sailor's exterior apparel, white *jumper* and white duck trousers, each more or less soiled, dimly glimmered in the obscure light of the bay like

a patch of discolored snow in early April lingering at some upland cave's black mouth. In
effect he is already in his shroud or the garments that shall serve him in lieu of one. Over
him but scarce illuminating him, two battle-
lanterns swing from two massive beams of the
deck above. Fed with the oil supplied by the
war-contractors (whose gains, honest or otherwise, are in every land an anticipated portion of
the harvest of death) with flickering splashes
of dirty yellow light they pollute the pale moonshine, all but ineffectually struggling in obstructed flecks thro' the open ports from which
the tompioned cannon protrude. Other lanterns at intervals serve but to bring out somewhat the obscurer bays which like small confessionals or side-chapels in a cathedral branch
from the long dim-vistaed broad aisle between
the two batteries of that covered tier.

Such was the deck where now lay the Handsome Sailor. Through the rose-tan of his complexion, no pallor could have shown. It would
have taken days of sequestration from the winds
and the sun to have brought about the efface-
ment of that. But the skeleton in the cheek-
bone at the point of its angle was just beginning delicately to be defined under the warm-
tinted skin. In fervid hearts self-contained
some brief experiences devour our human tissue as secret fire in a ship's hold consumes
cotton in the bale.

But now lying between the two guns, as
nipped in the vice of fate, Billy's agony, mainly
proceeding from a generous young heart's virgin
experience of the diabolical incarnate and effective in some men — the tension of that
agony was over now. It survived not the something healing in the closeted interview with
Captain Vere. Without movement, he lay as
in a trance. That adolescent expression previously noted as his, taking on something akin to
the look of a slumbering child in the cradle
when the warm hearth-glow of the still chamber at night plays on the dimples that at whiles
mysteriously form in the cheek, silently coming
and going there. For now and then in the
gyved one's trance a serene happy light born of
some wandering reminiscence or dream would
diffuse itself over his face, and then wane away
only anew to return.

The Chaplain coming to see him and finding
him thus, and perceiving no sign that he was
conscious of his presence, attentively regarded
him for a space, then slipping aside, withdrew

for the time, peradventure feeling that even he
the minister of Christ tho' receiving his stipend
from Mars had no consolation to proffer which
could result in a peace transcending that which
he beheld. But in the small hours he came
again. And the prisoner now awake to his surroundings noticed his approach and civilly, all
but cheerfully, welcomed him. But it was to
little purpose that in the interview following
the good man sought to bring Billy Budd to
some godly understanding that he must die,
and at dawn. True, Billy himself freely referred
to his death as a thing close at hand;
but it was something in the way that children
will refer to death in general, who yet among
their other sports will play a funeral with hearse
and mourners.

Not that like children Billy was incapable of
conceiving what death really is. No, but he was
wholly without irrational fear of it, a fear more
prevalent in highly civilized communities than
those so-called barbarous ones which in all respects stand nearer to unadulterate Nature.
And, as elsewhere said, a barbarian Billy radically was; as much so, for all the costume, as his
countrymen the British captives, living trophies,
made to march in the Roman triumph of Ger-
manicus. Quite as much so as those later barbarians, young men probably, and picked specimens among the earlier British converts to
Christianity, at least nominally such and taken
to Rome (as today converts from lesser isles of
the sea may be taken to London) of whom the
Pope of that time, admiring the strangeness
of their personal beauty so unlike the Italian
stamp, their clear ruddy complexion and curled
flaxen locks, exclaimed, "Angles" (meaning
English the modern derivative) "Angles do you
call them? And is it because they look so like
angels?" Had it been later in time one would
think that the Pope had in mind Fra Angelico's
seraphs some of whom, plucking apples in
gardens of the Hesperides, have the faint rose-
bud complexion of the more beautiful English
girls.

If in vain the good Chaplain sought to impress the young barbarian with ideas of death
akin to those conveyed in the skull, dial, and
cross-bones on old tombstones; equally futile to
all appearance were his efforts to bring home
to him the thought of salvation and a Saviour.
Billy listened, but less out of awe or reverence
perhaps than from a certain natural politeness;
doubtless at bottom regarding all that in much

the same way that most mariners of his class take any discourse abstract or out of the common tone of the work-a-day world. And this sailor-way of taking clerical discourse is not wholly unlike the way in which the pioneer of Christianity full of transcendent miracles was received long ago on tropic isles by any superior *savage* so called — a Tahitian say of Captain Cook's time or shortly after that time. Out of natural courtesy he received, but did not appropriate. It was like a gift placed in the palm of an outreached hand upon which the fingers do not close.

But the *Indomitable's* Chaplain was a discreet man possessing the good sense of a good heart. So he insisted not in his vocation here. At the instance of Captain Vere, a lieutenant had apprised him of pretty much everything as to Billy; and since he felt that innocence was even a better thing than religion wherewith to go to Judgement, he reluctantly withdrew; but in his emotion not without first performing an act strange enough in an Englishman, and under the circumstances yet more so in any regular priest. Stooping over, he kissed on the fair cheek his fellow-man, a felon in martial law, one who though on the confines of death he felt he could never convert to a dogma; nor for all that did he fear for his future.

Marvel not that having been made acquainted with the young sailor's essential innocence (an irruption of heretic thought hard to suppress) the worthy man lifted not a finger to avert the doom of such a martyr to martial discipline. So to do would not only have been as idle as invoking the desert, but would also have been an audacious transgression of the bounds of his function, one as exactly prescribed to him by military law as that of the boatswain or any other naval officer. Bluntly put, a chaplain is the minister of the Prince of Peace serving in the host of the God of War — Mars. As such, he is incongruous as that musket of Blücher etc. at Christmas. Why then is he there? Because he indirectly subserves the purpose attested by the cannon; because he too lends the sanction of the religion of the meek to that which practically is the abrogation of everything but brute Force.

26

The night so luminous on the spar-deck but otherwise on the cavernous ones below, level so like the tiered galleries in a coal-mine — the luminous night passed away. But, like the prophet in the chariot disappearing in heaven and dropping his mantle to Elisha, the withdrawing night transferred its pale robe to the breaking day. A meek shy light appeared in the East, where stretched a diaphanous fleece of white furrowed vapor. That light slowly waxed. Suddenly *eight bells* was struck aft, responded to by one louder metallic stroke from forward. It was four o'clock in the morning. Instantly the silver whistles were heard summoning all hands to witness punishment. Up through the great hatchways rimmed with racks of heavy shot, the watch below came pouring overspreading with the watch already on deck the space between the mainmast and foremast including that occupied by the capacious *launch* and the black booms tiered on either side of it, boat and booms making a summit of observation for the powder-boys and younger tars. A different group comprising one watch of topmen leaned over the rail of that sea-balcony, no small one in a seventy-four, looking down on the crowd below. Man or boy none spake but in whisper, and few spake at all. Captain Vere — as before, the central figure among the assembled commissioned officers — stood nigh the break of the poop-deck facing forward. Just below him on the quarter-deck the marines in full equipment were drawn up much as at the scene of the promulgated sentence.

At sea in the old time, the execution by halter of a military sailor was generally from the fore-yard. In the present instance, for special reasons the main-yard was assigned. Under an arm of that lee yard the prisoner was presently brought up, the Chaplain attending him. It was noted at the time and remarked upon afterwards, that in this final scene the good man evinced little or nothing of the perfunctory. Brief speech indeed he had with the condemned one, but the genuine Gospel was less on his tongue than in his aspect and manner towards him. The final preparations personal to the latter being speedily brought to an end by two boatswain's-mates, the consummation impended. Billy stood facing aft. At the penultimate moment, his words, his only ones, words wholly unobstructed in the utterance were these — "God bless Captain Vere!" Syllables so unanticipated coming from one with the ignominious hemp about his neck — a conventional felon's benediction directed aft towards the quarters of honor; syllables too delivered in the clear melody of a singing-bird on the point of launching from the twig, had a phenomenal effect, not unenhanced by the rare personal beauty of the young sailor spiritualized now thro' late experiences so poignantly profound.

Without volition as it were, as if indeed the ship's populace were but the vehicles of some vocal current electric, with one voice from alow and aloft came a resonant sympathetic echo — "God bless Captain Vere!" And yet at that instant Billy alone must have been in their hearts, even as he was in their eyes.

At the pronounced words and the spontaneous echo that voluminously rebounded them, Captain Vere, either thro' stoic self-control or a sort of momentary paralysis induced by emotional shock, stood erectly rigid as a musket in the ship-armorer's rack.

The hull, deliberately recovering from the periodic roll to leeward was just regaining an even keel, when the last signal, a preconcerted dumb one, was given. At the same moment it chanced that the vapory fleece hanging low in the East, was shot thro' with a soft glory as of the fleece of the Lamb of God seen in mystical vision, and simultaneously therewith, watched by the wedged mass of upturned faces, Billy ascended; and, ascending, took the full rose of the dawn.

In the pinioned figure, arrived at the yard-end, to the wonder of all no motion was apparent, none save that created by the ship's motion, in moderate weather so majestic in a great ship ponderously cannoned.

27

A digression

When some days afterward in reference to the singularity just mentioned, the Purser, a rather ruddy rotund person more accurate as an accountant than profound as a philosopher, said at mess to the Surgeon, "What testimony to the force lodged in will-power" the latter — saturnine, spare and tall, one in whom a discreet causticity went along with a manner less genial than polite, replied, "Your pardon, Mr. Purser. In a hanging scientifically conducted — and under special orders I myself directed how Budd's was to be effected — any movement following the completed suspension and originating in the body suspended, such move-ment indicates mechanical spasm in the muscular system. Hence the absence of that is no more attributable to will-power as you call it than to horse-power — begging your pardon."

"But this muscular spasm you speak of, is not that in a degree more or less invariable in these cases?"

"Assuredly so, Mr. Purser."

"How then, my good sir, do you account for its absence in this instance?"

"Mr. Purser, it is clear that your sense of the singularity in this matter equals not mine. You account for it by what you call will-power, a term not yet included in the lexicon of science. For me I do not, with my present knowledge, pretend to account for it at all. Even should we assume the hypothesis that at the first touch of the halyards the action of Budd's heart, intensified by extraordinary emotion at its climax, abruptly stopt — much like a watch when in carelessly winding it up you strain at the finish, thus snapping the chain — even under that hypothesis how account for the phenomenon that followed."

"You admit then that the absence of spasmodic movement was phenomenal."

"It was phenomenal, Mr. Purser, in the sense that it was an appearance the cause of which is not immediately to be assigned."

"But tell me, my dear Sir," pertinaciously continued the other, "was the man's death effected by the halter, or was it a species of euthanasia?"

"*Euthanasia*, Mr. Purser, is something like your *will-power*: I doubt its authenticity as a scientific term — begging your pardon again. It is at once imaginative and metaphysical, — in short, Greek. But" abruptly changing his tone "there is a case in the sick-bay that I do not care to leave to my assistants. Beg your pardon, but excuse me." And rising from the mess he formally withdrew.

28

The silence at the moment of execution and for a moment or two continuing thereafter, a silence but emphasized by the regular wash of the sea against the hull or the flutter of a sail caused by the helmsman's eyes being tempted astray, this emphasized silence was gradually disturbed by a sound not easily to be verbally rendered. Whoever has heard the freshet-wave of a torrent suddenly swelled by pouring showers in tropical mountains, showers not shared by the plain; whoever has heard the first muffled murmur of its sloping advance through precipitous woods, may form some conception of the sound now heard. The seeming remoteness of its source was because of its murmurous indistinctness since it came from close-by, even from the men massed on the ship's open deck. Being inarticulate, it was dubious in significance further than it seemed to indicate some capricious revulsion of thought or feeling such as mobs ashore are liable to, in the present instance possibly implying a sullen revocation on the men's part of their involuntary echoing of Billy's benediction. But ere the murmur had time to wax into clamor it was met by a strategic command, the more telling that it came with abrupt unexpectedness.

"Pipe down the starboard watch, Boatswain, and see that they go."

Shrill as the shriek of the sea-hawk the whistles of the Boatswain and his Mates pierced that ominous low sound, dissipating it; and yielding to the mechanism of discipline the throng was thinned by one half. For the remainder most of them were set to temporary employments connected with trimming the yards and so forth, business readily to be got up to serve occasion by an officer-of-the-deck.

Now each proceeding that follows a mortal sentence pronounced at sea by a drum-head court is characterized by promptitude not perceptibly merging into hurry, tho' bordering that. The hammock, the one which had been Billy's bed when alive, having already been ballasted with shot and otherwise prepared to serve for his canvas coffin, the last offices of the sea-undertakers, the Sail-Makers Mates, were now speedily completed. When everything was in readiness a second call for all hands made necessary by the strategic movement before mentioned was sounded and now to witness burial.

The details of this closing formality it needs not to give. But when the tilted plank let slide its freight into the sea, a second strange human murmur was heard, blended now with another inarticulate sound proceeding from certain larger sea-fowl whose attention having been attracted by the peculiar commotion in the water resulting from the heavy sloped dive of the shotted hammock into the sea, flew screaming to the spot. So near the hull did they come, that the stridor or bony creak of their gaunt double-jointed pinions was audible. As the ship under light airs passed on, leaving the burial-spot astern, they still kept circling it low down with the moving shadow of their outstretched wings and the croaked requiem of their cries.

Upon sailors as superstitious as those of the age preceding ours, men-of-war's men too who had just beheld the prodigy of repose in the form suspended in air and now foundering in the deeps; to such mariners the action of the sea-fowl tho' dictated by mere animal greed for prey, was big with no prosaic significance. An uncertain movement began among them, in which some encroachment was made. It was tolerated but for a moment. For suddenly the drum beat to quarters, which familiar sound happening at least twice every day, had upon the present occasion a signal peremptoriness in it. True martial discipline long continued superinduces in average man a sort of impulse of docility whose operation at the official sound of command much resembles in its promptitude the effect of an instinct.

The drum-beat dissolved the multitude, distributing most of them along the batteries of the two covered gun-decks. There, as wont, the guns' crews stood by their respective cannon erect and silent. In due course the First Officer, sword under arm and standing in his place on the quarter-deck, formally received the successive reports of the sworded Lieutenants commanding the section of batteries below; the last of which reports being made, the summed report he delivered with the customary salute to the Commander. All this occupied time, which in the present case, was the object of beating to quarters at an hour prior to the customary one. That such variance from usage was authorized by an officer like Captain Vere, a martinet as some deemed him, was evidence of the necessity for unusual action implied in what he deemed to be temporarily the mood of his men. "With mankind" he would say "forms, measured forms are everything; and that is the import couched in the story of Orpheus with his lyre spell-binding the wild denizens of the wood." And this he once applied to the disruption of forms going on across the Channel and the consequences thereof.

At this unwonted muster at quarters, all proceeded as at the regular hour. The band on the quarter-deck played a sacred air. After which the Chaplain went thro' the customary morning service. That done, the drum beat the retreat,

and toned by music and religious rites subserv-
ing the discipline and purpose of war, the men
in their wonted orderly manner, dispersed to
the places allotted them when not at the guns.

And now it was full day. The fleece of low-
hanging vapor had vanished, licked up by the
sun, that late had so glorified it. And the circumambient air in the clearness of its serenity
was like smooth white marble in the polished
block not yet removed from the marble-dealer's
yard.

29

The symmetry of form attainable in pure fiction can not so readily be achieved in a narration essentially having less to do with fable
than with fact. Truth uncompromisingly told
will always have its ragged edges; hence the
conclusion of such a narration is apt to be less
finished than an architectural finial.

How it fared with the Handsome Sailor during the year of the Great Mutiny has been
faithfully given. But tho' properly the story
ends with his life, something in way of sequel
will not be amiss. Three brief chapters will
suffice.

In the general re-christening under the Directory of the craft originally forming the navy
of the French monarchy, the St. Louis line-of-
battle ship was named the Athéiste. Such a
name, like some other substituted ones in the
Revolutionary fleet while proclaiming the infidel audacity of the ruling power was yet, tho'
not so intended to be, the aptest name, if one
consider it, ever given to a war-ship, far more
so indeed than the Devastation, the Erebus
(the Hell) and similar names bestowed upon
fighting-ships.

On the return-passage to the English fleet
from the detached cruise during which occurred
the events already recorded, the Indomitable
fell in with the Athéiste. An engagement ensued; during which Captain Vere in the act of
putting his ship alongside the enemy with a
view of throwing his boarders across her bulwarks, was hit by a musket-ball from a port-hole
of the enemy's main cabin. More than disabled
he dropped to the deck and was carried below
to the same cock-pit where some of his men
already lay. The senior Lieutenant took command. Under him the enemy was finally captured and though much crippled was by rare
good fortune successfully taken into Gibraltar,
an English port not very distant from the scene

of the fight. There, Captain Vere with the rest
of the wounded was put ashore. He lingered
for some days, but the end came. Unhappily
he was cut off too early for the Nile and Trafalgar. The spirit that spite its philosophic
austerity may yet have indulged in the most
secret of all passions, ambition, never attained
to the fulness of fame.

Not long before death while lying under the
influence of that magical drug which soothing
the physical frame mysteriously operates on the
subtler element in man, he was heard to murmur words inexplicable to his attendant —
"Billy Budd, Billy Budd." That these were not
the accents of remorse, would seem clear from
what the attendant said to the Indomitable's
senior officer of marines who, as the most reluctant to condemn of the members of the
drum-head court, too well knew, tho' here he
kept the knowledge to himself, who Billy Budd
was.

30

Some few weeks after the execution, among
other matters under the head of News from the
Mediterranean, there appeared in a naval chronicle of the time, an authorized weekly publication, an account of the affair. It was doubtless
for the most part written in good faith, tho' the
medium, partly rumor, through which the facts
must have reached the writer, served to deflect
and in part falsify them. The account was as
follows: —

"On the tenth of the last month a deplorable occurrence took place on board H.M.S.
Indomitable. John Claggart, the ship's master-
at-arms, discovering that some sort of plot was
incipient among an inferior section of the ship's
company, and that the ring-leader was one William Budd; he, Claggart, in the act of arraigning
the man before the Captain was vindictively
stabbed to the heart by the suddenly drawn
sheath-knife of Budd.

The deed and the implement employed, sufficiently suggest that tho' mustered into the service under an English name the assassin was no
Englishman, but one of those aliens adopting
English cognomens whom the present extraordinary necessities of the Service have caused
to be admitted into it in considerable numbers.

The enormity of the crime and the extreme
depravity of the criminal, appear the greater in
view of the character of the victim, a middle-

aged man respectable and discreet, belonging to that minor official grade, the petty-officers, upon whom, as none know better than the commissioned gentlemen, the efficiency of His Majesty's navy so largely depends. His function was a responsible one; at once onerous and thankless and his fidelity in it the greater because of his strong patriotic impulse. In this instance as in so many other instances in these days, the character of this unfortunate man signally refutes, if refutation were needed, that peevish saying attributed to the late Dr. Johnson, that patriotism is the last refuge of a scoundrel.

The criminal paid the penalty of his crime. The promptitude of the punishment has proved salutary. Nothing amiss is now apprehended aboard H.M.S. *Indomitable*."

The above, appearing in a publication now long ago superannuated and forgotten, is all that hitherto has stood in human record to attest what manner of men respectively were John Claggart and Billy Budd.

31

Everything is for a term remarkable in navies. Any tangible object associated with some striking incident of the service is converted into a monument. The spar from which the Foretopman was suspended, was for some few years kept trace of by the bluejackets. Their knowledge followed it from ship to dock-yard and again from dock-yard to ship, still pursuing it even when at last reduced to a mere dock-yard boom. To them a chip of it was a piece of the Cross. Ignorant tho' they were of the secret facts of the tragedy, and not thinking but that the penalty was somehow unavoidably inflicted from the naval point of view, for all that they instinctively felt that Billy was a sort of man as incapable of mutiny as of wilful murder. They recalled the fresh young image of the Handsome Sailor, that face never deformed by a sneer or subtler vile freak of the heart within. Their impression of him was doubtless deepened by the fact that he was gone, and in a measure mysteriously gone. At the time on the gun decks of the *Indomitable* the general estimate of his nature and its unconscious simplicity eventually found rude utterance from another foretopman, one of his own watch, gifted, as some sailors are, with an artless poetic tempera-

ment; the tarry hands made some lines which after circulating among the shipboard crew for a while, finally got rudely printed at Portsmouth as a ballad. The title given to it was the sailor's.

Billy in the Darbies

Good of the Chaplain to enter Lone Bay
And down on his marrow-bones here and pray
For the likes just o' me, Billy Budd. — But
    look:
Through the port comes the moonshine astray!
It tips the guard's cutlas and silvers this nook;
But 'twill die in the dawning of Billy's last day.
A jewel-block they'll make of me tomorrow,
Pendant pearl from the yard-arm-end
Like the ear-drop I gave to Bristol Molly —
O, 'tis me, not the sentence they'll suspend.
Ay, Ay, all is up; and I must up too
Early in the morning, aloft from alow.
On an empty stomach, now, never it would do.
They'll give me a nibble — bit o' biscuit ere I
    go.
Sure, a messmate will reach me the last parting
    cup;
But, turning heads away from the hoist and the
    belay,
Heaven knows who will have the running of me
    up!
No pipe to those halyards. — But aren't it all
    sham?
A blur's in my eyes; it is dreaming that I am.
A hatchet to my hawser? all adrift to go?
The drum roll to grog, and Billy never know?
But Donald he has promised to stand by the
    plank;
So I'll shake a friendly hand ere I sink.
But — no! It is dead then I'll be, come to
    think. —
I remember Taff the Welshman when he sank.
And his cheek it was like the budding pink.
But me they'll lash me in hammock, drop me
    deep.
Fathoms down, fathoms down, how I'll dream
    fast asleep.
I feel it stealing now. Sentry, are you there?
Just ease this darbies at the wrist, and roll me
    over fair,
I am sleepy, and the oozy weeds about me
    twist.

John Greenleaf Whittier [1807–1892]

Brought up on a farm tilled by his ancestors as far back as 1647, Whittier lived his span of eighty-three years at Haverhill and Amesbury in northeastern Massachusetts. Life meant to him for many years hard toil and poverty, and always frail health, but also the charms of nature, the happiness of human affection, and the consolation of the Quaker faith of his fathers. It meant, too, dedicated service in the cause of abolition of slavery, and the satisfaction of poetic creation.

At the age of fourteen Whittier read Robert Burns and began to scribble verses. Some of them appeared in *The Free Press*, a weekly edited in Newburyport by William Lloyd Garrison. Garrison became interested in his young contributor and urged the boy's parents to send him to Haverhill Academy. There he studied for only two terms; mainly he was self-educated. By turns he was a shoemaker, a teacher, an editor of journals in Boston and Hartford. In 1831 he published his first book, *Legends of New England*, and two years later entered the lists for abolition with a pamphlet on *Justice and Expediency*.

The next three decades, the most vigorous of his life, Whittier gave to his "opinion mill." He was a delegate to the anti-slavery convention in 1833 in Philadelphia. He was in the Massachusetts legislature in 1835 and 1836. He argued against slavery in prose, verse, and speech, risked his life before hostile mobs, gave up his political career, edited *The Pennsylvania Freeman*. In 1846 he published *Voices of Freedom*, two years later a collected edition of his *Poems*, and after two more years *Songs of Labor and Other Poems*.

The War of the Secession ended, Whittier settled down to the peaceful years he had earned. *Snow-Bound*, a deservedly popular success, was his first financially rewarding volume. Many other publications followed, including one of his best, *The Pennsylvania Pilgrim*, and at length the Riverside Edition of his verse and prose in seven volumes.

His poetry shows clearly the modern concern with "the near, the low, the common" of which Emerson had spoken. It is largely a poetry of the humble: of the pleasures of labor, of the evil of slavery; a poetry of simple home life on the farm; a poetry of popular, regional legends; a poetry of simple religion, the love of God and of man. The spirit of Whittier was close to that of Burns, Scotland's poet of the people, and to that of John Woolman, the Quaker tailor whose *Journal* he edited. Because his verse was often sentimental and moralistic, as well as facile and diffuse, it now seems to us to have been long overvalued. Yet he rose above his usual mediocrity often enough to achieve a small body of genuine poetry that has latterly been undervalued. The best of his poems are given below, together with a few others of special interest.

Further reading: *The Pennsylvania Pilgrim*; other poems. Whitman Bennett, *Whittier, Bard of Freedom*, 1941. J. A. Pollard, *Whittier, Friend of Man*, 1949. F. M. Pray, *A Study of Whittier's Apprenticeship as a Poet*, 1930. George Arms, "Whittier," in *The Fields Were Green*, 1953.

Proem

(w. 1847)

🐝 Whittier wrote this proem (preface) for the first collected edition of his *Poems*.

I love the old melodious lays
Which softly melt the ages through,
   The songs of Spenser's golden days,
   Arcadian Sidney's silvery phrase,
Sprinkling our noon of time with freshest
    morning dew.   5

Yet, vainly in my quiet hours
To breathe their marvellous notes I try;
   I feel them, as the leaves and flowers
   In silence feel the dewy showers,
And drink with glad, still lips the blessing of
    the sky.   10

The rigor of a frozen clime,
The harshness of an untaught ear,
   The jarring words of one whose rhyme
   Beat often Labor's hurried time,
Or Duty's rugged march through storm and
    strife, are here.   15

Of mystic beauty, dreamy grace,
No rounded art the lack supplies;
   Unskilled the subtle lines to trace,
   Or softer shades of Nature's face,
I view her common forms with unanointed
    eyes.   20

Nor mine the seer-like power to show
The secrets of the heart and mind;
   To drop the plummet-line below
   Our common world of joy and woe,
A more intense despair or brighter hope to
    find.   25

Yet here at least an earnest sense
Of human right and weal is shown;
   A hate of tyranny intense,
   And hearty in its vehemence,
As if my brother's pain and sorrow were my
    own.   30

O Freedom! if to me belong
Nor mighty Milton's gift divine,
   Nor Marvell's wit and graceful song,
   Still with a love as deep and strong
As theirs, I lay, like them, my best gifts on thy
    shrine!   35

Song of Slaves in the Desert

(1847)

🐝 *Sebah, Oasis of Fezzan, 10th March, 1846.* — This evening the female slaves were unusually excited in singing, and I had the curiosity to ask my negro servant Said, what they were singing about. . . . "Oh, they sing of *Rubee* (God) . . . they say, 'Where are we going?' . . . They remember their country, Bornou, and say, '*Bornou was a pleasant country, full of all good things; but this is a bad country, and we are miserable!*'" . . .— *Richardson's Journal in Africa.* (from Whittier's note)

Where are we going? where are we going,
   Where are we going, Rubee?

Lord of peoples, lord of lands,
Look across these shining sands,
Through the furnace of the noon,   5
Through the white light of the moon.
Strong the Ghiblee wind is blowing,
Strange and large the world is growing!
Speak and tell us where we are going,
   Where are we going, Rubee?   10

Bornou land was rich and good,
Wells of water, fields of food,
Dourra fields, and bloom of bean,
And the palm-tree cool and green:
Bornou land we see no longer,   15
Here we thirst and here we hunger,
Here the Moon-man smites in anger:
   Where are we going, Rubee?

When we went from Bornou land,
We were like the leaves and sand,   20
We were many, we are few;
Life has one, and death has two:
Whitened bones our path are showing,
Thou All-seeing, thou All-knowing!
Here us, tell us, where we are going,   25
   Where are we going, Rubee?

Moons of marches from our eyes
Bornou land behind us lies;
Stranger round us day by day
Bends the desert circle gray;   30
Wild the waves of sand are flowing,
Hot the winds above them blowing, —
Lord of all things! where are we going?
   Where are we going, Rubee?

We are weak, but Thou art strong;   35
Short our lives, but Thine is long;

We are blind, but Thou hast eyes;
We are fools, but Thou art wise!
Thou, our morrow's pathway knowing
Through the strange world round us growing,
Hear us, tell us where are we going,   41
    Where are we going, Rubee?

Ichabod

(w. *1850*)

"This poem," said Whittier, "was the outcome
of the surprise and grief and forecast of evil consequences which I felt on reading the Seventh of
March speech of Daniel Webster in support of the
'Compromise,' and the Fugitive Slave Law. No
partisan or personal enmity dictated it. On the
contrary my admiration of the splendid personality
and intellectual power of the great senator was never
stronger than when I laid down his speech, and, in
one of the saddest moments of my life, penned my
protest."

For the significance of the title, see 1 *Samuel* 4:
19–22 ("And she named the child Ichabod, saying,
The glory is departed from Israel").

So fallen! so lost! the light withdrawn
    Which once he wore!
The glory from his gray hairs gone
    Forevermore!

Revile him not, the Tempter hath   5
    A snare for all;
And pitying tears, not scorn and wrath,
    Befit his fall!

Oh, dumb be passion's stormy rage,
    When he who might   10
Have lighted up and led his age,
    Falls back in night.

Scorn! would the angels laugh, to mark
    A bright soul driven,
Fiend-goaded, down the endless dark,   15
    From hope and heaven!

Let not the land once proud of him
    Insult him now,
Nor brand with deeper shame his dim,
    Dishonored brow.   20

But let its humbled sons, instead,
    From sea to lake,
A long lament, as for the dead,
    In sadness make.

Of all we loved and honored, naught   25
    Save power remains;
A fallen angel's pride of thought,
    Still strong in chains.

All else is gone; from those great eyes
    The soul has fled: 30
When faith is lost, when honor dies,
    The man is dead!

Then pay the reverence of old days
    To his dead fame;
Walk backward, with averted gaze,   35
    And hide the shame!

First-Day Thoughts

(*1852*)

Christian attitudes and allusions enter into many
of Whittier's poems, regardless of subject, as, for
example, in "Ichabod." They also become the subject of a considerable group of poems. In "First-
Day Thoughts" we see Whittier take his place in a
Quaker meeting. The poem is essentially a prayer.

In calm and cool and silence, once again
    I find my old accustomed place among
    My brethren, where, perchance, no human
        tongue
Shall utter words; where never hymn is sung,
    Nor deep-toned organ blown, nor censer
        swung,   5
Nor dim light falling through the pictured
    pane!
There, syllabled by silence, let me hear
The still small voice which reached the
    prophet's ear;
Read in my heart a still diviner law
Than Israel's leader on his tables saw!   10
There let me strive with each besetting sin,
    Recall my wandering fancies, and restrain
    The sore disquiet of a restless brain;
And, as the path of duty is made plain,
May grace be given that I may walk therein,
    Not like the hireling, for his selfish gain,   16
With backward glances and reluctant tread,
Making a merit of his coward dread,
    But, cheerful, in the light around me thrown,
    Walking as one to pleasant service led;   20
    Doing God's will as if it were my own,
Yet trusting not in mine, but in his strength
    alone!

Skipper Ireson's Ride

(w. 1828, 1857)

"A Yankee ballad" Whittier called this poem when submitting it to Lowell, editor of the newly founded *Atlantic Monthly*. At Lowell's suggestion the refrain was put into dialect. The scene is Marblehead, Massachusetts, about 1808. Apparently Captain Ireson was actually blameless — does this affect the literary merit of the piece?

Of all the rides since the birth of time,
Told in story or sung in rhyme, —
On Apuleius's Golden Ass,
Or one-eyed Calender's horse of brass,
Witch astride of a human back,   5
Islam's prophet on Al-Borák, —
The strangest ride that ever was sped
Was Ireson's, out from Marblehead!
  Old Floyd Ireson, for his hard heart,
  Tarred and feathered and carried in a cart
    By the women of Marblehead!   11

Body of turkey, head of owl,
Wings a-droop like a rained-on fowl,
Feathered and ruffled in every part,
Skipper Ireson stood in the cart.   15
Scores of women, old and young,
Strong of muscle, and glib of tongue,
Pushed and pulled up the rocky lane,
Shouting and singing the shrill refrain:
  "Here's Flud Oirson, fur his horrd horrt,
  Torr'd an' furtherr'd an' corr'd in a corrt   21
    By the women o' Morble'ead!"

Wrinkled scolds with hands on hips,
Girls in bloom of cheek and lips,
Wild-eyed, free-limbed, such as chase   25
Bacchus round some antique vase,
Brief of skirt, with ankles bare,
Loose of kerchief and loose of hair,
With conch-shells blowing and fish-horns'
    twang,
Over and over the Maenads sang: 30
  "Here's Flud Oirson, fur his horrd horrt,
  Torr'd an' futherr'd an' corr'd in a corrt
    By the women o' Morble'ead!"

Small pity for him! — He sailed away
From a leaking ship in Chaleur Bay, —   35
Sailed away from a sinking wreck,
With his own town's-people on her deck!
"Lay by! lay by!" they called to him.
Back he answered, "Sink or swim!

Brag of your catch of fish again!"   40
And off he sailed through the fog and rain!
  Old Floyd Ireson, for his hard heart,
  Tarred and feathered and carried in a cart
    By the women of Marblehead!

Fathoms deep in dark Chaleur   45
That wreck shall lie forevermore.
Mother and sister, wife and maid,
Looked from the rocks of Marblehead
Over the moaning and rainy sea, —
Looked for the coming that might not be!   50
What did the winds and the sea-birds say
Of the cruel captain who sailed away — ?
  Old Floyd Ireson, for his hard heart,
  Tarred and feathered and carried in a cart
    By the women of Marblehead!   55

Through the street, on either side,
Up flew windows, doors swung wide;
Sharp-tongued spinsters, old wives gray,
Treble lent the fish-horn's bray.
Sea-worn grandsires, cripple-bound,   60
Hulks of old sailors run aground,
Shook head, and fist, and hat, and cane,
And cracked with curses the hoarse refrain:
  "Here's Flud Oirson, fur his horrd horrt,
  Torr'd an' futherr'd an' corr'd in a corrt   65
    By the women o' Morble'ead!"

Sweetly along the Salem road
Bloom of orchard and lilac showed.
Little the wicked skipper knew
Of the fields so green and the sky so blue.   70
Riding there in his sorry trim,
Like an Indian idol glum and grim,
Scarcely he seemed the sound to hear
Of voices shouting, far and near: 74
  "Here's Flud Oirson, fur his horrd horrt,
  Torr'd an' futherr'd an' corr'd in a corrt
    By the women o' Morble'ead!"

"Hear me, neighbors!" at last he cried, —
"What to me is this noisy ride?
What is the shame that clothes the skin   80
To the nameless horror that lives within?
Waking or sleeping, I see a wreck,
And hear a cry from a reeling deck!
Hate me and curse me, — I only dread
The hand of God and the face of the dead!"
  Said old Floyd Ireson, for his hard heart,   86
  Tarred and feathered and carried in a cart
    By the women of Marblehead!

Then the wife of the skipper lost at sea
Said, "God has touched him! why should we!"
Said an old wife mourning her only son,   91
"Cut the rogue's tether and let him run!"
So with soft relentings and rude excuse,
Half scorn, half pity, they cut him loose,
And gave him a cloak to hide him in,   95
And left him alone with his shame and sin.
　　Poor Floyd Ireson, for his hard heart,
　　Tarred and feathered and carried in a cart
　　　　By the women of Marblehead!

Laus Deo!

(w. 1865)

❧ "On hearing the bells ring on the passage of the constitutional amendment abolishing slavery." (Whittier's note.)

Laus Deo! (Praise be to God!). Whittier's emotion expressed itself in a strongly marked, trochaic meter and in Old Testament echoes. Lines 19–20: Job 38:1. Line 24: Psalms 107:16. Lines 27–30: Exodus 15:21. Lines 34–36: Isaiah 23:11. Lines 40–41: Numbers 17:8.

　　It is done!
　　Clang of bell and roar of gun
Send the tidings up and down.
　　How the belfries rock and reel!
　　How the great guns, peal on peal,   5
Fling the joy from town to town!

　　Ring, O bells!
　　Every stroke exulting tells
Of the burial hour of crime.
　　Loud and long, that all may hear,   10
　　Ring for every listening ear
Of Eternity and Time!

　　Let us kneel:
　　God's own voice is in that peal,
And this spot is holy ground.   15
　　Lord, forgive us! What are we,
　　That our eyes this glory see,
That our ears have heard the sound!

　　For the Lord
　　On the whirlwind is abroad;   20
In the earthquake He has spoken:
　　He has smitten with this thunder
　　The iron walls asunder,
And the gates of brass are broken!

　　Loud and long   25
　　Lift the old exulting song;
Sing with Miriam by the sea,
　　He has cast the mighty down;
　　Horse and rider sink and drown;
"He hath triumphed gloriously!"   30

　　Did we dare,
　　In our agony of prayer,
Ask for more than He has done?
　　When was ever his right hand
　　Over any time or land   35
Stretched as now beneath the sun?

　　How they pale,
　　Ancient myth and song and tale,
In this wonder of our days,
　　When the cruel rod of war   40
　　Blossoms white with righteous law
And the wrath of man is praise!

　　Blotted out!
　　All within and all about
Shall a fresher life begin;   45
　　Freer breathe the universe
　　As it rolls its heavy curse
On the dead and buried sin!

　　It is done!
　　In the circuit of the sun   50
Shall the sound thereof go forth.
　　It shall bid the sad rejoice,
　　It shall give the dumb a voice,
It shall belt with joy the earth!

　　Ring and swing,   55
　　Bells of joy! On morning's wing
Send the song of praise abroad!
　　With a sound of broken chains
　　Tell the nations that He reigns,
Who alone is Lord and God!   60

Snow-Bound

A *Winter Idyl*

❧ This idyl (little picture) of rural New England has the poetic warmth of a long cherished memory. "Out of his loyalty, not alone to vanished faces, but to the fulfillment of personal relationships which his boyhood home symbolized, he wrote *Snow-Bound* (1866), the finest of his Yankee idyls, a faultless integration of precisely remembered detail and tender devotion. In a general way this poem is the New England analogue of Burns' "The Cotter's Saturday Night," with which it compares favorably both for its wealth of homely description and for its genuineness of sentiment. . . . It is a quiet tribute to a form of civilized living that was passing. Here embodied in glowing terms was the Jeffersonian dream of the virtuous small landholder, beholden to no one and winning an honest, laborious livelihood from the soil" (G. F. Whicher in *Literary History of the United States*). Whittier prefaced the poem with the following quotations from an occult writer, Agrippa, and from Emerson.

As the Spirits of Darkness be stronger in the dark, so Good Spirits, which be Angels of Light, are augmented not only by the Divine light of the Sun, but also by our common VVood Fire: and as the Celestial Fire drives away dark spirits, so also this our Fire of VVood doth the same. — COR. AGRIPPA, *Occult Philosophy*, Book I. ch. v.

> Announced by all the trumpets of the sky,
> Arrives the snow, and, driving o'er the fields,
> Seems nowhere to alight: the whited air
> Hides hills and woods, the river and the heaven,
> And veils the farm-house at the garden's end.
> The sled and traveller stopped, the courier's feet
> Delayed, all friends shut out, the housemates sit
> Around the radiant fireplace, enclosed
> In a tumultuous privacy of storm.
> EMERSON, *The Snow-Storm*

The sun that brief December day
Rose cheerless over hills of gray,
And, darkly circled, gave at noon
A sadder light than waning moon.
Slow tracing down the thickening sky   5
Its mute and ominous prophecy,
A portent seeming less than threat,
It sank from sight before it set.
A chill no coat, however stout,
Of homespun stuff could quite shut out,   10
A hard, dull bitterness of cold,
That checked, mid-vein, the circling race
Of life-blood in the sharpened face,
The coming of the snow-storm told.
The wind blew east; we heard the roar   15
Of Ocean on his wintry shore,
And felt the strong pulse throbbing there
Beat with low rhythm our inland air.

Meanwhile we did our nightly chores, —
Brought in the wood from out of doors,   20
Littered the stalls, and from the mows
Raked down the herd's-grass for the cows:
Heard the horse whinnying for his corn;
And, sharply clashing horn on horn,
Impatient down the stanchion rows   25

The cattle shake their walnut bows;
While, peering from his early perch
Upon the scaffold's pole of birch,
The cock his crested helmet bent
And down his querulous challenge sent.   30

Unwarmed by any sunset light
The gray day darkened into night,
A night made hoary with the swarm
And whirl-dance of the blinding storm,
As zigzag, wavering to and fro,   35
Crossed and recrossed the wingèd snow:
And ere the early bedtime came
The white drift piled the window-frame,
And through the glass the clothes-line posts
Looked in like tall and sheeted ghosts.   40

So all night long the storm roared on:
The morning broke without a sun;
In tiny spherule traced with lines
Of Nature's geometric signs,
In starry flake, and pellicle,   45
All day the hoary meteor fell;
And, when the second morning shone,
We looked upon a world unknown,
On nothing we could call our own.
Around the glistening wonder bent   50
The blue walls of the firmament,
No cloud above, no earth below, —
A universe of sky and snow!
The old familiar sights of ours
Took marvellous shapes; strange domes and towers   55
Rose up where sty or corn-crib stood,
Or garden-wall, or belt of wood;
A smooth white mound the brush-pile showed,
A fenceless drift what once was road;
The bridle-post an old man sat   60
With loose-flung coat and high cocked hat;
The well-curb had a Chinese roof;
And even the long sweep, high aloof,
In its slant splendor, seemed to tell
Of Pisa's leaning miracle.   65

A prompt, decisive man, no breath
Our father wasted: "Boys, a path!"
Well pleased (for when did farmer boy
Count such a summons less than joy?)
Our buskins on our feet we drew;   70
With mittened hands, and caps drawn low,
To guard our necks and ears from snow,
We cut the solid whiteness through.
And, where the drift was deepest, made
A tunnel walled and overlaid   75

With dazzling crystal: we had read
Of rare Aladdin's wondrous cave,
And to our own his name we gave,
With many a wish the luck were ours
To test his lamp's supernal powers.   80
We reached the barn with merry din,
And roused the prisoned brutes within.
The old horse thrust his long head out,
And grave with wonder gazed about;
The cock his lusty greeting said,   85
And forth his speckled harem led;
The oxen lashed their tails, and hooked,
And mild reproach of hunger looked;
The hornèd patriarch of the sheep,
Like Egypt's Amun roused from sleep,   90
Shook his sage head with gesture mute,
And emphasized with stamp of foot.

All day the gusty north-wind bore
The loosening drift its breath before;
Low circling round its southern zone,   95
The sun through dazzling snow-mist shone.
No church-bell lent its Christian tone
To the savage air, no social smoke
Curled over woods of snow-hung oak.
A solitude made more intense   100
By dreary-voicèd elements,
The shrieking of the mindless wind,
The moaning tree-boughs swaying blind,
And on the glass the unmeaning beat
Of ghostly finger-tips of sleet.   105
Beyond the circle of our hearth
No welcome sound of toil or mirth
Unbound the spell, and testified
Of human life and thought outside.
We minded that the sharpest ear   110
The buried brooklet could not hear,
The music of whose liquid lip
Had been to us companionship,
And, in our lonely life, had grown
To have an almost human tone.   115

As night drew on, and, from the crest
Of wooded knolls that ridged the west,
The sun, a snow-blown traveller, sank
From sight beneath the smothering bank,
We piled, with care, our nightly stack   120
Of wood against the chimney-back, —
The oaken log, green, huge, and thick,
And on its top the stout back-stick;
The knotty forestick laid apart,
And filled between with curious art   125
The ragged brush; then, hovering near,
We watched the first red blaze appear,
Heard the sharp crackle, caught the gleam

On whitewashed wall and sagging beam,
Until the old, rude-furnished room   130
Burst, flower-like, into rosy bloom;
While radiant with a mimic flame
Outside the sparkling drift became,
And through the bare-boughed lilac-tree
Our own warm hearth seemed blazing free.
The crane and pendent trammels showed,   136
The Turks' heads on the andirons glowed:
While childish fancy, prompt to tell
The meaning of the miracle,
Whispered the old rhyme: "*Under the tree,*
When fire outdoors burns merrily,   141
There the witches are making tea."
The moon above the eastern wood
Shone at its full; the hill-range stood
Transfigured in the silver flood,   145
Its blown snows flashing cold and keen,
Dead white, save where some sharp ravine
Took shadow, or the sombre green
Of hemlocks turned to pitchy black
Against the whiteness at their back.   150
For such a world and such a night
Most fitting that unwarming light,
Which only seemed where'er it fell
To make the coldness visible.

Shut in from all the world without,   155
We sat the clean-winged hearth about,
Content to let the north-wind roar
In baffled rage at pane and door,
While the red logs before us beat
The frost-line back with tropic heat;   160
And ever, when a louder blast
Shook beam and rafter as it passed,
The merrier up its roaring draught
The great throat of the chimney laughed;
The house-dog on his paws outspread   165
Laid to the fire his drowsy head,
The cat's dark silhouette on the wall
A couchant tiger's seemed to fall;
And, for the winter fireside meet,
Between the andirons' straddling feet,   170
The mug of cider simmered slow,
The apples sputtered in a row,
And, close at hand, the basket stood
With nuts from brown October's wood.

What matter how the night behaved?   175
What matter how the north-wind raved?
Blow high, blow low, not all its snow
Could quench our hearth-fire's ruddy glow.
O Time and Change! — with hair as gray
As was my sire's that winter day,   180
How strange it seems, with so much gone

Of life and love, to still live on!
Ah, brother! only I and thou
Are left of all that circle now, —
The dear home faces whereupon   185
That fitful firelight paled and shone.
Henceforward, listen as we will,
The voices of that hearth are still;
Look where we may, the wide earth o'er
Those lighted faces smile no more.   190
We tread the paths their feet have worn,
　　We sit beneath their orchard trees,
　　We hear, like them, the hum of bees
And rustle of the bladed corn;
We turn the pages that they read,   195
　　Their written words we linger o'er,
But in the sun they cast no shade,
No voice is heard, no sign is made,
　　No step is on the conscious floor!
Yet Love will dream, and Faith will trust   200
(Since He who knows our need is just)
That somehow, somewhere, meet we must.
Alas for him who never sees
The stars shine through his cypress-trees!
Who, hopeless, lays his dead away,   205
Nor looks to see the breaking day
Across the mournful marbles play!
Who hath not learned, in hours of faith,
　　The truth to flesh and sense unknown,
That Life is ever lord of Death,   210
　　And Love can never lose its own!

We sped the time with stories old,
Wrought puzzles out, and riddles told,
Or stammered from our school-book lore
"The Chief of Gambia's golden shore."   215
How often since, when all the land
Was clay in Slavery's shaping hand,
As if a far-blown trumpet stirred
The languorous sin-sick air, I heard:
"Does not the voice of reason cry,   220
　　Claim the first right which Nature gave,
From the red scourge of bondage fly,
　　Nor deign to live a burdened slave!"
Our father rode again his ride
On Memphremagog's wooded side;   225
Sat down again to moose and samp
In trapper's hut and Indian camp;
Lived o'er the old idyllic ease
Beneath St. Francois' hemlock-trees;
Again for him the moonlight shone   230
On Norman cap and bodiced zone;
Again he heard the violin play
Which led the village dance away,
And mingled in its merry whirl
The grandam and the laughing girl.   235

Or, nearer home, our steps he led
Where Salisbury's level marshes spread
　　Mile-wide as flies the laden bee;
Where merry mowers, hale and strong,
Swept, scythe on scythe, their swaths along
　　The low green prairies of the sea.   241
We shared the fishing off Boar's Head,
　　And round the rocky Isles of Shoals
　　The hake-broil on the drift-wood coals;
The chowder on the sand-beach made,   245
Dipped by the hungry, steaming hot,
With spoons of clam-shell from the pot.
We heard the tales of witchcraft old,
And dream and sign and marvel told
To sleepy listeners as they lay   250
Stretched idly on the salted hay,
Adrift along the winding shores,
When favoring breezes deigned to blow
The square sail of the gundelow
And idle lay the useless oars.   255

Our mother, while she turned her wheel
Or run the new-knit stocking-heel,
Told how the Indian hordes came down
At midnight on Cocheco town,
And how her own great-uncle bore   260
His cruel scalp-mark to fourscore.
Recalling, in her fitting phrase,
　　So rich and picturesque and free
　　(The common unrhymed poetry
Of simple life and country ways),   265
The story of her early days, —
She made us welcome to her home;
Old hearths grew wide to give us room;
We stole with her a frightened look
At the gray wizard's conjuring-book,   270
The fame whereof went far and wide
Through all the simple country-side;
We heard the hawks at twilight play,
The boat-horn on Piscataqua,
The loon's weird laughter far away;   275
We fished her little trout-brook, knew
What flowers in wood and meadow grew,
What sunny hillsides autumn-brown
She climbed to shake the ripe nuts down,
Saw where in sheltered cove and bay   280
The ducks' black squadron anchored lay,
And heard the wild-geese calling loud
Beneath the gray November cloud.

Then, haply, with a look more grave,
And soberer tone, some tale she gave   285
From painful Sewel's ancient tome,
Beloved in every Quaker home,
Of faith fire-winged by martyrdom,

Or Chalkley's Journal, old and quaint, —
Gentlest of skippers, rare sea-saint! —   290
Who, when the dreary calms prevailed,
And water-butt and bread-cask failed,
And cruel, hungry eyes pursued
His portly presence mad for food,
With dark hints muttered under breath   295
Of casting lots for life or death,
Offered, if Heaven withheld supplies,
To be himself the sacrifice.
Then, suddenly, as if to save
The good man from his living grave,   300
A ripple on the water grew,
A school of porpoise flashed in view.
"Take, eat," he said, "and be content;
These fishes in my stead are sent
By Him who gave the tangled ram   305
To spare the child of Abraham."

Our uncle, innocent of books,
Was rich in lore of fields and brooks,
The ancient teachers never dumb
Of Nature's unhoused lyceum.   310
In moons and tides and weather wise,
He read the clouds as prophecies,
And foul or fair could well divine,
By many an occult hint and sign,
Holding the cunning-warded keys   315
To all the woodcraft mysteries;
Himself to Nature's heart so near
That all her voices in his ear
Of beast or bird had meanings clear,
Like Apollonius of old,   320
Who knew the tales the sparrows told,
Or Hermes, who interpreted
What the sage cranes of Nilus said;
A simple, guileless, childlike man,
Content to live where life began;   325
Strong only on his native grounds,
The little world of sights and sounds
Whose girdle was the parish bounds,
Whereof his fondly partial pride
The common features magnified,   330
As Surrey hills to mountains grew
In White of Selborne's loving view, —
He told how teal and loon he shot,
And how the eagle's eggs he got,
The feats on pond and river done,   335
The prodigies of rod and gun;
Till, warming with the tales he told,
Forgotten was the outside cold,
The bitter wind unheeded blew,
From ripening corn the pigeons flew,   340
The partridge drummed i' the wood, the mink
Went fishing down the river-brink;

In fields with bean or clover gay,
The woodchuck, like a hermit gray,
    Peered from the doorway of his cell;   345
The muskrat plied the mason's trade,
And tier by tier his mud-walls laid;
And from the shagbark overhead
    The grizzled squirrel dropped his shell.

Next, the dear aunt, whose smile of cheer   350
And voice in dreams I see and hear —
The sweetest woman ever Fate
Perverse denied a household mate,
Who, lonely, homeless, not the less
Found peace in love's unselfishness,   355
And welcome whereso'er she went,
A calm and gracious element,
Whose presence seemed the sweet income
And womanly atmosphere of home —
Called up her girlhood memories,   360
The huskings and the apple-bees,
The sleigh-rides and the summer sails,
Weaving through all the poor details
And homespun warp of circumstance
A golden woof-thread of romance.   365
For well she kept her genial mood
And simple faith of maidenhood;
Before her still a cloud-land lay,
The mirage loomed across her way;
The morning dew, that dries so soon   370
With others, glistened at her noon;
Through years of toil and soil and care,
From glossy tress to thin gray hair,
All unprofaned she held apart
The virgin fancies of the heart.   375
Be shame to him of woman born
Who hath for such but thought of scorn.

There, too, our elder sister plied
Her evening task the stand beside;
A full, rich nature, free to trust,   380
Truthful and almost sternly just,
Impulsive, earnest, prompt to act,
And make her generous thought a fact,
Keeping with many a light disguise
The secret of self-sacrifice.   385
O heart sore-tried! thou hast the best,
That Heaven itself could give thee, — rest,
Rest from all bitter thoughts and things!
    How many a poor one's blessing went
    With thee beneath the low green tent   390
Whose curtain never outward swings!

As one who held herself a part
Of all she saw, and let her heart
    Against the household bosom lean,

Upon the motley-braided mat   395
Our youngest and our dearest sat,
Lifting her large, sweet, asking eyes,
　　Now bathed in the unfading green
And holy peace of Paradise.
Oh, looking from some heavenly hill,   400
　　Or from the shade of saintly palms,
　　Or silver reach of river calms,
Do those large eyes behold me still?
With me one little year ago: —
The chill weight of the winter snow   405
　　For months upon her grave has lain;
And now, when summer south-winds blow
　　And brier and harebell bloom again,
I tread the pleasant paths we trod,
I see the violet-sprinkled sod   410
Whereon she leaned, too frail and weak
The hillside flowers she loved to seek,
Yet following me where'er I went
With dark eyes full of love's content.
The birds are glad; the brier-rose fills   415
The air with sweetness; all the hills
Stretch green to June's unclouded sky;
But still I wait with ear and eye
For something gone which should be nigh,
A loss in all familiar things,   420
In flower that blooms, and bird that sings.
And yet, dear heart! remembering thee,
　　Am I not richer than of old?
Safe in thy immortality,   424
　　What change can reach the wealth I hold?
　　What chance can mar the pearl and gold
Thy love hath left in trust with me?
And while in life's late afternoon,
　　Where cool and long the shadows grow,
I walk to meet the night that soon   430
　　Shall shape and shadow overflow,
I cannot feel that thou art far,
Since near at need the angels are;
And when the sunset gates unbar,
　　Shall I not see thee waiting stand,   435
And, white against the evening star,
　　The welcome of thy beckoning hand?

Brisk wielder of the birch and rule,
The master of the district school
Held at the fire his favored place,   440
Its warm glow lit a laughing face
Fresh-hued and fair, where scarce appeared
The uncertain prophecy of beard.
He teased the mitten-blinded cat,
Played cross-pins on my uncle's hat,   445
Sang songs, and told us what befalls
In classic Dartmouth's college halls.
Born the wild Northern hills among,

From whence his yeoman father wrung
By patient toil subsistence scant,   450
Not competence and yet not want,
He early gained the power to pay
His cheerful, self-reliant way;
Could doff at ease his scholar's gown
To peddle wares from town to town;   455
Or through the long vacation's reach
In lonely lowland districts teach,
Where all the droll experience found
At stranger hearths in boarding round,
The moonlit skater's keen delight,   460
The sleigh-drive through the frosty night,
The rustic-party, with its rough
Accompaniment of blind-man's-bluff,
And whirling-plate, and forfeits paid,
His winter task a pastime made.   465
Happy the snow-locked homes wherein
He tuned his merry violin,
Or played the athlete in the barn,
Or held the good dame's winding-yarn,
Or mirth-provoking versions told   470
Of classic legends rare and old,
Wherein the scenes of Greece and Rome
Had all the commonplace of home,
And little seemed at best the odds
'Twixt Yankee pedlers and old gods;   475
Where Pindus-born Arachthus took
The guise of any grist-mill brook,
And dread Olympus at his will
Became a huckleberry hill.

A careless boy that night he seemed;   480
　　But at his desk he had the look
And air of one who wisely schemed,
　　And hostage from the future took
　　In trainèd thought and lore of book.
Large-brained, clear-eyed, of such as he   485
Shall Freedom's young apostles be,
Who, following in War's bloody trail,
Shall every lingering wrong assail:
All chains from limb and spirit strike,
Uplift the black and white alike;   490
Scatter before their swift advance
The darkness and the ignorance,
The pride, the lust, the squalid sloth,
Which nurtured Treason's monstrous growth,
Made murder pastime, and the hell   495
Of prison-torture possible;
The cruel lie of caste refute,
Old forms remould, and substitute
For Slavery's lash the freeman's will,
For blind routine, wise-handed skill;   500
A school-house plant on every hill,
Stretching in radiate nerve-lines thence

The quick wires of intelligence;
Till North and South together brought
Shall own the same electric thought,   505
In peace a common flag salute,
And, side by side in labor's free
And unresentful rivalry,
Harvest the fields wherein they fought.

Another guest that winter night   510
Flashed back from lustrous eyes the light.
Unmarked by time, and yet not young,
The honeyed music of her tongue
And words of meekness scarcely told
A nature passionate and bold,   515
Strong, self-concentred, spurning guide,
Its milder features dwarfed beside
Her unbent will's majestic pride.
She sat among us, at the best,
A not unfeared, half-welcome guest,   520
Rebuking with her cultured phrase
Our homeliness of words and ways.
A certain pard-like, treacherous grace
Swayed the lithe limbs and dropped the lash,
Lent the white teeth their dazzling flash;   525
And under low brows, black with night,
Rayed out at times a dangerous light;
The sharp heat-lightnings of her face
Presaging ill to him whom Fate
Condemned to share her love or hate.   530
A woman tropical, intense
In thought and act, in soul and sense,
She blended in a like degree
The vixen and the devotee,
Revealing with each freak or feint   535
    The temper of Petruchio's Kate,
The raptures of Siena's saint.
Her tapering hand and rounded wrist
Had facile power to form a fist;
The warm, dark languish of her eyes   540
Was never safe from wrath's surprise.
Brows saintly calm and lips devout
Knew every change of scowl and pout;
And the sweet voice had notes more high
And shrill for social battle-cry.   545

Since then what old cathedral town
Has missed her pilgrim staff and gown,
What convent-gate has held its lock
Against the challenge of her knock!
Through Smyrna's plague-hushed thorough-
    fares,   550
Up sea-set Malta's rocky stairs,
Gray olive slopes of hills that hem
    Thy tombs and shrines, Jerusalem,

Or startling on her desert throne
The crazy Queen of Lebanon   555
With claims fantastic as her own,
Her tireless feet have held their way;
And still, unrestful, bowed, and gray,
She watches under Eastern skies,
    With hope each day renewed and fresh,
    The Lord's quick coming in the flesh,   561
Whereof she dreams and prophesies!

Where'er her troubled path may be,
    The Lord's sweet pity with her go!
The outward wayward life we see,   565
    The hidden springs we may not know.
Nor is it given us to discern
    What threads the fatal sisters spun,
    Through what ancestral years has run
The sorrow with the woman born,   570
What forged her cruel chain of moods,
What set her feet in solitudes,
    And held the love within her mute,
What mingled madness in the blood,
    A life-long discord and annoy,   575
    Waters of tears with oil of joy,
And hid within the folded bud
    Perversities of flower and fruit.
It is not ours to separate
    The tangled skein of will and fate,   580
To show what metes and bounds should stand
Upon the soul's debatable land,
And between choice and Providence
Divide the circle of events;
But He who knows our frame is just,   585
Merciful and compassionate,
And full of sweet assurances
And hope for all the language is,
That He remembereth we are dust!

At last the great logs, crumbling low,   590
Sent out a dull and duller glow,
The bull's-eye watch that hung in view,
Ticking its weary circuit through,
Pointed with mutely warning sign
Its black hand to the hour of nine.   595
That sign the pleasant circle broke:
My uncle ceased his pipe to smoke,
Knocked from its bowl the refuse gray,
And laid it tenderly away;
Then roused himself to safely cover   600
The dull red brands with ashes over.
And while, with care, our mother laid
The work aside, her steps she stayed
One moment, seeking to express
Her grateful sense of happiness   605

For food and shelter, warmth and health,
And love's contentment more than wealth,
With simple wishes (not the weak,
Vain prayers which no fulfilment seek,
But such as warm the generous heart,   610
O'er-prompt to do with Heaven its part)
That none might lack, that bitter night,
For bread and clothing, warmth and light.

Within our beds awhile we heard
The wind that round the gables roared,   615
With now and then a ruder shock,
Which made our very bedsteads rock.
We heard the loosened clapboards tost,
The board-nails snapping in the frost;
And on us, through the unplastered wall,   620
Felt the light sifted snow-flakes fall.
But sleep stole on, as sleep will do
When hearts are light and life is new;
Faint and more faint the murmurs grew,
Till in the summer-land of dreams   625
They softened to the sound of streams,
Low stir of leaves, and dip of oars,
And lapsing waves on quiet shores.

Next morn we wakened with the shout
Of merry voices high and clear;   630
And saw the teamsters drawing near
To break the drifted highways out.
Down the long hillside treading slow
We saw the half-buried oxen go,
Shaking the snow from heads uptost,   635
Their straining nostrils white with frost.
Before our door the straggling train
Drew up, an added team to gain.
The elders threshed their hands a-cold,
   Passed, with the cider-mug, their jokes   640
   From lip to lip; the younger folks
Down the loose snow-banks, wrestling, rolled,
Then toiled again the cavalcade
   O'er windy hill, through clogged ravine,
   And woodland paths that wound between   645
Low drooping pine-boughs winter-weighed.
From every barn a team afoot,
At every house a new recruit,
Where, drawn by Nature's subtlest law,
Haply the watchful young men saw   650
Sweet doorway pictures of the curls
And curious eyes of merry girls,
Lifting their hands in mock defence
Against the snow-ball's compliments,
And reading in each missive tost   655
The charm with Eden never lost.

We heard once more the sleigh-bells' sound;
   And, following where the teamsters led,
The wise old Doctor went his round,
Just pausing at our door to say,   660
In the brief autocratic way
Of one who, prompt at Duty's call,
Was free to urge her claim on all,
   That some poor neighbor sick abed
At night our mother's aid would need.   665
For, one in generous thought and deed,
   What mattered in the sufferer's sight
   The Quaker matron's inward light,
The Doctor's mail of Calvin's creed?
All hearts confess the saints elect   670
   Who, twain in faith, in love agree,
And melt not in an acid sect
   The Christian pearl of charity!

So days went on: a week had passed
Since the great world was heard from last.   675
The Almanac we studied o'er,
Read and reread our little store
Of books and pamphlets, scarce a score;
One harmless novel, mostly hid
From younger eyes, a book forbid,   680
And poetry (or good or bad,
A single book was all we had),
Where Ellwood's meek, drab-skirted Muse,
   A stranger to the heathen Nine,
   Sang, with a somewhat nasal whine,   685
The wars of David and the Jews.
At last the floundering carrier bore
The village paper to our door.
Lo! broadening outward as we read,
To warmer zones the horizon spread;   690
In panoramic length unrolled
We saw the marvels that it told.
Before us passed the painted Creeks,
   And daft McGregor on his raids
   In Costa Rica's everglades.   695
And up Taygetos winding slow
Rode Ypsilanti's Mainote Greeks,
A Turk's head at each saddle-bow!
Welcome to us its week-old news,
Its corner for the rustic Muse,   700
   Its monthly gauge of snow and rain,
Its record, mingling in a breath
The wedding bell and dirge of death:
Jest, anecdote, and love-lorn tale,
The latest culprit sent to jail;   705
Its hue and cry of stolen and lost,
Its vendue sales and goods at cost,
   And traffic calling loud for gain.
We felt the stir of hall and street,

The pulse of life that round us beat; 710
The chill embargo of the snow
Was melted in the genial glow;
Wide swung again our ice-locked door,
And all the world was ours once more!

Clasp, Angel of the backward look 715
And folded wings of ashen gray
And voice of echoes far away,
The brazen covers of thy book;
The weird palimpsest old and vast,
Wherein thou hid'st the spectral past; 720
Where, closely mingling, pale and glow
The characters of joy and woe;
The monographs of outlived years,
Or smile-illumed or dim with tears,
    Green hills of life that slope to death, 725
And haunts of home, whose vistaed trees
Shade off to mournful cypresses
    With the white amaranths underneath.
Even while I look, I can but heed
    The restless sands' incessant fall, 730
Importunate hours that hours succeed,
Each clamorous with its own sharp need,
    And duty keeping pace with all.
Shut down and clasp the heavy lids;
I hear again the voice that bids 735
The dreamer leave his dream midway
For larger hopes and graver fears;
Life greatens in these later years,
The century's aloe flowers to-day!
Yet, haply, in some lull of life, 740
Some Truce of God, which breaks its strife,
The worldling's eyes shall gather dew,
    Dreaming in throngful city ways
Of winter joys his boyhood knew;
And dear and early friends — the few 745
Who yet remain — shall pause to view
    These Flemish pictures of old days;
Sit with me by the homestead hearth,
And stretch the hands of memory forth
    To warm them at the wood-fire's blaze!
And thanks untraced to lips unknown 751
Shall greet me like the odors blown
From unseen meadows newly mown,
Or lilies floating in some pond,
Wood-fringed, the wayside gaze beyond; 755
The traveller owns the grateful sense
Of sweetness near, he knows not whence,
And, pausing, takes with forehead bare
The benediction of the air.

Abraham Davenport

(1866)

✵ In blank verse — a form he rarely used —
Whittier here shows a terseness and ironic undertone in keeping with a New England type of character he evidently relished. It is a type that much
later found a poetic voice in the "wisdom and grace"
and "shrewd dry humor" of Robert Frost.

"The famous Dark Day of New England, May 19,
1780, was a physical puzzle for many years to our
ancestors, but its occurrence brought something
more than philosophical speculation into the minds
of those who passed through it. The incident of
Colonel Abraham Davenport's sturdy protest is a
matter of history" (Whittier).

In the old days (a custom laid aside
With breeches and cocked hats) the people
    sent
Their wisest men to make the public laws.
And so, from a brown homestead, where the
    Sound
Drinks the small tribute of the Mianas, 5
Waved over by the woods of Rippowams,
And hallowed by pure lives and tranquil deaths,
Stamford sent up to the councils of the State
Wisdom and grace in Abraham Davenport.

'Twas on a May-day of the far old year 10
Seventeen hundred eighty, that there fell
Over the bloom and sweet life of the Spring,
Over the fresh earth and the heaven of noon,
A horror of great darkness, like the night
In day of which the Norland sagas tell, — 15
The Twilight of the Gods. The low-hung sky
Was black with ominous clouds, save where its
    rim
Was fringed with a dull glow, like that which
    climbs
The crater's sides from the red hell below.
Birds ceased to sing, and all the barn-yard
    fowls 20
Roosted; the cattle at the pasture bars
Lowed, and looked homeward; bats on leathern
    wings
Flitted abroad; the sounds of labor died;
Men prayed, and women wept; all ears grew
    sharp
To hear the doom-blast of the trumpet shat-
    ter 25
The black sky, that the dreadful face of Christ
Might look from the rent clouds, not as he
    looked

A loving guest at Bethany, but stern
As Justice and inexorable Law.

Meanwhile in the old State House, dim as
    ghosts   30
Sat the lawgivers of Connecticut,
Trembling beneath their legislative robes.
"It is the Lord's Great Day! Let us adjourn,"
Some said; and then, as if with one accord,
All eyes were turned to Abraham Davenport. 35
He rose, slow cleaving with his steady voice
The intolerable hush. "This well may be
The Day of Judgment which the world awaits;
But be it so or not, I only know
My present duty, and my Lord's command
To occupy till He come. So at the post   41
Where He hath set me in his providence,
I choose, for one, to meet Him face to face, —
No faithless servant frightened from my task,
But ready when the Lord of the harvest calls; 45
And therefore, with all reverence, I would say,
Let God do his work, we will see to ours."

Bring in the candles." And they brought them
    in.

Then by the flaring lights the Speaker read,
Albeit with husky voice and shaking hands,
An act to amend an act to regulate   51
The shad and alewive fisheries. Whereupon
Wisely and well spake Abraham Davenport,
Straight to the questions, with no figures of
    speech
Save the ten Arab signs, yet not without   55
The shrewd dry humor natural to the man:
His awe-struck colleagues listening all the while,
Between the pauses of his argument,
To hear the thunder of the wrath of God   59
Break from the hollow trumpet of the cloud.

And there he stands in memory to this day,
Erect, self-poised, a rugged face, half seen
Against the background of unnatural dark,
A witness to the ages as they pass,
That simple duty hath no place for fear.   65

Henry Wadsworth Longfellow [1807–1882]

Today we should be ready to read Longfellow justly, now that his fame has been, by turns, inflated and deflated. It was inflated at least till the end of the nineteenth century. He was the most widely read poet in the English language. He was the first American poet to be memorialized by a bust in Westminster Abbey. He was translated into a score of foreign tongues, from Russian to Portuguese. He brought the color and richness of the European past, as well as the vigorous native tradition, home to American readers, and at the same time he won the applause of most critics and men of letters. Unfortunately Longfellow's great fame rested largely on his inferior work, such as "The Psalm of Life," "The Wreck of the Hesperus," "The Village Blacksmith," and "Excelsior," short poems that are sentimental or didactic or both, shallow in feeling and feeble in technique. It rested also on several long poems, *Evangeline, Hiawatha, The Courtship of Miles Standish,* not only long but long-winded, tame and artificial, despite their frequent charm and metrical proficiency.

As late as 1929, according to a national poll of newspaper readers, America's favorite poem was still Longfellow's "Psalm of Life," and the other poems named above still ranked high in popular favor. But among critics and men of letters generally, his fame rapidly subsided after 1900, and in the rebellious and tumultuous 1920's he was mercilessly attacked as Victorian, genteel, preachy, silly, unreal — out of touch with the realities of American life. By the early 1930's a critic like Ludwig Lewisohn was saying: "Am I slaying the thrice slain? Who, except wretched schoolchildren, now reads Longfellow? . . . The thing to establish in America is not that Longfellow was a very small poet, but that he did not partake of the poetic character at all."

This critic erred twice: Longfellow *was* still esteemed popularly, and he *was* certainly a poet — a good one. His true accomplishments had already been apparent to Paul Elmer More at the time of the centenary in 1907 (*Shelburne Essays*, Fifth Series). Later came discerning essays by G. R. Elliott (*The Cycle of Modern Poetry*) and H. M. Jones (*American Writers on American Literature*, ed. John Macy), and the able introduction in the Longfellow volume of the American Writers Series by Odell Shepard. These and other critics have gradually enabled us to avoid the excesses of both the nineteenth century inflation and the twentieth century deflation, and to focus attention upon what seems, in sober afterthought, to be Longfellow's best achievement.

Longfellow came from Portland, Maine. His mother was a descendant of John Alden, a *Mayflower* Pilgrim, his father a lawyer and trustee of Bowdoin College, where the boy Henry entered as a sophomore. One of his classmates was Hawthorne. When he graduated in 1825 he had already shown enough ability at writing verse to make him desire a literary career. His father wished him to have a legal career. Bowdoin settled the matter by establishing a professorship in modern languages and sending him to Europe for three years to prepare himself for it. He returned with knowledge of German, French, Italian, and Spanish, and, late in 1829, joined the faculty at his alma mater in Maine.

He had been teaching at Bowdoin for six years when Harvard offered him the Smith professorship of modern languages. For further preparation he spent another year in Europe — where his first wife, Mary Potter, died in childbirth — and then began his long residence in Cambridge. In 1843 he married Frances Appleton, whom he had met in Switzerland and courted for seven years. She was the daughter of one of Boston's wealthiest merchants, who bought beautiful Craigie House for the young professor and his bride. In this house their six children were born.

The professor was soon a successful author. His early Irvingesque prose work, *Outre-Mer: A Pilgrimage Beyond the Sea*, was followed by the Germanic romance *Hyperion*. In the same year (1839) came his first book of poems, *Voices of the Night*, including the vastly popular "Psalm of Life" and the far superior "Hymn to the Night." Other volumes of poems quickly followed, including *Ballads and Other Poems, Poems on Slavery, The Belfry of Bruges and Other Poems*, and the first of his highly popular long narrative poems, *Evangeline*. In 1854 the poet was chafing at the professor's duties, and he resigned from Harvard after eighteen years of service during which he had introduced thousands of young men to the literatures of Europe. The next year came *Hiawatha*, his long Indian poem, and three years later *The Courtship of Miles Standish*, in which he used his Puritan background. But the even tenor of his life and writings was broken when his wife was burned to death. After this he brought out *Tales of a Wayside Inn*, largely done before his wife's death, and buried himself and his pain in the discipline of translating Dante's *Divina Commedia*. Another trip abroad brought him honorary degrees from Oxford and Cambridge and a private audience with Queen Victoria.

Further reading: *Evangeline, Hiawatha*, or *The Courtship of Miles Standish*. Odell Shepard, ed., *Henry Wadsworth Longfellow* (American Writers Series), 1934. Lawrance Thompson, *Young Longfellow*, 1938. H. S. Gorman, *A Victorian American: Henry Wadsworth Longfellow*, 1926. Critical essays by P. E. More, G. R. Elliott, and H. M. Jones (see third paragraph of the introductory note above).

Hymn to the Night

Ασπασίη, τρίλλιστος

(w. 1839)

"Welcome, thrice prayed-for" (*Iliad*, VIII, 488) seemed the repose of the Night to Longfellow, "while sitting at my chamber window, on one of the balmiest nights of the year. I endeavored to reproduce the impression of the hour and scene."

Despite the Homeric quotation and the reference to Orestes — in the tragedies of Aeschylus he is pursued by the Furies but at length finds peace — this poem is one of romantic mood. The title and the mood are reminiscent of the *Hymns to the Night* by the German poet Novalis, who had praised "holy, ineffable, mysterious night" as a symbol of the inner life. Common in romanticism was the preference of night to day.

The mood is conveyed chiefly through metaphors, beginning with one of which Poe said in his wholesale way, "No poem ever opened with a beauty more august."

I heard the trailing garments of the Night
  Sweep through her marble halls!
I saw her sable skirts all fringed with light
  From the celestial walls!

I felt her presence, by its spell of might,   5
  Stoop o'er me from above;
The calm, majestic presence of the Night,
  As of the one I love.

I heard the sounds of sorrow and delight,
  The manifold, soft chimes,   10
That fill the haunted chambers of the Night,
  Like some old poet's rhymes.

From the cool cisterns of the midnight air
  My spirit drank repose;
The fountain of perpetual peace flows
    there, —   15
  From those deep cisterns flows.

O holy Night! from thee I learn to bear
  What man has borne before!
Thou layest thy finger on the lips of Care,
  And they complain no more.   20

Peace! Peace! Orestes-like I breathe this prayer!
  Descend with broad-winged flight,
The welcome, the thrice-prayed for, the most
    fair,
  The best-beloved Night!

The Skeleton In Armor

(w. 1840)

In his bookish way, Longfellow had "been looking," as he said, "at the old Northern Sagas, and thinking of a series of ballads or a romantic poem on the deeds of the first bold Viking who crossed to this western world." Noting the discovery of the skeleton of a supposed Norseman at Fall River, Massachusetts, Longfellow wrote this ballad. It attracted romantic readers such as Poe, who said: "In 'The Skeleton in Armor' we find a pure and perfect thesis artistically treated. We find the beauty of bold courage and self-confidence, of love and maiden devotion, of reckless adventure, and finally of life contemning grief. . . . The meter is simple, sonorous, well-balanced, and fully adapted to the subject."

"Speak! speak! thou fearful guest!
  Who, with thy hollow breast,
  Still in rude armor drest,
    Comest to daunt me!
Wrapt not in Eastern balms,   5
  But with thy fleshless palms
  Stretched, as if asking alms,
    Why dost thou haunt me?"

Then from those cavernous eyes
  Pale flashes seemed to rise,   10
  As when the Northern skies
    Gleam in December;
And, like the water's flow
  Under December's snow,
  Came a dull voice of woe   15
    From the heart's chamber.

"I was a Viking old!
  My deeds, though manifold,
  No Skald in song has told,
    No Saga taught thee!   20
Take heed that in thy verse
  Thou dost the tale rehearse,
  Else dread a dead man's curse;
    For this I sought thee.

"Far in the Northern Land,   25
  By the wild Baltic's strand,
  I, with my childish hand,
    Tamed the gerfalcon;
And, with my skates fast-bound,
  Skimmed the half-frozen Sound,   30
  That the poor whimpering hound
    Trembled to walk on.

"Oft to his frozen lair
Tracked I the grisly bear,
While from my path the hare   35
    Fled like a shadow;
Oft through the forest dark
Followed the were-wolf's bark,
Until the soaring lark
    Sang from the meadow.   40

"But when I older grew,
Joining a corsair's crew,
O'er the dark sea I flew
    With the marauders.
Wild was the life we led;   45
Many the souls that sped,
Many the hearts that bled,
    By our stern orders.

"Many a wassail-bout
Wore the long winter out;   50
Often our midnight shout
    Set the cocks crowing,
As we the Berserk's tale
Measured in cups of ale,
Draining the oaken pail   55
    Filled to o'erflowing.

"Once as I told in glee
Tales of the stormy sea,
Soft eyes did gaze on me,
    Burning yet tender;   60
And as the white stars shine
On the dark Norway pine,
On that dark heart of mine
    Fell their soft splendor.

"I wooed the blue-eyed maid,   65
Yielding, yet half afraid,
And in the forest's shade
    Our vows were plighted.
Under its loosened vest
Fluttered her little breast,   70
Like birds within their nest
    By the hawk frighted.

"Bright in her father's hall
Shields gleamed upon the wall,
Loud sang the minstrels all,   75
    Chanting his glory;
When of old Hildebrand
I asked his daughter's hand,
Mute did the minstrels stand
    To hear my story.   80

"While the brown ale he quaffed,
Loud then the champion laughed,
And as the wind-gusts waft
    The sea-foam brightly,
So the loud laugh of scorn   85
Out of those lips unshorn,
From the deep drinking-horn
    Blew the foam lightly.

"She was a Prince's child,
I but a Viking wild,   90
And though she blushed and smiled,
    I was discarded!
Should not the dove so white
Follow the sea-mew's flight?
Why did they leave that night   95
    Her nest unguarded?

"Scarce had I put to sea,
Bearing the maid with me,
Fairest of all was she
    Among the Norsemen!   100
When on the white sea-strand,
Waving his armèd hand,
Saw we old Hildebrand,
    With twenty horsemen.

"Then launched they to the blast,   105
Bent like a reed each mast,
Yet we were gaining fast,
    When the wind failed us;
And with a sudden flaw
Came round the gusty Skaw,   110
So that our foe we saw
    Laugh as he hailed us.

"And as to catch the gale
Round veered the flapping sail,
'Death!' was the helmsman's hail,   115
    'Death without quarter!'
Midships with iron keel
Struck we her ribs of steel;
Down her black hulk did reel
    Through the black water!   120

"As with his wings aslant,
Sails the fierce cormorant,
Seeking some rocky haunt,
    With his prey laden, —
So toward the open main,   125
Beating to sea again,
Through the wild hurricane,
    Bore I the maiden.

"Three weeks we westward bore,
And when the storm was o'er,   130
Cloud-like we saw the shore
   Stretching to leeward;
There for my lady's bower
Built I the lofty tower,
Which, to this very hour,   135
   Stands looking seaward.

"There lived we many years;
Time dried the maiden's tears;
She had forgot her fears,
   She was a mother;   140
Death closed her mild blue eyes;
Under that tower she lies;
Ne'er shall the sun arise
   On such another!

"Still grew my bosom then,   145
Still as a stagnant fen!
Hateful to me were men,
   The sunlight hateful!
In the vast forest here,
Clad in my warlike gear,   150
Fell I upon my spear,
   Oh, death was grateful!

"Thus, seamed with many scars,
Bursting these prison bars
Up to its native stars   155
   My soul ascended!
There from the flowing bowl
Deep drinks the warrior's soul,
Skoal! to the Northland! *skoal!*"
   Thus the tale ended.   160

Nuremberg

Longfellow visited the old Bavarian city in 1842, and two years later communicated his delight to his readers in the New World.

From Longfellow's notes: Line 12: "Melchior Pfinzing was one of the most celebrated poets of the sixteenth century. The hero of his *Teuerdank* was the reigning Emperor, Maximilian." Line 38: "The Twelve Wise Masters was the title of the original corporation of the Mastersingers. Hans Sachs, the cobbler of Nuremberg, though not one of the original twelve, was the most renowned of the Mastersingers, as well as the most voluminous."

In the valley of the Pegnitz, where across broad
   meadow-lands
Rise the blue Franconian mountains, Nuremberg, the ancient, stands.

Quaint old town of toil and traffic, quaint old
   town of art and song,
Memories haunt thy pointed gables, like the
   rooks that round them throng:

Memories of the Middle Ages, when the emperors, rough and bold,   5
Had their dwelling in thy castle, time-defying,
   centuries old;

And thy brave and thrifty burghers boasted, in
   their uncouth rhyme,
That their great imperial city stretched its hand
   through every clime.

In the court-yard of the castle, bound with
   many an iron band,
Stands the mighty linden planted by Queen
   Cunigunde's hand;   10

On the square the oriel window, where in old
   heroic days
Sat the poet Melchior singing Kaiser Maximilian's praise,

Everywhere I see around me rise the wondrous
   world of Art:
Fountains wrought with richest sculpture standing in the common mart;

And above cathedral doorways saints and bishops
   carved in stone,   15
By a former age commissioned as apostles to
   our own.

In the church of sainted Sebald sleeps enshrined his holy dust,
And in bronze the Twelve Apostles guard from
   age to age their trust;

In the church of sainted Lawrence stands a pix
   of sculpture rare,
Like the foamy sheaf of fountains, rising
   through the painted air.   20

Here, when Art was still religion, with a simple,
   reverent heart,
Lived and labored Albrecht Dürer, the Evangelist of Art;

Hence in silence and in sorrow, toiling still with
   busy hand,
Like an emigrant he wandered, seeking for the
   Better Land.

Emigravit is the inscription on the tombstone
    where he lies;   25
Dead he is not, but departed, — for the artist
    never dies.

Fairer seems the ancient city, and the sunshine
    seems more fair,
That he once has trod its pavement; that he
    once has breathed its air!

Through these streets so broad and stately, these
    obscure and dismal lanes,
Walked of yore the Mastersingers, chanting
    rude poetic strains.   30

From remote and sunless suburbs came they
    to the friendly guild,
Building nests in Fame's great temple, as in
    spouts the swallows build.

As the weaver plied the shuttle, wove he too
    the mystic rhyme,
And the smith his iron measures hammered to
    the anvil's chime;

Thanking God, whose boundless wisdom makes
    the flowers of poesy bloom   35
In the forge's dust and cinders, in the tissues
    of the loom.

Here Hans Sachs, the cobbler-poet, laureate of
    the gentle craft,
Wisest of the Twelve Wise Masters, in huge
    folios sang and laughed.

But his house is now an ale-house, with a
    nicely sanded floor,
And a garland in the window, and his face
    above the door;   40

Painted by some humble artist, as in Adam
    Puschman's song,
As the old man gray and dove-like, with his
    great beard white and long.

And at night the swart mechanic comes to
    drown his cark and care,
Quaffing ale from pewter tankards, in the
    master's antique chair.

Vanished is the ancient splendor, and before
    my dreamy eye   45
Wave these mingled shapes and figures, like a
    faded tapestry.

Not thy Councils, not thy Kaisers, win for thee
    the world's regard;
But thy painter, Albrecht Dürer, and Hans
    Sachs thy cobbler bard.

Thus, O Nuremberg, a wanderer from a region
    far away,
As he paced thy streets and court-yards, sang
    in thought his careless lay: 50

Gathering from the pavement's crevice, as a
    floweret of the soil,
The nobility of labor, — the long pedigree of
    toil.

The Arsenal at Springfield
(1844)

On his wedding journey Longfellow passed through Springfield, Massachusetts, and visited the United States arsenal in company with Charles Sumner. "While Mr. Sumner was endeavoring," says S. Longfellow, "to impress upon the attendant that the money expended upon these weapons of war would have been much better spent upon a great library, Mrs. Longfellow pleased her husband by remarking how like an organ looked the ranged and shining gun-barrels which covered the walls from floor to ceiling, and suggesting what mournful music Death would bring from them. 'We grew quite warlike against war,' she wrote, 'and I urged H. to write a peace poem.'"

This is the Arsenal. From floor to ceiling,
    Like a huge organ, rise the burnished arms;
But from their silent pipes no anthem pealing
    Startles the villages with strange alarms.

Ah! what a sound will rise, how wild and
    dreary,   5
    When the death-angel touches those swift
        keys!
What loud lament and dismal Miserere
    Will mingle with their awful symphonies!

I hear even now the infinite fierce chorus,
    The cries of agony, the endless groan,   10
Which, through the ages that have gone before
    us,
    In long reverberations reach our own.

On helm and harness rings the Saxon hammer,
    Through Cimbric forest roars the Norseman's
        song,

And loud, amid the universal clamor, 15
  O'er distant deserts sounds the Tartar gong.

I hear the Florentine, who from his palace
  Wheels out his battle-bell with dreadful din,
And Aztec priests upon their teocallis
  Beat the wild war-drum made of serpent's
    skin; 20

The tumult of each sacked and burning village:
  The shout that every prayer for mercy drowns;
The soldiers' revels in the midst of pillage;
  The wail of famine in beleaguered towns;

The bursting shell, the gateway wrenched
    asunder, 25
  The rattling musketry, the clashing blade;
And ever and anon, in tones of thunder,
  The diapason of the cannonade.

Is it, O man, with such discordant noises,
  With such accursed instruments as these,
Thou drownest Nature's sweet and kindly
    voices, 31
  And jarrest the celestial harmonies?

Were half the power, that fills the world with
    terror,
  Were half the wealth, bestowed on camps
    and courts, 34
Given to redeem the human mind from error,
  There were no need of arsenals nor forts:

The warrior's name would be a name ab-
    horrèd!
  And every nation, that should lift again
Its hand against a brother, on its forehead
  Would wear forevermore the curse of
    Cain! 40

Down the dark future, through long genera-
    tions,
  The echoing sounds grow fainter and then
    cease;
And like a bell, with solemn, sweet vibrations,
  I hear once more the voice of Christ say,
    "Peace!"

Peace! and no longer from its brazen por-
    tals 45
  The blast of War's great organ shakes the
    skies!
But beautiful as songs of the immortals,
  The holy melodies of love arise.

The Day is Done

(1844)

Proem to *The Waif*, a collection of poems in which Longfellow represented the "humbler" poets. He suggests that a mood of restlessness and longing can be quieted by reading aloud some simple heart-felt poem. Is his own poem an example of this? Is it marred by sentimentalism? As in his "Hymn to the Night," the metaphors win attention.

The day is done, and the darkness
  Falls from the wings of Night,
As a feather is wafted downward
  From an eagle in his flight.

I see the lights of the village 5
  Gleam through the rain and the mist,
And a feeling of sadness comes o'er me
  That my soul cannot resist:

A feeling of sadness and longing,
  That is not akin to pain, 10
And resembles sorrow only
  As the mist resembles the rain.

Come, read to me some poem,
  Some simple and heartfelt lay,
That shall soothe this restless feeling, 15
  And banish the thoughts of day.

Not from the grand old masters,
  Not from the bards sublime,
Whose distant footsteps echo
  Through the corridors of Time. 20

For, like strains of martial music,
  Their mighty thoughts suggest
Life's endless toil and endeavor;
  And to-night I long for rest.

Read from some humbler poet, 25
  Whose songs gushed from his heart,
As showers from the clouds of summer,
  Or tears from the eyelids start;

Who, through long days of labor,
  And nights devoid of ease, 30
Still heard in his soul the music
  Of wonderful melodies.

Such songs have power to quiet
  The restless pulse of care,
And come like the benediction 35
  That follows after prayer.

Then read from the treasured volume
   The poem of thy choice,
And lend to the rhyme of the poet
   The beauty of thy voice.   40

And the night shall be filled with music,
   And the cares, that infest the day,
Shall fold their tents, like the Arabs,
   And as silently steal away.

The Fire of Drift-Wood

Devereux Farm, near Marblehead

(1848)

Though not widely familiar, this clearly seems
to be one of Longfellow's successful poems. It states
no obtrusive "moral." It manages without the aid
of elaborate figures of speech. Within a firmly developed unity, it harmonizes a striking scene, a complex retrospective mood, a sensitively simple diction,
and the subdued music of the verse. Less immediately obvious is the use of contrast (the turbulence
of sea and wind vs. the quiet talk indoors) and of
similarity (the old farmhouse, old wrecks, old times,
also the two fires brought together at the end).

We sat within the farm-house old,
   Whose windows, looking o'er the bay,
Gave to the sea-breeze damp and cold
   An easy entrance, night and day.

Not far away we saw the port,   5
   The strange, old-fashioned, silent town,
The lighthouse, the dismantled fort,
   The wooden houses, quaint and brown.

We sat and talked until the night,
   Descending, filled the little room;   10
Our faces faded from the sight,
   Our voices only broke the gloom.

We spake of many a vanished scene,
   Of what we once had thought and said,
Of what had been, and might have been,   15
   And who was changed, and who was dead;

And all that fills the hearts of friends,
   When first they feel, with secret pain,
Their lives henceforth have separate ends,
   And never can be one again;   20

The first slight swerving of the heart,
   That words are powerless to express,
And leave it still unsaid in part,
   Or say it in too great excess.

The very tones in which we spake   25
   Had something strange, I could but mark;
The leaves of memory seemed to make
   A mournful rustling in the dark.

Oft died the words upon our lips,
   As suddenly, from out the fire   30
Built of the wreck of stranded ships,
   The flames would leap and then expire.

And, as their splendor flashed and failed,
   We thought of wrecks upon the main,
Of ships dismasted, that were hailed   35
   And sent no answer back again.

The windows, rattling in their frames,
   The ocean, roaring up the beach,
The gusty blast, the bickering flames,
   All mingled vaguely in our speech;   40

Until they made themselves a part
   Of fancies floating through the brain,
The long-lost ventures of the heart,
   That send no answers back again.

O flames that glowed! O hearts that yearned!
   They were indeed too much akin,   46
The drift-wood fire without that burned,
   The thoughts that burned and glowed within.

The Jewish Cemetery at Newport

(w. 1852)

At Newport, Rhode Island, on July 9, 1852,
Longfellow wrote in his diary: "Went this morning
into the Jewish burying-ground, with a polite old
gentleman who keeps the key. There are few graves;
nearly all are low tombstones of marble with Hebrew
inscriptions, and a few words added in English or
Portuguese."
   Odell Shepard comments: "The poem . . . is written in the difficult stanza of Gray's 'Elegy' and in
the mood of that poem. Comparison will show that
Longfellow is as much superior to Gray in thought-
structure and 'sense of the whole' as he is inferior
in vividness and intensity of phrase and image."

How strange it seems! These Hebrews in their
      graves,
   Close by the street of this fair seaport town,
Silent beside the never-silent waves,
   At rest in all this moving up and down!

The trees are white with dust, that o'er their
    sleep   5
Wave their broad curtains in the southwind's
    breath,
While underneath these leafy tents they keep
    The long, mysterious Exodus of Death.

And these sepulchral stones, so old and brown,
    That pave with level flags their burial-
    place,   10
Seem like the tablets of the Law, thrown down
    And broken by Moses at the mountain's base.

The very names recorded here are strange,
    Of foreign accent, and of different climes;
Alvares and Rivera interchange   15
    With Abraham and Jacob of old times.

"Blessed be God! for he created Death!"
    The mourners said, "and Death is rest and
    peace;"
Then added, in the certainty of faith,   19
    "And giveth Life that nevermore shall cease."

Closed are the portals of their Synagogue,
    No Psalms of David now the silence break,
No Rabbi reads the ancient Decalogue
    In the grand dialect the Prophets spake.

Gone are the living, but the dead remain,   25
    And not neglected; for a hand unseen,
Scattering its bounty, like a summer rain,
    Still keeps their graves and their remembrance
    green.

How came they here? What burst of Christian
    hate,
What persecution, merciless and blind,   30
Drove o'er the sea — that desert desolate —
    These Ishmaels and Hagars of mankind?

They lived in narrow streets and lanes obscure,
    Ghetto and Judenstrass, in mirk and mire;
Taught in the school of patience to endure
    The life of anguish and the death of fire.   36

All their lives long, with the unleavened bread
    And bitter herbs of exile and its fears,
The wasting famine of the heart they fed,   39
    And slaked its thirst with marah of their tears.

Anathema maranatha! was the cry
    That rang from town to town, from street to
    street;

At every gate the accursed Mordecai
    Was mocked and jeered, and spurned by
    Christian feet.

Pride and humiliation hand in hand   45
    Walked with them through the world
    where'er they went;
Trampled and beaten were they as the sand,
    And yet unshaken as the continent.

For in the background figures vague and vast
    Of patriarchs and of prophets rose sublime,
And all the great traditions of the Past   51
    They saw reflected in the coming time.

And thus forever with reverted look
    The mystic volume of the world they read,
Spelling it backward, like a Hebrew book,   55
    Till life became a Legend of the Dead.

But ah! what once has been shall be no more!
    The groaning earth in travail and in pain
Brings forth its races, but does not restore,
    And the dead nations never rise again.   60

My Lost Youth

❧ Longfellow's *Journal:* "March 29, 1855 — At
night as I lie in bed, a poem comes into my mind,
— a memory of Portland, — my native town, the
city by the sea. . . ." "March 30 — Wrote the
poem; and am rather pleased with it, and with
the bringing in of the two lines of the old Lapland
song.
    A boy's will is the wind's will,
And the thoughts of youth are long, long thoughts."
These two lines Longfellow translated literally from
the German rendering of the Lapland song by
Herder, precursor of the German romantic school.
    The sea-fight referred to in the fifth stanza oc-
curred in 1813: it "was the engagement," Longfellow said, "between the Enterprise and Boxer off
the harbor of Portland, in which both captains were
slain. They were buried side by side in the cemetery
on Mountjoy."

Often I think of the beautiful town
    That is seated by the sea;
Often in thought go up and down
The pleasant streets of that dear old town,
    And my youth comes back to me.   5
      And a verse of a Lapland song
      Is haunting my memory still:
      "A boy's will is the wind's will,
And the thoughts of youth are long, long
    thoughts."

I can see the shadowy lines of its trees,   10
  And catch, in sudden gleams,
The sheen of the far-surrounding seas,
And islands that were the Hesperides
  Of all my boyish dreams.
    And the burden of that old song,   15
    It murmurs and whispers still:
    "A boy's will is the wind's will,
And the thoughts of youth are long, long
    thoughts."

I remember the black wharves and the slips,
  And the sea-tides tossing free;   20
And Spanish sailors with bearded lips,
And the beauty and mystery of the ships,
  And the magic of the sea.
    And the voice of that wayward song
    Is singing and saying still: 25
    "A boy's will is the wind's will,
And the thoughts of youth are long, long
    thoughts."

I remember the bulwarks by the shore,
  And the fort upon the hill;
The sunrise gun, with its hollow roar,   30
The drum-beat repeated o'er and o'er,
  And the bugle wild and shrill.
    And the music of that old song
    Throbs in my memory still:
    "A boy's will is the wind's will,   35
And the thoughts of youth are long, long
    thoughts."

I remember the sea-fight far away,
  How it thundered o'er the tide!
And the dead captains, as they lay
In their graves, o'erlooking the tranquil bay   40
  Where they in battle died.
    And the sound of that mournful song
    Goes through me with a thrill:
    "A boy's will is the wind's will,
And the thoughts of youth are long, long
    thoughts."   45

I can see the breezy dome of groves,
  The shadows of Deering's Woods;
And the friendships old and the early loves
Come back with a Sabbath sound, as of doves
  In quiet neighborhoods.   50
    And the verse of that sweet old song,

It flutters and murmurs still:
    "A boy's will is the wind's will,
And the thoughts of youth are long, long
    thoughts."   54

I remember the gleams and glooms that dart
  Across the school-boy's brain;
The song and the silence in the heart,
That in part are prophecies, and in part
  Are longings wild and vain.
    And the voice of that fitful song   60
    Sings on, and is never still:
    "A boy's will is the wind's will,
And the thoughts of youth are long, long
    thoughts."

There are things of which I may not speak;
  There are dreams that cannot die;   65
There are thoughts that make the strong heart
  weak,
And bring a pallor into the cheek,
  And a mist before the eye.
    And the words of that fatal song
    Come over me like a chill: 70
    "A boy's will is the wind's will,
And the thoughts of youth are long, long
    thoughts."

Strange to me now are the forms I meet
  When I visit the dear old town;
But the native air is pure and sweet,   75
And the trees that o'ershadow each well-known
  street,
  As they balance up and down,
    Are singing the beautiful song,
    Are sighing and whispering still:
    "A boy's will is the wind's will,   80
And the thoughts of youth are long, long
    thoughts."

And Deering's Woods are fresh and fair,
  And with joy that is almost pain
My heart goes back to wander there,
And among the dreams of the days that were,
  I find my lost youth again.   86
    And the strange and beautiful song,
    The groves are repeating it still:
    "A boy's will is the wind's will,
And the thoughts of youth are long, long
    thoughts."   90

Sonnets

Mezzo Cammin

(w. 1842)

The title is taken from Dante's *Divine Comedy*, meaning "Midway upon the journey of life." Longfellow here assesses his own life at mid-point.

In line 7, "a care" refers to the death of his first wife.

Half of my life is gone, and I have let
  The years slip from me and have not fulfilled
  The aspiration of my youth, to build
  Some tower of song with lofty parapet.
Not indolence, nor pleasure, nor the fret   5
  Of restless passions that would not be stilled,
  But sorrow, and a care that almost killed,
  Kept me from what I may accomplish yet;
Though, half-way up the hill, I see the Past
  Lying beneath me with its sounds and sights, —   10
A city in the twilight dim and vast,
With smoking roofs, soft bells, and gleaming lights, —
And hear above me on the autumnal blast
The cataract of Death far thundering from the heights.

Divina Commedia

(w. 1864–1867)

Longfellow wrote these sonnets during the long labor of translating the *Divine Comedy*. He thinks of Dante's magnificent imaginative structure as the poetic equivalent of a medieval cathedral. Building and poem alike have an architectural grandeur, a correspondence of form and function, a unity dominating an endless variety. At the same time the cathedral image suggests the spiritual refuge which the poem afforded Longfellow, a contemplative retreat from the harsh realities of "the Time" (to be specific, the Civil War and the death of his wife by fire).

I

All men carry burdens, as Longfellow intimates by beginning not with himself but with a laborer who has come to the cathedral door. In the quiet of the church, laborer and poet alike will pray and find peace, forgetting the clamor and sorrows of the world. Time yields to the higher reality of the eternal.

Oft have I seen at some cathedral door
A laborer, pausing in the dust and heat,
Lay down his burden, and with reverent feet
Enter, and cross himself, and on the floor
Kneel to repeat his paternoster o'er;   5
Far off the noises of the world retreat;
The loud vociferations of the street
Become an undistinguishable roar.
So, as I enter here from day to day,
And leave my burden at this minster gate,   10
Kneeling in prayer, and not ashamed to pray,
The tumult of the time disconsolate
To inarticulate murmurs dies away,
While the eternal ages watch and wait.

II

The poet is outside the cathedral, marveling at its rich sculptural adornments. The evil of the world is emphasized by the gargoyles, the dead Christ, the thieves, the traitor Judas, since the first two sonnets were prefixed to the *Inferno*. In the last six lines Longfellow indicates that the *Divine Comedy*, like the medieval cathedral, was the creation not of one man but of a whole people, a whole age.

How strange the sculptures that adorn these towers!   15
This crowd of statues, in whose folded sleeves
Birds build their nests; while canopied with leaves
Parvis and portal bloom like trellised bowers,
And the vast minster seems a cross of flowers!
But fiends and dragons on the gargoyled eaves
Watch the dead Christ between the living thieves,   21
And, underneath, the traitor Judas lowers!
Ah! from what agonies of heart and brain,
What exultations trampling on despair,
What tenderness, what tears, what hate of wrong,   25
What passionate outcry of a soul in pain,
Uprose this poem of the earth and air,
This mediaeval miracle of song!

III

The poet is now in the twilight of the cathedral interior. This sonnet and the next were prefixed to the *Purgatory*.

I enter, and I see thee in the gloom
Of the long aisles, O poet saturnine!   30
And strive to make my steps keep pace with
        thine.
The air is filled with some unknown perfume;
The congregation of the dead make room
For thee to pass; the votive tapers shine;
Like rooks that haunt Ravenna's groves of
        pine   35
The hovering echoes fly from tomb to tomb.
From the confessionals I hear arise
Rehearsals of forgotten tragedies,
And lamentations from the crypts below;
And then a voice celestial that begins   40
With the pathetic words, "Although your sins
As scarlet be," and ends with "as the snow."

IV

🙰 Longfellow imagines a meeting of Dante with
Beatrice. She, whom Dante had loved spiritually,
from afar, became, in the *Divine Comedy*, his guide
through Paradise. In line 12, Lethe is the river of
forgetfulness, Eunoë that of the good.

With snow-white veil and garments as of flame,
She stands before thee, who so long ago
Filled thy young heart with passion and the
        woe   45
From which thy song and all its splendors came;
And while with stern rebuke she speaks thy
        name,
The ice about thy heart melts as the snow
On mountain heights, and in swift overflow
Comes gushing from thy lips in sobs of shame.
Thou makest full confession; and a gleam,   51
As of the dawn on some dark forest cast,
Seems on thy lifted forehead to increase;
Lethe and Eunoë — the remembered dream
And the forgotten sorrow — bring at last   55
That perfect pardon which is perfect peace.

V

🙰 This sonnet and the last were prefixed to the
Paradise. For Longfellow, the glorious windows, one
of them rose-shaped, typify this part of Dante's
work. The Rose refers to the end of Dante's journey,
when he beholds the Trinity and the Blessed in the
form of a rose. The elevation of the Host is the
supreme moment of the Mass, when the elements
of the Lord's Supper are lifted from the altar by the
priest.

I lift mine eyes, and all the windows blaze
With forms of Saints and holy men who died,
Here martyred and hereafter glorified;
And the great Rose upon its leaves displays   60
Christ's Triumph, and the angelic roundelays,
With splendor upon splendor multiplied;
And Beatrice again at Dante's side
No more rebukes, but smiles her words of praise.
And then the organ sounds, and unseen choirs 65
Sing the old Latin hymns of peace and love
And benedictions of the Holy Ghost;
And the melodious bells among the spires
O'er all the house-tops and through heaven
        above
Proclaim the elevation of the Host!   70

VI

🙰 Longfellow describes Dante, the builder of the
poetic edifice, as also a poet of freedom and prophet
of the soul.

O star of morning and of liberty!
O bringer of the light, whose splendor shines
Above the darkness of the Apennines,
Forerunner of the day that is to be!
The voices of the city and the sea,   75
The voices of the mountains and the pines,
Repeat thy song, till the familiar lines
Are footpaths for the thought of Italy!
Thy flame is blown abroad from all the heights,
Through all the nations, and a sound is heard,
As of a mighty wind, and men devout,   81
Strangers of Rome, and the new proselytes,
In their own language hear the wondrous word,
And many are amazed and many doubt.

Chaucer

(w. 1873)

An old man in a lodge within a park;
The chamber walls depicted all around
With portraitures of huntsman, hawk, and
        hound,
And the hurt deer. He listeneth to the lark,
Whose song comes with the sunshine through
        the dark   5
Of painted glass in leaden lattice bound;
He listeneth and he laugheth at the sound,
Then writeth in a book like any clerk.
He is the poet of the dawn, who wrote
The Canterbury Tales, and his old age   10
Made beautiful with song; and as I read

I hear the crowing cock, I hear the note
Of lark and linnet, and from every page
Rise odors of ploughed field or flowery mead.

Milton

(w. 1873)

Maeonides, in line 11, stands for Homer.

I pace the sounding sea-beach and behold
  How the voluminous billows roll and run,
  Upheaving and subsiding, while the sun
  Shines through their sheeted emerald far un-
    rolled,
And the ninth wave, slow gathering fold by
    fold   5
  All its loose-flowing garments into one,
  Plunges upon the shore, and floods the dun
  Pale reach of sands, and changes them to
    gold.
So in majestic cadence rise and fall
  The mighty undulations of thy song,   10
  O sightless bard, England's Maeonides!
And ever and anon, high over all
  Uplifted, a ninth wave superb and strong,
  Floods all the soul with its melodious seas.

Venice

(1875)

White swan of cities, slumbering in thy nest
  So wonderfully built among the reeds
  Of the lagoon, that fences thee and feeds,
  As sayeth thy old historian and thy guest!
White water-lily, cradled and caressed   5
  By ocean streams, and from the silt and
    weeds
  Lifting thy golden filaments and seeds,
  Thy sun-illumined spires, thy crown and
    crest!
White phantom city, whose untrodden streets
  Are rivers, and whose pavements are the
    shifting   10
  Shadows of palaces and strips of sky;
I wait to see thee vanish like the fleets
  Seen in mirage, or towers of cloud uplifting
  In air their unsubstantial masonry.

The Three Silences of Molinos

TO JOHN GREENLEAF WHITTIER

(w. 1877)

Three Silences there are: the first of speech,
The second of desire, the third of thought;
This is the lore a Spanish monk, distraught
With dreams and visions, was the first to teach.
These Silences, commingling each with each,   5
Made up the perfect Silence that he sought
And prayed for, and wherein at times he caught
Mysterious sounds from realms beyond our
    reach.
O thou, whose daily life anticipates
The life to come, and in whose thoughts and
    word   10
The spiritual world preponderates,
Hermit of Amesbury! thou too hast heard
Voices and melodies from beyond the gates,
And speakest only when thy soul is stirred!

The Cross of Snow

(w. 1879)

The burden Longfellow carried, barely alluded
to in the first sonnet of "Divina Commedia," became the subject of this sonnet, many years after
the death of his wife.

In the long, sleepless watches of the night,
A gentle face — the face of one long dead —
Looks at me from the wall, where round its
    head
The night-lamp casts a halo of pale light.
Here in this room she died; and soul more
    white   5
Never through martyrdom of fire was led
To its repose; nor can in books be read
The legend of a life more benedight.
There is a mountain in the distant West,
That, sun-defying, in its deep ravines   10
Displays a cross of snow upon its side.
Such is the cross I wear upon my breast
These eighteen years, through all the changing
    scenes
And seasons, changeless since the day she died.

James Russell Lowell [1819–1891]

Lowell was born and bred in Cambridge, and at his pleasant colonial house "Elm-wood" spent most of his life. He came of one of the old, distinguished families of New England, and his home was rich in accumulated books. As an undergraduate at Harvard he read, he said, "nearly everything except the books prescribed by the faculty." When a senior he edited the college magazine, *Harvardiana*, and wrote the class poem. After graduation in 1838 he studied law, for no good reason. He was not interested.

Then he engaged to marry Maria White, of Watertown, Mass., who communicated to him her enthusiasms. Miss White wrote good poetry, was an ardent liberal and abolitionist, and inclined to mysticism. "They say," he reported, "that she is 'transcen-dental.'" Her influence and that of her romantic associates — "the Band" — is clear in two books of verse that Lowell published in the period before their marriage in 1844. Briefly he was an editor of the unsuccessful *Pioneer*, and he did anti-slavery writing for other periodicals. In 1848 he brought out *Poems* (second series), *The Biglow Papers* (first series), *A Fable for Critics*, and *The Vision of Sir Launfal* — all these in one year. He was now successfully launched as a poet. More than that, he had already written most of his best poetry.

He traveled in Europe, with his wife, two children, a nurse, and a goat, in 1851–52. The next year his wife died. He gave a course of lectures in Boston on the English poets, and this led to his Harvard appointment as Smith professor of French and Spanish and of belles-lettres at age thirty-five. After a second sojourn in Europe, 1855–56, he began the life of a teacher, scholar, critic, and, less frequently, poet. By this time his humanitarian ardors had cooled, and he had moved toward nationalism and a conservative humanism, impressed, as H. H. Clark puts it, with the need of "tradition, permanence, and inner control."

In 1857 he married Frances Dunlap, who had been his daughter's governess, and in the same year was made first editor of the *Atlantic Monthly*. Two years later he shifted to the *North American Review*. During the Civil War he wrote the second series of *The Biglow Papers*, and when the war was over delivered his "Commemoration Ode." Then came his long series of critical essays, beginning with *Among My Books* and *My Study Windows*. Before the middle of the 1870's he had been given honorary degrees by Oxford and Cambridge.

He was appointed Minister to Spain in 1877, as Irving had been thirty-five years before. After three years in Madrid, he was made minister to England, where he served till 1885. "During my reign no ambassador or minister has created so much interest or won so much regard," said Queen Victoria. After 1885 Lowell traveled widely, returned to Elmwood, and died.

It was a good life, and he won fame as poet, critic, essayist, professor, editor, diplomat. But he had never quite integrated his abounding talents.

Like Whittier and Longfellow, Lowell has a diminished reputation. This is partly because he had been overrated, and partly because he does not satisfy our twentieth-century attitudes and taste. While some of Whittier's and Longfellow's poetry commands our warm admiration, none of Lowell's does, not even *The Biglow Papers*, in the main closely tied to events and attitudes now remote. His prose essays on European writers of various periods do impress many readers with his admirable standards and frequent insight. But he is too casual in method greatly to serve the literary intellectuals of today, absorbed as they are in specialized historical studies and acute aesthetic analysis.

Further reading: More of *The Biglow Papers*; essays on Chaucer, Shakespeare, Dryden, Wordsworth; *Letters*. Ferris Greenslet, *James Russell Lowell*, 1905. Leon Howard, *Victorian Knight-Errant*, 1952. H. H. Clark and Norman Foerster eds., *James Russell Lowell* (American Writers Series), 1947.

From *A Fable for Critics*

(w. 1847-48)

This piece of high-spirited, often penetrating banter may remind the reader of such earlier satires as Pope's *Dunciad*, Byron's *English Bards and Scotch Reviewers*, and Leigh Hunt's *The Feast of the Poets*, as well as *A Critical Fable* by Amy Lowell in the twentieth century.

The "fable" is almost non-existent. Essentially the poem presents critical sketches of American authors, such as those below. In the sketch of Whittier, line 30, *Anne* etc., is the Latin version of Genesis 37:32.

[Emerson]

THERE comes Emerson first, whose rich
    words, every one,
Are like gold nails in temples to hang trophies
    on,
Whose prose is grand verse, while his verse, the
    Lord knows,
Is some of it pr—— No, 'tis not even prose;
I'm speaking of meters; some poems have
    welled   5
From those rare depths of soul that have ne'er
    been excelled;
They're not epics, but that doesn't matter a
    pin,
In creating, the only hard thing's to begin;
A grass-blade's no easier to make than an oak,
If you've once found the way, you've achieved
    the grand stroke;   10
In the worst of his poems are mines of rich
    matter,
But thrown in a heap with a crash and a clatter;
Now it is not one thing nor another alone
Makes a poem, but rather the general tone,
The something pervading, uniting the whole,   15
The before unconceived, unconceivable soul,
So that just in removing this trifle or that, you

Take away, as it were, a chief limb of the
    statue;
Roots, wood, bark, and leaves, singly perfect
    may be,
But, clapt hodge-podge together, they don't
    make a tree.   20

But to come back to Emerson (whom by the
    way,
I believe we left waiting), — his is, we may
    say
A Greek head on right Yankee shoulders, whose
    range
Has Olympus for one pole, for t'other the Ex-
    change;
He seems, to my thinking, (although I'm
    afraid   25
The comparison must, long ere this, have been
    made),
A Plotinus-Montaigne, where the Egyptian's
    gold mist
And the Gascon's shrewd wit cheek-by-jowl
    coexist;
All admire, and yet scarcely six converts he's
    got
To I don't (nor they either) exactly know
    what;   30
For though he builds glorious temples, 'tis odd
He leaves never a doorway to get in a god.
'Tis refreshing to old-fashioned people like me,
To meet such a primitive Pagan as he,
In whose mind all creation is duly respected   35
As parts of himself — just a little projected;
And who's willing to worship the stars and the
    sun,
A convert to — nothing but Emerson.
So perfect a balance there is in his head,
That he talks of things sometimes as if they
    were dead;   40
Life, nature, love, God, and affairs of that sort,
He looks at as merely ideas; in short,
As if they were fossils stuck round in a cabinet,

Of such vast extent that our earth's a mere dab
   in it;
Composed just as he is inclined to conjecture
   her,   45
Namely, one part pure earth, ninety-nine parts
   pure lecturer;
You are filled with delight at his clear demonstration,
Each figure, word, gesture, just fits the occasion,
With the quiet precision of science he'll sort
   'em,
But you can't help suspecting the whole a *post
mortem.****   50

He has imitators in scores, who omit
No part of the man but his wisdom and wit, —
Who go carefully o'er the sky-blue of his brain,
And when he has skimmed it once, skim it
   again;
If at all they resemble him, you may be sure
   it is   55
Because their shoals mirror his mists and ob-
   scurities,
As a mud-puddle seems deep as heaven for a
   minute,
While a cloud that floats o'er is reflected
   within it.

[Whittier]

There is Whittier, whose swelling and ve-
   hement heart
Strains the strait-breasted drab of the Quaker
   apart,
And reveals the live Man, still supreme and
   erect,
Underneath the bemummying wrappers of sect;
There was ne'er a man born who had more of
   the swing   5
Of the true lyric bard and all that kind of
   thing;
And his failures arise (though he seem not to
   know it)
From the very same cause that has made him
   a poet, —
A fervor of mind which knows no separation
'Twixt simple excitement and pure inspira-
   tion,   10
As my Pythoness erst sometimes erred from not
   knowing
If 'twere I or mere wind through her tripod
   was blowing;
Let his mind once get head in its favorite
   direction

And the torrent of verse bursts the dams of
   reflection,
While, borne with the rush of the meter
   along,   15
The poet may chance to go right or go wrong,
Content with the whirl and delirium of song;
Then his grammar's not always correct, nor his
   rhymes,
And he's prone to repeat his own lyrics some-
   times,
Not his best, though, for those are struck off
   at white-heats   20
When the heart in his breast like a trip-ham-
   mer beats,
And can ne'er be repeated again any more
Than they could have been carefully plotted
   before:
Like old what's-his-name there at the battle of
   Hastings
(Who, however, gave more than mere rhythmi-
   cal bastings),   25
Our Quaker leads off metaphorical fights
For reform and whatever they call human
   rights,
Both singing and striking in front of the war
And hitting his foes with the mallet of Thor;
Anne haec, one exclaims, on beholding his
   knocks,   30
Vestis filii tui, O, leather-clad Fox?
Can that be thy son, in the battle's mid din,
Preaching brotherly love and then driving it in
To the brain of the tough old Goliath of sin,
With the smoothest of pebbles from Castaly's
   spring,   35
Impressed on his hard moral sense with a sling?

All honor and praise to the right-hearted
   bard
Who was true to The Voice when such service
   was hard,
Who himself was so free he dared sing for the
   slave
When to look but a protest in silence was
   brave;   40
All honor and praise to the women and men
Who spoke out for the dumb and the down-
   trodden then!

[Hawthorne]

There is Hawthorne, with genius so shrinking and rare
That you hardly at first see the strength that is
   there;

A frame so robust, with a nature so sweet,
So earnest, so graceful, so lithe and so fleet,
Is worth a descent from Olympus to meet;   5
'Tis as if a rough oak that for ages had stood,
With his gnarled bony branches like ribs of the
    wood,
Should bloom, after cycles of struggle and
    scathe,
With a single anemone trembly and rathe;
His strength is so tender, his wildness so
    meek,   10
That a suitable parallel sets one to seek, —
He's a John Bunyan Fouqué, a Puritan Tieck;
When Nature was shaping him, clay was not
    granted
For making so full-sized a man as she wanted,
So, to fill out her model, a little she spared   15
From some finer-grained stuff for a woman pre-
    pared,
And she could not have hit a more excellent
    plan
For making him fully and perfectly man.
The success of her scheme gave her so much de-
    light,   19
That she tried it again, shortly after, in Dwight;
Only, while she was kneading and shaping the
    clay,
She sang to her work in her sweet childish way,
And found, when she'd put the last touch to
    his soul,
That the music had somehow got mixed with
    the whole.

[Lowell]

There is Lowell, who's striving Parnassus to
    climb
With a whole bale of *isms* tied together with
    rhyme,
He might get on alone, spite of branches and
    boulders,
But he can't with that bundle he has on his
    shoulders,
The top of the hill he will ne'er come nigh
    reaching   5
Till he learns the distinction 'twixt singing and
    preaching;
His lyre has some chords that would ring pretty
    well,
But he'd rather by half make a drum of the
    shell,
And rattle away till he's old as Methusalem,
At the head of a march to the last new Jerusa-
    lem.   10

From *The Biglow Papers*

🐝 Lowell published the First Series of *The Biglow Papers* (1848) without his own name, as the
verses of a young Yankee farmer, "Hosea Biglow,"
laboriously edited by "Homer Wilbur, A.M., Pastor
of the First Church in Jaalam."

In these poems Lowell used humor and dialect
for propagandist ends, with great popular success.
He found his verses, he said, "copied everywhere;
I saw them pinned up in workshops; I heard them
quoted and their authorship debated." Whittier
declared that the laugh caused by Hosea Biglow was
alone enough to have "shaken half the walls of
Slavery down." There had been popular "crackerbox philosophers" before, notably Seba Smith ("Major Downing"), but Lowell showed a grasp of
character and a literary skill that gave his work a
deeper interest.

The First Series concerned the Mexican War and
slavery. Lowell said later: "Thinking the Mexican
War, as I think it still, a national crime committed
in behoof of slavery, our common sin, and wishing
to put the feeling of those who thought as I did in
a way that would tell, I imagined to myself such an
up-country man as I had often seen at antislavery
gatherings, capable of district school English, but
always instinctively falling back into the natural
stronghold of his homely dialect when heated to the
point of self-forgetfulness. . . .

"In choosing the Yankee dialect, I did not act
without forethought. It had long seemed to me that
the great vice of American writing and speaking was
a studied want of simplicity, that we were in danger
of coming to look on our mother-tongue as a dead
language, to be sought in the grammar and dictionary rather than in the heart, and that our only chance
of escape was by seeking it at its living sources
among those who were, as Scottowe says of Major-
General Gibbons, 'divinely illiterate.'"

A Letter

🐝 Lowell represented Ezekiel Biglow, Hosea's
father, as writing a letter to the editor of the *Boston
Courier*, enclosing a poem by Hosea. This letter
begins:

                    "Jaylem, june 1846.

"MISTER EDDYTER, — Our Hosea wuz down to
Boston last week, and he see a cruetin Sarjunt a
struttin round as popler as a hen with 1 chicking,
with 2 fellers a drummin and fifin arter him like all
nater. the sarjunt he thout Hosea hedn't gut his
teeth cut cos he loked a kindo's though he'd jest
com down, so he cal'lated to hook him in, but
Hosy woodn't take none o' his sarse. . . .

"Hosea he com home considerabal riled, and arter
I'd gone to bed I heern Him a thrashin round like
a short-tailed Bull in flitime. The old Woman ses

she to me ses she, Zekle, ses she, our Hosee's gut the
chollery or suthin anuther ses she, don't you Bee
skeered, ses I, he's oney amakin pottery ses i. . . ."
   The "pottery" he wrote:

Thrash away, you'll *hev* to rattle
   On them kittle-drums o' yourn, —
'Taint a knowin' kind o' cattle
   Thet is ketched with mouldy corn;
Put in stiff, you fifer feller,   5
   Let folks see how spry you be, —
Guess you'll toot till you are yeller
   'Fore you git ahold o' me!

Thet air flag's a leetle rotten,
   Hope it aint your Sunday's best; —   10
Fact! it takes a sight o' cotton
   To stuff out a soger's chest:
Sence we farmers hev to pay fer't,
   Ef you must wear humps like these,
S'posin' you should try salt hay fer't,   15
   It would du ez slick ez grease.

Twouldn't suit them Suthun fellers,
   They're a dreffle graspin' set,
We must ollers blow the bellers
   Wen they want their irons het;   20
May be it's all right ez preachin',
   But *my* narves it kind o' grates,
Wen I see the overreachin'
   O' them nigger-drivin' States.

Them thet rule us, them slave-traders,   25
   Haint they cut a thunderin' swarth
(Helped by Yankee renegaders),
   Thru the vartu o' the North!
We begin to think it's nater
   To take sarse an' not be riled. —   30
Who'd expect to see a tater
   All on eend at bein' biled?

Ez fer war, I call it murder, —
   There you hev it plain an' flat;
I don't want to go no furder   35
   Than my Testament fer that;
God hez sed so plump an' fairly,
   It's ez long ez it is broad,
An' you've gut to git up airly
   Ef you want to take in God.   40

'Taint your eppyletts an' feathers
   Make the thing a grain more right;
'Taint afollerin' your bell-wethers
   Will excuse ye in His sight;

Ef you take a sword an' dror it,   45
   An' go stick a feller thru,
Guv'ment aint to answer for it,
   God'll send the bill to you.

Wut's the use o' meetin'-goin'
   Every Sabbath, wet or dry,   50
Ef it's right to go amowin'
   Feller-men like oats an' rye?
I dunno but wut it's pooty
   Trainin' round in bobtail coats, —
But it's curus Christian dooty   55
   This 'ere cuttin' folks's throats.

They may talk o' Freedom's airy
   Tell they're pupple in the face, —
It's a grand gret cemetary
   Fer the barthrights of our race;   60
They jest want this Californy
   So's to lug new slave-States in
To abuse ye, an' to scorn ye,
   An' to plunder ye like sin.

Aint it cute to see a Yankee   65
   Take sech everlastin' pains,
All to get the Devil's thankee
   Helpin' on 'em weld their chains?
Wy, it's jest ez clear ez figgers,
   Clear ez one an' one make two,   70
Chaps thet make black slaves o' niggers
   Want to make wite slaves o' you.

Tell ye jest the eend I've come to
   Arter cipherin' plaguy smart,
An' it makes a handy sum, tu,   75
   Any gump could larn by heart;
Laborin' man an' laborin' woman
   Hev one glory an' one shame.
Ev'y thin' thet's done inhuman
   Injers all on 'em the same.   80

'Taint by turnin' out to hack folks
   You're agoin' to git your right,
Nor by lookin' down on black folks
   Coz you're put upon by wite;
Slavery aint o' nary color,   85
   'Taint the hide thet makes it wus,
All it keers fer in a feller
   'S jest to make him fill its pus.

Want to tackle *me* in, du ye?
   I expect you'll hev to wait;   90
Wen cold lead puts daylight thru ye
   You'll begin to kal'late;

S'pose the crows wun't fall to pickin'
  All the carkiss from your bones,
Coz you helped to give a lickin'   95
To them poor half-Spanish drones?

Jest go home an' ask our Nancy
  Wether I'd be sech a goose
Ez to jine ye, — guess you'd fancy
  The etarnal bung wuz loose!   100
She wants me fer home consumption,
  Let alone the hay's to mow, —
Ef you're arter folks o' gumption,
  You've a darned long row to hoe.

Take them editors that's crowin'   105
  Like a cockerel three months old, —
Don't ketch any on 'em goin',
  Though they *be* so blasted bold;
*A*int they a prime lot o' fellers?
  'Fore they think on't guess they'll sprout
(Like a peach thet's got the yellers),   111
  With the meanness bustin' out.

Wall, go' long to help 'em stealin'
  Bigger pens to cram with slaves,
Help the men thet's ollers dealin'   115
  Insults on your fathers' graves;
Help the strong to grind the feeble,
  Help the many agin the few,
Help the men thet call your people
  Witewashed slaves an' peddlin' crew!   120

Massachusetts, God forgive her,
  She's akneelin' with the rest,
She, thet ough' to ha' clung ferever
  In her grand old eagle-nest;
She thet ough' to stand so fearless   125
  W'ile the wracks are round her hurled,
Holdin' up a beacon peerless
  To the oppressed of all the world!

Ha'n't they sold your colored seamen?
  Ha'n't they made your env'ys w'iz?   130
W*ut*'ll make ye act like freemen?
  W*ut*'ll git your dander riz?
Come, I'll tell ye wut I'm thinkin'
  Is our dooty in this fix,
They'd ha' done't ez quick ez winkin'   135
  In the days o' seventy-six.

Clang the bells in every steeple,
  Call all true men to disown
The tradoocers of our people,
  The enslavers o' their own;   140

Let our dear old Bay State proudly
  Put the trumpet to her mouth,
Let her ring this message loudly
  In the ears of all the South: —

"I'll return ye good fer evil   145
  Much ez we frail mortils can,
But I wun't go help the Devil
  Makin' man the cus o' man;
Call me coward, call me traiter,
  Jest ez suits your mean idees, —   150
Here I stand a tyrant-hater,
  An' the friend o' God an' Peace!"

Ef I'd *my* way I hed ruther
  We should go to work an' part,
They take one way, we take t'other,   155
  Guess it wouldn't break my heart;
Man hed ough' to put asunder
  Them thet God has noways jined;
An' I shouldn't gretly wonder
  Ef there's thousands o' my mind.   160

What Mr. Robinson Thinks

In 1847 George Nixon Briggs, Whig governor of Massachusetts, was up for re-election. He was opposed by General Caleb Cushing, the Democratic candidate, then serving in Mexico.

John P. Robinson, lawyer and Whig politician, who had previously supported Briggs, published an open letter announcing his switch to the Democratic candidate.

Lowell prefaced the poem with some remarks on the nature of satire: "In attacking bad principles he [the satirist] is obliged to select some individual who has made himself their exponent. . . . A bad principle is comparatively harmless while it continues to be an abstraction, nor can the general mind comprehend it fully till it is printed in that large type which all men can read at sight, namely, the life and character, the sayings and doings, of particular persons. . . . Meanwhile, let us not forget that the aim of the true satirist is not to be severe upon persons, but only upon falsehood. . . ."

Guvener B. is a sensible man;
  He stays to his home an' looks arter his
    folks;
He draws his furrer ez straight ez he can,
An' into nobody's tater-patch pokes;
      But John P.   5
    Robinson he
Sez he wunt vote fer Guvener B.

My! ain't it terrible? Wut shall we du?
  We can't never choose him o' course, —
    thet's flat;
Guess we shall hev to come round (don't
    you?)   10
An' go in fer thunder an' guns, an' all that;
      Fer John P.
      Robinson he
Sez he wunt vote fer Guvener B.

Gineral C. is a dreffle smart man: 15
  He's ben on all sides thet give places or pelf;
But consistency still wuz a part of his plan, —
  He's been true to *one* party, — an' thet is
    himself; —
      So John P.
      Robinson he   20
Sez he shall vote fer Gineral C.

Gineral C. he goes in fer the war;
  He don't vally princerple more'n an old cud;
Wut did God make us raytional creeturs fer,
  But glory an' gunpowder, plunder an' blood?
      So John P.   26
      Robinson he
Sez he shall vote fer Gineral C.

We were gittin' on nicely up here to our village,
  With good old idees o' wut's right an' wut
    aint,   30
We kind o' thought Christ went agin war an'
    pillage,
  An' thet eppyletts worn't the best mark of
    a saint;
      But John P.
      Robinson he
Sez this kind o' thing's an exploded idee.   35

The side of our country must ollers be took,
  An' President Polk, you know, *he* is our
    country.
An' the angel thet writes all our sins in a book
  Puts the *debit* to him, an' to us the *per
    contry*
      An' John P.   40
      Robinson he
Sez this is the view o' the thing to a T.

Parson Wilbur he calls all these argimunts lies;
  Sez they're nothin' on airth but just *fee, faw,
    fum*
An' thet all this big talk of our destinies   45
  Is half on it ign'ance, an' t'other half rum;
      But John P.
      Robinson he

Sez it ain't no sech thing; an' of course, so
    must we.

Parson Wilbur sez *he* never heerd in his life   50
  Thet th' Apostles rigged out in their swaller
    tail coats,
An' marched round in front of a drum an' a fife,
  To git some on 'em office, an' some on 'em
    votes;
      But John P.
      Robinson he   55
Sez they didn't know everythin' down in
    Judee.

Wal, it's a marcy we've gut folks to tell us
  The rights an' the wrongs o' these matters,
    I vow, —
God sends country lawyers, an' other wise fel-
    lers,
  To start the world's team wen it gits in a
    slough;   60
      Fer John P.
      Robinson he
Sez the world'll go right, ef he hollers out
    Gee!

The Courtin'

"The Courtin'" appeared in a brief form in
the First Series. Expanded — as given below — it
opened the Second Series, which was launched
fourteen years after the First, at the time of the
Civil War. "Cried," at the end, refers to the announcing of intention to marry.

God makes sech nights, all white an' still
  Fur'z you can look or listen,
Moonshine an' snow on field an' hill,
  All silence an' all glisten.

Zekle crep' up quite unbeknown   5
  An' peeked in thru' the winder,
An' there sot Huldy all alone,
  'ith no one nigh to hender.

A fireplace filled the room's one side
  With half a cord o' wood in —   10
There warn't no stoves (tell comfort died)
  To bake ye to a puddin'.

The wa'nut logs shot sparkles out
  Towards the pootiest, bless her,
An' leetle flames danced all about   15
  The chiny on the dresser.

Agin the chimbley crook-necks hung,
  An' in amongst 'em rusted
The ole queen's-arm thet gran'ther Young
  Fetched back f'om Concord busted.   20

The very room, coz she was in,
  Seemed warm f'om floor to ceilin',
An' she looked full ez rosy agin
  Ez the apples she was peelin'.

'Twas kin' o' kingdom-come to look   25
  On such a blessed cretur,
A dogrose blushin' to a brook
  Ain't modester nor sweeter.

He was six foot o' man, A 1,
  Clear grit an' human natur'.   30
None couldn't quicker pitch a ton
  Nor dror a furrer straighter.

He'd sparked it with full twenty gals,
  Hed squired 'em, danced 'em, druv 'em,
Fust this one, an' then thet, by spells —   35
  All is, he couldn't love 'em.

But long o' her his veins 'ould run
  All crinkly like curled maple,
The side she breshed felt full o' sun
  Ez a south slope in Ap'il.   40

She thought no v'ice hed sech a swing
  Ez hisn in the choir;
My! when he made Ole Hundred ring,
  She *knowed* the Lord was nigher.

An' she'd blush scarlit, right in prayer,   45
  When her new meetin'-bunnet
Felt somehow thru' its crown a pair
  O' blue eyes sot upun it.

Thet night, I tell ye, she looked *some!*
  She seemed to 've gut a new soul,   50
For she felt sartin-sure he'd come,
  Down to her very shoe-sole.

She heered a foot, an' knowed it tu,
  A-raspin' on the scraper, —
All ways to once her feelin's flew   55
  Like sparks in burnt-up paper.

He kin' o' l'itered on the mat,
  Some doubtfle o' the sekle,
His heart kep' goin' pity-pat,
  But hern went pity Zekle.   60

An' yit she gin her cheer a jerk
  Ez though she wished him furder,
An' on her apples kep' to work,
  Parin' away like murder.

"You want to see my Pa, I s'pose?"   65
  "Wal . . . no . . . I come dasignin' " —
"To see my Ma? She's sprinklin' clo'es
  Agin to-morrer's i'nin'."

To say why gals acts so or so,
  Or don't, 'ould be persumin';   70
Mebby to mean *yes* an' say *no*
  Comes nateral to women.

He stood a spell on one foot fust,
  Then stood a spell on t'other,
An' on which one he felt the wust   75
  He couldn't ha' told ye nuther.

Says he, "I'd better call agin!"
  Says she, "Think likely, Mister":
Thet last word pricked him like a pin,
  An' . . . . Wal, he up an' kist her.   80

When Ma bimeby upon 'em slips,
  Huldy sot pale ez ashes,
All kin' o' smily roun' the lips
  An' teary roun' the lashes.

For she was jes' the quiet kind   85
  Whose naturs never vary,
Like streams that keep a summer mind
  Snowhid in Jenooary.

The blood clost roun' her heart felt glued
  Too tight for all expressin',   90
Tell mother see how metters stood,
  An' gin 'em both her blessin'.

Then her red come back like the tide
  Down to the Bay o' Fundy,
An' all I know is they was cried   95
  In meetin' come nex' Sunday.

Emerson the Lecturer

This essay was first published in the *Atlantic Monthly* in 1861, as a review of *The Conduct of Life*, and was revised in 1868. It may be compared with Lowell's thumbnail sketch of Emerson in *A Fable for Critics* 20 years earlier (see page 555).

In the opening paragraph Lowell contrasts Emerson with lecturers who create a brief sensation and then become "disregarded King Logs." According to Aesop, Jupiter, petitioned by the frogs for a king, cast a log among them, which ruled satisfactorily till the frogs lost their fright and knew the log for what it was. In the last paragraph, Lowell compares Emerson with the magician Prospero addressing the spirit Ariel in Shakespeare's *Tempest*, V, i.

It is a singular fact that Mr. Emerson is the most steadily attractive lecturer in America. Into that somewhat cold-waterish region adventurers of the sensational kind come down now and then with a splash, to become disregarded King Logs before the next season. But Mr. Emerson always draws. A lecturer now for something like a third of a century, one of the pioneers of the lecturing system, the charm of his voice, his manner, and his matter has never lost its power over his earlier hearers, and continually winds new ones in its enchanting meshes. What they do not fully understand they take on trust, and listen, saying to themselves, as the old poet of Sir Philip Sidney, —

A sweet, attractive, kind of grace,
A full assurance given by looks,
Continual comfort in a face,
The lineaments of gospel books.

We call it a singular fact, because we Yankees are thought to be fond of the spread-eagle style, and nothing can be more remote from that than his. We are reckoned a practical folk, who would rather hear about a new air-tight stove than about Plato; yet our favorite teacher's practicality is not in the least of the Poor Richard variety. If he have any Buncombe constituency, it is that unrealized commonwealth of philosophers which Plotinus proposed to establish; and if he were to make an almanac, his directions to farmers would be something like this: "OCTOBER: *Indian Summer*; now is the time to get in your early Vedas." What, then, is his secret? Is it not that he out-Yankees us all? that his range includes us all? that he is equally at home with the potato-disease and

original sin, with pegging shoes and the Over-Soul? that, as we try all trades, so has he tried all cultures? and above all, that his mysticism gives us a counterpoise to our super-practicality?

There is no man living to whom, as a writer, so many of us feel and thankfully acknowledge so great an indebtedness for ennobling impulses, — none whom so many cannot abide. What does he mean? ask these last. Where is his system? What is the use of it all? What the deuce have we to do with Brahma? I do not propose to write an essay on Emerson at this time. I will only say that one may find grandeur and consolation in a starlit night without caring to ask what it means, save grandeur and consolation; one may like Montaigne, as some ten generations before us have done, without thinking him so systematic as some more eminently tedious (or shall we say tediously eminent?) authors; one may think roses as good in their way as cabbages, though the latter would make a better show in the witness-box, if cross-examined as to their usefulness; and as for Brahma, why, he can take care of himself, and won't bite us at any rate.

The bother with Mr. Emerson is, that, though he writes in prose, he is essentially a poet. If you undertake to paraphrase what he says, and to reduce it to words of one syllable for infant minds, you will make as sad work of it as the good monk with his analysis of Homer in the *Epistolæ Obscurorum Virorum* [Letters of Obscure Men]. We look upon him as one of the few men of genius whom our age has produced, and there needs no better proof of it than his masculine faculty of fecundating other minds. Search for his eloquence in his books and you will perchance miss it, but meanwhile you will find that it has kindled all your thoughts. For choice and pith of language he belongs to a better age than ours, and might rub shoulders with Fuller and Browne, — though he does use that abominable word *reliable*. His eye for a fine, telling phrase that will carry true is like that of a backwoodsman for a rifle; and he will dredge you up a choice word from the mud of Cotton Mather himself. A diction at once so rich and so homely as his I know not where to match in these days of writing by the page; it is like homespun cloth-of-gold. The many cannot miss his meaning, and only the few can find it. It is the open secret of all true genius. It is wholesome to angle in those profound pools, though one be rewarded with nothing more than the leap of a fish that flashes his freckled side in the sun and as suddenly absconds in the dark and dreamy waters again. There is keen excitement, though there be no ponderable acquisition. If we carry nothing home in our baskets, there is ample gain in dilated lungs and stimulated blood. What does he mean, quotha? He means inspiring hints, a divining-rod to your deeper nature. No doubt, Emerson, like all original men, has his peculiar audience, and yet I know none that can hold a promiscuous crowd in pleased attention so long as he. As in all original men, there is something for every palate. "Would you know," says Goethe, "the ripest cherries? Ask the boys and the blackbirds."

The announcement that such a pleasure as a new course of lectures by him is coming, to people as old as I am, is something like those forebodings of spring that prepare us every year for a familiar novelty, none the less novel, when it arrives, because it is familiar. We know perfectly well what we are to expect from Mr. Emerson, and yet what he says always penetrates and stirs us, as is apt to be the case with genius, in a very unlooked-for fashion. Perhaps genius is one of the few things which we gladly allow to repeat itself, — one of the few that multiply rather than weaken the force of their impression by iteration? Perhaps some of us hear more than the mere words, are moved by something deeper than the thoughts? If it be so, we are quite right, for it is thirty years and more of "plain living and high thinking" that speak to us in this altogether unique lay-preacher. We have shared in the beneficence of this varied culture, this fearless impartiality in criticism and speculation, this masculine sincerity, this sweetness of nature which rather stimulates than cloys, for a generation long. If ever there was a standing testimonial to the cumulative power and value of Character (and we need it sadly in these days), we have it in this gracious and dignified presence. What an antiseptic is a pure life! At sixty-five (or two years beyond his grand climacteric, as he would prefer to call it) he has that privilege of soul which abolishes the calendar, and presents him to us always the unwasted contemporary of his own prime. I do not know if he seem old to his younger hearers, but we who have known him so long wonder at the tenacity with which he maintains himself even in the outposts of youth. I suppose it is not the Emerson of 1868 to whom we listen.

For us the whole life of the man is distilled in the clear drop of every sentence, and behind each word we divine the force of a noble character, the weight of a large capital of thinking and being. We do not go to hear what Emerson says so much as to hear Emerson. Not that we perceive any falling-off in anything that ever was essential to the charm of Mr. Emerson's peculiar style of thought or phrase. The first lecture, to be sure, was more disjointed even than common. It was as if, after vainly trying to get his paragraphs into sequence and order, he had at last tried the desperate expedient of *shuffling* them. It was chaos come again, but it was a chaos full of shooting-stars, a jumble of creative forces. The second lecture, on "Criticism and Poetry," was quite up to the level of old times, full of that power of strangely subtle association whose indirect approaches startle the mind into almost painful attention, of those flashes of mutual understanding between speaker and hearer that are gone ere one can say it lightens. The vice of Emerson's criticism seems to be, that while no man is so sensitive to what is poetical, few men are less sensible than he of what makes a poem. He values the solid meaning of thought above the subtler meaning of style. He would prefer Donne, I suspect, to Spenser, and sometimes mistakes the queer for the original.

To be young is surely the best, if the most precarious, gift of life; yet there are some of us who would hardly consent to be young again, if it were at the cost of our recollection of Mr. Emerson's first lectures during the consulate of Van Buren. We used to walk in from the country to the Masonic Temple (I think it was), through the crisp winter night, and listen to that thrilling voice of his, so charged with subtle meaning and subtle music, as shipwrecked men on a raft to the hail of a ship that came with unhoped-for food and rescue. Cynics might say what they liked. Did our own imaginations transfigure dry remainder-biscuit into ambrosia? At any rate, he brought us *life*, which, on the whole, is no bad thing. Was it all transcendentalism? magic-lantern pictures on mist? As you will. Those, then, were just what we wanted. But it was not so. The delight and the benefit were that he put us in communication with a larger style of thought, sharpened our wits with a more pungent phrase, gave us ravishing glimpses of an ideal under the dry husk of our New England; made us conscious of the supreme and everlasting originality of whatever bit of soul might be in any of us; freed us, in short, from the stocks of prose in which we had sat so long that we had grown well-nigh contented in our cramps. And who that saw the audience will ever forget it, where every one still capable of fire, or longing to renew in himself the half-forgotten sense of it, was gathered? Those faces, young and old, agleam with pale intellectual light, eager with pleased attention, flash upon me once more from the deep recesses of the years with an exquisite pathos. Ah, beautiful young eyes, brimming with love and hope, wholly vanished now in that other world we call the Past, or peering doubtfully through the pensive gloaming of memory, your light impoverishes these cheaper days! I hear again that rustle of sensation, as they turned to exchange glances over some pithier thought, some keener flash of that humor which always played about the horizon of his mind like heat-lightning, and it seems now like the sad whisper of the autumn leaves that are whirling around me. But would my picture be complete if I forgot that ample and vegete countenance of Mr. R—— of W——, — how, from its regular post at the corner of the front bench, it turned in ruddy triumph to the profaner audience as if he were the inexplicably appointed fugleman of appreciation? I was reminded of him by those hearty cherubs in Titian's Assumption that look at you as who should say, "Did you ever see a Madonna like *that?* Did you ever behold one hundred and fifty pounds of womanhood mount heavenward before like a rocket?"

To some of us that long-past experience remains as the most marvellous and fruitful we have ever had. Emerson awakened us, saved us from the body of this death. It is the sound of the trumpet that the young soul longs for, careless what breath may fill it. Sidney heard it in the ballad of "Chevy Chase," and we in Emerson. Nor did it blow retreat, but called to us with assurance of victory. Did they say he was disconnected? So were the stars, that seemed larger to our eyes, still keen with that excitement, as we walked homeward with prouder stride over the creaking snow. And were *they* not knit together by a higher logic than our mere sense could master? Were we enthusiasts? I hope and believe we were, and am thankful to the man who made us worth something for once in our lives. If asked what was left? what we carried home? we should not have been care-

ful for an answer. It would have been enough if we had said that something beautiful had passed that way. Or we might have asked in return what one brought away from a symphony of Beethoven? Enough that he had set that ferment of wholesome discontent at work in us. There is one, at least, of those old hearers, so many of whom are now in the fruition of that intellectual beauty of which Emerson gave them both the desire and the foretaste, who will always love to repeat: —

Che in la mente m' è fitta, ed or m' accuora
La cara e buona immagine paterna
Di voi, quando nel mondo ad ora ad ora
M' insegnavaste come l' uom s' eterna.

[For in my mind is fixed, and touches now
  My heart, the dear and good paternal image
  Of you, when in the world from hour to hour
You taught me how a man becomes eternal.
  — Dante, Longfellow's translation.]

I am unconsciously thinking, as I write, of the third lecture of the present course, in which Mr. Emerson gave some delightful reminiscences of the intellectual influences in whose movement he had shared. It was like hearing Goethe read some passages of the *Wahrheit aus seinem Leben* [Truths from his Life]. Not that there was not a little *Dichtung* [Poetry], too, here and there, as the lecturer built up so lofty a pedestal under certain figures as to lift them into a prominence of obscurity, and seem to masthead them there. Everybody was asking his neighbor who this or that recondite great man was, in the faint hope that somebody might once have heard of him. There are those who call Mr. Emerson cold. Let them revise their judgment in presence of this loyalty of his that can keep warm for half a century, that never forgets a friendship, or fails to pay even a fancied obligation to the uttermost farthing. This substantiation of shadows was but incidental, and pleasantly characteristic of the man to those who know and love him. The greater part of the lecture was devoted to reminiscences of things substantial in themselves. He spoke of Everett, fresh from Greece and Germany; of Channing; of the translations of Margaret Fuller, Ripley, and Dwight; of the *Dial* and Brook Farm. To what he said of the latter an undertone of good-humored irony gave special zest. But what every one of his hearers felt was that the protagonist in the drama was left out.

The lecturer was no Æneas to babble the *quorum magna pars fui* [in which events I had a great share], and, as one of his listeners, I cannot help wishing to say how each of them was commenting the story as it went along, and filling up the necessary gaps in it from his own private store of memories. His younger hearers could not know how much they owed to the benign impersonality, the quiet scorn of everything ignoble, the never-sated hunger of self-culture, that were personified in the man before them. But the older knew how much the country's intellectual emancipation was due to the stimulus of his teaching and example, how constantly he had kept burning the beacon of an ideal life above our lower region of turmoil. To him more than to all other causes together did the young martyrs of our civil war owe the sustaining strength of thoughtful heroism that is so touching in every record of their lives. Those who are grateful to Mr. Emerson, as many of us are, for what they feel to be most valuable in their culture, or perhaps I should say their impulse, are grateful not so much for any direct teachings of his as for that inspiring lift which only genius can give, and without which all doctrine is chaff.

This was something like the *caret* which some of us older boys wished to fill up on the margin of the master's lecture. Few men have been so much to so many, and through so large a range of aptitudes and temperaments, and this simply because all of us value manhood beyond any or all other qualities of character. We may suspect in him, here and there, a certain thinness and vagueness of quality, but let the waters go over him as they list, this masculine fibre of his will keep its lively color and its toughness of texture. I have heard some great speakers and some accomplished orators, but never any that so moved and persuaded men as he. There is a kind of undertow in that rich baritone of his that sweeps our minds from their foothold into deeper waters with a drift we cannot and would not resist. And how artfully (for Emerson is a long-studied artist in these things) does the deliberate utterance, that seems waiting for the fit word, appear to admit us partners in the labor of thought and make us feel as if the glance of humor were a sudden suggestion, as if the perfect phrase lying written there on the desk were as unexpected to him as to us! In that closely filed speech of his at the Burns centenary dinner, every word seemed to have just dropped down to him from the clouds. He looked far away over the heads of his hearers, with a vague kind of expectation, as into some private heaven of invention, and the winged period came at last obedient to his spell. "My dainty Ariel!" he seemed murmuring to himself as he cast down his eyes as if in deprecation of the frenzy of approval and caught another sentence from the Sibylline leaves that lay before him, ambushed behind a dish of fruit and seen only by nearest neighbors. Every sentence brought down the house, as I never saw one brought down before, — and it is not so easy to hit Scotsmen with a sentiment that has no hint of native brogue in it. I watched, for it was an interesting study, how the quick sympathy ran flashing from face to face down the long tables, like an electric spark thrilling as it went, and then exploded in a thunder of plaudits. I watched till tables and faces vanished, for I, too, found myself caught up in the common enthusiasm, and my excited fancy set me under the *bema* listening to him who fulmined over Greece. I can never help applying to him what Ben Jonson said of Bacon: "There happened in my time one noble speaker, who was full of gravity in his speaking. His language was nobly censorious. No man ever spake more neatly, more pressly, more weightily, or suffered less emptiness, less idleness, in what he uttered. No member of his speech but consisted of his own graces. His hearers could not cough, or look aside from him, without loss. He commanded where he spoke." Those who heard him while their natures were yet plastic, and their mental nerves trembled under the slightest breath of divine air, will never cease to feel and say: —

Was never eye did see that face,
Was never ear did hear that tongue,
Was never mind did mind his grace,
 That ever thought the travail long;
But eyes, and ears, and every thought,
Were with his sweet perfections caught.

Oliver Wendell Holmes [1809–1894]

As Dr. Johnson felt about London — "When a man is tired of London, he is tired of life" — so did Oliver Wendell Holmes feel about Boston. "Boston State-House," he said, "is the hub of the solar system." He was city-bred, unlike Emerson and Thoreau who belonged to rural Concord, and he loved to wander through the streets of his native city or to take his recreation with the oars along the Charles River. He belonged to that level of society which lived in brownstone houses in the Back Bay and went to the sea-shore for the warm months in the summer. It was a different world from the solitude and comparative simplicity of Concord or Walden Pond.

In literature Holmes's tastes ran to gentle satire and witty social comment both in prose and in verse. He admired Pope and "that wise and charming" Roman, Horace. But literature was not his life; it was his avocation. His wit sparkled on many an "occasion" with clever verses reminiscent of Pope and Goldsmith. He was his own Boswell in *The Autocrat of the Breakfast Table* and its sequels, and he liked to think that his own life paralleled that of Dr. Johnson in the previous century. "I felt more intimately acquainted with him than I do with many of my living friends."

Holmes enjoyed a distinguished ancestry that included Anne Bradstreet, and he belonged to the self-styled "Brahmin caste of New England," which he described as a "harmless, inoffensive, untitled aristocracy." It was a society based partly upon wealth, but more upon good taste and the love of refinement, good manners, old books, old wines, and mellowed meerschaum pipes. For him, conversation was one of the fine arts. And he felt that the best societies were based upon family traditions and "the cumulative humanities of at least four or five generations."

Although socially a conservative, Holmes was too much the scientist and rationalist to accept the Calvinism of his father, the Rev. Abdiel Holmes. He devoted many essays to attacking the concept of hereditary sin and its social consequences. As a student of Darwin and evolution, he believed that evil was not a theological abstraction, but came from immediate environmental influences, drunken ancestors, abuse in childhood, and bad company, and that criminals, like the insane, should therefore be treated in hospitals. His ideas anticipated those of modern psychologists and sociologists.

After graduating from Harvard in 1829, he had a year in law school, and at this time wrote a fiery lyric, "Old Ironsides," that made his name known throughout the country. Giving up the law, Holmes prepared himself in medicine at Harvard and in Paris. In 1835 he began to practice (he took as his motto, "the smallest fevers thankfully received") and wrote and lectured on the side. His first book of poems had been issued in 1833, and he continued to produce occasional verse and essays, as well as medical articles. His most valuable medical contribution was "The Contagiousness of

Puerperal Fever." Turning from practice to teaching, Holmes was briefly professor of anatomy at Dartmouth College, and then, in 1847, entered upon thirty-five years of successful teaching as professor of anatomy and physiology in the Harvard Medical School.

In 1831 he had published in the *New England Magazine* two essays called "The Autocrat of the Breakfast-Table." Now, twenty-six years later, using the same title, he resumed with a new series, in which his first words were: "I was just going to say, when I was interrupted. . . ." In book form, *The Autocrat of the Breakfast-Table* was followed by *The Professor at the Breakfast-Table, The Poet at the Breakfast-Table,* and *Over the Tea-Cups.* Along with these sparkling monologues, he wrote excellent familiar verse, and also several novels, the best known of which was *Elsie Venner: A Romance of Destiny.* Not important as works of art, his "medicated novels" have acquired interest because they foreshadowed psychological attitudes toward crime and punishment typical of the twentieth century. We doctors, he wrote, "have nothing but compassion for a large class of persons condemned as sinners by theologians, but considered by us as invalids."

Further reading: *The Autocrat of the Breakfast-Table, Oliver Wendell Holmes,* eds. S. I. Hayakawa and H. M. Jones (American Writers Series), 1939. M. A. DeW. Howe, *Holmes of the Breakfast-Table,* 1939. E. M. Tilton, *Amiable Autocrat,* 1947.

The Ballad of the Oysterman

(1830)

In this mock-heroic poem, the Greek legend referred to in line 12 (summarized in college dictionaries under "Hero and Leander") is to be remembered to the end of the ballad. What is the effect of the suggested parallel?

It was a tall young oysterman lived by the river-
    side,
His shop was just upon the bank, his boat was
    on the tide;
The daughter of a fisherman, that was so straight
    and slim,
Lived over on the other bank, right opposite to
    him.

It was the pensive oysterman that saw a lovely
    maid,   5
Upon a moonlight evening, a-sitting in the
    shade:
He saw her wave her handkerchief, as much as
    if to say,
"I'm wide awake, young oysterman, and all the
    folks away."

Then up arose the oysterman, and to himself
    said he,
"I guess I'll leave the skiff at home, for fear that
    folks should see;   10
I read it in the story-book, that, for to kiss his
    dear,
Leander swam the Hellespont, — and I will
    swim this here."

And he has leaped into the waves, and crossed
    the shining stream,
And he has clambered up the bank, all in the
    moonlight gleam;
Oh there were kisses sweet as dew, and words
    as soft as rain, —   15
But they have heard her father's step, and in he
    leaps again!

Out spoke the ancient fisherman, — "Oh, what
    was that, my daughter?"
" 'Twas nothing but a pebble, sir, I threw into
    the water."
"And what is that, pray tell me, love, that
    paddles off so fast?"
"It's nothing but a porpoise, sir, that's been
    a-swimming past."   20

Out spoke the ancient fisherman, — "Now
    bring me my harpoon!
I'll get into my fishing-boat, and fix the fellow
    soon."
Down fell that pretty innocent, as falls a snow-
    white lamb,
Her hair drooped round her pallid cheeks, like
    seaweed on a clam.

Alas for those two loving ones! she waked not
    from her swound,   25
And he was taken with the cramp, and in the
    waves was drowned:
But Fate has metamorphosed them, in pity of
    their woe,
And now they keep an oyster-shop for mermaids
    down below.

My Aunt

(1831)

Humor, wit, and sentiment are here gently commingled in a way that was characteristic of Holmes.

My aunt! my dear unmarried aunt!
    Long years have o'er her flown;
Yet still she strains the aching clasp
    That binds her virgin zone;
I know it hurts her, — though she looks   5
    As cheerful as she can;
Her waist is ampler than her life,
    For life is but a span.

My aunt! my poor deluded aunt!
    Her hair is almost gray;   10
Why will she train that winter curl
    In such a spring-like way?
How can she lay her glasses down,
    And say she reads as well,
When through a double convex lens   15
    She just makes out to spell?

Her father — grandpapa! forgive
    This erring lip its smiles —
Vowed she should make the finest girl
    Within a hundred miles;   20
He sent her to a stylish school;
    'Twas in her thirteenth June;
And with her, as the rules required,
    "Two towels and a spoon."

They braced my aunt against a board,   25
    To make her straight and tall;

They laced her up, they starved her down,
    To make her light and small;
They pinched her feet, they singed her hair,
    They screwed it up with pins; —   30
Oh, never mortal suffered more
    In penance for her sins.

So, when my precious aunt was done,
    My grandsire brought her back
(By daylight, lest some rabid youth   35
    Might follow on the track);
"Ah!" said my grandsire, as he shook
    Some powder in his pan,
"What could this lovely creature do
    Against a desperate man!"   40

Alas! nor chariot, nor barouche,
    Nor bandit cavalcade,
Tore from the trembling father's arms
    His all-accomplished maid.
For her how happy had it been!   45
    And Heaven had spared to me
To see one sad, ungathered rose
    On my ancestral tree.

The Last Leaf

(1831)

The poem was suggested by the figure of Major Thomas Melville (grandfather of Herman Melville), known as "the last of the cocked hats" of the Revolutionary period.

I saw him once before,
    As he passed by the door,
        And again
The pavement stones resound,
As he totters o'er the ground   5
        With his cane.

They say that in his prime,
Ere the pruning-knife of Time
        Cut him down,
Not a better man was found   10
By the Crier on his round
        Through the town.

But now he walks the streets,
And he looks at all he meets
        Sad and wan,   15
And he shakes his feeble head,
That it seems as if he said,
        "They are gone."

The mossy marbles rest
On the lips that he has prest   20
   In their bloom,
And the names he loved to hear
Have been carved for many a year
   On the tomb.

My grandmamma has said   25
Poor old lady, she is dead
   Long ago —
That he had a Roman nose,
And his cheek was like a rose
   In the snow;   30

But now his nose is thin,
And it rests upon his chin
   Like a staff,
And a crook is in his back,
And a melancholy crack   35
   In his laugh.

I know it is a sin
For me to sit and grin
   At him here;
But the old three-cornered hat,   40
And the breeches, and all that,
   Are so queer!

And if I should live to be
The last leaf upon the tree
   In the spring,   45
Let them smile, as I do now,
At the old forsaken bough
   Where I cling.

The Chambered Nautilus

(1858)

In introducing this poem in *The Autocrat of the Breakfast-Table*, Holmes remarked, somewhat in the manner of Emerson in *Nature*, "Did I not say to you a little while ago that the universe swam in an ocean of similitudes and analogies?" Though Holmes usually made scant use of Emerson's thought, he may have remembered in writing the poem that Emerson, in "Compensation," had compared man's growth to that of the shell-fish which "crawls out of its beautiful but stony case, because it no longer admits of its growth, and slowly forms itself a new house." In Holmes's poem, the shell-fish is the Pearly Nautilus. As it grows it develops its shell, living successively in a series of compartments or chambers, each larger than the one before.

This is the ship of pearl, which, poets feign,
   Sails the unshadowed main, —
   The venturous bark that flings
On the sweet summer wind its purpled wings
In gulfs enchanted, where the Siren sings,   5
   And coral reefs lie bare,
Where the cold sea-maids rise to sun their
   streaming hair.

Its webs of living gauze no more unfurl;
   Wrecked is the ship of pearl!
   And every chambered cell,   10
Where its dim dreaming life was wont to dwell,
As the frail tenant shaped his growing shell,
   Before thee lies revealed, —
Its irised ceiling rent, its sunless crypt unsealed!

Year after year beheld the silent toil   15
   That spread his lustrous coil;
   Still, as the spiral grew,
He left the past year's dwelling for the new,
Stole with soft step its shining archway through,
   Built up its idle door,   20
Stretched in his last-found home, and knew the
   old no more.

Thanks for the heavenly message brought by
   thee,
   Child of the wandering sea,
   Cast from her lap, forlorn!
From thy dead lips a clearer note is born   25
Than ever Triton blew from wreathèd horn!
   While on mine ear it rings,
Through the deep caves of thought I hear a
   voice that sings: —

Build thee more stately mansions, O my soul,
   As the swift seasons roll!   30
   Leave thy low-vaulted past!
Let each new temple, nobler than the last,
Shut thee from heaven with a dome more vast,
   Till thou at length art free,
Leaving thine outgrown shell by life's unresting
   sea!

Contentment

(1858)

Like the one before, this poem was embedded in the prose of *The Autocrat*. "Should you like to hear," he asks, "what moderate wishes life brings one to at last?" He answers, for himself, with light irony.

"Brown stone" (line 3) was then the fashionable building material among the rich. "Plenipo" (line 21), a diplomat with full power; most important was the minister to the court of St. James in London.

"Man wants but little here below."

Little I ask; my wants are few;
    I only wish a hut of stone
(A *very plain* brown stone will do)
    That I may call my own; —
And close at hand is such a one,   5
In yonder street that fronts the sun.

Plain food is quite enough for me;
    Three courses are as good as ten; —
If Nature can subsist on three,
    Thank Heaven for three. Amen!   10
I always thought cold victual nice; —
My *choice* would be vanilla-ice.

I care not much for gold or land; —
    Give me a mortgage here and there, —
Some good bank-stock, some note of hand,   15
    Or trifling railroad share, —
I only ask that Fortune send
A *little* more than I shall spend.

Honors are silly toys, I know,
    And titles are but empty names;   20
I would, *perhaps*, be Plenipo, —
    But only near St. James;
I'm very sure I should not care
To fill our Gubernator's chair.

Jewels are baubles; 'tis a sin   25
    To care for such unfruitful things; —
One good-sized diamond in a pin, —
    Some, *not so large*, in rings, —
A ruby, and a pearl, or so,
Will do for me; — I laugh at show.   30

My dame should dress in cheap attire
    (Good, heavy silks are never dear); —
I own perhaps I *might* desire
    Some shawls of true Cashmere, —
Some marrowy crapes of China silk,   35
Like wrinkled skins on scalded milk.

I would not have the horse I drive
    So fast that folks must stop and stare;
An easy gait — two forty-five —
    Suits me; I do not care; —   40
Perhaps, for just a *single spurt*,
Some seconds less would do no hurt.

Of pictures, I should like to own
    Titians and Raphaels three or four, —
I love so much their style and tone,   45
    One Turner, and no more
(A landscape, — foreground golden dirt, —
The sunshine painted with a squirt).

Of books but few, — some fifty score
    For daily use, and bound for wear;   50
The rest upon an upper floor; —
    Some *little* luxury *there*
Of red morocco's gilded gleam
And vellum rich as country cream.

Busts, cameos, gems, — such things as these,
    Which others often show for pride,   56
I value for their power to please,
    And selfish churls deride; —
One Stradivarius, I confess
Two Meerschaums, I would fain possess.   60

Wealth's wasteful tricks I will not learn,
    Nor ape the glittering upstart fool; —
Shall not carved tables serve my turn,
    But *all* must be of buhl?
Give grasping pomp its double share, —   65
I ask but *one* recumbent chair.

Thus humble let me live and die,
    Nor long for Midas' golden touch;
If Heaven more generous gifts deny,
    I shall not miss them *much*, —   70
Too grateful for the blessing lent
Of simple tastes and mind content!

From *The Autocrat of the Breakfast-Table*

(1857–1858)

🦋 Lowell showed remarkable editorial judgment when he insisted, before editing the *Atlantic Monthly*, that Holmes become a contributor. Here was a man forty-eight years old, with a reputation in the field of medicine, but "outside the charmed circle," as he said later, "drawn around the scholars and poets of Cambridge and Concord." He had won fame with "Old Ironsides" but that was twenty-seven years ago. Now he was to achieve a more substantial fame as a prose writer. Beginning with the first number of the *Atlantic*, the Autocrat papers ran for twelve months.

A brilliant conversationalist, Holmes hit upon the plan — foreshadowed by his early *New England*

Magazine essays — of writing good talk, table talk. His rambling monologue touched on any topic that came to mind, never dwelt too long on anything, and revealed a mature mind notable for charm, wit, the free play of intelligence, and a style as firm and vivid as it was informal. The apparently inexhaustible flow of monologue is occasionally interrupted by one or another of the boarders at the table. Holmes used the fictional device of a "breakfast club," a group of characters of diverse types, whose responses contribute a little dramatic interest. There is even a thin thread of story. But we never forget the alert autocrat who commands the table.

The autocrat may well be more learned than his readers. But to trace all his allusions and translate his foreign phrases might be too much like explaining a joke.

— What if, instead of talking this morning, I should read you a copy of verses, with critical remarks by the author? Any of the company can retire that like.

ALBUM VERSES

When Eve had led her lord away,
    And Cain had killed his brother,
The stars and flowers, the poets say,
    Agreed with one another

To cheat the cunning tempter's art,
    And teach the race its duty,
By keeping on its wicked heart
    Their eyes of light and beauty.

A million sleepless lids, they say,
    Will be at least a warning;
And so the flowers would watch by day,
    The stars from eve to morning.

On hill and prairie, field and lawn,
    Their dewy eyes upturning,
The flowers still watch from reddening dawn
    Till western skies are burning.

Alas! each hour of daylight tells
    A tale of shame so crushing,
That some turn white as sea-bleached shells,
    And some are always blushing.

But when the patient stars look down
    On all their light discovers,
The traitor's smile, the murderer's frown,
    The lips of lying lovers,

They try to shut their saddening eyes,
    And in the vain endeavor
We see them twinkling in the skies,
    And so they wink forever.

What do *you* think of these verses, my friends? — Is that piece an impromptu? said my landlady's daughter. (Act. 19+. Tender-eyed blonde. Long ringlets. Cameo pin. Gold pencil-case on a chain. Locket. Bracelet. Album. Autograph book. Accordeon. Reads Byron, Tupper, and Sylvanus Cobb, Junior, while her mother makes the puddings. Says "Yes?" when you tell her anything.) — *Oui et non, ma petite,* — Yes and no, my child. Five of the seven verses were written off-hand; the other two took a week, — that is, were hanging round the desk in a ragged, forlorn, unrhymed condition as long as that. All poets will tell you just such stories. *C'est le* DERNIER *pas qui coûte.* Don't you know how hard it is for some people to get out of a room after their visit is really over? They want to be off, and you want to have them off, but they don't know how to manage it. One would think they had been built in your parlor or study, and were waiting to be launched. I have contrived a sort of ceremonial inclined plane for such visitors, which being lubricated with certain smooth phrases, I back them down, metaphorically speaking, stern-foremost, into their "native element," the great ocean of out-doors. Well, now, there are poems as hard to get rid of as these rural visitors. They come in glibly, use up all the serviceable rhymes, *day, ray, beauty, duty, skies, eyes, other, brother, mountain, fountain,* and the like; and so they go on until you think it is time for the wind-up, and the wind-up won't come on any terms. So they lie about until you get sick of the sight of them, and end by thrusting some cold scrap of a final couplet upon them, and turning them out of doors. I suspect a good many "impromptus" could tell just such a story as the above. — Here turning to our landlady, I used an illustration which pleased the company much at the time, and has since been highly commended. "Madam," I said, "you can pour three gills and three quarters of honey from that pint jug, if it is full, in less than one minute; but, Madam, you could not empty that last quarter of a gill though you were turned into a marble Hebe, and held the vessel upside down for a thousand years."

One gets tired to death of the old, old rhymes, such as you see in that copy of verses — which I don't mean to abuse, or to praise either. I always feel as if I were a cobbler, putting new top-leathers to an old pair of boot-soles and bodies, when I am fitting sentiments to these venerable jingles.

. . . . youth
. . . . morning
. . . . truth
. . . . warning.

Nine tenths of the "Juvenile Poems" written spring out of the above musical and suggestive coincidences.

"Yes?" said our landlady's daughter.

I did not address the following remark to her, and I trust, from her limited range of reading, she will never see it; I said it softly to my next neighbor.

When a young female wears a flat circular side-curl, gummed on each temple, — when she walks with a male, not arm in arm, but his arm against the back of hers, — and when she says "Yes?" with the note of interrogation, you are generally safe in asking her what wages she gets, and who the "feller" was you saw her with.

"What were you whispering?" said the daughter of the house, moistening her lips, as she spoke, in a very engaging manner.

"I was only laying down a principle of social diagnosis."

"Yes?"

***I really believe some people save their bright thoughts as being too precious for conversation. What do you think an admiring friend said the other day to one that was talking good things, — good enough to print? "Why," said he, "you are wasting merchantable literature, a cash article, at the rate, as nearly as I can tell, of fifty dollars an hour." The talker took him to the window and asked him to look out and tell what he saw.

"Nothing but a very dusty street," he said, "and a man driving a sprinkling-machine through it."

"Why don't you tell the man he is wasting that water? What would be the state of the highways of life, if we did not drive our thought-sprinklers through them with the valves open, sometimes?

"Besides, there is another thing about this talking, which you forget. It shapes our thoughts for us; — the waves of conversation roll them as the surf rolls the pebbles on the shore. Let me modify the image a little. I rough out my thoughts in talk as an artist models in clay. Spoken language is so plastic, — you can pat and coax, and spread and shave, and rub out, and fill up, and stick on so easily, when you work that soft material, that there is nothing

like it for modelling. Out of it come the shapes which you turn into marble or bronze in your immortal books, if you happen to write such. Or, to use another illustration, writing or printing is like shooting with a rifle; you may hit your reader's mind, or miss it; — but talking is like playing at a mark with the pipe of an engine; if it is within reach, and you have time enough, you can't help hitting it."

The company agreed that this last illustration was of superior excellence, or, in the phrase used by them, "Fust-rate." I acknowledged the compliment, but gently rebuked the expression. "Fust-rate," "prime," "a prime article," "a superior piece of goods," "a handsome garment," "a gent in a flowered vest," — all such expressions are final. They blast the lineage of him or her who utters them, for generations up and down.***

The whole force of conversation depends on how much you can take for granted. Vulgar chess-players have to play their game out; nothing short of the brutality of an actual checkmate satisfies their dull apprehensions. But look at two masters of that noble game! White stands well enough, so far as you can see; but Red says, Mate in six moves; — White looks, — nods; — the game is over. Just so in talking with first-rate men; especially when they are good-natured and expansive, as they are apt to be at table. That blessed clairvoyance which sees into things without opening them, — that glorious license, which, having shut the door and driven the reporter from its keyhole, calls upon Truth, majestic virgin! to get down from her pedestal and drop her academic poses, and take a festive garland and the vacant place on the *medicus letus*, — that carnival-shower of questions and replies and comments, large axioms bowled over the mahogany like bomb-shells from professional mortars, and explosive wit dropping its trains of many-colored fire, and the mischief-making rain of *bon-bons* pelting everybody that shows himself, — the picture of a truly intellectual banquet is one which the old Divinities might well have attempted to reproduce in their —

— "Oh, oh, oh!" cried the young fellow whom they call John, — "that is from one of your lectures!"

I know it, I replied, — I concede it, I confess it, proclaim it.***

Just as we find a mathematical rule at the bottom of many of the bodily movements, just so thought may be supposed to have its regular cycles. Such or such a thought comes round periodically, in its turn. Accidental suggestions, however, so far interfere with the regular cycles, that we may find them practically beyond our power of recognition. Take all this for what it is worth, but at any rate you will agree that there are certain particular thoughts which do not come up once a day, nor once a week, but that a year would hardly go round without your having them pass through your mind. Here is one which comes up at intervals in this way. Some one speaks of it, and there is an instant and eager smile of assent in the listener or listeners. Yes, indeed; they have often been struck by it:

All at once a conviction flashes through us that we have been in the same precise circumstances as at the present instant, once or many times before.

O, dear, yes! — said one of the company, — everybody has had that feeling.

The landlady didn't know anything about such notions; it was an idee in folks' heads, she expected.

The schoolmistress said, in a hesitating sort of way, that she knew the feeling well, and didn't like to experience it; it made her think she was a ghost, sometimes.

The young fellow whom they call John said he knew all about it; he had just lighted a cheroot the other day, when a tremendous conviction all at once came over him that he had done just the same thing ever so many times before. I looked severely at him, and his countenance immediately fell — *on the side toward me;* I cannot answer for the other, for he can wink and laugh with either half of his face without the other half's knowing it.

— I have noticed — I went on to say — the following circumstances connected with these sudden impressions. First, that the condition which seems to be the duplicate of a former one is often very trivial, — one that might have presented itself a hundred times. Secondly, that the impression is very evanescent, and that it is rarely, if ever, recalled by any voluntary effort, at least after any time has elapsed. Thirdly, that there is a disinclination to record the circumstances, and a sense of incapacity to reproduce the state of mind in words. Fourthly, I have often felt that the duplicate condition had not only occurred once before, but that it was familiar and, as it seemed, habitual. Lastly, I

have had the same convictions in my dreams.

How do I account for it — Why, there are several ways that I can mention, and you may take your choice. The first is that which the young lady hinted at; — that these flashes are sudden recollections of a previous existence. I don't believe that; for I remember a poor student I used to know told me he had such a conviction one day when he was blacking his boots, and I can't think he had ever lived in another world where they use Day and Martin.

Some think that Dr. Wigan's doctrine of the brain's being a double organ, its hemispheres working together like the two eyes, accounts for it. One of the hemispheres hangs fire, they suppose, and the small interval between the perceptions of the nimble and the sluggish half seems an indefinitely long period and therefore the second perception appears to be the copy of another, ever so old. But even allowing the center of perception to be double, I can see no good reason for supposing this indefinite lengthening of the time, nor any analogy that bears it out. It seems to me most likely that the coincidence of circumstances is very partial, but that we take this partial resemblance for identity, as we occasionally do resemblances of persons. A momentary posture of circumstances is so far like some preceding one that we accept it as exactly the same, just as we accost a stranger occasionally, mistaking him for a friend. The apparent similarity may be owing perhaps, quite as much to the mental state at that time, as to the outward circumstances.***

— There is a natural tendency in many persons to run their adjectives together in *triads,* as I have heard them called, — thus He was honorable, courteous, and brave; she was graceful, pleasing, and virtuous. Dr. Johnson is famous for this; I think it was Bulwer who said you could separate a paper in the "Rambler" into three distinct essays. Many of our writers show the same tendency, — my friend, the Professor, especially. Some think it is in humble imitation of Johnson, — some that it is for the sake of the stately sound only. I don't think they get to the bottom of it. It is, I suspect, an instinctive and involuntary effort of the mind to present a thought or image with the *three dimensions* which belong to every solid, — an unconscious handling of an idea as if it had length, breadth, and thickness. It is a great deal easier to say this than to prove it, and a great deal easier to dispute it than to disprove it. But mind this: the more we observe and study, the wider we find the range of the automatic and instinctive principles in body, mind, and morals, and the narrower the limits of the self-determining conscious movement.

— I have often seen piano-forte players and singers make such strange motions over their instruments or song-books that I wanted to laugh at them. "Where did our friends pick up all these fine ecstatic airs?" I would say to myself. Then I would remember My Lady in "Marriage à la Mode," and amuse myself with thinking how affectation was the same thing in Hogarth's time and in our own. But one day I bought me a Canary-bird and hung him up in a cage at my window. By-and-by he found himself at home, and began to pipe his little tunes; and there he was, sure enough, swimming and waving about, with all the droopings and liftings and languishing side-turnings of the head that I had laughed at. And now I should like to ask, WHO taught him all this? — and me, through him, that the foolish head was not the one swinging itself from side to side and bowing and nodding over the music, but that other which was passing its shallow and self-satisfied judgment on a creature made of finer clay than the frame which carried that same head upon its shoulders?

— Do you want an image of the human will or the self-determining principle, as compared with its pre-arranged and impassable restrictions? A drop of water, imprisoned in a crystal; you may see such a one in any mineralogical collection. One little fluid particle in the crystalline prism of the solid universe!

— Weaken moral obligations? — No, not weaken but define them. When I preach that sermon I spoke of the other day, I shall have to lay down some principles not fully recognized in some of your textbooks.

I should have to begin with one most formidable preliminary. You saw an article the other day in one of the journals, perhaps, in which some old Doctor or other said quietly that patients were very apt to be fools and cowards. But a great many of the clergyman's patients are not only fools and cowards, but also liars.

[Immense sensation at the table. — Sudden retirement of the angular female in oxydated bombazine. Movement of adhesion — as they say in the Chamber of Deputies — on the part of the young fellow they call John. Falling of the old-gentleman-opposite's lower jaw — (gravitation is beginning to get the better of him.) Our landlady to Benjamin Franklin, briskly, — Go to school right off, there's a good boy! Schoolmistress curious. — takes a quick glance at divinity-student, Divinity-student slightly flushed; draws his shoulders back a little, as if a big falsehood, — or truth, — had hit him in the forehead. Myself calm.]

— I should not make such a speech as that, you know, without having pretty substantial indorsers to fall back upon, in case my credit should be disputed. Will you run upstairs, Benjamin Franklin (for B. F. had *not* gone right off, of course), and bring down a small volume from the left upper corner of the right-hand shelves?

[Look at the precious little black, ribbed backed, clean-typed, vellum-papered 32mo. "DESIDERII ERASMI COLLOQUIA. Amstelodami. Typis Ludovici Elzevirii. 1650." Various names written on title-page. Most conspicuous this: Gul. Cookeson, E. Coll. Omn. Anim. 1725. Oxon.

— O William Cookeson, of All-Souls College, Oxford, — then writing as I now write, — now in the dust, where I shall lie, — is this line all that remains to thee of earthly remembrance? Thy name is at least once more spoken by living men; — is it a pleasure to thee? Thou shalt share with me my little draught of immortality, — its week, its month, its year, — whatever it may be, — and then we will go together into the solemn archives of Oblivion's Uncatalogued Library!]

— If you think I have used rather strong language, I shall have to read something to you out of the book of this keen and witty scholar, — the great Erasmus, — who "laid the egg of the Reformation which Luther hatched." Oh, you never read his *Naufragium*, or "Shipwreck," did you? Of course not; for, if you had, I don't think you would have given me credit, — or discredit, — for entire originality in that speech of mine. That men are cowards in the contemplation of futurity he illustrates by the extraordinary antics of many on board the sinking vessel; that they are fools, by their praying to the sea, and making promises to bits of wood from the true cross, and all manner of similar nonsense; that they are fools, cowards, and liars all at once, by this story: I will put it into rough English for you. — "I couldn't help laughing to hear one fellow bawling out, so that he might be sure to be heard, a promise to Saint Christopher of Paris — the monstrous statue in the great church there, — that he would give him a wax taper as big as himself. 'Mind what you promise!' said an acquaintance who stood near him, poking him with his elbow; 'you couldn't pay for it, if you sold all your things at auction.' 'Hold your tongue, you donkey!' said the fellow, — but softly, so that Saint Christopher should not hear him, — 'do you think I'm in earnest? If I once get my foot on dry ground, catch me giving him so much as a tallow candle!' "

Now, therefore, remembering that those who have been loudest in their talk about the great subject of which we were speaking have not necessarily been wise, brave, and true men, but, on the contrary, have very often been wanting in one or two or all of the qualities these words imply, I should expect to find a good many doctrines current in the schools which I should be obliged to call foolish, cowardly, and false.

— So you would abuse other people's beliefs, Sir, and yet not tell us your own creed! — said the divinity-student, coloring up with a spirit for which I liked him all the better.

— I have a creed, — I replied; — none better, and none shorter. It is told in two words, — the two first of the Paternoster. And when I say these words I mean them. And when I compared the human will to a drop in a crystal, and said I meant to *define* moral obligations, and not weaken them, this was what I intended to express: that the fluent, self-determining power of human beings is a very strictly limited agency in the universe. The chief planes of its enclosing solid are, of course, organization, education, condition. Organization may reduce the power of the will to nothing, as in some idiots; and from this zero the scale mounts upwards by slight gradations. Education is only second to nature. Imagine all the infants born this year in Boston and Timbuctoo to change places! Condition does less, but "Give me neither poverty nor riches" was the prayer of Agur, and with good reason. If there is any improvement in modern theology, it is in getting out of the region of pure abstractions and taking these every-day working forces into account. The great theological question now heaving and throbbing in the minds of Christian men is this: —

No, I won't talk about these things now. My remarks might be repeated, and it would give my friends pain to see with what personal incivilities I should be visited. Besides, what business has a mere boarder to be talking about such things at a breakfast-table? Let him make puns. To be sure, he was brought up among the Christian fathers, and learned his alphabet out of a quarto "Concilium Tridentinum." He has also heard many thousand theological lectures by men of various denominations; and it is not at all to the credit of these teachers, if he is not fit by this time to express an opinion on theological matters.

I know well enough that there are some of you who had a great deal rather see me stand on my head than use it for any purpose of thought. Does not my friend, the Professor, receive at least two letters a week, requesting him to ...., — on the strength of some youthful antic of his, which, no doubt, authorizes the intelligent constituency of autograph-hunters to address him as a harlequin?

— Well, I can't be savage with you for wanting to laugh, and I like to make you laugh well enough, when I can. But then observe this: if the sense of the ridiculous is one side of an impressible nature, it is very well; but if that is all there is in a man, he had better have been an ape at once, and so have stood at the head of his profession. Laughter and tears are meant to turn the wheels of the same machinery of sensibility; one is windpower, and the other waterpower; that is all. I have often heard the Professor talk about hysterics as being Nature's cleverest illustration of the reciprocal convertibility of the two states of which these acts are the manifestations. But you may see it every day in children; and if you want to choke with stifled tears at the sight of the transition, as it shows itself in older years, go and see Mr. Blake play *Jesse Rural*.

It is a very dangerous thing for a literary man to indulge his love for the ridiculous. People laugh *with* him just so long as he amuses them; but if he attempts to be serious, they must still have their laugh, and so they laugh *at* him. There is in addition, however, a deeper reason for this than would at first appear. Do you know that you feel a little superior to every man who makes you laugh, whether by making faces or verses? Are you aware that you have a pleasant sense of patronizing him, when you condescend so far as to let him turn somersets, literal or literary, for your royal delight? Now if a man can only be allowed to stand on a daïs, or raised platform, and look down on his neighbor who is exerting his talent for him, oh, it is all right! — first-rate performance! — and all the rest of the fine phrases. But if all at once the performer asks the gentleman to come upon the floor, and, stepping upon the platform, begins to talk down at him, — ah, that wasn't in the programme!

I have never forgotten what happened when Sydney Smith — who, as everybody knows, was an exceedingly sensible man, and a gentleman, every inch of him — ventured to preach a sermon on the Duties of Royalty. The "Quarterly," "so savage and tartarly," came down upon him in the most contemptuous style, as "a joker of jokes," a "diner-out of the first water," in one of his own phrases; sneering at him, insulting him, as nothing but a toady of a court, sneaking behind the anonymous, would ever have been mean enough to do to a man of his position and genius, or to any decent person even. — If I were giving advice to a young fellow of talent, with two or three facets to his mind, I would tell him by all means to keep his wit in the background until after he had made a reputation by his more solid qualities. And so to an actor: *Hamlet* first, and *Bob Logic* afterwards, if you like; but don't think, as they say poor Liston used to, that people will be ready to allow that you can do anything great with *Macbeth's* dagger after flourishing about with *Paul Pry's* umbrella. Do you know, too, that the majority of men look upon all who challenge their attention, — for a while, at least, — as beggars, and nuisances? They always try to get off as cheaply as they can; and the cheapest of all things they can give a literary man — pardon the forlorn pleasantry! — is the *funny*-bone. That is all very well so far as it goes, but satisfies no man, and makes a good many angry, as I told you on a former occasion.

— Oh, indeed, no! — I am not ashamed to make you laugh, occasionally. I think I could read you something I have in my desk which would probably make you smile. Perhaps I will read it one of these days, if you are patient with me when I am sentimental and reflective; not just now. The ludicrous has its place in the universe; it is not a human invention, but one of the Divine ideas, illustrated in the practical jokes of kittens and monkeys long before Aristophanes or Shakspeare. How curious it is that we always consider solemnity and the absence of all gay surprises and encounter of wits as essential to the idea of the future life of those whom we thus deprive of half their faculties and then call *blessed!* There are not a few who, even in this life, seem to be preparing themselves for that smileless eternity to which they look forward, by banishing all gayety from their hearts and all joyousness from their countenances. I meet one such in the street not unfrequently, a person of intelligence and education, but who gives me (and all that he passes) such a rayless and chilling look of recognition, — something as if he were one of Heaven's assessors, come down to "doom" every acquaintance he met, — that I have sometimes begun to sneeze on the spot, and gone home with a violent cold, dating from that instant. I don't doubt he would cut his kitten's tail off, if he caught her playing with it. Please tell me, who taught her to play with it?

No, no! — give me a chance to talk to you, my fellow-boarders, and you need not be afraid that I shall have any scruples about entertaining you, if I can do it, as well as giving you some of my serious thoughts, and perhaps my sadder fancies. I know nothing in English or any other literature more admirable than that sentiment of Sir Thomas Browne, "EVERY MAN TRULY LIVES, SO LONG AS HE ACTS HIS NATURE, OR SOME WAY MAKES GOOD THE FACULTIES OF HIMSELF."***

Now I tell you a poem must be kept *and used*, like a meerschaum, or a violin. A poem is just as porous as the meerschaum; — the more porous it is, the better. I mean to say that a genuine poem is capable of absorbing an indefinite amount of the essence of our own humanity, — its tenderness, its heroism, its regrets, its aspirations, so as to be gradually stained through with a divine secondary color derived from ourselves. So you see it must take time to bring the sentiment of a poem into harmony with our nature, by staining ourselves through every thought and image our being can penetrate.

Then again as to the mere music of a new poem, why, who can expect anything more from that than from the music of a violin fresh from the maker's hands? Now you know very well that there are no less than fifty-eight different pieces in a violin. These pieces are strangers to each other, and it takes a century, more or less, to make them thoroughly acquainted. At last they learn to vibrate in harmony and the instrument becomes an organic whole, as if it were a great seed-capsule which had grown from a garden-bed in Cremona, or elsewhere. Besides, the wood is juicy and full of sap for fifty years or so, but at the end of fifty or a hundred more gets tolerably dry and comparatively resonant.

Don't you see that all this is just as true of a poem? Counting each word as a piece, there are more pieces in an average copy of verses than in a violin. The poet has forced all these words together, and fastened them, and they don't understand it at first. But let the poem be repeated aloud and murmured over in the mind's muffled whisper often enough, and at length the parts become knit together in such absolute solidarity that you could not change a syllable without the whole world's crying out against you for meddling with the harmonious fabric.***

Did you never, in walking in the fields, come across a large flat stone, which had lain, nobody knows how long, just where you found it, with the grass forming a little hedge, as it were, all round it, close to its edges, — and have you not, in obedience to a kind of feeling that told you it had been lying there long enough, insinuated your stick or your foot or your fingers under its edge and turned it over as a housewife turns a cake, when she says to herself, "It's done brown enough by this time"? What an odd revelation, and what an unforseen and unpleasant surprise to a small community, the very existence of which you had not suspected, until the sudden dismay and scattering among its members produced by your turning the old stone over! Blades of grass flattened down, colorless, matted together, as if they had been bleached and ironed; hideous crawling creatures, some of them coleopterous or hornyshelled, — turtle-bugs one wants to call them; some of them softer, but cunningly spread out and compressed like Lepine watches; (Nature never loses a crack or a crevice, mind you, or a joint in a tavern bedstead, but she always has one of her flat-pattern live timekeepers to slide into it); black, glossy crickets, with their long filaments sticking out like the whips of four-horse stage-coaches; motionless, slug-like creatures, young larvæ, perhaps more horrible in their pulpy stillness than even in the infernal wriggle of maturity! But no sooner is the stone turned and the wholesome light of day let upon this compressed and blinded community of creeping things, than all of them which enjoy the luxury of legs — and some of them have a good many — rush round wildly, butting each other and everything in their way, and end in a general stampede for underground retreats from the region poisoned by sunshine. *Next year* you will find the grass growing tall and green where the stone lay; the ground-bird builds her nest where the beetle had his hole; the dandelion and the buttercup are growing there, and the broad fans of insect-angels open and shut their golden disks, as the rhythmic waves of blissful consciousness pulsate through their glorified being.

— The young fellow whom they call John saw fit to say, in his very familiar way, — at which I do not choose to take offence, but which I sometimes think it necessary to repress, that I was coming it rather strong on the butterflies.

No, I replied; there is meaning in each of those images, — the butterfly as well as the others. The stone is ancient error. The grass is human nature borne down and bleached of all its color by it. The shapes which are found beneath are the crafty beings that thrive in darkness, and the weaker organisms kept helpless by it. He who turns the stone over is whosoever puts the staff of truth to the old lying incubus, no matter whether he do it with a serious face or a laughing one. The next year stands for the coming time. Then shall the nature which had lain blanched and broken rise in its full stature and native hues in the sunshine. Then shall God's minstrels build their nests in the hearts of a newborn humanity. Then shall beauty — Divinity taking outlines and color — light upon the souls of men as the butterfly, image of the beautiful spirit rising from the dust, soars from the shell that held a poor grub, which would never have found wings had not the stone been lifted.

You never need think you can turn over any old falsehood without a terrible squirming and scattering of the horrid little population that dwells under it.***

Sin has many tools, but a lie is the handle which fits them all.

— I think, Sir, — said the divinity-student, — you must intend that for one of the sayings of the Seven Wise Men of Boston you were speaking of the other day.

I thank you, my young friend, — was my reply, — but I must say something better than that, before I could pretend to fill out the number.

— The schoolmistress wanted to know how many of these sayings there were on record, and what, and by whom said.

— Why, let us see, — there is that one of Benjamin Franklin, "the great Bostonian," after whom this lad was named. To be sure, he said a great many wise things, — and I don't feel sure he didn't borrow this, — he speaks as if it were old. But then he applied it so neatly! —

"He that has once done you a kindness will be more ready to do you another than he whom you yourself have obliged."

Then there is that glorious Epicurean paradox, uttered by my friend, the Historian, in one of his flashing moments: —

"Give us the luxuries of life, and we will dispense with its necessaries."

To these must certainly be added that other saying of one of the wittiest of men: —

"Good Americans, when they die, go to Paris."

— The divinity-student looked grave at this, but said nothing.

The schoolmistress spoke out, and said she didn't think the wit meant any irreverence. It was only another way of saying, Paris is a heavenly place after New York or Boston.

A jaunty-looking person, who had come in with the young fellow they call John, — evidently a stranger, — said there was one more wise man's saying that he had heard; it was about our place, but he didn't know who said it. — A civil curiosity was manifested by the company to hear the fourth wise saying. I heard him distinctly whispering to the young fellow who brought him to dinner, *Shall I tell it?* To which the answer was, *Go ahead!* — Well, — he said, — this was what I heard: —

"Boston State-House is the hub of the solar system. You couldn't pry that out of a Boston man if you had the tire of all creation straightened out for a crowbar."

Sir, — said I, — I am gratified with your remark. It expresses with pleasing vivacity that which I have sometimes heard uttered with malignant dulness. The satire of the remark is essentially true of Boston, — and of all other considerable, — and inconsiderable, — places with which I have had the privilege of being acquainted. Cockneys think London is the only place in the world. Frenchmen — you remember the line about Paris, the Court, the World, etc. — I recollect well, by the way, a sign in that city which ran thus: "Hotel de l'Univers et des États Unis"; and as Paris *is* the universe to a Frenchman, of course the United States are outside of it. — "See Naples and then die." It is quite as bad with smaller places. I have been about, lecturing, you know, and have found the following propositions to hold true of all of them.

1. The axis of the earth sticks out visibly through the center of each and every town or city.

2. If more than fifty years have passed since its foundation, it is affectionately styled by the inhabitants the "*good old* town of" — (whatever its name may happen to be).

3. Every collection of its inhabitants that comes together to listen to a stranger is invariably declared to be a "remarkably intelligent audience."

4. The climate of the place is particularly favorable to longevity.

5. It contains several persons of vast talent little known to the world. (One or two of them, you may perhaps chance to remember, sent short pieces to the "Pactolian" some time since, which were "respectfully declined.")

Boston is just like other places of its size; — only, perhaps, considering its excellent fish-market, paid fire-department, superior monthly publications, and correct habit of spelling the English language, it has some right to look down on the mob of cities. I'll tell you, though, if you want to know it, what is the real offence of Boston. It drains a large water-shed of its intellect, and will not itself be drained. If it would only send away its first-rate men, instead of its second-rate ones (no offence to the well-known exceptions, of which we are always proud), we should be spared such epigrammatics remarks as that which the gentleman has quoted. There can never be a real metropolis in this country, until the biggest center can drain the lesser ones of their talent and wealth. — I have observed, by the way, that the people who really live in two great cities are by no means so jealous of each other as are those of smaller cities situated within the intellectual basin, or *suction-range*, of one large one, of the pretensions of any other. Don't you see why? Because their promising young author and rising lawyer and large capitalist have been drained off to the neighboring big city, their prettiest girl has been exported to the same market; all their ambition points there, and all their thin gilding of glory comes from there. I hate little toad-eating cities.

— Would I be so good as to specify any particular example? — Oh, — an example? Did you ever see a bear-trap? Never? Well, shouldn't you like to see me put my foot into one? With sentiments of the highest consideration I must beg leave to be excused.

Besides, some of the smaller cities are charming. If they have an old church or two, a few stately mansions of former grandees, here and there an old dwelling with the second story projecting (for the convenience of shooting the Indians knocking at the front-door with their tomahawks), — if they have, scattered about, those mighty square houses built something more than half a century ago, and standing like architectural boulders dropped by the former diluvium of wealth, whose refluent wave has left them as its monument, — if they have gardens with elbowed apple-trees that push their branches over the high board-fence and drop their fruit on the side-walk, — if they have a little grass in the side-streets, enough to betoken quiet without proclaiming decay, — I think I could go to pieces, after my life's work were done, in one of those tranquil places, as sweetly as in any cradle that an old man may be rocked to sleep in. I visit such spots always with infinite delight. My friend, the Poet, says that rapidly growing towns are most unfavorable to the imaginative and reflective faculties. Let a man live in one of these old quiet places, he says, and the wine of his soul which is kept thick and turbid by the rattle of busy streets, settles, and, as you hold it up, you may see the sun through it by day and the stars by night.

— Do I think that the little villages have the conceit of the great towns? — I don't believe there is much difference. You know how they read Pope's line in the smallest town in our State of Massachusetts? — Well, they read it

"All are but parts of one stupendous HULL!"

***And since I am talking of early recollections, I don't know why I shouldn't mention some others that still cling to me, — not that you will attach any very particular meaning to these same images so full of significance to me, but that you will find something parallel to them in your own memory. You remember, perhaps, what I said one day about smells. There were certain *sounds* also which had a mysterious suggestiveness to me, — not so intense, perhaps, as that connected with the other sense, but yet peculiar, and never to be forgotten.

The first was the creaking of the woodsled, bringing their loads of oak and walnut from the country, as the slow-swinging oxen trailed them along over the complaining snow, in the cold, brown light of early morning. Lying in bed and listening to their dreary music had a pleasure in it akin to the Lucretian luxury, or that which Byron speaks of as to be enjoyed in looking on at a battle by one "who hath no friend, no brother there."

There was another sound, in itself so sweet, and so connected with one of those simple and curious superstitions of childhood of which I have spoken, that I can never cease to cherish a sad sort of love for it. — Let me tell the superstitious fancy first. The Puritan "Sabbath," as everybody knows, began at "sundown" on Saturday evening. To such observance of it I was born and bred. As the large, round disk of day declined, a stillness, a solemnity, a somewhat melancholy hush came over us all. It was time for work to cease, and for playthings to be put away. The world of active life passed into the shadow of an eclipse, not to emerge until the sun should sink again beneath the horizon.

It was in this stillness of the world without and of the soul within that the pulsating lullaby of the evening crickets used to make itself most distinctly heard — so that I well remember I used to think that the purring of these little creatures, which mingled with the batrachian hymns from the neighboring swamps, *was peculiar to Saturday evenings*. I don't know that anything could give a clearer idea of the quieting and subduing effect of the old habit of observance of what was considered holy time, than this strange, childish fancy.

Yes, and there was still another sound which mingled its solemn cadences with the waking and sleeping dreams of my boyhood. It was heard only at times, — a deep, muffled roar, which rose and fell, not loud, but vast, — a whistling boy would have drowned it for his next neighbor, but it must have been heard over the space of a hundred square miles. I used to wonder what this might be. Could it be the roar of the thousand wheels and the ten thousand footsteps jarring and trampling along the stones of the neighboring city? That would be continuous; but this, as I have said, rose and fell in regular rhythm. I remember being told, and I suppose this to have been the true solution, that it was the sound of the waves, after a high wind, breaking on the long beaches many miles distant. I should really like to know whether any observing people living ten miles, more or less, inland from long beaches, — in such a town, for instance, as Cantabridge, in the eastern part of the Territory of the Massachusetts, — have ever observed any such sound, and whether it was rightly accounted for as above.***

[The company looked a little flustered one morning when I came in, — so much so, that I inquired of my neighbor, the divinity-student, what had been going on. It appears that the young fellow whom they call John had taken advantage of my being a little late (I having been rather longer than usual dressing that morning) to circulate several questions involving a quibble or play upon words, — in short, containing that indignity to the human understanding, condemned in the passage from the distinguished moralist of the last century and the illustrious historian of the present, which I cited on a former occasion, and known as a *pun*. After breakfast, one of the boarders handed me a small roll of paper containing some of the questions and their answers. I subjoin two or three of them, to show what a tendency there is to frivolity and meaningless talk in young persons of a certain sort, when not restrained by the presence of more reflective natures. — It was asked, "Why tertian and quartan fevers were like certain short-lived insects." Some interesting physiological relation would be naturally suggested. The inquirer blushes to find that the answer is in the paltry equivocation, that they *skip* a day or two. — "Why an Englishman must go to the Continent to weaken his grog or punch." The answer proves to have no relation whatever to the temperance-movement, as no better reason is given than that island- (or, as it is absurdly written, *ile and*) water won't mix. — But when I came to the next question and its answer, I felt that patience ceased to be a virtue. "Why an onion is like a piano" is a query that a person of sensibility would be slow to propose; but that in an educated community an individual could be found to answer it in these words, — "Because it smell odious," *quasi*, it's melodious, — is not credible, but too true. I can show you the paper.

Dear reader, I beg your pardon for repeating such things. I know most conversations reported in books are altogether above such trivial details, but folly will come up at every table

as surely as purslain and chickweed and sorrel will come up in gardens. This young fellow ought to have talked philosophy, I know perfectly well; but he didn't, — he made jokes.]

I am willing, — I said, — to exercise your ingenuity in a rational and contemplative manner. — No, I do not proscribe certain forms of philosophical speculation which involve an approach to the absurd or the ludicrous, such as you may find, for example, in the folio of the Reverend Father Thomas Sanchez, in his famous Disputations, "De Sancto Matrimonio." I will therefore turn this levity of yours to profit by reading you a rhymed problem, wrought out by my friend the Professor:

THE DEACON'S MASTERPIECE:
OR THE WONDERFUL "ONE-HOSS-SHAY"
A LOGICAL STORY

Have you heard of the wonderful one-hoss-shay,
That was built in such a logical way
It ran a hundred years to a day,
And then, of a sudden, it — ah, but stay,
I'll tell you what happened without delay,
Scaring the parson into fits,
Frightening people out of their wits, —

Have you ever heard of that, I say?
Seventeen hundred and fifty-five,
Georgius Secundus was then alive, —
Snuffy old drone from the German hive;
That was the year when Lisbon-town
Saw the earth open and gulp her down,
And Braddock's army was done so brown,
Left without a scalp to its crown.
It was on the terrible earthquake-day
That the Deacon finished the one-hoss-shay.

Now in building of chaises, I tell you what,
There is always *somewhere* a weakest spot, —
In hub, tire, felloe, in spring or thill,
In panel, or crossbar, or floor, or sill,
In screw, bolt, thoroughbrace, — lurking still,
Find it somewhere you must and will, —
Above or below, or within or without, —
And that's the reason, beyond a doubt,
A chaise *breaks down*, but doesn't *wear out*.

But the Deacon swore (as Deacons do,
With an "I dew vum," or an "I tell *yeou*,")
He would build one shay to beat the taown
'n' the keounty 'n' all the kentry raoun';
It should be so built that it *couldn'* break daown,
— "Fur," said the Deacon, "'t's mighty plain
Thut the weakes' place mus' stan' the strain;
'n' the way t' fix it, uz I maintain,
        Is only jest
T' make that place uz strong uz the rest."

So the Deacon inquired of the village folk
Where he could find the strongest oak,
That couldn't be split nor bent nor broke, —
That was for spokes and floor and sills;
He sent for lancewood to make the thills;
The crossbars were ash, from the straightest trees,
The panels of white-wood, that cuts like cheese,
But lasts like iron for things like these;
The hubs of logs from the "Settler's ellum," —
Last of its timber, — they couldn't sell 'em,
Never an axe had seen their chips,
And the wedges flew from between their lips,
Their blunt ends frizzled like celery-tips;
Step and prop-iron, bolt and screw,
Spring, tire, axle, and linchpin too,
Steel of the finest, bright and blue;
Thoroughbrace bison-skin, thick and wide;
Boot, top, dasher, from tough old hide
Found in the pit when the tanner died.
That was the way he "put her through." —
"There!" said the Deacon, "naow she'll dew."

Do! I tell you, I rather guess
She was a wonder, and nothing less!
Colts grew horses, beards turned gray,
Deacon and deaconess dropped away,
Children and grand-children — where were they?
But there stood the stout old one-hoss-shay
As fresh as on Lisbon-earthquake-day!

EIGHTEEN HUNDRED; — it came and found
The Deacon's Masterpiece strong and sound.
Eighteen hundred increased by ten; —
"Hahnsum kerridge" they called it then.
Eighteen hundred and twenty came; —
Running as usual; much the same.
Thirty and forty at last arrive,
And then come fifty, and FIFTY-FIVE.

Little of all we value here
Wakes on the morn of its hundredth year
Without both feeling and looking queer.
In fact, there's nothing that keeps its youth,
So far as I know, but a tree and truth.
(This is a moral that runs at large;
Take it. — You're welcome. — No extra charge.)
FIRST OF NOVEMBER, — the Earthquake-day. —
There are traces of age in the one-hoss-shay.

A general flavor of mild decay,
But nothing local, as one may say.
There couldn't be, — for the Deacon's art
Had made it so like in every part
That there wasn't a chance for one to start.
For the wheels were just as strong as the thills,
And the floor was just as strong as the sills,
And the panels were just as strong as the floor,
And the whippletree neither less nor more,
And the back-crossbar as strong as the fore,
And spring and axle and hub encore.

And yet, as a whole, it is past a doubt
In another hour it will be worn out!

First of November, 'Fifty-five!
This morning the parson takes a drive.
Now, small boys, get out of the way!
Here comes the wonderful one-hoss-shay,
Drawn by a rat-tailed, ewe-necked bay.
"Huddup!" said the parson. — Off went they.
The parson was working his Sunday's text, —
Had got to fifthly, and stopped perplexed
At what the — Moses — was coming next.
All at once the horse stood still,
Close by the meet'n'-house on the hill.
— First a shiver, and then a thrill,
Then something decidedly like a spill, —
And the parson was sitting upon a rock,
At half-past nine by the meet'n'-house clock, —
Just the hour of the Earthquake shock!
— What do you think the parson found,
When he got up and stared around?
The poor old chaise in a heap or mound,
As if it had been to the mill and ground.
You see, of course, if you're not a dunce,
How it went to pieces all at once, —
All at once, and nothing first, —
Just as bubbles do when they burst.

End of the wonderful one-hoss-shay.
Logic is logic. That's all I say.

* * *

It was my last breakfast as a boarder, and
I could not leave them in utter silence.

Good-by, — I said, — my dear friends, one
and all of you! I have been long with you, and
I find it hard parting. I have to thank you for
a thousand courtesies, and above all for the
patience and indulgence with which you have
listened to me when I have tried to instruct or
amuse you. My friend the Professor (who, as
well as my friend the Poet, is unavoidably absent on this interesting occasion) has given me
reason to suppose that he would occupy my
empty chair about the first of January next. If
he comes among you, be kind to him, as you
have been to me. May the Lord bless you all!
— And we shook hands all round the table.

Half an hour afterwards the breakfast things
and the cloth were gone. I looked up and down
the length of the bare boards over which I had
so often uttered my sentiments and experiences
— and — Yes, I am a man, like another.

All sadness vanished, as, in the midst of
these old friends of mine, whom you know, and
others a little more up in the world, perhaps,
to whom I have not introduced you, I took
the schoolmistress before the altar from the

hands of the old gentleman who used to sit opposite, and who would insist on giving her away.

And now we two are walking the long path in peace together. The "schoolmistress" finds

her skill in teaching called for again, without going abroad to seek little scholars. Those visions of mine have all come true.

I hope you all love me none the less for any- 5 thing I have told you. Farewell.

ROMANTIC AND REALIST

Walt Whitman [1819–1892]

The pulse of the nation beat strong in New York, a city of over half a million souls in 1855 when Whitman published *Leaves of Grass.* But its literary life could not vie with that of Concord and Cambridge. Whitman was its only great writer, and for many years few recognized his greatness. During the late 1850's and early 1860's he fraternized with the "Bohemians" who met at Pfaff's restaurant on — or under — Broadway, among them no writers larger than Fitz James O'Brien and William Winter. They were more congenial to Whitman than another group associated with the city: Taylor, Stedman, Stoddard, Aldrich, poets of romanticism in its decline. But in the decades when the romantic impulse was fading away in a tame conventionality, Whitman gave it a last vigorous expression.

Walter Whitman was born at West Hills, Long Island. His ancestors were English and Dutch, some of them Quakers. The Whitmans moved to Brooklyn when Walt was small, and he felt the dual influence of a large city and a pleasant countryside near enough to be always available. He left school at the age of eleven. Office-boy, typesetter, occasional author, he became an itinerant country school teacher in 1836 and continued in this position until 1841 except for one brief flier in newspaper editing. In his spare time he learned the printing business, and in 1841 he definitely cast his lot with journalism in New York.

In five years he rose to be editor of the *Daily Brooklyn Eagle,* but lost his position in 1848 and was glad to accept another on a paper just starting in New Orleans. Three months in the South and he resigned his position and returned, by way of Chicago, to Brooklyn. Here he made his headquarters until 1862, as journalist, proprietor of a book store, builder, and poet. In 1855 he collected the verse he had recently been writing and published it in a thin volume.

Whitman himself seems to have expected *Leaves of Grass* to be a bombshell. The book, however, was scarcely noticed. It received one important comment: Emerson wrote, "I greet you at the beginning of a great career." Whitman used this sentence, without permission, to advertise the second edition published the next year. This edition contained thirty-two poems, twenty more than the first edition. All his life Whitman continued to supplement, rewrite, and revise *Leaves of Grass.*

Late in 1862 he went down to Fredericksburg to care for a younger brother who had been slightly wounded. The next three years he gave freely of his health and heart as a nurse among the wounded in hospitals in and near Washington. He still found time to write vivid accounts of what he saw, and occasional poems. He gathered the poems in *Drum-Taps* in 1865. The same year he was forced out of a governmental clerkship because a superior thought his poems indecent. His friends came to his aid, — one of them with a pamphlet entitled *The Good Gray Poet,* a name which stuck to Whitman thereafter — and he was established as a clerk in another department. Whitman never married; toward men he apparently had an abnormal attraction.

In 1873, two years after he had issued *Democratic Vistas,* he was stricken with paralysis and settled in Camden, New Jersey, where he lived nearly twenty years until his death. He revised his work, sent out a few articles, received many letters from friends in Europe and America, and made occasional journeys. In 1891–92 he approved the ninth edition of *Leaves of Grass,* the last which he supervised before his death.

Whitman's ideas and attitudes were chiefly those of the Romantic Movement. In his response to nature, his mystical desire for immediacy of experience, his cultivation of the senses, feelings, and imagination, his subjective individualism, his celebration of the common man, he was akin to such predecessors as Rousseau, Wordsworth, Shelley, and Emerson. To Emerson, in fact, he was deeply indebted, saying, "I was simmering, simmering, simmering; Emerson brought me to a boil." Even more than the author of "The American Scholar" he felt the romantic desire for a native experience, a national genius, and he tried to make himself spokesman for all America. With his nationalistic vision he combined a faith in progress, which in his day seemed to be supported by the theory of evolution. Into his romanticism he fused what were later to be traits of the developing realistic movement, such as his quest of a living speech coming out of American life, his generous inclusion of the commonplace and trivial, his incorporation of the ugly, his frank emphasis on sex and on bold sexual terms, and his hearty acceptance of science (though he was not really impregnated with its spirit).

To communicate all this Whitman felt it necessary to achieve a new poetic form. He rejected the time-hallowed marks of English verse: rhymes, regular meters, stanza patterns, elaborate similes, frequent allusions to the Bible, the Classics, the Middle Ages, etc. Instead, he aimed at a freer verse form based on the organic principle, a form not imposed upon but growing out of content. One of his least successful experiments was the cataloguing method, coordinating his materials as if to reflect the equality of all things or the complex miscellaneity of modern life. Most successful are features suggested by the art of music, which are indicated in notes to the poems given below.

The reputation of Whitman grew after his death, till it reached a high point during the lusty literary movement of the 1920's. For example, Lewis Mumford in *The Golden Day* (1926) said: "He is more than a single writer: he is almost a literature"; at his best he wrote "poetry of the first rank"; his poems "belong to sacred literature." Most critics would be less sweeping in their praise, but however Whitman is rated, there is no question of his profound influence on twentieth-century poets, obviously in the case of Carl Sandburg, more subtly in the case of many others, European as well as American. As a rule the influence of Whitman arose from his poetic technique more than from his vision of life.

Further reading: *Complete Poetry, and Selected Prose and Letters,* ed. Emory Holloway, 1938. H. S. Canby, *Walt Whitman, an American,* 1943. G. W. Allen, *The Solitary Singer: A Critical Biography of Walt Whitman,* 1955. F. O. Matthiessen, *American Renaissance,* 1941, pages 517–625.

From *Preface to Leaves of Grass*

(1855)

Leaves of Grass originally contained a dozen untitled poems headed by a long Preface — a ten page double-column essay. Believing that it was time "to break down the barriers of form between prose and poetry," Whitman wrote poetry with prominent prose qualities, and prose with prominent poetic qualities. Some of the prose of the Preface he actually incorporated later, with slight change, in various poems.

Whether or not the Preface is good prose, it is valuable (like Wordsworth's Preface to *Lyrical Ballads*) as a statement of what the poet was up to: a poetic revolution. The following extracts will prove illuminating, especially if read both before and after the poems. The rows of periods (. . .) are Whitman's, serving a function similar to that of dashes.

The opening paragraphs recall Emerson's desire for a truly American poet and his conception of America as itself a poem.

America does not repel the past or what it has produced under its forms or amid other politics or the idea of castes or the old religions . . . accepts the lesson with calmness . . . is not so impatient as has been supposed that the slough still sticks to opinions and manners and literature while the life which served its requirements has passed into the new life of the new forms . . . perceives that the corpse is slowly borne from the eating and sleeping rooms of the house . . . perceives that it waits a little while in the door . . . that it was fittest for its days . . . that its action has descended to the stalwart and wellshaped heir who approaches . . . and that he shall be fittest for his days.

The Americans of all nations at any time upon the earth have probably the fullest poetical nature. The United States themselves are essentially the greatest poem. In the history of the earth hitherto the largest and most stirring appear tame and orderly to their ampler largeness and stir. Here at last is something in the doings of man that corresponds with the broadcast doings of the day and night. Here is not merely a nation but a teeming nation of nations. Here is action united from strings necessarily blind to particulars and details magnificently moving in vast masses. Here is the hospitality which forever indicates heroes. . . . Here are the roughs and beards and space and ruggedness and nonchalance that the soul loves. Here the performance disdaining the trivial unapproached in the tremendous audacity of its crowds and groupings and the push of its perspective spreads with crampless and flowing breadth and showers its prolific and splendid extravagance. One sees it must indeed own the riches of the summer and winter, and need never be bankrupt while corn grows from the ground or the orchards drop apples or the bays contain fish or men beget children upon women.

Other states indicate themselves in their deputies . . . but the genius of the United States is not best or most in its executives or legislatures, nor in its ambassadors or authors or colleges or churches or parlors, nor even in its newspapers or inventors . . . but always most in the common people. Their manners speech dress friendships — the freshness and candor of their physiognomy — the picturesque looseness of their carriage . . . their deathless attachment to freedom — their aversion to anything indecorous or soft or mean — the practical acknowledgment of the citizens of one state by the citizens of all other states — the fierceness of their roused resentment — their curiosity and welcome of novelty — their self-esteem and wonderful sympathy — their susceptibility to a slight — the air they have of persons who never knew how it felt to stand in the presence of superiors — the fluency of their speech — their delight in music, the sure symptom of manly tenderness and native elegance of soul . . . their good temper and open-handedness — the terrible significance of their elections — the President's taking off his hat to them not they to him — these too are unrhymed poetry. It awaits the gigantic and generous treatment worthy of it.

The largeness of nature or the nation were monstrous without a corresponding largeness and generosity of the spirit of the citizen. Not nature nor swarming states nor streets and steamships nor prosperous business nor farms nor capital nor learning may suffice for the ideal of man . . . nor suffice the poet. No reminiscences may suffice either. A live nation can always cut a deep mark and can have the best authority the cheapest . . . namely from its own soul. This is the sum of the profitable uses of individuals or states and of present action and grandeur and of the subjects of poets. — As if it were necessary to trot back generation after generation to the eastern records! As if the beauty and sacredness of the demonstrable must fall behind that of the mythical!

As if men do not make their mark out of any times! As if the opening of the western continent by discovery and what has transpired since in North and South America were less than the small theatre of the antique or the aimless sleepwalking of the middle ages! The pride of the United States leaves the wealth and finesse of the cities and all returns of commerce and agriculture and all the magnitude of geography or shows of exterior victory to enjoy the breed of fullsized men or one fullsized man unconquerable and simple.

The American poets are to enclose old and new for America is the race of races. Of them a bard is to be commensurate with a people. To him the other continents arrive as contributions . . . he gives them reception for their sake and his own sake. His spirit responds to his country's spirit . . . he incarnates its geography and natural life and rivers and lakes. Mississippi with annual freshets and changing chutes, Missouri and Columbia and Ohio and Saint Lawrence with the falls and beautiful masculine Hudson, do not embouchure where they spend themselves more than they embouchure into him. The blue breadth over the inland sea of Virginia and Maryland and the sea off Massachusetts and Maine and over Manhattan bay and over Champlain and Erie and over Ontario and Huron and Michigan and Superior, and over the Texan and Mexican and Floridian and Cuban seas and over the seas off California and Oregon, is not tallied by the blue breadth of the waters below more than the breadth of above and below is tallied by him. When the long Atlantic coast stretches longer and the Pacific coast stretches longer he easily stretches with them north or south. He spans between them also from east to west and reflects what is between them. On him rise solid growths that offset the growths of pine and cedar and hemlock and live-oak and locust and chestnut and cypress and hickory and limetree and cottonwood and tuliptree and cactus and wildvine and tamarind and persimmon . . . and tangles as tangled as any canebreak or swamp . . . and forests coated with transparent ice and icicles hanging from the boughs and crackling in the wind . . . and sides and peaks of mountains . . . and pasturage sweet and free as savannah or upland or prairie . . . with flights and songs and screams that answer those of the wildpigeon and highhold and orchard-oriole and coot and surf-duck and redshouldered-hawk and fish-hawk

and white-ibis and indian-hen and cat-owl and water-pheasant and qua-bird and pied-sheldrake and blackbird and mockingbird and buzzard and condor and night-heron and eagle. To him the hereditary countenance descends both mother's and father's. To him enter the essences of the real things and past and present events — of the enormous diversity of temperature and agriculture and mines — the tribes of red aborigines — the weather-beaten vessels entering new ports or making landings on rocky coasts — the first settlements north or south — the rapid stature and muscle — the haughty defiance of '76, and the war and peace and formation of the constitution . . . the union always surrounded by blatherers and always calm and impregnable — the perpetual coming of immigrants — the wharfhem'd cities and superior marine — the unsurveyed interior — the loghouses and clearings and wild animals and hunters and trappers . . . the free commerce — the fisheries and whaling and gold-digging — the endless gestation of new states — the convening of Congress every December, the members duly coming up from all climates and the uttermost parts . . . the noble character of the young mechanics and of all free American workmen and workwomen . . . the general ardor and friendliness and enterprise — the perfect equality of the female with the male . . . the large amativeness — the fluid movement of the population — the factories and mercantile life and laborsaving machinery — the Yankee swap — the New-York firemen and the target excursion — the southern plantation life — the character of the northeast and the northwest and southwest — slavery and the tremulous spreading of hands to protect it, and the stern opposition to it which shall never cease till it ceases or the speaking of tongues and the moving of lips cease. For such the expression of the American poet is to be transcendant and new. It is to be indirect and not direct or descriptive or epic. Its quality goes through these to much more. Let the age and wars of other nations be chanted and their eras and characters be illustrated and that finish the verse. Not so the great psalm of the republic. Here the theme is creative and has vista. Here comes one among the wellbeloved stonecutters and plans with decision and science and sees the solid and beautiful forms of the future where there are now no solid forms.***

The land and sea, the animals fishes and

birds, the sky of heaven and the orbs, the forests mountains and rivers, are not small themes . . . but folks expect of the poet to indicate more than the beauty and dignity which always attach to dumb real objects . . . they expect him to indicate the path between reality and their souls. Men and women perceive the beauty well enough . . . probably as well as he. The passionate tenacity of hunters, woodmen, early risers, cultivators of gardens and orchards and fields, the love of healthy women for the manly form, seafaring persons, drivers of horses, the passion for light and the open air, all is an old varied sign of the unfailing perception of beauty and of a residence of the poetic in outdoor people. They can never be assisted by poets to perceive . . . some may but they never can. The poetic quality is not marshalled in rhyme or uniformity or abstract addresses to things nor in melancholy complaints or good precepts, but is the life of these and much else and is in the soul. The profit of rhyme is that it drops seeds of a sweeter and more luxuriant rhyme, and of uniformity that it conveys itself into its own roots in the ground out of sight. The rhyme and uniformity of perfect poems show the free growth of metrical laws and bud from them as unerringly and loosely as lilacs or roses on a bush, and take shapes as compact as the shapes of chestnuts and oranges and melons and pears, and shed the perfume impalpable to form. The fluency and ornaments of the finest poems or music or orations or recitations are not independent but dependent. All beauty comes from beautiful blood and a beautiful brain. If the greatnesses are in conjunction in a man or woman it is enough . . . the fact will prevail through the universe . . . but the gaggery and gilt of a million years will not prevail. Who troubles himself about his ornaments or fluency is lost. This is what you shall do: Love the earth and sun and the animals, despise riches, give alms to every one that asks, stand up for the stupid and crazy, devote your income and labor to others, hate tyrants, argue not concerning God, have patience and indulgence toward the people, take off your hat to nothing known or unknown or to any man or number of men, go freely with powerful uneducated persons and with the young and with the mothers of families, read these leaves in the open air every season of every year of your life, re-examine all you have been told at school or church or in any book, dismiss whatever insults your own soul,

and your very flesh shall be a great poem and have the richest fluency not only in its words but in the silent lines of its lips and face and between the lashes of your eyes and in every motion and joint of your body. . . . The poet shall not spend his time in unneeded work. He shall know that the ground is always ready plowed and manured . . . others may not know it but he shall. He shall go directly to the creation. His trust shall master the trust of everything he touches . . . and shall master all attachment.***

The art of art, the glory of expression and the sunshine of the light of letters is simplicity. Nothing is better than simplicity . . . nothing can make up for excess or for the lack of definiteness. To carry on the heave of impulse and pierce intellectual depths and give all subjects their articulations are powers neither common nor very uncommon. But to speak in literature with the perfect rectitude and insouciance of the movements of animals and the unimpeachableness of the sentiment of trees in the woods and grass by the roadside is the flawless triumph of art. If you have looked on him who has achieved it you have looked on one of the masters of all nations and times. You shall not contemplate the flight of the graygull over the bay or the mettlesome action of the blood horse or the tall leaning of sunflowers on their stalk or the appearance of the sun journeying through heaven or the appearance of the moon afterward with any more satisfaction than you shall contemplate him. The greatest poet has less a marked style and is more the channel of thoughts and things without increase or diminution, and is the free channel of himself. He swears to his art, I will not be meddlesome, I will not have in my writing any elegance or effect or originality to hang in the way between me and the rest like curtains. I will have nothing hang in the way, not the richest curtains. What I tell I tell for precisely what it is. Let who may exalt or startle or fascinate or soothe I will have purposes as health or heat or snow has and be as regardless of observation. What I experience or portray shall go from my composition without a shred of my composition. You shall stand by my side and look in the mirror with me.***

The direct trial of him who would be the greatest poet is today. If he does not flood himself with the immediate age as with vast oceanic tides . . . and if he does not attract his own land body and soul to himself and hang on its neck with incomparable love and plunge his semitic muscle into its merits and demerits . . . and if he be not himself the age transfigured . . . and if to him is not opened the eternity which gives similitude to all periods and locations and processes and animate and inanimate forms, and which is the bond of time, and rises up from its inconceivable vagueness and infiniteness in the swimming shape of today, and is held by the ductile anchors of life, and makes the present spot the passage from what was to what shall be, and commits itself to the representation of this wave of an hour and this one of the sixty beautiful children of the wave — let him merge in the general run and wait his development. . . . Still the final test of poems or any character or work remains. The prescient poet projects himself centuries ahead and judges performer or performance after the changes of time. Does it live through them? Does it still hold on untired? Will the same style and the direction of genius to similar points be satisfactory now? Has no new discovery in science or arrival at superior planes of thought and judgment and behaviour fixed him or his so that either can be looked down upon? Have the marches of tens and hundreds and thousands of years made willing detours to the right hand and the left hand for his sake? Is he beloved long and long after he is buried? Does the young man think often of him? and the young woman think often of him? and do the middle-aged and the old think of him?

A great poem is for ages and ages in common and for all degrees and complexions and all departments and sects and for a woman as much as a man and a man as much as a woman. A great poem is no finish to a man or woman but rather a beginning. Has any one fancied he could sit at last under some due authority and rest satisfied with explanations and realize and be content and full? To no such terminus does the greatest poet bring . . . he brings neither cessation or sheltered fatness and ease. The touch of him tells in action. Whom he takes he takes with firm sure grasp into live regions previously unattained . . . thenceforward is no rest . . . they see the space and ineffable sheen that turn the old spots and lights into dead vacuums. The companion of him beholds the birth and progress of stars and learns one of the meanings. Now there shall be a man cohered

out of tumult and chaos . . . the elder encourages the younger and shows him how . . . they two shall launch off fearlessly together till the new world fits an orbit for itself and looks unabashed on the lesser orbits of the stars and sweeps through the ceaseless rings and shall never be quiet again.

There will soon be no more priests. Their work is done. They may wait awhile . . . perhaps a generation or two . . . dropping off by degrees. A superior breed shall take their place . . . the gangs of kosmos and prophets en masse shall take their place. A new order shall arise and they shall be the priests of man, and every man shall be his own priest. The churches built under their umbrage shall be the churches of men and women. Through the divinity of themselves shall the kosmos and the new breed of poets be interpreters of men and women and of all events and things. They shall find their inspiration in real objects today, symptoms of the past and future . . . They shall not deign to defend immortality or God or the perfection of things or liberty or the exquisite beauty and reality of the soul. They shall arise in America and be responded to from the remainder of the earth.

The English language befriends the grand American expression . . . it is brawny enough and limber and full enough. On the tough stock of a race who through all change of circumstances was never without the idea of political liberty, which is the animus of all liberty, it has attracted the terms of daintier and gayer and subtler and more elegant tongues. It is the powerful language of resistance . . . it is the dialect of common sense. It is the speech of the proud and melancholy races and of all who aspire. It is the chosen tongue to express growth faith self-esteem freedom justice equality friendliness amplitude prudence decision and courage. It is the medium that shall well nigh express the inexpressible.

No great literature nor any like style of behaviour or oratory or social intercourse or household arrangements or public institutions or the treatment by bosses of employed people, nor executive detail or detail of the army or navy, nor spirit of legislation or courts or police or tuition or architecture or songs or amusements or the costumes of young men, can long elude the jealous and passionate instinct of American standards. Whether or no the sign appears from the mouths of the people, it throbs a live interrogation in every freeman's and freewoman's heart after that which passes by or this built to remain. Is it uniform with my country? Are its disposals without ignominious distinctions? Is it for the evergrowing communes of brothers and lovers, large, well-united, proud beyond the old models, generous beyond all models? Is it something grown fresh out of the fields or drawn from the sea for use to me today here? I know that what answers for me an American must answer for any individual or nation that serves for a part of my materials. Does this answer? or is it without reference to universal needs? or sprung of the needs of the less developed society of special ranks? or old needs of pleasure overlaid by modern science and forms? Does this acknowledge liberty with audible and absolute acknowledgement, and set slavery at naught for life and death? Will it help breed one good-shaped and wellhung man, and a woman to be his perfect and independent mate? Does it improve manners? Is it for the nursing of the young of the republic? Does it solve readily with the sweet milk of the nipples of the breasts of the mother of many children? Has it too the old ever-fresh forbearance and impartiality? Does it look with the same love on the last born and on those hardening toward stature, and on the errant, and on those who disdain all strength of assault outside of their own?

The poems distilled from other poems will probably pass away. The coward will surely pass away. The expectation of the vital and great can only be satisfied by the demeanor of the vital and great. The swarms of the polished deprecating and reflectors and the polite float off and leave no remembrance. America prepares with composure and goodwill for the visitors that have sent word. It is not intellect that is to be their warrant and welcome. The talented, the artist, the ingenious, the editor,

the statesman, the erudite . . . they are not unappreciated . . . they fall in their place and do their work. The soul of the nation also does its work. No disguise can pass on it . . . no disguise can conceal from it. It rejects none, it permits all. Only toward as good as itself and toward the like of itself will it advance half-way. An individual is as superb as a nation when he has the qualities which make a superb nation. The soul of the largest and wealthiest and proudest nation may well go half-way to meet that of its poets. The signs are effectual. There is no fear of mistake. If the one is true the other is true. The proof of a poet is that his country absorbs him as affectionately as he has absorbed it.

One's-Self I Sing
(1867, 1871)

This poem has commonly been placed first in editions of *Leaves of Grass*. It sums up the general theme of the poems. In using the formula "I sing," Whitman implies that his book is the rough equivalent of the old epics. Whitman announces that he sings of "Modern Man" — that is, the individual common man in a democratic society.

One's-Self I sing, a simple separate person,
Yet utter the word Democratic, the word En-
    Masse.
Of physiology from top to toe I sing,
Not physiognomy alone nor brain alone is
    worthy for the Muse,
    I say the Form complete is worthier far,   5
The Female equally with the Male I sing.

Of Life immense in passion, pulse, and power,
Cheerful, for freest action form'd under the laws
    divine,
The Modern Man I sing.

From Song of Myself
(1855)

The opening poem, untitled, in the first edition of *Leaves of Grass* (later called "Poem of Walt Whitman, an American") expresses the poet's strange mixture of pantheism, mysticism, and leveling materialism and his celebration of the body on an equal basis with the soul. "Myself" could just as well have been "Yourself," since Whitman's object is to identify himself with all men and to picture a representative American. The grandeur of the "divine average" is made clear to the poet in a passage of mystical revelation (section 5) which followed an experience of physical contact. Whitman's frankness in matters of sex, latent here, became, to Victorian minds, shockingly explicit in later poems and caused one reader to remark that he had celebrated every leaf but the fig leaf.

In form and method the poem is "organic" — shaped by natural laws of growth, like a leaf or a tree, according to its purpose and function. The style is conversational, talking "to you whoever you are," and at times employs the tone of public address, as Whitman was fascinated by the art of oratory. His meaning is best come by from reading him aloud, not inspecting the lines too closely at first or looking for a clear outline of thought until one has grasped his spirit and drift. Good, bad, and indifferent passages jostle each other, but the total impression is that of a vast, turbulent, equalitarian America of the nineteenth century.

Within the fifty-two free-verse sections of "Song of Myself," however, there are many passages of deliberate verse form and pattern — parallelisms, grammatical rhythms, Biblical repetitions, superb imagery, and verse "envelopes" such as the eight-line unit (section 21) beginning "Smile, O voluptuous cool-breath'd earth!"

1

I celebrate myself, and sing myself,
And what I assume you shall assume,
For every atom belonging to me as good belongs to you.

I loafe and invite my soul,
I lean and loafe at my ease observing a spear of summer grass. 5

My tongue, every atom of my blood, form'd from this soil, this air,
Born here of parents born here from parents the same, and their parents the same,
I, now thirty-seven years old in perfect health begin,
Hoping to cease not till death.

Creeds and schools in abeyance, 10
Retiring back a while sufficed at what they are, but never forgotten,
I harbor for good or bad, I permit to speak at every hazard,
Nature without check with original energy.

2

Houses and rooms are full of perfumes, the shelves are crowded with perfumes,
I breathe the fragrance myself and know it and like it, 15
The distillation would intoxicate me also, but I shall not let it.

The atmosphere is not a perfume, it has no taste of the distillation, it is odorless,
It is for my mouth forever, I am in love with it,
I will go to the bank by the wood and become undisguised and naked,
I am mad for it to be in contact with me. 20

The smoke of my own breath,
Echoes, ripples, buzz'd whispers, love-root, silk-thread, crotch and vine,
My respiration and inspiration, the beating of my heart, the passing of blood and air through my lungs,
The sniff of green leaves and dry leaves, and of the shore and dark-color'd sea-rocks, and of hay in the barn,
The sound of the belch'd words of my voice loos'd to the eddies of the wind, 25
A few light kisses, a few embraces, a reaching around of arms,
The play of shine and shade on the trees as the supple boughs wag,
The delight alone or in the rush of the streets, or along the fields and hill-sides,
The feeling of health, the full-noon trill, the song of me rising from bed and meeting the sun.

Have you reckon'd a thousand acres much? have you reckon'd the earth much? 30
Have you practis'd so long to learn to read?
Have you felt so proud to get at the meaning of poems?

Stop this day and night with me and you shall possess the origin of all poems,
You shall possess the good of the earth and sun, (there are millions of suns left.)
You shall no longer take things at second or third hand, nor look through the eyes of
    the dead, nor feed on the spectres in books, **35**
You shall not look through my eyes either, nor take things from me,
You shall listen to all sides and filter them from your self.

3

I have heard what the talkers were talking, the talk of the beginning and the end,
But I do not talk of the beginning or the end.

There was never any more inception than there is now, **40**
Nor any more youth or age than there is now,
And will never be any more perfection than there is now,
Nor any more heaven or hell than there is now.

Urge and urge and urge,
Always the procreant urge of the world. **45**
Out of the dimness opposite equals advance, always substance and increase, always sex,
Always a knit of identity, always distinction, always a breed of life.

To elaborate is no avail, learn'd and unlearn'd feel that it is so.

Sure as the most certain sure, plumb in the uprights, well entretied, braced in the beams,
Stout as a horse, affectionate, haughty, electrical, **50**
I and this mystery here we stand.

Clear and sweet is my soul, and clear and sweet is all that is not my soul.

Lack one lacks both, and the unseen is proved by the seen,
Till that becomes unseen and receives proof in its turn.

Showing the best and dividing it from the worst age vexes age, **55**
Knowing the perfect fitness and equanimity of things, while they discuss I am silent,
    and go bathe and admire myself.

Welcome is every organ and attribute of me, and of any man hearty and clean,
Not an inch nor a particle of an inch is vile, and none shall be less familiar than the rest.

I am satisfied — I see, dance, laugh, sing;
As the hugging and loving bed-fellow sleeps at my side through the night, and withdraws
    at the peep of the day with stealthy tread, **60**
Leaving the baskets cover'd with white towels swelling the house with their plenty,
Shall I postpone my acceptation and realization and scream at my eyes,
That they turn from gazing after and down the road,
And forthwith cipher and show me to a cent,
Exactly the value of one and exactly the value of two, and which is ahead? **65**

4

Trippers and askers surround me,
People I meet, the effect upon me of my early life or the ward and city I live in, or the
    nation,
The latest dates, discoveries, inventions, societies, authors old and new,
My dinner, dress, associates, looks, compliments, dues,
The real or fancied indifference of some man or woman I love, **70**

The sickness of one of my folks or of myself, or ill-doing or loss or lack of money, or
    depressions or exaltations,
Battles, the horrors of fratricidal war, the fever of doubtful news, the fitful events;
These come to me days and nights and go from me again,
But they are not the Me myself.

Apart from the pulling and hauling stands what I am,   75
Stands amused, complacent, compassionating, idle, unitary,
Looks down, is erect, or bends an arm on an impalpable certain rest
Looking with side-curved head curious what will come next,
Both in an out of the game and watching and wondering at it.

Backward I see in my own days where I sweated through fog with linguists and
    contenders,   80
I have no mockings or arguments, I witness and wait.

5

I believe in you my soul, the other I am must not abase itself to you,
And you must not be abased to the other.

Loafe with me on the grass, loose the stop from your throat,
Not words, not music or rhyme I want, not custom or lecture, not even the best,   85
Only the lull I like, the hum of your valvèd voice.

I mind how once we lay such a transparent summer morning,
How you settled your head athwart my hips and gently turn'd over upon me,
And parted the shirt from my bosom-bone, and plunged your tongue to my bare-stript
    heart,
And reach'd till you felt my beard, and reach'd till you held my feet.   90

Swiftly arose and spread around me the peace and knowledge that pass all the argument
    of the earth,
And I know that the hand of God is the promise of my own,
And I know that the spirit of God is the brother of my own,
And that all the men ever born are also my brothers, and the women my sisters and
    lovers,
And that a kelson of the creation is love,   95
And limitless are leaves stiff or drooping in the fields,
And brown ants in the little wells beneath them,
And mossy scabs of the worm fence, heap'd stones, elder, mullein and poke-weed.

6

A child said What is the grass? fetching it to me with full hands,
How could I answer the child? I do not know what it is any more than he.   100

I guess it must be the flag of my disposition, out of hopeful green stuff woven.
Or I guess it is the handkerchief of the Lord,
A scented gift and remembrancer designedly dropt,
Bearing the owner's name someway in the corners, that we may see and remark, and
    say Whose?

Or I guess the grass is itself a child, the produced babe of the vegetation.   105

Or I guess it is a uniform hieroglyphic,
And it means, Sprouting alike in broad zones and narrow zones,
Growing among black folks as among white,

Kanuck, Tuckahoe, Congressman, Cuff, I give them the same, I receive them the same.
And now it seems to me the beautiful uncut hair of graves.   110

Tenderly will I use you curling grass,
It may be you transpire from the breasts of young men,
It may be if I had known them I would have loved them,
It may be you are from old people, or from offspring taken soon out of their mothers'
     laps,
And here you are the mothers' laps.   115

This grass is very dark to be from the white heads of old mothers,
Darker than the colorless beards of old men,
Dark to come from under the faint red roofs of mouths.

O I perceive after all so many uttering tongues,
And I perceive they do not come from the roofs of mouths for nothing.   120

I wish I could translate the hints about the dead young men and women,
And the hints about old men and mothers, and the offspring taken soon out of their laps.

What do you think has become of the young and old men?
And what do you think has become of the women and children?

They are alive and well somewhere,   125
The smallest sprout shows there is really no death,
And if ever there was it led forward life, and does not wait at the end to arrest it,
And ceas'd the moment life appear'd.

All goes onward and outward, nothing collapses,
And to die is different from what any one supposed, and luckier.   130

7

Has any one supposed it lucky to be born?
I hasten to inform him or her it is just as lucky to die, and I know it.

I pass death with the dying and birth with the new-wash'd babe, and am not contain'd
     between my hat and boots,
And peruse manifold objects, no two alike and every one good,
The earth good and the stars good, and their adjuncts all good.   135

I am not an earth nor an adjunct of an earth,
I am the mate and companion of people, all just as immortal and fathomless as myself,
(They do not know how immortal, but I know.)

Every kind for itself and its own, for me mine male and female,
For me those that have been boys and that love women,   140
For me the man that is proud and feels how it stings to be slighted,
For me the sweet-heart and the old maid, for me mothers and the mothers of mothers,
For me lips that have smiled, eyes that have shed tears,
For me children and the begetters of children.

Undrape! you are not guilty to me, nor stale nor discarded,   145
I see through the broadcloth and gingham whether or no,
And am around, tenacious, acquisitive, tireless, and cannot be shaken away.

*   *   *   *   *   *

10

* * * *

The runaway slave came to my house and stopt outside,
I heard his motions crackling the twigs of the woodpile,   190
Through the swung half-door of the kitchen I saw him limpsy and weak,
And went where he sat on a log and led him in and assured him,
And brought water and fill'd a tub for his sweated body and bruis'd feet,
And gave him a room that enter'd from my own, and gave him some coarse clean
    clothes,
And remember perfectly well his revolving eyes and his awkwardness,   195
And remember putting plasters on the galls of his neck and ankles;
He staid with me a week before he was recuperated and pass'd north,
I had him sit next me at table, my fire-lock lean'd in the corner.

11

Twenty-eight young men bathe by the shore,
Twenty-eight young men and all so friendly;   200
Twenty-eight years of womanly life and all so lonesome.

She owns the fine house by the rise of the bank,
She hides handsome and richly drest aft the blinds of the window.
Which of the young men does she like the best?
Ah the homeliest of them is beautiful to her.   205

Where are you off to, lady? for I see you,
You splash in the water there, yet stay stock still in your room.

Dancing and laughing along the beach came the twenty-ninth bather,
The rest did not see her, but she saw them and loved them.

The beards of the young men glisten'd with wet, it ran from their long hair, 210
Little streams pass'd all over their bodies.

An unseen hand also pass'd over their bodies,
It descended tremblingly from their temples and ribs.

The young men float on their backs, their white bellies bulge to the sun, they do not ask
    who seizes fast to them,
They do not know who puffs and declines with pendant and bending arch,   215
They do not think whom they souse with spray.

12

The butcher-boy put off his killing-clothes, or sharpens his knife at the stall in the
    market,
I loiter enjoying his repartee and his shuffle and break-down.

Blacksmiths with grimed and hairy chests environ the anvil,
Each has his main-sledge, they are all out, there is a great heat in the fire. 220

From the cinder-strew'd threshold I follow their movements,
The lithe sheer of their waists plays even with their massive arms,
Overhand the hammers swing, overhand so slow, overhand so sure,
They do not hasten, each man hits in his place.

14

*　　*　　*　　*

What is commonest, cheapest, nearest, easiest, is Me,
Me going in for my chances, spending for vast returns,　　260
Adorning myself to bestow myself on the first that will take me,
Not asking the sky to come down to my good will,
Scattering it freely forever.

17

These are really the thoughts of all men in all ages and lands, they are not original
　　　　with me,　　355
If they are not yours as much as mine they are nothing, or next to nothing,
If they are not the riddle and the untying of the riddle they are nothing,
If they are not just as close as they are distant they are nothing.

This is the grass that grows wherever the land is and the water is,
This the common air that bathes the globe.　　360

18

With music strong I come, with my cornets and my drums,
I play not marches for accepted victors only, I play marches for conquer'd and slain
　　　　persons.

Have you heard that it was good to gain the day?
I also say it is good to fall, battles are lost in the same spirit in which they are won.

I beat and pound for the dead,　　365
I blow through my embouchures my loudest and gayest for them.

Vivas to those who have fail'd!
And to those whose war-vessels sank in the sea!
And to those themselves who sank in the sea!
And to all generals that lost engagements, and all overcome heroes!　　370
And the numberless unknown heroes equal to the greatest heroes known!

19

This is the meal equally set, this the meat for natural hunger,
It is for the wicked just the same as the righteous, I make appointment with all,
I will not have a single person slighted or left away,
The kept-woman, sponger, thief, are hereby invited,　　375
The heavy-lipp'd slave is invited, the venerealee is invited;
There shall be no difference between them and the rest.

This is the press of a bashful hand, this the float and odor of hair,
This is the touch of my lips to yours, this the murmur of yearning,
This the far-off depth and height reflecting my own face,　　380
This the thoughtful merge of myself, and the outlet again.

Do you guess I have some intricate purpose?
Well I have, for the Fourth-month showers have, and the mica on the side of a rock
　　　　has.

Do you take it I would astonish?
Does the daylight astonish? does the early redstart twittering through the woods?　　385

Do I astonish more than they?
This hour I tell things in confidence,
I might not tell everybody, but I will tell you.

20

Who goes there? hankering, gross, mystical, nude;
How is it I extract strength from the beef I eat?   390
What is a man anyhow? what am I? what are you?

All I mark as my own you shall offset it with your own,
Else it were time lost listening to me.

I do not snivel that snivel the world over,
That months are vacuums and the ground but wallow and filth.   395

Whimpering and truckling fold with powders for invalids, conformity goes to the fourth
    remov'd,
I wear my hat as I please indoors or out.
Why should I pray? why should I venerate and be ceremonious?

Having pried through the strata, analyzed to a hair, counsel'd with doctors and calcu-
    lated close,
I find no sweeter fat than sticks to my own bones.   400

In all people I see myself, none more and not one a barley-corn less,
And the good or bad I say of myself I say of them.

I know I am solid and sound,
To me the converging objects of the universe perpetually flow,
All are written to me, and I must get what the writing means.   405

I know I am deathless,
I know this orbit of mine cannot be swept by a carpenter's compass,
I know I shall not pass like a child's carlacue cut with a burnt stick at night.

I know I am august,
I do not trouble my spirit to vindicate itself or be understood,   410
I see that the elementary laws never apologize,
(I reckon I behave no prouder than the level I plant my house by, after all.)

I exist as I am, that is enough,
If no other in the world be aware I sit content,
And if each and all be aware I sit content.

One world is aware and by the far largest to me, and that is myself,
And whether I come to my own to-day or in ten thousand or ten million years,
I can cheerfully take it now, or with equal cheerfulness I can wait.

My foothold is tenon'd and mortis'd in granite,
I laugh at what you call dissolution,   420
And I know the amplitude of time.

21

I am the poet of the Body and I am the poet of the Soul,
The pleasures of heaven are with me and the pains of hell are with me,

The first I graft and increase upon myself, the latter I translate into a new tongue.

I am the poet of the woman the same as the man,   425
And I say it is as great to be a woman as to be a man,
And I say there is nothing greater than the mother of men.

I chant the chant of dilation or pride,
We have had ducking and deprecating about enough,
I show that size is only development.   430

Have you outstript the rest? are you the President?
It is a trifle, they will more than arrive there every one, and still pass **on.**

I am he that walks with the tender and growing night,
I call to the earth and sea half-held by the night.

Press close bare-bosom'd night — press close magnetic nourishing night!   435
Night of south winds — night of the large few stars!
Still nodding night — mad naked summer night.

Smile O voluptuous cool-breath'd earth!
Earth of the slumbering and liquid trees!
Earth of departed sunset — earth of the mountains misty-topt!   440
Earth of the vitreous pour of the full moon just tinged with blue!
Earth of shine and dark mottling the tide of the river!
Earth of the limpid gray of clouds brighter and clearer for my sake!
Far-swooping elbow'd earth — rich apple-blossom'd earth!
Smile, for your lover comes.   445

Prodigal, you have given me love — therefore I to you give love!
O unspeakable passionate love.

22

You sea! I resign myself to you also — I guess what you mean,
I behold from the beach your crooked inviting fingers,
I believe you refuse to go back without feeling of me,   450
We must have a turn together, I undress, hurry me out of sight of the land,
Cushion me soft, rock me in billowy drowse,
Dash me with amorous wet, I can repay you.

Sea of stretch'd ground-swells,
Sea breathing broad and convulsive breaths,   455
Sea of the brine of life and of unshovell'd yet always-ready graves,
Howler and scooper of storms, capricious and dainty sea,
I am integral with you, I too am of one phase and of all phases.***

*   *   * *

24

Walt Whitman, a kosmos, of Manhattan the son,
Turbulent, fleshy, sensual, eating, drinking and breeding,
No sentimentalist, no stander above men and women or apart from them,
No more modest than immodest.   500

Unscrew the locks from the doors!
Unscrew the doors themselves from their jambs!

Whoever degrades another degrades me,
And whatever is done or said returns at last to me.

Through me the afflatus surging and surging, through me the current and index.   505

I speak the pass-word primeval, I give the sign of democracy,
By God! I will accept nothing which all cannot have their counterpart of on the same
    terms.

Through me many long dumb voices,
Voices of the interminable generations of prisoners and slaves,
Voices of the diseas'd and despairing and of thieves and dwarfs,   510
Voices of cycles of preparation and accretion,
And of the threads that connect the stars, and of wombs and of the father-stuff,
And of the rights of them the others are down upon,
Of the deform'd, trivial, flat, foolish, despised,
Fog in the air, beetles rolling balls of dung.   515

Through me forbidden voices,
Voices of sexes and lusts, voices veil'd and I remove the veil,
Voices indecent by me clarified and transfigur'd.

I do not press my fingers across my mouth,
I keep as delicate around the bowels as around the head and heart,   520
Copulation is no more rank to me than death is.

I believe in the flesh and the appetites,
Seeing, hearing, feeling, are miracles, and each part and tag of me is a miracle.
Divine am I inside and out, and I make holy whatever I touch or am touch'd from,
The scent of these arm-pits aroma finer than prayer,   525
This head more than churches, bibles, and all the creeds.

If I worship one thing more than another it shall be the spread of my own body, or any
    part of it.
Translucent mould of me it shall be you!
Shaded ledges and rests it shall be you!
Firm masculine colter it shall be you!   530
Whatever goes to the tilth of me it shall be you!
You my rich blood! your milky stream pale strippings of my life!
Breast that presses against other breasts it shall be you!
My brain it shall be your occult convolutions!
Root of wash'd sweet-flag! timorous pond-snipe! nest of guarded duplicate eggs! it shall
    be you!   535

Mix'd tussled hay of head, beard, brawn, it shall be you!
Trickling sap of maple, fibre of manly wheat, it shall be you!
Sun so generous it shall be you!
Vapors lighting and shading my face it shall be you!
You sweaty brooks and dews it shall be you!   540
Winds whose soft-tickling genitals rub against me it shall be you!
Broad muscular fields, branches of live oak, loving lounger in my winding paths, it shall
    be you!
Hands I have taken, face I have kiss'd, mortal I have ever touch'd, it shall be you.

I dote on myself, there is that lot of me and all so luscious,
Each moment and whatever happens thrills me with joy,   545
I cannot tell how many ankles bend, nor whence the cause of my faintest wish,
Nor the cause of the friendship I emit, nor the cause of the friendship I take again.

That I walk up my stoop, I pause to consider if it really be,
A morning-glory at my window satisfies me more than the metaphysics of books.

To behold the day-break!   550
The little light fades the immense and diaphanous shadows,
The air tastes good to my palate.

Hefts of the moving world at innocent gambols silently rising, freshly exuding,
Scooting obliquely high and low.

Something I cannot see puts upward libidinous prongs,   555
Seas of bright juice suffuse heaven.

The earth by the sky staid with, the daily close of their junction,
The heav'd challenge from the east that moment over my head,
The mocking taunt, See then whether you shall be master!

                    *   *   *   *   *

27

To be in any form, what is that?
(Round and round we go, all of us, and ever come back thither,)
If nothing lay more develop'd the quahaug in its callous shell were enough.
Mine is no callous shell,
I have instant conductors all over me whether I pass or stop,   615
They seize every object and lead it harmlessly through me.

I merely stir, press, feel with my fingers, and am happy,
To touch my person to some one else's is about as much as I can stand.

28

Is this then a touch? quivering me to a new identity,
Flames and ether making a rush for my veins,   620
Treacherous tip of me reaching and crowding to help them,
My flesh and blood playing out lightning to strike what is hardly different from
    myself,
On all sides prurient provokers stiffening my limbs,
Straining the udder of my heart for its withheld drip,
Behaving licentious toward me, taking no denial,   625
Depriving me of my best as for a purpose,
Unbuttoning my clothes, holding me by the bare waist,
Deluding my confusion with the calm of the sunlight and pasture-fields,
Immodestly sliding the fellow-senses away,
They bribed to swap off with touch and go and graze at the edges of me, 630
No consideration, no regard for my draining strength or my anger,
Fetching the rest of the herd around to enjoy them a while,
Then all uniting to stand on a headland and worry me.

The sentries desert every other part of me,
They have left me helpless to a red marauder,   635
They all come to the headland to witness and assist against me.

I am given up by traitors,
I talk wildly, I have lost my wits, I and nobody else am the greatest traitor,
I went myself first to the headland, my own hands carried me there.

You villain touch! what are you doing? my breath is tight in its throat,   640
Unclench your floodgates, you are too much for me.

29

Blind loving wrestling touch, sheath'd hooded sharp-tooth'd touch!
Did it make you ache so, leaving me?

Parting track'd by arriving, perpetual payment of perpetual loan,
Rich showering rain, and recompense richer afterward.   645

Sprouts take and accumulate, stand by the curb prolific and vital,
Landscapes projected masculine, full-sized and golden.

30

All truths wait in all things,
They neither hasten their own delivery nor resist it,
They do not need the obstetric forceps of the surgeon,   650
The insignificant is as big to me as any,
(What is less or more than a touch?)

Logic and sermons never convince,
The damp of the night drives deeper into my soul.

(Only what proves itself to every man and woman is so,   655
Only what nobody denies it so.)

A minute and a drop of me settle my brain,
I believe the soggy clods shall become my lovers and lamps,
And a compend of compends is the meat of a man or woman,
And a summit and flower there is the feeling they have for each other,   660
And they are to branch boundlessly out of that lesson until it becomes omnific,
And until one and all shall delight us, and we them.

31

I believe a leaf of grass is no less than the journey-work of the stars,
And the pismire is equally perfect, and a grain of sand, and the egg of the wren,
And the tree-toad is a chef-d'œuvre for the highest,   665
And the running blackberry would adorn the parlors of heaven,
And the narrowest hinge in my hand puts to scorn all machinery,
And the cow crunching with depress'd head surpasses any statue,
And a mouse is a miracle enough to stagger sextillions of infidels.

I find I incorporate gneiss, coal, long-threaded moss, fruits, grains, esculent roots,   670
And am stucco'd with quadrupeds and birds all over,
And have distanced what is behind me for good reasons,
But call any thing back again when I desire it.

In vain the speeding or shyness,
In vain the plutonic rocks send their old heat against my approach,   675
In vain the mastodon retreats beneath its own powder'd bones,
In vain objects stand leagues off and assume manifold shapes,
In vain the ocean settling in hollows and the great monsters lying low,

In vain the buzzard houses herself with the sky,
In vain the snake slides through the creepers and logs,   680
In vain the elk takes to the inner passes of the woods,
In vain the razor-bill'd auk sails far north to Labrador,
I follow quickly, I ascend to the nest in the fissure of the cliff.

32

I think I could turn and live with animals, they are so placid and self contain'd,
I stand and look at them long and long.   685

They do not sweat and whine about their condition,
They do not lie awake in the dark and weep for their sins,
They do not make me sick discussing their duty to God,
Not one is dissatisfied, not one is demented with the mania of owning things,
Not one kneels to another, nor to his kind that lived thousands of years ago,   690
Not one is respectable or unhappy over the whole earth.

So they show their relations to me and I accept them,
They bring me tokens of myself, they evince them plainly in their possession.
I wonder where they get those tokens,
Did I pass that way huge times ago and negligently drop them?   695

Myself moving forward then and now and forever,
Gathering and showing more always and with velocity,
Infinite and omnigenous, and the like of these among them,
Not too exclusive toward the reachers of my remembrancers,
Picking out here one that I love, and now go with him on brotherly terms.   700

A gigantic beauty of a stallion, fresh and responsive to my caresses,
Head high in the forehead, wide between the ears,
Limbs glossy and supple, tail dusting the ground,
Eyes full of sparkling wickedness, ears finely cut, flexibly moving.

His nostrils dilate as my heels embrace him,   705
His well-built limbs tremble with pleasure as we race around and return.
I but use you a minute, then I resign you, stallion,
Why do I need your paces when I myself out-gallop them?
Even as I stand or sit passing faster than you.

33

Space and Time! now I see it is true, what I guess'd at,   710
What I guess'd when I loaf'd on the grass,
What I guess'd while I lay alone in my bed,
And again as I walk'd the beach under the paling stars of the morning.

My ties and ballasts leave me, my elbows rest in sea-gaps,
I skirt sierras, my palms cover continents,   715
I am afoot with my vision.***

I visit the orchards of spheres and look at the product,
And look at quintillions ripen'd and look at quintillions green.

I fly those flights of a fluid and swallowing soul,   800
My course runs below the soundings of plummets.

I help myself to material and immaterial,
No guard can shut me off, no law prevent me.***

I am a free companion, I bivouac by invading watchfires,
I turn the bridegroom out of bed and stay with the bride myself,
I tighten her all night to my thighs and lips.

My voice is the wife's voice, the screech by the rail of the stairs,   820
They fetch my man's body up dripping and drown'd.

I understand the large hearts of heroes,
The courage of present times and all times ***

*   *   *   *   *

You laggards there on guard! look to your arms!   945
In at the conquer'd doors they crowd! I am possess'd!
Embody all presences outlaw'd or suffering,
See myself in prison shaped like another man,
And feel the dull unintermitted pain.

For me the keepers of convicts shoulder their carbines and keep watch,   950
It is I let out in the morning and barr'd at night.

Not a mutineer walks handcuff'd to jail but I am handcuff'd to him and walk by his side,
(I am less the jolly one there, and more the silent one with sweat on my twitching lips.)

Not a youngster is taken for larceny but I go up too, and am tried and sentenced.

Not a cholera patient lies at the last gasp but I also lie at the last gasp,   955
My face is ash-color'd, my sinews gnarl, away from me people retreat.

Askers embody themselves in me and I am embodied in them,
I project my hat, sit shame-faced, and beg.

38

Enough! enough! enough!
Somehow I have been stunn'd. Stand back!   960
Give me a little time beyond my cuff'd head, slumbers, dreams, gaping,
I discover myself on the verge of a usual mistake.

That I could forget the mockers and insults!
That I could forget the trickling tears and the blows of the bludgeons and hammers!
That I could look with a separate look on my own crucifixion and bloody crowning.   965

I remember now,
I resume the overstaid fraction,
The grave of rock multiplies what has been confided to it, or to any graves,
Corpses rise, gashes heal, fastenings roll from me.   969

I troop forth replenish'd with supreme power, one of an average unending procession,
Inland and sea-coast we go, and pass all boundary lines,
Our swift ordinances on their way over the whole earth,
The blossoms we wear in our hats the growth of thousands of years.

Eleves, I salute you! come forward!
Continue your annotations, continue your questionings.   975

39

The friendly and flowing savage, who is he?
Is he waiting for civilization, or past it and mastering it?

Is he some Southwesterner rais'd out-doors? is he Kanadian?
Is he from the Mississippi country? Iowa, Oregon, California?
The mountains? prairie-life? bush-life? or sailor from the sea?   980

Wherever he goes men and women accept and desire him,
They desire he should like them, touch them, speak to them, stay with them.

Behavior lawless as snow-flakes, words simple as grass, uncomb'd head, laughter, and
       naïveté,
Slow-stepping feet, common features, common modes and emanations,
They descend in new forms from the tips of his fingers,   985
They are wafted with the odor of his body or breath, they fly out of the glance of his
       eyes.

40

Flaunt of the sunshine I need not your bask — lie over!
You light surfaces only, I force surfaces and depths also.

Earth! you seem to look for something at my hands,
Say, old top-knot, what do you want?   990

Man or woman, I might tell how I like you, but cannot,
And might tell what it is in me and what it is in you, but cannot,
And might tell that pining I have, that pulse of my nights and days.

Behold, I do not give lectures or a little charity,
When I give I give myself.   995

You there, impotent, loose in the knees,
Open your scarf'd chops till I blow grit within you,
Spread your palms and lift the flaps of your pockets,
I am not to be denied, I compel, I have stores plenty and to spare,
And any thing I have I bestow.   1000

I do not ask who you are, that is not important to me,
You can do nothing and be nothing but what I will infold you.

To cotton-field drudge or cleaner of privies I lean,
On his right cheek I put the family kiss,
And in my soul I swear I never will deny him.   1005

On women fit for conception I start bigger and nimbler babes,
(This day I am jetting the stuff of far more arrogant republics.)

To any one dying, thither I speed and twist the knob of the door,
Turn the bed-clothes toward the foot of the bed,
Let the physician and the priest go home.   1010

I seize the descending man and raise him with resistless will,
O despairer, here is my neck,
By God, you shall not go down! hang your whole weight upon me.

I dilate you with tremendous breath, I buoy you up,
Every room of the house do I fill with an arm'd force,   1015
Lovers of me, bafflers of graves.

Sleep — I and they keep guard all night,
Not doubt, not decease shall dare to lay finger upon you,
I have embraced you, and henceforth possess you to myself,
And when you rise in the morning you will find what I tell you is so.   1020

41

I am he bringing help for the sick as they pant on their backs,
And for strong upright men I bring yet more needed help.

I heard what was said of the universe,
Heard it and heard it of several thousand years;
It is middling well as far as it goes — but is that all?   1025
Magnifying and applying come I,
Outbidding at the start the old cautious hucksters,
Taking myself the exact dimensions of Jehovah,
Lithographing Kronos, Zeus his son, and Hercules his grandson,
Buying drafts of Osiris, Isis, Belus, Brahma, Buddha,   1030
In my portfolio placing Manito loose, Allah on a leaf, the crucifix engraved,
With Odin and the hideous-faced Mexitli and every idol and image,
Taking them all for what they are worth and not a cent more,
Admitting they were alive and did the work of their days,
(They bore mites as for unfledg'd birds who have now to rise and fly and sing for them-
        selves,)   1035
Accepting the rough deific sketches to fill out better in myself, bestowing them freely
        on each man and woman I see,
Discovering as much or more in a framer framing a house,
Putting higher claims for him there with his roll'd-up sleeves driving the mallet and
        chisel,
Not objecting to special revelations, considering a curl of smoke or a hair on the back
        of my hand just as curious as any revelation,
Lads ahold of fire-engines and hook-and-ladder ropes no less to me than the gods of the
        antique wars,   1040
Minding their voices peal through the crash of destruction,
Their brawny limbs passing safe over charr'd laths, their white foreheads whole and
        unhurt out of the flames;
By the mechanic's wife with her babe at her nipple interceding for every person born,
Three scythes at harvest whizzing in a row from three lusty angels with shirts bagg'd
        out at their waists,
The snag-tooth'd hostler with red hair redeeming sins past and to come,   1045
Selling all he possesses, travelling on foot to fee lawyers for his brother and sit by him
        while he is tried for forgery;
What was strewn in the amplest strewing the square rod about me, and not filling the
        square rod then,
The bull and the bug never worshipp'd half enough,
Dung and dirt more admirable than was dream'd,   1049
The supernatural of no account, myself waiting my time to be one of the supremes,
The day getting ready for me when I shall do as much good as the best, and be as
        prodigious;

By my life-lumps! becoming already a creator,
Putting myself here and now to the ambush'd womb of the shadows.

42

A call in the midst of the crowd,
My own voice, orotund sweeping and final.   1055

Come my children,
Come my boys and girls, my women, household and intimates,
Now the performer launches his nerve, he has pass'd his prelude on the reeds within.

Easily written loose-finger'd chords — I feel the thrum of your climax and close.

My head slues round on my neck,   1060
Music rolls, but not from the organ,
Folks are around me, but they are no household of mine.

Ever the hard unsunk ground,
Ever the eaters and drinkers, ever the upward and downward sun, ever the air and the
        ceaseless tides,
Ever myself and my neighbors, refreshing, wicked, real,   1065
Ever the old inexplicable query, ever that thorn'd thumb, that breath of itches and
        thirsts,
Ever the vexer's *hoot! hoot!* till we find where the sly one hides and bring him forth,
Ever love, ever the sobbing liquid of life,
Ever the bandage under the chin, ever the trestles of death.

Here and there with dimes on the eyes walking,   1070
To feed the greed of the belly the brains liberally spooning,
Tickets buying, taking, selling, but in to the feast never once going,
Many sweating, ploughing, thrashing, and then the chaff for payment receiving,
A few idly owning, and they the wheat continually claiming.

This is the city and I am one of the citizens,   1075
Whatever interests the rest interests me, politics, wars, markets, newspapers, schools,
The mayor and councils, banks, tariffs, steamships, factories, stocks, stores, real estate
        and personal estate.

The little plentiful manikins skipping around in collars and tail'd coats,
I am aware who they are, (they are positively not worms or fleas,)
I acknowledge the duplicates of myself, the weakest and shallowest is deathless with me,
What I do and say the same waits for them,   1081
Every thought that flounders in me the same flounders in them.

I know perfectly well my own egotism,
Know my omnivorous lines and must not write any less,
And would fetch you whoever you are flush with myself.   1085

Not words of routine this song of mine,
But abruptly to question, to leap beyond yet nearer bring;
This printed and bound book — but the printer and the printing-office boy?
The well-taken photographs — but your wife or friend close and solid in your arms?
The black ship mail'd with iron, her mighty guns in her turrets — but the pluck of the
        captain and engineers?   1090
In the houses the dishes and fare and furniture — but the host and hostess, and the
        look out of their eyes?

The sky up there — yet here or next door, or across the way?
The saints and sages in history — but you yourself?
Sermons, creeds, theology — but the fathomless human brain,
And what is reason? and what is love? and what is life?   **1095**

43

I do not despise you priests, all time, the world over,
My faith is the greatest of faiths and the least of faiths,
Enclosing worship ancient and modern and all between ancient and modern,
Believing I shall come again upon the earth after five thousand years,
Waiting responses from oracles, honoring the gods, saluting the sun,   **1100**
Making a fetich of the first rock or stump, powowing with sticks in the circle of obis,
Helping the llama or brahmin as he trims the lamps of the idols,
Dancing yet through the streets in a phallic procession, rapt and austere in the woods
     a gymnosophist,
Drinking mead from the skull-cup, to Shastas and Vedas admirant, minding the Koran,
Walking the teokallis, spotted with gore from the stone and knife, beating the serpent-
     skin drum,   **1105**
Accepting the Gospels, accepting him that was crucified, knowing assuredly that he is
     divine,
To the mass kneeling or the puritan's prayer rising, or sitting patiently in a pew,
Ranting and frothing in my insane crisis, or waiting dead-like till my spirit arouses me,
Looking forth on pavement and land, or outside of pavement and land,
Belonging to the winders of the circuit of circuits.   **1110**

One of that centripetal and centrifugal gang I turn and talk like a man leaving charges
     before a journey.

Down-hearted doubters dull and excluded,
Frivolous, sullen, moping, angry, affected, dishearten'd, atheistical,
I know every one of you, I know the sea of torment, doubt, despair and unbelief.

How the flukes splash!   **1115**
How they contort rapid as lightning, with spasms and spouts of blood!

Be at peace bloody flukes of doubters and sullen mopers,
I take my place among you as much as among any,
The past is the push of you, me, all, precisely the same,
And what is yet untried and afterward is for you, me, all, precisely the same.   **1120**

I do not know what is untried and afterward,
But I know it will in its turn prove sufficient, and cannot fail.

Each who passes is consider'd, each who stops is consider'd, not a single one can it fail.

It cannot fail the young man who died and was buried,
Nor the young woman who died and was put by his side,   **1125**
Nor the little child that peep'd in at the door, and then drew back and was never seen
     again,
Nor the old man who has lived without purpose, and feels it with bitterness worse than
     gall,
Nor him in the poor house tubercled by rum and the bad disorder,
Nor the numberless slaughter'd and wreck'd, nor the brutish koboo call'd the ordure of
     humanity,
Nor the sacs merely floating with open mouths for food to slip in,   **1130**
Nor any thing in the earth, or down in the oldest graves of the earth,

Nor any thing in the myriads of spheres, nor the myriads of myriads that inhabit them,
Nor the present, nor the least wisp that is known.

44

It is time to explain myself — let us stand up.

What is known I strip away,   1135
I launch all men and women forward with me into the Unknown.

The clock indicates the moment — but what does eternity indicate?

We have thus far exhausted trillions of winters and summers,
There are trillions ahead, and trillions ahead of them.

Births have brought us richness and variety,   1140
And other births will bring us richness and variety.

I do not call one greater and one smaller,
That which fills its period and place is equal to any.

Were mankind murderous or jealous upon you, my brother, my sister?
I am sorry for you, they are not murderous or jealous upon me,   1145
All has been gentle with me, I keep no account with lamentation,
(What have I to do with lamentation?)

I am an acme of things accomplish'd, and I an encloser of things to be.

My feet strike an apex of the apices of the stairs,
On every step bunches of ages, and larger bunches between the steps,   1150
All below duly travel'd, and still I mount and mount.

Rise after rise bow the phantoms behind me,
Afar down I see the huge first Nothing, I know I was even there,
I waited unseen and always, and slept through the lethargic mist,
And took my time, and took no hurt from the fetid carbon.   1155

Long I was hugg'd close — long and long.

Immense have been the preparations for me,
Faithful and friendly the arms that have help'd me.

Cycles ferried my cradle, rowing and rowing like cheerful boatmen,
For room to me stars kept aside in their own rings,   1160
They sent influences to look after what was to hold me.

Before I was born out of my mother generations guided me,
My embryo has never been torpid, nothing could overlay it.

For it the nebula cohered to an orb,
The long slow strata piled to rest it on,   1165

Vast vegetables gave it sustenance,
Monstrous sauroids transported it in their mouths and deposited it with care.
All forces have been steadily employ'd to complete and delight me,
Now on this spot I stand with my robust soul.

45

O span of youth! ever-push'd elasticity. 1170
O manhood, balanced, florid and full.

My lovers suffocate me,
Crowding my lips, thick in the pores of my skin,
Jostling me through streets and public halls, coming naked to me at night,
Crying by day *Ahoy!* from the rocks of the river, swinging and chirping over my head,
Calling my name from flower-beds, vines, tangled underbrush, 1176
Lighting on every moment of my life,
Bussing my body with soft balsamic busses,
Noiselessly passing handfuls out of their hearts and giving them to be mine.

Old age superbly rising! O welcome, ineffable grace of dying days! 1180

Every condition promulges not only itself, it promulges what grows after and out of
    itself,
And the dark hush promulges as much as any.

I open my scuttle at night and see the far-sprinkled systems,
And all I see multiplied as high as I can cipher edge but the rim of the farther systems.

Wider and wider they spread, expanding, always expanding, 1185
Outward and outward and forever outward.

My sun has his sun and round him obediently wheels,
He joins with his partners a group of superior circuit,
And greater sets follow, making specks of the greatest inside them.

There is no stoppage and never can be stoppage, 1190
If I, you, and the worlds, and all beneath or upon their surfaces, were this moment
    reduced back to a pallid float, it would not avail in the long run,
We should surely bring up again where we now stand,
And surely go as much farther, and then farther and farther.

A few quadrillions of eras, a few octillions of cubic leagues, do not hazard the span or
    make it impatient,
They are but parts, any thing is but a part. 1195

See ever so far, there is limitless space outside of that,
Count ever so much, there is limitless time around that.

My rendezvous is appointed, it is certain,
The Lord will be there and wait till I come on perfect terms,
The great Camerado, the lover true for whom I pine will be there. 1200

46

I know I have the best of time and space, and was never measured and never will be
    measured.

I tramp a perpetual journey, (come listen all!)
My signs are a rain-proof coat, good shoes, and a staff cut from the woods,
No friend of mine takes his ease in my chair,
I have no chair, no church, no philosophy,
I lead no man to a dinner-table, library, exchange, 1205
But each man and each woman of you I lead upon a knoll,

My left hand hooking you round the waist,
My right hand pointing to landscapes of continents and the public road.

Not I, not any one else can travel that road for you,   1210
You must travel it for yourself.

It is not far, it is within reach,
Perhaps you have been on it since you were born and did not know,
Perhaps it is everywhere on water and on land.

Shoulder your duds dear son, and I will mine, and let us hasten forth,   1215
Wonderful cities and free nations we shall fetch as we go.

If you tire, give me both burdens, and rest the chuff of your hand on my hip,
And in due time you shall repay the same service to me,
For after we start we never lie by again.

This day before dawn I ascended a hill and look'd at the crowded heaven,   1220
And I said to my spirit *When we become the enfolders of those orbs, and the pleasure
    and knowledge of every thing in them, shall we be fill'd and satisfied then?*
And my spirit said *No, we but level that lift to pass and continue beyond.*

You are also asking me questions and I hear you,
I answer that I cannot answer, you must find out for yourself.

Sit a while dear son,   1225
Here are biscuits to eat and here is milk to drink,
But as soon as you sleep and renew yourself in sweet clothes, I kiss you with a good-
    by kiss and open the gate for your egress hence.

Long enough have you dream'd contemptible dreams,
Now I wash the gum from your eyes,   1229
You must habit yourself to the dazzle of the light and of every moment of your life.

Long have you timidly waded holding a plank by the shore,
Now I will you to be a bold swimmer,
To jump off in the midst of the sea, rise again, nod to me, shout, and laughingly dash
    with your hair.

47

I am the teacher of athletes,
He that by me spreads a wider breast than my own proves the width of my own,   1235
He most honors my style who learns under it to destroy the teacher.

The boy I love, the same becomes a man not through derived power, but in his own
    right,
Wicked rather than virtuous out of conformity or fear,
Fond of his sweetheart, relishing well his steak,
Unrequited love or a slight cutting him worse than sharp steel cuts,   1240
First-rate to ride, to fight, to hit the bull's eye, to sail a skiff, to sing a song or play on
    the banjo,
Preferring scars and the beard and faces pitted with small-pox over all latherers,
And those well-tann'd to those that keep out of the sun.

I teach straying from me, yet who can stray from me?
I follow you whoever you are from the present hour,   1245

My words itch at your ears till you understand them.
I do not say these things for a dollar or to fill up the time while I wait for a boat,
(It is you talking just as much as myself, I act as the tongue of you,
Tied in your mouth, in mine it begins to be loosen'd.)

I swear I will never again mention love or death inside a house,   1250
And I swear I will never translate myself at all, only to him or her who privately stays
        with me in the open air.
If you would understand me go to the heights or water-shore,
The nearest gnat is an explanation, and a drop or motion of waves a key,
The maul, the oar, the hand-saw, second my words.

No shutter'd room or school can commune with me,   1255
But roughs and little children better than they.

The young mechanic is closest to me, he knows me well,
The woodman that takes his axe and jug with him shall take me with him all day,
The farm-boy ploughing in the field feels good at the sound of my voice,
In vessels that sail my words sail, I go with fishermen and seamen and love them.   1260

The soldier camp'd or upon the march is mine,
On the night ere the pending battle many seek me, and I do not fail them,
On that solemn night (it may be their last) those that know me seek me.

My face rubs to the hunter's face when he lies down alone in his blanket,
The driver thinking of me does not mind the jolt of his wagon,   1265
The young mother and old mother comprehend me,
The girl and the wife rest the needle a moment and forget where they are,
They and all would resume what I have told them.

48

I have said that the soul is not more than the body,
And I have said that the body is not more than the soul,   1270
And nothing, not God, is greater to one than one's self is,
And whoever walks a furlong without sympathy walks to his own funeral drest in his
        shroud,
And I or you pocketless of a dime may purchase the pick of the earth,
And to glance with an eye or show a bean in its pod confounds the learning of all times,
And there is no trade or employment but the young man following it may become a
        hero,   1275
And there is no object so soft but it makes a hub for the wheel'd universe,
And I say to any man or woman, Let your soul stand cool and composed before a
        million universes.

And I say to mankind, Be not curious about God,
For I who am curious about each am not curious about God,
(No array of terms can say how much I am at peace about God and about death.)   1280

I hear and behold God in every object, yet understand God not in the least,
Nor do I understand who there can be more wonderful than myself.

Why should I wish to see God better than this day?
I see something of God each hour of the twenty-four, and each moment then,
In the faces of men and women I see God, and in my own face in the glass,   1285
I find letters from God dropt in the street, and every one is sign'd by God's name,

And I leave them where they are, for I know that wheresoe'er I go,
Others will punctually come for ever and ever.

49

And as to you Death, and you bitter hug of mortality, it is idle to try to alarm me.

To his work without flinching the accoucheur comes,   1290
I see the elder-hand pressing receiving supporting,
I recline by the sills of the exquisite flexible doors,
And mark the outlet, and mark the relief and escape.

And as to you Corpse I think you are good manure, but that does not offend me,
I smell the white roses sweet-scented and growing,   1295
I reach to the leafy lips, I reach to the polish'd breasts of melons.

And as to you Life I reckon you are the leavings of many deaths,
(No doubt I have died myself ten thousand times before.)

I hear you whispering there O stars of heaven,
O suns — O grass of graves — O perpetual transfers and promotions,   1300
If you do not say any thing how can I say any thing?

Of the turbid pool that lies in the autumn forest,
Of the moon that descends the steeps of the soughing twilight,
Toss, sparkles of day and dusk — toss on the black stems that decay in the muck,
Toss to the moaning gibberish of the dry limbs.   1305

I ascend from the moon, I ascend from the night,
I perceive that the ghastly glimmer is noonday sunbeams reflected,
And debouch to the steady and central from the offspring great or small.

50

There is that in me — I do not know what it is — but I know it is in me.

Wrench'd and sweaty — calm and cool then my body becomes,   1310
I sleep — I sleep long.

I do not know it — it is without name — it is a word unsaid,
It is not in any dictionary, utterance, symbol.

Something it swings on more than the earth I swing on,
To it the creation is the friend whose embracing awakes me.   1315

Perhaps I might tell more. Outlines! I plead for my brothers and sisters.

Do you see O my brothers and sisters?
It is not chaos or death — it is form, union, plan — it is eternal life — it is Happiness.

51

The past and present wilt — I have fill'd them, emptied them,
And proceed to fill my next fold of the future.   1320

Listener up there! what have you to confide to me?
Look in my face while I snuff the sidle of evening,
(Talk honestly, no one else hears you, and I stay only a minute longer.)

Do I contradict myself?
Very well then I contradict myself,   1325
(I am large, I contain multitudes.)

I concentrate toward them that are nigh, I wait on the door-slab.

Who has done his day's work? who will soonest be through with his supper?
Who wishes to walk with me?

Will you speak before I am gone? will you prove already too late?   1330

52

The spotted hawk swoops by and accuses me, he complains of my gab and my loitering.

I too am not a bit tamed, I too am untranslatable,
I sound my barbaric yawp over the roofs of the world.

The last scud of day holds back for me,
It flings my likeness after the rest and true as any on the shadow'd wilds, 1335
It coaxes me to the vapor and the dusk.

I depart as air, I shake my white locks at the runaway sun,
I effuse my flesh in eddies, and drift it in lacy jags.

I bequeath myself to the dirt to grow from the grass I love,
If you want me again look for me under your boot-soles.   1340

You will hardly know who I am or what I mean,
But I shall be good health to you nevertheless,
And filter and fibre your blood.

Failing to fetch me at first keep encouraged,
Missing me one place search another,   1345
I stop somewhere waiting for you.

There Was a Child Went Forth

(1855, 1871)

     Like "Song of Myself," this poem was among the twelve
of the first edition of *Leaves of Grass*. Here, quite evidently,
Whitman is speaking of his own experience: his parents, the men
and women in the streets, the wonderful life of nature inland
and by the sea — the shaping influences on the child that went
forth into the world.

There was a child went forth every day,
And the first object he look'd upon, that object he became,
And that object became part of him for the day or a certain part of the day,
Or for many years or stretching cycles of years.

The early lilacs became part of this child,   5
And grass and white and red morning-glories, and white and red clover, and the song
    of the phœbe-bird,
And the Third-month lambs and the sow's pink-faint litter, and the mare's foal and
    the cow's calf,

And the noisy brood of the barnyard or by the mire of the pond-side,
And the fish suspending themselves so curiously below there, and the beautiful curious liquid,
And the water-plants with their graceful flat heads, all became part of him.   10

The field-sprouts of Fourth-month and Fifth-month became part of him,
Winter-grain sprouts and those of the light-yellow corn, and the esculent roots of the garden,
And the apple-trees cover'd with blossoms and the fruit afterward, and wood-berries, and the commonest weeds by the road,
And the old drunkard staggering home from the outhouse of the tavern whence he had lately risen,
And the schoolmistress that pass'd on her way to the school,   15
And the friendly boys that pass'd, and the quarrelsome boys,
And the tidy and fresh-cheek'd girls, and the barefoot Negro boy and girl,
And all the changes of city and country wherever he went.

His own parents, he that had father'd him and she that had conceiv'd him in her womb and birth'd him,
They gave this child more of themselves than that,   20
They gave him afterward every day, they became part of him.

The mother at home quietly placing the dishes on the supper-table,
The mother with mild words, clean her cap and gown, a wholesome odor falling off her person and clothes as she walks by,
The father, strong, self-sufficient, manly, mean, anger'd, unjust,
The blow, the quick loud word, the tight bargain, the crafty lure,   25
The family usages, the language, the company, the furniture, the yearning and swelling heart,
Affection that will not be gainsay'd, the sense of what is real, the thought if after all it should prove unreal,
The doubts of day-time and the doubts of night-time, the curious whether and how,
Whether that which appears so is so, or is it all flashes and specks?
Men and women crowding fast in the streets, if they are not flashes and specks what are they?   30
The streets themselves and the façades of houses, and goods in the windows,
Vehicles, teams, the heavy-plank'd wharves, the huge crossing at the ferries,
The village on the highland seen from afar at sunset, the river between,
Shadows, aureola and mist, the light falling on roofs and gables of white or brown two miles off,
The schooner near by sleepily dropping down the tide, the little boat slack-tow'd astern,
The hurrying tumbling waves, quick-broken crests, slapping,   36
The strata of color'd clouds, the long bar of maroon-tint away solitary by itself, the spread of purity it lies motionless in,
The horizon's edge, the flying sea-crow, the fragrance of salt marsh and shore mud,
These became part of that child who went forth every day, and who now goes, and will always go forth every day.

Crossing Brooklyn Ferry

(1856, 1881)

Like "Song of Myself," this poem makes no pretence of developing a logical progress of ideas. But it does have more form. There is a single scene: New York harbor. A single situation: the poet is crossing on the ferry between Manhattan and Brooklyn. And a single dominant idea: the mystical unity of men, between those living in the present and those who will follow in the future.

It also has a number of the formal elements of the art of music. Note the repetition, with variations, of themes and of perceptions. Note the method of expansion — adding as well as repeating, building up a cumulous impression of the scene and what it means. Whitman speaks with a bold rhetorical delivery that suggests musical recitative with orchestration. There are quiet passages, many passages that suggest trumpets and trombones. How effective is this musical technique?

1

Flood-tide below me! I see you face to face!
Clouds of the west — sun there half an hour high — I see you also face to face.

Crowds of men and women attired in the usual costumes, how curious you are to me!
On the ferry-boats the hundreds and hundreds that cross, returning home, are more curious to me than you suppose,
And you that shall cross from shore to shore years hence are more to me, and more in my meditations, than you might suppose.   5

2

The impalpable sustenance of me from all things at all hours of the day,
The simple, compact, well-join'd scheme, myself disintegrated, every one disintegrated yet part of the scheme,
The similitudes of the past and those of the future,
The glories strung like beads on my smallest sights and hearings, on the walk in the street and the passage over the river,
The current rushing so swiftly and swimming with me far away,   10
The others that are to follow me, the ties between me and them,
The certainty of others, the life, love, sight, hearing of others.

Others will enter the gates of the ferry and cross from shore to shore,
Others will watch the run of the flood-tide,
Others will see the shipping of Manhattan north and west, and the heights of Brooklyn to the south and east,   15
Others will see the islands large and small;
Fifty years hence, others will see them as they cross, the sun half an hour high,
A hundred years hence, or ever so many hundred years hence, others will see them,
Will enjoy the sunset, the pouring-in of the flood-tide, the falling-back to the sea of the ebb-tide.

3

It avails not, time nor place — distance avails not,   20
I am with you, you men and women of a generation, or ever so many generations hence,
Just as you feel when you look on the river and sky, so I felt,
Just as any of you is one of a living crowd, I was one of a crowd,
Just as you are refresh'd by the gladness of the river and the bright flow, I was refresh'd,
Just as you stand and lean on the rail, yet hurry with the swift current, I stood yet was hurried,   25
Just as you look on the numberless masts of ships and the thick-stemm'd pipes of steamboats, I look'd.

I too many and many a time cross'd the river of old,
Watched the Twelfth-month sea-gulls, saw them high in the air floating with motionless wings, oscillating their bodies,
Saw how the glistening yellow lit up parts of their bodies and left the rest in strong shadow,
Saw the slow-wheeling circles and the gradual edging toward the south,   30
Saw the reflection of the summer sky in the water,
Had my eyes dazzled by the shimmering track of beams,

Look'd at the fine centrifugal spokes of light round the shape of my head in the sunlit
  water,
Look'd on the haze on the hills southward and south-westward,
Look'd on the vapor as it flew in fleeces tinged with violet, 35
Look'd toward the lower bay to notice the vessels arriving,
Saw their approach, saw aboard those that were near me,
Saw the white sails of schooners and sloops, saw the ships at anchor,
The sailors at work in the rigging or out astride the spars,
The round masts, the swinging motion of the hulls, the slender serpentine pennants, 40
The large and small steamers in motion, the pilots in their pilot-houses,
The white wake left by the passage, the quick tremulous whirl of the wheels,
The flags of all nations, the falling of them at sunset,
The scallop-edged waves in the twilight, the ladled cups, the frolicsome crests and
  glistening,
The stretch afar growing dimmer and dimmer, the gray walls of the granite storehouses
  by the docks, 45
On the river the shadowy group, the big steam-tug closely flank'd on each side by the
  barges, the hay-boat, the belated lighter,
On the neighboring shore the fires from the foundry chimneys burning high and glar-
  ingly into the night,
Casting their flicker of black contrasted with wild red and yellow light over the tops
  of houses and down into the clefts of streets.

4

These and all else were to me the same as they are to you,
I loved well those cities, loved well the stately and rapid river, 50
The men and women I saw were all near to me,
Others the same — others who look back on me because I look'd forward to them,
(The time will come, though I stop here to-day and to-night.)

5

What is it then between us?
What is the count of the scores or hundreds of years between us? 55

Whatever it is, it avails not — distance avails not, and place avails not,
I too lived, Brooklyn of ample hills was mine,
I too walk'd the streets of Manhattan island, and bathed in the waters around it,
I too felt the curious abrupt questionings stir within me,
In the day among crowds of people sometimes they came upon me, 60
In my walks home late at night or as I lay in my bed they came upon me,
I too had been struck from the float forever held in solution,
I too had receiv'd identity by my body,
That I was I knew was of my body, and what I should be I knew I should be of my body.

6

It is not upon you alone the dark patches fall, 65
The dark threw its patches down upon me also,
The best I had done seem'd to me blank and suspicious,
My great thoughts as I supposed them, were they not in reality meagre?
Nor is it you alone who know what it is to be evil,
I am he who knew what it was to be evil, 70
I too knitted the old knot of contrariety,
Blabb'd, blush'd, resented, lied, stole, grudg'd,
Had guile, anger, lust, hot wishes I dared not speak,
Was wayward, vain, greedy, shallow, sly, cowardly, malignant,
The wolf, the snake, the hog, not wanting in me, 75
The cheating look, the frivolous word, the adulterous wish, not wanting,

Refusals, hates, postponements, meanness, laziness, none of these wanting,
Was one with the rest, the days and haps of the rest,
Was call'd my nighest name by clear loud voices of young men as they saw me approaching or passing,
Felt their arms on my neck as I stood, or the negligent leaning of their flesh against me as I sat, 80
Saw many I loved in the street or ferry-boat or public assembly, yet never told them a word,
Lived the same life with the rest, the same old laughing, gnawing, sleeping,
Play'd the part that still looks back on the actor or actress,
The same old role, the role that is what we make it, as great as we like,
Or as small as we like, or both great and small. 85

7

Closer yet I approach you,
What thought you have of me now, I had as much of you — I laid in my stores in advance,
I consider'd long and seriously of you before you were born.
Who was to know what should come home to me?
Who knows but I am enjoying this? 90
Who knows, for all the distance, but I am as good as looking at you now, for all you cannot see me?

8

Ah, what can ever be more stately and admirable to me than mast-hemm'd Manhattan?
River and sunset and scallop-edg'd waves of flood-tide?
The sea-gulls oscillating their bodies, the hay-boat in the twilight, and the belated lighter?
What gods can exceed these that clasp me by the hand, and with voices I love call me promptly and loudly by my nighest name as I approach? 95

What is more subtle than this which ties me to the woman or man that looks in my face?
Which fuses me into you now, and pours my meaning into you?

We understand then do we not?
What I promis'd without mentioning it, have you not accepted?
What the study could not teach — what the preaching could not accomplish is accomplish'd, is it not? 100

9

Flow on, river! flow with the flood-tide, and ebb with the ebb-tide!
Frolic on, crested and scallop-edg'd waves!
Gorgeous clouds of the sunset! drench with your splendor me, or the men and women generations after me!
Cross from shore to shore, countless crowds of passengers!
Stand up, tall masts of Mannahatta! stand up, beautiful hills of Brooklyn! 105
Throb, baffled and curious brain! throw out questions and answers!
Suspend here and everywhere, eternal float of solution!
Gaze, loving and thirsting eyes, in the house or street or public assembly!
Sound out, voices of young men! loudly and musically call me by my nighest name!
Live, old life! play the part that looks back on the actor or actress! 110
Play the old role, the role that is great or small according as one makes it!
Consider, you who peruse me, whether I may not in unknown ways be looking upon you;
Be firm, rail over the river, to support those who lean idly, yet haste with the hasting current;

Fly on, sea-birds! fly sideways, or wheel in large circles high in the air;
Receive the summer sky, you water, and faithfully hold it till all downcast eyes have
　　　time to take it from you!   115
Diverge, fine spokes of light, from the shape of my head, or any one's head, in the
　　　sunlit water!
Come on, ships from the lower bay! pass up or down, white-sail'd schooners, sloops,
　　　lighters!
Flaunt away, flags of all nations! be duly lower'd at sunset!
Burn high your fires, foundry chimneys! cast black shadows at nightfall! cast red and
　　　yellow light over the tops of the houses!
Appearances, now or henceforth, indicate what you are,   120
You necessary film, continue to envelop the soul,
About my body for me, and your body for you, be hung our divinest aromas,
Thrive, cities — bring your freight, bring your shows, ample and sufficient rivers,
Expand, being than which none else is perhaps more spiritual,
Keep your places, objects than which none else is more lasting.   125

You have waited, you always wait, you dumb, beautiful ministers,
We receive you with free sense at last, and are insatiate henceforward,
Not you any more shall be able to foil us, or withhold yourselves from us,
We use you, — and do not cast you aside — we plant you permanently within us,
We fathom you not — we love you — there is perfection in you also,   130
You furnish your parts toward eternity,
Great or small, you furnish your parts toward the soul.

Out of the Cradle Endlessly Rocking

(1859, 1860, 1881)

❧ Here we have Whitman at his best, full of his theme, concentrating on an artistic aim from beginning to end, rich in images, sounds, and symbolic meanings, shaping his verse patterns to fit the sense. Psychologically, the poem relates itself to the group of sex poems, "Children of Adam." It is a reminiscence of a boy's inner turmoil, with meanings infused by maturity.

The scene is the seashore of Long Island (Whitman liked its Indian name Paumanok). The time is May to September (he preferred the Quaker Fifth-Month, Ninth-Month). The "characters" are the boy, a pair of mockingbirds, and the sea ("fierce old Mother"). An introduction, a periodic sentence of 22 lines (with the epic predicate "I . . . sing"), lightly touches upon the happenings and significance we are to find in the poem. The poem proper is in two parts. The first part, extending to line 143, gives the story of the birds. The rest, line 143 to the end, interprets the influence of the male bird's song on the "outsetting bard."

What was this influence? One may answer vaguely that the bird's song stirred up a tumult of feeling and awoke the boy's poetic impulse. But like many another good poem, this poem of life and love and death, of the springs that feed the creative spirit, has invited a variety of specific interpretations. To indicate just one example, Leo Spitzer, in a full-length explication of the poem (ELH, September 1949), wrote:

"Nature wills sorrow and joy, life and death, and it may be that death will become or foster life. 'Out of the cradle endlessly rocking,' that is (we understand it now), out of the cradle of *death*, the poet will sing life. . . . A poet is born by the death of the bird who is a brother and a demon. A brother because he teaches the boy love; a demon [daemon], because he 'projects' the poet, anticipates, and heralds him, stirs up in him those creative faculties which must partake of the frightening and the daemonic. But while the bird was destined to teach the boy love ('death' being a reality the bird was not able to reconcile with love), the sea, wiser than the bird and the 'aroused child's heart,' has another message to bring to the boy: 'Death, death, death, death, death.' This line is the counterpart of the mockingbird's 'loved loved loved loved loved,' and it is couched in the same exclamational style, as though it were the organic continuation thereof . . . once he has discovered this *meaning* of life, which is death, he is no longer the boy of the beginning ('never again leave me to the peaceful boy I was before'). He has become the poet, the 'uniter' of here and hereafter. . . ."

Absorption in the ideas and symbols of the poem should not blind us to Whitman's mastery of his type of free verse, a mastery he had not attained in the first *Leaves of Grass* a few years earlier. A close technical study of his medium would prove rewarding.

Out of the cradle endlessly rocking,
Out of the mocking-bird's throat, the musical shuttle,
Out of the Ninth-month midnight,
Over the sterile sands and the fields beyond, where the child leaving his bed wander'd
    alone, bareheaded, barefoot,
Down from the shower'd halo,   5
Up from the mystic play of shadows twining and twisting as if they were alive,
Out from the patches of briers and blackberries,
From the memories of the bird that chanted to me,
From your memories sad brother, from the fitful risings and fallings I heard,
From under that yellow half-moon late-risen and swollen as if with tears,   10
From those beginning notes of yearning and love there in the mist,
From the thousand responses of my heart never to cease,
From the myriad thence-arous'd words
From the word stronger and more delicious than any,
From such as now they start the scene revisiting,   15
As a flock, twittering, rising, or overhead passing,
Borne hither, ere all eludes me, hurriedly,
A man, yet by these tears a little boy again,
Throwing myself on the sand, confronting the waves,
I, chanter of pains and joys, uniter of here and hereafter,   20
Taking all hints to use them, but swiftly leaping beyond them,
A reminiscence sing.

Once Paumanok,
When the lilac-scent was in the air and Fifth-month grass was growing,
Up this seashore in some briers,   25
Two feather'd guests from Alabama, two together,
And their nest, and four light-green eggs spotted with brown,
And every day the he-bird to and fro near at hand,
And every day the she-bird crouch'd on her nest, silent, with bright eyes,
And every day I, a curious boy, never too close, never disturbing them,   30
Cautiously peering, absorbing, translating.

Shine! shine! shine!
Pour down your warmth, great sun!
While we bask, we two together.

Two together!   35
Winds blow south, or winds blow north,
Day come white, or night come black,
Home, or rivers and mountains from home,
Singing all time, minding no time,
While we two keep together.   40

Till of a sudden,
May-be kill'd, unknown to her mate,
One forenoon that she-bird crouch'd not on the nest,
Nor return'd that afternoon, nor the next,
Nor ever appear'd again.   45

And thenceforward all summer in the sound of the sea,
And at night under the full of the moon in calmer weather,
Over the hoarse surging of the sea,
Or flitting from brier to brier by day,
I saw, I heard at intervals the remaining one, the he-bird,   50
The solitary guest from Alabama.

Blow! blow! blow!
Blow up sea-winds along Paumanok's shore;
I wait and I wait till you blow my mate to me.

Yes, when the stars glisten'd,   55
All night long on the prong of a moss-scallop'd stake,
Down almost amid the slapping waves,
Sat the lone singer wonderful causing tears.

He call'd on his mate,
He pour'd forth the meanings which I of all men know.   60

Yes my brother I know,
The rest might not, but I have treasur'd every note,
For more than once dimly down to the beach gliding,
Silent, avoiding the moonbeams, blending myself with the shadows,
Recalling now the obscure shapes, the echoes, the sounds and sights after their sorts,
The white arms out in the breakers tirelessly tossing,   66
I, with bare feet, a child, the wind wafting my hair,
Listen'd long and long.

Listen'd to keep, to sing, now translating the notes,
Following you my brother.   70

Soothe! soothe! soothe!
Close on its wave soothes the wave behind,
And again another behind embracing and lapping, every one close,
But my love soothes not me, not me.

Low hangs the moon, it rose late,   75
It is lagging — O I think it is heavy with love, with love.

O madly the sea pushes upon the land,
With love, with love.

O night! do I not see my love fluttering out among the breakers?
What is that little black thing I see there in the white?   80

Loud! loud! loud!
Loud I call to you, my love!
High and clear I shoot my voice over the waves,
Surely you must know who is here, is here,
You must know who I am, my love.   85

Low-hanging moon!
What is that dusky spot in your brown yellow?

O it is the shape, the shape of my mate!
O moon do not keep her from me any longer.

Land! land! O land!   90
Whichever way I turn, O I think you could give me my mate back again if you only
*   would,*
For I am almost sure I see her dimly whichever way I look.

O rising stars!
Perhaps the one I want so much will rise, will rise with one of you.

O throat! O trembling throat!   95
Sound clearer through the atmosphere!
Pierce the woods, the earth,
Somewhere listening to catch you must be the one I want.

Shake out carols!
Solitary here, the night's carols!   100
Carols of lonesome love! death's carols!
Carols under that lagging, yellow, waning moon!
O under that moon where she droops almost down into the sea!
O reckless despairing carols.

But soft! sink low!   105
Soft! let me just murmur,
And do you wait a moment you husky-nois'd sea,
For somewhere I believe I heard my mate responding to me,
So faint, I must be still, be still to listen,
But not altogether still, for then she might not come immediately to me.   110

Hither my love!
Here I am! here!
With this just-sustain'd note I announce myself to you,
This gentle call is for you my love, for you.

Do not be decoy'd elsewhere,   115
That is the whistle of the wind, it is not my voice,
That is fluttering, the fluttering of the spray,
Those are the shadows of leaves.

O darkness! O in vain!
O I am very sick and sorrowful.   120

O brown halo in the sky near the moon, drooping upon the sea!
O troubled reflection in the sea!
O throat! O throbbing heart!
And singing uselessly, uselessly all the night.

O past! O happy life! O song of joy!   125
In the air, in the woods, over fields,
Loved! loved! loved! loved! loved!
But my mate no more, no more with me!
We two together no more.

The aria sinking,   130
All else continuing, the stars shining,
The winds blowing, the notes of the bird continuous echoing,
With angry moan the fierce old mother incessantly moaning,
On the sands of Paumanok's shore gray and rustling,
The yellow half-moon enlarged, sagging down, drooping, the face of the sea almost
     touching,   135
The boy ecstatic, with his bare feet the waves, with his hair the atmosphere dallying,
The love in the heart long pent, now loose, now at last tumultuously bursting,
The aria's meaning, the ears, the soul, swiftly depositing,
The strange tears down the cheeks coursing,
The colloquy there, the trio, each uttering,   140
The undertone, the savage old mother incessantly crying,
To the boy's soul's questions sullenly timing, some drown'd secret hissing,
To the outsetting bard.

Demon or bird! (said the boy's soul,)
Is it indeed toward your mate you sing? or is it really to me? 145
For I, that was a child, my tongue's use sleeping, now I have heard you,
Now in a moment I know what I am for, I awake,
And already a thousand singers, a thousand songs, clearer, louder, and more sorrowful
    than yours,
A thousand warbling echoes have started to life within me, never to die.

O you singer solitary, singing by yourself, projecting me, 150
O solitary me listening, never more shall I cease perpetuating you,
Never more shall I escape, never more the reverberations,
Never more the cries of unsatisfied love be absent from me,
Never again leave me to be the peaceful child I was before what there in the night,
By the sea under the yellow and sagging moon, 155
The messenger there arous'd, the fire, the sweet hell within,
The unknown want, the destiny of me.

O give me the clew! (it lurks in the night here somewhere,)
O if I am to have so much, let me have more!

A word then, (for I will conquer it,) 160
The word final, superior to all,
Subtle, sent up — what is it? — I listen;
Are you whispering it, and have been all the time, you sea-waves?
Is that it from your liquid rims and wet sands?

Whereto answering, the sea, 165
Delaying not, hurrying not,
Whisper'd me through the night, and very plainly before daybreak,
Lisp'd to me the low and delicious word death,
And again death, death, death, death,
Hissing melodious, neither like the bird nor like my arous'd child's heart, 170
But edging near as privately for me rustling at my feet,
Creeping thence steadily up to my ears and laving me softly all over,
Death, death, death, death, death.

Which I do not forget,
But fuse the song of my dusky demon and brother, 175
That he sang to me in the moonlight on Paumanok's gray beach,
With the thousand responsive songs at random,
My own songs awaked from that hour,
And with them the key, the word up from the waves,
The word of the sweetest song and all songs, 180
That strong and delicious word which, creeping to my feet,
(Or like some old crone rocking the cradle, swathed in sweet garments, bending aside,)
The sea whisper'd me.

Once I Pass'd Through a Populous City
(1860, 1867)

✦ The following three poems are from the "Children of Adam" and the "Calamus" series of *Leaves of Grass* in which Whitman treats love for woman ("amativeness") and love for man ("adhesiveness") in erotic and ambivalent terms. In the original draft of the first poem, the lover was not a woman but "the man who wandered with me there," "one rude and ignorant man." H. S. Canby writes: "One of Whitman's great services was to restore sexuality to literature, but it is equally true that he was afflicted by his sexuality."

Once I pass'd through a populous city imprinting my brain for future use with its shows,
  architecture, customs, traditions,
Yet now of all that city I remember only a woman I casually met there who detain'd
  me for love of me,
Day by day and night by night we were together — all else has long been forgotten by
  me,
I remember I say only that woman who passionately clung to me,
Again she holds me by the hand, I must not go,
I see her close beside me with silent lips sad and tremulous.

When I Heard at the Close of the Day

(1867)

When I heard at the close of the day how my name had been receiv'd with plaudits in
  the capitol, still it was not a happy night for me that follow'd,
And else when I carous'd, or when my plans were accomplish'd, still I was not happy,
But the day when I rose at dawn from the bed of perfect health, refresh'd, singing,
  inhaling the ripe breath of autumn,
When I saw the full moon in the west grow pale and disappear in the morning light,
When I wander'd alone over the beach, and undressing bathed, laughing with the
  cool waters, and saw the sun rise,   5
And when I thought how my dear friend my lover was on his way coming, O then I
  was happy,
O then each breath tasted sweeter, and all that day my food nourish'd me more, and
  the beautiful day pass'd well,
And the next came with equal joy, and with the next at evening came my friend,
And that night while all was still I heard the waters roll slowly continually up the shores,
I heard the hissing rustle of the liquid and sands as directed to me whispering to
  congratulate me,   10
For the one I love most lay sleeping by me under the same cover in the cool night,
In the stillness in the autumn moonbeams his face was inclined toward me,
And his arm lay lightly around my breast — and that night I was happy.

A Glimpse

(1867)

A glimpse through an interstice caught,
Of a crowd of workmen and drivers in a bar-room around the stove late of a winter
  night, and I unremark'd seated in a corner,
Of a youth who loves me and whom I love, silently approaching and seating himself
  near, that he may hold me by the hand,
A long while amid the noises of coming and going, of drinking and oath and smutty jest,
There we two, content, happy in being together, speaking little, perhaps not a word.   5

A Noiseless Patient Spider

(1862–63, 1881)

A noiseless patient spider,
I mark'd where on a little promontory it stood isolated,
Mark'd how to explore the vacant vast surrounding,
It lauch'd forth filament, filament, filament, out of itself,
Ever unreeling them, ever tirelessly speeding them.

And you O my soul where you stand,
Surrounded, detached, in measureless oceans of space,
Ceaselessly musing, venturing, throwing, seeking the spheres to connect them,
Till the bridge you will need be form'd, till the ductile anchor hold,
Till the gossamer thread you fling catch somewhere, O my soul.   10

When I Heard the Learn'd Astronomer

(1865, 1867)

When I heard the learn'd astronomer;
When the proofs, the figures, were ranged in columns before me;
When I was shown the charts and the diagrams, to add, divide, and measure them,
When I, sitting, heard the astronomer, where he lectured with much applause in the
    lecture-room,
How soon, unaccountable, I became tired and sick;   5
Till rising and gliding out, I wander'd off by myself,
In the mystical moist night-air, and from time to time,
Look'd up in perfect silence at the stars.

Cavalry Crossing a Ford

This, like the next three poems evoked by the war, was
published in *Drum-Taps*, 1865.

A line in long array where they wind betwixt green islands,
They take a serpentine course, their arms flash in the sun — hark to the musical clank,
Behold the silvery river, in it the splashing horses loitering stop to drink,
Behold the brown-faced men, each group, each person a picture, the negligent rest
    on the saddles,
Some emerge on the opposite bank, others are just entering the ford — while,   5
Scarlet and blue and snowy white,
The guidon flags flutter gayly in the wind.

Come Up from the Fields Father

Come up from the fields father, here's a letter from our Pete,
And come to the front door mother, here's a letter from thy dear son,

Lo, 'tis autumn,
Lo, where the trees, deeper green, yellower and redder,
Cool and sweeten Ohio's villages with leaves fluttering in the moderate wind,   5
Where apples ripe in the orchards hang and grapes on the trellis'd vines,
(Smell you the smell of the grapes on the vines?
Smell you the buckwheat where the bees were lately buzzing?)

Above all, lo, the sky so calm, so transparent after the rain, and with wondrous clouds,
Below too, all calm, all vital and beautiful, and the farm prospers well.   10

Down in the fields all prospers well,
But now from the fields come father, come at the daughter's call,
And come to the entry mother, to the front door come right away.
Fast as she can she hurries, something ominous, her steps trembling,
She does not tarry to smooth her hair nor adjust her cap.   15

Open the envelope quickly,
O this is not our son's writing, yet his name is sign'd,
O a strange hand writes for our dear son, O stricken mother's soul!
All swims before her eyes, flashes with black, she catches the main words only,
Sentences broken, *gunshot wound in the breast, cavalry skirmish, taken to hospital,*   20
At present low, but will soon be better.

Ah now the single figure to me,
Amid all teeming and wealthy Ohio with all its cities and farms,
Sickly white in the face and dull in the head, very faint,
By the jamb of a door leans.   25

Grieve not so, dear mother, (the just-grown daughter speaks through her sobs,
The little sisters huddle around speechless and dismay'd,)
See, dearest mother, the letter says Pete will soon be better.

Alas poor boy, he will never be better, (nor may-be needs to be better, that brave and
    simple soul,)
While they stand at home at the door he is dead already,   30
The only son is dead.

But the mother needs to be better,
She with thin form presently drest in black,
By day her meals untouch'd, then at night fitfully sleeping, often waking,
In the midnight waking, weeping, longing with one deep longing,   35
O that she might withdraw unnoticed, silent from life escape and withdraw,
To follow, to seek, to be with her dear dead son.

A March in the Ranks Hard-Prest,
and The Road Unknown

A march in the ranks hard prest, and the road unknown,
A route through a heavy wood with muffled steps in the darkness,
Our army foil'd with loss severe, and the sullen remnant retreating,
Till after midnight glimmer upon us the lights of a dim-lighted building,
We come to an open space in the woods, and halt by the dim-lighted building,   5
'Tis a large old church at the crossing roads, now an impromptu hospital,
Entering but for a minute I see a sight beyond all the pictures and poems ever made,
Shadows of deepest, deepest black, just lit by moving candles and lamps,
And by one great pitchy torch stationary with wild red flame and clouds of smoke,
By these, crowds, groups of forms vaguely I see on the floor, some in the pews laid
    down,   10
At my feet more distinctly a soldier, a mere lad, in danger of bleeding to death, (he is
    shot in the abdomen,)
I stanch the blood temporarily, (the youngster's face is white as a lily,)
Then before I depart I sweep my eyes o'er the scene fain to absorb it all,
Faces, varieties, postures beyond description, most in obscurity, some of them dead,
Surgeons operating, attendants holding lights, the smell of ether, the odor of blood,   15
The crowd, O the crowd of the bloody forms, the yard outside also fill'd,
Some on the bare ground, some on planks or stretchers, some in the death-spasm sweat-
    ing,
An occasional scream or cry, the doctor's shouted orders or calls,
The glisten of the little steel instruments catching the glint of the torches,
These I resume as I chant, I see again the forms, I smell the odor,   20
Then hear outside the orders given, *Fall in, my men, fall in;*

But first I bend to the dying lad, his eyes open, a half-smile gives he me,
Then the eyes close, calmly close, and I speed forth to the darkness,
Resuming, marching, ever in darkness marching, on in the ranks,
The unknown roads still marching.   25

A Sight in Camp in the Daybreak
Gray and Dim

A sight in camp in the daybreak gray and dim,
As from my tent I emerge so early sleepless,
As slow I walk in the cool fresh air the path near by the hospital tent,
Three forms I see on stretchers lying, brought out there untended lying,
Over each the blanket spread, ample brownish woolen blanket,   5
Gray and heavy blanket, folding, covering all.

Curious I halt and silent stand,
Then with light fingers I from the face of the nearest the first just lift the blanket;
Who are you elderly man so gaunt and grim, with well-gray'd hair, and flesh all sunken
     about the eyes?
Who are you my dear comrade?   10

Then to the second I step — and who are you my child and darling?
Who are you sweet boy with cheeks yet blooming?

Then to the third — a face nor child nor old, very calm, as of beautiful yellow-white
     ivory;
Young man I think I know you — I think this face is the face of the Christ himself,
Dead and divine and brother of all, and here again he lies.   15

When Lilacs Last in the Dooryard Bloom'd
(1865–66, 1881)

✻ This is a poem about Lincoln, the best of many in American literature.

In Washington, during the year of Gettysburg, Whitman wrote: "I see the President almost every day, as I happen to live where he passes to or from his lodgings out of town. . . . the deep-cut lines, the eyes, always to me with a deep latent sadness in the expression. We have got so that we exchange bows."

On the second inauguration, March 4, 1865: "I saw him on his return, at three o'clock, after the performance was over. He was in his plain two-horse barouche, and look'd very much worn and tired; . . . yet all the old goodness, tenderness, sadness, and canny shrewdness, underneath the furrows. . . . By his side sat his little boy, of ten years. There were no soldiers."

The next month the President was murdered. It was lilac time in Brooklyn when Whitman heard the news — April 15, early in the morning. "Mother prepared breakfast — and other meals afterward — as usual; but not a mouthful was eaten all day by either of us. We each drank half a cup of coffee; that was all. Little was said. We got every newspaper morning and evening, and the frequent extras of that period, and pass'd them silently to each other."

A funeral train left Washington on April 21, carrying Lincoln's body to his home town, Springfield, Illinois, halting on the way at Philadelphia, New York, Chicago, and other cities.

The poem which Whitman was moved to write does not mention Lincoln's name, or dwell upon "the man I love." Instead, it unites two broad themes that absorbed him: America, "my land" (typified by its great President) and death, the "dark mother" of all of us. The solemn sense of bereavement that runs through the poem and the remarkable song to "lovely and soothing death" are not so much personal as national. As the funeral train moves on, and the bells toll in cities draped in black, the poet's emotion is that of a people, his tribute only his "sprig of lilac."

The poem is developed largely through three symbols: the star (Lincoln), the lilac (love), the hermit thrush (the poet singing of death). They keep reappearing, like themes in a musical recitative, and at the end are brought together in one phrase — "Lilac and star and bird."

1

When lilacs last in the dooryard bloom'd
And the great star early droop'd in the western sky in the night,
I mourn'd, and yet shall mourn with ever-returning spring.

Ever-returning spring, trinity sure to me you bring,
Lilac blooming perennial and drooping star in the west,   5
And thought of him I love.

2

O powerful western fallen star!
O shades of night — O moody, tearful night!
O great star disappear'd — O the black murk that hides the star!
O cruel hands that hold me powerless — O helpless soul of me!   10
O harsh surrounding cloud that will not free my soul.

3

In the dooryard fronting an old farm-house near the white-wash'd palings,
Stands the lilac-bush tall-growing with heart-shaped leaves of rich green,
With many a pointed blossom rising delicate, with the perfume strong I love,
With every leaf a miracle — and from this bush in the dooryard,   15
With delicate-color'd blossoms and heart-shaped leaves of rich green,
A sprig with its flower I break.

4

In the swamp in secluded recesses,
A shy and hidden bird is warbling a song.

Solitary the thrush,   20
The hermit withdrawn to himself, avoiding the settlements
Sings by himself a song.

Song of the bleeding throat,
Death's outlet song of life, (for well dear brother I know,
If thou wast not granted to sing thou would'st surely die.)   25

5

Over the breast of the spring, the land, amid cities,
Amid lanes and through old woods, where lately the violets peep'd from the ground,
     spotting the gray debris,
Amid the grass in the fields each side of the lanes, passing the endless grass,
Passing the yellow-spear'd wheat, every grain from its shroud in the dark-brown
     fields uprisen,
Passing the apple-tree blows of white and pink in the orchards,   30
Carrying a corpse to where it shall rest in the grave,
Night and day journeys a coffin.

6

Coffin that passes through lanes and streets,
Through day and night with the great cloud darkening the land,
With the pomp of the inloop'd flags with the cities draped in black,   35
With the show of the states themselves as of crape-veil'd women standing,
With processions long and winding and the flambeaus of the night,
With the countless torches lit, with the silent sea of faces and the unbared heads,
With the waiting depot, the arriving coffin, and the sombre faces,
With dirges through the night, with the thousand voices rising strong and solemn,   40
With all the mournful voices of the dirges pour'd around the coffin,

The dim-lit churches and the shuddering organs — where amid these you journey,
With the tolling tolling bells' perpetual clang,
Here, coffin that slowly passes,
I give you my sprig of lilac.   45

7

(Nor for you, for one alone,
Blossoms and branches green to coffins all I bring,
For fresh as the morning, thus would I chant a song for you O sane and sacred death.

All over bouquets of roses,
O death, I cover you over with roses and early lilies,   50
But mostly and now the lilac that blooms the first,
Copious I break, I break the sprigs from the bushes,
With loaded arms I come, pouring for you,
For you and the coffins all of you O death.)

8

O western orb sailing the heaven,   55
Now I know what you must have meant as a month since I walk'd,
As I walk'd in silence the transparent shadowy night,
As I saw you had something to tell as you bent to me night after night,
As you droop'd from the sky low down as if to my side, (while the other stars all
        look'd on,)
As we wander'd together the solemn night, (for something I know not what kept me
        from sleep,)   60
As the night advanced, and I saw on the rim of the west how full you were of woe,
As I stood on the rising ground in the breeze in the cool transparent night,
As I watch'd where you pass'd and was lost in the netherward black of night,
As my soul in its trouble dissatisfied sank, as where you sad orb,
Concluded, dropt in the night, and was gone.   65

9

Sing on there in the swamp,
O singer bashful and tender, I hear your notes, I hear your call,
I hear, I come presently, I understand you,
But a moment I linger, for the lustrous star has detain'd me,
The star my departing comrade holds and detains me.   70

10

O how shall I warble myself for the dead one there I loved?
And how shall I deck my song for the large sweet soul that has gone?
And what shall my perfume be for the grave of him I love?

Sea-winds blown from east and west,
Blown from the Eastern sea and blown from the Western sea, till there on the prairies
        meeting,   75
These and with these and the breath of my chant,
I'll perfume the grave of him I love.

11

O what shall I hang on the chamber walls?
And what shall the pictures be that I hang on the walls,
To adorn the burial-house of him I love?   80

Pictures of growing spring and farms and homes,
With the Fourth-month eve at sundown, and the gray smoke lucid and bright,

With floods of the yellow gold of the gorgeous indolent, sinking sun, burning, expanding the air,
With the fresh sweet herbage under foot, and the pale green leaves of the trees prolific,
In the distance the flowing glaze, the breast of the river, with a wind-dapple here and
there,   85
With ranging hills on the banks, with many a line against the sky, and shadows,
And the city at hand with dwellings so dense, and stacks of chimneys,
And all the scenes of life and the workshops, and the workmen homeward returning.

12

Lo, body and soul — this land,
My own Manhattan with spires, and the sparkling and hurrying tides, and the ships,   90
The varied and ample land, the South and the North in the light, Ohio's shores and
flashing Missouri,
And ever the far-spreading prairies cover'd with grass and corn.

Lo, the most excellent sun so calm and haughty,
The violet and purple morn with just-felt breezes,
The gentle soft-brown measureless light,   95
The miracle spreading bathing all, the fulfill'd noon,
The coming eve delicious, the welcome night and the stars,
Over my cities shining all, enveloping man and land.

13

Sing on, sing on you gray-brown bird,
Sing from the swamps, the recesses, pour your chant from the bushes,   100
Limitless out of the dusk, out of the cedars and pines.
Sing on dearest brother, warble your reedy song,
Loud human song, with voice of uttermost woe.
O liquid and free and tender!
O wild and loose to my soul — O wondrous singer!   105
You only I hear — yet the star holds me, (but will soon depart,)
Yet the lilac with mastering odor holds me.

14

Now while I sat in the day and look'd forth,
In the close of the day with its light and the fields of spring, and the farmers preparing
their crops,
In the large unconscious scenery of my land with its lakes and forests,   110
In the heavenly aerial beauty, (after the perturb'd winds and the storms,)
Under the arching heavens of the afternoon swift passing, and the voices of children
and women,
The many-moving sea-tides, and I saw the ships how they sail'd,
And the summer approaching with richness, and the fields all busy with labor,
And the infinite separate houses, how they all went on, each with its meals and minutia
of daily usages,   115
And the streets how their throbbings throbb'd, and the cities pent — lo, then and
there,
Falling upon them all and among them all, enveloping me with the rest,
Appear'd the cloud, appear'd the long black trail,
And I knew death, its thought, and the sacred knowledge of death.

Then with the knowledge of death as walking one side of me,   120
And the thought of death close-walking the other side of me,
And I in the middle as with companions, and as holding the hands of companions,

I fled forth to the hiding receiving night that talks not,
Down to the shores of the water, the path by the swamp in the dimness,
To the solemn shadowy cedars and ghostly pines so still.   125

And the singer so shy to the rest receiv'd me,
The gray-brown bird I know receiv'd us comrades three,
And he sang the carol of death, and a verse for him I love.

From deep secluded recesses,
From the fragrant cedars and the ghostly pines so still,   130
Came the carol of the bird.

And the charm of the carol rapt me,
As I held as if by their hands my comrades in the night,
And the voice of my spirit tallied the song of the bird.

Come lovely and soothing death,   135
Undulate round the world, serenely arriving, arriving,
In the day, in the night, to all, to each,
Sooner or later delicate death.

Prais'd be the fathomless universe,
For life and joy, and for objects and knowledge curious,   140
And for love, sweet love — but praise! praise! praise!
For the sure-enwinding arms of cool-enfolding death.

Dark mother always gliding near with soft feet,
Have none chanted for thee a chant of fullest welcome?
Then I chant it for thee, I glorify thee above all,   145
I bring thee a song that when thou must indeed come, come unfalteringly.

Approach strong deliveress,
When it is so, when thou hast taken them, I joyously sing the dead,
Lost in the loving floating ocean of thee,
Laved in the flood of thy bliss O death.   150

From me to thee glad serenades,
Dances for thee I propose saluting thee, adornments and feastings for thee,
And the sights of the open landscape and the high-spread sky are fitting,
And life and the fields, and the huge and thoughtful night.

The night in silence under many a star,   155
The ocean shore and the husky whispering wave whose voice I knew,
And the soul turning to thee O vast and well-veil'd death,
And the body gratefully nestling close to thee.

Over the tree-tops I float thee a song,
Over the rising and sinking waves, over the myriad fields and the prairies wide, 160
Over the dense-pack'd cities all and the teeming wharves and ways,
I float this carol with joy, with joy to thee O death.

15

To the tally of my soul,
Loud and strong kept up the gray-brown bird,
With pure deliberate notes spreading filling the night.   165
Loud in the pines and cedars dim,

Clear in the freshness moist and swamp-perfume,
And I with my comrades there in the night.

While my sight that was bound in my eyes unclosed,
As to long panoramas of visions.   170

And I saw askant the armies,
I saw as in noiseless dreams hundreds of battle-flags,
Borne through the smoke of the battles and pierc'd with missiles I saw them,
And carried hither and yon through the smoke, and torn and bloody,
And at last but a few shreds left on the staffs, (and all in silence,)   175
And the staffs all splinter'd and broken.

I saw battle-corpses, myriads of them,
And the white skeletons of young men, I saw them,
I saw the debris and debris of all the slain soldiers of the war,
But I saw they were not as was thought,   180
They themselves were fully at rest, they suffer'd not,
The living remain'd and suffer'd, the mother suffer'd,
And the wife and the child and the musing comrade suffer'd,
And the armies that remain'd suffer'd.

16

Passing the visions, passing the night,   185
Passing, unloosing the hold of my comrades' hands,
Passing the song of the hermit bird and the tallying song of my soul,
Victorious song, death's outlet song, yet varying ever-altering song,
As low and wailing, yet clear the notes, rising and falling, flooding the night,
Sadly sinking and fainting, as warning and warning, and yet again bursting with joy,
Covering the earth and filling the spread of the heaven,   191
As that powerful psalm in the night I heard from recesses,
Passing, I leave thee lilac with heart-shaped leaves,
I leave thee there in the door-yard, blooming, returning with spring.

I cease from my song for thee,   195
From my gaze on thee in the west, fronting the west, communing with thee,
O comrade lustrous with silver face in the night.
Yet each to keep and all, retrievements out of the night,
The song, the wondrous chant of the gray-brown bird,
And the tallying chant, the echo arous'd in my soul,   200
With the lustrous and drooping star with the countenance full of woe,
With the holders holding my hand hearing the call of the bird,
Comrades mine and I in the midst, and their memory ever to keep, for the dead I loved
    so well,
For the sweetest, wisest soul of all my days and lands — and this for his dear sake,
Lilac and star and bird twined with the chant of my soul,   205
There in the fragrant pines and the cedars dusk and dim.

Pioneers! O Pioneers!

(1865, 1881)

The spirit of the Westward Movement, while romanticized,
is admirably conveyed in this popular piece. Unlike most of
Whitman's poems, it is fairly regular and conventional in meter,
stanza, and refrain. What did Whitman gain and lose by departing from his usual form?

Come my tan-faced children,
Follow well in order, get your weapons ready,
Have you your pistols? have you your sharp-edged axes?
        Pioneers! O pioneers!

For we cannot tarry here,   5
We must march my darlings, we must bear the brunt of danger,
We the youthful sinewy races, all the rest on us depend,
        Pioneers! O pioneers!

O you youths, Western youths,
So impatient, full of action, full of manly pride and friendship,   10
Plain I see you Western youths, see you tramping with the foremost,
        Pioneers! O pioneers!

Have the elder races halted?
Do they droop and end their lesson, wearied over there beyond the seas?
We take up the task eternal, and the burden and the lesson,   15
        Pioneers! O pioneers!

All the past we leave behind,
We debouch upon a newer mightier world, varied world,
Fresh and strong the world we seize, world of labor and the march,
        Pioneers! O pioneers!   20

We detachments steady throwing,
Down the edges, through the passes, up the mountains steep,
Conquering, holding, daring, venturing as we go the unknown ways,
        Pioneers! O pioneers!

We primeval forests felling,   25
We the rivers stemming, vexing we and piercing deep the mines within,
We the surface broad surveying, we the virgin soil upheaving,
        Pioneers! O pioneers!

Colorado men are we,
From the peaks gigantic, from the great sierras and the high plateaus,   30
From the mine and from the gully, from the hunting trail we come,
        Pioneers! O pioneers!

From Nebraska, from Arkansas,
Central inland race are we, from Missouri, with the continental blood intervein'd,
All the hands of comrades clasping, all the Southern, all the Northern,   35
        Pioneers! O pioneers!

O resistless restless race!
O beloved race in all! O my breast aches with tender love for all!
O I mourn and yet exult, I am rapt with love for all,
        Pioneers! O pioneers!   40

Raise the mighty mother mistress,
Waving high the delicate mistress, over all the starry mistress, (bend your heads all,)
Raise the fang'd and warlike mistress, stern, impassive, weapon'd mistress,
        Pioneers! O pioneers!

See my children, resolute children,   45
By those swarms upon our rear we must never yield or falter,

Ages back in ghostly millions frowning there behind us urging,
           Pioneers! O pioneers!

        On and on the compact ranks,
With accessions ever waiting, with the places of the dead quickly fill'd,   50
Through the battle, through defeat, moving yet and never stopping,
           Pioneers! O pioneers!

        O to die advancing on!
Are there some of us to droop and die? has the hour come?
Then upon the march we fittest die, soon and sure the gap is fill'd,   55
           Pioneers! O pioneers!

        All the pulses of the world,
Falling in they beat for us, with the Western movement beat,
Holding single or together, steady moving to the front, all for us,
           Pioneers! O pioneers!   60

        Life's involv'd and varied pageants,
All the forms and shows, all the workmen at their work,
All the seamen and the landsmen, all the masters with their slaves,
           Pioneers! O pioneers!

        All the hapless silent lovers,   65
All the prisoners in the prisons, all the righteous and the wicked,
All the joyous, all the sorrowing, all the living, all the dying,
           Pioneers! O pioneers!

        I too with my soul and body,
We, a curious trio, picking, wandering on our way,   70
Through these shores amid the shadows, with the apparitions pressing,
           Pioneers! O pioneers!

        Lo, the darting bowling orb!
Lo, the brother orbs around, all the clustering suns and planets,
All the dazzling days, all the mystic nights with dreams,   75
           Pioneers! O pioneers!

        These are of us, they are with us,
All for primal needed work, while the followers there in embryo wait behind,
We to-day's procession heading, we the route for travel clearing,
           Pioneers! O pioneers!   80

        O you daughters of the West!
O you young and elder daughters! O you mothers and you wives!
Never must you be divided, in our ranks you move united,
           Pioneers! O pioneers!

        Minstrels latent on the prairies!   85
(Shrouded bards of other lands, you may rest, you have done your work),
Soon I hear you coming warbling, soon you rise and tramp amid us,
           Pioneers! O pioneers!

        Not for delectations sweet,
Not the cushion and the slipper, not the peaceful and the studious,   90
Not the riches safe and palling, not for us the tame enjoyment,
           Pioneers! O pioneers!

Do the feasters gluttonous feast?
Do the corpulent sleepers sleep? Have they lock'd and bolted doors?
Still be ours the diet hard, and the blanket on the ground,   95
    Pioneers! O pioneers!

        Has the night descended?
Was the road of late so toilsome? did we stop discouraged nodding on our way?
Yet a passing hour I yield you in your tracks to pause oblivious,
    Pioneers! O pioneers!   100

        Till with sound of trumpet,
Far, far off the daybreak call — hark! how loud and clear I hear it wind,
Swift! to the head of the army! — swift! spring to your places,
    Pioneers! O pioneers!

On the Beach at Night

(1856, 1871)

❧ The 1856 version, entitled "On the Beach at Night Alone,"
was composed of 14 lines and developed by the cataloguing
method. The 1871 version, given here, is developed as a dramatic situation, and is poetically far superior.

On the beach at night,
Stands a child with her father,
Watching the east, the autumn sky.

Up through the darkness,
While ravening clouds, the burial clouds, in black masses spreading,   5
Lower sullen and fast athwart and down the sky,
Amid a transparent clear belt of ether yet left in the east,
Ascends large and calm the lord-star Jupiter,
And nigh at hand, only a very little above,
Swim the delicate sisters the Pleiades.   10

From the beach the child holding the hand of her father,
Those burial clouds that lower victorious soon to devour all,
Watching, silently weeps.

Weep not, child,
Weep not, my darling,   15
With these kisses let me remove your tears,
The ravening clouds shall not long be victorious,
They shall not long possess the sky, they devour the stars only in apparition,
Jupiter shall emerge, be patient, watch again another night, the Pleiades shall emerge,
They are immortal, all those stars both silvery and golden shall shine out again,   20
The great stars and the little ones shall shine out again, they endure,
The vast immortal suns and the long-enduring pensive moons shall again shine.

Then dearest child mournest thou only for Jupiter?
Considerest thou alone the burial of the stars?
Something there is,   25
(With my lips soothing thee, adding I whisper,
I give thee the first suggestion, the problem and indirection,)
Something there is more immortal even than the stars,

(Many the burials, many the days and nights, passing away,)
Something that shall endure longer even than lustrous Jupiter,   30
Longer than sun or any revolving satellite,
Or the radiant sisters the Pleiades.

Passage to India

(1871)

Columbus, when discovering America, was looking for a passage to India. Centuries later, says Whitman (line 67), America has verified Columbus's dream. In 1869 the railroad tracks, laid west from Omaha and east from San Francisco, were joined in Utah. The same year, the Suez canal was opened. And three years earlier the Atlantic cable had been successfully laid (line 7). "Works of engineers" had thus outdone the ancient Seven Wonders of the World. It was now, physically, one world.

The burden of the poem, Whitman once remarked, is "evolution — . . . the unfolding of cosmic purposes." For him, evolution meant far more than material development. The world has been welded together

"not for trade or transportation only,
But in God's name, and for thy sake O soul."

Far in the past, India led the way in poetry and religion. This will be the way of the future. The world will be circumnavigated by the soul. "Finally shall come the poet worthy that name." He it is who will show how truly, how deeply, the world is one, that Spirit and Matter, Nature and Men, are one. In section 8 we see Whitman taking ship, launching out on trackless seas in an ecstatic adventure of the soul, a voyage to far more than India, more than stars or suns, a voyage whose destination is God.

1

Singing my days,
Singing the great achievements of the present,
Singing the strong light work of engineers,
Our modern wonders, (the antique ponderous Seven outvied,)
In the Old World the east the Suez canal,   5
The New by its mighty railroad spann'd,
The seas inlaid with eloquent gentle wires;
Yet first to sound, and ever sound, the cry with thee O soul,
The Past! the Past! the Past!

The Past — the dark unfathom'd retrospect!   10
The teeming gulf — the sleepers and the shadows!
The past — the infinite greatness of the past!
For what is the present after all but a growth out of the past?
(As a projectile form'd, impell'd, passing a certain line, still keeps on,
So the present, utterly form'd, impell'd by the past.)   15

2

Passage O soul to India!
Eclaircise the myths Asiatic, the primitive fables.

Not you alone proud truths of the world,
Nor you alone ye facts of modern science,
But myths and fables of eld, Asia's, Africa's fables,
The far-darting beams of the spirit, the unloos'd dreams,   20
The deep diving bibles and legends,
The daring plots of the poets, the elder religions;
O you temples fairer than lilies pour'd over by the rising sun!
O you fables spurning the known, eluding the hold of the known, mounting to heaven!
You lofty and dazzling towers, pinnacled, red as roses, burnish'd with gold!   25
Towers of fables immortal fashion'd from mortal dreams!
You too I welcome and fully the same as the rest!
You too with joy I sing.

Passage to India!   **30**
Lo, soul, seest thou not God's purpose from the first?
The earth to be spann'd, connected by network,
The races, neighbors, to marry and be given in marriage,
The oceans to be cross'd, the distant brought near,
The lands to be welded together.   **35**

A worship new I sing,
You captains, voyagers, explorers, yours,
You engineers, you architects, machinists, yours,
You, not for trade or transportation only,
But in God's name, and for thy sake O soul.   **40**

3

Passage to India!
Lo soul for thee of tableaus twain,
I see in one the Suez canal initiated, open'd,
I see the procession of steamships, the Empress Eugenie's leading the van,
I mark from on deck the strange landscape, the pure sky, the level sand in the distance,
I pass swiftly the picturesque groups, the workmen gather'd,   **46**
The gigantic dredging machines.

In one again, different, (yet thine, all thine, O soul, the same,)
I see over my own continent the Pacific railroad surmounting every barrier,   **49**
I see continual trains of cars winding along the Platte carrying freight and passengers,
I hear the locomotives rushing and roaring, and the shrill steam-whistle,
I hear the echoes reverberate through the grandest scenery in the world,
I cross the Laramie plains, I note the rocks in grotesque shapes, the buttes,
I see the plentiful larkspur and wild onions, the barren, colorless, sage-deserts,
I see in glimpses afar or towering immediately above me the great mountains, I see the
     Wind river and the Wahsatch mountains,   **55**
I see the Monument mountain and the Eagle's Nest, I pass the promontory, I ascend
     the Nevadas,
I scan the noble Elk mountain and wind around its base,
I see the Humboldt range, I thread the valley and cross the river,
I see the clear waters of lake Tahoe, I see forests of majestic pines,
Or crossing the great desert, the alkaline plains, I behold enchanting mirages of waters
     and meadows,   **60**
Marking through these and after all, in duplicate slender lines,
Bridging the three or four thousand miles of land travel,
Tying the Eastern to the Western sea,
The road between Europe and Asia.

(Ah Genoese thy dream! thy dream!   **65**
Centuries after thou art laid in thy grave,
The shore thou foundest verifies thy dream.)

4

Passage to India!
Struggles of many a captain, tales of many a sailor dead,
Over my mood stealing and spreading they come,   **70**
Like clouds and cloudlets in the unreach'd sky.

Along all history, down the slopes,
As a rivulet running, sinking now, and now again to the surface rising,

A ceaseless thought, a varied train — lo, soul, to thee, thy sight, they rise,
The plans, the voyages again, the expeditions;   75
Again Vasco de Gama sails forth,
Again the knowledge gain'd, the mariner's compass,
Lands found and nations born, thou born America,
For purpose vast, man's long probation fill'd,
Thou rondure of the world at last accomplish'd.   80

5

O vast Rondure, swimming in space,
Cover'd all over with visible power and beauty,
Alternate light and day and the teeming spiritual darkness,
Unspeakable high processions of sun and moon and countless stars above,
Below, the manifold grass and waters, animals, mountains, trees,   85
With inscrutable purpose, some hidden prophetic intention,
Now first it seems my thought begins to span thee.
Down from the gardens of Asia descending radiating,
Adam and Eve appear, then their myriad progeny after them,
Wandering, yearning, curious, with restless explorations,   90
With questionings, baffled, formless, feverish, with never-happy hearts.
With that sad incessant refrain, *Wherefore unsatisfied soul?* and *Whither O mocking
        life?*

Ah who shall soothe these feverish children?
Who justify these restless explorations?
Who speak the secret of impassive earth?   95
Who bind it to us? what is this separate Nature so unnatural?
What is this earth to our affections? (unloving earth, without a throb to answer ours,
Cold earth, the place of graves.)

Yet soul be sure the first intent remains, and shall be carried out,
Perhaps even now the time has arrived.   100

After the seas are all cross'd, (as they seem already cross'd,)
After the great captains and engineers have accomplish'd their work,
After the noble inventors, after the scientists, the chemists, the geologist, ethnologist,
Finally shall come the poet worthy that name,
The true son of God shall come singing his songs.   105

Then not your deeds only O voyagers, O scientists and inventors, shall be justified,
All these hearts as of fretted children shall be sooth'd,
All affection shall be fully responded to, the secret shall be told,
All these separations and gaps shall be taken up and hook'd and link'd together,
The whole earth, this cold, impassive, voiceless earth, shall be completely justified, 110
Trinitas divine shall be gloriously accomplish'd and compacted by the true son of God,
        the poet,
(He shall indeed pass the straits and conquer the mountains,
He shall double the cape of Good Hope to some purpose,)
Nature and Man shall be disjoin'd and diffused no more,
The true son of God shall absolutely fuse them.   115

6

Year at whose wide-flung door I sing!
Year of the purpose accomplish'd!
Year of the marriage of continents, climates and oceans!
(No mere doge of Venice now wedding the Adriatic,)

I see O year in you the vast terraqueous globe given and giving all,   120
Europe to Asia, Africa join'd, and they to the New World,
The lands, geographies, dancing before you, holding a festival garland,
As brides and bridegroom hand in hand.

Passage to India!
Cooling airs from Caucasus, far, soothing cradle of man,   125
The river Euphrates flowing, the past lit up again.

Lo soul, the retrospect brought forward,
The old, most populous, wealthiest of earth's lands,
The streams of the Indus and the Ganges and their many affluents,
(I my shores of America walking to-day behold, resuming all,)   130
The tale of Alexander on his warlike marches suddenly dying,
On one side China and on the other side Persia and Arabia,
To the south the great seas and the bay of Bengal,
The flowing literatures, tremendous epics, religions, castes,
Old occult Brahma interminably far back, the tender and junior Buddha,   135
Central and southern empires and all their belongings, possessors,
The wars of Tamerlane, the reign of Aurungzebe,
The trades, rulers, explorers, Moslems, Venetians, Byzantium, the Arabs, Portuguese,
The first travelers famous yet, Marco Polo, Batouta the Moor,
Doubts to be solv'd, the map incognita, blanks to be fill'd,   140
The foot of man unstay'd, the hands never at rest,
Thyself O soul that will not brook a challenge.

The mediæval navigators rise before me.
The world of 1492, with its awaken'd enterprise,
Something swelling in humanity now like the sap of the earth in spring,   145
The sunset splendor of chivalry declining.

And who art thou sad shade?
Gigantic, visionary, thyself a visionary,
With majestic limbs and pious beaming eyes,
Spreading around with every look of thine a golden world,   150
Enhuing it with gorgeous hues.

As the chief histrion,
Down to the footlights walks in some great scena,
Dominating the rest I see the Admiral himself,
(History's type of courage, action, faith,)   155
Behold him sail from Palos leading his little fleet,
His voyage behold, his return, his great fame,
His misfortunes, calumniators, behold him a prisoner, chain'd,
Behold his dejection, poverty, death.

(Curious in time I stand, noting the efforts of heroes,   160
Is the deferment long? bitter the slander, poverty, death?
Lies the seed unreck'd for centuries in the ground? lo, to God's due occasion,
Uprising in the night, it sprouts, blooms,
And fills the earth with use and beauty.)

7

Passage indeed O soul to primal thought,   165
Not lands and seas alone, thy own clear freshness,
The young maturity of brood and bloom,
To realms of budding bibles.

O soul, repressless, I with thee and thou with me,
Thy circumnavigation of the world begin,   170
Of man, the voyage of his mind's return,
To reason's early paradise,
Back, back to wisdom's birth, to innocent intuitions,
Again with fair creation.

8

O we can wait no longer,   175
We too take ship O soul,
Joyous we too launch out on trackless seas,
Fearless for unknown shores on waves of ecstasy to sail,
Amid the wafting winds, (thou pressing me to thee, I thee to me, O soul,)
Caroling free, singing our song of God,   180
Chanting our chant of pleasant exploration.

With laugh and many a kiss,
(Let others deprecate, let others weep for sin, remorse, humiliation,)
O soul thou pleasest me, I thee,

Ah more than any priest O soul we too believe in God,   185
But with the mystery of God we dare not dally.

O soul thou pleasest me, I thee.
Sailing these seas or on the hills, or waking in the night,
Thoughts, silent thoughts, of Time and Space and Death, like waters flowing,
Bear me indeed as through the regions infinite,   190
Whose air I breathe, whose ripples hear, lave me all over,
Bathe me O God in thee, mounting to thee,
I and my soul to range in range of thee.

O Thou transcendent,
Nameless, the fibre and the breath,   195
Light of the light, shedding forth universes, thou centre of them,
Thou mightier centre of the true, the good, the loving,
Thou moral, spiritual fountain — affection's source — thou reservoir,
(O pensive soul of me — O thirst unsatisfied — waitest not there?
Waitest not haply for us somewhere there the Comrade perfect?)   200
Thou pulse — thou motive of the stars, suns, systems,
That, circling, move in order, safe, harmonious,
Athwart the shapeless vastnesses of space,
How should I think, how breathe a single breath, how speak, if, out of myself,
I could not launch, to those, superior universes?   205

Swiftly I shrivel at the thought of God,
At Nature and its wonders, Time and Space and Death,
But that I, turning, call to thee O soul, thou actual Me,
And lo, thou gently masterest the orbs,
Thou matest Time, smilest content at Death,   210
And fillest, swellest full the vastnesses of Space.

Greater than stars or suns,
Bounding O soul thou journeyest forth;
What love than thine and ours could wider amplify?
What aspirations, wishes, outvie thine and ours O soul?   215
What dreams of the ideal? what plans of purity, perfection, strength,

What cheerful willingness for others' sake to give up all?
For others' sake to suffer all?

Reckoning ahead O soul, when thou, the time achiev'd,
The seas all cross'd, weather'd the capes, the voyage done,   220
Surrounded, copest, frontest God, yieldest, the aim attain'd,
As fill'd with friendship, love complete, the Elder Brother found,
The Younger melts in fondness in his arms.

9

Passage to more than India!
Are thy wings plumed indeed for such far flights?   225
O soul, voyagest thou indeed on voyages like those?
Disportest thou on waters such as those?
Soundest below the Sanscrit and the Vedas?
Then have thy bent unleash'd.

Passage to you, your shores, ye aged fierce enigmas!   230
Passage to you, to mastership of you, ye strangling problems!
You, strew'd with the wrecks of skeletons, that, living, never reach'd you.

Passage to more than India!
O secret of the earth and sky!
Of you O waters of the sea! O winding creeks and rivers!   235
Of you O woods and fields! of you strong mountains of my land!
Of you O prairies! of you gray rocks!
O morning red! O clouds! O rain and snows!
O day and night, passage to you!
O sun and moon and all you stars! Sirius and Jupiter!   240
Passage to you!

Passage, immediate passage! the blood burns in my veins!
Away O soul! hoist instantly the anchor!
Cut the hawsers — haul out — shake out every sail!
Have we not stood here like trees in the ground long enough?   245
Have we not grovel'd here long enough, eating and drinking like mere brutes?
Have we not darken'd and dazed ourselves with books long enough?

Sail forth — steer for the deep waters only,
Reckless O soul, exploring, I with thee, and thou with me,
For we are bound where mariner has not yet dared to go,   250
And we will risk the ship, ourselves and all.

O my brave soul!
O farther farther sail!
O daring joy, but safe! are they not all the seas of God?
O farther, farther, farther sail!   255

To a Locomotive in Winter

(1876, 1881)

Welcoming modern science and technology, Whitman
here makes the locomotive of the 1870's "serve the Muse," in
human and symbolical terms. There is an article on "Walt
Whitman and the Locomotive," by G. F. Cronkhite, in the
American Quarterly, Summer 1954.

Thee for my recitative,
Thee in the driving storm even as now, the snow, the winter-day declining,
Thee in thy panoply, thy measur'd dual throbbing and thy beat convulsive,
Thy black cylindric body, golden brass and silvery steel,
Thy ponderous side-bars, parallel and connecting rods, gyrating, shuttling at thy sides, 5
Thy metrical, now swelling pant and roar, now tapering in the distance,
Thy great protruding head-light fix'd in front,
Thy long, pale, floating vapor-pennants, tinged with delicate purple,
Thy knitted frame, thy springs and valves, the tremulous twinkle of thy wheels, 10
The dense and murky clouds out-belching from thy smoke-stack,
Thy train of cars behind, obedient, merrily following,
Through gale or calm, now swift, now slack, yet steadily careering;
Type of the modern — emblem of motion and power — pulse of the continent,
For once come serve the Muse and merge in verse, even as here I see thee,
With storm and buffeting gusts of wind and falling snow, 15
By day thy warning ringing bell to sound its notes,
By night thy silent signal lamps to swing.
Fierce-throated beauty!
Roll through my chant with all thy lawless music, thy swinging lamps at night,
Thy madly-whistled laughter, echoing, rumbling like an earthquake, rousing all, 20
Law of thyself complete, thine own track firmly holding,
(No sweetness debonair of tearful harp or glib piano thine,)
Thy trills of shrieks by rocks and hills return'd,
Launch'd o'er the prairies wide, across the lakes,
To the free skies unpent and glad and strong. 25

To the Man-of-War-Bird
(1876, 1881)

At the close Whitman departs, in a striking manner, from the romantic tendency to treat nature as equal or superior to man.

Thou who has slept all night upon the storm,
Waking renew'd on thy prodigious pinions,
(Burst the wild storm? above it thou ascended'st,
And rested on the sky, thy slave that cradled thee,)
Now a blue point, far, far in heaven floating, 5
As to the light emerging here on deck I watch thee,
(Myself a speck, a point on the world's floating vast.)
Far, far at sea,
After the night's fierce drifts have strewn the shore with wrecks,
With reappearing day as now so happy and serene, 10
The rosy and elastic dawn, the flashing sun,
The limpid spread of air cerulean,
Thou also reappearest.

Thou born to match the gale, (thou art all wings,)
To cope with heaven and earth and sea and hurricane, 15
Thou ship of air that never furl'st thy sails,
Days, even weeks untired and onward, through spaces, realms gyrating,
At dusk that look'st on Senegal, at morn America,
That sport'st amid the lightning-flash and thunder-cloud,
In them, in thy experiences, had'st thou my soul, 20
What joys! what joys were thine!

From *Democratic Vistas*

(1871)

After the Civil War, the moral corruption of politics and business, and the low tone of life generally, might well have disillusioned a romantic like Whitman. Instead, he sharply characterized what he saw around him, and bravely offered his specifications for a mature democracy in the future.

[American Democracy, Actual and Ideal]

We had best look our times and lands searchingly in the face, like a physician diagnosing some deep disease. Never was there, perhaps, more hollowness at heart than at present, and here in the United States. Genuine belief seems to have left us. The underlying principles of the States are not honestly believ'd in, (for all this hectic glow, and these melo-dramatic screamings,) nor is humanity itself believ'd in. What penetrating eye does not everywhere see through the mask? The spectacle is appalling. We live in an atmosphere of hypocrisy throughout. The men believe not in the women, nor the women in the men. A scornful superciliousness rules in literature. The aim of all the *littérateurs* is to find something to make fun of. A lot of churches, sects, etc., the most dismal phantasms I know, usurp the name of religion. Conversation is a mass of badinage. From deceit in the spirit, the mother of all false deeds, the offspring is already incalculable. An acute and candid person, in the revenue department in Washington, who is led by the course of his employment to regularly visit the cities, north, south and west, to investigate frauds, has talk'd much with me about his discoveries. The depravity of the business classes of our country is not less than has been supposed, but infinitely greater. The official services of America, national, state, and municipal, in all their branches and departments, except the judiciary, are saturated in corruption, bribery, falsehood, maladministration; and the judiciary is tainted. The great cities reek with respectable as much as non-respectable robbery and scoundrelism. In fashionable life, flippancy, tepid amours, weak infidelism, small aims, or no aims at all, only to kill time. In business, (this all-devouring modern word, business,) the one sole object is, by any means, pecuniary gain. The magician's serpent in the fable ate up all the other serpents; and money-making is our magician's serpent,

remaining to-day sole master of the field. The best class we show, is but a mob of fashionably dress'd speculators and vulgarians. True, indeed, behind this fantastic farce, enacted on the visible stage of society, solid things and stupendous labors are to be discover'd, existing crudely and going on in the background, to advance and tell themselves in time. Yet the truths are none the less terrible. I say that our New World democracy, however great a success in uplifting the masses out of their sloughs, in materialistic development, products, and in a certain highly-deceptive superficial popular intellectuality, is, so far, an almost complete failure in its social aspects, and in really grand religious, moral, literary, and esthetic results. In vain do we march with unprecedented strides to empire so colossal, outvying the antique, beyond Alexander's, beyond the proudest sway of Rome. In vain have we annex'd Texas, California, Alaska, and reach north for Canada and south for Cuba. It is as if we were somehow being endow'd with a vast and more and more thoroughly-appointed body, and then left with little or no soul.

Let me illustrate further, as I write, with current observations, localities, etc. The subject is important, and will bear repetition. After an absence, I am now again (September, 1870) in New York city and Brooklyn, on a few weeks' vacation. The splendor, picturesqueness, and oceanic amplitude and rush of these great cities, the unsurpass'd situation, rivers and bay, sparkling sea-tides, costly and lofty new buildings, façades of marble and iron, of original grandeur and elegance of design, with the masses of gay color, the preponderance of white and blue, the flags flying, the endless ships, the tumultuous streets, Broadway, the heavy, low, musical roar, hardly ever intermitted, even at night; the jobbers' houses, the rich shops, the wharves, the great Central Park, and the Brooklyn Park of hills, (as I wander among them this beautiful fall weather, musing, watching, absorbing) — the assemblages of the citizens in their groups, conversations, trades, evening amusements, or along the by-quarters — these, I say, and the like of these, completely satisfy my senses of power, fulness, motion, etc., and give me, through such senses and appetites, and through my esthetic conscience, a continued exaltation and absolute fulfilment. Always and more and more, as I cross the East and North rivers, the ferries, or with the pilots in their pilot-houses, or pass an hour in Wall street, or the gold exchange, I realize, (if we must admit such partialisms,) that not Nature alone is great in her fields of freedom and the open air, in her storms, the shows of night and day, the mountains, forests, seas — but in the artificial, the work of man too is equally great — in this profusion of teeming humanity — in these ingenuities, streets, goods, houses, ships — these hurrying, feverish, electric crowds of men, their complicated business genius, (not least among the geniuses,) and all this mighty, many-threaded wealth and industry concentrated here.

But sternly discarding, shutting our eyes to the glow and grandeur of the general superficial effect, coming down to what is of the only real importance, Personalities, and examining minutely, we question, we ask, Are there, indeed, *men* here worthy the name? Are there athletes? Are there perfect women, to match the generous material luxuriance? Is there a pervading atmosphere of beautiful manners? Are there crops of fine youths, and majestic old persons? Are there arts worthy freedom and a rich people? Is there a great moral and religious civilization — the only justification of a great material one? Confess that to severe eyes, using the moral microscope upon humanity, a sort of dry and flat Sahara appears, these cities, crowded with petty grotesques, malformations, phantoms, playing meaningless antics. Confess that everywhere, in shop, street, church, theatre, barroom, official chair, are pervading flippancy and vulgarity, low cunning, infidelity — everywhere the youth puny, impudent, foppish, prematurely ripe — everywhere an abnormal libidinousness, unhealthy forms, male, female, painted, padded, dyed, chignon'd, muddy complexions, bad blood, the capacity for good motherhood deceasing or deceas'd, shallow notions of beauty, with a range of manners, or rather lack of manners, (considering the advantages enjoy'd,) probably the meanest to be seen in the world.

Of all this, and these lamentable conditions, to breathe into them the breath recuperative of sane and heroic life, I say a new founded literature, not merely to copy and reflect existing surfaces, or pander to what is called taste — not only to amuse, pass away time, celebrate the beautiful, the refined, the past, or exhibit technical, rhythmic, or grammatical dexterity — but a literature underlying life, religious, consistent with science, handling the elements and forces with competent power, teaching and training men — and, as perhaps the most precious of its

results, achieving the entire redemption of woman out of these incredible holds and webs of silliness, millinery, and every kind of dyspeptic depletion — and thus insuring to the States a strong and sweet Female Race, a race of perfect Mothers — is what is needed.

And now, in the full conception of these facts and points, and all that they infer, pro and con — with yet unshaken faith in the elements of the American masses, the composites, of both sexes, and even consider'd as individuals — and ever recognizing in them the broadest bases of the best literary and esthetic appreciation — I proceed with my speculations, Vistas.

First, let us see what we can make out of a brief, general, sentimental consideration of political democracy, and whence it has arisen, with regard to some of its current features, as an aggregate, and as the basic structure of our future literature and authorship. We shall, it is true, quickly and continually find the origin-idea of the singleness of man, individualism, asserting itself, and cropping forth, even from the opposite ideas. But the mass, or lump character, for imperative reasons, is to be ever carefully weigh'd, borne in mind, and provided for. Only from it, and from its proper regulation and potency, comes the other, comes the chance of individualism. The two are contradictory, but our task is to reconcile them.

The political history of the past may be summ'd up as having grown out of what underlies the words, order, safety, caste, and especially out of the need of some prompt deciding authority, and of cohesion at all cost. Leaping time, we come to the period within the memory of people now living, when, as from some lair where they had slumber'd long, accumulating wrath, sprang up and are yet active, (1790, and on even to the present, 1870,) those noisy eructations, destructive iconoclasms, a fierce sense of wrongs, amid which moves the form, well known in modern history, in the old world, stain'd with much blood, and mark'd by savage reactionary clamors and demands. These bear, mostly, as on one inclosing point of need.

For after the rest is said — after the many time-honor'd and really true things for subordination, experience, rights of property, etc., have been listen'd to and acquiesced in — after the valuable and well-settled statement of our duties and relations in society is thoroughly conn'd over and exhausted — it remains to bring forward and modify everything else with the idea of that Something a man is, (last precious consolation of the drudging poor,) standing apart from all else, divine in his own right, and a woman in hers, sole and untouchable by any canons of authority, or any rule derived from precedent, state-safety, the acts of legislatures, or even from what is called religion, modesty, or art. The radiation of this truth is the key of the most significant doings of our immediately preceding three centuries, and has been the political genesis and life of America. Advancing visibly, it still more advances invisibly. Underneath the fluctuations of the expressions of society, as well as the movements of the politics of the leading nations of the world, we see steadily pressing ahead and strengthening itself, even in the midst of immense tendencies toward aggregation, this image of completeness in separatism, of individual personal dignity, of a single person, either male or female, characterized in the main, not from extrinsic acquirements or position, but in the pride of himself or herself alone; and, as an eventual conclusion and summing up, (or else the entire scheme of things is aimless, a cheat, a crash,) the simple idea that the last, best dependence is to be upon humanity itself, and its own inherent, normal, full-grown qualities, without any superstitious support whatever.***

[What Is an American?]

And, if we think of it, what does civilization itself rest upon — and what object has it, with its religions, arts, schools, etc., but rich, luxuriant, varied personalism? To that, all bends; and it is because toward such result democracy alone, on anything like Nature's scale, breaks up the limitless fallows of humankind, and plants the seed, and gives fair play, that its claims now precede the rest. The literature, songs, esthetics, etc., of a country are of importance principally because they furnish the materials and suggestions of personality for the women and men of that country, and enforce them in a thousand effective ways.***

America has yet morally and artistically originated nothing. She seems singularly unaware that the models of persons, books, manners, etc., appropriate for former conditions and for European lands, are but exiles and exotics here. No current of her life, as shown on the surfaces of what is authoritatively called her society, accepts or runs into social or esthetic democracy; but all

the currents set squarely against it. Never, in the Old World, was thoroughly upholster'd exterior appearance and show, mental and other, built entirely on the idea of caste, and on the sufficiency of mere outside acquisition — never were glibness, verbal intellect, more the test, the emulation — more loftily elevated as head and sample — than they are on the surface of our republican States this day. The writers of a time hint the mottoes of its gods. The word of the modern, say these voices, is the word Culture.

We find ourselves abruptly in close quarters with the enemy. This word Culture, or what it has come to represent, involves, by contrast, our whole theme, and has been, indeed, the spur, urging us to engagement. Certain questions arise. As now taught, accepted and carried out, are not the processes of culture rapidly creating a class of supercilious infidels, who believe in nothing? Shall a man lose himself in countless masses of adjustments, and be so shaped with reference to this, that, and the other, that the simply good and healthy and brave parts of him are reduced and clipp'd away, like the bordering of box in a garden? You can cultivate corn and roses and orchards — but who shall cultivate the mountain peaks, the ocean, and the tumbling gorgeousness of the clouds? Lastly — is the readily-given reply that culture only seeks to help, systematize, and put in attitude, the elements of fertility and power, a conclusive reply?

I do not so much object to the name, or word, but I should certainly insist, for the purposes of these States, on a radical change of category, in the distribution of precedence. I should demand a programme of culture, drawn out, not for a single class alone, or for the parlors or lecture-rooms, but with an eye to practical life, the West, the working-men, the facts of farms and jack-planes and engineers, and of the broad range of the women also of the middle and working strata, and with reference to the perfect equality of women, and of a grand and powerful motherhood. I should demand of this programme or theory a scope generous enough to include the widest human area. It must have for its spinal meaning the formation of a typical personality of character, eligible to the uses of the high average of men — and *not* restricted by conditions ineligible to the masses. The best culture will always be that of the manly and courageous instincts, and loving perceptions, and of self-respect — aiming to form, over this continent, an idiocrasy of universalism, which, true child of America, will bring joy to its mother, returning to her in her own spirit, recruiting myriads of offspring, able, natural, perceptive, tolerant, devout believers in her, America, and with some definite instinct why and for what she has arisen, most vast, most formidable of historic births, and is, now and here, with wonderful step, journeying through Time.***

[An American Literature]

What is the reason our time, our lands, that we see no fresh local courage, sanity, of our own — the Mississippi, stalwart Western men, real mental and physical facts, Southerners, etc., in the body of our literature? especially the poetic part of it. But always, instead, a parcel of dandies and ennuyees, dapper little gentlemen from abroad, who flood as with their thin sentiment of parlors, parasols, piano-songs, tinkling rhymes, the five-hundredth importation — or whimpering and crying about something, chasing one aborted conceit after another, and forever occupied in dyspeptic amours with dyspeptic women. While, current and novel, the grandest events and revolutions, and stormiest passions of history, are crossing to-day with unparallel'd rapidity and magnificence over the stages of our own and all the continents, offering new materials, opening new vistas, with largest needs, inviting the daring launching forth of conceptions in literature, inspired by them, soaring in highest regions, serving art in its highest, (which is only the other name for serving God, and serving humanity,) where is the man of letters, where is the book, with any nobler aim than to follow in the old track, repeat what has been said before — and, as its utmost triumph, sell well, and be erudite or elegant?

Mark the roads, the processes, through which these States have arrived, standing easy, henceforth ever-equal, ever-compact, in their range to-day. European adventures? the most antique? Asiatic or African? old history — miracles — romances? Rather, our own unquestion'd facts. They hasten, incredible, blazing bright as fire. From the deeds and days of Columbus down to the present, and including the present — and especially the late Secession war — when I con them, I feel, every leaf, like stopping to see if I

have not made a mistake, and fall'n on the splendid figments of some dream. But it is no dream. We stand, live, move, in the huge flow of our age's materialism — in its spirituality. We have had founded for us the most positive of lands. The founders have pass'd to other spheres — but what are these terrible duties they have left us?

Their politics the United States have, in my opinion, with all their faults, already substantially establish'd, for good, on their own native, sound, long-vista'd principles, never to be over-turn'd, offering a sure basis for all the rest. With that, their future religious forms, sociology, literature, teachers, schools, costumes, etc., are of course to make a compact whole, uniform, on tallying principles. For how can we remain, divided, contradicting ourselves, this way? I say we can only attain harmony and stability by consulting ensemble and the ethic purports, and faithfully building upon them. For the New World, indeed, after two grand stages of preparation-strata, I perceive that now a third stage, being ready for, (and without which the other two were useless,) with unmistakable signs appears. The First stage was the planning and putting on record the political foundation rights of immense masses of people — indeed all people — in the organization of republican National, State, and municipal governments, all constructed with reference to each, and each to all. This is the American programme, not for classes, but for universal man, and is embodied in the compacts of the Declaration of Independence, and, as it began and has now grown, with its amendments, the Federal Constitution — and in the State governments, with all their interiors, and with general suffrage; those having the sense not only of what is in themselves, but that their certain several things started, planted, hundreds of others in the same direction duly arise and follow. The Second stage relates to material prosperity, wealth, produce, labor-saving machines, iron, cotton, local, State and continental railways, intercommunication and trade with all lands, steamships, mining, general employment, organization of great cities, cheap appliances for comfort, numberless technical schools, books, newspapers, a currency for money circulation, etc. The Third stage, rising out of the previous ones, to make them and all illustrious, I, now, for one, promulge, announcing a native expression-spirit, getting into form, adult, and through mentality, for these States, self-contain'd, different from others, more expansive, more rich and free, to be evidenced by original authors and poets to come, by American personalities, plenty of them, male and female traversing the States, none excepted — and by native superber tableaux and growths of language, songs, operas, orations, lectures, architecture — and by a sublime and serious Religious Democracy sternly taking command, dissolving the old, sloughing off surfaces, and from its own interior and vital principles, reconstructing, democratizing society.***

America demands a poetry that is bold, modern, and all-surrounding and kosmical, as she is herself. It must in no respect ignore science or the modern, but inspire itself with science and the modern. It must bend its vision toward the future, more than the past. Like America, it must extricate itself from even the greatest models of the past, and, while courteous to them, must have entire faith in itself, and the products of its own democratic spirit only. Like her, it must place in the van, and hold up at all hazards, the banner of the divine pride of man in himself, (the radical foundation of the new religion.) Long enough have the People been listening to poems in which common humanity, deferential, bends low, humiliated, acknowledging superiors. But America listens to no such poems. Erect, inflated, and fully self-esteeming be the chant; and then America will listen with pleased ears.***

In the prophetic literature of these States (the reader of my speculations will miss their principal stress unless he allows well for the point that a new Literature, perhaps a new Metaphysics, certainly a new Poetry, are to be, in my opinion, the only sure and worthy supports and expressions of the American Democracy,) Nature, true Nature, and the true idea of Nature, long absent, must, above all, become fully restored, enlarged and must furnish the pervading atmosphere to poems, and the test of all high literary and esthetic compositions. I do not mean the smooth walks, trimm'd hedges, poseys and nightingales of the English poets, but the whole orb, with its geologic history, the kosmos, carrying fire and snow, that rolls through the illimitable areas, light as a feather, though weighing billions of tons. Furthermore, as by what we now partially call Nature is intended, at most, only what is entertainable by the physical conscience, the sense of matter, and

of good animal health — on these it must be distinctly accumulated, incorporated, that man, comprehending these, has, in towering superaddition, the moral and spiritual consciences, indicating his destination beyond the ostensible, the mortal.

To the heights of such estimate of Nature indeed ascending, we proceed to make observations for our Vistas, breathing rarest air. What is I believe called Idealism seems to me to suggest, (guarding against extravagance, and ever modified even by its opposite,) the course of inquiry and desert of favor for our New World metaphysics, their foundation of and in literature, giving hue to all.

The elevating and etherealizing ideas of the unknown and of unreality must be brought forward with authority, as they are the legitimate heirs of the known, and of reality, and at least as great as their parents. Fearless of scoffing, and of the ostent, let us take our stand, our ground, and never desert it, to confront the growing excess and arrogance of realism. To the cry, now victorious — the cry of sense, science, flesh, incomes, farms, merchandise, logic, intellect, demonstrations, solid perpetuities, buildings of brick and iron, or even the facts of the shows of trees, earth, rocks, etc., fear not, my brethren, my sisters, to sound out with equally determin'd voice, that conviction brooding within the recesses of every envision'd soul — illusions! apparitions! figments all! True, we must not condemn the show, neither absolutely deny it, for the indispensability of its meanings; but how clearly we see that, migrate in soul to what we can already conceive of superior and spiritual points of view, and, palpable as it seems under present relations, it all and several might, nay certainly would, fall apart and vanish.

I hail with joy the oceanic, variegated, intense practical energy, the demand for facts, even the business materialism of the current age, our States. But woe to the age or land in which these things, movements, stopping at themselves, do not tend to ideas. As fuel to flame, and flame to the heavens, so must wealth, science, materialism — even this democracy of which we make so much — unerringly feed the highest mind, the soul. Infinitude the flight: fathomless the mystery. Man, so diminutive, dilates beyond the sensible universe, competes with, outcopes space and time, meditating even one great idea. Thus, and thus only, does a human being, his spirit, ascend above, and justify, objective Nature, which, probably nothing in itself, is incredibly and divinely serviceable, indispensable, real, here. And as the purport of objective Nature is doubtless folded, hidden, somewhere here — as somewhere here is what this globe and its manifold forms, and the light of day, and night's darkness, and life itself, with all its experiences, are for — it is here the great literature, especially verse, must get its inspiration and throbbing blood. Then may we attain to a poetry worthy the immortal soul of man, and which, while absorbing materials, and, in their own sense, the shows of Nature, will, above all, have, both directly and indirectly, a freeing, fluidizing, expanding, religious character, exulting with science, fructifying the moral elements, and stimulating aspirations, and meditations on the unknown.

CIVIL WAR AND AFTER

Abraham Lincoln [1809–1865]

To Lincoln's brief autobiography printed below only a few facts need here be added. As he says, "What I have done since that is pretty well known." There was the senatorial campaign of 1858, the great debates with Douglas. Lincoln lost the election, but when the Republican national convention met in Chicago two years later he was nominated for the Presidency on the third ballot. With 180 electoral votes to his opponents' 123, he was elected to the office and began four stormy years in the White House.

Lincoln's part in the war need not be discussed here. When the result of the conflict was still in doubt, he was re-elected to the Presidency by an overwhelming majority in the electoral college. Inaugurated March 4, 1865, he had served little more than a month of his second term when an assassin's bullet ended his life.

Lincoln has won a place in American letters by salient ideas expressed in a style free of the bombastic oratory of the frontier, a style that ranged from the simply direct to the quietly firm or the harmoniously elevated.

Further reading: Any book of selected addresses and letters of Lincoln. Carl Sandburg, *Abraham Lincoln: The Prairie Years and the War Years* (one volume abridgement of his six volume work), 1954. D. Donald, *Lincoln Reconsidered*, 1956.

Autobiography

✿ Lincoln sent this short sketch of his life to J. W. Fell on December 20, 1859, in order that it might be used for campaign purposes.

I was born February 12, 1809, in Hardin County, Kentucky. My parents were both born in Virginia, of undistinguished families — second families, perhaps I should say. My mother, who died in my tenth year, was of a family of the name of Hanks, some of whom now reside in Adams, and others in Macon County, Illinois. My paternal grandfather, Abraham Lincoln, emigrated from Rockingham County, Virginia, to Kentucky about 1781 or 1782, where a year or two later he was killed by the Indians, not in battle, but by stealth, when he was laboring to open a farm in the forest. His ancestors, who were Quakers, went to Virginia from Berks County, Pennsylvania. An effort to identify them with the New England family of the same name ended in nothing more definite than a similarity of Christian names in both families, such as Enoch, Levi, Mordecai, Solomon, Abraham, and the like.

My father, at the death of his father, was but six years of age, and he grew up literally without education. He removed from Kentucky to what is now Spencer County, Indiana, in my eighth year. We reached our new home about the time the state came into the Union. It was a wild region, with many bears and other wild animals still in the woods. There I grew up. There were some schools, so called, but no qualification was ever required of a teacher beyond "readin', writin', and cipherin'," to the rule of three. If a straggler supposed to understand Latin happened to sojourn in the neighborhood, he was looked upon as a wizard. There was absolutely nothing to excite ambition for education. Of course, when I came of age I did not know much. Still, somehow, I could read, write, and cipher to the rule of three, but that was all. I have not been to school since. The little advance I now have upon this store of education, I have picked up from time to time under the pressure of necessity.

I was raised to farm work, which I continued till I was twenty-two. At twenty-one I came to Illinois, Macon County. Then I got to New Salem, at that time in Sangamon, now in Menard County, where I remained a year as a sort of clerk in a store. Then came the Black Hawk War; and I was elected a captain of volunteers, a success which gave me more pleasure than any I have had since. I went the campaign, was elated, ran for the legislature the same year (1832), and was beaten — the only time I ever have been beaten by the people. The next and three succeeding biennial elections I was elected to the legislature. I was not a candidate afterward. During this legislative period I had studied law, and removed to Springfield to practice it. In 1846 I was once elected to the lower House of Congress. Was not a candidate for reëlection. From 1849 to 1854, both inclusive, practiced law more assiduously than ever before. Always a Whig in politics; and generally on the Whig electoral tickets,

making active canvasses. I was losing interest in politics when the repeal of the Missouri Compromise aroused me again. What I have done since that is pretty well known.

If any personal description of me is thought desirable, it may be said I am, in height, six feet four inches, nearly; lean in flesh, weighing on an average one hundred and eighty pounds; dark complexion, with coarse black hair and gray eyes. No other marks or brands recollected.

Reply to Horace Greeley

EXECUTIVE MANSION, WASHINGTON,
August 22, 1862

HON. HORACE GREELEY.

Dear Sir: I have just read yours of the 19th, addressed to myself through the New York *Tribune.* If there be in it any statements or assumptions of fact which I may know to be erroneous, I do not, now and here, controvert them. If there be in it any inferences which I may believe to be falsely drawn, I do not, now and here, argue against them. If there be perceptible in it an impatient and dictatorial tone, I waive it in deference to an old friend whose heart I have always supposed to be right.

As to the policy I "seem to be pursuing," as you say, I have not meant to leave any one in doubt.

I would save the Union. I would save it the shortest way under the Constitution. The sooner the national authority can be restored, the nearer the Union will be "the Union as it was." If there be those who would not save the Union unless they could at the same time save slavery, I do not agree with them. If there be those who would not save the Union unless they could at the same time destroy slavery, I do not agree with them. My paramount object in this struggle is to save the Union, and is not either to save or to destroy slavery. If I could save the Union without freeing any slave, I would do it; and if I could save it by freeing all the slaves, I would do it; and if I could save it by freeing some and leaving others alone, I would also do that. What I do about slavery and the colored race, I do because I believe it helps to save the Union; and what I forbear, I forbear because I do not believe it would help to save the Union. I shall do less whenever I shall believe what I am doing hurts the cause, and I shall do more whenever I shall believe doing more will help the cause. I shall try to correct errors when shown to be errors, and I shall adopt new views so fast as they shall appear to be true views.

I have here stated my purpose according to my view of official duty; and I intend no modification of my oft-expressed personal wish that all men everywhere could be free.

Yours,

A. LINCOLN

Gettysburg Address

(1863)

"In a photographer's studio eleven days before delivering the speech at Gettysburg, Lincoln had held in his hands the lengthy address of Edward Everett, the designated orator of the day, the printed two-hour discourse covering nearly two sides of a one-sheet supplement of a Boston newspaper. To a young newspaper correspondent from California he said his own speech at Gettysburg would be 'short, short, short' — as it proved to be, ten sentences spoken in less than five minutes. In its implicative qualities, it stands among the supreme utterances of democratic peoples of the world." (Carl Sandburg, in *Literary History of the United States*.)

To grasp the *literary* qualities of this masterpiece one might contrast its language with that of a modern government report, as satirized in the *Harvard Alumni Bulletin* in 1951: "Eight and seven tenths decades ago the pioneer workers in this continental area implemented a new group based on an ideology of free boundaries and initial conditions of equality. We are now actively engaged in an over-all evaluation of conflicting factors in order to determine whether or not the life expectancy of this group or of any group operating under the stated conditions is significant. . . ."

Fourscore and seven years ago our fathers brought forth on this continent a new nation, conceived in liberty, and dedicated to the proposition that all men are created equal.

Now we are engaged in a great civil war, testing whether that nation, or any nation so conceived and so dedicated, can long endure. We are met on a great battlefield of that war. We have come to dedicate a portion of that field as a final resting place for those who here gave their lives that that nation might live. It is altogether fitting and proper that we should do this.

But, in a larger sense, we cannot dedicate — we cannot consecrate — we cannot hallow — this ground. The brave men, living and dead, who struggled here, have consecrated it far above our poor power to add or detract. The world will little note nor long remember what we say here, but it can never forget what they did here. It is for us, the living, rather, to be dedicated here to the unfinished work which they who fought here have thus far so nobly advanced. It is rather for us to be here dedicated to the great task remaining before us — that from these honored dead we take increased devotion to that cause for which they gave the last full measure of devotion; that we here highly resolve that these dead shall not have died in vain; that this nation, under God, shall have a new birth of freedom; and that government of the people, by the people, for the people, shall not perish from the earth.

Letter to Mrs. Bixby

"The War Department records showed a Boston woman to have lost five sons in combat actions. The number was less than five, as later research revealed, but Lincoln spoke through her to all families that had lost a boy or man in the war." (Sandburg.)

EXECUTIVE MANSION, WASHINGTON, *November 21, 1864*

MRS. BIXBY, Boston, Massachusetts.

DEAR MADAM: I have been shown in the files of the War Department a statement of the Adjutant-General of Massachusetts that you are the mother of five sons who have died gloriously on the field of battle. I feel how weak and fruitless must be any words of mine which should attempt to beguile you from the grief of a loss so overwhelming. But I cannot refrain from tendering to you the consolation that may be found in the thanks of the Republic they died to save. I pray that our heavenly Father may assuage the anguish of your bereavement, and leave you only the cherished memory of the loved and lost, and the solemn pride that must be yours to have laid so costly a sacrifice upon the altar of freedom.

Yours very sincerely and respectfully,

ABRAHAM LINCOLN

Second Inaugural Address

(1865)

FELLOW-COUNTRYMEN: At this second appearing to take the oath of the presidential office, there is less occasion for an extended address than there was at the first. Then a statement, somewhat in detail, of a course to be pursued, seemed fitting and proper. Now, at the expiration of four years, during which public declarations have been constantly called forth on every point and phase of the great contest which still absorbs the attention and engrosses the energies of the nation, little that is new could be presented. The progress of our arms, upon which all else chiefly depends, is as well known to the public as to myself; and it is, I trust, reasonably satisfactory and encouraging to all. With high hope for the future, no prediction in regard to it is ventured.

On the occasion corresponding to this four years ago, all thoughts were anxiously directed to an impending civil war. All dreaded it — all sought to avert it. While the inaugural address was being delivered from this place, devoted altogether to saving the Union without war, insurgent agents were in the city seeking to destroy it without war — seeking to dissolve the Union, and divide effects, by negotiation. Both parties deprecated war; but one of them would make war rather than let the nation survive; and the other would accept war rather than let it perish. And the war came.

One-eighth of the whole population were colored slaves, not distributed generally over the Union, but localized in the Southern part of it. These slaves constituted a peculiar and powerful interest. All knew that this interest was, somehow, the cause of the war. To strengthen, perpetuate, and extend this interest was the object for which the insurgents would rend the Union, even by war; while the government claimed no right to do more than to restrict the territorial enlargement of it.

Neither party expected for the war the magnitude or the duration which it has already attained. Neither anticipated that the cause of the conflict might cease with, or even before, the conflict itself should cease. Each looked for an easier triumph, and a result less fundamental and astounding. Both read the same Bible, and pray to the same God; and each invokes his aid against the other. It may seem strange that any men should dare to ask a just God's assistance in wringing their bread from the sweat of other men's faces; but let us judge not, that we be not judged. The prayers of both could not be answered — that of neither has been answered fully.

The Almighty has his own purposes. "Woe unto the world because of offences! for it must needs be that offences come; but woe to that man by whom the offence cometh." If we shall suppose that American slavery is one of those offences which, in the providence of God, must needs come, but which, having continued through his appointed time, he now wills to remove, and that he gives to both North and South this terrible war, as the woe due to those by whom the offence came, shall we discern therein any departure from those divine attributes which the believers in a living God always ascribe to him? Fondly do we hope — fervently do we pray — that this mighty scourge of war may speedily pass away. Yet, if God wills that it continue until all the wealth piled by the bondmen's two hundred and fifty years of unrequited toil shall be sunk, and until every drop of blood drawn with the lash shall be paid by another drawn with the sword, as was said three thousand years ago, so still it must be said, "The judgments of the Lord are true and righteous altogether."

With malice toward none; with charity for all; with firmness in the right, as God gives us to see the right, let us strive on to finish the work we are in; to bind up the nation's wounds; to care for him who shall have borne the battle, and for his widow, and his orphan — to do all which may achieve and cherish a just and lasting peace among ourselves, and with all nations.

$Henry$ Timrod [1828–1867]

Timrod was a member of the Charleston literary group in the heart of the South. Born in Charleston, he studied for a year and a half at the University of Georgia. After reading some law, he did tutoring and took to writing. A book of poems emerged in 1860. He enlisted as a volunteer in the armies of the Confederacy, but his frail constitution soon forced him out of service. He was editing a newspaper in Columbia, S.C., when Sherman's army arrived. His fortunes and his health ruined, he died of tuberculosis two years later.

In the "mood of exalted devotion which characterized the Confederacy at its best" (to use J. B. Hubbell's phrase) Timrod quickly matured as a poet. What he had written by 1860 was thinly romantic; his best poems came in the few years left to him. They showed a fine sensibility, at once passionate and controlled. They endure, as Matthiessen said, with a classic hardness.

Further reading: Selections in E. W. Parks, ed., *Southern Poets* (American Writers Series), 1936. J. B. Hubbell, *The South in American Literature*, 1954, pp. 466–74.

Ethnogenesis

The Greek title means "The Birth of a Nation." Written in February 1861 while the First Confederate Congress was in session at Montgomery, Alabama, this poem reflects the spirit of the South on the verge of armed conflict. Fort Sumter was bombarded April 12.

The reference in lines 34 and 35 is to Satan in Milton's *Paradise Lost*. Moultrie and Eutaw, line 42, were Revolutionary conflicts. "Redder sea," line 83: Exodus 14:15. "Gulf" in line 105: the Gulf Stream.

I

Hath not the morning dawned with added light?
And shall not evening call another star
Out of the infinite regions of the night,
To mark this day in Heaven? At last, we are
A nation among nations; and the world   5
Shall soon behold in many a distant port
  Another flag unfurled!
Now, come what may, whose favor need we
  court?
And, under God, whose thunder need we fear?
  Thank him who placed us here   10
Beneath so kind a sky — the very sun

Takes part with us; and on our errands run
All breezes of the ocean; dew and rain
Do noiseless battle for us; and the Year,
And all the gentle daughters in her train,   15
March in our ranks, and in our service wield
Long spears of golden grain!
A yellow blossom as her fairy shield,
June flings her azure banner to the wind,
  While in the order of their birth   20
Her sisters pass, and many an ample field
Grows white beneath their steps, till now, be-
  hold,
  Its endless sheets unfold
THE SNOW OF SOUTHERN SUMMERS! Let the
  earth
Rejoice! beneath those fleeces soft and
  warm   25
  Our happy land shall sleep
  In repose as deep
As if we lay intrenched behind
Whole leagues of Russian ice and Arctic storm!

II

And what if, mad with wrongs themselves have
  wrought,   30
  In their own treachery caught,

By their own fears made bold,
And leagued with him of old,
Who long since in the limits of the North
Set up his evil throne, and warred with
    God —   35
What if, both mad and blinded in their rage,
Our foes should fling us down their mortal
    gage,
And with a hostile step profane our sod!
We shall not shrink, my brothers, but go
    forth
To meet them, marshaled by the Lord of
    Hosts,   40
And overshadowed by the mighty ghosts
Of Moultrie and Eutaw — who shall foil
Auxiliars such as these? Not these alone,
    But every stock and stone
    Shall help us; but the very soil,   45
And all the generous wealth it gives to toil,
And all for which we love our noble land,
Shall fight beside, and through us; sea and
    strand,
    The heart of woman, and her hand,
Tree, fruit, and flower, and every influence,   50
    Gentle, or grave, or grand;
    The winds in our defence
Shall seem to blow; to us the hills shall lend
    Their firmness and their calm;
And in our stiffened sinews we shall blend   55
    The strength of pine and palm!

III

Nor would we shun the battleground,
    Though weak as we are strong;
Call up the clashing elements around,
    And test the right and wrong!   60
On one side, creeds that dare to teach
What Christ and Paul refrained to preach;
Codes built upon a broken pledge,
And Charity that whets a poniard's edge;
Fair schemes that leave the neighboring
    poor   65
To starve and shiver at the schemer's door
While in the world's most liberal ranks enrolled,
He turns some vast philanthropy to gold;
Religion, taking every mortal form
But that a pure and Christian faith makes
    warm,   70
Where not to vile fanatic passion urged,
Or not in vague philosophies submerged,
Repulsive with all Pharisaic leaven,
And making laws to stay the laws of Heaven!
And on the other, scorn of sordid gain,   75

Unblemished honor, truth without a stain,
Faith, justice, reverence, charitable wealth,
And, for the poor and humble, laws which give,
Not the mean right to buy the right to live,
    But life, and home, and health!   80
To doubt the end were want of trust in God,
    Who, if he has decreed
    That we must pass a redder sea
Than that which rang to Miriam's holy glee,
    Will surely raise at need   85
    A Moses with his rod!

IV

But let our fears — if fears we have — be still,
And turn us to the future! Could we climb
Some mighty Alp, and view the coming time,
    The rapturous sight would fill   90
    Our eyes with happy tears!
Not only for the glories which the years
Shall bring us; not for lands from sea to sea,
And wealth, and power, and peace, though these
    shall be;
But for the distant peoples we shall bless,   95
And the hushed murmurs of a world's distress:
For, to give labor to the poor,
    The whole sad planet o'er,
And save from want and crime the humblest
    door,
Is one among the many ends for which   100
    God makes us great and rich!
The hour perchance is not yet wholly ripe
When all shall own it, but the type
Whereby we shall be known in every land
Is that vast gulf which lips our Southern
    strand,   105
And through the cold, untempered ocean pours
Its genial streams, that far off Arctic shores
May sometimes catch upon the softened breeze
Strange tropic warmth and hints of summer
    seas.

The Cotton Boll

(1861)

"The Woodlands," in line 98, was the country
estate of Simms, the novelist and poet.

While I recline
    At ease beneath
This immemorial pine,
Small sphere!
(By dusky fingers brought this morning here

And shown with boastful smiles),   6
I turn thy cloven sheath,
Through which the soft white fibers peer,
That, with their gossamer bands,
Unite, like love, the sea-divided lands,   10
And slowly, thread by thread,
Draw forth the folded strands,
Than which the trembling line,
By whose frail help yon startled spider fled
Down the tall spear-grass from his swinging
          bed,   15
Is scarce more fine;
And as the tangled skein
Unravels in my hands,
Betwixt me and the noonday light,
A veil seems lifted, and for miles and miles   20
The landscape broadens on my sight,
As, in the little boll, there lurked a spell
Like that which, in the ocean shell,
With mystic sound,
Breaks down the narrow walls that hem us
          round,   25
And turns some city lane
Into the restless main,
With all his capes and isles!

Yonder bird,
Which floats, as if at rest,   30
In those blue tracts above the thunder, where
No vapors cloud the stainless air,
And never sound is heard,
Unless at such rare time
When, from the City of the Blest,   35
Rings down some golden chime,
Sees not from his high place
So vast a cirque of summer space
As widens round me in one mighty field,
Which, rimmed by seas and sands,   40
Doth hail its earliest daylight in the beams
Of gray Atlantic dawns;
And, broad as realms made up of many lands,
Is lost afar
Behind the crimson hills and purple lawns   45
Of sunset, among plains which roll their
          streams
Against the Evening Star!

And lo!
To the remotest point of sight,
Although I gaze upon no waste of snow,   50
The endless field is white;
And the whole landscape glows,
For many a shining league away,
With such accumulated light

As Polar lands would flash beneath a tropic
          day!   55
Nor lack there (for the vision grows,
And the small charm within my hands —
More potent even than the fabled one,
Which oped whatever golden mystery
Lay hid in fairy wood or magic vale,   60
The curious ointment of the Arabian tale —
Beyond all mortal sense
Doth stretch my sight's horizon, and I see,
Beneath its simple influence,
As if with Uriel's crown,   65
I stood in some great temple of the Sun,
And looked, as Uriel, down!)
Nor lack there pastures rich and fields all green
With all the common gifts of God,
For temperate airs and torrid sheen   70
Weave Edens of the sod;
Through lands which look one sea of billowy
          gold
Broad rivers wind their devious ways;
A hundred isles in their embraces fold
A hundred luminous bays;   75
And through yon purple haze
Vast mountains lift their plumed peaks cloud-
          crowned;
And, save where up their sides the plowman
          creeps
An unhewn forest girds them grandly round,
In whose dark shades a future navy sleeps!   80
Ye Stars, which, though unseen, yet with me
          gaze
Upon this loveliest fragment of the earth!
Thou Sun, that kindlest all thy gentlest rays
Above it, as to light a favorite hearth!
Ye Clouds, that in your temples in the West   85
See nothing brighter than its humblest flowers!
And you, ye Winds, that on the ocean's breast
Are kissed to coolness ere ye reach its bowers!
Bear witness with me in my song of praise,
And tell the world that, since the world began,
No fairer land hath fired a poet's lays,   91
Or given a home to man!

But these are charms already widely blown!
His be the meed whose pencil's trace
Hath touched our very swamps with grace,   95
And round whose tuneful way
All Southern laurels bloom;
The Poet of "The Woodlands," unto whom
Alike are known
The flute's low breathing and the trumpet's
          tone,   100
And the soft west wind's sighs;

But who shall utter all the debt,
O land wherein all powers are met
That bind a people's heart,
The world doth owe thee at this day,   105
And which it never can repay,
Yet scarcely deigns to own!
Where sleeps the poet who shall fitly sing
The source wherefrom doth spring
That mighty commerce which, confined   110
To the mean channels of no selfish mart,
Goes out to every shore
Of this broad earth, and throngs the sea with
    ships
That bear no thunders; hushes hungry lips
In alien lands;   115
Joins with a delicate web remotest strands;
And gladdening rich and poor,
Doth gild Parisian domes,
Or feed the cottage-smoke of English homes,
And only bounds its blessings by mankind!   120
In offices like these, thy mission lies,
My Country! and it shall not end
As long as rain shall fall and Heaven bend
In blue above thee; though thy foes be hard
And cruel as their weapons, it shall guard   125
Thy hearth-stones as a bulwark; make thee great
In white and bloodless state;
And haply, as the years increase —
Still working through its humbler reach   129
With that large wisdom which the ages teach —
Revive the half-dead dream of universal peace!
As men who labor in that mine
Of Cornwall, hollowed out beneath the bed
Of ocean, when a storm rolls overhead,
Hear the dull booming of the world of brine
Above them, and a mighty muffled roar   136
Of winds and waters, yet toil calmly on,
And split the rock, and pile the massive ore,
Or carve a niche, or shape the archèd roof;
So I, as calmly, weave my woof   140
Of song, chanting the days to come,
Unsilenced, though the quiet summer air
Stirs with the bruit of battles, and each dawn
Wakes from its starry silence to the hum
Of many gathering armies. Still,   145
In that we sometimes hear,
Upon the Northern winds, the voice of woe
Not wholly drowned in triumph, though I know
The end must crown us, and a few brief years
Dry all our tears,   150
I may not sing too gladly. To thy will
Resigned, O Lord! we cannot all forget
That there is much even Victory must regret.
And, therefore, not too long

From the great burthen of our country's wrong
Delay our just release!   156
And, if it may be, save
These sacred fields of peace
From stain of patriot or of hostile blood!
Oh, help us, Lord! to roll the crimson flood 160
Back on its course, and while our banners wing
Northward, strike with us! till the Goth shall
    cling
To his own blasted altar-stones, and crave
Mercy; and we shall grant it, and dictate
The lenient future of his fate   165
There, where some rotting ships and crumbling
    quays
Shall one day mark the Port which ruled the
    Western seas.

Charleston

(1862)

"Calpe" in line 9 is Gibraltar.

Calm as that second summer which precedes
    The first fall of the snow,
In the broad sunlight of heroic deeds
    The City bides the foe.

As yet, behind their ramparts stern and proud,
    Her bolted thunders sleep —   6
Dark Sumter like a battlemented cloud
    Looms o'er the solemn deep.

No Calpe frowns from lofty cliff or scar
    To guard the holy strand;   10
But Moultrie holds in leash her dogs of war
    Above the level sand.

And down the dunes a thousand guns lie
    couched
    Unseen beside the flood,
Like tigers in some Orient jungle crouched,   15
    That wait and watch for blood.

Meanwhile, through streets still echoing with
    trade,
    Walk grave and thoughtful men
Whose hands may one day wield the patriot's
    blade
    As lightly as the pen.   20

And maidens with such eyes as would grow dim
    Over a bleeding hound

Seem each one to have caught the strength of
    him
  Whose sword she sadly bound.

Thus girt without and garrisoned at home, 25
  Day patient following day,
Old Charleston looks from roof and spire and
    dome
  Across her tranquil bay.

Ships, through a hundred foes, from Saxon
    lands
  And spicy Indian ports   30
Bring Saxon steel and iron to her hands
  And Summer to her courts.

But still, along yon dim Atlantic line
  The only hostile smoke
Creeps like a harmless mist above the brine 35
  From some frail, floating oak.

Shall the Spring dawn, and she, still clad in
    smiles
  And with an unscathed brow,
Rest in the strong arms of her palm-crowned
    isles
  As fair and free as now?   40

We know not: in the temple of the Fates
  God has inscribed her doom;
And, all untroubled in her faith, she waits
  The triumph or the tomb.

Ode
(1867)

Sung at the occasion of decorating the graves of the Confederate dead, at Magnolia Cemetery, Charleston.

Sleep sweetly in your humble graves,
  Sleep, martyrs of a fallen cause;
Though yet no marble column craves
  The pilgrim here to pause.

In seeds of laurel in the earth   5
  The blossom of your fame is blown,
And somewhere, waiting for its birth,
  The shaft is in the stone!

Meanwhile, behalf the tardy years
  Which keep in trust your storied tombs, 10
Behold! your sisters bring their tears,
  And these memorial blooms.

Small tributes! but your shades will smile
  More proudly on these wreaths to-day,
Than when some cannon-molded pile 15
  Shall overlook this bay.

Stoop, angels, hither from the skies!
  There is no holier spot of ground
Than where defeated valor lies,
  By mourning beauty crowned! 20

Sidney Lanier [1842–1881]

Lanier's was the first poetic work of high promise to emerge from the desolate South of the Reconstruction days. Timrod was dead, Hayne's powers were frustrate through disease, and Lanier, a dozen years younger than they, found himself at the close of the war with impaired health and without a career. Born in Macon, Georgia, graduated from Oglethorpe College, Georgia, in 1860, he had served four years in the Confederate army, had been captured running a blockade, and emerged from a Federal prison at the end of the war with tuberculosis. He tried school teaching, he tried the law, he wrote a novel (*Tiger Lilies*, 1867), he wrote and printed poems. An excellent musician, he was appointed first flutist of the Peabody Symphony Orchestra of Baltimore in 1873, and two years later he drew considerable attention to his writing with the poem "Corn," which he published in *Lippincott's Magazine*.

He published a volume of *Poems* in 1877, and was made lecturer on English Literature in Johns Hopkins University in 1879. The next year appeared *The Science of English Verse*. But tuberculosis was upon him. He fled to the Carolina mountains, and died there at the age of thirty-nine.

Like Poe and Whitman and many other moderns, Lanier held music to be the supreme art. His flute-playing vied with his writing as a medium of expression; the relation of music to verse was the theme of *The Science of English Verse*; and his own experiments in the writing of musical poetry are noteworthy.

Further reading: *Selected Poems of Sidney Lanier* (ed. Stark Young). A. H. Starke, *Sidney Lanier*, 1933. *Southern Poets*, ed. E. W. Parks (American Writers Series), 1936. J. B. Hubbell, *The South in American Literature*, 1954, pp. 758–77.

The Symphony

(w.[1] 1875)

🙽🙽 In letters written before the poem Lanier had said: "I have so many fair dreams and hopes about music in these days. It is a gospel whereof the people are in great need. As Christ gathered up the ten commandments and re-distilled them into the clear liquid of that wondrous eleventh — Love God utterly, and thy neighbor as thyself — so I think the time will come when music, rightly developed to its now-little-foreseen grandeur, will be found to be a later revelation of all gospels in one."

"Trade, Trade, Trade: pah, are we not all sick? A man cannot walk down a green alley of woods, in these days, without unawares getting his mouth and nose and eyes covered with some web or other that Trade has stretched across, to catch some gain or other. 'Tis an old spider that has crawled all over our modern life, and covered it with a flimsy web that conceals the Realities."

"O Trade! O Trade! would thou wert dead!
The Time needs heart — 'tis tired of head:
We're all for love," the violins said.
"Of what avail the rigorous tale
Of bill for coin and box for bale?   5
Grant thee, O Trade! thine uttermost hope:
Level red gold with blue sky-slope,
And base it deep as devils grope:
When all's done, what hast thou won
Of the only sweet that's under the sun?   10
Ay, canst thou buy a single sigh
Of true love's least, least ecstasy?"
Then, with a bridegroom's heart-beats trembling,
All the mightier strings assembling

Ranged them on the violin's side   15
As when the bridegroom leads the bride,
And, heart in voice, together cried:
"Yea, what avail the endless tale
Of gain by cunning and plus by sale?
Look up the land, look down the land,   20
The poor, the poor, the poor, they stand
Wedged by the pressing of Trade's hand
Against an inward-opening door
That pressure tightens evermore:
They sigh a monstrous foul-air sigh   25
For the outside leagues of liberty,
Where Art, sweet lark, translates the sky
Into a heavenly melody.
'Each day, all day' (these poor folks say),
'In the same old year-long, drear-long way,   30
We weave in the mills and heave in the kilns,
We sieve mine-meshes under the hills,
And thieve much gold from the Devil's bank tills,
To relieve, O God, what manner of ills? —
The beasts, they hunger, and eat, and die;   35
And so do we, and the world's a sty;
Hush, fellow-swine: why nuzzle and cry?
Swinehood hath no remedy
Say many men, and hasten by,
Clamping the nose and blinking the eye.   40
But who said once, in the lordly tone,
Man shall not live by bread alone
But all that cometh from the Throne?
Hath God said so?
But Trade saith No: 45
And the kilns and the curt-tongued mills say Go!
There's plenty that can, if you can't: we know.
Move out, if you think you're underpaid.
The poor are prolific; we're not afraid;
*Trade is trade.'"   50
Thereat this passionate protesting
Meekly changed, and softened till

[1] A "w" before the date of a selection indicates that the year is that in which the piece was written. Otherwise the years are those of publication.

It sank to sad requesting
And suggesting sadder still:
"And oh, if men might sometime see 55
How piteous-false the poor decree
That trade no more than trade must be!
Does business mean, *Die, you — live, I?*
Then 'Trade is trade' but sings a lie:
'Tis only war grown miserly. 60
If business is battle, name it so:
War-crimes less will shame it so,
And widows less will blame it so.
Alas, for the poor to have some part
In yon sweet living lands of Art, 65
Makes problem not for head, but heart.
Vainly might Plato's brain revolve it:
Plainly the heart of a child could solve it."

And then, as when from words that seem but
rude
We pass to silent pain that sits abroad 70
Back in our heart's great dark and solitude,
So sank the strings to gentle throbbing
Of long chords change-marked with sobbing —
Motherly sobbing, not distinctlier heard
Than half wing-openings of the sleeping bird 75
Some dream of danger to her young hath
stirred.
Then stirring and demurring ceased, and lo!
Every least ripple of the strings' song-flow
Died to a level with each level bow
And made a great chord tranquil-surfaced so, 80
As a brook beneath his curving bank doth go
To linger in the sacred dark and green
Where many boughs the still pool overlean
And many leaves make shadow with their sheen.
        But presently 85
A velvet flute-note fell down pleasantly
Upon the bosom of that harmony,
And sailed and sailed incessantly,
As if a petal from a wild-rose blown
Had fluttered down upon that pool of tone 90
And boatwise dropped o' the convex side
And floated down the glassy tide
And clarified and glorified
The solemn spaces where the shadows bide.
From the warm concave of that fluted note 95
Somewhat, half song, half odor, forth did float,
As if a rose might somehow be a throat:
"When Nature from her far-off glen
Flutes her soft messages to men,
        The flute can say them o'er again; 100
        Yea, Nature, singing sweet and lone,
Breathes through life's strident polyphone
The flute-voice in the world of tone.

Sweet friends,
        Man's love ascends 105
To finer and diviner ends
Than man's mere thought e'er comprehends:
For I, e'en I,
As here I lie,
A petal on a harmony, 110
Demand of Science whence and why
Man's tender pain, man's inward cry,
When he doth gaze on earth and sky?
I am not overbold:
        I hold 115
Full powers from Nature manifold.
I speak for each no-tonguèd tree
That, spring by spring, doth nobler be,
And dumbly and most wistfully
His mighty prayerful arms outspreads 120
Above men's oft-unheeding heads,
And his big blessing downward sheds.
I speak for all-shaped blooms and leaves,
Lichens on stones and moss on eaves,
Grasses and grains in ranks and sheaves; 125
Broad-fronded ferns and keen-leaved canes,
And briery mazes bounding lanes,
And marsh-plants, thirsty-cupped for rains,
And milky stems and sugary veins;
For every long-armed woman-vine 130
That round a piteous tree doth twine;
For passionate odors, and divine
Pistils, and petals crystalline;
All purities of shady springs,
All shynesses of film-winged things 135
That fly from tree-trunks and bark-rings;
All modesties of mountain-fawns,
That leap to covert from wild lawns,
And tremble if the day but dawns;
All sparklings of small beady eyes 140
Of birds, and sidelong glances wise
Wherewith the jay hints tragedies;
All piquancies of prickly burs,
And smoothnesses of downs and furs,
Of eiders and of minevers; 145
All limpid honeys that do lie
At stamen-bases, nor deny
The humming-birds' fine roguery,
Bee-thighs, nor any butterfly;
All gracious curves of slender wings, 150
Bark-mottlings, fibre-spiralings,
Fern-wavings and leaf-flickerings;
Each dial-marked leaf and flower-bell
Wherewith in every lonesome dell
Time to himself his hours doth tell; 155
All tree-sounds, rustlings of pine-cones,
Wind-sighings, doves' melodious moans,

And night's unearthly under-tones;
All placid lakes and waveless deeps,
All cool reposing mountain-steeps,   160
Vale-calms and tranquil lotos-sleeps; —
Yea, all fair forms, and sounds, and lights,
And warmths, and mysteries, and nights,
Of Nature's utmost depths and heights.
— These doth my timid tongue present,   165
Their mouthpiece and leal instrument
And servant, all love-eloquent.
I heard, when 'All for love' the violins cried:
So, Nature calls through all her system wide,
Give me thy love, O man, so long denied.   170
Much time is run, and man hath changed his
      ways,
Since Nature, in the antique fable-days,
Was hid from man's true love by proxy fays,
False fauns and rascal gods that stole her praise.
The nymphs, cold creatures of man's colder
      brain,   175
Chilled Nature's streams till man's warm heart
      was fain
Never to lave its love in them again.
Later, a sweet Voice *Love thy neighbor* said,
Then first the bounds of neighborhood out-
      spread
Beyond all confines of old ethnic dread.   180
Vainly the Jew might wag his covenant head:
'*All men are neighbors,*' so the sweet Voice said.
So, when man's arms had circled all man's race,
The liberal compass of his warm embrace
Stretched bigger yet in the dark bounds of
      space;   185
With hands a-grope he felt smooth Nature's
      grace,
Drew her to breast and kissed her sweet-heart
      face:
Yea, man found neighbors in great hills and
      trees
And streams and clouds and suns and birds and
      bees,
And throbbed with neighbor-loves in loving
      these.   190
But oh, the poor! the poor! the poor!
That stand by the inward-opening door
Trade's hand doth tighten ever more,
And sigh their monstrous foul-air sigh
For the outside hills of liberty,   195
Where Nature spreads her wild blue sky
For Art to make into melody!
Thou Trade! thou king of the modern days!
      Change thy ways,
      Change thy ways;   200
Let the sweaty laborers file

      A little while,
      A little while,
Where Art and Nature sing and smile.
Trade! is thy heart all dead, all dead?   205
And hast thou nothing but a head?
I'm all for heart," the flute-voice said.
And into sudden silence fled,
Like as a blush that while 'tis red
Dies to a still, still white instead.   210

Thereto a thrilling calm succeeds,
Till presently the silence breeds
A little breeze among the reeds
That seems to blow by sea-marsh weeds:
Then from the gentle stir and fret   215
Sings out the melting clarionet,
Like as a lady sings while yet
Her eyes with salty tears are wet.
"O Trade! O Trade!" the Lady said,
"I too will wish thee utterly dead   220
If all thy heart is in thy head.
For O my God! and O my God!
What shameful ways have women trod
At beckoning of Trade's golden rod!
Alas when sighs are traders' lies,   225
And heart's-ease eyes and violet eyes
      Are merchandise!
O purchased lips that kiss with pain!
O cheeks coin-spotted with smirch and stain!
O trafficked hearts that break in twain!   230
— And yet what wonder at my sisters' crime?
So hath Trade withered up Love's sinewy prime,
Men love not women as in olden time.
Ah, not in these cold merchantable days
Deem men their life an opal gray, where plays
The one red Sweet of gracious ladies'-praise. 236
Now, comes a suitor with sharp prying eye —
Says, *Here, you Lady, if you'll sell, I'll buy:
Come, heart for heart — a trade? What! weep-
      ing? why?*
Shame on such wooers' dapper mercery!   240
I would my lover kneeling at my feet
In humble manliness should cry, O sweet!
*I know not if thy heart my heart will greet;
I ask not if thy love my love can meet:
Whate'er thy worshipful soft tongue shall say,
I'll kiss thine answer, be it yea or nay:*   246
*I do but know I love thee, and I pray
To be thy knight until my dying day.*
Woe him that cunning trades in hearts contrives!
Base love good women to base loving drives.   250
If men loved larger, larger were our lives;
And wooed they nobler, won they nobler
      wives."

There thrust the bold straightforward horn
To battle for that lady lorn,
With heartsome voice of mellow scorn,   255
Like any knight in knighthood's morn.
  "Now comfort thee," said he,
      "Fair Lady.
For God shall right thy grievous wrong,
And man shall sing thee a true-love song,   260
Voiced in act his whole life long,
    Yea, all thy sweet life long,
      Fair Lady.
Where's he that craftily hath said,
The day of chivalry is dead?   265
I'll prove that lie upon his head,
    Or I will die instead,
      Fair Lady.
Is Honor gone into his grave?
Hath Faith become a caitiff knave,   270
And Selfhood turned into a slave
    To work in Mammon's cave,
      Fair Lady?
Will Truth's long blade ne'er gleam again?
Hath Giant Trade in dungeons slain   275
All great contempts of mean-got gain
    And hates of inward stain,
      Fair Lady?
For aye shall name and fame be sold,
And place be hugged for the sake of gold,   280
And smirch-robed Justice feebly scold
    At Crime all money-bold,
      Fair Lady?
Shall self-wrapt husbands aye forget
Kiss-pardons for the daily fret   285
Wherewith sweet wifely eyes are wet —
    Blind to lips kiss-wise set —
      Fair Lady?
Shall lovers higgle, heart for heart,
Till wooing grows a trading mart   290
Where much for little, and all for part,
    Make love a cheapening art,
      Fair Lady?
Shall woman scorch for a single sin
That her betrayer may revel in,   295
And she be burnt, and he but grin
    When that the flames begin,
      Fair Lady?
Shall ne'er prevail the woman's plea,
We maids would far, far whiter be   300
If that our eyes might sometimes see
    Men maids in purity,
      Fair Lady?
Shall Trade aye salve his conscience-aches
With jibes at Chivalry's old mistakes —   305
The wars that o'erhot knighthood makes

For Christ's and ladies' sakes,
      Fair Lady?
Now by each knight that e'er hath prayed
To fight like a man and love like a maid,   310
Since Pembroke's life, as Pembroke's blade,
    I' the scabbard, death, was laid,
      Fair Lady,
I dare avouch my faith is bright
That God doth right and God hath might.   315
Nor time hath changed His hair to white,
    Nor His dear love to spite,
      Fair Lady.
I doubt no doubts: I strive, and shrive my clay,
And fight my fight in the patient modern
      way   320
For true love and for thee — ah me! and pray
    To be thy knight until my dying day,
      Fair Lady."
Made end that knightly horn, and spurred away
Into the thick of the melodious fray.   325
And then the hautboy played and smiled,
And sang like any large-eyed child,
    Cool-hearted and all undefiled.
  "Huge Trade!" he said,
"Would thou wouldst lift me on thy head   330
And run where'er my finger led!
Once said a Man — and wise was He —
Never shalt thou the heavens see,
Save as a little child thou be."
Then o'er sea-lashings of commingling tunes
The ancient wise bassoons,   336
    Like weird,
    Gray-beard
Old harpers sitting on the high sea-dunes,
    Chanted runes: 340
"Bright-waved gain, gray-waved loss,
The sea of all doth lash and toss,
One wave forward and one across:
But now 'twas trough, now 'tis crest,
And worst doth foam and flash to best,   345
    And curst to blest.

"Life! Life! thou sea-fugue, writ from east to
      west,
    Love, Love alone can pore
    On thy dissolving score
    Of harsh half-phrasings,   350
      Blotted ere writ,
    And double erasings
      Of chords most fit.
Yea, Love, sole music-master blest,
May read thy weltering palimpsest.   355
To follow Time's dying melodies through,
And never to lose the old in the new,

And ever to solve the discords true —
    Love alone can do.
And ever Love hears the poor-folks' crying,   360
And ever Love hears the women's sighing,
And ever sweet knighthood's death-defying,
And ever wise childhood's deep implying,
But never a trader's glozing and lying.

"And yet shall Love himself be heard,   365
Though long deferred, though long deferred:
O'er the modern waste a dove hath whirred:
Music is Love in search of a word."

Song of the Chattahoochee

(w. 1877)

Out of the hills of Habersham,
    Down the valleys of Hall,
I hurry amain to reach the plain,
Run the rapid and leap the fall,
Split at the rock and together again,   5
Accept my bed, or narrow or wide,
And flee from folly on every side
With a lover's pain to attain the plain
    Far from the hills of Habersham,
    Far from the valleys of Hall.   10

All down the hills of Habersham,
    All through the valleys of Hall,
The rushes cried *Abide, abide,*
The willful waterweeds held me thrall,
The laving laurel turned my tide,   15
The ferns and the fondling grass said *Stay,*
The dewberry dipped for to work delay,
And the little reeds sighed *Abide, abide,*
    Here in the hills of Habersham,
    Here in the valleys of Hall.   20

High o'er the hills of Habersham,
    Veiling the valleys of Hall,
The hickory told me manifold
Fair tales of shade, the poplar tall
Wrought me her shadowy self to hold,   25
The chestnut, the oak, the walnut, the pine,
Overleaning, with flickering meaning and sign,
Said, *Pass not, so cold, these manifold*
    Deep shades of the hills of Habersham,
    These glades in the valleys of Hall.   30

And oft in the hills of Habersham,
    And oft in the valleys of Hall,
The white quartz shone, and the smooth brook-
    stone
Did bar me of passage with friendly brawl,

And many a luminous jewel lone   35
— Crystals clear or a-cloud with mist,
Ruby, garnet and amethyst —
Made lures with the lights of streaming stone
    In the clefts of the hills of Habersham,
    In the beds of the valleys of Hall.   40

    But oh, not the hills of Habersham,
    And oh, not the valleys of Hall
Avail: I am fain for to water the plain.
Downward the voices of Duty call —   44
Downward, to toil and be mixed with the main,
The dry fields burn, and the mills are to turn,
And a myriad flowers mortally yearn,
And the lordly main from beyond the plain
    Calls o'er the hills of Habersham,
    Calls through the valleys of Hall.   50

The Marshes of Glynn

(w. 1878)

Glooms of the live-oaks, beautiful-braided and
    woven
With intricate shades of the vines that myriad-
    cloven
    Clamber the forks of the multiform boughs, —
        Emerald twilights, —
        Virginal shy lights,   5
Wrought of the leaves to allure to the whisper
    of vows,
When lovers pace timidly down through the
    green colonnades
Of the dim sweet woods, of the dear dark woods,
    Of the heavenly woods and glades,
That run to the radiant marginal sand-beach
    within   10
    The wide sea-marshes of Glynn; —

Beautiful glooms, soft dusks in the noonday
    fire, —
Wildwood privacies, closets of lone desire,
Chamber from chamber parted with wavering
    arras of leaves, —
Cells for the passionate pleasure of prayer to
    the soul that grieves,   15
Pure with a sense of the passing of saints
    through the wood,
Cool for the dutiful weighing of ill with
    good; —

O braided dusks of the oak and woven shades
    of the vine,
While the riotous noon-day sun of the June-
    day long did shine

Ye held me fast in your heart and I held you
    fast in mine;   20
But now when the noon is no more, and riot
    is rest,
And the sun is a-wait at the ponderous gate
    of the West,
And the slant yellow beam down the wood-
    aisle doth seem
Like a lane into heaven that leads from a
    dream, —
Ay, now, when my soul all day hath drunken
    the soul of the oak,   25
And my heart is at ease from men, and the
    wearisome sound of the stroke
    Of the scythe of time and the trowel of
      trade is low,
    And belief overmasters doubt, and I know
      that I know,
    And my spirit is grown to a lordly great
      compass within,
That the length and the breadth and the
    sweep of the Marshes of Glynn   30
Will work me no fear like the fear they have
    wrought me of yore
When length was fatigue, and when breadth
    was but bitterness sore,
And when terror and shrinking and dreary
    unnamable pain
Drew over me out of the merciless miles of
    the plain, —
Oh, now, unafraid, I am fain to face   35
    The vast sweet visage of space.
To the edge of the wood I am drawn, I am
    drawn,
Where the gray beach glimmering runs, as a
    belt of the dawn,
    For a mete and a mark
      To the forest-dark: —   40
        So:
Affable live-oak, leaning low, —
Thus — with your favor — soft, with a reverent
    hand
(Not lightly touching your person, Lord of the
    land!),
Bending your beauty aside, with a step I
    stand   45
On the firm-packed sand,
    Free
By a world of marsh that borders a world of sea.
    Sinuous southward and sinuous northward
      the shimmering band
    Of the sand-beach fastens the fringe of the
      marsh to the folds of the land.   50
Inward and outward to northward and south-
    ward the beach-lines linger and curl

As a silver-wrought garment that clings to and
    follows the firm sweet limbs of a
    girl.
Vanishing, swerving, evermore curving again
    into sight,
Softly the sand-beach wavers away to a dim
    gray looping of light.
And what if behind me to westward the wall
    of the woods stands high?   55
The world lies east: how ample, the marsh and
    the sea and the sky!
A league and a league of marsh-grass, waist-
    high, broad in the blade,
Green, and all of a height, and unflecked with
    a light or a shade,
Stretch leisurely off, in a pleasant plain,
To the terminal blue of the main.   60

Oh, what is abroad in the marsh and the
    terminal sea?
    Somehow my soul seems suddenly free
From the weighing of fate and the sad discus-
    sion of sin,
By the length and the breadth and the sweep
    of the marshes of Glynn.

Ye marshes, how candid and simple and
    nothing-withholding and free   65
Ye publish yourselves to the sky and offer your-
    selves to the sea!
Tolerant plains, that suffer the sea and the
    rains and the sun,
Ye spread and span like the catholic man who
    hath mightily won
God out of knowledge and good out of infinite
    pain
And sight out of blindness and purity out of
    a stain.   70

As the marsh-hen secretly builds on the watery
    sod,
Behold I will build me a nest on the greatness
    of God:
I will fly in the greatness of God as the marsh-
    hen flies
In the freedom that fills all the space 'twixt
    the marsh and the skies:
By so many roots as the marsh-grass sends in
    the sod   75
I will heartily lay me a-hold on the greatness
    of God:
Oh, like to the greatness of God is the greatness
    within
The range of the marshes, the liberal marshes
    of Glynn.

And the sea lends large, as the marsh: lo, out
    of his plenty the sea
Pours fast: full soon the time of the floodtide
    must be: 80
Look how the grace of the sea doth go
About and about through the intricate channels
    that flow
    Here and there,
      Everywhere,
Till his waters have flooded the uttermost creeks
    and the low-lying lanes,   85
And the marsh is meshed with a million veins,
That like as with rosy and silvery essences flow
    In the rose-and-silver evening glow.
      Farewell, my lord Sun!
The creeks overflow: a thousand rivulets run 90
'Twixt the roots of the sod; the blades of the
    marsh-grass stir;
Passeth a hurrying sound of wings that west-
    ward whirr;

Passeth, and all is still; and the currents cease
    to run;
And the sea and the marsh are one.

How still the plains of the waters be! 95
The tide is in his ecstasy.
The tide is at his highest height:
    And it is night.

And now from the Vast of the Lord will the
    waters of sleep
Roll in on the souls of men,   100
But who will reveal to our waking ken
The forms that swim and the shapes that creep
    Under the waters of sleep?
And I would I could know what swimmeth
    below when the tide comes in
On the length and the breadth of the marvellous
    marshes of Glynn. 105

The age of steel heralded a new realism in literature.

THE RISE OF REALISM

The Texture of Ordinary Living

❧

"Ah! poor Real Life, which I love" — HOWELLS

From the *Golden Age* to the *Gilded Age* — this is how social and cultural historians have often conceived of the change that came after the Civil War. They have looked upon the romantic period before the war as a Golden Age when farm and factory were still happily adjusted, when regional culture throve North and South, when mind and spirit flourished in an idealistic literature, and "plain living and high thinking" still had prestige. On the other hand the quarter century following the war has been viewed as a Gilded Age when the new machines of the Industrial Revolution facili-

tated a scramble for wealth and power, when our natural resources — farm lands, forests, and mines — were exploited and ravaged, when a continent was developed without fear of enemies beyond two broad oceans, when individualism was "rugged" and materialism unbridled and unashamed, when political and moral corruption proceeded unchecked, when science and invention seemed to point to an irresistible law of progress, when artistic and literary taste was vulgarized and debased, when, in a word, plain living and high thinking became high living and plain thinking.

The Gilded Age

Big business had been restrained before the war by the agrarian interests under the leadership of the Southern planting aristocracy. When this leadership was destroyed by the war and the horrors of "Reconstruction," Northern industrialists and financiers, finding themselves with a free hand, transformed the country with a rush, as we have seen, by the use of machines, natural resources, and labor constantly augmented by immigration — also by the use of government not to restrain but to speed up their activities (land grants, a protective tariff, etc.). In this process the capitalist class was, paradoxically enough, weaving the web of interdependence and centralization destined to be enlarged in the twentieth century, while it was following the *laissez-faire* philosophy that assured free opportunity to the individual. Certainly the most prominent feature of the early machine age was what came to be called rugged individualism.

Rugged individualism meant every man for himself and the devil take the hindmost. Life was a struggle for existence, a scramble for wealth and power. With many, the struggle meant a step toward the "good life" — but the good life itself would have to wait. The first step upward in the world, it seemed, must assure material success. It was not merely restlessness that drew Americans to the West and to the cities. As G. W. Pierson has put it in an article on "The Moving American," "lateral movement was no good without vertical movement, too." Both were included in the famous advice of Horace Greeley: "Go West, young man, and grow up with the country." To an aggressive person with an eye to the main chance, city life, East or West, offered the best opportunity to move upward. Individualism, self-reliance, was no longer understood as it had been in Concord. It now magnified Yankee canniness beyond all recognition, and dropped the old Puritan concept of a higher self to which the Transcendentalists had given new life. Or it kept a merely conventional respect for Christian morals and religion, which must not get in the way of a shrewd deal. "Business is busi-

New York Slum Scene

Often too poor to go west, immigrants flooded New York and multiplied misery on breathless summer nights.

ness." If a man of wealth and power, a "hero in the strife," felt the need of easing his conscience, a pleasant way was offered by philanthropic benefactions.

The rugged individualists of the Gilded Age were tough-minded men who proposed to deal with life realistically. In practice this largely meant — to borrow plain words from the historians — trickery, dishonesty, lying, bribery, stealing. A good way to understand the wild speculation and widespread moral corruption that attended the rush of exploitation is to read Mark Twain's and Charles Dudley Warner's satirical novel *The Gilded Age.* A few quotations will indicate the collusion between business men and politicians:

Duff Brown, the great railroad contractor, . . . a very pleasant man if you were not in his way, . . . managed to get out of Congress, in appropriations,
(continued on page 665)

Emily Dickinson Portrait

Retiring, sensitive, and perceptive, the face of Emily Dickinson reflects rare qualities of poet and person.

Brooklyn Bridge

Few structures have represented the aspiration, sturdiness, and sheer strength of America as Brooklyn Bridge has done — and still does. One of the world's great suspension structures, completed in 1883, it became for a poet of a later generation (Hart Crane, 1899–1932) a symbol of much that is both good and evil in America and in life.

Henry James

One of America's great writers of fiction, Henry James was a New Yorker who spent much of his life in England. One of his main themes was the impact of European culture on the American.

"Long Branch, New Jersey,"
by Winslow Homer, 1869

Like her best writers, America's best painters in the later nineteenth century strove to capture the quintessence of her civilization through faithful portrayal of externals.

"Harvesting on a Bonanza Farm,"
from Harper's Weekly, *1891*

The great plains and mechanized farming briefly made possible the "bonanza farm," yielding immense crops of grain to the growing, hungry nation.

"Snags on the Missouri River," aquatint after Bodmer

River navigation — hazardous, romantic, and profitable — helped to spread culture widely along the great western streams.

Mark Twain

In his early days a pilot, Mark Twain loved the rivers and the rich life they helped to create.

Victorian Mansion, Eureka, California

Turreted mansions frosted with wooden gingerbread became a mark of wealth and elegance in the late nineteenth century.

"Emigrant Train," by Samuel Colman, 1872

Hope of finding gold or rich lands beckoned thousands to California and the Oregon country. The vastness of the plains is beautifully suggested in Colman's painting.

about weight for weight of gold for the stone furnished.

[On bribery] A Congressional appropriation costs money. . . . A majority of the House committee, say $10,000 apiece — $40,000; a majority of the Senate committee, the same each — say $40,000; a little extra to one or two chairmen, [etc. etc., down to] gimcracks for Congressmen's wives and children.

[Senator Dilworthy] He's an able man, Dilworthy, and a good man. A man has got to be good to succeed as he has. He's only been in Congress a few years, and he must be worth a million.

[An alleged newspaper statement] We are now reminded of a note which we have received from the notorious burglar Murphy, in which he finds fault with a statement of ours to the effect that he has served one term in the penitentiary and also one in the U. S. Senate. He says, "The latter statement is untrue and does me great injustice."

Sometimes the fictional representation falls short of the actual facts. Thus, *The Gilded Age* tells of "William M. Weed," said to have stolen $20,000,000 from the city of New York. But the fact, as reported by the historian James Truslow Adams, is that the Tweed Ring in Tammany Hall had in three years "carried off loot from the city treasury to an amount variously estimated from $45,000,000 to $200,000,-000." How this was done may be indicated by an example. A county courthouse supposed to cost half a million actually cost sixteen times that sum. The taxpayers' money was quickly used up when chairs were listed at $470 and safes for storing papers at $400,000 apiece. Dissensions in the ring led to exposure and Tweed died in jail.

Kings of Fortune. By fair means or foul, millionaires began to abound. There were only three in the country in 1861, but before the end of the century they numbered 3800. Admiration for this new type of hero was not wholly uncritical; as Wecter pointed out, none was ever honored with the Presidency, nor had his birthplace or tomb been made into a national shrine. Yet they were vastly admired, or at least envied. These magnates came to be known as "kings of fortune" (ruling the "empire of business"), or, in our own time, as tycoons, moguls, or robber barons. Nearly all had begun at the bottom of the ladder, as farm boys or office boys, clerks or bookkeepers. The railroads had their Gould, Vanderbilt, Huntington; oil had its Rockefeller; steel its Carnegie; finance its Cooke and Morgan; meat-packing its Armour. Merely to reprobate them as "robber barons" is misleading. While they often engaged in methods that are unethical by any high standard, they presided, with a genius for construction and organization, over the building of great railroads, the peopling of the West, the formation of large corporations, the introduction of mass production. They gave the United States the material strength which makes many immaterial goods possible.

One of the more benevolent despots was James J. Hill, of Minnesota, the railroad king who labored to fill the Northwest with people and farms. Sending his agents to the East to advertise the rich opportunities of the region, bringing Eastern farmers out to inspect the land, he caused many thousands to migrate, and transported them, with livestock and household possessions, to the localities they chose. He interested himself in their communities, in problems of farming, drainage, roads, financing, etc. His rail system, extending to the Pacific Coast, was lined with thriving farms, growing towns, and industries. And across the Pacific he explored the possibilities of markets in the Orient. On the material plane, his vision matched that of Whitman in "A Passage to India."

A very different figure is that of the financial manipulator Jim Fisk. He had had a job with a circus, then became a peddler driving through the country-side with jingling bells in a gilded cart circus-style. During the war he went to Washington, drumming up contracts for blankets. Becoming a stock-broker in New York, he soon found his natural vocation of financial swindling. In the bitter struggle for control of the Erie Railroad, he and Jay Gould ("the Skunk of Wall Street") engaged in shameless operations too complicated to detail here. They were summed up at the time in the *Nation:*

By a fraudulent over issue of stock these men had depressed the price of Erie stock . . . reaping an enormous profit; and with the money so obtained they had run up the price of gold and made another large profit; they had then again advanced the price of Erie . . . and made a larger profit than ever. In the course of these operations they had ruined hundreds . . . had arrested the whole business of the country . . . had brought the banks to the verge of suspension and seriously threatened the national credit.

Jim Fisk's malefactions were interspersed with strutting as colonel in the militia, as Hudson River "admiral," as producer of operas and supporter of mistresses. He was only thirty-seven when a rival shot him dead. Six horses drew the hearse up Fifth Avenue preceded by hundreds of police, two bands, the Ninth Regiment, and followed by no end of carriages and pedestrians. At the railroad stations thousands turned out to see the funeral train as it bore him back to his native Vermont.

In spending as in getting, the plutocracy was elaborate and acquisitive. Unabashed by the disdainful social class that had inherited "background," it enjoyed its own version of flair, display, grandeur. Chicago had it fashionable district, the "Gold Coast," and men like Potter Palmer, king of dry goods and real estate. For his wife, whom her friends called "the Queen," Palmer erected a royal palace, a great Gothic castle with turrets, containing a Louis Quatorze salon, a Japanese room, a Moorish music-room. But the capital city of the plutocracy was actually New York. Here uprose a meaningless incongruity of English castles, Italian mansions, and French châteaux. On the corner of Fifth Avenue and 52nd Street, W. K. Vanderbilt constructed a $3,000,000 château, greatly admired in its time, replete with Medieval and Renaissance furniture, tapestry, and armor. With no desire to patronize anything vitally American or contemporary, the kings of fortune and their children turned their dwellings into museums, despoiling the cultural treasures of the Old World. Charles and Mary Beard, in their history of American civilization, have well described how the predatory wealthy bought their culture: "ransacked the palaces, churches, abbeys, castles, and ateliers of Europe for statuary, paintings, pottery, rugs, and every other form of art. Even the Orient was forced to yield up graven goddesses of mercy and complacent Buddhas to decorate the buildings of men absorbed in making soap, steel rails, whisky, and cotton bagging and to please the women who spent the profits of business enterprise. . . . Mandarin coats from Peking sprawled on the pianos of magnates who knew not Ming or Manchu and perhaps could not tell whether their hired musicians were grinding out Wagner or Chopin." If it did not come into their way to read books, at least they could build private libraries of rare editions and fine bindings. Their wives spared no expense in adorning themselves: "Grand ladies, who remembered with a blush the days when they laundered the fam-

ily clothes, shone idly resplendent in jewels garnered by a search of two hemispheres." There was increasing interest in the importation of family glory through genealogies and coats of arms — not always well authenticated — and through marriages of heiresses to foreign nobility.

❧ *Middle Class Taste and Morals.* At the other extreme, the urban poor — far behind in the materialistic scramble — lived in ugly, flimsy tenements where dirt and disease abounded. Many immigrants who had come to the Promised Land found only squalor. Yet America's poor did not constitute a fixed proletarian class. Most of them could hope to move up. And at least they could derive help of various sorts from the public schools, the political machines, and the Catholic Church. Above such workers living in or near poverty was the large middle class, dominantly of old American stock and Protestant, merging at the top into the plutocracy. Characteristically the middle class was urban, but its traits were shared by the small town and country population. More than ever, the United States was a land of the middle class. And it was this class that gave to the Gilded Age the prevailing tone of American life, of morals and manners, of literary and artistic taste.

Middle class taste was bad, above all, in domestic architecture and interior decoration. In the building of residences, dignity was sought not through the simple stately lines of the colonial period, but through mere size and highly complicated irregularity. It was an expensive way to build, and the greater the expense the worse the result. The more pretentious residences came close to including, incongruously, everything possible: a riot of Gothic arches, classical columns, towers, cupolas, manifold gables, bay windows, stained glass windows, balconies, verandas, etc., with a profusion of hideous "gingerbread" fretwork and openwork turned out by the jigsaw. On the lawn, if there was one, often stood an iron deer or two, or perhaps Diana the huntress. Inside, the large rooms were heavy with massive furniture of black walnut, tastelessly embellished with carving — uncomfortable sofas, ugly rockers, chairs with antimacassars, whatnots loaded with bric-a-brac, tables with padded albums of family photographs, marble mantles with fancy clocks, small statues, wax flowers, and the like. At its plainer best, the middle class house could have some real dignity and grace, but the worst was excessively common.

In the middle class people who lived in such surroundings one could easily find much to admire, or to deplore. During recent decades it has been customary to ridicule them. They had a set of characteristics that came to be called "Victorian," characteristics that appeared not only in England but also on the European continent, and that prevailed most fully in the United States. Our Victorians were, in part, heirs of the Puritans; and Puritans and Victorians were dismissed in one breath in the jazz age. The middle class took pride in "respectability," i.e. a combination of moral solidity (reflected in substantial worldly possessions), a strong sense of propriety and etiquette, and fastidious modesty and reticence — to us, prudishness. Though families were large, sex was scarcely recognized. (American ladies could sympathize with the English matron who commented on a performance of *Antony and Cleopatra*: "How unlike the home life of our dear Queen!") Religion itself was often little more than respectability in formal observance, or bigoted orthodoxy without inwardness. In general there was much hypocrisy, complacency, and pomposity. With moral assurance went a practical turn of mind — a high esteem for diligence, thrift, prudence, and their material rewards. As a relief from both morals and practicality there was the easy escape of sentimentality.

🌿 *The Pursuit of Culture.* Thus, while the plutocracy exploited and spent grandly, the middle class enjoyed its material solidity and moral decorum. Yet an important place was given to cultural activities. In western New York the 1870's saw the beginnings of the Chautauqua movement for adult education. At the Assembly Grounds, segregated from the world, for a summer term one could hear inspiring lectures on the humanities and sciences, and in the winters one could pursue a home reading course. Other Chautauquas bobbed up in many localities, and hundreds of thousands of middle-class Americans were soon absorbing enlightenment and enjoying good music. Meanwhile the education of the young was developed by compulsory school attendance, free textbooks, a huge increase in the number of high schools, more and more colleges public and private. The land grant colleges gave education a practical and vocational turn. Coeducation, started at Oberlin College in 1837, was widely extended in this period, and separate colleges for women were established at Vassar, Wellesley, and elsewhere. Harvard, under the leadership of Charles

W. Eliot, was transformed into a modern university, and Johns Hopkins University was started as a school for graduate study only. Among the plutocracy, Andrew Carnegie had read Shakespeare when a bobbin boy in a textile factory at $1.20 a week, and while making his $350,000,000 took time out for Plato and Confucius. By founding 2800 libraries and giving 7689 organs to churches he contributed much to popular culture.

Along with this widening of cultural assimilation, was there also a creative spirit? We have already seen how, in this vibrant period, the creative spirit showed itself in business. According to Lord Bryce's observation in 1888, business was absorbing the best brains of the country. But there were exceptionally endowed men in nearly every field of activity. Even in architecture and the arts — despite the general bad taste — the two decades attained excellence. To this day we can point with pride to the beauty of Brooklyn Bridge, begun in 1869 and completed in 1883, the work of Roebling, a German-born engineer. In the Middle West, the sterile imitation of old European architectural styles was offset by Louis Sullivan's interest in functional form and in the use of steel and plate glass. His Wainwright Building (1890) at St. Louis is spoken of as the first skyscraper. In the art of painting, the landscapes of Inness, Martin, and Homer far surpassed those of the preceding period, despite the romantic enthusiasm for nature. In portraiture the fashionable painter of the day was Sargent, superficial but brilliant, who placed on canvas well-bred men and lovely women caught in a moment when twiddling watch-chains or flashing fans. If they had souls he did not hint, content to suggest their standard and style of living. As for the art of literature, we shall consider presently how Mark Twain, Howells, James, and others created a new movement known as realism, expressive of contemporary life and impregnated with the spirit of science.

SCIENCE AS THE MEASURE

The master key to the Gilded Age is science. It changed the scene of life, the way of life, and the life of the mind. It concerned everyone. To the man in the street it meant material progress, a dazzling succession of technical inventions that saved labor, multiplied production, reduced distances, contributed to comfort, convenience, and health, with no end in sight. Especially in the cities, all these tangible evidences of the power and value of science gave it high prestige, and strengthened material values at the expense of the spiritual values offered by traditional Christianity.

The most momentous contribution of science was the theory of organic evolution. The biology of Darwin, as basic for the late nineteenth century as the physics of Newton had been for the eighteenth, established a new intellectual climate, to which our own time is thoroughly accustomed. But to men living in the 1860's and 70's *The Origin of Species* and *The Descent of Man* presented a startling challenge. Men suddenly felt called upon to abandon the exalted concept of the human species which had been held, through the ages, by the humanistic and religious traditions. It had been clearly understood that man was specially created in the image of God, endowed with a soul or faculty of reason that marked him off from the lower animals. Now science, the new evangel, pronounced him a monkey, or a descendant of apelike progenitors — it mattered little which! Ministers thundered denunciation of this appalling degradation of man, and laymen, even the less pious, resented the imposition of such forebears. In America as in Europe, educated and thoughtful people, though long accustomed to the general idea of evolution, were deeply disturbed when it was accounted for in purely natural terms. On the other hand, there were "free thinkers" who berated the churches for their superstition and pig-headed dogmatism. Controversy abounded for many years in addresses, books, magazines, newspapers.

Notorious was Robert G. Ingersoll, a cheap and superficial assailant of religion whose popular lectures, oral and printed, had a widespread influence on the ignorant. At Harvard a fine scientist, Agassiz, called Darwin's theory "mischievous" and never accepted it, while the botanist Gray gave it his support. One of the most effective preachers of the day, Henry Ward Beecher, also supported it. The ablest American advocate of Darwinism was John Fiske, who sought to give evolution a philosophic formulation that would allow a place for the religious principle. His *Outlines of Cosmic Philosophy Based on the Doctrine of Evolution* (1874) actually went through sixteen editions. But it was an English philosopher, Herbert Spencer, who most profoundly shaped American speculation. On the idea of evolution, or "development" from the simple to the complex, he tried to erect a complete system of philosophy, viewing man and his ideals as merely a product of nature as understood by science. With much reason, Spencer was felt to be as basically signifi-

cant for his time as Locke had been for the Age of Reason and Kant for the romantic period.

Gradually the conflict between science and religion came to an end. After all, each had its own realm, and if a man chose he could live in both realms; a good Christian — Catholic or Protestant — could also be a good scientist. Yet on the whole the result of the conflict was a victory for science. Except in the more isolated rural districts, people came to think largely in terms of evolution — "the struggle for existence," "the survival of the fittest." Man was a biological creature, part of nature. Many must have thought (though few said so in print) that Darwinism had sanctioned the fierce competition of rugged individualism. Much of the public, especially the more prosperous, found a new faith in Progress, a concept vital ever since the eighteenth century and now supposedly firmly grounded in evolutionary science. People no longer sustained by the old belief in another world derived enthusiasm by believing in the glorious future of this world. Ignoring the fact that evolution, being neutral, meant only change, they assumed that it meant improvement and that progress had the authority of a natural law. Since the future is conveniently vacant one could conceive, with Herbert Spencer, that what it had in store for us was a thoroughgoing individualism, or with Karl Marx that it would inevitably bring a thoroughgoing collectivism — though as yet Marx was only thunder on the left.

Facing the Facts. Belief in progress, to many intellectuals, was only one feature, however prominent, of a general faith in science. Dazzled by the achievements and promises of exact investigation, "pretending" (as the Beards put it) "to possess the one true key to the riddle of the universe," they made of science "a kind of dogmatic religion." This modern religion has been called *scientism*, that is, a love of verifiable truth excluding all other approaches to truth. Its scorn for the inner life was roundly expressed by a writer who began publishing late in the period, John Dewey, who said: "What is termed spiritual culture has usually been futile, with something rotten about it." Scientism rejected not only the spiritual standards of Christianity and Transcendentalism but at the same time all the constructions of systematic philosophy. As viewed by a recent philosopher, A. N. Whitehead, science itself, ever since the Renaissance, has been "predominantly an anti-rationalistic movement, based upon a naive faith. . . . Science repudiates philosophy. In other words, it has never cared to justify its faith." The intellectual portion of the public was content, like the scientists, with a mentality absorbed in number, space, time, motion, force, and the like. Even the common man, confused by the conflict between science and traditional religion, was increasingly impressed when he encountered, in newspapers, magazines, and books, the words "Science says . . ." used as if this phrase were the modern equivalent of the Biblical "And God said . . .".

The science of the nineteenth century came like a revelation. Here, as the public mind gradually conceived, was a solid structure of proved facts in place of antiquated religious doctrines and romantic dreams. It seemed necessary to face the facts. Men have always found it hard to give their attention to more than one thing at a time. This generation focused increasingly on science — the senses — observation — facts. What could be more refreshing than objective facts, anything actual, honestly observed, substantial and trustworthy, even if not always exciting or flattering? The interesting world around us, natural and human, is full of facts. What can be more satisfying than to look at them closely, patiently? If reason was at the center of the neo-classic period, and feeling at the center of the romantic, facts came to be at the center of the realistic period.

REALISM IN LITERATURE

The aim of the nineteenth and twentieth century literary movement known as realism is the representation of the realities of life. What *are* the realities — what is most certainly real? A little reflection will remind us that this is not merely a modern question. From Homer and Aeschylus in the ancient world to the novelists and dramatists of our own time in Europe and America, writers have represented what seemed to them real, but with very different results. We have seen how, in American literature, the Puritans were overwhelmed with a supernatural reality, a personal God and Satan, a human soul; how in the neo-classic period men turned away from this conception to a faith in the high reality of a dependable human reason matching the order of nature; and how the romantics, disparaging reason, sought an ideal reality through feeling, imagination, symbolism. Now so-called realists in turn rejected the romantic vision of life as unreal, and proposed instead, as *their* conception of reality, the world of

actual experience which modern science was so patiently and fruitfully exploring.

Triumphing earlier and more clearly in Europe than in America, realism was most consciously developed in France. There it arrived as early as the 1830's. The realistic prose fiction of Stendhal, Merimée, and Balzac soon led to the pessimistic realism (or naturalism) of Flaubert and Zola, and by 1885 this vigorous movement had virtually completed its course. From the critical and creative work of such writers it is not difficult to outline the characteristics of realism in contrast with those of romanticism.

Realism implies a scientific outlook upon life, sociological and psychological, instead of the artistic and poetic outlook of romanticism; it implies cool impersonality, self-effacement, instead of warm, personal feeling, confidences, confessions. Other characteristics are patient observation instead of flashes of intuition and insight; facts — detailed, documentary, verifiable — instead of guesses, dreams, visions; a materialistic instead of idealistic interpretation of life. Realism, typically, has aimed at definiteness and solidity, instead of indefiniteness and suggestiveness; the local and familiar instead of the remote and strange; contemporary life — everyday living, however humdrum or sordid — instead of the rich traditions and legends of the past. Realism has meant the use of commonplace or sub-normal characters instead of exceptional characters and the humble glorified, and it has meant the use of prose instead of verse as the prevailing medium, the novel becoming the typical form instead of the lyric. So far-reaching was this change that little was retained from the romantic regime, in the realistic theory, except keen senses, the concrete and specific, and the life of the humble.

For so bold and wide a departure from the conventions of the romantic period, American writers and especially middle-class readers were not ready. Most of the old romantic group of writers — Emerson, Longfellow, Lowell, etc. — were still active and in high esteem, and a younger generation — such writers as Bayard Taylor, R. H. Stoddard, E. C. Stedman, Thomas Bailey Aldrich — devotedly but unimportantly continued the romantic quest of beauty. The Victorian middle class, with its Puritan prejudices, still regarded the novel with suspicion, and naturally tolerated it most readily when it satisfied the standards of virtue and delicacy, as in the productions of E. P. Roe. This ministerial novelist, writing with a strong moral and religious purpose, turned out a series of novels, sentimental, didactic, melodramatic, that were immensely popular. One can guess their contents from such titles as *Barriers Burned Away*, *What Can She Do?*, *A Face Illumined*, *He Fell in Love with his Wife*. Sentimentally moral fiction, both serial novels and short stories, abounded in the magazines, *Harper's*, *Scribner's*, *Lippincott's*, *Putnam's*, largely the work of women writing for women. Said the *Nation*: "Our band of heart-wrenching female dealers in false fiction was never, we think, so numerous as now." Dime novels were issued by various publishers, the most famous being those for boys written by Horatio Alger, some 135 of them, which are said to have sold close to 200,000,000 copies. As befitted the Gilded Age, the Alger books were at once materialistic and sanctimonious, picturing clean poor boys who were honest and cheerful, had a good eye for the main chance, and rose through trials to the top. The young growing up in the Gilded Age had been edified in the schools by the standard literature and pious words of the McGuffey Readers, which, according to A. M. Schlesinger, did more to influence the general literary taste and standards of the period than Emerson and all the other Concord and Cambridge authors. Clearly, so conventional a public was in no mood to welcome a resolute and thoroughgoing realism of the French or Russian sort.

🔖 *Local Color.* A kind of bridge between romanticism and realism was, however, offered by writers of "local color" fiction. In novels and short stories of this kind emphasis is laid on the setting: the natural scenery, the human geography, the customs, the dress, the manners, the way of thinking, the mode of speech (often a dialect), treated in such a way as to bring out the picturesque peculiarities of a limited region. If Americans, as Henry James said, were "fond of local color," had "a hungry passion for the picturesque," it was partly because they prized regional peculiarity much as they had prized individual peculiarity in romantic literature. Regional peculiarity, when measured against the increasing standardization of life in an age of multiplying machines, seemed charmingly quaint and remote, as well as satisfyingly real. But the old provincial differences were in fact fast disappearing, vanishing in the irresistible currents of national life. The local color writer was impelled by a romantic desire to preserve a golden time when simple folk lived in happy brotherhood close to nature. At the same time he had a realistic desire to transcribe faithfully the look and feel of a region he had lived in and

understood. Thus Harriet Beecher Stowe in her preface to *Oldtown Folks* said: "I have tried to make my mind as still and passive as a looking-glass, or a mountain lake, and then to give you merely the images reflected there." Furthermore, she declared that her "studies" were "taken from real characters, real scenes, and real incidents. And some of those things in the story which may appear most romantic and like fiction are simple renderings and applications of facts."

The exploitation of natural resources that was going forward was thus matched by an exploitation of literary resources. Opening up various regions, the local color writers, with varying degrees of fidelity, achieved in terms of imaginative representation the final settlement of America, from the Atlantic to the Pacific, from Maine and Minnesota to Louisiana. In the 1870's the reading public for the first time became acquainted with a variety of native scenes and cultures. In the 1880's every American who read books and magazines was traveling, so to speak, throughout this continental nation. He could focus his attention upon New England, its attractions and oddities, in the pages of Mrs. Stowe and Miss Jewett, upon the South in Cable and Miss Murfree, upon the Pacific West in Harte, upon the Middle West in Eggleston. While the spirit in which these and other authors wrote was regional, the collective effect was national. As Eggleston said in his 1892 preface to *The Hoosier Schoolmaster*, "The taking up of life in this regional way has made our literature really national by the only process possible. The Federal nation has at length manifested a consciousness of the continental diversity of its forms of life."

As a rule the local color authors depicted life in the sympathetic and engaging manner desired by the public, romantically closing their eyes to many unpleasant facts. A remarkable exception was E. W. Howe, far in advance of his time, who wrote an acid description of the Middle West, *The Story of a Country Town*, in which the men were surly, the women fretful, nobody was happy, and "all hated each other in secret, there being much satisfaction when one of them failed." It would be hazardous, however, to assume that Howe told the truth while the typical local colorists did not: nothing is harder than to tell the truth, the whole truth, and nothing but the truth.

We can see the drift toward realism not only in local color writing but also in various folk expressions. Popular songs and ballads represented common human experience in a variety of scenes and occupations — the life of the plains, lumber camps, mines, railroads, homesteads, etc. They originated spontaneously, orally, and spread far and wide in differing versions, serving for amusement during or after work. There was also much oral story-telling, based on actual experience but embroidered. On the moving frontier there was vast delight in the shameless exaggerations of the tall tale. Hardships and hard labor were alleviated by humor. "The secret source of humor," said Mark Twain, "is not joy but sorrow; there is no humor in heaven." Professional comedians, following the homespun tradition, were highly popular: Artemus Ward, Petroleum Vesuvius Nasby, Josh Billings, and others. Their folk wisdom was often realistic in a hard-headed fashion, as when Josh Billings said, "There may cum a time when the Lion and the Lam will lie down together — i shall be az glad to see it as enny boddy — but i am still betting on the Lion." Another realistic saying of Josh Billings is virtually an expression of the spirit of science: "It ain't the things we don't know that makes such fools of us, but a whole lot of things that we know that ain't *so*." In a more literary way humor abounded in the local color fiction. Indeed, we may observe in this period interrelationships among folklore, humor, and local color, in a kind of democratic earthiness. This provided a vital American foundation for the development of a realistic movement open to foreign influences.

Mark Twain. An American democrat close to the soil — a plain man even in his days of splendor — Mark Twain was both humorist and local colorist. In journalism and lecturing he early displayed a talent for lowbrow humor like that of Artemus Ward, acquiring a lasting reputation as a "funny man." And certainly the author of *Huckleberry Finn* and *Life on the Mississippi* was a genius of regionalism. A regional novelist, in his view, "lays before you the ways and speech and life of a few people grouped in one place — his own place," and novelists in other places do the same, till in time you have "the life and the people of the whole nation."

But Mark Twain himself rose above the limitations of both lowbrow humor and local color, impresses us far more as an American, an expresser of the nation. He had many traits that Americans like to consider typically American, such as his high spirits, his plain-spokenness, his hatred of pretence, his irreverence toward many things one is supposed to admire. Issuing from Southern stock, briefly a Confederate soldier,

this Missourian with the wild red hair became a Westerner, but a Westerner who spanned the nation, from California to Connecticut, in his imagination as in the course of his life.

Unlike the New Englanders of the romantic period, he threw himself into the turbid currents of his time. Even while satirizing the Gilded Age he could share its defects, e.g. its get-rich-quick impulse. He used the American language of his day, the words and rhythms of native speech, testing his manuscripts by reading aloud. He aimed to reach the masses, he said, and he succeeded — was and still is the most widely read great American writer. He was not interested in trying "to help cultivate the cultivated classes." How far he differed from the cultivated literati of the vicinity of Boston is suggested by a Whittier birthday dinner at which he spoke. In harmless high spirits he told the select company about three drunks in the Sierras — Emerson, Longfellow, and Holmes. The select company listened in shocked silence, while Mark stood there (as Howells puts it) "with his joke dead on his hands." Perhaps the failure of the joke hurt him more than the needless offence he gave. The gap between West and East was shown again, years later, when *Huckleberry Finn* was removed from the town library of Concord because Huck had chosen to "go to Hell" rather than betray his runaway Negro friend.

A mere man, Mark, in frontier style, idolized woman, the eternal feminine that draws the rude male upward — up a little bit, anyway. This led him, easygoing rationalist-realist though he was, to write a book on Joan of Arc, "by far the most extraordinary person the human race has ever produced." *The Adventures of Huckleberry Finn*, as the full title suggests, has its romantic aspect, and the realistic Huck is set off by a romantic Tom. In his great work on his cub-pilot days he showed a romantic nostalgia for the "old times on the Mississippi" (he used this for a title, later changed to *Life on the Mississippi*). Writing from fond memories, he dropped out, as De Voto reminds us, most of the sinister features of the steamboating epoch: the jerry-built — though ornate and gilded — floating palaces that invited disaster, the cutthroat, corrupt competition, the sabotage, bribery, fraud, robbery, murder, the courtesans and harlots.

Yet his conscious attitude toward romanticism was hostile. Loving actual life, he was a foe of sentimentalism, idealism, any moonshine illusion. Romantic literature — Scott, Byron, Cooper — he persistently ridiculed, with a special animus against the "pernicious" "Sir Walter disease" of the South. He showed his colors, the flag of realism, plainly in his early travel sketches. If one dates American romanticism from 1819, with the publication of Irving's *Sketch Book* recounting the worshipful musings of an American dreamer in the Old World, one may date realism from 1869, with Mark Twain's *Innocents Abroad*, recounting the irreverent observations of a fact-finding American in the Old World. For example: speaking of Florence, where the glories of the Middle Ages and Renaissance come alive to the eye, he wrote, "It is popular to admire the Arno. It is a great historical creek with four feet of water in the channel and some scows floating around." He thought of himself as a "vandal" in Europe, deflating what he saw instead of gaping like most tourists or collecting marbles and tapestries like the new rich.

He wanted to be what he called "authentic." His hearty realism is akin to that of the English humorists of the eighteenth century. He said he "had read *Tom Jones* and *Roderick Random*, and other books of that kind," and though he was nobody's disciple he reminds us often of such writers as Fielding, Smollett, Goldsmith. His masterpiece, *Huckleberry Finn*, resembles a type popular in the eighteenth century, the picaresque novel (the adventures of a rogue). In his later years his cheerful realism darkened into the pessimism of *The Mysterious Stranger*, a pessimism as black as Jonathan Swift's, though he probably owed more to a shallow American free-thinker, Bob Ingersoll. "What a shabby poor ridiculous thing man is," he concluded, "and how mistaken he is in his estimate of his character and powers and qualities and his place among the animals." But one does not go to Mark Twain for speculative profundity; he scorned philosophy, gave little thought even to aesthetic theory. For the aesthetic theory of realism we may turn to his two chief contemporaries: Howells and James.

🎗 *Howells and James.* William Dean Howells admired deeply men as different as Mark Twain and Henry James. He wrote an essay on James and a book on *My Mark Twain*. Like Twain he came from west of the Appalachians. In his Ohio years he took part in democratic small-town life: "all had enough," he said, "and few too much." He early showed a dislike of the crude, the violent, the ugly which indicated the genial coloring his pictures of American life were to take. Geniality was encouraged, and urbanity added, when he went East — visited Boston, served as consul in Italy during the American Civil War, settled in Boston as an editor of the *Atlantic Monthly*.

Howells's early literary taste was largely classical. As a boy he wrote verse imitating Pope, and when he developed his characteristic prose style it took on, as W. F. Taylor has remarked, such neo-classic qualities as lucidity, restraint, and smoothness. His favorite English novelist was one bred in the eighteenth century, Jane Austen, whose sense of reality and of the comic in social manners seems to have fascinated him. As he reacted against the excesses of romantic idealization in the popular English and American novels, he reacted against the opposite extreme, the naturalistic degradation of man in many Continental novels. Instead he proposed ordinary actuality, a cheerful realism of the commonplace. In his first novel, *Their Wedding Journey*, he stated what was to prove his governing conception:

The sincere observer of man will not desire to look upon his heroic or occasional phases, but will seek him in his habitual moods of vacancy and tiresomeness. To me, at any rate, he is at such times very precious; and I never perceive him to be so much a man and a brother as when I feel the pressure of his vast, natural, unaffected dullness. . . . Yet it is a very amusing world, if you do not refuse to be amused.

Howells's extended statement of his theory of realism came much later. Removing to New York, the new literary capital of the country, he conducted in *Harper's Magazine* "The Editor's Study" (1886–91), from which he extracted material for a book on *Criticism and Fiction*. Like Walt Whitman before him, he felt that both science and democracy pointed to the value of the common. The true realist, he asserts, "cannot look upon human life and declare this thing or that thing unworthy of notice, any more than the scientist can declare a fact of the material world beneath the dignity of his inquiry." No less does democratic life as it is lived in America invite the artist "to the study and the appreciation of the common. . . . The arts must become democratic." Both his scientific and democratic criteria ruled out romanticism, the "mania of romanticism," which seized upon all Europe and caused novelists to idealize their characters, "take the life-likeness out of them." At the same time he saw in the texture of American life, with its prevailing wholesomeness and decency, no justification for adoption of the "tradition of indecency," which the French realists had established, though he admired them on other grounds. Life with us is not all "erotic shivers and fervors." Let the artist "front the every-day world and catch the charm of its work-worn, care-worn, brave, kindly face." Often Howells spoke as if this implied a direct transcript from fact, objective in the manner of science, without the intrusion of the author's personality and mind, but he stated better his own full view and practice when he called for "that sort of truth which fact precipitates after passing through the alembic of a friendly imagination." His own imagination, as shown in his novels, was indeed "friendly," rather than neutral or embittered. In his view of man he took sides with morals, and he had no desire to reject idealism altogether, long preferring, even, to speak of "romances" rather than "novels." Whatever his insistence on observed facts, his personality was engaged.

As Howells left the West for the culturally superior East, so his friend Henry James, born in New York city, left the East, escaped from the thinness of American civilization and the crudeness of the Gilded Age, made himself at home in the denser refinements of life in Paris and London, and eventually became a British subject. At the same time his imagination always had a bearing upon his nation land. He thus found himself qualified for his special theme, the American in Europe.

In his concept of the art of fiction James owed much, at first, to Hawthorne, thereafter to English (George Eliot) and especially Continental realists (Turgenev, Flaubert). Holding aloof from much "so-called realism," he aimed at a realism leavened by ideal elements: "an ideal of joy" and "an ideal of delicacy." As a work of art a novel should not lose itself in a moral intention, and yet should show "a sense of morality" used with discretion, "as a kind of essential perfume." "Joy" suggested to him appreciation of the quality of life itself and penetration to the finest experience that life offers. What he attempted was a psychological realism, "guessing" "what goes on beneath the vast smug surface" of life as it is experienced by this and that individual. In this exploratory process he anticipated much of our latter-day science of psychology, while escaping the doctrinaire rigidity which was to handicap later psychological novelists and dramatists. He simply relied upon the artist's tools of perception, awareness, imaginative insinuation into personalities, tools that he commanded with expert subtlety and refinement. The type of

personality in which the meanings and possibilities of life seemed to him most richly involved was the artist type — the writer, the painter. James thus preserved, in terms of a highly sophisticated realistic analysis, the romantic exaltation of the individual and especially the individual artist. In aesthetic sensibility he found relief from the limitations of modern society and the dilemmas of the modern mind. In respect to form, he was dissatisfied even with some of the greatest realistic fiction, such as "large loose baggy monsters" like Tolstoy's *War and Peace*. "I delight," he said in one of his prefaces, "in a deep-breathing economy and an organic form."

How could James reconcile realism, as a search for what "really" goes on in people, with the limiting effect of personality in the searcher, the individual artist? If each artist sees differently, is a valid result possible? He gave his answer to this question in a brilliant essay, a critical essay which considers the problems of "The Art of Fiction" from the artist's inside viewpoint. The writer of fiction should try "to represent life," with "beauty and truth." These are relative terms. "The province of art is all life," but the writer has only his own. Beauty must vary because art is organic: "a novel is a living thing," different from all others. And truth is not something fixed and standard, for "reality has a myriad forms." Hence the writer can properly use only the impressions arising from his own experience. He will possess an "air of reality" only when he conveys faithfully a personal impression of life. What counts above all is "the quality of the mind of the producer," his imaginative penetration, his "power to guess the unseen from the seen, to trace the implications of things." He is exactly like a painter ("his brother the painter"), for both attempt "to render the look of things, the look that conveys their meaning." Who shall say that a novel must follow a certain set of prescriptions? "There is no impression of life, no manner of seeing it and feeling it, to which the plan of the novelist may not offer a place." "There are all sorts of tastes." James's position is that of the impressionist, the relativist. He refuses to say what the artist should see, or feel, or like, requiring only that he sincerely try "to catch the color of life." James could have offered himself as an example: his ardor and expertness in pursuit of truth, especially the complicated facts of mind, equal in integrity the search of the scientist for objective truth. In James, artist and critic, realism at length reached maturity.

FOLK SONGS AND BALLADS

One of the foundations of realism was the folk literature of America. Folk songs and ballads are a kind of poetry of, by, and for the common man. Generally begun by individuals, they are transmitted orally, built up and altered, becoming the possession of a social group: pioneers, or cowboys, or railroad men, or sailors, or lumberjacks, etc. The purely literary value of most of them is slight. But capably sung (a number of phonograph records are available), they have vivid musical qualities. A sample of the music is given with the first selection below.

Among many collections are one made by the poet Carl Sandburg, *The American Songbag*, and one edited by B. A. Botkin, *A Treasury of American Folklore*. A good general account is chapter 43 of *Literary History of the United States*, volume 2.

Sweet Betsy from Pike

Despite hardships and dangers, as the wagon train jolted westward, emigrants enjoyed singing ballads such as this one about Betsy from Pike. In California a "Pike" was an emigrant from Pike County, Missouri, or anywhere around there, a type once defined by Bayard Taylor as "an Anglo-Saxon relapsed into semi-barbarism."

Collected, adapted & arranged by John A. & Alan Lomax. Copyright 1934 by John A. & Alan Lomax in the book *American Ballads and Folk Songs*. Copyright assigned 1958 to Ludlow Music, Inc., New York. Used by permission.

Oh, do you remember Sweet Betsy from Pike,
Who crossed the wide prairie with her lover Ike,
With two yoke of cattle and one spotted hog,
A tall Shanghai rooster, an old yaller dog.

Refrain

Sing too ra li oo ra li oo ra li ay,　　　5
Sing too ra li oo ra li oo ra li ay.

One evening quite early they camped on the
　　　Platte,
'Twas near by the road on a green shady flat;
Where Betsy, sore-footed, lay down to repose —
With wonder Ike gazed on his Pike County
　　　rose.　　　10

They swam the wide rivers and crossed the tall
　　　peaks,
And camped on the prairies for weeks upon
　　　weeks,
Starvation and cholera and hard work and
　　　slaughter,
They reached California spite of hell and high
　　　water.

Out on the prairie one bright starry night　　　15
They broke out the whiskey and Betsy got tight;
She sang and she shouted and danced o'er the
　　　plain,
And she put on a show for the whole wagon
　　　train.

Their wagon broke down with a terrible
    crash,   19
And out on the prairie rolled all sorts of trash;
A few little baby clothes done up with care —
'Twas rather suspicious, though all on the
    square.

The Injuns came down in a wild yelling horde,
And Betsy was skeered they would scalp her
    adored;   24
Behind the front wagon wheel Betsy did crawl,
And there fought the Injuns with musket and
    ball.

The alkali desert was burning and bare,
And Isaac's soul shrank from the death that
    lurked there:
"Oh, Dear Old Pike County, I'll go back to
    you."   29
Says Betsy, "You'll go by yourself if you do."

The Shanghai ran off and the cattle all died,
The last piece of bacon that morning was fried;
Poor Ike got discouraged, and Betsy got mad,
The dog wagged his tail and looked wonder-
    fully sad.

One morning they stopped on a very high hill,
And with wonder looked down upon old Placer-
    ville;   36
Ike shouted and said, as he cast his eyes down,
"Sweet Betsy, my darling, we'll go to Hang-
    town."

Long Ike and Sweet Betsy attended a dance, 39
Where Ike wore a pair of his Pike County pants;
Sweet Betsy was covered with ribbons and rings;
Says Ike, "you're an angel but where are your
    wings?"

A miner said, "Betsy, will you dance with me?"
"I will that, old hoss, if you don't make too free;
But don't dance me hard. Do you want to know
    why?   45
Dog on ye! I'm chock full of strong alkali!"

Long Ike and Sweet Betsy got married of course,
And Ike became jealous — obtained a divorce;
Sweet Betsy, well satisfied, said with a shout,
"Good-by, you big lummox, I'm glad you backed
    out!"   50

O Bury Me Not on the Lone Prairie

⚜ This cowboy classic exists in many forms, some
of them longer, some shorter, than the stanzas given
here. These stanzas, however, are the very heart of
every version — the cowboy's plea, and his misfortune, and his grave "on the lone prairie."

"O bury me not on the lone prairie,"
These words came slow and mournfully
From the pallid lips of a youth who lay
On his dying bed at the close of day.

He had wailed in pain till o'er his brow   5
Death's shadows fast were gathering now;
He thought of his home and his loved ones
    nigh
As the cowboys gathered to see him die.

"O bury me not on the lone prairie
Where the wild coyotes will howl o'er me, 10
In a narrow grave just six by three,
O bury me not on the lone prairie.

"In fancy I listen to the well known words
Of the free, wild winds and the song of the
    birds;
I think of home and the cottage in the bower
And the scenes I loved in my childhood's
    hour.   16

"It matters not, I've oft been told,
Where the body lies when the heart grows
    cold;
Yet grant, O grant this wish to me,
O bury me not on the lone prairie.   20

"O then bury me not on the lone prairie,
In a narrow grave six foot by three,
Where a buffalo paws o'er a prairie sea,
O bury me not on the lone prairie.

"I've always wished to be laid when I died 25
In the little churchyard on the green hillside;
By my father's grave, there let mine be,
And bury me not on the lone prairie.

"Let my death slumber be where my mother's
    prayer
And a sister's tear will mingle there,   30
Where my friends can come and weep o'er me;
O bury me not on the lone prairie.

"O bury me not on the lone prairie
In a narrow grave just six by three,

Where the buzzard waits and the wind blows
  free;   35
Then bury me not on the lone prairie.

"There is another whose tears may be shed
For one who lies on a prairie bed;
It pained me then and it pains me now; —
She has curled these locks, she has kissed this
  brow.   40

"These locks she has curled, shall the rattlesnake kiss?
This brow she has kissed, shall the cold grave
  press?
For the sake of the loved ones that will weep
  for me
O bury me not on the lone prairie.

"O bury me not on the lone prairie   45
Where the wild coyotes will howl o'er me,
Where the blizzard beats and the wind goes
  free,
O bury me not on the lone prairie.

"O bury me not," and his voice failed there,
But we took no heed of his dying prayer;   50
In a narrow grave just six by three
We buried him there on the lone prairie.

Where the dew-drops glow and the butterflies
  rest,
And the flowers bloom o'er the prairie's crest;
Where the wild coyote and winds sport free   55
On a wet saddle blanket lay a cowboy-ee.

"O bury me not on the lone prairie
Where the wild coyotes will howl o'er me,
Where the rattlesnakes hiss and the crow flies
  free,
O bury me not on the lone prairie."   60

O we buried him there on the lone prairie
Where the wild rose blooms and the wind blows
  free,
O his pale young face nevermore to see, —
For we buried him there on the lone prairie.

Yes, we buried him there on the lone prairie
Where the owl all night hoots mournfully,   66
And the blizzard beats and the winds blow free
O'er his lonely grave on the lone prairie.

And the cowboys now as they roam the plain, —
For they marked the spot where his bones were
  lain, —   70

Fling a handful of roses o'er his grave,
With a prayer to Him who his soul will save.

"O bury me not on the lone prairie
Where the wolves can howl and growl o'er
  me;
Fling a handful of roses o'er my grave   75
With a prayer to Him who my soul will
  save."

Whoopee, Ti Yi Yo, Git Along, Little Dogies

Many a cowboy has ridden the long Chisholm
Trail from Texas to the northwest while he sang this
ballad. "Dogies" are yearling steers.

As I was a-walking one morning for pleasure,
I saw a cowpuncher come riding alone.
His hat was throwed back and his spurs was
  a-jingling,
And as he approached he was singing this song:

Refrain

Whoopee, ti yi yo, git along, little dogies! 5
It's your misfortune and none of my own.
Whoopee, ti yi yo, git along, little dogies,
For you know Wyoming will be your new
  home!

Early in the spring we round up the dogies,
Mark and brand and bob off their tails,   10
Round up our horses, load up the chuck wagon,
Then throw the dogies up on the trail:
Whoopee, ti yi yo, git along, little dogies, etc.

It's whooping and yelling and driving the dogies;
O how I wish they would go on!   15
It's whooping and punching and go on little
  dogies,
For you know Wyoming will be your new home;
Whoopee, ti yi yo, git along, little dogies, etc.

When the night comes on we heard them on
  the bedground,
These little dogies that roll so slow;   20
Roll up the herd and cut out the strays,
And roll the little dogies that never rolled be-
  fore:
Whoopee, ti yi yo, git along, little dogies, etc.

Your mother she was raised way down in Texas,
Where the jimson weed and sand burrs grow. 25

Now we'll fill you up on prickly pears and
    cholla
Till you are ready for the trail to Idaho:
Whoopee, ti yi yo, git along, little dogies, etc.

Oh, you'll be soup for Uncle Sam's Injuns;
It's "beef, heap beef," I hear them cry. 30
Git along, git along, git along, little dogies,
You're going to be beef steers by and by.
Whoopee, ti yi yo, git along, little dogies, etc.

Casey Jones

✻✻ The spirit of Casey Jones is the spirit of the
early railroad engineers who laughed at death on
their runs with inefficient equipment through floods,
landslides, storms and holdups.

Come all you rounders, for I want you to hear,
The story of a brave engineer.
Casey Jones was the rounder's name.
On a big eight wheeler of a mighty fame.

Caller called Casey 'bout half-past four, 5
He kissed his wife at the station door,
Climbed to the cab with the orders in his hand,
He says, "This is my trip to the holy land."

Out of South Memphis yard on the fly,
Heard the fireman say, "You got a white eye." 10
Well, the switchmen knew by the engine moan
That the man at the throttle was Casey Jones.

The rain was comin' down five or six weeks.
The railroad track was like the bed of a creek.
They slowed her down to a thirty mile gait
And the south-bound mail was eight hours
    late. 16

Fireman says, "Casey, you're runnin' too fast,
You run that block board the last station you
    passed."
Casey says, "I believe we'll make it though,
For she steams a lot better than I ever know."

Casey says, "Fireman, don't you fret, 21
Keep knocking at the fire door, don't give up
    yet,
I'm going to run her till she leaves the rail,
Or make it on time with the south-bound
    mail."

Around the curve and down the dump, 25
Two locomotives was a bound to jump,

Fireman hollered, "Casey, it's just ahead,
We might jump and make it but we'll all be
    dead."

Around the curve comes a passenger train,
Casey blows the whistle, tells the fireman, "Ring
    the bell," 30
Fireman jumps and says "Goodby,
Casey Jones, you're bound to die."

Well Casey Jones was all right.
He stuck to his duty day and night.
They loved his whistle and his ring number
    three, 35
And he came into Memphis on the old I. C.

Fireman goes down the depot track,
Begging his honey to take him back,
She says, "Oranges on the table, peaches on the
    shelf,
You're goin' to get tired sleepin' by yourself."

Mrs. Casey Jones was a sittin' on the bed. 41
Telegram comes that Casey is dead.
She says, "Children, go to bed, and hush your
    cryin',
Cause you got another papa on the Frisco line."

Headaches and heartaches and all kinds of
    pain. 45
They ain't apart from a railroad train.
Stories of brave men, noble and grand,
Belong to the life of a railroad man.

Go Down, Moses

✻✻ This song and the one following are examples of
Negro spirituals. "In time-hallowed associations and
power of emotional evocation and expression for
millions, the spirituals have no serious rivals among
the types of American folksong" (A. P. Hudson).

When Israel was in Egypt's land,
    Let my people go;
Oppressed so hard dey could not stand,
    Let my people go.

    Go down, Moses, 5
        Way down in Egypt land,
    Tell ole Pharaoh
        Let my people go.

Thus saith the Lord, bold Moses said,
    Let my people go; 10

If not I'll smite your first-born dead,
  Let my people go.
      Go down, Moses, etc.

No more shall dey in bondage toil,
  Let my people go;   15
Let dem come out wid Egypt's spoil,
  Let my people go.
      Go down, Moses, etc.

Swing Low, Sweet Chariot

Swing low, sweet chariot,
  Comin' for to carry me home.

I looked over Jordan and what did I see,
Comin' for to carry me home?

A band of angels comin' aftah me,   5
Comin' for to carry me home.

If you git there before I do,
Comin' for to carry me home,
Tell all my frien's I'm a-comin', too,
Comin' for to carry me home.   10

The brightes' day that ever I saw,
Comin' for to carry me home,
When Jesus washed my sins away,
Comin' for to carry me home.

I'm sometimes up an' sometimes down,   15
Comin' for to carry me home,
But still my soul feel heavenly-boun',
Comin' for to carry me home.

MARK TWAIN — AMERICAN

Samuel L. Clemens [1835–1910]

"An American" — "authentic American" — "representative American": such has been the commonest characterization of Mark Twain. It seems to suit his writings, the man himself, the course of his life. In describing the variety of that life to a friend he wrote: "I was a *soldier* two weeks once in the beginning of the war, and was hunted like a rat the whole time. . . . Yes and I have shoveled silver tailings in a quartz mill a couple of weeks, and acquired the last possibilities of culture in *that* direction. . . . And I've been a prospector and know pay rock from poor when I find it — just with a touch of the tongue. . . . And I was some years a Mississippi pilot and familiarly knew all the different kinds of steamboatmen — a race apart and not like other folk. . . . And I was a lecturer on the public platform a number of seasons and was a responder to toasts at all the different kinds of banquets — and so I know a great many secrets about audiences — secrets not to be got out of books but only acquirable by experience. . . . And I have been an author for twenty years and an ass for 55. *Now* then: as the most valuable capital, or culture, or education usable in the building of novels is personal experience, I ought to be well equipped for that trade. I surely have the equipment, a wide culture and all of it real, none of it artificial, for I don't know anything about books."

As no previous author had done, he traveled all over the world, including his own country from coast to coast — first the Mississippi Valley, then Nevada and California, finally Connecticut. "The evolution of the frontier-born Samuel Clemens into the rural printer's apprentice, the tramp typesetter, the reporter; into 'Mark Twain' the newspaper humorist, the river pilot, the Gold Coast adventurer, the newspaper man; into Mark Twain the lecturer, the *Atlantic Monthly* contributor, the adopted New Englander, the recipient of the Oxford University degree; into Mark Twain the world littérateur and universal classic, — all this is a phenomenon peculiarly American. . . . Only in America and in the generation born in the eighteen-thirties and ending its career in the 'gilded age' following the Civil War could there have been evolved a Mark Twain" (F. L. Pattee).

When Samuel Clemens was born, Missouri and Louisiana were the only states west of the Mississippi. His birthplace was a village in Missouri less than fifty miles from the river. His parents, John Clemens and Jane Lampton, came of good Virginia and Kentucky stock. John Clemens was a lawyer and merchant, rarely far from disaster. Trying to improve his fortunes, he kept moving from place to place. When Sam was four, the family settled in Hannibal, Missouri. There, among the hills and beside the great river, a few miles above Pike County and a hundred miles from St. Louis, he lived the adventurous life described in his best-loved novels.

After the death of his father, the boy of twelve was apprenticed to the printer of his brother's paper in Hannibal. In 1853 he set out to see the world, working as a printer in St. Louis, then Chicago, Philadelphia, Keokuk, Cincinnati. In the spring of 1857 he took passage for New Orleans, with the intention of going to Brazil. On this trip he met the pilot, Horace Bixby, and with typical impulsiveness engaged himself as apprentice. Under Bixby for eighteen months, he "learned the river," all 1,200 miles of the Mississippi. Then as a pilot he was a king among the river men. His four years on the steamboats were his "brief, sharp schooling," he wrote later. "I got personally and familiarly acquainted with all the different types of human nature that are to be found in fiction, biography or history." Using his leisure time to advantage, he came to be recognized by his fellow pilots as a great reader.

Steamboating ended abruptly when traffic was blocked by the Civil War. Briefly he served as second lieutenant in a hastily formed Confederate militia company; picturesquely equipped, he rode a small yellow mule. Then with his brother Orion, who had been appointed Territorial Secretary of Nevada, he set out by stage, behind six galloping horses, over the plains and the Rockies, a journey later described in *Roughing It*. He tried some silver and gold prospecting and speculating, but did better in journalism, adopting the humorous variety popular in the West. In Virginia City and San Francisco he came to know Artemus Ward and Bret Harte, to both of whom he was indebted for encouragement and suggestions, and in 1865 he attained national success with his story of the Jumping Frog. The next year he first contributed to *Harper's*, and in the same year, after a sojourn in the Hawaiian Islands, discovered his talent for a new vocation when he lectured to a convulsed audience in San Francisco. After that there was no stopping his career.

Complete public recognition came with *Innocents Abroad* (1869), an account of his frolicsome invasion of the Old World, much of which reads rather languidly today. The next year he married Olivia Langdon, daughter of a wealthy business man of Elmira, New York; in 1872 they settled in Hartford, Connecticut. Meanwhile he had published *Roughing It*, a vivid narrative of his Western experiences, and in 1873 came *The Gilded Age*, written jointly with Charles Dudley Warner, a novel worth reading if only for its famous optimist, Colonel Sellers.

The finest of his writings followed: three works filled with joyous living along or on the Mississippi River. Two were novels based on his boyhood in the river town, *Tom Sawyer* (1876) and *Huckleberry Finn* (1884). The third described his life as a cubpilot — *Old Times on the Mississippi*, which reappeared eight years later as the first part of *Life on the Mississippi* (1883). Other books followed, including *Joan of Arc*, which seems to have been his own favorite, though his friend Howells inferred it was rather *Life on the Mississippi*. Before the turn of the century Mark Twain had formed a somber, pessimistic view of life, expressed in works published after his death: *The Man that Corrupted Hadleyburg, What is Man?, The Mysterious Stranger*. Realism (with a large admixture of romanticism) had led him, as it was leading others, to the disillusionment of naturalism.

Through his immensely popular books and his equally popular lectures Mark Twain acquired a fortune, lost when his ventures in the publishing business brought him to bankruptcy. "At the age of sixty" (as Stuart Sherman summed up his response) "he girded himself anew and made another fortune in three years and repaid his creditors to the last dollar, and in a few years more had accumulated a third fortune for himself, and drew annual royalties equal to the salary of the President of the United States."

Throughout his career Mark Twain showed the journalist's inclination to improvise, rather than the artist's solicitude for form. Yet he managed to convey, in cold type, his warm gusto, his keen powers of perception, his broad understanding, his ever refreshing humor. To the masses for whom he wrote he was at first, and remained, a "funny man." But a more critical audience came to realize that his rich humanity and contagious vitality, along with his play of humor, made him secure among the great writers of the United States.

Further reading: *Roughing It, Huckleberry Finn, The Mysterious Stranger*. A. B. Paine, *Mark Twain: a Biography*, 3 vols., 1912. W. D. Howells, *My Mark Twain*, 1910. Dixon Wecter, *Sam Clemens of Hannibal*, 1952. Bernard De Voto, *Mark Twain's America*, 1932. E. C. Wagenknecht, *Mark Twain: The Man and His Work*, 1935.

The Celebrated Jumping Frog of Calaveras County

(1865)

🎏 "Under the name of Mark Twain the wild-haired Southwesterner began to contribute to the press yarns swapped about the legislative halls of Carson City, the bars and billiard parlors of San Francisco, and the hot stoves of miners on Jackass Hill. From these last, about February, 1865, he first heard the old folk tale of the Jumping Frog. To the anecdote he added the salt of human values which the genre usually lacked, in garrulous Simon Wheeler and simple Jim Smiley the frog's owner." (Dixon Wecter in *Literary History of the United States*.)

In compliance with the request of a friend of mine, who wrote me from the East, I called on good-natured, garrulous old Simon Wheeler, and inquired after my friend's friend, *Leonidas*

W. Smiley, as requested to do, and I hereunto append the result. I have a lurking suspicion that *Leonidas* W. Smiley is a myth; that my friend never knew such a personage; and that he only conjectured that, if I asked old Wheeler about him, it would remind him of his infamous *Jim* Smiley, and he would go to work and bore me nearly to death with some infernal reminiscence of him as long and tedious as it should be useless to me. If that was the design, it certainly succeeded.

I found Simon Wheeler dozing comfortably by the bar-room stove of the old, dilapidated tavern in the ancient mining camp of Angel's, and I noticed that he was fat and bald-headed, and had an expression of winning gentleness and simplicity upon his tranquil countenance. He roused up and gave me good-day. I told him a friend of mine had commissioned me to make some inquiries about a cherished companion of his boyhood named *Leonidas* W. Smiley —

Rev. Leonidas W. Smiley — a young minister of the Gospel, who he had heard was at one time a resident of Angel's Camp. I added that, if Mr. Wheeler could tell me anything about this Rev. Leonidas W. Smiley, I would feel under many obligations to him.

Simon Wheeler backed me into a corner and blockaded me there with his chair, and then sat me down and reeled off the monotonous narrative which follows this paragraph. He never smiled, he never frowned, he never changed his voice from the gentle-flowing key to which he tuned the initial sentence, he never betrayed the slightest suspicion of enthusiasm; but all through the interminable narrative there ran a vein of impressive earnestness and sincerity, which showed me plainly that, so far from his imagining that there was anything ridiculous or funny about his story, he regarded it as a really important matter, and admired its two heroes as men of transcendent genius in *finesse*. To me, the spectacle of a man drifting serenely along through such a queer yarn without ever smiling, was exquisitely absurd. As I said before, I asked him to tell me what he knew of Rev. Leonidas W. Smiley, and he replied as follows. I let him go on in his own way, and never interrupted him once:

There was a feller here once by the name of *Jim* Smiley, in the winter of '49 — or may be it was the spring of '50 — I don't recollect exactly, somehow, though what makes me think it was one or the other is because I remember the big flume wasn't finished when he first came to the camp; but any way, he was the curiosest man about always betting on any thing that turned up you ever see, if he could get any body to bet on the other side; and if he couldn't, he'd change sides. Any way that suited the other man would suit him — any way just so's he got a bet, *he* was satisfied. But still he was lucky, uncommon lucky; he most always come out winner. He was always ready and laying for a chance; there couldn't be no solitary thing mentioned but that feller'd offer to bet on it, and take any side you please, as I was just telling you. If there was a horse-race, you'd find him flush, or you'd find him busted at the end of it; if there was a dog-fight, he'd bet on it; if there was a cat-fight, he'd bet on it; if there was a chicken-fight, he'd bet on it; why, if there was two birds setting on a fence, he would bet you which one would fly first; or if there was a

camp-meeting, he would be there reg'lar, to bet on Parson Walker, which he judged to be the best exhorter about there, and so he was, too, and a good man. If he even seen a straddle-bug start to go anywheres, he would bet you how long it would take him to get wherever he was going to, and if you took him up, he would follow that straddle-bug to Mexico but what he would find out where he was bound for and how long he was on the road. Lots of the boys here has seen that Smiley, and can tell you about him. Why, it never made no difference to *him* — he would bet on *any* thing — the dangdest feller. Parson Walker's wife laid very sick once, for a good while, and it seemed as if they warn't going to save her; but one morning he come in, and Smiley asked how she was, and he said she was considerable better — thank the Lord for his inf'nit mercy — and coming on so smart that, with the blessing of Prov'dence she'd get well yet; and Smiley, before he thought, says, "Well, I'll risk two-and-a-half that she won't, any way."

Thish-yer Smiley had a mare — the boys called her the fifteen-minute nag, but that was only in fun, you know, because, of course, she was faster than that — and he used to win money on that horse, for all she was so slow and always had the asthma, or the distemper, or the consumption, or something of that kind. They used to give her two or three hundred yards start, and then pass her under way; but always at the fag-end of the race she'd get excited and desperate-like, and come cavorting and straddling up, and scattering her legs around limber, sometimes in the air, and sometimes out to one side amongst the fences, and kicking up m-o-r-e dust, and raising m-o-r-e racket with her coughing and sneezing and blowing her nose — and always fetch up at the stand just about a neck ahead, as near as you could cypher it down.

And he had a little small bull pup, that to look at him you'd think he wa'n't worth a cent, but to set around and look ornery, and lay for a chance to steal something. But as soon as money was up on him, he was a different dog; his under-jaw'd begin to stick out like the fo'castle of a steamboat, and his teeth would uncover, and shine savage like the furnaces. And a dog might tackle him, and bully-rag him, and bite him, and throw him over his shoulder two or three times, and Andrew Jackson — which was the name of the pup — Andrew Jackson would never let on but what *he* was satisfied, and hadn't expected nothing else — and the bets being doubled and doubled on the other side all the time, till the money was all up; and then all of a sudden he would grab that other dog jest by the j'int of his hind leg and freeze to it — not chaw, you understand, but only jest grip and hang on till they throwed up the sponge, if it was a year. Smiley always come out winner on that pup, till he harnessed a dog once that didn't have no hind legs, because they'd been sawed off by a circular saw, and when the thing had gone along far enough, and the money was all up, and he come to make a snatch for his pet holt, he saw in a minute how he'd been imposed on, and how the other dog had him in the door, so to speak, and he 'peared surprised, and then he looked sorter discouraged-like, and didn't try no more to win the fight, and so he got shucked out bad. He give Smiley a look, as much as to say his heart was broke, and it was *his* fault, for putting up a dog that hadn't no hind legs for him to take holt of, which was his main dependence in a fight, and then he limped off a piece and laid down and died. It was a good pup, was that Andrew Jackson, and would have made a name for hisself if he'd lived, for the stuff was in him, and he had genius — I know it, because he hadn't had no opportunity to speak of, and it don't stand to reason that a dog could make such a fight as he could under them circumstances, if he hadn't no talent. It always makes me feel sorry when I think of that last fight of his'n, and the way it turned out.

Well, thish-yer Smiley had rat-tarriers, and chicken cocks, and tom-cats, and all them kind of things, till you couldn't rest, and you couldn't fetch nothing for him to bet on but he'd match you. He ketched a frog one day, and took him home, and said he cal'klated to edercate him; and so he never done nothing for three months but set in his back yard and learn that frog to jump. And you bet he *did* learn him, too. He'd give him a little punch behind, and the next minute you'd see that frog whirling in the air like a doughnut — see him turn one summerset, or may be a couple, if he got a good start, and come down flat-footed and all right, like a cat. He got him up so in the matter of catching flies, and kept him in practice so constant, that he'd nail a fly every time as far as he could see him. Smiley said all a frog wanted was education, and he could do most anything — and I believe him. Why, I've seen him set Dan'l Webster down here on this floor — Dan'l Webster was the name of the frog — and sing out, "Flies, Dan'l, flies!" and quicker'n you could wink, he'd spring straight up, and snake a fly off'n the counter there, and flop down on the floor again as solid as a gob of mud, and fall to scratching the side of his head with his hind foot as indifferent as if he hadn't no idea he'd been doin' any more'n any frog might do. You never see a frog so modest and straightfor'ard as he was, for all he was so gifted. And when it come to fair and square jumping on a dead level, he could get over more ground at one straddle than any animal of his breed you ever see. Jumping on a dead level was his strong suit, you understand; and when it come to that, Smiley would ante up money on him as long as he had a red. Smiley was monstrous proud of his frog, and well he might be, for fellers that had traveled and been everywheres, all said he laid over any frog that ever *they* see.

Well Smiley kept the beast in a little lattice box, and he used to fetch him down town sometimes and lay for a bet. One day a feller — a stranger in the camp, he was — come across him with his box, and says:

"What might it be that you've got in the box?"

And Smiley says, sorter indifferent like, "It might be a parrot, or it might be a canary, may be, but it ain't — it's only just a frog."

And the feller took it, and looked at it careful, and turned it round this way and that, and says, "H'm — so 'tis. Well, what's *he* good for?"

"Well," Smiley says, easy and careless, "he's good enough for *one* thing, I should judge — he can outjump ary frog in Calaveras county."

The feller took the box again, and took another long, particular look, and give it back to Smiley, and says, very deliberate, "Well, I don't see no p'ints about that frog that's any better'n any other frog."

"May be you don't," Smiley says. "May be you understand frogs, and may be you don't understand 'em; may be you've had experience, and may be you an't only a amature, as it were. Anyways, I've got *my* opinion, and I'll risk forty dollars he can outjump any frog in Calaveras county."

And the feller studied a minute, and then says, kinder sad like, "Well, I'm only a stranger here, and I ain't got no frog, but if I had a frog, I'd bet you."

And then Smiley says, "That's all right —
that's all right — if you'll hold my box a minute, I'll go and get you a frog." And so the feller
took the box, and put up his forty dollars along
with Smiley's, and set down to wait.

So he set there a good while thinking and
thinking to hisself, and then he got the frog out
and prized his mouth open and took a teaspoon
and filled him full of quail shot — filled him
pretty near up to his chin — and set him on the
floor. Smiley he went to the swamp and slopped
around in the mud for a long time, and finally
he ketched a frog, and fetched him in, and give
him to this feller, and says:

"Now, if you're ready, set him alongside of
Dan'l, with his fore-paws just even with Dan'l,
and I'll give the word." Then he says, "one —
two — three — jump!" and him and the feller
touched up the frogs from behind, and the new
frog hopped off, but Dan'l give a heave, and
hysted up his shoulders — so — like a Frenchman, but it want no use — couldn't budge; he
was planted as solid as an anvil, and he couldn't
no more stir than if he was anchored out. Smiley
was a good deal surprised, and he was disgusted
too, but he didn't have no idea what the matter
was, of course.

The feller took the money and started away;
and when he was going out of the door, he
sorter jerked his thumb over his shoulders —
this way — at Dan'l, and says again, very deliberate, "Well, I don' see no p'ints about that
frog that's any better'n any other frog."

Smiley he stood scratching his head and looking down at Dan'l a long time, and at last he
says, "I do wonder what in the nation that frog
throw'd off for — I wonder if there ain't something the matter with him — he 'pears to look
mighty baggy, somehow." And he ketched
Dan'l by the nap of the neck, and lifted him up
and says, "Why, blame my cats, if he don't
weigh five pound!" and turned him upside
down, and he belched out a double handful of
shot. And then he see how it was, and he was
the maddest man — he set the frog down and
took out after that feller, but he never ketched
him. And —

(Here Simon Wheeler heard his name called
from the front yard, and got up to see what was
wanted.) And turning to me as he moved away,
he said: "Just set where you are, stranger, and
rest easy — I ain't going to be gone a second."

But, by your leave, I did not think that a continuation of the history of the enterprising vagabond *Jim* Smiley would be likely to afford me
much information concerning the Rev. *Leonidas
W.* Smiley, and so I started away.

At the door I met the sociable Wheeler returning, and he buttonholed me and recom-
menced:

"Well, thish-yer Smiley had a yaller one-eyed
cow that didn't have no tail, only jest a short
stump like a bannanner, and —"

"Oh! hang Smiley and his afflicted cow!" I
muttered, good-naturedly, and bidding the old
gentleman good-day, I departed.

From *Innocents Abroad*

(1869)

Mark Twain's journalistic account of travel in
Europe, Egypt, and the Holy Land was first published as letters to the San Francisco *Alta California*
and the New York *Tribune*. He saw the Old World
shrines of the romantic imagination with eyes very
different from those of Irving, Longfellow, and
Lowell. Himself a product of the frontier in Missouri and the Far West, he chose to represent Americans as complacent democrats, with scant respect
for anything abroad. While cultivated readers were
likely to call his work crude (as it often was), plain
Americans, in a wholesome reaction against foreign
condescension and native veneration, were delighted
with his jibes.

[Italian Guides]

We have taken it out of this guide. He has
marched us through miles of pictures and sculpture in the vast corridors of the Vatican; and
through miles of pictures and sculpture in
twenty other palaces; he has shown us the great
picture in the Sistine Chapel, and frescoes
enough to fresco the heavens — pretty much all
done by Michael Angelo. So with him we have
played that game which has vanquished so
many guides for us — imbecility and idiotic
questions. These creatures never suspect —
they have no idea of a sarcasm.

He shows us a figure and says: "Statoo
brunzo." (Bronze statue.)

We look at it indifferently and the doctor
asks: "By Michael Angelo?"

"No — not know who."

Then he shows us the ancient Roman Forum.
The doctor asks: "Michael Angelo?"

A stare from the guide. "No — a thousan'
year before he is born."

Then an Egyptian obelisk. Again: "Michael Angelo?"

"Oh, *mon dieu*, genteelmen! Zis is *two* thousan' years before he is born!"

He grows so tired of that unceasing question sometimes, that he dreads to show us anything at all. The wretch has tried all the ways he can think of to make us comprehend that Michael Angelo is only responsible for the creation of a *part* of the world, but somehow he has not succeeded yet. Relief for overtasked eyes and brain from study and sight-seeing is necessary, or we shall become idiotic sure enough. Therefore this guide must continue to suffer. If he does not enjoy it, so much the worse for him. We do.

In this place I may as well jot down a chapter concerning those necessary nuisances, European guides. Many a man has wished in his heart he could do without his guide; but knowing he could not, has wished he could get some amusement out of him as a remuneration for the affliction of his society. We accomplished this latter matter, and if our experience can be made useful to others they are welcome to it.

Guides know about enough English to tangle everything up so that a man can make neither head nor tail of it. They know their story by heart — the history of every statue, painting, cathedral, or other wonder they show you. They know it and tell it as a parrot would — and if you interrupt, and throw them off the track, they have to go back and begin over again. All their lives long, they are employed in showing strange things to foreigners and listening to their bursts of admiration. It is human nature to take delight in exciting admiration. It is what prompts children to say "smart" things, and do absurd ones, and in other ways "show off" when company is present. It is what makes gossips turn out in rain and storm to go and be the first to tell a startling bit of news. Think, then, what a passion it becomes with a guide, whose privilege it is, every day, to show to strangers wonders that throw them into perfect ecstasies of admiration! He gets so that he could not by any possibility live in a soberer atmosphere. After we discovered this, we *never* went into ecstasies any more — we never admired anything — we never showed any but impassible faces and stupid indifference in the presence of the sublimest wonders a guide had to display. We had found their weak point. We have made good use of it ever since. We have made some of those

people savage, at times, but we have never lost our own serenity.

The doctor asks the questions, generally, because he can keep his countenance, and look more like an inspired idiot, and throw more imbecility into the tone of his voice than any man that lives. It comes natural to him.

The guides in Genoa are delighted to secure an American party, because Americans so much wonder, and deal so much in sentiment and emotion before any relic of Columbus. Our guide there fidgeted about as if he had swallowed a spring mattress. He was full of animation — full of impatience. He said:

"Come wis me, genteelmen! — come! I show you ze letterwriting by Christopher Colombo! — write it himself! — write it wis his own hand! — come!"

He took us to the municipal palace. After much impressive fumbling of keys and opening of locks, the stained and aged document was spread before us. The guide's eyes sparkled. He danced about us and tapped the parchment with his finger:

"What I tell you, genteelmen! Is it not so? See! handwriting Christopher Colombo! — write it himself!"

We looked indifferent — unconcerned. The doctor examined the document very deliberately, during a painful pause. Then he said, without any show of interest:

"Ah — Ferguson — what — what did you say was the name of the party who wrote this?"

"Christopher Colombo! ze great Christopher Colombo!"

Another deliberate examination.

"Ah — did he write it himself, or — or how?"

"He write it himself! — Christopher Colombo! he's own handwriting, write by himself!"

Then the doctor laid the document down and said:

"Why, I have seen boys in America only fourteen years old that could write better than that."

"But zis is ze great Christo —"

"I don't care who it is! It's the worst writing I ever saw. Now you mustn't think you can impose on us because we are strangers. We are not fools, by a good deal. If you have got any specimens of penmanship of real merit, trot them out! — and if you haven't, drive on!"

We drove on. The guide was considerably shaken up, but he made one more venture. He had something which he thought would overcome us. He said:

"Ah, genteelmen, you come wis me! I show you beautiful, oh, magnificent bust Christopher Colombo! — splendid, grand, magnificent!"

He brought us before the beautiful bust — for it *was* beautiful — and sprang back and struck an attitude:

"Ah, look, genteelmen! — beautiful, grand, — bust Christopher Colombo! — beautiful bust, beautiful pedestal!"

The doctor put up his eyeglass — procured for such occasions:

"Ah — what did you say this gentleman's name was?"

"Christopher Colombo! — ze great Christopher Colombo!"

"'Christopher Colombo! ze great Christopher Colombo!' Well, what did *he* do?"

"Discover America! — discover America, oh, ze devil!"

"Discover America. No — that statement will hardly wash. We are just from America ourselves. We heard nothing about it. Christopher Colombo — pleasant name — is — is he dead?"

"Oh, *corpo di Baccho!* — three hundred years!"

"What did he die of?"

"I do not know! — I cannot tell."

"Smallpox, think?"

"I do not know, genteelmen! — I do not know *what* he die of!"

"Measles, likely?"

"Maybe — maybe — I do *not* know — I think he die of something."

"Parents living?"

"Im-posseeble!"

"Ah — which is the bust and which is the pedestal?"

"Santa Maria! — *zis* ze bust! — *zis* ze pedestal!"

"Ah, I see, I see — happy combination — very happy combination, indeed. Is — is this the first time this gentleman was ever on a bust?"

That joke was lost on the foreigner — guides cannot master the subtleties of the American joke.

We have made it interesting for this Roman guide. Yesterday we spent three or four hours in the Vatican again, that wonderful world of curiosities. We came very near expressing interest, sometimes — even admiration — it was

very hard to keep from it. We succeeded though. Nobody else ever did, in the Vatican museums. The guide was bewildered — nonplussed. He walked his legs off, nearly, hunting up extraordinary things, and exhausted all his ingenuity on us, but it was a failure; we never showed any interest in anything. He had reserved what he considered to be his greatest wonder till the last — a royal Egyptian mummy, the best-preserved in the world, perhaps. He took us there. He felt so sure, this time, that some of his old enthusiasm came back to him:

"See, genteelmen! — Mummy! Mummy!"

The eyeglasses came up as calmly, as deliberately as ever.

"Ah, — Ferguson — what did I understand you to say the gentleman's name was?"

"Name? — he got no name! — Mummy! — 'Gyptian mummy!"

"Yes, yes. Born here?"

"No! 'Gyptian mummy!"

"Ah, just so. Frenchman, I presume?"

"No! — *not* Frenchman, not Roman! — born in Egypta!"

"Born in Egypta. Never heard of Egypta before. Foreign locality, likely. Mummy — mummy. How calm he is — how self-possessed. Is, ah — is he dead?"

"Oh, *sacré bleu,* been dead three thousan' year!"

The doctor turned on him savagely:

"Here, now, what do you mean by such conduct as this? Playing us for Chinamen because we are strangers and trying to learn! Trying to impose your vile second-hand carcasses on *us!* — thunder and lightning, I've a notion to — to — if you've got a nice *fresh* corpse, fetch him out! — or, by George, we'll brain you!"

We make it exceedingly interesting for this Frenchman. However, he has paid us back, partly, without knowing it. He came to the hotel this morning to ask if we were up, and he endeavored as well as he could to describe us, so that the landlord would know which persons he meant. He finished with the casual remark that we were lunatics. The observation was so innocent and so honest that it amounted to a very good thing for a guide to say.

There is one remark (already mentioned) which never yet has failed to disgust these guides. We use it always, when we can think of nothing else to say. After they have exhausted their enthusiasm pointing out to us and praising the beauties of some ancient bronze image or broken-legged statue, we look at it stupidly and in silence for five, ten, fifteen minutes — as long as we can hold out, in fact — and then ask: "Is — is he dead?"

That conquers the serenest of them. It is not what they are looking for — especially a new guide. Our Roman Ferguson is the most patient, unsuspecting, long-suffering subject we have had yet. We shall be sorry to part with him. We have enjoyed his society very much. We trust he has enjoyed ours, but we are harassed with doubts.

[We Were Americans!]

Wherever we went, in Europe, Asia, or Africa, we made a sensation, and, I suppose I may add, created a famine. None of us had ever been anywhere before; we all hailed from the interior; travel was a wild novelty to us, and we conducted ourselves in accordance with the natural instincts that were in us, and trammeled ourselves with no ceremonies, no conventionalities. We always took care to make it understood that we were Americans — Americans! When we found that a good many foreigners had hardly ever heard of America, and that a good many more knew it only as a barbarous province away off somewhere, that had lately been at war with somebody, we pitied the ignorance of the Old World, but abated no jot of our importance. Many and many a simple community in the Eastern hemisphere will remember for years the incursion of the strange horde in the year of our Lord 1867, that called themselves Americans, and seemed to imagine in some unaccountable way that they had a right to be proud of it. We generally created a famine, partly because the coffee on the *Quaker City* was unendurable, and sometimes the more substantial fare was not strictly first class; and partly because one naturally tires of sitting long at the same board and eating from the same dishes.

The people of those foreign countries are very, very ignorant. They looked curiously at the costumes we had brought from the wilds of America. They observed that we talked loudly at table sometimes. They noticed that we looked out for expenses, and got what we conveniently could out of a franc, and wondered where in the mischief we came from. In Paris they just simply opened their eyes and stared when we spoke to them in French! We never did succeed in making those idiots understand their own language. One of our passengers said to a shopkeeper, in reference to a proposed return to buy a pair of gloves, "*Allong restray trankeel — maybe ve coom Moonday*," and would you believe it, that shopkeeper, a born Frenchman, had to ask what it was that had been said. Sometimes it seems to me, somehow, that there must be a difference between Parisian French and *Quaker City* French.

The people stared at us everywhere, and we stared at them. We generally made them feel rather small, too, before we got done with them, because we bore down on them with America's greatness until we crushed them. And yet we took kindly to the manners and customs, and especially to the fashions of the various people we visited. When we left the Azores, we wore awful capotes and used fine-tooth combs — successfully. When we came back from Tangier, in Africa, we were topped with fezzes of the bloodiest hue, hung with tassels like an Indian's scalp-lock. In France and Spain we attracted some attention in these costumes. In Italy they naturally took us for distempered Garibaldians, and set a gunboat to look for anything significant in our changes of uniform. We made Rome howl. We could have made any place howl when we had all our clothes on. We got no fresh raiment in Greece — they had but little there of any kind. But at Constantinople, how we turned out! Turbans, simitars, fezzes, horse-pistols, tunics, sashes, baggy trousers, yellow slippers — Oh, we were gorgeous! The illustrious dogs of Constantinople barked their under-jaws off, and even then failed to do us justice. They are all dead by this time. They could not go through such a run of business as we gave them and survive.

And then we went to see the Emperor of Russia. We just called on him as comfortably as if we had known him a century or so, and when we had finished our visit we variegated ourselves with selections from Russian costumes and sailed away again more picturesque than ever. In Smyrna we picked up camel's-hair shawls and other dressy things from Persia; but in Palestine — ah, in Palestine — our splendid career ended. They didn't wear any clothes to speak of. We were satisfied, and stopped. We made no experiments. We did not try their costume. But we astonished the natives of that country. We astonished them with such eccentricities of dress as we could muster. We prowled through the Holy Land, from Cesarea

Philippi to Jerusalem and the Dead Sea, a weird procession of pilgrims, gotten up regardless of expense, solemn, gorgeous, green-spectacled, drowsing under blue umbrellas, and astride of a sorrier lot of horses, camels, and asses than those that came out of Noah's ark, after eleven months of seasickness and short rations. If ever those children of Israel in Palestine forget when Gideon's Band went through there from America, they ought to be cursed once more and finished. It was the rarest spectacle that ever astounded mortal eyes, perhaps.

Well, we were at home in Palestine. It was easy to see that that was the grand feature of the expedition. We had cared nothing much about Europe. We galloped through the Louvre, the Pitti, the Uffizzi, the Vatican — all the galleries — and through the pictured and frescoed churches of Venice, Naples, and the cathedrals of Spain; some of us said that certain of the great works of the old masters were glorious creations of genius (we found it out in the guide-book, though we got hold of the wrong picture sometimes), and the others said they were disgraceful old daubs. We examined modern and ancient statuary with a critical eye in Florence, Rome, or anywhere we found it, and praised it if we saw fit, and if we didn't we said we preferred the wooden Indians in front of the cigar stores of America. But the Holy Land brought out all our enthusiasm. We fell into raptures by the barren shores of Galilee; we pondered at Tabor and at Nazareth; we exploded into poetry over the questionable loveliness of Esdraelon; we meditated at Jezreel and Samaria over the missionary zeal of Jehu; we rioted — fairly rioted among the holy places of Jerusalem; we bathed in Jordan and the Dead Sea, reckless whether our accident-insurance policies were extra-hazardous or not, and brought away so many jugs of precious water from both places that all the country from Jericho to the mountains of Moab will suffer from drought this year, I think. Yes, the pilgrimage part of the excursion was its pet feature — there is no question about that. After dismal, smileless Palestine, beautiful Egypt had few charms for us. We merely glanced at it and were ready for home. They wouldn't let us land at Malta — quarantine; they would not let us land in Sardinia; nor at Algiers, Africa, nor at Malaga, Spain, nor Cadiz, nor at the Madeira Islands. So we got offended at all foreigners and turned our backs upon them and came home. I suppose we only stopped at the Bermudas because they were in the program. We did not care anything about any place at all. We wanted to go home. Homesickness was abroad in the ship — it was epidemic. If the authorities of New York had known how badly we had it, they would have quarantined us here.

The grand pilgrimage is over. Good-bye to it, and a pleasant memory to it, I am able to say in all kindness. I bear no malice, nor ill will toward any individual that was connected with it, either as passenger or officer. Things I did not like at all yesterday I like very well to-day, now that I am home, and always hereafter I shall be able to poke fun at the whole gang if the spirit so moves me to do, without ever saying a malicious word. The expedition accomplished all that its program promised that it should accomplish, and we ought all to be satisfied with the management of the matter, certainly. By-by!

MARK TWAIN

From *Roughing It*
(1872)

In *Roughing It* Mark Twain tells the story of his first public lecture. Just returned from "half a year's luxurious vagrancy" in the Sandwich Islands (now the Hawaiian Islands), he used them as the subject for a lecture in San Francisco.

[Trouble Will Begin at 8]

I was home again, in San Francisco, without means and without employment. I tortured my brain for a saving scheme of some kind, and at last a public lecture occurred to me! I sat down and wrote one, in a fever of hopeful anticipation. I showed it to several friends, but they all shook their heads. They said nobody would come to hear me, and I would make a humiliating failure of it. They said that as I had never spoken in public, I would break down in the delivery, anyhow. I was disconsolate now. But at last an editor slapped me on the back and told me to "go ahead." He said, "Take the largest house in town, and charge a dollar a ticket." The audacity of the proposition was charming; it seemed fraught with practical worldly wisdom, however. The proprietor of the several theaters endorsed the advice, and said I might have his handsome new opera house at half price — fifty dollars. In sheer desperation I took it — on credit, for sufficient reasons. In three days I did a hundred and fifty dollars' worth of printing and advertising, and was the most distressed and frightened creature on the Pacific coast. I could not sleep — who could, under such circumstances? For other people there was facetiousness in the last line of my posters, but to me it was plaintive with a pang when I wrote it:

> "Doors open at 7½. The trouble will begin at 8."

That line has done good service since. Showmen have borrowed it frequently. I have even seen it appended to a newspaper advertisement reminding school pupils in vacation what time next term would begin. As those three days of suspense dragged by, I grew more and more unhappy. I had sold two hundred tickets among my personal friends, but I feared they might not come. My lecture, which had seemed "humorous" to me, at first, grew steadily more and more dreary, till not a vestige of fun seemed left, and I grieved that I could not bring a coffin on the stage and turn the thing into a funeral. I was so panic-stricken, at last, that I went to three old friends, giants in stature, cordial by nature, and stormy-voiced, and said:

"This thing is going to be a failure; the jokes in it are so dim that nobody will ever see them; I would like to have you sit in the parquette, and help me through."

They said they would. Then I went to the wife of a popular citizen, and said that if she was willing to do me a very great kindness, I would be glad if she and her husband would sit prominently in the left-hand stage-box, where the whole house could see them. I explained that I should need help, and would turn toward her and smile, as a signal, when I had been delivered of an obscure joke — "and then," I added, "don't wait to investigate, but *respond!*"

She promised. Down the street I met a man I never had seen before. He had been drinking, and was beaming with smiles and good nature. He said:

"My name's Sawyer. You don't know me, but that don't matter. I haven't got a cent, but if you knew how bad I wanted to laugh, you'd give me a ticket. Come, now, what do you say?"

"Is your laugh hung on a hair-trigger? — that is, is it critical, or can you get it off *easy?*"

My drawling infirmity of speech so affected him that he laughed a specimen or two that struck me as being about the article I wanted, and I gave him a ticket, and appointed him to sit in the second circle, in the center, and be responsible for that division of the house. I gave him minute instructions about how to detect indistinct jokes, and then went away, and left him chuckling placidly over the novelty of the idea.

I ate nothing on the last of the three eventful days — I only suffered. I had advertised that on this third day the box-office would be opened for the sale of reserved seats. I crept down to the theater at four in the afternoon to see if any sales had been made. The ticket-seller was gone, the box-office was locked up. I had to swallow suddenly, or my heart would have got out. "No sales," I said to myself; "I might have known it." I thought of suicide, pretended illness, flight. I thought of these things in earnest, for I was very miserable and scared. But of course I had to drive them away, and prepare to meet my fate. I could not wait for half-past seven — I wanted to face the horror, and end it — the feeling of many a man doomed to hang, no doubt. I went down back streets at six o'clock, and entered the theater by the back door. I stumbled my way in the dark among the ranks of canvas scenery, and stood on the stage. The house was gloomy and silent, and its emptiness depressing. I went into the dark among the scenes again, and for an hour and a half gave myself up to the horrors, wholly unconscious of everything else. Then I heard a murmur; it rose higher and higher, and ended in a crash, mingled with cheers. It made my hair raise, it was so close to me, and so loud. There was a pause, and then another; presently came a third, and before I well knew what I was about, I was in the middle of the stage, staring at a sea of faces, bewildered by the fierce glare of the lights, and quaking in every limb with a terror that seemed like to take my life away. The house was full, aisles and all!

The tumult in my heart and brain and legs continued a full minute before I could gain any command over myself. Then I recognized the charity and the friendliness in the faces before me, and little by little my fright melted away, and I began to talk. Within three or four minutes I was comfortable, and even content. My three chief allies, with three auxiliaries, were on hand, in the parquette, all sitting together, all armed with bludgeons, and all ready to make an onslaught upon the feeblest joke that might show its head. And whenever a joke did fall, their bludgeons came down and their faces seemed to split from ear to ear; Sawyer, whose hearty countenance was seen looming redly in the center of the second circle, took it up, and the house was carried handsomely. Inferior jokes never fared so royally before. Presently, I delivered a bit of serious matter with impressive unction (it was my pet), and the audience listened with an absorbed hush that gratified me more than any applause; and as I dropped the last word of the clause, I happened to turn and catch Mrs. ——'s intent and waiting eye; my conversation with her flashed upon me and in spite of all I could do I smiled. She took it for the signal, and promptly delivered a mellow laugh that touched off the whole audience; and the explosion that followed was the triumph of the evening. I thought that that honest man Sawyer would choke himself; and as for the bludgeons, they performed like pile-drivers. But my poor little morsel of pathos was ruined. It was taken in good faith as an intentional joke, and the prize one of the entertainment, and I wisely let it go at that.

All the papers were kind in the morning; my appetite returned; I had abundance of money. All's well that ends well.

Baker's Blue-Jay Yarn

(1880)

Mark Twain often reproduced in print the oral characteristics of frontier story-telling. One may compare his practice in the Jumping Frog story or this tall tale of the Blue-Jay with his theory in the essay "How to Tell a Story." He says that while the comic story is English and the witty story is French, the humorous story is American. "The humorous story depends for its effect upon the *manner* of the telling." It "may be spun out to great lengths, and may wander around as much as it pleases, and arrive nowhere in particular." It "is told gravely; the teller does his best to conceal the fact that he even dimly suspects that there is anything funny about it." "Very often, of course, the rambling and disjointed humorous story finishes with a nub, point, snapper, or whatever you like to call it. Then the listener must be alert, for in many cases the teller will divert attention from that nub by dropping it in a carefully casual and indifferent way."

Animals talk to each other, of course. There can be no question about that; but I suppose there are very few people who can understand them. I never knew but one man who could. I knew he could, however, because he told me so himself. He was a middle-aged, simple-hearted miner who had lived in a lonely corner of California, among the woods and mountains, a good many years, and had studied the ways of his only neighbors, the beasts and the birds, until he believed he could accurately translate any remark which they made. This was Jim Baker. According to Jim Baker, some animals have only a limited education, and use only very simple words, and scarcely ever a comparison or a flowery figure; whereas, certain other animals have a large vocabulary, a fine command of language and a ready and fluent delivery; consequently these latter talk a great deal; they like it, they are conscious of their talent, and they enjoy "showing off." Baker said, that after long and careful observation, he had come to the conclusion that the blue-jays were the best talkers he had found among birds and beasts. Said he: —

"There's more *to* a blue-jay than any other creature. He has got more moods, and more different kinds of feelings than other creatures; and mind you, whatever a blue-jay feels, he can put into language. And no mere commonplace language, either, but rattling, out-and-out book-talk — and bristling with metaphor, too — just bristling! And as for command of language — why *you* never see a blue-jay get stuck for a word. No man ever did. They just boil out of him! And another thing: I've noticed a good deal, and there's no bird, or cow, or anything that uses as good grammar as a blue-jay. You may say a cat uses good grammar. Well, a cat does — but you let a cat get excited, once; you let a cat get to pulling fur with another cat on a shed, nights, and you'll hear grammar that will give you the lockjaw. Ignorant people think it's the *noise* which fighting cats make that is so aggravating, but it ain't so; it's the sickening grammar they use. Now I've never heard a jay use bad grammar but very seldom; and when they do, they are as ashamed as a human; they shut right down and leave.

"You may call a jay a bird. Well, so he is, in a measure — because he's got feathers on him, and don't belong to no church, perhaps; but otherwise he is just as much a human as you be. And I'll tell you for why. A jay's gifts, and instincts, and feelings, and interests, cover the whole ground. A jay hasn't got any more principle than a Congressman. A jay will lie, a jay will steal, a jay will deceive, a jay will betray; and four times out of five, a jay will go back on his solemnest promise. The sacredness of an obligation is a thing which you can't cram into no blue-jay's head. Now on top of all this, there's another thing: a jay can out-swear any gentleman in the mines. You think a cat can swear. Well, a cat can; but you give a blue-jay a subject that calls for his reserve-powers, and where is your cat? Don't talk to *me* — I know too much about this thing. And there's yet another thing: in the one little particular of scolding — just good, clean, out-and-out scolding — a blue-jay can lay over anything, human or divine. Yes, sir, a jay is everything that a man is. A jay can cry, a jay can laugh, a jay can feel shame, a jay can reason and plan and discuss, a jay likes gossip and scandal, a jay has got a sense of humor, a jay knows when he is an ass just as well as you do — maybe better. If a jay ain't human, he better take in his sign, that's all. Now I'm going to tell you a perfectly true fact about some blue-jays.

"When I first begun to understand jay language correctly, there was a little incident happened here. Seven years ago, the last man in this region but me, moved away. There stands his house, — been empty ever since; a log house, with a plank roof — just one big room, and no more; no ceiling — nothing between the rafters and the floor. Well, one Sunday morning I was sitting out here in front of my cabin, with my cat, taking the sun, and looking at the blue hills, and listening to the leaves rustling so lonely in the trees, and thinking of the home away yonder in the States, that I hadn't heard from in thirteen years, when a blue-jay lit on that house, with an acorn in his mouth, and says, 'Hello, I reckon I've struck something.' When he spoke, the acorn dropped out of his mouth and rolled down the roof, of course, but he didn't care; his mind was all on the thing he had struck. It was a knot-hole in the roof. He cocked his head to one side, shut one eye and put the other one to the hole, like a 'possum looking down a jug; then he glanced up with his bright eyes, gave a wink or two with his wings — which signifies gratification, you understand, — and says, 'It looks like a hole, it's located like a hole, — blamed if I don't believe it *is* a hole!'

"Then he cocked his head down and took another look; he glances up perfectly joyful, this time; winks his wings and his tail both, and says, 'O, no, this ain't no fat thing, I reckon! If I ain't in luck! — why it's a perfectly elegant hole!' So he flew down and got that acorn, and fetched it up and dropped it in, and was just tilting his head back, with the heavenliest smile on his face, when all of a sudden he was paralyzed into a listening attitude and that smile faded gradually out of his countenance like a breath off'n a razor, and the queerest look of surprise took its place. Then he says, 'Why, I didn't hear it fall!' He cocked his eye at the hole again, and took a long look; raised up and shook his head; stepped around to the other side of the hole and took another look from that side; shook his head again. He studied a while, then he just went into the *de-tails* — walked round and round the hole and spied into it from every point of the compass. No use. Now he took a thinking attitude on the comb of the roof and scratched the back of his head with his right foot a minute, and finally says, 'Well, it's too many for me, that's certain; must be a mighty long hole; however, I ain't got no time to fool around here, I got to 'tend to business; I reckon it's all right — chance it, anyway.'

"So he flew off and fetched another acorn and dropped it in, and tried to flirt his eye to the hole quick enough to see what become of it, but he was too late. He held his eye there as much as a minute; then he raised up and sighed, and says, 'Consound it, I don't seem to understand this thing, no way; however, I'll tackle her again.' He fetched another acorn, and done his level best to see what become of it, but he couldn't. He says, 'Well, I never struck no such hole as this, before; I'm of the opinion it's a totally new kind of a hole.' Then he begun to get mad. He held in for a spell, walking up and down the comb of the roof and shaking his head and muttering to himself; but his feelings got the upper hand of him, presently, and he broke loose and cussed himself black in the face. I never see a bird take on so about a little thing. When he got through he walks to the hole and looks in again for half a minute; then he says, 'Well, you're a long hole, and a deep hole, and a mighty singular hole altogether — but I've started in to fill you, and I'm d — d if I *don't* fill you, if it takes a hundred years!'

"And with that, away he went. You never

see a bird work so since you was born. He laid into his work like a nigger, and the way he hove acorns into that hole for about two hours and a half was one of the most exciting and astonishing spectacles I ever struck. He never stopped to take a look any more — he just hove 'em in and went for more. Well, at last he could hardly flop his wings, he was so tuckered out. He comes a-drooping down, once more, sweating like an ice-pitcher, drops his acorn in and says, 'Now I guess I've got the bulge on you by this time!' So he bent down for a look. If you'll believe me, when his head come up again he was just pale with rage. He says, 'I've shoveled acorns enough in there to keep the family thirty years, and if I can see a sign of one of 'em I wish I may land in a museum with a belly full of sawdust in two minutes!'

"He just had strength enough to crawl up on to the comb and lean his back agin the chimbly, and then he collected his impressions and begun to free his mind. I see in a second that what I had mistook for profanity in the mines was only just the rudiments, as you may say.

"Another jay was going by, and heard him doing his devotions, and stops to inquire what was up. The sufferer told him the whole circumstance, and says, 'Now yonder's the hole, and if you don't believe me, go and look for yourself.' So this fellow went and looked, and comes back and says, 'How many did you say you put in there?' 'Not less than two tons,' says the sufferer. The other jay went and looked again. He couldn't seem to make it out, so he raised a yell, and three more jays come. They all examined the hole, they all made the sufferer tell it over again, then they all discussed it, and got off as many leather-headed opinions about it as an average crowd of humans could have done.

"They called in more jays; then more and more, till pretty soon this whole region 'peared to have a blue flush about it. There must have been five thousand of them; and such another jawing and disputing and ripping and cussing, you never heard. Every jay in the whole lot put his eye to the hole and delivered a more chuckle-headed opinion about the mystery than the jay that went there before him. They examined the house all over, too. The door was standing half open, and at last one old jay happened to go and light on it and look in. Of course that knocked the mystery galley-west in a second. There lay the acorns, scattered all over the floor. He flopped his wings and raised a whoop. 'Come here!' he says, 'Come here, everybody; hang'd if this fool hasn't been trying to fill up a house with acorns!' They all came a-swooping down like a blue cloud, and as each fellow lit on the door and took a glance, the whole absurdity of the contract that that first jay had tackled hit him home and he fell over backwards suffocating with laughter, and the next jay took his place and done the same.

"Well, sir, they roosted around here on the house-top and the trees for an hour, and guffawed over that thing like human beings. It ain't any use to tell me a blue-jay hasn't got a sense of humor, because I know better. And memory, too. They brought jays here from all over the United States to look down that hole, every summer for three years. Other birds too. And they could all see the point except an owl that come from Nova Scotia to visit the Yo Semite, and he took this thing in on his way back. He said he couldn't see anything funny in it. But then he was a good deal disappointed about Yo Semite, too."

From *Life on the Mississippi*
(1875, 1883)

"Old Times on the Mississippi" appeared in the *Atlantic Monthly* in 1875. Eight years later it became chapters IV–XVII in *Life on the Mississippi*, occupying about one-third of the book. The rest is markedly inferior, save for a few stretches. But the chapters from the *Atlantic* (six of which are reprinted below) constitute, as the official biographer put it, "a memorial seemingly as enduring as the river itself."

Looking back when forty years old, Mark Twain told of his own early experience in the great, booming days of the Mississippi — for him, says Paine, "four marvelous, sunlit years, the glory of which would color all that followed them." They in turn were colored by memory and imagination. He was twenty-two when the adventure began, but gave the impression of being a romantic youth of perhaps seventeen. Mark Twain must have altered much else, if only by omitting the dull and sordid elements of his experience. Yet his account has the general tone and aspect of realistic art.

Here we have his writing at its best — at once vigorous and effortless, plain-spoken and high spirited, with the flash and sparkle of actual life. His humor is no longer that of the showman on the platform. It now seems not only unpremeditated but inevitable; it leaps, like a fish, out of the stream of description and narration. If never solemn he is, however, serious enough: he has obligations to discharge to the Father of Waters and the wonderful old times.

CHAPTER IV

The Boys' Ambition

When I was a boy, there was but one permanent ambition among my comrades in our village [1] on the west bank of the Mississippi River. That was, to be a steamboatman. We had transient ambitions of other sorts, but they were only transient. When a circus came and went, it left us all burning to become clowns; the first negro minstrel show that ever came to our section left us all suffering to try that kind of life; now and then we had a hope that, if we lived and were good, God would permit us to be pirates. These ambitions faded out, each in its turn; but the ambition to be a steamboatman always remained.

Once a day a cheap, gaudy packet arrived upward from St. Louis, and another downward from Keokuk. Before these events, the day was glorious with expectancy; after them, the day was a dead and empty thing. Not only the boys, but the whole village, felt this. After all these years I can picture that old time to myself now, just as it was then: the white town drowsing in the sunshine of a summer's morning; the streets empty, or pretty nearly so; one or two clerks sitting in front of the Water Street stores, with their splint-bottomed chairs tilted back against the walls, chins on breasts, hats slouched over their faces, asleep — with shingle-shavings enough around to show what broke them down; a sow and a litter of pigs loafing along the sidewalk, doing a good business in watermelon rinds and seeds; two or three lonely little freight piles scattered about the "levee"; a pile of "skids" on the slope of the stone-paved wharf, and the fragrant town drunkard asleep in the shadow of them; two or three wood flats at the head of the wharf, but nobody to listen to the peaceful lapping of the wavelets against them; the great Mississippi, the majestic, the magnificent Mississippi, rolling its mile-wide tide along, shining in the sun; the dense forest away on the other side; the "point" above the town, and the "point" below, bounding the river-glimpse and turning it into a sort of sea, and withal a very still and brilliant and lonely one. Presently a film of dark smoke appears above one of those

[1] Hannibal, Missouri. [Author's note.]

remote "points"; instantly a negro drayman, famous for his quick eye and prodigious voice, lifts up the cry, "S-t-e-a-m-boat a-comin'!" and the scene changes! The town drunkard stirs, the clerks wake up, a furious clatter of drays follows, every house and store pours out a human contribution, and all in a twinkling the dead town is alive and moving. Drays, carts, men, boys, all go hurrying from many quarters to a common center, the wharf. Assembled there, the people fasten their eyes upon the coming boat as upon a wonder they are seeing for the first time. And the boat is rather a handsome sight, too. She is long and sharp and trim and pretty; she has two tall, fancy-topped chimneys, with a gilded device of some kind swung between them; a fanciful pilot-house, all glass and "ginger-bread," perched on top of the "texas" deck behind them; the paddle-boxes are gorgeous with a picture or with gilded rays above the boat's name; the boiler-deck, the hurricane-deck, and the texas deck are fenced and ornamented with clean while railings; there is a flag gallantly flying from the jack-staff; the furnace doors are open and the fires glaring bravely; the upper decks are black with passengers; the captain stands by the big bell, calm, imposing, the envy of all; great volumes of the blackest smoke are rolling and tumbling out of the chimneys — a husbanded grandeur created with a bit of pitchpine just before arriving at a town; the crew are grouped on the forecastle; the broad stage is run far out over the port bow, and an envied deck-hand stands picturesquely on the end of it with a coil of rope in his hand; the pent steam is screaming through the gauge-cocks; the captain lifts his hand, a bell rings, the wheels stop; then they turn back, churning the water to foam, and the steamer is at rest. Then such a scramble as there is to get aboard, and to get ashore, and to take in freight and to discharge freight, all at one and the same time; and such a yelling and cursing as the mates facilitate it all with! Ten minutes later the steamer is under way again, with no flag on the jack-staff and no black smoke issuing from the chimneys. After ten more minutes the town is dead again, and the town drunkard asleep by the skids once more.

My father was a justice of the peace, and I supposed he possessed the power of life and death over all men, and could hang anybody that offended him. This was distinction enough for me as a general thing; but the desire to be a steamboatman kept intruding, nevertheless. I first wanted to be a cabin-boy, so that I could come out with a white apron on and shake a table-cloth over the side, where all my old comrades could see me; later I thought I would rather be the deckhand who stood on the end of the stage-plank with the coil of rope in his hand, because he was particularly conspicuous. But these were only day-dreams — they were too heavenly to be contemplated as real possibilities. By and by one of our boys went away. He was not heard of for a long time. At last he turned up as apprentice engineer or "striker" on a steamboat. This thing shook the bottom out of all my Sunday-school teachings. That boy had been notoriously worldly, and I just the reverse; yet he was exalted to this eminence, and I left in obscurity and misery. There was nothing generous about this fellow in his greatness. He would always manage to have a rusty bolt to scrub while his boat tarried at our town, and he would sit on the inside guard and scrub it, where we all could see him and envy him and loathe him. And whenever his boat was laid up he would come home and swell around the town in his blackest and greasiest clothes, so that nobody could help remembering that he was a steamboatman; and he used all sorts of steamboat technicalities in his talk, as if he were so used to them that he forgot common people could not understand them. He would speak of the "labboard" side of a horse in an easy, natural way that would make one wish he was dead. And he was always talking about "St. Looy" like an old citizen; he would refer casually to occasions when he was "coming down Fourth Street," or when he was "passing by the Planter's House," or when there was a fire and he took a turn on the brakes of "the old Big Missouri"; and then he would go on and lie about how many towns the size of ours were burned down there that day. Two or three of the boys had long been persons of consideration among us because they had been to St. Louis once and had a vague general knowledge of its wonders, but the day of their glory was over now. They lapsed into a humble silence, and learned to disappear when the ruthless "cub"-engineer approached. This fellow had money, too, and hair-oil. Also an ignorant silver watch and a showy brass watch-chain. He wore a leather belt and used no suspenders. If ever a youth was cordially admired and hated by his comrades, this one was. No girl could withstand his charms.

He "cut out" every boy in the village. When his boat blew up at last, it diffused a tranquil contentment among us such as we had not known for months. But when he came home the next week, alive, renowned, and appeared in church all battered up and bandaged, a shining hero, stared at and wondered over by everybody, it seemed to us that the partiality of Providence for an undeserving reptile had reached a point where it was open to criticism.

This creature's career could produce but one result, and it speedily followed. Boy after boy managed to get on the river. The minister's son became an engineer. The doctor's and the postmaster's sons became "mud clerks"; the wholesale liquor dealer's son became a barkeeper on a boat; four sons of the chief merchant, and two sons of the county judge, became pilots. Pilot was the grandest position of all. The pilot, even in those days of trivial wages, had a princely salary — from a hundred and fifty to two hundred and fifty dollars a month, and no board to pay. Two months of his wages would pay a preacher's salary for a year. Now some of us were left disconsolate. We could not get on the river — at least our parents would not let us.

So, by and by, I ran away. I said I would never come home again till I was a pilot and could come in glory. But somehow I could not manage it. I went meekly aboard a few of the boats that lay packed together like sardines at the long St. Louis wharf, and humbly inquired for the pilots, but got only a cold shoulder and short words from mates and clerks. I had to make the best of this sort of treatment for the time being, but I had comforting day-dreams of a future when I should be a great and honored pilot, with plenty of money, and could kill some of these mates and clerks and pay for them.

CHAPTER V

I Want to be a Cub-Pilot

Months afterward the hope within me struggled to a reluctant death, and I found myself without an ambition. But I was ashamed to go home. I was in Cincinnati, and I set to work to map out a new career. I had been reading about the recent exploration of the river Amazon by an expedition sent out by our government. It was said that the expedition, owing to difficulties, had not thoroughly explored a part of the country lying about the headwaters, some four thousand miles from the mouth of the river. It was only about fifteen hundred miles from Cincinnati to New Orleans, where I could doubtless get a ship. I had thirty dollars left; I would go and complete the exploration of the Amazon. This was all the thought I gave to the subject. I never was great in matters of detail. I packed my valise, and took passage on an ancient tub called the *Paul Jones*, for New Orleans. For the sum of sixteen dollars I had the scarred and tarnished splendors of "her" main saloon principally to myself, for she was not a creature to attract the eye of wiser travelers.

When we presently got under way and went poking down the broad Ohio, I became a new being, and the subject of my own admiration. I was a traveler! A word never had tasted so good in my mouth before. I had an exultant sense of being bound for mysterious lands and distant climes which I never have felt in so uplifting a degree since. I was in such a glorified condition that all ignoble feelings departed out of me, and I was able to look down and pity the untraveled with a compassion that had hardly a trace of contempt in it. Still, when we stopped at villages and wood-yards, I could not help lolling carelessly upon the railings of the boiler-deck to enjoy the envy of the country boys on the bank. If they did not seem to discover me, I presently sneezed to attract their attention, or moved to a position where they could not help seeing me. And as soon as I knew they saw me I gaped and stretched, and gave other signs of being mightily bored with traveling.

I kept my hat off all the time, and stayed where the wind and the sun could strike me, because I wanted to get the bronzed and weather-beaten look of an old traveler. Before the second day was half gone I experienced a joy which filled me with the purest gratitude; for I saw that the skin had begun to blister and peel off my face and neck. I wished that the boys and girls at home could see me now.

We reached Louisville in time — at least the neighborhood of it. We stuck hard and fast on the rocks in the middle of the river, and lay there four days. I was now beginning to feel a strong sense of being a part of the boat's family, a sort of infant son to the captain and younger brother to the officers. There is no estimating the pride I took in this grandeur, or the affection that began to swell and grow in me for those people. I could not know how the lordly steamboatman scorns that sort of presumption in a mere landsman. I particularly longed to acquire the least trifle of notice from the big stormy mate, and I was on the alert for an opportunity to do him a service to that end. It came at last. The riotous pow-wow of setting a spar was going on down on the forecastle, and I went down there and stood around in the way — or mostly skipping out of it — till the mate suddenly roared a general order for somebody to bring him a capstan bar. I sprang to his side and said: "Tell me where it is — I'll fetch it!"

If a rag-picker had offered to do a diplomatic service for the Emperor of Russia, the monarch could not have been more astounded than the mate was. He even stopped swearing. He stood and stared down at me. It took him ten seconds to scrape his disjointed remains together again. Then he said impressively: "Well, if this don't beat h—l!" and turned to his work with the air of a man who had been confronted with a problem too abstruse for solution.

I crept away, and courted solitude for the rest of the day. I did not go to dinner; I stayed away from supper until everybody else had finished. I did not feel so much like a member of the boat's family now as before. However, my spirits returned, in instalments, as we pursued our way down the river. I was sorry I hated the mate so, because it was not in (young) human nature not to admire him. He was huge and muscular, his face was bearded and whiskered all over; he had a red woman and a blue woman tattooed on his right arm — one on each side of a blue anchor with a red rope to it; and in the matter of profanity he was sublime. When he was getting out cargo at a landing, I was always where I could see and hear. He felt all the majesty of his great position, and made the world feel it, too. When he gave even the simplest order, he discharged it like a blast of lightning, and sent a long, reverberating peal of profanity thundering after it. I could not help contrasting the way in which the average landsman would give an order with the mate's way of doing it. If the landsman should wish the gangplank moved a foot farther forward, he would probably say: "James, or William, one of you push that plank forward, please"; but put the mate in his place, and he would roar out: "Here, now, start that gang-plank for'ard! Lively, now! *What*'re you about? Snatch it! *snatch* it! There! there! Aft again! aft again! Don't you hear me? Dash it to dash! are you going to *sleep* over it! 'Vast heaving. 'Vast heaving, I tell you! Going to heave it clear astern? WHERE're you going with that barrel! *for'ard* with it 'fore I make you swallow it, you dash-dash-dash-*dashed* split between a tired mud-turtle and a crippled hearse-horse!"

I wished I could talk like that.

When the soreness of my adventure with the mate had somewhat worn off, I began timidly to make up to the humblest official connected with the boat — the night watchman. He snubbed my advances at first, but I presently ventured to offer him a new chalk pipe, and that softened him. So he allowed me to sit with him by the big bell on the hurricane-deck, and in time he melted into conversation. He could not well have helped it, I hung with such homage on his words and so plainly showed that I felt honored by his notice. He told me the names of dim capes and shadowy islands as we glided by them in the solemnity of the night, under the winking stars, and by and by got to talking about himself. He seemed over-sentimental for a man whose salary was six dollars a week — or rather he might have seemed so to an older person than I. But I drank in his words hungrily, and with a faith that might have moved mountains if it had been applied judiciously. What was it to me that he was soiled and seedy and fragrant with gin? What was it to me that his grammar was bad, his construction worse, and his profanity so void of art that it was an element of weakness rather than strength in his conversation? He was a wronged man, a man who had seen trouble, and that was enough for me. As he mellowed into his plaintive history his tears dripped upon the lantern in his lap, and I cried, too, from sympathy. He said he was the son of an English nobleman — either an earl or an alderman, he could not remember which, but believed was both; his father, the nobleman, loved him, but his mother hated him from the cradle; and so while he was still a little boy he was sent to "one of them old, ancient colleges" — he couldn't remember which; and by and by his father died and his mother seized the property and "shook" him, as he phrased it. After his mother shook him, members of the nobility with whom he was acquainted used their influence to get him the position of "loblolly-boy in a ship"; and from that point my watchman threw off all trammels of date and locality and branched out into a narrative that bristled all along with incredible adventures; a narrative that was so reeking with bloodshed, and so crammed with hair-breadth escapes and the most engaging and unconscious personal villainies, that I sat speechless, enjoying, shuddering, wondering, worshiping.

It was a sore blight to find out afterward that he was a low, vulgar, ignorant, sentimental, half-witted humbug, an untraveled native of the wilds of Illinois, who had absorbed wildcat literature and appropriated its marvels, until in time he had woven odds and ends of the mess into this yarn, and then gone on telling it to fledglings like me, until he had come to believe it himself.

CHAPTER VI

A Cub-Pilot's Experience

What with lying on the rocks four days at Louisville, and some other delays, the poor old *Paul Jones* fooled away about two weeks in making the voyage from Cincinnati to New Orleans. This gave me a chance to get acquainted with one of the pilots, and he taught me how to steer the boat, and thus made the fascination of river life more potent than ever for me.

It also gave me a chance to get acquainted with a youth who had taken deck passage — more's the pity; for he easily borrowed six dollars of me on a promise to return to the boat and pay it back to me the day after we should arrive. But he probably died or forgot, for he never came. It was doubtless the former, since he had said his parents were wealthy, and he only traveled deck passage because it was cooler.[1]

I soon discovered two things. One was that a vessel would not be likely to sail for the mouth of the Amazon under ten or twelve years; and the other was that the nine or ten dollars still left in my pocket would not suffice for so impossible an exploration as I had planned, even if I could afford to wait for a ship. Therefore it followed that I must contrive a new career. The *Paul Jones* was now bound for St. Louis. I planned a siege against my pilot, and at the end of three hard days he surrendered. He agreed to teach me the Mississippi River from

1 "Deck" passage — *i.e.*, steerage passage. [Author's note.]

New Orleans to St. Louis for five hundred dollars, payable out of the first wages I should receive after graduating. I entered upon the small enterprise of "learning" twelve or thirteen hundred miles of the great Mississippi River with the easy confidence of my time of life. If I had really known what I was about to require of my faculties, I should not have had the courage to begin. I supposed that all a pilot had to do was to keep his boat in the river, and I did not consider that that could be much of a trick, since it was so wide.

The boat backed out from New Orleans at four in the afternoon, and it was "our watch" until eight. Mr. Bixby, my chief, "straightened her up," plowed her along past the sterns of the other boats that lay at the Levee, and then said, "Here, take her; shave those steamships as close as you'd peel an apple." I took the wheel, and my heartbeat fluttered up into the hundreds; for it seemed to me that we were about to scrape the side off every ship in the line, we were so close. I held my breath and began to claw the boat away from the danger; and I had my own opinion of the pilot who had known no better than to get us into such peril, but I was too wise to express it. In half a minute I had a wide margin of safety intervening between the *Paul Jones* and the ships; and within ten seconds more I was set aside in disgrace, and Mr. Bixby was going into danger again and flaying me alive with abuse of my cowardice. I was stung, but I was obliged to admire the easy confidence with which my chief loafed from side to side of his wheel, and trimmed the ships so closely that disaster seemed ceaselessly imminent. When he had cooled a little he told me that the easy water was close ashore and the current outside, and therefore we must hug the bank, up-stream, to get the benefit of the former, and stay well out, down-stream, to take advantage of the latter. In my own mind I resolved to be a downstream pilot and leave the up-streaming to people dead to prudence.

Now and then Mr. Bixby called my attention to certain things. Said he, "This is Six-Mile Point." I assented. It was pleasant enough information, but I could not see the bearing of it. I was not conscious that it was a matter of any interest to me. Another time he said, "This is Nine-Mile Point." Later he said, "This is Twelve-Mile Point." They were all about level with the water's edge; they all looked about alike to me; they were monotonously unpicturesque. I hoped Mr. Bixby would change the subject. But no; he would crowd up around a point, hugging the shore with affection, and then say: "The slack water ends here, abreast this bunch of China trees; now we cross over." So he crossed over. He gave me the wheel once or twice, but I had no luck. I either came near chipping off the edge of a sugar-plantation, or I yawed too far from shore, and so dropped back into disgrace again and got abused.

The watch was ended at last, and we took supper and went to bed. At midnight the glare of a lantern shone in my eyes, and the night watchman said:

"Come, turn out!"

And then he left. I could not understand this extraordinary procedure; so I presently gave up trying to, and dozed off to sleep. Pretty soon the watchman was back again, and this time he was gruff. I was annoyed. I said:

"What do you want to come bothering around here in the middle of the night for? Now, as like as not, I'll not get to sleep again to-night."

The watchman said:

"Well, if this ain't good, I'm blessed."

The "off-watch" was just turning in, and I heard some brutal laughter from them, and such remarks as "Hello, watchman! ain't the new cub turned out yet? He's delicate, likely. Give him some sugar in a rag, and send for the chambermaid to sing 'Rock-a-by Baby,' to him."

About this time Mr. Bixby appeared on the scene. Something like a minute later I was climbing the pilot-house steps with some of my clothes on and the rest in my arms. Mr. Bixby was close behind, commenting. Here was something fresh — this thing of getting up in the middle of the night to go to work. It was a detail in piloting that had never occurred to me at all. I knew that boats ran all night, but somehow I had never happened to reflect that somebody had to get up out of a warm bed to run them. I began to fear that piloting was not quite so romantic as I had imagined it was; there was something very real and worklike about this new phase of it.

It was a rather dingy night, although a fair number of stars were out. The big mate was at the wheel, and he had the old tub pointed at a star and was holding her straight up the middle of the river. The shores on either hand were not much more than half a mile apart, but they seemed wonderfully far away and ever so vague and indistinct. The mate said:

"We've got to land at Jones's plantation, sir."

The vengeful spirit in me exulted. I said to myself, "I wish you joy of your job, Mr. Bixby; you'll have a good time finding Mr. Jones's plantation such a night as this; and I hope you never *will* find it as long as you live."

Mr. Bixby said to the mate:

"Upper end of the plantation, or the lower?"

"Upper."

"I can't do it. The stumps there are out of water at this stage. It's no great distance to the lower, and you'll have to get along with that."

"All right, sir. If Jones don't like it, he'll have to lump it, I reckon."

And then the mate left. My exultation began to cool and my wonder to come up. Here was a man who not only proposed to find this plantation on such a night, but to find either end of it you preferred. I dreadfully wanted to ask a question, but I was carrying about as many short answers as my cargo-room would admit of, so I held my peace. All I desired to ask Mr. Bixby was the simple question whether he was ass enough to really imagine he was going to find that plantation on a night when all plantations were exactly alike and all of the same color. But I held in. I used to have fine inspirations of prudence in those days.

Mr. Bixby made for the shore and soon was scraping it, just the same as if it had been daylight. And not only that, but singing:

"Father in heaven, the day is declining," etc.

It seemed to me that I had put my life in the keeping of a peculiarly reckless outcast. Presently he turned on me and said:

"What's the name of the first point above New Orleans?"

I was gratified to be able to answer promptly, and I did. I said I didn't know.

"Don't *know?*"

This manner jolted me. I was down at the foot again, in a moment. But I had to say just what I had said before.

"Well, you're a smart one!" said Mr. Bixby. "What's the name of the *next* point?"

Once more I didn't know.

"Well, this beats anything. Tell me the name of *any* point or place I told you."

I studied awhile and decided that I couldn't.

"Look here! What do you start out from, above Twelve-Mile Point, to cross over?"

"I — I — don't know."

"You — you — don't know?" mimicking my drawling manner of speech. "What *do* you know?"

"I — I — nothing, for certain."

"By the great Cæsar's ghost, I believe you! You're the stupidest dunderhead I ever saw or ever heard of, so help me Moses! The idea of *you* being a pilot — *you!* Why, you don't know enough to pilot a cow down a lane."

Oh, but his wrath was up! He was a nervous man, and he shuffled from one side of his wheel to the other as if the floor was hot. He would boil awhile to himself, and then overflow and scald me again.

"Look here! What do you suppose I told you the names of those points for?"

I tremblingly considered a moment, and then the devil of temptation provoked me to say:

"Well to — to — be entertaining, I thought."

This was a red rag to the bull. He raged and stormed so (he was crossing the river at the time) that I judged it made him blind, because he ran over the steering-oar of a trading-scow. Of course the traders sent up a volley of red-hot profanity. Never was a man so grateful as Mr. Bixby was; because he was brimful, and here were subjects who could *talk back*. He threw open a window, thrust his head out, and such an irruption followed as I never had heard before. The fainter and farther away the scow-men's curses drifted, the higher Mr. Bixby lifted his voice and the weightier his adjectives grew. When he closed the window he was empty. You could have drawn a seine through his system and not caught curses enough to disturb your mother with. Presently he said to me in the gentlest way:

"My boy, you must get a little memorandum-book; and every time I tell you a thing, put it down right away. There's only one way to be a pilot, and that is to get this entire river by heart. You have to know it just like A B C."

That was a dismal revelation to me; for my memory was never loaded with anything but blank cartridges. However, I did not feel discouraged long. I judged that it was best to make some allowance, for doubtless Mr. Bixby was "stretching." Presently he pulled a rope and struck a few strokes on the big bell. The stars were all gone now, and the night was as black as ink. I could hear the wheels churn along the bank, but I was not entirely certain that I could see the shore. The voice of the invisible watchman called up from the hurricane-deck:

"What's this, sir?"

"Jones's plantation."

I said to myself, "I wish I might venture to offer a small bet that it isn't." But I did not chirp. I only waited to see. Mr. Bixby handled the engine-bells, and in due time the boat's nose came to the land, a torch glowed from the forecastle, a man skipped ashore, a darkey's voice on the bank said: "Gimme de k'yarpet-bag, Mass' Jones," and the next moment we were standing up the river again, all serene. I reflected deeply awhile, and then said — but not aloud — "Well, the finding of that plantation was the luckiest accident that ever happened; but it couldn't happen again in a hundred years." And I fully believed it *was* an accident, too.

By the time we had gone seven or eight hundred miles up the river, I had learned to be a tolerably plucky up-stream steersman, in daylight; and before we reached St. Louis I had made a trifle of progress in night work, but only a trifle. I had a note-book that fairly bristled with the names of towns, "points," bars, islands, bends, reaches, etc.; but the information was to be found only in the note-book — none of it was in my head. It made my heart ache to think I had only got half of the river set down; for as our watch was four hours off and four hours on, day and night, there was a long four-hour gap in my book for every time I had slept since the voyage began.

My chief was presently hired to go on a big New Orleans boat, and I packed my satchel and went with him. She was a grand affair. When I stood in her pilot-house I was so far above the water that I seemed perched on a mountain; and her decks stretched so far away, fore and aft, below me, that I wondered how I could ever have considered the little *Paul Jones* a large craft. There were other differences, too. The *Paul Jones*'s pilot-house was a cheap, dingy, battered rattle trap, cramped for room; but here was a sumptuous glass temple; room enough to have a dance in; showy red and gold window-curtains; an imposing sofa; leather cushions and a back to the high bench where visiting pilots sit, to spin yarns and "look at the river"; bright, fanciful "cuspidores," instead of a broad wooden box filled with sawdust; nice new oilcloth on the floor; a hospitable big stove for winter; a wheel as high as my head, costly with inlaid work; a wire tiller-rope; bright brass knobs for the bells; and a tidy, white-aproned, black "texas-tender," to bring up tarts and ices and coffee during mid-watch, day and night. Now this was "something like"; and so I began to take heart once more to believe that piloting was a romantic sort of occupation after all. The moment we were under way I began to prowl about the great steamer and fill myself with joy. She was as clean and as dainty as a drawing-room; when I looked down her long, gilded saloon, it was like gazing through a splendid tunnel; she had an oil-picture, by some gifted sign-painter, on every stateroom door; she glittered with no end of prism-fringed chandeliers; the clerk's office was elegant, the bar was marvelous, and the bar-keeper had been barbered and upholstered at incredible cost. The boiler-deck (*i.e.*, the second story of the boat, so to speak) was as spacious as a church, it seemed to me; so with the forecastle; and there was no pitiful handful of deck-hands, firemen, and roustabouts down there, but a whole battalion of men. The fires were fiercely glaring from a long row of furnaces, and over them were eight huge boilers! This was unutterable pomp. The mighty engines — but enough of this. I had never felt so fine before. And when I found that the regiment of natty servants respectfully "sir'd" me, my satisfaction was complete.

CHAPTER VII

A Daring Deed

When I returned to the pilot-house St. Louis was gone, and I was lost. Here was a piece of river which was all down in my book, but I could make neither head nor tail of it: you understand, it was turned around. I had seen it when coming up-stream, but I had never faced about to see how it looked when it was behind me. My heart broke again, for it was plain that I had got to learn this troublesome river *both ways*.

The pilot-house was full of pilots, going down to "look at the river." What is called the "upper river" (the two hundred miles between St. Louis and Cairo, where the Ohio comes in) was low; and the Mississippi changes its channel so constantly that the pilots used to always find it necessary to run down to Cairo to take a fresh look, when their boats were to lie in port a week; that is, when the water was at a low stage. A deal of this "looking at the river" was done by poor fellows who seldom had a berth, and whose only hope of getting one lay in their being always freshly posted and therefore ready to drop into the shoes of some reputable pilot, for a single trip, on account of such pilot's sudden illness, or some other necessity. And a good many of them constantly ran up and down inspecting the river, not because they ever really hoped to get a berth, but because (they being guests of the boat) it was cheaper to "look at the river" than stay ashore and pay board. In time these fellows grew dainty in their tastes, and only infested boats that had an established reputation for setting good tables. All visiting pilots were useful, for they were always ready and willing, winter or summer, night or day, to go out in the yawl and help buoy the channel or assist the boat's pilots in any way they could. They were likewise welcomed because all pilots are tireless talkers, when gathered together, and as they talk only about the river they are always understood and are always interesting. Your true pilot cares nothing about anything on earth but the river, and his pride in his occupation surpasses the pride of kings.

We had a fine company of these river inspectors along this trip. There were eight or ten, and there was abundance of room for them in our great pilot-house. Two or three of them wore polished silk hats, elaborate shirt-fronts, diamond breastpins, kid gloves, and patent-leather boots. They were choice in their English, and bore themselves with a dignity proper to men of solid means and prodigious reputation as pilots. The others were more or less loosely clad, and wore upon their heads tall felt cones that were suggestive of the days of the Commonwealth.

I was a cipher in this august company, and felt subdued, not to say torpid. I was not even of sufficient consequence to assist at the wheel when it was necesary to put the tiller hard down in a hurry; the guest that stood nearest did that when occasion required — and this was pretty much all the time, because of the crookedness of the channel and the scant water. I stood in a corner; and the talk I listened to took the hope all out of me. One visitor said to another:

"Jim, how did you run Plum Point, coming up?"

"It was in the night, there, and I ran it the way one of the boys on the *Diana* told me; started out about fifty yards above the woodpile on the false point, and held on the cabin under Plum Point till I raised the reef — quarter less twain — then straightened up for the middle bar till I got well abreast the old one-limbed cottonwood in the bend, then got my stern on the cottonwood, and head on the low place above the point, and came through a-booming — nine and a half."

"Pretty square crossing, ain't it?"

"Yes, but the upper bar's working down fast."

Another pilot spoke up and said:

"I had better water than that, and ran it lower down; started out from the false point — marked twain — raised the second reef abreast the big snag in the bend, and had quarter less twain."

One of the gorgeous ones remarked:

"I don't want to find fault with your leadsmen, but that's a good deal of water for Plum Point, it seems to me."

There was an approving nod all around as this quiet snub dropped on the boaster and "settled" him. And so they went on talk-talk-talking. Meantime, the thing that was running in my mind was, "Now, if my ears hear aright, I have not only to get the names of all the towns and islands and bends, and so on, by heart, but I must even get up a warm personal acquaintanceship with every old snag and one-limbed cottonwood and obscure wood-pile that ornaments the banks of this river for twelve hundred miles; and more than that, I must actually know where these things are in the dark, unless these guests are gifted with eyes that can pierce through two miles of solid blackness. I wish the piloting business was in Jericho and I had never thought of it."

At dusk Mr. Bixby tapped the big bell three times (the signal to land), and the captain emerged from his drawing-room in the forward end of the "texas," and looked up inquiringly. Mr. Bixby said:

"We will lay up here all night, captain."

"Very well, sir."

That was all. The boat came to shore and was tied up for the night. It seemed to me a fine thing that the pilot could do as he pleased, without asking so grand a captain's permission. I took my supper and went immediately to bed, discouraged by my day's observations and experiences. My late voyage's note-booking was but a confusion of meaningless names. It had tangled me all up in a knot every time I had looked at it in the daytime. I now hoped for respite in sleep; but no, it reveled all through my head till sunrise again, a frantic and tireless nightmare.

Next morning I felt pretty rusty and low-spirited. We went booming along, taking a good many chances, for we were anxious to "get out of the river" (as getting out to Cairo was called) before night should overtake us. But Mr. Bixby's partner, the other pilot, presently grounded the boat, and we lost so much time getting her off that it was plain the darkness would overtake us a good long way above the mouth. This was a great misfortune, especially to certain of our visiting pilots, whose boats would have to wait for their return, no matter how long that might be. It sobered the pilot-house talk a good deal. Coming up-stream, pilots did not mind low water or any kind of darkness; nothing stopped them but fog. But down-stream work was different; a boat was too nearly helpless, with a stiff current pushing behind her; so it was not customary to run down-stream at night in low water.

There seemed to be one small hope, however: if we could get through the intricate and dangerous Hat Island crossing before night, we could venture the rest, for we would have plainer sailing and better water. But it would be insanity to attempt Hat Island at night. So there was a deal of looking at watches all the rest of the day, and a constant ciphering upon the speed we were making; Hat Island was the eternal subject; sometimes hope was high and sometimes we were delayed in a bad crossing, and down it went again. For hours all hands lay under the burden of this suppressed excitement; it was even communicated to me, and I got to feeling so solicitous about Hat Island, and under such an awful pressure of responsibility, that I wished I might have five minutes on shore to draw a good, full, relieving breath, and start over again. We were standing no regular watches. Each of our pilots ran such portions of the river as he had run when coming up-stream, because of his greater familiarity with it; but both remained in the pilot-house constantly.

An hour before sunset Mr. Bixby took the wheel, and Mr. W. stepped aside. For the next thirty minutes every man held his watch in his hand and was restless, silent, and uneasy. At last somebody said, with a doomful sigh:

"Well, yonder's Hat Island — and we can't make it."

All the watches closed with a snap, everybody sighed and muttered something about its being "too bad, too bad — ah, if we could *only* have got here half an hour sooner!" and the place was thick with the atmosphere of disappointment. Some started to go out, but loitered, hearing no bell-tap to land. The sun dipped behind the horizon, the boat went on. Inquiring looks passed from one guest to another; and one who had his hand on the door-knob and had turned it, waited, then presently took away his hand and let the knob turn back again. We bore steadily down the bend. More looks were exchanged and nods of surprised admiration — but no words. Insensibly the men drew together behind Mr. Bixby, as the sky darkened and one or two dim stars came out. The dead silence and sense of waiting became oppressive. Mr. Bixby pulled the cord, and two deep, mellow notes from the big bell floated off on the night. Then a pause, and one more note was struck. The watchman's voice followed, from the hurricane-deck:

"Labboard lead, there! Stabbord lead!"

The cries of the leadsmen began to rise out of the distance, and were gruffly repeated by the word-passers on the hurricane-deck.

"M-a-r-k three! M-a-r-k three! Quarter-less-three! Half twain! Quarter twain! M-a-r-k twain! Quarter-less —— "

Mr. Bixby pulled two bell-ropes, and was answered by faint jinglings far below in the engine-room, and our speed slackened. The steam began to whistle through the gauge-cocks. The cries of the leadsmen went on — and it is a weird sound, always, in the night. Every pilot in the lot was watching now, with fixed eye, and talking under his breath. Nobody was calm and easy but Mr. Bixby. He would put his wheel down and stand on a spoke, and as the steamer swung into her (to me) utterly invisible marks — for we seemed to be in the midst of a wide and gloomy sea — he would meet and fasten her there. Out of the murmur of half-audible talk, one caught a coherent sentence now and then — such as:

"There; she's over the first reef all right!"

After a pause, another subdued voice:

"Her stern's coming down just *exactly* right, by *George!*"

"Now she's in the marks; over she goes!"

Somebody else muttered:

"Oh, it was done beautiful — *beautiful!*"

Now the engines were stopped altogether, and we drifted with the current. Not that I could see the boat drift, for I could not, the stars being all gone by this time. This drifting was the dismalest work; it held one's heart still. Presently I discovered a blacker gloom than that which surrounded us. It was the head of the island. We were closing right down upon it. We entered its deeper shadow, and so imminent seemed the peril that I was likely to suffocate; and I had the strongest impulse to do *something*, anything, to save the vessel. But still Mr. Bixby stood by his wheel, silent, intent as a cat, and all the pilots stood shoulder to shoulder at his back.

"She'll not make it!" somebody whispered.

The water grew shoaler and shoaler, by the leadsman's cries, till it was down to:

"Eight-and-a-half! E-i-g-h-t feet! E-i-g-h-t feet! Seven-and —— "

Mr. Bixby said warningly through his speaking-tube to the engineer:

"Stand by, now!"

"Ay, ay, sir!"

"Seven-and-a-half! Seven feet! Six-and —— "

We touched bottom! Instantly Mr. Bixby set a lot of bells ringing, shouted through the tube, "*Now*, let her have it — every ounce you've got!" then to his partner, "Put her hard down! snatch her! snatch her!" The boat rasped and ground her way through the sand, hung upon the apex of disaster a single tremendous instant, and then over she went And such a shout as went up at Mr. Bixby's back never loosened the roof of a pilot-house before!

There was no more trouble after that. Mr. Bixby was a hero that night; and it was some little time, too, before his exploit ceased to be talked about by river-men.

Fully to realize the marvelous precision required in laying the great steamer in her marks in that murky waste water, one should know that not only must she pick her intricate way through snags and blind reefs, and then shave the head of the island so closely as to brush the overhanging foliage with her stern, but at one place she must pass almost within arm's reach of a sunken and invisible wreck that would snatch the hull timbers from under her if she should strike it, and destroy a quarter of a million dollars' worth of steamboat and cargo in five minutes, and maybe a hundred and fifty human lives into the bargain.

The last remark I heard that night was a compliment to Mr. Bixby, uttered in soliloquy and with unction by one of our guests. He said:

"By the Shadow of Death, but he's a lightning pilot!"

Chapter VIII

Perplexing Lessons

At the end of what seemed a tedious while, I had managed to pack my head full of islands, towns, bars, "points," and bends; and a curiously inanimate mass of lumber it was, too. However, inasmuch as I could shut my eyes and reel off a good long string of these names without leaving out more than ten miles of river in every fifty, I began to feel that I could take a boat down to New Orleans if I could make her skip those little gaps. But of course my complacency could hardly get start enough to lift my nose a trifle into the air, before Mr. Bixby would think of something to fetch it down again. One day he turned on me suddenly with this settler:

"What is the shape of Walnut Bend?"

He might as well have asked me my grandmother's opinion of protoplasm. I reflected respectfully, and then said I didn't know it had any particular shape. My gun-powdery chief went off with a bang, of course, and then went on loading and firing until he was out of adjectives.

I had learned long ago that he only carried just so many rounds of ammunition, and was sure to subside into a very placable and even remorseful old smoothbore as soon as they were all gone. That word "old" is merely affectionate; he was not more than thirty-four. I waited. By and by he said:

"My boy, you've got to know the *shape* of the river perfectly. It is all there is left to steer by on a very dark night. Everything else is blotted out and gone. But mind you, it hasn't the same shape in the night that it has in the daytime."

"How on earth am I ever going to learn it, then?"

"How do you follow a hall at home in the dark? Because you know the shape of it. You can't see it."

"Do you mean to say that I've got to know all the million trifling variations of shape in the banks of this interminable river as well as I know the shape of the front hall at home?"

"On my honor, you've got to know them *better* than any man ever did know the shapes of the halls in his own house."

"I wish I was dead!"

"Now I don't want to discourage you, but —"

"Well, pile it on me; I might as well have it now as another time."

"You see, this has got to be learned; there isn't any getting around it. A clear starlight night throws such heavy shadows that, if you didn't know the shape of a shore perfectly, you would claw away from every bunch of timber, because you would take the black shadow of it for a solid cape; and you see you would be getting scared to death every fifteen minutes by the watch. You would be fifty yards from shore all the time when you ought to be within fifty feet of it. You can't see a snag in one of those shadows, but you know exactly where it is, and the shape of the river tells you when you are coming to it. Then there's your pitch-dark night; the river is a very different shape on a pitch-dark night from what it is on a starlight night. All shores seem to be straight lines, then, and mighty dim ones, too; and you'd *run* them for straight lines, only you know better. You boldly drive your boat right into what seems to be a solid, straight wall (you knowing very well that in reality there is a curve there), and that wall falls back and makes way for you. Then there's your gray mist. You take a night when there's one of these grisly, drizzly, gray mists, and then there isn't *any* particular shape to a shore. A gray mist would tangle the head of the oldest man that ever lived. Well, then, different kinds of *moonlight* change the shape of the river in different ways. You see — "

"Oh, don't say any more, please! Have I got to learn the shape of the river according to all these five hundred thousand different ways? If I tried to carry all that cargo in my head it would make me stoop-shouldered."

"No! you only learn *the* shape of the river; and you learn it with such absolute certainty that you can always steer by the shape that's *in your head,* and never mind the one that's before your eyes."

"Very well, I'll try it; but, after I have learned it, can I depend on it? Will it keep the same form and not go fooling around?"

Before Mr. Bixby could answer, Mr. W. came in to take the watch, and he said:

"Bixby, you'll have to look out for President's Island, and all that country clear away up above the Old Hen and Chickens. The banks are caving and the shape of the shores changing like everything. Why, you wouldn't know the point above 40. You can go up inside the old sycamore snag, now." [1]

So that question was answered. Here were leagues of shore changing shape. My spirits were down in the mud again. Two things seemed pretty apparent to me. One was, that in order to be a pilot a man had got to learn more than any one man ought to be allowed to know; and the other was, that he must learn it all over again in a different way every twenty-four hours.

That night we had the watch until twelve. Now it was an ancient river custom for the two pilots to chat a bit when the watch changed. While the relieving pilot put on his gloves and lit his cigar, his partner, the retiring pilot, would say something like this:

"I judge the upper bar is making down a little at Hale's Point; had quarter twain with the lower lead and mark twain [2] with the other."

"Yes, I thought it was making down a little, last trip. Meet any boats?"

"Met one abreast the head of 21, but she was away over hugging the bar, and I couldn't make her out entirely. I took her for the *Sunny South* — hadn't any skylights forward of the chimneys."

And so on. And as the relieving pilot took the wheel his partner [3] would mention that we were in such-and-such a bend, and say we were abreast of such-and-such a man's woodyard or plantation. This was courtesy; I supposed it was *necessity*. But Mr. W. came on watch full twelve minutes late on this particular night — a tremendous breach of etiquette; in fact, it is the unpardonable sin among pilots. So Mr. Bixby gave him no greeting whatever, but simply surrendered the wheel and marched out of the pilot-house without a word. I was appalled; it was a villainous night for blackness, we were in a particularly wide and blind part of the river, where there was no shape or sub-

[1] It may not be necessary, but still it can do no harm to explain that "inside" means between the snag and the shore. [Author's note.]

[2] Two fathoms. Quarter twain is 2¼ fathoms, 13½ feet. Mark three is three fathoms. [Author's note.]

[3] "Partner" is technical for "the other pilot." [Author's note.]

stance to anything, and it seemed incredible that Mr. Bixby should have left that poor fellow to kill the boat, trying to find out where he was. But I resolved that I would stand by him anyway. He should find that he was not wholly friendless. So I stood around, and waited to be asked where we were. But Mr. W. plunged on serenely through the solid firmament of black cats that stood for an atmosphere, and never opened his mouth. "Here is a proud devil!" thought I; "here is a limb of Satan that would rather send us all to destruction than put himself under obligations to me, because I am not yet one of the salt of the earth and privileged to snub captains and lord it over everything dead and alive in a steamboat." I presently climbed up on the bench; I did not think it was safe to go to sleep while this lunatic was on watch.

However, I must have gone to sleep in the course of time, because the next thing I was aware of was the fact that day was breaking, Mr. W. gone, and Mr. Bixby at the wheel again. So it was four o'clock and all well — but me; I felt like a skinful of dry bones, and all of them trying to ache at once.

Mr. Bixby asked me what I had stayed up there for. I confessed that it was to do Mr. W. a benevolence — tell him where he was. It took five minutes for the entire preposterousness of the thing to filter into Mr. Bixby's system, and then I judge it filled him nearly up to the chin; because he paid me a compliment — and not much of a one either. He said:

"Well, taking you by and large, you do seem to be more different kinds of an ass than any creature I ever saw before. What did you suppose he wanted to know for?"

I said I thought it might be a convenience to him.

"Convenience! D——nation! Didn't I tell you that a man's got to know the river in the night the same as he'd know his own front hall?"

"Well, I can follow the front hall in the dark if I know it *is* the front hall; but suppose you set me down in the middle of it in the dark and not tell me which hall it is; how am *I* to know?"

"Well, you've *got* to, on the river!"

"All right. Then I'm glad I never said anything to Mr. W."

"I should say so! Why, he'd have slammed you through the window and utterly ruined a hundred dollars' worth of windowsash and stuff."

I was glad this damage had been saved, for it would have made me unpopular with the owners. They always hated anybody who had the name of being careless and injuring things.

I went to work now to learn the shape of the river; and of all the eluding and ungraspable objects that ever I tried to get mind or hands on, that was the chief. I would fasten my eyes upon a sharp, wooded point that projected far into the river some miles ahead of me, and go to laboriously photographing its shape upon my brain; and just as I was beginning to succeed to my satisfaction, we would draw up toward it and the exasperating thing would begin to melt away and fold back into the bank! If there had been a conspicuous dead tree standing upon the very point of the cape, I would find that tree inconspicuously merged into the general forest, and occupying the middle of a straight shore, when I got abreast of it! No prominent hill would stick to its shape long enough for me to make up my mind what its form really was, but it was as dissolving and changeful as if it had been a mountain of butter in the hottest corner of the tropics. Nothing ever had the same shape when I was coming down-stream that it had borne when I went up. I mentioned these little difficulties to Mr. Bixby. He said:

"That's the very main virtue of the thing. If the shapes didn't change every three seconds they wouldn't be of any use. Take this place where we are now, for instance. As long as that hill over yonder is only one hill, I can boom right along the way I'm going; but the moment it splits at the top and forms a V, I know I've got to scratch to starboard in a hurry, or I'll bang this boat's brains out against a rock; and then the moment one of the prongs of the V swings behind the other, I've got to waltz to larboard again, or I'll have a misunderstanding with a snag that would snatch the keelson out of this steamboat as neatly as if it were a sliver in your hand. If that hill didn't change its shape on bad nights there would be an awful steamboat graveyard around here inside of a year."

It was plain that I had got to learn the shape of the river in all the different ways that could be thought of — upside down, wrong end first, inside out, fore-and-aft, and "thort-ships" — and then know what to do on gray nights when it hadn't any shape at all. So I set about it. In the course of time I began to get the best of this knotty lesson, and my self-complacency moved to the front once more. Mr. Bixby was all fixed, and ready to start it to the rear again. He opened on me after this fashion:

"How much water did we have in the middle crossing at Hole-in-the-Wall, trip before last?"

I considered this an outrage. I said:

"Every trip, down and up, the leadsmen are singing through that tangled place for three-quarters of an hour on a stretch. How do you reckon I can remember such a mess as that?"

"My boy, you've got to remember it. You've got to remember the exact spot and the exact marks the boat lay in when we had the shoalest water, in every one of the five hundred shoal places between St. Louis and New Orleans; and you mustn't get the shoal soundings and marks of one trip mixed up with the shoal soundings and marks of another, either, for they're not often twice alike. You must keep them separate."

When I came to myself again, I said:

"When I get so that I can do that, I'll be able to raise the dead, and then I won't have to pilot a steamboat to make a living. I want to retire from this business. I want a slush bucket and a brush; I'm only fit for a roustabout. I haven't got brains enough to be a pilot; and if I had I wouldn't have strength enough to carry them around, unless I went on crutches."

"Now drop that! When I say I'll learn [1] a man the river, I mean it. And you can depend on it, I'll learn him or kill him."

CHAPTER IX

Continued Perplexities

THERE was no use in arguing with a person like this. I promptly put such a strain on my memory that by and by even the shoal water and the countless crossing-marks began to stay with me. But the result was just the same. I never could more than get one knotty thing learned before another presented itself. Now I had often seen pilots gazing at the water and pretending to read it as if it were a book; but it was a book that told me nothing. A time came at last, however, when Mr. Bixby seemed to think me far enough advanced to bear a lesson on water-reading. So he began:

"Do you see that long, slanting line on the

[1] "Teach" is not in the river vocabulary. [Author's note.]

face of the water? Now, that's a reef. Moreover, it's a bluff reef. There is a solid sand-bar under it that is nearly as straight up and down as the side of a house. There is plenty of water close up to it, but mighty little on top of it. If you were to hit it you would knock the boat's brains out. Do you see where the line fringes out at the upper end and begins to fade away?"

"Yes, sir."

"Well, that is a low place; that is the head of the reef. You can climb over there, and not hurt anything. Cross over, now, and follow along close under the reef — easy water there — not much current."

I followed the reef along till I approached the fringed end. Then Mr. Bixby said:

"Now get ready. Wait till I give the word. She won't want to mount the reef; a boat hates shoal water. Stand by — wait — *wait* — keep her well in hand. *Now* cramp her down! Snatch her! snatch her!"

He seized the other side of the wheel and helped to spin it around until it was hard down, and then we held it so. The boat resisted, and refused to answer for a while, and next she came surging to starboard, mounted the reef, and sent a long, angry ridge of water foaming away from her bows.

"Now watch her; watch her like a cat, or she'll get away from you. When she fights strong and the tiller slips a little, in a jerky, greasy sort of way, let up on her a trifle; it is the way she tells you at night that the water is too shoal; but keep edging her up, little by little, toward the point. You are well up on the bar now; there is a bar under every point, because the water that comes down around it forms an eddy and allows the sediment to sink. Do you see those fine lines on the face of the water that branch out like the ribs of a fan? Well, those are little reefs; you want to just miss the ends of them, but run them pretty close. Now look out — look out! Don't you crowd that slick, greasy-looking place; there ain't nine feet there; she won't stand it. She begins to smell it; look sharp, I tell you! Oh, blazes, there you go! Stop the starboard wheel! Quick! Ship up to back! Set her back!"

The engine bells jingled and the engines answered promptly, shooting white columns of steam far aloft out of the 'scape-pipes, but it was too late. The boat had "smelt" the bar in good earnest; the foamy ridges that radiated from her bows suddenly disappeared, a great dead swell came rolling forward, and swept ahead of her, she careened far over to larboard, and went tearing away toward the shore as if she were about scared to death. We were a good mile from where we ought to have been when we finally got the upper hand of her again.

During the afternoon watch the next day, Mr. Bixby asked me if I knew how to run the next few miles. I said:

"Go inside the first snag above the point, outside the next one, start out from the lower end of Higgins's woodyard, make a square crossing, and — "

"That's all right. I'll be back before you close up on the next point."

But he wasn't. He was still below when I rounded it and entered upon a piece of the river which I had some misgivings about. I did not know that he was hiding behind a chimney to see how I would perform. I went gaily along, getting prouder and prouder, for he had never left the boat in my sole charge such a length of time before. I even got to "setting" her and letting the wheel go entirely, while I vaingloriously turned my back and inspected the stern marks and hummed a tune, a sort of easy indifference which I had prodigiously admired in Bixby and other great pilots. Once I inspected rather long, and when I faced to the front again my heart flew into my mouth so suddenly that if I hadn't clapped my teeth together I should have lost it. One of those frightful bluff reefs was stretching its deadly length right across our bows! My head was gone in a moment; I did not know which end I stood on; I gasped and could not get my breath; I spun the wheel down with such rapidity that it wove itself together like a spider's web; the boat answered and turned square away from the reef, but the reef followed her! I fled, but still it followed, still it kept — right across my bows! I never looked to see where I was going, I only fled. The awful crash was imminent. Why didn't that villain come? If I committed the crime of ringing a bell I might get thrown overboard. But better that than kill the boat. So in blind desperation, I started such a rattling "shivaree" down below as never had astounded an engineer in this world before, I fancy. Amidst the frenzy of the bells the engines began to back and fill in a curious way, and my reason forsook its throne — we were about to crash into the woods on the other side of the river. Just then Mr. Bixby stepped calmly into view

on the hurricane-deck. My soul went out to him in gratitude. My distress vanished; I would have felt safe on the brink of Niagara with Mr. Bixby on the hurricane-deck. He blandly and sweetly took his toothpick out of his mouth between his fingers, as if it were a cigar — we were just in the act of climbing an overhanging big tree, and the passengers were scudding astern like rats — and lifted up these commands to me ever so gently:

"Stop the starboard! Stop the larboard! Set her back on both!"

The boat hesitated, halted, pressed her nose among the boughs a critical instant, then reluctantly began to back away.

"Stop the larboard! Come ahead on it! Stop the starboard! Come ahead on it! Point her for the bar!"

I sailed away as serenely as a summer's morning. Mr. Bixby came in and said, with mock simplicity:

"When you have a hail, my boy, you ought to tap the big bell three times before you land, so that the engineers can get ready."

I blushed under the sarcasm, and said I hadn't had any hail.

"Ah! Then it was for wood, I suppose. The officer of the watch will tell you when he wants to wood up."

I went on consuming, and said I wasn't after wood.

"Indeed? Why, what could you want over here in the bend, then? Did you ever know of a boat following a bend up-stream at this stage of the river?"

"No, sir — and I wasn't trying to follow it. I was getting away from a bluff reef."

"No, it wasn't a bluff reef; there isn't one within three miles of where you were."

"But I saw it. It was as bluff as that one yonder."

"Just about. Run over it!"

"Do you give it as an order?"

"Yes. Run over it!"

"If I don't, I wish I may die."

"All right; I am taking the responsibility."

I was just as anxious to kill the boat, now, as I had been to save it before. I impressed my orders upon my memory, to be used at the inquest, and made a straight break for the reef. As it disappeared under our bows I held my breath; but we slid over it like oil.

"Now, don't you see the difference? It wasn't anything but a *wind* reef. The wind does that."

"So I see. But it is exactly like a bluff reef. How am I ever going to tell them apart?"

"I can't tell you. It is an instinct. By and by you will just naturally *know* one from the other, but you never will be able to explain why or how you know them apart."

It turned out to be true. The face of the water, in time, became a wonderful book — a book that was a dead language to the uneducated passenger, but which told its mind to me without reserve, delivering its most cherished secrets as clearly as if it uttered them with a voice. And it was not a book to be read once and thrown aside, for it had a new story to tell every day. Throughout the long twelve hundred miles there was never a page that was void of interest, never one that you could leave unread without loss, never one that you would want to skip, thinking you could find higher enjoyment in some other thing. There never was so wonderful a book written by man; never one whose interest was so absorbing, so unflagging, so sparklingly renewed with every reperusal. The passenger who could not read it was charmed with a peculiar sort of faint dimple on its surface (on the rare occasions when he did not overlook it altogether); but to the pilot that was an *italicized* passage; indeed, it was more than that, it was a legend of the largest capitals, with a string of shouting exclamation-points at the end of it, for it meant that a wreck or a rock was buried there that could tear the life out of the strongest vessel that ever floated. It is the faintest and simplest expression the water ever makes, and the most hideous to a pilot's eye. In truth, the passenger who could not read this book saw nothing but all manner of pretty pictures in it, painted by the sun and shaded by the clouds, whereas to the trained eye these were not pictures at all, but the grimmest and most dead-earnest of reading-matter.

Now when I had mastered the language of this water, and had come to know every trifling feature that bordered the great river as familiarly as I knew the letters of the alphabet, I had made a valuable acquisition. But I had lost something, too. I had lost something which could never be restored to me while I lived. All the grace, the beauty, the poetry, had gone out of the majestic river! I still kept in mind a certain wonderful sunset which I witnessed when steamboating was new to me. A broad expanse of the river was turned to blood; in the middle distance the red hue brightened into gold, through which a solitary log came floating, black and conspicuous; in one place a long, slanting mark lay sparkling upon the water; in another the surface was broken by boiling, tumbling rings, that were as many-tinted as an opal; where the ruddy flush was faintest, was a smooth spot that was covered with graceful circles and radiating lines, ever so delicately traced; the shore on our left was densely wooded, and the somber shadow that fell from this forest was broken in one place by a long, ruffled trail that shone like silver; and high above the forest wall a clean-stemmed dead tree waved a single leafy bough that glowed like a flame in the unobstructed splendor that was flowing from the sun. There were graceful curves, reflected images, woody heights, soft distances; and over the whole scene, far and near, the dissolving lights drifted steadily, enriching it every passing moment with new marvels of coloring.

I stood like one bewitched. I drank it in, in a speechless rapture. The world was new to me, and I had never seen anything like this at home. But as I have said, a day came when I began to cease from noting the glories and the charms which the moon and the sun and the twilight wrought upon the river's face; another day came when I ceased altogether to note them. Then, if that sunset scene had been repeated, I should have looked upon it without rapture, and should have commented upon it, inwardly, after this fashion: "This sun means that we are going to have wind to-morrow; that floating log means that the river is rising, small thanks to it; that slanting mark on the water refers to a bluff reef which is going to kill somebody's steamboat one of these nights, if it keeps on stretching out like that; those tumbling 'boils' show a dissolving bar and a changing channel there; the lines and circles in the slick water over yonder are a warning that that troublesome place is shoaling up dangerously; that silver streak in the shadow of the forest is the 'break' from a new snag, and he has located himself in the very best place he could have found to fish for steamboats; that tall dead tree, with a single living branch, is not going to last long, and then how is a body ever going to get through this blind place at night without the friendly old landmark?"

No, the romance and beauty were all gone from the river. All the value any feature of it had for me now was the amount of usefulness it could furnish toward compassing the safe piloting of a steamboat. Since those days, I have pitied doctors from my heart. What does the lovely flush in a beauty's cheek mean to a doctor but a "break" that ripples above some deadly disease? Are not all her visible charms sown thick with what are to him the signs and symbols of hidden decay? Does he ever see her beauty at all, or doesn't he simply view her professionally, and comment upon her unwholesome condition all to himself? And doesn't he sometimes wonder whether he has gained most or lost by learning his trade?

The Man that Corrupted Hadleyburg

Written in the 1890's, a period of family disasters, financial bankruptcy, and declining health for Clemens, this story illustrates the phase of pessimism and despair of the later Mark Twain when he expressed his bitterness in exposing the gullibility of "the damned human race." To this period also belong the misanthropic *What Is Man?* and *The Mysterious Stranger.* The picture of a whole town made mutually suspicious through greed may reflect, according to Russel Nye, Mark Twain's experience as a lecturer at Oberlin, Ohio, in 1885 when his performance met with some unfavorable criticism in the newspapers. The belief still exists in Oberlin. The effects of wealth or the illusion of wealth on human beings provided a theme for many of Twain's narratives.

1

It was many years ago. Hadleyburg was the most honest and upright town in all the region round about. It had kept that reputation unsmirched during three generations, and was prouder of it than of any other of its possessions. It was so proud of it, and so anxious to insure its perpetuation, that it began to teach the principles of honest dealing to its babies in the cradle, and made the like teachings the staple of their culture thenceforward through all the years devoted to their education. Also, throughout the formative years temptations were kept out of the way of the young people, so that their honesty could have every chance to harden and solidify, and become a part of their very bone. The neighboring towns were jealous of this honorable supremacy, and affected to sneer at Hadleyburg's pride in it and call it vanity; but all the same they were obliged to acknowledge that Hadleyburg was in reality an incorruptible town; and if pressed they would also acknowledge that the mere fact that a young man hailed from Hadleyburg was all the recommendation he needed when he went forth from his natal town to seek for responsible employment.

But at last, in the drift of time, Hadleyburg had the ill luck to offend a passing stranger — possibly without knowing it, certainly without caring, for Hadleyburg was sufficient unto itself, and cared not a rap for strangers or their opinions. Still, it would have been well to make an exception in this one's case, for he was a bitter man and revengeful. All through his wanderings during a whole year he kept his injury in mind, and gave all his leisure moments to trying to invent a compensating satisfaction for it. He contrived many plans, and all of them were good, but none of them was quite sweeping enough; the poorest of them would hurt a great many individuals, but what he wanted was a plan which would comprehend the entire town, and not let so much as one person escape unhurt. At last he had a fortunate idea, and when it fell into his brain it lit up his whole head with an evil joy. He began to form a plan at once, saying to himself, "That is the thing to do — I will corrupt the town."

Six months later he went to Hadleyburg, and arrived in a buggy at the house of the old cashier of the bank about ten at night. He got a sack out of the buggy, shouldered it, and staggered with it through the cottage yard, and knocked at the door. A woman's voice said "Come in," and he entered, and set his sack behind the stove in the parlor, saying politely to the old lady who sat reading the *Missionary Herald* by the lamp:

"Pray keep your seat, madam, I will not disturb you. There — now it is pretty well concealed; one would hardly know it was there. Can I see your husband a moment, madam?"

No, he was gone to Brixton, and might not return before morning.

"Very well, madam, it is no matter. I merely wanted to leave that sack in his care, to be delivered to the rightful owner when he shall be found. I am a stranger; he does not know me; I am merely passing through the town tonight to discharge a matter which has been long in my mind. My errand is now completed, and I go pleased and a little proud, and you will never see me again. There is a paper attached to the sack which will explain everything. Good-night, madam."

The old lady was afraid of the mysterious big stranger, and was glad to see him go. But her curiosity was roused, and she went straight to the sack and brought away the paper. It began as follows:

"TO BE PUBLISHED; *or, the right man sought out by private inquiry — either will answer. This sack contains gold coin weighing a hundred and sixty pounds four ounces —* "

"Mercy on us, and the door not locked!"

Mrs. Richards flew to it all in a tremble and locked it, then pulled down the window-shades and stood frightened, worried, and wondering if there was anything else she could do toward making herself and the money more safe. She listened awhile for burglars, then surrendered to curiosity and went back to the lamp and finished reading the paper:

"*I am a foreigner, and am presently going back to my own country, to remain there permanently. I am grateful to America for what I have received at her hands during my stay under her flag; and to one of her citizens — a citizen of Hadleyburg — I am especially grateful for a great kindness done me a year or two ago. Two great kindnesses, in fact. I will explain. I was a gambler. I say I WAS. I was a ruined gambler. I arrived in this village at night, hungry and without a penny. I asked for help — in the dark; I was ashamed to beg in the light. I begged of the right man. He gave me twenty dollars — that is to say, he gave me life, as I considered it. He also gave me fortune; for out of that money I have made myself rich at the gaming-table. And finally, a remark which he made to me has remained with me to this day, and has at last conquered me; and in conquering has saved the remnant of my morals; I shall gamble no more. Now I have no idea who that man was, but I want him found, and I want him to have this money, to give away, throw away, or keep, as he pleases. It is merely my way of testifying my gratitude to him. If I could stay, I would find him myself; but no matter, he will be found. This is an honest town, an incorruptible town, and I know I can trust it without fear. This man can be identified by the remark which he made to me; I feel persuaded that he will remember it.*

"*And now my plan is this: If you prefer to conduct the inquiry privately, do so. Tell the contents of this present writing to any one who is likely to be the right man. If he shall answer, 'I am the man; the remark I made was so-and-so,' apply the test*

to wit: open the sack, and in it you will find a sealed envelope containing that remark. If the remark mentioned by the candidate tallies with it, give him the money, and ask no further questions, for he is certainly the right man.

"*But if you shall prefer a public inquiry, then publish this present writing in the local paper — with these instructions added, to wit: Thirty days from now, let the candidate appear at the town-hall at eight in the evening (Friday), and hand his remark, in a sealed envelope, to the Rev. Mr. Burgess (if he will be kind enough to act); and let Mr. Burgess there and then destroy the seals on the sack, open it, and see if the remark is correct; if correct, let the money be delivered, with my sincere gratitude, to my benefactor thus identified.*"

Mrs. Richards sat down, gently quivering with excitement, and was soon lost in thinking — after this pattern: "What a strange thing it is! . . . And what a fortune for that kind man who set his bread afloat upon the waters! . . . If it had only been my husband that did it! — for we are so poor, so old and poor! . . . ." Then, with a sigh — "But it was not my Edward; no, it was not he that gave a stranger twenty dollars. It is a pity too; I see it now. . . . ." Then, with a shudder — "But it is *gambler's* money! the wages of sin; we couldn't take it; we couldn't touch it. I don't like to be near it; it seems a defilement." She moved to a farther chair. . . . "I wish Edward would come, and take it to the bank; a burglar might come at any moment; it is dreadful to be here all alone with it."

At eleven Mr. Richards arrived, and while his wife was saying, "I am *so* glad you've come!" he was saying, "I'm so tired — tired clear out; it is dreadful to be poor, and have to make these dismal journeys at my time of life. Always at the grind, grind, grind, on a salary — another man's slave, and he sitting at home in his slippers, rich and comfortable."

"I am so sorry for you, Edward, you know that; but be comforted; we have our livelihood; we have our good name ——"

"Yes, Mary, and that is everything. Don't mind my talk — it's just a moment's irritation and doesn't mean anything. Kiss me — there, it's all gone now, and I am not complaining any more. What have you been getting? What's in the sack?"

Then his wife told him the great secret. It dazed him for a moment; then he said:

"It weighs a hundred and sixty pounds? Why, Mary, it's for-ty thou-sand dollars — think of it — a whole fortune! Not ten men in this village are worth that much. Give me the paper."

He skimmed through it and said:

"Isn't it an adventure! Why, it's a romance; it's like the impossible things one reads about in books, and never sees in life." He was well stirred up now; cheerful, even gleeful. He tapped his old wife on the cheek, and said, humorously, "Why, we're rich, Mary, rich; all we've got to do is to bury the money and burn the papers. If the gambler ever comes to inquire, we'll merely look coldly upon him and say: 'What is this nonsense you are talking? We have never heard of you and your sack of gold before;' and then he would look foolish, and ——"

"And in the mean time, while you are running on with your jokes, the money is still here, and it is fast getting along toward burglar-time."

"True. Very well, what shall we do — make the inquiry private? No, not that; it would spoil the romance. The public method is better. Think what a noise it will make! And it will make all the other towns jealous; for no stranger would trust such a thing to any town but Hadleyburg, and they know it. It's a great card for us. I must get to the printing-office now, or I shall be too late."

"But stop — stop — don't leave me here alone with it, Edward!"

But he was gone. For only a little while, however. Not far from his own house he met the editor-proprietor of the paper, and gave him the document, and said, "Here is a good thing for you, Cox — put it in."

"It may be too late, Mr. Richards, but I'll see."

At home again he and his wife sat down to talk the charming mystery over; they were in no condition for sleep. The first question was, Who could the citizen have been who gave the stranger the twenty dollars? It seemed a simple one; both answered it in the same breath —

"Barclay Goodson."

"Yes," said Richards, "he could have done it, and it would have been like him, but there's not another in the town."

"Everybody will grant that, Edward — grant it privately, anyway. For six months, now, the village has been its own proper self once more — honest, narrow, self-righteous, and stingy."

"It is what he always called it, to the day of his death — said it right out publicly, too."

"Yes, and he was hated for it."

"Oh, of course; but he didn't care. I reckon he was the best-hated man among us, except the Reverend Burgess."

"Well, Burgess deserves it — he will never get another congregation here. Mean as the town is, it knows how to estimate *him*. Edward, doesn't it seem odd that the stranger should appoint Burgess to deliver the money?"

"Well, yes — it does. That is — that is ——"

"Why so much that-*is*-ing? Would *you* select him?"

"Mary, maybe the stranger knows him better than this village does."

"Much *that* would help Burgess!"

The husband seemed perplexed for an answer; the wife kept a steady eye upon him, and waited. Finally Richards said, with the hesitancy of one who is making a statement which is likely to encounter doubt,

"Mary, Burgess is not a bad man."

His wife was certainly surprised.

"Nonsense!" she exclaimed.

"He is not a bad man. I know. The whole of his unpopularity had its foundation in that one thing — the thing that made so much noise."

"That 'one thing,' indeed! As if that 'one thing' wasn't enough, all by itself."

"Plenty. Plenty. Only he wasn't guilty of it."

"How you talk! Not guilty of it! Everybody knows he *was* guilty."

"Mary, I give you my word — he was innocent."

"I can't believe it, and I don't. How do you know?"

"It is a confession. I am ashamed, but I will make it. I was the only man who knew he was innocent. I could have saved him, and — and — well, you know how the town was wrought up — I hadn't the pluck to do it. It would have turned everybody against me. I felt mean, ever so mean; but I didn't dare; I hadn't the manliness to face that."

Mary looked troubled, and for a while was silent. Then she said, stammeringly:

"I — I don't think it would have done for you to — to — One mustn't — er — public opinion — one has to be so careful — so —" It was a difficult road, and she got mired; but after a little she got started again. "It was a great pity, but — Why, we couldn't afford it, Edward — we couldn't indeed. Oh, I wouldn't have had you do it for anything!"

"It would have lost us the good-will of so many people, Mary; and then — and then —"

"What troubles me now is, what *he* thinks of us, Edward."

"He? *He* doesn't suspect that I could have saved him."

"Oh," exclaimed the wife, in a tone of relief, "I am glad of that. As long as he doesn't know that you could have saved him, he — he — well, that makes it a great deal better. Why, I might have known he didn't know, because he is always trying to be friendly with us, as little encouragement as we give him. More than once people have twitted me with it. There's the Wilsons, and the Wilcoxes, and the Harknesses, they take a mean pleasure in saying, '*Your friend* Burgess,' because they know it pesters me. I wish he wouldn't persist in liking us so; I can't think why he keeps it up."

"I can explain it. It's another confession. When the thing was new and hot, and the town made a plan to ride him on a rail, my conscience hurt me so that I couldn't stand it, and I went privately and gave him notice, and he got out of the town and staid out till it was safe to come back."

"Edward! If the town had found it out — "

"*Don't!* It scares me yet, to think of it. I repented of it the minute it was done; and I was even afraid to tell you, lest your face might betray it to somebody. I didn't sleep any that night, for worrying. But after a few days I saw that no one was going to suspect me, and after that I got to feeling glad I did it. And I feel glad yet, Mary — glad through and through."

"So do I, now, for it would have been a dreadful way to treat him. Yes, I'm glad; for really you did owe him that, you know. But, Edward, suppose it should come out yet, some day!"

"It won't."

"Why!"

"Because everybody thinks it was Goodson."

"Of course they would!"

"Certainly. And of course *he* didn't care. They persuaded poor old Sawlsberry to go and charge it on him, and he went blustering over there and did it. Goodson looked him over, like as if he was hunting for a place on him that he could despise the most, then he says, 'So you are the Committee of Inquiry, are you?'

Sawlsberry said that was about what he was. 'Hm. Do they require particulars, or do you reckon a kind of a *general* answer will do?' 'If they require particulars, I will come back, Mr. Goodson; I will take the general answer first.' 'Very well, then, tell them to go to hell — I reckon that's general enough. And I'll give you some advice, Sawlsberry; when you come back for the particulars, fetch a basket to carry the relics of yourself home in.'"

"Just like Goodson; it's got all the marks. He had only vanity; he thought he could give advice better than any other person."

"It settled the business, and saved us, Mary. The subject was dropped."

"Bless you, I'm not doubting *that*."

Then they took up the gold-sack mystery again, with strong interest. Soon the conversation began to suffer breaks — interruptions caused by absorbed thinkings. The breaks grew more and more frequent. At last Richards lost himself wholly in thought. He sat long, gazing vacantly at the floor, and by-and-by he began to punctuate his thoughts with little nervous movements of his hands that seemed to indicate vexation. Meantime his wife too had relapsed into a thoughtful silence, and her movements were beginning to show a troubled discomfort. Finally Richards got up and strode aimlessly about the room, ploughing his hands through his hair, much as a somnambulist might do who was having a bad dream. Then he seemed to arrive at a definite purpose; and without a word he put on his hat and passed quickly out of the house. His wife sat brooding, with a drawn face, and did not seem to be aware that she was alone. Now and then she murmured, "Lead us not into t . . . but — but — we are so poor, so poor! . . . Lead us not into . . . Ah, who would be hurt by it? — and no one would ever know. . . . Lead us . . . ." The voice died out in mumblings. After a little she glanced up and muttered in a half-frightened, half-glad way —

"He is gone! But, oh dear, he may be too late — too late. . . . Maybe not — maybe there is still time." She rose and stood thinking, nervously clasping and unclasping her hands. A slight shudder shook her frame, and she said, out of a dry throat, "God forgive me — it's awful to think such things — but . . . Lord, how we are made — how strangely we are made!"

She turned the light low, and slipped stealthily over and kneeled down by the sack and felt of its ridgy sides with her hands, and fondled them lovingly; and there was a gloating light in her poor old eyes. She fell into fits of absence; and came half out of them at times to mutter, "If we had only waited! — oh, if we had only waited a little, and not been in such a hurry!"

Meantime Cox had gone home from his office and told his wife all about the strange thing that had happened, and they had talked it over eagerly, and guessed that the late Goodson was the only man in the town who could have helped a suffering stranger with so noble a sum as twenty dollars. Then there was a pause, and the two became thoughtful and silent. And by-and-by nervous and fidgety. At last the wife said, as if to herself,

"Nobody knows this secret but the Richardses . . . and us . . . nobody."

The husband came out of his thinkings with a slight start, and gazed wistfully at his wife, whose face was become very pale; then he hesitatingly rose, and glanced furtively at his hat, then at his wife — a sort of mute inquiry. Mrs. Cox swallowed once or twice, with her hand at her throat, then in place of speech she nodded her head. In a moment she was alone, and mumbling to herself.

And now Richards and Cox were hurrying through the deserted streets, from opposite directions. They met, panting, at the foot of the printing-office stairs; by the night-light there they read each other's face. Cox whispered,

"Nobody knows about this but us?"

The whispered answer was,

"Not a soul — on honor, not a soul!"

"If it isn't too late to —"

The men were starting up-stairs; at this moment they were overtaken by a boy, and Cox asked,

"Is that you, Johnny?"

"Yes, sir."

"You needn't ship the early mail — nor *any* mail; wait till I tell you."

"It's already gone, sir."

"*Gone?*" It had the sound of an unspeakable disappointment in it.

"Yes, sir. Time-table for Brixton and all the towns beyond changed to-day, sir — had to get the papers in twenty minutes earlier than common. I had to rush; if I had been two minutes later —"

The men turned and walked slowly away, not waiting to hear the rest. Neither of them spoke

during ten minutes; then Cox said, in a vexed tone,

"What possessed you to be in such a hurry, I can't make out."

The answer was humble enough:

"I see it now, but somehow I never thought, you know, until it was too late. But the next time —"

"Next time be hanged! It won't come in a thousand years."

Then the friends separated without a good-night, and dragged themselves home with the gait of mortally stricken men. At their homes their wives sprang up with an eager "Well?" — then saw the answer with their eyes and sank down sorrowing, without waiting for it to come in words. In both houses a discussion followed of a heated sort — a new thing; there had been discussions before, but not heated ones, not ungentle ones. The discussions to-night were a sort of seeming plagiarisms of each other. Mrs. Richards said,

"If you had only waited, Edward — if you had only stopped to think; but no, you must run straight to the printing-office and spread it all over the world."

"It *said* publish it."

"That is nothing; it also said do it privately, if you liked. There, now — is that true, or not?"

"Why, yes — yes, it is true; but when I thought what a stir it would make, and what a compliment it was to Hadleyburg that a stranger should trust it so —"

"Oh, certainly, I know all that; but if you had only stopped to think, you would have seen that you *couldn't* find the right man, because he is in his grave, and hasn't left chick nor child nor relation behind him; and as long as the money went to somebody that awfully needed it, and nobody would be hurt by it, and — and —"

She broke down, crying. Her husband tried to think of some comforting thing to say, and presently came out with this:

"But after all, Mary, it must be for the best — it *must* be; we know that. And we must remember that it was so ordered —"

"Ordered! Oh, everything *ordered*, when a person has to find some way out when he has been stupid. Just the same, it was *ordered* that the money should come to us in this special way, and it was you that must take it on yourself to go meddling with the designs of Providence — and who gave you the right? It was wicked, that is what it was — just blasphemous presumption, and no more becoming to a meek and humble professor of —"

"But, Mary, you know how we have been trained all our lives long, like the whole village, till it is absolutely second nature to us to stop not a single moment to think when there's an honest thing to be done —"

"Oh, I know it, I know it — it's been one everlasting training and training and training in honesty — honesty shielded, from the very cradle, against every possible temptation, and so it's *artificial* honesty, and weak as water when temptation comes, as we have seen this night. God knows I never had shade nor shadow of a doubt of my petrified and indestructible honesty until now — and now, under the very first big and real temptation, I — Edward, it is my belief that this town's honesty is as rotten as mine is; as rotten as yours is. It is a mean town, a hard, stingy town, and hasn't a virtue in the world but this honesty it is so celebrated for and so conceited about; and so help me, I do believe that if ever the day comes that its honesty falls under great temptation, its grand reputation will go to ruin like a house of cards. There, now, I've made confession, and I feel better; I am a humbug, and I've been one all my life, without knowing it. Let no man call me honest again — I will not have it."

"I — Well, Mary, I feel a good deal as you do; I certainly do. It seems strange, too, so strange. I never could have believed it — never."

A long silence followed; both were sunk in thought. At last the wife looked up and said, "I know what you are thinking, Edward."

Richards had the embarrassed look of a person who is caught.

"I am ashamed to confess it, Mary, but —"

"It's no matter, Edward, I was thinking the same question myself."

"I hope so. State it."

"You were thinking, if a body could only guess out *what the remark was* that Goodson made to the stranger."

"It's perfectly true. I feel guilty and ashamed. And you?"

"I'm past it. Let us make a pallet here; we've got to stand watch till the bank vault opens in the morning and admits the sack. . . . Oh, dear, oh, dear — if we hadn't made the mistake!"

The pallet was made, and Mary said:

"The open sesame — what could it have been? I do wonder what that remark could have been? But come; we will get to bed now."

"And sleep?"

"No; think."

"Yes, think."

By this time the Coxes too had completed their spat and their reconciliation, and were turning in — to think, to think, and toss, and fret, and worry over what the remark could possibly have been which Goodson made to the stranded derelict: that golden remark; that remark worth forty thousand dollars, cash.

The reason that the village telegraph-office was open later than usual that night was this: The foreman of Cox's paper was the local representative of the Associated Press. One might say its honorary representative, for it wasn't four times a year that he could furnish thirty words that would be accepted. But this time it was different. His despatch stating what he had caught got an instant answer:

"*Send the whole thing — all the details — twelve hundred words.*"

A colossal order! The foreman filled the bill; and he was the proudest man in the State. By breakfast-time the next morning the name of Hadleyburg the Incorruptible was on every lip in America, from Montreal to the Gulf, from the glaciers of Alaska to the orange-groves of Florida; and millions and millions of people were discussing the stranger and his money-sack, and wondering if the right man would be found, and hoping some more news about the matter would come soon — right away.

2

Hadleyburg village woke up world-celebrated — astonished — happy — vain. Vain beyond imagination. Its nineteen principal citizens and their wives went about shaking hands with each other, and beaming, and smiling, and congratulating, and saying *this* thing adds a new word to the dictionary — *Hadleyburg*, synonym for *incorruptible* — destined to live in dictionaries forever! And the minor and unimportant citizens and their wives went around acting in much the same way. Everybody ran to the bank to see the gold-sack; and before noon grieved and envious crowds began to flock in from Brixton and all neighboring towns; and that afternoon and next day reporters began to arrive from everywhere to verify the sack and its history and write the whole thing up anew, and make dashing free-hand pictures of the sack and of Richards's house, and the bank, and the Presbyterian church, and the Baptist church, and the public square, and the town-hall where the test would be applied and the money delivered; and damnable portraits of the Richardses, and Pinkerton the banker, and Cox, and the foreman, and Reverend Burgess, and the postmaster — and even of Jack Halliday, who was the loafing, good-natured, no-account, irreverent fisherman, hunter, boys' friend, stray-dogs' friend, typical "Sam Lawson" of the town. The little mean, smirking, oily Pinkerton showed the sack to all comers, and rubbed his sleek palms together pleasantly, and enlarged upon the town's fine old reputation for honesty and upon this wonderful endorsement of it, and hoped and believed that the example would now spread far and wide over the American world, and be epoch-making in the matter of moral regeneration. And so on, and so on.

By the end of a week things had quieted down again; the wild intoxication of pride and joy had sobered to a soft, sweet, silent delight — a sort of deep, nameless, unutterable content. All faces bore a look of peaceful, holy happiness.

Then a change came. It was a gradual change: so gradual that its beginnings were hardly noticed; maybe were not noticed at all, except by Jack Halliday, who always noticed everything; and always made fun of it, too, no matter what it was. He began to throw out chaffing remarks about people not looking quite so happy as they did a day or two ago; and next he claimed that the new aspect was deepening to positive sadness; next, that it was taking on a sick look; and finally he said that everybody was become so moody, thoughtful, and absent-minded that he could rob the meanest man in town of a cent out of the bottom of his breeches pocket and not disturb his revery.

At this stage — or at about this stage — a saying like this was dropped at bedtime — with a sigh, usually — by the head of each of the nineteen principal households:

"Ah, what *could* have been the remark that Goodson made!"

And straightway — with a shudder — came this, from the man's wife:

"Oh, *don't!* What horrible thing are you mulling in your mind? Put it away from you, for God's sake!"

But that question was wrung from those men again the next night — and got the same retort. But weaker.

And the third night the men uttered the question yet again — with anguish, and absently. This time — and the following night — the wives fidgeted feebly, and tried to say something. But didn't.

And the night after that they found their tongues and responded — longingly,

"Oh, if we *could* only guess!"

Halliday's comments grew daily more and more sparklingly disagreeable and disparaging. He went diligently about, laughing at the town, individually and in mass. But his laugh was the only one left in the village: it fell upon a hollow and mournful vacancy and emptiness. Not even a smile was findable anywhere. Halliday carried a cigar-box around on a tripod, playing that it was a camera, and halted all passers and aimed the thing and said, "Ready! — now look pleasant, please," but not even this capital joke could surprise the dreary faces into any softening.

So three weeks passed — one week was left. It was Saturday evening — after supper. Instead of the aforetime Saturday-evening flutter and bustle and shopping and larking, the streets were empty and desolate. Richards and his old wife sat apart in their little parlor — miserable and thinking. This was become their evening habit now: the life-long habit which had preceded it, of reading, knitting, and contented chat, or receiving or paying neighborly calls, was dead and gone and forgotten, ages ago — two or three weeks ago; nobody talked now, nobody read, nobody visited — the whole village sat at home, sighing, worrying, silent. Trying to guess out that remark.

The postman left a letter. Richards glanced listlessly at the superscription and the post-mark — unfamiliar, both — and tossed the letter on the table and resumed his might-have-beens and his hopeless dull miseries where he had left them off. Two or three hours later his wife got wearily up and was going away to bed without a goodnight — custom now — but she stopped near the letter and eyed it awhile with a dead interest, then broke it open, and began to skim it over. Richards, sitting there with his chair tilted back against the wall and his chin between his knees, heard something fall. It was his wife. He sprang to her side, but she cried out:

"Leave me alone, I am too happy. Read the letter — read it!"

He did. He devoured it, his brain reeling. The letter was from a distant State, and it said:

"I am a stranger to you, but no matter: I have something to tell. I have just arrived home from Mexico, and learned about that episode. Of course you do not know who made that remark, but I know, and I am the only person living who does know. It was GOODSON. *I knew him well, many years ago. I passed through your village that very night, and was his guest till the midnight train came along. I overheard him make that remark to the stranger in the dark — it was in Hale Alley. He and I talked of it the rest of the way home, and while smoking in his house. He mentioned many of your villagers in the course of his talk — most of them in a very uncomplimentary way, but two or three favorably: among these latter yourself. I say 'favorably' — nothing stronger. I remember his saying he did not actually* LIKE *any person in the town — not one; but that you — I* THINK *he said you — am almost sure — had done him a very great service once, possibly without knowing the full value of it, and he wished he had a fortune, he would leave it to you when he died, and a curse apiece for the rest of the citizens. Now, then, if it was you that did him that service, you are his legitimate heir, and entitled to the sack of gold. I know that I can trust to your honor and honesty, for in a citizen of Hadleyburg these virtues are an unfailing inheritance, and so I am going to reveal to you the remark, well satisfied that if you are not the right man you will seek and find the right one and see that poor Goodson's debt of gratitude for the service referred to is paid. This is the remark:* 'YOU ARE FAR FROM BEING A BAD MAN: GO, AND REFORM.'*

"HOWARD L. STEVENSON."*

"Oh, Edward, the money is ours, and I am so grateful, *oh*, so grateful — kiss me, dear, it's forever since we kissed — and we needed it so — the money — and now you are free of Pinkerton and his bank, and nobody's slave any more; it seems to me I could fly for joy."

It was a happy half-hour that the couple spent there on the settee caressing each other; it was the old days come again — days that had begun with their courtship and lasted without a break till the stranger brought the deadly money. By-and-by the wife said:

"Oh, Edward, how lucky it was you did him that grand service, poor Goodson! I never liked him, but I love him now. And it was fine and beautiful of you never to mention it or brag about it." Then, with a touch of reproach, "But you ought to have told *me*, Edward, you ought to have told your wife, you know."

"Well, I — er — well, Mary, you see ——"

"Now stop hemming and hawing, and tell me about it, Edward. I always loved you, and now I'm proud of you. Everybody believes there was only one good generous soul in this village, and now it turns out that you — Edward, why don't you tell me?"

"Well — er — er — Why, Mary, I can't!"

"You *can't*? *Why* can't you?"

"You see, he — well, he — he made me promise I wouldn't."

The wife looked him over, and said, very slowly,

"Made — you — promise? Edward, what do you tell me that for?"

"Mary, do you think I would lie?"

She was troubled and silent for a moment, then she laid her hand within his and said:

"No . . . no. We have wandered far enough from our bearings — God spare us that! In all your life you have never uttered a lie. But now — now that the foundations of things seem to be crumbling from under us, we — we —" She lost her voice for a moment, then said, brokenly, "Lead us not into temptation. . . . I think you made the promise, Edward. Let it rest so. Let us keep away from that ground. Now — that is all gone by; let us be happy again; it is no time for clouds."

Edward found it something of an effort to comply, for his mind kept wandering — trying to remember what the service was that he had done Goodson.

The couple lay awake the most of the night, Mary happy and busy, Edward busy, but not so happy. Mary was planning what she would do with the money. Edward was trying to recall that service. At first his conscience was sore on account of the lie he had told Mary — if it was a lie. After much reflection — suppose it *was* a lie? What then? Was it such a great matter? Aren't we always *acting* lies? Then why not *tell* them? Look at Mary — look what she had done. While he was hurrying off on his honest errand, what was she doing? Lamenting because the papers hadn't been destroyed and the money kept! Is theft better than lying?

That point lost its sting — the lie dropped into the background and left comfort behind it. The next point came to the front: *had* he rendered that service? Well, here was Goodson's own evidence as reported in Stephenson's letter; there could be no better evidence than that — it was even *proof* that he had rendered it. Of course. So that point was settled. . . . No, not quite. He recalled with a wince that this unknown Mr. Stephenson was just a trifle unsure as to whether the performer of it was Richards or some other — and, oh dear, he had put Richards on his honor! He must himself decide whither that money must go — and Mr. Stephenson was not doubting that if he was the wrong man he would go honorably and find the right one. Oh, it was odious to put a man in such a situation — ah, why couldn't Stephenson have left out that doubt! What did he want to intrude that for?

Further reflection. How did it happen that *Richards's* name remained in Stephenson's mind as indicating the right man, and not some other man's name? That looked good. Yes, that looked very good. In fact, it went on looking better and better, straight along — until by-and-by it grew into positive *proof*. And then Richards put the matter at once out of his mind, for he had a private instinct that a proof once established is better left so.

He was feeling reasonably comfortable now, but there was still one other detail that kept pushing itself on his notice: of course, he had done that service — that was settled; but what *was* that service? He must recall it — he would not go to sleep till he had recalled it; it would make his peace of mind perfect. And so he thought and thought. He thought of a dozen things — possible services, even probable services — but none of them seemed adequate, none of them seemed large enough, none of them seemed worth the money — worth the fortune Goodson had wished he could leave in his will. And besides, he couldn't remember having done them, anyway. Now, then — now, then — what *kind* of a service would it be that would make a man so inordinately grateful? Ah — the saving of his soul! That must be it. Yes, he could remember, now, how he once set himself the task of converting Goodson, and labored at it as much as — he was going to say three months; but upon closer examination it shrunk to a month, then to a week, then to a day, then to nothing. Yes, he remembered now, and with unwelcome vividness, that Goodson had told him to go to thunder and mind his own business — *he* wasn't hankering to follow Hadleyburg to heaven!

So that solution was a failure — he hadn't saved Goodson's soul. Richards was discouraged. Then after a little came another idea:

had he saved Goodson's property? No, that wouldn't do — he hadn't any. His life? That is it! Of course. Why, he might have thought of it before. This time he was on the right track, sure. His imagination mill was hard at work in a minute, now.

Thereafter during a stretch of two exhausting hours he was busy saving Goodson's life. He saved it in all kinds of difficult and perilous ways. In every case he got it saved satisfactorily up to a certain point; then, just as he was beginning to get well persuaded that it had really happened, a troublesome detail would turn up which made the whole thing impossible. As in the matter of drowning, for instance. In that case he had swum out and tugged Goodson ashore in an unconscious state with a great crowd looking on and applauding, but when he had got it all thought out and was just beginning to remember all about it a whole swarm of disqualifying details arrived on the ground: the town would have known of it, it would glare like a limelight in his own memory instead of being an inconspicuous service which he had possibly rendered "without knowing its full value." And at this point he remembered that he couldn't swim, anyway.

Ah — *there* was a point which he had been overlooking from the start: it had to be a service which he had rendered "possibly without knowing the full value of it." Why, really, that ought to be an easy hunt — much easier than those others. And sure enough, by-and-by he found it. Goodson, years and years ago, came near marrying a very sweet and pretty girl, named Nancy Hewitt, but in some way or other the match had been broken off; the girl died, Goodson remained a bachelor, and by-and-by became a soured one and a frank despiser of the human species. Soon after the girl's death the village found out, or thought it had found out, that she carried a spoonful of Negro blood in her veins. Richards worked at these details a good while, and in the end he thought he remembered things concerning them which must have gotten mislaid in his memory through long neglect. He seemed to dimly remember that it was *he* that found out about the Negro blood; that it was he that told the village; that the village told Goodson where they got it; that he thus saved Goodson from marrying the tainted girl; that he had done him this great service "without knowing the full value of it," in fact without knowing that he *was* doing it; but that

Goodson knew the value of it, and what a narrow escape he had had, and so went to his grave grateful to his benefactor and wishing he had a fortune to leave him. It was all clear and simple now, and the more he went over it the more luminous and certain it grew; and at last, when he nestled to sleep satisfied and happy, he remembered the whole thing just as if it had been yesterday. In fact, he dimly remembered Goodson's *telling* him his gratitude once. Meantime Mary had spent six thousand dollars on a new house for herself and a pair of slippers for her pastor, and then had fallen peacefully to rest.

That same Saturday evening the postman had delivered a letter to each of the other principal citizens — nineteen letters in all. No two of the envelopes were alike, and no two of the superscriptions were in the same hand, but the letters inside were just like each other in every detail but one. They were exact copies of the letter received by Richards — handwriting and all — and were all signed by Stephenson, but in place of Richards's name each receiver's own name appeared.

All night long eighteen principal citizens did what their caste-brother Richards was doing at the same time — they put in their energies trying to remember what notable service it was that they had unconsciously done Barclay Goodson. In no case was it a holiday job; still they succeeded.

And while they were at this work, which was difficult, their wives put in the night spending the money, which was easy. During that one night the nineteen wives spent an average of seven thousand dollars each out of the forty thousand in the sack — a hundred and thirty-three thousand altogether.

Next day there was a surprise for Jack Halliday. He noticed that the faces of the nineteen chief citizens and their wives bore that expression of peaceful and holy happiness again. He could not understand it, neither was he able to invent any remarks about it that could damage it or disturb it. And so it was his turn to be dissatisfied with life. His private guesses at the reasons for the happiness failed in all instances, upon examination. When he met Mrs. Wilcox and noticed the placid ecstasy in her face, he said to himself, "Her cat has had kittens" — and went and asked the cook; it was not so; the cook had detected the happiness, but did not know the cause. When Halliday found the duplicate ecstasy in the face of "Shadbelly"

Billson (village nickname), he was sure some neighbor of Billson's had broken his leg, but inquiry showed that this had not happened. The subdued ecstasy in Gregory Yates's face could mean but one thing — he was a mother-in-law short; it was another mistake. "And Pinkerton — Pinkerton — he has collected ten cents that he thought he was going to lose." And so on, and so on. In some cases the guesses had to remain in doubt, in the others they proved distinct errors. In the end Halliday said to himself, "Anyway, it foots up that there's nineteen Hadleyburg families temporarily in heaven: I don't know how it happened; I only know Providence is off duty to-day."

An architect and builder from the next State had lately ventured to set up a small business in this unpromising village, and his sign had now been hanging out a week. Not a customer yet; he was a discouraged man, and sorry he had come. But his weather changed suddenly now. First one and then another chief citizen's wife said to him privately:

"Come to my house Monday week — but say nothing about it for the present. We think of building."

He got eleven invitations that day. That night he wrote his daughter and broke off her match with her student. He said she could marry a mile higher than that.

Pinkerton the banker and two or three other well-to-do men planned country-seats — but waited. That kind don't count their chickens until they are hatched.

The Wilsons devised a grand new thing — a fancy-dress ball. They made no actual promises, but told all their acquaintanceship in confidence that they were thinking the matter over and thought they should give it — "and if we do, you will be invited, of course." People were surprised, and said, one to another, "Why, they are crazy, those poor Wilsons, they can't afford it." Several among the nineteen said privately to their husbands, "It is a good idea, we will keep still till their cheap thing is over, then *we* will give one that will make it sick."

The days drifted along, and the bill of future squanderings rose higher and higher, wilder and wilder, more and more foolish and reckless. It began to look as if every member of the nineteen would not only spend his whole forty thousand dollars before receiving-day, but be actually in debt by the time he got the money. In some cases light-headed people did not stop with planning to spend, they really spent — on credit. They bought land, mortgages, farms, speculative stocks, fine clothes, horses, and various other things, paid down the bonus, and made themselves liable for the rest — at ten days. Presently the sober second thought came, and Halliday noticed that a ghastly anxiety was beginning to show up in a good many faces. Again he was puzzled, and didn't know what to make of it. "The Wilcox kittens aren't dead, for they weren't born; nobody's broken a leg; there's no shrinkage in mother-in-laws; *nothing* has happened — it is an insolvable mystery."

There was another puzzled man, too — the Rev. Mr. Burgess. For days, wherever he went, people seemed to follow him or to be watching out for him; and if he ever found himself in a retired spot, a member of the nineteen would be sure to appear, thrust an envelope privately into his hand, whisper "To be opened at the town-hall Friday evening," then vanish away like a guilty thing. He was expecting that there might be one claimant for the sack — doubtful, however, Goodson being dead — but it never occurred to him that all this crowd might be claimants. When the great Friday came at last, he found that he had nineteen envelopes.

3

The town-hall had never looked finer. The platform at the end of it was backed by a showy draping of flags; at intervals along the walls were festoons of flags; the gallery fronts were clothed in flags; the supporting columns were swathed in flags; all this was to impress the stranger, for he would be there in considerable force, and in a large degree he would be connected with the press. The house was full. The 412 fixed seats were occupied; also the 68 extra chairs which had been packed into the aisles; the steps of the platform were occupied; some distinguished strangers were given seats on the platform; at the horseshoe of tables which fenced the front and sides of the platform sat a strong force of special correspondents who had come from everywhere. It was the best-dressed house the town had ever produced. There were some tolerably expensive toilets there, and in several cases the ladies who wore them had the look of being unfamiliar with that kind of clothes. At least the town thought they had that look, but the notion could have arisen from the town's knowledge of the fact that these ladies had never inhabited such clothes before.

The gold-sack stood on a little table at the front of the platform where all the house could see it. The bulk of the house gazed at it with a burning interest, a mouth-watering interest, a wistful and pathetic interest; a minority of nineteen couples gazed at it tenderly, lovingly, proprietarily, and the male half of this minority kept saying over to themselves the moving little impromptu speeches of thankfulness for the audience's applause and congratulations which they were presently going to get up and deliver. Every now and then one of these got a piece of paper out of his vest pocket and privately glanced at it to refresh his memory.

Of course there was a buzz of conversation going on — there always is; but at last when the Rev. Mr. Burgess rose and laid his hand on the sack he could hear his microbes gnaw, the place was so still. He related the curious history of the sack, then went on to speak in warm terms of Hadleyburg's old and well-earned reputation for spotless honesty, and of the town's just pride in this reputation. He said that this reputation was a treasure of priceless value; that under Providence its value had now become inestimably enhanced, for the recent episode had spread this fame far and wide, and thus had focussed the eyes of the American world upon this village, and made its name for all time, as he hoped and believed, a synonym for commercial incorruptibility. [*Applause.*] "And who is to be the guardian of this noble treasure — the community as a whole? No! The responsibility is individual, not communal. From this day forth each and every one of you is in his own person its special guardian, and individually responsible that no harm shall come to it. Do you — does each of you — accept this great trust? [*Tumultuous assent.*] Then all is well. Transmit it to your children and to your children's children. To-day your purity is beyond reproach — see to it that it shall remain so. To-day there is not a person in your community who could be beguiled to touch a penny not his own — see to it that you abide in this grace. ["*We will! we will!*"] This is not the place to make comparisons between ourselves and other communities — some of them ungracious toward us; they have their ways, we have ours; let us be content. [*Applause.*] I am done. Under my hand, my friends, rests a stranger's eloquent recognition of what we are: through him the world will always henceforth know what we are. We do not know who he is, but in your name I utter your gratitude, and ask you to raise your voices in endorsement."

The house rose in a body and made the walls quake with the thunders of its thankfulness for the space of a long minute. Then it sat down, and Mr. Burgess took an envelope out of his pocket. The house held its breath while he slit the envelope open and took from it a slip of paper. He read its contents — slowly and impressively — the audience listening with tranced attention to this magic document, each of whose words stood for an ingot of gold:

" *'The remark which I made to the distressed stranger was this: "You are very far from being a bad man; go, and reform."' "* Then he continued: "We shall know in a moment now whether the remark here quoted corresponds with the one concealed in the sack; and if that shall prove to be so — and it undoubtedly will — this sack of gold belongs to a fellow-citizen who will henceforth stand before the nation as the symbol of the special virtue which has made our town famous throughout the land — Mr. Billson!"

The house had gotten itself all ready to burst into a proper tornado of applause; but instead of doing it, it seemed stricken with a paralysis; there was a deep hush for a moment or two, then a wave of whispered murmurs swept the place — of about this tenor: *"Billson! oh, come, this is too thin! Twenty dollars to a stranger — or anybody — Billson! Tell it to the marines!"* And now at this point the house caught its breath all of a sudden in a new access of astonishment, for it discovered that whereas in one part of the hall Deacon Billson was standing up with his head meekly bowed, in another part of it Lawyer Wilson was doing the same. There was a wondering silence now for a while. Everybody was puzzled, and nineteen couples were surprised and indignant.

Billson and Wilson turned and stared at each other. Billson asked, bitingly,

"Why do *you* rise, Mr. Wilson?"

"Because I have a right to. Perhaps you will be good enough to explain to the house why *you* rise?"

"With great pleasure. Because I wrote that paper."

"It is an impudent falsity! I wrote it myself."

It was Burgess's turn to be paralyzed. He stood looking vacantly at first one of the men and then the other, and did not seem to know what to do. The house was stupefied. Lawyer Wilson spoke up, now, and said,

"I ask the Chair to read the name signed to that paper."

That brought the Chair to itself, and it read out the name,

" 'John Wharton *Billson*.' "

"There!" shouted Billson, "what have you got to say for yourself, now? And what kind of apology are you going to make to me and to this insulted house for the imposture which you have attempted to play here?"

"No apologies are due, sir; and as for the rest of it, I publicly charge you with pilfering my note from Mr. Burgess and substituting a copy of it signed with your own name. There is no other way by which you could have gotten hold of the test-remark; I alone, of living men, possessed the secret of its wording."

There was likely to be a scandalous state of things if this went on; everybody noticed with distress that the short-hand scribes were scribbling like mad; many people were crying "Chair, Chair! Order! order!" Burgess rapped with his gavel, and said:

"Let us not forget the proprieties due. There has evidently been a mistake somewhere, but surely that is all. If Mr. Wilson gave me an envelope — and I remember now that he did — I still have it."

He took one out of his pocket, opened it, glanced at it, looked surprised and worried, and stood silent a few moments. Then he waved his hand in a wandering and mechanical way, and made an effort or two to say something, then gave it up, despondently. Several voices cried out:

"Read it! read it! What is it?"

So he began in a dazed and sleep-walker fashion:

" *'The remark which I made to the unhappy stranger was this: "You are far from being a bad man.* [The house gazed at him, marvelling.] *Go, and reform."'* [Murmurs: "Amazing! what can this mean?"] This one," said the Chair, "is signed Thurlow G. Wilson."

"There!" cried Wilson, "I reckon that settles it! I knew perfectly well my note was purloined."

"Purloined!" retorted Billson. "I'll let you know that neither you nor any man of your kidney must venture to —"

The Chair. "Order, gentlemen, order! Take your seats, both of you, please."

They obeyed, shaking their heads and grumbling angrily. The house was profoundly puzzled; it did not know what to do with this curious emergency. Presently Thompson got up. Thompson was the hatter. He would have liked to be a Nineteener; but such was not for him; his stock of hats was not considerable enough for the position. He said:

"Mr. Chairman, if I may be permitted to make a suggestion, can both of these gentlemen be right? I put it to you, sir, can both have happened to say the very same words to the stranger? It seems to me—"

The tanner got up and interrupted him. The tanner was a disgruntled man; he believed himself entitled to be a Nineteener, but he couldn't get recognition. It made him a little unpleasant in his ways and speech. Said he:

"Sho, *that's* not the point! *That* could happen—twice in a hundred years—but not the other thing. *Neither* of them gave the twenty dollars!" [*A ripple of applause.*]

Billson. "I did!"

Wilson. "I did!"

Then each accused the other of pilfering.

The Chair. "Order! Sit down, if you please—both of you. Neither of the notes has been out of my possession at any moment."

A Voice. "Good—that settles *that!*"

The Tanner. "Mr. Chairman, one thing is now plain: one of these men has been eavesdropping under the other one's bed, and filching family secrets. If it is not unparliamentary to suggest it, I will remark that both are equal to it. [*The Chair.* "Order! order!"] I withdraw the remark, sir, and will confine myself to suggesting that if one of them has overheard the other reveal the test-remark to his wife, we shall catch him now."

A Voice. "How?"

The Tanner. "Easily. The two have not quoted the remark in exactly the same words. You would have noticed that, if there hadn't been a considerable stretch of time and an exciting quarrel inserted between the two readings."

A Voice. "Name the difference."

The Tanner. "The word *very* is in Billson's note, and not in the other."

Many Voices. "That's so—he's right."

The Tanner. "And so, if the Chair will examine the test-remark in the sack, we shall know which of these two frauds—[*The Chair.* "Order!"]—which of these two adventurers—[*The Chair.* "Order! order!"]—which of these two gentlemen—[*laughter and applause*]—is entitled to wear the belt as being the first dishonest blatherskite ever bred in this town—which he has dishonored, and which will be a sultry place for him from now out!" [*Vigorous applause.*]

Many Voices. "Open it!—open the sack!"

Mr. Burgess made a slit in the sack, slid his hand in and brought out an envelope. In it were a couple of folded notes. He said:

"One of these is marked, 'Not to be examined until all written communications which have been addressed to the Chair—if any—shall have been read.' The other is marked 'The Test.' Allow me. It is worded—to wit:

"'I do not require that the first half of the remark which was made to me by my benefactor shall be quoted with exactness, for it was not striking, and could be forgotten; but its closing fifteen words are quite striking, and I think easily rememberable; unless *these* shall be accurately reproduced, let the applicant be regarded as an impostor. My benefactor began by saying he seldom gave advice to any one, but that it always bore the hall-mark of high value when he did give it. Then he said this—and it has never faded from my memory: "*You are far from being a bad man*—'"

Fifty Voices. "That settles it—the money's Wilson's! Wilson! Wilson! Speech! Speech!"

People jumped up and crowded around Wilson, wringing his hand and congratulating fervently—meantime the Chair was hammering with the gavel and shouting:

"Order, gentlemen! Order! Order! Let me finish reading, please." When quiet was restored, the reading was resumed—as follows:

"'"Go, and reform—or, mark my words—some day, for your sins, you will die and go to hell or Hadleyburg—TRY AND MAKE IT THE FORMER."'"

A ghastly silence followed. First an angry cloud began to settle darkly upon the faces of the citizenship; after a pause the cloud began to rise, and a tickled expression tried to take its place; tried so hard that it was only kept under with great and painful difficulty; the reporters, the Brixtonites, and other strangers bent their heads down and shielded their faces with their hands, and managed to hold in by main strength and heroic courtesy. At this most inopportune time burst upon the stillness the roar of a solitary voice—Jack Halliday's:

"*That's* got the hall-mark on it!"

Then the house let go, strangers and all. Even Mr. Burgess's gravity broke down presently, then the audience considered itself officially absolved from all restraint, and it made the most of its privilege. It was a good long laugh, and a tempestuously whole-hearted one, but it ceased at last — long enough for Mr. Burgess to try to resume, and for the people to get their eyes partially wiped; then it broke out again; and afterward yet again; then at last Burgess was able to get out these serious words:

"It is useless to try to disguise the fact — we find ourselves in the presence of a matter of grave import. It involves the honor of your town, it strikes at the town's good name. The difference of a single word between the test-remarks offered by Mr. Wilson and Mr. Billson was itself a serious thing, since it indicated that one or the other of these gentlemen had committed a theft — "

The two men were sitting limp, nerveless, crushed; but at these words both were electrified into movement, and started to get up —

"Sit down!" said the Chair, sharply, and they obeyed. "That, as I have said, was a serious thing. And it was — but for only one of them. But the matter has become graver; for the honor of *both* is now in formidable peril. Shall I go even further, and say in inextricable peril? *Both* left out the crucial fifteen words." He paused. During several moments he allowed the pervading stillness to gather and deepen its impressive effects, then added: "There would seem to be but one way whereby this could happen. I ask these gentlemen — Was there *collusion? — agreement?*"

A low murmur sifted through the house; its import was, "He's got them both."

Billson was not used to emergencies; he sat in a helpless collapse. But Wilson was a lawyer. He struggled to his feet, pale and worried, and said:

"I ask the indulgence of the house while I explain this most painful matter. I am sorry to say what I am about to say, since it must inflict irreparable injury upon Mr. Billson, whom I have always esteemed and respected until now, and in whose invulnerability to temptation I entirely believed — as did you all. But for the preservation of my own honor I must speak — and with frankness. I confess with shame — and I now beseech your pardon for it — that I

said to the ruined stranger all of the words contained in the test-remark, including the disparaging fifteen. [*Sensation.*] When the late publication was made I recalled them, and I resolved to claim the sack of coin, for by every right I was entitled to it. Now I will ask you to consider this point, and weigh it well: that stranger's gratitude to me that night knew no bounds; he said himself that he could find no words for it that were adequate, and that if he should ever be able he would repay me a thousandfold. Now, then, I ask you this: could I expect — could I believe — could I even remotely imagine — that, feeling as he did, he would do so ungrateful a thing as to add those quite unnecessary fifteen words to his test? — set a trap for me? — expose me as a slanderer of my own town before my own people assembled in a public hall? It was preposterous; it was impossible. His test would contain only the kindly opening clause of my remark. Of that I had no shadow of doubt. You would have thought as I did. You would not have expected a base betrayal from one whom you had befriended and against whom you had committed no offence. And so, with perfect confidence, perfect trust, I wrote on a piece of paper the opening words — ending with 'Go, and reform,' — and signed it. When I was about to put it in an envelope I was called into my back office, and without thinking I left the paper lying open on my desk." He stopped, turned his head slowly toward Billson, waited a moment, then added: "I ask you to note this: when I returned, a little later, Mr. Billson was retiring by my street door." (*Sensation.*)

In a moment Billson was on his feet and shouting:

"It's a lie! It's an infamous lie!"

The Chair. "Be seated, sir! Mr. Wilson has the floor."

Billson's friends pulled him into his seat and quieted him, and Wilson went on:

"Those are the simple facts. My note was now lying in a different place on the table from where I had left it. I noticed that, but attached no importance to it, thinking a draught had blown it there. That Mr. Billson would read a private paper was a thing which could not occur to me; he was an honorable man, and he would be above that. If you will allow me to say it, I think his extra word '*very*' stands explained; it is attributable to a defect of memory. I was the only man in the world who could furnish here any detail of the test-mark — by *honorable* means. I have finished."

There is nothing in the world like a persuasive speech to fuddle the mental apparatus and upset the convictions and debauch the emotions of an audience not practised in the tricks and delusions of oratory. Wilson sat down victorious. The house submerged him in tides of approving applause; friends swarmed to him and shook him by the hand and congratulated him, and Billson was shouted down and not allowed to say a word. The Chair hammered and hammered with its gavel, and kept shouting,

"But let us proceed, gentlemen, let us proceed!"

At last there was a measurable degree of quiet, and the hatter said,

"But what is there to proceed with, sir, but to deliver the money?"

Voices. "That's it! That's it! Come forward, Wilson!"

The Hatter. "I move three cheers for Mr. Wilson, Symbol of the special virtue which — "

The cheers burst forth before he could finish; and in the midst of them — and in the midst of the clamor of the gavel also — some enthusiasts mounted Wilson on a big friend's shoulder and were going to fetch him in triumph to the platform. The Chair's voice now rose above the noise —

"Order! To your places! You forget that there is still a document to be read." When quiet had been restored he took up the document, and was going to read it, but laid it down again, saying, "I forgot; this is not to be read until all written communications received by me have first been read." He took an envelope out of his pocket, removed its enclosure, glanced at it — seemed astonished — held it out and gazed at it — stared at it.

Twenty or thirty voices cried out:

"What is it? Read it! read it!"

And he did — slowly, and wondering:

" 'The remark which I made to the stranger — [*Voices.* "Hello! how's this?"] — was this: "You are far from being a bad man. [*Voices.* "Great Scott!"] Go, and reform." ' [*Voice.* "Oh, saw my leg off!"] Signed by Mr. Pinkerton the banker."

The pandemonium of delight which turned itself loose now was of a sort to make the judicious weep. Those whose withers were unwrung laughed till the tears ran down; the reporters, in throes of laughter, set down disordered pot-

hooks which would never in the world be decipherable; and a sleeping dog jumped up, scared out of its wits, and barked itself crazy at the turmoil. All manner of cries were scattered through the din: "We're getting rich — *two* Symbols of Incorruptibility! — without counting Billson!" "*Three!* — count Shadbelly in — we can't have too many!" "All right — Billson's elected!" "Alas, poor Wilson — victim of *two* thieves!"

A Powerful Voice. "Silence! The Chair's fished up something more out of its pocket."

Voices. "Hurrah! Is it something fresh? Read it! read! read!"

The Chair [*reading*]. " 'The remark which I made,' etc. 'You are far from being a bad man. Go,' etc. Signed, 'Gregory Yates.' "

Tornado of Voices. "Four Symbols!" " 'Rah for Yates!" "Fish again!"

The house was in a roaring humor now, and ready to get all the fun out of the occasion that might be in it. Several Nineteeners, looking pale and distressed, got up and began to work their way toward the aisles, but a score of shouts went up:

"The doors, the doors — close the doors; no Incorruptible shall leave this place! Sit down, everybody!"

The mandate was obeyed.

"Fish again! Read! read!"

The Chair fished again, and once more the familiar words began to fall from its lips —

" 'You are far from being a bad man — ' "

"Name! name! What's his name?"

" 'L. Ingoldsby Sargent.' "

"Five elected! Pile up the Symbols! Go on, go on!"

" 'You are far from being a bad — ' "

"Name! name!"

" 'Nicholas Whitworth.' "

"Hooray! hooray! it's a symbolical day!"

Somebody wailed in, and began to sing this rhyme (leaving out "it's") to the lovely "Mikado" tune of "When a man's afraid of a beautiful maid"; the audience joined in, with joy; then, just in time, somebody contributed another line —

"And don't you this forget —— "

The house roared it out. A third line was at once furnished —

"Corruptibles far from Hadleyburg are —— "

The house roared that one too. As the last

note died, Jack Halliday's voice rose high and clear, freighted with a final line —

"But the Symbols are here, you bet!"

That was sung, with booming enthusiasm. Then the happy house started in at the beginning and sang the four lines through twice, with immense swing and dash, and finished up with a crashing three-times-three and a tiger for "Hadleyburg the Incorruptible and all Symbols of it which we shall find worthy to receive the hallmark to-night."

Then the shoutings at the Chair began again, all over the place:

"Go on! go on! Read! read some more! Read all you've got!"

"That's it — go on! We are winning eternal celebrity!"

A dozen men got up now and began to protest. They said that this farce was the work of some abandoned joker, and was an insult to the whole community. Without a doubt these signatures were all forgeries —

"Sit down! sit down! Shut up! You are confessing. We'll find *your* names in the lot."

"Mr. Chairman, how many of those envelopes have you got?"

The Chair counted.

"Together with those that have been already examined, there are nineteen."

A storm of derisive applause broke out.

"Perhaps they all contain the secret. I move that you open them all and read every signature that is attached to a note of that sort — and read also the first eight words of the note."

"Second the motion!"

It was put and carried — uproariously. Then poor old Richards got up, and his wife rose and stood at his side. Her head was bent down, so that none might see that she was crying. Her husband gave her his arm, and so supporting her, he began to speak in a quavering voice:

"My friends, you have known us two — Mary and me — all our lives, and I think you have liked us and respected us — "

The Chair interrupted him:

"Allow me. It is quite true — that which you are saying, Mr. Richards; this town *does* know you two; it *does* like you; it *does* respect you; more — it honors you and *loves* you — "

Halliday's voice rang out:

"That's the hall-marked truth, too! If the Chair is right, let the house speak up and say

it. Rise! Now, then — hip! hip! hip! — all together!"

The house rose in mass, faced toward the old couple eagerly, filled the air with a snowstorm of waving handkerchiefs, and delivered the cheers with all its affectionate heart.

The Chair then continued:

"What I was going to say is this: We know your good heart, Mr. Richards, but this is not a time for the exercise of charity toward offenders. [Shouts of "Right! right!"] I see your generous purpose in your face, but I cannot allow you to plead for these men — "

"But I was going to — "

"Please take your seat, Mr. Richards. We must examine the rest of these notes — simple fairness to the men who have already been exposed requires this. As soon as that has been done — I give you my word for this — you shall be heard."

Many Voices. "Right! — the Chair is right — no interruption can be permitted at this stage! Go on! — the names! the names! — according to the terms of the motion!"

The old couple sat reluctantly down, and the husband whispered to the wife, "It is pitifully hard to have to wait; the shame will be greater than ever when they find we were only going to plead for *ourselves*."

Straightway the jollity broke loose again with the reading of the names.

" 'You are far from being a bad man — ' Signature, 'Robert J. Titmarsh.' "

" 'You are far from being a bad man — ' Signature, 'Eliphalet Weeks.' "

" 'You are far from being a bad man — ' Signature, 'Oscar B. Wilder.' "

At this point the house lit upon the idea of taking the eight words out of the Chairman's hands. He was not unthankful for that. Thenceforward he held up each note in its turn, and waited. The house droned out the eight words in a massed and measured and musical deep volume of sound (with a daringly close resemblance to a well-known church chant) — " 'You are f-a-r from being a b-a-a-a-d man.' " Then the Chair said, "Signature, 'Archibald Wilcox.' " And so on, and so on, name after name, and everybody had an increasingly and gloriously good time except the wretched Nineteen. Now and then, when a particularly shining name was called, the house made the Chair wait while it chanted the whole of the test-remark from the beginning to the closing words,

"And go to hell or Hadleyburg — try and make it the for-or-m-e-r!" and in these special cases they added a grand and agonized and imposing "A-a-a-a-men!"

The list dwindled, dwindled, dwindled, poor old Richards keeping tally of the count, wincing when a name resembling his own was pronounced, and waiting in miserable suspense for the time to come when it would be his humiliating privilege to rise with Mary and finish his plea, which he was intending to word thus: ". . . for until now we have never done any wrong thing, but have gone our humble way unreproached. We are very poor, we are old, and have no chick nor child to help us; we were sorely tempted, and we fell. It was my purpose when I got up before to make confession and beg that my name might not be read out in this public place, for it seemed to us that we could not bear it; but I was prevented. It was just; it was our place to suffer with the rest. It has been hard for us. It is the first time we have ever heard our name fall from any one's lips — sullied. Be merciful — for the sake of the better days; make our shame as light to bear as in your charity you can." At this point in his revery Mary nudged him, perceiving that his mind was absent. The house was chanting, "You are f-a-r," etc.

"Be ready," Mary whispered. "Your name comes now; he has read eighteen."

The chant ended.

"Next! next! next!" came volleying from all over the house.

Burgess put his hand into his pocket. The old couple, trembling, began to rise, Burgess fumbled a moment, then said,

"I find I have read them all."

Faint with joy and surprise, the couple sank into their seats, and Mary whispered,

"Oh, bless God, we are saved! — he has lost ours — I wouldn't give this for a hundred of those sacks!"

The house burst out with its "Mikado" travesty, and sang it three times with ever-increasing enthusiasm, rising to its feet when it reached for the third time the closing line —

"But the Symbols are here, you bet!"

and finishing up with cheers and a tiger for "Hadleyburg purity and our eighteen immortal representatives of it."

Then Wingate, the saddler, got up and proposed cheers "for the cleanest man in town, the one solitary important citizen in it who didn't try to steal that money — Edward Richards."

They were given with great and moving heartiness; then somebody proposed that Richards be elected sole Guardian and Symbol of the now Sacred Hadleyburg Tradition, with power and right to stand up and look the whole sarcastic world in the face.

Passed, by acclamation; then they sang the "Mikado" again, and ended it with,

"And there's *one* Symbol left, you bet!"

There was a pause; then —

A Voice. "Now, then, who's to get the sack?"

The Tanner (with bitter sarcasm). "That's easy. The money has to be divided among the eighteen Incorruptibles. They gave the suffering stranger twenty dollars apiece — and that remark — each in his turn — it took twenty-two minutes for the procession to move past. Staked the stranger — total contribution, $360. All they want is just the loan back — and interest — forty thousand dollars altogether."

Many Voices [derisively]. "That's it! Divvy! divvy! Be kind to the poor — don't keep them waiting!"

The Chair. "Order! I now offer the stranger's remaining document. It says: 'If no claimant shall appear [*grand chorus of groans*], I desire that you open the sack and count out the money to the principal citizens of your town, they to take it in trust [*Cries of "Oh! Oh! Oh!"*], and use it in such ways as to them shall seem best for the propagation and preservation of your community's noble reputation for incorruptible honesty [*more cries*] — a reputation to which their names and their efforts will add a new and far-reaching lustre.' [*Enthusiastic outburst of sarcastic applause.*] That seems to be all. No — here is a postscript:

"'P.S. — CITIZENS OF HADLEYBURG: There *is* no test-remark — nobody made one. [*Great sensation.*] There wasn't any pauper stranger, nor any twenty-dollar contribution, nor any accompanying benediction and compliment — these are all inventions. [*General buzz and hum of astonishment and delight.*] Allow me to tell my story — it will take but a word or two. I passed through your town at a certain time, and received a deep offense which I had not earned. Any other man would have been content to kill one or two of you and call it square, but to me that would have been a trivial revenge, and inadequate; for the dead do not *suffer*. Besides, I could not kill you all — and, anyway, made as I am, even that would not have satisfied me. I wanted to damage every man in the place, and every woman — and not in their bodies or in their estate, but in their vanity — the place where feeble and foolish people are most vulnerable. So I disguised myself and came back and studied you. You were easy game. You had an old and lofty reputation for honesty, and naturally you were proud of it — it was your treasure of treasures, the very apple of your eye. As soon as I found out that you carefully and vigilantly kept yourselves and your children *out of temptation*, I knew how to proceed. Why, you simple creatures, the weakest of all weak things is a virtue which has not been tested in the fire. I laid a plan, and gathered a list of names. My project was to corrupt Hadleyburg the Incorruptible. My idea was to make liars and thieves of nearly half a hundred smirchless men and women who had never in their lives uttered a lie or stolen a penny. I was afraid of Goodson. He was neither born nor reared in Hadleyburg. I was afraid that if I started to operate my scheme by getting my letter laid before you, you would say to yourselves, "Goodson is the only man among us who would give away twenty dollars to a poor devil" — and then you might not bite at my bait. But Heaven took Goodson; then I knew I was safe, and I set my trap and baited it. It may be that I shall not catch all the men to whom I mailed the pretended test secret, but I shall catch the most of them, if I know Hadleyburg nature. [*Voices*. "Right — he got every last one of them."] I believe they will even steal ostensible *gamble-money*, rather than miss, poor, tempted, and mistrained fellows. I am hoping to eternally and everlastingly squelch your vanity and give Hadleyburg a new renown — one that will *stick* — and spread far. If I have succeeded, open the sack and summon the Committee on Propagation and Preservation of the Hadleyburg Reputation.'"

A Cyclone of Voices. "Open it! Open it! The Eighteen to the front! Committee on Propagation of the Tradition! Forward — the Incorruptibles!"

The Chair ripped the sack wide, and gathered up a handful of bright, broad, yellow coins, shook them together, then examined them —

"Friends, they are only gilded disks of lead!"

There was a crashing outbreak of delight over this news, and when the noise had subsided, the tanner called out:

"By right of apparent seniority in this business, Mr. Wilson is Chairman of the Committee on Propagation of the Tradition. I suggest that he step forward on behalf of his pals, and receive in trust the money."

A Hundred Voices. "Wilson! Wilson! Wilson! Speech! Speech!"

Wilson [*in a voice trembling with anger*]. "You will allow me to say, and without apologies for my language, *damn* the money!"

A Voice. "Oh, and him a Baptist!"

A Voice. "Seventeen Symbols left! Step up, gentlemen, and assume your trust!"

There was a pause — no response.

The Saddler. "Mr. Chairman, we've got *one* clean man left, anyway, out of the late aristocracy; and he needs money, and deserves it. I move that you appoint Jack Halliday to get up there and auction off that sack of gilt twenty-dollar pieces, and give the result to the right man — the man whom Hadleyburg delights to honor — Edward Richards."

This was received with great enthusiasm, the dog taking a hand again; the saddler started the bids at a dollar, the Brixton folk and Barnum's representative fought hard for it, the people cheered every jump that the bids made, the excitement climbed moment by moment higher and higher, the bidders got on their mettle and grew steadily more and more daring, more and more determined, the jumps went from a dollar up to five, then to ten, then to twenty, then fifty, then to a hundred, then —

At the beginning of the auction Richards whispered in distress to his wife: "Oh, Mary, can we allow it? It — it — you see, it is an honor-reward, a testimonial to purity of character, and — and — can we allow it? Hadn't I better get up and — Oh, Mary, what ought we to do? — what do you think we —" [*Halliday's voice*. "Fifteen I'm bid! — fifteen for the sack! — twenty! — ah, thanks! — thirty — thanks again! Thirty, thirty, thirty! — do I hear forty? — forty it is! Keep the ball rolling, gentlemen, keep it rolling! — fifty! — thanks, noble Roman! — going at fifty, fifty, fifty! — seventy! — ninety! — splendid! — a hundred! — pile it up, pile it up! — hundred and twenty — forty! — just in time! — hundred and fifty! — two hundred! — superb! Do I hear two h — thanks! — two hundred and fifty! ——"]

"It is another temptation, Edward — I'm all

in a tremble — but, oh, we've escaped *one* temptation, and that ought to warn us, to — ["*Six did I hear? — thanks! — six fifty, six f— SEVEN hundred!*"] And yet, Edward, when you think — nobody susp — ["*Eight hundred dollars! — hurrah! — make it nine! — Mr. Parsons, did I hear you say — thanks! — nine! — this noble sack of virgin lead going at only nine hundred dollars, gilding and all — come! do I hear — a thousand! — gratefully yours! — did some one say eleven? — a sack which is going to be the most celebrated in the whole Uni——*"] Oh, Edward" (*beginning to sob*), "we are *so* poor! — but — but — do as you think best — do as you think best."

Edward fell — that is, he sat still; sat with a conscience which was not satisfied, but which was overpowered by circumstances.

Meantime a stranger, who looked like an amateur detective gotten up as an impossible English earl, had been watching the evening's proceedings with manifest interest, and with a contented expression in his face; and he had been privately commenting to himself. He was now soliloquizing somewhat like this: "None of the Eighteen are bidding; that is not satisfactory; I must change that — the dramatic unities require it; they must buy the sack they tried to steal; they must pay a heavy price, too — some of them are rich. And another thing, when I make a mistake in Hadleyburg nature the man that puts that error upon me is entitled to a high honorarium, and some one must pay it. This poor old Richards has brought my judgment to shame; he is an honest man; — I don't understand it, but I acknowledge it. Yes, he saw my deuces — *and* with a straight flush, and by rights the pot is his. And it shall be a jackpot, too, if I can manage it. He disappointed me, but let that pass."

He was watching the bidding. At a thousand, the market broke; the prices tumbled swiftly. He waited — and still watched. One competitor dropped out; then another, and another. He put in a bid or two, now. When the bids had sunk to ten dollars, he added a five; some one raised him a three; he waited a moment, then flung in a fifty-dollar jump, and the sack was his — at $1282. The house broke out in cheers — then stopped; for he was on his feet, and had lifted his hand. He began to speak.

"I desire to say a word, and ask a favor. I am a speculator in rarities, and I have dealings with persons interested in numismatics all over the world. I can make a profit on this purchase, just as it stands; but there is a way, if I can get your approval, whereby I can make every one of these leaden twenty-dollar pieces worth its face in gold, and perhaps more. Grant me that approval, and I will give part of my gains to your Mr. Richards, whose invulnerable probity you have so justly and so cordially recognized to-night; his share shall be ten thousand dollars, and I will hand him the money to-morrow. [*Great applause from the house.* But the "invulnerable probity" made the Richardses blush prettily; however, it went for modesty, and did no harm.] If you will pass my proposition by a good majority — I would like a two-thirds vote — I will regard that as the town's consent, and that is all I ask. Rarities are always helped by any device which will rouse curiosity and compel remark. Now if I may have your permission to stamp upon the faces of each of these ostensible coins the names of the eighteen gentlemen who — "

Nine-tenths of the audience were on their feet in a moment — dog and all — and the proposition was carried with a whirlwind of approving applause and laughter.

They sat down, and all the Symbols except "Dr." Clay Harkness got up, violently protesting against the proposed outrage, and threatening to —

"I beg you not to threaten me," said the stranger, calmly. "I know my legal rights, and am not accustomed to being frightened at bluster." [*Applause.*] He sat down. "Dr." Harkness saw an opportunity here. He was one of the two very rich men of the place, and Pinkerton was the other. Harkness was proprietor of a mint; that is to say, a popular patent medicine. He was running for the Legislature on one ticket, and Pinkerton on the other. It was a close race and a hot one, and getting hotter every day. Both had strong appetites for money; each had bought a great tract of land, with a purpose; there was going to be a new railway, and each wanted to be in the Legislature and help locate the route to his own advantage; a single vote might make the decision, and with it two or three fortunes. The stake was large, and Harkness was a daring speculator. He was sitting close to the stranger. He leaned over while one or another of the other Symbols was entertaining the house with protests and appeals, and asked, in a whisper,

"What is your price for the sack?"

"Forty thousand dollars."

"I'll give you twenty."

"No."

"Twenty-five."

"No."

"Say thirty."

"The price is forty thousand dollars; not a penny less."

"All right, I'll give it. I will come to the hotel at ten in the morning. I don't want it known; will see you privately."

"Very good." Then the stranger got up and said to the house:

"I find it late. The speeches of these gentlemen are not without merit, not without interest, not without grace; yet if I may be excused I will take my leave. I thank you for the great favor which you have shown me in granting my petition. I ask the Chair to keep the sack for me until to-morrow, and to hand these three five-hundred-dollar notes to Mr. Richards." They were passed up to the Chair. "At nine I will call for the sack, and at eleven will deliver the rest of the ten thousand to Mr. Richards in person, at his home. Good-night."

Then he slipped out, and left the audience making a vast noise, which was composed of a mixture of cheers, the "Mikado" song, dog-disapproval, and the chant, "You are f-a-r from being a b-a-a-d man — a-a-a-a-men!"

At home the Richardses had to endure congratulations and compliments until midnight. Then they were left to themselves. They looked a little sad, and they sat silent and thinking. Finally Mary sighed and said,

"Do you think we are to blame, Edward — *much* to blame?" and her eyes wandered to the accusing triplet of big bank-notes lying on the table, where the congratulations had been gloating over them and reverently fingering them. Edward did not answer at once; then he brought out a sigh and said, hesitatingly:

"We — we couldn't help it, Mary. It — well, it was ordered. *All* things are."

Mary glanced up and looked at him steadily, but he didn't return the look. Presently she said:

"I thought congratulations and praises always tasted good. But — it seems to me, now — Edward?"

"Well?"

"Are you going to stay in the bank?"

"N-no."

"Resign?"

"In the morning — by note."

"It does seem best."

Richards bowed his head in his hands and muttered:

"Before, I was not afraid to let oceans of people's money pour through my hands, but — Mary, I am so tired, so tired — "

"We will go to bed."

At nine in the morning the stranger called for the sack and took it to the hotel in a cab. At ten Harkness had a talk with him privately. The stranger asked for and got five checks on a metropolitan bank — drawn to "Bearer," — four for $1500 each, and one for $34,000. He put one of the former in his pocket-book, and the remainder, representing $38,500, he put in an envelope, and with these he added a note, which he wrote after Harkness was gone. At eleven he called at the Richards house and knocked. Mrs. Richards peeped through the shutters, then went and received the envelope, and the stranger disappeared without a word. She came back flushed and a little unsteady on her legs, and gasped out:

"I am sure I recognized him! Last night it seemed to me that maybe I had seen him somewhere before."

"He is the man that brought the sack here?"

"I am almost sure of it."

"Then he is the ostensible Stephenson too, and sold every important citizen in this town with his bogus secret. Now if he has sent checks instead of money, we are sold too, after we thought we had escaped. I was beginning to feel fairly comfortable once more, after my night's rest, but the look of that envelope makes me sick. It isn't fat enough; $8500 in even the largest bank-notes makes more bulk than that."

"Edward, why do you object to checks?"

"Checks signed by Stephenson! I am resigned to take the $8500 if it could come in bank-notes — for it does seem that it was so ordered, Mary — but I have never had much courage, and I have not the pluck to try to market a check signed with that disastrous name. It would be a trap. That man tried to catch me; we escaped somehow or other; and now he is trying a new way. If it is checks —— "

"Oh, Edward, it is *too* bad!" and she held up the checks and began to cry.

"Put them in the fire! quick! we mustn't be tempted. It is a trick to make the world laugh at *us*, along with the rest, and — Give them to *me*, since you can't do it!" He snatched them and tried to hold his grip till he could get to the stove; but he was human, he was a cashier, and he stopped a moment to make sure of the signature. Then he came near to fainting.

"Fan me, Mary, fan me! They are the same as gold!"

"Oh, how lovely, Edward! Why?"

"Signed by Harkness. What can the mystery of that be, Mary?"

"Edward, do you think ——— "

"Look here — look at this! Fifteen — fifteen — fifteen — thirty-four. Thirty-eight thousand five hundred! Mary, the sack isn't worth twelve dollars, and Harkness — apparently — has paid about par for it."

"And does it all come to us, do you think — instead of the ten thousand?"

"Why, it looks like it. And the checks are made to 'Bearer,' too."

"Is that good, Edward? What is it for?"

"A hint to collect them at some distant bank, I reckon. Perhaps Harkness doesn't want the matter known. What is that — a note?"

"Yes. It was with the checks."

It was in the "Stephenson" handwriting, but there was no signature. It said:

"I am a disappointed man. Your honesty is beyond the reach of temptation. I had a different idea about it, but I wronged you in that, and I beg pardon, and do it sincerely. I honor you — and that is sincere, too. This town is not worthy to kiss the hem of your garment. Dear sir, I made a square bet with myself that there were nineteen debauchable men in your self-righteous community. I have lost. Take the whole pot, you are entitled to it."

Richards drew a deep sigh, and said:

"It seems written with fire — it burns so. Mary — I am miserable again."

"I, too. Ah, dear, I wish ——— "

"To think, Mary — he believes in me."

"Oh, don't, Edward — I can't bear it."

"If those beautiful words were deserved, Mary — and God knows I believed I deserved them once — I think I could give the forty thousand dollars for them. And I would put that paper away, as representing more than gold and jewels, and keep it always. But now — We could not live in the shadow of its accusing presence, Mary."

He put it in the fire.

A messenger arrived and delivered an envelope. Richards took from it a note and read it; it was from Burgess.

"You saved me, in a difficult time. I saved you last night. It was at cost of a lie, but I made the sacrifice freely, and out of a grateful heart. None in this village knows so well as I know how brave and good and noble you are. At bottom you cannot respect me, knowing as you do of that matter of which I am accused, and by the general voice condemned; but I beg that you will at least believe that I am a grateful man; it will help me to bear my burden.

[Signed] "BURGESS."

"Saved, once more. And on such terms!" He put the note in the fire. "I — I wish I were dead, Mary, I wish I were out of it all."

"Oh, these are bitter, bitter days, Edward. The stabs, through their very generosity, are so deep — and they come so fast!"

Three days before the election each of two thousand voters suddenly found himself in possession of a prized memento — one of the renowned bogus double-eagles. Around one of its faces was stamped these words: "THE REMARK I MADE TO THE POOR STRANGER WAS — " Around the other face was stamped these: "GO, AND REFORM. [SIGNED] PINKERTON." Thus the entire remaining refuse of the renowned joke was emptied upon a single head, and with calamitous effect. It revived the recent vast laugh and concentrated it upon Pinkerton; and Harkness's election was a walk-over.

Within twenty-four hours after the Richardses had received their checks their consciences were quieting down, discouraged; the old couple were learning to reconcile themselves to the sin which they had committed. But they were to learn, now, that a sin takes on new and real terrors when there seems a chance that it is going to be found out. This gives it a fresh and most substantial and important aspect. At church the morning sermon was of the usual pattern; it was the same old things said in the same old way; they had heard them a thousand times and found them innocuous, next to meaningless, and easy to sleep under; but now it was different: the sermon seemed to bristle with accusations; it seemed aimed straight and specially at people who were concealing deadly sins. After church they got away from the mob of congratulators as soon as they could, and hurried homeward, chilled to the bone at they did not know what — vague, shadowy, indefinite fears. And by chance they caught a glimpse of Mr. Burgess as he turned a corner. He paid no attention to their nod of recognition! He hadn't seen it; but they did not know that. What could his conduct mean? It might mean — it might mean — oh, a dozen dreadful things. Was it possible that he knew that Richards could have cleared him of guilt in that bygone time, and had been silently waiting for a chance to even up accounts? At home, in their distress they got to imagining that their servant might have been in the next room listening when Richards revealed the secret to his wife that he knew of Burgess's innocence; next, Richards began to imagine that he had heard the swish of a gown in there at that time; next, he was sure he *had* heard it. They would call Sarah in, on a pretext, and watch her face: if she had been betraying them to Mr. Burgess, it would show in her manner. They asked her some questions — questions which were so random and incoherent and seemingly purposeless that the girl felt sure that the old people's minds had been affected by their sudden good fortune; the sharp and watchful gaze which they bent upon her frightened her, and that completed the business. She blushed, she became nervous and confused, and to the old people these were plain signs of guilt — guilt of some fearful sort or other — without doubt she was a spy and a traitor. When they were alone again they began to piece many unrelated things together and get horrible results out of the combination. When things had got about to the worst, Richards was delivered of a sudden gasp, and his wife asked,

"Oh, what is it? — what is it?"

"The note — Burgess's note! Its language was sarcastic, I see it now." He quoted: "'At bottom you cannot respect me, *knowing,* as you do, of *that matter* of which I am accused' — oh, it is perfectly plain, now, God help me! He knows that I know! You see the ingenuity of the phrasing. It was a trap — and like a fool, I walked into it. And Mary — ?"

"Oh, it is dreadful — I know what you are going to say — he didn't return your transcript of the pretended test-remark."

"No — kept it to destroy us with. Mary, he has exposed us to some already. I know it — I know it well. I saw it in a dozen faces after church. Ah, he wouldn't answer our nod of recognition — *he* knew what he had been doing!"

In the night the doctor was called. The news went around in the morning that the old couple were rather seriously ill — prostrated by the exhausting excitement growing out of their great windfall, the congratulations, and the late hours, the doctor said. The town was sincerely distressed; for these old people were about all it had left to be proud of, now.

Two days later the news was worse. The old couple were delirious, and were doing strange things. By witness of the nurses, Richards had exhibited checks — for $8500? No — for an amazing sum — $38,500! What could be the explanation of this gigantic piece of luck?

The following day the nurses had more news — and wonderful. They had concluded to hide the checks, lest harm come to them; but when they searched they were gone from under the patient's pillow — vanished away. The patient said:

"Let the pillow alone; what do you want?"

"We thought it best that the checks ——"

"You will never see them again — they are destroyed. They came from Satan. I saw the hell-brand on them, and I knew they were sent to betray me to sin." Then he fell to gabbling strange and dreadful things which were not clearly understandable, and which the doctor admonished them to keep to themselves.

Richards was right; the checks were never seen again.

A nurse must have talked in her sleep, for within two days the forbidden gabblings were the property of the town; and they were of a surprising sort. They seemed to indicate that Richards had been a claimant for the sack himself, and that Burgess had concealed that fact and then maliciously betrayed it.

Burgess was taxed with this and stoutly denied it. And he said it was not fair to attach weight to the chatter of a sick old man who was out of his mind. Still, suspicion was in the air, and there was much talk.

After a day or two it was reported that Mrs. Richards's delirious deliveries were getting to be duplicates of her husband's. Suspicion flamed up into conviction, now, and the town's pride in the purity of its one undiscredited important citizen began to dim down and flicker toward extinction.

Six days passed, then came more news. The old couple were dying. Richards's mind cleared in his latest hour, and he sent for Burgess. Burgess said:

"Let the room be cleared. I think he wishes to say something in privacy."

"No!" said Richards; "I want witnesses. I want you all to hear my confession, so that I

may die a man, and not a dog. I was clean —
artificially — like the rest; and like the rest I fell
when temptation came. I signed a lie, and
claimed the miserable sack. Mr. Burgess remembered that I had done him a service, and in
gratitude (and ignorance) he suppressed my
claim and saved me. You know the thing that
was charged against Burgess years ago. My testimony, and mine alone, could have cleared him,
and I was a coward, and left him to suffer
disgrace —"

"No — no — Mr. Richards, you ——"

"My servant betrayed my secret to him —"

"No one has betrayed anything to me ——"

— "and then he did a natural and justifiable
thing, he repented of the saving kindness which
he had done me, and he *exposed* me — as I
deserved —"

"Never! — I make oath ——"

"Out of my heart I forgive him."

Burgess's impassioned protestations fell upon
deaf ears; the dying man passed away without
knowing that once more he had done poor
Burgess a wrong. The old wife died that night.

The last of the sacred Nineteen had fallen a
prey to the fiendish sack; the town was stripped
of the last rag of its ancient glory. Its mourning
was not showy, but it was deep.

By act of the Legislature — upon prayer and
petition — Hadleyburg was allowed to change
its name to (never mind what — I will not give
it away), and leave one word out of the motto
that for many generations had graced the town's
official seal.

It is an honest town once more, and the man
will have to rise early that catches it napping
again.

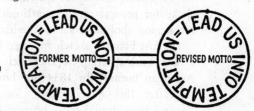

NATIVE HUMOR AND LOCAL COLOR

As the nation moved westward, regions and sections became aware of themselves, and
writers began to exploit local peculiarities, habits, and dialects (see introduction, page
670). Regional differences lent themselves easily to humorous treatment. Seba Smith
of Maine, the creator of "Jack Downing," had given us the first down-east Yankee, and
Lowell developed it toward the New England cracker-barrel philosopher in his *Biglow
Papers*. The rustic Yankee countryman, beginning with Yankee-Doodle, evolved into
Brother Jonathan and finally Uncle Sam.

The old Southwest produced a frontiersman of a rougher sort, such as Davy Crockett,
the bear-hugging gamecock of the wilderness, or the crude and red-necked Georgia
crackers of A. B. Longstreet's *Georgia Scenes* (1835). Of the ante-bellum humorists
who influenced Mark Twain, George Washington Harris, the inventor of a Tennessee-
mountain character named Sut Lovingood, was by all odds the earthiest, raciest, and
most Rabelaisian. Frontier humor of this sort was an important factor in the later
development of realism in American fiction.

After the war, however, came a group of literary comedians who were less authentic
and more professional in their methods. Artemus Ward, Josh Billings, Petroleum V.
Nasby, Bill Nye, and others employed such tricks of the trade as misspelling, slang,
dialect, and sly political commentary to appeal to a wider, newspaper-reading audience.
In some of the most successful stories of Bret Harte the western local-color tale and the
native humor tradition blended to produce a new and highly appealing combination of
realism and romance.

George Washington Harris [1814–1869]

Although born in Pennsylvania, Harris was the son of a native Virginian and a life-long southern confederate. At the age of six, he moved with his family to Knoxville, Tennessee, where he spent most of his life. He was a metal worker and jeweler and, like Mark Twain, learned to follow the river, becoming a steamboat captain at the age of 21. He was postmaster at Knoxville for a while and was active in politics and local affairs, writing articles for the Knoxville *Argus*. Politically a democrat, Harris vigorously spoke for pre-war southern attitudes, advocated secessionism, and wrote scathing attacks upon abolitionists and Abraham Lincoln.

His first fictional sketch appeared in 1845 in William T. Porter's *Spirit of the Times*, a New York sporting weekly which was to become famous for its publication of early American humor. In 1854 Sut Lovingood sprang vividly into life in the *Spirit* and thereafter this queer-looking, long-legged, small-headed, hog-eyed, practical-joking "nat'ral born durn'd fool" became the spokesman and the butt of Harris's humorous tales. An illiterate mountainer, early forerunner of Li'l Abner, Sut's chief loves are telling stories in racy and colorful dialect, drinking kill-devil whisky, hugging pretty girls, and "breeding scares among durn'd fools." He hates Yankee peddlers, Yankee lawyers, sheriffs, revenue officers, reformers, preachers, and polite language of all kinds. His favorite situation is one in which a swarm of angry hornets, an enraged bull, or a wild horse is let loose at a wedding or a quilting party with general chaos and physical discomfiture or worse as a result.

Harris's style is difficult at first because of his use of heavy dialect, coined words, slang, and vernacular spellings, but when slightly simplified the humor, vigor, and swift pace of his writing, with its many colorful figures of speech, come across easily to the modern reader. Some of his sniggering about sex and sheer animality make Sut, at his worst, too strong medicine for genteel readers, but in recent years he has come into his own as a humorist second only to Mark Twain for vivid imagination and earthy good fun. In the stream of southern humor he has his modern equivalent in some of the episodes in the work of Wolfe, Caldwell, and Faulkner.

Further reading: Stories and introduction in Brom Weber, ed., *Sut Lovingood*, 1954. F. J. Meine, *Tall Tales of the Southwest*, 1930. Walter Blair, *Native American Humor*, 1937. Bernard DeVoto, *Mark Twain's America*, 1932.

Blown Up With Soda

(1867)

🦅 This story contains most of the elements of a typical Sut Lovingood tale — the framed story, rough practical joke, racy description of the girl, Sicily Burns, Sut's dislike of circuit-riding preachers (Clapshaw), and vivid language in dialect. More often Sut is the one who sets the joke in motion, whereas here he is the butt.

"George, did you ever see Sicily Burns? Her dad lives at the Rattlesnake Spring, out on the Georgia line."

"Yes, a very handsome girl."

5 " 'Handsome!' That-there word don't cover the case. It sounds sorta like callin good whiskey 'strong water' when you are ten mile from a stillhouse, it's a-rainin, and your flask only half-full. She shows among women like a sunflower 10 among dog fennel, or a hollyhock in a patch of

smartweed. Such a bosom! Just think of two snowballs with a strawberry stuck butt-ended into both on 'em. She takes exactly fifteen inches of garter clear of the knot, stands sixteen and a half-hands high, and weighs one hundred and twenty-six in her petticoat-tail afore breakfast. She couldn't crawl through a whiskey-barrel with both heads stove out, nor sit in a common armchair, while you could lock the top hoop of a churn, or big dog collar, round the huggin place."

"The *what*, Sut?"

"The *waist*, you durn uninitiated gourd you! Her hair's as black as a crow's wing at midnight, or a nigger handlin charcoal when he's had no breakfast; it am as slick as this-here bottle, and as long as a hoss's tale. I've seed her jump over a split-bottom chair without showin her ankles, or ketchin her dress onto the knobs. She could cry and laugh at the same time, and either loved or hated you all over. If her hate fell onto you, you'd feel like you'd been whipped with a poison vine — or a broom made outen nettles — when your britches and shirt were both in the washtub. She carried enough devil about her to run crazy a big settlement of Job's children. Her skin were as white as the inside of a frogstool, and her cheeks and lips as rosy as a perch's gills in dogwood-blossom time. And such a smile! Why, when it struck you fair and square, it felt just like a big horn of unrectified ole Monongahela after you'd been sober for a month, attendin of a ten-hoss prayer-meetin twice't a day and most of the nites.

"Three of her smiles when she were a-tryin of herself, taken carefully ten minutes apart, would make the grand captain of a temp'rance society so durned drunk he wouldn't know his britches from a pair of bellowses, or a pledge from a — a — water-pot.

"Oh! I be durned if it's any use talkin. That-there gal could make me murder ole Bishop Soul hisself, or kill Mam, not to speak of Dad, if she just hinted she wanted such a thing done. Such a woman could do more devilment nor a loose stud-horse at a musterground, if she only knew what tools she totes; and I'se sorta beginnin to think she knows the use of the last durned one to a dot. Her ankles were as round and not much bigger nor the wrist of a rifle gun; and when she were a-dancin, or makin up a bed, or gittin over a fence — oh, durn such women! Why ain't they all made on the hempbrake plan, like Mam or Betts Carr or Suke Miller, so

they wouldn't bother a feller's thinker at all.

"George, this world am all wrong anyhow. More temptation than preventative. If it were equal, I'd stand it. What kin the old preachers and the ugly women expect of us, exposed as we are to such inventions as Sicily am? Oh, it's just no use in their talkin and groanin and sweatin theirselves about it; they must just upset nature onto her head and keep her there, or shet up. Let's taste this-here whiskey."

Sut continued, wipin his mouth on his shirt-sleeve: "I'se heerd in the mountains a first-rate, fourth-proof smash of thunder come unexpected and shake the earth, bringin along a string of lightnin as long as a quarter-track and as bright as a welding heat, a-racin down a big pine tree, tearin it into broom splits and toothpickers, and raisin a cloud of dust and bark and a army of limbs with a smell sorta like the Devil were about, and the long darning-needle leaves fallin round with a *tith — tith* quiet sorta sound and then a-quiverin on the earth as little snakes die. And I felt queer in my innards, sorta half-comfort, with a little glad and right-smart of sorry mixed with it.

"I'se seed the rattlesnake square hisself to come at me, a-saying 'Z-e-e-e-e' with that noisy tail of his'n, and I felt queer agin — monstrous queer. I've seed the Oconee River jumpin mad from rock to rock with its clear, cool water. . . . white foam. . . . and music —"

"What, Sut?"

"Music. The rushin water does make music. So does the wind, and the fire in the mountain, and it give me an uneasy queerness again. But every time I looked at that gal Sicily Burns, I had all the feelins mixed up — of the lightnin, the river, and the snake — with a touch of the quick-silver sensation a-huntin through all my veins for the ticklish place.

"To gather it all in a bunch and tie it, she were gal all over, from the point of her toe-nails to the end of the longest hair on the highest knob on her head — gal all the time, everywhere, and one of the excitingest kind. Of course I leaned up to her, as close't as I dare to, and in spite of these-here legs and my appetite for whiskey, that-there shirt-skinnin business and Dad's actin hoss, she sorta leaned to me just a scrimption, sorta like a careful man salts other people's cattle in the mountain, barely enough to bring 'em back to the lick-log some day — that's the way she salted me, and I attended the lick-log as regular as the old bell cow. *And* I were just beginnin to think I were onto the right trail to as much comfort and stayin awake a-purpose as ole Brigham Young with all his saddle-colored women, and the papers to fetch more if he wants 'em.

"Well, one day a cussed, palaverin, onion-eatin Yankee peddler — all jack-knife and jaw — came to ole man Burns with a carry-all full of apple-parin machines, jews-harps, calico, ribbons, sody-powder, and other durned truck.

"Now mind, I'd never heerd tell of sody-powder in *my* borned days; I didn't know it from Belshazzar's off ox. But I knows now that it am worse nor gunpowder for hurtin, and durned nigh as smart to go off.

"That-there Yankee peddler has my pious-est prayer: I just wish I had a keg of powder into his cussed paunch, with a slow match comin out at his mouth, and I had a chunk of fire. The feller what found a morsel of him big enough to feed a cockroach oughta be turned loose to pasture among seventy-five pretty women and set up in whiskey for life, because of his good eyes in huntin lost things. George, a Yankee peddler's soul would have more room in a turnip-seed to fly around in than a leatherwing bat has in a meetin-house. That's just so.

"Sicily had bought a tin box of the cold boiling truck and hid it till I come to the lick-log agin, you know. Well, I just happened to pass next day, and of course stopped to enjoy a look at the temptation and she were mighty lovin to me. I never felt the like — put one arm round my neck and t'other where the surcingle goes round a hoss, took the inturn onto me with her left foot, and give me a kiss.

"Says she, 'Sutty, love, I'se got somethin fur you: *a new sensation. . . .*'

"And I b'lieve in it strong, for I begun to feel it pow'ful. My toes felt like I were in a warm crick with minnows a-nibblin at 'em. A cold streak were a-racin up and down my back like a lizard with a turkey hen after him. My hands took the ague, and my heart felt hot and un-satisfied-like. Then it were that I'd a-cut ole Soul's throat with a handsaw and never batted my eye, if she'd a-hinted the necessity.

"Then she poured about ten blue papers of the fizzling powder into a great big tumbler, and as many white papers into another; and put nigh onto a pint of water into both of 'em; stirred em up with a caseknife and gritted a morsel of nutmeg on top — the deceitful she-torment lookin as solemn as a jackass in a snowstorm when the fodder give out.

"She held one tumbler and told me to drink t'other. I swallered it at one run; tasted sorta salty-like, but I thought it were part of the 'sensation.' But I were slightly mistakened; it were yet to come, and weren't long about it, hoss, better b'lieve. 'Ternally durn all sensations of every spot and stripe! I say. Then she give me t'other, and I sent it a-chasin the first installment to the sag of my paunch, racehoss way. You see, I'd got the idea under my hair that it were *love powders*, and I'd swallered the Devil red-hot from home a-thinkin that. Love powders *from her!* Just think of it yourself solemnly a minute, and sit still if you kin.

"Just 'bout the time I were ketchin my breath, I thought I'd swallered a threshin-machine in full blast with a couple of bull-dogs, and they had set into fightin; and I felt somethin comin up my swaller monstrous like a high pressure steamboat. I could hear it a-snortin, and sizzin.

"'*Ketched agin, by the great golly!*' thought I. 'Same family disposition to make a durned fool of myself just as often as the sun sets, and fifteen times oftener if there's half a chance.' Durn Dad everymore, amen! I say.

"I happened to think of my hoss, and I broke for him. I stole a hangdog look back and there lay Sicily, flat of her back in the porch, clappin her hands, screamin with laughin, her feet up in the air, a-kickin 'em a-past each other like she were tryin to kick her slippers off. I'se pow'ful sorry I were too busy to look at 'em.

"There were a road of foam from the house to the hoss two-foot wide and shoemouth deep — looked like it had been snowin — a-poppin and a-hissin and a-boilin like a tub of soapsuds with a red-hot mole-board in it. I gathered a cherry-tree limb as I run, and I lit a-straddle of ole Blacky, a-thrashin his hide like the Devil beatin tanbark and a-hissin worse nor four thousand mad ganders outen my mouth, eyes, nose, and ears. All this waked the ole hoss, and he fetched one rear, one kick, and then he went — he just mizzled, scared. Oh, lordy! How the foam rolled and the hoss flew!

"As we turned the corner of the garden lot, I heerd Sicily call as clear as a bugle: 'Hole hit down, Mister Lovingood! Hole hit down! Hit's a cure fur puppy love. Hole hit *down!*'

"'Hole hit down!' Who ever heard such a unpossible — why, *right then* I were a-feelin the bottom of my paunch coming up after it, inside out, just like the bottom of a green champagne bottle. I were expectin to see it every blast. That, with what Sicily said, were a-hurtin my thinker pow'ful bad; and then the ice-water idea that it weren't a love-powder — after all that hurtin, taken all together, I were sorta wishin it might keep on till I were all boiled to foam, plumb to my heelstrings.

"I were aimin for Doctor Goodman's at the Hiwassee Copper Mine — to git somethin to simmer it down with, when I met ole Clapshaw, the circuit rider, a-travellin toward somebody's hot biscuit and fried chicken. As I come tearin along, he held up his hands like he wanted to pray for me. But as I wanted somethin to reach further, and take a ranker hold nor his prayers could, I just rambled ahead. I were hot after a ten-hoss, double-actin, steam paunch-pump with one end socked deep into my soda lake and a strong man-body doctor at t'other; it were my *big want* just then.

"Ole Clapshaw took a scare as I were comin straight for him. His faith give out and he dodged — flat hat, hoss, and saddle-bags — into the thicket. I seed his hoss's tail fly up over his back as he disappeared into the bushes; there musta been spurrin going on 'bout there. I liked his motions under a scare right well; he made that dodge just like a mud-turtle drops offen a log when a big steamboat comes tearin a-past.

"As he passed ole man Burns's, Sicily hailed him to ask if he met anybody goin up the road in a sorta hurry. The poor devil thought that perhaps he might; weren't sure but he had seed a dreadful forewarnin, or a ghost, or ole Beelzebub, or the Tariff. Takin all things together, however, in the little time spared to him for reflection, it musta been a crazy, long-legged, shakin Quaker fleein from the wrath to come on a black-and-white spotted hoss, a-whippin him with a big brush . . . and he had a white beard which come from just under his eyes down to the pommel of the saddle, and then

forked and went to his knees, and from there dropped in bunches as big as a crow's nest to the ground . . . and Clapshaw heerd a sound like the rushin of mighty waters, and he were pow'fully exercised 'bout it anyhow. Well, I guess he were, and so were his fat hoss, and so were ole Blacky, and more so by a durned sight were me myself.

"After Clapshaw composed hisself, he writ out his fool notions for Sicily: that it were a new steam invention to spread the Catholic doctrine and tote the Pope's bulls to pasture in distant lands — made outen sheet iron, injun rubber, tanned leather, ice cream, and fat pine — and that the hoss's tail were made outen wire red-hot at the point, and a stream of sparks as long as the steerin oar of a flatboat follered thereafter; and taken it all together, it weren't a safe thing to meet in a lane of a dark night; and he thought he had a call over the mountain to another circuit; that chickens weren't as plenty over there, but then he were a self-denyin man.

"Now, George, all this beard and spotted hoss and steam and fire and snow and wire tails were durned-scared-circuit-rider's humbug. It all come outen my paunch, without any vomitin or coaxin; and if it hadn', I'd a done been busted into more scraps nor there's eggs in a big catfish.

"'Hole hit down, Mister Lovingood! Hole hit down!' Now weren't that just the durndest unreasonable request ever a woman made of man? She might just as well asked me to swaller my hoss, and then skin the cat on a cobweb. She's pow'ful on doctorin, though, I'll swear to that."

"Why, Sut?"

"Cause she cured my puppy-love with one dose, durn her! George, am sody *poison?*"

"No. Why?"

"I sorta 'spected it were; and I set in and ate yarbs and grass and roots till I'se punched out like onto a ole cow; my whole swaller and paunch am tanned hard as sole leather. I asks rot-gut no odds now. Here's a drink to the durndest fool in the world — just me!" And the bottom of Sut's flask flashed in the sunlight.

Bret Harte [1836–1902]

Interest in local color fiction was given spectacular impetus by a Western story of Bret Harte's in 1868. Ever since, the West has been a favorite theme, in fiction, motion picture, television.

Harte was an Easterner who lived in the West for seventeen years. Born in Albany, he was nineteen when he followed his mother to California. Here he lived a varied life, in city and country, but it would be hard to say how much his writings owed to direct experience. In 1862 he married Anna Griswold in San Francisco. A hard-working journalist, he attracted attention through his writings in the San Francisco *Golden Era* and the *Northern Californian*. As editor of the latter, he secured regular contributions from Mark Twain. In 1868 he became editor of a new Western magazine, the *Overland Monthly*, in which he printed the mining story, "The Luck of Roaring Camp." Received coolly at first in California, it produced sensational enthusiasm in the East. With this endorsement, Harte went on to write for the *Overland* "The Outcasts of Poker Flat" (1869) and other skilful stories in the rich vein he had opened. After the book publication of *The Luck of Roaring Camp and Other Sketches* (1870), he enjoyed great popular favor throughout the United States and in England.

Leaving California for good in 1871, Harte returned in triumph to the East. Looked upon as a new genius, he received a $10,000 contract from the *Atlantic Monthly* for twelve stories. But his best work had already been done. In the California stories that he went on writing to the end of his life he seemed to be imitating himself. In 1878 he left America (and his family), never to return. At Crefeld, Germany, he was commercial agent of the United States; in Glasgow, Scotland, he was United States consul. In 1885 he began residence in London, where he somehow contrived, in one or two stories, to recapture the flair he had shown in the *Overland*. And in London he died.

Bret Harte's achievement, if less than his fame, was not small. He sensed the literary possibilities of the picturesque life of the farthest west frontier. Here was real life of a sort quite unfamiliar to most Americans. "Ditches and claims" — "gamblers" — "French Pete and Kanaka Joe," who "shot each other to death" — "bar" — "Cherokee Sal": these came flocking in the very first paragraph of his first famous story. And, as Wallace Stegner remarks, "Harte was no prude; he drew no morals and preached no sermons; he painted prostitutes and foul-mouthed children and drunken sots without apology." However, he chose to describe this startling world, not in the scientific spirit of an accurate record, but with the freedom of the romancer. In character portrayal he apparently drew hints from Dickens, a master of sentiment and humor, and he learned much from the humorists of the frontier. He told his stories deftly, with a sense of the dramatic and with directness and economy. Only a leaning toward the theatrical prevented his coming to close grips with life and attaining a full aesthetic effect. Western local color was not his only forte. His brilliant parodies of Dickens, Cooper, Dumas, and others in *Condensed Novels* (1871) are more frequently reprinted now than are his stories, and his skill both as satirist and as humorist derived in part from the native tradition of yarn-spinners and tellers of tall tales.

Further reading: Poems and further stories (and the introduction) in J. B. Harrison, *Bret Harte*, American Writers Series, 1941. G. R. Stewart, Jr., *Bret Harte: Argonaut and Exile*, 1931.

The Outcasts of Poker Flat
(1869)

Heroism among gamblers and honor among thieves are themes often associated with romantic and sentimental literature. What qualities of sophistication, realism, and humor help raise this tale above the conventional, didactic treatment of such themes?

As Mr. John Oakhurst, gambler, stepped into the main street of Poker Flat on the morning of the 23d of November, 1850, he was conscious of a change in its moral atmosphere since the preceding night. Two or three men, conversing earnestly together, ceased as he approached, and exchanged significant glances. There was a Sabbath lull in the air, which, in a settlement unused to Sabbath influences, looked ominous.

Mr. Oakhurst's calm, handsome face betrayed small concern in these indications. Whether he was conscious of any predisposing cause was another question. "I reckon they're after somebody," he reflected; "likely it's me." He returned to his pocket the handkerchief with which he had been whipping away the red dust of Poker Flat from his neat boots, and quietly discharged his mind of any further conjecture.

In point of fact, Poker Flat was "after somebody." It had lately suffered the loss of several thousand dollars, two valuable horses, and a prominent citizen. It was experiencing a spasm of virtuous reaction, quite as lawless and ungovernable as any of the acts that had provoked it. A secret committee had determined to rid the town of all improper persons. This was done permanently in regard of two men who were then hanging from the boughs of a sycamore in the gulch, and temporarily in the banishment of certain other objectionable characters. I regret to say that some of these were ladies. It is but due to the sex, however, to state that their impropriety was professional, and it was only in such easily established standards of evil that Poker Flat ventured to sit in judgment.

Mr. Oakhurst was right in supposing that he was included in this category. A few of the committee had urged hanging him as a possible example and a sure method of reimbursing themselves from his pockets of the sums he had won from them. "It's agin justice," said Jim Wheeler, "to let this yer young man from Roaring Camp — an entire stranger — carry away our money." But a crude sentiment of equity residing in the breasts of those who had been fortunate enough to win from Mr. Oakhurst overruled this narrower local prejudice.

Mr. Oakhurst received his sentence with philosophic calmness, none the less coolly that he was aware of the hesitation of his judges. He was too much of a gambler not to accept fate. With him life was at best an uncertain game, and he recognized the usual percentage in favor of the dealer.

A body of armed men accompanied the deported wickedness of Poker Flat to the outskirts of the settlement. Besides Mr. Oakhurst, who was known to be a coolly desperate man, and for whose intimidation the armed escort was intended, the expatriated party consisted of a young woman familiarly known as "The Duchess"; another who had won the title of "Mother Shipton"; and "Uncle Billy," a suspected sluice-robber and confirmed drunkard. The cavalcade provoked no comments from the spectators, nor was any word uttered by the escort. Only when the gulch which marked the uttermost limit of Poker Flat was reached, the leader spoke briefly and to the point. The exiles were forbidden to return at the peril of their lives.

As the escort disappeared, their pent-up feelings found vent in a few hysterical tears from the Duchess, some bad language from Mother Shipton, and a Parthian volley of expletives from Uncle Billy. The philosophic Oakhurst alone remained silent. He listened calmly to Mother Shipton's desire to cut somebody's heart out, to the repeated statements of the Duchess that she would die in the road, and to the alarming oaths that seemed to be bumped out of Uncle Billy as he rode forward. With the easy good humor characteristic of his class, he insisted upon exchanging his own riding-horse, "Five-Spot," for the sorry mule which the Duchess rode. But even this act did not draw the party into any closer sympathy. The young woman readjusted her somewhat draggled plumes with a feeble, faded coquetry; Mother Shipton eyed the possessor of "Five-Spot" with malevolence, and Uncle Billy included the whole party in one sweeping anathema.

The road to Sandy Bar — a camp that, not having as yet experienced the regenerating influences of Poker Flat, consequently seemed to offer some invitation to the emigrants — lay over a steep mountain range. It was distant a day's severe travel. In that advanced season the party soon passed out of the moist, temperate regions of the foothills into the dry, cold, bracing air of the Sierras. The trail was narrow and difficult. At noon the Duchess, rolling out of her saddle upon the ground, declared her intention of going no farther, and the party halted.

The spot was singularly wild and impressive. A wooded amphitheatre, surrounded on three sides by precipitous cliffs of naked granite, sloped gently toward the crest of another precipice that overlooked the valley. It was, undoubtedly, the most suitable spot for a camp, had camping been advisable. But Mr. Oakhurst knew that scarcely half the journey to Sandy Bar was accomplished, and the party were not equipped or provisioned for delay. This fact he pointed out to his companions curtly, with a philosophic commentary on the folly of "throwing up their hand before the game was played out." But they were furnished with liquor, which in this emergency stood them in place of food, fuel, rest, and prescience. In spite of his remonstrances, it was not long before they were more or less under its influence. Uncle Billy passed rapidly from a bellicose state into one of stupor, the Duchess became maudlin, and Mother Shipton snored. Mr. Oakhurst alone remained erect leaning against a rock calmly surveying them.

Mr. Oakhurst did not drink. It interfered with a profession which required coolness, impassiveness and presence of mind and in his own language he "couldn't afford it." As he gazed at his recumbent fellow exiles, the loneliness begotten of his pariah trade, his habits of life, his very vices, for the first time seriously oppressed him. He bestirred himself in dusting his black clothes, washing his hands and face, and other acts characteristic of his studiously neat habits and for a moment forgot his annoyance. The thought of deserting his weaker and more pitiable companions never perhaps occurred to him. Yet he could not help feeling the want of that excitement which, singularly enough, was most conducive to that calm equanimity for which he was notorious. He looked at the gloomy walls that rose a thousand feet sheer above the circling pines around him, at the sky ominously clouded, at the valley below, already deepening into shadow; and, doing so, suddenly he heard his own name called.

A horseman slowly ascended the trail. In the fresh, open face of the newcomer Mr. Oakhurst recognized Tom Simson, otherwise known as "The Innocent," of Sandy Bar. He had met him some months before over a "little game," and had, with perfect equanimity, won the entire fortune — amounting to some forty dollars — of that guileless youth. After the game was finished, Mr. Oakhurst drew the youthful speculator behind the door and thus addressed him: "Tommy, you're a good little man, but you can't gamble worth a cent. Don't try it over again." He then handed him his money back, pushed him gently from the room, and so made a devoted slave of Tom Simson.

There was a remembrance of this in his boyish and enthusiastic greeting of Mr. Oakhurst. He had started, he said, to go to Poker Flat to seek his fortune. "Alone?" No, not exactly alone; in fact (a giggle), he had run away with Piney Woods. Didn't Mr. Oakhurst remember Piney? She that used to wait on the table at the Temperance House? They had been engaged a long time, but old Jake Woods had objected, and so they had run away, and were going to Poker Flat to be married, and here they were. And they were tired out, and how lucky it was they had found a place to camp, and company. All this the Innocent delivered rapidly, while Piney, a stout, comely damsel of fifteen emerged from behind the pine-tree, where she had been blushing unseen, and rode to the side of her lover.

Mr. Oakhurst seldom troubled himself with sentiment, still less with propriety; but he had a vague idea that the situation was not fortunate. He retained, however, his presence of mind sufficiently to kick Uncle Billy, who was about to say something, and Uncle Billy was sober enough to recognize in Mr. Oakhurst's kick a superior power that would not bear trifling. He then endeavored to dissuade Tom Simson from delaying further, but in vain. He even pointed out the fact that there was no provision, nor means of making a camp. But, unluckily, the Innocent met his objection by assuring the party that he was provided with an extra mule loaded with provisions, and by the discovery of a rude attempt at a log house near the trail. "Piney can stay with Mrs. Oakhurst," said the Innocent, pointing to the Duchess, "and I can shift for myself."

Nothing but Mr. Oakhurst's admonishing foot saved Uncle Billy from bursting into a roar of laughter. As it was, he felt compelled to retire up the cañon until he could recover his gravity. There he confided the joke to the tall pine-trees, with many slaps of his leg, contortions of his face, and the usual profanity. But when he returned to the party, he found them seated by a fire — for the air had grown strangely chill and the sky overcast — in apparently amicable conversation. Piney was actually talking in an impulsive girlish fashion to the Duchess, who was listening with an interest and animation she had not shown for many days. The Innocent was holding forth, apparently with equal effect, to Mr. Oakhurst and Mother Shipton, who was actually relaxing into amiability. "Is this yer a d—d picnic?" said Uncle Billy, with inward scorn, as he surveyed the sylvan group, the glancing firelight, and the tethered animals in the foreground. Suddenly an idea mingled with the alcoholic fumes that disturbed his brain. It was apparently of a jocular nature, for he felt impelled to slap his leg again and cram his fist into his mouth.

As the shadows crept slowly up the mountain, a slight breeze rocked the tops of the pine-trees and moaned through their long and gloomy aisles. The ruined cabin, patched and covered with pine boughs, was set apart for the ladies. As the lovers parted, they unaffectedly exchanged a kiss, so honest and sincere that it might have been heard above the swaying pines. The frail Duchess and the malevolent Mother Shipton were probably too stunned to remark upon this last evidence of simplicity, and so turned without a word to the hut. The fire was replenished, the men lay down before the door, and in a few minutes were asleep.

Mr. Oakhurst was a light sleeper. Toward morning he awoke benumbed and cold. As he stirred the dying fire, the wind, which was now blowing strongly, brought to his cheek that which caused the blood to leave it, — snow!

He started to his feet with the intention of awakening the sleepers, for there was no time to lose. But turning to where Uncle Billy had been lying, he found him gone. A suspicion leaped to his brain, and a curse to his lips. He ran to the spot where the mules had been tethered — they were no longer there. The tracks were already rapidly disappearing in the snow.

The momentary excitement brought Mr. Oakhurst back to the fire with his usual calm. He did not waken the sleepers. The Innocent slumbered peacefully, with a smile on his good-humored, freckled face; the virgin Piney slept beside her frailer sisters as sweetly as though attended by celestial guardians; and Mr. Oakhurst, drawing his blanket over his shoulders, stroked his mustaches and waited for the dawn. It came slowly in a whirling mist of snowflakes that dazzled and confused the eye. What could be seen of the landscape appeared magically changed. He looked over the valley, and summed up the present and future in two words, "Snowed in!"

A careful inventory of the provisions, which, fortunately for the party, had been stored within the hut, and so escaped the felonious fingers of Uncle Billy, disclosed the fact that with care and prudence they might last ten days longer. "That is," said Mr. Oakhurst *sotto voce* to the Innocent, "if you're willing to board us. If you ain't — and perhaps you'd better not — you can wait till Uncle Billy gets back with provisions." For some occult reason, Mr. Oakhurst could not bring himself to disclose Uncle Billy's rascality, and so offered the hypothesis that he had wandered from the camp and had accidentally stampeded the animals. He dropped a warning to the Duchess and Mother Shipton, who of course knew the facts of their associate's defection. "They'll find out the truth about us *all* when they find out anything," he added significantly, "and there's no good frightening them now."

Tom Simson not only put all his worldly store at the disposal of Mr. Oakhurst, but seemed to enjoy the prospect of their enforced seclusion. "We'll have a good camp for a week, and then the snow'll melt, and we'll all go back together." The cheerful gayety of the young man and Mr. Oakhurst's calm infected the others. The Innocent with the aid of pine boughs, extemporized a thatch for the roofless cabin, and the Duchess directed Piney in the rearrangement of the interior with a taste and tact that opened the blue eyes of that provincial maiden to their fullest extent. "I reckon now you're used to fine things at Poker Flat," said Piney. The Duchess turned away sharply to conceal something that reddened her cheeks through their professional tint, and Mother Shipton requested Piney not to "chatter." But when Mr. Oakhurst returned from a weary search for the trail, he heard the sound of happy laughter echoed from the rocks. He stopped in some alarm, and his thoughts first naturally reverted to the whiskey, which he had prudently cachéd. "And yet it don't somehow sound like whiskey," said the gambler. It was not until he caught sight of the blazing fire through the still blinding storm, and the group around it, that he settled to the conviction that it was "square fun."

Whether Mr. Oakhurst had cachéd his cards with the whiskey as something debarred the free access of the community, I cannot say. It was certain that, in Mother Shipton's words, he "didn't say 'cards' once" during that evening. Haply the time was beguiled by an accordion, produced somewhat ostentatiously by Tom Simson from his pack. Notwithstanding some difficulties attending the manipulation of this instrument, Piney Woods managed to pluck several reluctant melodies from its keys, to an accompaniment by the Innocent on a pair of bone castanets. But the crowning festivity of the evening was reached in a rude camp-meeting hymn, which the lovers, joining hands, sang with great earnestness and vociferation. I fear that a certain defiant tone and Covenanter's swing to its chorus, rather than any devotional quality, caused it speedily to infect the others, who at last joined in the refrain:

"I'm proud to live in the service of the Lord,
    And I'm proud to die in His army."

The pines rocked, the storm eddied and whirled above the miserable group, and the flames of their altar leaped heavenward, as if in token of the vow.

At midnight the storm abated, the rolling clouds parted, and the stars glittered keenly above the sleeping camp. Mr. Oakhurst, whose professional habits had enabled him to live on the smallest possible amount of sleep, in dividing the watch with Tom Simson somehow managed to take upon himself the greater part of the duty. He excused himself to the Innocent by saying that he had "often been a week without sleep." "Doing what?" asked Tom. "Poker!" replied Oakhurst sententiously. "When a man gets a streak of luck — nigger-luck — he don't get tired. The luck gives in first. Luck," continued the gambler reflectively, "is a mighty queer thing. All you know about it for certain is that it's bound to change. And it's finding out when it's going to change that makes you. We've had a streak of bad luck since we left Poker Flat — you come along, and slap you get into it, too. If you can hold your cards right along you're all right. For," added the gambler, with cheerful irrelevance —

"I'm proud to live in the service of the Lord,
    And I'm bound to die in His army."

The third day came, and the sun, looking through the white-curtained valley, saw the outcasts divide their slowly decreasing store of provisions for the morning meal. It was one of the peculiarities of that mountain climate that its rays diffused a kindly warmth over the wintry landscape, as if in regretful commiseration of the past. But it revealed drift on drift of snow piled high around the hut — a hopeless, uncharted, trackless sea of white lying below the rocky shores to which the castaways still clung. Through the marvelously clear air the smoke of the pastoral village of Poker Flat rose miles away. Mother Shipton saw it, and from a remote pinnacle of her rocky fastness hurled in that direction a final malediction. It was her last vituperative attempt, and perhaps for that reason was invested with a certain degree of sublimity. It did her good, she privately informed the Duchess. "Just you go out there and cuss, and see." She then set herself to the task of amusing "the child," as she and the Duchess were pleased to call Piney. Piney was no chicken, but it was a soothing and original theory of the pair thus to account for the fact that she didn't swear and wasn't improper.

When night crept up again through the gorges, the reedy notes of the accordion rose and fell in fitful spasms and long-drawn gasps by the flickering campfire. But music failed to fill entirely the aching void left by insufficient food, and a new diversion was proposed by Piney — story-telling. Neither Mr. Oakhurst nor his female companions caring to relate their personal experiences, this plan would have failed too, but for the Innocent. Some months before he had chanced upon a stray copy of Mr. Pope's ingenious translation of the Iliad. He now proposed to narrate the principal incidents of that poem — having thoroughly mastered the argument and fairly forgotten the words — in the current vernacular of Sandy Bar. And so for the rest of that night the Homeric demigods again walked the earth. Trojan bully and wily Greek wrestled in the winds, and the great pines in the cañon seemed to bow to the wrath of the son of Peleus. Mr. Oakhurst listened with quiet satisfaction. Most especially was he interested in the fate of "Ash-heels," as the Innocent persisted in denominating the "swift-footed Achilles."

So, with small food and much of Homer and the accordion, a week passed over the heads of the outcasts. The sun again forsook them, and again from leaden skies the snowflakes were sifted over the land. Day by day closer around them drew the snowy circle, until at last they looked from their prison over drifted walls of dazzling white, that towered twenty feet above their heads. It became more and more difficult to replenish their fires, even from the fallen trees beside them, now half hidden in the drifts. And yet no one complained. The lovers turned from the dreary prospect and looked into each other's eyes, and were happy. Mr. Oakhurst settled himself coolly to the losing game before him. The Duchess, more cheerful than she had been, assumed the care of Piney. Only Mother Shipton — once the strongest of the party — seemed to sicken and fade. At midnight on the tenth day she called Oakhurst to her side. "I'm going," she said, in a voice of querulous weakness, "but don't say anything about it. Don't waken the kids. Take the bundle from under my head, and open it." Mr. Oakhurst did so. It contained Mother Shipton's rations for the last week, untouched. "Give 'em to the child," she said, pointing to the sleeping Piney. "You've starved yourself," said the gambler. "That's what they call it," said the woman querulously, as she lay down again, and, turning her face to the wall, passed quietly away.

The accordion and the bones were put aside that day, and Homer was forgotten. When the body of Mother Shipton had been committed to the snow, Mr. Oakhurst took the Innocent aside, and showed him a pair of snow shoes, which he had fashioned from the old pack-saddle. "There's one chance in a hundred to save her yet," he said, pointing to Piney; "but it's there," he added, pointing toward Poker Flat. "If you can reach there in two days she's safe." "And you?" asked Tom Simson. "I'll stay here," was the curt reply.

The lovers parted with a long embrace. "You are not going, too?" said the Duchess, as she saw Mr. Oakhurst apparently waiting to accompany him. "As far as the cañon," he replied. He turned suddenly and kissed the Duchess, leaving her pallid face aflame, and her trembling limbs rigid with amazement.

Night came, but not Mr. Oakhurst. It brought the storm again and the whirling snow. Then the Duchess, feeding the fire, found that some one had quietly piled beside the hut enough fuel to last a few days longer. The tears rose to her eyes, but she hid them from Piney.

The women slept but little. In the morning, looking into each other's faces, they read their fate. Neither spoke, but Piney, accepting the position of the stronger, drew near and placed her arm around the Duchess's waist. They kept this attitude for the rest of the day. That night the storm reached its greatest fury, and, rending asunder the protecting vines, invaded the very hut.

Toward morning they found themselves unable to feed the fire, which gradually died away. As the embers slowly blackened, the Duchess crept closer to Piney, and broke the silence of many hours: "Piney, can you pray?" "No, dear," said Piney simply. The Duchess, without knowing exactly why, felt relieved, and, putting her head upon Piney's shoulder, spoke no more. And so reclining, the younger and purer pillowing the head of her soiled sister upon her virgin breast, they fell asleep.

The wind lulled as if it feared to waken them. Feathery drifts of snow, shaken from the long pine boughs, flew like white winged birds, and settled about them as they slept. The moon through the rifted clouds looked down upon what had been the camp. But all human stain, all trace of earthly travail, was hidden beneath the spotless mantle mercifully flung from above.

They slept all that day and the next, nor did they waken when voices and footsteps broke the silence of the camp. And when pitying fingers brushed the snow from their wan faces, you could hardly have told from the equal peace that dwelt upon them which was she that had sinned. Even the law of Poker Flat recognized this, and turned away, leaving them still locked in each other's arms.

But at the head of the gulch, on one of the largest pine-trees, they found the deuce of clubs pinned to the bark with a bowie-knife. It bore the following, written in pencil in a firm hand:

†

BENEATH THIS TREE
LIES THE BODY
OF
JOHN OAKHURST,
WHO STRUCK A STREAK OF BAD LUCK
ON THE 23D OF NOVEMBER 1850,
AND
HANDED IN HIS CHECKS
ON THE 7TH DECEMBER, 1850.
†

And pulseless and cold, with a Derringer by his side and a bullet in his heart, though still calm as in life, beneath the snow lay he who at once was the strongest and yet the weakest of the outcasts of Poker Flat.

Joel Chandler Harris [1848–1908]

The great popularity of Uncle Remus is indicated by the number of languages into which the stories of Joel Chandler Harris have been translated — more than twenty-five — and their continued appeal in recent reprintings, movie versions, and comic strips. The animal fable with moral implications is as old as Aesop, Chaucer, or La Fontaine and as new as Walt Disney. Harris used the fable for moral and political purposes, skillfully disguised behind his authentic portrayal of Old Plantation life and the Negro character and dialect; only recently have historians recognized that the stories about Brer Rabbit, Brer Fox, the Tar Baby, and many other memorable characters had an underlying motive of bringing about a reconciliation of North and South after the war. Other undertones of meaning may be discerned in the stories; for instance, the outwitting by Brer Rabbit of his stronger enemies has something in it of the experience and wisdom gained by the Negro race under slavery and by the South under Reconstruction.

Harris was born near Eatonton, Georgia, the son of an Irish laborer who deserted his wife. He earned a living from an early age in printing shops and as an editorial writer on local newspapers, educating himself by reading in the Bible, Shakespeare, and other English classics. He knew plantation life intimately. In 1877 he joined the staff of the Atlanta *Constitution*, with which he was connected the rest of his life, and his first sketches of Negro life appeared there. Uncle Remus became a popular figure in the late seventies, and Harris was quickly invited to write for such important periodicals as *The Century* and *The Saturday Evening Post*. At first only a mouthpiece for the author's opinions, Uncle Remus developed into a story-teller without peer when Harris began to collect and re-tell the stories he had learned from the field hands on the plantations of central Georgia.

In 1880 the first collection of these, *Uncle Remus: His Songs and Sayings*, was published, followed in 1883 by *Nights with Uncle Remus*. Three more collections were published, one posthumously, but the best and most familiar stories belong to the early volumes. Harris wrote other books about slavery and southern life, including as a fictional account of his own life on a plantation and a novel, *Gabriel Tolliver* (1902).

Harris was a careful student of folklore and Negro dialects; his transcriptions have been recognized as authentic. His stories came from various sources: from his own experiences among the Negroes, from friends or readers who sent him versions from other sections of the South, and from literary sources in volumes of Kaffir legends, Amazonian Indian myths, or Hottentot fables. But he did not invent any of them. All were first learned by him through native sources before he accepted them, and he stated that his only original contribution was the dialect and the setting, including Uncle Remus and the little boy listener.

Further reading: Stories in *Nights with Uncle Remus*, 1883. Julia C. Harris, *The Life and Letters of Joel Chandler Harris*, 1918. J. B. Hubbell, *The South in American Literature*, 1954, pages 782–795. P. H. Buck, *The Road to Reunion*, 1937.

Mr. Benjamin Ram and His Wonderful Fiddle

(1883)

"I 'speck you done year tell er ole man Benjermun Ram," said Uncle Remus, with a great affectation of indifference, after a pause.

"Old man who?" asked the little boy.

"Old man Benjermun Ram. I 'speck you done year tell er him too long 'go ter talk 'bout."

"Why, no, I haven't, Uncle Remus!" exclaimed the little boy, protesting and laughing. "He must have been a mighty funny old man."

"Dat's ez may be," responded Uncle Remus, sententiously. "Fun deze days wouldn't er counted fer fun in dem days; en many's de time w'at I see folks laughin'," continued the old man, with such withering sarcasm that the little boy immediately became serious, — "many's de time w'at I sees um laughin' en laughin', w'en I lay dey ain't kin tell w'at deyer laughin' at deyse'f. En 'tain't der laughin' w'at pesters me, nudder," — relenting a little, — "hit's dish yer ev'lastin' snickle en giggle, giggle en snickle."

Having thus mapped out, in a dim and uncertain way, what older people than the little boy might have been excused for accepting as a sort of moral basis, Uncle Remus proceeded:

"Dish yer Mr. Benjermun Ram, w'ich he done come up inter my min', was one er deze yer ole-timers. Dey tells me dat he 'uz a fiddler fum away back yander — one er dem ar kinder fiddlers w'at can't git de chune down fine 'less dey pats der foot. He stay all by he own-alone se'f 'way out in the middle un a big new-groun', en he sech a handy man fer ter have at a frolic dat de yuther creeturs like 'im mighty well, en w'en dey tuck a notion fer ter shake der foot, w'ich de notion tuck'n' struck um eve'y once in a w'ile, nuthin' 'ud do but dey mus' sen' fer ole man Benjermun Ram en he fiddle; en dey do say," continued Uncle Remus, closing his eyes in a sort of ecstasy, "dat w'en he squar' hisse'f back in a cheer, en git in a weavin' way, he kin des snatch dem old-time chunes fum who lay de rail.[1] En den, w'en de frolic wuz done, dey'd all fling in, dem yuther creeturs would, en fill up a bag er peas fer old Mr. Benjermun Ram fer ter kyar home wid 'im.

[1] That is, from the foundation, or beginning. [Author's note.]

"One time, des 'bout Christmas, Miss Meadows en Miss Motts en de gals dey up 'n' say dat dey'd sorter gin a blow-out, en dey got wud ter ole man Benjermun Ram w'ich dey 'speckted 'im fer ter be on han'. W'en de time come fer Mr. Benjermun Ram fer ter start, de win' blow cole en de cloud 'gun ter spread out 'cross de elements — but no marter fer dat; ole man Benjermun Ram tuck down he walkin'-cane, he did, en tie up de fiddle in a bag, en sot out fer Miss Meadows. He thunk he know de way, but hit keep on gittin' col'er, en col'er, en mo' cloudy, twel bimeby, fus' news you know, ole Mr. Benjermun Ram done lose de way. Ef he'd er kep' on down de big road fum de start, it moughter bin diffunt, but he tuck a nigh-cut, en he ain't git fur 'fo' he done los' sho' 'nuff. He go dis away, en he go dat away, en he go de yuther way, yit all de same he was done los'. Some folks would er sot right flat down whar dey wus en study out de way, but ole man Benjermun Ram ain't got wrinkle on he hawn fer nothin', kaze he done got de name er ole Billy Hardhead long 'fo' dat. Den ag'in, some folks would er stop right still in der tracks en holler en bawl fer ter see ef dey can't roust up some er de neighbors, but ole Mr. Benjermun Ram, he des stick he jowl in de win', he did, en he march right on des 'zackly like he know he ain't gwine de wrong way. He keep on, but 'twan't long 'fo' he 'gun ter feel right lonesome, mo' speshually w'en hit come up in he min' how Miss Meadows en de gals en all de comp'ny be bleedz ter do de bes' dey kin bidout any fiddlin'; en hit kinder make he marrer git cole w'en he study 'bout how he gotter sleep out dar in de woods by hisse'f.

"Yit, all de same, he keep on twel de dark 'gun ter drap down, en den he keep on still, en bimeby he come ter a little rise whar dey wuz a clay-gall. W'en he git dar he stop en look 'roun', he did, en 'way off down in de holler, dar he see a light shinin', en w'en he see dis, ole man Benjermun Ram tuck he foot in he han', en make he way todes it des lak it de ve'y place w'at he bin huntin'. 'Twan't long 'fo' he come ter de house whar de light is, en, bless you soul, he don't make no bones er knockin'. Den somebody holler out:

" 'Who dat?'

" 'I'm Mr. Benjermun Ram, en I done lose de way, en I come fer ter ax you ef you can't take me in fer de night,' sezee.

"In common," continued Uncle Remus, "ole

Mr. Benjermun Ram wuz a mighty rough-en-spoken somebody, but you better b'leeve he talk monst'us perlite dis time.

"Den some un on t'er side er de do' ax Mr. Benjermun Ram fer ter walk right in, en wid dat he open de do' en walk in, en make a bow like fiddlin' folks does w'en dey goes in comp'ny; but he ain't so sooner made he bow en look 'roun' twel he 'gun ter shake en shiver lak he done bin stricken wid de swamp-ager, kaze, settin' right dar 'fo' de fier wuz ole Brer Wolf, wid his toofies showin' up all w'ite en shiny like dey wuz bran new. Ef ole Mr. Benjermun Ram ain't bin so ole en stiff I boun' you he'd er broke en run, but 'mos' fo' he had time fer ter study 'bout gittin' 'way, ole Brer Wolf done bin jump up en shet de do' en fassen' 'er wid a great big chain. Ole Mr. Benjermun Ram he know he in fer't, en he tuck'n put on a bol' face ez he kin, but he des nat'ally hone[1] fer ter be los' in de woods some mo'. Den he make 'n'er low bow, en he hope Brer Wolf and all his folks is well, en den he say, sezee, dat he des drap in fer ter wom hisse'f, en 'quire uv de way ter Miss Meadows', en ef Brer Wolf be so good ez ter set 'im in de road ag'in, he be off putty soon en be much 'blige in de bargains.

" 'Tooby sho', Mr. Ram,' sez Brer Wolf, sezee, w'iles he lick he chops en grin; 'des put yo' walkin'-cane in de cornder over dar, en set y' bag down on de flo', en make yo'se'f at home,' sezee. 'We ain't got much,' sezee, 'but w'at we is got is yone w'iles you stays, en I boun' we'll take good keer un you,' sezee; en wid dat Brer Wolf laugh en show his toofies so bad dat ole man Benjermun Ram come mighty nigh havin' n'er ager.

"Den Brer Wolf tuck'n flung 'n'er lighter'd-knot on de fier, en den he slip inter de back room, en present'y, w'iles ole Mr. Benjermun Ram wuz settin' dar shakin' in he shoes, he year Brer Wolf whispun' ter he ole 'oman:

" 'Ole 'oman! ole 'oman! Fling 'way yo' smoke meat — fresh meat fer supper! Fling 'way yo' smoke meat — fresh meat fer supper!'

"Den ole Miss Wolf, she talk out loud, so Mr. Benjermun Ram kin year:

" 'Tooby sho' I'll fix 'im some supper. We er 'way off yer in de woods, so fur fum comp'ny

[1] To pine or long for anything. This is a good old English word which has been retained in the plantation vocabulary. [Author's note.]

dat goodness knows I'm mighty glad ter see Mr. Benjermun Ram.'

"Den Mr. Benjermun Ram year ole Miss Wolf whettin' 'er knife on a rock — *shirrah! shirrah! shirrah!* — en ev'y time he year de knife say *shirrah!* he know he dat much nigher de dinner-pot. He know he can't git 'way, en w'iles he settin' dar studyin', hit 'come 'cross he min' dat he des mought ez well play one mo' chune on he fiddle 'fo' de wuss come ter de wuss. Wid dat he ontie de bag en take out de fiddle, en 'gun ter chune 'er up — *plink, plank, plunk, plink! plunk, plank, plink, plunk!*"

Uncle Remus's imitation of the tuning of a fiddle was marvellous enough to produce a startling effect upon a much less enthusiastic listener than the little boy. It was given in perfect good faith, but the serious expression on the old man's face was so irresistibly comic that the child laughed until the tears ran down his face. Uncle Remus very properly accepted this as a tribute to his wonderful resources as a storyteller, and continued, in great good-humor:

"W'en ole Miss Wolf year dat kinder fuss, co'se she dunner w'at is it, en she drap 'er knife en lissen. Ole Mr. Benjermun Ram ain't know dis, en he keep on chunin' up — *plank, plink, plunk, plank!* Den ole Miss Wolf, she tuck'n' hunch Brer Wolf wid'er elbow, en she say, sez she:

" 'Hey, ole man! w'at dat?'

"Den bofe un um cock up der years en lissen, en des 'bout dat time, ole Mr. Benjermun Ram he sling de butt er de fiddle up und' he chin, en struck up one er dem ole-time chunes."

"Well, what tune was it, Uncle Remus?" the little boy asked, with some display of impatience.

"Ef I ain't done gone en fergit dat chune off'n my min'," continued Uncle Remus; "hit sorter went like dat ar song 'bout 'Sheep shell co'n wid de rattle er his ho'n;' en yit hit mout er been dat ar yuther one 'bout 'Roll de key, ladies, roll dem keys.' Brer Wolf en ole Miss Wolf, dey lissen en lissen, en de mo' w'at dey lissen de skeerder dey git, twel bimeby dey tuck ter der heels en make a break fer de swamp at de back er de house des lak de patter-rollers wuz atter um.

"W'en ole man Benjermun Ram sorter let up wid he fiddlin', he don't see no Brer Wolf, en he don't year no ole Miss Wolf. Den he look in de back room; no Wolf dar. Den he look in de back po'ch; no Wolf dar. Den he look in de closet en de cubberd; no Wolf ain't dar yit. Den ole Mr. Benjermun Ram, he tuck 'n' shot all de do's en lock um, en he s'arch 'round en he fine some peas en fodder in de lof', w'ich he et um fer he supper, en den he lie down front er de fier en sleep soun' ez a log. [5]

"Nex' mawnin' he 'uz up en stirrin' 'monst'us soon, en he put out fum dar, en he fine de way ter Miss Meadows' time 'nuff fer ter play at de frolic. W'en he git dar, Miss Meadows en de [10] gals, dey run ter de gate fer ter meet 'im, en dis un tuck he hat, en dat un tuck he cane, en

t'er 'n tuck he fiddle, en den dey up 'n' say: "'Law, Mr. Ram! whar de name er goodness is you bin? We so glad you come. Stir 'roun' yer, folks, en git Mr. Ram a cup er hot coffee.' "Dey make a mighty big ter-do 'bout Mr. Benjermun Ram, Miss Meadows en Miss Motts en de gals did, but 'twix' you en me en de bed-pos', honey, dey'd er had der frolic wh'er de ole chap 'uz dar er not, kaze de gals done made 'rangements wid Brer Rabbit fer ter pat fer um, en in dem days Brer Rabbit wuz a patter, mon. He mos' sho'ly wuz."

Sarah Orne Jewett [1849–1909]

Miss Jewett was born at Berwick, Maine, the daughter of a physician (the doctor of her book *A Country Doctor*) who was a Bowdoin graduate and a man of culture, and who became for her a companion and guide. "When I was perhaps fifteen," she said, "the first city boarders began to make their appearance near Berwick, and the way they misconstrued the country people and made game of their peculiarities fired me with indignation. I determined to teach the world that country people were not the awkward, ignorant set those people seemed to think. I wanted the world to know their grand simple lives; and, as far as I had a mission, when I first began to write, I think that was it."

She caught these plain people at a time when the old order, described in her stories, was passing away in consequence of the Industrial Revolution and the Civil War. Her characters, as Willa Cather said, were "everyday people who grew out of the soil." She observed them closely, with affectionate understanding, and disciplined herself to convey in words the "low tone" and unhurried pace suited to ordinary life. Her literary taste was formed, as well as expressed, through reading Harriet Beecher Stowe and William Dean Howells, and such realists of European fiction as Jane Austen, Thackeray, Balzac, and Flaubert.

She was only twenty when she published her first stories in the *Atlantic*. Later stories she collected in *Deephaven* (1877), and a succession of volumes followed, including her strongest book, *The Country of the Pointed Firs* (1896).

Further reading: *The Best Short Stories of Sarah Orne Jewett*, ed. by Willa Cather, 2 vols., 1925. F. O. Matthiessen, *Sarah Orne Jewett*, 1929.

Miss Tempy's Watchers

(1888)

The time of year was April; the place was a small farming town in New Hampshire, remote

from any railroad. One by one the lights had been blown out in the scattered houses near Miss Tempy Dent's; but as her neighbors took a last look out-of-doors, their eyes turned with instinctive curiosity toward the old house, where a lamp burned steadily. They gave a little sigh. "Poor Miss Tempy!" said more than one bereft acquaintance; for the good woman lay dead in her north chamber, and the light was a watcher's light. The funeral was set for the next day, at one o'clock.

The watchers were two of the oldest friends, Mrs. Crowe and Sarah Ann Binson. They were sitting in the kitchen, because it seemed less awesome than the unused best room, and they beguiled the long hours by steady conversation. One would think that neither topics nor opinions would hold out, at that rate, all through the long spring night; but there was a certain degree of excitement just then, and the two women had risen to an unusual level of expressiveness and confidence. Each had already told the other more than one fact that she had determined to keep secret; they were again and again tempted into statements that either would have found impossible by daylight. Mrs. Crowe was knitting a blue yarn stocking for her husband; the foot was already so long that it seemed as if she must have forgotten to narrow it at the proper time. Mrs. Crowe knew exactly what she was about, however; she was of a much cooler disposition than Sister Binson, who made futile attempts at some sewing, only to drop her work into her lap whenever the talk was most engaging.

Their faces were interesting, — of the dry, shrewd, quick-witted New England type, with thin hair twisted neatly back out of the way. Mrs. Crowe could look vague and benignant, and Miss Binson was, to quote her neighbors, a little too sharp-set; but the world knew that she had need to be, with the load she must carry of supporting an inefficient widowed sister and six unpromising and unwilling nieces and nephews. The eldest boy was at last placed with a good man to learn the mason's trade. Sarah Ann Binson, for all her sharp, anxious aspect, never defended herself, when her sister whined and fretted. She was told every week of her life that the poor children never would have had to lift a finger if their father had lived, and yet she had kept her steadfast way with the little farm, and patiently taught the young people many useful things, for which, as everybody said, they would live to thank her. However pleasureless her life appeared to outward view, it was brimful of pleasure to herself.

Mrs. Crowe, on the contrary, was well to do, her husband being a rich farmer and an easygoing man. She was a stingy woman, but for all that she looked kindly; and when she gave away anything, or lifted a finger to help anybody, it was thought a great piece of beneficence, and a compliment, indeed, which the recipient accepted with twice as much gratitude as double the gift that came from a poor and more generous acquaintance. Everybody liked to be on good terms with Mrs. Crowe. Socially she stood much higher than Sarah Ann Binson. They were both old schoolmates and friends of Temperance Dent, who had asked them, one day, not long before she died, if they would not come together and look after the house, and manage everything, when she was gone. She may have had some hope that they might become closer friends in this period of intimate partnership, and that the richer woman might better understand the burdens of the poorer. They had not kept the house the night before; they were too weary with the care of their old friend, whom they had not left until all was over.

There was a brook which ran down the hillside very near the house, and the sound of it was much louder than usual. When there was silence in the kitchen, the busy stream had a strange insistence in its wild voice, as if it tried to make the watchers understand something that related to the past.

"I declare, I can't begin to sorrow for Tempy yet. I am so glad to have her at rest," whispered Mrs. Crowe. "It is strange to set here without her, but I can't make it clear that she has gone. I feel as if she had got easy and dropped off to sleep, and I'm more scared about waking her up than knowing any other feeling."

"Yes," said Sarah Ann. "It's just like that, ain't it? But I tell you we are goin' to miss her worse than we expect. She's helped me through with many a trial, has Temperance. I ain't the only one who says the same, neither."

These words were spoken as if there were a third person listening; somebody beside Mrs. Crowe. The watchers could not rid their minds of the feeling that they were being watched themselves. The spring wind whistled in the window crack, now and then, and buffeted the little house in a gusty way that had a sort of companionable effect. Yet, on the whole, it was a very still night, and the watchers spoke in a half-whisper.

"She was the freest-handed woman that ever I knew," said Mrs. Crowe, decidedly. "According to her means, she gave away more than anybody. I used to tell her 't wa'n't right. I used really to be afraid that she went without too much, for we have a duty to ourselves."

Sister Binson looked up in a half-amused, unconscious way, and then recollected herself.

Mrs. Crowe met her look with a serious face. "It ain't so easy for me to give as it is for some," she said simply, but with an effort which was made possible only by the occasion. "I should like to say, while Tempy is laying here yet in her own house, that she has been a constant lesson to me. Folks are too kind, and shame me with thanks for what I do. I ain't such a generous woman as poor Tempy was, for all she had nothin' to do with, as one may say."

Sarah Binson was much moved at this confession, and was even pained and touched by the unexpected humility. "You have a good many calls on you" — she began, and then left her kind little compliment half finished.

"Yes, yes, but I've got means enough. My disposition's more of a cross to me as I grow older, and I made up my mind this morning that Tempy's example should be my pattern henceforth." She began to knit faster than ever.

"'T ain't no use to get morbid: that's what Tempy used to say herself," said Sarah Ann, after a minute's silence. "Ain't it strange to say 'used to say'?" and her own voice choked a little. "She never did like to hear folks git goin' about themselves."

"'T was only because they're apt to do it so as other folks will say 't was n't so, an' praise 'em up," humbly replied Mrs. Crowe, "and that ain't my object. There wa'n't a child but what Tempy set herself to work to see what she could do to please it. One time my brother's folks had been stopping here in the summer, from Massachusetts. The children was all little, and they broke up a sight of toys, and left 'em when they were going away. Tempy come right up after they rode by, to see if she could n't help me set the house to rights, and she caught me just as I was going to fling some of the clutter into the stove. I was kind of tired out, starting 'em off in season. 'Oh, give me them!' says she, real pleading; and she wropped 'em up and took 'em home with her when she went, and she mended 'em up and stuck 'em together, and made some young one or other happy with every blessed one. You'd thought I'd done her the biggest favor. 'No thanks to me. I should ha' burnt 'em, Tempy,' says I."

"Some of 'em came to our house, I know,"

said Miss Binson. "She'd take a lot o' trouble to please a child, 'stead o' shoving of it out o' the way, like the rest of us when we're drove."

"I can tell you the biggest thing she ever gave, and I don't know's there's anybody left but me to tell it. I don't want it forgot," Sarah Binson went on, looking up at the clock to see how the night was going. "It was that pretty-faced Trevor girl, who taught the Corners school, and married so well afterward, out in New York State. You remember her, I dare say?"

"Certain," said Mrs. Crowe, with an air of interest.

"She was a splendid scholar, folks said, and give the school a great start; but she'd overdone herself getting her education, and working to pay for it, and she all broke down one spring, and Tempy made her come and stop with her a while, — you remember that? Well, she had an uncle, her mother's brother, out in Chicago, who was well off and friendly, and used to write to Lizzie Trevor, and I dare say make her some presents; but he was a lively, driving man, and did n't take time to stop and think about his folks. He had n't seen her since she was a little girl. Poor Lizzie was so pale and weakly that she just got through the term o' school. She looked as if she was just going straight off in a decline. Tempy, she cosseted her up a while, and then, next thing folks knew, she was tellin' round how Miss Trevor had gone to see her uncle, and meant to visit Niagary Falls on the way, and stop over night. Now I happened to know, in ways I won't dwell on to explain, that the poor girl was in debt for her schoolin' when she come here, and her last quarter's pay had just squared it off at last, and left her without a cent ahead, hardly; but it had fretted her thinking of it, so she paid it all; they might have dunned her that she owed it to. An' I taxed Tempy about the girl's goin' off on such a journey till she owned up, rather 'n have Lizzie blamed, that she'd given her sixty dollars, same's if she was rolling in riches, and sent her off to have a good rest and vacation."

"Sixty dollars!" exclaimed Mrs. Crowe. "Tempy only had ninety dollars a year that came in to her; rest of her livin' she got by helpin' about, with what she raised off this little piece o' ground, sand one side an' clay the other. An' how often I've heard her tell, years ago, that she'd rather see Niagary than any other sight in the world!"

The women looked at each other in silence;

the magnitude of the generous sacrifice was almost too great for their comprehension.

"She was just poor enough to do that!" declared Mrs. Crowe at last, in an abandonment of feeling. "Say what you may, I feel humbled to the dust," and her companion ventured to say nothing. She never had given away sixty dollars at once, but it was simply because she never had it to give. It came to her very lips to say in explanation, "Tempy was so situated"; but she checked herself in time, for she would not betray her own loyal guarding of her dependent household.

"Folks say a great deal of generosity, and this one's being public-spirited, and that one free-handed about giving," said Mrs. Crowe, who was a little nervous in the silence. "I suppose we can't tell the sorrow it would be to some folks not to give, same's 't would be to me not to save. I seem kind of made for that, as if 't was what I'd got to do. I should feel sights better about it if I could make it evident what I was savin' for. If I had a child, now, Sarah Ann," and her voice was a little husky, — "if I had a child, I should think I was heapin' of it up because he was the one trained by the Lord to scatter it again for good. But here's Crowe and me, we can't do anything with money, and both of us like to keep things same's they've always been. Now Priscilla Dance was talking away like a mill-clapper, week before last. She'd think I would go right off and get one o' them new-fashioned gilt-and-white papers for the best room, and some new furniture, an' a marble-top table. And I looked at her, all struck up. 'Why,' says I, 'Priscilla, that nice old velvet paper ain't hurt a mite. I should n't feel 't was my best room without it. Dan'el says 't is the first thing he can remember rubbin' his little baby fingers on to it, and how splendid he thought them red roses was.' I maintain," continued Mrs. Crowe stoutly, "that folks wastes sights o' good money doin' just such foolish things. Tearin' out the insides o' meetin'-houses, and fixin' the pews different; 't was good enough as 't was with mendin'; then times come, an' they want to put it all back same's 't was before."

This touched upon an exciting subject to active members of that parish. Miss Binson and Mrs. Crowe belonged to opposite parties, and had at one time come as near hard feelings as they could, and yet escape them. Each hastened to speak of other things and to show her untouched friendliness.

"I do agree with you," said Sister Binson, "that few of us know what use to make of money, beyond every-day necessities. You've seen more o' the world than I have, and know what's expected. When it comes to taste and judgment about such things, I ought to defer to others"; and with this modest avowal the critical moment passed when there might have been an improper discussion.

In the silence that followed, the fact of their presence in a house of death grew more clear than before. There was something disturbing in the noise of a mouse gnawing at the dry boards of a closet wall near by. Both the watchers looked up anxiously at the clock; it was almost the middle of the night, and the whole world seemed to have left them alone with their solemn duty. Only the brook was awake.

"Perhaps we might give a look up-stairs now," whispered Mrs. Crowe, as if she hoped to hear some reason against their going just then to the chamber of death; but Sister Binson rose, with a serious and yet satisfied countenance, and lifted the small lamp from the table. She was much more used to watching than Mrs. Crowe, and much less affected by it. They opened the door into a small entry with a steep stairway; they climbed the creaking stairs, and entered the cold upper room on tiptoe. Mrs. Crowe's heart began to beat very fast as the lamp was put on a high bureau, and made long, fixed shadows about the walls. She went hesitatingly toward the solemn shape under its white drapery, and felt a sense of remonstrance as Sarah Ann gently, but in a business-like way, turned back the thin sheet.

"Seems to me she looks pleasanter and pleasanter," whispered Sarah Ann Binson impulsively, as they gazed at the white face with its wonderful smile. "To-morrow 't will all have faded out. I do believe they kind of wake up a day or two after they die, and it's then they go." She replaced the light covering, and they both turned quickly away; there was a chill in this upper room.

" 'T is a great thing for anybody to have got through, ain't it?" said Mrs. Crowe softly, as she began to go down the stairs on tiptoe. The warm air from the kitchen beneath met them with a sense of welcome and shelter.

"I don't know why it is, but I feel as near again to Tempy down here as I do up there," replied Sister Binson. "I feel as if the air was full of her, kind of. I can sense things, now and then, that she seems to say. Now I never was one to take up with no nonsense of sperits and such, but I declare I felt as if she told me just now to put some more wood into the stove."

Mrs. Crowe preserved a gloomy silence. She had suspected before this that her companion was of a weaker and more credulous disposition than herself. " 'T is a great thing to have got through," she repeated, ignoring definitely all that had last been said. "I suppose you know as well as I that Tempy was one that always feared death. Well, it's all put behind her now; she knows what 't is." Mrs. Crowe gave a little sigh, and Sister Binson's quick sympathies were stirred toward this other old friend, who also dreaded the great change.

"I'd never like to forgit almost those last words Tempy spoke plain to me," she said gently, like the comforter she truly was. "She looked up at me once or twice, that last after- noon after I come to set by her, and let Mis' Owen go home; and I says, 'Can I do anything to ease you, Tempy?' and the tears come into my eyes so I could n't see what kind of a nod she give me. 'No, Sarah Ann, you can't, dear,' says she; and then she got her breath again, and says she, looking at me real meanin', 'I'm only a-gettin' sleepier and sleepier; that's all there is,' says she, and smiled up at me kind of wishful, and shut her eyes. I knew well enough all she meant. She'd been lookin' out for a chance to tell me, and I don' know's she ever said much afterwards."

Mrs. Crowe was not knitting; she had been listening too eagerly. "Yes, 't will be a comfort to think of that sometimes," she said, in acknowledgment.

"I know that old Dr. Prince said once, in evenin' meetin', that he'd watched by many a dyin' bed, as we well knew, and enough o' his sick folks had been scared o' dyin' their whole lives through; but when they come to the last, he'd never seen one but was willin', and most were glad, to go. ' 'T is as natural as bein' born or livin' on,' he said. I don't know what had moved him to speak that night. You know he wa'n't in the habit of it, and 't was the monthly concert of prayer for foreign missions anyways," said Sarah Ann; "but 't was a great stay to the mind to listen to his words of experience."

"There never was a better man," responded Mrs. Crowe, in a really cheerful tone. She had recovered from her feeling of nervous dread, the kitchen was so comfortable with lamplight and firelight; and just then the old clock began to tell the hour of twelve with leisurely whirring strokes.

Sister Binson laid aside her work, and rose quickly and went to the cupboard. "We'd better take a little to eat," she explained. "The night will go fast after this. I want to know if you went and made some o' your nice cupcake, while you was home to-day?" she asked, in a pleased tone; and Mrs. Crowe acknowledged such a gratifying piece of thoughtfulness for this humble friend who denied herself all luxuries. Sarah Ann brewed a generous cup of tea, and the watchers drew their chairs up to the table presently, and quelled their hunger with good country appetites. Sister Binson put a spoon into a small, old-fashioned glass of preserved quince, and passed it to her friend. She was most familiar with the house, and played the part of hostess. "Spread some o' this on your bread and butter," she said to Mrs. Crowe. "Tempy wanted me to use some three or four times, but I never felt to. I know she'd like to have us comfortable now, and would urge us to make a good supper, poor dear."

"What excellent preserves she did make!" mourned Mrs. Crowe. "None of us has got her light hand at doin' things tasty. She made the most o' everything, too. Now, she only had that one old quince-tree down in the far corner of the piece, but she'd go out in the spring and tend to it, and look at it so pleasant, and kind of expect the old thorny thing into bloomin'."

"She was just the same with folks," said Sarah Ann. "And she'd never git more'n a little apernful o' quinces, but she'd have every mite o' goodness out o' those, and set the glasses up onto her best-room closet shelf, so pleased. 'T wa'n't but a week ago to-morrow mornin' I fetched her a little taste o' jelly in a teaspoon; and she says 'Thank ye,' and took it, an' the minute she tasted it she looked up at me as worried as could be. 'Oh, I don't want to eat that,' says she. 'I always keep that in case o' sickness.' 'You're goin' to have the good o' one tumbler yourself,' says I. 'I'd just like to know who's sick now, if you ain't!' An' she could n't help laughin', I spoke up so smart. Oh, dear me, how I shall miss talkin' over things with her! She always sensed things, and got just the p'int you meant."

"She didn't begin to age until two or three years ago, did she?" asked Mrs. Crowe. "I never saw anybody keep her looks as Tempy did. She looked young long after I begun to feel like an old woman. The doctor used to say 't was her young heart, and I don't know but what he was right. How she did do for other folks! There was one spell she was n't at home a day to a fortnight. She got most of her livin' so, and that made her own potatoes and things last her through. None o' the young folks could get married without her, and all the old ones was disappointed if she wa'n't round when they was down with sickness and had to go. An' cleanin', or tailorin' for boys, or rug-hookin', — there was nothin' but what she could do as handy as most. 'I do love to work,' — ain't you heard her say that twenty times a week?"

Sarah Ann Binson nodded, and began to clear away the empty plates. "We may want a taste o' somethin' more towards mornin'," she said. "There's plenty in the closet here; and in case some comes from a distance to the funeral, we'll have a little table spread after we get back to the house."

"Yes, I was busy all the mornin'. I've cooked up a sight o' things to bring over," said Mrs. Crowe. "I felt 't was the last I could do for her."

They drew their chairs near the stove again, and took up their work. Sister Binson's rocking-chair creaked as she rocked; the brook sounded louder than ever. It was more lonely when nobody spoke, and presently Mrs. Crowe returned to her thoughts of growing old.

"Yes, Tempy aged all of a sudden. I remember I asked her if she felt as well as common, one day, and she laughed at me good. There, when Dan'el begun to look old, I could n't help feeling as if somethin' ailed him, and like as not 't was somethin' he was goin' to git right over, and I dosed him for it stiddy, half of one summer."

"How many things we shall be wanting to ask Tempy!" exclaimed Sarah Ann Binson, after a long pause. "I can't make up my mind to doin' without her. I wish folks could come back just once, and tell us how 't is where they've gone. Seems then we could do without 'em better."

The brook hurried on, the wind blew about the house now and then; the house itself was a silent place, and the supper, the warm fire, and an absence of any new topics for conversation made the watchers drowsy. Sister Binson closed her eyes first, to rest them for a minute; and Mrs. Crowe glanced at her compassionately, with a new sympathy for the hard-worked little woman. She made up her mind to let Sarah Ann have a good rest, while she kept watch alone; but in a few minutes her own knitting was dropped, and she, too, fell asleep. Overhead, the pale shape of Tempy Dent, the outworn body of that generous, loving-hearted, simple soul, slept on also in its white raiment. Perhaps Tempy herself stood near, and saw her own life and its surroundings with new understanding. Perhaps she herself was the only watcher.

Later, by some hours, Sarah Ann Binson woke with a start. There was a pale light of dawn outside the small windows. Inside the kitchen, the lamp burned dim. Mrs. Crowe awoke, too.

"I think Tempy'd be the first to say 't was just as well we both had some rest," she said, not without a guilty feeling.

Her companion went to the outer door, and opened it wide. The fresh air was none too cold, and the brook's voice was not nearly so loud as it had been in the midnight darkness. She could see the shapes of the hills, and the great shadows that lay across the lower country. The east was fast growing bright.

" 'T will be a beautiful day for the funeral," she said, and turned again, with a sigh, to follow Mrs. Crowe up the stairs.

THE ART OF FICTION

William Dean Howells [1837–1920]

The first great realistic American novelist, "in himself almost an entire literary movement, almost an academy," was born in ante-bellum Ohio and lived there, as printer, newspaper correspondent, and editor, until after he had reached manhood. His early life and the environment that partly shaped him are the subjects of two charming and revealing books, *A Boy's Town*, 1890, and *Years of My Youth*, 1916. He virtually educated himself, by a long course of devoted reading described in *My Literary Passions*, 1895. In 1860, Howells had become well enough known as a journalist in Ohio to be asked to write a campaign biography of Lincoln. The following year he was appointed consul to Venice, and during the Civil War years went on reading, especially in Dante, Goldoni, and other Italians. He returned to America in 1865, served for a short time on the staff of the *Nation*, and then went to Boston to serve on the staff of the *Atlantic*. In 1872, at the age of thirty-five, he was made editor.

The young editor soon proved to be a leader, in criticism and fiction alike, away from romance and toward realism. In 1871 he had published *Suburban Sketches*, which mingled essay and story in a gracious delineation of New England life. Later in the 70's came several New England novels. After he had resigned from the *Atlantic* in 1881, he produced his finest creations: *A Modern Instance*, 1882, and *The Rise of Silas Lapham*, 1885, both of them gently accurate pictures of New England life and character which illustrate plainly his conception of the art of fiction. That conception was similar to Jane Austen's, his "divine Jane," rather than to that of Tolstoy, whom he later extolled in the highest terms but never really emulated.

Howells settled in New York in 1885, when it had become apparent that Boston was no longer the literary capital of the country. He served on the staff of *Harper's* and wrote a long series of novels, without excelling the two named above. He tried his hand at the short story and the drama, doing acceptable but not distinguished work. He was made president of the American Academy, received the gold medal of the National Institute, and lived to see realism at its height in America.

As a novelist and as a force for realism Howells will probably be best remembered. He "produced in his fourscore books," said Carl Van Doren, "the most considerable transcript of American life yet made by one man." As a realistic critic of literature he wrote urbanely, as in the little book *Criticism and Fiction*, which shows a mind sensitive to both American democracy and modern science. He came to be known as the "dean of American letters," and he was useful in sponsoring the work of such young realists as Frank Norris, Stephen Crane, and Hamlin Garland.

Further reading: *The Rise of Silas Lapham*. C. M. Kirk and R. Kirk, eds., *William*

Dean Howells (American Writers Series), 1950. Mildred Howells, ed., *Life in Letters*, 2 vols., 1928. O. W. Firkins, *William Dean Howells, A Study*, 1924. W. F. Taylor, *The Economic Novel in America*, 1942, chapter 6. Everett Carter, *Howells and the Age of Realism*, 1954.

From *Criticism and Fiction*

(1892)

[Criticism and Realism]

"As for those called critics," the author [Burke] says, "they have generally sought the rule of the arts in the wrong place; they have sought among poems, pictures, engravings, statues, and buildings; but art can never give the rules that make an art. This is, I believe, the reason why artists in general, and poets principally, have been confined in so narrow a circle; they have been rather imitators of one another than of nature. Critics follow them, and therefore can do little as guides. I can judge but poorly of anything while I measure it by no other standard than itself. The true standard of the arts is in every man's power; and an easy observation of the most common, sometimes of the meanest things, in nature will give the truest lights, where the greatest sagacity and industry that slights such observation must leave us in the dark, or, what is worse, amuse and mislead us by false lights."

If this should happen to be true — and it certainly commends itself to acceptance — it might portend an immediate danger to the vested interests of criticism, only that it was written a hundred years ago; and we shall probably have the "sagacity and industry that slights the observation" of nature long enough yet to allow most critics the time to learn some more useful trade than criticism as they pursue it. Nevertheless, I am in hopes that the communistic era in taste foreshadowed by Burke is approaching, and that it will occur within the lives of men now over-awed by the foolish old superstition that literature and art are anything but the expression of life, and are to be judged by any other test than that of their fidelity to it. The time is coming, I hope, when each new author, each new artist, will be considered, not in his proportion to any other author or artist, but in his relation to the human nature, known to us all, which it is his privilege, his high duty, to interpret. "The true standard of the artist is in every man's power" already, as Burke says; Michelangelo's "light of the piazza," the glance of the common eye, is and always was the best light on a statue; Goethe's "boys and black-birds" have in all ages been the real connoisseurs of berries; but hitherto the mass of common men have been afraid to apply their own simplicity, naturalness, and honesty to the appreciation of the beautiful. They have always cast about for the instruction of some one who professed to know better, and who browbeat wholesome common-sense into the self-distrust that ends in sophistication. They have fallen generally to the worst of this bad species, and have been "amused and misled" (how pretty that quaint old use of amuse is!) "by the false lights" of critical vanity and self-righteousness. They have been taught to compare what they see and what they read, not with the things that they have observed and known, but with the things that some other artist or writer has done. Especially if they have themselves the artistic impulse in any direction they are taught to form themselves, not upon life, but upon the masters who became masters only by forming themselves upon life. The seeds of death are planted in them, and they can produce only the still-born, the academic. They are not told to take their work into the public square and see if it seems true to the chance passer, but to test it by the work of the very men who refused and decried any other test of their own work. The young writer who attempts to report the phrase and carriage of every-day life, who tries to tell just how he has heard men talk and seen them look, is made to feel guilty of something low and unworthy by the stupid people who would like to have him show how Shakespeare's men talked and looked, or Scott's, or Thackeray's, or Balzac's, or Hawthorne's, or Dickens's; he is instructed to idealize his personages, that is, to take the life-likeness out of them, and put the book-likeness into them. He is approached in the spirit of the wretched pedantry into which learning, much or little, always decays when it withdraws itself and stands apart from experience in an attitude of imagined superiority, and which would say with the same confidence to the scientist: "I see that you are looking at a grasshopper there which you have found in the grass, and I suppose you intend to describe it. Now don't waste your time and sin against culture in that way. I've got a grasshopper here, which has been evolved at considerable pains and expense out of the grasshopper in general; in fact, it's a type. It's made up of wire and card-board, very prettily painted in a conventional tint, and it's perfectly indestructible. It isn't very much like a real grasshopper, but it's a great deal nicer, and it's served to represent the notion of a grasshopper ever since man emerged from barbarism. You may say that it's artificial. Well, it is artificial; but then it's ideal too; and what you want to do is to cultivate the ideal. You'll find the books full of my kind of grasshopper, and scarcely a trace of yours in any of them. The thing that you are proposing to do is commonplace; but if you say that it isn't commonplace, for the very reason that it hasn't been done before, you'll have to admit that it's photographic."

As I said, I hope the time is coming when not only the artist, but the common, average man, who always "has the standard of the arts in his power," will have also the courage to apply it, and will reject the ideal grasshopper wherever he finds it, in science, in literature, in art, because it is not "simple, natural, and honest," because it is not like a real grasshopper. But I will own that I think the time is yet far off, and that the people who have been brought up on the ideal grasshopper, the heroic grasshopper, the impassioned grasshopper, the self-devoted, adventureful, good old romantic card-board grasshopper, must die out before the simple, honest, and natural grasshopper can have a fair field. I am in no haste to compass the end of these good people, whom I find in the mean time very amusing. It is delightful to meet one of them, either in print or out of it — some sweet elderly lady or excellent gentleman whose youth was pastured on the literature of thirty or forty years ago — and to witness the confidence with which they preach their favorite authors as all the law and the prophets. They have commonly read little or nothing since, or, if they have, they have judged it by a standard taken from these authors, and never dreamed of judging it by nature; they are destitute of the documents in the case of the later writers; they suppose that Balzac was the beginning of real-

ism, and that Zola is its wicked end; they are quite ignorant, but they are ready to talk you down, if you differ from them, with an assumption of knowledge sufficient for any occasion. The horror, the resentment, with which they receive any question of their literary saints is genuine; you descend at once very far in the moral and social scale, and anything short of offensive personality is too good for you; it is expressed to you that you are one to be avoided, and put down even a little lower than you have naturally fallen.

These worthy persons are not to blame; it is part of their intellectual mission to represent the petrifaction of taste, and to preserve an image of a smaller and cruder and emptier world than we now live in, a world which was feeling its way towards the simple, the natural, the honest, but was a good deal "amused and misled" by lights now no longer mistakable for heavenly luminaries. They belong to a time, just passing away, when certain authors were considered authorities in certain kinds, when they must be accepted entire and not questioned in any particular. Now we are beginning to see and to say that no author is an authority except in those moments when he held his ear close to Nature's lips and caught her very accent. These moments are not continuous with any authors in the past, and they are rare with all. Therefore I am not afraid to say now that the greatest classics are sometimes not at all great, and that we can profit by them only when we hold them, like our meanest contemporaries, to a strict accounting, and verify their work by the standard of the arts which we all have in our power, the simple, the natural, and the honest.

Those good people, these curious and interesting if somewhat musty back-numbers, must always have a hero, an idol of some sort, and it is droll to find Balzac, who suffered from their sort such bitter scorn and hate for his realism while he was alive, now become a fetich in his turn, to be shaken in the faces of those who will not blindly worship him. But it is no new thing in the history of literature: whatever is established is sacred with those who do not think. At the beginning of the century, when romance was making the same fight against effete classicism which realism is making to-day against effete romanticism, the Italian poet Monti declared that "the romantic was the cold grave of the Beautiful," just as the realistic is now supposed to be. The romantic of that day and the real of this are in certain degree the same. Romanticism then sought, as realism seeks now, to widen the bounds of sympathy, to level every barrier against æsthetic freedom, to escape from the paralysis of tradition. It exhausted itself in this impulse; and it remained for realism to assert that fidelity to experience and probability of motive are essential conditions of a great imaginative literature. It is not a new theory, but it has never before universally characterized literary endeavor. When realism becomes false to itself, when it heaps up facts merely, and maps life instead of picturing it, realism will perish too. Every true realist instinctively knows this, and it is perhaps the reason why he is careful of every fact, and feels himself bound to express or to indicate its meaning at the risk of over-moralizing. In life he finds nothing insignificant; all tells for destiny and character; nothing that God has made is contemptible. He cannot look upon human life and declare this thing or that thing unworthy of notice, any more than the scientist can declare a fact of the material world beneath the dignity of his inquiry. He feels in every nerve the equality of things and the unity of men; his soul is exalted, not by vain shows and shadows and ideals, but by realities, in which alone the truth lives. In criticism it is his business to break the images of false gods and misshapen heroes, to take away the poor silly toys that many grown people still like to play with. He cannot keep terms with Jack the Giant-killer or Puss in Boots, under any name or in any place, even when they reappear as the convict Vautrec, or the Marquis de Montrivaut, or the Sworn Thirteen Noblemen. He must say to himself that Balzac, when he imagined these monsters, was not Balzac, he was Dumas; he was not realistic, he was romantic.***

[The English Novel since Jane Austen]

Which brings us again, after this long way about, to the divine Jane and her novels, and that troublesome question about them. She was great and they were beautiful, because she and they were honest, and dealt with nature nearly a hundred years ago as realism deals with it to-day. Realism is nothing more and nothing less than the truthful treatment of material, and Jane Austen was the first and the last of the English novelists to treat material with entire truthfulness. Because she did this, she remains the most artistic of the English novelists, and alone worthy to be matched with the great Scandinavian and Slavic and Latin artists. It is not a question of intellect, or not wholly that. The English have mind enough; but they have not taste enough; or, rather, their taste has been perverted by their false criticism, which is based upon personal preference, and not upon principle; which instructs a man to think that what he likes is good, instead of teaching him first to distinguish what is good before he likes it. The art of fiction, as Jane Austen knew it, declined from her through Scott, and Bulwer, and Dickens, and Charlotte Brontë, and Thackeray, and even George Eliot, because the mania of romanticism had seized upon all Europe, and these great writers could not escape the taint of their time; but it has shown few signs of recovery in England, because English criticism, in the presence of the Continental masterpieces, has continued provincial and special and personal, and has expressed a love and a hate which had to do with the quality of the artist rather than the character of his work. It was inevitable that in their time the English romanticists should treat, as Señor Valdés says, "the barbarous customs of the Middle Ages, softening and disfiguring them, as Walter Scott and his kind did"; that they should "devote themselves to falsifying nature, refining and subtilizing sentiment, and modifying psychology after their own fancy," like Bulwer and Dickens, as well as like Rousseau and Madame de Staël, not to mention Balzac, the worst of all that sort at his worst. This was the natural course of the disease; but it really seems as if it were their criticism that was to blame for the rest: not, indeed, for the performance of this writer or that, for criticism can never affect the actual doing of a thing; but for the esteem in which this writer or that is held through the perpetuation of false ideals. The only observer of English middle-class life since Jane Austen worthy to be named with her was not George Eliot, who was first ethical and then artistic, who transcended her in everything but the form and method most essential to art, and there fell hopelessly below her. It was Anthony Trollope who was most like her in simple honesty and instinctive truth, as unphilosophized as the light of common day; but he was so warped from a wholesome ideal as to wish at times to be like the caricaturist Thackeray, and to stand about in his scene, talking it over with his hands in his pockets, interrupting the action, and spoiling the illusion in which alone the truth of art resides. Mainly, his instinct was too much for his ideal, and with a low view of life in its civic relations and a thoroughly bourgeois soul, he yet produced works whose beauty is surpassed only by the effect of a more poetic writer in the novels of Thomas Hardy. Yet if a vote of English criticism even at this late day, when all continental Europe has the light of æsthetic truth, could be taken, the majority against these artists would be overwhelmingly in favor of a writer who had so little artistic sensibility, that he never hesitated on any occasion, great or small, to make a foray among his characters, and catch them up to show them to the reader and tell him how beautiful or ugly they were; and cry out over their amazing properties.

Doubtless the ideal of those poor islanders will be finally changed. If the truth could become a fad it would be accepted by all their "smart people," but truth is something rather too large for that; and we must await the gradual advance of civilization among them. Then they will see that their criticism has misled them; and that it is to this false guide they owe, not precisely the decline of fiction among them, but its continued debasement as an art.***

[Democracy and the American Novel]

I would have our American novelists be as American as they unconsciously can. Matthew Arnold complained that he found no "distinction" in our life, and I would gladly persuade all artists intending greatness in any kind among us that the recognition of the fact pointed out by Mr. Arnold ought to be a source of inspiration to them, and not discouragement. We have been now some hundred years building up a state on the affirmation of the essential equality of men in their rights and duties, and whether we have been right or been wrong the gods have taken us at our word, and have responded to us with a civilization in which there is no "distinction" perceptible to the eye that loves and values it. Such beauty and such grandeur as we have is common beauty, common grandeur, or the beauty and grandeur in which the quality of solidarity so prevails that neither distinguishes itself to the disadvantage of anything else. It seems to me that these conditions invite the artist to the study and the appreciation of the common, and to the por-

trayal in every art of those finer and higher aspects which unite rather than sever humanity, if he would thrive in our new order of things. The talent that is robust enough to front the every-day world and catch the charm of its work-worn, care-worn, brave, kindly face, need not fear the encounter, though it seems terrible to the sort nurtured in the superstition of the romantic, the bizarre, the heroic, the distinguished, as the things alone worthy of painting or carving or writing. The arts must become democratic, and then we shall have the expression of America in art; and the reproach which Mr. Arnold was half right in making us shall have no justice in it any longer; we shall be "distinguished."***

[Decency and the American Novel]

One of the great newspapers the other day invited the prominent American authors to speak their minds upon a point in the theory and practice of fiction which had already vexed some of them. It was the question of how much or how little the American novel ought to deal with certain facts of life which are not usually talked of before young people, and especially young ladies. Of course the question was not decided, and I forget just how far the balance inclined in favor of a larger freedom in the matter. But it certainly inclined that way; one or two writers of the sex which is somehow supposed to have purity in its keeping (as if purity were a thing that did not practically concern the other sex, preoccupied with serious affairs) gave it a rather vigorous tilt to that side. In view of this fact it would not be the part of prudence to make an effort to dress the balance; and indeed I do not know that I was going to make any such effort. But there are some things to say, around and about the subject, which I should like to have some one else say, and which I may myself possibly be safe in suggesting.

One of the first of these is the fact, generally lost sight of by those who censure the Anglo-Saxon novel for its prudishness, that it is really not such a prude after all; and that if it is sometimes apparently anxious to avoid those experiences of life not spoken of before young people, this may be an appearance only. Sometimes a novel which has this shuffling air, this effect of truckling to propriety, might defend itself, if it could speak for itself, by saying that such experiences happened not to come within its scheme, and that, so far from maiming or mutilating itself in ignoring them, it was all the more faithfully representative of the tone of modern life in dealing with love that was chaste, and with passion so honest that it could be openly spoken of before the tenderest society bud at dinner. It might say that the guilty intrigue, the betrayal, the extreme flirtation even, was the exceptional thing in life, and unless the scheme of the story necessarily involved it, that it would be bad art to lug it in, and as bad taste as to introduce such topics in a mixed company. It could say very justly that the novel in our civilization now always addresses a mixed company, and that the vast majority of the company are ladies, and that very many, if not most, of these ladies are young girls. If the novel were written for men and for married women alone, as in continental Europe, it might be altogether different. But the simple fact is that it is not written for them alone among us, and it is a question of writing, under cover of our universal acceptance, things for young girls to read which you would be put out-of-doors for saying to them, or frankly giving notice of your intention, and so cutting yourself off from the pleasure — and it is a very high and sweet one — of appealing to these vivid, responsive intelligences, which are none the less brilliant and admirable because they are innocent.

One day a novelist who liked, after the manner of other men, to repine at his hard fate, complained to his friend, a critic, that he was tired of the restriction he had put upon himself in this regard; for it is a mistake, as can be readily shown, to suppose that others impose it. "See how free those French fellows are!" he rebelled. "Shall we always be shut up to our tradition of decency?"

"Do you think it's much worse than being shut up to their tradition of indecency?" said his friend.

Then that novelist began to reflect, and he remembered how sick the invariable motive of the French novel made him. He perceived finally that, convention for convention, ours was not only more tolerable, but on the whole was truer to life, not only to its complexion, but also to its texture. No one will pretend that there is not vicious love beneath the surface of our society; if he did, the fetid explosions of the divorce trials would refute him; but if he pretended that it was in any just sense characteristic of our society, he could be still more easily refuted. Yet it exists, and it is unquestionably the material of tragedy, the stuff from which intense effects are wrought. The question, after owning this fact, is whether these intense effects are not rather cheap effects. I incline to think they are, and I will try to say why I think so, if I may do so without offence. The material itself, the mere mention of it, has an instant fascination; it arrests, it detains, till the last word is said, and while there is anything to be hinted. This is what makes a love intrigue of some sort all but essential to the popularity of any fiction. Without such an intrigue the intellectual equipment of the author must be of the highest, and then he will succeed only with the highest class of readers. But any author who will deal with a guilty love intrigue holds all readers in his hand, the highest with the lowest, as long as he hints the slightest hope of the smallest potential naughtiness. He need not at all be a great author; he may be a very shabby wretch, if he has but the courage or the trick of that sort of thing. The critics will call him "virile" and "passionate"; decent people will be ashamed to have been limed by him; but the low average will only ask another chance of flocking into his net. If he happens to be an able writer, his really fine and costly work will be unheeded, and the lure to the appetite will be chiefly remembered. There may be other qualities which make reputations for other men, but in his case they will count for nothing. He pays this penalty for his success in that kind; and every one pays some such penalty who deals with some such material. It attaches in like manner to the triumphs of the writers who now almost form a school among us, and who may be said to have established themselves in an easy popularity simply by the study of erotic shivers and fervors. They may find their account in the popularity, or they may not; there is no question of the popularity.

But I do not mean to imply that their case covers the whole ground. So far as it goes, though, it ought to stop the mouths of those who complain that fiction is enslaved to propriety among us. It appears that of a certain kind of impropriety it is free to give us all it will, and more. But this is not what serious men and women writing fiction mean when they rebel against the limitations of their art in our civilization. They have no desire to deal with nakedness, as painters and sculptors freely do in the worship of beauty; or with certain facts of life, as the stage does, in the service of sensation. But they ask why, when the conventions of the plastic and histrionic arts liberate their followers to the portrayal of almost any phase of the physical or of the emotional nature, an American novelist may not write a story on the lines of Anna Karenina or Madame Bovary. Sappho they put aside, and from Zola's work they avert their eyes. They do not condemn him or Daudet, necessarily, or accuse their motives; they leave them out of the question: they do not want to do that kind of thing. But they do sometimes wish to do another kind, to touch one of the most serious and sorrowful problems of life in the spirit of Tolstoi and Flaubert, and they ask why they may not. At one time, they remind us, the Anglo-Saxon novelist did deal with such problems — De Foe in his spirit, Richardson in his, Goldsmith in his. At what moment did our fiction lose this privilege? In what fatal hour did the Young Girl arise and seal the lips of Fiction, with a touch of her finger, to some of the most vital interests of life?

Whether I wished to oppose them in their aspiration for greater freedom, or whether I wished to encourage them, I should begin to answer them by saying that the Young Girl had never done anything of the kind. The manners of the novel have been improving with those of its readers; that is all. Gentlemen no longer swear or fall drunk under the table, or abduct young ladies and shut them up in lonely country-houses, or so habitually set about the ruin of their neighbors' wives, as they once did. Generally, people now call a spade an agricultural implement; they have not grown decent without having also grown a little squeamish, but they have grown comparatively decent; there is no doubt about that. They require of a novelist whom they respect unquestionable proof of his seriousness, if he proposes to deal with certain phases of life; they require a sort of scientific decorum. He can no longer expect to be received on the ground of entertainment only; he assumes a higher function, something like that of a physician or a priest, and they expect him to be bound by laws as sacred as those of such professions; they hold him solemnly pledged not to betray them or abuse their confidence. If he will accept the conditions, they give him their confidence, and he may then treat to his greater honor, and not at all to his disadvantage, of such experiences, such relations of men and women as George Eliot treats in Adam Bede, in Daniel Deronda, in Romola, in almost all her books; such as Hawthorne treats in the Scarlet Letter; such as Dickens treats in David Copperfield; such as Thackeray treats in Pendennis, and glances at in every one of his fictions; such as most of the masters of English fiction have at some time treated more or less openly. It is quite false or quite mistaken to suppose that our novels have left untouched these most important realities of life. They have only not made them their stock in trade; they have kept a true perspective in regard to them; they have relegated them in their pictures of life to the space and place they occupy in life itself, as we know it in England and America. They have kept a correct proportion, knowing perfectly well that unless the novel is to be a map, with everything scrupulously laid down in it, a faithful record of life in far the greater extent could be made to the exclusion of guilty love and all its circumstances and consequences.

I justify them in this view not only because I hate what is cheap and meretricious, and hold in peculiar loathing the cant of the critics who require "passion" as something in itself admirable and desirable in a novel, but because I prize fidelity in the historian of feeling and character. Most of these critics who demand "passion" would seem to have no conception of any passion but one. Yet there are several other passions; the passion of grief, the passion of avarice, the passion of pity, the passion of ambition, the passion of hate, the passion of envy, the passion of devotion, the passion of friendship; and all these have a greater part in the drama of life than the passion of love, and infinitely greater than the passion of guilty love. Wittingly or unwittingly, English fiction and American fiction have recognized this truth, not fully, not in the measure it merits, but in greater degree than most other fiction.

Henry James [1843–1916]

Born in New York, Henry James, brother of William James, the distinguished psychologist and philosopher, grew up in a turbulent period of American history — the period of westward expansion, the Civil War, enormous commercial and industrial developments, and the usual run of lively chapters in American politics. Yet, though he was unquestionably the major American novelist of his time, James's several thousand pages rarely touch any of these events. The reasons for this extraordinary omission constitute the significant facts of his career.

His father, a writer of theological and philosophical tracts, having rebelled against his own strict Calvinistic upbringing, and enjoying the freedom of an independent income, gave his sons an eclectic, purposefully haphazard education which would not limit their intellectual freedom by even so much as predisposing them to a particular profession. Exposed early to their father's Swedenborgian mysticism, the boys subsequently sampled many religions but subscribed to none, studied under various tutors and at various schools, and dipped into art, literature, science, law, and — most important — European travel. Henry James came to feel more at home and more sure of himself abroad than in the United States; in 1876 he took up permanent residence in England; and in 1915 he became a British citizen. He was further removed from the main currents of American life by a back injury which kept him self-consciously on the sidelines during the Civil War and perhaps intensified those elements in his temperament which were to keep him forever from the active life and from marriage, and make of him a detached, dedicated, increasingly skilled observer.

Thus it was perhaps inevitable that when, after writing some critical essays and reviews and a few stories showing the influence of Hawthorne, James began to develop his own brand of fiction, he should turn his back on most of American life. "One writes as one *can*," he said. He wrote of what he knew — a very small segment of American society at home and the American traveler abroad. His characters are in professional retirement or live on apparently sourceless incomes, or are writers or painters or jobless fortune-hunters. Thus freed from the concrete details of American life, James proceeded to free himself also from nearly all other concrete details, writing of the subtle relationships between mind and mind, and between one level of moral awareness or moral strength and another. His characters do not act so much as they observe, feel, realize, and — at the most — resolve. They are extraordinarily sensitive; James said in "The Art of Fiction" — "Try to be one of the people on whom nothing is lost," and he tried himself to be one, and his characters did, too. Their stories end in renunciation and loss oftener than in achievement, and their only victories are moral victories — themes plainly inappropriate to the temper of James's country and his time. This intense subjectivity is the source both of his richness and his difficulty. Many readers admire what they consider to be his intricate and accurate psychological analysis and profound ethical concerns, particularly in such great novels as *The Wings of the Dove*, *The Ambassadors*, and *The Golden Bowl*. Many others, who may enjoy the relatively straightforward earlier works, such as *The American*, *Daisy Miller*, and *The Portrait of a Lady,* are repelled by the later work, which they feel pursues moral problems so tenuous as to be mere hallucinations, problems more fussy than rigorous, more obscure than profound.

A self-conscious, devoted artist and a careful student of the French novelists, James achieved standards of style and form unprecedented in the American novel. In his critical writings, which make him a leading American critic, he analyzed in detail his own theories and techniques, and made the plea that the novel be taken — and take itself — seriously. Banishing the chatty author and writing from the point of view of a single character, a "filter," an observer-participant, he gave his work unity, form, and dramatic intensity. His narratives unfold in a realistic series of impressions — misconceptions, partial glimpses, and revelations. He was trying to catch the inconclusiveness and shapelessness of life — the Truth of the impressionist — in a firmly-shaped literary form. The resultant difficulties of exposition and analysis he solved with great ingenuity. Indeed, over the years his style and technique became so ingenious and complex that many readers found him hopelessly indirect and involved and tediously mystifying, though a few admired him more than ever. A careful analysis of this later style as it appears in the revisions he made of earlier works, shows that his elaborations are always purposeful and controlled — that *he,* at least, knew what he was doing.

His latter years were darkened by the unpopularity which came to him when he felt he was doing his best work, by illness, and by the moral and intellectual catastrophe of the first World War: "*This* is what we were so fondly working for!" But he predicted hopefully — and accurately — that one day "all my buried prose will kick off its various tombstones all at once." Whatever his final rating, his influence is unquestionably immense. Modern fiction has followed paths which celebrate his own. He is currently respected for his devotion to moral problems, his pioneering in subjective and symbolic drama, and his immense artistic integrity. Edith Wharton's remark is generally taken now as both an accurate description and a tribute: "For him every great novel must first of all be based on a profound sense of moral values and then constructed with a classical unity and economy of means."

Further reading: *The Portrait of a Lady. The American. The Ambassadors. Henry James: Selected Fiction,* ed. Leon Edel, 1953. Michael Swan, *Henry James* (biography), 1952. F. W. Dupee, *Henry James* (biography), 1951. Leon Edel, *Henry James: The Untried Years,* 1953. F. O. Matthiessen, *Henry James: The Major Phase,* 1944. F. W. Dupee, ed., *The Question of Henry James,* 1945.

From *Hawthorne*

(1879)

❦ James wrote his life of Hawthorne for the English Men of Letters series published by Macmillan and Co. of London. Hawthorne was the first American writer to be included in this well-known series.

The following passages are interesting for their revelation of James's attitude toward the "crude and simple society," the "large juvenility," of a land where history had left only a thin deposit.

[The Thinness of American Life]

Hawthorne, on the one side is so subtle and slender and unpretending, and the American world, on the other, is so vast and various and substantial, that it might seem to the author of *The Scarlet Letter* and the *Mosses from an Old Manse,* that we render him a poor service in 5 contrasting his proportions with those of a great civilization. But our author must accept the awkward as well as the graceful side of his fame; for he has the advantage of pointing a valuable moral. This moral is that the flower of art 10 blooms only where the soil is deep, that it takes a great deal of history to produce a little literature, that it needs a complex social machinery to set a writer in motion. American civilization has hitherto had other things to do than to pro- 15 duce flowers, and before giving birth to writers it has wisely occupied itself with providing something for them to write about. Three or four beautiful plants of trans-Atlantic growth are the sum of what the world usually recognises, and in this modest nosegay the genius of Hawthorne is admitted to have the rarest and sweetest fragrance.

His very simplicity has been in his favour; it has helped him to appear complete and homogeneous. To talk of his being national would be to force the note and make a mistake of proportion; but he is, in spite of the absence of the realistic quality, intensely and vividly local. Out of the soil of New England he sprang — in a crevice of that immitigable granite he sprouted and bloomed. Half of the interest that he possesses for an American reader with any turn for analysis must reside in his latent New England savour.*** The cold, bright air of New England seems to blow through his pages, and these, in the opinion of many people, are the medium in which it is most agreeable to make the acquaintance of that tonic atmosphere. As to whether it is worth while to seek to know something of New England in order to extract a more intimate quality from *The House of the Seven Gables* and *The Blithedale Romance*, I need not pronounce; but it is certain that a considerable observation of the society to which these productions were more directly addressed is a capital preparation for enjoying them. I have alluded to the absence in Hawthorne of that quality of realism which is now so much in fashion, an absence in regard to which there will of course be more to say; and yet I think I am not fanciful in saying that he testifies to the sentiments of the society in which he flourished almost as pertinently (proportions observed) as Balzac and some of his descendants — MM. Flaubert and Zola — testify to the manners and morals of the French people. He was not a man with a literary theory; he was guiltless of a system, and I am not sure that he had ever heard of Realism, this remarkable compound having (although it was invented some time earlier) come into general use only since his death. He had certainly not proposed to himself to give an account of the social idiosyncrasies of his fellow-citizens, for his touch on such points is always light and vague, he has none of the apparatus of an historian, and his shadowy style of portraiture never suggests a rigid standard of accuracy. Nevertheless, he virtually offers the most vivid reflection of New England life that has found its way into literature. His value in this respect is not diminished by the fact that he has not attempted to portray the usual Yankee of comedy, and that he has been almost culpably indifferent to his opportunities for commemorating the variations of colloquial English that may be observed in the New World. His characters do not express themselves in the dialect of the *Biglow Papers* — their language, indeed, is apt to be too elegant, too delicate. They are not portraits of actual types, and in their phraseology there is nothing imitative. But none the less, Hawthorne's work savours thoroughly of the local soil — it is redolent of the social system in which he had his being.***

In quiet provincial Salem, Nathaniel Hawthorne passed the greater part of his boyhood, as well as many years of his later life. Mr. Lathrop has much to say about the ancient picturesqueness of the place, and about the mystic influences it would project upon such a mind and character as Hawthorne's. These things are always relative, and in appreciating them everything depends upon the point of view. Mr. Lathrop writes for American readers, who in such a matter as this are very easy to please. Americans have, as a general thing, a hungry passion for the picturesque, and they are so fond of local colour that they contrive to perceive it in localities in which the amateurs of other countries would detect only the most neutral tints. History, as yet, has left in the United States but so thin and impalpable a deposit that we very soon touch the hard substratum of nature, and nature herself, in the Western World, has the peculiarity of seeming rather crude and immature. The very air looks new and young; the light of the sun seems fresh and innocent, as if it knew as yet but few of the secrets of the world and none of the weariness of shining; the vegetation has the appearance of not having reached its majority. A large juvenility is stamped upon the face of things, and in the vividness of the present, the past, which died so young and had time to produce so little, attracts but scanty attention. I doubt whether English observers would discover any very striking trace of it in the ancient town of Salem. Still, with all respect to a York and a Shrewsbury, to a Toledo and a Verona, Salem has a physiognomy in which the past plays a more important part than the present. It is of course a very recent past; but one must remember that the dead of yesterday are not more alive than those of a century ago. I know not of what picturesqueness Hawthorne was conscious in his respectable birthplace; I suspect his perception of it was less keen than his biographer assumes it to have been; but he must have felt at least that, of whatever complexity of earlier life there had been in the country, the elm-shadowed streets of Salem were a recognizable memento. He has made considerable mention of the place, here and there, in his tales; but he has nowhere dilated upon it very lovingly, and it is noteworthy that in The House of the Seven Gables, the only one of his novels of which the scene is laid in it, he has by no means availed himself of the opportunity to give a description of it. He had of course a filial fondness for it — a deep-seated sense of connection with it; but he must have spent some very dreary years there, and the two feelings, the mingled tenderness and rancour, are visible in the Introduction to The Scarlet Letter.

The old town of Salem, he writes — my native place, though I have dwelt much away from it, both in boyhood and in maturer years — possesses, or did possess, a hold on my affections, the force of which I have never realized during my seasons of actual residence here. Indeed, so far as the physical aspect is concerned, with its flat, unvaried surface, covered chiefly with wooden houses, few or none of which pretend to architectural beauty; its irregularity, which is neither picturesque nor quaint, but only tame; its long and lazy street, lounging wearisomely through the whole extent of the peninsula, with Gallows Hill and New Guinea at one end, and a view of the almshouse at the other — such being the features of my native town, it would be quite as reasonable to form a sentimental attachment to a disarranged chequer-board.

But he goes on to say that he has never divested himself of the sense of intensely belonging to it — that the spell of the continuity of his life with that of his predecessors has never been broken. "It is no matter that the place is joyless for him; that he is weary of the old wooden houses, the mud and the dust, the dead level of site and sentiment, the chill east wind, and the chilliest of social atmosphere; — all these, and whatever faults besides he may see or imagine, are nothing to the purpose. The spell survives, and just as powerfully as if the natal spot were an earthly paradise." There is a very American quality in this perpetual consciousness of a spell on Hawthorne's part; it is only in a country where newness and change and brevity of tenure are the common substance of life, that the fact of one's ancestors having lived for a hundred and seventy years in a single spot would become an element of one's morality. It is only an imaginative American that would feel urged to keep reverting to this circumstance, to keep analysing and cunningly considering it.***

I know not at what age he began to keep a diary; the first entries in the American volumes are of the summer of 1835. There is a phrase in the preface to his novel of Transformation [The Marble Faun] which must have lingered in the minds of many Americans who have tried to write novels, and to lay the scene of them in the Western world. "No author, without a trial, can conceive of the difficulty of writing a romance about a country where there is no shadow, no antiquity, no mystery, no picturesque and gloomy wrong, nor anything but a commonplace prosperity, in broad and simple daylight, as is happily the case with my dear native land." The perusal of Hawthorne's American Note-Books operates as a practical commentary upon this somewhat ominous text. It does so at least to my own mind; it would be too much, perhaps, to say that the effect would be the same for the usual English reader. An American reads between the lines — he completes the suggestions — he constructs a picture. I think I am not guilty of any gross injustice in saying that the picture he constructs from Hawthorne's American diaries, though by no means without charms of its own, is not, on the whole, an interesting one. It is characterised by an extraordinary blankness — a curious paleness of colour and paucity of detail. Hawthorne, as I have said, has a large and healthy appetite for detail, and one is, therefore, the more struck with the lightness of the diet to which his observation was condemned. For myself, as I turn the pages of his journals, I seem to see the images of the crude and simple society in which he lived. I use these epithets, of course, not invidiously, but descriptively; if one desire to enter as closely as possible into Hawthorne's situation, one must endeavour to reproduce his circumstances. We are struck with the large number of elements that were absent from them, and the coldness, the thinness, the blankness, to repeat my epithet, present themselves so vividly that our foremost feeling is that of compassion for a romancer looking for subjects in such a field. It takes so many things, as Hawthorne must have felt later in life, when he made the acquaintance of the denser, richer, warmer European spectacle — it takes such an accumulation of history and custom, such a complexity of manners and types, to form a fund of suggestion for a novelist. If Hawthorne had been a young Englishman, or a young Frenchman of the same degree of genius, the same cast of mind, the same habits, his consciousness of the world around him would have been a very different affair; however obscure, however reserved, his own personal life, his sense of the life of his fellow-mortals would have been almost infinitely more various. The negative side of the spectacle on which Hawthorne looked out, in his contemplative saunterings and reveries, might, indeed, with a little ingenuity, be made almost ludicrous; one might enumerate the items of high civilization, as it exists in other countries, which are absent from the texture of American life, until it should become a wonder to know what was left. No State, in the European sense of the word, and indeed barely a specific national name. No sovereign, no court, no personal loyalty, no aristocracy, no church, no clergy, no army, no diplomatic service, no country gentlemen, no palaces, no castles, nor manors, nor old country-houses, nor parsonages, nor thatched cottages, nor ivied ruins; no cathedrals, nor abbeys, nor little Norman churches; no great Universities nor public schools — no Oxford, nor Eton, nor Harrow; no literature, no novels, no museums, no pictures, no political society, no sporting class — no Epsom nor Ascot! Some such list as that might be drawn up of the absent things in American life — especially in the American life of forty years ago, the effect of which, upon an English or a French imagination, would probably, as a general thing, be appalling. The natural remark, in the almost lurid light of such an indictment, would be that if these things are left out, everything is left out. The American knows that a good deal remains; what it is that remains — that is his secret, his joke, as one may say. It would be cruel, in this terrible denudation, to deny him the consolation of his natural gift, that "American humour" of which of late years we have heard so much.

But in helping us to measure what remains,

our author's diaries, as I have already intimated, would give comfort rather to persons who might have taken the alarm from the brief sketch I have just attempted of what I have called the negative side of the American social situation, than to those reminding themselves of its fine compensations. Hawthorne's entries are to a great degree accounts of walks in the country, drives in stage-coaches, people he met in taverns. The minuteness of the things that attract his attention, and that he deems worthy of being commemorated, is frequently extreme, and from this fact we get the impression of a general vacancy in the field of vision. "Sunday evening, going by the jail, the setting sun kindled up the windows most cheerfully; as if there were a bright, comfortable light within its darksome stone wall." "I went yesterday with Monsieur S— to pick raspberries. He fell through an old log-bridge, thrown over a hollow; looking back, only his head and shoulders appeared through the rotten logs and among the bushes. A shower coming on, the rapid running of a little barefooted boy, coming up unheard, and dashing swiftly past us, and showing us the soles of his naked feet as he ran adown the path and up the opposite side." In another place he devotes a page to a description of a dog whom he saw running round after its tail; in still another he remarks, in a paragraph by itself, — "The aromatic odor of peat-smoke in the sunny autumnal air is very pleasant." The reader says to himself that when a man turned thirty gives a place in his mind — and his inkstand — to such trifles as these, it is because nothing else of superior importance demands admission. Everything in the Notes indicates a simple, democratic, thinly-composed society; there is no evidence of the writer finding himself in any variety or intimacy of relations with any one or with anything.

The Real Thing

(1893)

🦋 James's notebooks tell us that his stories often originated in some simple irony, some curious paradox or reversal. "The Real Thing" deals with the obvious paradox that the real thing is not as good as a substitute. Yet stories take their quality more from the author's mind than from the simple idea or "plot" from which they spring, and here James's wit and irony produce a sharp satire upon a social type which must have been common in the tourist and country-house world he knew so well. He also says something here about the function of art. What is the significance of the idea that realistic art does not consist of a literal copy of "the real thing"? In relation to this, why did James give his young model the name of "Miss Churm"?

I

When the porter's wife (she used to answer the house-bell), announced "A gentleman — with a lady, sir," I had, as I often had in those days, for the wish was father to the thought, an immediate vision of sitters. Sitters my visitors in this case proved to be; but not in the sense I should have preferred. However, there was nothing at first to indicate that they might have come for a portrait. The gentleman, a man of fifty, very high and very straight, with a moustache slightly grizzled and a dark grey walking-coat admirably fitted, both of which I noted professionally — I don't mean as a barber or yet as a tailor — would have struck me as a celebrity if celebrities often were striking. It was a truth of which I had for some time been conscious that a figure with a good deal of frontage was, as one might say, almost never a public institution. A glance at the lady helped to remind me of this paradoxical law: she also looked too distinguished to be a "personality." Moreover one would scarcely come across two variations together.

Neither of the pair spoke immediately — they only prolonged the preliminary gaze which suggested that each wished to give the other a chance. They were visibly shy; they stood there letting me take them in — which, as I afterwards perceived, was the most practical thing they could have done. In this way their embarrassment served their cause. I had seen people painfully reluctant to mention that they desired anything so gross as to be represented on canvas; but the scruples of my new friends appeared almost insurmountable. Yet the gentleman might have said "I should like a portrait of my wife," and the lady might have said "I should like a portrait of my husband." Perhaps they were not husband and wife — this naturally would make the matter more delicate. Perhaps they wished to be done together — in which case they ought to have brought a third person to break the news.

"We come from Mr. Rivet," the lady said at last, with a dim smile which had the effect of a moist sponge passed over a "sunk" piece of painting, as well as of a vague allusion to vanished beauty. She was as tall and straight, in her degree, as her companion, and with ten years less to carry. She looked as sad as a woman could look whose face was not charged with expression; that is, her tinted oval mask showed friction as an exposed surface shows it. The hand of time had played over her freely, but only to simplify. She was slim and stiff, and so well-dressed, in dark blue cloth, with lappets and pockets and buttons, that it was clear she employed the same tailor as her husband. The couple had an indefinable air of prosperous thrift — they evidently got a good deal of luxury for their money. If I was to be one of their luxuries it would behove me to consider my terms.

"Ah, Claude Rivet recommended me?" I inquired; and I added that it was very kind of him, though I could reflect that, as he only painted landscape, this was not a sacrifice.

The lady looked very hard at the gentleman, and the gentleman looked round the room. Then staring at the floor a moment and stroking his moustache, he rested his pleasant eyes on me with the remark: "He said you were the right one."

"I try to be, when people want to sit."

"Yes, we should like to," said the lady anxiously.

"Do you mean together?"

My visitors exchanged a glance. "If you could do anything with *me*, I suppose it would be double," the gentleman stammered.

"Oh, yes, there's naturally a higher charge for two figures than for one."

"We should like to make it pay," the husband confessed.

"That's very good of you," I returned, appreciating so unwonted a sympathy — for I supposed he meant pay the artist.

A sense of strangeness seemed to dawn on the lady. "We mean for the illustrations — Mr. Rivet said you might put one in."

"Put one in — an illustration?" I was equally confused.

"Sketch her off, you know," said the gentleman, colouring.

It was only then that I understood the service Claude Rivet had rendered me; he had told them that I worked in black and white, for magazines, for story-books, for sketches of contemporary life, and consequently had frequent employment for models. These things were true, but it was not less true (I may confess it now — whether because the aspiration was to lead to everything or to nothing I leave the reader to guess), that I couldn't get the honours, to say nothing of the emoluments, of a great painter of portraits out of my head. My "illustrations" were my pot-boilers; I looked to a different branch of art (far and away the most interesting it had always seemed to me), to perpetuate my fame. There was no shame in looking to it also to make my fortune; but that fortune was by so much further from being made from the moment my visitors wished to be "done" for nothing. I was disappointed; for in the pictorial sense I had immediately *seen* them. I had seized their type — I had already settled what I would do with it. Something that wouldn't absolutely have pleased them, I afterwards reflected.

"Ah, you're — you're — a — ?" I began, as soon as I had mastered my surprise. I couldn't bring out the dingy word "models"; it seemed to fit the case so little.

"We haven't had much practice," said the lady.

"We've got to *do* something, and we've thought that an artist in your line might perhaps make something of us," her husband threw off. He further mentioned that they didn't know many artists and that they had gone first, on the off-chance (he painted views of course, but sometimes put in figures — perhaps I remembered), to Mr. Rivet, whom they had met a few years before at a place in Norfolk where he was sketching.

"We used to sketch a little ourselves," the lady hinted.

"It's very awkward, but we absolutely *must* do something," her husband went on.

"Of course, we're not so *very* young," she admitted, with a wan smile.

With the remark that I might as well know something more about them, the husband had handed me a card extracted from a neat new pocket-book (their appurtenances were all of the freshest) and inscribed with the words "Major Monarch." Impressive as these words were they didn't carry my knowledge much further; but my visitor presently added: "I've left the army, and we've had the misfortune to lose our money. In fact our means are dreadfully small."

"It's an awful bore," said Mrs. Monarch.

They evidently wished to be discreet — to take care not to swagger because they were gentlefolks. I perceived they would have been willing to recognise this as something of a drawback, at the same time that I guessed at an underlying sense — their consolation in adversity — that they *had* their points. They certainly had; but these advantages struck me as preponderantly social; such for instance as would help to make a drawing-room look well. However, a drawing-room was always, or ought to be, a picture.

In consequence of his wife's allusion to their age Major Monarch observed: "Naturally, it's more for the figure that we thought of going in. We can still hold ourselves up." On the instant I saw that the figure was indeed their strong point. His "naturally" didn't sound vain, but it lighted up the question. "*She* has got the best," he continued, nodding at his wife, with a pleasant after-dinner absence of circumlocution. I could only reply, as if we were in fact sitting over our wine, that this didn't prevent his own from being very good; which led him in turn to rejoin: "We thought that if you ever have to do people like us, we might be something like it. *She,* particularly — for a lady in a book, you know."

I was so amused by them that, to get more of it, I did my best to take their point of view; and though it was an embarrassment to find myself appraising physically, as if they were animals on hire or useful blacks, a pair whom I should have expected to meet only in one of the relations in which criticism is tacit, I looked at Mrs. Monarch judicially enough to be able to exclaim, after a moment, with conviction: "Oh yes, a lady in a book!" She was singularly like a bad illustration.

"We'll stand up, if you like," said the Major; and he raised himself before me with a really grand air.

I could take his measure at a glance — he was six feet two and a perfect gentleman. It would have paid any club in process of formation and in want of a stamp to engage him at a salary to stand in the principal window. What struck me immediately was that in coming to me they had rather missed their vocation; they could surely have been turned to better account for advertising purposes. I couldn't of course see the thing in detail, but I could see them make someone's fortune — I don't mean their own. There was something in them for a waistcoat maker, an hotel-keeper or a soap-vendor. I could imagine "We always use it" pinned on their bosoms with the greatest effect; I had a vision of the promptitude with which they would launch a table d'hôte.

Mrs. Monarch sat still, not from pride but from shyness, and presently her husband said 5 to her: "Get up my dear and show how smart you are." She obeyed, but she had no need to get up to show it. She walked to the end of the studio, and then she came back blushing, with her fluttered eyes on her husband. I was 10 reminded of an incident I had accidentally had a glimpse of in Paris — being with a friend there, a dramatist about to produce a play — when an actress came to him to ask to be intrusted with a part. She went through her 15 paces before him, walked up and down as Mrs. Monarch was doing. Mrs. Monarch did it quite as well, but I abstained from applauding. It was very odd to see such people apply for such poor pay. She looked as if she had ten thousand a 20 year. Her husband had used the word that described her: she was, in the London current jargon, essentially and typically "smart." Her figure was, in the same order of ideas, conspicuously and irreproachably "good." For a woman 25 of her age her waist was surprisingly small; her elbow moreover had the orthodox crook. She held her head at the conventional angle; but why did she come to *me*! She ought to have tried on jackets at a big shop. I feared my 30 visitors were not only destitute, but "artistic" — which would be a great complication. When she sat down again I thanked her, observing that what a draughtsman most valued in his model was the faculty of keeping quiet. 35

"Oh, *she* can keep quiet," said Major Monarch. Then he added, jocosely: "I've always kept her quiet."

"I'm not a nasty fidget, am I?" Mrs. Monarch appealed to her husband. 40

He addressed his answers to me. "Perhaps it isn't out of place to mention — because we ought to be quite business-like, oughtn't we? — that when I married her she was known as the Beautiful Statue." 45

"Oh dear!" said Mrs. Monarch, ruefully.

"Of course I should want a certain amount of expression," I rejoined.

"Of *course!*" they both exclaimed.

"And then I suppose you know that you'll 50 get awfully tired."

"Oh, we *never* get tired!" they eagerly cried.

"Have you had any kind of practice?"

They hesitated — they looked at each other.

"We've been photographed, *immensely*," said Mrs. Monarch.

"She means the fellows have asked us," added the Major.

"I see — because you're so good-looking."

"I don't know what they thought, but they were always after us."

"We always got our photographs for nothing," smiled Mrs. Monarch.

"We might have brought some, my dear," her husband remarked.

"I'm not sure we have any left. We've given quantities away," she explained to me.

"With our autographs and that sort of thing," said the Major.

"Are they to be got in the shops?" I inquired, as a harmless pleasantry.

"Oh, yes; *hers* — they used to be."

"Not now," said Mrs. Monarch, with her eyes on the floor.

II

I could fancy the "sort of thing" they put on the presentation-copies of their photographs, and I was sure they wrote a beautiful hand. It was odd how quickly I was sure of everything that concerned them. If they were now so poor as to have to earn shillings and pence, they never had had much of a margin. Their good looks had been their capital, and they had good-humouredly made the most of the career that this resource marked out for them. It was in their faces, the blankness, the deep intellectual repose of the twenty years of country-house visiting which had given them pleasant intonations. I could see the sunny drawing-rooms, sprinkled with periodicals she didn't read, in which Mrs. Monarch had continuously sat; I could see the wet shrubberies in which she had walked, equipped to admiration for either exercise. I could see the rich covers the Major had helped to shoot and the wonderful garments in which, late at night, he repaired to the smoking-room to talk about them. I could imagine their leggings and waterproofs, their knowing tweeds and rugs, their rolls of sticks and cases of tackle and neat umbrellas; and I could evoke the exact appearance of their servants and the compact variety of their luggage on the platforms of country stations.

They gave small tips, but they were liked; they didn't do anything themselves, but they were welcome. They looked so well everywhere; they gratified the general relish for stature, complexion and "form." They knew it without fatuity or vulgarity, and they respected themselves in consequence. They were not superficial; they were thorough and kept themselves up — it had been their line. People with such a taste for activity had to have some line. I could feel how, even in a dull house, they could have been counted upon for cheerfulness. At present something had happened — it didn't matter what, their little income had grown less, it had grown least — and they had to do something for pocket-money. Their friends liked them, but didn't like to support them. There was something about them that represented credit — their clothes, their manners, their type; but if credit is a large empty pocket in which an occasional chink reverberates, the chink at least must be audible. What they wanted of me was to help to make it so. Fortunately they had no children — I soon divined that. They would also perhaps wish our relations to be kept secret: this was why it was "for the figure" — the reproduction of the face would betray them.

I liked them — they were so simple; and I had no objection to them if they would suit. But, somehow, with all their perfections I didn't easily believe in them. After all they were amateurs, and the ruling passion of my life was the detestation of the amateur. Combined with this was another perversity — an innate preference for the represented subject over the real one: the defect of the real one was so apt to be a lack of representation. I liked things that appeared; then one was sure. Whether they *were* or not was a subordinate and almost always a profitless question. There were other considerations, the first of which was that I already had two or three people in use, notably a young person with big feet, in alpaca, from Kilburn, who for a couple of years had come to me regularly for my illustrations and with whom I was still — perhaps ignobly — satisfied. I frankly explained to my visitors how the case stood; but they had taken more precautions than I supposed. They had reasoned out their opportunity, for Claude Rivet had told them of the projected *édition de luxe* of one of the writers of our day — the rarest of the novelists — who, long neglected by the multitudinous vulgar and dearly prized by the attentive (need I mention Philip Vincent?) had had the happy fortune of seeing, late in life, the dawn and then the full light of a higher

criticism — an estimate in which, on the part of the public, there was something really of expiation. The edition in question, planned by a publisher of taste, was practically an act of high reparation; the woodcuts with which it was to be enriched were the homage of English art to one of the most independent representatives of English letters. Major and Mrs. Monarch confessed to me that they had hoped I might be able to work *them* into my share of the enterprise. They knew I was to do the first of the books, "Rutland Ramsay," but I had to make clear to them that my participation in the rest of the affair — this first book was to be a test — was to depend on the satisfaction I should give. If this should be limited my employers would drop me without a scruple. It was therefore a crisis for me, and naturally I was making special preparations, looking about for new people, if they should be necessary, and securing the best types. I admitted however that I should like to settle down to two or three good models who would do for everything.

"Should we have often to — a — put on special clothes?" Mrs. Monarch timidly demanded.

"Dear, yes — that's half the business."

"And should we be expected to supply our own costumes?"

"Oh, no; I've got a lot of things. A painter's models put on — or put off — anything he likes."

"And do you mean — a — the same?"

"The same?"

Mrs. Monarch looked at her husband again.

"Oh, she was just wondering," he explained, "if the costumes are in *general* use." I had to confess that they were, and I mentioned further that some of them (I had a lot of genuine, greasy last-century things), had served their time, a hundred years ago, on living, world-stained men and women. "We'll put on anything that *fits*," said the Major.

"Oh, I arrange that — they fit in the pictures."

"I'm afraid I should do better for the modern books. I would come as you like," said Mrs. Monarch.

"She has got a lot of clothes at home: they might do for contemporary life," her husband continued.

"Oh, I can fancy scenes in which you'd be quite natural." And indeed I could see the slipshod rearrangements of stale properties —

the stories I tried to produce pictures for without the exasperation of reading them — whose sandy tracts the good lady might help to people. But I had to return to the fact that for this sort of work — the daily mechanical grind — I was already equipped; the people I was working with were fully adequate.

"We only thought we might be more like *some* characters," said Mrs. Monarch mildly, getting up.

Her husband also rose; he stood looking at me with a dim wistfulness that was touching in so fine a man. "Wouldn't it be rather a pull sometimes to have — a — to have?" He hung fire; he wanted me to help him by phrasing what he meant. But I couldn't — I didn't know. So he brought it out, awkwardly: "The *real* thing; a gentleman, you know, or a lady." I was quite ready to give a general assent — I admitted that there was a great deal in that. This encouraged Major Monarch to say, following up his appeal with an unacted gulp: "It's awfully hard — we've tried everything." The gulp was communicative; it proved too much for his wife. Before I knew it Mrs. Monarch had dropped again upon a divan and burst into tears. Her husband sat down beside her, holding one of her hands; whereupon she quickly dried her eyes with the other, while I felt embarrassed as she looked up at me. "There isn't a confounded job I haven't applied for — waited for — prayed for. You can fancy we'd be pretty bad first. Secretaryships and that sort of thing? You might as well ask for a peerage. I'd be *anything* — I'm strong; a messenger or a coalheaver. I'd put on a gold-laced cap and open carriage-doors in front of the haberdasher's; I'd hang about a station, to carry portmanteaus; I'd be a postman. But they won't *look* at you; there are thousands, as good as yourself, already on the ground. *Gentlemen*, poor beggars, who have drunk their wine, who have kept their hunters!"

I was as reassuring as I knew how to be, and my visitors were presently on their feet again while, for the experiment, we agreed on an hour. We were discussing it when the door opened and Miss Churm came in with a wet umbrella. Miss Churm had to take the omnibus to Maida Vale and then walk half-a-mile. She looked a trifle blowsy and slightly splashed. I scarcely ever saw her come in without thinking afresh how odd it was that, being so little in herself, she should yet be so much in others.

She was a meagre little Miss Churm, but she was an ample heroine of romance. She was only a freckled cockney, but she could represent everything, from a fine lady to a shepherdess; she had the faculty, as she might have had a fine voice or long hair. She couldn't spell, and she loved beer, but she had two or three "points," and practice, and a knack, and mother-wit, and a kind of whimsical sensibility, and a love of the theatre, and seven sisters, and not an ounce of respect, especially for the *h*. The first thing my visitors saw was that her umbrella was wet, and in their spotless perfection they visibly winced at it. The rain had come on since their arrival.

"I'm all in a soak; there *was* a mess of people in the 'bus. I wish you lived near a stytion," said Miss Churm. I requested her to get ready as quickly as possible, and she passed into the room in which she always changed her dress. But before going out she asked me what she was to get into this time.

"It's the Russian princess, don't you know?" I answered; "the one with the 'golden eyes,' in black velvet, for the long thing in the *Cheapside*."

"Golden eyes? I *say!*" cried Miss Churm, while my companions watched her with intensity as she withdrew. She always arranged herself, when she was late, before I could turn round; and I kept my visitors a little, on purpose, so that they might get an idea, from seeing her, what would be expected of themselves. I mentioned that she was quite my notion of an excellent model — she was really very clever.

"Do you think she looks like a Russian princess?" Major Monarch asked, with lurking alarm.

"When I make her, yes."

"Oh, if you have to *make* her — !" he reasoned, acutely.

"That's the most you can ask. There are so many that are not makeable."

"Well now, *here's* a lady" — and with a persuasive smile he passed his arm into his wife's — "who's already made!"

"Oh, I'm not a Russian princess," Mrs. Monarch protested, a little coldly. I could see that she had known some and didn't like them. There, immediately, was a complication of a kind that I never had to fear with Miss Churm.

This young lady came back in black velvet — the gown was rather rusty and very low on her lean shoulders — and with a Japanese fan in her red hands. I reminded her that in the scene I was doing she had to look over someone's head. "I forget whose it is; but it doesn't matter. Just look over a head."

"I'd rather look over a stove," said Miss Churm; and she took her station near the fire. She fell into position, settled herself into a tall attitude, gave a certain backward inclination to her head and a certain forward droop to her fan, and looked, at least to my prejudiced sense, distinguished and charming, foreign and dangerous. We left her looking so, while I went downstairs with Major and Mrs. Monarch.

"I think I could come about as near it as that," said Mrs. Monarch.

"Oh, you think she's shabby, but you must allow for the alchemy of art."

However, they went off with an evident increase of comfort, founded on their demonstrable advantage in being the real thing. I could fancy them shuddering over Miss Churm. She was very droll about them when I went back, for I told her what they wanted.

"Well, if *she* can sit I'll tyke to bookkeeping," said my model.

"She's very lady-like," I replied, as an innocent form of aggravation.

"So much the worse for *you*. That means she can't turn round."

"She'll do for the fashionable novels."

"Oh yes, she'll *do* for them!" my model humorously declared. "Ain't they bad enough without her?" I had often sociably denounced them to Miss Churm.

III

It was for the elucidation of a mystery in one of these works that I first tried Mrs. Monarch. Her husband came with her, to be useful if necessary — it was sufficiently clear that as a general thing he would prefer to come with her. At first I wondered if this were for "propriety's" sake — if he were going to be jealous and meddling. The idea was too tiresome, and if it had been confirmed it would speedily have brought our acquaintance to a close. But I soon saw there was nothing in it and that if he accompanied Mrs. Monarch it was (in addition to the chance of being wanted), simply because he had nothing else to do. When she was away from him his occupation was gone — she never *had* been away from him. I judged, rightly, that in their awkward situation their close union was their main comfort and that this union had

no weak spot. It was a real marriage, an encouragement to the hesitating, a nut for pessimists to crack. Their address was humble (I remember afterwards thinking it had been the only thing about them that was really professional), and I could fancy the lamentable lodgings in which the Major would have been left alone. He could bear them with his wife — he couldn't bear them without her.

He had too much tact to try and make himself agreeable when he couldn't be useful; so he simply sat and waited, when I was too absorbed in my work to talk. But I liked to make him talk — it made my work, when it didn't interrupt it, less sordid, less special. To listen to him was to combine the excitement of going out with the economy of staying at home. There was only one hindrance: that I seemed not to know any of the people he and his wife had known. I think he wondered extremely, during the term of our intercourse, whom the deuce I *did* know. He hadn't a stray sixpence of an idea to fumble for; so we didn't spin it very fine — we confined ourselves to questions of leather and even of liquor (saddlers and breeches-makers and how to get good claret cheap), and matters like "good trains" and the habits of small game. His lore on these last subjects was astonishing, he managed to interweave the station-master with the ornithologist. When he couldn't talk about greater things he could talk cheerfully about smaller, and since I couldn't accompany him into reminiscences of the fashionable world he could lower the conversation without a visible effort to my level.

So earnest a desire to please was touching in a man who could so easily have knocked one down. He looked after the fire and had an opinion on the draught of the stove, without my asking him, and I could see that he thought many of my arrangements not half clever enough. I remember telling him that if I were only rich I would offer him a salary to come and teach me how to live. Sometimes he gave a random sigh, of which the essence was: "Give me even such a bare old barrack as *this*, and I'd do something with it!" When I wanted to use him he came alone; which was an illustration of the superior courage of women. His wife could bear her solitary second floor, and she was in general more discreet; showing by various small reserves that she was alive to the propriety of keeping our relations markedly professional — not letting them slide into sociability. She wished it to remain clear that she and the Major were employed, not cultivated, and if she approved of me as a superior, who could be kept in his place, she never thought me quite good enough for an equal.

She sat with great intensity, giving the whole of her mind to it, and was capable of remaining for an hour almost as motionless as if she were before a photographer's lens. I could see she had been photographed often, but somehow the very habit that made her good for that purpose unfitted her for mine. At first I was extremely pleased with her lady-like air, and it was a satisfaction, on coming to follow her lines, to see how good they were and how far they could lead the pencil. But after a few times I began to find her too insurmountably stiff; do what I would with it my drawing looked like a photograph or a copy of a photograph. Her figure had no variety of expression — she herself had no sense of variety. You may say that this was my business, was only a question of placing her. I placed her in every conceivable position, but she managed to obliterate their differences. She was always a lady certainly, and into the bargain was always the same lady. She was the real thing, but always the same thing. There were moments when I was oppressed by the serenity of her confidence that she *was* the real thing. All her dealings with me and all her husband's were an implication that this was lucky for *me*. Meanwhile I found myself trying to invent types that approached her own, instead of making her own transform itself — in the clever way that was not impossible, for instance, to poor Miss Churm. Arrange as I would and take the precautions I would, she always, in my pictures, came out too tall — landing me in the dilemma of having represented a fascinating woman as seven feet high, which, out of respect perhaps to my own very much scantier inches, was far from my idea of such a personage.

The case was worse with the Major — nothing I could do would keep *him* down, so that he became useful only for the representation of brawny giants. I adored variety and range, I cherished human accidents, the illustrative note; I wanted to characterise closely, and the thing in the world I most hated was the danger of being ridden by a type. I had quarrelled with some of my friends about it — I had parted company with them for maintaining that one

had to be, and that if the type was beautiful (witness Raphael and Leonardo), the servitude was only a gain. I was neither Leonardo nor Raphael; I might only be a presumptuous young modern searcher, but I held that everything was to be sacrificed sooner than character. When they averred that the haunting type in question could easily *be* character, I retorted, perhaps superficially: "Whose?" It couldn't be everybody's — it might end in being nobody's.

After I had drawn Mrs. Monarch a dozen times I perceived more clearly than before that the value of such a model as Miss Churm resided precisely in the fact that she had no positive stamp, combined of course with the other fact that what she did have was a curious and inexplicable talent for imitation. Her usual appearance was like a curtain which she could draw up at request for a capital performance. This performance was simply suggestive; but it was a word to the wise — it was vivid and pretty. Sometimes, even, I thought it, though she was plain herself, too insipidly pretty; I made it a reproach to her that the figures drawn from her were monotonously (*bêtement*, as we used to say) graceful. Nothing made her more angry: it was so much her pride to feel that she could sit for characters that had nothing in common with each other. She would accuse me at such moments of taking away her "reputytion."

It suffered a certain shrinkage, this queer quantity, from the repeated visits of my new friends. Miss Churm was greatly in demand, never in want of employment, so I had no scruple in putting her off occasionally, to try them more at my ease. It was certainly amusing at first to do the real thing — it was amusing to do Major Monarch's trousers. They *were* the real thing, even if he did come out colossal. It was amusing to do his wife's back hair (it was so mathematically neat,) and the particular "smart" tension of her tight stays. She lent herself especially to positions in which the face was somewhat averted or blurred; she abounded in ladylike back views and *profils perdus*. When she stood erect she took naturally one of the attitudes in which court-painters represent queens and princesses; so that I found myself wondering whether, to draw out this accomplishment, I couldn't get the editor of the *Cheapside* to publish a really royal romance, "A Tale of Buckingham Palace." Sometimes, however, the real thing and the make-believe came into contact; by which I mean that Miss

Churm, keeping an appointment or coming to make one on days when I had much work in hand, encountered her invidious rivals. The encounter was not on their part, for they noticed her no more than if she had been the house- maid; not from intentional loftiness, but sim- ply because, as yet, professionally, they didn't know how to fraternise, as I could guess that they would have liked — or at least that the Major would. They couldn't talk about the omnibus — they always walked; and they didn't know what else to try — she wasn't interested in good trains or cheap claret. Besides, they must have felt — in the air — that she was amused at them, secretly derisive of their ever knowing how. She was not a person to conceal her scepticism if she had had a chance to show it. On the other hand Mrs. Monarch didn't think her tidy; for why else did she take pains to say to me (it was going out of the way, for Mrs. Monarch), that she didn't like dirty women?

One day when my young lady happened to be present with my other sitters (she even dropped in, when it was convenient, for a chat), I asked her to be so good as to lend a hand in getting tea — a service with which she was familiar and which was one of a class that, living as I did in a small way, with slender domestic resources, I often appealed to my models to render. They liked to lay hands on my prop- erty, to break the sitting, and sometimes the china — I made them feel Bohemian. The next time I saw Miss Churm after this incident she surprised me greatly by making a scene about it — she accused me of having wished to humiliate her. She had not resented the outrage at the time, but had seemed obliging and amused, enjoying the comedy of asking Mrs. Monarch, who sat vague and silent, whether she would have cream and sugar, and putting an exaggerated simper into the question. She had tried intonations — as if she too wished to pass for the real thing; till I was afraid my other visitors would take offence.

Oh, *they* were determined not to do this; and their touching patience was the measure of their great need. They would sit by the hour, uncomplaining, till I was ready to use them; they would come back on the chance of being wanted and would walk away cheerfully if they were not. I used to go to the door with them to see in what magnificent order they retreated. I tried to find other employment for them —

I introduced them to several artists. But they didn't "take," for reasons I could appreciate, and I became conscious, rather anxiously, that after such disappointments they fell back upon me with a heavier weight. They did me the honour to think that it was I who was most *their* form. They were not picturesque enough for the painters, and in those days there were not so many serious workers in black and white. Besides, they had an eye to the great job I had mentioned to them — they had secretly set their hearts on supplying the right essence for my pictorial vindication of our fine novelist. They knew that for this undertaking I should want no costume-effects, none of the frippery of past ages — that it was a case in which every- thing would be contemporary and satirical and, presumably, genteel. If I could work them into it their future would be assured, for the labour would of course be long and the occupation steady.

One day Mrs. Monarch came without her husband — she explained his absence by his having had to go to the City. While she sat there in her usual anxious stiffness there came, at the door, a knock which I immediately rec- ognised as the subdued appeal of a model out of work. It was followed by the entrance of a young man whom I easily perceived to be a foreigner and who proved in fact an Italian acquainted with no English word but my name, which he uttered in a way that made it seem to include all others. I had not then visited his country, nor was I proficient in his tongue; but as he was not so meanly constituted — what Italian is? — as to depend only on that member for expression he conveyed to me, in familiar but graceful mimicry, that he was in search of exactly the employment in which the lady before me was engaged. I was not struck with him at first, and while I continued to draw I emitted rough sounds of discouragement and dismissal. He stood his ground, however, not importu- nately, but with a dumb, dog-like fidelity in his eyes which amounted to innocent impudence — the manner of a devoted servant (he might have been in the house for years), unjustly suspected. Suddenly I saw that this very atti- tude and expression made a picture, whereupon I told him to sit down and wait till I should be free. There was another picture in the way he obeyed me, and I observed as I worked that there were others still in the way he looked wonderingly, with his head thrown back, about the high studio. He might have been crossing himself in St. Peter's. Before I finished I said to myself: "The fellow's a bankrupt orange-monger, but he's a treasure."

When Mrs. Monarch withdrew he passed across the room like a flash to open the door for her, standing there with the rapt, pure gaze of the young Dante spellbound by the young Beatrice. As I never insisted, in such situations, on the blankness of the British domestic, I reflected that he had the making of a servant (and I needed one, but couldn't pay him to be only that), as well as of a model; in short I made up my mind to adopt my bright adventurer if he would agree to officiate in the double capacity. He jumped at my offer, and in the event my rashness (for I had known nothing about him) was not brought home to me. He proved a sympathetic though a desultory minis-trant, and had in a wonderful degree the *senti-ment de la pose*. It was uncultivated, instinc-tive; a part of the happy instinct which had guided him to my door and helped him to spell out my name on the card nailed to it. He had had no other introduction to me than a guess, from the shape of my high north window, seen outside, that my place was a studio and that as a studio it would contain an artist. He had wandered to England in search of fortune, like other itinerants, and had embarked, with a partner and a small green handcart, on the sale of penny ices. The ices had melted away and the partner had dissolved in their train. My young man wore tight yellow trousers with reddish stripes and his name was Oronte. He was sallow but fair, and when I put him into some old clothes of my own he looked like an Englishman. He was as good as Miss Churm, who could look, when required, like an Italian.

IV

I thought Mrs. Monarch's face slightly con-vulsed when, on her coming back with her husband, she found Oronte installed. It was strange to have to recognise in a scrap of a lazzarone a competitor to her magnificent Ma-jor. It was she who scented danger first, for the Major was anecdotically unconscious. But Oronte gave us tea, with a hundred eager con-fusions (he had never seen such a queer proc-ess), and I think she thought better of me for having at last an "establishment." They saw a couple of drawings that I had made of the establishment, and Mrs. Monarch hinted that

it never would have struck her that he had sat for them. "Now the drawings you make from *us*, they look exactly like us," she reminded me, smiling in triumph; and I recognised that this was indeed just their defect. When I drew the Monarchs I couldn't, somehow, get away from them — get into the character I wanted to represent; and I had not the least desire my model should be discoverable in my picture. Miss Churm never was, and Mrs. Monarch thought I hid her, very properly, because she was vulgar; whereas if she was lost it was only as the dead who go to heaven are lost — in the gain of an angel the more.

By this time I had got a certain start with "Rutland Ramsay," the first novel in the great projected series; that is, I had produced a dozen drawings, several with the help of the Major and his wife, and I had sent them in for approval. My understanding with the publish-ers, as I have already hinted, had been that I was to be left to do my work, in this particular case, as I liked, with the whole book committed to me; but my connection with the rest of the series was only contingent. There were mo-ments when, frankly, it *was* a comfort to have the real thing under one's hand; for there were characters in "Rutland Ramsay" that were very much like it. There were people presumably as straight as the Major and women of as good a fashion as Mrs. Monarch. There was a great deal of country-house life — treated, it is true, in a fine, fanciful, ironical, generalised way — and there was a considerable implication of knickerbockers and kilts. There were certain things I had to settle at the outset; such things for instance as the exact appearance of the hero, the particular bloom of the heroine. The au-thor of course gave me a lead, but there was a margin for interpretation. I took the Monarchs into my confidence, I told them frankly what I was about, I mentioned my embarrassments and alternatives. "Oh, take *him*!" Mrs. Mon-arch murmured sweetly, looking at her husband; and "What could you want better than my wife?" the Major inquired, with the comfort-able candour that now prevailed between us.

I was not obliged to answer these remarks — I was only obliged to place my sitters. I was not easy in mind, and I postponed, a little timidly perhaps, the solution of the question. The book was a large canvas, the other figures were numerous, and I worked off at first some of the episodes in which the hero and the heroine were not concerned. When once I had set *them* up I should have to stick to them — I couldn't make my young man seven feet high in one place and five feet nine in another. I inclined on the whole to the latter measurement, though the Major more than once reminded me that *he* looked about as young as anyone. It was indeed quite possible to arrange him, for the figure, so that it would have been difficult to detect his age. After the spontaneous Oronte had been with me a month, and after I had given him to understand several different times that his native exuberance would presently constitute an insurmountable barrier to our further intercourse, I waked to a sense of his heroic capacity. He was only five feet seven, but the remaining inches were latent. I tried him almost secretly at first, for I was really rather afraid of the judgment my other models would pass on such a choice. If they regarded Miss Churm as little better than a snare, what would they think of the representation by a person so little the real thing as an Italian street-vendor of a protagonist formed by a public school?

If I went a little in fear of them it was not because they bullied me, because they had got an oppressive foothold, but because in their really pathetic decorum and mysteriously permanent newness they counted on me so intensely. I was therefore very glad when Jack Hawley came home: he was always of such good counsel. He painted badly himself, but there was no one like him for putting his finger on the place. He had been absent from England for a year; he had been somewhere — I don't remember where — to get a fresh eye. I was in a good deal of dread of any such organ, but we were old friends; he had been away for months and a sense of emptiness was creeping into my life. I hadn't dodged a missile for a year.

He came back with a fresh eye, but with the same old black velvet blouse, and the first evening he spent in my studio we smoked cigarettes till the small hours. He had done no work himself, he had only got the eye; so the field was clear for the production of my little things. He wanted to see what I had done for the *Cheapside*, but he was disappointed in the exhibition. That at least seemed the meaning of two or three comprehensive groans which, as he lounged on my big divan, on a folded leg, looking at my latest drawings, issued from his lips with the smoke of the cigarette.

"What's the matter with you?" I asked.

"What's the matter with *you!*"

"Nothing save that I'm mystified."

"You are indeed. You're quite off the hinge. What's the meaning of this new fad?" And he tossed me, with visible irreverence, a drawing in which I happened to have depicted both my majestic models. I asked if he didn't think it good, and he replied that it struck him as execrable, given the sort of thing I had always represented myself to him as wishing to arrive at; but I let that pass, I was so anxious to see exactly what he meant. The two figures in the picture looked colossal, but I supposed this was *not* what he meant, inasmuch as, for aught he knew to the contrary, I might have been trying for that. I maintained that I was working exactly in the same way as when he last had done me the honour to commend me. "Well, there's a big hole somewhere," he answered; "wait a bit and I'll discover it." I depended upon him to do so; where else was the fresh eye? But he produced at last nothing more luminous than "I don't know — I don't like your types." This was lame, for a critic who had never consented to discuss with me anything but the question of execution, the direction of strokes and the mystery of values.

"In the drawings you've been looking at I think my types are very handsome."

"Oh, they won't do!"

"I've had a couple of new models."

"I see you have. *They* won't do."

"Are you very sure of that?"

"Absolutely — they're stupid."

"You mean *I* am — for I ought to get round that."

"You *can't* — with such people. Who are they?"

I told him, as far as was necessary, and he declared, heartlessly: "*Ce sont des gens qu'il faut mettre à la porte.*"

"You've never seen them; they're awfully good," I compassionately objected.

"Not seen them? Why, all this recent work of yours drops to pieces with them. It's all I want to see of them."

"No one else has said anything against it — the *Cheapside* people are pleased."

"Everyone else is an ass, and the *Cheapside* people the biggest asses of all. Come, don't pretend, at this time of day, to have pretty illusions about the public, especially about publishers and editors. It's not for *such* animals you work — it's for those who know, *coloro che sanno;* so keep straight for *me* if you can't keep straight for yourself. There's a certain sort of thing you tried for from the first — and a very good thing it is. But this twaddle isn't *in it.*" When I talked with Hawley later about "Rutland Ramsay" and its possible successors he declared that I must get back into my boat again or I would go to the bottom. His voice in short was the voice of warning.

I noted the warning, but I didn't turn my friends out of doors. They bored me a good deal; but the very fact that they bored me admonished me not to sacrifice them — if there was anything to be done with them — simply to irritation. As I look back at this phase they seem to me to have pervaded my life not a little. I have a vision of them as most of the time in my studio, seated, against the wall, on an old velvet bench to be out of the way, and looking like a pair of patient courtiers in a royal ante-chamber. I am convinced that during the coldest weeks of the winter they held their ground because it saved them fire. Their newness was losing its gloss, and it was impossible not to feel that they were objects of charity. Whenever Miss Churm arrived they went away, and after I was fairly launched in "Rutland Ramsay" Miss Churm arrived pretty often. They managed to express to me tacitly that they supposed I wanted her for the low life of the book, and I let them suppose it, since they had attempted to study the work — it was lying about the studio — without discovering that it dealt only with the highest circles. They had dipped into the most brilliant of our novelists without deciphering many passages. I still took an hour from them, now and again, in spite of Jack Hawley's warning: it would be time enough to dismiss them, if dismissal should be necessary, when the rigour of the season was over. Hawley had made their acquaintance — he had met them at my fireside — and thought them a ridiculous pair. Learning that he was a painter they tried to approach him, to show him too that they were the real thing; but he looked at them, across the big room, as if they were miles away: they were a compendium of everything that he most objected to in the social system of his country. Such people as that, all convention and patent-leather, with ejaculations that stopped conversation, had no business in a studio. A studio was a place to learn to see, and how could you see through a pair of feather beds?

The main inconvenience I suffered at their hands was that, at first, I was shy of letting them discover how my artful little servant had begun to sit to me for "Rutland Ramsay." They knew that I had been odd enough (they were prepared by this time to allow oddity to artists,) to pick a foreign vagabond out of the streets, when I might have had a person with whiskers and credentials; but it was some time before they learned how high I rated his accomplishments. They found him in an attitude more than once, but they never doubted I was doing him as an organ-grinder. There were several things they never guessed, and one of them was that for a striking scene in the novel, in which a footman briefly figured, it occurred to me to make use of Major Monarch as the menial. I kept putting this off, I didn't like to ask him to don the livery — besides the difficulty of finding a livery to fit him. At last, one day late in the winter, when I was at work on the despised Oronte (he caught one's idea in an instant), and was in the glow of feeling that I was going very straight, they came in, the Major and his wife, with their society laugh about nothing (there was less and less to laugh at), like country-callers — they always reminded me of that — who have walked across the park after church and are presently persuaded to stay to luncheon. Luncheon was over, but they could stay to tea — I knew they wanted it. The fit was on me, however, and I couldn't let my ardour cool and my work wait, with the fading daylight, while my model prepared it. So I asked Mrs. Monarch if she would mind laying it out — a request which, for an instant, brought all the blood to her face. Her eyes were on her husband's for a second, and some mute telegraphy passed between them. Their folly was over the next instant; his cheerful shrewdness put an end to it. So far from pitying their wounded pride, I must add, I was moved to give it as complete a lesson as I could. They bustled about together and got out the cups and saucers and made the kettle boil. I know they felt as if they were waiting on my servant, and when the tea was prepared I said: "He'll have a cup, please — he's tired." Mrs. Monarch brought him one where he stood, and he took it from her as if he had been a gentleman at a party, squeezing a crush-hat with an elbow.

Then it came over me that she had made a great effort for me — made it with a kind of nobleness — and that I owed her a compensation. Each time I saw her after this I wondered what the compensation could be. I couldn't go on doing the wrong thing to oblige them. Oh, it *was* the wrong thing, the stamp of the work for which they sat — Hawley was not the only person to say it now. I sent in a large number of the drawings I had made for "Rutland Ramsay," and I received a warning that was more to the point than Hawley's. The artistic adviser of the house for which I was working was of opinion that many of my illustrations were not what had been looked for. Most of these illustrations were the subjects in which the Monarchs had figured. Without going into the question of what *had* been looked for, I saw at this rate I shouldn't get the other books to do. I hurled myself in despair upon Miss Churm, I put her through all her paces. I not only adopted Oronte publicly as my hero, but one morning when the Major looked in to see if I didn't require him to finish a figure for the *Cheapside*, for which he had begun to sit the week before, I told him that I had changed my mind — I would do the drawing from my man. At this my visitor turned pale and stood looking at me. "Is *he* your idea of an English gentleman?" he asked.

I was disappointed, I was nervous, I wanted to get on with my work; so I replied with irritation: "Oh, my dear Major — I can't be ruined for *you!*"

He stood another moment; then, without a word, he quitted the studio. I drew a long breath when he was gone, for I said to myself that I shouldn't see him again. I had not told him definitely that I was in danger of having my work rejected, but I was vexed at his not having felt the catastrophe in the air, read with me the moral of our fruitless collaboration, the lesson that, in the deceptive atmosphere of art, even the highest respectability may fail of being plastic.

I didn't owe my friends money, but I did see them again. They re-appeared together, three days later, and under the circumstances there was something tragic in the fact. It was a proof to me that they could find nothing else in life to do. They had threshed the matter out in a dismal conference — they had digested the bad news that they were not in for the series. If they were not useful to me even for the *Cheapside* their function seemed difficult to determine, and I could only judge at first that they had come, forgivingly, decorously, to take

a last leave. This made me rejoice in secret that I had little leisure for a scene; for I had placed both my other models in position together and I was pegging away at a drawing from which I hoped to derive glory. It had been suggested by the passage in which Rutland Ramsay, drawing up a chair to Artemisia's piano-stool, says extraordinary things to her while she ostensibly fingers out a difficult piece of music. I had done Miss Churm at the piano before — it was an attitude in which she knew how to take on an absolutely poetic grace. I wished the two figures to "compose" together, intensely, and my little Italian had entered perfectly into my conception. The pair were vividly before me, the piano had been pulled out; it was a charming picture of blended youth and murmured love, which I had only to catch and keep. My visitors stood and looked at it, and I was friendly to them over my shoulder.

They made no response, but I was used to silent company and went on with my work, only a little disconcerted (even though exhilarated by the sense that *this* was at least the ideal thing), at not having got rid of them after all. Presently I heard Mrs. Monarch's sweet voice beside, or rather above me: "I wish her hair was a little better done." I looked up and she was staring with a strange fixedness at Miss Churm whose back was turned to her. "Do you mind my just touching it?" she went on — a question which made me spring up for an instant, as with the instinctive fear that she might do the young lady a harm. But she quieted me with a glance I shall never forget — I confess I should like to have been able to paint *that* — and went for a moment to my model. She spoke to her softly, laying a hand upon her shoulder and bending over her; and as the girl, understandingly, gratefully assented, she disposed her rough curls, with a few quick passes, in such a way as to make Miss Churm's head twice as charming. It was one of the most heroic personal services I have ever seen rendered. Then Mrs. Monarch turned away with a low sigh and, looking about her as if for something to do, stooped to the floor with a noble humility and picked up a dirty rag that had dropped out of my paint-box.

The Major meanwhile had also been looking for something to do and, wandering to the other end of the studio, saw before him my breakfast things, neglected, unremoved. "I say, can't I be useful *here?*" he called out to me with an irrepressible quaver. I assented with a laugh that I fear was awkward and for the next ten minutes, while I worked, I heard the light clatter of china and the tinkle of spoons and glass. Mrs. Monarch assisted her husband — they washed up my crockery, they put it away. They wandered off into my little scullery, and I afterwards found that they had cleaned my knives and that my slender stock of plate had an unprecedented surface. When it came over me, the latent eloquence of what they were doing, I confess that my drawing was blurred for a moment — the picture swam. They had accepted their failure, but they couldn't accept their fate. They had bowed their heads in bewilderment to the perverse and cruel law in virtue of which the real thing could be so much less precious than the unreal; but they didn't want to starve. If my servants were my models, my models might be my servants. They would reverse the parts — the others would sit for the ladies and gentlemen, and *they* would do the work. They would still be in the studio — it was an intense dumb appeal to me not to turn them out. "Take us on," they wanted to say — "we'll do *anything*."

When all this hung before me the *afflatus* vanished — my pencil dropped from my hand. My sitting was spoiled and I got rid of my sitters, who were also evidently rather mystified and awestruck. Then, alone with the Major and his wife, I had a most uncomfortable moment. He put their prayer into a single sentence: "I say, you know — just let *us* do for you, can't you?" I couldn't — it was dreadful to see them emptying my slops; but I pretended I could, to oblige them, for about a week. Then I gave them a sum of money to go away; and I never saw them again. I obtained the remaining books, but my friend Hawley repeats that Major and Mrs. Monarch did me a permanent harm, got me into a second-rate trick. If it be true I am content to have paid the price — for the memory.

The Death of the Lion
(1894, 1895, 1909)

✻ In its technique and in its wit and irony this story resembles the preceding story, but it is more in James's later manner. The style is more figurative, more mannered; the narrative unfolds more slowly and indirectly, imitating the patternlessness of life and throwing the reader more off-guard,

yet keeping strictly to the point and achieving, in small compass, a many-faceted satire on the literary world. (Test the first section of the story in this respect.) Something of the intensity of feeling here, the mixture of bitterness and sympathy, results from the fact that James is writing about himself, for he in many particulars resembles Neil Paraday. James too was an artist of integrity who kept apart from the grotesque, popular Dora Forbeses; he too was neglected and misunderstood, and he doubtless had many small experiences which resembled Paraday's last minute encounter with a perverse public, and he could reflect upon the fact that he had been applauded on the publication of *Daisy Miller* and ignored in the time of his greatest work. Jamesian too are Paraday's excessive imagination — "What a pity that he has such a lot of it!" — and the "amorous plan" of his next novel, that "great gossiping eloquent letter," which suggests one of the preliminary accounts James prepared for the novels he was going to write. James nearly always wrote about himself — as most writers do — but in this story he does so with unusual directness, showing his confidence in his own worth, his strong sense of neglect, and what he might have called "the great good humor" with which he accepted this situation.

I

I had simply, I suppose, a change of heart, and it must have begun when I received my manuscript back from Mr. Pinhorn. Mr. Pinhorn was my "chief," as he was called in the office: he had accepted the high mission of bringing the paper up. This was a weekly periodical, which had been supposed to be almost past redemption when he took hold of it. It was Mr. Deedy who had let the thing down so dreadfully: he was never mentioned in the office now save in connexion with that misdemeanour. Young as I was I had been in a manner taken over from Mr. Deedy, who had been owner as well as editor; forming part of a promiscuous lot, mainly plant and office-furniture, which poor Mrs. Deedy, in her bereavement and depression, parted with at a rough valuation. I could account for my continuity but on the supposition that I had been cheap. I rather resented the practice of fathering all flatness on my late protector, who was in his unhonoured grave; but as I had my way to make I found matter enough for complacency in being on a "staff." At the same time I was aware of my exposure to suspicion as a product of the old lowering system. This made me feel I was doubly bound to have ideas, and had doubtless been at the bottom of my proposing to Mr. Pinhorn that I should lay my lean hands on Neil Paraday. I remember how he looked at me — quite, to begin with, as if he had never heard of this celebrity, who indeed at that moment was by no means in the centre of the heavens; and even when I had knowingly explained he expressed but little confidence in the demand for any such stuff. When I had reminded him that the great principle on which we were supposed to work was just to create the demand we required, he considered a moment and then returned: "I see — you want to write him up."

"Call it that if you like."

"And what's your inducement?"

"Bless my soul — my admiration!"

Mr. Pinhorn pursed his mouth. "Is there much to be done with him?"

"Whatever there is we should have it all to ourselves, for he hasn't been touched."

This argument was effective and Mr. Pinhorn responded. "Very well, touch him." Then he added: "But where can you do it?"

"Under the fifth rib!"

Mr. Pinhorn stared. "Where's that?"

"You want me to go down and see him?" I asked when I had enjoyed his visible search for the obscure suburb I seemed to have named.

"I don't 'want' anything — the proposal's your own. But you must remember that that's the way we do things *now*," said Mr. Pinhorn with another dig at Mr. Deedy.

Unregenerate as I was I could read the queer implications of this speech. The present owner's superior virtue as well as his deeper craft spoke in his reference to the late editor as one of that baser sort who deal in false representations. Mr. Deedy would as soon have sent me to call on Neil Paraday as he would have published a "holiday-number"; but such scruples presented themselves as mere ignoble thrift to his successor, whose own sincerity took the form of ringing door-bells and whose definition of genius was the art of finding people at home. It was as if Mr. Deedy had published reports without his young men's having, as Mr. Pinhorn would have said, really been there. I was unregenerate, as I have hinted, and couldn't be concerned to straighten out the journalistic morals of my chief, feeling them indeed to be an abyss over the edge of which it was better not to peer. Really to be there this time moreover was a vision that made the idea of writing something subtle about Neil Paraday only the more inspiring. I would be as considerate as even Mr. Deedy could have wished, and yet I should be as present as only Mr. Pinhorn could conceive. My allusion to the sequestered manner in which Mr. Paraday lived — it had formed part of my explanation, though I knew of it only by hearsay — was, I could divine, very much what had made Mr. Pinhorn nibble. It struck him as inconsistent with the success of his paper that any one should be so sequestered as that. And then wasn't an immediate exposure of everything just what the public wanted? Mr. Pinhorn effectually called me to order by reminding me of the promptness with which I had met Miss Braby at Liverpool on her return from her fiasco in the States. Hadn't we published, while its freshness and flavour were unimpaired, Miss Braby's own version of that great international episode? I felt somewhat uneasy at this lumping of the actress and the author, and I confess that after having enlisted Mr. Pinhorn's sympathies I procrastinated a little. I had succeeded better than I wished, and I had, as it happened, work nearer at hand. A few days later I called on Lord Crouchley and carried off in triumph the most unintelligible statement that had yet appeared of his lordship's reasons for his change of front. I thus set in motion in the daily papers columns of virtuous verbiage. The following week I ran down to Brighton for a chat, as Mr. Pinhorn called it, with Mrs. Bounder, who gave me, on the subject of her divorce, many curious particulars that had not been articulated in court. If ever an article flowed from the primal fount it was that article on Mrs. Bounder. By this time, however, I became aware that Neil Paraday's new book was on the point of appearing and that its approach had been the ground of my original appeal to Mr. Pinhorn, who was now annoyed with me for having lost so many days. He bundled me off — we would at least not lose another. I've always thought his sudden alertness a remarkable example of the journalistic instinct. Nothing had occurred, since I first spoke to him, to create a visible urgency, and no enlightenment could possibly have reached him. It was a pure case of professional *flair* — he had smelt the coming glory as an animal smells its distant prey.

II

I may as well say at once that this little record pretends in no degree to be a picture either of my introduction to Mr. Paraday or of certain proximate steps and stages. The scheme of my narrative allows no space for these things, and in any case a prohibitory sentiment would hang about my recollection of so rare an hour. These meagre notes are essentially private, so that if they see the light the insidious forces that, as my story itself shows, make at present for publicity will simply have overmastered my precautions. The curtain fell lately enough on the lamentable drama. My memory of the day I alighted at Mr. Paraday's door is a fresh memory of kindness, hospitality, compassion, and of the wonderful illuminating talk in which the welcome was conveyed. Some voice of the air had taught me the right moment, the moment of his life at which an act of unexpected young allegiance might most come home to him. He had recently recovered from a long, grave illness. I had gone to the neighbouring inn for the night, but I spent the evening in his company, and he insisted the next day on my sleeping under his roof. I hadn't an indefinite leave: Mr. Pinhorn supposed us to put our victims through on the gallop. It was later, in the office, that the rude motions of the jig were set to music. I fortified myself, however, as my training had taught me to do, by the conviction that nothing could be more advantageous for my article than to be written in the very atmosphere. I said nothing to Mr. Paraday about it, but in the morning, after my removal from the inn, while he was occupied in his study, as he had notified me he should need to be, I committed to paper the main heads of my impression. Then thinking to commend myself to Mr. Pinhorn by my celerity, I walked out and posted my little packet before luncheon. Once my paper was written I was free to stay on, and if it was calculated to divert attention from my levity in so doing I could reflect with satisfaction that I had never been so clever. I don't mean to deny of course that I was aware it was much too good for Mr. Pinhorn; but I was equally conscious that Mr. Pinhorn had the supreme shrewdness of recognising from time to time the cases in which an article was not too bad only because it was too good. There was nothing he loved so much as to print on the right occasion a thing he hated. I had begun my visit to the great man on a Monday, and on the Wednesday his book came out. A copy of it arrived by the first post, and he let me go out into the garden with it immediately after breakfast. I read it from beginning to end that day, and in the evening he asked me to remain with him the rest of the week and over the Sunday.

That night my manuscript came back from Mr. Pinhorn, accompanied with a letter the gist of which was the desire to know what I meant by trying to fob off on him such stuff. That was the meaning of the question, if not exactly its form, and it made my mistake immense to me. Such as this mistake was I could not only look it in the face and accept it. I knew where I had failed, but it was exactly where I couldn't have succeeded. I had been sent down to be personal and then in point of fact hadn't been personal at all: what I had dispatched to London was just a little finicking feverish study of my author's talent. Anything less relevant to Mr. Pinhorn's purpose couldn't well be imagined, and he was visibly angry at my having (at his expense, with a second-class ticket), approached the subject of our enterprise only to stand off so helplessly. For myself, I knew but too well what had happened, and how a miracle — as pretty as some old miracle of legend — had been wrought on the spot to save me. There had been a big brush of wings, the flash of an opaline robe, and then, with a great cool stir of the air, the sense of an angel's having swooped down and caught me to his bosom. He held me only till the danger was over, and it all took place in a minute. With my manuscript back on my hands I understood the phenomenon better, and the reflexions I made on it are what I meant, at the beginning of this anecdote, by my change of heart. Mr. Pinhorn's note was not only a rebuke decidedly stern, but an invitation immediately to send him — it was the case to say so — the genuine article, the revealing and reverberating sketch to the promise of which, and of which alone, I owed my squandered privilege. A week or two later I recast my peccant paper and, giving it a particular application to Mr. Paraday's new book, obtained for it the hospitality of another journal, where, I must admit, Mr. Pinhorn was so far vindicated as that it attracted not the least attention.

III

I was frankly, at the end of three days, a very prejudiced critic, so that one morning when, in the garden, my great man had offered to read me something I quite held my breath as I listened. It was the written scheme of another book — something put aside long ago, before his illness, but that he had lately taken out again to reconsider. He had been turning it round when I came down on him, and it had grown magnificently under this second hand. Loose liberal confident, it might have passed for a great gossiping eloquent letter — the overflow into talk of an artist's amorous plan. The theme I thought singularly rich, quite the strongest he had yet treated; and this familiar statement of it, full too of fine maturities, was really, in summarised splendour, a mine of gold, a precious independent work. I remember rather profanely wondering whether the ultimate production could possibly keep at the pitch. His reading of the fond epistle, at any rate, made me feel as if I were, for the advantage of posterity, in close correspondence with him — were the distinguished person to whom it had been affectionately addressed. It was a high distinction simply to be told such things. The idea he now communicated had all the freshness, the flushed fairness, of the conception untouched and untried: it was Venus rising from the sea and before the airs had blown upon her. I had never been so throbbingly present at such an unveiling. But when he had tossed the last bright word after the others, as I had seen cashiers in banks, weighing mounds of coin, drop a final sovereign into the tray, I knew a sudden prudent alarm.

"My dear master, how, after all, are you going to do it? It's infinitely noble, but what time it will take, what patience and independence, what assured, what perfect conditions! Oh for a lone isle in a tepid sea!"

"Isn't this practically a lone isle, and aren't you, as an encircling medium, tepid enough?" he asked, alluding with a laugh to the wonder of my young admiration and the narrow limits of his little provincial home. "Time isn't what I've lacked hitherto: the question hasn't been to find it, but to use it. Of course my illness made, while it lasted, a great hole — but I dare say there would have been a great hole at any rate. The earth we tread has more pockets than a billiard-table. The great thing is now to keep on my feet."

"That's exactly what I mean."

Neil Paraday looked at me with eyes — such pleasant eyes as he had — in which, as I now recall their expression, I seem to have seen a dim imagination of his fate. He was fifty years old, and his illness had been cruel, his convalescence slow. "It isn't as if I weren't all right."

"Oh if you weren't all right I wouldn't look at you!" I tenderly said.

We had both got up, quickened as by this clearer air, and he had lighted a cigarette. I had taken a fresh one, which with an intenser smile, by way of answer to my exclamation, he applied to the flame of his match. "If I weren't better I shouldn't have thought of *that!*" He flourished his script in his hand.

"I don't want to be discouraging, but that's not true," I returned. "I'm sure that during the months you lay here in pain you had visitations sublime. You thought of a thousand things. You think of more and more all the while. That's what makes you, if you'll pardon my familiarity, so respectable. At a time when so many people are spent you come into your second wind. But, thank God, all the same, you're better! Thank God too you're not, as you were telling me yesterday, 'successful.' If *you* weren't a failure what would be the use of trying? That's my one reserve on the subject of your recovery — that it makes you 'score,' as the newspapers say. It looks well in the newspapers, and almost anything that does that's horrible. 'We are happy to announce that Mr. Paraday, the celebrated author, is again in the enjoyment of excellent health.' Somehow I shouldn't like to see it."

"You won't see it; I'm not in the least celebrated — my obscurity protects me. But couldn't you bear even to see I was dying or dead?" my host enquired.

"Dead — *passe encore*; [1] there's nothing so safe. One never knows what a living artist may do — one has mourned so many. However, one must make the worst of it. You must be as dead as you can."

"Don't I meet that condition in having just published a book?"

"Adequately, let us hope; for the book's verily a masterpiece."

At this moment the parlour-maid appeared in the door that opened from the garden: Paraday lived at no great cost, and the frisk of petticoats, with a timorous "Sherry, sir?" was about his modest mahogany. He allowed half his income to his wife, from whom he had succeeded in separating without redundancy of legend. I had a general faith in his having

[1] Admitted, granted.

behaved well, and I had once, in London, taken Mrs. Paraday down to dinner. He now turned to speak to the maid, who offered him, on a tray, some card or note, while, agitated, excited, I wandered to the end of the precinct. The idea of his security became supremely dear to me, and I asked myself if I were the same young man who had come down a few days before to scatter him to the four winds. When I retraced my steps he had gone into the house, and the woman — the second London post had come in — had placed my letters and a newspaper on a bench. I sat down there to the letters, which were a brief business, and then, without heeding the address, took the paper from its envelope. It was the journal of highest renown, *The Empire* of that morning. It regularly came to Paraday, but I remembered that neither of us had yet looked at the copy already delivered. This one had a great mark on the "editorial" page, and, uncrumpling the wrapper, I saw it to be directed to my host and stamped with the name of his publishers. I instantly divined that *The Empire* had spoken of him, and I've not forgotten the odd little shock of the circumstance. It checked all eagerness and made me drop the paper a moment. As I sat there conscious of a palpitation I think I had a vision of what was to be. I had also a vision of the letter I would presently address to Mr. Pinhorn, breaking, as it were, with Mr. Pinhorn. Of course, however, the next minute the voice of *The Empire* was in my ears.

The article wasn't, I thanked heaven, a review; it was a "leader," the last of three, presenting Neil Paraday to the human race. His new book, the fifth from his hand, had been but a day or two out, and *The Empire*, already aware of it, fired, as if on the birth of a prince, a salute of a whole column. The guns had been booming these three hours in the house without our suspecting them. The big blundering newspaper had discovered him, and now he was proclaimed and anointed and crowned. His place was assigned him as publicly as if a fat usher with a wand had pointed to the topmost chair; he was to pass up and still up, higher and higher, between the watching faces and the envious sounds — away up to the dais and the throne. The article was "epoch-making," a landmark in his life; he had taken rank at a bound, waked up a national glory. A national glory was needed, and it was an immense convenience he was there. What all this meant

rolled over me, and I fear I grew a little faint — it meant so much more than I could say "yea" to on the spot. In a flash, somehow, all was different; the tremendous wave I speak of had swept something away. It had knocked down, I suppose, my little customary altar, my twinkling tapers and my flowers, and had reared itself into the likeness of a temple vast and bare. When Neil Paraday should come out of the house he would come out a contemporary. That was what had happened: the poor man was to be squeezed into his horrible age. I felt as if he had been overtaken on the crest of the hill and brought back to the city. A little more and he would have dipped down the short cut to posterity and escaped.

IV

When he came out it was exactly as if he had been in custody, for beside him walked a stout man with a big black beard, who, save that he wore spectacles, might have been a policeman, and in whom at a second glance I recognised the highest contemporary enterprise. "This is Mr. Morrow," said Paraday, looking, I thought, rather white: "he wants to publish heaven knows what about me."

I winced as I remembered that this was exactly what I myself had wanted. "Already?" I cried with a sort of sense that my friend had fled to me for protection.

Mr. Morrow glared, agreeably, through his glasses: they suggested the electric headlights of some monstrous modern ship, and I felt as if Paraday and I were tossing terrified under his bows. I saw his momentum was irresistible. "I was confident that I should be the first in the field. A great interest is naturally felt in Mr. Paraday's surroundings," he heavily observed.

"I hadn't the least idea of it," said Paraday, as if he had been told he had been snoring.

"I find he hasn't read the article in *The Empire*," Mr. Morrow remarked to me. "That's so very interesting — it's something to start with," he smiled. He had begun to pull off his gloves, which were violently new, and to look encouragingly round the little garden. As a "surrounding" I felt how I myself had already been taken in; I was a little fish in the stomach of a bigger one. "I represent," our visitor continued, "a syndicate of influential journals, no less than thirty-seven, whose public — whose publics, I may say — are in peculiar sympathy with Mr. Paraday's line of thought. They would greatly appreciate any expression of his views on the subject of the art he so nobly exemplifies. In addition to my connexion with the syndicate just mentioned I hold a particular commission from *The Tatler*, whose most prominent department, 'Smatter and Chatter' — I dare say you've often enjoyed it — attracts such attention. I was honoured only last week, as a representative of *The Tatler*, with the confidence of Guy Walsingham, the brilliant author of 'Obsessions.' She pronounced herself thoroughly pleased with my sketch of her method; she went so far as to say that I had made her genius more comprehensible even to herself."

Neil Paraday had dropped on the garden-bench and sat there at once detached and confounded; he looked hard at a bare spot in the lawn, as if with an anxiety that had suddenly made him grave. His movement had been interpreted by his visitor as an invitation to sink sympathetically into a wicker chair that stood hard by, and while Mr. Morrow so settled himself I felt he had taken official possession and that there was no undoing it. One had heard of unfortunate people's having "a man in the house," and this was just what *we* had. There was a silence of a moment, during which we seemed to acknowledge in the only way that was possible the presence of universal fate; the sunny stillness took no pity, and my thought, as I was sure Paraday's was doing, performed within the minute a great distant revolution. I saw just how emphatic I should make my rejoinder to Mr. Pinhorn, and that having come, like Mr. Morrow, to betray, I must remain as long as possible to save. Not because I had brought my mind back, but because our visitor's last words were in my ear, I presently enquired with gloomy irrelevance if Guy Walsingham were a woman.

"Oh yes, a mere pseudonym — rather pretty, isn't it? — and convenient, you know, for a lady who goes in for the larger latitude. 'Obsessions, by Miss So-and-so,' would look a little odd, but men are more naturally indelicate. Have you peeped into 'Obsessions'?" Mr. Morrow continued sociably to our companion.

Paraday, still absent, remote, made no answer, as if he hadn't heard the question; a form of intercourse that appeared to suit the cheerful Mr. Morrow as well as any other. Imperturbably bland, he was a man of resources — he

only needed to be on the spot. He had pocketed the whole poor place while Paraday and I were wool-gathering, and I could imagine that he had already got his "heads." His system, at any rate, was justified by the inevitability with which I replied, to save my friend the trouble: "Dear no — he hasn't read it. He doesn't read such things!" I unwarily added.

"Things that are *too* far over the fence, eh?" I was indeed a godsend to Mr. Morrow. It was the psychological moment; it determined the appearance of his note-book, which, however, he at first kept slightly behind him, even as the dentist approaching his victim keeps the horrible forceps. "Mr. Paraday holds with the good old proprieties — I see!" And thinking of the thirty-seven influential journals, I found myself, as I found poor Paraday, helplessly assisting at the promulgation of this ineptitude. "There's no point on which distinguished views are so acceptable as on this question — raised perhaps more strikingly than ever by Guy Walsingham — of the permissibility of the larger latitude. I've an appointment, precisely in connexion with it, next week, with Dora Forbes, author of 'The Other Way Round,' which everybody's talking about. Has Mr. Paraday glanced at 'The Other Way Round'?" Mr. Morrow now frankly appealed to me. I took on myself to repudiate the supposition, while our companion, still silent, got up nervously and walked away. His visitor paid no heed to his withdrawal, but opened out the notebook with a more fatherly pat. "Dora Forbes, I gather, takes the ground, the same as Guy Walsingham's, that the larger latitude has simply got to come. He holds that it has got to be squarely faced. Of course his sex makes him a less prejudiced witness. But an authoritative word from Mr. Paraday — from the point of view of *his* sex, you know — would go right round the globe. He takes the line that we *haven't* got to face it?"

I was bewildered: it sounded somehow as if there were three sexes. My interlocutor's pencil was poised, my private responsibility great. I simply sat staring, none the less, and only found presence of mind to say: "Is this Miss Forbes a gentleman?"

Mr. Morrow had a subtle smile. "It wouldn't be 'Miss' — there's a wife!"

"I mean is she a man?"

"The wife?" — Mr. Morrow was for a moment as confused as myself. But when I explained that I alluded to Dora Forbes in person he informed me, with visible amusement at my being so out of it, that this was the "pen-name" of an indubitable male — he had a big red moustache. "He goes in for the slight mys-tification because the ladies are such popular favourites. A great deal of interest is felt in his acting on that idea — which *is* clever, isn't it? — and there's every prospect of its being widely imitated." Our host at this moment joined us again, and Mr. Morrow remarked invitingly that he should be happy to make a note of any observation the movement in question, the bid for success under a lady's name, might suggest to Mr. Paraday. But the poor man, without catching the allusion, excused himself, plead-ing that, though greatly honoured by his visitor's interest, he suddenly felt unwell and should have to take leave of him — have to go and lie down and keep quiet. His young friend might be trusted to answer for him, but he hoped Mr. Morrow didn't expect great things even of his young friend. His young friend, at this moment, looked at Neil Paraday with an anxious eye, greatly wondering if he were doomed to be ill again; but Paraday's own kind face met his question reassuringly, seemed to say in a glance intelligible enough: "Oh I'm not ill, but I'm scared; get him out of the house as quietly as possible." Getting newspapermen out of the house was odd business for an emis-sary of Mr. Pinhorn, and I was so exhilarated by the idea of it that I called after him as he left us: "Read the article in *The Empire* and you'll soon be all right!"

V

"Delicious my having come down to tell him of it!" Mr. Morrow ejaculated. "My cab was at the door twenty minutes after *The Empire* had been laid on my breakfast-table. Now what have you got for me?" he continued, dropping again into his chair, from which, how-ever, he the next moment eagerly rose. "I was shown into the drawing-room, but there must be more to see — his study, his literary sanc-tum, the little things he has about, or other domestic objects and features. He wouldn't be lying down on his study-table? There's a great interest always felt in the scene of an author's labours. Sometimes we're favoured with very delightful peeps. Dora Forbes showed me all his table-drawers, and almost jammed my hand into one into which I made a dash! I don't ask that of you, but if we could talk things over right there where he sits I feel as if I should get the keynote."

I had no wish whatever to be rude to Mr. Morrow, I was too much initiated not to tend to more diplomacy; but I had a quick inspiration, and I entertained an insurmountable, an almost superstitious objection to his crossing the thresh-old of my friend's little lonely shabby conse-crated workshop. "No, no — we shan't get at his life that way," I said. "The way to get at his life is to — But wait a moment!" I broke off and went quickly into the house, whence I in three minutes reappeared before Mr. Morrow with the two volumes of Paraday's new book. "His life's here," I went on, "and I'm so full of this admirable thing that I can't talk of any-thing else. The artist's life's his work, and this is the place to observe him. What he has to tell us he tells us with *this* perfection. My dear sir, the best interviewer's the best reader."

Mr. Morrow good-humouredly protested. "Do you mean to say that no other source of infor-mation should be open to us?"

"None other till this particular one — by far the most copious — has been quite exhausted. Have you exhausted it, my dear sir? Had you exhausted it when you came down here? It seems to me in our time almost wholly ne-glected, and something should surely be done to restore its ruined credit. It's the course to which the artist himself at every step, and with such pathetic confidence, refers us. This last book of Mr. Paraday's is full of revelations."

"Revelations?" panted Mr. Morrow, whom I had forced again into his chair.

"The only kind that count. It tells you with a perfection that seems to me quite final all the author thinks, for instance, about the advent of the 'larger latitude.' "

"Where does it do that?" asked Mr. Morrow, who had picked up the second volume and was insincerely thumbing it.

"Everywhere — in the whole treatment of his case. Extract the opinion, disengage the answer — those are the real acts of homage."

Mr. Morrow, after a minute, tossed the book away. "Ah but you mustn't take me for a reviewer."

"Heaven forbid I should take you for any-thing so dreadful! You came down to perform a little act of sympathy, and so, I may confide to you, did I. Let us perform our little act to-gether. These pages overflow with the testimony we want: let us read them and taste them and interpret them. You'll of course have perceived for yourself that one scarcely does read Neil Paraday till one reads him aloud; he gives out to the ear an extraordinary full tone, and it's only when you expose it confidently to that test that you really get near his style. Take up your book again and let me listen, while you pay it out, to that wonderful fifteenth chapter. If you feel you can't do it justice, compose yourself to attention while I produce for you — I think I can! — this scarcely less admirable ninth."

Mr. Morrow gave me a straight look which was as hard as a blow between the eyes; he had turned rather red, and a question had formed itself in his mind which reached my sense as distinctly as if he had uttered it: "What sort of damned fool are *you*?" Then he got up, gathering together his hat and gloves, buttoning his coat, projecting hungrily all over the place the big transparency of his mask. It seemed to flare over Fleet Street and somehow made the actual spot distressingly humble: there was so little for it to feed on unless he counted the blisters of our stucco or saw his way to do something with the roses. Even the poor roses were common kinds. Presently his eyes fell on the manuscript from which Paraday had been reading to me and which still lay on the bench. As my own followed them I saw it looked promising, looked pregnant, as if it gently throbbed with the life the reader had given it. Mr. Morrow indulged in a nod at it and a vague thrust of his umbrella. "What's that?"

"Oh, it's a plan — a secret."

"A secret!" There was an instant's silence, and then Mr. Morrow made another movement. I may have been mistaken, but it affected me as the translated impulse of the desire to lay hands on the manuscript, and this led me to indulge in a quick anticipatory grab which may very well have seemed ungraceful, or even impertinent, and which at any rate left Mr. Paraday's two admirers very erect, glaring at each other while one of them held a bundle of papers well behind him. An instant later Mr. Morrow quitted me abruptly, as if he had really carried something off with him. To reassure myself, watching his broad back recede, I only grasped my manuscript the tighter. He went to the back door of the house, the one he had come out from, but on trying the handle he appeared to find it fastened. So he passed round into the front garden, and by listening intently enough I could presently hear the outer gate close behind him

with a bang. I thought again of the thirty-seven influential journals and wondered what would be his revenge. I hasten to add that he was magnanimous: which was just the most dreadful thing he could have been. *The Tatler* published a charming chatty familiar account of Mr. Paraday's "Home-life," and on the wings of the thirty-seven influential journals it went, to use Mr. Morrow's own expression, right round the globe.

VI

A week later, early in May, my glorified friend came up to town, where, it may be veraciously recorded, he was the king of the beasts of the year. No advancement was ever more rapid, no exaltation more complete, no bewilderment more teachable. His book sold but moderately, though the article in *The Empire* had done unwonted wonders for it; but he circulated in person to a measure that the libraries might well have envied. His formula had been found — he was a "revelation." His momentary terror had been real, just as mine had been — the overclouding of his passionate desire to be left to finish his work. He was far from unsociable, but he had the finest conception of being let alone that I've ever met. For the time, none the less, he took his profit where it seemed most to crowd on him, having in his pocket the portable sophistries about the nature of the artist's task. Observation too was a kind of work and experience a kind of success; London dinners were all material and London ladies were fruitful soil. "No one has the faintest conception of what I'm trying for," he said to me, "and not many have read three pages that I've written; but I must dine with them first — they'll find out why when they've time." It was rather rude justice perhaps; but the fatigue had the merit of being a new sort, while the phantasmagoric town was probably after all less of a battlefield than the haunted study. He once told me that he had had no personal life to speak of since his fortieth year, but had had more than was good for him before. London closed the parenthesis and exhibited him in relations; one of the most inevitable of these being that in which he found himself to Mrs. Weeks Wimbush, wife of the boundless brewer and proprietress of the universal menagerie. In this establishment, as everybody knows, on occasions when the crush is great, the animals rub shoulders freely with the spectators and the lions sit down for whole evenings with the lambs.

It had been ominously clear to me from the first that in Neil Paraday this lady, who, as all the world agreed, was tremendous fun, considered that she had secured a prime attraction, a creature of almost heraldic oddity. Nothing could exceed her enthusiasm over her capture, and nothing could exceed the confused apprehensions it excited in me. I had an instinctive fear of her which I tried without effect to conceal from her victim, but which I let her notice with perfect impunity. Paraday heeded it, but she never did, for her conscience was that of a romping child. She was a blind violent force to which I could attach no more idea of responsibility than to the creaking of a sign in the wind. It was difficult to say what she conduced to but circulation. She was constructed of steel and leather, and all I asked of her for our tractable friend was not to do him to death. He had consented for a time to be of indiarubber, but my thoughts were fixed on the day he should resume his shape or at least get back into his box. It was evidently all right, but I should be glad when it was well over. I had a special fear — the impression was ineffaceable of the hour when, after Mr. Morrow's departure, I had found him on the sofa in his study. That pretext of indisposition had not in the least been meant as a snub to the envoy of *The Tatler* — he had gone to lie down in very truth. He had felt a pang of his old pain, the result of the agitation wrought in him by this forcing open of a new period. His old programme, his old ideal even had to be changed. Say what one would, success was a complication and recognition had to be reciprocal. The monastic life, the pious illumination of the missal in the convent-cell were things of the gathered past. It didn't engender despair, but at least it required adjustment. Before I left him on that occasion we had passed a bargain, my part of which was that I should make it my business to take care of him. Let whoever would represent the interest in his presence (I must have had a mystical prevision of Mrs. Weeks Wimbush) I should represent the interest in his work — or otherwise expressed in his absence. These two interests were in their essence opposed; and I doubt, as youth is fleeting, if I shall ever again know the intensity of joy with which I felt that in so good a cause I was willing to make myself odious.

One day in Sloane Street I found myself questioning Paraday's landlord, who had come to the door in answer to my knock. Two vehicles, a barouche and a smart hansom, were drawn up before the house.

"In the drawing-room, sir? Mrs. Weeks Wimbush."

"And in the dining-room?"

"A young lady, sir — waiting: I think a foreigner."

It was three o'clock, and on days when Paraday didn't lunch out he attached a value to these appropriated hours. On which days, however, didn't the dear man lunch out? Mrs. Wimbush, at such a crisis, would have rushed round immediately after her own repast. I went into the dining-room first, postponing the pleasure of seeing how, upstairs, the lady of the barouche would, on my arrival, point the moral of my sweet solicitude. No one took such an interest as herself in his doing only what was good for him, and she was always on the spot to see that he did it. She made appointments with him to discuss the best means of economising his time and protecting his privacy. She further made his health her special business, and had so much sympathy with my own zeal for it that she was the author of pleasing fictions on the subject of what my devotion had led me to give up. I gave up nothing (I don't count Mr. Pinhorn) because I had nothing, and all I had as yet achieved was to find myself also in the menagerie. I had dashed in to save my friend, but I had only got domesticated and wedged; so that I could do little more for him than exchange with him over people's heads looks of intense but futile intelligence.

VII

The young lady in the dining-room had a brave face, black hair, blue eyes, and in her lap a big volume. "I've come for his autograph," she said when I had explained to her that I was under bonds to see people for him when he was occupied. "I've been waiting half an hour, but I'm prepared to wait all day." I don't know whether it was this that told me she was American, for the propensity to wait all day is not in general characteristic of her race. I was enlightened probably not so much by the spirit of the utterance as by some quality of its sound. At any rate I saw she had an individual patience and a lovely frock, together with an expression that played among her pretty features like a breeze among flowers. Putting her book on the table she showed me a massive album, showily bound and full of autographs of price. The collection of faded notes, of still more faded "thoughts," of quotations, platitudes, signatures, represented a formidable purpose.

I could only disclose my dread of it. "Most people apply to Mr. Paraday by letter, you know."

"Yes, but he doesn't answer. I've written three times."

"Very true," I reflected; "the sort of letter you mean goes straight into the fire."

"How do you know the sort I mean?" My interlocutress had blushed and smiled, and in a moment she added: "I don't believe he gets many like them!"

"I'm sure they're beautiful, but he burns without reading." I didn't add that I had convinced him he ought to.

"Isn't he then in danger of burning things of importance?"

"He would perhaps be so if distinguished men hadn't an infallible nose for nonsense."

She looked at me a moment — her face was sweet and gay. "Do *you* burn without reading too?" — in answer to which I assured her that if she'd trust me with her repository I'd see that Mr. Paraday should write his name in it.

She considered a little. "That's very well, but it wouldn't make me see him."

"Do you want very much to see him?" It seemed ungracious to catechise so charming a creature, but somehow I had never yet taken my duty to the great author so seriously.

"Enough to have come from America for the purpose."

I stared. "All alone?"

"I don't see that that's exactly your business, but if it will make me more seductive I'll confess that I'm quite by myself. I had to come alone or not come at all."

She was interesting; I could imagine she had lost parents, natural protectors — could conceive even she had inherited money. I was at a pass of my own fortunes when keeping hansoms at doors seemed to me pure swagger. As a trick of this bold and sensitive girl, however, it became romantic — a part of the general romance of her freedom, her errand, her innocence. The confidence of young Americans was notorious, and I speedily arrived at a conviction that no impulse could have been more generous than the impulse that had operated here. I foresaw at the moment that it would make her my peculiar charge, just as circum-

stances had made Neil Paraday. She would be another person to look after, so that one's honour would be concerned in guiding her straight. These things became clearer to me later on; at the instant I had scepticism enough to observe to her, as I turned the pages of her volume, that her net had all the same caught many a big fish. She appeared to have had fruitful access to the great ones of the earth; there were people moreover whose signatures she had presumably secured without a personal interview. She couldn't have worried George Washington and Friedrich Schiller and Hannah More. She met this argument, to my surprise, by throwing up the album without a pang. It wasn't even her own; she was responsible for none of its treasures. It belonged to a girl-friend in America, a young lady in a western city. This young lady had insisted on her bringing it, to pick up more autographs: she thought they might like to see, in Europe, in what company they would be. The "girl-friend," the western city, the immortal names, the curious errand, the idyllic faith, all made a story as strange to me, and as beguiling, as some tale in the Arabian Nights. Thus it was that my informant had encumbered herself with the ponderous tome; but she hastened to assure me that this was the first time she had brought it out. For her visit to Mr. Paraday it had simply been a pretext. She didn't really care a straw that he should write his name; what she did want was to look straight into his face.

I demurred a little. "And why do you require to do that?"

"Because I just love him!" Before I could recover from the agitating effect of this crystal ring my companion had continued: "Hasn't there ever been any face that *you've* wanted to look into?"

How could I tell her so soon how much I appreciated the opportunity of looking into hers? I could only assent in general to the proposition that there were certainly for every one such yearnings, and even such faces; and I felt the crisis demanded all my lucidity, all my wisdom. "Oh yes, I'm a student of physiognomy. Do you mean," I pursued, "that you've a passion for Mr. Paraday's books?"

"They've been everything to me and a little more beside — I know them by heart. They've completely taken hold of me. There's no author about whom I'm in such a state as I'm in about Neil Paraday."

"Permit me to remark then," I presently returned, "that you're one of the right sort."

"One of the enthusiasts? Of course I am!"

"Oh there are enthusiasts who are quite of the wrong. I mean you're one of those to whom an appeal can be made."

"An appeal?" Her face lighted as with the chance of some great sacrifice.

If she was ready for one it was only waiting for her, and in a moment I mentioned it. "Give up this crude purpose of seeing him. Go away without it. That will be far better."

She looked mystified, then turned visibly pale. "Why, hasn't he any personal charm?" The girl was terrible and laughable in her bright directness.

"Ah that dreadful word 'personal'!" I wailed; "we're dying of it, for you women bring it out with murderous effect. When you meet with a genius as fine as this idol of ours let him off the dreary duty of being a personality as well. Know him only by what's best in him and spare him for the same sweet sake."

My young lady continued to look at me in confusion and mistrust, and the result of her reflexion on what I had just said was to make her suddenly break out: "Look here, sir — what's the matter with him?"

"The matter with him is that if he doesn't look out people will eat a great hole in his life."

She turned it over. "He hasn't any disfigurement?"

"Nothing to speak of!"

"Do you mean that social engagements interfere with his occupations?"

"That but feebly expresses it."

"So that he can't give himself up to his beautiful imagination?"

"He's beset, badgered, bothered — he's pulled to pieces on the pretext of being applauded. People expect him to give them his time, his golden time, who wouldn't themselves give five shillings for one of his books."

"Five? I'd give five thousand!"

"Give your sympathy — give your forbearance. Two thirds of those who approach him only do it to advertise themselves."

"Why it's too bad!" the girl exclaimed with the face of an angel. "It's the first time I was ever called crude!" she laughed.

I followed up my advantage. "There's a lady with him now who's a terrible complication, and who yet hasn't read, I'm sure, ten pages he ever wrote."

My visitor's wide eyes grew tenderer. "Then how does she talk ——"

"Without ceasing. I only mention her as a single case. Do you want to know how to show a superlative consideration? Simply avoid him."

"Avoid him?" she despairingly breathed.

"Don't force him to have to take account of you; admire him in silence, cultivate him at a distance and secretly appropriate his message. Do you want to know," I continued, warming to my idea, "how to perform an act of homage really sublime?" Then as she hung on my words: "Succeed in never seeing him at all!"

"Never at all?" — she suppressed a shriek for it.

"The more you get into his writings the less you'll want to, and you'll be immensely sustained by the thought of the good you're doing him."

She looked at me without resentment or spite, and at the truth I had put before her with candour, credulity, pity. I was afterwards happy to remember that she must have gathered from my face the liveliness of my interest in herself. "I think I see what you mean."

"Oh I express it badly, but I should be delighted if you'd let me come to see you — to explain it better!"

She made no response to this, and her thoughtful eyes fell on the big album, on which she presently laid her hands as if to take it away. "I did use to say out West that they might write a little less for autographs — to all great poets, you know — and study the thoughts and style a little more."

"What do they care for the thoughts and style? They didn't even understand you. I'm not sure," I added, "that I do myself, and I dare say that you by no means make me out."

She had got up to go, and though I wanted her to succeed in not seeing Neil Paraday I wanted her also, inconsequently, to remain in the house. I was at any rate far from desiring to hustle her off. As Mrs. Weeks Wimbush, upstairs, was still saving our friend in her own way, I asked my young lady to let me briefly relate, in illustration of my point, the little incident of my having gone down into the country for a profane purpose and been converted on the spot to holiness. Sinking again into her chair to listen she showed a deep interest in the anecdote. Then thinking it over gravely she returned with her odd intonation: "Yes, but you do see him!" I had to admit that this was the case; and I wasn't so prepared with an effective attenuation as I could have wished. She eased the situation off, however, by the charming quaintness with which she finally said: "Well, I wouldn't want him to be lonely!" This time she rose in earnest, but I persuaded her to let me keep the album to show Mr. Paraday. I assured her I'd bring it back to her myself. "Well, you'll find my address somewhere in it on a paper!" she sighed all resignedly at the door.

VIII

I blush to confess it, but I invited Mr. Paraday that very day to transcribe into the album one of his most characteristic passages. I told him how I had got rid of the strange girl who had brought it — her ominous name was Miss Hunter and she lived at an hotel; quite agreeing with him moreover as to the wisdom of getting rid with equal promptitude of the book itself. This was why I carried it to Albemarle Street no later than on the morrow. I failed to find her at home, but she wrote to me and I went again: she wanted so much to hear more about Neil Paraday. I returned repeatedly, I may briefly declare, to supply her with this information. She had been immensely taken, the more she thought of it, with that idea of mine about the act of homage: it had ended by filling her with a rapturous rapture. She positively desired to do something sublime for him, though indeed I could see that, as this particular flight was difficult, she appreciated the fact that my visits kept her up. I had it on my conscience to keep her up; I neglected nothing that would contribute to it, and her conception of our cherished author's independence became at last as fine as his very own. "Read him, read him — — *that* will be an education in decency," I constantly repeated; while, seeking him in his works even as God in nature, she represented herself as convinced that, according to my assurance, this was the system that had, as she expressed it, weaned her. We read him together when I could find time, and the generous creature's sacrifice was fed by our communion. There were twenty selfish women about whom I told her and who stirred her to a beautiful rage. Immediately after my first visit her sister, Mrs. Milsom, came over from Paris, and the two ladies began to present, as they called it, their letters. I thanked our stars that none had been presented to Mr. Paraday. They received invita-

tions and dined out, and some of these occasions enabled Fanny Hunter to perform, for consistency's sake, touching feats of submission. Nothing indeed would now have induced her even to look at the object of her admiration. Once, hearing his name announced at a party, she instantly left the room by another door and then straightway quitted the house. At another time when I was at the opera with them — Mrs. Milsom had invited me to their box — I attempted to point Mr. Paraday out to her in the stalls. On this she asked her sister to change places with her and, while that lady devoured the great man through a powerful glass, presented, all the rest of the evening, her inspired back to the house. To torment her tenderly I pressed the glass upon her, telling her how wonderfully near it brought our friend's handsome head. By way of answer she simply looked at me in charged silence, letting me see that tears had gathered in her eyes. These tears, I may remark, produced an effect on me of which the end is not yet. There was a moment when I felt it my duty to mention them to Neil Paraday, but I was deterred by the reflexion that there were questions more relevent to his happiness.

These questions indeed, by the end of the season, were reduced to a single one — the question of reconstituting so far as might be possible the conditions under which he had produced his best work. Such conditions could never all come back, for there was a new one that took up too much place; but some perhaps were not beyond recall. I wanted above all things to see him sit down to the subject he had, on my making his acquaintance, read me that admirable sketch of. Something told me there was no security but in his doing so before the new factor, as we used to say at Mr. Pinhorn's, should render the problem incalculable. It only half-reassured me that the sketch itself was so copious and so eloquent that even at the worst there would be the making of a small but complete book, a tiny volume which, for the faithful, might well become an object of adoration. There would even not be wanting critics to declare, I foresaw, that the plan was a thing to be more thankful for than the structure to have been reared on it. My impatience for the structure, none the less, grew and grew with the interruptions. He had on coming up to town begun to sit for his portrait to a young painter, Mr. Rumble, whose little game, as we also used to say at Mr. Pinhorn's, was to be the first to perch on the shoulders of renown. Mr. Rumble's studio was a circus in which the man of the hour, and still more the woman, leaped through the hoops of his showy frames almost as electrically as they burst into telegrams and "specials." He pranced into the exhibitions on their back; he was the reporter on canvas, the Vandyke up to date, and there was one roaring year in which Mrs. Bounder and Miss Braby, Guy Walsingham and Dora Forbes proclaimed in chorus from the same pictured walls that no one had yet got ahead of him.

Paraday had been promptly caught and saddled, accepting with characteristic good humour his confidential hint that to figure in his show was not so much a consequence as a cause of immortality. From Mrs. Wimbush to the last "representative" who called to ascertain his twelve favourite dishes, it was the same ingenuous assumption that he would rejoice in the repercussion. There were moments when I fancied I might have had more patience with them if they hadn't been so fatally benevolent. I hated at all events Mr. Rumble's picture, and had my bottled resentment ready when, later on, I found my distracted friend had been stuffed by Mrs. Wimbush into the mouth of another cannon. A young artist in whom she was intensely interested, and who had no connexion with Mr. Rumble, was to show how far *he* could make him go. Poor Paraday, in return, was naturally to write something somewhere about the young artist. She played her victims against each other with admirable ingenuity, and her establishment was a huge machine in which the tiniest and the biggest wheels went round to the same treadle. I had a scene with her in which I tried to express that the function of such a man was to exercise his genius — not to serve as a hoarding for pictorial posters. The people I was perhaps angriest with were the editors of magazines who had introduced what they called new features, so aware were they that the newest feature of all would be to make him grind their axes by contributing his views on vital topics and taking part in the periodical prattle about the future of fiction. I made sure that before I should have done with him there would scarcely be a current form of words left me to be sick of; but meanwhile I could make surer still of my animosity to bustling ladies for whom he drew the water that irrigated their social flower-beds.

I had a battle with Mrs. Wimbush over the artist she protected, and another over the question of a certain week, at the end of July, that Mr. Paraday appeared to have contracted to spend with her in the country. I protested against this visit; I intimated that he was too unwell for hospitality without a *nuance*, for caresses without imagination; I begged he might rather take the time in some restorative way. A sultry air of promises, of ponderous parties, hung over his August, and he would greatly profit by the interval of rest. He hadn't told me he was ill again — that he had had a warning; but I hadn't needed this, for I found his reticence his worst symptom. The only thing he said to me was that he believed a comfortable attack of something or other would set him up: it would put out of the question everything but the exemptions he prized. I'm afraid I shall have presented him as a martyr in a very small cause if I fail to explain that he surrendered himself much more liberally than I surrendered him. He filled his lungs, for the most part, with the comedy of his queer fate: the tragedy was in the spectacles through which I chose to look. He was conscious of inconvenience, and above all of a great renouncement; but how could he have heard a mere dirge in the bells of his accession? The sagacity and the jealousy were mine, and his the impressions and the harvest. Of course, as regards Mrs. Wimbush, I was worsted in my encounters, for wasn't the state of his health the very reason for his coming to her at Prestidge? Wasn't it precisely at Prestidge that he was to be coddled, and wasn't the dear Princess coming to help her coddle him? The dear Princess, now on a visit to England, was of a famous foreign house, and, in her gilded cage, with her retinue of keepers and feeders, was the most expensive specimen in the good lady's collection. I don't think her august presence had had to do with Paraday's consenting to go, but it's not impossible he had operated as a bait to the illustrious stranger. The party had been made up for him, Mrs. Wimbush averred, and every one was counting on it, the dear Princess most of all. If he was well enough he was to read them something absolutely fresh, and it was on that particular prospect the Princess had set her heart. She was so fond of genius in *any* walk of life, and was so used to it and understood it so well: she was the greatest of Mr. Paraday's admirers, she devoured everything he wrote. And then he read like an angel. Mrs. Wimbush reminded me that he had again and again given her, Mrs. Wimbush, the privilege of listening to him.

I looked at her a moment. "What has he read to you?" I crudely enquired.

For a moment too she met my eyes, and for the fraction of a moment she hesitated and coloured. "Oh all sorts of things!"

I wondered if this were an imperfect recollection or only a perfect fib, and she quite understood my unuttered comment on her measure of such things. But if she could forget Neil Paraday's beauties she could of course forget my rudeness, and three days later she invited me, by telegraph, to join the party at Prestidge. This time she might indeed have had a story about what I had given up to be near the master. I addressed from that fine residence several communications to a young lady in London, a young lady whom, I confess, I quitted with reluctance and whom the reminder of what she herself could give up was required to make me quit at all. It adds to the gratitude I owe her on other grounds that she kindly allows me to transcribe from my letters a few of the passages in which that hateful sojourn is candidly commemorated.

IX

"I suppose I ought to enjoy the joke of what's going on here," I wrote, "but somehow it doesn't amuse me. Pessimism on the contrary possesses me and cynicism deeply engages. I positively feel my own flesh sore from the brass nails in Neil Paraday's social harness. The house is full of people who like him, as they mention, awfully, and with whom his talent for talking nonsense has prodigious success. I delight in his nonsense myself; why is it therefore that I grudge these happy folk their artless satisfaction? Mystery of the human heart — abyss of the critical spirit! Mrs. Wimbush thinks she can answer that question, and as my want of gaiety has at last worn out her patience she has given me a glimpse of her shrewd guess. I'm made restless by the selfishness of the insincere friend — I want to monopolise Paraday in order that he may push me on. To be intimate with him's a feather in my cap; it gives me an importance that I couldn't naturally pretend to, and I seek to deprive him of social refreshment because I fear that meeting more disinterested people may enlighten him as to my real motive. All the disinterested people here are his particular admirers and have been carefully selected as such. There's supposed to be a copy of his last book in the house, and in the hall I come upon ladies, in attitudes, bending gracefully over the first volume. I discreetly avert my eyes, and when I next look round the precarious joy has been superseded by the book of life. There's a sociable circle or a confidential couple, and the relinquished volume lies open on its face and as dropped under extreme coercion. Somebody else presently finds it and transfers it, with its air of momentary desolation, to another piece of furniture. Every one's asking every one about it all day, and every one's telling every one where they put it last. I'm sure it's rather smudgy about the twentieth page. I've a strong impression too that the second volume is lost — has been packed in the bag of some departing guest; and yet everybody has the impression that somebody else has read to the end. You see therefore that the beautiful book plays a great part in our existence. Why should I take the occasion of such distinguished honours to say that I begin to see deeper into Gustave Flaubert's doleful refrain about the hatred of literature? I refer you again to the perverse constitution of man.

"The Princess is a massive lady with the organisation of an athlete and the confusion of tongues of a *valet de place*. She contrives to commit herself extraordinarily little in a great many languages, and is entertained and conversed with in detachments and relays, like an institution which goes on from generation to generation or a big building contracted for under a forfeit. She can't have a personal taste any more than, when her husband succeeds, she can have a personal crown, and her opinion in any matter is rusty and heavy and plain — made, in the night of ages, to last and be transmitted. I feel as if I ought to 'tip' some *custode* for my glimpse of it. She has been told everything in the world and has never perceived anything, and the echoes of her education respond awfully to the rash footfall — I mean the casual remark — in the cold Valhalla of her memory. Mrs. Wimbush delights in her wit and says there's nothing so charming as to hear Mr. Paraday draw it out. He's perpetually detailed for this job, and he tells me it has a peculiarly exhausting effect. Every one's beginning — at the end of two days — to sidle obsequiously away from her, and Mrs. Wimbush pushes him again and again into the breach. None of the uses I have yet seen him put to infuriate me quite so much. He looks very fagged and has at last confessed to me that his condition makes him uneasy —

has even promised me he'll go straight home instead of returning to his final engagements in town. Last night I had some talk with him about going to-day, cutting his visit short; so sure am I that he'll be better as soon as he's shut up in his lighthouse. He told me that this is what he would like to do; reminding me, however, that the first lesson of his greatness has been precisely that he can't do what he likes. Mrs. Wimbush would never forgive him if he should leave her before the Princess has received the last hand. When I hint that a violent rupture with our hostess would be the best thing in the world for him he gives me to understand that if his reason assents to the proposition his courage hangs woefully back. He makes no secret of being mortally afraid of her, and when I ask what harm she can do him that she hasn't already done he simply repeats: 'I'm afraid, I'm afraid! Don't enquire too closely,' he said last night; 'only believe that I feel a sort of terror. It's strange, when she's so kind! At any rate, I'd as soon overturn that piece of priceless Sèvres as tell her I must go before my date.' It sounds dreadfully weak, but he has some reason, and he pays for his imagination, which puts him (I should hate it) in the place of others and makes him feel, even against himself, their feelings, their appetites, their motives. It's indeed inveterately against himself that he makes his imagination act. What a pity he has such a lot of it! He's too beastly intelligent. Besides, the famous reading's still to come off, and it has been postponed a day to allow Guy Walsingham to arrive. It appears this eminent lady's staying at a house a few miles off, which means of course that Mrs. Wimbush has forcibly annexed her. She's to come over in a day or two — Mrs. Wimbush wants her to hear Mr. Paraday.

"To-day's wet and cold, and several of the company, at the invitation of the Duke, have driven over to luncheon at Bigwood. I saw poor Paraday wedge himself, by command, into the little supplementary seat of a brougham in which the Princess and our hostess were already ensconced. If the front glass isn't open on his dear old back perhaps he'll survive. Bigwood, I believe, is very grand and frigid, all marble and precedence, and I wish him well out of the adventure. I can't tell you how much more and more *your* attitude to him, in the midst of all this, shines out by contrast. I never willingly talk to these people about him, but see what a comfort I find it to scribble to you! I appreciate

it — it keeps me warm; there are no fires in the house. Mrs. Wimbush goes by the calendar, the temperature goes by the weather, the weather goes by God knows what, and the Princess is easily heated. I've nothing but my acrimony to restore my circulation. Coming in an hour ago I found Lady Augusta Minch rummaging about the hall. When I asked her what she was looking for she said she had mislaid something that Mr. Paraday had lent her. I ascertained in a moment that the article in question is a manuscript, and I've a foreboding that it's the noble morsel he read me six weeks ago. When I expressed my surprise that he should have bandied about anything so precious (I happen to know it's his only copy — in the most beautiful hand in all the world) Lady Augusta confessed to me that she hadn't had it from himself, but from Mrs. Wimbush, who had wished to give her a glimpse of it as a salve for her not being able to stay and hear it read.

" 'Is that the piece he's to read,' I asked, 'when Guy Walsingham arrives?'

" 'It's not for Guy Walsingham they're waiting now, it's Dora Forbes,' Lady Augusta said. 'She's coming, I believe, early to-morrow. Meanwhile Mrs. Wimbush has found out about *him*, and is actively wiring to him. She says he also must hear him.'

" 'You bewilder me a little,' I replied; 'in the age we live in one gets lost among the genders and the pronouns. The clear thing is that Mrs. Wimbush doesn't guard such a treasure so jealously as she might.'

" 'Poor dear, she has the Princess to guard! Mr. Paraday lent her the manuscript to look over.'

" 'She spoke, you mean, as if it were the morning paper?'

"Lady Augusta stared — my irony was lost on her. 'She didn't have time, so she gave me a chance first; because unfortunately I go to-morrow to Bigwood.'

" 'And your chance has only proved a chance to lose it?'

" 'I haven't lost it. I remember now — it was very stupid of me to have forgotten. I told my maid to give it to Lord Dorimont — or at least to his man.'

" 'And Lord Dorimont went away directly after luncheon.'

" 'Of course he gave it back to my maid — or else his man did,' said Lady Augusta. 'I dare say it's all right.'

"The conscience of these people is like a summer sea. They haven't time to look over a priceless composition; they've only time to kick it about the house. I suggested that the 'man,' fired with a noble emulation, has perhaps kept the work for his own perusal; and her ladyship wanted to know whether, if the thing shouldn't reappear for the grand occasion appointed by our hostess, the author wouldn't have something else to read that would do just as well. Their questions are too delightful! I declared to Lady Augusta briefly that nothing in the world can ever do so well as the thing that does best; and at this she looked a little disconcerted. But I added that if the manuscript had gone astray our little circle would have the less of an effort of attention to make. The piece in question was very long — it would keep them three hours.

" 'Three hours! Oh the Princess will get up!' said Lady Augusta.

" 'I thought she was Mr. Paraday's greatest admirer.'

" 'I dare say she is — she's so awfully clever. But what's the use of being a Princess —'

" 'If you can't dissemble your love?' I asked as Lady Augusta was vague. She said at any rate that she'd question her maid; and I'm hoping that when I go down to dinner I shall find the manuscript has been recovered."

X

"It has *not* been recovered," I wrote early the next day, "and I'm moreover much troubled about our friend. He came back from Bigwood with a chill and, being allowed to have a fire in his room, lay down a while before dinner. I tried to send him to bed and indeed thought I had put him in the way of it; but after I had gone to dress Mrs. Wimbush came up to see him, with the inevitable result that when I returned I found him under arms and flushed and feverish, though decorated with the rare flower she had brought him for his buttonhole. He came down to dinner, but Lady Augusta Minch was very shy of him. To-day he's in great pain, and the advent of *ces dames* — I mean of Guy Walsingham and Dora Forbes — doesn't at all console me. It does Mrs. Wimbush, however, for she has consented to his remaining in bed so that he may be all right to-morrow for the listening circle. Guy Walsingham's already on the scene, and the doctor for Paraday also arrived early. I haven't yet seen the author of 'Obsessions,' but of course I've had a moment by myself with the

Doctor. I tried to get him to say that our invalid must go straight home — I mean to-morrow or next day; but he quite refuses to talk about the future. Absolute quiet and warmth and the regular administration of an important remedy are the points he mainly insists on. He returns this afternoon, and I'm to go back to see the patient at one o'clock, when he next takes his medicine. It consoles me a little that he certainly won't be able to read — an exertion he was already more than unfit for. Lady Augusta went off after breakfast, assuring me her first care would be to follow up the lost manuscript. I can see she thinks me a shocking busybody and doesn't understand my alarm, but she'll do what she can, for she's a good-natured woman. 'So are they all honourable men.' That was precisely what made her give the thing to Lord Dorimont and made Lord Dorimont bag it. What use *he* has for it God only knows. I've the worst forebodings, but somehow I'm strangely without passion — desperately calm. As I consider the unconscious, the well-meaning ravages of our appreciative circle I bow my head in submission to some great natural, some universal accident; I'm rendered almost indifferent, in fact quite gay (ha-ha!) by the sense of immitigable fate. Lady Augusta promises me to trace the precious object and let me have it through the post by the time Paraday's well enough to play his part with it. The last evidence is that her maid did give it to his lordship's valet. One would suppose it some thrilling number of *The Family Budget*. Mrs. Wimbush, who's aware of the accident, is much less agitated by it than she would doubtless be were she not for the hour inevitably engrossed with Guy Walsingham."

Later in the day I informed my correspondent, for whom indeed I kept a loose diary of the situation, that I had made the acquaintance of this celebrity and that she was a pretty little girl who wore her hair in what used to be called a crop. She looked so juvenile and so innocent that if, as Mr. Morrow had announced, she was resigned to the larger latitude, her superiority to prejudice must have come to her early. I spent most of the day hovering about Neil Paraday's room, but it was communicated to me from below that Guy Walsingham, at Prestidge, was a success. Toward evening I became conscious somehow that her superiority was contagious, and by the time the company had separated for the night I was sure the larger latitude had been generally accepted. I thought of Dora Forbes and felt that he had no time to lose. Before dinner I received a telegram from Lady Augusta Minch. "Lord Dorimont thinks he must have left bundle in train — enquire." How could I enquire — if I was to take the word as a command? I was too worried and now too alarmed about Neil Paraday. The Doctor came back, and it was an immense satisfaction to me to be sure he was wise and interested. He was proud of being called to so distinguished a patient, but he admitted to me that night that my friend was gravely ill. It was really a relapse, a recrudescence of his old malady. There could be no question of moving him: we must at any rate see first, on the spot, what turn his condition would take. Meanwhile, on the morrow, he was to have a nurse. On the morrow the dear man was easier, and my spirits rose to such cheerfulness that I could almost laugh over Lady Augusta's second telegram: "Lord Dorimont's servant been to station — nothing found. Push enquiries." I did laugh, I'm sure, as I remembered this to be the mystic scroll I had scarcely allowed poor Mr. Morrow to point his umbrella at. Fool that I had been: the thirty-seven influential journals wouldn't have destroyed it, they'd only have printed it. Of course I said nothing to Paraday.

When the nurse arrived she turned me out of the room, on which I went downstairs. I should premise that at breakfast the news that our brilliant friend was doing well excited universal complacency, and the Princess graciously remarked that he was only to be commiserated for missing the society of Miss Collop. Mrs. Wimbush, whose social gift never shone brighter than in the dry decorum with which she accepted this fizzle in her fireworks, mentioned to me that Guy Walsingham had made a very favourable impression on her Imperial Highness. Indeed I think every one did so, and that, like the money-market or the national honour, her Imperial Highness was constitutionally sensitive. There was a certain gladness, a perceptible bustle in the air, however, which I thought slightly anomalous in a house where a great author lay critically ill. "Le roy est mort — vive le roy": I was reminded that another great author had already stepped into his shoes. When I came down again after the nurse had taken possession I found a strange gentleman hanging about the hall and pacing to and fro by the closed door of the drawing-room. This personage was florid and bald; he had a big red moustache and wore showy knickerbockers — characteristics all that fitted to my conception of the identity of Dora Forbes. In a moment I saw what had happened: the author of "The Other Way Round" had just alighted at the portals of Prestidge, but had suffered a scruple to restrain him from penetrating further. I recognised his scruple when, pausing to listen at his gesture of caution, I heard a shrill voice lifted in a sort of rhythmic uncanny chant. The famous reading had begun, only it was the author of "Obsessions" who now furnished the sacrifice. The new visitor whispered to me that he judged something was going on he oughtn't to interrupt.

"Miss Collop arrived last night," I smiled, "and the Princess has a thirst for the *inédit*." [1]

Dora Forbes raised his bushy brows. "Miss Collop?"

"Guy Walsingham, your distinguished confrère — or shall I say your formidable rival?"

"Oh!" growled Dora Forbes. Then he added: "Shall I spoil it if I go in?"

"I should think nothing could spoil it!" I ambiguously laughed.

Dora Forbes evidently felt the dilemma; he gave an irritated crook to his moustache. "*Shall I go in?*" he presently asked.

We looked at each other hard a moment; then I expressed something bitter that was in me, expressed it in an infernal "Do!" After this I got out into the air, but not so fast as not to hear, when the door of the drawing-room opened, the disconcerted drop of Miss Collop's public manner: she must have been in the midst of the larger latitude. Producing with extreme rapidity, Guy Walsingham has just published a work in which amiable people who are not initiated have been pained to see the genius of a sister-novelist held up to unmistakable ridicule; so fresh an exhibition does it seem to them of the dreadful way men have always treated women. Dora Forbes, it's true, at the present hour, is immensely pushed by Mrs. Wimbush and has sat for his portrait to the young artists she protects, sat for it not only in oils but in monumental alabaster.

What happened at Prestidge later in the day is of course contemporary history. If the interruption I had whimsically sanctioned was almost a scandal, what is to be said of that general scatter of the company which, under the Doctor's rule, began to take place in the evening? His rule was soothing to behold, small comfort

1 Unpublished.

as I was to have at the end. He decreed in the interest of his patient an absolutely soundless house and a consequent break-up of the party. Little country practitioner as he was, he literally packed off the Princess. She departed as promptly as if a revolution had broken out, and Guy Walsingham emigrated with her. I was kindly permitted to remain, and this was not denied even to Mrs. Wimbush. The privilege was withheld indeed from Dora Forbes; so Mrs. Wimbush kept her latest capture temporarily concealed. This was so little, however, her usual way of dealing with her eminent friends that a couple of days of it exhausted her patience and she went up to town with him in great publicity. The sudden turn for the worse her afflicted guest had, after a brief improvement, taken on the third night, raised an obstacle to her seeing him before her retreat; a fortunate circumstance doubtless, for she was fundamentally disappointed in him. This was not the kind of performance for which she had invited him to Prestidge, let alone invited the Princess. I must add that none of the generous acts marking her patronage of intellectual and other merit have done so much for her reputation as her lending Neil Paraday the most beautiful of her numerous homes to die in. He took advantage to the utmost of the singular favour. Day by day I saw him sink, and I roamed alone about the empty terraces and gardens. His wife never came near him, but I scarcely noticed it: as I paced there with rage in my heart I was too full of another wrong. In the event of his death it would fall to me perhaps to bring out in some charming form, with notes, with the tenderest editorial care, that precious heritage of his written project. But where *was* that precious heritage, and were both the author and the book to have been snatched from us? Lady Augusta wrote me she had done all she could and that poor Lord Dorimont, who had really been worried to death, was extremely sorry. I couldn't have the matter out with Mrs. Wimbush, for I didn't want to be taunted by her with desiring to aggrandise myself by a public connexion with Mr. Paraday's sweepings. She had signified her willingness to meet the expense of all advertising, as indeed she was always ready to do. The last night of the horrible series, the night before he died, I put my ear closer to his pillow.

"That thing I read you that morning, you know."

"In your garden that dreadful day? Yes?"

"Won't it do as it is?"

"It would have been a glorious book."

"It *is* a glorious book," Neil Paraday murmured. "Print it as it stands — beautifully."

"Beautifully!" I passionately promised.

It may be imagined whether, now that he's gone, the promise seems to me less sacred. I'm convinced that if such pages had appeared in his lifetime the Abbey would hold him to-day. I've kept the advertising in my own hands, but the manuscript has not been recovered. It's impossible, and at any rate intolerable, to suppose it can have been wantonly destroyed. Perhaps some hazard of a blind hand, some brutal fatal ignorance has lighted kitchen-fires with it. Every stupid and hideous accident haunts my meditations. My undiscourageable search for the lost treasure would make a long chapter. Fortunately I've a devoted associate in the person of a young lady who has every day a fresh indignation and a fresh idea, and who maintains with intensity that the prize will still turn up. Sometimes I believe her, but I've quite ceased to believe it myself. The only thing for us at all events is to go on seeking and hoping together, and we should be closely united by this firm tie even were we not at present by another.

Maud-Evelyn

(1900)

Especially in his later years James was attracted to psychological themes. He dealt in various stories with the supernatural, the frustration of sex relations, and "the sense of the past." All three, as L. N. Richardson remarks, merge in "Maud-Evelyn." The odd subject, inherently difficult to treat, called for the sort of subtlety — of perception, attitude, and technique — of which James was a master.

On some allusion to a lady who, though unknown to myself, was known to two or three of the company, it was asked by one of these if we had heard the odd circumstance of what she had just "come in for" — the piece of luck suddenly overtaking, in the gray afternoon of her career, so obscure and lonely a personage. We were at first, in our ignorance, mainly reduced to crude envy; but old Lady Emma, who for a while had said nothing, scarcely even appearing to listen and letting the chatter, which was indeed plainly beside the mark, subside of itself, came back from a mental absence to observe that if what had happened to Lavinia was wonderful, certainly, what had for years gone before it, led up to it, had likewise not been without some singular features. From this we perceived that Lady Emma had a story — a story moreover out of the ken even of those of her listeners acquainted with the quiet person who was the subject of it. Almost the oddest thing — as came out afterwards — was that such a situation should, for the world, have remained so in the background of this person's life. By "afterwards" I mean simply before we separated; for what came out came on the spot, under encouragement and pressure, our common, eager solicitation. Lady Emma, who always reminded me of a fine old instrument that has first to be tuned, agreed, after a few of our scrapings and fingerings, that, having said so much, she couldn't without wantonly tormenting us, forbear to say all. She had known Lavinia, whom she mentioned throughout only by that name, from far away, and she had also known —— But what she had known I must give as nearly as possible as she herself gave it. She talked to us from her corner of the sofa, and the flicker of the firelight in her face was like the glow of memory, the play of fancy, from within.

I

"Then why on earth don't you take him?" I asked. I think that was the way that, one day when she was about twenty — before some of you perhaps were born — the affair, for me, must have begun. I put the question because I knew she had had a chance, though I didn't know how great a mistake her failure to embrace it was to prove. I took an interest because I liked them both — you see how I like young people still — and because, as they had originally met at my house, I had in a manner to answer to each for the other. I'm afraid I'm thrown baldly back on the fact that if the girl was the daughter of my earliest, almost my only governess, to whom I had remained much attached and who, after leaving me, had married — for a governess — "well," Marmaduke (it isn't *his* real name!) was the son of one of the clever men who had — I was charming then, I assure you I was — wanted, years before, and this one as a widower, to marry me. I hadn't cared, somehow, for widowers, but even after I had taken somebody else I was conscious of a pleasant link with the boy whose stepmother it had been open to me to become and to whom it was perhaps a little a matter of vanity with me to show that I should have been for him one of the kindest. This was what the woman his father eventually did marry was not, and that threw him upon me the more.

Lavinia was one of nine, and her brothers and sisters, who have never done anything for her, help, actually, in different countries and on something, I believe, of that same scale, to people the globe. There were mixed in her then, in a puzzling way, two qualities that mostly exclude each other — an extreme timidity and, as the smallest fault that could qualify a harmless creature for a world of wickedness, a self-complacency hard in tiny, unexpected spots, for which I used sometimes to take her up, but which, I subsequently saw, would have done something for the flatness of her life had they not evaporated with everything else. She was at any rate one of those persons as to whom you don't know whether they might have been attractive if they had been happy, or might have been happy if they had been attractive. If I was a trifle vexed at her not jumping at Marmaduke, it was probably rather less because I expected wonders of him than because I thought she took her own prospect too much for granted. She had made a mistake and, before long, admitted it; yet I remember that when she expressed to me a conviction that he would ask her again, I also thought this highly probable, for in the meantime I had spoken to him. "She does care for you," I declared; and I can see at this moment, long ago though it be, his handsome, empty young face look, on the words, as if, in spite of itself for a little, it really thought. I didn't press the matter, for he had, after all, no great things to offer; yet my conscience was easier, later on, for having not said less. He had three hundred and fifty a year from his mother, and one of his uncles had promised him something — I don't mean an allowance, but a place, if I recollect, in a business. He assured me that he loved as a man loves — a man of twenty-two! — but once. He said it, at all events, as a man says it but once.

"Well, then," I replied, "your course is clear."

"To speak to her again, you mean?"

"Yes — try it."

He seemed to try it a moment in imagination; after which, a little to my surprise, he asked:

"Would it be very awful if she should speak to *me*?"

I stared. "Do you mean pursue you — overtake you? Ah, if you're running away ——"

"I'm not running away!" — he was positive as to that. "But when a fellow has gone so far ——"

"He can't go any further? Perhaps," I replied dryly. "But in that case he shouldn't talk of 'caring.'"

"Oh, but I do, I do."

I shook my head. "Not if you're too proud!" On which I turned away, looking round at him again, however, after he had surprised me by a silence that seemed to accept my judgment. Then I saw he had not accepted it; I perceived it indeed to be essentially absurd. He expressed more, on this, than I had yet seen him do — had the queerest, frankest, and, for a young man of his conditions, saddest smile.

"I'm *not* proud. It isn't *in* me. If you're not, you're not, you know. I don't think I'm proud enough."

It came over me that this was, after all, probable; yet somehow I didn't at the moment like him the less for it, though I spoke with some sharpness. "Then what's the matter with you?"

He took a turn or two about the room, as if what he had just said had made him a little happier. "Well, how can a man say more?" Then, just as I was on the point of assuring him that I didn't know what he had said, he went on: "I swore to her that I would never marry. Oughtn't that to be enough?"

"To make her come after you?"

"No — I suppose scarcely that; but to make her feel sure of me — to make her wait."

"Wait for what?"

"Well, till I come back."

"Back from where?"

"From Switzerland — haven't I told you? I go there next month with my aunt and my cousin."

He was quite right about not being proud — this was an alternative distinctly humble.

II

And yet see what it brought forth — the beginning of which was something that, early in the autumn, I learned from poor Lavinia. He had written to her, they were still such friends; and thus it was that she knew his aunt and his cousin to have come back without him. He had stayed on — stayed much longer and traveled much further: he had been to the Italian lakes and to Venice; he was now in Paris. At this I vaguely wondered, knowing that he was always short of funds and that he must, by his uncle's beneficence, have started on the journey on a basis of expense paid. "Then whom has he picked up?" I asked; but feeling sorry, as soon as I had spoken, to have made Lavinia blush. It was almost as if he had picked up some improper lady, though in this case he wouldn't have told her, and it wouldn't have saved him money.

"Oh, he makes acquaintance so quickly, knows people in two minutes," the girl said. "And everyone always wants to be nice to him."

This was perfectly true, and I saw what she saw in it. "Ah, my dear, he will have an immense circle ready for you!"

"Well," she replied, "if they do run after us I'm not likely to suppose it will ever be for me. It will be for *him,* and they may do to me what they like. My pleasure will be — but you'll see." I already saw — saw at least what she supposed she herself saw: her drawing room crowded with female fashion and her attitude angelic. "Do you know what he said to me again before he went?" she continued.

I wondered; he *had* then spoken to her. "That he will never, never marry ——"

"Anyone but *me!*" She ingenuously took me up. "Then you knew?"

It might be. "I guessed."

"And don't you believe it?"

Again I hesitated. "Yes." Yet all this didn't tell me why she had changed color. "Is it a secret — whom he's with?"

"Oh, no, they seem so nice. I was only struck with the way you know him — your seeing immediately that it must be a new friendship that has kept him over. It's the devotion of the Dedricks," Lavinia said. "He's traveling with them."

Once more I wondered. "Do you mean they're taking him about?"

"Yes — they've invited him."

No, indeed, I reflected — he wasn't proud. But what I said was: "Who in the world are the Dedricks?"

"Kind, good people whom, last month, he accidentally met. He was walking some Swiss pass — a long, rather stupid one, I believe, without his aunt and his cousin, who had gone round some other way and were to meet him somewhere. It came on to rain in torrents, and while he was huddling under a shelter he was overtaken by some people in a carriage, who kindly made him get in. They drove him, I gather, for several hours; it began an intimacy, and they've continued to be charming to him."

I thought a moment. "Are they ladies?"

Her own imagination meanwhile had also strayed a little. "I think about forty."

"Forty ladies?"

She quickly came back. "Oh, no; I mean Mrs. Dedrick is."

"About forty? Then Miss Dedrick——"

"There isn't any Miss Dedrick."

"No daughter?"

"Not with them, at any rate. No one but the husband."

I thought again. "And how old is *he?*"

Lavinia followed my example. "Well, about forty, too."

"About forty-two?" We laughed, but "That's all right!" I said; and so, for the time, it seemed.

He continued absent, none the less, and I saw Lavinia repeatedly, and we always talked of him, though this represented a greater concern with his affairs than I had really supposed myself committed to. I had never sought the acquaintance of his father's people, nor seen either his aunt or his cousin, so that the account given by these relatives of the circumstances of their separation reached me at last only through the girl, to whom, also — for she knew them as little — it had circuitously come. They considered, it appeared, the poor ladies he had started with, that he had treated them ill and thrown them over, sacrificing them selfishly to company picked up on the road — a reproach deeply resented by Lavinia, though about the company too I could see she was not much more at her ease. "How can he help it if he's so taking?" she asked; and to be properly indignant in one quarter she had to pretend to be delighted in the other. Marmaduke *was* "taking"; yet it also came out between us at last that the Dedricks must certainly be extraordinary. We had scant added evidence, for his letters stopped, and that naturally was one of our signs. I had meanwhile leisure to reflect — it was a sort of study of the human scene I always liked — on what to be taking consisted of. The upshot of my meditations, which experience has only confirmed, was that it consisted simply of itself. It was a quality implying

no others. Marmaduke *had* no others. What indeed was his need of any?

III

He at last, however, turned up; but then it happened that if, on his coming to see me, his immediate picture of his charming new friends quickened even more than I had expected my sense of the variety of the human species, my curiosity about them failed to make me respond when he suggested I should go to see them. It's a difficult thing to explain, and I don't pretend to put it successfully, but doesn't it often happen that one may think well enough of a person without being inflamed with the desire to meet — on the ground of any such sentiment — other persons who think still better? Somehow — little harm as there was in Marmaduke — it was but half a recommendation of the Dedricks that they were crazy about him. I didn't say this — I was careful to say little; which didn't prevent his presently asking if he mightn't then bring them to *me.* "If not, why not?" he laughed. He laughed about everything.

"Why not? Because it strikes me that your surrender doesn't require any backing. Since you've done it you must take care of yourself."

"Oh, but they're as safe," he returned, "as the Bank of England. They're wonderful — for respectability and goodness."

"Those are precisely qualities to which my poor intercourse can contribute nothing." He hadn't, I observed, gone so far as to tell me they would be "fun," and he *had*, on the other hand, promptly mentioned that they lived in Westbourne Terrace. They were not forty — they were forty-five; but Mr. Dedrick had already, on considerable gains, retired from some primitive profession. They were the simplest, kindest, yet most original and unusual people, and nothing could exceed, frankly, the fancy they had taken to him. Marmaduke spoke of it with a placidity of resignation that was almost irritating. I suppose I should have despised him if, after benefits accepted, he had said they bored him; yet their not boring him vexed me even more than it puzzled. "Whom do they know?"

"No one but me. There are people in London like that."

"Who know no one but you?"

"No — I mean no one at all. There are extraordinary people in London, and awfully nice. You haven't an idea. You people don't know everyone. They lead their lives — they go their way. One finds — what do you call it? — refinement, books, cleverness, don't you know, and music, and pictures, and religion, and an excellent table — all sorts of pleasant things. You only come across them by chance; but it's all perpetually going on."

I assented to this: the world was very wonderful, and one must certainly see what one could. In my own quarter too I found wonders enough. "But are you," I asked, "as fond of them — "

"As they are of *me?*" He took me up promptly, and his eyes were quite unclouded. "I'm quite sure I shall become so."

"Then are you taking Lavinia —— ?"

"Not to see them — no." I saw, myself, the next minute, of course, that I had made a mistake. "On what footing *can* I?"

I bethought myself. "I keep forgetting you're not engaged."

"Well," he said after a moment, "I shall never marry another."

It somehow, repeated again, gave on my nerves. "Ah, but what good will that do her, or me either, if you don't marry *her?*"

He made no answer to this — only turned away to look at something in the room; after which, when he next faced me, he had a heightened color. "She ought to have taken me that day," he said gravely and gently; fixing me also as if he wished to say more.

I remember that his very mildness irritated me; some show of resentment would have been a promise that the case might still be righted. But I dropped it, the silly case, without letting him say more, and, coming back to Mr. and Mrs. Dedrick, asked him how in the world, without either occupation or society, they passed so much of their time. My question appeared for a moment to leave him at a loss, but he presently found light; which, at the same time, I saw on my side, really suited him better than further talk about Lavinia. "Oh, they live for Maud-Evelyn."

"And who's Maud-Evelyn?"

"Why, their daughter."

"Their daughter?" I had supposed them childless.

He partly explained. "Unfortunately they've lost her."

"Lost her?" I required more.

He hesitated again. "I mean that a great many people would take it that way. But *they* don't — they won't."

I speculated. "Do you mean other people would have given her up?"

"Yes — perhaps even tried to forget her. But the Dedricks can't."

I wondered what she had done: had it been anything very bad? However, it was none of my business, and I only said: "They communicate with her?"

"Oh, all the while."

"Then why isn't she with them?"

Marmaduke thought. "She *is* — now."

" 'Now?' Since when?"

"Well, this last year."

"Then why do you say they've lost her?"

"Ah," he said, smiling sadly, "*I* should call it that. I, at any rate," he went on, "don't see her."

Still more I wondered. "They keep her apart?"

He thought again. "No, it's not that. As I say, they live for her."

"But they don't want *you* to — is that it?"

At this he looked at me for the first time, as I thought, a little strangely. "How *can* I?"

He put it to me as if it were bad of him, somehow, that he shouldn't; but I made, to the best of my ability, a quick end of that. "You can't. Why in the world *should* you? Live for *my* girl. Live for Lavinia."

IV

I had unfortunately run the risk of boring him again with that idea, and, though he had not repudiated it at the time, I felt in my having returned to it the reason why he never reappeared for weeks. I saw "my girl," as I had called her, in the interval, but we avoided with much intensity the subject of Marmaduke. It was just this that gave me my perspective for finding her constantly full of him. It determined me, in all the circumstances, not to rectify her mistake about the childlessness of the Dedricks. But whatever I left unsaid, her naming the young man was only a question of time, for at the end of a month she told me he had been twice to her mother's and that she had seen him on each of these occasions.

"Well then?"

"Well then, he's very happy."

"And still taken up —— "

"As much as ever, yes, with those people. He didn't tell me so, but I could see it."

I could, too, and her own view of it. "What, in that case, did he tell you?"

"Nothing — but I think there's something he wants to. Only not what *you* think," she added.

I wondered then if it were what I had had from him the last time. "Well, what prevents him?" I asked.

"From bringing it out? I don't know."

It was in the tone of this that she struck, to my ear, the first note of an acceptance so deep and a patience so strange that they gave me, at the end, even more food for wonderment than the rest of the business. "If he can't speak, why does he come?"

She almost smiled. "Well, I think I *shall* know."

I looked at her; I remember that I kissed her. "You're admirable; but it's very ugly."

"Ah," she replied, "he only wants to be kind!"

"To *them*? Then he should let others alone. But what I call ugly is his being content to be so 'beholden' —— "

"To Mr. and Mrs. Dedrick?" She considered as if there might be many sides to it. "But mayn't he do them some good?"

The idea failed to appeal to me. "What good can Marmaduke do? There's one thing," I went on, "in case he should want you to know them. Will you promise me to refuse?"

She only looked helpless and blank. "Making their acquaintance?"

"Seeing them, going near them — ever, ever."

Again she brooded. "Do you mean *you* won't?"

"Never, never."

"Well, then, I don't think I want to."

"Ah, but that's not a promise." I kept her up to it. "I want your word."

She demurred a little. "But why?"

"So that at least he shan't make use of you," I said with energy.

My energy overbore her, though I saw how she would really have given herself. "I promise, but it's only because it's something I know he will never ask."

I differed from her at the time, believing the proposal in question to have been exactly the subject she had supposed him to be wishing to broach; but on our very next meeting I heard from her of quite another matter, upon which, as soon as she came in, I saw her to be much excited.

"You know then about the daughter without having told me? He called again yesterday,"
she explained as she met my stare at her unconnected plunge, "and now I know that he *has* wanted to speak to me. He at last brought it out."

I continued to stare. "Brought what?"

"Why, everything." She looked surprised at my face. "Didn't he tell you about Maud-Evelyn?"

I perfectly recollected, but I momentarily wondered. "He spoke of there being a daughter, but only to say that there's something the matter with her. What is it?"

The girl echoed my words. "What 'is' it? — you dear, strange thing! The matter with her is simply that she's dead."

"Dead?" I was naturally mystified. "When, then, did she die?"

"Why, years and years ago — fifteen, I believe. As a little girl. Didn't you understand it so?"

"How *should* I? — when he spoke of her as 'with' them and said that they lived for her!"

"Well," my young friend explained, "that's just what he meant — they live for her memory. She *is* with them in the sense that they think of nothing else."

I found matter for surprise in this correction, but also, at first, matter for relief. At the same time it left, as I turned it over, a fresh ambiguity. "If they think of nothing else, how can they think so much of Marmaduke?"

The difficulty struck her, though she gave me even then a dim impression of being already, as it were, rather on Marmaduke's side, or, at any rate — almost as against herself — in sympathy with the Dedricks. But her answer was prompt: "Why, that's just their reason — that they can talk to him so much about her."

"I see." Yet still I wondered. "But what's *his interest* —— ?"

"In being drawn into it?" Again Lavinia met her difficulty. "Well, that she was so interesting! It appears she was lovely."

I doubtless fairly gaped. "A little girl in a pinafore?"

"She was out of pinafores; she was, I believe, when she died, about fourteen. Unless it was sixteen! She was at all events wonderful for beauty."

"That's the rule. But what good does it do him if he has never seen her?"

She thought a moment, but this time she had no answer. "Well, you must ask him!"

I determined without delay to do so; but I had before me meanwhile other contradictions. "Hadn't I better ask him on the same occasion what he means by their 'communicating'?"

Oh, this was simple. "They go in for 'mediums,' don't you know, and raps, and sittings. They began a year or two ago."

"Ah, the idiots!" I remember, at this, narrowmindedly exclaiming. "Do they want to drag *him* in —— ?"

"Not in the least; they don't desire it, and he has nothing to do with it."

"Then where does his fun come in?"

Lavinia turned away; again she seemed at a loss. At last she brought out: "Make him show you her little photograph."

But I remained unenlightened. "Is her little photograph his fun?"

Once more she colored for him. "Well, it represents a young loveliness!"

"That he goes about showing?"

She hesitated. "I think he has only shown it to *me*."

"Ah, you're just the last one!" I permitted myself to observe.

"Why so, if I'm also struck?"

There was something about her that began to escape me, and I must have looked at her hard. "It's very good of you to be struck!"

"I don't only mean by the beauty of the face," she went on; "I mean by the whole thing — by that also of the attitude of the parents, their extraordinary fidelity and the way that, as she says, they have made of her memory a real religion. That was what, above all, he came to tell me about."

I turned away from her now, and she soon afterwards left me; but I couldn't help its dropping from me before we parted that I had never supposed him to be *that* sort of fool.

V

If I were really the perfect cynic you probably think me, I should frankly say that the main interest of the rest of this matter lay for me in fixing the sort of fool I *did* suppose him. But I'm afraid, after all, that my anecdote amounts mainly to a presentation of my own folly. I shouldn't be so in possession of the whole spectacle had I not ended by accepting it, and I shouldn't have accepted it had it not, for my imagination, been saved somehow from grotesqueness. Let me say at once, however, that grotesqueness, and even indeed something worse, did at first appear to me strongly to season it. After that talk with Lavinia I immediately addressed to our friend a request that he would come to see me; when I took the liberty of challenging him outright on everything she had told me. There was one point in particular that I desired to clear up and that seemed to me much more important than the color of Maud-Evelyn's hair or the length of her pinafores: the question, I of course mean, of my young man's good faith. Was he altogether silly or was he only altogether mercenary? I felt my choice restricted for the moment to these alternatives.

After he had said to me "It's as ridiculous as you please, but they've simply adopted me," I had it out with him, on the spot, on the issue of common honesty, the question of what he was conscious, so that his self-respect should be saved, of being able to give such benefactors in return for such bounty. I'm obliged to say that to a person so inclined at the start to quarrel with him his amiability could yet prove persuasive. His contention was that the equivalent he represented was something for his friends alone to measure. He didn't for a moment pretend to sound deeper than the fancy they had taken to him. He had not, from the first, made up to them in any way: it was all their own doing, their own insistence, their own eccentricity, no doubt, and even, if I liked, their own insanity. Wasn't it enough that he was ready to declare to me, looking me straight in the eye, that he was "really and truly" fond of them and that they didn't bore him a mite? I had evidently — didn't I see? — an ideal for him that he wasn't at all, if I didn't mind, the fellow to live up to. It was he himself who put it so, and it drew from me the pronouncement that there *was* something irresistible in the refinement of his impudence. "I don't go near Mrs. Jex," he said — Mrs. Jex was their favorite medium: "I do find *her* ugly and vulgar and tiresome, and I hate that part of the business. Besides," he added in words that I afterwards remembered, "I don't require it: I do beautifully without it. But my friends themselves," he pursued, "though they're of a type you've never come within miles of, are not ugly, are not vulgar, are not in any degree whatever any sort of a 'dose.' They're, on the contrary, in their own unconventional way, the very best company. They're endlessly amusing. They're delightfully queer and quaint and kind — they're like people in some old story of some old time. It's at any rate our own affair — mine and theirs — and I beg you to believe that I should make short work of a remonstrance on the subject from anyone but you."

I remember saying to him three months later: "You've never yet told me what they really want of you"; but I'm afraid this was a form of criticism that occurred to me precisely because I had already begun to guess. By that time indeed I had had great initiations, and poor Lavinia had had them as well — hers in fact throughout went further than mine — and we shared them together, and I had settled down to a tolerably exact sense of what I was to see. It was what Lavinia added to it that really made the picture. The portrait of the little dead girl had evoked something attractive, though one had not lived so long in the world without hearing of plenty of little dead girls; and the day came when I felt as if I had actually sat with Marmaduke in each of the rooms converted by her parents — with the aid not only of the few small, cherished relics, but that of the fondest figments and fictions, ingenious imaginary mementoes and tokens, the unexposed make-believes of the sorrow that broods and the passion that clings — into a temple of grief and worship. The child, incontestably beautiful, had evidently been passionately loved, and in the absence from their lives — I suppose originally a mere accident — of such other elements, either new pleasures or new pains, as abound for most people, their feeling had drawn to itself their whole consciousness: it had become mildly maniacal. The idea was fixed, and it kept others out. The world, for the most part, allows no leisure for such a ritual, but the world had consistently neglected this plain, shy couple, who were sensitive to the wrong things and whose sincerity and fidelity, as well as their tameness and twaddle, were of a rigid, antique pattern.

I must not represent that either of these objects of interest, or my care for their concerns, took up all my leisure; for I had many claims to meet and many complications to handle, a hundred preoccupations and much deeper anxieties. My young woman, on her side, had other contacts and contingencies — other troubles too, poor girl; and there were stretches of time in which I neither saw Marmaduke nor heard a word of the Dedricks. Once, only once, abroad, in Germany at a railway station, I met him in their company. They were colorless, commonplace, elderly Britons, of the kind you identify by the livery of their footman or the labels of their luggage, and the mere sight of them justified me to my conscience in having avoided, from the first, the stiff problem of conversation with them. Marmaduke saw me on the spot and came over to me. There was no doubt whatever of *his* vivid bloom. He had grown fat — or almost, but not with grossness — and might perfectly have passed for the handsome, happy, full-blown son of doting parents who couldn't let him out of view and to whom he was a model of respect and solicitude. They followed him with placid, pleased eyes when he joined me, but asking nothing at all for themselves and quite fitting into his own manner of saying nothing about them. It had its charm, I confess, the way he could be natural and easy, and yet intensely conscious too, on such a basis. What he was conscious of was that there were things I by this time knew; just as, while we stood there and good-humoredly sounded each other's faces — for, having accepted everything at last, I was only a little curious — I knew that he measured my insight. When he returned again to his doting parents I had to admit that, doting as they were, I felt him not to have been spoiled. It was incongruous in such a career, but he was rather more of a man. There came back to me with a shade of regret after I had got on this occasion into my train, which was not theirs, a memory of some words that, a couple of years before, I had uttered to poor Lavinia. She had said to me, speaking in reference to what was then our frequent topic and on some fresh evidence that I have forgotten: "He feels now, you know, about Maud-Evelyn quite as the old people themselves do."

"Well," I had replied, "it's only a pity he's paid for it!"

"Paid?" She had looked very blank.

"By all the luxuries and conveniences," I had explained, "that he comes in for through living with them. For that's what he practically does."

At present I saw how wrong I had been. He was paid, but paid differently, and the mastered wonder of that was really what had been between us in the waiting room of the station. Step by step, after this, I followed.

VI

I can see Lavinia, for instance, in her ugly new mourning immediately after her mother's death. There had been long anxieties connected with this event, and she was already faded, already almost old. But Marmaduke, on her bereavement, had been to her, and she came straightway to me.

"Do you know what he thinks now?" she soon began. "He thinks he knew her."

"Knew the child?" It came to me as if I had half expected it.

"He speaks of her now as if she hadn't been a child." My visitor gave me the strangest fixed smile. "It appears that she wasn't so young — it appears she had grown up."

I started. "How can it 'appear'? They *know* at least! There were the facts."

"Yes," said Lavinia, "but they seem to have come to take a different view of them. He talked to me a long time, and all about *her*. He told me things."

"What kind of things? Not trumpery stuff, I hope, about 'communicating' — about his seeing or hearing her?"

"Oh, no, he doesn't go in for that; he leaves it to the old couple, who, I believe, cling to their mediums, keep up their sittings and their rappings and find in it all a comfort, an amusement, that he doesn't grudge them and that he regards as harmless. I mean anecdotes — memories of his own. I mean things she said to him and that they did together — places they went to. His mind is full of them."

I turned it over. "Do you think he's decidedly mad?"

She shook her head with her bleached patience. "Oh, no, it's too beautiful!"

"Then are *you* taking it up? I mean the preposterous theory ——"

"It *is* a theory," she broke in, "but it isn't necessarily preposterous. Any theory has to suppose something," she sagely pursued, "and it depends at any rate on what it's a theory *of*. It's wonderful to see this one work."

"Wonderful always to see the growth of a legend!" I laughed. "This is a rare chance to watch one in formation. They're all three in good faith building it up. Isn't that what you made out from him?"

Her tired face fairly lighted. "Yes — you understand it; and you put it better than I. It's the gradual effect of brooding over the past; the past, that way, grows and grows. They make it and make it. They've persuaded each other — the parents — of so many things that they've at last also persuaded *him*. It has been contagious."

"It's you who put it well," I returned. "It's the oddest thing I ever heard of, but it is, in its way, a reality. Only we mustn't speak of it to others."

She quite accepted that precaution. "No — to nobody. *He* doesn't. He keeps it only for me."

"Conferring on you thus," I again laughed, "such a precious privilege!"

She was silent a moment, looking away from me. "Well, he has kept his vow."

"You mean of not marrying? Are you very sure?" I asked. "Didn't he perhaps ——?" But I faltered at the boldness of my joke.

The next moment I saw I needn't. "He *was* in love with her," Lavinia brought out.

I broke now into a peal which, however provoked, struck even my own ear at the moment as rude almost to profanity. "He literally tells you outright that he's making believe?"

She met me effectively enough. "I don't think he *knows* he is. He's just completely in the current."

"The current of the old people's twaddle?"

Again my companion hesitated; but she knew what she thought. "Well, whatever we call it, I like it. It isn't so common, as the world goes, for anyone — let alone for two or three — to feel and to care for the dead as much as that. It's self-deception, no doubt, but it comes from something that — well," she faltered again, "is beautiful when one does hear of it. They make her out older, so as to imagine they had her longer; and they make out that certain things really happened to her, so that she shall have had more life. They've invented a whole experience for her, and Marmaduke has become a part of it. There's one thing, above all, they want her to have had." My young friend's face, as she analyzed the mystery, fairly grew bright with her vision. It came to me with a faint dawn of awe that the attitude of the Dedricks *was* contagious. "And she did have it!" Lavinia declared.

I positively admired her, and if I could yet perfectly be rational without being ridiculous, it was really, more than anything else, to draw from her the whole image. "She had the bliss of knowing Marmaduke? Let us agree to it, then, since she's not here to contradict us. But what I don't get over is the scant material for *him!*" It may easily be conceived how little, for the moment, I could get over it. It was the last time my impatience was to be too much for me, but I remember how it broke out. "A man who might have had *you!*"

For an instant I feared I had upset her — thought I saw in her face the tremor of a wild wail. But poor Lavinia was magnificent. "It wasn't that he might have had 'me' — that's nothing: it was, at the most, that I might have had *him*. Well, isn't that just what has happened? He's mine from the moment no one else has him. I give up the past, but don't you see what it does for the rest of life? I'm surer than ever that he won't marry."

"Of course, he won't — to quarrel, with those people!"

For a minute she answered nothing; then, "Well, for whatever reason!" she simply said. Now, however, I had gouged out of her a couple of still tears, and I pushed away the whole obscure comedy.

VII

I might push it away, but I couldn't really get rid of it; nor, on the whole, doubtless, did I want to, for to have in one's life, year after year, a particular question or two that one couldn't comfortably and imposingly make up one's mind about was just the sort of thing to keep one from turning stupid. There had been little need of my enjoining reserve upon Lavinia: she obeyed, in respect to impenetrable silence save with myself, an instinct, an interest of her own. We never therefore gave poor Marmaduke, as you call it, "away"; we were much too tender, let alone that she was also too proud; and, for himself, evidently, there was not, to the end, in London, another person in his confidence. No echo of the queer part he played ever came back to us; and I can't tell you how this fact, just by itself, brought home to me little by little a sense of the charm he was under. I met him "out" at long intervals — met him usually at dinner. He had grown like a person with a position and a history. Rosy and rich-looking, fat, moreover, distinctly fat at last, there was almost in him something of the bland — yet not too bland — young head of an hereditary business. If the Dedricks had been bankers he might have constituted the future of the house. There was none the less a long middle stretch during which, though we were all so much in London, he dropped out of my talks with Lavinia. We were conscious, she and I, of his absence from them; but we clearly felt in each quarter that there are things after all unspeakable, and the fact, in any case, had nothing to do with her seeing or not seeing our friend. I was sure, as it happened, that she

did see him. But there were moments that for myself still stand out.

One of these was a certain Sunday afternoon when it was so dismally wet that, taking for granted I should have no visitors, I had drawn up to the fire with a book — a successful novel of the day — that I promised myself comfortably to finish. Suddenly, in my absorption, I heard a firm rat-tat-tat; on which I remember giving a groan of inhospitality. But my visitor proved in due course Marmaduke, and Marmaduke proved — in a manner even less, at the point we had reached, to have been counted on — still more attaching than my novel. I think it was only an accident that he became so; it would have been the turn of a hair either way. He hadn't come to speak — he had only come to talk, to show once more that we could continue good old friends without his speaking. But somehow there were the circumstances: the insidious fireside, the things in the room, with their reminders of his younger time; perhaps even too the open face of my book, looking at him from where I had laid it down for him and giving him a chance to feel that he could supersede Wilkie Collins. There was at all events a promise of intimacy, of opportunity for him in the cold lash of the windows by the storm. We should be alone, it was cosy; it was safe.

The action of these impressions was the more marked that what was touched by them, I afterwards saw, was not at all a desire for an effect — was just simply a spirit of happiness that needed to overflow. It had finally become too much for him. His past, rolling up year after year, had grown too interesting. But he was, all the same, directly stupefying. I forget what turn of our preliminary gossip brought it out, but it came, in explanation of something or other, as it had not yet come: "When a man has had for a few months what *I* had, you know!" The moral appeared to be that nothing in the way of human experience of the exquisite could again particularly matter. He saw, however, that I failed immediately to fit his reflection to a definite case, and he went on with the frankest smile: "You look as bewildered as if you suspected me of alluding to some sort of thing that isn't usually spoken of; but I assure you I mean nothing more reprehensible than our blessed engagement itself."

"Your blessed engagement?" I couldn't help the tone in which I took him up; but the way he disposed of that was something of which I feel to this hour the influence. It was only a look, but it put an end to my tone forever. It made me, on my side, after an instant, look at the fire — look hard and even turn a little red. During this moment I saw my alternatives and I chose; so that when I met his eyes again I was fairly ready. "You still feel," I asked with sympathy, "how much it did for you?"

I had no sooner spoken than I saw that that would be from that moment the right way. It instantly made all the difference. The main question would be whether I could keep it up. I remember that only a few minutes later, for instance, this question gave a flare. His reply had been abundant and imperturbable — had included some glance at the way death brings into relief even the faintest things that have preceded it; on which I felt myself suddenly as restless as if I had grown afraid of him. I got up to ring for tea; he went on talking — talking about Maud-Evelyn and what she had been for him; and when the servant had come up I prolonged, nervously, on purpose, the order I had wished to give. It made time, and I could speak to the footman sufficiently without thinking: what I thought of really was the risk of turning right round with a little outbreak. The temptation was strong; the same influences that had worked for my companion just worked, in their way, during that minute or two, for me. *Should* I, taking him unaware, flash at him a plain "I say, just settle it for me once for all. *Are* you the boldest and basest of fortune hunters, or have you only, more innocently and perhaps more pleasantly, suffered your brain slightly to soften?" But I missed the chance — which I didn't in fact afterwards regret. My servant went out, and I faced again to my visitor, who continued to converse. I met his eyes once more, and their effect was repeated. If anything had happened to his brain this effect was perhaps the domination of the madman's stare. Well, he was the easiest and gentlest of madmen. By the time the footman came back with tea I was in for it; I was in for everything. By "everything" I mean my whole subsequent treatment of the case. It *was* — the case was — really beautiful. So, like all the rest, the hour comes back to me: the sound of the wind and the rain; the look of the empty, ugly, cabless square and of the stormy spring light; the way that, uninterrupted and absorbed, we had tea together by my fire. So it was that he found me receptive

and that I found myself able to look merely grave and kind when he said, for example: "Her father and mother, you know, really, that first day — the day they picked me up on the Splügen — recognized me as the proper one."

"The proper one?"

"To make their son-in-law. They wanted her so," he went on, "to have had, don't you know, just everything."

"Well, if she did have it" — I tried to be cheerful — "isn't the whole thing then all right?"

"Oh, it's all right *now*," he replied — "now that we've got it all there before us. You see, they couldn't like me so much" — he wished me thoroughly to understand — "without wanting me to have been the man."

"I see — that was natural."

"Well," said Marmaduke, "it prevented the possibility of anyone else."

"Ah, that would never have done!" I laughed.

His own pleasure at it was impenetrable, splendid. "You see, they couldn't do much, the old people — and they can do still less now — with the future; so they had to do what they could with the past."

"And they seem to have done," I concurred, "remarkably much."

"Everything, simply. Everything," he repeated. Then he had an idea, though without insistence or importunity — I noticed it just flicker in his face. "If you *were* to come to Westbourne Terrace——"

"Oh, don't speak of that!" I broke in. "It wouldn't be decent now. I should have come, if at all, ten years ago."

But he saw, with his good humor, further than this. "I see what you mean. But there's much more in the place now than then."

"I daresay. People get new things. All the same——" I was at bottom but resisting my curiosity.

Marmaduke didn't press me, but he wanted me to know. "There are our rooms — the whole set; and I don't believe you ever saw anything more charming, for *her* taste was extraordinary. I'm afraid too that I myself have had much to say to them." Then as he made out that I was again a little at sea, "I'm talking," he went on, "of the suite prepared for her marriage." He "talked" like a crown prince. "They were ready, to the last touch — there was nothing more to be done. And they're just as they were — not an object moved, not an arrangement altered, not a person but ourselves coming in: they're only exquisitely kept. All our presents are there — I should have liked you to see them."

It had become a torment by this time — I saw that I had made a mistake. But I carried it off. "Oh, I couldn't have borne it!"

"They're not sad," he smiled — "they're too lovely to be sad. They're happy. And the things —!" He seemed, in the excitement of our talk, to have them before him.

"They're so very wonderful?"

"Oh, selected with a patience that makes them almost priceless. It's really a museum. There was nothing they thought too good for her."

I had lost the museum, but I reflected that it could contain no object so rare as my visitor. "Well, you've helped them — you could do *that*."

He quite eagerly assented. "I could do that, thank God — I could do that! I felt it from the first, and it's what I *have* done." Then as if the connection were direct: "All *my* things are there."

I thought a moment. "Your presents?"

"Those I made her. She loved each one, and I remember about each the particular thing she said. Though I do say it," he continued, "none of the others, as a matter of fact, come near mine. I look at them every day, and I assure you I'm not ashamed." Evidently, in short, he had spared nothing, and he talked on and on. He really quite swaggered.

VIII

In relation to times and intervals I can only recall that if this visit of his to me had been in the early spring it was one day in the late autumn — a day, which couldn't have been in the same year, with the difference of hazy, drowsy sunshine and brown and yellow leaves — that, taking a short cut across Kensington Gardens, I came, among the untrodden ways, upon a couple occupying chairs under a tree, who immediately rose at the sight of me. I had been behind them at recognition, the fact that Marmaduke was in deep mourning having perhaps, so far as I had observed it, misled me. In my desire both not to look flustered at meeting them and to spare their own confusion I bade them again be seated and asked leave, as a third chair was at hand, to share a little their rest. Thus it befell that after a minute Lavinia

and I had sat down, while our friend, who had looked at his watch, stood before us among the fallen foliage and remarked that he was sorry to have to leave us. Lavinia said nothing, but I expressed regret; I couldn't, however, as it struck me, without a false or a vulgar note speak as if I had interrupted a tender passage or separated a pair of lovers. But I could look him up and down, take in his deep mourning. He had not made, for going off, any other pretext than that his time was up and that he was due at home. "Home," with him now, had but one meaning: I knew him to be completely quartered in Westbourne Terrace. "I hope nothing has happened," I said — "that you've lost no one whom *I* know."

Marmaduke looked at my companion, and she looked at Marmaduke. "He has lost his wife," she then observed.

Oh, this time, I fear, I had a small quaver of brutality; but it was at him I directed it. "Your wife? I didn't know you had *had* a wife!"

"Well," he replied, positively gay in his black suit, his black gloves, his high hatband, "the more we live in the past, the more things we find in it. That's a literal fact. You would see the truth of it if your life had taken such a turn."

"*I* live in the past," Lavinia put in gently and as if to help us both.

"But with the result, my dear," I returned, "of not making, I hope, such extraordinary discoveries!" It seemed absurd to be afraid to be light.

"May none of her discoveries be more fatal than mine!" Marmaduke wasn't uproarious, but his treatment of the matter had the good taste of simplicity. "They've wanted it so for her," he continued to me wonderfully, "that we've at last seen our way to it — I mean to what Lavinia has mentioned." He hesitated but three seconds — he brought it brightly out. "Maud-Evelyn had *all* her young happiness."

I stared, but Lavinia was, in her peculiar manner, as brilliant. "The marriage *did* take place," she quietly, stupendously explained to me.

Well, I was determined not to be left. "So you're a widower," I gravely asked, "and these are the signs?"

"Yes; I shall wear them always now."

"But isn't it late to have begun?"

My question had been stupid, I felt the next

instant; but it didn't matter — he was quite equal to the occasion. "Oh, I had to wait, you know, till all the facts about my marriage had given me the right." And he looked at his watch again. "Excuse me — I *am* due. Good-by, good-by." He shook hands with each of us, and as we sat there together watching him walk away I was struck with his admirable manner of looking the character. I felt indeed as our eyes followed him that we were at one on this, and I said nothing till he was out of sight. Then by the same impulse we turned to each other.

"I thought he was never to marry!" I exclaimed to my friend.

Her fine wasted face met me gravely. "He isn't — ever. He'll be still more faithful."

"Faithful this time to whom?"

"Why, to Maud-Evelyn." I said nothing — I only checked an ejaculation; but I put out a hand and took one of hers, and for a minute we kept silence. "Of course it's only an idea," she began again at last, "but it seems to me a beautiful one." Then she continued resignedly and remarkably: "And now *they* can die."

"Mr. and Mrs. Dedrick?" I pricked up my ears. "Are they dying?"

"Not quite, but the old lady, it appears, is failing, steadily weakening; less, as I understand it, from any definite ailment than because she just feels her work done and her little sum of passion, as Marmaduke calls it, spent. Fancy, with her convictions, all her reasons for wanting to die! And if she goes, he says, Mr. Dedrick won't long linger. It will be quite 'John Anderson my jo.'"

"Keeping her company down the hill, to lie beside her at the foot?"

"Yes, having settled all things."

I turned these things over as we walked away, and how they had settled them — for Maud-Evelyn's dignity and Marmaduke's high advantage; and before we parted that afternoon — we had taken a cab in the Bayswater Road and she had come home with me — I remember saying to her: "Well then, when they die won't he be free?"

She seemed scarce to understand. "Free?"

"To do what he likes?"

She wondered. "But he does what he likes now."

"Well then, what *you* like!"

"Oh, you know what *I* like ——!"

Ah, I closed her mouth! "You like to tell horrid fibs — yes, I know it!"

What she had then put before me, however, came in time to pass: I heard in the course of the next year of Mrs. Dedrick's extinction, and some months later, without, during the interval, having seen a sign of Marmaduke, wholly taken up with his bereaved patron, learned that her husband had touchingly followed her. I was out of England at the time; we had had to put into practice great economies and let our little place; so that, spending three winters successively in Italy, I devoted the periods between, at home, altogether to visits among people, mainly relatives, to whom these friends of mine were not known. Lavinia of course wrote to me — wrote, among many things, that Marmaduke was ill and had not seemed at all himself since the loss of his "family," and this in spite of the circumstance, which she had already promptly communicated, that they had left him, by will, "almost everything." I knew before I came back to remain that she now saw him often and, to the extent of the change that had overtaken his strength and his spirits, greatly ministered to him. As soon as we at last met I asked for news of him; to which she replied: "He's gradually going." Then on my surprise: "He has had his life."

"You mean that, as he said of Mrs. Dedrick, his sum of passion is spent?"

At this she turned away. "You've never understood."

I *had*, I conceived; and when I went subsequently to see him I was moreover sure. But I only said to Lavinia on this first occasion that I would immediately go; which was precisely what brought out the climax, as I feel it to be, of my story. "He's not now, you know," she turned round to admonish me, "in Westbourne Terrace. He has taken a little old house in Kensington."

"Then he hasn't kept the things?"

"He has kept everything." She looked at me still more as if I had never understood.

"You mean he has moved them?"

She was patient with me. "He has moved nothing. Everything is as it was, and kept with the same perfection."

I wondered. "But if he doesn't live there?"

"It's just what he does."

"Then how can he be in Kensington?"

She hesitated, but she had still more than her old grasp of it. "He's in Kensington — without living."

"You mean that at the other place ——?"

"Yes, he spends most of his time. He's driven

over there every day — he remains there for hours. He keeps it for that."

"I see — it's still the museum."

"It's still the temple!" Lavinia replied with positive austerity.

"Then why did he move?"

"Because, you see, there" — she faltered again — "I could come to him. And he wants me," she said with admirable simplicity.

Little by little I took it in. "After the death of the parents, even, you never went?"

"Never."

"So you haven't seen anything?"

"Anything of hers? Nothing."

I understood, oh perfectly; but I won't deny that I was disappointed: I had hoped for an account of his wonders and I immediately felt that it wouldn't be for me to take a step that she had declined. When, a short time later, I saw them together in Kensington Square — there were certain hours of the day that she regularly spent with him — I observed that everything about him was new, handsome, and simple. They were, in their strange, final union — if union it could be called — very natural and very touching; but he was visibly stricken — he had his ailment in his eyes. She moved about him like a sister of charity — at all events like a sister. He was neither robust nor rosy now, nor was his attention visibly very present, and I privately and fancifully asked myself where it wandered and waited. But poor Marmaduke was a gentleman to the end — he wasted away with an excellent manner. He died twelve days ago; the will was opened; and last week, having meanwhile heard from her of its contents, I saw Lavinia. He leaves her everything that he himself had inherited. But she spoke of it all in a way that caused me to say in surprise: "You haven't yet been to the house?"

"Not yet. I've only seen the solicitors, who tell me there will be no complications."

There was something in her tone that made me ask more. "Then you're not curious to see what's there?"

She looked at me with a troubled — almost a pleading — sense, which I understood; and presently she said: "Will you go with me?"

"Some day, with pleasure — but not the first time. You must go alone then. The 'relics' that you'll find there," I added — for I had read her look — "you must think of now not as hers —"

"But as his?"

"Isn't that what his death — with his so close relation to them — has made them for you?" Her face lighted — I saw it was a view she could thank me for putting into words. "I see — I see. They are his. I'll go."

She went, and three days ago she came to me. They're really marvels, it appears, treasures extraordinary, and she has them all. Next week I go with her — I shall see them at last. Tell *you* about them you say? My dear man, everything.

The Art of Fiction

(1884)

This fine essay was written in reply to a lecture by Walter Besant, Victorian novelist and historian. It is at once a declaration of the coming of age of the novel as an art form, an admirable essay in definition of that art form, and an illuminating discussion of some of James's own principles and techniques. Much of this essay also applies with particular force to the novel of the twentieth century.

I should not have affixed so comprehensive a title to these few remarks, necessarily wanting in any completeness upon a subject the full consideration of which would carry us far, did I not seem to discover a pretext for my temerity in the interesting pamphlet lately published under this name by Mr. Walter Besant. Mr. Besant's lecture at the Royal Institution — the original form of his pamphlet — appears to indicate that many persons are interested in the art of fiction, and are not indifferent to such remarks, as those who practise it may attempt to make about it. I am therefore anxious not to lose the benefit of this favourable association, and to edge in a few words under cover of the attention which Mr. Besant is sure to have excited. There is something very encouraging in his having put into form certain of his ideas on the mystery of story-telling.

It is a proof of life and curiosity — curiosity on the part of the brotherhood of novelists as well as on the part of their readers. Only a short time ago it might have been supposed that the English novel was not what the French call *discutable*. It had no air of having a theory, a conviction, a consciousness of itself behind it — of being the expression of an artistic faith, the result of choice and comparison. I do not say it was necessarily the worse for that: it would take much more courage than I possess to intimate that the form of the novel as Dickens and

Thackeray (for instance) saw it had any taint of incompleteness. It was, however, *naïf* (if I may help myself out with another French word); and evidently if it be destined to suffer in any way for having lost its *naïveté* it has now an idea of making sure of the corresponding advantages. During the period I have alluded to there was a comfortable, good-humoured feeling abroad that a novel is a novel, as a pudding is a pudding, and that our only business with it could be to swallow it. But within a year or two, for some reason or other, there have been signs of returning animation — the era of discussion would appear to have been to a certain extent opened. Art lives upon discussion, upon experiment, upon variety of attempt, upon the exchange of views and the comparison of standpoints; and there is a presumption that those times when no one has anything particular to say about it, and has no reason to give for practice or preference, though they may be times of honour, are not times of development — are times, possibly even, a little of dulness. The successful application of any art is a delightful spectacle, but the theory too is interesting; and though there is a great deal of the latter without the former I suspect there has never been a genuine success that has not had a latent core of conviction. Discussion, suggestion, formulation, these things are fertilising when they are frank and sincere. Mr. Besant has set an excellent example in saying what he thinks, for his part, about the way in which fiction should be written, as well as about the way in which it should be published; for his view of the "art," carried on into an appendix, covers that too. Other labourers in the same field will doubtless take up the argument, they will give it the light of their experience, and the effect will surely be to make our interest in the novel a little more what it had for some time threatened to fail to be — a serious, active, inquiring interest, under protection of which this delightful study may, in moments of confidence, venture to say a little more what it thinks of itself.

It must take itself seriously for the public to take it so. The old superstition about fiction being "wicked" has doubtless died out in England; but the spirit of it lingers in a certain oblique regard directed toward any story which does not more or less admit that it is only a joke. Even the most jocular novel feels in some degree the weight of the proscription that was formerly directed against literary levity: the jocularity does not always succeed in passing for orthodoxy. It is still expected, though perhaps people are ashamed to say it, that a production which is after all only a "make-believe" (for what else is a "story"?) shall be in some degree apologetic — shall renounce the pretension of attempting really to represent life. This, of course, any sensible, wide-awake story declines to do, for it quickly perceives that the tolerance granted to it on such a condition is only an attempt to stifle it disguised in the form of generosity. The old evangelical hostility to the novel, which was as explicit as it was narrow, and which regarded it as little less favourable to our immortal part than a stage-play, was in reality far less insulting. The only reason for the existence of a novel is that it does attempt to represent life. When it relinquishes this attempt, the same attempt that we see on the canvas of the painter, it will have arrived at a very strange pass. It is not expected of the picture that it will make itself humble in order to be forgiven; and the analogy between the art of the painter and the art of the novelist is, so far as I am able to see, complete. Their inspiration is the same, their process (allowing for the different quality of the vehicle) is the same, their success is the same. They may learn from each other, they may explain and sustain each other. Their cause is the same, and the honour of one is the honour of another. The Mahometans think a picture an unholy thing, but it is a long time since any Christian did, and it is therefore the more odd that in the Christian mind the traces (dissimulated though they may be) of a suspicion of the sister art should linger to this day. The only effectual way to lay it to rest is to emphasise the analogy to which I just alluded — to insist on the fact that as the picture is reality, so the novel is history. That is the only general description (which does it justice) that we may give of the novel. But history also is allowed to represent life; it is not, any more than painting, expected to apologise. The subject-matter of fiction is stored up likewise in documents and records, and if it will not give itself away, as they say in California, it must speak with assurance, with the tone of the historian. Certain accomplished novelists have a habit of giving themselves away which must often bring tears to the eyes of people who take their fiction seriously. I was lately struck, in reading over many pages of Anthony Trollope, with his want of discretion in this particular. In a digression, a parenthesis or an aside, he concedes to the reader that he and this trusting friend are only "making believe." He admits that the events he narrates have not really happened, and that he can give his narrative any turn the reader may like best. Such a betrayal of a sacred office seems to me, I confess, a terrible crime; it is what I mean by the attitude of apology, and it shocks me every whit as much in Trollope as it would have shocked me in Gibbon or Macaulay. It implies that the novelist is less occupied in looking for the truth (the truth, of course I mean, that he assumes, the premises that we must grant him, whatever they may be), than the historian, and in doing so it deprives him at a stroke of all his standing-room. To represent and illustrate the past, the actions of men, is the task of either writer, and the only difference that I can see is, in proportion as he succeeds, to the honour of the novelist, consisting as it does in his having more difficulty in collecting his evidence, which is so far from being purely literary. It seems to me to give him a great character, the fact that he has at once so much in common with the philosopher and the painter; this double analogy is a magnificent heritage.

It is of all this evidently that Mr. Besant is full when he insists upon the fact that fiction is one of the *fine* arts, deserving in its turn of all the honours and emoluments that have hitherto been reserved for the successful profession of music, poetry, painting, architecture. It is impossible to insist too much on so important a truth, and the place that Mr. Besant demands for the work of the novelist may be represented, a trifle less abstractly, by saying that he demands not only that it shall be reputed artistic, but that it shall be reputed very artistic indeed. It is excellent that he should have struck this note, for his doing so indicates that there was need of it, that his proposition may be to many people a novelty. One rubs one's eyes at the thought; but the rest of Mr. Besant's essay confirms the revelation. I suspect in truth that it would be possible to confirm it still further, and that one would not be far wrong in saying that in addition to the people to whom it has never occurred that a novel ought to be artistic, there are a great many others who, if this principle were urged upon them, would be filled with an indefinable mistrust. They would find it difficult to explain their repugnance, but it would operate strongly to put them on their guard. "Art," in our Protestant communities, where so many things have

got so strangely twisted about, is supposed in certain circles to have some vaguely injurious effect upon those who make it an important consideration, who let it weigh in the balance. It is assumed to be opposed in some mysterious manner to morality, to amusement, to instruction. When it is embodied in the work of the painter (the sculptor is another affair!) you know what it is: it stands there before you, in the honesty of pink and green and a gilt frame; you can see the worst of it at a glance, and you can be on your guard. But when it is introduced into literature it becomes more insidious — there is danger of its hurting you before you know it. Literature should be either instructive or amusing, and there is in many minds an impression that these artistic preoccupations, the search for form, contribute to neither end, interfere indeed with both. They are too frivolous to be edifying, and too serious to be diverting; and they are moreover priggish and paradoxical and superfluous. That, I think, represents the manner in which the latent thought of many people who read novels as an exercise in skipping would explain itself if it were to become articulate. They would argue, of course, that a novel ought to be "good," but they would interpret this term in a fashion of their own, which indeed would vary considerably from one critic to another. One would say that being good means representing virtuous and aspiring characters, placed in prominent positions; another would say that it depends on a "happy ending," on a distribution at the last of prizes, pensions, husbands, wives, babies, millions, appended paragraphs, and cheerful remarks. Another still would say that it means being full of incident and movement, so that we shall wish to jump ahead, to see who was the mysterious stranger, and if the stolen will was ever found, and shall not be distracted from this pleasure by any tiresome analysis or "description." But they would all agree that the "artistic" idea would spoil some of their fun. One would hold it accountable for all the description, another would see it revealed in the absence of sympathy. Its hostility to a happy ending would be evident, and it might even in some cases render any ending at all impossible. The "ending" of a novel is, for many persons, like that of a good dinner, a course of dessert and ices, and the artist in fiction is regarded as a sort of meddlesome doctor who forbids agreeable aftertastes. It is therefore true that this conception of Mr.

Besant's of the novel as a superior form encounters not only a negative but a positive indifference. It matters little that as a work of art it should really be as little or as much of its essence to supply happy endings, sympathetic characters, and an objective tone, as if it were a work of mechanics: the association of ideas, however incongruous, might easily be too much for it if an eloquent voice were not sometimes raised to call attention to the fact that it is at once as free and as serious a branch of literature as any other.

Certainly this might sometimes be doubted in presence of the enormous number of works of fiction that appeal to the credulity of our generation, for it might easily seem that there could be no great character in a commodity so quickly and easily produced. It must be admitted that good novels are much compromised by bad ones, and that the field at large suffers discredit from overcrowding. I think, however, that this injury is only superficial, and that the superabundance of written fiction proves nothing against the principle itself. It has been vulgarised, like all other kinds of literature, like everything else to-day, and it has proved more than some kinds accessible to vulgarisation. But there is as much difference as there ever was between a good novel and a bad one: the bad is swept with all the daubed canvases and spoiled marble into some unvisited limbo, or infinite rubbish-yard beneath the back-windows of the world, and the good subsists and emits its light and stimulates our desire for perfection. As I shall take the liberty of making but a single criticism of Mr. Besant, whose tone is so full of the love of his art, I may as well have done with it at once. He seems to me to mistake in attempting to say so definitely beforehand what sort of an affair the good novel will be. To indicate the danger of such an error as that has been the purpose of these few pages; to suggest that certain traditions on the subject, applied *a priori*, have already had much to answer for, and that the good health of an art which undertakes so immediately to reproduce life must demand that it be perfectly free. It lives upon exercise, and the very meaning of exercise is freedom. The only obligation to which in advance we may hold a novel, without incurring the accusation of being arbitrary, is that it be interesting. That general responsibility rests upon it, but it is the only one I can think of. The ways in which it is at liberty to accomplish this result (of interesting us) strike me as innumerable, and such as can only suffer from being marked out or fenced in by prescription. They are as various as the temperament of man, and they are successful in proportion as they reveal a particular mind, different from others. A novel is in its broadest definition a personal, a direct impression of life: that, to begin with, constitutes its value, which is greater or less according to the intensity of the impression. But there will be no intensity at all, and therefore no value, unless there is freedom to feel and say. The tracing of a line to be followed, of a tone to be taken, of a form to be filled out, is a limitation of that freedom and a suppression of the very thing that we are most curious about. The form, it seems to me, is to be appreciated after the fact; then the author's choice has been made, his standard has been indicated; then we can follow lines and directions and compare tones and resemblances. Then in a word we can enjoy one of the most charming of pleasures, we can estimate quality, we can apply the test of execution. The execution belongs to the author alone; it is what is most personal to him, and we measure him by that. The advantage, the luxury, as well as the torment and responsibility of the novelist, is that there is no limit to what he may attempt as an executant — no limit to his possible experiments, efforts, discoveries, successes. Here it is especially that he works, step by step, like his brother of the brush, of whom we may always say that he has painted his picture in a manner best known to himself. His manner is his secret, not necessarily a jealous one. He cannot disclose it as a general thing if he would; he would be at a loss to teach it to others. I say this with a due recollection of having insisted on the community of method of the artist who paints a picture and the artist who writes a novel. The painter *is* able to teach the rudiments of his practice, and it is possible, from the study of good work (granted the aptitude), both to learn how to paint and to learn how to write. Yet it remains true, without injury to the *rapprochement*, that the literary artist would be obliged to say to his pupil much more than the other, "Ah, well, you must do it as you can!" It is a question of degree, a matter of delicacy. If there are exact sciences, there are also exact arts, and the grammar of painting is so much more definite that it makes the difference.

I ought to add, however, that if Mr. Besant says at the beginning of his essay that the "laws of fiction may be laid down and taught with as much precision and exactness as the laws of harmony, perspective, and proportion," he mitigates what might appear to be an extravagance by applying his remark to "general" laws, and by expressing most of these rules in a manner with which it would certainly be unaccommodating to disagree. That the novelist must write from his experience, that his "characters must be real and such as might be met with in actual life"; that "a young lady brought up in a quiet country village should avoid descriptions of garrison life," and "a writer whose friends and personal experiences belong to the lower middle-class should carefully avoid introducing his characters into society"; that one should enter one's notes in a common-place book; that one's figures should be clear in outline; that making them clear by some trick of speech or of carriage is a bad method, and "describing them at length" is a worse one; that English Fiction should have a "conscious moral purpose"; that "it is almost impossible to estimate too highly the value of careful workmanship — that is, of style"; that "the most important point of all is the story," that "the story is everything": these are principles with most of which it is surely impossible not to sympathise. That remark about the lower middle-class writer and his knowing his place is perhaps rather chilling; but for the rest I should find it difficult to dissent from any one of these recommendations. At the same time, I should find it difficult positively to assent to them, with the exception, perhaps, of the injunction as to entering one's notes in a common-place book. They scarcely seem to me to have the quality that Mr. Besant attributes to the rules of the novelist — the "precision and exactness" of "the laws of harmony, perspective, and proportion." They are suggestive, they are even inspiring, but they are not exact, though they are doubtless as much so as the case admits of: which is a proof of that liberty of interpretation for which I just contended. For the value of these different injunctions — so beautiful and so vague — is wholly in the meaning one attaches to them. The characters, the situation, which strike one as real will be those that touch and interest one most, but the measure of reality is very difficult to fix. The reality of Don Quixote or of Mr. Micawber is a very delicate shade; it is a reality so coloured by the author's vision that, vivid as it may be, one would hesitate to propose it as a model: one would expose one's

self to some very embarrassing questions on the part of a pupil. It goes without saying that you will not write a good novel unless you possess the sense of reality; but it will be difficult to give you a recipe for calling that sense into being. Humanity is immense, and reality has a myriad forms; the most one can affirm is that some of the flowers of fiction have the odour of it, and others have not; as for telling you in advance how your nosegay should be composed, that is another affair. It is equally excellent and inconclusive to say that one must write from experience; to our supposititious aspirant such a declaration might savour of mockery. What kind of experience is intended, and where does it begin and end? Experience is never limited, and it is never complete; it is an immense sensibility, a kind of huge spiderweb of the finest silken threads suspended in the chamber of consciousness, and catching every air-borne particle in its tissue. It is the very atmosphere of the mind; and when the mind is imaginative — much more when it happens to be that of a man of genius — it takes to itself the faintest hints of life, it converts the very pulses of the air into revelations. The young lady living in a village has only to be a damsel upon whom nothing is lost to make it quite unfair (as it seems to me) to declare to her that she shall have nothing to say about the military. Greater miracles have been seen than that, imagination assisting, she should speak the truth about some of these gentlemen. I remember an English novelist, a woman of genius, telling me that she was much commended for the impression she had managed to give in one of her tales of the nature and way of life of the French Protestant youth. She had been asked where she learned so much about this recondite being, she had been congratulated on her peculiar opportunities. These opportunities consisted in her having once, in Paris, as she ascended a staircase, passed an open door where, in the household of a *pasteur*, some of the young Protestants were seated at table round a finished meal. The glimpse made a picture; it lasted only a moment, but that moment was experience. She had got her direct personal impression, and she turned out her type. She knew what youth was, and what Protestantism; she also had the advantage of having seen what it was to be French, so that she converted these ideas into a concrete image and produced a reality. Above all, however, she was blessed with the faculty which when you give it an inch takes an ell, and which for the artist is a much greater source of strength than any accident of residence or of place in the social scale. The power to guess the unseen from the seen, to trace the implication of things, to judge the whole piece by the pattern, the condition of feeling life in general so completely that you are well on your way to knowing any particular corner of it — this cluster of gifts may also be said to constitute experience, and they occur in country and in town, and in the most differing stages of education. If experience consists of impressions, it may be said that impressions *are* experience, just as (have we not seen it?) they are the very air we breathe. Therefore, if I should certainly say to a novice, "Write from experience and experience only," I should feel that this was rather a tantalising monition if I were not careful immediately to add, "Try to be one of the people on whom nothing is lost!"

I am far from intending by this to minimise the importance of exactness — of truth of detail. One can speak best from one's own taste, and I may therefore venture to say that the air of reality (solidity of specification) seems to me to be the supreme virtue of a novel — the merit on which all its other merits (including that conscious moral purpose of which Mr. Besant speaks) helplessly and submissively depend. If it be not there they are all as nothing, and if these be there, they owe their effect to the success with which the author has produced the illusion of life. The cultivation of this success, the study of this exquisite process, form, to my taste, the beginning and the end of the art of the novelist. They are his inspiration, his despair, his reward, his torment, his delight. It is here in very truth that he competes with life; it is here that he competes with his brother the painter in *his* attempt to render the look of things, the look that conveys their meaning, to catch the colour, the relief, the expression, the surface, the substance of the human spectacle. It is in regard to this that Mr. Besant is well inspired when he bids him take notes. He cannot possibly take too many, he cannot possibly take enough. All life solicits him, and to "render" the simplest surface, to produce the most momentary illusion, is a very complicated business. His case would be easier, and the rule would be more exact, if Mr. Besant had been able to tell him what notes to take. But this, I fear, he can never learn in any manual; it is the business of his life. He has to take a great many

in order to select a few, he has to work them up as he can, and even the guides and philosophers who might have most to say to him must leave him alone when it comes to the application of precepts, as we leave the painter in communion with his palette. That his characters "must be clear in outline," as Mr. Besant says — he feels that down to his boots; but how he shall make them so is a secret between his good angel and himself. It would be absurdly simple if he could be taught that a great deal of "description" would make them so, or that on the contrary the absence of description and the cultivation of dialogue, or the absence of dialogue and the multiplication of "incident," would rescue him from his difficulties. Nothing, for instance, is more possible than that he be of a turn of mind for which this odd, literal opposition of description and dialogue, incident and description, has little meaning and light. People often talk of these things as if they had a kind of internecine distinctness, instead of melting into each other at every breath, and being intimately associated parts of one general effort of expression. I cannot imagine composition existing in a series of blocks, nor conceive, in any novel worth discussing at all, of a passage of description that is not in its intention narrative, a passage of dialogue that is not in its intention descriptive, a touch of truth of any sort that does not partake of the nature of incident, or an incident that derives its interest from any other source than the general and only source of the success of a work of art — that of being illustrative. A novel is a living thing, all one and continuous, like any other organism, and in proportion as it lives will it be found, I think, that in each of the parts there is something of each of the other parts. The critic who over the close texture of a finished work shall pretend to trace a geography of items will mark some frontiers as artificial, I fear, as any that have been known to history. There is an old-fashioned distinction between the novel of character and the novel of incident which must have cost many a smile to the intending fabulist who was keen about his work. It appears to me as little to the point as the equally celebrated distinction between the novel and the romance — to answer as little to any reality. There are bad novels and good novels, as there are bad pictures and good pictures; but that is the only distinction in which I see any meaning, and I can as little imagine speaking of a novel of character as I can imagine speaking of a picture of character. When one says picture one says of character, when one says novel one says of incident, and the terms may be transposed at will. What is character but the determination of incident? What is incident but the illustration of character? What is either a picture or a novel that is *not* of character? What else do we seek in it and find in it? It is an incident for a woman to stand up with her hand resting on a table and look out at you in a certain way; or if it be not an incident I think it will be hard to say what it is. At the same time it is an expression of character. If you say you don't see it (character in *that — allons donc!*), this is exactly what the artist who has reasons of his own for thinking he *does* see it undertakes to show you. When a young man makes up his mind that he has not faith enough after all to enter the church as he intended, that is an incident, though you may not hurry to the end of the chapter to see whether perhaps he doesn't change once more. I do not say that these are extraordinary or startling incidents. I do not pretend to estimate the degree of interest proceeding from them, for this will depend upon the skill of the painter. It sounds almost puerile to say that some incidents are intrinsically much more important than others, and I need not take this precaution after having professed my sympathy for the major ones in remarking that the only classification of the novel that I can understand is into that which has life and that which has it not.

The novel and the romance, the novel of incident and that of character — these clumsy separations appear to me to have been made by critics and readers for their own convenience, and to help them out of some of their occasional queer predicaments, but to have little reality or interest for the producer, from whose point of view it is of course that we are attempting to consider the art of fiction. The case is the same with another shadowy category which Mr. Besant apparently is disposed to set up — that of the "modern English novel"; unless indeed it be that in this matter he has fallen into an accidental confusion of standpoints. It is not quite clear whether he intends the remarks in which he alludes to it to be didactic or historical. It is as difficult to suppose a person intending to write a modern English as to suppose him writing an ancient English novel: that is a label which begs the question. One writes the novel, one paints the picture, of one's language and of

one's time, and calling it modern English will not, alas! make the difficult task any easier. No more, unfortunately, will calling this or that work of one's fellow-artist a romance — unless it be, of course, simply for the pleasantness of the thing, as for instance when Hawthorne gave this heading to his story of *Blithedale*. The French, who have brought the theory of fiction to remarkable completeness, have but one name for the novel, and have not attempted smaller things in it, that I can see, for that. I can think of no obligation to which the "romancer" would not be held equally with the novelist; the standard of execution is equally high for each. Of course it is of execution that we are talking — that being the only point of a novel that is open to contention. This is perhaps too often lost sight of, only to produce interminable confusions and cross-purposes. We must grant the artist his subject, his idea, his *donnée*: our criticism is applied only to what he makes of it. Naturally I do not mean that we are bound to like it or find it interesting: in case we do not our course is perfectly simple — to let it alone. We may believe that of a certain idea even the most sincere novelist can make nothing at all, and the event may perfectly justify our belief; but the failure will have been a failure to execute, and it is in the execution that the fatal weakness is recorded. If we pretend to respect the artist at all, we must allow him his freedom of choice, in the face, in particular cases, of innumerable presumptions that the choice will not fructify. Art derives a considerable part of its beneficial exercise from flying in the face of presumptions, and some of the most interesting experiments of which it is capable are hidden in the bosom of common things. Gustave Flaubert has written a story about the devotion of a servant-girl to a parrot, and the production, highly finished as it is, cannot on the whole be called a success. We are perfectly free to find it flat, but I think it might have been interesting; and I, for my part, am extremely glad he should have written it; it is a contribution to our knowledge of what can be done — or what cannot. Ivan Turgenev has written a tale about a deaf and dumb serf and a lap-dog, and the thing is touching, loving, a little masterpiece. He struck the note of life where Gustave Flaubert missed it — he flew in the face of a presumption and achieved a victory.

Nothing, of course, will ever take the place of the good old fashion of "liking" a work of art or not liking it: the most improved criticism will not abolish that primitive, that ultimate test. I mention this to guard myself from the accusation of intimating that the idea, the subject, of a novel or a picture, does not matter. It matters, to my sense, in the highest degree, and if I might put up a prayer it would be that artists should select none but the richest. Some, as I have already hastened to admit, are much more remunerative than others, and it would be a world happily arranged in which persons intending to treat them should be exempt from confusions and mistakes. This fortunate condition will arrive only, I fear, on the same day that critics become purged from error. Meanwhile, I repeat, we do not judge the artist with fairness unless we say to him, "Oh, I grant you your starting-point, because if I did not I should seem to prescribe to you, and heaven forbid I should take that responsibility. If I pretend to tell you what you must not take, you will call upon me to tell you then what you must take; in which case I shall be prettily caught. Moreover, it isn't till I have accepted your data that I can begin to measure you. I have the standard, the pitch; I have no right to tamper with your flute and then criticise your music. Of course I may not care for your idea at all; I may think it silly, or stale, or unclean; in which case I wash my hands of you altogether. I may content myself with believing that you will not have succeeded in being interesting, but I shall, of course, not attempt to demonstrate it, and you will be as indifferent to me as I am to you. I needn't remind you that there are all sorts of tastes: who can know it better? Some people, for excellent reasons, don't like to read about carpenters; others, for reasons even better, don't like to read about courtesans. Many object to Americans. Others (I believe they are mainly editors and publishers) won't look at Italians. Some readers don't like quiet subjects; others don't like bustling ones. Some enjoy a complete illusion, others the consciousness of large concessions. They choose their novels accordingly, and if they don't care about your idea they won't, *a fortiori*, care about your treatment."

So that it comes back very quickly, as I have said, to the liking: in spite of M. Zola, who reasons less powerfully than he represents, and who will not reconcile himself to this absoluteness of taste, thinking that there are certain things that people ought to like, and that they can be made to like. I am quite at a loss to imagine anything (at any rate in this matter of fiction) that people *ought* to like or to dislike. Selection will be sure to take care of itself, for it has a constant motive behind it. That motive is simply experience. As people feel life, so they will feel the art that is most closely related to it. This closeness of relation is what we should never forget in talking of the effort of the novel. Many people speak of it as a factitious, artificial form, a product of ingenuity, the business of which is to alter and arrange the things that surround us, to translate them into conventional, traditional moulds. This, however, is a view of the matter which carries us but a very short way, condemns the art to an eternal repetition of a few familiar *clichés*, cuts short its development, and leads us straight up to a dead wall. Catching the very note and trick, the strange irregular rhythm of life, that is the attempt whose strenuous force keeps Fiction upon her feet. In proportion as in what she offers us we see life *without* rearrangement do we feel that we are touching the truth; in proportion as we see it *with* rearrangement do we feel that we are being put off with a substitute, a compromise and convention. It is not uncommon to hear an extraordinary assurance of remark in regard to this matter of rearranging, which is often spoken of as if it were the last word of art. Mr. Besant seems to me in danger of falling into the great error with his rather unguarded talk about "selection." Art is essentially selection, but it is a selection whose main care is to be typical, to be inclusive. For many people art means rose-coloured window-panes, and selection means picking a bouquet for Mrs. Grundy. They will tell you glibly that artistic considerations have nothing to do with the disagreeable, with the ugly; they will rattle off shallow commonplaces about the province of art and the limits of art till you are moved to some wonder in return as to the province and the limits of ignorance. It appears to me that no one can ever have made a seriously artistic attempt without becoming conscious of an immense increase — a kind of revelation — of freedom. One perceives in that case — by the light of a heavenly ray — that the province of art is all life, all feeling, all observation, all vision. As Mr. Besant so justly intimates, it is all experience. That is a sufficient answer to those who maintain that it must not touch the sad things of life, who stick into its divine unconscious bosom little prohibitory inscriptions on the end of sticks, such as we see in public gardens — "It is forbidden to walk on the grass; it is forbidden to touch the flowers; it is not allowed to introduce dogs or to remain after dark; it is requested to keep to the right." The young aspirant in the line of fiction whom we continue to imagine will do nothing without taste, for in that case his freedom would be of little use to him; but the first advantage of his taste will be to reveal to him the absurdity of the little sticks and tickets. If he have taste, I must add, of course he will have ingenuity, and my disrespectful reference to that quality just now was not meant to imply that it is useless in fiction. But it is only a secondary aid; the first is a capacity for receiving straight impressions.

Mr. Besant has some remarks on the question of "the story" which I shall not attempt to criticise, though they seem to me to contain a singular ambiguity, because I do not think I understand them. I cannot see what is meant by talking as if there were a part of a novel which is the story and part of it which for mystical reasons is not — unless indeed the distinction be made in a sense in which it is difficult to suppose that any one should attempt to convey anything. "The story," if it represents anything, represents the subject, the idea, the *donnée* of the novel; and there is surely no "school" — Mr. Besant speaks of a school — which urges that a novel should be all treatment and no subject. There must assuredly be something to treat; every school is intimately conscious of that. This sense of the story being the idea, the starting-point, of the novel, is the only one that I see in which it can be spoken of as something different from its organic whole; and since in proportion as the work is successful the idea permeates and penetrates it, informs and animates it, so that every word and every punctuation-point contribute directly to the expression, in that proportion do we lose our sense of the story being a blade which may be drawn more or less out of its sheath. The story and the novel, the idea and the form, are the needle and thread, and I never heard of a guild of tailors who recommended the use of the thread without the needle, or the needle without the thread. Mr. Besant is not the only critic who may be observed to have spoken as if there were certain things in life which constitute stories, and certain others which do not. I find the same odd implication in an entertaining article

in the *Pall Mall Gazette*, devoted, as it happens, to Mr. Besant's lecture. "The story is the thing!" says this graceful writer, as if with a tone of opposition to some other idea. I should think it was, as every painter who, as the time for "sending in" his picture looms in the distance, finds himself still in quest of a subject — as every belated artist not fixed about his theme will heartily agree. There are some subjects which speak to us and others which do not, but he would be a clever man who should undertake to give a rule — an index expurgatorius — by which the story and the no story should be known apart. It is impossible (to me at least) to imagine any such rule which shall not be altogether arbitrary. The writer in the *Pall Mall* opposes the delightful (as I suppose) novel of *Margot la Balafrée* to certain tales in which "Bostonian nymphs" appear to have "rejected English dukes for psychological reasons." I am not acquainted with the romance just designated, and can scarcely forgive the *Pall Mall* critic for not mentioning the name of the author, but the title appears to refer to a lady who may have received a scar in some heroic adventure. I am inconsolable at not being acquainted with this episode, but am utterly at a loss to see why it is a story when the rejection (or acceptance) of a duke is not, and why a reason, psychological or other, is not a subject when a cicatrix is. They are all particles of the multitudinous life with which the novel deals, and surely no dogma which pretends to make it lawful to touch the one and unlawful to touch the other will stand for a moment on its feet. It is the special picture that must stand or fall, according as it seem to possess truth or to lack it. Mr. Besant does not, to my sense, light up the subject by intimating that a story must, under penalty of not being a story, consist of "adventures." Why of adventures more than of green spectacles? He mentions a category of impossible things, and among them he places "fiction without adventure." Why without adventure, more than without matrimony, or celibacy, or parturition, or cholera, or hydropathy, or Jansenism? This seems to me to bring the novel back to the hapless little *rôle* of being an artificial, ingenious thing — bring it down from its large, free character of an immense and exquisite correspondence with life. And what *is* adventure, when it comes to that, and by what sign is the listening pupil to recognise it? It is an adventure — an immense one — for me to write this little article; and for a Bostonian nymph to reject an English duke is an adventure only less stirring, I should say, than for an English duke to be rejected by a Bostonian nymph. I see dramas within dramas in that, and innumerable points of views. A psychological reason is, to my imagination, an object adorably pictorial; to catch the tint of its complexion — I feel as if that idea might inspire one to Titianesque efforts. There are few things more exciting to me, in short, than a psychological reason, and yet, I protest, the novel seems to me the most magnificent form of art. I have just been reading, at the same time, the delightful story of *Treasure Island*, by Mr. Robert Louis Stevenson and, in a manner less consecutive, the last tale from M. Edmond de Goncourt, which is entitled *Chérie*. One of these works treats of murders, mysteries, islands of dreadful renown, hair-breadth escapes, miraculous coincidences and buried doubloons. The other treats of a little French girl who lived in a fine house in Paris, and died of wounded sensibility because no one would marry her. I call *Treasure Island* delightful, because it appears to me to have succeeded wonderfully in what it attempts; and I venture to bestow no epithet upon *Chérie*, which strikes me as having failed deplorably in what it attempts — that is in tracing the development of the moral consciousness of a child. But one of these productions strikes me as exactly as much of a novel as the other, and as having a "story" quite as much. The moral consciousness of a child is as much a part of life as the islands of the Spanish Main, and the one sort of geography seems to me to have those "surprises" of which Mr. Besant speaks quite as much as the other. For myself (since it comes back in the last resort, as I say, to the preference of the individual), the picture of the child's experience has the advantage that I can at successive steps (an immense luxury, near to the "sensual pleasure" of which Mr. Besant's critic in the *Pall Mall* speaks) say Yes or No, as it may be, to what the artist puts before me. I have been a child in fact, but I have been on a quest for a buried treasure only in supposition, and it is a simple accident that with M. de Goncourt I should have for the most part to say No. With George Eliot, when she painted that country with a far other intelligence, I always said Yes.

The most interesting part of Mr. Besant's lecture is unfortunately the briefest passage — his very cursory allusion to the "conscious moral purpose" of the novel. Here again it is not very clear whether he be recording a fact or laying down a principle; it is a great pity that in the latter case he should not have developed his idea. This branch of the subject is of immense importance, and Mr. Besant's few words point to considerations of the widest reach, not to be lightly disposed of. He will have treated the art of fiction superficially who is not prepared to go every inch of the way that these considerations will carry him. It is for this reason that at the beginning of these remarks I was careful to notify the reader that my reflections on so large a theme have no pretension to be exhaustive. Like Mr. Besant, I have left the question of the morality of the novel till the last, and at the last I find I have used up my space. It is a question surrounded with difficulties, as witness the very first that meets us, in the form of a definite question, on the threshold. Vagueness, in such a discussion, is fatal, and what is the meaning of your morality and your conscious moral purpose? Will you not define your terms and explain how (a novel being a picture) a picture can be either moral or immoral? You wish to paint a moral picture or carve a moral statue: will you not tell us how you would set about it? We are discussing the Art of Fiction; questions of art are questions (in the widest sense) of execution; questions of morality are quite another affair, and will you not let us see how it is that you find it so easy to mix them up? These things are so clear to Mr. Besant that he has deduced from them a law which he sees embodied in English Fiction, and which is "a truly admirable thing and a great cause for congratulation." It is a great cause for congratulation indeed when such thorny problems become as smooth as silk. I may add that in so far as Mr. Besant perceives that in point of fact English Fiction has addressed itself preponderantly to these delicate questions he will appear to many people to have made a vain discovery. They will have been positively struck, on the contrary, with the moral timidity of the usual English novelist; with his (or with her) aversion to face the difficulties with which on every side the treatment of reality bristles. He is apt to be extremely shy (whereas the picture that Mr. Besant draws is a picture of boldness), and the sign of his work, for the most part, is a cautious silence on certain subjects. In the English novel (by which of course I mean the American as well), more than in any other, there is a traditional difference between that which people know and that which they agree to admit that they know, that which they see and that which they speak of, that which they feel to be a part of life and that which they allow to enter into literature. There is the great difference, in short, between what they talk of in conversation and what they talk of in print. The essence of moral energy is to survey the whole field, and I should directly reverse Mr. Besant's remark and say not that the English novel has a purpose, but that it has a diffidence. To what degree a purpose in a work of art is a source of corruption I shall not attempt to inquire; the one that seems to me least dangerous is the purpose of making a perfect work. As for our novel, I may say lastly on this score that as we find it in England to-day it strikes me as addressed in a large degree to "young people," and that this in itself constitutes a presumption that it will be rather shy. There are certain things which it is generally agreed not to discuss, not even to mention, before young people. That is very well, but the absence of discussion is not a symptom of the moral passion. The purpose of the English novel — "a truly admirable thing, and a great cause for congratulation" — strikes me therefore as rather negative.

There is one point at which the moral sense and the artistic sense lie very near together; that is in the light of the very obvious truth that the deepest quality of a work of art will always be the quality of the mind of the producer. In proportion as that intelligence is fine will the novel, the picture, the statue partake of the substance of beauty and truth. To be constituted of such elements is, to my vision, to have purpose enough. No good novel will ever proceed from a superficial mind; that seems to me an axiom which, for the artist in fiction, will cover all needful moral ground: if the youthful aspirant take it to heart it will illuminate for him many of the mysteries of "purpose." There are many other useful things that might be said to him, but I have come to the end of my article, and can only touch them as I pass. The critic in the *Pall Mall Gazette*, whom I have already quoted, draws attention to the danger, in speaking of the art of fiction, of generalising. The danger that he has in mind is rather, I imagine, that of particularising, for there are some comprehensive remarks which, in addi-

tion to those embodied in Mr. Besant's suggestive lecture, might without fear of misleading him be addressed to the ingenuous student. I should remind him first of the magnificence of the form that is open to him, which offers to sight so few restrictions and such innumerable opportunities. The other arts, in comparison, appear confined and hampered; the various conditions under which they are exercised are so rigid and definite. But the only condition that I can think of attaching to the composition of the novel is, as I have already said, that it be sincere. This freedom is a splendid privilege, and the first lesson of the young novelist is to learn to be worthy of it. "Enjoy it as it deserves," I should say to him; "take possession of it, explore it to its utmost extent, publish it, rejoice in it. All life belongs to you, and do not listen either to those who would shut you up into corners of it and tell you that it is only here and there that art inhabits, or to those who would persuade you that this heavenly messenger wings her way outside of life altogether, breathing a superfine air, and turning away her head from the truth of things. There is no impression of life, no manner of seeing it and feeling it, to which the plan of the novelist may not offer a place; you have only to remember that talents so dissimilar as those of Alexandre Dumas and Jane Austen, Charles Dickens and Gustave Flaubert have worked in this field with equal glory. Do not think too much about optimism and pessimism; try and catch the colour of life itself. In France to-day we see a prodigious effort (that of Emile Zola, to whose solid and serious work no explorer of the capacity of the novel can allude without respect), we see an extraordinary effort, vitiated by a spirit of pessimism on a narrow basis. M. Zola is magnificent, but he strikes an English reader as ignorant; he has an air of working in the dark; if he had as much light as energy, his results would be of the highest value. As for the aberrations of a shallow optimism, the ground (of English fiction especially) is strewn with their brittle particles as with broken glass. If you must indulge in conclusions, let them have the taste of a wide knowledge. Remember that your first duty is to be as complete as possible — to make as perfect a work. Be generous and delicate and pursue the prize."

Edith **Wharton** [1862–1937]

Like her literary model and master, Henry James, Edith Wharton was more at home in Europe than in America. Aside from the fashionable society of New York and Newport into which she was born, she knew little of her native land, spending much of her life in European residence and travel.

The characteristic material for her fiction she had at hand in the leisure class to which she had been bred, a vanishing aristocracy which she cherished while gently but firmly satirizing its defects — its narrow pride, its fear of both ideas and emotions. In such novels as *The House of Mirth* (1905) and *The Age of Innocence* (1920) she revealed this formal little world with fine realistic craftsmanship. The breadth of her appeal is indicated by the respect in which she was held by the somewhat journalistic Sinclair Lewis, who dedicated his *Babbitt* to her, and by the warm interest of Henry James, whose example of artistic austerity had helped her in her apprentice years. She also felt kinship with English and French realists and "the great Russians," but not with the novelists who "beat their brains out against the blank wall of 'Naturalism.' "

She had approached the novel by way of the short story, and kept returning to the short form. In her novels she concentrated on characters; in her short stories on situations, "the disengaging of crucial moments from the welter of existence." Sometimes these moments involved choices in the life of art or of science, more often in the experience of love, as in "The Choice."

Further reading: *The House of Mirth* or *The Age of Innocence*. A *Backward Glance* (autobiography). Percy Lubbock, *Portrait of Edith Wharton* (1947). Blake Nevius, *Edith Wharton*, 1954.

The Choice

(1916)

I

Stilling, that night after dinner, had surpassed himself. He always did, Wrayford reflected, when the small fry from Highfield came to dine. He, Cobham Stilling, who had to find his bearings, keep to his level, in the big, heedless, oppressive world of New York, dilated and grew vast in the congenial medium of Highfield. The Red House was the biggest house of the Highfield summer colony, as Cobham Stilling was its biggest man. No one else within a radius of a hundred miles (on a conservative estimate) had as many horses, as many greenhouses, as many servants, and assuredly no one else had two motors, or a motor-boat for the lake.

The motor-boat was Stilling's latest hobby, and he rode — or sailed — it in and out of the conversation all the evening, to the obvious edification of every one present save his wife and his visitor, Austin Wrayford. The interest of the latter two, who, from opposite ends of the drawing-room, exchanged a fleeting glance when Stilling again launched his craft on the thin current of the talk — the interest of Mrs. Stilling and Wrayford, had already lost its edge by protracted conversational contact with the subject.

But the dinner-guests — the Rector, Mr. Swordsley, and Mrs. Swordsley, Lucy and Agnes Granger and their brother Addison, and young Jack Emmerton from Harvard — were all, for divers reasons, stirred to the proper pitch of feeling. Mr. Swordsley, no doubt, was saying to himself: "If my good parishioner here can afford to buy a motor-boat, in addition to all the other expenditures which an establishment like this must entail, I certainly need not scruple to appeal to him again for a contribution toward our Galahad Club." The Granger girls, meanwhile, were evoking visions of lakeside picnics, not unadorned with the presence of young Mr. Emmerton; while that youth himself speculated as to whether his affable host would let him, when he came back on his next vacation, "learn to run the thing himself"; and Mr. Addison Granger, the elderly bachelor brother of the volatile Lucy and Agnes, mentally formulated the precise phrase in which, in his next letter to his cousin Professor Spildyke of the University of East Latmos, he should allude to "our last delightful trip in my old friend Cobham Stilling's ten-thousand-dollar motor-launch" — for East Latmos was still in that primitive stage of social culture on which such figures impinge.

Isabel Stilling, sitting beside Mrs. Swordsley, her head slightly bent above the needlework with which, on such occasions, it was her old-fashioned habit to be engaged — Isabel also had doubtless her reflections to make. As Wrayford leaned back in his corner, and looked at her across the bright, flower-filled drawing-room, he noted first of all — for the hundredth time — the flexible play of her hands above the embroidery-frame, the shadow of the dusky, wavy hair on her forehead, the tired droop of the lids over her somewhat full gray eyes. He noted this, taking in unconsciously, at the same time, the indescribable quality in her attitude, in the fall of her dress and the turn of her head, that set her, for him, in a separate world; then he said to himself: "She's certainly thinking 'Where on earth will he get the money to pay for it?' "

But at the same moment, from his inevitable position on the hearth-rug, cigar in mouth, his hands in his waistcoat pockets, Stilling was impressively perorating.

"I said, 'If I have the thing at all, I want the best that can be got.' That's my way, you know, Swordsley; I suppose I'm what you'd call fastidious. Always was, about everything, from cigars to wom-" — his eye met the apprehensive glance of Mrs. Swordsley, who looked, in evening dress, like her husband with his clerical coat cut slightly lower — "So I said, 'If I have the thing at all, I want the best that can be got.' Nothing makeshift for me, no second-best. I never cared for the cheap and showy. I always say frankly to a man, 'If you can't give me a first-rate cigar, for the Lord's sake, let me smoke my own.' Well, if you have *my* standards, you can't buy a thing in a minute. You must look round, compare, select. I found there were lots of motor-boats on the market, just as there's

lots of stuff called champagne. But I said to myself, 'Ten to one there's only one fit to buy, just as there's only one champagne fit for a gentleman to drink.' Argued like a lawyer, eh, Austin?" He tossed this jovially toward Wrayford. "Take me for one of your own trade, wouldn't you? Well, I'm not such a fool as I look. I suppose you fellows who are tied to the treadmill, — oh, excuse me, Swordsley, but that's work, isn't it? — I suppose you think a man like me has nothing to do but take it easy — loll through life like a woman. By George, sir, I'd like either of you to see the time it takes — I won't say the brains — but just the *time* it takes to pick out a good motor-boat. Why, I went —"

Mrs. Stilling set her embroidery-frame noiselessly on the low table at her side, and turned her head toward Wrayford. "Would you mind ringing for the tray?"

The interruption helped Mrs. Swordsley to waver to her feet. "I think we really ought to be going; my husband has an early service tomorrow."

Her host sounded an immediate protest. "Going already? Nothing of the sort! Why, the night's still young, as the poet says. Long way from here to the rectory? Nonsense! In our little twenty-horse motor we do it in five minutes — don't we, Belle? Ah, you're walking, to be sure —" Stilling's indulgent gesture seemed to concede that, in such a case, allowances must be made, and that he was the last man not to make them. "Well, then, Swordsley —" He held out a thick, red hand that seemed to exude beneficence, and the clergyman, pressing it, ventured to murmur a suggestion.

"What, that Galahad Club again? Why, I thought my wife — Isabel, didn't we — No? Well, it must have been my mother, then. And of course, you know, anything my good mother gives is — well —— virtually — You haven't asked her? Sure? I could have sworn; I get so many of these appeals. And in these times, you know, we have to go cautiously. I'm sure you recognize that yourself, Swordsley. With my obligations — here now, to show you don't bear malice, have a brandy and soda before you go. Nonsense, man! This brandy isn't liquor; it's *liqueur*. I picked it up last year in London — last of a famous lot from Lord St. Oswyn's cellar. Laid down here, it stood me at — Eh?" he broke off as his wife moved toward him. "Ah, yes, of course. Miss Lucy, Miss Agnes — a drop of soda-water? Look here, Addison, *you* won't refuse my tipple, I know. Well, take a cigar, at any rate, Swordsley. And, by the way, I'm afraid you'll have to go round the long way by the avenue to-night. Sorry, Mrs. Swordsley, but I forgot to tell them to leave the gate on the lane unlocked. Well, it's a jolly night, and I daresay you won't mind the extra turn along the lake. And, by Jove! if the moon's out, you can get a glimpse of the motor-boat, as you turn the point. She's moored just out beyond our boat-house; and it's a privilege to look at her, I can tell you!"

The dispersal of the remaining guests carried Stilling out into the hall, where his pleasantries echoed genially under the oak rafters while the Granger girls were being muffled for the drive and the carriages summoned from the stables.

By a common impulse Mrs. Stilling and Wrayford had moved together toward the hearth, which was masked from the door into the hall by a tall screen of lacquer. Wrayford leaned his elbow against the chimney-piece, and Mrs. Stilling stood motionless beside him, her clasped hands hanging down before her. The rose on her breast stirred slightly.

"Have you any more work to do with him to-night?" she asked below her breath.

Wrayford shook his head. "We wound it all up before dinner. He doesn't want to talk about it any more than he can help."

"It's so bad?"

"No; but he's got to pull up."

She paused, looking down at her clasped hands. He listened a moment, catching Stilling's farewell shout; then he changed his position slightly, and laid his hand on her arm.

"In an hour?"

She made a faint motion of assent.

"I'll tell you all about it then. The key's in the usual place?"

She nodded again, and walked away with her long, drifting motion as her husband came in from the hall. He went up to the tray, and poured himself a tall glass of brandy and soda.

"The weather's turning queer — black as pitch out now. I hope the Swordsleys won't walk into the lake — involuntary immersion, eh? He'd come out a Baptist, I suppose. What'd the Bishop do in such a case? There's a problem for a lawyer, my boy!"

He clapped Wrayford resoundingly on the thin shoulder and then walked over to his wife, who was gathering up her embroidery silks and dropping them into an old-fashioned work-bag.

Stilling took her by the arms and swung her playfully about so that she faced the lamp-light.

"What's the matter with you to-night?"

"The matter?" she echoed, blushing a little, and standing very erect in her desire not to appear to shrink from his touch.

"You never opened your lips. Left me the whole job of entertaining those blessed people. Didn't she, Austin?"

Wrayford laughed and lighted a cigarette. "She wasn't quite up to the mark."

"There! You see even Austin noticed it. What's the matter? Aren't they good enough for you? I don't pretend they're particularly exciting; but, hang it! I like to ask them here — I like to give pleasure."

"I didn't mean to be dull," said Isabel, appealingly.

"Well, you must learn to make an effort. Don't treat people as if they weren't in the room just because they don't happen to amuse you. Do you know what they'll think? They'll think it's because you've got a bigger house and more cash. Shall I tell you something? My mother said she'd noticed the same thing in you lately. She said she sometimes felt you looked down on her for living in a small house. Oh, she was half joking, of course; but you see you do give people that impression. I can't understand treating any one in that way. The more I have myself, the more I want to make other people happy."

Isabel gently freed herself and laid the work-bag on her embroidery-frame. "I have a headache; perhaps that made me stupid. I'm going to bed." She turned toward Wrayford and held out her hand. "Good night."

"Good night," he answered, opening the door for her.

When he turned back into the room, his host was pouring himself a third glass of brandy and soda.

"Here, have a nip? Gad, I need it badly, after the shaking up you gave me this afternoon." Stilling gave a short laugh, and carried his glass to the hearth, where he took up his usual commanding position. "Why the deuce don't you drink something, Austin? You look as glum as Isabel. One would think *you* were the chap that had been hit."

Wrayford threw himself into the chair from which Mrs. Stilling had lately risen. It was the one she habitually sat in, and to his fancy a faint scent of her always clung to it. He leaned back and looked up at Stilling.

"Want a cigar?" the latter continued. "Shall we go into the den and smoke?"

Wrayford hesitated. "If there's anything more you want to ask me about—"

"Gad, no! I had full measure and running over this afternoon. The deuce of it is, I don't see where the money's all gone to. Luckily I've got plenty of nerve; I'm not the kind of man to sit down and snivel because he's been touched in Wall Street."

Wrayford rose again. "Then, if you don't want me, I think I'll go up to my room and put some finishing touches to a brief before I turn in. I must get back to town to-morrow afternoon."

"All right, then." Stilling set down his empty glass, and held out his hand with a tinge of alacrity. "Good night, old man."

They shook hands, and Wrayford moved toward the door.

"I say, Austin—stop a minute!" his host called after him.

Wrayford turned, and the two men faced each other across the hearth-rug. Stilling's eyes shifted uneasily in his flushed face.

"There's one thing more you *can* do for me, like a good chap, before you go. Tell Isabel about that loan; explain to her she's got to sign a note for it."

Wrayford, in his turn, flushed slightly.

"You want *me* to tell her?"

"Hang it! I'm soft-hearted—that's the worst of me." Stilling moved toward the tray, and lifted the brandy decanter. "And she'll take it better from you; she'll *have* to take it from you. She's proud. You can take her out for a row to-morrow morning—you can take her out in the motor-launch, if you like. I meant to have a spin in it myself in the morning; but if you'll tell her——"

Wrayford hesitated. "All right. I'll tell her."

"Thanks a lot, my dear fellow. And you'll make her see it wasn't my fault, eh? Women are awfully vague about money, and if you appear to back me up, you know——"

Wrayford nodded. "As you please. Good night."

"Good night. Here, Austin—there's just one more thing. You needn't say anything to Isabel about the other business—I mean my mother's securities."

"Ah?" said Wrayford.

Stilling shifted from one foot to the other. "I'd rather put that to the old lady myself. I can make it clear to her. She idolizes me, you know—and, hang it! I've got a good record. Up to now, I mean. My mother's been in clover since I married; I may say she's been my first thought. And I don't want her to hear of this from Isabel. Isabel's a little harsh at times—and of course this isn't going to make her any easier to live with."

"Very well," Wrayford assented.

Stilling, with a look of relief, walked toward the window which opened on the terrace. "Gad! what a queer night! Hot as the kitchen-range. Shouldn't wonder if we had a squall before morning. I wonder if that infernal skipper took in the launch's awnings before he went home."

Wrayford paused a moment in the doorway. "Yes, I saw him do it. She's shipshape for the night."

"Good! That saves me a run down to the shore." Stilling strolled back into the room, whistling cheerfully.

"Good night then," said Wrayford.

"Good night, old man. You'll tell her?"

"I'll tell her," Wrayford answered from the threshold.

"And mum about my mother!" his host called after him.

II

The darkness had thinned a little when Wrayford scrambled down the steep path to the shore. Though the air was heavy, the threat of a storm seemed to have vanished, and now and then the moon's edge showed above a torn slope of cloud.

But in the densely massed shrubbery about the boat-house the night was still black, and Wrayford had to strike a match before he could find the lock and insert his key. He left the door unlatched, and groped his way in. How often he had crept into this warm pine-scented obscurity, guiding himself cautiously by the edge of the bench along the side wall, and hearing the stealthy lap of water through the gaps in the flooring! He knew just where one had to duck one's head to avoid the two canoes swung from the rafters, and just where to put his hand on the latch of the door that led to the balcony above the lake.

The boat-house represented one of Stilling's abandoned whims. He had built it some seven years before, and for a time it had been the scene of incessant nautical exploits. Stilling had rowed, sailed, paddled indefatigably, and all Highfield had been impressed to bear him company and admire his versatility. Then mo- 5 tors had come in, and he had forsaken aquatic sports for the guidance of the flying chariot. The canoes of birch-bark and canvas had been hoisted to the roof, the little sail-boat had rotted at her moorings, and the movable floor of the 10 boat-house, ingeniously contrived to slide back on noiseless runners, had lain undisturbed through several seasons. Even the key of the boat-house had been mislaid, — by Isabel's fault, her husband asserted — and the locksmith 15 had to be called in to make a new one when the purchase of the motor-boat made the lake once more the center of Stilling's activity.

As Wrayford entered he noticed that a strange oily odor overpowered the usual scent 20 of dry pine-wood; and at the next step his foot struck an object that rolled noisily across the boards. He lighted a match, and found he had overturned a can of grease which the boatman had no doubt been using to oil the runners 25 of the sliding-floor.

Wrayford felt his way down the length of the boat-house, and softly opening the balcony door, looked out on the lake. A few yards off the launch lay motionless in the veiled moon- 30 light; and just below him, on the black water, he saw the dim outline of the skiff which Stilling used to paddle out to her. The silence was so intense that Wrayford fancied he heard a faint rustling in the shrubbery on the high bank be- 35 hind the boat-house, and the crackle of gravel on the path descending to it.

He closed the door again and turned back; and as he did so the other door, on the land-side, swung inward, and a figure darkened the 40 dim opening. Just enough light entered through the round holes above the respective doors to reveal it as Mrs. Stilling's cloaked outline, and to guide her to him as he advanced. But before they met she stumbled and gave a little cry. 45

"What is it?" he exclaimed, springing toward her.

"My foot caught; the floor seemed to give way under me. Ah, of course —" She bent down in the darkness — "I saw the men oiling 50 it this morning."

Wrayford caught her to him. "Be careful, darling! It might be dangerous if it slid too easily. The water's deep under here."

"Yes; the water's very deep. I sometimes wish —" She leaned against him without finishing her sentence, and he tightened his arms about her.

"Hush!" he whispered, his lips on her hair.

Suddenly she threw back her head and seemed to listen.

"What's the matter?" he asked, listening also. "What did you hear?"

"I don't know." He felt her trembling. "I'm not sure this place is as safe as it used to be —"

Wrayford held her to him reassuringly. "But the boatman sleeps down at the village: and who else should come here at this hour?"

"My husband might. He thinks of nothing but the launch."

"He won't to-night, for I told him I'd seen the skipper roll up the awning, and put the launch shipshape, and that satisfied him."

"Ah, he *did* think of coming, then?"

"Only for a minute, when the sky looked so black half an hour ago, and he was afraid of a squall. It's clearing now, and there's no danger."

He drew her down on the bench, and they sat a moment or two in silence, her hands in his. Then she said wearily: "You'd better tell me."

Wrayford gave a faint laugh. "Yes, I suppose I had. In fact, he asked me to."

"He asked you to?"

"Yes."

She sounded a sharp note of contempt. "The coward! he's afraid!"

Wrayford made no reply, and she went on: "*I'm* not. Tell me everything, please."

"Well, he's chucked away a pretty big sum again —"

"How has he done it?"

"He says he doesn't know. He's been speculating, I suppose. The madness of making him your trustee!"

She drew her hands away quickly. "You know why I did it. When we married I didn't want to put him in the false position of the man who accepts everything; I wanted people to think the money was partly his."

"I don't know what you've made *people* think; but you've been eminently successful in one respect. *He* thinks it's his — and he loses it as if it were."

She shivered a little, drawing her cloak closer. "There are worse things. Go on."

"Isabel!" He bent over her. "Give me your

hand again." He lifted it and laid a long kiss on it.

"What was it — exactly — that he wished you to tell me?" she asked.

"That you've got to sign another promissory note — for fifty thousand this time."

She drew a deep breath. "Is that all?"

Wrayford hesitated; then he said: "Yes — for the present."

She sat motionless, her head bent, her hand resting passively in his.

He leaned nearer. "What did you mean, just now, by worse things?"

She paused a moment. "Haven't you noticed that he's been drinking a great deal lately?"

"Yes; I've noticed."

They were both silent again; then Wrayford said with sudden vehemence: "And *yet* you won't —"

"Won't?"

"Put an end to it. Good God! Save what's left of your life."

She made no answer, and in the deep stillness the *throb-throb* of the water underneath them was like the anxious beat of a heart.

"Isabel —" Wrayford murmured. He bent over to kiss her, and felt the tears on her face. "Isabel! I can't stand it! Listen to me —"

She interrupted him. "No; no. I've thought of everything. There's the boy — the boy's fond of him. He's not a bad father."

"Except in the trifling matter of ruining his son."

"And there's his poor old mother. He's a good son, at any rate; he's never hurt *her*. And I know her. If I left him she'd never touch a penny. What she has of her own is not enough to live on, and how could *he* provide for her? If I put him out of doors, I should be putting his mother out, too — out of the little house she's so happy in."

"But surely you could arrange — there are always ways."

"Not for her! She's proud. And then she believes in him. Lots of people believe in him, you know. It would kill her if she ever found out."

Wrayford made an impatient movement: "It will kill you, if you stay with him to prevent her finding out."

She turned toward him and laid her other hand on his. "Not while I have you."

"Have me? In this way?" he echoed with an exasperated laugh.

"In any way."

"My poor girl — poor child!"

She drew back from him suddenly, with a quick movement of fear. "You mean that *you'll* grow tired — your patience will give out soon?"

He answered her only by saying: "My poor Isabel!"

But she went on insistently: "Don't you suppose I've thought of that — foreseen it?"

"Well — and then?" he exclaimed with sudden passion.

"I've accepted that, too," she said.

He dropped her hands with a despairing gesture. "Then, indeed, I waste my breath!"

She made no answer, and for a time they sat silent, side by side, but with a space between. At length he asked in a contrite voice: "You're not crying, Isabel?"

"No."

"I can't see your face, it's grown so dark again."

"Yes. I hadn't noticed. The storm must be coming, after all." She made a motion as if to rise.

He drew close, and put his arm about her again. "Don't leave me yet, dear! You know I must go to-morrow." He broke off with a laugh. "I'm to break the news to you to-morrow morning, by the way; I'm to take you out in the motor-launch and break it to you." He dropped her hands and stood up. "Good God! How can I go away and leave you here alone with him?"

"You've done it often before."

"Yes; but each time it's more damnable. And then I've always had a hope —"

"A hope?" She rose up. "Give it up! Give it up!" she moaned.

"You've none, then, yourself?"

She was silent, drawing the folds of her cloak about her.

"None — none?" he insisted.

"Only one," she broke out passionately.

He bent over and sought for her in the darkness. "What is it, my dearest? What is it?"

"Don't touch me! That he may die!" she shuddered back.

He dropped his hands, and they drew apart instinctively, hearing each other's quick breathing through the obscurity.

"*You* wish that sometimes, too?" he said at length in a low voice.

"Sometimes? I wish it always — every day, every hour, every moment!" She paused, and then let the quivering words break out. "You'd better know it; you'd better know the worst of me. I'm not the saint you suppose; the duty I do is poisoned by the thoughts I think. Day by day, hour by hour, I wish him dead. When he goes out I pray for something to happen; when he comes back I say to myself: 'Are you here again?' When I hear of people being killed in accidents I think: 'Why wasn't he there?' When I read the death-notices in the paper I say: 'So-and-so was just his age.' When I see him taking such care of his health and his diet — as he does, you know, except when he gets reckless and begins to drink too much — when I see him exercising and resting, and eating only certain things, and weighing himself, and feeling his muscles, and boasting that he hasn't gained a pound, I think of the men who die from overwork, who throw their lives away for some big object, and I say to myself: 'What can kill a man who thinks only of himself?' And night after night I keep myself from going to sleep for fear I may dream that he's dead. When I dream that, and wake and find him there, it's worse than ever — and my thoughts are worse than ever, too!"

She broke off on a stifled sob, and the *thump-thump* of the water under the floor was like the beat of a loud, rebellious heart.

"There, you know the truth! Is it too bad for you?"

He answered in a low voice, as if unconscious of her question: "Such things do sometimes happen, you know."

"Do they?" She laughed. "Yes, I've seen it happen — in happy marriages!"

They were silent again, not approaching each other. Abruptly Isabel turned, feeling her way toward the door. As she did so, the profound stillness of the night was broken by the sound of a man's voice, caroling out somewhat unsteadily the refrain of a music-hall song.

The two in the boat-house darted toward each other with a simultaneous movement clutching hands as they met.

"He's coming!" Isabel breathed.

Wrayford detached himself hastily from her hold.

"He may only be out for a turn before he goes to bed. Wait a minute. I'll see if I can make out." He felt his way to the bench, scrambled up on it, and stretching his body forward, managed to bring his eyes in line with the opening above the door.

"It's as black as pitch. I can't see anything."

The refrain rang out nearer.

"Wait! I saw something twinkle. There it is again. It's coming this way — down the path. It's his cigar."

There was a long rattle of thunder through the stillness.

"It's the storm!" Isabel gasped. "He's coming to see about the launch."

Wrayford dropped noiselessly from the bench to her side.

"He's coming — yes."

She caught him by the arm.

"Isn't there time to get up the path and slip under the shrubbery?" she whispered.

"No, no; he's in the path now. He'll be here in two minutes. He'll find us."

He felt her hand tighten on his arm.

"You must go in the skiff, then. It's the only way."

"And let him find you here? And hear my oars? Isabel, listen — there's something I must say."

She flung herself against him, shaken with dry sobs.

"Isabel, just now I didn't tell you everything. He's ruined his mother — taken everything of hers, too. And he's got to tell her; it can't be kept from her."

She uttered a startled sound and drew away.

"Is this the truth? Why didn't you tell me before?"

"He forbade me. You were not to know."

Close above them, in the shrubbery, Stilling rolled out:

"Nita, Juanita,
    Ask thy soul if we must part!"

Wrayford caught her wrist in a hard grasp. "Understand this — if he comes in, he'll find us. And if there's a scandal you'll lose your boy."

She seemed not to hear him. "You — you — you — he'll kill you!" she cried out.

Wrayford laughed and released her. She drew away and stood shrinking close against the wall, her hands pressed to her breast. Wrayford straightened himself and listened intently. Then he dropped to his knees and laid his hands against the boards of the sliding-floor. It yielded at once with a kind of evil alacrity; and at their feet they saw, in the night, another night that moved and shimmered. Wrayford sprang up, and threw himself back against the wall, behind the door.

A key rattled, and after a moment's fumbling the door swung open noisily. Wrayford and Isabel saw a black bulk against the obscurity.

It moved a step, lurched forward, and vanished from them. In the depths there was a long cry and a splash.

"Go! go!" Wrayford cried out, feeling blindly for Isabel in the blackness.

"Go?" she shuddered back, wrenching herself away from him with horror.

He stood still a moment, as if dazed; then she saw him suddenly plunge from her side, and heard another splash far down, and a tumult in the beaten water.

In the darkness she cowered close to the opening, pressing her face over the edge, and frantically crying out the name of each in turn. Suddenly she began to see; the obscurity was less opaque, a faint moon-pallor diluted it. Isabel vaguely discerned the two shapes struggling in the black pit below her; once she saw the gleam of a face. Then she glanced up desperately for some means of rescue, and caught sight of the oars ranged on brackets against the wall. She snatched down the nearest, bent over the opening, and pushed the oar down into the blackness, calling her husband's name.

The clouds had swallowed up the moon again, and she could see nothing below her, but she still heard a tumult in the beaten water.

"Cobham! Cobham!" she screamed.

As if in answer, she felt a mighty clutch on the oar, a clutch that strained her arms to the breaking-point as she tried to brace her knees against the runners of the sliding-floor.

"Hold on! hold on! hold on!" a voice gasped out from below; and she held on, with racked muscles, with bleeding palms, with eyes straining from their sockets, and a heart that tugged at her like the weight on the oar.

Suddenly the weight relaxed, and the oar slipped up through her lacerated hands. She felt a wet bulk scrambling over the edge of the opening, and Stilling's voice, raucous and strange, groaned out, close to her: "God! I thought I was done for."

He staggered to his knees, coughing and sputtering, and the water dripped on her from his clothes.

She flung herself down, straining over the pit. Not a sound came up from it.

"Austin! Austin! Quick! Another oar!" she shrieked.

Stilling gave a cry. "My God! Was it Austin? What in hell — another oar? No, no; untie the skiff, I tell you. But it's no use. Nothing's any use. I felt him lose hold as I came up."

After that she remembered nothing more till, hours later, as it appeared to her, she became dimly aware of her husband's voice, high, hysterical and important, haranguing a group of scared lantern-struck faces that seemed to have sprung up mysteriously about them in the night.

"Poor Austin! Poor fellow . . . terrible loss to me . . . mysterious dispensation. Yes, I *do* feel gratitude — miraculous escape — but I wish he could have known that I was saved!"

NEW ENGLAND RECLUSE

Emily Dickinson [1830–1886]

In 1915 many readers would have agreed with Fred Lewis Pattee in dismissing the poems of Emily Dickinson as "mere conceits, vague jottings. . . . They should have been allowed to perish as their author intended." But only a few years later, in the

1920's, her poems were being widely read with enthusiasm. In 1939 George F. Whicher said of them: "No finer body of lyric poetry by an American author of the nineteenth century can be found." In 1955 Robert E. Spiller pronounced Miss Dickinson "one of the great poets of all time."

This startling change in taste came with recognition of her modernity, her critical and realistic side. Remote though she was from the outward life of the Gilded Age, she shared, as Stanley Williams put it, "the passion for actuality pervading America, expressed now not in the brawling of pioneers but in the gossamer strength of a woman's soul." At the same time she seems to have experienced, far in advance, something like the spirit of revolt, the skepticism, the freedom of expression that flourished after the First World War.

Yet her mind was mainly shaped by two great forces that had already shaped the New England mind. The newer one was the romantic and Transcendental idealism flourishing in her girlhood. It is worth remembering that when she was twenty a friend gave her a copy of Emerson's *Poems*, then out only three years. Like Emerson she came to think of the poet as a prophet of the soul. The other and more fundamental force was the Puritan tradition, very much alive in her immediate environment.

With seven generations of solid New Englanders behind her, Emily was born in Amherst, Massachusetts, in the Connecticut Valley, where the shadow of Jonathan Edwards was still firm. Her lawyer father, treasurer of Amherst College, was a pillar of the First Church, with a heart, said Emily, "pure and terrible." Describing the family, her sister Lavinia said that Emily "had to think — she was the only one of us that had that to do. Father believed; and mother loved; and Austin had Amherst; and I had the family to keep track of." The family observed morning devotions, and on Sundays attended church twice. After schooling at Amherst Academy, Emily went for a year to Mount Holyoke Female Seminary, where young ladies were divided into three groups: those who were professed Christians, those who "had hope," and those "without hope." Emily belonged, uncomfortably, in the third group; nor in later years did her preoccupation with the soul bring her into the fold. Yet she remained immersed, like her forebears, in the Word of God. As Thomas H. Johnson ventures to say, "in almost every poem she wrote, there are echoes of her sensitivity to the idiom of the Bible, and of her dependence upon its imagery for her own striking figures of speech." And her verse meters were based on the old English hymns of Isaac Watts, familiar to her as a child.

After her return from Mount Holyoke, she lived all her days in Amherst, except for some rare visits to Washington, Philadelphia, and Boston. Like her sister, she never married. In Ben Newton she had "a friend, who taught me Immortality," and who, till his early death, encouraged her ambition to write poetry. A few years later came an experience of love that, says her biographer, "may well have been the single most important event in her life" — her love of Charles Wadsworth, of Philadelphia, a married minister with a family. There seems to have been correspondence, and in 1860 he called on her in Amherst. The next year, when he accepted a pastorate in San Francisco, she was in a tumult of misery. It was at this time that she began to dress exclusively in immaculate white. The Queen Recluse (as her friend Bowles called her) was writing "bridal" poems, and many others: two-thirds of all her poems seem to have been composed within eight years.

By 1870 Miss Dickinson, isolated in her "dear home," saw only family and friends. "I do not cross my father's ground to any house or town." If not wide, her experience was deep and intense. "I find ecstasy in living," she said, and she found it also in writing about living, about the great themes: nature, love, death, immortality. In her lifetime only seven poems appeared in print, anonymously, but the total number eventually gathered into an authoritative edition of *The Poems of Emily Dickinson* (the work of Thomas H. Johnson, in three volumes) amounted to 1775 poems.

The 47 poems printed below are from the Johnson text, which follows, so far as possible, the order of composition. Perhaps a good way to begin is to read first poems 585 and 1463.

Further reading: More of the poems. *The Letters of Emily Dickinson*, ed. T. H. Johnson, 3 vols., 1958. T. H. Johnson, *Emily Dickinson: An Interpretive Biography*, 1955. G. F. Whicher, *This Was a Poet: A Critical Biography*, 1939.

Letters

The letters of Emily Dickinson share the qualities of coy and cryptic ambiguity found in her verse. Longing for poetic sympathy, she addressed the following to T. W. Higginson, a critic and essayist whose work she admired. The first letter contained four of her poems for his comment, and no signature. Instead her name was enclosed on a separate card. Note the changes in the signatures on succeeding letters.

15 April 1862

Mr. Higginson,

Are you too deeply occupied to say if my Verse is alive?

The Mind is so near itself — it cannot see, distinctly — and I have none to ask —

Should you think it breathed — and had you the leisure to tell me, I should feel quick gratitude —

If I make the mistake — that you dare to tell me — would give me sincerer honor — toward you —

I enclose my name — asking you, if you please — Sir — to tell me what is true?

That you will not betray me — it is needless to ask — since Honor is it's own pawn —

25 April 1862

Mr. Higginson,

Your kindness claimed earlier gratitude — but I was ill — and write today, from my pillow.

Thank you for the surgery — it was not so painful as I supposed. I bring you others — as you ask — though they might not differ —

While my thought is undressed — I can make the distinction, but when I put them in the Gown — they look alike, and numb.

You asked how old I was? I made no verse — but one or two — until this winter — Sir —

I had a terror — since September — I could tell to none — and so I sing, as the Boy does by the Burying Ground — because I am afraid — You inquire my Books — For Poets — I have Keats — and Mr and Mrs Browning. For Prose — Mr Ruskin — Sir Thomas Browne — and the Revelations. I went to school — but in your manner of the phrase — had no education. When a little Girl, I had a friend, who taught me Immortality — but venturing too near, himself — he never returned — Soon after, my Tutor, died — and for several years, my Lexicon — was my only companion — Then I found one more — but he was not contented I be his scholar — so he left the Land.

You ask of my Companions Hills — Sir — and the Sundown — and a Dog — large as myself, that my Father bought me — They are better than Beings — because they know — but do not tell — and the noise in the Pool, at Noon — excels my Piano. I have a Brother and Sister — My Mother does not care for thought — and Father, too busy with his Briefs — to notice what we do — He buys me many Books — but begs me not to read them — because he fears they joggle the Mind. They are religious — except me — and address an Eclipse, every morning — whom they call their "Father." But I fear my story fatigues you — I would like to learn — Could you tell me how to grow — or is it unconveyed — like Melody — or Witchcraft?

You speak of Mr. Whitman — I never read his Book — but was told that he was disgraceful —

I read Miss Prescott's "Circumstance," but it followed me, in the Dark — so I avoided her —

Two Editors of Journals came to my Father's House, this winter — and asked me for my Mind — and when I asked them "Why," they said I was penurious — and they, would use it for the World —

I could not weigh myself — Myself —

My size felt small — to me — I read your Chapter in the Atlantic — and experienced honor for you — I was sure you would not reject a confiding question —

Is this — Sir — what you asked me to tell you?

> Your friend,
> E — Dickinson.

7 June 1862

Dear friend.

Your letter gave no Drunkenness, because I tasted Rum before — Domingo comes but once — yet I have had few pleasures so deep as your opinion, and if I tried to thank you, my tears would block my tongue —

My dying Tutor told me that he would like to live till I had been a poet, but Death was much of Mob as I could master — then — And when far afterward — a sudden light on Orchards, or a new fashion in the wind troubled my attention — I felt a palsy, here — the Verses just relieve —

Your second letter surprised me, and for a moment, swung — I had not supposed it. Your first — gave no dishonor, because the True — are not ashamed — I thanked you for your justice — but could not drop the Bells whose jingling cooled my Tramp — Perhaps the Balm, seemed better, because you bled me, first.

I smile when you suggest that I delay "to publish" — that being foreign to my thought, as Firmament to Fin —

If fame belonged to me, I could not escape her — if she did not, the longest day would pass me on the chase — and the approbation of my Dog, would forsake me — then — My Barefoot-Rank is better —

You think my gait "spasmodic" — I am in danger — Sir —

You think me "uncontrolled" — I have no Tribunal.

Would you have time to be the "friend" you should think I need? I have a little shape — it would not crowd your Desk — nor make much Racket as the Mouse, that dents your Galleries — * * *

But, will you be my Preceptor, Mr Higginson?

> Your friend
> E Dickinson —

🐦 The following letter was in answer to a request by Higginson for a photograph of his "enigmatical correspondent."

July 1862

5 Could you believe me — without? I had no portrait, now, but am small, like the Wren, and my Hair is bold, like the Chestnut Bur — and my eyes, like the Sherry in the Glass, that the Guest leaves — Would this do just as well?

10 It often alarms Father — He says Death might occur, and he has Molds of all the rest — but has no Mold of me, but I noticed the Quick wore off those things, in a few days, and forestall the dishonor — You will think no caprice of 15 me —

You said "Dark." I know the Butterfly — and the Lizard — and the Orchis —

Are not those *your* Countrymen?

I am happy to be your scholar, and will de-20 serve the kindness, I cannot repay.

If you truly consent, I recite, now —

Will you tell me my fault, frankly as to yourself, for I had rather wince, than die. Men do not call the surgeon, to commend — the Bone, 25 but to set it, Sir, and fracture within, is more critical. And for this, Preceptor, I shall bring you — Obedience — the Blossom from my Garden, and every gratitude I know. Perhaps you smile at me. I could not stop for that — My 30 Business is Circumference — An ignorance, not of Customs, but if caught with the Dawn — or the Sunset see me — Myself the only Kangaroo among the Beauty, Sir, if you please, it afflicts me, and I thought that instruction would take 35 it away.

Because you have much business, beside the growth of me — you will appoint, yourself, how often I shall come — without your inconvenience. And if at any time — you regret you re-40 ceived me, or I prove a different fabric to that you supposed — you must banish me —

When I state myself, as the Representative of the Verse — it does not mean — me — but a supposed person. You are true, about the "per-45 fection."

Today, makes Yesterday mean.

You spoke of Pippa Passes — I never heard anybody speak of Pippa Passes — before.

You see my posture is benighted.

50 To thank you, baffles me. Are you perfectly powerful? Had I a pleasure you had not, I could delight to bring it.

> Your Scholar

Poems

67

"Her theme was precisely the perception of value won through deprivation. It was not sight, she knew, that could be won out of blindness, but a full appreciation of the miraculousness and preciousness of sight. So to 'comprehend' (not to taste) a nectar, to 'tell the definition' (not to have the experience) of victory, one must suffer thirst and defeat." (G. F. Whicher). The date of the poem is 1859.

Success is counted sweetest
By those who ne'er succeed.
To comprehend a nectar
Requires sorest need.

Not one of all the purple Host   5
Who took the Flag today
Can tell the definition
So clear of Victory

As he defeated — dying —
On whose forbidden ear   10
The distant strains of triumph
Burst agonized and clear!

76

Exultation is the going
Of an inland soul to sea,
Past the houses — past the headlands —
Into deep Eternity —

Bred as we, among the mountains,   5
Can the sailor understand
The divine intoxication
Of the first league out from land?

89

Some things that fly there be —
Birds — Hours — the Bumblebee —
Of these no Elegy.

Some things that stay there be —
Grief — Hills — Eternity —   5
Nor this behooveth me.

There are that resting, rise.
Can I expound the skies?
How still the Riddle lies!

126

To fight aloud, is very brave —
But *gallanter*, I know
Who charge within the bosom
The Cavalry of Wo —

Who win, and nations do not see —   5
Who fall — and none observe —
Whose dying eyes, no Country
Regards with patriot love —

We trust, in plumed procession
For such, the Angels go —   10
Rank after Rank, with even feet —
And Uniforms of Snow.

189

It's such a little thing to weep —
So short a thing to sigh —
And yet — by Trades — the size of *these*
We men and women die!

210

The thought beneath so slight a film —
Is more distinctly seen —
As laces just reveal the surge —
Or Mists — the Appenine —

214

I taste a liquor never brewed —
From Tankards scooped in Pearl —
Not all the Frankfort Berries
Yield such an Alcohol!

Inebriate of Air — am I —   5
And Debauchee of Dew —
Reeling — thro endless summer days —
From inns of Molten Blue —

When "Landlords" turn the drunken Bee
Out of the Foxglove's door —   10
When Butterflies — renounce their "drams" —
I shall but drink the more!

Till Seraphs swing their snowy Hats —
And Saints — to windows run —

To see the little Tippler   15
From Manzanilla come!

249

📯 This poem was written about 1861. In 1891
Col. Higginson wrote to Mrs. Todd (they were
editing a selection of the poems): "One poem only
I dread a little to print — that wonderful 'Wild
Nights,' — lest the malignant read into it more
than that virgin recluse ever dreamed of putting
there."

> Wild Nights — Wild Nights!
> Were I with thee
> Wild Nights should be
> Our luxury!
>
> Futile — the Winds —   5
> To a Heart in port —
> Done with the Compass —
> Done with the Chart!
>
> Rowing in Eden —
> Ah, the Sea!
> Might I but moor — Tonight —   10
> In Thee!

254

"Hope" is the thing with feathers —
That perches in the soul —
And sings the tune without the words —
And never stops — at all —

And sweetest — in the Gale — is heard —   5
And sore must be the storm —
That could abash the little Bird
That kept so many warm —

I've heard it in the chillest land —
And on the strangest Sea —   10
Yet, never, in Extremity,
It asked a crumb — of Me.

258

There's a certain Slant of light,
Winter Afternoons —

That oppresses, like the Heft
Of Cathedral Tunes —

Heavenly Hurt, it gives us —   5
We can find no scar,
But internal difference,
Where the Meanings, are —

None may teach it — Any —
'Tis the Seal Despair —   10
An imperial affliction
Sent us of the Air —

When it comes, the Landscape listens —
Shadows — hold their breath —
When it goes, 'tis like the Distance   15
On the look of Death —

265

Where Ships of Purple — gently toss —
On Seas of Daffodil —
Fantastic Sailors — mingle —
And then — the Wharf is still!

303

📯 Miss Dickinson wrote this poem about 1862,
when her seclusion was deepening. "She has in mind
a way of life," says Johnson, "and she will remain
unmoved even though chariots pause at her low
gate or an emperor kneels upon her mat, presumably to beg her to alter her convictions or to offer
inducements for accepting other close associations.
. . . The poem is universalized, but at the personal
level it states her intent to live by her convictions."
How does the rhythm itself suggest her decisiveness?

The Soul selects her own Society —
Then — shuts the Door —
To her divine Majority —
Present no more —

Unmoved — she notes the Chariots — paus-
ing —   , 5
At her low Gate —
Unmoved — an Emperor be kneeling
Upon her Mat —

I've known her — from an ample nation —
Choose One —   10
Then — close the Valves of her attention —
Like Stone —

304

How put in words a sunrise — its beauty, brilliance, freshness? Miss Dickinson's way, here, is to toss before us a series of metaphors, implied comparisons, that spring into her mind. They are not intended to cohere, but individually to play their part in the whole. Some of them describe the greater by means of the smaller (the rising sun — the flash of a fired musket; the wide landscape — the Victorian "parlor"). With what effect? Some may seem far-fetched, roguishly indecorous — or are they justified because poetry, like humor, rests largely on the unexpected?

The Day came slow — till Five o'clock —
Then sprang before the Hills
Like Hindered Rubies — or the Light
A Sudden Musket — spills —

The Purple could not keep the East —   5
The Sunrise shook abroad
Like Breadths of Topaz — packed a Night —
The Lady just unrolled —

The Happy Winds — their Timbrels took —
The Birds — in docile Rows   10
Arranged themselves around their Prince
The Wind — is Prince of Those —

The Orchard sparkled like a Jew —
How mighty 'twas — to be
A Guest in this stupendous place —   15
The Parlor — of the Day

338

I know that He exists.
Somewhere — in Silence —
He has hid his rare life
From our gross eyes.

'Tis an instant's play.   5
'Tis a fond Ambush —
Just to make Bliss
Earn her own surprise!

But — should the play
Prove piercing earnest —   10
Should the glee — glaze —
In Death's — stiff — stare —

Would not the fun
Look too expensive!
Would not the jest —   15
Have crawled too far!

410

The first Day's Night had come —
And grateful that a thing
So terrible — had been endured —
I told my Soul to sing —

She said her Strings were snapt —   5
Her Bow — to Atoms blown —
And so to mend her — gave me work
Until another Morn —

And then — a Day as huge
As Yesterdays in pairs,   10
Unrolled it's horror in my face —
Until it blocked my eyes —

My Brain — begun to laugh —
I mumbled — like a fool —
And tho' 'tis Years ago — that Day —   15
My Brain keeps giggling — still.

And Something's odd — within —
That person that I was —
And this One — do not feel the same —
Could it be Madness — this?   20

435

Much Madness is divinest Sense —
To a discerning Eye —
Much Sense — the starkest Madness —
'Tis the Majority
In this, as All, prevail —   5
Assent — and you are sane —
Demur — you're straightway dangerous —
And handled with a Chain —

441

This is my letter to the World
That never wrote to Me —
The simple News that Nature told —
With tender Majesty

Her Message is committed   5
To Hands I cannot see —
For love of Her — Sweet — countrymen —
Judge tenderly — of Me

465

I heard a Fly buzz — when I died —
The Stillness in the Room
Was like the Stillness in the Air —
Between the Heaves of Storm —

The Eyes around — had wrung them dry —
And Breaths were gathering firm
For that last Onset — when the King   6
Be witnessed — in the Room —

I willed my Keepsakes — Signed away
What portion of me be   10
Assignable — and then it was
There interposed a Fly —

With Blue — uncertain stumbling Buzz —
Between the light — and me —
And then the Windows failed — and then   15
I could not see to see —

466

'Tis little I — could care for Pearls —
Who own the ample sea —
Or Brooches — when the Emperor —
With Rubies — pelteth me —

Or Gold — who am the Prince of Mines —   5
Or Diamonds — when have I
A Diadem to fit a Dome —
Continual upon me —

511

If you were coming in the Fall,
I'd brush the Summer by
With half a smile, and half a spurn,
As Housewives do, a Fly.

If I could see you in a year,   5
I'd wind the months in balls —
And put them each in separate Drawers,
For fear the numbers fuse —

If only Centuries, delayed,
I'd count them on my Hand,   10
Subtracting, till my fingers dropped
Into Van Dieman's Land.

If certain, when this life was out —
That your's and mine, should be —
I'd toss it yonder, like a Rind,   15
And take Eternity —

But, now, uncertain of the length
Of this, that is between,
It goads me, like the Goblin Bee —
That will not state — it's sting.   20

526

The statement may be strictly the poet's own, or an echo from romanticism. Compare in Coleridge's Harz Forest poem:

> ". . . outward forms the loftiest, still receive
> Their finer influence from the Life within; —
> Fair cyphers else."

Or in Coleridge's "Dejection: An Ode":

> ". . . we receive but what we give,
> And in our life alone does Nature live."

To hear an Oriole sing
May be a common thing —
Or only a divine.

It is not of the Bird
Who sings the same, unheard,   5
As unto Crowd —

The Fashion of the Ear
Attireth that it hear
In Dun, or fair —

So whether it be Rune,   10
Or whether it be none
Is of within.

The "Tune is in the Tree —"
The Skeptic — showeth me —
"No Sir! In Thee!"   15

585

How successful was Emily Dickinson in her attempt to invest a mechanical product of science with aesthetic effects? This poem, written about 1862, is a charmingly Dickinsonian result of the coming of technology. Emily's father, Edward Dickinson, took part in 1853 in establishing the Amherst & Belchertown Railway — to us a perfect name to match Emily's dinkey engine! Her iron horse will remind us of Thoreau's in the chapter "Sounds" of *Walden*. The poem may be compared, illuminatingly, with Whitman's "To a Locomotive in Winter" (page 638) as to purpose, design, attitude, tone, verse medium.

Miss Dickinson was given to using words in more or less unusual senses. Examples in this poem: "prodigious," i.e. marvellous, out of the course of nature; "Boanerges" ("sons of thunder"), generally applied to preachers and orators, here made to serve for a mythical horse that hoots and neighs.

I like to see it lap the Miles —
And lick the Valleys up —
And stop to feed itself at Tanks —
And then — prodigious step

Around a Pile of Mountains —   5
And supercilious peer
In Shanties — by the sides of Roads —
And then a Quarry pare

To fit it's sides
And crawl between   10
Complaining all the while
In horrid — hooting stanza —
Then chase itself down Hill —

And neigh like Boanerges —
Then — prompter than a Star   15
Stop — docile and omnipotent
At it's own stable door —

609

I Years had been from Home
And now before the Door
I dared not enter, lest a Face
I never saw before

Stare stolid into mine   5
And ask my Business there —
"My Business but a Life I left
Was such remaining there?"

I leaned upon the Awe —
I lingered with Before —   10
The Second like an Ocean rolled
And broke against my ear —

I laughed a crumbling Laugh
That I could fear a Door
Who Consternation compassed   15
And never winced before.

I fitted to the Latch
My Hand, with trembling care
Lest back the awful Door should spring
And leave me in the Floor —   20

Then moved my Fingers off
As cautiously as Glass
And held my ears, and like a Thief
Fled gasping from the House —

632

The Brain — is wider than the Sky —
For — put them side by side —
The one the other will contain
With ease — and You — beside —

The Brain is deeper than the sea —   5
For — hold them — Blue to Blue —
The one the other will absorb —
As Sponges — Buckets — do —

The Brain is just the weight of God —
For — Heft them — Pound for Pound —   10
And they will differ — if they do —
As Syllable from Sound —

640

I cannot live with You —
It would be Life —
And Life is over there —
Behind the Shelf

The Sexton keeps the Key to —   5
Putting up
Our Life — His Porcelain —
Like a Cup —

Discarded of the Housewife —
Quaint — or Broke —   10
A newer Sevres pleases —
Old Ones crack —

I could not die — with You —
For One must wait
To shut the Other's Gaze down —   15
You — could not —

And I — Could I stand by
And see You — freeze —
Without my Right of Frost —
Death's privilege?   20

Nor could I rise — with You —
Because Your Face
Would put out Jesus' —
That New Grace

Glow plain — and foreign   25
On my homesick Eye —
Except that You than He
Shone closer by —

They'd judge Us — How —
For You — served Heaven — You know,   30
Or sought to —
I could not —

Because You saturated Sight —
And I had no more Eyes
For sordid excellence   35
As Paradise

And were You lost, I would be —
Though My Name
Rang loudest
On the Heavenly fame —   40

And were You — saved —
And I — condemned to be
Where You were not —
That self — were Hell to Me —

So We must meet apart —   45
You there — I — here —
With just the Door ajar
That Oceans are — and Prayer —
And that White Sustenance —
Despair —   50

701

A Thought went up my mind today —
That I have had before —
But did not finish — some way back —
I could not fix the Year —

Nor where it went — nor why it came   5
The second time to me —
Nor definitely, what it was —
Have I the Art to say —

But somewhere — in my Soul — I know —
I've met the Thing before —   10
It just reminded me — 'twas all —
And came my way no more —

712

This is one of Emily Dickinson's best poems.
Allen Tate, in *Reactionary Essays*, ventures to say it
"is one of the greatest in the English language; it is
flawless to the last detail. The rhythm charges with
movement the pattern of suspended action back of
the poem. Every image is precise and, moreover, not
merely beautiful, but inextricably fused with the
central idea. Every image extends and intensifies

every other. The third stanza especially shows Miss
Dickinson's power to fuse, into a single order of perception, a heterogeneous series: the children, the
grain, and the setting sun (time) have the same
degree of credibility; the first subtly preparing for the
last. The sharp *gazing* before *grain* instils into nature
a kind of cold vitality of which the qualitative richness has infinite depth. The content of death in the
poem eludes forever any explicit definition. He is a
gentleman taking a lady out for a drive. But note the
restraint that keeps the poet from carrying this so
far that it is ludicrous and incredible; and note the
subtly interfused erotic motive, which the idea of
death has presented to every romantic poet, love
being a symbol interchangeable with death. The
terror of death is objectified through this figure of
the genteel driver, who is made ironically to serve the
end of Immortality. This is the heart of the poem:
she has presented a typical Christian theme in all its
final irresolution, without making any final statement
about it."

Because I could not stop for Death —
He kindly stopped for me —
The Carriage held but just Ourselves —
And Immortality.

We slowly drove — He knew no haste   5
And I had put away
My labor and my leisure too,
For His Civility —

We passed the School, where Children strove
At Recess — in the Ring —   10
We passed the Fields of Gazing Grain —
We passed the Setting Sun —

Or rather — He passed Us —
The Dews drew quivering and chill —
For only Gossamer, my Gown —   15
My Tippet — only Tulle —

We paused before a House that seemed
A Swelling of the Ground —
The Roof was scarcely visible —
The Cornice — in the Ground —   20

Since then — 'tis Centuries — and yet
Feels shorter than the Day
I first surmised the Horses Heads
Were toward Eternity —

739

I many times thought Peace had come
When Peace was far away —

As Wrecked Men — deem they sight the
　　Land —
At Centre of the Sea —

And struggle slacker — but to prove 　5
As hopelessly as I —
How many the fictitious Shores —
Or any Harbor be —

747

It dropped so low — in my Regard —
I heard it hit the Ground —
And go to pieces on the Stones
At bottom of my Mind —

Yet blamed the Fate that fractured — *less* 　5
Than I reviled Myself,
For entertaining Plated Wares
Upon my Silver Shelf —

764

Presentiment — is that long Shadow — on the
　　Lawn —
Indicative that Suns go down —

The Notice to the startled Grass
That Darkness — is about to pass —

816

A Death blow is a Life blow to Some
Who till they died, did not alive become —
Who had they lived, had died but when
They died, Vitality begun.

986

A narrow Fellow in the Grass
Occasionally rides —
You may have met Him — did you not
His notice sudden is —

The Grass divides as with a Comb — 　5
A spotted shaft is seen —
And then it closes at your feet
And opens further on —

He likes a Boggy Acre
A Floor too cool for Corn — 　10
Yet when a Boy, and Barefoot —
I more than once at Noon
Have passed, I thought, a Whip lash

Unbraiding in the Sun
When stooping to secure it 　15
It wrinkled, and was gone —

Several of Nature's People
I know, and they know me —
I feel for them a transport
Of cordiality — 　20

But never met this Fellow
Attended, or alone
Without a tighter breathing
And Zero at the Bone —

1030

That Such have died enable Us
The tranquiller to die —
That Such have lived,
Certificate for Immortality.

1052

I never saw a Moor —
I never saw the Sea —
Yet know I how the Heather looks
And what a Billow be.

I never spoke with God 　5
Nor visited in Heaven —
Yet certain am I of the spot
As if the Checks were given —

1075

The Sky is low — the Clouds are mean.
A Travelling Flake of Snow
Across a Barn or through a Rut
Debates if it will go —

A Narrow Wind complains all Day 　5
How some one treated him
Nature, like Us is sometimes caught
Without her Diadem.

1078

❧ Facing a great fact, the poet uses simple words,
housekeeping allusions, and a touch of irony, in two
little but resonant stanzas.

The Bustle in a House
The Morning after Death
Is solemnest of industries
Enacted upon Earth —

The Sweeping up the Heart   5
And putting Love away
We shall not want to use again
Until Eternity.

1100

The last Night that She lived
It was a Common Night
Except the Dying — this to Us
Made Nature different

We noticed smallest things —   5
Things overlooked before
By this great light upon our Minds
Italicized — as 'twere.

As We went out and in
Between Her final Room   10
And Rooms where Those to be alive
Tomorrow were, a Blame

That Others could exist
While She must finish quite
A Jealousy for Her arose   15
So nearly infinite —

We waited while She passed —
It was a narrow time —
Too jostled were Our Souls to speak
At length the notice came.   20

She mentioned, and forgot —
Then lightly as a Reed
Bent to the Water, struggled scarce —
Consented, and was dead —

And We — We placed the Hair —   25
And drew the Head erect —
And then an awful leisure was
Belief to regulate —

1176

We never know how high we are
Till we are asked to rise
And then if we are true to plan
Our statures touch the skies —

The Heroism we recite   5
Would be a normal thing
Did not ourselves the Cubits warp
For fear to be a King —

1207

He preached upon "Breadth" till it argued him
    narrow —
The Broad are too broad to define
And of "Truth" until it proclaimed him a
    Liar —
The Truth never flaunted a Sign —

Simplicity fled from his counterfeit presence   5
As Gold the Pyrites would shun —
What confusion would cover the innocent
    Jesus
To meet so enabled a Man!

1463

🐾 The poem, like the hummingbird, is small and quickly gone — but rammed with life. "Here is the whole *sensation* of hummingbird: first, a dazzle of sudden sense impressions, movement, motion of wings, color, and whir (in the reiterated *r*'s), all at once; then (the bird's departure taken for granted) the emptiness emphasized by the clear picture of nodding blossoms; and finally the startled mind of the (assumed) spectator regaining its poise with a whimsical comment" (G. F. Whicher).

A Route of Evanescence
With a revolving Wheel —
A Resonance of Emerald —
A Rush of Cochineal —
And every Blossom on the Bush   5
Adjusts it's tumbled Head —
The mail from Tunis, probably,
An easy Morning's Ride —

1510

How happy is the little Stone
That rambles in the Road alone,
And does'nt care about Careers
And Exigencies never fears —
Whose Coat of elemental Brown   5
A passing Universe put on,
And independent as the Sun
Associates or glows alone,
Fulfilling absolute Decree
In casual simplicity —   10

1587

He ate and drank the precious Words —
His Spirit grew robust —
He knew no more that he was poor,
Nor that his frame was Dust —

He danced along the dingy Days   5
And this Bequest of Wings
Was but a Book — What Liberty
A loosened spirit brings —

1593

There came a Wind like a Bugle —
It quivered through the Grass
And a Green Chill upon the Heat
So ominous did pass
We barred the Windows and the Doors   5
As from an Emerald Ghost —
The Doom's electric Moccasin
That very instant passed —
On a strange Mob of panting Trees
And Fences fled away   10
And Rivers where the Houses ran
Those looked that lived — that Day —
The Bell within the steeple wild
The flying tidings told —
How much can come   15
And much can go,
And yet abide the World!

1624

Apparently with no surprise
To any happy Flower
The Frost beheads it at it's play —
In accidental power —
The blonde Assassin passes on —   5
The Sun proceeds unmoved
To measure off another Day
For an Approving God.

1732

"No autograph copy of this justly famous poem is known. Unless one eventually is found, any speculation about its autobiographical import is vain." (Johnson.)

My life closed twice before its close;
It yet remains to see
If Immortality unveil
A third event to me,

So huge, so hopeless to conceive   5
As these that twice befel.
Parting is all we know of heaven,
And all we need of hell.

1755

To make a prairie it takes a clover and one bee,
One clover, and a bee,
And revery.
The revery alone will do,
If bees are few.   5

1760

Elysium is as far as to
The very nearest Room
If in that Room a Friend await
Felicity or Doom —

What fortitude the Soul contains,   5
That it can so endure
The accent of a coming Foot —
The opening of a Door —

And this Bouquet of Wings

And Fences fled away

How much can come

If bees are few.

The realism of bleakness and desolation: "Landscape Near Chicago," by Aaron Bohrod, 1934

THE REALISTIC MOVEMENT
AND NEW DIRECTIONS

Disillusionment and the Search for Values

"A little farther into time and pain" — E. A. ROBINSON

In the eighteen-nineties defeated farmers headed east scrawled on their wagons: "In God we trusted, in Kansas we busted." In the West generally (and the South as well) the Gilded Age had finally brought them to despair. They could no longer endure their harsh struggle with nature, magnified by a series of drought years, and their economic plight, summed up by the phrase "10 cent corn and 10 per cent interest." For an understanding of the uprising of the farmers William Dean Howells pointed to Hamlin Garland's volume of short stories, *Main-Travelled Roads*, written in a new, bitter realism. "The stories," said Howells, "are full of those gaunt, grim, sordid, pathetic, ferocious figures, whom our satirists find so easy to caricature as Hayseeds, and whose blind groping for fairer conditions is so grotesque to the newspapers and so menacing to the politicians." The menace to the politicians was real. Working outside the Republican and Democratic parties, the farm group won in 1890 four seats in the Senate and over fifty in the House. Then they organized the Populist party and two years later held a national convention at St. Louis. In a preamble to their platform they denounced the abuses of irresponsible capitalism.

Industrial workers were as resentful as the farmers. In 1890 there were more strikes than in any other year of the century, and in the next years came two specially alarming strikes, that in the works of Carnegie's steel company at Homestead, Pennsylvania, and that at the Pullman Palace Car Company in Illinois. The stock market collapsed, rural banks fell like leaves, wages and prices dropped with a thud, strikes multiplied, and "Coxey's Army" of unemployed marched from the Middle West to the national capital. The year 1894 was the darkest the United States had known since the Civil War. Small wonder that thoughtful Americans, seeing the drift of economic individualism toward class conflict and anarchy, were attracted by the promises of socialism. Socialism had a winning aspect in Edward Bellamy's novel *Looking Backward* (1888), which reached a sale of at least 500,000 copies and inspired the Bellamy clubs that assailed the established disorder. Even the genial Howells, at fifty, took a new turn, writing a series of economic novels, hoping, like Bellamy, that democracy could peacefully introduce the principles of collectivism.

Life in the 1890's was not, of course, all disorder and conflict. There were curious or astonishing events, as when Elwood Haynes drove a horseless carriage through the streets of Chicago in 1895. At this time the bicycle craze was at its height; while older people might deplore, gay young things succumbed to the lure of the demon Speed, flashing, with tinkling bells, past the smartest horse-drawn equipages. For women there was one awkward feature — long skirts often caught in the wheels. The ideal young woman of the time, fully dressed even at the bathing resorts, was imaged in Gibson's pen-and-ink drawings, "a creature rather overwhelming in her perfections," as Isham, an art historian,

(*continued on page* 838)

William Faulkner

In a series of novels and stories, Faulkner has created an epitome of the history of the South and of Mississippi — and seen reality both comic and tragic.

Robert Frost in his Eighties

America's most popular and beloved poet in a characteristic pose, philosophizing on a stone wall in New England, "north of Boston."

Ernest Hemingway

Hemingway's masculine writing shows his love of action —a unique combination with his subtle perception of contemporary life.

Carl Sandburg's Chicago

A view of the Chicago River, artery of commerce running west and south from the heart of the city — "the nation's freight handler."

"Baptism in Kansas," by John Steuart Curry

Revivalist religion has lasted longest in rural communities where old customs cling.

put it, "with no occupation in life save to be adored by young athletes in tennis clothes or by disreputable foreign noblemen."

Literary taste was still romantic, well satisfied with the fiction of Marion Crawford, probably the highest paid novelist of the decade, or with that of such English novelists as Anthony Hope, whose entertaining *Prisoner of Zenda* dealt with a mythical kingdom, and George Du Maurier, whose *Trilby* told the story of an artist's model in what was to Americans far-away Paris. Yet American readers could also respond, as we have seen, to a thought-provoking novel like Bellamy's picture of a socialist utopia. They could even make a best seller of a deadly serious work, *Degeneration*, by Max Nordau, a Hungarian-German who announced that nervous exhaustion was about to bring about the collapse of Occidental civilization.

NATURALISM

Naturalism in Fiction. But the reading public was not prepared for the plain story of an everyday instance of degeneration right around the corner — in the slums. Brought up in a brutalized environment in lower Manhattan, a girl is driven from her home by her drunken mother, works in a sweatshop, is seduced by a bartender, lives with him till abandoned, becomes a prostitute, and drowns herself. This is the story of *Maggie: A Girl of the Streets.* Clearly the novelist, Stephen Crane, had chosen to ignore those pleasant aspects of life which to Howells were typically American, and to ignore equally the popular taste for romantic make-believe. Yet his dismal theme might have been tolerated, had Crane handled it with humanitarian sentiment or taught a moral lesson. Instead, he simply tried to tell the truth, amorally, without any judgment upon the characters' actions. The result was that he could not find a magazine editor or book publisher willing to risk such a radical departure. On borrowed money he had it privately printed in 1893. Hardly any copies were sold, and three more years elapsed before his success with his brilliantly impressionistic *Red Badge of Courage* made possible the publication of *Maggie*. In this awkward fashion a new type of realism was introduced into American literature, an advanced realism commonly called naturalism.

Main Street, Sauk Center, Minnesota

This is the "Main Street" Sinclair Lewis made famous. It happens to be his own Sauk Center, but it could be any of a thousand, anywhere in the U.S.A. Notice that "flivvers" and horses are still on speaking acquaintance.

How did our naturalism beginning in the 1890's (as well as the earlier naturalism in Europe) differ from the mild realism of the Gilded Age? Superficially, it differed in subject-matter. A realist like Howells, for example, was generally content to hold the mirror up to the everyday life of the "good society" in which he moved. In his forty volumes, as O. W. Firkins pointed out, "Adultery is never pictured; seduction never; divorce once and sparingly (*A Modern Instance*), marriage discordant to the point of cleavage, only once and in the same novel with the divorce; crime only once with any fullness." But it was precisely such "unpleasant" or "ugly" themes that the naturalists sought out and analyzed.

Still, unpleasant themes do not alone suffice to mark a work as naturalistic, for they have abounded in literature ever since Greek tragedy. The fundamental sign of naturalism is a certain interpretation of life, a particular philosophy. Realism, as Howells conceived of it, was as "unphilosophized as the light of common day." It wished to be in harmony with the spirit of science; it did not wish to be committed to any philosophy. But naturalism ventured to philosophize. Using scientific concepts as a basis, it assumed or declared that the forces at work in nature are in truth the only forces at work in man too. It held that the universe is completely indifferent to the preferences and desires that seem so important to us. It therefore threw out the possibility of anything in our experience that could be called peculiarly human (humanism) or supernatural (religion). Man is subject to the law of nature, and no other. He has no moral freedom to act as he chooses. "Build your own world"? Stuff and nonsense! — your world is built for you, by heredity and environment. We are all like Crane's Maggie, though perhaps more fortunate. With this biological determinism often went pessimism, the gloomiest view, as if the drift of things is always toward the worst. Nature is not only indifferent, it is hostile. Anatole France expressed the pessimistic mood when he said, "If we knew all, we could not endure life an hour."

Such are the ideas implied by a definition of naturalism in the *American College Dictionary*: "A theory, as practiced by Emile Zola, Stephen Crane and others, which applied scientific concepts and methods to such problems as plot development and characterization." Zola provided American writers with examples (such as *Nana*) and also a forthright statement of theory (*The Experimental Novel*). But the work of this French writer was only one of the forces making for naturalism in the United States.

A mood favorable to such a school was a waning optimism in the face of the darkening economic and social scene, already glanced at above — the distress of the farmers and industrial laborers, the bitter conflict between the haves and the have-nots, intensified by a drawn-out depression. At the same time various intellectual influences, the acids of modernity (chief among them Darwinism), were eating into the foundations of religious and moral standards, already weakened in the Gilded Age. In literature, the older realism, having stressed the commonplace and trivial, made it easy to pass on to the unpleasant and ugly, as Garland had shown in his stories and presently showed in his critical statement, *Crumbling Idols*. Instead of conforming to the superficial popular taste, the most vital writers of this time penetrated to deeper currents and produced fiction that in varying degrees expressed a stark naturalism. Hence we have Crane's *Maggie, The Red Badge of Courage, The Open Boat*; Frank Norris's *McTeague, The Octopus, The Pit*; Jack London's *Sea Wolf, The Call of the Wild*; Mark Twain's *The Mysterious Stranger*; Theodore Dreiser's *Sister Carrie* and *Jennie Gerhardt*. In the 1890's and early 1900's romantic dreams and Victorian prettiness and evasion encountered a thoroughgoing revolt.

The naturalistic emphasis on the unpleasant also played a part in the art of painting. This was the time of the so-called "Ash Can School" of Henri, Davies, Glackens, Sloan, Luks, and others. They revolted against Art for Art's Sake, immersed themselves in the turbid currents of life, and came up with canvases, usually dismal in coloring, depicting city streets, tenements, dance halls, barrooms, prizefights, drunks, slatterns. In 1908 they defied the official art of the time by holding in New York an exhibition daily attended by hundreds, including the horrified art critics.

Meanwhile "muckrakers" were pouring into the magazines — *McClure's, Collier's, Cosmopolitan* — sensational revelations of business and government scandals, the backwash of *laissez-faire*. Some of the ablest reappeared in book form: Ida M. Tarbell's *History of the Standard Oil Company*, Lincoln Steffens' *The Shame of the Cities*. Attacks were made on every front — railroads, insurance companies, patent medicines, juvenile delinquency, the delinquency of U. S. Senators. Novelists lent a hand. Frank Norris showed up the Southern Pacific Railroad and the wheat exchange. With fascinated abhorrence people read *The Jungle*, Upton Sinclair's novel exposing the Chicago meat packers, which caused the president, Theodore Roosevelt, to send for the author and to urge a meat-inspection bill in Congress. Yet in this same year, 1906, the heaping up of evidence of rottenness in American civilization caused Roosevelt to protest against the protesters. He called them muckrakers, deriving the word, as he explained, from a character in Bunyan's *Pilgrim's Progress* "who was offered the celestial crown for his muck-rake, but would neither look up nor regard the crown he was offered, but continued to rake the filth of the floor."

The Revival of Poetry

❧ *The "New Poetry."* This brings us, a long way around, to the creative renewal of poetry, a vigorous and varied outburst in the midst of an age of science and technology, when even philosophy (William James, John Dewey) stressed practicality. During and after the Gilded Age, it had looked as though prose was the natural vehicle for a realistic movement in harmony with the modern outlook. Poetry had seemed asleep, except for Crane's experiments, a few of Moody's poems, and the first three books of Edwin Arlington Robinson, scantly read before the revival. These were heralds of what turned out to be a fresh and vital period of American poetry, with a multiplicity of types and talents, and an impetus that carried it forward for decades.

The revival began (if one must choose a place and date) with the first number, October 1912, of *Poetry: A Magazine of Verse*, bravely published from Chicago, "Hog Butcher for the World." In the years surrounding 1912 Chicago was a focus of the literary activity of such men as Norris, Dreiser, Sinclair, Herrick, Anderson in prose, and Moody, Sandburg, Masters, Lindsay in poetry. And it had *Poetry*. This influential little magazine, originally financed by Chicago businessmen, was ably edited by Harriet Monroe with a view to giving genuine poets a chance to be heard. In its pages appeared, within the first three years, work by Ezra Pound, Hilda Doolittle, Vachel Lindsay, Amy Lowell, William Carlos Williams, John Gould Fletcher, Robert Frost, Carl Sandburg, Edna St. Vincent Millay, Wallace Stevens, Edgar Lee Masters, and Marianne Moore.

But the suddenness, volume, variety, and quality of the poetic revival can perhaps best be shown by a partial list of books of verse published within the span of only six years:

1912
Amy Lowell, *A Dome of Many-Coloured Glass*
Ezra Pound, *Ripostes*

1913
Robert Frost, *A Boy's Will*
Vachel Lindsay, *General William Booth Enters into Heaven*

1914
Robert Frost, *North of Boston*
Vachel Lindsay, *The Congo and Other Poems*
Amy Lowell, *Sword Blades and Poppy Seed*
Des Imagistes: An Anthology
James Oppenheim, *Songs for the New Age*

1915
Edgar Lee Masters, *Spoon River Anthology*
John Gould Fletcher, *Irradiations*

1916
Carl Sandburg, *Chicago Poems*
Edwin Arlington Robinson, *The Man Against the Sky*
Robert Frost, *Mountain Interval*
Ezra Pound, *Lustra*
John Gould Fletcher, *Goblins and Pagodas*
Amy Lowell, *Men, Women, and Ghosts*
Conrad Aiken, *Turns and Movies, The Jig of Forslin*

1917
Edna St. Vincent Millay, *Renascence*
Edwin Arlington Robinson, *Merlin*
Vachel Lindsay, *The Chinese Nightingale*
T. S. Eliot, *Prufrock and Other Observations*

What were the new poets trying to do? They agreed, in general, in reacting against the conventionalized romanticism of the Victorian age, which had lingered into the new century: against a poetry sweetly smooth and politely moral, the diminished legacy of Tennyson and Longfellow. They agreed in seeking fresh suggestions of technique, whether in Whitman, or French symbolism of the late nineteenth century, or English metaphysical poetry of the seventeenth century, or Oriental poetry, or the inconspicuous heritage of realistic art in such poets as Crabbe, Burns, and Cowper. Suggestions for substance, themes, attitudes came from some of these sources, and also from the fiction of the realistic movement (localism, naturalism). For a contemporary statement of the results of this reorientation we may return to Harriet Monroe, who, with Alice C. Henderson, edited an anthology of *The New Poets* (1917) with an explanatory introduction. Here, despite the diversity of the new poets' methods, is a fairly accurate statement of the shift from the old poetry to the new.

To avoid the vagueness of the old poetry, the new poets sought concreteness; e.g., Amy Lowell:

In the brown water,
Thick and silver-sheened in the sunshine,
Liquid and cool in the shade of the reeds,
A pike dozed.

To avoid eloquence, rhetoric, they sought simplicity, sincerity; e.g., E. A. Robinson:

Isaac and Archibald were two old men.
I knew them, and I may have laughed at them
A little; but I must have honored them,
For they were old, and they were good to me.

To avoid wordiness, diffuseness, they sought intensiveness, concentration; e.g., Carl Sandburg in "Fog," a poem of six lines:

The fog comes
on little cat feet.
It sits looking
over harbor and city
on silent haunches
and then moves on.

To avoid handed-down poetic diction, they sought the real speech of contemporary life; e.g., Sandburg:

You tell $6 a week department store girls all they
need is Jesus; you take a steel trust wop, dead
without having lived, gray and shrunken at forty
years of age, and you tell him to look at Jesus on
the cross and he'll be all right.

(For another kind of natural speaking see the lines from Robert Frost, below.)

To avoid imposed rhythm, patterned verse, most of them sought organic rhythm, "free verse"; e.g., all the extracts above except that from Robinson.

To avoid "poetical subjects," shop-worn themes, they felt free, like the realists in prose, to deal with anything, and found most of their substance in contemporary life; e.g., Vachel Lindsay:

Drum on your drums, batter on your banjos, sob on
the long cool winding saxaphones. Go to it, O
jazzmen.
Sling your knuckles on the bottoms of the happy tin
pans, let your trombones ooze, and go husha-
husha-hush with the slippery sandpaper.

or Robert Frost:

I'm going out to fetch the little calf
That's standing by the mother. It's so young
It totters when she licks it with her tongue.
I sha'n't be gone long. — You come too.

Such verse — alive, vivid, natural, understandable — earned its popularity. Once more as in the days of Tennyson and Longfellow, but in a twentieth-century way, poetry of a high order appealed to many classes of readers. Robinson, Frost, Sandburg, Lindsay, Millay could be enjoyed not only by "literary" people but also housewives, lawyers, machinists, beauty parlor workers, and truck drivers. But such widespread acceptance was denied to the brilliant expatriates Ezra Pound and T. S. Eliot, the forerunners of a long list of "difficult" and "obscure" poetic artists that flourished in the 1920's and 30's: for example, Wallace Stevens, Hart Crane, Marianne Moore, Archibald MacLeish, John Crowe Ransom. Experimenting on lines suggested mainly by the symbolist and metaphysical traditions, Pound and Eliot and their associates and disciples reached only a tiny portion of the reading public, those who welcomed the challenge of the tensely complex, difficult, and obscure. Naturally, modern poetry of this sort, like much of the most typical modern painting and music, bewildered and hence repelled the plain citizen.

While ordinary readers continued to think of Robinson and Frost as the major poets, typical intellectuals came to regard T. S. Eliot as the outstanding poetic voice of the first half of the twentieth century. He employed, in the work that established his reputation, a technique that called uncompromisingly for alert, flexible, sensitive reading. Characteristically he offered no specific setting, no progressive action, no progressive unfolding of logical statement. He attained form by developing a mood and attitude through striking images and symbols linked in free association, and by using subtly modulated repetition much as "themes" reappear in varying contexts in the art of music. His method was elliptical, allusive, condensed, full of overtones and hidden implications. He abounded in abrupt contrasts, often ironic, between the grand manner and the flatly colloquial, between the serious and the witty, the large and the trivial, the lovely and the repulsive.

Through an impersonal art, avoiding self-display, Eliot represented in poetic form a succession of attitudes toward the modern world, beginning in disgust and revulsion, ending in Christian faith. His earlier fame rested upon poems published in the beginning years of the 1920's. With history and myth as a backdrop, he pictured the contemporary disintegration of faith, the dissolving of tradition — a sterile waste land with memories but no hope, an "immense panorama of futility and anarchy." Human life as lived in our modern urban civilization — in London, his adopted home, as in his ancestral Boston — seemed devoid of all meaning and value. The "Lost Generation" who had survived what seemed a fruitless world war found in him a spokesman of their revolt and despair.

A Disillusioned Generation

Good-by to World Affairs. The revolt of the Roaring Twenties had been forming since about 1890, especially in the years just preceding the World War. But the war brought on a fresh access of disillusionment. To most Americans the outbreak of the conflict in 1914 had been simply incredible. Ignorant of European history and geography, many read eagerly the explanations offered by journalists and even the background works of historians (e.g. *Europe Since 1815*). Fatefully, the American people drifted into the vortex, repeating the slogans: "The world must be made safe for democracy," "A war to end war." After a vast mobilization of physical force and moral energy under the leadership of Woodrow Wilson, the nation embarked on the Great Crusade. Surely, when the Huns had been crushed, a new and better world would be built. Nothing would be as it had been.

But when the dizzy enthusiasm of victory subsided, reaction set in. The Great War soon began to look like a Great Interruption. Then, when the "four old men" at Versailles had finished their work, it looked like a Great Mistake. The vision was gone. The postwar generation, said Harold Stearns in 1920, no longer believed "a word about the ostensible aims for which the war was waged." Dos Passos in his novel *Three Soldiers* (1923) wrote: "So was civilization nothing but a vast edifice of sham, and the war, instead of its crumbling, was its fullest and most ultimate expression." Hemingway, in *A Farewell to Arms* (1929) wrote: "I was always embarrassed by the words *sacred, glorious*, and *sacrifice* and the expression *in vain*. We had heard them, sometimes standing in the rain

almost out of earshot, so that only the shouted words came through, and had read them, on proclamations that were slapped up by billposters over other proclamations, now for a long time, and I had seen nothing sacred, and the things that were glorious had no glory and the sacrifices were like the stockyards at Chicago if nothing was done with the meat except to bury it."

Not even science escaped the hysterical backwash of the war. Three states — Tennessee, Mississippi, and Arkansas — tried to abolish the idea of evolution, passing laws that forbade teaching, in any public school or college, "that man has descended from a lower order of animals." Fundamentalist obscurantism was soon dramatized in Dayton, Tennessee, by a "monkey trial" which became a national show. Clarence Darrow, a famous lawyer, defended the young teacher Scopes, while William Jennings Bryan endeavored — in his own passionate words — "to protect the word of God against the greatest atheist and agnostic in the United States."

Right behavior as well as right thinking was sought by legislation. State after state had gone "dry" before the World War, largely through the zeal of Methodist and other church groups, largely also through the concern of employers for the efficiency and safety of labor in the use of modern machinery. The war added a fresh motive: the saving of grain. In 1917 Congress, habituated to drastic measures, submitted the Prohibition Amendment to the states, and in 1920 a "bone-dry" law went into effect, at the very time when the country was in a mood for a spree. The twelve years that followed witnessed the flourishing of bootleggers, rumrunners, hijackers, gangsters (like Al Capone in his armored car), speak-easies, cocktail parties, and the hip-flask. While the national consumption of liquor was probably reduced, it was increased among the prosperous classes, and evasion of the law contributed much to the postwar relaxation of morals and manners.

The Big Boom. The great interruption over, President Harding, addressing an audience of business men, assured them that his administration favored "not nostrums but normalcy." This meant: not an adventure in an alien league of nations, nor any silly socialist ideas imported from Russia, but a return to the good old ways of free enterprise. And free enterprise meant, not Woodrow Wilson's "New Freedom" for the small folk, but the old freedom for big business, the "robust Republicanism" of the Hanna-McKinley school. The policy was continued by President Coolidge, who sagely observed, "The business of the United States is business."

After a mild recession the Big Boom started. By 1926 Stuart Chase was able to report that the United States was the economic and financial center of the world. "While Europe staggers and reels," he wrote, "national America is, beyond peradventure, the Eighth Wonder, and subject to the awe and the envy which all wonders command." With lyrical enthusiasm he spread out the statistics, like a miser counting his gold. The Age of the Machine was indeed in full career. Mechanical energy gave us the equivalent, as engineers were saying, of the labor of 3,000,000,000 slaves, or 30 for every man, woman, and child in the land. Around the middle of the decade there was, appropriately enough, a popular demand for the election of Henry Ford as President of the United States. Aided by mass production, high wages, blatant advertising, and installment purchasing, getting and spending vastly exceeded the extravagance of the Gilded Age. As the flood of prosperity rushed toward the Niagara of 1929, economists and business men were jubilantly announcing that henceforth prosperity would be permanent, perhaps ever-increasing.

For two years the nation's best-selling non-fiction book was one by Bruce Barton entitled *The Man Nobody Knows*: i.e. Jesus, "the founder of modern business," a great executive and advertiser who stood for "service." While professing to serve the country, business men and politicians were freely helping themselves, as they showed by their corruption and maladministration during the Harding regime, most flagrantly in the Teapot Dome and other oil scandals. When these scandals were exposed, the public was profoundly apathetic. Was it not unpatriotic to "rock the boat" of prosperity? Were not those who called for a searching investigation "nothing better than Bolsheviki"?

The Jazz Age. The average man had access to the new means of convenience and pleasure pouring from the factories of the Machine Age. A "car for the masses," achieved by Henry Ford, was in 1924 priced only $290. Three years later the fifteen millionth Tin Lizzy left the assembly line and sputtered efficiently in town and country. The automobile added immeasurably to the mobility of the American people, to standardized ways of living, to the subordination of the home to outside interests. Second only to the automobile, in altering habits of living and the tone of living, was the motion picture. In *Middletown*, the Lynds' study of a typical small city, we are informed that attendance reached, in one month of 1923, four and a half times the total population. To a people avid for entertainment the pictures offered, in the words of a *Saturday Evening Post* advertisement, "all the adventure, all the romance, all the excitement you lack in your daily life. If only for an afternoon or an evening — escape!" Who did not lose himself in Charlie Chaplin, Douglas Fairbanks, Theda Bara, Clara Bow, Rudolph Valentino? A third means of popular entertainment by machine came in 1920, when the first regular broadcasting station, KDKA, went on the air at Pittsburgh. By 1922 radio was a new craze, and the sales mounted from 60 million dollars in that year to over 842 in 1929. Life at home could now become, by the magic of a switch, the life of all America: a political convention, a philharmonic concert, a sermon by Dr. Fosdick, the crooning of Rudy Vallee. Dubiously, Willa Cather observed in 1921, "We have music by machines, we travel by machines — the American people are so submerged in them that sometimes I think they can only be made to laugh and cry by machinery."

Organized sport became a passion and a major industry. Prize fights, once outlawed, drew vast crowds, who, in two contests in which Dempsey fought, paid $4,545,000. Football came to be played in what Coach Stagg called "lunar craters," sometimes filled, says one historian, with the largest crowds of the sort since the fall of Rome. Charges of bribe-taking by the White Sox occasioned far more popular excitement than did charges of bribe-taking by members of the President's cabinet in Washington. Indoors, card-playing, once widely frowned upon, was possible even on Sundays, without drawn window curtains, and the game of bridge was all the rage.

Perhaps the dominating symbol of the decade was the flapper. She bobbed her hair, swore like a boy, smoked cigarettes, took to gin and corn and got drunk ("blotto"), made the most, or least, of the short skirts (they went up like the stock market, reached the knee in 1927), and often rolled her stockings on the calf. Like unmentionable women in an earlier time, she had, in her armory, powder, rouge, and lipstick. Outrageously, she spoke whatever came into her head. *He:* "How many Commandments are there?" *She:* "Ten." *He:* "Suppose you were to break one of them?" *She (hopefully)*: "There'd be nine."

The best account of Flaming Youth is Fitzgerald's novel *This Side of Paradise*, though it was published at the threshold of the decade of whoopee. Rosalind, nineteen and beautiful like all flappers, "once told a roomful of her mother's friends that the only excuse for women was the necessity for a disturbing element among men." "None of the Victorian mothers — and most of the mothers were Victorians — had any idea how casually their daughters were accustomed to being kissed. '*Servant*-girls are that way,' says Mrs. Huston-Carmelite to her popular daughter." "Amory found it rather fascinating to feel that any popular girl he met before eight he might quite possibly kiss before twelve." (Five minutes sufficed when he met Rosalind.) At the end of the novel, playing with the idea of socialism, Amory sums up: "I'm restless. My whole generation is restless," and, having returned to Princeton, he contemplates a new generation of students, "dedicated more than the last to the fear of poverty and the worship of success; grown up to find all Gods dead, all wars fought, all faiths in man shaken."

In their disillusionment, in their carnival of sex, dancing, jazz, and alcohol, the young and their elders tried to justify their behavior by the "New Psychology," especially the theory of the great Viennese psychoanalyst, Sigmund Freud. His name came to suggest the lowdown on human nature and a sanction for doing what one pleases. Attention was once more directed upon the inner life — this time not the Christian soul or the romantic ego but a subconscious activity dominated by sex. In life and in literature sex became an obsession; the repression of the nineteenth century became the expression of the twentieth, the old reticence became the new outspokenness, the former discussions of religion were replaced by chatter about sex. Typical enough is the brash girl in Fitzgerald's novel who says to the young hero: "Oh, just one person in fifty has any glimmer of what sex is. I'm hipped on Freud and all that. . . ." Few people bothered to read Freud's works, but his scientific ideas were in the air. In the glib columns of the daily press, in the patter of the dinner table and drinking sessions, the technical words of the new gospel were familiarly used and misused: *introvert, extrovert, inhibition, repression, expression, sublimation, libido, Oedipus complex, sadism, neuroses*. Religion itself was often looked upon as a neurosis: once a cure for the sick soul, it was now a sign of the soul's sickness. The general conclusion: all restraint is bad, mental health requires a free outlet of sexual impulses.

The impact of Freudian and other psychologies on the literature of the 1920's and 30's was tremendous. A whole new and exciting realm of interpretation was opened up, explored, and occupied, giving fresh impetus to the realistic and naturalistic movement. The analysis of complexes and maladjustments bulks large in the fiction of Sherwood Anderson (e.g. *Winesburg, Ohio*, 1919, *Dark Laughter*, 1925), in the plays of the leading American dramatist, Eugene O'Neill (*The Emperor Jones*, 1920, *Strange Interlude*, 1928), in the poems of Robinson Jeffers (*Tamar*, 1924, *Roan Stallion*, 1925). Few if any writers were untouched by the current explanations of human nature.

🐝 *Revolt of the Intellectuals.* In the just-named works by Anderson, O'Neill, and Jeffers; in the novels of Theodore Dreiser, Sinclair Lewis, and Ernest Hemingway; in the poems of T. S. Eliot, and in the essays and editorials of H. L. Mencken, the vague mood of disillusionment and revolt that pervaded the Jazz Age became more clear, conscious, and programmatic.

The critical spokesman was the rampaging H. L. Mencken. A raucous and hard-boiled journalist with a Germanic frankness and combativeness, a keen and ribald sense of humor, a tremendous gusto, and a talent for devastating phrase-making, he made short work of civilization in these United States. He despised the "mob," mercilessly ridiculed the middle class, scorned the aristocratic pretensions of the plutocracy. Waving the banner of the German philosopher Nietzsche, he damned both religion and democracy, proclaimed an aristocracy of intelligence, and demanded the right of the elite to live as they pleased and to be amused by the great American circus, an uproarious exhibition of ignorance, stupidity, bigotry, stuffiness, hypocrisy, sentimentalism. To a generation determined to be emancipated, to those who dimly and not always wisely desired a free, creative individualism, he spoke with the authority of a messiah in the pages of the *American Mercury* and the series of books named *Prejudices*. Here his countless readers learned that the grand evil bedeviling American civilization was the tyranny of "Puritan" or "Victorian" repression, epithets used by him and his followers more as swear-words than as historical symbols. The Puritan bogy stood for almost everything that the new elect did not like in the American heritage and environment. Yet much that Mencken said was just and needed saying, and unquestionably he played an important role in preparing the public mind and taste for acceptance of the vital prose fiction coming from the pens of Dreiser, Anderson, and Lewis. Appropriately enough, Lewis dedicated one of his novels "To H. L. Mencken, with profound admiration."

Sinclair Lewis's *Main Street*, published in 1920, was rated by P. W. Slosson, a historian at the end of the Jazz Age, as "the most important book written in the United States in the postwar decade," though several of Lewis's later books were much better novels. Gifted like Mencken with high spirits and a flair for satire, he also wrote with powers of close observation and vivid mimicry that his journalistic champion did not possess. Americans in a mood of vague disenchantment were suddenly given a sharply defined picture — all true if not all the truth — of a typical town, a Main Street that extended clear across the prosperous country. "This is America," said Lewis: "an unimaginatively standardized background, a sluggishness of speech and manners, a rigid ruling of the spirit by the desire to appear respectable. It is contentment . . . the contentment of the quiet dead, who are scornful of the living for their restless walking. It is negation canonized as the one positive virtue. It is the prohibition of happiness. It is slavery self-sought and self-defended. It is dullness made God."

Attached to his country, cherishing what H. S. Canby called "a fierce idealism for America," Lewis had brooded long upon the dismal reality achieved by a triumphant middle class, upon the symptoms of the Main Street virus that had infected village, town, and city. He described it again in later books, most notably in *Babbitt*, in which the central character, a realtor, comes dimly to see the American way of life for what it is: "Mechanical business — a brisk selling of badly built houses. Mechanical religion — a dry, hard church, shut off from the real life of the streets, inhumanly respectable as a top hat. Mechanized golf and dinner parties and bridge and conversation. Save with Paul Riesling, mechanical friendships — backslapping and jocular, never daring to essay the test of quietness." In such a society, intellectually and emotionally starved, inwardly insecure despite its complacency and demand for conformity, there could be only the shadow of culture, typified by the silly "Thanatopsis Club" in *Main Street*. The creative mind, Lewis seemed to be saying, must either accept frustration or make its escape.

In actual life many of the creatively minded escaped to a Bohemian freedom in one of the large cities, preferably New York. There the district known as Greenwich Village, ever since the turn of the century, had been attracting young writers and artists with or without talent. They could live cheaply in hall bedrooms or attics, and enjoy independence, companionship, and love accompanied by some work and much gay Prohibition drinking. Hither came Eugene O'Neill, getting into his stride as a playwright, Edna St. Vincent Millay, red-haired, sophisticated, innocent, darling of flappers everywhere, and the shy and ardent Floyd Dell, who in *Moon-Calf* and other novels spoke for young lovers seeking happiness in the machine age. In his *Love in Greenwich Village* a modern wife leaves her husband because he wants her to sew buttons on his shirts — "I've got a right to be *myself*," she said.

Or one could escape the dull mechanism of American life altogether by taking refuge in Europe. Seeking richer cultural currents, T. S. Eliot had been living in England since 1914 and in the 1920's became a British subject. Ezra Pound had gone abroad still earlier, sojourning in Spain, Italy, England, France. But after the war, when exchange rates were favorable, scores of American writers drifted over the Continent, many of them for five years or more, often doing little beyond trying to endure life. They were enticed, above all, to Paris, the center of Bohemianism and of modern artistic and literary experiments. They foregathered on the Left Bank, eating, drinking, adventuring in love or mere sex, doing some writing, meeting other free spirits, wandering from the Café du Dôme to the Cupole and other sidewalk cafés. For a picture of the Lost Generation one can go to *The Sun Also Rises*, a novel in which Hemingway described a group of American and English expatriates, pleasure-loving but dismally frustrated writers and artists, examples of the spiritual wreckage of the war. The book came out in 1926.

What was it that caused the intellectual class to fall into disillusionment, pessimism, and despair, the sense of futility, the grim philosophy of naturalism? Not the World War; that only intensified the crisis of the human spirit. The crisis had taken form, we will remember, with the impact of evolutionary science in the previous century. Could the Christian religion survive? Could a new outlook on the world satisfy the mind and provide the values that make life worth living? Many espoused the religion of Progress. But in the new century this too disintegrated, first in Europe, then in the United States. In 1918 the American book of the year, among intellectual readers, was the disillusioned and pessimistic *Education of Henry Adams*. Looking backward, Adams conceived of the thirteenth century as "the point of history when man held the highest idea of himself as a unit in a unified universe." Since that medieval century, as every educated person knew, science had taken a series of steps that might be understood as the degradation of man. Copernicus had dethroned our planet. Darwin had reduced physical man to one form of natural life among myriads. Finally Freud, it seemed, had placed even man's inner life in nature, finding it neither rational nor spiritual but impulsive and sexual. Equally depressing was the behaviorism of Watson, widely heralded in the 1920's, which made man the helpless subject of inherited and "determined" responses. Meanwhile the social scientists were commonly assuming that institutions and moral codes have no inherent or permanent validity but are determined and relative. Even the traditional political faith of America was suspect: "At no period since the French Revolution," said Laski at the close of the 20's, "has there been a skepticism of democracy so profound."

When science and scientism were busily deflating the dignity of man, it is scarcely surprising that innumerable thinking people no longer took seriously the Christian view of man or held the churches competent to guide men's morals. But instead of asserting disbelief in Christian doctrine, as many intellectuals had done through the ages, they did something far more devastating: they simply ignored it. They dismissed it with the bland assurance of many undergraduates objecting to chapel: "No intelligent person believes in God any more."

The modern mind had rejected the mysteries of religion and looked to science for clear truth, only to find science itself becoming mysterious and elusive. At this juncture, attention was arrested by the appearance in translation (1926–28) of an imposing German work, *The Decline of the West*, by Spengler, a philosophical pessimist, announcing the doom of Western civilization. Many reflective people

solemnly asked whether science, a great constructive force in the nineteenth century, was to become a great destructive force in the twentieth. Soon after came an American book, *The Modern Temper*, by Joseph Wood Krutch, an excellent statement of the predicament of those who found in science the only light of the world. Krutch was plainly restive under "the tyranny which scientific thought has come to exercise over the human spirit," — "science, once so much loved but now so much feared." Yet as a candid pessimist he could see only "such despair as must inevitably be ours."

The twenties were a strange decade: disillusioned and despairing yet abounding in zest for life; brash and cocksure yet insecure and bewildered; creative (in business, science, literature) yet intent upon deflating, debunking, destroying; asserting every manner of freedom yet picturing man in bondage to external and internal forces.

THE QUEST OF VALUES

Humanism and Religion. The collapse of the Big Boom in the fall of 1929 shattered the Roaring Twenties. The long weekend party was over, and the revellers and pessimists sobered in the cold gray light of the Great Depression, deepest and longest in American history. The irresponsible mood of the 20's was now passé. It was time to find — or to grope earnestly toward — values and standards that might once more make sense of life. The dark fears that beset the 30's must be countered by objects of hope and loyalty. This call to order and faith did not, of course, come suddenly. As grimly naturalistic literature still had a place in the 30's, so the quest for values had had a place in the 20's. Novels like Willa Cather's *Death Comes for the Archbishop* (1927), Thornton Wilder's *The Bridge of San Luis Rey* (1927), poems like those of Robert Frost in the 20's and earlier, and Stephen Vincent Benét's *John Brown's Body* (1928) ran counter to the mood of irresponsible self-expression. Perhaps it is also significant that in the very heart of the age of jazz, gin, and sex the best-selling book of 1926 (more than a million copies, surpassing even the popular novels) was Will Durant's *Story of Philosophy*.

Meanwhile, critics, scholars, and journalists were taking sides in a hot controversy over humanism. Irving Babbitt, at the center of the controversy, held that unless there was "a reaffirmation of the truths of the inner life in some form — traditional or critical, religious or humanistic — " civilization was "threatened at its base." Modernism had put man into nature, first emotionally (Rousseau, Wordsworth), then physically (Darwin), then in every way (Spencer, Freud). But were there not elements in human experience that refused to fit into this scheme? Was there not a "law for man" as well as a "law for thing"? Babbitt described it as a power of self-restraint, of imposing a limit to the flow of appetite and temperament, of selecting human ends to be served. This power he attributed not to reason or feeling but to will. He distinguished between a "higher will" and mere impulse, as love is distinguished from sex. It required moderation, proportion. It aimed — to state it in familiar terms — at the centered and well-rounded life often praised in college catalogues but often lacking in college graduates. As a critical modern, Babbitt stopped short of the divine realm; yet he acknowledged the need of humility toward something felt to be above man, and in the debate between naturalists and supernaturalists did not hesitate to range himself with the supernaturalists. While never a mere traditionalist, he nourished himself upon the "wisdom of the ages" — not only the humanistic doctrine of Aristotle and Confucius but the religious insight of Jesus and especially Buddha.

T. S. Eliot, when a student at Harvard, had been impressed with Professor Babbitt's attack on the subjection of man to nature in the sentimental and scientific forms of humanitarianism. As the author of The Waste Land (1922) he pictured the desolation wrought by the skeptical temper, the inner emptiness of life without faith. Then in 1927 he announced his conversion to Anglo-Catholicism. In an essay of this time he held that humanism depends on religion. "For us," he added, "religion is of course Christianity." He regretted that Babbitt could not take the same step he had taken: "Professor Babbitt knows too much," "knows too many religions and philosophies . . . to be able to give himself to any." Holding that humanism needs religion, he also held (in the humanist manifesto of 1930) that religion needs humanism. Both the Roman Catholic and the Protestant churches, when lacking humanistic criteria, he pronounced liable to "corruption," "stupidity," and "vulgarity." One wing of Protestantism, furthermore, tended to be "liberal, sloppy, hypocritical, and humanitarian." While announcing himself as a believer in Christian revelation, Eliot also announced himself as a classicist. What classicism meant to

him he had already indicated in the year after The Waste Land, when he contrasted it with romanticism: it was complete not fragmentary, adult not immature, orderly not chaotic. Accepting both the Christian and the classical disciplines, Eliot rejected the postwar skeptical emancipation, which had brought only a "meager, impoverished emotional life; in the end it is the Christian who can have the more varied, refined and intense enjoyment of life."

The return of typically modern minds to the Christian fold had seemed all but impossible ten years earlier. Yet here was Eliot — with a modern sensibility and artistic method that made him a commanding influence on the poets of his time — finding his essential meanings in revealed religion. Nor was this a merely private matter: it provided the substance of his public verse. With Ash Wednesday in 1930, Eliot became a Christian poet. So complex a person could not be expected to repeat in the twentieth century the utter certitude of Dante or simple piety of Chaucer. His choice of a Lenten theme for his sequence of six poems itself suggests the modern temper of his faith. He is concerned with self-examination and discipline, with temptation, doubt, penitence, renunciation, prayer, acutely aware of all the tensions of the inner life and the elusiveness of genuine affirmation. Poetry of this sort, interfused with religious dogma and ritual, caused consternation among some of his followers who now regarded him as a lost leader. Others deplored his retreat to tradition and authority while they admired his craftsmanship. The Four Quartets, published as a unit in 1943, marked a high point of Eliot's achievement in symphonic structure, as the title suggests. The four parts, each divided into five sections, give poetic expression to the Christian doctrines of revelation, incarnation, and annunciation in contrapuntal movements alternating between lyrical metaphors and colloquial statement. The essential subject is that of The Waste Land and Ash Wednesday — that man's history and experience have meaning only in a total identification of the temporal with the eternal achieved through faith in the traditional authority of such mysteries as Incarnation and Pentecost.

Toward the Left. To the religionist or humanist, the fundamental conflict is between good and evil within the human heart. To the ordinary modernist it is between the individual and society. Generally speaking, the nineteenth century was individualistic, and the twentieth has been socialistic. In the United States, the results of free enterprise (when kept within bounds by government) proved so pleasing to all classes that the individualistic pattern was by no means abandoned even by the reforming New Deal.

The Great Depression that spanned the whole of the 1930's seemed to offer an ideal chance for the growth of socialism. There were American roots to begin with. Ever since the days of Populism, political progressives and labor leaders had tended to propagate socialist theories and attitudes, with aid from such novelists as Upton Sinclair (especially in *The Jungle*, 1906), Jack London (*Martin Eden*, 1909), then Floyd Dell and Ernest Poole, as well as such poets as Sandburg and Lindsay. Could the ills of American democracy be cured by some simple patent medicine? Could not the best hints for a new beginning be derived from a great people across the seas, with a planned economy and full employment, moving by Five-Year Plans toward a happy, classless, peaceful society? While tempted by the example of Communist Russia, many Americans hesitated or drew back. Many others hoped that such blessedness could be attained, without violence, by gradual evolution. A much smaller number deliberately warmed their hearts at the fire of Marxism and determined to spread the flames of revolution. Something of the spirit of that day may be found at the end of the *Autobiography of Lincoln Steffens*, goateed veteran muckraker, to whom American evolution was less attractive than Russian revolution "ruthlessly" carried out by "a few thoughtful, feeling individuals." "Not the cunning, grasping possessors of things but the generous, industrious producers and the brave, imaginative leaders of the race shall be the fit to survive. Russia is the land of conscious, wilful hope."

The creative writers of the period had varying attitudes toward American failure and Russian hope, but most of them shared a sense of social sympathy and responsibility, as usual in the 1930's as rare in the 20's. They were ready to hail "the Century of the Common Man." No longer ridiculed as a boob or yokel, the common man was looked upon as a martyr, a victim of social forces beyond his control. A "Leftist" or "Proletarian" stand was evident in the little magazines such as the *Partisan Review*, in the theater (even Broadway), in such poets as Kenneth Fearing and Muriel Rukeyser, in critics like Granville Hicks and Edmund Wilson. The Communist Party of the United States, thriving in the 1930's, warmly endorsed writing about the working class, drearily approved ill-written representations of "the class struggle."

The better writers who pictured the plight of the common man were only briefly, if at all, Stalinists; rather they were independent Marxists, idealists who felt that the principles underlying communism held great hope for the world. As better writers, they subdued their radical opinions to their concern for artistic construction. One was James T. Farrell, author of the powerful *Studs Lonigan* trilogy of novels (1932–35) on the degeneration of an Irish Catholic youth in the lower middle class of Chicago, victim of a brutal environment in the Depression period. Another was John Steinbeck, whose best-selling novel *The Grapes of Wrath* (1939) pictured the Joad family of the Dust Bowl, tractored off their Oklahoma farm and lured in their jalopy to the uncertain promise of California, a family unquenchable in their love of life, resolute in the face of utter defeat. Plainly, the American Dream that had drawn generations of pioneers westward had turned into a nightmare.

The immediate American past was the subject of one of the most impressive literary achievements of the decade — *U.S.A.* (1930–37), a trilogy of novels by John Dos Passos. It is a panoramic view of the life of America for thirty years, from the pre-war time to the onset of the depression. Samples of public events, great and trivial, are flashed before us in headline fashion, famous leaders like Wilson, Debs, Morgan, Ford, and Hearst are scrutinized in thumbnail biographies, but the bulk of the work is fiction, the stories of a number of diverse men and women. In these characters are few signs of virtue; instead, a monotony of greed, cruelty, lust, drunkenness, bribery, and general cussedness. They can control neither themselves nor their circumstances. Those who strive and those who drift are alike swept to defeat by the destructive forces of society. The author's desire to be honest and forthright seems to lead him to a naturalistic determinism, the judgment that man is hopeless and life futile. Yet Dos Passos loved life and land enough to condemn them in more than 1400 pages, enough to desire a socialist revolution (while looking askance at Communists and other radicals), and enough to write later a book offering men like Jefferson, Franklin, and Roger Williams as *The Ground We Stand On* (1941).

Actually, the case for any sort of violent

revolution was undermined by the New Deal. This was much the largest step in a peaceful revolution begun by the Populists and propagated by Bryan, Theodore Roosevelt, La Follette, and finally Franklin D. Roosevelt. Under his leadership, the term *liberal* no longer signified leaving individuals as free as possible to control themselves (or not control themselves); it now meant extending social controls over individuals for the general welfare. The Democratic party, though traditionally associated with states' rights, sponsored a vast increase in centralized Federal government. Measure after measure was introduced that had the effect of tying the national economy, from big business down to "the forgotten man," far more closely to Washington. Bureaucracy developed apace; the population of the capital shifted from fourteenth among the cities in 1930 to ninth in 1940; the public debt mounted from $16 billion to $42 billion.

Part of the money appropriated to create jobs in this Depression era was spent in support of artists and writers. The Federal theater project supported thousands of actors, who put on the stage dramatizations of the slum problem, the TVA, the farmers' troubles, and the threat of fascism (Sinclair Lewis's *It Can't Happen Here* in play form). Another Federal project gave novelists, poets, journalists, and other writers a chance to go on writing. The most notable result of this literary project was a long series of detailed guide books to cities, states, and rivers, with attention to history, folkways, scenery, and practical information.

Regionalism and the South.

The New Deal not only sponsored this inventory of the parts that made the whole, but set up various regional administrative units and ventured a regional experiment involving seven states — the Tennessee Valley Authority. Yet its dominant tendency was plainly toward centralization, as many thoughtful Americans saw with growing alarm. They had shared in the revolt of the prosperous 20's against Main Street and all the dull uniformities of the machine age. Was there not now, in the depressed 30's, grave danger that an ever-increasing mechanical unity resting on Federal authority would in time completely destroy the organic diversity of the United States, a diversity resting on spontaneous differences in interests, customs, ways of looking at life? A spirited controversy arose. Whether regionalism could and should be fostered was discussed by critics, creative writers,

journalists, and scholars. Usually those who called themselves regionalists rejected the old term *sectionalism*, which seemed separatist and aloof, while *regionalism* implied the contribution of the parts to the whole.

Definitions and theories of regionalism did little more than rationalize a deep impulse at work in American literature since the rise of realism after the Civil War. The section of the United States that was most distinctive, and most wanted to be itself, had been for four years known as the Confederate States of America. Impoverished in those desperate years, resentful of the horrors of "Reconstruction," the South was long bewildered in its need for refinding itself — not restoring what had been shattered but creating a new economic and social order. It could not forget its own tradition when that tradition, notwithstanding slavery, contained so much that was admirable and charming; nor could it heartily adopt the modern industrial pattern, when this seemed (not without reason) so dubious an avenue to true fulfillment. Some Southerners faced toward the proud past, others accepted what the machine age promised, while many others looked both ways, hoping that an uncertain future would reconcile old and new. Increasingly divided, Southerners agreed at least in devotion to the region and the nation.

Even that boorish newspaperman, H. L. Mencken, Baltimorean born and bred, was attached to the South — the old South, with a civilization "perhaps the best that the Western Hemisphere has ever seen," original in political ideas, accomplished in culture and the art of living. The New South — the South ruined by the Civil War and fallen into the clutches of plutocrats and Protestant barbarians — he pronounced "almost as sterile artistically, intellectually, culturally, as the Sahara Desert" (*Prejudices*, second series, 1920). Had Mencken been a more alert journalist he might have suspected that the desert was about to blossom with talent and genius. An editor of the *American Mercury*, he presently found himself publishing, in the first two years of the magazine, fifty-five contributions by twenty-three Southern writers. And by the end of the 1920's writers of unmistakable genius, as we shall note later, had arisen to place the South in the forefront of American literature.

At the opening of the 1930's, just before the American way of life seemed discredited by the deepening Depression, twelve Southerners issued a critical manifesto entitled *I'll Take My Stand*. They took their stand in favor of "a Southern way of life against what may be called the American or prevailing way": "Agrarian *versus* Industrial." Agriculture, they said, is "the best and most sensitive of vocations," nourishing social amenities, religion, and the arts. They called upon the younger Southerners, led astray by an alien industrial gospel, to "come back to the support of the Southern tradition." Unfortunately, according to the historian of *The South in American Literature*, Jay B. Hubbell, "Their Old South was too much like the idealized picture in Page's *In Ole Virginia*." Among the contributors were John Crowe Ransom, Donald Davidson, Allen Tate, and Robert Penn Warren. They were a brilliant group, natives of Kentucky and Tennessee, who had gathered at Vanderbilt University and written for *The Fugitive*, a magazine of verse. After the agrarian episode, these men attained great distinction as poets without laurels, esteemed by adept readers of "pure" and "obscure" poems but regarded by the general public with indifference or hostility. From this group also came leadership in the "New Criticism," "exclusively," said Ransom, an "aesthetic criticism." The intent of the critic is to examine and define the poem (or prose work of art) with respect to "its structure and its texture." By doctrine and example, Southerners like Ransom, Tate, Warren, and Cleanth Brooks (along with Eliot and other critics in England) exerted a profound influence upon American literary criticism, scholarship, and teaching.

Meanwhile Southern fiction writers, like Southern historical and sociological scholars, were responding to the scientific and realistic temper of the time. In Thomas Wolfe the South possessed a writer with the vitality of genius, a realist-romanticist whose driving powers got beyond his control. His first novel, *Look Homeward, Angel* (1929), one of the major books of the period, is essentially an account of his own life and family in North Carolina. His later novels, coming out of the Depression decade, were also autobiographical, a torrential flow of memories, chants, lamentations: "his loss and loneliness, the furious, irremediable confusion of his huge unrest," as he put it in *Of Time and the River*. Something like his own turmoil he imputed to all America: "Immense and cruel skies bend over us, and all of us are driven on forever and we have no home." Yet he faced life, as Sinclair Lewis said, with great gusto, and, with the hope of the 30's, he loved his America. In the accent of Walt Whitman he exclaims: "I think the true fulfillment of our

spirit, of our people, of our mighty and immortal land, is yet to come." Wolfe early separated himself from the developing literary regionalism of the South, for, though devoted to North Carolina, he could not find there (could he find anywhere?) answers to his questions.

The greatest of Southern writers, William Faulkner, has lived since childhood — with few interruptions — in Oxford, Mississippi. Life in "Yoknapatawpha County," a fictional equivalent of Oxford and its surrounding countryside, became the theme of a dozen books that finally brought him international fame. To this immediate theme he gave wide extension: he covered a time span from the early nineteenth century to the present; he implied the experience of the entire South, with its social and moral complexities, its psychological frustrations; and by so doing he suggested the tragic plight of modern man, his soul all but lost in the mechanisms of his religion and his external affairs. Faulkner presents a fearful picture of perversions and acts of violence, till he implies to the casual reader that the abnormal is normal. A great artist, with a blazing imagination, an inexhaustible lyrical responsiveness, a rich fertility in structural devices, he makes the most of his horrors. But they grow out of and are sustained by an intense scrutiny of human nature. His horrors, in other words (the words of E. E. Sandeen) "do not occur in the vacuum of mere effects, whether romantic or naturalistic. In fact, his horrors are memorable exactly for the reason that they arouse the sense of moral outrage."

Faulkner's imagination is essentially historical, and the history he contemplates is human, has an ethical center which is permanent and absolute. He feels deeply that the moral law cannot be violated by a people or by an individual with impunity. He seems to think of history as the force which drives his characters, in the manner of the writers of the Old Testament: "The fathers have eaten sour grapes and the children's teeth are set on edge." Like Hawthorne, an artist preoccupied with moral reflection realized aesthetically through symbolism, Faulkner at length turned, in A *Fable* (1954), to a Christian allegory. To his readers in the atomic age he offered this long meditated fable of the premature armistice of 1918, suggesting, behind pacifism, the peace that passeth understanding, the peace of soul without which man is not truly human. The spirit in which he wrote it he had previously made plain enough in his address, in Sweden, upon receiving the Nobel Prize:

I decline to accept the end of man. . . . He is immortal, not because he alone among creatures has an inexhaustible voice, but because he has a soul, a spirit capable of compassion and sacrifice and endurance. The poet's, the writer's,

duty is to write about these things. It is his privilege to help man endure by lifting his heart, by reminding him of the courage and honor and hope and pride and compassion and pity and sacrifice which have been the glory of the past. The poet's voice need not merely be the record of man, it can be one of the props, the pillars to help him endure and prevail.

THE NATURALISTIC REVOLT

Henry Adams [1838–1918]

The book of the year in 1918 was an autobiography, *The Education of Henry Adams*. Privately printed back in 1907, it was not publicly available till the year of his death, which was also the last year of the war. By this time it had a quite unforeseen effect. Oddly enough, an intellectual old man of an old New England family was soon recognized as a spokesman for the rebellious, questioning young moderns who dominated the disillusioned 1920's.

The Adams Family is the title of a book by the historian James Truslow Adams. The family had long abounded in abilities and fame. It included two of the abler presidents of the United States: John Quincy Adams, the grandfather of Henry Adams, and John Adams, the great-grandfather of Henry Adams. On his mother's side, his grandfather was the wealthiest man in Boston, where Henry was appropriately born in the shadow of the State House. With brilliant intellectual gifts added to his heritage, he seemed a darling of the gods. He studied at Harvard and in Germany, was secretary to his father (Charles Francis Adams, minister to England), edited the *North American Review*, became an effective teacher of medieval history at Harvard, wrote a valuable nine-volume history of the administrations of Jefferson and Madison, a learned and fascinating book on French medieval cathedrals, *Mont-Saint-Michel and Chartres*, several biographies, and two novels.

By any ordinary measure, his career was a success, but his own measure was not ordinary. He conceived of his entire life as a process of education and a quest of values, the results of which he found disappointingly meager. He had a justified pride in the tradition of a family accustomed to lead as if public service were a trust, but his desire to contribute such service himself was frustrated, he felt, by the political life of the Grant period. Viewed more generally, his sense of failure sprang from his misfortune in living in an acquisitive period of American society to which, as an intellectual, he could not adjust. More generally still, he could not adjust to the universe. It seemed to him that while man dreamed of Order, "Chaos was the law of nature" — or rather the lawlessness of nature.

The universe apparently makes no sense, has no plan, certainly no purpose. "Every free energy of the universe" revolts against the artificial imposition of order and insists upon anarchy. Man cannot elude these forces. By 1863 Adams had reached a pessimistic, naturalistic conclusion: "My philosophy teaches me, and I firmly believe it," he said, "that the laws which govern animated beings will be ultimately found to be at bottom the same with those which rule inanimate nature." With "the curious enormity of creation" he contrasted "the littleness of our kind." Our vaunted discoveries and inventions do not enable man to control nature: nature controls man. Though living in the horse-and-buggy age, he foresaw the sinister role that science might play in our Age of the Atom. Writing to his brother Charles as early as 1862 he said: "Man has mounted science, and is now run away with. Some day science may have the existence of mankind in its power, and the human race commit suicide by blowing up the world." To this final catastrophe he indicated political preliminaries. In China, he predicted in 1903, "the last struggle for power is to come. . . . The only country now on the spot is Russia, and if Russia organizes China as an economical power, the little drama of history will end in the overthrow of our clumsy Western civilization."

Why did Adams write of himself in the third person instead of using the pronoun *I*? Mainly, perhaps, in the interest of objectivity: he wanted to look at himself as if he were somebody else. He tried to fathom the meaning of his experience and knowledge with the integrity proper to the historian or scientist. Yet he was never merely matter-of-fact, but alertly aware of his complexity, which he seems to have enjoyed. The signs of his enjoyment, in his style of writing, are indirection, irony, wit, unexpectedness of many sorts, the juxtaposition or blending of differing moods or tones. Candid, acute, intriguing, vivid, he reads well to this day.

Further reading: *The Education of Henry Adams; Mont-Saint-Michel and Chartres.* Elizabeth Stevenson, *Henry Adams,* 1955. R. E. Spiller, *The Cycle of American Literature,* 1955, pages 191–200.

From *The Education of Henry Adams*

Chaos (1870)

***He had been some weeks in London when he received a telegram from his brother-in-law at the Bagni di Lucca telling him that his sister had been thrown from a cab and injured, and that he had better come on. He started that night, and reached the Bagni di Lucca on the second day. Tetanus had already set in.

The last lesson — the sum and term of education — began then. He had passed through thirty years of rather varied experience without having once felt the shell of custom broken. He had never seen Nature — only her surface — the sugar-coating that she shows to youth. Flung suddenly in his face, with the harsh brutality of chance, the terror of the blow stayed by him thenceforth for life, until repetition made it more than the will could struggle with; more than he could call on himself to bear. He found his sister, a woman of forty, as gay and brilliant in the terrors of lockjaw as she had been in the careless fun of 1859, lying in bed in consequence of a miserable cab-accident that had bruised her foot. Hour by hour the muscles grew rigid, while the mind remained bright, until after ten days of fiendish torture she died in convulsions.

One had heard and read a great deal about death, and even seen a little of it, and knew by heart the thousand commonplaces of religion and poetry which seemed to deaden one's senses and veil the horror. Society being immortal, could put on immortality at will. Adams being mortal, felt only the mortality. Death took features altogether new to him, in these rich and sensuous surroundings. Nature enjoyed it, played with it, the horror added to her charm, she liked the torture, and smothered her victim with caresses. Never had one seen her so winning. The hot Italian summer brooded outside, over the market-place and the picturesque peasants, and, in the singular color of the Tuscan atmosphere, the hills and vineyards of the Apennines seemed bursting with mid-summer blood. The sick-room itself glowed with the Italian joy of life; friends filled it; no harsh northern lights pierced the soft shadows; even the dying woman shared the sense of the Italian summer, the soft, velvet air, the humor, the courage, the sensual fulness of Nature and man. She faced death, as women mostly do, bravely and even gaily, racked slowly to unconsciousness, but yielding only to violence, as a soldier sabred in battle. For many thousands of years, on these hills and plains, Nature had gone on sabring men and women with the same air of sensual pleasure.

Impressions like these are not reasoned or catalogued in the mind; they are felt as part of violent emotion; and the mind that feels them is a different one from that which reasons; it is thought of a different power and a different person. The first serious consciousness of Nature's gesture — her attitude towards life — took form then as a phantasm, a nightmare, an insanity of force. For the first time, the stage-scenery of the senses collapsed; the human mind felt itself stripped naked, vibrating in a void of shapeless energies, with resistless mass, colliding, crushing, wasting, and destroying what these same energies had created and labored from eternity to perfect. Society became fantastic, a vision of pantomime with a mechanical motion; and its so-called thought merged in the mere sense of life, and pleasure in the sense. The usual anodynes of social medicine became evident artifice. Stoicism was perhaps the best; religion was the most human; but the idea that any personal deity could find pleasure or profit in torturing a poor woman, by accident, with fiendish cruelty known to man only in perverted and insane temperaments, could not be held for a moment. For pure blasphemy, it made pure atheism a comfort. God might be, as the Church said, a Substance, but He could not be a Person.

With nerves strained for the first time beyond their power of tension, he slowly travelled northwards with his friends, and stopped for a few days at Ouchy to recover his balance in a new world; for the fantastic mystery of coincidences had made the world, which he thought real, mimic and reproduce the distorted nightmare of his personal horror. He did not yet know it, and he was twenty years in finding it out; but he had need of all the beauty of the Lake below and of the Alps above, to restore the finite to its place. For the first time in his life, Mont Blanc for a moment looked to him what it was — a chaos of anarchic and purposeless forces — and he needed days of repose to see it clothe itself again with the illusions of his senses, the white purity of its snows, the splendor of its light, and the infinity of its heavenly peace. Nature was kind; Lake Geneva was beautiful beyond itself, and the Alps put on charms real as terrors; but man became chaotic, and before the illusions of Nature were wholly restored, the illusions of Europe suddenly vanished, leaving a new world to learn.

On July 4, all Europe had been in peace; on July 14, Europe was in full chaos of war. One felt helpless and ignorant, but one might have been king or kaiser without feeling stronger to deal with the chaos. Mr. Gladstone was as astounded as Adams; the Emperor Napoleon was nearly as stupefied as either, and Bismarck himself hardly knew how he did it. As education, the outbreak of the war was wholly lost on a man dealing with death hand-to-hand, who could not throw it aside to look at it across the Rhine. Only when he got up to Paris, he began to feel the approach of catastrophe. Providence set up no *affiches* to announce the tragedy. Under one's eyes France cut herself adrift, and floated off, on an unknown stream, towards a less known ocean. Standing on the curb of the Boulevard, one could see as much as though one stood by the side of the Emperor or in command of an army corps. The effect was lurid. The public seemed to look on the war, as it had looked on the wars of Louis XIV and Francis I, as a branch of decorative art. The French, like true artists, always regarded war as one of the fine arts. Louis XIV practised it; Napoleon I perfected it; and Napoleon III had till then pursued it in the same spirit with singular success. In Paris, in July, 1870, the war was brought out like an opera of Meyerbeer. One felt one's self a supernumerary hired to fill the scene. Every evening at the theater the comedy was interrupted by order, and one stood up by order, to join in singing the *Mar-*

seillaise to order. For nearly twenty years one had been forbidden to sing the *Marseillaise* under any circumstances, but at last regiment after regiment marched through the streets shouting "Marchons!" while the bystanders cared not enough to join. Patriotism seemed to have been brought out of the Government stores, and distributed by grammes *per capita*. One had seen one's own people dragged unwillingly into a war, and had watched one's own regiments march to the front without sign of enthusiasm; on the contrary, most serious, anxious, and conscious of the whole weight of the crisis; but in Paris every one conspired to ignore the crisis, which every one felt at hand. Here was education for the million, but the lesson was intricate. Superficially Napoleon and his Ministers and marshals were playing a game against Thiers and Gambetta. A bystander knew almost as little as they did about the result. How could Adams prophesy that in another year or two, when he spoke of *his* Paris and its tastes, people would smile at his dotage?

As soon as he could, he fled to England, and once more took refuge in the profound peace of Wenlock Abbey. Only the few remaining monks, undisturbed by the brutalities of Henry VIII — three or four young Englishmen — survived there, with Milnes Gaskell acting as Prior. The August sun was warm; the calm of the Abbey was ten times secular; not a discordant sound — hardly a sound of any sort except the cawing of the ancient rookery at sunset — broke the stillness and, after the excitement of the last month, one felt a palpable haze of peace brooding over the Edge and the Welsh Marches. Since the reign of *Pteraspis*, nothing had greatly changed; nothing except the monks. Lying on the turf, the ground littered with newspapers, the monks studied the war correspondence. In one respect Adams had succeeded in educating himself; he had learned to follow a campaign.

While at Wenlock, he received a letter from President Eliot inviting him to take an Assistant Professorship of History, to be created shortly at Harvard College. After waiting ten or a dozen years for some one to show consciousness of his existence, even a *Terebratula* would be pleased and grateful for a compliment which implied that the new President of Harvard College wanted his help; but Adams knew nothing about history, and much less about teaching, while he knew more than enough about Harvard College; and wrote at once to thank President

Eliot, with much regret that the honor should be above his powers. His mind was full of other matters. The summer, from which he had expected only amusement and social relations with new people, had ended in the most intimate personal tragedy, and the most terrific political convulsion he had ever known or was likely to know. He had failed in every object of his trip. The Quarterlies had refused his best essay. He had made no acquaintances and hardly picked up the old ones. He sailed from Liverpool, on September 1, to begin again where he had started two years before, but with no longer a hope of attaching himself to a President or a party or a press. He was a free lance and no other career stood in sight or mind. To that point education had brought him.

Yet he found, on reaching home, that he had not done quite so badly as he feared. His article on the Session in the July *North American* had made a success. Though he could not quite see what partisan object it served, he heard with flattered astonishment that it had been reprinted by the Democratic National Committee and circulated as a campaign document by the hundred thousand copies. He was henceforth in opposition, do what he might; and a Massachusetts Democrat, say what he pleased; while his only reward or return for this partisan service consisted in being formally answered by Senator Timothy Howe, of Wisconsin, in a Republican campaign document, presumed to be also freely circulated, in which the Senator, besides refuting his opinions, did him the honor — most unusual and picturesque in a Senator's rhetoric — of likening him to a begonia.

The begonia is, or then was, a plant of such senatorial qualities as to make the simile, in intention, most flattering. Far from charming in its refinement, the begonia was remarkable for curious and showy foliage; it was conspicuous; it seemed to have no useful purpose; and it insisted on standing always in the most prominent positions. Adams would have greatly liked to be a begonia in Washington, for this was rather his ideal of the successful statesman, and he thought about it still more when the *Westminister Review* for October brought him his article on the Gold Conspiracy, which was also instantly pirated on a great scale. Piratical he was himself henceforth driven to be, and he asked only to be pirated, for he was sure not to be paid; but the honors of piracy resemble the colors of the begonia; they are showy but not useful. Here was a *tour de force* he had never dreamed himself equal to performing: two long, dry, quarterly, thirty or forty page articles, appearing in quick succession, and pirated for audiences running well into the hundred thousands; and not one person, man or woman, offering him so much as a congratulation, except to call him a begonia.

Had this been all, life might have gone on very happily as before, but the ways of America to a young person of literary and political tastes were such as the so-called evolution of civilized man had not before evolved. No sooner had Adams made at Washington what he modestly hoped was a sufficient success, than his whole family set on him to drag him away. For the first time since 1861 his father interposed; his mother entreated; and his brother Charles argued and urged that he should come to Harvard College. Charles had views of further joint operations in a new field. He said that Henry had done at Washington all he could possibly do; that his position there wanted solidity; that he was, after all, an adventurer; that a few years in Cambridge would give him personal weight; that his chief function was not to be that of teacher, but that of editing the *North American Review* which was to be coupled with the professorship, and would lead to the daily press. In short, that he needed the university more than the university needed him.

Henry knew the university well enough to know that the department of history was controlled by one of the most astute and ideal administrators in the world — Professor Gurney — and that it was Gurney who had established the new professorship, and had cast his net over Adams to carry the double load of mediaeval history and the *Review*. He could see, no relation whatever between himself and a professorship. He sought education; he did not sell it. He knew no history; he knew only a few historians; his ignorance was mischievous because it was literary, accidental, indifferent. On the other hand he knew Gurney, and felt much influenced by his advice. One cannot take one's self quite seriously in such matters; it could not much affect the sum of solar energies whether one went on dancing with girls in Washington, or began talking to boys at Cambridge. The good people who thought it did matter had a sort of right to guide. One could not reject their advice; still less disregard their wishes.

The sum of the matter was that Henry went out to Cambridge and had a few words with President Eliot which seemed to him almost as American as the talk about diplomacy with his father ten years before. "But, Mr. President," urged Adams, "I know nothing about Mediaeval History." With the courteous manner and bland smile so familiar for the next generation of Americans, Mr. Eliot mildly but firmly replied, "If you will point out to me any one who knows more, Mr. Adams, I will appoint him." The answer was neither logical nor convincing, but Adams could not meet it without overstepping his privileges. He could not say that, under the circumstances, the appointment of any professor at all seemed to him unnecessary.

So, at twenty-four hours' notice, he broke his life in halves again in order to begin a new education, on lines he had not chosen, in subjects for which he cared less than nothing; in a place he did not love, and before a future which repelled. Thousands of men have to do the same thing, but his case was peculiar because he had no need to do it. He did it because his best and wisest friends urged it, and he never could make up his mind whether they were right or not. To him this kind of education was always false. For himself he had no doubts. He thought it a mistake; but his opinion did not prove that it was one, since, in all probability, whatever he did would be more or less a mistake. He had reached cross-roads of education which all led astray. What he could gain at Harvard College he did not know, but in any case it was nothing he wanted. What he lost at Washington he could partly see, but in any case it was not fortune. Grant's administration wrecked men by thousands, but profited few. Perhaps Mr. Fish was the solitary exception. One might search the whole list of Congress, Judiciary, and Executive during the twenty-five years 1870 to 1895, and find little but damaged reputation. The period was poor in purpose and barren in results.

Henry Adams, if not the rose, lived as near it as any politician, and knew, more or less, all the men in any way prominent at Washington, or knew all about them. Among them, in his opinion, the best equipped, the most active-minded, and most industrious was Abram Hewitt, who sat in Congress for a dozen years, between 1874 and 1886, sometimes leading the House and always wielding influence second to none. With nobody did Adams form closer or longer relations than with Mr. Hewitt, whom he regarded as the most useful public man in Washington; and he was the more struck by Hewitt's saying, at the end of his laborious career as legislator, that he left behind him no permanent result except the Act consolidating the Surveys. Adams knew no other man who had done so much, unless Mr. Sherman's legislation is accepted as an instance of success. Hewitt's nearest rival would probably have been Senator Pendleton who stood father to civil service reform in 1882, an attempt to correct a vice that should never have been allowed to be born. These were the men who succeeded.

The press stood in much the same light. No editor, no political writer, and no public administrator achieved enough good reputation to preserve his memory for twenty years. A number of them achieved bad reputations, or damaged good ones that had been gained in the Civil War. On the whole, even for Senators, diplomats, and Cabinet officers, the period was wearisome and stale.

None of Adams's generation profited by public activity unless it were William C. Whitney, and even he could not be induced to return to it. Such ambitions as these were out of one's reach, but supposing one tried for what was feasible, attached one's self closely to the Garfields, Arthurs, Frelinghuysens, Blaines, Bayards, or Whitneys, who happened to hold office; and supposing one asked for the mission to Belgium or Portugal, and obtained it; supposing one served a term as Assistant Secretary or Chief of Bureau; or, finally, supposing one had gone as sub-editor on the *New York Tribune* or *Times* — how much more education would one have gained than by going to Harvard College? These questions seemed better worth an answer than most of the questions on examination papers at college or in the civil service; all the more because one never found an answer to them, then or afterwards, and because, to his mind, the value of American society altogether was mixed up with the value of Washington.

At first, the simple beginner, struggling with principles, wanted to throw off responsibility on the American people, whose bare and toiling shoulders had to carry the load of every social or political stupidity; but the American people had no more to do with it than with the customs of Peking. American character might perhaps account for it, but what accounted for

American character? All Boston, all New England, and respectable New York, including Charles Francis Adams the father and Charles Francis Adams the son, agreed that Washington was no place for a respectable young man. All Washington, including Presidents, Cabinet officers, Judiciary, Senators, Congressmen, and clerks, expressed the same opinion, and conspired to drive away every young man who happened to be there, or tried to approach. Not one young man of promise remained in the Government service. All drifted into opposition. The Government did not want them in Washington. Adams's case was perhaps the strongest because he thought he had done well. He was forced to guess it, since he knew no one who would have risked so extravagant a step as that of encouraging a young man in a literary career, or even in a political one; society forbade it, as well as residence in a political capital; but Harvard College must have seen some hope for him, since it made him professor against his will; even the publishers and editors of the *North American Review* must have felt a certain amount of confidence in him, since they put the *Review* in his hands. After all, the *Review* was the first literary power in America, even though it paid almost as little in gold as the United States Treasury. The degree of Harvard College might bear a value as ephemeral as the commission of a President of the United States; but the government of the college, measured by money alone, and patronage, was a matter of more importance than that of some branches of the national service. In social position, the college was the superior of them all put together. In knowledge, she could assert no superiority, since the Government made no claims, and prided itself on ignorance. The service of Harvard College was distinctly honorable; perhaps the most honorable in America; and if Harvard College thought Henry Adams worth employing at four dollars a day, why should Washington decline his services when he asked nothing? Why should he be dragged from a career he liked in a place he loved, into a career he detested, in a place and climate he shunned? Was it enough to satisfy him that all America should call Washington barren and dangerous? What made Washington more dangerous than New York?

The American character showed singular limitations which sometimes drove the student of civilized man to despair. Crushed by his own ignorance — lost in the darkness of his own gropings — the scholar finds himself jostled of a sudden by a crowd of men who seem to him ignorant that there is a thing called ignorance; who have forgotten how to amuse themselves; who cannot even understand that they are bored. The American thought of himself as a restless, pushing, energetic, ingenious person, always awake and trying to get ahead of his neighbors. Perhaps this idea of the national character might be correct for New York or Chicago; it was not correct for Washington. There the American showed himself, four times in five, as a quiet, peaceful, shy figure, rather in the mould of Abraham Lincoln, somewhat sad, sometimes pathetic, once tragic; or like Grant, inarticulate, uncertain, distrustful of himself, still more distrustful of others and awed by money. That the American, by temperament, worked to excess, was true; work and whiskey were his stimulants; work was a form of vice; but he never cared much for money or power after he earned them. The amusement of the pursuit was all the amusement he got from it; he had no use for wealth. Jim Fisk alone seemed to know what he wanted; Jay Gould never did. At Washington one met mostly such true Americans, but if one wanted to know them better, one went to study them in Europe. Bored, patient, helpless; pathetically dependent on his wife and daughters; indulgent to excess; mostly a modest, decent, excellent, valuable citizen; the American was to be met at every railway station in Europe, carefully explaining to every listener that the happiest day of his life would be the day he should land on the pier at New York. He was ashamed to be amused; his mind no longer answered to the stimulus of variety; he could not face a new thought. All his immense strength, his intense nervous energy, his keen analytic perceptions, were oriented in one direction, and he could not change it. Congress was full of such men; in the Senate, Sumner was almost the only exception; in the Executive, Grant and Boutwell were varieties of the type — political specimens — pathetic in their helplessness to do anything with power when it came to them. They knew not how to amuse themselves; they could not conceive how other people were amused. Work, whiskey, and cards were life. The atmosphere of political Washington was theirs — or was supposed by the outside world to be in their control — and this was the reason why the outside world judged

that Washington was fatal even for a young man of thirty-two, who had passed through the whole variety of temptations, in every capital of Europe, for a dozen years; who never played cards, and who loathed whiskey.

The Dynamo and the Virgin (1900)

Until the Great Exposition of 1900 closed its doors in November, Adams haunted it, aching to absorb knowledge, and helpless to find it. He would have liked to know how much of it could have been grasped by the best-informed man in the world. While he was thus meditating chaos, Langley came by, and showed it to him. At Langley's behest, the Exhibition dropped its superfluous rags and stripped itself to the skin, for Langley knew what to study, and why, and how; while Adams might as well have stood outside in the night, staring at the Milky Way. Yet Langley said nothing new, and taught nothing that one might not have learned from Lord Bacon, three hundred years before; but though one should have known the *Advancement of Science* as well as one knew the *Comedy of Errors*, the literary knowledge counted for nothing until some teacher should show how to apply it. Bacon took a vast deal of trouble in teaching King James I and his subjects, American or other, towards the year 1620, that true science was the development or economy of forces; yet an elderly American in 1900 knew neither the formula nor the forces; or even so much as to say to himself that his historical business in the Exposition concerned only the economies or developments of force since 1893, when he began the study at Chicago.

Nothing in education is so astonishing as the amount of ignorance it accumulates in the form of inert facts. Adams had looked at most of the accumulations of art in the storehouses called Art Museums; yet he did not know how to look at the art exhibits of 1900. He had studied Karl Marx and his doctrines of history with profound attention, yet he could not apply them at Paris. Langley, with the ease of a great master of experiment, threw out of the field every exhibit that did not reveal a new application of force, and naturally threw out, to begin with, almost the whole art exhibit. Equally, he ignored almost the whole industrial exhibit. He led his pupil directly to the forces. His chief interest was in new motors to make his airship feasible, and he taught Adams the astonishing complexities of the Daimler motor and of the automobile, which, since 1893, had become a nightmare at a hundred kilometres an hour, almost as destructive as the electric tram which was only ten years older; and threatening to become as terrible as the locomotive steam-engine itself, which was almost exactly Adams's own age.

Then he showed his scholar the great hall of dynamos, and explained how little he knew about electricity or force of any kind, even of his own special sun, which spouted heat in inconceivable volume, but which, as far as he knew, might spout less or more, at any time, for all the certainty he felt in it. To him, the dynamo itself was but an ingenious channel for conveying somewhere the heat latent in a few tons of poor coal hidden in a dirty engine-house carefully kept out of sight; but to Adams the dynamo became a symbol of infinity. As he grew accustomed to the great gallery of machines, he began to feel the forty-foot dynamos as a moral force, much as the early Christians felt the Cross. The planet itself seemed less impressive, in its old-fashioned, deliberate, annual or daily revolution, than this huge wheel, revolving within arm's-length at some vertiginous speed, and barely murmuring — scarcely humming an audible warning to stand a hair's-breadth farther for respect of power — while it would not wake the baby lying close against its frame. Before the end, one began to pray to it; inherited instinct taught the natural expression of man before silent and infinite force. Among the thousand symbols of ultimate energy, the dynamo was not so human as some, but it was the most expressive.

Yet the dynamo, next to the steam-engine, was the most familiar of exhibits. For Adams's objects its value lay chiefly in its occult mechanism. Between the dynamo in the gallery of machines and the engine-house outside, the break of continuity amounted to abysmal fracture for a historian's objects. No more relation could he discover between the steam and the electric current than between the Cross and the cathedral. The forces were interchangeable if not reversible, but he could see only an absolute *fiat* in electricity as in faith. Langley could not help him. Indeed, Langley seemed to be worried by the same trouble, for he constantly repeated that the new forces were anarchical, and especially that he was not responsible for the new rays, that were little short of parricidal in their wicked spirit towards science. His own rays, with which he had doubled the solar spectrum, were altogether harmless and beneficent; but Radium denied its God — or, what was to Langley the same thing, denied the truths of his Science. The force was wholly new.

A historian who asked only to learn enough to be as futile as Langley or Kelvin, made rapid progress under this teaching, and mixed himself up in the tangle of ideas until he achieved a sort of Paradise of ignorance vastly consoling to his fatigued senses. He wrapped himself in vibrations and rays which were new, and he would have hugged Marconi and Branly had he met them, as he hugged the dynamo; while he lost his arithmetic in trying to figure out the equation between the discoveries and the economies of force. The economies, like the discoveries, were absolute, super-sensual, occult; incapable of expression in horse-power. What mathematical equivalent could he suggest as the value of a Branly coherer? Frozen air, or the electric furnace, had some scale of measurement, no doubt, if somebody could invent a thermometer adequate to the purpose; but X-rays had played no part whatever in man's consciousness, and the atom itself had figured only as a fiction of thought. In these seven years man had translated himself into a new universe which had no common scale of measurement with the old. He had entered a super-sensual world, in which he could measure nothing except by chance collisions of movements imperceptible to his senses, perhaps even imperceptible to his instruments, but perceptible to each other, and so to some known ray at the end of the scale. Langley seemed prepared for anything, even for an indeterminable number of universes interfused — physics stark mad in metaphysics.

Historians undertake to arrange sequences — called stories, or histories — assuming in silence a relation of cause and effect. These assumptions, hidden in the depths of dusty libraries, have been astounding, but commonly unconscious and childlike; so much so, that if any captious critic were to drag them to light, historians would probably reply, with one voice, that they had never supposed themselves required to know what they were talking about. Adams, for one, had toiled in vain to find out what he meant. He had even published a dozen volumes of American history for no other purpose than to satisfy himself whether, by the severest process of stating, with the least possible comment, such facts as seemed sure, in such order as seemed rigorously consequent, he could fix for a familiar moment a necessary sequence of human movement. The result had satisfied him as little as at Harvard College. Where he saw sequence, other men saw something quite different, and no one saw the same unit of measure. He cared little about his experiments and less about his statesmen, who seemed to him quite as ignorant as himself and, as a rule, no more honest; but he insisted on a relation of sequence, and if he could not reach it by one method, he would try as many methods as science knew. Satisfied that the sequence of men led to nothing and that the sequence of their society could lead no further, while the mere sequence of time was artificial, and the sequence of thought was chaos, he turned at last to the sequence of force; and thus it happened that, after ten years' pursuit, he found himself lying in the Gallery of Machines at the Great Exposition of 1900, his historical neck broken by the sudden irruption of forces totally new.

Since no one else showed much concern, an elderly person without other cares had no need to betray alarm. The year 1900 was not the first to upset schoolmasters. Copernicus and Galileo had broken many professorial necks about 1600; Columbus had stood the world on its head towards 1500; but the nearest approach to the revolution of 1900 was that of 310, when Constantine set up the Cross. The rays that Langley disowned, as well as those which he fathered, were occult, supersensual, irrational; they were a revelation of mysterious energy like that of the Cross; they were what, in terms of mediaeval science, were called immediate modes of the divine substance.

The historian was thus reduced to his last resources. Clearly if he was bound to reduce all these forces to a common value, this common value could have no measure but that of their attraction on his own mind. He must treat them as they had been felt; as convertible, reversible, interchangeable attractions on thought. He made up his mind to venture it; he would risk translating rays into faith. Such a reversible process would vastly amuse a chemist, but the chemist could not deny that he, or some of his fellow physicists, could feel the force of both. When Adams was a boy in Boston, the best chemist in the place had probably never heard of Venus except by way of scandal, or of the Virgin except as idolatry; neither had he heard of dynamos or automobiles or radium; yet his mind was ready to feel the force of all, though rays were unborn and the women were dead.

Here opened another totally new education, which promised to be by far the most hazardous of all. The knife-edge along which he must crawl, like Sir Lancelot in the twelfth century, divided two kingdoms of force which had nothing in common but attraction. They were as different as a magnet is from gravitation, supposing one knew what a magnet was, or gravitation, or love. The force of the Virgin was still felt at Lourdes, and seemed to be as potent as X-rays; but in America neither Venus nor Virgin ever had value as force — at most as sentiment. No American had ever been truly afraid of either.

This problem in dynamics gravely perplexed an American historian. The Woman had once been supreme; in France she still seemed potent, not merely as a sentiment, but as a force. Why was she unknown in America? For evidently America was ashamed of her, and she was ashamed of herself, otherwise they would not have strewn fig-leaves so profusely all over her. When she was a true force, she was ignorant of fig-leaves, but the monthly-magazine-made American female had not a feature that would have been recognized by Adam. The trait was notorious, and often humorous, but any one brought up among Puritans knew that sex was sin. In any previous age, sex was strength. Neither art nor beauty was needed. Every one, even among Puritans, knew that neither Diana of the Ephesians nor any of the Oriental goddesses was worshipped for her beauty. She was goddess because of her force; she was the animated dynamo; she was reproduction — the greatest and most mysterious of all energies; all she needed was to be fecund. Singularly enough, not one of Adams's many schools of education had ever drawn his attention to the opening lines of Lucretius, though they were perhaps the finest in all Latin literature, where the poet invoked Venus exactly as Dante invoked the Virgin:

Quae quoniam rerum naturam *sola* gubernas.
[Thou who *alone* above all dost govern the things of nature.]

The Venus of Epicurean philosophy survived in the Virgin of the Schools:

Donna, sei tanto grande, e tanto vali,
Che qual vuol grazia, e a te non ricorre,
Sua disianza vuol volar senz' ali.

[Lady, thou art so great and hast such worth,
that if there be he who would have grace yet be-   5
taketh not himself to thee, his longing seeketh to
fly without wings.]

All this was to American thought as though it
had never existed. The true American knew   10
something of the facts, but nothing of the feelings; he read the letter but he never felt the law.
Before this historical chasm, a mind like that of
Adams felt itself helpless; he turned from the
Virgin to the Dynamo as though he were a   15
Branly coherer. On one side, at the Louvre and
at Chartres, as he knew by the record of work
actually done and still before his eyes, was the
highest energy ever known to man, the creator
of four-fifths of his noblest art, exercising vastly   20
more attraction over the human mind than all
the steam-engines and dynamos ever dreamed of;
and yet this energy was unknown to the American mind. An American Virgin would never
dare command; an American Venus would never   25
dare exist.

The question, which to any plain American
of the nineteenth century seemed as remote as
it did to Adams, drew him almost violently to
study, once it was posed; and on this point Lang-   30
leys were as useless as though they were Herbert
Spencers or dynamos. The idea survived only as
art. There one turned as naturally as though the
artist were himself a woman. Adams began to
ponder, asking himself whether he knew of any   35
American artist who had ever insisted on the
power of sex, as every classic had always done;
but he could think only of Walt Whitman;
Bret Harte, as far as the magazines would let
him venture; and one or two painters, for the   40
flesh-tones. All the rest had used sex for sentiment, never for force; to them, Eve was a tender
flower, and Herodias an unfeminine horror.
American art, like the American language and
American education, was as far as possible sex-   45
less. Society regarded this victory over sex as its
greatest triumph, and the historian readily admitted it, since the moral issue, for the moment,
did not concern one who was studying the relations of unmoral force. He cared nothing for   50
the sex of the dynamo until he could measure
its energy.

Vaguely seeking a clue, he wandered through
the art exhibit, and, in his stroll, stopped almost

every day before Saint-Gaudens's General Sherman, which had been given the central post of
honor. Saint-Gaudens himself was in Paris, putting on the work his usual interminable last
touches, and listening to the usual contradictory
suggestions of brother sculptors. Of all the
American artists who gave to American art whatever life it breathed in the seventies, Saint-
Gaudens was perhaps the most sympathetic, but
certainly the most inarticulate. General Grant
or Don Cameron had scarcely less instinct of
rhetoric than he. All the others — the Hunts,
Richardson, John La Farge, Stanford White —
were exuberant; only Saint-Gaudens could never
discuss or dilate on an emotion, or suggest artistic arguments for giving to his work the forms
that he felt. He never laid down the law, or
affected the despot, or became brutalized like
Whistler by the brutalities of his world. He
required no incense; he was no egoist; his simplicity of thought was excessive; he could not
imitate, or give any form but his own to the
creations of his hand. No one felt more strongly
than he the strength of other men, but the idea
that they could affect him never stirred an image
in his mind.

This summer his health was poor and his
spirits were low. For such a temper, Adams was
not the best companion, since his own gaiety
was not *folle*; but he risked going now and then
to the studio on Mont Parnasse to draw him out
for a stroll in the Bois de Boulogne, or dinner as
pleased his moods, and in return Saint-Gaudens
sometimes let Adams go about in his company.

Once Saint-Gaudens took him down to
Amiens, with a party of Frenchmen, to see the
cathedral. Not until they found themselves actually studying the sculpture of the western
portal, did it dawn on Adams's mind that, for
his purposes, Saint-Gaudens on that spot had
more interest to him than the cathedral itself.
Great men before great monuments express
great truths, provided they are not taken too
solemnly. Adams never tired of quoting the
supreme phrase of his idol Gibbon, before the
Gothic cathedrals: "I darted a contemptuous
look on the stately monuments of superstition."
Even in the footnotes of his history, Gibbon had
never inserted a bit of humor more human than
this, and one would have paid largely for a
photograph of the fat little historian, on the
background of Notre Dame of Amiens, trying to
persuade his readers — perhaps himself — that

he was darting a contemptuous look on the stately monument, for which he felt in fact the respect which every man of his vast study and active mind always feels before objects worthy of it; but besides the humor, one felt also the relation. Gibbon ignored the Virgin, because in 1789 religious monuments were out of fashion. In 1900 his remark sounded fresh and simple as the green fields to ears that had heard a hundred years of other remarks, mostly no more fresh and certainly less simple. Without malice, one might find it more instructive than a whole lecture of Ruskin. One sees what one brings, and at that moment Gibbon brought the French Revolution. Ruskin brought reaction against the Revolution. Saint-Gaudens had passed beyond all. He liked the stately monuments much more than he liked Gibbon or Ruskin; he loved their dignity; their unity; their scale; their lines; their lights and shadows; their decorative sculpture; but he was even less conscious than they of the force that created it all — the Virgin, the Woman — by whose genius "the stately monuments of superstition" were built, through which she was expressed. He would have seen more meaning in Isis with the cow's horns, at Edfoo, who expressed the same thought. The art remained, but the energy was lost even upon the artist.

Yet in mind and person Saint-Gaudens was a survival of the 1500; he bore the stamp of the Renaissance, and should have carried an image of the Virgin round his neck, or stuck in his hat, like Louis XI. In mere time he was a lost soul that had strayed by chance into the twentieth century, and forgotten where it came from. He writhed and cursed at his ignorance, much as Adams did at his own, but in the opposite sense. Saint-Gaudens was a child of Benvenuto Cellini, smothered in an American cradle. Adams was a quintessence of Boston, devoured by curiosity to think like Benvenuto. Saint-Gaudens's art was starved from birth, and Adams's instinct was blighted from babyhood. Each had but half of a nature, and when they came together before the Virgin of Amiens they ought both to have felt in her the force that made them one; but it was not so. To Adams she became more than ever a channel of force; to Saint-Gaudens she remained as before a channel of taste.

For a symbol of power, Saint-Gaudens instinctively preferred the horse, as was plain in his horse and Victory of the Sherman monument. Doubtless Sherman also felt it so. The attitude was so American that, for at least forty years, Adams had never realized that any other could be in sound taste. How many years had he taken to admit a notion of what Michaelangelo and Rubens were driving at? He could not say; but he knew that only since 1895 had he begun to feel the Virgin or Venus as force, and not everywhere even so. At Chartres — perhaps at Lourdes — possibly at Cnidos if one could still find there the divinely naked Aphrodite of Praxiteles — but otherwise one must look for force to the goddesses of Indian mythology. The idea died out long ago in the German and English stock. Saint-Gaudens at Amiens was hardly less sensitive to the force of the female energy than Matthew Arnold at the Grande Chartreuse. Neither of them felt goddesses as power — only as reflected emotion, human expression, beauty, purity, taste, scarcely even as sympathy. They felt a railway train as power; yet they, and all other artists, constantly complained that the power embodied in a railway train could never be embodied in art. All the steam in the world could not, like the Virgin, build Chartres.

Yet in mechanics, whatever the mechanician might think, both energies acted as interchangeable forces on man, and by action on man all known force may be measured. Indeed, few men of science measured force in any other way. After once admitting that a straight line was the shortest distance between two points, no serious mathematician cared to deny anything that suited his convenience, and rejected no symbol, unprobed or unprovable, that helped him to accomplish work. The symbol was force, as a compass-needle or a triangle was force, as the mechanist might prove by losing it, and nothing could be gained by ignoring their value. Symbol or energy, the Virgin had acted as the greatest force the Western world ever felt, and had drawn man's activities to herself more strongly than any other power, natural or super-natural, had ever done; the historian's business was to follow the track of the energy; to find where it came from and where it went to; its complex source and shifting channels; its values, equivalents, conversions. It could scarcely be more complex than radium; it could hardly be deflected, diverted, polarized, absorbed more perplexingly than other radiant matter. Adams knew nothing about any of them, but as a mathematical problem of influence on human progress, though all were occult, all reacted on his mind, and he rather inclined to think the Virgin easiest to handle.

The pursuit turned out to be long and tortuous, leading at last into the vast forests of scholastic science. From Zeno to Descartes, hand in hand with Thomas Aquinas, Montaigne, and Pascal, one stumbled as stupidly as though one were still a German student of 1860. Only with the instinct of despair could one force one's self into this old thicket of ignorance after having been repulsed at a score of entrances more promising and more popular. Thus far, no path had led anywhere, unless perhaps to an exceedingly modest living. Forty-five years of study had proved to be quite futile for the pursuit of power; one controlled no more force in 1900 than in 1850, although the amount of force controlled by society had enormously increased. The secret of education still hid itself somewhere behind ignorance, and one fumbled over it as feebly as ever. In such labyrinths, the staff is a force almost more necessary than the legs; the pen becomes a sort of blind-man's dog, to keep him from falling into the gutters. The pen works for itself, and acts like a hand, modelling the plastic material over and over again to the form that suits it best. The form is never arbitrary, but is a sort of growth like crystallization, as any artist knows too well; for often the pencil or pen runs into sidepaths and shapelessness, loses its relations, stops or is bogged. Then it has to return on its trail, and recover, if it can, its line of force. The result of a year's work depends more on what is struck out than on what is left in; on the sequence of the main lines of thought than on their play or variety. Compelled once more to lean heavily on this support, Adams covered more thousands of pages with figures as formal as though they were algebra, laboriously striking out, altering, burning, experimenting, until the year had expired, the Exposition had long been closed, and winter drawing to its end, before he sailed from Cherbourg, on January 19, 1901, for home.

Vis Nova (1903–1904)

***Ten years had passed since he last crossed the Mississippi, and he found everything new. In this great region from Pittsburgh through Ohio and Indiana, agriculture had made way for steam; tall chimneys reeked smoke on every horizon, and dirty suburbs filled with scrap-iron, scrap-paper and cinders, formed the setting of every town. Evidently, cleanliness was not to be the birthmark of the new American, but this matter of discards concerned the measure of force little, while the chimneys and cinders concerned it so much that Adams thought the Secretary of State should have rushed to the platform at every station to ask who were the people; for the American of the prime seemed to be extinct with the Shawnee and the buffalo.

The subject grew quickly delicate. History told little about these millions of Germans and Slavs, or whatever their race-names, who had overflowed these regions as though the Rhine and the Danube had turned their floods into the Ohio. John Hay was as strange to the Mississippi River as though he had not been bred on its shores, and the city of St. Louis had turned its back on the noblest work of nature, leaving it bankrupt between its own banks. The new American showed his parentage proudly; he was the child of steam and the brother of the dynamo, and already, within less than thirty years, this mass of mixed humanities, brought together by steam, was squeezed and welded into approach to shape; a product of so much mechanical power, and bearing no distinctive marks but that of its pressure. The new American, like the new European, was the servant of the powerhouse, as the European of the twelfth century was the servant of the Church, and the features would follow the parentage.

The St. Louis Exposition was its first creation in the twentieth century, and, for that reason, acutely interesting. One saw here a third-rate town of half-a-million people without history, education, unity, or art, and with little capital — without even an element of natural interest except the river which it studiously ignored — but doing what London, Paris, or New York would have shrunk from attempting. This new social conglomerate, with no tie but its steam-power and not much of that, threw away thirty or forty million dollars on a pageant as ephemeral as a stage flat. The world had never witnessed so marvellous a phantasm; by night Arabia's crimson sands had never returned a glow half so astonishing, as one wandered among long lines of white palaces, exquisitely lighted by thousands on thousands of electric candles, soft, rich, shadowy, palpable in their sensuous depths; all in deep silence, profound solitude, listening for a voice or a foot-fall or the plash of an oar, as though the Emir Mirza were displaying the beauties of this City of Brass, which could show nothing half so beautiful as this illumination, with its vast, white, monumental solitude, bathed in the pure light of setting suns. One enjoyed it with iniquitous rapture, not because of exhibits but rather because of their want. Here was a paradox like the stellar universe that fitted one's mental faults. Had there been no exhibits at all, and no visitors, one would have enjoyed it only the more.

Here education found new forage. That the power was wasted, the art indifferent, the economic failure complete, added just so much to the interest. The chaos of education approached a dream. One asked one's self whether this extravagance reflected the past or imaged the future; whether it was a creation of the old American or a promise of the new one. No prophet could be believed, but a pilgrim of power, without constituency to flatter, might allow himself to hope. The prospect from the Exposition was pleasant; one seemed to see almost an adequate motive for power; almost a scheme for progress. In another half-century, the people of the central valleys should have hundreds of millions to throw away more easily than in 1900 they could throw away tens; and by that time they might know what they wanted. Possibly they might even have learned how to reach it.

This was an optimist's hope, shared by few except pilgrims of World's Fairs, and frankly dropped by the multitude, for, east of the Mississippi, the St. Louis Exposition met a deliberate conspiracy of silence, discouraging, beyond measure, to an optimistic dream of future strength in American expression. The party got back to Washington on May 24, and before sailing for Europe, Adams went over, one warm evening, to bid goodbye on the garden-porch of the White House. He found himself the first person who urged Mrs. Roosevelt to visit the Exposition for its beauty, and, as far as he ever knew, the last.

He left St. Louis May 22, 1904, and on Sunday, June 5, found himself again in the town of Coutances, where the people of Normandy had built, towards the year 1250, an Exposition which architects still admired and tourists visited, for it was thought singularly expressive of force as well as of grace in the Virgin. On this Sunday, the Norman world was celebrating a pretty church-feast — the Fête Dieu — and the streets were filled with altars to the Virgin, covered with flowers and foliage; the pavements strewn with paths of leaves and the spring handiwork of nature; the cathedral densely thronged at mass. The scene was graceful. The Virgin did not shut her costly Exposition on Sunday, or any other day, even to American Senators who had shut the St. Louis Exposition to her — or for her; and a historical tramp would gladly have offered a candle, or even a candle-stick in her honor, if she would have taught him her relation with the deity of the Senators. The power of the Virgin had been plainly One, embracing all human activity; while the power of the Senate, or its deity, seemed — might one say — to be more or less ashamed of man and his work. The matter had no great interest as far as it concerned the somewhat obscure mental processes of Senators who could probably have given no clearer idea than priests of the deity they supposed themselves to honor — if that was indeed their purpose; but it interested a student of force, curious to measure its manifestations. Apparently the Virgin — or her Son — had no longer the force to build expositions that one cared to visit, but had the force to close them. The force was still real, serious, and, at St. Louis, had been anxiously measured in actual money-value.

That it was actual and serious in France as in the Senate Chamber at Washington, proved itself at once by forcing Adams to buy an automobile, which was a supreme demonstration because this was the form of force which Adams most abominated. He had set aside the summer for study of the Virgin, not as a sentiment but as a motive power, which had left monuments widely scattered and not easily reached. The automobile alone could unite them in any reasonable sequence, and although the force of the automobile, for the purposes of a commercial traveller, seemed to have no relation whatever to the force that inspired a Gothic cathedral, the Virgin in the twelfth century would have guided and controlled both bagman and architect, as she controlled the seeker of history. In his mind the problem offered itself as to Newton; it was a matter of mutual attraction, and he knew it, in his own case, to be a formula as precise as $s = gt^2/2$, if he could but experimentally prove it. Of the attraction he needed no proof on his own account; the costs of his automobile were more than sufficient: but as teacher he needed to speak for others than himself. For him, the Virgin was an adorable mistress, who led the automobile and its owner where she would, to her wonderful palaces and châteaux, from Chartres to Rouen, and thence to Amiens and Laon, and a score of others, kindly receiving, amusing, charming and dazzling her lover, as though she were Aphrodite herself, worth all else that man ever dreamed. He never doubted her force, since he felt it to the last fibre of his being, and could not more dispute its mastery than he could dispute the force of gravitation of which he knew nothing but the formula. He was only too glad to yield himself entirely, not to her charm or to any sentimentality of religion, but to her mental and physical energy of creation which had built up these World's Fairs of thirteenth-century force that turned Chicago and St. Louis pale.

"Both were faiths and both are gone," said Matthew Arnold of the Greek and Norse divinities; but the business of a student was to ask where they had gone. The Virgin had not even altogether gone; her fading away had been excessively slow. Her adorer had pursued her too long, too far, and into too many manifestations of her power, to admit that she had any equivalent, either of quantity or kind, in the actual world, but he could still less admit her annihilation as energy.

So he went on wooing, happy in the thought that at last he had found a mistress who could see no difference in the age of her lovers. Her own age had no time-measure. For years past, incited by John La Farge, Adams had devoted his summer schooling to the study of her glass at Chartres and elsewhere, and if the automobile had one *vitesse* more useful than another, it was that of a century a minute; that of passing from one century to another without break. The cen-

turies dropped like autumn leaves in one's road, and one was not fined for running over them too fast. When the thirteenth lost breath, the fourteenth caught on, and the sixteenth ran close ahead. The hunt for the Virgin's glass opened rich preserves. Especially the sixteenth century ran riot in sensuous worship. Then the ocean of religion, which had flooded France, broke into Shelley's light dissolved in star-showers thrown, which had left every remote village strewn with fragments that flashed like jewels, and were tossed into hidden clefts of peace and forgetfulness. One dared not pass a parish church in Champagne or Touraine without stopping to look for its window of fragments, where one's glass discovered the Christ-child in his manger, nursed by the head of a fragmentary donkey, with a Cupid playing into its long ears from the balustrade of a Venetian palace, guarded by a legless Flemish *Leibwache*, standing on his head with a broken halbert; all invoked in prayer by remnants of the donors and their children that might have been drawn by Fouquet or Pinturicchio, in colors as fresh and living as the day they were burned in, and with feeling that still consoled the faithful for the paradise they had paid for and lost. France abounds in sixteenth-century glass. Paris alone contains acres of it, and the neighborhood within fifty miles contains scores of churches where the student may still imagine himself three hundred years old, kneeling before the Virgin's window in the silent solitude of an empty faith, crying his culp, beating his breast, confessing his historical sins, weighed down by the rubbish of sixty-six years' education, and still desperately hoping to understand.

Stephen Crane [1871–1900]

The embittered stories of Hamlin Garland (see page 835) were followed by the unflinching naturalism of a far more gifted writer, in whose work the modern literary movement very definitely got under way.

Son of a Methodist minister, Stephen Crane was born in Newark, New Jersey, attended college for two years (Lafayette, Syracuse), then became a writer for newspapers and magazines. He had to his credit ten printed volumes, and others about to be added, when he was cut off by death at age twenty-nine.

Crane was the first naturalistic fiction writer in a series which would include, conventionally, Frank Norris, Jack London, Theodore Dreiser, and Sherwood Anderson. His first novel, *Maggie: A Girl of the Streets* (see the period introduction, page 838), was welcomed by Hamlin Garland in a review as "a story which deals with vice and poverty and crime . . . not out of salaciousness, but because of a distinct art impulse to utter in truthful phrase a certain rebellious cry. It is the voice of the slums." Encouraged by Garland and also by Howells, he proceeded to write a second novel, *The Red Badge of Courage*, published when he was still only twenty-four, yet a best seller. It is a brilliant psychological representation of a boy's first battle experience in the Civil War — a wholly imaginary construction, since the author had never been in any military engagement. Long before Dos Passos and Hemingway, Crane stripped war of all romance and meaning.

After this success, Crane set sail to report real war for a syndicate. Shipwrecked off Florida, he suffered from exposure, further weakened his condition by experiences as reporter in the Greek-Turkish war, and died of tuberculosis in Germany.

His special talents were perhaps best displayed in the short story, especially "The Open Boat" and "The Blue Hotel," powerful representations, in brief compass, of a naturalistic concept of fate. They also illustrate well his control of a style of writing that seems ahead of his time, a prose, as Carl Van Doren described it, with "rapid, flashing movement" and "bright, startling phrases." Similarly, his experimental poems pointed forward to the "free verse" that came into vogue a decade and a half later.

Further reading: *The Red Badge of Courage. Twenty Stories*, ed. Carl Van Doren. John Berryman, *Stephen Crane*, 1951. Maxwell Geismar, *Rebels and Ancestors*, 1953, pages 69–136.

The Open Boat

*A Tale Intended to be after the Fact:
Being the Experience of Four Men
from the Sunk Steamer* Commodore

As we have noted, Crane's *Red Badge of Courage* had no basis in direct personal experience. On the other hand, "The Open Boat," first published in 1897, rested entirely on such experience. The subtitle means exactly what it says: the events of this fine story follow closely an experience which Crane shared with three other shipwrecked men. In 1896 he was on his way, as war correspondent, to Cuba, then in insurrection against Spain, two years before the United States intervened. The *Commodore* went down off St. Augustine. Crane got into the last of the open boats. The story tells the rest.

But good fiction is not mere fact. How, without altering the events, has Crane achieved a memorable story? And just what makes it "naturalistic"?

I

None of them knew the color of the sky. Their eyes glanced level, and were fastened upon the waves that swept toward them. These waves were of the hue of slate, save for the tops, which were of foaming white, and all of the men knew the colors of the sea. The horizon narrowed and widened, and dipped and rose, and at all times its edge was jagged with waves that seemed thrust up in points like rocks. Many a man ought to have a bath-tub larger than the boat which here rode upon the sea. These waves were most wrongfully and barbarously abrupt and tall, and each froth-top was a problem in small-boat navigation.

The cook squatted in the bottom and looked with both eyes at the six inches of gunwale which separated him from the ocean. His sleeves were rolled over his fat forearms, and the two flaps of his unbuttoned vest dangled as he bent to bail out the boat. Often he said: "Gawd! That was a narrow clip." As he remarked it he invariably gazed eastward over the broken sea.

The oiler, steering with one of the two oars in the boat, sometimes raised himself suddenly to keep clear of water that swirled in over the stern. It was a thin little oar and it seemed often ready to snap.

The correspondent, pulling at the other oar, watched the waves and wondered why he was there.

The injured captain, lying in the bow, was at this time buried in that profound dejection and indifference which comes, temporarily at least, to even the bravest and most enduring when, willy nilly, the firm fails, the army loses, the ship goes down. The mind of the master of a vessel is rooted deep in the timbers of her, though he command for a day or a decade, and this captain had on him the stern impression of a scene in the grays of dawn of seven turned faces, and later a stump of a top-mast with a white ball on it that slashed to and fro at the waves, went low and lower, and down. Thereafter there was something strange in his voice. Although steady, it was deep with mourning, and of a quality beyond oration or tears.

"Keep 'er a little more south, Billie," said he.

"'A little more south,' sir," said the oiler in the stern.

A seat in this boat was not unlike a seat upon a bucking broncho, and by the same token, a broncho is not much smaller. The craft pranced and reared, and plunged like an animal. As each wave came, and she rose for it, she seemed like a horse making at a fence outrageously high. The manner of her scramble over these walls of water is a mystic thing, and, moreover, at the top of them were ordinarily these problems in white water, the foam racing down from the summit of each wave, requiring a new leap, and a leap from the air. Then, after scornfully bumping a crest, she would slide, and race, and splash down a long incline, and arrive bobbing and nodding in front of the next menace.

A singular disadvantage of the sea lies in the fact that after successfully surmounting one wave you discover that there is another behind it just as important and just as nervously anxious to do something effective in the way of swamping boats. In a ten-foot dingey one can get an idea of the resources of the sea in the line of waves that is not probable to the average experience which is never at sea in a dingey. As each slatey wall of water approached, it shut all else from the view of the men in the boat, and it was not difficult to imagine that this particular wave was the final outburst of the ocean, the last effort of the grim water. There was a terrible grace in the move of the waves, and they came in silence, save for the snarling of the crests.

In the wan light, the faces of the men must have been gray. Their eyes must have glinted in strange ways as they gazed steadily astern. Viewed from a balcony, the whole thing would doubtless have been weirdly picturesque. But the men in the boat had not time to see it, and if they had had leisure there were other things to occupy their minds. The sun swung steadily up the sky, and they knew it was broad day because the color of the sea changed from slate to emerald-green, streaked with amber lights, and the foam was like tumbling snow. The process of the breaking day was unknown to them. They were aware only of this effect upon the color of the waves that rolled toward them.

In disjointed sentences the cook and the correspondent argued as to the difference between a life-saving station and a house of refuge. The cook had said: "There's a house of refuge just north of the Mosquito Inlet Light, and as soon as they see us, they'll come off in their boat and pick us up."

"As soon as who see us?" said the correspondent.

"The crew," said the cook.

"Houses of refuge don't have crews," said the correspondent. "As I understand them, they are only places where clothes and grub are stored for the benefit of shipwrecked people. They don't carry crews."

"Oh, yes, they do," said the cook.

"No, they don't," said the correspondent.

"Well, we're not there yet, anyhow," said the oiler, in the stern.

"Well," said the cook, "perhaps it's not a house of refuge that I'm thinking of as being near Mosquito Inlet Light. Perhaps it's a life-saving station."

"We're not there yet," said the oiler, in the stern.

II

As the boat bounced from the top of each wave, the wind tore through the hair of the hatless men, and as the craft plopped her stern down again the spray splashed past them. The crest of each of these waves was a hill, from the top of which the men surveyed, for a moment, a broad tumultuous expanse, shining and wind-riven. It was probably splendid. It was probably glorious, this play of the free sea, wild with lights of emerald and white and amber.

"Bully good thing it's an on-shore wind," said the cook. "If not, where would we be? Wouldn't have a show."

"That's right," said the correspondent.

The busy oiler nodded his assent.

Then the captain, in the bow, chuckled in a way that expressed humor, contempt, tragedy, all in one.

"Do you think we've got much of a show now, boys?" said he.

Whereupon the three were silent, save for a trifle of hemming and hawing. To express any particular optimism at this time they felt to be childish and stupid, but they all doubtless possessed this sense of the situation in their minds. A young man thinks doggedly at such times. On the other hand, the ethics of their condition was decidedly against any open suggestion of hopelessness. So they were silent.

"Oh, well," said the captain, soothing his children, "we'll get ashore all right."

But there was that in his tone which made them think, so the oiler quoth: "Yes! If this wind holds!"

The cook was bailing: "Yes! If we don't catch hell in the surf."

Canton flannel gulls flew near and far. Sometimes they sat down on the sea, near patches of brown seaweed that rolled on the waves with a movement like carpets on a line in a gale. The birds sat comfortably in groups, and they were envied by some in the dingey, for the wrath of the sea was no more to them than it was to a covey of prairie chickens a thousand miles inland. Often they came very close and stared at the men with black bead-like eyes. At these times they were uncanny and sinister in their unblinking scrutiny, and the men hooted angrily at them, telling them to be gone.

One came, and evidently decided to alight on the top of the captain's head. The bird flew parallel to the boat and did not circle, but made short sidelong jumps in the air in chicken-fashion. His black eyes were wistfully fixed upon the captain's head. "Ugly brute," said the oiler to the bird. "You look as if you were made with a jack-knife." The cook and the correspondent swore darkly at the creature. The captain naturally wished to knock it away with the end of the heavy painter; but he did not dare do it, because anything resembling an emphatic gesture would have capsized this freighted boat, and so with his open hand, the captain gently and carefully waved the gull away. After it had been discouraged from the pursuit the captain breathed easier on account of his hair, and others breathed easier because the bird struck their minds at this time as being somehow gruesome and ominous.

In the meantime the oiler and the correspondent rowed. And also they rowed.

They sat together in the same seat, and each rowed an oar. Then the oiler took both oars; then the correspondent took both oars; then the oiler; then the correspondent. They rowed and they rowed. The very ticklish part of the business was when the time came for the reclining one in the stern to take his turn at the oars. By the very last star of truth, it is easier to steal eggs from under a hen than it was to change seats in the dingey. First the man in the stern slid his hand along the thwart and moved with care, as if he were of Sèvres. Then the man in the rowing seat slid his hand along the other thwart. It was all done with the most extraordinary care. As the two sidled past each other, the whole party kept watchful eyes on the coming wave, and the captain cried: "Look out now! Steady there!"

The brown mats of seaweed that appeared from time to time were like islands, bits of earth. They were traveling, apparently, neither one way nor the other. They were, to all intents, stationary. They informed the men in the boat that it was making progress slowly toward the land.

The captain, rearing cautiously in the bow, after the dingey soared on a great swell, said that he had seen the lighthouse at Mosquito Inlet. Presently the cook remarked that he had seen it. The correspondent was at the oars then, and for some reason he too wished to look at the lighthouse, but his back was toward the far shore and the waves were important, and for some time he could not seize an opportunity to turn his head. But at last there came a wave more gentle than the others, and when at the crest of it he swiftly scoured the western horizon.

"See it?" said the captain.

"No," said the correspondent slowly, "I didn't see anything."

"Look again," said the captain. He pointed. "It's exactly in that direction."

At the top of another wave, the correspondent did as he was bid, and this time his eyes chanced on a small still thing on the edge of the swaying horizon. It was precisely like the point of a pin. It took an anxious eye to find a lighthouse so tiny.

"Think we'll make it, captain?"

"If this wind holds and the boat don't swamp, we can't do much else," said the captain.

The little boat, lifted by each towering sea, and splashed viciously by the crests, made progress that in the absence of seaweed was not apparent to those in her. She seemed just a wee thing wallowing, miraculously top-up, at the mercy of five oceans. Occasionally, a great spread of water, like white flames, swarmed into her.

"Bail her, cook," said the captain serenely.

"All right, captain," said the cheerful cook.

III

It would be difficult to describe the subtle brotherhood of men that was here established on the seas. No one said that it was so. No one mentioned it. But it dwelt in the boat, and each man felt it warm him. They were a captain, an oiler, a cook, and a correspondent, and they were friends, friends in a more curiously iron-bound degree than may be common. The hurt captain, lying against the water-jar in the bow, spoke always in a low voice and calmly, but he could never command a more ready and swiftly obedient crew than the motley three of the dingey. It was more than a mere recognition of what was best for the common safety. There was surely in it a quality that was personal and heartfelt. And after this devotion to the commander of the boat there was this comradeship that the correspondent, for instance, who had been taught to be cynical of men, knew even at the time was the best experience of his life. But no one said that it was so. No one mentioned it.

"I wish we had a sail," remarked the captain. "We might try my overcoat on the end of an oar and give you two boys a chance to rest."

So the cook and the correspondent held the mast and spread wide the overcoat. The oiler steered, and the little boat made good way with her new rig. Sometimes the oiler had to scull sharply to keep a sea from breaking into the boat, but otherwise sailing was a success.

Meanwhile the lighthouse had been growing slowly larger. It had now almost assumed color, and appeared like a little gray shadow on the sky. The man at the oars could not be prevented from turning his head rather often to try for a glimpse of this little gray shadow.

At last, from the top of each wave the men in the tossing boat could see land. Even as the lighthouse was an upright shadow on the sky, this land seemed but a long black shadow on the sea. It certainly was thinner than paper. "We must be about opposite New Smyrna," said the cook, who had coasted this shore often in schooners. "Captain, by the way, I believe they abandoned that life-saving station there about a year ago."

"Did they?" said the captain.

The wind slowly died away. The cook and the correspondent were not now obliged to slave in order to hold high the oar. But the waves continued their old impetuous swooping at the dingey, and the little craft, no longer under way, struggled woundily over them. The oiler or the correspondent took the oars again.

Shipwrecks are à propos of nothing. If men could only train for them and have them occur when the men had reached pink condition, there would be less drowning at sea.

Of the four in the dingey none had slept any time worth mentioning for two days and two nights previous to embarking in the dingey, and in the excitement of clambering about the deck of a foundering ship they had also forgotten to eat heartily.

For these reasons, and for others, neither the oiler nor the correspondent was fond of rowing at this time. The correspondent wondered ingenuously how in the name of all that was sane could there be people who thought it amusing to row a boat. It was not an amusement; it was a diabolical punishment, and even a genius of mental aberrations could never conclude that it was anything but a horror to the muscles and a crime against the back. He mentioned to the boat in general how the amusement of rowing struck him, and the weary-faced oiler smiled in full sympathy. Previously to the foundering, by the way, the oiler had worked double-watch in the engine-room of the ship.

"Take her easy, now, boys," said the captain. "Don't spend yourselves. If we have to run a surf you'll need all your strength, because we'll sure have to swim for it. Take your time."

Slowly the land arose from the sea. From a black line it became a line of black and a line of white, trees and sand. Finally, the captain said that he could make out a house on the shore.

"That's the house of refuge, sure," said the cook. "They'll see us before long, and come out after us."

The distant lighthouse reared high. "The keeper ought to be able to make us out now, if he's looking through a glass," said the captain. "He'll notify the life-saving people."

"None of those other boats could have got ashore to give word of the wreck," said the oiler, in a low voice. "Else the life-boat would be out hunting us."

Slowly and beautifully the land loomed out of the sea. The wind came again. It had veered from the north-east to the south-east.

Finally, a new sound struck the ears of the men in the boat. It was the low thunder of the surf on the shore. "We'll never be able to make the lighthouse now," said the captain. "Swing her head a little more north, Billie," said he.

" 'A little more north,' sir," said the oiler.

Whereupon the little boat turned her nose once more down the wind, and all but the oarsman watched the shore grow. Under the influence of this expansion doubt and direful apprehension was leaving the minds of the men. The management of the boat was still most absorbing, but it could not prevent a quiet cheerfulness. In an hour, perhaps, they would be ashore.

Their backbones had become thoroughly used to balancing in the boat, and they now rode this wild colt of a dingey like circus men. The correspondent thought that he had been drenched to the skin, but happening to feel in the top pocket of his coat, he found therein eight cigars. Four of them were soaked with sea-water; four were perfectly scatheless. After a search, somebody produced three dry matches, and thereupon the four waifs rode impudently in their little boat, and with an assurance of an impending rescue shining in their eyes, puffed at the big cigars and judged well and ill of all men. Everybody took a drink of water.

IV

"Cook," remarked the captain, "there don't seem to be any signs of life about your house of refuge."

"No," replied the cook. "Funny they don't see us!"

A broad stretch of lowly coast lay before the eyes of the men. It was of dunes topped with dark vegetation. The roar of the surf was plain, and sometimes they could see the white lip of a wave as it spun up the beach. A tiny house was blocked out black upon the sky. Southward, the slim lighthouse lifted its little gray length.

Tide, wind, and waves were swinging the dingey northward. "Funny they don't see us," said the men.

The surf's roar was dulled, but its tone was, nevertheless, thunderous and mighty. As the boat swam over the great rollers, the men sat listening to this roar. "We'll swamp sure," said everybody.

It is fair to say here that there was not a life-saving station within twenty miles in either direction, but the men did not know this fact, and in consequence they made dark and opprobrious remarks concerning the eyesight of the nation's life-savers. Four scowling men sat in the dingey and surpassed records in the invention of epithets.

"Funny they don't see us."

The lightheartedness of a former time had completely faded. To their sharpened minds it was easy to conjure pictures of all kinds of incompetency and blindness and, indeed, cowardice. There was the shore of the populous land, and it was bitter and bitter to them that from it came no sign.

"Well," said the captain, ultimately, "I suppose we'll have to make a try for ourselves. If we stay out here too long, we'll none of us have strength left to swim after the boat swamps."

And so the oiler, who was at the oars, turned the boat straight for the shore. There was a sudden tightening of muscle. There was some thinking.

"If we don't all get ashore ——" said the captain. "If we don't all get ashore, I suppose you fellows know where to send news of my finish?"

They then briefly exchanged some addresses and admonitions. As for the reflections of the men, there was a great deal of rage in them. Perchance they might be formulated thus: "If I am going to be drowned — if I am going to be drowned — if I am going to be drowned, why, in the name of the seven mad gods who rule the sea, was I allowed to come thus far and contemplate sand and trees? Was I brought here merely to have my nose dragged away as I was about to nibble the sacred cheese of life? It is preposterous. If this old ninny-woman, Fate, cannot do better than this, she should be deprived of the management of men's fortunes. She is an old hen who knows not her intention. If she has decided to drown me, why did she not do it in the beginning and save me all this trouble? The whole affair is absurd. . . . . But no, she cannot mean to drown me. She dare not drown me. She cannot drown me. Not after all this work." Afterward the man might have had an impulse to shake his fist at the clouds: "Just you drown me, now, and then hear what I call you!"

The billows that came at this time were more formidable. They seemed always just about to break and roll over the little boat in a turmoil of foam. There was a preparatory and long growl in the speech of them. No mind unused to the sea would have concluded that the dingey could ascend these sheer heights in time. The shore was still afar.

The oiler was a wily surfman. "Boys," he said swiftly, "she won't live three minutes more,

and we're too far out to swim. Shall I take her to sea again, captain?"

"Yes! Go ahead!" said the captain.

This oiler, by a series of quick miracles, and fast and steady oarsmanship, turned the boat in the middle of the surf and took her safely to sea again.

There was a considerable silence as the boat bumped over the furrowed sea to deeper water. Then somebody in gloom spoke. "Well, anyhow, they must have seen us from the shore by now."

The gulls went in slanting flight up the wind toward the gray desolate east. A squall, marked by dingy clouds, and clouds brick-red, like smoke from a burning building, appeared from the south-east.

"What do you think of those life-saving people? Ain't they peaches?"

"Funny they haven't seen us."

"Maybe they think we're out here for sport! Maybe they think we're fishin'. Maybe they think we're damned fools."

It was a long afternoon. A changed tide tried to force them southward, but the wind and wave said northward. Far ahead, where coast-line, sea, and sky formed their mighty angle, there were little dots which seemed to indicate a city on the shore.

"St. Augustine?"

The captain shook his head. "Too near Mosquito Inlet."

And the oiler rowed, and then the correspondent rowed. Then the oiler rowed. It was a weary business. The human back can become the seat of more aches and pains than are registered in books for the composite anatomy of a regiment. It is a limited area, but it can become the theater of innumerable muscular conflicts, tangles, wrenches, knots, and other comforts.

"Did you ever like to row, Billie?" asked the correspondent.

"No," said the oiler. "Hang it!"

When one exchanged the rowing-seat for a place in the bottom of the boat, he suffered a bodily depression that caused him to be careless of everything save an obligation to wiggle one finger. There was cold sea-water swashing to and fro in the boat, and he lay in it. His head, pillowed on a thwart, was within an inch of the swirl of a wave crest, and sometimes a particularly obstreperous sea came in-board and drenched him once more. But these matters did not annoy him. It is almost certain that if the boat had capsized he would have tumbled comfortably out upon the ocean as if he felt sure that it was a great soft mattress.

"Look! There's a man on the shore!"

"Where?"

"There! See 'im? See 'im?"

"Yes, sure! He's walking along."

"Now he's stopped. Look! He's facing us!"

"He's waving at us!"

"So he is! By thunder!"

"Ah, now we're all right! Now we're all right! There'll be a boat out here for us in half-an-hour."

"He's going on. He's running. He's going up to that house there."

The remote beach seemed lower than the sea, and it required a searching glance to discern the little black figure. The captain saw a floating stick and they rowed to it. A bath-towel was by some weird chance in the boat, and, tying this on the stock, the captain waved it. The oarsman did not dare turn his head, so he was obliged to ask questions.

"What's he doing now?"

"He's standing still again. He's looking, I think . . . . There he goes again. Toward the house . . . . Now he's stopped again."

"Is he waving at us?"

"No, not now! he was, though."

"Look! There comes another man!"

"He's running."

"Look at him go, would you."

"Why, he's on a bicycle. Now he's met the other man. They're both waving at us. Look!"

"There comes something up the beach."

"What the devil is that thing?"

"Why, it looks like a boat."

"Why, certainly it's a boat."

"No, it's on wheels."

"Yes, so it is. Well, that must be the life-boat. They drag them along shore on a wagon."

"That's the life-boat, sure."

"No, by ———, it's — it's an omnibus."

"I tell you it's a life-boat."

"It is not! It's an omnibus. I can see it plain. See? One of these big hotel omnibuses."

"By thunder, you're right. It's an omnibus, sure as fate. What do you suppose they are doing with an omnibus? Maybe they are going around collecting the life-crew, hey?"

"That's it, likely. Look! There's a fellow waving a little black flag. He's standing on the steps of the omnibus. There comes those other two fellows. Now they're all talking together. Look at the fellow with the flag. Maybe he ain't waving it."

"That ain't a flag, is it? That's his coat. Why, certainly, that's his coat."

"So it is. It's his coat. He's taken it off and is waving it around his head. But would you look at him swing it."

"Oh, say, there isn't any life-saving station there. That's just a winter resort hotel omnibus that has brought over some of the boarders to see us drown."

"What's that idiot with the coat mean? What's he signaling, anyhow?"

"It looks as if he were trying to tell us to go north. There must be a life-saving station up there."

"No! He thinks we're fishing. Just giving us a merry hand. See? Ah, there, Willie!"

"Well, I wish I could make something out of those signals. What do you suppose he means?"

"He don't mean anything. He's just playing."

"Well, if he'd just signal us to try the surf again, or to go to sea and wait, or go north, or go south, or go to hell — there would be some reason in it. But look at him. He just stands there and keeps his coat revolving like a wheel. The ass!"

"There come more people."

"Now there's quite a mob. Look! Isn't that a boat?"

"Where? Oh, I see where you mean. No, that's no boat."

"That fellow is still waving his coat."

"He must think we like to see him do that. Why don't he quit it? It don't mean anything."

"I don't know. I think he is trying to make us go north. It must be that there's a life-saving station there somewhere."

"Say, he ain't tired yet. Look at 'im wave."

"Wonder how long he can keep that up. He's been revolving his coat ever since he caught sight of us. He's an idiot. Why aren't they getting men to bring a boat out? A fishing boat — one of those big yawls — could come out here all right. Why don't he do something?"

"Oh, it's all right, now."

"They'll have a boat out here for us in less than no time, now that they've seen us."

A faint yellow tone came into the sky over the low land. The shadows on the sea slowly deepened. The wind bore coldness with it, and the men began to shiver.

"Holy smoke!" said one, allowing his voice to express his impious mood, "if we keep on monkeying out here! If we've got to flounder out here all night!"

"Oh, we'll never have to stay here all night! Don't you worry. They've seen us now, and it won't be long before they'll come chasing out after us."

The shore grew dusky. The man waving a coat blended gradually into this gloom, and it swallowed in the same manner the omnibus and the group of people. The spray, when it dashed uproariously over the side, made the voyagers shrink and swear like men who were being branded.

"I'd like to catch the chump who waved the coat. I feel like soaking him one, just for luck."

"Why? What did he do?"

"Oh, nothing, but then he seemed so damned cheerful."

In the meantime the oiler rowed, and then the correspondent rowed, and then the oiler rowed. Gray-faced and bowed forward, they mechanically, turn by turn, plied the leaden oars. The form of the lighthouse had vanished from the southern horizon, but finally a pale star appeared, just lifting from the sea. The streaked saffron in the west passed before the all-merging darkness, and the sea to the east was black. The land had vanished, and was expressed only by the low and drear thunder of the surf.

"If I am going to be drowned — if I am going to be drowned — if I am going to be drowned, why, in the name of the seven mad gods who rule the sea, was I allowed to come this far and contemplate sand and trees? Was I brought here merely to have my nose dragged away as I was about to nibble the sacred cheese of life?"

The patient captain, drooped over the water-jar, was sometimes obliged to speak to the oarsman.

"Keep her head up! Keep her head up!"

" 'Keep her head up,' sir." The voices were weary and low.

This was surely a quiet evening. All save the oarsman lay heavily and listlessly in the boat's bottom. As for him, his eyes were just capable of noting the tall black waves that swept forward in a most sinister silence, save for an occasional subdued growl of a crest.

The cook's head was on a thwart, and he looked without interest at the water under his nose. He was deep in other scenes. Finally he spoke. "Billie," he murmured, dreamfully, "what kind of pie do you like best?"

V

"Pie," said the oiler and the correspondent, agitatedly. "Don't talk about those things, blast you!"

"Well," said the cook, "I was just thinking about ham sandwiches, and —— "

A night on the sea in an open boat is a long night. As darkness settled finally, the shine of the light, lifting from the sea in the south, changed to full gold. On the northern horizon a new light appeared, a small bluish gleam on the edge of the waters. These two lights were the furniture of the world. Otherwise there was nothing but waves.

Two men huddled in the stern, and distances were so magnificent in the dingey that the rower was enabled to keep his feet partly warmed by thrusting them under his companions. Their legs indeed extended far under the rowing-seat until they touched the feet of the captain forward. Sometimes, despite the efforts of the tired oarsmen, a wave came piling into the boat, an icy wave of the night, and the chilling water soaked them anew. They would twist their bodies for a moment and groan, and sleep the dead sleep once more, while the water in the boat gurgled about them as the craft rocked.

The plan of the oiler and the correspondent was for one to row until he lost the ability, and then arouse the other from his sea-water couch in the bottom of the boat.

The oiler plied the oars until his head dropped forward, and the overpowering sleep blinded him. And he rowed yet afterward. Then he touched a man in the bottom of the boat, and called his name. "Will you spell me for a little while?" he said, meekly.

"Sure, Billie," said the correspondent, awakening and dragging himself to a sitting position. They exchanged places carefully, and the oiler, cuddling down in the sea-water at the cook's side, seemed to go to sleep instantly.

The particular violence of the sea had ceased. The waves came without snarling. The obligation of the man at the oars was to keep the boat headed so that the tilt of the rollers would not capsize her, and to preserve her from filling when the crests rushed past. The black waves were silent and hard to be seen in the darkness. Often one was almost upon the boat before the oarsman was aware.

In a low voice the correspondent addressed the captain. He was not sure that the captain was awake, although this iron man seemed to be always awake. "Captain, shall I keep her making for that light north, sir?"

The same steady voice answered him. "Yes. Keep it about two points off the port bow."

The cook had tied a life-belt around himself in order to get even the warmth which this clumsy cork contrivance could donate, and he seemed almost stove-like when a rower, whose teeth invariably chattered wildly as soon as he ceased his labor, dropped down to sleep.

The correspondent, as he rowed, looked down at the two men sleeping under-foot. The cook's arm was around the oiler's shoulders, and, with their fragmentary clothing and haggard faces, they were the babes of the sea, a grotesque rendering of the old babes in the wood.

Later he must have grown stupid at his work, for suddenly there was a growling of water, and a crest came with a roar and a swash into the boat, and it was a wonder that it did not set the cook afloat in his lifebelt. The cook continued to sleep, but the oiler sat up, blinking his eyes and shaking with the new cold.

"Oh, I'm awful sorry, Billie," said the correspondent contritely.

"That's all right, old boy," said the oiler, and lay down again and was asleep.

Presently it seemed that even the captain dozed, and the correspondent thought that he was the one man afloat on all the oceans. The wind had a voice as it came over the waves, and it was sadder than the end.

There was a long, loud swishing astern of the boat, and a gleaming trail of phosphorescence, like blue flame, was furrowed on the black waters. It might have been made by a monstrous knife.

Then there came a stillness, while the correspondent breathed with the open mouth and looked at the sea.

Suddenly there was another swish and another long flash of bluish light, and this time it was alongside the boat, and might almost have been reached with an oar. The correspondent saw an enormous fin speed like a shadow through the water, hurling the crystalline spray and leaving the long glowing trail.

The correspondent looked over his shoulder at the captain. His face was hidden, and he seemed to be asleep. He looked at the babes of the sea. They certainly were asleep. So being bereft of sympathy, he leaned a little way to one side and swore softly into the sea.

But the thing did not then leave the vicinity of the boat. Ahead or astern, on one side or the other, at intervals long or short, fled the long sparkling streak, and there was to be heard the whirroo of the dark fin. The speed and power of the thing was greatly to be admired. It cut the water like a gigantic and keen projectile.

The presence of this biding thing did not affect the man with the same horror that it would if he had been a picnicker. He simply looked at the sea dully and swore in an undertone.

Nevertheless, it is true that he did not wish to be alone. He wished one of his companions to awaken by chance and keep him company with it. But the captain hung motionless over the water-jar and the oiler and the cook in the bottom of the boat were plunged in slumber.

VI

"If I am going to be drowned — if I am going to be drowned — if I am going to be drowned, why, in the name of the seven mad gods who rule the sea, was I allowed to come thus far and contemplate sand and trees?"

During this dismal night, it may be remarked that a man would conclude that it was really the intention of the seven mad gods to drown him, despite the abominable injustice of it. For it was certainly an abominable injustice to drown a man who had worked so hard, so hard. The man felt it would be a crime most unnatural. Other people had drowned at sea since galleys swarmed with painted sails, but still ——

When it occurs to a man that Nature does not regard him as important, and that she feels she would not maim the universe by disposing of him, he at first wishes to throw bricks at the temple, and he hates deeply the fact that there are no bricks and no temples. Any visible expression of Nature would surely be pelleted with jeers.

Then, if there be no tangible thing to hoot, he feels, perhaps, the desire to confront a personification and indulge in pleas, bowed to one knee, and with hands supplicant, saying: "Yes, but I love myself."

A high cold star on a winter's night is the

word he feels that she says to him. Thereafter he knows the pathos of his situation.

The men in the dingey had not discussed these matters, but each had, no doubt, reflected upon them in silence and according to his mind. There was seldom any expression upon their faces save the general one of complete weariness. Speech was devoted to the business of the boat.

To chime the notes of his emotion, a verse mysteriously entered the correspondent's head. He had even forgotten that he had forgotten this verse, but it suddenly was in his mind.

"A soldier of the Legion lay dying in Algiers,
There was lack of woman's nursing, there was dearth of woman's tears;
But a comrade stood beside him, and he took that comrade's hand,
And he said: 'I never more shall see my own, my native land.'"

In his childhood, the correspondent had been made acquainted with the fact that a soldier of the Legion lay dying in Algiers, but he had never regarded the fact as important. Myriads of his school-fellows had informed him of the soldier's plight, but the dinning had naturally ended by making him perfectly indifferent. He had never considered it his affair that a soldier of the Legion lay dying in Algiers, nor had it appeared to him as a matter for sorrow. It was less to him than the breaking of a pencil's point.

Now, however, it quaintly came to him as a human, living thing. It was no longer merely a picture of a few throes in the breast of a poet, meanwhile drinking tea and warming his feet at the grate; it was an actuality — stern, mournful, and fine.

The correspondent plainly saw the soldier. He lay on the sand with his feet out straight and still. While his pale left hand was upon his chest in an attempt to thwart the going of his life, the blood came between his fingers. In the far Algerian distance, a city of low square forms was set against a sky that was faint with the last sunset hues. The correspondent, plying the oars and dreaming of the slow and slower movements of the lips of the soldier, was moved by a profound and perfectly impersonal comprehension. He was sorry for the soldier of the Legion who lay dying in Algiers.

The thing which had followed the boat and waited, had evidently grown bored at the delay. There was no longer to be heard the slash of the cut-water, and there was no longer the flame of the long trail. The light in the north still glimmered, but it was apparently no nearer to the boat. Sometimes the boom of the surf rang in the correspondent's ears, and he turned the craft seaward then and rowed harder. Southward, some one had evidently built a watch-fire on the beach. It was too low and too far to be seen, but it made a shimmering, roseate reflection upon the bluff back of it, and this could be discerned from the boat. The wind came stronger, and sometimes a wave suddenly raged out like a mountain-cat, and there was to be seen the sheen and sparkle of a broken crest.

The captain, in the bow, moved on his water-jar and sat erect. "Pretty long night," he observed to the correspondent. He looked at the shore. "Those life-saving people take their time."

"Did you see that shark playing around?"

"Yes, I saw him. He was a big fellow, all right."

"Wish I had known you were awake."

Later the correspondent spoke into the bottom of the boat.

"Billie!" There was a slow and gradual disentanglement. "Billie, will you spell me?"

"Sure," said the oiler.

As soon as the correspondent touched the cold comfortable sea-water in the bottom of the boat, and had huddled close to the cook's life-belt he was deep in sleep, despite the fact that his teeth played all the popular airs. This sleep was so good to him that it was but a moment before he heard a voice call his name in a tone that demonstrated the last stages of exhaustion. "Will you spell me?"

"Sure, Billie."

The light in the north had mysteriously vanished, but the correspondent took his course from the wide-awake captain.

Later in the night they took the boat farther out to sea, and the captain directed the cook to take one oar at the stern and keep the boat facing the seas. He was to call out if he should hear the thunder of the surf. This plan enabled the oiler and the correspondent to get respite together. "We'll give those boys a chance to get into shape again," said the captain. They curled down and, after a few preliminary chatterings and trembles, slept once more the dead sleep. Neither knew they had bequeathed to the cook the company of another shark, or perhaps the same shark.

As the boat caroused on the waves, spray occasionally bumped over the side and gave them a fresh soaking, but this had no power to break their repose. The ominous slash of the wind and the water affected them as it would have affected mummies.

"Boys," said the cook, with the notes of every reluctance in his voice, "she's drifted in pretty close. I guess one of you had better take her to sea again." The correspondent, aroused, heard the crash of the toppled crests.

As he was rowing, the captain gave him some whisky-and-water, and this steadied the chills out of him. "If I ever get ashore and anybody shows me even a photograph of an oar —— "

At last there was a short conversation.

"Billie . . . Billie, will you spell me?"

"Sure," said the oiler.

VII

When the correspondent again opened his eyes, the sea and the sky were each of the gray hue of the dawning. Later, carmine and gold was painted upon the waters. The morning appeared finally, in its splendor, with a sky of pure blue, and the sunlight flamed on the tips of the waves.

On the distant dunes were set many little black cottages, and a tall white windmill reared above them. No man, nor dog, nor bicycle appeared on the beach. The cottages might have formed a deserted village.

The voyagers scanned the shore. A conference was held in the boat. "Well," said the captain, "if no help is coming we might better try a run through the surf right away. If we stay out here much longer we will be too weak to do anything for ourselves at all." The others silently acquiesced in this reasoning. The boat was headed for the beach. The correspondent wondered if none ever ascended the tall windtower, and if then they never looked seaward. This tower was a giant, standing with its back to the plight of the ants. It represented in a degree, to the correspondent, the serenity of Nature amid the struggles of the individual — Nature in the wind, and Nature in the vision of men. She did not seem cruel to him then, nor beneficent, nor treacherous, nor wise. But she was indifferent, flatly indifferent. It is, perhaps, plausible that a man in this situation, impressed with the unconcern of the universe, should see the innumerable flaws of his life, and have them taste wickedly in his mind and wish for another chance. A distinction between right and wrong seems absurdly clear to him, then, in this new ignorance of the grave-edge, and he understands that if he were given another opportunity he would mend his conduct and his words, and be better and brighter during an introduction or at a tea.

"Now, boys," said the captain, "she is going to swamp, sure. All we can do is to work her in as far as possible, and then, when she swamps, pile out and scramble for the beach. Keep cool now, and don't jump until she swamps sure."

The oiler took the oars. Over his shoulder he scanned the surf. "Captain," he said, "I think I'd better bring her about, and keep her head-on to the seas and back her in."

"All right, Billie," said the captain. "Back her in." The oiler swung the boat then and, seated in the stern, the cook and the correspondent were obliged to look over their shoulders to contemplate the lonely and indifferent shore.

The monstrous in-shore rollers heaved the boat high until the men were again enabled to see the white sheets of water scudding up the slanted beach. "We won't get in very close," said the captain. Each time a man could wrest his attention from the rollers, he turned his glance toward the shore, and in the expression of the eyes during this contemplation there was a singular quality. The correspondent, observing the others, knew that they were not afraid, but the full meaning of their glances was shrouded.

As for himself, he was too tired to grapple fundamentally with the fact. He tried to coerce his mind into thinking of it, but the mind was dominated at this time by the muscles, and the muscles said they did not care. It merely occurred to him that if he should drown it would be a shame.

There were no hurried words, no pallor, no plain agitation. The men simply looked at the shore. "Now, remember to get well clear of the boat when you jump," said the captain.

Seaward the crest of a roller suddenly fell with a thunderous crash, and the long white comber came roaring down upon the boat.

"Steady now," said the captain. The men were silent. They turned their eyes from the shore to the comber and waited. The boat slid up the incline, leaped at the furious top, bounced over it, and swung down the long back of the wave. Some water had been shipped and the cook bailed it out.

But the next crest crashed also. The tumbling, boiling flood of white water caught the boat and whirled it almost perpendicular. Water swarmed in from all sides. The correspondent had his hands on the gunwale at this time, and when the water entered at that place he swiftly withdrew his fingers, as if he objected to wetting them.

The little boat, drunken with this weight of water, reeled and snuggled deeper into the sea.

"Bail her out, cook! Bail her out!" said the captain.

"All right, captain," said the cook.

"Now, boys, the next one will do for us, sure," said the oiler. "Mind to jump clear of the boat."

The third wave moved forward, huge, furious, implacable. It fairly swallowed the dingey, and almost simultaneously the men tumbled into the sea. A piece of life-belt had lain in the bottom of the boat, and as the correspondent went overboard he held this to his chest with his left hand.

The January water was icy, and he reflected immediately that it was colder than he had expected to find it on the coast of Florida. This appeared to his dazed mind as a fact important enough to be noted at the time. The coldness of the water was sad; it was tragic. This fact was somehow so mixed and confused with his opinion of his own situation that it seemed almost a proper reason for tears. The water was cold.

When he came to the surface he was conscious of little but the noisy water. Afterward he saw his companions in the sea. The oiler was ahead in the race. He was swimming strongly and rapidly. Off to the correspondent's left, the cook's great white and corked back bulged out of the water, and in the rear the captain was hanging with his one good hand to the keel of the overturned dingey.

There is a certain immovable quality to a shore, and the correspondent wondered at it amid the confusion of the sea.

It seemed also very attractive, but the correspondent knew that it was a long journey, and he paddled leisurely. The piece of life preserver lay under him, and sometimes he whirled down the incline of a wave as if he were on a hand-sled.

But finally he arrived at a place in the sea where travel was beset with difficulty. He did not pause swimming to inquire what manner of current had caught him, but there his progress ceased. The shore was set before him like a bit of scenery on a stage, and he looked at it and understood with his eyes each detail of it.

As the cook passed, much farther to the left, the captain was calling to him, "Turn over on your back, cook! Turn over on your back and use the oar."

"All right, sir." The cook turned on his back, and, paddling with an oar, went ahead as if he were a canoe.

Presently the boat also passed to the left of the correspondent with the captain clinging with one hand to the keel. He would have appeared like a man raising himself to look over a board fence, if it were not for the extraordinary gymnastics of the boat. The correspondent marvelled that the captain could still hold to it.

They passed on, nearer to shore — the oiler, the cook, the captain — and following them went the water-jar, bouncing gaily over the seas.

The correspondent remained in the grip of this strange new enemy — a current. The shore, with its white slope of sand and its green bluff, topped with little silent cottages, was spread like a picture before him. It was very near to him then, but he was impressed as one who in a gallery looks at a scene from Brittany or Holland.

He thought: "I am going to drown? Can it be possible? Can it be possible? Can it be possible?" Perhaps an individual must consider his own death to be the final phenomenon of nature.

But later a wave perhaps whirled him out of this small, deadly current, for he found suddenly that he could again make progress toward the shore. Later still, he was aware that the captain, clinging with one hand to the keel of the dingey, had his face turned away from the shore and toward him, and was calling his name. "Come to the boat! Come to the boat!"

In his struggle to reach the captain and the boat, he reflected that when one gets properly wearied, drowning must really be a comfortable arrangement, a cessation of hostilities accompanied by a large degree of relief, and he was glad of it, for the main thing in his mind for some months had been horror of the temporary agony. He did not wish to be hurt.

Presently he saw a man running along the shore. He was undressing with most remarkable speed. Coat, trousers, shirt, everything flew magically off him.

"Come to the boat," called the captain.

"All right, captain." As the correspondent paddled, he saw the captain let himself down to bottom and leave the boat. Then the correspondent performed his one little marvel of the voyage. A large wave caught him and flung him with ease and supreme speed completely over the boat and far beyond it. It struck him even then as an event in gymnastics, and a true miracle of the sea. An overturned boat in the surf is not a plaything to a swimming man.

The correspondent arrived in water that reached only to his waist, but his condition did not enable him to stand for more than a moment. Each wave knocked him into a heap, and the undertow pulled at him.

Then he saw the man who had been running and undressing, and undressing and running, come bounding into the water. He dragged ashore the cook, and then waded towards the captain, but the captain waved him away, and sent him to the correspondent. He was naked, naked as a tree in winter, but a halo was about his head, and he shone like a saint. He gave a strong pull, and a long drag, and a bully heave at the correspondent's hand. The correspondent, schooled in the minor formulae, said: "Thanks, old man." But suddenly the man cried: "What's that?" He pointed a swift finger. The correspondent said: "Go."

In the shallows, face downward, lay the oiler. His forehead touched sand that was periodically, between each wave, clear of the sea.

The correspondent did not know all that transpired afterward. When he achieved safe ground he fell, striking the sand with each particular part of his body. It was as if he dropped from a roof, but the thud was grateful to him.

It seems that instantly the beach was populated with men with blankets, clothes, and flasks, and women with coffee-pots and all the remedies sacred to their minds. The welcome of the land to the men from the sea was warm and generous, but a still and dripping shape was carried slowly up the beach, and the land's welcome for it could only be the different and sinister hospitality of the grave.

When it came night, the white waves paced to and fro in the moonlight, and the wind brought the sound of the great sea's voice to the men on shore, and they felt that they could then be interpreters.

War Is Kind

✣ Crane published two slender volumes of poems: *The Black Riders* (1895) and *War is Kind* (1899), dedicating the former to Hamlin Garland. As in his prose fiction, he voiced his pessimistic reflections on the world and its lack of meaning. Men live in an abyss of loneliness; the universe cares nothing for them; aghast at their situation, men build up pretenses and hypocrisies to make existence tolerable, but only make themselves absurd.

Crane's revolt against current faiths and rationalizations was accompanied by a corresponding revolt against conventional poetic form. Using no rhyme or meter, he relied upon concentrated imagery, oracular statement, and pungent irony, in a manner unacceptable to his time but prophetic of the "New Poetry" of the twentieth century.

The two poems given here are from *War is Kind*.

Do not weep, maiden, for war is kind.
Because your lover threw wild hands toward the
    sky
And the affrighted steed ran on alone,
Do not weep.
War is kind.   5

Hoarse, booming drums of the regiment,
Little souls who thirst for fight,
These men were born to drill and die.
The unexplained glory flies above them,
Great is the battle-god, great, and his king-
    dom —   10
A field where a thousand corpses lie.

Do not weep, babe, for war is kind.
Because your father tumbled in the yellow
    trenches,
Raged at his breast, gulped and died,
Do not weep.   15
War is kind.

Swift blazing flag of the regiment,
Eagle with crest of red and gold,
These men were born to drill and die.
Point for them the virtue of slaughter,   20
Make plain to them the excellence of killing
And a field where a thousand corpses lie.

Mother whose heart hung humble as a button
On the bright splendid shroud of your son,
Do not weep.   25
War is kind.

A Man Said to the Universe

A man said to the universe:
"Sir, I exist!"
"However," replied the universe,
"The fact has not created in me
A sense of obligation."   5

Theodore Dreiser [1871–1945]

A great writer of plebeian origins, said James T. Farrell, Dreiser "came from the wrong side of the tracks." Born in Indiana of German Catholic parents, he was the twelfth of thirteen children. From his early years he knew poverty and rootlessness, together with a yearning for wealth and social success, as the family moved from town to town. His schooling ended without a high school diploma; he presented himself to the world in Chicago, became a dishwasher, a hardware clerk, a scene-painter. Aided by a kindly teacher, he spent a year at Indiana University with scant profit. Back in Chicago, he started upon a career in journalism which later took him to St. Louis, Cleveland, Pittsburgh, and New York. He was twice married and divorced. In the year of his death he joined the Communist Party of the United States.

Despite this unpromising background, Dreiser became one of the major novelists of the first quarter of the century. Partly under the influence of Balzac and scientific thought (Huxley, Tyndall, Spencer) he made into powerful fiction the kind of experience he had seen and felt in American cities. His first novel was among his best: *Sister Carrie*, which Frank Norris recommended for publication. It appeared in 1900, but was promptly withdrawn; the public was not ready to learn that illicit love does not always lead to tragedy. Carrie, unlike Crane's Maggie, rises in the world. Like Crane, Dreiser tells his story amorally, without judging the conduct of his characters, intent only on truth to actual life. Yet to readers of a later and sex-obsessed time, it came to seem that he wrote with "the delicacy of a dewy-eyed Victorian bride knitting tiny garments." Eleven years passed before he published his second novel, *Jennie Gerhardt*, on a girl much like Carrie. Then came in quick succession three novels on men, or rather supermen striving for fulfillment: *The Financier, The Titan, The "Genius"*, the last of which was banned. After another decade *An American Tragedy* was a popular success and an impressive naturalistic novel, one of the landmarks of the 1920's.

Dreiser's naturalistic vision of life, plain in his fiction, was often stated in other writings, as in *A Book About Myself*: "Of one's ideals, struggles, deprivations, sorrows and joys, it could only be said that they were chemic compulsions, something which for some inexplicable but unimportant reason responded to and resulted from the hope of pleasure and the fear of pain. Man was a mechanism, undevised and uncreated, and a badly and carelessly driven one at that." A man is only material for the play of internal forces and external pressures. His acts are inevitable. Humanly speaking, life is a meaningless chaos, "a god-damned stinking game."

Despite his choice of the title *An American Tragedy*, Dreiser pictured life not tragically but pathetically. Man is a subject for pity, and no quality stands out more prominently in his work than his profound pity for the victims of the forces that misshape and destroy in that meaningless chaos we call life. This feeling of compassion is the more impressive because of the power of his lumbering art. His philosophy is naïve, his narrative structure clumsy, his sentences and diction an affront to the lover of good prose. Yet he is so earnest and honest in his determination to show us the truth as he sees it, so insistent on adding detail to detail to build his vision into words, that the reader is overborne by the sheer weight of the work and of the personality behind it.

There was a parallel between his fiction and his physical appearance: "A huge, ungainly figure," as Ernest Boyd described him, "whose heavy features were relieved only by the alert and kindly glance of those observant eyes which had seen everything and forgotten nothing."

Further reading: *An American Tragedy*. Robert Elias, *Theodore Dreiser: Apostle of Nature*, 1949. F. O. Matthiessen, *Theodore Dreiser*, 1951. *The Stature of Theodore Dreiser*, ed. A. Kazin and C. Shapiro, 1955.

The Lost Phoebe

(w. 1912)

While Dreiser was most characteristic in his novels, a story like the one below displays various aspects of his fiction. What is the quality of love pictured here? Of family life? Of the farm economy? What is the treatment of old age? Of death? What are we to infer as to the value of living?

They lived together in a part of the country which was not so prosperous as it had once been, about three miles from one of those small towns that, instead of increasing in population, is steadily decreasing. The territory was not very thickly settled; perhaps a house every other mile or so, with large areas of corn- and wheat-land and fallow fields that at odd seasons had been sown to timothy and clover. Their particular house was part log and part frame, the log portion being the old original home of Henry's grandfather. The new portion, of now rain-beaten, time-worn slabs, through which the wind squeaked in the chinks at times, and which several overshadowing elms and a butter-nut-tree made picturesque and reminiscently pathetic, but a little damp, was erected by Henry when he was twenty-one and just married.

That was forty-eight years before. The furniture inside, like the house outside, was old and mildewy and reminiscent of an earlier day. You have seen the what-not of cherry wood, perhaps, with spiral legs and fluted top. It was there. The old-fashioned four poster bed, with its ball-like protuberances and deep curving incisions, was there also, a sadly alienated descendant of an early Jacobean ancestor. The bureau of cherry was also high and wide and solidly built, but faded-looking, and with a musty odor. The rag carpet that underlay all these sturdy examples of enduring furniture was a weak, faded, lead-and-pink-colored affair woven by Phoebe Ann's own hands, when she was fifteen years younger than she was when she died. The creaky wooden loom on which it had been done now stood like a dusty, bony skeleton, along with a broken rocking-chair, a worm-eaten clothes-press — Heaven knows how old — a lime-stained bench that had once been used to keep flowers on outside the door, and other decrepit factors of household utility, in an east room that was a lean-to against this so-called main portion. All sorts of other broken-down furniture were about this place; an antiquated clothes-horse, cracked in two of its ribs; a broken mirror in an old cherry frame, which had fallen from a nail and cracked itself three days before their youngest son, Jerry, died; an extension hat-rack, which once had had porcelain knobs on the ends of its pegs; and a sewing-machine, long since outdone in its clumsy mechanism by rivals of a newer generation.

The orchard to the east of the house was full of gnarled old apple trees, worm-eaten as to trunks and branches, and fully ornamented with green and white lichens, so that it had a sad, greenish-white, silvery effect in moonlight. The low outhouses, which had once housed chickens, a horse or two, a cow, and several pigs, were covered with patches of moss as to their roof, and the sides had been free of paint for so long that they were blackish gray as to color, and a little spongy. The picket-fence in front, with its gate squeaky and askew, and the side fences of the stake-and-rider type were in an equally run-down condition. As a matter of fact, they had aged synchronously with the persons who lived here, old Henry Reifsneider and his wife Phoebe Ann.

They had lived here, these two, ever since their marriage, forty-eight years before, and Henry had lived here before that from his childhood up. His father and mother, well along in years when he was a boy, had invited him to bring his wife here when he had first fallen in love and decided to marry; and he had done so. His father and mother were the companions of himself and his wife for ten years after they were married, when both died; and then Henry and Phoebe were left with their five children growing lustily apace. But all sorts of things had happened since then. Of the seven children, all told, that had been born to them, three had died; one girl had gone to Kansas; one boy had gone to Sioux Falls, never even to be heard of after; another boy had gone to Washington; and the last girl lived five counties away in the same State; but was so burdened with cares of her own that she rarely gave them a thought. Time and a commonplace home life that had never been attractive had weaned them thoroughly, so that, wherever they were, they gave little thought as to how it might be with their father and mother.

Old Henry Reifsneider and his wife Phoebe were a loving couple. You perhaps know how it is with simple natures that fasten themselves like lichens on the stones of circumstance and weather their days to a crumbling conclusion. The great world sounds widely, but it has no call for them. They have no soaring intellect. The orchard, the meadow, the cornfield, the pig-pen, and the chicken-lot measure the range of their human activities. When the wheat is headed it is reaped and threshed; when the corn is browned and frosted it is cut and shocked; when the timothy is in full head it is cut, and the haycock erected. After that comes winter, with the hauling of grain to market, the sawing and splitting of wood, the simple chores of fire-building, meal-getting, occasional repairing and visiting. Beyond these and the changes of weather — the snows, the rains, and the fair days — there are no immediate significant things. All the rest of life is a far-off, clamorous phantasmagoria, flickering like Northern lights in the night, and sounding as faintly as cow-bells tinkling in the distance.

Old Henry and his wife Phoebe were as fond of each other as it is possible for two old people to be who have nothing else in this life to be fond of. He was a thin old man, seventy when she died, a queer, crotchety person with coarse gray-black hair and beard, quite straggly and unkempt. He looked at you out of dull, fishy, watery eyes that had deep-brown crow's-feet at the sides. His clothes, like the clothes of many farmers, were aged and angular and baggy, standing out at the pockets, not fitting about the neck, protuberant and worn at elbow and knee. Phoebe Ann was thin and shapeless, a very umbrella of a woman, clad in shabby black, and with a black bonnet for her best wear. As time had passed, and they had only themselves to look after, their movements had become slower and slower, their activities fewer and fewer. The annual keep of pigs had been reduced from five to one grunting porker, and the single horse which Henry now retained was a sleepy animal, not over-nourished and not very clean. The chickens, of which formerly there was a large flock, had almost disappeared, owing to ferrets, foxes, and the lack of proper care, which produces disease. The former healthy garden was now a straggling memory of itself, and the vines and flowerbeds that formerly ornamented the windows and dooryard had now become choking thickets. A will had been made which divided the small tax-eaten property equally among the remaining four, so that it was really of no interest to any of them. Yet these two lived together in peace and sympathy, only that now and then old Henry would become unduly cranky, complaining almost invariably that something had been neglected or mislaid which was of no importance at all.

"Phoebe, where's my corn-knife? You ain't never minded to let my things alone no more."

"Now you hush, Henry," his wife would caution him in a cracked and squeaky voice. "If you don't, I'll leave yuh. I'll git up and walk out of here some day, and then where would y' be? Y' ain't got anybody but me to look after yuh, so yuh just behave yourself. Your corn knife's on the mantel where it's allus been unless you've gone an' put it summers else."

Old Henry, who knew his wife would never leave him in any circumstances, used to speculate at times as to what he would do if she were to die. That was the one leaving that he really feared. As he climbed on the chair at night to wind the old, long-pendulumed, double-weighted clock, or went finally to the front and the back door to see that they were safely shut in, it was a comfort to know that Phoebe was there, properly ensconced on her side of the bed, and that if he stirred restlessly in the night, she would be there to ask what he wanted.

"Now, Henry, do lie still! You're as restless as a chicken."

"Well, I can't sleep, Phoebe."

"Well, yuh needn't roll so, anyhow. Yuh kin let me sleep."

This usually reduced him to a state of somnolent ease. If she wanted a pail of water, it was a grumbling pleasure for him to get it; and if she did rise first to build the fires, he saw that the wood was cut and placed within easy reach. They divided this simple world nicely between them.

As the years had gone on, however, fewer and fewer people had called. They were well-known for a distance of as much as ten square miles as old Mr. and Mrs. Reifsneider, honest, moderately Christian, but too old to be really interesting any longer. The writing of letters had become an almost impossible burden too difficult to continue or even negotiate via others, although an occasional letter still did arrive from the daughter in Pemberton County. Now and then some old friend stopped with a pie or cake or a roasted chicken or duck, or merely to see that they were well; but even these kindly minded visits were no longer frequent.

One day in the early spring of her sixty-fourth year Mrs. Reifsneider took sick, and from a low fever passed into some indefinable ailment which, because of her age, was no longer curable. Old Henry drove to Swinnerton, the neighboring town, and procured a doctor. Some friends called, and the immediate care of her was taken off his hands. Then one chill spring night she died, and old Henry, in a fog of sorrow and uncertainty, followed her body to the nearest graveyard, an unattractive space with a few pines growing in it. Although he might have gone to the daughter in Pemberton or sent for her, it was really too much trouble and he was too weary and fixed. It was suggested to him at once by one friend and another that he come to stay with them awhile, but he did not see fit. He was so old and so fixed in his notions and so accustomed to the exact surroundings he had known all his days, that he could not think of leaving. He wanted to remain near where they had put his Phoebe; and the fact that he would have to live alone did not trouble him in the least. The living children were notified and the care of him offered if he would leave, but he would not.

"I kin make a shift for myself," he continually announced to old Dr. Morrow, who had attended his wife in this case. "I kin cook a

little, and besides, it don't take much more'n coffee an' bread in the mornin's to satisfy me. I'll get along now well enough. Yuh just let me be." And after many pleadings and proffers of advice, with supplies of coffee and bacon and baked bread duly offered and accepted, he was left to himself. For a while he sat idly outside his door brooding in the spring sun. He tried to revive his interest in farming, and to keep himself busy and free from thought by looking after the fields, which of late had been much neglected. It was a gloomy thing to come in of an evening, however, or in the afternoon and find no shadow of Phoebe where everything suggested her. By degrees he put a few of her things away. At night he sat beside his lamp and read in the papers that were left him occasionally or in a Bible that he had neglected for years, but he could get little solace from these things. Mostly he held his hand over his mouth and looked at the floor as he sat and thought of what had become of her, and how soon he himself would die. He made a great business of making his coffee in the morning and frying himself a little bacon at night; but his appetite was gone. The shell in which he had been housed so long seemed vacant, and its shadows were suggestive of immedicable griefs. So he lived quite dolefully for five long months, and then a change began.

It was one night, after he had looked after the front and the back door, wound the clock, blown out the light, and gone through all the selfsame motions that he had indulged in for years, that he went to bed not so much to sleep as to think. It was a moonlight night. The green-lichen-covered orchard just outside and to be seen from his bed where he now lay was a silvery affair sweetly spectral. The moon shone through the east windows, throwing the pattern of the panes on the wooden floor, and making the old furniture, to which he was accustomed, stand out dimly in the room. As usual he had been thinking of Phoebe and the years when they had been young together, and of the children who had gone, and the poor shift he was making of his present days. The house was coming to be in a very bad state indeed. The bed-clothes were in disorder, and not clean, for he made a wretched shift of washing. It was a terror to him. The roof leaked, causing things, some of them, to remain damp for weeks at a time, but he was getting into that brooding state where he would accept anything rather than exert himself. He preferred to pace slowly to and fro or to sit and think.

By twelve o'clock of this particular night he was asleep, however, and by two had waked again. The moon by this time had shifted to a position on the western side of the house, and it now shone in through the windows of the living-room and those of the kitchen beyond. A certain combination of furniture — a chair near a table, with his coat on it, the half-open kitchen door casting a shadow, and the position of a lamp near a paper — gave him an exact representation of Phoebe leaning over the table as he had often seen her do in life. It gave him a great start. Could it be she — or her ghost? He had scarcely ever believed in spirits; and still —— He looked at her fixedly in the feeble half-light, his old hair tingling oddly at the roots, and then sat up. The figure did not move. He put his thin legs out of the bed and sat looking at her, wondering if this could really be Phoebe. They had talked of ghosts often in their lifetime, of apparitions and omens; but they had never agreed that such things could be. It had never been a part of his wife's creed that she could have a spirit that could return to walk the earth. Her after-world was quite a different affair, a vague heaven, no less, from which the righteous did not trouble to return. Yet here she was now, bending over the table in her black skirt and gray shawl, her pale profile outlined against the moonlight.

"Phoebe," he called, thrilling from head to toe and putting out one bony hand, "have yuh come back?"

The figure did not stir, and he arose and walked uncertainly to the door, looking at it fixedly the while. As he drew near, however, the apparition resolved itself into its primal content — his old coat over the high-backed chair, the lamp by the paper, the half-open door.

"Well," he said to himself, his mouth open, "I thought shore I saw her." And he ran his hand strangely and vaguely through his hair, the while his nervous tension relaxed. Vanished as it had, it gave him the idea that she might return.

Another night, because of this first illusion, and because his mind was now constantly on her and he was old, he looked out of the window that was nearest his bed and commanded a hen-coop and pig-pen and a part of the wagon-shed, and there, a faint mist exuding from the damp of the ground, he thought he saw her again. It was one of those little wisps of mist, one of those faint exhalations of the earth, that rise in a cool night after a warm day, and flicker like small white cypresses of fog before they disappear. In life it had been a custom of hers to cross this lot from her kitchen door to the pig-pen to throw in any scrap that was left from her cooking, and here she was again. He sat up and watched it strangely, doubtfully, because of his previous experience, but inclined, because of the nervous titillation that passed over his body, to believe that spirits really were, and that Phoebe, who would be concerned because of his lonely state, must be thinking about him, and hence returning. What other way would she have? How otherwise could she express herself? It would be within the province of her charity so to do, and like her loving interest in him. He quivered and watched it eagerly; but, a faint breath of air stirring, it wound away toward the fence and disappeared.

A third night, as he was actually dreaming, some ten days later, she came to his bedside and put her hand on his head.

"Poor Henry!" she said. "It's too bad."

He roused out of his sleep, actually to see her, he thought, moving from his bed-room into the one living-room, her figure a shadowy mass of black. The weak straining of his eyes caused little points of light to flicker about the outlines of her form. He arose, greatly astonished, walked the floor in the cool room, convinced that Phoebe was coming back to him. If he only thought sufficiently, if he made it perfectly clear by his feeling that he needed her greatly, she would come back, this kindly wife, and tell him what to do. She would perhaps be with him much of the time, in the night, anyhow; and that would make him less lonely, this state more endurable.

In age and with the feeble it is not such a far cry from the subtleties of illusion to actual hallucination, and in due time this transition was made for Henry. Night after night he waited, expecting her return. Once in his weird mood he thought he saw a pale light moving about the room, and another time he thought he saw her walking in the orchard after dark. It was one morning when the details of his lonely state were virtually unendurable that he woke with the thought that she was not dead.

How he had arrived at this conclusion it is hard to say. His mind had gone. In its place was a fixed illusion. He and Phoebe had had a senseless quarrel. He had reproached her for not leaving his pipe where he was accustomed to find it, and she had left. It was an aberrated fulfillment of her old jesting threat that if he did not behave himself she would leave him.

"I guess I could find yuh ag'in," he had always said. But her cackling threat had always been:

"Yuh'll not find me if I ever leave yuh. I guess I kin git some place where yuh can't find me."

This morning when he arose he did not think to build the fire in the customary way or to grind his coffee and cut his bread, as was his wont, but solely to meditate as to where he should search for her and how he should induce her to come back. Recently the one horse had been dispensed with because he found it cumbersome and beyond his needs. He took down his soft crush hat after he had dressed himself, a new glint of interest and determination in his eye, and taking his black crook cane from behind the door, where he had always placed it, started out briskly to look for her among the nearest neighbors. His old shoes clumped soundly in the dust as he walked, and his gray-black locks, now grown rather long, straggled out in a dramatic fringe or halo from under his hat. His short coat stirred busily as he walked, and his hands and face were peaked and pale.

"Why, hello, Henry! Where're yuh goin' this mornin'?" inquired Farmer Dodge, who, hauling a load of wheat to market, encountered him on the public road. He had not seen the aged farmer in months, not since his wife's death, and he wondered now, seeing him looking so spry.

"Yuh ain't seen Phoebe, have yuh?" inquired the old man, looking up quizzically.

"Phoebe who?" inquired Farmer Dodge, not for the moment connecting the name with Henry's dead wife.

"Why, my wife Phoebe, o'course. Who do yuh s'pose I mean?" He stared up with a pathetic sharpness of glance from under his shaggy, gray eyebrows.

"Wall, I'll swan, Henry, yuh ain't jokin', are yuh?" said the solid Dodge, a pursy man, with a smooth, hard red face. "It can't be your wife yuh're talkin' about. She's dead."

"Dead! Shucks!" retorted the demented Reifsneider. "She left me early this mornin', while I was sleepin'. She allus got up to build the fire, but she's gone now. We had a little spat last night, an' I guess that's the reason. But I guess I kin find her. She's gone over to Matilda Race's; that's where she's gone."

He started briskly up the road, leaving the amazed Dodge to stare in wonder after him.

"Well, I'll be switched!" he said aloud to himself. "He's clean out'n his head. That poor old feller's been livin' down there till he's gone outen his mind. I'll have to notify the authorities." And he flicked his whip with great enthusiasm. "Geddap!" he said, and was off.

Reifsneider met no one else in this poorly populated region until he reached the whitewashed fence of Matilda Race and her husband three miles away. He had passed several other houses en route, but these not being within the range of his illusion were not considered. His wife, who had known Matilda well, must be here. He opened the picket-gate which guarded the walk, and stamped briskly up to the door.

"Why, Mr. Reifsneider," exclaimed old Matilda herself, a stout woman, looking out of the door in answer to his knock, "what brings yuh here this mornin'?"

"Is Phoebe here?" he demanded eagerly.

"Phoebe who? What Phoebe?" replied Mrs. Race, curious as to this sudden development of energy on his part.

"Why, my Phoebe, o'course. My wife Phoebe. Who do yuh s'pose? Ain't she here now?"

"Lawsy me!" exclaimed Mrs. Race, opening her mouth. "Yuh pore man! So you're clean out'n your mind now. Yuh come right in and sit down. I'll git yuh a cup o' coffee. O' course your wife ain't here; but yuh come in an' sit down. I'll find her fer yuh after a while. I know where she is."

The old farmer's eyes softened, and he entered. He was so thin and pale a specimen, pantalooned and patriarchal, that he aroused Mrs. Race's extremest sympathy as he took off his hat and laid it on his knees quite softly and mildly.

"We had a quarrel last night, an' she left me," he volunteered.

"Laws! laws!" sighed Mrs. Race, there being no one present with whom to share her astonishment as she went to her kitchen. "The pore man! Now somebody's just got to look after him. He can't be allowed to run around the country this way lookin' for his dead wife. It's turrible."

She boiled him a pot of coffee and brought in some of her new-baked bread and fresh butter. She set out some of her best jam and put a couple of eggs to boil, lying whole-heartedly the while.

"Now yuh stay right there, Uncle Henry, till Jake comes in, an' I'll send him to look for Phoebe. I think it's more'n likely she's over to Swinnerton with some o' her friends. Anyhow, we'll find out. Now yuh just drink this coffee an' eat this bread. Yuh must be tired. Yuh've had a long walk this mornin'." Her idea was to take counsel with Jake, "her man," and perhaps have him notify the authorities.

She bustled about, meditating on the uncertainties of life, while old Reifsneider thrummed on the rim of his hat with his pale fingers and later ate abstractedly of what she offered. His mind was on his wife, however, and since she was not here, or did not appear, it wandered vaguely away to a family by the name of Murray, miles away in another direction. He decided after a time that he would not wait for Jake Race to hunt his wife but would seek her for himself. He must be on, and urge her to come back.

"Well, I'll be goin'," he said, getting up and looking strangely about him. "I guess she didn't come here after all. She went over to the Murrays', I guess. I'll not wait any longer, Mis' Race. There's a lot to do over to the house to-day." And out he marched in the face of her protests, taking to the dusty road again in the warm spring sun, his cane striking the earth as he went.

It was two hours later that this pale figure of a man appeared in the Murrays' doorway, dusty, perspiring, eager. He had tramped all of five miles, and it was noon. An amazed husband and wife of sixty heard his strange query, and realized also that he was mad. They begged him to stay to dinner, intending to notify the authorities later and see what could be done; but though he stayed to partake of a little something, he did not stay long, and was off again to another distant farmhouse, his idea of many things to do and his need of Phoebe impelling him. So it went for that day and the next and the next, the circle of his inquiry ever widening.

The process by which a character assumes the significance of being peculiar, his antics weird, yet harmless, in such a community is often in-volute and pathetic. This day, as has been said, saw Reifsneider at other doors, eagerly asking his unnatural question, and leaving a trail of amazement, sympathy, and pity in his wake. Although the authorities were informed — the county sheriff, no less — it was not deemed advisable to take him into custody; for when those who knew old Henry, and had for so long, reflected on the condition of the county insane asylum, a place which, because of the poverty of the district, was of staggering aberration and sickening environment, it was decided to let him remain at large; for, strange to relate, it was found on investigation that at night he returned peaceably enough to his lonesome domicile there to discover whether his wife had returned, and to brood in loneliness until the morning. Who would lock up a thin, eager, seeking old man with iron-gray hair and an attitude of kindly, innocent inquiry, particularly when he was well-known for a past of only kindly servitude and reliability? Those who had known him best rather agreed that he should be allowed to roam at large. He could do no harm. There were many who were willing to help him as to food, old clothes, the odds and ends of his daily life — at least at first. His figure after a time became not so much a commonplace as an accepted curiosity, and the replies, "Why, no, Henry; I ain't see her," or "No, Henry; she ain't been here to-day," more customary.

For several years thereafter then he was an odd figure in the sun and rain, on dusty roads and muddy ones, encountered occasionally in strange and unexpected places, pursuing his endless search. Undernourishment, after a time, although the neighbors and those who knew his history gladly contributed from their store, affected his body; for he walked much and ate little. The longer he roamed the public highway in this manner, the deeper became his strange hallucination; and finding it harder and harder to return from his more and more distant pilgrimages, he finally began taking a few utensils with him from his home, making a small package of them, in order that he might not be compelled to return. In an old tin coffee-pot of large size he placed a small tin cup, a knife, fork, and spoon, some salt and pepper, and to the outside of it, by a string forced through a pierced hole, he fastened a plate, which could be released, and which was his woodland table. It was no trouble for him to secure the little food that he needed, and with a strange, almost religious dignity, he had no hesitation in asking for that much. By degrees his hair became longer and longer, his once black hat became an earthen brown, and his clothes threadbare and dusty.

For all of three years he walked, and none knew how wide were his perambulations, nor how he survived the storms and cold. They could not see him, with homely rural understanding and forethought, sheltering himself in haycocks, or by the sides of cattle, whose warm bodies protected him from the cold, and whose dull understandings were not opposed to his harmless presence. Overhanging rocks and trees kept him at times from the rain, and a friendly hay-loft or corn-crib was not above his humble consideration.

The involute progression of hallucination is strange. From asking at doors and being constantly rebuffed or denied, he finally came to the conclusion that although his Phoebe might not be in any of the houses at the doors of which he inquired, she might nevertheless be within the sound of his voice. And so, from patient inquiry, he began to call sad, occasional cries, that ever and anon waked the quiet landscapes and ragged hill regions, and set to echoing his thin "O-o-o Phoebe! O-o-o Phoebe!" It had a pathetic, albeit insane, ring, and many a farmer or plowboy came to know it even from afar and say, "There goes old Reifsneider."

Another thing that puzzled him greatly after a time and after many hundreds of inquiries was, when he no longer had any particular dooryard in view and no special inquiry to make, which way to go. These crossroads, which occasionally led in four or even six directions, came after a time to puzzle him. But to solve this knotty problem, which became more and more of a puzzle, there came to his aid another hallucination. Phoebe's spirit or some power of the air or wind or nature would tell him. If he stood at the center of the parting of the ways, closed his eyes, turned thrice about, and called "O-o-o Phoebe!" twice, and then threw his cane straight before him, that would surely indicate which way to go for Phoebe, or one of these mystic powers would surely govern its direction and fall! In whichever direction it went, even though, as was not infrequently the case, it took him back along the path he had already come, or across fields, he was not so far gone in his mind but that he gave himself ample time to search before he called again. Also the halluci-

nation seemed to persist that at some time he would surely find her. There were hours when his feet were sore, and his limbs weary, when he would stop in the heat to wipe his seamed brow, or in the cold to beat his arms. Sometimes, after throwing away his cane, and finding it indicating the direction from which he had just come, he would shake his head wearily and philosophically, as if contemplating the unbelievable or an untoward fate, and then start briskly off. His strange figure came finally to be known in the farthest reaches of three or four counties. Old Reifsneider was a pathetic character. His fame was wide.

Near a little town called Watersville, in Green County, perhaps four miles from that minor center of human activity, there was a place or precipice locally known as the Red Cliff, a sheer wall of red sandstone, perhaps a hundred feet high, which raised its sharp face for half a mile or more above the fruitful cornfields and orchards that lay beneath and which was surmounted by a thick grove of trees. The slope that slowly led up to it from the opposite side was covered by a rank growth of beech, hickory, and ash, through which threaded a number of wagontracks crossing at various angles. In fair weather it had become old Reifsneider's habit, so inured was he by now to the open, to make his bed in some such patch of trees as this to fry his bacon or boil his eggs at the foot of some tree before laying himself down for the night. Occasionally, so light and inconsequential was his sleep, he would walk at night. More often, the moonlight or some sudden wind stirring in the trees or a reconnoitering animal arousing him, he would sit up and think, or pursue his quest in the moonlight or the dark, a strange, unnatural, half wild, half savage-looking but utterly harmless creature, calling at lonely road crossings, staring at dark and shuttered houses, and wondering where, where Phoebe could really be.

That particular lull that comes in the systole-diastole of this earthly ball at two o'clock in the morning invariably aroused him, and though he might not go any farther he would sit up and contemplate the darkness or the stars, wondering. Sometimes in the strange processes of his mind he would fancy that he saw moving among the trees the figure of his lost wife, and then he would get up to follow, taking his utensils, always on a string, and his cane. If she seemed to evade him too easily he would run, or plead, or, suddenly losing track of the fancied figure, stand awed or disappointed, grieving for the moment over the almost insurmountable difficulties of his search.

It was in the seventh year of these hopeless peregrinations, in the dawn of a similar springtime to that in which his wife had died, that he came at last one night to the vicinity of this selfsame patch that crowned the rise to the Red Cliff. His far-flung cane, used as a divining-rod at the last crossroads, had brought him hither. He had walked many, many miles. It was after ten o'clock at night, and he was very weary. Long wandering and little eating had left him but a shadow of his former self. It was a question now not so much of physical strength but of spiritual endurance which kept him up. He had scarcely eaten this day, and now, exhausted, he set himself down in the dark to rest and possibly to sleep.

Curiously on this occasion a strange suggestion of the presence of his wife surrounded him. It would not be long now, he counseled with himself, although the long months had brought him nothing, until he should see her, talk to her. He fell asleep after a time, his head on his knees. At midnight the moon began to rise, and at two in the morning, his wakeful hour, was a large silver disk shining through the trees to the east. He opened his eyes when the radiance became strong, making a silver pattern at his feet and lighting the woods with strange lusters and silvery, shadowy forms. As usual, his old notion that his wife must be near occurred to him on this occasion, and he looked about him with a speculative, anticipatory eye. What was it that moved in the distant shadows along the path by which he had entered — a pale, flickering will-o'-the wisp that bobbed gracefully among the trees and riveted his expectant gaze? Moonlight and shadows combined to give it a strange form and a stranger reality, this fluttering of bogfire or dancing of wandering fireflies. Was it truly his lost Phoebe? By a circuitous route it passed about him, and in his fevered state he fancied that he could see the very eyes of her, not as she was when he last saw her in the black dress and shawl but now a strangely younger Phoebe, gayer, sweeter, the one whom he had known years before as a girl. Old Reifsneider

got up. He had been expecting and dreaming of this hour all these years, and now as he saw the feeble light dancing lightly before him he peered at it questioningly, one thin hand in his gray hair.

Of a sudden there came to him now for the first time in many years the full charm of her girlish figure as he had known it in boyhood, the pleasing, sympathetic smile, the brown hair, the blue sash she had once worn about her waist at a picnic, her gay, graceful movements. He walked around the base of the tree, straining with his eyes, forgetting for once his cane and utensils, and following eagerly after. On she moved before him, a will-o'-the-wisp of the spring, a little flame above her head, and it seemed as though among the small saplings of ash and beech and the thick trunks of hickory and elm that she signaled with a young, a lightsome hand.

"O Phoebe! Phoebe!" he called. "Have yuh really come? Have yuh really answered me?" And hurrying faster, he fell once, scrambling lamely to his feet, only to see the light in the distance dancing illusively on. On and on he hurried until he was fairly running, brushing his ragged arms against the trees, striking his hands and face against impending twigs. His hat was gone, his lungs were breathless, his reason quite astray, when coming to the edge of the cliff he saw her below among a silvery bed of apple-trees now blooming in the spring.

"O Phoebe!" he called. "O Phoebe! Oh, no, don't leave me!" And feeling the lure of a world where love was young and Phoebe as this vision presented her, a delightful epitome of their quondam youth, he gave a gay cry of "Oh, wait, Phoebe!" and leaped.

Some farmer-boys, reconnoitering this region of bounty and prospect some few days afterward, found first the tin utensils tied together under the tree where he had left them, and then later at the foot of the cliff, pale, broken, but elate, a molded smile of peace and delight upon his lips, his body. His old hat was discovered lying under some low-growing saplings the twigs of which had held it back. No one of all the simple population knew how eagerly and joyously he had found his lost mate.

THE REVIVAL OF POETRY

Edwin Arlington Robinson [1869–1935]

Twenty years before the flowering of the "New Poetry" (refer to page 840, above), Robinson was writing, albeit in old forms, a strikingly new kind of verse. It was intellectual, realistic in attitude, penetrating as a comment on life, free of the conventional poetic diction of the time, close to the rhythms of actual speech. Quietly going his own way, he was not widely recognized till the poetic revival came. In that revival he was to play a major role.

His detachment, together with his austerity, reticence, and hardness of fiber, may be partly explained by his New England ancestry and his early environment in the town of Gardiner on the Kennebec, where he came to know the folk of his "Tilbury" portraits. He was born at Head Tide, Maine, but his family removed to Gardiner when he was one year old. After two years at Harvard he was obliged to terminate his formal education upon the death of his father. During a decade of intense discouragement, Robinson tried to publish his poems and maintain himself in the business world. In neither did he succeed, and by 1905 he was reduced to working as a checker of loads of shale during the building of the New York subway. He had all but abandoned his poetry when President Theodore Roosevelt became interested in him and gave him a position in the New York Custom House.

Once established as a successful poet, Robinson lived quietly in New York in the winters, and spent the summers at the MacDowell colony in New Hampshire. He was never married. His death in New York occurred a few hours after he had completed correction of the page proofs of his last volume.

Robinson's first volume was privately printed in 1896. The next year came *The Children of the Night*, including "Richard Cory"; in 1902 the first of his long monographs, *Captain Craig*; in 1910 *The Town Down the River*, which contained "Miniver Cheevy." But Robinson's high distinction was not clearly recognized till *The Man Against the Sky*, 1916, a work regarded by many critics as his finest. Responding to the lure that the Arthurian legend has held for poets from Spenser and Milton down to our own times, he then wrote *Merlin*, and *Lancelot*, and his greatest popular success, *Tristram*. During the last fourteen years of his life he devoted himself to long blank verse narratives, each with only three or four characters, such as *Avon's Harvest*, *Dionysus in Doubt*, *Cavender's House*, *Matthias at the Door*, *King Jasper*.

The turn of mind most prominent in the poetry of Robinson is evident also in some of his literary admirations, which included Hardy and Zola, also the late eighteenth-century realist poet, Crabbe. Robinson himself had the cool integrity of the realist, not the warm or facile emotionality of the romanticist. With an inquiring spirit, he analyzed people and the forces that move them to success or failure. In his gray world happiness is won hardly, or at a price, or not at all. But Robinson recoiled from the abyss of sheer naturalism. He would not subscribe to the new dogmas that were displacing the old. He found "gleams" of high meaning in life which he would have regarded it blindness to ignore.

Further reading: *Collected Poems*. Emery Neff, *Edward Arlington Robinson*, 1948 (biography). Ellsworth Barnard, *Edwin Arlington Robinson: A Critical Study*, 1952.

The Children of the Night

(1897)

🐾 In many of Robinson's poems, light and darkness represent contrasting aspects of human experience, with variations in application, associated imagery, attitude, effect. Examples in early poems are "The Children of the Night," "Luke Havergal," and "Credo."

For those that never know the light,
  The darkness is a sullen thing;
And they, the Children of the Night,
  Seem lost in Fortune's winnowing.

But some are strong and some are weak, — 5
  And there's the story. House and home
Are shut from countless hearts that seek
  World-refuge that will never come.

And if there be no other life,
  And if there be no other chance   10
To weigh their sorrow and their strife
  Than in the scales of circumstance,

'T were better, ere the sun go down
  Upon the first day we embark,
In life's imbittered sea to drown,   15
  Than sail forever in the dark.

Let us, the Children of the Night,
  Put off the cloak that hides the scar!
Let us be Children of the Light,
  And tell the ages what we are!   20

George Crabbe

(1896)

🐾 Crabbe, English poet of the late eighteenth and early nineteenth centuries, is still remembered for his darksome portrayal of the everyday life of ordinary people in such works as *The Village* and *The Borough*. Byron called him "nature's sternest painter."

Give him the darkest inch your shelf allows,
Hide him in lonely garrets, if you will, —
But his hard, human pulse is throbbing still
With the sure strength that fearless truth endows.
In spite of all fine science disavows,   5
Of his plain excellence and stubborn skill
There yet remains what fashion cannot kill,
Though years have thinned the laurel from his brows.

Whether or not we read him, we can feel
From time to time the vigor of his name   10
Against us like a finger for the shame
And emptiness of what our souls reveal
In books that are as altars where we kneel
To consecrate the flicker, not the flame.

John Evereldown

(w. 1894?)

🐾 "Then there is old John Evereldown who had all the women of Tilbury Town under his wing, or thought he had." (Robinson, in a letter.)

"Where are you going to-night, to-night, —
  Where are you going, John Evereldown?
There's never the sign of a star in sight,
  Nor a lamp that's nearer than Tilbury Town.
Why do you stare as a dead man might?   5
Where are you pointing away from the light?
And where are you going to-night, to-night, —
  Where are you going, John Evereldown?"

"Right through the forest, where none can see,   9
  There's where I'm going, to Tilbury Town.
The men are asleep, — or awake, may be, —
  But the women are calling John Evereldown.
Ever and ever they call for me,
And while they call can a man be free?
So right through the forest, where none can see,   15
  There's where I'm going, to Tilbury Town."

"But why are you going so late, so late, —
   Why are you going, John Evereldown?
Though the road be smooth and the way be
    straight,
   There are two long leagues to Tilbury Town.
Come in by the fire, old man, and wait!   21
Why do you chatter out there by the gate?
And why are you going so late, so late, —
   Why are you going, John Evereldown?"

"I follow the women wherever they call, — 25
   That's why I'm going to Tilbury Town.
God knows if I pray to be done with it all,
   But God is no friend to John Evereldown.
So the clouds may come and the rain may fall,
The shadows may creep and the dead men
    crawl, —   30
But I follow the women wherever they call,
   And that's why I'm going to Tilbury Town."

Cliff Klingenhagen

(w. 1893–96)

Cliff Klingenhagen had me in to dine
With him one day; and after soup and meat,
And all the other things there were to eat,
Cliff took two glasses and filled one with wine
And one with wormwood. Then, without a sign
For me to choose at all, he took the draught 6
Of bitterness himself, and lightly quaffed
It off, and said the other one was mine.

And when I asked him what the deuce he meant
By doing that, he only looked at me   10
And smiled, and said it was a way of his.
And though I know the fellow, I have spent
Long time a-wondering when I shall be
As happy as Cliff Klingenhagen is.

Richard Cory

(w. 1893–96)

When Theodore Roosevelt wrote his review
of the poetry of Robinson for a periodical, *The
Outlook,* he quoted "Richard Cory" entire.

In this firm little sketch Robinson conveys how
"we people" regarded Richard Cory, and, in the last
two lines, how he regarded himself. The ironic
contrast startles, but, looking back, one notes some
preparation for it.

Whenever Richard Cory went down town,
We people on the pavement looked at him:
He was a gentleman from sole to crown,
Clean favored, and imperially slim.

And he was always quietly arrayed,   5
And he was always human when he talked;
But still he fluttered pulses when he said,
  "Good-morning," and he glittered when he
    walked.

And he was rich — yes, richer than a king —
And admirably schooled in every grace: 10
In fine, we thought that he was every thing
To make us wish that we were in his place.

So on we worked, and waited for the light,
And went without the meat, and cursed the
    bread;
And Richard Cory, one calm summer night, 15
Went home and put a bullet through his head.

Luke Havergal

(w. 1894?)

This poem, written in a symbolist manner,
was referred to in one of Robinson's letters as "a
piece of deliberate degeneration called 'Luke Havergal,' which is not at all funny." Certainly it is
serious enough to exemplify an attitude that is present in much of Robinson's poetry.

Havergal, bereaved and in blinding despair, hears
a voice out of a grave that bids him relinquish renewal of the past ("a dawn in eastern skies") and
face the darkness ("western glooms"), the bitter
truth, which must be known before faith is possible
— before "she will call" (to a life after death?).

Go to the western gate, Luke Havergal,
There where the vines cling crimson on the wall,
And in the twilight wait for what will come.
The leaves will whisper there of her, and some,
Like flying words, will strike you as they fall;
But go, and if you listen she will call. 6
Go to the western gate, Luke Havergal —
Luke Havergal.

No, there is not a dawn in eastern skies
To rift the fiery night that's in your eyes;   10
But there, where western glooms are gathering,
The dark will end the dark, if anything:
God slays Himself with every leaf that flies,
And hell is more than half of paradise.
No, there is not a dawn in eastern skies — 15
In eastern skies.

Out of a grave I come to tell you this,
Out of a grave I come to quench the kiss
That flames upon your forehead with a glow
That blinds you to the way that you must go.

Yes, there is yet one way to where she is,   21
Bitter, but one that faith may never miss.
Out of a grave I come to tell you this —
To tell you this.

There is the western gate, Luke Havergal,   25
There are the crimson leaves upon the wall.
Go, for the winds are tearing them away, —
Nor think to riddle the dead words they say,
Nor any more to feel them as they fall;
But go, and if you trust her she will call.   30
There is the western gate, Luke Havergal —
Luke Havergal.

Credo

(w. 1894?)

I cannot find my way: there is no star
In all the shrouded heavens anywhere;
And there is not a whisper in the air
Of any living voice but one so far
That I can hear it only as a bar   5
Of lost, imperial music, played when fair
And angel fingers wove, and unaware,
Dead leaves to garlands where no roses are.

No, there is not a glimmer, nor a call,
For one that welcomes, welcomes when he fears,
The black and awful chaos of the night;   11
For through it all — above, beyond it all —
I know the far-sent message of the years,
I feel the coming glory of the Light.

Isaac and Archibald

(w. 1899)

Isaac and Archibald were two old men.
I knew them, and I may have laughed at them
A little; but I must have honored them
For they were old, and they were good to me.

I do not think of either of them now,   5
Without remembering, infallibly,
A journey that I made one afternoon
With Isaac to find out what Archibald
Was doing with his oats. It was high time
Those oats were cut, said Isaac; and he feared
That Archibald — well, he could never feel   11
Quite sure of Archibald. Accordingly
The good old man invited me — that is,
Permitted me — to go along with him;
And I, with a small boy's adhesiveness   15
To competent old age, got up and went.

I do not know that I cared overmuch
For Archibald's or anybody's oats,
But Archibald was quite another thing,
And Isaac yet another; and the world   20
Was wide, and there was gladness everywhere.
We walked together down the River Road
With all the warmth and wonder of the land
Around us, and the wayside flash of leaves, —
And Isaac said the day was glorious;   25
But somewhere at the end of the first mile
I found that I was figuring to find
How long those ancient legs of his would keep
The pace that he had set for them. The sun
Was hot, and I was ready to sweat blood;   30
But Isaac, for aught I could make of him,
Was cool to his hat-band. So I said then
With a dry gasp of affable despair,
Something about the scorching days we have
In August without knowing it sometimes;   35
But Isaac said the day was like a dream,
And praised the Lord, and talked about the
    breeze.
I made a fair confession of the breeze,
And crowded casually on his thought
The nearness of a profitable nook   40
That I could see. First I was half inclined
To caution him that he was growing old,
But something that was not compassion soon
Made plain the folly of all subterfuge.
Isaac was old, but not so old as that.   45

So I proposed, without an overture,
That we be seated in the shade a while,
And Isaac made no murmur. Soon the talk
Was turned on Archibald, and I began
To feel some premonitions of a kind   50
That only childhood knows; for the old man
Had looked at me and clutched me with his
    eye,
And asked if I had ever noticed things.
I told him that I could not think of them,
And I knew then, by the frown that left his face
Unsatisfied, that I had injured him.   56
"My good young friend," he said, "you cannot
    feel
What I have seen so long. You have the eyes —
Oh, yes — but you have not the other things:
The sight within that never will deceive,   60
You do not know — you have no right to know;
The twilight warning of experience,
The singular idea of loneliness, —
These are not yours. But they have long been
    mine,
And they have shown me now for seven years

That Archibald is changing. It is not   66
So much that he should come to his last hand,
And leave the game, and go the old way down;
But I have known him in and out so long,
And I have seen so much of good in him   70
That other men have shared and have not seen,
And I have gone so far through thick and thin,
Through cold and fire with him, that now it
      brings
To this old heart of mine an ache that you
Have not yet lived enough to know about.   75
But even unto you, and your boy's faith,
Your freedom, and your untried confidence,
A time will come to find out what it means
To know that you are losing what was yours,
To know that you are being left behind;   80
And then the long contempt of innocence —
God bless you, boy! — don't think the worse of it
Because an old man chatters in the shade —
Will all be like a story you have read   84
In childhood and remembered for the pictures.
And when the best friend of your life goes down,
When first you know in him the slackening
That comes, and coming always tells the end, —
Now in a common word that would have passed
Uncaught from any other lips than his,   90
Now in some trivial act of every day,
Done as he might have done it all along
But for a twinging little difference
That nips you like a squirrel's teeth — oh, yes,
Then you will understand it well enough.   95
But oftener it comes in other ways;
It comes without your knowing when it comes;
You know that he is changing, and you know
That he is going — just as I know now
That Archibald is going, and that I   100
Am staying. . . . Look at me, my boy,
And when the time shall come for you to see
That I must follow after him, try then
To think of me, to bring me back again,
Just as I was to-day. Think of the place   105
Where we are sitting now, and think of me —
Think of old Isaac as you knew him then,
When you set out with him in August once
To see old Archibald." — The words come back
Almost as Isaac must have uttered them,   110
And there comes with them a dry memory
Of something in my throat that would not move.

If you had asked me then to tell just why
I made so much of Isaac and the things
He said, I should have gone far for an answer;
For I knew it was not sorrow that I felt,   116
Whatever I may have wished it, or tried then

To make myself believe. My mouth was full
Of words, and they would have been comforting
To Isaac, spite of my twelve years, I think;   120
But there was not in me the willingness
To speak them out. Therefore I watched the
      ground;
And I was wondering what made the Lord
Create a thing so nervous as an ant,
When Isaac, with commendable unrest,   125
Ordained that we should take the road again —
For it was yet three miles to Archibald's,
And one to the first pump. I felt relieved
All over when the old man told me that;
I felt that he had stilled a fear of mine   130
That those extremities of heat and cold
Which he had long gone through with Archibald
Had made the man impervious to both;
But Isaac had a desert somewhere in him,   134
And at the pump he thanked God for all things
That He had put on earth for men to drink,
And he drank well, — so well that I proposed
That we go slowly lest I learn too soon
The bitterness of being left behind,
And all those other things. That was a joke
To Isaac, and it pleased him very much;   141
And that pleased me — for I was twelve years
      old.

At the end of an hour's walking after that
The cottage of old Archibald appeared.
Little and white and high on a smooth round
      hill   145
It stood, with hackmatacks and apple-trees
Before it, and a big barn-roof beyond;
And over the place — trees, houses, fields and
      all —
Hovered an air of still simplicity
And a fragrance of old summers — the old style
That lives the while it passes. I dare say   151
That I was lightly conscious of all this
When Isaac, of a sudden, stopped himself,
And for the long first quarter of a minute
Gazed with incredulous eyes, forgetful quite   155
Of breezes and of me and of all else
Under the scorching sun but a smooth-cut field,
Faint yellow in the distance. I was young,
But there were a few things that I could see,
And this was one of them. — "Well, well!" said
      he;   160
And "Archibald will be surprised, I think,"
Said I. But all my childhood subtlety
Was lost on Isaac, for he strode along
Like something out of Homer — powerful
And awful on the wayside, so I thought.   165

Also I thought how good it was to be
So near the end of my short-legged endeavor
To keep the pace with Isaac for five miles.

Hardly had we turned in from the main road
When Archibald, with one hand on his back   170
And the other clutching his huge-headed cane,
Came limping down to meet us. — "Well! well!
    well!"
Said he; and then he looked at my red face,
All streaked with dust and sweat, and shook my
    hand,   174
And said it must have been a right smart walk
That we had had that day from Tilbury
    Town. —
"Magnificent," said Isaac; and he told
About the beautiful west wind there was
Which cooled and clarified the atmosphere.
"You must have made it with your legs, I guess,"
Said Archibald; and Isaac humored him   181
With one of those infrequent smiles of his
Which he kept in reserve, apparently,
For Archibald alone. "But why," said he,
"Should Providence have cider in the world   185
If not for such an afternoon as this?"
And Archibald, with a soft light in his eyes,
Replied that if he chose to go down cellar,
There he would find eight barrels — one of
    which
Was newly tapped, he said, and to his taste   190
An honor to the fruit. Isaac approved
Most heartily of that, and guided us
Forthwith, as if his venerable feet
Were measuring the turf in his own door-yard,
Straight to the open rollway. Down we went,
Out of the fiery sunshine to the gloom,   196
Grateful and half sepulchral, where we found
The barrels, like eight potent sentinels,
Close ranged along the wall. From one of them
A bright pine spile stuck out alluringly,   200
And on the black flat stone, just under it,
Glimmered a late-spilled proof that Archibald
Had spoken from unfeigned experience.
There was a fluted antique water-glass
Close by, and in it, prisoned, or at rest,   205
There was a cricket, of the brown soft sort
That feeds on darkness. Isaac turned him out,
And touched him with his thumb to make him
    jump,
And then composedly pulled out the plug
With such a practised hand that scarce a drop
Did even touch his fingers. Then he drank   211
And smacked his lips with a slow patronage
And looked along the line of barrels there

With a pride that may have been forgetfulness
That they were Archibald's and not his own.
"I never twist a spigot nowadays,"   216
He said, and raised the glass up to the light,
"But I thank God for orchards." And that glass
Was filled repeatedly for the same hand
Before I thought it worth while to discern   220
Again that I was young, and that old age,
With all his woes, had some advantages.
"Now, Archibald," said Isaac, when we stood
Outside again, "I have it in my mind
That I shall take a sort of little walk —   225
To stretch my legs and see what you are doing.
You stay and rest your back and tell the boy
A story: Tell him all about the time
In Stafford's cabin forty years ago,   229
When four of us were snowed up for ten days
With only one dried haddock. Tell him all
About it, and be wary of your back.
Now I will go along." — I looked up then
At Archibald, and as I looked I saw
Just how his nostrils widened once or twice   235
And then grew narrow. I can hear to-day
The way the old man chuckled to himself —
Not wholesomely, not wholly to convince
Another of his mirth, — as I can hear   239
The lonely sigh that followed. — But at length
He said: "The orchard now's the place for us;
We may find something like an apple there,
And we shall have the shade, at any rate."
So there we went and there we laid ourselves
Where the sun could not reach us; and I
    champed   245
A dozen of worm-blighted astrakhans
While Archibald said nothing — merely told
The tale of Stafford's cabin, which was good,
Though "master chilly" — after his own
    phrase —
Even for a day like that. But other thoughts
Were moving in his mind, imperative,   251
And writhing to be spoken: I could see
The glimmer of them in a glance or two,
Cautious, or else unconscious, that he gave
Over his shoulder: . . . "Stafford and the
    rest —   255
But that's an old song now, and Archibald
And Isaac are old men. Remember, boy,
That we are old. Whatever we have gained,
Or lost, or thrown away, we are old men.
You look before you and we look behind,   260
And we are playing life out in the shadow —
But that's not all of it. The sunshine lights
A good road yet before us if we look,
And we are doing that when least we know it;

For both of us are children of the sun, 265
Like you, and like the weed there at your feet.
The shadow calls us, and it frightens us —
We think; but there's a light behind the stars
And we old fellows who have dared to live,
We see it — and we see the other things, 270
The other things. . . . Yes, I have seen it come
These eight years, and these ten years, and I
    know
Now that it cannot be for very long
That Isaac will be Isaac. You have seen —
Young as you are, you must have seen the
    strange 275
Uncomfortable habit of the man?
He'll take my nerves and tie them in a knot
Sometimes, and that's not Isaac. I know that —
And I know what it is: I get it here
A little, in my knees, and Isaac — here." 280
The old man shook his head regretfully
And laid his knuckles three times on his fore-
    head.
"That's what it is: Isaac is not quite right.
You see it, but you don't know what it means:
The thousand little differences — no, 285
You do not know them, and it's well you don't;
You'll know them soon enough — God bless
    you, boy! —
You'll know them, but not all of them — not
    all.
So think of them as little as you can:
There's nothing in them for you, or for me —
But I am old and I must think of them; 291
I'm in the shadow, but I don't forget
The light, my boy, — the light behind the
    stars.
Remember that: remember that I said it;
And when the time that you think far away 295
Shall come for you to say it — say it, boy;
Let there be no confusion or distrust
In you, no snarling of a life half lived,
Nor any cursing over broken things
That your complaint has been the ruin of. 300
Live to see clearly and the light will come
To you, and as you need it. — But there, there,
I'm going it again, as Isaac says,
And I'll stop now before you go to sleep. —
Only be sure that you growl cautiously, 305
And always where the shadow may not reach
    you."

Never shall I forget, long as I live,
The quaint thin crack in Archibald's voice,
The lonely twinkle in his little eyes,
Or the way it made me feel to be with him. 310

I know I lay and looked for a long time
Down through the orchard and across the road,
Across the river and the sun-scorched hills
That ceased in a blue forest, where the world
Ceased with it. Now and then my fancy caught
A flying glimpse of a good life beyond — 316
Something of ships and sunlight, streets and
    singing,
Troy falling, and the ages coming back,
And ages coming forward: Archibald
And Isaac were good fellows in old clothes, 320
And Agamemnon was a friend of mine;
Ulysses coming home again to shoot
With bows and feathered arrows made another,
And all was as it should be. I was young.

So I lay dreaming of what things I would, 325
Calm and incorrigibly satisfied
With apples and romance and ignorance,
And the still smoke from Archibald's clay pipe.
There was a stillness over everything,
As if the spirit of heat had laid its hand 330
Upon the world and hushed it; and I felt
Within the mightiness of the white sun
That smote the land around us and wrought out
A fragrance from the trees, a vital warmth
And fullness for the time that was to come, 335
And a glory for the world beyond the forest.
The present and the future and the past,
Isaac and Archibald, the burning bush,
The Trojans and the walls of Jericho,
Were beautifully fused; and all went well 340
Till Archibald began to fret for Isaac
And said it was a master day for sunstroke.
That was enough to make a mummy smile,
I thought; and I remained hilarious,
In face of all precedence and respect, 345
Till Isaac (who had come to us unheard)
Found he had no tobacco, looked at me
Peculiarly, and asked of Archibald
What ailed the boy to make him chirrup so.
From that he told us what a blessed world 350
The Lord had given us. — "But, Archibald,"
He added, with a sweet severity
That made me think of peach-skins and goose-
    flesh,
"I'm half afraid you cut those oats of yours
A day or two before they were well set." 355
"They were set well enough," said Archibald, —
And I remarked the process of his nose
Before the words came out. "But never mind
Your neighbor's oats: you stay here in the shade
And rest yourself while I go find the cards. 360
We'll have a little game of seven-up

And let the boy keep count." — "We'll have
    the game,
Assuredly," said Isaac; "and I think
That I will have a drop of cider, also."

They marched away together towards the house
And left me to my childish ruminations   366
Upon the ways of men. I followed them
Down cellar with my fancy, and then left them
For a fairer vision of all things at once
That was anon to be destroyed again   370
By the sound of voices and of heavy feet —
One of the sounds of life that I remember,
Though I forget so many that rang first
As if they were thrown down to me from Sinai.

So I remember, even to this day,   375
Just how they sounded, how they placed them-
    selves,
And how the game went on while I made marks
And crossed them out, and meanwhile made
    some Trojans.
Likewise I made Ulysses, after Isaac,
And a little after Flaxman. Archibald   380
Was injured when he found himself left out,
But he had no heroics, and I said so:
I told him that his white beard was too long
And too straight down to be like things in
    Homer.   384
"Quite so," said Isaac. — "Low," said Archibald;
And he threw down a deuce with a deep grin
That showed his yellow teeth and made me
    happy.
So they played on till a bell rang from the door,
And Archibald said, "Supper." — After that
The old men smoked while I sat watching them
And wondered with all comfort what might
    come   391
To me, and what might never come to me;
And when the time came for the long walk
    home
With Isaac in the twilight, I could see
The forest and the sunset and the sky-line,   395
No matter where it was that I was looking:
The flame beyond the boundary, the music,
The foam and the white ships, and two old men
Were things that would not leave me. — And
    that night   399
There came to me a dream — a shining one,
With two old angels in it. They had wings,
And they were sitting where a silver light
Suffused them, face to face. The wings of one
Began to palpitate as I approached,
But I was yet unseen when a dry voice   405

Cried thinly, with unpatronizing triumph,
"I've got you, Isaac; high, low, jack, and the
    game."

Isaac and Archibald have gone their way
To the silence of the loved and well-forgotten.
I knew them, and I may have laughed at them;
But there's a laughing that has honor in it,   411
And I have no regret for light words now.
Rather I think sometimes they may have made
Their sport of me; — but they would not do
    that,   414
They were too old for that. They were old men,
And I may laugh at them because I knew them.

Miniver Cheevy

(w. 1908?)

Miniver Cheevy, child of scorn,
    Grew lean while he assailed the seasons;
He wept that he was ever born,
    And he had reasons.

Miniver loved the days of old   5
    When swords were bright and steeds were
        prancing;
The vision of a warrior bold
    Would set him dancing.

Miniver sighed for what was not,
    And dreamed, and rested from his labors;
He dreamed of Thebes and Camelot,   11
    And Priam's neighbors.

Miniver mourned the ripe renown
    That made so many a name so fragrant;
He mourned Romance, now on the town,   15
    And Art, a vagrant.

Miniver loved the Medici,
    Albeit he had never seen one;
He would have sinned incessantly
    Could he have been one.   20

Miniver cursed the commonplace
    And eyed a khaki suit with loathing:
He missed the mediaeval grace
    Of iron clothing.

Miniver scorned the gold he sought,   25
    But sore annoyed was he without it;
Miniver thought, and thought, and thought
    And thought about it.

Miniver Cheevy, born too late,　29
　Scratched his head and kept on thinking;
Miniver coughed, and called it fate,
　And kept on drinking.

For a Dead Lady

(1909)

No more with overflowing light
Shall fill the eyes that now are faded,
Nor shall another's fringe with night
Their woman-hidden world as they did.
No more shall quiver down the days　5
The flowing wonder of her ways,
Whereof no language may requite
The shifting and the many-shaded.

The grace, divine, definitive,
Clings only as a faint forestalling;　10
The laugh that love could not forgive
Is hushed, and answers to no calling;
The forehead and the little ears
Have gone where Saturn keeps the years;
The breast where roses could not live　15
Has done with rising and with falling.

The beauty, shattered by the laws
That have creation in their keeping,
No longer trembles at applause,
Or over children that are sleeping;　20
And we who delve in beauty's lore
Know all that we have known before
Of what inexorable cause
Makes Time so vicious in his reaping.

Ben Jonson Entertains a Man from Stratford

(w. 1914?)

You are a friend then, as I make it out,
Of our man Shakespeare, who alone of us
Will put an ass's head in Fairyland
As he would add a shilling to more shillings,
All most harmonious, — and out of his　5
Miraculous inviolable increase
Fills Ilion, Rome, or any town you like
Of olden time with timeless Englishmen;
And I must wonder what you think of him —
All you down there where your small Avon
　flows　10
By Stratford, and where you're an Alderman.

Some, for a guess, would have him riding back
To be a farrier there, or say a dyer;
Or maybe one of your adept surveyors;
Or like enough the wizard of all tanners.　15
Not you — no fear of that; for I discern
In you a kindling of the flame that saves —
The nimble element, the true caloric;
I see it, and was told of it, moreover,
By our discriminate friend himself, no other.
Had you been one of the sad average,　21
As he would have it, — meaning, as I take it,
The sinew and the solvent of our Island,
You'd not be buying beer for this Terpander's
Approved and estimated friend Ben Jonson;　25
He'd never foist it as a part of his
Contingent entertainment of a townsman
While he goes off rehearsing, as he must,
If he shall ever be the Duke of Stratford.　29
And my words are no shadow on your town —
Far from it; for one's town's as like another
As all are unlike London. Oh, he knows it, —
And there's the Stratford in him; he denies it,
And there's the Shakespeare in him. So, God
　　help him!
I tell him he needs Greek; but neither God　35
Nor Greek will help him. Nothing will help
　　that man.
You see the fates have given him so much,
He must have all or perish, — or look out
Of London, where he sees too many lords.　39
They're part of half what ails him: I suppose
There's nothing fouler down among the demons
Than what it is he feels when he remembers
The dust and sweat and ointment of his calling
With his lords looking on and laughing at him.
King as he is, he can't be king *de facto*,　45
And that's as well, because he wouldn't like it;
He'd frame a lower rating of men then
Than he has now; and after that would come
An abdication or an apoplexy.
He can't be king, not even king of Strat-
　　ford, —　50
Though half the world, if not the whole of it,
May crown him with a crown that fits no king
Save Lord Apollo's homesick emissary:
Not there on Avon, or on any stream
Where Naiads and their white arms are no
　　more,　55
Shall he find home again. It's all too bad.
But there's a comfort, for he'll have that
　　House —
The best you ever saw; and he'll be there
Anon, as you're an Alderman. Good God!
He makes me lie awake o'nights and laugh.　60

And you have known him from his origin,
You tell me; and a most uncommon urchin
He must have been to the few seeing ones —
A trifle terrifying, I dare say,
Discovering a world with his man's eyes,   65
Quite as another lad might see some finches,
If he looked hard and had an eye for nature.
But this one had his eyes and their foretelling,
And he had you to fare with, and what else?
He must have had a father and a mother —   70
In fact I've heard him say so — and a dog,
As a boy should, I venture; and the dog,
Most likely, was the only man who knew
    him.
A dog, for all I know, is what he needs
As much as anything right here to-day,   75
To counsel him about his disillusions,
Old aches, and parturitions of what's com-
    ing, —
A dog of orders, an emeritus,
To wag his tail at him when he comes home,
And then to put his paws up on his knees   80
And say, "For God's sake, what's it all about?"
I don't know whether he needs a dog or not —
Or what he needs. I tell him he needs Greek;
I'll talk of rules and Aristotle with him,
And if his tongue's at home he'll say to that,   85
"I have your word that Aristotle knows,
And you mine that I don't know Aristotle."
He's all at odds with all the unities,
And what's yet worse, it doesn't seem to matter;
He treads along through Time's old wilderness
As if the tramp of all the centuries   91
Had left no roads — and there are none, for
    him;
He doesn't see them, even with those eyes, —
And that's a pity, or I say it is.
Accordingly we have him as we have him —
Going his way, the way that he goes best,   96
A pleasant animal with no great noise
Or nonsense anywhere to set him off —
Save only divers and inclement devils
Have made of late his heart their dwelling
    place.   100
A flame half ready to fly out sometimes
At some annoyance may be fanned up in him,
But soon it falls, and when it falls goes out;
He knows how little room there is in there
For crude and futile animosities,   105
And how much for the joy of being whole,
And how much for long sorrow and old pain.
On our side there are some who may be given
To grow old wondering what he thinks of us
And some above us, who are, in his eyes,   110

Above himself, — and that's quite right and
    English.
Yet here we smile, or disappoint the gods
Who made it so: the gods have always eyes
To see men scratch; and they see one down
    here
Who itches, manor-bitten to the bone,   115
Albeit he knows himself — yes, yes, he knows —
The lord of more than England and of more
Than all the seas of England in all time
Shall ever wash. D'ye wonder that I laugh?
He sees me, and he doesn't seem to care;   120
And why the devil should he? I can't tell you.

I'll meet him out alone of a bright Sunday,
Trim, rather spruce, and quite the gentleman.
"What ho, my lord!" say I. He doesn't hear
    me;
Wherefore I have to pause and look at him.   125
He's not enormous, but one looks at him.
A little on the round if you insist,
For now, God save the mark, he's growing old;
He's five and forty, and to hear him talk
These days you'd call him eighty; then you'd
    add   130
More years to that. He's old enough to be
The father of a world, and so he is.
"Ben, you're a scholar, what's the time of day?"
Says he; and there shines out of him again
An aged light that has no age or station —
The mystery that's his — a mischievous   136
Half-mad serenity that laughs at fame
For being won so easy, and at friends
Who laugh at him for what he wants the
    most,   139
And for his dukedom down in Warwickshire; —
By which you see we're all a little jealous. . . .
Poor Greene! I fear the color of his name
Was even as that of his ascending soul;
And he was one where there are many
    others, —   144
Some scrivening to the end against their fate,
Their puppets all in ink and all to die there;
And some with hands that once would shade
    an eye
That scanned Euripides and Æschylus
Will reach by this time for a pot-house mop
To slush their first and last of royalties.   150
Poor devils! and they all play to his hand;
For so it was in Athens and old Rome.
But that's not here or there; I've wandered
    off.
Greene does it, or I'm careful. Where's that
    boy?

Yes, he'll go back to Stratford. And we'll miss
   him?   155
Dear sir, there'll be no London here without
   him.
We'll all be riding, one of these fine days,
Down there to see him — and his wife won't
   like us;
And then we'll think of what he never said
Of women — which, if taken all in all   160
With what he did say, would buy many horses.
Though nowadays he's not so much for women:
"So few of them," he says, "are worth the
   guessing."
But there's a worm at work when he says that,
And while he says it one feels in the air   165
A deal of circumambient hocus-pocus.
They've had him dancing till his toes were
   tender,
And he can feel 'em now, come chilly rains.
There's no long cry for going into it,   169
However, and we don't know much about it.
But you in Stratford, like most here in London,
Have more now in the *Sonnets* than you paid
   for;
He's put one there with all her poison on,
To make a singing fiction of a shadow   174
That's in his life a fact, and always will be.
But she's no care of ours, though Time, I fear,
Will have a more reverberant ado
About her than about another one
Who seems to have decoyed him, married him,
And sent him scuttling on his way to
   London, —   180
With much already learned, and more to learn,
And more to follow. Lord! how I see him now,
Pretending, maybe trying, to be like us.
Whatever he may have meant, we never had
   him;
He failed us, or escaped, or what you will, —
And there was that about him (God knows
   what, —   186
We'd flayed another had he tried it on us)
That made as many of us as had wits
More fond of all his easy distances
Than one another's noise and clap-your-
   shoulder.   190
But think you not, my friend, he'd never talk!
Talk? He was eldritch at it; and we listened —
Thereby acquiring much we knew before
About ourselves, and hitherto had held
Irrelevant, or not prime to the purpose.   195
And there were some, of course, and there be
   now,
Disordered and reduced amazedly

To resignation by the mystic seal
Of young finality the gods had laid
On everything that made him a young demon;
And one or two shot looks at him already   201
As he had been their executioner;
And once or twice he was, not knowing it, —
Or knowing, being sorry for poor clay
And saying nothing. . . . Yet, for all his engines,
You'll meet a thousand of an afternoon   206
Who strut and sun themselves and see around
   'em
A world made out of more that has a reason
Than his, I swear, that he sees here to-day;
Though he may scarcely give a Fool an exit
But we mark how he sees in everything   211
A law that, given we flout it once too often,
Brings fire and iron down on our naked heads.
To me it looks as if the power that made
   him,   214
For fear of giving all things to one creature,
Left out the first, — faith, innocence, illusion,
Whatever 'tis that keeps us out o' Bedlam, —
And thereby, for his too consuming vision,
Empowered him out of nature; though to see
   him,
You'd never guess what's going on inside him.
He'll break out some day like a keg of ale   221
With too much independent frenzy in it;
And all for cellaring what he knows won't keep,
And what he'd best forget — but that he can't.
You'll have it, and have more than I'm fore-
   telling;   225
And there'll be such a roaring at the Globe
As never stunned the bleeding gladiators.
He'll have to change the color of its hair
A bit, for now he calls it Cleopatra.
Black hair would never do for Cleopatra.   230

But you and I are not yet two old women,
And you're a man of office. What he does
Is more to you than how it is he does it, —
And that's what the Lord God has never told
   him.
They work together, and the Devil helps 'em;
They do it of a morning, or if not,   236
They do it of a night; in which event
He's peevish of a morning. He seems old;
He's not the proper stomach or the sleep —
And they're two sovran agents to conserve him
Against the fiery art that has no mercy   241
But what's in that prodigious grand new House.
I gather something happening in his boyhood
Fulfilled him with a boy's determination
To make all Stratford 'ware of him. Well, well,

I hope at last he'll have his joy of it,   246
And all his pigs and sheep and bellowing beeves,
And frogs and owls and unicorns, moreover,
Be less than hell to his attendant ears.
Oh, past a doubt we'll all go down to see
    him.   250

He may be wise. With London two days off,
Down there some wind of heaven may yet re-
    vive him;
But there's no quickening breath from anywhere
Shall make of him again the poised young faun
From Warwickshire, who'd made, it seems
    already   255
A legend of himself before I came
To blink before the last of his first lightning.
Whatever there be, there'll be no more of that;
The coming on of his old monster Time   259
Has made him a still man; and he has dreams
Were fair to think on once, and all found
    hollow.
He knows how much of what men paint them-
    selves
Would blister in the light of what they are;
He sees how much of what was great now
    shares
An eminence transformed and ordinary;   265
He knows too much of what the world has
    hushed
In others, to be loud now for himself;
He knows now at what height low enemies
May reach his heart, and high friends let him
    fall;
But what not even such as he may know   270
Bedevils him the worst: his lark may sing
At heaven's gate how he will, and for as long
As joy may listen, but he sees no gate,
Save one whereat the spent clay waits a little
Before the churchyard has it, and the worm. 275
Not long ago, late in an afternoon,
I came on him unseen down Lambeth way,
And on my life I was afear'd of him:
He gloomed and mumbled like a soul from
    Tophet,
His hands behind him and his head bent
    solemn.   280
"What is it now," said I, — "another woman?"
That made him sorry for me, and he smiled.
"No, Ben," he mused; "it's Nothing. It's all
    Nothing.
We come, we go; and when we're done, we're
    done.
Spiders and flies — we're mostly one or
    t'other —   285

We come, we go; and when we're done, we're
    done."
"By God, you sing that song as if you knew it!"
Said I, by way of cheering him; "what ails ye?"
"I think I must have come down here to think,"
Says he to that, and pulls his little beard;   290
"Your fly will serve as well as anybody,
And what's his hour? He flies, and flies, and
    flies,
And in his fly's mind has a brave appearance;
And then your spider gets him in her net,
And eats him out, and hangs him up to dry.   295
That's Nature, the kind mother of us all.
And then your slattern housemaid swings her
    broom,
And where's your spider? And that's Nature,
    also.
It's Nature, and it's Nothing. It's all Nothing.
It's all a world where bugs and emperors   300
Go singularly back to the same dust,
Each in his time; and the old, ordered stars
That sang together, Ben, will sing the same
Old stave to-morrow."   304

                          When he talks like that,
There's nothing for a human man to do
But lead him to some grateful nook like this
Where we be now, and there to make him drink.
He'll drink, for love of me, and then be sick;
A sad sign always in a man of parts,   310
And always very ominous. The great
Should be as large in liquor as in love, —
And our great friend is not so large in either:
One disaffects him, and the other fails him;
Whatso he drinks that has an antic in it,   315
He's wondering what's to pay in his insides;
And while his eyes are on the Cyprian
He's fribbling all the time with that damned
    House.
We laugh here at his thrift, but after all
It may be thrift that saves him from the
    devil;
God gave it, anyhow, — and we'll suppose   321
He knew the compound of his handiwork.
To-day the clouds are with him, but anon
He'll out of 'em enough to shake the tree
Of life itself and bring down fruit unheard-
    of, —   325
And, throwing in the bruised and whole to-
    gether,
Prepare a wine to make us drunk with wonder;
And if he live, there'll be a sunset spell
Thrown over him as over a glassed lake
That yesterday was all a black wild water.   330

God send he live to give us, if no more,
What now's a-rampage in him, and exhibit,
With a decent half-allegiance to the ages
An earnest of at least a casual eye
Turned once on what he owes to Gutenberg,
And to the fealty of more centuries   336
Than are as yet a picture in our vision.
"There's time enough, — I'll do it when I'm old,
And we're immortal men," he says to that;
And then he says to me, "Ben, what's 'im-
    mortal'?   340
Think you by any force of ordination
It may be nothing of a sort more noisy
Than a small oblivion of component ashes
That of a dream-addicted world was once   344
A moving atomy much like your friend here?"
Nothing will help that man. To make him
    laugh,
I said then he was a mad mountebank, —
And by the Lord I nearer made him cry.
I could have eat an eft then, on my knees,
Tail, claws, and all of him; for I had stung 350
The king of men, who had no sting for me,
And I had hurt him in his memories;
And I say now, as I shall say again,
I love the man this side idolatry.

He'll do it when he's old, he says. I wonder. 355
He may not be so ancient as all that.
For such as he, the thing that is to do
Will do itself, — but there's a reckoning;
The sessions that are now too much his own,
The roiling inward of a stilled outside,   360
The churning out of all those blood-fed lines,
The nights of many schemes and little sleep,
The full brain hammered hot with too much
    thinking,
The vexed heart over-worn with too much ach-
    ing, —
This weary jangling of conjoined affairs   365
Made out of elements that have no end,
And all confused at once, I understand,
Is not what makes a man to live forever.
O no, not now! He'll not be going now:
There'll be time yet for God knows what
    explosions   370
Before he goes. He'll stay awhile. Just wait:
Just wait a year or two for Cleopatra,
For she's to be a balsam and a comfort;
And that's not all a jape of mine now, either.
For granted once the old way of Apollo   375
Sings in a man, he may then, if he's able,
Strike unafraid whatever strings he will
Upon the last and wildest of new lyres;

Nor out of his new magic, though it hymn
The shrieks of dungeoned hell, shall he create
A madness or a gloom to shut quite out   381
A cleaving daylight, and a last great calm
Triumphant over shipwreck and all storms.
He might have given Aristotle creeps,   384
But surely would have given him his *katharsis*.

He'll not be going yet. There's too much yet
Unsung within the man. But when he goes,
I'd stake ye coin o' the realm his only care
For a phantom world he sounded and found
    wanting
Will be a portion here, a portion there,   390
Of this or that thing or some other thing
That has a patent and intrinsical
Equivalence in those egregious shillings.
And yet he knows, God help him! Tell me, now,
If ever there was anything let loose   395
On earth by gods or devils heretofore
Like this mad, careful, proud, indifferent Shake-
    speare!
Where was it, if it ever was? By heaven,
'Twas never yet in Rhodes or Pergamon —
In Thebes or Nineveh, a thing like this!   400
No thing like this was ever out of England;
And that he knows. I wonder if he cares.
Perhaps he does. . . . O Lord, that House in
    Stratford!

The Man Against the Sky

(w. 1914?)

Upon a round hill, against the dazzling sunset, stands and moves the solitary figure of a man, glorified ("with fire all round him") as if he were a god. Over the crest of the hill this figure vanishes.
   "Where was he going, this man against the sky?" We can only guess. Various guesses are given and summed up in lines 183–187. This leads the poet to confront the darkness which life is, but a darkness not without "gleams" that seem to explain why we do not choose to destroy ourselves.

Between me and the sunset, like a dome
Against the glory of a world on fire,
Now burned a sudden hill,
Bleak, round, and high, by flame-lit height made
    higher,
With nothing on it for the flame to kill   5
Save one who moved and was alone up there
To loom before the chaos and the glare
As if he were the last god going home
Unto his last desire.

Dark, marvelous, and inscrutable he moved on
Till down the fiery distance he was gone, 11
Like one of those eternal, remote things
That range across a man's imaginings
When a sure music fills him and he knows
What he may say thereafter to few men, — 15
The touch of ages having wrought
An echo and a glimpse of what he thought
A phantom or a legend until then;
For whether lighted over ways that save,
Or lured from all repose, 20
If he go on too far to find a grave,
Mostly alone he goes.

Even he, who stood where I had found him,
On high with fire all round him,
Who moved along the molten west, 25
And over the round hill's crest
That seemed half ready with him to go down,
Flame-bitten and flame-cleft,
As if there were to be no last thing left
Of a nameless unimaginable town, — 30
Even he who climbed and vanished may have
  taken
Down to the perils of a depth not known,
From death defended though by men forsaken,
The bread that every man must eat alone;
He may have walked while others hardly dared
Look on to see him stand where many fell; 36
And upward out of that, as out of hell,
He may have sung and striven
To mount where more of him shall yet be given,
Bereft of all retreat, 40
To sevenfold heat, —
As on a day when three in Dura shared
The furnace, and were spared
For glory by that king of Babylon
Who made himself so great that God, who
  heard, 45
Covered him with long feathers, like a bird.

Again, he may have gone down easily,
By comfortable altitudes, and found,
As always, underneath him solid ground
Whereon to be sufficient and to stand 50
Possessed already of the promised land,
Far stretched and fair to see:
A good sight, verily,
And one to make the eyes of her who bore him
Shine glad with hidden tears. 55
Why question of his ease of who before him,
In one place or another where they left
Their names as far behind them as their bones,
And yet by dint of slaughter toil and theft,

And shrewdly sharpened stones, 60
Carved hard the way for his ascendency
Through deserts of lost years?
Why trouble him now who sees and hears
No more than what his innocence requires,
And therefore to no other height aspires 65
Than one at which he neither quails nor tires?
He may do more by seeing what he sees
Than others eager for iniquities;
He may, by seeing all things for the best,
Incite futurity to do the rest. 70

Or with an even likelihood,
He may have met with atrabilious eyes
The fires of time on equal terms and passed
Indifferently down, until at last
His only kind of grandeur would have been, 75
Apparently, in being seen.
He may have had for evil or for good
No argument; he may have had no care
For what without himself went anywhere
To failure or to glory, and least of all 80
For such a stale, flamboyant miracle;
He may have been the prophet of an art
Immovable to old idolatries;
He may have been a player without a part,
Annoyed that even the sun should have the
  skies 85
For such a flaming way to advertise;
He may have been a painter sick at heart
With Nature's toiling for a new surprise;
He may have been a cynic, who now, for all
Of anything divine that his effete 90
Negation may have tasted,
Saw truth in his own image, rather small,
Forbore to fever the ephemeral,
Found any barren height a good retreat
From any swarming street, 95
And in the sun saw power superbly wasted;
And when the primitive old-fashioned stars
Came out again to shine on joys and wars
More primitive, and all arrayed for doom,
He may have proved a world a sorry thing 100
In his imagining,
And life a lighted highway to the tomb.

Or, mounting with infirm unsearching tread,
His hopes to chaos led, 104
He may have stumbled up there from the past,
And with an aching strangeness viewed the last
Abysmal conflagration of his dreams, —
A flame where nothing seems
To burn but flame itself, by nothing fed;
And while it all went out, 110

Not even the faint anodyne of doubt
May then have eased a painful going down
From pictured heights of power and lost renown,
Revealed at length to his outlived endeavor
Remote and unapproachable forever;   115
And at his heart there may have gnawed
Sick memories of a dead faith foiled and flawed
And long dishonored by the living death
Assigned alike by chance
To brutes and hierophants;   120
And anguish fallen on those he loved around
     him
May once have dealt the last blow to confound
     him,
And so have left him as death leaves a child,
Who sees it all too near;
And he who knows no young way to forget   125
May struggle to the tomb unreconciled.
Whatever suns may rise or set
There may be nothing kinder for him here
Than shafts and agonies;
And under these   130
He may cry out and stay on horribly;
Or, seeing in death too small a thing to fear,
He may go forward like a stoic Roman
Where pangs and terrors in his pathway lie, —
Or, seizing the swift logic of a woman,   135
Curse God and die.

Or maybe there, like many another one
Who might have stood aloft and looked ahead,
Black-drawn against wild red,
He may have built, unawed by fiery gules   140
That in him no commotion stirred,
A living reason out of molecules
Why molecules occurred,
And one for smiling when he might have sighed
Had he seen far enough,   145
And in the same inevitable stuff
Discovered an odd reason too for pride
In being what he must have been by laws
Infrangible and for no kind of cause.
Deterred by no confusion or surprise   150
He may have seen with his mechanic eyes
A world without a meaning, and had room,
Alone amid magnificence and doom,
To build himself an airy monument
That should, or fail him in his vague intent,   155
Outlast an accidental universe —
To call it nothing worse —
Or, by the burrowing guile
Of Time disintegrated and effaced,
Like once-remembered mighty trees go down   160
To ruin, of which by man may now be traced
No part sufficient even to be rotten,

And in the book of things that are forgotten
Is entered as a thing not quite worth while.
He may have been so great   165
That satraps would have shivered at his frown,
And all he prized alive may rule a state
No larger than a grave that holds a clown;
He may have been a master of his fate,
And of his atoms, — ready as another   170
In his emergence to exonerate
His father and his mother;
He may have been a captain of a host,
Self-eloquent and ripe for prodigies,
Doomed here to swell by dangerous degrees,   175
And then give up the ghost.
Nahum's great grasshoppers were such as these,
Sun-scattered and soon lost.

Whatever the dark road he may have taken,
This man who stood on high   180
And faced alone the sky,
Whatever drove or lured or guided him, —
A vision answering a faith unshaken,
An easy trust assumed of easy trials,
A sick negation born of weak denials,   185
A crazed abhorrence of an old condition,
A blind attendance on a brief ambition, —
Whatever stayed him or derided him,
His way was even as ours;   189
And we, with all our wounds and all our powers,
Must each await alone at his own height
Another darkness or another light;
And there, of our poor self dominion reft,
If inference and reason shun
Hell, Heaven, and Oblivion,   195
May thwarted will (perforce precarious,
But for our conservation better thus)
Have no misgiving left
Of doing yet what here we leave undone?
Or if unto the last of these we cleave,   200
Believing or protesting we believe
In such an idle and ephemeral
Florescence of the diabolical, —
If, robbed of two fond old enormities,
Our being had no onward auguries,   205
What then were this great love of ours to say
For launching other lives to voyage again
A little farther into time and pain,
A little faster in a futile chase
For a kingdom and a power and a Race   210
That would have still in sight
A manifest end of ashes and eternal night?
Is this the music of the toys we shake
So loud, — as if there might be no mistake
Somewhere in our indomitable will?   215
Are we no greater than the noise we make

Along one blind atomic pilgrimage
Whereon by crass chance billeted we go
Because our brains and bones and cartilage
Will have it so?   220
If this we say, then let us all be still
About our share in it, and live and die
More quietly thereby.

Where was he going, this man against the sky?
You know not, nor do I.   225
But this we know, if we know anything:
That we may laugh and fight and sing
And of our transience here make offering
To an orient Word that will not be erased,
Or, save in incommunicable gleams   230
Too permanent for dreams,
Be found or known.
No tonic and ambitious irritant
Of increase or of want
Has made an otherwise insensate waste   235
Of ages overthrown
A ruthless, veiled, implacable foretaste
Of other ages that are still to be
Depleted and rewarded variously
Because a few, by fate's economy,   240
Shall seem to move the world the way it goes;
No soft evangel of equality,
Safe-cradled in a communal repose
That huddles into death and may at last
Be covered well with equatorial snows —   245
And all for what, the devil only knows —
Will aggregate an inkling to confirm
The credit of a sage or of a worm,
Or tell us why one man in five
Should have a care to stay alive   250
While in his heart he feels no violence
Laid on his humor and intelligence
When infant Science makes a pleasant face
And waves again that hollow toy, the Race;
No planetary trap where souls are wrought   255
For nothing but the sake of being caught
And sent again to nothing will attune
Itself to any key of any reason
Why man should hunger through another sea-
    son
To find out why 'twere better late than soon   260
To go away and let the sun and moon
And all the silly stars illuminate
A place for creeping things,
And those that root and trumpet and have wings,
And herd and ruminate,   265
Or dive and flash and poise in rivers and seas,
Or by their loyal tails in lofty trees
Hang screeching lewd victorious derision
Of man's immortal vision.

Shall we, because Eternity records   270
Too vast an answer for the time-born words
We spell, whereof so many are dead that once
In our capricious lexicons
Were so alive and final, hear no more
The Word itself, the living word   275
That none alive has ever heard
Or ever spelt,
And few have ever felt
Without the fears and old surrenderings
And terrors that began   280
When Death let fall a feather from his wings
And humbled the first man?
Because the weight of our humility,
Wherefrom we gain
A little wisdom and much pain,   285
Falls here too sore and there too tedious,
Are we in anguish or complacency,
Not looking far enough ahead
To see by what mad couriers we are led
Along the roads of the ridiculous,   290
To pity ourselves and laugh at faith
And while we curse life bear it?
And if we see the soul's dead end in death,
Are we to fear it?
What folly is here that has not yet a name   295
Unless we say outright that we are liars?
What have we seen beyond our sunset fires
That lights again the way by which we came?
Why pay we such a price, and one we give
So clamoringly, for each racked empty day   300
That leads one more last human hope away,
As quiet fiends would lead past our crazed eyes
Our children to an unseen sacrifice?
If after all that we have lived and thought,
All comes to Nought, —   305
If there be nothing after Now,
And we be nothing anyhow,
And we know that, — why live?
'Twere sure but weaklings' vain distress
To suffer dungeons where so many doors   310
Will open on the cold eternal shores
That look sheer down
To the dark tideless floods of Nothingness
Where all who know may drown.

Flammonde

(w. 1915–16)

This psychological portrait of a Tilbury Town
character invites interpretation through the man's
bearing, manner, acts. "What small satanic sort of
kink . . . in his brain" withheld him from being
what it seems he might have been?

The man Flammonde, from God knows where,
With firm address and foreign air,
With news of nations in his talk
And something royal in his walk,
With glint of iron in his eyes,   5
But never doubt, nor yet surprise,
Appeared, and stayed, and held his head
As one by kings accredited.

Erect, with his alert repose
About him, and about his clothes,   10
He pictured all tradition hears
Of what we owe to fifty years.
His cleansing heritage of taste
Paraded neither want nor waste;
And what he needed for his fee   15
To live, he borrowed graciously.

He never told us what he was,
Or what mischance, or other cause,
Had banished him from better days
To play the Prince of Castaways.   20
Meanwhile he played surpassing well
A part, for most, unplayable;
In fine, one pauses, half afraid
To say for certain that he played.

For that, one may as well forego   25
Conviction as to yes or no;
Nor can I say just how intense
Would then have been the difference
To several, who, having striven
In vain to get what he was given,   30
Would see the stranger taken on
By friends not easy to be won.

Moreover, many a malcontent
He soothed and found munificent;
His courtesy beguiled and foiled   35
Suspicion that his years were soiled;
His mien distinguished any crowd,
His credit strengthened when he bowed;
And women, young and old, were fond
Of looking at the man Flammonde.   40

There was a woman in our town
On whom the fashion was to frown;
But while our talk renewed the tinge
Of a long-faded scarlet fringe,
The man Flammonde saw none of that,   45
And what he saw we wondered at —
That none of us, in her distress,
Could hide or find our littleness.

There was a boy that all agreed
Had shut within him the rare seed   50
Of learning. We could understand,
But none of us could lift a hand.
The man Flammonde appraised the youth,
And told a few of us the truth;
And thereby, for a little gold,   55
A flowered future was unrolled.

There were two citizens who fought
For years and years, and over nought;
They made life awkward for their friends,
And shortened their own dividends.   60
The man Flammonde said what was wrong
Should be made right; nor was it long
Before they were again in line,
And had each other in to dine.

And these I mention are but four   65
Of many out of many more.
So much for them. But what of him —
So firm in every look and limb?
What small satanic sort of kink
Was in his brain? What broken link   70
Withheld him from the destinies
That came so near to being his?

What was he, when we came to sift
His meaning, and to note the drift
Of incommunicable ways   75
That make us ponder while we praise?
Why was it that his charm revealed
Somehow the surface of a shield?
What was it that we never caught?
What was he, and what was he not?   80

How much it was of him we met
We cannot ever know; nor yet
Shall all he gave us quite atone
For what was his, and his alone;
Nor need we now, since he knew best,   85
Nourish an ethical unrest:
Rarely at once will nature give
The power to be Flammonde and live.

We cannot know how much we learn
From those who never will return,   90
Until a flash of unforeseen
Remembrance falls on what has been.
We've each a darkening hill to climb;
And this is why, from time to time
In Tilbury Town, we look beyond   95
Horizons for the man Flammonde.

Cassandra

(w. 1915–16)

I heard one who said: "Verily,
　What word have I for children here?
Your Dollar is your only Word,
　The wrath of it your only fear.

"You build it altars tall enough   5
　To make you see, but you are blind;
You cannot leave it long enough
　To look before you or behind.

"When Reason beckons you to pause,
　You laugh and say that you know best;   10
But what it is you know, you keep
　As dark as ingots in a chest.

"You laugh and answer, 'We are young;
　O leave us now, and let us grow.' —
Not asking how much more of this   15
　Will Time endure or Fate bestow.

"Because a few complacent years
　Have made your peril of your pride,
Think you that you are to go on
　Forever pampered and untried?   20

"What lost eclipse of history,
　What bivouac of the marching stars,
Has given the sign for you to see
　Millenniums and last great wars?

"What unrecorded overthrow   25
　Of all the world has ever known,
Or ever been, has made itself
　So plain to you, and you alone?

"Your Dollar, Dove and Eagle make
　A Trinity that even you   30
Rate higher than you rate yourselves;
　It pays, it flatters, and it's new.

"And though your very flesh and blood
　Be what your Eagle eats and drinks,
You'll praise him for the best of birds, 35
　Not knowing what the Eagle thinks.

"The power is yours, but not the sight;
　You see not upon what you tread;
You have the ages for your guide,
　But not the wisdom to be led.   40

"Think you to tread forever down
　The merciless old verities?
And are you never to have eyes
　To see the world for what it is?

"Are you to pay for what you have   45
　With all you are?" — No other word
We caught, but with a laughing crowd
　Moved on. None heeded, and few heard.

Mr. Flood's Party

(w. 1919?)

⚜ Mr. Flood has outlived his welcome in the
world, the little world of Tilbury Town. He is reduced to drinking by himself and talking to himself, under the harvest moon. Thus he alleviates the
loneliness of an old age that finds the younger
generation unfriendly.

Pathos and humor alternate or blend, as in the
bizarre comparison of Mr. Flood with Roland, the
heroic knight of French romance who, when ambushed, raised his enchanted horn to his lips to
summon Charlemagne.

Old Eben Flood, climbing alone one night
Over the hill between the town below
And the forsaken upland hermitage
That held as much as he should ever know
On earth again of home, paused warily.   5
The road was his with not a native near;
And Eben, having leisure, said aloud,
For no man else in Tilbury Town to hear:

"Well, Mr. Flood, we have the harvest moon
Again, and we may not have many more;   10
The bird is on the wing, the poet says,
And you and I have said it here before.
Drink to the bird." He raised up to the light
The jug that he had gone so far to fill,
And answered huskily: "Well, Mr. Flood,   15
Since you propose it, I believe I will."

Alone, as if enduring to the end
A valiant armor of scarred hopes outworn,
He stood there in the middle of the road
Like Roland's ghost winding a silent horn.   20
Below him, in the town among the trees,
Where friends of other days had honored him,
A phantom salutation of the dead
Rang thinly till old Eben's eyes were dim.

Then, as a mother lays her sleeping child   25
Down tenderly, fearing it may awake,

He set the jug down slowly at his feet
With trembling care, knowing that most things
   break.
And only when assured that on firm earth
It stood, as the uncertain lives of men   30
Assuredly did not, he paced away,
And with his hand extended paused again:

"Well, Mr. Flood, we have not met like this
In a long time; and many a change has come
To both of us, I fear, since last it was   35
We had a drop together. Welcome home!"
Convivially returning with himself,
Again he raised the jug up to the light;
And with an acquiescent quaver said:
"Well, Mr. Flood, if you insist, I might.   40

"Only a very little, Mr. Flood —
For auld lang syne. No more, sir; that will do."
So, for the time, apparently it did,
And Eben evidently thought so too;
For soon amid the silver loneliness   45
Of night he lifted up his voice and sang,
Secure, with only two moons listening,
Until the whole harmonious landscape rang —

"For auld lang syne." The weary throat gave
   out,
The last word wavered; and the song being done,

He raised again the jug regretfully   51
And shook his head, and was again alone.
There was not much that was ahead of him,
And there was nothing in the town below —
Where strangers would have shut the many
   doors   55
That many friends had opened long ago.

Karma

(w. 1923)

Christmas was in the air and all was well
With him, but for a few confusing flaws
In divers of God's images. Because
A friend of his would neither buy nor sell,
Was he to answer for the axe that fell?   5
He pondered; and the reason for it was,
Partly, a slowly freezing Santa Claus
Upon the corner, with his beard and bell.

Acknowledging an improvident surprise,
He magnified a fancy that he wished   10
The friend whom he had wrecked were here
   again.
Not sure of that, he found a compromise;
And from the fulness of his heart he fished
A dime for Jesus who had died for men.

Robert Frost [1875–]

Like Robinson, Frost was an unrecognized new poet long before the New Poetry.
For twenty years he kept sending his poems to magazines and getting them back — all
but a handful that brought him about $200. In 1912, the very year, as it happened,
that *Poetry: A Magazine of Verse* signalized the revival, he decided to settle in England
in order to "write and be poor without further scandal in the family."

Though his family had been New Englanders for nine generations, Robert Lee Frost
was born in San Francisco and lived there till he was ten, when, his father having died,
his mother took her children to live with their grandfather in Lawrence, Massachusetts.
He graduated from high school there, studied for a few months at Dartmouth, married,
spent two years at Harvard. Then in a long struggle with poverty he took up school
teaching, shoemaking, journalism, and farming. He sold his farm when he went, with
wife and children, to England. There it was that he published his first two volumes of
verse, *A Boy's Will* (1913) and *North of Boston* (1914). Republished the next year in
New York, these books established him as one of the leading poets of the revival. In
this same year (1915) he returned from wartime England and began dividing his time

between farming in Vermont, writing, and serving as "tame poet" at Amherst, Michigan, Harvard, and Breadloaf. *Mountain Interval* appeared in 1916, *New Hampshire* in 1923, and other volumes kept coming, including, in his late years, two "masques." Repeatedly a Pulitzer Prize winner, he also received many honorary degrees. His popularity, having begun during the first World War, persisted through the succeeding decades. He is America's best loved poet of the twentieth century.

In one aspect, Frost's poetry is an expression of rural New England, akin to that of Whittier and Robinson, and to the prose stories of Sarah Orne Jewett and others. It has the reality known by one "versed in country things," intimate, in the way of a farmer, with the facts of nature and the traits of his neighbors north of Boston. A spoken kind of poetry, it is based on a selection of the language, idioms, intonations, rhythms — the actual speech habits — of the region. But what counts is the selection, or rather the poet selecting. No typical farmer ever spoke so happily, conveyed so simply so intricate and intriguing a personality.

For in its main aspect the poetry of Frost is personal and universal. While rooted in his region, it comes to flower and fruit in his art, the registration of his personal quality and outlook upon the human lot. Like Robinson, he faced, in its modern form, the endless conflict between skepticism and faith, and was too honest for a one-sided choice. He would doubt without denying, believe without affirming; see the worst in life without making it worse still and see the best without wishing for something better; insist upon winning his truths by discovery instead of tradition, yet freely recognize that there are "truths we keep coming back and back to." This ambivalent attitude he sustains through kindliness of spirit, through a shrewd common sense, and through sly humor, the elements in which his work as a whole is bathed.

Like Robinson, Frost accepted the long established metrical forms, but to them he gave a subtly informal turn as close to conversation as to regular verse. In harmony with the realistic spirit, he developed his poems chiefly with direct observation and reflection, relying surprisingly little on metaphor and simile. As he conceived, "A poem begins in delight and ends in wisdom. . . . It assumes direction with the first line laid down, it runs a course of lucky events, and ends in a clarification of life. . . . It has an outcome that though unforeseen was predestined from the first image of the original mood — and indeed from the very mood." "Like a piece of ice on a hot stove the poem must ride on its own melting."

Further reading: *Complete Poems*. G. R. Elliott, *The Cycle of Modern Poetry*, 1929, chapter 8. Lawrance Thompson, *Fire and Ice: The Art and Thought of Robert Frost*, 1942.

Mowing

🌠 This poem and the two following were in *A Boy's Will*. Frost said that he wrote "Mowing" about 1900, the year in which he settled on a farm near Derry, New Hampshire. In this poem he touches upon the relation of labor to "the truth," "the fact."

There was never a sound beside the wood but one,
And that was my long scythe whispering to the ground.

What was it it whispered? I knew not well myself;
Perhaps it was something about the heat of the sun,   4
Something, perhaps, about the lack of sound —
And that was why it whispered and did not speak.
It was no dream of the gift of idle hours,
Or easy gold at the hand of fay or elf:
Anything more than the truth would have seemed too weak   9
To the earnest love that laid the swale in rows,

Not without feeble-pointed spikes of flowers
(Pale orchises), and scared a bright green snake.
The fact is the sweetest dream that labor knows.
My long scythe whispered and left the hay to
make.

The Tuft of Flowers

(w. 1904)

Solitary labor need not be lonely. The whispering scythe (in the preceding poem) was some sort of company. In "The Tuft of Flowers" the farmer poet holds "brotherly speech" with an absent worker. The apartness and the togetherness of men are reconciled.

Even in his early work Frost gave a free and easy flexibility to conventional verse patterns — to the sonnet in "Mowing," to heroic couplets in "The Tuft of Flowers."

I went to turn the grass once after one
Who mowed it in the dew before the sun.

The dew was gone that made his blade so keen
Before I came to view the levelled scene.

I looked for him behind an isle of trees;   5
I listened for his whetstone on the breeze.

But he had gone his way, the grass all mown,
And I must be, as he had been, — alone,

"As all must be," I said within my heart,
"Whether they work together or apart."   10

But as I said it, swift there passed me by
On noiseless wing a bewildered butterfly,

Seeking with memories grown dim o'er night
Some resting flower of yesterday's delight.

And once I marked his flight go round and
     round,   15
As where some flower lay withering on the
     ground.

And then he flew as far as eye could see,
And then on tremulous wing came back to me.

I thought of questions that have no reply,   19
And would have turned to toss the grass to dry;

But he turned first, and led my eye to look
At a tall tuft of flowers beside a brook,

A leaping tongue of bloom the scythe had spared
Beside a reedy brook the scythe had bared.

I left my place to know them by their name,   25
Finding them butterfly weed when I came.

The mower in the dew had loved them thus,
By leaving them to flourish, not for us,

Nor yet to draw one thought of ours to him,
But from sheer morning gladness at the brim.   30

The butterfly and I had lit upon,
Nevertheless, a message from the dawn,

That made me hear the wakening birds around,
And hear his long scythe whispering to the
     ground,

And feel a spirit kindred to my own;   35
So that henceforth I worked no more alone;

But glad with him, I worked as with his aid,
And weary, sought at noon with him the shade;

And dreaming, as it were, held brotherly speech
With one whose thought I had not hoped to
     reach.   40

"Men work together," I told him from the
     heart,
"Whether they work together or apart."

Reluctance

(w. 1901)

Out through the fields and the woods
     And over the walls I have wended;
I have climbed the hills of view
     And looked at the world, and descended;
I have come by the highway home,   5
     And lo, it is ended.

The leaves are all dead on the ground,
     Save those that the oak is keeping
To ravel them one by one
     And let them go scraping and creeping   10
Out over the crusted snow,
     When others are sleeping.

And the dead leaves lie huddled and still,
     No longer blown hither and thither;
The last lone aster is gone;   15
     The flowers of the witch-hazel wither;

The heart is still aching to seek,
   But the feet question "Whither?"

Ah, when to the heart of man
   Was it ever less than a treason   20
To go with the drift of things,
   To yield with a grace to reason,
And bow and accept the end
   Of a love or a season?

The Death of the Hired Man

Written in 1905, the poem was first published
nine years later in *North of Boston*.

The center of interest, in this dialogue, can hardly
be dramatic suspense, since the title foretells the conclusion. Is it, then, dramatic irony — our awareness
of the incongruity between the words of husband
and wife and the death of Silas? Or is it character —
the character of Silas? the differing characters of
Mary and Warren? Or, behind the characters, differing attitudes toward life?

Mary sat musing on the lamp-flame at the table
Waiting for Warren. When she heard his step,
She ran on tip-toe down the darkened passage
To meet him in the doorway with the news
And put him on his guard. "Silas is back."   5
She pushed him outward with her through the
      door
And shut it after her. "Be kind," she said.
She took the market things from Warren's arms
And set them on the porch, then drew him down
To sit beside her on the wooden steps.   10

"When was I ever anything but kind to him?
But I'll not have the fellow back," he said.
"I told him so last haying, didn't I?
'If he left then,' I said, 'that ended it.'
What good is he? Who else will harbour him   15
At his age for the little he can do?
What help he is there's no depending on.
Off he goes always when I need him most.
'He thinks he ought to earn a little pay,
Enough at least to buy tobacco with,   20
So he won't have to beg and be beholden.'
'All right,' I say, 'I can't afford to pay
Any fixed wages, though I wish I could.'
'Someone else can.' 'Then someone else will
      have to.'
I shouldn't mind his bettering himself   25
If that was what it was. You can be certain,
When he begins like that, there's someone at
      him

Trying to coax him off with pocket-money, —
In haying time, when any help is scarce.
In winter he comes back to us. I'm done."   30
"Sh! not so loud: he'll hear you," Mary said.

"I want him to: he'll have to soon or late."

"He's worn out. He's asleep beside the stove.
When I came up from Rowe's I found him here,
Huddled against the barn-door fast asleep,   35
A miserable sight, and frightening, too —
You needn't smile — I didn't recognise him —
I wasn't looking for him — and he's changed.
Wait till you see."

         "Where did you say he'd been?"

"He didn't say. I dragged him to the house,
And gave him tea and tried to make him smoke.
I tried to make him talk about his travels.
Nothing would do: he just kept nodding off."

"What did he say? Did he say anything?"

"But little."

         "Anything? Mary, confess   45
He said he'd come to ditch the meadow for me."

"Warren!"

         "But did he? I just want to know."

"Of course he did. What would you have him
      say?
Surely you wouldn't grudge the poor old man
Some humble way to save his self-respect.   50
He added, if you really care to know,
He meant to clear the upper pasture, too.
That sounds like something you have heard
      before?
Warren, I wish you could have heard the way
He jumbled everything. I stopped to look   55
Two or three times — he made me feel so
      queer —
To see if he was talking in his sleep.
He ran on Harold Wilson — you remember —
The boy you had in haying four years since.   59
He's finished school, and teaching in his college.

"Silas declares you'll have to get him back.
He says they two will make a team for work:
Between them they will lay this farm as smooth!
The way he mixed that in with other things.

He thinks young Wilson a likely lad, though
daff   65
On education — you know how they fought
All through July under the blazing sun,
Silas up on the cart to build the load,
Harold along beside to pitch it on."

"Yes, I took care to keep well out of earshot." 70

"Well, those days trouble Silas like a dream.
You wouldn't think they would. How some
things linger!
Harold's young college boy's assurance piqued
him.
After so many years he still keeps finding
Good arguments he sees he might have used. 75
I sympathise. I know just how it feels
To think of the right thing to say too late.
Harold's associated in his mind with Latin.
He asked me what I thought of Harold's saying
He studied Latin like the violin   80
Because he liked it — that an argument!
He said he couldn't make the boy believe
He could find water with a hazel prong —
Which showed how much good school had ever
done him.
He wanted to go over that. But most of all 85
He thinks if he could have another chance
To teach him how to build a load of hay — "

"I know, that's Silas' one accomplishment.
He bundles every forkful in its place,
And tags and numbers it for future reference,
So he can find and easily dislodge it   91
In the unloading. Silas does that well.
He takes it out in bunches like birds' nests.
You never see him standing on the hay
He's trying to lift, straining to lift himself." 95

"He thinks if he could teach him that, he'd be
Some good perhaps to someone in the world.
He hates to see a boy the fool of books.
Poor Silas, so concerned for other folks,
And nothing to look backward to with pride,
And nothing to look forward to with hope, 101
So now and never any different."

Part of a moon was falling down the west,
Dragging the whole sky with it to the hills.
Its light poured softly in her lap. She saw 105
And spread her apron to it. She put out her
hand
Among the harp-like morning-glory strings,
Taut with the dew from garden bed to eaves,

As if she played unheard the tenderness
That wrought on him beside her in the night.
"Warren," she said, "he has come home to
die: 111
You needn't be afraid he'll leave you this time."

"Home," he mocked gently.

                "Yes, what else but home?
It all depends on what you mean by home. 115
Of course he's nothing to us, any more
Than was the hound that came a stranger to us
Out of the woods, worn out upon the trail."

"Home is the place where, when you have to
go there,
They have to take you in."   120

                "I should have called it
Something you somehow haven't to deserve."

Warren leaned out and took a step or two,
Picked up a little stick, and brought it back
And broke it in his hand and tossed it by. 125
"Silas has better claim on us you think
Than on his brother? Thirteen little miles
As the road winds would bring him to his door.
Silas has walked that far no doubt to-day.
Why didn't he go there? His brother's rich, 130
A somebody — director in the bank."

"He never told us that."

                "We know it though."

"I think his brother ought to help, of course.
I'll see to that if there is need. He ought of
right   135
To take him in, and might be willing to —
He may be better than appearances.
But have some pity on Silas. Do you think
If he'd had any pride in claiming kin
Or anything he looked for from his brother, 140
He'd keep so still about him all this time?"

"I wonder what's between them."

                "I can tell you.
Silas is what he is — we wouldn't mind him —
But just the kind that kinsfolk can't abide. 145
He never did a thing so very bad.
He don't know why he isn't quite as good
As anyone. He won't be made ashamed
To please his brother, worthless though he is."

"*I can't think Si ever hurt anyone.*" 150

"No, but he hurt my heart the way he lay
And rolled his old head on that sharp-edged
    chair-back.
He wouldn't let me put him on the lounge.
You must go in and see what you can do.
I made the bed up for him there to-night. 155
You'll be surprised at him — how much he's
    broken.
His working days are done; I'm sure of it."

"I'd not be in a hurry to say that."

"I haven't been. Go, look, see for yourself.
But, Warren, please remember how it is: 160
He's come to help you ditch the meadow.
He has a plan. You mustn't laugh at him.
He may not speak of it, and then he may.
I'll sit and see if that small sailing cloud
Will hit or miss the moon." 165

                It hit the moon.
Then there were three there, making a dim row,
The moon, the little silver cloud, and she.

Warren returned — too soon, it seemed to her,
Slipped to her side, caught up her hand and
    waited. 170

"Warren?" she questioned.

          "Dead," was all he answered.

Dust of Snow
(w. 1906)

The way a crow
Shook down on me
The dust of snow
From a hemlock tree

Has given my heart 5
A change of mood
And saved some part
Of a day I had rued.

Mending Wall

This poem, one of the best known in *North of Boston*, was written in England in 1913.

A familiar feature of farms in the stony New England landscape is the loose stone wall used as a fence.

After hunters and the frosts of winter have disordered the wall, neighbors may "walk the line" to make the boundary clear again by restoring fallen stones. Taking an instance of this custom as a theme, the poem contrasts two attitudes: that of the neighbor, who has a blind faith in fences, and the "I" of the poem, who wants them only when they serve a clear purpose and yet teasingly humors his neighbor.

The reader, too, is humored: not told what general conclusion is to be drawn, but left free to decide this for himself. Many years later Frost observed, of this poem, "I played exactly fair in it. Twice I say 'Good fences make good neighbors' and twice 'Something there is that doesn't love a wall.'" These sayings represent opposed principles that, in many forms, keep recurring in Frost's poems (beginning with "The Tuft of Flowers," with its correlative recognition that all men are essentially alone and all men are essentially one).

Something there is that doesn't love a wall,
That sends the frozen-ground-swell under it,
And spills the upper boulders in the sun;
And makes gaps even two can pass abreast.
The work of hunters is another thing: 5
I have come after them and made repair
Where they have left not one stone on a stone,
But they would have the rabbit out of hiding,
To please the yelping dogs. The gaps I mean,
No one has seen them made or heard them
    made, 10
But at spring mending-time we find them there.
I let my neighbor know beyond the hill;
And on a day we meet to walk the line
And set the wall between us once again.
We keep the wall between us as we go. 15
To each the boulders that have fallen to each.
And some are loaves and some so nearly balls
We have to use a spell to make them balance:
"Stay where you are until our backs are turned!"
We wear our fingers rough with handling them.
Oh, just another kind of outdoor game, 21
One on a side. It comes to little more:
There where it is we do not need the wall:
He is all pine and I am apple-orchard.
My apple trees will never get across 25
And eat the cones under his pines, I tell him.
He only says, "Good fences make good neigh-
    bors."
Spring is the mischief in me, and I wonder
If I could put a notion in his head:
"*Why* do they make good neighbors? Isn't it 30
Where there are cows? But here there are no
    cows.
Before I built a wall I'd ask to know
What I was walling in or walling out,

And **to whom** I was like to give offence.
Something there is that doesn't love a wall,   35
That wants it down." I could say "Elves" to
    him,
But it's not elves exactly, and I'd rather
He said it for himself. I see him there,
Bringing a stone grasped firmly by the top
In each hand, like an old-stone savage armed.
He moves in darkness as it seems to me,   41
Not of woods only and the shade of trees.
He will not go behind his father's saying,
And he likes having thought of it so well
He says again, "Good fences make good neigh-
    bors."   45

The Pasture

(w. 1912?)

I'm going out to clean the pasture spring;
I'll only stop to rake the leaves away
(And wait to watch the water clear, I may):
I sha'n't be gone long. — You come too.

I'm going out to fetch the little calf   5
That's standing by the mother. It's so young,
It totters when she licks it with her tongue.
I sha'n't be gone long. — You come too.

Home Burial

(w. 1913)

He saw her from the bottom of the stairs
Before she saw him. She was starting down,
Looking back over her shoulder at some fear.
She took a doubtful step and then undid it
To raise herself and look again. He spoke   5
Advancing toward her: "What is it you see
From up there always — for I want to know."
She turned and sank upon her skirts at that,
And her face changed from terrified to dull.
He said to gain time: "What is it you see,"   10
Mounting until she cowered under him.
"I will find out now — you must tell me, dear."
She, in her place, refused him any help
With the least stiffening of her neck and silence.
She let him look, sure that he wouldn't see,   15
Blind creature; and a while he didn't see.
But at last he murmured, "Oh," and again,
    "Oh."

"What is it — what?" she said.

                    "Just that I see."

"You don't," she challenged. "Tell me what
    it is."   20

"The wonder is I didn't see at once.
I never noticed it from here before.
I must be wonted to it — that's the reason.
The little graveyard where my people are!
So small the window frames the whole of it.
Not so much larger than a bedroom, is it?   26
There are three stones of slate and one of
    marble,
Broad-shouldered little slabs there in the sun-
    light
On the sidehill. We haven't to mind *those*.
But I understand: it is not the stones,   30
But the child's mound —"

        "Don't, don't, don't, don't," she cried.

She withdrew shrinking from beneath his arm
That rested on the banister, and slid downstairs;
And turned on him with such a daunting look,
He said twice over before he knew himself: 36
"Can't a man speak of his own child he's lost?"

"Not you! Oh, where's my hat? Oh, I don't
    need it!
I must get out of here. I must get air.
I don't know rightly whether any man can."

"Amy! Don't go to someone else this time.   41
Listen to me. I won't come down the stair."
He sat and fixed his chin between his fists.
"There's something I should like to ask you,
    dear."

"You don't know how to ask it."   45

                    "Help me, then."

Her fingers moved the latch for all reply.

"My words are nearly always an offence.
I don't know how to speak of anything
So as to please you. But I might be taught   50
I should suppose. I can't say I see how.
A man must partly give up being a man
With women-folk. We could have some ar-
    rangement
By which I'd bind myself to keep hands off
Anything special you're a-mind to name.   55
Though I don't like such things 'twixt those
    that love.
Two that don't love can't live together without
    them.

But two that do can't live together with them."
She moved the latch a little. "Don't — don't
    go
Don't carry it to someone else this time.   60
Tell me about it if it's something human.
Let me into your grief. I'm not so much
Unlike other folks as your standing there
Apart would make me out. Give me my chance.
I do think, though, you overdo it a little.   65
What was it brought you up to think it the thing
To take your mother-loss of a first child
So inconsolably — in the face of love.
You'd think his memory might be satisfied —"

"There you go sneering now!"   70

                        "I'm not, I'm not!
You make me angry. I'll come down to you.
God, what a woman. And it's come to this,
A man can't speak of his own child that's dead."

"You can't because you don't know how to
    speak.   75
If you had any feelings, you that dug
With your own hand — how could you? —
    his little grave;
I saw you from that very window there,
Making the gravel leap and leap in air,   79
Leap up, like that, like that, and land so lightly
And roll back down the mound beside the hole.
I thought, Who is that man? I didn't know you.
And I crept down the stairs and up the stairs
To look again, and still your spade kept lifting.
Then you came in. I heard your rumbling
    voice   85
Out in the kitchen, and I don't know why,
But I went near to see with my own eyes.
You could sit there with the stains on your shoes
Of the fresh earth from your own baby's grave
And talk about your everyday concerns.   90
You had stood the spade up against the wall
Outside there in the entry, for I saw it."

"I shall laugh the worst laugh I ever laughed.
I'm cursed. God, if I don't believe I'm cursed."

"I can repeat the very words you were saying.   95
'Three foggy mornings and one rainy day
Will rot the best birch fence a man can build.'
Think of it, talk like that at such a time!
What had how long it takes a birch to rot
To do with what was in the darkened parlor.   100
You *couldn't* care! The nearest friends can go
With any one to death, comes so far short

They might as well not try to go at all.
No, from the time when one is sick to death,
One is alone, and he dies more alone.   105
Friends make pretence of following to the grave,
But before one is in it, their minds are turned
And making the best of their way back to life
And living people, and things they understand.
But the world's evil. I won't have grief so   110
If I can change it. Oh, I won't, I won't!"

"There, you have said it all and you feel better.
You won't go now. You're crying. Close the
    door.
The heart's gone out of it: why keep it up.
Amy! There's something coming down the
    road!"   115

"*You* — oh, you think the talk is all. I must
    go —
Somewhere out of this house. How can I make
    you —"

"If — you — do!" She was opening the door
    wider.
"Where do you mean to go? First tell me that.
I'll follow and bring you back by force. I
    will! —"   120

The Black Cottage

(1914)

We chanced in passing by that afternoon
To catch it in a sort of special picture
Among tar-banded ancient cherry trees,
Set well back from the road in rank lodged
    grass,
The little cottage we were speaking of,   5
A front with just a door between two windows,
Fresh painted by the shower a velvet black.
We paused, the minister and I, to look.
He made as if to hold it at arm's length
Or put the leaves aside that framed it in.   10
"Pretty," he said. "Come in. No one will care."
The path was a vague parting in the grass
That led us to a weathered window-sill.
We pressed our faces to the pane. "You see,"
    he said,
"Everything's as she left it when she died.   15
Her sons won't sell the house or the things in it.
They say they mean to come and summer here
Where they were boys. They haven't come this
    year.
They live so far away — one is out West —

It will be hard for them to keep their word.   20
Anyway they won't have the place disturbed."
A buttoned hair-cloth lounge spread scrolling
    arms
Under a crayon portrait on the wall
Done sadly from an old daguerreotype.
"That was the father as he went to war.   25
She always, when she talked about war,
Sooner or later came and leaned, half knelt,
Against the lounge beside it, though I doubt
If such unlifelike lines kept power to stir
Anything in her after all the years.   30
He fell at Gettysburg or Fredericksburg,
I ought to know — it makes a difference which:
Fredericksburg wasn't Gettysburg, of course.
But what I'm getting to is how forsaken
A little cottage this has always seemed;   35
Since she went more than ever, but before —
I don't mean altogether by the lives
That had gone out of it, the father first,
Then the two sons, till she was left alone.
(Nothing could draw her after those two
    sons.   40
She valued the considerate neglect
She had at some cost taught them after years.)
I mean by the world's having passed it by —
As we almost got by this afternoon.
It always seems to me a sort of mark   45
To measure how far fifty years have brought us.
Why not sit down if you are in no haste?
These doorsteps seldom have a visitor.
The warping boards pull out their own old nails
With none to tread and put them in their place.
She had her own idea of things, the old lady.   51
And she liked talk. She had seen Garrison
And Whittier, and had her story of them.
One wasn't long in learning that she thought
Whatever else the Civil War was for   55
It wasn't just to keep the States together,
Nor just to free the slaves, though it did both.
She wouldn't have believed those ends enough
To have given outright for them all she gave.
Her giving somehow touched the principle   60
That all men are created free and equal.
And to hear her quaint phrases — so removed
From the world's view today of all those things.
That's a hard mystery of Jefferson's.
What did he mean? Of course the easy way   65
Is to decide it simply isn't true.
It may not be. I heard a fellow say so.
But never mind, the Welshman got it planted
Where it will trouble us a thousand years.
Each age will have to reconsider it.   70
You couldn't tell her what the West was saying,

And what the South to her serene belief.
She had some art of hearing and yet not
Hearing the latter wisdom of the world.
White was the only race she ever knew.   75
Black she had scarcely seen, and yellow never.
But how could they be made so very unlike
By the same hand working in the same stuff?
She had supposed the war decided that.
What are you going to do with such a person?   80
Strange how such innocence gets its own way.
I shouldn't be surprised if in this world
It were the force that would at last prevail.
Do you know but for her there was a time
When to please younger members of the
    church,   85
Or rather say non-members in the church,
Whom we all have to think of nowadays,
I would have changed the Creed a very little?
Not that she ever had to ask me not to;
It never got so far as that; but the bare thought
Of her old tremulous bonnet in the pew,   91
And of her half asleep was too much for me.
Why, I might wake her up and startle her.
It was the words "descended into Hades"
That seemed too pagan to our liberal youth.   95
You know they suffered from a general on-
    slaught.
And well, if they weren't true, why keep right
    on
Saying them like the heathen? We could drop
    them.
Only — there was the bonnet in the pew.
Such a phrase couldn't have meant much to
    her.   100
But suppose she had missed it from the Creed
As a child misses the unsaid Good-night,
And falls asleep with heartache — how should
    I feel?
I'm just as glad she made me keep hands off,
For, dear me, why abandon a belief   105
Merely because it ceases to be true.
Cling to it long enough, and not a doubt
It will turn true again, for so it goes.
Most of the change we think we see in life
Is due to truths being in and out of favor.   110
As I sit here, and oftentimes, I wish
I could be monarch of a desert land
I could devote and dedicate forever
To the truths we keep coming back and back
    to.
So desert it would have to be, so walled   115
By mountain ranges half in summer snow,
No one would covet it or think it worth
The pains of conquering to force change on.

Scattered oases where men dwelt, but mostly
Sand dunes held closely in tamarisk   120
Blown over and over themselves in idleness.
Sand grains should sugar in the natal dew
The babe born to the desert, the sand storm
Retard mid-waste my cowering caravans——

"There are bees in this wall." He struck the
    clapboards,   125
Fierce heads looked out; small bodies pivoted.
We rose to go. Sunset blazed on the windows.

Birches

(w. 1915)

When I see birches bend to left and right
Across the line of straighter darker trees,
I like to think some boy's been swinging them.
But swinging doesn't bend them down to stay.
Ice-storms do that. Often you must have seen
    them   5
Loaded with ice a sunny winter morning
After a rain. They click upon themselves
As the breeze rises, and turn many-colored
As the stir cracks and crazes their enamel.
Soon the sun's warmth makes them shed crystal
    shells   10
Shattering and avalanching on the snow-crust —
Such heaps of broken glass to sweep away
You'd think the inner dome of heaven had
    fallen.
They are dragged to the withered bracken by
    the load,
And they seem not to break; though once they
    are bowed   15
So low for long, they never right themselves:
You may see their trunks arching in the woods
Years afterwards, trailing their leaves on the
    ground
Like girls on hands and knees that throw their
    hair   19
Before them over their heads to dry in the sun.
But I was going to say when Truth broke in
With all her matter-of-fact about the ice-storm
(Now am I free to be poetical?)
I should prefer to have some boy bend them
As he went out and in to fetch the cows —   25
Some boy too far from town to learn baseball,
Whose only play was what he found himself,
Summer or winter, and could play alone.
One by one he subdued his father's trees
By riding them down over and over again   30
Until he took the stiffness out of them,

And not one but hung limp, not one was left
For him to conquer. He learned all there was
To learn about not launching out too soon
And so not carrying the tree away   35
Clear to the ground. He always kept his poise
To the top branches, climbing carefully
With the same pains you use to fill a cup
Up to the brim, and even above the brim.   39
Then he flung outward, feet first, with a swish,
Kicking his way down through the air to the
    ground.
So was I once myself a swinger of birches.
And so I dream of going back to be.
It's when I'm weary of considerations,
And life is too much like a pathless wood   45
Where your face burns and tickles with the
    cobwebs
Broken across it, and one eye is weeping
From a twig's having lashed across it open.
I'd like to get away from earth awhile
And then come back to it and begin over.   50
May no fate wilfully misunderstand me
And half grant what I wish and snatch me
    away
Not to return. Earth's the right place for love:
I don't know where it's likely to go better.
I'd like to go by climbing a birch tree,   55
And climb black branches up a snow-white
    trunk
Toward heaven, till the tree could bear no more,
But dipped its top and set me down again.
That would be good both going and coming
    back.
One could do worse than be a swinger of
    birches.   60

The Road Not Taken

(w. 1915)

Two roads diverged in a yellow wood,
And sorry I could not travel both
And be one traveler, long I stood
And looked down one as far as I could
To where it bent in the undergrowth;   5

Then took the other, as just as fair,
And having perhaps the better claim,
Because it was grassy and wanted wear;
Though as for that the passing there
Had worn them really about the same,   10

And both that morning equally lay
In leaves no step had trodden black.

Oh, I kept the first for another day!
Yet knowing how way leads on to way,
I doubted if I should ever come back.   15

I shall be telling this with a sigh
Somewhere ages and ages hence:
Two roads diverged in a wood, and I —
I took the one less traveled by,
And that has made all the difference.   20

An Old Man's Winter Night

(w. 1915)

All out-of-doors looked darkly in at him
Through the thin frost, almost in separate stars,
That gathers on the pane in empty rooms.
What kept his eyes from giving back the gaze
Was the lamp tilted near them in his hand. 5
What kept him from remembering the need
That brought him to that creaking room was
          age.
He stood with barrels round him — at a loss.
And having scared the cellar under him
In clomping there, he scared it once again   10
In clomping off: — and scared the outer night,
Which has its sounds, familiar, like the roar
Of trees and crack of branches, common things,
But nothing so like beating on a box.
A light he was to no one but himself   15
Where now he sat, concerned with he knew
          what,
A quiet light, and then not even that.
He consigned to the moon, such as she was,
So late-arising, to the broken moon
As better than the sun in any case   20
For such a charge, his snow upon the roof,
His icicles along the wall to keep;
And slept. The log that shifted with a jolt
Once in the stove, disturbed him and he shifted,
And eased his heavy breathing, but still slept. 25
One aged man — one man — can't fill a house,
A farm, a countryside, or if he can,
It's thus he does it of a winter night.

Not to Keep

(w. 1915)

They sent him back to her. The letter came
Saying . . . And she could have him. And be-
          fore
She could be sure there was no hidden ill

Under the formal writing, he was in her sight,
Living. They gave him back to her alive — 5
How else? They are not known to send the
          dead —
And not disfigured visibly. His face?
His hands? She has to look, to ask,
"What is it, dear?" And she has given all
And still she had all — they had — they the
          lucky!   10
Wasn't she glad now? Everything seemed won,
And all the rest for them permissible ease.
She had to ask, "What was it, dear?"
                                        "Enough,
Yet not enough. A bullet through and through,
High in the breast. Nothing but what good
          care   15
And medicine and rest, and you a week,
Can cure me of to go again." The same
Grim giving to do over for them both.
She dared no more than ask him with her
          eyes
How was it with him for a second trial.   20
And with his eyes he asked her not to ask.
They had given him back to her, but not to
          keep.

The Oven Bird

(1916)

There is a singer everyone has heard,
Loud, a mid-summer and a mid-wood bird,
Who makes the solid tree trunks sound again.
He says that leaves are old and that for flowers
Mid-summer is to spring as one to ten.   5
He says the early petal-fall is past
When pear and cherry bloom went down in
          showers
On sunny days a moment overcast;
And comes that other fall we name the fall.
He says the highway dust is over all.   10
The bird would cease and be as other birds
But that he knows in singing not to sing.
The question that he frames in all but words
Is what to make of a diminished thing.

"Out, Out —"

(1916)

The buzz-saw snarled and rattled in the yard
And made dust and dropped stove-length sticks
          of wood,

Sweet-scented stuff when the breeze drew across
  it.
And from there those that lifted eyes could
  count
Five mountain ranges one behind the other 5
Under the sunset far into Vermont.
And the saw snarled and rattled, snarled and
  rattled,
As it ran light, or had to bear a load.
And nothing happened: day was all but done.
Call it a day, I wish they might have said   10
To please the boy by giving him the half hour
That a boy counts so much when saved from
  work.
His sister stood beside them in her apron
To tell them "Supper." At the word, the saw,
As if to prove saws knew what supper meant, 15
Leaped out at the boy's hand, or seemed to
  leap —
He must have given the hand. However it was,
Neither refused the meeting. But the hand!
The boy's first outcry was a rueful laugh,
As he swung toward them holding up the hand
Half in appeal, but half as if to keep   21
The life from spilling. Then the boy saw all —
Since he was old enough to know, big boy
Doing a man's work, though a child at heart —
He saw all spoiled. "Don't let him cut my hand
  off —   25
The doctor, when he comes. Don't let him,
  sister!"
So. But the hand was gone already.
The doctor put him in the dark of ether.
He lay and puffed his lips out with his breath.
And then — the watcher at his pulse took
  fright.   30
No one believed. They listened at his heart.
Little — less — nothing! — and that ended it.
No more to build on there. And they, since they
Were not the one dead, turned to their affairs.

Fire and Ice

(w. 1919?)

Some say the world will end in fire,
Some say in ice.
From what I've tasted of desire
I hold with those who favor fire.
But if it had to perish twice,   5
I think I know enough of hate
To say that for destruction ice
Is also great
And would suffice.

New Hampshire

(1923)

🚩 In this poem we can foresee the reflective, conversational tendency of Frost in his late years. He
is talking freely, but cagily, about the goods and ills
of life as he has known them in his own experience.
There is more humor than before, a humor, as G. R.
Elliott suggests, not of the effervescent sort popular
in the 1920's, but quietly efficient. "It is ripe northern whisky. To imbibe his work slowly and completely, with decent intervals for meditation between
drams, is to feel his humor gradually seeping through
one's whole system."

I met a lady from the South who said
(You won't believe she said it, but she said it):
"None of my family ever worked, or had
A thing to sell." I don't suppose the work
Much matters. You may work for all of me. 5
I've seen the time I've had to work myself.
The having anything to sell is what
Is the disgrace in man or state or nation.

I met a traveller from Arkansas
Who boasted of his state as beautiful   10
For diamonds and apples. "Diamonds
And apples in commercial quantities?"
I asked him, on my guard. "Oh yes," he an-
  swered,
Off his. The time was evening in the Pullman.
"I see the porter's made your bed," I told him.

I met a Californian who would   16
Talk California — a state so blessed,
He said, in climate, none had ever died there
A natural death, and Vigilance Committees
Had had to organize to stock the graveyards 20
And vindicate the state's humanity.
"Just the way Steffanson runs on," I murmured,
"About the British Arctic. That's what comes
Of being in the market with a climate."

I met a poet from another state,   25
A zealot full of fluid inspiration,
Who in the name of fluid inspiration,
But in the best style of bad salesmanship,
Angrily tried to make me write a protest
(In verse I think) against the Volstead Act. 30
He didn't even offer me a drink
Until I asked for one to steady *him*.
This is called having an idea to sell.

It never could have happened in New Hampshire.

The only person really soiled with trade   35
I ever stumbled on in old New Hampshire
Was someone who had just come back ashamed
From selling things in California.
He'd built a noble mansard roof with balls
On turrets like Constantinople, deep   40
In woods some ten miles from a railroad station,
As if to put forever out of mind
The hope of being, as you say, received.
I found him standing at the close of day
Inside the threshold of his open barn,   45
Like a lone actor on a gloomy stage —
And recognized him through the iron grey
In which his face was muffled to the eyes
As an old boyhood friend, and once indeed
A drover with me on the road to Brighton.   50
His farm was "grounds," and not a farm at all;
His house among the local sheds and shanties
Rose like a factor's at a trading station.
And he was rich, and I was still a rascal.
I couldn't keep from asking impolitely,   55
Where had he been and what had he been do-
ing?
How did he get so? (Rich was understood.)
In dealing in "old rags" in San Francisco.
Oh it was terrible as well could be.
We both of us turned over in our graves.   60
Just specimens is all New Hampshire has,
One each of everything as in a show-case
Which naturally she doesn't care to sell.

She had one President (pronounce him Purse,
And make the most of it for better or worse.   65
He's your one chance to score against the state).
She had one Daniel Webster. He was all
The Daniel Webster ever was or shall be.
She had the Dartmouth needed to produce him.

I call her old. She has one family   70
Whose claim is good to being settled here
Before the era of colonization,
And before that of exploration even.
John Smith remarked them as he coasted by
Dangling their legs and fishing off a wharf   75
At the Isles of Shoals, and satisfied himself
They weren't Red Indians, but veritable
Pre-primitives of the white race, dawn people,
Like those who furnished Adam's sons with
wives;
However uninnocent they may have been   80
In being there so early in our history.
They'd been there then a hundred years or
more.
Pity he didn't ask what they were up to

At that date with a wharf already built,
And take their name. They've since told me
their name —   85
Today an honored one in Nottingham.
As for what they were up to more than fish-
ing —
Suppose they weren't behaving Puritanly,
The hour had not yet struck for being good,
Mankind had not yet gone on the Sabbatical.   90
It became an explorer of the deep
Not to explore too deep in others' business.

Did you but know of him, New Hampshire has
One real reformer who would change the world
So it would be accepted by two classes,   95
Artists the minute they set up as artists,
Before, that is, they are themselves accepted,
And boys the minute they get out of college.
I can't help thinking those are tests to go by.

And she has one I don't know what to call
him,   100
Who comes from Philadelphia every year
With a great flock of chickens of rare breeds
He wants to give the educational
Advantages of growing almost wild
Under the watchful eye of hawk and eagle —   105
Dorkings because they're spoken of by Chaucer,
Sussex because they're spoken of by Herrick.

She has a touch of gold. New Hampshire
gold —
You may have heard of it. I had a farm
Offered me not long since up Berlin way   110
With a mine on it that was worked for gold;
But not gold in commercial quantities.
Just enough gold to make the engagement rings
And marriage rings of those who owned the
farm.
What gold more innocent could one have asked
for?   115
One of my children ranging after rocks
Lately brought home from Andover or Canaan
A specimen of beryl with a trace
Of radium. I know with radium
The trace would have to be the merest trace   120
To be below the threshold of commercial;
But trust New Hampshire not to have enough
Of radium or anything to sell.

A specimen of everything, I said.
She has one witch — old style. She lives in
Colebrook.   125
(The only other witch I ever met

Was lately at a cut-glass dinner in Boston.
There were four candles and four people present.
The witch was young, and beautiful (new style),
And open-minded. She was free to question 130
Her gift for reading letters locked in boxes.
Why was it so much greater when the boxes
Were metal than it was when they were wooden?
It made the world seem so mysterious.
The S'ciety for Psychical Research 135
Was cognizant. Her husband was worth millions.
I think he owned some shares in Harvard College.)

New Hampshire *used* to have at Salem
A company we called the White Corpuscles,
Whose duty was at any hour of night 140
To rush in sheets and fools' caps where they smelled
A thing the least bit doubtfully perscented
And give someone the Skipper Ireson's Ride.

One each of everything as in a show-case.
More than enough land for a specimen 145
You'll say she has, but there there enters in
Something else to protect her from herself.
There quality makes up for quantity.
Not even New Hampshire farms are much for sale.
The farm I made my home on in the mountains 150
I had to take by force rather than buy.
I caught the owner outdoors by himself
Raking up after winter, and I said,
"I'm going to put you off this farm: I want it."
"Where are you going to put me? In the road?" 155
"I'm going to put you on the farm next to it."
"Why won't the farm next to it do for you?"
"I like this better." It was really better.

Apples? New Hampshire has them, but unsprayed,
With no suspicion in stem-end or blossom-end
Of vitriol or arsenate of lead, 161
And so not good for anything but cider.
Her unpruned grapes are flung like lariats
Far up the birches out of reach of man.

A state producing precious metals, stones, 165
And — writing; none of these except perhaps

The precious literature in quantity
Or quality to worry the producer
About disposing of it. Do you know,
Considering the market, there are more 170
Poems produced than any other thing?
No wonder poets sometimes have to *seem*
So much more business-like than business men.
Their wares are so much harder to get rid of. 174

She's one of the two best states in the Union.
Vermont's the other. And the two have been
Yoke-fellows in the sap-yoke from of old
In many Marches. And they lie like wedges,
Thick end to thin end and thin end to thick end,
And are a figure of the way the strong 180
Of mind and strong of arm should fit together,
One thick where one is thin and vice versa.
New Hampshire raises the Connecticut
In a trout hatchery near Canada,
But soon divides the river with Vermont. 185
Both are delightful states for their absurdly
Small towns — Lost Nation, Bungey, Muddy Boo,
Poplin, Still Corners (so called not because
The place is silent all day long, nor yet
Because it boasts a whisky still — because 190
It set out once to be a city and still
Is only corners, cross-roads in a wood).
And I remember one whose name appeared
Between the pictures on a movie screen
Election night once in Franconia, 195
When everything had gone Republican
And Democrats were sore in need of comfort:
Easton goes Democratic, Wilson 4
Hughes 2. And everybody to the saddest
Laughed the loud laugh, the big laugh at the little. 200
New York (five million) laughs at Manchester,
Manchester (sixty or seventy thousand) laughs
At Littleton (four thousand), Littleton
Laughs at Franconia (seven hundred), and
Franconia laughs, I fear, — did laugh that night — 205
At Easton. What has Easton left to laugh at,
And like the actress exclaim, "Oh my God" at?
There's Bungey; and for Bungey there are towns,
Whole townships named but without population.

Anything I can say about New Hampshire 210
Will serve almost as well about Vermont,
Excepting that they differ in their mountains.

The Vermont mountains stretch extended
straight;
New Hampshire mountains curl up in a coil.

I had been coming to New Hampshire moun-
tains.   215
And here I am and what am I to say?
Here first my theme becomes embarrassing.
Emerson said, "The God who made New
Hampshire
Taunted the lofty land with little men."
Another Massachusetts poet said,   220
"I go no more to summer in New Hampshire.
I've given up my summer place in Dublin."
But when I asked to know what ailed New
Hampshire,
She said she couldn't stand the people in it,
The little men (it's Massachusetts speaking).
And when I asked to know what ailed the
people,   226
She said, "Go read your own books and find
out."
I may as well confess myself the author
Of several books against the world in general.
To take them as against a special state   230
Or even nation's to restrict my meaning.
I'm what is called a sensibilitist,
Or otherwise an environmentalist.
I refuse to adapt myself a mite
To any change from hot to cold, from wet   235
To dry, from poor to rich, or back again.
I make a virtue of my suffering
From nearly everything that goes on round
me.
In other words, I know wherever I am,
Being the creature of literature I am,   240
I shall not lack for pain to keep me awake.
Kit Marlowe taught me how to say my prayers:
"Why, this is Hell, nor am I out of it."
Samoa, Russia, Ireland I complain of,
No less than England, France and Italy.   245
Because I wrote my novels in New Hampshire
Is no proof that I aimed them at New Hamp-
shire.

When I left Massachusetts years ago
Between two days, the reason why I sought
New Hampshire, not Connecticut,   250
Rhode Island, New York, or Vermont was this:
Where I was living then, New Hampshire
offered
The nearest boundary to escape across.
I hadn't an illusion in my hand-bag
About the people being better there   255

Than those I left behind. I thought they
weren't.
I thought they couldn't be. And yet they
were.
I'd sure had no such friends in Massachusetts
As Hall of Windham, Gay of Atkinson,
Bartlett of Raymond (now of Colorado),   260
Harris of Derry, and Lynch of Bethlehem.

The glorious bards of Massachusetts seem
To want to make New Hampshire people over.
They taunt the lofty land with little men.
I don't know what to say about the people. 265
For art's sake one could almost wish them worse
Rather than better. How are we to write
The Russian novel in America
As long as life goes so unterribly?
There is the pinch from which our only out-
cry
In literature to date is heard to come.   271
We get what little misery we can
Out of not having cause for misery.
It makes the guild of novel writers sick
To be expected to be Dostoievskis   275
On nothing worse than too much luck and
comfort.
This is not sorrow, though; it's just the vapors,
And recognized as such in Russia itself
Under the new regime, and so forbidden.
If well it is with Russia, then feel free   280
To say so or be stood against the wall
And shot. It's Pollyanna now or death.
This, then, is the new freedom we hear tell of;
And very sensible. No state can build
A literature that shall at once be sound   285
And sad on a foundation of well-being.

To show the level of intelligence
Among us: it was just a Warren farmer
Whose horse had pulled him short up in the
road
By me, a stranger. This is what he said,   290
From nothing but embarrassment and want
Of anything more sociable to say:
"You hear those hound-dogs sing on Moosi-
lauke?
Well they remind me of the hue and cry
We've heard against the Mid-Victorians   295
And never rightly understood till Bryan
Retired from politics and joined the chorus.
The matter with the Mid-Victorians
Seems to have been a man named John L.
Darwin."

"Go 'long," I said to him, he to his horse. 300

I knew a man who failing as a farmer
Burned down his farmhouse for the fire insur-
    ance,
And spent the proceeds on a telescope
To satisfy a life-long curiosity
About our place among the infinities.   305
And how was that for other-worldliness?

If I must choose which I would elevate —
The people or the already lofty mountains,
I'd elevate the already lofty mountains.   309
The only fault I find with old New Hampshire
Is that her mountains aren't quite high enough.
I was not always so; I've come to be so.
How, to my sorrow, how have I attained
A height from which to look down critical   314
On mountains? What has given me assurance
To say what height becomes New Hampshire
    mountains,
Or any mountains? Can it be some strength
I feel as of an earthquake in my back
To heave them higher to the morning star?
Can it be foreign travel in the Alps?   320
Or having seen and credited a moment
The solid moulding of vast peaks of cloud
Behind the pitiful reality
Of Lincoln, Lafayette and Liberty?
Or some such sense as says how high shall jet
The fountain in proportion to the basin?   326
No, none of these has raised me to my throne
Of intellectual dissatisfaction,
But the sad accident of having seen
Our actual mountains given in a map   330
Of early times as twice the height they are —
Ten thousand feet instead of only five —
Which shows how sad an accident may be.
Five thousand is no longer high enough.
Whereas I never had a good idea   335
About improving people in the world,
Here I am over-fertile in suggestion,
And cannot rest from planning day or night
How high I'd thrust the peaks in summer snow
To tap the upper sky and draw a flow   340
Of frosty night air on the vale below
Down from the stars to freeze the dew as starry.

The more the sensibilitist I am
The more I seem to want my mountains wild;
The way the wiry gang-boss liked the log-
    jam.   345
After he'd picked the lock and got it started,
He dodged a log that lifted like an arm
Against the sky to break his back for him,
Then came in dancing, skipping, with his life

Across the roar and chaos, and the words   350
We saw him say along the zigzag journey
Were doubtless as the words we heard him say
On coming nearer: "Wasn't she an *i*-deal
Son-of-a-bitch? You bet she was an *i*-deal."

For all her mountains fall a little short,   355
Her people not quite short enough for Art,
She's still New Hampshire, a most restful state.

Lately in converse with a New York alec
About the new school of the pseudo-phallic,
I found myself in a close corner where   360
I had to make an almost funny choice.
"Choose you which you will be — a prude, or
    puke,
Mewling and puking in the public arms."
"Me for the hills where I don't have to choose."
"But if you had to choose, which would you
    be?"   365
I wouldn't be a prude afraid of nature.
I know a man who took a double axe
And went alone against a grove of trees;
But his heart failing him, he dropped the axe
And ran for shelter quoting Matthew Arnold:
"Nature is cruel, man is sick of blood;   371
There's been enough shed without shedding
    mine.
Remember Birnam Wood! The wood's in flux!"
He had a special terror of the flux
That showed itself in dendrophobia.   375
The only decent tree had been to mill
And educated into boards, he said.
He knew too well for any earthly use
The line where man leaves off and nature starts,
And never over-stepped it save in dreams.   380
He stood on the safe side of the line talking;
Which is sheer Matthew Arnoldism,
The cult of one who owned himself "a foiled,
Circuitous wanderer," and "took dejectedly
His seat upon the intellectual throne."   385
Agreed in frowning on these improvised
Altars the woods are full of nowadays,
Again as in the days when Ahaz sinned
By worship under green trees in the open.
Scarcely a mile but that I come on one,   390
A black-cheeked stone and stick of rain-washed
    charcoal.
Even to say the groves were God's first temples
Comes too near to Ahaz' sin for safety.
Nothing not built with hands of course is sacred.
But here is not a question of what's sacred;   395
Rather of what to face or run away from.
I'd hate to be a runaway from nature.

And neither would I choose to be a puke
Who cares not what he does in company,
And, when he can't do anything, falls back   400
On words, and tries his worst to make words
      speak
Louder than actions, and sometimes achieves it.
It seems a narrow choice the age insists on.
How about being a good Greek, for instance?
That course, they tell me, isn't offered this year.
"Come, but this isn't choosing — puke or
      prude?"   406
Well, if I have to choose one or the other,
I choose to be a plain New Hampshire farmer
With an income in cash of say a thousand
(From say a publisher in New York City).   410
It's restful to arrive at a decision,
And restful just to think about New Hampshire.
At present I am living in Vermont.

Stopping by Woods on a Snowy Evening
(w. 1923)

🜲 Practical people, like the practical little horse,
might think it queer to stop at the woods on a dark,
snowy evening. The reason given in line 4, along
with everything else in the first three stanzas, is kept
close to matter-of-fact. Then, in a final stanza, as
simple in language as the rest, the poem becomes
richly imaginative and symbolic. It perhaps involves,
if one cares to specify, nature, beauty, duty, action,
time, death. Frost himself said that the poem contains "all I ever knew."
    Lines 9 and 10 should be read rapidly, jinglingly;
the last line of the poem, slowly, broodingly.

Whose woods these are I think I know.
His house is in the village though;
He will not see me stopping here
To watch his woods fill up with snow.

My little horse must think it queer   5
To stop without a farmhouse near
Between the woods and frozen lake
The darkest evening of the year.

He gives his harness bells a shake
To ask if there is some mistake.   10
The only other sound's the sweep
Of easy wind and downy flake.

The woods are lovely, dark and deep.
But I have promises to keep,
And miles to go before I sleep,   15
And miles to go before I sleep.

Once by the Pacific
(1926)

The shattered water made a misty din.
Great waves looked over others coming in,
And thought of doing something to the shore
That water never did to land before.
The clouds were low and hairy in the skies,   5
Like locks blown forward in the gleam of eyes.
You could not tell, and yet it looked as if
The shore was lucky in being backed by cliff,
The cliff in being backed by continent;
It looked as if a night of dark intent   10
Was coming, and not only a night, an age.
Someone had better be prepared for rage.
There would be more than ocean-water broken
Before God's last *Put out the Light* was spoken.

Tree at My Window
(w. 1928)

Tree at my window, window tree,
My sash is lowered when night comes on;
But let there never be curtain drawn
Between you and me.

Vague dream-head lifted out of the ground,   5
And thing next most diffuse to cloud,
Not all your light tongues talking aloud
Could be profound.

But tree, I have seen you taken and tossed,
And if you have seen me when I slept,   10
You have seen me when I was taken and swept
And all but lost.

That day she put our heads together,
Fate had her imagination about her,
Your head so much concerned with outer,   15
Mine with inner, weather.

Desert Places
(1934)

Snow falling and night falling fast, oh, fast
In a field I looked into going past,
And the ground almost covered smooth in snow,
But a few weeds and stubble showing last.

The woods around it have it — it is theirs.   5
All animals are smothered in their lairs.
I am too absent-spirited to count;
The loneliness includes me unawares.

And lonely as it is that loneliness
Will be more lonely ere it will be less —   10
A blanker whiteness of benighted snow
With no expression, nothing to express.

They cannot scare me with their empty spaces
Between stars — on stars where no human race
    is.
I have it in me so much nearer home   15
To scare myself with my own desert places.

Two Tramps in Mud Time

Or, A Full-Time Interest

(w. 1934)

Out of the mud two strangers came
And caught me splitting wood in the yard.
And one of them put me off my aim
By hailing cheerily "Hit them hard!"
I knew pretty well why he dropped behind   5
And let the other go on a way.
I knew pretty well what he had in mind:
He wanted to take my job for pay.

Good blocks of beech it was I split,
As large around as the chopping block;   10
And every piece I squarely hit
Fell splinterless as a cloven rock.
The blows that a life of self-control
Spares to strike for the common good
That day, giving a loose to my soul,   15
I spent on the unimportant wood.

The sun was warm but the wind was chill.
You know how it is with an April day
When the sun is out and the wind is still,
You're one month on in the middle of May.
But if you so much as dare to speak,   21
A cloud comes over the sunlit arch,
A wind comes off a frozen peak,
And you're two months back in the middle of
    March.

A bluebird comes tenderly up to alight   25
And fronts the wind to unruffle a plume,
His song so pitched as not to excite
A single flower as yet to bloom.
It is snowing a flake: and he half knew
Winter was only playing possum.   30
Except in color he isn't blue,
But he wouldn't advise a thing to blossom.

The water for which we may have to look
In summertime with a witching-wand,
In every wheelrut's now a brook,   35
In every print of a hoof a pond.
Be glad of water, but don't forget
The lurking frost in the earth beneath
That will steal forth after the sun is set
And show on the water its crystal teeth.   40

The time when most I loved my task
These two must make me love it more
By coming with what they came to ask.
You'd think I never had felt before
The weight of an axe-head poised aloft,   45
The grip on earth of outspread feet,
The life of muscles rocking soft
And smooth and moist in vernal heat.

Out of the woods two hulking tramps
(From sleeping God knows where last night,
But not long since in the lumber camps).   51
They thought all chopping was theirs of right.
Men of the woods and lumberjacks,
They judged me by their appropriate tool.
Except as a fellow handled an axe,   55
They had no way of knowing a fool.

Nothing on either side was said.
They knew they had but to stay their stay
And all their logic would fill my head:
As that I had no right to play   60
With what was another man's work for gain.
My right might be love but theirs was need.
And where the two exist in twain
Theirs was the better right — agreed.

But yield who will to their separation,   65
My object in living is to unite
My avocation and my vocation
As my two eyes make one in sight.
Only where love and need are one,
And the work is play for mortal stakes,   70
Is the deed ever really done
For Heaven and the future's sakes.

Departmental

Or, My Ant Jerry

(1936)

An ant on the table-cloth
Ran into a dormant moth

Of many times his size.
He showed not the least surprise.
His business wasn't with such. 5
He gave it scarcely a touch,
And was off on his duty run.
Yet if he encountered one
Of the hive's enquiry squad
Whose work is to find out God 10
And the nature of time and space,
He would put him onto the case.
Ants are a curious race;
One crossing with hurried tread
The body of one of their dead 15
Isn't given a moment's arrest —
Seems not even impressed.
But he no doubt reports to any
With whom he crosses antennae,
And they no doubt report 20
To the higher up at court.
Then word goes forth in Formic:
"Death's come to Jerry McCormic,
Our selfless forager Jerry.
Will the special Janizary 25
Whose office it is to bury
The dead of the commissary
Go bring him home to his people.
Lay him in state on a sepal.
Wrap him for shroud in a petal. 30
Embalm him with ichor of nettle.
This is the word of your Queen."
And presently on the scene
Appears a solemn mortician;
And taking formal position 35
With feelers calmly atwiddle,
Seizes the dead by the middle,
And heaving him high in air,
Carries him out of there.
No one stands round to stare. 40
It is nobody else's affair.

It couldn't be called ungentle.
But how thoroughly departmental.

A Considerable Speck

(1942)

A speck that would have been beneath my sight
On any but a paper sheet so white
Set off across what I had written there,
And I had idly poised my pen in air
To stop it with a period of ink, 5
When something strange about it made me
    think
This was no dust speck by my breathing blown,
But unmistakably a living mite
With inclinations it could call its own.
It paused as with suspicion of my pen, 10
And then came racing wildly on again
To where my manuscript was not yet dry,
Then paused again and either drank or smelt —
With horror, for again it turned to fly.
Plainly with an intelligence I dealt. 15
It seemed too tiny to have room for feet,
Yet must have had a set of them complete
To express how much it didn't want to die.
It ran with terror and with cunning crept.
It faltered! I could see it hesitate — 20
Then in the middle of the open sheet
Cower down in desperation to accept
Whatever I accorded it of fate.
I have none of the tenderer-than-thou
Political collectivistic love 25
With which the modern world is being swept —
But this poor microscopic item now!
Since it was nothing I knew evil of
I let it lie there till I hope it slept.
I have a mind myself, and recognize 30
Mind where I meet with it in any guise.
No one can know how glad I am to find
On any sheet the least display of mind.

The Gift Outright

Read in 1941 before the Alpha Chapter of the
Phi Beta Kappa Society at the College of William
and Mary.

The land was ours before we were the land's.
She was our land more than a hundred years
Before we were her people. She was ours
In Massachusetts, in Virginia,
But we were England's, still colonials, 5
Possessing what we still were unpossessed by,
Possessed by what we now no more possessed.
Something we were withholding made us weak
Until we found out that it was ourselves
We were withholding from our land of living,
And forthwith found salvation in surrender. 11
Such as we were we gave ourselves outright
(The deed of gift was many deeds of war)
To the land vaguely realizing westward,
But still unstoried, artless, unenhanced, 15
Such as she was, such as she would become.

Come In

(1942)

As I came to the edge of the woods,
Thrush music — hark!
Now if it was dusk outside,
Inside it was dark.

Too dark in the woods for a bird
By sleight of wing
To better its perch for the night,
Though it still could sing.

The last of the light of the sun
That had died in the west   10

Still lived for one song more
In a thrush's breast.

Far in the pillared dark
Thrush music went —
Almost like a call to come in   15
To the dark and lament.

But no, I was out for stars:
I would not come in.
I meant not even if asked;
And I hadn't been.   20

Carl Sandburg [1878–   ]

Of the many poets who sounded their "barbaric yawp over the roofs of the world" (the phrase is Whitman's), none secured a larger audience of admirers and detractors than Carl Sandburg, "laureate of industrial America." Born in Galesburg, Illinois, son of an uneducated Swedish immigrant, he was trained chiefly in the school of experience. Beginning at the age of thirteen, he was driver of a milk wagon, porter in a barber shop, scene-shifter in a theater, truck-handler in a brick-yard, turner apprentice in a pottery, dish-washer in hotels, harvest hand in Kansas, soldier in Puerto Rico, "self-help" student at Lombard College, advertising manager for a department store, "Safety First" expert for a business magazine, district organizer for the Social-Democratic Party of Wisconsin, secretary to Mayor Seidel of Milwaukee, etc. Poetic expression of this experience came late. In a pamphlet of twenty-two poems privately printed in 1904, Sandburg was feeling his way, and it was not until 1914, when he was thirty-six, that he found the way — in "Chicago" and other poems printed in the new magazine Poetry. Two years later his Chicago Poems provoked widespread discussion, and Sandburg had "arrived."

In these, as in much of his later work, there are "two Sandburgs," says Louis Untermeyer: "the muscular, heavy-fisted, hard-hitting son of the streets, and his almost unrecognizable twin, the shadow-painter, the haunter of mists, the lover of implications and overtones." The latter Sandburg — cf. "Fog" — is a relative of the Imagists; the first Sandburg — who wrote "Chicago" — is the more typically Whitmanesque, and the one that has elicited more warm praise and dispraise.

He followed his initial success of 1916 with Cornhuskers (1918), Smoke and Steel (1920), Slabs of the Sunburnt West (1922), Good Morning, America (1928), The People, Yes (1936). He wrote both tales and lyrics for children, and edited a collection of ballads, The American Songbag (1927). A major achievement was his six-volume life of Lincoln: *Abraham Lincoln, The Prairie Years*, 1926, *Abraham Lincoln, The War Years*, 1939.

Further reading: *Chicago Poems; The People, Yes*. Karl Detzer, *Carl Sandburg: A Study in Personality and Background*, 1941.

Nocturne in a Deserted Brickyard
(1916)

Stuff of the moon
Runs on the lapping sand
Out to the longest shadows.
Under the curving willows,
And round the creep of the wave line,
Fluxions of yellow and dusk on the waters
Make a wide dreaming pansy on an old pond in the night.

Fog
(1916)

The fog comes
on little cat feet.
It sits looking
over harbor and city
on silent haunches
and then moves on.

Chicago
(1914, 1916)

Hog Butcher for the World,
Tool Maker, Stacker of Wheat,
Player with Railroads and the Nations' Freight Handler;
Stormy, husky, brawling,
City of the Big Shoulders: 5

They tell me you are wicked and I believe them, for I have seen your painted women
    under the gas lamps luring the farm boys.
And they tell me you are crooked and I answer: Yes, it is true I have seen the gunman
    kill and go free to kill again.
And they tell me you are brutal and my reply is: On the faces of women and children
    I have seen the marks of wanton hunger.
And having answered so I turn once more to those who sneer at this my city, and I give
    them back the sneer and say to them:
Come and show me another city with lifted head singing so proud to be alive and coarse
    and strong and cunning.   10
Flinging magnetic curses amid the toil of piling job on job, here is a tall bold slugger
    set vivid against the little soft cities;

Fierce as a dog with tongue lapping for action, cunning as a savage pitted against the
    wilderness,
        Bareheaded,
        Shoveling,
        Wrecking,   15
        Planning,
        Building, breaking, rebuilding,
Under the smoke, dust all over his mouth, laughing with white teeth,
Under the terrible burden of destiny laughing as a young man laughs,
Laughing even as an ignorant fighter laughs who has never lost a battle,   20
Bragging and laughing that under his wrist is the pulse, and under his ribs the heart of
    the people,
        Laughing!
Laughing the stormy, husky, brawling laughter of Youth, half-naked, sweating, proud
        to be Hog Butcher, Tool Maker, Stacker of Wheat, Player with Railroads
        and Freight Handler to the Nation.

I Am the People, the Mob

(1916)

I am the people — the mob — the crowd — the mass.
Do you know that all the great work of the world is done through me?
I am the workingman, the inventor, the maker of the world's food and clothes.
I am the audience that witnesses history. The Napoleons come from me and the
    Lincolns. They die. And then I send forth more Napoleons and Lincolns.   5
I am the seed ground. I am a prairie that will stand for much plowing. Terrible storms
    pass over me. I forget. The best of me is sucked out and wasted. I forget.
    Everything but Death comes to me and makes me work and give up what I have.
    And I forget.
Sometimes I growl, shake myself and spatter a few red drops for history to remember.
    Then — I forget.   11
When I, the People, learn to remember, when I, the People, use the lessons of yester-
    day and no longer forget who robbed me last year, who played me for a fool, —
    then there will be no speaker in all the world say the name: "The People," with
    any fleck of a sneer in his voice or any far-off smile of derision.   15
The mob — the crowd — the mass — will arrive then.

Cool Tombs

(w. 1916)

When Abraham Lincoln was shoveled into the tombs, he forgot the copperheads and
    the assassin . . . in the dust, in the cool tombs.

And Ulysses Grant lost all thought of con men and Wall Street, cash and collateral
    turned ashes . . . in the dust, in the cool tombs.

Pocahontas' body, lovely as a poplar, sweet as a red haw in November or a pawpaw in
    May, did she wonder? does she remember? . . . in the dust, in the cool tombs?

Take any streetful of people buying clothes and groceries, cheering a hero or throwing
    confetti and blowing tin horns . . . tell me if the lovers are losers . . . tell me if
    any get more than the lovers . . . in the dust . . . in the cool tombs.

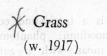

Grass

(w. *1917*)

Pile the bodies high at Austerlitz and Waterloo.
Shovel them under and let me work —
                I am the grass; I cover all.

And pile them high at Gettysburg
And pile them high at Ypres and Verdun.   5
Shovel them under and let me work.
Two years, ten years, and passengers ask the
        conductor:
                What place is this?
                Where are we now?

                I am the grass.   10
                Let me work.

From *The People, Yes*

(*1936*)

The Man in the Street is Fed

The man in the street is fed
    with lies in peace, gas in war,
    and he may live now
    just around the corner from you
    trying to sell   5
    the only thing he has to sell,
    the power of his hand and brain
    to labor for wages, for pay,
    for cash of the realm.
And there are no takers, he can't connect.   10
Maybe he says, "Some pretty good men are on
        the street."
Maybe he says, "I'm just a palooka . . . all
        washed up."
Maybe he's a wild kid ready for his first stickup.
Maybe he's bummed a thousand miles and has
        a diploma.
Maybe he can take whatever the police can
        hand him,   15
Too many of him saying in their own wild way,
"The worst they can give you is lead in the
        guts."
Whatever the wild kids want to do they'll do
And whoever gives them ideas, faiths, slogans,
Whoever touches the bottom flares of them,   20
Connects with something prouder than all
        deaths
For they can live on hard corn and like it.
They are the original sons of the wild jackass
Crowned and clothed with what the Unknown
        Soldier had   24

If he went to his fate in a pride over all deaths.
Give them a cause and they are a living dyna-
        mite.
They are the game fighters who will die fighting.

Here and there a man in the street
is young, hard as nails,
cold with questions he asks   30
from his burning insides.
        Bred in a motorized world of trial and error
        He measures by millionths of an inch,
        Knows ball bearings from spiral gearings,   34
        Chain transmission, heat treatment of steel,
        Speeds and feeds of automatic screw ma-
            chines,
        Having handled electric tools
        With pistol grip and trigger switch.
Yet he can't connect and he can name thousands
Like himself idle amid plants also idle.   40
He studies the matter of what is justice
And revises himself on money, comfort, good
        name.
He doesn't know what he wants
And says when he gets it he'll know it.
        He asks, "Why is this what it is?"   45
        He asks, "Who is paying for this propa-
            ganda?"
        He asks, "Who owns the earth and why?"
Here and there a wife or sweetheart sees with
        him
The pity of being sold down the river in a smoke
Of confusions taken from the mouths of the
        dead   50
And spoken as though those dead are alive now
And would say now what they said then.

"Let him go as far as he likes," says one lawyer
        who sits on several heavy directorates.
"What do we care? Is he any of our business?
        If he knew how he could manage.   55
"There are exceptional cases but where there is
        poverty you will generally find they were
        improvident and lacking in thrift and
        industry.
"The system of free competition we now have
        has made America the greatest and rich-
        est country on the face of the globe.   61
"You will seek in vain for any land where so
        large a number of people have had so
        many of the good things of life.
"The malcontents who stir up class feeling and
        engender class hatred are the foremost
        enemies of our republic and its constitu-
        tional government."   66

And so on and so on in further confusions taken
    from the mouths of the dead and spoken
    as though those dead are alive now and
    would say now what they said then.   **70**

Like the form of a seen and unheard
    prowler,
Like a slow and cruel violence,
is the known unspoken menace:
Do what we tell you or go hungry;
listen to us or you don't eat.   **75**

He walks and walks and walks
and wonders why the hell he built the road.

Once I built a railroad
. . . now . . .
brother, can you spare a dime?   **80**

To his dry well a man carried
all the water he could carry,
primed the pump, drew out the water,
and now
he has all the water he can carry.   **85**

We asked the cyclone
to go around our barn
but it didn't hear us.

The People Will Live On

      The people will live on.
The learning and blundering people will live on.
They will be tricked and sold and again sold
And go back to the nourishing earth for root-
    holds,
The people so peculiar in renewal and come-
    back,   **5**
You can't laugh off their capacity to take it.
The mammoth rests between his cyclonic
    dramas.

The people so often sleepy, weary, enigmatic,
is a vast huddle with many units saying:
    "I earn my living.   **10**
    I make enough to get by
    and it takes all my time.
    If I had more time
    I could do more for myself
    and maybe for others.   **15**
    I could read and study
    and talk things over
    and find out about things.
    It takes time.
    I wish I had the time."   **20**

The people is a tragic and comic two-face:
hero and hoodlum: phantom and gorilla
twisting to moan with a gargoyle mouth:
"They buy me and sell me . . . it's a
game . . . sometime I'll break loose . . ."
    Once having marched
Over the margins of animal necessity,
Over the grim line of sheer subsistence,
    Then man came
To the deeper rituals of his bones,   **30**
To the lights lighter than any bones,
To the time for thinking things over,
To the dance, the song, the story,
Or the hours given over to dreaming,
    Once having so marched.   **35**

Between the finite limitations of the five
senses and the endless yearnings of man for
the beyond the people hold to the humdrum bidding of work and food while reaching out when it comes their way for lights
beyond the prison of the five senses, for keepsakes lasting beyond any hunger or death.
    This reaching is alive.
The panderers and liars have violated and
smutted it.
    Yet this reaching is alive yet   **45**
for lights and keepsakes.

The people know the salt of the sea
and the strength of the winds
lashing the corners of the earth.
The people take the earth   **50**
as a tomb of rest and a cradle of hope.
Who else speaks for the Family of Man?
They are in tune and step
with constellations of universal law.
The people is a polychrome,   **55**
a spectrum and a prism
held in a moving monolith,
a console organ of changing themes,
a clavilux of color poems
wherein the sea offers fog   **60**
and the fog moves off in rain
and the labrador sunset shortens
to a nocturne of clear stars
serene over the shot spray
of northern lights   **65**
The steel mill sky is alive.
The fire breaks white and zigzag
shot on a gun-metal gloaming.
Man is a long time coming.
Man will yet win.   **70**
Brother may yet line up with brother:

This old anvil laughs at many broken ham-
   mers.
There are men who can't be bought.
The fireborn are at home in fire.
The stars make no noise.   75
You can't hinder the wind from blowing.
Time is a great teacher.
Who can live without hope?

In the darkness with a great bundle of grief
   the people march.
In the night, and overhead a shovel of stars
   for keeps, the people march: 80
           "Where to? what next?"

Ezra Pound [1885–   ]

Carl Sandburg was one of many who came to feel that Pound was "the greatest single influence in American poetry." This is not to say the greatest poet.

Certainly he proved to be the most irreconcilable of all the expatriates. Born in Idaho, he was brought up in the East, studied romance languages at the University of Pennsylvania and Hamilton College, went abroad to get material for his thesis. In 1907 he was teaching at Wabash College in Indiana, but after a few months was dismissed. He left the United States, to return only once in thirty-one years and then only for a brief visit. For more than a decade he lived in London. Rebelling against England as he had rebelled against America, he felt drawn to Latin civilization. For four years he lived in Paris, and in 1924 he established himself in Italy. There, in the 1930's he became interested in economic theory, and, while writers in America were turning toward Communism, he espoused Fascism and exalted Mussolini. In 1941 he began broadcasting over Radio Roma's "American Hour," in 1945 he was arrested, flown to the United States, but instead of being tried for treason was placed in a federal hospital for the insane. In 1958 the charges against him were dropped, and he was released to return to Italy where he now lives.

Eager literary activities accompanied his life at each stage. The years beginning in 1908 were full of learning and experiment, of volumes of original verse and translations. In London he was foregathering with a group led by T. E. Hulme, who, reacting against the enfeebled romantic tradition of poetry, felt the need of a severe discipline in "accurate, precise, and definite description" and a mode of poetic speech reflecting the complicated modern mind. Pound proceeded to make himself champion of the school of "Imagists" (he is said to have invented the name), and from this time on was active in ever-changing poetic speculation, experiment, and propaganda.

He edited a volume, *Des Imagistes*, 1914, of the writing of this school of poets, and the same year became editor of *Blast*, a magazine of the still newer school of "Vorticists." From 1912 to 1919 he served as foreign correspondent of *Poetry: A Magazine of Verse*. To it he sent some of his own work and verse by other American poets not yet recognized, such as Frost, "H. D.," Eliot, as well as non-American writers who had a great reputation ahead, such as Lawrence, Tagore, Yeats, Joyce. His own later volumes include *Cathay* (1915), *Lustra* (1916), *A Draft of XXX Cantos* (1933), *Pisan Cantos* (1948). The last volume precipitated a national controversy when it was awarded the Bollingen prize for poetry in 1949. In 1955 appeared *Rock-Drill*, another section of the Cantos. Pound continues to issue new parts of that epical undertaking. A selection of his prose is *The Literary Essays of Ezra Pound* (1954).

Pound's brilliant virtuosity deeply impressed T. S. Eliot, Archibald MacLeish, Hart Crane, and many other poets and students of poetry. Quite as remarkable as his poetry were his practical services in the discovery of fresh talent, in winning recognition for it, and the impregnating effect of his successive theories of verse during the years of the poetic revival. Typically, he called for a mode of expression "austere, direct, free from emotional slither." Pound's own poetry, like Eliot's, reflects his wide reading in the verse of many countries, including Latin, Anglo-Saxon, Provençal, Chinese, Japanese, and French symbolism. It is often obscure to any but the specialist. His shorter poems are largely experiments in translating the rhythms of older civilizations into English. A prevailing theme of his longer works, especially the *Cantos*, is the degeneracy and materialism of modern culture.

Further reading: *Selected Poems*, ed. by T. S. Eliot, 1928. *The Cantos of Ezra Pound*, 1948. R. P. Blackmur, "Masks of Ezra Pound," *Hound and Horn*, March, 1934. H. Kenner, *The Poetry of Ezra Pound*, 1951. J. J. Espey, *Ezra Pound's Mauberley*, 1955.

A Virginal

(1909)

🦋 An early poem in the traditional sonnet form, containing, in the last lines the imaginative tone-color of Provence. The woman-tree image is a favorite of Pound.

No, no! Go from me. I have left her lately.
I will not spoil my sheath with lesser brightness,
For my surrounding air has a new lightness;
Slight are her arms, yet they have bound me
    straitly
And left me cloaked as with a gauze of ether;   5
As with sweet leaves; as with a subtle clearness.
Oh, I have picked up magic in her nearness
To sheathe me half in half the things that
    sheathe her.

No, no! Go from me. I have still the flavor,
Soft as spring wind that's come from birchen
    bowers.   10
Green come the shoots, aye April in the
    branches,
As winter's wound with her sleight hand she
    staunches,
Hath of the trees a likeness of the savor:
As white their bark, so white this lady's hours.

Sestina: Altaforte

(1909)

🦋 This poem is a re-creation into English of a number of passages of the joys of war in the *sirventes* of the twelfth-century troubadour of Provence, Bertrans

de Born. In a Browningesque monologue, Pound reveals the quality of this knight and warrior, one of the damned souls to whom Dante spoke in the *Inferno*. Note the complicated rime scheme of the sestina form.

Loquitur: *En* Bertrans de Born.
  Dante Alighieri put this man in hell for that
    he was a stirrer up of strife.
  Eccovi!
  Judge ye!
  Have I dug him up again?
The scene is at his castle, Altaforte. "Papiols"
  is his jongleur.
"The Leopard," the *device* of Richard Coeur
  de Lion.

1

Damn it all! all this our South stinks peace.
You whoreson dog, Papiols, come! Let's to
    music!
I have no life save when the swords clash.
But ah! when I see the standards gold, vair,[1]
    purple, opposing
And the broad fields beneath them turn crimson,
Then howls my heart nigh mad with rejoicing.   6

2

In hot summer have I great rejoicing
When the tempests kill the earth's foul peace,
And the lightnings from black heav'n flash
    crimson,
And the fierce thunders roar me their music   10
And the winds shriek through the clouds mad,
    opposing,
And through all the riven skies God's swords
    clash.

1 heraldic term for blue and silver.

3

Hell grant soon we hear again the swords clash!
And the shrill neighs of destriers [2] in battle re-
    joicing,
Spiked breast to spiked breast opposing!   15
Better one hour's stour [3] than a year's peace
With fat boards, bawds, wine and frail music!
Bah! there's no wine like the blood's crimson!

4

And I love to see the sun rise blood-crimson.
And I watch his spears through the dark clash 20
And it fills all my heart with rejoicing
And pries wide my mouth with fast music
When I see him so scorn and defy peace,
His lone might 'gainst all darkness opposing.

5

The man who fears war and squats opposing 25
My words for stour, hath no blood of crimson
But is fit only to rot in womanish peace
Far from where worth's won and the swords
    clash
For the death of such sluts I go rejoicing;
Yea, I fill all the air with my music.   30

6

Papiols, Papiols, to the music!
There's no sound like to swords swords opposing,
No cry like the battle's rejoicing
When our elbows and swords drip the crimson
And our charges 'gainst "The Leopard's" rush
    clash.   35
May God damn for ever all who cry "Peace!"

7

And let the music of the swords make them
    crimson!
Hell grant soon we hear again the swords clash!
Hell blot black for alway the thought "Peace"!

The Return

(1912)

Inspired by a French poem, *"J'ai feint que des deux m'aient parlé,"* from Henri de Régnier's *Médailles d'Argile*, it indicates the influence of French symbolism upon Pound. He has compressed 51 lines into a brief poem, using only hints from the original, and has caught the classical tone and strophe form to perfection. A moment of weary exhaustion, following the excitements of the hunt, or a vision of rare beauty, is captured on canvas in these few lines.

2 war horses
3 combat

See, they return; ah, see the tentative
Movements, and the slow feet,
The trouble in the pace and the uncertain
Wavering!

See, they return, one, and by one,   5
With fear, as half-awakened;
As if the snow should hesitate
And murmur in the wind,
    and half turn back;
These were the "Wing'd-with-Awe,"
    Inviolable.   10

Gods of the wingèd shoe!
With them the silver hounds,
    sniffing the trace of air!

Haie! Haie!
    These were the swift to harry;
These the keen-scented;   15
These were the souls of blood.

Slow on the leash,
    pallid the leash-men!

The River Merchant's Wife

A Letter

(1915)

When Pound received the manuscripts of Ernest Fenollosa containing many literal translations from the Chinese, he reworked them to catch both the visual and rhythmical qualities of the Chinese poems. This was from Li Po, a Chinese poet of the T'ang dynasty (*Rihaku* is the Japanese form of the name), and it illustrates Pound's theory of "the exact word" to render a visual image.

While my hair was still cut straight across my
    forehead
I played about the front gate, pulling flowers.
You came by on bamboo stilts, playing horse,
You walked about my seat, playing with blue
    plums.   4
And we went on living in the village of Chokan:
Two small people, without dislike or suspicion.

At fourteen I married My Lord you.
I never laughed, being bashful.
Lowering my head, I looked at the wall.   9
Called to, a thousand times, I never looked back.[1]

1 A reference to the teasing of the bride in a Chinese wedding ceremony. Her eyes lowered, she makes no reply to bawdy remarks made to her.

At fifteen I stopped scowling,
I desired my dust to be mingled with yours
For ever and for ever and for ever.
Why should I climb the lookout?

At sixteen you departed,   15
You went into far Ku-to-yen, by the river of
          swirling eddies,
And you have been gone five months.
The monkeys make sorrowful noise overhead.
You dragged your feet when you went out.
By the gate now, the moss is grown, the differ-
          ent mosses,   20
Too deep to clear them away!

The leaves fall early this autumn, in wind.
The paired butterflies are already yellow with
          August
Over the grass in the West garden;
They hurt me. I grow older.   25
If you are coming down through the narrows of
          the river Kiang,
Please let me know beforehand,
And I will come out to meet you
          As far as Cho-fu-sa.
                              By Rihaku.

In a Station at the Metro
(1913)

❧ This brief imagistic poem was first written in 36
lines, then reduced to 18, then to just two. Pound's
account of its inception and composition reveals much
about his dislike for verbal excess, as well as his interest
in Japanese poetry and the association in his mind
between poetry and painting.

    Once on getting out of a "metro" train in Paris,
Pound says, he saw a beautiful face, then others, a
woman's and a child's, and he sought all that day
for words to express his sudden and lovely emotion.
None offered until at length there came to him an
"equation" — not in speech, but in "little splotches
of color." This he called an "image," or "vortex."
An image he defined as "that which presents an
intellectual and emotional complex in an instant of
time." A vortex, similarly, comes to the consciousness
in some "primary form." In this case it was felt in
color as a single image, like the Japanese *hokku*,
which Pound described as "one idea set on top of
another." Like Japanese verse, vorticism is art before
it has spread itself into flaccidity:
          "The fallen blossom flies
                back to its branch:
          A butterfly."
That, Pound says, is the substance of a well-known
hokku. His experience in Paris belonged to that kind

of inspiration and should have gone into paint. "In
a poem of this sort," he wrote, "one is trying to record
the precise instant when a thing outward and objective
transforms itself into a thing inward and subjective."

The apparition of these faces in the crowd;
Petals on a wet, black bough.

The Rest
(1913)

❧ The following two poems illustrate different viewpoints on the expatriate theme. The first reflects
Pound's revolt against the materialism of America —
the exiled artist. The second finds him in a more
conciliatory mood toward his fellow American poet.

O helpless few in my country,
O remnant enslaved!

Artists broken against her,
Astray, lost in the villages,
Mistrusted, spoken against,   5

Lovers of beauty, starved,
Thwarted with systems,
Helpless against the control;

You who cannot wear yourselves out
By persisting to successes,   10
You who can only speak,
Who cannot steel yourselves into reiteration;

You of the finer sense,
Broken against false knowledge,
You who can know at first hand,   15
Hated, shut in, mistrusted:

Take thought:
I have weathered the storm,
I have beaten out my exile.

A Pact
(1913)

I make a pact with you, Walt Whitman —
I have detested you long enough.
I come to you as a grown child
Who has had a pig-headed father;
I am old enough now to make friends.   5
It was you that broke the new wood,
Now is a time for carving.
We have one sap and one root —
Let there be commerce between us.

From *Hugh Selwyn Mauberley*

(*Life and Contacts*)

(1920)

In this poem Pound again, in a far more complex way, deals with the theme of the exiled artist out of tune with the times. E.P. is Pound himself; Mauberley, a sort of alter-ego of Pound and a minor artist, reflecting the failure of genuine devotion to art in a diseased age. The full poem contains eighteen separate sections, of which the first twelve and "Envoi" are reprinted here. The poem marks the final expatriation of Pound from America and England and the beginning of his life in Rapallo, Italy, where he was to spend many years of alienation. *Mauberley* depicts various phases of the poet's "life" and his literary "contacts" — both living and dead. The subject of the poet, ignored by his age and rebellious against it, is held together by a parallel with the journey of Odysseus through temptations and dangers toward his ultimate goal, "Penelope." It is a kind of summing up, midway in his career, of his relation to the aestheticism of the 1890's and the cultural sterility of the era of World War I. A further aim of Pound, here and elsewhere, was to purge poetry of excessively romantic diction and rhetoric and to restore the exact word — an aim of the Imagists and new poets of the 1912 movement — "to purify the dialect of the tribe." The epitaph to himself, quoted from a Carthaginian poet, suggest Pound's and Mauberley's withdrawal from the world and may be translated: "The heat calls us into the shade."

Vocat Aestus in Umbram
Nemesianus Ec. IV.

I

E. P. Ode pour l'Election de son Sepulchre [1]

For three years, out of key with his time,
He strove to resuscitate the dead art
Of poetry; to maintain "the sublime"
In the old sense. Wrong from the start —

No, hardly, but seeing he had been born   5
In a half-savage country, out of date;
Bent resolutely on wringing lilies from the acorn;
Capaneus; trout for factitious bait; [2]

[1] "Ode on the Choice of his Tomb" — from an ode by Ronsard, French poet (1534–1585).
[2] Pound says that two opposing views of his career may be the heroic one (like Capaneus, one of the Seven Against Thebes, who was struck down by Zeus for his rebellion) or the ridiculous view (like that of a fish taking an artificial bait).

''Ἴδμεν γάρ τοι πάνθ', ὅσ' ἐνὶ Τροίη
Caught in the unstopped ear;   10
Giving the rocks small lee-way
The chopped seas held him, therefore, that year.

His true Penelope was Flaubert,
He fished by obstinate isles;
Observed the elegance of Circe's hair   15
Rather than the mottoes on sun-dials. [3]

Unaffected by "the march of events,"
He passed from men's memory in *l'an trentiesme*
De son eage; the case presents
No adjunct to the Muses' diadem. [4]   20

II

The age demanded an image
Of its accelerated grimace,
Something for the modern stage,
Not, at any rate, an Attic grace;

Not, not certainly, the obscure reveries   25
Of the inward gaze;
Better mendacities
Than the classics in paraphrase!

The "age demanded" chiefly a mould in plaster,
Made with no loss of time,   30
A prose kinema, not, not assuredly, alabaster
Or the "sculpture" of rhyme.

III

The tea-rose tea-gown, etc.
Supplants the mousseline of Cos,
The pianola "replaces"   35
Sappho's barbitos.

Christ follows Dionysus,
Phallic and ambrosial

[3] The above two stanzas portray the poet as Odysseus who heard the Siren's song ("For we know all the things that are in Troy") and who has fished in "obstinate isles" — the many languages of Pound's study — and who admired the beauty of Circe's hair, despite its danger, instead of reading the clichés found on sundials. Penelope was Odysseus' wife who remained faithful to him for many years of his absence. Flaubert, French novelist and author of *Madame Bovary*, whom Pound admired for the purity of his diction — *le mot juste*.
[4] Pound points up the irony of contrast between his wasted life and that of François Villon whose *Grand Testament* began with the line "In the thirtieth year of my age."

Made way for macerations;
Caliban casts out Ariel.[5]   40

All things are a flowing,
Sage Heracleitus says; [6]
But a tawdry cheapness
Shall outlast our days.

Even the Christian beauty   45
Defects — after Samothrace; [7]
We see τὸ καλὸν[8]
Decreed in the market-place.

Faun's flesh is not to us,
Nor the saint's vision.   50
We have the Press for wafer;
Franchise for circumcision.

All men, in law, are equals.
Free of Pisistratus,[9]
We choose a knave or an eunuch   55
To rule over us.

O bright Apollo,
τίν' ἄνδρα, τίν' ἥρωα, τίνα θεόν[1]
What god, man, or hero
Shall I place a tin wreath upon!   60

IV

These fought in any case,
and some believing,
        pro domo, in any case . . .

Some quick to arm,
some for adventure,   65
some from fear of weakness,
some from fear of censure,
some for love of slaughter, in imagination,
learning later . . .
some in fear, learning love of slaughter;   70

Died some, pro patria,
        non "dulce" non "et decor" [2] . . .
walked eye-deep in hell
believing in old men's lies, then unbelieving
came home, home to a lie,   75
home to many deceits,
home to old lies and new infamy;
usury age-old and age-thick
and liars in public places.   79
Daring as never before, wastage as never before.
Young blood and high blood,
fair cheeks, and fine bodies;

fortitude as never before,

frankness as never before,
disillusions as never told in the old days,   85
hysterias, trench confessions,
laughter out of dead bellies.

V

There died a myriad,
And of the best, among them,
For an old bitch gone in the teeth,   90
For a botched civilization,

Charm, smiling at the good mouth,
Quick eyes gone under earth's lid,

For two gross of broken statues,
For a few thousand battered books.   95

Yeux Glauques [3]

Gladstone was still respected,
When John Ruskin produced
"King's Treasuries"; Swinburne
And Rossetti still abused.

Fœtid Buchanan lifted up his voice   100
When that faun's head of hers
Became a pastime for
Painters and adulterers.

---

5 In above two stanzas "mousseline" is a costly silk from the Greek island of Cos, used in the tunic; "barbitos" — lyre; Dionysus — Greek god worshipped in phallic rites; Ariel and Caliban — ethereal beauty and bestial ignorance (see Shakespeare's The Tempest).

6 Greek philosopher whose work emphasized the concept of an eternally changing universe.

7 The Nike of Samothrace, a statue which Pound uses as the essence of classic beauty, as opposed to Christian beauty (or beauties?).

8 "The Beautiful."

9 Athenian dictator who enforced rigid conformity to the law.

1 From Pindar's Second Olympian Ode, meaning: "What man, what hero, what god . . ." Pound disliked Pindar as the "prize windbag of all ages," and the lines which follow are contemptuous: i.e., a "tin" god.

2 That is, they died, but not as Horace wrote: "Dulce et decorum est pro patria mori" ("It is sweet and appropriate to die for one's country").

3 This section returns to the 19th century suggesting that the beginning of the present "botched civilization" lay in the period of Gladstone and Ruskin. In the '90's pre-Raphaelite poets like Swinburne and Rossetti were indifferently received and harshly treated by critics like Buchanan who especially singled out "Jenny," a London harlot and the subject of a Rossetti poem. The girl with the yeux glauques ("glaucous eyes") was Elizabeth Siddal, an English model and later Rossetti's wife. Pound says she was painted by Burne-Jones in his "Cophetua and the Beggar Maid" (1884). FitzGerald translated the Rubáiyát of Omar Khayyám (1859).

The Burne-Jones cartons
Have preserved her eyes;   105
Still, at the Tate, they teach
Cophetua to rhapsodize;

Thin like brook-water,
With a vacant gaze.
The English Rubaiyat was still-born   110
In those days.

The thin, clear gaze, the same
Still darts out faun-like from the half-ruin'd face,
Questing and passive. . . .
"Ah, poor Jenny's case" . . .   115

Bewildered that a world
Shows no surprise
At her last maquero's
Adulteries.

"Siena Mi Fe; Disfecemi Maremma" [4]

Among the pickled fœtuses and bottled bones,
Engaged in perfecting the catalogue,   121
I found the last scion of the
Senatorial families of Strasbourg, Monsieur
Verog.[5]

For two hours he talked of Gallifet; [6]
Of Dowson; of the Rhymers' Club;   125
Told me how Johnson (Lionel) died
By falling from a high stool in a pub . . .[7]

But showed no trace of alcohol
At the autopsy, privately performed —
Tissue preserved — the pure mind   130
Arose toward Newman as the whisky warmed.

Dowson found harlots cheaper than hotels;
Headlam [8] for uplift; Image [9] impartially imbued

With raptures for Bacchus, Terpsichore and the
    Church.
So spoke the author of "The Dorian Mood," 135

M. Verog, out of step with the decade,
Detached from his contemporaries,
Neglected by the young,
Because of these reveries.

Brennbaum [1]

The sky-like limpid eyes,   140
The circular infant's face,
The stiffness from spats to collar
Never relaxing into grace;

The heavy memories of Horeb, Sinai and the
    forty years,
Showed only when the daylight fell   145
Level across the face
Of Brennbaum "The Impeccable."

Mr. Nixon [2]

In the cream gilded cabin of his steam yacht
Mr. Nixon advised me kindly, to advance with
    fewer
Dangers of delay. "Consider   150
    Carefully the reviewer.

"I was as poor as you are;
When I began I got, of course,
Advance on royalties, fifty at first," said Mr.
    Nixon,
"Follow me and take a column,   155
Even if you have to work free.

"Butter reviewers. From fifty to three hundred
I rose in eighteen months;
The hardest nut I had to crack
Was Dr. Dundas.[3]   160

"I never mentioned a man but with the view
Of selling my own works.
The tip's a good one, as for literature
It gives no man a sinecure.

[4] Dante's *Purgatorio*. Among those violently slain who repented before death was Pia de Tolomei whose husband, in love with another woman, had her murdered in his castle at Maremma. "Siena made me; Maremma unmade me."

[5] Identified as Victor Plarr, biographer of Dowson and author of a book of poems, *In the Dorian Mood* (1896).

[6] French general of the Franco-Prussian War at the battle of Sedan.

[7] Ernest Dowson and Lionel Johnson were poets of the '90's and members of the Rhymers' Club whom Pound admired. Strongly addicted to drugs and alcohol, both died young.

[8] Rev. Stewart Headlam of Gloucester, who held festive parties with dancers and revelry for church and literary people.

[9] Professor Selwyn Image co-edited *The Hobby Horse*, literary periodical of the '90's.

[1] Literary portrait of a Jewish intellectual of the '90's. J. J. Espey suggests he was modeled after Max Beerbohm, though the Beerbohm family is not Jewish.

[2] Portrait of a literary man who publicly stated that his real interest in letters was to make money. A fictitious name, he was probably, in real life, the novelist, Arnold Bennett (see Studies by H. Kenner and J. J. Espey).

[3] A literary editor — a type name.

"And no one knows, at sight, a masterpiece. 165
And give up verse, my boy,
There's nothing in it."

*   *   *   *

Likewise a friend of Bloughram's [4] once advised
      me:
Don't kick against the pricks,
Accept opinion. The "Nineties" tried your
      game   170
And died, there's nothing in it.

X

Beneath the sagging roof
The stylist has taken shelter,
Unpaid, uncelebrated,
At last from the world's welter   175

Nature receives him;
With a placid and uneducated mistress
He exercises his talents
And the soil meets his distress.

The haven from sophistications and contentions
Leaks through its thatch;   181
He offers succulent cooking;
The door has a creaking latch.[5]

XI

"Conservatrix of Milésien"
Habits of mind and feeling,   185
Possibly. But in Ealing
With the most bank-clerkly of Englishmen?

No, "Milesian" is an exaggeration.
No instinct has survived in her
Older than those her grandmother   190
Told her would fit her station.[6]

XII

"Daphne with her thighs in bark
Stretches toward me her leafy hands," —

4 See Browning's "Bishop Blougram's Apology" for
Pound's original. He misspells "Blougram."
5 The true artist is forced to retire from a commercial
world and live in a Bohemian way in the country.
6 These two stanzas are an ironic statement of the
tame love-making of the modern woman, "conservatrix
Milésien." The *Milésien Tales* were highly erotic stories
by Aristides of Milesia, an ancient city of Asia Minor.
The stories are mostly lost, as is their tradition of
eroticism, in such "proper" surroundings as Ealing (or
any other small town) near the city of London. Pound
takes the quotation from Rémy de Gourmont's *Histoires
Magiques* (1894) where, as J. J. Espey has shown, the
meaning is frankly sexual.

Subjectively. In the stuffed-satin drawing room
I await the Lady Valentine's [7] commands,   195

Knowing that my coat has never been
Of precisely the fashion
To stimulate, in her,
A durable passion;

Doubtful, somewhat, of the value   200
Of well-gowned approbation
Of literary effort,
But never of the Lady Valentine's vocation:

Poetry, her border of ideas,
The edge, uncertain, but a means of blending
With other strata   206
Where the lower and higher have ending:

A hook to catch the Lady Jane's attention,
A modulation toward the theatre,
Also, in case of revolution,   210
A possible friend and comforter.

*   *   *   *

Conduct, on the other hand, the soul
"Which the highest cultures have nourished"
To Fleet St. where
Dr. Johnson flourished;   215

Beside this thoroughfare
The sale of half-hose has
Long since superseded the cultivation
Of Pierian roses.[8]

Envoi (1919) [9]

Go, dumb-born book,   220
Tell her that sang me once that song of Lawes:

7 Pound compares the legend of Daphne, a nymph
changed into a laurel tree while pursued by Apollo, to
the modern society patroness of the artist — Lady Valentine. The quotation is from Gautier's "Le Château de
Souvenir."
8 The theme of patronage is carried further by the
reference to Dr. Johnson, whose famous letter to
Chesterfield marked the end of the earlier tradition of
support for the artist by the wealthy. Johnson retired to
Fleet Street, now a purely business section unconcerned
with art. Haberdashery shops have taken the place of
the worship of Muses, as once in Pieria, Greece, where
art was celebrated. The quotation is a translation by
Pound of a line from a poem by Laforgue, "*Com-
plainte des Pianos qu'on Entend dans les Quartiers
Aisés.*"
9 The "Farewell" sings the triumph of beauty and
love over all material things in the accents of Edmund
Waller's "Go, Lovely Rose!", set to music by the English
composer, Henry Lawes.

Hadst thou but song
As thou hast subjects known,
Then were there cause in thee that should con-
*   done*
Even my faults that heavy upon me lie,   225
And build her glories their longevity.

Tell her that sheds
Such treasure in the air,
Recking naught else but that her graces give
Life to the moment,   230
I would bid them live
As roses might, in magic amber laid,
Red overwrought with orange and all made
One substance and one colour
Braving time.   235

Tell her that goes
With song upon her lips
But sings not out the song, nor knows
The maker of it, some other mouth,
May be as fair as hers,   240
Might, in new ages, gain her worshippers,
When our two dusts with Waller's shall be laid,
Siftings on siftings in oblivion,
Till change hath broken down
All things save Beauty alone.   245

Canto I
(1925)

Pound's *Cantos*, begun in 1917, are the work of over forty years and have reached 100 in number. They have been published in separate sequences, but were evidently intended as a kind of modern epic or intellectual diary into which he poured the sum total of his preoccupations and aspirations, as well as his criticism of modern society. The overall unity or structure of the *Cantos* is a complicated subject of scholarship, and the beginning student is advised to approach a selection of the poems, such as the two opening *Cantos* here reprinted, to discover something of Pound's method and explore a few of the motifs or themes which re-appear throughout the whole. Certain major themes (Pound called them "vortices") may be distinguished, out of which various lines of thought and emotional attitudes emerge. The plan involved an interweaving of modern themes and events with scenes and characters drawn from classical and Renaissance literature, from American history, European history, and Oriental thought. The poet Yeats in 1928 described the structure of the *Cantos* as follows: "There will be no plot, no chronicle of events, no logic of discourse, but two themes, the descent

into Hades from Homer, a metamorphosis from Ovid, and mixed with these medieval or modern historical characters." *Canto I* introduces Odysseus, who represented for Pound the many-sided man, resourceful and self-reliant. There is an implied parallel between Odysseus' journey through many dangers toward home and the poet's search through remote literature for a new kind of poetry. Book XI of *The Odyssey* describes the hero's descent to the underworld in search of the prophet, Tiresias. Pound is translating this episode, covering the first 67 lines of the poem, from a Renaissance Latin translation of Homer by Andreas Divus (mentioned in l. 67). At this point Pound introduces a new theme, beauty and desire, or perhaps the emotional element in poetry as compared with the elements of will and action as seen in Odysseus. Circe's fatal beauty and that of Aphrodite, goddess of beauty, may (according to E. M. Glenn) signify the alluring but destructive power of sex, which, when properly managed by the poet, can be productive of high accomplishment.

And then went down to the ship,
Set keel to breakers, forth on the godly sea, and
We [1] set up mast and sail on that swart ship,
Bore sheep aboard her, and our bodies also
Heavy with weeping, and winds from sternward
Bore us out onward with bellying canvas,   6
Circe's this craft, the trim-coifed goddess.[2]
Then sat we amidships, wind jamming the tiller,
Thus with stretched sail, we went over sea till
    day's end.   9
Sun to his slumber, shadows o'er all the ocean,
Came we then to the bounds of deepest water,
To the Kimmerian lands, and peopled cities
Covered with close-webbed mist, unpierced ever
With glitter of sun-rays
Nor with stars stretched, nor looking back from
    heaven   15
Swartest night stretched over wretched men
    there.
The ocean flowing backward, came we then to
    the place
Aforesaid by Circe.
Here did they rites, Perimedes and Eurylochus,[3]
And drawing sword from my hip   20
I dug the ell-square pitkin;

[1] The episode is related by Odysseus at the court of Alcinous, King of the Phaeacians. "We" refers to himself and his companions.

[2] Circe, the sorceress, had turned Odysseus' men into swine. He persuades her to disenchant them, lives with her a year, then departs to Ithaca, but first upon her advice he goes to the world of the dead to seek the aid of the soothsayer, Tiresias. His ship is speeded by the wind, provided by Circe's magic.

[3] Two of Odysseus' companions.

Poured we libations unto each the dead,
First mead and then sweet wine, water mixed
    with white flour.
Then prayed I many a prayer to the sickly
    death's-heads;
As set in Ithaca, sterile bulls of the best   25
For sacrifice, heaping the pyre with goods,
A sheep to Tiresias only, black and a bell-sheep.
Dark blood flowed in the fosse,
Souls out of Erebus, cadaverous dead, of brides
Of youths and of the old who had borne much;
Souls stained with recent tears, girls tender, 31
Men many, mauled with bronze lance heads,
Battle spoil, bearing yet dreory [4] arms,
These many crowded about me; with shouting,
Pallor upon me, cried to my men for more
    beasts;   35
Slaughtered the herds, sheep slain of bronze;
Poured ointment, cried to the gods,
To Pluto the strong, and praised Proserpine;
Unsheathed the narrow sword,
I sat to keep off the impetuous impotent dead,
Till I should hear Tiresias.   41
But first Elpenor came, our friend Elpenor,[5]
Unburied, cast on the wide earth,
Limbs that we left in the house of Circe,
Unwept, unwrapped in sepulchre, since toils
    urged other.   45
Pitiful spirit. And I cried in hurried speech:
"Elpenor, how art thou come to this dark coast?
"Cam'st thou afoot, outstripping seamen?"
    And he in heavy speech:
"Ill fate and abundant wine. I slept in Circe's
    ingle.   50
"Going down the long ladder unguarded,
"I fell against the buttress,
"Shattered the nape-nerve, the soul sought
    Avernus.
"But thou, O King, I bid remember me, unwept,
    unburied,
"Heap up mine arms, be tomb by sea-bord, and
    inscribed: 55
"A man of no fortune, and with a name to come.
"And set my oar up, that I swung mid fellows."

And Anticlea [6] came, whom I beat off, and then
    Tiresias Theban,

4 bloody.
5 The youngest of Odysseus' companions, killed in
a fall from Circe's house. His ghost reminds Odysseus
that his body was left unburied. See line 67 where
Tiresias prophesies that Odysseus would "lose all companions."
6 Mother of Odysseus, who has died in his absence.
He weeps over her spirit in Hades.

Holding his golden wand, knew me, and spoke
    first:
"A second time? why? man of ill star,   60
"Facing the sunless dead and this joyless region?
"Stand from the fosse, leave me my bloody bever
"For soothsay."
    And I stepped back,
And he strong with the blood, said then:
    "Odysseus   65
"Shalt return through spiteful Neptune, over
    dark seas,
"Lose all companions." And then Anticlea came.
Lie quiet Divus. I mean, that is Andreas Divus,
In officina Wecheli, 1538, out of Homer.[7]
And he sailed, by Sirens and thence outward and
    away   70
And unto Circe.
    Venerandam,[8]
In the Cretan's phrase, with the golden crown,
    Aphrodite,
Cypri munimenta sortita est, mirthful, oricalchi,
    with golden
Girdles and breast bands, thou with dark eye-
    lids   75
Bearing the golden bough of Argicida.[9] So
    that:[10]

Canto II

🦋 The Canto opens with a reference to Browning's
poem *Sordello*, dealing with an Italian troubadour of
the Provence. Pound is interested both in the obscure
dramatic method of Browning and in the life and
poetry of Sordello, perhaps as a model for his own
work. The theme of destructive feminine beauty,
begun in Canto I, is continued here with allusions to
Helen of Troy, Eleanor of Aquitaine, and Atalanta
("Schoeney's" daughter) — all of whom caused war
and discord and the death of men. The literary source
then shifts to Ovid's *Metamorphosis* III in which

7 Indicating the end of the translation from Andreas
Divus. "Officina Wecheli" is from the imprint of
Pound's volume of Divus: "at the workshop of
Wechel."
8 "Compelling admiration" — a phrase from the
Latin translation of the second Homeric Hymn to
Aphrodite by the Cretan, Georgius Dartona. This and
other details describing Aphrodite are from the hymn.
"Cypri . . .": "the citadels of Cyprus were her appointed realm." "Oricalchi" (Latin "of copper").
9 The god Hermes was slayer of Argus who guarded
Io, whom Zeus loved. E. M. Glenn suggests "Argicida"
might also apply to Aphrodite as slayer of the Greeks
because she was responsible for the Trojan War and
sided against the Greeks. On the whole, the reference
carries out the theme of the fatal power of passion.
10 May simply be the Latin "ut" meaning "so
that . . ."

the story of Acoetes is related. On the ship bearing Dionysus to Naxos, the crew attempts to abduct the god, disguised as a young boy, into slavery. Dionysus causes tigers and leopards to appear, sets vines around the oarshafts, and changes the crew into dolphins.

Hang it all, Robert Browning,
    there can be but the one "Sordello."
But Sordello, and my Sordello?
    Lo Sordels si fo di Mantovana.[1]
So-shu churned in the sea.[2]   5
Seal sports in the spray-whited circles of cliff-
    wash,
Sleek head, daughter of Lir,[3]
    eyes of Picasso
Under black fur-hood, lithe daughter of Ocean;
And the wave runs in the beach-groove: 10
"Eleanor, ἑλέναυς and ἑλέπτολις"[4]
    And poor old Homer blind, blind, as a bat,
Ear, ear for the sea-surge, murmur of old men's
    voices:
"Let her go back to the ships,
Back among Grecian faces, lest evil come on our
    own,   15
Evil and further evil, and a curse cursed on our
    children,
Moves, yes she moves like a goddess
And has the face of a god
    and the voice of Schoeney's daughters,
And doom goes with her in walking,   20
Let her go back to the ships,
    back among Grecian voices."[5]
And by the beach-run, Tyro,[6]
    Twisted arms of the sea-god,   24
Lithe sinews of water, gripping her, cross-hold,
And the blue-gray glass of the wave tents them,
Glare azure of water, cold-welter, close cover.

Quiet sun-tawny sand-stretch,
The gulls broad out their wings,
    nipping between the splay feathers;   30
Snipe come for their bath,
    bend out their wing-joints,
Spread wet wings to the sun-film,
And by Scios,[7]
    to left of the Naxos [8] passage,   35
Naviform rock overgrown,
    algæ cling to its edge,
There is a wine-red glow in the shallows,
    a tin flash in the sun-dazzle.

The ship landed in Scios,   40
    men wanting spring-water,
And by the rock-pool a young boy loggy with
    vine-must,
"To Naxos? Yes, we'll take you to Naxos,
Com' along lad." "Not that way!"
"Aye, that way is Naxos."   45
    And I said: "It's a straight ship."
And an ex-convict out of Italy
    knocked me into the fore-stays,
(He was wanted for manslaughter in Tuscany)
    And the whole twenty against me,   50
Mad for a little slave money.
    And they took her out of Scios
And off her course . . . .
    And the boy came to, again, with the racket,
And looked out over the bows,   55
    and to eastward, and to the Naxos passage.
God-sleight then, god-sleight:
    Ship stock fast in sea-swirl,
Ivy upon the oars, King Pentheus,[9]
    grapes with no seed but sea-foam,   60
Ivy in scupper-hole.
Aye, I, Acœtes, stood there,
    and the god stood by me,
Water cutting under the keel,
Sea-break from stern forrards,   65
    wake running off from the bow,
And where was gunwale, there now was vine-
    trunk,
And tenthril where cordage had been,
    grape-leaves on the rowlocks,
Heavy vine on the oarshafts,   70
And, out of nothing, a breathing,
    hot breath on my ankles,

---

[1] "Sordello was from the region around Mantua." In Dante's *Purgatorio*, VI, the poet Virgil is recognized by Sordello as a fellow-Mantuan and is embraced with enthusiasm by the poet-patriot.

[2] Perhaps a Chinese Taoist philosopher, Chuang Tzŭ (So-Shu is the Japanese version). Pound wrote a poem "Ancient Wisdom, Rather Cosmic" about So-Shu.

[3] A Celtic sea-god. These lines, 6–10, describe the seal in imagistic language.

[4] Pound is quoting words used to describe Helen of Troy by Aeschylus: "destroyer of ships" and "breaker of cities." But he refers at the same time to Eleanor of Aquitaine, queen of France and later of England, wife of Henry II, whose possessions caused war between the two countries. Her name is likewise a pun on the Greek word *elander* (man-destroyer).

[5] The words in quotation marks are from *The Iliad*, III, 158–160, in which the old men of Troy speak of Helen as they watch Paris and Menelaus fight.

[6] In *The Odyssey*, XI, 235–259, is the story of Tyro, daughter of Salmoneus, ravished by the sea-god, Poseidon, in the waves (cf. also ll. 132–137).

[7] Scios, or Chios, is a large Ionian island off the coast of Asia Minor, northeast of Naxos.

[8] Greek island devoted to worship of Bacchus (Dionysus), famous for its wines.

[9] In Ovid the story of Acoetes, the only survivor, is told to Pentheus, King of Thebes, as a warning against the failure to worship the god Bacchus.

Beasts like shadows in glass,
    a furred tail upon nothingness.
Lynx-purr, and heathery smell of beasts,   75
    where tar smell had been,
Sniff and pad-foot of beasts,
    eye-glitter out of black air.
The sky overshot, dry, with no tempest,
Sniff and pad-foot of beasts,   80
    fur brushing my knee-skin,
Rustle of airy sheaths,
    dry forms in the *aether*.
And the ship like a keel in ship-yard,
    slung like an ox in smith's sling,   85
Ribs stuck fast in the ways,
    grape-cluster over pin-rack,
    void air taking pelt.
Lifeless air become sinewed,
    feline leisure of panthers,   90
Leopards sniffing the grape shoots by scupper-
    hole,
Crouched panthers by fore-hatch,
And the sea blue-deep about us,
    green-ruddy in shadows,
And Lyæus: [1] "From now, Acœtes, my altars, 95
Fearing no bondage,
    fearing no cat of the wood,
Safe with my lynxes,
    feeding grapes to my leopards,
Olibanum is my incense,   100
    the vines grow in my homage."

The back-swell now smooth in the rudder-chains,
Black snout of a porpoise
    where Lycabs [2] had been,
Fish-scales on the oarsmen.   105
    And I worship.
I have seen what I have seen.
    When they brought the boy I said:
"He has a god in him,
    though I do not know which god."   110
And they kicked me into the fore-stays.
I have seen what I have seen:
    Medon's [3] face like the face of a dory,
Arms shrunk into fins. And you, Pentheus,
Had as well listen to Tiresias, and to Cadmus,[4]

[1] Another name for Bacchus-Dionysus.
[2] Lycabas was one of the shipmates of Acoetes who tried to abduct Dionysus. He is the "ex-convict" of line 47 who knocked Acoetes into the forestays.
[3] Another of the shipmates.
[4] Founder of Thebes and grandfather of Pentheus. Cadmus and Tiresias had both advised Pentheus not to ignore the worship of Dionysus.

or your luck will go out of you.   116
Fish-scales over groin muscles,
    lynx-purr amid sea . . .
And of a later year,
    pale in the wine-red algæ,   120
If you will lean over the rock,
    the coral face under wave-tinge,
Rose-paleness under water-shift,
    Ileuthyeria, fair Dafne of sea-bords,[5]
The swimmer's arms turned to branches,   125
Who will say in what year,
    fleeing what band of tritons,
The smooth brows, seen, and half seen,
    now ivory stillness.

And So-shu churned in the sea, So-shu also,   130
    using the long moon for a churn-stick . . .
Lithe turning of water,
    sinews of Poseidon,
Black azure and hyaline,
    glass wave over Tyro,   135
Close cover, unstillness,
    bright welter of wave-cords,
Then quiet water,
    quiet in the buff sands,
Sea-fowl stretching wing-joints,   140
    splashing in rock-hollows and sand-hollows
In the wave-runs by the half-dune;
Glass-glint of wave in the tide-rips against sun-
    light,
    pallor of Hesperus,
Gray peak of the wave,   145
    wave, colour of grape's pulp.

Olive gray in the near,
    far, smoke gray of the rock-slide,
Salmon-pink wings of the fish-hawk
    cast gray shadows in water,   150
The tower like a one-eyed great goose
    cranes up out of the olive-grove,

And we have heard the fauns chiding Proteus
    in the smell of hay under the olive-trees,
And the frogs singing against the fauns in the
    half light.   155
And . . .

[5] Ileuthyeria is a sea-nymph who was turned into coral, like Daphne who was turned into a laurel tree when she was pursued by Apollo. The name is Pound's own coinage, based on the Greek word for "freedom."

T. S. Eliot [1888-   ]

"When the history of American poetry in our time comes to be written," said F. O. Matthiessen in 1950, "the central figures will probably be Frost and Eliot." The differences between the two largely grow out of the fact that the one is a poet of "man in nature," the other of "man in the metropolitan desert."

The particular "metropolitan desert" into which Thomas Stearns Eliot was born was St. Louis. There his father, Henry Ware Eliot, was a businessman, and there his grandfather, the Reverend William Greenleaf Eliot, had founded Washington University. But it was a New England family. T. S. Eliot came to see, he said, that he had "always been a New Englander in the South West, and a South Westerner in New England." As a college undergraduate he edited the *Harvard Advocate* and printed in it some of his own poems. After taking the A.B. and A.M. degrees, he went on with philosophy: for a year at the University of Paris, for three more years at Harvard, and for one year at Oxford.

The year at Oxford began just after the war broke out in 1914. Then a learned young man of twenty-six, he was to reside the rest of his life in England. In 1915 he married an Englishwoman, a dancer, and tried school-teaching. A few years later he was employed at Lloyds Bank. In 1922 he began editing *The Criterion*, an influential literary magazine. Three years later he joined the board of the publishing house of Faber and Gwyer (later Faber and Faber). In 1927 he became a British subject, and was confirmed as a communicant of the Church of England. From this point on, Eliot placed himself more and more against the current of liberal-democratic ideas generated in the nineteenth century, declaring himself, in 1928, a "royalist in politics, a classicist in literature, and an Anglo-Catholic in religion." He rejected the standards of the commercial-minded, American middle-class as boring, decadent, and without spiritual meaning, but unlike many of his contemporaries who were experimenting with an idealistic form of international communism, he turned, instead, to the authority of the early Church and the intangible goals of a mystical Christianity. The direction of his thought has been steadily toward asceticism, contemplation, and a denial of the self and, like Henry Adams, he has preferred the simpler faith of an early, irrational age to the "benefits" of science, reason, progress, and modern conveniences.

Beginning with *Prufrock and Other Observations*, 1917, Eliot published several slim volumes of verse in which the poetic techniques of seventeenth-century English metaphysical poets such as Donne and Marvell, the French symbolists such as Laforgue and Corbière, the early Imagists (especially Ezra Pound to whom Eliot acknowledged his debt in the dedication to *The Waste Land* and elsewhere), and other influences were brought together to form a style as "new" for our time as was Whitman's for his. Humor and seriousness mingle strangely in Eliot's work; scraps of popular songs, slang, scenes from low and high life, and even parody stand side by side with allusions to Ecclesiastes, Dante, Shakespeare, and classical myths. The result, in the longer poems, is a complex patchwork of cultural references, quotations, and literary echoes held together by an underlying thematic unity — a criticism of modern life. Taken as a whole, his *Poems* (1919), *The Waste Land* (1922), *Ash Wednesday* (1930), and *Four Quartets* (1943) form an integrated sequence, voicing more profoundly than the work of any other modern poet the mood of the twenties and thirties. (See also page 847.) When he turned to verse drama, he was less original and less influential, though his *Murder in the Cathedral* (1935), based on the life of Thomas à Becket, was a moving expression of the theme of religious affirmation; it was followed by *The Cocktail Party* (1950), and *The Confidential Clerk* (1953), both more adequate as philosophical disquisitions than as stage performances.

Eliot's great influence upon his generation of poets, critics, and scholars cannot be questioned. If his poetry helped shape the work of his contemporaries in England and America, such as Spender, Auden, MacLeish, Hart Crane, Aiken, and others, his criticism almost literally gave birth to the kind of analysis of separate works which is loosely described as the "New Criticism." In *The Sacred Wood* (1920), *Selected Essays* (1932, 1959), and *The Use of Poetry and the Use of Criticism* (1933), he helped re-define the uses of the past, set up new literary gods, and challenged the supremacy of romantic and subjective poetry. His prose is cool, precise, almost prim, and (to use his own word) pontifical. His other work is directed toward establishing certain standards of belief and conduct in a Christian society: *The Idea of a Christian Society* (1939) and *Notes Toward the Definition of Culture* (1948).

Further reading: *Complete Poems and Plays. Selected Essays.* F. O. Matthiessen, *The Achievement of T. S. Eliot*, 1935, revised 1947. George Williamson, *A Reader's Guide to T. S. Eliot*, 1953. *T. S. Eliot: A Selected Critique*, ed. Leonard Unger, 1948. Elizabeth Drew, *T. S. Eliot, The Design of his Poetry*, 1949.

The Love Song of J. Alfred Prufrock

(1915)

In this self-portrait of Prufrock we have the portrait of a society, a society of shallow tea-and-coffee talk and uncomprehending art talk and other lifeless formulae of conversation, a sophisticated, world-weary society which has grown away from all genuine emotions and serious thought, and which lies sunken in the life-in-death sea of its artificiality. This society is here observed by one of its members who, more sensitive than his fellows, senses the truth that they miss. Yet he is too much a member of this society to rebel successfully against it. His sensitivity threatens only to make him incapable of enduring this life any longer. For if, aware of his submersion, he gasps for life, he drowns.

The poem says none of these things directly. In this dramatic monologue the character of this society emerges gradually through the opening image of desensitized passivity, through the primitive, unthinking, somnolent cat-life of the fog, which symbolically blinds and enshrouds the city, through glimpses of its members in action, talking of Michelangelo, and through the ludicrous ineffectuality of Prufrock. The appropriate tone is set by the calculated flatness of the understatements, the hesitating, groping repetitions, and the ironic contrasts between Prufrock's portentously described impulses and his actual achievements. Even his death is debunked. His society scarcely provides an adequate context for tragedy.

S'io credesse che mia risposta fosse
A persona che mai tornasse al mondo,
Questa fiamma staria senza piu scosse.
Ma perciocche giammai di questo fondo
Non torno vivo alcun, s'i'odo il vero,
Senza tema d'infamia ti rispondo.[1]

Let us go then, you and I,
When the evening is spread out against the sky
Like a patient etherised upon a table;
Let us go, through certain half-deserted streets,
The muttering retreats   5
Of restless nights in one-night cheap hotels
And sawdust restaurants with oyster-shells:
Streets that follow like a tedious argument
Of insidious intent
To lead you to an overwhelming question . . .
Oh, do not ask, "What is it?"   11
Let us go and make our visit.

[1] Dante's *Inferno*: "If I thought my answer were to one who ever could return to the world, this flame should gleam no more [i.e. this spirit should speak no more]; but since, if what I hear be true, none ever did return alive from this depth, without fear of infamy, I answer thee." Spoken by the shade of Guido de Montefeltro confessing his sins of betrayal of the Colonna family and his unrepentant death to Dante in Hades. Prufrock, too, would not bare his soul to the world, but keep his desires hidden between his inner self ("I") and outer ("you").

In the room the women come and go
Talking of Michelangelo.

The yellow fog that rubs its back upon the
    window-panes,   15
The yellow smoke that rubs its muzzle on the
    window-panes
Licked its tongue into the corners of the eve-
    ning,
Lingered upon the pools that stand in drains,
Let fall upon its back the soot that falls from
    chimneys,
Slipped by the terrace, made a sudden leap, 20
And seeing that it was a soft October night,
Curled once about the house, and fell asleep.

And indeed there will be time
For the yellow smoke that slides along the street,
Rubbing its back upon the window-panes; 25
There will be time, there will be time
To prepare a face to meet the faces that you
    meet;
There will be time to murder and create,
And time for all the works and days of hands
That lift and drop a question on your plate;
Time for you and time for me,   31
And time yet for a hundred indecisions,
And for a hundred visions and revisions,
Before the taking of a toast and tea.

In the room the women come and go   35
Talking of Michelangelo.

And indeed there will be time
To wonder, "Do I dare?" and, "Do I dare?"
Time to turn back and descend the stair,
With a bald spot in the middle of my hair — 40
(They will say: "How his hair is growing thin!")
My morning coat, my collar mounting firmly to
    the chin,
My necktie rich and modest, but asserted by a
    simple pin —
(They will say: "But how his arms and legs are
    thin!")
Do I dare   45
Disturb the universe?
In a minute there is time
For decisions and revisions which a minute will
    reverse.

For I have known them all already, known them
    all: 49
Have known the evenings, mornings, afternoons,
I have measured out my life with coffee spoons;

I know the voices dying with a dying fall
Beneath the music from a farther room.
  So how should I presume?

And I have known the eyes already, known them
    all —   55
The eyes that fix you in a formulated phrase,
And when I am formulated, sprawling on a pin,
When I am pinned and wriggling on the wall,
Then how should I begin
To spit out all the butt-ends of my days and
    ways?   60
  And how should I presume?

And I have known the arms already, known
    them all —
Arms that are braceleted and white and bare
(But in the lamplight, downed with light brown
    hair!)
Is it perfume from a dress   65
That makes me so digress?
Arms that lie among a table, or wrap about a
    shawl.
  And should I then presume?
  And how should I begin?

    .   .   .   .   .   .

Shall I say, I have gone at dusk through narrow
    streets   70
And watched the smoke that rises from the pipes
Of lonely men in shirt-sleeves, leaning out of
    windows? . . .

I should have been a pair of ragged claws
Scuttling across the floors of silent seas.

And the afternoon, the evening, sleeps so peace-
    fully!   75
Smoothed by long fingers,
Asleep . . . tired . . . or it malingers,
Stretched on the floor, here beside you and me.
Should I, after tea and cakes and ices,
Have the strength to force the moment to its
    crisis? [2]   80
But though I have wept and fasted, wept and
    prayed,

[2] This line seems to draw together several other references in the poem indicating a half-concealed account of Prufrock's fear of making love to the woman in the poem (see title and ll. 62–69, 107–110). Also, what is "the overwhelming question," l. 10? F. O. Matthiessen writes: "the point of calling the poem a 'Love Song' lies in the irony that it will never be sung; that Prufrock will never dare to voice what he feels." For interpretations see Brooks and Warren, *Understanding Poetry*, and R. P. Basler, *Sex, Symbolism and Psychology in Literature*.

Though I have seen my head (grown slightly
    bald) brought in upon a platter,[3]
I am no prophet — and here's no great matter;
I have seen the moment of my greatness flicker,
And I have seen the eternal Footman hold my
    coat, and snicker,   85
And in short, I was afraid.

And would it have been worth it, after all,
After the cups, the marmalade, the tea,
Among the porcelain, among some talk of you
    and me,
Would it have been worth while,   90
To have bitten off the matter with a smile,
To have squeezed the universe into a ball,
To roll it toward some overwhelming question,
To say: "I am Lazarus, come from the dead,[4]
Come back to tell you all, I shall tell you all" —
If one, settling a pillow by her head,   96
    Should say: "That is not what I meant at all.
    That is not it, at all."

And would it have been worth it, after all,
Would it have been worth while,   100
After the sunsets and the dooryards and the
    sprinkled streets,
After the novels, after the teacups, after the
    skirts that trail along the floor —
And this, and so much more? —
It is impossible to say just what I mean!
But as if a magic lantern threw the nerves in
    patterns on a screen: 105
Would it have been worth while
If one, settling a pillow or throwing off a shawl,
And turning toward the window, should say:
    "That is not it at all,
    That is not what I meant, at all."   110

   .   .   .   .   .   .

No! I am not Prince Hamlet, nor was meant
    to be;
Am an attendant lord, one that will do
To swell a progress, start a scene or two,
Advise the prince; no doubt, an easy tool,
Deferential, glad to be of use,   115
Politic, cautious, and meticulous;
Full of high sentence, but a bit obtuse;
At times, indeed, almost ridiculous —
Almost, at times, the Fool.[5]

---

[3] Refer to Matt. 14:3–11.
[4] For the resurrection of Lazarus, see John 10:1–44.
[5] Polonius, in *Hamlet*, seems partially to fit the description of ll. 114–119. Chaucer in the *Canterbury Tales* describes the Clerk of Oxenford's speech as "full of high sentence." Eliot uses the phrase in the sense of windy or pompous.

I grow old . . . I grow old . . .   120
I shall wear the bottoms of my trousers rolled.

Shall I part my hair behind? Do I dare to eat a
    peach?
I shall wear white flannel trousers, and walk
    upon the beach.
I have heard the mermaids singing, each to each.

I do not think that they will sing to me.   125

I have seen them riding seaward on the waves
Combing the white hair of the waves blown
    back
When the wind blows the water white and
    black.

We have lingered in the chambers of the sea
By sea-girls wreathed with seaweed red and
    brown   130
Till human voices wake us, and we drown.

The Hippopotamus

(1917)

This derisive treatment of the Catholic Church takes its effect largely from the sudden, unannounced, flippant reversal in the seventh stanza, and from the ironic contrast between its malicious comment and its assumed naïveté of form and language. The regular stanzaic pattern, the simple diction, and the frequent childish flatness of understatement suggest the nursery rhyme; but the sophisticated, double-edged allusions, the keenly pointed phrasing, and the rugged cynicism betray the satirist.

The two mottoes, Jane Worthington has remarked in *American Literature* (March, 1949), "come from that period, historically known as the Apostolic Age, when the foundations of the church were still to be laid." Miss Worthington's translation of the first motto, from the epistle of St. Ignatius to the Trallians, reads: "And likewise let all the deacons be reverenced, as commanded by Jesus Christ; and let the bishop be reverenced, as Jesus Christ, the living son of the Father; also let the presbyters be reverenced, as the council of God and the assembly of the apostles. Without these there can be no church; of these things I persuade you as I can."

The second motto is from St. Paul, Colossians 4:16. Like the Trallians, the Laodiceans were "unstable in their practice of Christianity."

---

*Similiter et omnes revereantur Diaconos, ut
mandatum Jesu Christi; et Episcopum, ut Jesum*

Christum, existentem filium Patris; Presbyteros autem, ut concilium Dei et conjunctionem Apostolorum. Sine his Ecclesia non vocatur; de quibus suadeo vos sic habeo.
                                  S. IGNATII AD TRALLIANOS

And when this epistle is read among you, cause that it be read also in the church of the Laodiceans.

The broad-backed hippopotamus
Rests on his belly in the mud;
Although he seems so firm to us
He is merely flesh and blood.

Flesh and blood is weak and frail,   5
Susceptible to nervous shock;
While the True Church can never fail
For it is based upon a rock.

The hippo's feeble steps may err
In compassing material ends,   10
While the True Church need never stir
To gather in its dividends.

The 'potamus can never reach
The mango on the mango-tree;
But fruits of pomegranate and peach   15
Refresh the Church from over sea.

At mating time the hippo's voice
Betrays inflexions hoarse and odd;
But every week we hear rejoice
The Church at being one with God.   20

The hippopotamus's day
Is passed in sleep; at night he hunts;
God works in a mysterious way —
The Church can sleep and feed at once.

I saw the 'potamus take wing   25
Ascending from the damp savannas,
And quiring angels round him sing
The praise of God, in loud hosannas.

Blood of the Lamb shall wash him clean
And him shall heavenly arms enfold,   30
Among the saints he shall be seen
Performing on a harp of gold.

He shall be washed as white as snow,
By all the martyr'd virgins kist,
While the True Church remains below   35
Wrapt in the old miasmal mist.

Gerontion[1]
(1920)

Like "Prufrock," this is a monologue in which the speaker, in characterizing himself, characterizes his society. Modern society, the poem tells us, has lost its faith and therefore been deprived of God's grace, which is symbolized as the life-giving rain.

The first section evokes the torpid, spiritually arid modern scene in concrete images which are at once sharply particularized and universal. In the second section the speaker cries out for a sign — a sign of coming rain, of God's grace — and he recalls the one great sign from God, the birth of Christ, who came as an infant (swaddled now in earth's darkness and ignorance), God's Word incarnate in an infant unable to speak a word. But the world has neglected this sign and has devoted itself to spiritually false or shallow faiths. The next section tells us why. It shows us the intricate hazards which Truth faces in this life of the flesh; man's boldness and cowardice alike betray him into error. The speaker sees himself as one of those who have lost Christ and who are thus disinherited. But unlike those about him, he does not seek life in the titillation of his jaded senses, for he knows that the sensual life is mortal and will not lead him to God. It faces destruction in relentless nature — the relentless spider and weevil. Unlike others in his society, the speaker recognizes the immense difficulties of the spiritual life, faces honestly and without sentimentality his present deprivation, and *desires*, at least, to return to God. This is the necessary first step to spiritual regeneration.

Thus this poem develops compactly and dramatically its spiritual argument, and for what it lacks in rigid logical coherence and explicit argument, offers an unusual richness of connotation, and an unusual freshness and vigor of rhythm.

——————————

Thou hast nor youth nor age
But as it were an after dinner sleep
Dreaming of both.[2]

Here I am, an old man in a dry month,
Being read to by a boy, waiting for rain.[3]

[1] From the Greek *geron*, meaning "old" or "old man."
[2] In Shakespeare's *Measure for Measure*, the Duke, disguised as a friar, advises a young man condemned to die not to fear death and tells him life is deceptive, empty of value, full of bitterness. He closes with these lines, carrying the theme of Eliot's poem.
[3] Compare A. C. Benson's *Life of Edward FitzGerald* (1905), 142: "Here he sits, in a dry month, old and blind, being read to by a country boy, longing for rain." FitzGerald wrote the immensely popular free poetic translation, *The Rubáiyát of Omar Khayyám* (1859), which expressed the mood of 19th-century melancholy and pessimism for many readers. "Hot gates" (l. 3) refers to Thermopylae where a small band of Spartans defeated the Persian host under Xerxes (480 B.C.) in a famous battle told by Herodotus.

I was neither at the hot gates
Nor fought in the warm rain,
Nor knee deep in the salt marsh, heaving a
    cutlass,   5
Bitten by flies, fought.
My house is a decayed house,
And the jew squats on the window sill, the
    owner,
Spawned in some estaminet 4 of Antwerp,
Blistered in Brussels, patched and peeled in
    London.   10
The goat coughs at night in the field overhead;
Rocks, moss, stonecrop, iron, merds.5
The woman keeps the kitchen, makes tea,
Sneezes at evening, poking the peevish gutter.
                        I an old man,   15
A dull head among windy spaces.

Signs are taken for wonders. "We would see a
    sign!"
The word within a word, unable to speak a word,
Swaddled with darkness. In the juvescence of
    the year
Came Christ the tiger 6   20
In depraved May, dogwood and chestnut, flow-
    ering judas,7
To be eaten, to be divided, to be drunk
Among whispers; by Mr. Silvero
With caressing hands, at Limoges
Who walked all night in the next room;   25

By Hakagawa, bowing among the Titians;
By Madame de Tornquist, in the dark room
Shifting the candles; Fräulein von Kulp 8
Who turned in the hall, one hand on the door.
    Vacant shuttles   30
Weave the wind. I have no ghosts,

An old man in a draughty house
Under a windy knob.

After such knowledge, what forgiveness? Think
    now
History has many cunning passages, contrived
    corridors   35
And issues, deceives with whispering ambitions,
Guides us by vanities. Think now
She gives when our attention is distracted
And what she gives, gives with such supple
    confusions
That the giving famishes the craving.9 Gives too
    late   40
What's not believed in, or if still believed,
In memory only, reconsidered passion. Gives
    too soon
Into weak hands, what's thought can be dis-
    pensed with
Till the refusal propagates a fear. Think
Neither fear nor courage saves us. Unnatural
    vices   45
Are fathered by our heroism. Virtues
Are forced upon us by our impudent crimes.
These tears are shaken from the wrath-bearing
    tree.1

The tiger springs in the new year. Us he de-
    vours.2 Think at last
We have not reached conclusion, when I   50
Stiffen in a rented house. Think at last
I have not made this show purposelessly
And it is not by any concitation
Of the backward devils.3
I would meet you upon this honestly.   55
I that was near your heart was removed there-
    from
To lose beauty in terror, terror in inquisition.
I have lost my passion: why should I need to
    keep it
Since what is kept must be adulterated?
I have lost my sight, smell, hearing, taste and
    touch: 60
How should I use them for your closer contact?

4 small café.   5 dung.
6 The Biblical echoes in these lines suggest the mysteries of Christianity, once passionately understood, and
now become empty rituals. "In the beginning was the
Word . . ." (John 1:1); "the babe wrapped in swad-
dling clothes" (Luke 2:12). Eliot admired the sermons
of Lancelot Andrewes (1555–1626), Bishop of Chi-
chester under James I, and in his essay on Andrewes,
he quotes the lines: "the word within a word, unable
to speak a word." Also, the unusual "Christ the tiger"
may be a variant of Andrewes' "Christ is no wildcat. . . ."
7 May is "depraved" because it is associated with the
crucifixion and betrayal of Christ. The theme is carried
out in the flowering "judas" tree and the "blood-twig"
dogwood. Compare this passage with the first paragraph of Ch. 18 in The Education of Henry Adams
where the same blooms suggest the "intermixture of
delicate grace and passionate depravity" of May.
8 The names are persons in Gerontion's reminiscences. But each, in a different way, represents a distortion of the true Christian meaning of the "Word".

9 A Shakespearean echo: "she makes hungry/ Where
she most satisfies." — Antony and Cleopatra, II, ii,
245–6.
1 Gerontion's own tree of knowledge or betrayal —
the "judas."
2 See ll. 20–23. Christ came in the "juvescence" of
the year (the Christian era) bringing hope; now, in
the "new" age (Second Coming) he brings vengeance
and judgment, "us he devours."
3 In this passage he attempts to justify himself to
Christ, at the day of Judgment, at the same time trying
to be "honest," and admitting his betrayal of Christ
(the "you" of the poem).

These with a thousand small deliberations
Protract the profit of their chilled delirium,
Excite the membrane, when the sense has
    cooled,
With pungent sauces, multiply variety   65
In a wilderness of mirrors. What will the spider
    do,
Suspend its operations, will the weevil
Delay? De Bailhache, Fresca, Mrs. Cammel,
    whirled
Beyond the circuit of the shuddering Bear
In fractured atoms.[4] Gull against the wind, in
    the windy straits   70
Of Belle Isle, or running on the Horn,[5]
White feathers in the snow, the Gulf claims,
And an old man driven by the Trades
To a sleepy corner.

                   Tenants of the house,[6]
Thoughts of a dry brain in a dry season.   75

The Waste Land

(1922)

This is one of the most discussed and most influential poems of our time. In it Eliot makes his most complex use of allusions, fitting together quotations from many sources in order to bring to bear upon his present statements numerous literary associations in a medley of parallels and ironic contrasts. Many of these references are explained in Eliot's own "Notes on 'The Waste Land,' " in his *Collected Poems*, pages 91–98. Eliot stated: "Not only the title, but the plan and a good deal of the incidental symbolism of the poem were suggested by Miss Jessie L. Weston's book on the Grail legend: *From Ritual to Romance*." He also used parts of Frazer's *The Golden Bough* for certain references to vegetation ceremonies. Miss Weston had connected the Fisher King of the fertility cults with the Grail legend in which the Lance and the Grail, the sacred vessel of the Last Supper, were sex symbols similar to those found in the Tarot pack. The interweaving of these symbols constitutes the central meaning of the poem, as they are applied to the modern waste land.

4 The names may be fictitious or, as Leavis suggests, names in the news of the day — "finance, crime, and divorce". All are destroyed in the final judgment of man — "fractured atoms."
5 "Bear": Ursa Minor, the northermost of the constellations. Belle Isle: straits of Newfoundland in the far north. Horn: Cape Horn, southernmost point of South America.
6 "Tenants" repeats the idea of the rented house (l. 51) and suggests the borrowed, transient aspect of Gerontion's life.

As in *Gerontion*, the poet is concerned with the problem of spiritual barrenness, or dryness — the loss of religion — but also with the remedies to this condition, represented variously as death and liberation, and as suffering followed by liberation and transformation. The inhabitants of the Waste Land, which is the present-day world, are at present incapable of these experiences. By mingling references to the Christian rites, to the legend of the Fisher King (a king who was sexually maimed and whose land was put under a curse and made a Waste Land), and to other fertility myths, the death act of liberation is further associated with the liberating of life-giving forces of water, which would relieve the drought of the Waste Land, while spiritual sterility is associated with sexual sterility. In the act of drowning — death by water — two of these symbols are fused into a major symbol. Other frequent symbols are roots, rocks, winter, spring, rubbish, rats, broken images, blindness, burial, bones, thunder. In addition, Eliot half-quotes or echoes many literary sources, especially Dante, Shakespeare, and the Bible.

"NAM Sibyllam quidem Cumis ego ipse oculis meis vidi in ampulla pendere, et cum illi pueri dicerent: Σίβυλλα τί θέλεις; respondebat illa: ἀποθανεῖν θέλω." [1]

For Ezra Pound
il miglior fabbro [2]

I. *The Burial of the Dead*

Here we see present day society, deprived of God's grace, sterile, torpid, reluctant to awaken from its torpidity (lines 1–7), and afraid of death. A series of literary, Biblical, and historical allusions add parallels to this spiritual situation, and develop the symbols outlined above. The spurious Madame Sosostris, like Madame de Tornquist, appears to be a fraudulent substitute for true spiritual vision. The last lines (60–70) suggest parallels between the Waste Land and London, Baudelaire's Paris, and Dante's Limbo, and sound the theme of the fertility myths.

1 The epigraph, from Petronius' *Satyricon*, tells of a dinner party presided over by the drunken Trimalchio in which he tells the guests he has seen the Cumaean Sybil (a prophetess) hanging in a cage with boys taunting her. When the boys cried: "Sybil, what do you want?" she replied: "I long to die." The Sybil had been granted eternal life, but had forgotten to ask for eternal youth. In Eliot's poem she is associated with Madame Sosostris, another false prophetess of the Waste Land, and Tiresias, the blind prophet, who has experienced love of both sexes. G. Williamson says: "Reduced to its simplest terms, *The Waste Land* is a statement of the experience that drives a character to the fortune-teller, the fortune that is told, and the unfolding of that fortune."
2 The Italian dedication (taken from Dante's description of Arnaut Daniel) to Ezra Pound may be rendered: "the better craftsman." Eliot indicated his debt to Pound who helped him revise the poem.

April is the cruelest month, breeding
Lilacs out of the dead land,[3] mixing
Memory and desire, stirring
Dull roots with spring rain.
Winter kept us warm, covering   5
Earth in forgetful snow, feeding
A little life with dried tubers.
Summer surprised us, coming over the Starn-
        bergersee
With a shower of rain; we stopped in the
        colonnade,
And went on in sunlight, into the Hofgarten, 10
And drank coffee, and talked for an hour.
Bin gar keine Russin, stamm' aus Litauen, echt
        deutsch.[4]
And when we were children, staying at the
        archduke's,
My cousin's, he took me out on a sled,
And I was frightened. He said, Marie,   15
Marie, hold on tight. And down we went.
In the mountains, there you feel free.
I read, much of the night, and go south in the
        winter.

What are the roots that clutch, what branches
        grow
Out of this stony rubbish? Son of man,   20
You cannot say, or guess, for you know only
A heap of broken images, where the sun beats,
And the dead tree gives no shelter, the cricket
        no relief,
And the dry stone no sound of water.[5] Only
There is shadow under this red rock,   25
(Come in under the shadow of this red rock),
And I will show you something different from
        either
Your shadow at morning striding behind you
Or your shadow at evening rising to meet you;
I will show you fear in a handful of dust.   30
        Frisch weht der Wind
        Der Heimat zu
        Mein Irisch Kind,
        Wo weilest du?[6]

"You gave me hyacinths first a year ago;   35
"They called me the hyacinth girl."
— Yet when we came back, late, from the
        Hyacinth garden,
Your arms full, and your hair wet, I could not
Speak, and my eyes failed, I was neither
Living nor dead, and I knew nothing,   40
Looking into the heart of light, the silence.[7]
Oed' und leer das Meer.

Madame Sosostris,[8] famous clairvoyante,
Had a bad cold, nevertheless
Is known to be the wisest woman in Europe, 45
With a wicked pack of cards. Here, said she,
Is your card, the drowned Phoenician Sailor,
(Those are pearls that were his eyes.[9] Look!)
Here is Belladonna, the Lady of the Rocks,
The lady of situations.   50
Here is the man with three staves, and here the
        Wheel,
And here is the one-eyed merchant, and this
        card,
Which is blank, is something he carries on his
        back,
Which I am forbidden to see. I do not find
The Hanged Man. Fear death by water.   55
I see crowds of people, walking round in a ring.
Thank you. If you see dear Mrs. Equitone,
Tell her I bring the horoscope myself:
One must be so careful these days.

Unreal City,[1]   60
Under the brown fog of a winter dawn,
A crowd flowed over London Bridge, so many,

---

[3] An ironic reversal of the Vegetation rites where spring restored the Fisher King to potency. Lilacs symbolized fertility in the primitive legends.

[4] Chance talk overheard in a café in Munich, reflecting post-World War I conditions in Germany: "I am not a Russian, but pure German from Lithuania."

[5] Cf. Ecclesiastes 12:5. The Preacher warns of the days to come when "the almond tree shall flourish, and the grasshopper shall be a burden, and desire shall fail. . . . Then shall the dust return to the earth as it was."

[6] From Wagner's Tristan und Isolde, Act I: "Fresh blows the wind/ To home, and now/ My Irish maid/ Where waitest thou?" For the unhappy love experiences etched here, see C. Brooks, p. 1164, below.

[7] Describes the effect of the vision of the Holy Grail (a symbol of purity and holiness) upon the impure. — G. Williamson.

[8] Madame Sosostris is an example of the way true prophecy has been perverted in the Waste Land to mere fortune-telling. The Tarot cards, once used for purposes of divining the coming of the waters, have now fallen into disuse, their significance forgotten. "The Hanged Man, a member of the traditional pack, fits my purpose in two ways: because he is associated in my mind with the Hanged God of Frazer, and because I associate him with the hooded figure in the passage of the disciples to Emmaus in Part V. The Phoenician Sailor and the Merchant appear later. . . . The Man with Three Staves (an authentic member of the Tarot pack) I associate, quite arbitrarily, with the Fisher King himself" (Eliot's note). He has also noted that "all the women are one woman," suggesting the connection between Marie (l. 15), Belladonna (l. 49), and the various ladies of "situations" in Part II.

[9] Shakespeare's The Tempest, I, ii, 398 in which there is also a death and transformation by drowning.

[1] See Brooks, p. 1165, below, for identification of "The Unreal City" as Baudelaire's Paris, London, and Dante's Purgatory.

I had not thought death had undone so many.[2]
Sighs, short and infrequent, were exhaled,
And each man fixed his eyes before his feet.   65
Flowed up the hill and down King William
    Street
To where Saint Mary Woolnoth kept the hours
With a dead sound on the final stroke of nine.
There I saw one I knew, and stopped him cry-
    ing: "Stetson! [3]   69
"You who were with me in the ships at Mylae! [4]
"That corpse you planted last year in your
    garden,
"Has it begun to sprout? Will it bloom this
    year?
"Or has the sudden frost disturbed its bed?
"Oh keep the Dog far hence, that's friend to
    men,
"Or with his nails he'll dig it up again! [5]   75
"You! hypocrite lecteur! — mon semblable, —
    mon frère!" [6]

II. A *Game of Chess* [7]

❧ The opening description of material ("synthetic") splendor and the references to the Philomela
legend, which presents one aspect of the theme of
suffering and transformation — of beauty out of
violence, suffering, or death — lead to the two concluding scenes, in which modern sexual and intellectual sterility image the spiritual sterility of the
modern world.

The Chair she sat in, like a burnished throne,[8]
Glowed on the marble, where the glass
Held up by standards wrought with fruited vines
From which a golden Cupidon peeped out   80
(Another hid his eyes behind his wing)
Doubled the flames of sevenbranched cande-
    labra
Reflecting light upon the table as
The glitter of her jewels rose to meet it,
From satin cases poured in rich profusion;   85
In vials of ivory and colored glass
Unstoppered, lurked her strange synthetic per-
    fumes,
Unguent, powdered, or liquid — troubled, con-
    fused
And drowned the sense in odors; stirred by the
    air
That freshened from the window, these
    ascended   90
In fattening the prolonged candle-flames,
Flung their smoke into the laquearia,
Stirring the pattern on the coffered ceiling.
Huge sea-wood fed with copper
Burned green and orange, framed by the colored
    stone,   95
In which sad light a carvèd dolphin swam.
Above the antique mantel was displayed
As though a window gave upon the sylvan scene
The change of Philomel, by the barbarous king
So rudely forced; yet there the nightingale   100
Filled all the desert with inviolable voice
And still she cried, and still the world pursues,
"Jug Jug" to dirty ears.[9]
And other withered stumps of time
Were told upon the walls; staring forms   105
Leaned out, leaning, hushing the room enclosed.
Footsteps shuffled on the stair.
Under the firelight, under the brush, her hair
Spread out in fiery points   109
Glowed into words, then would be savagely still.

[2] Dante, *Inferno*, iii, 55–57. Watching a crowd of people crossing London Bridge, the poet is reminded of Dante, seeing a crowd in hell and saying: "So great a crowd of people. I had not believed Death had undone so many."

[3] Stetson is any man in the Waste Land, a friend of the protagonist, or one of the crowd of damned whom Dante recognizes in purgatory.

[4] At the battle of Mylae (260 B.C.) the Romans defeated the Carthaginians on the sea. By linking Stetson with the ancient battle, Eliot associates modern wars with all wars, equally destructive.

[5] In Webster's *The White Devil*, a play of murder, passion, fratricide, and betrayal, a mad woman, Cornelia, sings a dirge while burying her son who has been murdered by his brother: "But keep the wolf far thence that's foe to men/Or with his nails he'll dig them [i.e. the friendless bodies of unburied men] up again." Eliot alters "wolf" to "Dog," capitalizing the word to refer to Sirius, the Dogstar which, according to Frazer's *The Golden Bough*, appeared at its brightest at the rising of the waters of the Nile — hence a *friend* to man.

[6] In Baudelaire's *Les Fleurs du Mal*, the poet describes himself as sunk in suffering and boredom and addresses the reader as like himself: "You, hypocrite reader, my likeness, my brother!"

[7] The title and later references in this section to a chess-game draw on the play of Middleton, *Women Beware Women*, Act II, in which a mother is kept playing chess in one room while her daughter is being seduced in another. Middleton has both scenes take place at once on the stage and arranges for the mother to be checkmated at the same moment the daughter, Bianca, is seduced by the Duke. See ll. 137–8 below.

[8] Cf. Shakespeare's *Antony and Cleopatra*, II, ii, 199 ff., where Cleopatra is described lying in splendor on a barge "like a burnished throne" going to meet Antony. The lady is Belladonna, "lady of situations," a woman of the Waste Land. Eliot alters "barge" to "Chair," suggesting the constellation Cassiopeia, shaped like a chair, and named for a mythical queen whose vanity brought destruction to her country.

[9] Ovid, *Metamorphoses*, VI, 412 ff., describes the rape of Philomela by King Tereus of Thrace who then cut out her tongue to silence her. The gods, in pity, changed her into a nightingale. The "jug-jug" was common in Elizabethan songs comparing a ravished woman to Philomela. "Tereu" is Tereus. See Part III, ll. 203–206.

"My nerves are bad tonight. Yes, bad. Stay
    with me.
"Speak to me. Why do you never speak. Speak.
"What are you thinking of? What thinking?
    What?
"I never know what you are thinking. Think."

I think we are in rats' alley [1]   115
Where the dead men lost their bones.

"What is that noise?"
        The wind under the door.
"What is that noise now? What is the wind
    doing?"
        Nothing again nothing.[2]   120
            "Do
"You know nothing? Do you see nothing? Do
    you remember
"Nothing?"

    I remember
Those are pearls that were his eyes.[3]   125
"Are you alive or not? Is there nothing in your
    head?"
                But
O O O O that Shakespeherian Rag — [4]
It's so elegant
So intelligent   130
"What shall I do now? What shall I do?"
"I shall rush out as I am, and walk the street
"With my hair down, so. What shall we do
    tomorrow?
"What shall we ever do?"
        The hot water at ten.   135
And if it rains, a closed car at four.
And we shall play a game of chess,
Pressing lidless eyes and waiting for a knock
    upon the door.[5]

When Lil's husband got demobbed, I said —
I didn't mince my words, I said to her myself,   140

1 Another image of the sterility and spiritual death
of the Waste Land.
2 Echoes of lines in two of Webster's plays. In The
Devil's Law Case, the dying Duke is saved when his
enemy stabs him a second time, opening the wound to
allow it to drain. The surgeon, hearing him breathe,
says: "Is the wind in that doore still?" — i.e. is he still
living? In The White Devil, when Flamineo is about to
be killed, his murderer asks: "What dost think on?" and
he replies: "Nothing; of nothing."
3 Shakespeare's The Tempest. Cf. note to l. 48.
4 Eliot parodies a popular song of 1912, "The Shake-
spearian Rag," by way of comment on the modern distortion of the classics.
5 The lady, neurotic and bored, like the woman in
Webster's play, waits for some similar experience or
sign. Cf. note to "A Game of Chess" (Part II).

HURRY UP PLEASE ITS TIME [6]
Now Albert's coming back, make yourself a bit
    smart.
He'll want to know what you done with that
    money he gave you
To get yourself some teeth. He did, I was there.
You have them all out, Lil, and get a nice set,   145
He said, I swear, I can't bear to look at you.
And no more can't I, I said, and think of poor
    Albert,
He's been in the army four years, he wants a
    good time,
And if you don't give it him, there's others will,
    I said.
Oh is there, she said. Something o' that, I said.
Then I'll know who to thank, she said, and
    give me a straight look.   151
HURRY UP PLEASE ITS TIME
If you don't like it you can get on with it, I
    said.
Others can pick and choose if you can't.
But if Albert makes off, it won't be for lack of
    telling.   155
You ought to be ashamed, I said, to look so
    antique
(And her only thirty-one.)
I can't help it, she said, pulling a long face,
It's them pills I took, to bring it off, she said.
(She's had five already, and nearly died of young
    George.)   160
The chemist said it would be all right, but I've
    never been the same.
You are a proper fool, I said.
Well, if Albert won't leave you alone, there it
    is, I said,
What you get married for if you don't want
    children?
HURRY UP PLEASE ITS TIME   165
Well, that Sunday Albert was home, they had
    a hot gammon,[7]
And they asked me in to dinner, to get the
    beauty of it hot —
HURRY UP PLEASE ITS TIME
HURRY UP PLEASE ITS TIME
Goonight Bill. Goonight Lou. Goonight May.
    Goonight.   170
Ta ta. Goonight. Goonight.
Good night, ladies, good night, sweet ladies,
    good night, good night.[8]

6 The customary call of the bartender in a London
"pub" telling the customers that it is closing time.
7 A side of ham.
8 In Hamlet, IV, v, 67 ff., Ophelia, out of her mind,
sings songs and ends her wild talk with: "Good-night,
ladies; good-night, sweet ladies; good-night, good-night."

III. *The Fire Sermon* [9]

Here references to Spenser's *Prothalamion* appear among scenes in the Waste Land and scenes along the twentieth-century river bank, and among references to *The Tempest*, to the nightingale, and to the grail rituals and their vulgar parallel in the Mrs. Porter song. Then present-day society is adumbrated again in the dubious proposition of Mr. Eugenides and the scenes of sterile, casual, joyless lust, with interjections of the themes of spiritual regeneration (lines 257–265) and the songs of the Rhine Daughters. The conclusion cites the writings of Buddha and Augustine on lust.

The river's tent is broken: the last fingers of leaf
Clutch and sink into the wet bank. The wind
Crosses the brown land, unheard. The nymphs are departed.   175
Sweet Thames, run softly, till I end my song.[1]
The river bears no empty bottles, sandwich papers,
Silk handkerchiefs, cardboard boxes, cigarette ends
Or other testimony of summer nights. The nymphs are departed.
And their friends, the loitering heirs of city directors;   180
Departed, have left no addresses.
By the waters of Leman I sat down and wept [2] . . .
Sweet Thames, run softly till I end my song,
Sweet Thames, run softly, for I speak not loud or long.
But at my back in a cold blast I hear   185
The rattle of the bones, and chuckle spread from ear to ear.
A rat crept softly through the vegetation
Dragging its slimy belly on the bank
While I was fishing in the dull canal
On a winter evening round behind the gashouse   190
Musing upon the king my brother's wreck
And on the king my father's death before him.
White bodies naked on the low damp ground

And bones cast in a little low dry garret,
Rattled by the rat's foot only, year to year.   195
But at my back from time to time I hear [3]
The sound of horns and motors, which shall bring
Sweeney to Mrs. Porter in the spring.
O the moon shone bright on Mrs. Porter
And on her daughter   200
They wash their feet in soda water [4]
Et O ces voix d'enfants, chantant dans la coupole! [5]

Twit twit twit
Jug jug jug jug jug jug
So rudely forc'd.   205
Tereu

Unreal City
Under the brown fog of a winter noon
Mr. Eugenides, the Smyrna merchant
Unshaven, with a pocket full of currants   210
C.i.f. London: [6] documents at sight,
Asked me in demotic French
To luncheon at the Cannon Street Hotel
Followed by a weekend at the Metropole.

At the violet hour, when the eyes and back   215
Turn upward from the desk, when the human engine waits
Like a taxi throbbing waiting,

9 Cf. note to l. 307.
1 Eliot compares the tawdry scene along the Thames river at present (c. 1920) with the beautiful wedding hymn of Edmund Spenser's "Prothalamion" (1596) describing a procession of nymphs on the same river. This is one line from the poem.
2 In Psalm 137, the Jews weep over their exile from Palestine: "By the rivers of Babylon, there we sat down, yea, we wept, when we remembered Zion." Lac Leman is the French name for Lake Geneva in Switzerland.

3 This and the following lines contain a medley of quotations and echoes. In Marvell's "To His Coy Mistress" are the lines: "But at my back I always hear/ Time's winged chariot hurrying near." The poet urges his mistress not to be coy, as time is passing and beauty fades.
4 Sweeney appears in a number of Eliot's poems, always as a type of the debased human animal, living on the lowest plane of sex and appetite. Mrs. Porter and her daughter were part of a vulgar ballad sung by soldiers in World War I. They kept a bawdy house in Cairo and practiced precautionary ablutions.
5 From Paul Verlaine's sonnet, "Parsifal," which translated reads: "And, O those children's voices chanting in the dome!" In the story of the Grail, Parsifal, having resisted the seductions of the temptress, Kundry, is granted power to enter the castle and to heal the wounds of the king with his lance. First, however, his feet are washed by Kundry, whose taint is thus cleansed. Parsifal becomes king and receives the Holy Grail. In celebration, the children sing from the choir loft, as in the lines from Verlaine's poem. Eliot ironically places this line alongside the vulgar foot-washing of Mrs. Porter.
6 "Carriage and insurance free to London" — a banking phrase. Mr. Eugenides, Eliot says in a note, "melts into the Phoenician sailor, and the latter is not wholly distinct from Ferdinand Prince of Naples." He is a "one-eyed" business man, making the protagonist an indecent proposal — thus bringing the ideas of lust, perversion, and profit into a single character.

I Tiresias,[7] though blind, throbbing between two
    lives,
Old man with wrinkled female breasts, can see
At the violet hour, the evening hour that strives
Homeward, and brings the sailor home from the
    sea,   221
The typist home at teatime, clears her breakfast,
    lights
Her stove, and lays out food in tins.
Out of the window perilously spread
Her drying combinations touched by the sun's
    last rays,   225
On the divan are piled (at night her bed)
Stockings, slippers, camisoles, and stays.
I Tiresias, old man with wrinkled dugs
Perceived the scene, and foretold the rest —
I too awaited the expected guest.   230
He, the young man carbuncular, arrives,
A small house agent's clerk, with one bold stare,
One of the low on whom assurance sits
As a silk hat on a Bradford millionaire.
The time is now propitious, as he guesses, 235
The meal is ended, she is bored and tired,
Endeavors to engage her in caresses
Which still are unreproved, if undesired.
Flushed and decided, he assaults at once;
Exploring hands encounter no defense;   240
His vanity requires no response,
And makes a welcome of indifference.
(And I Tiresias have foresuffered all
Enacted on this same divan or bed;
I who have sat by Thebes below the wall   245
And walked among the lowest of the dead.)
Bestows one final patronizing kiss,
And gropes his way, finding the stairs unlit . . .

She turns and looks a moment in the glass,
Hardly aware of her departed lover;   250
Her brain allows one half-formed thought to
    pass:

[7] Eliot explains that the two sexes meet in Tiresias, the blind prophet, and "what Tiresias *sees*, in fact, is the substance of the poem." He cites the passage from Ovid's *Metamorphoses*, III, 316 ff., describing how Tiresias was turned into a woman when he struck two serpents coupling in the forest. Seven years later, seeing the same serpents, he struck them again and was restored to manhood. Having experienced both sexes, he was asked to judge an argument between Jove and Juno as to which sex experienced most pleasure in love. When he supported Jove, Juno punished him by blinding him. Jove, in compensation, gave him the gift of prophecy. Thus Eliot places Tiresias in a central position in the poem, as one who sees the lust and boredom of such scenes as the following between the typist and the young man carbuncular. Tiresias lived at Thebes and was consulted where he sat near the wall. After his death he went to Hades, still retaining his powers, and was visited by Ulysses. Cf. ll. 245–246.

"Well now that's done: and I'm glad it's over."
When lovely woman stoops to folly [8] and
Paces about her room again, alone,
She smooths her hair with automatic hand, 255
And puts a record on the gramophone.

"This music crept by me upon the waters" [9]
And along the Strand, up Queen Victoria Street.
O City city, I can sometimes hear
Beside a public bar in Lower Thames Street, 260
The pleasant whining of a mandolin
And a clatter and a chatter from within
Where fishermen lounge at noon: where the
    walls
Of Magnus Martyr [1] hold   264
Inexplicable splendor of Ionian white and gold.

The river sweats [2]
Oil and tar
The barges drift
With the turning tide
Red sails   270
Wide
To leeward, swing on the heavy spar.
The barges wash
Drifting logs
Down Greenwich reach   275
Past the Isle of Dogs.
       Weialala leia
       Wallala leialala

Elizabeth and Leicester [3]
Beating oars   280

[8] The phrase comes from Goldsmith's *The Vicar of Wakefield* where Olivia, who has been seduced, sings a song which says that "when lovely woman stoops to folly" her only course is to die. Eliot makes the contrast between her thought and the resigned acceptance of the typist.

[9] This line, like ll. 48, 191–192, is from Shakespeare's *The Tempest:* "Sitting on a bank/ Weeping again the king my father's wrack/ This music crept by me upon the waters."

[1] Church built by Christopher Wren which was regarded by Eliot as having a particularly fine interior. It is located near London Bridge among bars where fishermen congregate.

[2] "The Song of the (three) Thames-daughters begins here. From line 292 to 306 inclusive they speak in turn. V. *Götterdämmerung*, III, i: the Rhine-daughters" (Eliot's note). In the Wagner opera the three Rhine-daughters lament the theft of their gold and the loss of the beauty of the river. The two introductory stanzas describe the Thames in the present time and at the time of Elizabeth.

[3] The scene depicted here is taken by Eliot from Froude's life of *Elizabeth*, Vol. I, Ch. iv, in which the Bishop De Quadra, ambassador of Spain to England, writes a letter recounting Elizabeth's love for Lord Robert Leicester. Eliot, in a note, quotes the De Quadra letter: "In the afternoon we were in a barge,

The stern was formed
A gilded shell
Red and gold
The brisk swell
Rippled both shores   285
Southwest wind
Carried down stream
The peal of bells
White towers
      Weialala leia   290
      Wallala leialala

"Trams and dusty trees.
Highbury bore me. Richmond and Kew
Undid me.[4] By Richmond I raised my knees
Supine on the floor of a narrow canoe."   295

"My feet are at Moorgate, and my heart
Under my feet. After the event
He wept. He promised 'a new start.'
I made no comment. What should I resent?"

"On Margate Sands.   300
I can connect
Nothing with nothing
The broken fingernails of dirty hands.
My people humble people who expect
Nothing."   305
      la la

To Carthage then I came [5]

Burning burning burning burning [6]

watching the games on the river. (The queen) was
alone with Lord Robert and myself on the poop, when
they began to talk nonsense, and went so far that Lord
Robert at last said, as I was on the spot there was no
reason why they should not be married if the queen
pleased." Eliot places this courtly flirtation alongside
the three episodes of seduction which follow.
  4 The three stanzas which follow are the laments of
three daughters of the Thames, Waste Land counter-
parts of the Rhine maidens, recounting their love-ex-
periences in the park and resort areas near London such
as Richmond and Kew. Highbury is a working-class
neighborhood; Moorgate, a warehouse district near London Bridge. Margate Sands is a popular resort on the
Thames estuary.
  5 From St. Augustine's *Confessions*, III, i. Carthage,
notorious as a place of lust and unholy love, was the
scene of Augustine's confession of his own impure desires. He called on God's help to pluck him out of the
cauldron of passions of his youth; cf. ll. 309–310.
  6 Eliot refers the reader to the complete text of Buddha's Fire Sermon from which this line is taken. The
passage (which Eliot says "corresponds in importance
to the Sermon on the Mount") calls for a life free from
burning passions and all depravity and a dedication to
the pure and holy way. Eliot adds: "The collocation
of these two representatives of eastern and western asceticism, as the culmination of this part of the poem,
is not an accident."

O Lord Thou pluckest me out
O Lord Thou pluckest   310

burning

IV. *Death by Water* [7]

Death by water brings a kind of peace, brings an
end to the lust, fear, and pettiness of the first three
parts.

Phlebas the Phoenician, a fortnight dead,
Forgot the cry of gulls, and the deep sea swell
And the profit and loss.
         A current under sea 315
Picked his bones in whispers. As he rose and
    fell
He passed the stages of his age and youth
Entering the whirlpool.
            Gentile or Jew
O you who turn the wheel [8] and look to wind-
    ward,   320
Consider Phlebas, who was once handsome and
    tall as you.

V. *What the Thunder Said*

We return here to the Christ theme. Christ is
not yet risen, but there is thunder over distant mountains. Then the arid Waste Land is again described.
Abruptly we are on the journey to Emmaus, with
Christ risen but not yet seen or recognized. Nightmare visions of the decay of eastern Europe and of
death and destruction and aridity lead to a vision of
the long awaited rain. The thunder speaks the formula for the removal of the curse — give, sympathise, control. But this formula has not yet been
satisfied by the society. The protagonist sits by his
still arid plain, considering the task of setting at least
his own affairs in order. He sees the problem clearly

  7 Part IV is an adaptation of part of an earlier poem
by Eliot in French called *Dans le Restaurant* in which
an old waiter describes to a patron his earliest sex experience at the age of seven. The lecherous waiter is
identified with Phlebas the Phoenician, the drowned
sailor of Madame Sosostris' Tarot cards. Both are purified by death in water, as was the fertility god of the
pagan rituals whose image was thrown into the water as
a symbol of fertility and resurrected again in the spring.
Here the waiter, Phlebas, and Ferdinand of *The Tempest* seem to represent the purification of the lust depicted in Part III.
  8 The wheel: one of the Tarot cards allegorizing the
wheel of fortune. The god, Anubis, in the figure of a
jackal, is represented on one side and Typhon, as a
serpent, on the other. The wheel itself is turned by a
figure holding a sword and a crown. The "whirlpool"
is the mystery of man's fate, his death and cleansing
in the water.

enough now, but the great task, the great ordeal
lies before him. The last line signifies the peace to
be achieved through the formula.

After the torchlight red on sweaty faces
After the frosty silence in the gardens [9]
After the agony in stony places
The shouting and the crying   325
Prison and palace and reverberation
Of thunder of spring over distant mountains
He who was living is now dead
We who were living are now dying
With a little patience   330

Here is no water but only rock [1]
Rock and no water and the sandy road
The road winding above among the mountains
Which are mountains of rock without water
If there were water we should stop and drink 335
Amongst the rock one cannot stop or think
Sweat is dry and feet are in the sand
If there were only water amongst the rock
Dead mountain mouth of carious teeth that
          cannot spit
Here one can neither stand nor lie nor sit   340
There is not even silence in the mountains
But dry sterile thunder without rain
There is not even solitude in the mountains
But red sullen faces sneer and snarl
From doors of mudcracked houses   345
                    If there were water
  And no rock
  If there were rock
  And also water
  And water   350
  A spring
  A pool among the rock
  If there were the sound of water only
  Not the cicada
  And dry grass singing   355
  But sound of water over a rock
  Where the hermit-thrush sings in the pine
          trees
  Drip drop drip drop drop drop drop
  But there is no water   359

Who is the third who walks always beside you? [2]

9 The Garden of Gethsemane and that of Golgotha,
scenes of Christ's betrayal, crucifixion, and burial.
1 The Journey to Emmaus begins here and proceeds
through a bleak and sterile country in which images
of the Waste Land and echoes of Ecclesiastes prevail,
relieved only by the song of the thrush (l. 357) and the
illusion of dripping water to relieve the drought.
2 Christ, risen from the dead, accompanies the disciples to Emmaus, but (cf. Luke 24:16) "their eyes

When I count, there are only you and I together
But when I look ahead up the white road
There is always another one walking beside you
Gliding wrapped in a brown mantle, hooded
I do not know whether a man or woman   364
— But who is that on the other side of you?

What is that sound high in the air [3]
Murmur of maternal lamentation
Who are those hooded hordes swarming
Over endless plains, stumbling in cracked earth
Ringed by the flat horizon only   370
What is the city over the mountains
Cracks and reforms and bursts in the violet air
Falling towers
Jerusalem Athens Alexandria
Vienna London   375
Unreal

A woman drew her long black hair out tight [4]
And fiddled whisper music on those strings
And bats with baby faces in the violet light
Whistled, and beat their wings   380
And crawled head downward down a blackened
          wall
And upside down in air were towers
Tolling reminiscent bells, that kept the hours
And voices singing out of empty cisterns and
          exhausted wells.

In this decayed hole among the mountains 385
In the faint moonlight, the grass is singing
Over the tumbled graves, about the chapel [5]
There is the empty chapel, only the wind's
          home.

were holden that they should not know him." Eliot's
note cites one of the Antarctic expeditions of the time
in which the explorers, nearly exhausted, had a delusion
that there was one more member with them than could
actually be counted.
3 This passage depicts a nightmare vision of the decay of eastern Europe, stimulated by Eliot's reading of
Hermann Hesse's German book, A Glimpse into Chaos.
The passage records the fear of Europe over the turbulence of the Russian revolution, presaging a general
cracking up of western civilization.
4 For an interpretation of the images and meaning of
this passage, see the essay by Brooks (p. 1172).
5 To the theme of Christ's trial and agony is now
added the strange initiation of the knight of the Grail
legends approaching the Chapel Perilous and the Perilous Cemetery, prior to his vision of the Grail. In the
legends recounted in From Ritual to Romance there is
a storm and great wind, an altar in the chapel, a dead
body upon it, sometimes candles and a Black Hand
which extinguishes them. The significance of the
knight's ordeal seems lost in the Waste Land where
only an empty chapel is seen with a weathercock in
place of the prophetic crowing of the cock in Luke
22, which announces Peter's denial of Christ.

It has no windows, and the door swings,
Dry bones can harm no one.   390
Only a cock stood on the rooftree
Co co rico co co rico
In a flash of lightning. Then a damp gust
Bringing rain

Ganga was sunken,[6] and the limp leaves   395
Waited for rain, while the black clouds
Gathered far distant, over Himavant
The jungle crouched, humped in silence.
Then spoke the thunder
DA   400
Datta: [7] what we given?
My friend, blood shaking my heart
The awful daring of a moment's surrender
Which an age of prudence can never retract
By this, and this only, we have existed [8]   405
Which is not to be found in our obituaries
Or in memories draped by the beneficent spider
Or under seals broken by the lean solicitor
In our empty rooms
DA   410
Dayadhvam: I have heard the key
Turn in the door once and turn once only [9]
We think of the key, each in his prison
Thinking of the key, each confirms a prison
Only at nightfall, ethereal rumors   415
Revive for a moment a broken Coriolanus [1]
DA
Damyata: The boat responded
Gaily, to the hand expert with sail and oar
The sea was calm, your heart would have re-
    sponded   420
Gaily, when invited, beating obedient
To controlling hands

I sat upon the shore
Fishing,[2] with the arid plain behind me
Shall I at least set my lands in order? [3]   425
London Bridge is falling down falling down
    falling down
Poi s'ascose nel foco che gli affina [4]
Quando fiam uti chelidon — O swallow swallow [5]
Le Prince d' Aquitaine à la tour abolie [6]
These fragments I have shored against my
    ruins   430
Why then Ile fit you. Hieronymo's mad againe.[7]
Datta. Dayadhvam. Damyata.
          Shantih   shantih   shantih [8]

Animula

(w. 1929)

This poem, like the fourth part of "Gerontion,"
is concerned with spiritual hazards of this world. The
soul as it comes from God is symbolized in the simple
life of the infant, who responds forthrightly to his
world and takes pleasure in its beauty. But time in
this life of the flesh has its way with him. He becomes misshapen, distrustful, self-conscious, and no
longer simple; he engages in futile and self-destroy-

6 The Ganges River, scene of the early vegetation
myths, had its source in the Himalaya mountains
("Himavant"). The thunder and rain were the promise of spring and fertility over the land.
7 " 'Datta, dayadhvam, damyata' (Give, sympathise,
control). The fable of the meaning of the Thunder is
found in the *Brihadaranyaka — Upanishad*, 5, 1"
(Eliot's note). Here the thunder speaks the words of
the wise man to the protagonist of the poem: self-giving,
self-control, and compassion.
8 Giving in the Waste Land has been only a
momentary surrender, that of sex, but even that is
some evidence of existence and a sign of forgiveness.
9 Eliot cites Dante, *Inferno,* xxxiii, 46: "And below
I heard the door of the horrible tower being locked."
Count Ugolino had been imprisoned by Archbishop
Ruggieri along with his sons and grandsons. The door
was locked and the keys of the prison thrown away.
In the ninth circle of hell, he is found gnawing upon
the head of the archbishop. The incident is a type of
all self-imprisonment.
1 Coriolanus of Shakespeare's play is another type
of self-pride and self-interest told under the admonish-
ment of "sympathise."

2 Eliot's note here refers the reader to Miss Weston's
chapter "The Fisher King" in which Christian symbolism of "fish," as applied to Christ and the Apostles is
likewise derived from pagan symbols in which the
fish is a life-force and indicates fertility and birth.
3 Cf. Isaiah 38:1: "Set thine house in order: for
thou shalt die, not live."
4 The quotation is from Dante, *Purgatorio,* xxvi, 148.
Arnaut Daniel, a Provençal poet who has sinned in
lust, asks Dante to remember his pain when he ascends
the stairway leading to Paradise. Then, says Dante,
"he disappeared into the purifying flame."
5 Eliot's note on the swallow refers to a medieval
poem called "Pervigilium Veneris" ("Nights of Venus")
in which all nature celebrates the time of love. The
nightingale (symbol of betrayed beauty, and likewise
the voiceless artist) cries: "when shall I be as the
swallow and cease to be voiceless?"
6 Eliot's note refers to a sonnet by Gerard de Nerval,
entitled *El Desdichado,* in which the poet, bereaved
and inconsolable, bewails his fate in melancholy strain
and compares himself to "the Prince of Acquitaine in
the ruined tower."
7 From Thomas Kyd's *Spanish Tragedy,* an Elizabethan play of murder, madness, and violence, sub-
titled "Hieronymo Is Mad Again." Hieronymo is asked
by the king to perform a play. Seeking revenge for the
murder of his son, he says to the king: "Why, then, I'll
fit you!" — i.e. he will do the play and revenge himself at the same time, which he does, but is killed himself during the performance. Earlier, he has bitten off
his tongue to avoid confessing, an incident which recalls the theme of the nightingale, Philomela, referred
to in the lines about the swallow, above.
8 "Shantih. Repeated as here, a formal ending to an
Upanishad. 'The Peace which passeth understanding' is
our equivalent to this word" (Eliot's note).

ing pursuits. Note how the characteristic Eliot image in line 30 compactly symbolizes much human shabbiness and futility. And note, too, how the alteration of the traditional prayer in the last line points up the argument.

"Issues from the hand of God, the simple soul"
To a flat world of changing lights and noise,
To light, dark, dry or damp, chilly or warm;
Moving between the legs of tables and of chairs,
Rising or falling, grasping at kisses and toys, 5
Advancing boldly, sudden to take alarm,
Retreating to the corner of arm and knee,
Eager to be reassured, taking pleasure
In the fragrant brilliance of the Christmas tree,
Pleasure in the wind, the sunlight and the sea;
Studies the sunlit pattern on the floor 11
And running stags around a silver tray;
Confounds the actual and the fanciful,
Content with playing-cards and kings and
    queens,
What the fairies do and what the servants
    say. 15
The heavy burden of the growing soul
Perplexes and offends more, day by day;
Week by week, offends and perplexes more
With the imperatives of "is and seems"
And may and may not, desire and control. 20
The pain of living and the drug of dreams
Curl up the small soul in the window seat
Behind the *Encyclopaedia Britannica.*
Issues from the hand of time the simple soul
Irresolute and selfish, misshapen, lame, 25
Unable to fare forward or retreat,
Fearing the warm reality, the offered good,
Denying the importunity of the blood,
Shadow of its own shadows, spectre in its own
    gloom,
Leaving disordered papers in a dusty room; 30
Living first in the silence after the viaticum.

Pray for Guiterriez,[9] avid of speed and power,
For Boudin, blown to pieces,
For this one who made a great fortune,
And that one who went his own way. 35
Pray for Floret, by the boarhound slain between
    the yew trees,
Pray for us now and at the hour of our birth.

[9] "As for the references about which you ask in the poem Animula . . . the third of these figures is so entirely imaginary that there is really no identification to be made. . . . Of the first two, it is only necessary to say they represent different types of career, the successful person of the machine age and someone who was killed in the last war." — Eliot.

Ash Wednesday
(1930)

The ritual of Ash Wednesday is the anointing of the forehead with ashes, while the priest recites: "Remember, man, that thou art dust, and unto dust thou shalt return." The student who wishes to understand this poem fully must trace the many other scriptural references and give the poem careful study, probably with the aid of one of the many published explications. See, for example, George Williamson, *A Reader's Guide to T. S. Eliot,* pp. 168–185, or Leonard Unger, *T. S. Eliot: A Selected Critique,* pp. 349–394.

1

The poem begins in despair. The poet is weary of the things of this world, but he is not yet able to turn to God. Nevertheless he rejoices at least in the certainty of his present position, in his honest acceptance even of his negation of God, upon which he can begin to construct something positive. Like Gerontion, he is spiritually at the bottom and ready to start up. Having ceased to care about himself, he may now perhaps care about God with proper unselfishness and humility — if he can manage the ticklish separation of these two concerns. Eliot sees despair as a kind of necessary first step in spiritual regeneration. Note how, throughout the poem, the spiritual life is interpreted in terms of these and other such paradoxes.

Because I do not hope to turn again [1]
Because I do not hope
Because I do not hope to turn
Desiring this man's gift and that man's scope [2]
I no longer strive to strive towards such things 5
(Why should the agèd eagle [3] stretch its wings?)
Why should I mourn
The vanished power of the usual reign?

[1] The central motif of "turning" recalls the spiraling circles by which Dante ascends through Purgatory to Paradise and thence to union with God. Eliot is also echoing the first line of Guido Cavalcanti's ballad, "In Exile at Saranza," in which the poet, near death and deprived of all hope, addresses his lady in tears. The translated lines are "Because I think not ever to return/ Ballad, to Tuscany." Eliot applies the more worldly plea of Cavalcanti to his central theme of the penitent soul and the desire for mystical union with God.
[2] An altered line from Shakespeare's 29th sonnet, in which the poet reveals a mood of wavering desires and a spirit depressed by being outcast from hope and faith. Again, whereas Shakespeare addresses a lady, Eliot speaks to God.
[3] In the Middle Ages the rejuvenation of the aged eagle was a symbol of spiritual rebirth. He was said to fly up in old age into a circle of fire where his feathers were burnt off. Then he fell into a fountain of baptismal grace, his youth renewed.

Because I do not hope to know again
The infirm glory of the positive hour 10
Because I do not think
Because I know I shall not know
The one veritable transitory power
Because I cannot drink
There, where trees flower, and springs flow, for
    there is nothing again 15

Because I know that time is always time
And place is always and only place
And what is actual is actual only for one time
And only for one place
I rejoice that things are as they are and 20
I renounce the blessèd face
And renounce the voice
Because I cannot hope to turn again
Consequently I rejoice, having to construct
    something
Upon which to rejoice 25

And pray to God to have mercy upon us
And I pray that I may forget
These matters that with myself I too much
    discuss
Too much explain
Because I do not hope to turn again 30
Let these words answer
For what is done, not to be done again
May the judgment not be too heavy upon us

Because these wings are no longer wings to fly
But merely vans to beat the air 35
The air which is now thoroughly small and dry
Smaller and dryer than the will
Teach us to care and not to care
Teach us to sit still.

Pray for us sinners now and at the hour of our
    death 40
Pray for us now and at the hour of our death.[4]

2

The death of the flesh appears here as cleansing
and releasing. The speaker submits to annihilation
and anonymity, permits his self-sick flesh to be dispersed from his bones, and achieves a reflection of
the contemplative selflessness of the Lady, image
of love, who honors the Virgin. The bones sing of
the Virgin in the paradoxes of Christ, who suffers
and despairs over mankind, but remains whole and
peaceful and offers endless hope and solace; and they

[4] From the *Ave Maria*: "Holy Mary, mother of God,
pray for us sinners now and at the hour of our death."

sing of the Garden, where all earthly loves end and
all divine love reposes. The desert here is the world;
the garden is God.

Lady, three white leopards [5] sat under a juniper-
    tree
In the cool of the day, having fed to satiety
On my legs my heart my liver and that which
    had been contained 44
In the hollow round of my skull. And God said
Shall these bones live? shall these
Bones live? [6] And that which had been con-
    tained
In the bones (which were already dry) said
    chirping:
Because of the goodness of this Lady
And because of her loveliness, and because 50
She honors the Virgin in meditation,
We shine with brightness. And I who am here
    dissembled
Proffer my deeds to oblivion, and my love
To the posterity of the desert and the fruit of
    the gourd.
It is this which recovers 55
My guts the strings of my eyes and the indi-
    gestible portions
Which the leopards reject. The lady is with-
    drawn
In a white gown, to contemplation, in a white
    gown.
Let the whiteness of bones atone to forgetful-
    ness.
There is no life in them. As I am forgotten 60
And would be forgotten, so I would forget
Thus devoted, concentrated in purpose. And
    God said
Prophesy to the wind,[7] to the wind only for only
The wind will listen. And the bones sang
    chirping
With the burden of the grasshopper, saying 65

[5] "The opening lines suggest Elijah (1 Kings 19)
when, having been threatened with death by Jezebel,
he sat down under a juniper tree and prayed that he
might die." — G. Williamson. The leopards, like the
leopard, the lion, and the wolf in Dante's *Inferno*, perform here a double function of feeding on the organs
of lust and the senses and providing a purging of the
sins of the flesh. Hence they are "white," the color
of purity. The Lady is an idealized woman like
Dante's Beatrice and at the same time symbolizes
the Virgin Mary.
[6] Ezekiel 37:3: "And he said unto me, Son of Man,
can these bones live?" Ezekiel is commanded to prophesy that the bones will be covered with flesh, and
he does so, marveling at the power of God.
[7] Ezekiel 37:9: "Then he said unto me, Prophesy unto
the wind, prophesy, son of man. . . . and breathe upon
these slain that they may live."

Lady of silences
Calm and distressed
Torn and most whole
Rose of memory
Rose of forgetfulness   70
Exhausted and life-giving
Worried reposeful
The single Rose
Is now the Garden [8]
Where all loves end   75
Terminate torment
Of love unsatisfied
The greater torment
Of love satisfied
End of the endless   80
Journey to no end
Conclusion of all that
Is inconclusible
Speech without word and
Word of no speech   85
Grace to the Mother
For the Garden
Where all love ends.

Under a juniper-tree the bones sang, scattered
    and shining
We were glad to be scattered, we did little good
    to each other,   90
Under a tree in the cool of the day, with the
    blessing of sand,
Forgetting themselves and each other, united
In the quiet of the desert. This is the land
    which ye
Shall divide by lot. And neither division nor
    unity
Matters. This is the land. We have our in-
    heritance.[9]   95

3

On the second stair of his ascent to love of God,
the speaker sees below him that part of himself
which still struggles in a darkness which precedes
even the first section of the poem, and then he
mounts on through renewed misgivings, passes en-
ticing images of sensuality, and comes finally to a
strength beyond weak doubts and irresponsible hopes.
He can now half voice a prayer for God's help.

[8] For an understanding of the sexual-religious significance of the image of the Rose and the Garden in
Eliot, cf. Leonard Unger's "T. S. Eliot's Rose Garden:
A Persistent Theme," *Southern Review*, Spring, 1942.
The rose was also a symbol of the Virgin in Dante,
Paradiso.
[9] Ezekiel 45:1 and 48:29: "This is the land which
ye shall divide by lot unto the tribes of Israel for inheritance, and these are their portions, saith the Lord
God." This section ends on a note of hope for "these
bones."

At the first turning of the second stair [1]
I turned and saw below
The same shape twisted on the banister
Under the vapor in the fetid air
Struggling with the devil of the stairs who wears
The deceitful face of hope and of despair.   101

At the second turning of the second stair
I left them twisting, turning below;
There were no more faces and the stair was dark,
Damp, jagged, like an old man's mouth drivel-
    ling, beyond repair,   105
Or the toothed gullet of an agèd shark.

At the first turning of the third stair
Was a slotted window bellied like the fig's fruit
And beyond the hawthorn blossom and a pas-
    ture scene   109
The broadbacked figure drest in blue and green
Enchanted the maytime with an antique flute.
Blown hair is sweet, brown hair over the mouth
    blown,
Lilac and brown hair;
Distraction, music of the flute, stops and steps
    of the mind over the third stair,
Fading, fading; strength beyond hope and
    despair   115
Climbing the third stair.

Lord, I am not worthy
Lord, I am not worthy

        but speak the word only.

4

The Lady of Love becomes an image of the
mediator, between man and God, recalling Dante's
Beatrice, and merging with Our Lady of Sorrow
(Mary). She renews the fountains and springs in
the desert. The years now bear away the garden of
sensuality, and bring the new song of the redemption
of the dream. After exile will come the return to
God, which is led up to and then left unvoiced at
the end of the section.

Who walked between the violet and the violet
Who walked between   121
The various ranks of varied green
Going in white and blue, in Mary's color,

[1] The ascending stairway again recalls the words of
Arnaut Daniel, the poet, to Dante (*Purgatorio*, xxvi,
146): "Now I pray you, by that Goodness which
guideth you to the summit of the stairway, be mindful
in due time of my pain." Part 3 of *Ash Wednesday*
was first published under the title of *Som de l'Escalina*
(The Summit of the Stairway).

Talking of trivial things   124
In ignorance and in knowledge of eternal dolor
Who moved among the others as they walked,
Who then made strong the fountains and made
    fresh the springs [2]

Made cool the dry rock and made firm the sand
In blue of larkspur, blue of Mary's color,
Sovegna vos [3]   130

Here are the years that walk between, bearing
Away the fiddles and the flutes, restoring
One who moves in the time between sleep and
    waking, wearing

White light folded, sheathed about her, folded.
The new years walk, restoring   135
Through a bright cloud of tears, the years, re-
    storing
With a new verse the ancient rhyme. Redeem
The time.[4] Redeem
The unread vision in the higher dream
While jewelled unicorns draw by the gilded
    hearse.[5]   140

The silent sister veiled in white and blue
Between the yews,[6] behind the garden god,
Whose flute is breathless, bent her head and
    signed but spoke no word

But the fountain sprang up and the bird sang
    down
Redeem the time, redeem the dream   145
The token of the word unheard, unspoken

Till the wind shake a thousand whispers from
    the yew

And after this our exile [7]

2 The scene is closely related to that in which Dante
meets Beatrice in the Earthly Paradise. E. E. Duncan-
Jones points out: "The colours used in this poem are
all capable of symbolical meanings: the violet of penance, the green of hope, the white of purity, the blue
of celestial things."
3 "Remember" — cf. note to line 96, above.
4 Cf. Ephesians 5:14-16: "Awake, thou that sleep-
est, and arise from the dead, and Christ shall give thee
light. See that ye walk circumspectly, not as fools,
but as wise, Redeeming the time, because the days
are evil."
5 The unicorn was a symbol of chastity in religious
literature and jewelled unicorns drawing a car in which
sat the Virgin were a part of the pageantry of Mary-
worship.
6 The yew suggests the Tree of Life and typifies
death and the resurrection.
7 From the prayer of the Mass, "Salve Regina": "And
after this our exile show unto us the blessed fruit of
thy womb, Jesus."

5

O my people, what have I done unto thee.

    The Word of God fares badly in the world.
The world is against it. Man avoids the Word;
busily self-distracted, he gives it no empty, silent
space to enter his soul. Now the exact question becomes this: Will the mediatress pray for those who
choose God, but are incapable of coming to him —
who, in the perverse structure of their human souls,
offend that which they desire? There is clearly a
final limit to what man can do for himself, even
though he labor painfully and long.

If the lost word is lost, if the spent word is spent
If the unheard, unspoken   150
Word is unspoken, unheard;
Still is the unspoken word, the Word unheard,
The Word without a word, the Word within
The world and for the world;
And the light shone in darkness and   155
Against the Word the unstilled world still
    whirled
About the center of the silent Word.[8]

O my people, what have I done unto thee.

Where shall the word be found, where will the
    word
Resound? Not here, there is not enough silence
Not on the sea or on the islands, not   161
On the mainland, in the desert or the rain land,
For those who walk in darkness
Both in the day time and in the night time
The right time and the right place are not
    here   165
No place of grace for those who avoid the face
No time to rejoice for those who walk among
    noise and deny the voice

Will the veiled sister pray for
Those who walk in darkness, who chose thee
    and oppose thee,
Those who are torn on the horn between season
    and season, time and time, between   170
Hour and hour, word and word, power and
    power, those who wait
In darkness? Will the veiled sister pray
For children at the gate
Who will not go away and cannot pray:
Pray for those who chose and oppose   175

8 John 1:1–6: "In the beginning was the Word, and
the Word was with God, and the Word was God. . . .
And the light shineth in darkness; and the darkness
comprehended it not." Note the distinction between
the "Word," which is God, and the "word" which Eliot
uses in the sense of the language of God to man.

O my people, what have I done unto thee.[9]

Will the veiled sister between the slender
Yew trees pray for those who offend her
And are terrified and cannot surrender
And affirm before the world and deny between
    the rocks   180
In the last desert between the last blue rocks
The desert in the garden the garden in the desert
Of drouth, spitting from the mouth the withered
    apple-seed.[1]

O my people.

6

⚜ Although the speaker does not want to return to
the world to which he has died, he now hears again
its call to him, and drifts again toward its blindness.
"This is the time of tension," before his final death
to the world and his spiritual rebirth. He prays that
even in this world, this desert, he shall learn to care
wisely, to find his peace in God's will, and not be
separated from God. Thus he has come from spiritual desiccation and despair, up through the tangled
difficulties of spiritual ascent, to the supplication of
the last line.

Although I do not hope to turn again   185
Although I do not hope
Although I do not hope to turn

Wavering between the profit and the loss
In this brief transit where the dreams cross
The dreamcrossed twilight between birth and
    dying [2]   190
(Bless me father) though I do not wish to wish
    these things
From the wide window towards the granite shore
The white sails still fly seaward, seaward flying
Unbroken wings

And the lost heart stiffens and rejoices   195
In the lost lilac and the lost sea voices
And the weak spirit quickens to rebel
For the bent golden-rod and the lost sea smell
Quickens to recover

9 Micah 6:3, in which God speaks to the people of
Israel: "O my people, what have I done unto thee?
and wherein have I wearied thee? testify against me."

1 Possibly a reference to the apple of the tree of
knowledge and a sign that sin is diminishing by the
act of casting out the seed.

2 The dreams of this world, like the hope and despair
of man, are the "empty forms" (l. 202) which emerged
from one of the Gates of Sleep in the *Aeneid*, VI, and
which are false dreams.

The cry of quail and the whirling plover   200
And the blind eye creates
The empty forms between the ivory gates
And smell renews the salt savor of the sandy
    earth

This is the time of tension between dying and
    birth
The place of solitude where three dreams cross
Between blue rocks   206
But when the voices shaken from the yew tree
    drift away
Let the other yew be shaken and reply.

Blessèd sister, holy mother, spirit of the foun-
    tain, spirit of the garden,
Suffer us not to mock ourselves with falsehood
Teach us to care and not to care   211
Teach us to sit still
Even among these rocks,
Our peace in His will [3]
And even among these rocks   215
Sister, mother
And spirit of the river, spirit of the sea,
Suffer me not to be separated

And let my cry come unto Thee.[4]

From *Four Quartets*
(1943)
The Dry Salvages, V

⚜ *Four Quartets*, like *Ash Wednesday*, should be
read as a whole. The following brief selection, however, gives some idea of the characteristic themes,
techniques, and tone of this long and difficult poem.

In this passage, a catalogue of common but mistaken methods for divining spiritual truths is contrasted with the method of the saint, who contemplates directly and with constancy a vision of Truth.
Most of us never see this vision, but catch only
transient hints of it in those unattended moments
when a tremor of feeling, a half-recognition of some-

3 This line and some of the surrounding imagery of
the sea derive from Dante's *Paradiso*, iii, 85, where
the poet is told that all spirits accept their sphere in
heaven and do not aspire to higher ones: "And his will
is our peace: it is the sea to which all moves that it
createth and that nature maketh."

4 The closing lines are from an ancient prayer, the
Anima Christi: "Suffer me not to be separated from
thee." Also, the verse: "Lord, hear our prayer: and let
our cry come unto Thee."

thing beyond ourselves, touches us. For the rest, we who are not saints must follow the church ritual laid out for us, go on trying to see the vision, and remain at the last content with "The life of significant soil."

To communicate with Mars, converse with spirits,
To report the behaviour of the sea monster,
Describe the horoscope, haruspicate or scry,
Observe disease in signatures, evoke
Biography from the wrinkles of the palm   5
And tragedy from fingers; release omens
By sortilege, or tea leaves, riddle the inevitable
With playing cards, fiddle with pentagrams
Or barbituric acids, or dissect
The recurrent image into pre-conscious ter-
rors —   10
To explore the womb, or tomb, or dreams; all
these are usual
Pastimes and drugs, and features of the press:
And always will be, some of them especially
When there is distress of nations and perplexity
Whether on the shores of Asia, or in the
Edgware Road.   15
Men's curiosity searches past and future
And clings to that dimension. But to apprehend
The point of intersection of the timeless
With time, is an occupation for the saint —
No occupation either, but something given   20
And taken, in a lifetime's death in love,
Ardour and selflessness and self-surrender.
For most of us, there is only the unattended
Moment, the moment in and out of time,   24
The distraction fit, lost in a shaft of sunlight,
The wild thyme unseen, or the winter lightning
Or the waterfall, or music heard so deeply
That it is not heard at all, but you are the music
While the music lasts. These are only hints and
guesses,
Hints followed by guesses; and the rest   30
Is prayer, observance, discipline, thought and
action.
The hint half guessed, the gift half understood,
is Incarnation.
Here the impossible union
Of spheres of existence is actual,
Here the past and future   35
Are conquered, and reconciled,
Where action were otherwise movement
Of that which is only moved
And has in it no source of movement —
Driven by daemonic, chthonic   40
Powers. And right action is freedom
From past and future also.

For most of us, this is the aim
Never here to be realised;
Who are only undefeated   45
Because we have gone on trying;
We, content at the last
If our temporal reversion nourish
(Not too far from the yew tree)
The life of significant soil.   50

The Metaphysical Poets

(1921)

Eliot's essay on the seventeenth-century metaphysical poets (together with Wilson's essay on the nineteenth-century symbolist poets, page 1154) offers a perceptive survey of the examples to whom many twentieth-century poets looked for guidance.

At the time this essay was written, the metaphysical poets were doubtless "more often named than read," and, when read, were likely to be abused with prejudice, or relished merely with "antiquarian affection." But for Eliot they counted importantly. If he could make them count importantly for others, he would be doing much toward justifying the difficult and complex poets of his own time.

Eliot rests his case for the seventeenth-century poets on their technique. He does not concern himself with their philosophical truth or ethical values. He concerns himself with the processes of historical change, only to argue that what happened should not have happened — that the virtue of these poets "ought not to have disappeared." Centrally, his interest is in poetic technique, in relation to the psychology of poetic experience.

By collecting these poems [1] from the work of a generation more often named than read, and more often read than profitably studied, Professor Grierson has rendered a service of some importance. Certainly the reader will meet with many poems already preserved in other anthologies, at the same time that he discovers poems such as those of Aurelian Townshend or Lord Herbert of Cherbury here included. But the function of such an anthology as this is neither that of Professor Saintsbury's admirable edition of Caroline poets nor that of the *Oxford Book of English Verse*. Mr. Grierson's book is in itself a piece of criticism and a provocation of criticism; and we think that he was right in

[1] *Metaphysical Lyrics and Poems of the Seventeenth Century:* Donne to Butler. Selected and edited, with an Essay, by Herbert J. C. Grierson (Oxford: Clarendon Press. London: Milford). [Author's note.]

including so many poems of Donne, elsewhere (though not in many editions) accessible, as documents in the case of "metaphysical poetry." The phrase has long done duty as a term of abuse or as the label of a quaint and pleasant taste. The question is to what extent the so-called metaphysicals formed a school (in our own time we should say a "movement"), and how far this so-called school or movement is a digression from the main current.

Not only is it extremely difficult to define metaphysical poetry, but difficult to decide what poets practice it and in which of their verses. The poetry of Donne (to whom Marvell and Bishop King are sometimes nearer than any of the other authors) is late Elizabethan, its feeling often very close to that of Chapman. The "courtly" poetry is derivative from Jonson, who borrowed liberally from the Latin; it expires in the next century with the sentiment and witticism of Prior. There is finally the devotional verse of Herbert, Vaughan, and Crashaw (echoed long after by Christina Rossetti and Francis Thompson); Crashaw, sometimes more profound and less sectarian than the others, has a quality which returns through the Elizabethan period to the early Italians. It is difficult to find any precise use of metaphor, simile, or other conceit, which is common to all the poets and at the same time important enough as an element of style to isolate these poets as a group. Donne, and often Cowley, employ a device which is sometimes considered characteristically "metaphysical"; the elaboration (contrasted with the condensation) of a figure of speech to the farthest stage to which ingenuity can carry it. Thus Cowley develops the commonplace comparison of the world to a chess-board through long stanzas ("To Destiny"), and Donne, with more grace, in "A Valediction," the comparison of two lovers to a pair of compasses. But elsewhere we find, instead of the mere explication of the content of a comparison, a development by rapid association of thought which requires considerable agility on the part of the reader.

> On a round ball
> A workman that hath copies by, can lay
> An Europe, Afrique, and an Asia,
> And quickly make that, which was nothing, All,
>   So doth each teare,
>   Which thee doth weare,
> A globe, yea, world by that impression grow,
> Till thy tears mixt with mine doe overflow

This world, by waters sent from thee, my heaven dissolved so.

Here we find at least two connections which are not implicit in the first figure, but are forced upon it by the poet: from the geographer's globe to the tear, and the tear to the deluge. On the other hand, some of Donne's most successful and characteristic effects are secured by brief words and sudden contrasts:

> A bracelet of bright hair about the bone,

where the most powerful effect is produced by the sudden contrast of associations of "bright hair" and of "bone." This telescoping of images and multiplied associations is characteristic of the phrase of some of the dramatists of the period which Donne knew: not to mention Shakespeare, it is frequent in Middleton, Webster, and Tourneur, and is one of the sources of the vitality of their language.

Johnson, who employed the term "metaphysical poets," apparently having Donne, Cleveland, and Cowley chiefly in mind, remarks of them that "the most heterogeneous ideas are yoked by violence together." The force of this impeachment lies in the failure of the conjunction, the fact that often the ideas are yoked but not united; and if we are to judge of styles of poetry by their abuse, enough examples may be found in Cleveland to justify Johnson's condemnation. But a degree of heterogeneity of material compelled into unity by the operation of the poet's mind is omnipresent in poetry. We need not select for illustration such a line as:

> Notre âme est un trois-mâts cherchant son Icarie;

we may find it in some of the best lines of Johnson himself ("The Vanity of Human Wishes"):

> His fate was destined to a barren strand,
> A petty fortress, and a dubious hand;
> He left a name at which the world grew pale,
> To point a moral, or adorn a tale—

where the effect is due to a contrast of ideas, different in degree but the same in principle, as that which Johnson mildly reprehended. And in one of the finest poems of the age (a poem which could not have been written in any other age), the "Exequy" of Bishop King, the extended comparison is used with perfect success: the idea and the simile become one in the passage in which the Bishop illustrates his impatience to see his dead wife, under the figure of a journey:

> Stay for me there; I will not faile
> To meet thee in that hollow Vale.
> And think not much of my delay;
> I am already on the way,
> And follow thee with all the speed
> Desire can make, or sorrows breed.
> Each minute is a short degree,
> And ev'ry houre a step towards thee.
> At night when I betake to rest,
> Next morn I rise nearer my West
> Of life, almost by eight houres sail,
> Than when sleep breath'd his drowsy gale . . .
> But heark! My Pulse, like a soft Drum
> Beats my approach, tells Thee I come;
> And slow howere my marches be,
> I shall at last sit down by Thee.

(In the last few lines there is that effect of terror which is several times attained by one of Bishop King's admirers, Edgar Poe.) Again, we may justly take these quatrains from Lord Herbert's "Ode," stanzas which would, we think, be immediately pronounced to be of the metaphysical school:

> So when from hence we shall be gone,
> And be no more, nor you, nor I,
> As one another's mystery,
> Each shall be both, yet both but one.

> This said, in her up-lifted face,
> Her eyes, which did that beauty crown,
> Were like two stars, that having faln down,
> Look up again to find their place:

> While such a moveless silent peace
> Did seize on their becalmed sense,
> One would have thought some influence
> Their ravished spirits did possess.

There is nothing in these lines (with the possible exception of the stars, a simile not at once grasped, but lovely and justified) which fits Johnson's general observations on the metaphysical poets in his essay on Cowley. A good deal resides in the richness of association which is at the same time borrowed from and given to the word "becalmed"; but the meaning is clear, the language simple and elegant. It is to be observed that the language of these poets is as

a rule simple and pure; in the verse of George Herbert this simplicity is carried as far as it can go — a simplicity emulated without success by numerous modern poets. The *structure* of the sentences, on the other hand, is sometimes far from simple, but this is not a vice; it is a fidelity to thought and feeling. The effect, at its best, is far less artificial than that of an ode by Gray. And as this fidelity induces variety of thought and feeling, so it induces variety of music. We doubt whether, in the eighteenth century, could be found two poems in nominally the same metre, so dissimilar as Marvell's "Coy Mistress" and Crashaw's "Saint Teresa"; the one producing an effect of great speed by the use of short syllables, and the other an ecclesiastical solemnity by the use of long ones:

> Love, thou art absolute sole lord
> Of life and death.

If so shrewd and sensitive (though so limited) a critic as Johnson failed to define metaphysical poetry by its faults, it is worth while to inquire whether we may not have more success by adopting the opposite method: by assuming that the poets of the seventeenth century (up to the Revolution) were the direct and normal development of the precedent age; and, without prejudicing their case by the adjective "metaphysical," consider whether their virtue was not something permanently valuable, which subsequently disappeared, but ought not to have disappeared. Johnson has hit, perhaps by accident, on one of their peculiarities, when he observes that "their attempts were always analytic"; he would not agree that, after the dissociation, they put the material together again in a new unity.

It is certain that the dramatic verse of the later Elizabethan and early Jacobean poets expresses a degree of development of sensibility which is not found in any of the prose, good as it often is. If we except Marlowe, a man of prodigious intelligence, these dramatists were directly or indirectly (it is at least a tenable theory) affected by Montaigne. Even if we except also Jonson and Chapman, these two were notably erudite, and were notably men who incorporated their erudition into their sensibility: their mode of feeling was directly and freshly altered by their reading and thought. In Chapman especially there is a direct sensuous apprehension of thought, or a re-creation of thought into feeling, which is exactly what we find in Donne:

> in this one thing, all the discipline
> Of manners and of manhood is contained;
> A man to join himself with th' Universe
> In his main sway, and make in all things fit
> One with that All, and go on, round as it;
> Not plucking from the whole his wretched part,
> And into straits, or into nought revert,
> Wishing the complete Universe might be
> Subject to such a rag of it as he;
> But to consider great Necessity.

We compare this with some modern passage:

> No, when the fight begins within himself,
> A man's worth something. God stoops o'er his head.
> Satan looks up between his feet — both tug —
> He's left, himself, i' the middle; the soul wakes
> And grows. Prolong that battle through his life!

It is perhaps somewhat less fair, though very tempting (as both poets are concerned with the perpetuation of love by offspring), to compare with the stanzas already quoted from Lord Herbert's "Ode" the following from Tennyson:

> One walked between his wife and child,
> With measured footfall firm and mild,
> And now and then he gravely smiled.
>   The prudent partner of his blood
>   Leaned on him, faithful, gentle, good,
>   Wearing the rose of womanhood.
> And in their double love secure,
> The little maiden walked demure,
> Pacing with downward eyelids pure.
> These three made unity so sweet,
> My frozen heart began to beat,
> Remembering its ancient heat.

The difference is not a simple difference of degree between poets. It is something which had happened to the mind of England between the time of Donne or Lord Herbert of Cherbury and the time of Tennyson and Browning; it is the difference between the intellectual poet and the reflective poet. Tennyson and Browning are poets, and they think; but they do not feel their thought as immediately as the odour of a rose. A thought to Donne was an experience; it modified his sensibility. When a poet's mind is perfectly equipped for its work, it is constantly amalgamating disparate experience; the ordinary man's experience is chaotic, irregular, fragmentary. The latter falls in love, or reads Spinoza,

and these two experiences have nothing to do with each other, or with the noise of the typewriter or the smell of cooking; in the mind of the poet these experiences are always forming new wholes.

We may express the difference by the following theory: The poets of the seventeenth century, the successors of the dramatists of the sixteenth, possessed a mechanism of sensibility which could devour any kind of experience. They are simple, artificial, difficult, or fantastic, as their predecessors were; no less nor more than Dante, Guido Cavalcanti, Guinizelli, or Cino. In the seventeenth century a dissociation of sensibility set in, from which we have never recovered; and this dissociation, as is natural, was aggravated by the influence of the two most powerful poets of the century, Milton and Dryden. Each of these men performed certain poetic functions so magnificently well that the magnitude of the effect concealed the absence of others. The language went on and in some respects improved; the best verse of Collins, Gray, Johnson, and even Goldsmith satisfies some of our fastidious demands better than that of Donne or Marvell or King. But while the language became more refined, the feeling became more crude. The feeling, the sensibility, expressed in the "Country Churchyard" (to say nothing of Tennyson and Browning) is cruder than that in the "Coy Mistress."

The second effect of the influence of Milton and Dryden followed from the first, and was therefore slow in manifestation. The sentimental age began early in the eighteenth century, and continued. The poets revolted against the ratiocinative, the descriptive; they thought and felt by fits, unbalanced; they reflected. In one or two passages of Shelley's "Triumph of Life," in the second "Hyperion," there are traces of a struggle toward unification of sensibility. But Keats and Shelley died, and Tennyson and Browning ruminated.

After this brief exposition of a theory — too brief, perhaps, to carry conviction — we may ask, what would have been the fate of the "metaphysical" had the current of poetry descended in a direct line from them, as it descended in a direct line to them? They would not, certainly, be classified as metaphysical. The possible interests of a poet are unlimited; the more intelligent he is the better; the more intelligent he is the more likely that he will have interests: our only condition is that he turn them into poetry, and not merely meditate on them poetically. A philosophical theory which has entered into poetry is established, for its truth or falsity in one sense ceases to matter, and its truth in another sense is proved. The poets in question have, like other poets, various faults. But they were, at best, engaged in the task of trying to find the verbal equivalent for states of mind and feeling. And this means both that they are more mature, and that they wear better, than later poets of certainly not less literary ability.

It is not a permanent necessity that poets should be interested in philosophy, or in any other subject. We can only say that it appears likely that poets in our civilization, as it exists at present, must be *difficult*. Our civilization comprehends great variety and complexity, and this variety and complexity, playing upon a refined sensibility, must produce various and complex results. The poet must become more and more comprehensive, more allusive, more indirect, in order to force, to dislocate if necessary, language into his meaning. (A brilliant and extreme statement of this view, with which it is not requisite to associate oneself, is that of M. Jean Epstein, "La Poésie d'aujourd'hi.") Hence we get something which looks very much like the conceit — we get, in fact, a method curiously similar to that of the "metaphysical poets," similar also in its use of obscure words of simple phrasing.

O géraniums diaphanes, guerroyeurs sortiléges,
Sacriléges monomanes!
Emballages, dévergondages, douches! O pressoirs
Des vendanges des grands soirs!
Layettes aux abois,
Thyrses au fond des bois!
Transfusions, représailles,
Relevailles, compresses et l'éternal potion,
Angélus! n'en pouvoir plus
De débâcles nuptiales! de débâcles nuptiales!

The same poet could write also simply:

Elle est bien loin, elle pleure,
Le grand vent se lamente aussi . . .

Jules Laforge, and Tristan Corbière in many of his poems, are nearer to the "school of Donne" than any modern English poet. But poets more classical than they have the same essential quality of transmuting ideas into sensations, of transforming an observation into a state of mind.

Pour l'enfant, amoureux de cartes et d'estampes,
L'univers est égal à son vaste appétit.
Ah, que le monde est grand à la clarté des lampes!
Aux yeux du souvenir que le monde est petit!

In French literature the great master of the seventeenth century — Racine — and the great master of the nineteenth — Baudelaire — are in some ways more like each other than they are like any one else. The greatest two masters of diction are also the greatest two psychologists, the most curious explorers of the soul. It is interesting to speculate whether it is not a misfortune that two of the greatest masters of diction in our language, Milton and Dryden, triumph with a dazzling disregard of the soul. If we continued to produce Miltons and Drydens it might not so much matter, but as things are it is a pity that English poetry has remained so incomplete. Those who object to the "artificiality" of Milton or Dryden sometimes tell us to "look into our hearts and write." But that is not looking deep enough; Racine or Donne looked into a good deal more than the heart. One must look into the cerebral cortex, the nervous system, and the digestive tracts.

May we not conclude, then, that Donne, Crashaw, Vaughan, Herbert and Lord Herbert, Marvell, King, Cowley at his best, are in the direct current of English poetry, and that their faults should be reprimanded by this standard rather than coddled by antiquarian affection? They have been enough praised in terms which are implicit limitations because they are "metaphysical" or "witty," "quaint" or "obscure," though at their best they have not these attributes more than other serious poets. On the other hand, we must not reject the criticism of Johnson (a dangerous person to disagree with) without having mastered it, without having assimilated the Johnsonian canons of taste. In reading the celebrated passage in his essay on Cowley we must remember that by wit he clearly means something more serious than we usually mean today; in his criticism of their versification we must remember in what a narrow discipline he was trained, but also how well trained; we must remember that Johnson tortures chiefly the chief offenders, Cowley and Cleveland. It would be a fruitful work, and one requiring a substantial book, to break up the classification of Johnson (for there has been none since) and exhibit these poets in all their difference of kind and of degree, from the massive music of Donne to the faint, pleasing tinkle of Aurelian Townshend — whose "Dialogue Between a Pilgrim and Time" is one of the few regrettable omissions from the excellent anthology of Professor Grierson.

Literature and the Modern World

(1935)

People may be conscious of their age without knowing very much about it. I believe that most of us are influenced, more than we realize, by a kind of deterministic conception of history. That may be all right for the Marxian, who has a reasoned theory about it; but it has no advantage as an unconscious assumption. The assumption of the inevitability of progress has, we all know, been discarded in its nineteenth-century form: it is the butt of popular philosophers like Dean Inge. But actually, what we have discarded is a particular variety of the theory of progress: that which is associated with Darwin, Tennyson, free trade, and the industrial development of the latter part of the last century: in short, with Liberalism. Our beliefs have been shaken in detail: for instance, no one now is convinced of the automatic beneficence of scientific invention. Invention may be applied to destructive, rather than to creative activity; and it throws people out of work and it stimulates production while it diminishes consumption: these are commonplaces. Nevertheless, we retain the essential of the doctrine of progress: we have no faith in the present.

In popularizing the belief in the future in a crude form we have, I think, a good deal for which to thank Mr. H. G. Wells. His superficial philosophy has had an extensive influence. Whatever Mr. Wells may explicitly disclaim, I think that the effect of his writing has been something like this: to propagate a belief that the value of the present resides in its service to the future, and nowhere else. Morality consists in working to forward the happiness of future generations, "happiness" of a not remarkably spiritualized kind. We are to find our happiness in scientific work which will benefit future humanity, and for the rest get anything out of life that we can. I do not want to let my words be twisted to suggest that we should take no concern with the lives of future generations. It is very much our business. What I object to is the complete dislocation of values. It is impor-

tant not only that we should try to want the right things for the future. It is important also that we should have just as much respect for ourselves; and remember that we, as human beings, are individually just as valuable as the men of the future. Mr. Wells seems to propagate a strange false humility of evolutionism: as the higher apes are to us, he says in effect, so are we to the men of the future; and as we regard our animal ancestors, whether apes, lemurs, or opossums, so will they of the future regard us. This is, of course, the quite natural corollary of a naïf faith in perpetual evolution, combined with a denial of any sharp dividing line between the human and the animal: that is, a denial of the human soul.

Now, one effect of this is to justify a contempt for humanity as we find it today, and the admission of any means, at whatever cost to human dignity, which will bring about the kind of future which Mr. Wells contemplates with such rapture. I confess that I cannot see why we should take such pains to produce a race of men, millennia hence, who will only look down upon *us* as apes, lemurs, or opossums. It seems a thankless labor. We must affirm that there is no more value in the future than there is in the present. That is to say, we must affirm the eternal against the transient; the eternal which has been realized in the past can be realized in the present; and it is our business to try to bring about a future in which the obstacles to this realization will be less, for the mass of humanity, than they are today. And these obstacles are not all of a material kind; they are in ourselves too. Our attitude may seem less ambitious than that of Mr. Wells; but it is more definite. It is simply that of the humble parent who wants his child to have a better chance in life than he had, and to lead a better life than he has led.

I said at the beginning that this modern eschatology begins in optimism and easily ends in despair. But I do not draw the moral of the proprietor whose granary was full. We are obviously at the end of an age, oppressed by the sense of corruption and decay, and fearful of the kinds of change which may come, since some change must. And since our minds must needs be filled with thought about the future, thought affecting our own action tomorrow perhaps, and our consciences disturbed by what we find about us and within us, it is all the more important to keep our heads, our sense of values; all the more important that we should hold fast to the things which were, and are, and shall be, world without end.

My immediate occupation, however, is with the effect upon modern literature of this dislocation of values and this moral subservience of the present to the future. As a kind of consultant, as well as a potential impresario, I have to see a good deal of what is being written, in some forms, by those much younger than myself. In the better writers there is strongly developed a kind of social conscience, a notion that literature ought to be useful to society. In the inferior writers this conscience may, of course, take the form merely of a determination not to miss the boat; but I confidently assure you of the existence of a fair proportion of sincerity. Now this devotion to society may involve precisely the same dislocation of values as the devotion to the future; and I propose to try to come to a conclusion about the proper relation of the poet today to himself and to society. The preoccupation of which I speak is inevitable, it is right; but how is it to be adjusted to the permanent values which literature is supposed to realize?

Here we get to the point. Should a literary artist have this acute sense of a social duty obliging him to convey a message; and if so, when is the "message" beneficial and when detrimental to the "art"?

I believe that the man of letters at the present day ought to have this sense. But the great danger for the artist is always that of conscientiously trying to feel what he does not feel. I will venture the following formulation: What is desirable is a harmony between the individual and sub-individual passions of the artist, and the social ideas and feelings which he wishes to propagate. In this harmony, he neither exploits the conscious doctrine as a vehicle for his personality, nor cramps or distorts his personality to adapt it to a social doctrine. This requires some little amplification.

A man is both an individual and a member. Instead of "individual" I shall use the word "person." His *personality* is unique and not to be violated; but he is equally created to be a *member* of society. When society is conceived as merely a sum of individuals, you get the chaos of liberal democracy. When the person is wholly subordinated to society, you get the dehumanization of fascism or communism. The extremes, however, may meet. For what liberal democracy really recognizes is a sum, not of persons, but of individuals: that is to say, not the variety and uniqueness of persons, but the purely material individuation of the old-fashioned or Democritean atom. And this is a disrespect to the person. For the person is no longer a person if wholly isolated from the community; and the community is no longer a community if it does not consist of persons. A man is not himself unless he is a member; and he cannot be a member unless he is also something alone. Man's membership and his solitude must be taken together. There are moments, perhaps not known to everyone, when a man may be nearly crushed by the terrible awareness of his isolation from every other human being; and I pity him if he finds himself only alone with himself and his meanness and futility, alone without God. It is after these moments, alone *with* God and aware of our worthiness, but for Grace, of nothing but damnation, that we turn with most thankfulness and appreciation to the awareness of our *membership*: for we appreciate and are thankful for nothing fully until we see where it begins and where it ends. All that I have been saying is recognized by the Church, and the balance is maintained only by the Church: it is not recognized, but is made manifest by, the endless seesaw of political tendency between anarchy and tyranny: a seesaw which, in the secular world, I believe has no end.

Now all this may sound perfectly irrelevant to my subject; but it is not so. This same balance ought to exist, on its plane, in the activity of the artist. For the artist cannot devote himself truly to any cause unless by that devotion he is also most truly being, and becoming, himself. The artist may, as Remy de Gourmont profoundly says, "in writing himself, write his age"; but I think that we should add that he may sometimes, in writing his age, write himself: which will come to the same thing. But it is from himself that he must start. It is sometimes helpful to put things in an extreme, and therefore dangerous way. So I may say that in one aspect the true artist may be said to be simply *exploiting* the things he believes in for the purpose of making art: only if he does this *consciously* is he a false artist.

Whereas a man like D. H. Lawrence is in danger of manipulating his philosophy to fit his private needs and to justify his private weaknesses, the adherent of an objective creed is in danger of denying or distorting himself to fit his beliefs; and the opposite insincerity becomes possible. This is equally a danger for the Christian and for the communist, and especially at those moments when personal inspiration fails. How far can one go in identifying a creed with oneself, or oneself with a creed? The development of the person may be twisted, or the purity of the creed may be polluted. I believe, naturally, that the Christian, if he understands his Christianity, has safeguards which the mere social revolutionist cannot have: safeguards of the personal emotion. For instance: social enthusiasm alone, however intense, does not seem to have the substance needed to make poetry. What is the difference between Dante's denunciation of the vices of his time and Shelley's denunciation of kings, tyrants, and priests? Shelley's excitement is in his head, and therefore emits rather shrill and inapplicable head noises; whereas Dante's is involved with all his own sufferings — definite grievances and definite humiliations at the hands of particular people, of all of which he is conscious: self-interested grudges and deprivations, earthly if you like, but primarily *real*, and that is the first thing. Only the greatest, the Hebrew prophets, seem to be utterly caught up and possessed by God as mouthpieces; in ordinary human poets the human personal loss, the private grievance and bitterness and loneliness, must be present. Even when the poet is aware of nothing, interested in nothing, beyond his personal feelings, these may have, by their intensity, a representative value, so that we envisage him, like Villon, not as wrapped up in his private griefs, but reliving them, holding nothing back, in a passionate cry to God — and there is, in the end, no one else to cry to. But in the greatest poets these private passions are completed in a passionate belief in objective moral values, in a striving towards justice and the life of the spirit among men.

Now the tendency of secular revolution today seems to me to be to diminish the value of the person. Of what importance, we may say currently, is all this expression of personal feeling and private suffering, in a world of so much general injustice and oppression? and this is the secular point of view: of what importance one man, when the life of society is at stake! We are back with the modern eschatology of which Mr. Wells is the popular preacher. The present order is damned, let us snatch what satisfaction we can, say some; and, the present order is

damned, let us sacrifice — not our pleasure, but our *selves* — to the future, say others; and one may perhaps maintain both conclusions at once. And behind is the master idea which has been working unobtrusively throughout our time, an idea which in the forms of heresy has always been waiting for us: the idea of the *"group consciousness"* — modest, and scientific and certain it sounds under that name.

In a recent article called "The Real Issue," which I have read with interest and approval, Mr. Christopher Dawson makes some pertinent remarks about the position of the individual in the classless society:

. . . the orthodox Communist will deny that this total subordination and sacrifice of humanity to the State machine is of the essence of Communism, for did not Marx and Lenin expressly teach that the dictatorship of the proletariat is only a temporary phase, and that the State itself will eventually wither away and give place to a classless and Stateless society? But how will this end be attained? Only when the individual is so completely socialized that he will instinctively devote all his energies to working for society and will be unable to conceive of any other end than that of the economic organism of which he forms part. In such an order there will be no need for a State any more than it is necessary for ants or bees to have a State. But it is a human order, and is it possible for humanity to rise or sink to such a level?

I do not, any more than Mr. Dawson, think such a consummation likely; but if I did not think it possible I should not take the trouble of attacking the idea of it. It would be brought about, not by the diabolic cleverness of scheming philosophers and politicians, but by the natural aversion of human beings to the responsibility and strain of being *human*. For we must remember that it *is* a great strain for the erect animal to persist in being erect, a physical and still more a moral strain. With or without mechanical aids of movement and noise, most people spend a good deal of their time avoiding the human responsibility; and we only remain human because of the continual vicarious sacrifice of a few dedicated lives. And the "group consciousness," the heresy bred within the antithetical heresy of liberalism, has a great seductive charm; for it helps to release us from the burden of responsibility. It would more likely, I think, be a reversion to a lower kind of consciousness than an ascent to a higher one; it is largely, in fact, to the speculations, which profess to be based on the study of primitive races, of such writers as Durkheim and Lévy-Bruhl, that we owe the conceptions. That such a state of humanity would be unfavorable to poetry follows from what I have said earlier. That is not perhaps of the utmost importance in itself; there are matters more important than the perpetual production of new poetry, though we must remember that a people which ceases to create the new will also lose the power to appreciate the *old*. What is important is that the creation of poetry depends upon the maintenance of the person, of the person in relation to other individuals, to God, and to society.

There is much, however, in the aspirations of poetry today with which I am in full sympathy. When we compare the state of poetry now with that of forty years ago, towards the end of the last century, I think we may see, without drawing any comparison between the merits of individual poets (and even if that comparison were to result to our disadvantage), that the social earnestness and dissatisfaction which have been lately expressing themselves have been all to the good; and poetry has taken on a new seriousness and a new social importance. It is perhaps not insignificant that the one great poet we have who belongs to both periods, Mr. William Butler Yeats, has been writing his finest poetry within recent years. With all we owe him, I find it difficult to regard Mr. Yeats as anything but a *contemporary*; and if anyone said that of me, when I arrive at his present age, I should consider it the highest of compliments. What I think we have missed, and have been struggling for, is the recognition of poetry as something other than exquisite pleasure for a small number of people who have the taste for it — as something having a function of social value. The poet must assume his rôle of moralist, and thus manifest his relation to society.

I think, however, that the passion for social righteousness will prove in the end not enough in itself. The danger of what I have called the modern eschatology, the danger of neglecting the permanent for the transitory, the personal for the social, is one to which the poet is exposed in common with everyone else: but he has a peculiar responsibility not to be deluded. Yet I would ask you to have some sympathy with his difficulties. An age of change, and a period of incessant apprehension of war, do not form a favorable environment. There is a temptation to welcome change for its own sake, to sink our minds in some desperate philosophy of *action;* and several such philosophies are being urged upon us. Contempt for the past, and even ignorance of it, is on the increase, and many are ready for the unlimited experiment. We cannot effect intelligent change unless we hold fast to the permanent essentials; and a clear understanding of what we should hold fast to, and what abandon, should make us all the better prepared to carry out the changes that are needed. Thus we can look back upon the past without regret, and to the future without fear.

Robinson Jeffers [1887–   ]

While granting that Eliot's *Waste Land* was one of the finest poems of the century, Jeffers deplored the trend of contemporary poetry: "the self-consciousness and naïve learnedness, the undergraduate irony, unnatural metaphors, hiatuses and labored obscurity." From his aerie on the California coast he sent forth a very different kind of verse.

California has so long been the home of Robinson Jeffers and is so much a part of his writing that it seems irrelevant now that he was born in Pittsburgh and lived much in Europe until he was sixteen. After graduating from Occidental College when only eighteen, he studied at the University of Southern California (three years in medicine) and the University of Washington (a year of forestry). But actually, he says, "I wasn't deeply interested in anything but poetry." "I married Una Call Kuster in 1913. We were going to England in the autumn of 1914. But the August news turned us to this village of Carmel instead; and when the stagecoach topped the hill from Monterey, and we looked down through pines and sea-fog on Carmel Bay, it was evident that we had come without knowing it to our inevitable place." Here, on Point Sur, he built with his own hands a stone house and near it a high tower in which he works — his secluded home ever since.

In 1924 *Tamar and Other Poems*, his third book of verse, created a sensation. The sensation was deepened into a substantial reputation by *Roan Stallion, Tamar, and Other Poems* (1925), *The Women at Point Sur* (1927), *Cawdor and Other Poems* (1928), *Dear Judas and Other Poems* (1929), *Thurso's Landing and Other Poems* (1932). *Give Your Heart to the Hawks and Other Poems* (1933) and later volumes including *Selected Poetry of Robinson Jeffers* (1939). These volumes maintained the characteristics of Jeffers' verse — a loose but strong musical line, daring choice of subjects (in the long poems), and an elemental imagination akin to the strength of his own California rock cliffs. The magnificence of his landscape, the beauty of its detail, give some measure of relief to his dark reading of human destiny. This contrast is carried out by two favorite symbols: the stone, or enduring, immemorial earth, and the hawk, the wild, undirected spirit of man, marked for destruction. His attachment is to the granite rocks, the clean beating surf, the redwoods towering in their strength.

In his stark naturalism, the immense universe itself is God, the God of physics, "praised adequately," as Yvor Winters put it, "only by the screaming demons that make up the atom." Nature is completely indifferent to what we call "humanity." Indeed, Jeffers symbolizes man's self-regard as incest, which leads him, helpless, to his doom. The poet has expressed his aversion to man and human society by saying: "Cut humanity out of my being, that is the wound that festers," and by conjecturing that the stars, which seem to be fleeing outward from the solar system, are fleeing "the contagion of consciousness that infects this corner of space." Contemptuous of "the animals Christ was rumored to have died for," he looks forward to a time when the earth will have got rid of man and have reached a "white and most clean, colorless quietness." For "civilization is a transient sickness." Not without satisfaction did he view the destruction of 1914–18, the ensuing international chaos, the economic disorder, the resumption of world conflict. The disillusioned mood of the period between the wars could not go much farther.

Further reading: *Selected Poetry*. L. C. Powell, *Robinson Jeffers: The Man and His Work*, revised 1940.

Robinson Jeffers [1887–   ]

Roan Stallion

(w. 1925)

This early narrative poem is a good introduction to Jeffers, illustrating his storm and seacoast settings, his preoccupation with violence, pain, and sexuality, his aversion toward humanity and affection for death, and his scientific vision. Inspired partly by an Italian legend about an equine statue with a woman lover and partly by the Leda myth, it was intended as a detached, amoral Freudian narrative. But the vision at the ford and the somewhat labored deification of the stallion give a measure of divine sanction to the concluding brutality — in spite of the psychological reduction of religion in the passage beginning, "The fire threw up figures . . .", and the philosophical reduction of man in the passage beginning, "Humanity is the start of the race . . ." Later, disturbed by the implications of such a narrative, Jeffers wrote *The Women at Point Sur* "to show in action the danger of that Roan Stallion idea of 'breaking out of humanity' misinterpreted in the mind of a fool or a lunatic."

The dog barked; then the woman stood in the doorway, and hearing iron strike stone
    down the steep road
Covered her head with a black shawl and entered the light rain; she stood at the turn
    of the road.
A nobly formed woman; erect and strong as a new tower; the features stolid and dark
But sculptured into a strong grace; straight nose with a high bridge, firm and wide eyes,
    full chin,
Red lips; she was only a fourth part Indian; a Scottish sailor had planted her in young
    native earth,   5
Spanish and Indian, twenty-one years before. He had named her California when she
    was born;
That was her name; and had gone north.

                        She heard the hooves and
    wheels come nearer, up the steep road.
The buckskin mare, leaning against the breastpiece, plodded into sight round the wet
    bank.
The pale face of the driver followed; the burnt-out eyes; they had fortune in them.
    He sat twisted   10
On the seat of the old buggy, leading a second horse by a long halter, a roan, a big one,
That stepped daintily; by the swell of the neck, a stallion. "What have you got,
    Johnny?" "Maskerel's stallion.
Mine now. I won him last night, I had very good luck." He was quite drunk. "They
    bring their mares up here now.
I keep this fellow. I got money besides, but I'll not show you." "Did you buy some-
    thing, Johnny,
For our Christine? Christmas comes in two days, Johnny." "By God, forgot," he
    answered laughing.   15
"Don't tell Christine it's Christmas; after while I get her something, maybe." But
    California:
"I shared your luck when you lost: you lost *me* once, Johnny, remember? Tom Dell
    had me two nights
Here in the house: other times we've gone hungry: now that you've won, Christine
    will have her Christmas.
We share your luck, Johnny. You give me money, I go down to Monterey to-morrow,
Buy presents for Christine, come back in the evening. Next day Christmas." "You have
    wet ride," he answered   20
Giggling. "Here money. Five dollar; ten; twelve dollar. You buy two bottles of rye
    whisky for Johnny."
"All right. I go to-morrow."

                     He was an outcast Hollander; not old, but
    shriveled with bad living.
The child Christine inherited from his race blue eyes, from his life a wizened forehead;
    she watched
From the house-door her father lurch out of the buggy and lead with due respect the
    stallion   25
To the new corral, the strong one; leaving the wearily breathing buckskin mare to his
    wife to unharness.

Storm in the night; the rain on the thin shakes of the roof like the ocean on rock
    streamed battering; once thunder
Walked down the narrow canyon into Carmel valley and wore away westward; Christine
    was wakeful
With fears and wonders; her father lay too deep for storm to touch him.
           Dawn comes late in the year's dark,   30
Later into the crack of a canyon under redwoods; and California slipped from bed
An hour before it; the buckskin would be tired; there was little barley, and why should
    Johnny

Feed all the barley to his stallion? That is what he would do. She tiptoed out of the
    room.
Leaving her clothes, he'd waken if she waited to put them on, and passed from the door
    of the house
Into the dark of the rain; the big black drops were cold through the thin shift, but
    the wet earth   35
Pleasant under her naked feet. There was a pleasant smell in the stable; and moving
    softly,
Touching things gently with the supple bend of the unclothed body, was pleasant. She
    found a box,
Filled it with sweet dry barley and took it down to the old corral. The little mare
    sighed deeply
At the rail in the wet darkness; and California returning between two redwoods up to
    the house
Heard the happy jaws grinding the grain. Johnny could mind the pigs and chickens.
    Christine called to her   40
When she entered the house, but slept again under her hand. She laid the wet night-
    dress on a chair-back
And stole into the bedroom to get her clothes. A plank creaked, and he wakened. She
    stood motionless
Hearing him stir in the bed. When he was quiet she stooped after her shoes, and he
    said softly,
"What are you doing? Come back to bed." "It's late, I'm going to Monterey, I must
    hitch up."
"You come to bed first. I been away three days. I give you money, I take back the
    money   45
And what you do in town then?" She sighed sharply and came to the bed.
                He reaching his hands from it
Felt the cool curve and firmness of her flank, and half rising caught her by the long
    wet hair.
She endured, and to hasten the act she feigned desire; she had not for long, except in
    dream, felt it.
Yesterday's drunkenness made him sluggish and exacting; she saw, turning her head
    sadly,   50
The windows were bright gray with dawn; he embraced her still, stopping to talk about
    the stallion.
At length she was permitted to put on her clothes. Clear daylight over the steep hills;
Gray-shining cloud over the tops of the redwoods; the winter stream sang loud; the
    wheels of the buggy
Slipped in deep slime, ground on washed stones at the road-edge. Down the hill the
    wrinkled river smothered the ford.
You must keep to the bed of stones: she knew the way by willow and alder: the buckskin
    halted mid-stream,   55
Shuddering, the water her own color washing up to the traces; but California, drawing up
Her feet out of the whirl onto the seat of the buggy swung the whip over the yellow
    water
And drove to the road.
                               All morning the clouds were racing north-
    ward like a river. At noon they thickened.
When California faced the southwind home from Monterey it was heavy with level
    rainfall.   60
She looked seaward from the foot of the valley; red rays cried sunset from a trumpet
    of streaming
Cloud over Lobos, the southwest occident of the solstice. Twilight came soon, but the
    tired mare
Feared the road more than the whip. Mile after mile of slow gray twilight.
           Then, quite suddenly, darkness.

"Christine will be asleep. It is Christmas Eve. The ford. That hour of daylight wasted
    this morning!"   65
She could see nothing; she let the reins lie on the dashboard and knew at length by
    the cramp of the wheels
And the pitch down, they had reached it. Noise of wheels on stones, plashing of
    hooves in water; a world
Of sounds; no sight; the gentle thunder of water; the mare snorting, dipping her head,
    one knew,
To look for footing, in the blackness, under the stream. The hushing and creaking
    of the sea-wind
In the passion of invisible willows.   70
                                                          The mare stood still; the woman
                    shouted to her; spared whip,
For a false leap would lose the track of the ford. She stood. "The baby's things,"
    thought California,
"Under the seat: the water will come over the floor"; and rising in the midst of the water
She tilted the seat; fetched up the doll, the painted wooden chickens, the woolly bear,
    the book
Of many pictures, the box of sweets: she brought them all from under the seat and
    stored them, trembling,   75
Under her clothes, about the breasts, under the arms; the corners of the cardboard boxes
Cut into the soft flesh; but with a piece of rope for a girdle and wound about the
    shoulders
All was made fast. The mare stood still as if asleep in the midst of the water. Then
    California
Reached out a hand over the stream and fingered her rump; the solid wet convexity of it
Shook like the beat of a great heart. "What are you waiting for?" But the feel of the
    animal surface   80
Had wakened a dream, obscured real danger with a dream of danger. "What for? for
    the water-stallion
To break out of the stream, that is what the rump strains for, him to come up flinging
    foam sidewise,
Fore-hooves in air, crush me and the rig and curl over his woman." She flung out with
    the whip then;
The mare plunged forward. The buggy drifted sidelong: was she off ground? Swim-
    ming? No: by the splashes.
The driver, a mere prehensile instinct, clung to the sideirons of the seat and felt the force
But not the coldness of the water, curling over her knees, breaking up to the waist   86
Over her body. They'd turned. The mare had turned up stream and was wallowing
    back into shoal water.
Then California dropped her forehead to her knees, having seen nothing, feeling a
    danger,
And felt the brute weight of a branch of alder, the pendulous light leaves brush her
    bent neck
Like a child's fingers. The mare burst out of water and stopped on the slope to the
    ford. The woman climbed down   90
Between the wheels and went to her head. "Poor Dora," she called her by her name,
    "there, Dora. Quietly,"
And led her around, there was room to turn on the margin, the head to the gentle
    thunder of the water.
She crawled on hands and knees, felt for the ruts, and shifted the wheels into them.
    "You can see, Dora.
I can't. But this time you'll go through it." She climbed into the seat and shouted
    angrily. The mare
Stopped, her two forefeet in the water. She touched with the whip. The mare plodded
    ahead and halted.   95
Then California thought of prayer: "Dear little Jesus,

Dear baby Jesus born to-night, your head was shining
Like silver candles. I've got a baby too, only a girl. You had light wherever you walked.
Dear baby Jesus give me light." Light streamed: rose, gold, rich purple, hiding the
    ford like a curtain.
The gentle thunder of water was a noise of wing-feathers, the fans of paradise lifting
    softly.   100
The child afloat on radiance had a baby face, but the angels had birds' heads, hawks'
    heads,
Bending over the baby, weaving a web of wings about him. He held in the small fat hand
A little snake with golden eyes, and California could see clearly on the under radiance
The mare's pricked ears, a sharp black fork against the shining light-fall. But it dropped;
    the light of heaven
Frightened poor Dora. She backed; swung up the water,   105
And nearly oversetting the buggy turned and scrambled backward; the iron wheel-tires
    rang on boulders.

Then California weeping climbed between the wheels. Her wet clothes and the toys
    packed under
Dragged her down with their weight; she stripped off cloak and dress and laid the baby's
    things in the buggy;
Brought Johnny's whisky out from under the seat; wrapped all in the dress, bottles and
    toys, and tied them
Into a bundle that would sling over her back. She unharnessed the mare, hurting her
    fingers   110
Against the swollen straps and the wet buckles. She tied the pack over her shoulders,
    the cords
Crossing her breasts, and mounted. She drew up her shift about her waist and knotted
    it, naked thighs
Clutching the sides of the mare, bare flesh to the wet withers, and caught the mane
    with her right hand,
The looped-up bridle-reins in the other. "Dora, the baby gives you light." The blind-
    ing radiance   114
Hovered the ford. "Sweet baby Jesus give us light." Cataracts of light and Latin singing
Fell through the willows; the mare snorted and reared: the roar and thunder of the
    invisible water;
The night shaking open like a flag, shot with the flashes; the baby face hovering; the
    water
Beating over her shoes and stockings up to the bare thighs; and over them, like a
    beast
Lapping her belly; the wriggle and pitch of the mare swimming; the drift, the sucking
    water; the blinding
Light above and behind with not a gleam before, in the throat of darkness; the shock
    of the forehooves   120
Striking bottom, the struggle and surging lift of the haunches. She felt the water
    streaming off her
From the shoulders down; heard the great strain and sob of the mare's breathing, heard
    the horseshoes grind on gravel.
When California came home the dog at the door snuffed at her without barking;
    Christine and Johnny
Both were asleep; she did not sleep for hours, but kindled fire and knelt patiently over it,
Shaping and drying the dear-bought gifts for Christmas morning.   125

    She hated (she thought) the proud-necked stallion.
He'd lean the big twin masses of his breast on the rail, his red-brown eyes flash the
    white crescents,
She admired him then, she hated him for his uselessness, serving nothing

But Johnny's vanity. Horses were too cheap to breed. She thought, if he could range in freedom,

Shaking the red-roan mane for a flag on the bare hills.   130

                                                                                A man

    brought up a mare in April;

Then California, though she wanted to watch, stayed with Christine indoors. When the child fretted

The mother told her once more about the miracle of the ford; her prayers to the little Jesus

The Christmas Eve when she was bringing the gifts home; the appearance, the lights, the Latin singing,

The thunder of wing-feathers and water, the shining child, the cataracts of splendor down the darkness.   135

"A little baby," Christine asked, "the God is a baby?" "The child of God. That was his birthday.

His mother was named Mary: we pray to her too: God came to her. He was not the child of a man

Like you or me. God was his father: she was the stallion's wife — what did I say — God's wife,"

She said with a cry, lifting Christine aside, pacing the planks of the floor. "She is called more blessed

Than any woman. She was so good, she was more loved." "Did God live near her house?" "He lives   140

Up high, over the stars; he ranges on the bare blue hill of the sky." In her mind a picture

Flashed, of the red-roan mane shaken out for a flag on the bare hills, and she said quickly, "He's more

Like a great man holding the sun in his hand." Her mind giving her words the lie, "But no one

Knows, only the shining and the power. The power, the terror, the burning fire covered her over . . ."

"Was she burnt up, mother?" "She was so good and lovely, she was the mother of the little Jesus.   145

If you are good nothing will hurt you." "What did she think?" "She loved, she was not afraid of the hooves —

Hands that had made the hills and sun and moon, and the sea and the great redwoods, the terrible strength,

She gave herself without thinking." "You only saw the baby, mother?" "Yes, and the angels about him,

The great wild shining over the black river." Three times she had walked to the door, three times returned,

And now the hand that had thrice hung on the knob, full of prevented action, twisted the cloth   150

Of the child's dress that she had been mending. "Oh, Oh, I've torn it." She struck at the child and then embraced her

Fiercely, the small blond sickly body.

                                                        Johnny came in, his face reddened as if he had stood

Near fire, his eyes triumphing. "Finished," he said, and looked with malice at Christine. "I go

Down valley with Jim Carrier; owes me five dollar, fifteen I charge him, he brought ten in his pocket.   155

Has grapes on the ranch, maybe I take a barrel red wine instead of money. Be back to-morrow.

To-morrow night I tell you — Eh, Jim," he laughed over his shoulder, "I say to-morrow evening

I show her how the red fellow act, the big fellow. When I come home." She answered
     nothing, but stood
In front of the door, holding the little hand of her daughter, in the path of sun between
     the redwoods,
While Johnny tied the buckskin mare behind Carrier's buggy, and bringing saddle and
     bridle tossed them   160
Under the seat. Jim Carrier's mare, the bay, stood with drooped head and started
     slowly, the men
Laughing and shouting at her; their voices could be heard down the steep road, after
     the noise
Of the iron-hooped wheels died from the stone. Then one might hear the hush of the
     wind in the tall redwoods,
The tinkle of the April brook, deep in its hollow.
                                                             Humanity is the
          start of the race; I say   165
Humanity is the mold to break away from, the crust to break through, the coal to break
     into fire,
The atom to be split.
                                   Tragedy that breaks man's face and a white
          fire flies out of it; vision that fools him
Out of his limits, desire that fools him out of his limits, unnatural crime, inhuman
     science,
Slit eyes in the mask; wild loves that leap over the walls of nature, the wild fence-
     vaulter science,   170
Useless intelligence of far stars, dim knowledge of the spinning demons that make an
     atom,
These break, these pierce, these deify, praising their God shrilly with fierce voices: not
     in man's shape
He approves the praise, he that walks lightning-naked on the Pacific, that laces the
     suns with planets,
The heart of the atom with electrons: what is humanity in this cosmos? For him,
     the last
Least taint of a trace in the dregs of the solution; for itself, the mold to break away
     from, the coal   175
To break into fire, the atom to be split.

                              After the child slept, after
          the leopard-footed evening
Had glided oceanward, California turned the lamp to its least flame and glided from
     the house.
She moved sighing, like a loose fire, backward and forward on the smooth ground by
     the door.
She heard the night-wind that draws down the valley like the draught in a flue under
     clear weather   180
Whisper and toss in the tall redwoods; she heard the tinkle of the April brook deep
     in its hollow.
Cooled by the night the odors that the horses had left behind were in her nostrils;
     the night
Whitened up the bare hill; a drift of coyotes by the river cried bitterly against moonrise;
Then California ran to the old corral, the empty one where they kept the buckskin
     mare,
And leaned, and bruised her breasts on the rail, feeling the sky whiten. When the
     moon stood over the hill   185
She stole to the house. The child breathed quietly. Herself: to sleep? She had seen
     Christ in the night at Christmas.
The hills were shining open to the enormous night of the April moon: empty and empty,

The vast round backs of the bare hills? If one should ride up high might not the Father himself

Be seen brooding His night, cross-legged, chin in hand, squatting on the last dome? More likely

Leaping the hills, shaking the red-roan mane for a flag on the bare hills. She blew out the lamp. 190

Every fiber of flesh trembled with faintness when she came to the door; strength lacked, to wander

Afoot into the shining of the hill, high enough, high enough . . . the hateful face of a man had taken

The strength that might have served her, the corral was empty. The dog followed her, she caught him by the collar,

Dragged him in fierce silence back to the door of the house, latched him inside. It was like daylight 195

Out-doors and she hastened without faltering down the footpath, through the dark fringe of twisted oak-brush,

To the open place in a bay of the hill. The dark strength of the stallion had heard her coming; she heard him

Blow the shining air out of his nostrils, she saw him in the white lake of moonlight

Move like a lion along the timbers of the fence, shaking the nightfall

Of the great mane; his fragrance came to her; she leaned on the fence; 200

He drew away from it, the hooves making soft thunder in the trodden soil.

Wild love had trodden it, his wrestling with the stranger, the shame of the day

Had stamped it into mire and powder when the heavy fetlocks

Strained the soft flanks. "Oh, if I could bear you!

If I had the strength. O great God that came down to Mary, gently you came. But I will ride him 205

Up into the hill, if he throws me, if he tramples me, is it not my desire

To endure death?" She climbed the fence, pressing her body against the rail, shaking like fever,

And dropped inside to the soft ground. He neither threatened her with his teeth nor fled from her coming,

And lifting her hand gently to the upflung head she caught the strap of the headstall,

That hung under the quivering chin. She unlooped the halter from the high strength of the neck 210

And the arch the storm-cloud mane hung with live darkness. He stood; she crushed her breasts

On the hard shoulder, an arm over the withers, the other under the mass of his throat, and murmuring

Like a mountain dove, "If I could bear you." No way, no help, a gulf in nature. She murmured, "Come,

We will run on the hill. O beautiful, O beautiful," and led him to the gate and flung the bars on the ground. He threw his head downward

To snuff at the bars; and while he stood, she catching mane and withers with all sudden contracture 215

And strength of her lithe body, leaped, clung hard, and was mounted. He had been ridden before; he did not

Fight the weight but ran like a stone falling;

Broke down the slope into the moon-glass of the stream, and flattened to his neck

She felt the branches of a buck-eye tree fly over her, saw the wall of the oak-scrub

End her world: but he turned there, the matted branches 220

Scraped her right knee, the great slant shoulders

Laboring the hill-slope, up, up, the clear hill. Desire had died in her

At the first rush, the falling like death, but now it revived,

She feeling between her thighs the labor of the great engine, the running muscles, the hard swiftness,

She riding the savage and exultant strength of the world. Having topped the thicket
    he turned eastward,   225

Running less wildly; and now at length he felt the halter when she drew on it; she
    guided him upward;

He stopped and grazed on the great arch and pride of the hill, the silent calvary. A
    dwarfish oakwood

Climbed the other slope out of the dark of the unknown canyon beyond; the last
    wind-beaten bush of it

Crawled up to the height, and California slipping from her mount tethered him to it.
    She stood then,

Shaking. Enormous films of moonlight   230

Trailed down from the height. Space, anxious whiteness, vastness. Distant beyond
    conception the shining ocean

Lay light like a haze along the ledge and doubtful world's end. Little vapors gleaming,
    and little

Darknesses on the far chart underfoot symbolized wood and valley; but the air was the
    element, the moon-

Saturate arcs and spires of the air.

                      Here is solitude, here on the
    calvary, nothing conscious   235

But the possible God and the cropped grass, no witness, no eye but that misformed one,
    the moon's past fullness.

Two figures on the shining hill, woman and stallion, she kneeling to him, brokenly
    adoring.

He cropping the grass, shifting his hooves, or lifting the long head to gaze over the
    world,

Tranquil and powerful. She prayed aloud, "O God, I am not good enough, O fear, O
    strength, I am draggled.

Johnny and other men have had me, and O clean power! Here am I," she said falling
    before him,   240

And crawled to his hooves. She lay a long while, as if asleep, in reach of the fore-hooves,
    weeping. He avoided

Her head and the prone body. He backed at first; but later plucked the grass that grew
    by her shoulder.

The small dark head under his nostrils: a small round stone, that smelt human, black
    hair growing from it:

The skull shut the light in it: it was not possible for any eyes

To know what throbbed and shone under the sutures of the skull, or a shell full of
    lightning   245

Had scared the roan strength, and he'd have broken tether, screaming, and run for the
    valley.

                      The atom bounds-breaking,

Nucleus to sun, electrons to planets, with recognition

Not praying, self-equaling, the whole to the whole, the microcosm

Not entering nor accepting entrance, more equally, more utterly, more incredibly
    conjugate   250

With the other extreme and greatness; passionately perceptive of identity. . . .
               The fire threw up figures

And symbols meanwhile, racial myths formed and dissolved in it, the phantom rulers
    of humanity

That without being are yet more real than what they are born of, and without shape,
    shape that which makes them:

The nerves and the flesh go by shadowlike, the limbs and the lives shadowlike, these
    shadows remain, these shadows   255

To whom temples, to whom churches, to whom labors and wars, visions and dreams
    are dedicate:

Out of the fire in the small round stone that black moss covered, a crucified man
      writhed up in anguish;
A woman covered by a huge beast in whose mane the stars were netted, sun and moon
      were his eyeballs,
Smiled under the unendurable violation, her throat swollen with the storm and blood-
      flecks gleaming
On the stretched lips; a woman — no, a dark water, split by jets of lightning, and after
      a season   260
What floated up out of the furrowed water, a boat, a fish, a fire-globe?
      It had wings, the creature,
And flew against the fountain of lightning, fell burnt out of the cloud back to the
      bottomless water . . . .
Figures and symbols, castlings of the fire, played in her brain; but the white fire was
      the essence,
The burning in the small round shell of bone that black hair covered, that lay by the
      hooves on the hilltop.   265

She rose at length, she unknotted the halter; she walked and led the stallion; two
      figures, woman and stallion,
Came down the silent emptiness of the dome of the hill, under the cataract of the
      moonlight.

The next night there was moon through cloud. Johnny had returned half drunk
      toward evening, and California
Who had known him for years with neither love nor loathing to-night hating him had
      let the child Christine
Play in the light of the lamp for hours after her bedtime; who fell asleep at length on
      the floor   270
Beside the dog; then Johnny: "Put her to bed." She gathered the child against her
      breasts, she laid her
In the next room, and covered her with a blanket. The window was white, the moon
      had risen. The mother
Lay down by the child, but after a moment Johnny stood in the doorway. "Come
      drink." He had brought home
Two jugs of wine slung from the saddle, part payment for the stallion's service; a
      pitcher of it
Was on the table, and California sadly came and emptied her glass. Whisky, she
      thought,   275
Would have erased him till to-morrow; the thin red wine. . . . "We have a good
      evening," he laughed, pouring it.
"One glass yet then I show you what the red fellow did." She moving toward the
      house-door his eyes
Followed her, the glass filled and the red juice ran over the table. When it struck the
      floor-planks
He heard and looked. "Who stuck the pig?" he muttered stupidly, "here's blood, here's
      blood," and trailed his fingers
In the red lake under the lamplight. While he was looking down the door creaked, she
      had slipped out-doors,   280
And he, his mouth curving like a faun's, imagined the chase under the solemn redwoods,
      the panting
And unresistant victim caught in a dark corner. He emptied the glass and went out-doors
Into the dappled lanes of moonlight. No sound but the April brook's. "Hey Bruno,"
      he called, "find her.
Bruno, go find her." The dog after a little understood and quested, the man following.
When California crouching by an oak-bush above the house heard them come near she
      darted   285

To the open slope and ran down hill. The dog barked at her heels, pleased with the
    game, and Johnny
Followed in silence. She ran down to the new corral, she saw the stallion
Move like a lion along the timbers of the fence, the dark arched neck shaking the
    nightfall
Of the great mane; she threw herself prone and writhed under the bars, his hooves
    backing away from her
Made muffled thunder in the soft soil. She stood in the midst of the corral, panting,
    but Johnny   290
Paused at the fence. The dog ran under it, and seeing the stallion move, the woman
    standing quiet,
Danced after the beast, with white-toothed feints and dashes. When Johnny saw the
    formidable dark strength
Recoil from the dog, he climbed up over the fence.

The child Christine waked when her mother left her
And lay half-dreaming, in the half-waking dream she saw the ocean come up out of the
    west   295
And cover the world, she looked up through clear water at the tops of the redwoods.
    She heard the door creak
And the house empty; her heart shook her body, sitting up on the bed, and she heard
    the dog
And crept toward light, where it gleamed under the crack of the door. She opened the
    door, the room was empty,
The table-top was a red lake under the lamplight. The color of it was terrible to her;
She had seen the red juice drip from a coyote's muzzle, her father had shot one day
    in the hills   300
And carried him home over the saddle: she looked at the rifle on the wall-rack: it was
    not moved:
She ran to the door, the dog was barking and the moon was shining: she knew wine
    by the odor
But the color frightened her, the empty house frightened her, she followed down hill
    in the white lane of moonlight
The friendly noise of the dog. She saw in the big horse's corral, on the level shoulder
    of the hill,
Black on white, the dark strength of the beast, the dancing fury of the dog, and the
    two others.   305
One fled, one followed; the big one charged, rearing; one fell under his forehooves.
    She heard her mother
Scream: without thought she ran to the house, she dragged a chair past the red pool
    and climbed to the rifle,
Got it down from the wall and lugged it somehow through the door and down the
    hillside, under the hard weight
Sobbing. Her mother stood by the rails of the corral, she gave it to her. On the far side
The dog flashed at the plunging stallion; in the midst of the space the man, slow-moving,
    like a hurt worm   310
Crawling, dragged his body by inches toward the fence-line. Then California, resting
    the rifle
On the top rail, without doubting, without hesitance,
Aimed for the leaping body of the dog, and when it stood, fired. It snapped, rolled
    over, lay quiet.
"O mother, you've hit Bruno!" "I couldn't see the sights in the moonlight," she
    answered quietly. She stood
And watched, resting the rifle-butt on the ground. The stallion wheeled, freed from his
    torment, the man   315
Lurched up to his knees, wailing a thin and bitter bird's cry, and the roan thunder

Struck; hooves left nothing alive but teeth tore up the remnant. "O mother, shoot,
   shoot!" Yet California
Stood carefully watching, till the beast having fed all his fury stretched neck to utmost,
   head high,
And wrinkled back the upper lip from the teeth, yawning obscene disgust over — not
   a man —
A smear on the moon-lake earth: then California moved by some obscure human fidelity
Lifted the rifle. Each separate nerve-cell of her brain flaming the stars fell from their
   places
Crying in her mind: she fired three times before the haunches crumpled sidewise, the
   forelegs stiffening,
And the beautiful strength settled to earth: she turned then on her little daughter the
   mask of a woman
Who has killed God. The night-wind veering, the smell of the spilt wine drifted down
   hill from the house.

Gale in April

(w. 1921?)

⚜ The theme of the inseparable beauty and pain of life is
central to Jeffers' thought. Compare his attitude toward death
with that found in Walt Whitman.

Intense and terrible beauty, how has our race with the frail naked nerves,
So little a craft swum down from its far launching?
Why now, only because the northwest blows and the headed grass billows,
Great seas jagging the west and on the granite
Blanching, the vessel is brimmed, this dancing play of the world is too much passion. 5
A gale in April so overfilling the spirit,
Though his ribs were thick as the earth's, arches of mountain, how shall one dare to live,
Though his blood were like the earth's rivers and his flesh iron,
How shall one dare to live? One is born strong, how do the weak endure it?
The strong lean upon death as on a rock,   10
After eighty years there is shelter and the naked nerves shall be covered with deep
   quietness.
O beauty of things go on, go on, O torture
Of intense joy I have lasted out my time, I have thanked God and finished,
Roots of millennial trees fold me in the darkness,
Northwest wind shake their tops, not to the root, not to the root, I have passed   15
From beauty to the other beauty, peace, the night splendor.

To the Stone-Cutters

(w. 1922?)

Stone-cutters fighting time with marble, you foredefeated
Challengers of oblivion
Eat cynical earnings, knowing rock splits, records fall down,
The square-limbed Roman letters
Scale in the thaws, wear in the rain.   5
   The poet as well
Builds his monument mockingly;
For man will be blotted out, the blithe earth die, the brave sun
Die blind, his heart blackening:
Yet stones have stood for a thousand years, and pained thoughts found   10
The honey peace in old poems.

Archibald MacLeish [1892 —   ]

Disciplined, in his expatriate years, in the verse modes of Pound and Eliot, preoccupied with the poetic registration of his own sensibility, Archibald MacLeish eventually turned outward to his land and people and to the great crises of his time — the depression, the rise of fascism, the peril of a second World War, the need of a lasting peace, the meaning and destiny of America.

Born in Glencoe, Illinois, MacLeish spent his boyhood on the lake shore, was educated in the local schools and in Connecticut, attended Yale College (where the literary group included Benét and Wilder) and the Harvard Law School. In the first World War he served in France in the field artillery, rising to the rank of captain. For three years he tried the practice of law in Boston, but boldly gave it up in favor of a career as poet. Setting forth with his family, he established himself in Paris, 1923–28, to write and read. Back in America, he lived on a farm, made a trip to Mexico (in preparation for his poem *Conquistador*), became one of the editors of *Fortune*, was appointed Librarian of Congress by President Roosevelt in 1939. During the war he served as director of the Office of Facts and Figures, then as assistant Secretary of State. In 1949 he became professor of English at Harvard.

All along, he had been publishing freely. His first significant poetry, showing the influence of Robinson and Eliot, and revealing him as one of the "Lost Generation" after the first World War, appeared in three books in 1924–25, and the next year he emerged fully in *Streets in the Moon*. *The Hamlet of A. MacLeish*, 1928, strongly colored by T. S. Eliot, was a long, subjective poem of spiritual disintegration.

A new attitude began with *New Found Land*, 1930, and *Frescoes for Mr. Rockefeller's City*, 1933, more independent in poetic style, more responsive to his national and cultural tradition. Directing his new social consciousness to the contemporary world, he wrote the verse drama *Panic*, the poems of *Public Speech*, the poetic commentary of a book of photographs *Land of the Free*, the radio verse plays *The Fall of the City* and *Air Raid*. In 1940 came *America Was Promises*, and the same year a public address (quickly published as a book) *The Irresponsibles*, denouncing the writers of the 1920's for having "done more to disarm democracy in the face of Fascism than any other single influence." Other books followed in the 1940's and 1950's, notably the poetic drama, *J.B.* (1958), a modern reinterpretation of the story of Job.

Further reading: *Collected Poems, 1917–1952.*

'Ars Poetica

(w. 1924)

🔌 The Latin title of this "Art of Poetry" is a reminder of the famous discourse on the subject by Horace. Like the Roman poet, MacLeish loved fine craftsmanship. When he wrote this miniature *ars*

poetica he was an expatriate in Paris, fascinated by the symbolist school, reading Laforgue, Rimbaud, Valéry, Ezra Pound, T. S. Eliot.

In a notebook he wrote: "The purpose of the expression of emotion in a poem is not to recreate the poet's emotion in some one else. . . . The poem itself is a finality, an end, a creation." A good poem, he conceived, is self-sufficient; it *is*, it does not "mean." One might as well ask the meaning of a friend or brother. A poem is not a statement or demonstration but an experience, and its medium is metaphor, "the conviction of the senses."

In the version first published there were few commas and no periods.

A poem should be palpable and mute
As a globed fruit,

Dumb
As old medallions to the thumb,

Silent as the sleeve-worn stone   5
Of casement ledges where the moss has grown —

A poem should be wordless
As the flight of birds.

A poem should be motionless in time
As the moon climbs,   10

Leaving, as the moon releases
Twig by twig the night-entangled trees,

Leaving, as the moon behind the winter leaves,
Memory by memory the mind —

A poem should be motionless in time   15
As the moon climbs

A poem should be equal to:
Not true.

For all the history of grief
An empty doorway and a maple leaf.   20

For love
The leaning grasses and two lights above the
        sea —

A poem should not mean
But be.

You, Andrew Marvell
(w. 1926)

❧ The seventeenth-century poem by Andrew Marvell "To His Coy Mistress" contains the lines
        "But at my back I always hear
        Time's winged chariot hurrying near"
to which Eliot had alluded in *The Waste Land*, and to which MacLeish alludes through the title and idea of his poem, and also in a note written on the Mediterranean as he was returning from Persia. This is the note: "The unforeseen experience — conscious-

ness now of the other side of the earth: the always westward coming on of the night. . . ."

And here face down beneath the sun
And here upon earth's noonward height
To feel the always coming on
The always rising of the night:

To feel creep up the curving east   5
The earthy chill of dusk and slow
Upon those under lands the vast
And ever climbing shadow grow

And strange at Ecbatan the trees
Take leaf by leaf the evening strange   10
The flooding dark about their knees
The mountains over Persia change

And now at Kermanshah the gate
Dark empty and the withered grass
And through the twilight now the late   15
Few travelers in the westward pass

And Baghdad darken and the bridge
Across the silent river gone
And through Arabia the edge
Of evening widen and steal on   20

And deepen on Palmyra's street
The wheel rut in the ruined stone
And Lebanon fade out and Crete
High through the clouds and overblown

And over Sicily the air   25
Still flashing with the landward gulls
And loom and slowly disappear
The sails above the shadowy hulls

And Spain go under and the shore
Of Africa the gilded sand   30
And evening vanish and no more
The low pale light across that land

Nor now the long light on the sea

And here face downward in the sun
To feel how swift how secretly   35
The shadow of the night comes on

American Letter
For Gerald Murphy
(1929)

❧ Having lived himself in "the old lands" for five years, the expatriate poet returns to his native country. Psychologically, the poem oscillates between puzzled reawareness of America and swift, warm memories of southern France. It might be compared to the verses Emerson wrote on returning from a much briefer sojourn in Europe (page 297).

The wind is east but the hot weather continues,
Blue and no clouds, the sound of the leaves thin,
Dry like the rustling of paper, scored across
With the slate-shrill screech of the locusts.
            The tossing of
Pines is the low sound. In the wind's running   5
The wild carrots smell of the burning sun.
Why should I think of the dolphins at Capo di Mele?
Why should I see in my mind the taut sail
And the hill over St.-Tropez and your hand on the tiller?
Why should my heart be troubled with palms still?   10
I am neither a sold boy nor a Chinese official
Sent to sicken in Pa for some Lo-Yang dish.
This is my own land, my sky, my mountain:
This — not the humming pines and the surf and the sound
At the Ferme Blanche, nor Port Cros in the dusk and the harbor   15
Floating the motionless ship and the sea-drowned star.
I am neither Po Chü-i nor another after
Far from home, in a strange land, daft
For the talk of his own sort and the taste of his lettuces.
This land is my native land. And yet   20
I am sick for home for the red roofs and the olives,
And the foreign words and the smell of the sea fall.
How can a wise man have two countries?
How can a man have the earth and the wind and want
A land far off, alien, smelling of palm-trees   25
And the yellow gorse at noon in the long calms?

It is a strange thing — to be an American.
Neither an old house it is with the air
Tasting of hung herbs and the sun returning
Year after year to the same door and the churn   30
Making the same sound in the cool of the kitchen
Mother to son's wife, and the place to sit

Marked in the dusk by the worn stone at the wellhead —
That — nor the eyes like each other's eyes and the skull
Shaped to the same fault and the hands' sameness.   35
Neither a place it is nor a blood name.
America is West and the wind blowing.
America is a great word and the snow,
A way, a white bird, the rain falling,
A shining thing in the mind and the gulls' call.   40
America is neither a land nor a people,
A word's shape it is, a wind's sweep —
America is alone: many together,
Many of one mouth, of one breath,
Dressed as one — and none brothers among them: 45
Only the taught speech and the aped tongue.
America is alone and the gulls calling.

It is a strange thing to be an American.
It is strange to live on the high world in the stare   49
Of the naked sun and the stars as our bones live.
Men in the old lands housed by their rivers.
They built their towns in the vales in the earth's shelter.
We first inhabit the world. We dwell
On the half earth, on the open curve of a continent.
Sea is divided from sea by the day-fall. The dawn   55
Rides the low east with us many hours;
First are the capes, then are the shorelands, now
The blue Appalachians faint at the day rise;
The willows shudder with light on the long Ohio:
The Lakes scatter the low sun: the prairies 60
Slide out of the dark: in the eddy of clean air
The smoke goes up from the high plains of Wyoming:
The steep Sierras rise: the struck foam
Flames at the wind's heel on the far Pacific:
Already the noon leans to the eastern cliff: 65
The elms darken the door and the dust-heavy lilacs.

It is strange to sleep in the bare stars and to die
On an open land where few bury before us:
(From the new earth the dead return no more.)

It is strange to be born of no race and no
    people.   70
In the old lands they are many together. They
    keep
The wise past and the words spoken in com-
    mon.
They remember the dead with their hands,
    their mouths dumb.
They answer each other with two words in their
    meeting.
They live together in small things. They eat 75
The same dish, their drink is the same and
    their proverbs.
Their youth is like. They are like in their ways
    of love.
They are many men. There are always others
    beside them.
Here it is one man and another and wide
On the darkening hills the faint smoke of the
    houses.   80
Here it is one man and the wind in the boughs.

Therefore our hearts are sick for the south
    water.
The smell of the gorse comes back to our night
    thought.
We are sick at heart for the red roofs and the
    olives;
We are sick at heart for the voice and the foot-
    fall . . .   85

Therefore we will not go though the sea call
    us.
This, this is our land, this is our people,
This that is neither a land nor a race. We must
    reap
The wind here in the grass for our soul's harvest:
Here we must eat our salt or our bones starve.
Here we must live or live only as shadows.   91
This is our race, we that have none, that have
    had
Neither the old walls nor the voices around us,
This is our land, this is our ancient ground —
The raw earth, the mixed bloods and the
    strangers,   95
The different eyes, the wind, and the heart's
    change.
These we will not leave though the old call us.
This is our country-earth, our blood, our kind.
Here we will live our years till the earth blind
    us —
The wind blows from the east. The leaves
    fall.   100

Where of faring men the eyes   5
At oar bench at the rising bow
Have seen — torn shrouds between — the Wain
And that star's changelessness, not changing:

There upon that intent star,
Trust of wandering men, of truth   10
The most reminding witness, we
Fix our eyes also, waylost, the wanderers:

We too turn now to that star:
We too in whose trustless hearts
All truth alters and the lights   15
Of earth are out now turn to that star:

Liberty of man and mind
That once was mind's necessity
And made the West blaze up has burned
To bloody embers and the lamp's out: 20

Hope that was a noble flame
Has fanned to violence and feeds
On cities and the flesh of men
And chokes where unclean smoke defiles it:

Even the small spark of pride   25
That taught the tyrant once is dark
Where gunfire rules the starving street
And justice cheats the dead of honor:

Liberty and pride and hope
And every guide-mark of the mind   30
That led our blindness once has vanished.
This star will not. Love's star will not.

Love that has beheld the face
A man has with a man's eyes in it
Bloody from the slugger's blows   35
Or heard the cold child cry for hunger —

Love that listens where the good,
The virtuous, the men of faith,
Proclaim the paradise on earth
And murder starve and burn to make it —   40

Love that cannot either sleep
Or keep rich music in the ear
Or lose itself for the wild beat
The anger in the blood makes raging —

Love that hardens into hate,   45
Love like hatred and as bright,
Love is that one waking light
That leads now when all others darken.

Wallace Stevens [1879-1955]

In an age when many poets found it difficult to breathe in the commercial atmosphere of America, Wallace Stevens wrote remarkably fine poetry while serving as a successful New York lawyer and then as vice-president of a large Hartford insurance company. Furthermore, he became exactly what the aloof poets wanted to be, a poet's poet, far removed from the taste and understanding of the masses. "It gives a man character as a poet to have a daily contact with a job," he said. "I doubt whether I've lost a thing by leading an exceedingly regular and disciplined life."

Born in Pennsylvania and educated there and at Harvard, Stevens early began writing poetry, but he had no intention of letting it interfere with the business of making a living. He wrote so slowly and was so reticent and so reluctant to publish that he became something of a myth to other poets and for long remained totally unknown, as a poet, to his business confreres and the public at large. Four poems were published in *Poetry* in 1914, but not until 1923, when he was forty-four, did he publish his first volume, *Harmonium*. Then he again lapsed into silence and, it is said, forgot poetry for a while — until it came back in spite of him. In 1931 appeared an enlarged version of *Harmonium*, and in 1935 *Ideas of Order*. Thereafter he published a new volume every few years until 1948. His *Collected Poems* appeared in 1954.

The various prose pieces in which Stevens discusses his art constitute a defense of poetry in the high tone of a Sir Philip Sidney or a Milton. "Poetry increases our feeling for reality," he says, and "the search for reality is as momentous as the search for God." Particularly "in an age of disbelief . . . it is for the poet to supply the satisfactions of belief, in his measure and his style." Therefore the poet should discover his own "particular quality," his particular vision of the world, and then develop this quality "in intensity and volume." It is thus that he may become a "light in the minds of others . . . to help people live their lives." For the true creator of the world we live in, be it bright or dull, is the *imagination*, that "necessary angel," the "only true genius." The world of Plato and the world of Shakespeare are not ours; different imaginations brought them into being. This aesthetic subjectivism, which may have seemed perversely fanciful in the days when Things seemed irrevocably in the saddle, looks more reasonable now that science tells us Things are really nothing at all, and thought, in the last analysis, is as solid as rock. Science seems once more to have caught up with the poet.

Because poetry is for Stevens no mere verbalization of other modes of thought, but a mode of thought in itself, a way of seeing and a way of creating, his poems do not lend themselves readily to paraphrase and are therefore considered difficult and obscure. He has in fact said that poems, "having their origins in the imagination or the emotions . . . very often have meanings that differ in nature from the meanings of things that have their origin in reason . . . It is not possible to [give them] a single rational meaning . . ." If we keep these remarks in mind we will find that he makes the kind of sense that he sets out to make. To reproach him for not being readily paraphrasable is a little like accusing Picasso of not being able to draw a straight line. Moreover, though he is a highly intellectual poet and though he feels that the extreme achievement of the imagination "lies in abstraction," his poems are packed with concrete imagery. Imagination, he says, must begin with the real. From the richly sensuous *Harmonium* down to the *Collected Poems*, which opens with a poem called "An Earthy Anecdote" and closes with a poem called "Not Ideas About the Thing but the Thing Itself," Stevens feeds our senses on a colored world of fire-cats and snowmen and pears and parrots. And like all great artists he does not simply share with us the particular perceptions recorded in his poems, but sends us on our way with a heightened sensitivity of our own, a sharpened imagination for the world at hand.

Further reading: *Collected Poems*, 1954. William Van O'Connor, *The Shaping Spirit: A Study of Wallace Stevens*, 1950.

Domination of Black

(1924)

The following remarks are not a paraphrase but a searching of the poem. In the colored firelight the autumn leaves spin again, but the darkness of the hemlocks (and of death?) comes striding upon this fire-image as it did upon the leaves themselves — as winter comes upon autumn, night upon day, and eventually (lines 29–36) darkness upon the stars themselves — and the ill-omened cry of the peacock is heard, remembered. The peacocks sweep through the room: a premonition of the coming darkness, their cry a cry of disaster. But they too resemble the leaves and must perish. Is their cry then the voice of the darkness or a protest against it?

At night, by the fire,
The colors of the bushes
And of the fallen leaves,
Repeating themselves,
Turned in the room,   5
Like the leaves themselves
Turning in the wind.
Yes: but the color of the heavy hemlocks
Came striding.
And I remembered the cry of the peacocks.   10

The colors of their tails
Were like the leaves themselves
Turning in the wind,
In the twilight wind.
They swept over the room,   15
Just as they flew from the boughs of the hemlocks
Down to the ground.
I heard them cry — the peacocks.
Was it a cry against the twilight
Or against the leaves themselves   20
Turning in the wind,
Turning as the flames

Turned in the fire,
Turning as the tails of the peacocks
Turned in the loud fire,   25
Loud as the hemlocks
Full of the cry of the peacocks?
Or was it a cry against the hemlocks?

Out of the window,
I saw how the planets gathered   30
Like the leaves themselves
Turning in the wind.
I saw how the night came,
Came striding like the color of the heavy hemlocks.
I felt afraid.   35
And I remembered the cry of the peacocks.

The Emperor of Ice-Cream

(1923)

This poem has been much discussed and given many interpretations, but, in the light of certain of Stevens' remarks in connection with it, we are probably mistaken to seek an exact paraphrase. Certain attitudes, however, are clear. At this funeral (or wake) there is to be neither the pretense nor the fact of morbid grief. Life will pursue honestly (and commendably) the festive, concupiscent moods by which it survives, recognizing as emperor, not crape, but ice-cream. At the same time there will be neither disrespect for the dead — for whom a solid kindness somehow comes through the dispassionate lines — nor a blinking of the facts of poverty and death ("Let the lamp affix its beam"). The particular quality of the poem lies in the contrast, without contradiction, of these moods. One feels that the attitude of the poet is a realistic and stable one.

Call the roller of big cigars,
The muscular one, and bid him whip
In kitchen cups concupiscent curds.

Let the wenches dawdle in such dress
As they are used to wear, and let the boys **5**
Bring flowers in last month's newspapers.
Let be be finale of seem.
The only emperor is the emperor of ice-cream.

Take from the dresser of deal,
Lacking the three glass knobs, that sheet **10**
On which she embroidered fantails once
And spread it so as to cover her face.
If her horny feet protrude, they come
To show how cold she is, and dumb.
Let the lamp affix its beam. **15**
The only emperor is the emperor of ice-cream.

Sunday Morning

(1923)

This poem has been called by more than one critic "the greatest poem of the twentieth century," and it is indeed an impressive dramatization of a state of mind characteristic of our time. Here a modern hedonist, a person who does not believe in the spiritual nature of man and therefore sees man's sole purpose and sole reward to be the pleasures of this earthly life, he reexamines this philosophy in the light of other, more comforting faiths. Because the poet rejects these other faiths in spite of his great longing for them, and accepts forthrightly the painful limitations of the one he feels compelled to accept, the poem is a moving one and is good evidence for the fact that we needn't share the opinions of the author in order to appreciate the poetry he writes. For this poem a brief paraphrase may be useful.

I. In the complacent luxury of a Sunday morning, amid the grim associations of Christian worship, a woman comes again upon the thought of death, which again calls into question the faith she lives by.

II. Why should she turn from her pleasures to a faith of suffering and sacrifice, merely for the ghost-promises of an after-life? She must find her divinity here, in the broad rich range of human emotions.

III. If man will accept his earthly divinity, he will find himself at home on earth instead of in exile, and will have a faith which is both realistic and "next in glory," at least, "to enduring love."

IV. The woman protests that her pleasures are transient rather than eternal, and she is told that no concept of spiritual heaven has endured as this earth and its pleasures endure in the endless renewal of seasons and generations.

V, VI. When the woman says she craves a more personal permanence, she is told that "death is the mother of beauty," for without death and change all sensuous experience would cloy, like the "insipid lutes."

VII. The poet envisages a religion wherein man will worship the elements from which he sprang, accepting his perishable nature for what it is.

VIII. In this beautiful stanza the woman learns that Jesus was but a man, no spirit, and sees this earthly life in both its beauty and its poignant isolation from all the comforting sponsorships man has invented for it — a lonely immortality of endless and impersonal generations.

I

Complacencies of the peignoir, and late
Coffee and oranges in a sunny chair,
And the green freedom of a cockatoo
Upon a rug mingle to dissipate
The holy hush of ancient sacrifice. **5**
She dreams a little, and she feels the dark
Encroachment of that old catastrophe,
As a calm darkens among water-lights.
The pungent oranges and bright, green wings
Seem things in some procession of the dead,
Winding across wide water, without sound. **11**
The day is like wide water, without sound,
Stilled for the passing of her dreaming feet
Over the seas, to silent Palestine,
Dominion of the blood and sepulchre. **15**

II

Why should she give her bounty to the dead?
What is divinity if it can come
Only in silent shadows and in dreams?
Shall she not find in comforts of the sun,
In pungent fruit and bright, green wings, or
     else **20**
In any balm or beauty of the earth,
Things to be cherished like the thought of
     heaven?
Divinity must live within herself:
Passions of rain, or moods in falling snow;
Grievings in loneliness, or unsubdued **25**
Elations when the forest blooms; gusty
Emotions on wet roads on autumn nights;
All pleasures and all pains, remembering
The bough of summer and the winter branch.
These are the measures destined for her soul.

III

Jove in the clouds had his inhuman birth. **31**
No mother suckled him, no sweet land gave
Large-mannered motions to his mythy mind.
He moved among us, as a muttering king,
Magnificent, would move among his hinds, **35**
Until our blood, commingling, virginal,
With heaven, brought such requital to desire
The very hinds discerned it, in a star.
Shall our blood fail? Or shall it come to be

The blood of paradise? And shall the earth 40
Seem all of paradise that we shall know?
The sky will be much friendlier then than now,
A part of labor and a part of pain,
And next in glory to enduring love,
Not this dividing and indifferent blue. 45

IV

She says, "I am content when wakened birds,
Before they fly, test the reality
Of misty fields, by their sweet questionings;
But when the birds are gone, and their warm
    fields
Return no more, where, then, is paradise?" 50
There is not any haunt of prophecy,
Nor any old chimera of the grave,
Neither the golden underground, nor isle
Melodious, where spirits gat them home,
Nor visionary south, nor cloudy palm 55
Remote on heaven's hill, that has endured
As April's green endures; or will endure
Like her remembrance of awakened birds,
Or her desire for June and evening, tipped 59
By the consummation of the swallow's wings.

V

She says, "But in contentment I still feel
The need of some imperishable bliss."
Death is the mother of beauty; hence from her,
Alone, shall come fulfilment to our dreams 64
And our desires. Although she strews the leaves
Of sure obliteration on our paths,
The path sick sorrow took, the many paths
Where triumph rang its brassy phrase, or love
Whispered a little out of tenderness,
She makes the willow shiver in the sun 70
For maidens who were wont to sit and gaze
Upon the grass, relinquished to their feet.
She causes boys to pile new plums and pears
On disregarded plate. The maidens taste 74
And stray impassioned in the littering leaves.

VI

Is there no change of death in paradise?
Does ripe fruit never fall? Or do the boughs
Hang always heavy in that perfect sky,
Unchanging, yet so like our perishing earth,
With rivers like our own that seek for seas 80
They never find, the same receding shores
That never touch with inarticulate pang?
Why set the pear upon those river-banks
Or spice the shores with odors of the plum?
Alas, that they should wear our colors there,
The silken weavings of our afternoons, 86

And pick the strings of our insipid lutes!
Death is the mother of beauty, mystical,
Within whose burning bosom we devise
Our earthly mothers waiting, sleeplessly. 90

VII

Supple and turbulent, a ring of men
Shall chant in orgy on a summer morn
Their boisterous devotion to the sun,
Not as a god, but as a god might be,
Naked among them, like a savage source. 95
Their chant shall be a chant of paradise,
Out of their blood, returning to the sky;
And in their chant shall enter, voice by voice,
The windy lake wherein their lord delights,
The trees, like serafin, and echoing hills, 100
That choir among themselves long afterward.
They shall know well the heavenly fellowship
Of men that perish and of summer morn.
And whence they came and whither they shall go
The dew upon their feet shall manifest. 105

VIII

She hears, upon that water without sound,
A voice that cries, "The tomb in Palestine
Is not the porch of spirits lingering.
It is the grave of Jesus, where he lay."
We live in an old chaos of the sun, 110
Or old dependency of day and night,
Or island solitude, unsponsored, free,
Of that wide water, inescapable.
Deer walk upon our mountains, and the quail
Whistle about us their spontaneous cries; 115
Sweet berries ripen in the wilderness;
And, in the isolation of the sky,
At evening, casual flocks of pigeons make
Ambiguous undulations as they sink,
Downward to darkness, on extended wings. 120

Peter Quince at the Clavier

(1923)

❦ For this poem the student should read the story
of Susanna and the Elders in the Biblical Apocrypha.

How does the identification of music, feeling, and
beauty throughout the poem contribute to the culminating statement in section IV? Compare the
idea of permanence given here with that given in
stanza IV of "Sunday Morning."

I

Just as my fingers on these keys
Make music, so the selfsame sounds
On my spirit make a music, too.

Music is feeling, then, not sound;
And thus it is that what I feel,   5
Here in this room, desiring you,

Thinking of your blue-shadowed silk,
Is music. It is like the strain
Waked in the elders by Susanna.

Of a green evening, clear and warm,   10
She bathed in her still garden, while
The red-eyed elders, watching, felt

The basses of their beings throb
In witching chords, and their thin blood
Pulse pizzicati of Hosanna.   15

II

In the green water, clear and warm,
Susanna lay.

She searched
The touch of springs,
And found   20
Concealed imaginings.
She sighed,
For so much melody.

Upon the bank, she stood
In the cool   25
Of spent emotions.
She felt, among the leaves,
The dew
Of old devotions.

She walked upon the grass,   30
Still quavering.
The winds were like her maids,
On timid feet,
Fetching her woven scarves,
Yet wavering.   35

A breath upon her hand
Muted the night.
She turned —
A cymbal crashed,
And roaring horns.   40

III

Soon, with a noise like tambourines,
Came her attendant Byzantines.

They wondered why Susanna cried
Against the elders by her side;

And as they whispered, the refrain   45
Was like a willow swept by rain.

Anon, their lamps' uplifted flame
Revealed Susanna and her shame.

And then, the simpering Byzantines
Fled, with a noise like tambourines.   50

IV

Beauty is momentary in the mind —
The fitful tracing of a portal;
But in the flesh it is immortal.

The body dies; the body's beauty lives.
So evenings die, in their green going,   55
A wave, interminably flowing.
So gardens die, their meek breath scenting
The cowl of winter, done repenting.
So maidens die, to the auroral
Celebration of a maiden's choral.   60

Susanna's music touched the bawdy strings
Of those white elders; but, escaping,
Left only Death's ironic scraping.
Now, in its immortality, it plays
On the clear viol of her memory,   65
And makes a constant sacrament of praise.

The Death of a Soldier
(1924)

🐝 This poem is far simpler than most of Stevens'
poems, but by expanding it into an explicit prose
statement you will see how much of its particular
quality lies beyond paraphrase.

Life contracts and death is expected,
As in a season of autumn.
The soldier falls.

He does not become a three-days' personage,
Imposing his separation,   5
Calling for pomp.

Death is absolute and without memorial,
As in a season of autumn,
When the wind stops.

When the wind stops and, over the heavens,
The clouds go, nevertheless,   11
In their direction.

The Idea of Order at Key West

(1935)

This is one of Stevens' most explicit poetic statements of his concept of the function of art. "Oh! Blessed rage for order," he cries, and the paradox is a tribute to the artist, who combines passion and control, who gives order, pattern, and meaning to the material flux, which, until it is thus shaped by the creative imagination, is "all body," and no spirit, but an empty garment "fluttering its empty sleeves." The artist here is the singing woman who articulates and gives being to the sea and sky and the hour. She is thus "the single artificer of the world in which she sang," the world "she sang and, singing, made" — just as the lights in the fishing boats (lines 45–50) bound the unbounded night, giving it order and meaning.

She sang beyond the genius of the sea.
The water never formed to mind or voice,
Like a body wholly body, fluttering
Its empty sleeves; and yet its mimic motion
Made constant cry, caused constantly a cry, 5
That was not ours although we understood,
Inhuman, of the veritable ocean.

The sea was not a mask. No more was she.
The song and water were not medleyed sound
Even if what she sang was what she heard, 10
Since what she sang was uttered word by word.
It may be that in all her phrases stirred
The grinding water and the gasping wind;
But it was she and not the sea we heard.

For she was the maker of the song she sang. 15
The ever-hooded, tragic-gestured sea
Was merely a place by which she walked to
      sing.
Whose spirit is this? we said, because we knew
It was the spirit that we sought and knew
That we should ask this often as she sang. 20

If it was only the dark voice of the sea
That rose, or even colored by many waves;
If it was only that outer voice of sky
And cloud, of the sunken coral water-walled,
However clear, it would have been deep
      air, 25
The heaving speech of air, a summer sound
Repeated in a summer without end
And sound alone. But it was more than that,
More even than her voice, and ours, among
The meaningless plungings of water and the
wind, 30

Theatrical distances, bronze shadows heaped
On high horizons, mountainous atmospheres
Of sky and sea.

                    It was her voice that made
The sky acutest at its vanishing.
She measured to the hour its solitude. 35
She was the single artificer of the world
In which she sang. And when she sang, the sea,
Whatever self it had, became the self
That was her song, for she was the maker.
      Then we,
As we beheld her striding there alone, 40
Knew that there never was a world for her
Except the one she sang and, singing, made.

Ramon Fernandez, tell me, if you know,
Why, when the singing ended and we turned
Toward the town, tell why the glassy lights, 45
The lights in the fishing boats at anchor there,
As the night descended, tilting in the air,
Mastered the night and portioned out the
      sea,
Fixing emblazoned zones and fiery poles,
Arranging, deepening, enchanting night. 50

Oh! Blessed rage for order, pale Ramon,
The maker's rage to order words of the sea,
Words of the fragrant portals, dimly-starred,
And of ourselves and of our origins,
In ghostlier demarcations, keener sounds. 55

A Postcard from the Volcano

(1935)

How does this poem extend the statement of "Idea of Order at Key West"?

Children picking up our bones
Will never know that these were once
As quick as foxes on the hill;

And that in autumn, when the grapes
Made sharp air sharper by their smell 5
These had a being, breathing frost;

And least will guess that with our bones
We left much more, left what still is
The look of things, left what we felt

At what we saw. The spring clouds blow 10
Above the shuttered mansion-house,
Beyond our gate and the windy sky

Cries out a literate despair.
We knew for long the mansion's look
And what we said of it became   15

A part of what it is . . . . Children,
Still weaving budded aureoles,
Will speak our speech and never know,

Will say of the mansion that it seems
As if he that lived there left behind   20
A spirit storming in blank walls,

A dirty house in a gutted world,
A tatter of shadows peaked to white,
Smeared with the gold of the opulent sun.

Study of Two Pears

This poem is useful in further defining Stevens' aesthetics. Note how he remains faithful to the objective fact and rules out loose impressionistic fancies. Study the first and last stanzas in the light of Stevens' belief that the imagination, though creative, must start with the real, and that "the essential fault of surrealism is that it invents without discovery. To make a clam play an accordion is to invent, not to discover."

How would you say the poem has been influenced by modern painting?

The first line may be translated: "A little job of pedagogy" — a humorous description of the task assumed by the poet in the poem.

I

Opusculum paedagogum.
The pears are not viols,
Nudes or bottles.
They resemble nothing else.

II

They are yellow forms   5
Composed of curves
Bulging toward the base.
They are touched red.

III

They are not flat surfaces
Having curved outlines.   10
They are round
Tapering toward the top.

IV

In the way they are modelled
There are bits of blue.
A hard dry leaf hangs   15
From the stem.

V

The yellow glistens.
It glistens with various yellows,
Citrons, oranges and greens
Flowering over the skin.   20

VI

The shadows of the pears
Are blobs on the green cloth.
The pears are not seen
As the observer wills.

Of Modern Poetry

Here Stevens describes the problem of poetry in our time. What historical considerations lie behind this statement, and what is the aesthetic basis of lines 10–26?

The poem of the mind in the act of finding
What will suffice. It has not always had
To find: the scene was set; it repeated what
Was in the script.
                    Then the theatre was changed   5
To something else. Its past was a souvenir.

It has to be living, to learn the speech of the
        place.
It has to face the men of the time and to meet
The women of the time. It has to think about
        war
And it has to find what will suffice. It has   10
To construct a new stage. It has to be on that
        stage
And, like an insatiable actor, slowly and
With meditation speak words that in the ear,
In the delicatest ear of the mind, repeat,
Exactly, that which it wants to hear, at the
        sound   15
Of which, an invisible audience listens,
Not to the play, but to itself, expressed
In an emotion as of two people, as of two
Emotions becoming one. The actor is
A metaphysician in the dark, twanging   20
An instrument, twanging a wiry string that gives
Sounds passing through sudden rightnesses,
        wholly
Containing the mind, below which it cannot
        descend,
Beyond which it has no will to rise.
                                It must   25
Be the finding of a satisfaction, and may
Be of a man skating, a woman dancing, a woman
Combing. The poem of the act of the mind.

Hart Crane [1899–1932]

Hart Crane's life was one of turbulence and rebellion. Reared on "the bloody-battle-ground" of his parents' breaking marriage, all his life he felt alienated from his father. He rebelled against the Midwest — he was born at Garretsville, Ohio — and fled periodically to New York and to a family plantation in the West Indies. He alternately rebelled against and tried to accept and express his mercantilistic, materialistic society. He rebelled against his jobs in advertising and in his father's candy business, longing for freedom in which to write. He refused a chance to go to college and later regretted his refusal. His moods fluctuated violently in accordance with his immediate material prospects, his love affairs, and his confidence in his talent. For all his brilliant gifts, he was uncertain of himself, perhaps discouraged by his lack of formal education, certainly isolated by his assertive genius, his broken home, and his homosexuality. He died in 1932, when he leaped from the steamer on which he was returning from Mexico to the United States.

Crane started writing poetry when he was thirteen. Schooled in the literary circles of *The Little Review* and *The Seven Arts*, and counseled by such friends as Allen Tate, Gorham Munson, and Waldo Frank, he passed through many of the crowded influences of his time and of his wide reading, and eventually developed a personal idiom which frequently has great power and depth, but which has proved almost unvaryingly obscure to friends, editors, and fellow poets alike. This obscurity may be in some measure due to his erratic punctuation and his occasional lack of control, but it is due more largely to his layered symbolism and to his implicit leaps of metaphor. He argued for "the logic of metaphor" and "the so-called illogical impingements of the connotations of words," as against the ordinary continuity of logical syntax. As a result he leaves gaps in his chains of images, and forces words into unaccustomed grammatical functions. Perhaps his obscurity is also due to the mysticism — compounded of Christian Science, Rimbaud, Whitman, Ouspensky, and others — with which he tried to order his doubt-tormented life and time. He is a poet of great passages, rather than great poems. *The Bridge* fails as an epic but contains excellent passages. Some of his poems, however, such as "Voyages II" and "Repose of Rivers," seem in every way successful.

Further reading: *Collected Poems*. Brom Weber, *Hart Crane: A Biographical and Critical Study*, 1948. Allen Tate, essay in *Reactionary Essays*, 1936.

From *The Bridge*

(1930)

Crane meant *The Bridge* to be a "mystical synthesis of 'America,'" an epic of man's "conquest of space and knowledge." He intended not a chronological resumé of American history, but "a more organic panorama, showing the continuous and living evidence of the past in the . . . present." There-fore the poem, though patterned roughly on a day in the city, glides from era to era and the images and personages merge into one another with no explicit transitions. *The Bridge* was obviously much influenced by *The Waste Land* of T. S. Eliot.

To Brooklyn Bridge

This section sketches the poet's day: dawn, noon, and night (though line 8, a late alteration, upsets this sequence). There are glimpses of the dull, futile, imperceptive life of the city. Starting in the fourth stanza, the poet addresses the bridge, and seeks in its soaring form an order, a myth for the chaos of his time. Crane wrote of this section: "That little prelude . . . I think to be almost the best thing I have ever written . . ." Note throughout that some lines (lines 4, 6 and 7), though perfectly comprehensible, are so compressed that there is no explicit logical coherence between their images.

How many dawns, chill from his rippling rest
The seagull's wings shall dip and pivot him,
Shedding white rings of tumult, building high
Over the chained bay waters Liberty —

Then, with inviolate curve, forsake our eyes 5
As apparitional as sails that cross
Some page of figures to be filed away;
— Till elevators drop us from our day . . .

I think of cinemas, panoramic sleights
With multitudes bent toward some flashing
    scene   10
Never disclosed, but hastened to again,
Foretold to other eyes on the same screen;

And Thee, across the harbor, silver-paced
As though the sun took step of thee, yet left
Some motion ever unspent in thy stride, —
Implicitly thy freedom staying thee!   16

Out of some subway scuttle, cell or loft
A bedlamite speeds to thy parapets,
Tilting there momently, shrill shirt ballooning,
A jest falls from the speechless caravan.   20

Down Wall, from girder into street noon leaks,
A rip-tooth of the sky's acetylene;
All afternoon the cloud-flown derricks turn . . .
Thy cables breathe the North Atlantic still.

And obscure as that heaven of the Jews,   25
Thy guerdon . . . Accolade thou dost bestow
Of anonymity time cannot raise:
Vibrant reprieve and pardon thou dost show.

O harp and altar, of the fury fused,
(How could mere toil align thy choiring
    strings!)   30
Terrific threshold of the prophet's pledge,
Prayer of pariah, and the lover's cry, —

Again the traffic lights that skim thy swift
Unfractioned idiom, immaculate sigh of stars,

Beading thy path — condense eternity: 35
And we have seen night lifted in thine arms.

Under thy shadow by the piers I waited;
Only in darkness is thy shadow clear.
The City's fiery parcels all undone,
Already snow submerges an iron year . . .   40

O Sleepless as the river under thee,
Vaulting the sea, the prairies' dreaming sod,
Unto us lowliest sometime sweep, descend
And of the curveship lend a myth to God.

Van Winkle

🥀 As the poet walks through the streets on his way to work, a hurdy-gurdy takes him back into his own past and into America's past. Like Rip Van Winkle, he is of two times, and of all times. He *is* Rip Van Winkle (just as Rip, in this blur and merge of time, is a twentieth-century janitor), and he momentarily forgets his daily responsibilities and remembers his childhood of cruelty and alienation. Finally, he boards the subway, which, like the streets, is part of the flow of transportation that "leaps," bridges the nation.

Macadam, gun-gray as the tunny's belt,
Leaps from Far Rockaway to Golden Gate:
Listen! the miles a hurdy-gurdy grinds —
Down gold arpeggios mile on mile unwinds.

Times earlier, when you hurried off to school, 5
— It is the same hour though a later day —
You walked with Pizarro in a copybook,
And Cortes rode up, reining tautly in —
Firmly as coffee grips the taste, — and away!

There was Priscilla's cheek close in the wind, 10
And Captain Smith, all beard and certainty,
And Rip Van Winkle, bowing by the way, —
"Is this Sleepy Hollow, friend — ?" And he —

And Rip forgot the office hours,
                and he forgot the pay; 15
Van Winkle sweeps a tenement
                down town on Avenue A, —

The grind-organ says . . . Remember, remember
The cinder pile at the end of the backyard
Where we stoned the family of young   20
Garter snakes under . . . And the monoplanes
We launched — with paper wings and twisted

Rubber bands. . . . Recall —
                           the rapid tongues
That flittered from under the ash heap day   25
After day whenever your stick discovered
Some sunning inch of unsuspecting fiber —
It flashed back at your thrust, as clean as fire.

And Rip was slowly made aware
        that he, Van Winkle, was not here   30
Nor there. He woke and swore he'd seen Broad-
        way a Catskill daisy chain in May —

So memory, that strikes a rhyme out of a
        box,
Or splits a random smell of flowers through
        glass —
Is it the whip stripped from the lilac tree   35
One day in spring my father took to me,
Or is it the Sabbatical, unconscious smile
My mother almost brought me once from
        church
And once only, as I recall — ?

It flickered through the snow screen, blindly   40
It forsook her at the doorway; it was gone
Before I had left the window. It
Did not return with the kiss in the hall.

Macadam, gun-gray as the tunny's belt,
Leaps from Far Rockaway to Golden Gate . . . 45
Keep hold of that nickel for car-change, Rip, —
Have you got your paper — ?
And hurry along, Van Winkle — it's getting
        late!

The River

❧ The subway becomes a transcontinental train and
roars "past the din and slogans of the year." Abruptly
the poet is among some tramps beside the railroad
tracks. These tramps are "the left-overs of the
pioneers in at least this respect — that their wanderings carry the reader through an experience parallel to that of Boone and others." These men
know the land with special directness and intimacy,
"knowing her without name." The poet has known
her too, and sensed her past. Again in the train, we
ride on to the Mississippi River. The final superb
tribute to the river raises it as another image of the
bridge, spanning and netting the continent, spanning and embodying the present and the past. Note
here the virtually unparaphrasable metaphors, and
the unusual grammatical function of certain words:
"alluvial march of days," "the basalt surface drags
a jungle grace." (Cf. line 44 of "Cutty Sark."
"Then you may laugh and dance the axle-tree.")

Stick your patent name on a signboard
brother — all over — going west — young man
Tintex — Japalac — Certain-teed Overalls ads
and lands sakes! under the new playbill ripped
in the guaranteed corner — see Bert Williams
        what?   5
Minstrels when you steal a chicken just
save me the wing, for if it isn't
Erie it ain't for miles around a
Mazda — and the telegraphic night coming on
        Thomas

a Ediford — and whistling down the tracks   10
a headlight rushing with the sound — can you
imagine — while an EXPRESS makes time like
SCIENCE — COMMERCE and the HOLYGHOST
RADIO ROARS IN EVERY HOME WE HAVE THE
        NORTHPOLE
WALLSTREET AND VIRGINBIRTH WITHOUT STONES
        OR   15
WIRES OR EVEN RUNNING brooks connecting ears
and no more sermons windows flashing roar
Breathtaking — as you like it . . . eh?

                    So the 20th Century — so
whizzed the Limited — roared by and left   20
three men, still hungry on the tracks, plod-
        dingly
watching the tail lights wizen and converge,
slipping gimleted and neatly out of sight.
The last bear, shot drinking in the Dakotas,
Loped under wires that span the mountain
        stream.   25
Keen instruments, strung to a vast precision
Bind town to town and dream to ticking
        dream.
But some men take their liquor slow — and
        count —
Though they'll confess no rosary nor clue —
The river's minute by the far brook's year.   30
Under a world of whistles, wires and steam
Caboose-like they go ruminating through
Ohio, Indiana — blind baggage —
To Cheyenne tagging . . . Maybe Kalamazoo.

Time's renderings, time's blendings they con-
        strue   35
As final reckonings of fire and snow;
Strange bird-wit, like the elemental gist
Of unwalled winds they offer, singing low
My Old Kentucky Home and Casey Jones,
Some Sunny Day. I heard a road-gang chant-
        ing so.   40

And afterwards, who had a colt's eyes — one
said,
"Jesus! Oh I remember watermelon days!"
And sped
High in a cloud of merriment, recalled
" — And when my Aunt Sally Simpson smiled,"
he drawled —
"It was almost Louisiana, long ago."   45

"There's no place like Booneville though,
Buddy,"
One said, excising a last burr from his vest,
" — For early trouting." Then peering in the
can,
" — But I kept on the tracks." Possessed, re-
signed,
He trod the fire down pensively and grinned, 50
Spreading dry shingles of a beard. . . .

Behind
My father's cannery works I used to see
Rail-squatters ranged in nomad raillery,
The ancient men — wifeless or runaway   55
Hobo-trekkers that forever search
An empire wilderness of freight and rails.
Each seemed a child, like me, on a loose perch.
Holding to childhood like some termless play.
John, Jake, or Charley, hopping the slow
freight   60
— Memphis to Tallahassee — riding the rods,
Blind fists of nothing, humpty-dumpty clods.

Yet they touch something like a key perhaps.
From pole to pole across the hills, the states
— They know a body under the wide rain;   65
Youngsters with eyes like fjords, old reprobates
With racetrack jargon, — dotting immensity
They lurk across her, knowing her yonder breast
Snow-silvered, sumac-stained or smoky blue,
Is past the valley-sleepers, south or west.   70
— As I have trod the rumorous midnights, too,

And past the circuit of the lamp's thin flame
(O Nights that brought me to her body bare!)
Have dreamed beyond the print that bound her
name.
Trains sounding the long blizzards out — I
heard   75
Wail into distances I knew were hers.
Papooses crying on the wind's long mane
Screamed redskin dynasties that fled the brain,
— Dead echoes! But I knew her body there,
Time like a serpent down her shoulder, dark, 80
And space, an eaglet's wing, laid on her hair.

Under the Ozarks, domed by Iron Mountain,
The old gods of the rain lie wrapped in pools
Where eyeless fish curvet a sunken fountain   84
And re-descend with corn from querulous crows.
Such pilferings make up their timeless eatage,
Propitiate them for their timber torn
By iron, iron — always the iron dealt cleavage!
They doze now, below axe and powder horn.   89

And Pullman breakfasters glide glistening steel
From tunnel into field — iron strides the dew —
Straddles the hill, a dance of wheel on wheel.
You have a half-hour's wait at Siskiyou,
Or stay the night and take the next train
through.
Southward, near Cairo passing, you can see   95
The Ohio merging, — borne down Tennessee;
And if it's summer and the sun's in dusk
Maybe the breeze will lift the River's musk
— As though the waters breathed that you
might know
Memphis Johnny, Steamboat Bill, Missouri Joe.
Oh, lean from the window, if the train slows
down,   101
As though you touched hands with some ancient
clown,
— A little while gaze absently below
And hum Deep River with them while they go.

Yes, turn again and sniff once more — look
see,   105
O Sheriff, Brakeman and Authority —
Hitch up your pants and crunch another quid,
For you, too, feed the River timelessly.
And few evade full measure of their fate;
Always they smile out eerily what they seem. 110
I could believe he joked at heaven's gate —
Dan Midland — jolted from the cold brake-
beam.

Down, down — born pioneers in time's despite,
Grimed tributaries to an ancient flow —
They win no frontier by their wayward plight,
But drift in stillness, as from Jordan's brow. 116

You will not hear it as the sea; even stone
Is not more hushed by gravity . . . But slow,
As loth to take more tribute — sliding prone
Like one whose eyes were buried long ago 120

The River, spreading, flows — and spends your
dream.
What are you, lost within this tideless spell?
You are your father's father, and the stream —

A liquid theme that floating niggers swell.

Damp tonnage and alluvial march of days — 125
Nights turbid, vascular with silted shale
And roots surrendered down of moraine clays:
The Mississippi drinks the farthest dale.

O quarrying passion, undertowed sunlight!
The basalt surface drags a jungle grace 130
Ochreous and lynx-barred in lengthening might;
Patience! and you shall reach the biding place!

Over DeSoto's bones the freighted floors
Throb past the City storied of three thrones.
Down two more turns the Mississippi pours
(Anon tall ironsides up from salt lagoons)

And flows within itself, heaps itself free.
All fades but one thin skyline 'round . . . Ahead
No embrace opens but the stinging sea;
The River lifts itself from its long bed, 140

Poised wholly on its dream, a mustard glow,
Tortured with history, its one will — flow!
— The Passion spreads in wide tongues, chocked
     and slow,
Meeting the Gulf, hosannas silently below.

Cutty Sark

The poet drinks with an old man of the sea late at night. The rhythm here is meant to suggest intoxication, the lurch of a boat in heavy seas, and the grinding interjections of a mechanical piano. This section is a fugue of two voices: the sailor and the narrator are the voice of Time; the piano-Atlantis theme is the voice of Eternity. On his way home across Brooklyn Bridge the poet sees the phantoms of the clipper ships of the past, and slips into a rich, keenly phrased fantasy of the old sailing days. Thus again, this time in the image of the ageless sea, past and present have been interfused.

O, the navies old and oaken,
     O, the Temeraire no more!
          — MELVILLE.

I met a man in South Street, tall —
a nervous shark tooth swung on his chain.
His eyes pressed through green grass
— green glasses, or bar lights made them
so — 5
     shine —
GREEN —
     eyes —

stepped out — forgot to look at you
or left you several blocks away — 10
in the nickel-in-the-slot piano jogged
"Stamboul   Nights" — weaving   somebody's
     nickel — sang —

O Stamboul Rose — dreams weave the rose!

     Murmurs of Leviathan he spoke,
     and rum was Plato in our heads . . . 15
"It's S.S. *Ala* — Antwerp, — now remember kid
to put me out at three she sails on time.
I'm not much good at time any more keep
weakeyed watches sometimes snooze — " his
     bony hands
got to beating time . . . "A whaler once — 20
I ought to keep time and get over it — I'm a
Democrat — I know what time it is — No
I don't want to know what time it is — that
damned white Arctic killed my time . . ."

     O Stamboul Rose — drums weave — 25

"I ran a donkey engine down there on the Canal
in Panama — got tired of that —
then Yucatan selling kitchenware — beads —
have you seen Popocatepetl — birdless mouth
with ashes sifting down — ? 30
               and then the coast again . . ."

*Rose of Stamboul O coral Queen —
teased remnants of the skeletons of cities —
and galleries, galleries of watergutted lava
snarling stone — green — drums — drown* 35
Sing!
" — that spiracle!" he shot a finger out the
     door . . .
"O life's a geyser — beautiful — my lungs —
No — I can't live on land — !"

I saw the frontiers gleaming of his mind; 40
or are there frontiers — running sands some-
     times
running sands — somewhere — sands run-
     ning . . .
Or they may start some white machine that
     sings.
Then you may laugh and dance the axletree —
steel — silver — kick the traces — and
     know — 45

ATLANTIS ROSE *drums wreathe the rose,
the star floats burning in a gulf of tears*

and sleep another thousand —
                              interminably
long since somebody's nickel — stopped — 50
playing —

A wind worried those wicker-neat lapels, the
swinging summer entrances to cooler hells . . .
Outside a wharf truck nearly ran him down
— he lunged up Bowery way while the dawn 55
was putting the Statue of Liberty out — that
torch of hers you know —

I started walking home across the Bridge . . .
                      . . . . . .

Blithe Yankee vanities, turreted sprites, winged
                      British repartees, skil-
ful savage sea-girls   61
that bloomed in the spring — Heave, weave
those bright designs the trade winds drive . . .

Sweet opium and tea, Yo-ho!
Pennies for porpoises that bank the keel! 65
Fins whip the breeze around Japan!

Bright skysails ticketing the line, wink round
    the Horn

to Frisco, Melbourne . . . .
                      Pennants, parabolas —
clipper dreams indelible and ranging,   70
baronial white on lucky blue!
Perrenial-*Cutty*-trophied-*Sark*!

Thermopylae, Black Prince, Flying Cloud
    through Sunda
— scarfed of foam, their bellies veered green
    esplanades,
locked in wind-humors, ran their eastings
    down;   75

    at Java Head freshened the nip
    (*sweet opium and tea!*)
    and turned and left us on the lee . . .

Buntlines tusseling (91 days, 20 hours and an-
    chored!)
                      Rainbow, Leander
(last trip a tragedy) — where can you be
Nimbus? and you rivals two —

                      a long tack keeping —

                                    Taeping?
                                    Ariel?

THE PLAYS OF O'NEILL

Eugene O'Neill [1888–1953]

American drama strode forward with seven-league boots in the early twentieth century, but before that time its progress was so slow and tortuous that one realizes with
difficulty that dramatic performances had been given in this country as early as 1703,
and that the first professional company of actors exhibited in 1752. To this company
Thomas Godfrey offered *The Prince of Parthia*, but Godfrey was dead before the tragedy was first acted in Philadelphia in 1767. Twenty years elapsed before a native comedy
was acted professionally. This play, Royall Tyler's *The Contrast*, came after the Revolution. Further development of the American drama was hindered not only by the

long-continued prejudice against the theater but also by the lyrical and reflective rather than dramatic spirit of the romantic movement. It was not till after the rise of realism that the United States had playwrights of even moderate distinction: Clyde Fitch, Augustus Thomas, Percy MacKaye, William Vaughn Moody. Then at length came Eugene O'Neill, of whom Sinclair Lewis, on receiving the Nobel Prize, said that it might appropriately have been bestowed on this dramatic genius. Had not O'Neill, taking hold of the American drama, contrived "to transform it utterly, in ten or twelve years, from a false world of neat and competent trickery to a world of splendor and fear and greatness," revealing life "as a terrifying, magnificent, and often quite horrible thing akin to the tornado, the earthquake, the devastating fire"?

Born in New York City, son of a celebrated actor, O'Neill accompanied his father on theatrical tours. After attending Catholic schools and Betts Academy, he entered Princeton, but was suspended at the end of a year and never returned. He worked for a mail-order firm in New York, made an ill-fated marriage (the first of three), and then began a career of reckless living and diverse occupations. He prospected for gold in Honduras, shipped before the mast to Buenos Aires, worked as mule-tender on a cattle-boat bound for South Africa, signed up as seaman for the return to New York, worked on ships between New York and Southampton, presented himself as a prodigal to his father in New Orleans and acted with the company for fifteen weeks, was cub reporter for a Connecticut newspaper, and came down with tuberculosis.

This illness, in 1912–13, was the turning-point in his life; it gave him time to reflect upon his experience and decide what to make of himself. He tells us that he now read widely: "the Greeks, the Elizabethans — practically all the classics — and of course all the moderns. Ibsen and Strindberg, especially Strindberg." He began to write one-act plays; then, for technical training, enrolled in 1914 in George Pierce Baker's famous "47 Workshop" at Harvard, deriving little from it, he thought. Next year he joined a radical group in Greenwich Village, and in 1916 associated himself with the Provincetown Players, who, in the course of the three years following, put on many of his one-act plays, including *Bound East for Cardiff* (1916) and *The Moon of the Caribbees* (1918). When his first full-length play, an impressive realistic tragedy, *Beyond the Horizon*, was produced in New York in 1920, it brought him the Pulitzer Prize and recognition as the foremost American playwright of his time.

In the decade of the 1920's his fame rose to new heights. His fecundity and brilliance are apparent in a mere list of his plays in these years: *Beyond the Horizon* was followed by *Gold, The Emperor Jones, Diff'rent, The Straw, The Hairy Ape, Anna Christie, The First Man, All God's Chillun Got Wings, Welded, Desire Under the Elms, The Great God Brown, The Fountain, Marco Millions, Lazarus Laughed, Strange Interlude, Dynamo.* Assuredly O'Neill did more than his share to make the 1920's a remarkable decade in American letters.

Maintaining his pace in the first half of the 1930's, he added *Mourning Becomes Electra, Ah, Wilderness!, Days Without End,* and in 1934–35 saw *The Plays of Eugene O'Neill* published in 12 volumes. Then his career was all but ended. Only after an interval of twelve years did he return to Broadway with a new play, *The Iceman Cometh,* not one of his best. At his death he left a play that he had completed in 1940, *Long Day's Journey into Night,* concerning the O'Neill family, a harsh and painful drama "of old sorrow, written in tears and blood," which had its world première in Stockholm, Sweden, in 1956.

In all his work O'Neill showed a strong "sense of the theater." He explored the possibilities of the stage, presenting the dramatic conflict, typically, through such experiments as the use of symbolic masks, or parallel asides, or the device of a chorus, or the beat of tom-toms. So strong is his attachment to stage-craft that his work leans toward a melodramatic straining for effect. Freely shifting his method and emphasis, he may be said to be a realist in *Beyond the Horizon*, a naturalist in *Desire Under the Elms*, a symbolist in *The Great God Brown*, an expressionist in *The Emperor Jones*, though the traits of the realistic movement appear everywhere, as well as an admixture of romanticism. In general, the mood of his plays is that of the disillusioned period after the first World War, a disillusionment deepened by the Freudian psychology. Human life, as he reads it, is unhappy; men and women are maladjusted, frustrated, spiritually starved, despairing, or tripped up by fate. "In the midst of this general unhappiness," he said, "art alone is happy" — art which finds beauty even in ugliness.

Further reading: *The Hairy Ape. Desire Under the Elms. The Great God Brown. Strange Interlude.* B. H. Clark, *Eugene O'Neill*, revised 1947. A. H. Quinn, *A History of the American Drama from the Civil War to the Present Day*, revised 1936.

The Emperor Jones
(w. 1920)

🦋 This study of fear is one of O'Neill's most original and skilful plays, highly effective on the stage. It is "perfectly constructed and artistically inevitable. The settings and plot contribute with as inexorable an art as that of Poe to the single effect, and that effect is bound up with a clear problem in character. The theme is the regression of a Negro to savagery; and as we watch the succession of weird visions and feel the emotional crescendo of the tom-toms, at the same time we see the disintegration of the Negro's mind. The parallel progress of inner and outer events is beautifully executed" (Alan Reynolds Thompson).

CHARACTERS

BRUTUS JONES . . . . *Emperor*
HENRY SMITHERS . . . . *A Cockney Trader*
AN OLD NATIVE WOMAN
LEM . . . . *A Native Chief*
SOLDIERS . . . . *Adherents of Lem*
The Little Formless Fears; Jeff; The Negro Convicts; The Prison Guard; The Planters; The Auctioneer; The Slaves; The Congo Witch-Doctor; The Crocodile God.

The action of the play takes place on an island in the West Indies as yet not self-determined by White Marines. The form of native government is, for the time being, an Empire.

SCENE ONE

SCENE — *The audience chamber in the palace of the Emperor — a spacious, high-ceilinged room with bare, white-washed walls. The floor is of white tiles. In the rear, to the left of center, a wide archway giving out on a portico with white pillars. The palace is evidently situated on high ground, for beyond the portico nothing can be seen but a vista of distant hills, their summits crowned with thick groves of palm trees. In the right wall, center, a smaller arched doorway leading to the living quarters of the palace. The room is bare of furniture with the exception of one huge chair made of uncut wood which stands at center, its back to rear. This is very apparently the Emperor's throne. It is painted a dazzling, eye-smiting scarlet. There is a brilliant orange cushion on the seat and another smaller one is placed on the floor to serve as a footstool. Strips of matting, dyed scarlet, lead from the foot of the throne to the two entrances.*

It is late afternoon but the sunlight still blazes yellowly beyond the portico and there is an oppressive burden of exhausting heat in the air.

As the curtain rises, a native Negro woman sneaks in cautiously from the entrance on the right. She is very old, dressed in cheap calico, bare-footed, a red bandana handkerchief covering all but a few stray wisps of white hair. A bundle bound in colored cloth is carried over her shoulder on the end of a stick. She hesitates beside the doorway, peering back as if in extreme dread of being discovered. Then she begins to glide noiselessly, a step at a time, toward the doorway in the rear. At this moment, SMITHERS appears beneath the portico.

SMITHERS is a tall, stoop-shouldered man about forty. His bald head, on a long neck with an enormous Adam's apple, looks like an egg. The tropics have tanned his naturally pasty face with its small, sharp features to a sickly yellow, and native rum has painted his pointed nose to a startling red. His little, washy-blue eyes are red-rimmed and dart about him like a ferret's. His expression is one of unscrupulous meanness, cowardly and dangerous. He is dressed in a worn riding suit of dirty white drill, puttees, spurs, and wears a white cork helmet. A cartridge belt with an automatic revolver is around his waist. He carries a riding whip in his hand. He sees the woman and stops to watch her suspiciously. Then, making up his mind, he steps quickly on tiptoe into the room. The woman, looking back over her shoulder continually, does not see him until it is too late. When she does SMITHERS springs forward and grabs her firmly by the shoulder. She struggles to get away, fiercely but silently.

SMITHERS [Tightening his grasp — roughly]: Easy! None o' that, me birdie. You can't wriggle out now. I got me 'ooks on yer.

WOMAN [Seeing the uselessness of struggling, gives way to frantic terror, and sinks to the ground, embracing his knees supplicatingly]: No tell him! No tell him, Mister!

SMITHERS [With great curiosity]: Tell 'im? [Then scornfully.] Oh, you mean 'is bloomin' Majesty. What's the gaime, any'ow? What are you sneakin' away for? Been stealin' a bit, I s'pose. [He taps her bundle with his riding whip significantly.]

WOMAN [Shaking her head vehemently]: No, me no steal.

SMITHERS: Bloody liar! But tell me what's up. There's somethin' funny goin' on. I smelled it in the air first thing I got up this mornin'. You blacks are up to some devilment. This palace of 'is is like a bleedin' tomb. Where's all the 'ands? [The woman keeps sullenly silent. SMITHERS raises his whip threateningly.] Ow, yer won't, won't yer? I'll show yer what's what.

WOMAN [Coweringly]: I tell, Mister. You no hit. They go — all go. [She makes a sweeping gesture toward the hills in the distance.]

SMITHERS: Run away — to the 'ills?

WOMAN: Yes, Mister. Him Emperor — Great Father. [She touches her forehead to the floor with a quick mechanical jerk.] Him sleep after eat. Then they go — all go. Me old woman. Me left only. Now me go too.

SMITHERS [His astonishment giving way to an immense, mean satisfaction]: Ow! So that's the ticket! Well, I know bloody well wot's in the air — when they runs orf to the 'ills. The tom-tom 'll be thumping out there bloomin' soon. [With extreme vindictiveness.] And I'm bloody glad of it, for one! Serve 'im right! Puttin' on airs, the stinkin' nigger! 'Is Majesty! Gowd blimey! I only 'opes I'm there when they takes 'im out to shoot 'im. [Suddenly.] 'E's still 'ere all right, ain't 'e?

WOMAN: Yes. Him sleep.

SMITHERS: 'E's bound to find out soon as 'e wakes up. 'E's cunnin' enough to know when 'is time's come. [He goes to the doorway on right and whistles shrilly with his fingers in his mouth. The old woman springs to her feet and runs out of the doorway, rear. SMITHERS goes after her, reaching for his revolver.] Stop or I'll shoot! [Then stopping — indifferently.] Pop orf then, if yer like, yer black cow. [He stands in the doorway, looking after her.]

[JONES enters from the right. He is a tall, powerfully-built, full-blooded Negro of middle age. His features are typically Negroid, yet there is something decidedly distinctive about his face — an underlying strength of will, a hardy, self-reliant confidence in himself that inspires respect. His eyes are alive with a keen, cunning intelligence. In manner he is shrewd, suspicious, evasive. He wears a light blue uniform coat, sprayed with brass buttons, heavy gold chevrons on his shoulders, gold braid on the collar, cuffs, etc. His pants are bright red with a light blue stripe down the side. Patent leather laced boots with brass spurs, and a belt with a long-barreled, pearl-handled revolver in a holster complete his make-up. Yet there is something not altogether ridiculous about his grandeur. He has a way of carrying it off.]

JONES [Not seeing anyone — greatly irritated and blinking sleepily — shouts]: Who dare whistle dat way in my palace? Who dare wake up de Emperor? I'll git de hide frayled off some o' you niggers sho'!

SMITHERS [Showing himself — in a manner half-afraid and half-defiant]: It was me whistled to yer. [*As* JONES *frowns angrily*.] I got news for yer.

JONES [*Putting on his suavest manner, which fails to cover up his contempt for the white man*]: Oh, it's you, Mister Smithers. [*He sits down on his throne with easy dignity.*] What news you got to tell me?

SMITHERS [*Coming close to enjoy his discomfiture:*] Don't yer notice nothin' funny today?

JONES [*Coldly*]: Funny? No. I ain't perceived nothin' of de kind!

SMITHERS: Then yer ain't so foxy as I thought yer was. Where's all your court? [*Sarcastically*] the Generals and the Cabinet Ministers and all?

JONES [*Imperturbably*]: Where dey mostly runs to minute I close my eyes — drinkin' rum and talkin' big down in de town. [*Sarcastically.*] How come you don't know dat? Ain't you sousin' with 'em most every day?

SMITHERS [*Stung but pretending indifference — with a wink*]: That's part of the day's work. I got ter — ain't I — in my business?

JONES [*Contemptuously*]: Yo' business!

SMITHERS [*Impudently enraged*]: Gawd blimey, you was glad enough for me ter take yer in on it when you landed here first. You didn't 'ave no 'igh and mighty airs in them days!

JONES [*His hand going to his revolver like a flash — menacingly*]: Talk polite, white man! Talk polite, you heah me! I'm boss heah now, is you fergettin'? [*The Cockney seems about to challenge this last statement with the facts but something in the other's eyes holds and cows him.*]

SMITHERS [*In a cowardly whine*]: No 'arm meant, old top.

JONES [*Condescendingly*]: I accepts yo' apology. [*Lets his hand fall from his revolver.*] No use'n you rakin' up ole times. What I was den is one thing. What I is now's another. You didn't let me in on yo' crooked work out o' no kind feelin's dat time. I done de dirty work fo' you — and most o' de brain work, too, fo' dat matter — and I was wu'th money to you, dat's de reason.

SMITHERS: Well, blimey, I give yer a start, didn't I — when no one else would. I wasn't afraid to 'ire yer like the rest was — 'count of the story about your breakin' jail back in the States.

JONES: No, you didn't have no s'cuse to look down on me fo' dat. You been in jail you'self more'n once.

SMITHERS [*Furiously*]: It's a lie! [*Then trying to pass it off by an attempt at scorn.*] Garn! Who told yer that fairy tale?

JONES: Dey's some tings I ain't got to be tole. I kin see 'em in folks' eyes. [*Then after a pause — meditatively.*] Yes, you sho' give me a start. And it didn't take long from dat time to git dese fool, woods' niggers right where I wanted dem. [*With pride.*] From stowaway to Emperor in two years! Dat's goin' some!

SMITHERS [*With curiosity*]: And I bet you got yer pile o' money 'id safe some place.

JONES [*With satisfaction*]: I sho' has! And it's in a foreign bank where no pusson don't ever git it out but me no matter what come. You didn't s'pose I was holdin' down dis Emperor job for de glory in it, did you? Sho'! De fuss and glory part of it, dat's only to turn de heads o' de low-flung, bush niggers dat's here. Dey wants de big circus show for deir money. I gives it to 'em an' I gits de money. [*With a grin.*] De long green, dat's me every time! [*Then rebukingly.*] But you ain't got no kick agin me, Smithers. I'se paid you back all you done for me many times. Ain't I pertected you and winked at all de crooked tradin' you been doin' right out in de broad day? Sho' I has — and me makin' laws to stop it at de same time! [*He chuckles.*]

SMITHERS [*Grinning*]: But, meanin' no 'arm, you been grabbin' right and left yourself, ain't yer? Look at the taxes you've put on 'em! Blimey! You've squeezed 'em dry!

JONES [*Chuckling*]: No, dey ain't *all* dry yet. I'se still heah, ain't I?

SMITHERS [*Smiling at his secret thought*]: They're dry right now, you'll find out. [*Changing the subject abruptly.*] And as for me breakin' laws, you've broke 'em all yerself just as fast as yer made 'em.

JONES: Ain't I de Emperor? De laws don't go for him. [*Judicially.*] You heah what I tells you, Smithers. Dere's little stealin' like you does, and dere's big stealin' like I does. For de little stealin' dey gits you in jail soon or late. For de big stealin' dey makes you Emperor and puts you in de Hall o' Fame when you croaks. [*Reminiscently.*] If dey's one thing I learns in ten years on de Pullman ca's listenin' to de white quality talk, it's dat same fact. And when I gits a chance to use it I winds up Emperor in two years.

SMITHERS [*Unable to repress the genuine admiration of the small fry for the large*]: Yes, yer turned the bleedin' trick, all right. Blimey, I never seen a bloke 'as 'ad the bloomin' luck you 'as.

JONES [*Severely*]: Luck? What you mean — luck?

SMITHERS: I suppose you'll say as that swank about the silver bullet ain't luck — and that was what first got the fool blacks on yer side the time of the revolution, wasn't it?

JONES [*With a laugh*]: Oh, dat silver bullet! sho was luck! But I makes dat luck, you heah? I loads de dice! Yessuh! When dat murderin' nigger ole Lem hired to kill me takes aim ten feet away and his gun misses fire and I shoots him dead, what you heah me say?

SMITHERS: You said yer'd got a charm so's no lead bullet'd kill yer. You was so strong only a silver bullet could kill yer, you told 'em. Blimey, wasn't that swank for yer — and plain, fat-'eaded luck?

JONES [*Laughing*]: And dere all dem fool, bush niggers was kneelin' down and bumpin' deir heads on de ground like I was a miracle out o' de Bible. Oh Lawd, from dat time on I has dem eatin out' of my hand. I cracks de whip and dey jumps through.

SMITHERS [*With a sniff*]: Yankee bluff done it.

JONES: Ain't a man's talkin' big what makes him big — long as he makes folks believe it? Sho', I talks large when I ain't got nothin' to back it up, but I ain't talkin' wild just de same. I knows I kin fool 'em — I *knows* it — and dat's backin' enough fo' my game. And ain't I got to learn deir lingo and teach some of dem English befo' I kin talk to 'em? Ain't dat wuk? You ain't never learned any word er it, Smithers, in de ten years you been heah, dough you' knows it's money in yo' pocket tradin' wid 'em if you does. But you'se too shiftless to take de trouble.

SMITHERS [*Flushing*]: Never mind about me. What's this I've 'eard about yer really 'avin' a silver bullet moulded for yourself?

JONES: It's playin' out my bluff. I has de silver bullet moulded and I tells 'em when de time comes I kills myself wid it. I tells 'em dat's 'cause I'm de on'y man in de world big enuff to git me. No use'n deir tryin'. And dey falls down and bumps deir heads. [*He laughs.*] I does dat so's I kin take a walk in peace widout no jealous nigger gunnin' at me from behind de trees.

SMITHERS [*Astonished*]: Then you 'ad it made — 'onest?

JONES: Sho' did. Heah she be. [*He takes out his revolver, breaks it, and takes the silver bullet out of one chamber.*] Five lead an' dis silver baby at de last. Don't she shine pretty? [*He holds it in his hand, looking at it admiringly, as if strangely fascinated.*]

SMITHERS: Let me see. [*Reaches out his hand for it.*]

JONES [*Harshly*]: Keep yo' hands whar dey b'long, white man. [*He replaces it in the chamber and puts the revolver back on his hip.*]

SMITHERS [*Snarling*]: Gawd blimey! Think I'm a bleedin' thief, you would.

JONES: No, 'tain't dat. I knows you'se scared to steal from me. On'y I ain't 'lowin' nary body to touch dis baby. She's my rabbit's foot.

SMITHERS [*Sneering*]: A bloomin' charm, wot? [*Venomously.*] Well, you'll need all the bloody charms you 'as before long, s' 'elp me!

JONES [*Judicially*]: Oh, I'se good for six months yit 'fore dey gits sick o' my game. Den, when I sees trouble comin', I makes my get-away.

SMITHERS: Ho! You got it all planned, ain't yer?

JONES: I ain't no fool. I knows dis Emperor's time is sho't. Dat why I make hay when de sun shine. Was you thinkin' I'se aimin' to hold down dis job for life? No, suh! What good is gittin' money if you stays back in dis raggedy country? I wants action when I spends. And when I sees dese niggers gittin' up deir nerve to tu'n me out, and I'se got all de money in sight, I resigns on de spot and beats it quick.

SMITHERS: Where to?

JONES: None o' yo' business.

SMITHERS: Not back to the bloody States, I'll lay my oath.

JONES [*Suspiciously*]: Why don't I? [*Then with an easy laugh.*] You mean 'count of dat story 'bout me breakin' from jail back dere? Dat's all talk.

SMITHERS [*Skeptically*]: Ho, yes!

JONES [*Sharply*]: You ain't 'sinuatin' I'se a liar, is you?

SMITHERS [*Hastily*]: No, Gawd strike me! I was only thinkin' o' the bloody lies you told the blacks 'ere about killin' white men in the States.

JONES [*Angered*]: How come dey're lies?

SMITHERS: You'd 'ave been in jail if you 'ad, wouldn't yer then? [*With venom.*] And from what I've 'eard, it ain't 'ealthy for a black to kill a white man in the States. They burns 'em in oil, don't they?

JONES [*With cool deadliness*]: You mean lynchin' 'd scare me? Well, I tells you, Smithers, maybe I does kill one white man back dere. Maybe I does. And maybe I kills another right heah 'fore long if he don't look out.

SMITHERS [*Trying to force a laugh*]: I was on'y spoofin' yer. Can't yer take a joke? And you was just sayin' you'd never been in jail.

JONES [*In the same tone — slightly boastful*]: Maybe I goes to jail dere for gettin' in an argument wid razors ovah a crap game. Maybe I gits twenty years when dat colored man die. Maybe I gits in 'nother argument wid de prison guard was overseer ovah us when we're wukin' de roads. Maybe he hits me wid a whip and I splits his head wid a shovel and runs away and files de chain off my leg and gits away safe. Maybe I does all dat an' maybe I don't. It's a story I tells you so's you knows I'se de kind of man dat if you evah repeats one word of it, I ends yo' stealin' on dis yearth mighty damn quick!

SMITHERS [*Terrified*]: Think I'd peach on yer? Not me! Ain't I always been yer friend?

JONES [*Suddenly relaxing*]: Sho' you has — and you better be.

SMITHERS [*Recovering his composure — and with it his malice*]: And just to show yer I'm yer friend, I'll tell yer that bit o' news I was goin' to.

JONES: Go ahead! Shoot de piece. Must be bad news from de happy way you look.

SMITHERS [*Warningly*]: Maybe it's gettin' time for you to resign — with that bloomin' silver bullet, wot? [*He finishes with a mocking grin.*]

JONES [*Puzzled*]: What's dat you say? Talk plain.

SMITHERS: Ain't noticed any of the guards or servants about the place today, I 'aven't.

JONES [*Carelessly*]: Dey're all out in de garden sleepin' under de trees. When I sleeps, dey sneaks a sleep, too, and I pretends I never suspicions it. All I got to do is to ring de bell and dey come flyin', makin' a bluff dey was wukin' all de time.

SMITHERS [*In the same mocking tone*]: Ring the bell now an' you'll bloody well see what I means.

JONES [*Startled to alertness, but preserving the same careless tone*]: Sho' I rings. [*He reaches below the throne and pulls out a big, common dinner bell which is painted the same vivid scarlet as the throne. He rings this vigorously — then stops to listen. Then he goes to both doors, rings again, and looks out.*]

SMITHERS [*Watching him with malicious satisfaction, after a pause — mockingly*]: The bloody ship is sinkin' an' the bleedin' rats 'as slung their 'ooks.

JONES [*In a sudden fit of anger flings the bell clattering into a corner*]: Low-flung, woods' niggers! [*Then catching Smithers' eye on him, he controls himself and suddenly bursts into a low chuckling laugh.*] Reckon I overplays my hand dis once! A man can't take de pot on a bob-tailed flush all de time. Was I sayin' I'd sit in six months mo'? Well, I'se changed my mind den. I cashes in and resigns de job of Emperor right dis minute.

SMITHERS [*With real admiration*]: Blimey, but you're a cool bird, and no mistake.

JONES: No use'n fussin'. When I knows de game's up I kisses it good-bye widout no long waits. Dey've all run off to de hills, ain't dey?

SMITHERS: Yes — every bleedin' man jack of 'em.

JONES: Den de revolution is at de post. And de Emperor better git his feet smokin' up de trail. [*He starts for the door in rear.*]

SMITHERS: Goin' out to look for your 'orse? Yer won't find any. They steals the 'orses first thing. Mine was gone when I went for 'im this mornin'. That's wot first give me a suspicion of wot was up.

JONES [*Alarmed for a second, scratches his head, then philosophically*]: Well, den I hoofs it. Feet, do yo' duty! [*He pulls out a gold watch and looks at it.*] Three-thuty. Sundown's at six-thuty or dere-abouts. [*Puts his watch back — with cool confidence.*] I got plenty o' time to make it easy.

SMITHERS: Don't be so bloomin' sure of it. They'll be after you 'ot and 'eavy. Ol' Lem is at the bottom o' this business an' 'e 'ates you like 'ell. 'E'd rather do for you than eat 'is dinner, 'e would!

JONES [*Scornfully*]: Dat fool no-count nigger! Does you think I'se scared o' him? I stands him on his thick head more'n once befo' dis, and I does it again if he come in my way . . . [*Fiercely.*] And dis time I leave him a dead nigger fo' sho'!

SMITHERS: You'll 'ave to cut through the big forest — an' these blacks 'ere can sniff and follow a trail in the dark like 'ounds. You'd 'ave to 'ustle to get through that forest in twelve hours even if you knew all the bloomin' trails like a native.

JONES [*With indignant scorn*]: Look-a-heah, white man! Does you think I'se a natural bo'n fool? Give me credit fo' havin' some sense, fo' Lawd's sake! Don't you s'pose I'se looked ahead and made sho' of all de chances? I'se gone out in dat big forest, pretendin' to hunt, so many times dat I knows it high an' low like a book. I could go through on dem trails wid my eyes shut. [*With great contempt.*] Think dese ign'rent bush niggers dat ain't got brains enuff to know deir own names even can catch Brutus Jones? Huh, I s'pects not! Not on yo' life! Why, man, de white men went after me wid bloodhounds where I come from an' I jes' laughs at 'em. It's a shame to fool dese black trash around heah, dey're so easy. You watch me, man. I'll make dem look sick, I will. I'll be 'cross de plain to de edge of de forest by time dark comes. Once in de woods in de night, dey got a swell chance o' findin' dis baby! Dawn tomorrow I'll be out at de oder side and on de coast whar dat French gunboat is stayin'. She picks me up, take me to Martinique when she go dar, and dere I is safe wid a mighty big bankroll in my jeans. It's easy as rollin' off a log.

SMITHERS [*Maliciously*]: But s'posin' somethin' 'appens wrong an' they do nab yer?

JONES [*Decisively*]: Dey don't — dat's de answer.

SMITHERS: But, just for argyment's sake — what'd you do?

JONES [*Frowning*]: I'se got five lead bullets in dis gun good enuff fo' common bush niggers — and after dat I got de silver bullet left to cheat 'em out o' gittin' me.

SMITHERS [*Jeeringly*]: Ho, I was fergettin' that silver bullet. You'll bump yourself orf in style, won't yer? Blimey!

JONES [*Gloomily*]: You kin bet yo' whole roll on one thing, white man. Dis baby plays out his string to de end and when he quits, he quits wid a bang de way he ought. Silver bullet ain't none too good for him when he go, dat's a fac'! [*Then shaking off his nervousness — with a confident laugh.*] Sho'! What is I talkin' about? Ain't come to dat yit and I never will — not wid trash niggers like dese yere. [*Boastfully.*] Silver bullet bring me luck anyway. I kin outguess, outrun, outfight, an'

outplay de whole lot o' dem all ovah de board any time o' de day er night! You watch me! [*From the distant hills comes the faint, steady thump of a tom-tom, low and vibrating. It starts at a rate exactly corresponding to normal pulse beat — 72 to the minute — and continues at a gradually accelerating rate from this point uninterruptedly to the very end of the play.*]

[JONES *starts at the sound. A strange look of apprehension creeps into his face for a moment as he listens. Then he asks, with an attempt to regain his most casual manner.*] What's dat drum beatin' fo'?

SMITHERS [*With a mean grin*]: For you. That means the bleedin' ceremony 'as started. I've 'eard it before and I knows.

JONES: Cer'mony? What cer'mony?

SMITHERS: The blacks is 'oldin' a bloody meetin', 'avin' a war dance, gettin' their courage worked up b'fore they starts after you.

JONES: Let dem! Dey'll sho' need it!

SMITHERS: And they're there 'oldin' their 'eathen religious service — makin' no end of devil spells and charms to 'elp 'em against your silver bullet. [*He guffaws loudly.*] Blimey, but they're balmy as 'ell!

JONES [*A tiny bit awed and shaken in spite of himself*]: Huh! Takes more'n dat to scare dis chicken!

SMITHERS [*Scenting the other's feeling — maliciously*]: Ternight when it's pitch black in the forest, they'll 'ave their pet devils and ghosts 'oundin' after you. You'll find yer bloody 'air 'll be standin' on end before termorrow mornin'. [*Seriously.*] It's a bleedin' queer place, that stinkin' forest, even in daylight. Yer don't know what might 'appen in there, it's that rotten still. Always sends the cold shivers down my back minute I gets in it.

JONES [*With a contemptuous sniff*]: I ain't no chicken-liver like you is. Trees an' me, we'se friends, and dar's a full moon comin' bring me light. And let dem po' niggers make all de fool spells dey'se a min' to. Does yo' s'pect I'se silly enuff to b'lieve in ghosts an' ha'nts an' all dat ole women's talk? G'long, white man! You ain't talkin' to me. [*With a chuckle.*] Doesn't you know dey's got to do wid a man was member in good standin' o' de Baptist Church? Sho' I was dat when I was porter on de Pullmans, befo' I gits into my little trouble. Let dem try deir heathen tricks. De Baptist Church done pertect me and land dem all in hell. [*Then with more confident satisfaction.*] And I'se got little silver bullet o' my own, don't forgit.

SMITHERS: Ho! You 'aven't give much 'eed to your Baptist Church since you been down 'ere. I've 'eard myself you 'ad turned yer coat an' was takin' up with their blarsted witch-doctors, or whatever the 'ell yer calls the swine.

JONES [*Vehemently*]: I pretends to! Sho' I pretends! Dat's part o' my game from de fust. If I finds out dem niggers believes dat black is white, den I yells it out louder 'n deir loudest. It don't git me nothin' to do mission-ary work for de Baptist Church. I'se after de coin, an' I lays my Jesus on de shelf for de time bein'. [*Stops abruptly to look at his watch — alertly.*] But I ain't got de time to waste no more fool talk wid you. I'se gwine away from heah dis secon'. [*He reaches in under the throne and pulls out an expensive Panama hat with a bright multi-colored band and sets it jauntily on his head.*] So long, white man! [*With a grin.*] See you in jail sometime, maybe!

SMITHERS: Not me, you won't. Well, I wouldn't be in yer bloody boots for no bloomin' money, but 'ere's wishin' yer luck just the same.

JONES [*Contemptuously*]: You're de fright-enedest man evah I see! I tells you I'se safe's 'f I was in New York City. It takes dem nig-gers from now to dark to git up de nerve to start somethin'. By dat time, I'se got a head start dey never kotch up wid.

SMITHERS [*Maliciously*]: Give my regards to any ghosts yer meets up with.

JONES [*Grinning*]: If dat ghost got money, I'll tell him never ha'nt you less'n he wants to lose it.

SMITHERS [*Flattered*]: Garn! [*Then curi-ously.*] Ain't yer takin' no luggage with yer?

JONES: I travels light when I wants to move fast. And I got tinned grub buried on de edge o' de forest. [*Boastfully.*] Now say dat I don't look ahead an' use my brains! [*With a wide, lib-eral gesture.*] I will all dat's left in de palace to you — and you better grab all you kin sneak away wid befo' dey gits here.

SMITHERS [*Gratefully*]: Righto — and thanks ter yer. [*As JONES walks toward the door in rear — cautioningly.*] Say! Look 'ere, you ain't goin' out that way, are yer?

JONES: Does you think I'd slink out de back door like a common nigger? I'se Emperor yit,

ain't I? And de Emperor Jones leaves de way he comes, and dat black trash don't dare stop him — not yit, leastways. [*He stops for a mo-ment in the doorway, listening to the far-off but insistent beat of the tom-tom.*] Listen to dat roll-call, will you? Must be mighty big drum carry dat far. [*Then with a laugh.*] Well, if dey ain't no whole brass band to see me off, I sho' got de drum part of it. So long, white man. [*He puts his hands in his pockets and with studied carelessness, whistling a tune, he saun-ters out of the doorway and off to the left.*]

SMITHERS [*Looks after him with a puzzled admiration*]: 'E's got 'is bloomin' nerve with 'im, s'elp me! [*Then angrily.*] Ho — the bleed-in' nigger — puttin' on 'is bloody airs! I 'opes they nabs 'im an' gives 'im what's what! [*Then putting business before the pleasure of this thought, looking around him with cupidity.*] A bloke ought to find a 'ole lot in this palace that'd go for a bit of cash. Let's take a look, 'Arry, me lad. [*He starts for the doorway on right as*

[*The curtain falls.*]

SCENE TWO

SCENE — *Nightfall. The end of the plain where the Great Forest begins. The foreground is sandy, level ground dotted by a few stones and clumps of stunted bushes cowering close against the earth to escape the buffet-ing of the trade wind. In the rear the forest is a wall of darkness dividing the world. Only when the eye becomes accustomed to the gloom can the outlines of separate trunks of the nearest trees be made out, enormous pillars of deeper blackness. A somber monotone of wind lost in the leaves moans in the air. Yet this sound serves but to intensify the impression of the forest's relentless immobility, to form a back-ground throwing into relief its brooding, implacable silence.*

[JONES *enters from the left, walking rap-idly. He stops as he nears the edge of the forest, looks around him quickly, peering into the dark as if searching for some fa-miliar landmark. Then, apparently satisfied that he is where he ought to be, he throws himself on the ground, dog-tired.*]

Well, heah I is. In de nick o' time, too! Little mo' an' it'd be blacker'n de ace of spades heah-abouts. [*He pulls a bandana handker-*

chief from his hip pocket and mops off his perspiring face.] Sho'! Gimme air! I'se tuckered out sho' 'nuff. Dat soft Emperor job ain't no trainin' for a long hike ovah dat plain in de brilin' sun. [Then with a chuckle.] Cheah up, nigger, de worst is yet to come. [He lifts his head and stares at the forest. His chuckle peters out abruptly. In a tone of awe.] My goodness, look at dem woods, will you? Dat no-count Smithers said dey'd be black an' he sho' called de turn. [Turning away from them quickly and looking down at his feet, he snatches at a chance to change the subject — solicitously.] Feet, you is holdin' up yo' end fine an' I sutinly hopes you ain't blisterin' none. It's time you git a rest. [He takes off his shoes, his eyes studiously avoiding the forest. He feels of the soles of his feet gingerly.] You is still in de pink — on'y a little mite feverish. Cool yo'selfs. Remember you done got a long journey yit befo' you. [He sits in a weary attitude, listening to the rhythmic beating of the tom-tom. He grumbles in a loud tone to cover up a growing uneasiness.] Bush niggers! Wonder dey wouldn't git sick o' beatin' dat drum. Sound louder, seem like. I wonder if dey's startin' after me? [He scrambles to his feet, looking back across the plain.] Couldn't see dem now, nohow, if dey was hundred feet away. [Then shaking himself like a wet dog to get rid of these depressing thoughts.] Sho', dey's miles an' miles behind. What you gittin' fidgety about? [But he sits down and begins to lace up his shoes in great haste, all the time muttering reassuringly.] You know what? Yo' belly is empty, dat's what's de matter wid you. Come time to eat! Wid nothin' but wind on yo' stumach, o' course you feels jiggedy. Well, we eats right heah an' now soon's I gits dese pesky shoes laced up! [He finishes lacing up his shoes.] Dere! Now le's see. [Gets on his hands and knees and searches the ground around him with his eyes.] White stone, white stone, where is you? [He sees the first white stone and crawls to it — with satisfaction.] Heah you is! I knowed dis was de right place. Box of grub, come to me. [He turns over the stone and feels in under it — in a tone of dismay.] Ain't heah! Gorry, is I in de right place or isn't I? Dere's 'nother stone. Guess dat's it. [He scrambles to the next stone and turns it over.] Ain't heah, neither! Grub, whar is you? Ain't heah. Gorry, has I got to go hungry into dem woods — all de night? [While he is talking he scrambles from one stone to another, turning them over in

frantic haste. Finally, he jumps to his feet excitedly.] Is I lost de place? Must have! But how dat happen when I was followin' de trail across de plain in broad daylight? [Almost plaintively.] I'se hungry, I is! I gotta git my feed. What's my strength gonna come from if I doesn't? Gorry, I gotta find dat grub high an' low somehow! Why it come dark so quick like dat? Can't see nothin'. [He scratches a match on his trousers and peers about him. The rate of the beat of the far-off tom-tom increases perceptibly as he does so. He mutters in a bewildered voice.] How come all dese white stones come heah when I only remembers one? [Suddenly, with a frightened gasp, he flings the match on the ground and stamps on it.] Nigger, is you gone crazy mad? Is you lightin' matches to show dem whar you is? Fo' Lawd's sake, use yo' haid. Gorry, I'se got to be careful! [He stares at the plain behind him apprehensively, his hand on his revolver.] But how come all dese white stones? And whar's dat tin box o' grub I hid all wrapped up in oil cloth?

[While his back is turned, the LITTLE FORMLESS FEARS creep out from the deeper blackness of the forest. They are black, shapeless, only their glittering little eyes can be seen. If they have any describable form at all, it is that of a grubworm about the size of a creeping child. They move noiselessly, but with deliberate, painful effort, striving to raise themselves on end, failing and sinking prone again. JONES turns about to face the forest. He stares up at the tops of the trees, seeking vainly to discover his whereabouts by their conformation.]

Can't tell nothin' from dem trees! Gorry, nothin' round heah look like I evah seed it befo'. I'se done lost de place sho' 'nuff! [With mournful foreboding.] It's mighty queer! It's mighty queer! [With sudden forced defiance — in an angry tone.] Woods, is you tryin' to put somethin' ovah on me?

[From the formless creatures on the ground in front of him comes a tiny gale of low mocking laughter like a rustling of leaves. They squirm upward toward him in twisted attitudes. JONES looks down, leaps backward with a yell of terror, yanking out his revolver as he does so — in a quavering voice.] What's dat? Who's dar? What is you? Git away from me befo' I shoots you up! You don't? . . .

[He fires. There is a flash, a loud report, then silence broken only by the far-off, quickened throb of the tom-tom. The formless creatures *have scurried back into the forest. JONES remains fixed in his position, listening intently. The sound of the shot, the reassuring feel of the revolver in his hand, have somewhat restored his shaken nerve. He addresses himself with renewed confidence.]*

Dey're gone. Dat shot fix 'em. Dey was only little animals — little wild pigs, I reckon. Dey've maybe rooted out yo' grub an' eat it. Sho', you fool nigger, what you think dey is — ha'nts? *[Excitedly.]* Gorry, you give de game away when you fire dat shot. Dem niggers heah dat fo' su'tin! Time you beat it in de woods widout no long waits. *[He starts for the forest — hesitates before the plunge — then urging himself in with manful resolution.]* Git in, nigger! What you skeered at? Ain't nothin' dere but de trees! Git in! *[He plunges boldly into the forest.]*

SCENE THREE

SCENE — *Nine o'clock. In the forest. The moon has just risen. Its beams, drifting through the canopy of leaves, make a barely perceptible, suffused, eerie glow. A dense low wall of underbrush and creepers is in the nearer foreground, fencing in a small triangular clearing. Beyond this is the massed blackness of the forest like an encompassing barrier. A path is dimly discerned leading down to the clearing from left, rear, and winding away from it again toward the right. As the scene opens nothing can be distinctly made out. Except for the beating of the tom-tom, which is a trifle louder and quicker than in the previous scene, there is silence, broken every few seconds by a queer, clicking sound. Then gradually the figure of the Negro, JEFF, can be discerned crouching on his haunches at the rear of the triangle. He is middle-aged, thin, brown in color, is dressed in a Pullman porter's uniform, cap, etc. He is throwing a pair of dice on the ground before him, picking them up, shaking them, casting them out with the regular, rigid, mechanical movements of an automaton. The heavy, plodding foot-steps of someone approaching along the trail from the left are heard and JONES' voice, pitched in a slightly higher key and strained in a cheering effort to overcome its own tremors.]*

De moon's rizen. Does you heah dat, nigger? You gits more light from dis out. No mo' but-

tin' yo' fool head agin' de trunks an' scratchin' de hide off yo' legs in de bushes. Now you sees whar yo'se gwine. So cheer up! From now on you has a snap. *[He steps just to the rear of the triangular clearing and mops off his face on his sleeve. He has lost his Panama hat. His face is scratched, his brilliant uniform shows several large rents.]* What time's it gittin' to be, I wonder? I dassent light no match to find out. Phoo. It's wa'm an' dat's a fac'! *[Wearily.]* How long I been makin' tracks in dese woods? Must be hours an' hours. Seems like fo'evah! Yit can't be, when de moon's jes' riz. Dis am a long night fo' yo', yo' Majesty! *[With a mournful chuckle.]* Majesty! Der ain't much majesty 'bout dis baby now. *[With attempted cheerfulness.]* Never min'. It's all part o' de game. Dis night come to an end like everything else. And when you gits dar safe and has dat bankroll in yo' hands you laughs at all dis. *[He starts to whistle but checks himself abruptly.]* What yo' whistlin' for, you po' dope! Want all de worl' to heah you? *[He stops talking to listen.]* Heah dat ole drum! Sho' gits nearer from de sound. Dey're packin' it along wid 'em. Time fo' me to move. *[He takes a step forward, then stops — worriedly.]* What's dat odder queer clickety sound I heah? Dere it is! Sound close! Sound like — sound like — Fo' God sake, sound like some nigger was shootin' crap! *[Frightenedly.]* I better beat it quick when I gits dem notions. *[He walks quickly into the clear space — then stands transfixed as he sees JEFF — in a terrified gasp.]* Who dar? Who dat? Is dat you, Jeff? *[Starting toward the other, forgetful for a moment of his surroundings and really believing it is a living man that he sees — in a tone of happy relief.]* Jeff! I's sho' mighty glad to see you! Dey tol' me you done died from dat razor cut I gives you. *[Stopping suddenly, bewilderedly.]* But how you come to be heah, nigger? *[He stares fascinatedly at the other who continues his mechanical play with the dice. JONES' eyes begin to roll wildly. He stutters.]* Ain't you gwine — look up — can't you speak to me? Is you — is you — a ha'nt? *[He jerks out his revolver in a frenzy of terrified rage.]* Nigger, I kills you dead once. Has I got to kill you agin? You take it den. *[He fires. When the smoke clears away JEFF has disappeared. JONES stands trembling — then with a certain reassurance.]* He's gone, anyway. Ha'nt or no ha'nt, dat shot fix him. *[The beat of the far-off tom-tom is perceptibly louder and*

more rapid. JONES *becomes conscious of it —*
with a start, looking back over his shoulder.]
Dey's gittin' near! Dey's comin' fast! And
heah I is shootin' shots to let 'em know jes'
whar I is. Oh, Gorry, I'se got to run. [*Forget-*
ting the path he plunges wildly into the under-
brush in the rear and disappears in the shadow.]

SCENE FOUR

SCENE — *Eleven o'clock. In the forest. A wide*
dirt road runs diagonally from right, front,
to left, rear. Rising sheer on both sides
the forest walls it in. The moon is now
up. Under its light the road glimmers
ghastly and unreal. It is as if the forest
had stood aside momentarily to let the road
pass through and accomplish its veiled pur-
pose. This done, the forest will fold in
upon itself again and the road will be no
more. JONES *stumbles in from the forest*
on the right. His uniform is ragged and
torn. He looks about him with numbed
surprise when he sees the road, his eyes
blinking in the bright moonlight. He flops
down exhaustedly and pants heavily for a
while. Then with sudden anger.

I'm meltin' wid heat! Runnin' an' runnin'
an' runnin'! Damn dis heah coat! Like a strait-
jacket! [*He tears off his coat and flings it away*
from him, revealing himself stripped to the
waist.] Dere! Dat's better! Now I kin breathe!
[*Looking down at his feet, the spurs catch his*
eye.] And to hell wid dese high-fangled spurs.
Dey're what's been a-trippin' me up an' breakin'
my neck. [*He unstraps them and flings them*
away disgustedly.] Dere! I gits rid o' dem frip-
pety Emperor trappin's an' I travels lighter.
Lawd! I'se tired! [*After a pause, listening to the*
insistent beat of the tom-tom in the distance.]
I must 'a put some distance between myself an'
dem — runnin' like dat — and yit — dat damn
drum sound jes' de same — nearer, even. Well,
I guess I a'most holds my lead anyhow. Dey
won't never catch up. [*With a sigh.*] If on'y
my fool legs stand up. Oh, I'se sorry I evah
went in for dis. Dat Emperor job is sho' hard
to shake. [*He looks around him suspiciously.*]
How'd dis road evah git heah? Good level road,
too. I never remembers seein' it befo'. [*Shak-*
ing his head apprehensively.] Dese woods is
sho' full o' de queerest things at night. [*With*
a sudden terror.] Lawd God, don't let me see
no more o' dem ha'nts! Dey gits my goat!

[*Then trying to talk himself into confidence.*]
Ha'nts! You fool nigger, dey ain't no such
things! Don't de Baptist parson tell you dat
many time? Is you civilized, or is you like dese
ign'rent black niggers heah? Sho'! Dat was
all in yo' own head. Wasn't nothin' dere.
Wasn't no Jeff! Know what? You jus' get seein'
dem things 'cause yo' belly's empty and you's
sick wid hunger inside. Hunger 'fects yo' head
and yo' eyes. Any fool know dat. [*Then plead-*
ing fervently.] But bless God, I don't come
across no more o' dem, whatever dey is! [*Then*
cautiously.] Rest! Don't talk! Rest! You
needs it. Den you gits on yo' way again. [*Look-*
ing at the moon.] Night's half gone a'most.
You hits de coast in de mawnin'! Den you'se all
safe.

[*From the right forward a small gang of*
Negroes enter. They are dressed in striped con-
vict suits, their heads are shaven, one leg drags
limpingly, shackled to a heavy ball and chain.
Some carry picks, the others shovels. They are
followed by a white man dressed in the uniform
of a prison guard. A Winchester rifle is slung
across his shoulders and he carries a heavy whip.
At a signal from the GUARD *they stop on the*
road opposite where JONES *is sitting.* JONES,
who has been staring up at the sky, unmindful
of their noiseless approach, suddenly looks
down and sees them. His eyes pop out, he tries
to get to his feet and fly, but sinks back, too
numbed by fright to move. His voice catches
in a choking prayer.]

Lawd Jesus!

[*The* PRISON GUARD *cracks his whip — noise-*
lessly — and at that signal all the convicts start
to work on the road. They swing their picks,
they shovel, but not a sound comes from their
labor. Their movements, like those of JEFF *in*
the preceding scene, are those of automatons,
— rigid, slow, and mechanical. The PRISON
GUARD *points sternly at* JONES *with his whip,*
motions him to take his place among the other
shovelers. JONES *gets to his feet in a hypnotized*
stupor. He mumbles subserviently.]

Yes, suh! Yes, suh! I'se comin'.

[*As he shuffles, dragging one foot, over to his*
place, he curses under his breath with rage and
hatred.]

God damn yo' soul, I gits even wid you yit,
sometime.

[*As if there were a shovel in his hands he goes*
through weary, mechanical gestures of digging
up dirt, and throwing it to the roadside. Sud-

denly the GUARD *approaches him angrily, threateningly. He raises his whip and lashes* JONES *viciously across the shoulders with it.* JONES *winces with pain and cowers abjectly. The* GUARD *turns his back on him and walks away contemptuously. Instantly* JONES *straightens up. With arms upraised as if his shovel were a club in his hands, he springs murderously at the unsuspecting* GUARD. *In the act of crashing down his shovel on the white man's skull,* JONES *suddenly becomes aware that his hands are empty. He cries despairingly.*]

Whar's my shovel? Gimme my shovel 'till I splits his damn head! [*Appealing to his fellow convicts.*] Gimme a shovel, one o' you, fo' God's sake!

They stand fixed in motionless attitudes, their eyes on the ground. The GUARD *seems to wait expectantly, his back turned to the attacker.* JONES *bellows with baffled, terrified rage, tugging frantically at his revolver.*]

I kills you, you white debil, if it's de last thing I evah does! Ghost or debil, I kill you again!

[*He frees the revolver and fires point-blank at the* GUARD's *back. Instantly the walls of the forest close in from both sides, the road and the figures of the convict gang are blotted out in an enshrouding darkness. The only sounds are a crashing in the underbrush as* JONES *leaps away in mad flight and the throbbing of the tom-tom still far distant, but increased in volume of sound and rapidity of beat.*]

SCENE FIVE

SCENE — *One o'clock. A large circular clearing, enclosed by the serried ranks of gigantic trunks of tall trees whose tops are lost to view. In the center is a big dead stump worn by time into a curious resemblance to an auction block. The moon floods the clearing with a clear light.* JONES *forces his way in through the forest on the left. He looks wildly about the clearing with hunted, fearful glances. His pants are in tatters, his shoes cut and misshapen, flapping about his feet. He slinks cautiously to the stump in the center and sits down in a tense position, ready for instant flight. Then he holds his head in his hands and rocks back and forth, moaning to himself miserably.*]

Oh Lawd, Lawd! Oh Lawd, Lawd! [*Suddenly he throws himself on his knees and raises his clasped hands to the sky — in a voice of agonized pleading.*] Lawd Jesus, heah my prayer! I'se a po' sinner, a po' sinner! I knows I done wrong, I knows it! When I cotches Jeff cheatin' wid loaded dice my anger overcomes me and I kills him dead! Lawd, I done wrong! When dat guard hits me wid de whip, my anger overcomes me, and I kills him dead. Lawd, I done wrong! And down heah whar dese fool bush niggers raises me up to the seat o' de mighty, I steals all I could grab. Lawd, I done wrong! I knows it! I'se sorry! Forgive me, Lawd! Forgive dis po' sinner! [*Then beseeching terrifiedly.*] And keep dem away, Lawd! Keep dem away from me! And stop dat drum soundin' in my ears! Dat begin to sound ha'nted, too. [*He gets to his feet, evidently slightly reassured by his prayer — with attempted confidence.*] De Lawd'll preserve me from dem ha'nts after dis. [*Sits down on the stump again.*] I ain't skeered o' real men. Let dem come. But dem odders . . . [*He shudders — then looks down at his feet, working his toes inside the shoes — with a groan.*] Oh, my po' feet! Dem shoes ain't no use no more 'ceptin' to hurt. I'se better off without dem. [*He unlaces them and pulls them off — holds the wrecks of the shoes in his hands and regards them mournfully.*] You was real, A-one patin' leather, too. Look at you now. Emperor, you'se gittin' mighty low!

[*He sits dejectedly and remains with bowed shoulders, staring down at the shoes in his hands as if reluctant to throw them away. While his attention is thus occupied, a crowd of figures silently enters the clearing from all sides. All are dressed in Southern costumes of the period of the fifties of the last century. There are middle-aged men who are evidently well-to-do planters. There is one spruce, authoritative individual — the* AUCTIONEER. *There is a crowd of curious spectators, chiefly young belles and dandies who have come to the slave-market for diversion. All exchange courtly greetings in dumb show and chat silently together. There is something stiff, rigid, unreal, marionettish about their movements. They group themselves about the stump. Finally a batch of slaves are led in from the left by an attendant — three men of different ages, two women, one with a baby in her arms, nursing. They are placed to the left of the stump, beside* JONES.

The white planters look them over appraisingly as if they were cattle, and exchange judgments on each. The dandies point with their fingers and make witty remarks. The belles titter bewitchingly. All this in silence save for the ominous throb of the tom-tom. The Auc-TIONEER holds up his hand, taking his place at the stump. The groups strain forward atten- 5 tively. He touches JONES on the shoulder per-emptorily, motioning for him to stand on the stump — the auction block.

JONES looks up, sees the figures on all sides, looks wildly for some opening to escape, sees 10 none, screams and leaps madly to the top of the stump to get as far away from them as possible. He stands there, cowering, paralyzed with hor-ror. The AUCTIONEER begins his silent spiel. He points to JONES, appeals to the planters to 15 see for themselves. Here is a good field hand, sound in wind and limb as they can see. Very strong still in spite of his being middle-aged. Look at that back. Look at those shoulders. Look at the muscles in his arms and his sturdy 20 legs. Capable of any amount of hard labor. Moreover, of a good disposition, intelligent and tractable. Will any gentleman start the bid-ding? The PLANTERS raise their fingers, make their bids. They are apparently all eager to 25 possess JONES. The bidding is lively, the crowd interested. While this has been going on, JONES has been seized by the courage of des-peration. He dares to look down and around him. Over his face abject terror gives way to 30 mystification, to gradual realization — stutter-ingly.]

What you all doin', white folks? What's all dis? What you all lookin' at me fo'? What you doin' wid me, anyhow? [Suddenly con- 35 vulsed with raging hatred and fear.] Is dis a auction? Is you sellin' me like dey uster befo' de war? [Jerking out his revolver just as the AUCTIONEER knocks him down to one of the planters — glaring from him to the purchaser.] 40 And you sells me? And you buys me? I shows you I'se a free nigger, damn yo' souls! [He fires at the AUCTIONEER and at the PLANTER with such rapidity that the two shots are almost simultaneous. As if this were a signal the walls 45 of the forest fold in. Only blackness remains and silence broken by JONES as he rushes off, crying with fear — and by the quickened, ever louder beat of the tom-tom.]

SCENE SIX

SCENE — Three o'clock. A cleared space in the forest. The limbs of the trees meet over it

forming a low ceiling about five feet from the ground. The interlocked ropes of creep-ers reaching upward to entwine the tree trunks give an arched appearance to the sides. The space thus enclosed is like the dark, noisome hold of some ancient vessel. The moonlight is almost completely shut out and only a vague, wan light filters through. There is the noise of someone approaching through the undergrowth. JONES' voice is heard between chattering moans.

Oh, Lawd, what I gwine do now? Ain't got no bullet left on'y de silver one. If mo' o' dem ha'nts come after me, how I gwine skeer dem away? Oh, Lawd, on'y de silver one left — an' I gotta save dat fo' luck. If I shoots dat one I'm a goner sho'! Lawd, it's black heah! Whar's de moon? Oh, Lawd, don't dis night evah come to an end? [By the sounds, he is feeling his way cautiously forward.] Dere! Dis feels like a clear space. I gotta lie down an' rest. I don't care if dem niggers does cotch me. I gotta rest.

[He is well forward now where his figure can be dimly made out. His pants have been so torn away that what is left of them is no better than a breech cloth. He flings himself full length, face downward on the ground, panting with exhaustion. Gradually it seems to grow lighter in the enclosed space and two rows of seated figures can be seen behind JONES. They are sitting in crumpled, despairing attitudes, hunched, facing one another with their backs touching the forest walls as if they were shackled to them. All Negroes, naked save for loin cloths. At first they are silent and motionless. Then they begin to sway slowly forward toward each and back again in unison, as if they were laxly letting themselves follow the long roll of a ship at sea. At the same time, a low, melancholy murmur rises among them, increasing grad-ually by rhythmic degrees which seem to be directed and controlled by the throb of the tom-tom in the distance, to a long, tremulous wail of despair that reaches a certain pitch, unbearably acute, then falls by slow gradations of tone into silence and is taken up again. JONES starts, looks up, sees the figures, and throws himself down again to shut out the sight. A shudder of terror shakes his whole body as the wail rises up about him again. But the next time, his voice, as if under some uncanny compulsion, starts with the others. As their chorus lifts he rises to a sitting posture similar to the others, swaying back and forth. *His voice reaches the highest pitch of sorrow, of desolation. The light fades out, the other voices cease, and only darkness is left.* JONES *can be heard scrambling to his feet and running off, his voice sinking down the scale and receding as he moves farther and farther away in the forest. The tom-tom beats louder, quicker, with a more insistent, triumphant pulsation.*]

SCENE SEVEN

SCENE — *Five o'clock. The foot of a gigantic tree by the edge of a great river. A rough structure of boulders, like an altar, is by the tree. The raised river bank is in the nearer background. Beyond this the surface of the river spreads out, brilliant and unruffled in the moonlight, blotted out and merged into a veil of bluish mist in the distance.* JONES' *voice is heard from the left rising and falling in the long, despairing wail of the chained slave, to the rhythmic beat of the tom-tom. As his voice sinks into silence, he enters the open space. The expression of his face is fixed and stony, his eyes have an obsessed glare, he moves with a strange deliberation like a sleep-walker or one in a trance. He looks around at the tree, the rough stone altar, the moonlit surface of the river beyond, and passes his hand over his head with a vague gesture of puzzled bewilderment. Then, as if in obedience to some obscure impulse, he sinks into a kneeling, devotional posture before the altar. Then he seems to come to himself partly, to have an uncertain realization of what he is doing, for he straightens up and stares about him horrifiedly — in an incoherent mumble.*

What — what is I doin'? What is — dis place? Seems like — seems like I know dat tree — an' dem stones — an' de river. I remember — seems like I been heah befo'. [*Tremblingly.*] Oh, Gorry, I'se skeered in dis place! I'se skeered! Oh, Lawd, perfect dis sinner!

[*Crawling away from the altar, he cowers close to the ground, his face hidden, his shoulders heaving with sobs of hysterical fright. From behind the trunk of the tree, as if he had sprung out of it, the figure of the* CONGO WITCH-DOCTOR *appears. He is wizened and old, naked except for the fur of some small animal tied about his waist, its bushy tail hanging down in front. His body is stained all over a bright red.*

Antelope horns are on each side of his head, branching upward. In one hand he carries a bone rattle, in the other a charm stick with a bunch of white cockatoo feathers tied to the end. A great number of glass beads and bone ornaments are about his neck, ears, wrists, and ankles. He struts noiselessly with a queer prancing step to a position in the clear ground between JONES *and the altar. Then with a preliminary, summoning stamp of his foot on the earth, he begins to dance and to chant. As if in response to his summons the beating of the tom-tom grows to a fierce, exultant boom whose throbs seem to fill the air with vibrating rhythm.* JONES *looks up, starts to spring to his feet, reaches a half-kneeling, half-squatting position and remains rigidly fixed there, paralyzed with awed fascination by this new apparition. The* WITCH-DOCTOR *sways, stamping with his foot, his bone rattle clicking the time. His voice rises and falls in a weird, monotonous croon, without articulate word divisions. Gradually his dance becomes clearly one of a narrative in pantomime, his croon is an incantation, a charm to allay the fierceness of some implacable deity demanding sacrifice. He flees, he is pursued by devils, he hides, he flees again. Even wilder and wilder becomes his flight, nearer and nearer draws the pursuing evil, more and more the spirit of terror gains possession of him. His croon, rising to intensity, is punctuated by shrill cries.* JONES *has become completely hypnotized. His voice joins in the incantation, in the cries, he beats time with his hands and sways his body to and fro from the waist. The whole spirit and meaning of the dance has entered into him, has become his spirit. Finally the theme to the pantomime halts on a howl of despair, and is taken up again in a note of savage hope. There is a salvation. The forces of evil demand sacrifice. They must be appeased. The* WITCH-DOCTOR *points with his wand to the sacred tree, to the river beyond, to the altar, and finally to* JONES *with a ferocious command.* JONES *seems to sense the meaning of this. It is he who must offer himself for sacrifice. He beats his forehead abjectly to the ground, moaning hysterically.*]

Mercy, Oh Lawd! Mercy! Mercy on dis po' sinner.

[*The* WITCH-DOCTOR *springs to the river bank. He stretches out his arms and calls to some God within its depths. Then he starts backward slowly, his arms remaining out. A huge head of a crocodile appears over the bank, and its eyes, glittering greenly, fasten upon* JONES. *He stares into them fascinatedly. The* WITCH-DOCTOR *prances up to him, touches him with his wand, motions him with hideous command toward the waiting monster.* JONES *squirms on his belly nearer and nearer, moaning continually.*]

Mercy, Lawd! Mercy!

[*The crocodile heaves more of his enormous hulk onto the land.* JONES *squirms toward him. The* WITCH-DOCTOR'S *voice shrills out in furious exaltation, the tom-tom beats madly.* JONES *cries out in a fierce, exhausted spasm of anguished pleading.*]

Lawd, save me! Lawd Jesus, heah my prayer!

[*Immediately, in answer to his prayer, comes the thought of the one bullet left him. He snatches at his hip, shouting defiantly.*]

De silver bullet! You don't git me yit!

[*He fires at the green eyes in front of him. The head of the crocodile sinks back behind the river bank, the* WITCH-DOCTOR *springs behind the sacred tree and disappears.* JONES *lies with his face to the ground, his arms outstretched, whimpering with fear as the throb of the tom-tom fills the silence about him with a somber pulsation, a baffled but revengeful power.*]

SCENE EIGHT

SCENE — *Dawn. Same as Scene Two. The dividing line of forest and plain. The nearest tree trunks are dimly revealed but the forest behind them is still a mass of glooming shadow. The tom-tom seems on the very spot, so loud and continuously vibrating are its beats.* LEM *enters from the left, followed by a small squad of his soldiers, and by the Cockney trader,* SMITHERS. LEM *is a heavy-set, ape-faced old savage of the extreme African type, dressed only in a loin cloth. A revolver and cartridge belt are about his waist. His soldiers are in different degrees of rag-concealed nakedness. All wear broad palm-leaf hats. Each one carries a rifle.* SMITHERS *is the same as in Scene One. One of the soldiers, evidently a tracker, is peering about keenly on the ground. He grunts and points to the spot where* JONES *entered the forest.* LEM *and* SMITHERS *come to look.*]

SMITHERS [*After a glance, turns away in disgust*]: That's where 'e went in right enough. Much good it'll do yer. 'E's miles orf by this an' safe to the Coast, damn 'is 'ide! I tole yer yer'd lose 'im, didn't I? — wastin' the 'ole bloomin' night beatin' yer bloody drum and castin' yer silly spells! Gawd blimey, wot a pack!

LEM [*Gutturally*]: We cotch him. You see. [*He makes a motion to his soldiers who squat down on their haunches in a semicircle.*]

SMITHERS [*Exasperatedly*]: Well, ain't yer goin' in an' 'unt 'im in the woods? What the 'ell's the good of waitin'?

LEM [*Imperturbably — squatting down himself*]: We cotch him.

SMITHERS [*Turning away from him contemptuously*]: Aw! Garn! 'E's a better man than the lot o' you put together. I 'ates the sight o' 'im but I'll say that for 'im. [*A sound of snapping twigs comes from the forest. The soldiers jump to their feet, cocking their rifles alertly.* LEM *remains sitting with an imperturbable expression, but listening intently. The sound from the woods is repeated.* LEM *makes a quick signal with his hand. His followers creep quickly but noiselessly into the forest, scattering so that each enters at a different spot.*]

SMITHERS [*In the silence that follows — in a contemptuous whisper*]: You ain't thinkin' that would be 'im, I 'ope?

LEM [*Calmly*]: We cotch him.

SMITHERS: Blarsted fat 'eads! [*Then after a second's thought — wonderingly.*] Still an' all, it might 'appen. If 'e lost 'is bloody way in these stinkin' woods 'e'd likely turn in a circle without 'is knowin' it. They all does.

LEM [*Peremptorily*]: Sssh! [*The reports of several rifles sound from the forest, followed a second later by savage, exultant yells. The beating of the tom-tom abruptly ceases.* LEM *looks up at the white man with a grin of satisfaction:*] We cotch him. Him dead.

SMITHERS [*With a snarl*]: 'Ow d'yer know it's 'im an' 'ow d'yer know 'e's dead?

LEM: My mens dey got 'um silver bullets. Dey kill him shore.

SMITHERS [*Astonished*]: They got silver bullets?

LEM: Lead bullet no kill him. He got um strong charm. I cook um money, make um silver bullet, make um strong charm, too.

SMITHERS [*Light breaking upon him*]: So that's wot you was up to all night, wot? You was scared to put after 'im till you'd molded silver bullets, eh?

LEM [*Simply stating a fact*]: Yes. Him got strong charm. Lead no good.

SMITHERS [*Slapping his thigh and guffawing*]: Haw-haw! If yer don't beat all 'ell! [*Then recovering himself — scornfully.*] I'll bet yer it ain't 'im they shot at all, yer bleedin' looney!

LEM [*Calmly*]: Dey come bring him now. [*The soldiers come out of the forest, carrying* JONES' *limp body. There is a little reddish-purple hole under his left breast. He is dead. They carry him to* LEM, *who examines his body with great satisfaction.*]

SMITHERS [*leans over his shoulder — in a tone of frightened awe*]: Well, they did for yer right enough, Jonesey, me lad! Dead as a 'erring! 15

[*Mockingly.*] Where's yer 'igh an' mighty airs now, yer bloomin' Majesty? [*Then with a grin.*] Silver bullets! Gawd blimey, but yer died in the 'eight o' style, any'ow! [LEM *makes a motion to the soldiers to carry the body out left.* SMITHERS *speaks to him sneeringly.*]

SMITHERS: And I s'pose you think it's yer bleedin' charms and yer silly beatin' the drum that made 'im run in a circle when 'e'd lost 'imself, don't yer? [*But* LEM *makes no reply, does not seem to hear the question, walks out left after his men.* SMITHERS *looks after him with contemptuous scorn.*] Stupid as 'ogs, the lot of 'em! Blarsted niggers!

[*Curtain falls.*]

FICTION OF THE TWENTIES AND LATER

Willa Cather [1873-1947]

"When I strike the open plains," said Miss Cather, ". . . I breathe differently. That love of great spaces, of rolling open country like the sea — it's the grand passion of my life." As a child of nine she had been taken from her native Virginia to a windswept Nebraska farm near Red Cloud, a town of about a thousand people. There she was fortunate in her high school teachers, with one of whom she continued to read Greek and Latin during vacations from college. At the University of Nebraska she was editor of a literary periodical and wrote for the Lincoln *State Journal*. Graduating in 1895, she spent the next year at home in Red Cloud. Then, eager for wider experience, she embraced a chance to work for a magazine in Pittsburgh, Pennsylvania, and to enjoy concerts, opera, and the theater. Half of her decade in the city she spent in journalism (her chief position was on the *Daily Leader*), the second half in teaching in the high schools. In this period, too, she had a summer in Europe, and published a book of poems and her first collection of short stories. In 1906 she went to New York to join the staff of *McClure's Magazine*, of which she was managing editor from 1908 to 1912.

At this point she cast aside all distractions, and gave herself henceforth to writing. Making her home in New York, often returning for vacations to the prairies of her girlhood, she wrote quiet novels that attained startling successes. She was already thirty-nine when her first novel appeared. In the novels that followed — notably in *O Pioneers!*, *My Ántonia*, and *A Lost Lady* — she found the most vital source of her materials, the spacious landscape and the people of Nebraska and the Southwest, long close to her heart. Quite out of sympathy with the easygoing later generation there ("They want to buy everything ready-made: clothes, food, education, music, pleasure"), she loved to reflect on the generation that had known hardships and looked upon life with a certain noble largeness. This led her imagination back to the Spanish Southwest of one of her finest works, *Death Comes for the Archbishop* (1927). From this it was not a long way, except geographically, to old French Quebec, the scene of *Shadows on the Rock*, a picture drawn with delicate pastel art.

Highly selective in her art, Willa Cather deplored the tendency of realists deliberately to pile up details, to catalogue material objects, physical sensations, and the like. Should not realism be, above all, "an attitude of mind on the part of the writer toward his material, a vague indication of the sympathy and candor with which he accepts, rather than chooses, his theme?" Instead of the massiveness of a Balzac or Dreiser she pointed to the economy of Hawthorne. "The higher processes of art are all processes of simplification." The structure and texture of her own fiction are characterized by strict simplicity, largely achieved by symbols, suggestions, overtones, and a pure, quiet style.

These qualities, as well as her balanced concern with human evil and human excellence, are also well illustrated by her short stories. She published in all about three dozen stories, and three collections: *The Troll Garden*, 1905; *Youth and the Bright Medusa*, 1920; *Obscure Destinies*, 1932. "Neighbor Rosicky," the example printed below, was included in *Obscure Destinies* and translated into Czech the next year (Prague, 1933).

Further reading: *My Ántonia*. *Death Comes for the Archbishop*. E. K. Brown, *Willa Cather: A Critical Biography* (completed by Leon Edel), 1953. E. K. Brown, "Homage to Willa Cather," *Yale Review*, Autumn 1946.

Neighbor Rosicky

(w. 1928)

❧ Willa Cather's early novels (*O Pioneers!*, *My Ántonia*) showed how much she admired and enjoyed the Swedes and Czechs of her prairie girlhood. Later she wrote: "When I stop at one of the graveyards in my own county, and see on the headstones the names of fine old men I used to know, . . . I have always the hope that something went into the ground with those pioneers that will one day come out again. Something that will come out not only in sturdy traits of character, but in elasticity of mind, in an honest attitude toward the realities of life, in certain qualities of feeling and imagination." Many of the Czech immigrants were persons of superior culture, but for this story she chose a simpler type, an old man she knew in her first Nebraska years. He was much in her mind during the time of her own father's illness and death (of angina pectoris) when she wrote the story.

Even a casual reading will reveal, beneath the plain surface of Miss Cather's art, her intimate development of her material and the depth of her sympathetic understanding. A more thoughtful reading will note the specific values of living that appear to be admired, in contrast with those disapproved.

I

When Doctor Burleigh told neighbor Rosicky he had a bad heart, Rosicky protested.

"So? No, I guess my heart was always pretty good. I got a little asthma, maybe. Just a awful
5 short breath when I was pitchin' hay last summer, dat's all."

"Well now, Rosicky, if you know more about it than I do, what did you come to me for? It's your heart that makes you short of breath, I tell
10 you. You're sixty-five years old, and you've always worked hard, and your heart's tired. You've got to be careful from now on, and you

can't do heavy work any more. You've got five boys at home to do it for you."

The old farmer looked up at the Doctor with a gleam of amusement in his queer triangular-shaped eyes. His eyes were large and lively, but the lids were caught up in the middle in a curious way, so that they formed a triangle. He did not look like a sick man. His brown face was creased but not wrinkled, he had a ruddy color in his smooth-shaven cheeks and in his lips, under his long brown moustache. His hair was thin and ragged around his ears, but very little grey. His forehead, naturally high and crossed by deep parallel lines, now ran all the way up to his pointed crown. Rosicky's face had the habit of looking interested — suggested a contented disposition and a reflective quality that was gay rather than grave. This gave him a certain detachment, the easy manner of an on-looker and observer.

"Well, I guess you ain't got no pills fur a bad heart, Doctor Ed. I guess the only thing is fur me to git me a new one."

Doctor Burleigh swung round in his desk-chair and frowned at the old farmer. "I think if I were you I'd take a little care of the old one, Rosicky."

Rosicky shrugged. "Maybe I don't know how. I expect you mean fur me not to drink my coffee no more."

"I wouldn't, in your place. But you'll do as you choose about that. I've never yet been able to separate a Bohemian from his coffee or his pipe. I've quit trying. But the sure thing is you've got to cut out farm work. You can feed the stock and do chores about the barn, but you can't do anything in the fields that makes you short of breath."

"How about shelling corn?"

"Of course not!"

Rosicky considered with puckered brows.

"I can't make my heart go no longer'n it wants to, can I, Doctor Ed?"

"I think it's good for five or six years yet, maybe more, if you'll take the strain off it. Sit around the house and help Mary. If I had a good wife like yours, I'd want to stay around the house."

His patient chuckled. "It ain't no place fur a man. I don't like no old man hanging round the kitchen too much. An' my wife, she's a awful hard worker her own self."

"That's it; you can help her a little. My Lord, Rosicky, you are one of the few men I know who has a family he can get some comfort out of; happy dispositions, never quarrel among yourselves, and they treat you right. I want to see you live a few years and enjoy them."

"Oh, they're good kids, all right," Rosicky assented.

The Doctor wrote him a prescription and asked him how his oldest son, Rudolph, who had married in the spring, was getting on. Rudolph had struck out for himself, on rented land. "And how's Polly? I was afraid Mary mightn't like an American daughter-in-law, but it seems to be working out all right."

"Yes, she's a fine girl. Dat widder woman bring her daughters up very nice. Polly got lots of spunk, an' she got some style, too. Da's nice, for young folks to have some style." Rosicky inclined his head gallantly. His voice and his twinkly smile were an affectionate compliment to his daughter-in-law.

"It looks like a storm, and you'd better be getting home before it comes. In town in the car?" Doctor Burleigh rose.

"No, I'm in de wagon. When you got five boys, you ain't got much chance to ride round in de Ford. I ain't much for cars, noway."

"Well, it's a good road out to your place; but I don't want you bumping around in a wagon much. And never again on a hay-rake, remember!"

Rosicky placed the Doctor's fee delicately behind the desk-telephone, looking the other way, as if this were an absent-minded gesture. He put on his plush cap and his corduroy jacket with a sheepskin collar, and went out.

The Doctor picked up his stethoscope and frowned at it as if he were seriously annoyed with the instrument. He wished it had been telling tales about some other man's heart, some old man who didn't look the Doctor in the eye so knowingly, or hold out such a warm brown hand when he said good-bye. Doctor Burleigh had been a poor boy in the country before he went away to medical school; he had known Rosicky almost ever since he could remember, and he had a deep affection for Mrs. Rosicky.

Only last winter he had had such a good breakfast at Rosicky's, and that when he needed it. He had been out all night on a long, hard confinement case at Tom Marshall's — a big rich farm where there was plenty of stock and plenty of feed and a great deal of expensive farm machinery of the newest model, and no comfort whatever. The woman had too many children and too much work, and she was no manager. When the baby was born at last, and handed over to the assisting neighbor woman, and the mother was properly attended to, Burleigh refused any breakfast in that slovenly house, and drove his buggy — the snow was too deep for a car — eight miles to Anton Rosicky's place. He didn't know another farm-house where a man could get such a warm welcome, and such good strong coffee with rich cream. No wonder the old chap didn't want to give up his coffee!

He had driven in just when the boys had come back from the barn and were washing up for breakfast. The long table, covered with a bright oilcloth, was set out with dishes waiting for them, and the warm kitchen was full of the smell of coffee and hot biscuit and sausage. Five big handsome boys, running from twenty to twelve, all with what Burleigh called natural good manners — they hadn't a bit of the painful self-consciousness he himself had to struggle with when he was a lad. One ran to put his horse away, another helped him off with his fur coat and hung it up, and Josephine, the youngest child and the only daughter, quickly set another place under her mother's direction.

With Mary, to feed creatures was the natural expression of affection — her chickens, the calves, her big hungry boys. It was a rare pleasure to feed a young man whom she seldom saw and of whom she was as proud as if he belonged to her. Some country housekeepers would have stopped to spread a white cloth over the oilcloth, to change the thick cups and plates for their best china, and the wooden-handled knives for plated ones. But not Mary.

"You must take us as you find us, Doctor Ed. I'd be glad to put out my good things for you if you was expected, but I'm glad to get you any way at all."

He knew she was glad — she threw back her head and spoke out as if she were announcing him to the whole prairie. Rosicky hadn't said anything at all; he merely smiled his twinkling smile, put some more coal on the fire, and went into his own room to pour the Doctor a little drink in a medicine glass. When they were all seated, he watched his wife's face from his end of the table and spoke to her in Czech. Then, with the instinct of politeness which seldom failed him, he turned to the Doctor and said slyly: "I was just tellin' her not to ask you no questions about Mrs. Marshall till you eat some breakfast. My wife, she's terrible fur to ask questions."

The boys laughed, and so did Mary. She watched the Doctor devour her biscuit and sausage, too much excited to eat anything herself. She drank her coffee and sat taking in everything about her visitor. She had known him when he was a poor country boy, and was boastfully proud of his success, always saying: "What do people go to Omaha for, to see a doctor, when we got the best one in the State right here?" If Mary liked people at all, she felt physical pleasure in the sight of them, personal exultation in any good fortune that came to them. Burleigh didn't know many women like that, but he knew she was like that.

When his hunger was satisfied, he did, of course, have to tell them about Mrs. Marshall, and he noticed what a friendly interest the boys took in the matter.

Rudolph, the oldest one (he was still living at home then), said: "The last time I was over there, she was lifting them big heavy milkcans, and I knew she oughtn't to be doing it."

"Yes, Rudolph told me about that when he come home, and I said it wasn't right," Mary put in warmly. "It was all right for me to do them things up to the last, for I was terrible strong, but that woman's weakly. And do you think she'll be able to nurse it, Ed?" She sometimes forgot to give him the title she was so proud of. "And to think of your being up all night and then not able to get a decent breakfast! I don't know what's the matter with such people."

"Why, Mother," said one of the boys, "if Doctor Ed had got breakfast there, we wouldn't have him here. So you ought to be glad."

"He knows I'm glad to have him, John, any time. But I'm sorry for that poor woman, how bad she'll feel the Doctor had to go away in the cold without his breakfast."

"I wish I'd been in practice when these were getting born." The Doctor looked down the row of close-clipped heads. "I missed some good breakfasts by not being."

The boys began to laugh at their mother because she flushed so red, but she stood her ground and threw up her head. "I don't care, you wouldn't have got away from this house without breakfast. No doctor ever did. I'd have had something ready fixed that Anton could warm up for you."

The boys laughed harder than ever, and exclaimed at her: "I'll bet you would!" "She would, that!"

"Father, did you get breakfast for the Doctor when we were born?"

"Yes, and he used to bring me my breakfast, too, mighty nice. I was always awful hungry!" Mary admitted with a guilty laugh.

While the boys were getting the Doctor's horse, he went to the window to examine the house plants. "What do you do to your geraniums to keep them blooming all winter, Mary? I never pass this house that from the road I don't see your windows full of flowers."

She snapped off a dark red one, and a ruffled new green leaf, and put them in his buttonhole. "There, that looks better. You look too solemn for a young man, Ed. Why don't you git married? I'm worried about you. Settin' at breakfast, I looked at you real hard, and I seen you've got some grey hairs already."

"Oh, yes! They're coming. Maybe they'd come faster if I married."

"Don't talk so. You'll ruin your health eating at the hotel. I could send your wife a nice loaf of nut bread, if you only had one. I don't like to see a young man getting grey. I'll tell you something, Ed; you make some strong black tea and keep it handy in a bowl, and every morning just brush it into your hair, an' it'll keep the grey from showin' much. That's the way I do!"

Sometimes the Doctor heard the gossipers in the drug-store wondering why Rosicky didn't get on faster. He was industrious, and so were his boys, but they were rather free and easy, weren't pushers, and they didn't always show good judgment. They were comfortable, they were out of debt, but they didn't get much ahead. Maybe, Doctor Burleigh reflected, people as generous and warm-hearted and affectionate as the Rosickys never got ahead much; maybe you couldn't enjoy your life and put it into the bank, too.

II

When Rosicky left Doctor Burleigh's office he went into the farm-implement store to light his pipe and put on his glasses and read over the list Mary had given him. Then he went into the general merchandise place next door and stood about until the pretty girl with the plucked eyebrows, who always waited on him, was free. Those eyebrows, two thin India-ink strokes, amused him, because he remembered how they used to be. Rosicky always prolonged his shopping by a little joking; the girl knew the old fellow admired her, and she liked to chaff with him.

"Seems to me about every other week you buy ticking, Mr. Rosicky, and always the best quality," she remarked as she measured off the heavy bolt with red stripes.

"You see, my wife is always makin' goose-fedder pillows, an' de thin stuff don't hold in dem little down-fedders."

"You must have lots of pillows at your house."

"Sure. She makes quilts of dem, too. We sleeps easy. Now she's makin' a fedder quilt for my son's wife. You know Polly, that married my Rudolph. How much my bill, Miss Pearl?"

"Eight eighty-five."

"Chust make it nine, and put in some candy fur de woman."

"As usual. I never did see a man buy so much candy for his wife. First thing you know, she'll be getting too fat."

"I'd like dat. I ain't much for all dem slim women like what de style is now."

"That's one for me, I suppose, Mr. Bohunk!" Pearl sniffed and elevated her India-ink strokes.

When Rosicky went out to his wagon, it was beginning to snow — the first snow of the season, and he was glad to see it. He rattled out of town and along the highway through a wonderfully rich stretch of country, the finest farms in the country. He admired this High Prairie, as it was called, and always liked to drive through it. His own place lay in a rougher territory, where there was some clay in the soil and it was not so productive. When he bought his land, he hadn't the money to buy on High Prairie; so he told his boys, when they grumbled, that if their land hadn't some clay in it, they wouldn't own it at all. All the same, he enjoyed looking at these fine farms, as he enjoyed looking at a prize bull.

After he had gone eight miles, he came to the graveyard, which lay just at the edge of his own hay-land. There he stopped his horses and sat still on his wagon seat, looking about at the snowfall. Over yonder on the hill he could see his own house, crouching low, with the clump of orchard behind and the windmill before, and all down the gentle hill-slope the rows of pale gold cornstalks stood out against the white field. The snow was falling over the cornfield and the pasture and the hay-land, steadily, with very little wind — a nice dry snow. The graveyard had only a light wire fence about it and was all overgrown with long red grass. The fine snow, settling into this red grass and upon the few little evergreens and the headstones, looked very pretty.

It was a nice graveyard, Rosicky reflected, sort of snug and homelike, not cramped or mournful — a big sweep all round it. A man could lie down in the long grass and see the complete arch of the sky over him, hear the wagons go by; in summer the mowing-machine rattled right up to the wire fence. And it was so near home. Over there across the cornstalks his own roof and windmill looked so good to him that he promised himself to mind the Doctor and take care of himself. He was awful fond of his place, he admitted. He wasn't anxious to leave it. And it was a comfort to think that he would never have to go farther than the edge of his own hay-field. The snow, falling over his barnyard and the graveyard, seemed to draw things together like. And they were all old neighbors in the graveyard, most of them friends; there was nothing to feel awkward or embarrassed about. Embarrassment was the most disagreeable feeling Rosicky knew. He didn't often have it — only with certain people whom he didn't understand at all.

Well, it was a nice snowstorm; a fine sight to see the snow falling so quietly and graciously over so much open country. On his cap and shoulders, on the horses' backs and manes, light, delicate, mysterious it fell; and with it a dry cool fragrance was released into the air. It meant rest for vegetation and men and beasts, for the ground itself; a season of long nights for sleep, leisurely breakfasts, peace by the fire. This and much more went through Rosicky's mind, but he merely told himself that winter was coming, clucked to his horses, and drove on.

When he reached home, John, the youngest boy, ran out to put away his team for him, and he met Mary coming up from the outside cellar with her apron full of carrots. They went into the house together. On the table, covered with oilcloth figured with clusters of blue grapes, a place was set, and he smelled hot coffee-cake of some kind. Anton never lunched in town; he thought that extravagant, and anyhow he didn't like the food. So Mary always had something ready for him when he got home.

After he was settled in his chair, stirring his coffee in a big cup, Mary took out of the oven a pan of *kolache* stuffed with apricots, examined them anxiously to see whether they had got too dry, put them beside his plate, and then sat down opposite him.

Rosicky asked her in Czech if she wasn't going to have any coffee.

She replied in English, as being somehow the right language for transacting business: "Now what did Doctor Ed say, Anton? You tell me just what."

"He said I was to tell you some compliments, but I forgot 'em." Rosicky's eyes twinkled.

"About you, I mean. What did he say about your asthma?"

"He says I ain't got no asthma." Rosicky took one of the little rolls in his broad brown fingers. The thickened nail of his right thumb told the story of his past.

"Well, what is the matter? And don't try to put me off."

"He don't say nothing much, only I'm a little older, and my heart ain't so good like it used to be."

Mary started and brushed her hair back from her temples with both hands as if she were a little out of her mind. From the way she glared, she might have been in a rage with him.

"He says there's something the matter with your heart? Doctor Ed says so?"

"Now don't yell at me like I was a hog in de garden, Mary. You know I always did like to hear a woman talk soft. He didn't say anything de matter wid my heart, only it ain't so young like it used to be, an' he tell me not to pitch hay or run de corn-sheller."

Mary wanted to jump up, but she sat still. She admired the way he never under any circumstances raised his voice or spoke roughly. He was city-bred, and she was country-bred; she often said she wanted her boys to have their papa's nice ways.

"You never have no pain there, do you? It's your breathing and your stomach that's been wrong. I wouldn't believe nobody but Doctor Ed about it. I guess I'll go see him myself. Didn't he give you no advice?"

"Chust to take it easy like, an' stay round de house dis winter. I guess you got some carpenter work for me to do. I kin make some new shelves for you, and I want dis long time to build a closet in de boys' room and make dem two little fellers keep dere clo'es hung up."

Rosicky drank his coffee from time to time, while he considered. His moustache was of the soft long variety and came down over his mouth like the teeth of a buggy-rake over a bundle of hay. Each time he put down his cup, he ran his blue handkerchief over his lips. When he took a drink of water, he managed very neatly with the back of his hand.

Mary sat watching him intently, trying to find any change in his face. It is hard to see anyone who has become like your own body to you. Yes, his hair had got thin, and his high forehead had deep lines running from left to right. But his neck, always clean-shaved except in the busiest seasons, was not loose or baggy. It was burned a dark reddish brown, and there were deep creases in it, but it looked firm and full of blood. His cheeks had a good color. On either side of his mouth there was a half-moon down the length of his cheek, not wrinkles, but two lines that had come there from his habitual expression. He was shorter and broader than when she married him; his back had grown broad and curved, a good deal like the shell of an old turtle, and his arms and legs were short.

He was fifteen years older than Mary, but she had hardly ever thought about it before. He was her man, and the kind of man she liked. She was rough, and he was gentle — city-bred, as she always said. They had been shipmates on a rough voyage and had stood by each other in trying times. Life had gone well with them because, at bottom, they had the same ideas about life. They agreed, without discussion, as to what was most important and what was secondary. They didn't often exchange opinions, even in Czech — it was as if they had thought the same thought together. A good deal had to be sacrificed and thrown overboard in a hard life like theirs, and they had never disagreed as to the things that could go. It had been a hard life, and a soft life, too. There wasn't anything brutal in the short, broad-backed man with the three-cornered eyes and the forehead that went on to the top of his skull. He was a city man, a gentle man, and though he had married a rough farm girl, he had never touched her without gentleness.

They had been at one accord not to hurry through life, not to be always skimping and saving. They saw their neighbors buy more land and feed more stock than they did, without discontent. Once when the creamery agent came to the Rosickys to persuade them to sell him their cream, he told them how much money the Fasslers, their nearest neighbors, had made on their cream last year.

"Yes," said Mary, "and look at them Fassler children! Pale, pinched little things, they look like skimmed milk. I'd rather put some color into my children's faces than put money into the bank."

The agent shrugged and turned to Anton.

"I guess we'll do like she says," said Rosicky.

III

Mary very soon got into town to see Doctor Ed, and then she had a talk with her boys and set a guard over Rosicky. Even John, the youngest, had his father on his mind. If Rosicky went to throw hay down from the loft, one of the boys ran up the ladder and took the fork from him. He sometimes complained that though he was getting to be an old man, he wasn't an old woman yet.

That winter he stayed in the house in the afternoons and carpentered, or sat in the chair between the window full of plants and the wooden bench where the two pails of drinking-water stood. This spot was called "Father's corner," though it was not a corner at all. He had a shelf there, where he kept his Bohemian papers and his pipes and tobacco, and his shears and needles and thread and tailor's thimble. Having been a tailor in his youth, he couldn't bear to see a woman patching at his clothes, or at the boys'. He liked tailoring, and always patched all the overalls and jackets and work shirts. Occasionally he made over a pair of pants one of the older boys had outgrown, for the little fellow.

While he sewed, he let his mind run back over his life. He had a good deal to remember, really; life in three countries. The only part of his youth he didn't like to remember was the two years he had spent in London, in Cheapside, working for a German tailor who was wretchedly poor. Those days, when he was nearly always hungry, when his clothes were dropping off him for dirt, and the sound of a strange language kept him in continual bewilderment, had left a sore spot in his mind that wouldn't bear touching.

He was twenty when he landed at Castle Garden in New York, and he had a protector who got him work in a tailor shop in Vesey Street, down near the Washington Market. He looked upon that part of his life as very happy. He became a good workman, he was industrious, and his wages were increased from time to time. He minded his own business and envied nobody's good fortune. He went to night school and learned to read English. He often did overtime work and was well paid for it, but somehow he never saved anything. He couldn't refuse a loan to a friend, and he was self-indulgent. He liked a good dinner, and a little went for beer, a little for tobacco; a good deal went to the girls. He often stood through an opera on Saturday nights; he could get standing-room for a dollar. Those were the great days of opera in New York, and it gave a fellow something to think about for the rest of the week. Rosicky had a quick ear, and a childish love of all the stage splendor; the scenery, the costumes, the ballet. He usually went with a chum, and after the performance they had beer and maybe some oysters somewhere. It was a fine life; for the first five years or so it satisfied him completely. He was never hungry or cold or dirty, and everything amused him: a fire, a dog fight, a parade, a storm, a ferry ride. He thought New York the finest, richest, friendliest city in the world.

Moreover, he had what he called a happy home life. Very near the tailor shop was a small furniture factory, where an old Austrian, Loeffler, employed a few skilled men and made unusual furniture, most of it to order, for the rich German housewives uptown. The top floor of Loeffler's five-storey factory was a loft, where he kept his choice lumber and stored the odd pieces of furniture left on his hands. One of the young workmen he employed was a Czech, and he and Rosicky became fast friends. They persuaded Loeffler to let them have a sleeping-room in one corner of the loft. They bought good beds and bedding and had their pick of the furniture kept up there. The loft was low-pitched, but light and airy, full of windows, and good-smelling by reason of the fine lumber put up there to season. Old Loeffler used to go down to the docks and buy wood from South America and the East from the sea captains. The young men were as foolish about their house as a bridal pair. Zichec, the young cabinet-maker, devised every sort of convenience, and Rosicky kept their clothes in order. At night and on Sundays, when the quiver of machinery underneath was still, it was the quietest place in the world, and on summer nights all the sea winds blew in. Zichec often practised on his flute in the evening. They were both fond of music and went to the opera together. Rosicky thought he wanted to live like that forever.

But as the years passed, all alike, he began to get a little restless. When spring came round, he would begin to feel fretted, and he got to drinking. He was likely to drink too much of a Saturday night. On Sunday he was languid and heavy, getting over his spree. On Monday he plunged into work again. So he never had time to figure out what ailed him, though he knew something did. When the grass turned green in Park Place, and the lilac hedge at the back of Trinity churchyard put out its blossoms, he was tormented by a longing to run away. That was why he drank too much; to get a temporary illusion of freedom and wide horizons.

Rosicky, the old Rosicky, could remember as if it were yesterday the day when the young Rosicky found out what was the matter with him. It was on a Fourth of July afternoon, and he was sitting in Park Place in the sun. The lower part of New York was empty. Wall Street, Liberty Street, Broadway, all empty. So much stone and asphalt with nothing going on, so many empty windows. The emptiness was intense, like the stillness in a great factory when the machinery stops and the belts and bands cease running. It was too great a change, it took all the strength out of one. Those blank buildings, without the stream of life pouring through them, were like empty jails. It struck young Rosicky that this was the trouble with big cities; they built you in from the earth itself, cemented you away from any contact with the ground. You lived in an unnatural world, like the fish in an aquarium, who were probably much more comfortable than they ever were in the sea.

On that very day he began to think seriously about the articles he had read in the Bohemian papers, describing prosperous Czech farming communities in the West. He believed he would like to go out there as a farmhand; it was hardly possible that he could ever have land of his own. His people had always been workmen; his father and grandfather had worked in shops. His mother's parents had lived in the country, but they rented their farm and had a hard time to get along. Nobody in his family had ever owned any land — that belonged to a different station of life altogether. Anton's mother died when he was little, and he was sent into the country to her parents. He stayed with them until he was twelve, and formed those ties with the earth and the farm animals and growing things which are never made at all unless they are made early. After his grandfather died, he went back to live with his father and step-mother, but she was very hard on him, and his father helped him to get passage to London.

After that Fourth of July day in Park Place, the desire to return to the country never left him. To work on another man's farm would be all he asked; to see the sun rise and set and to plant things and watch them grow. He was a very simple man. He was like a tree that has not many roots, but one taproot that goes down deep. He subscribed for a Bohemian paper printed in Chicago, then for one printed in Omaha. His mind got farther and farther west. He began to save a little money to buy his liberty. When he was thirty-five, there was a great meeting in New York of Bohemian athletic societies, and Rosicky left the tailor shop and went home with the Omaha delegates to try his fortune in another part of the world.

IV

Perhaps the fact that his own youth was well over before he began to have a family was one reason why Rosicky was so fond of his boys. He had almost a grandfather's indulgence for them. He had never had to worry about any of them — except, just now, a little about Rudolph.

On Saturday night the boys always piled into the Ford, took little Josephine, and went to town to the moving-picture show. One Saturday morning they were talking at the breakfast table about starting early that evening, so that they would have an hour or so to see the Christmas things in the stores before the show began. Rosicky looked down the table.

"I hope you boys ain't disappointed, but I want you to let me have de car tonight. Maybe some of you can go in with de neighbors."

Their faces fell. They worked hard all week, and they were still like children. A new jack-knife or a box of candy pleased the older ones as much as the little fellow.

"If you and Mother are going to town," Frank said, "maybe you could take a couple of us along with you, anyway."

'No, I want to take de car down to Rudolph's, and let him an' Polly go in to de show. She don't git into town enough, an' I'm afraid she's gettin' lonesome, an' he can't afford no car yet."

That settled it. The boys were a good deal dashed. Their father took another piece of

apple-cake and went on: "Maybe next Saturday night de two little fellers can go along wid dem."

"Oh, is Rudolph going to have the car every Saturday night?"

Rosicky did not reply at once; then he began to speak seriously: "Listen, boys; Polly ain't lookin' so good. I don't like to see nobody lookin' sad. It comes hard fur a town girl to be a farmer's wife. I don't want no trouble to start in Rudolph's family. When it starts, it ain't so easy to stop. An American girl don't git used to our ways all at once. I like to tell Polly she and Rudolph can have the car every Saturday night till after New Year's, if it's all right with you boys."

"Sure it's all right, Papa," Mary cut in. "And it's good you thought about that. Town girls is used to more than country girls. I lay awake nights, scared she'll make Rudolph discontented with the farm."

The boys put as good a face on it as they could. They surely looked forward to their Saturday nights in town. That evening Rosicky drove the car the half-mile down to Rudolph's new, bare little house.

Polly was in a short-sleeved gingham dress, clearing away the supper dishes. She was a trim, slim little thing, with blue eyes and shingled yellow hair, and her eyebrows were reduced to a mere brush-stroke, like Miss Pearl's.

"Good evening, Mr. Rosicky. Rudolph's at the barn, I guess." She never called him father, or Mary mother. She was sensitive about having married a foreigner. She never in the world would have done it if Rudolph hadn't been such a handsome, persuasive fellow and such a gallant lover. He had graduated in her class in the high school in town, and their friendship began in the ninth grade.

Rosicky went in, though he wasn't exactly asked. "My boys ain't goin' to town tonight, an' I brought de car over fur you two to go in to de picture show."

Polly, carrying dishes to the sink, looked over her shoulder at him. "Thank you. But I'm late with my work tonight, and pretty tired. Maybe Rudolph would like to go in with you."

"Oh, I don't go to de shows! I'm too old-fashioned. You won't feel so tired after you ride in de air a ways. It's a nice clear night, an' it ain't cold. You go an' fix yourself up, Polly, an' I'll wash de dishes an' leave everything nice fur you."

Polly blushed and tossed her bob. "I couldn't let you do that, Mr. Rosicky. I wouldn't think of it."

Rosicky said nothing. He found a bib apron on a nail behind the kitchen door. He slipped it over his head and then took Polly by her two elbows and pushed her gently toward the door of her own room. "I washed up de kitchen many times for my wife, when de babies was sick or somethin'. You go an' make yourself look nice. I like you to look prettier'n any of dem town girls when you go in. De young folks must have some fun, an' I'm goin' to look out fur you, Polly."

That kind, reassuring grip on her elbows, the old man's funny bright eyes, made Polly want to drop her head on his shoulder for a second. She restrained herself, but she lingered in his grasp at the door of her room, murmuring tearfully: "You always lived in the city when you were young, didn't you? Don't you ever get lonesome out here?"

As she turned round to him, her hand fell naturally into his, and he stood holding it and smiling into her face with his peculiar, knowing, indulgent smile without a shadow of reproach in it. "Dem big cities is all right fur de rich, but dey is terrible hard fur de poor."

"I don't know. Sometimes I think I'd like to take a chance. You lived in New York, didn't you?"

"An' London. Da's bigger still. I learned my trade dere. Here's Rudolph comin', you better hurry."

"Will you tell me about London sometime?"

"Maybe. Only I ain't no talker, Polly. Run an' dress yourself up."

The bedroom door closed behind her, and Rudolph came in from the outside, looking anxious. He had seen the car and was sorry any of his family should come just then. Supper hadn't been a very pleasant occasion. Halting in the doorway, he saw his father in a kitchen apron, carrying dishes to the sink. He flushed crimson and something flashed in his eye. Rosicky held up a warning finger.

"I brought de car over fur you an' Polly to go to de picture show, an' I made her let me finish here so you won't be late. You go put on a clean shirt, quick!"

"But don't the boys want the car, Father?"

"Not tonight dey don't." Rosicky fumbled under his apron and found his pants pocket. He took out a silver dollar and said in a hurried

whisper: "You go an' buy dat girl some ice cream an' candy tonight, like you was courtin'. She's awful good friends wid me."

Rudolph was very short of cash, but he took the money as if it hurt him. There had been a crop failure all over the country. He had more than once been sorry he'd married this year.

In a few minutes the young people came out, looking clean and a little stiff. Rosicky hurried them off, and then he took his own time with the dishes. He scoured the pots and pans and put away the milk and swept the kitchen. He put some coal in the stove and shut off the draughts, so the place would be warm for them when they got home late at night. Then he sat down and had a pipe and listened to the clock tick.

Generally speaking, marrying an American girl was certainly a risk. A Czech should marry a Czech. It was lucky that Polly was the daughter of a poor widow woman; Rudolph was proud, and if she had a prosperous family to throw up at him, they could never make it go. Polly was one of four sisters, and they all worked; one was bookkeeper in the bank, one taught music, and Polly and her younger sister had been clerks, like Miss Pearl. All four of them were musical, had pretty voices, and sang in the Methodist choir, which the eldest sister directed.

Polly missed the sociability of a store position. She missed the choir, and the company of her sisters. She didn't dislike housework, but she disliked so much of it. Rosicky was a little anxious about this pair. He was afraid Polly would grow so discontented that Rudy would quit the farm and take a factory job in Omaha. He had worked for a winter up there, two years ago, to get money to marry on. He had done very well, and they would always take him back at the stockyards. But to Rosicky that meant the end of everything for his son. To be a landless man was to be a wage-earner, a slave, all your life; to have nothing, to be nothing.

Rosicky thought he would come over and do a little carpentering for Polly after the New Year. He guessed she needed jollying. Rudolph was a serious sort of chap, serious in love and serious about his work.

Rosicky shook out his pipe and walked home across the fields. Ahead of him the lamplight shone from his kitchen windows. Suppose he were still in a tailor shop on Vesey Street, with a bunch of pale, narrow-chested sons working on machines, all coming home tired and sullen to eat supper in a kitchen that was a parlour also; with another crowded, angry family quarrelling just across the dumb-waiter shaft, and squeaking pulleys at the windows where dirty washings hung on dirty lines above a court full of old brooms and mops and ashcans . . .

He stopped by the windmill to look up at the frosty winter stars and draw a long breath before he went inside. That kitchen with the shining windows was dear to him; but the sleeping fields and bright stars and the noble darkness were dearer still.

V

On the day before Christmas the weather set in very cold; no snow, but a bitter, biting wind that whistled and sang over the flat land and lashed one's face like fine wires. There was baking going on in the Rosicky kitchen all day and Rosicky sat inside, making over a coat that Albert had outgrown into an overcoat for John. Mary had a big red geranium in bloom for Christmas, and a row of Jerusalem cherry trees, full of berries. It was the first year she had ever grown these; Doctor Ed brought her the seed from Omaha when he went to some medical convention. They reminded Rosicky of plants he had seen in England; and all afternoon, as he stitched, he sat thinking about those two years in London, which his mind usually shrank from even after all this while.

He was a lad of eighteen when he dropped down into London, with no money and no connections except the address of a cousin who was supposed to be working at a confectioner's. When he went to the pastry shop, however, he found that the cousin had gone to America. Anton tramped the streets for several days, sleeping in doorways and on the Embankment, until he was in utter despair. He knew no English, and the sound of the strange language all about him confused him. By chance he met a poor German tailor who had learned his trade in Vienna, and could speak a little Czech. This tailor, Lifschnitz, kept a repair shop in a Cheapside basement, underneath a cobbler. He didn't much need an apprentice, but he was sorry for the boy and took him in for no wages but his keep and what he could pick up. The pickings were supposed to be coppers given you when you took work home to a customer. But most of the customers called for their clothes themselves, and the coppers that came Anton's way were very few. He had, however, a place to sleep. The tailor's family lived upstairs in three rooms; a kitchen, a bedroom, where Lifschnitz and his wife and five children slept, and a living-room. Two corners of this living-room were curtained off for lodgers; in one Rosicky slept on an old horsehair sofa, with a feather quilt to wrap himself in. The other corner was rented to a wretched, dirty boy, who was studying the violin. He actually practised there. Rosicky was dirty, too. There was no way to be anything else. Mrs. Lifschnitz got the water she cooked and washed with from a pump in a brick court, four flights down. There were bugs in the place, and multitudes of fleas, though the poor woman did the best she could. Rosicky knew she often went empty to give another potato or a spoonful of dripping to the two hungry, sad-eyed boys who lodged with her. He used to think he would never get out of there, never get a clean shirt to his back again. What would he do, he wondered, when his clothes actually dropped to pieces and the worn cloth wouldn't hold patches any longer?

It was still early when the old farmer put aside his sewing and his recollections. The sky had been a dark grey all day, with not a gleam of sun, and the light failed at four o'clock. He went to shave and change his shirt while the turkey was roasting. Rudolph and Polly were coming over for supper.

After supper they sat round in the kitchen, and the younger boys were saying how sorry they were it hadn't snowed. Everybody was sorry. They wanted a deep snow that would lie long and keep the wheat warm, and leave the ground soaked when it melted.

"Yes, sir!" Rudolph broke out fiercely; "if we have another dry year like last year, there's going to be hard times in this country."

Rosicky filled his pipe. "You boys don't know what hard times is. You don't owe nobody, you got plenty to eat an' keep warm, an' plenty water to keep clean. When you got them, you can't have it very hard."

Rudolph frowned, opened and shut his big right hand, and dropped it clenched upon his knee. "I've got to have a good deal more than that, Father, or I'll quit this farming gamble. I can always make good wages railroading, or at the packing house, and be sure of my money."

"Maybe so," his father answered dryly.

Mary, who had just come in from the pantry

and was wiping her hands on her roller towel, thought Rudy and his father were getting too serious. She brought her darning-basket and sat down in the middle of the group.

"I ain't much afraid of hard times, Rudy," she said heartily. "We've had a plenty, but we've always come through. Your father wouldn't never take nothing very hard, not even hard times. I got a mind to tell you a story on him. Maybe you boys can't hardly remember the year we had that terrible hot wind, that burned everything up on the Fourth of July? All the corn an' the gardens. An' that was in the days when we didn't have alfalfa yet — I guess it wasn't invented.

"Well, that very day your father was out cultivatin' corn, and I was here in the kitchen makin' plum preserves. We had bushels of plums that year. I noticed it was terrible hot, but it's always hot in the kitchen when you're preservin', an' I was too busy with my plums to mind. Anton come in from the field about three o'clock, an' I asked him what was the matter.

"'Nothin',' he says, 'but it's pretty hot, an' I think I won't work no more today.' He stood round for a few minutes, an' then he says: 'Ain't you near through? I want you should git up a nice supper for us tonight. It's Fourth of July.'

"I told him to git along, that I was right in the middle of preservin', but the plums would taste good on hot biscuit. 'I'm goin' to have fried chicken, too,' he says, and he went off an' killed a couple. You three oldest boys was little fellers, playin' round outside, real hot an' sweaty, an' your father took you to the horse tank down by the windmill an' took off your clothes an' put you in. Them two box-elder trees was little then, but they made shade over the tank. Then he took off all his own clothes, an' got in with you. While he was playin' in the water with you, the Methodist preacher drove into our place to say how all the neighbors was goin' to meet at the schoolhouse that night, to pray for rain. He drove right to the windmill, of course, and there was your father and you three with no clothes on. I was in the kitchen door, an' I had to laugh, for the preacher acted like he ain't never seen a naked man before. He surely was embarrassed, an' your father couldn't git to his clothes; they was all hangin' up on the windmill to let the sweat dry out of 'em. So he laid in the tank where he was, an' put one of you boys on top of him

to cover him up a little, an' talked to the preacher.

"When you got through playin' in the water, he put clean clothes on you and a clean shirt on himself, an' by that time I'd begun to get supper. He says: 'It's too hot in here to eat comfortable. Let's have a picnic in the orchard. We'll eat our supper behind the mulberry hedge, under them linden trees.'

"So he carried our supper down, an' a bottle of my wild-grape wine, an' everything tasted good, I can tell you. The wind got cooler as the sun was goin' down, and it turned out pleasant, only I noticed how the leaves was curled up on the linden trees. That made me think, an' I asked your father if that hot wind all day hadn't been terrible hard on the gardens an' the corn.

"'Corn,' he says, 'there ain't no corn.'

"'What you talkin' about?' I said. 'Ain't we got forty acres?'

"'We ain't got an ear,' he says, 'nor nobody else ain't got none. All the corn in this country was cooked by three o'clock today, like you'd roasted it in an oven.'

"'You mean you won't get no crop at all?' I asked him. I couldn't believe it, after he'd worked so hard.

"'No crop this year,' he says. 'That's why we're havin' a picnic. We might as well enjoy what we got.'

"An' that's how your father behaved, when all the neighbors was so discouraged they couldn't look you in the face. An' we enjoyed ourselves that year, poor as we was, an' our neighbors wasn't a bit better off for bein' miserable. Some of 'em grieved till they got poor digestions and couldn't relish what they did have."

The younger boys said they thought their father had the best of it. But Rudolph was thinking that, all the same, the neighbors had managed to get ahead more, in the fifteen years since that time. There must be something wrong about his father's way of doing things. He wished he knew what was going on in the back of Polly's mind. He knew she liked his father, but he knew, too, that she was afraid of something. When his mother sent over coffee-cake or prune tarts or a loaf of fresh bread, Polly seemed to regard them with a certain suspicion. When she observed to him that his brothers had nice manners, her tone implied that it was remarkable they should have. With his mother she was stiff and on her guard. Mary's hearty frankness and gusts of good humor irritated her. Polly was afraid of being unusual or conspicuous in any way, of being "ordinary," as she said!

When Mary had finished her story, Rosicky laid aside his pipe.

"You boys like me to tell you about some of dem hard times I been through in London?" Warmly encouraged, he sat rubbing his forehead along the deep creases. It was bothersome to tell a long story in English (he nearly always talked to the boys in Czech), but he wanted Polly to hear this one.

"Well, you know about dat tailor shop I worked in in London? I had one Christmas dere I ain't never forgot. Times was awful bad before Christmas; de boss ain't got much work, an' have it awful hard to pay his rent. It ain't so much fun, bein' poor in a big city like London, I'll say! All de windows is full of good t'ings to eat, an' all de pushcarts in de streets is full, an' you smell 'em all de time, an' you ain't got no money — not a damn bit. I didn't mind de cold so much, though I didn't have no overcoat, chust a short jacket I'd outgrowed so it wouldn't meet on me, an' my hands was chapped raw. But I always had a good appetite, like you all know, an' de sight of dem pork pies in de windows was awful fur me!

"Day before Christmas was terrible foggy dat year, an' dat fog gits into your bones and makes you all damp like. Mrs. Lifschnitz didn't give us nothin' but a little bread an' drippin' for supper, because she was savin' to try for to give us a good dinner on Christmas Day. After supper de boss say I can go an' enjoy myself, so I went into de streets to listen to de Christmas singers. Dey sing old songs an' make very nice music, an' I run round after dem a good ways, till I got awful hungry. I t'ink maybe if I go home, I can sleep till morning an' forgit my belly.

"I went into my corner real quiet, and roll up in my fedder quilt. But I ain't got my head down, till I smell somet'ing good. Seem like it git stronger an' stronger, an' I can't git to sleep noway. I can't understand dat smell. Dere was a gas light in a hall across de court, dat always shine in at my window a little. I got up an' look round. I got a little wooden box in my corner fur a stool, 'cause I ain't got no chair. I picks up dat box, and under it dere is a roast goose on a platter! I can't believe my eyes. I carry it to de window where de light

comes in, an' touch it and smell it to find out, an' den I taste it to be sure. I say, I will eat chust one little bite of dat goose, so I can go to sleep, and tomorrow I won't eat none at all. But I tell you, boys, when I stop, one half of dat goose was gone!"

The narrator bowed his head, and the boys shouted. But little Josephine slipped behind his chair and kissed him on the neck beneath his ear.

"Poor little Papa, I don't want him to be hungry!"

"Da's long ago, child. I ain't never been hungry since I had your mudder to cook fur me."

"Go on and tell us the rest, please," said Polly.

"Well, when I come to realize what I done, of course, I felt terrible. I felt better in de stomach, but very bad in de heart. I set on my bed wid dat platter on my knees, an' it all come to me; how hard dat poor woman save to buy dat goose, and how she get some neighbor to cook it dat got more fire, an' how she put it in my corner to keep it away from dem hungry children. Dey was a old carpet hung up to shut my corner off, an' de children wasn't allowed to go in dere. An' I know she put it in my corner because she trust me more'n she did de violin boy. I can't stand it to face her after I spoil de Christmas. So I put on my shoes and go out into de city. I tell myself I better throw myself in de river; but I guess I ain't dat kind of a boy.

"It was after twelve o'clock, an' terrible cold, an' I start out to walk about London all night. I walk along de river awhile, but dey was lots of drunks all along; men, and women too. I chust move along to keep away from de police. I git onto de Strand, an' den over to New Oxford Street, where dere was a big German restaurant on de ground floor, wid big windows all fixed up fine, an' I could see de people having parties inside. While I was lookin' in, two men and two ladies come out, laughin' and talkin' and feelin' happy about all dey been eatin' an' drinkin', and dey was speakin' Czech — not like de Austrians, but like de home folks talk it.

"I guess I went crazy, an' I done what I ain't never done before nor since. I went right up to dem gay people an' begun to beg dem: 'Fellow-countrymen, for God's sake give me money enough to buy a goose!'

"Dey laugh, of course, but de ladies speak

awful kind to me, an' dey take me back into de restaurant and give me hot coffee and cakes, an' make me tell all about how I happened to come to London, an' what I was doin' dere. Dey take my name and where I work down on paper, an' both of dem ladies give me ten shillings.

"De big market at Covent Garden ain't very far away, an' by dat time it was open. I go dere an' buy a big goose an' some pork pies, an' potatoes and onions, an' cakes an' oranges fur de children — all I could carry! When I git home, everybody is still asleep. I pile all I bought on de kitchen table, an' go in an' lay down on my bed, an' I ain't waken up till I hear dat woman scream when she come out into her kitchen. My goodness, but she was surprise! She laugh an' cry at de same time, an' hug me and waken all de children. She ain't stop fur no breakfast; she git de Christmas dinner ready dat morning, and we all sit down an' eat all we can hold. I ain't never seen dat violin boy have all he can hold before.

"Two three days after dat, de two men come to hunt me up, an' dey ask my boss, and he give me a good report an' tell dem I was steady boy all right. One of dem Bohemians was very smart an' run a Bohemian newspaper in New York, an' de odder was a rich man, in de importing business, an' dey been travelling togedder. Dey told me how t'ings was easier in New York, an' offered to pay my passage when dey was goin' home soon on a boat. My boss say to me: 'You go. You ain't got no chance here, an' I like to see you git ahead, fur you always been a good boy to my woman, and fur dat fine Christmas dinner you give us all.' An' da's how I got to New York."

That night when Rudolph and Polly, arm in arm, were running home across the fields with the bitter wind at their backs, his heart leaped for joy when she said she thought they might have his family come over for supper on New Year's Eve. "Let's get up a nice supper, and not let your mother help at all; make her be company for once."

"That would be lovely of you, Polly," he said humbly. He was a very simple, modest boy, and he, too, felt vaguely that Polly and her sisters were more experienced and worldly than his people.

VI

The winter turned out badly for farmers. It was bitterly cold, and after the first light snows before Christmas there was no snow at all — and no rain. March was as bitter as February. On those days when the wind fairly punished the country, Rosicky sat by his window. In the fall he and the boys had put in a big wheat planting, and now the seed had frozen in the ground. All that land would have to be ploughed up and planted over again, planted in corn. It had happened before, but he was younger then, and he never worried about what had to be. He was sure of himself and of Mary; he knew they could bear what they had to bear, that they would always pull through somehow. But he was not so sure about the young ones, and he felt troubled because Rudolph and Polly were having such a hard start.

Sitting beside his flowering window while the panes rattled and the wind blew in under the door, Rosicky gave himself to reflection as he had not done since those Sundays in the loft of the furniture factory in New York, long ago. Then he was trying to find what he wanted in life for himself; now he was trying to find what he wanted for his boys, and why it was he so hungered to feel sure they would be here, working this very land, after he was gone.

They would have to work hard on the farm, and probably they would never do much more than make a living. But if he could think of them as staying here on the land, he wouldn't have to fear any great unkindness for them. Hardships, certainly; it was a hardship to have the wheat freeze in the ground when seed was so high; and to have to sell your stock because you had no feed. But there would be other years when everything came along right, and you caught up. And what you had was your own. You didn't have to choose between bosses and strikers, and go wrong either way. You didn't have to do with dishonest and cruel people. They were the only things in his experience he had found terrifying and horrible; the look in the eyes of a dishonest and crafty man, of a scheming and rapacious woman.

In the country, if you had a mean neighbor, you could keep off his land and make him keep off yours. But in the city, all the foulness and misery and brutality of your neighbors was part of your life. The worst things he had come upon in his journey through the world were human — depraved and poisonous specimens of man. To this day he could recall certain terrible faces in the London streets. There were mean people everywhere, to be sure, even in their own country town here. But they weren't tempered, hardened, sharpened, like the treacherous people in cities who live by grinding or cheating or poisoning their fellow-men. He had helped to bury two of his fellow-workmen in the tailoring trade, and he was distrustful of the organized industries that see one out of the world in big cities. Here, if you were sick, you had Doctor Ed to look after you; and if you died, fat Mr. Haycock, the kindest man in the world, buried you.

It seemed to Rosicky that for good, honest boys like his, the worst they could do on the farm was better than the best they would be likely to do in the city. If he'd had a mean boy, now, one who was crooked and sharp and tried to put anything over on his brothers, then town would be the place for him. But he had no such boy. As for Rudolph, the discontented one, he would give the shirt off his back to anyone who touched his heart. What Rosicky really hoped for his boys was that they could get through the world without ever knowing much about the cruelty of human beings. "Their mother and me ain't prepared them for that," he sometimes said to himself.

These thoughts brought him back to a grateful consideration of his own case. What an escape he had had, to be sure! He, too, in his time, had had to take money for repair work from the hand of a hungry child who let it go so wistfully; because it was money due his boss. And now, in all these years, he had never had to take a cent from anyone in bitter need — never had to look at the face of a woman become like a wolf's from struggle and famine. When he thought of these things, Rosicky would put on his cap and jacket and slip down to the barn and give his work-horses a little extra oats, letting them eat it out of his hand in their slobbery fashion. It was his way of expressing what he felt, and made him chuckle with pleasure.

The spring came warm, with blue skies — but dry, dry as a bone. The boys began ploughing up the wheat-fields to plant them over in corn. Rosicky would stand at the fence corner and watch them, and the earth was so dry it blew up in clouds of brown dust that hid the horses and the sulky plough and the driver. It was a bad outlook.

The big alfalfa field that lay between the home place and Rudolph's came up green, but Rosicky was worried because during that open windy winter a great many Russian thistle plants had blown in there and lodged. He kept asking the boys to rake them out; he was afraid their seed would root and "take the alfalfa." Rudolph said that was nonsense. The boys were working so hard planting corn, their father felt he couldn't insist about the thistles, but he set great store by that big alfalfa field. It was a feed you could depend on — and there was some deeper reason, vague but strong. The peculiar green of that clover woke early memories in old Rosicky, went back to something in his childhood in the old world. When he was a little boy, he had played in fields of that strong blue-green color.

One morning, when Rudolph had gone to town in the car, leaving a work-team idle in his barn, Rosicky went over to his son's place, put the horses to the buggy-rake, and set about quietly raking up those thistles. He behaved with guilty caution, and rather enjoyed stealing a march on Doctor Ed, who was just then taking his first vacation in seven years of practice and was attending a clinic in Chicago. Rosicky got the thistles raked up, but did not stop to burn them. That would take some time, and his breath was pretty short, so he thought he had better get the horses back to the barn.

He got them into the barn and to their stalls, but the pain had come on so sharp in his chest that he didn't try to take the harness off. He started for the house, bending lower with every step. The cramp in his chest was shutting him up like a jack-knife. When he reached the windmill, he swayed and caught at the ladder. He saw Polly coming down the hill, running with the swiftness of a slim greyhound. In a flash she had her shoulder under his armpit.

"Lean on me, Father, hard! Don't be afraid. We can get to the house all right."

Somehow they did, though Rosicky became blind with pain; he could keep on his legs, but he couldn't steer his course. The next thing he was conscious of was lying on Polly's bed, and Polly bending over him wringing out bathtowels in hot water and putting them on his chest. She stopped only to throw coal into the stove, and she kept the tea-kettle and the black pot going. She put these hot applications on him for nearly an hour, she told him afterwards, and all that time he was drawn up stiff and blue, with the sweat pouring off him.

As the pain gradually loosed its grip, the stiffness went out of his jaws, the black circles round his eyes disappeared, and a little of his natural color came back. When his daughter-in-law buttoned his shirt over his chest at last, he sighed.

"Da's fine, de way I feel now, Polly. It was a awful bad spell, an' I was so sorry it all come on you like it did."

Polly was flushed and excited. "Is the pain really gone? Can I leave you long enough to telephone over to your place?"

Rosicky's eyelids fluttered. "Don't telephone, Polly. It ain't no use to scare my wife. It's nice and quiet here, an' if I ain't too much trouble to you, just let me lay still till I feel like myself. I ain't got no pain now. It's nice here."

Polly bent over him and wiped the moisture from his face. "Oh, I'm glad it's over!" she broke out impulsively. "It just broke my heart to see you suffer so, Father."

Rosicky motioned her to sit down on the chair where the tea-kettle had been, and looked up at her with that lively affectionate gleam in his eyes. "You was awful good to me, I won't never forgit dat. I hate it to be sick on you like dis. Down at de barn I say to myself, dat young girl ain't had much experience in sickness, I don't want to scare her, an' maybe she's got a baby comin' or somet'ing."

Polly took his hand. He was looking at her so intently and affectionately and confidingly; his eyes seemed to caress her face, to regard it with pleasure. She frowned with her funny streaks of eyebrows, and then smiled back at him.

"I guess maybe there is something of that kind going to happen. But I haven't told anyone yet, not my mother or Rudolph. You'll be the first to know."

His hand pressed hers. She noticed that it was warm again. The twinkle in his yellow-brown eyes seemed to come nearer.

"I like mighty well to see dat little child, Polly," was all he said. Then he closed his eyes and lay half-smiling. But Polly sat still, thinking hard. She had a sudden feeling that nobody in the world, not her mother, not Rudolph, or anyone, really loved her as much as old Rosicky did. It perplexed her. She sat frowning and trying to puzzle it out. It was as if Rosicky had a special gift for loving people, something that was like an ear for music or an eye for color. It was quiet, unobtrusive; it was merely there. You saw it in his eyes — perhaps that was why they were merry. You felt it in his hands, too. After he dropped off to sleep, she sat holding his warm, broad, flexible brown hand. She had never seen another in the least like it. She wondered if it wasn't a kind of gypsy hand, it was so alive and quick and light in its communications — very strange in a farmer. Nearly all the farmers she knew had huge lumps of fists, like mauls, or they were knotty and bony and uncomfortable-looking, with stiff fingers. But Rosicky's was like quicksilver, flexible, muscular, about the color of a pale cigar, with deep, deep creases across the palm. It wasn't nervous, it wasn't a stupid lump; it was a warm brown human hand, with some cleverness in it, a great deal of generosity, and something else which Polly could only call "gypsy-like" — something nimble and lively and sure, in the way that animals are.

Polly remembered that hour long afterwards; it had been like an awakening to her. It seemed to her that she had never learned so much about life from anything as from old Rosicky's hand. It brought her to herself; it communicated some direct and untranslatable message.

When she heard Rudolph coming in the car, she ran out to meet him.

"Oh, Rudy, your father's been awful sick! He raked up those thistles he's been worrying about, and afterwards he could hardly get to the house. He suffered so I was afraid he was going to die."

Rudolph jumped to the ground. "Where is he now?"

"On the bed. He's asleep. I was terribly scared, because, you know, I'm so fond of your father." She slipped her arm through his and they went into the house. That afternoon they took Rosicky home and put him to bed, though he protested that he was quite well again.

The next morning he got up and dressed and sat down to breakfast with his family. He told Mary that his coffee tasted better than usual to him, and he warned the boys not to bear any tales to Doctor Ed when he got home. After breakfast he sat down by his window to do some patching and asked Mary to thread several needles for him before she went to feed her chickens — her eyes were better than his, and her hands steadier. He lit his pipe and took up John's overalls. Mary had been watching him anxiously all morning, and as she went out of the door with her bucket of scraps, she saw that he was smiling. He was thinking, indeed, about Polly, and how he might never have known what a tender heart she had if he hadn't got sick over there. Girls nowadays didn't wear their heart on their sleeve. But now he knew Polly would make a fine woman after the foolishness wore off. Either a woman had that sweetness at her heart or she hadn't. You couldn't always tell by the look of them; but if they had that, everything came out right in the end.

After he had taken a few stitches, the cramp began in his chest, like yesterday. He put his pipe cautiously down on the windowsill and bent over to ease the pull. No use — he had better try to get to his bed if he could. He rose and groped his way across the familiar floor, which was rising and falling like the deck of a ship. At the door he fell. When Mary came in, she found him lying there, and the moment she touched him she knew that he was gone.

Doctor Ed was away when Rosicky died, and for the first few weeks after he got home he was hard driven. Every day he said to himself that he must get out to see that family that had lost their father. One soft, warm moonlight night in early summer he started for the farm. His mind was on other things, and not until his road ran by the graveyard did he realize that Rosicky wasn't over there on the hill where the red lamplight shone, but here, in the moonlight. He stopped his car, shut off the engine, and sat there for a while.

A sudden hush had fallen on his soul. Everything here seemed strangely moving and significant, though signifying what, he did not know. Close by the wire fence stood Rosicky's mowing-machine, where one of the boys had been cutting hay that afternoon; his own work-horses had been going up and down there. The new-cut hay perfumed all the night air. The moonlight silvered the long, billowy grass that grew over the graves and hid the fence; the few little evergreens stood out black in it, like shadows in a pool. The sky was very blue and soft, the stars rather faint because the moon was full.

For the first time it struck Doctor Ed that this was really a beautiful graveyard. He thought of city cemeteries; acres of shrubbery and heavy stone, so arranged and lonely and unlike anything in the living world. Cities of the dead, indeed; cities of the forgotten, of the "put away." But this was open and free, this little square of long grass which the wind forever stirred. Nothing but the sky overhead, and the many-colored fields running on until they met that sky. The horses worked here in summer; the neighbors passed on their way to town; and over yonder, in the cornfield, Rosicky's own cattle would be eating fodder as winter came on. Nothing could be more undeathlike than this place; nothing could be more right for a man who had helped to do the work of great cities and had always longed for the open country and had got to it at last. Rosicky's life seemed to him complete and beautiful.

Sherwood Anderson [1876–1941]

Against the bleakness and pettiness of life in industrial America, Willa Cather held up the sturdy qualities of the frontier and the rich humanity brought from Europe. Sherwood Anderson, hating the machine age, extolled, in a manner suggested by the Freudian psychology, self-expression through the creative spirit of handicraftsmanship and art, and, most insistently, through the mystical ministrations of sex.

He was born in Camden, Ohio, into a family which was "a wandering, gypsy sort of tribe," often moving from place to place just ahead of the collector — each of the seven children was born in a different town. He went to work when he was twelve, ended his schooling when he was fourteen. He served in Cuba during the Spanish war, returned to Ohio, married, and became a successful paint manufacturer in Elyria. One day (he was now thirty-six) he suddenly walked out of the factory, deserted his family, and went to Chicago. Writing for an advertising agency, he met the "Chicago group" — Dreiser, Sandburg, Floyd Dell, Ben Hecht, and others. After many rejections his first novel was published in 1916. Two other books followed, and then came *Winesburg, Ohio* (1919), a collection of short stories which established his reputation. His later novels included *Poor White* (1920) and *Dark Laughter* (1925), and his later short story collections *The Triumph of the Egg* (1921) and *Horses and Men* (1923). Moving to New York, he wrote for *The Masses, The Little Review, The Seven Arts, The Nation, The New Republic.* Later he moved to a farm near Marion, Virginia, and edited the town's two newspapers, one Democratic and one Republican! He was married four times.

In the novels and short stories of Anderson, the chief characters were all "slip-off sections of himself." They were small-town people, tame and dull in aspect, but inwardly tortured and craving, worked upon by forces only dimly realized. It was his purpose to uncover and reveal this hidden life. The clues he found in himself, puzzled and unhappy, warped and thwarted by the pressures of a soulless machine civilization. He hated the machine as the symbol of standardized living, of a corrupting material prosperity, of the suppression of primal forces in man's nature. "If any man can find beauty in an American factory town," he said, "I wish he would show me the way. For myself, I cannot find it. To me, and I am living in industrial life, the whole thing is as ugly as modern war." G. F. Whicher summed up the two sides of Anderson's writing by saying that "In all his work from first to last one can sense his worship of the egg, the life-force, and his antipathy to the machine."

In structure, his novels have obvious faults. The short stories are better works of art. Typically they are all but plotless, but build up suspense and concentrate upon a crucial moment. He devised a style based not on literary tradition but on the living speech of small-town folk, which he shaped into a medium homely and low-pitched, subtle in its rhythms and repetitions. In this he may have been helped by Gertrude Stein. He in turn influenced such young authors as Ernest Hemingway and James T. Farrell.

Further reading: *Winesburg, Ohio.* Irving Howe, *Sherwood Anderson,* 1951. James Schevill, *Sherwood Anderson,* 1951. Maxwell Geismar, *The Last of the Provincials,* 1947, chapter on Anderson.

"Queer"

(w. 1918)

From his seat on a box in the rough board shed that stuck like a burr on the rear of Cowley & Son's store in Winesburg, Elmer Cowley, the junior member of the firm, could see through a dirty window into the printshop of the *Winesburg Eagle.* Elmer was putting new shoelaces in his shoes. They did not go in readily and he had to take the shoes off. With the shoes in his hand he sat looking at a large hole in the heel of one of his stockings. Then looking quickly up he saw George Willard, the only newspaper reporter in Winesburg, standing at the back door of the *Eagle* printshop and staring absent-mindedly about.

"Well, well, what next!" exclaimed the young man with the shoes in his hand, jumping to his feet and creeping away from the window.

A flush crept into Elmer Cowley's face and his hands began to tremble. In Cowley & Son's store a Jewish traveling salesman stood by the counter talking to his father. He imagined the reporter could hear what was being said and the thought made him furious. With one of the shoes still held in his hand he stood in a corner of the shed and stamped with a stockinged foot upon the board floor.

Cowley & Son's store did not face the main street of Winesburg. The front was on Maumee Street and beyond it was Voight's wagon shop and a shed for the sheltering of farmers' horses. Beside the store an alleyway ran behind the main street stores and all day drays and delivery wagons, intent on bringing in and taking out goods, passed up and down. The store itself was indescribable. Will Henderson once said of it that it sold everything and nothing. In the window facing Maumee Street stood a chunk of coal as large as an apple barrel, to indicate that orders for coal were taken, and beside the black mass of the coal stood three combs of honey grown brown and dirty in their wooden frames.

The honey had stood in the store window for six months. It was for sale as were also the coat hangers, patent suspender buttons, cans of roof paint, bottles of rheumatism cure and a substitute for coffee that companioned the honey in its patient willingness to serve the public.

Ebenezer Cowley, the man who stood in the store listening to the eager patter of words that fell from the lips of the traveling man, was tall and lean and looked unwashed. On his scrawny neck was a large wen partially covered by a grey beard. He wore a long Prince Albert coat. The coat had been purchased to serve as a wedding garment. Before he became a merchant Ebenezer was a farmer and after his marriage he wore the Prince Albert coat to church on Sundays and on Saturday afternoons when he came into town to trade. When he sold the farm to become a merchant he wore the coat constantly. It had become brown with age and was covered with grease spots, but in it Ebenezer always felt dressed up and ready for the day in town.

As a merchant Ebenezer was not happily placed in life and he had not been happily placed as a farmer. Still he existed. His family, consisting of a daughter named Mabel and the son, lived with him in rooms above the store and it did not cost them much to live. His troubles were not financial. His unhappiness as a merchant lay in the fact that when a traveling man with wares to be sold came in at the front door he was afraid. Behind the counter he stood shaking his head. He was afraid, first that he would stubbornly refuse to buy and thus lose the opportunity to sell again; second that he would not be stubborn enough and would in a moment of weakness buy what could not be sold.

In the store on the morning when Elmer Cowley saw George Willard standing and apparently listening at the back door of the *Eagle* printshop, a situation had arisen that always stirred the son's wrath. The traveling man talked and Ebenezer listened, his whole figure expressing uncertainty. "You see how quickly it is done," said the traveling man who had for sale a small flat metal substitute for collar buttons. With one hand he quickly unfastened a collar from his shirt and then fastened it on again. He assumed a flattering wheedling tone. "I tell you what, men have come to the end of all this fooling with collar buttons and you are the man to make money out of the change that is coming. I am offering you the exclusive agency for this town. Take twenty dozen of these fasteners and I'll not visit any other store. I'll leave the field to you."

The traveling man leaned over the counter and tapped with his finger on Ebenezer's breast. "It's an opportunity and I want you to take it," he urged. "A friend of mine told me about you. 'See that man Cowley,' he said. 'He's a live one.'"

The traveling man paused and waited. Taking a book from his pocket he began writing out the order. Still holding the shoe in his hand Elmer Cowley went through the store, past the two absorbed men, to a glass showcase near the front door. He took a cheap revolver from the case and began to wave it about.

"You get out of here!" he shrieked. "We don't want any collar fasteners here." An idea came to him. "Mind, I'm not making any threat," he added. "I don't say I'll shoot. Maybe I just took this gun out of the case to look at it. But you better get out. Yes sir, I'll say that. You better grab up your things and get out."

The young storekeeper's voice rose to a scream and going behind the counter he began to advance upon the two men. "We're through being fools here!" he cried. "We ain't going to buy any more stuff until we begin to sell. We ain't going to keep on being queer and have folks staring and listening. You get out of here!"

The traveling man left. Raking the samples of collar fasteners off the counter into a black leather bag, he ran. He was a small man and very bow-legged and he ran awkwardly. The black bag caught against the door and he stumbled and fell. "Crazy, that's what he is — crazy!" he sputtered as he arose from the sidewalk and hurried away.

In the store Elmer Cowley and his father stared at each other. Now that the immediate object of his wrath had fled, the younger man was embarrassed. "Well, I meant it. I think

we've been queer long enough," he declared,
going to the showcase and replacing the revolver.
Sitting on a barrel he pulled on and fastened
the shoe he had been holding in his hand. He
was waiting for some word of understanding
from his father, but when Ebenezer spoke his
words only served to reawaken the wrath in the
son and the young man ran out of the store
without replying.

Scratching his grey beard with his long dirty
fingers, the merchant looked at his son with the
same wavering uncertain stare with which he
had confronted the traveling man. "I'll be
starched," he said softly. "Well, well, I'll be
washed and ironed and starched!"

Elmer Cowley went out of Winesburg and
along a country road that paralleled the railroad track. He did not know where he was going or what he was going to do. In the shelter
of a deep cut where the road, after turning
sharply to the right, dipped under the tracks
he stopped and the passion that had been the
cause of his outburst in the store began to
again find expression.

"I will not be queer — one to be looked at
and listened to," he declared aloud. "I'll be
like other people. I'll show that George Willard. He'll find out. I'll show him!"

The distraught young man stood in the middle of the road and glared back at the town.
He did not know the reporter George Willard
and had no special feeling concerning the tall
boy who ran about town gathering the town
news. The reporter had merely come, by his
presence in the office and in the printshop of
the Winesburg Eagle, to stand for something
in the young merchant's mind. He thought the
boy who passed and repassed Cowley & Son's
store and who stopped to talk to people in the
street must be thinking of him and perhaps
laughing at him. George Willard, he felt, belonged to the town, typified the town, represented in his person the spirit of the town.

Elmer Cowley could not have believed that
George Willard had also his days of unhappiness, that vague hungers and secret unnam-
able desires visited also his mind. Did he not
represent public opinion and had not the public opinion of Winesburg condemned the Cow-
leys to queerness? Did he not walk whistling
and laughing through Main Street? Might not
one by striking his person strike also the greater
enemy — the thing that smiled and went its
own way — the judgment of Winesburg?

Elmer Cowley was extraordinarily tall and his
arms were long and powerful. His hair, his eyebrows, and the downy beard that had begun
to grow upon his chin, were pale almost to
whiteness. His teeth protruded from between
his lips and his eyes were blue with the colorless
blueness of the marbles called "aggies" that the
boys of Winesburg carried in their pockets. Elmer had lived in Winesburg for a year and had
made no friends. He was, he felt, one condemned to go through life without friends and
he hated the thought.

Sullenly the tall young man tramped along
the road with his hands stuffed into his trou-
ser pockets. The day was cold with a raw wind,
but presently the sun began to shine and the
road became soft and muddy. The tops of the
ridges of frozen mud that formed the road began to melt and the mud clung to Elmer's
shoes. His feet became cold. When he had
gone several miles he turned off the road,
crossed a field and entered a wood. In the wood
he gathered sticks to build a fire by which he
sat trying to warm himself, miserable in body
and in mind.

For two hours he sat on the log by the fire
and then, arising and creeping cautiously
through a mass of underbrush, he went to a
fence and looked across fields to a small farm-
house surrounded by low sheds. A smile came
to his lips and he began making motions with
his long arms to a man who was husking corn
in one of the fields.

In his hour of misery the young merchant had
returned to the farm where he had lived
through boyhood and where there was another
human being to whom he felt he could explain himself. The man on the farm was a
half-witted old fellow named Mook. He had
once been employed by Ebenezer Cowley and
had stayed on the farm when it was sold. The
old man lived in one of the unpainted sheds
back of the farmhouse and puttered about all
day in the fields.

Mook the half-wit lived happily. With childlike faith he believed in the intelligence of the
animals that lived in the sheds with him, and
when he was lonely held long conversations
with the cows, the pigs, and even with the
chickens that ran about the barnyard. He it
was who had put the expression regarding being "laundered" into the mouth of his former
employer. When excited or surprised by anything he smiled vaguely and muttered: "I'll be

washed and ironed. Well, well, I'll be washed and ironed and starched."

When the half-witted old man left his husking of corn and came into the wood to meet Elmer Cowley, he was neither surprised nor especially interested in the sudden appearance of the young man. His feet also were cold and he sat on the log by the fire, grateful for the warmth and apparently indifferent to what Elmer had to say.

Elmer talked earnestly and with great freedom, walking up and down and waving his arms about. "You don't understand what's the matter with me so of course you don't care," he declared. "With me it's different. Look how it has always been with me. Father is queer and mother was queer, too. Even the clothes mother used to wear were not like other people's clothes, and look at that coat in which father goes about there in town, thinking he's dressed up, too. Why don't he get a new one? It wouldn't cost much. I'll tell you why. Father doesn't know and when mother was alive she didn't know either. Mabel is different. She knows but she won't say anything. I will, though. I'm not going to be stared at any longer. Why look here, Mook, father doesn't know that his store there in town is just a queer jumble, that he'll never sell the stuff he buys. He knows nothing about it. Sometimes he's a little worried that trade doesn't come and then he goes and buys something else. In the evenings he sits by the fire upstairs and says trade will come after a while. He isn't worried. He's queer. He doesn't know enough to be worried."

The excited young man became more excited. "He don't know but I know," he shouted, stopping to gaze down into the dumb, unresponsive face of the half-wit. "I know too well. I can't stand it. When we lived out here it was different. I worked and at night I went to bed and slept. I wasn't always seeing people and thinking as I am now. In the evening, there in town, I go to the post office, or to the depot to see the train come in, and no one says anything to me. Everyone stands around and laughs and they talk but they say nothing to me. Then I feel so queer that I can't talk either. I go away. I don't say anything. I can't."

The fury of the young man became uncontrollable.

"I won't stand it," he yelled, looking up at the bare branches of the trees. "I'm not made to stand it."

Maddened by the dull face of the man on the log by the fire, Elmer turned and glared at him as he had glared back along the road at the town of Winesburg. "Go on back to work," he screamed. "What good does it do me to talk to you?" A thought came to him and his voice dropped. "I'm a coward too, eh?" he muttered. "Do you know why I came clear out here afoot? I had to tell someone and you were the only one I could tell. I hunted out another queer one, you see. I ran away, that's what I did. I couldn't stand up to someone like that George Willard. I had to come to you. I ought to tell him and I will."

Again his voice arose to a shout and his arms flew about. "I will tell him. I won't be queer. I don't care what they think. I won't stand it."

Elmer Cowley ran out of the woods leaving the half-wit sitting on the log before the fire. Presently the old man arose and climbing over the fence went back to his work in the corn. "I'll be washed and ironed and starched," he declared. "Well, well, I'll be washed and ironed." Mook was interested. He went along a lane to a field where two cows stood nibbling at a straw stack. "Elmer was here," he said to the cows. "Elmer is crazy. You better get behind the stack where he don't see you. He'll hurt someone yet, Elmer will."

At eight o'clock that evening Elmer Cowley put his head in at the front door of the office of the *Winesburg Eagle* where George Willard sat writing. His cap was pulled down over his eyes and a sullen determined look was on his face. "You come on outside with me," he said, stepping in and closing the door. He kept his hand on the knob as though prepared to resist anyone else coming in. "You just come along outside. I want to see you."

George Willard and Elmer Cowley walked through the main street of Winesburg. The night was cold and George Willard had on a new overcoat and looked very spruce and dressed up. He thrust his hands into the overcoat pockets and looked inquiringly at his companion. He had long been wanting to make friends with the young merchant and find out what was in his mind. Now he thought he saw a chance and was delighted. "I wonder what he's up to? Perhaps he thinks he has a piece of news for the paper. It can't be a fire because I haven't heard the fire bell and there isn't anyone running," he thought.

In the main street of Winesburg, on the cold November evening, but few citizens appeared and these hurried along bent on getting to the stove at the back of some store. The windows of the stores were frosted and the wind rattled the tin sign that hung over the entrance to the stairway leading to Doctor Welling's office. Before Hearn's Grocery a basket of apples and a rack filled with new brooms stood on the sidewalk. Elmer Cowley stopped and stood facing George Willard. He tried to talk and his arms began to pump up and down. His face worked spasmodically. He seemed about to shout. "Oh, you go on back," he cried. "Don't stay out here with me. I ain't got anything to tell you. I don't want to see you at all."

For three hours the distracted young merchant wandered through the resident streets of Winesburg blind with anger, brought on by his failure to declare his determination not to be queer. Bitterly the sense of defeat settled upon him and he wanted to weep. After the hours of futile sputtering at nothingness that had occupied the afternoon and his failure in the presence of the young reporter, he thought he could see no hope of a future for himself.

And then a new idea dawned for him. In the darkness that surrounded him he began to see a light. Going to the now darkened store, where Cowley & Son had for over a year waited vainly for trade to come, he crept stealthily in and felt about in a barrel that stood by the stove at the rear. In the barrel beneath shavings lay a tin box containing Cowley & Son's cash. Every evening Ebenezer Cowley put the box in the barrel when he closed the store and went upstairs to bed. "They wouldn't never think of a careless place like that," he told himself, thinking of robbers.

Elmer took twenty dollars, two ten dollar bills, from the little roll containing perhaps four hundred dollars, the cash left from the sale of the farm. Then replacing the box beneath the shavings he went quietly out at the front door and walked again in the streets.

The idea that he thought might put an end to all of his unhappiness was very simple. "I will get out of here, run away from home," he told himself. He knew that a local freight passed through Winesburg at midnight and went on to Cleveland where it arrived at dawn.

He would steal a ride on the local and when he got to Cleveland would lose himself in the crowds there. He would get work in some shop and become friends with other workmen. Gradually he would become like other men and would be indistinguishable. Then he could talk and laugh. He would no longer be queer and would make friends. Life would begin to have warmth and meaning for him as it had for others.

The tall awkward young man, striding through the streets, laughed at himself because he had been angry and had been half afraid of George Willard. He decided he would have his talk with the young reporter before he left town, that he would tell him about things, perhaps challenge him, challenge all of Winesburg through him.

Aglow with new confidence Elmer went to the office of the New Willard House and pounded on the door. A sleepy-eyed boy slept on a cot in the office. He received no salary but was fed at the hotel table and bore with pride the title of "night clerk." Before the boy Elmer was bold, insistent. "You wake him up," he commanded. "You tell him to come down by the depot. I got to see him and I'm going away on the local. Tell him to dress and come on down. I ain't got much time."

The midnight local had finished its work in Winesburg and the trainsmen were coupling cars, swinging lanterns and preparing to resume their flight east. George Willard, rubbing his eyes and again wearing the new overcoat, ran down to the station platform afire with curiosity. "Well, here I am. What do you want? You've got something to tell me, eh?" he said.

Elmer tried to explain. He wet his lips with his tongue and looked at the train that had begun to groan and get under way. "Well, you see," he began, and then lost control of his tongue. "I'll be washed and ironed. I'll be washed and ironed and starched," he muttered half incoherently.

Elmer Cowley danced with fury beside the groaning train in the darkness of the station platform. Lights leaped into the air and bobbed up and down before his eyes. Taking the two ten dollar bills from his pocket he thrust them into George Willard's hand. "Take them," he cried. "I don't want them. Give them to father. I stole them." With a snarl of rage he turned and his long arms began to flay the air. Like one struggling for release from hands that held him he struck out, hitting George Willard blow after blow on the breast, the neck, the mouth. The young reporter rolled over on the platform half unconscious, stunned by the terrific force of the blows. Springing aboard the passing train and running over the tops of cars, Elmer sprang down to a flat car and lying on his face looked back, trying to see the fallen man in the darkness. Pride surged up in him. "I showed him," he cried. "I guess I showed him. I ain't so queer. I guess I showed him I ain't so queer."

Sinclair Lewis [1885–1951]

The rebellious spirit of American literature in the "Roaring Twenties" had its fullest expression in Sinclair Lewis.

Born in Sauk Center, Minnesota, he was a nonconformist almost from the beginning. He found the school curriculum not to his taste, read erratically on his own account, studied Greek with a clergyman, decided to get a college education in the East. "A gangling, pink-skinned, freckled, red-haired boy," he entered Yale, where he earned his way by doing newspaper work at night, read a great deal, edited the literary magazine, became a Socialist. Interrupting his college career, he worked as janitor of Upton Sinclair's Socialist colony in New Jersey, and sought jobs in New York and Panama. After finishing his course at Yale, he held miscellaneous positions in Iowa, in New York, in California, in Washington. By 1916 he felt it safe to become a free-lance writer, having sold a number of stories to the *Saturday Evening Post* and published two novels, *Our Mr. Wrenn* and *The Trail of the Hawk*. In both the stories and the novels he was writing according to the prevailing standards of entertainment.

Then he broke loose, wrote a novel to suit himself rather than the market, a novel he had planned, he says, in college: it was *Main Street*. This picture of small-town America, as he had seen it in the Middle West and everywhere, brought him sensational fame. The book has been translated into nearly every European language. Published in 1920, it was soon followed by the two novels commonly regarded as Lewis's best: *Babbitt* (1922), the American business man, and *Arrowsmith* (1925), the medical scientist. The latter novel won the Pulitzer Prize, which Lewis declined, saying that it represented an effort to make writers "safe, polite, obedient, and sterile." The other work, *Babbitt*, was the occasion of the award of the Nobel Prize in Literature, which he accepted — the first American thus recognized.

Among his later novels are *Elmer Gantry*, a harsh attack on shams in the church; *Dodsworth*, concerning a retired manufacturer who goes to Europe; *It Can't Happen Here* (1935), a forecast of American fascism played in dramatized version all over the country by the Federal Theater Project; *Kingsblood Royal* (1947), on the Negro problem.

Lewis's novels display an amazing aptness in catching behavior and in mimicking the color and texture of actual American speech. They are of course more than photographic: the details so accurately portrayed were selected and massed to serve the purpose of satire. The Lewis that the world applauded was not satisfied with the standardized America of the machine age, any more than Dreiser and Anderson were, but he voiced his criticism obliquely through satire that ranges from good-humored caricature to bitter condemnation. Within his limits he is a great satiric realist, though it must be admitted that the affirmations implied by satire are in his case all too uncertain, that his power in understanding and conveying character is not often remarkable, and that his spirited style is often "journalistic" in the bad sense of the word.

Further reading: *Main Street. Babbitt. Arrowsmith.* Carl Van Doren, *Sinclair Lewis, A Biographical Sketch,* 1933.

The Man Who Knew Coolidge

This monologue appeared in the January 1928 number of the *American Mercury,* a magazine edited by H. L. Mencken, one of Lewis's early champions. In 1943 it was reprinted in the place of honor in the *American Mercury Reader* (issued in celebration of the magazine's twentieth year), with the following note:

"Sinclair Lewis, during the twenties and thirties, said in lusty fiction what *The American Mercury* was saying in many of its articles and sketches. This long and hilarious story, which eventually became a book with the same title, displays Mr. Lewis in all his glory."

I certainly do enjoy listening to you gentlemen and getting your views. That's one of the nice things about being on a Pullman like this: you can guarantee that you'll meet a lot of regular he-Americans with sound opinions and ideas.

And now let me tell you: the way I look at these things —

I don't mean to suggest for one second that I've got any better bean than the plain, ordinary, average citizen, but I've given a whole lot of attention to politics and such matters and — In fact, strikes me that it's the duty of all the better-educated citizens to take an interest in the affairs of the State, for what, after all, as a fellow was saying to us at the Kiwanis Club the other day — what is the government but the union of all of us put together for mutual advantage and protection?

And me — why, say, I read the political editorials in the *Advocate* — that's the leading paper in my town — Zenith — I read 'em like most folks read the sporting page. And as a result of all this, and certain personal information that I can't disclose the sources of, I've come to the firm conclusion —

Here's something maybe you gentlemen never thought of:

They can say all they want to about how President Coolidge — good old silent Cal — isn't maybe as flashy as some of these statesmen. Maybe he isn't as much given to shooting off his mouth as certain other public figures that I could name. Maybe he isn't what my daughter would call Ritzy —

And say, by golly, it's beyond me where the young generation of today, taking them by and large, get all this slang that they pull. Why, here just the other day my daughter was talking to her brother, and Robby — That's the boy's name; only fifteen — three years younger than his sister, but smart's a whip. There's certainly one up-and-coming kid, if I do say so.

Why, say —

Now, I never put him up to it, y'understand. The Lord knows I can afford to give Robby the best the land affords, at least to a reasonable extent — I mean as much comfort and even luxury as is good for him. I'd never made a peep about his going out and earning a little money on the side. But he comes in one evening, just before supper — before dinner-time — with his hat on one side of his head, looking proud as Punch.

So I says to him, "Well, Robert Livingston —"

As a matter of fact, his middle name isn't Livingston at all, it's Otto, but we often call him Robert Livingston jokingly.

"Well, Robert Livingston," I says to him, "who do you think you are? Thomas Edison or Napoleon or somebody? Or maybe Red Grange! Sit down, Mr. Grange, and let me hang up your hat."

You know, jokingly.

Well, he just looks at me —

I'm afraid if the truth were known that kid is pretty gosh-awful fresh, but he's so darn' cute about it that you can't get sore at him, the darn' little cuss — just as up-and-coming as I was at his age. He just stands and looks at me and sticks his hands in his pants-pockets and then he says, "Dad," he says, "in me you behold the feline's *robe de nuit.* I've gone and ——"

Mind you, 's I said, I'd never even suggested to him that he get a job out of school-hours and earn a little money. I most certainly do believe that it's a mighty fine thing for a boy to do a little work, no matter how well fixed his folks are, and learn the value of money; learn how doggone hard it is to sneak up on ole Mr. Dollar and get a stranglehold on him.

I swear, a lot of the young folks today seem to think the Old Man is simply made of money and don't have to sweat for every cent he makes. But same time, I hadn't figured it was time yet to explain this to Robby, though maybe that was a mistake on my part, and if it was, I'm perfectly willing to admit it — confession is good for the soul, as they say.

Maybe I should have drummed it into him long ago. I've got it on mighty straight inside information — in fact, one of my best friends is acquainted with a man who knows the Rocke- fellers intimately — and he tells me that the Rockefellers — people with all their jack — they bring up their families to be just as careful of money as any of us: *they* don't let their kids run away with the notion that it don't take any trouble to collect the dough.

Well, this gentleman related a significant little incident regarding the Rockefellers that he heard personally. Seems he was right there at the time. Here was old John D., probably with half the money-kings in the world waiting to see him, talking to young John D., just as simple and quiet as any of us. And he said, and I've never forgotten his words — in fact I repeated them to Robby that day — he looked at young John D., and prob'ly, I imagine, he put his hand on his shoulder, and he looked at him and said, "My boy, waste not, want not!"

Yes sir!

But anyway ——

I'm afraid I'm getting a little off the subject of Coolidge, and if there's anything I hate it's a fellow that if he starts to talk about a subject he can't stick to it. I remember one time we had one of these book-authors speaking at the Kiwanis Club, and say, that fellow, maybe he could write all right (though at that I'd like to see him sit down and dictate a letter to some fellow that would make him pay his account and yet not make him sore!) — I don't know anything about his writing, but when it came to *talking*, why, say, he wandered all 'round Robin Hood's barn! Shows what a lack of business-

training does to these fellows that think they're so gosh-awful smart and superior!

Well, as I say, Robby looks at me, and he says, "Well, Dad, I've got me a job in Zabriskie's drug-store for every Saturday afternoon, and I draw down one and one-half bucks for each and every said same!"

Pretty good, eh? I'll say it is! And him only fifteen!

But what I started to say was: The way that boy and his sister torture the English language to death just about gets my goat. Here him and his sister was talking one time, and he starts kidding her about some bird she was sweet on, and he says, "That guy's all wet."

But she come back at him, quick's a flash: "Yeh, he's wet like a Methodist Sunday-school!"

Yes sir, it beats the cars how this new generation takes the Queen's English like you and I were brought up to speak it in the good old-fashioned schools, where there was some thoroughness and not a lot of these flashy fads, and they just practically ruin it, and as I was saying, if Sister — that's what we often call my daughter — if *she* was talking about Coolidge, she'd probably say he wasn't Ritzy.

Well, if you want to look at it that way, all right. Maybe he isn't as high-falutin as some people I could name, but I wonder if any of you gentlemen ever thought of this?

He may not shoot off a lot of fireworks, but do you know what he is? He's SAFE.

II

Yes sir, Cal is the President for real honest-to-God Americans like us.

There's a lot of folks that pan him, but what are they? You can bet your sweet life he isn't popular with the bums, or yeggs, or anarchists, or highbrows, or cynics ——

I remember our pastor saying one time, "A cynic is a man who sneers, and a man who sneers is setting himself up to tell God that he doesn't approve of God's handiwork!" No sir! You can bet Coolidge ain't popular with the Bolsheviks, or the lazy boob of a workman that wants fifteen bucks a day for doing nothing! No sir, nor with the cocaine fiends, or the drunkards, or the fellows that don't want the Prohibition law enforced ——

Not that I never take a drink. What I say about Prohibition is: Once a law has been passed by the duly elected and qualified representatives of the people of these United States, in fact once it's on the statute books, it's *there*, and it's there to be enforced. There hadn't ought to be any blind pigs or illegal stills. But the same time, that don't mean you got to be a fanatic.

If a fellow feels like making some good home-brewed beer or wine, or if you go to a fellow's house and he brings out some hootch or gin that *you* don't know where he got it and it isn't any of your business, or if you have a business acquaintance coming to your house and you figure he won't loosen up and talk turkey without a little spot and you know a good dependable bootlegger that you can *depend* on, well then, that's a different matter, and there ain't any reason on God's green earth that *I* can see why you shouldn't take advantage of it, always providing you aren't setting somebody a bad example or making it look like you sympathized with law-breaking.

No, sir!

But now to come down to the point of my story, I hope to be able to give you gentlemen an agreeable little surprise.

I know Coolidge personally!

Yes sir! In fact, I was a classmate of his! Sure as I'm telling you! I'll give you gentlemen an inside view of him, not only as I saw him in college, but as I've studied him at the White House!

When I say I was a classmate of his ——

Well, the fact is that certain unfortunate family circumstances that I needn't go into, and that wouldn't interest you, prevented me from completing my college course ——

My father, and a fine, upstanding, cultured gentleman of the old school he was too, always ready with a helping hand for any mortal that needed it, a man of A-1 standing in his community — Fall River, Mass. that was; in fact I was born and brought up in Fall River, which is, as you may know, one of the most beautiful and enterprising and go-ahead communities in the fair State of Massachusetts — he was, in fact, the leading corn and feed merchant in his section of Fall River.

But I'm afraid he put a little too much confidence in the advice of an alleged friend.

Fact is, he invested his savings in a perpetual-motion machine company that had little or no value. He died, and it was quite sudden, in December of my freshman year, so I had to go back home and take up the burden of helping support the family.

But I certainly got a lot of value out of even that comparatively short time at Amherst, and the fellows at the Kiwanis Club tell me that they can see my educational advantages in the quality of such speeches or motions as I may be called upon to deliver at the club, and welcomes to speakers.

So it was at college that I was able to get an inside view of Cal Coolidge that has maybe been denied to even his more intimate associates in these later busy years, when he has been so engrossed with the cares of the nation.

I don't suppose I could have been called one of Cal's closest friends in college, but I knew him pretty well. In fact, we lived not far from each other, and I used to see him frequently. I'll admit that I never had any notion he'd climb to his present high position and international and historical fame, but even in those days you could see from the way he worked, and the way he looked at a thing from all sides before he went off half-cocked, that in whatever department of life he might choose, he would make his mark. And the next time you hear one of these birds criticizing Coolidge, you just tell 'em *that*, will you, from one who knew him in the days when he wasn't surrounded with adulations.

I can remember just 's well as if it was yesterday, Cal and me happened to come out of a class together, and I said, "Well, it's going to be a cold Winter," and he came right back, "Yep."

Didn't waste a lot of time arguing and discussing! He *knew*!

And another time: I never could get along any too good in Latin — my talent, you might say, is more along practical lines. I asked Cal — we happened to be going into class together, and I asked him, "Say, what's the Latin for 'defy'?"

"Don't know," he said. No beating around the bush and pretending and four flushing, but coming right out with it, bang! That's the kind of man he is, you take it from one who *knows* him!

Yes sir, I knew the boy and had the greatest affection and respect for him, like all of us who had the rare opportunity of *understanding* him!

And to think that I might not have gotten acquainted with him, if we hadn't been chums together in one of the smaller colleges!

I tell you, gentlemen, the way I figure it: the great, you might say the invincible advantage of the smaller educational institutions is that they throw the boys together in such intimate contact and — as Dr. Frank Crane says in one of his pieces somewhere — they provide that profound knowledge of human beings that fits a boy for supremacy in the future walks and struggles of life.

Still, same time ——

These great modern universities with their laboratories and stadiums and everything — They *do* have an advantage; and fact is, my son is preparing to enter the State university.

But anyway!

III

Naturally, considering that I had the privilege — through no virtue of my own, mind you — of being in my modest way rather chummy with Coolidge, I've watched his rise to world-wide fame with peculiar interest, and after he became President I often said to my wife, "By golly, I'd like to see the boy and just shake hands with him again."

Not, mind you, because he was President. After all, I've reached a position where I'm just as independent as the next fellow. An American citizen doesn't have to bow down and kowtow to anybody, whether it be the President, or a millionaire, or Queen Marie of Bulgaria, or ——

By the way, Queen Marie made quite a stay at Zenith. She stopped over pretty near an hour between trains, and say, we certainly gave her a good time. The mayor read her an address and presented her with a gold-mounted polished cow's-foot combination ink-well, thermometer, and daily text calendar that I'll bet she's showing the folks in her palace right now. But I mean:

It wasn't because Cal was President, as I explained to the wife but ——

"Besides," I said to her, "just between you and I, I bet it would give the boy a real kick, after having to associate with ambassadors and generals and Frank Kellogg and all those high-up guys, to be able to let down for a minute, and shake the mitt of a fellow that he used to laugh and joke with in the old care-free days before we both assumed the responsibilities of our present careers."

So here about six months ago, when we were planning to take a little trip to New York ——

I had to go to New York to look over a new mimeographing machine. You see, I'm in the office-supply business, and let me tell you gentlemen that though I'm the first to respect other professions, though I honor the surgeon who can snatch you from the very gates of death, the lawyer who can so brilliantly argue your case — though personally I always think it's better to settle out of court — or the great banker or department-store owner, yet in all fairness, let me put this to you:

Who is it that enables these gentlemen to do business and get their great ideas across in an up-to-date, efficient, time-saving manner? Who is it but the office-supply man! Yes sir, I'm proud of my profession, and as a matter of fact, if I may say so, I have the honor of representing the office-supply classification in our great Zenith Kiwanis Club!

Just take filing-cabinets alone:

I always say, and sometimes the boys laugh at me at the Athletic Club — but good-naturedly, because I've got as fine a lot of friends as anybody I know, and believe me, I'm mighty good and proud of them, and I tell them, "Boys," I say, "excuse me if I get flowery, but you must always remember I'm a great reader of Colonel Bob Ingersoll, though I'm the first to deprecate the unfortunate religious ideas and skepticism that marred that otherwise great philosopher and public speaker, and probably it's from him that I got the idea of talking without having to resort to cheap and vulgar phrases, besides being a college man and ——

"Excuse me if I get high-falutin," I often say to them — you know, at lunch at the Athletic Club — you know how a lot of fellows will get to reminiscing and chewing the rag when maybe they ought to be beating it back to their offices, but ——

"Maybe you think I'm getting kind of woozy about it," I tell 'em, "but to me the beauties of modern filing-systems, which enable a man to instantly and without the least loss of time or effort find a letter on which, perhaps, depends the closing of an important deal, is in its practical way, to say nothing of the physical appearance of modern up-to-date filing cabinets, no longer mere wooden boxes but whether in steel or fireproofed wood, the finest example of the cabinetmaker's art and imitating perfectly the rarest woods ——

"To me," I often tell 'em, "these filing-systems are in every way as beautiful as the poet's song, as the flush on the maiden's cheek when she hears the first whispered words of love, or the soft chirp of the mother bird at eveningtide chirping to her birdlings! Yes sir, you bet your sweet life they are, and you can laugh all you want to!"

So as I say, I had to go on to New York to look over ——

I usually do my buying in Chicago but this was a new caper that the wholesalers in Chicago hadn't got hold of yet. I'd been working pretty hard, and my wife was kind of a little rundown from the after-effects of the 'flu ——

God, what a curse that is! I wonder if you gentlemen ever stopped to think that though the 'flu is in each individual case so much less fatal than diseases like the plague or brain-fever, yet considering the *number* of those afflicted with it — and after all, when you look at a subject, you've got to go into the statistics of it — of course, naturally an office-supply man has great advantages that way, being in the business — When you think how *many* folks get 'flu, it seems like one of the most important of all diseases.

I tell you, I'm as religious as the next fellow, and I'd never for one moment dream of criticizing the preachers' doctrines — let them figure out theology and religion, I say, and I'll stick to the office-supply business. But don't it sometimes almost make you question the workings of Providence when you see the mysterious way in which disease smites down the just with the unjust?

Why, my wife went on snivelling and subject to constant headaches for more than six weeks after the doctor *said* he'd got her all cured of the 'flu!

So I said to her, "Honey," as I often call her, "what say you and me and Almerine ——"

Almerine, that's my daughter's name. Don't know, by the way, that I've introduced myself, Lowell Schmaltz is my name ——

Funny! Whole lot of people take Schmaltz for a German name, but of course as a matter of fact when you look into the matter, it isn't German at all but Pennsylvania Dutch, which is almost the same as saying New England Yankee and ——

Well, I figured Almerine could get away all right, because she's finished high school.

I'd asked her if she wanted to go to college — I could perfectly well afford to send her, of course — but she thought it over, and she felt her talents lay more kind of along the musical line, and she was taking vocal and piano, but

I figured she could drop them all right for a few weeks and I said ——

Robby (that's my son), of course he couldn't get away, because he was in school, but ——

I says to my wife, "Mamie, how'd it strike you — I've simply got to go to New York on a business trip, and things are kind of slack now, and how'd it be if Almerine and you went along and saw the Big Town?"

Say she was tickled pink. She'd never seen New York, and of course ——

Not that I'd want to live there. What I always say is: New York is a swell burg for a few days' visit, and theaters and all like that, but when it comes to living there — say, I wouldn't live there if they gave me Times Square and threw in Riverside Drive to boot. Compared with Zenith ——

And believe me, gentlemen ——

IV

I don't believe in going around boosting your own burg all the time. I don't suppose Zenith is any better, practically, than Minneapolis or Cincinnati or Pittsburgh, say. But it certainly is one high-class city, and you may or may not know that not only do we lead the world in the manufacture of loud speakers and overalls but we have, since Lindbergh's flight, made all the planes and raised quite a lot of the money to construct the largest flying-field between Chicago and New York, excepting Detroit and Dayton, of course, and we plan to have a restaurant there serving short-orders twenty-four hours a day.

And I must say the wife and I are pretty well fixed there. Believe me, we don't have to travel any to get ideas how to live. Just a couple of years ago I finished building a dandy little Italian villa style bungalow, with a Spanish mission entrance. We've got two bathrooms, and a fireplace, and everything fixed up first-rate, and in the basement I've installed an electric washing-machine and a garbage-incinerator, and we got something that you don't find in many houses: in both bathrooms I've got a slit in the wall, right by the stationary bowls, for the disposal of safety-razor blades.

And of course I drive a Chrysler myself and I gave my wife a Chevrolet coop ——

Say, I certainly got a rise out of her. She's one darn' nice little woman, if I do say so: been an A 1 wife in every way, even if she does kick a little sometimes about my driving too fast. Well, here her last birthday I come home and I could see she was mooching around skittish as a wasp, because most always on her birthdays I've got something tucked in my inside pocket for her.

"Do you know what day this is?" I finally says to her, after I'd looked over the paper and listened in on the radio a little — though I remember there wasn't anything very interesting on them; nothing but the daily receipts reports from the Omaha stock-yards.

She brightens up and tries to look kittenish and makes out like she doesn't know, and she says, "No, what?"

"It's the day — or it will be the evening — of the Kid Milligan-Pooch Federstein fight, and we better invite some of the folks and listen to the fight on the radio," I says.

Well sir, the poor kid, she certainly did look awful' down in the mouth. I didn't know whether she was going to be plucky or whether she'd bawl me out. But she was game and didn't say anything, and pretty soon, long about fifteen, maybe twenty minutes, I suggested we go out and have a little walk before dinner. Well, meantime, you get me, I'd had the fellow bring this Chevrolet coop around and park it right in front of the house.

"Here's a nice little car," I says. "Wonder how she runs."

And I goes and gets in and starts it!

Well sir — You know how women carry on. She cusses me out, and she beefs, and she gets on a rampage, and she says, "Why, Lowell Schmaltz, what do you mean! What'll the owner say?"

"I'll bet he'll do a lot of saying," I laughs, "if he — or she — happens to see me!"

"Why, I never knew you to do a thing like that!" she says. "You get right out of that car!"

Say, I had her wild!

"So that's how a fellow gets treated, is it?" I says, and I pretended to look hurt, and I gets out, and then I draws her attention to a little card that I'd had tied on the door handle — 'd tied it on myself, matter of fact — and it reads sort of like this: "To Mamie on her birthday from Woofums" — Woofums — nut name, but that's what she calls me every now and then when we're kind of fooling around.

Say, maybe she didn't pretty nearly keel over!

Yes sir, you bet, both of us have our own cars, though mine ——

It ain't the fault of the Chrysler itself, I'm certain of that, but the garage got to fooling with it, and my car's got a squeak in it somewhere that I, by golly, simply can not locate, and say, if there's anything gets me wild when I'm driving ——

I can stand the big gaff — Why say, when I had a Sweeney tire blow out on me after only two thousand miles — Any of you gentlemen ever try the Sweeney?

Well don't, that's my advice to you, and believe me I know! I've tried two of 'em, and in my opinion this monkey-business they advertise of wrapping the fabric crosswise or whatever it is is all the bugs; don't get the result they claim at all.

I can stand those big things, but say, even the littlest squeak, it simply drives me crazy when I'm driving.

Why, here just last Sunday I was driving the family out to a cousin of ours that lives in Elmwood for Sunday dinner, and it was as fine a day as you ever saw, but just about the time I began to enjoy myself, and I was going past the Seven Corners and looking at the new filling-station they got there — Say, man, I'll bet that's one of the finest filling-stations in the United States: twelve pumps they got, and a comfort-station fixed up to look like an old-fashioned log cabin, and a supply store with a great big huge enormous fish-aquarium simply chucked full of goldfish right in the window. And geraniums!

And just when I was calling it to Mamie's attention — by golly, all of a sudden that squeak started again.

Well say, I couldn't enjoy anything all day. After dinner, I took Cousin Ed out for a drive, to see if he could locate the squeak, and we drove right down through a woods, a park they got there, mighty pretty and I'd of enjoyed it like the dickens — I always was a great believer in Nature — but every time I looked at a tree or a nice rustic bench or something, that darn' squeak would start in again, and Cousin Ed — he thinks he's such a wiz at cars, but Lord love you, he couldn't locate that squeak any more'n I could!

V

But's I say: I guess we're about as well fixed as most folks, and don't have to get away from home to enjoy ouselves, but when I said to my wife, "I kind of got an idea you and Almerine might come along with me and give New York the once-over," why she looked like somebody'd left her a million dollars.

And Almerine, she just hollers, "Oh boy! I'll give those Manhattan cabarets a look at a live one for once!"

"And we might stop at Cousin Walter's in Troy, on the way," I says.

"Oh no, let's not," says my wife.

"But we *got* to go there! Ain't Cousin Walter living there?" I says.

"Well, what of that?" she says. "Haven't you and he always hated each other?"

"Well, maybe we have," I says, "but he's a *relative*, ain't he? And when you travel you got to look up your relatives, ain't you?"

Well, make a long story short, we decided to stop at Cousin Walter's for a few days — and then — man! — then I springs the BIG surprise!

"And after New York," I says, "we'll come home by way of Washington, and we'll stop in and call on the President!"

"Oh, papa, we couldn't do *that*!" Almerine hollers.

"I'd like to know why not!" I says. "Ain't he and I classmates?"

"Yes, but maybe he wouldn't remember you," she says.

"Now you look here!" I says. "If you think for one moment that I wasn't just as important in college as he was, and maybe then some — they told me if I could of stayed till Spring I'd of been on the track team —

"But that isn't the point! Let me tell you right now that words like that are a direct insult not to me, my fine young lady, but to the Great Executive himself! What is it that more than any other one quality distinguishes leaders of men like Cal? It isn't merely his profound thought, his immovable courage, his genial and democratic manners, but it's the fact that he's so close a student of human nature that he quickly but thoroughly studies each man as he meets him, and so never *can* forget him!

"Understand now," I says to them, "I understand that the President is one of the busiest men in the United States what with having to sign documents and shake hands with delegations and so on, and I certainly don't intend to intrude, but we'll just drop in and give him a pleasant surprise — think how many years it is since we've seen each other! — and just shake hands and pass on. And you, Almerine, you'll

be able to tell your grandchildren that once you heard the voice of Calvin Coolidge!"

Well, of course when I made it all clear like that they were tickled to death at the prospect, and so we started making plans. Personally I was for just taking some suitcases, but my wife held out for the black trunk, and I must say — I'm always the first one to admit it when I'm licked, and Mamie certainly won that time — she pointed out I'd have to have my dress-suit in New York, and it wouldn't get wrinkled in a wardrobe trunk — and now say, while we're speaking of that, I'll bet it's struck you gentlemen as it has me: there's one of the highest class and most significant of modern inventions that do so much to make life happy, the wardrobe trunk, and what a lot it adds to ease of travel and seeing the world, yes sir, she sure won that time and ——

And just then ——

Say, isn't it funny how a fellow will remember comparatively unimportant details even regarding a critical moment? Happened just then that Robby — that's my son, he's only fifteen, and the little cuss had started smoking. Seems like I'd done everything I could to make him stop, but he's such a cute little beggar the way he comes back at you when you try to bawl him out that I never could get much more than a word in edgeways. Well, he comes in ——

And besides, I must say I still ain't sold on the idea of cigarettes.

I think I can with justification call myself what you might call a modern, up-to-date, liberal man. I was the first fellow in my neighborhood to put in a radio, and I never did believe they ought to have hung Sacco and Vanzetti if they were innocent. But when it comes to smoking, I still prefer a pipe or a good cigar.

But's I was saying, he comes in smoking a cigarette, and Almerine — that's my daughter, a girl that I want to tell you gentlemen can in my judgment sing just as good right this minute as Schumann-Heink or Sophie Tucker or any of these famous prima donnas — and she hollers at him, "Say, Dad's going to take us to see President Coolidge!"

Well, Robby gets fresh, and he says, "Are you going to give him enough warning so he can get away?"

Well, say, maybe I didn't light into him! I believe in giving kids their freedom, but I've told Robby time and time again that it's nice language and nice manners that enable a fellow to get along in this world, and if he'd study his mother and me a little more instead of a lot of these smart-aleck cigarette-sucking high-school fraternity yahoos, he'd be a lot better off! You bet! Every time!

Well, so we decided and got started. I don't want to bore you gentlemen with a lot of details of our trip. Of course what you want to hear about is the inside glimpse of Coolidge and the White House that I was privileged to have. So I'll cut it short and come right down to the real meat of the story.

VI

We got off on the noon train in about a week and — Say, it certainly is remarkable, ain't it, the conveniences of railroad travel today? In America, I mean. A fellow that knows every inch of Europe was telling me there ain't a what you might call really comfortable train in the whole length and breadth of the Old Country. But — there I sit in the club car, with every convenience and luxury — soft drinks (personally I always find the Loganberry highball the best drink on a Pullman) — soft drinks to be had just by touching a button, and a regular library of free magazines and everything, especially the *Saturday Evening Post*, which is, taking it by and large, my favorite magazine, especially the advertisements, now that they've taken to printing 'em in colors.

Say! they can keep their old masters; give me some of these advertisements!

Yes sir, it's wonderful what strides advertising has made these last few years. Of course I admire the really great and leading American authors — Mrs. Rinehart and Peter B. Kyne and Arthur Brisbane — but I doubt if even they can touch the fellows that get up these advertisements nowadays. And it was a mighty bright idea — I don't know who started it, but this idea of working in a girl with pretty legs in all sorts of ads; not only stocking ads, but auto ads, showing her climbing into a car; and machinery, showing her giving it the North and South, and so on. Yes sir, a fellow that wants to understand the United States, all he has to do is study the *Saturday Evening Post* ads, and he'll see why we're the most advanced nation in the world, and the most individual.

There's a lot of sorehead critics of America that claim we're standardized, but ——

Well, to take an example, let me take the fellow that I happened to be lunching with just before I caught this train — just take the differences between him and me. We both belong to the Athletic Club, we both belong to service clubs, we have our offices in the same block, we live within a quarter of a mile of each other, we both like golf and a good lively jazz on the radio. And yet this fellow and me — his name is Babbitt, G. F. Babbitt, fellow in the real estate game — we're as different as Moses and Gene Tunney.

Where these poor devils of Europeans are crushed down and prevented from having their characters developed by the wide and free initiative so characteristic of American life, him and me can be friendly yet as different ——

Well, like this, for instance: I drive a Chrysler, and Babbitt doesn't. I'm a Congregationalist, and Babbitt has no use whatsomever for anything but his old Presbyterian church. He wears these big round spectacles, and you couldn't hire me to wear anything but eyeglasses — much more dignified, *I* think. He's got so he likes golf for its own sake, and I'd rather go fishing, any day. And so on and so on. Yes sir, it's a wonderful thing how American civilization, as represented, you might say, by modern advertising, has encouraged the — as a speaker at the Kiwanis recently called it — the free play of individualism.

But as I say ——

Make a long story short, we got to Cousin Walter's at Troy all right, and on to New York ——

But say, Walt certainly did entertain us in fine style. I got to thinking he wasn't such a bad cuss after all. And he's got a new house that, and I'm the first to admit it, is just as modern as mine is. A modern homey home! Vacuum cleaner and gas clothes-dryer and one of these new noiseless electric refrigerators!

Man, what a convenience that is! I never could understand why they make so much fuss over Babe Ruth or even a real scientific pioneer like Lindbergh, when we haven't yet done anything to boost the honest-to-God master genius that invented the electric refrigerator!

Think of what it'll do! Give you every sort of frozen dessert! Get rid of the iceman that tracks mud on the back porch! What I always say is: these fellows can have their big libraries, their blinking art galleries, their private pipe organs, their rose gardens, but give me the *practical* things that make a home an inspiration and a solid comfort to a real family!

And I got to admit that Walt's radio shades mine just the least little bit. And there's mighty few things that indicate a fellow's social rank and progress better than his radio.

And what an invention *that* is! *What* an invention! Talk about miracles ——

Just think of it! Here you sit at home in the ole over-stuffed chair, happy as a clam at low tide (or is it high tide — whichever it is). You sit there and smoke your pipe and twiddle the knob and what do you get? *Think* of it! Right there at home you hear the best jazz bands in the country, bands in the best hotels in Chicago, and that wonderful orchestra at Zion City! Jokes by the best comedians in the country ——

Say, I heard a crackajack over the radio the other day. Seems there was a couple of fellows sitting chinning in a Pullman, just like we are. "Haven't I met you in Buffalo?" one fellow says to the other, and the other says, "I've never been in Buffalo," and the first fellow says, "Neither have I — must o' been a couple o' other fellows!"

Yes sir! and then think of the instructive lectures you get on the radio — why say, just the other night I heard that in the eye of the ordinary house-fly there are several thousand, I think it was, separate lenses. Ever know that?

And then the sermons on Sunday morning. Why, that alone would make the radio one of the most world-revolutionizing inventions the world has ever known.

I tell you, it gives a real spiritual uplift to a poor devil that all week, excepting maybe at the Kiwanis lunch, he's had to toil and moil amid the dust of busy affairs and forget higher things. You bet! I'll never forget one sermon that I wouldn't ever've heard, if I hadn't had the radio, being way off in Youngstown, Ohio — Reverend Wayo on how he didn't want to say that every atheist was a bootlegger, but you could bet your sweet life every bootlegger was an atheist!

Cute idea for a sermon, eh? and ——

But as I say, Walt's radio was every bit as good as mine, and we had some dandy drives around Troy and a big beer party Sunday evening — the only evening we stayed up late — I was mighty glad to find that Walt still kept regular hours and turned in about ten.

I tell you there never was a truer saying than "Early to bed, early to rise, makes a man healthy, wealthy, and wise." I've certainly found it true in my own case — and we drove out for a few rounds of golf ——

Now you take golf. By golly, if anybody'd told me fifteen years ago that I'd ever be out on the links chasing a little white pill around, I'd 've told 'em they were crazy, but let me tell you, I've found one of the best ways to get acquainted with customers is to play 'round with 'em, and I've got so I like the game itself a good deal — take like my playing there at Troy, even when I wasn't making any contacts — and even though the weather was pretty chilly and ——

Seems to me that on the whole the weather has gotten warmer than it used to be when we were kids. You read in the papers how it hasn't changed materially, but they can say what they want to, don't you remember how doggone cold it used to be mornings when we had to get up and chase off to school, and now it seems like we don't have any more old-fashioned winters? Maybe that's one reason why the kids today aren't as self-reliant as we were.

But to get back to my subject: As I say, I certainly did enjoy my stay with Walt, especially his stories and inside information about the war — he was a lieutenant in the quartermasters' corps at Camp Devon ——

You know, there's a lot of false ideas about the war. I don't want to criticize General Pershing — I know he ranks among the greatest generals we've ever had, right along with Grant and Lee and Israel Putnam, but same time, what we ought to 've done, what I'd 've done if I'd been running things, was to march right straight through to Berlin, and make them Germans suffer *good* — suffer like we did.

I was explaining this to my wife, and she says, "Why, Lowell T. Schmaltz," she says, "I'm ashamed of you! Don't we know some Germans that are awful' nice folks?"

"You don't know the Germans like I do," I says to her. "They haven't got any forward-looking ideas. They believe in rule by tyranny and despotism and compulsion and all that, and if they haven't understood our democratic ideas, they ought to of been *forced* to, that's what they ought to of been!" I told her. "But same time, you got to hand it to 'em — they certainly have buckled down to work ever since the war," I said. "Be a good thing if *our* workmen worked like that, 'stead of watching the clock and thinking about a raise all the time!"

But make a long story short, we certainly

enjoyed our stay, and we went on to New York.

I was kind of sore all the time I was in New York though. These damn' New Yorkers — I hope none of you gentlemen come from New York — they seem to think they run the nation, and what I always say is, as a matter of fact New York is the most provincial town in the country! Give me Chicago every time!

You see, when I go to Chicago, in the first place I always stay at the Hotel Grand Imperial Palace, it's a nice quiet little place and the clerks *know* me and try to give me a little service; but in those big New York hotels, they're so darn' independent, you'd think they were doing you a favor.

Then when it comes to business ——

In Chicago I usually do the bulk of my business, you might say, with Starbright, Horner, and Dodd; and Billy Dodd himself looks after me, and say, there's a man that it's a pleasure to do business with, a square-shooter if ever there was one, and always got a good story and a good cigar for you, and acts like he was glad to see you, and he isn't one of these fellows that throw seven kinds of cat-fits if maybe a fellow is temporarily a little short and wants an extension of a couple of days or a month or so. Yes sir, and many's the good lunch I've had with Billy in the old Palmer House before they tore it down, and though of course this new Palmer House is you might say a regular palace, still, there was a kind of an atmosphere about the old place, and say, they certainly did know how to cook a steak and fried onions to a turn. But in New York ——

All this darn' fancy French food, and the prices ——

"My God," I says to one of these smart-aleck headwaiters, or maybe he was what they call a captain — anyway he was the fellow that takes the order and then hands it on to the regular waiter — "My God," I said to him, when I looked at the prices on the bill of fare, "I just come in here to eat," I says. "I don't want to buy the hotel!"

And just the same way in the business world. Why say, the firm that was handling these new mimeograph machines, they said they were behind on their orders and they couldn't make a delivery right away. Oh, that's all right, I told 'em — why couldn't they fill my order and keep some other fellow waiting?

No sir, they said, they wouldn't do it. They were just naturally arbitrary, and when I tried to make 'em understand that with the class and

volume of business that *I* do, they ought to be willing to make some concessions, they acted like a bunch of human icicles. Some day I'm going to write a letter to the New York papers and tell 'em what a real he-American from the Middle West thinks about their town.

The noise, and traffic so thick you can't get anywhere, and the outrageous prices and ——

And no home life. Folks all out in the evening, hitting it up at these night clubs and everything. But back home — Now you take us, for instance. Evenings, except maybe when I have to be at the lodge or some Kiwanis committee meeting, or maybe Almerine or Roddy are at the movies or at a party or something, we all just settle down around the radio and have a real old-fashioned homey time together. But not in New York! No sir! I swear, I don't know what the nation's coming to ——

And too many foreigners — fellows with wop names and hunky names and Lord knows what all — and all this corrupt politics ——

Oh say, speaking of politics, if I may interrupt myself a moment and take the risk of straying from my story, I got to tell you what I heard at the Kiwanis luncheon just this past week. Our congressman, and I think it's pretty generally conceded even right in Washington that he's got one of the ablest minds in the entire House of Representatives, he got back from an extensive investigation of the European status — spent six weeks in Germany, France, and Italy, and he gave it as his measured opinion that all these countries are so prosperous now that we certainly ought to press for the payment of our debt in full! Why, he said that in the better class of hotels in those countries, you could get just as good food and nearly as expensive as in New York itself! And then complaining about being poor!

VII

But to get back to my story, I didn't think so much of New York, though we did have one dandy evening — we ran into some folks from home in the hotel lobby, and we all went to a Chink restaurant and got outside of some of the best chicken chow mein that I ever ate in my life, and then we went to a movie that I knew was good because I'd seen it in Zenith — Hoot Gibson in a crackajack Western film.

But Almerine, she liked New York, and my Lord, how that girl did keep nagging and teasing and complaining!

She wanted to go to one of these night clubs.

I pointed out to her that while I had to work all day, talking to a lot of different firms, she and her mother were free to enjoy themselves all day — go to a matinee or look over the stores and shop a little (though I didn't encourage 'em to buy too much; "why not wait till you get back home — the stores there are just as up-to-date as New York, far's I can see," I pointed out to 'em). But she kept insisting, and her mother more or less agreed with her, and so one night I took 'em to a swell night club that was recommended to me by one of the bellboys at the hotel, cute little lad, knew the town like a book.

Well, thinks I, here's where I have a punk evening, but I want to admit that I was wrong. Not but what it was expensive, and I certainly wouldn't want to go to one of those places more'n once or twice a year, but say, that was some place!

First, we was all kind of disappointed. We drives up to a house in the Fifties, just an ordinary-looking place, and all dark.

"This can't be the place," I says to the taxi driver.

"Sure, this is the joint all right," he says.

"Are you sure?" I says.

"Sure, you bet," he says. "I've driven lots of folks here. You just ring that basement bell and they'll let you in," he says.

Well, I figured he probably knew his business, so my wife and Almerine and I, we all piled out of the taxi, and I went and rang the bell at the basement door — well, they call it the basement; it was really practically the ground floor, but this was one of those houses that they got so many of in New York, or used to have anyway, though now a lot of 'em are being torn down to make way for modern apartment houses — graystone houses they call 'em, and you go up a flight of steps from the street to the parlor floor, so the door to this basement floor, as they call it, was really kind of under these steps practically on the ground level, only of course you go down into a kind of areaway that's a step or maybe it might have been two steps below the pavement level, but not more than that if I remember rightly, and there was a kind of iron grilled door but, 's I said, there weren't any lights or anything that we could see, and I wondered if the taxi-driver could of been right and —

But I rang the bell and pretty soon, sure enough, the door opened, and by golly, there was a fellow in one of these funny Lord High Admiral uniforms, and I says to him, "Is this the Nouvelle Desire?" That was the name of the joint I was looking for. "Is this the Nouvelle Desire?" I says.

"Yes, but I haven't the pleasure of knowing your face," he says — you know, some high-falutin comeback like that.

Well, I kidded him along — I told him it wasn't such a hard face to know when you put your mind to it. Almerine — she stood right back of me, and I must say, maybe it was just because she was my girl, but she wore a kind of light violet dress and shiny spangles and gold slippers and say, she certainly looked as elegant as anybody there that night, and my wife wasn't such a slouch herself, for a Midwestern girl and —

But as I was saying, Almerine was standing right near me, and she kind of whispers to me, "Say, you hadn't ought to kid the servants like that."

But I knew this guy in the uniform wasn't any ordinary servant and I wanted to show him I was just as used to the Gay Life as anybody (of course I was wearing my dress suit), and —

But anyway, he calls what I figured out to be the assistant manager — nice-looking fellow in a dress suit, kind of dark-complected, Italian I guess, but a nice-spoken fellow.

He explained that this Nouvelle Desire was a club and they couldn't let in nobody that didn't belong, but I introduced him to the wife and Almerine, and I explained we come from Zenith and was only in town for about a week, and I showed him my Elks card, and he looked us over good, and he said maybe he could fix it. The regular membership cost two hundred bucks a head a year, but finally he let me have a temporary membership for that week for only five bucks a head.

So we got in all safe and —

Maybe you couldn't see any lights outside, but inside, oh boy! It was fixed up as elegant as if it was the Vanderbilts' ballroom. They'd turned the whole parlor floor — that is, the floor above the basement — I guess they had the kitchen and all like that on the basement floor ——

And here was a funny thing: this assistant manager — he and I got to be quite chummy; he told me to call him Nick, and I said he was to call me Low, but he said that was against the rules — and Nick told me something that may surprise you gentlemen as it certainly surprised me at the time: he told me that they did all their cooking by electricity!

Then, as I say, there was this kind of ball-room. Halfway up, the walls was all red satin or silk or something, with a lot of what they call Modern Art decoration, or that's what Nick called it — all kinds of zigzags and big flowers and everything in gold; and then above that the walls was all hung with flowers. I found they was artificial flowers, but they looked so real you had to touch 'em before you'd believe it.

And some of the tables was in kind of booths fixed up so they looked like grape arbors and all like that. And at the end of the room there was some great big yellow marble columns — it looked like real genuine marble, though it may not have been — in front of where the orchestra played — and say, the boys in that orchestra certainly were some jazz babies, all coons but they had a regular high-class musical education, Nick told me later; and the fellow that played the saxophone — say, if they got anybody better'n him in Paul Whiteman's band, I want to hear him, that's all — Why say, he could make that ole saxophone sound like a fog horn or anything he wanted.

Well, before we got settled down — there weren't many folks there yet — Nick took me aside and said they had a regular sure-enough old-fashioned bar on the floor above, and he thought he could fix it so that I could go up and throw in a little real liquor. The rules of the club, or so he said anyway, the rules of the club made every fellow buy wine at his table, and when it comes to fizz, of course it's a grand high-class wine, but it ain't got the authority like hootch, like the fellow says.

Well, make a long story short, he went away and he fixed it so we could go up to the bar.

I'd just intended to let Almerine and her mother have some ginger ale up there, but seems they didn't stock any soft drinks, and anyway, Almerine put up a holler.

"I want a cocktail," she says, "and I'll bet so does Mama, if she tells the truth. Maybe we'll never get to another night club again," she says. "And besides," she says, "you've let me taste a sip of your cocktail when you've had 'em at home. And think of what my bunch will say if I go back home and tell 'em we went to a night club and I couldn't have a cocktail. I'm not a kid," she says.

Well, anyway, I kicked, and I pointed out her mother didn't want any — my wife's a great

believer in Prohibition — but her mother, dog-gone her, she went and laid right down on me and didn't back me up —— just kind of giggled, and said she wouldn't mind one herself, just this once. So, make a long story short, we all had a cocktail — Mame took a Bronx, and Al-merine took a side-car, if I remember rightly, and I ordered a Martini and then I said, "No sir, by golly, I believe I'll have a Manhattan. Must be five years since I've had a Manhattan cocktail." And so I had a Manhattan. And then I sneaked in a coupla highballs while Mame and the girl was in the ladies' dressing-room, and say, by that time I certainly did feel primed for one high, wide and fancy evening.

And I want to say that, think what you may of New York, we certainly had said evening.

Nick had fixed us up a nice little table almost right next to where they danced.

We looked around and there was a nice-looking lot of people there — they was just coming in. Almerine was just saying, "Oh, I wish we knew somebody here — I won't have anybody to dance with except you, Papa," and I was informing her that I was regarded as by golly just as good a dancer as anybody at the Country Club when — Say, you could've knocked me down with a feather! Yes sir, by golly I hears a familiar voice, and there stands Sam Geierstein, of the Mammoth Clothing Company of Zenith — fellow I'd often met at the Athletic Club.

Now, there's a whole lot of fellows I'd rather seen than Sam. To tell the truth, just between ourselves, he hasn't got any too good a reputation for square dealing, and I've heard some mighty queer rumors about the way him and his lady secretary carry on. But same time — you know how it is when you're away from home — espe-cially in a city like New York where they're such a chilly lot of stiffs: familiar face sure does look good to you.

So we invites Sam to sit down, and say, I will say one thing for him, he certainly did insist on buying his share of wine and then some. And he sure could dance. I never did like his looks — kind of too dark and good-looking, and big black eyes like you don't really like to see in a real he-male, but he certainly did spin Almerine and even the wife around that ole floor all right. And me, after I'd got a little champagne into my system, I guess I wouldn't 've hardly beefed much even if he'd kissed Almerine ——

Not that he did anything like that, you understand; he acted like a perfect gentleman, you understand; and once when I was dancing with Mame and I kind of slipped and almost fell down — they had that floor altogether too slippery for any use — why, it was Sam that grabbed me and kept me from falling.

Though I don't like the way he's been hanging around the house since we been back in Zenith — seems he's got a wife somewhere, only they're separated. Almerine, she says I'm crazy. She says she just discusses music with Sam — seems he knows a lot about it. But I don't like her being out late ——

Oh, I guess I'm an old crank. But Al is so young, and she thinks she knows everything, but she's innocent as a baby but — Oh, I'm a regular fusser, I guess. But anyway, we certainly did have one large round time that evening — evening, huh! Say, we certainly were high-rollers for once! I'll bet it was three o'clock before we hit the hay. I remember ——

It was comic! Here was Mame — that's my wife — supposed to be a good respectable dame, and me, a deacon in the church, and us coming down Broadway at three A.M., singing "We Won't Go Home Until Morning!"

You see Sam — he's got the nerve of the Devil — he picked up a couple from Fort Worth, Texas (and maybe she wasn't some baby; say, she had all the regular New York dames there beat a mile!), and somehow, I don't exactly remember how, we got acquainted with another couple from San José, California, a gentleman that was in the fruit-ranching business, and his wife and son; he took a shine to Almerine; up in the bar I got to talking to a gentleman and lady from Kansas City, Missouri — or it may have been Kansas City, Kansas, I can't exactly remember, at this late date — and the whole lot of us carried on like we'd always known each other, dancing and laughing and drinking toasts and singing and drinking and cutting up — Say! But I hate to think of what it cost me. But as I told my wife, that's the way of it, in New York.

But I don't need to tell you gentlemen about New York. Probably you know it better'n I do, and you want me to sing my little song and get it finished and get on to Washington and my experiences at the White House. Yes sir, the less said about New York the better. Money-mad, that's what the New Yorkers are.

If I wanted to sacrifice other more worth-while things, like our home life and friendships and reading worth-while literature, and getting in a good fish every Summer — And let me tell you that they can talk about Canada all they want to, but if they can show me any better fishing than I get up in Northern Michigan, right within you'd hardly call it more'n an overnight ride from Zenith, why just let 'em show it to me, that's all!

But the way I look at it, a fellow ought to be prosperous for his family's sake and that of his own position in the community, but money-making can be overdone, and what I always say is, Ideals before Dollars every time.

VIII

So that's what I think of New York and we packed up and went on to Washington, and say, Almerine pretended she didn't care, but she was so excited over the prospect of having a chat with the President that she couldn't hardly sit still. Well, so was I — hadn't seen Cal for so many years. I got to thinking maybe he might invite us to lunch or supper, but still, I knew that was unreasonable — having to entertain so many people — ambassadors and high officials of the Order of Moose and so on — but I guess I was pretty excited just the same.

I don't know how well you gentlemen know Washington, but the new station there is very handsome and up-to-date in every respect, with a great big open space — the Plaza I believe they call it — in front; and what I'd never known, you can see the dome of the Capitol right from the front of the station. I tell you I got a mighty big thrill out of that.

Well, Mame wanted us to get a room in the hotel first and get washed, but I says, "No sir, we better see the President first and see what his plans are; we'll just keep the taxi waiting and I don't care if it costs a dollar and a half; 'tisn't often in your life that you're going to sit in with a President of these United States!"

So we got into a taxi and we started off all het up and all of a sudden I says to my wife, "Say, do you notice anything funny about this taxi?"

"Why no," she says, "I don't know's I do; it looks all right to me. Why?"

"Looks all right!" I says, "I should say it does! Do you mean to tell me you don't notice something different about this taxi?"

"Why no," she says.

"Well, what make of car is it?" I says.

Of course Almerine has to horn in. "It's a Studebaker, isn't it?" she says.

"Oh it is, is it, Miss Smarty!" I says. "My God, and me teaching you to drive myself! It is not a Studebaker, and it isn't a Cadillac, no, and it isn't a flivver either! It's a Buick! See the significance?"

Well, they both stared at me — couldn't get the idea at all — just like women, even the brightest of 'em.

"Can't you see?" I says. "Here's the Buick, the biggest-selling six cylinder car in the United States, if not in the world. And yet how often do you see a Buick taxi? Not very often. Ever think of that? Yes sir, it's a mighty peculiar thing, and I'm sure I don't know why it is. At least, I'm practically certain it's a Buick — of course, with a taxi body on it — I didn't happen to notice the hood, but from the looks of the dashboard — Anyway ——"

So I tapped on the window, and the driver — he probably thought we were just ordinary tourists that wanted to see the town, and we were passing some building or other and he just hardly turns his head and says, "It's the Pensions Building." (Or it may have been the Patent Building — I didn't pay much attention, I was so worked up and excited about seeing the President, and I can't exactly remember at this late date.)

"No," I hollers at him, "what I want to know is: isn't this a Buick taxi?"

"Yeh," he says.

"There," I says to the girls, "what did I tell you!"

So we came to the White House and ——

Now, even you gentlemen that've been to Washington and seen the White House may not know that the offices, including the President's own private office, are in wings stretching out on either side of the old main structure. The wings are new, I should think, and they're so low that you wouldn't hardly notice 'em from the street in front — not hardly know they were there unless you'd happened, like I was, to be privileged to enter 'em.

So we came up the driveway to that famous old place ——

I tell you it was a mighty moving thing to think of the famous men that had inhabited that structure. Grant and McKinley and Harding and Garfield and everybody! By golly, as I told the Kiwanis when I addressed them about my trip, it certainly gave a fellow inspiration. For what, after all, is a greater inspiration than the lives of our heroes?

That reminds me that recently — why, in fact, it was just a couple of nights ago, and a neighbor and I were having a little visit, and he says to me, "Lowell, who do you think have been the greatest heroes of the United States since 1900, and the geniuses?"

Well, a question like that certainly makes a fellow think, and him and I, we began making lists, and it just happens I've still got mine in my pocket here, and here's how I figured out our leading intellects: Coolidge, Harding, Wilson (though I'm a Republican), Ford, Lindbergh, Billy Sunday, Pershing, Roosevelt, Judge Gary ——

Now here's a couple more names that may surprise you gentlemen. Maybe you never looked at it like this. I figured that what you might call the Arts ought to be represented, and I put in Anne Nichols — say, the author of a play like "Abie's Irish Rose," that can run five years, is in my mind — maybe it's highbrow and impractical to look at it that way, but the way I see it, she's comparable to any business magnate. And besides, they say she's made as much money as Jack Dempsey!

And here's a name that may surprise you still more: Samuel Gompers!

Yes, I knew that would surprise you, my putting in a man that lots of folks think he merely stood for union labor and labor disturbances and all those kind of Bolshevik activities. But it seems that Gompers — a fellow, some kind of professor he was, he was explaining this to us at the Kiwanis Club here just recently — Gompers stood right square against labor disturbances. He thought that laboring men ought to have their rights, and I suppose that's true, but the way he looked at it, he wanted employes and employers and the general public to join hands in one great brotherhood for the glory of the union and the extension of our markets into lands now unfairly monopolized by England and Germany. Yes sir!

So, as I say, we drove up to the White House ——

I'd told the chauffeur to go right up to the front door — just like I'd expect Cal Coolidge to come right up to *my* front door, if he came to call on me in Zenith. I didn't understand then about the arrangement of the White House.

But there was some kind of cop at the gate and he says, "What do you want, please?"

"What do I want, officer?" I says. "What do I *want*? Why, I just want to call on the President!" I says. "I'm just an old friend of his, that's all!" I says.

Well, I explains, and he tells me the proper caper is to go round to the office entrance, so I says all right; I'd be the last, I says, as a friend of the President, to want to break any proper regulations.

Well, make a long story short, at last there we were, in one of the waiting-rooms to the President's own offices, and a gentleman came in — fine-looking gentleman he was, all dressed up like Sunday morning, in a cutaway coat and striped pants, and seems he was practically the President's first main secretary, and I presented my wife and Almerine to him, and I explained about the President and me being classmates.

"I know the President's a busy man, but it'd be nice to have a look at the old kid," I tells him, "and I kind of thought I'd like to have my wife and daughter shake hands with him."

Well sir, he understood perfectly.

He went right in and saw the President — didn't keep me waiting one minute, no sir, not hardly a minute.

He came back and said the President was aw-ful' sorry he couldn't have us come in just that second, but seems he was all tied up with an important international conference about — I think it was about Geneva, he said — and would I wait? This secretary was mighty nice, too; he didn't let us sit there like bumps on a log; he sat and visited with us, and that's how I had the chance to get the real inside low-down on so many of the President's opinions and activities, but I don't want you gentlemen to give any of this stuff to the newspapers.

IX

I asked this secretary, Mr. Jones his name was — I said to him, "What does the President think about disarmament, Mr. Jones?"

"Well, it just happens," he says, "that I can tell you in the President's own words. I heard him talking to the Secretary of State," he says — say, maybe that didn't give me a kick, sitting in as it were on a conference between the President and the Secretary of State! But anyway: "I heard him talking to the Secretary," Mr. Jones told me, "and he said, 'Frank, big navies cost a lot of money, and in my opinion it would be a saving if we could get the different nations to reduce them.'"

"Well, well, I'm mighty glad to find that out, Mr. Jones," I said, "and it confirms my own opinion about disarmament. Say, tell me," I says, "how does the President live, in his personal life? What does he take for breakfast?"

Well, Mr. Jones explained that the President took a simple breakfast just like the rest of us — just some coffee and toast and eggs and porridge and so on. I was mighty proud and glad to hear that Cal was unspoiled by all his fame and was still just the same simple direct fellow he'd been when we were chums.

"What does the President think of the situation in China?" I asked Mr. Jones.

"Well I think I can say without violating any confidence that, in opposition to the opinion of certain Senators, the President feels the situation is serious and in fact almost critical, and that — but this mustn't go any further," Mr. Jones told me, "he feels decidedly that while the rights and properties of the Great Powers must be safeguarded, yet we must consider patiently and fairly the rights of the Chinese themselves."

"Well, sir, I certainly am interested to hear that," I told him. "There's no question about it. That's exactly how I feel myself."

You see, I'd had a kind of you might say special opportunity of getting the real inside dope about the Chinese situation and the Bolshevik influence there. I heard a missionary just recently back from the scene of disturbance in China, speak at the Wednesday Evening Supper at our church — the Pilgrim Congregational Church of Zenith — Dr. G. Prosper Edwards is the pastor, very famous pulpit orator, you've quite probably heard him on the radio, tunes in on WWWL every second Sunday morning at eleven-fifteen, very eloquent man and a ripsnorting good scholar, too — but very liberal. As he always says, he's more than ready to fellowship with any Christian body, no matter what their differences in theology are, providing they merely accept the fundamental and indisputable elements of Christianity, such as the Virgin Birth and the proven fact of after-life.

I tell you how I feel about religion, anyway.

I'm a Congregationalist myself, and it isn't for one second just because I happened to be born one, as one of these smart-aleck agnostics was trying to prove to me one day, but because of my deep reverence for the great leaders of the church, like Jonathan Edwards and Roger Baldwin — no, come to think of it, he was a Baptist, wasn't he, that Rhode Island guy?

But anyway: just the same today: fellows like Newell Dwight Hillis and S. Parks Cadman, that during the World War they did as much to win the struggle for world-wide democracy as any soldier, the way they showed up the secret plans of Germany to dominate the world — and the way Dr. Cadman writes this column in the newspapers; say, he knows just about everything, and he can clear up your troubles about anything, whether it's an incurable sickness or who wrote Shakespeare — yes sir, a real big typical American leader.

But same time, way I look at it, the other denominations — the Methodists and Baptists and Presbyterians and Campbellites — they're all working together to make a greater and purer America.

Our generation, I guess we still got a lot of the Old Harry in us. Me, I admit, I smoke and I sometimes take a little drink — but never to excess; if there's anything I despise it's a man that can't hold his liquor. And I do like a nice drive on Sunday, and sometimes I cuss a little, and I guess I ain't above looking at a pretty ankle even yet. But it's my firm belief — maybe you gentlemen never thought about it this way — if we'll just support the churches and give the preachers a chance, a generation will come which won't even *want* to do those things, and then America will stand forth before the world such a nation as has never been seen, yes sir, and I'm mighty glad to fellowship with Methodists or ——

Not that I think so much of these Christian Scientists and Seventh Day Adventists and all them, though. They carry things too far, and I don't believe in going to extremes in anything; and as for Catholics — I hope none of you gentlemen are Catholics and I wouldn't want this to go any further, but I've always felt the Catholics were too tolerant toward drinking and smoking, and so they aren't, you might say, really hardly typically American at all.

And as to religion in general, they tell me there's a lot of smart-aleck highbrows today that are calling the truth of Christianity in question. Well, I may not be any theologian, but I wish I could meet one of these fellows, and believe me, I'd settle his hash!

"Look here," I tell him; "in the first place it stands to reason, don't it, that fellows specially trained in theology, like the preachers, know more than us laymen, don't it? And in the second, if the Christian religion has lasted two thousand years and is today stronger than ever before — just look, for instance, at that skyscraper church they're building in New York — is it likely that a little handful of you smart galoots are going to be able to change it?"

I guess they never thought of that! Trouble with fellows like agnostics is that you simply can *not* get 'em to stop and think and use their minds!

And what have they got to put in the *place* of religion? Know what the trouble with those fellows is? *They're destructive and not constructive!*

But as I was saying, our church has a regular Wednesday Evening Supper before prayer-meeting, and say, the ladies of the church certainly do serve one of the nicest suppers you ever ate, and for only forty cents — Hamburg steak with Spanish sauce, or creamed chipped beef, or corn beef and cabbage, and sometimes ice cream for dessert, all A 1. And they usually have a speaker, and this evening I was speaking of, the speaker that spoke on China was a missionary, and he gave us the real lowdown on China, and he told us it was fierce the way the Chinks were carrying on, and not respecting either their trade treaties — and what a *damn* fool thing *that* was, because here they had a chance to get in contact with America and England and all, and get civilized, and give up worshipping idols — But he showed a real Christian spirit. He said that even though the Chinks had practically kicked him out, he believed they ought to be allowed to have another chance to try to run their own country.

Well, I could see that was fair, and I was real interested to see the President agreed with him, and then I asked Mr. Jones ——

"Mr. Jones," I said, "what's the real truth about the President's fishing? Is he a good fisherman?" I said.

"He's one of the best. His catch always compares favorably with that of any other member of the party, when he sets his mind to it, but you must remember that he's constantly weighed down by the cares of the world," Mr. Jones said.

"Yes, I can see that," I told him, "and personally, I think it's a shame for some of these newspapers that haven't got anything better to write to make fun of him. Say, another thing," I asked him, "does the President belong to any of the service clubs — Rotary and Kiwanis and so on?"

"No, in his position," Mr. Jones explained to me, "in his position he couldn't hardly discriminate between them, but I think I'm not betraying any secret when I say that the President has the highest admiration for the great service and ideals of all these organizations."

Well, I was mighty glad to hear that, and I think you gentlemen will be, too, whether you belong to 'em or not. For, after all, what organizations are doing a greater good and providing more real happiness today than the service clubs, all of them, though I myself am a Kiwanian and I can't help feeling that maybe our own organization has got the edge on the other fellows —— we aren't as darned snobbish as these Rotarians, and yet we aren't you might say as common as the Civitans and the Lions and — Yes sir!

Think what these clubs provide. A chance for a lot of the most responsible and forward-looking men of the community to get together once a week, and not only have a high old time, with all the dignity of our positions checked at the door, calling each other by our first names — Think of what that means! Say here's some high muckamuck of a judge; for that hour or so I can call him "Pete," and slap him on the back and kid him about his family, and stands to reason that any man enjoys having a chance to let down and be human like that.

And then the good we do! Why say, just this past year our Zenith Kiwanians have put up not less than two hundred and sixty-three highway markers within forty miles of Zenith, and we gave the kids at an orphan asylum a dandy auto ride and free feed. And believe me it was one fine ad for the Kiwanians, because we took the kids out in trucks, and each one had on it a great big red sign: "Free Outing for the Unfortunate Kiddies, Provided Free by Zenith Kiwanis Club."

But be that as it may, I was mighty glad to hear the President speak like that and to get his real inside view, and so I asks Mr. Jones, "What's, uh — what's the President's views on taxation, if it isn't impertinent to ask?"

Now, you gentlemen will be interested to learn what Mr. Jones told me, because of course that's one of the most important topics of the day, and Jones spoke right up, without hesitation:

"I know for a fact," he told me, "that the President feels that the burdens of taxation should be so equably distributed that they shall lay no undue burden on the poor and unfortunate yet at the same time they must in no sense be so prejudicial to honest business interests as to cramp the necessary conduct and expansion of commerce."

And some soreheads claim the President isn't really a deep thinker!

And then ——

Almerine had just been on pins and needles at the prospect of talking with the President; couldn't hardly keep still in her chair. Mr. Jones was real nice to her, and I certainly was proud of the way one of our home girls could answer up to a man in official position like that.

"So you come from Zenith, " he says to her. "Do you like it?"

"Oh, you bet," she said. "I just think Zenith is the nicest city in America. Of course I'd rather live in New York, but my, do you know we have the finest park system in the United States?"

"Is that a fact!" he says. "No, I didn't know that. And I guess you like to Charleston," he says. "Or have you gone out for the black bottom? Do you like it?"

"Do I?" she says. "Oh boy! I'd show you, but I guess this isn't the place."

"No, I'm afraid it isn't," he says, and we all four bust right out laughing together — wasn't that a comical idea — to dance the Charleston in the President's office!

X

I was just going to ask Mr. Jones how the President felt about Socialism when there was a messenger boy come out and called Mr. Jones in and he was gone about a couple minutes, it couldn't have been more than that, and he come back, and say, he did look real sorry.

"I've got terrible news," he told me. "The President was just ready to see you when the British ambassador come in with some specially important business, and then he has to hustle down to the *Mayflower* — that's his yacht — and be gone maybe forty-five days, on an important secret conference. But he hopes you'll drop in any time you're in Washington."

So you gentlemen can see that it isn't by accident but by real thinking and good fellowship that President Coolidge — yes, or any other President we've had recently — maintains his position, and I hope I haven't bored you, and now I'll dry up and let some other fellow talk and ——

But just to speak of Socialism a moment — I'm willing to give every man a fair square deal, 5

but when it comes to supporting a lot of loafers, the way I look at it is that constructive, practical people like ourselves, who control the country, ought, you might say ——

F. Scott Fitzgerald [1896–1940]

In literary circles the "Age of Anxiety" after World War II, the reckless period after World War I came to be remembered with a certain nostalgia. Scott Fitzgerald, a long undervalued spokesman of the Jazz Age, was revived with enthusiasm.

Born in St. Paul, Minnesota, he attended Princeton, where he played and wrote, but left college in his senior year in order to enlist in the army. Never sent overseas, he combined writing with soldiering, and after his discharge published *This Side of Paradise* (described above, page 844). He suddenly found himself famous and rich. He married Zelda Sayre, of Montgomery, Alabama, and together they threw themselves into the postwar revelry, "the greatest, gaudiest spree in history." "I had everything I wanted and knew I would never be so happy again." It cost $36,000 in one year.

In 1924, taking their four-year-old daughter abroad with them, they set up a still dizzier pace in Paris and on the Riviera. Four years later Zelda, fascinated by the ballet, was dancing like mad, and Scott, drinking heavily, was twice arrested for brawling. In 1931 they returned to America financially and emotionally spent. Zelda, in fact, had gone insane. He now drank uncontrollably, struggled with his writing, ran up a huge debt, worked for eighteen months at Hollywood, finally succumbed to a heart attack.

In a short life, he did not write many novels. After *This Side of Paradise* he published three more: *The Beautiful and Damned* (1922), *The Great Gatsby* (1925), *Tender Is the Night* (1934). The only one of these that is deftly, tightly built is *The Great Gatsby*, the theme of which is the love and death of an enormously wealthy bootlegger.

For the popular magazines Fitzgerald wrote many short stories, collecting most of them in *Flappers and Philosophers* (1920), *Tales of the Jazz Age* (1922), *All the Sad Young Men* (1926), and *Taps at Reveille* (1935). The story printed below is taken from the second of these.

Further reading: *The Great Gatsby*. Arthur Mizener, *The Far Side of Paradise: A Biography of F. Scott Fitzgerald*, 1951.

May Day

🐟 Published in the *Smart Set* in July 1920, this story relates a series of events which took place during the May Day riots in New York in 1919. Fitzgerald later said that the beginning of the Jazz Age could be dated from that time.

There had been a war fought and won and the great city of the conquering people was crossed with triumphal arches and vivid with thrown 10

flowers of white, red, and rose. All through the long spring days the returning soldiers marched up the chief highway behind the strump of drums and the joyous, resonant wind of the 5 brasses, while merchants and clerks left their bickerings and figurings and, crowding to the windows, turned their white-bunched faces gravely upon the passing battalions.

Never had there been such splendor in the great city, for the victorious war had brought plenty in its train, and the merchants had flocked thither from the South and West with their households to taste of all the luscious feasts and witness the lavish entertainments prepared — and to buy for their women furs against the next winter and bags of golden mesh and varicolored slippers of silk and silver and rose satin and cloth of gold.

So gaily and noisily were the peace and prosperity impending hymned by the scribes and poets of the conquering people that more and more spenders had gathered from the provinces to drink the wine of excitement, and faster and faster did the merchants dispose of their trinkets and slippers until they sent up a mighty cry for more trinkets and more slippers in order that they might give in barter what was demanded of them. Some even of them flung up their hands helplessly, shouting:

"Alas! I have no more slippers! and alas! I have no more trinkets! May Heaven help me, for I know not what I shall do!"

But no one listened to their great outcry, for the throngs were far too busy — day by day, the foot-soldiers trod jauntily the highway and all exulted because the young men returning were pure and brave, sound of tooth and pink of cheek, and the young women of the land were virgins and comely both of face and of figure.

So during all this time there were many adventures that happened in the great city, and, of these, several — or perhaps one — are here set down.

I

At nine o'clock on the morning of the first of May, 1919, a young man spoke to the room clerk at the Biltmore Hotel, asking if Mr. Philip Dean were registered there, and if so, could he be connected with Mr. Dean's rooms. The inquirer was dressed in a well-cut, shabby suit. He was small, slender, and darkly handsome; his eyes were framed above with unusually long eyelashes and below with the blue semicircle of ill health, this latter effect heightened by an unnatural glow which colored his face like a low, incessant fever.

Mr. Dean was staying there. The young man was directed to a telephone at the side.

After a second his connection was made; a sleepy voice hello'd from somewhere above.

"Mr. Dean?" — this very eagerly — "it's Gordon, Phil. It's Gordon Sterrett. I'm downstairs. I heard you were in New York and I had a hunch you'd be here."

The sleepy voice became gradually enthusiastic. Well, how was Gordy, old boy! Well, he certainly was surprised and tickled! Would Gordy come right up, for Pete's sake!

A few minutes later Philip Dean, dressed in blue silk pajamas, opened his door and the two young men greeted each other with a half-embarrassed exuberance. They were both about twenty-four, Yale graduates of the year before the war; but there the resemblance stopped abruptly. Dean was blond, ruddy, and rugged under his thin pajamas. Everything about him radiated fitness and bodily comfort. He smiled frequently, showing large and prominent teeth.

"I was going to look you up," he cried enthusiastically. "I'm taking a couple of weeks off. If you'll sit down a sec I'll be right with you. Going to take a shower."

As he vanished into the bathroom his visitor's dark eyes roved nervously around the room, resting for a moment on a great English travelling bag in the corner and on a family of thick silk shirts littered on the chairs amid impressive neckties and soft woollen socks.

Gordon rose and, picking up one of the shirts, gave it a minute examination. It was of very heavy silk, yellow with a pale blue stripe — and there were nearly a dozen of them. He stared involuntarily at his own shirt-cuffs — they were ragged and linty at the edges and soiled to a faint gray. Dropping the silk shirt, he held his coat-sleeves down and worked the frayed shirt-cuffs up till they were out of sight. Then he went to the mirror and looked at himself with listless, unhappy interest. His tie, of former glory, was faded and thumb-creased — it served no longer to hide the jagged buttonholes of his collar. He thought, quite without amusement, that only three years before he had received a scattering vote in the senior elections at college for being the best-dressed man in his class.

Dean emerged from the bathroom polishing his body.

"Saw an old friend of yours last night," he remarked.

"Passed her in the lobby and couldn't think of her name to save my neck. That girl you brought up to New Haven senior year."

Gordon started.

"Edith Bradin? That whom you mean?"

"'At's the one. Damn good looking. She's still sort of a pretty doll — you know what I mean: as if you touched her she'd smear."

He surveyed his shining self complacently in

the mirror, smiled faintly, exposing a section of teeth.

"She must be twenty-three anyway," he continued.

"Twenty-two last month," said Gordon absently.

"What? Oh, last month. Well, I imagine she's down for the Gamma Psi dance. Did you know we're having a Yale Gamma Psi dance to-night at Delmonico's? You better come up, Gordy. Half of New Haven'll probably be there. I can get you an invitation."

Draping himself reluctantly in fresh underwear, Dean lit a cigarette and sat down by the open window, inspecting his calves and knees under the morning sunshine which poured into the room.

"Sit down, Gordy," he suggested, "and tell me all about what you've been doing and what you're doing now and everything."

Gordon collapsed unexpectedly upon the bed; lay there inert and spiritless. His mouth, which habitually dropped a little open when his face was in repose, became suddenly helpless and pathetic.

"What's the matter?" asked Dean quickly.

"Oh, God!"

"What's the matter?"

"Every God damn thing in the world," he said miserably. "I've absolutely gone to pieces, Phil. I'm all in."

"Huh?"

"I'm all in." His voice was shaking.

Dean scrutinized him more closely with appraising blue eyes.

"You certainly look all shot."

"I am. I've made a hell of mess of everything." He paused. "I'd better start at the beginning — or will it bore you?"

"Not at all; go on." There was, however, a hesitant note in Dean's voice. This trip East had been planned for a holiday — to find Gordon Sterrett in trouble exasperated him a little.

"Go on," he repeated, and then added half under his breath, "Get it over with."

"Well," began Gordon unsteadily, "I got back from France in February, went home to Harrisburg for a month, and then came down to New York to get a job. I got one — with an export company. They fired me yesterday."

"Fired you?"

"I'm coming to that, Phil. I want to tell you frankly. You're about the only man I can turn to in a matter like this. You won't mind if I just tell you frankly, will you, Phil?"

Dean stiffened a bit more. The pats he was bestowing on his knees grew perfunctory. He felt vaguely that he was being unfairly saddled with responsibility; he was not even sure he wanted to be told. Though never surprised at finding Gordon Sterrett in mild difficulty, there was something in this present misery that repelled him and hardened him, even though it excited his curiosity.

"Go on."

"It's a girl."

"Hm." Dean resolved that nothing was going to spoil his trip. If Gordon was going to be depressing, then he'd have to see less of Gordon.

"Her name is Jewel Hudson," went on the distressed voice from the bed. "She used to be 'pure,' I guess, up to about a year ago. Lived here in New York — poor family. Her people are dead now and she lives with an old aunt. You see it was just about the time I met her that everybody began to come back from France in droves — and all I did was to welcome the newly arrived and go on parties with 'em. That's the way it started, Phil, just from being glad to see everybody and having them glad to see me."

"You ought to've had more sense."

"I know," Gordon paused, and then continued listlessly. "I'm on my own now, you know, and Phil, I can't stand being poor. Then came this darn girl. She sort of fell in love with me for a while and, though I never intended to get so involved, I'd always seem to run into her somewhere. You can imagine the sort of work I was doing for those exporting people — of course, I always intended to draw; do illustrating for magazines; there's a pile of money in it."

"Why didn't you? You've got to buckle down if you want to make good," suggested Dean with cold formalism.

"I tried, a little, but my stuff's crude. I've got talent, Phil; I can draw — but I just don't know how. I ought to go to art school and I can't afford it. Well, things came to a crisis about a week ago. Just as I was down to about my last dollar this girl began bothering me. She wants some money; claims she can make trouble for me if she doesn't get it."

"Can she?"

"I'm afraid she can. That's one reason I lost my job — she kept calling up the office all the time, and that was sort of the last straw down there. She's got a letter all written to send to my family. Oh, she's got me, all right. I've got to have some money for her."

There was an awkward pause. Gordon lay very still, his hands clenched by his side.

"I'm all in," he continued, his voice trembling. "I'm half crazy, Phil. If I hadn't known you were coming East, I think I'd have killed myself. I want you to lend me three hundred dollars."

Dean's hands, which had been patting his bare ankles, were suddenly quiet — and the curious uncertainty playing between the two became taut and strained.

After a second Gordon continued:

"I've bled the family until I'm ashamed to ask for another nickel."

Still Dean made no answer.

"Jewel says she's got to have two hundred dollars."

"Tell her where she can go."

"Yes, that sounds easy, but she's got a couple of drunken letters I wrote her. Unfortunately she's not at all the flabby sort of person you'd expect."

Dean made an expression of distaste.

"I can't stand that sort of woman. You ought to have kept away."

"I know," admitted Gordon wearily.

"You've got to look at things as they are. If you haven't got money you've got to work and stay away from women."

"That's easy for you to say," began Gordon, his eyes narrowing. "You've got all the money in the world."

"I most certainly have not. My family keep darn close tab on what I spend. Just because I have a little leeway I have to be extra careful not to abuse it."

He raised the blind and let in a further flood of sunshine.

"I'm no prig, Lord knows," he went on deliberately. "I like pleasure — and I like a lot of it on a vacation like this, but you're — you're in awful shape. I never heard you talk just this way before. You seem to be sort of bankrupt — morally as well as financially."

"Don't they usually go together?"

Dean shook his head impatiently.

"There's a regular aura about you that I don't understand. It's a sort of evil."

"It's an air of worry and poverty and sleepless nights," said Gordon, rather defiantly.

"I don't know."

"Oh, I admit I'm depressing. I depress myself. But, my God, Phil, a week's rest and a new suit and some ready money and I'd be like — like I was. Phil, I can draw like a streak, and you know it. But half the time I haven't had the money to buy decent drawing materials — and I can't draw when I'm tired and discouraged and all in. With a little ready money I can take a few weeks off and get started."

"How do I know you wouldn't use it on some other woman?"

"Why rub it in?" said Gordon quietly.

"I'm not rubbing it in. I hate to see you this way."

"Will you lend me the money, Phil?"

"I can't decide right off. That's a lot of money and it'll be darn inconvenient for me."

"It'll be hell for me if you can't — I know I'm whining, and it's all my own fault but — that doesn't change it."

"When could you pay it back?"

This was encouraging. Gordon considered. It was probably wisest to be frank.

"Of course, I could promise to send it back next month, but — I'd better say three months. Just as soon as I start to sell drawings."

"How do I know you'll sell any drawings?"

A new hardness in Dean's voice sent a faint chill of doubt over Gordon. Was it possible that he wouldn't get the money?

"I supposed you had a little confidence in me."

"I did have — but when I see you like this I begin to wonder."

"Do you suppose if I wasn't at the end of my rope I'd come to you like this? Do you think I'm enjoying it?" He broke off and bit his lip, feeling that he had better subdue the rising anger in his voice. After all, he was the suppliant.

"You seem to manage it pretty easily," said Dean angrily. "You put me in the position where, if I don't lend it to you, I'm a sucker — oh, yes, you do. And let me tell you it's no easy thing for me to get hold of three hundred dollars. My income isn't so big but that a slice like that won't play the deuce with it."

He left his chair and began to dress, choosing his clothes carefully. Gordon stretched out his arms and clenched the edges of the bed, fighting back a desire to cry out. His head was splitting and whirring, his mouth was dry and bitter and he could feel the fever in his blood resolving itself into innumerable regular counts like a slow dripping from a roof.

Dean tied his tie precisely, brushed his eyebrows, and removed a piece of tobacco from his teeth with solemnity. Next he filled his cigarette case, tossed the empty box thoughtfully into the waste basket, and settled the case in his vest pocket.

"Had breakfast?" he demanded.

"No; I don't eat it any more."

"Well, we'll go out and have some. We'll decide about that money later. I'm sick of the subject. I came East to have a good time.

"Let's go over to the Yale Club," he continued moodily, and then added with an implied reproof: "You've given up your job. You've got nothing else to do."

"I'd have a lot to do if I had a little money," said Gordon pointedly.

"Oh, for Heaven's sake drop the subject for a while! No point in glooming on my whole trip. Here, here's some money."

He took a five-dollar bill from his wallet and tossed it over to Gordon, who folded it carefully and put it in his pocket. There was an added spot of color in his cheeks, an added glow that was not fever. For an instant before they turned to go out their eyes met and in that instant each found something that made him lower his own glance quickly. For in that instant they quite suddenly and definitely hated each other.

II

Fifth Avenue and Forty-fourth Street swarmed with the noon crowd. The wealthy, happy sun glittered in transient gold through the thick windows of the smart shops, lighting upon mesh bags and purses and strings of pearls in gray velvet cases; upon gaudy feather fans of many colors; upon the laces and silks of expensive dresses; upon the bad paintings and the fine period furniture in the elaborate show rooms of interior decorators.

Working-girls, in pairs and groups and swarms, loitered by the windows, choosing their future boudoirs from some resplendent display which included even a man's silk pajamas laid domestically across the bed. They stood in front of the jewelry stores and picked out their engagement rings, and their wedding rings and their platinum wrist watches, and then drifted on to inspect the feather fans and opera cloaks; meanwhile digesting the sandwiches and sundaes they had eaten for lunch.

All through the crowd were men in uniform, sailors from the great fleet anchored in the Hudson, soldiers with divisional insignia from Massachusetts to California wanting fearfully to be noticed, and finding the great city thoroughly fed up with soldiers unless they were nicely massed into pretty formations and uncomfortable under the weight of a pack and rifle.

Through this medley Dean and Gordon wandered; the former interested, made alert by the display of humanity at its frothiest and gaudiest; the latter reminded of how often he had been one of the crowd, tired, casually fed, overworked, and dissipated. To Dean the struggle was significant, young, cheerful; to Gordon it was dismal, meaningless, endless.

In the Yale Club they met a group of their former classmates who greeted the visiting Dean vociferously. Sitting in a semicircle of lounges and great chairs, they had a highball all around.

Gordon found the conversation tiresome and interminable. They lunched together *en masse*, warmed with liquor as the afternoon began. They were all going to the Gamma Psi dance that night — it promised to be the best party since the war.

"Edith Bradin's coming," said some one to Gordon. "Didn't she used to be an old flame of yours? Aren't you both from Harrisburg?"

"Yes." He tried to change the subject. "I see her brother occasionally. He's sort of a socialistic nut. Runs a paper or something here in New York."

"Not like his gay sister, eh?" continued his eager informant. "Well, she's coming to-night with a junior named Peter Himmell."

Gordon was to meet Jewel Hudson at eight o'clock — he had promised to have some money for her. Several times he glanced nervously at his wrist watch. At four, to his relief, Dean rose and announced that he was going over to Rivers Brothers to buy some collars and ties. But as they left the Club another of the party joined them, to Gordon's great dismay. Dean was in a jovial mood now, happy, expectant of the evening's party, faintly hilarious. Over in Rivers' he chose a dozen neckties, selecting each one after long consultations with the other man. Did he think narrow ties were coming back? And wasn't it a shame that Rivers couldn't get any more Welsh Margotson collars? There never was a collar like the "Covington."

Gordon was in something of a panic. He wanted the money immediately. And he was now inspired also with a vague idea of attending the Gamma Psi dance. He wanted to see

Edith — Edith whom he hadn't met since one romantic night at the Harrisburg Country Club just before he went to France. The affair had died, drowned in the turmoil of the war and quite forgotten in the arabesque of these three months, but a picture of her, poignant, debonnaire, immersed in her own inconsequential chatter, recurred to him unexpectedly and brought a hundred memories with it. It was Edith's face that he had cherished through college with a sort of detached yet affectionate admiration. He had loved to draw her — around his room had been a dozen sketches of her — playing golf, swimming — he could draw her pert, arresting profile with his eyes shut.

They left Rivers' at five-thirty and paused for a moment on the sidewalk.

"Well," said Dean genially, "I'm all set now. Think I'll go back to the hotel and get a shave, haircut, and massage."

"Good enough," said the other man, "I think I'll join you."

Gordon wondered if he was to be beaten after all. With difficulty he restrained himself from turning to the man and snarling out, "Go on away, damn you!" In despair he suspected that perhaps Dean had spoken to him, was keeping him along in order to avoid a dispute about the money.

They went into the Biltmore — a Biltmore alive with girls — mostly from the West and South, the stellar débutantes of many cities gathered for the dance of a famous fraternity of a famous university. But to Gordon they were faces in a dream. He gathered together his forces for a last appeal, was about to come out with he knew not what, when Dean suddenly excused himself to the other man and taking Gordon's arm led him aside.

"Gordy," he said quickly, "I've thought the whole thing over carefully and I've decided that I can't lend you that money. I'd like to oblige you, but I don't feel I ought to — it'd put a crimp in me for a month."

Gordon, watching him dully, wondered why he had never before noticed how much those upper teeth projected.

"— I'm mighty sorry, Gordon," continued Dean, "but that's the way it is."

He took out his wallet and deliberately counted out seventy-five dollars in bills.

"Here," he said, holding them out, "here's seventy-five; that makes eighty all together. That's all the actual cash I have with me, besides what I'll actually spend on the trip."

Gordon raised his clenched hand automatically, opened it as though it were a tongs he was holding, and clenched it again on the money.

"I'll see you at the dance," continued Dean. "I've got to get along to the barber shop."

"So-long," said Gordon in a strained and husky voice.

"So-long."

Dean began to smile, but seemed to change his mind. He nodded briskly and disappeared.

But Gordon stood there, his handsome face awry with distress, the roll of bills clenched tightly in his hand. Then, blinded by sudden tears, he stumbled clumsily down the Biltmore steps.

III

About nine o'clock of the same night two human beings came out of a cheap restaurant in Sixth Avenue. They were ugly, ill-nourished, devoid of all except the very lowest form of intelligence, and without even that animal exuberance that in itself brings color into life; they were lately vermin-ridden, cold, and hungry in a dirty town of a strange land; they were poor, friendless; tossed as driftwood from their births, they would be tossed as driftwood to their deaths. They were dressed in the uniform of the United States Army, and on the shoulder of each was the insignia of a drafted division from New Jersey, landed three days before.

The taller of the two was named Carrol Key, a name hinting that in his veins, however thinly diluted by generations of degeneration, ran blood of some potentiality. But one could stare endlessly at the long, chinless face, the dull, watery eyes, and high cheek-bones, without finding a suggestion of either ancestral worth or native resourcefulness.

His companion was swart and bandy-legged, with rat-eyes and a much-broken hooked nose. His defiant air was obviously a pretense, a weapon of protection borrowed from that world of snarl and snap, of physical bluff and physical menace, in which he had always lived. His name was Gus Rose.

Leaving the café they sauntered down Sixth Avenue, wielding toothpicks with great gusto and complete detachment.

"Where to?" asked Rose, in a tone which implied that he would not be surprised if Key suggested the South Sea Islands.

"What you say we see if we can getta holda

some liquor?" Prohibition was not yet. The ginger in the suggestion was caused by the law forbidding the selling of liquor to soldiers.

Rose agreed enthusiastically.

"I got an idea," continued Key, after a moment's thought, "I got a brother somewhere."

"In New York?"

"Yeah. He's an old fella." He meant that he was an elder brother. "He's a waiter in a hash joint."

"Maybe he can get us some."

"I'll say he can!"

"B'lieve me, I'm goin' to get this darn uniform off me to-morra. Never get me in it again, neither. I'm goin' to get me some regular clothes."

"Say, maybe I'm not."

As their combined finances were something less than five dollars, this intention can be taken largely as a pleasant game of words, harmless and consoling. It seemed to please both of them, however, for they reinforced it with chuckling and mention of personages high in biblical circles, adding such further emphasis as "Oh, boy!" "You know!" and "I'll say so!" repeated many times over.

The entire mental pabulum of these two men consisted of an offended nasal comment extended through the years upon the institution — army, business, or poorhouse — which kept them alive, and toward their immediate superior in that institution. Until that very morning the institution had been the "government" and the immediate superior had been the "Cap'n" — from these two they had glided out and were now in the vaguely uncomfortable state before they should adopt their next bondage. They were uncertain, resentful, and somewhat ill at ease. This they hid by pretending an elaborate relief at being out of the army, and by assuring each other that military discipline should never again rule their stubborn, liberty-loving wills. Yet, as a matter of fact, they would have felt more at home in a prison than in this new-found and unquestionable freedom.

Suddenly Key increased his gait. Rose, looking up and following his glance, discovered a crowd that was collecting fifty yards down the street. Key chuckled and began to run in the direction of the crowd; Rose thereupon also chuckled and his short bandy legs twinkled beside the long, awkward strides of his companion.

Reaching the outskirts of the crowd they immediately became an indistinguishable part of it. It was composed of ragged civilians somewhat the worse for liquor, and of soldiers representing many divisions and many stages of sobriety, all clustered around a gesticulating little Jew with long black whiskers, who was waving his arms and delivering an excited but succinct harangue. Key and Rose, having wedged themselves into the approximate parquet, scrutinized him with acute suspicion, as his words penetrated their common consciousness.

" — What have you got outa the war?" he was crying fiercely. "Look arounja, look arounja! Are you rich? Have you got a lot of money offered you? — no; you're lucky if you're alive and got both your legs; you're lucky if you came back an' find your wife ain't gone off with some other fella that had the money to buy himself out of the war! That's when you're lucky! Who got anything out of it except J. P. Morgan an' John D. Rockefeller?"

At this point the little Jew's oration was interrupted by the hostile impact of a fist upon the point of his bearded chin and he toppled backward to a sprawl on the pavement.

"God damn Bolsheviki!" cried the big soldier-blacksmith who had delivered the blow. There was a rumble of approval, the crowd closed in nearer.

The Jew staggered to his feet, and immediately went down again before a half-dozen reaching-in fists. This time he stayed down, breathing heavily, blood oozing from his lip where it was cut within and without.

There was a riot of voices, and in a minute Rose and Key found themselves flowing with the jumbled crowd down Sixth Avenue under the leadership of a thin civilian in a slouch hat and the brawny soldier who had summarily ended the oration. The crowd had marvelously swollen to formidable proportions and a stream of more non-committal citizens followed it along the sidewalks lending their moral support by intermittent huzzas.

"Where we goin'?" yelled Key to the man nearest him.

His neighbor pointed up to the leader in the slouch hat.

"That guy knows where there's a lot of 'em! We're goin' to show 'em!"

"We're goin' to show 'em!" whispered Key delightedly to Rose, who repeated the phrase rapturously to a man on the other side.

Down Sixth Avenue swept the procession,

joined here and there by soldiers and marines, and now and then by civilians, who came up with the inevitable cry that they were just out of the army themselves, as if presenting it as a card of admission to a newly formed Sporting and Amusement Club.

Then the procession swerved down a cross street and headed for Fifth Avenue and the word filtered here and there that they were bound for a Red meeting at Tolliver Hall.

"Where is it?"

The question went up the line and a moment later the answer floated back. Tolliver Hall was down on Tenth Street. There was a bunch of other sojers who was goin' to break it up and was down there now!

But Tenth Street had a faraway sound and at the word a general groan went up and a score of the procession dropped out. Among these were Rose and Key, who slowed down to a saunter and let the more enthusiastic sweep on by.

"I'd rather get some liquor," said Key as they halted and made their way to the sidewalk amid cries of "Shell hole!" and "Quitters!"

"Does your brother work around here?" asked Rose, assuming the air of one passing from the superficial to the eternal.

"He oughta," replied Key. "I ain't seen him for a coupla years. I been out to Pennsylvania since. Maybe he don't work at night anyhow. It's right along here. He can get us some o'right if he ain't gone."

They found the place after a few minutes' patrol of the street — a shoddy tablecloth restaurant between Fifth Avenue and Broadway. Here Key went inside to inquire for his brother George, while Rose waited on the sidewalk.

"He ain't here no more," said Key emerging. "He's a waiter up to Delmonico's."

Rose nodded wisely, as if he'd expected as much. One should not be surprised at a capable man changing jobs occasionally. He knew a waiter once — there ensued a long conversation as they walked as to whether waiters made more in actual wages than in tips — it was decided that it depended on the social tone of the joint wherein the waiter labored. After having given each other vivid pictures of millionaires dining at Delmonico's and throwing away fifty-dollar bills after their first quart of champagne, both men thought privately of becoming waiters. In fact, Key's narrow brow was secreting a resolution to ask his brother to get him a job.

"A waiter can drink up all the champagne those fellas leave in bottles," suggested Rose with some relish, and then added as an afterthought, "Oh, boy!"

By the time they reached Delmonico's it was half past ten, and they were surprised to see a stream of taxis driving up to the door one after the other and emitting marvelous, hatless young ladies, each one attended by a stiff young gentleman in evening clothes.

"It's a party," said Rose with some awe. "Maybe we better not go in. He'll be busy."

"No, he won't. He'll be o'right."

After some hesitation they entered what appeared to them to be the least elaborate door and, indecision falling upon them immediately, stationed themselves nervously in an inconspicuous corner of the small dining-room in which they found themselves. They took off their caps and held them in their hands. A cloud of gloom fell upon them and both started when a door at one end of the room crashed open, emitting a comet-like waiter who streaked across the floor and vanished through another door on the other side.

There had been three of these lightning passages before the seekers mustered the acumen to hail a waiter. He turned, looked at them suspiciously, and then approached with soft, catlike steps, as if prepared at any moment to turn and flee.

"Say," began Key, "say, do you know my brother? He's a waiter here."

"His name is Key," annotated Rose.

Yes, the waiter knew Key. He was up-stairs, he thought. There was a big dance going on in the main ballroom. He'd tell him.

Ten minutes later George Key appeared and greeted his brother with the utmost suspicion; his first and most natural thought being that he was going to be asked for money.

George was tall and weak chinned, but there his resemblance to his brother ceased. The waiter's eyes were not dull, they were alert and twinkling, and his manner was suave, in-door, and faintly superior. They exchanged formalities. George was married and had three children. He seemed fairly interested, but not impressed by the news that Carrol had been abroad in the army. This disappointed Carrol.

"George," said the younger brother, these amenities having been disposed of, "we want to get some booze, and they won't sell us none. Can you get us some?"

George considered.

"Sure. Maybe I can. It may be half an hour, though."

"All right," agreed Carrol, "we'll wait."

At this Rose started to sit down in a convenient chair, but was hailed to his feet by the indignant George.

"Hey! Watch out, you! Can't sit down here! This room's all set for a twelve o'clock banquet."

"I ain't goin' to hurt it," said Rose resentfully. "I been through the delouser."

"Never mind," said George sternly, "if the head waiter seen me here talkin' he'd romp all over me."

"Oh."

The mention of the head waiter was full explanation to the other two; they fingered their overseas caps nervously and waited for a suggestion.

"I tell you," said George, after a pause, "I got a place you can wait; you just come here with me."

They followed him out the far door, through a deserted pantry and up a pair of dark winding stairs, emerging finally into a small room chiefly furnished by piles of pails and stacks of scrubbing brushes, and illuminated by a single dim electric light. There he left them, after soliciting two dollars and agreeing to return in half an hour with a quart of whiskey.

"George is makin' money, I bet," said Key gloomily as he seated himself on an inverted pail. "I bet he's making fifty dollars a week."

Rose nodded his head and spat.

"I bet he is, too."

"What'd he say the dance was of?"

"A lot of college fellas. Yale College."

They both nodded solemnly at each other.

"Wonder where that crowda sojers is now?"

"I don't know. I know that's too damn long to walk for me."

"Me too. You don't catch me walkin' that far."

Ten minutes later restlessness seized them.

"I'm goin' to see what's out here," said Rose, stepping cautiously toward the other door.

It was a swinging door of green baize and he pushed it open a cautious inch.

"See anything?"

For answer Rose drew in his breath sharply.

"Doggone! Here's some liquor I'll say!"

"Liquor?"

Key joined Rose at the door, and looked eagerly.

"I'll tell the world that's liquor," he said, after a moment of concentrated gazing.

It was a room about twice as large as the one they were in — and in it was prepared a radiant feast of spirits. There were long walls of alternating bottles set along two white covered tables; whiskey, gin, brandy, French and Italian vermouths, and orange juice, not to mention an array of syphons and two great empty punch bowls. The room was as yet uninhabited.

"It's for this dance they're just starting," whispered Key; "hear the violins playin'? Say, boy, I wouldn't mind havin' a dance."

They closed the door softly and exchanged a glance of mutual comprehension. There was no need of feeling each other out.

"I'd like to get my hands on a coupla those bottles," said Rose emphatically.

"Me too."

"Do you suppose we'd get seen?"

Key considered.

"Maybe we better wait till they start drinkin' 'em. They got 'em all laid out now, and they know how many of them there are."

They debated this point for several minutes. Rose was all for getting his hands on a bottle now and tucking it under his coat before any one came into the room. Key, however, advocated caution. He was afraid he might get his brother in trouble. If they waited till some of the bottles were opened it'd be all right to take one, and everybody'd think it was one of the college fellas.

While they were still engaged in argument George Key hurried through the room and, barely grunting at them, disappeared by way of the green baize door. A minute later they heard several corks pop, and then the sound of crackling ice and splashing liquid. George was mixing the punch.

The soldiers exchanged delighted grins.

"Oh, boy!" whispered Rose.

George reappeared.

"Just keep low, boys," he said quickly. "I'll have your stuff for you in five minutes."

He disappeared through the door by which he had come.

As soon as his footsteps receded down the stairs, Rose, after a cautious look, darted into the room of delights and reappeared with a bottle in his hand.

"Here's what I say," he said, as they sat radiantly digesting their first drink. "We'll wait till he comes up, and we'll ask him if we can't just stay here and drink what he brings us — see. We'll tell him we haven't got any place to drink it — see. Then we can sneak in there whenever there ain't nobody in that there room and tuck a bottle under our coats. We'll have enough to last us a coupla days — see?"

"Sure," agreed Rose enthusiastically. "Oh, boy! And if we want to we can sell it to sojers any time we want to."

They were silent for a moment thinking rosily of this idea. Then Key reached up and unhooked the collar of his O. D. coat.

"It's hot in here, ain't it?"

Rose agreed earnestly.

"Hot as hell."

IV

She was still quite angry when she came out of the dressing-room and crossed the intervening parlor of politeness that opened onto the hall — angry not so much at the actual happening which was, after all, the merest commonplace of her social existence, but because it had occurred on this particular night. She had no quarrel with herself. She had acted with that correct mixture of dignity and reticent pity which she always employed. She had succinctly and deftly snubbed him.

It had happened when their taxi was leaving the Biltmore — hadn't gone half a block. He had lifted his right arm awkwardly — she was on his right side — and attempted to settle it snugly around the crimson fur-trimmed opera cloak she wore. This in itself had been a mistake. It was inevitably more graceful for a young man attempting to embrace a young lady of whose acquiescence he was not certain, to first put his far arm around her. It avoided that awkward movement of raising the near arm.

His second *faux pas* was unconscious. She had spent the afternoon at the hairdresser's; the idea of any calamity overtaking her hair was extremely repugnant — yet as Peter made his unfortunate attempt the point of his elbow had just faintly brushed it. That was his second *faux pas*. Two were quite enough.

He had begun to murmur. At the first murmur she had decided that he was nothing but a college boy — Edith was twenty-two, and anyhow, this dance, first of its kind since the war, was reminding her, with the accelerating rhythm of its associations, of something else — of another dance and another man, a man for whom her feelings had been little more than a sad-

eyed, adolescent mooniness. Edith Bradin was falling in love with her recollection of Gordon Sterrett.

So she came out of the dressing-room at Delmonico's and stood for a second in the doorway looking over the shoulders of a black dress in front of her at the groups of Yale men who flitted like dignified black moths around the head of the stairs. From the room she had left drifted out the heavy fragrance left by the passage to and fro of many scented young beauties — rich perfumes and the fragile memory-laden dust of fragrant powders. This odor drifting out acquired the tang of cigarette smoke in the hall, and then settled sensuously down the stairs and permeated the ballroom where the Gamma Psi dance was to be held. It was an odor she knew well, exciting, stimulating, restlessly sweet — the odor of a fashionable dance.

She thought of her own appearance. Her bare arms and shoulders were powdered to a creamy white. She knew they looked very soft and would gleam like milk against the black backs that were to silhouette them tonight. The hairdressing had been a success; her reddish mass of hair was piled and crushed and creased to an arrogant marvel of mobile curves. Her lips were finely made of deep carmine; the irises of her eyes were delicate, breakable blue, like china eyes. She was a complete, infinitely delicate, quite perfect thing of beauty, flowing in an even line from a complex coiffure to two small slim feet.

She thought of what she would say to-night at this revel, faintly presaged already by the sounds of high and low laughter and slippered footsteps, and movements of couples up and down the stairs. She would talk the language she had talked for many years — her line — made up of the current expressions, bits of journalese and college slang strung together into an intrinsic whole, careless, faintly provocative, delicately sentimental. She smiled faintly as she heard a girl sitting on the stairs near her say: "You don't know the half of it, dearie!"

And as she smiled her anger melted for a moment, and closing her eyes she drew in a deep breath of pleasure. She dropped her arms to her side until they were faintly touching the sleek sheath that covered and suggested her figure. She had never felt her own softness so much nor so enjoyed the whiteness of her own arms.

"I smell sweet," she said to herself simply,

and then came another thought — "I'm made for love."

She liked the sound of this and thought it again; then in inevitable succession came her new-born riot of dreams about Gordon. The twist of her imagination which, two months before, had disclosed to her her unguessed desire to see him again, seemed now to have been leading up to this dance, this hour.

For all her sleek beauty, Edith was a grave, slow-thinking girl. There was a streak in her of that same desire to ponder, of that adolescent idealism that had turned her brother socialist and pacifist. Henry Bradin had left Cornell, where he had been an instructor in economics, and had come to New York to pour the latest cures for incurable evils into the columns of a radical weekly newspaper.

Edith, less fatuously, would have been content to cure Gordon Sterrett. There was a quality of weakness in Gordon that she wanted to take care of; there was a helplessness in him that she wanted to protect. And she wanted someone she had known a long while, someone who had loved her a long while. She was a little tired; she wanted to get married. Out of a pile of letters, half a dozen pictures and as many memories, and this weariness, she had decided that next time she saw Gordon their relations were going to be changed. She would say something that would change them. There was this evening. This was her evening. All evenings were her evenings.

Then her thoughts were interrupted by a solemn undergraduate with a hurt look and an air of strained formality who presented himself before her and bowed unusually low. It was the man she had come with, Peter Himmel. He was tall and humorous, with horned-rimmed glasses and an air of attractive whimsicality. She suddenly rather disliked him — probably because he had not succeeded in kissing her.

"Well," she began, "are you still furious at me?"

"Not at all."

She stepped forward and took his arm.

"I'm sorry," she said softly. "I don't know why I snapped out that way. I'm in a bum humor to-night for some strange reason. I'm sorry."

"S'all right," he mumbled, "don't mention it."

He felt disagreeably embarrassed. Was she rubbing in the fact of his late failure?

"It was a mistake," she continued, on the same consciously gentle key. "We'll both forget it." For this he hated her.

A few minutes later they drifted out on the floor while the dozen swaying, sighing members of the specially hired jazz orchestra informed the crowded ballroom that "if a saxophone and me are left alone why then two is com-pan-ee!"

A man with a mustache cut in.

"Hello," he began reprovingly. "You don't remember me."

"I can't just think of your name," she said lightly — "and I know you so well."

"I met you up at —" His voice trailed disconsolately off as a man with very fair hair cut in. Edith murmured a conventional "Thanks, loads — cut in later," to the *inconnu*.

The very fair man insisted on shaking hands enthusiastically. She placed him as one of the numerous Jims of her acquaintance — last name a mystery. She remembered even that he had a peculiar rhythm in dancing and found as they started that she was right.

"Going to be here long?" he breathed confidentially.

She leaned back and looked up at him.

"Couple of weeks."

"Where are you?"

"Biltmore. Call me up some day."

"I mean it," he assured her. "I will. We'll go to tea."

"So do I — Do."

A dark man cut in with intense formality.

"You don't remember me, do you?" he said gravely.

"I should say I do. Your name's Harlan."

"No-ope. Barlow."

"Well, I knew there were two syllables anyway. You're the boy that played the ukulele so well up at Howard Marshall's house party."

"I played — but not —"

A man with prominent teeth cut in. Edith inhaled a slight cloud of whiskey. She liked men to have had something to drink; they were so much more cheerful, and appreciative and complimentary — much easier to talk to.

"My name's Dean, Philip Dean," he said cheerfully. "You don't remember me, I know, but you used to come up to New Haven with a fellow I roomed with senior year, Gordon Sterrett."

Edith looked up quickly.

"Yes, I went up with him twice — to the Pump and Slipper and the Junior prom."

"You've seen him, of course," said Dean carelessly. "He's here to-night. I saw him just a minute ago."

Edith started. Yet she had felt quite sure he would be here.

"Why, no, I haven't —— "

A fat man with red hair cut in.

"Hello, Edith," he began.

"Why — hello there —— "

She slipped, stumbled lightly.

"I'm sorry, dear," she murmured mechanically.

She had seen Gordon — Gordon very white and listless, leaning against the side of a doorway, smoking and looking into the ballroom. Edith could see that his face was thin and wan — that the hand he raised to his lips with a cigarette was trembling. They were dancing quite close to him now.

" — They invite so darn many extra fellas that you — " the short man was saying.

"Hello, Gordon," called Edith over her partner's shoulder. Her heart was pounding wildly.

His large dark eyes were fixed on her. He took a step in her direction. Her partner turned her away — she heard his voice bleating ——

" — but half the stags get lit and leave before long, so —— "

Then a low tone at her side.

"May I, please?"

She was dancing suddenly with Gordon; one of his arms was around her; she felt it tighten spasmodically; felt his hand on her back with the fingers spread. Her hand holding the little lace handkerchief was crushed in his.

"Why Gordon," she began breathlessly.

"Hello, Edith."

She slipped again — was tossed forward by her recovery until her face touched the black cloth of his dinner coat. She loved him — she knew she loved him — then for a minute there was silence while a strange feeling of uneasiness crept over her. Something was wrong.

Of a sudden her heart wrenched, and turned over as she realized what it was. He was pitiful and wretched, a little drunk, and miserably tired.

"Oh — " she cried involuntarily.

His eyes looked down at her. She saw suddenly that they were blood-streaked and rolling uncontrollably.

"Gordon," she murmured, "we'll sit down, I want to sit down."

They were nearly in mid-floor, but she had seen two men start toward her from opposite sides of the room, so she halted, seized Gordon's limp hand and led him bumping through the crowd, her mouth tight shut, her face a little pale under her rouge, her eyes trembling with tears.

She found a place high up on the soft-carpeted stairs, and he sat down heavily beside her.

"Well," he began, staring at her unsteadily, "I certainly am glad to see you, Edith."

She looked at him without answering. The effect of this on her was immeasurable. For years she had seen men in various stages of intoxication, from uncles all the way down to chauffeurs, and her feelings had varied from amusement to disgust, but here for the first time she was seized with a new feeling — an unutterable horror.

"Gordon," she said accusingly and almost crying, "you look like the devil."

He nodded. "I've had trouble, Edith."

"Trouble?"

"All sorts of trouble. Don't you say anything to the family, but I'm all gone to pieces. I'm a mess, Edith."

His lower lip was sagging. He seemed scarcely to see her.

"Can't you — can't you," she hesitated, "can't you tell me about it, Gordon? You know I'm always interested in you."

She bit her lip — she had intended to say something stronger, but found at the end that she couldn't bring it out.

Gordon shook his head dully. "I can't tell you. You're a good woman. I can't tell a good woman the story."

"Rot," she said, defiantly. "I think it's a perfect insult to call any one a good woman in that way. It's a slam. You've been drinking, Gordon."

"Thanks." He inclined his head gravely. "Thanks for the information."

"Why do you drink?"

"Because I'm so damn miserable."

"Do you think drinking's going to make it any better?"

"What you doing — trying to reform me?"

"No; I'm trying to help you, Gordon. Can't you tell me about it?"

"I'm in an awful mess. Best thing you can do is to pretend not to know me."

"Why, Gordon?"

"I'm sorry I cut in on you — it's unfair to

you. You're pure woman — and all that sort of thing. Here, I'll get some one else to dance with you."

He rose clumsily to his feet, but she reached up and pulled him down beside her on the stairs.

"Here, Gordon. You're ridiculous. You're hurting me. You're acting like a — like a crazy man ——"

"I admit it. I'm a little crazy. Something's wrong with me, Edith. There's something left me. It doesn't matter."

"It does, tell me."

"Just that. I was always queer — little bit different from other boys. All right in college, but now it's all wrong. Things have been snapping inside me for four months like little hooks on a dress, and it's about to come off when a few more hooks go. I'm very gradually going loony."

He turned his eyes full on her and began to laugh, and she shrank away from him.

"What *is* the matter?"

"Just me," he repeated. "I'm going loony. This whole place is like a dream to me — this Delmonico's ——"

As he talked she saw he had changed utterly. He wasn't at all light and gay and careless — a great lethargy and discouragement had come over him. Revulsion seized her, followed by a faint, surprising boredom. His voice seemed to come out of a great void.

"Edith," he said, "I used to think I was clever, talented, an artist. Now I know I'm nothing. Can't draw, Edith. Don't know why I'm telling you this."

She nodded absently.

"I can't draw, I can't do anything. I'm poor as a church mouse." He laughed, bitterly and rather too loud. "I've become a damn beggar, a leech on my friends. I'm a failure. I'm poor as hell."

Her distaste was growing. She barely nodded this time, waiting for her first possible cue to rise.

Suddenly Gordon's eyes filled with tears.

"Edith," he said, turning to her with what was evidently a strong effort at self-control, "I can't tell you what it means to me to know there's one person left who's interested in me."

He reached out and patted her hand, and involuntarily she drew it away.

"It's mighty fine of you," he repeated.

"Well," she said slowly, looking him in the eye, "any one's always glad to see an old friend — but I'm sorry to see you like this, Gordon."

There was a pause while they looked at each other, and the momentary eagerness in his eyes wavered. She rose and stood looking at him, her face quite expressionless.

"Shall we dance?" she suggested, coolly.

— Love is fragile — she was thinking — but perhaps the pieces are saved, the things that hovered on lips, that might have been said. The new love words, the tendernesses learned, are treasured up for the next lover.

V

Peter Himmel, escort to the lovely Edith, was unaccustomed to being snubbed; having been snubbed, he was hurt and embarrassed, and ashamed of himself. For a matter of two months he had been on special delivery terms with Edith Bradin and knowing that the one excuse and explanation of the special delivery letter is its value in sentimental correspondence, he had believed himself quite sure of his ground. He searched in vain for any reason why she should have taken this attitude in the matter of a simple kiss.

Therefore when he was cut in on by the man with the mustache he went out into the hall and, making up a sentence, said it over to himself several times. Considerably deleted, this was it:

"Well, if any girl ever led a man on and then jolted him, she did — and she has no kick coming if I go out and get beautifully boiled."

So he walked through the supper room into a small room adjoining it, which he had located earlier in the evening. It was a room in which there were several large bowls of punch flanked by many bottles. He took a seat beside the table which held the bottles.

At the second highball, boredom, disgust, the monotony of time, the turbidity of events, sank into a vague background before which glittering cobwebs formed. Things became reconciled to themselves, things lay quietly on their shelves; the troubles of the day arranged themselves in trim formation and at his curt wish of dismissal, marched off and disappeared. And with the departure of worry came brilliant, permeating symbolism. Edith became a flighty, negligible girl, not to be worried over; rather to be laughed at. She fitted like a figure of his own dream into the surface world forming about him. He himself became in a measure symbolic, a type of the continent bacchanal, the brilliant dreamer at play.

Then the symbolic mood faded and as he sipped his third highball his imagination yielded to the warm glow and he lapsed into a state similar to floating on his back in pleasant water. It was at this point that he noticed that a green baize door near him was open about two inches, and that through the aperture a pair of eyes were watching him intently.

"Hm," murmured Peter calmly.

The green door closed — and then opened again — a bare half inch this time.

"Peek-a-boo," murmured Peter.

The door remained stationary and then he became aware of a series of tense intermittent whispers.

"One guy."

"What's he doin'?"

"He's sittin' lookin'."

"He better beat it off. We gotta get another li'l' bottle."

Peter listened while the words filtered into his consciousness.

"Now this," he thought, "is most remarkable."

He was excited. He was jubilant. He felt that he had stumbled upon a mystery. Affecting an elaborate carelessness he arose and walked around the table — then, turning quickly, pulled open the green door, precipitating Private Rose into the room.

Peter bowed.

"How do you do?" he said.

Private Rose set one foot slightly in front of the other, poised for fight, flight, or compromise.

"How do you do?" repeated Peter politely.

"I'm o'right."

"Can I offer you a drink?"

Private Rose looked at him searchingly, suspecting possible sarcasm.

"O'right," he said finally.

Peter indicated a chair.

"Sit down."

"I got a friend," said Rose, "I got a friend in there." He pointed to the green door.

"By all means let's have him in."

Peter crossed over, opened the door and welcomed in Private Key, very suspicious and uncertain and guilty. Chairs were found and the three took their seats around the punch bowl. Peter gave them each a highball and offered them a cigarette from his case. They accepted both with some diffidence.

"Now," continued Peter easily, "may I ask why you gentlemen prefer to lounge away your leisure hours in a room which is chiefly furnished, as far as I can see, with scrubbing brushes. And when the human race has progressed to the stage where seventeen thousand chairs are manufactured on every day except Sunday — " he paused. Rose and Key regarded him vacantly. "Will you tell me," went on Peter, "why you choose to rest yourselves on articles intended for the transportation of water from one place to another?"

At this point Rose contributed a grunt to the conversation.

"And lastly," finished Peter, "will you tell me why, when you are in a building beautifully hung with enormous candelabra, you prefer to spend these evening hours under one anemic electric light?"

Rose looked at Key; Key looked at Rose. They laughed; they laughed uproariously; they found it was impossible to look at each other without laughing. But they were not laughing with this man — they were laughing at him. To them a man who talked after this fashion was either raving drunk or raving crazy.

"You are Yale men, I presume," said Peter, finishing his highball and preparing another.

They laughed again.

"Na-ah."

"So? I thought perhaps you might be members of that lowly section of the university known as the Sheffield Scientific School."

"Na-ah."

"Hm. Well, that's too bad. No doubt you are Harvard men, anxious to preserve your incognito in this — this paradise of violet blue, as the newspapers say."

"Na-ah," said Key scornfully, "we was just waitin' for somebody."

"Ah," exclaimed Peter, rising and filling their glasses, "very interestin'. Had a date with a scrublady, eh?"

They both denied this indignantly.

"It's all right," Peter reassured them, "don't apologize. A scrublady's as good as any lady in the world. Kipling says 'Any lady and Judy O'Grady under the skin.'"

"Sure," said Key, winking broadly at Rose.

"My case, for instance," continued Peter, finishing his glass. "I got a girl up here that's spoiled. Spoildest darn girl I ever saw. Refused to kiss me; no reason whatsoever. Led me on deliberately to think sure I want to kiss you and then plunk! Threw me over! What's the younger generation comin' to?"

"Say tha's hard luck," said Key — "that's awful hard luck."

"Oh boy!" said Rose.

"Have another?" said Peter.

"We got in a sort of fight for a while," said Key after a pause, "but it was too far away."

"A fight? — tha's stuff!" said Peter, seating himself unsteadily. "Fight 'em all! I was in the army."

"This was with a Bolshevik fella."

"Tha's stuff!" exclaimed Peter, enthusiastic. "That's what I say! Kill the Bolshevik! Exterminate 'em!"

"We're Americuns," said Rose, implying a sturdy, defiant patriotism.

"Sure," said Peter. "Greatest race in the world! We're all Americuns! Have another."

They had another.

VI

At one o'clock a special orchestra, special even in a day of special orchestras, arrived at Delmonico's, and its members, seating themselves arrogantly around the piano, took up the burden of providing music for the Gamma Psi Fraternity. They were headed by a famous flute-player, distinguished throughout New York for his feat of standing on his head and shimmying with his shoulders while he played the latest jazz on his flute. During his performance the lights were extinguished except for the spotlight on the flute-player and another roving beam that threw flickering shadows and changing kaleidoscopic colors over the massed dancers.

Edith had danced herself into that tired, dreamy state habitual only with débutantes, a state equivalent to the glow of a noble soul after several long highballs. Her mind floated vaguely on the bosom of her music; her partners changed with the unreality of phantoms under the colorful shifting dusk, and to her present coma it seemed as if days had passed since the dance began. She had talked on many fragmentary subjects with many men. She had been kissed once and made love to six times. Earlier in the evening different undergraduates had danced with her, but now, like all the more popular girls there, she had her own entourage — that is, half a dozen gallants had singled her out or were alternating her charms with those of some other chosen beauty; they cut in on her in regular, inevitable succession.

Several times she had seen Gordon — he had been sitting a long time on the stairway with his palm to his head, his dull eyes fixed at an infinite speck on the floor before him, very depressed, he looked, and quite drunk — but Edith each time had averted her glance hurriedly. All that seemed long ago; her mind was passive now, her senses were lulled to trance-like sleep; only her feet danced and her voice talked on in hazy sentimental banter.

But Edith was not nearly so tired as to be incapable of moral indignation when Peter Himmel cut in on her, sublimely and happily drunk. She gasped and looked up at him.

"Why, *Peter!*"

"I'm a li'l' stewed, Edith."

"Why, Peter, you're a *peach*, you are! Don't you think it's a bum way of doing — when you're with me?"

Then she smiled unwillingly, for he was looking at her with owlish sentimentality varied with a silly spasmodic smile.

"Darlin' Edith," he began earnestly, "you know I love you, don't you?"

"You tell it well."

"I love you — and I merely wanted you to kiss me," he added sadly.

His embarrassment, his shame, were both gone. She was a mos' beautiful girl in whole worl'. Mos' beautiful eyes, like stars above. He wanted to 'pologize — firs', for presuming try to kiss her; second, for drinking — but he'd been so discouraged 'cause he had thought she was mad at him ——

The red-fat man cut in, and looking up at Edith smiled radiantly.

"Did you bring any one?" she asked.

No. The red-fat man was a stag.

"Well, would you mind — would it be an awful bother for you to — to take me home to-night?" (this extreme diffidence was a charming affectation on Edith's part — she knew that the red-fat man would immediately dissolve into a paroxysm of delight).

"Bother? Why, good Lord, I'd be darn glad to! You know I'd be darn glad to."

"Thanks *loads!* You're awfully sweet."

She glanced at her wrist-watch. It was half-past one. And, as she said "half-past one" to herself, it floated vaguely into her mind that her brother had told her at luncheon that he worked in the office of his newspaper until after one-thirty every evening.

Edith turned suddenly to her current partner.

"What street is Delmonico's on, anyway?"

"Street? Oh, why Fifth Avenue, of course."

"I mean, what cross street?"

"Why — let's see — it's on Forty-fourth Street."

This verified what she had thought. Henry's office must be across the street and just around the corner, and it occurred to her immediately that she might slip over for a moment and surprise him, float in on him, a shimmering marvel in her new crimson opera cloak and "cheer him up." It was exactly the sort of thing Edith revelled in doing — an unconventional, jaunty thing. The idea reached out and gripped at her imagination — after an instant's hesitation she had decided.

"My hair is just about to tumble entirely down," she said pleasantly to her partner; "would you mind if I go and fix it?"

"Not at all."

"You're a peach."

A few minutes later, wrapped in her crimson opera cloak, she flitted down a side-stairs, her cheeks glowing with excitement at her little adventure. She ran by a couple who stood at the door — a weak-chinned waiter and an over-rouged young lady, in hot dispute — and opening the outer door stepped into the warm May night.

VII

The over-rouged young lady followed her with a brief, bitter glance — then turned again to the weak-chinned waiter and took up her argument.

"You better go up and tell him I'm here," she said defiantly, "or I'll go up myself."

"No, you don't!" said George sternly.

The girl smiled sardonically.

"Oh, I don't, don't I? Well, let me tell you I know more college fellas and more of 'em know me, and are glad to take me out on a party, than you ever saw in your whole life."

"Maybe so ——"

"Maybe so," she interrupted. "Oh, it's all right for any of 'em like that one that just ran out — God knows where *she* went — it's all right for them that are asked here to come or go as they like — but when I want to see a friend they have some cheap, ham-slinging, bring-me-a-doughnut waiter to stand here and keep me out."

"See here," said the elder Key indignantly, "I can't lose my job. Maybe this fella you're talkin' about doesn't want to see you."

"Oh, he wants to see me all right."

"Anyway, how could I find him in all that crowd?"

"Oh, he'll be there," she asserted confidently. "You just ask anybody for Gordon Sterrett and they'll point him out to you. They all know each other, those fellas."

She produced a mesh bag, and taking out a dollar bill handed it to George.

"Here," she said, "here's a bribe. You find him and give him my message. You tell him if he isn't here in five minutes I'm coming up."

George shook his head pessimistically, considered the question for a moment, wavered violently, and then withdrew.

In less than the allotted time Gordon came down-stairs. He was drunker than he had been earlier in the evening and in a different way. The liquor seemed to have hardened on him like a crust. He was heavy and lurching — almost incoherent when he talked.

"'Lo, Jewel," he said thickly. "Came right away. Jewel, I couldn't get that money. Tried my best."

"Money nothing!" she snapped. "You haven't been near me for ten days. What's the matter?"

He shook his head slowly.

"Been very low, Jewel. Been sick."

"Why didn't you tell me if you were sick. I don't care about the money that bad. I didn't start bothering you about it at all until you began neglecting me."

Again he shook his head.

"Haven't been neglecting you. Not at all."

"Haven't! You haven't been near me for three weeks, unless you been so drunk you didn't know what you were doing."

"Been sick, Jewel," he repeated, turning his eyes upon her wearily.

"You're well enough to come and play with your society friends here all right. You told me you'd meet me for dinner, and you said you'd have some money for me. You didn't even bother to ring me up."

"I couldn't get any money."

"Haven't I just been saying that doesn't matter? I wanted to see *you*, Gordon, but you seem to prefer your somebody else."

He denied this bitterly.

"Then get your hat and come along," she suggested.

Gordon hesitated — and she came suddenly close to him and slipped her arms around his neck.

"Come on with me, Gordon," she said in a half whisper. "We'll go over to Devineries' and have a drink, and then we can go up to my apartment."

"I can't, Jewel, —— "

"You can," she said intensely.

"I'm sick as a dog!"

"Well, then, you oughtn't to stay here and dance."

With a glance around him in which relief and despair were mingled, Gordon hesitated; then she suddenly pulled him to her and kissed him with soft, pulpy lips.

"All right," he said heavily. "I'll get my hat."

VIII

When Edith came out into the clear blue of the May night she found the Avenue deserted. The windows of the big shops were dark; over their doors were drawn great iron masks until they were only shadowy tombs of the late day's splendor. Glancing down toward Forty-second Street she saw a commingled blue of lights from the all-night restaurants. Over on Sixth Avenue the elevated, a flare of fire, roared across the street between the glimmering parallels of light at the station and streaked along into the crisp dark. But at Forty-fourth Street it was very quiet.

Pulling her cloak close about her Edith darted across the Avenue. She started nervously as a solitary man passed her and said in a hoarse whisper — "Where bound, kiddo?" She was reminded of a night in her childhood when she had walked around the block in her pajamas and a dog had howled at her from a mystery-big back yard.

In a minute she had reached her destination, a two-story, comparatively old building on Forty-fourth, in the upper windows of which she thankfully detected a wisp of light. It was bright enough outside for her to make out the sign beside the window — the *New York Trumpet*. She stepped inside a dark hall and after a second saw the stairs in the corner.

Then she was in a long, low room furnished with many desks and hung on all sides with file copies of newspapers. There were only two occupants. They were sitting at different ends of the room, each wearing a green eye-shade and writing by a solitary desk light.

For a moment she stood uncertainly in the doorway, and then both men turned around simultaneously and she recognized her brother.

"Why, Edith!" He rose quickly and approached her in surprise, removing his eye-shade. He was tall, lean, and dark, with black, piercing eyes under very thick glasses. They were far-away eyes that seemed always fixed just over the head of the person to whom he was talking.

He put his hands on her arms and kissed her cheek.

"What is it?" he repeated in some alarm.

"I was at a dance across at Delmonico's, Henry," she said excitedly, "and I couldn't resist tearing over to see you."

"I'm glad you did." His alertness gave way quickly to a habitual vagueness. "You oughtn't to be out alone at night though, ought you?"

The man at the other end of the room had been looking at them curiously, but at Henry's beckoning gesture he approached. He was loosely fat with little twinkling eyes, and, having removed his collar and tie, he gave the impression of a Middle-Western farmer on a Sunday afternoon.

"This is my sister," said Henry. "She dropped in to see me."

"How do you do?" said the fat man, smiling. "My name's Bartholomew, Miss Bradin. I know your brother has forgotten it long ago."

Edith laughed politely.

"Well," he continued, "not exactly gorgeous quarters we have here, are they?"

Edith looked around the room.

"They seem very nice," she replied. "Where do you keep the bombs?"

"The bombs?" repeated Bartholomew, laughing. "That's pretty good — the bombs. Did you hear her, Henry? She wants to know where we keep the bombs. Say, that's pretty good."

Edith swung herself around onto a vacant desk and sat dangling her feet over the edge. Her brother took a seat beside her.

"Well," he asked, absent-mindedly, "how do you like New York this trip?"

"Not bad. I'll be over at the Biltmore with the Hoyts until Sunday. Can't you come to luncheon to-morrow?"

He thought a moment.

"I'm especially busy," he objected, "and I hate women in groups."

"All right," she agreed, unruffled. "Let's you and me have luncheon together."

"Very well."

"I'll call for you at twelve."

Bartholomew was obviously anxious to return to his desk, but apparently considered that it would be rude to leave without some parting pleasantry.

"Well" — he began awkwardly.

They both turned to him.

"Well, we — we had an exciting time earlier in the evening."

The two men exchanged glances.

"You should have come earlier," continued Bartholomew, somewhat encouraged. "We had a regular vaudeville."

"Did you really?"

"A serenade," said Henry. "A lot of soldiers gathered down there in the street and began to yell at the sign."

"Why?" she demanded.

"Just a crowd," said Henry, abstractedly. "All crowds have to howl. They didn't have anybody with much initiative in the lead, or they'd probably have forced their way in here and smashed things up."

"Yes," said Bartholomew, turning again to Edith, "you should have been here."

He seemed to consider this a sufficient cue for withdrawal, for he turned abruptly and went back to his desk.

"Are the soldiers all set against the Socialists?" demanded Edith of her brother. "I mean do they attack you violently and all that?"

Henry replaced his eye-shade and yawned.

"The human race has come a long way," he said casually, "but most of us are throw-backs; the soldiers don't know what they want, or what they hate, or what they like. They're used to acting in large bodies, and they seem to have to make demonstrations. So it happens to be against us. There've been riots all over the city to-night. It's May Day, you see."

"Was the disturbance here pretty serious?"

"Not a bit," he said scornfully. "About twenty-five of them stopped in the street about nine o'clock, and began to bellow at the moon."

"Oh" — She changed the subject. "You're glad to see me, Henry?"

"Why, sure."

"You don't seem to be."

"I am."

"I suppose you think I'm a — a waster. Sort of the World's Worst Butterfly."

Henry laughed.

"Not at all. Have a good time while you're young. Why? Do I seem like the priggish and earnest youth?"

"No —" She paused, " — but somehow I began thinking how absolutely different the party I'm on is from — from all your purposes. It seems sort of — of incongruous, doesn't it? — me being at a party like that, and you over here working for a thing that'll make that sort of party impossible ever any more, if your ideas work."

"I don't think of it that way. You're young, and you're acting just as you were brought up to act. Go ahead — have a good time."

Her feet, which had been idly swinging, stopped and her voice dropped a note.

"I wish you'd — you'd come back to Harrisburg and have a good time. Do you feel sure that you're on the right track —— "

"You're wearing beautiful stockings," he interrupted. "What on earth are they?"

"They're embroidered," she replied, glancing down. "Aren't they cunning?" She raised her skirts and uncovered slim, silk-sheathed calves. "Or do you disapprove of silk stockings?"

He seemed slightly exasperated, bent his dark eyes on her piercingly.

"Are you trying to make me out as criticizing you in any way, Edith?"

"Not at all —— "

She paused. Bartholomew had uttered a grunt. She turned and saw that he had left his desk and was standing at the window.

"What is it?" demanded Henry.

"People," said Bartholomew, and then after an instant: "Whole jam of them. They're coming from Sixth Avenue."

"People?"

The fat man pressed his nose to the pane.

"Soldiers, by God!" he said emphatically. "I had an idea they'd come back."

Edith jumped to her feet, and running over joined Bartholomew at the window.

"There's a lot of them!" she cried excitedly. "Come here, Henry!"

Henry readjusted his shade, but kept his seat.

"Hadn't we better turn out the lights?" suggested Bartholomew.

"No. They'll go away in a minute."

"They're not," said Edith, peering from the window. "They're not even thinking of going away. There's more of them coming. Look — there's a whole crowd turning the corner of Sixth Avenue."

By the yellow glow and blue shadows of the street lamp she could see that the sidewalk was crowded with men. They were mostly in uniform, some sober, some enthusiastically drunk, and over the whole swept an incoherent clamor and shouting.

Henry rose, and going to the window exposed himself as a long silhouette against the office lights. Immediately the shouting became a steady yell, and a rattling fusillade of small missiles, corners of tobacco plugs, cigarette-boxes, and even pennies beat against the window. The sounds of the racket now began floating up the stairs as the folding doors revolved.

"They're coming up!" cried Bartholomew.

Edith turned anxiously to Henry.

"They're coming up, Henry."

From down-stairs in the lower hall their cries were now quite audible.

" — God damn Socialists!"

"Pro-Germans! Boche-lovers!"

"Second floor, front! Come on!"

"We'll get the sons —— "

The next five minutes passed in a dream. Edith was conscious that the clamor burst suddenly upon the three of them like a cloud of rain, that there was a thunder of many feet on the stairs, that Henry had seized her arm and drawn her back toward the rear of the office. Then the door opened and an overflow of men were forced into the room — not the leaders, but simply those who happened to be in front.

"Hello, Bo!"

"Up late, ain't you?"

"You an' your girl. Damn *you!*"

She noticed that two very drunken soldiers had been forced to the front, where they wobbled fatuously — one of them was short and dark, the other was tall and weak of chin.

Henry stepped forward and raised his hand.

"Friends!" he said.

The clamor faded into a momentary stillness, punctuated with mutterings.

"Friends!" he repeated, his far-away eyes fixed over the heads of the crowd, "you're injuring no one but yourselves by breaking in here to-night. Do we look like rich men? Do we look like Germans? I ask you in all fairness —— "

"Pipe down!"

"I'll say you do!"

"Say, who's your lady friend, buddy?"

A man in civilian clothes, who had been pawing over a table, suddenly held up a newspaper.

"Here it is!" he shouted. "They wanted the Germans to win the war!"

A new overflow from the stairs was shouldered in and of a sudden the room was full of men all closing around the pale little group at the back. Edith saw that the tall soldier with the weak chin was still in front. The short dark one had disappeared.

She edged slightly backward, stood close to the open window, through which came a clear breath of cool night air.

Then the room was a riot. She realized that the soldiers were surging forward, glimpsed the fat man swinging a chair over his head — instantly the lights went out, and she felt the push of warm bodies under rough cloth, and her ears were full of shouting and trampling and hard breathing.

A figure flashed by her out of nowhere, tottered, was edged sideways, and of a sudden disappeared helplessly out through the open window with a frightened, fragmentary cry that died staccato on the bosom of the clamor. By the faint light streaming from the building backing on the area Edith had a quick impression that it had been the tall soldier with the weak chin.

Anger rose astonishingly in her. She swung her arms wildly, edged blindly toward the thickest of the scuffling. She heard grunts, curses, the muffled impact of fists.

"Henry!" she called frantically, "Henry!"

Then, it was minutes later, she felt suddenly that there were other figures in the room. She heard a voice, deep, bullying, authoritative; she saw yellow rays of light sweeping here and there in the fracas. The cries became more scattered. The scuffling increased and then stopped.

Suddenly the lights were on and the room was full of policemen, clubbing left and right. The deep voice boomed out:

"Here now! Here now! Here now!"

And then:

"Quiet down and get out! Here now!"

The room seemed to empty like a wash-bowl. A policeman fast-grappled in the corner released his hold on his soldier antagonist and started him with a shove toward the door. The deep voice continued. Edith perceived now that it came from a bull-necked police captain standing near the door.

"Here now! This is no way! One of your own sojers got shoved out of the back window an' killed hisself!"

"Henry!" called Edith, "Henry!"

She beat wildly with her fists on the back of the man in front of her; she brushed between two others; fought, shrieked, and beat her way to a very pale figure sitting on the floor close to a desk.

"Henry," she cried passionately, "what's the matter? What's the matter? Did they hurt you?"

His eyes were shut. He groaned and then looking up said disgustedly ——

"They broke my leg. My God, the fools!"

"Here now!" called the police captain. "Here now! Here now!"

IX

"Childs', Fifty-ninth Street," at eight o'clock of any morning differs from its sisters by less than the width of their marble tables or the degree of polish on the frying-pans. You will see there a crowd of poor people with sleep in the corners of their eyes, trying to look straight before them at their food so as not to see the other poor people. But Childs', Fifty-ninth, four hours earlier is quite unlike any Childs' restaurant from Portland, Oregon, to Portland, Maine. Within its pale but sanitary walls one finds a noisy medley of chorus girls, college boys, débutantes, rakes, *filles de joie* — a not unrepresentative mixture of the gayest of Broadway, and even of Fifth Avenue.

In the early morning of May the second it was unusually full. Over the marble-topped tables were bent the excited faces of flappers whose fathers owned individual villages. They were eating buckwheat cakes and scrambled eggs with relish and gusto, an accomplishment that it would have been utterly impossible for them to repeat in the same place four hours later.

Almost the entire crowd were from the Gamma Psi dance at Delmonico's except for several chorus girls from a midnight revue who sat at a side table and wished they'd taken off a little more make-up after the show. Here and there a drab, mouse-like figure, desperately out of place, watched the butterflies with a weary, puzzled curiosity. But the drab figure was the exception. This was the morning after May Day, and celebration was still in the air.

Gus Rose, sober but a little dazed, must be classed as one of the drab figures. How he had got himself from Forty-fourth Street to Fifty-ninth Street after the riot was only a hazy half-memory. He had seen the body of Carrol Key put in an ambulance and driven off, and then he had started up town with two or three soldiers. Somewhere between Forty-fourth Street and Fifty-ninth Street the other soldiers had met some women and disappeared. Rose had wandered to Columbus Circle and chosen the gleaming lights of Childs' to minister to his craving for coffee and doughnuts. He walked in and sat down.

All around him floated airy, inconsequential chatter and high-pitched laughter. At first he failed to understand, but after a puzzled five minutes he realized that this was the aftermath of some gay party. Here and there a restless, hilarious young man wandered fraternally and familiarly between the tables, shaking hands indiscriminately and pausing occasionally for a facetious chat, while excited waiters, bearing cakes and eggs aloft, swore at him silently, and bumped him out of the way. To Rose, seated at the most inconspicuous and least crowded table, the whole scene was a colorful circus of beauty and riotous pleasure.

He became gradually aware, after a few moments, that the couple seated diagonally across from him, with their backs to the crowd, were not the least interesting pair in the room. The man was drunk. He wore a dinner coat with a dishevelled tie and shirt swollen by spillings of water and wine. His eyes, dim and bloodshot, roved unnaturally from side to side. His breath came short between his lips.

"He's been on a spree!" thought Rose.

The woman was almost if not quite sober. She was pretty, with dark eyes and feverish high color, and she kept her active eyes fixed on her companion with the alertness of a hawk. From time to time she would lean and whisper intently to him, and he would answer by inclining his head heavily or by a particularly ghoulish and repellent wink.

Rose scrutinized them dumbly for some minutes, until the woman gave him a quick, resentful look; then he shifted his gaze to two of the most conspicuously hilarious of the promenaders who were on a protracted circuit of the tables. To his surprise he recognized in one of them the young man by whom he had been so ludicrously entertained at Delmonico's. This started him thinking of Key with a vague sentimentality, not unmixed with awe. Key was dead. He had fallen thirty-five feet and split his skull like a cracked cocoanut.

"He was a darn good guy," thought Rose mournfully. "He was a darn good guy, o'right. That was awful hard luck about him."

The two promenaders approached and started

down between Rose's table and the next, addressing friends and strangers alike with jovial familiarity. Suddenly Rose saw the fair-haired one with the prominent teeth stop, look unsteadily at the man and girl opposite, and then begin to move his head disapprovingly from side to side.

The man with the blood-shot eyes looked up.

"Gordy," said the promenader with the prominent teeth, "Gordy."

"Hello," said the man with the stained shirt thickly.

Prominent Teeth shook his finger pessimistically at the pair, giving the woman a glance of aloof condemnation.

"What'd I tell you Gordy?"

Gordon stirred in his seat.

"Go to hell!" he said.

Dean continued to stand there shaking his finger. The woman began to get angry.

"You go away!" she cried fiercely. "You're drunk, that's what you are!"

"So's he," suggested Dean, staying the motion of his finger and pointing it at Gordon.

Peter Himmel ambled up, owlish now and oratorically inclined.

"Here now," he began as if called upon to deal with some petty dispute between children. "Wha's all trouble?"

"You take your friend away," said Jewel tartly. "He's bothering us."

"What's 'at?"

"You heard me!" she said shrilly. "I said to take your drunken friend away."

Her rising voice rang out above the clatter of the restaurant and a waiter came hurrying up.

"You gotta be more quiet!"

"That fella's drunk," she cried. "He's insulting us."

"Ah-ha, Gordy," persisted the accused. "What'd I tell you." He turned to the waiter. "Gordy an' I friends. Been tryin' help him, haven't I, Gordy?"

Gordy looked up.

"Help me? Hell, no!"

Jewel rose suddenly, and seizing Gordon's arm assisted him to his feet.

"Come on, Gordy!" she said, leaning toward him and speaking in a half whisper. "Let's us get out of here. This fella's got a mean drunk on."

Gordon allowed himself to be urged to his feet and started toward the door. Jewel turned for a second and addressed the provoker of their flight.

"I know all about you!" she said fiercely. "Nice friend, you are, I'll say. He told me about you."

Then she seized Gordon's arm, and together they made their way through the curious crowd, paid their check, and went out.

"You'll have to sit down," said the waiter to Peter after they had gone.

"What's 'at? Sit down?"

"Yes — or get out."

Peter turned to Dean.

"Come on," he suggested. "Let's beat up this waiter."

"All right."

They advanced toward him, their faces grown stern. The waiter retreated.

Peter suddenly reached over to a plate on the table beside him and picking up a handful of hash tossed it into the air. It descended as a languid parabola in snowflake effect on the heads of those near by.

"Hey! Ease up!"

"Put him out!"

"Sit down, Peter!"

"Cut out that stuff!"

Peter laughed and bowed.

"Thank you for your kind applause, ladies and gents. If some one will lend me some more hash and a tall hat we will go on with the act."

The bouncer hustled up.

"You've gotta get out!" he said to Peter.

"Hell, no!"

"He's my friend!" put in Dean indignantly.

A crowd of waiters were gathering. "Put him out!"

"Better go, Peter."

There was a short struggle and the two were edged and pushed toward the door.

"I got a hat and a coat here!" cried Peter.

"Well, go get 'em and be spry about it!"

The bouncer released his hold on Peter, who, adopting a ludicrous air of extreme cunning, rushed immediately around to the other table, where he burst into derisive laughter and thumbed his nose at the exasperated waiters.

"Think I just better wait a l'il' longer," he announced.

The chase began. Four waiters were sent around one way and four another. Dean caught hold of two of them by the coat, and another struggle took place before the pursuit of Peter could be resumed; he was finally pinioned after overturning a sugar-bowl and several cups of coffee. A fresh argument ensued at the cashier's desk, where Peter attempted to buy another dish of hash to take with him and throw at policemen.

But the commotion upon his exit proper was dwarfed by another phenomenon which drew admiring glances and a prolonged involuntary "Oh-h-h!" from every person in the restaurant.

The great plate-glass front had turned to a deep creamy blue, the color of a Maxfield Parrish moonlight — a blue that seemed to press close upon the pane as if to crowd its way into the restaurant. Dawn had come up in Columbus Circle, magical, breathless dawn, silhouetting the great statue of the immortal Christopher, and mingling in a curious and uncanny manner with the fading yellow electric light inside.

X

Mr. In and Mr. Out are not listed by the census-taker. You will search for them in vain through the social register or the births, marriages, and deaths, or the grocer's credit list. Oblivion has swallowed them and the testimony that they ever existed at all is vague and shadowy, and inadmissible in a court of law. Yet I have it upon the best authority that for a brief space Mr. In and Mr. Out lived, breathed, answered to their names and radiated vivid personalities of their own.

During the brief span of their lives they walked in their native garments down the great highway of a great nation; were laughed at, sworn at, chased, and fled from. Then they passed and were heard of no more.

They were already taking form dimly, when a taxicab with the top open breezed down Broadway in the faintest glimmer of May dawn. In this car sat the souls of Mr. In and Mr. Out discussing with amazement the blue light that had so precipitately colored the sky behind the statue of Christopher Columbus, discussing with bewilderment the old, gray faces of the early risers which skimmed palely along the street like blown bits of paper on a gray lake. They were agreed on all things, from the absurdity of the bouncer in Childs' to the absurdity of the business of life. They were dizzy with the extreme maudlin happiness that the morning had awakened in their glowing souls. Indeed, so fresh and vigorous was their pleasure in living that they felt it should be expressed by loud cries.

"Ye-ow-ow!" hooted Peter, making a mega-phone with his hands — and Dean joined in with a call that, though equally significant and symbolic, derived its resonance from its very inarticulateness.

"Yo-ho! Yea! Yoho! Yo-buba!"

Fifty-third Street was a bus with a dark, bobbed-hair beauty atop; Fifty-second was a street cleaner who dodged, escaped, and sent up a yell of, "Look where you're aimin'!" in a pained and grieved voice. At Fiftieth Street a group of men on a very white sidewalk in front of a very white building turned to stare after them, and shouted:

"Some party, boys!"

At Forty-ninth Street Peter turned to Dean. "Beautiful morning," he said gravely, squinting up his owlish eyes.

"Probably is."

"Go get some breakfast, hey?"

Dean agreed — with additions.

"Breakfast and liquor."

"Breakfast and liquor," repeated Peter, and they looked at each other, nodding. "That's logical."

Then they both burst into loud laughter.

"Breakfast and liquor! Oh, gosh!"

"No such thing," announced Peter.

"Don't serve it? Ne'mind. We force 'em serve it. Bring pressure bear."

"Bring logic bear."

The taxi cut suddenly off Broadway, sailed along a cross street, and stopped in front of a heavy tomb-like building in Fifth Avenue.

"What's idea?"

The taxi-driver informed them that this was Delmonico's.

This was somewhat puzzling. They were forced to devote several minutes to intense concentration, for if such an order had been given there must have been a reason for it.

"Somep'm 'bouta coat," suggested the taxi-man.

That was it. Peter's overcoat and hat. He had left them at Delmonico's. Having decided this, they disembarked from the taxi and strolled toward the entrance arm in arm.

"Hey!" said the taxi-driver.

"Huh?"

"You better pay me."

They shook their heads in shocked negation.

"Later, not now — we give orders, you wait."

The taxi-driver objected; he wanted his money now. With the scornful condescension of men exercising tremendous self-control they paid him.

Inside Peter groped in vain through a dim, deserted check-room in search of his coat and derby.

"Gone, I guess. Somebody stole it."

"Some Sheff student."

"All probability."

"Never mind," said Dean, nobly. "I'll leave mine here too — then we'll both be dressed the same."

He removed his overcoat and hat and was hanging them up when his roving glance was caught and held magnetically by two large squares of cardboard tacked to the two coat-room doors. The one on the left-hand door bore the word "In" in big black letters, and the one on the right-hand door flaunted the equally emphatic word "Out."

"Look!" he exclaimed happily ——

Peter's eyes followed his pointing finger.

"What?"

"Look at the signs. Let's take 'em."

"Good idea."

"Probably pair very rare an' valuable signs. Probably come in handy."

Peter removed the left-hand sign from the door and endeavored to conceal it about his person. The sign being of considerable proportions, this was a matter of some difficulty. An idea flung itself at him, and with an air of dignified mystery he turned his back. After an instant he wheeled dramatically around, and stretching out his arms displayed himself to the admiring Dean. He had inserted the sign in his vest, completely covering his shirt front. In effect, the word "In" had been painted upon his shirt in large black letters.

"Yoho!" cheered Dean. "Mister In."

He inserted his own sign in like manner.

"Mister Out!" he announced triumphantly. "Mr. In meet Mr. Out."

They advanced and shook hands. Again laughter overcame them and they rocked in a shaken spasm of mirth.

"Yoho!"

"We probably get a flock of breakfast."

"We'll go — go to the Commodore."

Arm in arm they sallied out the door, and turning east in Forty-fourth Street set out for the Commodore.

As they came out a short dark soldier, very pale and tired, who had been wandering listlessly along the sidewalk, turned to look at them.

He started over as though to address them, but as they immediately bent on him glances of withering unrecognition, he waited until they had started unsteadily down the street, and then followed at about forty paces, chuckling to himself and saying, "Oh, boy!" over and over under his breath, in delighted, anticipatory tones.

Mr. In and Mr. Out were meanwhile exchanging pleasantries concerning their future plans.

"We want liquor; we want breakfast. Neither without the other. One and indivisible."

"We want both 'em!"

"Both 'em!"

It was quite light now, and passers-by began to bend curious eyes on the pair. Obviously they were engaged in a discussion, which afforded each of them intense amusement, for occasionally a fit of laughter would seize upon them so violently that, still with their arms interlocked, they would bend nearly double.

Reaching the Commodore, they exchanged a few spicy epigrams with the sleepy-eyed doorman, navigated the revolving door with some difficulty, and then made their way through a thinly populated but startled lobby to the dining-room, where a puzzled waiter showed them an obscure table in a corner. They studied the bill of fare helplessly, telling over the items to each other in puzzled mumbles.

"Don't see any liquor here," said Peter reproachfully.

The waiter became audible but unintelligible.

"Repeat," continued Peter, with patient tolerance, "that there seems to be unexplained and quite distasteful lack of liquor upon bill of fare."

"Here!" said Dean confidently, "let me handle him." He turned to the waiter — "Bring us — bring us —" he scanned the bill of fare anxiously. "Bring us a quart of champagne and a — a — probably ham sandwich."

The waiter looked doubtful.

"Bring it!" roared Mr. In and Mr. Out in chorus.

The waiter coughed and disappeared. There was a short wait during which they were subjected without their knowledge to a careful scrutiny by the headwaiter. Then the champagne arrived, and at the sight of it Mr. In and Mr. Out became jubilant.

"Imagine their objecting to us having champagne for breakfast — jus' imagine."

They both concentrated upon the vision of such an awesome possibility, but the feat was too much for them. It was impossible for their joint imaginations to conjure up a world where any one might object to any one else having champagne for breakfast. The waiter drew the cork with an enormous *pop* — and their glasses immediately foamed with pale yellow froth.

"Here's health, Mr. In."

"Here's the same to you, Mr. Out."

The waiter withdrew; the minutes passed; the champagne became low in the bottle.

"It's — it's mortifying," said Dean suddenly.

"Wha's mortifying?"

"The idea their objecting us having champagne breakfast."

"Mortifying?" Peter considered. "Yes, tha's word — mortifying."

Again they collapsed into laughter, howled, swayed, rocked back and forth in their chairs, repeating the word "mortifying" over and over to each other — each repetition seeming to make it only more brilliantly absurd.

After a few more gorgeous minutes they decided on another quart. Their anxious waiter consulted his immediate superior, and this discreet person gave implicit instructions that no more champagne should be served. Their check was brought.

Five minutes later, arm in arm, they left the Commodore and made their way through a curious, staring crowd along Forty-second Street, and up Vanderbilt Avenue to the Biltmore. There, with sudden cunning, they rose to the occasion and traversed the lobby, walking fast and standing unnaturally erect.

Once in the dining-room they repeated their performance. They were torn between intermittent convulsive laughter and sudden spasmodic discussions of politics, college, and the sunny state of their dispositions. Their watches told them that it was now nine o'clock, and a dim idea was born in them that they were on a memorable party, something that they would remember always. They lingered over the second bottle. Either of them had only to mention the word "mortifying" to send them both into riotous gasps. The dining-room was whirring and shifting now; a curious lightness permeated and rarefied the heavy air.

They paid their check and walked out into the lobby.

It was at this moment that the exterior doors revolved for the thousandth time that morning, and admitted into the lobby a very pale young beauty with dark circles under her eyes, attired in a much-rumpled evening dress. She was accompanied by a plain stout man, obviously not an appropriate escort.

At the top of the stairs this couple encountered Mr. In and Mr. Out.

"Edith," began Mr. In, stepping toward her hilariously and making a sweeping bow, "darling, good morning."

The stout man glanced questioningly at Edith, as if merely asking her permission to throw this man summarily out of the way.

"'Scuse familiarity," added Peter, as an afterthought. "Edith, good-morning."

He seized Dean's elbow and impelled him into the foreground.

"Meet Mr. In, Edith, my bes' frien'. Inseparable. Mr. In and Mr. Out."

Mr. Out advanced and bowed; in fact, he advanced so far and bowed so low that he tipped slightly forward and only kept his balance by placing a hand lightly on Edith's shoulder.

"I'm Mr. Out, Edith," he mumbled pleasantly, "S'misterin Misterout."

"'Smisterinanout," said Peter proudly.

But Edith stared straight by them, her eyes fixed on some infinite speck in the gallery above her. She nodded slightly to the stout man, who advanced bull-like and with a sturdy brisk gesture pushed Mr. In and Mr. Out to either side. Through this alley he and Edith walked.

But ten paces farther on Edith stopped again — stopped and pointed to a short, dark soldier who was eyeing the crowd in general, and the tableau of Mr. In and Mr. Out in particular, with a sort of puzzled, spell-bound awe.

"There," cried Edith. "See there!"

Her voice rose, became somewhat shrill. Her pointing finger shook slightly.

"There's the soldier who broke my brother's leg."

There were a dozen exclamations; a man in a cutaway coat left his place near the desk and advanced alertly; the stout person made a sort of lightning-like spring toward the short, dark soldier, and then the lobby closed around the little group and blotted them from the sight of Mr. In and Mr. Out.

But to Mr. In and Mr. Out this event was merely a particolored iridescent segment of a whirring, spinning world.

They heard loud voices; they saw the stout man spring; the picture suddenly blurred.

Then they were in an elevator bound skyward.

"What floor, please?" said the elevator man.

"Any floor," said Mr. In.

"Top floor," said Mr. Out.

"This is the top floor," said the elevator man.

"Have another floor put on," said Mr. Out.

"Higher," said Mr. In.

"Heaven," said Mr. Out.

XI

In a bedroom of a small hotel just off Sixth Avenue Gordon Sterrett awoke with a pain in the back of his head and a sick throbbing in all his veins. He looked at the dusky gray shadows in the corners of the room and at a raw place on a large leather chair in the corner where it had long been in use. He saw clothes, dishevelled, rumpled clothes on the floor and he smelt stale cigarette smoke and stale liquor. The windows were tight shut. Outside the bright sunlight had thrown a dust-filled beam across the sill — a beam broken by the head of the wide wooden bed in which he had slept. He lay very quiet — comatose, drugged, his eyes wide, his mind clicking wildly like an unoiled machine.

5   It must have been thirty seconds after he perceived the sunbeam with the dust on it and the rip on the large leather chair that he had the sense of life close beside him, and it was another thirty seconds after that before he 10 realized he was irrevocably married to Jewel Hudson.

He went out half an hour later and bought a revolver at a sporting goods store. Then he took a taxi to the room where he had been living on 15 East Twenty-seventh Street, and, leaning across the table that held his drawing materials, fired a cartridge into his head just behind the temple.

Ernest Hemingway [1898–]

Spokesman of the disillusioned Lost Generation at the close of the first World War, yet with an enormous zest for life, Hemingway possessed a magical power and an infectious literary style.

He was born in the year of the Spanish-American war, at Oak Park, Illinois, son of a physician. As a boy and youth, he enjoyed hunting trips with his father in northern Michigan, boxed and played football in high school, and after graduation got a job as reporter for the Kansas City *Star*. Upon the entry of the United States into the war, he volunteered in an American ambulance unit, then served in an Italian combat unit, was severely wounded, and decorated by the Italian Government for valor. Back in America after the war, he married (the first of four wives) and returned to newspaper work. In 1920 he was in the Near East and Greece as correspondent for the Toronto *Star*, and became Paris correspondent for the Hearst papers. Thus Hemingway was schooled in the two things he cared most for: action and writing.

From reportorial journalism he turned to fiction writing, contributing short stories to *Transition*, *This Quarter*, the *Atlantic* and *Scribners*. In 1924 he brought out, in Paris, a collection of fifteen short stories, *In Our Time*, chiefly on themes arising from his Middle Western boyhood and youth, but also others concerned with the lives of such expatriates as he was associating with. The moral plight of postwar expatriates was likewise the theme of a novel, *The Sun Also Rises* (1926).

In 1927 he returned from Paris to his own country, bought a house in Key West, Florida, wrote *A Farewell to Arms* (1929), generally regarded as the best of his own novels and the best of all the novels arising from the first World War. It was followed by a book on the art of bullfighting, *Death in the Afternoon*. In 1936 he went as a writer to Spain, then in its civil war, the setting of his play *The Fifth Column* and of the most popular of his novels, *For Whom the Bell Tolls* (1940), which Paramount

Pictures bought for $150,000. Of his later writings the most warmly received was *The Old Man and the Sea*, a long short story. He made expeditions to China and Africa, and during the years at Key West acquired his reputation as a redoubtable fisherman, big-game hunter, boxer, and sportsman in general. He finally settled in Cuba.

Hemingway wrote his books as if asking, "What is possible for us after the war?" Not the values of civilization as they had been conceived, not the "idealism" which had prettified literature. At least there could be a frank intensity of living. Easily available were the physical satisfactions of the Lost Generation, drinking and sex. But love — as in *A Farewell to Arms* — could be a vastly greater experience. And the life of action which he celebrated was full of goods, such as honesty, courage, skill, endurance, most readily revealed in violence and death. Such goods are basic, the values of primitivism, and indeed Hemingway well illustrates the passion of modern art in many fields to seek to renew its strength by descending to the primitive and trying to build up, once more, differently from the old way. In later books — e.g. *For Whom the Bell Tolls* — Hemingway made affirmations more explicitly and in new directions — the values of democracy, the responsibility of the individual. And always, in his own practice as a writer, he assumed the values of artistic integrity. Aesthetic values, like moral, must be candid ("no faking"). His most admired fiction is stripped clean, with no commentary by the author and no self-analysis by the characters. He simply tells us what was said and done, leaving the rest to implication.

Hence, too, his famous style. He wanted the clearness, the cleanness, of a style unmuddied by vague abstractions and pompous complexity. The syntax of his sentences must be elementally plain, a procession of simple and compound sentences, stringing *and* clauses one after another as a child does (but a very artful child). When he did use complex sentences he commonly placed the subordinate after the main clause. He defied the rhetoric books and the tradition on which they are based; in style, as in many other things, we should go back to the primitively natural and build upon that. In short, the art of the writer will be much like that of the bullfighter: Pedro Romero, in *The Sun Also Rises*, "never made any contortions, always it was straight and pure and natural in line."

Further reading: *Men Without Women. A Farewell to Arms.* Carlos Baker, *Hemingway: The Writer as Artist*, 1952. Philip Young, *Ernest Hemingway*, 1952.

A
Clean, Well-Lighted Place

(1933)

It was late and every one had left the café except an old man who sat in the shadow the leaves of the tree made against the electric light. In the day time the street was dusty, but at night the dew settled the dust and the old man liked to sit late because he was deaf and now at night it was quiet and he felt the difference. The two waiters inside the café knew that the old man was a little drunk, and while he was a good client they knew that if he became too drunk he would leave without paying, so they kept watch on him.

"Last week he tried to commit suicide," one waiter said.

"Why?"

"He was in despair."

"What about?"

"Nothing."

"How do you know it was nothing?"

"He has plenty of money."

They sat together at a table that was close against the wall near the door of the café and looked at the terrace where the tables were all empty except where the old man sat in the shadow of the leaves of the tree that moved slightly in the wind. A girl and a soldier went by in the street. The street light shone on the brass number on his collar. The girl wore no head covering and hurried beside him.

"The guard will pick him up," one waiter said.

"What does it matter if he gets what he's after?"

"He had better get off the street now. The guard will get him. They went by five minutes ago."

The old man sitting in the shadow rapped on his saucer with his glass. The younger waiter went over to him.

"What do you want?"

The old man looked at him. "Another brandy," he said.

"You'll be drunk," the waiter said. The old man looked at him. The waiter went away.

"He'll stay all night," he said to his colleague. "I'm sleepy now. I never get into bed before three o'clock. He should have killed himself last week."

The waiter took the brandy bottle and another saucer from the counter inside the café and marched out to the old man's table. He put down the saucer and poured the glass full of brandy.

"You should have killed yourself last week," he said to the deaf man. The old man motioned with his finger. "A little more," he said. The waiter poured on into the glass so that the brandy slopped over and ran down the stem into the top saucer of the pile. "Thank you," the old man said. The waiter took the bottle back inside the café. He sat down at the table with his colleague again.

"He's drunk now," he said.

"He's drunk every night."

"What did he want to kill himself for?"

"How should I know."

"How did he do it?"

"He hung himself with a rope."

"Who cut him down?"

"His niece."

"Why did they do it?"

"Fear for his soul."

"How much money has he got?"

"He's got plenty."

"He must be eighty years old."

"Anyway I should say he was eighty."

"I wish he would go home. I never get to bed before three o'clock. What kind of hour is that to go to bed?"

"He stays up because he likes it."

"He's lonely. I'm not lonely. I have a wife waiting in bed for me."

"He had a wife once too."

"A wife would be no good to him now."

"You can't tell. He might be better with a wife."

"His niece looks after him."

"I know. You said she cut him down."

"I wouldn't want to be that old. An old man is a nasty thing."

"Not always. This old man is clean. He drinks without spilling. Even now, drunk. Look at him."

"I don't want to look at him. I wish he would go home. He has no regard for those who must work."

The old man looked from his glass across the square, then over at the waiters.

"Another brandy," he said, pointing to his glass. The waiter who was in a hurry came over.

"Finished," he said, speaking with that omission of syntax stupid people employ when talking to drunken people or foreigners. "No more tonight. Close now."

"Another," said the old man.

"No. Finished." The waiter wiped the edge of the table with a towel and shook his head.

The old man stood up, slowly counted the saucers, took a leather coin purse from his pocket and paid for the drinks, leaving half a peseta tip.

The waiter watched him go down the street, a very old man walking unsteadily but with dignity.

"Why didn't you let him stay and drink?" the unhurried waiter asked. They were putting up the shutters. "It is not half-past two."

"I want to go home to bed."

"What is an hour?"

"More to me than to him."

"An hour is the same."

"You talk like an old man yourself. He can buy a bottle and drink at home."

"It's not the same."

"No, it is not," agreed the waiter with a wife. He did not wish to be unjust. He was only in a hurry.

"And you? You have no fear of going home before your usual hour?"

"Are you trying to insult me?"

"No, hombre, only to make a joke."

"No," the waiter who was in a hurry said, rising from pulling down the metal shutters. "I have confidence. I am all confidence."

"You have youth, confidence, and a job," the older waiter said. "You have everything."

"And what do you lack?"

"Everything but work."

"You have everything I have."

"No. I have never had confidence and I am not young."

"Come on. Stop talking nonsense and lock up."

"I am of those who like to stay late at the café," the older waiter said. "With all those who do not want to go to bed. With all those who need a light for the night."

"I want to go home and into bed."

"We are of two different kinds," the older waiter said. He was now dressed to go home. "It is not only a question of youth and confidence although those things are very beautiful. Each night I am reluctant to close up because there may be some one who needs the café."

"Hombre, there are bodegas open all night long."

"You do not understand. This is a clean and pleasant café. It is well lighted. The light is very good and also, now, there are shadows of the leaves."

"Good night," said the younger waiter.

"Good night," the other said. Turning off the electric light he continued the conversation with himself. It is the light of course but it is necessary that the place be clean and pleasant. You do not want music. Certainly you do not want music. Nor can you stand before a bar with dignity although that is all that is provided for these hours. What did he fear? It was not fear or dread. It was a nothing that he knew too well. It was all a nothing and a man was noth-

ing too. It was only that and light was all it needed and a certain cleanness and order. Some lived in it and never felt it but he knew it all was nada y pues nada y nada y pues nada.[1] Our nada who art in nada, nada be thy name thy kingdom nada thy will be nada in nada as it is in nada. Give us this nada our daily nada and nada us our nada as we nada our nadas and nada us not into nada but deliver us from nada; pues nada. Hail nothing full of nothing, nothing is with thee. He smiled and stood before a bar with a shining steam pressure coffee machine.

"What's yours?" asked the barman.

"Nada."

"Otro loco mas," [2] said the barman and turned away.

"A little cup," said the waiter.

The barman poured it for him.

"The light is very bright and pleasant but the bar is unpolished," the waiter said.

The barman looked at him but did not answer. It was too late at night for conversation.

"You want another copita?" the barman asked.

"No, thank you," said the waiter and went out. He disliked bars and bodegas. A clean, well-lighted café was a very different thing. Now, without thinking further, he would go home to his room. He would lie in the bed and finally, with daylight, he would go to sleep. After all, he said to himself, it is probably only insomnia. Many must have it.

[1] Nothing, nothing at all.
[2] Another crazy one.

Thomas Wolfe [1900–1938]

Thomas Wolfe was born and brought up in Asheville, North Carolina. His father was a stone-cutter with a passion for Shakespearean rhetoric, his mother a shrewd business woman who dealt in real-estate and managed a boarding house. His early years are described in thinly disguised autobiography in the lives of Oliver and Eliza Gant, the parents of Eugene, in *Look Homeward, Angel.* The novel also deals with his life at the University of North Carolina which he attended from 1916 to 1920, editing the college paper and magazine, writing three plays, and acting with the famous Carolina Players. At Harvard (A.M., 1922) he studied playwriting in the famous "English 47 Workshop" of George Pierce Baker, but his dramatic career produced no original work. Instead, he turned to teaching and the writing of fiction. From 1924 to 1930 he taught

English at New York University, traveled, and wrote prodigiously, pouring his own experience into the passionate and poetic prose for which he has become famous.

Everything about Wolfe was of the grand scale. He was 6′ 6″ in height, weighed 200 pounds, and had a gargantuan appetite for all kinds of life and knowledge. His books were inordinately long and written in furious spurts of composition, and he left them in states of chaotic organization which required the careful and devoted editing of Maxwell Perkins of Scribner's to bring them into marketable shape. His insatiably romantic temperament, his love for the swollen rhetoric of the English classics, his Wagnerian self-dramatization, romantic egoism, lack of discipline, and unquestioned genius produced material enough for ten ordinary-sized novels. After *Look Homeward, Angel* (1929) struck literary America with force enough to elicit extremes of critical praise and abuse, he published in 1935 a sequel entitled *Of Time and the River*. His work was compared to that of Melville and Whitman, both as to its torrential recollection and its lack of disciplined form.

Wolfe's travel in Europe, especially the Germany of the early Hitler days, provided material for two further novels, both published after his early death, *The Web and the Rock* (1939) and *You Can't Go Home Again* (1940). A third posthumous novel, *The Hills Beyond* (1941), a collection of short stories, *From Death to Morning* (1935), and a long critical essay defending himself from unfavorable critical appraisal, *The Story of a Novel* (1936), complete the record of his major work.

Wolfe never belonged to the economic-naturalist school of writers of the 1930's, but found his true ancestry in the earlier pattern of the archetypal romantic individualist whose quest is self-understanding rather than social justice. The central theme of his work may be described as the search for an image of wisdom and fulfillment, external to his own hunger and need, to which he could ally himself.

Further reading: *Look Homeward, Angel*, 1929. *Of Time and the River*, 1935. Edward C. Aswell, "A Note on Thomas Wolfe," in *The Hills Beyond*, 1941. *The Letters of Thomas Wolfe*, ed. Elizabeth Nowell, 1956.

From You Can't Go Home Again
Enter Mr. Lloyd McHarg

This passage from *You Can't Go Home Again* is a skillful portrayal of Sinclair Lewis (Lloyd McHarg). Lewis was an important influence upon Wolfe's writing, helping to turn his style from the poetic exuberances of his early work to a more dramatic and satiric maturity. The passage describes the first meeting of the older writer and the younger in London.

During the late autumn and early winter of that year occurred an event which added to Webber's chronicle the adventure of an extraordinary experience. He had received no news from America for several weeks when, suddenly in November, he began to get excited letters from his friends, informing him of a recent incident that bore directly on his own career.

The American novelist, Mr. Lloyd McHarg, had just published a new book which had been instantly and universally acclaimed as a monument of national significance, as well as the crowning achievement in McHarg's brilliant literary career. George had read in the English press brief accounts of the book's tremendous success, but now he began to receive enlargements on the news from his friends at home. Mr. McHarg, it seemed, had given an interview to reporters, and to the astonishment of everyone had begun to talk, not about his own book, but about Webber's. Cuttings of the interview were sent to George. He read them with astonishment, and with the deepest and most earnest gratitude.

George had never met Mr. Lloyd McHarg. He had never had occasion to communicate with him in any way. He knew him only through his books. He was, of course, one of the chief figures in American letters, and now, at the zenith of his career, when he had won the greatest ovation one could win, he had seized the occasion, which most men would have employed for purposes of self-congratulation, to praise enthusiastically the work of an obscure young writer who was a total stranger to him and who had written only one book.

It seemed to George then, as it seemed to him ever afterwards, one of the most generous acts he had ever known, and when he had somewhat recovered from the astonishment and joy which this unexpected news had produced in him, he sat down and wrote to Mr. McHarg and told him how he felt. In a short time he had an answer from him — a brief note, written from New York. Mr. McHarg said that he had spoken as he had because he felt that way about Webber's book, and that he was happy to have had the opportunity of giving public acknowledgement to his feeling. He said that he was about to be awarded an honorary degree by one of America's leading universities — an event which, he confessed with pardonable pride, pleased him all the more because the award was to be made out of season, in special recognition of his last book, and because the ceremony attending it was not to be part of the usual performance of trained seals at commencement time. He said that he was sailing for Europe immediately afterwards and would spend some time on the Continent, that he would be in England a little later, and that he hoped to see Webber then. George wrote back and told him he was looking forward to their meeting, gave him his address, and there for a time the matter rested.***

After that they waited daily for McHarg's coming. Week lengthened into week. They searched the papers every morning for news of him. He seemed to be making a tour of Europe, and everywhere he went he was entertained and fêted and interviewed and photographed in the company of other famous men. Now he was in Copenhagen. Now he was staying in Berlin a week or two. Later he had gone to Baden-Baden for a cure.

* * * *

There were three men in the room, but so astonishing was the sight of McHarg that at first George did not notice the other two. McHarg was standing in the middle of the floor with a glass in one hand and a bottle of Scotch whiskey in the other, preparing to pour himself a drink. When he saw George he looked up quickly, put the bottle down, and advanced with his hand extended in greeting. There was something almost terrifying in his appearance. George recognized him instantly. He had seen McHarg's pictures many times, but he now realized how beautifully unrevealing are the uses of photography. He was fantastically ugly, and to this ugliness was added a devastation of which George had never seen the equal.

The first and most violent impression was his astonishing redness. Everything about him was red — hair, large protuberant ears, eyebrows, eyelids, even his bony, freckled, knuckly hands. (As George noticed the hands he understood why everyone who knew him called him "Knuckles.") Moreover, it was a most alarming redness. His face was so red that it seemed to throw off heat, and if at that moment smoke had begun to issue from his nostrils and he had burst out in flames all over, George would hardly have been surprised.

His face did not have that fleshy and high-colored floridity that is often seen in men who have drunk too long and too earnestly. It was not like that at all. McHarg was thin to the point of emaciation. He was very tall, six feet two or three, and his excessive thinness and angularity made him seem even taller. George thought he looked ill and wasted. His face, which was naturally a wry, puckish sort of face — as one got to know it better, a pugnacious but very attractive kind of face, full of truculence, but also with an impish humor and a homely, Yankee, freckled kind of modesty that were wonderfully engaging — this face now looked as puckered up as if it were permanently about to swallow a half-green persimmon, and it also seemed to be all dried out and blistered by the fiery flames that burned in it. And out of this face peered two of the most remarkable-looking eyes in all the world. Their color must originally have been light blue, but now they were so bleached and faded that they looked as if they had been poached.

He came toward George quickly, with his bony, knuckled hand extended in greeting, his lips twitching and bared nervously over his large teeth, his face turned wryly upward and to one side in an expression that was at once truculent, nervously apprehensive, and yet movingly eloquent of something fiercely and permanently wounded, something dreadfully lacerated, something so tender and unarmed in the soul and spirit of the man that life had got in on him at a thousand points and slashed him to ribbons. He took George's hand and shook it vigorously, at the same time bristling up to him with his wry and puckered face like a small boy to another before the fight begins, as if to say: "Go on, now, go on. Knock that chip off my shoulder. I dare and double-dare you." This was precisely his manner now, except that he said:

"Why you — why you monkeyfied — why you monkeyfied bastard, you! Just look at him!" he cried suddenly in a high-pitched voice, half turning to his companions. "Why you — who the hell ever told you you could write, anyway?" Then cordially: "George, how are you? Come on in, come on over here!"

And, still holding Webber's hand in his bony grip, and taking his arm with his other hand, he led him across the room toward his other guests. Then, suddenly releasing him, and striking a pompous oratorical attitude, he began to declaim in the florid accents of an after-dinner speaker:

"Ladies and gentlemen, it is my peculiar privilege, and I may even say my distinguished honor, to present to the members of the Hog Head Hollow Ladies Leeterary, Arteestic, and Mutual Culshural Society our esteemed guest of honor — a man who writes books that are so God-damned long that few people can even pick 'em up. A man whose leeterary style is distinguished by such a command of beautiful English as she is wrote that he has rarely been known to use less than twenty-one adjectives where four would do."

He changed abruptly, dropped his oratorical attitude, and laughed a sudden, nervous, dry, falsetto laugh, at the same time mauling Webber in the ribs with a bony finger. "How do you like that, George?" he said with immediate friendly warmth. "Does that get 'em? Is that the way they do it? Not bad, eh?" He was obviously pleased with his effort.

"George," he now continued in a natural tone of voice, "I want you to meet two friends of mine. Mr. Bendien, of Amsterdam," he said, presenting Webber to a heavy-set, red-faced, elderly Dutchman, who sat by the table within easy reaching distance of a tall brown crock of Holland gin, of which, to judge from his complexion, he had already consumed a considerable quantity.

"Ladies and gentlemen," cried McHarg, striking another attitude, "allow me to introduce that stupendous, that death-defying, that thrill-packed wonder of the ages, that hair-raising and spine-tingling act which has thrilled most of the crowned heads of Europe and all of the dead-heads of Amsterdam. Now appearing absolutely for the first time under the big tent. Ladies and gentlemen, I now take pleasure in introducing Mynheer Cornelius Bendien, the Dutch maestro, who will perform for you his celebrated act of balancing an eel on the end of his nose while he swallows in rapid succession, without pausing for breath, three — count 'em — three brown jugs of the finest imported Holland gin. Mr. Bendien, Mr. Webber. . . . How was that, boy, how was that?" said McHarg, laughing his shrill falsetto, and turning and prodding Webber again with an eager finger.

Then, somewhat more curtly, he said: "You may have met Mr. Donald Stoat before. He tells me that he knows you."

The other man looked out from underneath his heavy eyebrows and inclined his head pompously. "I believe," he said, "I have had the honor of Mr. Webber's acquaintance."

George remembered him, although he had seen him only once or twice, and that some years before. Mr. Stoat was not the kind of man one easily forgets.

It was plain to see that McHarg was on edge, terribly nervous, and also irritated by Stoat's presence. He turned away abruptly, muttering: "Too — too — too much — too much." And then, wheeling about suddenly: "All right, George. Have a drink. What's it going to be?"

"My own experience," said Mr. Stoat with unctuous pomposity, "is that the best drink in the morning —" he leered significantly with his bushy eyebrows — "a gentleman's drink, if I may say so — is a glawss of dry sherry." He had a "glawss" of this beverage in his hand at the moment, and, lifting it with an air of delicate connoisseurship, at the same time working his eyebrows appraisingly, he sniffed it — an action which seemed to irritate McHarg no end. "Allow me," continued Mr. Stoat, with rotund deliberation, "to recommend it to your consideration."

McHarg began to pace rapidly up and down. "Too much — too much," he muttered. "All right, George," he said irritably, "what'll you have to drink — Scotch?"

Mynheer Bendien put in his oar at this point. Holding up his glass and leaning forward with a hand on one fat knee, he said with guttural solemnity: "You should trink chin. Vy don't you try a trink of Holland chin?"

This advice also seemed to annoy Mr. Mc-Harg. He glared at Bendien with his flaming face, then, throwing up his bony hands with a quick, spasmodic movement, he cried, "Oh, for God's sake!" He turned and began to pace up and down again, muttering: "Too much — too much — too — too — too much." Then abruptly, in a voice shrill with irritation: "Let him drink what he wants, for Christ's sake! Go ahead, Georgie," he said roughly. "Drink what you like. Pour yourself some Scotch." And suddenly turning to Webber, his whole face lighting up with an impish smile, his lips flickering nervously above his teeth: "Isn't it wonderful, Georgie? Isn't it marvelous? K-k-k-k-k —" prodding Webber in the ribs with bony forefinger, and laughing a high, dry, feverish laugh — "Can you beat it?"

"I confess," said Mr. Donald Stoat at this point, with rotund unction, "that I have not read our young friend's opus, which, I believe —" unction here deepening visibly into rotund sarcasm — "which, I believe, has been hailed by certain of our cognoscenti as a masterpiece. After all, there are so many masterpieces now-adays, aren't there? Scarcely a week goes by but what I pick up my copy of *The Times* — I refer, of course, to *The Times* of London, as distinguished from its younger and somewhat more immature colleague, *The New York Times* — to find that another of our young men has enriched English literature with another masterpiece of im—per—ish—able prose."

All this was uttered in ponderous periods with leerings and twitchings of those misplaced mustaches that served the gentleman for eyebrows. McHarg was obviously becoming more and more annoyed, and kept pacing up and down, muttering to himself. Mr. Stoat, however, was too obtuse by nature, and too entranced by the rolling cadences of his own rhetoric, to observe the warning signals. After leering significantly with his eyebrows again, he went on:

"I can only hope, however, that our young friend here is a not too enthusiastic devotee of the masters of what I shall call The School of Bad Taste."

"What are you talking about?" said McHarg, pausing suddenly, half turning, and glaring fiercely. "I suppose you mean Hugh Walpole, and John Galsworthy, and other dangerous radicals of that sort, eh?"

"No, sir," said Mr. Stoat deliberately. "I was not thinking of them. I was referring to that concocter of incoherent nonsense, that purveyor of filth, that master of obscenity, who wrote that book so few people can read, and no one can understand, but which some of our young men are hailing enthusiastically as the greatest masterpiece of the century."

"What book are you talking about anyway?" McHarg said irritably.

"Its name, I believe," said Mr. Stoat pompously, "is *Ulysses*. Its author, I have heard, is an Irishman."

"Oh," cried McHarg with an air of enlightenment, and with an impish gleam in his eye that was quite lost on Mr. Stoat. "You're speaking of George Moore, aren't you?"

"That's it! That's it!" cried Mr. Stoat quickly, nodding his head with satisfaction. He was getting excited now. His eyebrows twitched more rapidly than ever. "That's the fellow! And the book —" he sputtered — "pah!" He spat out the word as though it had been brought up by an emetic, and screwed his eyebrows around across his domy forehead in an expression of nausea. "I tried to read a few pages of it once," he whispered sonorously and dramatically, "but I let it fall. I let it fall. As though I had touched a tainted thing, I let it fall. And then," he said hoarsely, "I washed my hands, with a very — strong — soap."

"My dear sir," cried McHarg suddenly, with an air of sincere conviction, at the same time being unable to keep his eye from gleaming more impishly than ever, "you are absolutely right. I absolutely agree with you."

Mr. Stoat, who had been very much on his dignity up to now, thawed visibly under the seducing cajolery of this unexpected confirmation of his literary judgment.

"You are positively and unanswerably correct," said Knuckles, now standing in the middle of the room with his long legs spread wide apart, his bony hands hanging to the lapels of his coat. "You have hit the nail right smack — dead — square on the top of its head." As he uttered these words, he jerked his wry face from side to side to give them added emphasis. "There has never been a dirtier — filthier — more putrid — and more corrupt writer than George Moore. And as for that book of his, *Ulysses*," McHarg shouted, "that is unquestionably the vilest ——"

"— the rottenest —" shouted Mr. Stoat ——

"— the most obscene —" shrilled McHarg —

"— the most vicious —" panted Mr. Stoat

"— unadulterated ——"

"— piece of tripe —" choked Mr. Stoat with rapturous agreement ——

"— that has ever polluted the pages, defiled the name, and besmirched the record ——"

"— of English literature!" gasped Mr. Stoat happily, and paused, panting for breath. "Yes," he went on when he had recovered his power of speech, "and that other thing — that play of his — that rotten, vile, vicious, so-called tragedy in five acts — what was the name of that thing, anyway?"

"Oh," cried McHarg with an air of sudden recognition — "you mean *The Importance of Being Earnest*, don't you?"

"No, no," said Mr. Stoat impatiently. "Not that one. This one came later on."

"Oh yes!" McHarg exclaimed, as if it had suddenly come to him. "You're speaking of *Mrs. Warren's Profession*, aren't you?"

"That's it, that's it!" cried Mr. Stoat. "I took my wife to see it — I took my *wife* — my *own* wife ——"

"His *own* wife!" McHarg repeated, as if astounded. "Well I'll be God-damned," he said. "What do you know about that!"

"And would you believe it, sir?" Mr. Stoat's voice again sank to a whisper of loathing and revulsion, and his eyebrows worked ominously about his face. "I was so ashamed — I was *so ashamed* — that I could not look at her. We got up and left, sir, before the end of the first act — before anyone could see us. I went away with head bowed, as one who had been forced to take part in some nasty thing."

"Well what do you know about that?" said McHarg sympathetically. "Wasn't that just too damned bad? *I call it perfectly damned awful!*" he shouted suddenly, and turned away, his jaw muscles working convulsively as he muttered again, "Too much — too much." He halted abruptly in front of Webber with his puckered face aflame and his lips twitching nervously, and began to prod him in the ribs, laughing his high, falsetto laugh. "He's a publisher," he squeaked. "He publishes books. K-k-k-k-k — Can you beat it, Georgie?" he squeaked almost inaudibly. Then, jerking a bony thumb in the direction of the astonished Stoat, he shrieked: "In the name of Christ Almighty — a *publisher!*" — and resumed his infuriated pacing of the room.

[What Is Man?]

🙌 In his poetic and romantic vein, Wolfe sought to emulate the purple rhetoric of the English classics. Here he mingles the tone of contemporary disillusion with rhythmic prose in a final affirmation about man. The passage, modeled after the Seven Ages of Man in *As You Like It*, is from *You Can't Go Home Again*.

If George Webber had never gone beyond the limits of the neighborhood in which he lived, the whole chronicle of the earth would have been there for him just the same. South Brooklyn was a universe.

The people in the houses all around him, whose lives in the cold, raw days of winter always seemed hermetic, sterile, and remote, as shut out from him as though they were something sealed up in a tin, became in spring and summer so real to him it seemed that he had known them from his birth. For, as the days and nights grew warmer, everybody kept their windows open, and all the dwellers in these houses conducted their most intimate affairs in loud and raucous voices which carried to the street and made the casual passer-by a confidant of every family secret.

God knows he saw squalor and filth and misery and despair enough, violence and cruelty and hate enough, to crust his lips forever with the hard and acrid taste of desolation. He found a sinister and demented Italian grocer whose thin mouth writhed in a servile smile as he cringed before his customers, and the next moment was twisted in a savage snarl as he dug his clawlike fingers into the arm of his wretched little son. And on Saturdays the Irishmen would come home drunk, and then would beat their wives and cut one another's throats, and the whole course and progress of their murderous rages would be published nakedly from their open windows with laugh, shout, scream, and curse.

But he found beauty in South Brooklyn, too. There was a tree that leaned over into the narrow alley where he lived, and George could stand at his basement window and look up at it and watch it day by day as it came into its moment's glory of young and magic green. And then toward sunset, if he was tired, he could lie down to rest a while upon his iron bed and listen to the dying birdsong in the tree. Thus, each spring, in that one tree, he found all April and the earth. He also found devotion, love, and wisdom in a shabby little Jewish tailor and his wife, whose dirty children were always tumbling in and out of the dingy suffocation of his shop.

In the infinite variety of such common, accidental, oft-unheeded things one can see the web of life as it is spun. Whether we wake at morning in the city, or lie at night in darkness in the country towns, or walk the streets of furious noon in all the dusty, homely, and enduring lights of present time, the universe around us is the same. Evil lives forever — so does good. Man alone has knowledge of these two, and he is such a little thing.

For what is man?

First, a child, soft-boned, unable to support itself on its rubbery legs, befouled with its excrement, that howls and laughs by turns, cries for the moon but hushes when it gets its mother's teat; a sleeper, eater, guzzler, howler, laugher, idiot, and a chewer of its toe; a little tender thing all blubbered with its spit, a reacher into fires, a beloved fool.

After that, a boy, hoarse and loud before his companions, but afraid of the dark; will beat the weaker and avoid the stronger; worships strength and savagery, loves tales of war and murder, and violence done to others; joins gangs and hates to be alone; makes heroes out of soldiers, sailors, prize fighters, football players, cowboys, gunmen, and detectives; would rather die than not out-try and out-dare his companions, wants to beat them and always to win, shows his muscle and demands that it be felt, boasts of his victories and will never own defeat.

Then the youth: goes after girls, is foul behind their backs among the drugstore boys, hints at a hundred seductions, but gets pimples on his face; begins to think about his clothes, becomes a fop, greases his hair, smokes cigarettes with a dissipated air, reads novels, and writes poetry on the sly. He sees the world now as a pair of legs and breasts; he knows hate, love, and jealousy; he is cowardly and foolish, he cannot endure to be alone; he lives in a crowd, thinks with the crowd, is afraid to be marked off from his fellows by an eccentricity. He joins clubs and is afraid of ridicule; he is bored and unhappy and wretched most of the time. There is a great cavity in him, he is dull.

Then the man: he is busy, he is full of plans and reasons, he has work. He gets children, buys and sells small packets of everlasting earth, intrigues against his rivals, is exultant when he cheats them. He wastes his little three score years and ten in spendthrift and inglorious liv-ing; from his cradle to his grave he scarcely sees the sun or moon or stars; he is unconscious of the immortal sea and earth; he talks of the future and he wastes it as it comes. If he is lucky, he saves money. At the end his fat purse buys him flunkeys to carry him where his shanks no longer can; he consumes rich food and golden wine that his wretched stomach has no hunger for; his weary and lifeless eyes look out upon the scenery of strange lands for which in youth his heart was panting. Then the slow death, prolonged by costly doctors, and finally the graduate undertakers, the perfumed carrion, the suave ushers with palms outspread to leftwards, the fast motor hearses, and the earth again.

This is man: a writer of books, a putter-down of words, a painter of pictures, a maker of ten thousand philosophies. He grows passionate over ideas, he hurls scorn and mockery at another's work, he finds the one way, the true way, for himself, and calls all others false — yet in the billion books upon the shelves there is not one that can tell him how to draw a single fleeting breath in peace and comfort. He makes histories of the universe, he directs the destiny of nations, but he does not know his own history, and he cannot direct his own destiny with dignity or wisdom for ten consecutive minutes.

This is man: for the most part a foul, wretched, abominable creature, a packet of decay, a bundle of degenerating tissues, a creature that gets old and hairless and has a foul breath, a hater of his kind, a cheater, a scorner, a mocker, a reviler, a thing that kills and murders in a mob or in the dark, loud and full of brag surrounded by his fellows, but without the courage of a rat alone. He will cringe for a coin, and show his snarling fangs behind the giver's back; he will cheat for two sous, and kill for forty dollars, and weep copiously in court to keep another scoundrel out of jail.

This is man, who will steal his friend's woman, feel the leg of his host's wife below the table cloth, dump fortunes on his whores, bow down in worship before charlatans, and let his poets die. This is man, who swears he will live only for beauty, for art, for the spirit, but will live only for fashion, and will change his faith and his convictions as soon as fashion changes. This is man, the great warrior with the flaccid gut, the great romantic with the barren loins, the eternal knave devouring the eternal fool, the most glorious of all the animals, who uses his brain for the most part to make himself a stench in the nostrils of the Bull, the Fox, the Dog, the Tiger, and the Goat.

Yet, this is man, and it is impossible to say the worst of him, for the record of his obscene existence, his baseness, lust, cruelty, and treachery, is illimitable. His life is also full of toil, tumult, and suffering. His days are mainly composed of a million idiot repetitions — in goings and comings along hot streets, in sweatings and freezings, in the senseless accumulation of fruitless tasks, in decaying and being patched, in grinding out his life so that he may buy bad food, in eating bad food so that he may grind his life out in distressful defecations. He is the dweller in that ruined tenement who, from one moment's breathing to another, can hardly forget the bitter weight of his uneasy flesh, the thousand diseases and distresses of his body, the growing incubus of his corruption. This is man, who, if he can remember ten golden moments of joy and happiness out of all his years, ten moments unmarked by care, unseamed by aches or itches, has power to lift himself with his expiring breath and say: "I have lived upon this earth and known glory!"

This is man, and one wonders why he wants to live at all. A third of his life is lost and deadened under sleep; another third is given to a sterile labor; a sixth is spent in all his goings and his comings, in the moil and shuffle of the streets, in thrusting, shoving, pawing. How much of him is left, then, for a vision of the tragic stars? How much of him is left to look upon the everlasting earth? How much of him is left for glory and the making of great songs? A few snatched moments only from the barren glut and suck of living.

Here, then, is man, this moth of time, this dupe of brevity and numbered hours, this travesty of waste and sterile breath. Yet if the gods could come here to a desolate, deserted earth where only the ruin of man's cities remained, where only a few marks and carvings of his hand were legible upon his broken tablets, where only a wheel lay rusting in the desert sand, a cry would burst out of their hearts and they would say: "He lived, and he was here!"

Behold his works:

He needed speech to ask for bread — and he had Christ! He needed songs to sing in battle — and he had Homer! He needed words to curse his enemies — and he had Dante, he had Voltaire, he had Swift! He needed cloth to cover up his hairless, puny flesh against the seasons — and he wove the robes of Solomon, he made the garments of great kings, he made the samite for the young knights! He needed walls and a roof to shelter him — and he made Blois! He needed a temple to propitiate his God — and he made Chartres and Fountains Abbey! He was born to creep upon the earth — and he made great wheels, he sent great engines thundering down the rails, he launched great wings into the air, he put great ships upon the angry sea!

Plagues wasted him, and cruel wars destroyed his strongest sons, but fire, flood, and famine could not quench him. No, nor the inexorable grave — his sons leaped shouting from his dying loins. The shaggy bison with his thews of thunder died upon the plains; the fabled mammoths of the unrecorded ages are vast scaffoldings of dry, insensate loam; the panthers have learned caution and move carefully among tall grasses to the water hole; and man lives on amid the senseless nihilism of the universe.

For there is one belief, one faith, that is man's glory, his triumph, his immortality — and that is his belief in life. Man loves life, and, loving life, hates death, and because of this he is great, he is glorious, he is beautiful, and his beauty is everlasting. He lives below the senseless stars and writes his meanings in them. He lives in fear, in toil, in agony, and in unending tumult, but if the blood foamed bubbling from his wounded lungs at every breath he drew, he would still love life more dearly than an end of breathing. Dying, his eyes burn beautifully, and the old hunger shines more fiercely in them — he has endured all the hard and purposeless suffering, and still he wants to live.

Thus it is impossible to scorn this creature. For out of his strong belief in life, this puny man made love. At his best, he *is* love. Without him there can be no love, no hunger, no desire.

So this is man — the worst and best of him — this frail and petty thing who lives his day and dies like all the other animals, and is forgotten. And yet, he is immortal, too, for both the good and evil that he does live after him. Why, then, should any living man ally himself with death, and, in his greed and blindness, batten on his brother's blood?

Katherine Anne Porter [1890–   ]

Great-great-great-granddaughter of Daniel Boone's brother, Miss Porter was born at Indian Creek, Texas, and educated in small convent schools in Texas and Louisiana. "As soon as I learned," she says, "to form letters on paper, at about three years, I began to write stories, and this has been the basic and absorbing occupation, the intact line of my life which directs my actions, determines my point of view, and profoundly affects my character and personality, my social beliefs and economic status, and the kind of friendships I form." Miss Porter grew up in literary isolation, having no contact with literary centers or with writers. Up to her twenty-fifth year, she read "a grand sweep of all English and translated classics from the beginning up to about 1800"; after that immersion in tradition she went on to the moderns. Till she was thirty she did not attempt to publish. She was in Mexico during the revolution, and has lived in Europe, in New York, in California.

Miss Porter built a solid reputation on a small published output. *Flowering Judas*, 1930, when it appeared in 1935 as *Flowering Judas and Other Stories*, established her as one of America's finest short-story writers. Other collections of stories followed: *Hacienda*, 1934; *Pale Horse, Pale Rider* (three short novels), 1939; *The Leaning Tower and Other Stories*, 1944; and a novel, *Ship of Fools*, 1960.

Through high standards and hard discipline her art became pure and strong, subtle and delicate, a fit vehicle for her penetrating understanding of human values. In all her stories, says Robert Penn Warren, there is "the same underlying structure of contrast and tension, the same paradoxical problems of definition, the same delicate balancing of rival considerations, the same scrupulous development of competing claims to attention and action, the same interplay of the humorous and the serious, the same refusal to take the straight line, the formula, through the matter at hand."

Further reading: *Pale Horse, Pale Rider*. R. P. Warren, "Katherine Anne Porter: Irony with a Center," *Kenyon Review*, Winter 1942.

María Concepción

(1930)

María Concepción walked carefully, keeping to the middle of the white dusty road, where the maguey thorns and the treacherous curved spines of organ cactus had not gathered so profusely. She would have enjoyed resting for a moment in the dark shade by the roadside, but she had no time to waste drawing cactus needles from her feet. Juan and his chief would be waiting for their food in the damp trenches of the buried city.

She carried about a dozen living fowls slung over her right shoulder, their feet fastened together. Half of them fell upon the flat of her back, the balance dangled uneasily over her breast. They wriggled their benumbed and swollen legs against her neck, they twisted their stupefied eyes and peered into her face inquiringly. She did not see them or think of them. Her left arm was tired with the weight of the food basket, and she was hungry after her long morning's work.

Her straight back outlined itself strongly under her clean bright blue cotton rebozo. Instinctive serenity softened her black eyes, shaped like almonds, set far apart, and tilted a bit endwise. She walked with the free, natural, guarded ease of the primitive woman carrying an unborn child. The shape of her body was easy, the swelling life was not a distortion, but the right inevitable proportions of a woman. She was entirely contented. Her husband was at work and she was on her way to market to sell her fowls.

Her small house sat half-way up a shallow hill, under a clump of pepper-trees, a wall of organ cactus enclosing it on the side nearest to the road. Now she came down into the valley, divided by the narrow spring, and crossed a bridge of loose stones near the hut where María Rosa the beekeeper lived with her old godmother, Lupe the medicine woman. María Concepción had no faith in the charred owl bones, the singed rabbit fur, the cat entrails, the messes and ointments sold by Lupe to the ailing of the village. She was a good Christian, and drank simple herb teas for headache and stomachache, or bought her remedies bottled, with printed directions that she could not read, at the drugstore near the city market, where she went almost daily. But she often bought a jar of honey from young María Rosa, a pretty, shy child only fifteen years old.

María Concepción and her husband, Juan Villegas, were each a little past their eighteenth year. She had a good reputation with the neighbors as an energetic religious woman who could drive a bargain to the end. It was commonly known that if she wished to buy a new rebozo for herself or a shirt for Juan, she could bring out a sack of hard silver coins for the purpose.

She had paid for the license, nearly a year ago, the potent bit of stamped paper which permits people to be married in the church. She had given money to the priest before she and Juan walked together up to the altar the Monday after Holy Week. It had been the adventure of the villagers to go, three Sundays one after another, to hear the banns called by the priest for Juan de Dios Villegas and María Concepción Manriquez, who were actually getting married in the church, instead of behind it, which was the usual custom, less expensive, and as binding as any other ceremony. But María Concepción was always as proud as if she owned a hacienda.

She paused on the bridge and dabbled her feet in the water, her eyes resting themselves from the sun-rays in a fixed gaze to the far-off

mountains, deeply blue under their hanging drift of clouds. It came to her that she would like a fresh crust of honey. The delicious aroma of bees, their slow thrilling hum, awakened a pleasant desire for a flake of sweetness in her mouth.

"If I do not eat it now, I shall mark my child," she thought, peering through the crevices in the thick hedge of cactus that sheered up nakedly, like bared knife blades set protectingly around the small clearing. The place was so silent she doubted if María Rosa and Lupe were at home.

The leaning jacal of dried rush-withes and corn sheaves, bound to tall saplings thrust into the earth, roofed with yellow maguey leaves flattened and overlapping like shingles, hunched drowsy and fragrant in the warmth of noonday. The hives, similarly made, were scattered towards the back of the clearing, like small mounds of clean vegetable refuse. Over each mound there hung a dusty golden shimmer of bees.

A light gay scream of laughter rose from behind the hut; a man's short laugh joined in. "Ah, hahahaha!" went the voices together high and low, like a song.

"So María Rosa has a man!" María Concepción stopped short, smiling, shifted her burden slightly, and bent forward shading her eyes to see more clearly through the spaces of the hedge.

María Rosa ran, dodging between beehives, parting two stunted jasmine bushes as she came, lifting her knees in swift leaps, looking over her shoulder and laughing in a quivering, excited way. A heavy jar, swung to her wrist by the handle, knocked against her thighs as she ran. Her toes pushed up sudden spurts of dust, her half-raveled braids showered around her shoulders in long crinkled wisps.

Juan Villegas ran after her, also laughing strangely, his teeth set, both rows gleaming behind the small soft black beard growing sparsely on his lips, his chin, leaving his brown cheeks girl-smooth. When he seized her, he clenched so hard her chemise gave way and ripped from her shoulder. She stopped laughing at this, pushed him away and stood silent, trying to pull up the torn sleeve with one hand. Her pointed chin and dark red mouth moved in an uncertain way, as if she wished to laugh again; her long black lashes flickered with the quick-moving lights in her hidden eyes.

María Concepción did not stir nor breathe

for some seconds. Her forehead was cold, and yet boiling water seemed to be pouring slowly along her spine. An unaccountable pain was in her knees, as if they were broken. She was afraid Juan and María Rosa would feel her eyes fixed upon them and would find her there, unable to move, spying upon them. But they did not pass beyond the enclosure, nor even glance towards the gap in the wall opening upon the road.

Juan lifted one of María Rosa's loosened braids and slapped her neck with it playfully. She smiled softly, consentingly. Together they moved back through the hives of honey-comb. María Rosa balanced her jar on one hip and swung her long full petticoats with every step. Juan flourished his wide hat back and forth, walking proudly as a game-cock.

María Concepción came out of the heavy cloud which enwrapped her head and bound her throat, and found herself walking onward, keeping the road without knowing it, feeling her way delicately, her ears strumming as if all María Rosa's bees had hived in them. Her careful sense of duty kept her moving toward the buried city where Juan's chief, the American archeologist, was taking his midday rest, waiting for his food.

Juan and María Rosa! She burned all over now, as if a layer of tiny fig-cactus bristles, as cruel as spun glass, had crawled under her skin. She wished to sit down quietly and wait for her death, but not until she had cut the throats of her man and that girl who were laughing and kissing under the cornstalks. Once when she was a young girl she had come back from market to find her jacal burned to a pile of ash and her few silver coins gone. A dark empty feeling had filled her; she kept moving about the place, not believing her eyes, expecting it all to take shape again before her. But it was gone, and though she knew an enemy had done it, she could not find out who it was, and could only curse and threaten the air. Now here was a worse thing, but she knew her enemy. María Rosa, that sinful girl, shameless! She heard herself saying a harsh, true word about María Rosa, saying it aloud as if she expected someone to agree with her: "Yes, she is a whore! She has no right to live."

At this moment the gray untidy head of Givens appeared over the edges of the newest trench he had caused to be dug in his field of excavations. The long deep crevasses, in which a man might stand without being seen, lay criss-crossed like orderly gashes of a giant scalpel. Nearly all of the men of the community worked for Givens, helping him to uncover the lost city of their ancestors. They worked all the year through and prospered, digging every day for those small clay heads and bits of pottery and fragments of painted walls for which there was no good use on earth, being all broken and encrusted with clay. They themselves could make better ones, perfectly stout and new, which they took to town and peddled to foreigners for real money. But the unearthly delight of the chief in finding these worn-out things was an endless puzzle. He would fairly roar for joy at times, waving a shattered pot or a human skull above his head, shouting for his photographer to come and make a picture of this!

Now he emerged, and his young enthusiast's eyes welcomed María Concepción from his old-man face, covered with hard wrinkles and burned to the color of red earth. "I hope you've brought me a nice fat one." He selected a fowl from the bunch dangling nearest him as María Concepción, wordless, leaned over the trench. "Dress it for me, there's a good girl. I'll broil it."

María Concepción took the fowl by the head, and silently, swiftly drew her knife across its throat, twisting the head off with the casual firmness she might use with the top of a beet.

"Good God, woman, you do have nerve," said Givens, watching her. "I can't do that. It gives me the creeps."

"My home country is Guadalajara," explained María Concepción, without bravado as she picked and gutted the fowl.

She stood and regarded Givens condescendingly, that diverting white man who had no woman of his own to cook for him, and moreover appeared not to feel any loss of dignity in preparing his own food. He squatted now, eyes squinted, nose wrinkled to avoid the smoke, turning the roasting fowl busily on a stick. A mysterious man, undoubtedly rich, and Juan's chief, therefore to be respected, to be placated.

"The tortillas are fresh and hot, señor," she murmured gently. "With your permission I will now go to market."

"Yes, yes, run along; bring me another of these tomorrow." Givens turned his head to look at her again. Her grand manner sometimes reminded him of royalty in exile. He noticed her unnatural paleness. "The sun is too hot, eh?" he asked.

"Yes, sir. Pardon me, but Juan will be here soon?"

"He ought to be here now. Leave his food. The others will eat it."

She moved away; the blue of her rebozo became a dancing spot in the heat waves that rose from the gray-red soil. Givens liked his Indians best when he could feel a fatherly indulgence for their primitive childish ways. He told comic stories of Juan's escapades, of how often he had saved him, in the past five years, from going to jail, and even from being shot, for his varied and always unexpected misdeeds.

"I am never a minute too soon to get him out of one pickle or another," he would say. "Well, he's a good worker, and I know how to manage him."

After Juan was married, he used to twit him, with exactly the right shade of condescension, on his many infidelities to María Concepción. "She'll catch you yet, and God help you!" he was fond of saying, and Juan would laugh with immense pleasure.

It did not occur to María Concepción to tell Juan she had found him out. During the day her anger against him died, and her anger against María Rosa grew. She kept saying to herself, "When I was a young girl like María Rosa, if a man had caught hold of me so, I would have broken my jar over his head." She forgot completely that she had not resisted even so much as María Rosa, on the day that Juan had first taken hold of her. Besides she had married him afterwards in the church, and that was a very different thing.

Juan did not come home that night, but went away to war and María Rosa went with him. Juan had a rifle at his shoulder and two pistols at his belt. María Rosa wore a rifle also, slung on her back along with the blankets and the cooking pots. They joined the nearest detachment of troops in the field, and María Rosa marched ahead with the battalion of experienced women of war, which went over the crops like locusts, gathering provisions for the army. She cooked with them, and ate with them what was left after the men had eaten. After battles she went out on the field with the others to salvage clothing and ammunition and guns from the slain before they should begin to swell in the heat. Sometimes they would encounter the women from the other army, and a second battle as grim as the first would take place.

There was no particular scandal in the village. People shrugged, grinned. It was far better that they were gone. The neighbors went around saying that María Rosa was safer in the army than she would be in the same village with María Concepción.

María Concepción did not weep when Juan left her; and when the baby was born, and died within four days, she did not weep. "She is mere stone," said old Lupe, who went over and offered charms to preserve the baby.

"May you rot in hell with your charms," said María Concepción.

If she had not gone so regularly to church, lighting candles before the saints, kneeling with her arms spread in the form of a cross for hours at a time, and receiving holy communion every month, there might have been talk of her being devil-possessed, her face was so changed and blind-looking. But this was impossible when, after all, she had been married by the priest. It must be, they reasoned, that she was being punished for her pride. They decided that this was the true cause for everything: she was altogether too proud. So they pitied her.

During the year that Juan and María Rosa were gone, María Concepción sold her fowls and looked after her garden and her sack of hard coins grew. Lupe had no talent for bees, and the hives did not prosper. She began to blame María Rosa for running away, and to praise María Concepción for her behavior. She used to see María Concepción at the market or at church, and she always said that no one could tell by looking at her now that she was a woman who had such a heavy grief.

"I pray God everything goes well with María Concepción from this out," she would say, "for she has had her share of trouble."

When some idle person repeated this to the deserted woman, she went down to Lupe's house and stood within the clearing and called to the medicine woman, who sat in her doorway stirring a mess of her infallible cure for sores: "Keep your prayers to yourself, Lupe, or offer them for others who need them. I will ask God for what I want in this world."

"And will you get it, you think, María Concepción?" asked Lupe, tittering cruelly and smelling the wooden mixing spoon. "Did you pray for what you have now?"

Afterward everyone noticed that María Concepción went oftener to church, and ever seldomer to the village to talk with the other women as they sat along the curb, nursing their babies and eating fruit, at the end of the market-day.

"She is wrong to take us for enemies," said old Soledad, who was a thinker and a peacemaker. "All women have these troubles. Well, we should suffer together."

But María Concepción lived alone. She was gaunt, as if something were gnawing her away inside, her eyes were sunken, and she would not speak a word if she could help it. She worked harder than ever, and her butchering knife was scarcely ever out of her hand.

Juan and María Rosa, disgusted with military life, came home one day without asking permission of anyone. The field of war had unrolled itself, a long scroll of vexations, until the end had frayed out within twenty miles of Juan's village. So he and María Rosa, now lean as a wolf, burdened with a child daily expected, set out with no farewells to the regiment and walked home.

They arrived one morning about daybreak. Juan was picked up on sight by a group of military police from the small barracks on the edge of town, and taken to prison, where the officer in charge told him with impersonal cheerfulness that he would add one to a catch of ten waiting to be shot as deserters the next morning.

María Rosa, screaming and falling on her face in the road, was taken under the armpits by two guards and helped briskly to her jacal, now sadly run down. She was received with professional importance by Lupe, who helped the baby to be born at once.

Limping with foot soreness, a layer of dust concealing his fine new clothes got mysteriously from somewhere, Juan appeared before the captain at the barracks. The captain recognized him as head digger for his good friend Givens, and dispatched a note to Givens saying: "I am holding the person of Juan Villegas awaiting your further disposition."

When Givens showed up, Juan was delivered to him with the urgent request that nothing be made public about so humane and sensible an operation on the part of military authority.

Juan walked out of the rather stifling atmosphere of the drumhead court, a definite air of swagger about him. His hat, of unreasonable dimensions and embroidered with silver thread, hung over one eyebrow, secured at the back by a cord of silver dripping with bright blue tassels. His shirt was of a checkerboard pattern in green and black, his white cotton trousers were bound by a belt of yellow leather tooled in red. His feet were bare, full of stone bruises, and sadly ragged as to toenails. He removed his cigarette from the corner of his full-lipped wide mouth. He removed the splendid hat. His black dusty hair, pressed moistly to his forehead, sprang up suddenly in a cloudy thatch on his crown. He bowed to the officer, who appeared to be gazing at a vacuum. He swung his arm wide in a free circle upsoaring towards the prison window, where forlorn heads poked over the window sill, hot eyes following after the lucky departing one. Two or three of the heads nodded, and a half dozen hands were flipped at him in an effort to imitate his own casual and heady manner.

Juan kept up this insufferable pantomime until they rounded the first clump of fig-cactus. Then he seized Givens' hand and burst into oratory. "Blessed be the day your servant Juan Villegas first came under your eyes. From this day my life is yours without condition, ten thousand thanks with all my heart!"

"For God's sake stop playing the fool," said Givens irritably. "Some day I'm going to be five minutes too late."

"Well, it is nothing much to be shot, my chief — certainly you know I was not afraid — but to be shot in a drove of deserters, against a cold wall, just in the moment of my homecoming, by order of that . . ."

Glittering epithets tumbled over one another like explosions of a rocket. All the scandalous analogies from the animal and vegetable worlds were applied in a vivid, unique and personal way to the life, loves, and family history of the officer who had just set him free. When he had quite cursed himself dry, and his nerves were soothed, he added: "With your permission, my chief!"

"What will María Concepción say to all this?" asked Givens. "You are very informal, Juan, for a man who was married in the church."

Juan put on his hat.

"Oh, María Concepción! That's nothing. Look, my chief, to be married in the church is a great misfortune for a man. After that he is not himself any more. How can that woman complain when I do not drink even at fiestas enough to be really drunk? I do not beat her; never,

never. We were always at peace. I say to her, Come here, and she comes straight. I say, Go there, and she goes quickly. Yet sometimes I looked at her and thought, Now I am married to that woman in the church, and I felt a sinking inside, as if something were lying heavy on my stomach. With María Rosa it is all different. She is not silent; she talks. When she talks too much, I slap her and say, Silence, thou simpleton! and she weeps. She is just a girl with whom I do as I please. You know how she used to keep those clean little bees in their hives? She is like their honey to me. I swear it. I would not harm María Concepción because I am married to her in the church; but also, my chief, I will not leave María Rosa, because she pleases me more than any other woman."

"Let me tell you, Juan, things haven't been going as well as you think. You be careful. Some day María Concepción will just take your head off with that carving knife of hers. You keep that in mind."

Juan's expression was the proper blend of masculine triumph and sentimental melancholy. It was pleasant to see himself in the role of hero to two such desirable women. He had just escaped from the threat of a disagreeable end. His clothes were new and handsome, and they had cost him just nothing. María Rosa had collected them for him here and there after battles. He was walking in the early sunshine, smelling the good smells of ripening cactus-figs, peaches, and melons, of pungent berries dangling from the pepper-trees, and the smoke of his cigarette under his nose. He was on his way to civilian life with his patient chief. His situation was ineffably perfect, and he swallowed it whole.

"My chief," he addressed Givens handsomely, as one man of the world to another, "women are good things, but not at this moment. With your permission, I will now go to the village and eat. My God, *how* I shall eat! Tomorrow morning very early I will come to the buried city and work like seven men. Let us forget María Concepción and María Rosa. Each one in her place. I will manage them when the time comes."

News of Juan's adventure soon got abroad, and Juan found many friends about him during the morning. They finally commended his way of leaving the army. It was in itself the act of a hero. The new hero ate a great deal and drank somewhat, the occasion being better than a feast-day. It was almost noon before he returned to visit María Rosa.

He found her sitting on a clean straw mat, rubbing fat on her three-hour-old son. Before this felicitous vision Juan's emotions so twisted him that he returned to the village and invited every man in the "Death and Resurrection" pulque shop to drink with him.

Having thus taken leave of his balance, he started back to María Rosa, and found himself unaccountably in his own house, attempting to beat María Concepción by way of re-establishing himself in his legal household.

María Concepción, knowing all the events of that unhappy day, was not in a yielding mood, and refused to be beaten. She did not scream nor implore; she stood her ground and resisted; she even struck at him. Juan, amazed, hardly knowing what he did, stepped back and gazed at her inquiringly through a leisurely whirling film which seemed to have lodged behind his eyes. Certainly he had not even thought of touching her. Oh, well, no harm done. He gave up, turned away, half-asleep on his feet. He dropped amiably in a shadowed corner and began to snore.

María Concepción, seeing that he was quiet, began to bind the legs of her fowls. It was market-day and she was late. She fumbled and tangled the bits of cord in her haste, and set off across the plowed fields instead of taking the accustomed road. She ran with a crazy panic in her head, her stumbling legs. Now and then she would stop and look about her, trying to place herself, then go on a few steps, until she realized that she was not going towards the market.

At once she came to her senses completely, recognized the thing that troubled her so terribly, was certain of what she wanted. She sat down quietly under a sheltering thorny bush and gave herself over to her long devouring sorrow. The thing which had for so long squeezed her whole body into a tight dumb knot of suffering suddenly broke with shocking violence. She jerked with the involuntary recoil of one who receives a blow, and the sweat poured from her skin as if the wounds of her whole life were shedding their salt ichor. Drawing her rebozo over her head, she bowed her forehead on her updrawn knees, and sat there in deadly silence and immobility. From time to time she lifted her head where the sweat formed steadily and poured down her face, drenching the front of her chemise, and her mouth had the shape of crying, but there were no tears and no sound. All her being was a dark confused memory of grief burning in her at night, of deadly baffled anger eating at her by day, until her very tongue tasted bitter, and her feet were as heavy as if she were mired in the muddy roads during the time of rains.

After a great while she stood up and threw the rebozo off her face, and set out walking again.

Juan awakened slowly, with long yawns and grumblings, alternated with short relapses into sleep full of visions and clamors. A blur of orange light seared his eyeballs when he tried to unseal his lids. There came from somewhere a low voice weeping without tears, saying meaningless phrases over and over. He began to listen. He tugged at the leash of his stupor, he strained to grasp those words which terrified him even though he could not quite hear them. Then he came awake with frightening suddenness, sitting up and staring at the long sharpened streak of light piercing the corn-husk walls from the level disappearing sun.

María Concepción stood in the doorway, looming colossally tall to his betrayed eyes. She was talking quickly, and calling his name. Then he saw her clearly.

"God's name!" said Juan, frozen to the marrow, "here I am facing my death!" for the long knife she wore habitually at her belt was in her hand. But instead, she threw it away, clear from her, and got down on her knees, crawling toward him as he had seen her crawl many times toward the shrine at Guadalupe Villa. He watched her approach with such horror that the hair of his head seemed to be lifting itself away from him. Falling forward upon her face, she huddled over him, lips moving in a ghostly whisper. Her words became clear, and Juan understood them all.

For a second he could not move nor speak. Then he took her head between both his hands, and supported her in this way, saying swiftly, anxiously reassuring, almost in a babble:

"Oh, thou poor creature! Oh, mad-woman! Oh, my María Concepción, unfortunate! Listen. . . . Don't be afraid. Listen to me! I will hide thee away. I thy own man will protect thee! Quiet! Not a sound!"

Trying to collect himself, he held her and cursed under his breath for a few moments in the gathering darkness. María Concepción bent over, face almost on the ground, her feet folded under her, as if she would hide behind him. For the first time in his life Juan was aware of danger. This was danger. María Concepción would be dragged away between two gendarmes, with him following helpless and unarmed, to spend the rest of her days in Belén Prison, maybe. Danger! The night swarmed with threats. He stood up and dragged her up with him. She was silent and perfectly rigid, holding to him with resistless strength, her hands stiffened on her arms.

"Get me the knife," he told her in a whisper. She obeyed, her feet slipping along the hard earth floor, her shoulders straight, her arms close to her side. He lighted a candle. María Concepción held the knife out to him. It was stained and dark even to the handle with drying blood.

He frowned at her harshly, noting the same stains on her chemise and hands.

"Take off thy clothes and wash thy hands," he ordered. He washed the knife carefully, and threw the water wide of the doorway. She watched him and did likewise with the bowl in which she had bathed.

"Light the brasero and cook food for me," he told her in the same peremptory tone. He took her garments and went out. When he returned, she was wearing an old soiled dress, and was fanning the fire in the charcoal burner. Seating himself cross-legged near her, he stared at her as at a creature unknown to him, who bewildered him utterly, for whom there was no possible explanation. She did not turn her head, but kept silent and still, except for the movements of her strong hands fanning the blaze which cast sparks and small jets of white smoke, flaring and dying rhythmically with the motion of the fan lighting her face and darkening it by turns.

Juan's voice barely disturbed the silence: "Listen to me carefully, and tell me the truth, and when the gendarmes come here for us, thou shalt have nothing to fear. But there will be something for us to settle between us afterward."

The light from the charcoal burner shone in her eyes; a yellow phosphorescence glimmered behind the dark iris.

"For me everything is settled now," she answered, in a tone so tender, so grave, so heavy with suffering, that Juan felt his vitals contract.

He wished to repent openly, not as a man, but as a very small child. He could not fathom her, nor himself, nor the mysterious fortunes of life grown so instantly confused where all had seemed so gay and simple. He felt too that she had become invaluable, a woman without equal among a million women, and he could not tell why. He drew an enormous sigh that rattled in his chest.

"Yes, yes, it is all settled. I shall not go away again. We must stay here together."

Whispering, he questioned her and she answered whispering, and he instructed her over and over until she had her lesson by heart. The hostile darkness of the night encroached upon them, flowing over the narrow threshold, invading their hearts. It brought with it sighs and murmurs, the pad of secretive feet in the near-by road, the sharp staccato whimper of wind through the cactus leaves. All these familiar, once friendly cadences were now invested with sinister terrors; a dread, formless, and uncontrollable, took hold of them both.

"Light another candle," said Juan, loudly, in too resolute, too sharp a tone. "Let us eat now."

They sat facing each other and ate from the same dish, after their old habit. Neither tasted what they ate. With food half-way to his mouth, Juan listened. The sound of voices rose, spread, widened at the turn of the road along the cactus wall. A spray of lantern light shot through the hedge, a single voice slashed the blackness, ripped the fragile layer of silence suspended above the hut.

"Juan Villegas!"

"Pass, friends!" Juan roared back cheerfully.

They stood in the doorway, simple cautious gendarmes from the village, mixed-bloods themselves with Indian sympathies, well known to all the community. They flashed their lanterns almost apologetically upon the pleasant, harmless scene of a man eating supper with his wife.

"Pardon, brother," said the leader. "Someone has killed the woman María Rosa, and we must question her neighbors and friends." He paused, and added with an attempt at severity, "Naturally!"

"Naturally," agreed Juan. "You know that I was a good friend of María Rosa. This is bad news."

They all went away together, the men walking in a group, María Concepción following a few steps in the rear, near Juan. No one spoke.

The two points of candlelight at María Rosa's head fluttered uneasily; the shadows shifted and dodged on the stained darkened walls. To María Concepción everything in the smothering enclosing room shared an evil restlessness. The watchful faces of those called as witnesses, the faces of old friends, were made alien by the look of speculation in their eyes. The ridges of the rose-colored rebozo thrown over the body varied continually, as though the thing it covered was not perfectly in repose. Her eyes swerved over the body in the open painted coffin, from the candle tips at the head to the feet, jutting up thinly, the small scarred soles protruding, freshly washed, a mass of crooked, half-healed wounds, thorn-pricks and cuts of sharp stones. Her gaze went back to the candle flame, to Juan's eyes warning her, to the gendarmes talking among themselves. Her eyes would not be controlled.

With a leap that shook her, her gaze settled upon the face of María Rosa. Instantly her blood ran smoothly again: there was nothing to fear. Even the restless light could not give a look of life to that fixed countenance. She was dead. María Concepción felt her muscles give way softly; her heart began beating steadily without effort. She knew no more rancor against that pitiable thing, lying indifferently in its blue coffin under the fine silk rebozo. The mouth drooped sharply at the corners in a grimace of weeping arrested half-way. The brows were distressed; the dead flesh could not cast off the shape of its last terror. It was all finished. María Rosa had eaten too much honey and had had too much love. Now she must sit in hell, crying over her sins and her hard death forever and ever.

Old Lupe's cackling voice arose. She had spent the morning helping María Rosa and it had been hard work. The child had spat blood the moment it was born, a bad sign. She thought then that bad luck would come to the house. Well, about sunset she was in the yard at the back of the house grinding tomatoes and peppers. She had left mother and babe asleep. She heard a strange noise in the house, a choking and smothered calling, like someone wailing in sleep. Well, such a thing is only natural. But there followed a light, quick, thudding sound —

"Like the blows of a fist?" interrupted an officer.

"No, not at all like such a thing."

"How do you know?"

"I am well acquainted with that sound,

friends," retorted Lupe. "This was something else."

She was at a loss to describe it exactly. A moment later, there came the sound of pebbles rolling and slipping under feet; then she knew someone had been there and was running away.

"Why did you wait so long before going to see?"

"I am old and hard in the joints," said Lupe. "I cannot run after people. I walked as fast as I could to the cactus hedge, for it is only by this way that anyone can enter. There was no one in the road, sir, no one. Three cows, with a dog driving them; nothing else. When I got to María Rosa, she was lying all tangled up, and from her neck to her middle she was full of knife-holes. It was a sight to move the Blessed Image Himself! Her eyes were —"

"Never mind. Who came oftenest to her house before she went away? Did you know her enemies?"

Lupe's face congealed, closed. Her spongy skin drew into a network of secretive wrinkles. She turned withdrawn and expressionless eyes upon the gendarmes.

"I am an old woman. I do not see well. I cannot hurry on my feet. I know no enemy of María Rosa. I did not see anyone leave the clearing."

"You did not hear splashing in the spring near the bridge?"

"No, sir."

"Why, then, do our dogs follow a scent there and lose it?"

"God only knows, my friend. I am an old wo —"

"Yes. How did the footfalls sound?"

"Like the tread of an evil spirit!" Lupe broke forth in a swelling oracular tone that startled them. The Indians stirred uneasily, glanced at the dead, then at Lupe. They half expected her to produce the evil spirit among them at once. The gendarme began to lose his temper.

"No, poor unfortunate; I mean, were they heavy or light? The footsteps of a man or of a woman? Was the person shod or barefoot?"

A glance at the listening circle assured Lupe of their thrilled attention. She enjoyed the dangerous importance of her situation. She could have ruined that María Concepción with a word, but it was even sweeter to make fools of these gendarmes who went about spying on honest people. She raised her voice again. What she had not seen she could not describe,

thank God! No one could harm her because her knees were stiff and she could not run even to seize a murderer. As for knowing the difference between footfalls, shod or bare, man or woman, nay, between devil and human, who heard of such madness?

"My eyes are not ears, gentlemen," she ended grandly, "but upon my heart I swear those footsteps fell as the tread of the spirit of evil!"

"Imbecile!" yapped the leader in a shrill voice. "Take her away, one of you! Now, Juan Villegas, tell me —"

Juan told his story patiently, several times over. He had returned to his wife that day. She had gone to market as usual. He had helped her prepare her fowls. She had returned about mid-afternoon, they had talked, she had cooked, they had eaten, nothing was amiss. Then the gendarmes came with the news about María Rosa. That was all. Yes, María Rosa had run away with him, but there had been no bad blood between him and his wife on this account, nor between his wife and María Rosa. Everybody knew that his wife was a quiet woman.

María Concepción heard her own voice answering without a break. It was true at first she was troubled when her husband went away, but after that she had not worried about him. It was the way of men, she believed. She was a church-married woman and knew her place. Well, he had come home at last. She had gone to market, but had come back early, because now she had her man to cook for. That was all.

Other voices broke in. A toothless old man said: "She is a woman of good reputation among us, and María Rosa was not." A smiling young mother, Anita, baby at breast, said: "If no one thinks so, how can you accuse her? It was the loss of her child and not of her husband that changed her so." Another: "María Rosa had a strange life, apart from us. How do we know who might have come from another place to do her evil?" And old Soledad spoke up boldly: "When I saw María Concepción in the market today, I said, 'Good luck to you, María Concepción, this is a happy day for you!'" and she gave María Concepción a long easy stare, and the smile of a born wisewoman.

María Concepción suddenly felt herself guarded, surrounded, upborne by her faithful friends. They were around her, speaking for her, defending her, the forces of life were ranged invincibly with her against the beaten dead. María Rosa had thrown away her share of strength in them, she lay forfeited among them. María Concepción looked from one to the other of the circling, intent faces. Their eyes gave back reassurance, understanding, a secret and mighty sympathy.

The gendarmes were at a loss. They, too, felt that sheltering wall cast impenetrably around her. They were certain she had done it, and yet they could not accuse her. Nobody could be accused; there was not a shred of true evidence. They shrugged their shoulders and snapped their fingers and shuffled their feet. Well, then, good night to everybody. Many pardons for having intruded. Good health!

A small bundle lying against the wall at the head of the coffin squirmed like an eel. A wail, a mere sliver of sound, issued. María Concepción took the son of María Rosa in her arms.

"He is mine," she said clearly, "I will take him with me."

No one assented in words, but an approving nod, a bare breath of complete agreement, stirred among them as they made way for her.

María Concepción, carrying the child, followed Juan from the clearing. The hut was left with its lighted candles and a crowd of old women who would sit up all night, drinking coffee and smoking and telling ghost stories.

Juan's exaltation had burned out. There was not an ember of excitement left in him. He was tired. The perilous adventure was over. María Rosa had vanished, to come no more forever. Their days of marching, of eating, of quarreling and making love between battles, were all over. Tomorrow he would go back to dull and endless labor, he must descend into the trenches of the buried city as María Rosa must go into her grave. He felt his veins fill up with bitterness, with black unendurable melancholy. Oh, Jesus! what bad luck overtakes a man!

Well, there was no way out of it now. For· the moment he craved only to sleep. He was so drowsy he could scarcely guide his feet. The occasional light touch of the woman at his elbow was as unreal, as ghostly as the brushing of a leaf against his face. He did not know why he had fought to save her, and now he forgot her. There was nothing in him except a vast blind hurt like a covered wound.

He entered the jacal, and without waiting to light a candle, threw off his clothing, sitting just within the door. He moved with lagging, half-awake hands, to strip his body of its heavy finery. With a long groaning sigh of relief he fell straight back on the floor, almost instantly asleep, his arms flung up and outward.

María Concepción, a small clay jar in her hand, approached the gentle little mother goat tethered to a sapling, which gave and yielded as she pulled at the rope's end after the farthest reaches of grass about her. The kid, tied up a few feet away, rose bleating, its feathery fleece shivering in the fresh wind. Sitting on her heels, holding his tether, she allowed him to suckle a few moments. Afterward — all her movements very deliberate and even — she drew a supply of milk for the child.

She sat against the wall of her house, near the doorway. The child, fed and asleep, was cradled in the hollow of her crossed legs. The silence overfilled the world, the skies flowed down evenly to the rim of the valley, the stealthy moon crept slantwise to the shelter of the mountains. She felt soft and warm all over; she dreamed that the newly born child was her own, and she was resting deliciously.

María Concepción could hear Juan's breathing. The sound vapored from the low doorway, calmly; the house seemed to be resting after a burdensome day. She breathed, too, very slowly and quietly, each inspiration saturating her with repose. The child's light, faint breath was a mere shadowy moth of sound in the silver air. The night, the earth under her, seemed to swell and recede together with a limitless, unhurried, benign breathing. She drooped and closed her eyes, feeling the slow rise and fall within her own body. She did not know what it was, but it eased her all through. Even as she was falling asleep, head bowed over the child, she was still aware of a strange, wakeful happiness.

William Faulkner [1897-   ]

In 1950, when he accepted the Nobel Prize for literature in Stockholm and spoke of the duties of the writer in serious terms, Faulkner placed "Yoknapatawpha County" (the fictional name for his home territory of northern Mississippi) authoritatively on the world literary map and at the same time succeeded, in his own laconic phrase, in making a small "scratch on the face of anonymity." Behind his modest words lies a brilliant, if uneven, record of some sixteen novels and enough short fiction to fill seven volumes.

Faulkner comes of an old and proud Mississippi family which included a governor, a colonel in the Confederate army, bankers, and railroad builders all of whom helped build Lafayette County and the town of Oxford. He portrays them and the other "old families" with mingled pride and scorn in his books — the Sartorises, the Compsons, the Sutpens, the De Spains, the Benbows — once-aristocratic planters whose present descendants are reduced to a genteel poverty and worse, alcoholism, insanity, despair. Although cultivated and well-born, these families are weak and have suffered deeply from the sin of slavery on their land. They expiate this sin by watching the country being invaded by the pushing and lower-class Snopeses who have appropriated to themselves and their children the rivers, forests, and farms, wasting and abusing their newly-won title. Faulkner's Negro and Indian characters are mostly treated with sympathy and respect and a feeling that both, having been deprived of their birthright by the whites, have won from suffering a measure of dignity and peace.

Most of Faulkner's life has been lived in Oxford, where he went to school through the fifth grade, and spasmodically attended high school and later, 1919–21, the University of Mississippi. His education, like his personality, has been private and independent. His early reading was in romantic poetry of the Swinburne kind; later came the modern Imagists and the standard classics, such as Shakespeare, Keats, Dickens, Thackeray, and Balzac. He also read Joyce, whose work has left a mark upon his own. During the First World War he joined the Canadian Air Force but was not sent to France. He returned to Oxford, working at odd jobs in desultory fashion, painting university buildings, and acting as postmaster at the university. He preferred to regard himself as a poet turning out quantities of verse in the Imagist manner; some of it was later published. In 1925 en route to Europe, he went to New Orleans, where he met Sherwood Anderson and decided to stay and write novels. His first novel, *Soldiers' Pay*, was written there and published through Anderson's help. Now embarked on a writing career he produced sketches, poetry, and criticism in the *Times-Picayune* and the *Double Dealer*, an experimental magazine of writers and artists in the Bohemian group of the French Quarter.

After a short trip to Europe, Faulkner settled again to writing. He finished *Sartoris* and *The Sound and the Fury* (1929), the latter a critical success, but neither book brought any financial return. In need of money to finance his marriage, he deliberately undertook to produce a pot-boiling "shocker," *Sanctuary*, which brought him instant popularity, huge sales, a Hollywood contract, and notoriety.

Sartoris had introduced the pattern of his later work, the "Yoknapatawpha Saga," a kind of microcosm of the South in which the pattern of the old and new people, the town of "Jefferson," and the geographical details form a mythical domain and family tree. His succeeding work filled in, incompletely but with the fascination of a puzzle, further episodes and periods in this legend extending from before the Civil War down to the 1930's. This tapestry seems to have been woven without a deliberate plan, but Faulkner gradually came to regard all his work as a single "book." With one or two exceptions his novels contributed to the story — notably *Light in August* (1931), *Absalom, Absalom!* (1936), *The Unvanquished* (1938), *Intruder in the Dust* (1959). Outside the saga was *The Fable* (1954), a story of the First World War in France and an allegory of the crucifixion. In 1957 he returned to the Snopes-story with *The Town*, part of a trilogy with *The Hamlet*.

Faulkner's style is versatile, often fulsome and rhetorical, but likewise racy and realistic. His experiments in time-sequence, point of view, and perspective remind one of Wolfe and Joyce. Violence and frankness in describing sexual perversion are qualities balanced by his somber and brooding sense of the past and his broad humor. Despite faults and over-writing, his work has struck a chord in our time and has found readers in many other languages than his own.

Further reading: *Light in August. The Sound and the Fury. William Faulkner: Two Decades of Criticism*, 1951, ed. F. J. Hoffman and O. W. Vickery. Irving Howe, *William Faulkner: A Critical Study*, 1952.

The Bear

Like *Moby Dick*, "The Bear" is an epic story of a hunt for a legendary beast. It is also a symbolic tale of man's relation to the land which has been cursed by the traffic in slaves and the fierce economic strife among men. Published in its final form in *Go Down, Moses* (1942), it had appeared in two earlier versions in *Harper's* (1935) as "Lion" and in *The Saturday Evening Post* (1942) as "The Bear." The central theme of the young Ike McCaslin learning to be faithful to the wilderness and finding his heritage of manhood in a "pageant-rite" of the hunt has its beginnings in the earlier stories, but its full development in the final version involves the secondary theme of white injustice to the Negro and a Faulknerian interpretation of the entire tragic history of the South. The first three sections and the fifth are concerned primarily with the hunt for Old Ben and the wisdom to be learned from the wilderness under the tutelage of Sam Fathers. The long fourth section, omitted here, moves ahead in time to Ike McCaslin's twenty-first year.

The "wilderness theme" contains two contrasting strands. It is the source of moral and spiritual knowledge, Ike's "college," where he learns courage, humility, pity, and pride — in short, his heritage of responsible manhood. The wilderness is likewise the victim of man's greed and the encroachment of a corrupt civilization. Old Ben's death signalizes the end of an era, corresponding in time to the defeat of the South and the beginning of its decline. Thus Ike fatalistically takes part in God's predestined plan when he abandons his watch, gun,

and compass and submits himself, almost sacrificially, to the forces which will teach him humanity through suffering.

It is a mistake to search too pointedly for a symbolic reading of the story. As in all profound literature, the meanings are suggested, not stated. Sam Fathers, by his name, his part-Negro, part-Indian blood, bears several relationships to the story and to his young "novitiate," Ike. Boon Hogganbeck, the half-savage hunter; Lion, the dog whom Ike "should have hated and feared"; the one-eyed mule "which would not spook at the smell of blood"; and the taste of brass in Ike's mouth at the sight of Old Ben — all these have overtones of meaning to the reader. In the end when Ike finds Boon frenziedly hammering at the parts of his gun beneath the Gum Tree full of squirrels and shouting, "Don't touch a one of them! They're mine!" the reader senses that Boon, as a blind and ignorant part of humanity, has helped to destroy the spirit of the wilderness and hastened the coming of the new age, fiercely competitive and devoted to trivial and possessive ends.

1

There was a man and a dog too this time. Two beasts, counting Old Ben, the bear, and two men, counting Boon Hogganbeck, in whom some of the same blood ran which ran in Sam Fathers, even though Boon's was a plebeian strain of it and only Sam and Old Ben and the mongrel Lion were taintless and incorruptible.

He was sixteen. For six years now he had

been a man's hunter. For six years now he had heard the best of all talking. It was of the wilderness, the big woods, bigger and older than any recorded document; of white man fatuous enough to believe he had bought any fragment of it, of Indian ruthless enough to pretend that any fragment of it had been his to convey; bigger than Major de Spain and the scrap he pretended to, knowing better; older than old Thomas Sutpen of whom Major de Spain had had it and who knew better; older even than old Ikkemotubbe, the Chickasaw chief, of whom old Sutpen had had it and who knew better in his turn. It was of the men, not white nor black nor red but men, hunters, with the will and hardihood to endure and the humility and skill to survive, and the dogs and the bear and deer juxtaposed and reliefed against it, ordered and compelled by and within the wilderness in the ancient and unremitting contest according to the ancient and immitigable rules which voided all regrets and brooked no quarter; — the best game of all, the best of all breathing and forever the best of all listening, the voices quiet and weighty and deliberate for retrospection and recollection and exactitude among the concrete trophies — the racked guns and the heads and skins — in libraries of town houses or the offices of plantation houses or (and best of all) in the camps themselves where the intact and still-warm meat yet hung, the men who had slain it sitting before the burning logs on hearths when there were houses and hearths or about the smoky blazing of piled wood in front of stretched tarpaulins when there were not. There was always a bottle present, so that it would seem to him that those fine fierce instants of heart and brain and courage and wiliness and speed were concentrated and distilled into that brown liquor which not women, not boys and children, but only hunters drank, drinking not of the blood they spilled but some condensation of the wild immortal spirit, drinking it moderately, humbly even, not with the pagan's base and baseless hope of acquiring thereby the virtues of cunning and strength and speed but in salute to them. Thus it seemed to him on this December morning not only natural but actually fitting that this should have begun with whisky.

He realized later that it had begun long before that. It had already begun on that day when he first wrote his age in two ciphers and his cousin McCaslin brought him for the first time to the camp, the big woods, to earn for himself from the wilderness the name and state of hunter provided he in his turn were humble and enduring enough. He had already inherited then, without ever having seen it, the big old bear with one trap-ruined foot that in an area almost a hundred miles square had earned for himself a name, a definite designation like a living man: — the long legend of corn-cribs broken down and rifled, of shoats and grown pigs and even calves carried bodily into the woods and devoured and traps and deadfalls overthrown and dogs mangled and slain and shotgun and even rifle shots delivered at point-blank range yet with no more effect than so many peas blown through a tube by a child — a corridor of wreckage and destruction beginning back before the boy was born, through which sped, not fast but rather with the ruthless and irresistible deliberation of a locomotive, the shaggy tremendous shape. It ran in his knowledge before he ever saw it. It loomed and towered in his dreams before he even saw the unaxed woods where it left its crooked print, shaggy, tremendous, red-eyed, not malevolent but just big, too big for the dogs which tried to bay it, for the horses which tried to ride it down, for the men and the bullets they fired into it; too big for the very country which was its constricting scope. It was as if the boy had already divined what his senses and intellect had not encompassed yet: that doomed wilderness whose edges were being constantly and punily gnawed at by men with plows and axes who feared it because it was wilderness, men myriad and nameless even to one another in the land where the old bear had earned a name, and through which ran not even a mortal beast but an anachronism indomitable and invincible out of an old dead time, a phantom, epitome and apotheosis of the old wild life which the little puny humans swarmed and hacked at in a fury of abhorrence and fear like pygmies about the ankles of a drowsing elephant; — the old bear, solitary, indomitable, and alone; widowered childless and absolved of mortality — old Priam reft of his old wife and outlived all his sons.

Still a child, with three years then two years then one year yet before he too could make one of them, each November he would watch the wagon containing the dogs and the bedding and food and guns and his cousin McCaslin and Tennie's Jim and Sam Fathers too until Sam moved to the camp to live, depart for the Big

Bottom, the big woods. To him, they were going not to hunt bear and deer but to keep yearly rendezvous with the bear which they did not even intend to kill. Two weeks later they would return, with no trophy, no skin. He had not expected it. He had not even feared that it might be in the wagon this time with the other skins and heads. He did not even tell himself that in three years or two years or one year more he would be present and that it might even be his gun. He believed that only after he had served his apprenticeship in the woods which would prove him worthy to be a hunter, would he even be permitted to distinguish the crooked print, and that even then for two November weeks he would merely make another minor one, along with his cousin and Major de Spain and General Compson and Walter Ewell and Boon and the dogs which feared to bay it and the shotguns and rifles which failed even to bleed it, in the yearly pageant-rite of the old bear's furious immortality.

His day came at last. In the surrey with his cousin and Major de Spain and General Compson he saw the wilderness through a slow drizzle of November rain just above the ice point as it seemed to him later he always saw it or at least always remembered it — the tall and endless wall of dense November woods under the dissolving afternoon and the year's death, sombre, impenetrable (he could not even discern yet how, at what point they could possibly hope to enter it even though he knew that Sam Fathers was waiting there with the wagon), the surrey moving through the skeleton stalks of cotton and corn in the last of open country, the last trace of man's puny gnawing at the immemorial flank, until, dwarfed by that perspective into an almost ridiculous diminishment, the surrey itself seemed to have ceased to move (this too to be completed later, years later, after he had grown to a man and had seen the sea) as a solitary small boat hangs in a lonely immobility, merely tossing up and down, in the infinite waste of the ocean while the water and then the apparently impenetrable land which it nears without appreciable progress, swings slowly and opens the widening inlet which is the anchorage. He entered it. Sam was waiting, wrapped in a quilt on the wagon seat behind the patient and steaming mules. He entered his novitiate to the true wilderness with Sam beside him as he had begun his apprenticeship in miniature to manhood after the rabbits and such with Sam

beside him, the two of them wrapped in the damp, warm, Negro-rank quilt, while the wilderness closed behind his entrance as it had opened momentarily to accept him, opening before his advancement as it closed behind his progress, no fixed path the wagon followed but a channel non-existent ten yards ahead of it and ceasing to exist ten yards after it had passed, the wagon progressing not by its own volition but by attrition of their intact yet fluid circumambiance, drowsing, earless, almost lightless.

It seemed to him that at the age of ten he was witnessing his own birth. It was not even strange to him. He had experienced it all before, and not merely in dreams. He saw the camp — a paintless six-room bungalow set on piles above the spring high-water — and he knew already how it was going to look. He helped in the rapid orderly disorder of their establishment in it and even his motions were familiar to him, foreknown. Then for two weeks he ate the coarse, rapid food — the shapeless sour bread, the wild strange meat, venison and bear and turkey and coon which he had never tasted before — which men ate, cooked by men who were hunters first and cooks afterward; he slept in harsh sheetless blankets as hunters slept. Each morning the gray of dawn found him and Sam Fathers on the stand, the crossing, which had been allotted him. It was the poorest one, the most barren. He had expected that; he had not dared yet to hope even to himself that he would even hear the running dogs this first time. But he did hear them. It was on the third morning — a murmur, sourceless, almost indistinguishable, yet he knew what it was although he had never before heard that many dogs running at once, the murmur swelling into separate and distinct voices until he could call the five dogs which his cousin owned from among the others. "Now," Sam said, "slant your gun up a little and draw back the hammers and then stand still."

But it was not for him, not yet. The humility was there; he had learned that. And he could learn the patience. He was only ten, only one week. The instant had passed. It seemed to him that he could actually see the deer, the buck, smoke-colored, elongated with speed, vanished, the woods, the gray solitude still ringing even when the voices of the dogs had died away; from far away across the sombre woods and the gray half-liquid morning there came two shots. "Now let your hammers down," Sam said.

He did so. "You knew it too," he said.

"Yes," Sam said. "I want you to learn how to do when you didn't shoot. It's after the chance for the bear or the deer has done already come and gone that men and dogs gets killed."

"Anyway, it wasn't him," the boy said. "It wasn't even a bear. It was just a deer."

"Yes," Sam said, "it was just a deer."

Then one morning, it was in the second week, he heard the dogs again. This time before Sam even spoke he readied the too-long, too-heavy, man-size gun as Sam had taught him, even though this time he knew the dogs and the deer were coming less close than ever, hardly within hearing even. They didn't sound like any running dogs he had ever heard before even. Then he found that Sam, who had taught him first of all to cock the gun and take position where he could see best in all directions and then never to move again, had himself moved up beside him. "There," he said. "Listen." The boy listened, to no ringing chorus strong and fast on a free scent but, a moiling yapping an octave too high and with something more than indecision and even abjectness in it which he could not yet recognize, reluctant, not even moving very fast, taking a long time to pass out of hearing, leaving even then in the air that echo of thin and almost human hysteria, abject, almost humanly grieving, with this time nothing ahead of it, no sense of a fleeing unseen smoke-colored shape. He could hear Sam breathing at his shoulder. He saw the arched curve of the old man's inhaling nostrils.

"It's Old Ben!" he cried, whispering.

Sam didn't move save for the slow gradual turning of his head as the voices faded on and the faint steady rapid arch and collapse of his nostrils. "Hah," he said. "Not even running. Walking."

"But up here!" the boy cried. "Way up here!"

"He do it every year," Sam said. "Once. Ash and Boon say he comes up here to run the other little bears away. Tell them to get to hell out of here and stay out until the hunters are gone. Maybe." The boy no longer heard anything at all, yet still Sam's head continued to turn gradually and steadily until the back of it was toward him. Then it turned back and looked down at him — the same face, grave, familiar, expressionless until it smiled, the same old man's eyes from which as he watched there faded slowly a quality darkly and fiercely lambent, passionate and proud. "He don't care no more for bears than he does for dogs or men neither. He come to see who's here, who's new in camp this year, whether he can shoot or not, can stay or not. Whether we got the dog yet that can bay and hold him until a man gets there with a gun. Because he's the head bear. He's the man." It faded, was gone; again they were the eyes as he had known them all his life. "He'll let them follow him to the river. Then he'll send them home. We might as well go too; see how they look when they get back to camp."

The dogs were there first, ten of them huddled back under the kitchen, himself and Sam squatting to peer back into the obscurity where they crouched, quiet, the eyes rolling and luminous, vanishing, and no sound, only that effluvium which the boy could not quite place yet, of something more than dog, stronger than dog and not just animal, just beast even. Because there had been nothing in front of the abject and painful yapping except the solitude, the wilderness, so that when the eleventh hound got back about mid-afternoon and he and Tennie's Jim held the passive and still trembling bitch while Sam daubed her tattered ear and raked shoulder with turpentine and axle-grease, it was still no living creature but only the wilderness which, leaning for a moment, had patted lightly once her temerity. "Just like a man," Sam said. "Just like folks. Put off as long as she could having to be brave, knowing all the time that sooner or later she would have to be brave once so she could keep on calling herself a dog, and knowing beforehand what was going to happen when she done it."

He did not know just when Sam left. He only knew that he was gone. For the next three mornings he rose and ate breakfast and Sam was not waiting for him. He went to his stand alone; he found it without help now and stood on it as Sam had taught him. On the third morning he heard the dogs again, running strong and free on a true scent again, and he readied the gun as he had learned to do and heard the hunt sweep past on since he was not ready yet, had not deserved other yet in just one short period of two weeks as compared to all the long life which he had already dedicated to the wilderness with patience and humility; he heard the shot again, one shot, the single clapping report of Walter Ewell's rifle. By now he could not only find his stand and then return to camp without guidance, by using the compass his cousin had given him he reached Walter, waiting beside the buck and the moiling of dogs over the cast entrails before any of the others except Major de Spain and Tennie's Jim on the horses, even before Uncle Ash arrived with the one-eyed wagon-mule which did not mind the smell of blood or even, so they said, of bear.

It was not Uncle Ash on the mule. It was Sam, returned. And Sam was waiting when he finished his dinner and, himself on the one-eyed mule and Sam on the other one of the wagon team, they rode for more than three hours through the rapid shortening sunless afternoon, following no path, no trail even that he could discern, into a section of country he had never seen before. Then he understood why Sam had made him ride the one-eyed mule which would not spook at the smell of blood, of wild animals. The other one, the sound one, stopped short and tried to whirl and bolt even as Sam got down, jerking and wrenching at the rein while Sam held it, coaxing it forward with his voice since he did not dare risk hitching it, drawing it forward while the boy dismounted from the marred one which would stand. Then, standing beside Sam in the thick great gloom of ancient woods and the winter's dying afternoon, he looked quietly down at the rotted log scored and gutted with claw-marks and, in the wet earth beside it, the print of the enormous warped two-toed foot. Now he knew what he had heard in the hounds' voices in the woods that morning and what he had smelled when he peered under the kitchen where they huddled. It was in him too, a little different because they were brute beasts and he was not, but only a little different — an eagerness, passive; an abjectness, a sense of his own fragility and impotence against the timeless woods, yet without doubt or dread; a flavor like brass in the sudden run of saliva in his mouth, a hard sharp constriction either in his brain or his stomach, he could not tell which and it did not matter; he knew only that for the first time he realized that the bear which had run in his listening and loomed in his dreams since before he could remember and which therefore must have existed in the listening and the dreams of his cousin and Major de Spain and even old General Compson before they began to remember in their turn, was a mortal animal and that they had departed for the camp each November with no actual intention of slaying it, not because it could not be slain but because so far

they had no actual hope of being able to. "It will be tomorrow," he said.

"You mean we will try tomorrow," Sam said. "We aint got the dog yet."

"We've got eleven," he said. "They ran him Monday."

"And you heard them," Sam said. "Saw them too. We aint got the dog yet. It won't take but one. But he aint there. Maybe he aint nowhere. The only other way will be for him to run by accident over somebody that had a gun and knowed how to shoot it."

"That wouldn't be me," the boy said. "It would be Walter or Major or —"

"It might," Sam said. "You watch close tomorrow. Because he's smart. That's how come he has lived this long. If he gets hemmed up and has got to pick out somebody to run over, he will pick out you."

"How?" he said. "How will he know . . ." He ceased. "You mean he already knows me, that I aint never been to the big bottom before, aint had time to find out yet whether I . . ." He ceased again, staring at Sam; he said humbly, not even amazed: "It was me he was watching. I dont reckon he did need to come but once."

"You watch tomorrow," Sam said. "I reckon we better start back. It'll be long after dark now before we get to camp."

The next morning they started three hours earlier than they had ever done. Even Uncle Ash went, the cook, who called himself by profession a camp cook and who did little else save cook for Major de Spain's hunting and camping parties, yet who had been marked by the wilderness from simple juxtaposition to it until he responded as they all did, even the boy who until two weeks ago had never even seen the wilderness, to a hound's ripped ear and shoulder and the print of a crooked foot in a patch of wet earth. They rode. It was too far to walk: the boy and Sam and Uncle Ash in the wagon with the dogs, his cousin and Major de Spain and General Compson and Boon and Walter and Tennie's Jim riding double on the horses; again the first gray light found him, as on that first morning two weeks ago, on the stand where Sam had placed and left him. With the gun which was too big for him, the breech-loader which did not even belong to him but to Major de Spain and which he had fired only once, at a stump on the first day to learn the recoil and how to reload it with the paper shells, he stood against a big gum tree beside a little bayou whose black still water crept without motion out of a cane-brake, across a small clearing and into the cane again, where, invisible, a bird, the big woodpecker called Lord-to-God by Negroes, clattered at a dead trunk. It was a stand like any other stand, dissimilar only in incidentals to the one where he had stood each morning for two weeks; a territory new to him yet no less familiar than that other one which after two weeks he had come to believe he knew a little — the same solitude, the same loneliness through which frail and timorous man had merely passed without altering it, leaving no mark nor scar, which looked exactly as it must have looked when the first ancestor of Sam Fathers' Chickasaw predecessors crept into it and looked about him, club or stone axe or bone arrow drawn and ready, different only because, squatting at the edge of the kitchen, he had smelled the dogs huddled and cringing beneath it and saw the raked ear and side of the bitch that, as Sam had said, had to be brave once in order to keep on calling herself a dog, and saw yesterday in the earth beside the gutted log, the print of the living foot. He heard no dogs at all. He never did certainly hear them. He only heard the drumming of the woodpecker stop short off, and knew that the bear was looking at him. He never saw it. He did not know whether it was facing him from the cane or behind him. He did not move, holding the useless gun which he knew now he would never fire at it, now or ever, tasting in his saliva that taint of brass which he had smelled in the huddled dogs when he peered under the kitchen.

Then it was gone. As abruptly as it had stopped, the woodpecker's dry hammering set up again, and after a while he believed he even heard the dogs — a murmur, scarce a sound even, which he had probably been hearing for a time, perhaps a minute or two, before he remarked it, drifting into hearing and then out again, dying away. They came nowhere near him. If it was dogs he heard, he could not have sworn to it; if it was a bear they ran, it was another bear. It was Sam himself who emerged from the cane and crossed the bayou, the injured bitch following at heel as a bird dog is taught to walk. She came and crouched against his leg, trembling. "I didn't see him," he said. "I didn't, Sam."

"I know it," Sam said. "He done the looking. You didn't hear him neither, did you?"

"No," the boy said. "I — "

"He's smart," Sam said. "Too smart." Again the boy saw in his eyes that quality of dark and brooding lambence as Sam looked down at the bitch trembling faintly and steadily against the boy's leg. From her raked shoulder a few drops of fresh blood clung like bright berries. "Too big. We aint got the dog yet. But maybe some day."

Because there would be a next time, after and after. He was only ten. It seemed to him that he could see them, the two of them, shadowy in the limbo from which time emerged and became time: the old bear absolved of mortality and himself who shared a little of it. Because he recognised now what he had smelled in the huddled dogs and tasted in his own saliva, recognised fear as a boy, a youth, recognises the existence of love and passion and experience which is his heritage but not yet his patrimony, from entering by chance the presence or perhaps even merely the bedroom of a woman who has loved and been loved by many men. *So I will have to see him,* he thought, without dread or even hope. *I will have to look at him.* So it was in June of the next summer. They were at the camp again, celebrating Major de Spain's and General Compson's birthdays. Although the one had been born in September and the other in the depth of winter and almost thirty years earlier, each June the two of them and McCaslin and Boon and Walter Ewell (and the boy too from now on) spent two weeks at the camp, fishing and shooting squirrels and turkey and running coons and wildcats with the dogs at night. That is, Boon and the Negroes (and the boy too now) fished and shot squirrels and ran the coons and cats, because the proven hunters, not only Major de Spain and old General Compson (who spent those two weeks sitting in a rocking chair before a tremendous iron pot of Brunswick stew, stirring and tasting, with Uncle Ash to quarrel with about how he was making it and Tennie's Jim to pour whisky into the tin dipper from which he drank it), but even McCaslin and Walter Ewell who were still young enough, scorned such other shooting the wild gobblers with pistols for wagers or to test their marksmanship.

That is, his cousin McCaslin and the others thought he was hunting squirrels. Until the third evening he believed that Sam Fathers thought so too. Each morning he would leave the camp right after breakfast. He had his own gun now, a new breech-loader, a Christmas gift; he would own and shoot it for almost seventy years, through two new pairs of barrels and locks and one new stock, until all that remained of the original gun was the silver-inlaid trigger-guard with his and McCaslin's engraved names and the date in 1878. He found the tree beside the little bayou where he had stood that morning. Using the compass he ranged from that point; he was teaching himself to be better than a fair woodsman without even knowing he was doing it. On the third day he even found the gutted log where he had first seen the print. It was almost completely crumbled now, healing with unbelievable speed, a passionate and almost visible relinquishment, back into the earth from which the tree had grown. He ranged the summer woods now, green with gloom, if anything actually dimmer than they had been in November's gray dissolution, where even at noon the sun fell only in windless dappling upon the earth which never completely dried and which crawled with snakes — moccasins and watersnakes and rattlers, themselves the color of the dappled gloom so that he would not always see them until they moved; returning to camp later and later and later, first day, second day, passing in the twilight of the third evening the little log pen enclosing the log barn where Sam was putting up the stock for the night. "You aint looked right yet," Sam said.

He stopped. For a moment he didn't answer. Then he said peacefully, in a peaceful rushing burst, as when a boy's miniature dam in a little brook gives way: "All right. Yes. But how? I went to the bayou. I even found that log again. I —"

"I reckon that was all right. Likely he's been watching you. You never saw his foot?"

"I . . ." the boy said. "I didn't . . . I never thought . . ."

"It's the gun," Sam said. He stood beside the fence, motionless, the old man, son of a Negro slave and a Chickasaw chief, in the battered and faded overalls and the frayed five-cent straw hat which had been the badge of the Negro's slavery and was now the regalia of his freedom. The camp — the clearing, the house, the barn and its tiny lot with which Major de Spain in his turn had scratched punily and evanescently at the wilderness — faded in the dusk, back into the immemorial darkness of the woods. *The gun*, the boy thought. *The gun.* "You will have to choose," Sam said.

He left the next morning before light, without breakfast, long before Uncle Ash would wake in his quilts on the kitchen floor and start the fire. He had only the compass and a stick for the snakes. He could go almost a mile before he would need to see the compass. He sat on a log, the invisible compass in his hand, while the secret night-sounds which had ceased at his movements, scurried again and then fell still for good and the owls ceased and gave over to the waking day birds and there was light in the gray wet woods and he could see the compass. He went fast yet still quietly, becoming steadily better and better as a woodsman without yet having time to realise it; he jumped a doe and a fawn, walked them out of the bed, close enough to see them — the crash of undergrowth, the white scut, the fawn scudding along behind her, faster than he had known it could have run. He was hunting right, upwind, as Sam had taught him, but that didn't matter now. He had left the gun; by his own will and relinquishment he had accepted not a gambit, not a choice, but a condition in which not only the bear's heretofore inviolable anonymity but all the ancient rules and balances of hunter and hunted had been abrogated. He would not even be afraid, not even in the moment when the fear would take him completely: blood, skin, bowels, bones, memory from the long time before it even became his memory — all save that thin clear quenchless lucidity which alone differed him from this bear and from all the other bears and bucks he would follow during almost seventy years, to which Sam had said: "Be scared. You cant help that. But dont be afraid. Aint nothing in the woods going to hurt you if you dont corner it or it dont smell that you are afraid. A bear or a deer has got to be scared of a coward the same as a brave man has got to be."

By noon he was far beyond the crossing on the little bayou, farther into the new and alien country than he had ever been, travelling now not only by the compass but by the old, heavy, biscuit-thick silver watch which had been his father's. He had left the camp nine hours ago; nine hours from now, dark would already have been an hour old. He stopped, for the first time since he had risen from the log when he could see the compass face at last, and looked about, mopping his sweating face on his sleeve. He had already relinquished, of his will, because of his need, in humility and peace and without regret, yet apparently that had not been enough, the leaving of the gun was not enough. He stood for a moment — a child, alien and lost in the green and soaring gloom of the markless wilderness. Then he relinquished completely to it. It was the watch and the compass. He was still tainted. He removed the linked chain of the one and the looped thong of the other from his overalls and hung them on a bush and leaned the stick beside them and entered it.

When he realised he was lost, he did as Sam had coached and drilled him: made a cast to cross his back-track. He had not been going very fast for the last two or three hours, and he had gone even less fast since he left the compass and watch on the bush. So he went slower till now, since the tree could not be very far; in fact, he found it before he really expected to and turned and went to it. But there was no bush beneath it, no compass nor watch, so he did next as Sam had coached and drilled him: made this next circle in the opposite direction and much larger, so that the pattern of the two of them would bisect his track somewhere, but crossing no trace nor mark anywhere of his feet or any feet, and now he was going faster though still not panicked, his heart beating a little more rapidly but strong and steady enough, and this time it was not even the tree because there was a down log beside it which he had never seen before and beyond the log a little swamp, a seepage of moisture somewhere between earth and water, and he did what Sam had coached and drilled him as the next and the last, seeing as he sat down on the log the crooked print, the warped indentation in the wet ground which while he looked at it continued to fill with water until it was level full and the water began to overflow and the sides of the print began to dissolve away. Even as he looked up he saw the next one, and, moving, the one beyond it; moving, not hurrying, running, but merely keeping pace with them as they appeared before him as though they were being shaped out of thin air just one constant pace short of where he would lose them forever and be lost forever himself, tireless, eager, without doubt or dread, panting a little above the strong rapid little hammer of his heart, emerging suddenly into a little glade and the wilderness coalesced. It rushed, soundless, and solidified — the tree, the bush, the compass and the watch glinting where a ray of sunlight touched them. Then he saw the bear. It did not emerge,

appear: it was just there, immobile, fixed in the green and windless noon's hot dappling, not as big as he had dreamed it but as big as he had expected, bigger, dimensionless against the dappled obscurity, looking at him. Then it moved. It crossed the glade without haste, walking for an instant into the sun's full glare and out of it, and stopped again and looked back at him across one shoulder. Then it was gone. It didn't walk into the woods. It faded, sank back into the wilderness without motion as he had watched a fish, a huge old bass, sink back into the dark depths of its pool and vanish without even any movement of its fins.

2

So he should have hated and feared Lion. He was thirteen then. He had killed his buck and Sam Fathers had marked his face with the hot blood, and in the next November he killed a bear. But before that accolade he had become as competent in the woods as many grown men with the same experience. By now he was a better woodsman than most grown men with more. There was no territory within twenty-five miles of the camp that he did not know — bayou, ridge, landmark trees and path; he could have led anyone direct to any spot in it and brought him back. He knew game trails that even Sam Fathers had never seen; in the third fall he found a buck's bedding-place by himself and unbeknown to his cousin he borrowed Walter Ewell's rifle and lay in wait for the buck at dawn and killed it when it walked back to the bed as Sam had told him how the old Chickasaw fathers did.

By now he knew the old bear's footprint better than he did his own, and not only the crooked one. He could see any one of the three sound prints and distinguish it at once from any other, and not only because of its size. There were other bears within that fifty miles which left tracks almost as large, or at least so near that the one would have appeared larger only by juxtaposition. It was more than that. If Sam Fathers had been his mentor and the backyard rabbits and squirrels his kindergarten, then the wilderness the old bear ran was his college and the old male bear itself, so long unwifed and childless as to have become its own ungendered progenitor, was his alma mater.

He could find the crooked print now whenever he wished, ten miles or five miles or sometimes closer than that, to the camp. Twice while on stand during the next three years he heard the dogs strike its trail and once even jump it by chance, the voices high, abject, almost human in their hysteria. Once, still-hunting with Walter Ewell's rifle, he saw it cross a long corridor of down timber where a tornado had passed. It rushed through rather than across the tangle of trunks and branches as a locomotive would, faster than he had ever believed it could have moved, almost as fast as a deer even because the deer would have spent most of that distance in the air; he realised then why it would take a dog not only of abnormal courage but size and speed too ever to bring it to bay. He had a little dog at home, a mongrel, of the sort called fyce by Negroes, a ratter, itself not much bigger than a rat and possessing that sort of courage which had long since stopped being bravery and had become fool-hardiness. He brought it with him one June and, timing them as if they were meeting an appointment with another human being, himself carrying the fyce with a sack over its head and Sam Fathers with a brace of the hounds on a rope leash, they lay downwind of the trail and actually ambushed the bear. They were so close that it turned at bay although he realised later this might have been from surprise and amazement at the shrill and frantic uproar of the fyce. It turned at bay against the trunk of a big cypress, on its hind feet; it seemed to the boy that it would never stop rising, taller and taller, and even the two hounds seemed to have taken a kind of desperate and despairing courage from the fyce. Then he realised that the fyce was actually not going to stop. He flung the gun down and ran. When he overtook and grasped the shrill, frantically pinwheeling little dog, it seemed to him that he was directly under the bear. He could smell it, strong and hot and rank. Sprawling, he looked up where it loomed and towered over him like a thunderclap. It was quite familiar, until he remembered: this was the way he had used to dream about it.

Then it was gone. He didn't see it go. He knelt, holding the frantic fyce with both hands, hearing the abased wailing of the two hounds drawing further and further away, until Sam came up, carrying the gun. He laid it quietly down beside the boy and stood looking down at him. "You've done seed him twice now, with a gun in your hands," he said. "This time you couldn't have missed him."

The boy rose. He still held the fyce. Even in his arms it continued to yap frantically, surging and straining toward the fading sound of the hounds like a collection of live-wire springs. The boy was panting a little. "Neither could you," he said. "You had the gun. Why didn't you shoot him?"

Sam didn't seem to have heard. He put out his hand and touched the little dog in the boy's arms which still yapped and strained even though the two hounds were out of hearing now. "He's done gone," Sam said. "You can slack off and rest now, until next time." He stroked the little dog until it began to grow quiet under his hand. "You's almost the one we wants," he said. "You just aint big enough. We aint got that one yet. He will need to be just a little bigger than smart, and a little braver than either." He withdrew his hand from the fyce's head and stood looking into the woods where the bear and the hounds had vanished. "Somebody is going to, some day."

"I know it," the boy said. "That's why it must be one of us. So it wont be until the last day. When even he dont want it to last any longer."

So he should have hated and feared Lion. It was in the fourth summer, the fourth time he had made one in the celebration of Major de Spain's and General Compson's birthday. In the early spring Major de Spain's mare had foaled a horse colt. One evening when Sam brought the horses and mules up to stable them for the night, the colt was missing and it was all he could do to get the frantic mare into the lot. He had thought at first to let the mare lead him back to where she had become separated from the foal. But she would not do it. She would not even feint toward any particular part of the woods or even in any particular direction. She merely ran, as if she couldn't see, still frantic with terror. She whirled and ran at Sam once, as if to attack him in some ultimate desperation, as if she could not for the moment realise that he was a man and a long-familiar one. He got her into the lot at last. It was too dark by that time to back-track her, to unravel the erratic course she had doubtless pursued.

He came to the house and told Major de Spain. It was an animal, of course, a big one, and the colt was dead now, wherever it was. They all knew that. "It's a panther," General Compson said at once. "The same one. That doe and fawn last March." Sam had sent Major de Spain word of it when Boon Hogganbeck came to the camp on a routine visit to see how the stock had wintered — the doe's throat torn out, and the beast had run down the helpless fawn and killed it too.

"Sam never did say that was a panther," Major de Spain said. Sam said nothing now, standing behind Major de Spain where they sat at supper, inscrutable, as if he were just waiting for them to stop talking so he could go home. He didn't even seem to be looking at anything. "A panther might jump a doe, and he wouldn't have much trouble catching the fawn afterward. But no panther would have jumped that colt with the dam right there with it. It was Old Ben," Major de Spain said. "I'm disappointed in him. He has broken the rules. I didn't think he would have done that. He has killed mine and McCaslin's dogs, but that was all right. We gambled the dogs against him; we gave each other warning. But now he has come into my house and destroyed my property, out of season too. He broke the rules. It was Old Ben, Sam." Still Sam said nothing, standing there until Major de Spain should stop talking. "We'll back-track her tomorrow and see," Major de Spain said.

Sam departed. He would not live in the camp; he had built himself a little hut something like Joe Baker's, only stouter, tighter, on the bayou a quarter-mile away, and a stout log crib where he stored a little corn for the shoat he raised each year. The next morning he was waiting when they waked. He had already found the colt. They did not even wait for breakfast. It was not far, not five hundred yards from the stable — the three-months' colt lying on its side, its throat torn out and the entrails and one ham partly eaten. It lay not as if it had been dropped but as if it had been struck and hurled, and no cat-mark, no claw-mark where a panther would have gripped it while finding its throat. They read the tracks where the frantic mare had circled and at last rushed in with that same ultimate desperation with which she had whirled on Sam Fathers yesterday evening, and the long tracks of dead and terrified running and those of the beast which had not even rushed at her when she advanced but had merely walked three or four paces toward her until she broke, and General Compson said, "Good God, what a wolf!"

Still Sam said nothing. The boy watched him while the men knelt, measuring the tracks. There was something in Sam's face now. It was neither exultation nor joy nor hope. Later, a man, the boy realised what it had been, and that Sam had known all the time what had made the tracks and what had torn the throat out of the doe in the spring and killed the fawn. It had been foreknowledge in Sam's face that morning. *And he was glad*, he told himself. *He was old. He had no children, no people, none of his blood anywhere above earth that he would ever meet again. And even if he were to, he could not have touched it, spoken to it, because for seventy years now he had had to be a Negro. It was almost over now and he was glad.*

They returned to camp and had breakfast and came back with guns and the hounds. Afterward the boy realised that they also should have known then who killed the colt as well as Sam Fathers did. But that was neither the first nor the last time he had seen men rationalise from and even act upon their misconceptions. After Boon, standing astride the colt, had whipped the dogs away from it with his belt, they snuffed at the tracks. One of them, a young dog hound without judgment yet, bayed once, and they ran for a few feet on what seemed to be a trail. Then they stopped, looking back at the men, eager enough, not baffled, merely questioning, as if they were asking, "Now what?" Then they rushed back to the colt, where Boon, still astride it, slashed at them with the belt.

"I never knew a trail to get cold that quick," General Compson said.

"Maybe a single wolf big enough to kill a colt with the dam right there beside it dont leave scent," Major de Spain said.

"Maybe it was a hant," Walter Ewell said. He looked at Tennie's Jim. "Hah, Jim?"

Because the hounds would not run it, Major de Spain had Sam hunt out and find the tracks a hundred yards further on and they put the dogs on it again and again the young one bayed and not one of them realised then that the hound was not baying like a dog striking game but was merely bellowing like a country dog whose yard has been invaded. General Compson spoke to the boy and Boon and Tennie's Jim: to the squirrel hunters. "You boys keep the dogs with you this morning. He's probably hanging around somewhere, waiting to get his breakfast off the colt. You might strike him."

But they did not. The boy remembered how Sam stood watching them as they went into the woods with the leashed hounds — the Indian face in which he had never seen anything until it smiled except that faint arching of the nostrils on that first morning when the hounds had found Old Ben. They took the hounds with them on the next day, though when they reached the place where they hoped to strike a fresh trail, the carcass of the colt was gone. Then on the third morning Sam was waiting again, this time until they had finished breakfast. He said, "Come." He led them to his house, his little hut, to the corn-crib beyond it. He had removed the corn and had made a dead-fall of the door, baiting it with the colt's carcass; peering between the logs, they saw an animal almost the color of a gun or pistol barrel, what little time they had to examine its color or shape. It was not crouched nor even standing. It was in motion, in the air, coming toward them — a heavy body crashing with tremendous force against the door so that the thick door jumped and clattered in its frame, the animal, whatever it was, hurling itself against the door again seemingly before it could have touched the floor and got a new purchase to spring from. "Come away," Sam said, "fore he break his neck." Even when they retreated the heavy and measured crashes continued, the stout door jumping and clattering each time, and still no sound from the beast itself — no snarl, no cry.

"What in hell's name is it?" Major de Spain said.

"It's a dog," Sam said, his nostrils arching and collapsing faintly and steadily and that faint, fierce milkiness in his eyes again as on that first morning when the hounds had struck the old bear. "It's the dog."

"*The* dog?" Major de Spain said.

"That's gonter hold Old Ben."

"Dog the devil," Major de Spain said. "I'd rather have Old Ben himself in my pack than that brute. Shoot him."

"No," Sam said.

"You'll never tame him. How do you ever expect to make an animal like that afraid of you?"

"I don't want him tame," Sam said; again the boy watched his nostrils and the fierce milky light in his eyes. "But I almost rather he be tame than scared, of me or any man or any thing. But he won't be neither, of nothing."

"Then what are you going to do with it?"

"You can watch," said Sam.

Each morning through the second week they would go to Sam's crib. He had removed a few shingles from the roof and had put a rope on the colt's carcass and had drawn it out when the trap fell. Each morning they would watch him lower a pail of water into the crib while the dog hurled itself tirelessly against the door and dropped back and leaped again. It never made any sound and there was nothing frenzied in the act but only a cold and grim indomitable determination. Toward the end of the week it stopped jumping at the door. Yet it had not weakened appreciably and it was not as if it had rationalised the fact that the door was not going to give. It was as if for that time it simply disdained to jump no longer. It was not down. None of them had ever seen it down. It stood, and they could see it now — part mastiff, something of Airedale and something of a dozen other strains probably, better than thirty inches at the shoulders and weighing as they guessed almost ninety pounds, with cold yellow eyes and a tremendous chest and over all that strange color like a blued gun-barrel.

Then the two weeks were up. They prepared to break camp. The boy begged to remain and his cousin let him. He moved into the little hut with Sam Fathers. Each morning he watched Sam lower the pail of water into the crib. By the end of that week the dog was down. It would rise and half stagger, half crawl to the water and drink and collapse again. One morning it could not even reach the water, could not raise its forequarters even from the floor. Sam took a short stick and prepared to enter the crib. "Wait," the boy said. "Let me get the gun —"

"No," Sam said. "He cant move now." Nor could it. It lay on its side while Sam touched it, its head and the gaunted body, the dog lying motionless, the yellow eyes open. They were not fierce and there was nothing of petty malevolence in them, but a cold and almost impersonal malignance like some natural force. It was not even looking at Sam nor at the boy peering at it between the logs.

Sam began to feed it again. The first time he had to raise its head so it could lap the broth. That night he left a bowl of broth containing lumps of meat where the dog could reach it. The next morning the bowl was empty and the dog was lying on its belly, its head up, the cold yellow eyes watching the door as Sam entered, no change whatever in the cold yellow eyes and still no sound from it even when it sprang, its aim and co-ordination still bad from weakness so that Sam had time to strike it down with the stick and leap from the crib and slam the door as the dog, still without having had time to get its feet under it to jump again seemingly, hurled itself against the door as if the two weeks of starving had never been.

At noon that day someone came whooping through the woods from the direction of the camp. It was Boon. He came and looked for a while between the logs, at the tremendous dog lying again on its belly, its head up, the yellow eyes blinking sleepily at nothing: the indomitable and unbroken spirit. "What we better do," Boon said, "is to let that son of a bitch go and catch Old Ben and run him on the dog." He turned to the boy his weather-reddened and beetling face. "Get your traps together. Cass says for you to come on home. You been in here fooling with that horse-eating varmint long enough."

Boon had a borrowed mule at the camp; the buggy was waiting at the edge of the bottom. He was at home that night. He told McCaslin about it. "Sam's going to starve him again until he can go in and touch him. Then he will feed him again. Then he will starve him again, if he has to."

"But why?" McCaslin said. "What for? Even Sam will never tame that brute."

"We dont want him tame. We want him like he is. We just want him to find out at last that the only way he can get out of that crib and stay out of it is to do what Sam or somebody tells him to do. He's the dog that's going to stop Old Ben and hold him. We've already named him. His name is Lion."

Then November came at last. They returned to the camp. With General Compson and Major de Spain and his cousin and Walter and Boon he stood in the yard among the guns and bedding and boxes of food and watched Sam Fathers and Lion come up the lane from the lot — the Indian, the old man in battered overalls and rubber boots and a worn sheepskin coat and a hat which had belonged to the boy's father; the tremendous dog pacing gravely beside him. The hounds rushed out to meet them and stopped, except the young one which still had but little of judgment. It ran up to Lion, fawning. Lion didn't snap at it. He

didn't even pause. He struck it rolling and yelping for five or six feet with a blow of one paw as a bear would have done and came on into the yard and stood, blinking sleepily at nothing, looking at no one, while Boon said, "Jesus. Jesus. — Will he let me touch him?"

"You can touch him," Sam said. "He dont care. He dont care about nothing or nobody."

The boy watched that too. He watched it for the next two years from that moment when Boon touched Lion's head and then knelt beside him, feeling the bones and muscles, the power. It was as if Lion were a woman — or perhaps Boon was the woman. That was more like it — the big, grave, sleepy-seeming dog which, as Sam Fathers said, cared about no man and no thing; and the violent, insensitive, hard-faced man with his touch of remote Indian blood and the mind almost of a child. He watched Boon take over Lion's feeding from Sam and Uncle Ash both. He would see Boon squatting in the cold rain beside the kitchen while Lion ate. Because Lion neither slept nor ate with the other dogs though none of them knew where he did sleep until in the second November, thinking until then that Lion slept in his kennel beside Sam Fathers' hut, when the boy's cousin McCaslin said something about it to Sam by sheer chance and Sam told him. And that night the boy and Major de Spain and McCaslin with a lamp entered the back room where Boon slept — the little, tight, airless room rank with the smell of Boon's unwashed body and his wet hunting-clothes — where Boon, snoring on his back, choked and waked and Lion raised his head beside him and looked back at them from his cold, slumbrous yellow eyes.

"Damn it, Boon," McCaslin said. "Get that dog out of here. He's got to run Old Ben tomorrow morning. How in hell do you expect him to smell anything fancier than a skunk after breathing you all night?"

"The way I smell aint hurt my nose none that I ever noticed," Boon said.

"It wouldn't matter if it had," Major de Spain said. "We're not depending on you to trail a bear. Put him outside. Put him under the house with the other dogs."

Boon began to get up. "He'll kill the first one that happens to yawn or sneeze in his face or touches him."

"I reckon not," Major de Spain said. "None of them are going to risk yawning in his face or touching him either, even asleep. Put him outside. I want his nose right tomorrow. Old Ben fooled him last year. I dont think he will do it again."

Boon put on his shoes without lacing them; in his long soiled underwear, his hair still tousled from sleep, he and Lion went out. The others returned to the front room and the poker game where McCaslin's and Major de Spain's hands waited for them on the table. After a while McCaslin said, "Do you want me to go back and look again?"

"No," Major de Spain said. "I call," he said to Walter Ewell. He spoke to McCaslin again. "If you do, dont tell me. I am beginning to see the first sign of my increasing age: I dont like to know that my orders have been disobeyed, even when I knew when I gave them that they would be. — A small pair," he said to Walter Ewell.

"How small?" Walter said.

"Very small," Major de Spain said.

And the boy, lying beneath his piled quilts and blankets waiting for sleep, knew likewise that Lion was already back in Boon's bed, for the rest of that night and the next one and during all the nights of the next November and the next one. He thought then: *I wonder what Sam thinks. He could have Lion with him, even if Boon is a white man. He could ask Major or McCaslin either. And more than that. It was Sam's hand that touched Lion first and Lion knows it.* Then he became a man and he knew that too. It had been all right. That was the way it should have been. Sam was the chief, the prince; Boon, the plebeian, was his huntsman. Boon should have nursed the dogs.

On the first morning that Lion led the pack after Old Ben, seven strangers appeared in the camp. They were swampers: gaunt, malaria-ridden men appearing from nowhere, who ran trap-lines for coons or perhaps farmed little patches of cotton and corn along the edge of the bottom, in clothes but little better than Sam Fathers' and nowhere near as good as Tennie's Jim's, with worn shotguns and rifles, already squatting patiently in the cold drizzle in the side yard when day broke. They had a spokesman; afterward Sam Fathers told Major de Spain how all during the past summer and fall they had drifted into the camp singly or in pairs and threes, to look quietly at Lion for a while and then go away: "Mawnin, Major. We heerd you was aimin to put that ere blue dawg on that old two-toed bear this mawnin. We figgered we'd come up and watch, if you dont mind. We wont do no shooting, lessen he runs over us."

"You are welcome," Major de Spain said. "You are welcome to shoot. He's more your bear than ours."

"I reckon that aint no lie. I done fed him enough cawn to have a sheer in him. Not to mention a shoat three years ago."

"I reckon I got a sheer too," another said. "Only it aint in the bear." Major de Spain looked at him. He was chewing tobacco. He spat. "Hit was a heifer calf. Nice un too. Last year. When I finally found her, I reckon she looked about like that colt of yourn looked last June."

"Oh," Major de Spain said. "Be welcome. If you see game in front of my dogs, shoot it."

Nobody shot Old Ben that day. No man saw him. The dogs jumped him within a hundred yards of the glade where the boy had seen him that day in the summer of his eleventh year. The boy was less than a quarter-mile away. He heard the jump but he could distinguish no voice among the dogs that he did not know and therefore would be Lion's, and he thought, believed, that Lion was not among them. Even the fact that they were going much faster than he had ever heard them run behind Old Ben before and that the high thin note of hysteria was missing now from their voices was not enough to disabuse him. He didn't comprehend until that night, when Sam told him that Lion would never cry on a trail. "He gonter growl when he catches Old Ben's throat," Sam said. "But he aint gonter never holler, no more than he ever done when he was jumping at that two-inch door. It's that blue dog in him. What you call it?"

"Airedale," the boy said.

Lion was there; the jump was just too close to the river. When Boon returned with Lion about eleven that night, he swore that Lion had stopped Old Ben once but that the hounds would not go in and Old Ben broke away and took to the river and swam for miles down it and he and Lion went down one bank for about ten miles and crossed and came up the other but it had begun to get dark before they struck any trail where Old Ben had come up out of the water, unless he was still in the water when he passed the ford where they crossed. Then he fell to cursing the hounds and ate the supper

Uncle Ash had saved for him and went off to bed and after a while the boy opened the door of the little stale room thunderous with snoring and the great grave dog raised its head from Boon's pillow and blinked at him for a moment and lowered its head again.

When the next November came and the last day, the day which it was now becoming traditional to save for Old Ben, there were more than a dozen strangers waiting. They were not all swampers this time. Some of them were townsmen, from other county seats like Jefferson, who had heard about Lion and Old Ben and had come to watch the great blue dog keep his yearly rendezvous with the old two-toed bear. Some of them didn't even have guns and the hunting-clothes and boots they wore had been on a store shelf yesterday.

This time Lion jumped Old Ben more than five miles from the river and bayed and held him and this time the hounds went in, in a sort of desperate emulation. The boy heard them; he was that near. He heard Boon whooping; he heard the two shots when General Compson delivered both barrels, one containing five buckshot, the other a single ball, into the bear from as close as he could force his almost unmanageable horse. He heard the dogs when the bear broke free again. He was running now; panting, stumbling, his lungs bursting, he reached the place where General Compson had fired and where Old Ben had killed two of the hounds. He saw the blood from General Compson's shots, but he could go no further. He stopped, leaning against a tree for his breathing to ease and his heart to slow, hearing the sound of the dogs as it faded on and died away.

In camp that night — they had as guests five of the still terrified strangers in new hunting coats and boots who had been lost all day until Sam Fathers went out and got them — he heard the rest of it: how Lion had stopped and held the bear again but only the one-eyed mule which did not mind the smell of wild blood would approach and Boon was riding the mule and Boon had never been known to hit anything. He shot at the bear five times with his pump gun, touching nothing, and Old Ben killed another hound and broke free once more and reached the river and was gone. Again Boon and Lion hunted as far down one bank as they dared. Too far; they crossed in the first of dusk and dark overtook them within a mile. And this time Lion found the broken trail, the

blood perhaps, in the darkness where Old Ben had come up out of the water, but Boon had him on a rope, luckily, and he got down from the mule and fought Lion hand-to-hand until he got him back to camp. This time Boon didn't even curse. He stood in the door, muddy, spent, his huge gargoyle's face tragic and still amazed. "I missed him," he said. "I was in twenty-five feet of him and I missed him five times."

"But we have drawn blood," Major de Spain said. "General Compson drew blood. We have never done that before."

"But I missed him," Boon said. "I missed him five times. With Lion looking right at me."

"Never mind," Major de Spain said. "It was a damned fine race. And we drew blood. Next year we'll let General Compson or Walter ride Katie, and we'll get him."

Then McCaslin said, "Where is Lion, Boon?"

"I left him at Sam's," Boon said. He was already turning away. "I aint fit to sleep with him."

So he should have hated and feared Lion. Yet he did not. It seemed to him that there was a fatality in it. It seemed to him that something, he didn't know what, was beginning; had already begun. It was like the last act on a set stage. It was the beginning of the end of something, he didn't know what except that he would not grieve. He would be humble and proud that he had been found worthy to be a part of it too or even just to see it too.

3

It was December. It was the coldest December he had ever remembered. They had been in camp four days over two weeks, waiting for the weather to soften so that Lion and Old Ben could run their yearly race. Then they would break camp and go home. Because of these unforeseen additional days which they had had to pass waiting on the weather, with nothing to do but play poker, the whisky had given out and he and Boon were being sent to Memphis with a suitcase and a note from Major de Spain to Mr Semmes, the distiller, to get more. That is, Major de Spain and McCaslin were sending Boon to get the whisky and sending him to see that Boon got back with it or most of it or at least some of it.

Tennie's Jim waked him at three. He dressed rapidly, shivering, not so much from the cold because a fresh fire already boomed and roared on the hearth, but in that dead winter hour when the blood and the heart are slow and sleep is incomplete. He crossed the gap between house and kitchen, the gap of iron earth beneath the brilliant and rigid night where dawn would not begin for three hours yet, tasting, tongue, palate, and to the very bottom of his lungs, the searing dark, and entered the kitchen, the lamp-lit warmth where the stove glowed, fogging the windows, and where Boon already sat at the table at breakfast, hunched over his plate, almost in his plate, his working jaws blue with stubble and his face innocent of water and his coarse, horse-mane hair innocent of comb — the quarter Indian, grandson of a Chickasaw squaw, who on occasion resented with his hard and furious fists the intimation of one single drop of alien blood and on others, usually after whisky, affirmed with the same fists and the same fury that his father had been the full-blood Chickasaw and even a chief and that even his mother had been only half white. He was four inches over six feet; he had the mind of a child, the heart of a horse, and little hard shoe-button eyes without depth or meanness or generosity or viciousness or gentleness or anything else, in the ugliest face the boy had ever seen. It looked like somebody had found a walnut a little larger than a football and with a machinist's hammer had shaped features into it and then painted it, mostly red; not Indian red but a fine bright ruddy color which whisky might have had something to do with but which was mostly just happy and violent out-of-doors, the wrinkles in it not the residue of the forty years it had survived but from squinting into the sun or into the gloom of cane-brakes where game had run, baked into it by the camp fires before which he had lain trying to sleep on the cold November or December ground while waiting for daylight so he could rise and hunt again, as though time were merely something he walked through as he did through air, aging him no more than air did. He was brave, faithful, improvident and unreliable; he had neither profession job nor trade and owned one vice and one virtue: whisky, and that absolute and unquestioning fidelity to Major de Spain and the boy's cousin McCaslin. "Sometimes I'd call them both virtues," Major de Spain said once. "Or both vices," McCaslin said.

He ate his breakfast, hearing the dogs under the kitchen, wakened by the smell of frying meat or perhaps by the feet overhead. He heard Lion once, short and peremptory, as the best hunter in any camp has only to speak once to all save the fools, and none other of Major de Spain's and McCaslin's dogs were Lion's equal in size and strength and perhaps even in courage, but they were not fools; Old Ben had killed the last fool among them last year.

Tennie's Jim came in as they finished. The wagon was outside. Ash decided he would drive them over to the log-line where they would flag the outbound log-train and let Tennie's Jim wash the dishes. The boy knew why. It would not be the first time he had listened to old Ash badgering Boon.

It was cold. The wagon wheels banged and clattered on the frozen ground; the sky was fixed and brilliant. He was not shivering, he was shaking, slow and steady and hard, the food he had just eaten still warm and solid inside him while his outside shook slow and steady around it as though his stomach floated loose. "They wont run this morning," he said. "No dog will have any nose today."

"Cep Lion," Ash said. "Lion dont need no nose. All he need is a bear." He had wrapped his feet in towsacks and he had a quilt from his pallet bed on the kitchen floor drawn over his head and wrapped around him until in the thin brilliant starlight he looked like nothing at all that the boy had ever seen before. "He run a bear through a thousand-acre ice-house. Catch him too. Them other dogs dont matter because they aint going to keep up with Lion nohow, long as he got a bear in front of him."

"What's wrong with the other dogs?" Boon said. "What the hell do you know about it anyway? This is the first time you've had your tail out of that kitchen since we got here except to chop a little wood."

"Aint nothing wrong with them," Ash said. "And long as it's left up to them, aint nothing going to be. I just wish I had knowed all my life how to take care of my health good as them hounds knows."

"Well, they aint going to run this morning," Boon said. His voice was harsh and positive. "Major promised they wouldn't until me and Ike get back."

"Weather gonter break today. Gonter soft up. Rain by night." Then Ash laughed, chuckled, somewhere inside the quilt which concealed even his face. "Hum up here, mules!" he said, jerking the reins so that the mules leaped forward and snatched the lurching and banging wagon for several feet before they slowed again into their quick, short-paced, rapid plodding. "Sides, I like to know why Major need to wait on you. It's Lion he aiming to use. I aint never heard tell of you bringing no bear nor no other kind of meat into this camp."

Now Boon's going to curse Ash or maybe even hit him, the boy thought. But Boon never did, never had; the boy knew he never would even though four years ago Boon had shot five times with a borrowed pistol at a Negro on the street in Jefferson, with the same result as when he had shot five times at Old Ben last fall. "By God," Boon said, "he aint going to put Lion or no other dog on nothing until I get back tonight. Because he promised me. Whip up them mules and keep them whipped up. Do you want me to freeze to death?"

They reached the log-line and built a fire. After a while the log-train came up out of the woods under the paling east and Boon flagged it. Then in the warm caboose the boy slept again while Boon and the conductor and brakeman talked about Lion and Old Ben as people later would talk about Sullivan and Kilrain and, later still, about Dempsey and Tunney. Dozing, swaying as the springless caboose lurched and clattered, he would hear them still talking, about the shoats and calves Old Ben had killed and the cribs he had rifled and the traps and deadfalls he had wrecked and the lead he probably carried under his hide — Old Ben, the two-toed bear in a land where bears with trap-ruined feet had been called Two-Toe or Three-Toe or Cripple-Foot for fifty years, only Old Ben was an extra bear (the head bear, General Compson called him) and so had earned a name such as a human man could have worn and not been sorry.

They reached Hoke's at sunup. They emerged from the warm caboose in their hunting clothes, the muddy boots and stained khaki and Boon's blue unshaven jowls. But that was all right. Hoke's was a sawmill and commissary and two stores and a loading-chute on a sidetrack from the main line, and all the men in it wore boots and khaki too. Presently the Memphis train came. Boon bought three packages of popcorn-and-molasses and a bottle of beer from the news butch and the boy went to sleep again to the sound of his chewing.

But in Memphis it was not all right. It was as if the high buildings and the hard pavements, the fine carriages and the horse cars and the men in starched collars and neckties made their boots and khaki look a little rougher and a little muddier and made Boon's beard look worse and more unshaven and his face look more and more like he should never have brought it out of the woods at all or at least out of reach of Major de Spain or McCaslin or someone who knew it and could have said, "Dont be afraid. He wont hurt you." He walked through the station, on the slick floor, his face moving as he worked the popcorn out of his teeth with his tongue, his legs spraddled and stiff in the hips as if he were walking on buttered glass, and that blue stubble on his face like the filings from a new gun-barrel. They passed the first saloon. Even through the closed doors the boy could seem to smell the sawdust and the reek of old drink. Boon began to cough. He coughed for something less than a minute. "Damn this cold," he said. "I'd sure like to know where I got it."

"Back there in the station," the boy said.

Boon had started to cough again. He stopped. He looked at the boy. "What?" he said.

"You never had it when we left camp nor on the train either." Boon looked at him, blinking. Then he stopped blinking. He didn't cough again. He said quietly:

"Lend me a dollar. Come on. You've got it. If you ever had one, you've still got it. I dont mean you are tight with your money because you aint. You just dont never seem to ever think of nothing you want. When I was sixteen a dollar bill melted off of me before I even had time to read the name of the bank that issued it." He said quietly: "Let me have a dollar, Ike."

"You promised Major. You promised McCaslin. Not till we get back to camp."

"All right," Boon said in that quiet and patient voice. "What can I do on just one dollar? You aint going to lend me another."

"You're damn right I aint," the boy said, his voice quiet too, cold with rage which was not at Boon, remembering: Boon snoring in a hard chair in the kitchen so he could watch the clock and wake him and McCaslin and drive them the seventeen miles in to Jefferson to catch the train to Memphis; the wild, never-bridled Texas paint pony which he had persuaded McCaslin to let him buy and which he and Boon had bought at auction for four dollars and seventy-five cents and fetched home wired between two gentle old mares with pieces of barbed wire and which had never even seen shelled corn before and didn't even know what it was unless the grains were bugs maybe and at last (he was ten and Boon had been ten all his life) Boon said the pony was gentled and with a towsack over its head and four Negroes to hold it they backed it into an old two-wheeled cart and hooked up the gear and he and Boon got up and Boon said, "All right, boys. Let him go" and one of the Negroes — it was Tennie's Jim — snatched the towsack off and leaped for his life and they lost the first wheel against a post of the open gate only at that moment Boon caught him by the scruff of the neck and flung him into the roadside ditch so he only saw the rest of it in fragments: the other wheel as it slammed through the side gate and crossed the back yard and leaped up onto the gallery and scraps of the cart here and there along the road and Boon vanishing rapidly on his stomach in the leaping and spurting dust and still holding the reins until they broke too and two days later they finally caught the pony seven miles away still wearing the hames and the headstall of the bridle around its neck like a duchess with two necklaces at one time. He gave Boon the dollar.

"All right," Boon said. "Come on in out of the cold."

"I aint cold," he said.

"You can have some lemonade."

"I dont want any lemonade."

The door closed behind him. The sun was well up now. It was a brilliant day, though Ash had said it would rain before night. Already it was warmer; they could run tomorrow. He felt the old lift of the heart, as pristine as ever, as on the first day; he would never lose it, no matter how old in hunting and pursuit: the best, the best of all breathing, the humility and the pride. He must stop thinking about it. Already it seemed to him that he was running, back to the station, to the tracks themselves: the first train going south, he must stop thinking about it. The street was busy. He watched the big Norman draft horses, the Percherons; the trim carriages from which the men in the fine overcoats and the ladies rosy in furs descended and entered the station. (They were still next door to it but one.) Twenty years ago his father had ridden into Memphis as a member of Colonel Sartoris' horse in Forrest's command, up Main street and (the tale told) into the lobby of the Gayoso Hotel where the Yankee officers sat in the leather chairs spitting into the tall bright cuspidors and then out again, scot-free —

The door opened behind him. Boon was wiping his mouth on the back of his hand. "All right," he said. "Let's go tend to it and get the hell out of here."

They went and had the suitcase packed. He never knew where or when Boon got the other bottle. Doubtless Mr Semmes gave it to him. When they reached Hoke's again at sundown, it was empty. They could get a return train to Hoke's in two hours; they went straight back to the station as Major de Spain and then McCaslin had told Boon to do and then ordered him to do and had sent the boy along to see that he did. Boon took the first drink from his bottle in the wash room. A man in a uniform cap came to tell him he couldn't drink there and looked at Boon's face once and said nothing. The next time he was pouring into his water glass beneath the edge of a table in the restaurant when the manager (she was a woman) did tell him he couldn't drink there and he went back to the washroom. He had been telling the Negro waiter and all the other people in the restaurant who couldn't help but hear him and who had never heard of Lion and didn't want to, about Lion and Old Ben. Then he happened to think of the zoo. He had found out that there was another train to Hoke's at three oclock and so they would spend the time at the zoo and take the three oclock train until he came back from the washroom for the third time. Then they would take the first train back to camp, get Lion and come back to the zoo where, he said, the bears were fed on ice cream and lady fingers and he would match Lion against them all.

So they missed the first train, the one they were supposed to take, but he got Boon onto the three oclock train and they were all right again, with Boon not even going to the washroom now but drinking in the aisle and talking about Lion and the men he buttonholed no more daring to tell Boon he couldn't drink there than the man in the station had dared.

When they reached Hoke's at sundown, Boon was asleep. The boy waked him at last and got him and the suitcase off the train and he even persuaded him to eat some supper at the sawmill commissary. So he was all right when they got in the caboose of the log-train to go back into the woods, with the sun going down red and the sky already overcast and the ground would not freeze tonight. It was the boy who slept now, sitting behind the ruby stove while the springless caboose jumped and clattered and Boon and the brakeman and the conductor talked about Lion and Old Ben because they knew what Boon was talking about because this was home. "Overcast and already thawing," Boon said. "Lion will get him tomorrow."

It would have to be Lion, or somebody. It would not be Boon. He had never hit anything bigger than a squirrel that anybody ever knew, except the Negro woman that day when he was shooting at the Negro man. He was a big Negro and not ten feet away but Boon shot five times with the pistol he had borrowed from Major de Spain's Negro coachman and the Negro he was shooting at outed with a dollar-and-a-half mail-order pistol and would have burned Boon down with it only it never went off, it just went snicksnicksnicksnicksnick five times and Boon still blasting away and he broke a plate-glass window that cost McCaslin forty-five dollars and hit a Negro woman who happened to be passing in the leg only Major de Spain paid for that; he and McCaslin cut cards, the plate-glass window against the Negro woman's leg. And the first day on stand this year, the first morning in camp, the buck ran right over Boon; he heard Boon's old pump gun go whow. whow. whow. whow. whow. and then his voice: "God damn, here he comes! Head him! Head him!" and when he got there the buck's tracks and the five exploded shells were not twenty paces apart.

There were five guests in camp that night from Jefferson: Mr. Bayard Sartoris and his son and General Compson's son and two others. And the next morning he looked out the window, into the gray thin drizzle of daybreak which Ash had predicted, and there they were, standing and squatting beneath the thin rain, almost two dozen of them who had fed Old Ben corn and shoats and even calves for ten years, in their worn hats and hunting coats and overalls which any town Negro would have thrown away or burned and only the rubber boots strong and sound, and the worn and blue-less guns, and some even without guns. While they ate breakfast a dozen more arrived, mounted and on foot: loggers from the camp thirteen miles below and sawmill men from Hoke's and the only gun among them that one which the log-train conductor carried: so that when they went into the woods this morning Major de Spain led a party almost as strong, excepting that some of them were not armed, as some he had led in the last darkening days of '64 and '65. The little yard would not hold them. They overflowed it, into the lane where Major de Spain sat his mare while Ash in his dirty apron thrust the greasy cartridges into his carbine and passed it up to him and the great grave blue dog stood at his stirrup not as a dog stands but as a horse stands, blinking his sleepy topaz eyes at nothing, deaf even to the yelling of the hounds which Boon and Tennie's Jim held on leash.

"We'll put General Compson on Katie this morning," Major de Spain said. "He drew blood last year; if he'd had a mule then that would have stood, he would have —"

"No," General Compson said. "I'm too old to go helling through the woods on a mule or a horse or anything else any more. Besides, I had my chance last year and missed it. I'm going on a stand this morning. I'm going to let that boy ride Katie."

"No, wait," McCaslin said. "Ike's got the rest of his life to hunt bears in. Let somebody else —"

"No," General Compson said. "I want Ike to ride Katie. He's already a better woodsman than you or me either and in another ten years he'll be as good as Walter."

At first he couldn't believe it, not until Major de Spain spoke to him. Then he was up, on the one-eyed mule which would not spook at wild blood, looking down at the dog motionless at Major de Spain's stirrup, looking in the gray streaming light bigger than a calf, bigger than he knew it actually was — the big head, the chest almost as big as his own, the blue hide beneath which the muscles flinched or quivered to no touch since the heart which drove blood to them loved no man and no thing, standing as a horse stands yet different from a horse which infers only weight and speed while Lion inferred not only courage and all else that went to make up the will and desire to pursue and kill, but endurance, the will and desire to endure beyond all imaginable limits of flesh in order to overtake and slay. Then the dog looked at him. It moved its head and looked at him across the trivial uproar of the hounds, out of the yellow eyes as depthless as Boon's, as free as Boon's of meanness or generosity or gentleness or viciousness. They were just cold and sleepy. Then it blinked, and he knew it was not looking at him and never had been, without even bothering to turn its head away.

That morning he heard the first cry. Lion had already vanished while Sam and Tennie's Jim were putting saddles on the mule and horse which had drawn the wagon and he watched the hounds as they crossed and cast, snuffing and whimpering, until they too disappeared. Then he and Major de Spain and Sam and Tennie's Jim rode after them and heard the first cry out of the wet and thawing woods not two hundred yards ahead, high, with that abject, almost human quality he had come to know, and the other hounds joining in until the gloomed woods rang and clamored. They rode then. It seemed to him that he could actually see the big blue dog boring on, silent, and the bear too: the thick, locomotive-like shape which he had seen that day four years ago crossing the blow-down, crashing on ahead of the dogs faster than he had believed it could have moved, drawing away even from the running mules. He heard a shotgun, once. The woods had opened, they were going fast, the clamor faint and fading on ahead; they passed the man who had fired — a swamper, a pointing arm, a gaunt face, the small black orifice of his yelling studded with rotten teeth.

He heard the changed note in the hounds' uproar and two hundred yards ahead he saw them. The bear had turned. He saw Lion drive in without pausing and saw the bear strike him aside and lunge into the yelling hounds and kill one of them almost in its tracks and whirl and run again. Then they were in a streaming tide of dogs. He heard Major de Spain and Tennie's Jim shouting and the pistol sound of Tennie's Jim's leather thong as he tried to turn them. Then he and Sam Fathers were riding alone. One of the hounds had kept on with Lion though. He recognised its voice. It was the young hound which even a year ago had had no judgment and which, by the lights of the other hounds anyway, still had none. *Maybe that's what courage is*, he thought. "Right," Sam said behind him. "Right. We got to turn him from the river if we can."

Now they were in cane: a brake. He knew the path through it as well as Sam did. They came out of the undergrowth and struck the entrance almost exactly. It would traverse the brake and come out onto a high open ridge above the river. He heard the flat clap of Walter Ewell's rifle, then two more. "No," Sam said. "I can hear the hound. Go on."

They emerged from the narrow roofless tunnel of snapping and hissing cane, still galloping, onto the open ridge below which the thick yellow river, reflectionless in the gray and streaming light, seemed not to move. Now he could hear the hound too. It was not running. The cry was a high frantic yapping and Boon was running along the edge of the bluff, his old gun leaping and jouncing against his back on its sling made of a piece of cotton plow-line. He whirled and ran up to them, wild-faced, and flung himself onto the mule behind the boy. "That damn boat!" he cried. "It's on the other side! He went straight across! Lion was too close to him! That little hound too! Lion was so close I couldn't shoot! Go on!" he cried, beating his heels into the mule's flanks. "Go on!"

They plunged down the bank, slipping and sliding in the thawed earth, crashing through the willows and into the water. He felt no shock, no cold, he on one side of the swimming mule, grasping the pommel with one hand and holding his gun above the water with the other, Boon opposite him. Sam was behind them somewhere, and then the river, the water about them, was full of dogs. They swam faster than the mules; they were scrabbling up the bank before the mules touched bottom. Major de Spain was whooping from the bank they had just left and, looking back, he saw Tennie's Jim and the horse as they went into the water.

Now the woods ahead of them and the rain-heavy air were one uproar. It rang and clamored; it echoed and broke against the bank behind them and reformed and clamored and rang until it seemed to the boy that all the hounds which had ever bayed game in this land were yelling down at him. He got his leg over the mule as it came up out of the water. Boon didn't try to mount again. He grasped one stirrup as they went up the bank and crashed through the undergrowth which fringed the bluff and saw the bear, on its hind feet, its back against a tree while the bellowing hounds swirled around it and once more Lion drove in, leaping clear of the ground.

This time the bear didn't strike him down. It caught the dog in both arms, almost lover-like, and they both went down. He was off the mule now. He drew back both hammers of the gun but he could see nothing but moiling spotted houndbodies until the bear surged up again. Boon was yelling something, he could not tell what; he could see Lion still clinging to the bear's throat and he saw the bear, half erect, strike one of the hounds with one paw and hurl it five or six feet and then, rising and rising as though it would never stop, stand erect again and begin to rake at Lion's belly with its forepaws. Then Boon was running. The boy saw the gleam of the blade in his hand and watched him leap among the hounds, hurdling them, kicking them aside as he ran, and fling himself astride the bear as he had hurled himself onto the mule, his legs locked around the bear's belly, his left arm under the bear's throat where Lion clung, and the glint of the knife as it rose and fell.

It fell just once. For an instant they almost resembled a piece of statuary: the clinging dog, the bear, the man astride its back, working and probing the buried blade. Then they went down, pulled over backward by Boon's weight, Boon underneath. It was the bear's back which reappeared first but at once Boon was astride it again. He had never released the knife and again the boy saw the almost infinitesimal movement of his arm and shoulder as he probed and sought; then the bear surged erect, raising with it the man and the dog too, and turned and still carrying the man and the dog it took two or three steps toward the woods on its hind feet as a man would have walked and crashed down. It didn't collapse, crumple. It fell all of a piece, as a tree falls, so that all three of them, man, dog, and bear, seemed to bounce once.

He and Tennie's Jim ran forward. Boon was kneeling at the bear's head. His left ear was shredded, his left coat sleeve was completely gone, his right boot had been ripped from knee to instep; the bright blood thinned in the thin rain down his leg and hand and arm and down the side of his face which was no longer wild but was quite calm. Together they prized Lion's jaws from the bear's throat. "Easy, god-damn it," Boon said. "Can't you see his guts are all out of him?" He began to remove his coat. He spoke to Tennie's Jim in that calm voice: "Bring the boat up. It's about a hundred yards down the bank there. I saw it." Tennie's Jim rose and went away. Then, and he could not remember if it had been a call or an exclamation from Tennie's Jim or if he had glanced up by chance, he saw Tennie's Jim stooping and saw Sam Fathers lying motionless on his face in the trampled mud.

The mule had not thrown him. He remembered that Sam was down too even before Boon began to run. There was no mark on him what-

ever and when he and Boon turned him over, his eyes were open and he said something in that tongue which he and Joe Baker had used to speak together. But he couldn't move. Tennie's Jim brought the skiff up; they could hear him shouting to Major de Spain across the river. Boon wrapped Lion in his hunting coat and carried him down to the skiff and they carried Sam down and returned and hitched the bear to the one-eyed mule's saddle-bow with Tennie's Jim's leash-thong and dragged him down to the skiff and got him into it and left Tennie's Jim to swim the horse and the two mules back across. Major de Spain caught the bow of the skiff as Boon jumped out and past him before it touched the bank. He looked at Old Ben and said quietly: "Well." Then he walked into the water and leaned down and touched Sam and Sam looked up at him and said something in that old tongue he and Joe Baker spoke. "You dont know what happened?" Major de Spain said.

"No, sir," the boy said. "It wasn't the mule. It wasn't anything. He was off the mule when Boon ran in on the bear. Then we looked up and he was lying on the ground." Boon was shouting at Tennie's Jim, still in the middle of the river.

"Come on, goddam it!" he said. "Bring me that mule!"

"What do you want with a mule?" Major de Spain said.

Boon didn't even look at him. "I'm going to Hoke's to get the doctor," he said in that calm voice, his face quite calm beneath the steady thinning of the bright blood.

"You need a doctor yourself," Major de Spain said. "Tennie's Jim —"

"Damn that," Boon said. He turned on Major de Spain. His face was still calm, only his voice was a pitch higher. "Cant you see his goddamn guts are all out of him?"

"Boon!" Major de Spain said. They looked at one another. Boon was a good head taller than Major de Spain; even the boy was taller now than Major de Spain.

"I've got to get the doctor," Boon said. "His goddamn guts —"

"All right," Major de Spain said. Tennie's Jim came up out of the water. The horse and the sound mule had already scented Old Ben; they surged and plunged all the way up to the top of the bluff, dragging Tennie's Jim with them, before he could stop them and tie them and come back. Major de Spain unlooped the leather thong of his compass from his button-hole and gave it to Tennie's Jim. "Go straight to Hoke's," he said. "Bring Doctor Crawford back with you. Tell him there are two men to be looked at. Take my mare. Can you find the road from here?"

"Yes, sir," Tennie's Jim said.

"All right," Major de Spain said. "Go on." He turned to the boy. "Take the mules and the horse and go back and get the wagon. We'll go on down the river in the boat to Coon bridge. Meet us there. Can you find it again?"

"Yes, sir," the boy said.

"All right. Get started."

He went back to the wagon. He realised then how far they had run. It was already afternoon when he put the mules into the traces and tied the horse's lead-rope to the tail-gate. He reached Coon bridge at dusk. The skiff was already there. Before he could see it and almost before he could see the water he had to leap from the tilting wagon, still holding the reins, and work around to where he could grasp the bit and then the ear of the plunging sound mule and dig his heels and hold it until Boon came up the bank. The rope of the led horse had already snapped and it had already disappeared up the road toward camp. They turned the wagon around and took the mules out and he led the sound mule a hundred yards up the road and tied it. Boon had already brought Lion up to the wagon and Sam was sitting up in the skiff now and when they raised him he tried to walk, up the bank and to the wagon and he tried to climb into the wagon but Boon did not wait; he picked Sam up bodily and set him on the seat. Then they hitched Old Ben to the one-eyed mule's saddle again and dragged him up the bank and set two skid-poles into the open tail-gate and got him into the wagon and he went and got the sound mule and Boon fought it into the traces, striking it across its hard hollow-sounding face until it came into position and stood trembling. Then the rain came down, as though it had held off all day waiting on them.

They returned to camp through it, through the streaming and sightless dark, hearing long before they saw any light the horn and the spaced shots to guide them. When they came to Sam's dark little hut he tried to stand up. He spoke again in the tongue of the old fathers; then he said clearly: "Let me out. Let me out."

"He hasn't got any fire," Major said. "Go on!" he said sharply.

But Sam was struggling now, trying to stand up. "Let me out, master," he said. "Let me go home."

So he stopped the wagon and Boon got down and lifted Sam out. He did not wait to let Sam try to walk this time. He carried him into the hut and Major de Spain got light on a paper spill from the buried embers on the hearth and lit the lamp and Boon put Sam on his bunk and drew off his boots and Major de Spain covered him and the boy was not there, he was holding the mules, the sound one which was trying again to bolt since when the wagon stopped Old Ben's scent drifted forward again along the streaming blackness of air, but Sam's eyes were probably open again on that profound look which saw further than them or the hut, further than the death of a bear and the dying of a dog. Then they went on, toward the long wailing of the horn and the shots which seemed each to linger intact somewhere in the thick streaming air until the next spaced report joined and blended with it, to the lighted house, the bright streaming windows, the quiet faces as Boon entered, bloody and quite calm, carrying the bundled coat. He laid Lion, blood coat and all, on his stale sheetless pallet bed which not even Ash, as deft in the house as a woman, could ever make smooth.

The sawmill doctor from Hoke's was already there. Boon would not let the doctor touch him until he had seen to Lion. He wouldn't risk giving Lion chloroform. He put the entrails back and sewed him up without it while Major de Spain held his head and Boon his feet. But he never tried to move. He lay there, the yellow eyes open upon nothing while the quiet men in the new hunting clothes and in the old ones crowded into the little airless room rank with the smell of Boon's body and garments, and watched. Then the doctor cleaned and disinfected Boon's face and arm and leg and bandaged them and, the boy in front with a lantern and the doctor and McCaslin and Major de Spain and General Compson following, they went to Sam Fathers' hut. Tennie's Jim had built up the fire; he squatted before it, dozing. Sam had not moved since Boon had put him in the bunk and Major de Spain had covered him with the blankets, yet he opened his eyes and looked from one to another of the faces and when McCaslin touched his shoulder and said,

"Sam. The doctor wants to look at you," he even drew his hands out of the blanket and began to fumble at his shirt buttons until Mc-Caslin said, "Wait. We'll do it." They undressed him. He lay there — the copper-brown, almost hairless body, the old man's body, the old man, the wild man not even one generation from the woods, childless, kinless, peopleless — motionless, his eyes open but no longer looking at any of them, while the doctor examined him and drew the blankets up and put the stethoscope back into his bag and snapped the bag and only the boy knew that Sam too was going to die.

"Exhaustion," the doctor said. "Shock maybe. A man his age swimming rivers in December. He'll be all right. Just make him stay in bed for a day or two. Will there be somebody here with him?"

"There will be somebody here," Major de Spain said.

They went back to the house, to the rank little room where Boon still sat on the pallet bed with Lion's head under his hand while the men, the ones who had hunted behind Lion and the ones who had never seen him before today, came quietly in to look at him and went away. Then it was dawn and they all went out into the yard to look at Old Ben, with his eyes open too and his lips snarled back from his worn teeth and his mutilated foot and the little hard lumps under his skin which were the old bullets (there were fifty-two of them, buckshot rifle and ball) and the single almost invisible slit under his left shoulder where Boon's blade had finally found his life. Then Ash began to beat on the bottom of the dishpan with a heavy spoon to call them to breakfast and it was the first time he could remember hearing no sound from the dogs under the kitchen while they were eating. It was as if the old bear, even dead there in the yard, was a more potent terror still than they could face without Lion between them.

The rain had stopped during the night. By midmorning the thin sun appeared, rapidly burning away mist and cloud, warming the air and the earth; it would be one of those windless Mississippi December days which are a sort of Indian summer's Indian summer. They moved Lion out to the front gallery, into the sun. It was Boon's idea. "Goddamn it," he said, "he never did want to stay in the house until I made him. You know that." He took a crowbar and loosened the floor boards under his pallet bed so it could be raised, mattress and all, without disturbing Lion's position, and they carried him out to the gallery and put him down facing the woods.

Then he and the doctor and McCaslin and Major de Spain went to Sam's hut. This time Sam didn't open his eyes and his breathing was so quiet, so peaceful that they could hardly see that he breathed. The doctor didn't even take out his stethoscope nor even touch him. "He's all right," the doctor said. "He didn't even catch cold. He just quit."

"Quit?" McCaslin said.

"Yes. Old people do that sometimes. Then they get a good night's sleep or maybe it's just a drink of whisky, and they change their minds."

They returned to the house. And then they began to arrive — the swamp-dwellers, the gaunt men who ran trap-lines and lived on quinine and coons and river water, the farmers of little corn- and cotton-patches along the bottom's edge whose fields and cribs and pig-pens the old bear had rifled, the loggers from the camp and the sawmill men from Hoke's and the town men from further away than that, whose hounds the old bear had slain and whose traps and deadfalls he had wrecked and whose lead he carried. They came up mounted and on foot and in wagons, to enter the yard and look at him and then go on to the front where Lion lay, filling the little yard and over-flowing it until there were almost a hundred of them squatting and standing in the warm and drowsing sunlight, talking quietly of hunting, of the game and the dogs which ran it, of hounds and bear and deer and men of yesterday vanished from the earth, while from time to time the great blue dog would open his eyes, not as if he were listening to them but as though to look at the woods for a moment before closing his eyes again, to remember the woods or to see that they were still there. He died at sundown.

Major de Spain broke camp that night. They carried Lion into the woods, or Boon carried him that is, wrapped in a quilt from his bed, just as he had refused to let anyone else touch Lion yesterday until the doctor got there; Boon carrying Lion, and the boy and General Compson and Walter and still almost fifty of them following with lanterns and lighted pine-knots — men from Hoke's and even further, who would have to ride out of the bottom in the dark, and swampers and trappers who would have to walk even, scattering toward the little hidden huts where they lived. And Boon would let nobody else dig the grave either and lay Lion in it and cover him and then General Compson stood at the head of it while the blaze and smoke of the pine-knots streamed away among the winter branches and spoke as he would have spoken over a man. Then they returned to camp. Major de Spain and McCaslin and Ash had rolled and tied all the bedding. The mules were hitched to the wagon and pointed out of the bottom and the wagon was already loaded and the stove in the kitchen was cold and the table was set with scraps of cold food and bread and only the coffee was hot when the boy ran into the kitchen where Major de Spain and McCaslin had already eaten. "What?" he cried. "What? I'm not going."

"Yes," McCaslin said, "we're going out to-night. Major wants to get on back home."

"No!" he said. "I'm going to stay."

"You've got to be back in school Monday. You've already missed a week more than I intended. It will take you from now until Monday to catch up. Sam's all right. You heard Doctor Crawford. I'm going to leave Boon and Tennie's Jim both to stay with him until he feels like getting up."

He was panting. The others had come in. He looked rapidly and almost frantically around at the other faces. Boon had a fresh bottle. He upended it and started the cork by striking the bottom of the bottle with the heel of his hand and drew the cork with his teeth and spat it out and drank. "You're damn right you're going back to school," Boon said. "Or I'll burn the tail off of you myself if Cass dont, whether you are sixteen or sixty. Where in hell do you expect to get without education? Where would Cass be? Where in hell would I be if I hadn't never went to school?"

He looked at McCaslin again. He could feel his breath coming shorter and shorter and shallower and shallower, as if there were not enough air in the kitchen for that many to breathe. "This is just Thursday. I'll come home Sunday night on one of the horses. I'll come home Sunday, then. I'll make up the time I lost studying Sunday night, McCaslin," he said, without even despair.

"No, I tell you," McCaslin said. "Sit down here and eat your supper. We're going out to —"

"Hold up, Cass," General Compson said. The boy did not know General Compson had moved until he put his hand on his shoulder. "What is it, bud?" he said.

"I've got to stay," he said. "I've got to."

"All right," General Compson said. "You can stay. If missing an extra week of school is going to throw you so far behind you'll have to sweat to find out what some hired pedagogue put between the covers of a book, you better quit altogether. — And you shut up, Cass," he said, though McCaslin had not spoken. "You've got one foot straddled into a farm and the other foot straddled into a bank; you aint even got a good hand-hold where this boy was already an old man long before you damned Sartorises and Edmondses invented farms and banks to keep yourselves from having to find out this boy was born knowing and fearing too maybe but without being afraid, that could go ten miles on a compass because he wanted to look at a bear none of us had ever got near enough to put a bullet in and looked at the bear and came the ten miles back on the compass in the dark; maybe by God that's the why and the wherefore of farms and banks. — I reckon you still aint going to tell what it is?"

But still he could not. "I've got to stay," he said.

"All right," General Compson said. "There's plenty of grub left. And you'll come home Sunday, like you promised McCaslin? Not Sunday night: Sunday."

"Yes, sir," he said.

"All right," General Compson said. "Sit down and eat, boys," he said. "Let's get started. It's going to be cold before we get home."

They ate. The wagon was already loaded and ready to depart; all they had to do was to get into it. Boon would drive them out to the road, to the farmer's stable where the surrey had been left. He stood beside the wagon, in silhouette on the sky, turbaned like a Paythan and taller than any there, the bottle tilted. Then he flung the bottle from his lips without even lowering it, spinning and glinting in the faint starlight, empty. "Them that's going," he said, "get in the goddamn wagon. Them that aint, get out of the goddamn way." The others got in. Boon mounted to the seat beside General Compson and the wagon moved, on into the obscurity until the boy could no longer see it, even the moving density of it amid the greater night. But he could still hear it, for a long while: the slow, deliberate banging of the wooden frame as it lurched from rut to rut. And he could hear Boon even when he could no longer hear the wagon. He was singing, harsh, tuneless, loud.

That was Thursday. On Saturday morning Tennie's Jim left on McCaslin's woods-horse which had not been out of the bottom one time now in six years, and late that afternoon rode through the gate on the spent horse and on to the commissary where McCaslin was rationing the tenants and the wage-hands for the coming week, and this time McCaslin forestalled any necessity or risk of having to wait while Major de Spain's surrey was being horsed and harnessed. He took their own, and with Tennie's Jim already asleep in the back seat he drove in to Jefferson and waited while Major de Spain changed to boots and put on his overcoat, and they drove the thirty miles in the dark of that night and at daybreak on Sunday morning they swapped to the waiting mare and mule and as the sun rose they rode out of the jungle and onto the low ridge where they had buried Lion: the low mound of unannealed earth where Boon's spade-marks still showed, and beyond the grave the platform of freshly cut saplings bound between four posts and the blanket-wrapped bundle upon the platform and Boon and the boy squatting between the platform and the grave until Boon, the bandage removed, ripped from his head so that the long scoriations of Old Ben's claws resembled crusted tar in the sunlight, sprang up and threw down upon them with the old gun with which he had never been known to hit anything although McCaslin was already off the mule, kicked both feet free of the irons and vaulted down before the mule had stopped, walking toward Boon.

"Stand back," Boon said. "By God, you wont touch him. Stand back, McCaslin." Still McCaslin came on, fast yet without haste.

"Cass!" Major de Spain said. Then he said, "Boon! You, Boon!" and he was down too and the boy rose too, quickly, and still McCaslin came on not fast but steady and walked up to the grave and reached his hand steadily out, quickly yet still not fast, and took hold the gun by the middle so that he and Boon faced one another across Lion's grave, both holding the gun, Boon's spent indomitable amazed and frantic face almost a head higher than McCaslin's beneath the black scoriations of beast's claws and then Boon's chest began to heave as though there were not enough air in all the woods, in all the wilderness, for all of them, for him and anyone else, even for him alone.

"Turn it loose, Boon," McCaslin said.

"You damn little spindling—" Boon said. "Dont you know I can take it away from you? Dont you know I can tie it around your neck like a damn cravat?"

"Yes," McCaslin said. "Turn it loose, Boon."

"This is the way he wanted it. He told us. He told us exactly how to do it. And by God you aint going to move him. So we did it like he said, and I been sitting here ever since to keep the damn wildcats and varmints away from him and by God —" Then McCaslin had the gun, downslanted while he pumped the slide, the five shells snicking out of it so fast that the last one was almost out before the first one touched the ground and McCaslin dropped the gun behind him without once having taken his eyes from Boon's.

"Did you kill him, Boon?" he said. Then Boon moved. He turned, he moved like he was still drunk and then for a moment blind too, one hand out as he blundered toward the big tree and seemed to stop walking before he reached the tree so that he plunged, fell toward it, flinging up both hands and catching himself against the tree and turning until his back was against it, backing with the tree's trunk his wild spent scoriated face and the tremendous heave and collapse of his chest, McCaslin following, facing him again, never once having moved his eyes from Boon's eyes. "Did you kill him, Boon?"

"No!" Boon said. "No!"

"Tell the truth," McCaslin said. "I would have done it if he had asked me to." Then the boy moved. He was between them, facing McCaslin; the water felt as if it had burst and sprung not from his eyes alone but from his whole face, like sweat.

"Leave him alone!" he cried. "Goddamn it! Leave him alone!"

⚜ The long Part 4, omitted here, moves ahead in time to Ike McCaslin's twenty-first year when he refuses to inherit the property bequeathed to him by his grandfather, Carothers McCaslin, because it is stained by the guilt of slavery and mixed blood. Ike broods over his family history, the sufferings of mulatto kindred and descendants of Carothers McCaslin who were bought and sold and freed and who suffered with their freedom, his father and uncle who likewise refused to live in the family mansion. He recalls his marriage which was tainted by his wife's desire for the property he has disclaimed. In this section Faulkner appears to draw a parallel between the fall of man, his loss of Eden, and the sin of the McCaslin family and indeed of the South as a whole. "Don't you see? This whole land, the whole South, is cursed, and all of us who derive from it, whom it ever suckled, white and black both, lie under the curse?" Ike's relinquishment of his lands, the wisdom learned from the wilderness, may be a beginning of a slow regeneration.

5

He went back to the camp one more time before the lumber company moved in and began to cut the timber. Major de Spain himself never saw it again. But he made them welcome to use the house and hunt the land whenever they liked, and in the winter following the last hunt when Sam Fathers and Lion died, General Compson and Walter Ewell invented a plan to corporate themselves, the old group, into a club and lease the camp and the hunting privileges of the woods — an invention doubtless of the somewhat childish old General but actually worthy of Boon Hogganbeck himself. Even the boy, listening, recognised it for the subterfuge it was: to change the leopard's spots when they could not alter the leopard, a baseless and illusory hope to which even McCaslin seemed to subscribe for a while, that once they had persuaded Major de Spain to return to the camp he might revoke himself, which even the boy knew he would not do. And he did not. The boy never knew what occurred when Major de Spain declined. He was not present when the subject was broached and McCaslin never told him. But when June came and the time for the double birthday celebration there was no mention of it and when November came no one spoke of using Major de Spain's house and he never knew whether or not Major de Spain knew they were going on the hunt though without doubt old Ash probably told him: he and McCaslin and General Compson (and that one was the General's last hunt too) and Walter and Boon and Tennie's Jim and old Ash loaded two wagons and drove two days and almost forty miles beyond any country the boy had ever seen before and lived in tents for the two weeks. And the next spring they heard (not from Major de Spain) that he had sold the timber-rights to a Memphis lumber company and in June the boy came to town with McCaslin one Saturday and went to Major de Spain's office —

the big, airy, book-lined, second-storey room with windows at one end opening upon the shabby hinder purlieus of stores and at the other a door giving onto the railed balcony above the Square, with its curtained alcove where sat a cedar water-bucket and a sugar-bowl and spoon and tumbler and a wicker-covered demijohn of whisky, and the bamboo-and-paper punkah swinging back and forth above the desk while old Ash in a tilted chair beside the entrance pulled the cord.

"Of course," Major de Spain said. "Ash will probably like to get off in the woods himself for a while, where he wont have to eat Daisy's cooking. Complain about it, anyway. Are you going to take anybody with you?"

"No sir," he said. "I thought that maybe Boon — " For six months now Boon had been town-marshal at Hoke's; Major de Spain had compounded with the lumber company — or perhaps compromised was closer, since it was the lumber company who had decided that Boon might be better as a town-marshal than head of a logging gang.

"Yes," Major de Spain said. "I'll wire him today. He can meet you at Hoke's. I'll send Ash on by the train and they can take some food in and all you will have to do will be to mount your horse and ride over."

"Yes sir," he said. "Thank you." And he heard his voice again. He didn't know he was going to say it yet he did know, he had known it all the time: "Maybe if you . . ." His voice died. It was stopped, he never knew how because Major de Spain did not speak and it was not until his voice ceased that Major de Spain moved, turned back to the desk and the papers spread on it and even that without moving because he was sitting at the desk with a paper in his hand when the boy entered, the boy standing there looking down at the short plumpish gray-haired man in sober fine broadcloth and an immaculate glazed shirt whom he was used to seeing in boots and muddy corduroy, unshaven, sitting the shaggy powerful long-hocked mare with the worn Winchester carbine across the saddlebow and the great blue dog standing motionless as bronze at the stirrup, the two of them in that last year and to the boy anyway coming to resemble one another somehow as two people competent for love or for business who have been in love or in business together for a long time sometimes do. Major de Spain did not look up again.

"No. I will be too busy. But good luck to you. If you have it, you might bring me a young squirrel."

"Yes sir," he said. "I will."

He rode his mare, the three-year-old filly he had bred and raised and broken himself. He left home a little after midnight and six hours later, without even having sweated her, he rode into Hoke's, the tiny log-line junction which he had always thought of as Major de Spain's property too although Major de Spain had merely sold the company (and that many years ago) the land on which the sidetracks and loading-platforms and the commissary store stood, and looked about in shocked and grieved amazement even though he had had forewarning and had believed himself prepared: a new planing-mill already half completed which would cover two or three acres and what looked like miles and miles of stacked steel rails red with the light bright rust of newness and of piled crossties sharp with creosote, and wire corrals and feeding-troughs for two hundred mules at least and the tents for the men who drove them; so that he arranged for the care and stabling of his mare as rapidly as he could and did not look any more, mounted into the log-train caboose with his gun and climbed into the cupola and looked no more save toward the wall of wilderness ahead within which he would be able to hide himself from it once more anyway.

Then the little locomotive shrieked and began to move: a rapid churning of exhaust, a lethargic deliberate clashing of slack couplings traveling backward along the train, the exhaust changing to the deep slow clapping bites of power as the caboose too began to move and from the cupola he watched the train's head complete the first and only curve in the entire line's length and vanish into the wilderness, dragging its length of train behind it so that it resembled a small dingy harmless snake vanishing into weeds, drawing him with it too until soon it ran once more at its maximum clattering speed between the twin walls of unaxed wilderness as of old. It had been harmless once. Not five years ago Walter Ewell had shot a six-point buck from this same moving caboose, and there was the story of the half-grown bear: the train's first trip in to the cutting thirty miles away, the bear between the rails, its rear end elevated like that of a playing puppy while it dug to see what sort of ants or bugs they might contain or perhaps just to examine the curious symmetrical squared barkless logs which had appeared apparently from nowhere in one endless mathematical line overnight, still digging until the driver on the braked engine not fifty feet away blew the whistle at it, whereupon it broke frantically and took the first tree it came to: an ash sapling not much bigger than a man's thigh and climbed as high as it could and clung there, its head ducked between its arms as a man (a woman perhaps) might have done while the brakeman threw chunks of ballast at it, and when the engine returned three hours later with the first load of outbound logs the bear was halfway down the tree and once more scrambled back up as high as it could and clung again while the train passed and was still there when the engine went in again in the afternoon and still there when it came back out at dusk; and Boon had been in Hoke's with the wagon after a barrel of flour that noon when the train-crew told about it and Boon and Ash, both twenty years younger then, sat under the tree all that night to keep anybody from shooting it and the next morning Major de Spain had the log-train held at Hoke's and just before sundown on the second day, with not only Boon and Ash but Major de Spain and General Compson and Walter and McCaslin, twelve then, watching, it came down the tree after almost thirty-six hours without even water and McCaslin told him how for a minute they thought it was going to stop right there at the barrow-pit where they were standing and drink, how it looked at the water and paused and looked at them and at the water again, but did not, gone, running, as bears run, the two sets of feet, front and back, tracking two separate though parallel courses.

It had been harmless then. They would hear the passing log-train sometimes from the camp; sometimes, because nobody bothered to listen for it or not. They would hear it going in, running light and fast, the light clatter of the trucks, the exhaust of the diminutive locomotive and its shrill peanut-parcher whistle flung for one petty moment and absorbed by the brooding and inattentive wilderness without even an echo. They would hear it going out, loaded, not quite so fast now yet giving its frantic and toylike illusion of crawling speed, not whistling now to conserve steam, flinging its bitten laboring miniature puffing into the immemorial woodsface with frantic and bootless vainglory, empty and noisy and puerile, carrying to no destination or purpose sticks which left nowhere any scar or stump as the child's toy loads and transports and unloads its dead sand and rushes back for more, tireless and unceasing and rapid yet never quite so fast as the Hand which plays with it moves the toy burden back to load the toy again. But it was different now. It was the same train, engine cars and caboose, even the same enginemen brakeman and conductor to whom Boon, drunk then sober then drunk again then fairly sober once more all in the space of fourteen hours, had bragged that day two years ago about what they were going to do to Old Ben tomorrow, running with its same illusion of frantic rapidity between the same twin walls of impenetrable and impervious woods, passing the old landmarks, the old game crossings over which he had trailed bucks wounded and not wounded and more than once seen them, anything but wounded, bolt out of the woods and up and across the embankment which bore the rails and ties then down and into the woods again as the earth-bound supposedly move but crossing as arrows travel, groundless, elongated, three times its actual length and even paler, different in color, as if there were a point between immobility and absolute motion where even mass chemically altered, changing without pain or agony not only in bulk and shape but in color too, approaching the color of wind, yet this time it was as though the train (and not only the train but himself, not only his vision which had seen it and his memory which remembered it but his clothes too, as garments carry back into the clean edgeless blowing of air the lingering effluvium of a sick-room or of death) had brought with it into the doomed wilderness even before the actual axe the shadow and portent of the new mill not even finished yet and the rails and ties which were not even laid; and he knew now what he had known as soon as he saw Hoke's this morning but had not yet thought into words: why Major de Spain had not come back, and that after this time he himself, who had had to see it one time other, would return no more.

Now they were near. He knew it before the engine-driver whistled to warn him. Then he saw Ash and the wagon, the reins without doubt wrapped once more about the brake-lever as within the boy's own memory Major de Spain had been forbidding him for eight years to do, the train slowing, the slackened couplings jolt-

ing and clashing again from car to car, the caboose slowing past the wagon as he swung down with his gun, the conductor leaning out above him to signal the engine, the caboose still slowing, creeping, although the engine's exhaust was already slatting in mounting tempo against the unechoing wilderness, the crashing of drawbars once more traveling backward along the train, the caboose picking up speed at last. Then it was gone. It had not been. He could no longer hear it. The wilderness soared, musing, inattentive, myriad, eternal, green; older than any mill-shed, longer than any spurline. "Mr. Boon here yet?" he said.

"He beat me in," Ash said. "Had the wagon loaded and ready for me at Hoke's yistiddy when I got there and setting on the front steps at camp last night when I got in. He already been in the woods since fo daylight this morning. Said he gwine up to the Gum Tree and for you to hunt up that way and meet him." He knew where that was: a single big sweet-gum just outside the woods, in an old clearing; if you crept up to it very quietly this time of year and then ran suddenly into the clearing, sometimes you caught as many as a dozen squirrels in it, trapped, since there was no other tree near they could jump to. So he didn't get into the wagon at all.

"I will," he said.

"I figured you would," Ash said, "I fotch you a box of shells." He passed the shells down and began to unwrap the lines from the brake-pole.

"How many times up to now do you reckon Major has told you not to do that?" the boy said.

"Do which?" Ash said. Then he said: "And tell Boon Hogganbeck dinner gonter be on the table in a hour and if yawl want any to come on and eat it."

"In an hour?" he said. "It aint nine oclock yet." He drew out his watch and extended it face-toward Ash. "Look." Ash didn't even look at the watch.

"That's town time. You aint in town now. You in the woods."

"Look at the sun then."

"Nemmine the sun too," Ash said. "If you and Boon Hogganbeck want any dinner, you better come on in and get it when I tole you. I aim to get done in that kitchen because I got my wood to chop. And watch your feet. They're crawling."

"I will," he said.

Then he was in the woods, not alone but solitary; the solitude closed about him, green with summer. They did not change, and, timeless, would not, any more than would the green of summer and the fire and rain of fall and the iron cold and sometimes even snow

The day, the morning when he killed the buck and Sam marked his face with its hot blood, they returned to camp and he remembered old Ash's blinking and disgruntled and even outraged disbelief until at last McCaslin had had to affirm the fact that he had really killed it: and that night Ash sat snarling and unapproachable behind the stove so that Tennie's Jim had to serve the supper and waked them with breakfast already on the table the next morning and it was only half-past one oclock and at last out of Major de Spain's angry cursing and Ash's snarling and sullen rejoinders the fact emerged that Ash not only wanted to go into the woods and shoot a deer also but he intended to and Major de Spain said, "By God, if we dont let him we will probably have to do the cooking from now on:" and Walter Ewell said, "Or get up at midnight to eat what Ash cooks:" and since he had already killed his buck for this hunt and was not to shoot again unless they needed meat, he offered his gun to Ash until Major de Spain took command and allotted that gun to Boon for the day and gave Boon's unpredictable pump gun to Ash, with two buckshot shells but Ash said, "I got shells:" and showed them, four: one buck, one of number three shot for rabbits, two of bird-shot and told one by one their history and their origin and he remembered not Ash's face alone but Major de Spain's and Walter's and General Compson's too, and Ash's voice: "Shoot? In course they'll shoot! Genl Cawmpson guv me this un" — the buckshot — "right outen the same gun he kilt that big buck with eight years ago. And this un" — it was rabbit shell: triumphantly ——— "is oldern thisyer boy!" And that morning he loaded the gun himself, reversing the order: the bird-shot, the rabbit, then the buck so that the buckshot would feed first into the chamber, and himself without a gun, he and Ash walked beside Major de Spain's and Tennie's Jim's horses and the dogs (that was the snow) until they cast and struck, the sweet strong cries ringing away into the muffled falling air and gone almost immediately, as if the constant and unmurmuring flakes had already buried even the unformed echoes beneath their myriad and weightless falling, Major

de Spain and Tennie's Jim gone too, whooping on into the woods; and then it was all right, he knew as plainly as if Ash had told him that Ash had now hunted his deer and that even his tender years had been forgiven for having killed one, and they turned back toward home through the falling snow — that is, Ash said, "Now whut?" and he said, "This way" — himself in front because, although they were less than a mile from camp, he knew that Ash, who had spent two weeks of his life in the camp each year for the last twenty, had no idea whatever where they were, until quite soon the manner in which Ash carried Boon's gun was making him a good deal more than just nervous and he made Ash walk in front, striding on, talking now, an old man's garrulous monologue beginning with where he was at the moment then of the woods and of camping in the woods and of eating in camps then of eating then of cooking it and of his wife's cooking then briefly of his old wife and almost at once and at length of a new light-colored woman who nursed next door to Major de Spain's and if she didn't watch out who she was switching her tail at he would show her how old was an old man or not if his wife just didn't watch him all the time, the two of them in a game trail through a dense brake of cane and brier which would bring them out within a quarter-mile of camp, approaching a big fallen tree-trunk lying athwart the path and just as Ash, still talking, was about to step over it the bear, the yearling rose suddenly beyond the log, sitting up, its forearms against its chest and its wrists limply arrested as if it had been surprised in the act of covering its face to pray: and after a certain time Ash's gun yawed jerkily up and he said, "You haven't got a shell in the barrel yet. Pump it:" but the gun already snicked and he said, "Pump it. You haven't got a shell in the barrel yet:" and Ash pumped the action and in a certain time the gun steadied again and snicked and he said, "Pump it:" and watched the buckshot shell jerk, spinning heavily, into the cane. This is the rabbit shot: he thought and the gun snicked and he thought: The next is bird-shot: and he didn't have to say Pump it; he cried, "Dont shoot! Dont shoot!" but that was already too late too, the light dry vicious snick! before he could speak and the bear turned and dropped to all-fours and then was gone and there was only the log, the cane, the velvet and constant snow and Ash said, "Now whut?" and he said, "This way. Come on:" and

began to back away down the path and Ash said,
"I got to find my shells:" and he said, "God-
damn it, goddamn it, come on:" but Ash leaned
the gun against the log and returned and stooped
and fumbled among the cane roots until he 5
came back and stooped and found the shells
and they rose and at that moment the gun, un-
touched, leaning against the log six feet away
and for that while even forgotten by both of
them, roared, bellowed and flamed, and ceased: 10
and he carried it now, pumped out the last
mummified shell and gave that one also to Ash
and, the action still open, himself carried the
gun until he stood it in the corner behind
Boon's bed at the camp 15

— ; summer, and fall, and snow, and wet and
sap-rife spring in their ordered immortal sequence, the deathless and immemorial phases of
the mother who had shaped him if any had
toward the man he almost was, mother and 20
father both to the old man born of a Negro
slave and a Chickasaw chief who had been his
spirit's father if any had, whom he had revered
and harkened to and loved and lost and grieved:
and he would marry someday and they too 25
would own for their brief while that brief un-
substanced glory which inherently of itself cannot last and hence why glory: and they would,
might, carry even the remembrance of it into
the time when flesh no longer talks to flesh 30
because memory at least does last: but still the
woods would be his mistress and his wife.

He was not going toward the Gum Tree.
Actually he was getting farther from it. Time
was and not so long ago either when he would 35
not have been allowed here without someone
with him, and a little later, when he had begun
to learn how much he did not know, he would
not have dared be here without someone with
him, and later still, beginning to ascertain, even 40
if only dimly, the limits of what he did not
know, he could have attempted and carried it
through with a compass, not because of any
increased belief in himself but because McCaslin and Major de Spain and Walter and General 45
Compson too had taught him at last to believe
the compass regardless of what it seemed to
state. Now he did not even use the compass but
merely the sun and that only subconsciously,
yet he could have taken a scaled map and 50
plotted at any time to within a hundred feet of
where he actually was; and sure enough, at
almost the exact moment when he expected it,
the earth began to rise faintly, he passed one

of the four concrete markers set down by the
lumber company's surveyor to establish the four
corners of the plot which Major de Spain had
reserved out of the sale, then he stood on the
crest of the knoll itself, the four corner-markers
all visible now, blanched still even beneath the
winter's weathering, lifeless and shockingly alien
in that place where dissolution itself was a
seething turmoil of ejaculation tumescence conception and birth, and death did not even exist.
After two winters' blanketings of leaves and the
flood-waters of two springs, there was no trace
of the two graves any more at all. But those
who would have come this far to find them
would not need headstones but would have
found them as Sam Fathers himself had taught
him to find such: by bearings on trees: and did,
almost the first thrust of the hunting knife finding (but only to see if it was still there) the
round tin box manufactured for axle-grease and
containing now Old Ben's dried mutilated paw,
resting above Lion's bones.

He didn't disturb it. He didn't even look for
the other grave where he and McCaslin and
Major de Spain and Boon had laid Sam's body,
along with his hunting horn and his knife and
his tobacco-pipe, that Sunday morning two years
ago; he didn't have to. He had stepped over it,
perhaps on it. But that was all right. *He prob-*
ably knew I was in the woods this morning long
before I got here, he thought, going on to the
tree which had supported one end of the platform where Sam lay when McCaslin and Major
de Spain found them — the tree, the other axle-
grease tin nailed to the trunk, but weathered,
rusted, alien too yet healed already into the
wilderness' concordant generality, raising no
tuneless note, and empty, long since empty of
the food and tobacco he had put into it that
day, as empty of that as it would presently be
of this which he drew from his pocket — the
twist of tobacco, the new bandanna handkerchief, the small paper sack of the peppermint
candy which Sam had used to love; that gone
too, almost before he had turned his back, not
vanished but merely translated into the myriad
life which printed the dark mold of these secret
and sunless places with delicate fairy tracks,
which, breathing and biding and immobile,
watched him from beyond every twig and leaf
until he moved, moving again, walking on; he
had not stopped, he had only paused, quitting
the knoll which was no abode of the dead
because there was no death, not Lion and not

Sam: not held fast in earth but free in earth and not in earth but of earth, myriad yet undiffused of every myriad part, leaf and twig and particle, air and sun and rain and dew and night, acorn oak and leaf and acorn again, dark and dawn and dark and dawn again in their immutable progression and, being myriad, one: and Old Ben too, Old Ben too; they would give him his paw back even, certainly they would give him his paw back: then the long challenge and the long chase, no heart to be driven and outraged, no flesh to be mauled and bled — Even as he froze himself, he seemed to hear Ash's parting admonition. He could even hear the voice as he froze, immobile, one foot just taking his weight, the toe of the other just lifted behind him, not breathing, feeling again and as always the sharp shocking inrush from when Isaac McCaslin long yet was not, and so it was fear all right but not fright as he looked down at it. It had not coiled yet and the buzzer had not sounded either, only one thick rapid contraction, one loop cast sideways as though merely for purchase from which the raised head might start slightly backward, not in fright either, not in threat quite yet, more than six feet of it, the head raised higher than his knee and less than his knee's length away, and old, the once-bright markings of its youth dulled now to a monotone concordant too with the wilderness it crawled and lurked: the old one, the ancient and accursed about the earth, fatal and solitary and he could smell it now: the thin sick smell of rotting cucumbers and something else which had no name, evocative of all knowledge and an old weariness and of pariah-hood and of death. At last it moved. Not the head. The elevation of the head did not change as it began to glide away from him, moving erect yet off the perpendicular as if the head and that elevated third were complete and all: an entity walking on two feet and free of all laws of mass and balance and should have been because even now he could not quite believe that all that shift and flow of shadow behind that walking head could have been one snake: going and then gone; he put the other foot down at last and didn't know it, standing with one hand raised as Sam had stood that afternoon six years ago when Sam led him into the wilderness and showed him and he ceased to be a child, speaking the old tongue which Sam had spoken that day without premeditation either: "Chief," he said: "Grandfather."

He couldn't tell when he first began to hear the sound, because when he became aware of it, it seemed to him that he had been already hearing it for several seconds — a sound as though someone were hammering a gun-barrel against a piece of railroad iron, a sound loud and heavy and not rapid yet with something frenzied about it, as the hammerer were not only a strong man and an earnest one but a little hysterical too. Yet it couldn't be on the logline because, although the track lay in that direction, it was at least two miles from him and this sound was not three hundred yards away. But even as he thought that, he realised where the sound must be coming from: whoever the man was and whatever he was doing, he was somewhere near the edge of the clearing where the Gum Tree was and where he was to meet Boon. So far, he had been hunting as he advanced, moving slowly and quietly and watching the ground and the trees both. Now he went on, his gun unloaded and the barrel slanted up and back to facilitate its passage through brier and undergrowth, approaching as it grew louder and louder that steady savage somehow queerly hysterical beating of metal on metal, emerging from the woods, into the old clearing, with the solitary gum tree directly before him. At first glance the tree seemed to be alive with frantic squirrels. There appeared to be forty or fifty of them leaping and darting from branch to branch until the whole tree had become one green maelstrom of mad leaves, while from time to time, singly or in twos and threes, squirrels would dart down the trunk then whirl without stopping and rush back up again as though sucked violently back by the vacuum of their fellows' frenzied vortex. Then he saw Boon, sitting, his back against the trunk, his head bent, hammering furiously at something on his lap. What he hammered with was the barrel of his dismembered gun, what he hammered at was the breech of it. The rest of the gun lay scattered about him in a half-dozen pieces while he bent over the piece on his lap his scarlet and streaming walnut face, hammering the disjointed barrel against the gun-breech with the frantic abandon of a madman. He didn't even look up to see who it was. Still hammering, he merely shouted back at the boy in a hoarse strangled voice:

"Get out of here! Dont touch them! Dont touch a one of them! They're mine!"

Dry September

Through the bloody September twilight, after-math of sixty-two rainless days, it had gone like a fire in dry grass — the rumor, the story, what-ever it was. Something about Miss Minnie Cooper and a Negro. Attacked, insulted, fright-ened: none of them, gathered in the barber shop on that Saturday evening where the ceiling fan stirred, without freshening it, the vitiated air, 10 sending back upon them, in recurrent surges of stale pomade and lotion, their own stale breath and odors, knew exactly what had happened.

"Except it wasn't Will Mayes," a barber said. He was a man of middle age; a thin, sand-colored 15 man with a mild face, who was shaving a client. "I know Will Mayes. He's a good nigger. And I know Miss Minnie Cooper, too."

"What do you know about her?" a second barber said.

"Who is she?" the client said. "A young 20 girl?"

"No," the barber said. "She's about forty, I reckon. She aint married. That's why I dont be-lieve —"

"Believe, hell!" a hulking youth in a sweat-25 stained silk shirt said. "Wont you take a white woman's word before a nigger's?"

"I dont believe Will Mayes did it," the barber said. "I know Will Mayes."

"Maybe you know who did it, then. Maybe 30 you already got him out of town, you damn niggerlover."

"I dont believe anybody did anything. I dont believe anything happened. I leave it to you fel-lows if them ladies that get old without getting 35 married dont have notions that a man cant —"

"Then you are a hell of a white man," the client said. He moved under the cloth. The youth had sprung to his feet.

"You dont?" he said. "Do you accuse a white 40 woman of lying?"

The barber held the razor poised above the half-risen client. He did not look around.

"It's this durn weather," another said. "It's enough to make a man do anything. Even to 45 her."

Nobody laughed. The barber said in his mild, stubborn tone: "I aint accusing nobody of nothing. I just know and you fellows know how 50 a woman that never —"

"You damn niggerlover!" the youth said.

"Shut up, Butch," another said. "We'll get the facts in plenty of time to act."

"Who is? Who's getting them?" the youth said. "Facts, hell! I —"

"You're a fine white man," the client said. "Aint you?" In his frothy beard he looked like 5 a desert rat in the moving pictures. "You tell them, Jack," he said to the youth. "If there aint any white men in this town, you can count on me, even if I aint only a drummer and a stranger."

"That's right, boys," the barber said. "Find 10 out the truth first. I know Will Mayes."

"Well, by God!" the youth shouted. "To think that a white man in this town —"

"Shut up, Butch," the second speaker said. 15 "We got plenty of time."

The client sat up. He looked at the speaker. "Do you claim that anything excuses a nigger attacking a white woman? Do you mean to tell me you are a white man and you'll stand for it? 20 You better go back North where you came from. The South dont want your kind here."

"North what?" the second said. "I was born and raised in this town."

"Well, by God!" the youth said. He looked 25 about with a strained, baffled gaze, as if he was trying to remember what it was he wanted to say or to do. He drew his sleeve across his sweat-ing face. "Damn if I'm going to let a white woman —"

30 "You tell them, Jack," the drummer said. "By God, if they —"

The screen door crashed open. A man stood in the floor, his feet apart and his heavy-set body poised easily. His white shirt was open at the 35 throat; he wore a felt hat. His hot, bold glance swept the group. His name was McLendon. He had commanded troops at the front in France and had been decorated for valor.

"Well," he said, "are you going to sit there 40 and let a black son rape a white woman on the streets of Jefferson?"

Butch sprang up again. The silk of his shirt clung flat to his heavy shoulders. At each arm-pit was a dark halfmoon. "That's what I been 45 telling them! That's what I —"

"Did it really happen?" a third said. "This aint the first man scare she ever had, like Hawk-shaw says. Wasn't there something about a man on the kitchen roof, watching her undress, about 50 a year ago?"

"What?" the client said. "What's that?" The barber had been slowly forcing him back into the chair; he arrested himself reclining, his head lifted, the barber still pressing him down.

McLendon whirled on the third speaker. "Happen? What the hell difference does it make? Are you going to let the black sons get away with it until one really does it?"

"That's what I'm telling them!" Butch shouted. He cursed, long and steady, pointless.

"Here, here," a fourth said. "Not so loud. Dont talk so loud."

"Sure," McLendon said; "no talking necessary at all. I've done my talking. Who's with me?" He poised on the balls of his feet, roving his gaze.

The barber held the drummer's face down, the razor poised. "Find out the facts first, boys. I know Willy Mayes. It wasn't him. Let's get the sheriff and do this thing right."

McLendon whirled upon him his furious, rigid face. The barber did not look away. They looked like men of different races. The other barbers had ceased also above their prone clients. "You mean to tell me," McLendon said, "that you'd take a nigger's word before a white woman's? Why, you damn niggerloving —"

The third speaker rose and grasped McLendon's arm; he too had been a soldier. "Now, now. Let's figure this thing out. Who knows anything about what really happened?"

"Figure out hell!" McLendon jerked his arm free. "All that're with me get up from there. The ones that aint —" He roved his gaze, dragging his sleeve across his face.

Three men rose. The drummer in the chair sat up. "Here," he said, jerking at the cloth about his neck; "get this rag off me. I'm with him. I dont live here, but by God, if our mothers and wives and sisters —" He smeared the cloth over his face and flung it to the floor. McLendon stood in the floor and cursed the others. Another rose and moved toward him. The remainder sat uncomfortable, not looking at one another, then one by one they rose and joined him.

The barber picked the cloth from the floor. He began to fold it neatly. "Boys, dont do that. Will Mayes never done it. I know."

"Come on," McLendon said. He whirled. From his hip pocket protruded the butt of a heavy automatic pistol. They went out. The screen door crashed behind them reverberant in the dead air.

The barber wiped the razor carefully and swiftly, and put it away, and ran to the rear, and took his hat from the wall. "I'll be back as soon as I can," he said to the other barbers. "I cant

let —" He went out, running. The two other barbers followed him to the door and caught it on the rebound, leaning out and looking up the street after him. The air was flat and dead. It had a metallic taste at the base of the tongue.

"What can he do?" the first said. The second one was saying "Jees Christ, Jees Christ" under his breath. "I'd just as lief be Will Mayes as Hawk, if he gets McLendon riled."

"Jees Christ, Jees Christ," the second whispered.

"You reckon he really done it to her?" the first said.

II

She was thirty-eight or thirty-nine. She lived in a small frame house with her invalid mother and a thin, sallow, unflagging aunt, where each morning between ten and eleven she would appear on the porch in a lace-trimmed boudoir cap, to sit swinging in the porch swing until noon. After dinner she lay down for a while, until the afternoon began to cool. Then, in one of the three or four new voile dresses which she had each summer, she would go downtown to spend the afternoon in the stores with the other ladies, where they would handle the goods and haggle over the prices in cold, immediate voices, without any intention of buying.

She was of comfortable people — not the best in Jefferson, but good people enough — and she was still on the slender side of ordinary looking, with a bright, faintly haggard manner and dress. When she was young she had had a slender, nervous body and a sort of hard vivacity which had enabled her for a time to ride upon the crest of the town's social life as exemplified by the high school party and church social period of her contemporaries while still children enough to be unclassconscious.

She was the last to realize that she was losing ground; that those among whom she had been a little brighter and louder flame than any other were beginning to learn the pleasure of snobbery — male — and retaliation — female. That was when her face began to wear that bright, haggard look. She still carried it to parties on shadowy porticoes and summer lawns, like a mask or a flag, with that bafflement of furious repudiation of truth in her eyes. One evening at a party she heard a boy and two girls, all schoolmates, talking. She never accepted another invitation.

She watched the girls with whom she had grown up as they married and got homes and children, but no man ever called on her steadily until the children of the other girls had been calling her "aunty" for several years, the while their mothers told them in bright voices about how popular Aunt Minnie had been as a girl. Then the town began to see her driving on Sunday afternoons with the cashier in the bank. He was a widower of about forty — a high-colored man, smelling always faintly of the barber shop or of whisky. He owned the first automobile in town, a red runabout; Minnie had the first motoring bonnet and veil the town ever saw. Then the town began to say: "Poor Minnie." "But she is old enough to take care of herself," others said. That was when she began to ask her old schoolmates that their children call her "cousin" instead of "aunty."

It was twelve years now since she had been relegated into adultery by public opinion, and eight years since the cashier had gone to a Memphis bank, returning for one day each Christmas, which he spent at an annual bachelors' party at a hunting club on the river. From behind their curtains the neighbors would see the party pass, and during the over-the-way Christmas day visiting they would tell her about him, about how well he looked, and how they heard that he was prospering in the city, watching with bright, secret eyes her haggard, bright face. Usually by that hour there would be the scent of whisky on her breath. It was supplied her by a youth, a clerk at the soda fountain: "Sure; I buy it for the old gal. I reckon she's entitled to a little fun."

Her mother kept to her room altogether now; the gaunt aunt ran the house. Against that background Minnie's bright dresses, her idle and empty days, had a quality of furious unreality. She went out in the evenings only with women now, neighbors, to the moving pictures. Each afternoon she dressed in one of the new dresses and went downtown alone, where her young "cousins" were already strolling in the late afternoons with their delicate, silken heads and thin, awkward arms and conscious hips, clinging to one another or shrieking and giggling with paired boys in the soda fountain when she passed and went on along the serried store fronts, in the doors of which the sitting and lounging men did not even follow her with their eyes any more.

III

The barber went swiftly up the street where the sparse lights, insect-swirled, glared in rigid and violent suspension in the lifeless air. The day had died in a pall of dust; above the dark-ened square, shrouded by the spent dust, the sky was as clear as the inside of a brass bell. Below the east was a rumor of the twice-waxed moon.

When he overtook them McLendon and three others were getting into a car parked in an alley. McLendon stooped his thick head, peering out beneath the top. "Changed your mind, did you?" he said. "Damn good thing; by God, tomorrow when this town hears about how you talked tonight —"

"Now, now," the other ex-soldier said. "Hawkshaw's all right. Come on, Hawk; jump in."

"Will Mayes never done it, boys," the barber said. "If anybody done it. Why, you all know well as I do there aint any town where they got better niggers than us. And you know how a lady will kind of think things about men when there aint any reason to, and Miss Minnie anyway —"

"Sure, sure," the soldier said. "We're just going to talk to him a little; that's all."

"Talk hell!" Butch said. "When we're through with the —"

"Shut up, for God's sake!" the soldier said. "Do you want everybody in town —"

"Tell them, by God!" McLendon said. "Tell every one of the sons that'll let a white woman —"

"Let's go; let's go: here's the other car." The second car slid squealing out of a cloud of dust at the alley mouth. McLendon started his car and took the lead. Dust lay like fog in the street. The street lights hung nimbused as in water. They drove on out of town.

A rutted lane turned at right angles. Dust hung above it too, and above all the land. The dark bulk of the ice plant, where the Negro Mayes was night watchman, rose against the sky. "Better stop here, hadn't we?" the soldier said. McLendon did not reply. He hurled the car up and slammed to a stop, the headlights glaring on the blank wall.

"Listen here, boys," the barber said; "if he's here, dont that prove he never done it? Dont it? If it was him, he would run. Dont you see he would?" The second car came up and stopped. McLendon got down; Butch sprang down beside him. "Listen, boys," the barber said.

"Cut the lights off!" McLendon said. The breathless dark rushed down. There was no sound in it save their lungs as they sought air in the parched dust in which for two months they had lived; then the diminishing crunch of McLendon's and Butch's feet, and a moment later McLendon's voice:

"Will! . . . Will!"

Below the east the wan hemorrhage of the moon increased. It heaved above the ridge, silvering the air, the dust, so that they seemed to breathe, live, in a bowl of molten lead. There was no sound of nightbird nor insect, no sound save their breathing and a faint ticking of contracting metal about the cars. Where their bodies touched one another they seemed to sweat dryly, for no more moisture came. "Christ!" a voice said; "let's get out of here."

But they didn't move until vague noises began to grow out of the darkness ahead; then they got out and waited tensely in the breathless dark. There was another sound: a blow, a hissing expulsion of breath and McLendon cursing in undertone. They stood a moment longer, then they ran forward. They ran in a stumbling clump, as though they were fleeing something. "Kill him, kill the son," a voice whispered. McLendon flung them back.

"Not here," he said. "Get him into the car." "Kill him, kill the black son!" the voice murmured. They dragged the Negro to the car. The barber had waited beside the car. He could feel himself sweating and he knew he was going to be sick at the stomach.

"What is it, captains?" the Negro said. "I aint done nothing. 'Fore God, Mr John." Someone produced handcuffs. They worked busily about the Negro as though he were a post, quiet, intent, getting in one another's way. He submitted to the handcuffs, looking swiftly and constantly from dim face to dim face. "Who's here, captains?" he said, leaning to peer into the faces until they could feel his breath and smell his sweaty reek. He spoke a name or two. "What you all say I done, Mr John?"

McLendon jerked the car door open. "Get in!" he said.

The Negro did not move. "What you all going to do with me, Mr John? I aint done nothing. White folks, captains, I aint done nothing: I swear 'fore God." He called another name.

"Get in!" McLendon said. He struck the Negro. The others expelled their breath in a dry hissing and struck him with random blows and he whirled and cursed them, and swept his manacled hands across their faces and slashed the barber upon the mouth, and the barber struck him also. "Get him in there," McLendon said. They pushed at him. He ceased struggling and got in and sat quietly as the others took their places. He sat between the barber and the soldier, drawing his limbs in so as not to touch

them, his eyes going swiftly and constantly from face to face. Butch clung to the running board. The car moved on. The barber nursed his mouth with his handkerchief.

"What's the matter, Hawk?" the soldier said.

"Nothing," the barber said. They regained the highroad and turned away from town. The second car dropped back out of the dust. They went on, gaining speed; the final fringe of houses dropped behind.

"Goddamn, he stinks!" the soldier said.

"We'll fix that," the drummer in front beside McLendon said. On the running board Butch cursed into the hot rush of air. The barber leaned suddenly forward and touched McLendon's arm.

"Let me out, John," he said.

"Jump out, niggerlover," McLendon said without turning his head. He drove swiftly. Behind them the sourceless lights of the second car glared in the dust. Presently McLendon turned into a narrow road. It was rutted with disuse. It led back to an abandoned brick kiln — a series of reddish mounds and weed- and vine-choked vats without bottom. It had been used for pasture once, until one day the owner missed one of his mules. Although he prodded carefully in the vats with a long pole, he could not even find the bottom of them.

"John," the barber said.

"Jump out, then," McLendon said, hurling the car along the ruts. Beside the barber the Negro spoke:

"Mr Henry."

The barber sat forward. The narrow tunnel of the road rushed up and past. Their motion was like an extinct furnace blast: cooler, but utterly dead. The car bounded from rut to rut.

"Mr Henry," the Negro said.

The barber began to tug furiously at the door. "Look out, there!" the soldier said, but the barber had already kicked the door open and swung onto the running board. The soldier leaned across the Negro and grasped at him, but he had already jumped. The car went on without checking speed.

The impetus hurled him crashing through dust-sheathed weeds, into the ditch. Dust puffed about him, and in a thin, vicious crackling of sapless stems he lay choking and retching until the second car passed and died away. Then he rose and limped on until he reached the highroad and turned toward town, brushing at his clothes with his hands. The moon was higher, riding high and clear of the dust at last, and after a while the town began to glare beneath the dust. He went on, limping. Presently he heard cars and the glow of them grew in the dust behind him and he left the road and crouched again in the weeds until they passed. McLendon's car came last now. There were four people in it and Butch was not on the running board.

They went on; the dust swallowed them; the glare and the sound died away. The dust of them hung for a while, but soon the eternal dust absorbed it again. The barber climbed back onto the road and limped on toward town.

IV

As she dressed for supper on that Saturday evening, her own flesh felt like fever. Her hands trembled among the hooks and eyes, and her eyes had a feverish look, and her hair swirled crisp and crackling under the comb. While she was still dressing the friends called for her and sat while she donned her sheerest underthings and stockings and a new voile dress. "Do you feel strong enough to go out?" they said, their eyes bright too, with a dark glitter. "When you have had time to get over the shock, you must tell us what happened. What he said and did; everything."

In the leafed darkness, as they walked toward the square, she began to breathe deeply, something like a swimmer preparing to dive, until she ceased trembling, the four of them walking slowly because of the terrible heat and out of solicitude for her. But as they neared the square she began to tremble again, walking with her head up, her hands clenched at her sides, their voices about her murmurous, also with that feverish, glittering quality of their eyes.

They entered the square, she in the center of the group, fragile in her fresh dress. She was trembling worse. She walked slower and slower, as children eat ice cream, her head up and her eyes bright in the haggard banner of her face, passing the hotel and the coatless drummers in chairs along the curb looking around at her: "That's the one: see? The one in pink in the middle." "Is that her? What did they do with the nigger? Did they—?" "Sure. He's all right." "All right, is he?" "Sure. He went on a little trip." Then the drug store, where even the young men lounging in the doorway tipped their hats and followed with their eyes the motion of her hips and legs when she passed.

They went on, passing the lifted hats of the gentlemen, the suddenly ceased voices, deferent, protective. "Do you see?" the friends said.

Their voices sounded like long, hovering sighs of hissing exultation. "There's not a Negro on the square. Not one."

They reached the picture show. It was like a miniature fairyland with its lighted lobby and colored lithographs of life caught in its terrible and beautiful mutations. Her lips began to tingle. In the dark, when the picture began, it would be all right; she could hold back the laughing so it would not waste away so fast and so soon. So she hurried on before the turning faces, the undertones of low astonishment, and they took their accustomed places where she could see the aisle against the silver glare and the young men and girls coming in two and two against it.

The lights flicked away; the screen glowed silver, and soon life began to unfold, beautiful and passionate and sad, while still the young men and girls entered, scented and sibilant in the half dark, their paired backs in silhouette delicate and sleek, their slim, quick bodies awkward, divinely young, while beyond them the silver dream accumulated, inevitably on and on. She began to laugh. In trying to suppress it, it made more noise than ever; heads began to turn. Still laughing, her friends raised her and led her out, and she stood at the curb, laughing on a high, sustained note, until the taxi came up and they helped her in.

They removed the pink voile and the sheer underthings and the stockings, and put her to bed, and cracked ice for her temples, and sent for the doctor. He was hard to locate, so they ministered to her with hushed ejaculations, renewing the ice and fanning her. While the ice was fresh and cold she stopped laughing and lay still for a time, moaning only a little. But soon the laughing welled again and her voice rose screaming.

"Shhhhhhhhhhh! Shhhhhhhhhhhhhhh!" they said, freshening the icepack, smoothing her hair, examining it for gray; "poor girl!" Then to one another: "Do you suppose anything really happened?" their eyes darkly aglitter, secret and passionate. "Shhhhhhhhhhh! Poor girl! Poor Minnie!"

V

It was midnight when McLendon drove up to his neat new house. It was trim and fresh as a birdcage and almost as small, with its clean, green-and-white paint. He locked the car and mounted the porch and entered. His wife rose from a chair beside the reading lamp. McLendon stopped in the floor and stared at her until she looked down.

"Look at that clock," he said, lifting his arm, pointing. She stood before him, her face lowered, a magazine in her hands. Her face was pale, strained, and weary-looking. "Haven't I told you about sitting up like this, waiting to see when I come in?"

"John," she said. She laid the magazine down. Poised on the balls of his feet, he glared at her with his hot eyes, his sweating face.

"Didn't I tell you?" He went toward her. She looked up then. He caught her shoulder. She stood passive, looking at him.

"Don't, John. I couldn't sleep . . . The heat; something. Please, John. You're hurting me."

"Didn't I tell you?" He released her and half

struck, half flung her across the chair, and she lay there and watched him quietly as he left the room.

He went on through the house, ripping off his shirt, and on the dark, screened porch at the rear he stood and mopped his head and shoulders with the shirt and flung it away. He took the pistol from his hip and laid it on the table beside the bed, and sat on the bed and removed his shoes, and rose and slipped his trousers off. He was sweating again already, and he stooped and hunted furiously for the shirt. At last he found it and wiped his body again, and, with his body pressed against the dusty screen, he stood panting. There was no movement, no sound, not even an insect. The dark world seemed to lie stricken beneath the cold moon and the lidless stars.

AN AGE OF CRITICISM

The recovery of the past, especially through literature, has become one of the distinguishing marks of our time. The process of reinterpretation of the older literature and the discovery of values in the new has become a significant part of the literary revival which may be dated roughly from 1912. Like poetry, fiction, and the drama, criticism shared the revolt and excitement of the 1920's, took Freud and Marx to its bosom, and adapted to its own uses certain of the scientific insights of psychology and sociology. It has become a truism to describe the twentieth century as an age of criticism.

In the selections which follow, a number of the most distinct lines of critical activity are represented. H. L. Mencken was the spokesman for the intellectual revolt of the twenties in journalistic and *impressionistic* criticism. Irving Babbitt thundered to his classes at Harvard the gospel of the *New Humanism.* Edmund Wilson has continued to investigate the social and cultural background of literature from a *historical* point of view, influenced by the theories of both Marx and Freud. *Analytical criticism* in which the text of a poem or prose work is subjected to an intense and careful scrutiny, with a minimum of reference to biography or history, has become the hallmark of the "New Criticism" and is often associated with Cleanth Brooks and Robert Penn Warren. Brooks's essay on "The Waste Land" is printed here for the twofold purpose of illustrating the analytical method and illuminating that difficult poem for the student.

Two further approaches in modern criticism are illustrated by the essays of Lionel Trilling, a liberal, post-Marxist critic who has interested himself in the Freudian approach (with reservations), and Malcolm Cowley, an independent observer of the literary situation.

Further reading: *Literary Opinion in America,* ed. M. D. Zabel, 1951. *The Development of American Literary Criticism,* ed. F. Stovall, 1955.

H. L. Mencken [1880–1956]

The oracle of Flaming Youth and other rebels of the Jazz Age (see page 844) was born in Baltimore and graduated from the Baltimore Polytechnic Institute in 1896. After three years in his father's tobacco business, he started his long career as a newspaperman. On the Baltimore *Morning Herald* he was successively reporter, city editor, and editor. In 1906 he began his thirty-five years' connection with the Baltimore *Sun*. Within this time he was also associated with the *Smart Set*, as reviewer, then literary editor, and finally co-editor with George Jean Nathan. The two, in 1923, left the *Smart Set* to start the *American Mercury*, and when Nathan dropped out a year later, Mencken remained as editor-in-chief till 1935, making it a magazine famous for its witty skepticism and boisterous criticism of almost everything American. When the Depression ended the Jazz Age, Mencken's vast popularity quickly evaporated.

Among his books were a study of Bernard Shaw's plays (1905) and one on Nietzsche's philosophy (1908); *A Book of Prefaces* (1917); six series of *Prejudices* (1919–27); and *The American Language* (4th edition, 1936), an important contribution to learning.

Further reading: *Selected Prefaces.*

Footnote on Criticism

(1922)

🦋 In a well-known essay by Matthew Arnold, three types of criticism are described. There is the *historical estimate*, the importance of a work in relation to its time and place; the *personal estimate*, based on our individual likings and limitations; and the *real estimate*, the attempt to judge what is really great and valuable to mankind. The personal estimate is the foundation of impressionistic criticism, which grew out of the romantic emphasis on sympathy and self-expression. In English literature, this type of criticism suggests the names of Hazlitt (mentioned by Mencken) and Pater; in French, Anatole France and Lemaître. Mencken was in agreement with the most radical of these, Anatole France, whose skeptical turn of mind led him to discard any objective or "real" estimate as impossible, since "one never gets out of oneself" and the good critic is merely one "who relates the adventures of his soul among masterpieces." Accordingly, Mencken says that the critic is "simply trying to express himself" — that, like an artist (or a hen) he enjoys creation.

Nearly all the discussions of criticism that I am acquainted with start off with a false assumption, to wit, that the primary motive of the critic, the impulse which makes a critic of him instead of, say, a politician, or a stockbroker, is pedagogical — that he writes because he is possessed by a passion to advance the enlightenment, to put down error and wrong, to disseminate some specific doctrine: psychological, epistemological, historical, or aesthetic. This is true, it seems to me, only of bad critics, and its degree of truth increases in direct ratio of their badness. The motive of the critic who is really worth reading — the only critic of whom, indeed, it may be said truthfully that it is at all possible to read him, save as an act of mental discipline — is something quite different. That motive is not the motive of the pedagogue, but the motive of the artist. It is no more and no less than the simple desire to function freely and beautifully, to give outward and objective form to ideas that bubble inwardly and have a fascinating lure in them, to get rid of them dramatically and make an articulate noise in the world. It was for this reason that Plato wrote the "Republic," and for this reason that Beethoven wrote the Ninth Symphony, and it is for this reason, to drop a million miles, that I am writing the present essay. Everything else is afterthought, mock-modesty, messianic delusion — in brief, affectation and folly. Is the contrary conception of criticism widely cherished? Is it almost universally held that the thing is a brother to jurisprudence, advertising, laparotomy, chautauqua lecturing and the art of the schoolmarm? Then certainly the fact that it is so held should be sufficient to set up an overwhelming probability of its lack of truth and sense. If I speak with some heat, it is as one who has suffered. When, years ago, I devoted myself diligently to critical pieces upon the writings of Theodore Dreiser, I found that practically every one who took any notice of my proceedings at all fell into either one of two assumptions about my underlying purpose: (*a*) that I had a fanatical devotion for Mr. Dreiser's ideas and desired to propagate them, or (*b*) that I was an ardent patriot, and yearned to lift up American literature. Both assumptions were false. I had then, and I have now, very little interest in many of Mr. Dreiser's main ideas; when we meet, in fact, we usually quarrel about them. And I am wholly devoid of public spirit, and haven't the least lust to improve American literature; if it ever came to what I regard as perfection my job would be gone. What, then, was my motive in writing about Mr. Dreiser so copiously? My motive, well known to Mr. Dreiser himself and to every one else who knew me as intimately as he did, was simply and solely to sort out and give coherence to the ideas of Mr. Mencken, and to put them into suave and ingratiating terms, and to discharge them with a flourish, and maybe with a phrase of pretty song, into the dense fog that blanketed the Republic.

The critic's choice of criticism rather than of what is called creative writing is chiefly a matter of temperament — perhaps, more accurately of hormones — with accidents of education and environment to help. The feelings that happen to be dominant in him at the moment the scribbling frenzy seizes him are feelings inspired, not directly by life itself, but by books, pictures, music, sculpture, architecture, religion, philosophy — in brief, by some other man's feelings about life. They are thus, in a sense, second-hand, and it is no wonder that creative artists so easily fall into the theory that they are also second-rate. Perhaps they usually are. If, indeed, the critic continues on this plane — if he lacks the intellectual agility and enterprise needed to make the leap from the work of art to the vast and mysterious complex of phenomena behind it — then they *always* are, and he remains no more than a fugelman or policeman to his betters. But if a genuine artist is concealed within him — if his feelings are in any sense profound and original, and his capacity for self-expression is above the average of educated men — then he moves inevitably from the

work of art to life itself, and begins to take on a dignity that he formerly lacked. It is impossible to think of a man of any actual force and originality, universally recognized as having those qualities, who spent his whole life appraising and describing the work of other men. Did Goethe, or Carlyle, or Matthew Arnold, or Sainte-Beuve, or Macaulay, or even, to come down a few pegs, Lewes, or Lowell, or Hazlitt? Certainly not. The thing that becomes most obvious about the writings of all such men, once they are examined carefully, is that the critic is always being swallowed up by the creative artist — that what starts out as the review of a book, or a play, or other work of art, usually develops very quickly into an independent essay upon the theme of that work of art, or upon some theme that it suggests — in a word, that it becomes a fresh work of art, and only indirectly related to the one that suggested it. This fact, indeed, is so plain that it scarcely needs statement. What the pedagogues always object to in, for example, the *Quarterly* reviewers is that they forgot the books they were supposed to review, and wrote long papers — often, in fact, small books — expounding ideas suggested (or not suggested) by the books under review. Every critic who is worth reading falls inevitably into the same habit. He cannot stick to his task: what is before him is always infinitely less interesting to him than what is within him. If he is genuinely first-rate — if what is within him stands the test of type, and wins an audience, and produces the reactions that every artist craves — then he usually ends by abandoning the criticism of specific works of art altogether, and setting up shop as a merchant in general ideas, *i.e.*, as an artist working in the materials of life itself.

Mere reviewing, however conscientiously and competently it is done, is plainly a much inferior business. Like writing poetry, it is chiefly a function of intellectual immaturity. The young literatus just out of the university, having as yet no capacity for grappling with the fundamental mysteries of existence, is put to writing reviews of books, or plays, or music, or painting. Very often he does it extremely well; it is, in fact, not hard to do well, for even decayed pedagogues often do it, as such graves of the intellect as the New York *Times* bear witness. But if he continues to do it, whether well or ill, it is a sign to all the world that his growth ceased when they made him *Artium Baccalau-*

reus. Gradually he becomes, whether in or out of the academic grove, a professor, which is to say, a man devoted to diluting and retailing the ideas of his superiors — not an artist, not even a bad artist, but almost the antithesis of an artist. He is learned, he is sober, he is painstaking and accurate — but he is as hollow as a jug. Nothing is in him save the ghostly echoes of other men's thoughts and feelings. If he were a genuine artist he would have thoughts and feelings of his own, and the impulse to give them objective form would be irresistible. An artist can no more withstand that impulse than a politician can withstand the temptations of a job. There are no mute, inglorious Miltons, save in the hallucinations of poets. The one sound test of a Milton is that he functions as a Milton. His difference from other men lies precisely in the superior vigor of his impulse to self-expression, not in the superior beauty and loftiness of his ideas. Other men, in point of fact, often have the same ideas, or perhaps even loftier ones, but they are able to suppress them, usually on grounds of decorum, and so they escape being artists, and are respected by right-thinking persons, and die with money in the bank, and are forgotten in two weeks.

Obviously, the critic whose performance we are commonly called upon to investigate is a man standing somewhere along the path leading from the beginning that I have described to the goal. He has got beyond being a mere cataloguer and valuer of other men's ideas, but he has not yet become an autonomous artist — he is not yet ready to challenge attention with his own ideas alone. But it is plain that his motion, in so far as he is moving at all, must be in the direction of that autonomy — that is, unless one imagines him sliding backward into senile infantilism: a spectacle not unknown to literary pathology, but too pathetic to be discussed here. Bear this motion in mind, and the true nature of his aims and purposes becomes clear; more, the incurable falsity of the aims and purposes usually credited to him becomes equally clear. He is not actually trying to perform an impossible act of arctic justice upon the artist whose work gives him a text. He is not trying with mathematical passion to find out exactly what was in that artist's mind at the moment of creation, and to display it precisely and in an ecstasy of appreciation. He is not trying to bring the work discussed into accord with some transient theory of aesthetics, or ethics, or truth, or to determine its degree of departure from that theory. He is not trying to lift up the fine arts, or to defend democracy against sense, or to promote happiness at the domestic hearth, or to convert sophomores into right-thinkers, or to serve God. He is not trying to fit a group of novel phenomena into the orderly process of history. He is not even trying to discharge the catalytic office that I myself, in a romantic moment, once sought to force upon him. He is, first and last, simply trying to express himself. He is trying to arrest and challenge a sufficient body of readers, to make them pay attention to him, to impress them with the charm and novelty of his ideas, to provoke them into an agreeable (or shocked) awareness of him, and he is trying to achieve thereby for his own inner ego the grateful feeling of a function performed, a tension relieved, a *katharsis* attained which Wagner achieved when he wrote "Die Walküre," and a hen achieves every time she lays an egg.

Joseph Conrad is moved by that necessity to write romances; Bach was moved to write music; poets are moved to write poetry; critics are moved to write criticism. The form is nothing; the only important thing is the motive power, and it is the same in all cases. It is the pressing yearning of every man who has ideas in him to empty them upon the world, to hammer them into plausible and ingratiating shapes, to compel the attention and respect of his equals, to lord it over his inferiors. So seen, the critic becomes a far more transparent and agreeable fellow than ever he was in the discourses of the psychologists who sought to make him a mere appraiser in an intellectual customs house, a gauger in a distillery of the spirit, a just and infallible judge upon the cosmic bench. Such offices, in point of fact, never fit him. He always bulges over their confines. So labelled and estimated, it inevitably turns out that the specific critic under examination is a very bad one, or no critic at all. But when he is thought of, not as pedagogue, but as artist, then he begins to take on reality, and, what is more, dignity. Carlyle was surely no just and infallible judge; on the contrary, he was full of prejudices, biles, naïvetés, humors. Yet he is read, consulted, attended to. Macaulay was unfair, inaccurate, fanciful, lyrical — yet his essays live. Arnold had his faults too, and so did Sainte-Beuve, and so did Goethe, and so did many another of that line — and yet they are remembered today, and all the learned and conscientious critics of their time, laboriously concerned with the precise intent of the artists under review, and passionately determined to set it forth with god-like care and to relate it exactly to this or that great stream of ideas — all these pedants are forgotten. What saved Carlyle, Macaulay and company is as plain as day. They were first-rate artists. They could make the thing charming, and that is always a million times more important than making it true.

Truth, indeed, is something that is believed in completely only by persons who have never tried personally to pursue it to its fastnesses and grab it by the tail. It is the adoration of second-rate men — men who always receive it at secondhand. Pedagogues believe in immutable truths and spend their lives trying to determine them and propagate them; the intellectual progress of man consists largely of a concerted effort to block and destroy their enterprise. Nine times out of ten, in the arts as in life, there is actually no truth to be discovered; there is only error to be exposed. In whole departments of human inquiry it seems to me quite unlikely that the truth ever *will* be discovered. Nevertheless, the rubber stamp thinking of the world always makes the assumption that the exposure of an error is identical with the discovery of the truth — that error and truth are simple opposites. They are nothing of the sort. What the world turns to when it has been cured of one error, is usually simply another error, and maybe one worse than the first one. This is the whole history of the intellect in brief. The average man of today does not believe in precisely the same imbecilities that the Greek of the fourth century before Christ believed in, but the things that he *does* believe in are often quite as idiotic. Perhaps this statement is a bit too sweeping. There is, year by year, a gradual accumulation of what may be called, provisionally, truths — there is a slow accretion of ideas that somehow manage to meet all practicable human tests, and so survive. But even so, it is risky to call them absolute truths. All that one may safely say of them is that no one, as yet, has demonstrated that they are errors. Soon or late, if experience teaches us anything, they are likely to succumb too. The profoundest truths of the Middle Ages are now laughed at by schoolboys. The profoundest truths of democracy will be laughed at, a few centuries hence, even by schoolteachers.

In the department of aesthetics, wherein critics mainly disport themselves, it is almost impossible to think of a so-called truth that shows any sign of being permanently true. The most profound of principles begins to fade and quiver almost as soon as it is stated. But the work of art, as opposed to the theory behind it, has a longer life, particularly if that theory be obscure and questionable, and so cannot be determined accurately. "Hamlet," the Mona Lisa, "Faust," "Dixie," "Parsifal," "Mother Goose," "Annabel Lee," "Huckleberry Finn" — these things, so baffling to pedagogy, so contumacious to the categories, so mysterious in purpose and utility — these things live. And why? Because there is in them the flavor of salient, novel and attractive personality, because the quality that shines from them is not that of correct demeanor but that of creative passion, because they pulse and breathe and speak, because they are genuine works of art. So with criticism. Let us forget all the heavy effort to make a science of it; it is a fine art, or nothing. If the critic, retiring to his cell to concoct his treatise upon a book or play or what-not, produces a piece of writing that shows sound structure, and brilliant color, and the flash of new and persuasive ideas, and civilized manners, and the charm of an uncommon personality in free function, then he has given something to the world that is worth having, and sufficiently justified his existence. Is Carlyle's "Frederick" true? Who cares? As well ask if the Parthenon is true, or the C Minor Symphony, or "Wiener Blut." Let the critic who is an artist leave such necropsies to professors of aesthetics, who can no more determine the truth than he can, and will infallibly make it unpleasant and a bore.

It is, of course, not easy to practice this abstention. Two forces, one within and one without, tend to bring even a Hazlitt or a Huneker under the campus pump. One is the almost universal human susceptibility to messianic delusions — the irresistible tendency of practically every man, once he finds a crowd in front of him, to strut and roll his eyes. The other is the public demand, born of such long familiarity with pedagogical criticism that no other kind is readily conceivable, that the critic teach something as well as say something — in the popular phrase, that he be constructive. Both operate powerfully against his free functioning, and especially the former. He finds it hard to resist the flattery of his customers, however little he may actually esteem it. If he knows anything at all, he knows that his following, like that of every other artist in ideas, is chiefly made up of the congenitally subaltern type of man and woman — natural converts, lodge joiners, me-toos, stragglers after circus parades. It is precious seldom that he ever gets a positive idea out of them; what he usually gets is mere unintelligent ratification. But this troop, despite its obvious failings, corrupts him in various ways. For one thing, it enormously reënforces his belief in his own ideas, and so tends to make him stiff and dogmatic — in brief, precisely everything that he ought not to be. And for another thing, it tends to make him (by a curious contradiction) a bit pliant and politic: he begins to estimate new ideas, not in proportion as they are amusing or beautiful, but in proportion as they are likely to please. So beset, front and rear, he sometimes sinks supinely to the level of a professor, and his subsequent proceedings are interesting no more. The true aim of a critic is certainly not to make converts. He must know that very few of the persons who are susceptible to conversion are worth converting. Their minds are intrinsically flabby and parasitical, and it is certainly not sound sport to agitate minds of that sort. Moreover, the critic must always harbor a grave doubt about most of the ideas that they lap up so greedily — it must occur to him not infrequently, in the silent watches of the night, that much that he writes is sheer buncombe. As I have said, I can't imagine any idea — that is, in the domain of aesthetics — that is palpably and incontrovertibly sound. All that I am familiar with, and in particular all that I announce most vociferously, seem to me to contain a core of quite obvious nonsense. I thus try to avoid cherishing them too lovingly, and it always gives me a shiver to see any one else gobble them at one gulp. Criticism, at bottom, is indistinguishable from skepticism. Both launch themselves, the one by aesthetic presentations and the other by logical presentations, at the common human tendency to accept whatever is approved, to take in ideas ready-made, to be responsive to mere rhetoric and gesticulation. A critic who believes in anything absolutely is bound to that something quite as helplessly as a Christian is bound to the Freudian garbage in the Book of Revelation. To that extent, at all events, he is unfree and unintelligent, and hence a bad critic.

The demand for "constructive" criticism is based upon the same false assumption that immutable truths exist in the arts, and that the artist will be improved by being made aware of them. This notion, whatever the form it takes, is always absurd — as much so, indeed, as its brother delusion that the critic, to be competent, must be a practitioner of the specific art he ventures to deal with, i.e., that a doctor, to cure a belly-ache, must have a belly-ache. As practically encountered, it is disingenuous as well as absurd, for it comes chiefly from bad artists who tire of serving as performing monkeys, and crave the greater ease and safety of sophomores in class. They demand to be taught in order to avoid being knocked about. In their demand is the theory that instruction, if they could get it, would profit them — that they are capable of doing better work than they do. As a practical matter, I doubt that this is ever true. Bad poets never actually grow any better; they invariably grow worse and worse. In all history there has never been, to my knowledge, a single practitioner of any art who, as a result of "constructive" criticism, improved his work. The curse of all the arts, indeed, is the fact that they are constantly invaded by persons who are not artists at all — persons whose yearning to express their ideas and feelings is unaccompanied by the slightest capacity for charming expression — in brief, persons with absolutely nothing to say. This is particularly true of the art of letters, which interposes very few technical obstacles to the vanity and garrulity of such invaders. Any effort to teach them to write better is an effort wasted, as every editor discovers for himself; they are as incapable of it as they are of jumping over the moon. The only sort of criticism that can deal with them to any profit is the sort that employs them frankly as laboratory animals. It cannot cure them, but it can at least make an amusing and perhaps edifying show of them. It is idle to argue that the good in them is thus destroyed with the bad. The simple answer is that there is no good in them. Suppose Poe had wasted his time trying to dredge good work out of Rufus Dawes, author of "Geraldine." He would have failed miserably — and spoiled a capital essay, still diverting after three quarters of a century. Suppose Beethoven, dealing with Gottfred Weber, had tried laboriously to make an intelligent music critic of him. How much more apt, useful and durable the simple note: "Arch-ass! Double-barrelled ass!" Here was absolutely sound criticism.

Here was a judgment wholly beyond challenge. Moreover, here was a small but perfect work of art.

Upon the low practical value of so-called constructive criticism I can offer testimony out of my own experience. My books are commonly reviewed at great length, and many critics devote themselves to pointing out what they conceive to be my errors, both of fact and of taste. Well, I cannot recall a case in which any suggestion offered by a constructive critic has helped me in the slightest, or even actively interested me. Every such wet-nurse of letters has sought fatuously to make me write in a way differing from that in which the Lord God Almighty, in His infinite wisdom, impels me to write — that is, to make me write stuff which, coming from me, would be as false as an appearance of decency in a Congressman. All the benefits I have ever got from the critics of my work have come from the destructive variety. A hearty slating always does me good, particularly if it be well written. It begins by enlisting my professional respect; it ends by making me examine my ideas coldly in the privacy of my chamber. Not, of course, that I usually revise them, but I at least examine them. If I decide to hold fast to them, they are all the dearer to me thereafter, and I expound them with a new passion and plausibility. If, on the contrary, I discern holes in them, I shelve them in a *pianissimo* manner, and set about hatching new ones to take their place. But constructive criticism irritates me. I do not object to being denounced, but I can't abide being school-mastered, especially by men I regard as imbeciles.

I find, as a practicing critic, that very few men who write books are even as tolerant as I am — that most of them, soon or late, show signs of extreme discomfort under criticism, however polite its terms. Perhaps this is why enduring friendships between authors and critics are so rare. All artists, of course, dislike one another more or less, but that dislike seldom rises to implacable enmity, save between opera singer and opera singer, and creative author and critic. Even when the latter two keep up an outward show of good-will, there is always bitter antagonism under the surface. Part of it, I daresay, arises out of the impossible demands of the critic, particularly if he be tinged with the constructive madness. Having favored an author with his good opinion, he expects the poor fellow to live up to that good opinion without the slightest compromise or faltering, and this is commonly beyond human power. He feels that any let-down compromises *him* — that his hero is stabbing him in the back, and making him ridiculous — and this feeling rasps his vanity. The most bitter of all literary quarrels are those between critics and creative artists, and most of them arise in just this way. As for the creative artist, he on his part naturally resents the critic's air of pedagogical superiority and he resents it especially when he has an uneasy feeling that he has fallen short of his best work, and that the discontent of the critic is thus justified. Injustice is relatively easy to bear; what stings is justice. Under it all, of course, lurks the fact that I began with: the fact that the critic is himself an artist, and that his creative impulse, soon or late, is bound to make him neglect the punctilio. When he sits down to compose his criticism, his artist ceases to be a friend, and becomes mere raw material for his work of art. It is my experience that artists invariably resent this cavalier use of them. They are pleased so long as the critic confines himself to the modest business of interpreting them — preferably in terms of their own estimate of themselves — but the moment he proceeds to adorn their theme with variations of his own, the moment he brings new ideas to the enterprise and begins contrasting them with their ideas, that moment they grow restive. It is precisely at this point, of course, that criticism becomes genuine criticism; before that it was mere reviewing. When a critic passes it he loses his friends. By becoming an artist, he becomes the foe of all other artists.

But the transformation, I believe, has good effects upon him: it makes him a better critic. Too much *Gemütlichkeit* is as fatal to criticism as it would be to surgery or politics. When it rages unimpeded it leads inevitably either to a dull professorial sticking on of meaningless labels or to log-rolling, and often it leads to both. One of the most hopeful symptoms of the new *Aufklärung* in the Republic is the revival of acrimony in criticism — the renaissance of the doctrine that aesthetic matters are important, and that it is worth the while of a healthy male to take them seriously, as he takes business, sport and amour. In the days when American literature was showing its first vigorous growth, the native criticism was extraordinarily violent and even vicious; in the days when American literature swooned upon the tomb of the Puritan

Kultur it became flaccid and childish. The typical critic of the first era was Poe, as the typical critic of the second was Howells. Poe carried on his critical jehads with such ferocity that he often got into law-suits, and sometimes ran no little risk of having his head cracked. He regarded literary questions as exigent and momentous. The lofty aloofness of the don was simply not in him. When he encountered a book that seemed to him to be bad, he attacked it almost as sharply as a Chamber of Commerce would attack a fanatic preaching free speech, or the corporation of Trinity Church would attack Christ. His opponents replied in the same Berserker manner. Much of Poe's surviving illfame, as a drunkard and dead-beat, is due to their inordinate denunciations of him. They were not content to refute him; they constantly tried to dispose of him altogether. The very ferocity of that ancient row shows that the native literature, in those days, was in a healthy state. Books of genuine value were produced. Literature always thrives best, in fact, in an atmosphere of hearty strife. Poe, surrounded by admiring professors, never challenged, never aroused to the emotions of revolt, would probably have written poetry indistinguishable from the hollow stuff of, say, Prof. Dr. George E. Woodberry. It took the persistent (and often grossly unfair and dishonorable) opposition of Griswold *et al.* to stimulate him to his highest endeavors. He needed friends, true enough, but he also needed enemies.

Today, for the first time in years, there is strife in American criticism, and the Paul Elmer Mores and Hamilton Wright Mabies are no longer able to purr in peace. The instant they fall into stiff professorial attitudes they are challenged, and often with anything but urbanity. The *ex cathedra* manner thus passes out, and free discussion comes in. Heretics lay on boldly, and the professors are forced to make some defense. Often, going further, they attempt counter-attacks. Ears are bitten off. Noses are bloodied. There are wallops both above and below the belt. I am, I need not say, no believer in any magical merit in debate, no matter how free it may be. It certainly does not necessarily establish the truth; both sides, in fact, may be wrong, and they often are. But it at least accomplishes two important effects. On the one hand, it exposes all the cruder fallacies to hostile examination, and so disposes of many of them. And on the other hand, it melodramatizes the business of the critic, and so convinces thousands of bystanders, otherwise quite inert, that criticism is an amusing and instructive art, and that the problems it deals with are important. What men will fight for seems to be worth looking into.

Irving Babbitt [1865–1933]

Irving Babbitt was born in Dayton, Ohio, but the family often moved. He attended school in East Orange, New Jersey, sold newspapers on the streets of New York, was a farm boy in Ohio, a reporter in Cincinnati, a cowboy in Wyoming. With help from his uncles he entered Harvard, and graduated in 1889. After two years of teaching Latin and Greek at the University of Montana, he spent a year in Paris studying Sanskrit, then continued in this Oriental field as a graduate student at Harvard. The philosophy of Greece and the religion of ancient India henceforth constituted the foundations of his thought. But he was also devoted to French literature, and it was in the French department (and later in comparative literature) that he taught at Harvard — beginning in 1894 — for nearly forty years. His strong influence as a teacher was exerted chiefly through his courses on the history of literary criticism and the Romantic Movement in England, France, and Germany. The governing ideas of his teaching and writing have been suggested in a paragraph on pages 846–847, above.

Aside from articles in such periodicals as the *Atlantic Monthly* and the *Yale Review*, he wrote a series of books, at once learned and trenchant, of which the first was *Literature and the American College* (1908). His ablest works were perhaps *Masters of Modern French Criticism* (1912), *Rousseau and Romanticism* (1919), and *Democracy and Leadership* (1924). After his death came *The Dhammapada*, translated from the Pali, with an essay on Buddha and the Occident.

Further reading: *Rousseau and Romanticism* or *Democracy and Leadership*.

The Critic and American Life

Serious criticism, Babbitt held, is something other than the temperamental self-expression of "our half-baked intelligentsia." "A thoroughgoing and complete modern" will not be satisfied either with "the latest thing" because it is fashionable, nor with any handed-down tradition or creed taken on "authority." As examples of the full and free use of "the critical spirit" he points, in this essay, to Socrates, elsewhere to Petrarch, Goethe, Sainte-Beuve, Renan, and Matthew Arnold. Himself a general or cultural critic, he was largely concerned with ethical and philosophical problems even when dealing with literature, neglecting its aesthetic aspect.

Provoked by Menckenism, this essay first appeared in the *Forum* in 1928, during the humanist controversy. It involves many contrasting ideas, some of which may be indicated by a few questions. What does Babbitt say for and against Mencken as critic? What does he say for and against the Puritans? What, according to Babbitt, is the main issue in modern thought, and on this issue what stand did he take? How does Babbitt distinguish among the three types of "realism"? Why did he attack certain creative writers of the period, rather than others?

A frequent remark of the French about Americans is: "They're children"; which, interpreted, means that from the French point of view Americans are childishly uncritical. The remark is relevant only in so far as it refers to general critical intelligence. In dealing with the special problems of a commercial and industrial society, Americans have shown that they can be abundantly critical. Certain Americans, for example, have developed a critical keenness in estimating the value of stocks and bonds that is nothing short of uncanny.[1] The very persons, however, who are thus keen in some particular field are, when confronted with questions that call for general critical intelligence, often puerile. Yet in an age like the present, which is being subjected to a constant stream of propaganda in everything from the choice of its religion to its cigarettes, general critical intelligence would seem desirable.

As a matter of fact, most persons nowadays aspire to be not critical but creative. We have not merely creative poets and novelists, but creative readers and listeners and dancers. Lately a form of creativeness has appeared that may in time swallow up all the others — creative salesmanship. The critic himself has caught the contagion and also aspires to be creative. He is supposed to become so when he receives from the creation of another, conceived as pure temperamental overflow, so vivid an impression that, when passed through his temperament, it issues forth as a fresh creation. What is eliminated in both critic and creator is any standard that is set above temperament and that therefore might interfere with their eagerness to get themselves expressed.

This notion of criticism as self-expression is important for our present subject, for it has been adopted by the writer who is, according to the *Encyclopædia Britannica*,[2] "the greatest critical force in America" — Mr. H. L. Mencken. Creative self-expression, as practiced by himself and others, has, according to Mr. Mencken, led to a salutary stirring up of the stagnant pool of American letters: "Today for the first time in years there is strife in American criticism. . . .

[1] This was written before the collapse of the great common stock bubble in the autumn of 1929. It then became evident that what the financial leaders of the "boom" period lacked was not so much expertness in their own field as general critical intelligence — especially some working knowledge of the way of Nemesis. There were of course honorable exceptions. The late Paul M. Warburg showed that he was one of them when he remarked, apropos of the so-called business cycle, that "it is a subject for psychologists rather than for economists." [What is involved] "is the answer to the question: How long — in industry, commerce and finance — does the memory of painful experiences prevent human greed and conceit from regaining control, etc." [Author's note.]

[2] Thirteenth edition. In the fourteenth edition we are informed that Mr. Mencken is a satirist rather than a critic. [Author's note.]

Heretics lay on boldly and the professors are forced to make some defence. Often going further they attempt counter-attacks. Ears are bitten off, noses are bloodied. There are wallops both above and below the belt."

But it may be that criticism is something more than Mr. Mencken would have us believe, more in short than a squabble between Bohemians, each eager to capture the attention of the public for his brand of self-expression. To reduce criticism indeed to the satisfaction of a temperamental urge, to the uttering of one's gustos and disgustos (in Mr. Mencken's case chiefly the latter) is to run counter to the very etymology of the word which implies discrimination and judgment. The best one would anticipate from a writer like Mr. Mencken, possessing an unusual verbal virtuosity and at the same time temperamentally irresponsible, is superior intellectual vaudeville. One must grant him, however, certain genuine critical virtues — for example, a power of shrewd observation within rather narrow limits. Yet the total effect of his writing is nearer to intellectual vaudeville than to serious criticism.

The serious critic is more concerned with achieving a correct scale of values and so seeing things proportionately than with self-expression. His essential virtue is poise. The specific benefit he confers is to act as a moderating influence on the opposite insanities between which mankind in the lump is constantly tending to oscillate — oscillations that Luther compares to the reelings of a drunken peasant on horseback. The critic's survey of any particular situation may very well seem satirical. The complaint that Mr. Mencken is too uniformly disgruntled in his survey of the American situation rather misses the point. Behind the pleas for more constructiveness it is usually easy to detect the voice of the booster. A critic who did not get beyond a correct diagnosis of existing evils might be very helpful. If Mr. Mencken has fallen short of being such a diagnostician, the failure is due not to his excess of severity but to his lack of discrimination.

The standards with reference to which men have discriminated in the past have been largely traditional. The outstanding fact of the present period, on the other hand, has been the weakening of traditional standards. An emergency has arisen not unlike that with which Socrates sought to cope in ancient Athens. Anyone who is untraditional and seeks at the same time to be discriminating must almost necessarily own Socrates as his master. As is well known, Socrates sought above all to be discriminating in his use of general terms. Before allowing one's imagination and finally one's conduct to be controlled by a general term, it would seem wise to submit it to a Socratic scrutiny.

It is therefore, unfortunate that at a time like the present, which plainly calls for a Socrates, we should instead have got a Mencken. One may take as an example of Mr. Mencken's failure to discriminate adequately, his attitude towards the term that for several generations past has been governing the imagination of multitudes — democracy. His view of democracy is simply that of Rousseau turned upside down, and nothing, as has been remarked, resembles a hollow so much as a swelling. A distinction of which he has failed to recognize the importance is that between a direct or unlimited and a constitutional democracy. In the latter we probably have the best thing in the world. The former, on the other hand, as all thinkers of any penetration from Plato and Aristotle down have perceived, leads to the loss of liberty and finally to the rise of some form of despotism. The two conceptions of democracy involve not merely incompatible views of government but ultimately of human nature. The desire of the constitutional democrat for institutions that act as checks on the immediate will of the people implies a similar dualism in the individual — a higher self that acts restrictively on his ordinary and impulsive self. The partisan of unlimited democracy on the other hand is an idealist in the sense the term assumed in connection with the so-called romantic movement. His faith in the people is closely related to the doctrine of natural goodness proclaimed by the sentimentalists of the eighteenth century and itself marking an extreme recoil from the dogma of total depravity. The doctrine of natural goodness favors the free temperamental expansion that I have already noticed in speaking of the creative critic.

It is of the utmost importance, however, if one is to understand Mr. Mencken, to discriminate between two types of temperamentalist — the soft and sentimental type, who cherishes various "ideals," and the hard, or Nietzschean type, who piques himself on being realistic. As a matter of fact, if one sees in the escape from traditional controls merely an opportunity to live temperamentally, it would seem advantageous to pass promptly from the idealistic to the Nietzschean phase, sparing oneself as many as possible of the intermediary disillusions. It is at all events undeniable that the rise of Menckenism has been marked by a certain collapse of romantic idealism in the political field and elsewhere. The numerous disillusions that have supervened upon the War have provided a favoring atmosphere.

The symptoms of Menckenism are familiar: a certain hardness and smartness and disposition to rail at everything that, rightly or wrongly, is established and respected; a tendency to identify the real with what Mr. Mencken terms "the cold and clammy facts" and to assume that the only alternative to facing these facts is to fade away into sheer romantic unreality. These and similar traits are becoming so widely diffused that, whatever one's opinion of Mr. Mencken as a writer and thinker, one must grant him representativeness. He is a chief prophet at present of those who deem themselves emancipated but who are, according to Mr. Brownell, merely unbuttoned.

The crucial point in any case is one's attitude towards the principle of control. Those who stand for this principle in any form or degree are dismissed by the emancipated as reactionaries or, still graver reproach, as Puritans. Mr. Mencken would have us believe that the historical Puritan was not even sincere in his moral rigorism, but was given to "lamentable transactions with loose women and fiery jugs." This may serve as a sample of the assertions, picturesquely indiscriminate, by which a writer wins immediate notoriety at the expense of his permanent reputation. The facts about the Puritan happen to be complex and need to be dealt with very Socratically. It has been affirmed that the point of view of the Puritan was stoical rather than truly Christian, and the affirmation is not wholly false. The present discussion of the relationship between Puritanism and the rise of capitalism with its glorification of the acquisitive life also has its justification. It is likewise a fact that the Puritan was from the outset unduly concerned with reforming others as well as himself, and this trait relates him to the humanitarian meddler or "wowser" of the present day, who is Mr. Mencken's pet aversion. Yet it remains true that awe and reverence and humility are Christian virtues and that there was some survival of these virtues in the Puritan. For a representative Puritan like Jona-

than Edwards they were inseparable from the illumination of grace, from what he terms "a divine and supernatural light." In the passage from the love and fear of God of an Edwards to the love and service of man professed by the humanitarian, something has plainly dropped out, something that is very near the center. What has tended to disappear is the inner life with the special type of control it imposes. With the decline of this inner control there has been an increasing resort to outer control. Instead of the genuine Puritan we then have the humanitarian legalist who passes innumerable laws for the control of people who refuse to control themselves. The activity of our uplifters is scarcely suggestive of any "divine and supernatural light." Here is a discrimination of the first importance that has been obscured by the muddy thinking of our half-baked intelligentsia. One is thus kept from perceiving the real problem, which is to retain the inner life, even though one refuse to accept the theological nightmare with which the Puritan associated it. More is involved in the failure to solve this problem than the Puritan tradition. It is the failure of our contemporary life in general. Yet, unless some solution is reached by a full and free exercise of the critical spirit, one remains a mere modernist and not a thoroughgoing and complete modern; for the modern spirit and the critical spirit are in their essence one.

What happens, when one sets out to deal with questions of this order without sufficient depth of reflection and critical maturity, may be seen in Mr. Sinclair Lewis's *Elmer Gantry*. He has been lured from art into the writing of a wild diatribe which, considered even as such, is largely beside the mark. If the Protestant Church is at present threatened with bankruptcy, it is not because it has produced an occasional Elmer Gantry. The true reproach it has incurred is that, in its drift toward modernism, it has lost its grip not merely on certain dogmas but, simultaneously, on the facts of human nature. It has failed above all to carry over in some modern and critical form the truth of a dogma that unfortunately receives much support from these facts — the dogma of original sin. At first sight Mr. Mencken would appear to have a conviction of evil — when, for example, he reduces democracy in its essential aspect to a "combat between jackals and jackasses" — that establishes at least one bond between him and the austere Christian.

The appearance, however, is deceptive. The Christian is conscious above all of the "old Adam" in himself: hence his humility. The effect of Mr. Mencken's writing, on the other hand, is to produce pride rather than humility, a pride ultimately based on flattery. The reader, especially the young and callow reader, identifies himself imaginatively with Mr. Mencken and conceives of himself as a sort of morose and sardonic divinity surveying from some superior altitude an immeasurable expanse of "boobs." This attitude will not seem especially novel to anyone who has traced the modern movement. One is reminded in particular of Flaubert, who showed a diligence in collecting bourgeois imbecilities comparable to that displayed by Mr. Mencken in his *Americana*. Flaubert's discovery that one does not add to one's happiness in this way would no doubt be dismissed by Mr. Mencken as irrelevant, for he has told us that he does not believe in happiness. Another discovery of Flaubert's may seem to him more worthy of consideration. "By dint of railing at idiots," Flaubert reports, "one runs the risk of becoming idiotic oneself."

It may be that the only way to escape from the unduly complacent cynicism of Mr. Mencken and his school is to reaffirm once more the truths of the inner life. In that case it would seem desirable to disengage, so far as possible, the principle of control on which the inner life finally depends from mere creeds and traditions and assert it as a psychological fact; a fact, moreover, that is neither "cold" nor "clammy." The coldness and clamminess of much so-called realism arises from its failure to give this fact due recognition. A chief task, indeed, of the Socratic critic would be to rescue the noble term "realist" from its present degradation. A view of reality that overlooks the element in man that moves in an opposite direction from mere temperament, the specifically human factor in short, may prove to be singularly one-sided. Is the Puritan, John Milton, when he declares that "he who reigns within himself and rules passions, desires, and fears is more than a king," less real than Mr. Theodore Dreiser when he discourses in his peculiar dialect of "those rearranging chemisms upon which all the morality or immorality of the world is based"?

As a matter of fact, according to the degree and nature of the exercise of the principle of control, one may distinguish two main types of realism which may be denominated respectively religious and humanistic: as the principle of control falls into abeyance, a third type tends to emerge, which may be termed naturalistic realism. That the decline of the traditional controls has been followed by a lapse to the naturalistic level is indubitable. The characteristic evils of the present age arise from unrestraint and violation of the law of measure and not, as our modernists would have us believe, from the tyranny of taboos and traditional inhibitions. The facts cry to heaven. The delicate adjustment that is required between the craving of emancipation and the need of control has been pointed out once for all by Goethe, speaking not as a Puritan but as a clear-eyed man of the world. Everything, he says, that liberates the spirit without a corresponding growth in self-mastery is pernicious. This one sentence would seem to cover the case of our "flaming youth" rather completely.

The movement in the midst of which we are still living was from its inception unsound in its dealing with the principle of control. It is vain to expect from the dregs of this movement what its "first sprightly running failed to give." Mr. Carl Sandburg speaks of the "marvelous rebellion of man at all signs reading 'Keep off.'" An objection to this purely insurrectional attitude is that as a result of its endless iteration during the past century and more, it has come to savor too strongly of what has been called "the humdrum of revolt." A more serious objection to the attitude is that it encourages an unrestricted and merely temperamental liberty which, paradoxically enough at first sight, affords the modern man no avenue of escape from the web that is being woven about him by the scientific determinist.

Realists of the current type are in point of fact intimately allied with the psychologists — glandular, behavioristic, and psychoanalytical — who, whatever their divergences among themselves, unite in their deterministic trend and therefore clash fundamentally with both religious and humanistic realists. The proper method of procedure in defending the freedom of the will would seem to be to insist upon it as a fact of experience, a fact so primary that the position of the determinist involves an evasion of one of the immediate data of consciousness in favor of a metaphysical dream. What is genuinely experimental in naturalistic psychology should of course be received with respect; but the facts of which it takes account in its experiments are unimportant compared with the facts it either neglects or denies. Practically it is running into grotesque extremes of pseudo-science that make of it a shining mark for the Socratic critic.

Here at all events is the issue on which all other issues finally hinge; for until the question of moral freedom — the question whether man is a responsible agent or only the plaything of his impulses and impressions — is decided, nothing is decided; and to decide the question under existing circumstances calls for the keenest critical discrimination. Creation that is not sufficiently supported by such discrimination is likely to prove premature.

One may illustrate from Mr. Dreiser's *American Tragedy*, hailed in certain quarters as the "Mount Everest" of recent fiction. He has succeeded in producing in this work something genuinely harrowing; but one is harrowed to no purpose. One has in more than full measure the tragic qualm but without the final relief and enlargement of spirit that true tragedy succeeds somehow in giving, and that without resort to explicit moralizing. It is hardly worth while to struggle through eight hundred and more very pedestrian pages to be left at the end with a feeling of sheer oppression. The explanation of this oppression is that Mr. Dreiser does not rise sufficiently above the level of "rearranging chemisms," in other words, of animal behavior. Tragedy may admit fate — Greek tragedy admits it — but not of the naturalistic variety. Confusion on this point may compromise in the long run the reputation of writers more eminent than Mr. Dreiser — for example, of Thomas Hardy. Fatalism of the naturalistic type is responsible in large measure for the atmosphere of futility and frustration that hangs heavily over so much contemporary writing. One finally comes to feel with a recent poet that "dust" is the common source from which

stream

The cricket's cry and Dante's dream.

Anyone who admits reality only in what derives from the dust, whether in a cricket or a Dante, must, from the point of view of the religious or the humanistic realist, be prepared to make substantial sacrifices. In the first place, he must sacrifice the depth and subtlety that arise from the recognition in some form of the duality of man's nature. For the interest that may arise from the portrayal of the conflict between a law of the spirit and a law of the mem-

bers, the inordinate interest in sex for its own sake promoted by most of the so-called realists is a rather shabby substitute. A merely naturalistic realism also involves the sacrifice of beauty in almost any sense of that elusive term. Closely related to this sacrifice is the sacrifice of delicacy, elevation, and distinction. The very word realism has come to connote the opposite of these qualities. When we learn, for example, that someone has written a realistic study of a great man, we are sure in advance that he has devoted his main effort to proving that "Plutarch lied." The more the great man is reduced to the level of commonplace or worse, the more we feel he has been "humanized."

Mr. Sherwood Anderson has argued ingeniously that, inasmuch as we ourselves are crude, our literature, if it is not to be unreal and factitious, should be crude likewise. But the writer who hopes to achieve work of importance cannot afford to be too deeply immersed in the atmosphere of the special place and passing moment. Still less can he afford to make us feel, as writers like Mr. Anderson and Mr. Dreiser and Mr. Sinclair Lewis do, that, if there were any lack of vulgarity in what they are depicting, they would be capable of supplying the defect from their own abundance. More is involved here than mere loss of distinction. We have come, indeed, to the supreme sacrifice that every writer must make who does not transcend a naturalistic realism. He must forego the hope of the enduring appeal — the hope that every writer worthy of his salt cherishes in some degree. In the absence of humanistic or religious standards, he is prone to confound the real with the welter of the actual, and so to miss the "grandeur of generality."

Certain books in the current mode are so taken up with the evanescent surfaces of life that they will survive, if at all, not as literature but as sociological documents. The very language in which they are written will, in a generation or two, require a glossary. So far from imposing an orderly pattern on the raw material of experience, they rather emphasize the lack of pattern. The resulting effect, to borrow a phrase from the late Stephen Crane, who has had a marked influence on the recent movement, is that of a "cluttered incoherency." As an extreme example of the tendency one may cite *Manhattan Transfer* by John Dos Passos. In the name of reality, Mr. Dos Passos has perpetrated a literary nightmare. Such a work would seem to have slight value even as a sociological document; unless, indeed, one is prepared to admit that contemporary Manhattan is inhabited chiefly by epileptic Bohemians.

"It is as much a trade," says La Bruyère, "to make a book as it is to make a clock"; in short, literature is largely a matter of technique. The technique of *Manhattan Transfer* is as dubious as its underlying philosophy. Neither can be justified save on the assumption that the aim of art is to exaggerate the clutter and incoherency of the mundane spectacle instead of eliciting its deeper meaning. Technique counts for even more in poetry than in prose. It would be possible to base on technical grounds alone a valid protest against the present preposterous overestimate of Walt Whitman. Fundamental questions need, in these very untraditional days, to be critically elucidated with a view to right definition if the poet is not to lack technique or still worse, if he is not, like certain recent practitioners of free verse, to be hagridden by a false technique. It evidently concerns both the form and substance of poetry, whether one define it with Aristotle as the portrayal of representative human action, or whether one define it with Mr. Carl Sandburg as a "mystic, sensuous mathematics of fire, smokestacks, waffles, pansies, people, and purple sunsets."

There is no doubt much in the America of to-day that suggests a jazzy impressionism. Still our naturalistic deliquescence has probably not gone so far as one might infer from poetry like that of Mr. Sandburg or fiction like that of Mr. Dos Passos. The public response to some of the realistic novels has been considerable: allowance must be made however for the *succès de scandale*, also for the skill attained by the modern publisher in the art of merchandizing. The reputation of certain books one might mention may be regarded as a triumph of "creative" advertising. What has been created is a mirage of masterpieces where no masterpieces are. It is well also to remember in regard to some of the works that have been most discussed that, so far from being an authentic reflection of the American scene, they are rather a belated echo of certain European movements. For it is as certain that in our literary and artistic modes we follow Europe — usually at an interval of from five to forty years — as it is that we lead Europe in our bathtubs and sanitary plumbing. Anyone who resided in Paris in the nineties and later in America, will, as I can testify from personal experience, have the sense of having lived through the same literary fads twice. Mr. Dreiser reminds one of Zola and his school. The technique of Mr. Dos Passos recalls that of the Goncourts. Our experimenters in free verse have followed in the wake not merely of Walt Whitman but of the French symbolists, and so on.

We shall presently begin to hear of certain new developments in French literature and critical thought that point, though indecisively as yet, to a radical departure from what has been the main current since the eighteenth century and in some respects since the Renaissance. It is well that we should become familiar with the writers who reveal in different ways this latest trend — notably with Maritain, Maurras, Lasserre, Seillière, and Benda; for they give evidence of a quality of cerebration that is rare in our own literati. At the same time we should not adopt with our usual docility the total outlook of any of these writers: for no one of them has worked out a point of view exactly adapted to our requirements. In general, it is not fitting that a great nation at the very height of its power should go on indefinitely trailing after Europe. It is time for us to initiate something of our own. This does not mean that we should proceed forthwith to inbreed our own "originality." It means almost the exact opposite. The most original thing one could do nowadays would be to question the whole theory of originality as mere temperamental overflow and self-expression that has prevailed from the "geniuses" of the eighteenth century down to one of our youthful and very minor bards who aspires to "spill his bright illimitable soul."

A genuinely critical survey would make manifest that the unsatisfactoriness of our creative effort is due to a lack of the standards that culture alone can supply. Our cultural crudity and insignificance can be traced in turn to the inadequacy of our education, especially our higher education. Mr. Mencken's attack on the "professors" is therefore largely justified; for if the professors were performing their function properly Mr. Mencken himself would not be possible. One must add in common justice that the professors themselves, or at least some of them, are becoming aware that all is not well with existing conditions. One could not ask anything more perspicacious than the following paragraph from a recent report of Committee G to the American Association of University Professors:

American education has suffered from the domination, conscious or unconscious, direct or indirect, of political and sentimental, as well as educational, theories that are demonstrably false. If the views of some men are to prevail the intellectual life of the country is doomed; everybody except the sheer idiot is to go to college and pursue chiefly sociology, nature study, child study, and community service — and we shall have a society unique only in its mediocrity, ignorance, and vulgarity. It will not do to dismiss lightly even so extreme a view as this; it is too indicative. Such influences are very strong, their pressure is constant; and if education has largely failed in America it has been due primarily to them.

In short, as a result of the encroachments of an equalitarian democracy, the standards of our higher education have suffered in two distinct particulars: first, as regards the quality of students; second, as regards the quality of the studies these students pursue. The first of these evils is generally recognized. There is even some prospect of remedial measures. Certain institutions, Harvard, for example, without being as yet severely selective, are becoming more critical of the incompetent student. On the other hand, there seems to be less hope than ever of any righting of the second and more serious evil — the failure to distinguish qualitatively between studies. The main drift is still towards what one may term the blanket degree. (Dartmouth for example, has just merged its bachelor of arts and bachelor of science.) Yet rather than blur certain distinctions it would have been better, one might suppose, to use up all the letters of the alphabet devising new degrees to meet the real or supposed educational needs of the modern man. To bestow the A.B. degree indiscriminately on a student for whom education has meant primarily a specialization in chemistry and on one for whom it has meant primarily an assimilation of the masterpieces of Greek literature is to empty it of any effective meaning. At the present rate, indeed, the time may come when the A.B. will not throw much more light on the cultural quality of its recipient than it would, if, as has been suggested, it were bestowed on every American child at birth.

It goes without saying that those who have been lowering and confusing educational standards have been profuse in their professions of "service." A critical examination, not merely of American education but of American life at the present time will almost necessarily hinge on this term. The attitude of the Socratic critic

towards it is not to be confounded with that of Mr. Mencken and the "hard-boiled" contingent. "When a gang of real estate agents," says Mr. Mencken, "bond salesmen, and automobile dealers gets together to sob for Service, it takes no Freudian to surmise that someone is about to be swindled." But if one entertain doubts about this current American gospel, why waste one's ammunition on any such small fry? Other and more exalted personages than the members of the Rotary Club at Zenith have, in Mr. Sinclair Lewis's elegant phrase, been "yipping for Service." If one is to deal with this idea of service Socratically, one needs to consider it in its relation to the two figures who have rightly been taken to be the most representative in our cultural background — Benjamin Franklin and Jonathan Edwards. Franklin's idea of service is already humanitarian. Edwards' idea is still traditionally Christian — service not of man but of God. What Franklin stood for is flourishing prodigiously at the present moment, so much so that he may perhaps be defined in his chief line of influence as the great superrotarian. What Edwards stood for is, on the other hand, largely obsolete or survives only in the form of habits, which, lacking doctrinal support, are steadily declining along with the whole Puritan culture.

Intermediary types are possible. One may in one's character reflect the Puritan background and at the same time in one's idea of service derive rather from Franklin. Precisely that combination is found in the most influential of our recent educational leaders — the late President Eliot. A legitimate admiration for his personal qualities should not interfere with the keenest critical scrutiny of his views about education, for the two things stand in no necessary connection. Practically this means to scrutinize the humanitarian idealism that he probably did more than any other man of his generation to promote. In this respect most of the heads of our institutions of learning have been and still are understudies of President Eliot.

In an address on the occasion of his ninetieth birthday President Eliot warned his hearers against introspection, lest it divert them from a whole-hearted devotion to service. Between this attitude and a religious or humanistic attitude there is a clash of first principles. Both humanism and religion require introspection as a prerequisite of the inner life and its appropriate activity. With the disappearance of this activity what is left is the outer activity of the utilitarian, and this leads straight to the one-sided cult of material efficiency and finally to the standardization that is, according to nearly all foreign critics and many of our own, a chief American danger. We cannot return to the introspection of the Puritan. We shudder at the theology an Edwards would impose as the condition of his "divine and supernatural light." Yet it does not follow, as I have already suggested, that we should reject the inner life itself along with this theology. One may recognize innumerable incidental advantages in the gospel of service and yet harbor an uneasy suspicion withal that in the passage from the older religion to the modern humanitarian dispensation something vital has disappeared, something for which neither the outer working of the utilitarian nor again the expansive sympathy of the sentimentalist can offer an equivalent.

The problem of the inner life is very much bound up with two other problems that are now pressing for solution in our higher education and have as yet found none: the problem of the specialist and the problem of leisure. The man of leisure is engaged in an inner and specifically human form of activity, a form that is, according to Aristotle, needful if he is to compass the end of ends — his own happiness. The question is whether one should consent like the specialist to forego this activity and to live partially and as a mere instrument for the attainment of some outer end — even though this end be the progress of humanity. We are beginning to hear a great deal nowadays about the "menace" of leisure. It has been estimated that with the perfecting of mechanical devices the man of the future will be able to satisfy his material wants by working not more than four hours a day. It is vain to anticipate that the rank and file will use this release from outer activity intelligently unless the leaders, notably those in high academic station, show the way. The notion of true leisure is the ultimate source of the standards of any education that deserves to be called liberal. When even a few of our college and university presidents show that they are thinking to some purpose on the nature of leisure it will be time enough to talk of "America's coming of age."

As it is, our institutions of learning seem to be becoming more and more hotbeds of "idealism." Their failure, on the whole, to achieve standards as something quite distinct from ideals, on the one hand, and standardization,

on the other, may prove a fact of sinister import for the future of American civilization. The warfare that is being waged at the present time by Mr. Sinclair Lewis and others against a standardized Philistinism continues in the main the protest that has been made for several generations past by the temperamentalists, hard or soft, against the mechanizing of life by the utilitarian. This protest has been, and is likely to continue to be, ineffectual. The fruitful opposite of the standardized Philistine is not the Bohemian, nor again the hard temperamentalist or superman, as Mr. Mencken conceives him, but the man of leisure. Leisure involves an inner effort with reference to standards that is opposed to the sheer expansion of temperament, as it is to every other form of sheer expansion.

Perhaps a reason why the standards of the humanist are less popular in this country than the ideals of the humanitarian is that these standards set bounds to the acquisitive life; whereas it seems possible to combine a perfect idealism with an orgy of unrestricted commercialism. It is well for us to try to realize how we appear to others in this matter. Our growing unpopularity abroad is due no doubt in part to envy of our material success, but it also arises from the proneness of the rest of the world to judge us, not by the way we feel about ourselves, but by our actual performance. If we are in our own eyes a nation of idealists, we are, according to a recent French critic, M. André Siegfried [1] a "nation of Pharisees." The European, M. Siegfried would have us believe, still has a concern for the higher values of civilization, whereas the American is prepared to sacrifice these values ruthlessly to mass production and material efficiency.

It is easy to detect under this assumption the latest form of a "certain condescension in foreigners." The breakdown of cultural standards is European as well as American. It is not clear that M. Siegfried himself has an adequate notion of the form of effort that can alone serve as a counterpoise to the one-sided activity of the utilitarian. At the same time his anatomy of our favorite ideal of service is not without interest. This ideal opposes no effective barrier to our expansiveness. An unchecked expansiveness on the national scale is always imperialistic. Among the ingredients of a possible Ameri-

[1] See his volume *Les Etats-Unis d'aujourd'hui* (1927), translated under the title *America Comes of Age*. [Author's note.]

can imperialism. M. Siegfried enumerates the American's "great self-satisfaction, his rather brutal sense of his own interests, and *the consciousness, still more dangerous, of his 'duties' towards humanity."* M. Siegfried admits however that our imperialism is likely to be of a new and subtle essence, not concerned primarily with territorial aggrandizement.

A proper discussion of M. Siegfried's position as well as of other issues I have been raising would transcend the limits of an essay. My end has been accomplished if I have justified in some measure the statement with which I started as to the importance of cultivating a general critical intelligence. James Russell Lowell's dictum that before having an American literature we must have an American criticism was never truer than it is today. The obvious reply to those who call for more creation and less criticism is that one needs to be critical above all in examining what now passes for creation.

A scrutiny of this kind would, I have tried to show, extend beyond the bounds of literature to various aspects of our national life and would converge finally on our higher education.

We cannot afford to accept as a substitute for this true criticism the self-expression of Mr. Mencken and his school, unless indeed we are to merit the comment that is, I am told, made on us by South Americans: "They are not a very serious people!" To be sure, the reader may reflect that I am myself a critic, or would-be critic. I can only express the hope that, in my magnifying of the critical function, I do not offer too close a parallel to the dancing-master in Molière who averred, it will be remembered, that "all the mistakes of men, the fatal reverses that fill the world's annals, the shortcomings of statesmen, and the blunders of great captains arise from not knowing how to dance."

Edmund Wilson [1895–   ]

Born in New Jersey, Edmund Wilson attended the Hill School and Princeton, from which he graduated in 1916. For a year he was a reporter on the New York *Evening Sun*. Then he entered the army, serving for a year and a half in a hospital unit in France. Back in America, he joined the staff of *Vanity Fair*, of which he became managing editor. From 1926 to 1931 he was an associate editor of the *New Republic*. Later he became book editor on the *New Yorker*.

His standing as a literary critic was established by a study of the Symbolist movement, *Axel's Castle*, 1931. A large part of his writing, however, he devoted to forwarding his left-wing economic and social opinions. His attitude toward Marxism underwent several marked changes, revealed more or less clearly in *The American Jitters*, 1932; *Travels in Two Democracies* (Soviet Russia and the United States), 1936; "Marxism and Literature," in *The Triple Thinkers*, 1938; *To the Finland Station*, 1940. He tried verse, the novel, short stories, plays. His literary essays have been collected in *The Triple Thinkers*; *The Wound and the Bow*, 1941; and other volumes.

In critical theory he numbers himself among the descendants of the nineteenth-century French critic Taine, who viewed literary works as products of three large factors: the race, the place, and the time. Wilson found fresh means of historical interpretation in the dialectical materialism of Marx and the "case history" method of Freud. Criticism, he believes, is essentially a form of history. Whether a piece of literature is good or bad art can only be settled, in a relative way, by the critic's "emotional reaction." To this extent Wilson is an impressionist, showing, as such, considerable freshness, directness, and sanity.

Further reading: *Axel's Castle*. Stanley Hyman, *The Armed Vision*, 1948.

Symbolism

❦ The historical interpretation of literature has long been the favorite province of scholars in our colleges and universities. Under the nineteenth-century influences of the method of science, the theory of evolution, and the example of German scholarship, literature was studied in the light of literary history or even for the sake of literary history. And literary history was usually conceived of as a branch of historical science, resting upon demonstrable facts. Of course there were many scholars, like Christian Gauss of Princeton, who employed the historical approach flexibly and imaginatively. To Professor Gauss, Edmund Wilson inscribed a letter, printed at the beginning of his *Axel's Castle*: "You will see how these essays have grown out of your lectures of fifteen years ago. . . . It was principally from you that I acquired then my idea of what literary criticism ought to be — a history of man's ideas and imaginings in the setting of the conditions which have shaped them. . . ."

First published as "A Preface to Modern Literature" in the *New Republic* in 1929, this historical-critical essay formed the opening chapter of *Axel's Castle: A Study in the Imaginative Literature of 1870–1930* (1931).

It is my purpose in this book to try to trace the origins of certain tendencies in contemporary literature and to show their development in the work of six contemporary writers. To persons already familiar with the field, my explanations in this first chapter will seem rudimentary; but I believe that it is still true in general, for reasons which I shall suggest, that the sources and fundamental principles of many of the books which have excited most discussion during the period since the War are singularly little understood. It is not usually recognized that writers such as W. B. Yeats, James Joyce, T. S. Eliot, Gertrude Stein, Marcel Proust and Paul Valéry represent the culmination of a self-conscious and very important literary movement; and even when we have become aware that these writers have something in common, that they belong to a common school, we are likely to be rather vague as to what its distinguishing features are.

We do, however, to-day as a rule have a pretty clear idea of the issues which were raised by the Romantic Movement of the beginning of the nineteenth century. We still debate Classicism and Romanticism, and when we attempt to deal with contemporary literary problems, we often tend to discuss them in those terms. Yet the movement of which in our own day we are witnessing the mature development is not merely a degeneration or an elaboration of Romanticism, but rather a counterpart to it, a second flood of the same tide. And even the metaphor of a tide is misleading: what we have to-day is an entirely distinct movement, which has arisen from different conditions and must be dealt with in different terms.

Romanticism, as everyone has heard, was a revolt of the individual. The "Classicism" against which it was a reaction meant, in the domain of politics and morals, a preoccupation with society as a whole; and, in art, an ideal of objectivity. In *Le Misanthrope*, in *Bérénice*, in *The Way of the World*, in *Gulliver's Travels*, the artist is out of the picture: he would consider it artistic bad taste to identify his hero with himself and to glorify himself with his hero, or to intrude between the reader and the story and give vent to his personal emotions. But in *René*, in *Rolla*, in *Childe Harold*, in *The Prelude*, the writer is either his own hero, or unmistakably identified with his hero, and the personality and emotions of the writer are presented as the principal subject of interest. Racine, Molière, Congreve and Swift ask us to be interested in what they have made; but Chateaubriand, Musset, Byron, and Wordsworth ask us to be interested in themselves. And they ask us to be interested in themselves by virtue of the intrinsic value of the individual: they vindicate the rights of the individual against the claims of society as a whole — against government, morals, conventions, academy or church. The Romantic is nearly always a rebel.

In this connection, it is illuminating to consider the explanation of the Romantic Movement given by A. N. Whitehead in his *Science and the Modern World*. The Romantic Movement, Whitehead says, was really a reaction against scientific ideas, or rather against the mechanistic ideas to which certain scientific discoveries gave rise. The seventeenth and eighteenth centuries were in Europe the great period of the development of mathematical and physical theory; and in the literature of the so-called Classical period, Descartes and Newton were influences as important as those of the classics themselves. The poets, like the astronomers and mathematicians, had come to regard the universe as a machine, obeying logical laws and susceptible of reasonable explanation: God figured merely as the clockmaker who must have existed to make the clock. People applied this conception also to society, which, from the point of view of Louis XIV and of the American Constitution alike, had the character of a planetary system or a well-regulated machine; and they examined human nature dispassionately, in the same lucid and reasonable spirit, to find the principles on which it worked. Thus the theorems of the physicist were matched by the geometrical plays of Racine and the balanced couplets of Pope.

But this conception of a fixed mechanical order came eventually to be felt as a constraint: it excluded too much of life — or rather, the description it supplied did not correspond to actual experience. The Romantics had become acutely conscious of aspects of their experience which it was impossible to analyze or explain on the theory of a world run by clock-work. The universe was not a machine, after all, but something more mysterious and less rational.

> The atoms of Democritus,
> And Newton's particles of light
> Are sands upon the Red Sea shore,
> Where Israel's tents do shine so bright!

Blake had already contradicted contemptuously the physical theory of the eighteenth century. And to Wordsworth, the countryside of his boyhood meant neither agriculture nor neoclassic idylls, but a light never seen on land or sea. When the poet looked into his own soul, he beheld something which did not seem to him reducible to a set of principles of human nature such, for example, as La Rochefoucauld's *Maxims:* he saw fantasy, conflict, confusion. And he either set himself, like Wordsworth and Blake, to affirm the superior truth of this vision as compared to the mechanical universe of the physicists; or, accepting this mechanical universe, like Byron or Alfred de Vigny, as external to and indifferent to man, he pitted against it, in defiance, his own turbulent insubordinate soul.

In any case, it is always, as in Wordsworth, the individual sensibility, or, as in Byron, the individual will, with which the Romantic poet is preoccupied; and he has invented a new language for the expression of its mystery, its conflict and confusion. The arena of literature has been transferred from the universe conceived as a machine, from society conceived as an organization, to the individual soul.

What has really taken place, says Whitehead, is a philosophical revolution. The scientists of the seventeenth century who presented the universe as a mechanism had caused people to draw the conclusion that man was something apart from nature, something introduced into the universe from outside and remaining alien to all that he found. But a Romantic poet like Wordsworth has come to feel the falsity of this assumption: he has perceived that the world is an organism, that nature includes planets, mountains, vegetation and people alike, that what we are and what we see, what we hear, what we feel and what we smell, are inextricably related, that all are involved in the same great entity. Those who make fun of the Romantics are mistaken in supposing that there is no intimate connection between the landscape and the poet's emotions. There is no real dualism, says Whitehead, between external lakes and hills, on the one hand, and personal feelings, on the other: human feelings and inanimate objects are interdependent and developing together in some fashion of which our traditional notions of laws of cause and effect, of dualities of mind and matter or of body and soul, can give us no true idea. The Romantic poet, then, with his turbid or opalescent language, his sympathies and passions which cause him to seem to merge with his surroundings, is the prophet of a new insight into nature: he is describing things as they really are; and a revolution in the imagery of poetry is in reality a revolution in metaphysics.

Whitehead drops the story at this point; but he has provided the key to what follows. In the middle of the nineteenth century, science made new advances, and mechanistic ideas were brought back into fashion again. But they came this time from a different quarter — not from physics and mathematics, but from biology. It was the effect of the theory of Evolution to reduce man from the heroic stature to which the Romantics had tried to exalt him, to the semblance of a helpless animal, again very small in the universe and at the mercy of the forces about him. Humanity was the accidental product of heredity and environment, and capable of being explained in terms of these. This doctrine in literature was called Naturalism, and it was put into practice by novelists like Zola, who believed that composing a novel was like performing a laboratory experiment: you had only to supply your characters with a specific environment and heredity and then watch their automatic reactions; and by historians and critics like Taine, who asserted that virtue and vice were as much the products of automatic processes as alkalis and acids, and who attempted to account for masterpieces by studying the geographical and climatic conditions of the countries in which they had been produced.

Not, however, that the movement known as Naturalism arose directly from *The Origin of Species*. There had already set in, about the middle of the century, quite independent of the theory of Evolution, a reaction against the sentimentality and the looseness of Romanticism, and in the direction of the objectivity and the severity of Classicism again; and this reaction had already been characterized by a kind of scientific observation which closely corresponded to that of biological science. This reaction is seen most clearly in France. The Parnassian group of poets, who made their first appearance in the fifties — Gautier, Leconte de Lisle, Hérédia — seemed to have taken it for their aim merely to picture historical incidents and natural phenomena as objectively and accurately as possible in impassive perfect verse. Leconte de Lisle's elephants crossing the desert is a celebrated example: the elephants appear and disappear with a certain classical dignity and grandeur, and the poet leaves it at that.

It is less easy, in English poetry, to give clear examples of the reaction toward Naturalism: the English did not, after the Romantic Movement, take much interest in literary methods till toward the end of the nineteenth century. But the tendency toward what we call realism had set in, none the less: Browning, though he had, of course, nothing of the classical form of the Parnassians, was addicted to historical reconstruction of a kind more pedantic and less flamboyant than that of the true Romantics, and when he dealt with contemporary life, did so at least as realistically as any of the Victorian novelists — themselves going in Zola's direction without quite being aware of the fact. And we can see very plainly in Tennyson, who was much preoccupied with the doctrines of Evolution, something of the same exactitude of description combined with something of the same severity of verse — though with less hardness and more grace — that we find in the French poets.

Nor wilt thou snare him in the white ravine,
Nor find him dropt upon the firths of ice,
That huddling slant in furrow-cloven fells
To roll the torrent out of dusky doors:

But follow; let the torrent dance thee down
To find him in the valley; let the wild
Lean-headed eagles yelp alone.

And it is interesting to compare Tennyson, in this connection, with Pope on the rare occasions (though not so rare as people sometimes suppose) when he is describing natural objects:

The silver eel, in shining volumes roll'd,
The yellow carp, in scales bedropp'd with gold.

These lines have the technical perfection and the precise observation of Tennyson, but they are heavier and more metallic. Pope is often, as a matter of fact, very close to the French Parnassians. The latter represent, in reality, a second classical-scientific movement, the counterpart to that represented by Pope.

But the highest development of Naturalism took place, not in poetry, but in prose. The plays of Ibsen and the novels of Flaubert are the masterpieces of this second period of modern classicism, as Racine and Swift are of the first. The art of Flaubert and Ibsen is again, like the art of the seventeenth-century writers, scrupulously non-personal and objective, and it insists upon precision of language and economy of form. Compare the lucidity, the logic and the limited number of characters of such a tragedy of Ibsen's as *Rosmersholm* with the rigorous conventions of Racine; or compare *Gulliver's Travels* with *Bouvard et Pécuchet* or *L'Education Sentimentale*. Yet, though the earlier works resemble the later ones in many obvious ways, they differ from them in this: where a seventeenth-century moralist like La Rochefoucauld would have sought to discover and set forth the universal principles of human behavior, a nineteenth-century writer like Ibsen or Flaubert has begun to study man in relation to his particular environment and time. The method of approach in both cases, however, may be described as "scientific," and it tends to lead us to mechanistic conclusions.

Now Flaubert and Ibsen both had been suckled on Romanticism. Flaubert had begun by writing a Romantic *Saint-Antoine* before he chastened it and cut it down to the more sober one which he published; and Ibsen had written in verse his Faustian *Brand* and *Peer Gynt* before he arrived at his realistic plays in prose. Each, beginning in Romanticism, had evolved for himself a new discipline and developed a new point of view. For *Madame Bovary* is not merely arranged and written differently from a novel by Victor Hugo: it also constitutes an objective criticism of a case of Romantic personality; and Ibsen was occupied all his life with situations produced by the conflict of the essentially Romantic conception of one's duty to one's own personality with the conception of one's duty to society.

But in the later prose plays of Ibsen, the trolls and ghosts of his early dramatic poems have begun to creep back into the bourgeois drawing-rooms: the Naturalist has been finally compelled to make cracks in his own mold. All that vaporous, confused and grandiose world of Romanticism had been resolutely ordered and compressed; but now the objective point of view of Naturalism, the machine-like technique which went with it, begin to cramp the poet's imagination, to prove inadequate to convey what he feels. The reader begins to chafe at the strain, and the artist begins to betray it. Huysmans described Leconte de Lisle as "the sonorous hardware man"; we remember Wordsworth's strictures on Pope. Literature is rebounding again from the scientific-classical pole to the poetic-romantic one. And this second reaction at the end of the century, this counterpart to the Romantic reaction of the end of the century before, was known in France as Symbolism.

Now in attempting to write literary history, one must guard against giving the impression that these movements and counter-movements necessarily follow one another in a punctual and well-generalled fashion — as if eighteenth-century reason had been cleanly put to rout by nineteenth-century Romanticism, which then proceeded to hold the field till it was laid by the heels by Naturalism, and as if Mallarmé and Rimbaud had then blown up Naturalism with bombs. What really happens, of course, is that one set of methods and ideas is not completely superseded by another; but that, on the contrary, it thrives in its teeth — so that, on the one hand, Flaubert's prose has learned to hear, see and feel with the delicate senses of Romanticism at the same time that Flaubert is disciplining and criticizing the Romantic temperament; and so that, on the other hand, certain members of a school, unaffected by new influences abroad, will continue to practise its methods and to exploit its possibilities further and further, when nearly everybody else has abandoned it.

I have here purposely been selecting writers who seemed to represent some tendency or

school in its purest or most highly developed form. We must, however, now consider some Romantics who, in certain ways, carried Romanticism further than even Chateaubriand or Musset, or than Wordsworth or Byron, and who became the first precursors of Symbolism and were afterwards placed among its saints.

One of these was the French writer who called himself Gérard de Nerval. Gérard de Nerval suffered from spells of insanity; and, partly no doubt as a result of this, habitually confused his own fancies and feelings with external reality. He believed, even in his lucid periods — and no doubt Whitehead would approve his metaphysics — that the world which we see about us is involved in some more intimate fashion than is ordinarily supposed with the things that go on in our minds, that even our dreams and hallucinations are somehow bound up with reality. And in one of his sonnets he outdoes Wordsworth, with his "Presences of Nature in the sky" and his "Souls of lonely places," by imagining shuttered eyes coming to life in the very walls and "a pure spirit under the bark of stones."

But a more important prophet of Symbolism was Edgar Allan Poe. It was in general true that, by the middle of the century, the Romantic writers in the United States — Poe, Hawthorne, Melville, Whitman, and even Emerson — were, for reasons which it would be interesting to determine, developing in the direction of Symbolism; and one of the events of prime importance in the early history of the Symbolist Movement was the discovery of Poe by Baudelaire. When Baudelaire, a late Romantic, first read Poe in 1847, he "experienced a strange commotion." When he began to look up Poe's writings in the files of American magazines, he found among them stories and poems which he said that he himself had already "thought vaguely and confusedly" of writing, and his interest became a veritable passion. In 1852, Baudelaire published a volume of translations of Poe's tales; and from then on the influence of Poe played an important part in French literature. Poe's critical writings provided the first scriptures of the Symbolist Movement, for he had formulated what amounted to a new literary programme which corrected the Romantic looseness and lopped away the Romantic extravagance, at the same time that it aimed, not at Naturalistic, but at ultra-Romantic effects. There was, of course, a good deal in common between Poe's poetry and such Romantic poetry as Coleridge's *Kubla Khan,* as there was between his poems in prose and such Romantic prose as that of De Quincey. But Poe, by insisting on and specially cultivating certain aspects of Romanticism, helped to transform it into something different. "I *know,*" we find Poe writing, for example, "that indefiniteness is an element of the true music [of poetry] — I mean of the true musical expression . . . a suggestive indefiniteness of vague and therefore of spiritual *effect.*" And to approximate the indefiniteness of music was to become one of the principal aims of Symbolism.

This effect of indefiniteness was produced not merely by the confusion I have mentioned between the imaginary world and the real; but also by means of a further confusion between the perceptions of the different senses.

Comme de longs échos qui de loin se confondent . . .
Les parfums, les couleurs et les sons se répondent,

wrote Baudelaire. And we find Poe, in one of his poems, *hearing* the approach of the darkness, or writing such a description as the following of the sensations which follow death: "Night arrived; and with its shadows a heavy discomfort. It oppressed my limbs with the oppression of some dull weight, and was palpable. There was also a moaning sound, not unlike the distant reverberation of surf, but more continuous, which beginning with the first twilight, had grown in strength with the darkness. Suddenly lights were brought into the room . . . and issuing from the flame of each lamp, there flowed unbrokenly into my ears a strain of melodious monotone."

This notation of super-rational sensations was a novelty in the forties of the last century — as was the dream-like irrational musical poetry of *Annabel Lee* and *Ulalume;* and they helped to effect a revolution in France. For an English-speaking reader of to-day Poe's influence may be hard to understand; and even when such a reader comes to examine the productions of French Symbolism it may surprise him that they should have caused amazement. The medley of images; the deliberately mixed metaphors; the combination of passion and wit — of the grand and the prosaic manners; the bold amalgamation of material with spiritual — all these may seem to him quite proper and familiar. He has always known them in the English poetry of the sixteenth and seventeenth centuries — Shake-speare and the other Elizabethans did all these things without theorizing about them. Is this not the natural language of poetry? Is it not the norm against which, in English literature, the eighteenth century was a heresy and to which the Romantics did their best to return?

But we must remember that the development of French poetry has been quite different from that of English. Michelet says that in the sixteenth century the future of French literature had hung in the balance between Rabelais and Ronsard, and he regrets that it was Ronsard who triumphed. For Rabelais in France was a sort of equivalent to our own Elizabethans, whereas Ronsard, who represented to Michelet all that was poorest, dryest and most conventional in the French genius, was one of the fathers of that classical tradition of lucidity, sobriety and purity which culminated in Molière and Racine. In comparison with the Classicism of the French, which has dominated their whole literature since the Renaissance, the English Classicism of the eighteenth century, the age of Dr. Johnson and Pope, was a brief ineffective deviation. And from the point of view of English readers, the most daring innovations of the Romantic revolution in France, in spite of all the excitement which accompanied them, must appear of an astonishingly moderate character. But the age and the rigor of the tradition were the measure of the difficulty of breaking out of it. After all, Coleridge, Shelley, and Keats — in spite of Pope and Doctor Johnson — had only to look back to Milton and Shakespeare, whose dense forests had all along been in view beyond the formal eighteenth-century gardens. But to an eighteenth-century Frenchman like Voltaire, Shakespeare was incomprehensible; and to the Frenchman of the classical tradition of the beginning of the nineteenth century, the rhetoric of Hugo was a scandal: the French were not used to such rich colors or to so free a vocabulary; moreover, the Romantics broke metrical rules far stricter than any we have had in English. Yet Victor Hugo was still very far from the variety and freedom of Shakespeare. It is enlightening to compare Shelley's lyric which begins "O World! O Life! O Time!" with the poem of Alfred de Musset's which begins, "J'ai perdu ma force et ma vie." These two lyrics are in some ways curiously similar: each is the breath of a Romantic sigh over the passing of the pride of youth. Yet the French poet, even in his wistfulness, makes epigrammatic points: his language is always logical and precise; whereas the English poet is vague and gives us images unrelated by logic. And it will not be till the advent of the Symbolists that French poetry will really become capable of the fantasy and fluidity of English.

The Symbolist Movement broke those rules of French metrics which the Romantics had left intact, and it finally succeeded in throwing overboard completely the clarity and logic of the French classical tradition, which the Romantics had still to a great extent respected. It was nourished from many alien sources — German, Flemish, modern Greek — and especially, precisely, from English. Verlaine had lived in England, and knew English well; Mallarmé was a professor of English; and Baudelaire, as I have said, had provided the movement with its first programs by translating the essays of Poe. Two of the Symbolist poets, Stuart Merrill and Francis Vielé-Griffin, were Americans who lived in Paris and wrote French; and an American, reading to-day the latter's *Chevauchée d'Yeldis*, for example, may wonder how, when Symbolism was new, such a poem could ever have been regarded as one of the movement's acknowledged masterpieces: to us, it seems merely agreeable, not in the least revolutionary or novel, but like something which might not impossibly have been written by Thomas Bailey Aldrich if he had been influenced by Browning. We are surprised to learn that Vielé-Griffin is still considered an important poet. But the point was that he had performed a feat which astonished and impressed the French and of which it is probable that no Frenchman was capable: he had succeeded in wrecking once for all the classical Alexandrine, hitherto the basis of French poetry — or rather, as an English reader at once recognizes, he had dispensed with it altogether and begun writing English metres in French. The French called this "vers libre," but it is "free" only in the sense of being irregular, like many poems of Matthew Arnold and Browning.

What made Poe particularly acceptable to the French, however, was what had distinguished him from most of the other Romantics of the English-speaking countries: his interest in æsthetic theory. The French have always reasoned about literature far more than the English have; they always want to know what they are doing and why they are doing it: their literary criticism has acted as a constant interpreter and guide to the rest of their literature.

And it was in France that Poe's literary theory, to which no one seems to have paid much attention elsewhere, was first studied and elucidated. So that, though the effects and devices of Symbolism were of a kind that was familiar in English, and though the Symbolists were sometimes indebted to English literature directly — the Symbolist Movement itself, by reason of its origin in France, had a deliberate self-conscious aesthetic which made it different from anything in English. One must go back to Coleridge to find in English a figure comparable to the Symbolist leader Stéphane Mallarmé. Paul Valéry says of Mallarmé that, as he was the greatest French poet of his time, he could also have been one of the most popular. But Mallarmé was an unpopular poet: he taught English for a living, and wrote little and published less. Yet, ridiculed and denounced by the public, who reiterated that his poetry was nonsense and yet were irritated by his seriousness and obstinacy, he exercised, from his little Paris apartment, where he held Tuesday receptions, an influence curiously far-reaching over the young writers — English and French alike — of the end of the century. There in the sitting-room which was also the dining-room on the fourth floor in the Rue de Rome, where the whistle of locomotives came in through the windows to mingle with the literary conversation, Mallarmé, with his shining pensive gaze from under his long lashes and always smoking a cigarette "to put some smoke," as he used to say, "between the world and himself," would talk about the theory of poetry in a "mild, musical and unforgettable voice." There was an atmosphere "calm and almost religious." Mallarmé had "the pride of the inner life," said one of his friends; his nature was "patient, disdainful and imperiously gentle." He always reflected before he spoke and always put what he said in the form of a question. His wife sat beside him embroidering; his daughter answered the door. Here came Huysmans, Whistler, Degas, Moréas, Laforgue, Vielé-Griffin, Paul Valéry, Henri de Régnier, Pierre Louis, Paul Claudel, Remy de Gourmont, André Gide, Oscar Wilde, Arthur Symons, George Moore and W. B. Yeats. For Mallarmé was a true saint of literature: he had proposed to himself an almost impossible object, and he pursued it without compromise or distraction. His whole life was dedicated to the effort to do something with the language of poetry which had never been done before. "Donner un sens plus pur," he had written in a sonnet on Poe, "aux mots de la tribu." He was, as Albert Thibaudet has said, engaged in "a disinterested experiment on the confines of poetry, at a limit where other lungs would find the air unbreathable."

What, then, was this purer sense which Mallarmé believed he was following Poe in wishing to give to the words of the tribe? What, precisely, was the nature of this experiment on the confines of poetry which Mallarmé found so absorbing and which so many other writers tried to repeat? What, precisely, did the Symbolists propose? I have called attention, in speaking of Poe, to the confusion between the perceptions of the different senses, and to the attempt to make the effects of poetry approximate to those of music. And I should add, in this latter connection, that the influence on Symbolist poetry of Wagner was as important as that of any poet: at the time when Romantic music had come closest to literature, literature was attracted toward music. I have also spoken, in connection with Gérard de Nerval, of the confusion between the imaginary and the real, between our sensations and fancies, on the one hand, and what we actually do and see, on the other. It was the tendency of Symbolism — that second swing of the pendulum away from a mechanistic view of nature and from a social conception of man — to make poetry even more a matter of the sensations and emotions of the individual than had been the case with Romanticism: Symbolism, indeed, sometimes had the result of making poetry so much a private concern of the poet's that it turned out to be incommunicable to the reader. The peculiar subtlety and difficulty of Symbolism is indicated by the name itself. This name has often been complained of as being inadequate for the movement to which it was given and inappropriate to certain of its aspects; and it may prove misleading to English readers. For the symbols of Symbolism have to be defined a little differently from symbols in the ordinary sense — the sense in which the Cross is the symbol of Christianity or the Stars and Stripes the symbol of the United States. This symbolism differs even from such symbolism as Dante's. For the familiar kind of symbolism is conventional and fixed; the symbolism of the *Divine Comedy* is conventional, logical and definite. But the symbols of the Symbolist school are usually chosen arbitrarily by the poet to stand for special ideas

of his own — they are a sort of disguise for these ideas. "The Parnassians, for their part," wrote Mallarmé, "take the thing just as it is and put it before us — and consequently they are deficient in mystery: they deprive the mind of the delicious joy of believing that it is creating. To name an object is to do away with the three-quarters of the enjoyment of the poem which is derived from the satisfaction of guessing little by little: to suggest it, to evoke it — that is what charms the imagination."

To intimate things rather than state them plainly was thus one of the primary aims of the Symbolists. But there was more involved in their point of view than Mallarmé here explains. The assumptions which underlay Symbolism lead us to formulate some such doctrine as the following: Every feeling or sensation we have, every moment of consciousness, is different from every other; and it is, in consequence, impossible to render our sensations as we actually experience them through the conventional and universal language of ordinary literature. Each poet has his unique personality; each of his moments has its special tone, its special combination of elements. And it is the poet's task to find, to invent, the special language which will alone be capable of expressing his personality and feelings. Such a language must make use of symbols: what is so special, so fleeting and so vague cannot be conveyed by direct statement or description, but only by a succession of words, of images, which will serve to suggest it to the reader. The Symbolists themselves, full of the idea of producing with poetry effects like those of music, tended to think of these images as possessing an abstract value like musical notes and chords. But the words of our speech are not musical notation, and what the symbols of Symbolism really were, were metaphors detached from their subjects — for one cannot, beyond a certain point, in poetry, merely enjoy color and sound for their own sake: one has to guess what the images are being applied to. And Symbolism may be defined as an attempt by carefully studied means — a complicated association of ideas represented by a medley of metaphors — to communicate unique personal feelings.

The Symbolist Movement proper was first largely confined to France and principally limited to poetry of rather an esoteric kind; but it was destined, as time went on, to spread to the whole western world and its principles

to be applied on a scale which the most enthusiastic of its founders could scarcely have
foreseen. Remy de Gourmont, who was eventually to become the most distinguished critical
champion of the movement, tells of his excitement, one afternoon in the eighties, at discovering the new poetry in a little magazine which
he had picked up at a book-stall in the Odéon:
"As I looked through it, I experienced the little
æsthetic thrill and that exquisite impression of
novelty which has so much charm for youth. I
seemed to myself to have been dreaming rather
than reading. The Luxembourg was pink with
early April: I crossed it toward the Rue d'Assas,
thinking a great deal more about the new literature which was coinciding for me that day
with the renewal of the world than about the
business which had brought me to that part of
Paris. All that I had written up to that time
inspired me with profound disgust. . . . In less
than an hour my literary orientation was radically modified." And Yeats wrote in 1897:
"The reaction against the rationalism of the
eighteenth century has mingled with a reaction
against the materialism of the nineteenth century, and the symbolical movement, which has
come to perfection in Germany in Wagner, in
England in the Pre-Raphaelites, and in France
in Villiers de L'Isle-Adam and Mallarmé and
Maeterlinck, and has stirred the imagination of
Ibsen and D'Annunzio, is certainly the only
movement that is saying new things."

We do not talk about Symbolism to-day in
dealing with English literature; we do not even,
as Yeats did at the end of the last century, think
of writers whom he mentions as all belonging to
a "symbolical movement"; yet the influence of
Mallarmé and his fellow poets was felt widely
and deeply outside of France, and it is difficult
to understand certain of the things which have
been happening lately in English literature
without some knowledge of the Symbolist
school. I believe, in fact, that if English and
American criticism have sometimes shown themselves at a loss when confronted with the work
of certain recent writers, it is partly because the
work of these writers is the result of a literary
revolution which occurred outside English literature. The case of the Romantic Movement
was different: Wordsworth's prefaces were English manifestoes; Lockhart's attack on Keats
and Byron's attack on Jeffrey were blows struck
in an English civil war. But in spite of the Pre-
Raphaelites, who were launched by an impulse

somewhat similar to that of the Symbolists, and
in spite of the English "æsthetics" and "de-
cadents," who for the most part imitated the
French without very much originality, the battle
of Symbolism has never properly been fought
out in English. So that whereas French writers
like Valéry and Proust who have grown out of
the Symbolist Movement are well understood
and appreciated by French literary criticism, the
critics of the English-speaking countries have
often seemed not to know how to deal with
writers such as Eliot and Joyce. Even when
these writers have brought back into English
qualities which are natural to it and resources
which it originally possessed, these elements have
returned by way of France and have taken on
the complexion of the French mind — critical,
philosophical, much occupied with æsthetic
theory and tending always to aim self-consciously
at particular effects and to study scrupulously
appropriate means.

It has perhaps been peculiarly easy for certain
of the leaders of contemporary English literature — that is, of the literature since the War
— to profit by the example of Paris, because
they have themselves not been English. Of the
writers in English I shall discuss in this book,
Yeats is an Irishman who turns almost as easily
toward Paris as toward London; Joyce an Irishman who has done most of his work on the
Continent and who has scarcely lived in England at all; and T. S. Eliot and Gertrude Stein
are Americans living abroad. The work of these
writers has been largely a continuance or extension of Symbolism. Yeats, the ablest of the
fin de siècle group who tried in London to
emulate the French, managed to make Symbolism flourish triumphantly by transplanting it
to the more favorable soil of Ireland. T. S.
Eliot in his earliest poems seems to have been
as susceptible to the influence of the Symbolists
as to that of the English Elizabethans. Joyce,
a master of Naturalism as great as Flaubert, has
at the same time succeeded in dramatizing
Symbolism by making use of its methods for
differentiating between his various characters
and their varying states of mind. And Gertrude
Stein has carried Mallarmé's principles so far in
the direction of that limit where other lungs
find the air unbreathable as perhaps finally to
reduce them to absurdity. It is true, however,
that under proper conditions, these principles
remain valid; and both the strength and the
weaknesses characteristic of much of the litera-

ture since the War derive naturally from the Symbolist poets and may already be studied in their work. The literary history of our time is to a great extent that of the development of Symbolism and of its fusion or conflict with Naturalism.

Cleanth Brooks [1906–   ]

Among contemporary critics, Cleanth Brooks has been the most consistent follower of the principles of T. S. Eliot in his rejection of "biographical irrelevancies," "historical explanation," and "sociological theory" as approaches to literary criticism. As such, he has become one of the central figures in the vigorous debate over the values of the so-called "New Criticism." For him the text is everything. The critic's function is to inspect it closely for subtle felicities of irony, "wit," paradox, ambiguity, and the clash of metaphors. In an early essay, "The Language of Paradox," he described poetry as "words perpetually juxtaposed in new and sudden combination," and stated that the task and challenge of the poet is to gain precision and new meaning from the paradoxical nature of language. By close textual scrutiny of a complex poem, the critic may discover levels of meaning beneath the conscious surface-intention of the poet. Like Eliot, he has traced the line of descent in modern poetry to the school of Donne and the Metaphysicals of the seventeenth century, preferring their intellectual conceits and their sense of irony to the rhythmic affirmations of romantic verse. Brooks's influence has been especially marked upon the methods of teaching literature at advanced levels. His texts, *Understanding Poetry* (1938) and *Understanding Fiction* (1943), co-edited with Robert Penn Warren, have supplied a vocabulary and a technique which have had a widespread effect on the classroom analysis of difficult verse and prose.

Brooks's career has been wholly within the academic world. He graduated from Vanderbilt University in 1928, went to Oxford as a Rhodes Scholar, and took his B. Litt. degree there in 1932. While teaching literature at Louisiana State University in the 1930's he began publishing in the *Southern Review*, of which he was an editor. Since 1947 he has been a Professor of English at Yale University.

His essays, published in *Poetry*, the *Kenyon Review*, the *New Republic*, the *American Scholar*, and other periodicals, have been collected in two volumes, *Modern Poetry and the Tradition* (1939) and *The Well-Wrought Urn* (1947). Also in 1947 he collaborated with Robert Heilman on a third textbook, *Understanding Drama*.

Further reading: "The New Criticism: A Brief for the Defense," *American Scholar*, Summer, 1944. *Modern Poetry and the Tradition*, 1939.

The Waste Land: An Analysis

To venture to write anything further on *The Waste Land*, particularly after the work of F. R. Leavis and F. O. Matthiessen, may call for some explanation and even apology. I am obviously indebted to both critics. The justification for such a commentary as this must be made primarily in terms of a difference of intention. Leavis is interested predominantly in Eliot's method of organization. One or two passages in the poem are treated in detail and are highly valuable for a knowledge of the "meaning" of the poem, but the bulk of the poem does not receive this kind of examination. Moreover, I believe, Leavis makes some positive errors. Matthiessen examines more of the poem in detail, and, as far as it goes, his account is excellent. But the plan of his *Achievement of T. S. Eliot* does not allow for a consecutive examination either. He puts his finger on the basic theme, death-in-life, but I do not think that he has given it all the salience which it deserves.

I prefer not to raise here the question of how important it is for the reader of the poem to have an explicit intellectual account of the various symbols, and a logical account of their relationships. It may well be that such rationalization is no more than a scaffolding to be got out of the way before we contemplate the poem itself as a poem. But many readers (including myself) find the erection of such a scaffolding valuable — if not absolutely necessary — and if some readers will be tempted to lay more stress on the scaffolding than they properly should, there are perhaps still more readers who will be prevented from getting at the poem at all without the help of such a scaffolding. Furthermore, an interest attaches to Mr. Eliot's own mental processes, and whereas Mr. Matthiessen has quite properly warned us that Eliot's poetry cannot be read as autobiography, many of the symbols and ideas which occur in *The Waste Land* are ideas which are definitely central to Eliot's general intellectual position.

The basic symbol used, that of the waste land, is taken, of course, from Miss Jessie Weston's *From Ritual to Romance*. In the legends which she treats there, the land has been blighted by a curse. The crops do not grow, and the animals cannot reproduce. The plight of the land is summed up by, and connected with, the plight of the lord of the land, the Fisher King, who has been rendered impotent by maiming or sickness. The curse can only be removed by the appearance of a knight who will ask the meanings of the various symbols which are displayed to him in the castle. The shift in meaning from physical to spiritual sterility is easily made, and was, as a matter of fact, made in certain of the legends. A knowledge of this symbolism is, as Eliot has already pointed out, essential for an understanding of the poem.

Of hardly less importance to the reader, however, is a knowledge of Eliot's basic method. *The Waste Land* is built on a major contrast — a device which is a favourite of Eliot's and to be found in many of his poems, particularly his later poems. The contrast is between two kinds of life and two kinds of death. Life devoid of meaning is death; sacrifice, even the sacrificial death, may be life-giving, an awakening to life. The poem occupies itself to a great extent with this paradox, and with a number of variations on it.

Eliot has stated the matter quite explicitly himself in one of his essays. In his "Baudelaire" he says:

One aphorism which has been especially noticed is the following: *la volupté unique et suprême de l'amour gît dans la certitude de faire le mal.* This means, I think, that Baudelaire has perceived that what distinguishes the relations of man and woman from the copulation of beasts is the knowledge of Good and Evil (of *moral* Good and Evil which are not natural Good and Bad or puritan Right and Wrong). Having an imperfect, vague romantic conception of Good, he was at least able to understand that the sexual act as evil is more dignified, less boring than as the natural, 'life-giving,' cheery automatism of the modern world. . . . So far as we are human, what we do must be either evil or good; so far as we do evil or good, we are human; and it is better, in a paradoxical way, to do evil than to do nothing: at least, *we exist* [italics mine].

The last statement is highly important for an understanding of *The Waste Land*. The fact that men have lost the knowledge of good and evil keeps them from being alive, and is the justification for viewing the modern waste land as a realm in which people do not even exist.

This theme is stated in the quotation which prefaces the poem. The Sybil says: "I wish to die." Her statement has several possible interpretations. For one thing, she is saying what the people who inhabit the waste land are saying. But she also may be saying what the speaker says in *The Journey of the Magi*, . . . "this Birth was/Hard and bitter agony for us, like Death, our death/. . . . I should be glad of another death."

I

The first section of "The Burial of the Dead" develops the theme of the attractiveness of death, or of the difficulty in rousing oneself from the death-in-life in which the people of the waste land live. Men are afraid to live in reality. April, the month of rebirth, is not the most joyful season but the cruellest. Winter at least kept us warm in forgetful snow. The idea is one which Eliot has stressed elsewhere. Earlier in *Gerontion* he had written

In the juvescence of the year
Came Christ the tiger

. . . .

The tiger springs in the new year. Us he devours.   5

More lately, in *Murder in the Cathedral*, he has the chorus say

We do not wish anything to happen.
Seven years we have lived quietly,   10
Succeeded in avoiding notice,
Living and partly living.

And in another passage: "Now I fear disturbance of the quiet seasons." Men dislike to be aroused   15
from their death-in-life.

The first part of "The Burial of the Dead" introduces this theme through a sort of reverie on the part of the protagonist — a reverie in which speculation on life glides off into memory of an   20
actual conversation in the Hofgarten and back into speculation again. The function of the conversation is to establish to some extent the class and character of the protagonist. The reverie is resumed with line 19.   25

What are the roots that clutch, what branches grow
Out of this stony rubbish?

The protagonist answers for himself: 30

Son of man,
You cannot say, or guess, for you know only
A heap of broken images, where the sun beats,
And the dead tree gives no shelter, the cricket no
      relief,   35
And the dry stone no sound of water.

In this passage there are references to Ezekiel and to Ecclesiastes, and these references indicate what it is that men no longer know: the passage referred to in Ezekiel ii pictures a   40
world thoroughly secularized:

1. And he said unto me, Son of man, stand upon thy feet, and I will speak unto thee. 2. And the spirit entered into me when he spake unto me, and set me   45
upon my feet, that I heard him that spake unto me. 3. And he said unto me, Son of man, I send thee to the children of Israel, to a rebellious nation that hath rebelled against me: they and their fathers have transgressed against me, even unto this very day.   50

The following passage, from Eccleciastes xii, is not only referred to in this passage; a reference to it also is evidently made in the nightmare vision of Section V of the poem:

1. Remember now thy Creator in the days of thy youth, while the evil days come not, nor the years draw nigh, when thou shalt say, I have no pleasure in them; 2. While the sun, or the light, or the moon, or the stars, be not darkened, nor the clouds return after the rain: 3. In the day when the keepers of the house shall tremble, and the strong men shall bow themselves, and the grinders cease because they are few, and those that look out of the windows be darkened, 4. And the doors shall be shut in the streets, when the sound of the grinding is low, and he shall rise up at the voice of the bird, and all the daughters of musick shall be brought low; 5. Also when they shall be afraid of that which is high, and fears shall be in the way, and the almond tree shall flourish, and the grasshopper shall be a burden, *and desire shall fail* [italics mine]: because man goeth to his long home, and the mourners go about the streets: 6. Or ever the silver cord be loosed, or the golden bowl be broken, or the pitcher be broken at the fountain, or the wheel broken at the cistern. 7. Then shall the dust return to the earth as it was: and the spirit shall return unto God who gave it. 8. Vanity of vanities, saith the preacher; all is vanity.

The next section which begins with the scrap of song quoted from Wagner (perhaps another item in the reverie of the protagonist), states the opposite half of the paradox which underlies the poem: namely, that life at its highest moments of meaning and intensity resembles death. The song from Act I of Wagner's *Tristan and Isolde*, "Frisch weht der Wind," is sung in the opera by a young sailor aboard the ship which is bringing Isolde to Cornwall. The *"Irisch Kind"* of the song does not properly apply to Isolde at all. The song is merely one of happy and naïve love. It brings to the mind of the protagonist an experience of love — the vision of the hyacinth girl as she came back from the hyacinth garden. The poet says

. . . my eyes failed, I was neither
Living nor dead, and I knew nothing,
Looking into the heart of light, the silence.

The line which immediately follows this passage, "Oed' und leer das Meer," seems at first to be simply an extension of the last figure: that is, "Empty and wide the sea (of silence)." The line, however, as a matter of fact, makes an ironic contrast; for the line as it occurs in Act III of the opera, is the reply of the watcher who reports to the wounded Tristan that Isolde's ship is nowhere in sight; the sea is empty. And, though the *"Irisch Kind"* of the first quotation is not Isolde, the reader familiar with the opera will apply it to Isolde when he comes to the line "Oed' und leer das Meer." For the question in the song is in essence Tristan's question in Act III: My Irish child, where dwellest thou? The two quotations from the opera which frame the ecstasy-of-love passage thus take on a new meaning in the altered context. In the first, love is happy: the boat rushes on with a fair wind behind it. In the second, love is absent; the sea is wide and empty. And the last quotation reminds us that even love cannot exist in the waste land.

The next passage, that in which Madame Sosostris figures, calls for further reference to Miss Weston's book. As Miss Weston has shown, the Tarot cards were originally used to determine the event of the highest importance to the people, the rising of the waters. Madame Sosostris has fallen a long way from the high function of her predecessors. She is engaged merely in vulgar fortune-telling — is merely one item in a generally vulgar civilization. But the symbols of the Tarot pack are still unchanged. The various characters are still inscribed on the cards, and she is reading in reality, though she does not know it, the fortune of the protagonist. She finds that his card is that of the drowned Phoenician Sailor, and so she warns him against death by water, not realizing any more than do the other inhabitants of the modern waste land that the way into life may be by death itself. The drowned Phoenician Sailor is a type of the fertility god whose image was thrown into the sea annually as a symbol of the death of summer. As for the other figures in the pack: Belladonna, the Lady of the Rocks, is woman in the waste land. The man with three staves Eliot says he associates rather arbitrarily with the Fisher King. The term 'arbitrarily' indicates that we are not to attempt to find a logical connection here.

The Hanged Man, who represents the hanged god of Frazer (including the Christ), Eliot states in a note, is associated with the hooded figure who appears in "What the Thunder Said." That he is hooded accounts for Madame Sosostris' inability to see him; or rather, here again the palaver of the modern fortune-teller is turned to new and important accounts by the poet's shifting the matter into a new and serious context. The Wheel and the one-eyed merchant will be discussed later.

After the Madame Sosostris passage, Eliot proceeds to complicate his symbols for the sterility and unreality of the modern waste land by associating it with Baudelaire's *fourmillante cité* and with Dante's Limbo. The passages already quoted from Eliot's essay on Baudelaire will indicate one of the reasons why Baudelaire's lines are evoked here. In Baudelaire's city, dream and reality seem to mix, and it is interesting that Eliot in *The Hollow Men* refers to this same realm of death-in-life as "death's dream kingdom" in contradistinction to "death's other kingdom."

The references to Dante are most important. The line, "I had not thought death had undone so many," is taken from the Third Canto of the *Inferno*; the line, "Sighs, short and infrequent, were exhaled," from the Fourth Canto. Mr. Matthiessen has already pointed out that the Third Canto deals with Dante's Limbo which is occupied by those who on earth had "lived without praise or blame." They share this abode with the angels, "Who were not rebels, nor were faithful to God, but were for themselves." They exemplify almost perfectly the secular attitude which dominates the modern world. Their grief, according to Dante, arises from the fact that they "have no hope of death; and their blind life is so debased, that they are envious of every other lot." But though they may not hope for death, Dante calls them "these wretches who never were alive." The people who are treated in the Fourth Canto are those who lived virtuously but who died before the proclamation of the Gospel — they are the unbaptized. This completes the categories of people who inhabit the modern waste land: those who are secularized and those who have no knowledge of the faith. Without a faith their life is in reality a death. To repeat the sentence from Eliot previously quoted: "So far as we do evil or good, we are human; and it is better, in a paradoxical way, to do evil than to do nothing: at least, we exist."

The Dante and Baudelaire references, then, come to the same thing as the allusion to the waste land of the medieval legends; and these various allusions drawn from widely differing sources enrich the comment on the modern city so that it becomes "unreal" on a number of levels: as seen through "the brown fog of a winter dawn"; as the medieval waste land and Dante's Limbo and Baudelaire's Paris are unreal.

The reference to Stetson stresses again the connection between the modern London of the poem and Dante's hell. After the statement, "I could never have believed death had undone so many," follow the words "After I had distinguished some among them, I saw and knew the shade of him who made, through cowardice, the great refusal." The protagonist, like Dante, sees among the inhabitants of the contemporary waste land one whom he recognizes. (The name "Stetson" I take to have no ulterior significance. It is merely an ordinary name such as might be borne by the friend one might see in a crowd in a great city.) Mylae, as Mr. Matthiessen has pointed out to us, is the name of a battle between the Romans and the Carthaginians in the Punic War. The Punic War was a trade war — might be considered a rather close parallel to the war of 1914–18. At any rate, it is plain that Eliot in having the protagonist address the friend in a London street as one who was with him in the Punic War rather than as one who was with him in the World War is making the point that all the wars are one war; all experience, one experience. As Eliot put the idea in *Murder in the Cathedral*:

> We do not know very much of the future
> Except that from generation to generation
> The same things happen again and again.

I am not sure that Leavis and Matthiessen are correct in inferring that the line, "That corpse you planted last year in your garden," refers to the attempt to bury a memory. But whether or not this is true, the line certainly refers also to the buried god of the old fertility rites. It also is to be linked with the earlier passage — "What are the roots that clutch, what branches grow," etc. This allusion to the buried god will account for the ironical, almost taunting tone of the passage. The burial of the dead is now a sterile planting — without hope. But the advice to "keep the Dog far hence," in spite of the tone, is, I believe, well taken and serious. The passage in Webster goes as follows:

> O keep the wolf far hence, that's foe to men,
> Or with his nails he'll dig it up again.

Why does Eliot turn the wolf into a dog? And why does he reverse the point of importance from the animal's normal hostility to men to its friendliness? If, as some critics have suggested, he is merely interested in making a reference to Webster's darkest play, why alter the line? I am inclined to take the Dog (the capital letter is Eliot's) as Humanitarianism and the related

philosophies which in their concern for man extirpate the supernatural — dig up the corpse of the buried god and thus prevent the rebirth of life. For the general idea, see Eliot's essay, "The Humanism of Irving Babbitt."

The last line of "The Burial of the Dead" — "You! hypocrite lecteur! — mon semblable, — mon frère!" — the quotation from Baudelaire, completes the universalization of Stetson begun by the reference to Mylae. Stetson is every man, including the reader and Mr. Eliot himself.

II

If "The Burial of the Dead" gives the general abstract statement on the situation, the second part of *The Waste Land*, "A Game of Chess," gives a more concrete illustration. The easiest contrast in this section — and one which may easily blind the casual reader to a continued emphasis on the contrast between the two kinds of life, or the two kinds of death, already commented on — is the contrast between life in a rich and magnificent setting, and life in the low and vulgar setting of a London pub. But both scenes, however antithetical they may appear superficially, are scenes taken from the contemporary waste land. In both of them life has lost its meaning.

I am particularly indebted to Mr. Allen Tate's brilliant comment on the first part of this section. To quote from him, "the woman . . . is, I believe, the symbol of man at the present time. He is surrounded by the grandeurs of the past, but he does not participate in them; they don't sustain him." And to quote from another section of his commentary: "The rich experience of the great tradition depicted in the room receives a violent shock in contrast with a game that symbolizes the inhuman abstraction of the modern mind." Life has no meaning; history has no meaning; there is no answer to the question: "What shall we ever do?" The only thing that has meaning is the abstract game which they are to play, a game in which the meaning is assigned and arbitrary, meaning by convention only — in short, a game of chess.

This interpretation will account in part for the pointed reference to Cleopatra in the first lines of the section. But there is, I believe, a further reason for the poet's having compared the lady to Cleopatra. The queen in Shakespeare's drama — "Age cannot wither her, nor custom stale/Her infinite variety" — is perhaps the extreme exponent of love for love's sake — the feminine member of the pair of lovers who threw away an empire for love. But the infinite variety of the life of the woman in "A Game of Chess" *has* been staled. There is indeed no variety at all, and love simply does not exist. The function of the sudden change in the description of the carvings and paintings in the room from the heroic and magnificent to the characterization of the rest of them as "other withered stumps of time" is obvious. But the reference to Philomela is particularly important, for Philomela, it seems to me, is one of the major symbols of the poem.

Miss Weston points out that a section of one of the Grail manuscripts, which is apparently intended as a gloss of the Grail story, tells how the court of the rich Fisher King was withdrawn from the knowledge of men when certain of the maidens who frequented the shrine were raped and had their golden cups taken from them. The curse on the land follows from this act. Miss Weston conjectures that this may be a statement, in the form of parable, of the violation of the older mysteries which were probably once celebrated openly, but were later forced underground into secrecy. Whether or not Mr. Eliot intends a reference to this passage, the violation of a woman makes a very good symbol of the process of secularization. John Crowe Ransom makes the point very neatly for us in his *God Without Thunder*. Love is the aesthetic of sex; lust is the science. Love implies a deferring of the satisfaction of the desire; it implies even a certain asceticism and a ritual. Lust drives forward urgently and scientifically to the immediate extirpation of the desire. Our contemporary waste land is in a large part the result of our scientific attitude — of our complete secularization. Needless to say, lust defeats its own ends. The portrayal of "The change of Philomel, by the barbarous kind" is a fitting commentary on the scene which it ornaments. The waste land of the legend came in this way — the modern waste land has come in this way.

That this view is not mere fine-spun ingenuity is borne out somewhat by the change of tense which Eliot employs here and which Mr. Edmund Wilson has commented upon: "And still she cried, and still the world pursues." Apparently the "world" partakes in the barbarous king's action, and still partakes in that action.

To "dirty ears" the nightingale's song is not that which filled all the desert with inviolable voice — it is "jug, jug." Edmund Wilson has pointed out that the rendition of the bird's song here represents not merely the Elizabethan neutral notation of the bird's song, but carries associations of the ugly and coarse. The passage is therefore one of many instances of Eliot's device of using something which in one context is innocent but in another context becomes loaded with a special meaning.

The Philomela passage has another importance, however. If it is a commentary on how the waste land became waste, it also repeats the theme of the death which is the door to life — the theme of the dying god. The raped woman becomes transformed through suffering into the nightingale; through the violation comes the "inviolable voice." The thesis that suffering is action, and that out of suffering comes poetry is a favourite one of Eliot's. For example, "Shakespeare, too, was occupied with the struggle — which alone constitutes life for a poet — to transmute his personal and private agonies into something rich and strange, something universal and impersonal." Consider also his statement with reference to Baudelaire: "Indeed, in his way of suffering is already a kind of presence of the supernatural and of the superhuman. He rejects always the purely natural and the purely human; in other words, he is neither 'naturalist' nor 'humanist.'" The theme of the life which is death is stated specifically in the conversation between the man and the woman. She asks the question "Are you alive, or not?" and this time we are sufficiently prepared by the Dante references in "The Burial of the Dead" for the statement here to bear a special meaning. (She also asks "Is there nothing in your head?" He is one of the Hollow Men — "headpiece stuffed with straw.") These people, as people in the waste land, know nothing, see nothing, do not even live.

But the protagonist, after this reflection that in the waste land of modern life even death is sterile — "I think we are in rats' alley/Where the dead men lost their bones" — remembers a death which was not sterile, remembers a death that was transformed into something rich and strange, the death described in the song from *The Tempest* — "Those are pearls that were his eyes."

The reference to this section of *The Tempest* is, like the Philomela reference, one of Eliot's major symbols. We are to meet it twice more, in later sections of the poem. Some more general comment on it is therefore appropriate here. The song, one remembers, was sung by Ariel in luring Ferdinand, Prince of Naples, on to meet Miranda, and thus to find love, and through this love, to effect the regeneration and deliverance of all the people on the island. Ferdinand says of the song.

> The ditty doth remember my drowned father
> This is no mortal business, nor no sound
> That the earth owes. . . .

The allusion is an extremely interesting example of the device of Eliot's already commented upon, that of taking an item from one context and shifting it into another in which it assumes a new and powerful meaning. This description of a death which is a portal into a realm of the rich and strange — a death which becomes a sort of birth — assumes in the mind of the protagonist an association with that of the drowned god whose effigy was thrown into the water as a symbol of the death of the fruitful powers of nature but which was taken out of the water as a symbol of the revivified god. (See *From Ritual to Romance*.) The passage therefore represents the perfect antithesis to the passage in "The Burial of the Dead": "That corpse you planted last year in your garden," etc. It also, as we have already pointed out, finds its antithesis in the sterile and unfruitful death "in rats' alley" just commented upon. (We shall find that this contrast between the death in rats' alley and the death in *The Tempest* is made again in "The Fire Sermon.")

We have yet to treat the relation of the title of the section, "A Game of Chess," to Middleton's play, *Women beware Women*, from which the game of chess is taken. In the play, the game is used as a device to keep the widow occupied while her daughter-in-law is being seduced. The seduction amounts almost to a rape, and in a *double entendre* the rape is actually described in terms of the game. We have one more connection with the Philomela symbol therefore. The abstract game is being used in the contemporary waste land, as in the play, to cover up a rape and is a description of the rape itself.

In the second part of "A Game of Chess" we are given a picture of spiritual emptiness, but this time, at the other end of the social scale, as reflected in the talk between two cockney women in a London pub. The account here is straightforward enough and the only matter which calls for comment is the line spoken by Ophelia in *Hamlet* which ends the passage. Ophelia, too, was very much concerned about love, the theme of conversation of the two ladies. As a matter of fact, she was in very much the same position as that of the woman who has been the topic of conversation between the two good ladies we have just heard. She had remarked too once that

> Young men will do't, if they come to't!
> By cock, they are to blame.

And her poetry (including the line quoted from her here), like Philomela's had come out of suffering. I think that we are probably to look for the relevance of the allusion to her in some such matter as this rather than in an easy satiric contrast between Elizabethan glories and modern sordidness. After all (in spite of the Marxists) Eliot's objection to the present world is not merely the sentimental one that this happens to be the twentieth century after Christ and not the seventeenth.

III

"The Fire Sermon" makes much use of several of the symbols already developed. The fire is the sterile burning of lust, and the section is a sermon, although a sermon by example only. This section of the poem also contains some of the most easily apprehended uses of literary allusion. The poem opens on a vision of the modern river. In Spenser's *Prothalamion* the scene described is also a river scene at London, and it is dominated by nymphs and their paramours, and the nymphs are preparing for a bridal. The contrast between Spenser's scene and its twentieth-century equivalent is jarring. The paramours are now "the loitering heirs of city directors," and, as for the bridals of Spenser's Elizabethan maidens, in the stanzas which follow we learn a great deal about those. At the end of the section the speech of the third of the Thames-nymphs summarizes the whole matter for us.

The waters of the Thames are also associated with those of Leman — the poet in the contemporary waste land is in a sort of Babylonian Captivity.

The castle of the Fisher King was always located on the banks of a river or on the sea shore. The title "Fisher King," Miss Weston shows, originates from the use of the fish as a fertility or life symbol. This meaning, however, was often forgotten, and so the title in many of the later Grail romances is accounted for by describing the king as fishing. Eliot uses the reference to fishing for reverse effect. The reference to fishing is part of the realistic detail of the scene — "While I was fishing in the dull canal." But to the reader who knows the Weston references, the reference is to that of the Fisher King of the Grail legends. The protagonist is the maimed and impotent King of the legends.

Eliot proceeds now to tie the waste-land symbol to that of *The Tempest*, by quoting one of the lines spoken by Ferdinand, Prince of Naples, which occurs just before Ariel's song, "Full Fathom Five," is heard. But he alters the passage from *The Tempest* somewhat, writing not, "Weeping again the king my father's wreck," but

Musing upon the king my brother's wreck
And on the king my father's death before him.

It is possible that the alteration has been made to bring the account taken from *The Tempest* into accord with the situation in the Percival stories. In Wolfram von Eschenbach's *Parzival*, for instance, Trevrezent, the hermit, is the brother of the Fisher King, Anfortas. He tells Parzival, "His name all men know as Anfortas, and I weep for him evermore." Their father, Frimutel, is of course, dead.

The protagonist in the poem, then, imagines himself not only in the situation of Ferdinand in *The Tempest* but also in that of one of the characters in the Grail legend; and the wreck, to be applied literally in the first instance, applies metaphorically in the second.

After the lines from *The Tempest*, appears again the image of a sterile death from which no life comes, the bones, "rattled by the rat's foot only, year to year." (The collocation of this figure with the vision of the death by water in Ariel's song has already been commented on. The lines quoted from *The Tempest* come just before the song.)

The allusion to Marvell's *To His Coy Mistress* is of course one of the easiest allusions in the poem. Instead of "Time's winged chariot" the poet hears "the sound of horns and motors" of contemporary London. But the passage has been further complicated. The reference has been combined with an allusion to Day's *Par-liament of Bees*. "Time's winged chariot" of Marvell has not only been changed to the modern automobile; Day's "sound of horns and hunting" has changed to the horns of the motors. And Actaeon will not be brought face to face with Diana, goddess of chastity; Sweeney, type of the vulgar bourgeois, is to be brought to Mrs. Porter, hardly a type of chastity. The reference in the ballad to the feet "washed in soda water" reminds the poet ironically of another sort of foot-washing, the sound of the children singing in the dome heard at the ceremony of the foot-washing which precedes the restoration of the wounded Anfortas (the Fisher King) by Parzival and the taking away of the curse from the waste land. The quotation thus completes the allusion to the Fisher King commenced in line 189 — "While I was fishing in the dull canal."

The pure song of the children also reminds the poet of the song of the nightingale which we have heard in "The Game of Chess." The recapitulation of symbols is continued with a repetition of "Unreal city" and with the reference to the one-eyed merchant.

Mr. Eugenides, the Smyrna merchant, is the one-eyed merchant mentioned by Madame Sosostris. The fact that the merchant is one-eyed apparently means in Madame Sosostris' speech no more than that the merchant's face on the card is shown in profile. But Eliot applies the term to Mr. Eugenides for a totally different effect. The defect corresponds somewhat to Madame Sosostris' bad cold. The Syrian merchants, we learn from Miss Weston's book, were, with slaves and soldiers, the principal carriers of the mysteries which lie at the core of the Grail legends. But in the modern world we find both the representatives of the Tarot divining and the mystery cults in decay. What he carries on his back and what the fortune-teller was forbidden to see is evidently the knowledge of the mysteries (although Mr. Eugenides himself is hardly likely to be more aware of it than Madame Sosostris is aware of the importance of her function). Mr. Eugenides, in terms of his former function, ought to be inviting the protagonist to an initiation into the esoteric cult which holds the secret of life, but on the realistic surface of the poem, in his invitation to "a weekend at the Metropole" he is really inviting him to a homosexual debauch. The homosexuality is "secret" and now a "cult," but a very different cult from that which Mr.

Eugenides ought to represent. The end of the new cult is not life, but ironically, sterility.

In the modern waste land, however, even the relation between man and woman is also sterile. The incident between the typist and the carbuncular young man is a picture of "love" so exclusively and practically pursued that it is not love at all. The scene, as Allen Tate puts it, is one of our most terrible insights into Western civilization. The tragic chorus to the scene is Tiresias, into whom perhaps Mr. Eugenides may be said to modulate, Tiresias, the historical "expert" on the relation between the sexes.

The allusions to Sappho's lines and to Goldsmith's made in this passage need little comment. The hour of evening, which in Sappho's poem brings rest to all and brings the sailor home, brings the typist to her travesty of home — "On the divan . . . at night her bed" — and brings the carbuncular young man, the meeting with whom ends not in peace but in sterile burning.

The reminiscence of the lines from Goldsmith's song in the description of the young woman's actions after the departure of her lover gives concretely and ironically the utter breakdown of traditional standards.

It is the music of her gramophone which the protagonist hears "creep by" him "upon the waters." Far from the music which Ferdinand heard bringing him to Miranda and love, it is, one is tempted to think, the music of "O O O O that Shakespeherian Rag" of "A Game of Chess."

But the protagonist says that he *sometimes* hears "The pleasant whining of a mandoline." Significantly enough, it is the music of the fishmen (the fish again as a life symbol) and it comes from beside a church (though — if this is not to rely too much on Eliot's note — the church has been marked for destruction). Life on Lower Thames Street, if not on the Strand, still has meaning as it cannot have meaning for either the typist or the rich woman of "A Game of Chess."

The song of the Thames-daughters brings us back to the opening section of "The Fire Sermon" again, and once more we have to do with the river and the river-nymphs. Indeed, the typist incident is framed by the two river-nymph scenes.

The connection of the river-nymphs with the Rhine-daughters of Wagner's *Götterdämmerung* is easily made. In the passage in Wagner's opera to which Eliot refers in his note, the opening of Act III, the Rhine-daughters bewail the loss of the beauty of the Rhine occasioned by the theft of the gold, and then beg Siegfried to give them back the Ring made from this gold, finally threatening him with death if he does not give it up. Like the Thames-daughters they too have been violated; and like the maidens mentioned in the Grail legend, the violation has brought a curse on gods and men. The first of the songs depicts the modern river, soiled with oil and tar. (Compare also with the description of the river in the first part of "The Fire Sermon.") The second song depicts the Elizabethan river, also evoked in the first part of "The Fire Sermon." (Leicester and Elizabeth ride upon it in a barge of state. Incidentally, Spenser's *Prothalamion*, from which quotation is made in the first part of "The Fire Sermon," mentions Leicester as having formerly lived in the house which forms the setting of that poem.)

In this second song there is also a definite allusion to the passage in *Antony and Cleopatra* already referred to in the opening line of "A Game of Chess."

> Beating oars
> The stern was formed
> A gilded shell.

And if we still have any doubt of the allusion, Eliot's note on the passage with its reference to the "barge" and "poop" should settle the matter. We have already commented on the earlier allusion to Cleopatra as the prime example of love for love's sake. The symbol bears something of the same meaning here, and the note which Eliot supplies does something to reinforce the "Cleopatra" aspect of Elizabeth. Elizabeth in the presence of the Spaniard De Quadra, though negotiations were going on for a Spanish marriage, "went so far that Lord Robert at last said, as I [De Quadra was a bishop] was on the spot there was no reason why they should not be married if the queen pleased." The passage has a sort of double function. It reinforces the general contrast between Elizabethan magnificence and modern sordidness: in the Elizabethan age love for love's sake had some meaning and therefore some magnificence. But the passage gives something of an opposed effect too: the same sterile love, emptiness of love, obtained in this period too: Elizabeth and the Typist are alike as well as different.

The third Thames-daughter's song depicts another sordid "love" affair, and unites the themes of the first two songs. It begins "Trams and *dusty* trees." With it we are definitely in the waste land again. Pia, whose words she echoes in saying "Highbury bore me. Richmond and Kew/Undid me" was in Purgatory and had hope. The woman speaking here has no hope — she too is in the Inferno: "I can connect/ Nothing with nothing." She has just completed, floating down the river in the canoe, what Eliot has described in *Murder in the Cathedral* as

... the effortless journey, to the empty land ... . Where the soul is no longer deceived, for there are no objects, no tones, Where those who were men can no longer turn the mind To distraction, delusion, escape into dream, pretence, No colours, no forms to distract, to divert the soul From seeing itself, foully united forever, nothing with nothing, Nor what we call death, but what beyond death is not death ... .

Now, "on Margate sands," like the Hollow Men, she stands "on this beach of the tumid river."

The songs of the three Thames-daughters, as a matter of fact, epitomize this whole section of the poem. With reference to the quotations from St. Augustine and Buddha at the end of "The Fire Sermon" Eliot states that "The collocation of these two representatives of eastern and western asceticism, as the culmination of this part of the poem, is not an accident."

It is certainly not an accident. The moral of all the incidents which we have been witnessing is that there must be an asceticism — something to check the drive of desire. The wisdom of the East and the West comes to the same thing on this point. Moreover, the image which both St. Augustine and Buddha use for lust is fire. What we have witnessed in the various scenes of "The Fire Sermon" is the sterile burning of lust. Modern man, freed from all restraints, in his cultivation of experience for experience's sake burns, but not with a "hard and gemlike flame." One ought not to pound the point home in this fashion, but to see that the imagery of this section of the poem furnishes illustrations leading up to "The Fire Sermon" is the necessary requirement for feeling the force of the brief allusions here at the end to Buddha and St. Augustine.

IV

Whatever the specific meaning of the symbols, the general function of the section, "Death by Water," is readily apparent. The section forms a contrast with "The Fire Sermon" which precedes it — a contrast between the symbolism of fire and that of water. Also readily apparent is its force as a symbol of surrender and relief through surrender.

Some specific connections can be made, however. The drowned Phoenician Sailor recalls the drowned god of the fertility cults. Miss Weston tells that each year at Alexandria an effigy of the head of the god was thrown into the water as a symbol of the death of the powers of nature, and that this head was carried by the current to Byblos where it was taken out of the water and exhibited as a symbol of the reborn god.

Moreover, the Phoenician Sailor is a merchant — "Forgot ... the profit and loss." The vision of the drowned sailor gives a statement of the message which the Syrian merchants originally brought to Britain and which the Smyrna merchant, unconsciously and by ironical negatives, has brought. One of Eliot's notes states that the "merchant . . . melts into the Phoenician Sailor, and the latter is not wholly distinct from Ferdinand Prince of Naples." The death by water would seem to be equated with the death described in Ariel's song in *The Tempest*. There is a definite difference in the tone of the description of this death — "A current under sea/Picked his bones in whispers," as compared with the "other" death — "bones cast in a little low dry garret,/Rattled by the rat's foot only, year to year."

Farther than this it would not be safe to go, but one may point out that whirling (the whirlpool here, the Wheel of Madame Sosostris' palaver) is one of Eliot's symbols frequently used in other poems (*Ash Wednesday*, *Gerontion*, *Murder in the Cathedral*, and *Burnt Norton*) to denote the temporal world. And one may point out, the following passage from *Ash Wednesday*:

Although I do not hope to turn again
. . . .
Wavering between the profit and the loss
In this brief transit where the dreams cross
The dreamcrossed twilight between birth and dying.

At least, with a kind of hindsight, one may

suggest that Section IV gives an instance of the conquest of death and time — the "perpetual recurrence of determined seasons," the "world of spring and autumn, birth and dying" — through death itself.

V

The reference to the "torchlight red on sweaty faces" and to the "frosty silence in the gardens" obviously associates, as we have already pointed out, Christ in Gethsemane with the other hanged gods. The god has now died, and in referring to this, the basic theme finds another strong restatement:

> He who was living is now dead
> We who were living are now dying
> With a little patience

The poet does not say "We who *are* living." It is "We who *were* living." It is the death-in-life of Dante's Limbo. Life in the full sense had been lost.

The passage on the sterility of the waste land and the lack of water which follows, provides for the introduction later of two highly important passages:

> There is not even silence in the mountains
> But dry sterile thunder without rain

— lines which look forward to the introduction later of "what the thunder said" when the thunder, no longer sterile, but bringing rain speaks.

The second of these passages is, "There is not even solitude in the mountains," which looks forward to the reference to the Journey to Emmaus theme a few lines later: "Who is the third who walks always beside you?" The god has returned, has risen, but the travellers cannot tell whether it is really he, or mere illusion induced by their delirium.

The parallelism between the "hooded" figure who walks "always . . . beside you" and the "hooded hordes" is another instance of the sort of parallelism that is really a contrast, one of the type of which Eliot is fond. In the first case, the figure is indistinct because spiritual; in the second, the hooded hordes are indistinct because completely *unspiritual* — they are the people of the waste land —

> Shape without form, shade without colour,
> Paralysed force, gesture without motion

— to take two lines from "The Hollow Men,"

where the people of the waste land once more appear. Or to take another line from the same poem, perhaps their hoods are the "deliberate disguises" which the Hollow Men, the people of the waste land, wear.

Eliot, as his notes tell us, has particularly connected the description here with the "decay of eastern Europe." The hordes represent then the general waste land of the modern world with a special application to the break-up of Eastern Europe, the region with which the fertility cults were especially connected and in which to-day the traditional values are thoroughly discredited. The cities, Jerusalem, Athens, Alexandria, Vienna, like the London of the first section of the poem are "unreal," and for the same reason.

The passage which immediately follows develops the unreality into nightmare, but it is a nightmare vision which is not only an extension of the passage beginning, "What is the city over the mountains" — in it appear other figures from earlier in the poem: the lady of "A Game of Chess" who, surrounded by the glory of history and art, sees no meaning in either and threatens to rush out into the street "With my hair down, so," has here let down her hair and fiddles "whisper music on those strings." One remembers in "A Game of Chess" that it was the woman's hair that spoke:

> . . . her hair
> Spread out in fiery points
> Glowed into words, then would be savagely still.

The hair has been immemorially a symbol of fertility, and Miss Weston and Frazer mention sacrifices of hair in order to aid the fertility god.

As we have pointed out earlier in dealing with "The Burial of the Dead," this whole passage is to be connected with the twelfth chapter of Ecclesiastes. The doors "of mudcracked houses," and the cisterns in this passage are to be found in Ecclesiastes, and the woman fiddling music from her hair is one of "the daughters of music" brought low. The towers and bells from the Elizabeth and Leicester passage of "The Fire Sermon" also appear here, but the towers are upside down, and the bells, far from pealing for an actual occasion or ringing the hours, are "reminiscent." The civilization is breaking up.

The "violet light" also deserves comment. In "The Fire Sermon" it is twice mentioned as the "violet hour," and there it has little more than a physical meaning. It is a description of the hour of twilight. Here it indicates the twilight of the civilization, but it is perhaps something more. Violet is one of the liturgical colours of the Church. It symbolizes repentance and it is the colour of baptism. The visit to the Perilous Chapel, according to Miss Weston, was an initiation — that is, a baptism. In the nightmare vision, the bats wear baby faces.

The horror built up in this passage is a proper preparation for the passage on the Perilous Chapel which follows it. The journey has not been merely an agonized walk in the desert, though it is that, or merely the journey after the god has died and hope has been lost; it is also the journey to the Perilous Chapel of the Grail story. In Miss Weston's account, the Chapel was part of the ritual, and was filled with horrors to test the candidate's courage. In some stories the perilous cemetery is also mentioned. Eliot has used both: "Over the tumbled graves, about the chapel." In many of the Grail stories the Chapel was haunted by demons.

The cock in the folk-lore of many peoples is regarded as the bird whose voice chases away the powers of evil. It is significant that it is after his crow that the flash of lightning comes and the "damp gust/Bringing rain." It is just possible that the cock has a connection also with *The Tempest* symbols. The first song which Ariel sings to Ferdinand as he sits "Weeping again the king my father's wreck" ends

> The strain of strutting chanticleer,
> Cry, cock-a-doodle-doo.

The next stanza is the "Full Fathom Five" song which Eliot has used as a vision of life gained through death. If this relation holds, here we have an extreme instance of an allusion, in itself innocent, forced into serious meaning through transference to a new context.

As Miss Weston has shown, the fertility cults go back to a very early period and are recorded in Sanskrit legends. Eliot has been continually in the poem linking up the Christian doctrine with the beliefs of as many peoples as he can. Here he goes back to the very beginnings of Aryan culture, and tells the rest of the story of the rain's coming, not in terms of the setting already developed but in its earliest form. The passage is thus a perfect parallel in method to the passage in "The Burial of the Dead."

> You who were with me in the ships at Mylae!
> That corpse you planted last year in your garden. . . .

The use of Sanskrit in what the thunder says

is thus accounted for. In addition, there is of course a more obvious reason for casting what the thunder said into Sanskrit here: onomatopoeia.

The comments on the three statements of the thunder imply an acceptance of them. The protagonist answers the first question, "What have we given?" with the statement:

> The awful daring of a moment's surrender
> Which an age of prudence can never retract
> By this, and this only, we have existed.

Here the larger meaning is stated in terms which imply the sexual meaning. Man cannot be absolutely self-regarding. Even the propagation of the race — even mere "existence" — calls for such a surrender. Living calls for — see the passage already quoted from Eliot's essay on Baudelaire — belief in something more than "life."

The comment on *dayadhvam* (sympathize) is obviously connected with the foregoing passage. The surrender to something outside the self is an attempt (whether on the sexual level or some other) to transcend one's essential isolation. The passage gathers up the symbols previously developed in the poem just as the foregoing passage reflects, though with a different implication, the numerous references to sex made earlier in the poem. For example, the woman in the first part of "A Game of Chess" has also heard the key turn in the door, and confirms her prison by thinking of the key:

> Speak to me. Why do you never speak. Speak.
> What are you thinking of? What thinking? What?
> I never know what you are thinking. Think.

The third statement made by the thunder, *damyata* (control) follows the logical condition for control, sympathy. The figure of the boat catches up the figure of control already given in "Death by Water" — "O you who turn the wheel and look to windward" — and from "The Burial of the Dead" the figure of happy love in which the ship rushes on with a fair wind behind it: *Frisch weht der Wind. . . .*

I cannot accept Mr. Leavis's interpretation of the passage, "I sat upon the shore/Fishing, with the arid plain behind me," as meaning that the poem "exhibits no progression." The comment upon what the thunder says would indicate, if other passages did not, that the poem does not "end where it began." It is true that the protagonist does not witness a revival of the waste land; but there are two important relationships involved in his case; a personal one as well as a general one. If secularization has destroyed, or is likely to destroy, modern civilization, the protagonist still has a private obligation to fulfil. Even if the civilization is breaking up — "London Bridge is falling down falling down falling down" — there remains the personal obligation: "Shall I at least set my lands in order?" Consider in this connection the last sentences of Eliot's "Thoughts After Lambeth": "The World is trying the experiment of attempting to form a civilized but non-Christian mentality. The experiment will fail; but we must be very patient in awaiting its collapse; meanwhile redeeming the time: so that the Faith may be preserved alive through the dark ages before us; to renew and rebuild civilization, and save the World from suicide."

The bundle of quotations with which the poem ends has a very definite relation to the general theme of the poem and to several of the major symbols used in the poem. Before Arnaut leaps back into the refining fire of Purgatory with joy he says: "I am Arnaut who weep and go singing; contrite I see my past folly, and joyful I see before me the day I hope for. Now I pray you by that virtue which guides you to the summit of the stair, at times be mindful of my pain." This note is carried forward by the quotation from *Pervigilium Veneris*: "When shall I be like the swallow?" The allusion also connects with the Philomela symbol. (Eliot's note on the passage indicates this clearly.) The sister of Philomela was changed into a swallow as Philomela was changed into a nightingale. The protagonist is asking therefore when shall the spring, the time of love return, but also when will he be reborn out of his sufferings, and — with the special meaning which the symbol takes on from the preceding Dante quotation and from the earlier contexts already discussed — he is asking what is asked at the end of one of the minor poems: "When will Time flow away?"

The quotation from "El Desdichado," as Edmund Wilson has pointed out, indicates that the protagonist of the poem has been disinherited, robbed of his tradition. The ruined tower is perhaps also the Perilous Chapel, "only the wind's home," and it is also the whole tradition in decay. The protagonist resolves to claim his tradition and rehabilitate it.

The quotation from *The Spanish Tragedy* — "When then Ile fit you. Hieronymo's mad againe" — is perhaps the most puzzling of all these quotations. It means, I believe, this: the protagonist's acceptance of what is in reality the deepest truth will seem to the present world mere madness. ("And still she cried, and still the world pursues,/'Jug Jug' to dirty ears.") Hieronymo in the play, like Hamlet, was "mad" for a purpose. The protagonist is conscious of the interpretation which will be placed on the words which follow — words which will seem to many apparently meaningless babble, but which contain the oldest and most permanent truth of the race:

Datta. Dayadhvam. Damyata.

After this statement comes the benediction:

Shantih Shantih Shantih

The foregoing account of *The Waste Land* is, of course, not to be substituted for the poem itself. Moreover, it certainly is not to be considered as representing *the method by which the poem was composed*. Much which the prose expositor must represent as though it had been consciously contrived, obviously was arrived at unconsciously and concretely.

The account given above is a statement merely of the "prose meaning," and bears the same relation to the poem as does the "prose meaning" of any other poem. But one need not perhaps apologize for setting forth such a statement explicitly, for *The Waste Land* has been almost consistently misinterpreted since its first publication. Even a critic so acute as Edmund Wilson has seen the poem as essentially a statement of despair and disillusionment, and this account sums up the stock interpretation of the poem. Indeed, the phrase, "the poetry of drouth," has become a cliché of left-wing criticism. It is such a misrepresentation of *The Waste Land* as this which allows Eda Lou Walton to entitle an essay on contemporary poetry, "Death in the Desert"; or which causes Waldo Frank to misconceive of Eliot's whole position and personality. But more than the meaning of one poem is at stake. If *The Waste Land* is not a world-weary cry of despair or a sighing after the vanished glories of the past, then not only the popular interpretation of the poem will have to be altered but also the general interpretations of post-war poetry which begin with such a misinterpretation as a premise.

Such misinterpretations involve also misconceptions of Eliot's technique. Eliot's basic method may be said to have passed relatively unnoticed. The popular view of the method used in *The Waste Land* may be described as follows: Eliot makes use of ironic contrasts between the glorious past and the sordid present — the crashing irony of

But at my back from time to time I hear
The sound of horns and motors, which shall bring
Sweeney to Mrs. Porter in the spring.

But this is to take the irony of the poem at the most superficial level, and to neglect the other dimensions in which it operates. And it is to neglect what are essentially more important aspects of his method. Moreover, it is to overemphasize the difference between the method employed by Eliot in his poem and that employed by him in later poems.

The basic method used in *The Waste Land* may be described as the application of the principle of complexity. The poet works in terms of surface parallelisms which in reality make ironical contrasts, and in terms of surface contrasts which in reality constitute parallelisms. (The second group sets up effects which may be described as the obverse of irony.) The two aspects taken together give the effect of chaotic experience ordered into a new whole though the realistic surface of experience is faithfully retained. The complexity of the experience is not violated by the apparent forcing upon it of a predetermined scheme.

The fortune-telling of "The Burial of the Dead" will illustrate the general method very satisfactorily. On the surface of the poem the poet reproduces the patter of the charlatan, Madame Sosostris, and there is the surface irony: the contrast between the original use of the Tarot cards and the use made here. But each of the details (justified realistically in the palaver of the fortune-teller) assumes a new meaning in the general context of the poem. There is then in addition to the surface irony something of a Sophoclean irony too, and the "fortune-telling" which is taken ironically by a twentieth-century audience becomes true as the poem develops — true in a sense in which Madame Sosostris herself does not think it true. The surface irony is thus reversed and becomes an irony on a deeper level. The items of her speech have only one reference in terms of the context of her speech: the "man with three staves," and "one-eyed merchant," and "crowds

of people, walking round in a ring," etc. But transferred to other contexts they become loaded with special meanings. To sum up, all the central symbols of the poem head up here, but here, in the only section in which they are explicitly bound together, the binding is slight and accidental. The deeper lines of association only emerge in terms of the total context as the poem develops — and this is, of course, exactly the effect which the poet intends.

This transference of items from an "innocent" context into a context in which they become charged and transformed in meaning will account for many of the literary allusions in the poem. For example, the "change of Philomel" is merely one of the items in the decorative detail in the room in the opening of "A Game of Chess." But the violent change of tense — "And still she cried, and still the world pursues" — makes it a comment upon, and a symbol of, the modern world. And further allusions to it through the course of the poem gradually equate it with the general theme of the poem. The allusions to *The Tempest* display the same method. The parallelism between Dante's Hell and the waste land of the Grail legends is fairly close; even the equation of Baudelaire's Paris to the waste land is fairly obvious. But the parallelism between the death by drowning in *The Tempest* and the death of the fertility god is, on the surface, merely accidental, and the first allusion to Ariel's song is merely an irrelevant and random association of the stream-of-consciousness:

Is your card, the drowned Phoenician Sailor,
(Those are pearls that were his eyes. Look!)

And on its second appearance in "A Game of Chess" it is still only an item in the protagonist's abstracted reverie. Even the association of *The Tempest* symbol with the Grail legends in the lines

While I was fishing in the dull canal
. . . .
Musing upon the king my brother's wreck.

and in the passage which follows, is ironical merely. But the associations have been established, even though they may seem to be made in ironic mockery, and when we come to the passage "Death by Water," with its change of tone, they assert themselves positively. We have a sense of revelation out of material apparently accidentally thrown together. I have called the effect the obverse of irony, for the method like that of irony, is indirect, though the effect is positive rather than negative.

The "melting" of the characters into each other is, of course, an aspect of this general process. Elizabeth and the girl born at Highbury both ride on the Thames, one in the barge of state, the other supine in a narrow canoe, and they are both Thames-nymphs, who are violated and thus are like the Rhine-nymphs who have also been violated, etc. With the characters as with the other symbols, the surface relationships may be accidental and apparently trivial and they may be made either ironically or through random association or in hallucination, but in the total context of the poem the deeper relationships are revealed. The effect is a sense of the oneness of experience, and of the unity of all periods, and with this, a sense that the general theme of the poem is true. But the theme has not been imposed — it has been revealed.

This complication of parallelisms and contrasts makes, of course, for ambiguity, but the ambiguity, in part, resides in the poet's fidelity to the complexity of experience. The symbols resist complete equation with a simple meaning. To take an example, "rock" throughout the poem seems to be one of the "desert" symbols. For example, the "dry stone" gives "no sound of water"; woman in the waste land is "the Lady of the Rocks," and most pointed of all, there is the long delirium passage in "What the Thunder Said": "Here is no water but only rock," etc. So much for its general meaning, but in "The Burial of the Dead" occur the lines

Only

There is shadow under this red rock,
(Come in under the shadow of this red rock).

Rock here is a place of refuge. (Moreover, there may also be a reference to the Grail symbolism. In *Parzival*, the Grail is a stone: "And this stone all men call the grail. . . . As children the Grail doth call them, 'neath its shadow they wax and grow.") The paradox, life through death, penetrates the symbol itself.

To take an even clearer case of this paradoxical use of symbols, consider the lines which occur in the hyacinth-girl passage. The vision gives obviously a sense of the richness and beauty of life. It is a moment of ecstasy (the basic imagery is obviously sexual); but the moment in its intensity is like death. The protagonist looks in that moment into the "heart of light, the silence," and so looks into — not richness — but blankness: he is neither "living nor dead." The symbol of life stands also for a kind of death. This duality of function may, of course, extend to a whole passage. For example, consider:

Where fishmen lounge at noon: where the walls
Of Magnus Martyr hold
Inexplicable splendour of Ionian white and gold.

The function of the passage is to indicate the poverty into which religion has fallen: the splendid church now surrounded by the poorer districts. But the passage has an opposed effect also: the fishmen in the "public bar in Lower Thames Street" next to the church have a meaningful life which has been largely lost to the secularized upper and middle classes.

The poem would undoubtedly be "clearer" if every symbol had one, unequivocal, meaning; but the poem would be thinner, and less honest. For the poet has not been content to develop a didactic allegory in which the symbols are two-dimensional items adding up directly to the sum of the general scheme. They represent dramatized instances of the theme, embodying in their own nature the fundamental paradox of the theme.

We shall better understand why the form of the poem is right and inevitable if we compare Eliot's theme to Dante's and to Spenser's. Eliot's theme is not the statement of a faith held and agreed upon (Dante's *Divine Comedy*) nor is it the projection of a "new" system of beliefs (Spenser's *Faerie Queene*). Eliot's theme is the rehabilitation of a system of beliefs, known but now discredited. Dante did not have to "prove" his statement; he could assume it and move within it about a poet's business. Eliot does not care, like Spenser, to force the didacticism. He prefers to stick to the poet's business. But, unlike Dante, he cannot assume acceptance of the statement. A direct approach is calculated to elicit powerful "stock responses" which will prevent the poem's being *read* at all. Consequently, the only method is to work by indirection. The "Christian" material is at the centre, but the poet never deals with it directly. The theme of resurrection is made on the surface in terms of the fertility rites; the words which the thunder speaks are Sanskrit words.

We have been speaking as if the poet were a strategist trying to win acceptance from a hostile audience. But of course this is true only in a sense. The poet himself is audience as well as speaker; we state the problem more exactly if we state it in terms of the poet's integrity rather than in terms of his strategy. He is so much a man of his own age that he can indicate his attitude toward the Christian tradition without falsity only in terms of the difficulties of a rehabilitation; and he is so much a poet and so little a propagandist that he can be sincere only as he presents his theme concretely and dramatically.

To put the matter in still other terms: the Christian terminology is for the poet here a mass of *clichés*. However "true" he may feel the terms to be, he is still sensitive to the fact that they operate superficially as *clichés,* and his method of necessity must be a process of bringing them to life again. The method adopted in *The Waste Land* is thus violent and radical, but thoroughly necessary. For the renewing and vitalizing of symbols which have been crusted over with a distorting familiarity demands the type of organization which we have already commented on in discussing particular passages: the statement of surface similarities which are ironically revealed to be dissimilarities, and the association of apparently obvious dissimilarities which culminates in a later realization that the dissimilarities are only superficial — that the chains of likeness are in reality fundamental. In this way the statement of beliefs emerges *through* confusion and cynicism — not in spite of them.

Lionel Trilling [1905–   ]

Lionel Trilling belongs to that group of contemporary liberal critics, influenced by the depression-economics of the thirties, for whom literature and politics are closely connected. But the newer liberalism of the forties, he felt, must be less dogmatic than the old and, above all, it must take fuller account of the aesthetic and emotional content of literature. A native of New York City, he has been a teacher, scholar, and critic of literature at Columbia University since 1931. His first book, *Matthew Arnold* (1939), revealed his interest in the tradition of English criticism and evidenced a somewhat tentative application of Freudian methods in biography. A study, *E. M. Forster* (1943), made a contribution to the revived interest in that English writer in America. Trilling has written short stories and one novel, *The Middle of the Journey* (1947), which is concerned with the conflict of ideas faced in the post-war years by liberals who can no longer accept the doctrinaire Marxism of the 1930's.

As a critic, he has written essays on Mark Twain, Sherwood Anderson, Henry James, the Kinsey Report, and the relation of Freudian concepts to literature, published in such influential periodicals as the *Kenyon Review* and the *Partisan Review.* The best of these were collected in 1950 under the title, *The Liberal Imagination.* The unifying theme of this volume was to recall liberalism to its proper function in literary criticism by emphasizing the emotional, subconscious, and imaginative areas of experience as a corrective to the tendency among social critics to reduce everything to the level of abstract ideas. *The Opposing Self* (1955) is another collection of essays giving further evidence of Trilling's use of the methods of historical and aesthetic criticism without going to the extremes of either technique. Instead, he subordinates them to devote himself to literature as an expression of man's moral life. He has been called both "divided" in his position as critic (by one reviewer) and one of the "best critical intelligences in America" (by another)

His interest in the effect of psychology upon literature has led him to write on Freud and upon such modern theories as the origin of all art in disease and neurosis. Although he has accepted some of the perceptions which Freudian criticism affords, he has likewise pointed out its deficiencies, especially its exaggeration of the element of neurosis in art and its undisguised contempt for the literary mind. Literature must be measured by literary standards, he feels, and not by an elaborate analysis of the neurotic symptoms of the writer.

Further reading: *The Liberal Imagination,* 1950. *The Opposing Self,* 1955.

Freud and Literature
(1940, 1950)

🎣 Originally published as "The Legacy of Sigmund Freud: Literary and Aesthetic" in the *Kenyon Review* (Spring, 1940), and in a revised version, as "Freud and Literature," *Horizon,* September, 1947. The present text is from the essay as printed in *The Liberal Imagination,* 1950.

I. The Freudian psychology is the only sys- 10 tematic account of the human mind which, in point of subtlety and complexity, of interest and tragic power, deserves to stand beside the chaotic mass of psychological insights which literature has accumulated through the centuries. To pass 15 from the reading of a great literary work to a treatise of academic psychology is to pass from one order of perception to another, but the human nature of the Freudian psychology is exactly the stuff upon which the poet has always 20 exercised his art. It is therefore not surprising that the psychoanalytical theory has had a great effect upon literature. Yet the relationship is reciprocal, and the effect of Freud upon litera- ture has been no greater than the effect of 25 literature upon Freud. When, on the occasion of the celebration of his seventieth birthday, Freud was greeted as the "discoverer of the un- conscious," he corrected the speaker and dis- claimed the title. "The poets and philosophers 30 before me discovered the unconscious," he said. "What I discovered was the scientific method by which the unconscious can be studied."

A lack of specific evidence prevents us from considering the particular literary "influences" 35 upon the founder of psychoanalysis; and, besides, when we think of the men who so clearly antic- ipated many of Freud's own ideas — Schopen- hauer and Nietzsche, for example — and then learn that he did not read their works until after 40 he had formulated his own theories, we must see that particular influences cannot be in question

here but that what we must deal with is nothing less than a whole *Zeitgeist,* a direction of thought. For psychoanalysis is one of the culminations of the Romanticist literature of the nineteenth cen- tury. If there is perhaps a contradiction in the idea of a science standing upon the shoulders of a literature which avows itself inimical to science in so many ways, the contradiction will be re- solved if we remember that this literature, de- spite its avowals, was itself scientific in at least the sense of being passionately devoted to a re- search into the self.

In showing the connection between Freud and this Romanticist tradition, it is difficult to know where to begin, but there might be a cer- tain aptness in starting even back of the tradition, as far back as 1762 with Diderot's *Rameau's Nephew.* At any rate, certain men at the heart of nineteenth-century thought were agreed in finding a peculiar importance in this brilliant little work: Goethe translated it, Marx admired it, Hegel — as Marx reminded Engels in the letter which announced that he was sending the book as a gift — praised and expounded it at length, Shaw was impressed by it, and Freud himself, as we know from a quotation in his *Introductory Lectures,* read it with the pleasure of agreement.

The dialogue takes place between Diderot him- self and a nephew of the famous composer. The protagonist, the younger Rameau, is a despised, outcast, shameless fellow; Hegel calls him the "disintegrated consciousness" and credits him with great wit, for it is he who breaks down all the normal social values and makes new combi- nations with the pieces. As for Diderot, the deuteragonist, he is what Hegel calls the "honest consciousness," and Hegel considers him reason- able, decent, and dull. It is quite clear that the author does not despise his Rameau and does not mean us to. Rameau is lustful and greedy, arrogant yet self-abasing, perceptive yet "wrong," like a child. Still, Diderot seems actually to be giving the fellow a kind of superiority over himself, as though Rameau represents the elements which, dangerous but wholly necessary, lie beneath the reasonable decorum of social life. It would perhaps be pressing too far to find in Rameau Freud's id and in Diderot Freud's ego; yet the connection does suggest itself; and at least we have here the perception which is to be the common characteristic of both Freud and Romanticism, the perception of the hidden element of human nature and of the opposition between the hidden and the visible. We have too the bold perception of just what lies hidden: "If the little savage [i.e., the child] were left to himself, if he preserved all his foolishness and combined the violent passions of a man of thirty with the lack of reason of a child in the cradle, he'd wring his father's neck and go to bed with his mother."

From the self-exposure of Rameau to Rousseau's account of his own childhood is no great step; society might ignore or reject the idea of the "immorality" which lies concealed in the beginning of the career of the "good" man, just as it might turn away from Blake struggling to expound a psychology which would include the forces beneath the propriety of social man in general, but the idea of the hidden thing went forward to become one of the dominant notions of the age. The hidden element takes many forms and it is not necessarily "dark" and "bad"; for Blake the "bad" was the good, while for Wordsworth and Burke what was hidden and unconscious was wisdom and power, which work in despite of the conscious intellect.

The mind has become far less simple; the devotion to the various forms of autobiography — itself an important fact in the tradition — provides abundant examples of the change that has taken place. Poets, making poetry by what seems to them almost a freshly discovered faculty, find that this new power may be conspired against by other agencies of the mind and even deprived of its freedom; the names of Wordsworth, Coleridge, and Arnold at once occur to us again, and Freud quotes Schiller on the danger to the poet that lies in the merely analytical reason. And it is not only the poets who are threatened; educated and sensitive people throughout Europe become aware of the depredations that reason might make upon the affective life, as in the classic instance of John Stuart Mill.

We must also take into account the preoccupation — it began in the eighteenth century, or even in the seventeenth — with children, women, peasants, and savages, whose mental life, it is felt, is less overlaid than that of the educated adult male by the proprieties of social habit. With this preoccupation goes a concern with education and personal development, so consonant with the historical and evolutionary bias of the time. And we must certainly note the revolution in morals which took place at the instance (we might almost say) of the Bildungsroman, for in the novels fathered by Wilhelm Meister we get the almost complete identification of author and hero and of the reader with both, and this identification almost inevitably suggests a leniency of moral judgment. The autobiographical novel has a further influence upon the moral sensibility by its exploitation of all the modulations of motive and by its hinting that we may not judge a man by any single moment in his life without taking into account the determining past and the expiating and fulfilling future.

It is difficult to know how to go on, for the further we look the more literary affinities to Freud we find, and even if we limit ourselves to bibliography we can at best be incomplete. Yet we must mention the sexual revolution that was being demanded — by Shelley, for example, by the Schlegel of Lucinde, by George Sand, and later and more critically by Ibsen; the belief in the sexual origin of art, badly stated by Tieck, more subtly by Schopenhauer; the investigation of sexual maladjustment by Stendhal, whose observations on erotic feeling seem to us distinctly Freudian. Again and again we see the effective, utilitarian ego being relegated to an inferior position and a plea being made on behalf of the anarchic and self-indulgent id. We find the energetic exploitation of the idea of the mind as a divisible thing, one part of which can contemplate and mock the other. It is not a far remove from this to Dostoevski's brilliant instances of ambivalent feeling. Novalis brings in the preoccupation with the death wish, and this is linked on the one hand with sleep and on the other hand with the perception of the perverse, self-destroying impulses, which in turn leads us to that fascination by the horrible which we find in Shelley, Poe, and Baudelaire. And always there is the profound interest in the dream — "Our dreams," said Gerard de Nerval, "are a second life" — and in the nature of metaphor, which reaches its climax in Rimbaud and the later Symbolists, metaphor becoming less and less communicative as it approaches the relative autonomy of the dream life.

But perhaps we must stop to ask, since these are the components of the *Zeitgeist* from which Freud himself developed, whether it can be said that Freud did indeed produce a wide literary effect. What is it that Freud added that the tendency of literature itself would not have developed without him? If we were looking for a writer who showed the Freudian influence, Proust would perhaps come to mind as readily as anyone else; the very title of his novel, in French more than in English, suggests an enterprise of psychoanalysis and scarcely less so does his method — the investigation of sleep, of sexual deviation, of the way of association, the almost obsessive interest in metaphor; at these and at many other points the "influence" might be shown. Yet I believe it is true that Proust did not read Freud. Or again, exegesis of *The Waste Land* often reads remarkably like the psychoanalytic interpretation of a dream, yet we know that Eliot's methods were prepared for him not by Freud but by other poets.

Nevertheless, it is of course true that Freud's influence on literature has been very great. Much of it is so pervasive that its extent is scarcely to be determined; in one form or another, frequently in perversions or absurd simplifications, it has been infused into our life and become a component of our culture of which it is now hard to be specifically aware. In biography its first effect was sensational but not fortunate. The early Freudian biographers were for the most part Guildensterns who seemed to know the pipes but could not pluck out the heart of the mystery, and the same condemnation applies to the early Freudian critics. But in recent years, with the acclimatization of psychoanalysis and the increased sense of its refinements and complexity, criticism has derived from the Freudian system much that is of great value, most notably the license and the injunction to read the work of literature with a lively sense of its latent and ambiguous meanings, as if it were, as indeed it is, a being no less alive and contradictory than the man who created it. And this new response to the literary work has had a corrective effect upon our conception of literary biography. The literary critic or biographer who makes use of the Freudian theory is no less threatened by the dangers of theoretical systematization than he was in the early days, but he is likely to be more aware of these dangers; and I think it is true to say that now the motive of his interpretation is not that of exposing the secret shame of the writer and limiting the meaning of his work, but, on the contrary, that of finding grounds for sympathy with the writer and for increasing the possible significances of the work.

The names of the creative writers who have been more or less Freudian in tone or assumption would of course be legion. Only a relatively small number, however, have made serious use of the Freudian ideas. Freud himself seems to have thought this was as it should be: he is said to have expected very little of the works that were sent to him by writers with inscriptions of gratitude for all they had learned from him. The Surrealists have, with a certain inconsistency, depended upon Freud for the "scientific" sanction of their program. Kafka, with an apparent awareness of what he was doing, has explored the Freudian conceptions of guilt and punishment, of the dream, and of the fear of the father. Thomas Mann, whose tendency, as he himself says, was always in the direction of Freud's interests, has been most susceptible to the Freudian anthropology, finding a special charm in the theories of myths and magical practices. James Joyce, with his interest in the numerous states of receding consciousness, with his use of words as things and of words which point to more than one thing, with his pervading sense of the interrelation and interpenetration of all things, and, not least important, his treatment of familial themes, has perhaps most thoroughly and consciously exploited Freud's ideas.

II. It will be clear enough how much of Freud's thought has significant affinity with the anti-rationalist element of the Romanticist tradition. But we must see with no less distinctness how much of his system is militantly rationalistic. Thomas Mann is at fault when, in his first essay on Freud, he makes it seem that the "Apollonian," the rationalistic, side of psychoanalysis is, while certainly important and wholly admirable, somehow secondary and even accidental. He gives us a Freud who is committed to the "night side" of life. Not at all: the rationalistic element of Freud is foremost; before everything else he is positivistic. If the interpreter of dreams came to medical science through Goethe, as he tells us he did, he entered not by way of the *Walpurgisnacht* but by the essay which played so important a part in the lives of so many scientists of the nineteenth century, the famous disquisition on Nature.

This correction is needed not only for accuracy but also for any understanding of Freud's attitude to art. And for that understanding we must see how intense is the passion with which Freud believes that positivistic rationalism, in its golden-age pre-Revolutionary purity, is the very form and pattern of intellectual virtue. The aim of psychoanalysis, he says, is the control of the night side of life. It is "to strengthen the ego, to make it more independent of the super-ego, to widen its field of vision, and so to extend the organization of the id." "Where id was," — that is, where all the irrational, non-logical, pleasure-seeking dark forces were — "there shall ego be," — that is, intelligence and control. "It is," he concludes, with a reminiscence of Faust, "reclamation work, like the draining of the Zuyder Zee." This passage is quoted by Mann when, in taking up the subject of Freud a second time, he does indeed speak of Freud's positivistic program; but even here the bias induced by Mann's artistic interest in the "night side" prevents him from giving the other aspect of Freud its due emphasis. Freud would never have accepted the role which Mann seems to give him as the legitimizer of the myth and the dark irrational ways of the mind. If Freud discovered the darkness for science he never endorsed it. On the contrary, his rationalism supports all the ideas of the Enlightenment that deny validity to myth or religion; he holds to a simple materialism, to a simple determinism, to a rather limited sort of epistemology. No great scientist of our day has thundered so articulately and so fiercely against all those who would sophisticate with metaphysics the scientific principles that were good enough for the nineteenth century. Conceptualism or pragmatism is anathema to him through the greater part of his intellectual career, and this, when we consider the nature of his own brilliant scientific methods, has surely an element of paradox in it.

From his rationalistic positivism comes much of Freud's strength and what weakness he has. The strength is the fine, clear tenacity of his positive aims, the goal of therapy, the desire to bring to men a decent measure of earthly happiness. But upon the rationalism must also be placed the blame for the often naïve scientific principles which characterize his early thought — they are later much modified — and which consist largely of claiming for his theories a perfect correspondence with an external reality, a position which, for those who admire Freud and especially for those who take seriously his views on art, is troublesome in the extreme.

Now Freud has, I believe, much to tell us about art, but whatever is suggestive in him is not likely to be found in those of his works in which he deals expressly with art itself. Freud is not insensitive to art — on the contrary — nor does he ever intend to speak of it with contempt. Indeed, he speaks of it with a real tenderness and counts it one of the true charms of the good life. Of artists, especially of writers, he speaks with admiration and even a kind of awe, though perhaps what he most appreciates in literature are specific emotional insights and observations; as we have noted, he speaks of literary men, because they have understood the part played in life by the hidden motives, as the precursors and coadjutors of his own science.

And yet eventually Freud speaks of art with what we must indeed call contempt. Art, he tells us, is a "substitute gratification," and as such is "an illusion in contrast to reality." Unlike most illusions, however, art is "almost always harmless and beneficent" for the reason that "it does not seek to be anything but an illusion. Save in the case of a few people who are, one might say, obsessed by Art, it never dares make any attack on the realm of reality." One of its chief functions is to serve as a "narcotic." It shares the characteristics of the dream, whose element of distortion Freud calls a "sort of inner dishonesty." As for the artist, he is virtually in the same category with the neurotic. "By such separation of imagination and intellectual capacity," Freud says of the hero of a novel, "he is destined to be a poet or a neurotic, and he belongs to that race of beings whose realm is not of this world."

Now there is nothing in the logic of psychoanalytical thought which requires Freud to have these opinions. But there is a great deal in the practice of the psychoanalytical therapy which makes it understandable that Freud, unprotected by an adequate philosophy, should be tempted to take the line he does. The analytical therapy deals with illusion. The patient comes to the physician to be cured, let us say, of a fear of walking in the street. The fear is real enough, there is no illusion on that score, and it produces all the physical symptoms of a more rational fear, the sweating palms, pounding heart, and shortened breath. But the patient knows there is no cause for fear, or rather that there is, as he says, no "real cause": there are no machine guns, man traps, or tigers in the street. The physician knows, however, that there is indeed a "real" cause for the fear, though it has nothing at all to do with what is or is not in the street; the cause is within the patient, and the process of the therapy will be to discover, by gradual steps, what this real cause is and so free the patient from its effects.

Now the patient in coming to the physician, and the physician in accepting the patient, make a tacit compact about reality; for their purpose they agree to the limited reality by which we get our living, win our loves, catch our trains and our colds. The therapy will undertake to train the patient in proper ways of coping with this reality. The patient, of course, has been dealing with this reality all along, but in the wrong way. For Freud there are two ways of dealing with external reality. One is practical, effective, positive; this is the way of the conscious self, of the ego which must be made independent of the super-ego and extend its organization over the id, and it is the right way. The antithetical way may be called, for our purpose now, the "fictional" way. Instead of doing something about, or to, external reality, the individual who uses this way does something to, or about, his affective states. The most common and "normal" example of this is daydreaming, in which we give ourselves a certain pleasure by imagining our difficulties solved or our desires gratified. Then, too, as Freud discovered, sleeping dreams are, in much more complicated ways, and even though quite unpleasant, at the service of this same "fictional" activity. And in ways yet more complicated and yet more unpleasant, the actual neurosis from which our patient suffers deals with an external reality which the mind considers still more unpleasant than the painful neurosis itself.

For Freud as psychoanalytic practitioner there are, we may say, the polar extremes of reality and illusion. Reality is an honorific word, and it means what is *there*; illusion is a pejorative word, and it means a response to what is *not there*. The didactic nature of a course of psychoanalysis no doubt requires a certain firm crudeness in making the distinction; it is after all aimed not at theoretical refinement but at practical effectiveness. The polar extremes are practical reality and neurotic illusion, the latter judged by the former. This, no doubt, is as it should be; the patient is not being trained in metaphysics and epistemology.

This practical assumption is not Freud's only view of the mind in its relation to reality. Indeed what may be called the essentially Freudian view assumes that the mind, for good as well as bad, helps create its reality by selection and evaluation. In this view, reality is malleable and subject to creation; it is not static but is rather a series of situations which are dealt with in their own terms. But beside this conception of the mind stands the conception which arises from Freud's therapeutic-practical assumptions; in this view, the mind deals with a reality which is quite fixed and static, a reality that is wholly "given" and not (to use a phrase of Dewey's) "taken." In his epistemological utterances, Freud insists on this second view, although it is not easy to see why he should do so. For the reality to which he wishes to reconcile the neurotic patient is, after all, a "taken" and not a "given" reality. It is the reality of social life and of value, conceived and maintained by the human mind and will. Love, morality, honor, esteem — these are the components of a created reality. If we are to call art an illusion then we must call most of the activities and satisfactions of the ego illusions; Freud, of course, has no desire to call them that.

What, then, is the difference between, on the one hand, the dream and the neurosis, and, on the other hand, art? That they have certain common elements is of course clear; that unconscious processes are at work in both would be denied by no poet or critic; they share too, though in different degrees, the element of fantasy. But there is a vital difference between them which Charles Lamb saw so clearly in his defense of the sanity of true genius: "The . . . poet dreams being awake. He is not possessed by his subject but he has dominion over it."

That is the whole difference: the poet is in command of his fantasy, while it is exactly the mark of the neurotic that he is possessed by his fantasy. And there is a further difference which Lamb states; speaking of the poet's relation to reality (he calls it Nature), he says, "He is beautifully loyal to that sovereign directress, even when he appears most to betray her"; the illusions of art are made to serve the purpose of a closer and truer relation with reality. Jacques Barzun, in an acute and sympathetic discussion of Freud, puts the matter well: "A good analogy between art and *dreaming* has led him to a false one between art and *sleeping*. But the difference between a work of art and a dream is precisely this, that the work of art *leads us back to the outer reality by taking account of it*." Freud's assumption of the almost exclusively hedonistic nature and purpose of art bar him from the perception of this.

Of the distinction that must be made between the artist and the neurotic Freud is of course aware; he tells us that the artist is not like the neurotic in that he knows how to find a way back from the world of imagination and "once more get a firm foothold in reality." This however seems to mean no more than that reality is to be dealt with when the artist suspends the practice of his art; and at least once when Freud speaks of art dealing with reality he actually means the rewards that a successful artist can win. He does not deny to art its function and its usefulness; it has a therapeutic effect in releasing mental tension; it serves the cultural purpose of acting as a "substitute gratification" to reconcile men to the sacrifices they have made for culture's sake; it promotes the social sharing of highly valued emotional experiences; and it recalls men to their cultural ideals. This is not everything that some of us would find that art does, yet even this is a good deal for a "narcotic" to do.

III. I started by saying that Freud's ideas could tell us something about art, but so far I have done little more than try to show that Freud's very conception of art is inadequate. Perhaps, then, the suggestiveness lies in the application of the analytic method to specific works of art or to the artist himself? I do not think so, and it is only fair to say that Freud himself was aware both of the limits and the limitations of psychoanalysis in art, even though he does not always in practice submit to the former or admit the latter.

Freud has, for example, no desire to encroach upon the artist's autonomy; he does not wish us to read his monograph on Leonardo and then say of the "Madonna of the Rocks" that it is a fine example of homosexual, autoerotic painting. If he asserts that in investigation the "psychiatrist cannot yield to the author," he immediately insists that the "author cannot yield to the psychiatrist," and he warns the latter not to "coarsen everything" by using for all human manifestations the "substantially useless and awkward terms" of clinical procedure. He admits, even while asserting that the sense of beauty probably derives from sexual feeling, that psychoanalysis "has less to say about beauty than about

most other things." He confesses to a theoretical indifference to the form of art and restricts himself to its content. Tone, feeling, style, and the modification that part makes upon part he does not consider. "The layman," he says, "may expect perhaps too much from analysis . . . for it must be admitted that it throws no light upon the two problems which probably interest him the most. It can do nothing toward elucidating the nature of the artistic gift, nor can it explain the means by which the artist works — artistic technique."

What, then, does Freud believe that the analytical method can do? Two things: explain the "inner meanings" of the work of art and explain the temperament of the artist as man.

A famous example of the method is the attempt to solve the "problem" of *Hamlet* as suggested by Freud and as carried out by Dr. Ernest Jones, his early and distinguished follower. Dr. Jones's monograph is a work of painstaking scholarship and of really masterly ingenuity. The research undertakes not only the clearing up of the mystery of Hamlet's character, but also the discovery of "the clue to much of the deeper workings of Shakespeare's mind." Part of the mystery in question is of course why Hamlet, after he had so definitely resolved to do so, did not avenge upon his hated uncle his father's death. But there is another mystery to the play — what Freud calls "the mystery of its effect," its magical appeal that draws so much interest toward it. Recalling the many failures to solve the riddle of the play's charm, he wonders if we are to be driven to the conclusion "that its magical appeal rests solely upon the impressive thoughts in it and the splendor of its language." Freud believes that we can find a source of power beyond this.

We remember that Freud has told us that the meaning of a dream is its intention, and we may assume that the meaning of a drama is its intention, too. The Jones research undertakes to discover what it was that Shakespeare intended to say about Hamlet. It finds that the intention was wrapped by the author in a dreamlike obscurity because it touched so deeply both his personal life and the moral life of the world; what Shakespeare intended to say is that Hamlet cannot act because he is incapacitated by the guilt he feels at his unconscious attachment to his mother. There is, I think, nothing to be quarreled with in the statement that there is an Oedipus situation in *Hamlet*; and if psychoanalysis has indeed added a new point of interest to the play, that is to its credit.[1] And, just so, there is no reason to quarrel with Freud's conclusion when he undertakes to give us the meaning of *King Lear* by a tortuous tracing of the mythological implications of the theme of the three caskets, of the relation of the caskets to the Norns, the Fates, and the Graces, of the connection of these triadic females with Lear's daughters, of the transmogrification of the death goddess into the love goddess and the identification of Cordelia with both, all to the conclusion that the meaning of *King Lear* is to be found in the tragic refusal of an old man to "renounce love, choose death, and make friends with the necessity of dying." There is something both beautiful and suggestive in this, but it is not *the* meaning of *King Lear* any more than the Oedipus motive is *the* meaning of *Hamlet*.

I do not think that anything I have said about the inadequacies of the Freudian method of interpretation limits the number of ways we can deal with a work of art. Bacon remarked that experiment may twist nature on the rack to wring out its secrets, and criticism may use any instruments upon a work of art to find its meanings. The elements of art are not limited to the world of art. They reach into life, and whatever extraneous knowledge of them we gain — for example, by research into the historical context of the work — may quicken our feelings for the work itself and even enter legitimately into those feelings. Then, too, anything we may learn about the artist himself may be enriching and legitimate. But one research into the mind of the artist is simply not practicable, however legitimate it may theoretically be. That is, the investigation of his unconscious intention as it exists apart from the work itself. Criticism understands that the artist's statement of his conscious intention, though it is sometimes useful, cannot finally determine meaning. How much less can we know from his unconscious inten-

tion considered as something apart from the whole work? Surely very little that can be called conclusive or scientific. For, as Freud himself points out, we are not in a position to question the artist; we must apply the technique of dream analysis to his symbols, but, as Freud says with some heat, those people do not understand his theory who think that a dream may be interpreted without the dreamer's free association with the multitudinous details of his dream.

We have so far ignored the aspect of the method which finds the solution to the "mystery" of such a play as *Hamlet* in the temperament of Shakespeare himself and then illuminates the mystery of Shakespeare's temperament by means of the solved mystery of the play. Here it will be amusing to remember that by 1935 Freud had become converted to the theory that it was not Shakespeare of Stratford but the Earl of Oxford who wrote the plays, thus invalidating the important bit of evidence that Shakespeare's father died shortly before the composition of *Hamlet*. This is destructive enough to Dr. Jones's argument, but the evidence from which Dr. Jones draws conclusions about literature fails on grounds more relevant to literature itself. For when Dr. Jones, by means of his analysis of *Hamlet*, takes us into "the deeper workings of Shakespeare's mind," he does so with a perfect confidence that he knows what *Hamlet* is and what its relation to Shakespeare is. It is, he tells us, Shakespeare's "chief masterpiece," so far superior to all his other works that it may be placed on "an entirely separate level." And then, having established his ground on an entirely subjective literary judgment, Dr. Jones goes on to tell us that *Hamlet* "probably expresses the core of Shakespeare's philosophy and outlook as no other work of his does." That is, all the contradictory or complicating or modifying testimony of the other plays is dismissed on the basis of Dr. Jones's acceptance of the peculiar position which, he believes, *Hamlet* occupies in the Shakespeare canon. And it is upon this quite inadmissible judgment that Dr. Jones bases his argument: "It may be expected *therefore* that anything which will give us the key to the inner meaning of the play will *necessarily* give us the clue to much of the deeper workings of Shakespeare's mind." (The italics are mine.)

I should be sorry if it appeared that I am trying to say that psychoanalysis can have nothing to do with literature. I am sure that the opposite

---

[1] However, A. C. Bradley, in his discussion of Hamlet (*Shakespearean Tragedy*), states clearly the intense sexual disgust which Hamlet feels and which, for Bradley, helps account for his uncertain purpose; and Bradley was anticipated in this view by Löning. It is well known, and Dover Wilson has lately emphasized the point, that to an Elizabethan audience Hamlet's mother was not merely tasteless, as to a modern audience she seems, in hurrying to marry Claudius, but actually adulterous in marrying him at all because he was, as her brother-in-law, within the forbidden degrees. [Author's note.]

is so. For example, the whole notion of rich ambiguity in literature, of the interplay between the apparent meaning and the latent — not "hidden" — meaning, has been reinforced by the Freudian concepts, perhaps even received its first impetus from them. Of late years, the more perceptive psychoanalysts have surrendered the early pretensions of their teachers to deal "scientifically" with literature. That is all to the good, and when a study as modest and precise as Dr. Franz Alexander's essay on *Henry IV* comes along, an essay which pretends not to "solve" but only to illuminate the subject, we have something worth having. Dr. Alexander undertakes nothing more than to say that in the development of Prince Hal we see the classic struggle of the ego to come to normal adjustment, beginning with the rebellion against the father, going on to the conquest of the super-ego (Hotspur, with his rigid notions of honor and glory), then to the conquests of the *id* (Falstaff, with his anarchic self-indulgence), then to the identification with the father (the crown scene) and the assumption of mature responsibility. An analysis of this sort is not momentous and not exclusive of other meanings; perhaps it does no more than point up and formulate what we all have already seen. It has the tact to *accept* the play and does not, like Dr. Jones's study of *Hamlet*, search for a "hidden motive" and a "deeper working," which implies that there is a reality to which the play stands in the relation that a dream stands to the wish that generates it and from which it is separable; it is this reality, this "deeper working," which, according to Dr. Jones, produced the play. But *Hamlet* is not merely the product of Shakespeare's thought, it is the very instrument of his thought, and if meaning is intention, Shakespeare did not intend the Oedipus motive or anything less than *Hamlet*; if meaning is effect then it is *Hamlet* which affects us, not the Oedipus motive. *Coriolanus* also deals, and very terribly, with the Oedipus motive, but the effect of the one drama is very different from the effect of the other.

IV. If, then, we can accept neither Freud's conception of the place of art in life nor his application of the analytical method, what is it that he contributes to our understanding of art or to its practice? In my opinion, what he contributes outweighs his errors; it is of the greatest importance, and it lies in no specific statement that he makes about art but is, rather,

implicit in his whole conception of the mind.

For, of all mental systems, the Freudian psychology is the one which makes poetry indigenous to the very constitution of the mind. Indeed, the mind, as Freud sees it, is in the greater part of its tendency exactly a poetry-making organ. This puts the case too strongly, no doubt, for it seems to make the working of the unconscious mind equivalent to poetry itself, forgetting that between the unconscious mind and the finished poem there supervene the social intention and the formal control of the conscious mind. Yet the statement has at least the virtue of counterbalancing the belief, so commonly expressed or implied, that the very opposite is true, and that poetry is a kind of beneficent aberration of the mind's right course.

Freud has not merely naturalized poetry; he has discovered its status as a pioneer settler, and he sees it as a method of thought. Often enough he tries to show how, as a method of thought, it is unreliable and ineffective for conquering reality; yet he himself is forced to use it in the very shaping of his own science, as when he speaks of the topography of the mind and tells us with a kind of defiant apology that the metaphors of space relationship which he is using are really most inexact since the mind is not a thing of space at all, but that there is no other way of conceiving the difficult idea except by metaphor. In the eighteenth century Vico spoke of the metaphorical, imagistic language of the early stages of culture; it was left to Freud to discover how, in a scientific age, we still feel and think in figurative formations, and to create, what psychoanalysis is, a science of tropes, of metaphor and its variants, synecdoche and metonymy.

Freud showed, too, how the mind, in one of its parts, could work without logic, yet not without that directing purpose, that control of intent from which, perhaps it might be said, logic springs. For the unconscious mind works without the syntactical conjunctions which are logic's essence. It recognizes no *because*, no *therefore*, no *but*; such ideas as similarity, agreement, and community are expressed in dreams imagistically by compressing the elements into a unity. The unconscious mind in its struggle with the conscious always turns from the general to the concrete and finds the tangible trifle more congenial than the large abstraction. Freud discovered in the very organization of the mind those mechanisms by which art makes its effects, such devices as the condensations of meanings and the displacement of accent.

All this is perhaps obvious enough and, though I should like to develop it in proportion both to its importance and to the space I have given to disagreement with Freud, I will not press it further. For there are two other elements in Freud's thought which, in conclusion, I should like to introduce as of great weight in their bearing on art.

Of these, one is a specific idea which, in the middle of his career (1920), Freud put forward in his essay *Beyond the Pleasure Principle*. The essay itself is a speculative attempt to solve a perplexing problem in clinical analysis, but its relevance to literature is inescapable, as Freud sees well enough, even though his perception of its critical importance is not sufficiently strong to make him revise his earlier views of the nature and function of art. The idea is one which stands beside Aristotle's notion of the catharsis, in part to supplement, in part to modify it.

Freud has come upon certain facts which are not to be reconciled with his earlier theory of the dream. According to his theory, all dreams, even the unpleasant ones, could be understood upon analysis to have the intention of fulfilling the dreamer's wishes. They are in the service of what Freud calls the pleasure principle, which is opposed to the reality principle. It is, of course, this explanation of the dream which had so largely conditioned Freud's theory of art. But now there is thrust upon him the necessity for reconsidering the theory of the dream, for it was found that in cases of war neurosis — what we once called shellshock — the patient, with the utmost anguish, recurred in his dreams to the very situation, distressing as it was, which had precipitated his neurosis. It seemed impossible to interpret these dreams by any assumption of a hedonistic intent. Nor did there seem to be the usual amount of distortion in them: the patient recurred to the terrible initiatory situation with great literalness. And the same pattern of psychic behavior could be observed in the play of children; there were some games which, far from fulfilling wishes, seemed to concentrate upon the representation of those aspects of the child's life which were most unpleasant and threatening to his happiness.

To explain such mental activities Freud evolved a theory for which he at first refused to claim much but to which, with the years, he attached an increasing importance. He first makes the assumption that there is indeed in the psychic life a repetition-compulsion which goes beyond the pleasure principle. Such a compulsion cannot be meaningless, it must have an intent. And that intent, Freud comes to believe, is exactly and literally the developing of fear. "These dreams," he says, "are attempts at restoring control of the stimuli by developing apprehension, the pretermission of which caused the traumatic neurosis." The dream, that is, is the effort to reconstruct the bad situation in order that the failure to meet it may be recouped; in these dreams there is no obscured intent to evade but only an attempt to meet the situation, to make a new effort of control. And in the play of children it seems to be that "the child repeats even the unpleasant experiences because through his own activity he gains a far more thorough mastery of the strong impression than was possible by mere passive experience."

Freud, at this point, can scarcely help being put in mind of tragic drama; nevertheless, he does not wish to believe that this effort to come to mental grips with a situation is involved in the attraction of tragedy. He is, we might say, under the influence of the Aristotelian tragic theory which emphasizes a qualified hedonism through suffering. But the pleasure involved in tragedy is perhaps an ambiguous one; and sometimes we must feel that the famous sense of cathartic resolution is perhaps the result of glossing over terror with beautiful language rather than an evacuation of it. And sometimes the terror even bursts through the language to stand stark and isolated from the play, as does Oedipus's sightless and bleeding face. At any rate, the Aristotelian theory does not deny another function for tragedy (and for comedy, too) which is suggested by Freud's theory of the traumatic neurosis — what might be called the mithridatic function, by which tragedy is used as the homeopathic administration of pain to inure ourselves to the greater pain which life will force upon us. There is in the cathartic theory of tragedy, as it is usually understood, a conception of tragedy's function which is too negative and which inadequately suggests the sense of active mastery which tragedy can give.

In the same essay in which he sets forth the conception of the mind embracing its own pain for some vital purpose, Freud also expresses a provisional assent to the idea (earlier stated, as he reminds us, by Schopenhauer) that there is perhaps a human drive which makes of death the final and desired goal. The death instinct is a conception that is rejected by many of even the most thoroughgoing Freudian theorists (as, in his last book, Freud mildly noted); the late Otto Fenichel in his authoritative work on the neurosis argues cogently against it. Yet even if we reject the theory as not fitting the facts in any operatively useful way, we still cannot miss its grandeur, its ultimate tragic courage in acquiescence to fate. The idea of the reality principle and the idea of the death instinct form the crown of Freud's broader speculation on the life of man. Their quality of grim poetry is characteristic of Freud's system and the ideas it generates for him.

And as much as anything else that Freud gives to literature, this quality of his thought is important. Although the artist is never finally determined in his work by the intellectual systems about him, he cannot avoid their influence; and it can be said of various competing systems that some hold more promise for the artist than others. When, for example, we think of the simple humanitarian optimism which, for two decades, has been so pervasive, we must see that not only has it been politically and philosophically inadequate, but also that it implies, by the smallness of its view of the varieties of human possibility, a kind of check on the creative faculties. In Freud's view of life no such limitation is implied. To be sure, certain elements of his system seem hostile to the usual notions of man's dignity. Like every great critic of human nature — and Freud is that — he finds in human pride the ultimate cause of human wretchedness, and he takes pleasure in knowing

that his ideas stand with those of Copernicus and Darwin in making pride more difficult to maintain. Yet the Freudian man is, I venture to think, a creature of far more dignity and far more interest than the man which any other modern system has been able to conceive. Despite popular belief to the contrary, man, as Freud conceives him, is not to be understood by any simple formula (such as sex) but is rather an inextricable tangle of culture and biology. And not being simple, he is not simply good; he has, as Freud says somewhere, a kind of hell within him from which rise everlastingly the impulses which threaten his civilization. He has the faculty of imagining for himself more in the way of pleasure and satisfaction than he can possibly achieve. Everything that he gains he pays for in more than equal coin; compromise and the compounding with defeat constitute his best way of getting through the world. His best qualities are the result of a struggle whose outcome is tragic. Yet he is a creature of love; it is Freud's sharpest criticism of the Adlerian psychology that to aggression it gives everything and to love nothing at all.

One is always aware in reading Freud how little cynicism there is in his thought. His desire for man is only that he should be human, and to this end his science is devoted. No view of life to which the artist responds can insure the quality of his work, but the poetic qualities of Freud's own principles, which are so clearly in the line of the classic tragic realism, suggest that this is a view which does not narrow and simplify the human world for the artist but on the contrary opens and complicates it.

Malcolm Cowley [1898–   ]

The social and economic problems confronting the American writer, his cultural environment, the literary situation in its year-to-year changes of mood and tone — such are the areas in which Malcolm Cowley has practiced the art of criticism. He began his career in the expatriate days in Paris, in 1920; he shared the literary radicalisms of the twenties and thirties; he was himself a literary exile who returned. At present a publisher's adviser and editor, he has remained contemporary in interest, in harmony with the time, and his critical approach is inquiring and pragmatic.

Born in Pennsylvania near Pittsburgh, Cowley served in the American Ambulance Service in France in 1917. He graduated from Harvard two years later, returned to

Europe on a fellowship, and remained abroad until 1923. In France he was a free-lance reviewer, translator, and editor of small magazines. In 1930 he became book editor for the *New Republic*. He has written several volumes of poetry. In criticism his first important book was *Exile's Return* (1934; revised and enlarged in 1951), an informative portrait of the literary atmosphere of the 1920's. This was followed by *After the Genteel Tradition* (1937), of which he was both an editor and a co-author. During the forties Cowley edited a number of important collections of American writers, notably Hawthorne, Hemingway, and Faulkner for the Viking Press, and since 1948 he has acted as literary adviser for the Viking "Portable" editions. Cowley's essays on Hemingway and Faulkner, originating as introductions to editions of their work, are among his best criticism, going beyond the conventional introduction to open up fresh approaches and throw new light on America's two foremost living novelists. In *The Literary Situation* (1954) he analyzes the changing taste in fiction and portrays the newer generation of young novelists whose work seems moving in a direction quite different from that of the naturalists and social realists of the twenties and thirties.

Further reading: Introduction to *The Portable Hemingway*, 1944. *The Literary Situation*, 1954.

William Faulkner's Legend of the South

William Faulkner is one of the writers who reward and even in a sense demand a second reading. When you return to one of his books years after its publication, the passages that had puzzled you are easier to understand and each of them takes its proper place in the picture. Moreover, you lose very little by knowing the plot in advance. Faulkner's stories are not the sort that unwind in celluloid ribbons until the last inch of them has been reflected on a flat screen, with nothing to imagine and nothing more to see except the newsreel, the animated cartoon and the Coming Repulsions; instead his books are sculptural, as if you could walk round them for different views of the same solid object. But it is not merely a statue that he presents: rather it is a whole monument or, let us say, a city buried in the jungle, to which the author wishes to guide us, but not at once or by following a single path. We start out along one road, winding between walls of jungle growth in the humid afternoon, and it is not long until we catch a glimpse of our destination. Just beyond us, however, is a swamp filled with snakes, and the guide makes us turn back. We take another road; we gain a clearer picture of the city; but this time there are other dangers in front of us, quicksands or precipices, and again the guide makes us return. By whatever road we travel, we always

catch sight of our goal, always learn more about it and are always forced back; till at last we find the proper path and reach the heart of the city just as it is about to be overwhelmed by fire or earthquake. . . . Reading the same book a second time is like soaring over the jungle in a plane, with every section of the landscape falling into its proper perspective.

And there is another respect in which our judgment of the author changes when we return to not one but several of his novels in succession. On a first reading what had chiefly impressed us may have been their violence, which sometimes seemed to have no justification in art or nature. We had remembered incidents and figures like the violating of Temple Drake, in *Sanctuary*; like the pursuit and castration of Joe Christmas, in *Light in August*; like the idiot boy who fell in love and eloped with a cow, in *The Hamlet*; and like the nameless woman, in *The Wild Palms*, who bore her child unaided in the midst of a Mississippi River flood, on an Indian mound where all the snakes in the Delta had taken refuge. After a second reading, most of these nightmares retain their power to shock, but at the same time they merge a little into the background, as if they were the almost natural product of the long unbearable Mississippi summers; as if they were thunder showers brewed in the windless heat. We pay less attention to the horrors as such, and more to the old situation out of which they developed and the new disasters it seems to foreshadow. The situation itself, and not the violence to which it leads, is Faulkner's real subject. It is, moreover, the same situation in all his books — or, let us say, in all the novels and stories belonging to his Yoknapatawpha County series. Briefly it is the destruction of the old Southern order, by war and military occupation and still more by finance capitalism that tempts and destroys it from within. "Tell about the South," says Quentin Compson's roommate at Harvard, who comes from Edmonton, Alberta, and is curious about the unknown region beyond the Ohio. "What's it like there?" Shreve McCannon goes on to ask. "What do they do there? Why do they live there? Why do they live at all?" And Quentin, whose background is a little like that of the author and who often seems to speak for him — Quentin answers, "You can't understand it. You would have to be born there." Nevertheless, he tells a long and violent story that he regards as the essence of the Deep South, which is not so much a region as it is, in Quentin's mind, an incomplete and frustrated nation trying to recover its own identity, trying to relive its legendary past.

There was a boy, Quentin says — I am giving the plot of *Absalom, Absalom!* — a mountain boy named Thomas Sutpen whose family drifted into the Virginia tidewater. There his father found odd jobs on a plantation. One day the father sent him with a message to the big house, but he was turned away at the door by a black man in livery. The mountain boy, puzzled and humiliated, was seized upon by the ambition to which he would afterwards refer as "the design." He would own a plantation, with slaves and a liveried butler; he would build a mansion as big as any in the tidewater; and he would have a son to inherit his wealth.

A dozen years later, Sutpen appeared in the frontier town of Jefferson, Mississippi and, by some transaction the nature of which was never explained — though it certainly wasn't by honest purchase — he obtained a hundred square miles of land from the Chickasaws. He disappeared again, and this time he returned with twenty wild Negroes from the jungle and a French architect. On the day of his reappearance, he set about building the largest house in northern Mississippi, with timbers from the forest and bricks that his Negroes molded and baked on the spot; it was as if his mansion, Sutpen's Hundred, had been literally torn from the soil.

Only one man in Jefferson — he was Quentin's grandfather, General Compson — ever learned how and where Sutpen had acquired his slaves. He had shipped to Haiti from Virginia, worked as an overseer on a sugar plantation and married the rich planter's daughter, who had borne him a son. Then, finding that his wife had Negro blood, he had simply put her away, with her child and her fortune, while keeping the twenty slaves as a sort of indemnity. He explained to General Compson in the stilted speech he had taught himself that she could not be "adjunctive to the forwarding of the design."

"Jesus, the South is fine, isn't it?" says Shreve McCannon. "It's better than the theatre, isn't it? It's better than Ben Hur, isn't it? No wonder you have to come away now and then, isn't it?"

Sutpen married again, Quentin continues. This time his wife belonged to a pious family of the neighborhood, and she bore him two children, Henry and Judith. He became the biggest landowner and cotton planter in the county, and it seemed that his "design" had already been fulfilled. At this moment, however — it was Christmas in 1859 — Henry came home from the University of Mississippi with an older and worldlier new friend, Charles Bon, who was in reality Sutpen's son by his first marriage. Charles became engaged to Judith. Sutpen learned his identity and, without making a sign of recognition, ordered him to leave the house. Henry, who refused to believe that Charles was his half-brother, renounced his birthright and followed him to New Orleans. In 1861 all the male Sutpens went off to war, and all of them survived four years of fighting. Then, in the spring of 1865, Charles suddenly decided to marry Judith, even though he was certain by now that she was his half-sister. Henry rode beside him all the way back to Sutpen's Hundred, but tried to stop him at the gate, killed him when he insisted on going ahead with his plan, told Judith what he had done, and disappeared.

"The South," Shreve McCannon says as he listens to the story. "The South. Jesus. No wonder you folks all outlive yourselves by years and years." And Quentin says, remembering his own sister with whom he was in love — just as Charles Bon, and Henry too, were in love with Judith — "I am older at twenty than a lot of people who have died."

But Quentin's story of the Deep South does not end with the war. Colonel Sutpen came home, he says, to find his wife dead, his son a fugitive, his slaves dispersed (they had run away even before they were freed by the Union army) and most of his land about to be seized for debt. But still determined to carry out "the design," he did not even pause for breath before undertaking to restore his house and plantation as nearly as possible to what they had been. The effort failed; he lost most of his land and was reduced to keeping a crossroads store. Now in his sixties, he tried again to beget a son; but his wife's younger sister, Miss Rosa Coldfield, was outraged by his proposal ("Let's try it," he had said, "and if it's a boy we'll get married"); and later poor Milly Jones, with whom he had an affair, gave birth to a baby girl. At that Sutpen abandoned hope and provoked Milly's grandfather into killing him. Judith survived her father for a time, as did the half-caste son of Charles Bon by a New Orleans octoroon. After the death of these two by yellow fever, the great house was haunted rather than inhabited by an ancient mulatto woman, Sutpen's daughter by one of his slaves. The fugitive Henry Sutpen came home to die; the townspeople heard of his illness and sent an ambulance after him; but old Clytie thought they were arresting him for murder and set fire to Sutpen's Hundred. The only survivor of the conflagration was Jim Bond, a half-witted, saddle-colored creature who was Charles Bon's grandson.

"Do you know what I think?" says Shreve McCannon after the story has ended. "I think that in time the Jim Bonds are going to conquer the western hemisphere. Of course it won't be quite in our time and of course as they spread toward the poles they will bleach out again like the rabbits and the birds do, so they won't show up so sharp against the snow. But it will still be Jim Bond; and so in a few thousand years, I who regard you will also have sprung from the loins of African kings. Now I want you to tell me just one thing more. Why do you hate the South?"

"I don't hate it," Quentin says quickly, at once. "I don't hate it," he repeats, speaking for the author as well as himself. *I don't hate it*, he thinks, panting in the cold air, the iron New England dark; *I don't. I don't! I don't hate it! I don't hate it!*

The reader cannot help wondering why this somber and, at moments, plainly incredible story had so seized upon Quentin's mind that he trembled with excitement when telling it and felt that it revealed the essence of the Deep South. It seems to belong in the realm of Gothic romances, with Sutpen's Hundred taking the place of the haunted castle on the Rhine, with Colonel Sutpen as Faust and Charles Bon as Manfred. Then slowly it dawns on you that most of the characters and incidents have a double meaning; that besides their place in the story, they also serve as symbols or metaphors with a general application. Sutpen's great design, the land he stole from the Indians, the French architect who built his house with the help of wild Negroes from the jungle, the woman of mixed blood whom he married and disowned, the unacknowledged son who ruined him, the poor white whom he wronged and who killed him in anger, the final destruction of his mansion like the downfall of a social order: all these might belong to a tragic fable of Southern history. With a little cleverness, the whole novel might be explained as a connected and logical allegory, but this, I think, would be going beyond the author's intention. First of all he was writing a story, and one that affected him deeply, but he was also brooding over a social situation. More or less unconsciously, the incidents in the story came to represent the forces and elements in the social situation, since the mind naturally works in terms of symbols and parallels. In Faulkner's case, this form of parallelism is not confined to *Absalom, Absalom!* It can be found in the whole fictional framework that he has been elaborating in novel after novel, until his work has become a myth or legend of the South.

I call it a legend because it is obviously no more intended as a historical account of the country south of the Ohio than *The Scarlet Letter* is intended as a history of Massachusetts Bay or *Paradise Lost* as a factual description of the Fall. Briefly stated, the legend might run something like this: The Deep South was settled partly by aristocrats like the Sartoris clan and partly by new men like Colonel Sutpen. Both types of planters were determined to establish a lasting social order on the land they had seized from the Indians (that is, to leave sons behind them). They had the virtue of living single-mindedly by a fixed code; but there was also an inherent guilt in their "design," their way of life, that put a curse on the land and brought about the Civil War. After the War was lost, partly as a result of their own mad heroism (for who else but men as brave as Jackson and Stuart could have frightened the Yankees into standing together and fighting back?) they tried to restore "the design" by other methods. But they no longer had the strength to achieve more than a partial success, even after they had freed their land from the carpetbaggers who followed the Northern armies. As time passed, moreover, the men of the old order found that they had Southern enemies too: they had to fight against a new exploiting class descended from the landless whites of slavery days. In this struggle between the clan of Sartoris and the unscrupulous tribe of Snopes, the Sartorises were defeated in advance by a traditional code that prevented them from using the weapons of the enemy. But the Snopeses as price of their victory had to serve the mechanized civilization of the North, which was morally impotent in itself, but which, with the aid of its Southern retainers, ended by corrupting the Southern nation. In our own day, the problems of the South are still unsolved, the racial conflict is becoming more acute; and Faulkner's characters in their despairing moments foresee or forebode some catastrophe of which Jim Bond and his like will be the only survivors.

This legend of Faulkner's, if I have stated it correctly, is clearly not a scientific interpretation of Southern history (if such a thing exists); but neither is it the familiar plantation legend that has been embodied in hundreds of romantic novels. Faulkner presents the virtues of the old order as being moral rather than material. There is no baronial pomp in his novels; no profusion of silk and silver, mahogany and moonlight and champagne. The big house on Mr. Hubert Beauchamp's plantation (in *Go Down, Moses*) had a rotted floorboard in the back gallery that Mr. Hubert never got round to having fixed. Visitors used to find him sitting in the springhouse with his boots off and his feet in the water while he drank a morning toddy, which he invited them to share. Visitors to Sutpen's Hundred were offered champagne: it was the best, doubtless, and yet it was "crudely dispensed out of the burlesqued pantomime elegance of Negro butlers who (and likewise the drinkers who gulped it down like neat whiskey between flowery and unsubtle toasts) would have treated lemonade the same way." All the planters lived comfortably, with plenty of servants, but Faulkner never lets us forget that they were living on what had recently been the frontier. What he admires about them is not their wealth or their manners or their fine houses, but rather their

unquestioning acceptance of a moral code that taught them "courage and honor and pride, and pity and love of justice and of liberty." Living with single hearts, they were, says Quentin Compson's father:

. . . people too as we are, and victims too as we are, but victims of a different circumstance, simpler and therefore, integer for integer, larger, more heroic and the figures therefore more heroic too, not dwarfed and involved but distinct, uncomplex, who had the gift of living once or dying once instead of being diffused and scattered creatures drawn blindly limb from limb from a grab bag and assembled, author and victim too of a thousand homicides and a thousand copulations and divorcements.

The old order was a moral order: that was **its** strength and the secret lost by its heirs. But also — and here is another respect in which Faulkner's legend differs from the plantation legend as presented in a novel like *Gone with the Wind* — it bore the moral burden of a guilt so great that the War and even Reconstruction were in some sense a merited punishment. There is madness, but there is a metaphorical meaning too, in Miss Rosa Coldfield's belief that Sutpen was a demon and that his sins were the real reason ". . . why God let us lose the War: that only through the blood of our men and the tears of our women could He stay this demon and efface his name and lineage from the earth." Quentin's father is quite sane, in his sober moments, and yet he expresses almost the same idea about Sutpen's guilt and its consequences. He is telling the story of the Sutpens when he remarks that the Civil War was ". . . a stupid and bloody aberration in the high (and impossible) destiny of the United States, maybe instigated by that family fatality which possessed, along with all circumstance, that curious lack of economy between cause and effect which is always a characteristic of fate when reduced to using human materials."

Colonel Sutpen himself has a feeling, not exactly of guilt, since he has never questioned the rightness of his design, but rather of amazement that so many misfortunes have fallen on him. Sitting in General Compson's office, he goes back over his career, trying to see where he had made his "mistake," for that is what he calls it. Sometimes the author seems to be implying that the sin for which Sutpen and his class are being punished is simply the act of cohabiting with Negroes. But before the end of *Absalom, Absalom!* we learn that miscegenation is only part of it. When Charles Bon's curious actions are explained, we find that he was taking revenge on his father for having refused to recognize him by so much as a single glance. Thus, heartlessness was the "mistake" that had ruined Sutpen, not the taking of a partly Negro wife and Negro concubines. And the point becomes clearer in a long story called *The Bear* (in *Go Down, Moses*), probably the best single piece that Faulkner has written. When Isaac McCaslin is twenty-one, he insists on relinquishing the big plantation that is his by inheritance; he thinks that the land is cursed. It is cursed in his eyes by the deeds of his grandfather: "that evil and unregenerate old man who could summon, because she was his property, a human being because she was old enough and female, to his widower's house and get a child on her and then dismiss her because she was of an inferior race, and then bequeath a thousand dollars to the infant because he would be dead then and wouldn't have to pay it." It follows that the land was cursed — and the War was part of the curse — because its owners had treated human beings as instruments; in a word, it was cursed by slavery.

All through his boyhood, Faulkner must have dreamed of fighting in the Civil War. It was a Sartoris war and not a Snopes war, like the one in which he afterwards risked his life in a foreign army. And yet his sympathies did not wholly lie with the slaveholding clan of Sartoris, even though it was his own clan. The men he most admired and must have pictured himself as resembling were the Southern soldiers — after all, they were the vast majority — who owned no slaves themselves and suffered from the institution of slavery. The men he would praise in his novels were those "who had fought for four years and lost . . . not because they were opposed to freedom as freedom, but for the old reasons for which man (not the generals and politicians but man) has always fought and died in wars: to preserve a status quo or to establish a better future one to endure for his children." You might define his position as that of an anti-slavery Southern nationalist.

His attitude toward Negroes will seem surprising only to Northerners. It seems to have developed from the attitude of the slaveholders, which was often inhuman but never impersonal — that is, the slave might be treated as a domestic animal, but not as a machine or the servant of a machine. Apparently the slaveholding class had little or no feeling of racial animosity. Fred-

erick Law Olmsted, a sharp and by no means a friendly observer, was struck by what he called "the close cohabitation and association of black and white." In his *Journal in the Seaboard Slave States*, the record of his travels in 1853–54, he said: "Negro women are carrying black and white babies together in their arms; black and white children are playing together (not going to school together); black and white faces are constantly thrust together out of doors, to see the train go by." He described the relation between masters and servants as having "a familiarity and closeness of intimacy that would have been noticed with astonishment, if not with manifest displeasure, in almost any chance company at the North." In Faulkner's historical novels, we find this closeness of intimacy compounded with closeness of blood, for the servants are very often the illegitimate half-brothers or sisters of their white companions — not only more often than in life, a mild way of putting it, but also more often than in any Abolitionist tract. He describes the old South as inhabited by two races that lived essentially the same life, if on different levels. Thus, he says in *Absalom, Absalom!* that the young planters were

. . . only in the surface matter of food and clothing and daily occupation any different from the Negro slaves who supported them — the same sweat, the only difference being that on the one hand it went for labor in fields where on the other it went as the price of the spartan and meagre pleasures which were available to them because they did not have to sweat in the fields: the hard violent hunting and riding; the same pleasures: the one, gambling for worn knives and brass jewelry and twists of tobacco and buttons and garments because they happened to be easiest and quickest to hand; on the other for the money and horses, the guns and watches, and for the same reason; the same parties: the identical music from identical instruments, crude fiddles and guitars, now in the big house with candles and silk dresses and champagne, now in dirt-floored cabins with smoking pine knots and calico and water sweetened with molasses.

"They will endure. They are better than we are," Ike McCaslin says of the Negroes, although he finds it more painful to utter this heresy than it is to surrender his plantation. "Stronger than we are," he continues. "Their vices are vices aped from white men or that white men and bondage have taught them: improvidence and intemperance and evasion — not laziness . . . and their virtues are their own: endurance and pity and tolerance and forbearance and fidelity and love of children, whether their own or not or black or not." In Faulkner's novels, the Negroes are an element of stability and endurance, just as the octoroons (like Charles Bon and Joe Christmas) are an element of tragic instability. His favorite characters are the Negro cooks and matriarchs who hold a white family together: Elnora and Dilsey and Clytie and Aunt Mollie Beauchamp. After the Compson family has gone to pieces (in *The Sound and the Fury*), it is Dilsey the cook who endures and is left behind to mourn. Looking up at the square, unpainted house with its rotting portico, she thinks, "Ise seed de first and de last"; and later in the kitchen, looking at the cold stove, "I seed de first en de last."

The increasing hatred between two races is explained in Faulkner's novels partly by the heritage of slavery and Reconstruction; partly by the coming into power of a new class which, so far as it consists of families with landless and slaveless ancestors, has a tradition of hostility to the Negroes. But Faulkner also likes to think that the lynch mobs were often led by the descendants of his old enemies, the carpetbaggers —

. . . that race threefold in one and alien even among themselves save for a single fierce will for rapine and pillage, composed of the sons of middle-aged Quartermaster lieutenants and Army sutlers and contractors in military blankets and shoes and transport mules, who followed the battles they themselves had not fought and inherited the conquest they themselves had not helped to gain . . . and left their bones and in another generation would be engaged in a fierce economic competition of small sloven farms with the black men they were supposed to have freed and the white descendants of fathers who had owned no slaves anyway whom they were supposed to have disinherited, and in the third generation would be back once more in the little lost county seats as barbers and garage mechanics and deputy sheriffs and mill and gin hands and power-plant firemen, leading, first in mufti then later in an actual formalized regalia of hooded sheets and passwords and fiery Christian symbols, lynching mobs against the race their ancestors had come to save.

Faulkner's novels of contemporary Southern life continue the legend into a period that he regards as one of moral confusion and social decay. He is continually seeking in them for violent images to convey his sense of despair. *Sanctuary* is the most violent of all his novels; it is also the most popular and by no means the least important (in spite of Faulkner's comment that it was "a cheap idea . . . deliberately con-

ceived to make money"). The story of Popeye and Temple Drake has more meaning than appears on a first hasty reading — the only reading that most of the critics have been willing to grant it. George Marion O'Donnell went over the novel more carefully and decided that it formed a coherent allegory. Writing in the *Kenyon Review*, he said that the pattern of the allegory was something like this:

Southern Womanhood Corrupted but Undefiled (Temple Drake), in the company of the Corrupted Tradition (Gowan Stevens, a professional Virginian), falls into the clutches of amoral Modernism (Popeye), which is itself impotent, but which with the aid of its strong ally Natural Lust ("Red") rapes Southern Womanhood unnaturally and then seduces her so satisfactorily that her corruption is total, and she becomes the tacit ally of Modernism. Meanwhile Pore White Trash (Goodwin) has been accused of the crime which he, with the aid of the Naif Faithful (Tawmmy), actually tried to prevent. The Formalized Tradition (Horace Benbow), perceiving the true state of affairs, tries vainly to defend Pore White Trash. However, Southern Womanhood is so hopelessly corrupted that she willfully sees Pore White Trash convicted and lynched; she is then carried off by Wealth (Judge Drake) to meaningless escape in European luxury. Modernism, carrying in it from birth its own impotence and doom, submits with masochistic pleasure to its own destruction for the one crime that it has not yet committed — Revolutionary Destruction of Order (the murder of the Alabama policeman, for which the innocent Popeye is executed).

Mr. O'Donnell deserves very great credit as the first critic to discuss Faulkner as a moralist, the first to compare him in passing with Hawthorne, and almost the first to see that he is engaged in creating Southern myths. In his comments on *Sanctuary*, however, he has been entirely too ingenious. There is no doubt that his allegorical scheme can be read into the novel, but it hardly seems possible that the author intended to put it there. Faulkner tells us that *Sanctuary* was written "in about three weeks." It was completely rewritten two years later, in the effort "to make out of it something which would not shame *The Sound and the Fury* and *As I Lay Dying* too much"; but I doubt that Faulkner had or took the time to give every character a double meaning. Lee Goodwin, for example, is not Pore White Trash, capitalized, but a tough, frightened moonshiner dishonorably discharged from the Army. Tawmmy is not the Naif Faithful, capitalized; he is simply faithful and stupid. If

Temple Drake has any symbolic value, she represents the South as a whole, or the younger generation in the South, rather than Southern Womanhood (a phrase that makes Faulkner wince); but it is also quite possible that she represents nothing but a rather silly co-ed. Popeye, however, is another question; and at this point Mr. O'Donnell's reading is not only ingenious but comes very close to Faulkner's conscious or unconscious intention.

Popeye is one of several characters in Faulkner's novels who stand for something that might be called "amoral Modernism," considering that they are creatures of the time and have no social morality whatever; but it might also be called — more accurately, I think — the mechanical civilization that has invaded and partly conquered the South. Popeye is always described in mechanical terms: his eyes "looked like rubber knobs"; his face "just went awry, like the face of a wax doll set too near a hot fire and forgotten"; his tight suit and stiff hat were "all angles, like a modernistic lampshade"; and in general he had "that vicious depthless quality of stamped tin." He was the son of a professional strikebreaker, from whom he inherited syphilis, and the grandson of a pyromaniac. Like two other villains in Faulkner's novels, Joe Christmas and Januarius Jones, he had spent most of his childhood in an institution. He was the man "who made money and had nothing he could do with it, spend it for, since he knew that alcohol would kill him like poison, who had no friends and had never known a woman" — in other words, he was the compendium of all the hateful qualities that Faulkner assigns to finance capitalism. *Sanctuary* is not the connected allegory that Mr. O'Donnell presents in outline (he doesn't approve of allegorical writing by novelists), but neither is it the accumulation of pointless horrors as which it has been dismissed by other critics. It is an example of the Freudian method turned backwards, being full of sexual nightmares that are in reality social symbols. In the author's mind, the novel is somehow connected with what he regards as the rape and corruption of the South.

And the descendants of the old ruling caste, in Faulkner's novels, have the wish but not the courage or the strength of will to prevent this new disaster. They are defeated by Popeye (like Horace Benbow), or they run away from him (like Gowan Stevens, who had gone to school at Virginia and learned to drink like a gentleman,

but not to fight for his principles), or they are robbed and replaced in their positions of influence by the Snopeses (like old Bayard Sartoris, the president of the bank), or they drug themselves with eloquence and alcohol (like Mr. Compson), or they retire into the illusion of being inviolable Southern ladies (like Mrs. Compson, who says, "It can't be simply to flout and hurt me. Whoever God is, He would not permit that. I'm a lady"), or they dwell so much on the past that they are incapable of facing the present (like Reverend Hightower, of *Light in August*, who loses his wife and his church through living in a dream world), or they run from danger to danger (like young Bayard Sartoris) frantically seeking their own destruction. Faulkner's novels are full of well-meaning and even admirable people, not only the grandsons of the cotton aristocracy, but also pine-hill farmers and storekeepers and sewing-machine agents and Negro cooks and sharecroppers; but they are almost all of them defeated by circumstances and they carry with them a sense of their own doom.

They also carry, whether heroes or villains, a curious sense of submission to their fate. "There is not one of Faulkner's characters," says André Gide in his dialogue on *The New American Novelists*, "who, properly speaking, has a soul"; and I think he means that not one of them exercises the faculty of conscious choice between good and evil. They are haunted, obsessed, driven forward by some inner necessity. Like Miss Rosa Coldfield (in *Absalom, Absalom!*), they exist in "that dream state in which you run without moving from a terror in which you cannot believe, toward a safety in which you have no faith." Or, like the slaves freed by General Sherman's army (in *The Unvanquished*), they follow the roads toward any river, believing that it will be their Jordan:

They were singing, walking along the road singing, not even looking to either side. The dust didn't even settle for two days, because all that night they still passed; we sat up listening to them, and the next morning every few yards along the road would be the old ones who couldn't keep up any more, sitting or lying down and even crawling along, calling to the others to help them; and the others — the young strong ones — not stopping, not even looking at them. "Going to Jordan," they told me. "Going to cross Jordan."

All Faulkner's characters, black and white, are

a little like that. They dig for gold frenziedly after they have lost their hope of finding it (like Henry Armstid in *The Hamlet* and Lucas Beauchamp in *Go Down, Moses*); or they battle against and survive a Mississippi flood for the one privilege of returning to the state prison farm (like the tall convict in *The Wild Palms*); or, a whole family together, they carry a body through flood and fire and corruption to bury it in the cemetery at Jefferson (like the Bundrens in *As I Lay Dying*); or they tramp the roads week after week in search of men who had promised to marry them (like Lena Grove, the pregnant woman of *Light in August*); or, pursued by a mob, they turn at the end to meet and accept death (like Joe Christmas in the same novel). Even when they seem to be guided by a conscious design, like Colonel Sutpen, it is not something they have chosen by an act of will, but something that has taken possession of them: ". . . not what he wanted to do but what he just had to do, had to do it whether he wanted to or not, because if he did not do it he knew that he could never live with himself for the rest of his life." In the same way, Faulkner himself writes, not what he wants to, but what he just has to write whether he wants to or not. And the effect produced on us by all these haunted characters, described in hypnagogic prose, is that of myths or fairy tales or dreams, where again the people act under compulsion, toward fatally predetermined ends.

In addition to being a fatalist, Faulkner is also an idealist, more strongly so than any other American writer of our time. The idealism disguises itself as its own opposite, but that is because he is deeply impressed by and tends to exaggerate the contrast between the life around him and the ideal picture in his mind. No other American writer makes such a use of negative turns of speech: his stories abound in words like "paintless," "lightless," "windowless," "not-feeling," "unvisioned." He speaks of "that *roadless* and even *pathless* waste of *unfenced* fallow and wilderness jungle — *no* barn, *no* stable, *not so much as* a hen-coop; just a log cabin built by hand and *no* clever hand either, a meagre pile of clumsily cut firewood sufficient for about one day and *not even* a gaunt hound to come bellowing out from under the house when he rode up." In the same story (*The Bear*), he speaks of ". . . the empty fields without plow or seed to work them, fenceless against the stock which did not exist within or without the walled stable which likewise was not there." He speaks of faces watching "without alarm, without recognition, without hope," and he speaks of the South under Reconstruction as "a lightless and gutted and empty land." Always in his mind he has an ideal picture of how the land and the people should be — a picture of painted, many-windowed houses, fenced fields, overflowing barns, eyes lighting up with recognition; and always, being honest, he measures that picture against the land and people he has seen. And both pictures are not only physical but moral; for always in the background of his novels is a sense of moral standards and a feeling of outrage at their being violated or simply pushed aside. Seeing little hope in the future, he turns to the past, where he hopes to discover a legendary and recurrent pattern that will illuminate and lend dignity to the world about him. So it is that Reverend Hightower, dying in the dingy ruin of his plans, sees a vision of Bedford Forrest's troopers, who lived without question by a single and universally accepted code:

He hears above his heart the thunder increase, myriad and drumming. Like a long sighing of wind in trees it begins, then they sweep into sight, borne now upon a cloud of phantom dust. They rush past, forwardleaning in the saddles, with brandished arms, beneath whipping ribbons from slanted and eager lances; with tumult and soundless yelling they sweep past like a tide whose crest is jagged with the wild heads of horses and the brandished arms of men like the crater of the world in explosion. They rush past, are gone; the dust swirls skyward sucking, fades away into the night which has fully come. Yet, leaning forward in the window . . . it seems to him that he still hears them: the wild bugles and the clashing sabres and the dying thunder of hooves.

THREE POETS

William Carlos Williams
[1883–   ]

William Carlos Williams was born in New Jersey, took the M.D. degree at Pennsylvania, and, while practicing medicine, published many small volumes of verse, *Complete Collected Poems 1906–1938*, *Paterson*, 1951, etc.

Tract
(w. 1916)

This poem flouts conventional poetic form and achieves a tone of bluff independence and colloquial vigor appropriate to its statement. It is written in "free verse": the lines do not rhyme and they do not contain an equal number of syllables. They nevertheless fit a carefully controlled rhythm. Read the poem aloud and listen for the rhythm of the dominant accents.

The poet holds forth against the polite, formal elegance of funerals. Do you think the funeral decorations which he suggests are more appropriate or more sincere? How do lines 63–67 help define the poet's attitude toward grief and mourning?

I will teach you my townspeople
how to perform a funeral —
for you have it over a troop
of artists —
unless one should scour the world —   5
you have the ground sense necessary.

See! the hearse leads.
I begin with a design for a hearse.
For Christ's sake not black —
nor white either — and not polished!   10
Let it be weathered — like a farm wagon —

with gilt wheels (this could be
applied fresh at small expense)
or no wheels at all:
a rough dray to drag over the ground.   15

Knock the glass out!
My God — glass, my townspeople!
For what purpose? Is it for the dead
to look out or for us to see
how well he is housed or to see   20
the flowers or the lack of them —
or what?
To keep the rain and snow from him?
He will have a heavier rain soon:
pebbles and dirt and what not.   25
Let there be no glass —
and no upholstery! phew!
and no little brass rollers
and small easy wheels on the bottom —
my townspeople what are you thinking of!   30

A rough plain hearse then
with gilt wheels and no top at all.
On this the coffin lies
by its own weight. No wreaths please —
especially no hot-house flowers.   35
Some common memento is better,
something he prized and is known by:
his old clothes — a few books perhaps —
God knows what! You realize
how we are about these things,   40
my townspeople —
something will be found — anything —
even flowers if he had come to that.
So much for the hearse.

For heaven's sake though see to the driver!   45
Take off the silk hat! In fact
that's no place at all for him
up there unceremoniously
dragging our friend out to his own dignity!
Bring him down — bring him down!   50
Low and inconspicuous! I'd not have him ride

on the wagon at all — damn him —
the undertaker's understrapper!
Let him hold the reins
and walk at the side   55
and inconspicuously too!

Then briefly as to yourselves:
Walk behind — as they do in France,
seventh class, or if you ride
Hell take curtains! Go with some show   60
of inconvenience; sit openly —
to the weather as to grief.
Or do you think you can shut grief in?
What — from us? We who have perhaps
nothing to lose? Share with us   65
share with us — it will be money
in your pockets.
                    Go now
I think you are ready.

The Yachts

(1935)

This poem begins (lines 1–15) with accurate,
compact objective description. Then (lines 15–18) it
gives a first subjective impression of the yachts as
images of certain gay qualities of experience. The
poem becomes increasingly subjective as it moves to
the impression at the end (lines 25–33), where the
sea is no longer formidable and merciless (as it was
in lines 1–5), but an image of the suffering which
must support the luxurious, scintillant gaiety of the
yachts. Our vision has been reversed.

Contend in a sea which the land partly en-
        closes
shielding them from the too heavy blows
of an ungoverned ocean which when it chooses
tortures the biggest hulls, the best man knows
to pit against its beatings, and sinks them piti-
        lessly.   5
Mothlike in mists, scintillant in the minute

brilliance of cloudless days, with broad bellying
        sails
they glide to the wind tossing green water
from their sharp prows while over them the
        crew crawls

ant-like, solicitously grooming them, releasing,
making fast as they turn, lean far over and hav-
        ing   11
caught the wind again, side by side, head for
        the mark.
In a well guarded arena of open water sur-
        rounded by
lesser and greater craft which, sycophant, lum-
        bering

and flittering follow them they appear youthful,
        rare   15
as the light of a happy eye, live with the grace
of all that in the mind is feckless, free and
naturally to be desired. Now the sea which
        holds them

is moody, lapping their glossy sides, as if feeling
for some slightest flaw but fails completely.   20
Today no race. Then the wind comes again.
        The yachts

move, jockeying for a start, the signal is set and
        they
are off. Now the waves strike at them but they
        are too
well made, they slip through, though they take
        in canvas.

Arms with hands grasping seek to clutch at the
        prows.   25
Bodies thrown recklessly in the way are cut
        aside.
It is a sea of faces about them in agony, in
        despair

until the horror of the race dawns staggering
        the mind,
the whole sea becomes an entanglement of
        watery bodies
lost to the world, bearing what they cannot hold.
        Broken   30

beaten, desolate, reaching from the dead to be
        taken up
they cry out, failing, failing! their cries rising
in waves still as the skillful yachts pass over.

Marianne Moore [1887–

Born in St. Louis and educated at Bryn Mawr, Marianne Moore was an editor of *The Dial* from 1925 to 1929, and became the author of small volumes of verse (beginning 1921) brought together in *Collected Poems* (1951).

The Steeple-Jack
(1932)

The poet finds in a seaport town a certain quality of light and line, a certain formality, which is characteristic of the paintings of the German artist, Albrecht Dürer, and illustrates it with many sharply perceived concrete details. Then the poet ascribes to the town an order, "an elegance of which the source is not bravado," and assigns certain qualities to life in such a town (lines 38–39, 44–45, 57–61, 65–73). What relationship do you find between these qualities and the concrete visual details?

Dürer would have seen a reason for living
    in a town like this, with eight stranded whales
to look at; with the sweet sea air coming into your house
      on a fine day, from water etched
  with waves as formal as the scales   5
    on a fish.

One by one in two's, in three's, the seagulls keep
    flying back and forth over the town clock,
or sailing around the lighthouse without moving the wings —
      rising steadily with a slight   10
    quiver of the body — or flock
mewing where

a sea the purple of the peacock's neck is
    paled to greenish azure as Dürer changed
the pine green of the Tyrol to peacock blue and guinea   15
gray. You can see a twenty-five-
    pound lobster; and fishnets arranged
to dry. The

whirlwind fife-and-drum of the storm bends the salt
    marsh grass, disturbs stars in the sky and the   20
star on the steeple; it is a privilege to see so
much confusion. Disguised by what
    might seem austerity, the sea-
side flowers and

trees are favoured by the fog so that you have   25
    the tropics at first hand: the trumpet-vine,

fox-glove, giant snap-dragon, a salpiglossis that has
spots and stripes; morning-glories, gourds,
   or moon-vines trained on fishing-twine
at the back   30

door. There are no banyans, frangipani, nor
   jack-fruit trees; nor an exotic serpent
life. Ring lizard and snake-skin for the foot, or crocodile;
but here they've cats, not cobras, to
   keep down the rats. The diffident   35
little newt

with white pin-dots on black horizontal spaced
   out bands lives here; yet there is nothing that
ambition can buy or take away. The college student
named Ambrose sits on the hillside   40
   with his not-native books and hat
and sees boats

at sea progress white and rigid as if in
   a groove. Liking an elegance of which
the source is not bravado, he knows by heart the antique   45
sugar-bowl-shaped summer-house of
   interlacing slats, and the pitch
of the church

spire, not true, from which a man in scarlet lets
   down a rope as a spider spins a thread;
he might be part of a novel, but on the sidewalk a   50
sign says C. J. Poole, Steeple Jack,
   in black and white; and one in red
and white says

Danger. The church portico has four fluted   55
   columns, each a single piece of stone, made
modester by white-wash. This would be a fit haven for
waifs, children, animals, prisoners,
   and presidents who have repaid
sin-driven   60

senators by not thinking about them. There
   are a school-house, a post-office in a
store, fish-houses, hen-houses, a three-masted
   schooner on
the stocks. The hero, the student,   65
   the steeple-jack, each in his way,
is at home.

It could not be dangerous to be living
   in a town like this, of simple people,
      star of David, star of Bethlehem,
while he is gilding the solid-   70
   pointed star, which on a steeple
stands for hope.

In Distrust of Merits
(1944)

🐾 This poem describes the poet's personal relationship to the war which is being fought by her countrymen. Note that she describes the enemy as "the blind man who thinks he sees." Compare to this, and to lines 28–33, 75–78, Yeats's lines:

> "The best lack all conviction, while the worst
> Are full of passionate intensity."

The enemy in this war (and perhaps in all wars) is actually within us. The soldiers, by their sacrifice, by their reaffirmation of eternal Christian values, do not defeat him for us, but give us the opportunity to defeat him for ourselves. It is to the definition of this "inward" war that the poem is devoted.

Re-read the poem in the light of the last two lines in order to account for the strong emotion of the speaker.

Strengthened to live, strengthened to die for medals
      and position victories?
They're fighting, fighting, fighting the blind man
     who thinks he sees, —
who cannot see that the enslaver is
enslaved; the hater, harmed. O shining O
    firm star, O tumultuous   **5**
      ocean lashed till small things go
    as they will, the mountainous
      wave makes us who look, know

depth. Lost at sea before they fought! O
    star of David, star of Bethlehem,   **10**
O black imperial lion
    of the Lord — emblem
of a risen world — be joined at last, be
joined. There is hate's crown beneath which all is
      death; there's love's without which none   **15**
        is king; the blessed deeds bless
    the halo. As contagion
      of sickness makes sickness,

contagion of trust can make trust. They're
    fighting in deserts and caves, one by   **20**
one, in battalions and squadrons;
    they're fighting that I
may yet recover from the disease, My
Self; some have it lightly, some will die. "Man's
      wolf to man" and we devour   **25**
      ourselves. The enemy could not
    have made a greater breach in our
      defenses. One pilot-

ing a blind man can escape him, but
    Job disheartened by false comfort knew   **30**
that nothing can be so defeating
    as a blind man who

can see. O alive who are dead, who are
proud not to see, O small dust of the earth
   that walks so arrogantly,   35
      trust begets power and faith is
   an affecting thing. We
     vow, we make this promise

to the fighting — it's a promise — "We'll
   never hate black, white, red, yellow, Jew,   40
Gentile, Untouchable." We are
   not competent to
make our vows. With set jaw they are fighting,
fighting, fighting, — some we love whom we know,
   some we love but know not — that   45
     hearts may feel and not be numb.
   It cures me; or am I what
    I can't believe in? Some

in snow, some on crags, some in quicksands,
   little by little, much by much, they   50
are fighting fighting fighting that where
   there was death there may
be life. "When a man is prey to anger,
he is moved by outside things; when he holds
   his ground in patience patience   55
     patience, that is action or
   beauty," the soldier's defense
    and hardest armor for

the fight. The world's orphans' home. Shall
   we never have peace without sorrow?   60
without pleas of the dying for
   help that won't come? O
quiet form upon the dust, I cannot
look and yet I must. If these great patient
   dyings — all these agonies   65
    and woundbearings and bloodshed —
   can teach us how to live, these
    dyings were not wasted.

Hate-hardened heart, O heart of iron,
   iron is iron till it is rust.
There never was a war that was   70
   not inward; I must
fight till I have conquered in myself what
causes war, but I would not believe it.
   I inwardly did nothing.
    O Iscariotlike crime!   75
   Beauty is everlasting
    and dust is for a time.

Ɛ. Ɛ. Cummings [1894–   ]

"e. e. cummings" was born in Cambridge, Mass., educated at Harvard, served in the war, lived in Paris after 1920, later in New York, and published *The Enormous Room* (among the best prose books of the war), and then small volumes of verse eventually assembled in *Poems 1923–1954*.

20

❧ Cummings, like Emily Dickinson earlier, employs images which are not "realistic," which cannot be visualized. Note, for example, the curious combination of concrete and abstract diction in the phrase, "the petal of somewhere." Poetry can communicate, of course, even when it cannot be paraphrased; indeed, it can never be wholly paraphrased. How successfully do the images of this poem communicate the emotional quality of the poet's experience?

a wind has blown the rain away and blown
the sky away and all the leaves away,
and the trees stand. I think i too have known
autumn too long
        (and what have you to say,   5
wind wind wind—did you love somebody
and have you the petal of somewhere in your heart
pinched from dumb summer?
                  O crazy daddy
of death dance cruelly for us and start   10

the last leaf whirling in the final brain
of air!) Let us as we have seen see
doom's integration . . . . a wind has blown the rain

away and the leaves and the sky and the   15
trees stand:
        the trees stand. The trees,
suddenly wait against the moon's face.

30

❧ This is a simple poem, but note what happens in line 20. How well does the diction throughout catch the point of view of childhood?

       in Just-
       spring   when the world is mud-
       luscious the little
       lame balloonman

whistles   far   and wee   5

and eddieandbill come
running from marbles and
piracies and it's
spring

when the world is puddle-wonderful   10

the queer
old balloonman whistles
far   and   wee
and bettyandisbel come dancing

from hop-scotch and jump-rope and   15

it's
spring
and
       the

           goat-footed   20

balloonMan   whistles
far
and
wee

31

(1923)

This poem talks of the death of Buffalo Bill with a dashing
irreverence appropriate to the way of life of such a man — a
way of life which the diction, the meter, the typography, and
the images all combine to epitomize in a single characteristic
glimpse of Buffalo Bill on horseback, dashing onstage and off.
Do the other selections from Cummings display similar unity
and concentration?

Buffalo Bill's
defunct
      who used to
      ride a watersmooth-silver
                stallion   5
and break onetwothreefourfive pigeonsjustlikethat
                                    Jesus

he was a handsome man
                   and what i want to know is
how do you like your blueeyed boy   10
Mister Death

225

(1931)

❧ In this poem Cummings' diction is again faintly reminiscent of Emily Dickinson. In a way not wholly paraphrasable the poet describes the power held over him by another person. How do the images develop the paradox of strength-in-fragility?

somewhere i have never travelled,gladly beyond
any experience,your eyes have their silence:
in your most frail gesture are things which enclose me,
or which i cannot touch because they are too near

your slightest look easily will unclose me   5
though i have closed myself as fingers,
you open always petal by petal myself as Spring opens
(touching skilfully,mysteriously)her first rose

or if your wish be to close me,i and
my life will shut very beautifully,suddenly,   10
as when the heart of this flower imagines
the snow carefully everywhere descending;

nothing which we are to perceive in this world equals
the power of your intense fragility:whose texture
compels me with the colour of its countries,   15
rendering death and forever with each breathing

(i do not know what it is about you that closes
and opens;only something in me understands
the voice of your eyes is deeper than all roses)
nobody,not even the rain,has such small hands   20

312

may my heart always be open to little
birds who are the secrets of living
whatever they sing is better than to know
and if men should not hear them men are old

may my mind stroll about hungry   5
and fearless and thirsty and supple
and even if it's sunday may i be wrong
for whenever men are right they are not young

and may myself do nothing usefully
and love yourself so more than truly   10
there's never been quite such a fool who could fail
pulling all the sky over him with one smile

XXXIX

(1944)

The first eleven lines develop a coherent general statement about the life of the human race. Why does the poet regard this life as winter and the afterlife as spring? The paradoxes of the last three lines provide a kind of climax to this lively poem, but are they meaningful? Do they seem characteristic of Cummings?

all ignorance toboggans into know
and trudges up to ignorance again:
but winter's not forever,even snow
melts;and if spring should spoil the game,what then?

all history's a winter sport or three: 5
but were it five,i'd still insist that all
history is too small for even me;
for me and you,exceedingly too small.

Swoop(shrill collective myth)into thy grave
merely to toil the scale to shrillerness   10
per every madge and mabel dick and dave
— tomorrow is our permanent address

and there they'll scarcely find us(if they do,
we'll move away still further:into now

SELECTED BIBLIOGRAPHY

The bibliographical suggestions in the text, labeled "Further Reading," are intended to encourage students both to read more of the primary material than the limited space of an anthology permits and to consult especially relevant secondary works of biography or criticism. For those who wish to pursue still further a critical study of the literature, the following highly selective bibliography has been compiled.

General Reference and Background

For extensive bibliographies of American letters, see the listings in R. E. Spiller and others, eds., *Literary History of the United States*, III (1948) and A. H. Quinn and others, eds., *The Literature of the American People* (1951). On twentieth-century authors the most complete listing is F. B. Millett, *Contemporary American Authors: A Critical Survey and 219 Bio-bibliographies* (1940). Another authoritative work, still in progress, is the *Bibliography of American Literature* (1955–), ed. J. Blanck.

Valuable for biographical entries are J. D. Hart, *The Oxford Companion to American Literature* (1948; revised 1956) and the *Dictionary of American Biography*, 20 vols., ed. A. Johnson and D. Malone (1928–36; 2 suppl. vols. 1944, 1958). For periodical articles and essays on individual authors and limited aspects of their work, Lewis Leary, ed., *Articles on American Literature Appearing in Current Periodicals, 1900–1950* (1954) is an indispensable source, though not annotated. Its use should be supplemented, for more recent articles, by the "American Bibliography" published annually in *Publications of the Modern Language Association* and by "Articles on American Literature Appearing in Current Periodicals" to be found in every issue of the quarterly magazine *American Literature*. For extensive and critically annotated entries on major American writers (Emerson to Henry James), F. Stovall, ed., *Eight American Authors: A Review of Research and Criticism* (1956) is recommended highly for its completeness and judicial tone.

The student should have access to a good, brief guide to American history, such as R. B. Morris, ed., *Encyclopedia of American History* (1953) or the *Harvard Guide to American History* (1954), ed. O. Handlin and others, which covers many aspects and issues of importance to the student of literature. An excellent general history is S. E. Morison and H. S. Commager, *The Growth of the American Republic*, 2 vols. (revised 1950).

LITERARY HISTORY *

American Writers Series, H. H. Clark, general editor, 1934– , contains 28 volumes, each devoted to a single author (occasionally to a school or regional

* For comprehensive period studies, see the first paragraph under each period heading, pp. 1208ff., below.

group) and is notable for full historical-critical introductions, chronologies, and bibliographies.

Blair, Walter, *Native American Humor*, 1937. History and selections from the beginnings to 1900; historical introduction.

Clark, H. H., ed., *Transitions in American Literary History*, 1954. Contains chapters of joint authorship on each of the major phases of literary and intellectual history; detailed notes.

Parrington, V. L., *Main Currents in American Thought: An Interpretation of American Literature from the Beginnings to 1920*, 3 vols., 1927–30. Ideas and literature from the socio-economic point of view; skillful and important.

Quinn, A. H., ed. (and others), *The Literature of the American People, An Historical and Critical Survey*, 1951. A recent, complete history; thorough bibliographies, critical as well as descriptive.

Spiller, R., ed. (and others), *Literary History of the United States*, 3 vols., 1948. Includes chapters on many aspects of the subject as well as on major writers. The third volume is entirely bibliography. Available in one volume, minus bibliography.

LITERARY TYPES

POETRY

Blackmur, R. P., *Form and Value in Modern Poetry*, 1957.

Bogan, L., *Achievement in American Poetry, 1900–1950*, 1951.

Clark, H. H., ed., *Major American Poets*, 1934. Anthology with full critical and historical annotations; from Freneau to Frost.

Deutsch, Babette, *Poetry in Our Time*, 1956.

Friar, K., and J. M. Brinnin, eds., *Modern Poetry: American and British*, 1951. Detailed interpretive notes, especially helpful on Pound and Eliot.

Gregory, H., and M. Zaturenska, *A History of American Poetry, 1900–1940*, 1946.

Kreymborg, A., *A History of American Poetry*, 1934. From the beginnings to the present; a general history.

O'Connor, W. V., *Sense and Sensibility in Modern Poetry*, 1948.

Poetry Explication: A Checklist of Interpretations since 1925, compiled by G. Arms and J. M. Kunitz,

1950. A valuable guide to critical interpretations of many difficult poems from all periods.

Stedman, E. C., *Poets of America*, 1885. A standard authority on the earlier poets.

Weirick, B., *From Whitman to Sandburg in American Poetry: A Critical Survey*, 1924.

PROSE FICTION

Beach, J. W., *American Fiction, 1920–1940*, 1941. A study of eight contemporary writers.

Brown, H. R., *The Sentimental Novel in America, 1789–1860*, 1940.

Chase, R., *The American Novel and Its Tradition*, 1957. An interpretation and history in terms of realism and romance, Charles Brockden Brown to William Faulkner.

Cowie, A., *The Rise of the American Novel*, 1948. Full chapters on the major novelists from the beginnings to 1900.

Cowley, M., ed., *After the Genteel Tradition: American Writers since 1910*, 1937. Estimates, by a number of critics, on the major novelists of the period covered; anti-Victorianism is the theme.

Geismar, M., *Rebels and Ancestors: The American Novel, 1890–1915*, 1953; and *Writers in Crisis: The American Novel between Two Wars*, 1942.

Kazin, A., *On Native Grounds: An Interpretation of Modern American Prose Literature*, 1942, revised 1955. Historical and critical in method, it extends from Howells to the present.

Leisy, E. E., *The American Historical Novel*, 1950.

Quinn, A. H., *American Fiction: An Historical and Critical Survey*, 1936. Detailed summaries, inclusive history of the subject, but needs to be balanced by recent critical appraisals.

Taylor, W. F., *The Economic Novel in America*, 1942. Sound and thorough to date of publication.

Van Doren, C., *The American Novel*, 1921, revised 1940. Useful as a reference; touches on major movements and figures.

CRITICISM

Brooks, C., and R. P. Warren, *Understanding Poetry*, 1938, revised 1950. Selections and critical essays in the analytical technique of the "new criticism."

Brown, C. A., ed., *The Achievement of American Criticism*, 1954. Representative essays from the whole field, with interpretive introductions.

Burke, K., *The Philosophy of Literary Form*, 1941. Literature as "symbolic action."

De Mille, G. E., *Literary Criticism in America: A Preliminary Survey*, 1931. A partial history of the subject.

Foerster, N., *American Criticism*, 1928. Detailed essays on major nineteenth-century critics from the humanist point of view.

Hyman, S. E., *The Armed Vision: A Study in the Methods of Modern Literary Criticism*, 1948, revised 1955. Detailed and critical chapters on the recent critics and their techniques.

O'Connor, W. V., *An Age of Criticism, 1900–1950*, 1952. Historical survey of the subject.

Rahv, P., *Literature in America*, 1957. An anthology of some of the best criticism, with a twentieth-century emphasis.

Ransome, J. C., *The New Criticism*, 1941. Essays on the "new critics," with special emphasis on textual analysis of literature.

Smith, B., *Forces in American Criticism*, 1939. A history of the subject from the social and economic viewpoint.

Stauffer, D. A., ed., *The Intent of the Critic*, 1941. A group of essays representing different critical philosophies.

Stovall, F., ed., *The Development of American Literary Criticism*, 1955. Five chapters of joint authorship cover the history of the subject to about 1930.

Zabel, M. D., *Literary Opinion in America*, 1937, revised 1951. Selections, interpretive introduction, and full bibliographies on the problems of criticism in the present century.

A Guide to Scholarship
Concerning the Authors Represented in "American Poetry and Prose" *

THE PURITAN AGE

The best general literary history of the colonial period as a whole is still M. C. Tyler, *A History of*

* Originally prepared by Roger B. Stein for the Fourth Edition of *American Poetry and Prose* (1957), this guide has been revised to take account of recent scholarship and of the particular scope of this New Shorter Edition.

American Literature During the Colonial Time, 1607–1765, 2 vols. (1878, rev. ed. 1897; reissued in one volume, 1949). K. B. Murdock's *Literature and Theology in Colonial New England* (1949) is an excellent, concise survey of the first century. P. Miller, *The New England Mind: The Seventeenth Century* (1939) is an authoritative study of the period, with emphasis on intellectual history; see especially chs. XI and XII for the rationale behind Puritan literature.

S. E. Morison, *Intellectual Life in Colonial New England* (1956) has basic material. V. L. Parrington's *The Colonial Mind, 1620–1800* (1927; vol. I of *Main Currents in American Thought*) is excellent, if used with awareness of its socioeconomic orientation, and is available in a paperback edition. For the southern writers, see L. B. Wright, *The First Gentlemen of Virginia* (1940). For individual authors the following studies are useful:

For WILLIAM BRADFORD see W. Walker, *Ten New England Leaders* (1901), pp. 3–45, and G. F. Willison, *Saints and Strangers* (1945), an account of the Plymouth colony.

The standard life of JOHN WINTHROP is still R. C. Winthrop, *Life and Letters of John Winthrop*, 2 vols. (1864–67). Cotton Mather has an account of Winthrop in his *Magnalia Christi Americana*, Bk. II, ch. IV. The *Winthrop Papers*, 5 vols. (1927–47), is the definitive edition of Winthrop's Journal and other papers.

The account of ANNE BRADSTREET by Lyon Richardson in the *Dictionary of American Biography* can be supplemented by the old full-length study by H. S. Campbell, *Anne Bradstreet and Her Times* (1891). A recent study is E. W. White, "The Tenth Muse — A Tercentenary Appraisal of Anne Bradstreet," *William & Mary Quarterly*, VIII (1951), pp. 355–377.

The poetry of EDWARD TAYLOR is examined critically and in relation to other Puritan poets in K. B. Murdock, *Literature and Theology*, ch. V. Among articles on Taylor are H. Blau, "Heaven's Sugar Cake: Theology and Imagery in the Poetry of Edward Taylor," *New England Quarterly*, XXVI (1953), pp. 337–360, and N. Wright, "The Morality Tradition in the Poetry of Edward Taylor," *American Literature*, XVIII (1946), pp. 1–17. Also Austin Warren, "Edward Taylor's Poetry: Colonial Baroque," in *Rage for Order* (1948).

On JONATHAN EDWARDS there is O. E. Winslow's narrative biography, *Jonathan Edwards: 1703–1758* (1940), and P. Miller's *Jonathan Edwards* (1949) which combines biographical material with a critical analysis of Edwards' ideas. For Edwards' thought, see also C. H. Faust and T. H. Johnson, eds., *Jonathan Edwards: Representative Selections* (1935), especially the critical introduction. P. Miller's introduction to his edition of *Images or Shadows of Divine Things* (1948), in treating the history and significance of that work, suggests the relationship of Edwards' thought to Emerson and transcendentalism. E. H. Cady, "The Artistry of Jonathan Edwards," *New England Quarterly*, XXII (1949), pp. 61–72, is a good literary analysis.

For JOHN WOOLMAN see W. L. Sperry, "The Journal of John Woolman," in *Strangers and Pilgrims: Studies in Classics of Christian Devotion* (1939), and John Greenleaf Whittier's introduction

to *The Journal of John Woolman* (1871). Also G. M. Trevelyan, "John Woolman, the Quaker," in *Clio, a Muse, and Other Essays* (1913).

WILLIAM BYRD as diarist is the subject of L. B. Wright and M. Tinling, "William Byrd of Westover, an American Pepys," *South Atlantic Quarterly*, XXXIX (1940), pp. 259–274. The same authors have published *The Secret Diary of William Byrd of Westover, 1709–1712* (1941).

THE NEO–CLASSIC AGE

❧ M. C. Tyler, *The Literary History of the American Revolution, 1763–1783*, 2 vols. (1897; reissued in facsimile, 1941), is still the standard work on the period. L. Howard, *The Connecticut Wits* (1943) treats broad currents of thought of the time, as well as the individuals of the Hartford group. Since purely literary studies of the neo-classic age are few, the student is referred to the general literary histories and the special studies of major writers, some of which are suggested below:

BENJAMIN FRANKLIN: C. Becker's sketch in the *Dictionary of American Biography* is an excellent brief account of Franklin's life and work. F. L. Mott and C. E. Jorgensen, eds., *Benjamin Franklin: Representative Selections* (1936) has a sound critical introduction and thorough bibliography. For a comparison of Franklin and Edwards, see F. Davidson, "Three Patterns of Living," in *AAUP Bulletin*, XXXIV (1948), pp. 364–374. See also the interesting selection of essays on Franklin in C. L. Sanford, ed., *Benjamin Franklin and the American Character* in the Problems in American Civilization Series (1955).

CRÈVECOEUR receives penetrating analysis in D. H. Lawrence, *Studies in Classic American Literature* (1922), ch. III. H. N. Smith, *Virgin Land* (1950), Bk. III, considers Crèvecoeur's contribution to ideas about the American West. The literature of foreign residents and travelers in America is very large and often very rewarding. Two good collections of travelers' accounts are O. Handlin, ed., *This Was America* (1949), and H. S. Commager, ed., *America in Perspective* (1947).

A detailed analysis of THOMAS PAINE is in H. H. Clark, ed., *Thomas Paine: Representative Selections* (1944); see the introduction. M. D. Conway, *The Life of Thomas Paine* (1892) is a substantial biography. See also the sketch in the *Dictionary of American Biography*. For Paine's literary theory and religious thought there are two essays by H. H. Clark: "Thomas Paine's Theories of Rhetoric," *Wis. Acad. Transactions*, XXVIII (1933), pp. 307–339, and "An Historical Interpretation of Thomas Paine's Religion," *Univ. of Calif. Chron.*, XXXV (1933), pp. 56–87.

Two studies of THOMAS JEFFERSON which emphasize his ideas and literary quality are C. Becker, *The Declaration of Independence* (1922), a good account of the style and background of that document, and K. Lehrmann, *Thomas Jefferson: American Humanist* (1947).

A combined approach to HAMILTON and JEFFERSON, with a comparison of their viewpoints, is in F. C. Prescott, ed., *Hamilton and Jefferson: Representative Selections* (1934).

A good biography of PHILIP FRENEAU is L. Leary, *That Rascal Freneau* (1941). See also the sketch in the *Dictionary of American Biography*. P. E. More, "Philip Freneau," in *Shelburne Essays*, 5th series (1908), is still sound. An illuminating critical introduction is provided in H. H. Clark, ed., *Poems of Freneau* (1929).

THE ROMANTIC MOVEMENT

🏴 Studies of various aspects of the romantic movement are legion. Book-length treatments include F. O. Matthiessen's important study, *American Renaissance: Art and Expression in the Age of Emerson and Whitman* (1941); V. L. Parrington, *The Romantic Revolution in America, 1800–1860* (1927; Vol. II of *Main Currents in American Thought*); and G. Boas, *Romanticism in America* (1940), a symposium. Briefer accounts are R. P. Adams, "Romanticism and the American Renaissance," *American Literature* (Jan., 1952) and P. Kaufman, "The Romantic Movement," in N. Foerster, ed., *The Reinterpretation of American Literature* (1928; reissued 1959). See several chapters in H. H. Clark, ed., *Transitions in American Literary History* (1954).

WASHINGTON IRVING: A good account by a contemporary is William Cullen Bryant, *A Discourse on the Life . . . of Washington Irving* (1860). For a more recent life, see that by S. T. Williams, 2 vols. (1935). An interesting essay on Irving's famous story is J. B. Thompson, "The Genesis of the Rip Van Winkle Legend," *Harper's Magazine* (Sept., 1883), pp. 617–622.

JAMES FENIMORE COOPER: A biography discussing briefly many of Cooper's novels is J. Grossman, *James Fenimore Cooper* (1949). Cooper's attitude towards the West is subject to penetrating analysis in H. N. Smith, *Virgin Land* (1950), especially ch. VI. Two other provocative studies are D. H. Lawrence, *Studies in Classic American Literature* (1922), chs. IV and V, and R. H. Pearce, "The Leatherstocking Tales Re-Examined," *South Atlantic Quarterly*, XLVI (1947), pp. 524–536. Cooper as social critic is treated in introductory notes by both H. L. Mencken and R. Spiller in the latest reprint of *The American Democrat* (1956).

A sound introduction to WILLIAM CULLEN BRYANT is T. McDowell, ed., *William Cullen Bryant: Representative Selections* (1935), introduction and bibliography. Poe reviewed Bryant's poems in the *Southern Literary Messenger* in 1837. More recently, see F. L. Pattee, *Sidelights on American Literature* (1922), pp. 293–326, and W. C. Bryant, II, "The Genesis of Thanatopsis," *New England Quarterly*, XXI (1948), pp. 163–184.

EDGAR ALLAN POE: Critical opinion on Poe has been extremely diverse. A good short discussion is F. O. Matthiessen's chapter on Poe in the *Literary History of the United States* (1948), I, pp. 321–342. J. W. Krutch presents a Freudian thesis in his *Edgar Allan Poe: A Study in Genius* (1926). Baudelaire's perceptive criticism has been translated by L. and F. E. Hyslop, *Baudelaire on Poe* (1952). Two good articles by A. Tate are reprinted in his *The Forlorn Demon* (1953), chs. IV and V. Y. Winters, *In Defense of Reason* (1947), pp. 234–261, is highly critical. Very useful for the understanding of this complex personality are *The Letters of Edgar Allan Poe*, 2 vols. (1948), edited by J. Ostrom. A stimulating psychological study is Marie Bonaparte, *The Life and Works of Edgar Allan Poe, A Psycho-Analytic Interpretation* (1949), with a foreword by Sigmund Freud.

RALPH WALDO EMERSON: F. I. Carpenter, *Emerson Handbook* (1953), is a topical summary and guide to much of the literature on Emerson. A rewarding study of Emerson's ideas, treated synthetically rather than chronologically, is S. Paul, *Emerson's Angle of Vision* (1952). F. O. Matthiessen's treatment of Emerson as artist in *American Renaissance* (1941), pp. 3–175, is one of the best. K. S. Cameron, *Emerson the Essayist*, 2 vols. (1945), contains both criticism and primary materials. Valuable for both Emerson and Thoreau are P. Miller, ed., *The Transcendentalists: An Anthology* (1950), and a special study, A. Christy, *The Orient in American Transcendentalism* (1932).

HENRY DAVID THOREAU: J. W. Krutch, *Henry David Thoreau* (1948), is biographical and critical. Thoreau is discussed in relation to Emerson in Matthiessen, *American Renaissance*, pp. 3–175. Helpful for a study of *Walden* are G. F. Whicher, *Walden Revisited* (1945), and R. Cook, *Passage to Walden* (1949). A specific study of Thoreau's literary technique is S. Paul, "The Wise Silence: Sound as an Agency of Correspondence in Thoreau," *New England Quarterly*, XXII (1949), pp. 511–527. E. Seybold deals with Thoreau's use of classical literature in her *Thoreau: The Quest and The Classics* (1951).

NATHANIEL HAWTHORNE: A reading of the *American Notebooks*, ed. R. Stewart (1932), is a rewarding background for the stories. A *Study of Hawthorne* (1876) by his son-in-law, G. Lathrop, is still one of the best. Henry James' *Hawthorne* (1879) contains some masterly comment on the novels. Recent analytical criticism of six stories and the four novels is in R. Fogle, *Hawthorne's Fiction: The Light and the Dark* (1952). H. von Abele, *The Death of the Artist* (1955) has a penetrating discussion of the stories in chs. II and III. R. P. Adams has a good discussion of "Hawthorne's Provincial Tales" in the *New England Quarterly*, XXX (1957), pp. 39–57. Hawthorne and Melville are considered in relation to one another in Matthiessen's *American Renaissance*, pp. 179–380. A perceptive study of comparison between Hawthorne and Henry James is M. Bewley, *The Complex Fate* (1952).

HERMAN MELVILLE: On his life, see the year-by-year chronology in J. Leyda, *The Melville Log* (1952), 2 vols., and the illuminating life by L. Howard, *Herman Melville, A Biography* (1951). Critical essays on *Moby Dick* are legion; a sound, book-length interpretation is H. Vincent, *The Trying-Out of Moby Dick* (1949). On *Billy Budd*, see C. R. Anderson, "The Genesis of *Billy Budd*," *American Literature*, XII (1940), pp. 329–346; and E. L. Watson, "Melville's Testament of Acceptance," *New England Quarterly*, VI (1933), pp. 318–326, a good discussion of the symbolism. A critical study of all the works is R. Chase, *Herman Melville* (1949).

JOHN GREENLEAF WHITTIER: For his relation to the anti-slavery movement read T. W. Higginson's *Contemporaries* (1899), pp. 60–71, or a good introductory biography such as G. R. Carpenter, *John Greenleaf Whittier* (1903). V. L. Parrington in *The Romantic Revolution*, pp. 361–370, stresses his reform writing. A collection of Whittier's literary opinions is found in H. H. Clark and E. H. Cady, *Whittier on Writers and Writing* (1950), with a good introduction. For Whittier as a poet, see W. T. Scott, "Poetry in America: a New Consideration of Whittier's Verse," *New England Quarterly*, VII (1934), pp. 258–275.

HENRY WADSWORTH LONGFELLOW: For earlier interpretations, see E. C. Stedman, *Poets of America* (1885), pp. 180–224, and James Russell Lowell, *The Function of the Poet, and Other Essays* (ed. A. Mordell, 1920), pp. 115–126. Significant revaluations include H. M. Jones, "The Longfellow Nobody Knows," *Outlook*, vol. 149 (1928), pp. 577–579 and 586, and Lawrance Thompson, *Young Longfellow, 1807–1843* (1938). A recent extended study is E. Wagenknecht, *Longfellow* (1955).

JAMES RUSSELL LOWELL: Interesting early estimates of Lowell include those of Henry James in *Essays in London and Elsewhere* (1893), pp. 44–80, and W. D. Howells, *Literary Friends and Acquaintances* (1900), pp. 212–250, the latter a warmly personal appreciation. On Lowell's criticism, see the introduction to H. H. Clark and N. Foerster, eds., *James Russell Lowell: Representative Selections* (1947); the most complete and rounded study of Lowell in all phases, this useful edition has ample selections and an extensive bibliography. J. Tandy, *Crackerbox Philosophers in American Humor and Satire* (1925)

discusses *The Biglow Papers* in their relation to native humor.

WALT WHITMAN: For direct comment on and analysis of "Song of Myself" and other major poems, see G. W. Allen, *Walt Whitman Handbook* (1946), especially ch. II on the growth and structure of *Leaves of Grass*. Also on this subject read C. F. Strauch, "The Structure of Walt Whitman's 'Song of Myself,'" *English Journal*, XXVII (1938), pp. 597–607. G. W. Allen and C. T. Davis, eds., *Walt Whitman's Poems* (1955) provides notes and critical aids. The development of the poems in successive editions of *Leaves of Grass* was studied by F. Schyberg in his *Walt Whitman* (1933), since translated by E. Allen (1951). F. Stovall's "Main Drifts in Whitman's Poetry," *American Literature*, IV (1932), pp. 3–21, is a sound exegesis of the main ideas of Whitman. R. Chase, *Walt Whitman Reconsidered* (1955) is a recent critical study.

ABRAHAM LINCOLN: R. P. Basler's one-volume *Abraham Lincoln: His Speeches and His Writings* (1946) has a good critical introduction. *The Lincoln Reader*, ed. P. M. Angle (1947), is a selection of key chapters from a number of biographies of Lincoln. Carl Sandburg's chapter in Spiller, *Literary History of the United States*, is a brief statement distilled from his longer works on Lincoln. A useful and available study is B. P. Thomas, *Abraham Lincoln* (1952).

SOUTHERN POETS: Both TIMROD and LANIER are discussed fully in the introduction to E. W. Parks, *Southern Poets* (1936). A. H. Starke, *Sidney Lanier* (1933) is a thorough one-volume study (see review of this by R. P. Warren in *American Review*, II (Nov. 1933), pp. 27–45, for a critical view of Lanier's poetry). A volume of joint authorship, *I'll Take My Stand: The South and the Agrarian Tradition* (1930) elucidates the position of modern Southern critics. Also note M. J. Moses, *The Literature of the South* (1910).

THE RISE OF REALISM

The social and economic backgrounds of the post-Civil War years are characterized in V. L. Parrington, *The Beginnings of Critical Realism in America, 1860–1920* (1930; vol. III of *Main Currents in American Thought*), especially the chapter called "The Great Barbecue." The literary origins of realism are traced in R. P. Falk, "The Rise of Realism, 1870–1890," in H. H. Clark, ed., *Transitions in American Literary History* (1954). Mark Twain's novel *The Gilded Age* (1874) described some of the aspects of the 1870's and suggested to historians a name for the era. See C. A. and M. R. Beard, *The Rise of Ameri-*

can Civilization (rev. ed. 1933) for social history, and R. Hofstadter, *Social Darwinism in American Thought, 1860–1915* (1945) for intellectual backgrounds. Literary trends are treated in F. L. Pattee, *A History of American Literature Since 1870* (1915).

FOLKSONGS AND BALLADS: Two good collections edited by J. A. and A. Lomax are *American Ballads and Folksongs* (1934), and *Our Singing Country* (1941). A recent collection, A. B. Friedman, ed., *The Viking Book of Folk Ballads of the English Speaking World* (1956), is particularly interesting in tracing the changes in ballads from England to this country. On folklore in general see M. A. Beckwith, *Folklore in America, Its Scope and Method* (1931).

SAMUEL L. CLEMENS: M. M. Brashear, *Mark Twain, Son of Missouri* (1934) deals with Twain's Western background; K. R. Andrews, *Nook Farm: Mark Twain's Hartford Circle* (1950), with Twain's period of residence in Connecticut. Van W. Brooks, *The Ordeal of Mark Twain* (rev. ed. 1933) has many insights, though it should be read in conjunction with other biographical studies; see those by D. Wecter and B. De Voto. De Voto, in the introduction to his *Mark Twain in Eruption* (1940), discusses the pessimism of Clemens in the 1890's; and in his *Mark Twain at Work* (1942) shows Clemens as literary craftsman, with evidence from unpublished manuscripts of *Huckleberry Finn* and *The Mysterious Stranger*. For recent comment on *Huckleberry Finn*, see H. N. Smith's introduction to the Riverside edition (1958); T. S. Eliot's introduction to the Chanticleer Press edition (1950); and L. Trilling's introduction to the Rinehart edition (1948), later reprinted in *The Liberal Imagination* (1950). Clemens learning his craft is the subject of E. M. Branch, *The Literary Apprenticeship of Mark Twain* (1950), and G. C. Bellamy, *Mark Twain as Literary Artist* (1950). His letters have been collected in two volumes by A. B. Paine. A useful compendium is M. L. Scott, ed., *Mark Twain, Selected Criticism* (1955).

HUMOR AND LOCAL COLOR: The two best historical books on humor are Constance Rourke, *American Humor* (1931), on the themes and backgrounds of the subject, and Walter Blair, *Native American Humor, 1800–1900* (1937), containing a long introduction and selections. Also, types of American humor are traced historically in J. R. Tandy, *Crackerbox Philosophers in American Humor and Satire* (1925). On the local color story, useful comment is found in F. L. Pattee, *A History of American Literature Since 1870* (1915) and *The Development of the American Short Story* (1923). On GEORGE WASHINGTON HARRIS, see the introduction to Brom Weber, ed., *Sut Lovingood* (1954). On BRET HARTE, see J. B. Harrison, ed., *Bret Harte: Representative Selections* (1941) for its detailed introduction and bibliography. JOEL CHANDLER HARRIS is the subject of articles by R. I. Cline, "The Tar-Baby Story," *American Literature*, II (1930), pp. 72–78, and L. Dauner, "Myth and Humor in the Uncle Remus Fables," *American Literature*, XX (1948), pp. 129–143. The only extensive treatment of SARAH ORNE JEWETT is that of F. O. Matthiessen (1929).

WILLIAM DEAN HOWELLS: E. H. Cady's is the most recent biography, in two volumes: *The Road to Realism* (1956) and *The Realist at War* (1958). A good general introduction to Howells' whole career is C. M. and R. Kirk, eds., *William Dean Howells: Representative Selections* (1950). On his novels of social criticism, see G. Arms, "The Literary Background of Howells's Social Criticism," *American Literature*, XIV (1942), pp. 260–276. For an analysis of his literary theory, see E. Carter's article in the *Journal of English Literary History*, XVI (1949), pp. 151–166. A long and perceptive study is in A. Cowie, *The Rise of the American Novel* (1948). H. Edwards, "Howells and the Controversy over Realism in American Fiction," *American Literature*, III (1931), pp. 237–248, analyzes the concept of realism. See also L. Trilling's perceptive study of Howells and the modern temper in *The Opposing Self* (1955), pp. 76–103.

HENRY JAMES: James' background and his relation to the other members of his distinguished family are examined by F. O. Matthiessen in *The James Family* (1947). The same author wrote a study of James' later fiction, *Henry James, The Major Phase* (1944). F. R. Leavis, *The Great Tradition* (1949), and M. Bewley, *The Complex Fate* (1952), present contrasting views. In many ways James was his own best commentator. See F. O. Matthiessen and K. B. Murdock, eds., *The Notebooks of Henry James* (1947), and R. P. Blackmur, ed., *The Art of the Novel* (1935), a collection of the critical prefaces which James wrote for the New York edition of his works. A good recent collection of his critical essays is Leon Edel, ed., *The American Essays of Henry James* (1956). A useful volume containing key essays in James criticism is F. W. Dupee, ed., *The Question of Henry James* (1945). The Autumn, 1943, issue of the *Kenyon Review* contained nine essays by appreciators of James.

EDITH WHARTON: Edith Wharton's comments on her own art are in *The Writing of Fiction* (1925). Recent studies include A. Kazin, *On Native Grounds* (1942), ch. III, and B. Nevius, *Edith Wharton: A Study of Her Fiction* (1953).

EMILY DICKINSON: *The Poems of Emily Dickinson*, 3 vols. (1955), ed. T. H. Johnson, is a variorum edition of all the known poems and supersedes all previous editions. It is indispensable to any serious student of the poet. Helpful as commentary on the poetry are the letters, also definitively edited by T. H. Johnson with T. V. W. Ward in 3 volumes (1958). For a selection, see T. V. W. Ward, ed., *Emily Dickinson's Letters to Dr. and Mrs. Josiah Gilbert*

Holland (1951). An account of the early letters to T. W. Higginson is in Higginson's *Carlyle's Laugh and Other Surprises* (1909). For interpretations of some of the difficult poems, see *Poetry Explication: A Checklist.*

THE REALISTIC MOVEMENT
AND NEW DIRECTIONS

Although there are many good specialized studies of separate authors and limited aspects, it is difficult to suggest broad histories of the complex contemporary period. A few, however, may be mentioned here. H. S. Commager, *The American Mind: An Interpretation of American Thought and Character since the 1880's* (1950) is a good intellectual-historical introduction. Two decade studies that explore the relationship of literature and society are F. J. Hoffman, *The Twenties: American Writing in the Postwar Decade* (1955) and D. Wecter, *The Age of the Great Depression, 1929–1941* (1948). An influential study of the American psyche is D. Reisman, *The Lonely Crowd* (1950). For studies of literary types, see the relevant listings on page 1207, above.

HENRY ADAMS: The brief biographical introduction to the collection of Adams' letters, H. Cater, ed., *Henry Adams and His Friends* (1947), is helpful. A good study of Adams' intellectual development is E. Samuels, *The Young Henry Adams* (1948) and *Henry Adams: The Middle Years* (1958). On his theories of history see R. Nichols, "The Dynamic Interpretation of History," *New England Quarterly,* VIII (1935), pp. 163–178. R. E. Spiller's essay in *Literary History of the United States,* II, ch. LXV, is excellent. Also, R. A. Hume, "The Style and Literary Background of Henry Adams," *American Literature,* XVI (1945), pp. 296–315.

STEPHEN CRANE: There is critical comment on separate stories of Crane in R. W. Stallman, ed., *Stephen Crane: Stories and Tales* (1955) and in G. C. Knight, *The Critical Period in American Literature, 1890–1900* (1951). L. Åhnebrink, *The Beginnings of Naturalism in American Fiction, 1891–1903* (1950) is the most complete study of the movement and of Crane's part in it. See H. G. Wells, "Stephen Crane from an English Standpoint," *North American Review,* vol. 171, pp. 233–242, reprinted in *The Shock of Recognition,* ed. Edmund Wilson (1943).

THEODORE DREISER: L. Åhnebrink (cited above) discusses Dreiser. C. C. Walcutt, "The Three Stages of Dreiser's Naturalism," *PMLA,* LV (1940), pp. 266–289, is a sound study. See also J. T. Flanagan, "Theodore Dreiser in Retrospect," *Southwest Review,* XXXI (1946), pp. 408–411. Dreiser's

own views on writing are given in his *Hey Rub-a-Dub-Dub* (1920).

EDWIN ARLINGTON ROBINSON: Robert Frost's introduction to Robinson's *King Jasper* (1935) is an excellent comment on the poetry. Y. Winters, *Edwin Arlington Robinson* (1947) is a brief critical study. A good recent volume is E. S. Fussell, *Edwin Arlington Robinson: The Literary Background of a Traditional Poet* (1954). Analyses of several poems included in the present text are to be found in *The Explicator,* vols. 3, 4, 5, and 7 (1944–48); see also W. D. Jacobs, "E. A. Robinson's 'Mr. Flood's Party,'" *College English,* XII (1950), p. 110.

ROBERT FROST: Early critical articles on Frost's poetry are collected in R. Thornton, ed., *Recognition of Robert Frost* (1937). More recent criticism includes G. F. Whicher, "Out for Stars: A Meditation on Robert Frost," *Atlantic Monthly,* vol. 171 (1943), pp. 64–67, and his "Frost at Seventy," *American Scholar,* XVI (1947), pp. 171–182. Useful critical notes are in R. and E. Mertens, *The Intervals of Robert Frost* (1947), a collection. M. Van Doren, "The Permanence of Robert Frost," *American Scholar,* V (1936), pp. 190–198, is a valuable essay. See *The Explicator,* vols. 3, 8, and *passim,* for analyses of separate poems.

CARL SANDBURG: Two good early evaluations are T. K. Whipple, *Spokesmen* (1928), pp. 161–183, and Amy Lowell, *Tendencies in Modern American Poetry* (1917), pp. 139–232. On his mystic quality see O. Cargill, "Carl Sandburg: Crusader and Mystic," *College English,* XI (1950), pp. 365–372, and B. S. Oldsey, "Sandburg's 'Broken-Faced Gargoyles,'" *Explicator* (1949), p. 50.

EZRA POUND: J. J. Espey's *Ezra Pound's "Mauberley": A Study in Composition* (1955) is a fine, perceptive treatment of the poem. P. Russell, ed., *An Examination of Ezra Pound: A Collection of Essays* (1950) is a cross-section of criticism. An early introductory study is A. Amdur, *The Poetry of Ezra Pound* (1936). Two valuable studies of the Cantos are H. Watts, *Ezra Pound and the Cantos* (1951) and L. Leary, ed., *Motive and Method in the Cantos of Ezra Pound* (1954). See also the *Quarterly Review of Literature,* V (1949), an Ezra Pound issue.

T. S. ELIOT: The diversity of criticism on Eliot can be seen in two collections, B. Rajan, ed., *T. S. Eliot . . .* (1947), and L. Unger, ed., *T. S. Eliot: A Selected Critique* (1948). H. L. Gardner, *The Art of T. S. Eliot* (1950) deals principally with the *Four Quartets.* There are full explanatory notes on "The Waste Land" and other poems in K. Friar and M. Brinnin, eds., *Modern Poetry* (1951). For critical explications of "Ash Wednesday," "Gerontion," and other poems, see issues of *The Explicator,* vols. 2, 3, 4, 7, and 11. For a Freudian reading of "The Love Song of J. Alfred Prufrock," see R. P. Basler, *Sex, Symbolism, and Psychology in Literature* (1948), pp. 203–221. Williamson and Matthiessen (cited in the biographical sketch of Eliot in the text, page 942 above) are the best for detailed discussions of the poetry.

ROBINSON JEFFERS: H. H. Waggoner, *The Heel of Elohim* (1950), ch. V, and F. I. Carpenter, "The Values of Robinson Jeffers," *American Literature*, X (1940), pp. 355–366, deal with the poet's thought.

ARCHIBALD MACLEISH: D. Kohler, "MacLeish and the Modern Temper," *South Atlantic Quarterly*, XXXVIII (1939), pp. 416–426, and M. D. Zabel, "The Poet on Capitol Hill," *Partisan Review*, VIII (1941), pp. 2–19 and 128–145, are recommended.

WALLACE STEVENS: Y. Winters, *The Anatomy of Nonsense* (1943), pp. 88–119, M. Bewley, *The Complex Fate* (1952), pp. 171–192, and R. Jarrell, *Poetry and the Age* (1953), pp. 133–149, present three different viewpoints.

HART CRANE: Philip Horton, *Hart Crane: The Life of a Poet* (1937) is narrative and interpretive. The poet's own statements on his art can be found in B. Weber, ed., *Letters of Hart Crane: 1916–1932* (1952). Two critical studies are R. P. Blackmur, *The Double Agent* (1935), pp. 121–140, and H. H. Waggoner, *The Heel of Elohim* (1950), ch. VII.

EUGENE O'NEILL: A general study of most of O'Neill's work is J. W. Krutch, *The American Drama Since 1918* (1939), pp. 73–133. A European debt is assessed in C. Blackburn, "Continental Influences on Eugene O'Neill's Expressionistic Drama," *American Literature*, XIII (1941), pp. 109–133. A full-length critical study is E. A. Engle, *The Haunted Heroes of Eugene O'Neill* (1953).

WILLA CATHER: M. R. Bennett, *The World of Willa Cather* (1951), treats Cather's Nebraska background; E. Lewis, *Willa Cather Living* (1953), is a personal memoir; D. Daiches, *Willa Cather: A Critical Introduction* (1951), is valuable. *Willa Cather on Writing* (1949), contains her essay on "The Novel Démeublé."

SHERWOOD ANDERSON: H. M. Jones and W. B. Rideout have edited *Letters of Sherwood Anderson* (1953). Critical appraisals appear in L. Trilling, *The Liberal Imagination* (1950), pp. 22–33, and A. Kazin, *On Native Grounds* (1942), ch. VIII.

SINCLAIR LEWIS: G. H. Lewis, *With Love from Gracie* (1956), is a valuable study of his personality and life up to about 1930 by his former wife. F. Hoffman, *The Twenties* (1955), pp. 304–370, is interesting background and deals with Lewis as a social critic. H. E. Maule and M. H. Cane have edited Lewis's non-fictional writings in *The Man from Main Street* (1953).

F. SCOTT FITZGERALD: A. Kazin, ed., *F. Scott Fitzgerald: the Man and His Work* (1951), is a good collection of critical and biographical essays which can be supplemented by the excellent recent article on *Gatsby* by M. Bewley, "Scott Fitzgerald's Criticism of America," *Sewanee Review*, XLII (1954), pp. 223–246. E. Wilson has edited *The Crack-Up* (1945), a collection of stories, notebooks, and letters by Fitzgerald which are invaluable to any student of the writer's life and work.

ERNEST HEMINGWAY: An interesting study of Hemingway's training as a writer before 1923 is C. Fenton, *The Apprenticeship of Ernest Hemingway* (1954). J. K. M. McCaffrey, *Ernest Hemingway, The Man and his Work* (1950), is a useful collection. To it should be added R. P. Warren, "Hemingway," *Kenyon Review*, IX (1947), pp. 1–28.

THOMAS WOLFE: T. C. Pollock and O. Cargill, *Thomas Wolfe at Washington Square* (1954), details one phase of his life. H. Muller, *Thomas Wolfe* (1947), is a concise critical study, and W. Walser, ed., *The Enigma of Thomas Wolfe* (1953), collects critical and biographical essays.

WILLIAM FAULKNER: Two books helpful as background for Faulkner and other modern writers are L. Edel, *The Psychological Novel: 1900–1950* (1955), and R. Humphrey, *Stream of Consciousness in the Modern Novel* (1954). Recent critical appraisals include H. M. Campbell and R. E. Foster, *William Faulkner* (1951), and W. V. O'Connor, *The Tangled Fire of William Faulkner* (1954). For "The Bear" see R. W. B. Lewis, "The Hero in the New World: William Faulkner's *The Bear*," *Kenyon Review*, XIII (1951), pp. 641–660.

SCHOOLS OF CRITICISM: None of the biographies of H. L. MENCKEN to date is really adequate, though E. Kemler, *The Irreverent Mr. Mencken* (1950), is useful. M. Geismar, *The Last of the Provincials* (1947), ch. I, places Mencken within the context of the twenties, and M. Bewley, "Mencken and the American Language," in his *The Complex Fate* (1952), pp. 193–210, examines Mencken as critic and philologist from a moral point of view. F. Leander, *Humanism and Naturalism* (1937), is a Swedish critic's comparative analysis of IRVING BABBITT and Paul Elmer More in relation to European humanism. F. Manchester and O. Shepard, eds., *Irving Babbitt, Man and Teacher* (1941), is a collective portrait. R. P. Blackmur, "Humanism and the Symbolic Imagination," *Southern Review*, VII (1941), pp. 309–325, is valuable. Most recent on Babbitt is A. Warren, *New England Saints* (1956), pp. 143–164. A. Tate, "The Fallacy of Humanism," *Hound and Horn*, III (1930), pp. 234–258, is a criticism of the movement. For EDMUND WILSON's critical theory, see his essay "The Historical Interpretation of Literature," contributed to a symposium edited by D. A. Stauffer, *The Intent of the Critic* (1941). Wilson's development is best seen through examination of his own work: *To the Finland Station* (1940) is a high point in his career as interpreter of history; *The Shores of Light* (1952) and *Classics and Commercials* (1950) are collections of his short critical pieces of the 1920's, '30's, and '40's; most recent is *A Piece of My Mind* (1956). Similarly, for TRILLING and COWLEY, see their books mentioned on pages 1177 and 1188, above. For the New Criticism, see S. Hyman, *The Armed Vision* (1948) and M. D. Zabel, *Literary Opinion in America* (1937).

WILLIAM CARLOS WILLIAMS: A good full-length analysis is V. Koch, *William Carlos Williams* (1950); an earlier article is Ezra Pound, *Polite Essays* (1937), pp. 67–81. Williams' *Autobiography* was published in 1951.

E. E. CUMMINGS: E. Wilson, ed., *The Collected Essays of John Peale Bishop* (1948), pp. 83–95, has a perceptive article on Cummings by another poet. R. P. Blackmur, *The Double Agent* (1935), pp. 1–29, is helpful. Cummings discusses his own art and poetry in general in *i: six non-lectures* (1953).

MARIANNE MOORE: Among the many good articles on Miss Moore are R. Jarrell, *Poetry and the Age* (1953), pp. 179–207, the Marianne Moore issue of *Quarterly Review of Literature*, IV (1948), and R. P. Blackmur, *The Double Agent* (1935), pp. 141–171.

PICTURE CREDITS

"Sperm Whaling, No. 2 — The Capture," from drawings by A. Van Best & R. S. Gifford, corrected by Benj. Russell. Goodspeed's Book Shop, Boston

Carson House, Eureka, California, built in 1886. Pacific Gas and Electric Company
"Emigrant Train," by Samuel Colman, 1872. Courtesy of Hall Park McCullough

Page 661

A trip hammer at the Nashua Iron Company, Nashua, New Hampshire, 1859. Lithograph by Endicott and Company after photographs by J. S. Miller. The Harry Shaw Newman Gallery

Page 835

"Landscape Near Chicago," by Aaron Bohrod, 1934. Collection of Whitney Museum of American Art, New York

Page 662

New York Slum Scene. Bettmann Archive
Emily Dickinson, portrait. Harvard College Library

Page 836

William Faulkner. Black Star
Robert Frost. Black Star

Page 663

Brooklyn Bridge. Courtesy of Dr. D. B. Steinman
Henry James, London, 1912. Harvard College Library
"Long Branch, New Jersey," by Winslow Homer. Museum of Fine Arts, Boston
"Harvesting on a Bonanza Farm," engraving after a drawing by W. A. Rogers, *Harper's Weekly*, 1891. Library of Congress

Page 837

Ernest Hemingway. Black Star
Scene on the Chicago River. Wide World
"Baptism in Kansas," by John Steuart Curry, 1928. Collection of Whitney Museum of American Art, New York

Page 664

Mark Twain. Bettmann Archive
"Snags on the Missouri River," Carl Bodmer, 1841. New York Public Library

Page 838

Main Street, Sauk Center, Minnesota, 1920. Bettmann Archive

INDEX OF AUTHORS AND TITLES

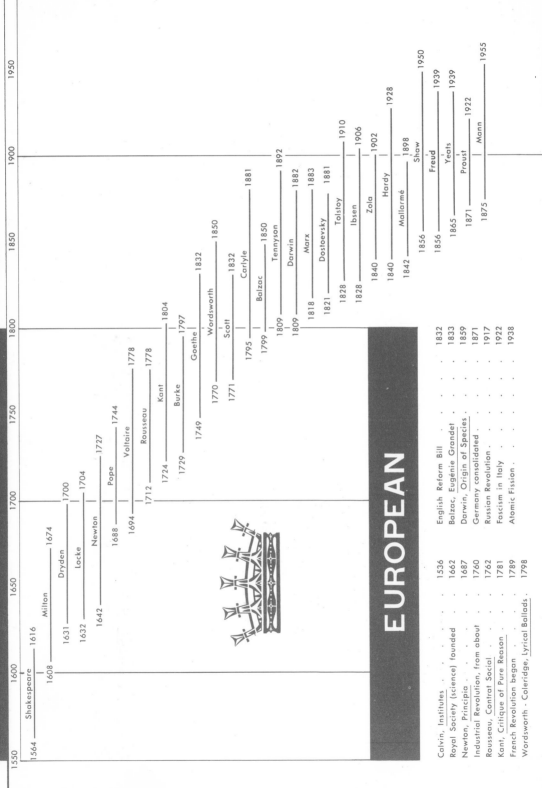

TIME CHART

EUROPEAN

1550　1600　1650　1700　1750　1800　1850　1900　1950

1564

Shakespeare

1616

1608

Milton

1674

1631

Dryden

Locke

1632

1700

1704

Newton

1642

1727

Pope

1688

1744

Voltaire

1694

1778

Rousseau

1712

1778

Kant

1724

1804

Burke

1729

1797

Goethe

1749

1832

Wordsworth

1770

1850

Scott

1771

1832

Carlyle

1795

1881

Balzac

1799

1850

Tennyson

1809

1892

Darwin

1809

1882

Marx

1818

1883

Dostoevsky

1821

1881

Tolstoy

1828

1910

Ibsen

1828

1906

Zola

1840

1902

Hardy

1840

1928

Mallarmé

1842

1898

Shaw

1856

1950

Freud

1856

1939

Yeats

1865

1939

Proust

1871

1922

Mann

1875

1955

Calvin, Institutes	1536	English Reform Bill 1832
Royal Society (science) founded . .	1662	Balzac, Eugénie Grandet . . 1833
Newton, Principia	1687	Darwin, Origin of Species . . 1859
Industrial Revolution, from about . .	1760	Germany consolidated . . . 1871
Rousseau, Contrat Social . . .	1762	Russian Revolution 1917
Kant, Critique of Pure Reason . .	1781	Fascism in Italy 1922
French Revolution began . . .	1789	Atomic Fission 1938
Wordsworth - Coleridge, Lyrical Ballads .	1798	